Æthelflæd, Lady of the Mercians;
the battle of Tettenhall 910AD;
and other West Mercian studies.

To the memory of
Margaret Gelling, 1924-2009
scholar and friend.

Æthelflæd, Lady of the Mercians; the battle of Tettenhall 910AD; and other West Mercian studies.

David Horovitz

2017

ISBN 978-1-5272-0619-9

Typeset and published by
David Horovitz
Kiddemore Cottage
Brewood, Stafford ST19 9BH

© David Horovitz 2017

The moral rights of the author are asserted.
No part of this book may be reproduced
in any form or by any means
without permission in writing
from the author.

Contents

Abbreviations		3
Preface		7
	Prologue.	11
1.	The Vikings.	12
2.	The siege of Buttington, 893.	23
3.	The wintering of the Danes at *Cwatbrycge* in 895-6.	34
4.	The Danish camp at *Cwatbrycge*.	41
5.	Geology and hydrology of the Bridgnorth area.	57
6.	Quatford and its two castles.	62
7.	*Cwatbrycge* and its bridge.	81
8.	The bridge at Bridgnorth.	110
9.	Æthelflæd's *burh* at *Cwatbrycge*.	114
10.	*Scergeat*.	131
11.	The tenth-century topography around Quatford, Wednesfield and Tettenhall.	146
12.	Wednesfield and Woden: pagans and Christianity.	161
13.	Early routeways in the Wolverhampton area.	176
14.	Early tenth-century warfare.	182
15.	Anglo-Saxon armies.	189
16.	Tenth-century warriors: clothing, arms and armour.	193
17.	Viking armies.	202
18.	Viking strategy and tactics.	206
19.	Viking allies.	210
20.	Mounted forces or cavalry?	211
21.	Medical matters.	214
22.	Treatment of defeated enemies.	217
23.	Wales in the late ninth and early tenth centuries.	220
24.	Supposed tumuli in the Wolverhampton, Wednesfield and Tettenhall area.	232
25.	Willenhall and its chapel.	241
26.	Accounts of the battle of Tettenhall.	248
27.	Analysis of the documentary evidence relating to the battle of Tettenhall.	278
28.	Opinions as to the site of the battle of Tettenhall.	303
29.	Clues to the site of the battle of Tettenhall?	311
30.	Archaeological evidence of the battle of Tettenhall.	342
31.	The Tong fragment.	356
32.	The Quatford spearhead.	361
33.	The prelude to the battle of Tettenhall.	366
34.	The battle of Tettenhall – possible scenario.	418
35.	The aftermath of the battle of Tettenhall.	465
36.	The enigma of the *Three Fragments* and other problems.	495

Continued overleaf

Contents (*continued*)

Appendix I:	The Morfe 'tumuli'.	521
Appendix II:	Ancient sites.	531
Appendix III:	The Royal Free Chapels, Wulfrun, and the early history of the church of Wolverhampton.	540
Appendix IV:	The Wolverhampton cross-shaft.	568
Bibliography		626
Index		669

Abbreviations

AC	*Archaeologia Cambrensis.*
ADS	Archaeological Data Services website.
AJ	*Archaeological Journal.*
ASC	*Anglo-Saxon Chronicle.*
ASSAH	*Anglo-Saxon Studies in Archaeology and History*, Oxford: Oxford University School of Archaeology.
BCA	Birmingham City Archives.
BCSMR	Black Country Sites and Monuments Record.
BDS	*Bagshaw's Directory of Shropshire.*
BL	British Library.
BM	British Museum
CA	*Current Archaeology.*
CCALSS	Cheshire and Chester Archives and Local Studies Service.
CPAT	Clwyd-Powys Archaeological Trust.
CPR	*Calendar of Patent Rolls.*
DB	Domesday Book.
DNB	*Oxford Dictionary of National Biography.*
EDD	*The English Dialect Dictionary.*
EHD	Dorothy Whitelock (ed.), *English Historical Documents, c.500-1042*, Vol. I, London: Eyre & Spottiswoode Ltd., 1955.
EHR	*English Historical Review*
EPNE	A. H. Smith, *English Place-Name Elements*, 2 vols., Cambridge: Cambridge University Press, 1956.
HE	Bede, *Historia Ecclesiastica*.
HER	Historic Environment Record.
HLSL	Deed in Harvard Law School Library.
HM	BBC *History* Magazine.
JBAA	*Journal of the British Archaeological Association.*
JBHS	*Journal of Broseley History Society.*
JEPNS	*Journal of the English Place-Name Society.*
LiDAR	Environment Agency LiDAR Composite Digital Surface website.
LMM	*Lawyer's and Magistrate's Magazine.*
MA	*Medieval Archaeology.*
ME	Middle English.
MED	Henry Bradley (ed.), *A Middle-English Dictionary*, by Francis Henry Stratmann, Oxford: Oxford University Press, 1891.
NLW	National Library of Wales.
OE	Old English.
OED	*Oxford English Dictionary.*
ON	Old Norse.
O.S.	Ordnance Survey.
Oxford DNB	*Oxford Dictionary of National Biography*, Oxford: Oxford University Press, 2004.
PAS	Portable Antiquities Scheme.
P.R.	Parish Register.
PMSANRP	Public Monument and Sculpture Association National Recording Project.
PN Sa	M. Gelling in collaboration with H. D. G. Foxall, *The Place-Names of Shropshire*, Nottingham: English Place-Name Society, 1990 and ongoing.
PN Warks	J. E. B. Gover, A. Mawer and F. M. Stenton, in collaboration with F. T. S. Houghton, *The Place-Names of Warwickshire*, Cambridge: Cambridge University Press.
PODS	*Post Office Directory for Shropshire.*
PSA	*Proceedings of the Society of Antiquaries.*
PTRSL	*Philosophical Transactions of the Royal Society of London.*
RCAHMW	Royal Commission on the Ancient and Historical Monuments of Wales.

RCHM	Royal Commission on Historical Manuscripts.
RMLWL	R. E. Latham, *Revised Medieval Latin Word-List*, London: British Academy, 1965.
RRAN	*Regesta Regum Anglo-Normannorum 1066-1154*: Vol. II *Regesta Henrici Primi 1100-1135*, Oxford: Oxford University Press.
S.	Charter (with relevant number given) listed in P. H. Sawyer (1968), *Anglo-Saxon Charters: An Annotated List and Bibliography*, London: Royal Historical Society.
SA	Shropshire Archives (formerly Shropshire Records and Research Centre).
SHC	*Staffordshire Historical Collections* (formerly *Transactions of the William Salt Society*).
SRO	Staffordshire Record Office.
SSMR	Shropshire County Council Sites and Monuments Record (now Shropshire County Historic Environment Record).
TA	Tithe Award.
TBAS	*Transactions of Birmingham Archaeological Society.*
TNSFC	*Transactions of the North Staffordshire Field Club.*
TOE	Jane Roberts and Christian Kay with Lynne Grundy, *A Thesaurus of Old English*, 2 vols., London: King's College London Centre for Late Antique and Medieval Studies, 1995.
TSAHS	*Transactions of the Shropshire Archaeological and Historical Society.*
TSANHS	*Transactions of the Shropshire Archaeological and Natural History Society.*
TSAS	*Transactions of the Shropshire Archaeological Society.*
TSSAHS	*Transactions of the South Staffordshire Archaeological and Historical Society.*
TStAHS	*Transactions of the Staffordshire Archaeological and Historical Society.*
VCH	*Victoria County History* (of the county of Stafford unless otherwise indicated).
WA	G. P. Mander, *The Wolverhampton Antiquary: being collections for a history of the town gathered by Gerald Poynton Mander*, Whitehead Brothers (Wolverhampton) Limited, 1933 etc.
WAN	*Worcestershire Archaeological Newsletter.*
WC	*The Wolverhampton Chronicle.*
WLHC	Walsall Local History Centre.
WMANS	*West Midlands Archaeological News Sheet.*
VEPN	David N. Parsons and Tania Styles, *The Vocabulary of English Place-Names*, Nottingham: Centre for English Name-Studies, 2000, etc.
WJ	*The Wolverhampton Journal.*
WSL	William Salt Library, Stafford.
YAJ	*Yorkshire Archaeological Journal.*

The elaborately-carved cross-shaft in the churchyard of St Peter's church, Wolverhampton, held to be one of the finest surviving monuments of the Anglo-Saxon period, from a drawing published in *The Builder* journal, 5th October 1872.

Preface

Coacervavi omne quod inveni
'I have made a heap of everything I have found': the anonymous compiler
known as Nennius, in the preface to his *Historia Brittonum*, c.800 AD.

Underlying its title, the main theme of this book is essentially an ongoing investigation into large-scale violent and premeditated killings which took place over eleven hundred years ago in what was to become south Staffordshire. The episode is generally known as the battle of Tettenhall. The spark that ignited that research occurred in the early 1950s when, as a child, the awestruck author was told that beneath an unkempt grassy mound serving as a traffic island at the junction of Wergs Road and Yew Tree Lane, Tettenhall – or it may have been Woodthorne Road (memories fade) – lay the bodies of Viking warriors killed long ago in a great battle. Who were they? Who were they fighting? Why were they at Tettenhall? What led to the battle? Where was it? Had any relics been found? What were the consequences of the battle? The memory of that nondescript grassy mound eventually led to over half a century of sporadic research, rummaging for and sifting clues which might help illuminate the great battle and its participants.

As the chronicler William of Malmesbury recognised with incontestable clarity over 900 years ago, the ambition of historians is 'to bring to light things lost in the midden of the past',[1] and this work sets out to provide a synthesis of such information as can be gleaned from the sparse and often contradictory evidence – archaeological, documentary, cartographic, numismatic, place-name, topographical, and legendary – relating directly and indirectly to a conflict which has been all but ignored by many authorities, and to consider the background to, and consequences of, what was a momentous Anglo-Saxon military victory against a predominantly Scandinavian force. If the battle of Agincourt has been described as a battle whose reputation far outranked its importance,[2] Tettenhall might fairly be said to be a battle the importance of which far outranks its obscurity. The expression 'battle of Tettenhall' is used throughout this work as a matter of convenience, since that is how the great conflict is generally referred to (if at all) in our history books, but is not intended to imply that the battle necessarily took place at Tettenhall.

If the conclusions to be drawn from this research are less than certain, it should be remembered that locating early battlefields is not as straightforward as might be imagined. The quest is necessarily founded on informed speculation rather than stark certainty. Despite centuries of meticulous study by many generations of historians, the site in the Midlands where tens of thousands of Boudica's rebellious forces were, we are told, butchered by the Romans in 60 AD has never been found; the battlefield of Bannockburn (1314) remains untraced; and the site of the battle of Bosworth, fought in 1485 – well over half a millennium after the battle of Tettenhall – was only identified positively in 2009 following extensive archaeological research costing over £1 million after large-scale field investigations by metal detectorists. It was the discovery of lead shot and cannon balls – artefacts hardly to be found on an Anglo-Saxon battlefield – which showed that the engagement had actually taken place some two miles south-west of the traditional site. In 2010 it was announced that the Civil War battle of Stow-on-the-Wold, fought in 1646, may have taken place two miles south of the long-recognised site near Donnington, Gloucestershire. Indeed, apart from the site of the battle of Hastings (from which, except

---

[1] Holland 2016: 93.
[2] Cornwell 2009: afterword.

for a corroded axe-head of dubious authenticity, not a single military artefact has ever been recorded), no Anglo-Saxon battlefield has been identified precisely,[3] and even in that case a startling claim has recently been made that the battle may have taken place not at Senlac Hill, but at Crowhurst, 2½ miles away.

Few cases illustrate the problems better than ongoing academic skirmishes over the battle of *Brunanburh*, arguably the greatest of all Anglo-Saxon conflicts, when Æthelstan's English forces annihilated a formidable coalition army from Dublin, Scotland and Strathclyde in 937. The enemy slain included at least five kings and seven earls. Accounts of the clash are found in at least 53 sources in Old English, Anglo-Norman, Irish, Welsh, Scots, Middle English, Latin, and Icelandic, including a famous Old English poem in the *Anglo-Saxon Chronicle*. A consensus of scholarly opinion now favours a site in the west at Bromborough on The Wirral, but supporters continue to press a case for locations as far apart as Lanchester (County Durham), Tinsley Wood (South Yorkshire), Burnswark (Dumfries and Galloway), Axminster (Devon), and indeed many other far-flung places.[4]

What these examples reveal is the extraordinary and to some extent inexplicable truth that local – and national – memories of particularly traumatic historical events can simply dissipate entirely with the passage of time, demonstrating (if proof were needed) the widespread fallacy of long-lived folk-memory. Nevertheless, the sites of early – even Anglo-Saxon – battles do occasionally come to light. A notable example, emphasising the value of place-name research in such investigations, is the battlefield of *Æthelingadene*, where in 1001 a Viking force defeated an Anglo-Saxon militia. A suspected (though not the favoured) site for the engagement was conclusively confirmed in 1987 by the early spellings of nothing less than an ancient rabbit warren.[5]

No historical event can properly be understood in isolation from the age in which it occurred. For the local, national and international context for the battle of Tettenhall the only primary sources from which knowledge can be gleaned, apart from surviving documents such as charters and wills, are early English (and occasional Continental) chronicles, invariably based at best on third-party information almost certainly partisan, incomplete, exaggerated, and in some cases inadvertently – or even deliberately – misleading or simply wrong, providing a distorted picture.[6] The nature of the distortions is, very often, impossible to identify, and almost every statement in such chronicles as do survive raises unanswered questions. Even the *Anglo-Saxon Chronicle*, the most important authority for the period, is memorably described by one authority as an 'entrancing fraud'.[7] To add to the difficulties, the chronicles and annals tend to imply that incidents and events followed consecutively, whereas many must have overlapped or occurred simultaneously, forcing rulers to constantly fight several fires on several fronts in different parts of their territory, and often elsewhere, with scriptorium-based scribes doing their best to discover afterwards – perhaps long afterwards – what may have occurred, and in what sequence, at great distances from their quills and ink galls. All this is compounded by the complete absence of Scandinavian written evidence from the period: in contrast to the relative wealth of surviving Anglo-Saxon documentation from England (though a mere fraction of

---

[3] Williams 2016: 36-7, 51 fn.21.
[4] Livingston 2011; Foot 2011: 178-9.
[5] Gardiner and Coates 1987: 251-2; Marren 2006: 3, 163, 190.
[6] For an outstanding survey of the chronicles of medieval England and Scotland see Gransden 1992: 199-238.
[7] Campbell 2003: 5

what must have one existed) it is sobering to reflect that not a single pre-Conquest Scandinavian document exists.[8] It goes without saying, therefore, that anyone enquiring into obscure events that occurred well over a thousand years ago is entitled – indeed, forced – to speculate on possibilities without necessarily having evidence beyond reasonable plausibility.

It was originally intended that this study would serve merely as an unpublished quarry of material for a much shorter volume, but the unpolished notes were in the event published in 2010 in some haste to mark the eleven-hundredth anniversary of the battle. Ironically, at the very moment the book was published – the first devoted to the subject in over a thousand years – historians were immersed in a reassessment of the events leading up to the engagement. Perversely, recent research has clouded rather than clarified the position, and much of what we believed we knew has been cast into the melting pot. This second edition has accordingly been heavily rewritten to take account, inter alia, of that research, not least that of Dr John Quanrud of Nottingham University, to whom I am indebted for making available and discussing points arising from a pre-publication copy of his seminal paper on the battle. The traditional analysis of the conflict as set out in the first edition of this work must now be seen in a new light, after a paradigm shift in centuries-old conclusions about significant aspects of the battle. Moreover, just as that reassessment was taking place, ground-breaking research became available on the nature of Viking fortifications. That, too, has led to revised conclusions on the subject in this volume which, as will be painfully apparent, is essentially a compilation or agglomeration of material that has been amassed over several decades of intermittent research, a commonplace-book added-to haphazardly from time to time, which explains the head-spinning blizzard of details, cacophony of references and tedious repetition, which could only be avoided by even more distracting cross-referencing or interminable editing. To quote Benjamin Franklin, writing to a correspondent in 1750: 'I have already made this paper too long, for which I crave pardon, not having time to make it shorter'.

Over the course of more than half a century during which this work has been in the making, help and advice have been given freely by friends and others beyond count. They will understand, I hope, that any attempt to list all their names would greatly increase the size of this already cumbersome work, and would be quite impossible. Nevertheless their assistance and support (and especially that of my ever-patient wife Sylvia) has been gratefully appreciated, and is now formally acknowledged. Responsibility for all errors, infelicities and irrational interpretations rests, of course, entirely with the publisher and not the author.

Needless to say, there is not the slightest evidence that the grassy mound at the end of Yew Tree Lane in Tettenhall ever covered any dead soldiers – which is not to say, of course, that it did not.

David Horovitz,
Brewood
5th August 2017.

---

[8] Graves 1975: 351-7.

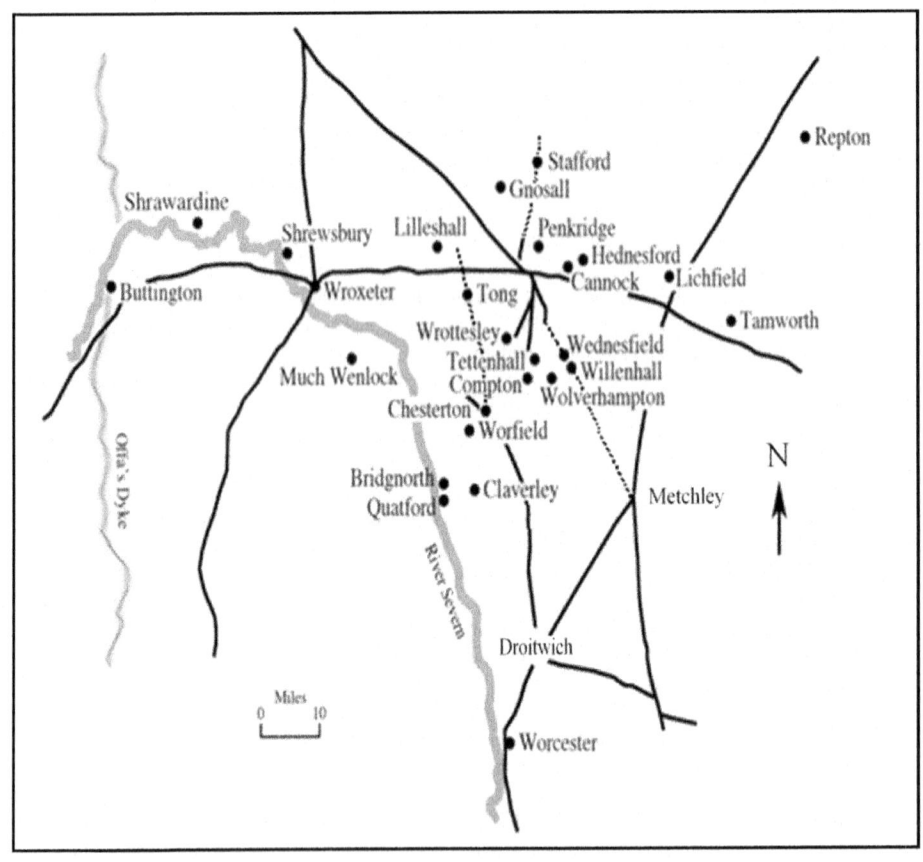

Map showing places mentioned in the text. The solid black lines represent certain Roman roads, the broken black lines probable Roman roads.

Prologue

In 893 AD a Viking raiding army taking refuge in a fortification at *Butting tune*, probably near Welshpool, was besieged by pusuing English forces. Many Vikings were killed, and the rest fled.

In 895 other Vikings fleeing English forces wintered in a fortification at or near Bridgnorth on the river Severn, before leaving peacefully the following year.

In 909 Edward the Elder launched a devasting raid into the kingdom of Northumbria, killing and plundering.

The following year a Northumbrian raiding army attacked and looted deep within Mercia. On its return it was intercepted by English forces and crushed. The clash became known as the battle of Tettenhall.

That is what the chronicles tell us; whether to be accepted as 'facts' is open to debate.

This work seeks to investigate in detail this period and the historical topography of those areas in an attempt to throw more light on those events.

1. The Vikings.

Vikings is the name commonly applied today to all Scandinavians who lived during the expansive era of raiding, trading and colonisation that dawned around 800 AD.[9] Yet long before they gained a reputation as bloody marauders, the Scandinavians were energetic traders, and for centuries had been hosting foreign merchants at bustling Scandinavian market towns. Trade exposed them to the wealth of others and fed dreams of plunder and conquest.

In 793, according to the *Anglo-Saxon Chronicle*,[10] ominous symbols of pending doom affected England, including lightning and fiery dragons in the sky, with dreadful famine in Northumbria. These omens were afterwards recognised as portents of imminent catastrophe, and indeed presaged the last of the great barbarian incursions into Britain, the coming of the Vikings. The Chronicle tells that the omens were followed by 'the harrying of the heathen [who] miserably destroyed God's church in Lindisfarne by rapine and slaughter'. These Viking raids would continue intermittently for over two centuries and not cease until the early decades of the twelfth century.

The annalists knew these raiders not only as 'the northmen', 'the Danes', and 'the Vikings', but also as 'the heathen', 'the barbarians', 'the pirates', 'the host', 'the foreigners', 'the gentiles', and 'the pagans', and to the Welsh and Irish as 'the black gentiles', 'the black host', 'the black foreigners', 'the white foreigners', and 'the black pagans', a reminder that the annalists themselves were Christian clerics whose objectivity when recording incidents in which the Vikings were involved is unlikely to have been been untainted, and all Scandinavian raiders were included in the general term 'Danes' or 'heathen' in Old English records: those who attacked Lindisfarne were actually Norwegians, and the distribution of metalwork finds from Britain and Ireland suggests that the early raids came from western and south-western Norway.[11] We must also remember that the only sources we have of the Viking raids is from their victims: the Norsemen themselves left no written records.

The word 'Viking' (*wicenga*), a term still not completely understood, was not a synonym for Dane, Norwegian, Swede, or Scandinavian. It represented a specific occupational meaning 'pirate or robber', not 'warrior' or 'soldier', and was not an ethnic classification: it is likely that many Viking warbands consisted of mercenaries of various nationalities, including sometimes (and perhaps more often than we might suppose) Englishmen, and even on occasion women and children. Contemporary Irish sources recording Scandinavian activity never use the term Viking, but it is sometimes found in later Old Icelandic accounts to describe freebooters and pirates just as likely to raid settled communities in the Scandinavian homeland as in the Christian West. The term Viking did not refer to the Nordic peoples who stayed at home; those who shared a similar language (Old Norse) and cultural traditions that distinguished them from other linguistic or ethnic

---

[9] For a comprehensive and well-researched account of the Viking world see Parker 2014. A detailed and scholarly analysis of the Vikings is contained in papers published in Brink and Price 2008.

[10] The *Anglo-Saxon Chronicle* (hereafter ASC), versions 'E' and 'F'. Three Danish ships arrived on the south coast, perhaps Dorset, four years earlier. The king's reeve and his men who rode to meet the strangers were killed by them: Whitelock 1955: 166.

[11] Williams, Pentz and Wemhoff 2014: 238 fn.2.

groups were known by various ethnic names, such as Goths, Svear (Swedes), Norwegians (who spoke East Norse), or Danes (who spoke West Norse).[12]

By the middle of the ninth century the term Viking is not appropriate for settled communities in the Danelaw – a misleading term first recorded c.1050 for the area in the north and east of England under the control or law of the Danes,[13] which gives a false impression of unity for territories that were, like the Scandinavian homelands, politically fragmented – but is reserved for raiding bands in the earliest stages of the Norse period or for one-off later raiders who sacked established communities – including those of earlier Scandinavian settlers – and then departed.[14] Downham uses the term Vikings to describe those of Scandinavian culture active outside Scandinavia whose colonies affiliated themselves more strongly with the culture of their homelands than with that of the indigenous population.[15]

Whatever the derivation, it is clear that the majority of Scandinavians were not Vikings: probably relatively few Scandinavian males in the ninth century went 'a-Viking'. Likewise not all Vikings were Scandinavians,[16] and indeed some historians now use the word Viking without a capital letter to reflect the fact that the Vikings are a historical construct, rather than a nation,[17] but to avoid overly pedantic distinctions, terms such as Danes, Norse, Scandinavians and Vikings (with the usual V) are used in some cases interchangeably in this work.

Abundant archaeological and documentary evidence shows that in many ways the Vikings shared a similar social structure with the Anglo Saxons. Their way of life was mainly agricultural, with strong family units built around loyalty to a lord, sophisticated law codes, and a lively artistic culture with designs based around animal forms. Even their language shared a common root with and was not totally dissimilar to the Old English

---

[12] The Appendix to the *Chronicon ex chronicis* of Florence (John) of Worcester notes that the pagan force active in England in 867 included 'Danis, Norreganis, Suanis, Goutis et quarundum aliarum natione populis': Quanrud 2015: 76.
[13] OED; Holman 2001; Hart 1992; Hadley 2012.The Danelaw originated in the 9th-century settlements of the Great Danish Army in and after 875, and is given implicit recognition in the undated treaty made at some time between 886 and 890 between Alfred and Guthrum. Various lists dating from the second half of the 12th century probably define with reasonable accuracy the extent of the Danelaw, and list counties subject to West Saxon law, Mercian law (Herefordshire, Gloucestershire, Worcestershire, Shropshire, Cheshire, Staffordshire, Warwickshire, Oxfordshire), and the Danelaw (Yorkshire, Nottinghamshire, Derbyshire, Leicestershire, Lincolnshire, Northamptonshire, Huntingdonshire, Cambridgeshire, Bedfordshire, Norfolk, Suffolk, Essex, Hertfordshire, Middlesex, Buckinghamshire): Hart 1992: 8; Riley 1860: II 505, 625.
[14] Smyth 1998a: 38; Abrams 2001; and especially Brink 2008: 4-7.
[15] Downham 2009: xv. The definition has been slightly paraphrased.
[16] Scholars are still undecided about the derivation of the term Viking, which occurs several times in the OE poem Widsith, usually dated to the end of the 7th century, and in the 8th-century Exodus, where the tribe of Reuben are described as *sæwicingas*, meaning 'sea-warriors', as they cross the Red Sea on their way out of Egypt. The ASC uses the term only four times before 1066, in the native English forms *wicenga* or *wicinga*, in 879, 885, 921 and 982. It is not even certain that Viking is Scandinavian in origin: one theory is that both the OE and ON forms are parallel developments from a common Germanic verb meaning 'to withdraw, leave or depart'; that it is related to the Old Icelandic *vik*, meaning 'a bay or creek'; that it is derived from the area of Vik or Viken around the Oslofjord from where many left to escape Danish hegemony; that it comes from *vika*, meaning 'a turn on duty or relay oarsmen'; that it derives from an Old Icelandic verb *vika*, meaning 'to turn aside'; or the OE *wic*, or armed camp: Richards 2005: 4; Williams, Pentz and Wemhoff 2014: 17-20.
[17] See e.g. Abels 2003: 265; Brink and Price 2008: 3.

spoken by the Anglo-Saxons. But they were very different from their Anglo-Saxon contemporaries in one important respect. They were expansionist and aggressive seafaring adventurers, and by the eighth century had evolved a formidable sailing vessel, the longship – fast, nimble, seaworthy, which could be beached along coasts, rowed far up rivers, and even dragged overland. Often decorated with fabulous carving and brightly painted, the longship opened up the world to the Vikings. Driven from their homelands by a lack of good farming land, overpopulation, internal political disputes, and especially by the lure of accessible and portable wealth in various forms to be found in unprotected monasteries, the Vikings were exceedingly mobile, whether on land or, especially, by sea, able to range widely, raiding far beyond their homelands. But perhaps the greatest strength of the Vikings was their flexibility: if conditions prevented raiding and looting in England, they simply turned their attention to Ireland or Francia[18] or elsewhere (and *vice-versa*), and displayed remarkable versatility in their military operations. Armies would split up, with warbands striking simultaneously in different parts of the country, re-forming when necessary to mount more intensive campaigns. This was a period when the Baltic islands, notably Gotland, became remarkably wealthy as a result of looted wealth taken to the Viking homelands.

The decision by the Christian church to establish communities of monks on small islands and at isolated coastal sites in Britain and Ireland so that holy men could live in seclusion and peace, devoting themselves to duty and prayer, was to prove disastrous. If we can rely on the chroniclers,[19] the earliest recorded raids on Britain consisted of hit-and-run attacks targetingthose same undefended communities and monasteries to snatch easily portable booty. Thegreatest asset of the Vikings was surprise. Appearing without warning, they sacked a target and fled in their longships before any slow-moving local defences could be mustered. No local fleets were available to confront them or cut off their retreat, but that does not mean that there were no forces in England to meet the threat: as early as 792 Offa of Mercia is said to have imposed the three common burdens (army-service, fortresswork and bridgework) in response to the threat from seaborne Viking armies, and organised coastal defences for his kingdom *contra paganos*,[20] though no details are known.

The *Anglo-Saxon Chronicle* accounts of Viking raids are certainly incomplete:[21] it is only chance references in charters, for example, that tell us that the people of Lyminge needed a refuge from Vikings within the walls of Canterbury in 804, and that before 811 Viking armies had not only been campaigning in Kent but even building themselves fortresses there.[22] Despite attempts in recent years to rehabilitate their reputation, it is clear that sudden and savage raids by Vikings might result in torture, mutilation, death, ransoming or

---

[18] Francia was the Germanic kingdom that developed out of what was Roman Gaul, with the term is used to differentiate it from the medieval kingdom of France that emerged from the 11th century onwards.

[19] Those chronicles are all from areas which suffered from Viking attacks, with none from Scandinavia itself: compared with other parts of Western Europe, Scandinavia is poorly provided with written evidence for its early medieval history. Before the 11th century the only texts produced in Scandinavia were runic inscriptions, generally on memorial stones, domestic objects, and coin legends. The oldest surviving historical document fron Denmark is a deed of 1085 (Hart 1992: 4); the earliest original Scandinavian charter is a Danish fragment of 1135; and the earliest Swedish charter is from 1165. By comparison, scholars of the later Anglo-Saxon period in England have a wealth of contemporary written material, though representing the smallest fraction of what once existed.

[20] Haywood 1995: 4-5; Brooks 2000: 43.

[21] For references to Vikings in insular chronicles see Dumville 2008: 350-67.

[22] Brooks 2000: 43.

sale into slavery far from home,[23] and brought additional tragedy to the lives of Anglo-Saxon communities already beset by hazards such as communal warfare, harvest failure, virulent and deadly disease, accident, poisoning from putrid food, enslavement for debt and family blood feud.

Monasteries, the primary targets for looting, were attacked without warning, often on the feast days of the Christian calendar, including Christmas Day, when the Vikings knew that their isolated monastic communities would be distracted by religious duties. Night raids were common, as well as surprise attacks across frozen lakes and rivers. Religious sites were targeted not because the Vikings were filled with a ferocious pagan hostility to Christianity, but for their undefended wealth in the form of portable booty, for example shrines made from precious metals and other high-status ecclesiastical cult objects such as gem-studded gospel books and reliquaries, in the knowledge that their custodians would pay almost any ransom to recover their holy relics and the bones of their holy patrons and founders – which may be how the illuminated manuscript known as the Lichfield Gospels found its way from the church of Llandeilo Fawr in Dyfed – but also to undermine the morale of their victims. Centuries-old libraries with books of great scholarship were put to the torch – a memorandum dating between 883 and 911 of a renewed grant of King Burgred records an ancient landbook (the legal title to an estate) carried off from Marcliff in Cleeve Prior in Worcestershire by the pagans[24] – and learned clerics slain without mercy or captured for ransom.[25] Indeed, the devastation of church buildings was so severe that there was a real fear among church leaders about the very survival of the Christian faith, since many Irishmen were known to have abandoned Christianity in favour of the pagan gods of their persecutors,[26] and many Christian Irish groups are known to have attacked monasteries.[27] Yet there is no evidence that the Vikings were bent on eradicating Christianity: it was the portable riches from the churches that they sought, and monasteries were often left to rebuild their wealth, so providing future targets. The Vikings were not conducting a religious crusade; they treated all victims and their property, religious or lay, with equal savagery. Indeed, they were not above punishing their own for supposed impiety: a record of a Viking raid in Francia in 860 tells how Viking chiefs themselves piled their loot for safe-keeping on a church altar and entrusted it to a monk who had chosen not to flee. Other Vikings who tried to steal the loot were hypocritically condemned by their own chiefs for sacrilege, and hanged from the monastery gate, 'a divine manifestation, even through the judgement of infidels'.[28] But sacrilege is unlikely to have been the primary transgression in the minds of the Viking chiefs.

---

[23] The Vikings took slaves especially from the Celtic peoples – a single raid in Ireland took over 700 slaves – and from the Scandinavians themselves, though most were used by the Vikings rather than sold on: Carroll et al 2014: 126. Large numbers of Welsh and Irish were taken in captivity to Iceland to supplement the labour force during the period of settlement, and were also taken in large numbers by Norwegians to restore the manpower denuded by emigration to Iceland. As well as victims, the Welsh were also dealers in the slave trade, with two major centres at Bristol and Dublin, as well as Scandinavian bases such as Hedeby, from where Scandinavian merchants sold their human cargo all over Western Europe and by river and overland routes to Muslims in the Middle East and Central Asia: Patterson 1982: 154; Walvin 2006: 28.
[24] S.222. It should be noted, however, that the memorandum cannot be genuine in its present form: Finberg 1972; 107, No. 270.
[25] In 914 Edward the Elder paid forty pounds in ransom to the Vikings to obtain the release of bishop Cameleac of Archenfield: ASC 'A', Swanton 1996: 98.
[26] Higham 1993: 176.
[27] Kirwan 2014: 5.
[28] Nelson 1999: I 64.

Ireland proved a particularly attractive focus for Viking attacks. Unsurprisingly, it was the wealthy monasteries that attracted the first recorded raid on Ireland in 794. It became the first foreign country to be threatened with deliberate conquest, as opposed to short-term raiding. By the 830s, using the Orkneys and Western Isles as a staging post, the Vikings had moved inland along Ireland's river systems, and shortly after 840 they established coastal colonies at Dublin (the principal *longphort* or 'ship-port' of the Vikings in Ireland),[29] and other locations. That activity is mirrored by the Vikings on the continent. But from the mid 840s the major Irish kings turned on the Vikings, and defeated them in a number of battles, and there is evidence of major clashes between the Scandinavians themselves. In 849 120 ships reached Ireland from 'the king of the Foreigners' to exact obedience from the Vikings, and in 851-2 major conflicts took place between the Vikings of Ireland and the incoming Danes, who were eventually driven off. In 853 Amláib, son of the king of Laithlind, came to Ireland, and the Foreigners of Ireland submitted to him. For the next 20 years he and two others, Ímar (Ivarr) and Auisle (a name we will meet again), who are called his brothers or kinsmen, became the most prominent of the Dublin-based Vikings, in 866 overrunning Pictland, and capturing Dumbarton in 871, smashing the British of Strathclyde. From the mid-ninth century the Vikings had become well-established in their coastal settlements, but unlike in Scotland, England and Francia, they failed to pacify the native population and acquire large territories outside those areas.

To the Vikings the Irish Sea was no more than an inland lake, and native annals from Wales, though meagre, suggest that the Welsh coastal monasteries were plundered from the Irish Sea before the Vikings attacked the royal stronghold on Anglesey in 853/4, and Rhodri, king of Gwynedd, with its island of Anglesey recognised as the principal Welsh kingdom, killed their leader Horm in 856. The absence of easily navigable rivers providing access to the interior of Wales almost certainly explains the absence of Viking archaeology in central Wales. From Irish annals we learn that Rhodri was forced to flee to Ireland in 877 and was killed by the English when he returned to Wales in 878. The Vikings wintered in Dyfed that year. Other than isolated burials from Anglesey and north-east Wales which may provide evidence of pagan Scandinavian burials, there is little archaeological evidence for Vikings in Wales before the tenth century: many place-names incorporating Scandinavian elements have been identified in Wales, but cannot be dated with certainty, and could be explained by contact with seaborne Scandinavian traders rather than settlers.[30]

By about the middle of the ninth century the Swedes had sailed eastwards to the Gulf of Finland and penetrated via rivers to the Black Sea to develop trading links into Russia with a presence in Byzantium and beyond, establishing a dynasty of rulers which lasted until the thirteenth century. In about 860 Vikings reached Iceland, then inhabited by a few intrepid Irish monks, and from 874 began to colonise it so vigorously that two generations later there were 20,000 or more Norwegians settled there, using it as a base to colonise Greenland in about 985, and soon after to reach Labrador and Nova Scotia. Elsewhere, Viking raiders spread devastation at all the major towns and cities that were accessible by water: sailing up the Thames they sacked London, went up the Seine to besiege Paris four times, up the Loire to Nantes, up the Gironde to Bordeaux. They sailed into the Bay of

---

[29] Charles-Edwards 2013: 469.
[30] Maund 2005: 81-2.

Biscay and attacked areas bordering the Mediterranean.[31] Their use of rivers to raid far from the coast is well evidenced.

Eloquent testimony of the terror inspired by Viking raiders is provided by an ecclesiastical chronicler, Ermentarius of Noirmoutier, whose own monastery was attacked repeatedly, who noted despairingly that:

> 'the number of ships increases, the endless flood of Vikings never ceases to grow bigger. Everywhere Christ's people are the victims of massacre, burning and plunder. The Vikings over-run all that lies before them, and none can withstand them ...'.[32]

Again, a monk from Arras records in 884:

> 'The Northmen never stopped enslaving and killing the Christian people, pulling down churches, demolishing fortifications and burning towns. And on every road lay the corpses of clergy and laity, noblemen and commoners, women, youngsters and babies. Indeed there was no village or highway where the dead did not lie, and all were filled with grief and torment as they saw the Christian populace being destroyed to the point of extinction'.[33] The tombs of the Merovingian kings were broken open and their bones scattered.[34]

Little wonder that in the mid-ninth century a new supplication was introduced into the Gallican liturgies: *A furore Normannorum libera nos, Domine* – 'Lord, deliver us from the wrath of the Norsemen'.[35]

Historians have in the past tended to conclude that the key to Danish attacks, certainly in the early years, was not the use of English rivers to carry troops inland, but the straight Roman military roads. The Danes did not require roads in good repair, merely roads or tracks good enough for horses to use, and although neglected for some half a millennium, the Roman roads may well have provided fast direct routes across much of England, although there is evidence that parts at least of even the major Roman roads became impassable at a relatively early stage in the post-Roman period as a result of trees and shrubs taking root in the paved or gravelled surfaces. Many of those sections were only reinstated as highways – if at all – in the road-making boom of the eighteenth century, and it would be unsafe to assume that all Roman roads in use today were available to the Vikings during the ninth and tenth centuries, although there were probably many that are lost or disused today which were in use at that period.[36]

But Vikings were legendarily associated from birth with rivers, seas and ships, and Viking camps in England invariably lie close to or alongside rivers. Since there is abundant evidence that the Vikings raided far up the major rivers of Ireland and Francia, by the late ninth century the Scandinavians (probably including some involved in raids overseas) were accustomed to venturing far inland by ship. It must be safe to assume that they adopted the same practice in England: there is little firm evidence in the chronicles of inland raids by

---

[31] Sayles 1964: 87-93.
[32] Parker 2014: 39.
[33] From the *Annales Vedastini*, 54-5, quoted in Coupland 1995: 200.
[34] Palgrave 1851: I 460.
[35] Palgrave 1851: I 460.
[36] See, for example, Rackham 1986: 253.

water, but they certainly reached Repton in Derbyshire, about as far from the coast as it is possible to get, in 874; wintered at Gloucester in 877-8; and were some twenty miles north of London on the river Lea in 895.[37] In rivers such as the Severn, shallows and the many fish-weirs may have served to obstruct journeys into the higher reaches, but we might suppose that major Roman cities such as Viroconium (Wroxeter), well upstream, were accessible by ships in the Roman period, and the Vikings were adept at hauling their vessels considerable distances on rollers around obstructions. Even strongly-built fish-weirs, designed to resist occasionally violent flood-waters, could easily be ripped down to allow passage, and the few bridges that may have existed over the Severn in the Anglo-Saxon period will have proved a minor hindrance. On occasions the Vikings split their forces, with one force travelling overland and another by sea, to meet up at an agreed location, allowing the land force to travel unencumbered with supplies moved by sea, which would be safe from counter-attack, if vulnerable to the weather.[38]

By 851, hit-and-run attacks had given way to better-organised large-scale incursions designed to occupy land as well as take booty, and a Danish army was sufficiently confident to spend the winter in England.[39] Thereafter, Viking raiding parties became larger and more determined, their intention to secure permanent occupation, though not conquest: even in later decades, when Viking leaders 'made peace' with Carolingian or Anglo-Saxon rulers, they consistently sought tribute rather than political power.[40] This transition from raiding to full-scale invasion and settlement was marked by war parties wintering in estuaries and offshore islands in the 840s and 850s, and by the new tactic of pillaging across great tracts of countryside, usually on commandeered horses but occasionally on foot, leaving their vessels secured in fortified bases.

The arrival in England of the Danish Great Army in 865 marked a turning point in the Viking wars. This was the period of the so-called Heptarchy, when England was divided into seven kingdoms, each with its own king: Northumbria, East Anglia, Mercia, Sussex, Essex, Kent and Wessex. The northern kingdom of Northumbria, with its capital at York, the Roman legionary fortress which had been reoccupied in the sixth century as a royal, ecclesiastical and mercantile centre by the Anglo-Saxons, but which had been long distracted by anarchy, accepted as king a Danish nominee between 867 and 869, so becoming a powerful Viking kingdom controlling most of northern England between the rivers Humber and Tees. By 868 Mercia was in danger of being overrun after the Danish army moved south to seize Nottingham. Joining forces, the Mercians and West Saxons laid siege to the Viking army, but the enemy refused to be drawn into battle, and a peace was concluded,[41] presumably by payment to the Vikings of tribute – coin, precious metals, livestock, and, doubtless, food and drink. This payment is not recorded by the chroniclers, but is well evidenced in contemporary Frankish sources elsewhere,[42] and it is reasonable to assume that similar payments were frequently demanded by, and made to, Viking armies in England. Indeed, in 872 the bishop of Worcester granted a lease of land at Nuthurst

---

[37] ASC 'A' and 'E'; Swanton 1996: 72-3; Campbell 1962: 42; ASC 'A'; Swanton 1996: 88-9. We might note that ASC 'A' says that the Danes 'went overland' from their camp on the Lea to *Cwatbrycge* (Bateley 1986: 59), perhaps implying that the Danes sometimes travelled by ship.
[38] Williams 2008: 197, citing events at Exeter in 876.
[39] Coupland 1995: 190-201.
[40] Coupland 1995: 199.
[41] Swanton 1996: 68-70. It was during the Nottingham campaign that Alfred is assumed to have married Ealhswith, a Mercian nobleman's daughter, about whom little is known: see especially Smyth 1995: 24-8.
[42] Smyth 1995: 24.

(Warwickshire) to obtain money to pay tribute to the Danes, doubtless associated with the treaty made by the Mercians the previous year with Danes who had taken up winter quarters in London.[43]

Turning their attention to Wessex in 871, the Danish army met strong resistance from Alfred, King of the West Saxons, newly crowned after the death of his brother, and the *Anglo-Saxon Chronicle* records no fewer than nine battles in that year, most of which Alfred lost, probably buying off the attackers by tribute. By 878 the heathen not only had control over most of Northumbria, but also eastern Mercia and East Anglia, and had temporarily taken London and struck far into Wessex, the heartland of Anglo-Saxon England. This was the crux of the Viking threat, and Alfred was forced to make a last-ditch stand from the marshland island of Athelney in the Somerset levels. By some means gathering together an army strong enough to turn the tide,[44] he almost miraculously forced the Danes back. Historians have long accepted that the division between English England and Danish-controlled territory was fixed in 886 under the Treaty of Wedmore along the line of the eastern part of the Roman Watling Street, with the Danes and their Northern Army (a term with which modern historians are not entirely comfortable) holding the Danelaw (as we have seen, another term which has attracted modern criticism) with the Five Boroughs (a term first recorded in 942 for Nottingham, Lincoln, Stamford, Derby and Leicester) to the east of that frontier.[45] In fact, as David Dumville has cogently argued, this treaty probably represents not the terms of a permanent treaty concluded at Wedmore in 886, but only a temporary peace agreed after the battle of Edington in 878.[46] The idea that the Danelaw enabled the Danes to retreat into friendly territory if at risk of a military reverse when raiding outside Danish-controlled territory is almost certainly misplaced: the treaty boundaries were unmarked as such and unpatrolled, and are unlikely to have deterred military incursions and pursuits by either side into the territory of the other when deemed necessary.[47]

---

[43] S.1278; Dumville 1992: 33 fn.12; ASC 'A' and 'E': Swanton 1996: 72-3. A translation of the lease is printed in Whitelock 1979: 532.
[44] Alfred may have hired contingents of Viking mercenaries to swell his troops: Asser, whose account of the King's life has been questioned, says that 'many Franks, Frisians, Gauls, Vikings, Welshmen, Irishmen and Bretons' flocked to the King's court (chapter 76; see also Williams 1999: 77), and the *Anglo-Saxon Chronicle* records that at a naval engagement between Alfred's fleet and the Danes in 896 a number of Frisians who were part of the English forces were killed, including three who are named and presumably held positions of some importance: Whitelock 1955: 189. The loyalty of some English landowners may not have been beyond doubt, for a suit heard c.975 suggests that Edward the Elder, after the defeat of the southern Danelaw, confiscated the lands of those Englishmen who had taken the Danish side in the recent war: Stenton 1970: 123.
[45] Some historians feel uncomfortable with long-established and convenient terms such as Northern Army, the Danelaw and the Five Boroughs, since they convey misleading connotations: Williams 2013.
[46] Dumville 1992: 1-24.
[47] Scholars now take the view that Watling Street formed the boundary of the Danelaw only as far west as the northern tip of Warwickshire, after which it turned north along what became the boundary separating Staffordshire, Cheshire and Lancashire from Derbyshire and Yorkshire (Gelling 1992: 128): there is no evidence that any part of Staffordshire ever lay within the Danelaw: see Hart 1992: 9 map, correcting the O.S.*Map of Britain Before the Norman Conquest*, 1973, which shows the boundary running west along Watling Street as far as the river Penk; see now the map in Hunt 2016: 119. Evidence to support the boundary line might be seen in a charter (S.224) by Æthelflæd to Ealhhelm of land at Stanton, near Burton-on-Trent, Derbyshire (assumed to be 900, but see Sawyer 1979: 1-2, which argues for a later dating), and in a charter of 926 (S.397) of lands at Hope and Ashford in Derbyshire which a certain Uhtred 'had bought from the pagans on the orders of King Edward and Ealdorman Æthelred', showing that between 899 (when Edward became king) and 9112

By this time, the great kingdom of Mercia, which had been the dominant Anglo-Saxon kingdom during the eighth and early part of the ninth century under the long reigns of Æthelbald (716-757) and Offa (757-796), and latterly under Coenwulf (796-821), was at risk of disintegration under the weight of the Viking onslaught. In 873 the Danes of Northumbria launched an assault on Mercia, wintering in 873/4 at the historic monastery which served as the royal burial ground of many Mercian kings at Repton in Derbyshire near the Staffordshire border. Ravaging Mercia in 874, they forced king Burgred of Mercia to seek sanctuary in Rome.

After the death in 879 of his successor Ceolwulf II, supposedly a Viking nominee but in all likelihood a powerful Mercian ruler, there emerges from amongst the Mercian ealdormanry a leader by the name of Æthelred, to become known as Lord of the Mercians.[48] His background is uncertain – Alex Woolf has suggested that he was probably the son of Æthelswith, daughter of King Æthelwulf of Kent (825-39, 856-58) and Wessex (839-855),[49] and Ian Walker that he might tentatively be seen as a relative and successor of Æthelmund, ealdorman of the Hwicce, who was killed in battle in 802[50] – but he probably led the Mercian forces defeated at the battle of Conwy in 881,[51] and he appears in history for the first time in a charter of 883,[52] becoming in all but title king of Mercia,[53] in 886/7 sealing an allegiance to the West Saxons by marrying Æthelflæd, the first-born child and

---

(when Æthelred died), Englishmen were being encouraged to recover territory from the Danes: Wainwright 1975: 297. Sihtric Cáech, King of York from 920 to 926, married the sister of King Æthelstan in a Christian ceremony at Tamworth in 926 (Higham 1993: 189), implying that Tamworth then lay on the boundary of his kingdom and that of Æthelstan, a boundary that may have been may decades old at that date. Watling Street, or part of it, was evidently the boundary between the English and Danish territory of Edmund and Olaf c.940 if we are to believe the chronicle of Simeon of Durham (who had access to much Northern material): Stevenson 1855: 482.

[48] David Dumville pertinently observes that the *Anglo-Saxon Chronicle*, our principal source for this perioed, does not tell us which parts of Mercia the Danes settled under Coelwulf, nor which parts they directly controlled but did not settle, nor which parts they gave to Coelwulf; and other sources do not assist in defining the borders between such areas: Dumville 1992: 18 fn.18.

[49] Woolf 2001: 98. Whatever his lineage, it is clear that he (and his wife) had or developed particularly strong attachments to Gloucester.

[50] Walker 2000: 69, 210; Williams, Smyth and Kirby 1991: 24.

[51] Charles Edwards 2013: 490-1.

[52] S. 218, which confirms that Æthelred even then regarded Alfred as his overlord: Keynes and Lapidge 1983: 84. If Woolf is correct, Æthelred's father would have been King Burgred of Mercia c.852-74, his grandfather a King of Wessex, his great-grandfather Charles the Bald, King of the Franks, who was grandson of Charlemagne, and Æthelflæd would have been Æthelred's first cousin: Keynes and Lapidge 1983: 252; Woolf 2001: 98. Political marriages between Wessex and Mercia were not uncommon: not only did King Burgred of Mercia marry Æthelswith, daughter of Æthelwulf of Wessex, but King Alfred's wife Ealhswith was a Mercian royal woman, probably a descendant on her mother's side of King Coenwulf: Williams, Smyth and Kirby 1991: 41; Sharp 2001: 81; Stafford 2003: 259. For a discussion of an untrustworthy charter of 883x911 (S.222) which mentions Æthelred, *dux Merciorum*, renewing a grant of King Burgred, see Stenton 1971: 259 fn.2; Finberg 1971: 107, No. 270. Several daughters of Edward the Elder became brides for Frankish, Saxon and Viking rulers and aristocrats: Sharp 2001: 79-88; MacLean 2008: 167-90.

[53] Indeed, a Mercian king-list preserved at Worcester includes Æthelred, placing him after Ceolwulf II, which suggests that he was seen as a king, at least by the Mercians, at some stage in his reign (Cumberledge 2002: 3), and the chronicler Æthelweard describes Æthelred as *rex Myrciorum* 'king of the Mercians' (Campbell 1962: 50), with Irish annals calling him 'King of the Saxons': O'Donovan 1860: 230-7.

daughter of Alfred the Great,[54] who he had evidently regarded as his overlord from at least 883.[55] In 886 he was entrusted by Alfred with the city of London, re-taken from the Danes, a city which had previously long pertained to Mercia.[56]

Together, Æthelred, Æthelflæd, Alfred, and Æthelflæd's brother Edward the Elder were to play leading roles in this momentous period in the history of England, with Æthelflæd formally taking up her role as Lady of the Mercians – *Æpelflæd Myrcna hlæfdige* – on the death of her husband in 911, although evidence from the *Anglo-Saxon Chronicle* and elsewhere suggests that from at least 902 Æthelflæd was acting largely on her own initiative, wielding authority and not merely influence, as a result of the increasing incapacity of Æthelred – later Irish sources tell us that at the siege of Chester c.905 he was 'in disease ... and it was from this disease that [Æthelred] died' – from an unidentified but evidently progressive disability which may have caused his death, perhaps prematurely, in 911.[57] On the other hand, the *Mercian Register*, a set of annals inserted into the *Anglo-Saxon Chronicle* intended to glorify the exploits of Æthelflæd, does not mention her name before 912, which might suggest that Æthelred was not especially incapacitated before his death in 911.

At this point it is necessary to stress that the Vikings who settled in Ireland from the 840s were predominantly Norwegians. The Danes had temporarily captured Dublin in 851, but were quickly driven out by Olaf, son of a Norwegian king, who became an active participant in Irish political life, forming alliances with local rulers. Ireland then remained relatively free from Viking attacks during the so-called 'Forty Years Rest', with the Irish Vikings concentrating their raiding on Francia and England.

By this date the Danes were stongly established in the northern and eastern part of England within the Northumbrian Danelaw, divided from the English by Watling Street in the east and in the Midlands by the rivers Trent and Dove to the Mersey, thus leaving Staffordshire outside the Danelaw.[58] It was the Danes of York who were especially troublesome in England and Wales, but in 902 the Hiberno-Scandinavians, sometimes called the Irish

---

[54] Alfred married in 868, and Æthelflæd was his oldest child, described as *coniux* (wife) of Æthelred in a Worcester charter of 887 (S.217), when she could have been no more than 19: Dumville 1992: 18 fn.86; Williams, Smyth and Kirby 1991: 27. Little is known of Æthelflæd's early life, but in her father's will she is left just one bequest, *pæne ham æt welewe*, compared with 2 estates to the second daughter and 3 to the youngest. Harmer notes that the use of the term *ham* rather than *land* found in earlier entries perhaps denotes the idea of a residence, particularly the residence of the owner of the estate: Harmer 1914: 17, 98. It is tempting to speculate that that residence may have had special significance for Æthelflæd, possibly even the place where she was born. *Welewe* is identified as Birch as Wiley (Wiltshire), but that appears as *Wilig* in ealdorman Æthelwold's will, c.946-7: Harmer 1914: 33. Harmer identifies *Welewe* as Wellow (4 miles south of Bath, Somerset, in Wessex close to the border with Mercia), and Keynes and Lapidge (1983: 321, fn.58) as that place or East Wellow (3 miles west of Romsey, Hampshire), held of the king in DB, or nearby West Wellow, or Wellow (Somerset). Sawyer is undecided as to the identification: Sawyer 1968: 422. A meeting of the king's counsellors was held at *Welowe* in 931 (S.1604), which Birch identifies as 'Welowe in Co. Hants' [East or West Wellow?]: Birch 1887: II 362; Keynes and Lapidge 1983: 321 fn.58.
[55] As revealed by a charter from the Worcester archives (S.218): Keynes and Lapidge 1983: 228.
[56] Dumville 1992: 7.
[57] O'Donovan 1860: 230-7; Wainwright 1975: 79-83; VCH Cheshire: I 249.
[58] The maps showing the boundary of the Danelaw in 892 in Graham Campbell et al 1994: 134, Hart 1992: 9, and now especially Hunt 2016: 119, are to be preferred to the maps showing the Danelaw c.900 and in 902 in Lapidge et al 1999: 519 and McKitterick 2003: 67, the latter showing Staffordshire within the Danelaw.

North-Sea Vikings, were driven out of Dublin by the Irish and found refuge in the Wirral, cementing a secure foothold with long-settled Norse communities in the region to the north-west. By this date the uncomfortable alliance between the Hiberno-Norse on the one hand and the Danes of York and East Anglia on the other seems to have been disintegrating, with considerable suspicion and animosity, even hatred, between the two groups, which came to see each other as foes.[59]

Until this time England could be roughly divided into various kingdoms under two principal factions: the English, and the Danes of York, both Christian – or at least (in the case of the Danes of York) Christianised. To this was now added a third dimension on the English mainland: the still-pagan Irish North-Sea Hiberno-Scandinavians who helped to swell the Scandinavian population on the western edge of Northumbria. That meant that the great kingdom of Northumbria housed two main groups with Scandinavian roots or connections, but we have seen that not all Scandinavians were Vikings, just as not all Vikings were Scandinavian. These problems of terminology have a direct bearing on the battle of Tettenhall, and the existence of the two Scandinavian groupings greatly complicates our understanding of the circumstances surrounding the events of August, 910, adding a new facet to the previous interpretation – as set out in the first edition of this work – of the limited evidence on the battle, further complicated by the evolving and sometimes capricious Welsh elements.

Finally, it is worth making the point that despite their differing ethnic origins, the various English and Scandinavian factions with which we are concerned in this study all shared languages of Germanic origin, and philogists have established that English was probably intelligible to those of Scandinavian origin, though the degree of mutual comprehensibility must remain uncertain.[60]

---

[59] Walker 2000: 90.
[60] Thompson 2002: 4, 29, citing Townend 2000: 90; Townend 2002.

2. The siege of Buttington, 893 AD.

The *Anglo-Saxon Chronicles* record that in 893 two Danish armies, one which had landed in England from a fleet of 250 ships and built a fort at Appledore, the other led by Hæsten,[61] which had arrived in 80 ships, camped at a stronghold at Shoebury in Essex, where they were joined by a 'great reinforcement' (*micel eaca*) of troops from Northumbria and East Anglia. This mixed horde of Danes began to plunder along the Thames and up the Severn[62] until it reached *Butting tune*.[63]

There are two places with the name Buttington in England, and both lie close to the Severn. One is near the confluence of the Severn and Wye in Gloucestershire; the other two miles north-west of Welshpool. Each place has attracted distinguished academic support as the site of *Butting tune*, but in recent years, though the question has not been resolved with certainty, the scales have tipped quite strongly in favour of Buttington on Offa's Dyke near Welshpool in Powys,[64] on the English/Welsh border, where the Danish

---

[61] Hæsten was the OE version of the name of one of the most prominent Viking leaders of the ninth century who became a legend in medieval Norman-French folklore for his barbarous exploits. A veteran who had fought with the Danish Great Army against the Anglo-Saxons, in 859 he was joint leader of a fleet from the Loire bound for Spain with the intention, no less, of sacking Rome, and became one of the the first Vikings to enter the Mediterranean from the west. Looting en route in north Africa his forces reached Rome and achieved the prize – or so they thought. They had actually sacked Lucca in error. Hæsten gained notoriety as a church looter and military campaigner on the Loire in the late 860s, pillaging monasteries and villages and acting as a mercenary in border wars. He is probably the same person as Alstigus, a Frankish Viking who after a bloody campaign in Francia in which the Vikings suffered a heavy defeat in 891, withdrew to Boulogne and left for England in 892, probably intending to settle, supposedly in a fleet of 250 ships carrying horses and supplies. Those forces landed in Kent and Hæsten built a fortress at Milton, near Sittingbourne. After various campaigns by both the West Saxons and the Vikings, Alfred launched a successful attack on a Danish camp built by Hæsten at Benfleet in Essex. There is no evidence that Hæsten ever accepted Christianity, but Alfred and his son-in-law Æthelred had earlier sponsored his two children as godsons when Alfred had received oaths and hostages from Hæsten in return for money. But Hæsten began raiding into Mercia and Alfred was again forced to pay off Hæsten and his surviving forces. See, e.g., Keynes and Lapidge 1983: 282; Logan 1991: 126-7, 133; Haywood 2000: 58; Price 2008a: 465-6. Irish annals known as *The Three Fragments*, considered in more detail in Chapter 36, mention Jarl Sihfric who led one of the contingents from Dublin in 893, perhaps fighting at the battle at which *Annals of Ulster* records in that year a major defeat of 'dark foreigners' at the hands of the English, and which Claire Downham suggests was the siege of Buttington: Downham 2009: 72.

[62] The source of the Thames lies a few miles south-west of Cirencester, and the Severn is some 17 miles further west. Travelling along the west bank of the Severn will have taken the Danes to the religious sites and treasures at Gloucester, Tewkesbury, Hereford and Worcester: Hill 1984: 56.

[63] ASC 'A': Earle and Plummer 1892-99: 87

[64] Sir John Edward Lloyd concluded that 'Buttington by Chepstow tallies much better with the data of the *Chronicle* – especially with the composition of the English army and its leader – than does Buttington near Welshpool': Lloyd 1948: 329 fn.32, following Earle and Plummer 1892-1899: ii 109-10. Eilert Ekwall came to question whether he was right to have dismissed the southern Buttington as the site of the battle: Ekwall 1959: 23-5. The scholarly consensus today, however, is that the site is to be identified as Buttington near Welshpool: see e.g. Toller 1898: 136-7; Fox 1955: 90 fn.3; Stenton 1971: 267; VCH Gloucestershire 10: 65; Wainwright 1975: 74 fn.2; Swanton 1996: 87 fn.13; a view perhaps supported by the statement in the *Bruty Tywysogion* that in 890 (895) the 'black Normans' (Danes) came a second time to 'gastell Baldwin' (Montgomery): Williams ab Ithel 1860: 16-17. The RCAHMW, however, prefers the site near Chepstow, citing Lloyd 1948 and Charles 1938: 189. It seems to have gone unnoticed, but may not be a coincidence, that the only two places in England and Wales called Buttington both lie on Offa's Dyke. At Buttington near Welshpool a long section of the Dyke running north comes to an end at the school house, and indeed Sir Cyril Fox believed it marked

army is said to have taken refuge in a fortification. That the Danish camp lay near Welshpool seems to be supported by other Danish activity at Chester and *Cwatbrycge* (near Bridgnorth), both far from the Gloucestershire Buttington (which is hardly 'up' the Severn), at the same period. North-western Mercia was to become for two or three years a region of exceptional events involving the Danes. What happened at Buttington is recorded in the *Anglo-Saxon Chronicle* in the following terms:

' ... [The Danes] went up along the Thames until they reached the Severn, then up along the Severn. Then there gathered Ealdorman Æthelred and Ealdorman Æthelhelm and Ealdorman Æthelnoth, and the king's thegns who were occupying the fortifications, from every stronghold east of the Parret, both west and east of Selwood, and also north of the Thames and west of the Severn, and also a certain part of the Welsh race. Then, when they were all gathered, they overtook the raiding-army from behind at Buttington on Severn shore, and besieged them on every side in a fortification. Then when they had settled for many weeks on the two sides of the river, and the king was west in Devon against the raiding ship-army, they were weighed down with lack of food, and had devoured the greater part of their horses, and the others were perishing with hunger; then they went out to the men camped on the east side of the river and fought against them, and the Christians had the victory. And Ordheah, the king's thegn, was killed there, and also many other king's thegns killed, and very great slaughter was made there of the Danish, and the part that came away there were saved by flight.'[65]

Since Æthelred is named first in the account, followed by two named *ealdormen* from Wessex, he might be thought to have taken the leading role in this episode.[66]

However, the chronicler Æthelweard, writing in the later tenth century, gives a slightly different version of events, apparently derived from some Northumbrian source, recording that 'Hæsten made a rush with a large force from Benfleet, and ravaged savagely through the all lands of the Mercians, until he and his men reached the borders of the Welsh; the army stationed then in the east of the country gave them support, and the Northumbrian one similarly. The famous Ealdorman Æthelhelm made open preparations with a cavalry force, and gave pursuit together with the West-Saxon army under the generalship of Æthelnoth. And King [*sic*] Æthelred of the Mercians was afterwards present with them, being at hand with a large army. They launched mutual strife with a clash of the two nations, the young Englishmen on that occasion kept possession of the field of victory in the end.' In an uncharacteristic comment on the period of Alfred's reign, Æthelweard adds that 'These events, which occurred at Buttington, are vaunted by ancient men.'[67]

---

the northern extremity of the earliest section of the Dyke, running some 34 miles from Rushock Hill, Herefordshire (Fox 1955: 89, 286; Ray and Bapty 2016: 39-41), and at Buttington, which lies close to the southern extremity of the Dyke where it runs across the Beachley Peninsula near Chepstow in Gloucestershire, 'a well preserved portion of the bank, known as Buttington Tump, survives ... it is unusually large ...' (Fox 1955: 197; Ray and Bapty 2016: 177, 182, 186, 213, 249; see also VCH Gloucestershire X 50-62). It has been suggested that OE **butta*, or a variant **butt* or **butte*, is probably the etymon of ME *butt* 'the thick end of something', for example the two Buttington names, which would seem to be appropriate for the Dyke at both places: Horovitz 2015: 38-54.
[65] Swanton 1996: 87-8.
[66] Charles-Edwards 2013: 507-8.
[67] Campbell 1962: 50; Stenton 1970: 9; Keynes and Lapidge 1983: 190. It is noteworthy that Æthelweard refers to Æthelred as King (and later Æthelflæd as Queen) of the Mercians, and that Æthelred and his forces apparently arrived after the West Saxon contingent, a curious observation which remains unexplained.

Whether the Danes travelled to Buttington by land or water is unstated, but since the Thames and the Severn are unjoined it is likely that they travelled on horseback following the course of those rivers. Whether they were aware of the English forces following in their tracks is unclear, and it seems unlikely that they would have built any fortifications during their campaign: though there is evidence that the Vikings had been building fortresses in England even before 811, when one is recorded in Kent.[68] Such a structure would require time, manpower, tools and materials, and would certainly take many days, possibly weeks, to construct. We must suppose that the Danes at Buttington utilised an existing naturally defensive feature such as an island, or taken over an appropriately-sized existing fortification, which would have needed to be large enough to contain the Danish force, but small enough to allow all parts of the perimeter to be adequately manned and defended.[69]

Roger of Wendover, a monk of St Albans abbey who died c.1236, helpfully records that the Danish camp was 'washed on all sides by the waters of the Severn',[70] indicating that it was on an island (a conclusion shared unhesitatingly by Sir Frank Stenton),[71] which may be seen to be of particular relevance in a later episode involving a Danish encampment.[72] Roger also adds that Alfred surrounded the pagans both with sea and land forces.[73] Roger's work is of value because, if it is to be trusted, it seems to incorporate material from other sources, many of which can no longer be traced, but must be treated with considerable caution.[74]

Wherever it lay, it is clear that the Danish camp, on the border of Powys, ruled by the Merfynion (a dynasty named after the legendary Merfyn Frych who took the kingship of

---

[68] Brooks 2000: 43.

[69] Why Buttington was chosen as the site of the Danish camp is unexplained, but the Danes invariably chose sites on navigable rivers, and Buttington lies at the point where Offa's Dyke, a major landscape feature of great political and military significance, meets the Severn to mark a 5-mile gap in the Dyke before it reappears at Derwas to the north. It is likely that the Danes were familiar with the Severn from earlier expeditions along the river (or Dyke) which remain unrecorded. But Buttington also lies on an important ford of the Severn (Rhyd y Groes), and would be an obvious location for an early fortification: see Davies 2006: 23-6, who cites Henry Owen (ed.), *The Description of Pembrokeshire* 4 (London 1936) 617. It has been noted that 'the valley of the river Severn reaches at Buttington its narrowest point in the whole 27 miles ... between Abermule, 10 miles to the south-west, and Shrawardine 17 miles [upriver]. Between Buttington and Derwas the Severn is, or has been historically, fordable in one or two places, but the valley is broad and full of former back-channels and marshy areas, that in the eighth century may well have been impassable in all but the very driest conditions': Ray and Bapty 2016: 39-40.

[70] Giles 1892: 231; Gransden 1996: 359. 'Roger of Wendover, a deplorable person, but still an assiduous searcher out of materials ...': Stenton 1970: 373.

[71] Stenton 1971: 267, who records that there were still traces of an island between two branches of the Severn, but that the construction of a railway across the site had changed its character.

[72] Marren 2006: 113 says that the Danes established what he calls a ship-fortress (presumably a fortification to protect ships) at Buttington inside a meander of the river Severn, but no authority is given for that statement.

[73] Giles 1892: 231. The nature of the 'sea forces' is not immediately apparent, but perhaps indicates that boats were deployed. In that respect the expression might be seen to support Buttington near Chpepstow, between the Wye and the Severn Estuary, as the site of the Danish camp. .

[74] See Luard's editorial note to the chronicle of Matthew Paris (which incorporates the work of Roger of Wendover), pointing out that the account of Hastein's defeat at Buttington is 'altogether falsified' as a result of the ASC being used and misunderstood: Luard 1872: lii, though on p.431fn6 Luard refers only to the introduction to the siege. His reference in that fn. to Earle's notes on the ASC has not been traced.

Gwynedd in about 825),[75] was besieged by a combined army of West Saxons and Mercians who blockaded it from both sides of the river for several weeks. The Mercian army, which Æthelweard tells us arrived after the West-Saxon army (suggesting perhaps that the Mercians were on foot), was led by *ealdorman* Æthelred, Lord of the Mercians. The Mercians had been gathered from 'north of the Thames and west of the Severn', and were reinforced by 'some portion of the Welsh people' – *sum dæl þæs Norð wealcynnes*[76] – but whether Welsh levies from within English districts along the Welsh border, or Welshmen from one of the Welsh kingdoms, is unclear.[77] The ancient animosity between the Merfynion of Gwynedd, led by Anarawd ap Rhodri (who with his brothers controlled all of North Wales from Anglesey as far south as Ceredigion and Powys), and the Mercians seems to have been set aside in the face of the Viking threat; indeed Charles-Edwards has concluded that in 893 King Alfred's authority had extended over all Wales, and that Æthelred and Æthelflæd must have come to an arrangement with Anarawd by which he accepted Mercian overlordship in return for the freedom to make further conquests in south-west Wales.[78]

The West Saxon contingent was led by two *ealdormen*, Æthelhelm of Wiltshire and Æthelnoth of Somerset, who controlled a force of thegns and warriors gathered 'from every borough east of the river Parret, and both east and west of Selwood'.[79] The details of the composition of the English forces speak of a highly sophisticated call-up and assembly process, details of which we can only guess.

Roger of Wendover, in describing the events leading up to the siege at Buttington, tells us that 'the wicked Hastein and the rest of the pagans, whom King Alfred's army had driven from Beamfleot, resolved to cross over 'to their countrymen who dwelt in the western part of England. Stealing, therefore, a hasty march through the province of the Mercians, they reached a certain village named Buttingetune, situated on the river Severn, 'where they were honourably received by their brethren, and admitted to the town they had built there' [emphasis added].[80] The idea that there were Danes and an existing Danish settlement or fortification at Buttington (and perhaps others elsewhere in the region) is most curious and unexplained, but might suppport the observation of Florence (John) of Worcester that the Danes retreated into a fortification at Buttington, and reminds us that for a time there had been an alliance between Gwynedd and the Viking rulers of Northumbria, probably from

---

[75] Charles-Edwards 2013: 467.
[76] The term *Norð wealcynnes* does not mean that the Welsh were from North Wales, but was used to distinguish the people of Wales from those of Devon and Cornwall, the West Welsh: Wainwright 1975: 75 fn.3.
[77] See Smyth 1995: 359. It has been suggested that the Welsh contingent at Buttington was led by an allied Welsh army under Merfyn of Powys (who died in 904), brother of Anarawd (Peddie 1999: 180), or was from South Wales (Ó Corráin 1995: 61).
[78] Charles-Edwards 2013: 507-8.
[79] Alfred was otherwise occupied pursuing Northumbrian and East Anglian forces across western Wessex: Smyth 1995: 132. The West Saxon leaders were close associates of Alfred. According to the chronicler Æthelweard, Æthelhelm had led the party which carried the alms of King Alfred and the West Saxons to Rome in 887, and Æthelnoth had shared the tribulations of Alfred when the king was forced to seek refuge in the marshes of Athelney in 878, and in 894 led a force to York, probably to negotiate with Sigeferth *piraticus*, who held a large territory to the west of Stamford, between the Welland and Kesteven, though the outcome is unknown: Campbell 1962: 42, 47, 51; Stenton 1970: 10.
[80] Giles 1892: I 231.

the early 880s until Anarawd submitted to Alfred c.890. That alliance of a decade or so could well have led to the establishment of small enclaves of Vikings in the wider area.[81]

From a puzzling reference in a charter of 855 by Burgred, King of the Mercians, we are told that the charter was granted *quando fuerunt pagani Wreocensetun* 'when the pagans were in the province of the Wrekin-dwellers'.[82] Those *pagani* are generally understood to have been transient Danish raiders rather than established Scandinavian colonists[83] (although that conclusion may be open to question), and it is not certain whether Buttington was within or outside the territory of the *Wreocensæte*,[84] but Roger of Wendover's claim – perhaps originating in northern annals now lost originating from York[85] – that there were Danes living at or near Buttington in 893, a claim not found in any other chronicle, cannot be lightly dismissed. We can probably rule out the possibility that the details were invented by Roger, who is generally held to be a reliable chronicler, but we cannot know how trustworthy his sources were.[86] Roger's claims are however reinforced to some degree by entries in the Irish *Annals of Ulster*, which record under the year 855 that a certain Orm, 'leader of the Black Gentiles' (*Dubgennti*, i.e. Dark Foreigners or *Dubhgaill*) was slain by Rhodri Mawr (father of Anarawd),[87] an episode perhaps associated with the reference to the *pagani* in the territory of the *Wreocensæte* mentioned above (in which case the *pagani* were Hiberno-Norse rather than Danes), or linked to the devastion of Anglesey by the 'Black Gentiles' recorded two years earlier in Welsh sources. Those same sources show that the Danes continued to harass the country between Caernarvon and the Dee.[88] In 853 king Beorhtwulf of Mercia (840-52) and king Æthelwulf of Wessex (839-58) launched a joint assault against the Welsh,[89] perhaps in part to deal with a Viking presence. Other Welsh annals (though in manuscripts written much later)[90] also mention Danes in Wales: *Brenhinedd y Saesson* records under the year 890 (correctly 892): 'the Black Norsemen came again to Gwyn',[91] an event also recorded in *Brut y Tywysogion* which notes that in 890 'the Black Normans came a second time to Castle Baldwin', which can be identified as Hen Domen (also known as Old Montgomery, not to be confused with the present town of Montgomery), lying at the strategically important ford of Rhydwhiman[92] on the river Severn, some seven miles from Buttington.[93] Neither

---

[81] Charles-Edwards 2013: 482, 489-90. The reference to the *pagani* recorded in the territory of the *Wreocensæte*, 'the people associated with the Wrekin', in a Mercian charter of 855 (S.206), may also be noted: see Gelling 1992: 83; also Whitelock 1955: I 90; 485-6; Finberg 1961: 48 no. 77. Peddie 1999: 179 suggests that the Buttington area may have been settled in about 890 by Danes infiltrating up the river from the Bristol Channel.
[82] S.206.
[83] See for example Gelling 1992: 134. For a brief discussion of the reference to the *pagani* see Hill 2001: 175.
[84] See for example Hart 1977: 48, 50, 53-4, where Offa's Dyke, which passes through Buttington, is taken as the western boundary of the *Wreocensæte*.
[85] Gransden 1996: 359; Graves 1975: 297. Wendover's history of this period has been described as 'a mere collection of elegant extracts, transcribed from earlier books': Galbraith 1982: X 15.
[86] The idea that the nucleas of his chronicle was a compilation, extending to 1188, of John de Cella, abbot of St Albans 1195-1214, is still debated, but even if it was, Cella's work must have been a compilation and not an original work: Gross 1900: 310; Graves 1975: 451-2; Gransden 1996: 359.
[87] *Annales Cambriæ* and *Brut y Tywysogion*, s.a. 853; Wainwright 1975: 86-7.
[88] Wainwright 1975: 87.
[89] Williams, Smyth and Kirby 1991: 68.
[90] Jack 1972: 25-32.
[91] Jones 1971: 24-5.
[92] Rhydwhiman is the anglicised Welsh name Rhyd Chwima: Davies 2006: 23.

annal indicates when the Danes first came to the area,[94] but there were Hiberno-Norse settlers in the Wirral and Southern Lancashire at this period,[95] and the Vikings are known to have ravaged Gwynedd and other parts of Wales in the mid-890s.[96] In the same year (855) that *pagani* are recorded in the territory of the *Wreocensæte* is a reference in another charter to 'those men called in Saxon *Walhfæreld*', a term meaning literally 'Welsh expedition',[97] which is not fully understood by historians, but might well be connected with the presence of the *pagani*, perhaps denoting a mobile force created to react quickly to Viking incursions into Wales and the Welsh Marches.

The *Anglo-Saxon Chronicle* records how after a siege of 'many weeks' some of the Danes at Buttington starved to death,[98] and others, having eaten their horses to survive, made a

---

[93] Both place-names were transferred to the new castle at Montgomery Trefaldwyn, which lies a little under two miles away, c.1224: Morgan 2001: 137-8; Owen and Morgan 2007: 328.
[94] Williams ab Ithel 1860a: 16-17.
[95] Bu'lock 1972: 51.
[96] Downham 2009: 205. Further evidence to support a possible Viking presence in Wales is found in Asser's *Life* of king Alfred, where we are told that in 895 the sons of Rhodri were trying to control Ceredigion, which lay between Gwynedd and Dyfed in south-west Wales. This curious entry remains unexplained, but led David Dumville to wonder whether the Scandinavians may have taken control: Smyth 2002: 129. The action is presumably to be associated with the puzzling entry in the *Annales Cambriae* which records that in the same year 'Anarawd came with the English – *cum Anglis* – to lay waste Ceredigion and Ystrad Tywi': Smyth 2002: 128. Smyth has concluded that Asser's chapter on Welsh rulers in the 880s and 890s, perhaps based on a set of Welsh king-lists, may be the most valuable section of the entire work, conspicuous for its density of apparently genuine information, the 'consistency of its Welshness and the consistency of content in regard to dynastic information', in contrast with the remainder of this 'vague and derivative biography' and 'the poverty and glaring ignorance of the rest of the *Life*'. Asser provides the names of six Welsh rulers, four king's fathers and names four Welsh territories: Smyth 2002: 125-6, 130. Wendy Davies has concluded that between c.960 and 1015 Scandinavians were actually controlling Gwynedd, either from the Isle of Man or Dublin or indeed from bases within Wales itself: the various members of the Gwynedd dynasty were referred to as 'holding' Gwynedd. They were not called 'kings', and were paying tribute to the Vikings: Davies 1990: 59. It may be added that no place-names incorporating Norse elements have been traced by the present author in the wider area around Buttington, but Professor Hywel Wyn Owen considers that the place-name Bretton, attached to a village in Flintshire close to the Cheshire border, incorporates the ON *Bretar* 'Britons', implying that Bretton was settled by Scandinavianised Welsh speakers: Wyn Owen 1994: 20-21; Wyn Owen: 2013: 324-5.
[97] S.207; Whitelock 1979: 527-8.
[98] The O.S. 6" map of 1890-1 shows, in addition to 'Site of Battle fought between the Saxons and the Danes A.D. 984' on the north-east side of Buttington Bridge, the words 'Human Remains found here A.D. 1838' on the east side of the Severn at Buttington Green, between the old vicarage and the river Severn. All archaeological notices of this kind on O.S. maps of the period must be treated with suspicion, but there is some evidence of the discovery of human bones here. One of the earliest reports, if not the first, is found in GM,1837 [*sic*], page 638: 'At Buttington, near [Welsh]Pool, Montgomeryshire, in digging the foundation for a school-house, near the church, the workmen's labours were lately interrupted by the discovery of imense quantities of human skulls huddled together in holes, with other bones of the human frame scattered around, to the amount of several cartloads. Ninety skulls were taken from one hole, and upwards of 300 are ranged in grisly show in the church. In many the teeth are perfect, and most of them exhibit symptoms of having belonged to men in the prime of life...'. *The Shrewsbury Chronicle* of 1838 recorded the discovery in the following terms: 'A workman having been employed in the churchyard of Buttington, Montgomeryshire, to dig the foundation for a school-room, was interrupted in his labour by a very extraordinary discovery of immense quantities of human skulls, and several cartloads of human bones. In one circular hole, three feet and a half in diameter and three feet and a half deep, were found one hundred skulls, all arranged in mechanical order, facing the east, and covered with a single range of thigh and leg bones, belonging respectively to each other. In the other two holes, about the

desperate attempt to break out on the eastern side of the river and fought their way through the besieging army, killing Ordheah and many other king's thegns, and despite 'many thousands' of casualties, managed to make their escape and journey to Essex. Roger of Wendover's account tells us that the faithful (the English) drowned numbers of the pagans and put others to the sword, with those who escaped fleeing to Chester, whose English name is *Wyrhale* (Wirral) where they found numbers of their countrymen in a certain town, and were admitted by them into their fraternity.[99] Perhaps significantly, it was the great victory of Æthelred 'in which countless numbers were slain' which was recorded in contemporary Irish annals, rather than those won elsewhere by Alfred.[100]

Yet the *Anglo-Saxon Chronicle* account of the action at Buttington leaves many questions unanswered, and indeed suggests that this was a campaign where the so-called victory was of a curious nature, inferring that at this period anything other than outright defeat may have been seen as a victory, for it records an enemy so weakened by hunger that it was reduced to eating its horses,[101] but sufficiently strong to break through the English lines,

---

same depth, but very irregularly formed, were deposited in each about one hundred skulls, intermixed with a great number of bones, and all the cavities, containing a space of fourteen feet by five feet, were completely overlaid by bones. The teeth in very many of the jaw-bones were as perfect and fresh as though they had recently been interred. Nearly three hundred skulls, all appearing in the same stage of decomposition, are arranged in the church for inspection of visitors, great numbers of whom have seen the above remains of mortality. ...': Boyd Dawkins 1873: 141-2. These early accounts of the discovery of skulls and bones (mentioned in various versions in many publications thereafter, for example Musson and Spurgeon 1988: 106-7) do not mention any cuts or other damage to the bones (despite later references to the contrary: see Musson andSpurgeon 1988: 106), but Boyd Dawkins 1873: 142 says that some of the skulls had been fractured, and the men to whom they belonged had evidently come to a violent death. He also notes that the jaw-bone of a horse and some teeth were found in one of the pits. One would like to know more about the source for his statements, made some 35 years after the discovery. The accounts of the siege of Buttington say that many Danes died of starvation, which would have left no trace on skeletal remains. Two skulls (one illustrated on the cover of this volume, both lacking teeth) now in the Powysland Museum in Welshpool are reputed to be from the discovery of 1837 (Redknap 2000: 32). It has been suggested that Buttington was the scene in 1039 of the battle of Rhyd-y-Groes, the important initial victory of Gruffydd ap Llewlyn over the English, and that the bones may have been associated with that battle: Musson and Spurgeon 1998: 106. However, recent scientific analysis at the National Museum of Wales has revealed that two skulls from Buttington, presumably those mentioned above, are of more recent date than the battles of 893 or 1039: CPATReport 1134 (2012). The CPAT SMR gives the date of the present church building at Buttington as perhaps 14th century, but there has been a church on the site from at least 1265, when it was part of the manor of Strata Marcella (Ystrad Marchall), an abbey founded originally in 1170 at an unknown location thought to be near Welshpool, and relocated in 1172 to the west bank of the Severn a little over a mile south of Buttington (at SJ25131042). The bones might perhaps be associated with that relocation. It may also be noted that in 1892 large quantities of human bones were found in the nave of Llanmerewig church, a few miles up the Severn from Buttington, and at Bettws Cedewain in 1906: Riggings and Evans Jones 1910: 98.

[99] Giles 1892: 231. Roger has evidently conflated the aftermath of the battle with the return of the Danes after they had regrouped as mentioned below.

[100] Smyth 1995: 132; Walker 2000: 85. In 893 the *Annals of Ulster* records the major defeat of 'dark foreigners' at the hands of the English, which Claire Downham suggests was the battle of Buttington, a party of Vikings having left Dublin the same year: Downham 2009: 72. Jarl Sihfric, who led one of the contingents from Dublin, has been tentatively identified with Sihfric, leader of a Northumbrian fleet that attacked Wessex the same year. A useful summary of the siege of Buttington and its background is found in Earle and Plummer 1892-99: II 108.

[101] Whilst there is some slight archaeological evidence that the Anglo-Saxons ate horsemeat (see Page 1970: 90), the *Sagas of the Norse Kings* suggests that the practice was frowned upon by the

slaying many high-ranking Englishmen in the process. Furthermore, despite the reported loss of 'many thousands',[102] it is clear that a significant proportion of those escaping Danes managed to make their way, presumably on foot (if, as claimed, their horses had starved and been eaten), through the encircling Anglo-Saxons, and travelled unharmed through hostile Mercia to reach Danish territory, for later in the year they had regrouped and assembled a great army drawn from East Anglia and Northumbria, and, placing their women and ships and property in safety in East Anglia,[103] returned to their offensive in the north-west Midlands.

Before the onset of winter, moving 'continuously by day and night', they evaded the English forces led by lieutenants of Alfred and Æthelred trying to overtake them (presumably using Watling Street and the arrow-straight Roman road, now partly traceable only as cropmarks, which ran from *Pennocrucium* (Water Eaton, south of Penkridge)[104] to Chester, then described as 'a deserted city in the Wirral', which place they occupied.[105] According to Roger of Wendover and Matthew Paris (the latter's work based on the former),[106] they were admitted by numbers of their countrymen, indicating that there were Danes then living within the city.[107] Laying siege to the fortification, the English forces seized cattle and stocks of corn in the neighbourhood to deny them to the enemy, and slaughtered those Danes who ventured outside the fortification, but, for reasons which remain unexplained, apparently lifted the siege after only two days, evidently having agreed terms with the enemy. Quite why the English concluded a pact with the Danes, who would seem to have been in a perilously weak position, is unclear, but the Danes were forced by lack of supplies to raid Wales in 894. According to early Welsh annals such as *Brut y Tywysogion, Brenhinedd y Saesson* and the thirteenth-century collection known as the *Annales Cambriae*, there were Viking attacks on England, Brycheiniog, Morgannwg,

---

Vikings: Griffith 1995: 104. For reference to a papal prohibition on the eating of horseflesh see Lavelle 2010: 229, fn.75.

[102] It has been suggested that the Viking Great Army that was active from 892 to 896 could scarcely have exceeded a few thousand troops, with the other Viking armies probably considerably less: Logan 1991: 167.

[103] See Smyth 1995: 121, who suggests that this and similar *Chronicle* references point towards a genuine migration of peoples intent on settlement rather than an isolated raiding party.

[104] Margary route 19: Margary 1973: 293.

[105] The comment may simply mean that its citizens had fled in the face of the Scandinavian advance, for there is evidence of occupation in Chester at this period, in particular the supposed transfer of the relics of St Werburgh from Hanbury in 874 to prevent them falling into the hands of Danes from Repton, which if true would indicate a functioning church and associated community, and some churches may have had a much earlier history: see Bu'lock 1972: 51-2; VCH Cheshire I 250, 252, 268; Griffiths 2001: 169. However, the tradition of the transfer of the saint's relics has not been traced to an earlier date than Ranulph Higden's *Polychronicon* completed in 1352, and a more likely date for the translation is after the refortification of Chester in 907: Lewis 2008: 114-5. A mint may have been operating in Chester during the last years of the tenth century, possibly in a *wic* outside the walls, as in London (Lyon 2001: 75), which might indicate a period of relative peace, since a mint is unlikely to have been established in an unprotected location in unsettled times. Furthermore, the Irish *Three Fragments*, though of dubious historical value, record that Ingimund, expelled from Dublin with his forces in 901, coveted the wealth and rich lands of Chester: O'Donovan 1860: 230-7; Wainwright 1975: 79-87. There is considerable evidence of Roman saltworking at Middlewich but less at Northwich and Nantwich in the Roman period, though by the time of Domesday these and other nearby places in Cheshire were clearly thriving salt-producing centres and the focus of established long-distance route-ways: VCH Cheshire I 198-211, 328-9. The significance of salt production to the Scandinavians is unclear.

[106] See e.g. Galbraith 1982: X 5-48.

[107] Luard 1872: 431; Giles 1892: 231; Bu'lock 1972: 51.

Gwent, Buellt and Gwynllwg in south Wales,[108] with the raiders reaching as far as Monmouthshire and Glamorganshire,[109] before the Danes returned to east Essex and Mersea Island via Danish-held Northumbria and East Anglia.

It will be noted that the *Chronicle* accounts of the siege of Buttington do not suggest that the Danes built a fortification, merely that they took refuge in a fortification. Since the episode closely mirrors another pursuit of the Danes to the Severn at Shropshire two years' later, it is worth examining the nature of the Danish camp in some detail.

In his account of this episode, Florence (John) of Worcester says that the English and Welsh army pursued the Danes and came up to them at Buttington and besieged the fortress to which they had retreated,[110] implying that the Danes took refuge in an existing fortification. Buttington churchyard, which lies just above the flood level, is raised, and the north-west side distinctively curved. A local scholar born at Buttington vicarage in 1838 noted that: 'Buttington is said to be on the east bank of the Severn. Since [the siege of Buttington] the river source has passed to the westward to a distance of about a quarter of a mile. Its ancient course, however, is still marked by a small brook running close under the churchyard, and which finds its way into the Severn by the "main ditch" ... It is quite possible to trace at the present time the boundaries of the Danish camp. It was defended on the north-west by the river Severn; on the east by a rampart running parallel, or nearly so, with the road to Forden; on the north-east by the churchyard wall; and on the south by the depression which runs down from the present line of the Forden road behind the Vicarage garden down to what was then the old course of the Severn. It may also have included the site of the out-buildings opposite to the Green Dragon Inn.'.[111]

Another writer in 1900 says: 'Here are plainly to be seen the remains of a camp answering exactly to the requirements of the Danish position, now occupied by the churchyard and the vicarage grounds. Offa's dyke (since leveled at that place, to form the Leighton road) fenced it on the east. On the south side, at right angles to the dyke, there remain a strong bank and a broad deep ditch, partly filled in. The western bank has been leveled into its ditch, with a slope to the swampy ground between it and the river. The northern defences were destroyed in the making of the Welshpool-Shrewsbury road.'[112] An examination of

---

[108] Downham 2009: 206.
[109] Wainwright 1975: 75-6.
[110] Stevenson 1853: 69.
[111] Boyd Dawkins 1873: 145.
[112] Dymond 1900: 346. Swanton 1996: 87 mentions the remains of a sub-rectangular elevated area, formerly entrenched, of almost 5 acres recorded in 1899 and 1912, evidently the earthwork mentioned by Musson and Spurgeon 1988: 106-7; Gelling 1992: 111-12; Peddie 1999: 180. Redknap 2000: 32-33, having noted references in 1870 to a 'rampart' on the east side of the church running almost parallel with the road to Forden, says that the site of a supposed rectangular fortification of about 120 metres by 170 metres remains unproven. Although the various nineteenth century accounts suggest that there were indeed earthworks of some type to be seen, their age and original purpose must remain uncertain, and it is worth noting that modern maps show no island at Buttington, but the 1890-16" O.S. map indicates that the land adjoining the Severn in this area is liable to flooding, which may suggest that the river course has changed since 893. Indeed, in the context of an investigation into the line of Offa's Dyke as it approached the river Severn at Buttington it has been noted that: 'The area of the floodplain at Buttington has a very complex depositional history with at least two former channels of the River Severn ... and silts up to several metres deep as the present river channel is approached.'.[112] The investigation concluded that the Dyke probably did not cross the Severn at Buttington but continued somewhere on the higher ground of the old river terrace on the east side of the river between Buttington and Llandrinio, although the precise route was not

the area by the present author in 2008 failed to detect any obvious earthworks, and it seems unlikely that it will ever be possible to throw further light on the accounts of earlier commentators.[113]

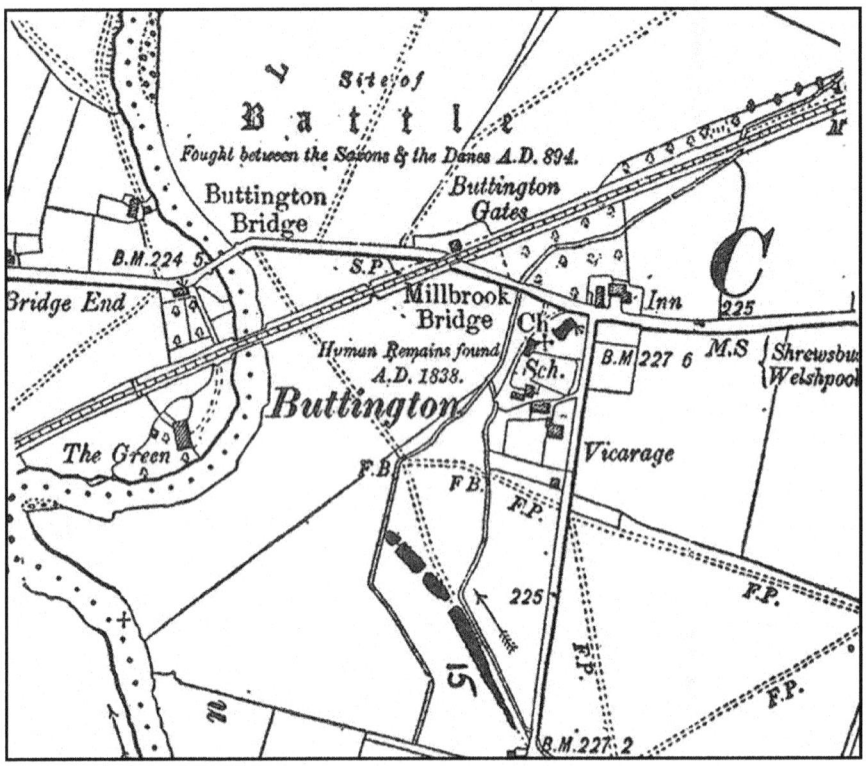

Extract from the 1934 6" Ordnance Survey map of Buttington showing the supposed site of the battle between the English and the Danes in 893 [sic] and the place where a vast quantity of human bones was found in 1837 [sic]. The heavy broken black line lower centre marks what was thought to be the line of Offa's Dyke, which is now believed to have continued north along the higher ground on the east side of the river.

The years around 893 were clearly a wretched period for at least some of the Welsh kingdoms, for English troops appear to have allied with Anarawd to ravage other Welsh

---

identified. It was noted that the river Severn 'is easily fordable in a number of places' at Buttington: Hill and Worthington 2003: 64-5. Investigations after the discovery of ancient timbers exposed in the banks of the Severn after flooding in 2001, probably part of a mill constructed some time after 1175, showed that this part of the river Severn has been extremely active, and a number of abandoned river channels were identified, one to the east apparently contemporary with Offa's Dyke. The meander on which the timbers were found had moved some 150 feet to the south-east since the early 1960s: *Buttington Medieval Mill Report*, CPAT.
[113] An interesting suggestion is that a fortification built in 915 at Chirbury, near Offa's Dyke, by Æthelflæd, Lady of Mercia, may have been a restoration of a temporary fortress built by English forces in 893 as a base during their siege of the Viking camp at Buttington (Walker 2000: 105), although Chirbury lies over 6 miles south of Buttington.

territories, perhaps as a reward for Anarawd's support at Buttington.[114] But it was not only the Welsh who were living in fear, for after the siege at Buttington a certain Sihtric, leading a large fleet from Northumbria, made two raids against Wessex before returning to Northumbria, and in 894, so Æthelweard tells us, a huge Viking fleet from Boulogne reached Kent.[115] That led to Alfred despatching *ealdorman* Æthelnoth, who had led the West Saxon forces at Buttington and was evidently a crucial figure in Alfred's entourage at that time, as an emissary to York to negotiate a peace treaty, though there is no record of what, if anything, was agreed.[116]

---

[114] Smyth 2002: 124-6; Downham 2009: 204.
[115] Campbell 1962: 51.
[116] Downham 2009: 74. The event demonstrates that diplomatic relations continued despite ongoing warfare.

3. The wintering of the Danes at *Cwatbrycge* in 895-6.

The next major campaign – unless the Chronicles have overlooked some important event, which cannot be ruled out – occurred in the late autumn or early winter of 895 when those Vikings who had escaped from the siege of Buttington and returned to east Essex and Mersea Island earlier that year after wintering in Chester and ravaging parts of Wales, carrying off 'immense booty',[117] 'rowed their ships up the Thames and up the Lea' and established a fortress by the Lea, some 20 miles north of London,[118] perhaps to procure supplies for the great army, and overwintered there. The following summer 'a great part of the [English] citizens (*burgwara*)', presumably from London, and many others, tried unsuccessfully to storm the fortress, with four king's thegns dying in the process. That led Alfred to lead an army to the Lea to protect the English harvesters.[119] Those forces, almost certainly supported by Mercian forces (London lying in Mercia), began to build two forts, one on either side of the river, perhaps part of a barrier in the form of a chain stretched between the forts to deny the Vikings the use of their ships. Realising that their vessels were trapped, the Danes sent their womenfolk – whose existence suggests that this was no mere raiding-army – to East Anglia for safety, and fled, probably on horseback,[120] since the *Chronicle* recounts that 'the English army rode after the enemy'. The Danes may have been led by a battle-hardened commander, Hun(c)deus,[121] or perhaps even Haesten, who had led the Danes to Buttington in 893. In the meantime the serviceable Danish ships were taken to London, showing that the English utilised captured vessels, and the others (which the Danes may have disabled) were destroyed.[122]

Doubtless guided by warriors who had campaigned along the Severn only two years' previously, the Danish forces, pursued by the English army,[123] reached a place by the river

---

[117] Stevenson 1853: 70.

[118] Unidentified; not at Hertford, as sometimes suggested: see Williams 1999: 187 fn.106; Dumville 1992: 8-9 note 47.

[119] It is worth noting that the river Lea formed the boundary between the East and West Saxons, but more importantly in the late ninth century it (with the section upon which Hertford lay) was part of the Danelaw boundary negotiated at some date between 878 and 890 by King Alfred and Guthrum: Keynes and Lapidge 1983: 171-2, 311-12; Cubitt 1995: 298-300 (with map). Unless the Danes had constructed a fortress on the west side of the Lea (which seems unlikely), it is difficult to see upon what basis Alfred took exception to the Danish presence, which was not prohibited by the boundary treaty, though seems seems to have survived for no more than seven years:: Keynes and Lapidge 1983: 171-2; Davis 1991: 50. It may have been their use of the Lea and their intimidating presence on the boundary or provocations across it which led Alfred to use force against them.

[120] But note that the *Chronicle* of Florence (John) of Worcester (sometimes known as the *Worcester Latin Chronicle*: Smyth 2002: 69) clearly says 'on foot', possibly inferring that the Danes normally travelled by horse or by ship. The use of horses does not of course infer the existence of cavalry. Smyth 1995: 127 says however, without citing references: 'The Danes were almost certainly horsed'. It is known that the Vikings fought on horseback in Francia: there is a reference to Viking cavalry at a battle near Maastricht in 891: Davis 1957: 174, citing a translation of the *Chronicles of Regino of Prüm*, ed. Kurze, 1890: 136 ff. In contrast to the Anglo-Saxons, the Franks relied on cavalry almost exclusively: ibid. 175 fn.2.

[121] He was named as the leader of the contingent that reached the Seine in 893 in five large ships (*barchis*), according to the *Annals of St Vast*: Keynes and Lapidge 1983: 288. The Danes under Hun(c)deus caused much damage, but in 894 he was baptised with King Charles (the Simple) as sponsor, and may subsequently have returned to Northumbria: ibid.

[122] ASC 'A' 89; Swanton 1996: 89.

[123] The identity of the English forces is uncertain: the West Saxon royal army seems to have completed its service, and Walker sees a Mercian or mixed West Saxon and Mercian force under Æthelred's command (Walker 2000: 87), but there is little likelihood that West Saxons would have

Severn recorded in the *Anglo-Saxon Chronicle* as *(æt) Brycge* ['bridge'] or *(æt) Cwatbrycge*.[124] There they built a *geweorc*, or work, an entrenched and pallisaded camp – or reinforced an existing fortification, previously constructed by the Anglo-Saxons, or even the Danes[125] – and spent the whole of the winter of 895 and the spring of 896, before leaving in the summer.[126]

Why should the Danes have retreated under attack at the Lea in the direction of the West Midlands, rather than the (comparative) safety of the Danish-controlled Danelaw? The answer is probably to be associated with the river Severn, at which the Danes fleeing from the river Lea two years' earlier had dug-in against their Anglo-Saxon pursuers. The evidence seems to point towards a small but growing Danish presence somewhere in the central and northern Marches area (if the admittedly opaque and later comments of the chronicler Roger of Wendover are to be believed), perhaps near Buttington and probably adjoining or close to the Severn, as well as the greater Scandinavian presence in the north-west, an area which was becoming increasingly attractive to the Irish North Sea Vikings towards the end of the ninth and, especially, the early years of the tenth century. One specific area associated with the Vikings at this period was centred on and around the Wirral which, if the annals are to be believed, was to be granted by Æthelflæd to Hiberno-Scandinavian immigrants fleeing Dublin, but that was c.903, after they had been forced by the Welsh to abandon plans to settle in parts of North Wales, including Anglesey, a scenario discussed in more detail elsewhere in this volume. The Danes at *Cwatbrycge* in 895 had perhaps been prevented by English (and perhaps Welsh) forces from reaching allies in North Wales and were forced to seek refuge as they were attempting to cross the Severn at one of the few bridges across this major river.

---

served under Æthelred. Henry of Huntingdon says King Alfred led the army (Forester 1853: 159), which is possible but unlikely: Alfred is not mentioned in other chronicles, and it has been suggested that some of the details in Henry of Huntingdon not found elsewhere are likely to be figments of the imagination: Gross 1900: 292.

[124] ASC 'B' and 'C'; ASC 'A'. For a discussion on OE *æt* in this context see Lundskær-Nelson 1993: 81-94. Davis 1991: 50 notes that Watling Street would have been the shortest route from the River Lea to *Cwatbrycge*, but that is debateable: a deviation along the Roman road to Eatington, Alcester, Droitwich and Greensforge may have been more direct (Margary 1973), though the absence of maps probably ensured that major roads were preferred, and in any event Davis's statement assumes that the Danes had a specific destination in mind, which may not have been the case. Powel records that the Danes '... passed spoiling the land to Quadbryge vpon Seaverne, and so passed the river, and spoiled the counties of Brecknock, Gwentland, and Gwentlhwg': Powel 1584: 34.

[125] The reference to the 'countrymen [of the Danes] who dwelt in the western part of England' and the inference that there was an existing Danish settlement or fortification at Buttington and perhaps others elsewhere in the region has been mentioned previously, and is perhaps to be connected with a reference to the *pagani* recorded in the territory of the *Wreocensæte*, 'the people associated with the Wrekin', in a Mercian charter of 855 (S.206; see Gelling 1992: 83; also Whitelock 1955: I 90; 485-6; Finberg 1961: 48 no. 77), though entries in the *Brut y Tywysogion* record at about this date an attack against Anglesey by the Black Pagans (ab Ithel 1860: 12-13), in which case the *pagani* were Hiberno-Norse rather than Danes. If Peddie is correct in suggesting that the Buttington area may have been settled in about 890 by Danes infiltrating up the river from the Bristol Channel (Peddie 1999: 179), a pre-existing Danish fortification at *Cwatbrycge*, perhaps incorporating an earlier – possibly a much earlier – Anglo-Saxon fortress at this major river-crossing, would be readily explicable. The Welsh annals record a campaign by Æthelred and Ananrawd of Gwynedd against Ceredigion and Ystrad Tywi in central Wales in 895: Smyth 2002: 128-9. That campaign may have been connected with the wintering of the Danes at *Cwatbrycge*: Walker suggests that it may have been designed in part to to prevent supplies or help reaching the Danes (Walker 2000: 87), though there is no evidence that they were denied supplies, as was clearly the case at Buttington.

[126] Earle and Plummer 1894-9: I 89.

During the wintering of the Danes at *Cwatbrycge* we can be certain that a sizeable English force would have been encamped nearby – possibly at the still impressive Iron-Age earthworks at Chesterton, some 4½ miles north-west of Quatford – watching nervously for signs that the enemy might be on the move. King Alfred himself may conceivably have been present for at least some of the time during the Danes' sojourn at *Cwatbrycge*, since he had been in command at the siege at the Lea, and we know that the English army had followed the Danes to *Cwatbrycge*. Alfred might have been at its head, but it is far more likely that (as at Buttington) a senior West Saxon *earldorman*, supported by a senior Mercian *ealdorman*, almost certainly Æthelred himself, took control of the West Saxon and Mercian forces respectively.

Neither English nor Danes will have relished a full-scale battle at *Cwatbrycge* – such encounters were generally avoided by both sides – but why the English forces chose not to lay siege to and starve out the Danish camp, as they had done half-successfully at the Lea and (perhaps even less successfully, despite the upbeat account in the *Chronicle*) at Buttington, remains a puzzle, as does the protracted stay by the Danes. Certainly the wintering of the Danes at *Cwatbrycge* will have created serious supply problems for both Danish and English forces. A powerful Mercian and West Saxon army would have been well-placed to successfully besiege an encircled Danish warband far from the Danelaw which had fled without, one assumes, the usual accoutrements of a warband acting in attack mode. Since the Danes remained for several months, one is forced to conclude that there must have been some sort of accommodation or pact between the leaders of the English and Danish forces, whereby the Danes were perhaps provided with supplies – and doubtless coin and bullion – and given assurances that they would not be attacked, in return for the usual sworn oaths (almost invariably worthless) that they would depart peacefully. Yet it is difficult to understand why the English forces should have allowed – indeed perhaps supported – the Danes to winter at *Cwatbrycge*, and thereafter leave with impunity.[127]

One possible explanation may be found in the *Anglo-Saxon Chronicle*, which, after recording the wintering of the Danes on the Severn, continues: 'The raiding-army, by the grace of God, had not altogether crushed the English race [doubtless meaning the West Saxon kingdom]; but they were a great deal more crushed in those three years with pestilence among cattle and men, most of all by the fact that many of the best of the king's thegns there were in the land passed away in those three years', and then names eight *ealdormen*, bishops, thegns and a reeve who had all died, adding that there were many others in addition.[128] In an age when murrain and epidemics were the norm, the *Chronicle* account can only be explained by an exceptionally virulent and widespread outbreak of disease affecting man and beast. Deaths from pestilence – probably plague, more specifically perhaps anthrax or some similar murrain, which is known to have broken out in the 890s[129] – of *ealdormen* who were leading military officers, added to the loss in 893 of the king's thegn and many other senior figures fighting at Buttington, evidently

---

[127] The scenario is in some ways reminiscent of events in 914, discussed more fully elsewhere in this volume, when the men of Gloucestershire and Herefordshire defeated a fleeing Danish raiding army at the battle of Archenfield and cornered the survivors in an enclosure, taking hostages to guarantee the oaths of the Danes to leave peacefully, although we might assume that the English forces could easily have stormed the enclosure and killed the enemy: ASC 'A'; Swanton 1996: 98.
[128] Swanton 1996: 89-91.
[129] Cantor 2001: 11-21, 63-; Hinton 1990: 68. Evidence from subsequent epidemics of plague suggests that a high mortality is likely: see generally Cantor 2001. Stewart Lyon has noted what may have been an economic downturn during this period: Lyon 2001: 75.

persuaded Alfred to abandon thoughts of any attack on the besieged Danes at *Cwatbrycge*.[130] The Welsh annals record the harrying of Ceredigion and Ystrad Tywi at about this time by Anarawd and the English,[131] but whether this is to be associated with the events at *Cwatbrycge* – perhaps one of the measures taken by Æthelred to prevent supplies or reinforcements reaching the trapped Danes – is unknown.

The wintering of the Danes might be seen as confirmation that the human cost to the English of the siege at Buttington two years' earlier (when plague was evidently even then affecting at least some parts of the country) had been far greater than we are led to suppose from the chronicles, and that the escape of so many Danes had been in reality no victory for the English. Attacking the Danes at *Cwatbrycge* must have been judged by the English commanders as simply too risky. But perhaps we are trying to make sense of a jigsaw where too many pieces are missing.

It is not impossible, though hardly likely, that the Danes built ships during their wintering to replace those lost in Alfred's blockade as the renowned Shropshire medievalist R. W. Eyton evidently believed.[132] Indeed, their long stay could plausibly be explained by that activity, which would have permitted a ready escape down the Severn, although the presence of numerous fish-weirs which existed in the Anglo-Saxon period may have made such navigation tricky – it is said that as late as the mid-fifteenth century the Severn was navigable upstream only as far as Bewdley,[133] though the Danes were adept at hauling their ships for surprising distances around obstacles. We might imagine that if they were in need of ships they would have been demanded from the English in return for an agreement to depart. English ships by this date are likely to have come close to the impressively seaworthy longships of the Danes, if we are to believe the *Chronicle* accounts that speak of a new design of vessels ordered to be built by King Alfred in 896,[134] but we have seen that the seaworthy vessels left by the Danes at the river Lea before they fled to *Cwatbrycge* had been taken to London, and it is not inconceivable (though in truth hardly likely) that the Danes negotiated their return before leaving *Cwatbrycge*. Whatever the case, when they left their wintering camp, one part of the Danish force went to East Anglia, the other to Northumbria,[135] where 'those that were moneyless/without treasure' (*feohlease*, from Old English *feoh* 'money, treasure, wealth'), perhaps implying a pay-off negotiated to secure their withdrawal,[136] 'got themselves ships, and went south across the sea to the Seine'.[137]

---

[130] It is of course possible that the Danes successfully resisted attacks on their camp, a scenario that is unlikely to have been reported in the chronicles.
[131] Ab Ithel 1860: 15.
[132] Eyton 1854-60: I 105 fn.4; III 214.
[133] VCH Worcester II 250. In the 18th century the river was said to be navigable to within a mile of Welshpool: Gough 1806: I 389.
[134] ASC 'A'; Swanton 1996: 90. The Sutton Hoo ship-burial attests to the ship-building skills of the 6th century, but a century after Alfred's shipbuilding refinements, the Viking fleet still had the edge over those of its enemies: Lapidge et al 2001: 419-20.
[135] It may be noted that the ASC 'A' records that in 896 the coast of Wessex was greatly harassed by forces from East Anglia and Northumbria, most of all with 'askrs' (warships) they had built many years before. There follows an extraordinarily detailed account of new, larger, English warships said to have been designed by Alfred and a battle at sea between English and Danes naming some of the English dead and the capture of two Danish ships, whose crews were taken before Alfred at Winchester who ordered them to be hanged: Swanton 1996: 90-1. We cannot know whether Danes who had wintered at *Cwatbrycge* were involved in that campaign.
[136] It has been suggested that *feohleas* means the proceeds of the Danish raiding, that is, money and valuable goods, and possibly even livestock [although whether a fleeing army under siege will have been encumbered by livestock must be debateable]. 'Those who had 'property' would have been able

The most straightforward explanation of the phrase 'those that were moneyless/without treasure', and the (presumably) peaceful conclusion to the wintering and departure of the Danes, suggest they had shared their looted coinage and other booty less than equally, and that some will have benefited at the expense of others from any payments made by Alfred and Æthelred. Another interpretation, however, is that those who elected not to receive *feoh* and leave overland were provided instead with vessels to make their escape. This is the last knowledge we have of the infamous Hæsten, who thereafter disappears from history, but not perhaps of those who wintered at Cwatbrycge, for when writing of a Viking raid into the Severn estuary in 914, Florence (John) of Worcester describes the Danes as the 'pagan pirates, who nearly nineteen years before had quitted Britain and gone to Gaul',[138] presumably those who had wintered at *Cwatbrycge* in 895-6.[139] The Norman monk Dudo of St. Quentin, evidently no great admirer, tells us that '[Hæsten] was a man accursed: fierce, mightily cruel, and savage, hostile, sombre, truculent, given to outrage, pestilent and untrustworthy, fickle and lawless. Death-dealing, uncouth, fertile in ruses, warmonger, general, traitor, fomenter of evil, and double-dyed dissimulator ...'.[140]

Little is known of other matters affecting the Severn region at this period, but a reference in the Welsh chronicle *Brenhinedd y Saesson* to England and Brycheiniog and Gwent and Gwynllwg being ravaged in 896[141] hints at other actions about which we have no other details (but probably not by Danes from *Cwatbrycge*, who will have been carefully cordoned by the English), and there were doubtless very many more episodes which have been lost in history. Yet an account of a Mercian assembly held in 896 at Gloucester,

---

to use it to acquire land on which to settle, where they might still hope to make their fortunes': Keynes and Lapidge 1983: 288. The reference to those without money might imply that tribute was paid by the English in return for the Danes leaving peacefully, which would further explain why the English chose not to attack the Danish camp. Payment of what is usually called Danegeld (an expression not recorded during the Anglo-Saxon period, when the term *heregeld* 'army tax', or sometimes *gafol* 'tribute', was used, but a concept which, as tribute, existed in the early Anglo-Saxon kingdoms: Oswiu of Northumbria attempted to buy peace from the pagan Mercian king Penda c.655) is well-evidenced in other cases in contemporary Frankish sources. In 861 Charles the Bald made a payment of 5,000 lbs of silver and large quantities of livestock and corn 'so the realm should not be looted', and it is reasonable to assume that similar payments were demanded by Viking armies in England. In 882 the Vikings extorted from Francia 2,412 lbs of 'purest gold and silver', and two years later 12,000 lbs of gold and silver. Between 845 and 886 at least 39,700 lbs of silver was paid to the Vikings by the Franks: Logan 1991: 122. References to buying off the Danes appear in the *Anglo-Saxon Chroniclesubanno*. 865, 872, and 876, although the entry for 991 wrongly assigns the first payment of tribute to the Danes to the reign of Æthelred II. James Graham-Campbell has estimated that the geld paid by England to Viking raiders between 991 and 1014 alone amounted to 36 million coins: Carver 1987: 77; Williams 2003: 151-3.

[137] The Frankish Annals of 896 record Viking ravages recommencing on the south coast of the Channel after a gap of four summers: Oman 1913: 489. It has been suggested that the Danes who reached the Seine formed the core of the Viking army which after many years of fighting eventually forced Charles the Simple to conclude the Treaty of St-Clair-sur-Epte in 911, which created the region of the Northmen, Normandy, providing many Vikings with a permanent home: Hart 1992: 36.

[138] Stevenson 1853: 75.

[139] It was in 897 (*recte* 896), according to Florence (John) of Worcester, that 'king Alfred ordered ships to be built, of twice the length and twice as deep, which were swifter [than Viking ships] and did not heel so much, so that by their weight they might destroy the enemy's ships. These were put to sea, with orders from the king to take as many prisoners as they could, and to kill such of the enemy as they could not take alive. So in that year twenty ships full of Danish pirates were taken, some of whom were slain, and the rest were brought to the king alive, and hanged on gibbets': Stevenson 1853: 71.

[140] Dudo of St. Quentin's *Gesta Normannorum*, Book 1, Chapter 3.

[141] Jones 1971: 19.

chosen by *ealdorman* Æthelred as the principal Mercian town in place of Tamworth – now dangerously close to, if not on, the border with the Danelaw – has survived and provides a fascinating insight into matters of concern to the Mercian Council at that time.[142] A document recording the assembly tells how the Council, with the consent of king Alfred, 'deliberated there how they could most justly govern their people, both in spiritual and temporal matters, and also do justice to many men, both clerical and lay, with regards to land and other things in which they had been wronged'.[143] Sadly, we are denied details of those deliberations, or of the grievances which were addressed, or at least discussed, but the account goes on to record particular disputes about specific estates in Gloucestershire, with the boundaries of one estate given in some detail. Yet the reference to 'other things in which ... many men, both clerical and lay ... had been wronged' might be seen to be unresolved grievances. Could it be the case that those grievances had contributed in some way to the decision not to attack the Danes at *Cwatbrycge*, or were associated with the disease and murrain that had so badly affected the country?

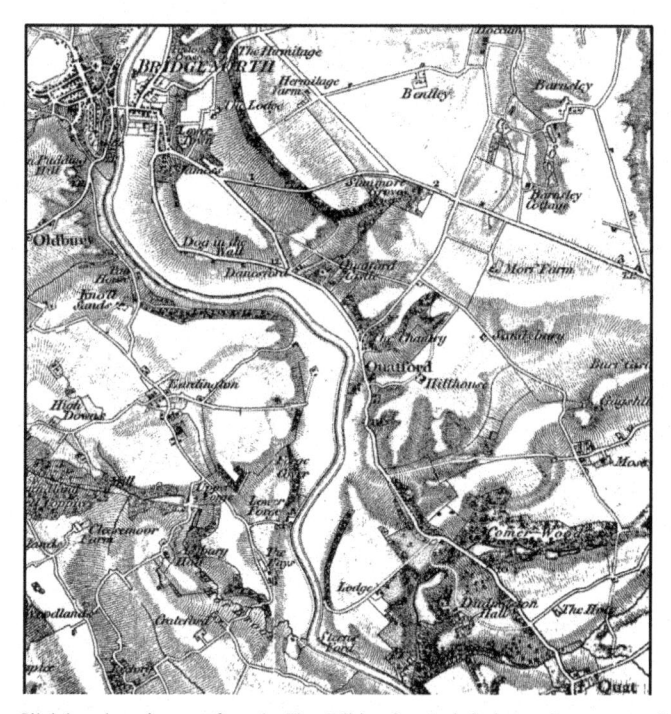

Slightly enlarged extract from the First Edition One-Inch Ordnance Survey map of 1834 on two sheets showing Bridgnorth and the area to the east and south.

Whether the assembly was held before or after the Danes left *Cwatbrycge* is unknown. If before, it shows (if we can take it to be a complete record of the proceedings, which is unlikely) remarkable indifference to the threat posed by the pagans, and if after, it contains

---

[142] S.1441. The document is printed in translation in Thorpe 1853: 122-4; the OE text in Harmer 1914: 24-5, with a translation at 56-7, and notes at 107-9.
[143] Harmer 1914: 56.

nothing which might suggest military activity in the region, and leads us to imagine that there was little concern about how the threat of future raids was to be dealt with. Reading the document, no-one would imagine that any hostilities were taking place, or had recently occurred, less than fifty miles from Gloucester, posing a serious threat to the kingdom. The account might almost suggest, extraordinarily, that the Danes were seen as a temporary local irritation rather than a very real military threat not only to Mercia, but to the whole of England outside the Danelaw. It can only be said that a study of surviving charters from the late ninth and early tenth centuries (as opposed to entries in the *Anglo-Saxon Chronicle*) provides little, if any, evidence to paint English-controlled kingdoms on a war footing. Indeed, the superficially mundane account of the Mercian assembly indicates, on the contrary, that it was 'business as usual', and is notable in particular not for what it contains, but for what it fails to mention.

4. The Danish camp at *Cwatbrycge*.

The location of the place where the Danes wintered in 895-6 has not been identified with certainty. Our only clue, as we have seen, is that the camp is said by the chroniclers, probably writing soon after the events, to have been at *Cwatbrycge* or *Brycge*.[144] Very possibly Eyton was correct in suggesting that the place chosen by the Danes, who invariably selected a strong defensive position for their camps, had no specific name at the time, and *Cwatbrycge* may have been the nearest named place,[145] or perhaps more accurately the nearest structure with a name. Yet in the mid-nineteenth century local people had little doubt where the Danes had camped, for the sandstone crag dominating the village of Quatford, on the east bank of the Severn two miles south-east of Bridgnorth, had supposedly been known from time immemorial – probably meaning 'for longer than we remember' – as Danish Camp and Camp Hill.[146] Could that belief – almost certainly far less long-lived than supposed – have any foundation?

Over the last two centuries or more much has been written about Viking fortifications, one of the best known being the Danish fortification on the east bank of the river Trent at Repton where the Danes wintered in 873-4.[147] The fortification consisted of a D-shaped earthwork with a ditch about 13' deep and 26' wide incorporating the Anglo-Saxon church and encompassing an area of just over 3½ acres (which Martin Biddle has estimated to have taken two hundred men five weeks to construct), incorporating a slipway for ships to the river Trent that then formed the western defences.[148] The Danish camp built at Stamford c.877 lay on the north bank of the river Welland and may have been no more than 2½ acres in area.[149] But these may have represented fall-back defences for use in emergencies, rather than defended encampments, since the Danes were prepared when necessary to create significant defensive earthworks: Asser records that in 871 the Danish leaders Haldan and Bacsecg had their entire camp at Reading defended with a rampart built between the Thames and Kennett,[150] and the wintering camp at Torksey is some 64 acres in area, though no defences have been traced.[151]

---

[144] ASC 'A' gives *Cwatbrycge*, ASC 'B' and 'C' give *Bricge*, ASC 'D' gives *Brygce*, Florence (John) of Worcester gives *Quatbricg*, and Roger of Wendover gives *Quantebregge*. Æthelweard and William of Malmesbury do not mention the matter. Earle and Plummer 1892-99: II 358 confidently asserts that *Cwatbrycge* = Bridgnorth.

[145] Eyton 1854-60: I 104-5.

[146] Wasey 1859: 17. The hill was known as Danish Camp in 1830 (title on watercolour of Quatford Castle produced for John Smalman by Joseph Powell, part of Lot 338, Dreweatt & Bloomsbury Auctions, London, 13 November 2014), and Camp Hill appears on the Tithe Map of 1842. Neither name has been traced before the 19th century. It is noteworthy that the c.1560 map of Bridgnorth identifies the outcrop as *a Rock*, and the 1842 Tithe Map shows the meadow opposite on the east side of the Severn as *Meadow opposite the rock*. Mason claims that the hill was known as Broomy Leasow (*Bromilesoe* 1598 SA 2922/2/23), though his conclusion is unexplained: see TSAS LVII 1961-4 39. An early 13th-century grant mentions 'a selion called *ettecrug* [at *crug*] at Parva Quatford' (SA BB/E/1/2/38), suggesting perhaps that the earliest name of the rock outcrop was Welsh*crug* 'hillock, heap, cairn', although the exact location of 'Little Quatford' remains uncertain.

[147] ASC 'A' and 'E'; Swanton 1996: 72-3.

[148] But see Hadley 2000: 223, where a Viking origin for the earthworks is questioned.

[149] Taylor 1979: 98; Hall 1995: 23; Biddle and Kjølbye-Biddle 2001: 59. Crawford 2003: 61 mentions a D-shaped enclosure on the north bank of the river Fye in Norwich which is thought to represent a Danish fortified base, but further information has not been traced.

[150] Smyth 2002: 18.

[151] Hadley and Richards 2016.

Historically, various sites for the Danish camp at *Cwatbrycge* have been proposed, and before discussing Quatford in more detail in a later chapter it is appropriate to consider those sites, which include Panpudding Hill (the end of a natural hillspur reshaped into a large motte on the south-west side of Bridgnorth);[152] Castle Hill on the sandstone outcrop on the west side of the Severn in Bridgnorth; the flat ground on the east side of the river (now known as Low Town)[153] at Bridgnorth; Quatford Castle, near Quatford, two miles south-east of Bridgnorth; and Burf Castle, a little over a mile to the east of Quatford.[154] It is necessary to comment briefly on those locations.

Panpudding Hill, quite simply, is not the type of earthwork one would expect to find from the Danish period: there is no evidence that the Vikings created camps in such form, and

---

[152] The circular mound, 346 yards south-west of Bridgnorth Castle, is some 160 feet in diameter with an earth-covered gravel and stone rampart rising about 10' above the outside ground level, with a narrow bailey to the west separated from the mound by a shallow ditch: see Duckers 2006: 33 and Plate 32. It is recorded on the 1560 map of Bridgnorth as *Old Castell hill*, and in 1571 as *le Tirrett alias le Old Castle* (PN Sa I 227, which suggests that the name Panpudding is an inversion of pudding-pan, although a panpudding was a pudding cooked in a pudding-pan). Panpudding Hill (sometimes mentioned as *Pampudding Hill*, see e.g. Timmins 1899: 177) is a natural feature which was adapted as a ringwork or motte by Henry I during the three-week siege of Robert de Bellême's fortification in 1102: see Eyton 1854-60: I 242; TSAHS 1961-4 222. The attribution of this work to Henry I's campaign is supported by Florence (John) of Worcester, who records that in 1102 '[the King] with almost all the army of England laid siege to Bridgnorth, and there built siege engines and a strong castle': McGurk 1998: 101. Furthermore, Henry of Huntingdon tells us that Henry I 'laid siege to [Robert de Belême's] castle at Arundel, but finding it difficult to reduce, he built forts against it, and besieged Bridgnorth': Forester 1853: 241. Those forts can be identified as the ringwork-and-bailey type siege castles at Lyminster and Rackham Bank, near Arundel, both castles being of very similar design to the earthworks at Panpudding Hill: Kenyon 2005: 24; see also Purton 1998. Watkins-Pitchford 1937 claims that the mound was called Old Castle during the Civil War and until the 19th century, but the name may not have been ancient at the date it is first recorded. 'A mention of the pan puddings of Shropshire occurs in Taylor's *Workes*, 1630, I 146' (Halliwell-Phillipps 1881: 602), and a small mound on the top of the Laxton Motte in Nottinghamshire is known as Pan Pudding Hill: Wright 2004. A flat-topped artificial eminence (at SO 715923; SSMR PRN 02974), 200 yards south of Panpudding Hill more or less surrounded by the remains of a low earthern rampart enclosing an area larger than the mound, was excavated in advance of the construction of the Bridgnorth By-Pass c.1991. A man-made rampart of gravel and packed stone on the north and east sides showed that the site had been defended or consolidated. Seventeenth-century pottery was found, but no evidence of medieval occupation or activity, and it was concluded that the feature may have been associated with the 26-day siege of Bridgnorth Castle in 1646.

[153] Known as *Bassa Villa* in 'old documents': TSAS XLIX 1937-8 191; see also SA 796/20.

[154] For completeness, it may be noted a so-called 'Danish camp' near Gatacre Park is recorded in Scott 1832: 330 (about which nothing is known); a 'Danish fortification' is said to have stood on Long Common near Claverley 'from which the summit takes its name of Apers Castle hill [Abbot's Castle Hill]' (Anon. 1824: 824), perhaps the sub-circular earthwork c.150' in diameter with low raised mound identified c.¾ mile E.S.E. of Little Aston (HER 31297); and that the insignificant hamlet of Ewdness, some two miles north of Bridgnorth, on the east side of the Severn less than a mile from the river, has been said to take its name from the Welsh *Hen Dinas* 'the old city' (Ekwall 1960: 170; Coates and Breeze 2000: 326), which might be seen as a clue to the site of the Danish camp. But any name incorporating Welsh elements must date from a time when the local population was still Welsh-speaking, which would give a date much earlier than the ninth century (Jackson 1953). It is clear that whether or not any 'city' lay at or near Ewdness (cropmarks of enclosures have been located nearby, but do not support the existence of any sizeable early settlement), if the derivation of the name is correct, it was centuries old when the Danes first visited the area. The philological evidence, indeed, points towards an English origin for the name (see PN Sa 6: 74-5, which suggests the generic OE *næss* 'promontory', which is topographically appropriate, with an uncertain first element), but whether Welsh or English, Ewdness can be excluded from our search for the Danish camp.

the mound, as will be seen, is more readily explained as a mount for use as a siege-castle associated with the siege of Bridgnorth Castle by Henry I in 1102. Orderic Vitalis (1075-c.1142), a reliable and prolific contemporary historian born at Atcham in Shropshire, tell us that to avoid committing large numbers of men to a lengthy siege, attacking forces built temporary castles in which small troops of knights could keep watch and prevent supplies being brought in, though great timber catapults were known to have been used in such situations, and may have been placed on the mound.[155]

So far as Castle Hill in Bridgnorth is concerned, there is no archaeological or other evidence that it was utilised at that early period,[156] although that does not of course rule out such use, and a prehistoric hill fort may have existed on the hill, even if no evidence has been traced. The rocky outcrop can almost certainly be ruled out from its scale and nature: the Danes had an instinctive compulsion to site their camps alongside rivers, to which they required convenient access, and that would not have been be possible from the sheer size of the 200' sandstone formation at Bridgnorth. Low Town on the east bank has produced no archaeological or other evidence to show that it was occupied before the twelfth century.[157] But another reason for eliminating Bridgnorth is the chroniclers' insistence that the Danish camp lay at *Cwatbrycge*, which (if the identification set out in a later chapter is accepted) is two miles from Bridgnorth.

Gerald P. Mander, the Wolverhampton antiquary and scion of the Mander family of Wightwick Manor, who wrote in the first half of the last century, recorded in 1908 that '... as the Stourbridge road ascends the hill from the Severn valley, and about 1½ miles from Bridgnorth [the distance is in reality some 1,500 yards], are to be seen some strong lines of entrenchment. These curve round the hill and are cut through by the road: they are easily traced to the north, but south of the road their outline is shadowy to say the least. Three valla and their fosses at least are presented: their depth and heights vary ... It will be noticed that these works are some distance from the ridge of the hill, being about half-way down it, and that their position points to an anticipated invasion from the west. Being therefore a defence against the Britons, we may assume that they were not made by the Britons...'.[158] The greatest of these 'strong lines of entrenchments' was said to be 18' deep with an escarpment 20' high.[159]

---

[155] Chibnall 2000: XVI 49; WMANS 1983 86.

[156] Though Bridgnorth is not mentioned in the Domesday Book, the relationship of St Leonard's churchyard, some distance from the castle and borough founded in the early 12th century, implies that it predates the expansion of the town in the later 12th to early 13th century, and and it is very possible that there was a settlement in the area of the High Town before the 12th century, with St Leonard's church an Anglo-Saxon foundation: Slater 1988; Croom 1989.

[157] Excavations at the rear of The Falcon Hotel in St John's Street have revealed no evidence of pre-Conquest settlement: TSAS Vol. LXXVII 2002 128. It is evident that Lilley 2002: 140-142, who concludes that Bridgnorth was founded c.1082, and whose work is cited in Hooke 2006: 60, has misdated events recorded by Orderic Vitalis, (see Chibnall 1968-80: II 224-5; 1991: 20-21), perhaps as a result of a misreading of the entry for Quatford in Domesday Book which led Rowley 1983: 99 to imagine that Bridgnorth could have been meant by the reference to a *novus burgus*: in fact Domesday refers to a *noua dom'* [*nova domus*] and a *burgu'*, or new house and borough, and the borough is named as Quatford. Orderic makes it clear that after the siege of Arundel castle by Henry I in 1102, Robert de Bellême was in the process of building a very strong castle at Bridgnorth: Chibnall 1968-80: VI book XI 20-21.

[158] WJ, October 1908, 265-8, which includes a sketch of a cross-section of the earthworks, described as being 'between Stanmore Grove and Bridgnorth in the parish of Worfield'.

[159] See also VCH Shropshire: I 410.

The three ditches of Mander's earthwork survive intact, readily identiable on LiDAR surveys as two close parallel east-west ditches and a third a little further north with a slightly more sinuous plan, and form an impressive and substantial feature at the southern end of the belt of woodland which runs first south, and then south-east, from the sandstone cliff-dwellings long known as The Hermitage on the south side of the Bridgnorth-Wolverhampton road. The ditches lie on the north side of and adjoin the Bridgnorth-Stourbridge road (which seems to have been driven though them), are exceptionally well preserved, and run for a distance of 550 feet or so, fading away at the lower (west) end of the woodland, and stopping below the summit of the long escarpment. The earthworks are curious, for prehistoric earthworks (which they certainly resemble, both in scale and profile) would normally be expected to follow the contours of a hill, whereas these run steeply upwards from east to west, and have no obvious corners at their extremities. No investigation appears to have been made into this mysterious earthwork, but its nature and its distance from the river make it difficult to explain as Anglo-Saxon – or even medieval – in date.[160]

In the early nineteenth century the Shropshire historian William Hardwicke (1772-1843) records in his manuscript *Collections for a History of Bridgnorth*: '...under Barnet's Hill, corruptly so named from Mount Barnard, which was the hill's appellation in the reign of Edward II; on or near this eminence in that reign was a spot called Barrow,[161] probably a military place of interment for such who had fallen in some great battle; and within the last 50 years human skeletons and bones have been dug up near the summit and almost at the south-east extremity'.[162] Barnet's Hill[163] is evidently the hill forming the high escarpment running from The Hermitage to Gatacre Plantation, but who the eponymous Barnard was remains unknown. He is remembered in the road name Bernards Hill in Low Town. The 'south-east extremity' is not easy to identify, but may be the northern side of Spring Valley near Essex Fall.

It is a matter of particular regret that we have no more information about the skeletal remains mentioned by Hardwicke, but he was a generally reliable antiquary, and from the words he uses we are entitled to assume that he had personal knowledge of the finds, or

---

[160] No feature which might be intended to represent the earthwork appears on the 1613 map of Morfe Forest (SA 4296). *Broad Ditch*, mentioned in a lease of 1739 (Griffith 1880: 88-9) may possibly be associated with the earthwork, as could 'the olde Diche under the gybet' marked on the c.1560 map of Bridgnorth, which is almost certainly 'the certain ancient ditch under the Gyhet [gibbet]' recorded in the perambulation of Morfe Forest in 1300: Bellet 1856: 212. The 1815 O.S. survey produced by Robert Dawson (BL map collection) marks *The [?]ulwark* at the midpoint of Hermitage Hill ridge south-west of Hermitage Farm. The name is unexplained, but may be associated with a record in 1642 of 'tooles for pioners to make fortificacions upon Morffe and bulwarkes to keep out enemies from this Town' (TSAHS X (1887) 153; *Manuscripts of the Earl of Westmorland, etc.*, HMSO, 1906: 434), or with the rifle-range which existed here in the nineteenth century, with targets on the crest of the hill (1891 and 1903 1:10,560 O.S. maps). Dawson's map marks no earthworks along the Bridgnorth-Stourbridge road.
[161] Probably the place called Barrow recorded in 1654: SA BB/F/3/5/13. The name may have derived from OE *beorg*, often meaning 'a hill', and sometimes applied to tumuli: the reference to human skeletons suggests that the second meaning cannot be dismissed entirely. It is also possible that the name is from OE *bearu* 'a grove or small wood'.
[162] Page 191; see TSAS XLIX 1937-8 189-217. The location is typical of an Anglo-Saxon execution cemetery: cf. cemeteries at Sutton Hoo and Ridgeway Hill, Dorset.
[163] Recorded in 1694 as *Barnett Hill*: SA 796/79, but a 19th century plan gives the name *Barnard's Hill* (SA DA2/709/2/8). A *Barnett's Meadow* is shown on the east bank of the Severn north-west of Quatford on the 1842 Tithe Map.

was satisfied as to the veracity of his informant, otherwise we might have expected him to have used words such as 'it is reported that ...'. But he could occasionally be inclined to wild romanticism, and despite his depth of learning and deep knowledge of the local area, was not immune from occasional flights of fantasy.[164] We cannot know how old the remains might have been, or what they represented, but it is very unusual to find numbers of skeletons buried away from a graveyard, especially on a hill, and it is not impossible that they are to be associated in some way with the military events that took place in the area in the late ninth and early tenth century, although the sandy soil might point towards a more recent deposition, since bones do not survive well in sand, and the idea can probably be discounted.

Indeed, it must be more likely that the burials from Barnet's Hill were perhaps connected with the gibbet which seems to have stood on the crest of the ridge above the Hermitage: 'The old Diche under the gybet' is shown, with a sketch of the gibbet, on an ancient map of Bridgnorth c.1560, and what would appear to be a thumbnail sketch of a gibbet in this same area is marked on a 1613 map of Morfe Forest produced by Samuel Parsons.[165] Gibbets were used to publicly display the corpses of executed criminals. The place of execution is still marked on maps as *Gallows Field* between Bridgnorth and Quatford to the north of Danesford.

What other explanation might account for the presence of these skeletons? It is difficult to imagine that the burials might have been associated with the two medieval hospitals which lay on the east side of the Severn: the Hospital of Holy Trinity and St John the Baptist, founded in the late twelfth century, lay in the angle formed by Mill Street and St John's Street, commemorated in the name Hospital Street, and the leper hospital of St James, first recorded in 1224, which stood further south, on the south side of the junction of Hospital Street and the road to Stourbridge.[166] The leper hospital was made a priory in the reign of Edward IV, and in the 1830s the priory buildings were converted into the private house known as St James's Priory. During the creation of the shrubbery at the north of the house in 1823, 37 skeletons were discovered lying in rows within eighteen inches of the surface. They had been buried in widing sheets without coffins, and were well preserved.[167] Such a discovery at an ancient priory is not unusual.

Midway between Quatford and Bridgnorth is an area formerly called Dog-on-the-Wall from an inn of that name which became in recent times Danesford Grange Nursing

---

[164] One example might be seen in his references to the supposed and unexplained castle or 'palace' at Hallon near Worfield.

[165] SA 4296; SA X5586/5/3/31. The c.1560 map of Bridgnorth shows the gibbet to the south of The Hermitage. Ogilby's road book of 1675 shows *Gallowes* in approximately the same position: Ogilby 1675 Plate 13. Eyton 1854-60 III: 19 mentions *Gibbet Hill*. According to Watkins-Pitchford 'The gibbet stood near the old Quatford road – a road which is very little used now – in the second field on the right, just after you have turned off the Stourbridge road just above St James' Priory' (Watkins-Pitchford 1932: 24), but he appears to have confused the gibbet with the gallows, though early dictionaries show that the two terms were often used interchangeably. *Gallows Field* appears in Gothic script on modern maps at SO 728919. There was, of course, a distinction between gallows and gibbet: executions were carried out on gallows, and the bodies displayed on gibbets. On 22 April 1643 the Bridgnorth Chamberlain's Accounts record payments made 'for carryinge the postes of the gibbet together which were thrown abroade by souldiers', and 'for gathering part thereof out of the water': TSAHS X (1885) 155.

[166] Bellett 1856: 80-7; VCH Shropshire II 98-101. There is no reason to believe that the 'skeletons of former inmates ... found from time to time' (TSAS 4th series VIII 1920-1 59) were discovered at any distance from the site of the hospital.

[167] Lewis 1849: I 366.

Home.[168] Towards the end of the nineteenth century G. T. 'Castle' Clark (1809-98), an engineer and ironmaster who had worked with Brunel and edited the charters of Glamorgan, seen as the founding father of castle studies in Britain, and who should have been eminently qualified to survey early fortifications, mentions a ditch cutting off the tail of a piece of detached highish ground near this place, with the suggestion that it seemed to have been a light temporary work for the accommodation of a small body of men.[169] Clark has been shown to be an unreliable authority (certainly in respect of the Quatford area), and subsequent investigations by an Ordnance Survey field investigator in the 1970s failed to identify the 'highish ground' or the ditch, but recent LiDAR surveys show a deep roadway across the hill-spur enclosed by the junction of the Bridgnorth-Quatford road and the Old Worcester Road which could well be Clark's ditch.[170]

Although, bizarrely, Clark denied its existence,[171] Burf Castle,[172] mentioned elsewhere in this volume, is a small prehistoric earthwork near the edge of a high escarpment overlooking the Severn a mile-and-a-half to the east of Quatford. The site has never been excavated, and no finds have been recorded from the vicinity, but the earthwork remains are readily discernible and have the appearance of an Iron-Age hillfort. Certainly it would have been sensible for the Danes to have adapted an existing fortification rather than involve themselves in the construction of a new camp, but there is no evidence that the Danes (unlike the Anglo-Saxons) ever utilised prehistoric earthworks, and since Burf Castle (which enjoys no obvious water supply) lies some distance from the river Severn, and the Danes tended to build their camps on rivers and streams, it can probably be dismissed as a site likely to have been used by the Danes.[173] The site of the Danish camp must be sought elsewhere.[174]

The identification of Viking camps has recently been methodically analysed by Benjamin Raffield.[175] His research, which renders valuable service to historians of the Viking age,

---

[168] The name *Dog on the Wall* (sic) appears on Robert Dawson's 1815 map produced for the O.S. (BL map collection); *Dog in the Wall* 1833 O.S.; *Dog-in-the-wall Meadow* is shown on the 1840 Tithe Map on the north bank of the Severn opposite Cliff Coppice and to the west of the old ford at Danesford (SO 725914). For a map of Dog-in-the-Wall c.1850 see SA DA2/709/2/13.

[169] Clark 1884: I 181-2; SSMR PRN 00203. Clark's reputation as a historian of military architecture has not stood the test of time, and many of his other observations must be treated with caution.

[170] It is possible that the highish ground, if not a figment of Clark's imagination, was the tongue of land to the west of Quatford Castle at SO733918, but no ditch has been identified there.

[171] 'Burf Castle, placed a mile and a half to the west [of Quatford] on that record [i.e. the O.S. map] does not exist, and it is pretty clear from the character and surface of the hill that there never was any kind of earthwork upon it': Clark 1874: 276.

[172] The name is from OE *burh* 'fortified place', with the common dialectical confusion between *f* and *th*. The name may perhaps be found in the surname *de Burgh'* recorded in 1327, and *de Bury* and *ate Bury*, recorded 1344-1360: PN Sa 6: 23.

[173] Eyton had little doubt that this was the site of the Danish wintering, for he writes: 'At Burf Castle, eastward of Quatford, the Danes lay intrenched for one winter.': Eyton 1854-60 III 213-4. Watkins-Pitchford 1932: 6 held the same view, and indeed suggests that Heathen's Ditch may have been a ship-building slip for the launching of vessels constructed by the Danes at Burf Castle. The idea cannot be dismissed out of hand: it should be remembered that in the early 7th century a 90' vessel weighing perhaps 10 tons was dragged some 500 yards from the river Deben to the top of a 100' hill at Sutton Hoo for use as a sepulchre. Robert Dawson's 1815 survey for the O.S. (BL map collection) suggests that a long wide valley running south-west from west of The Burf would have been the most convenient route to haul a vessel to the Severn.

[174] Burf Castle may, however, have been utilised by the English forces keeping watch over the Danish camp, wherever it may have been.

[175] Raffield 2010; Raffield 2013.

includes a schedule of sites hitherto identified as possible Viking fortifications (including Quatford), as well as a detailed analysis of earlier writings on the subject. He concludes that the criteria used by earlier historians to identify such sites – which often assumed that Viking fortifications were D-shaped – are wrong or spurious; that there is no formula for identifying Viking fortifications; and many sites once thought to be Viking are now held to be prehistoric, Roman, Anglo-Saxon or post-Conquest in origin. There is no reason why the Vikings should have consistently built fortifications of similar shape, and no evidence that they did. Indeed, some examples are cited where camps take advantage of naturally occurring defences, such as watercourses, which produce singularly irregular plans. A Viking camp could be defended by v-shaped ditches with banks, probably topped by a palisade, but undefended sites also seem to have existed, presumably served by sentries and pickets to warn of an approaching enemy. But one particular conclusion reached by Raffield deserves to be quoted verbatim: 'Fortified sites may utilise a natural barrier such as a river cliff or rock outcrop so as to improve the defensive capabilities of the site as well as ensuring that less 'digging in' had to take place'.[176]

Any search for the Danish camp at *Cwatbrycge* must now be conducted in the light of Raffield's conclusions, reinforced by remarkable discoveries made over the last two decades at Torksey in Lincolnshire which are providing invaluable knowledge about wintering camps of the Vikings.[177] In 865 a Viking warband landed in East Anglia. After many battles, in 871 the raiders were reinforced by a 'summer army' under the leadership of Guthrum. Following the death of his brother Æthelred, King Alfred became king of Wessex in the same year, and bought time by making peace with the Vikings. It was against this backdrop that the Danes returned northwards in 872 and, in the terse record of the *Anglo-Saxon Chronicle*, 'Here the army took winter quarters at *Turcesige*'. Recent finds from the Torksey site include over 350 coins, including more than 100 Arabic dirhams and over 50 pieces of hacksilver and cut fragments of Anglo-Saxon, Frankish and Irish copper-alloy jewellery. The finds were concentrated on the east side of the river Trent in a natural oval of higher land overlooking the river floodplain. But what is especially noteworthy is that at its highest point a near-vertical cliff edge plunges down to the river, confirming Raffield's conclusion that waterside outcrops were sites favoured by the Vikings. The surrounding land is still prone to flooding, and the site will have formed a natural defensive position of some 65 acres with the cliff on one side and marshy or flooded land on the other, factors which evidently appealed to earlier settlers, for a Romano-British farmstead has also been identified on the site.

As will be seen, not only is the topography of Torksey similar in some ways to the site at Quatford, but it is evident that even though Torksey sheltered the great army, it had no defensive ditches,[178] perhaps explaining why no such ditches have been identified at Quatford, or indeed anywhere else in the area. Furthermore, like Quatford, Torksey later became an Anglo-Saxon *burh*, or borough, perhaps one of the seven mentioned in an entry in the *Anglo-Saxon Chronicle* for 1015,[179] and, like Quatford, was an area that had previously attracted an Iron Age/Romano-British community, the prehistoric site at Quatford lying on the west side of the river north of Slade Lane. The great number of

---

[176] Raffield 2010: 105. There is no evidence that Raffield was writing with any detailed knowledge of the topography of Quatford.
[177] See especially Hadley and Richards 2016.
[178] The ASC does not mention any fortifications either at Torksey or at Repton, where the Danes wintered the following year and where fortifications have been found: Swanton 1996: 72-3.
[179] Swanton 1996: 146.

artifacts from Torksey form an impressively comprehensive collection of booty of all types gathered during campaigning not only in Wessex and Northumbria, but also in Ireland and on the Continent, in Francia, and perhaps further east.[180] Research and excavation is ongoing, but the evidence suggests that this winter camp at least was of considerable size, perhaps housing women and children, and is likely to have been a place of dense occupation with bustling industrial and commercial activity, possibly one of the largest settlements, albeit temporary, in the region, paving the way for the tenth century urban development of the site.

But Torksey was the camp of a substantial army: at *Cwatbrycge* we seek the camp of a smaller raiding party which had sent its women and children to safety before fleeing to *Cwatbrycge*. We might imagine that the Danes at *Cwatbrycge* could have utilised some sort of fortification previously built by Danes, for it seems a reasonable assumption that they had explored and were familiar with the upper reaches of the Severn by the later ninth century. We might picture the Danes fleeing their fortification on the river Lea in 895 and heading directly for *Cwatbrycge*, in the knowledge that it would offer the best defensive position for the least labour, with the benefit of an escape route via the river in case of emergency: Vikings will rarely if ever have built their camps far from rivers. The suitability of Quatford as a fortification implies that the Danes did not stumble across the place by chance, but taking flight from Mercian forces at the River Lea (the Thames forming the boundary here between Mercia and Wessex) made directly to Quatford and the Severn. That presupposes that at least some of the Danes in the warband possessed a good knowledge of the area, perhaps having utilised the site previously, an idea that ties in with other slight evidence discussed previously for a Danish presence in the central Marches region in the later part of the ninth century.

Raffield's conclusion that the Danes utilised natural features such as a river cliff or rock outcrop, combined with the same topography at Torksey, exactly reflects the topography at Quatford, with its prominent riverside sandstone outcrop. Apart from a spearhead discussed elsewhere in this volume, no finds from the Viking period are known to have been recorded from the wider area, but the absence of expected finds at other known and suspected Viking wintering sites is well established: Thanet, where Vikings are recorded in 850 and 864, and Sheppey in 854, have produced virtually no traces of occupation. It must not be forgotten, either, that the sandstone outcrop was heavily worked and remodelled during the construction of the Norman motte and church, and the nineteenth-century 'restoration' of the former which is discussed later in this volume.

Even ignoring the phonetic similarities between the names *Cwatbrycge* and Quatford, we can be reasonably confident in concluding that the Danish camp was centred on the sandstone bluff overlooking the Severn at Quatford and covered only a few acres, at most, presumably the summit of the wide ridge extending east towards and including the present church. A camp at Quatford would have enabled the Danes to control a strategic bridgehead, assuming that a bridge then existed, or at least an important ford, denying its use to the English, and ensured that in the event of attack they could if necessary make a river crossing or escape by water.[181]

---

[180] Hadley and Richards 2016.
[181] A parallel for a Danish fortification defending a ford may be the earthwork known as Beeston Berrys at Beeston near Sandy in Bedfordshire: Dyer 1972: 225-6. It will also be noted that the Danish fortification at Buttington lay adjacent to a major ford over the river Severn.

One other possibility is that the Danish camp was also sited on a bylet or island: the Danes had a propensity to place their encampments on islands. It will be recalled that Roger of Wendover described the Danish camp at Buttington 'washed on all sides by the waters of the Severn', clearly referring to an island.[182] The attraction of islands to the Danes is well-recorded. The *Anglo-Saxon Chronicle* tells us that after suffering defeat at Farnham in 893, the Danish army fled across the Thames and was besieged by King Alfred's son Edward at an island named Thorney. This may be Thorney in Buckinghamshire, where the river Colne flows to the Thames in several channels, which intersect to form islands.[183] The Danes are also associated with the Isles of Thanet and Sheppey (850s), Mersea Island (880), Steepholme (915),[184] and Northey Island (991). On the Continent the Vikings built a fort on an island in the Seine called Oscellus,[185] fortified the island of Oiselle in the Seine, not far from Rouen, and the peninsula of Fossa Givaldi near Bougivae protected by a marsh. The encampment at Noimoutier was an island in the Loire, and other island fortifications were at La Camargue in the Rhone, Walcheren in the Scheldt, and an island near Neuss in the Rhine. Near Louvain, about 50 miles west of Maastricht, the Danes built a fortification 'of wood and piled-up earth in their usual manner' surrounded by marsh in a loop of the river Dyle in 891.[186]

The use by the Danes of an island in the Severn at Quatford in this way would have an interesting parallel, even if from a different era. In 1041 a royal army was sent to ravage Worcester after two of the king's tax collectors had been murdered in the town. The *Anglo-Saxon Chronicle* records that a 'great number' of citizens took refuge on 'a certain small island which is called Bevere [which still exists], situated in the middle of the Severn, and having made a fortification, defended themselves manfully against their enemies until peace was restored and they were allowed to return home freely'.[187] Evidently Bevere was fortified in a very short time – sadly we have no details of the form of the defences – and we might wonder whether the citizens were prompted at short notice to make use of the island by some distant memory of its use by others for the same purpose in the past.

Evidence for islands in the Severn at Quatford is not lacking. The 1842 Tithe Map shows an area on the west bank named *The Island* (field number 99) in the field called *Meadow Opposite the Rock* (field number 92), suggesting that the river may have once divided there to create a bylet.[188] One island or bylet is recorded by Wasey in 1859, when he writes that 'the present sexton [of Quatford], Richard Turley, tells me that there was within his

---

[182] Modern maps show no island at Buttington, but the 1890-1 6" O.S. map indicates that the land adjoining the Severn in this area is liable to flooding, which may suggest that the river course has changed since 893.
[183] See Whitelock 1955: 186; Stenton 1970: 14-5.
[184] Legg 1993: 54-6. For Scomer, Gateholm, Caldy or Burry Holm, Flatholm, Sully, Ramsey, Emsger, Skokholm, and Grassholm, all in Pembrokeshire with Scandinavian names, see Loyn 1976: 8, 17.
[185] Whitelock 1955: 315.
[186] Davis 1957: 175; Bradbury 1992: 25.
[187] Whitelock 1955: 291-2; the episode is also recorded by Florence (John) of Worcester: Stevenson 1853: 116. Bevere Island lies three miles north of Worcester, and is some 250 yards long and 100 yards wide. Roman and 13th century pottery and an enclosure thought to be of Roman date are said to have been discovered on the island by archaeologists in 1958. We may also note that an important meeting between Cnut and Eadmund took place in 1016 on an island in the Severn called *Olanege* at Deerhurst in Gloucestershire: Stevenson 1853: 106.
[188] The area may be associated with the *Water Meadow and the Byletts* recorded in 1741: SA 2922/3/80. The area marked *Ilan/ds* on the east bank of the Severn opposite the former island on the 1632 map of Morfe Forest (SRO 4296) may also be noted.

recollection, forty years ago, an Islet of nearly a quarter of an acre on which grew alders and willow bushes among which he has often played ...'.[189] This is evidently the bylet which Bellet says in 1855 was remembered in his day as almost ¼ acre in size and covered with alders and willows.[190] It may well have been a remnant of the bylet which appears on the map of the Bridgnorth area, supposedly a copy of an original dating from c.1560,[191] and on a map of Morfe Common made in 1613,[192] and was doubtless associated with the widening of the Severn which is clearly shown on the 1613 map. The large flat area to the west side of the river may have had a very different profile and indeed been a large island in the tenth century.[193] It is true that the ground is low-lying and prone to regular flooding, especially in the winter and spring, but the area may then have been higher – perhaps considerably higher – and also possible that the Danes raised earthern embankments to protect the island from inundation, with the area having since been eroded and levelled by a millenium of Severn floods.

One further possibility that cannot be discounted in the quest for the Danish camp at *Cwatbrycge* is that the Danes utilised a pre-existing Anglo-Saxon fortification, since we know that the duty of building or maintaining fortresses is recorded from 749 in Mercia, and gradually becomes more frequent thereafter,[194] and a fortification would be a natural adjunct to protect an important Anglo-Saxon river crossing, especially if that crossing took the form of a bridge, which almost certainly existed at *Cwatbrycge* in 910, and probably earlier. It is doubtful whether any earlier Anglo-Saxon fortification will have incorporated the sandstone outcrop, since early *burhs* seem to have taken the form of relatively level ditched and banked areas, and an area dominated by a large outcrop would be atypical.[195]

---

[189] Wasey 1859: 25.
[190] Bellett 1855: 3. The bylet, still prominent on LiDAR surveys, may well have been considerably larger in the early medieval period, for islands are continuously scoured and eroded by the river, and may indeed be the ½ acre meadow called *the Bylett* recorded in 1683 (SA 2922/2/40).
[191] TSAS LVII 1961-4 38. A rendering of the map, which Croom 1989 inadvertently (or possibly more accurately) dates to 1650, is printed in Bellett 1855. A large photographic reproduction of what was evidently a copy of the original is in Bridgnorth Northgate Museum. That copy has now perished. An extract from what seems to be a very similar map appears in TSAHS LXXI 1996 78, where it is described as 17th century, but the text on the previous page describes it as late 16th century, and cites Bridgnorth Borough Collection SRR 4001/P/1/39. Eyton evidently believed it to have been made shortly after the Dissolution (Eyton 1854-60: I 369, fn.505), and VCH Shropshire II 1973: 98 fn.1 suggests a date of c.1555-74. From its depiction of crosses in the town and monastic houses with their fields it would certainly seem to be pre-Reformation in date. For convenience, in this work the map is called the c.1560 map of Bridgnorth, but it is important to emphasise that the authenticity and precise date of the map remain uncertain.
[192] SA 4296. No bylet appears on the Tithe Map of 1842, but that may not be significant: the purpose of the map would not call for such features to be included. Since Bellett speaks in 1855 of a memory of the bylet, it seems likely, however, that it had indeed disappeared by 1842.
[193] Thirteenth and fourteenth century records (e.g. NLW Otley (Pitchford Hall) Estate I 1295, 1240) mention a parcel of land called *le Ree* or *la Rye* or similar opposite the rock of Quatford. The name is almost certainly from OE *(æt) þære ēa* '(at) the river', which developed into ME *atter ē*, which became wrongly divided as *atte Re*, denoting a watercourse which is evidently not the Severn, since the river-name was normally used in such records. No watercourse is marked on modern maps. Is it possible that the Ree/Rye was a secondary channel of the Severn which served to create an island in the flat ground to the west of Quatford?
[194] Lapidge et al 1999: 191.
[195] The multiple meanings of OE and ME *burh*, far from synonymous, have been highlighted in Hill and Rumble 1996: 3. In the present work the term may be taken to mean 'fortification'.

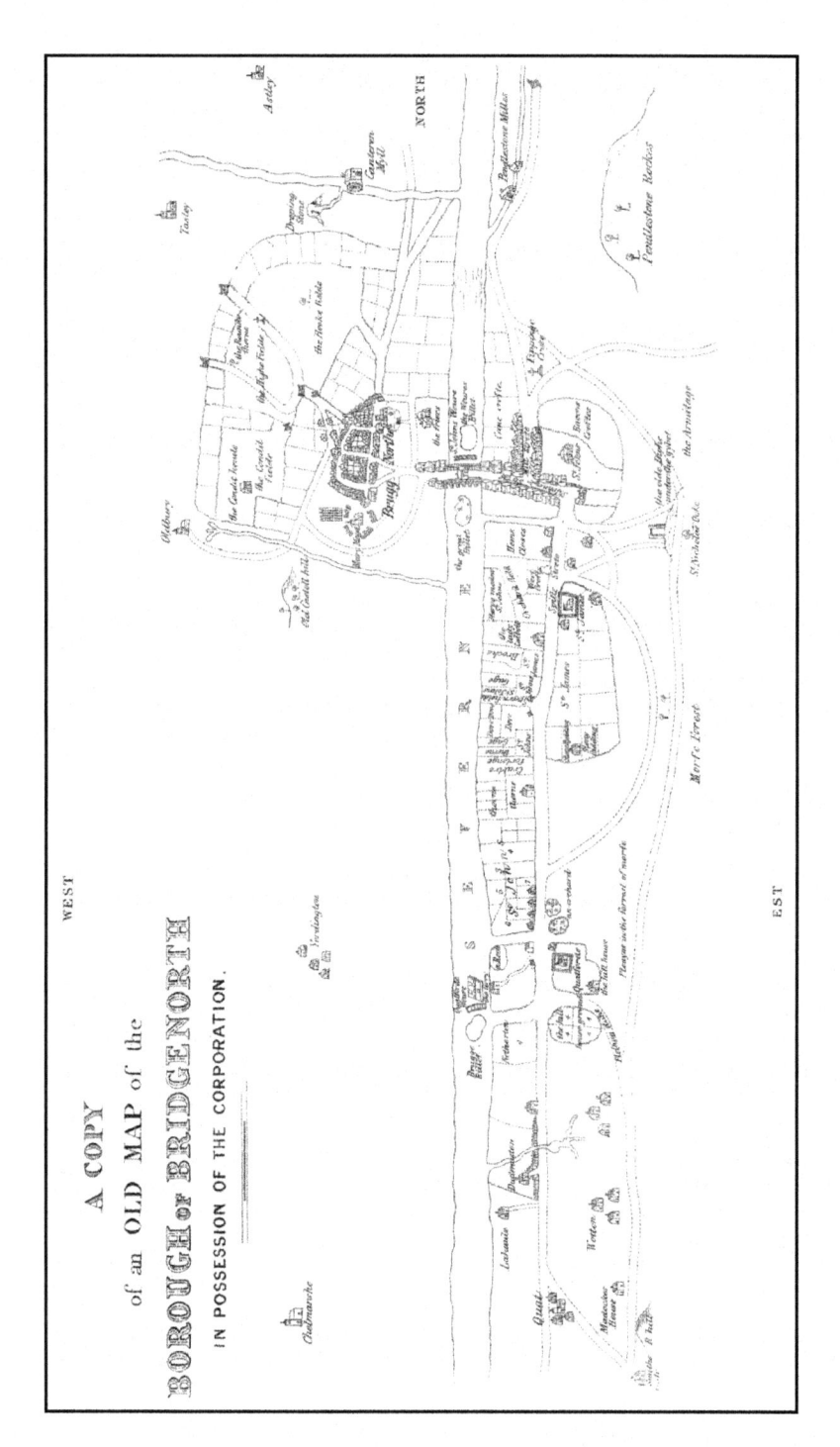

The well-known but enigmatic 'ancient map' of Bridgnorth and the river Severn to the south-east of the town, as reproduced in the Reverend G. Bellet's *Antiquities of Bridgnorth* in 1856. The original map, said to date from c.1560, has perished, but copies exist in various versions. An island ('Brugge Billet'), weir and ferry are shown at Quatford, with the eleventh century motte labelled 'a Rock'.

Other evidence which is almost certainly to be associated with a river crossing at Quatford, and which has been linked to the Danes, must also be considered. A ditch known as *Hethenedich*, generally interpreted as 'Heathens' Ditch' (i.e. 'the ditch associated with the pagan Danes') is recorded in formal perambulations written in Latin of the bounds of Morfe Forest in 1298 and 1300. The 1298 survey records (in translation): '... to *haleweyeslydesete* and thus by a certain path which leads as far as Quatford as far as *le hethenedict*. And thus by the said ditch as far as the fish-weir of Quatford ...', and the 1300 survey records (in translation): '...to *Halyweyes-lydyat*; and so by a certain path to the *Hethenedich*, going down by the *Hethenedich* to the fish-weir of Quatford, and so going up By the Severn to a certain ancient ditch between the field of Brugge and the vill of Quatford'.[196] The word ditch comes from Old English *dīc*, which generally carried the meaning 'excavated trench', created for defence or drainage, and both meanings are found in place-names. The word is also found in Middle English applied to an embankment or bank of earth – a dyke – created when a ditch is excavated, but tends to be found in low-lying areas in the north-east of England.[197] Offa's Dyke and Wat's Dyke are perhaps the best known examples of several along the Welsh Marches.

J. F. A. Mason, commenting on *Hethenedich* in the 1960s, states that it ran from Mose in the direction of Quatford weir, and raises the possibility that it may be identified with a trackway labelled *flethug diche* on the map of the Bridgnorth area c.1560.[198] The earlier perambulations show that *Hethenedich* deviated from the path between *haleweyeslydesete* (which is found as *Holloeway Liddeat* on the 1613 map of Morfe Forest,[199] a place that evidently lay on the west side of Gags Rock at a point where a trackway crosses a minor road running from Sandybury and Mose),[200] and Quatford. The point at which the ditch deviated from the path is uncertain, but it evidently ran to the now vanished Quatford fish-weir, which was at or close to the site of the former ferry just south of the sandstone bluff. All we know from the documentary evidence is that a path from *Holloeway Liddeat* towards Quatford ran to the ditch, which then continued to the fish-weir.

In summary, therefore, the riverside sandstone outcrop at Quatford almost certainly formed the core of the Viking wintering camp in 895/6, a conclusion possibly supported by the discovery of what may – but might not – be a Viking spearhead in the area in recent times, a find discussed in more detail in Chapter 32 of this volume.

The nature, route and extent of the 'Heathen's Ditch' are unclear. If the name was of pre-Conquest date, which is unlikely but not impossible, it might provide tantalising evidence for the presence of the Danes. Remains of the ditch were apparently still visible, and mentioned by William Hardwicke, a generally reliable local historian, in the nineteenth century,[201] but sadly he offers no clues as to where it was located. In 1874 G. T. Clark described the area to the east of Quatford motte, assumed to be the bailey, as defended on

---

[196] For the 1298 perambulation see TSAHS LXX 1996 27: ... haleweyeslydesete. et sic inde per quandum semitam que ducit usque quatforde usque le hethenedict. et sic per dictum fossatum usque gurgitem de quatford .... For the 1300 perambulation see Eyton 1854-60: III 219.
[197] EPNE i 131-2.
[198] TSAS LVII 1961-4 38.
[199] SA 4296. The name *Holloeway Liddeat* incorporates OE *hlid-geat* 'swing-gate', so marking the site of such a gate associated with a hollow-way. No such holloway has been identified in the immediate area, although the trackway between Hill House Farm and Gag's Hill runs through a shallow valley in the woodland between those two places.
[200] At SO 75458060.
[201] William Hardwicke's M.S. *Parochial Histories*, vol. iv 'Quatford' (unpaginated), WSL.

the north and south sides by a ditch, which on the south was deep and wide.[202] Dr W. Watkins-Pitchford, who researched much of the history of the Bridgnorth area in the early twentieth century, describes the ditch as 'a shallow ravine which led down to the weir at Quatford',[203] but gives no further details.[204] Although it has been claimed that no trace of Heathen's Ditch is now to be seen,[205] the 1883-4 1:2,500 Ordnance Survey map and succeeding maps clearly show a sunken road, still existing, on the south side of the 'bailey', exactly opposite the church, as described by Clark. That road seems to be the sinuous track marked on the c.1560 map of Bridgnorth which forms the western end of *flethug diche*. The track surface may have been raised in fairly recent times, quite possibly from material from twentieth-century road widening at Quatford, or even with fill from the motte trench, though it is still in use, and appears clearly on LiDAR surveys. There can be little doubt that this is the western end of the trackway once known as Heathen's Ditch.

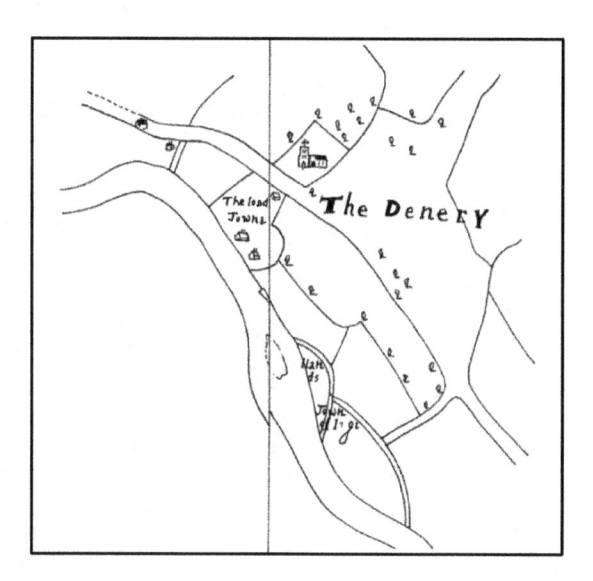

A redrawn extract (with some detail omitted) showing Quatford and the River Severn, on two sheets which do not align precisely, from the huge and extraordinarily detailed, but much worn, map of Morfe Common and the surrounding villages made in 1613. The semi-circular boundary cut by the join of the sheets echoes the perimeter of the eleventh-century motte. *The load Towne* incorporates the early Modern English word *lode*, a term for a ferry found only along the River Severn: a ferry is recorded here in the twelfth century. Reproduced by permission of Shropshire Archives, Collection No. 4296.

If the ditch was so-named after the Danes, it might be thought to commemorate the Danish wintering of 895-6, or perhaps the crossing of the Severn by the Danes in 910 before the battle of Tettenhall/Wednesfield – or, indeed, some other long-forgotten event or events of which we have no knowledge: there must have been many incidents, some of major

---

[202] 'Bridgenorth, Oldbury, and Quatford', AC 29 (1874) 275-6, reprinted in Clark 1884: 281-2.
[203] Watkins-Pitchford 1932: 6.
[204] The eye of faith might detect a trackway running east along the bottom of the shallow valley that runs towards Hillhouse on the 1st edition 1" O.S. map of 1833.
[205] Buteux 1995: 3.

significance, which the chroniclers failed to record, or if they did, their accounts have not survived.

As noted above, Mason has suggested that a feature on the map of the Bridgnorth area c.1560 labelled (he believed) *flethug diche* might be a corrupt version of the name Heathen's Ditch,[206] but a careful examination of a photograph of the map in the Northgate Museum in Bridgnorth suggests that the name is written *Flethuey diche* or indeed *Hethuey diche*. Heath Farm lies 1,000 yards or so to the south-east of Quatford, its name well-describing the nature of the landscape hereabouts, and the name *Flethuey diche* may simply be a mistranscription or misreading of the more prosaic 'heath-way ditch', a ditch serving as a trackway to the heath. The line of the ditch as marked on the c.1560 map suggests that it ran from the river in an easterly direction and curved southwards on the south side of Hill House (Farm) and continued to the east of Wootton. The route from the Severn appears to be marked by boundaries on the 1613 map of Morfe Forest, and is shown on the 1883 1:2,500 Ordnance Survey map.[207]

So, although *Hethenedich*, mentioned in the 1298 and 1300 perambulations, could mean 'heathens' ditch' (and that possibility cannot be completely excluded here), a more likely explanation must be that the name contains Old English *hæðen* 'heathy, growing with heather'.[208] We must conclude that the name *Hethenedich* is almost certainly an unfortunate and long-lived red herring in the search for the site of the Danish camp. But perhaps not a complete red-herring, for if the rocky outcrop is to be identified as the Danish camp, the ditch on the south which was 'deep and wide',[209] also described as 'a shallow ravine which led down to the weir at Quatford',[210] and which seems to have been the western end of 'Heathen's Ditch', could have been created originally – or at least adopted as a defensive feature – by the Danes in 895 (though a Norman origin must be more likely), even if the name of the ditch is unlikely to record their presence.[211] Indeed, the sunken main Bridgnorth-Quatt road (the A442) that separates the supposed bailey site from the church may disguise a rock-cut defensive ditch created by the Danes (or more likely the Normans) before the church was built.[212] The excavations of the supposed bailey

---

[206] TSAS LVII 1961-4 38 and 45 fn.10.
[207] SA 4296.
[208] Personal communication from Margaret Gelling dated 2nd August 2008. We may also note that *Heathen Field* is the name attached to several fields to the east and south-east of Claverley on the 1613 map of Morfe Common, there with the meaning Heathton Field; Heathton lies two miles south-east of Claverley: SA 4296; see also PN Sa 6 29. *Heathen Grene* recorded in 1603 refers to Heathton Green: ibid. 29.
[209] 'Bridgenorth, Oldbury, and Quatford', AC 29 (1874) 275-6, reprinted in Clark 1884: 281-2.
[210] Watkins-Pitchford 1932: 6.
[211] Matt Edgeworth notes that the Viking fortification at Tempsford was located at the point where an old but significant routeway, possibly a former course of the great North Road, once crossed the river Ouse: Edgeworth 2014: 51-2.
[212] Another ditch, the line of which has not been traced, lay, as we have seen, between the field or plain of Bridgnorth [Low Town?] and the vill of Quatford: '...ad quaddam vetus fossatum quod est inter campum de Bruges et villam de quatford' (TSAHS LXX 1996), almost certainly to be associated with 'a certain plain commencing at an ancient trench near Quatford...' recorded in the perambulation of Morfe Forest in 1300: Eyton 1854-60: III 114. It is unclear whether this is to be associated with 'the olde Diche under the gybet' which appears on the c.1560 map of Bridgnorth, and echoed in a reference in the perambulation of Morfe Forest in 1300, which refers to 'a certain ancient ditch under the Gybet': Eyton 1854-60: III 219. The Latin of the 1298 perambulation reads '... per dictum vetus fossatum subtus de Gybet ...': TSAHS LXXI 1996 27. The gibbet appears to have lain due east of

area in 1960 did not extend as far south as the sunken road leading to the river, and improvements to the A442 will have destroyed any early evidence on the line of that road.

We have seen that *Hethenedich* ran to the fish-weir at Quatford. References to Quatford weir by earlier researchers[213] are somewhat misleading, and may have led to the assumption that the weir-like feature was a conventional weir. But there was never a weir in the usual sense of that word at Quatford. The Latin word *gurgitem*, which is generally translated as 'weir', is more accurately a fish-weir or fish-trap.[214] Historically there were numerous fish weirs on the middle section of the Severn sited at places where the natural rock created shallows in the river certainly long before the Conquest, and probably from prehistoric times. They consisted in more recent times of a series of wickerwork fences and nets suspended from a substantial permanent structure of timbers and stakes, probably reinforced by stone foundations, driven into the bed of the river, arranged to form a series of V-shapes across the river channel. At the point of each V would be a wooden frame from which a net would be hung, apparently designed mainly to catch migrating eels. The fences would channel the water through these nets, so catching any passing fish. A walkway built across the top of the fences allowed access from the bank to haul in the catch. Some weirs ran across part of the river, others across the full width of the river.[215]

These fish weirs gradually fell out of use in the seventeenth and eighteenth centuries, although traces of a few remained until the latter part of the nineteenth century, and some may still be seen today. There are various references to a weir at Quatford from at least the thirteenth century, and a deed dated 1558 refers specifically to the fishing weir at Quatford.[216] We know that a ford lay close to the fish-weir (both of which are found where water is shallow), for a deed of 1296, which also records the fish-weir, mentions '... the road which leads to the ford of Severn, near the fishing-weir of Quatford ...'.[217] That tells us that *Hethenedich* which ran to the fishing-weir was also close to the ford, which indeed was its probable destination. The reported discovery at Netherton, just below the old ferry marked on early Ordnance Survey maps until recent times slightly south of a line running west from the church, close to two cottages on the east bank, one of which will have served as the ferryman's house, of large oak timbers and piers in and by the river in the late eighteenth and early nineteenth century has been held to be tentative evidence of a timber bridge of uncertain date some five feet wide,[218] but it is far more likely that the timbers

---

Bridgnorth and south of The Hermitage, to the west of St Nicholas' Oak, on the crest of the ridge along which ran a trackway running towards Gag's Hill: map of Bridgnorth c.1560.
[213] For example Eyton 1854-60: III 219; TSAS LVII 1961-4 38.
[214] RMLWL 218.
[215] The c.1560 map of the Bridgnorth area shows the fishing-weir at Quatford with a gap at each end at an angle across the river. Informative nineteenth century photograph of a fish weir at Preston Boats on the Severn are reproduced in Carr 1994 (unpaginated, plate number 8) and Jeremiah 1998: Plate 19. The c.1560 map of Bridgnorth also shows a fish-weir on the north side of the bridge at Bridgnorth.
[216] SA 2922/2/37.
[217] Eyton 1854-60: I 125. The *vado [ford] de Quatford* occurs before 1135, probably before 1127: Eyton 1854-60: III 166.
[218] TSAS LVII 1961-4: 43-4, which mentions that 'in about 1780 a very large piece of squared oak timber had been lifted out of the river at this point, and taken away, and that another piece of oak five feet long and eighteen inches square was still discernible about a foot deep in the earth on the east bank', and also mentions nineteenth century records of piers of the bridge visible at low water, of oak and two in number. Wasey records how 'Mr Bangham [from Bridgnorth], told me a short time before his death that he remembered seeing on one occasion at unusually low water the remains of two piers

were the remains of the fish weir: similar remains may still be seen at Arley and Alveley as substantial timbers in the river bank, with the infill of woven hazel stakes sometimes still visible at Arley.

But if these researches have identified with reasonable certainty the site of the Danish camp, there remains a further mystery to solve: seventeen years after the Danes wintered at *Cwatbrycge*, Æthelflæd, Lady of the Mercians, built a *burh*, or fortification, at a place called *Brycge* in the *Anglo-Saxon Chronicle*. That place was also known as *Cwatybrycge*. Its site remains undiscovered. In searching for clues to its location we might usefully consider in more detail the river Severn in the Bridgnorth area, and investigate whether other physical traces at Quatford might conceivably represent evidence of early fortifications.

---

of this very bridge. An old villager told Mr Smalman that he remembered beams of wood being raised from that part of the bed of the river ...': Wasey 1859: 25.

5. Geology and hydrology of the Bridgnorth area.

Dominating Bridgnorth and Quatford is the river Severn, at about 220 miles the longest river in the United Kingdom.

The Severn developed its present course during the melting of the Devensian ice sheets which encroached into the region from the west over 30,000 years ago.[219] Ralph Pee, who carried out detailed research into the river Severn in the Bridgnorth area,[220] observed that after each ice age vast quantities of gravel were deposited by the huge south-flowing torrents on areas where the valley widened, causing the current to slow. Remains of those deposits are found at Bridgnorth and Eardington. With warmer and drier conditions this composite river with a significant drop in its middle reaches – over three feet per mile between Ironbridge and Bridgnorth – carved out the river valley as we know it today, and has since reduced in size to fill only part of the old channel, depositing clay and silt in the remainder. The river has changed its course within the floodplain in many places, depositing scroll bars – curving ridges of silt – on the inside of bends opposite eroding banks. Backwater depressions are found in parts of the floodplain furthest away from the river and its deposited sediment, as at Quatford. In places its meanderings have carved out a flood plain some half a mile wide, sweeping away many of the gravel deposits except where shielded by features such as High Rock which protected the gravel terrace of The Grove, and the rise at Knowle which protected the deposits at Eardington, still a valuable source of building gravel.[221] The meadows of the flood plain, being separated from the main farm land, were invariably used as permanent pasture.

Pee makes the valuable observation that the sandstone over which the river flows is not uniformly hard. Had it been, at summer levels it would be swift and shallow throughout its course. If it had been uniformly soft, the river would have eroded its bed downwards and back upstream to the harder rocks above Linley, creating an impassable cataract between the lower and upper reaches. In fact hard bands appear at intervals running across the river roughly north-east to south-west. These hard bands, often connecting prominences like Queen's Parlour and High Town, Bridgnorth, provide fords which act as natural weirs so that the river descends in a number of shallow steps, with the water between these fords often very deep and slow-moving, while all the fords have a deep and comparatively narrow channel somewhere across their width. Barge operators on the Severn would of course have been aware of these. At Gadstone Ford near Apley, which is very long and shallow, the deep channel is so clearly defined that it appears to be, and probably is, artificial. We might wonder whether the earliest bridges were designed to cross such channels.

At Bridgnorth the original river valley was very wide and the hard band very prominent, which Pee believed had forced the river to break up into a number of channels. He suggested that one such ancient channel ran somewhere east of Mill Street, and along the route of the new (in the 1970s) by-pass. A ridge marking this channel (not be confused with the ridge marking the edge of of the flood plain, which extends beyond it), was

---

[219] This paragraph and the several paragraphs which follow incorporate much valuable material from a paper by David Pannett, 'The River Severn at Wroxeter', TSAHS LXVI 1989 48-55.
[220] JBHS 5 1977: 6-8; Vol. 6 1978: 4-8.
[221] Pee notes that a relic of gravel extraction can be seen on the side of Hermitage Hill, where the sandstone floor on which these gravels were laid has been cut into to provide a shute and wagon bay to enable gravel to be loaded into the once ubiquitous one-horse tipping cart.

visible in the fields below the town. It is said that in former times the road near the Fox public house was often flooded when the river was high.

In historic times another channel ran between Mill Street and the river, joining The Bylet channel via what is now the first arch of Bridgnorth bridge. The end of the island formed by this channel is marked by a gully at the bottom of Doctors Lane, which runs parallel to and just north of the bridge on the east side of the river. This gully has merely been left unfilled, not excavated for barges as sometimes asserted. The channel can be traced in the gardens behind Mill Street, but traces of its northern end may have been obliterated by rubbish from the former Hazeldine's Foundry. Pee concludes, not unreasonably, that this very wide and much divided ford may account for the otherwise most unlikely location for the bridge here.

In his survey of the Severn in the Wroxeter area, David Pannett has noted that where the river is generally some 150' wide, gravel banks known as riffles alternate with deeper pools.[222] Some of the gravel may underly the floodplain, and in other places is derived from the erosion of boulder clay leaving a lag deposit, sometimes found as a bed of stones set in clay with the appearance of a cobbled surface. Where riffles are found, the river is usually wider, since the water is shallower. These gravel banks were historically adopted as fords and bridging points, and in the medieval period some were used as sites for fish traps or fish weirs.

Since the Severn has long been busy with boats and barges which would be obstructed by the heavy timbering and wickerwork fences in the main river channel, by-pass channels were constructed alongside the main channel. These so-called barge gutters were dug through the adjacent floodplain, often by labour provided by monasteries, and leased to various proprietors, to create navigable side streams which could also be used by migrating fish such as salmon and eels. Gutters were found at many places along the Severn, including Dowles, Trimpley, Bewdley (mentioned in Domesday Book), Arley, Alveley, Chelmarsh, Quatford and Bridgnorth, although most of the weirs (28 are listed between Malverley and Dorles Weir in 1575) had fallen into disuse by 1650, every one, it is said, having been badly damaged by extreme flooding in 1635.[223] By 1700 only the weir at Alveley is still mentioned in documents, but may by then have been disused, and the gutter on the northernmost part of the Severn loop containing Shrewsbury was clearly visible until the 1960s, marked on Ordnance Survey maps as 'Barge Gutter'. The gutter channels were originally called bylets, but in time the word began to be applied to the islands so formed,[224] the best known probably being that on the south side of the bridge at Bridgnorth, although bylets are still to be found at Arley and Trimpley.

The situation at Wroxeter in the later medieval period appears to have mirrored in many respects that of Quatford, with a fish-weir, bylet and ford lying a short distance to the west of the church. At Wroxeter the old fish-weir lay at the head of Upper Bylet, which appears to have begun eroding when the timbers of the weir decayed. Erosion was accelerated with a loss of some 300 feet from the northern tip between 1842 and 1968, and deposition joined Lower Bylet to Upper Bylet. In other words, since 1842 two bylets have become

---

[222] Pannett 1989: 48-55.
[223] TSAS 1888 XI 425-6. See also Pannett 1981: 144,148.
[224] Jackson 1897: 61 defines bylet as 'A river island, land lying between the divergent branches of a stream, as, for instance, between the natural course of a brook and the mill-stream, or 'flem''. The term appears to be unique to Shropshire.

one, and the northern tip has been displaced 300 feet south, although the area of the newly formed bylet is no less than that of the two separate bylets.

The c.1560 map of Bridgnorth shows three features in the river at Quatford. One is what appears to be a square raft with sides, probably to be interpreted as a ferry. Nearby to the south is a slightly curved 'ladder' lying across the middle of the river but not reaching either bank, probably representing the fish weir, and nearby on the south a sub-circular shape which is evidently Bridge Bylet, a feature which seems to appear as a roughly lozenge-shaped island on the 1613 map of Morfe Forest.[225] The earlier map is highly schematic (for example, the river between Bridgnorth is greatly shortened and has no bends), and it is difficult to relate every feature to the modern topography, but it is probably significant that as at Wroxeter, the bylet lies to the south of the weir, but does not adjoin it. Possibly the weir was in a state of decay c.1560, and the northern end of the bylet had started to erode. It is possible that the disturbance to the current caused by fish weirs led to the deposition of silt and the gradual formation of bylets.

The river Severn at Quatford makes a sharp turn at the point where it is forced to deviate by the sandstone bluff. On the west side of the river is the large floodplain mentioned previously. A useful exercise will be to examine the sinuous meanders that are a characteristic feature of such floodplains.[226]

Meanders originate from the enlargement of river bends, and occur when the path of flow in a river is disturbed or obstructed. For example, on a straight stretch of river the growth of a sand bar, perhaps from the collapse of part of a river bank, a very common occurrence along the Severn, will deflect the line of flow towards the opposite bank, where undercutting results, and a bend will begin to form. Material from the undercut bank is carried a short distance downstream to form another bar, which in turn deflects the flow to the opposite bank to develop a second bend. Once a slight bend is produced, centrifugal force thrusts the flow towards the outside of the bend, until a meander loop is eventually created. On the inside of the bend a series of sand and gravel bars accumulate to produce a point-bar deposit. Because of the differences in erodibility in the materials that form the floodplain, a meander may become constricted, so as to have a narrow meander neck, which may be cut through by bank collapse or by overflow in times of flood, permitting the stream to bypass the bend and thereby produce a cut-off. The cut-off meander bend will quickly become detached from the main stream by silt deposits to become an oxbow lake. Gradual filling of the lake results in an oxbow swamp or marsh.

Many alluvial rivers such as the Severn have floods of such magnitude that the water can no longer be contained within the channel and inundates the floodplain. Such overbank flooding permits fine-grained sediment (silts and clays) suspended in the relatively slow-moving water to be deposited across the floodplain as 'overbank deposits'. The coarsest sediment – sand and coarse silt – is deposited in two belts, one on each side of the river channel, since the flow here will be relatively swift. After many floods there will thus be lateral zones of natural ground, termed natural levees, with their highest point close to the river bank and a very slight slope away from the river to a low lying, often marshy, area at

---

[225] SA 4296. The map, which is rubbed and illegible in some places, covers an area of several square miles on the east side of the Severn, and includes a colourful bird's-eye view of Quatford and useful details of field-boundaries, roads, buildings, etc., in the area around Quatford.
[226] The following paragraphs are based on Strahler 1963: 493-5.

the edge of the floodplain. Such an area lies on the west side of the Severn floodplain opposite Quatford, before the land rises steeply.

The presence of a natural levee along an alluvial river has a curious effect upon the junction of tributaries. Streams entering the floodplain cannot flow directly into the main stream because the levee acts as a barrier. Instead the tributary turns downstream and roughly parallel to the main river, often for many miles, before a junction is formed.

Studies have shown that rivers flowing across floodplains can migrate very considerably over a relatively short period as a result of the natural formation of meanders. As an example, the Mississippi is known to have changed its course by creating a series of new meanders and abandoning old ones between 1765 and 1942, and the phenomenon applies to all rivers and streams to a greater or lesser extent. At Repton, the Danish wintering camp was created in 874-5 on a prominent bluff of Bunter sandstone adjoining the river Trent. Since that time the course of the river has changed, and it is now over half a mile to the north of Repton.[227]

In the case of the river Severn, it is very clear that floodplains (often marked on nineteenth-century Ordnance Survey maps as 'Liable to Flooding') would have allowed the river to adopt a continually changing course over time, and the course of the river today cannot tell us what line it would have taken in the late ninth and early-tenth century. Since that date the river has almost certainly taken a variety of lines past Quatford, and we should be aware that the river at Quatford probably followed a different course at the period in question.[228] It is very possible that in the tenth century one or more islands existed in the Severn on what is now the wide floodplain to the east of Quatford, which would have formed ready-made defensive positions for a Viking camp.

In conclusion, it is likely that the Danish camp lay on the banks of the river Severn at Quatford, utilising the sandstone outcrop on the east bank, and possibly on an island in the river opposite that bluff, with any such island long since obliterated by successive floodwaters. Whilst we have reasons to explain why no remains of the Danish fortification have been detected – many were evidently undefended by ditches and banks – it is curious (but certainly not unusual) that no evidence has been found of any Anglo-Saxon encampment(s) created by the English forces during the several months they must have spent keeping a careful eye on the Danes in 895-6, or of the *burh* built by Æthelflæd in 912. Confirmation of the site of the Danish camp might yet materialise in the form of archaeological evidence of ninth-century English military sites overlooking the Severn, perhaps including the temporary re-use of The Walls at Chesterton and the Burf Castle earthworks.

Before closing this section, we might note, in connection with the subject of D-shaped enclosures lying against the Severn, once believed to signify Viking fortifications, that there are two overlapping semi-circular boundaries lying on the east bank of the river at the supposed site of the bridge which crossed the river at Quatford. These boundaries are clearly shown on the 1613 map of Morfe Forest,[229] proving that they are of some antiquity,

---

[227] Hall 2012: 82-5.
[228] Pee notes that one of Arthur Mees' encyclopaedias has a photograph which shows children in a spot which is now in the middle of the river.
[229] SA 4296. The northern area is marked *Ilan ds* (*sic*) on two lines, probably dictated by the limited space. Across the southern area is written *Town[e?] of In[ ]g[e*': the writing is worn and indistinct,

and were considered sufficiently prominent to be represented on a map at that date.[230] It is unclear whether the parallel lines of the interconnected curved areas on the 1613 map might be intended to represent banks or ditches, and those parts of the boundaries to the north have for many years been subsumed beneath a permanent caravan site, but the southern part of the southernmost arc is now marked by a modest ditch serving as an open drain carrying water from the higher ground on the east into the Severn. The lines represent the ghost of the artificial channels or barge gutters which were cut from the main river to allow boats to by-pass fish weirs or other obstructions in the main river channel. The 1613 map shows that they lay to the south of the Bridge Billet at Quatford, and well south of the weir, which might suggest that they were intended to circumvent the fallen remains of an obstruction, such as the old bridge or fish weir. Why they are interconnected is not entirely obvious, but it seems possible that the obstruction in the river shifted over the years, and a new channel became necessary.[231]

The interlocking D-shapes of the gutters at Quatford is reminiscent of the D-shaped enclosure banks and ditches recorded at Viking sites such as Woodstown in Waterford, near the coast in south-east Ireland (where two such D-shapes, one larger than the other, adjoin (as at Quatford), forming an enclosure some 450 yards long and 140 yards wide, enclosing some 7½ acres. There are no traces of defensive banks on the barge gutters at Quatford, but creating a bank would self-evidently give rise to a ditch, and we might wonder whether it could have been a Viking ditch that was later utilised as a gutter. But the gutters lie below higher ground to the east, which could affect their defensibility, would have been prone to flooding, and at roughly 290 yards wide and 48 yards deep (though both dimensions may have been reduced – perhaps considerably reduced – by river erosion) are of a smaller scale than other recognised Viking sites. However, the Danish camp was a wintering camp rather than a permanent settlement, and the possibility that they represent physical manifestations of the Viking wintering of 895-6 and later re-adapted can almost certainly be discounted.

---

but perhaps 'Towne of Ininge': the term *inning* is found fairly frequently in ME field names, meaning 'a piece of land taken in or enclosed': Smith 1956: i 304. The first name may indicate that the boundaries identify former bylets or channels associated with fisheries which effectively created islands in the Severn. The c.1560 map of Bridgnorth shows nothing that might represent the curved features.

[230] They also indicate that there has been little erosion of the adjoining river bank in almost 400 years.

[231] Satellite photographs taken in 2010 (Google Earth) show a sizeable D-shaped area to the south of Quatford on the east bank of the river. Field hedges and boundaries form five straight sides, with the sixth (northernmost) represented by a crop mark, all of similar length forming the angularly-curved part of the letter D. The lower end of the D is aligned exactly with a boundary of Eardington Lower Forge on the west side of the Severn. The forge was built in the 1780s and in was use until 1889 (TSAS LVIII 1965-8 235-43; Pevsner 2006: 255), and the upper end of the D is marked similarly by a cropmark on the east side of the river running directly east-west, which is identified as a hedgeline on the 6" O.S. map of 1884. The delineated D-shaped area might well be taken for a large defended area, with its northern and southern ends marked by boundaries extending from the west bank. However, the 1884 map shows that there were then no curves in the southern boundary (the continuing straight line of the old hedgerow can be made out on the 2010 satellite photograph), and the northernmost section of the D appears to be a channel associated with the former Dudmaston Mill (disused by 1903) which lay to the east.

6. Quatford and its two castles.

Before discussing the two castles at Quatford, it is necessary to consider the early administrative and ecclesiastical history of the place. From Domesday Book we seem to be told that Eardington (on the west bank of the Severn) lay in Shropshire and incorporated Quatford and its borough.[232] Quatford is normally recognised as an estate on the east bank of the river opposite Eardington, but including a small area adjoining the west bank. That will have placed Quatford, principally on the east side of the river, as an isolated projection into Staffordshire, assuming that Worfield (then in Staffordshire, but transferred to Shropshire before 1102)[233] included all the land up to the Severn. Later, and confusingly, the two estates became known as Quatford, which included Eardington, with the township of Quatford on the east bank including the small area of low-lying ground on the west bank opposite the ford. This unusual arrangement may have contributed to uncertainty and confusion as to the diocese in which Eardington and Quatford lay: in the first half of the eleventh century both were held to be in the see of Hereford, whereas Eyton placed Quatford in Lichfield diocese in 1086.[234] In summary, Eardington may have been a pre-Domesday estate on the west bank of the Severn incorporating a significant but smaller area on the east bank which included a settlement later known as Quatford; or Eardington was a pre-Domesday estate on the west bank of the Severn with another estate, Quatford, facing it on the east bank, with a small part of Quatford lying on the west side of the river. In either case land of one of those estates would have lain on both sides of the river, clear evidence of a major and ancient crossing of the Severn and the concern to ensure that both banks were held in the same ownership.

Together with Quatford church, the dominent feature of the historic landscape of Quatford is the motte, generally known as Quatford castle, not to be confused with the mock medieval house known as Quatford Castle half a mile north-west of Quatford built in little more than twelve months in 1829-30 by John Smalman, a wealthy architect and antiquary, on a rounded eminence called appropriately Round Hill.[235]

The site of Smalman's house is the subject of an enigmatic record made by William Hardwicke,[236] the Bridgnorth antiquary writing in the early nineteenth century, who says: 'About two hundred paces to the north-west of the New Castle [mentioned below] at Quatford, in the grounds of Miss Stanier of Saint James's in Bridgnorth, on the western

---

[232] Morris 1986: 4.1.32.
[233] Thorn and Thorn 2007.
[234] TSAS LVII 1961-4a: 45 fn.21.
[235] TSAS LVII 1961-4a: 46 fn.37. The 1842 Tithe Map shows Round Hill Side adjoining the south-east side of Quatford Castle. Scott 1832: 331 mentions 'the two lofty sandrocks, culivated and adorned by the proprietor of this demesne ... [one of which] is crowned with a rising castellated mansion, surrounded by woodlands'. The 1842 Tithe Map shows *Castle Trenches* as the name of a field north of Quatford and east of the nineteenth-century Quatford Castle. The name may have archaeological implications, but is perhaps more likely to be associated with the nineteenth-century castle. The field-name has not been traced in any other records, and the nature of the 'trenches' is unknown. Bowman's Hill, which lies above Quatford Castle, may have taken its name from the Beaumont, Beamon or Beaman family recorded in Bridgnorth from at least the 16th century: the house of Grey Friars in Bridgnorth was granted at the Dissolution to John Beaumont: Cruttwell 1801: III 365. The family name is said to be from one of five places in Normandy named Beaumont (Reaney 1997: 35), and Bowman's Hill is recorded as Beaumont hill in 1841, but is perhaps a 19th-century naming attributable to John Smalman, responsible for the construction of Quatford Castle in 1829-30: no earlier forms have been traced.
[236] MS *Parochial Histories of Shropshire*, Vol. IV, WSL. The volume is unpaginated.

extremity near the upper public road leading from Quatford to that town, is a natural and circular eminence, generally called the Round hill, in the centre of which have lain in quiet and undisturbed repose during the long protracted period of 900 years and upwards the warlike remains of some Danish leader.' Hardwicke goes on to record a stone over the body 6" thick and 7' long, on the upper surface 'the rude effigy of a Danish chief', and claims that the stone was removed in 1830 to the shrubbery above the garden of St James's (presumably near the 37 skeletons discovered in 1823), at the further end of the terrace, placed upright. Frustratingly, Hardwicke provides no further information about the supposed body he mentions: we do not know whether he himself witnessed any exhumation of some skeletal remains, or whether the tale was local folklore. One would like to know far more about the stone with its 'rude effigy' mentioned and evidently seen by Hardwicke,[237] but we can be reasonably certain that whatever might have appeared on the face of any stone, it was not of Danish origin. If ancient, a post-Conquest date must be assumed. Nothing more has been discovered about this intriguing find.

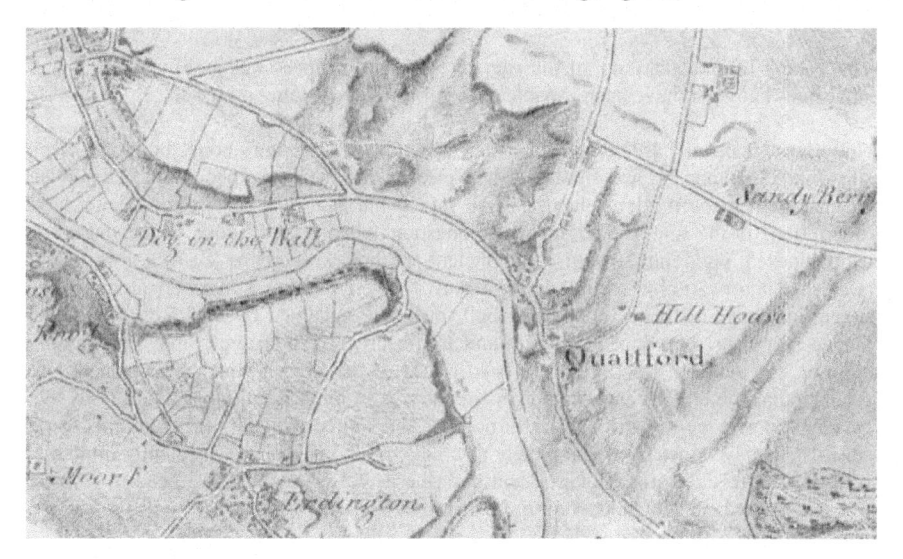

Indistinct but informative map of Quatford, from the draft survey of the Bridgnorth area produced by Robert Dawson for the Ordnance Survey in 1815 (British Library).

Smalman's house, said to have been called originally Morf Mount, is a 'mock fortalice, and example of the Oxford Goal type, of red sandstone and brick, of four storeys, embattled throughout. There are five Gothic glazed windows to the façade, a square tower of five stages, machiolations, arrow slits, etc. The curtain walls have corner bastions, and there are earth ramparts and catellated outbuildings. The interior is characteristic with a stone tunnel staircase approach, ribbed ceilings, oak doors with applied mouldings and oak well stair with brass rod balusters'.[238] Howard Colvin wrote of it as '... a castellated mansion ...

---

[237] Enquiries made via a letter from the author published in the *Bridgnorth Journal* on 13th February 2009 elicited only one response, from Mr John Dixon of St John Street, who generously provided a wealth of material relating to the Bridgnorth area from his family archive, but was unable to throw any light on the mysterious memorial stone, the area around St James's having been heavily re-developed since the early nineteenth century.
[238] Shropshire SMR SA 11640.

somewhat in the style of Wyatville's work at Windsor'.[239] The house and grounds were described by G. T. Clark in 1874 in the following terms: 'A short steep combe descends from the high ground to the north-east, and branching below includes a knoll of rock perhaps 150 ft. above the valley and 200 ft. above the river. The soft red rock has been paced [sic] and scarped, and a part of the material employed to give an artifical top to the hill. This is somewhat of an oval, and seems to have had a sort of mound at its east end, now occupied by a modern castellated house. The slopes are steep, especially towards the west, and they are broken by narrow terraces, now walks, but which may have been ditches. The approach is by a sort of causeway on the north-east or least steep side. The summit and sides of the work are converted into a house and gardens, but the general arrangement of the original hill can readily be detected. It must have been very strong, and resembles generally Devizes and similar works of English origin. Probably this is the site of the "nova domus" of Earl Roger, as it was the seat of his English predecessor. It is a very curious work, and deserves to be surveyed on a large scale by the officers of the ordnance.'[240]

The 'pacing [?] and scarping' of the site were evidently carried out by Smalman himself, since he is known to have been capable of significant landscaping projects.

Nowadays Quatford Castle tends to be seen as a nineteenth-century house built on a virgin site. John Smalman, as we shall see, was clearly disposed to expend time, labour and expense to reshape the local landscape to satisfy his historical sensibilities, but Clark's description of the site should make us question whether the house could indeed be superimposed upon and disguise an ancient earthwork, perhaps even a fortification (Danish and/or Anglo-Saxon) dating from the pre-Conquest period, although his suggestion that Smalman's house was built on a site occupied by Earl Roger's 'English predecessor' must be entirely fanciful, and Clark has proved an unreliable historian and reporter. No detailed description has been traced of the site on which Smalman's house stands before he built it, but Clark was supposedly an eminent antiquary with unrivalled personal knowledge of fortifications throughout the United Kingdom (although his dating conclusions have since been completely discredited), and if he was sufficiently impressed with the site to liken it to Devizes, and describe it as 'very strong', we need to consider whether it may be a contender for the site of Æthelflæd's *burh*.

The 1815 draft map of the area produced by Robert Dawson, an experienced and respected Ordnance Survey surveyor, shows no building on the site or any landscape feature that may have been man-made.[241] Hardwicke makes no mention of any prominent earthwork at Smalman's house, which he calls 'the New Castle', but his text is somewhat confusing, and it is unclear whether he may have been referring to the house known as The Chantry, also

---

[239] Colvin 1997: 930.
[240] AC 4th Series XX 1874 275. Clark's belief that Smalman's house was on the site of a very much older earthwork was not shared by Watkins-Pitchford 1937, who says: '... the site of Quatford Castle has no known historic associations'. Griffith 1870: 262 states that '[Quatford] castle stands on a natural mound upwards of one hundred feet high, and is surrounded by groves of oak, beech, fir and chestnut. These the proprietor planted with his own hands ...', but Burke refers enigmatically to 'Quatford Castle, a modern mansion, which [Smalman] erected on the site of the old Castle of Quatford': Burke 1884: 934.
[241] BL online gallery of first edition 1" O.S. draft surveys.

restored by Smalman,[242] which has a fifteenth-century core, with a nearby early nineteenth century brick watchtower, a folly on a sandstone rock having two small towers with battlements and arrow slits, rustic glazed windows in pointed arch recesses, and a diamond-shaped clock face.[243] It seems possible that Smalman built (or improved) the New Castle to use as a residence while he completed Quatford Castle – he was certainly living at Quatford from at least 1823, and is known to have lived at The Chantry before Quatford Castle was under construction.

An illustration from John Randall's *Tourists' Guide to Bridgnorth*, published in 1875, showing various Gothic Revival buildings in Quatford village viewed from the south, including the castellated watchtower, the folly on the hill above, and the dominating pile of Quatford Castle in the background.

An account of Smalman's house published in 1825 describes it as '... one of the most interesting spots in the county of Salop. The labour bestowed, the ingenuity and taste displayed, by its intelligent and enlightened proprietor, have given to a barren rock,

---

[242] SA 11635. Newman and Pevsner 2006: 482 suggest that the house may have been converted from a late medieval chapel, mentioning a piscina within the building. There were Smalmans living at The Chantry in 1884: Burke 1884: 934.

[243] SMR NO11638. The building is clearly not the structure labelled 'watch tower' in a watercolour produced for John Smalman by Joseph Powell (part of Lot 338, Dreweatt & Bloomsbury Auctions, London, 13 November 2014), which shows a slender three-storey undecorated tower of square plan, angular profile and central doorway with pointed arch, surmounted by an integral covered viewing platform.

loveliness and fertility'.[244] That description would seem appropriate for Quatford Castle, rather than The Chantry, but the date is a little earlier than the period generally ascribed to the building. The matter is certainly confused, for a recent commentator has noted that 'Smalman was listed in directories as of Quatford Castle, to which building he was said by contemporaries to have made 'considerable additions in 1830 with some reference to the national character of the place'. (The additions were comprehensive enough for Pevsner to imply rather that he built the castle entirely new.)'.[245] However, the reference to 'additions' referred to houses in Quatford village, many of which were built or renovated by Smalman, not specifically to Quatford Castle, and Pevsner would seem to be correct.[246]

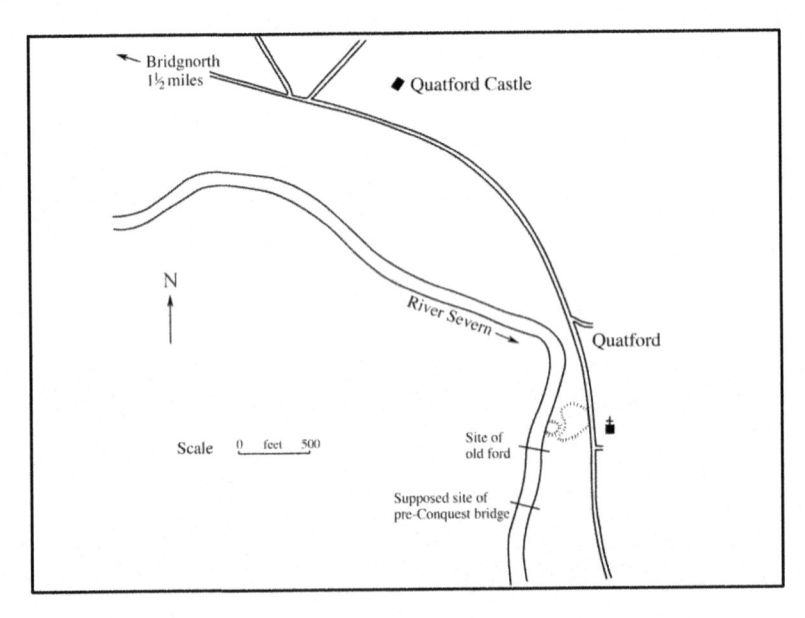

Map showing the location of the eleventh-century motte and supposed bailey between the church and the River Severn at Quatford. The nineteenth-century Quatford Castle lies some distance to the north-west.

Further to the south-east, Quatford church stands well back from and above the river Severn on a wide spur of sandstone which slopes down from the high ground on the east and ends abruptly as a vertical cliff when it reaches the Severn. On the south-east side of the churchyard, platforms, clearly once the site of structures but now devoid of buildings, have been carved out of the sandstone.[247] Between the church and the river stands Quatford castle, held to be a classic motte-and-bailey fortification, its topography succinctly described by Watkins-Pitchford in 1937: 'near the church the east bank of the

---

[244] Hulbert 1825: 461.
[245] TSAHS LXXXII 2007 17.
[246] Smalman is said to have 'built a handsome village, redeemed and planted the common, or rather the Desert of Morfe, and found employment for numbers of his fellow beings during a length of years ...': Griffith 1868: 113. 'Quatford Castle is a modern building' according to PODS 1863: 737.
[247] It is worth recording an ancient custom peculiar to Quatford whereby the maintenance of the churchyard wall, 270 yards in length, is apportioned between 9 properties in the parish, an obligation named Hayments: Wasey 1859: 65.

river rises somewhat abruptly into a rocky eminence, about 80' in height above the water, contrary to the statement made in several books, this elevation is not a promontory ... the whole of the summit of this eminence is artificial, and consists of about 15 feet of sandy soil piled upon the rock so as to produce a rounded mound, shaped like the top of a thimble; this is the motte of [Roger de] Montgomery's castle'.[248]

Raised on a natural sandstone knoll rising sheer from the river, the mound is D-shaped and tree grown, some 28 feet high, 120 feet by 155 feet at the base, and 35 feet across the top, which has been severely mutilated by a trench running north to south and another from that trench eastwards. The west side of the summit is broken and irregular.[249] An impressive flat-bottomed v-shaped rock-cut ditch some 15 feet wide at the base and 8 feet below the level of the ground to the east circles the mound, except on the west, where the sandstone cliff falls vertically to the Severn and has probably been eroded by the river.[250] The ditch separates the mound from what has been assumed to be the bailey, which is a little under an acre in area, defined on the northern and southern sides by scarps measuring about 6' and 3' 9" in height respectively. The spoil from the ditch around the motte was evidently used to create the mound.[251]

---

[248] Watkins-Pitchford 1937. It is unclear whether an enigmatic reference in BDS for 1851 might refer to this site. The entry reads: 'On the south-east side of the Morffe in early times was an important military station, which may still be traced; the ground is elevated, and the moat [sic] still visibly circumscribing a large area'.

[249] G. T. Clark describes the summit as 'much cut about, probably for modern purposes' (whatever that may mean): AC 4th Series XX (1874) 276.

[250] Any such erosion may explain early references in 1086, discussed in more detail elsewhere in this volume, to 'the land between the water and the mount': Eyton 1854-60: I 109.

[251] Confusingly, a report in 1832 (Scott 1832: 331) mentions the opening of what was described as a tumulus on the rock at Quatford three years earlier, although the account is not convincing. It reads: 'In August 1829 the writer of this article in company with a party of gentlemen, was present at the opening of a tumulus raised on a massive sand stone rock, protruding into the channel of the Severn. Transverse trenches had been opened by order of the proprietor of the domain, – Smallman, Esq., perforating the adventitious sandy soil. No human remains occurred, but the anxiety of the company was in some measure relieved by the appearance of several fragments of Roman pottery, both plain and striped. In 1830 a human skeleton was found in an adjacent field. The barrow is supposed to have been an exploratory station rather than a place of sepulture. A foss of nearly circular form is visible in an adjoining field, the contents of which have probably been transferred to the tumulus'. Later in the same volume (p.587) is an addendum: 'Tumulus, Quatford. From subsequent information, it appears, that a few human remains, not a human skeleton, occurred on opening this tumulus, 1830. A Norman spur, and an antique ring, with a cross attached, were also found'. It is clear that the writer has provided an account of an excavation on the summit of the motte a short time before the motte ditch was dug out, although the addendum leads one to question whether Scott was present at the excavation as he claims, and he seems, in his addendum, to have conflated the excavation of the mound with that of the related ditch. The reference to transverse trenches on the summit of the mound accords with what Watkins-Pitchford recorded in 1937: 'The domed top of the motte measures about 41 feet from north to south, and about 56 feet from east to west. Near the centre, this top is traversed from north to south by the remains of a trench, 2 to 3 feet deep and about 6 feet wide. From the middle of this trench another trench runs at right-angles towards the east, and opens out onto a cresent-shaped platform cut into the side of the mound', which he suggested marked the site of a ladder linking the lower and upper storeys of the timber tower. The description of the summit still holds good today. No other excavation of the mound has been recorded, but if the earth on the mound was indeed used to fill the surrounding ditch, as seems likely, any archaeological evidence may have been destroyed at that time, although if a tower was constructed on the sandstone rock it is very possible that traces remain within the artificial mound.

The rock outcrop is especially noteworthy in the light of Benjamin Raffield's study of Viking fortifications which concluded, inter alia, that '[Viking] fortified sites may utilise a natural barrier such as a river cliff or rock outcrop'.[252] It is difficult to believe that a Danish camp at *Cwatbrycge* in 895-6 was not centred on the outcrop, and it would not be unusual to find that the camp had no artificial defences, although those may have existed and remain untraced.

It was seemingly John Smalman who first identified the motte at Quatford with its infilled ditch as artificial and ancient – surprisingly, it is unrecorded before his time[253] – and it was certainly he who arranged for his workmen to dig out the ditch during the winter of 1830-1,[254] though there is no evidence that at the time the mound was seen as anything more than a stand-alone artificial mount.[255]

In *Salopia Antiqua*, published in 1841, the Shropshire antiquary and topographer C. H. Hartshorne gives a minute description of the mound and its ditch, and concludes that it is 'Altogether unlike any species of fortification with which I am acquainted; this ditch is cut in a curvilinear direction for nearly two hundred yards through the solid rock, and the marks of the workmen's tools upon it in several places are still distinctly visible. It is three yards wide at the bottom, and at least four in depth below the average level of the meadow above it, whilst the summit of the keep upon the top of the rock is about twenty-five feet above the same level ... there are faint indications of an inferior keep a little nearer to the ford, close to the present footpath leading to the ferry;[256] this was evidently designed for its special protection'.[257] He provides no details of the presumed bailey, but an oblique reference is found in his comment that 'the whole land occupied by the original castle comprises two acres. The rent of this land is at present appropriated to defray the charge of ferrying persons over the river when they attend the parish church'.[258]

---

[252] Raffield 2010: 105. A brief note on the history of Quatford and its church, seemingly in the hand of John Higgs, minister of Quatford, and probably dating from c.1734, notes the existence of '... a fortress which was built near ye church & which is now demolished', but whether he understood the mound to be the remains of the 'fortress' is uncertain: SA X7381/189/1072.

[253] Unless John Leland's reference to *great Tokens of a Pyle or Mannour Place* here, discussed below, was intended to refer to the mound.

[254] TSAS LVII 1961-4 42. Some 200 cartloads of fill from the ditch were removed. Unfortunately we have no information as to where this quantity of earth was deposited – it would surely have been sufficient to change the shape of the area in which it was deposited – and it is unclear whether the faces of the sandstone in the base of the ditch which have been carefully tooled and follow the profile and curve of the mound were formed when the motte was first created, or when the ditch was re-excavated in the 1830s.

[255] It is worth recording the observations of a traveller in 1808: 'We gained an eminence of sandy rock at Quatford, which being hewn for many feet on either side of the road, makes an avenue, through which the town of Bridgenorth is seen very happily. Of the collegiate church founded here by Roger de Bellesmo, earl of Shrewsbury, in the reign of William Rufus, not even the slightest vestiges are to be traced, neither of his residence, which is mentioned as being extant in the sixteenth century ...': Aitken 1808: 326. The reference to remains extant in the 16th century is presumably based on Leland's observation.

[256] No other mention of the feature has been traced elsewhere. LiDAR surveys show a flattish mound adjoining the south side of the sunken track (? Heathen's Ditch) running west towards the river. Could this be where spoil from the ditch was deposited in 1830-1?

[257] Hartshorne 1841: 225. The ferry ceased in 1940.

[258] Hartshorne 1841: 230; Randall 1863: 18. Randall 1875 says that among the old endowments of Quatford church was 'a piece of land, called Paradise, containing four acres and three quarters, and a house and garden, let at a low rent of 10s per annum on condition that the tenant performs the service gratuitously of rowing over at all times the parishioners to the parish church': cited in Jeremiah 1998:

G. T. Clark gives a description of the ditched motte in 1874, and adds: 'Outside this ditch and to the east of it is an area of irregular figure, governed by the outline of the ground. Its north and south sides are defended by a ditch, which to the south is deep and wide [doubtless *heathens ditch* referred to previously]. This probably included the east side, but is now superceded by the hollow road. The area is not very large, and would perhaps accommodate about two hundred men'.[259] We might presume that Clark had observed distinct traces of a bailey which were unnoticed by Hartshorne, notwithstanding the latter's careful inspection of the site, but as noted earlier Clark has proved to be an unreliable observer, and it may be unsafe to rely on his report: in 1889 he says of Quatford motte, in an account of moated mounds and *burhs* (*sic*), that it is 'A moated mound chiefly artificial, with a very curious and perfect well',[260] the latter comment puzzling and unexplained – no such well is mentioned by any other observer – unless the entry refers to the site of Smalman's neo-medieval house to the north.

From these accounts we must suppose that it is only since the 1820s that the mound has been recognised as artificial, and not until the 1840s that the existence of an associated bailey on the east side of the motte has been assumed, which is perhaps surprising given the typical scarp slopes readily discernible in the position one would expect in the case of a Norman bailey, and the higher ground between the motte and the church is not untypical of that chosen for baileys. At this point it is appropriate to mention another motte located on a ford on the Severn at Little Shrawardine, 7 miles west of Shrewsbury, which adjoins the Welsh border. The place is discussed in more detail in Chapter 10 in this volume, but is remarkably similar to Quatford. Since meetings were anciently held at mounds – and mounds were often created to mark meeting places – with assemblies often held at fords,[261] we might be justified in speculating that both mounds (and doubtless others elsewhere) could have been created originally to mark notable pre-Conquest boundary points and/or meeting places, and were adapted later by the Normans as ready-made mottes. But that idea can be no more than conjecture.[262]

In an attempt to identify the bailey to the motte, an archaeological excavation was undertaken prior to roadwidening in the 1960s. A narrow strip at the eastern end of the supposed bailey area was excavated, and topsoil removed to reveal a worn sandstone surface representing a footway on the line of the public path on the south side of the bailey area towards the river, but the excavators were puzzled to find that the apparent rampart and ditch did not exist as archaeological features, and concluded that the bailey area may have been fortified by a palisade alone, though no postholes to support the existence of a palisade were traced. The only real archaeological features were very shallow postholes in the sandstone surface, some of which had been packed with 'stones, tufa, slates, and other oddments foreign to the site'.[263]

The excavators conceded that the results of the excavation were baffling: ' ... [there were] no floors, nor hearths, nor any other evidence of continuous occupation, nor was there any

---

Plate 51. This seems to be a conflation of two endowments, one of 'Paradise and garden, 4 acres, 2 roods and 5 perches', followed by 'Ferry house and garden 1 rood 38 perches', the latter at a rent of 10s subject to the service of ferrying parishioners to the church: see Wasey 1859: 89.

[259] AC 4th Series XX 1874 276.
[260] Clark 1889: 211.
[261] For meeting places in the region see Pantos 1999: 91-112; see also Pantos and Semple 2004.
[262] It must be conceded that there is no mound at the ancient and important ford and meeting place at Rhydwhiman near Montgomery.
[263] TSAS LVII 1961-4 49; Eyton 1854-60: I 116, citing Hartshorne's *Salopia Antiqua* 232.

firm evidence of more than one period of construction ... The apparent rampart along the edge of the bailey had 17th/18th pottery in its base, there was no evidence of a stockade and there was no bailey ditch. It seems likely that the postholes represent out-buildings which were hardly used before being abandoned; there was nothing to connect them with the Danes or with Roger de Montgomery'.[264] This account, a summary of the more detailed report published subsequently, is slightly misleading, for the section through the apparent southern rampart bordering the public footpath which crossed the site showed that it was made up from disturbed sand overlying cleaner sand and contained unstratified pottery and objects of all dates from the twelfth to the nineteenth centuries, with a halfpenny of 1881 found a few inches above the natural rock in the deepest part of the supposed rampart. That feature was in fact illusory: it transpired that the bank had been formed by ploughing during the 1939-45 war.[265]

The discovery of tufa used as packing in some of the shallow postholes in the area of the supposed bailey at Quatford is of particular interest. Tufa, or travertine, is a type of limestone formed when spring-water laden with calcium carbonate bubbles through sphagnum moss, and the calcium carbonate is deposited in the form of precipitate which gradually hardens. When dry the rock has a characteristic pitted appearance, like a petrified sponge. The most remarkable feature of the church at Quatford is that it was apparently built entirely of tufa, probably from a narrow band of tufa-bearing limestone in an outcrop which runs from Harpswood, barely three miles to the north-west, along the side of Mor Brook, and down Corve Dale, skirting the foot of Brown Clee, with large deposits said to exist in Easthope parish below Wenlock Edge.[266]

The site of the original Norman church, which we know was founded (or possibly refounded) on 14th November 1086,[267] is not known for certain,[268] but is very likely to have been on or close to the site of the present church, which probably dates from the twelfth century,[269] and stands on a platform levelled out of the wide sandstone rib which falls to the Severn. We should remember that Domesday Book tells us that a borough existed at Quatford when the great survey was compiled in 1086, and a borough would normally include a church or chapel. There may have been a pre-1086 church or chapel – perhaps even a pre-Conquest foundation – somewhere in Quatford: Earl Roger may have seen an earlier church, with extraordinary rights and immunity from interference by bishops (if it could then have been a Royal Free Chapel), as an ideal base from which to

---

[264] TSAS LVI 1957-60 346; TSAS LVII 1961-64: 37-62. Randall 1863: 17 suggests that travertine was also used in the earliest church at Alveley, and it is also said to have been used at Chetton and Worfield: Murchison 1839: 565-7.

[265] Barker 1993: 226. As noted elsewhere, LiDAR surveys show extensive areas of mechanical ploughing in various parts of Quatford, including unbroken plough-lines to the north and east of the motte extending south into the 'bailey' area, showing that there was then no impediment to the plough on the north side of the bailey.

[266] Leonard 2004: 241; Swift 2008: 121. 'Calcareous tufa, a lime deposit found in restricted areas in various parts of the country (e.g. Kent and Herefordshire), was a material both extremely light in weight and easy to work [tufa in large blocks is used very freely in the eleventh-century east range of Westminster Abbey, and in a large number of buildings throughout Kent and Essex]. It was extensively used by the Romans, and much of the tufa used in early Anglo-Norman buildings is re-used Roman material. ... [T]he use of tufa continued well into the twelfth century.': Clapham 1934: II 114.

[267] TSAS LVII 1961-4 40, 45 fn.29.

[268] Watkins-Pitchford 1937 believed that the fabric of the original church was taken to Bridgnorth when the borough was transferred there by Robert de Bellême.

[269] Leonard 2004: 241-2.

control the south-eastern part of his territory, though we might have expected to see some reference to an earlier foundation in the much later digest of the founding of Quatford church, of which more shortly.[270]

The use of tufa is generally taken as a sign of relatively early Norman building, and seems to have been rarely used after c.1125, although the present Quatford church is generally held to date from c.1180.[271] Why tufa should have been used when the area is self-evidently rich in building stone will be readily apparent to anyone who visits the church, for the local sandstone is badly weathered, whereas the tufa is in very good order.[272] Tufa is not a good material for carving, but is surprisingly durable. John Smalman, the eminent architect who built and lived at the neo-medieval Quatford Castle, claimed that whenever he made alterations to any old church in the neighbourhood he found pieces of tufa in the foundations or elsewhere. Under the impression that tufa had been transported a considerable distance from the Stroud area,[273] he deduced that the Normans must have attached some special religious importance to it.[274] Its use is now more easily explained: the proximity of sources, its light weight, ease of working and durability probably made it the material of choice for high-status buildings such as Quatford church, which makes it puzzling that so few Shropshire churches show evidence of its use.

The discovery during the 1960s excavation of tufa in the shallow post-holes must mean that they almost certainly post-dated 1180 (assuming that the tufa was not used in the church founded in 1086), and may have been much later. The totality of the evidence might suggest that the excavated area is to be associated with the rebuilding of the church in the twelfth century, perhaps a masons' yard with temporary workshops or awnings, and that the bailey area was never utilised as a defensive adjunct to the motte in the eleventh cemtury – the transfer of the village to the new site at Bridgnorth perhaps interrupting the completion of a motte and bailey castle. Yet the sunken road running to the river was

---

[270] However, Jane Croom, in her study of the minster *parochiae* of south-east Shropshire, has concluded that Worfield may have been the original minster church serving a middle Saxon land unit which originally encompassed the parishes of Worfield, Claverley, Quatt, Quatford, Alveley, and St Mary Magdalene, Bridgnorth, to be eclipsed in the 10th century when Quatford emerged as the chapel of the royal *burh*, the forerunner of St Mary Magdalene, Bridgnorth: Croom 1989: 156, 163.
Other *ford* places with middle-Saxon minster churches include Stafford, Salford Priors (Warwickshire) and Stratford-upon-Avon: Jenkins 1988: 54-55.
[271] Leonard 2004: 7, 242-3. Tufa was used in Herefordshire churches for quoins, window and door surrounds in the Anglo-Saxon period: TSAS LXXX (2005) 15.
[272] The Norman builders at Quatford took precautions with the tufa they used, making the walls very thick, and extending the east wall of the nave to act as an abutment to the chancel arch. There is no evidence that any fabric of the 1086 church survives at Quatford, but a deeply splayed small round-headed window high in the north wall may date from the 11th century, in which case we may have some evidence (unless the window was reused later: Wasey believed it to be an insertion: JBAA 29 306) that the church probably stands on its original site. Eyton believed the present church preserved the floor plan of the original structure: Eyton 1854-60: I 116. Amongst works carried out to the church in 1857 was the construction of a new porch faced inside with coursed ashlar tufa: Wasey 1865: 31.
[273] Tufa used in Shropshire buildings was widely believed to have been obtained in the Stroud area, though what is claimed to be the largest deposit in the British Isles lies on the right bank of the river Teme between Tenbury and Knightwick Bridge, covering at least half an acre and 50 to 60 feet high: Murchison 1839: 565-7; Hartshorne 1841: 232; Eyton 1854-60: I 116; Wasey 1865: 23; Leonard 2004: 241-1. Symonds thought the tufa in Quatford church came from the source near Tenbury, but also says that it came from Ribbesford: Symonds 1872: 222, 405. Blocks of tufa are to be found in the fabric of Quatt church.
[274] Wasey 1859: 22-3.

evidently utilised – indeed perhaps created – as a defensive ditch forming the southern boundary of what may have been the bailey. LiDAR surveys confirm that the northern boundary of any bailey probably took the line shown on the 1883 1:2,500 Ordnance Survey map of 1883.

The absence of expected defences around the supposed bailey may not be especially surprising when we find that while 'there are a number of references in medieval deeds to the area of Quatford motte-and-bailey, these references are always to the rock (usually *rupis*) of Quatford, never to the castle ...'.[275] In other words, if the villagers of Quatford retained any memory that some sort of artificial structure once existed on the rocky hill at Quatford, that memory is not reflected in any of their field or other names, or by references in early deeds. Indeed, it is surprising to find that no unambiguous reference to any castle at Quatford has been traced in any medieval document: no castle at Quatford is mentioned before the nineteenth century. Domesday itself simply mentions a *noua dom'* [*nova domus*][276] and a *burgu'*,[277] or new house and what is usually translated as borough. Specifically, Domesday Book, under the entry for Eardington, then held by Roger of Montgomery, and in Edward the Confessor's time by the church of St Mildburh (Wenlock), concludes *Ibi molin de III oris 7 noua dom[us] 7 burgu[m] Quatford dictum[s] nil redd[it?]* – 'There is a mill rendering 3 orae, and a new house, and a borough of Quatford stated [i.e. in the original returns] to pay nothing', before recording that Eardington was worth 30s, and had been 40s at the time of Edward the Confessor. The wording is ambiguous and perplexing, since it is unclear whether both the house and the *burgus* were then new.

But a second authority survives to confirm that in 1086 a *burgus* existed at Quatford. That source is a very rare record, a much later abbreviated 'recitatory' précis of the founding (or possibly refounding) of Quatford church, incorporated in an early 18th century copy of a memorandum, possibly drawn up in the fourteenth or fifteenth century, supposedly 'found among the Archives of the Royal Peculiar and exempt jurisdiction of Bridgnorth'.[278] The memorandum tells us that the church [probably of timber][279] was dedicated on 14th November 1086[280] in the presence, inter alia, of Wulfstan, bishop of Worcester (then some 80 years of age, the last surviving pre-Conquest bishop), and the bishops of Hereford and

---

[275] TSAS LVII 1961-4 42. The rock of Quatford is recorded in the 13th century, and the word *Rupe* in 1343/4: NLW Otley (Pitchford Hall) Estate deeds 1258 and 1 120. The map of Bridgnorth c.1560 labels the mound as *a Rock*.

[276] Rowley mistakenly suggests that the term *novus burgus* was used in the Domesday Book entry for Quatford (as it was in Norwich), and that as there is no hint of urbanisation at Quatford, 'it may conceivably reflect an unfulfilled ambition, or it could refer instead to Bridgnorth ...': Rowley 1983: 99. Domesday Book states specifically that in Eardington is a *burgu* called Quatford.

[277] TSAS LVII 1961-4 40-1. Robert de Bellême is reported by Orderic to have 'transporta ailleurs la population de la place Quatfort, et bâtit sur la Saverne le château très-fort de Bridgenorth ... ' according to Guizot 1826: no fortification is indicated.

[278] Clark-Maxwell and Hamilton Thompson 1927: 1-23; VCH Shropshire II (1973) 123-8. On monastic foundation charters of the 11th and 12th centuries see Galbraith 1982: XVIII 205-25.

[279] That the church was of timber might be deduced from the fact that Robert de Bellême's new castle at Bridgnorth seems to have been of timber: the earliest surviving stonework, that of the keep, evidently dates from c.1170. In 1086 timber structures were the norm, though the presence of many dignitaries at the consecration of the new church might suggest a high-status structure, possibly of stone.

[280] The dedication of the church was formerly believed to have taken place on 22nd July 1086 (Clark-Maxwell and Hamilton Thompson 1927: 1), but that date has now been revised: TSAS, LVII (1961-4), 45 fn.29.

Chester, as well as six archdeacons, monks from Shrewsbury and Gloucester, two sheriffs, and many nobles and laymen, 26 of whom are named: a truly remarkable assembly. The digest records the grant to the church of Eardington, except the land of Walter the Smith, and the land upon which the borough (*burgus*) stands or was seated, and all their hays and chases free from all manner of service. It also records that Roger gave Millichope to the church of St Mildburh by way of compensation for its loss of Eardington, which included Quatford.[281] These are the only two documentary references to the borough of Quatford, and an analysis of their implications is clearly required.

The word *burgus* is commonly found in Domesday Book, and invariably translated as 'borough'. G. H. Martin has written that Domesday Book was called upon to record 'towns, in the sense of permanent settlements with multiple functions, too populous to live on their own agricultural resources and therefore dependant on a trade which might, and usually did, serve other and wider purposes. ... By the eleventh century regular trade needed the protection of a sovereign power, and in a society open to change protection is apt to confer a civil status on the settlement which enjoys it. A community so privileged was historically known in English as a borough. In eleventh-century England it was called variously a *burh* or a *port* by the English themselves, and sometimes a *tun*, meaning simply a place where people lived'. To the Normans an Anglo-Saxon *tun* was a *ville*, and a *burh* or *port* was a *bourg*, found as *burgus* in the Latin of Domesday Book.[282]

The reality behind the label borough, though, was complex. *Burh* and its cogeners originally signified a fortified place, large or small, and although it might be only a fortified house – referred to as a *domus defensabilis* in Domesday Book[283] – the term *burh* was generally applied from the early tenth century to the communal fortifications raised against the Scandinavians by the Anglo-Saxons. Many *burhs* so established were little more than campaigning quarters, but all had to be victualled, and many developed into important commercial centres. By the early eleventh century the larger Anglo-Saxon borough was a complex institution. The maintenance of its fortifications fell to the shire and its revenues were apportioned between the king and the earl in a way that emphasised its separation from the shire, paying seignorial dues to the king and containing burgesses and properties appurtenant to rural manors in the hands of a variety of lords, reflecting their origins as communal garrisons. In the case of Quatford we have no evidence of any charge falling on the shire and might suppose that the *burgus* was at the time of Domesday, like the new house and the church, a recently created construct, since it was given no taxable value, but destined to quickly wither when the borough was transferred to Bridgnorth in 1101.

That idea may be contradicted, however, by the endowment of Quatford church, when it received, inter alia, the tithes of tolls (presumably from the bridge) and a market in Quatford, which suggests that both tolls and markets were then in being.[284] Since the purpose of Domesday was essentially a schedule of income-producing assets, the idea that the expression *burgus* might refer simply to the Æthelflædian (and possibly pre-existing

---

[281] Eyton 1854-60: I 110-12. It is unclear when Millichope (which adjoined Wenlock's estate of Ticklerton, later Eaton-under-Haywood) passed to St Mildburh: Domesday Book records that it was held in 1086 by Helgot under Roger of Montgomery. Eyton concludes that it was transferred 'immediately succeeding' Domesday Book: Eyton 1864-60 IV 1; VCH Shropshire X 190.
[282] Martin 1985: 144-5.
[283] Higham and Barker 1992: 51; Erskine and Williams 2003: 107.
[284] VCH Shropshire II: 123-8.

Viking) fortification might be thought unlikely.[285] However, the doyen of medieval castle studies, R. Allen Brown, was confident that the *burh* at Quatford was to be distinguished from Domesday's *nova domus*, which he held certainly referred to a *domus defensabilis*,[286] a view shared by David Roffe, a leading expert on Domesday Book, who believes that that the *burgum* in question was indeed the physical borough – a fortification – and the fact that it rendered nothing presumably accounts for the terse entry, suggesting that it may well be that Quatford was the centre of the estate rather than Eardington which was clearly geldable.[287] Given that the endowment to Quatford church at its dedication excluded, inter alia, the lands on which the borough stood, it might be thought that clues to its location could be traced by identifying the areas which did not fall into the hands of the church, but that exercise has been thwarted by incomplete church archives. The evidence, tenuous though it is, might suggest that the borough at Quatford was of some age when recorded (twice) in 1086, perhaps originally benefiting in particular from traffic generated by the bridge. It is also worth making the point that a richly-endowed collegiate church is unlikely to have been constructed at this turbulent period (of which more below) without the protection of a fortification adjoining or nearby.

We now turn to a quite remarkable occurrence, extraordinarily and inexplicably unmentioned by any English chronicler – even by Florence of Worcester, esconced in his scriptorium less than 24 miles to the south – and found recorded only by a single Continental historian, without whom we would be in complete ignorance of the event. We owe our information about the event to the prolific and respected Anglo-Norman historian Orderic Vitalis, who was born at Atcham in Shropshire in 1075 to an English mother and Norman father, Odelerius of Orléans, a priest in the service of Roger de Montgomery, Earl of Shrewsbury.[288] Orderic was educated in Shrewsbury from the age of 5 until he was sent to Normandy when 11 to train for the church, and wrote a number of chronicles between 1123 and 1141. Unequalled amongst Anglo-Norman historians, he worked for over 30 years and was exceptionally well informed, researching all the extant histories he could find. It is known that at some date between 1114 and 1123 – the exact year is uncertain – he visited Worcester from Normandy for the express purpose of gathering material for his writings,[289] and it may have been during that visit that he acquired information found only in his history of the period, though why the episode about which he writes was not incorporated into Florence's own chronicle is baffling.

Orderic tells us that in 1101-2 Robert de Bellême transferred the *oppidum de Quatfort* to Bridgnorth.[290] This was not the first time Robert had moved an entire population to a new site: the episode mirrors his transfer only a decade earlier of the population of Vignats in

---

[285] See especially Martin 1985. Raymund and Allen *de Castell* are witnesses to a 12th century Grant of land in the field of Bruges near Quatford (NLW Otley (Pitchford Hall) Estate 1 1368), but *Castell* is almost certainly Bridgnorth castle.

[286] Erskine and Williams 2003: 107.

[287] Personal communication 9th January 2015. Roffe compares Quatford with the account of Bedford which was similarly quit: ibid. Armitage describes the motte at Quatford and a bean-shaped bailey, and concludes that the Domesday Book reference to a *burgu'* implies the existence of a Norman fortification: Armitage 1912: 58, 191, a view evidently shared by VCH Shropshire II: 123, where the expression *burgu'* in the foundation document of Quatford church is translated as 'castle'.

[288] The names of Earl Roger's household clergy would suggest that they were all Continental.

[289] Chibnall 1968-80: I 25; Gransden 1992: 117.

[290] The statement in VCH Shropshire II (1973) 123-8 that the castle is mentioned in the foundation documents of Quatford church in 1086 is based on the translation of *burgu'* as 'castle', which is highly debateable.

Maine, Normandy, to the nearby crag of Fourches, where (as at Bridgnorth), he built a castle with twin baileys.[291] It was the act of building a new castle without permission which was seen as rebellion by Henry I, who responded by besieging and capturing Robert's castles of Arundel, Blyth and Shrewsbury, as well as Bridgnorth, and forcing Robert into exile.

Whilst the use of the word *oppidum* to describe what was transferred from Quatford would normally suggest a fortified site, quite possibly Orderic's *oppidum* was no more than the *nova domus* (a view evidently held by Eyton, who refers to 'an incipient castle or fortified mansion', later adding that it was probable that before 1096 'this hunting lodge of the Earl assumed somewhat more of a castellated character'),[292] or even the borough, rather than a typical Norman motte-and-bailey castle, for which we might perhaps have expected Orderic to use words such as *castellum* or *munitissum*, both of which he indeed uses (but not of Quatford) in the sentence that refers to the *oppidum*. Perhaps significantly, he refers to the *castellum* of Bridgnorth, but the *oppidum* at Quatford.[293]

Orderic's most recent translator and editor tellingly observes that '... difficulty exists in translating his references to 'castles'. He uses a number of terms, including 'oppidum', 'castrum', and 'castellum', which may in different places mean 'castle', 'fortified town', or simply 'town'",[294] and 'Having wrestled with the translation of military terms in Orderic Vitalis I can only say that I wish the different words always meant something different; they depend upon all sorts of factors, such as whether the information came from an author who was trained in the classics and used Roman language, or whether he was trying to be literary by varying the terms he used for the same building or whether he was describing something he had actually seen, and could be specific'.[295] It is also noteworthy that both Thomas Forester and Thomas Auden chose to translate Orderic's word as 'town'.[296] The Domesday reference to a *nova domus* at Quatford (which G. T. Clark believed was on the site of Quatford Castle, Smalman's pseudo-medieval house, an idea which can almost certainly be discounted) remains to be satisfactorily explained. David Roffe considers the Domesday reference to the *nova domus* to be especially interesting, but is unable to offer any explanation, acknowledging that the term is unique: it does not appear anywhere else in Domesday Book.[297]

---

[291] Forester 1854: 504-5; Chibnall 1991: 271; Lilley 2000. Orderic, born at Atcham to a Norman father and English mother, was a prolific and highly respected historian based at Saint-Evroult (Orne) abbey who retained a particular interest in the county of his birth.

[292] TSAS LVII 1961-4: 41. No trace of the *Nova Domus* was found during the excavation of part of the bailey at Quatford, but it may have been taken in parts to Bridgnorth: the uplifting of halls to new locations is not unknown – the halls of Llywelyn ap Gruffyd at Aberffraw and Ystumgwern were removed by Edward I and re-erected, one inside Caernarvon Castle, the other inside Harlech. Neither survives at its new site, and excavation at Aberffraw has failed to find any trace of the original position of the hall: Peers 1921-2: 68-9.

[293] 'Oppidum de Quatford transtulit, et Brugiam munitissimum castellum super Sabrinam fluvium condidit'.

[294] Chibnall 1968-80: III xxxvi.

[295] Extract from undated letter written in 1995 to Nick Austin by Marjorie Chibnall: http://secretsofthenormaninvasion.com/corresp/chibnall.htm. See also Chibnall 2000: XVI 53-4.

[296] Forester 1854: III 220; Auden 1906: 32.

[297] Personal communication 9th January 2015. Roffe has also suggested that there is a parallel of sorts in the place-name Newbold, 'new building'. He notes that in Great Domesday Book it stands in for the major estates of Chesterfield in Derbyshire and Astbury in Cheshire, while it is associated with the soke of Groby in Leicestershire and a comital estate in Nottinghamshire. He has tentatively suggested that the preference for Newbold as against Astbury indicated that a dreng administered the

The concept of the medieval castle as we know it today has long been held to have been introduced into Britain by the Normans after 1066, although there is a handful of eleventh century Norman-type fortifications which can be shown to pre-date the Conquest.[298] Invariably the earliest castles took the form of ringworks or motte and bailey castles with the structure first of timber and later of stone. The motte was an artificial earthern mound, usually conical in shape with a flat top, on which the timber or stone keep was built. It is generally supposed that the keep was constructed as soon as the mound was raised, but clearly a newly-formed earthern mound would need to settle for a period, depending on the nature of the soil, before any structure could safely be set upon it. A motte of clay might deflect only slightly under load, providing air voids were removed by tamping as the layers were built up, but such tamping would not remove moisture, and such moisture would affect the stability of the mound. A mound of sand would not settle significantly, but would be difficult to construct with a slope exceeding 35 degrees without some sort of covering to prevent the sand from being washed away. It seems likely that a period of weeks in the case of a sand mound, or months or more in the case of a clay mound, would need to elapse before any attempt was made to build a structure on it, although there is archaeological evidence from the mottes at Abinger and South Mimms, as well as the famous illustration in the Bayeux Tapestry, that earth was piled up around at least some towers as they were being built:[299] if a timber keep or donjon had been built directly onto the rock at Quatford, earth could have been piled against it to form a motte. At Abinger the timber tower rose from four stout posts which allowed the defenders to move beneath it on the confined platform of the motte, in the manner illustrated in the Bayeux Tapestry, where soldiers are shown below the tower of Dinan.[300]

As noted previously, Quatford mound is composed of sandy soil piled on a knoll of natural sandstone, presumably thrown up as a motte *de novo* in the late eleventh century. A castle as such would not normally be expected to be mentioned in Domesday Book, and is not referred to in the foundation or refoundation document of Quatford church in 1086,[301] but we might reasonably assume that the mound was created at some date after 1066 and before 1101 (when Quatford was abandoned), and the ditch refilled with earth from the motte soon after,[302] with the transfer of the inhabitants of Quatford to Bridgnorth.[303]

---

royal estate and his rights were becoming territorialised on a different site to the *burh* in question. Clearly there is a significant phenomenon there and the Quatford 'new house' may be another example if *nova domus* is taken as a Latin translation of Newbold: ibid.

[298] Norman and French lords may have built castles in the 1050s at Ewyas Harold in the Black Mountains, at Richards Castle to the south of Ludlow, at Hereford, and at Clavering in Essex: Rowley 1986: 95; Brown 1992: 7; but see Higham and Barker 1992: 43-5. Abels 1988: 92 claims that Goltho Manor in Lincolnshire was a pre-Conquest castle, with its extensive rampart and ditch defences refurbished c.1000 AD, and may well prove typical when other aristocratic estates have been investigated.

[299] Anderson1980: 52; Brown 1992: 10; Hinton 1977: 133.

[300] Brown 1992: 10.

[301] The statement in VCH Shropshire 1973: 123-8 that the castle is mentioned in the foundation document is questionable: the expression *burgu'* is generally translated as 'borough' rather than 'castle'.

[302] The presence of burnt straw found in the fill of the ditch around the motte when it was dug out in 1830-1 might suggest that there was once a thatched timber structure on the motte destroyed by fire: TSAS LVII 1961-4 42. Or perhaps the straw was from thatched structures occupied by those who had built the motte – or the church?

[303] Watkins-Pitchford 1937 concluded that the ditch could not have been filled in until after c.1180 because Smalman found fragments of tufa in the filling of the ditch. The only references which have

The tenth century was a troubled period for the Welsh Marches, with Quatford lying on their eastern edge. Gruffydd ap Llywelyn succeeded to Gwynedd in 1039 and eventually became king of all Wales, the first and last ruler to achieve the position. In the 1050s he led many raids into England, and after King Harold attacked Gruffydd's residence in 1062 after the latter broke his sworn oath to Harold, Gruffydd escaped to raise an invasion by land and sea supported by his brother Tostig. The Welsh were defeated and Gruffydd slain.[304]

In 1067, immediately after the Conquest, an uprising throughout the region against the Normans was led by Eadric the Wild and Gruffydd, and during their rebellion of 1069-70 Shrewsbury was burned and the castle attacked, though not take, the rebels moving on to Stafford.[305] The 1090s saw a surge in savage military campaigns led by the Norman lords against central and south Wales, and the resulting Welsh outrage led to revolts which broke out in almost every part of Wales between 1094 and 1098, with the Welsh inflicting signal defeats on the Normans in many parts of Wales and capturing many of their outposts. The chronicler Roger de Hoveden records that in 1094 many castles in west Wales were destroyed, and towns burnt throughout Cheshire, Shropshire and Herefordshire.[306] In that year soon after entering holy orders Roger de Montgomery died, and was buried at Shrewsbury Abbey.[307]

The *Anglo-Saxon Chronicle* version 'E' records how a great raiding-army led by King William ventured deep into Wales in 1097 to quell the violence but was forced to retreat when many Welshmen and their leaders, including the nephew of Gruffydd, turned against him: 'When the king saw that he could achieve nothing ... he went back into his land, and

---

been traced to any such material having been found are in Bellett 1858: 21 and Wasey 1859: 27, where it is said that Smalman found in the bottom of the ditch 'fragments of the same stone of which the church was built' (if indeed tufa was meant). Those fragments are not mentioned in the otherwise detailed report compiled by Hardwicke, who was in little doubt that it was Robert de Bellême who ordered that the ditch be filled (TSAS LVII 1961-4 61-2), but Wasey was an acquaintance of Smalman, and was also told, apparently, that the ditch had been filled from the motte, which would mean that the motte was originally higher, and the summit smaller: Wasey 1859: 27-8. Hartshorne mentions information supplied to him by Smalman about the excavated ditch, which does not include any reference to tufa: Hartshorne 1841: 229. Hardwicke mentions a silver penny of Henry I (1100-35) found at the bottom of the ditch on 26 March 1831, a month or so after it had been cleared (TSAS LVII 1961-4 47, 61-2); the coin, now lost, could have been deposited at any time after 1100, and need not have been associated with the infilling of the ditch.

[304] A map showing waste recorded in DB concentrated along the Welsh border might be seen as evidence of Gruffedd's raiding, though other explanations are also available: Hill 1984: 73-4.

[305] ASC 'D'; Williams 1995: 37; Swanton 1996: 201 fn12. After the Conquest Eadric refused to submit and was attacked by Norman forces from Hereford Castle. He raised a rebellion and allying himself to the Welsh prince of Gwynedd (and Powys), Bleddyn ap Cynfyn, and his brother, Riwallon, unsuccessfully attacked Hereford in 1067. Involved in the widespread wave of English rebellions in 1069-70, he burned Shrewsbury and unsuccessfully besieged Shrewsbury Castle, again helped by his Welsh allies from Gwynedd and English rebels from Cheshire. It was probably this combination of forces which was decisively defeated by William in a battle at Stafford in late 1069. Thereafter his life becomes uncertain, but he appears to have submitted to William in 1070 and later participated in the invasion of Scotland in 1072. He may have held Wigmore Castle against Ranulph de Mortimer during the rebellion of 1075.

[306] Stubbs 1868: I 149. These events seem to have coincided with 'a mortality among the inhabitants' throughout England, if Florence (John) of Worcester is to be believed: Stevenson 1853: 154.

[307] Matthew Bennett claims that Roger died at Quatford (Bennett 2013: 63), but no evidence to support that claim has been traced.

quickly after that he had castles made along the border'.[308] In 1098 Earl Hugh of Shrewsbury, heir to Roger de Bellême, was killed in Anglesey by Norwegian invaders, to be succeeded (after payment to the king of the huge sum of £3,000) by Robert de Bellême, notorious for his sadism, who became the wealthiest magnate in both England and Normandy.

The continuing threat from the rebellious Welsh must have been directly related to Robert's immediate and dramatic decision to transfer the *oppidum de Quatfort* to the more easily defensible sandstone outcrop at Bridgnorth: the formidable new castle at Bridgnorth could not have been built overnight. Certainly the endowment (or re-endowment) of a new church at Quatford in 1086 tells us that at the time of Domesday there had been no thought of relocating the township of Quatford. Though unrecorded in any sources, we might wonder whether the strategic bridge and the *nova domus* at Quatford had attracted the hostility of the Welsh during their recent rebellion against the Normans.

Although the excavators in the early 1960s failed to detect any trace of the expected bailey rampart or ditch adjacent to the motte at Quatford, that may be because they were seeking evidence for something that never existed. The possibility that no bailey was there to be found must be strengthened by the subsequent discovery that the supposed rampart was apparently formed as a result of ploughing during the 1939-45 war,[309] although Clark's late nineteenth century description (if reliable) of ditches to the north and south of the bailey area might suggest that they could have been, like the motte ditch, dug out by John Smalman, at some date between 1841 and 1852, the year of his death.[310]

If we have no firm evidence that a bailey was created at Quatford when the motte was constructed, we need to reconsider the nature of the earthwork. There seem to be two possibilities: the first that what we have is an unfinished motte and bailey castle, in which case we might reasonably imagine, as previously noted, that it was begun shortly before 1086 and abandoned when the borough was moved to Bridgnorth, when the ditch is likely to have been refilled;[311] the second that the motte was always intended to stand alone, and there never was an associated bailey (and it should be noted that mottes are normally assumed to have been raised only after a defensive palisade creating a bailey was erected), in which case we may have here the site of the mysterious 'new house' mentioned in Domesday Book. That edifice, about which in truth we know nothing, could have taken the form of a substantial structure, possibly up to three stories high, almost certainly of timber

---

[308] Owen and Blakeway 1825: I 51; Swanton 1996: 233.
[309] Barker 1993: 226.
[310] Armitage 1912: 58, 191, describes the motte and a bean-shaped bailey. She also concludes that the Domesday Book reference to a *burgu'* implies the existence of a Norman fortification.
[311] In that respect, the chronicle of Fulk Fitz Warine, an Anglo-Norman poem dating from about 1320 of doubtful historiocity, seemingly based on an earlier English metrical version dating probably from 1256x1264, tells that Roger of Montgomery [who died in or about 1094] began but left unfinished the castles of Brugge and Dynan [Ludlow]: Wright 1855: x, xii-xiii. Eyton 1854-60: V 234-6 has shown that Roger could not have commenced work on any castle at Ludlow (see also Lloyd 2008), nor at Brugge. Although Brugge was the shortened name of *Cwatbycge*, there can be little doubt that in the 13th century the name will have referred to Bridgnorth, and the poem cannot therefore be used as evidence to support the view that Quatford castle was started by Roger de Montgomery at some date before 1094 and never completed, although that might well have been the case. However, we do not know where the chronicler obtained his information, and the possibility that Brugge indeed refers to *Cwatbrycge* cannot be discounted entirely.

rather than stone, atop the rocky knoll which had been ditched and artificially heightened, to form a sentinel post dominating the major ford and bridge across the Severn.[312]

It is difficult to imagine anyone other than Robert de Bellême having good reason and taking the trouble to fill in the ditch around the motte at Quatford: he would have been anxious to ensure that the structure on the mound and any defences should be denied to any enemy.[313] It seems reasonably certain that the timber structure would have been dismantled and transferred to the new borough of Bridgnorth. One possibility already considered is that it had been destroyed, deliberately (by the Welsh?) or accidentally, at some date before 1100, which might have encouraged Robert de Bellême to create his new castle at Bridgnorth. Doubtless the nearby *Cwatbrycge* across the Severn was destroyed in any event when the new bridge became operational at Bridgnorth, if indeed *Cwatbrycge* was then still in existence.

Much speculation has been caused by a puzzling reference in the writings of John Leland, the antiquary, who writing c.1540 mentions 'great Tokens of a Pyle or Mannour Place longing that tyme to Robert de Belesmo' at Quatford.[314] Although the expression Pyle could mean 'a mass, a heap', we can be reasonably certain that it did not refer to the motte, which was evidently unrecognisable as artificial since its ditch had been filled in almost half a millennia earlier. The more usual meaning of 'Pyle', found elsewhere in Leland's writings, was in the sense of an edifice or building, and that seems more likely in association with the expression 'Mannour Place', which probably refers to a structure, though at this period all kinds of major residences, including castles, were called 'manors' or 'manor places' simply because they were seats of lordly authority.[315] The words 'great Tokens' show that the remains were more than insignificant, and we can only guess at their nature, extent and location, but what Leland saw could scarcely have been associated with the *nova domus*, since that would almost certainly have been of timber, dismantled and taken to Bridgnorth in 1101, or long since destroyed or decayed in situ. We might suspect that what he saw were ashlar or rubble blocks associated with the construction or repair of the church, or even perhaps the remains of the church founded in 1086 which could have stood on a different site from the present building, but that is no more than guesswork.[316]

---

[312] Cf. Garewald's Tower in Shrewsbury, which may have been pre-Conquest, overlooking Garewald's Ford: PN Sa IV 2; Barker 2010: 96. Two structures described as *domus defensabilis* are recorded in the Herefordshire Domesday (the only two fortified houses mentioned in Domesday Book), one of which may be identified as Eardisley Camp, a circular mount about 14½ feet high with a platform about 40 feet in diameter surrounded by a shallow moat connected to a stream, within a roughly circular enclosure (but no ditch between the mound and the enclosure), the other perhaps Lemore Mount, an earthwork of similar configuration with a mound some 4½ to 6 feet high, with a circular platform 80 feet in diameter surrounded by a moat connected to a stream: VCH Herefordshire I 226-7. Neither is in a strong tactical position, and they may have been incipient fortifications which served essentially as places of refuge and defence. Clearly the earthworks at Quatford do not fall into the same category, but a sceptical observer might wonder whether the motte and its rock-cut ditch were not created de novo by Smalman, with his penchant for historical artifice and major landscaping works.

[313] A coin dated to early in the reign of Henry I is said to have been found in the bottom of the motte ditch during the excavations of 1830-1. The excavators concluded, quite reasonably, that this indicated that some part at least of the ditch was open after August 1100 when Henry took the throne: TSAS LVII 1961-4 47.

[314] Hearne 1744: IV 99.

[315] Goodall 2011: 5.

[316] Excavations of the easternmost part of the bailey in 1960 found no trace of stone buildings: TSAS LVII 1961-4: 37-62.

Furthermore, while it has been assumed that his comments referred to what he saw within the supposed bailey,[317] the 'great Tokens' could have been anywhere at Quatford, and it is noticeable that some old buildings in the village incorporate substantial blocks of ashlar.

Leland's report indeed brings to mind an observation by William Hardwicke, the Bridgnorth antiquary, who recorded in the early nineteenth century that 'large fragments of freestone', brought thither from some other place, had within living memory been revealed by the plough in the field to the east of the motte which has since been held to be the site of the bailey.[318] The freestone was clearly not sandstone, for Hardwicke would surely have described it as such. Could the large fragments have been associated with a restoration of the church in 1653,[319] or with the contract of 1714 for the building and restoration of the church which provided for the procurement of 'white stone' in the lands of Mr Spencer at Eardington to be carried to 'the old slade on Severn over against Quatford'?[320] That seems far more likely than Hardwicke having seen the 'great Tokens of a Pyle' noticed by Leland, and the discovery of fragments of floor tile, lead glazing strips and glass – all evidence to be expected of an eighteenth-century church rebuilding – during the 1960 excavation would seem to confirm it.[321] It may be assumed that the 'great Tokens' were recycled for use in the church or another nearby building – and may perhaps still be discoverable in unexpected places locally – at some date after Leland's visit.

Hardwicke's observation may be connected with a comment made by Watkins-Pitchford in 1937: 'There was, until recently, an ashlar [squared stone] of travertine [tufa] lying in the bailey near the path which leads from the moat to the high road and the church.'.[322] It seems just possible that what Leland records was the site of a builder's or mason's yard where imported tufa had been stockpiled for the repair of the church. However, Mason suggests that Hardwicke's freestone fragments, if not taken from or intended for Quatford church, may well have been the remains of Roger of Montgomery's *domus*.[323] We have seen that the idea is unlikely, not least because abandoned building stone, especially ashlar, tends to be appropriated quickly for use elsewhere.

---

[317] TSAS LVII 1961-4: 55.
[318] TSAS LVII 1961-4: 43. The area generally identified as the bailey is said to be recorded in 1841 as 'Two acres ... appropriated to defray the cost of ferrying persons over the river when they attend the parish church' (Hartshorne 1841: 230), but Wasey 1859: 89 shows that the service attached to the Ferry House and Garden, as confirmed by the Report from the Commissioners of Charities in England and Wales (4), Vol. 5, 1820: 247.
[319] NLW Pitchford Hall (Otley) Papers 1625-28.
[320] SA P225/B/2/2. It is noticeable that white stone is found at Eardington, for example in the garden walls of The Manor, but the stone of Quatford is red. Slade is a common field-name in Shropshire, often applied to a damp valley or ground in a ploughed field too wet for grain and left as greensward: Foxall 1980: 18. Old Slade Meadow is shown on the 1842 Tithe Map where Slade Lane, which runs from the the east side of Eardington, approaches the Severn to a ford known as Sladeford.
[321] TSAS LVII 1961-4 55. The existence of a chantry, said to incorporate a 15th-century core, to the north north of the church at Quatford should not be overlooked. The origin of the chantry, discussed elsewhere in this volume, is unknown.
[322] Watkins-Pitchford 1937.
[323] TSAS LVII 1961-4 43. Watkins-Pitchford 1937 notes that the site of the castle and its presumed bailey belongs to the incumbent of Quatford church, and surmises that it was probably given to the church by Henry II, the site having been forfeited to the crown when the English possessions of Robert de Bellême were confiscated in 1102.

7. *Cwatbrycge* and its bridge.

We have seen that the place-name *Cwatbrycge* is well-recorded in the *Anglo-Saxon Chronicle* as the place where the Danes wintered in 895-6; is named by Æthelweard (alone of the chroniclers) as the place where the Danish army crossed the Severn in 910 immediately before the battle of Tettenhall;[324] and is almost certainly the place where Æthelflæd built a *burh* in 912.

For obvious phonological reasons *Cwatbrycge* has long been associated with Quatford on the east bank of the river Severn, some two miles south-east of Bridgnorth. However, the picture is clouded by the fact that *Brycge* was also the early name of Bridgnorth. That has led historians to reach differing conclusions as to the location of *Cwatbrycge*, otherwise *Brycge*. For example, authorities such as Camden, Gibson, Thorpe, Plummer, Stenton, Whitelock, Garmonsway, Campbell, and Swanton identify the place as Bridgnorth, whereas Oman, Hodgkin, Ekwall and Webster prefer to place it at Quatford.[325] A more recent study by Margaret Gelling[326] opted for Bridgnorth, on the basis of a carefully researched and argued paper by J. F. A. Mason published in the early 1960s which, not unreasonably, concluded that *Quatbrycge*, *Brycge* and Bridgnorth were in reality the same place.[327]

That identification, which has influenced scholars for over half a century, was founded on the supposition that there was a bridge at Bridgnorth in 895 where the Danes established a camp; that a Danish army crossed that same bridge immediately before the battle of Tettenhall in 910; and that Æthelflæd built a *burh* in the same place two years later. The hypothesis assumed that the bridge (together with any associated settlement) at Bridgnorth had disappeared completely before the Conquest – it is not mentioned or alluded to in Domesday Book, or indeed in any pre-twelfth century record. What is certain is that a new settlement and bridge were established there in 1100-1 by Robert de Bellême, eldest son of Roger de Montgomery. In short, Mason proposed that *Cwatbrycge* was at Bridgnorth, which had disappeared by Domesday but reappeared in 1100-1.

The name *Cwatbrycge* has been of particular interest to philologists, and various theories have been put forward to explain the curious names Quatford and Quatt (the latter a village some two miles south-east of Quatford), all three evidently incorporating the Old English element *cwat(t)*.

A review of research into the names shows that the word *cwat(t)* seems first to have been recorded in the personal name Leofwine Cwatt, mentioned in the will of *æðeling* Æthelstan in 1015.[328] In the mid-nineteenth century the eminent Shropshire historian the

---

[324] Earle and Plummer 1892-99 I 89; Campbell 1962: 53. Curiously, Æthelweard makes no mention of the wintering of the Danes at Cwatbrycge in 895-6.

[325] Gough 1806: III 4, 18; Thorpe 1861: II 78; Earle and Plummer 1892-99: II 342 and 358 (*sub. nom. Brycg* and *Cwatbrycge*); Stenton 1971: 268, 326; Whitelock 1955: 188, 194; TSAS LVII 1961-4 37; Garmonsway 1953: 89, 96; Campbell 1962: 53; Swanton 1996: 89; Oman 1913: 489, 498; Ekwall 1960: 376-7; Webster 2003: 79. Watkins-Pitchford 1932 believed the Danes wintered in 895-6 on Castle Hill at Quatford, with another camp at Burf Castle, and that Æthelflæd's *burh* was at Bridgnorth. Beresford and Finberg 1957: 153 conclude that Æthelflæd's *burh* was at Bridgnorth.

[326] PN Sa I 56-9.

[327] TSAS LVII 1961-4 37-46.

[328] Searle 1897: 335; Whitelock 1930: 60, 173; see also Ekwall 1960: 376-7 *sub. nom.* Quatford, where Ekwall associates this byname with the place-name. However, Margaret Gelling (personal

Reverend R. W. Eyton confidently asserted that the place-name Quatt represented the Welsh *coed* ('trees, woodland'), identifying it with the local Forests of Morfe, Kinver and Wyre, a derivation now rejected with equal confidence by philologists. Max Förster took the view that a personal name might be involved,[329] and Eilert Ekwall, suggesting in the first edition (1936) of his *Concise Oxford Dictionary of English Place-Names* that a possible root was the Old English *cwead* 'mud, dung',[330] added the possibility in the 1960 (fourth and last) edition, on the basis of the byname in Leofwine Cwatt, that the element may have been a personal name, but noted that the genitive form should be Cwattes, and, as a further possibility, that there may have been an Old English word *cwatt* which could be used in place-names and could also give rise to a byname. He considered it doubtful that the place-names Quatt and Quatford contained a word which was the ancestor of Modern English *quat*, meaning a pimple. Subsequently he acknowledged that his own suggested derivation from *cwead* 'had better be abandoned', and wrote that 'the most reasonable explanation seems to me to be from a word cwatt, whose meaning rendered it liable to give rise both to a nickname and to a place-name. A word meaning 'a lump', 'a hump' or the like would be possible, though it has, so far as I know, no analogy in any Germanic language', and he went on to suggest further consideration of the local topography. He thought it doubtful, but not altogether impossible, that the place-names contain the nickname Cwatt.[331] It is unclear whether he was aware of G. Tengvik's observations on the name Leofwine Cwatt: 'in my opinion it is probably identical with an early M[iddle] E[nglish] (evidenced from 1579) and Mod[ern] Eng[lish] dialect quat 'pimple, boil', formed from the German stem *kwat- with the sense of 'something lumpy, protruding'.[332]

Margaret Gelling, in her exhaustive study of Shropshire place-names, encouraged by Mason's paper into identifying *Cwatbrycge* with Bridgnorth, concluded that the element *cwat(t)* must have been a district name, covering a sizeable area from Quatt to Bridgnorth. Noting that Ekwall was less than satisfied with his suggestion that the element derived from OE *cwead/cwēd* 'dirt, mud, dung', she also dismissed a derivation from a word *quat*, recorded in 1579, meaning 'a pimple', as not suitable for a district name, and concluded that no suggestion was available about its meaning, which appeared to have no parallel among other place-names.[333]

In that respect, we might usefully take up Ekwall's suggestion and consider the topography of Quatt. Quatt churchyard, which lies at the centre of the small settlement, is a slightly domed, roughly square plateau modelled out of a pronounced sandstone knoll or hillock,

---

comment) was unwilling to accept that the byname can be associated with Quatt, since in OE the formula for connecting a person with a place was to use the preposition *æt*, and if the addition is not preceded by a preposition, the addition is a nickname. That is illustrated by the names in Æðeling Æthelstan's will, which gives in the place-name category Lyfingce æt Tywingan, Leommære æt Biggrafan, and Ælfric æt Bertune, whereas the nickname group includes Æthelwerde Stameran ('stammerer') and Godwine Dref(e)lan ('driveller'). Although the reference to Leofwine Cwatt does not follow precisely the same format, for the will mentions ... *Leofstane Leofwines breðer. Cwattes* ... (... Leofstane, the brother of Leofwine Cwatt ...): Whitelock 1930: 60-1, 173, it is clear that the name is a nickname, and we must assume that Leofwine Cwatt was distinguished by some sort of disfigurement in the form of a pustule or lump.

[329] Förster 1941: 769.
[330] *Sub. nom.* Quatford.
[331] Letter of August 1961: see TSAS LVII 1961-4 45 fn.14.
[332] Tengvik 1938: 305.
[333] PN Sa I 56-9; Gelling 1992: 204.

with the church of St Andrew, which has traces of Anglo-Saxon fabric,[334] standing on its highest point. Indeed, the striking characteristic of the topography of Quatt and the immediately surrounding area is said to be the extraordinary rounded sandstone tumps or hillocks, aptly described by a commentator writing in 1874 who observed that '... the character of the surface of the country hereabouts is very favourable for the construction of these earthworks with mounds [similar to Quatford motte]. There are scores of natural rounded hillocks of red sandstone that have an artificial aspect, and that with a little scarping would be strong. There is one, especially, close east of the road between Quatford and Dudmaston Park, that looks like an English earthwork, and wants nothing but a ditch to make it perfect'.[335]

We can be reasonably confident, despite the reservations of Eilert Ekwall and Margaret Gelling, that the names Quatt and Quatford attest to an otherwise unrecorded Anglo-Saxon element *cwætt or similar, which survived until modern times as a dialect word (found in Shakespeare and well-recorded in more recent times in the Midland counties)[336] for a pustule or pimple, which, at some date before the tenth century was applied topographically to the rounded sandstone mounds in the area, or more specifically to the hillock on which Quatt church stands.[337] There is no reason to believe that the element was applied to a district, as Gelling had been led to believe, an idea that for half a century or more has served as a significant red herring. Quatt is recorded in Domesday Book under the name *Quatone*, which must surely mean 'the tūn at the pimple-like mound(s)', which (if an accurate record) evidently became abbreviated to the present name, though it is perhaps more likely that the Domesday spelling is one of the many place-name aberrations in the great survey.[338]

It is worth recording that in setting the scene for the battle of Tettenhall, the chronicler Æthelweard, writing probably between 978 and 988, some two generations or so after the battle, says that the Danes crossed a bridge on the Severn called *[ ]antbricge*.[339] His spelling of the first syllable (the first letter destroyed when the manuscript was badly damaged in the Cotton Library fire in 1731), or that of the copyist who transcribed the one surviving (badly burned) copy of the chronicle now surviving, may have attempted to rationalise the unintelligible name *Cwatbrycge*, but we should also note that Roger of Wendover's later account of the Danish wintering in 895 places their camp at *Quantebregge*.[340]

---

[334] TSAHS LXVI 1989 15-19.

[335] Clark 1874: 276-7. It must be said that no such hillocks have been traced by the present author, and Clark has proved a less than reliable observer.

[336] Horovitz 2005: 447-8.

[337] See Horovitz 2005: 447-8. The most recent comprehensive and scholarly study of English place-names suggests that the name Quatt is from an OE *cwætt of uncertain meaning and origin, possibly related to *quat*, a word meaning 'a pimple, a pustule, a small boil', but offers no further explanation: CDEPN 487 *sub nom* Quatt.

[338] The latter view was held by Margaret Gelling (personal comment).

[339] Campbell 1962: 53, who amends –*antbricge* to –*uatbricge*, and identifies the place as Bridgnorth. The single manuscript from which Æthelweard's *Chronicon* has passed down to us is a copy dating from the early eleventh century, perhaps the first fair copy made of the original: ibid. xii. The chronicle was charred in the great fire at Ashburnham House in 1731, but from fragments of the manuscript which survived it is clear that Æthelweard wrote *[ ]antbricge*: PN Sa I 57. CDEPN 85 states unequivocally and inexplicably that the name Bridgnorth is short for Quatbridge.

[340] Giles 1892: 232.

With that in mind, it may not be completely irrelevant to record that a stream from the east joining the Severn almost a mile north of Bridgnorth is called Cantern Brook. The name is of some antiquity, recorded from the end of the twelfth century.[341] The meaning of the name (which is also found in a lost mill name *Cantereyne* in Haughton township, High Ercall) is uncertain: there is a possibility that it might be a British stream-name containing the word meaning 'beautiful' found in Candover, Hampshire,[342] or 'border',[343] which may be found in the name of the river Ceint in Anglesey.[344] However, Professor Richard Coates has suggested that Cantreyn is a French name of a type common in France which combines the verb *chant* 'sing' with the name of a wild creature, in this case Old French *reine* 'frog', so giving 'sing frog', as found in the place-name C(h)antereine, found widely in France.[345] That suggestion might be paralleled by Cantlop, perhaps from a phrase meaning 'sing wolf', which has also given rise to many place-names in France.[346] If, on the other hand, the name Cantreyn is British in origin, one might consider whether Æthelweard was attempting in his chronicle to rationalise a place-name containing an obscure dialect element he did not recognise, by incorporating the first syllable of a stream name which was widely known in the area. But even if (which must be doubtful) the name Cantreyn pre-dates the time of Æthelweard, his slipshod recording of names is well attested – '[h]is Latin was poor, his chronology confused, and his transcription of proper names careless'[347] – and we can suppose that there was simply a mistranscription of the name *Cwatbrycge* by Æthelweard himself or an early copier.

Whilst it is usually assumed that the name Quatford means 'the ford leading to Quatt',[348] or 'the ford near Quatt', or 'the ford associated with Quatt', we should perhaps consider whether Quatford might possibly be a separate name in its own right,[349] since the most striking feature of the place is the 60-foot sandstone knoll which rises sheer from the Severn, now topped by the motte, which overlooks the ancient ford, and which would not be inappropriately described as 'the ford at the lump or mound'.[350] The knoll is made all the more prominent by the fact that it rises sharply from the flat meadows that adjoin the Severn to the north and south, and is very conspicuous when viewed across the wide flood plain that forms the west bank.[351] If that derivation might be correct, it would provide

---

[341] Recorded in 1194 as *Cantinunt* (TSAS IX 1886 47), c.1215 *Canterey* (*ibid.* 58), 1227 *Cantreia* (SA 1093/2/204), c.1277 *Cantreyne* (TSAS IX 1886 370), 1258, 1265 *Cantreyn* (*ibid.* 58), 1293 *Canteryn'* (SA 796/3), late 13th century *Contreyne* (TSAS IX 188645), *Cantrey* c.1300 (Deed in HLSL), early 14th century *Cantrey* (Rees 1997: 299), *Cauntreyn* 1327 (Subsidy Roll), *Canter broke* 1639 (TSAS L 1939-40 170), and *Canteren Mill* (?*Cantrey* c.1300) (Deed in HLSL) is shown on the stream on the c.1560 map of the area.
[342] See Ekwall 1928: 69; CDEPN 483 *sub nom* Preston Candover.
[343] See Owen and Morgan 2007: xxxi.
[344] Owen and Morgan 2007: 79.
[345] Personal communication from Margaret Gelling, 2nd August 2008.
[346] PN Sa I 69-70.
[347] Marsh 1970: 157.
[348] CDEPN 487. Quatford lies midway between Bridgnorth and Quatt – the ford led to both places.
[349] The name Quatford is not unique: It occurs twice in Gloucestershire in the 12th and 19th century (PN Gloucestershire 2 73, 3 186), and is also recorded in Ledbury, Herefordshire, in 1605 and 1722x1862: Joseph Foster, *Register of Admissions to Gray's Inn 1521-1889*, 1889; NA D1604/T1.
[350] It is worth noting that the very common *ford* element in place-names does not necessarily denote a water crossing: some occurrences may incorporate Welsh *ffordd* 'road, ford' (Owen and Morgan 2007: xliii), though 'shallow water crossing' is certain here.
[351] Margaret Gelling (personal communication) took the view that place-names are not so localised that a word is likely to appear twice in a small area and nowhere else, and considered it doubtful that

evidence that a mound on the clifftop at Quatford long predated the Norman Conquest.[352] But whatever the case, any association of the name with Bridgnorth is almost certainly illusory. Historians and philologists are released from the need to secure an explanation for the element *cwat* which would be applicable to an area extending well beyond Quatt and Quatford.

When considering the name *Cwatbrycge*, we need to note that the *brycg* element is not itself without interpretative difficulties. While the Old English word *brycg* usually meant what we would now think of as a bridge, that is 'a structure affording passage between two points at a height above [water or a gap]',[353] there are some contexts in which the word can only be interpreted as 'causeway' or similar.[354] Perhaps the best known example is in the Anglo-Saxon poem *The Battle of Maldon*, where the topography can easily be identified, and the *brycg* mentioned in the poem is without doubt the causeway from Northey Island to the mainland which floods at high tide. There has never been a bridge there. Again, at Dunklington, Oxfordshire, a feature described in the bounds of a charter of 958 as *stan ford*, and again in 969 as *stan bricge*, has been identified by excavation as a rubble-paved ford,[355] and a boundary mark in a charter of Oldswinford in Worcestershire mentions a feature described enigmatically as *eorth brycge* 'earth-bridge'.[356]

This makes it clear that places with names incorporating the element *brycg* may not have had any bridge construction in the conventional sense at the time the name was in use, even if other evidence makes it certain that a structure existed at a later date.[357] However, as will be seen, the tenth-century chronicler Æthelweard might remove any possible doubt by referring in his Latin text to the Danes crossing the Severn over a *pontem*, 'bridge', and it seems safe to assume that *Cwatbrycge*, wherever it was located, was indeed a bridge in the conventional sense of that word by that date.[358] This made it a crossing of exceptional regional as well as local importance, both for commercial and military purposes. Whilst there is no archaeological or documentary evidence for the existence of any pre-Conquest (including Roman) bridge over the Severn, it would be very surprising if the Romans had no bridges at Wroxeter and Gloucester, and a Roman bridge at Worcester may have been

---

the element would have been considered appropriate for the rock at Quatford. The present author is not altogether persuaded by that opinion.

[352] In that respect the existence of a similar riverside mound at a ford on the Severn at a place where the settlement boundary extended across the Severn might be noted: see the discussion on Shrawardine in Chapter 10 of this work.

[353] OED.

[354] See Parsons and Styles 2000: 517. A useful discussion on the subject can be found in Baker and Brookes 2013: 164-6.

[355] Blair and Millard 1992: 342-8.

[356] S 579; see Hooke 1990: 162-7. It has been suggested that the term *eord-brich*, found in a charter of Upper Arley (S.860, see Hooke 1983: 68-70) is to be read as *eorth brycge*, but it seems possible that the expression incorporates OE *bryce* 'breaking', used for newly cultivated land, commonly found in this area as breach, bratch.

[357] Hart 1992: 530 observes that 'It is clear from the Maldon poem that the O[ld] E[nglish] word bricg was used more often to describe such artificially constructed trackways, submerged by high tides and flooding, than as a term for bridges in the modern sense, which were rare in the Anglo-Saxon period'.

[358] It should not be overlooked, however, that Æthelweard, who almost certainly had no personal knowledge of *Cwatbrycge*, may have assumed from the name that it referred to a conventional *pontem*, a conclusion that might conceivably have been incorrect, though any doubts are probably removed by the reference to a bridge in the abbreviated 'recitatory' précis of the founding (or possibly refounding) of Quatford church in 1086: Clark-Maxwell and Hamilton Thompson 1927: 1-23; VCH Shropshire II (1973) 123-8.

repaired in 1088, rebuilt in the 1320s, and only demolished in 1781.[359] A bridge at Gloucester is first mentioned in 1119, and at Shrewsbury in the early twelfth century.[360] If bridges had existed in each of those towns in the later Saxon period, the distance as the crow flies from a bridge at Shrewsbury to Quatford would have been 20 miles; from Quatford to a bridge at Worcester 24 miles; and from Worcester to the bridge at Gloucester 24 miles, so conveniently spacing the crossings on this major watercourse.

Any search for the site of the bridge giving rise to the name *Cwatbrycge* must start with an analysis of the historic road pattern in the Bridgnorth region, for early roads will have converged on any river crossing.

For details of the early road system on the west side of the Severn we are greatly assisted by research undertaken by Jane Croom in the 1990s which revealed, on the basis of a detailed analysis of the early landscape and field patterns of south-eastern Shropshire, especially around Much Wenlock and Bridgnorth, a significant Roman presence, including a trackway or road from Wenlock Edge via Morville to Eardington, almost certainly in use during the Roman period, and quite possibly of prehistoric origin.[361] Evidence of a possible Romano-British villa site in Much Wenlock and a major concentration of Roman occupation debris at an unenclosed major Roman site at Upton Cresset fits this picture.[362] An enclosure has also been traced opposite Quatford on the west side of the Severn, probably of Iron Age or Romano-British date,[363] and close to Cliff Coppice to the north-north-west of Eardington a double-ditched rectilinear Iron-Age/Romano-British enclosure on a silt-covered gravel plateau, from the absence of imported pottery sherds probably a low-status native enclosure with a post-built gateway and traces of round houses within.[364] There can be little doubt that the cluster of Severn crossings at Quatford, Danesford and Sladeford were in use in the prehistoric and Roman period.

On the east side of the Severn, large-scale changes to the field and road pattern, particularly since the enclosure of the area in 1812,[365] do not allow a detailed study to balance that undertaken by Croom on the west, but historians have researched the possibility of Roman roads in the area.

---

[359] Carver 1980: 2. For the possibility of a Roman bridge surviving over the Wye nar Kenchester into the 7th century see Noble 1983: 23.
[360] Baker 2010: 97.
[361] Groom 1992: 18. The age of the routeway is demonstrated by the fact that it is aligned with and forms part of ancient rectilinear field systems: ibid. Croom's analysis of the roads in the area was based on the 1st edition 1" O.S. map of the area, without reference to earlier maps, e.g. Rocque's 1752 map of Shropshire. It would be a valuable exercise to transfer the roads shown on that map onto a modern map to help identify ancient (or at least pre-18th century) routeways.
[362] Webster 1991: 103; TSAHS LXXVI 2001 100; White and Barker 1998: 61; TSAHS 91 (2016) 135. Upton Cresset clearly lay in an area of some importance during the Roman period, though no traces of buildings have yet been found.
[363] Grid Reference SO 73229038, SMR NO04564.
[364] Howlett and Coxah 1992; Hunn 2000: 119-44; SSMR SA00202. The western corner of the enclosure appears clearly on satellite photographs taken in the 1990s on Google Earth. The corner points towards the west.
[365] Enclosure map of 1812: SA QE/1/2/29. The area east of Bridgnorth and south of The Hermitage is divided into rectangular fields called Inclosures on the Tithe Map: PN Sa 6 86. Not all evidence of earlier farming practices has been obliterated: traces of 'Celtic fields' have been detected on aerial photographs of Stanmore Farm: National Trust HBSMR.

Graham Webster noted in 1981 that a bridge across the Severn at Quatford (which he evidently accepted as *Cwatbrycge*) could only have been of Roman origin, implying a route from Greensforge, but the only possible trace he was able to detect was a track over Gag's Hill and at the south-east end a stretch of parish boundary.[366] He recognised that if a crossing had existed at Quatford the Romans would have faced the challenge of establishing a route through the Ironbridge gap for any road to Wroxeter, and thought the Roman army may have preferred to use the more open country on the west bank of the Severn and cut off the river bend, following, more or less, the line of the modern A58 from Morville to Cressage, which according to Ogilby was the route from London to Shrewsbury in the late seventeenth century. He also noted that the large fort at Eaton Constantine appeard to be guarding a north-south crossing of the river somewhere near the present bridge at Cressage.[367]

Oddly, Webster seems to have overlooked that some two decades earlier he had read and commented upon a paper by Dr A.W. J. Houghton describing a lost road Houghton had traced running north-west from the Roman sites at Greensforge and curving west to the south of Swancote Farm. Houghton identified the road as Roman, and suggested that it turned sharply west to cross the river Severn at or near Bridgnorth, continuing west and then south-west along the Corve Valley and ultimately into Mid-Wales.[368] The road from Morville towards Bridgnorth, which forms the westward extension of Houghton's road, is clearly superimposed over earlier field boundaries, which from their alignment are likely to be of pre-Roman Iron-Age date, but the possibility cannot be discounted that they are post-Roman, and even post-Conquest. All that can be said with confidence is that the road between Morville and Bridgnorth runs across earlier field-boundaries, which cannot be taken as evidence of a Roman origin for the road. Houghton's report itself provides little evidence to indicate a Roman origin for the road between Bridgnorth and Morville, and indeed the Roman road may have turned south-east from Morville following the existing road towards Eardington and Quatford.

An excavated section of Houghton's road at Winchester near Claverley revealed a relatively sophisticated construction with a side ditch on the south (the north side lay under a hedge, and was not excavated), which certainly points towards a Roman identification,[369] and the road would seem to run from Greensforge, with several Roman sites of some importance. However, the course of the road is not ruler-straight, as are sections of most (though certainly not all) Roman roads in the region, though deviations are normally due to significant topographical obstacles, few of which exist on the line of Houghton's road, and there must be some doubt whether it deviated sharply and inexplicably to the west in a far-

---

[366] Presumably the boundary running due west from Greensforge to Foucher's Pool; 1882 1:2,500 O.S. map. TSAHS 91 (2016) 72 describes Margary's route 193 as crossing the Severn at 'Quatt Bridge near Bridgnorth', but his supposed route crossed the Severn at 'Bridgenorth' (sic): Margary 1967: 73. The basis of the map showing a Roman road passing from west to east through Quatford in TSAHS 91 (2016) 100 is unclear, but seems to be Houghton's postulated route crossing the Severn at Bridgnorth.
[367] Webster 1981: 79.
[368] TSAHS LVI 1957-60 237; 241; SSMR PRN04076; Margary 1973: 296; the route is Margary 193.
[369] See WMANS 3/1960/8. A sherd of Roman pottery is said to have been found at Winchester Farm (SO 798923) in 1972: Shropshire SMR 436. The name Winchester, which appears on the 1840 Tithe Map, does not appear to incorporate OE *ceaster* 'town, city, Roman site' (as supposed by Webster 1981: 79) which might suggest a Roman origins, but is seemingly derived from a field-name *Wincestry Field*, recorded in 1651 (SA 972/2/1/16), which may incorporate the personal name Winsige.

from-Roman fashion to cross the Severn at or near Bridgnorth. The account provided by Houghton becomes admittedly speculative as the route approaches Roughton from the south-east, and apart from the existence of footpaths of indeterminate date no evidence is provided to support any turn to the west towards Bridgnorth.[370] In short, there is a gap between Roughton and Morville on each side of the Severn which may or may not have been linked by a Roman road, but no convincing evidence has been adduced to prove the existence of any such road.[371] Certainly no indication of any permanent Roman occupation in or close to Bridgnorth has been recorded elsewhere.[372] We are entitled to wonder why Houghton's road ran north-west, then swerved dramatically west at Swancote. Even if the course of the road from Greensforge was of Roman date, that turn may not have formed part of the original road, which could instead have continued northwards, perhaps towards Wroxeter, taking an earlier line than the road past The Walls mentioned below. From the west, any Roman road from Morville may have turned south-east and taken the line of the present road to Eardington, with a Severn crossing further south.[373]

What is indisputable is that a Roman road which ran arrow-straight from Greensforge has long been known to the north of Houghton's road to Swancote, traceable along the southern flank of Abbot's Castle Hill and passing the south side of the earthworks known as The Walls at Chesterton to Rudge Heath, Ackleton and Sutton Madock (with a typical Roman deviation to avoid difficult ground at Folley) in the general direction of the Roman settlement at *Uxacona* (Redhill, on Watling Street to the east of Telford), and is marked on modern Ordnance Survey maps as far as the Shropshire-Staffordshire boundary, though the northern part beyond Sutton Madock is untraced.[374] If Houghton's road had a Roman origin, quite why two Roman roads may have run from the same place in almost the same direction is unexplained, but the road to Abbot's Castle Hill reinforces doubts about a Roman attribution for Houghton's road through Winchester towards Swancote. But as we shall see, the indisputably Roman road from Greensforge passing The Walls may have played a major role in the events leading to the battle of Tettenhall, as perhaps did the fortification at The Walls.

---

[370] It has not proved possible to confirm the line of the road from early O.S. maps, satellite photographs, or LiDAR surveys.
[371] Dr Houghton's postulated Roman river crossing at Bridgnorth does not appear on the O.S. *Map of Roman Britain*, 4th edition, 1978, or in Jones and Mattingly 1990, or on the map of Roman roads in White and Barker 1998: 37, where a Severn crossing at or near Quatt is shown, with another further north near Leighton (where there was a vexillation fortress: see Jones and Mattingly 1990: 91) or Buildwas; see also White and Barker 1998: 39. A small marching camp of just over 3 acres has been located by aerial photography at Quatt (SO 73818898): Welfare and Swan 1995: 162. One would expect a permanent fort to protect a fixed river crossing.
[372] Some late third century Roman and Romano-British coins are recorded from Castle Hill (Mason 1957: 5); a single Roman coin is recorded from topsoil in the oval earthwork containing Bridgnorth castle keep (Bassett 2011: 18, fn.63); and a hoard of some 2,500 Roman coins (some of which are on display in Ludlow Museum) was found 'in the Bridgnorth area' by a metal detectorist in recent years.
[373] Dr Houghton's postulated Roman river crossing at Bridgnorth does not appear on the O.S. *Map of Roman Britain*, 4th edition, 1978, or in Jones and Mattingly 1990, or on the map of Roman roads in White and Barker 1998: 37, where a Severn crossing at or near Quatt is shown, with another further north near Leighton (where there was a vexillation fortress: see Jones and Mattingly 1990: 91) or Buildwas; see also White and Barker 1998: 39. A small marching camp of just over 3 acres has been located by aerial photography at Quatt (SO 73818898): Welfare and Swan 1995: 162. One would expect a permanent fort to protect a fixed river crossing.
[374] Curiously, the road is unrecorded in Margary 1973 and the 4th edition of the O.S. map of Roman Britain, though it is marked on the O.S. *Historical Map of Roman Britain*, 6th edition, 2011. The existing roads to Sutton Maddock are recorded on Robert Baugh's map of Shropshire, 1808.

Caesar records Gallic or British timber bridges on several of the major rivers of Gaul and Britain at the time of his campaigns, including a major bridge on the Thames, which was probably downstream from London.[375] Roman bridges in northern Europe typically took the form of stone piers and abutments with a timber superstructure.[376] The pier-foundations for the Roman bridge over the Medway at Rochester, which was probably about 500' long, and designed to cope with tidal levels differing by up to 17½ feet,[377] extended at least 13' and perhaps up to 25' beneath the Roman river bed.[378] In northern Europe the standard Roman practice was to construct timber coffer-dams in the river on the site of the intended bridge piers. The water was removed from within the coffer-dam and the alluvium excavated until a firm stratum was reached. Massive iron-shod timber piles were driven into that stratum and a rubble foundation rammed down around the piles to create footings on which ashlar-faced masonry piers could be built. There is no reason to suppose that any Roman bridge across the Severn in the Bridgnorth area would have deviated markedly from the standard Roman design, and fragmentary remains of a the foundations of a pier from a probable Roman bridge across the Severn to the south-west of St Andrew's church at Wroxeter have been traced in the form of a bed of concrete some 24' long and 4' wide,[379] with abutments protecting the pier from floodwater in the form of a series of sharply pointed piles holding in place vertical planking backed with clay.[380]

The superstructure of any Roman bridge across the Severn in the Bridgnorth area[381] will almost certainly have been of timber, and is very unlikely to have had arches of stone: the only major Roman bridge in northern Europe that remains in use to the present day crosses the river Mosel at Trier and dates from the second century, and together with its first century predecessor has been the subject of detailed architectural and archaeological investigation. Some 450' in length, it carried a timber superstructure and was only arched in stone in the eighteenth century.[382]

We might expect any Roman bridge across a major river to be associated with a military and civil presence on each bank. The fact that Roman remains have not been recorded at Bridgnorth cannot of course be taken as evidence that there was no Roman presence. It may be that there was a Roman or pre-Roman ford at or near Bridgnorth: the river can be forded without undue difficulty at various places in the driest weather, but would be impassable on foot or horseback at other times. It is inconceivable that if the Romans had a river crossing they would not have created a structure to cross the river whatever the water levels, and the idea of a seasonal 'Summerford', useable only in summer, can be discounted.

Dr Houghton's road towards Swancote must remain something of an enigma, but Roman engineers typically diverted and re-aligned roads to avoid difficult features,[383] and in this

---

[375] Brooks 2000: 20. On Roman bridges in Britain see especially Bishop 2014: 348.
[376] Brooks 2000: 238-9.
[377] Brooks 2000: 221.
[378] Brooks 2000: 226.
[379] Roman engineers had long been able to manufacture concrete which set underwater.
[380] TSAS 4th Series XI 1928 304-307; TSAS XLIX 1937-8 82. A supposed Roman bridge site 4½ miles south-west of Wroxeter on the line of the Roman road from Wroxeter to Acton Burnell is discussed in TSAS LV 1954-6 38-50.
[381] The only Roman bridges across the Severn downsteam from Quatford were at Gloucester and (probably) Worcester: Carver 1980: 2, 21-2.
[382] Brooks 2000: 223.
[383] See Taylor 1979: 72.

case, if the road crossed the Severn hereabouts, it may have utilised a river crossing to the north or south of Bridgnorth, since there must be serious doubt whether early bridge-builders would have selected Bridgnorth as a site of choice for an early river crossing.[384] The topography of the Severn in the Bridgnorth area in the Roman period will have consisted, as today, of low-lying areas alongside the river prone to flooding where the river is constrained by the high ground on both sides, and the difficulty of defending a river crossing between two areas of particularly high ground Cannock be ignored. Moreover, with cliffs on both sides of the river, it is far from an ideal place for a crossing, since traffic and travellers from both sides of the river will have been forced to take a path along the banks of the river or ascend or descend what are, even today, particularly steep routes which cut through the sandstone cliffs of Castle Hill (on the west) or Hermitage Hill (on the east), routes which are unlikely to have existed at an early period. It seems likely that they are contemporary with or post-date the creation of Bridgnorth in the early 12th century.[385] In that respect we may note the account of Orderic Vitalis, writing of matters that occurred in the early twelfth century:

'When Robert [de Bellême] heard that the strong fortress of Bridgnorth in which he had placed his trust had surrendered to the king [in 1102] he was in despair; almost insane with grief he did not know what course to take. The king [Henry I] commanded his troops to go by way of *Huvel hegen*,[386] and lay siege to the town of Shrewsbury, which stands on a hill encircled by the river Severn. The English call this way through the wood by the name *Huvel hegen*, which may be translated as 'evil path' or 'road'. For a whole mile the road passed through a deep cutting, strewn with huge boulders; it was so narrow that two horsemen could scarcely ride abreast, and was overshadowed on both sides by a thick wood, in which archers used to lie hidden and without warning send javelins or arrows whistling to take their toll of passers-by. At that time there were more than sixty thousand foot-soldiers in the army; these the king ordered to cut down the wood with axes and make a much wider road, both for his use and for all travellers ever afterwards. The royal command was soon obeyed: the road was cleared and many hands levelled out a very wide road.'[387]

Of this account Sir Frank Stenton observed that: 'There is very little evidence of deliberate road-making in medieval England. The road cut by Henry I in 1102 for the passage of his army across Wenlock Edge seems to be the only example of such work recorded in the Norman period'.[388]

---

[384] Martin Carver's observation that 'In general, shallow water and a wide channel are required for a ford, and a deep channel and short span for a bridge' (Carver 1980: 20) seems to reflect received wisdom which must be open to question: a sequence of Anglo-Saxon bridges crossed the Trent on a flood plain at Hemington Quarry, Lockington-Hemington, Leicestershire (Cooper, Ripper and Clay 1994: 316-21; Salisbury 1995: 34-7); the bridge at Buttington, recorded in the 13th century (Owen and Morgan 2007: 58), crosses the Severn on a floodplain, as does the early bridge at Gloucester.

[385] The road through the sandstone cutting on Hermitage Hill is recorded as *Sondy Wey* before 1327: TSAHS XLIX 1937-8 192. It seems likely to have been constructed by Henry I when he transferred the borough from Quatford to found Bridgnorth in 1101.

[386] Literally 'evil hege or undergrowth', from ME *uvel hege*. This would appear to be the 'narrow and rugged way called Evil-street [Mala Platea]' near Wenlock mentioned by Giraldus Cambrensis, evidently unimpressed by Henry's works, in his itinerary through Wales in 1187: Wright 1863: 467.

[387] Chibnall 1968-80: VI book X 28-31.

[388] Stenton 1970: 238.

If Orderic is to be believed (and whilst his estimate of the 60,000 troops is almost certainly exaggerated, there is no reason to doubt the rest of his account), is it fanciful to imagine that Houghton's road, and perhaps even the cliff-cut road descending into Bridgnorth from the east, may also have been created by Henry I during the same campaign? But if that were the case, it is not easy to put forward a convincing explanation for the subsequent abandonment of the road in many places between Highgate and Swancote, although there is some evidence that the road across Wenlock Edge may have fallen into disrepair less than a century after it had been widened and made good.[389]

Finally, before leaving Dr Houghton's lost road, which we have seen may have been created or improved in the early twelfth century, it may be noted that no evidence has been traced of any possible Roman road aligned with Bridgnorth branching off the better-known Roman road running from Greensforge to Chesterton and Sutton Maddock,[390] which one might have expected if any Severn crossing had existed. The evidence, such as it is, including the likelihood of a significant Roman population on the west side of the river, might point toward the probable existence of a Roman crossing over the Severn somewhere – possibly some distance – to the south of Bridgnorth.

Reverting to the possibility of an Anglo-Saxon bridge at Quatford, we should note that the Reverend R. W. Eyton, whose opinions cannot lightly be dismissed, was not willing to accept that any bridge existed in the area in the ninth century, writing: 'I cannot suppose for an instant that in the year 896 there was a bridge over the Severn at or near Quatford, nor that, if there were, would a contemporary Saxon have described it as 'Cwatbricge by Severn', words which are only referable to a period when there was both a bridge and a village in the locality. The word 'bridge' is therefore an interpolation by some one transcribing the older document at a time when there was a bridge at Quatford, and which was probably not till the end of the eleventh century. The chronicle formerly attributed to Florence (and, latterly, John) of Worcester, now known to scholars as the Worcester Latin Chronicle,[391] on the other hand, using the same original authority and writing, as we know, at the beginning of the twelfth century, interpolates the same passage much more truly and intelligibly. He describes the Danes as flying to the place (not town) which is called Quat-bridge – that is, called so at the time he was writing. This is not the only instance which I have met with, where the ipsissima verba of Florence convey a truth not deducible from any copy of the Saxon Chronicle ... All we can safely conclude on this subject is then, that the Danes in 895, having lost their fleet, came and wintered in the forest by the Severn; and the writer of the Worcester Latin Chronicle, two centuries after, understood the place then called Quatbridge, to have been the site of their encampment. Their object in coming to the 'forest by the river' when they had lost their ships is obvious[392] ... [t]hey probably came here with the purpose of building a fleet, but finding that, when built, it could not be got down the Severn, they abandoned their design'.[393]

Is Eyton's scepticism about an early (i.e. pre-tenth century) bridge at *Cwatbrycge* justified?

---

[389] Wright 1863: 467; TSAHS 3rd Series I (1901) 114-5.

[390] Jones and Mattingly 1990: 206 show two Roman pottery kilns to the east of the Severn which appear to lie somewhere near Badger, although the map is too small-scale to identify the area with any certaintly.

[391] See Smyth 2002: xix, 69-72. The tenth-century section of the *Chronicle* may have been compiled by Byrhtferth of Ramsey: ibid. xix.

[392] Eyton 1854-60: I 105, whose views were accepted by the antiquary W. D. G. Fletcher: TSAS 2nd Series V (1893) xiv.

[393] Eyton 1864-60: III 214.

The best evidence for a bridge existing in the late ninth and early tenth century in the Bridgnorth area comes from two sources: *Anglo-Saxon Chronicle* 'A' tells us that in 895/6 the Danes wintered at *Cwatbrycge be Sæfern* ('B', 'C' and 'D' name the place simply as *Bricge*, *Bricge* and *Brygcge* respectively),[394] and in the chronicler Æthelweard's account of the events leading up to the battle of Tettenhall in 910 we are told *Ast ubi pedem retraxere domi ouantes spoliis opimis parte in eoa fluuii Sefern etiam transmeabant pontem ordine litterato qui uulgo [ ]antbricge nuncupatur*: 'But when rejoicing in rich spoils they [the pagans] were still engaged in crossing to the east side of the river Severn over a pons to give the Latin spelling, which is called [ ]antbricge by the common people...'.[395]

The relevant extract from version 'A' of the *Chronicle* was probably entered between 911/914 and 930.[396] The date of Æthelweard's birth is not known, but he probably died c.998.[397] Eyton's doubts about a bridge at Quatford might properly be considered removed by these accounts which, uncharacteristically, he appears to have overlooked.

Assuming that the name *Cwatbrycge* refers to a physical structure over the Severn (a matter considered earlier in this chapter), we have evidence, then, that a bridge at *Cwatbrycge* probably existed in 910, and certainly existed by 930, the latest date by which the entry mentioning the bridge-name in *Chronicle* 'A' was written,[398] and definitely existed as a *pontem* before c.988, when Æthelweard died.[399] We can reasonably assume that the ninth/tenth-century bridge lay at or close to the site of the bridge recorded at Quatford in 1086, since a major structure such as a bridge is unlikely to have been relocated in the absence of any extraordinary upheaval such as the transfer en-bloc of the borough, bridge and fortress of Quatford to Bridgnorth. Later bridge builders would almost certainly use an existing river crossing, served by pre-existing routeways leading to the site, and utilise earlier bridge foundations which might well survive even if the superstructure had been destroyed. That might suggest that we should seek evidence for any Roman bridge on the site of the Anglo-Saxon bridge.

An indirect reference to a pre-Conquest bridge may conceivably be detected in the boundary between the dioceses of Hereford and of Lichfield recorded at some date in a self-styled *discretionem* recorded in a gospel-book during the episcopacy of Æthelstan, bishop of Hereford between 1012 and 1056,[400] which begins at Monmouth and ends when

---

[394] Thorpe 1861: I 174-5.
[395] Bateley 1986: 59; MS Coton Otho A x and xii; Campbell 1962: 53.
[396] Bateley 1996: xxxiii-xxxiv; Stafford 2008: 108.
[397] Campbell 1962: xii-xvi; Williams, Smyth and Kirby 1991: 30-31.
[398] Swanton 1996: xxi; Stafford 2008: 108.
[399] It is said that only two English bridges are named in the chronicles before the eleventh century: *Grantabricg* (Cambridge) is mentioned in 975 and 951 and *Cwatbrycge* in 895, 910 and 912: Cooper 2006: 12.
[400] Finberg 1972: 225-7; Hooke 1990: 442. The boundary was said to run 'along the edge of Carcdune' (Carton, a name now applied to a farm in the parish of Bayton), and 'from Carcdune to Eardigtun', probably following Dowles Brook, which falls into the Severn a mile or so above Bewdley, then 'up the Severn to Eardington', from where it runs 'up the Severn to Quattford': Finberg 1972: 225-7. This description poses certain difficulties, for Eardington lies a mile or so west of the Severn, and Quatford lies due east of Eardington on the opposite side of the river. Rowley suggests that the boundary 'obviously left the Severn at its confluence with the Mor brook and followed the straight road [*sic*] to Eardington', or (if the terminology is correct), that Quatford lay further upstream at this date: Rowley 1972: 45. Finberg may well be correct in his analysis, but the boundary wording is far from clear: it reads in part (according to Förster 1941: 775) ... *of Carc-dune in Eardig-tun, of Eardigtune est in Sæfern in Quatt-ford,* or (according to Hooke 1990: 442) ... *of carcdune in*

it comes to the Severn at Quatford, after reaching Eardington: the reference to Quatford may suggest that the place was of special importance, perhaps because it was an ancient Severn crossing point, possibly with a bridge. Of particular interest in that respect is the suggestion advanced by Eyton that the boundary of Hereford diocese (founded in 676, the time of St Mildburh),which does not follow the Severn as might be expected, but meanders to encompass Badger, Beckbury, Madeley and Little Wenlock,is attributable to the ancient boundary of Mildburh's lands having been adopted as that of the diocese.[401] If Eyton's supposition is correct, could that suggest that Wenlock's interest in Quatford also dated from the later seventh century?[402]

When the collegiate community of Quatford was transferred to Bridgnorth after the transfer of the borough in 1101 it moved from the diocese of Hereford to the diocese of Coventry and Lichfield.[403] It might be argued that if the boundary had deviated from the river at a bridge, the name Quatbridge or similar (or indeed a reference to the bridge itself) might have been expected in the eleventh-century *discretionem*, but there is no reason why the ancient (and presumably earlier) name Quatford should have changed even after a bridge had been built, as attested by many other place-names, with Oxford perhaps the best known. The bridge may have been known as *Cwatbrycge* and the associated settlement as Quatford.[404]

Whilst the account in *Chronicle* 'A' to *Cwatbrycge* and Æthelweard's reference to a *pontem* record a bridge at *[ ]antbricge*, we are given no clues to the precise location of *Cwatbrycge*, presumably because it was so well known in the tenth century. The only unambiguous evidence for a bridge at Quatford itself at any period (apart from the name *Cwatbrycge*, which as noted above might conceivably be misleading) is the single reference in the foundation document of Quatford church in 1086 mentioned earlier in this

---

eardigtun. of eardigtune eft in sæfern. in quattford, which can be translated: '... from Carton to Eardington and from Eardington again to the Severn to Quatford [or the ford at Quatt]'. There is no specific reference to the boundary running along the Severn between Carton and Eardington (the places lie over ten miles apart), but the Severn is mentioned in the earlier part of the boundary clause. Patrick Sims-Williams questions whether the boundary to Eardington may have run overland, and notes that some doubt has been expressed about the identification of *carcdune* as Carton in Bayton parish: Sims-Williams 1990: 392. Eyton places Quatford in Lichfield diocese in 1086 (1854-60: I 118), and notes that the boundary of Lichfield diocese incorporating Eardington was recognised in the *Valor Ecclesiasticus* of 1535 (ibid.). From the boundary description of 1012x1056 we might conclude that the boundaries of Lichfield, Hereford and Worcester met at Quatford, with the boundary between Worcester and Hereford to the west of the Severn (a conclusion that seems to have been accepted by J. F. A. Mason in TSAS LVII 1961-4 158, who suggests that Quatt, listed in Warwickshire in DB, lay in the diocese of Worcester), but note the boundary line shown in Hill 1984: 160. VCH Shropshire II 1 states that in the 13th century Quatford lay in the diocese of Hereford, though the bishop denied this in 1333 and by the 16th century it was territorially within Lichfield. The diocesan boundary between Hereford and Worcester may well have followed the boundary between the Mercians and the people known as the Hwicce. By the late 8th century Mercia had annexed the Hwicce: Bassett 2000: 1-27.

[401] Eyton 1854-60: III 326; see also VCH Shropshire 10 187-212.

[402] Bassett suggests that the diocesan boundary between Hereford and Worcester may well have followed the boundary between the Mercians and the people known as the Hwicce. By the late 8th century Mercia had annexed the Hwicce: Bassett 2000: 1-27.

[403] Barrow 2004: 47.

[404] A study of early *–ford* place-names in Shropshire suggests that almost a third were either on or associated with Roman roads: Laflin 2001: 1. The paper makes no mention of Quatford, or the Welsh *ffordd* (borrowed into Welsh from OE *ford*) meaning 'road', perhaps applied to sections of Roman roads constructed on causeways: see Jermy 1992: 229-9; Jermy and Breeze 20000: 109-10.

volume.[405] The foundation document is incorporated in a précis, likely to be authentic, which was probably drawn up in or after the thirteenth century,[406] and records that in 1086 Roger de Montgomery endowed Quatford church with, inter alia, 'Eardington, except the land of Walter the smith, and the land lying between the water [of the Severn] and the *monte*, near the bridge, and except the land on which the borough [of Quatford] stands'.[407] That description is puzzling, for if the *monte* is to be identified as Camp Hill, there is no land between it and the Severn, for it lies on a sheer cliff rising from the Severn, though it is very possible that during the course of a millennium or more the river has eroded ground at the foot of Camp Hill, as well as the cliff itself.

Eyton, who knew the area well as a boy,[408] states that all these features lay on the east side of the river, but Wasey is almost certainly correct in his belief that the *monte* refers to the higher ground to the west of the river – in the twelfth century the abbot of Lilleshall held land at Quatford and Netherton and on the west side of the Severn opposite, between what is described as the *monte de Erdinton* and the river near the ferry.[409] The history of that holding is of some interest. Eyton suggests that it could have been some purpresture or occupation of the royal demesne which had not been taken into account when the rent payable to the sheriff was settled: it is recorded as purpresture in 1168.[410] In 1177 the sheriff of Shropshire listed purprestures and escheats relating to certain crown lands in the borough of Bridgnorth. Those lands may perhaps have come into the hands of Henry I after the insurrection of Robert de Montgomery in 1101, and might possibly represent, at least in part, the land of Walter the Smith excluded from the endowment of Quatford

---

[405] Eyton 1854-60: I 109. The church may have replaced an earlier chapel: chapels have long been associated with bridges, and a chapel, variously known as The Holy Trinity and St Sythe, St Clement and St Syth, or St Sythe stood on Bridgnorth bridge from at least the 15th century until the eighteenth century: Harrison 2004: 199; TSAHS X (1885) 139; SSMR PRN 00423.
[406] VCH Shropshire II 123.
[407] SA Shrewsbury Free Library MS 292 20; see also Eyton 1854-60: I 109; Clark-Maxwell and A. Hamilton Thompson 1927: 1-4. The parish of Eardington, of which Quatford formed part (a reversal of the situation in 1086), was a Peculiar Jurisdiction, afterwards jealously guarded by the Crown (a status transferred to Bridgnorth when the settlement of Quatford was transferred there in 1101), and within the ancient diocese of Chester, the boundary of which crossed the Severn at this point: Eyton 1854-60: I 118 fn59. Several ancient estates within Eardington opposite Quatford are mentioned in early records. The Hay is recorded in 1226 and many times thereafter: Eyton I 123; NLW Otley (Pitchford Hall) Estate papers: The ford lay near the weir of Quatford. *Hamstodeshul* is recorded in the 12th century (probably to be associated with the field-name *Church Hampstead* on the 1842 Tithe Map on the south side of the track leading to the Severn), lay nearby: Eyton 1854-60: I 125; NLW Otley (Pitchford Hall) Estate 1 1214. The name is discussed in more detail elsewhere in this volume. Meadow called *le Ree in the field of Brug* is recorded frequently in this area from the late 13th century: Eyton 1854-60: I 126; NLW Otley (Pitchford Hall) Estate 1 1221. The name is from OE *æt þære ea* 'at the river' which became ME *atter e*, and was mis-divided as *atte re*. The name was often applied to rivers. *La Ho*, recorded in the 13th century (NLW Otley (Pitchford Hall) Estate 1 1225) is probably to be associated with the field-name *Far Hoo Bank* which appears on the Tithe Map at a headland, the name incorporating OE *hōh* 'heel; a headland': Gelling 1984: 167.
[408] Eyton 1854-60: I 109 fn.14, TSAS LVII 1961-4 46 fn.39.
[409] Eyton 1854-60: I 359-61; NLW Otley (Pitchford Hall) Estate 1 1368; SA 2922/2/20; SA 972/1/1/116. The author of a paper in the JBAA (vol 29, 229), believed that the deed of endowment of Quatford church specifically mentioned meadows on the low ground on the west side of the Severn. For other estates of St Alkmund's abbey in Shrewsbury granted by Roger de Montgomery to his clerk Godebold (who was amongst those at the dedication of Quatford church in 1086) which eventually passed to Lilleshall abbey, see VCH Shropshire II 70-80. Lilleshall's holdings in Eardington/Quatford are unmentioned in the history of the abbey in VCH Shropshire II 70-80.
[410] Eyton 1854-60: I 359-61.

church in 1086, perhaps now represented by Moor Farm, north-west of Eardington.[411] In the same year the lands were granted by Henry II to Walter de Linley. By 1199 these had passed to Sibil de Linley, who granted them to Lilleshall abbey, with the grant included in a confirmation of King John that year.[412] A confirmation by Pope Honorius III (1216-1227) to the abbey mentions a fishery of the abbey in the Severn at Bridgnorth, though the grantor is unnamed.[413] In 1535 the abbey held various leases of land, which included land at Netherton which probably relates to the Linley property.[414] A conveyance in 1598 of land at Netherton and *Bromilesoe* (the latter supposedly Camp Hill, on which stands the motte)[415] describes it as 'all of which once belonged to the late dissolved monastery of Lilleshall'.[416] If the identification of *Bromilesoe* is correct (which is far from certain), it suggests that at one time Lilleshall abbey held the motte of Quatford castle. The conveyance also suggests that the area of Netherton extended southwards beyond the boundary with Quatt.[417]

But Lilleshall was not the only religious foundation to hold land here, for Wenlock abbey evidently retained interests in Quatford after it had been granted Millichope in exchange for Quatford in 1086, for it still held Quatford fish-weir in 1538, when it was conveyed to Richard Lemm.[418] The conveyance of the fish-weir is puzzling evidence, and perhaps the last identifiable vestige of Wenlock's ancient holding in the area.

Having established that a bridge existed at Quatford in 1086, if not by 930 (by which date the name *Cwatbrycge* had been recorded in the Chronicle), the evidence pointing to the location of such bridge must be reviewed. The early routeway identified by Croom running from Wenlock Edge to Eardington (and the direct route from Wenlock) means that when considering the site of an ancient Severn crossing we need to concentrate on the topography of the area around Quatford. The very name, recorded as *quattford* between

---

[411] The Moor was a small property which, although part of Eardington, constituted a separate tenement *in capite* of the Crown from the earliest recorded period (Eyton 1854-60: I 126; Morris 1986: notes to 4,1,32) and has been suggested as the place identified in Domesday Book as *Bolebec*, which had half a hide of waste land, perhaps not far from Eardington, and has never been located (Eyton 1854-60: I 128-30); but see Morris 1986: Notes 4.1.33, which finds the evidence unconvincing. A very ancient tradition is associated with The Moors: 'The king's tenant at the More held his land (a virgate) by service of appearing yearly in the exchequer, on the morrow of Michaelmas Day, with a hazel rod of a year's growth and cubit's length, and two knives., The Treasurer and barons being present the tenant was to attempt to sever [split] the rod with one of the knives which was not to bend or break; the other knife was to do the same work at one stroke, and then to be given up to the king's champion for royal use': Anderson 1864: 10-11. Anderson believed the object of the ancient service was the acquision of a good knife by the king, but a split hazel represents the short hazel notched tallies used for centuries to record receipts in the Exchequer: Poole 1912: 89.
[412] NLW Otley (Pitchford Hall) Estate 1 1368; SA 2922/2/20.
[413] Eyton 1854-60: I 360 fn.465.
[414] Eyton 1854-60: I 359-61.
[415] Mason 1961-4: 39; SA 2922/2/23. *Bromilesoe* is evidently Broomy Leasow, from OE dative singular *læswe* 'pasture, meadowland'. It is noteworthy that the name provides no evidence for any ancient fortification or other man-made structure on the site. The 1842 Tithe Map gives the name *Rough Bank*, with *Camp Hill* adjoining to the east.
[416] SA 2922/2/23.
[417] SA 2922/2/23.
[418] BCA MS 3688/305. The Lemm(e) family appear to have been one of Quatford's most prominent families, mentioned frequently in local records over several generations.

1012 and 1056,[419] and as *Quatford* in Domesday Book, shows that a ford existed somewhere in the area in the late Anglo-Saxon period, and it does not seem unreasonable to suppose that it had its origins in the prehistoric period. Croom notes that fords can migrate upstream or downstream over time, and that view is emphasised by Matt Edgeworth, who observes that fords will have been much more common in Anglo-Saxon England than now, with rivers generally wider and shallower, and as part of the geomorphology fords would rarely stay in one place, being affected by the changes in the river-bed as rivers gradually altered their course. A weir downstream from a ford would deepen it, drowning it or making it difficult to use, and an obstruction upstream would create scouring and erosion of the river-bed or dangerous currents which impeded crossing.

Furthermore, there is some evidence of the natural upstream retreat of a few centimetres a year by some fords, a phenomenon affecting rapids known as headwater retreat,[420] but it is unclear whether such a phenomenon may have occurred at Quatford: Pee's researches suggest that fords are found where harder rock forms the river bed, and those features are hardly likely to migrate. Nevertheless, when a ford moves, it will take with it the configuration of roads and trackways that formerly led to it.[421] Having analysed the early routeways in the area, Croom concluded that the early ford was at or close to the point where Slade Lane (from Old English *slæd* 'valley') reaches the river, marked by the parish boundary crossing the Severn, presumably the site of the ford recorded in 1830 as Sladeford',[422] though the ford at Quatford would seem to be an equal, if not better, candidate, and in reality there were probably at least three fords in close proximity: Danesford, Sladeford and Quatford.

That conclusion is supported by Robert Dawson's plan of the area for the Ordnance Survey in 1815 which shows Slade Lane turning to the river crossing, and another lane running towards the ferry crossing opposite Quatford (which is downstream of the point where Slade Lane reaches the river), and we might suppose that the ford at Quatford has long been at the place where the river was crossed by a ferry in the nineteenth century, a little to the south of the rock above the river.[423] The ford at Quatford is almost certainly very much older than any bridge, but there is no reason why a bridge and a ford should not have co-existed in close proximity after a bridge had been built, for the movement of cattle, for example, will have been easier across a shallow ford[424] – even the Severn is fordable in

---

[419] S.1561; see Finberg 1972: 225-7; Hooke 1990: 422. It would appear that some Anglo-Saxon magnate temporarily transferred Quatt (and probably Romsley, Rudge and Shipley) from Staffordshire into Warwickshire for reasons which are unclear, but within 50 years of 1086 they (together with Worfield, Alveley, Nordley and Claverley, which undoubtedly lay in Staffordshire) were mised, or transferred, into Shropshire: Eyton 1881: 6; TSAHS LVII 1961-4 158. The name Quatford does not necessarily indicate a settlement, but suggests that in the first half of the 11th century the ford may have been a feature of some importance.

[420] Davies 2006: 23-6, citing Gregory 1992.

[421] Edgeworth 2014: 51-2. Indeed, Edgeworth notes that the Viking fortification at Tempsford was located at the point where an old but significant routeway, possibly a former course of the great North Road, once crossed the river Ouse: ibid.

[422] Watercolour of Quatford Castle from Sladeford Meadow by Joseph Powell made for John Smalman, sold with others of Bridgnorth and Quatford as Lot 338 by Dreweatts and Bloomsbury, London, 12th November 2014.

[423] O.S. 6" map 1890-1. It is worth noting that Quatt lies a mile or so from the ancient ferry crossing at Hampton Loade, but 2 miles from Quatford.

[424] A. R. B. Haldane has observed that bridges 'were not popular with drovers. Many of the early bridges were narrow wooden structures. To cattle being driven for the first time, and unused as many

many places in a dry summer – and a relatively narrow timber bridge of some antiquity may have offered a challenging crossing. A drover or horseman or cart driver would probably have been more confident taking his cattle or mount or cart across a shallow ford in dry weather than risk a bridge of doubtful strength, but a ford will have been of little use in all but the driest conditions.

Since Croom's early routeway to Eardington leads towards the river at or near to Quatford (though there is some uncertainty whether the route originally ran to the river or turned south before reaching the river) and may well be Roman or even pre-Roman in date, it is appropriate to mention a hollow-way from Eardington which approaches to within two or three hundred yards of the west bank of the river, with the trackway – perhaps the *Fordway* on the Eardington side of the river mentioned in medieval deeds[425] – continuing on the north side of a straight hedgeline across the level ground to the river Severn.[426] The Eardington parish boundary runs in a straight line slightly to the south of this hedgeline to a point a little to the north of where the 1891 6" Ordnance Survey map marks (arguably with misplaced certainty) the site of the old bridge. However, this straight length of boundary is unmarked in any way on the ground for the last few hundred yards before it reaches the Severn, and it seems surprising that if the boundary follows the line of an ancient trackway to a bridge that there is no visible evidence of such trackway, although the flat ground across the floodplain must have been affected by both erosion and deposition from the Severn.[427] The trackway and hedgeline to the north might mark the route to any bridge, but even that trackway shows no evidence of great age.[428]

It is worth noting that at river and stream crossings it is not uncommon to find parish and other boundaries deviating from the watercourse to encompass the end of such crossing. The site of the supposed 'old bridge' at Quatford lies on the southern edge of such a deviation, whereas we might have expected the deviation, if the boundary line is indeed ancient, to be centred on the river crossing. The centre of this deviation is the point where the Brignorth to Quatt road comes closest to the river, to the west of Quatford village. However, the present boundary may be relatively modern, since until the late nineteenth

---

of them were to anything but their native hills, crossing a bridge was a terrifying experience': Haldane 2008: 40.

[425] TSAS LVII 1961-4 46 fn.54. The route is recorded as *le Vordwey* in the 13th century (NLW Otley (Pitchford Hall) Estate 1 42), and *le Fodvey* in 1292/3 (ibid. 1090).

[426] This ground may be the area known as *le Heye* (13th century and frequently thereafter; cf. Hay House, 2 miles south-west of Quatford), and *la Ree* (c.1300), *le Reyhe* (1329), and *le Rye* (1408/9): NLW Otley (Pitchford Hall) Estate 1 1214, 76, 1618, 1212. These places seem to have formed part of one of the fields of Bridgnorth called Severn Field (*Saverne veld* 1346/7: ibid. 1296). Ree/Reyhe/Rye are evidently from OE *(æt) þære ēa* '(at) the river', which developed (with incorrect division) into *ate Re* – river names Rea, Ray, etc., are common in England: see Ekwall 1928: 337.

[427] A lease of meadow called *the Nead* or *Nealt* in 1672 required the lessee to plant withies and to endeavour to stop the meadow being eroded by water: SA BB/E/1/2/38. This is the meadow known as *Quatford Neald in Quatford Park* in 1774: SA BB/E/1/2/345. Worthy of mention is a 1683 reference to *the Bylett* (half an acre) at Quatford and adjoining meadow called *the Neyt*: SA 2922/2/40. The name *Neyt(e)* seems to be recorded only in Shropshire and Worcestershire, and is evidently a noun derived from the OE adjective **næt* 'wet, moist', although the precise meaning in place-names is uncertain: all other references traced appear to relate to land adjoining fisheries, and Neyt(e) may have some special technical meaning with that connection.

[428] Two public footpaths converge at the riverbank at a point one hundred feet or so to the north, evidently to the old ferry which is marked on the Tithe Map of 1842. No weir is shown on that map.

century the parish of Quatford extended across the river to include Eardington.[429] Assuming that the boundary follows its ancient course – an assumption supported by the fact that the ancient boundary of the diocese of Lichfield crossed the river Severn at Quatford to include Eardington[430] – the point where it reaches the Severn might indicate the site of the early bridge.

Mason observes that evidence for the existence of a bridge is found in references to field-names containing Brug or Bridge at Quatford from the time of Edward II, still called Ford or Bridge Meadow in the nineteenth century, and the name Bridge Bylet for an islet in the river at Quatford marked on the c.1560 map of the Bridgnorth area and on the 1613 map of Morfe Forest.[431] It is clear, however, that one of the great open fields of Bridgnorth was on the west side of the river at Quatford, and references to Brug and Bridge Field[432] almost certainly refer to Bridgnorth Field, and cannot be taken as evidence for any bridge at Quatford.

The previously-mentioned discovery at Netherton, just below the old ferry,[433] of large oak timbers and piers in and by the river in the late eighteenth and early nineteenth century has been held to be tentative evidence of a timber bridge of uncertain date some five feet wide,[434] but it must be more likely that the timbers were the remains of the well-recorded

---

[429] The O.S. 6" map of 1891-2 shows the modern boundary of Quatford on the west side of the Severn. It is worth recording that Robert Creighton's map for Samuel Lewis's *Topographical Dictionary* (1835) shows a detached area marked 'Part of Quatford Parish' which included Mose and Wootton.

[430] Eyton 1854-60: I 118. The same boundary was recognised in the *Valor Ecclesiasticus* of 1535: ibid. It is possible that the diocesan boundaries of Lichfield, Worcester and Hereford met at Quatford: see TSAS LVII 1961-4 157-60.

[431] TSAS LVII 1961-4: 43-4; SA 4296.

[432] E.g. *the field of Brugia opposite Quatford*, recorded in the early 13th century: NLW Otley (Pitchford Hall) Estate 1 1217. An estate called Hay (*la Hay* 12th century NLW Otley (Pitchford Hall) Estate 1 1214; *le heye opposite the rock of Quatford* 13th century ibid. 1258) evidently lay on the west side of the river, and was in the parish of Quatford: NLW Otley (Pitchford Hall) Estate 1231; see also Eyton 1854-60: I 123-6. If the boundaries have remained unchanged, the place must have lain on the flat floodplain opposite Quatford rock. The name is remembered in Haye House further south along the river and Hay Bridge over Mor Brook.

[433] TSAS LVII 1961-4 40; 44; Watkins-Pitchford 1937, where it is suggested that the bridge was built by Roger de Montgomery, and possibly destroyed by his son Robert de Bellême when he moved to Bridgnorth.

[434] TSAS LVII 1961-4: 43-4, which mentions that 'in about 1780 a very large piece of squared oak timber had been lifted out of the river at this point, and taken away, and that another piece of oak five feet long and eighteen inches square was still discernible about a foot deep in the earth on the east bank', and also mentions nineteenth century records of piers of the bridge visible at low water, of oak and two in number. PN Sa I 1990: 58, having cited the previous reference, concludes inexplicably that 'there is no reason to postulate a bridge at Quatford'. Wasey records how the 'excellent townsman Mr Bangham [from Bridgnorth], told me a short time before his death that he remembered seeing on one occasion at unusually low water the remains of two piers of this very bridge. An old villager told Mr Smalman that he remembered beams of wood being raised from that part of the bed of the river …': Wasey 1859: 25. The O.S. 6" map of 1891-2 shows 'Site of Bridge', the word Bridge in Gothic lettering to denote an antiquity, on the Severn to the south-west of Quatford (SO 736905), but should be treated with particular caution, since at that period archaeological features of particularly doubtful pedigree often found their way onto otherwise impressively accurate maps, and we have no record of the evidence that persuaded the Ordnance Surveyors to mark a bridge in the position shown on the map.

fish weir, badly damaged by extreme floods in 1635.[435] The existence of an islet or 'bylet' in the river at or near this point c.1560 and in 1613 (and still visible in about 1820)[436] might suggest that this place was chosen for a bridge because it was located on a floodplain and the divided river was easier to cross, with the bylet providing a firm foundation for bridge piers. Indeed, it is not inconceivable that the bylet itself was man-made – or at least artificially-modified – rather than a natural feature, a remnant of a pier and its foundations dividing the river at a convenient point to facilitate a crossing. If the bylet was formerly of any size, as seems quite possible – it would appear to have been a significant feature in 1613, where it seems to appear on the worn map of Morfe Forest at a point where the river is shown to widen markedly[437] – it is not inconceivable that it was used by the Danes as their winter base in 895-6. A bridge may have existed at that date – its existence at least implied by the record of the name *Cwatbrycge* in *Anglo-Saxon Chronicle* 'A', which we have seen probably dates to c.930 – making use of the bylet to house some of the piers. On the other hand it is possible that the bylet was created by natural turbulence from a bridge upstream, as seems to have been the case of an island recorded in the Severn at Worcester which could still be seen in the early nineteenth century.[438] It should also be remembered that fish-weir fences were often reinforced with stones, as at Montford and Preston, which will be all that remains after the timber decayed or was destroyed.

Mason makes the valid point that Florence (John) of Worcester is unlikely to have used the name *Cwatbrycge* for Quatford at a time when the name Quatford itself seems to have been already well established.[439] The explanation may be that a small hamlet known as *Cwatbrycge* developed at the east end of the bridge (possibly what became later known as Netherton),[440] to be distinguished from the community at Quatford, or that *Cwatbrycge* was simply the name of the structure and Quatford the name of the nearby settlement.

Mason also questions why Roger de Montgomery decided to develop Quatford with a church and borough, when he had a number of alternative sites open to him in Shropshire, not to mention Sussex.[441] One romantically fanciful explanation for the siting of the church at Quatford is supplied by the anonymous fourteenth-century chronicle once owned by John Brompton, after whom it is named,[442] who attributed the foundation of the church to a dream by a priest accompanying Roger's second wife, Adelais, beset by a storm in the Channel when returning to England, in which the price of a safe crossing was the promise to found a church in honour of St Mary Magdalene at the place where Adelais should meet

---

[435] TSAS 1888 XI 425-6. See also Pannett 1981: 144,148.
[436] TSAS LVII 1961-4: 43-4.
[437] SA 4296. Unfortunately the map is badly worn in places, and the island is drawn on the edge of two sheets pasted together to form one, with the boundaries of the island not aligning exactly, making it difficult to determine its size and shape.
[438] Carver 1980: 20, 282.
[439] TSAS LVII 1961-4 44 fn.8.
[440] In about 1280 John de Exton, clerk, sold to Richard Dammas of Bridgnorth, chaplain, land in the field opposite Quatford. In 1293-4 Richard founded a chantry in the King's Free Chapel of Bridgnorth, endowing it with two messuages, one at Bridgnorth, the other in Netherton by Quatford, perhaps the property acquired c.1280: Eyton 1864-60: I 113-14.
[441] TSAS LVII 1961-4 39.
[442] The *Chronicon* of John Brompton has been described as 'An untrustworthy Chronicle, made up of extracts from Bede, Henry of Huntingdon, Higden and other well-known sources. It is not certain that Brompton [elected abbot of Jervaux in 1437] wrote it': Gross 1900: 270. It has since been concluded that the *Chronicon* was not composed by Brompton.

her husband. That encounter supposedly took place at Quatford.[443] The real reason was doubtless far less imaginative: an existing bridge, known as *Cwatbrycge*, adjoining a much older ford, already the site of a Viking camp and an Æthelflædian *burh*, provided a major focus for travellers and the genesis for a new commercial centre. Since any major ford and bridge will have attracted traffic from a wide area, it must be supposed that the road on the east side of the Severn now passing through Bridnorth and Quatt will have been supplemented by trackways running across country from the east and/or north-east to meet the river at Quatford. Traces of those trackways have effectively been obliterated by the enclosure of Morfe Forest over recent centuries, clearly shown by straight field and parish boundaries, though those routeways will in any event have become largely redundant after 1101 when Quatford transferred to Bridgnorth.

The former existence of an important ford over the Severn with the evocative name Danesford, between Bridgnorth and Quatford, has been mentioned. The ford is recorded from at least the early fourteenth century,[444] is shown in Gothic script on the 1891 6" Ordnance Survey map, and in 2005 was marked by a dozen or so irregular sandstone rocks and boulders lying some eight feet or so below the top of the steeply sloping bank on the west side of the river. Hardcore and debris in the form of stones, small rocks and pieces of brick lie embedded in the riverbank some three feet or so below the top of the riverbank, and would seem to date from the nineteenth or earlier twentieth century. The boulders and hardcore extend over a width of no more than six or seven feet. There is no evidence on the ground of any trackway to the ford, which (according to the Ordnance Survey) crossed the river diagonally, running north-east to the opposite bank.[445] Despite popular folklore to the contrary, the name Danesford has no association with the Danes, but originated as 'the hidden ford', a commonly-found name from Old English *derne, dierne, dyrne* 'hidden, secret, obscure' (perhaps to distinguish it from the more prominent Cwat-ford, half a mile to the south-east), and doubtless developed into its present form as a result of later antiquarianism associating the place (and name) with the Danish presence in the area in 895-6 and 910.

It is difficult to identify a period during the sub-Roman or Anglo-Saxon period when, in the apparent absence of an adjoining settlement, a bridge across the Severn – a major civil engineering project by any standards – might have been built, and by whom, and why. Elsewhere in England there is evidence of significant projects of a similar nature during

---

[443] TSAS LVII 1961-4 39. Earl Roger endowed the college with its estates, and probably intended to use the six canonries as a means of providing livings for his household clerks. After Earl Roger's death in 1094, his sons Hugh (d.1098) and Robert, who were successively Earls, planned to make Quatford into a Benedictine monastery, dependant on the French abbey of Le Sauve Majeure. In 1102, however, after Earl Robert lost his earldom and property, the college fell into the hands of the Crown. Transferred to Bridgnorth, it was reconstituted with a dean and five canons, who served St Mary Magdalen's chapel in the royal castle there: Baugh and Cox 1982: 37-8.

[444] At SO 72909141. The name is recorded as *Darneford* in 1420 (TSAS LVII 1961-4 39; NLW Ottley (Pitchford Hall) Estate 1 536), but Rees 1997: 154 records the name with the same spelling in the early 14th century. The name also appears as *Daneford* in 1612 (SA 796/78), and as *Danesford* in 1833 (O.S.), but as *Darnford* in 1818 (SA 1190/3/55). The existence of a Sladeford nearby should also be noted: Old Slade Meadow is shown on the 1842 Tithe Map where Slade Lane, which runs from the the east side of Eardington, approaches the Severn.

[445] 1891 6" O.S. map; 1965 1:25,000 O.S. map. An excavated Anglo-Saxon weir dated to the 9th century which crossed the Trent at Colwick near Holme Pierrepoint, Nottinghamshire, was some 38 metres long and formed of boulders, posts and wattle, and extended very obliquely across the river. It was interpreted as a fish weir: Christopher Salisbury, 'The Trent, the story of a river', in CA 74, vol. VII no. 3, November 1980 90-91.

the Anglo-Saxon period, for example a complex timber causeway to the island of Mersea in Essex was built in the late seventh century, and a timber and clay causeway leading to the ford at Oxford has been scientifically dated to about the late eighth or early ninth century, i.e. during the reign of the Mercian kings Offa (757-96) or Coenwulf (796-821).

Bridge-building is often associated with the assertion of territorial rights, whether by kings or feudal lords. A new bridge would transform a region, allowing both banks to be integrated into one undivided holding. 'Borough-work', the obligation to build and repair fortifications, had first been introduced throughout the Mercian kingdom (and subsequently countrywide) under the *trinoda necessitas* (or more correctly the *trimoda necessitas*),[446] the great public 'three-fold obligations' of *expeditionam, burhbotam et brugbotam* (military service, fortress work and bridge work), probably in the eighth century: in 792 Offa of Mercia is said to have imposed the three existing common burdens in response to the threat from seaborne Viking armies and organised coastal defences for his kingdom *contra paganos*,[447] though no details are known. In essence, possession of land entailed an obligation of military service and the construction and upkeep of urban fortifications and bridges. It is therefore possible that the first bridge at Quatford was built, or restored, during the reign of one of the more powerful Mercian kings, such as Offa or his predecessor Æthelbald.[448] Bridging the Severn would have been a relatively straightforward exercise for a ruler such as Offa, who was capable of constructing the largest earthwork in Britain, Offa's Dyke.

If not a Mercian king, a bridge may well have been erected by local ruler.[449] The west side of the Severn at *Cwatbrycge* lay in the far north of the territory of the Anglo-Saxon people known as the *Magonsaete*, possibly an alternative name for the *Westerna*, perhaps to be associated with the considerable territory possibly granted by Penda after the battle of Maserfelth (Oswestry) in 642 to Merewalh, the first named Anglo-Saxon to rule the area.[450] To the north (it has indeed been suggested that the boundary may have followed Wenlock Edge)[451] lay the territory of the *Wreocansaetan* (perhaps a successor to the area held by the Iron-Age tribe known as the Cornovii), and their territory may have been within the diocese of both Hereford and Lichfield, since the medieval boundary of those dioceses runs straight across the Wrekin, although that may be a later extension northwards.[452] Their lands probably stretched from beyond Chester in the north and along the east side of the Severn to join that of the *Husmerœ*, a group centred on the Stour valley,[453] within the territory of the *Hwicce*, a powerful people who held territory

---

[446] John Selden was responsible for mistaking *trinoda* for *trimoda* in a forged 10th-century charter: Contamine 1986: 51 fn.33.
[447] Haywood 1995: 4-5; Brooks 2000: 43.
[448] Jeremy Haslam has argued that a series of Roman and non-Roman bridgehead sites were fortified by Offa and served thereafter as administrative and market centres: Haslam 1987.
[449] On the origins of Mercia and the early history of the folk-groups of the West Midlands, particularly in Herefordshire and Shropshire, see especially Hooke 1992: 47-64.
[450] See especially Pretty 1989; Featherstone 2001: 31; Hooke 1992: 47-64; Hooke 2002: 48-52. Pretty makes the point that the *Magonsaete* are associated strictly with the Lugg Valley and Leominster, and that the *Hecani* may have occupied territory in Corve Dale and around Clee Hill: ibid 182. It has been suggested that the *Westerna* were either the inhabitants of later Cheshire and north Staffordshire, or was a generic term for the Britons of Wales, the Isle of Man and Anglesey: Hill and Rumble 1996: 19 fn.4.
[451] Charles-Edwards 2013: 388, fn41, citing Sims-Williams 1990: 44.
[452] Hooke 1992: 52-6; Charles-Edwards 2013: 387-8.
[453] Hooke 1992: 48.

represented by the medieval diocese of Worcester (which included Gloucester),[454] perhaps meeting at *Cwatbrycge* itself, since the boundary of the diocese of Hereford, which came into being by 680, as noted previously, recorded in a document dated between 1012 and 1056 as deviating from the Severn – or crossing the river[455] – to turn east at Quatford – perhaps specifically at the bridge, since the boundary had been following the river northwards from a mile or so north of Bewdley.[456] From an early date *Cwatbrycge* may have been an important meeting point of the boundaries between the peoples of the *Wreocansaetan*, the *Magonsaete/Westerna*, and the *Husmeræ/Hwicce*.[457]

Although Bede evidently knew little about the Anglo-Saxon kingdoms in this region, in the sixth and seventh centuries, the pagan *Magonsaetan*, together with the *Hwicce*, occupied the frontier from Stratford-upon-Avon as far as the Welsh kingdoms west of Offa's Dyke, with their own kings, aristocracy and independent monasteries, into the eighth century. Patrick Sims-Williams has traced the early conversion to Christianity of these people, the origins of the dioceses of Worcester and Hereford, and the early growth of Anglo-Saxon monasticism, revealing a wide range of Continental, Irish and Anglo-Saxon influences on the church to show that the monasteries were as varied in character as their Northumbrian counterparts described by Bede.[458] A bridge benefiting parties on both sides of the Severn may even have been a shared project undertaken jointly by the *Magonsaete* and the *Wreocansaetan*. Or again, the bridge may have been constructed by some wealthy and powerful religious community.[459]

The most significant religious foundation within the Bridgnorth area was that of Wenlock.[460] Wenlock abbey had been founded c.685, possibly on the site of a Romano-British villa, at a place called *Wininicas*, under the tutelage of St Botwulf's minster at Iken (Suffolk),[461] as a monastery for both sexes ruled by an abbess with endowments of extensive estates given to Mildburh, daughter of King Merewalh (of whom more below) of the West Hecani,[462] whose father was King Penda's third son. Liobsynde (a Frankish name) became its first abbess until Mildburh took the role, and it survived through all the vicissitudes of the next four hundred years before being abandoned shortly after the Conquest by the Norman earl of Shrewsbury, who installed in its place a colony of Clunaic monks from France.

---

[454] It has also been suggested that the *Hwicce* may have been the 'western' branch of the *Hecani*: Ray and Bapty 2016: 412 fn.29.

[455] Patrick Sims-Williams suggests the boundary to Eardington may have run overland rather than followed the Severn, and notes that some doubt has been expressed about the identification of *carcdune* as Carton in Bayton parish: Sims-Williams 1990: 392.

[456] S.1561; Finberg 1972: 225-7; Hooke 1990: 422. The relevant section reads *of carcdunein eardigtun. of eardigtune eft in sæfern. in quattford*: Hooke 1990: 422.

[457] Gelling 1992: 97-100.

[458] See generally Sims-Williams 1990.

[459] Hart 1977: 50-51.

[460] See especially TSAS LXXXIX (2014) 1-14. A collegiate foundation representing an 'old minster' existed at Morville in the time of Edward the Confessor (1042-66) (Eyton 1854-60: I 32; Stenton 1971: 668 fn.3), and may have existed at an earlier date.

[461] Finberg 1972: 207-9; Thacker 1985.

[462] Mildburg (d. after 715) was niece of Werburgh whose remains were by tradition transferred from Hanbury to Chester to avoid them falling into the hands of the Danes: Griffiths 2001: 169; Lewis 2008: 114-5.

A hagiography of Mildburh, who became celebrated for her miracles and quickly became a saint, was produced c.1101 and is known as *St Mildburh's Testament*,[463] largely a narrative of miraculous events, from which we learn that the abbey was a daughter-house of Medehamstede abbey (Peterborough), the principal centre of clerical education in seventh-century Mercia. The Medehamstede charter of Mildburh's endowments was confirmed by her uncle, King Æthelred of Mercia (674-716). Merewalh's father remained a pagan until 660, when he founded a church at Leominster and subsequently a number of others, including Wenlock, ruling over territory from the Wye to the Wrekin, and west to the forests of Clun and Radnor. From an early date the abbey held many estates in Wales and what were to become Herefordshire and Worcestershire.[464] Part of the land confirmed by King Æthelred between 674 and 704 was in Chelmarsh, and probably included the adjacent manors of Quatford/Eardington and Deuxhill, both of which were held by Wenlock in 1066, although Chelmarsh itself had been lost by that date.[465] That suggests that Quatford (in Eardington) was held by Wenlock by 704.

H. P. R.Finberg, in a valuable paper on the early Anglo-Saxon history of the region,[466] paints a picture of an Anglian dynasty centred at Medehamstede reigning over a preponderantly Welsh-speaking population and introducing English settlers in relatively peaceful conditions. Merewalh (who from his name may have been a Briton rather than an Anglo-Saxon)[467] left two sons who succeeded jointly to his kingdom and in 704 with the consent of King Æthelred granted to the abbey 63 hides of land scattered in south Shropshire. One son was by tradition the founder of Worcester cathedral. After the death of Penda, Wulfhere eventually became king, and a charter he ostensibly granted in 664 to Medehamstede names four places in Shropshire among its possessions. Wenlock also received estates from Æthelred's son King Ceolred (709-16) and from a certain Sigeweard, a *comes* of King Æthelbald (716-57), who witnessed the charter.[468]

Wenlock was clearly 'a church of some significance in Mercia, probably associated with royal administration' which continued to function, though eventually as a college of priests, into the tenth century and beyond.[469] The community certainly existed in 901, run by a male superior, when the cult of St Mildburh (one of a number of such cults promoted by Æthelred, Lord of the Mercians, and his wife Æthelflæd within Mercia) was honoured by their gift to the house of a gold chalice weighing 30 *mancuses* and restoring land to the house to keep the community in food, though William of Malmesbury tells that at the Conquest 'the attacks of enemies [presumably the Danes] and of time had destroyed all the signs of the people of old'.[470]

The Wenlock estates in the Welsh Marches will have benefited considerably from crossings over the Severn, the river posing a major physical barrier to travel in all but the driest conditions. The passage of travellers, goods and commodities, especially salt from Droitwich doubtless transported along the Roman road which connected Droitwich with

---

[463] BM Add. MS. 34,633; Finberg 1972: 197-216; Whitelock 1972: 12-13; Gransden 1996: 108-11 (which notes that there is no direct evidence of Goscelin's authorship); Blair 2002: 464, 472, 544-5.
[464] PN Sa 1: 304; VCH Shropshire X 187. The Borough or Franchise of Much Wenlock included Bridgnorth in 1831: VCH Shropshire X map 188.
[465] VCH Shropshire II 39; Finberg 1972: 147-8.
[466] Finberg 1964: 66-82, which must now be read in the light of Pretty 1989.
[467] Pretty 1989: 176-7.
[468] Finberg 1972: 205-6, 212.
[469] Foot 2006: 276-7.
[470] S.221; TSAS 4th Series I 4-6; Preest 2002: 207; Blair 2005: 306.

Greensforge and Chesterton, the latter only 4½ miles from Quatford, would have been greatly facilitated by such a crossing.[471]

As we have seen, after the Conquest Quatford (included in Eardington) passed from Wenlock abbey to Roger de Montgomery, who, according to the foundation document of Quatford church, granted Millichope to Wenlock by way of exchange, but the abbey evidently retained interests in Quatford, and held Quatford fish-weir until 1538, perhaps the last identifiable vestige of Wenlock's holding. If Wenlock held the fish-weir (or weirs, for there are references to more than one), it seems just as likely that it held the nearby bridge, although if that were the case we would perhaps expect to find some documentary evidence, however slight. But if it did hold the bridge, we may be entitled to imagine that it was responsible for the construction of the original structure, and indeed it has been argued that although monasteries had always enjoyed immunity from providing army service, Æthelbald enforced their performance of fortification and bridge-building services, though early exemptions may have varied from one monastery to another.[472]

Certainly Wenlock abbey must be the most likely candidate as the builder of *Cwatbrycge* – a glance at a map will even show a road, incorporating Croom's supposed Roman road, running via Morville direct to Eardington, which may or may not be relevant – and it is quite possible that the piers of the former bridge were utilised to create a fish weir, in which case we would have a direct link between Wenlock and the bridge, but if the abbey built the bridge, the date of its probable construction is more problematic. We might hazard a guess that the bridge could have been built during the reign of Æthelbald, whose *comes* Sigeweard granted land to the abbey c.737,[473] but it must be conceded that there is simply no evidence before the *Anglo-Saxon Chronicle* reference, made before 930, to events at *Cwatbrycge* in 895/6. Indeed, Alan Cooper, in an intensive study of bridges in early medieval England, has concluded that 'the weight of evidence from charter bounds, from place-names, from the *Anglo-Saxon Chronicle* and from the formulae of the bridge-work clauses themselves, suggests that there were not many bridges in England until the tenth century', and that 'the six bridges for which evidence exists of widely distributed bridge-work can be traced back to around the year 900 ... [which] makes them very unusual; bridges were rare until the tenth century, and these bridges were great bridges at major river crossings'. Cooper also notes that 'a survey of recent archaeological scholarship has turned up no evidence of Anglo-Saxon bridges built [in England] prior to 900',[474] though of course that does not mean that none was built. *Cwatbrycge* might indeed have been one of the earliest major bridges – if not the first – to have been built in Anglo-Saxon England.

It is frequently noted that developments in Francia during the ninth century were often paralleled in England. From the 860s Charles the Bald began to put in place in Francia a defensive strategy against the Vikings which included the construction of fortified bridges on the Seine, Marne, Oise and possibly the Loire. The precise nature of these structures is

---

[471] It has been suggested that Ditton Priors, which was associated with salt rights at Droitwich in 1086 and had woodland 1 league by ½ league, may at one time have sent wood for fuel to Droitwich: Hooke 1992: 59; see also TSAS I (1978) 129. Hill 1984: 116 shows two bridges over the Severn in the Anglo-Saxon period, at Bridgnorth and Worcester, but it is almost certain that there was no bridge or settlement at Bridgnorth until the end of the 11th century. See also Baker 2010: 97.
[472] Campbell 2008: 38, where the various views are summarised.
[473] S.1802. Sigeweard is listed as *Sigeweard5* in the *Prosopography of Anglo-Saxon England*, accessed 19 September 2015. Nothing more is known about him.
[474] Cooper 2006: 13, 47.

uncertain, but it is known that they were placed at bends in rivers,[475] possibly for strategic reasons – in that respect the sharp 90° bend of the Severn at Quatford may be noted – and that timber and stone were used in their construction, perhaps to create a structure akin to a pontoon bridge, which would also serve as an obstacle to enemy ships. Stone forts were often created at each end of these Frankish bridges to act as defensive positions once the enemy was forced to disembark.[476] In 885 when the Vikings sailed up the Seine to Paris two fortified bridges blocked their way.[477] The Ile de la Cité in Paris was fortified so that the bridges connecting it with either bank could effectively prevent navigation further upstream.[478]

The bridge at Pitres, some ten miles north of Rouen on the lower Seine, may have been typical of these bridges. It was located at the site of the modern Pont de L'Arche, a place where the river could be easily forded (as at Quatford).[479] Considerable effort seems to have been required to build the bridge. Work began in 862 but proceeded slowly and intermittently, and the bridge, protected by large square-plan forts of wood and stone on both banks of the river, was only completed in 873 after Charles had been forced to draft in labourers from throughout his kingdom. After the loss of the national authority of the crown in the 880s,[480] local people in Francia took it upon themselves to fortify bridges and rebuild town defences,[481] but at Pitres both bridge and forts were destroyed by the Vikings in 885.

However, it is clear from a Kentish charter of 811 that the idea of using bridges to prevent Viking ships from using major rivers was recognised in England at least half a century before the concept was adopted in Francia, and the possibility that *Cwatbrycge* was a structure built during the latter part of the ninth century specifically as part of a campaign to thwart Viking raids via the river Severn – or to facilitate the movement of the Mercian army and its allies, which may have been the primary reason for building the bridge – cannot be excluded.[482] In England Viking warbands invariably travelled overland if we are to believe the chroniclers, but the written evidence may be misleading: it would be very surprising if the sea-going marauders had not made extensive use of the main rivers, including in particular the Severn, as routeways.

If *Cwatbrycge* was constructed during the late ninth century, the rulers responsible could have been Ceolwulf II (874-9, supposedly a Viking puppet, but perhaps misrepresented as such by a West-Saxon chronicler), or, perhaps more likely, *ealdorman* Æthelred, Lord of the Mercians (879-911) and his wife, Æthelflæd, whose traditional centre of authority had

---

[475] Quatford is at a bend in the river Severn, but the traditional site of the bridge is a short distance downstream from the bend. It must be remembered that the course of the river may have changed in the last 1,000 years.
[476] Halsall 2003: 219 suggests that there were fewer fortified bridges than some historians have imagined. Some accounts seem to show that the Frankish forces stationed themselves at bridges to prevent the passage of Vikings.
[477] Haywood 1995: 64. The siege was witnessed by a young monk, Abbo of Saint-Germain-des-Pres, who later recorded the event in a verse chronicle, *Bella Parisiacae urbis*. The account shows that the Vikings were adopting Roman military techniques, and deployed sophisticated seige engines.
[478] Davis 1957: 171.
[479] A ford has existed at Quatford since at least the eleventh century, as proved by the place-name itself. Curiously, the bridge is recorded at an earlier date than the ford.
[480] Charles the Fat's incompetence led to his deposition on 887.
[481] Logan 1991: 120-21.
[482] Cooper 2006: 45.

been transferred from Tamworth (dangerously exposed on the border of the Danelaw) to Gloucester, and who in 901 issued with her husband at least one charter from Shrewsbury, the first record of that town.[483] Æthelred is known to have led Mercian forces at the siege of Buttington on the Severn in 893, and the Severn must have figured largely in discussions about strategy to tackle Danish incursions. If the bridge at *Cwatbrycge* had been built at that period, it is quite possible that fortifications had been linked at each end along Francian lines and that the Danes chose to winter in a fortification there in 895/6. The totality of the evidence might point towards a bridge built by Wenlock abbey under the auspices of Æthelred and Æthelflæd at some date between 894 (after the successful siege of the Danes at Buttington), and 930 (by which date the name *Cwatbrycge* is first set down in the *Anglo-Saxon Chronicle*), to allow the rapid movement of troops into areas to the west of the Severn, and especially perhaps to protect the monastery at Much Wenlock housing the relics of Mildburh, one of the group of early saints they were vigorously promoting within Mercia.[484] That time-frame can probably be reduced further by supposing that a bridge probably existed by 910 (when it was used by the Scandinavians who were defeated at Tettenhall), and almost certainly existed when Æthelflæd built her *burh* at *Cwatbrycge* in 912.[485]

We might at this point usefully consider in more detail the area in and around Quatford. In the early thirteenth century Quatford was divided into *Quatford Maiore* (Greater Quatford), *Quatford Minore* (Smaller Quatford), and *Quatford Parva* (Little Quatford).[486] The rounded rib on which stand Quatford church and the motte may have been the natural dividing line between Greater Quatford and Smaller Quatford, with Greater Quatford to the north, but that is mere speculation. The site of Little Quatford remains quite unknown – it may even have lain on the west side of the Severn.

Netherton, associated with Quatford, is recorded (as *la Nethereton*) c.1284-92.[487] Eyton refers to 'Netherton Lane (now disused) ... part of the road which crossed the river Severn at Quatford',[488] quoting the Reverend George Leigh Wasey, who was vicar of Quatford in the mid-nineteenth century and knew the area and its history well, and who tells us that it was said to have been 'near the Deanery public house, now a mere approach to two fields'.[489] That lane 'led down to the bridge', and 'left the high road near the ... Danery Inn'.[490] The field-name *Netherton Piece* appears on the 1842 Tithe Map some 300 yards south of The Danery. From a conveyance of land at Netherton in 1598 it appears that Netherton may have extended southwards into Quatt.[491]

---

[483] It is impossible to know whether the presence of Æthelflæd and Æthelred at Shrewsbury in 901 might be connected with an important gathering called by Edward at Southampton in the same year attended by almost all the bishops of Edward's kingdom except apparently Wærferth, bishop of Worcester, and by several royals and thegns, but not by Æthelred and Æthelflæd or any West Saxon or Mercian *ealdormen*: Keynes 2001: 50-1. Could military matters affecting Mercia have prevented their attendance? Or was their absence a pointed reminder of their status as non-royals?

[484] If a bridge at *Cwatbrycge* had been built by Wenlock abbey c.900, might the donation to it of a gold chalice and the restoration of land to the abbey have been intended in part to reflect that benefit?

[485] It is worth recording that no evidence has been traced connecting Quatford with any of the saints whose cults were vigorously promoted by Æthelred and Æthelflæd.

[486] SA 972/1/1/29.

[487] SA 2922/2/1.

[488] 1854-60: I 114.

[489] Wasey 1859: 25.

[490] Watkins-Pitchford 1932: 20. It may be the feature marked by parallel lines on the map of the Bridgnorth area c.1560.

[491] SA 2922/2/23.

Wasey claimed, though on what authority is unclear, that part of the land excluded from the endowment of Quatford church by Roger de Montgomery in 1086 was an area, less than a quarter of an acre in extent, then identifiable on the south bank of the river at the supposed site of the old bridge.[492] This is almost certainly the area of broken ground (described by Croom as earthworks which she interpreted as former channels and islands)[493] still identifiable on the west bank of the Severn opposite a small landing stage or platform cut into the east bank, which has the appearance of a narrow islet which was once separated from the west bank by a narrow channel, although the ditch which might mark any such channel fades away to the north of the broken ground. That broken ground is evidently to be associated with a comment made by Wasey in 1865: 'When the monks of Wenlock gave up their property on the Severn at Eardington in exchange for Millichope, they reserved to themselves a small patch of ground on the South bank of the river as a weir for catching fish, an important part of their dietaries, – and this very small plot of ground, not above a quarter of an acre, remains distinct from the surrounding property, though unenclosed, and now belongs to the Dudmaston Estate, which has no other land on that side of the river'.[494] Wasey also notes that thirty-five acres on the Eardington side of the river between the river and the rising ground to the west [perhaps the area held by the abbot of Lilleshall in the twelfth century] belonged to Quatford township. That area could perhaps represent 'the land lying between the water and the monte and the land of Walter', mentioned previously, which was excluded from Roger's endowment.

Before leaving the subject of the bridge at Quatfordit is appropriate to review our knowledge of the form and construction of Anglo-Saxon bridges. On rivers such as the Severn any post-Roman bridge will almost certainly have consisted of a number of timber-reinforced stone or earthern piers connected by a timber roadway – bridges with stone arches were a post-Conquest development – but whatever the construction, any type of bridge over the Severn in the late ninth/early tenth century – or indeed at any other period – must perforce have been a substantial structure to cope with the winter flood-waters which discharge from the Welsh hills. Floods were always the main cause of bridge collapse, as they still are. The famed Severn Bore, a dramatic tidal surge that periodically sweeps up the Severn, will not have posed any challenge to the bridge-builders, for its force is virtually dissipated this far upriver.[495]

---

[492] Wasey 1865: 15. The area is said to have been held by the Dudmaston Estate in 1859, the only land it held on the west side of the river: ibid.
[493] Croom 1989: 302.
[494] Wasey 1865: 15. Frustratingly, the source from which Wasey extracted this observation is not known, but he was generally a sound and cautious historian, and it is most unlikely that his observation could be mere speculation. It may be noted that the *Report from the Charity Commissioners of England and Wales* (4), Vol 5 (1820) mentions 'a small parcel on the Eardington side of the river near the village, about one acre': p.248.
[495] The Severn estuary has the second largest tidal range in the world, and at about 45 feet is exceeded only by the Bay of Fundy in Canada. There are more than 60 bores around the world, including tidal surges on the Seine and Gironde in France, the Indus, Hooghly and Brahmaputra in India, the Araguari in the Amazon basin and the head of the Cook Inlet in Alaska. The world's biggest tidal bore is on the Qiantang river in China, where waves can reach up to 25 feet. The Severn bore, with its self-reinforcing solitary 4 foot wave (or soliton, as it is known to scientists) which occurs about 12 times a year at the spring and autumn equinoxes begins in the lower reaches of the river upstream of the port of Sharpness, and travels upstream at an average of 16 kph, is mentioned in the compilation known to us as Nennius, perhaps dating from the late eighth century, which records that 'There is another marvel [in Britain] called 'the two kings of the Severn'; when the tide rushes in at the mouth of the Severn, two heaps of foam gather separately and fight each other like battering-rams, hurling themselves on each other and colliding, then withdrawing and rushing together again.

Evidence of the method of construction of bridges that originated in the Anglo-Saxon period – as opposed to Roman bridges which may have been rebuilt at that period – is rare, but in the 1980s a sequence of three bridges was identified in workings in the flood-plain of the river Trent at Hemington Quarry, Lockington-Hemington, Leicestershire.

A drawing (based on Salisbury 1995) of a reconstructed late 11th-century trestle from Hemington, Leicestershire, with a decking width of 8' 7". The trestle would have been laid in the river bed with the base beam parallel with the flow of water. It is very likely that the pre-Conquest bridge at Quatford utilised trestles of similar design.

The bridges had spanned the former course of the river, and the earliest structure, dated dendrochronologically to about 1100, consisted of two similarly-shaped oak bases carrying the bridge superstructure. Each pier was a timber box, diamond-shaped in plan, measuring internally roughly 8' by 15', and at least 4' deep. Each box was filled with about five tonnes of sandstone rubble to act as ballast to secure the structure to the river-bed and as a platform to support the superstructure. Of particular interest was the discovery that though very solidly constructed, the bridge eventually collapsed into a scour pool formed by turbulence where the river flow met the pier bases. Directly over the collapsed remains of the pier base was the broken but still jointed timber trestle constructed from massive timbers which had formed the support for the bridge decking. The huge base plate, over 32' long, would have rested on the river bed parallel with the river flow. Two main posts were mortised through the base place, with their lower ends projecting by 3'. Each post was stabilised by bracing which ran down to the ends of the base plate. The presence of an edge peg hole in the side of one of the main posts suggests that a collar would have supported the bridge decking. It was calculated that the bridgeway – the track carried by the bridge – was some 8' wide and over 14' above the river bed. The bridgeway was also supported by a double row of posts some 9' apart, spaced at irregular intervals across the river between 14' and 20' apart. The dendrochronological dates for these posts showed that they may have been used as reinforcements for the pier base or bridge structure.[496]

And this they have done from the beginning of the world until this very day': Barber 1999: 85. William of Malmesbury records *higram ... Anglice uocant*, i.e. 'the eager ... so-called in English'. Eagre, first recorded in 1612 (OED), may be from OE *e(a)gor*- meaning 'flood' or the like, probably from a Latin root, and came to mean 'bore, a tidal wave of unusual height in a narrowing estuary'. The Severn at Shrewsbury in 1672 was about 3 feet deep in dry weather, but rose to 19 feet 7½ inches after particularly wet weather: Harrison 2004: 79.

[496] Cooper, Ripper and Clay 1994: 316-21; Salisbury 1995: 34-7.

There is good evidence that nearly all moat bridges from moated sites from the eleventh to the sixteenth centuries are structurally similar to the Hemington bridges, with their posts not earth-fast but framed in transverse sole plates. The form with lateral braces or shores, symetrically arranged, does not appear until the thirteenth century.[497] Any Anglo-Saxon bridge built over the Severn in the Bridgnorth/Quatford area in the later Anglo-Saxon period will almost certainly have resembled to a greater or lesser degree the Hemington bridge.

---

[497] Rigold 1995: 48-49.

8. The bridge at Bridgnorth.

According to a short history of Shropshire bridges, the first bridge at Bridgnorth, probably of timber on stone piers, was built by Robert de Bellême in about 1100.[498] That is certainly correct, for a bridge would have been needed when the township and borough of Quatford were transferred en bloc to Bridgnorth, created as a newly-established settlement c.1101. A bridge of stone arches existed in the reign of Edward II, and in 1324 Edward III granted the town pontage, or authority to collect tolls from users of the bridge, with further grants made in 1331, 1337 and 1381.[499] A stone bridge with eight arches is recorded at Bridgnorth c.1478 by William of Worcester (d.1480), and was in the same form in the late 1530s.[500]

The earliest certain references to Bridgnorth are dated to the twelfth century and appear as *Bruges*, *Brug'*, *Brugis*, *Brig'*, and *Briges*.[501] It has long been assumed that the element *north* in the name was attached to the simplex name to signify that it was the bridge to the north of the former Bridge at Quatford. Margaret Gelling, however, drew attention to the curious word-order in the dithematic name, and pointed out that if the first element was intended to distinguish the bridge at Bridgnorth from another bridge to the south, it would normally be expected to appear first, so Newbridge or Northbridge, concluding that the suffix North may have been applied by government officials to the most northerly of several places called 'Bridge' with which they had to deal.[502]

The use of the simplex name Brycge without a qualifier or descriptor for the new settlement at Bridgnorth suggests that in 1101-2 there was no other bridge across the Severn in the area: the old bridge at *Cwatbrycge* had decayed or been accidentally or

---

[498] Blackwall 1985: 7. The 'Collections for a History of Bridgnorth, Salop', a MS compiled by the Bridgnorth antiquary William Hardwicke in the early nineteenth century, contains the following: 'It is conjectured that a bridge was at an ancient period thrown over the Severn below the present, nearly in a straight line with a long narrow strip called the Bridge Acre', which was said then to be immediately south of the Textile Print Works, in Hospital Street. A continuation of the line crossed the lower end of the Bylet and cut Castle Hill near the Old Tower: see TSAS XLIX 1937-8 205. The copy of the ancient plan of Bridgnorth and the surrounding area c.1560 seems to show the bridge at that time in its present position, and there seems no reason to believe the present bridge has not been in the same position since 1101-2.
[499] Blackwall 1985: 7; Cooper 2006: 11-12,158-60, 165.
[500] ibid.
[501] PN Sa 1: 56. The conclusion in Lilley 2002: 140-142, followed by Hooke 2006: 60, that Bridgnorth dates from c.1080 appears to be based on a misdating of unequivocal evidence from Orderic Vitalis (see Chibnall 1968-80: II 224-5; 1991: 20-21), and may have originated from a misreading of the entry for Quatford in Domesday Book which led Rowley to imagine that Bridgnorth could have been meant by the reference to a *novus burgus* (Rowley 1983: 99): in fact Domesday refers not to a *novus burgus* but to a *noua dom'* [*nova domus*] and a *burgu'*, or new house and borough, and the borough is named as Quatford. There are various references (e.g. Rees 1997: 87-88) from at least the early 13th century to *terre in Brug'* iuxta Lutebrug, and *in Brugia foras lutebrug*, and to *Littlebridge* in 1255. Those references indicate a place known as 'Little Bridgnorth' (outside the town walls), also called 'Southbridge', rather than the existence of a lesser/narrower/lower/shorter/smaller bridge, from about 1200, and perhaps earlier: Eyton 1854-60: I 354. The place was thought by Gough to be Low Town: Gough 1806: III 18. The name was attached to a place in or close to Pound Street, at the lower end of Whitburn Street: see Dukes 1844: 51; TSAS XLIX 1937-8 195. Camden tells us that 'Ralph de Pickford had behaved himself so valiantly here [Bridgnorth], that Henry I gave him little Brug in this neighbourhood, "by the service of finding dry wood for the chamber in Brug castle when the king came hither"': Gough 1806: III 4.
[502] PN Sa I 58-9.

deliberately destroyed.[503] Assuming that *Cwatbrycge* lay near Quatford, there is no mention of any bridge, either directly or by implication, at Bridgnorth before 1100. Only the place-name *Brycge* (and variants) suggests that a bridge crossed the Severn at Bridgnorth, but such names are found only from the twelfth century onwards. No evidence has been traced to suggest that there were bridges existing at Quatford and Bridgnorth, only two miles apart, at the same time,[504] which would in any event be very unlikely. Once the borough and the simplex name had been transferred to Bridgnorth, it may have been considered difficult to place a new descriptive element before the name, since that may have suggested a new place altogether. Hence the so-called 'manorial suffix'.

The explanation for the name may be prosaic: the word 'north' may have been added spontaneously by a clerk who, having written the name *Bricge* or similar in an official document, realised that there was a possibility of confusion with *Brycge*, the alternative name for the old *Cwatbrycge* or *Brycge* (i.e. Quatford), and added almost casually, as if in parentheses, the clarificatory description 'north', and that name thereafter developed into the accepted or 'official' name. Although Bridgnorth as a dithematic name does not appear before the end of the twelfth century,[505] it seem reasonable to assume that the name had been in use for some time before first found in the records. The earliest name of Bridgnorth clearly meant 'The Bridge'. The terminal –*s* in the spellings is not an indication that the word was plural: the Normans often added an –*s* to English place-names, particularly to shorter names, for example Staines (Middlesex), and Barnes (Surrey).

In short, we have seen that there is evidence that a bridge certainly existed across the Severn in 930, presumably the bridge recorded at Quatford in 1086, whereas there is no evidence[506] of any kind for a pre-Conquest ford or a bridge (or indeed settlement) at Bridgnorth. A dispassionate observer might consider it puzzling that if *Cwatbrycge* were the original name for Bridgnorth, the distinctive and unique first element of the name had been totally lost and forgotten when the borough of Quatford moved there in 1101-2. It is

---

[503] Mason puts the same point conversely, suggesting that since the -north element is not found before 1282, there is an implication that a bridge still existed at Quatford, although he concedes that 'it is very difficult to believe that two bridges would continue in existence one within two miles of the other for very long in medieval conditions', and accepts that the difficuly is removed if -north came to distinguish Bridge in Shropshire from Bridge (Bridgwater) in Somerset: TSAS LVII 1961-4 44. A 12th century reference to a ferry at Quatford (NLW Otley (Pitchford Hall) Estate 1 1367 and 1368), may be taken as strong evidence that no bridge was then in existence. The situation at Quatford may be compared with the Roman bridge that carried the Great North Road over the river Ure which seems to have remained useable until the twelfth century, but when it collapsed a new site was found and the Great North Road had to be diverted. The Saxon borough of Aldborough near the old bridge declined, and the new town of Boroughbridge flourished by the new bridge: Beresford 1988: 118.

[504] According to William Hardwicke, writing at some date after 1823: 'It is conjectured that a bridge was at an ancient period thrown over the Severn below the present [bridge at Bridgnorth], nearly in a straight line with a long narrow strip called the Bridge Acre', which was said then to be immediately south of the Textile Print Works, in Hospital Street. A continuation of the line crossed the lower end of the Bylet and cut Castle Hill near the Old Tower: see TSAS XLIX 1937-8 205. The copy of the ancient plan of Bridgnorth c.1560 shows only one bridge at that time, in its present position, and no other references which might point towards a second bridge have been traced.

[505] PN Sa I: 56, which says 11th century, whilst citing a form c.1200. One unexplained oddity noted by the present author is the inclusion, in lists of places in the area, of both *Bridgnorth* and *Brugeys* in 1470, *Bridgnorth* and *Bruge* in 1521, and to *Bruge* and *Bridgnorth* in 1554: TSAS XLVI 1931-2 15-6.

[506] Other than the rather doubtful evidence of the supposed Roman road which was presumed to cross the Severn at or near Bridgnorth.

clear that J. F. A. Mason's theory that *Cwatbrycge* = *Brycge* = Bridgnorth cannot be sustained. Quite simply, there is no evidence, other than Florence (John) of Worcester which says that Robert de Bellême's castle – wherever that may have been – was built on the site of Æthelflæd's *burh*, to equate *Cwatbrycge* with Bridgnorth (and Florence (John) of Worcester may, as we shall see, be incorrect), but abundant evidence to equate *Cwatbrycge* with Quatford.

That evidence may include the boundaries of early estates in this area. At the time of Domesday, the river Severn formed a natural boundary for administrative units on each side of the Severn. However, we have seen that Eardington included Quatford in 1086. The fact that an estate lay on both sides of the river is a very strong indication that there was a river crossing, whether ford or bridge, at that point.[507] From an early period stream and river crossings were frequently marked by the same administrative unit holding both banks of the river, one example being Arley, where a part of Staffordshire lay on the west bank of the Severn until 1895, so ensuring that both sides of the crossing were within Staffordshire. Many county and parish boundaries deviate at water crossings to ensure common ownership of the crossing, and otherwise unexplained boundary deflections at watercourses often denote a lost ford or bridge. There is no evidence of any such early deviation (as at Quatford) at what became Bridgnorth.

For completeness it may be added that there is no evidence, despite assertions to the contrary,[508] of any mint at Bridgnorth in the pre-Conquest period, and Anglo-Saxon coins with the mint-name *Brycg* or *Bridian* are now attributed to Bridport, or possibly Breedy.[509] No coins are known which could be associated with *Cwatbrycge*. Furthermore, the Welsh had no name for Bridgnorth,[510] which implies a late foundation, as does the dependent status of the early church of the town which originally lay in Morville parish.[511]

Finally, it may be noted that as at many medieval bridges, a chapel, dedicated variously to The Holy Trinity and St Sythe, St Clement and St Syth, or St Sythe alone, stood on the bridge at Bridgnorth from at least the fifteenth century until the eighteenth century, probably above the fortified gateway above the second pier.[512] St Sythe (or Osyth or Osgyth) was the daughter of Redwald, the first Christian king of East Anglia, and Wilburga, the daughter of Penda, king of the Mercians. One of the more memorable incidents of her childhood, which was spent in the care of the Irish Abbess St Modwenna of Burton upon Trent (wrongly equated with an Irish saint called Monenna) at Polesworth, was when she fell from a bridge and drowned. She lay in the water for three days, but was restored to life by the prayers of St Modwenna. She married Sighere, king of the East

---

[507] As noted by S. A. H. Burne: TNSFC 1913-4 XLVIII 53.
[508] E.g. Rahtz 1977: 108; West 1983: 37, 50. Hill 1984: 116, 224, 230 ascribes a bridge, town and mint (Æthelred II 1st hand 978, last small cross 1009) to Bridgnorth, but that information must now be seen as incorrect.
[509] Oral information from Gareth Williams, Department of Coins and Medals, British Museum, May 2005; see also North 1994. R. H. M. Dolley attributed coins bearing the inscription BRY(G)GIN to a probable new Anglo-Saxon mint at Bridgnorth (*British Numismatic Journal*, Vol. 28 1955-1957 88-105), but that attribution can no longer be supported, and coins with that mint name are now held to have originated in the south of England: Hinton 1984: 151.
[510] Dukes 1844: 44. The old Welsh name for the area around Bridgnorth (which would include Quatford) is said to have been Meigion: Bromwich 2006: 158. The word has not been traced in any modern place-name.
[511] Beresford 1988: 480.
[512] Harrison 2004: 199; SSMR PRN 00423.

Saxons, but left him to take the veil, and founded and presided over a nunnery at Chich, on the estuary of the river Colne in Essex, until martyred at the hands of pirates in about 676 – she is said to have been beheaded for refusing to make a sacrifice to pagan gods – and was a favoured saint of Richard de Belmeis.[513] As sheriff of Shropshire, Robert de Bellême may well have been responsible for the dedication of a chapel on the new bridge at Bridgnorth. Sadly, any wild speculation that he may have had some first-hand experience of an unsafe bridge – possibly the ancient bridge at *Cwatbrycge* – must be discounted, since the river episode in the life of St Sythe was evidently part of a thirteenth-century interpolation into a late twelfth-century poetic account of the life of the saint, added long after the death of Robert and entirely without foundation.[514]

---

[513] SSMR PRN 00423; HER 00382; Sutcliffe 1993; Thacker and Sharpe 2002: 549. The monastery was refounded as an Augustinian Priory by Richard, bishop of London between 1108 and 1118, who retired to the priory before he died there in 1127: Eyton 1854-60 I 246; TSAS IX 1923-4 118-25; Yorke 2003: 21, 58.

[514] Bethell 1970: 102.

9. Æthelflæd's *burh* at *Cwatbrycge*.

The *Mercian Register*, a block of annals inserted into *Anglo-Saxon Chronicle* 'C' for the years 902 to at least 919, tells us that in 912 (two years after the English victory over the Danes at Tettenhall/Wednesfield), Æthelflæd, Lady of the Mercians, constructed a *burh* or fortification at *Bricge* on the Severn, her husband Æthelred presumably indisposed by his failing health.[515]

'Borough-work', the obligation to build and repair fortifications, had been imposed throughout the Mercian kingdom under the *trimoda necessitas*, the 'three-fold obligation' of military service, fortress work and bridge work imposed since the mid-eighth century – the obligation was usually imposed on every holder of land, even if he were exempt from every other service – and by the beginning of Alfred's reign in 871 all estates in midland and southern England had long been required to provide manpower to perform such labour.[516]

The Vikings were devastating hit-and-run raiders, but were less effective in conducting long sieges, and were particularly averse to attacking fortified centres and engaging in full-blooded battles, especially when English reinforcements might be readily available. Recognising this, Alfred launched a crash fortress-building programme during a lull in Viking activity from 879 to 892, restoring cities and towns and building others on new sites. It is sometimes said Æthelred and Æthelflæd were adopting this *burh*-building policy developed in Wessex by Alfred. But the *burhs* in Mercia created by Æthelred and Æthelflæd were certainly not a ninth- or tenth-century innovation.

We have seen that Charles the Bald had created a system of defensive fortifications in Western Francia, associated with fortified bridges over the Loire and Seine in the 860s, in order to obstruct the passage of Viking invaders, and the Danes themselves routinely fortified their camps. From his contacts in Francia Alfred certainly introduced Frankish institutions into his kingdom, and while the West Saxon *burhs* may have been based on the Frankish concept, Alfred could have taken the idea from an early fifth century Christian history which was translated during his reign, Orosius's *Seven Books of History Against the Pagans*, which proved extremely popular during the Middle Ages.

Yet there is reason to believe that some of the earliest *burhs*, possibly predating those in Francia, may have been constructed in Mercia.[517] At Hereford, for example, a *burh* town with traces of eighth century ditches and rampart defences, excavations have shown that the initial fortification took the form of an earthen bank, which included turves, consolidated with horizontal branches, which survived to a height of over 7', and which may have originally been some 10' high. This was fronted by a timber revetment and

---

[515] Whitelock 1955: 193-4; Earle and Plummer 1894-9: I 96.
[516] See Hollister 1962: 59-63; Brooks 2000: 11; Williams 2001: 296-309. No visible evidence has been traced of any fortified bridges or towns which can be positively dated to the eighth or ninth centuries, and only three Mercian *burhs* show any signs of defences from this period, with excavations at Hereford, Tamworth and Winchcombe revealing defences of the eighth or ninth century underlying those dating from the fortress building programme of Æthelflæd, Lady of the Mercians, in the early part of the tenth century: Brooks and Cubitt 1996: 155; Williams 2001: 301.
[517] See Lavelle 2010: 212 (where the 5th-century Theodosian Code is also mentioned), and Higham and Ryan 2013: 277-83, but see also the observations of Martin Carver, who is less convinced by the early dates suggested for fortifications at Gloucester, Hereford and Tamworth: Carver 2010: 130-1, 137.

breastwork, and another, smaller, wall of stone was constructed at the rear of the rampart. This design mirrored that at Tamworth, again with eighth-century ditches and ramparts, where Æthelflæd's defences consisted of a turf rampart held together with timber strapping. Near the gateway the rampart was twice the thickness, and may have been stepped up, with a platform across the gate creating a continuous walkway along the ramparts.[518] The *burh* at Runcorn seems to have been an enclosure of no more than 1.5 hectares in area on Castle Rock, a coastal headland on the south bank of the Mersey, surrounded by ramparts with a tidal water-filled ditch on the landward side.[519] At Towcester, Edward the Elder stayed in the *burh* there in 917 while a stone wall was constructed.[520]

The *burhs* provided a very effective solution to the problem of Danish attack. The Vikings quickly found that English towns were no longer easy targets for plunder and looting. *Burhs* heavily fortified with ditches and earthen ramparts reinforced with timber revetments and topped with heavy timber palisades were not easily stormed, and any attempt to starve out a garrison would allow time for the *fyrd* and garrisons from neighbouring *burhs* to come to the aid of a beleaguered town and put the attackers at great risk. The logistics of maintaining such a mounted force must have required considerable organisation. Presumably the force would be maintained at a state of high alert ready for action at short notice, and required enough horses, fodder and provisions for campaigns that might last for weeks. It is difficult to believe that it could be manned by the ordinary shire-levies, and may have been a mercenary force or a 'select *fyrd*', a group obliged to serve on military expeditions.[521]

In addition to the mobile mounted force was the main body of the army, which in the early part of Alfred's reign took the form of the shire-levies under the command of the *ealdormen*. The arrangement was probably similar towards the end of the ninth century, but by 893, according to the *Anglo-Saxon Chronicle*, King Alfred had divided his army into two, so that at any one time half its men were at home and half on service, apart from the men who guarded the *burhs*, which suggests permanent garrisons, and there is evidence that perhaps one in five of the able-bodied adult male population of Wessex was involved in garrison duty.[522] Alfred's intention was not merely to create a number of new fortifications, but to form a planned network of strategically inter-related *burhs* commanding all the major navigable rivers, estuaries, Roman roads and other major routeways, and some thirty fortified centres of varying sizes were either built on existing sites, such as Roman city walls,[523] or Iron Age hill-forts were refortified.[524] The intention was that no place was to be more than twenty miles, a day's march, from a *burh*.[525]

---

[518] Biddle 1976: 134-7; Laing 1982: 190; Abels 1988: 69.
[519] Griffiths 2001: 177. The headland, now destroyed, appears on the 1842 1" O.S. map: ibid.
[520] Whitelock 1955: 197.
[521] Lapidge et al 1999: 47-8.
[522] ASC 'A' refers in 921 (*recte* 920) to the 'called-up army' going home and 'the other [army]' travelling to Huntingdon to restore and reinforce the fortification there: Swanton 1996: 103.
[523] There is no evidence of any attempt to adapt or use Roman defence works before the repair of the walls of London and Colchester in 886 and 891 by Alfred and Edward the Elder, as recorded in the *Anglo-Saxon Chronicle*: Hill 1974: 17.
[524] Fox 1955: 260 fn.1 concludes that 'There is no satisfactory evidence that Early Iron Age forts were anywhere reused by [the Anglo-Saxons]'.
[525] Abels 1985: 203.

This strategy was not introduced a moment too soon, for the Viking Great Heathen Army had grown in size during the closing decades of the ninth century, and in 892-3 was reinforced by allies from Northumbria and East Anglia. But the *burhs* were not only defensive in nature, for they provided protected centres holding manpower available to supplement the field forces. Even if a Viking raiding party managed to evade English troops and ravage deep into English territory, it would face the risk of returning burdened with booty through the network of fortified *burhs*.

Communication between the *burhs* (and other parts of the country) would have been essential, and it is known that the Anglo-Saxons had developed a sophisticated signalling system using beacons, and probably a system of royal messengers.[526] That will have enabled the English to warn other areas of an approaching enemy, and to call up and co-ordinate reinforcements. The document known as the *Burghal Hidage*, perhaps dating from around 914 – the actual date remains the subject of continuing academic debate – is generally agreed to represent Alfred's original conception for the maintenance of his *burhs*. The text lists 29 West Saxon and two Mercian *burhs* and the number of hides belonging to each. The reason for listing the hidage is explained in an appendix that relates hidage allotments to the defensive requirements of the *burhs*: 'For the maintenance and defence of an acre's breadth of wall [4 poles or 22 yards], 16 hides are required. If every hide is represented by one man, then every pole [5½ yards] of wall can be manned by four men'. This formula allowed the length of wall for each *burh* and the number of men required to man it to be calculated. The theoretical length of wall and the actual length in places identifiable from the *Burghal Hidage* is in many cases remarkably accurate (e.g. Winchester), whereas in other cases the differences are significant and inexplicable (e.g. Exeter). In the main, however, the stated hidages accord fairly well with the actual measurements.[527]

Alfred's creation of a network of fortified *burhs* and burgal towns in Wessex was paralleled in English Mercia (where we have seen that the earliest *burhs*, such as Hereford and Tamworth, may have originated much earlier) during the late ninth and early tenth century by Æthelred and after his death in 911 by his widow Æthelflæd until her death in 918. Indeed, Æthelred and Æthelflæd issued a charter at some date between 884 and 899 'ordering the fortifications of Worcester to be constructed for the protection of all the people, and also that the worship of God may be celebrated therein [with security]' – though whether *eallum þæm folce* referred to the inhabitants of the nascent borough or of the burghal territory that was to become Worcestershire is unclear[528] – and it is likely that other similar charters were issued for other places of which we have no knowledge.[529] Certainly there is no reason to suppose that numerous unrecorded *burhs* were not built within Mercia by Æthelred and Æthelflæd before those specifically listed as bult by Æthelflæd with their dates of construction, starting in 910, in the *Mercian Register*.[530]

From 900 the programme was continued along the southern and central boundaries of the Danelaw by Edward the Elder, who continued Æthelflæd's advance into the Danelaw after her death, and eventually (if the chronicles are to be believed) gained control over the

---

[526] Hill and Sharpe 1997: 157-65. See also Hart 1992: 528-32.
[527] See especially Hill and Rumble 1996.
[528] For a useful discussion of the charter see Brooks 1996: 143.
[529] S.223; Harmer 1914: 22-3, 54-5, 106-7 (where the date of Alfred's death is mistakenly given as 901); Bassett 2007: 53-85.
[530] Whitelock 1961: 61-4.

whole of England. Yet while Alfred's son Edward the Elder is known for his extension of his father's *burh*-building programme, his role was dwarfed by the activities of Æthelred and Æthelflæd. The chronicles tell us the date on or by which many of the county towns of central England were fortified under Æthelred, Æthelflæd and Edward: Chester (907), Stafford (913), Hertford (913), Leicester (914), Warwick (914-5), Hereford (915), Buckingham (917), Bedford (918), Huntingdon (921), and Nottingham (922). The apparent (but perhaps fanciful) dearth of *burhs* in West Mercia in the first decade of the tenth century might explain why the Danes turned their attention to the area to the west of the Severn for their raid which ended in the battle of Tettenhall.

The apparent paucity of *burhs* along the western borders of Mercia seems to have been addressed as a matter of the greatest urgency after the great victory at Tettenhall. According to the *Mercian Register*, in 912 'Æthelflæd, lady of the Mercians, came on the holy eve of the Invention of the Cross to *Scergeat*, and built the borough there – *þær ða burh getimbrede* – and in the same year that at *Bricge*'.[531] The new *burh* at *Bricge*, evidently the same place as *Brycge* or *Cwatbrycge* where the Danes wintered in 895-6,[532] was not built until completion of the *burh* at *Scergeat*, and work on that did not start until 6th May.

Wherever *Scergeat* lay (a question considered more fully in Chapter 10), we might guess that work on the *burh* at *Cwatbrycge* was started in about August or September 912. The fortification was, it seems clear, designed to protect the important bridge crossing the Severn which had been used by the Scandinavians returning towards the Danelaw before the battle of Tettenhall only two years earlier, and perhaps on other occasions which are unrecorded.

At this point is is appropriate to emphasise that *burhs* were of two main types: *burh* fortifications and urban *burhs*. The former were not intended for permanent occupation, but merely to serve as defensive compounds from which English forces could take refuge from the Danes and from which they could launch attacks on the Scandinavians. They sometimes took the form of reworked and refortified Iron-Age earthworks or Roman fortifications, an example of the former being at Eddisbury in Cheshire, fortified by Æthelflæd in 914,[533] and of the latter the Roman fortification at Manchesterre, fortified by Edward the Elder in 919.[534] The urban *burhs* tended to be sited within pre-existing settlements, sometimes incorporating Roman fortifications, were often roughly square or rectangular in plan,[535] and were intended to protect permanent civil centres and encourage

---

[531] Whitelock 1955: 193-4; Earle and Plummer 1894-9: I 96. Though Dumville felt it unclear what distinction should be made between the various verbs used by the chroniclers to describe fortress building, such as *atimbran, getimbran, wyrcan, gewyrcan* (Dumville 1992: 12 fn.60), Pelteret suggests that the use of the expression *atimbren* and its variant *getimbran* has the specific meaning 'to provide a *burh* with a wooden palisade': Pelteret 2009: 321; see also Swanton 1996: 102 fn.7.
[532] Thorpe 1861: I 173-5.
[533] Swanton 1996: 98; VCH Cheshire I 110-11, 250, 252. An interesting curiosity is a note in *Walker's Hibernian Magazine* (Dublin 1788, 698) which tells us that Eddisbury is 'now the chamber in the forest of Cheshire', without further explanation. The *Burghal Hidage* lists a small number of hillforts which were re-used as *burhs* in the 9th century, including Halwell and possibly Pilton near Barnstaple, both in Devon.
[534] ASC 'A'; Swanton 1996: 104. The *Mercian Register* refers to restoration or repair (*betan*) rather than building anew (*settan*): Thorpe 1861: I 196.
[535] In that respect a large square area, with sides of roughly 300 yards, the northern boundary formed by Chantry Lane and a former track to the Severn (clearly marked on the 1842 Tithe Map), the

not only trade and commerce and the long-term prosperity of the place, but to promote Christian churches frequently associated with obscure saints promoted in particular by Æthelflæd.

What is very clear is that *burhs* created by Alfred, Æthelred, and Æthelflæd had no standard plan and took many forms.[536] The Alfredian *burh* at Chisbury in Wiltshire, for example, is assumed to have re-used a multivallate Iron Age hillfort, and the *burh* at Cricklade is a regular square in plan, but most *burhs* are irregular in shape, taking advantage of the local topography, many being no more than a simple rampart across an easily defended headland.[537] A consideration of other Æthelflædian *burhs* has an obvious relevance in this discussion. As noted above, in 914 Æthelflæd constructed a fortification at Eddisbury, generally understood to be Castle Ditches, the largest Iron Age hillfort in Cheshire, near Delamere. The earthworks, roughly oval in shape, some 1000' long and 600' broad, badly damaged by ploughing and quarrying, were excavated in 1935-8, and traces of a post-Dark Age rebuilding were identified, although there was no evidence of any long-lasting occupation at that period, and it has been suggested that once Derby had been captured in 917 and certainly once the *burh* at Manchester had been founded in 919, the *burh* at Eddisbury would have become obsolete.[538]

Research has shown that building *burh* fortifications of both types in the later ninth and early tenth century could have been completed relatively quickly. Construction may have been of simple dump construction with turf revetments built with material dug from a ditch or ditches. The average width of an earthen wall was perhaps 18-20', with a height c.7-8'. A team of four men could have built two cubic yards of bank in a day, suggesting that a perimeter bank of 2,280 yards could have been completed in 68,400 man/days, or by 1,000 men working for almost 70 days, or a little under 14 weeks of 5 working days – about four months. But that takes no account of additional features required in a *burh*, such as walkways and palisades, gateway and watchtowers. We should perhaps allow seven or eight months for a complete *burh*, but in the cases of Towcester and *Wigingamere* built in 917, the fortresses were completed and withstood sieges within three months, and the *Mercian Register* entry for 912 shows that *burhs* could be thrown up in a much shorter time: both *Scergeat* and *Cwatbrycge* were built after 6th May in that year, though it cannot be assumed that both were built by the same itinerant workforce. Even more remarkably, in 914 Edward went to Buckingham with his army and stayed four weeks while *burhs* on both sides of the river were completed before he left.[539] Manpower provided by the army doubtless explains the speed with which the fortifications were built – when the need arose *burhs* could be construed in a matter of weeks.

---

southern boundary slightly sinuous (but possibly once further south, marked by the track from the ferry to Hillhouse Farm), with the Norman motte and Quatford church near its south-west corner, may be noted. The area, which slopes upwards from east to west and from north to south, is divided into Churchyard Piece and Upper Piece on the Tithe Map, and at the end of the 20th century was occupied by a market garden. LiDAR surveys show that it was part of an area of intensive ploughing during the Second World War. It seems likely that any *burh* at Quatford lay in the area incorporating the bridge and fish weirs, to the south of the wide east-west rib on which stand the church and motte, but some part of the *burh* may have lain to the north.

[536] Martin Carver suggests that late Saxon *burhs* may have imitated the classical rectinear plan of typical Roman fortresses: Carver 2010: 143-4
[537] See especially Hill and Rumble 1996: 189-231.
[538] VCH Cheshire I 110-11, 250, 252; Swanton 1996: 98.
[539] Whitelock 1961: 64.

In 915 Æthelflæd built a *burh* at *Cyricbyrig*, generally identified as Chirbury in Shropshire, three miles east of Offa's Dyke.[540] The name means 'fortification associated with a church', and in the north-west corner of the village is a rectangular embanked platform, Chirbury Castle or King's Orchard, with traces of single banks up to 14' high forming a square enclosure with sides of about 180' lying some 250 yards west of the village on the bank of a stream. There are differing opinions as to whether the earthworks are to be associated with the site of the *burh*: excavations in 1958 failed to identify any trace of a palisade, defensive ditch or internal occupation, or indeed to produce any dating evidence. An Æthelflædian *burh*, though, is likely to have been considerably larger than the embanked platform, and it has been suggested that the *burh* may have been built around the village on an axis parallel with its roads.[541]

The failure to positively identify the exact position of the *burh* at Chirbury is echoed at Quatford, for the location of Æthelflæd's *burh* at *Cwatbrycge* has led to much speculation. Some or all of the sites already considered for the possible location of the Danish camp of 895-6 have also, at one time or another, been put forward as the site of Æthelflæd's *burh*, most commonly Castle Hill at Bridgnorth. Certainly the position, on Castle Rock, a prominent sandstone cliff on the west bank of the Severn, high above the river, is strategically impressive, and was the site of Robert de Bellême's castle – it replicates on a much larger scale the abandoned site of the motte at Quatford, built on a great sandstone outcrop rising above the Severn, and is the type of location favoured by Norman castle builders. However, the site is atypical of Anglo-Saxon *burhs* in the Midlands, where a relatively level site on lower ground, often adjoining a river at an important crossing point, is usually found. According to the *Mercian Register*, Æthelflæd constructed *burhs* at Tamworth, Stafford,[542] Eddisbury,[543] Warwick, Chirbury, and Runcorn, as well as others at places which remain unidentified. Tamworth adjoins the river Anker, Stafford lies on the river Sow, Warwick probably extended to the river Avon.[544] Worcester stands on the Severn.

Two other potential candidates have been proposed as the site of Æthelflæd's fortification.

The first is supposed traces of a rectangular earthwork identified by T. R. Slater on the east bank of the Severn at Bridgnorth centred on the existing bridge.[545] Slater saw the feature as a unified Anglo-Saxon defensive system incorporating the bridge and a fortified promontory designed to prevent Viking penetration up the Severn,[546] but further investigations have thrown doubt on both the nature and period of the earthwork, and for the moment the matter is unresolved. Given the probability that there was no bridge there

---

[540] Swanton 1996: 99.
[541] SO 258985; Shropshire SMR 00498; see VCH Shropshire I 378-0; Stanford 1991: 131; Duckers 2006: 50.
[542] On the *burh* at Stafford see Cutler, Hunt and Rátkai 2009. Our understanding of the pre-Conquest history of the town is likely to be greatly enhanced by the publication of Carver 2010.
[543] Higham has noted that Rainow, 2 miles north-east of Macclesfield, is also known as Eddisbury: Higham 1993a. It is generally assumed that Æthelflæd refortified the Iron Age hillfort at Eddisbury, but the *burh* may have been at Rainow.
[544] See Rumble and Hill 1996: 222-3; Bassett 2008.
[545] Slater 1988: 9.
[546] The feature is described as a slight break running from the bank of the river at SO 71909320, turning south at SO 72129304, west at SO 72099292, returning to the river at SO 79509293: SSMR PRN00424.

in the Anglo-Saxon period, it is very likely that Slater's feature has a post-Conquest origin.[547]

The second place is Oldbury, on the west side of the river, a little over half a mile southwest of Bridgnorth. The name is recorded in Domesday Book, and evidently incoporates Old English *byrig*, from *burh*,[548] a term meaning 'a defended place', but also 'defended manor house', and in late Old English, 'town'. Often the expression refers to a prehistoric earthwork. The name might suggest a fortification already ancient in 1086, although no traces of any conventional earthwork fortification have been found there. It is most unlikely that the name 'old fortification' would have been applied by the Anglo-Saxons to a fortification built by the Danes, and certainly not to a new *burh* built in the early tenth century. The name could not be 'old town' to distinguish it from the new town of Bridgnorth, since Bridgnorth was not in existence in 1086. However, before the place-name is dismissed from this enquiry as an unsolved red-herring, we need to note that the Old English word *ald* had at least one other meaning, which is 'old' in the sense 'disused'. If we can take the word as having that meaning in this case, we may have a reference to 'the disused or abandoned fortification', possibly with reference to a temporary fortification that has left no trace. But we must also remember that Panpudding Hill, with its twelfth-century siegework mound, lies within the parish of Oldbury, and those earthworks may have been remodelled from some pre-Conquest/prehistoric fortification. Having said that, any feature separated from the Severn is unlikely to represent the encampment of the Danes or the *burh* of Æthelflæd.

From what has been said above it is impossible to know what type of earthwork might have existed at *Cwatbrycge*, but a possible clue to help identify the site of the elusive *burh* may be found in the chronicle of Florence (John) of Worcester, who records that Æthelflæd built a *burh* – an *arcem munitam* – on the western bank of the Severn,[549] in the place called *Brycge* (*in occidentali plaga Sabrinae fluminis, in loco qui Brycge dicitur*). Because *Brycge* is the early name of Bridgnorth, it has long been held that Æthelflæd's *burh* was at Bridgnorth. That supposition, indeed, is reinforced by Florence's later statement that *arcem quam in occidentali Sabrinae fluminis plaga, in loco qui Brycge dicitur lingua Saxonica, Ægelfleda Merciorum domina quondam construxerat*:[550] 'Robert de Bellême, earl of Shrewsbury, son of Earl Roger, began to strengthen with a high and thick wall the fort on the western bank of the Severn, at the place called in the Saxon tongue Brycge. This had been built by the Lady of the Mercians, Ægelfleda':[551]

As we have seen, it is evident that *Brycge* was an alternative name for *Cwatbrycge*, which almost certainly lay at or very near Quatford,[552] and that name transferred to what is now

---

[547] As noted previously, though Bridgnorth is not mentioned in the Domesday Book, it is very possible that there was a settlement in the area of the High Town before the 12th century, with St Leonard's church an Anglo-Saxon foundation: Slater 1988; Croom 1989.
[548] PN Sa I: 226-7.
[549] Curiously, Simeon of Durham, whose work incorporates the chronicle of Florence (John) of Worcester, says that the *burh* was built on the south side of the Severn: Stevenson 1855: 583.
[550] From TSAS LVII 1961-4 38, citing B. Thorpe, *Florence of Worcester*, i (1848) 115.
[551] Mc Gurk 1998: 99-101; see also Stevenson 1853: 161 (where *arcem* 'fortification' is inadvertently translated as 'bridge').
[552] A fact accepted by the respected Shropshire historians Owen and Blakeway, who say simply that Æthelflæd 'built castles at Chirbury and Brugge, (i.e. Quatford near Bridgenorth)': Owen and Blakeway 1825: I 20. Untypically, the authors provide no evidence for the identification of Brugge as Quatford, implying that the fact is obvious.

Bridgnorth when the bridge at *Cwatbrycge* was replaced with a new bridge on the transfer of the borough of Quatford to Bridgnorth in 1101-2.[553] Whilst Florence (John) of Worcester might be expected to have had a particular interest in the Bridgnorth area, and indeed perhaps had personal knowledge of the locality, only 24 miles or so from Worcester, it is evident that his information was not taken from any version of the *Anglo-Saxon Chronicle* with which we are familiar. The source for the statement that Robert built his castle on the site of Æthelflæd's *burh* is unknown, and we are entitled to question its veracity.[554] Whilst Florence (John) of Worcester is normally considered a reliable historian, it is submitted that in linking Æthelflæd's *burh* – which we can assume was a *burh* fortification – with Robert de Bellême's castle, the chronicler is incorrect, but only as a result of confusion based on the understandable, but in this case mistaken, assumption that *Brycge* was a static place-name.

Is there any other evidence to support the claim that Florence (John) of Worcester's statement may be incorrect? Our main source of information for Robert de Bellême's rebellion against Henry I is the chronicler Orderic Vitalis, writing between 1123 and 1141.[555] He records the transfer in 1101-2 of Robert de Bellême's headquarters from Quatford to Bridgnorth: *Oppidum de Quatfort transtulit, et Brugiam, munitissmum castellum, super Sabrinam fluvium condidit*. The relocated oppidum is called *Brugiam* and *Brugiæ* in Orderic's subsequent account of its siege and capture by Henry I after Robert's rebellion.[556] It is noticeable that Orderic makes no claim that Robert's new castle was built on the site of Æthelflæd's *burh*, and indeed the claim is made by no-one other than Florence (John) of Worcester.[557]

It seems to the present writer that the chronicle associated with Florence (John) of Worcester, whoever the author and despite his geographical proximity to the area, reasonably but mistakenly assumed that *Brycge* where Æthelflæd built her *burh* was *Brycge* where Robert de Bellême built his castle,[558] and that view is perhaps strengthened by evidence that his chronicle from 1095 was written after about 1124,[559] that is, after Florence's death in 1118, and the observations of a recent editor of that chronicle who observes that 'It is possible that [the entry under 1094] ... and the entry under 1101 (describing Robert of Belême's fortifying of Bridgnorth and Quatford) were the result of

---

[553] In a short but typically perceptive analysis of the early history of Bridgnorth and Quatford, Beresford recognises '[t]he second town of "Brug" (Bridge)': Beresford 1988: 479-80.
[554] Eyton 1854-60: I 132 had no difficulty in concluding that Florence (John) of Worcester could be mistaken, for he does not accept that Bellême's castle was built on the site of Æthelflæd's *burh*, and was in no doubt that Panpudding Hill was the site of her fortification.
[555] See also Thompson 1990.
[556] Eyton 1854-60: I 57. Orderic evidently had access to details of the events in the area in the early 12th century, for he provides the names of the three Norman garrison commanders put in charge of Bridgnorth castle by Robert de Bellême: TSAS LVII 1961-4A 43.
[557] Watkins-Pitchford's belief that Anglo-Saxon work, evidently to be associated with Æthelflæd's *burh*, was to be identified in the stonework of Bridgnorth castle (see TSAS LII 1947-8 153-78) is now held to be mistaken, with the present square keep with sloping plinth, slighted during the Civil War, probably dating from between 1166 and 1174 (Croom 1992: 20), but with the coursed rubble section probably dating from, but certainly no earlier than, 1101-2: AC 4th Series XX 1874 268.
[558] Croom 1989: 300 puts forward another possible explanation, suggesting that Florence may have been entirely accurate but misunderstood: Robert de Bellême's castle of 1101-2 may have been 'a temporary affair, thrown up in the immediate run-up to the confiscation of de Belêsme's estates, on a different site to the later one on Castle Hill'. That suggestion seems very unlikely. Accounts of the siege make it clear that the castle was hardly a temporary structure.
[559] Gransden 2010: 144.

[the chronicler] inferring or of his editing of his text, and may not have been taken directly from his sources'.[560] Florence (John) of Worcester is the earliest source[561] for the statement that Æthelflæd built her *burh* on the west bank of the Severn (i.e. the site of Robert de Bellême's new fortification at Bridgnorth), and all the evidence leads us to believe that this part of his chronicle must be discounted. That conclusion is reinforced by the inexplicable failure of the chronicler to mention the transfer of the township of Quatford to create the new township Bridgnorth, a truly remarkable event that must have been widely known in the area and well beyond.[562]

There are, however, other references to Æthelflæd's *burh* which might be considered to add to the evidence for its location. The chronicles of Roger of Wendover and Matthew Paris tells us that Æthelflæd restored a fortification on the west bank of the river Severn at *Bregges*:[563] ... *et in plaga occidentali Sabrinæ fluminis, in loco qui Bregges dicitur, aliam restaurit*.[564] The use of the word 'restored' is clearly deliberate, and must suggest that Æthelflæd's fortification made use of an earlier fortification, perhaps the camp created by the Danes during their wintering in 895-6. That possibility cannot be ignored, for Æthelflæd is known to have rebuilt or refortified Danish camps elsewhere: the *burh* at Tamworth, for example, was built by Æthelflæd over earlier, possibly Danish, earthworks.[565]

If we are entitled to trust Roger of Wendover's statement – which may be derived from Florence (John) of Worcester – that Æthelflæd's *burh* was on the west bank of the Severn (bearing in mind that the Worcester chronicler's account may be untrustworthy as to the location of the *burh*), it is unthinkable that Æthelflæd would have built a new *burh* on the west bank of the Severn if there were no bridge across the river at that point. Quite apart from the difficulties of transporting engineers and other specialists to the western side of the Severn, constructing a new *burh* on that side of the river in the absence of a bridge would be strategically perilous, for in the event of attack or siege, the *burh* defenders would be denied rapid retreat to the east, and reinforcements prevented from reaching beleaguered troops, even though boats or rafts could have been made ready for emergency use. Quite simply it must be inconceivable from a military perspective that the *burh* could have been built on the west bank of the Severn, exposed to attack not only by the Danes but also the unpredictable Welsh, who might blockade, damage or destroy a timber bridge, and prevent access by English reinforcements.[566] Furthermore, the purpose of a *burh* was

---

[560] McGurk 1998: xxxi-xxxii.

[561] Roger of Wendover makes the same claim, but his chronicle incorporated that of Florence (John) of Worcester: Giles 1892: 241.

[562] Nor, surprisingly, is there any reference to an incident recorded by Simeon of Durham in 1118 when the congregation attending the dedication of Morville church by the bishop of Hereford were returning home. Sheltering from a sudden thunderstorm, a party of two women and three men were struck by lighning. The women and five horses were killed; the men were unscathed: Stevenson 1855: 598.

[563] Giles 1892: 241. It must be remembered, however, that Wendover's work, taken from numerous sources, may incorporate material from Florence (John) of Worcester.

[564] Coxe 1841: 375; Luard 1872: I 442.

[565] Those earthworks may, however, have been of 8th-century date, and associated with the palace complex: Gelling 1992: 149.

[566] Although 'the overwhelming tenor of the surviving written evidence is that it was the English who repeatedly launched attacks on Wales, and not the Welsh who attacked England. Despite popular belief, schoolbooks and the mythology that surrounds [Offa's] dyke, it is extremely difficult to find solid evidence of Welsh attacks on the English between the late seventh and mid-eleventh centuries': Davies 1990: 67.

to provide a fortified position on a major road or river or other strategic point. Since none of the chroniclers suggest that Æthelflæd constructed a bridge when the *burh* was built, but identify the *burh* as *Bricge*, we are surely safe in assuming that the *burh* was built at the site of an existing bridge. The only record of a bridge over the Severn in this area in the late ninth and early tenth century (and specifically in 1086) is that at *Cwatbrycge*. The possibility that two bridges existed across the Severn only a few miles apart in the early tenth century is so unlikely that it can be discounted. Moreover, Norman mottes were frequently thrown up within earlier Anglo-Saxon *burhs*, often within a corner. Working backwards in time from the motte at Quatford, we might suppose that the *burh* defences should be sought surrounding the motte.

If the statements of Florence (John) of Worcester and Roger of Wendover which tell us that Æthelflæd's *burh* was constructed on the west bank of the Severn can be trusted (which we have seen is unlikely), we need to search on the west side of the Severn at Quatford for traces of ancient earthworks. As noted above, the shape of Æthelflæd's *burhs* varied, but despite differences in the topography at Hereford, Tamworth and Worcester, the defences of these three urban *burhs* effectively formed a D-shape in plan alongside a river, including a substantial stretch of river frontage inside the defended area, and probably incorporating a bridgehead. That may have been to save resources – the rivers acting as ready-made defensive barriers – but the inclusion of a river bank and bridgehead is not likely to have been entirely due to military expediency, since waterside markets were often an early and significant element in the planning of urban centres.[567]

Just such a feature is readily identifiable on the most recent and indeed the earliest maps of the area, with the northern boundary marked by Slade Lane, which runs from east of Eardington in a conspicuous arc to a valley leading to the Severn (and Sladeford), at the point where the parish boundary deviates from the river.[568] The southern line runs from east of Eardington in an arc which is now marked for a short distance by the 19th-century railway to a sunken curving depression, shown very clearly on Robert Dawson's survey of the area made in 1815,[569] running to the Severn between the site of the presumed Quatford bridge and Lower Forge. The area, roughly the shape of a parrot's beak, encloses a plateau which rises to over 650 feet, and is neatly bisected by a trackway, now a paved road running due east to the supposed site of the old bridge. Before crossing the floodplain the road passes through a sunken gap in a wooded bank.[570] The area, probably far too large to be identified as a Danish camp, might be seen as the site of a classic Æthelflædian *burh*. The length of the boundary, some 5,700 feet (or less if the river then ran further to the west, and significantly shorter if the supposed rampart formed the eastern side of the defences), would equate well with the defences recorded for other such *burhs*. For example, the northern defences at Worcester have been assessed at some 4,650 feet,[571] Wallingford at some 5,500 feet,[572] Exeter over 7,500 feet,[573] and Wareham some 6,540 feet.[574] The *Burghal Hidage* assessment for Malmesbury assumes defences of almost 5,000

---

[567] Griffiths 1995a: 77.

[568] Slade Lane is shown leading to the west bank of the Severn on Robert Baugh's 1808 map of Shropshire.

[569] BL map collection. Dawson was perhaps the most talented and prolific of the O.S. cartographers of the period, and set the style for British military map-making.

[570] These various features are readily apparerent in LiDAR surveys.

[571] Hill and Rumble 1996: 227.

[572] Hill and Rumble 1996: 219-20.

[573] Hill and Rumble 1996: 205.

[574] Hill and Rumble 1996: 221-2.

feet.[575] However, those named towns were urban *burhs*, whereas the *burh* at *Cwatbrycge* is more likely to have been planned as a smaller military *burh*, perhaps for use in emergencies, which quickly became obsolete, though the borough mentioned in 1086 might suggest a much earlier urban status.

This leads to the possibility that the area to the south of Slade Lane might conceivably have been Æthelflæd's *burh*, incorporating the western bridgehead of the old bridge at Quatford. Some slight support to that idea might be found in the name *Hamstodeshul*, 'the hill called Hamstede', evidently the name of the plateau here, recorded from the twelfth century and clearly to be associated with the field-names *Church Hampstead*, *Big Hamstead* and *Little Hamstead* (*sic*) on the 1842 Tithe Map on the south side of the track from Eardington leading east to the Severn, the highest land in this immediate area.[576] *Big Hamstead* and *Little Hamstead* adjoin in the south of the area, and are separated from *Church Hampstead* further north, suggesting that the whole area was once named Hamstead.[577] The Anglo-Saxons regularly created compounds of two words. Old English *hām* generally meant 'a village, a village community, a homestead', but is a very rare element in West Midland place-names, and is unmentioned in the standard work on English field-names.[578] Old English *stede* meant 'a place, a site', sometimes 'a deserted site', and generally in compounds 'the site of a structure'.[579] In Old English *hām-stede* carried the meaning 'homestead, a manor', and in Middle English is held to mean 'a homestead; the site of a building; a hamlet, a village, a town'.[580] The name is of particular interest since although the date when *Hamstodeshul* was adopted is unknown, *ham-stede* is almost unrecorded in Middle English field-names, especially in the West Midlands.[581] The name raises the intriguing possibility that it commemorates the site of a deserted structure or habitation or manor, even perhaps, forcing the bounds of credibility, the Æthelflædian *burh*, or more realistically the borough recorded in 1086. The *Church* element in the 1842 name is unexplained and its age unknown: whether it refers to Quatford church or Bridgnorth church or some other religious foundation remains uncertain; there is no church at Eardington, which was probably served by Chelmarsh, although a chapel of St Lawrence, about which no information has been traced, is recorded at Eardington.[582] That leaves open the startling though admittedly unlikely possibility that the name marks the site of the first church of Quatford, but it would be very unsafe to base such speculations on a field-name found only once at such a recent date.

---

[575] Hill and Rumble 1996: 211-2.
[576] Eyton 1854-60: I 125; NLW Otley (Pitchford Hall) Estate 1 1214, 1249. It should be noted that Robert Dawson's O.S. map of 1815 (BL map collection) marks no field-boundaries in the plateau.
[577] The field to the south of the track leading east as it enters this area is named *Ludgate* on the 1842 Tithe Map, probably from OE *hlid-geat* 'a swing-gate': Foxall 1980: 39. Google Earth satellite photographs taken in 2009 show closely-spaced parallel lines running north-west to south-east across the northern half of the site, but with a break resembling a trackway, which does not coincide with a wide, low bank which appears to have run roughly north-south across the lower part of the area, with a parallel feature to the south-west. They appear to be drainage channels rather than ridge-and-furrow, but may repay further investigation.
[578] Gelling and Cole 2000: 48, citing Birmingham and Pattingham as examples; Field 1982.
[579] Sandred 1963: 59; Gardner 1968: 4, 106-8.
[580] Smith 1956: I 226-9, 232; II 147-8. Little evidence for any habitation in this immediate area was traced when parts of the area were examined archaeologically in 1992: Howlett and Coxah 1992; Hunn 2000: 119-44; SSMR SA00202.
[581] Smith 1956: I 232. The name Hampstead might be expected to be pronounced *home-steed* following the usual rules of sound-changes, but no shortening of vowels took place in compound words which were still regarded as such: Brook 1955: 24.
[582] AC lxxxiv (1927) 6; VCH Shropshire X 190.

It is noticeable that the southern boundary of *Church Hampstead* field appears to continue below the bank on its east to cross the lower-lying area towards the Severn. That is echoed to a degree by field boundaries to the north of the trackway which lead eastward to the Severn past Quatford Cottage. The entirety of the rectangular area so formed (or a narrower piece at the east edge of the high ground) might conceivably have formed a defensible area incorporating a *burh* on the plateau protecting the western bridgehead at *Cwatbrycge*, with the bisecting track running down between two modest hillocks which might be seen as an entranceway: a timber gateway at that entrance to the plateau might possibly explain the name. Alternatively, the name *Hamstodeshul* may reflect the existence of a *ham-stede* at the foot of the plateau, i.e. the plateau was named after some former structure on the flat ground on the south side of the east-west Quatford boundary presumed to mark the old trackway to the bridge. There is little likelihood that the structure could have been the bridge, for which a term such as *brycge-stede* might be expected.

It may be objected that an Æthelflædian *burh* here would lie in Eardington, not Quatford. But we have seen that early accounts, notably that of Florence (John) of Worcester,[583] tell us it was at *Bricge* or *Cwatbrycge*, not Quatford (though they may in reality have been the same place), and on the *west* side of the Severn. If those claims are correct, we might suspect that in the early tenth century Eardington had yet to come into existence.

Extensive archaeological survey of parts of this area (unconnected with any search for the Æthelflædian *burh*) carried out in 1992, detected some fragments of linear marks running north to south close to the central trackway to the supposed bridge site, one of which turned at a right angle at the northern end, but detected no significant archaeological features other than what was identified as an Iron Age/Romano-British rectangular enclosure to the north-west of Slade Lane, close to Cliff Coppice.[584] The speculation that

---

[583] Stephenson 1853: 74.
[584] Howlett and Coxah 1992; Hunn 2000: 119-44; SSMR SA00202. The area is undivided into fields on Robert Dawson's O.S. map of 1815 (BL map collection), but fields are shown on the 1842 Tithe Map. It is worth recording that a steep bank known variously as *Ougeres Klif*, *Oureges Klif* and *Eugeres Klif* near The Hay is recorded in the 12th century: NLW Otley (Pitchford Hall) Estate 1 438, 1256, 1317. The name appears to be from an unidentified personal name with OE *clif* 'steep slope': EPNE i 98. It is also appropriate to record a cryptic observation by Thomas Barns, a Staffordshire clergyman writing of the Roman*Limes Britannicus* in 1902, who observed in a paper claiming that the boundary of the *Limes* ran through Quatford that '[it] has a good claim to be a Roman castellum ... it is the site of a bridge, a ford, and a ferry, and a mile to the east is the hillfort of Burf Castle. There is also on the opposite bank of the river a camp, evidently an outwork of Roman times, against the Ordovices, like the Aldewarke [3½ miles east of Rotherham] on the Don. It may have been the station Maglovæ of the Notitia, the seat of the Præfectus numeri Solensium. Its immediate purpose was to hold in check the strongholds of the Brown Clee Hills beyond the Severn': TNSFC XXXVI (1901-2) 120. Barns was a knowledgeable historian but noted for wild flights of fancy (see for example TNSFC 1908), and his reference to a Roman camp remains unexplained: no earthworks, Roman or otherwise, have been traced on the west side of the Severn opposite Quatford – it is hardly likely to be the Roman fort at Wall Town, 3 miles north-east of Cleobury Mortimer, some 7½ miles south-west of Quatford – and indeed no evidence has been traced of any ancient fortification at Aldewarke, although the name, from OE *ald weorc* 'old fortification' suggests that one once existed. It is worth adding that aerial photographs appear to show a tumulus-like mound within the area at SO 72759059, but this was evidently the site of an electricity pylon. The 1999 edition of the 1:25,000 O.S. Explorer map shows a line of pylons, from cartographic evidence erected between 1954 and 1964 and since removed, aligned north-west to south-east running across the area. What is striking is that the pylons were sited on very prominent low mounds (on one of which is a square brick structure, perhaps of Second World War date) which continued from the mound nearest to Slade Lane as a wide low bank running north. Why the pylons should have required such large mounds is

Æthelflæd's *burh* and/or the Norman borough lay to the west of the Severn, it must be conceded, might be seen to be unlikely,[585] but it may be relevant to note that 'where ... defended [English] enclosures (or *burh*s) have been located, some appear to be almost empty inside, although occupation may be encountered nearby: Cricklade, Christchurch, Buckingham, Maldon and Wareham are examples'.[586]

Yet despite the chroniclers' claims that Æthelflæd's *burh* was constructed on the west bank of the Severn, doubtless based on the assumption that *Brycge/Cwatbrycge* were to be identified as Bridgnorth, with its castle on the west bank, it might be thought more likely that Æthelflæd's *burh* lay on the east side of and probably adjoining the Severn, and close to – almost certainly encompassing – the bridge at Quatford,[587] possibly facing or on the site of the earlier Danish camp, or even an island in the river.[588] The concept of double-*burhs* was followed by Alfred the Great in Wessex (e.g. at the as-yet unidentified site on the river Lea from which the Danes fled to *Cwatbrycge* in 895), and by his son Edward, who added a second *burh* to Hertford and Bedford in 912 and 914 respectively after each had been retaken from the Vikings. A *burh* at Nottingham captured in 918 had another fortification added in 920, joined by a bridge,[589] and fortifications on each side of the river were created at Buckingham in 918.[590] The submission of Stamford in the same year was apparently achieved by the building of an opposing fortification on its southern side. There is no reason to suppose that Æthelred and Æthelflæd would not also have adopted the same strategy in Mercia.

In considering whether the site of Æthelflæd's *burh* was at Quatford, we must reflect on Eyton's observation that '...there is little likelihood that a Saxon Queen [Æthelflæd] should have intruded her Castle upon the domain of a Saxon Saint [St Mildburh], though the forest-loving Norman and the heathen Dane had less or no such scruples'.[591]

The deliberate acquisition and transfer to secular control by Alfred, Edward, Æthelred and Æthelflæd of particular strategically important and defensible sites through exchange with

---

unclear. A possible Bronze Age barrow is recorded not far distant at SO72339090 (ADS), and the field-name *Founslow* or *Fonslow* is recorded south of Eardington on the 1842 Tithe Map, perhaps incorporating OE *hlāw* 'a mound, a tumulus', generally found as 'low': the field appears to incorporate a pronounced headland.
[585] The absence of surface traces of ancient earthworks is not unusual: many sections of Offa's Dyke, the ditch of which was at least 6' deep and 28' wide, cannot now be traced on the ground (see generally Hill and Worthington 2003), and the earthworks adjoining Repton church were only detected by excavation, but aerial photography will normally identify even minor disturbances in the earth.
[586] Carver 1989: 47.
[587] A supposition supported by Owen and Blakeway 1825: I 20, who state unequivocally that her *burh* was built at 'Brugge, (i.e. Quatford)'.
[588] The location of *Sceaftesege*, one of the Anglo-Saxon forts listed in the so-called *Burghal Hidage*, which dates perhaps to the years 911-919, has been identified as an island in the Thames at Cookham known as Sashes, now some 54 acres in area. The *Hidage* allots to Sashes 1,000 hides, which indicates that the length of defences to be manned can be calculated at 4,125 feet, which would have enclosed half the present island: Brooks 1964: 74-90.
[589] Laing 1982: 190; Lavelle 2003: 16.
[590] Swanton 1996: 100. Other double *burhs* or forts defending a bridgehead were created at Bedford, Hertford, Stamford, and perhaps London and Cambridge: Biddle 1976: 134-7; Haslam 1984: 184. Edward the Elder recaptured Nottingham from the Danes in 918, and two years later built a second *burh* on the south bank of the Trent, connecting the two with a bridge.
[591] Eyton 1854-60: I 106-7. It is of interest that Eyton should have seen Æthelflæd as a queen.

ecclesiastical communities for military reasons in the late ninth century is now well recognised, with numerous examples said to have been recognised in Mercia.[592] Direct and indirect evidence (not known to Eyton) suggests that in Alfred's reign and during the early years of Edward the Elder, the Crown was acquiring ecclesiastical lands for defensive purposes, with Edward engaged in the 'nationalisation' of church-lands where this was deemed strategically necessary,[593] and there is no reason to doubt that Æthelred and Æthelflæd did not likewise commandeer sites of crucial military importance.[594] Whilst this did not occur at Eardington and Quatford, which remained with the church of Wenlock until acquired by Roger de Montgomery in exchange for Millichope at some date between 1066 and 1086, the reality is that Æthelflæd had the power and authority to build her *burhs* wherever she considered it strategically necessary, and the defence of Mercia would necessarily have overridden any diplomatic niceties of the type mentioned by Eyton.[595] In the same way, there is little likelihood that Wenlock would have resisted any action taken in the national interest by the de facto ruler of the kingdom who had also been a generous benefactor to the house. Eyton's objections to the idea that Æthelflæd built her *burh* at *Brycge/Cwatbrycge* at or close to Quatford can be set aside: it is unnecessary imagine that Anglo-Saxon *burhs* are only to be found on pre-Domesday Crown land.[596]

In that respect, it is appropriate to recall the reference in the foundation charter of Quatford church with its grant of 'Ardintone [Eardington], except the land of Walter the smith and that land which lies between the water and the mount (*montē*, for *montem*, though the Latin for mount(ain) is *mons*) nigh to the bridge, and except that land where the borough is built, and all its hays and proper chaces quit of all service and thing'.[597]

'The water' mentioned in the 1086 church foundation charter can only refer to the Severn,[598] though whether it then took its present course is not known, but the identity of 'the mount' is less certain. G. T. Clark suggested that it may be part of the older earthwork of the nineteenth-century Quatford Castle built by John Smalman, but there is no evidence of any such older earthwork.[599] Eyton, who knew the area well, for he spent time at Quatford in his schooldays, says enigmatically that the spot between the water and the mount was then still to be identified (a comment not easy to explain, for if the mount was the motte, the latter falls sheer to the Severn), and that the site of the borough and probably the hays and chases were all on the Quatford side of the river.[600] Yet although hays and chases are features found in Forest areas – a hay an enclosure, and a chase the hunting ground of a non-royal – and so would not lie on the west of the Severn, it seems very

---

[592] Dumville 1992: 46.
[593] Dumville 1992: 29-30, 39.
[594] In the mid- and later tenth century, for example, the sites of former monasteries at Abingdon, Ely and Peterborough were all under royal control when Bishop Æthelwold (963-75) acquired them; King Edgar held Barrow-upon-Humber before he granted it to the same Bishop in 971; and there is slight evidence for many other similar cases: Dumville 1992: 40.
[595] For the compulsory acquisition of property in Anglo-Saxon England see especially Fleming 1985; Dumville 1992; Reynolds 2008.
[596] Though it will be noted that Chirbury was held by Edward the Confessor before 1066.
[597] SA P225/B/2/1;
[598] Eyton 1854-60: I 109 fn.14 had no doubt about this. The only other watercourse to appear on modern maps is a modest stream which flows along the southern part of the southernmost curved boundary shown on the 1613 map of Morfe Forest (SA4296), but it seems reasonable to suppose that water will have drained off the high ground to the east of Quatford (although the area is very sandy), and modern drainage may conceal the course of earlier watercourses.
[599] AC 4th Series xx 1874 270.
[600] 1854-60: I 109.

possible that the area excluded from the exchange with Wenlock in 1086 incorporated the area to the west of the river which is now encompassed by the modern Quatford boundary: no other record has been traced describing the motte (or indeed any other ground) on the east side of the river as a mount, and it must be more likely that 'the mount' is the high ground above the flood plain on the east side of the river. Wasey understood the mount to refer to this ground,[601] and his view is reinforced by the twelfth-century reference to *Monte de Erdintun* mentioned earlier, which is clearly 'the mount of Eardington' on the west side of the river opposite Quatford ferry, doubtless the *hill called Hamstede* discussed above.

While the location of the borough mentioned in Domesday Book and in the foundation (or re-foundation) charter of the church is not known, it is generally presumed to have been near the 1086 church.[602] As noted elsewhere, David Roffe believes that the *burgu[m]* mentioned in Domesday Book was indeed the *burh*, and the fact that it rendered nothing presumably accounts for the terse entry, suggesting that it may well be that Quatford was the centre of the estate rather than Eardington which clearly was geldable.[603] Most newly-planned boroughs of this period consist of a spine road with property boundaries running off at right angles, often with the church at one end. It is difficult to discern any such arrangement either from the physical topography or on early maps of Quatford, but recent LiDAR surveys reveal three banked sides of an intriguing platform, roughly 100 yards square, on the spur of higher ground some 150 yards east of Quatford church. The northern and southern banks extend westwards in a less pronounced way to incorporate the church, and indeed internal lines which the eye of faith might identify as traces of lanes. The eastern ends of the square feature deviate to continue as old field boundaries joining enclosure boundaries at a higher level. The square area calls to mind the *burh* built by Æthelflæd at Chirbury in 915, only three years after that at *Cwatbrycge*. As noted previously, in the north-west corner of Chirbury is a rectangular embanked platform with traces of single banks up to 14' high forming a square enclosure with sides of about 180'.[604]

An Æthelflædian *burh*, though, is likely to have been considerably larger than the platform at Chirbury, and probably also that at Quatford, although the eastern edge of the platform at Quatford is uncertain,[605] and we have seen that the *burh* at Runcorn was only 1½ acres in area. But we are forced to eliminate the square feature (though not necessarily the immediate area) from any search for the Æthelflædian *burh*, for the same LiDAR surveys show a large area of unbroken parallel plough lines extending northwards from the motte almost as far as the lane running east from the right-angled bend of the Severn, and east beyond Hillhouse Farm, covering what has been assumed to be the bailey to the east of the

---

[601] Wasey 1865: 24.

[602] As mentioned above, a large square area, the northern boundary formed by Chantry Lane and a track to the Severn, the southern boundary slightly sinuous, divided into Churchyard Piece and Upper Piece on the 1842 Tithe Map, with the Norman motte and Quatford church in its south-west corner, may be noted.

[603] Personal communication 9th January 2015. Roffe compares Quatford with the account of Bedford which was similarly quit: ibid. Armitage describes the motte at Quatford and a bean-shaped bailey, and concludes that the Domesday Book reference to a *burgu'* implies the existence of a Norman fortification: Armitage 1912: 58, 191,

[604] SO 258985; Shropshire SMR 00498; see VCH Shropshire I 378-0; Stanford 1991: 131; Duckers 2006: 50.

[605] Interestingly, the sides of the platform at Quatford do not correlate with hedgelines shown on the 1:2,500 O.S. map of 1883, or on the 1613 map of Morfe Common (SA 4296). Aerial photographs of the site show it to be largely concealed by trees.

motte, as well as the square area to the east of the church, the lines continuing southwards across the northern boundary of that square area. The LiDAR surveys show that the lines are markedly straight, close, and regular, and do not exhibit the aratral or 'reversed-S' curve at each end which marks the turning of oxen teams to create ridge-and-furrow, showing that they were machine-made, and probably date from the period of intensive arable production during the Second World War. The northern bank at least of the square area clearly post-dates those lines.[606]

Any Æthelflædian *burh* (and indeed Norman borough) at Quatford will almost certainly have incorporated a church, possibly on the site of the present church, the earliest fabric of which has been dated to the early twelfth century,[607] and research into the *burh* has quite properly concentrated on that area, with the spine road generally identified as the ancient road running north-south through Quatford, although there will have been steep climbs from both north and south which have since been alleviated though not removed by a wide cutting made through the solid sandstone.[608] The square platform above the church described above may indeed be a particularly significant feature in that respect.

Yet if we are correct in identifying the *monte* and the land of Walter the Smith as the hill on the west side of the river and Moor Farm respectively, that leads to the possibility that the new borough of Quatford, which was also excluded in the 1086 endowment to Quatford church, lay too on that side of the river. Certainly nothing in Domesday Book (which contains the only other record of the borough) serves to preclude the possibility. Furthermore, while the reference to hays and chases, both Forest terms,[609] is correctly taken to refer to areas within Morfe Forest on the east side of the Severn, it should not be overlooked that the ancient estate of The Hay (recorded in the twelfth century as *Haia*)[610]

---

[606] Traces of identical lines are also found on the north-facing slopes of the valley running east from The Danery public house, and on the west-facing slopes of the plateau further south, as well as the plateau itself, and on the high ground on the opposite side of the Severn.
[607] Cranage 1903.
[608] An intriguing reference in the first (1578) edition of Holinshed's *Chronicles* must be addressed. Holished says that 'From Bridgenorth our Sauerne descendeth to Woodburie, Quatford, and there taking in the Marbrooke beneath Eaton that riseth above Collaton…'. Eaton may be Eardington, and *Marbrooke* is presumably Mor Brook, which which rises near Callaughton and flows into the Severn from the west opposite Dudmaston,. but the location of Woodburie is less clear. Intriguingly, a modern public house known as the Woodberry Down lies on the north-west side of Bridgnorth, but the age and derivation of the name are untraced, and may be a recent red herring. The name Woodburie must be of some interest, however, for, if correctly represented, it means 'the timber fortification', or possibly 'the fortification associated with the wood'. It evidently lay between Bridgnorth and Quatford, perhaps on the west side of the river, for it is not included among names shown on the eastern side of the river on the c.1560 or 1613 maps of Bridgnorth, in the very area in which we seek Æthelflæd's *burh*. It would be fanciful to suggest that in the sixteenth century there was still a place named after a long-lost timber palisaded fortification, however, for the name of Oldbury, a village lying a mile or so south-west of Bridgnorth, was written *Wowbury* in 1576, *Oldbury alias Woberye* in 1600,[608] and as *Wobury* on Speed's map of Shropshire published in 1612. Since Oldbury village lies a mile of so west of the Severn, Holinshed's reference evidently refers to the parish, the boundary of which extends to the river. It may also be noted that Astbury Hall lies on the east side of Mor Brook, a little over a mile from Quatford. This common name, if ancient, normally means 'eastern fortification or manor house', but the history of Astbury Hall (*Asbury* 1815 draft 1" O.S. map by Robert Dawson, BL map collection) has not been traced before the nineteenth century, and the name may well be relatively modern.
[609] A hay was a Forest enclosure; a chase a Forest held by someone other than the king.
[610] Otley (Pitchford Hall) Estate/1367.

lies on the West side of the Severn a mile south of Quatford.[611] Could the intriguing and ancient field-names found on the headland opposite Quatford relate to the borough of Quatford, and perhaps even the *nova domus*? That historians and archaeologists searching for the borough (and possibly 'new house'), perhaps distracted by the Norman motte, church and more recent habitation on the east side of the river and its absence on the west, may have been concentrating on the wrong side of the Severn, cannot be entirely discounted.[612]

---

[611] The word *chacia* is translated by most authorities as 'chase', a term used in Forest areas, but the word is found in Latin dictionaries with reference to the short notched split hazel tally sticks used by the Exchequer to record receipts: Poole 1912: 89. It is doubtless coincidence that the ancient London custom (mentioned earlier in this chapter) of splitting two faggots of wood by way of service to the Exchequer is undertaken only by tenants of The Moors in Eardington, a mile north-west of Quatford on the east side of the Severn, and a mile or so north-west of The Hay: Anderson 1864: 10-11; Timmins 1899: 195-6.

[612] Mention might be made of the significant place-name Harpsford, alias Harpswood, where the road from Bridgnorth towards Neenton crosses the Mor Brook near Cross Houses. Early spellings suggest that the place incorporates OE *here-pæð* 'a military road, a highway', so 'the ford associated with the army-path' (EPNE i 244-5; Eyton 1854-60: I 78-9; PN Sa volume forthcoming), from which we may conclude that one of the roads nearby was used by warriors in the Anglo-Saxon period.

10. Scergeat.

We have seen that the *burh* at *Cwatbrycge* was built by Æthelflæd in 912, following that at *Scergeat*, which had been started on the eve of the Invention of the Holy Cross, 6th May, of that year, a day which may have had special resonance for a Mercian royal woman.[613] They were not the first of Æthelflæd's known *burhs* (though not all may have been recorded, and it is very likely that many were constructed by her husband before his death): that was *Bremesbyrig*, built soon after the battle of Tettenhall in 910, the location of which remains unidentified.[614] The speed with which Æthelflæd moved to create that *burh* might suggest that its position was dictated by the direction from which the Northumbrian raiding party which fought at Tettenhall approached the area, or from which it entered Mercia.

The location of *Scergeat*, first mentioned in the *Mercian Register*,[615] continues to perplex historians.[616] In the words of Roger of Wendover, in 913 'Alfleda, lady of the Mercians, came with a great force to Strengate, and built there a castle of defence'.[617] That fortification could have lain in almost any part of the West Midlands to the west of the line of the Danelaw, but is perhaps more likely to have been somewhere in Shropshire, the west side of Staffordshire, North Worcestershire or South Cheshire.[618] It could well have been at a pre-existing earthwork that could easily be refortified, and/or at a militarily strategic place such as river crossing.[619] Physical remains might not survive; notwithstanding the

---

[613] See Stafford 2008: 102-3.

[614] Swanton suggests possibly Bromsberrow in Gloucestershire or Bromesberrow near Ledbury in Herefordshire: (Swanton 1996: 95 fn.13, followed by Walker 2000: 93), though both seem to be the same place. It is rather remarkable that the place-name Quatford is also found in Ledbury: the name is recorded in 1605 and 1722x1862: *Register of Admissions to Gray's Inn 1521-1889*, Joseph Foster 1889; NA D1604/T1. Curiously, Robert Fabyan, writing in the early 16th century, tells us that Æthelflæd 'buylded a bridge ouer ye ryuer of Seuerne; whiche is, or was named Brymmysbury Bridge': Ellis 1811: 177. Frustratingly, the source of this intriguing comment (also found in other works, e.g. Heywoode 1624: 236 as 'Thatarne Brimsbury [*sic*], the bridge upon Seuerne') is unknown, but perhaps explained by *Brycge* (Quatford) following *Bremesbyrig* in *Chronicle* accounts, with the reference to the Severn an added gloss.

[615] ASC 'C'; Swanton 1996: 96.

[616] For a recent discussion on the possible location of Æthelflæd's *burhs* see Sharp 2016, which speculates that *Scergeat* may have lain on the Severn, perhaps in the Wyre Forest [Bewdley] area.

[617] Giles 1892: 241. Florence (John) of Worcester records the event in the same terms: Stevenson 1853: 74.

[618] Leland appears to have believed that *Scargate* (corrected by him to *Scorgate*) lay in Gloucestershire, possibly near Tewksbury, 'about Severn side', presumably knowing of a place of that name, and notes that it was 'repaired' by Ethelfleda: Toulmin Smith 1964: VI 40.

[619] For the suggestion that *Scergeat* controlled one of the supposed gaps in Offa's Dyke see Coates 1998: 9. Earle believed that 'One great object of this line of fortresses was to cut off the Danes of the Five Boroughs from the Welsh, and to prevent them from receiving reinforcements from their kinsmen in Ireland through the estuaries of the Severn, the Dee and the Mersey': Earle and Plummer 1892-9: ii 119. Since the eviction of the Hiberno-Norse from Dublin c.902 had effectively neutralised the threat from Ireland, that analysis seems improbable, though the Welsh may have been seen as the most immediate threat, especially after the death of Cadell ap Rhodri of Deheubarth in south-west Wales (to be succeeded by his son Hywel) in 909 or 910, described in the Irish *Chronicum Scotorum* as 'king of the Britons', a title the Irish annals generally reserved for the most powerful and wide-ruling kings among the Britons of Wales and Strathclyde, and a title also given by the Welsh chronicles to his uncle Anarawd ap Rhodri, who held Gwynedd and probably Powys. Both Hywel and Ananarwd had wider territorial ambitions, and Æthelflæd will not have forgotten that Ananarwd

(single) reference to some *burhs* in the *Mercian Register*, some of those fortifications may not have been completed or have been destroyed in the intervening period.

Cwatbrycge, as we have seen, is almost certainly to be identified as Quatford, and was the place where a Northumbrian force crossed the Severn before the battle of Tettenhall only twenty months earlier, and that crossing was almost certainly the main reason why the place was chosen as the site for a *burh*. Those traumatic events, and the over-wintering of the Danes at the same place in 895-6, were evidently major factors when Æthelflæd, following the death of her husband the previous year, decided where the second and third of the new *burhs* were to be constructed. It would not be surprising if *Scergeat*, built in the months before that at *Cwatbrycge*, had also been placed with the Tettenhall campaign still sharp in memory, elsewhere – but not far distant – on the Severn: it is readily apparent that Æthelflæd saw her western borders as the region that left her kingdom dangerously exposed to attack. Furthermore, we might assume that *Scergeat* is to be found (if traces of its name should still survive, an idea that could well be misplaced) at a location with a name now beginning Sh–: in Old English *Sc*– would be pronounced *Sh*–.

Little Shrawardine in central Shropshire stands at a major ford on the south bank of a loop of the Severn, seven miles west of Shrewsbury, with Shrawardine (sometimes recorded as Greater Shrawardine), part of the same estate, nearby on the opposite bank.[620] The place was a sizeable village in the post-Conquest period, and in Domesday Book was an 'outlier' of the manor of Ford (which took its name from a crossing over a minor stream, not from a Severn crossing), held, like Quatford, by Roger de Montgomery. To emphasise the strategic importance of the place, both Little Shrawardine and Shrawardine, unusually, have castles, barely 800 yards apart, the former a motte and bailey, the motte enjoying extensive views along the Severn valley, evidently superseded by that at Shrawardine, which eventually became the more substantial of the neighbouring estates.[621] In the pre-Conquest period Shrawardine and Little Shrawardine seem to have been associated vills, together responsible for safeguarding the important ford. Their existing earthworks are assumed to be post-Conquest, but it is possible that the origins of one or both predate that period. Pre-Conquest fortifications, Viking or Anglo-Saxon or both, are recorded at the strategic Severn fords at Buttington and Quatford,[622] and the possibility that Little Shrawardine had a similar fortification cannot be ignored.

In many ways Little Shrawardine mirrors Quatford, a probable *burh* site, and though that cannot be taken as evidence that the former was also the site of a *burh*, it might be suggestive of a possible location. Both lie on the outer bank of a right-angled bend in the

---

had at one stage formed an alliance, albeit decades earlier and short-lived, with the Northumbrians: Maund 2006: 58; Charles-Edwards 2013: 489-90.

[620] The ford seems to have used until the 1860s, when the cartway leading to it and the hedges on each side where obliterated: TSAHS VII (1895) 124. The name is pronounced Shraywardyne or Shrayden by older local residents, as noted in PN Sa I: 265-7.

[621] A castle is known to have existed since the mid 12th century and in 1212 was destroyed by the Welsh during Llewellyn's successful raid on Shrewsbury, after whih it was rebuilt by the Fitz Allens who renamed it Castle Isabel. It was sold in 1583 to Thomas Bromley, and during the Civil War was held for the Royalists. Soon after the fall of Shrewsbury in 1645 it was captured and the keep dismantled to provide stone for additional defences at Shrewsbury. Fragmentary remains of the base of the keep and one tower survive.

[622] However, pre-Conquest elements have not been recorded at Hen Domen, overlooking the important ford over the Severn at Rhywhiman.

Severn, and overlook a floodplain,[623] an early and strategic ford, an ancient fish weir, and a ferry, each with an imposing motte on the very edge of the river slightly upstream of the ford and with commanding views along the river.[624] The importance of the fords at both Quatford and Shrawardine[625] is shown by the boundaries of both places extending – unusually – across the Severn to include land isolated or 'cut off' – the common ownership of both banks at early and important fords, even when the river forms a major boundary, is well recorded. As noted above, though Little Shrawardine lies south of the Severn, its twin settlement Shrawardine is north of the river, lying within an artificial and irregular deviation some 2 miles wide and a mile deep that anciently formed part of the diocese of Hereford,[626] creating a gap in the diocesan boundary with St Asaph, formalised in 1291 on the basis of 'ancient usage', running along the Severn from Rhydwhiman near Montgomery.[627] This (and perhaps the existence of the two castles) might even imply that a pre-Conquest tenth-century double-*burh* once existed here.[628]

Little Shrawardine (*Parva Shretwardyn* in 1291-2)[629] is a little over two miles from the Welsh border, and is not only the site of the last upstream English ford on the Severn, with an ancient trackway from Rowton Castle in the south,[630] but also lies on the boundary between the Anglo-Saxon folk-groups of the *Wrocensæte*, centred on north Shropshire, and the *Magonsæte*, centred on south Shropshire and Herefordshire.[631] This mirrors to a

---

[623] The southern and western edge of the floodplain at Shrawardine is marked on aerial photographs by a line curving parallel with the river. It is worth recording that the Severn valley at Shrawardine is notably narrow, and the narrowest point in the 27 miles of river between Abermule and Shrawardine is Buttington: Ray and Bapty 2016: 40.

[624] No recorded excavation appears to have taken place at the motte at Little Shrawardine: Higham and Barker 2004: 357. Curiously, Shrawardine is recorded in Renn 1973: 311, but the motte at Little Shrawardine is unmentioned. The existence of the mound at Little Shrawardine raises the intriguing possibility that it (and perhaps the motte at Quatford) may have been a pre-Conquest feature associated with Anglo-Saxon fords and/or meeting places. Interestingly, the Shropshire historian J. E. Auden was in little doubt that the mound 'is a very perfect Saxon mound': TSAS 2nd Series VII 1895: 120.

[625] If the mound at Little Shrawardine lay at the ford across the Severn, the ford evidently later moved east, to the opposite side of the headland, presumably when the Norman castle at Shrawardine was established and a more direct connection was required.

[626] TSAS 2nd Series VII 1895 124. The 1728 map of Shawardine mentioned below (SA 552/8/306) shows a single tree just beyond the sharp angle at the north-west of the parish boundary with the words 'At this Tree Ends Three Bishopricks, St Asaph, Hereford, Litchfield & Cov.', but a tree seems an impermanent marker for such an important intersection, when a mound might have been expected.

[627] *Montgomeryshire Collections*, 40 (1922) 258; Baugh's map of Shropshire, 1808; O.S. map: *Monastic Britain*, 2nd edition, 1954; Gelling 1992: 98 fig.40; Morriss 2005: 133. Baugh's map and the O.S. map differ slightly; the former is to a much larger scale, is evidently based on local knowledge, and is to be preferred.

O.S. map: *Monastic Britain*, 2nd edition, 1954.

[628] We have seen that the concept of double-*burhs* was adopted by Alfred the Great in Wessex (e.g. at Southwark, at the as-yet unidentified site on the river Lea from which the Danes fled to *Cwatbrycge* in 895), and by Edward the Elder, where for example second *burhs* were added to Hertford and Bedford in 912 (the year *Scergeat* was built) and 914 respectively after each had been retaken from the Vikings. A *burh* at Nottingham captured in 918 had another fortification added in 920, linked by a bridge: Laing 1982: 190; Lavelle 2003: 16.

[629] PN Sa I 266-7.

[630] The trackway running south from the ford to the Shrewsbury-Alberbury road is clearly shown on the First Edition O.S. 1" map of 1833.

[631] Gelling 1989: 190.

degree the situation at Quatford, the meeting point of the *Wrocensæte*, the *Magonsæte*, and the *Hwicce*, the latter probably represented by the later diocese of Worcester.[632]

What information can be extracted from the name Shrawardine? First recorded (in Domesday Book) as *Saleurdine*, later spellings include *Seraordina* 1121, *Sera(w)ordina* 1155, *Scrawardin* 1166, *Scharwurdi* 1171, *Screwrdin* 1204, *Scawrðin* 1205, *Shrewardin* 1214, *Shrewrdin* 1220, *Shrewurthin* 1221, *Serewardin* 1272, *Schrewardyn* 1291, *Schyreveworthdin* 1292, *Schirewordyn* 1302, *Shrowardyne* 1397, and *Shrewardyn* 1528.[633] The second element of the name poses no difficulties: it is clearly Old English *worðign* – perhaps surprisingly at this location, since the word *ford* might have been expected for what was presumably an ancient, probably prehistoric, river crossing, though that element could have been found in an earlier Anglo-Saxon name, to be supplanted by *worðign*, as Tamworth was originally *Tomtūn* before *tūn* was replaced by *worðig*.[634]

Old English *worðig*, *worð*, and *worðign* all have the similar meaning 'enclosure, enclosed settlement', but are not necessarily synonymous, presumably carrying subtle distinctions in the Anglo-Saxon period which are not readily recognisable today.[635] *Worðig* appears to be a distinctively South-West place name element, with *Worðign* especially common in the West Midlands (usually in the later West Midland development *–wardine*), particularly in Herefordshire and Shropshire, often found in compounds with significant descriptive or topographical words or old place-names and river-names.[636] The element is never found as a first element in compound names.

Margaret Gelling has suggested that at a very early stage of Anglo-Saxon settlement in the West Midlands *worðig*, as well as meaning 'enclosure' or similar, may have developed a meaning akin to *burh*, 'fortification', applied to a site of considerable importance (there is no occurrence of *worth*, *worthig* or *worthign* in names recorded before 730),[637] and Professor Richard Coates has developed the idea by proposing that the same word was introduced to Mercia from Wessex 'through royal dynastic contacts to name places which were of particular significance to ruling families [Æthelflaed is expressly mentioned, with her *burhs* at *Tameworðig* (Tamworth) and *Norðworðig* (Northworthy = Derby)], and situated in a particular relation to other significant places nearby'.[638] There can be no argument that Little Shrawardine was situated in a particular relation to other significant places nearby, with Shrewsbury only seven miles away to the east. A charter issued from Shrewsbury by Æthelred and Æthelflæd, a decade or so before *Scergeat* and *Cwatbrycge* were built, calls it *civitate Scrobbensis*,[639] implying a place of considerable administrative, ecclesiastical and military significance,[640] probably of long standing and almost certainly

---

[632] Finberg 1972: 225-7; Gelling 1989: 192.
[633] Bowcock 1923: 212; PN Sa I 265-7. 'J.F.A.' (Probably J. F. Auden, the Shropshire historian), a contributor to *Bye-Gones Relating to Wales and the Border Counties*, 1911, 28, provides other spellings, including *Snewardin*, *Shrawarine*, *Schawurde*, *Szwardin*, *Sevewarden*, *Seraordin* (all 12th century), *Serewarden*, *Shrewurthin*, *Srewardin* (all 13th century), and *Shirewordan*, *Scrawarthyn*, and *Shrewgardyn* (all 14th century).
[634] Horovitz 2005: 529.
[635] PN Sa I 265-7; Watts 2004: 548.
[636] EPNE ii 277.
[637] EPNE ii 273-7; Gelling 1992: 147-8.
[638] Coates 2012: 40.
[639] S.221.
[640] Basset 1996: 156; Baker 2010: 89.

the location of an existing *burh*.[641] As Ray and Bapty observe in their recent study of Offa's Dyke, '... the names of places ending in –wardine may indicate those that were in some sense or another regarded as defensible settlements'.[642]

The first element in the name Shrawardine remains unidentified,[643] but the earliest forms *Saleurdine* (DB), *Seraordina* 1121, and *Sera(w)ordina* 1155, have been explained as showing the usual Norman-French vowel insertion. French speakers had difficulty pronouncing the cluster of initial consonants, which they simplified by inserting a vowel between the first two consonants, with the Domesday form showing the typical confusion of –*r*– with –*l*–, as found in early spellings of Shrewsbury,[644] though the 1272 form which seems to confirm the earliest spellings is noteworthy. Also worth noting is that unlike nearby Shrewsbury, the earliest spellings for Shrawardine providing evidence for *Scr*– begin only from 1166,[645] very much later than for Shrewsbury, though the earliest spellings allow us to reconstruct the name with reasonable confidence. Nevertheless, as with many places first recorded in Domesday Book, the name may be (very) considerably older, and its name corrupt by the time of Domesday. Here we have the presence of nearby Shrewsbury casting its shadow over local names, especially those that might have a resemblance to the spelling of the county town.

If the ending of *scræ*– in Shrawardine were –*w*, the first element would be Old English *screawa* 'shrew' – a word hinted at in some later spellings for Shrewsbury – though its use with *worðign* would be difficult to explain unless as a personal name or nickname,[646] and the hypothetical –*w* is very likely to be chimerical, a figment attributable to the first letter of the following word.

Around 1300 the spellings for Shrawardine develop a fanciful association with *sheriff* and *shire*,[647] and indeed the earliest authority on Shropshire place-names, E. W. Bocock, concluded in 1923 that the name meant 'sheriff's farm or estate',[648] but chose to overlook

---

[641] The earliest reference to the place-name Shrewsbury incorporating –*byrig* is in 1006: ASC 'E'; Swanton 1996: 137; PN Sa I 267; Baker 2010: 89. Rather remarkably, amongst various other idiosyncratic conclusions, Sharp casually dismisses the charter, S.221, as 'at least corrupt and probably fraudulent' (even though its authenticity is unquestioned by leading scholars), and not to be seen as evidence that Shrewsbury existed in 901: Sawyer 1968: 126; Sharp 2016. The existence in the Cuerdale hoard, dated to c.905, of coins likely to have been minted at Shrewsbury, and a small hoard of coins probably minted before 910 found in the town in 1936, confirms the existence of a mint, and therefore a *burh*, before c.905: Lyon 2001: 72-5. Coins were certainly minted at Shrewsbury during the reign of Æthelstan (925-39): Baker 2010: 89. For an interesting 19th-century discussion on the names Shrewsbury and Shrawardine (written without the benefit of modern toponymic knowledge) see Kerslake 1875: 161-2.

[642] Ray and Bapty 2016: 295. The line of place-names implying fortifications running south to from Stanwardine in the Wood, including Stanwordine in the Fields, Shrawardine, Alberbury, Westbury, Worthen and Chirbury, may denote part of a chain of military stations protecting Mercia to the east of the Severn and west of Shrewsbury. A useful map of early estate names (including *worð(ign)* names) in Herefordshire and Shropshire is found in Hooke 2002: 55.

[643] The idea that the name is from 'the Castle of the Shire-reeve or Sheriff' as put forward by Owen and Blakeway 1825: I 70 cannot be supported on philological grounds.

[644] PN Sa I 265-71.

[645] We might note that 'a few eccentric forms [for Shrawardine] which may be suspected of being misreadings' were omitted from PN Sa I 265-7.

[646] PN Sa I 265-7.

[647] PN Sa I 265-7.

[648] Bocock 1923: 212.

earlier spellings which showed that his explanation was philologically impossible. The superficial resemblance of some thirteenth-century spellings with the first element of the modern name Shrewsbury is illusory, and must be discounted, since the earliest forms for the name of the county town are very different from (but might well have influenced) those for Shrawardine.[649]

It was Eilert Ekwall, doyen of place-name scholars, who in the original (1936) edition of his *Concise Oxford Dictionary of English Place-Names* first proposed that the name Shrawardine might incorporate Old English *scræf, scref*, a word used with two primary senses, (1) 'a cave, a hollow place in the earth, ', sometimes in place-names 'a narrow valley, a ravine',[650] and (2) 'a hovel, a hut, a poor dwelling',[651] with the loss of the final consonant, perhaps in the first sense with reference to some landscape feature now obscured by Shrawardine Pool,[652] but that overgrown 44-acre mere half a mile north of the village is only a few feet deep, and the idea seems most unlikely. However, any derivation from *scræf, scref* poses difficulties, since there is no obvious cave or hollow at Shrawardine.

But other important evidence must now be thrown into the mix. As this chapter was being drafted, the author became aware quite by chance of a parchment estate map of Shrawardine[653] produced in 1728 by Joseph Dougharty of Worcester[654] that records land to

---

[649] During the drafting of this chapter, one element considered as the first element of Shrawardine was OE *scrēad(e)*, meaning 'a piece cut off, a cutting, a shred' (Toller 1898: 840; Oakden 1984: 137; Horovitz 2005: 493), with the loss of the final consonant, perhaps used in a similar way to Anglian Old English *snæd* (EPNE ii 277), with reference to the detached part of the parish north of the Severn. But the word *scrēad(e)* is rarely found in place-names (the element is unlisted in EPNE. though it may be the first element of Shredicote in Staffordshire, some 30 miles to the east, where the exact application there is unclear (Horovitz 2005: 493); cf. Scredington, Lincolnshire, which may incorporate the element, in which case it could refer to the position of Scredington on a strip of land cut off by streams: Watts 2004: 533. Another element considered was OE *scearu, scaru*, with the meaning 'a shearing, something cut off, a share of land, district, province or nation, boundary', not infrequently found in place-names (EPNE ii 109-11; EPNE ii 102; counties with places incorporating the element include Lancashire, North Yorkshire, Northamptonshire, Cheshire and Shropshire: Watts 2004: 539-40; EPNS 43 (1967) 213; EPNS 54 (1981) 331; EPNS 82 (2006) V 281. For a discussion of the name Skilgate in Somerset, formerly held to mean 'boundary gate', see Mills 1997: 241-3). J. J. Anderson notes that 'B[osworth] T[oller] has two articles, one for *scearu*, var. *scyru* 'tonsure', another for *scearu* 'groin', but it is reasonable to regard these as one word, with the basic sense 'cutting, division'; cf. *OED* s. Share, sb.² and sb.³': Anderson 1977: 104. OE *scearu, scaru*, like OE *scear, scer* either derive from or are intimately related to Old English *sceran* 'to cut'. Behind these words is the idea 'to divide or separate by cutting ... or (to cause) to deviate from a course': Partridge 1966: 613. Tetsuji Oda, in a paper on the sound symbolism of words beginning *sc-* in OE Heroic Poetry, concludes that 'Words begininning with the bilateral OE *sc-* (>ModE *sk-/sc-*) are traced back to their supposed IE roots [the majority of which have the meaning] 'to cut' and 'to cover': Oda 2010: 56.
[650] Ekwall 1960: 408 *sub nom* Scrafton, North Yorkshire; 414 *sub nom* Sharlston, Yorkshire West; 420 *sub nom* Shrawley, Worcs.
[651] Pages 394-5 (*sub nom* Sharlston, Yorkshire West), 400; Oakden 1984: 115-7; see also BT i 840. The derivation is also accepted by Smith: EPNE ii 113-4.
[652] Ekwall 1960: 420; PN Sa I 265-7.
[653] 'A Map of the township of Shrawardin in the Mannor of Shrawardin in the County of Salop belonging to Henry Bromley Esq; Accurately surveyed 1728 by Joseph Dougharty Esq.', at a scale of 4 chains to an inch: SA 552/8/306. J. E. Auden was evidently unaware of the 1728 map when he wrote his comprehensive history of Shrawardine in 1895: TSAS 2nd Series VII (1895) 120-202. An extract from the map showing the curved boundary is reproduced as Figure 2 in the online Report No. 436, Shrawardine Castle, produced on by the Clwyd-Powys Archaeological Trust in 2002. Henry

the south of the lane from Shrawardine to Montford between The Clamp (*sic*)[655] and Greenfields, ¼ mile south-east of the church, identified as *Old Camp*. The name refers to a substantial sickle-shapes linear feature running north to south.[656] The area lies a short distance down the south-facing headland of the highest land in the area.[657] On a map of 1826, the site is marked as *old entrenchment*,[658] and appears as *The Camp* on the 1842 Tithe Map.[659] Tentatively identified as the possible western boundary of a deer park – place-name evidence shows that a park existed here[660] – that idea no longer prevails, and its shape and the relative height of the ground has suggested that it may have been prehistoric or Anglo-Saxon in date, or possibly associated with the Norman castle, but both its date and function remain a mystery.[661]

What is clear is that the curved feature is no longer readily identifiable on the ground. Its position is now marked very approximately by a straight north-south hedgeline with a slight change of direction halfway along demarcating a slightly undulating plateau sloping slightly south towards the Severn from higher ground to the north. The ground to the east of the hedgeline is some 2'-3' lower than the plateau (a differential visible on LiDAR surveys that disappears at what seems to be a more recent continuation of the boundary to the south) and slopes down markedly to the east. Cartographic evidence suggests that the trench was obliterated during the nineteenth century, but LiDAR surveys show traces of a slight curving sunken trench perhaps 10' or so wide running parallel with and some 20' east of the hedgeline in its central section which could well be a ghost of the feature, though it does not extend along the continuation of the hedgeline mentioned above. The plateau has far-reaching views to the east, west and south across the nearby Severn (with views to the north from the summit of the hill), and falls away at the edge to the west. LiDAR surveys show a slightly curving raised linear feature to the south, modest in scale and parallel with the Severn,[662] unassociated with modern field boundaries, which 1728 map shows linked

---

Bromley (1705-55) was an MP who became Lord Montford in 1741 but ran up great debts and committed suicide in 1755. There is no evidence that he had any interest in antiquities.

[654] Dougharty (b.1699), 'an ingenious and reputable person', surveyor and architectural engraver, came from a family of prominent surveyors: both his father (John, 1677-1755) and brother (John, b. 1709) were known for their estate surveys. His father was an ambitious self-educated Irish surveyor and mathematician who published several successful books on mathematics and trained as a land surveyor, producing many fine estate maps. That skill and knowledge of mathematics was inherited by his sons, also famed for their maps and plans. The family lived above the massive stone gatehouse, King Edgard's Tower, in the precints of Worcester Cathedral, and c.1750 Joseph, who had produced fine architectural engravings and town maps, but is not known to have published any writings, was teaching mathematics at Worcester: Smith 1967.

[655] The Clamp is presumably a corruption of The Camp.

[656] HER (PRN) 04647. The feature is at Grid Reference SJ 403149.

[657] At just over 300'. LiDAR surveys indicate that the southern end of the feature appears to terminate at an enclosure-period east-west field boundary, but is continued by a similar straight boundary running south.

[658] SA 552/8/337. The feature appears as the straight bank with a slight bend near the centre running north-south which appears on LiDAR surveys. The area shows clear evidence of fields created during the enclosure period.

[659] SA 552/8/30 p7; SA LSL Tithe Apportionment 290.

[660] Names from the 1728 map includes *Red Deer Park* (SJ4060 1500); *Park* (SJ4085 1480); *Stag Park* (SJ4100 1480); *Fallow Deer Park* (SJ4055 1555); *Horse Park* (SJ4050 1520); and *Plain Park* (SJ4090 1535).

[661] It has been suggested that fields called *Big Camp* and *Long Camp* at the end of the nineteenth century were exercise grounds for the castle garrison during the Civil War (TSAS 2nd Series VII 149-50), but that seem unlikely.

[662] LiDAR surveys show that the feature incorporates a noticeable mound to the east.

up to the southern end of *Old Camp* entrenchment. That map also shows that the area to the east and south of both features was then wooded,[663] suggesting that the southern feature may have been a typical wood-bank, and that the present lane towards Montford continued little further than the north-south curved boundary (which we might doubt, for Montford and Shrawardine must anciently have had a direct link) – there were no properties along it in 1728.[664] A spring is said to have existed at the northern end of the curved trench,[665] and in 1728 a pool existed further the west within the angle formed by the lane towards Montford and a stopped lane running south, its site visible on LiDAR surveys, with a stream flowing south from it into the Severn. Those same surveys also show a curious wide channel or trench with a watercourse running towards the Severn from the headland, turning sharply west and then (at the end of a lane from the village) sharply south to the river.

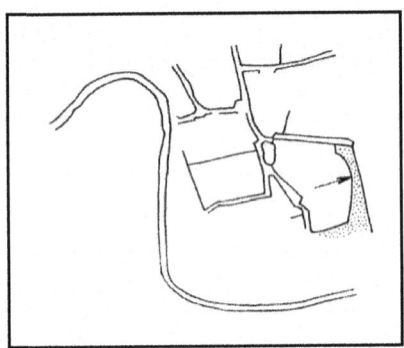

Redrawn and simplified extract from the 1728 estate map of Shrawardine to the north of the Severn with the site of *Old Camp* arrowed (Shropshire Archives SA 552/8/337).

Though the site remains an enigma, the 1728 map is especially notable for an extraordinary contemporary annotation: the curving feature (carefully shaded on the east, presumably to denote a ditch) is endorsed in minute and delicately neat script with the faint and barely-legible but startling words: *This trench was before the Conquest the Camp of the Mercians in Ye Saxon Heptarchy*,[666] presumably added by Joseph Dougharty, who certainly had an interest in antiquities. The Heptarchy (from Greek *hepta*, 'seven' and *arkho*, 'to rule') is a collective name applied to the Anglo-Saxon kingdoms of England during the early Middle Ages: East Anglia, Essex, Kent, Mercia, Northumbria, Sussex and Wessex. Those kingdoms eventually unified into the kingdom of England. The term has been in use since the 16th century, but the idea that there were seven Anglo-Saxon kingdoms is attributed to the chronicler Henry of Huntingdon in the 12th century and was first used in his *Historia Anglorum*. Particularly noteworthy is the fact that the feature on the 1728 map was identified not as a simple linear earthwork, but as an enclosure – an *Old*

---

[663] The curved trench would seem to have far more substantial than a typical wood bank, with which Joseph Dougharty would in any event have been very familiar.
[664] The First Edition 1" O.S. map of 1836 shows the lane continuing to Montford, and the headland running down towards the Severn.
[665] Information kindly supplied by Mr Tony Oliver, who moved to Greenfields in 1972, and who, with his neighbour at The Clamp, in 2017 had no knowledge of any supposed ancient entrenchment.
[666] This wording corrects that given in HER (PRN) 04647. The second word is particularly indistinct but has been identified under ultra-violet light.

Camp, which implies, intriguingly, that more extensive earthworks may once have existed, for a single ditch is hardly a camp. But what is most extraordinary is that some three centuries ago a connection should have been made not with the Romans or Britons or Druids, as was almost invariably the case with ancient earthworks at that period, but by the Anglo-Saxons, a connection made even more surprising when the village was and is dominated by the remains of a post-Conquest castle. That a trench at Shrawardine should have been associated with the Mercians during Anglo-Saxon Heptarchy cannot easily be explained.

The word *camp*, known in Old English, is discussed in more detail in Chapter 29 in connection with *Camp Feld* in Wednesfield, but in this context the appellation *Camp* is not ancient, but a term reintroduced in the early modern period from French as a term for a military encampment or fort,[667] and its use with reference to significant ancient earthworks was widespread. It would be dangerous to attach undue significance to the Mercian association claimed by the annotation on the map, since archaeology and knowledge of pre-Conquest *burhs* were subjects little understood in the early eighteenth century, but it is clear that some substantial feature(s) must have been detectable which indicated that the curved feature formed part of an enclosure, and in 1728 was held by local tradition – or from deductions made by Joseph Dougharty – be of considerable antiquity, to the extent that it could be firmly identified as Anglo-Saxon in date, and more specifically of the period of the Heptarchy. Whilst that conclusion must be seen as no more than interesting speculation – no empirical evidence could have been available in 1728 to justify such a dating – the feature is unlikely to have Roman, where curved earthworks are uncommon, but that does not preclude an Anglo-Saxon, even an Æthelflædian date, since many other known *burhs* from the period have curved boundaries.[668]

The feature might indeed provide a crucial key to assist in unravelling the name Shrawardine. That the name may incorporate Old English *scræf* in the sense 'a hollow feature', with reference to the substantial ancient curved trench, seems unlikely, since place-names incorporating OE *scræf* are found referring to natural features. Victoria Thompson has noted that *scræf* is a complex word found in connection with burials, often referring in prose to neutral [?natural] landscape features such as caves more frequently than man-made trenches. It does not appear in charters, but in poetry it often refers to hell,[669] although it is unclear to what extent her research may have extended to place-names. Nevertheless Old English *dīc* 'a ditch, an excavated trench', far more commonly found in place-names, might have been expected to refer to an artificial ditch or trench.[670] In short, there seems little evidence to support a case for *scræf* in the name Shrawardine, unless it might signify huts, as one suggestion for Shrawley in Herefordshire.[671]

Another possibility is Old English *scrēad(e)*, meaning 'a piece cut off, a cutting, a shred',[672] with the loss of the final consonant, perhaps used in a similar way to Anglian

---

[667] OED. No earlier name for *The Camp* at Shrawardine is known.
[668] See Hill and Rumble 1996: 189-227.
[669] Thompson 2002: 105, where it is noted that *scræf* is often found in compounds, most commonly *eorðscræf*, used to describe the grave in the OE poems *The Wanderer*, the damned body's grave in *Soul and Body*, and the ambiguous cave/grave space inhabited by the speaker in *The Wife's Lament*, citing Semple 1998: 109-26.
[670] EPNE i 131-3.
[671] Watts 2004: 548. One might imagine temporary huts occupied to those engaged in building *burhs*.
[672] Toller 1898: 840; Oakden 1984: 137; Horovitz 2005: 493.

Old English *snæd*,[673] with reference to the detached part of the parish (and diocese) north of the Severn. However, the word *scrēad(e)* is rarely found in place-names,[674] and the idea can probably be discounted. Other candidates are Old English *scearu, scaru*, an element more frequently found in place-names,[675] perhaps with the possible meaning here 'a shearing, something cut off, a share of land, district, province or nation, boundary', not infrequently found in place-names,[676] used in the sense 'the fortified settlement at the boundary', or possibly the Old English noun and adjective *sceard, scard* 'an incision, a notch, notched, a cleft, a gap, gashed, mutilated',[677] with reference to the gash-like trench of Old Camp, assuming that the feature is older than the place-name. A curved trench is perhaps more likely to have been seen as a gash than a straight ditch. Those elements of course would be pronounced sh–, rather than the Shr– of the place-name, but it might be imagined that the name could easily have been influenced by the proximity of Shrewsbury with its initial Shr–: we have noted that Shrawardine spellings with Scr– (pronounced Shr–) are not found until the mid twelfth century, although that is readily explicable.

Could the name Shrawardine (albeit with *worðign*, rather than *worðig*), a name evidently well-established by 1086, support the existence of a pre-Conquest *burh*, possibly even a double-*burh*, at a place then known as *Scergeat* (a name discussed in more detail below) on which work began on 6 May 912, the place subsequently becoming known as *scraef* or *sceard worðign*, which developed into Shrawardine?

The construction of *burhs* within a few months of each other in the same year at *Scergeat* and *Cwatbrycge* implies that they may have been in the same general area, or at least not far distant: in 913, the year following the construction of those fortifications, Æthelflæd built *burhs* at Tamworth (the core of *Ærest Myrcnaland*, 'first or original Mercia', as recorded in the *Tribal Hidage* probably between the seventh and ninth centuries)[678] and Stafford, in the same county. It is worth noting that those places (both on tributaries of the Trent) are some 20 miles apart, and that Little Shrawardine and Quatford (both on the Severn) are less than 27 miles apart and in the same county. And if Little Shrawardine might indeed be the same place as *Scergeat*, it is surely more than coincidence that as the second and third *burhs* respectively built by Æthelflæd following the battle of Tettenhall, both lay at important Severn crossings, one west of Shrewsbury, the other south-east of

---

[673] EPNE ii 277.
[674] The element is unlisted in EPNE, though it may be the first element of Shredicote in Staffordshire, some 30 miles to the east, where the exact application there is unclear: Horovitz 2005: 493; cf. Scredington, Lincolnshire, which may incorporate the element, in which case it could refer to the position of Scredington on a strip of land cut off by streams: Watts 2004: 533.
[675] For example Sharoe Green, Lancashire; Sharow, North Yorkshire: Watts 2004: 539-40.
[676] (EPNE ii 109-11; EPNE ii 102; counties with places incorporating the element include Lancashire, North Yorkshire, Northamptonshire, Cheshire and Shropshire: Watts 2004: 539-40; EPNS 43 (1967) 213; EPNS 54 (1981) 331; EPNS 82 (2006) V 281. For a discussion of the name Skilgate in Somerset, formerly held to mean 'boundary gate', see Mills 1997: 241-3). J. J. Anderson notes that 'B[osworth] T[oller] has two articles, one for *scearu*, var. *scyru* 'tonsure', another for *scearu* 'groin', but it is reasonable to regard these as one word, with the basic sense 'cutting, division'; cf. *OED* s. Share, sb.² and sb.³': Anderson 1977: 104. OE *scearu, scaru*, like OE *scear, scer* either derive from or are intimately related to Old English *sceran* 'to cut'. Behind these words is the idea 'to divide or separate by cutting ... or (to cause) to deviate from a course': Partridge 1966: 613. Tetsuji Oda, in a paper on the sound symbolism of words beginning *sc-* in OE Heroic Poetry, concludes that 'Words begininning with the bilateral OE *sc-* (>ModE *sk-/sc-*) are traced back to their supposed IE roots [the majority of which have the meaning] 'to cut' and 'to cover': Oda 2010: 56.
[677] Clark Hall 1960: 292.
[678] Hill and Rumble 1996: 19 fn.2; Featherstone 2001: 23-34.

Shrewsbury, with *Cwatbrycge* known to have been used by the Northumbrians as a crossing point before that conflict, as well as the site of a wintering camp fourteen years earlier.[679] Neither can the site of the strategic ford across the Severn at Buttington, where the Danes were besieged by English forces in 893, be overlooked. It is very clear that the river Severn was to be a – if not *the* – major factor in military planning 912, just as the Trent tributaries, the rivers Tame and Sow, would be when Tamworth and Stafford were fortified the following year.[680] It would be surprising if an important ford (especially Shrawardine) would have been left unprotected by a *burh*, and that such locations would not have been a pressing priority in Æthelflæd's *burh*-building campaign. It should also be remembered that Worcester, and its bishop, Werferth,[681] one of the greatest scholars of his age, were especially favoured by Æthelred and Æthelflæad, who may have chosen to be buried there before re-establishing St Peter's church at Gloucester, both places, like Shrewsbury, lying on the Severn and exposed to attack from the river.

But unlike Alfred's *burhs*, which formed an integrated and inter-related programme collectively designed to deter Danish aggression and provide defended bases from which to launch attacks on enemy raiding parties, the *burhs* of Mercia seem, rather, to have developed rather as a rolling programme of individual responses to specific Scandinavian (and possibly Welsh) threats, with *burhs* often lacking the relative proximity to other nearby *burhs* which was an important – indeed critical – element in the selection of *burh*-sites in Wessex. That conclusion about Æthelflæd's *burhs* should, however, be tempered by the realisation that our knowledge of Mercian *burhs* extracted from the various annals and chronicles is almost certainly incomplete, perhaps very significantly so: the north-west Midlands, for whatever reason, is not included in the so-called *Burghal Hidage* which concentrates mainly on *burhs* within Wessex,[682] and many minor, short-lived and incompleted *burhs* within Mercia – and some, perhaps many, probably constructed by Æthelred from the late ninth century – must remain unknown to us, though place-names may nevertheless offer a valuable clue to their former existence. Any such exercise, however, is fraught with problems, not least by the multifarious applications of (to take just one example) the element *burh* in place-names, ranging from abandoned prehistoric sites and Roman enclosures to (later) manor houses and monasteries.[683]

The location of the *burh* at *Cyric byrig*,[684] almost certainly Chirbury, 14 miles south of Little Shrawardine, shows that three years after *Cwatbrycge* and *Scergeat* were built – wherever the latter was located – Æthelflæd had particular reasons to further secure and reinforce her western border.[685] Those same reasons could well explain the construction of

---

[679] It is of course not inconceivable that during their raiding within Mercia before the battle of Tettenhall the Scandinavians had also crossed the Severn at Shrawardine.
[680] Whitelock 1961: 62.
[681] Werferth was bishop of Worcester from 872 to 914/5: Williams, Smyth and Kirby 1991: 235.
[682] See Hill and Rumble 1996.
[683] Parsons and Styles 2000: 74-85; Bapty and Ray 2016: 227.
[684] ASC 'C'; Earle and Plummer 1892-99: 99.
[685] Walker suggests that the *burh* at Chirbury may have been a reconstruction or extension of a temporary fortification created by the English as a base during the siege of Buttington, 9 miles away, in 893 (Walker 2000: 105), though the distance makes that unlikely. Wainwright concluded that relations between Mercia and the Welsh were not good during this period, with the *burh* at Chirbury built apparently in anticipation of trouble from Wales, but presumably based his conclusion about the relationship with the Welsh on the location of the *burh*: Wainwright 1975: 90. There is no evidence that the Welsh, almost certainly less well equipped than the English and Danes, posed any particular threat at this time, but the absence of evidence may be misleading.

an earlier *burh* at Shrawardine. In the absence of any evidence of significant Welsh threats against Mercia at this time – a presumably isolated episode in 916 when Æthelflæd sent an army to Brecon after an abbot and his companions were killed in mysterious circumstances[686] is noted elsewhere in this volume, but the background to this violent episode is unknown, and the disturbance may have been more serious than we are led to believe – it is reasonably clear that the *burh* was a response to the Northumbrian raid into the area to the west of the Severn in 910 and the great Viking fleet from Brittany which had entered the Severn estuary in 914 and raided along the Severn into Wales and around Archenfield, south of Hereford, before being driven off by the men of Hereford and Gloucester. There would also be memories of the siege of the Danish camp at Buttington on the Severn in 893, and doubtless other unrecorded lesser incursions.

Worthen, midway between Shrawardine and Chirbury on a Roman road from Viroconium heading towards the Roman fort at Forden Gaer, and equidistant from Buttington and Chirbury, is another place in the area incorporating *worðign* in its name which might be associated with Æthelflæd's *burh*-building programme. All these possibilities, though, can remain no more than conjecture.[687]

The quest for *Scergeat* is made no less difficult by the variety of spellings in various sources,[688] including *Sceargeat*,[689] *Scargate*,[690] *Sceargete*,[691] *Scoriate*,[692] *Scorgate*,[693] *Sceargate*,[694] and *Strengate*.[695] Those problems are compounded by different early copies of the same text giving variant spellings. But the derivation proposed above for the name Shrawardine might itself provide a solution to those difficulties, for what might be the first element in that name, Old English *scræf*, may sometimes be found in the metathesised form *scærf*.[696] That word (with the loss of its final syllable, as in the case of *scræf* in Shrawardine), would readily explain the first element of *Scergeat*, in which case we have evidence suggesting that the names Shrawardine and *Scergeat* might incorporate the same element and indeed be the same place. Alternatively, the word *sceard* may be found in both Shrawardine and *Scergeat*.

No less problematic is the second element of *Scergeat*, the meaning of which is in little doubt, for the spellings show it to be Old English *geat* 'a gate, a gap, an opening, a ravine or pass',[697] often used for physical gaps in earthworks or walls or entrances to parks,

---

[686] Whitelock 1979: 214.
[687] PN Sa: I 328; Ray and Bapty 2016: 294. For a discussion of various *burh* and *worðign* names in the wider region, including Westbury, Thornbury, Worthenbury, Buttington, and Berrington, some of which might be associated in some way with Æthelflæd's campaign at this period (but which could be much earlier), see Ray and Bapty 2016: 293-7. Curiously, that list omits the significant name Pontesbury, a place which has a road layout suggesting a pre-Conquest enclosure, perhaps the *byrig* or fortification in the place-name: PN Sa I 238-9. The name Westbury may denote a *byrig* west of Pontesbury: ibid. 306-7.
[688] A useful summary of variant spellings and sources is given in JBAA 31 (1875) 162-3 fn.2.
[689] Simeon of Durham.
[690] Florence (John) of Worcester.
[691] Roger de Hoveden.
[692] Henry of Huntingdon.
[693] John Leland, following Aelred of Rievaulx.
[694] Roger de Hoveden.
[695] Matthew Paris. See also Kerslake 1875: 161-2.
[696] EPNE ii 113-4.
[697] EPNE i 198.

enclosures and the like.[698] One very small clue that might link Shawardine and *Scergeat* is the obscure place-name Red Shore in Wiltshire, which incorporates *sceard* (conceivably found in the name Shrawardine) which has replaced *geat*, possibly suggesting that in some cases the terms were synonymous.[699] The problem is identifying any obvious *geat*-like (or *sceard*-like) feature at Shrawardine.

Since both Quatford and Little Shrawardine are notable, as we have seen, for great riverside mottes (usually seen as post-Conquest structures), and meetings were anciently (i.e. in the Anglo-Saxon period) held at mounds, and mounds were often created to mark meeting places, for practical as well as symbolic reasons, with assemblies often held at fords,[700] we might be justified in speculating that the mound at each ford may originally have been created to designate an important pre-Conquest feature, possibly a meeting-place (we have seen that Shrawardine lies on the boundary between the Anglo-Saxon peoples of the *Wrocensæte* and the *Magonsæte*, and the boundaries of three early dioceses meet there), and adapted later by the Normans as a ready-made motte.[701] We might speculate further, in attempting to identify what feature may have given rise to *geat* in *Scergeat*, that if *two* mounds might have existed at Shrawardine in the Anglo-Saxon period, as they certainly did later, one on each side of the river (the diocesan meeting point lies north of the river), and were later incorporated into Norman castles, that might explain the *geat* element, with the two mounds representing a gate or entrance. Or the *geat* may have referred to some impermanent feature long-since vanished. But those can be no more than rather wild, fanciful, and contentious speculations, and like the first element of Shrawardine, the *geat* in *Scergeat* must remain a mystery.

What is more clear is that if Shrawardine and *Scergeat* might be the same place, the enigmatic entrenchment at *The Camp* could even tentatively be associated with Æthelflæd's *burh* built in 913, as the extraordinary annotation on the 1728 map might imply. The original name *Scergeat* could have supplanted by the name Shrawardine when the *burh* had been completed, which would explain the element *worðign* and the disappearance of the name *Scergeat* after 912.

Little Shrawardine (with a ford that might be of Roman date or earlier) is 7 miles north of a major Roman road running from Viroconium via Forden Gaer to Caersws and mid-

---

[698] In that respect the introduction of the so-called tower coinage of Edward the Elder (or possibly Æthelflæd) at about this period should not be overlooked. The coinage is associated with the *burh*-building campaign, and features the image of a tower found mainly on Chester-minted coins of the period, perhaps to be associated with the refortification of Chester in 908: Walker 2000: 124; Karkov 2011: 128-9. However, the elaborate three-storey tower (or gatehouse) illustrated on such coins might denote a very much smaller object, such as a reliquary.

[699] EPNE ii 101.

[700] For meeting places in the region see Gelling 1992: 142-4; Pantos 1999: 91-112; and for assembly places generally Pantos and Semple 2004.

[701] Interestingly, the Shropshire historian J. E. Auden refers to 'a very perfect Saxon "mound", all that is left of the stronghold which probably gave its name [which he held to be 'Castle of the Shire-reeve or Sheriff'] to the village ...' (TSAS 2nd Series VII (1895) 120-1), and the eminent antiquary W. G. D. Fletcher mentions that 'the existence of an artificial look-out mound commanding the river, shows [Shrawardine's] importance when the "ford of Shrawardine" was in frequent use': TSAS Second Series X (1898) 116-7. Note also the recent discovery that the huge mound at Skipsea Castle near Bridlington, East Yorkshire, believed to be a Norman motte, is some 2,500 years old, and another mound at Marlborough School has been dated to 2,400 BC: *The Guardian* 3 October 2016. Many ancient mounds may be far older than hitherto believed.

Wales, with the *burh* at Chirbury, built in 915, some two miles from that same road.[702] Chirbury lies a mile from the English-Welsh border, is near Offa's Dyke, and is less than 4 miles east of the Severn. The *burh* controlled the main route through Montgomery into (and from) central Wales. The *burh* at Quatford was sited midway between Shrewsbury and Worcester, protecting an important Severn crossing that we know was used by the Danes, and a *burh* at Little Shrawardine would have provided protection for another important route and Severn crossing in the northernmost reaches of the Severn, virtually adjoining the western border of Mercia, and in particular serving as an outlying defence protecting Shrewsbury, certainly the most important centre between Chester and Worcester, which had probably been provided with *burh* defences by at least 901 when the Hiberno-Norse were attemting to settle in Anglesey and North Wales.[703] Those *burhs* might also tell of a greater threat from the west than hitherto supposed: Wainwright, though of course without knowledge of the site of *Scergeat*, noted that with Chirbury, *Bremesbyrig, Weardbyrig*,[704] Chester and *Cwatbrycge*, it could be used against the Welsh,[705] though Viking incursions via the Severn were certainly a major threat, as shown by the dramatic raid of 914,[706] which we might suppose was just one of many other less significant raids, both earlier and later, which have gone unrecorded.

---

[702] For the Roman road to mid-Wales see O.S. 1:625,000 map of Roman Britain, 6th edition, 2011. The road runs from Westbury to Forden Gaer, south of Margary route 64, but is unlisted in Margary 1977; see also ASC 'C'; Swanton 1996: 99. Westbury, a name likely to denote a military association, lies on that road. The place is at the junction of routes into Wales, and a small D-shaped enclosure in the centre of the village may preserve the outine of a fortification: PN Sa I 307.

[703] The presence of Æthelred and Æthelflæd at Shrewsbury in 901 (evidenced by S.221) may have been associated with the construction of a *burh* there at that time. Circumstantial evidence from coins of Æthelstan minted at Shrewsbury certainly imply a *burh* in existence between 925 and 939: Baker 2010: 89.

[704] Numismatic evidence shows that coins were minted at *Weardbyrig* (the name meaning 'watch or lookout stronghold') in the reigns of Æthelstan and Edgar, indicating that it was a place of some size which survived for some years, located perhaps in the general area of Chirbury or Runcorn with which it is listed (Whitelock 1961: 64), or in the general vicinity of Gloucester/Hereford/Shrewsbury: Elmore Jones and Blunt 1955-7: 494-8; Hill and Rumble 1996: 165; Coates 1998: 8-12; Naismith 2014: 73. The place has been tentatively identified with both the lost *Wæstbyrig* (ASC 'C' s.a. 1053) and Gwespyr in Llanasa, Flint, North Wales (Coates 1988), or Whitchurch (Carroll 2010: 251-4).

[705] The chronological sequence of *burh*-building in the West Midlands during the first decades of the tenth century was *Bremesbyrig* (910), *Scergeat* (912), Quatford (912), Tamworth (913), Stafford (913), Eddisbury (914), Warwick (914), Chirbury (915), *Weardbyrig* (915), Runcorn (915), and Thelwall (by Edward in 919). If Little Shrawardine is indeed the site of *Scergeat*, a map displaying the *burh*-building sequence (for example Gelling 1992: 129), but excluding the northern outliers Runcorn and Thelwall, shows a gradually expanding spiral running anti-clockwise (with Warwick an aberration), which if correct might suggest a long-term strategy executed by a mobile team of skilled military specialists, surveyors, carpenters, artisans, navvies and supervisors, planned well in advance by Æthelflæd, rather than a programme formulated on an ad-hoc basis, perhaps providing tenuous confirmation for the general area of *Scergeat*, and possibly implying that *Bremesbyrig* should be somewhere in north Shropshire, north Staffordshire or south Cheshire, and *Weardbyrig* could be in south Shropshire or north Herefordshire, though the crudeness of the hypothesis will be readily apparent, and indeed Professor Richard Coates has plausibly suggested that *Weardbyrig* might be Gwespyr at the mouth of the Dee near Prestatyn (which would place it in the Runcorn/Thelwall grouping): Coates 1988. For the possibility that *Wæstbyrig*, where according to ASC 'A' Welshmen killed many English guards (*weardmenn*) in 1053 might be Westbury in Shropshire or Gloucestershire, see PN Sa: I 306-7; Hill 2001: 182.

[706] ASC 'A' (917); 'C' and 'D' (915); Whitelock 1961: 63.

Many promising sites for *Scergeat* have been put forward over the years,[707] with the difficulties highlighted, for example, by various attempts, none entirely convincing, to identify conclusive archaeological evidence for the exact location of Æthelflæd's *burh* at Chirbury.[708]

Comparisons between Quatford and Shrawardine may usefully be summarised as follows:

Shrawardine	Quatford
- on a great loop of river Severn, 7 miles west of Shrewsbury	- on a great loop of river Severn, 20 miles south-east of Shrewsbury
- south-facing headland	- west-facing headland
- on major ancient ford	- on major ancient ford
- overlooks floodplain	- overlooks floodplain
- on no known Roman road	- on no known Roman road
- on boundary between folk-groups of the *Wrocensæte* and the *Magonsæte*	- meeting point of the folk-groups of the *Wrocensæte*, *Hwicce* and *Magonsæte*
- deviation in boundary to include land on opposite bank	- deviation in boundary to include land on opposite bank
- meeting point of dioceses of Hereford, Lichfield and St Asaph	- meeting point of dioceses of Hereford, Lichfield and Worcester
- motte high above river bank slightly upstream of ford	- motte high above river bank slightly upstream of ford

This chapter unapologetically incorporates much speculation, but has nevertheless adduced evidence which attempts to place *Scergeat* at Shrawardine. The philological evidence is admittedly at best equivocal, but the strategic location and importance of Shrawardine seem incontestable, and the site of *Old Camp* would have fulfilled all the necessary requirements for an Anglo-Saxon fortification. But most importantly, Shrawardine was ideally placed to serve as an Æthelflædian *burh*, forming a key part of Æthelflæd's strategy along the Severn in 912. It would be pleasing to think that the solution to the identity of the lost *Scergeat* was in reality solved some three centuries ago by Joseph Dougharty, a little-known map-maker and mathematician from Worcester, with the answer almost staring us in the face from a worn and faded but still captivating parchment map now slumbering in a Shropshire archive. If the mysterious *Scergeat* should prove to have been concealed for more than a millennium in the landscape at Shrawardine, credit for its discovery should properly rest, albeit belatedly, with the erudite Joseph Dougharty. But historians relish the hunt, and there is little doubt that the location of the elusive *Scergeat* will continue to excite their interest for many years to come.

---

[707] The first edition of this work, for example, discussed the possibility of an identification of *Scergeat* with Shugborough or The Walls at Chesterton.

[708] Another place which has not previously been considered as the site of an Anglo-Saxon or Danish fortification is the Roman site at *Letocetum*, which from the remains recorded in the eighteenth century, with walls up to 12' high, must have been of considerable strength, probably incorporating a *geat* or gateway astride Watling Street in the Anglo-Saxon period, and occupied a strategic position on the major Roman road close to the western edge of the Danelaw. Three separate finds of complete Viking cigar-shaped silver ingots and a fragment of a fourth from the area (PAS records WMID-F6EEFO, WMID-OB3FC7, and WMID-C36B61), discussed elsewhere in this volume, serve as hard evidence for a Scandinavian presence in the late ninth or early tenth century, and their significance should not be underestimated. Roman sites refortified by the Anglo-Saxons included Gloucester, Chester, and possibly the Roman fort at the confluence of the rivers Medlock and Irwell, in Manchester: Griffiths 2001: 177. In 917 four of Æthelflæd's thegns are said to have been killed within the gates of 'Derby' (ASC 'C'; Swanton 1996: 101); those defences were more accurately those of the Roman fort at Little Chester: Birss and Wheeler 1985: 11.

11. The tenth-century topography around Quatford, Wednesfield and Tettenhall.

Any consideration of the military events of 910 must take account of the topography of the area between Quatford and the Wednesfield/Tettenhall area, those places being historically associated with the battle of Tettenhall. In that respect, the absence of documentary evidence and paucity of archaeological sites and finds means that we are reliant to a great extent on what slight evidence can be gleaned from place-names and field-names. Minor place-names, including names that are likely to have been coined in the post-Conquest period but which could refer to archaeological features that cannot now be indentified, offer some tantalising clues which might provide some insight into the landscape in the Anglo-Saxon period, though such evidence must be used with considerable caution: the exercise demonstrates all too clearly how the interpretation of many place-name elements can be stretched, perhaps well beyond reasonable likelihood, to imply a scene of conflict. Nevertheless many current or former place-names, most of which cannot be dated with certainty but which may well be of Anglo-Saxon origin, have possible military associations. Those names include:

Burcote, two miles north-east of Bridgnorth (SO 747951), possibly from Old English *burh-cote* 'the cottage at the fortification'.[709]

Oldbury, a lost place recorded in field-names between Hopstone and Chicknell, a little under a mile north-west of Claverley (SO 782938)), from Old English *ald burh* 'the old or disused fortification'.[710] Wall Hill (1833 O.S.) is in the same area, but probably refers to a spring, from Mercian Old English *wælle*.

Burhall, a field-name recorded in the eighteenth century on the north-west side of Ewdness at SO 72709830. The antiquity of the name is unknown, but it may incorporate Old English *burh* 'a fortification'. Cropmarks of irregular enclosures have been noted here.

Broughton, 1½ miles south-east of Claverley (SO 8091), from Old English *burh-tūn* 'tūn near the fortified place'. *Burh-* became *Bruh-* owing to metathesis. The nature of the fortification is not known.[711]

Winchester, half a mile south-east of Claverley (SO 7992), which appears on the 1840 Tithe Award, but not the 1833 O.S. map, on the line of a supposed Roman road from Greensforge. The name is probably derived from a field-name *Wincestry Field*, recorded in 1651,[712] which may incorporate the personal name Winsige. The name does not incorporate Old English *ce(a)ster* '(Roman) city, camp'.

Danesford and Upper Danesford 1 mile north-east of Claverley (SO 8093).[713] The present name, which continues to be held as proof for the presence of Danes in the area, is influenced by local antiquarianism in the 18th or 19th century associating the place with the passage of the Danish army in 910. The name has no connection with the Danes, but means 'the hidden ford', from Old English *derne, dierne, dyrne* 'hidden, secret, obscure',[714]

---

[709] See also PN Sa 6: 73-4.
[710] See PN Sa: 6: 27.
[711] See PN Sa 6: 15; TSAS LVI 1957-60 237.
[712] SA 972/2/1/16.
[713] *Danesford* 1833 O.S. *Derneforde* 1291, *Darneford More* 1617.
[714] See PN Sa 6: 16, which gives the modern name Danford.

a common ford-name: cf. Danesford between Bridgnorth and Quatford, which has the same derivation (and mistaken modern association with the Danes).

Hartlebury, some two and a half miles north-west of Bridgnorth (probably a relatively modern name,[715] since early spellings have not been traced), was perhaps borrowed from Hartlebury in Worcestershire.

In addition, there is a cluster of names which may point towards the existence of a chain of look-out points on high ground with a view-field to the west, which includes Tuter's Hill, ½ mile west of Pattingham. The name, recorded as *Tootershill* in1683,[716] and *Tattershill* in 1686,[717] is perhaps from Old English *tōt-ærn hyll 'the look-out-house hill', related to Old English *tōtian* 'to peer, peep, look out', used in place-names for places with far-reaching views, as here, and normally indicative of an ancient hill-fort.[718] However, the 1686 spelling suggests 'Tāthere's hill'.[719] Although the place is the type of location at which one might expect to find a hill-fort, there are no traces or record of any such earthworks here, so the possibility of a derivation from the tutoring or dressing of hemp cannot be ruled out: a Hemp Yard is recorded 'at the back of the church', and one of the Pattingham fields was known as Hemp Field.[720] A field-name *Tutors Hill* is recorded in 1840 south-west of Claverley,[721] with *Little Tutor Hill* and *Big Tutor Hill* found in 1839 attached to the headland on the south-east side of Roughton,[722] and *Totters Bank* and *Totty's Meadow* are recorded at Chesterton (q.v.) near Worfield, which may be from Old English *tōt-ærn: the element *ærn* often becomes *-er-* in modern forms, and at Chesterton is the prehistoric earthwork known as The Walls.[723]

Moving closer to the possible scene of the battle, the landscape of the Tettenhall area is striking. The ancient parish church lies hard against the foot of a long sandstone bluff facing east that runs roughly north-east to south-west and is a watershed, with springs on the north-west side forming the headwaters of the river Penk, which flows north and ultimately to the Trent, and springs to the north-east flowing as Smestow Brook[724] south-east ultimately to the Severn. The land on the summit of the bluff is relatively level. It seems that the original settlement lay at the base of the bluff, although much of modern Tettenhall is on the high ground on the summit, marked as *Over Green* on Robert Dawson's map of the Wolverhampton area,[725] the earliest detailed map of Tettenhall and the surrounding area prepared for the Ordnance Survey in 1816.[726]

---

[715] *Hartlebury* 1815 draft 1st edition 1" O.S. map (B.L.). The name is unmentioned in PN Sa 6.
[716] Pattingham P.R.
[717] Horovitz 2005: 549.
[718] Cf. Tutbury; Toot Hill, Nottinghamshire; Toothill, Yorkshire; Tothill, Lincolnshire and Middlesex; Tuttle Hill, Warwickshire. See Gelling 1997: 147. A useful discussion of *tōt-ærn names is found in Baker and Brookes 2013: 185-8.
[719] Cf. Tattershall, Lincolnshire; Tatterford and Tattersett, Norfolk.
[720] Brighton 1942: 16-7.
[721] PN Sa 6: 28, but the name could well be from the tutoring of hemp, recorded in this area.
[722] Tithe Map.
[723] See Foxall 1980: 31, 54; Gelling 1997: 147; PN Sa 6: 88.
[724] Which rises at Showell (named from the old moated site of Seawall): Shaw 1801 II: 198.
[725] BL map collection.
[726] BL.

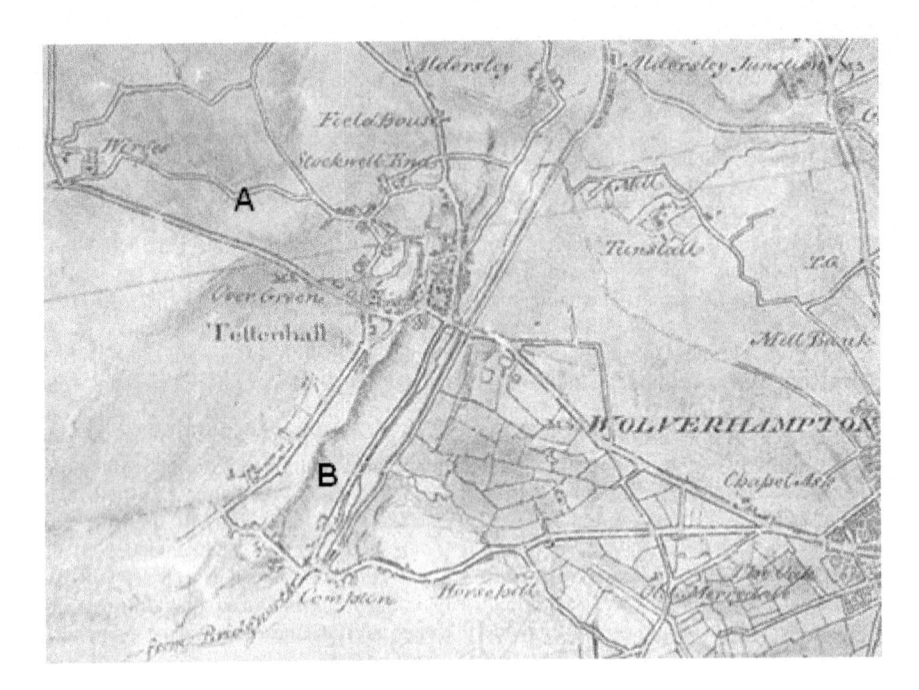

Indistinct but informative map of Tettenhall, from the draft survey of the Wolverhampton area produced by Robert Dawson for the Ordnance Survey in 1816 (British Library). The map shows the old road between Lower Green and Upper Green before the deep cutting was made in 1835. The lane from *Werges* towards *Stockwell End* fell into disuse soon after the survey was made. **A** marks the approximate site of Low Hill Field, and **B** the site of the mysterious mound at Compton.

In 910 the bluff will have formed an impressive and formidable landscape feature, as it does today. To the east, the ground falls away sharply to the valley of the Smestow, then rises gradually eastwards until the gradient increases sharply at the headland on which lies Wolverhampton church some two miles away. The modern road from the west runs through the bluff at Tettenhall via a deep cutting in a more or less direct line to Wolverhampton,[727] but in early times the main route through Tettenhall took a line to the south of the present road opposite the church and ascended the bluff at an angle. The bridge across the Smestow Brook at the foot of the bluff is evidently ancient: the name Newbridge is recorded as early as 1286,[728] and suggests the existence of an even older stream crossing.

---

[727] It is received wisdom locally that Thomas Telford was responsible for the deep cutting in the sandstone as part of his new Holyhead Road in 1835. In fact Telford planned a route from Wolverhampton to Aldersley, and then on to the Wergs, thereby bypassing the ridge altogether. But his plan required approval by the local Turnpike Trusts, and the Wolverhampton Turnpike Trustees rejected his idea, as well as another which envisaged a short tunnel through the ridge, and decided to proceed with their own scheme. They created a steep road in a deep cutting, lined with stone retaining walls, running through the ridge. The spoil was used to construct a rising embankment at the bottom of the cutting, and ramped side roads, and the work was completed in 1823. The old road, still in use, took a more circuitous route to the south: see Hancock 1991: 39-41. A view of Tettenhall before the cutting and embankment were created can be found in Shaw 1798: I facing 199.
[728] Horovitz 2005: 407.

The name Tettenhall is first recorded (as *(æt) Teotaheale*) in the Abingdon manuscript of the *Anglo-Saxon Chronicle* ('C'), which has been dated to c.1048, in the section relating to the battle of Tettenhall.[729] Other early spellings are *(æt) Totanheale*,[730] *Totehala, Totenhale* 1086,[731] *Tettenhala* 1169,[732] *Tettenhal* 1173,[733] *Totenhala* 1190,[734] *Teteneshal'* 1194,[735] *Tettenhale* 1195,[736] 1201,[737] *Tetenhalle* 1196,[738] *Totenhall* 1240 (1798),[739] *Totenhale* 1255,[740] *Tottenhale* 1286,[741] and *Tetnall* 1577.[742] As mentioned previously, William Camden (1551-1623) concluded that the early name *Theotenhall* meant 'the hall of nations or pagans',[743] his derivation based possibly on the Old English word *þēod* 'a people, a tribe, a region' (but not 'pagans'), used in place-names in some such sense as 'public, general',[744] and a second element which he interpreted as 'hall' (but which is from Old English *halh*, meaning 'a nook, a corner'), associating the place with dead Danes who fell at the battle of Tettenhall. Place-name scholars[745] are generally agreed that the forms indicate a derivation from the genitive singular Tēottan of the Old English personal name Tēotta, which is not on record except as Teoda and (in place-names) its diminutive Teodec, the latter representing pet-forms from names beginning *þēod-*. The personal name name Tēotta is also found in Teddington, Gloucestershire.[746]

However, the commanding views from the abrupt sandstone bluff here makes a possible connection with the Old English verb *totian*, Middle English *toten* 'to look-out, spy' difficult to ignore: a century ago the great philologist W. W. Skeat suggested that 'if we take the words as they stand (Anglo-Saxon *Totanhale*, Domesday spelling *Totehala*), then Anglo-Saxon *totan heall* means 'tout's corner'; i.e. a corner (or convenient spyplace) whence a spy looks out. Totan should be To'tan with long o, and is the genitive case of To'ta, a spy, or lookout man. Mod. Eng. Tout for custom. It means the Hall or Dwelling on a look out hill. We should call it Spy Hall if we had to make up the word nowadays'.[747]

That derivation cannot be entirely dismissed, notwithstanding the *Teot-* spellings in the *Anglo-Saxon Chronicle*, which are not found in other records, since there is sufficient evidence for early *Tot-* forms.[748] Indeed, there is a parallel for one of the earliest spellings: the name *totanlege* is recorded in a charter dated 681 of land at Pennard, Somerset,[749] and is evidently from Old English *$\bar{tot}(e)$, Middle English *tote* 'a look-out, a look-out hill', with

---

[729] Thorpe 1861: I 183.
[730] ASC 'D'.
[731] Domesday Book.
[732] Pipe Rolls.
[733] SHC I 68.
[734] SHC II 12.
[735] Pipe Rolls.
[736] SHC II 46.
[737] SHC II 108.
[738] SHC II 57.
[739] Shaw 1798: I xxx.
[740] SHC V (i) 113.
[741] SHC V (i) 166.
[742] Saxton's map of Staffordshire, 1577.
[743] Camden 1806: II 495.
[744] EPNE ii 203.
[745] E.g. Ekwall1960: 463-4, Watts 2004: 605, Horovitz 2005: 531-1.
[746] Watts 2004: 603.
[747] Jones 1894: 8; see also TBAS 1893: 55-6.
[748] A useful discussion of *$\bar{tot}(e)$ names can be found in Baker and Brookes 2013: 185-8.
[749] S.236; Birch 1885-93: I 96.

Old English *leah* 'a wood, woodland pasture'.[750] Somewhat later is *Totenhulle*, found in 1275 and 1327 for Tutnall (Mount), a lost name for a hill in Claines parish north of Worcester.[751] The meaning of the name Tettenhall is therefore likely to be 'Teotta's nook or corner' (with Teotta perhaps an occupational name denoting a look-out man), or 'the nook or corner associated with the look-out',[752] the latter perfectly-suited to the topography. Tettenhall was held by the clergy of Wolverhampton, which explains references to Tettenhall Clericorum,[753] and the king held the manor of Tettenhall Regis. Tettenhall is the name of the civil parish, Tettenhall Regis the ecclesiastical parish. *Tetenhalehome* or *Totenhalehome*, recorded in 1337,[754] incorporate Old English *hām* in the sense 'manor'.

It is important to recognise that some modern place-names may be misleading, which is why it is essential to identify early spellings before derivations can be adduced. A perfect example of a name which might lead the unwary astray is Danescourt (*Danescourt* 1922 O.S.), an area north-west of Tettenhall,[755] which is not of any great age but comes from a Victorian house-name, inspired by local antiquarianism commemorating the battle, attached to a large residence built in 1864 on what was formerly *Low Field* and demolished in 1958.[756]

The name *Tilbury Camp* is recorded in 1894, presumably remembered in, and perhaps located at or close to, Tilbury Close on Castlecroft Hill, and 'some remains of an old fort or earthwork' which seems to have been opposite Wightwick Mill.[757] No other reference to this earthwork has been traced, and the name is almost certainly of nineteenth century coinage. The place lies near *Castlecroft*, which is another name (recorded from at least 1647)[758] sometimes indicative of early earthworks. However, older maps show that the original place called Castlecroft is not on the highest point hereabouts,[759] and it is almost certain that the name derives from Old English *ceastel* 'a heap of stones':[760] Robert Plot records in 1686 peculiar coloured pebbles and stones here.[761]

---

[750] EPNE ii 18-22,184.
[751] Allies 1852: 232, 341; PN Wo 115, where the derivation is given as 'Tota's hill'. Tottenham (Court), *Pottanheale* 1000, *Totehele* DB, *Totenhale* 1254, held to be 'Tota's or Totta's halh' (Ekwall 1960: 478) and Tottenhill, south of King's Lynn in Norfolk, *Tottenhelle* DB, *Totehill* 1251, held to be 'Totta's hill' (Ekwall 1960) may also be noted.,
[752] It would be fanciful to imagine that the name might be associated in some way with the events of August, 910.
[753] See for example SHC XVIII 160.
[754] SHC VI NS (ii) 94-5.
[755] SJ 8800.
[756] VCH XX 8; 1887 1:2,500 O.S. map. The lodge to the house still stands. It is very possible that the house was built on the supposed tumulus in *Low Field*. Other houses named *Danes Hurst* and *Danes Croft* lay to the west on Wergs Road from c.1900 to c.1955.
[757] Jones 1894: 7, 10.
[758] Horovitz 2005: 178.
[759] The field-names *Great Castle Croft* and *Castle Croft* are shown as fields 811 and 796 on the Tithe Map of 1814 between Langley Hall Farm and Castlecroft Bridge at SO864973 and SO 868974 respectively. The 1816 draft 1" O.S. map (BL map collection) and 1834 1" O.S. map show *Castle Croft* at the junction of Radford Lane and Castlecroft Road.
[760] Smith 1956: I 82.
[761] Plot 1686: 156; Shaw 1801 II: *221. It is of interest that the word 'pebble' was used by Plot for stones of immense size: see Plot 1686: 169.

Early spellings show that the place-name Muchall (remembered in Muchall Road), two miles south-west of Wolverhampton, recorded from the end of the twelfth century), is probably derived from Middle English *muche* 'great', or, less likely, from Old English *mūs* 'mice', with Old English *halh*, 'a nook or corner', or *hall*: although the word hall is rarely found in place-names (notwithstanding modern names which appear to include the element, such as Codsall, Pelsall, Ettingshall, Walsall, Willenhall, but which early spellings show do not), there is evidence that during the medieval period the Chapter Court of Penkridge met at Muchall, presumably in some hall-like building.[762] Why it chose to meet there is unclear, but Richard Wilkes noted in the eighteenth century that Upper Penn, then a small town, 'was once of far greater extent and power; for, many of the neighbouring villages owe suit and service to this court, and come here to chuse their constables yearly'.[763] The history of Muchall may repay more intensive investigation: as noted elsewhere, a pre-Conquest routeway running north-west from Wolverhampton was called *penwie* or Penway, suggesting that Penn was at one time of greater significance than Wolverhampton.[764]

In Tettenhall itself no evidence has been traced of any field-names (other than *Lowe-hill Field* which is discussed elsewhere in this volume) which might relate to a battle, but the records are admittedly much fewer for Tettenhall than for other areas.[765]

The natural topography of Wednesfield is strikingly dissimilar to that of Tettenhall. Smallshire has described Wednesfield in the following terms: 'Wednesfield village with New Cross stands on a plain that gradually descends to Portobello and Moseley Hole, at the Wolverhampton to Willenhall road. There is a gradual ascent in general north east, north and northwest, to Essington and Bushbury Hill, but to the west lies the source of the Smestow Brook and tributary of the river Severn. To the south west is Springfield, a somewhat considerable descent after the plain of Heath Town. To the direct east and south east of Wednesfield village runs Waddensbrook, tributary of the river Thame, itself a main feeder to the Trent. Much of the area in the vicinity of the brook was formerly called the Moors or the Marsh from which March End is derived, and an earlier hamlet called Moor End (now untraceable).'[766] Nordley Hill lies on the north-west side of Wednesfield village, with another slight hill on the site of New Cross hospital and a third between the two. A wide raised irregular bank or escarpment runs through the area roughly north of the line of Deansfield Road.[767]

The plain of Wednesfield is lower on the south-east and rises gradually on the north and north-west.[768] Like Tettenhall the area is a watershed: on the extreme west lies the site of Showell (or Seawall) Moat, the source of Smestow Brook (which flows through Tettenhall), a tributary of the Severn. To the east and south runs Waddens Brook, a

---

[762] Horovitz 2005: 402.
[763] Shaw 1801 II: 218.
[764] Hooke 1983: 72-5.
[765] For field-names in Tettenhall see MA 1883 83-6.
[766] Smallshire 1978: 9. Could this be 'a certain hamlet ... called Mora' recorded in Wolverhampton (Stowheath) in 1242 (SHC 1911 144)? March End appears as *Marshend* on the 1st edition 1" O.S. map of 1834. At least three archaeological assessments have been made on areas in Wednesfield: Brereton 1996, Tyler 2010 and Tyler 2010a.
[767] McC. Bride 1997: map 2.
[768] Wednesfield town centre lies at 482', Amos Lane to the north rises to 500', the area on the north-east of New Cross hospital is 511', Heath Town is 480', Strawberry Lane 446', and the area along Waddens Brook 435' or thereabouts: www.daftlogic.com accessed 29 September 2015.

tributary of the river Tame which appears to rise at the site of the former Moat House Farm and flows southwards across Waddensbrook Lane and Watery Lane and joins another streem to flow eastwards through Willenhall and eventually into the Tame and Trent. Further west, a stream, perhaps known as Caldwall, appears to have risen close to Well Lane[769] (mentioned in 1642[770] and which probably took its name from the spring), and ran south before turning south-east towards the southern end of Neachells Lane near the former Neachells railway bridge.[771] Another minor watercourse seems to have run from near Well Lane via Neachells to join Waddens Brook to the south-east.[772] As will be seen, Waddens Brook, Caldwell or the minor un-named stream may be important clues in our search for the battlefield of Tettenhall.

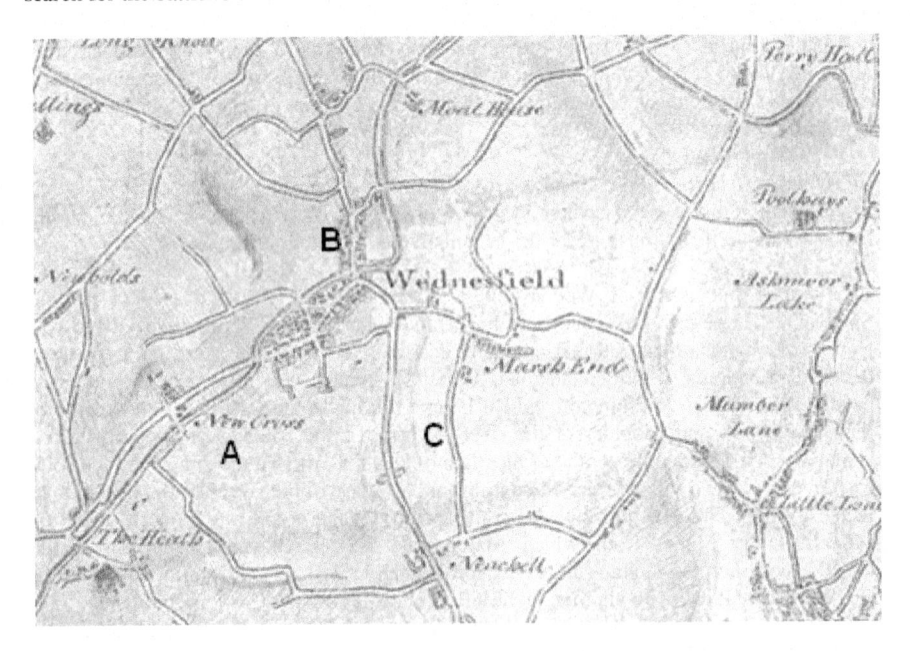

Indistinct map of Wednesfield, from the draft survey of the Wolverhampton area produced by Robert Dawson for the Ordnance Survey in 1816 (British Library). The principal roads are shown, but no watercourses (British Library). **A** marks the approximate position of The Great Low, **B** of North Low, **C** of Southlow.

The soil in Wednesfield is heavy clay,[773] with various types of volcanic stone, including dolerite and 'greenstone', lying close to the surface.[774] The area from Bushbury to New

---

[769] Recorded in 1702: Smallshire 1978: 94-6.
[770] Smallshire 1978: 94.
[771] 1895 1" O.S. map. Modern development has made it difficult to locate early watercourses in and around Wednesfield. The stream to Neachells Lane does not appear on the 1st edition 1" O.S. map of 1834.
[772] Curiously, Robert Dawson's detailed O.S. drawing, produced in 1816, and of inestimable value in any study of the history of Wednesfield, shows no watercourses around Wednesfield – even Waddens Brook is missing: BL online gallery of first edition 1" O.S. draft surveys.
[773] Smallshire 1978: 52.
[774] Problems encountered in the development of the area since c.1900, which in some cases necessitated the use of explosives to remove rock formations, are mentioned in Smallshire 1978: 9.

Cross Hospital overlies a thick band of chert, divided geologically by the Western Boundary Fault from the area to the east of the hospital to Perry Hall Estate, which overlies dolerite, from which it seems likely that the pre-Conquest landscape will have been marshland and heathland or moor with stunted bushes elsewhere, and areas of woodland to the north-west, later commemorated in the names Wood End, Wood Hayes, and especially Prestwood, the name applied to the Domesday woodland pannage ¾ mile long and 660 yards wide held by the canons of Wolverhampton in 1086.[775] However, the absence of names ending in *–ley* (from Old English *lēah*, denoting ancient woodland) are notable by their absence in the Wednesfield area. *La Hethe* in Wednesfield is recorded in 1262,[776] and it is known that North Low (Nordley) on the west side of Wednesfield lay in an area known as *The Old Heath*, recorded as *Norlowefeld Super le Oldehet* in 1347.[777] The same name was also attached to the area between Wolverhampton and Portobello, remembered in the name Old Heath Lane, In more recent times *Heath* is shown on William Yates' map of Staffordshire, 1775, as the earlier name of Heath Town, otherwise *Wednesfield Heath*. The same place is marked as *The Heath* on Robert Dawson's draft map of 1816.[778]

Considerable quarrying has been carried out in the Wednesfield area in recent centuries, which with the creation of canals and railways, mines and factories, has in many places greatly altered the landscape.[779] Further evidence that the area was in general terms bleak heathland interspersed with marshland, small woods and areas of higher land is provided by names such as *Quebbefield* (from Middle English *quabbe* 'marshy place, bog'), one of the great open fields in Stowheath to the east of Wolverhampton, Old Fallings (Park), Wood Hayes, Friezeland,[780] Wood End, Stowheath,[781] Short Heath, *Fennilydyat*,[782] *Croumore*,[783] *Salamonnes More*,[784] Ashmore, *The Moor*,[785] March End,[786] *le fen de la Heth*,[787] and Bentley.

The name Wednesfield has been associated with the battle of Tettenhall for over a thousand years, and is first recorded between c.978 and 988, as *Vuodnesfelda campo*. It is generally agreed by place-name scholars that the first word of the name means 'Woden's

---

[775] VCH IV 45. In 1286 a complaint was made against the Dean of Wolverhampton that he had 'made new destruction of the woods of Wednesfield': Smallshire 1978: 45.
[776] SHC 1999 33.
[777] SRO D593/B/1/26/6/2/4; SRO D593/B/1/26/6/2/17.
[778] BL map collection.
[779] See especially McC Bride et al 1997, which includes a map of made ground (map 16).
[780] From OE *fyrs* 'furze': Foxall 1980: 50. The place is remembered in the name Friesland Drive.
[781] Recorded as *Stowheth* c.1272: Horovitz 2005: 517. Some enclosure of the waste of Stowheath had occurred by 1623: SRO D593/J/22/7/17.
[782] Recorded in the 14th century: SRO D593/B/1/26/6/2/3.
[783] Recorded in 1365: SRO D593/B/1/26/6/19/17. *Quabbefield*, also called *Wyndmill Field* in 1614 (SRO D593/B/1/26/11/4) lay in *Croumore*, and adjoined *Redestret* in 1404: SRO D593/B/1/26/6/19/17; SRO D593/B/1/26/6/23/4.
[784] Recorded in 1493 in Wednesfield, 'on the road to Lichfield': SRO D593/B/1
[785] Recorded in Wednesfield in 1536: SRO D593/B/1/26/6/8-9.
[786] Recorded as *Marsh End* c.1658 (Smallshire 1978: 40), perhaps to be associated with *Marsh*, recorded in 1300 (ibid. 50), and William *Atte Mersshe* of Wednesfield, recorded in 1388 (SRO D593/B/1/26/6/36/10)).
[787] Recorded in 1317 (SRO D593/B/1/26/6/14/13), and probably *the Hethe alias the field of Diminsdale in Willenhall* (on the west side of what is now Heath Town) recorded in the late 13th century (SRO D593/B/1/26/6/39/5.

feld or open land'.[788] That word and *campo* are considered in more detail elsewhere in this volume.

In Wednesfield, *Le Palmeresberie* is recorded near *le Portwey*, probably somewhere near the junction of Amos Lane and Lower Prestwood Road, in the 14th century.[789] The name, doubtless associated with *Palmersknolle* in Wednesfield recorded in 1346,[790] is intriguing, for it would appear to be from *Palmer's burh*, meaning 'the fortification or fortified house or manor house associated with the palmer or a man (or indeed woman)[791] called Palmer'. The word (and name) Palmer is post-Conquest, from Old French *palmier, paumier*, and was applied to a pilgrim who had returned from the Holy Land, to signify which he carried a palm-branch or palm-leaf. The word was also applied to an itinerant monk under a perpetual vow of silence, and was also used as an alternative word for a pilgrim.[792] It may also be noted that *burh* may in some place-names refer to a monastery or manor house, with reference to a surrounding wall,[793] and the possibility cannot be excluded (though it is not likely) that the name refers to some early religious site, since the two elements can each have a religious connotation.

The spurious confirmation of the grant by Wulfrun to the monastery of Wolverhampton of estates including Wednesfield includes in the boundary clause of Wednesfield a reference to *Byri broc* – recorded as *Berrybrook* in 1588[794] – now Bury Brook or Waterhead Brook, which runs along the north-west corner of Wednesfield into Bushbury parish to join the river Penk.[795] The identity of the *burh* or fortification or manor house from which the stream takes its name is unknown, but might conceivably be *Le Palmeresberie* (above).

An intriguing field-name *Herebrekusbruche* is recorded in the area c.1320.[796] The precise meaning of the name is unclear, but the final element is Middle English *breche* 'land broken up for cultivation', a not uncommon element in this area. The first element is probably from an Old English personal name, many of which began *Here*,[797] and is unlikely to be Old English *here* 'army'. The middle element may be a corrupted fragment of a *Here*– name, but may be Old English *bræc* (the source of modern *brake*) 'copse, thicket'. It is probably safe to rule out any possibility that we have a minor name incorporating memories of the great battle.

One of the four open fields of Wednesfield was called *Luchfield*,[798] also found as *Lechefield* in 1840, and *Leachfield* in 1842,[799] which lay between the village and

---

[788] Ekwall 1960: 503; Gelling and Cole 2000: 269-74; CDEPN 658.
[789] SRO D593/B/1/26/6/2/3; Smallshire 1978: 60. It is unclear whether the street-name Palmer Close on the north-west side of Ashmore Park may have any association with this place.
[790] SRO D593/B/1/26/6/2/14.
[791] The Forest Pleas of 1262 and 1270 mention William Palmer of Wednesfield (SHC 1999 38, 87) and Margery the Palmer [of Wednesfield?] is recorded in 1314: SRO D593/B/1/26/6/35/3.
[792] Shorter OED.
[793] Parsons and Styles 2000: 77.
[794] Perambulation in Bushbury Manor Papers, Foxley Collection, Hereford Record Office.
[795] Hooke 1983: 72-5.
[796] SRO A/2/21.
[797] See Searle 1897: 292-5.
[798] Smallshire 1978: 53. For field-names in Wednesfield extracted from the Plea Rolls of 1430 see SHC 1896: 121. Frustratingly, the list concludes with the words 'Several other pieces of land are here mentioned'.
[799] TA.

Moathouse Lane, near the junction of Woodhouse Road and Lichfield Road.[800] The earliest spellings which have been traced are *le Lachefeyld* in 1303,[801] *le Lachefeld* in 1389,[802] *Lachefeild* in 1537[803] and 1614,[804] and *Latchfield* is also found.[805] The name is almost certain to derive from Old English **læc(c)*, **lec(c)*, **lece*, Middle English *lache*, *leche* 'a slow or boggy stream', a common element in the West Midlands, usually found as *lache* or *letch*, where the meaning 'swampy boggy ground' is sometimes more appropriate,[806] which would suit the topography here perfectly, for the place lies near the headwaters of the streams that join to form Waddens Brook. The name is found locally elsewhere,[807] but we may note that Old English **læcce*, Middle English *latch*, meant 'a trap' or similar,[808] which might arguably be appropriate for a place where an enemy army was cornered (though that is certainly stretching the interpretation here), and Old English *lāc* (pronounced 'larch') had a number of meanings, including 'play, sport', but also, more significantly, 'strife, battle', and 'sacrifice, offering'.[809] The possibility that the name records the site of a battle cannot be discounted entirely, and the possible association with sacrifice or offering is particularly noteworthy given the pagan associations of the name Wednesfield. It would be particularly unfortunate if the name were to be dismissed simply because a boggy stream existed in this area if (which must be quite possible) the same area also happened to be the site of a tenth-century battle. The name *Luchfield* is commemorated in Lakefield Road, in the centre of Wednesfield.[810]

One flatt (a narrow strip sometimes called a furlong) within *Luchfield*, adjacent to the Wolverhampton to Lichfield road, and possibly near the junction of Wood End Road and Lichfield Road, was known as *Battgate Flatt* in 1642. The name may be from Middle English *bat*, from *debat* 'debate, strife', so 'the disputed gate' or 'the gate where the dispute took place', but more likely from Middle English *bat* 'clod of earth', or with reference to a mineral called batt found in this area.[811]

---

[800] Smallshire 1978: 96; 53, at approximately SJ 954017 (although the Tithe Map shows *Leachfield* at SJ 950006). The other fields were Northlow Field (recorded as *Northlowfeld* in 1355: SRO D593/B/1/26/6/3/15), Southlow Field and Church Field.
[801] SRO D593/B/1/26/6/34/6.
[802] CCALSS DCR/19/11/5.
[803] SRO D4407.
[804] D440/85[SF102]. The name *Lachefolang* [*recte Lachefurlong?*] appears in the same document.
[805] SHC 1931: 82. The name is no doubt to be associated with *Lechmore* or *Lichmore* recorded in this area by Stebbing Shaw in 1801, and linked by him with the battle of Tettenhall (Shaw 1801 II: (147) fn.3), presumably in the belief that the names incorporated OE *līc* 'body, corpse'. Scott 1832: 332 records that 'On viewing the spot [Wednesfield], June, 1829, nothing worthy of observation occurred, though the attention of the visitor was directed to the field to which the inhabitants applied the term litch, or lech.'. Local residents doubtless became aware of the supposed significance of the name from Shaw's comments. But the name could arguably be from OE *lāc mōr* 'marshland associated with a battle', though *lache moor* 'the marshy land with the boggy stream' must be more likely..
[806] EPNE ii 10; PN Cheshire II 256.
[807] See for example The Laches in Brewood parish, 5 miles north-west of Wednesfield: Horovitz 2005: 351. The element *lēce* appears to be relatively uncommon, however: it is unmentioned in the standard work on English field names: Field 1982.
[808] Cf. Latchingdon, Essex: Watts 2004: 362.
[809] Clark Hall 1960: 208.
[810] Although *Luchfield* lay on the Lichfield Road, the name is clearly not derived from the name Lichfield. By coincidence (one assumes), a broad plain called Lechfeld near Augsburg in Southern Germany was the site of a great battle in August 955, when the forces of Otto the Great annihilated a huge army of Magyar archers.
[811] '... those substances which divide the strata of coals and iron ores are called Batts by the miners; they are generally black, consisting of a matter peculiar to themselves, and are of a texture nearest

The Wednesfield Tithe Apportionment of 1842 includes the name *Bellimore Piece*.[812] The name appears on the Sutherland Estate map of 1764 as *Bellmoor Lane*,[813] and *Bellemore House* is marked on the south side of Lower Prestwood Road, near its junction with Amos Lane, c.1888,[814] commemorated in the name Bellamy Lane.[815] The element *belli* or *bello* means in Latin 'war, battle', but it would be very unusual indeed to find a name incorporating both Latin and English elements, and place-names incorporating Latin terms are in any event extremely rare. It is possible that *Belli-* is the result of nineteenth century antiquarianism attempting to manipulate *Bellmoor* into a name to be associated with the great battle. However, the name *Bellmoor Lane* has an ancient and certain pedigree, unrelated to any battle, for it is recorded as *Belamyealone* in 1376,[816] evidently incorporating the surname Belami, from Old French *bel ami* 'fair friend', and indeed John Belami of Wednesfield is recorded in 1262.[817] *Lone* is the early form of lane.

The name *Sechmore Meadow* is recorded in Wednesfield in 1427. The meaning is probably 'the sedgey or reedy moor', from Old English *sedg*, but *sedg* could also mean 'a warrior', though that derivation can probably be ruled out here.[818] A personal name Sedg is also on record.

One puzzling reference is to *land called Newbold alias Ballyscyles* recorded in 1585,[819] with *Ballyscyles* or variants mentioned at various other dates. The meaning of *Ballyscyles* remains unclear.

The place-name *Wollesford* in Wednesfield is recorded in 1361.[820] The location is unknown, but the *ford* element shows that it lay on a watercourse, possibly Waddensbrook although that is far from certain. Without early spellings, on which all place-name research depends, it is not possible to identify the derivation of the first element, but it may well be from an Old English personal name Wiglāf or Wulflāf.[821]

A field-name *Wollmore Bruche* is recorded in Stowheath in 1325,[822] and as *Wolemerebruche* in 1351.[823] The names are puzzling, with their location uncertain, and despite their superficial similarity with the name *Wollesford*, mentioned above, seem to be unrelated to it. Old English *mere* meant 'a pool', and *mōr* 'a moor, marshland', probably relating to the same feature, a boggy pool. *Bruche* is from Old English *Bryce* 'newly broken ground', a very common element in this area. The names are unlikely to incorporate Mercian Old English *wælla*, *wælle* 'a well, a spring, a stream', since that element usually becomes *wall* in this region, but we may note that Old English *wæl* meant 'slaughter,

---

like marle, though some of them are fossile, and others have different substance, etc.': Shaw 1801 II: 13.
[812] TA number 871, lying at approximately SJ 946007.
[813] Smallshire 1978: 57. *Castle Inn* lay nearby: ibid.
[814] 1:2,500 O.S. map 1887-9.
[815] Smallshire 1978: 57.
[816] SRO D593/B/1/26/6/4/17.
[817] Reaney and Wilson 1997: 37; SHC 1999 36.
[818] Lawley 1868: 32; EPNE ii 117.
[819] SRO D593/B/1/26/11/10.
[820] SRO D593/B/1/26/6/3/20.
[821] Cf. Wollaston in Northamptonshire and Shropshire.Watts 2004: 693.
[822] SRO D593/B/1/26/6/14/7.
[823] SRO D593/B/1/26/6/3/7.

battle', which might conceivably give here 'the pool/marshland associated with a battle', though the spellings tend to refute that idea.[824]

Field-names incorporating the name *Chester Hill* appear in the 1842 Tithe Apportionment of Wednesfield in the area of what is now known as Nordley Hill.[825] The name is most unlikely to be from Old English *ceaster*, usually applied to old fortifications or Roman remains: no earlier spellings have been traced, and the name may be of nineteenth-century coinage. It is unlikely that the field-names are to be associated with *Palmeresberie*. Other field-names of interest are *Castle Grounds*[826] and *Castle Field*, probably named after the Castle Inn.[827]

At some date in the thirteenth century before 1269 is a reference to a place in the area described as the *fossatum Wulfrini* 'the entrenched place of Wulfrini',[828] who is surely to be identified (through the correction of a typical misreading of minims) as Wulfrun, the name Wulfrini being otherwise unrecorded. Indeed, it may not be too fanciful to consider whether the *fossatum* may not be the *valla monasterium* of a church pre-dating the monastic church refounded by Wulfrun in Wolverhampton c.994.[829]

A thirteenth-century reference to *le olde Borewardes Croft in territorio de Bentley*, 'the old fort-warden's or (more probably) boar-keeper's croft in the land pertaining to Bentley',[830] refers to land, said to have been bounded by a ditch, near *Kirnesford* (also found as *Curtlesford, Curtle(s)ford* or *Kirclesford*),[831] a place perhaps to be identified with Moseley Hole, the site of Stowman's Hill,[832] due east of Wolverhampton and south of Wednesfield: *Curtleford* is mentioned in the deed that includes the reference to *fossatum Wulfrini*. The former deed also mentions a *Horestan*, which lay somewhere not far distant from *byribroc*

---

[824] The existence of a rare OE word *wal* meaning 'a rod, a stick, a staff' has also been noted (Earle 1888: 462-3; Smith 1956: ii 245 records the existence of OE *walu*, 'a weal', used topographically of 'a ridge of earth or stone'), which brings to mind the claim in Egil's Saga that the battlefield of *Brunanburh* in 937 was marked out by hazel rods (Pálsson and Edwards 1976: 119), though the element *wal* has not apparently been noted in any other place-name, and it is not likely here: care must be taken to ensure that evidence is considered objectively, and that too much weight is not attached to illusory place-name associations.

[825] At approximately SJ 947005.

[826] At approximately SJ 963012.

[827] Smallshire 1978: 57. *Castlefields* is shown on the 1842 Tithe Map, but the Sutherland Collection map of 1764 (SRO 593/H/392) gives the name *Home Closes*: Smallshire 1978: 59.

[828] Mander and Tildesley 1960: 28, who suggest that it may have lain in the Blackhalve area, or somewhere in Short Heath. Smallshire suggests that it may have been in the Noose Lane/Portobello area: Smallshire 1978: 45.

[829] In that respect we might note that the name Wolverhampton may mean either 'the high *tūn* associated with Wulfrun', or 'the chief *tūn* associated with Wulfrun'. The name is first recorded as *Heantune*, with Wulfrun's name added a century or so after her time, and the former is generally accepted as the correct derivation, though Stenton preferred the latter.

[830] Reaney and Wilson 1997: 76 (sub nom Burward). Bentley lay in the parish of Wolverhampton; Bentley Hay was perhaps what became known as Short Heath: Mander and Tildesley 1960: 29. Cecily Bereward, widow, is recorded in the Wolverhampton area in 1454. The surname, if correct, means 'keeper of the bear' (Reaney and Wilson 1997: 34), but a connection with the Bentley name cannot be ruled out.

[831] A field-name *Curtlesford* is recorded in Cannock c.1290: PN Staffordshire I: 54. The name may incorporate the OE personal name *Cyrtla, probably found in Kirtling, Cambridgeshire, and Kirtlington, Oxfordshire, but otherwise unrecorded, though the dative –n– would normally have been expected rather than –s–.

[832] Mander and Tildesley 1960: 2, 28-9.

(Bury Brook or Waterhead Brook noted above, the stream mentioned in Wulfrun's charter that ran eastwards from Underhill near Bushbury)[833] and may be the *haran stan* which appears in that same charter, though *horestan* is a common name in charter boundaries, used generally of boundary stones.[834] It is difficult to know whether the 'boar warden's croft' may be connected with *Wardesleiheye*, recorded in 1273,[835] which would appear to be from Old English *weard* 'watch, watchman, look-out place', with Old English *lēah* 'clearing', and Mercian Old English *(ge)heg* 'fence, enclosure', so 'the enclosure associated with the watchman's clearing'.

Various references to *Le Burycroft*[836] and *Buricroft*[837] ('the croft or small field associated with the fortification or manor house') which possibly lay at Willenhall, are perhaps to be associated with the names *Far*, *Middle* and *Near Bury Field*[838] on the 1840 Tithe Map of Willenhall.[839] *Burilane* in Wolverhampton parish (which included Willenhall) is recorded in 1504.[840]

The royal manor of Wolverhampton, curiously unmentioned in Domesday Book given that Samson the Clerk, who may have been responsible for the compilation of the great record (the evidence continues to be debated)[841] held the church of Wolverhampton, and may have lived there,[842] is estimated to have been of three hides. Bilston was a royal manor in 1086, and had probably long been so. In the time of Henry II (1154-89) it is described as royal demesne with Bilston, Willenhall and Tettenhall, and c.1239 is said to have included Dunstall, Willenhall and Bilston.[843] Stowheath, a mile or so to the east of Wolverhampton, to the south of the road to Willenhall, is a name traced from at least 1272[844] – and is perhaps much older – formerly applied to one of the three manors of Wolverhamton (two belonging to the church and one to the king), formed probably in the early thirteenth-century by uniting the local royal manors of Bilston, part of Willenhall and one half of Wolverhampton, including the site of St Peter's church.[845] It was by far the largest of the three Wolverhampton manors, for it included not only a large part of Wolverhampton as far as the Halfway House between Wolverhampton and Tettenhall, but also Bilston and a considerable part of Willenhall, but the boundaries were always vague, and small islands of one manor are found scattered within others.[846]

Stowheath is a name which may be of considerable siginificance. The name incorporates Old English *Stow* which can mean simply 'place', but sometimes carries the particular

---

[833] Hooke 1983: 73-5.
[834] Mander and Tildesley 1960: 2, 28-9. Duignan identifies the stone as a boulder lying in a ditch on the south side of the road midway between Perry Hall and Marsh End: Duignan 1888: 12 fn.8. The place may have been somewhere near the western end of Pool Hayes Lane.
[835] SRO D1790/A/2/71.
[836] Temp. Ed.I/II SRO D593/B/1/26/6/92; 1362 SRO D593/B/1/26/6/19/17; 1413 SRO D593/B/1/26/6/24/1.
[837] 1323 SRO D593/B/1/26/6/9/7.
[838] At approximately SO 969998.
[839] *Burycroftlone* is recorded in 1438: SRO D593/B/1/26/6/25/1.
[840] SRO D/593/B/1/26/6/28/5.
[841] Harvey 2014: 111-12, which incorporates a useful summary of Samson's life.
[842] SHC 1916 185.
[843] VCH IV 5, 44.
[844] Horovitz 2005: 517.
[845] WA II 103. Pasture called *Stow-brook* is recorded in 1458 (Price 1835: 23), but has not been located.
[846] Mander and Tildesley 1960:26-7.

meaning 'place of assembly', specifically 'holy place', often associated with a religious site or building, a meaning which by the mid-tenth century was a normal term for a religious establishment.[847] The most obvious derivation is from the church founded or re-founded by Wulfrun, perhaps the predecessor to the present church, so 'the heath associated with the holy estate known as *stow*', and though the use of the word in that way has not been traced elsewhere, it is not inconceivable that Stowheath itself was the site of a Christian place of worship. In that respect we may note that one of the four great open fields of Wednesfield lay to the south-west of the village, on the west side of Neachells, south of New Cross,[848] and was known as Churchfield.[849] By this date the term *field* had evolved into its modern meaning of an enclosed area of cultivation or pasture. Could that name commemorate a church that once existed somewhere in this area?[850] It will be seen that other *Chirche*-names within Churchfield might tend to support that theory. The medieval capital messuage of Stowheath appears to have been at a moated site one mile to the south-east of Wolverhampton,[851] and such sites often incorporated a church, though none has not been traced in records relating to the area. The *stow* element is also found in Stowlawn and Stowman's Hill in the same area.[852]

The name New Cross, which attaches to an area some two miles south of Stowheath, is of uncertain age – it is first recorded on the 1" O.S. map of 1834 on the road between Wolverhampton and Wednesfield, and is shown as a cluster of half a dozen buildings on the Wednesfield Tithe Map of 1842 – and might suggest the possibility of an 'old' cross,[853] in which case one would like to know more about the origin and nature of such older monument. It is almost certain, however, that it marks a new crossing of the Wyrley and Essington canal, constructed under an Act of 1792: New Cross lay on the west bank of the canal, near a bridge, and the road across it is New Cross Avenue.

---

[847] Blair 2005: 217 fn.145, which contains a useful comment on *stow* names.
[848] It has been suggested that the field extended north of Wolverhampton road (Smallshire 1978: 53, 95), but that seems unlikely.
[849] Smallshire 1978: 53, 56.
[850] Since the name Stowheath has not been traced before the Conquest it could have originated in the ME period, when *stow* may have carried the meaning 'track' or 'passage' or similar, although other examples of that use come from Cambridgeshire and Lincolnshire in the east of England (EPNE ii 159-60), and that meaning here seems unlikely. Sawyer 1981: 162 suggests that in some names the meaning may be 'market'.
[851] At SO928982. It was subsumed by the Chillington Iron Works: Cockin 2000: 561. It might be mentioned that the river Smestow, which rises near Showell and runs south to the river Stour, does not incorporate the element *stow*, but was originally Smestall, from OE *smeðe* 'smooth' or 'a smithy', with Mercian OE *steall* 'a place for catching fish' or 'stagnant water': Horovitz 2005: 498.
[852] *Stouwe mylne* is also recorded in 1316: SRO D593/B/1/26/6/14/12.
[853] References to *Newcroste* in 1670 (SRO D4407/74[SF91], and *New Croste* in 1717 (BCA MS3145/31/4) are likely to be mistranscriptions of *New Crofte*. The name is evidently not to be associated with the curiously-named *Maiottys Crosse* recorded in 1481 between the Wolverhampton to Willenhall road and *Le Longacres* in Wolverhampton (SRO D593/B/1/26/6/13/8), recorded as *Madgetts Crosse* in Willenhall in 1614 (SRO D593/B/1/26/6/11/5), perhaps from the surname Madgett, derived from Magge or Madge (Margery): cf. *the lane called Maggebruche* recorded in Willenhall in 1348 (SRO D593/B/1/20/6/10/9), and *The More meadow (or Magge meadow)* in Willenhall, recorded in 1517 (SRO D593/B/1/26/6/39/10). *Crossbyrches*, recorded in the 14th or 15th century (Shaw 1801 II: 150), is found as *Crosbruche* in 1386 (doubtless associated with land called *Overcrosbruche* and *Nethercrosbruche* recorded in Wolverhampton in 1369: SRO D593/B/1/26/6/20/17, and *Crosbirch in Nechells* in 1669-1670: SRO 1798/666/34), and lay on the road from Wolverhampton to Essington: SRO D593/B/1/26/6/36/7.

On the south side of the road from Wolverhampton to Bilston, about a mile from Wolverhampton, lies Monmore, a name recorded from from the mid-thirteenth century, with the associated names *Monmere* (recorded in 1327),[854] *Monbruche* (recorded from 1386),[855] *Monnemedewe* (recorded from the 14th century) and *Monway (Field)* (recorded in the seventeenth century).[856] The names incorporate Old English *monn, mann*, generally meaning 'a person (male or female), vassal, people, mankind', often denoting common land and applied to land on boundaries,[857] but also with the meaning 'brave man, hero', or 'warrior'.[858] The second elements are Old English *mere* 'lake, pool' (of which all traces have now disappeared from the Monmore area), and *bryce* 'newly-cleared land', in the main a heathland term,[859] and 'meadow', so perhaps giving 'the people's pool', 'the people's newly-cleared land', 'the people's meadow', and 'the peoples way', but it is also possible (though not likely) that *mon-* denotes an association with heroes or warriors.

The place-name Bilston provides important evidence for an early and obscure Anglo-Saxon tribal group, for the name is first recorded as *Bilsetnatun* in 996, incorporating the Old English word *sæte* (genitive plural *sætena*) meaning 'settlers', so giving 'dwellers at the place called Bil'.[860] The meaning of Bil is uncertain, but it may be from Old English *bile* 'bill, beak', used topographically for a beak-like projection. The absence of such a feature at Bilston might indicate that the group originated elsewhere and eventually settled at Bilston. We have no knowledge of the period at which they arrived at Bilston, but since Bilston is barely one and a half miles from Willenhall, we may be entitled to speculate that when King Æthelbald visited the area in 732, he was in the territory of the *Bilsetna*, or (if they were not yet inhabiting the area), in territory which was to become their home and take their name.

---

[854] Mander and Tildesley 1960: 7.
[855] SRO D593/B/1/26/6/36/7.
[856] Horovitz 2005: 394.
[857] Field 1982: 133.
[858] Clark Hall 1960: 229; TOE I: 609; II 1165.
[859] PN Sa IV xviii.
[860] Horovitz 2005: 121.

12. Wednesfield and Woden: pagans and Christianity.

Wednesfield is a place-name of particular interest to toponymists since it has been held to be one of a relatively modest number that seem to provide evidence for religious practices before Christianity gradually permeated the country in an irregular fashion after Augustine's mission of 597.[861] The name is first recorded in Æthelweard's Latin *Chronicon*, written between c.978 and 988, as *Vuodnesfelda campo*, and found subsequently as *Wodnesfeld(e)* in 985,[862] *Wedingfeld* in 1248,[863] *Wudesfeud* 1250,[864] *Wednesfeld* 1251,[865] *Wodnesfeld* frequently 15th century,[866] *Wedffeld* 1532,[867] and *Weddesfeld* 1538.[868] The spurious post-Domesday confirmation, now lost, of Wulfrun's charter to the monastery of Wolverhampton purporting to date from 996 gives the spelling *Wodnesfeld*.[869]

It is generally agreed by place-name scholars that the name means 'Woden's *feld* or open land'.[870] The existence of the name when recorded in the late tenth-century does not indicate that there was a settlement at this date, since it is not in itself a habitative name (i.e. it does not contain any Old English habititive element such as *hām* or *tūn*, both meaning 'village, estate, homestead'), but is a topographical name referring to the nature of the landscape.[871] The conventional wisdom is that place-names incorporating the names of pagan gods (Woden was not used as a contemporary personal name) either date from the earliest period of Anglo-Saxon migration, when pagan gods were still worshipped, or were adopted a generation or so later to reflect local pockets of pagan worship which had managed to survive the introduction of Christianity.[872] Places of pagan worship 'which managed to survive for decades because they were not accessible to [early missionaries] would be more likely to give rise to place-names because they would by that time be felt to be remarkable, as they might not have been when paganism was the only form of religion among English speakers'.[873]

On that basis it has been held that such names in the West Midlands must date from the first half of the seventh century or earlier,[874] perhaps coined by the first Mercian immigrants moving into the area from the Trent and Tame valleys, or from the generation

---

[861] On pagan place-names see especially Gelling 1987; Semple 2013: Appendix 4, 262, which lists all recorded pre-Conquest Woden place and field-names in their literary context. A field-name *Wodnesfeld* is recorded in the north of Essex, but *Wedynsfeld* in the south of that county is now discounted: Stenton 1971: 100; Gelling 1987: 109.
[862] S.860.
[863] SHC IV 111
[864] SHC IV 120
[865] Charter Rolls.
[866] SRO
[867] SHC 4th Series 8 159
[868] SHC 1912 107
[869] S.1380.
[870] Ekwall 1960: 503; CDEPN 658.
[871] It is worth recording that the *feld* name *Wodnesfeld(e)* applying to an estate some 2 miles north-east of Wolverhampton is mirrored by the *feld* (usually identified as Finchfield, some 2 miles south-west of Wolverhampton, a name otherwise not recorded before the 13th century) found in King Æthelred's lost charter to Wulfrun supposedly dated 985: Hooke 1983: 63-5; Horovitz 2005: 256.
[872] See Gelling 1997: 159.
[873] Cameron 1987: 104.
[874] Stenton 1970: 287 observes that '... it is probable, if not certain, that most of the heathen names which can now be identified arose before rather than after the year 600'.

or so after the introduction of Christianity into central Mercia in the mid-seventh century.[875] The name Wednesfield (with that of Wednesbury and Weeford)[876] may indeed be surviving evidence of paganism from the time of the powerful pagan king Penda,[877] or possibly from the reign of Peada's brother Wulfhere, who ruled from 658 to c.674 and who, though a pagan, was not unsympathetic to the Christian mission in Mercia. In that respect we have seen that Lakefield Road, in the centre of Wednesfield, well-recorded in the late medieval period as *Luchfield*, may derive from Old English *lāc* (pronounced 'larch') which had a number of meanings, including 'play, sport', but also, perhaps more significantly, 'strife, battle', and 'sacrifice, offering'.[878] The possible association with sacrifice or offering may be particularly noteworthy in any discussion of pagan place-names, and the connection with battles must be of interest to anyone seeking an early battlefield. On the other hand, the name may (and probably does) incorporate Old English **læc(c)*, Middle English *lache*, most commonly found in the north-west Midlands, meaning 'a stream, a bog, a stream flowing through boggy land, a swampy pool',[879] which would be particularly appropriate for the area to the east and south of Wednesfield.

The second element of the name Wednesfield, Old English *feld*, is believed to have been used originally for a large area of open land, more specifically 'unencumbered ground ... land without trees as opposed to woodland, level ground as opposed to hills, or land without buildings'[880] – the most significant name containing the element locally must be Lichfield[881] – and it was only later that it developed the meaning 'arable land', and 'an enclosed piece of land'. Furthermore, *feld* meaning 'the ground on which a battle is fought' is well-attested in Old English, and as discussed elsewhere in this volume might have that meaning in the name Wednesfield, so giving 'the level tract of treeless open ground associated with the god Woden', or possibly 'the district associated with Woden',[882] or 'the field of battle associated with Woden'. Although, as noted above, the name may have been adopted in the mid-seventh century, we cannot assume that it would have been two centuries old, at least, at the date of the battle of Tettenhall, for the period of dating cannot be known: it is very possible that places acquired their names some time following, perhaps long after, the circumstances giving rise to the name, although Sir Frank Stenton took the view that most such names arose before rather than after the year 600, but that it was dominant in the Midlands until the fall of Penda in 654. He also concluded that 'most of the sites to which they relate were either on the verge of cultivable ground or on conspicuous features of the countryside. Some of them occupy outstanding hills; many are

---

[875] Gelling 1992: 92; Gelling 1997: 159.
[876] However, Sarah Semple suggests that the OE element *wēoh*, 'idol, image', found in Weeford, may have been applied to ancient prehistoric or Roman structures, ritual or otherwise: Semple 2013: 100. Weeford lies on the Roman Watling Street.
[877] Who reigned c.632-55 AD, and whose name may be commemorated in Pendeford, which lies less than four miles from Wednesfield. For a discussion on the possible association of Penda with Wednesbury see Ede 1962: 9-10.
[878] Clark Hall 1960: 208.
[879] Smith 1956: ii 10.
[880] Gelling and Cole 2000: 269-74.
[881] 'The open land at or called *Lyccid*': Watts 2004: 372. *Lyccid* is from Primitive Welsh **Luitgēd* 'the grey wood', from the British form of which the name Letocetum (Wall) derived: ibid; Rivet and Smith 1979: 387-8. The existence of Finchfield on the south-west side of Wolverhampton, probably to be associated with *ðone feld* recorded in 985 (S.860; Hooke 1983: 63-5; Horovitz 2005: 256), should also be noted.
[882] PN Sa 6: 75-6, where it is suggested that the *feld* element of Worfield in Shropshire may have been a district name. For a list of Anglo-Saxon charter boundary clauses incorporating the name Woden and other heathen gods see Semple 2013: Appendix 4.

within a short distance of Roman or other ancient roads, heathen burial grounds, or villages bearing names of an archaic type'.[883] Certainly Wednesfield can be associated with a conspicuous feature of the countryside (the *feld* or open ground on which it stands); it lies on or very close to a lost Roman road from *Pennocrucium* to Metchley and a possible heathen burial ground, as evidenced by at least four or five mounds or lows (*The (Great) Low, Northlow, Southlow, Dunnlow*, and possibly a *Little Low*), in the immedieate area, discussed elsewhere in this volume.

But while the literal meaning of Wednesfield seems clear, there are aspects that remain puzzling. In particular we are entitled to wonder why pagan place-names such as Wednesfield and Wednesbury – some three miles apart – continued to be tolerated in an area so close to a major Christian centre, and were not replaced as part of a cultural cleansing with the introduction of Christianity. Both Wednesfield and Wednesbury (the latter from 'the *burh* or fortification associated with Woden') lie within a dozen or so miles of Lichfield, the hub from which the Christian conversion of a huge area radiated under royal patronage and authority from the mid seventh century, and both places would have been readily accessible to early missionaries and their audiences.[884] Indeed, Willenhall, a mile and a half south-east of Wednesfield, was evidently a place of some importance in the eighth century and perhaps earlier: two charters of King Æthelbald[885] were attested at *Willanhalch*, usually identified as Willenhall in Staffordshire,[886] as early as c.732. These are some of the earliest references to any place in the county, and are of considerable significance, suggesting that there was a high-status, even royal, residence in the area in the first half of the eighth century of sufficient importance to serve as accommodation for the king and the important nobles and bishops in his retinue.[887] It seems likely that the place would also at that time have contained a church. Domesday Book records that the king retained an interest in Willenhall in 1086, and it may well be that we should see

---

[883] Stenton 1970: 286-7.

[884] Those places are even closer to the Roman sites at *Letocetum* (Wall) and it has been noted that in Wessex and elsewhere the pagan Anglo-Saxons generally occupied areas which probably had a substantial rural population in the Roman-British period: see Bonney 1979: 43. It is possible that if those place-names mark places where heathenism continued to a relatively late date, Lichfield may have been chosen as a suitable base for missionary work: Gelling 1992: 96. After careful analysis of Domesday Book estates in south Staffordshire, Dr David Roffe, a leading authority on the great survey, has concluded that *Wodnesfeld* was a vast royal estate extending from Bushbury to Norton Canes and Watling Street in the north, to Little Aston in the east, and to Upper Penn in the south, and Tettenhall to the west, encompassing a fortified nucleus at Wednesbury and other estates such as Wolverhampton, so including Ogley Hay and the site of the Staffordshire Hoard at its northern edge. The import of this sobering assessment, if correct, would be that the battle of Tettenhall could have taken place anywhere within an immense irregular area of perhaps 100 square miles or more. The present author is unpersuaded by the theory since places within such an enormous area would almost certainly have retained traces of the *feld*-name, even after the postulated estate ceased to exist as such, but research over several decades has discovered not one reference to the name *Wodnesfeld* in any early record for any place outside the area immediately surrounding Wednesfield. However, if not named after the battle, it is not impossible that the *feld* of *Wodnesfeld* incorporated both Tettenhall and Wolverhampton (and possibly Wednesbury) in 910. I am grateful to Dr Roffe for making available a copy of his important 2014 paper 'Sitting on the Fence: The Staffordshire Hoard find site in context'.

[885] S.86 and S.87; Horovitz 2005: 578.

[886] The charters are very similar, each being a grant by Æthelbald, king of Mercia, of the toll due on one ship at London to Mildred, abbess of Thanet.

[887] S.86 is attested by the king and 7 nobles or bishops, S.87 by the king and 8 nobles or bishops, being those who witnessed the former plus one other.

Willenhall as a centre of particular importance in earlier centuries.[888] Indeed, it has been suggested that as an Ancient Parish of Wolverhampton, Willenhall (like Wednesfield) had once been a member of Tettenhall.[889] Willenhall probably lay within the great open area or *feld* from which Wednesfield took its name.

Changes of pagan names are not unknown: *Wodnes beorge* in Wiltshire, for example, recorded in 825, is now identified as a neolithic long-barrow known as Adam's Grave,[890] but it is clear that the Church (including the clerical scribes) and a Christian population had no difficulty in preserving and perpetuating the provocative name of a major pagan deity in close vicinity to the centre of Mercian Christianity. Changing a minor place-name is hardly to be compared with the difficulties associated with the change of the name used in speech for a week-day incorporating the name of a pagan god, and it would have been a simple matter to create a new – and overtly Christian – name to replace those older, and presumably distasteful, place-names.

What alternative explanations might be put forward for some place-names involving the names of pagan deities? One possibility, which would admittedly run contrary to the great body of scholarly research which has built up over at least the last century, is that some place-names incorporating the names of pagan gods do not necessarily date from the pre-Christian era, and indeed may be considerably later. In that respect it should be emphasised that whilst place-name scholars have long held that a place-name incorporating the name of a pagan god is to be seen as firm evidence for the worship of that god at that place, no physical or documentary evidence of any kind has ever been adduced to support that conclusion.

Within the Danelaw the organisation of the Christian church had broken down in southern Northumbria and East Anglia during the Danish occupation of the later part of the ninth century, and many of the churches appear to have been dispossessed of their estates. Though the Vikings sacked York in 866, and a later chronicler claims they 'destroyed minsters and churches far and wide with sword and fire', some form of formalised Christianity seems to have survived.[891] The Danes certainly plundered and sacked the minsters within the Danelaw, and the influx of Scandinavian settlers may have introduced Óðinn as a new god, with a particular resurgance associated with the Great Army of Danes which invaded Eastern England in the 860s and 870s. They were followed by settlers from

---

[888] VCH IV 39.

[889] Thorn and Thorn 2007.

[890] S.272; S.1403. Thomas Williams has concluded that 'the name Wodnesbeorg, for example, implies an idea that a quasi-deific primogenitor like Woden could be the sole occupant of a colossal Neolithic chambered tomb. It seems plausible that legendary battles would also have taken on in the imagination the sort of epic proportions in which only landscapes forged at the hands of swollen supernatural entities could adequately contain. The places associated with these stories may well have thus represented exaggerated exempla that informed the ongoing association of conflicts with places symbolic of royal authority in the reigns of Alfred and those who came after him': Williams 2016: 40. Yorke 1995: 168 suggests that the name change may be evidence of a deliberate [Anglo-Saxon?] policy of substituting other place-names for pagan place-names, but the date of the substitution may be relatively recent: no early forms of Adam's Grave are recorded in PN Wiltshire 318. Furthermore, *Wodnes beorge*, together with nearby *Wodnesdene* and *Woddesgeat* (the former recorded in S.449, a charter of 939), lie on or near Wansdyke, found as *wodnes dic* in 903 (13th century, S.368; PN Wiltshire 17), and might be derived from the early name of Wansdyke, which may have been named from its supposed construction by the early king or god, without any direct pagan associations; see also Gelling 1997: 158-61.

[891] Blair 2005: 311-2.

Scandinavia in the later ninth and early tenth century, as evidenced later by some dismissive references in the tenth-century treatise *De falsis deis* by the scholar and homilist Ælfric to the cults of Óðinn, Thor and 'the shameless goddess' Frigg (alias Friya or Freya).[892]

Within Danish Northumbria York minster had evidently continued to function during this period, for 48 pieces of excavated funerary sculpture of all periods from the late seventh to the eleventh century from the cemetery which lies beneath it show uninterrupted Christianity within the city.[893] Wulfhere, Archbishop of York, who was appointed in 854 and held the position until 900, had evidently come to some accommodation with the Viking invaders, for he was temporarily expelled from the city during an anti-Northumbrian uprising in 872.[894] It appears that the Scandinavians of York, whatever their own beliefs, tolerated other religions, and indeed after the death of the Viking leader Halfdan in 883, a Scandinavian, Guthfrith, was chosen as king of York, apparently under the influence of the Abbot of Carlisle. The monks of Lindisfarne who had fled westwards to the Irish Sea with the bones of St Cuthbert could return and establish themselves at Chester-le-Street, presumably under the patronage of Guthfrith. A mid-eleventh century *History of St Cuthbert* describes Guthric's accession ceremony which involved with impressive pragmatism both the holy relics of Christian tradition and the holy gold armrings of Viking heathenism. Evidence of his conversion is shown by his burial in York minster after his death in 895.[895] Clearly Guthfrith's people were Christianised, though we may imagine that their beliefs were tempered with aspects of the old Viking paganism. The Siefred/Cnut coins issued in York at the turn of the ninth century (Siefred from c.895 with his name and the title king) contain Christian crosses, and some even contain Christian inscriptions: *Mirabilia fecit* ('He has done marvellous things'), and *Dominus deus omnipotens rex* ('Lord God, almighty King').[896] In 900, in circumstances which remain unclear, Æthelbald was consecrated in London as archbishop of York to succeed Wulfhere, indicating that the Christian faith continued to be promoted in the region, though there is no evidence that Æthelbald ever travelled to Northumbria.[897]

From 905 coinage from the mint at York Minster (the church of St Peter), carried for a decade or so Christian legends that abbreviate the Latin *Sancti Petri Moneta* ('St Peter's money').[898] The most recent theory suggests that the issue came to an end when the Norse pagan Ragnall secured control of York in 919. A second, less prolific, issue seems to have originated from the York mint in the period 910-19, and may reflect the local economic straits after the battle of Tettenhall had disrupted the commercial links between the

---

[892] Niles 1991: 127.
[893] Blair 2005: 313-4.
[894] Hall 2001: 188.
[895] Owen 1981: 175-6; and especially Downham 2009: 75-77. Æthelweard was evidently no great admirer of Guthfrith, calling him without explanation a 'hateful king': Campbell 1962: 51.
[896] Gooch 2012: 48, 160.
[897] Downton 2009: 82. On the fate of the Northumbrian episcopate see McGuigan 2015: 58-81. It is worth recording that Wulfstan, archbishop of York (931-56), collaborated enthusiastically with the pagan king Olaf (Anlafr) Guthfrithsson (one of the kings defeated at Brunanburh in 937) when he seised the moment and returned from Dublin to York at the death of Æthelstan in 939 to become ruler of Northumbria, with Wulstan's resentment of West Saxon rule said to have 'far outweighed any distaste he might have felt for a pagan warlord'. Olaf and Wulfstan led an army which stormed Mercia in 940 to capture Tamworth (and seize Wulfrun) and take Leicester, Lincoln, Nottingham and Derby from Mercian control: ASC 'D'; Swanton 1996: 111; Holland 2016: 87-8.
[898] Bailey 1980: 42; Logan 1991: 171; Gooch 2012: 60-70.

Hiberno-Scandinavians of the north-west and the Danes of York. The second issue (with sword, appropriate to St Peter, and with Thor's hammer) seems to reflect an ambiguous approach, then current, to the new faith and the old paganism.[899] That approach is emphasised by the enthusiastic collaboration between Wulfstan, archbishop of York (931-56), and the pagan king Olaf (Anlafr) Guthfrithsson (one of the kings defeated at Brunanburh in 937) when Olaf seised the moment and returned from Dublin to York at the death of Æthelstan in 939 to become ruler of Northumbria, with Wulstan's resentment of West Saxon rule said to have 'far outweighed any distaste he might have felt for a pagan warlord'. Indeed, Wulfstan accompanied Olaf when the latter led an army which stormed Mercia in 940 to capture Tamworth (and seize Wulfrun) and take Leicester, Lincoln, Nottingham and Derby from Mercian control.[900]

Evidence of Christian sympathies in other Viking-controlled areas of England may be found in coins with the legend 'Saint Edmund', referring to the king of East Anglia killed by the army of Ivar the Boneless in 869 after the battle of Hoxne in East Anglia. The Edmund coins were appararently produced by the Danish rulers before 900, which suggests that 'his cult was flourishing within a generation of his death, and certainly points to respect and veneration for a Christian martyr among descendants of the leaders of the [Viking] great army'.[901] That view is supported by the paucity of pagan graveyards, apart from Viking graves at Repton and Ingleby, and evidence from the Danelaw of burial in graveyards, most without the deposition of grave goods associated with pagan practices, which suggests that the Vikings who settled in the late 860s and 870s had accepted Christianity by c.900.[902]

Of the pagan deities, Óðinn (who succeeded the far more ancient Tiw, whose name is related to Roman Jupiter and Greek Zeus),[903] was the principal god of the 'official' or 'higher' religion of the Scandinavians in the Migration Age, at least amongst the aristocracy. He was an upper-class warrior god, with the kings playing a key role in the promotion of his cult,[904] although most of the evidence of pagan practices in Viking age Denmark comes from twelfth- and thirteenth-century Icelandic and Norse sagas of uncertain historical value.[905] Óðinn was regarded as higher in the social scale than the other gods, and was especially the god of professional warriors, held in such high esteem that even kings in Scandinavia were sacrificed to appease him in times of disaster. However, the worship of Óðinn is unlikely to have gained a firm foothold even in Northumbria, and there is certainly no evidence that the Northumbrians sought to impose paganism: they seem to have had no interest in restricting or prohibiting Christianity, for after the revanchism of the Danelaw no reconversion was necessary.[906] As Victoria Thompson has observed, 'The men who made up the late ninth-century *micel hæþen here* ('great heathen army') of the Anglo-Saxon Chronicles may have been behaving in a fashion

---

[899] Hall 1981: 134; Higham 1993: 199-200; Price 2014: 187.
[900] ASC 'D'; Swanton 1996: 111; Holland 2016: 87-8.
[901] Crawford 2003: 62.
[902] Pryce 2003: 160; and especially Downham 2009: 77-8. Within Sweden itself Chrisitianity gained a firm footing in the mid-9th century when the Danish chief Harold was baptised on a visit to Louis the Pious, the Frankish king, and on his return brought with him St Anskar: Cross 1971: 388.
[903] Owen 1981: 28.
[904] Hald 1963: 109. Traces of some 30 or so names associated with heathen religion have been recorded in Denmark, at least 600 in Norway, and well over 100 in Sweden: Hald 1963: 99. See also Grimm 1880.
[905] Abels 1998: 150. For examples of pagan practices see Sturlason 1930: 94.
[906] Lawrence 1965: 54.

the chroniclers found shockingly unchristian, but the phrase is not necessarily defining them as committed to a systematically pagan way of life, nor entirely ignorant of Christianity, nor indeed as foreigners.'

That situation was not reflected across the Irish Sea, however, where the Dublin Norsemen appear to have remained heathen until contacts with England and the Hebrides led them to Christianity in the late tenth and early eleventh century.[907] So if the Northumbrians fighting at the battle of Tettenhall were based at York, they were probably Christian, or at least Christianised;[908] if they were Hiberno-Scandinavians from the north-west, which we shall see is more likely, they were almost certainly pagan.[909]

To the Vikings, success in battle was paramount, and Óðinn became the all-important deity for the survival of the invaders. The sacrifice for victory was an age-old central feature of his cult. As early as the sixth century the Byzantine historian Procopius records that the sacrifice most valued by the people of Thule (Norway and Sweden) was that of the first man whom they captured in war, although it is unclear whether 'first' means the first man in number or the first in rank. To support the second interpretation is an account from *Egils saga ok Ásmundr* of the leader of a defeated army being sacrificed to Óðinn for victory, as was king Ælla of Northumbria: 'All Ásmundr's men had fallen and he was himself taken prisoner. It was then evening. They had decided to slay him at the morrow at Árán's tomb, and give him to Óðinn that they might themselves have victory'.[910] Procopius also tells of the human sacrifice of Goths by the Frankish King Theudebert in 539 AD as 'the first-fruits of the war. For these barbarians, though they have become Christians, preserve the greater part of their ancient religion'.

One source records that half those slain in battle belonged to Óðinn and half to the god Freya, the female deity who is sometimes said to have been his wife. According to the Icelandic writer Snorri Sturluson, who died in 1241, Freya 'rode to battle and took one half of the corpses and Óðinn the other half'.[911] As god of war he was not seen merely as a deity who glorified conflicts in their own right, but was above all the arbiter of victory as his alias Sigtyr, or 'victory-god', suggests.[912] Prior to battle near Uppsala, probably in the 980s, the Swedish King Erik the Victorious dedicated the army of his enemy Styrbjörn to Óðinn.[913] Adam of Bremen, writing in the second half of the eleventh century, confirms the Swedish practice of sacrificing to Óðinn before hostilities, and such ritual may well have been a significant feature for a Danish army wintering in England.[914]

Evidence from Irish annals for the ritual slaying of churchmen by the Vikings is ambiguous, since accounts which mention martyrdom are inconclusive. There is, however, considerable evidence of the ritual killing of Irish secular leaders by the Danes. In 859 King Maelguala of Munster was put to death by the Vikings. The *Cogadh Gaedhel* records

---

[907] Smyth 1977: 168; Smyth 1984: 210-14.
[908] Though Sihtric Caech, King of Northumbria 920-7, who married a sister of Æthelstan at Tamworth in 926 is said to have renounced his pagan beliefs at the ceremony, but when the marriage failed soon after 'restored the worship of idols: Giles 1892: 245; ASC 'D'; Swanton 1996: 105..
[909] 'The presumption is that Guthfrith [king of Dublin who unsuccessfully attempted to seize York in 927] was not a Christian': Charles-Edwards 2013: 522.
[910] Smyth 1977: 221.
[911] Branston 1974: 35.
[912] Smyth 1977: 192.
[913] Branston 1974: 39.
[914] Smyth 1977: 223.

that 'his back was broken on a stone', implying a ritual slaughter. The incident is referred to in a passage in the Norse *Eyrbyggja Saga* which describes a *thing*, or meeting place, in western Iceland before the introduction of Christianity in 1000 AD: 'There is yet to be seen the judgment-circle where men were condemned to be sacrificed. In that circle stands the Stone of Þórr, over which those men were broken who were to be sacrificed, and the colour of the blood on that stone is yet to be seen. At that thing was one of the holiest places'.[915] In 916 King Gébennach, who ruled a kingdom near Limerick, was slain and decapitated by a Scandinavian army led by Ragnall, king of York and Dublin.

On the other side of the coin, in pre-Christian times the pre-eminent pagan god of Anglo-Saxon England, adopted from the Germanic pantheon, was Woden, equivalent to Óðinn, and god of wisdom, divination and battle.[916] But of how such gods were worshipped we have little knowledge: there is little direct evidence of any worship of Woden in England, or of Thunor or the other deities of the old religion – indeed, Woden rarely appears in Old English literature, which was written entirely in the Christian epoch – though Bede mentions a chief priest, Coifi, who turned against his gods, and another priest mentioned in Stephen of Ripon's *Life of Wilfred* who behaved more as a magician.[917] The name Woden, however, is well evidenced in place-names both lost and current, and is not known to have been used by mere mortals.

The conversion to Christianity of the Anglo-Saxons of West Mercia, where Anglo-Saxon cemeteries are rarely found, is held by some historians to have come about by the acceptance of Christianity by the incoming Anglo-Saxons from the native British population, with the incomers otherwise retaining their cultural practices, principally language, but possibly also their ancient rites and superstitions, although others agree with Bede that the Britons made no effort to convert the Anglo-Saxons.[918] Enclaves of non-Christians may have co-existed in parts of the West Midlands late into the Anglo-Saxon period.[919] In fact there is surprisingly abundant evidence from references to pagan practices in laws from the time of Alfred[920] – i.e. after the Viking invasions – to explain why Pope Formosus found it necessary to write to the bishops of the English in the 890s, a mere decade or so before the battle of Tettenhall/Wednesfield, to warn that he had learned 'that the abominable rites of the pagans have sprouted again in your parts'.[921] It is uncertain whether the warning was associated with the burgeoning Hiberno-Scandinavian

---

[915] Smyth 1977: 217-8.
[916] Hald 1963: 108.
[917] Lapidge et al 1999: 351-2. Bede is seen by some modern scholars as a 'fundamentalist' who 'turned on the heroes of the English non-Christian past his unrivalled capacity for withering silence': Church 2008: 180.
[918] Higham 2002: 65.
[919] The *pagani* recorded in *Wreocensetun*, 'the territory of the Wrekin-dwellers', in a Mercian charter of 855, less than 60 years earlier than the date of the battle of Tettenhall/Wednesfield (S.206 – see Gelling 1992: 83; also Whitelock 1955: I 90; 485-6; Finberg 1961: 48 no. 77) are likely to have been Danish raiders, perhaps even the Danes described as the 'Black Gentiles' who devastated Anglesey c.853 and are recorded in the *Annals of Ulster* in 855 (Wainwright 1975: 86-7), rather than established occupiers, though whether a transient raiding party could be expected to have been referred to in those terms in a contemporary charter must be open to debate. See also Fletcher 1997: 369-416; Nelson 1999: I 52.
[920] See in particular Chaney 1970, on which much of the remainder of this paragraph is based, and North 1997.
[921] Whitelock 1955: 820. Pagan practices are also mentioned in the laws of Edward the Elder, Æthelstan, Edmund, Aethelred the Unready, and Cnut.

settlements in the north-west, greatly strengthened by the influx of Hiberno-Norse after their expulsion from Dublin c.901.

But Pope Formosus's warning was more likely to have been caused by activities associated with aspects of heathenism in Anglo-Saxon England which had almost certainly never died out completely: it seems likely (and should come as no surprise) that well into the Christian period – indeed until well after the Norman Conquest – a sizeable proportion of the Anglo-Saxon population retained a belief in some aspects of the ancient pagan religion whilst outwardly practising Christianity.[922] Cult survivals are evidenced by the continuation or resurfacing of superstitious practices such as incantations and auguries, the veneration of stones, trees and wells, magic potions, ancient customs concerning the sun and the moon, and witchcraft. King Æthelstan sought to combat pagan practices by declaring '... with regard to witchcraft and sorcery, and deadly spells, that if it causes death, and the accused is unable to deny it, then his life should be forfeit',[923] and as late as the early eleventh-century the laws of Cnut condemn the heathen practices of witchcraft, divination, or idolatry, with the latter helpfully described as 'if one worships heathen gods and the sun or the moon, fire or flood, wells or stones or any kind of forest trees'.[924] Those proscriptions were almost certainly directed not at the old Germanic paganism introduced from the Continent by the Angles, Saxons, Jutes, Frisians and Franks, but rather the pagan worship of the Scandinavians who had settled in England during the Viking age.[925] Proof that pagan practices continued in England notwithstanding the spread of Christianity may be revealed in an entry in the *Anglo-Saxon Chronicle* 'D', which records that in 926 – a decade-and-a-half after the battle of Tettenhall – King Æthelstan met with a number of sub-kings from Wales and Scotland at Eamont in Westmorland where they pledged peace to him, and 'they forbade all devil-worship and then parted in concord'.[926]

No semantic sophistry or casuistry can help to explain the apparent longevity of the place-names Wednesfield and Wednesbury if they were coined in the pagan Anglo-Saxon period, that is in the period from the first arrival of the Angles, Saxons and Jutes in the fifth century to about the mid seventh century. That the name Wednesfield could be interpreted as 'the field or plain upon which Woden gave victory to the English' (with reference to the battle of 910), or 'the field or plain upon which Woden was vanquished', coined after the Northumbrian defeat as a contemptuous memorial to the site where a great slaughter occurred of those who worshipped the god, with the deaths of the pagans seen as evidence of the derisory protection afforded by their god and of the supremacy of the

---

[922] Illuminating references to heathen activities are found in Anglo-Saxon Penitentials, catalogues of sins and of the penances demanded of the sinner, and in the secular law codes of the Anglo-Saxon kings, which, as well as predictable prohibitions on the worship of idols, the practice of witchcraft and the casting of spells, forbade more esoteric activities such as placing children on a roof or in an oven or drawing them through a hole of dug-out earth at cross-roads to cure fever or infirmity: see Meaney 2006: 147, 152-3.
[923] Laws 2 Æthelstan 6; Holland 2016: 70. For an estate in Ailsworth, Huntingdonshire, forfeited in 948 by a widow and her son for attempting to encompass a death by witchcraft, see Whitelock 1930: 129-30.
[924] EHD 455; Meaney 2002.
[925] Niles 1991: 127.
[926] Swanton 1981: 107. Charles-Edwards sees the *Chronicle* entry not as evidence that any of the parties to the treaty followed such practices, but as a reference to the cause of Christianity in opposition to Scandinavian paganism: Charles-Edwards 2013: 522.

Christian beliefs of the victors, can probably be dismissed as fanciful.[927] But whilst it might seem unthinkable that a supposedly Christian society would incorporate the name of a pagan god into a place-name, it is equally difficult to explain how pagan place-names supposedly coined in the earliest period of Anglo-Saxon occupation, or adopted later to record long-lived pagan practices, remained unchanged thoughout the centuries of Christianity,[928] and indeed why some large areas of Anglo-Saxon England, notably East Anglia, from which the pagan Angles gradually spread westwards into areas including Mercia, are devoid of such place-names.

That the pagans sacrificed to Óðinn for the acquisition of victory and courage was known among the English, as confirmed by the nobleman and chronicler Æthelweard.[929] But it should not be overlooked that Æthelweard, a highlyeducated ealdorman writing towards the end of the tenth century, believed that Woden had been a real king from whom Æthelweard himself was descended,[930] and that Woden had received divine honours after death.[931] There is no reason to imagine that during much of the Anglo-Saxon period that belief was not widely shared, perhaps at every level of society.[932] Indeed, Anglo-Saxon royal genealogies invariably, and with pride, traced lines of descent back to Woden: eschewing reservations about promoting a pagan deity, Bede noted that Woden was the ancestor of Æthelberht of Kent, and even Alfred the Great, 'that paragon of Christian kingship ... paraded a West Saxon genealogy which alleged he was descended from the bloodthirsty and cruellest of Germanic war-gods, Woden'.[933] John Nils has noted that in various parts of the *Anglo-Saxon Chronicle*, Woden is identified as the ancestral figure from whom kings of the Kentish, Northumbrian, Mercian and West Saxon lines claim descent. He believes that was attributable to a reinvention of pagan culture by Christian authors by euphemising the pagan gods as real humans, thus weaving them into Christian history. In the mid-ninth century the West Saxon royal genealogy was recreated whereby Woden was identified as the son of a certain Frithuwald, who in turn was descended via fifteen generations from the son of Noah, whose ancestor nine generations earlier was no less than Adam himself, and so linked directly to 'our father Christ'.[934] The pedigree of the kings of Mercia as set out in the so-called *Anglian Collection* (probably originating in Northumbria)[935] begins with a certain Wihtlæg, said variously to be the son (*Anglo-Saxon Chronicle*), grandson (*Anglian Collection*), or great-grandson (*Historia Brittonum*) of Woden, and the euhemerizing treatment of Woden is believed to be a late innovation within the genealogical tradition which arose during the Christianisation of the Anglo-Saxon kingdoms, the derivation of kingship from a god perhaps rooted in Germanic

---

[927] It is difficult to know what to make of Tom Holland's cryptic observation that an 'Infallible token of God's hand was to be found in the site of the great battle, for it preserved in its name the echo of earlier, darker times, before the light of Christ had purged the shadows: Woden's Field': Holland 2016: 41.
[928] Stenton 1970: 286 fn.2 recognised that names associated with pagan religious beliefs are likely to have been changed, citing Gadshill [Isle-of-Wight] as an example.
[929] Campbell 1962: 7.
[930] Cheney 1970: 39.
[931] Cheney 1970: xxi.
[932] See Yorke 2001: 17-18, who notes: 'Whether Woden was actually seen as a divine ancestor has been questioned', citing John 1992.
[933] Smyth 1998: 25. Hodgson 1939: 686. In East Francia the biographer of Otto the Great (912-973) thought Woden descent important: John 1992: 127.
[934] Niles 1991: 135. For the idea that the claim that English kings were descended from Woden is of Kentish origin see John 1992: 127-34.
[935] John 2002: 130-1.

paganism.[936] Woden descent was understood to be a necessary element of royal authority, with Woden conveniently mutating into the lineal progeny of Christ, and no stigma attaching to his descendants, including Alfred. This leads Niles to conclude that 'place-names like Wednesbury ... indicate sites where Woden was once important, whether as a god or an ancestral hero'.[937]

What is readily apparent is that place-name scholars have frequently – though not always – failed to recognise that Wednesfield was the site of a major Anglo-Saxon battle, or if they have, ignored the possibility that the place-name and the conflict might in some way be connected. Of particular interest is that Woden, as we have seen, was above all associated in Anglo-Saxon England (like Óðinn in Scandinavia and Scandianavianised parts of Britain and Ireland) with victory in battle, and his principal role was the god of battles,[938] more specifically a god of the dead killed in battle: we have seen the Continental evidence that one particular form of sacrifice to Woden was the dedication to him of war dead.[939] Like Óðinn, Woden was seen primarily as a haunter of battlefields, and described as *wælceasega*, 'chooser of the slain, carrion picker', in the Anglo-Saxon poem *Exodus*.[940] Belief in a historic Woden may have merged with memories of Woden the god: his name may have been incorporated by the Anglo-Saxons into particular place-names as that of a real king associated with victories, rather than in his capacity as a pagan deity, at the sites of great battles, with Wednesfield perhaps representing a particularly late manifestation of that practice.

Slight support for that idea may be found, albeit at an improbably early date, in the battle in 592 at *Wodnesbeorg*, 'Woden's mound or tumulus', and another battle in 715 at the same place.[941] The *Anglo-Saxon Chronicle* records a battle in 838 at *Hengestdune*, Hengests's or Stallion's Hill (Hingston Down in Cornwall),[942] and in 1006 tells of folklore associated with *Cwicchelmes hlaew* 'Cwichelm's Barrow' (now Scutchamer Knob or Cuckhamsley Hill, Oxfordshire).[943] One scholar has recently observed that 'all three of these place-names utilise personal or theophoric elements that have a particular significance in West Saxon genealogies,'[944] a comment that could include the name *Wodnesfeld* in Mercian nomenclature.

It might be considered a surprising coincidence if two battles at *Wodnesbeorg*, together with the great battle of *Wodnesfeld*, had all been fought at places already incorporating the name Woden. After studying Woden place-names one scholar has even expressed the

---

[936] Dumville 1976.
[937] Niles 1991: 129, 135.
[938] Cheney 1970: 35.
[939] Cheney 1970: 35, 39, 110; Branston 1974: 100.
[940] Branston 1974: 107.
[941] Swanton 1996: 42; Williams 2016: 44. Sir Cyril and Lady Fox held that Wandsdyke and the surrounding area in which place-names incorporating Woden's name are found was dedicated to the god Woden when it was constructed, whereas J. N. L. Myers felt that 'the name Wodnesdic is most naturally to be explained as a name given by the pagan Anglo-Saxons to an important monument whose origin and purpose they did not know and could not guess, and which was therefore attributed by them to supernatural agency': Cheney 1970: 36 fn.120.
[942] ASC 'A'; ASC 'E' gives *Hengestes dune*; Swanton 1996: 62. Hengest was the traditional founder of modern Kent in the 5th century: Williams, Smyth and Kirby 1991: 153.
[943] The *hlæw* may have been thought to be the burial-place of one of two West Saxon nobles named Cwichelm recorded in 593 and 636: ASC 'A' and 'E': Swanton 1996: 20, 26-7, 137.
[944] Williams 2016: 55 fn.86.

viewthat 'It is possible to imagine these ... as places set aside for violence, frequented by the beasts of battle and hallowed through blood and sacrifice',[945] implying that warring parties somehow contrived or orchestrated events whereby their armies fought on places already dedicated to the god of war, a remarkable theory that raises innumerable practical and other issues, but which, if correct (which seems unlikely), could admittedly explain why two armies that supposedly first clashed at *Cwatbrycge* (Quatford) concluded their engagement at Wednesfield, a dozen miles away.

The name Woden in particular amongst the pagan gods was therefore understood with some ambiguity in tenth-century England, and possibly much earlier, recognised as a legendary but real king associated with victory in battle, proudly claimed as a lineal ancestor of Anglo-Saxon kings, and also worshipped by the pagans. The particular royal associations with Woden might help to explain the relationship which, according to tradition, was made between Woden and the harvest: even in Christian times Wednesday was considered a propitious day for sowing and planting crops, even though for other activities it was generally considered to be unlucky.[946]

Whatever the case for associating pagan practices with the names of other pagan gods, a prosaic explanation for place-names incorporating the name Woden is that the name of the god of war, who was also an eminent royal ancestor, was applied to places where battles had been fought (though the battles in 592 at 'Woden's mound or tumulus', and in 715 between Ine and Ceolred at the same place, admittedly occurred long before Woden was incorporated into the royal genealogy), places which at the time might well have been unnamed: battles were presumably fought in open ground, rather than in named towns, villages or farmsteads. If the custom of dedicating the dead of battle to Woden were remembered well into the Christian period, the derivation of names such as Wednesfield might be self-evident. Place-name specialists have found no difficulty in accepting that Woden could be seen as a mythical figure rather than a god: Sir Frank Stenton was willing to accept that in some situations (specifically where the name Grim in place-names can be equated with Woden) his name could be applied to a landscape feature, natural or manmade, 'where it clearly represents him [Woden] as a figure of myth rather than an object of worship'.[947] King Alfred's claim to and pride in a genealogy including Woden made him no pagan, and by the same token there may be little reason to imagine that every place-name incorporating that name denoted paganism and could date only from the pagan period.

To add weight to that point, it is worth noting that in a paper discussing Danish place-names incorporating the name Óðinn, Kristian Hald suggested that the name Wansdyke, mentioned above and applied to the famous earthwork in south-east England, which incorporates the name Woden, may post-date the heathen Anglo-Saxon period, and was perhaps so-named 'simply because it was a venerable and impressive relic of antiquity which might fittingly be attributed to the chief heathen god'.[948]

The chronicler Simeon of Durham records in his *History of the Church of Durham* of the battle of *Brunanburh* that King Æthelstan defeated a combined army *apud Weondune*,

---

[945] Williams 2015: 193.
[946] Cheney 1970: 35.
[947] Stenton 1970: 295-6.
[948] Hald 1963: 107. A parallel may be Torsburgen, the name of Scandinavia's largest defensive earthwork on Gotland, probably built during the migration period: Hald 1963: 107.

quod alio nomine Aetbrunnanwerc vel Brunnanbyrig appellatur, which tells us that the site of the battle was also known as *æt Weondune*, a name which, according to Stenton, seems to contain an inflected form of the adjective which is substantivised in the noun *weoh* 'idol, image, shrine',[949] usually associated with pagan religious practices – a battle site with a pagan, rather than kingly, connection, and a name which may derive from, and not predate, the battle.[950] An example of the name of a battle site coined after a conflict may be *Fethanleag*, the location of which continues to engage academic debate, but where acording to the *Anglo-Saxon Chronicle*, King Ceawlin and a certain Cutha fought against the Britons in 584. W. H. Stevenson believed the name to be a compound of Old English *fēða* 'a band or troop', and Old English *lēah*, probably here 'a wood', coined to commemorate the battle, a suggestion held by Stenton to be 'highly probable'.[951]

The coining of new names after a battle was not completely unknown. In that respect an observation by Eric John, though applied to the Continental Saxons of the eighth century, may be of particular significance: 'If we recall Professor Turville-Petres' remarkable study of what it was like to believe in Woden in his *Myth and Religion of the Pagan North*, then luck, *fortuna*, was an important part of Woden's stock in trade. A decisive victory that established a*gens*[people] in a *patrie*[country] was a singularly appropriate time to celebrate Woden in a very permanent way, as the Saxon tradition suggests the Saxons did.'[952] A battle site named after Woden following *fortuna* on the Tettenhall battlefield would certainly 'celebrate Woden in a very permanent way'. Or is it simply coincidence that a great victory over a Scandinavian raiding army by a combined Anglo-Saxon forcein 910 was supposedly achieved at a place with an exceptionally rare name incorporating that of a pagan deity/ancestral king whose name was especially associated with victory in battle? In that respect we might note the judicious warnings of Thomas Williams that 'the attribution of a battle to a named place is no indicator of historicity – many early Chronicle entries are rife with flagrant invention.' He reminds us that there can rarely be certainty as to whether an event occurred at the place named, or (in an observation of significance) 'even whether the place existed before its invention as a forum for conflict'. Particularly noteworthy is his comment that 'it seems likely that some battles were 'moved' in the telling and ascribed to a location considered more appropriate, more likely to be known, or perhaps just a place that the chronicler knew to be the right sort of area.'[953] Whether that scenario might be applied to *Wodnesfeld campo*, named as the site of the battle of Tettenhall by Æthelweard no later than c.988 – some eight decades after the conflict – cannot of course be known.

A further observation might usefully be added in connection with Wednesfield. Thomas Williams has noted how Anglo-Saxon poetry emphasises the role of haunted and desolate places as loci for conflict with monstrous adversaries, citing not only the borderlands and wilderness represented as the home of monsters in Beowulf, but St Guthlac fighting demons within a burial mound and St Wilfrid confronting a pagan sorceror issuing heathen curses and directing his forces in battle from atop a tumulus. He concludes that battles were often associated with landscapes characterised by their sinister and marginal

---

[949] Stenton 1970: 290-1; Whitelock 1955: 200 fn.5. In his *Historia Regum*, Simeon of Durham gives the place of the battle as *Wendun*: Whitelock 1955: 253.
[950] See also Cavill 2010: 317.
[951] Stenton 1970: 279.
[952] John 1992: 128.
[953] Williams 2016: 37. Unfortunately no sources are provided for these interesting observations.

aspects.[954] Wednesfield seems likely to have been a marginal area in the early tenth century, but we must not overlook that the national population in the tenth century was a mere fraction of that of today, with many, if not most, rural areas considered marginal by modern historians. Many urban areas were of course little more than large villages, and a local population well removed from such a centre in the tenth century may not necessarily have considered itself marginal.

The foregoing analysis is further complicated by the place-name Wednesbury, attached to a settlement on a hill some four miles or so south-east of Wednesfield. We might assume that both names are associated, and were coined in roughly the same era. If the name Wednesfield could be associated with the battle of 910, how do we explain the name Wednesbury? On the face of it that name is straightforward – we have seen that it means 'the fortification associated with Woden', and indeed slight traces of landscape features which the eye of faith might identify as an earthwork have been recorded at various times in recent centuries around the summit of the hill on which the place stands,[955] though small-scale excavations have generally proved inconclusive and failed to produce any evidence for an ancient origin. Place-names of this type, where the name of a god or spirit figure is associated with an earthwork, are not uncommon, early spellings are numerous, and there is no reason to doubt that the derivation is correct. What is less clear is the date when the name was coined, and how the meaning of the name is to be understood. In other words, is Woden when found in place-names always to be seen as the pagan god? In the light of the analysis given above, the answer is surely 'no': the name can be seen, certainly after the mid-ninth century, as that of an eminent royal ancestor of the contemporary rulers but, perhaps from distant memories of his association with the pagan god, as linked particularly to prehistoric earthworks of a military appearance. It might be supposed that the names Wednesfield and Wednesbury both date from the same period, and that may well be the case. Various theories can be advanced to explain the two names and, importantly, their proximity, but one possibility is that the name of one gave rise to the other: that the name Wednesbury became attached to a hillfort – just as Woden's name became attached to Wansdyke – as a quasi-mythological but powerful personality linked by tradition with early earthworks, and the first element came in time to be applied to a vast, generally open, surrounding area, with the development within that area of a settlement named Wednesfield. Alternatively, and contrariwise, a large, generally level, area called Wednesfield incorporated a hillfort to which the name Woden also became attached. Which name was coined first must remain a matter of speculation.

However, the reference in Æthelweard's *Chronicon* to *Vuodnesfelda campo*, discussed in more detail elsewhere in this volume, is especially noteworthy, since the word *campo* is found nowhere else the *Chronicon*, and we might question why Æthelweard chose to refer to *Vuodnesfelda campo* and not simply *Vuodnesfelda*. One of the meanings of Latin *campo* is 'theatre of action, battlefield', but Æthelweard has already mentioned a battle, and the word *campo* is not found attached to the names of any other of the many battles or places he mentions. Its unique use may be to emphasise its other meaning 'a level place, a large plain', to give 'the place called *Vuodnesfelda* in the large tract of level treeless land'.[956] The element *felda* in *Vuodnesfelda* may have been understood by Æthelweard to mean 'area of

---

[954] Williams 2016: 44.
[955] See e.g. Shaw 1801: II 83; Erdeswick 1844: 398
[956] This is made explicit in the chronicles of Roger of Wendover and Matthew Paris: Cox 1841: 375; Luard 1872: I 440; Luard 1890: I 482.

open ground' or 'battlefield',[957] and *campo* must have been intended to supplement the name, presumably representing the literal translation of Old English *feld*, perhaps supporting the idea of an extensive area of open land known simply as *feld* incorporating Wednesfield to the east of Wolverhampton and extending to Finchfield (probably within *ðone feld* recorded in 985)[958] or beyond to the west, with both such *feld*-names perhaps adopted after the battle. The inference may be, then, that *Vuodnesfelda campo* was intended to refer to an area called *Vuodnesfelda*, perhaps without a settlement, which lay within a sizeable tract of open ground, possibly originally of much greater extent, with the Woden element adopted after 910, not as the name of a pagan god, but as the eponymous ancestor and god-hero who had been proudly adopted into Anglo-Saxon royal genealogies. This hypothesis might explain why the names Tettenhall and Wednesfield are both associated with the great battle, and perhaps provide an alternative explanation for Woden place-names elsewhere long believed to be associated with the pagan deity.

As we have seen, names incorporating Old English *byrig*, the dative singular of *burh* 'a stronghold', are frequently associated with prehistoric earthworks or medieval fortified manor-houses (the latter probably the case with Bushbury, 'the Bishop's *burh*', more likely to refer to a manor-house),[959] and that may be the case with Wednesbury, but it is possible that (if the name Wednesfield commemorates the great battle), any older, pre-English name for an earthwork at Wednesbury was replaced by the present name, but the possibility that the name refers to an Anglo-Saxon – even perhaps Æthelflædian – fortification cannot be discounted entirely.[960] Indeed, from superficial similiarities in the names, historians from at least the time of Camden have identified Wednesbury as the site of the *burh* built (according to the *Mercian Register*) by Æthelflæd in 915 at *Weardbyrig*.[961] However, there is in reality no philological connection between the name *Weardbyrig* and early spellings of the name Wednesbury, and the absence of a nearby river (a feature often, but not invariably, associated with Æthelflædian *burhs*) makes such an origin for the *byrig* in Wednesbury unlikely (though the place lies on or close to a Roman road from *Pennocrucium* to Metchley, and Æthelflædian *burhs* are often associated with Roman roads), but there is no reason to associate any possible *burh* there with *Weardbyrig*, which remains unidentified, and is probably on the western side of Mercia.

In truth, all that can really be said is that a degree of uncertainty surrounds the names Wednesfield and Wednesbury, and their dates and origins may not be as straightforward as might have been supposed.

---

[957] Clark Hall 1960: 113.Other notable *feld* names in the region include Morville (*Membrefelde* 1086 DB; PN Sa I 213-4), 3 miles west of Bridgnorth, Enville (*Efnefeld* 1086 DB; Horovitz 2005: 248), 8 miles south-east of Bridgnorth, Worfield, 3 miles north-east of Bridgnorth (PN Sa I: 326-7), and most notably Lichfield: Horovitz 2005: 18-21, 361.
[958] S.860; Hooke 1983: 63-5. It is worth recording a reference to *Campo de Tettenhall* (which J. P. Jones associated without explanation with military activity) supposedly 'found in old deeds of this land for several centuries': Jones 1894: 7.
[959] Horovitz 2005: 166.
[960] Large natural features or exceptional prehistoric man-made features probably carried British names which were replaced during the Anglo-Saxon period. We do not know the earliest names of Stonehenge or Silbury Hill, names coined in the Anglo-Saxon period, for example.
[961] Whitelock 1961: 64. Those histories include, for example, Camden 1695: 530; Shaw 1801: II 83; Erdeswick 1844: 398.

13. Early routeways in the Wolverhampton area.

The connection between the sites of historic battles and Roman roads has long been recognised, and is now supported by detailed research recently published by M. C. Bishop, who has attempted to identify Roman roads associated with no fewer than 157 battles fought between 455 and 1057 (though omitting the significant battle of the Holme in 903, doubtless because the location is not known with certainty), as well as 216 post-Conquest battles up to 1746. He concludes that such roads 'lay at the heart of medieval England, both in times of conflict when armies used the network ... and ... definitely had a profound effect on medieval life, both martial and peaceful, and that [they] probably still exerted some influence in the later periods, to the point where most of the post-Roman battles in England and Wales (and a good few in Scotland) were fought on or next to a Roman road ... [O]ur knowledge of the Roman road network can be a valuable tool in assessing the location of unknown or poorly attested battle sites'.[962] With that in mind it will be instructive to consider in some detail the early road system in the wider area around Tettenhall and Wednesfield.

Though some prehistoric trackways could well have remained in use into modern times, they have not been identified. The earliest identifiable routeways in the Wolverhampton area are probably the Roman roads radiating from the civil settlement and Roman forts at Water Eaton (*Pennocrucium*), where Watling Street crosses the river Penk, 2½ miles south-west of Penkridge. As well as roads running north-west direct to Chester and north through Stafford, others ran (i) south-west to Wrottesley Park Farm; (ii) south through Codsall to Heath House Lane; (iii) south through Upper Pendeford Farm towards the Roman forts at Greensforge (and – perhaps most significantly for our researches – passing close to Tettenhall); and (iv) south-east to the Roman fort at Metchley, running – equally significantly – through or close to Wednesfield. The road to Upper Pendeford Farm has not been traced further south than Pendeford, and little more can be said about it, except to note that its course (if indeed it was ever completed) may have run along the crest of the high ground above Tettenhall church.

The precise line of the postulated Roman road between *Pennocrucium* and Metchley has not been traced further south than Slade Heath, and Roman roads often deviated slightly, or even significantly, usually to avoid particularly difficult ground, but a straight line between Slade Heath, east of Coven, would have run close to Oakley Farm at Wood Hayes, across Waddens Brook Lane and along Wednesfield Road towards Wednesbury.[963] Traces of the road might perhaps be detected in *ye ould road from London to Salop* on a Sutherland Estate map of Prestwood Farm by William Forster made in 1661 running across Linthouse Lane parallel with Ridge Lane, said to be the right of way running north

---

[962] Bishop 2014: 133, who associates the battle of Tettenhall with the Roman road known as Margary 191 running south from Water Eaton through Upper Pendeford Farm, a conclusion evidently based on the generally-used name of the battle (Tettenhall) with the course of the road which ran towards Tettenhall. Bishop also notes that the other side of the coin is that well-known battle-sites might indicate previously unsuspected Roman roads, citing the battle at Stafford in 1069 when William the Conqueror defeated the Mercian Earl Edric (ibid: 76, 98, 133, 150-62), evidently unaware of the evidence for such a road running north-south through Stafford: Horovitz 2005: 36-41.

[963] Smallshire 1978: 33; O.S. map of Roman Britain, 4th edition; Horovitz 1992: 31-6. A line of Roman finds running south-west from *Letocetum* suggests that a Roman road may have run from there to Greensforge.

to Blackhalve Lane.[964] That routeway is almost certainly to be identified as that mentioned by the Staffordshire historian Stebbing Shaw in 1801, who writes: 'Tradition says, that a great road from Chester to London had its course formerly over Byshbury-hill, and from thence towards Wednesfield. However that may be, certain it is, that evident traces of a road yet remain in a field about half a mile North-West of the church, and which are still distinguished by the name London road'.[965] Shaw's road is evidently the ancient trackway known as Portway (a very common name for early routeways, meaning 'the routeway to the *port* or market town')[966] which is said to have run from London to Chester via Warwick, Oldbury and Stafford, passing Wednesfield and Stowheath, recorded by various authorities.[967] Duignan says 'it comes from Wednesbury, where it is still called the Portway, to Catherines Cross, Darlaston; thence by Bunker's Hill to Moseley Hole, where I think, it bifurcated (as is common in British ways), one branch passing through Heath Town, by the Newbolds and Old Fallings, and over Bushbury Hill, where it is now broken; the other by Nechells, Wednesfield, and the Pear Tree, uniting at Northicote and falling into the Stafford Road at Coven. This said to have been an old pack way from London to Chester'.[968] The routeway is evidently that mentioned (as *portstrete*) in the bounds of Wednesfield in the spurious confirmation of Wulfrun's grant of estates to the monastery of Wolverhampton,[969] and possibly as *Stamstre* (*?Stanstret*) in a survey of 1240,[970] and it seems very possible that it followed roughly, or was perhaps adopted as, the Roman road which ran from *Pennocrucium* (Water Eaton) on Watling Street south of Penkridge to Metchley Roman forts south-west of Birmingham. The section across Bushbury Hill is recorded as *the portway* in 1588,[971] and another part is described in the same year as the

---

[964] Smallshire 1978: 32-3, 43, 45-6, 64. An agreement of 1240 between Robert de Essington and Robert de Wyston (1) and the Dean of Wolverhampton (2) mentions a high road called *Stamstre*, running from Burybrook and Kirclesford (Moseley Hole), and a continuation of that road would follow Mattox Lane and Neachells Lane: ibid. *Stamstre* may be a corruption of *Stanstret*, 'Stone Street', meaning perhaps '(?Roman) paved road'.

[965] Shaw 1801 II: 181. A map by William Forster of 1661 shows a length of lane marked *the ould road from London to Salop* at what is now a footpath running south to north from Linthouse Lane to Blackhalve Lane on the east side of Prestwood Farm (Smallshire 1978: 32, 64), but it is difficult to see how it may relate to Portway.

[966] See, for example, Scott 1832: 334, PN Worcestershire 3; PN Warwickshire 9-10; Cockin 2000: 462; Horovitz 2005: 443.

[967] E.g. Price 1835: 83, WA II 103-4. *Portwey* near Monmore is mentioned in 1537: SHC 1912 113. As noted previously, Smallshire shows the line of the road running from Moseley Hole via Neachells Lane to the north (*sic*) of Wednesfield village and on to Amos Lane, Long Knowle, Underhill and Northicote, and notes that the southern part was called *Stamstre* in a deed of 1240: Smallshire 1978: 32, 43. The road is mentioned as *the highway from Stafford to Warwick* c.1275 (SHC 1928 108), and *Warrewickford* is recorded in 1506 (SHC 1928 96, 115), possibly where the stream that runs west from Old Mill Pool crosses Northicote Lane. A place called Portway (recorded in 1641: Horovitz 2005: 443) lies between Oldbury and Rowley Regis, and evidently took its name from the ancient road. Port is from OE *port*, meaning 'a town, a market town': EPNE ii 70-1.

[968] Duignan N/D 12 fn.11.

[969] Hooke 1983: 72-4; map on p.47. The road is not shown on the Bodleian Library map of Britain, c.1360 (Parsons and Stenton 1958), which includes the more important roads, and it is likely that this *portstrete* had local, rather than national, importance, and simply served to link two urban centres – possibly Stafford, or even Penkridge, in the north, with another place (evidently not Wednesfield, which the street bypasses) to the south-east. The OE element *strēte* was applied not only to Roman roads (e.g. Watling Street), but to paved ways: EPNE ii 161-2.

[970] Smallshire 1978: 45.

[971] Mander and Tildesley 1960: 8 fn.1; Perambulation in Bushbury Manor Papers, Foxley Collection, Hereford Record Office.

portwey that leads to Bilston.[972] It is likely to have been in existence as an important routeway in the early tenth century[973] – and indeed much later, from its eighteenth century name, London road – and it is noteworthy that it does not pass through Wolverhampton, suggesting that the road may be of greater age than the town. The local line of the *strēte* would seem to follow the approximate course of Moseley Road (Bilston), northwards along Deans Road, Church Street, Bushbury Road, and Old Fallings Lane.[974]

In attempting to identify other roads and trackways that may have been in existence in 910, we are fortunate to have access to the text of the two tenth-century charters relating to Wolverhampton, the first the royal grant to Wulfrun of 985, the second the supposed copy of Wulfrun's grant to the monastery of Wolverhampton c.994. The latter, undoubtedly spurious but with boundary clauses of the various estates likely to have been taken from a contemporary source, enables at least some elements of the pre-Conquest landscape to be set out. Here we have the benefit of the valuable research conducted by Della Hooke in her study of the pre-Conquest landscape of Staffordshire.[975]

That research has identified *penwie* 'Penn Way',[976] which may have run through Penn, in the upland area to the south of Wolverhampton, across Goldthorn Hill and towards what is now Wolverhampton, continuing in the direction of the royal centre of Cannock, which served (perhaps significantly for our enquiries) as the boundary between Wednesfield and Bushbury.[977] The line of the routeway probably followed what is now Park Lane into Cannock Road. The name *penwie* is of interest, for it implies, like the Portway mentioned above, that it was so-called before Wolverhampton became a place of any importance,

---

[972] SHC 1912 113. The section is presumably to be identified as Moseley Road.

[973] Indeed, it seems possible that the *strete* could have been prehistoric andserved as a section of the lost but presumed Roman road from Pennocrucium to Metchley Roman forts and civil settlement between Edgbaston and Selly Oak which has not been traced further south than Brinsford: see Hooke 1983: 83-6. In that respect Hartshorne 1841: 273 makes an observation that is worth recording in full: 'Port Way, two miles South East of Dudley, Co. Worcester, leading by Causeway Green, Harborne and Selly Oak. It seems very probable that this is part of a line of Roman communication from the Watling Street below Penkridge to Alcester, passing by Crateford, Standiford, the Ford Houses, Wolverhampton, Cockshut Colliery, Sedgeley Beacon, Sedgeley, Cotwall End, Dudley, Portway, Causeway Green, Harborne and Selly Oak, where it divided into two branches, one going to the West, through Bromgrove to Droitwich; the other taking the course of some bye-ways for a mile and a half to King's Norton at which place there is a straight line of road to Forhill, where it joins the Icknield Way, coming in directly from Alcester, due south.' Roman roads sometimes took a winding course to avoid difficult terrain, and it is noteworthy that Hartshorne's route takes in Harborne and Selly Oak. Hartshorne's theory seems to have been adopted by Hackwood (see Ede 1962: 4), but although miscellaneous finds from the Roman period have been recorded from Sedgley, Bilston, Wednesbury, and Walsall (Ede 1962: 4), no traces of permanent occupation have been traced, and there is no evidence that the routeway (if indeed it is anything more than connected local trackways) was of Roman origin.

[974] Based on the map in Hooke 1983: 75.

[975] Hooke 1983; Phillips and Phillips 2011: 32-3.

[976] Phillips and Phillips 2011: 33. The OE word *weg* 'a routeway' may denote a feature of greater age than a *strete*, although in the later Anglo-Saxon period *strete* routes seem to have been more important than *weg* routes, and many appear to have developed from Roman roads: Carver 1980: 46.

[977] See Mander and Tildesley 1960: 2; Hooke 1983: 72-5; Hooke 1993: 13. There were strong pre-Conquest manorial ties between Moseley and an un-named estate (probably Showell) in Bushbury, and Lower Penn: Domesday Book tells us that in 1086 they were held by Godgifu (who we know as Lady Godiva); Lower Penn was held by her son Alfgar. It seems likely that *penwie* was a long-distance routeway that continued southwards from Penn. This leaves in question the age of the present Penn road.

since one might have expected the road to be named *heantune weg* 'the trackway associated with [Wolver]hampton', or similar. Given the northerly direction in which the Northumbrians were probably heading when the conflict of 910 occurred, it does not seem unreasonable to imagine that the great battle may have occurred somewhere in the vicinity of that road, or possibly close to another trackway, known in the late tenth century as *alde strete*, the Lichfield road which led from Wolverhampton to Wednesfield (probably along the line now marked by Wednesfield Road, Wolverhampton Road, and Lichfield Road via New Invention),[978] and onwards north-east to Watling Street and then eastwards to Ryknield Street, which led into Derbyshire and the Danelaw[979] It seems likely that this is the old road between Wolverhampton and Wednesfield which, as noted previously, ran across what was effectively a causeway.[980]

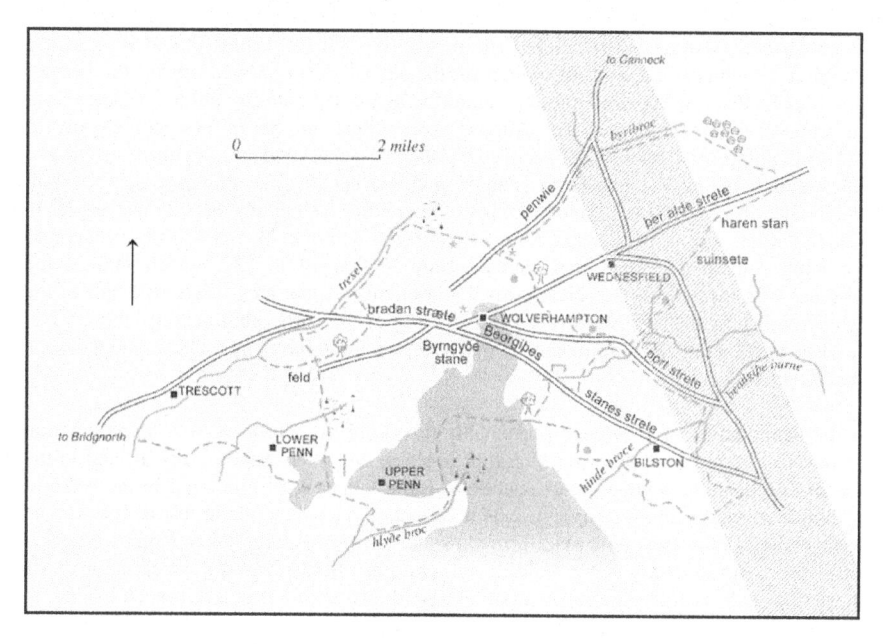

Tenth-century routeways in the Wolverhampton area from evidence found in early charters, based on a map created by Della Hooke and reproduced by permission. The shaded band on the right marks the approximate line of a lost Roman road running between Pennocrucium and Metchley.

The word *strete* in the Anglo-Saxon period normally denoted a paved road, often of Roman origin, and the word *alde* had two meanings, 'long in use' or 'disused'. Here we

---

[978] A note in Smallshire 1978: 31 claims that Duignan says the road ran (from east to west) across Pool Hayes towards Broad Lane South to Noose Lane, probably along Watery Lane to Neachells hamlet. The only cited work of Duignan is his paper on Wulfrun's charter (Duignan 1888), which does not mention those roads (see p.12). No evidence has been traced to suggest that *alde strete* ran south of Wednesfield.

[979] S.860. See also Hooke 1983: 47. The Staffordshire Hoard of Anglo-Saxon gold artefacts found in 2009 had been buried on the west side of the junction of this road with Watling Street.

[980] Phillips and Phillips 2011: 33. We might note that the name Stowheath could date from the ME period (it has not been traced before the 13th century), when *stōw* may have carried the meaning 'track or 'passage' or similar, though other examples are from Cambridgeshire and Lincolnshire: EPNE ii 158-60.

probably have 'the ancient paved road', and again it could have been a route used by the Northumbrians in 910. It is possible that *penwie* or *alde street* lay on the route intended to be taken by the Northumbrians on their return to the Danelaw: the nearest concentration of Scandinavian settlement to Quatford would seem to be the handful of villages with -*by* names to the east of Burton upon Trent, with Repton a few miles to the north, though if, as seems possible, indeed likely, the Northumbrians were Hiberno-Scandinavians from the north-west, we might have expected them to have headed in a northerly direction from Quatford, though they may have viewed any part of the Danelaw as friendly territory.

We do not know the route taken by the Northumbrians after crossing the Severn, but since rivers were often used for routefinding – the earliest maps show rivers rather than roads – they may have followed the rivers Worfe and Smestow, which would have taken them past Tettenhall and towards Wednesfield. The possibility that the Danes intended to sack a church at Tettenhall or a minster church on the site of, or in the vicinity of, the present church of St Peter at Wolverhampton, cannot be dismissed entirely, although (apart from the equivocal evidence of the Anglo-Saxon pillar in St Peter's churchyard at Wolverhampton, discussed in Appendix IV), there is scant evidence for the existence of either church before the late tenth century, and indeed the first reference to Tettenhall church is Domesday Book, although it is very likely that both churches had their origins in a much earlier period, as discussed elsewhere in this volume. We should also remember that King Æthelbald issued two charters from Willenhall in 732, which implies the existence of a high status – probably royal – residence in that area in the first half of the eighth century, which may have been in existence in the early tenth century, though had the place been of special significance at that time we might have expected to find a church recorded there.[981]

As the Scandinavian forces were presumably travelling in a north-easterly direction from the Severn, we must suppose that the joint Mercian and West Saxon army arrived in the area from the south, south-west or south-east (unless they were following in the wake of the Northumbrian raiding army), in which case they may have made use of the Roman roads leading to the area. One road from the south ran from Worcester to Greensforge and northwest towards *Uxacona* (Redhill, on Watling Street east of Wellington), via Chesterton with its Iron Age fortification at The Walls, with a northern branch leading to *Pennocrucium* on Watling Street, which would have passed to the west of Wolverhampton. We have seen that another road ran from Metchley Roman forts between Edgbaston and Selly Oak to *Pennocrucium*, the precise line of which is uncertain, but which is likely to have passed close to Wednesfield and Willenhall, and if it still remained serviceable in 910 may have been used by the English forces. Yet another major road, Icknield Street, (sometimes known as Ryknild Street) runs from Bourton-on-the-Water in the Cotswolds to Templeborough in South Yorkshire, and passed through Birmingham and close to Lichfield. It is noteworthy that the Portway (like the road to Metchley) led south-east from Wednesfield towards that road.

How the joint English army had been mustered from disparate parts of Wessex and Mercia (and even perhaps parts of Wales) is unknown. Our knowledge of muster procedures is slight, but they were clearly sophisticated, capable of rallying large numbers of fighting men and associated transport and provisions at short notice from the most remote corners of the two kingdoms, and it seems likely that hundredal meeting places – long-established

---

[981] S.86; S.87. Willenhall never became a separate parish, but was part of the large parish of Wolverhampton.

assembly sites – were often chosen for military musters.[982] The great mound of the ancient Staffordshire hundred meeting place at Offlow (a name perhaps associated with the great Mercian king, who died in 796, although not his place of burial)[983] lay close to the junction of the two principal Roman roads in the county, Watling Street and Ryknild Street, less than two miles east of the fortified Roman posting station of *Letocetum* (the 11-foot thick stone defences still visible at the end of the eighteenth century, and undoubtedly a far more impressive ruin in the tenth century).[984] Only a dozen miles from Wednesfield, it could have served as a strategic and prominent assembly point for the West Saxon and Mercian armies. It is not difficult to imagine the joint forces assembling south of Lichfield and moving south-west to confront the enemy, though there is of course not the slightest evidence that this is what happened: we have seen that the English forces may well have followed in the wake of the Scandinavian raiders or intercepted them at or close to *Cwatbrycge*, for example.

In that respect the location of the Staffordshire hundredal meeting place of Seisdon, just six miles north-east of Quatford and on a direct line to Tettenhall and Wednesfield, cannot be overlooked: it lies on high ground a mile from what must have been an important Roman road – which must have been crossed by the Scandinavians moving north-east from the Severn in 910 – running north-west along Abbot's Castle Hill to Rudge Heath and Ackleton from the Roman forts at Greensforge, three miles south-east.[985] The name Seisdon, first recorded in Domesday Book, is probably from Old English *Seax-dun* 'the hill of the Saxons', *Seax* being normally applied in the earlier stages of Anglo-Saxon penetration of England to those from the south, to distinguish them from Anglians permeating from the east, though the precise meaning of the place-name remains uncertain.[986] The possibility that the name arose from the joint English armies, or some elements of those forces, rallying at Seisdon in 910, so giving rise to 'the hill where the English assembled' can be ruled out, not least since Old English *Englisc* was the usual term for the English at that date, and the meeting place had probably carried its name long before 910 That the English forces might have mustered there or at The Walls, the fortification three miles north-west of Seisdon, lying on the same Roman road, is quite possible, however.

---

[982] Baker and Brookes 2016: 79. A number of shire muster sites have been identified from the OE term *here*, 'army', in their place-names: ibid. 80. Other than Harlow (Wood) near Mayfield on the river Dove, which serves as the Staffordshire-Derbyshire border (Horovitz 2005: 300-301), no such names have been identified in Staffordshire. It is worth noting, however, that some names such as Moat Farm and similar may derive not from a surrounding wet or dry ditch, but from OE *mōt*, denoting a moot or assembly site.

[983] Horovitz 2005: 48, 417.

[984] It is worth recording that the defended area might have been utilised at some date as a suitable *burh* in the 9th or 10th century.

[985] O.S. *Historical Map of Roman Britain*, 6th edition, 2011. The continuation of this road north is labelled X57 on Keith Brigg's *Map of Roman Britain* website.

[986] Horovitz 2005: 48-9, 482. Fields named Musters are recorded to the east of the village from 1298: ibid. 48.

14. Early tenth century warfare.[987]

It is important at the outset to emphasise that a state of war was the norm during much of the Anglo-Saxon period. Kings were expected not simply to defend their kingdoms, but to lead aggressive campaigns to conquer or weaken would-be aggressors and rival kingdoms and obtain treasure, money, slaves, cattle and other booty to reward those who took up arms for the king. With the coming of the Vikings the country faced an additional threat from overseas. As Richard Abels has aptly noted, 'Peace was simply the aftermath of one war and the prelude to another', with another author concluding that 'The destiny of the early medieval King, pagan or Christian, was to die on the field of battle'.[988] Aggressive warfare was essential to maintain a kingdom, and for a great part of the population death by violence was a perpetual possibility.

In the early tenth century, morale, tactics, discipline and weight of numbers tended to be the decisive factors in battle, since all armies fighting in England would probably have been very similarly equipped, although it is likely that the Danes wore mailshirts and probably iron helmets, which may not have been worn by many in English armies, though any apparent benefit in battle may have been arguable.

The age of participants in armed conflict is not easy to determine, but front line troops were probably hardened and experienced professional warriors, although written sources tell us that adolescents took part in battles,[989] and there is evidence that young men played a leading role in Anglo-Saxon warfare: in the siege of Buttington in 893, Æthelweard tells us that 'the young Englishmen on that occasion kept possession of the field of victory to the end'.[990] We might also be surprised at the numbers of relatively old warriors otherwise in good health who would be found on a battlefield.

Tactics on the battlefield have been the subject of much speculation. One authority on medieval warfare has concluded that 'The Saxons employed much the same kind of disorganised infantry tactics as the Franks, assaulting wildly and bravely in crowded orderless masses which hit the enemy line with great shock effect. The well-trained, disciplined and brave housecarls formed the nucleus of the later Saxon armies while the fyrd was an undisciplined, ill-trained and badly controlled militia who fought, man for man, as an orderless mob. During the seventh to the ninth centuries in Britain it is possible that the art of war sank to a lower level than anywhere else in the Western world. Strategy, tactics and discipline were unknown: disorderly mobs of opposing warriors formed in roughly parallel formations moved towards each other until they met in a jostling sprawling mêlée that went on until one side broke and fled, to be butchered by their pursuers'.[991] A more recent account of the life of Alfred the Great assures us that warfare at that time 'relied on numbers and morale more than tactics, and it would continue largely unchanged until the Norman Conquest'.[992]

---

[987] Lavelle 2010 now serves as an outstanding sourcebook for Anglo-Saxon warfare in the Viking Age.
[988] Abels 1988: 12; Adams 2013: 229.
[989] Lapidge et al 1999: 104.
[990] Campbell 1962: 50; Keynes and Lapidge 1983: 190.
[991] Featherstone 1997: 130-31.
[992] Horspool 2014: 55.

No evidence is adduced to support those views, and there is little proof to support them. The reality, indeed, was almost certainly the exact opposite, for warfare was an ever-present and significant part of virtually every aspect of life affecting almost everyone in Anglo-Saxon England, just as it was before and after. The Romans had been masters of military strategy, but there is no evidence that Roman tactics were widely familiar to commanders in the earlier Anglo-Saxon period, since military tracts such *De Re Militari* by Vegetius, written down in the early fifth century, were not available until the eleventh century in England.[993] Yet it would be surprising if warfare was not seen as sufficiently important – literally a matter of life and death – to ensure that those engaged in offensive or defensive campaigns during the later Anglo-Saxon period were properly trained in the martial arts. Whatever skills Anglo-Saxon warriors lacked, they were almost certainly far from the disorderly mobs described above. It seems fair to assume that from a very young age boys will have learnt rudimentary skills of basic weaponry, and those likely to have been called to fight will have practiced basic weapons handling, with military drills to instill morale and discipline, and military roleplays to acquaint them with situations they were likely to face in battle. Whilst it is dangerous to read too much into some aspects of the martial contents of the Staffordshire Hoard, with its wealth of astonishingly sophisticated gold and garnet military accoutrements, we would surely be mistaken to imagine that those who carried such weapons into war – and pieces from the Hoard showed clear evidence of heavy wear and impact damage[994] – were not skilled practitioners in the art of warfare, having practiced since childhood, and that members of their fighting forces, on which their lives and the very survival of their kingdoms depended, were not equally well trained and disciplined.

But as Sean Davies has observed (in the context of seventh-century battles, though his comments could equally be applied to the tenth-century), 'medieval warfare was characterised by the avoidance of battle wherever possible', with parties preferring small-scale clashes and ravaging.[995] The value of surprise and cunning and prudent generalship was recognised, with the key tactical objectives amounting to ravaging an opponent's land, stealing plunder, engineering favourable ambushes and clashes, and not least evading a full-blooded pitched battle. Such an approach to warfare would have been familiar to Roman military leaders and would continue into the industrial age. Leaders chose to fight battles only when both were equally confident of victory, or alternatively when one side was extremely confident, saw a strong advanage in fighting and was able to draw the enemy into the field. But however confident, every leader recognised that full-scale conflict carried the greatest possible risk, with the outcome often indecisive.

Once battle was joined, it would have been very difficult for commanders to control their forces in the general mêlée, and it is easy to imagine an unco-ordinated scrummage with warriors attacking anyone they could not instantly identify as an ally. Battlefields will have been very noisy places, with battle cries, howling and chanting intended to intimidate the enemy, as well as the screams of the injured and dying. Whether or not musical instruments, such as horns or drums, were used to communicate battle orders to the troops is uncertain, but is very possible.

---

[993] Lavelle 2010: 1.
[994] Such wear and damage is, however, less than might be expected on military equipment exposed to heavy use in warfare, and is perhaps more indicative of ceremonial usage.
[995] Davies 2010.

There is no evidence that members of individual warbands wore any distinguishing uniforms or emblems, but in the heat of battle it would be of crucial importance to readily distinguish friend from foe: perhaps to avoid premeditated confusion planned by the enemy, a particular coloured cloth or some similar identification was chosen at the outset of each campaign and worn by warriors to show at a glance which side they supported and avoid injury from 'friendly arms', always a hazard in any battle, although if, as we believe, mailshirts were commonly worn by the Danes, that may have been sufficient to identify the enemy. Moreover, it is said that the Vikings shaved their hair, leaving a tuft at the front,[996] perhaps so that they were instantly recognisable, as well as fearsome. Particular styles of beards and moustaches (or their absence) may also have identified an enemy, but little contemporary information is available for Scandinavian styles in the early tenth century.

In some battles where both parties were well-prepared, commanders may have drawn up relatively sophisticated battle plans in advance, and arrayed their forces carefully to their best tactical advantage in the light of the topography of the area, but we have seen that enemy forces were under no obligation to comply with those plans. We should also remember that divisions within tenth century English armies were generally led by *ealdormen*, who were the chief officials for their particular area, with many disparate responsibilities, not full-time military commanders, and military strategy may have been a tertiary, though far from unregarded, skill.

Battle tactics at this period are difficult to reconstruct for want of evidence, but could have been relatively unsophisticated, with armies approaching each other in divisions of orderly ranks, shield to shield, the leaders in the vanguard surrounded by their intimate cohort of warriors. Regimented slow marching towards the enemy, perhaps to the beat of a well-known anthem or rhythmic noises produced by the most simple percussion instrument, such as an iron pot or cymbal struck by a stick, may have inspired a collective confidence. The king or most senior *ealdorman*, acting as commander, carefully protected by specially chosen household warriors, may well have taken a central position towards the front of the army to take in the tactical aspects of the fight and to give orders and encouragement to his troops. Battle was supposedly commenced by sending a hail of missile weapons (the *beaduscūr* or 'battle shower') into the enemy forces, and in heathen and early Christian times it had been customary for a single warrior to hurl his spear over the heads of the opposing forces as a signal that the fighting should begin. That may have occurred at the battle of Tettenhall, for it is thought to have been common practice with the Vikings well into the medieval period.[997]

One of the most famed military procedures of the period was the formation of the shield-wall, so beloved of film producers and re-enactors. Whether the shield-wall was an invariable feature of Anglo-Saxon warfare continues to attract academic debate. From the poetic sources (which we might be unwise to treat as sound historical narratives) there is strong evidence that the shield-wall was a standard feature of late ninth and tenth-century warfare, along with the idea that maintaining the cohesion of the shield-wall was of critical

---

[996] Miles 2005: 200. There is certainly evidence from the Bayeux Tapestry that the Normans (descendants of course of the Danish 'north-men' from whom they acquired their name) shaved the back of the head. An undated fragment of an OE letter mentions the bared necks of the Danes: Whitelock 1955: 825.
[997] Pollington 1989: 140-1.

importance in Anglo-Saxon battle tactics.[998] But it has been suggested that the invariable use of the shield-wall, with warriors interlocking their shields, may be an exaggeration, for the circular shields of the period will have offered protection only to that part of the body between the thighs and the neck, and it seems more likely that warriors will have found it preferable to respond quickly by moving the shield to a position where it was able to deflect or protect against enemy weapons and incoming missiles. Indeed, one authority has questioned the advantages of a shield-wall created by 'untrained and, by Roman standards, atrociously undisciplined troops'.[999] For the moment, the perplexing question of the shield-wall must be seen as unresolved.

One tactic favoured by the Vikings for breaking through an enemy battle-line was the legendary *svinfylking* or 'swine-array', so-called from its comparison with a charging boar. Experienced troops would form a tight wedge-shaped formation some ten rows deep and charge into the enemy, maintaining formation to force a break in the line of opposing troops. By tradition the bravest warriors led the attack from the apex of the wedge, a manoeuvre which the *Liber Eliensis* tells us was employed by the Vikings to defeat the English forces of Ealdorman Byrhtnoth at the battle of Maldon in 991,[1000] and which may have been used at the battle of Ashdown in 871.[1001]

Any breaches in the enemy ranks caused by the battle shower or wedge attack could be exploited in the next phase, the *beaduræs* or 'battle rush', where a great shout went up from the two armies as the advance troops rushed forwards to clash with the foe. This was a critical phase, since the first onslaught, by fresh troops, eager for glory, was invariably the fiercest, and a concerted attack could sweep away the opposing shield-wall and leave the forces behind exposed to splitting into small groups which could be quickly overcome. Equally, a successful defence of a first attack could inflict heavy casualties and form a basis for a forceful counter-attack. But one must suppose that in most cases the battle rush made headway in some areas and was repulsed in others, and the gory work of the hand-to-hand hacking and butchery then began, with fighting taking the form of multiple skirmishes.

Once the enemy line was broken more troops would flood in and the enemy would find itself outflanked or even attacked from behind. Vegetius advised that the best way to deal with this threat was to 'swallow the charge' by allowing it to penetrate the line and then closing ranks to isolate and destroy the forces within the wedge.[1002] Face-to-face conflict involving sword and spear, dart and knife, must have been an exhausting affair, but it is difficult to believe, as some have suggested, that lulls in the melée will have been used as an opportunity where both armies 'caught their breath, rested and searched for replacements for damaged equipment'.[1003] The idea of leaders making their famous speeches of encouragement so graphically recorded in the poems such as *The Battle of Maldon* may derive entirely from the active imagination of poets with no battle experience. If there were such lulls, the fighting must have taken the form of a series of short and violent encounters in the 'killing ground' between the two armies.

---

[998] Brooks 1991: 215.
[999] Abels and Morillo 2005: 12-3, although that view has been questioned: see Bachrach 2007: 171.
[1000] Kennedy 1991: 63-8.
[1001] Lavelle 2010: 279.
[1002] Marren 2006: 12; 117.
[1003] Pollington 1989: 140-1.

A particularly informative account of the battle of Ashdown is found in the *Life of King Alfred* by the monk (and later bishop) Asser, who tells us that the Danish army split into two divisions with shield-walls of equal size, one under the command of two kings, the other under a number of earls, at the sight of which the West Saxons similarly divided their army into two, so that King Æthelred might engage the two Danish kings and their forces, leaving Alfred and his troops to take on the Danish earls and their army. Asser records that the Danes had taken the higher and better position on the battlefield first, with the English in a lower position. Of the two English armies, that of Alfred reached the battlefield sooner and in better order than that of his brother, King Æthelred, who refused to interrupt hearing Mass to begin battle, saying that he would not forsake divine service for that of men, an impressively moral tale if unconvincing. Alfred, whose army was in shield-wall position, realised that he had two choices: to concede the battle and retreat from the field, or engage the enemy battle-line without the support of his brother. Closing on his army's shield-wall, he led his troops against the Danes, and the conflict raged for some time around an isolated small thorn-tree,[1004] after which the two Danish kings and five of the earls and 'many thousands' of the Danish troops had been slain. Asser emphasises that bodies lay 'scattered everywhere, far and wide', with the remaining Danish forces put to flight 'right on to nightfall and into the following day'. The enemy fled back into the fortification near Reading from which they had come, and 'the Christians followed them till nightfall, cutting them down on all sides'.[1005] There is an implication in the poem recording the battle of *Brunanburh* in 937 that hostilities lasted from sunrise to sunset, and the victorious English pursued fleeing enemies 'all day long'.[1006] We may be entitled to take this as evidence that battles could last for some time, and that mopping-up operations might extend much longer over a very wide area.

In the Scandinavian saga known as *Egil's Saga*, probably written c.1230, perhaps by Snorri Sturluson (1179-1241), who lived for a time at Borg (where Egil farmed), we are given much detail about the build up to the battle of Vin Heath near Vin Forest, which is generally taken to be the battle of *Brunanburh*, fought between Æthelstan and his brother Edmund leading an army of West Saxons and Mercians which defeated a coalition of Vikings (led by Anlaf or Olaf, Viking king of Dublin), Strathclyde Welsh, and Scots. It is difficult to give much credence to the details provided in the saga,[1007] but it provides much interesting incidental information that may have a kernel of truth at its core.

The *Saga* tells us that once a field of battle had been identified by the king, he could not honourably wage war until that battle had been fought. The choice of ground was made with great care, for it had to be level, and big enough to line up a great army. Hazel rods were set up to fix the boundaries of the battlefield.[1008] Æthelstan is said to have arrived at *Brunanburh* several days before the conflict, and attempted to deceive the enemy into imagining that he had a much larger force than was the case. He also tried to buy off Olaf with silver coin, an offer that was greatly increased after days of negotiation which subsequently came to nothing.

[1004] Which Asser claims to have seen for himself, perhaps making him one of the first battlefield tourists: Keynes and Lapidge 1983: 79.
[1005] Keynes and Lapidge 1983: 79.
[1006] Swanton 1996: 106-10.
[1007] Whitelock concluded that Snorri had muddled the battle of Vin Heath with one by the Drina in Bjarmaland mentioned earlier in the saga: Whitelock 1955: 125.
[1008] Lavelle 2010: 301-2.

After the battle, where the English victory was decisive, Egil is said to have returned to the battlefield to find his brother Thorolf's body, which was washed and prepared for burial 'according to custom'. A grave was dug on the battlefield and Thorolf was laid in it with all his weapons and other clothing. Then Egil clasped a gold bracelet around each of Thorolf's arms, and covered the grave with earth and stones.[1009]

The suggestion that the battlefield was physically demarcated and that fallen warriors of high status were buried with treasure on the battlefield are two details of particular interest, though to what extent they are attributable to literary licence on the part of an author attempting to convince his readers of the veracity of the account is impossible to say, for while one leading authority on the battle has dismissed the saga as complete fiction which cannot serve as a credible source for details of the conflict,[1010] another renowned medievalist, writing about the battle of Hastings, has concluded that in his account of that battle in another of his works, the *Heimskringla*, Snorri may have had access to Norse accounts of events in England taken back to Scandinavia by Norsemen,[1011] and if that could be the case in respect of earlier battles, we may need to reconsider the value of Snorri's writings as evidence for battles in tenth-century England. It is surely highly improbable, to say the least, that a battlefield would have been marked out in the manner of a modern sportsfield, and equally unlikely that a Dane would have returned to a battlefield where a Danish coalition army had been decisively defeated, identified his brother amongst the dead, and buried him there with treasure.

It is generally recognised that a battle was won when one side gained control of the field of battle, most frequently by killing or putting to flight the most important leaders of the enemy force, allowing it to loot weaponry and anything else of value from the enemy dead and dying, although troops feigning retreat or returning to the attack led to a number of reverses for forces that believed a battle had gone in their favour.[1012] The *Anglo-Saxon Chronicle* and other records refer to victory in such terms as *wælstowe geweald habban* 'to have control of the place of slaughter'. The *Anglo-Saxon Chronicle* records how in 871, among several battles with the Danes, King Æthelred and his brother Alfred fought against the Danes 'and were victorious far on into the day; and there was a great slaughter on both sides; and the Danes had possession of the battle-field', and when Alfred became king later in the same year his army 'fought with a small force against the whole [Danish] army at Wilton and put it to flight far on into the day; and the Danes had possession of the battle-field'.[1013] It should come as no surprise that the chroniclers were often forced into ambivalence when attempting to identify which side took the victory in Anglo-Saxon battles.

At the battle of the Holme, probably fought in or shortly before 903,[1014] where many of high rank were killed from both sides – the Danes losing their leader, Edward's rebellious cousin Æthelwold, and Eohric, king of the East Anglians, who were challenging his

---

[1009] Pálsson and Edwards 1976: 119-127.
[1010] James Campbell, *Battle of Brunanburh*, 69-70, cited in Padel and Parsons 2008: 319.
[1011] Glover 1996: 178-9.
[1012] Based on Abels 1998: 128-9. Bately has noted that though in the ASC 'the victorious side is often (though not always) named, it is never described before 800 as having the victory, or before 833 as having control of the battlefield': Bately 1990: 277.
[1013] Whitelock 1955: 178. The same phrases 'The Christians/Vikings won the victory and were masters of the battlefield' were used by Asser in his account of the same battles: Keynes and Lapidge 1983: 78.
[1014] Dumville 1992: 10.

authority – it was the Danes who were deemed victors, notwithstanding the death of their leaders and that 'there were more of the Danish killed there ... they had possession of the place of slaughter'.[1015] These seemingly contradictory entries show how the English were prepared to claim victory even when the battlefield was admittedly held by the enemy, and conversely that the side that gained control of the battlefield was not necessarily seen as the victor, at least by the other side.[1016] The general impression is that however well planned, most battles soon became relatively uncontrolled, and that notwithstanding the expected rewards in the afterlife for both pagans and Christians, most warriors will have preferred to save themselves to wield arms another day rather than fight to the death. Many battles must have been fought where warriors and commanders on both sides left the field of battle uncertain whether they had lost – or won – the day.

Warfare in Anglo-Saxon England is likely to have been especially brutal and merciless but not necessarily because it was seen by participants as part of a long-term war of religion, in the later period by English Christian against Scandinavian pagan, for in truth the Vikings had no particular difficulty tolerating Christianity: a bold German monk named Ansgar proselytised at length in Scandinavia during the ninth century and lived to tell the tale, and we have seen that in Northumbria at the end of the ninth and beginning of the tenth century Christianity was widespread, with the coinage of York-based Danish kings incorporating Christian motifs and inscriptions.[1017] The Anglo-Saxons saw their wars as not only just, but a duty, for it was part of their culture that men of royal lineage had an obligation to defend their kin and country against a foreign invader, or indeed to invade territory of another English kingdom to avoid attack by that kingdom and to replenish their own coffers to meet the appreciable cost of defence. Offensive campaigns were the strongest and most effective forms of defence. Warfare was seen, quite simply, as a righteous necessity.

[1015] Swanton 1996: 94-5. Even the region where the battle took place remains uncertain.
[1016] ASC 'C' says of the battle of Fulford in 1066 (which it does not name) that the Norwegians 'had possession of the place of slaughter', and the same phrase is used in ASC 'D' to conclude its discussion of Hastings in the same year: Swanton 1991: 196, 199.
[1017] Gooch 2012: 48, 160.

15. Anglo-Saxon armies.

We know little of the means by which Anglo-Saxon armies were constituted and mustered.[1018] In particular, we have next to no information about the way in which fighting men were summoned, where they assembled – although hundred meeting places may have been chosen for the purpose – and how long they took to reach a muster point.[1019] We do not know whether they were inspected, what arms or provisions they may have been required to take with them,[1020] and whether only fighting men were called up. It may be supposed that a proportion of those mustered were unsuited for fighting – perhaps too young, too old, or with some physical disability – but could have supported the warriors by undertaking ancillary functions such as valets or cooks, smiths or carpenters, quartermasters or ostlers, medics or armourers.[1021] There is no reason to suppose that females were excluded from some of those roles.[1022]

Just how conscription was effected, and the arrangements for supplying and victualling the armed forces at this period, are uncertain, but illuminating evidence is available from the continent a century earlier: in 802 Charlemagne required that men summoned for army service must each have a lance, shield, bow with twelve arrows, breastplate and helmet, and in a circular letter of 806 required the recipient to provide men equipped with arms, gear, food and clothing. Each horseman was to have a shield, lance, sword, dagger, bow and quivers with arrows. Carts were to carry utensils of various kinds, including axes, planes, augers, adzes, trenching tools, iron spades or shovels, together with other tools necessary for an army. The supplies and equipment of the king were to be carried in carts, as were those of bishops, counts, abbots and nobles, and were to include flour, wine, pork and victuals in abundance, with tools such as adzes, axes, augers and slings, and men were to be supplied proficient in their use. King's marshalls were responsible for the whetstones, and each count was required to reserve a measure of fodder for the use of the army, and was also responsible for the maintenance of bridges and roads.[1023] To what extent the situation may have been mirrored in England a century later is unclear.

[1018] The so-called Grateley Code of King Æthelstan (924-39) does contain elements that may be read in a military context, but the precise meaning is uncertain: Clause 15 states that 'no shieldmaker is to put any sheepskin on a shield, and if he does so, he is to pay 30 shillings', and in Clause 16: 'every man is to have two mounted men for every plough', a demand that, if it relates to military service, is much higher than in later times, when one man from every five hides is generally found: Whitelock 1955: 384.

[1019] There is a unique reference to the time and place of an assembly in the *Anglo-Saxon Chronicle* (ASC 'A') and Asser (chapter 55), which records the raising of an army by King Alfred in 878 after the Danes had made a surprise attack at Chippenham after Twelfth Night. Alfred retreated to the marshes of Athelney 'after Easter', and seven weeks after Easter mustered an army which assembled at Egbert's Stone 'to the east of Selwood', the location of which is uncertain: see Peddie 1999: 135-44; Baker and Brookes 2016: 79-80.

[1020] Charlemagne, the most successful warleader of the early middle ages, paid particular attention to supplies for his armies, ordering those called up to bring with them provisions for three months in carts, together with other necessaries for war. Fresh meat was provided by beasts on the hoof, and supply trains were manned by labour which was provided in the main by the poor: Hooper 1989: 194.

[1021] See also Hooper 1989: 195.

[1022] One area on which we have no information is the existence or otherwise of camp followers. OE *forlegis, forlegisse, forlegnis, forlegystre* meant 'a harlot, a fornicatress, a prostitute' (BT i 314; Clark Hall 1960: 130; Pollington 1993: 95), but no reference to the subject has been found in association with armies or warfare, and it is ummentioned in Lavelle 2010.

[1023] McKitterick 2008: 228, 272-3.

The smallest Anglo-Saxon military grouping was the warband, usually of between six and ten men. A frequently-cited clause in the laws of Ine, King of Wessex (688-726), defined an army (*here*) as a band of more than 35 men, but *here* is probably best translated in that context as 'raid'.[1024] Nevertheless, we might suppose that early accounts of armies of many thousands are significant exaggerations.

The chronicles refer very frequently to armed forces which they describe as the king's *fyrds*. The expression meant originally 'a journey', but came to mean 'an armed expedition of force', and in 'official' documents such as charters and writs the word denoted a specific type of military expedition, one conducted by or in the name of the king.[1025] What is surprising is that given the numerous references to wars and battles in Anglo-Saxon England, remarkably little evidence has survived concerning the composition and organisation of Anglo-Saxon armies, which has led to differing views as to the nature of the *fyrds*. Sir Frank Stenton concluded that *fyrd* service was the duty of peasants, and the thegn's obligations arose from his rank – he was a warrior and a king's man from birth. Other academics, perhaps most notably Eric John, felt that the late Anglo-Saxon *fyrd* was essentially a feudal army of landed aristocrats and thegnly retainers whose military obligation derived from their possession of land.[1026] The latter view has now prevailed, and it is evident that the local *fyrds* were territorial forces made up from landowners and their followers – army service was an obligation imposed on free adult male landowners.

These local *fyrds* (which became the shire *fyrds* when shires came into being, in the case of Staffordshire probably during the second decade of the tenth century) were led by *ealdormen*, royal reeves and local king's thegns (many of whom were the king's personal followers, or those who had sworn to serve him, often found as witnesses to Anglo-Saxon charters in their capacity as thanes or *ealdormen*), and sometimes took the form of independent armies defending specific areas against raiders. But because they were raised on an *ad hoc* basis, local *fyrds* were ill-suited to meet the challenge presented by the Vikings, since by the time the *fyrd* had been gathered together from outlying areas of thinly populated countryside, a highly mobile enemy force is likely to have devastated a region and moved on.[1027] Furthermore, charter evidence suggests that not every local landed thegn was required to provide military service in response to a general summons of a shire *fyrd*.

Many questions about obligations relating to military service presently remain unanswered, but what is clear is that apart from Alfred the Great, and possibly his son Edward the Elder, Anglo-Saxon kings did not maintain standing armies. In pre-Viking England, royal armies were war bands consisting primarily of the king's noble retainers and their followers. The core of the army consisted of the royal household, supplemented by free landowners who recognised the king as their personal lord. Richard Abels has emphasised that when an Anglo-Saxon king went to war, his retainers would follow him into battle not necessarily because they felt a sense of duty to defend the kingdom, but because he was their lord: Anglo-Saxon institutions were built upon the over-riding obligation of retainers to their lord, to the extent that a warrior-retainer was obliged to share his lord's peril, so that if, for example, the lord was exiled, his followers were

---

[1024] Abels 1988: 35; Abels 2003: 269.
[1025] Abels 1988: 12-3.
[1026] Abels 1988: 97.
[1027] Abels 1998: 139.

morally obliged to follow him, and endure all his hardships.[1028] Armies were therefore composed of lords who carried an obligation to the king, and their followers.

During the reign of King Alfred the armies of Wessex consisted of select forces of the king's men and their retainers. Their core was made up of royal household thegns, perhaps fifty to one hundred strong, who, in return for the traditional gifts of gold rings, sumptuous clothes and feasts, repaid their royal lord with loyalty and service, and the support of their own followers. In response to the Viking threat, Alfred re-organised his military forces, and by 893, according to the *Anglo-Saxon Chronicle*, 'the king had seperated his army into two, so that there was always half at home and half out [on service], except for those men who had to hold the fortresses'.[1029] That meant that one half of the army was always ready for action and the other at home protecting its local territory and those undertaking the roles which enabled the community to function properly, for example working the land and bringing in the harvest. Since Alfred was effectively ruling English Mercia through his son-in-law Æthelred and his daughter Æthelflaed, it is very likely that by 910 similar arrangements applied in Mercia.[1030] These arrangements may have mirrored a similar creation in Danish Northumbria, where the organisation of territory subject to York into three 'ridings' (from Old Norse *þriðiungr* 'third part', with the initial consonant lost in combination with east, west, etc.) at about the same period implies a division of manpower available to the kings of York into three 'shifts', which would have allowed military campaigning at any time by a third of the military classes.[1031]

Military recruitment in Mercia is believed to have made particular demands on its population in order to maintain a large army which enabled it to dominate much of England when Mercia was at the height of its power, and Mercian forces are said to have included the *twelfhynde*, a noble class of landowner each equal in value or status to six *ceorls* who were themselves prosperous peasants rather than unfree serfs. From the tenth century the policy adopted in Wessex whereby one man was theoretically levied from each hide or specified acreage of land for the obligation to build and maintain fortresses and bridges, with one from every five hides for service in the army, was almost certainly introduced into Mercia; indeed may have originated there.[1032]

Although a large proportion of adult males may have served directly at one time or another in the English forces raised to deal with the Viking threat, for much of the population, especially the peasantry, military service probably meant indirect support in various forms, including financial support to maintain professional troops and their retainers who would act as what later became known as squires. Those likely to have been enlisted to fight will have received some type of formal training and practice in the use of arms, at least of spear and shield, although no evidence for the provision of such training has been traced. It should be remembered that many of those called up to fight may have suffered from some form of physical disability, for injuries of various types will have been common in Anglo-

---

[1028] Abels 1988: 16-17; 219 fn.128. For the confiscation of estates after the desertion of King Alfred by a certain ealdorman Wulfhere see S.362; Whitelock 1979: 541-2. The laws of Cnut (1016-35), Second Code, declared that if a warrior deserted his lord out of cowardice while on campaign, he was to lose his life and property, but if a man distinguished himself in battle by falling alongside his lord, his heriot was to be remitted and his heirs were to succeed to his landed estates: Abels 1988: 120.
[1029] ASC 'A'; Swanton 1996: 84.
[1030] By the reign of Æthelred the Unready (978-1016) royal armies had reverted to ad hoc forces raised on the command of the king or an ealdorman: Lapidge et al 1999: 47.
[1031] Higham 1993: 180.
[1032] Nicolle 1995: 60.

Saxon England. One area often unconsidered by historians is defective eyesight and hearing, and it seems likely from modern statistics that many strong and healthy warriors must have been unable to see or hear properly, a critical handicap on a battlefield. Other common disabilities, such as arthritis, will have been equally incapacitating.

Finally, it must not be supposed that the English armies consisted only of Englishmen, for as well as Welsh contingents, Alfred may have hired contingents of Viking mercenaries and Scandinavians to swell his troops: Asser says that 'many Franks, Frisians, Gauls, Vikings, Welshmen, Irishmen and Bretons' flocked to the King's court,[1033] and the *Anglo-Saxon Chronicle* records that at a naval engagement between Alfred's fleet and the Danes in 896 a number of Frisians who were part of the English forces were killed, including three who are named and presumably held positions of some importance.[1034] It is known that Æthelstan had Scandinavians, including Egill Skallagrimsson if *Egil's Saga* is to be believed, amongst his forces at the battle of *Brunanburh* in 937.[1035] Likewise, the loyalty of even royal family members could not be taken for granted, as illustrated by the bid for power made by Edward the Elder's cousin Æthelwold who, having failed to seize control of his Wessex homeland after his uncle Alfred's death in 899, went to 'the Danish army in Northumbria', who gave him their allegiance – and may even have recognised him as king – and was killed in battle at the Holme fighting against Edward c.903.[1036] In the same way, the loyalty of some English landowners may not have been beyond doubt, as shown by a suit heard c.975 which suggests that Edward the Elder, after the conquest of the southern Danelaw, confiscated the lands of those Englishmen who had taken the Danish side in the recent war.[1037] The Scottish chronicler John of Fordun, writing in 1363, records how a certain Alfred, opposed to Æthelstan (repeatedly described as illegitimate), 'speedily bound himself with King Constantine (of Scotland) and ... Sithric, in a close and faithful alliance'.[1038] This Alfred has analogies with a certain Alfred who, according to William of Malmesbury, conspired 'with his factious party' after the death of his father Edward to blind Æthelstan, to whose accession he objected on the grounds that Æthelstan was illegitimate, but the plan was exposed and Alfred sent to Rome to defend himself before the Pope, collapsing after taking the oath and dying soon after. His body was returned to England and allowed a Christian burial. Nothing further is known of this Alfred, but his estates (which fell to Æthelstan) are described as both great and small; evidently he was a person of some standing.[1039]

[1033] Chapter 76; see also Williams 1999: 77.
[1034] Whitelock 1955: 189.
[1035] Pálsson and Edwards 1976: 118-31; Livingstone 2011.
[1036] Swanton 1996: 92-5. Barbara Yorke has noted that until Edward reached his majority in the 890s, Æthelwold probably had a stronger claim to the throne: Yorke 2001. The Silverdale Hoard of silver jewellery and coins found wrapped in lead in Lancashire in September 2011, included a coin of AIWALDVS, perhaps representing the name Æthelwold, as well as another carrying the name AIRDECNVT, apparently the Scandinavian name Harthacnut, otherwise unrecorded at this period (but possibly the son of Guthfrith, who ruled 883-94 or 96, son of Harthacnut – there was a tradition of sons taking the name of their grandfather), with the inscription DNS [Dominus] Rex arranged in the form of a cross on the reverse, indicating a Christian affiliation. The design is related to coins issued by the Northumbrian Viking rulers Siefred and Cnut, probably in the earliest years of the tenth century. The hoard is dated to c.900: Gooch 2012: 48.
[1037] Stenton 1970: 123.
[1038] Skene 1872: 155.
[1039] Giles 1847: 128, 139; Smyth 1995: 440; Preest 2002: 274-5.

16. Tenth-century warriors: clothing, arms and armour.[1040]

Abundant evidence from surviving manuscript illustrations shows that lower-rank English warriors in the early tenth century wore belted tunics of natural unbleached linen or wool, sometimes with coloured braided trim around the edges, while wealthier warriors would wear coloured tunics. Popular colours were scarlet, red, brown, green, purple, indigo, deep blue and white (as depicted in the Bayeux Tapestry), but light blue and yellow clothing seems to have been much less fashionable, and indeed there may have been an aversion amongst the English to those colours. Trousers or leggings were generally in duller colours – brown, grey and reddish brown, with strips of cloth bound round the lower leg. Cloaks were common, often fastened by a circular brooch.

Like the English, Vikings of the tenth century wore knee-length linen or woollen tunics belted at the waist with a round or square neck and long sleeves. Decorative braid was sometimes applied around the neck-hole, hem and cuffs. Cloaks of rectangular or square shape appear to have been standard wear, though not in combat. The sagas refer to embroidered cloaks, which we must assume were only available to the wealthy. Some cloaks and tunics appear to have incorporated a hood. Other dress accessories included narrow leather belts with decorative copper-alloy buckles and strap-ends, and pouches hung from the belt seem to have served as purses. The baggy trousers of the early Viking period gave way in the tenth century to tight-fitting trousers of English fashion, bound mid-leg with strips of decorated material, the dominant colours red and blue.[1041] Shoes, boots and sandals would be of leather or hide, and a shapeless woollen sock was discovered at Coppergate.[1042] Surprisingly, some contemporary illustrations seem to show ploughmen, other agricultural workers and warriors barefoot,[1043] though it is hardly likely that battles will have involved unshod fighters.

There is reason to believe that, at least in the later Anglo-Saxon period, those Englishmen engaged in warfare were better equipped than we might imagine, for one of the laws of Æthelred the Unready (978-1016), admittedly later than the battle of Tettenhall, states that a ceorl (a free peasant) was not the equal to a thegn (which originally meant 'one who serves another', but came to apply to men who served the king and his lords),[1044] even when he possessed a helmet, mail shirt and a sword, unless he also held at least five hides of land. This tells us that even some humble ceorls possessed arms and armour, although the standard war-gear may have been no more than a leather jerkin, a close-fitting leather cap, a spear and a shield, and perhaps a knife and a cudgel, or even a bow.[1045] Yet those ceorls must have been in a minority, for an edict of the king is reported in 1008 that 'ships should be built unremittingly over all England, namely a warship from 310 hides, and a helmet and a mailshirt from eight hides'.[1046] On the other hand, at the battle of Farnham in 893 the forces of Alfred's son Edward were said to have included young men who 'slipped on their armour' and forced the Danes to disperse.[1047]

[1040] See Brooks 1991: 208-19; Clarke 1999: 42-4; Marren 2006: 6-11.
[1041] Chartrand et al 2006: 125-8; CA 305 (August 2015) 49.
[1042] Lapidge et al 1999: 107-8.
[1043] See, for example, illustrations from the 9th-century Utrecht Psalter, which provides a lively illustration to accompany each psalm.
[1044] Stenton 1971: 488-9.
[1045] It might be assumed that fighting men of the period will have carried some sort of backpack, but if they did we seem to have no evidence from contemporary illustrations or literary sources.
[1046] ASC 'E'; Swanton 1996: 138.
[1047] Campbell 1962: 49.

Evidence of Anglo-Saxon and Viking weaponry and armour can be obtained from archaeology, literature, and illustrations in surviving Anglo-Saxon manuscripts. When they first appeared in Britain in the late eighth century, the Vikings seem to have been very primitively armed, with the majority of raiders without the protection of mailshirts. Such helmets and mailshirts as they had were obtained from their slain victims or by trade, but within half a century the situation had changed completely. From their enemies they had not merely captured arms, armour and equipment superior to their own, but also the skills necessary to make them. By the middle of the ninth century many Viking warriors are likely to have worn mailshirts, based very much on the Frankish model, and they were probably better armed and armoured than their enemies,[1048] although the chronicler Æthelweard mentions young English warriors donning armour at the battle of Farnham in 894.[1049] Plate armour did not make an appearance until the late thirteenth century,[1050] but armour made from small overlapping plates sewn onto fabric or leather was being used by Carolingian forces from at least the later ninth century: a well-known illustration from the St Gall Psalter, dating from 890-920 – the period of the battle of Tettenhall – shows a group of mounted Carolingian warriors, some (perhaps those of higher rank) in armoured tunics of small overlapping plates, all wearing helmets, with spears raised over their shoulders, led by a single rider in armour with a large dragon banner.[1051] There is no reason to imagine that English and Viking warriors were less well armed.

Those of highest rank may have worn expensive knee-length tunics or byrnies of chain-mail or possibly lamellate plates, and simple conical helmets with nose-guards, although both are rare in the archaeological record, since chain-mail corrodes and rarely survives. It is noticeable that the incomplete Old English poem describing the battle of Maldon in 991 makes no mention of helmets,[1052] and we might suppose that they are unlikely to have been widely worn at the battle of Tettenhall earlier in the same century. Although many thousands – indeed tens of thousands – of helmets must have been produced in the Anglo-Saxon period, there are no certain survivals of pre-Conquest helmets, but in 2009 a heavily corroded conical four-plate iron helmet was found in a Midlands antiques shop with a label attached stating that it was found in the 1950s in the river Derwent at Stamford Bridge. Expert examination concluded that the style was consistent with an early medieval date, and the low-carbon iron from which it was made was typical of iron artefacts produced from the Iron Age to the Civil War,[1053] which does not indicate a pre-Conquest date, but does not preclude it. Whether it could have been a genuine Anglo-Saxon helmet remains unresolved.

[1048] Koch 1978: 30; Brooks 1991: 217; Griffith 1995: 172-3; but note that one commentator has suggested that 'the usage [of mail armour] among the Vikings may have been quite low', pointing to the paucity of surviving mail fragments: Chartrand et al 2006: 130. A hauberk perhaps pre-dating 935 is preserved in the treasury of Prague cathedral, and is said to have belonged to St Wenceslaus, who died in that year. All the iron rings are riveted and the cut and style are similar to those portrayed on the Bayeux Tapestry, although the skirt is split at the back only and the sleeves are almost full length. The only known authentic Viking helmet is the Gjermundbu helmet, which has a rounded dome with four ribs surmounted by a short rounded spike and an attached spectacle-like combined eye surround and nose-guard to the front, and which dates from c.880 AD: Griffiths 1995 cover illustration.
[1049] Campbell 1962: 49.
[1050] Nicholson 2004: 108.
[1051] Bullough 1965: 182.
[1052] Brooks 1991: 215-7.
[1053] *The Times*, 5th October 2009. The helmet was discovered by Nicholas Reeves, an Egyptologist, and the label was evidently written by a D. R. Lancaster, who has not been identified. The helmet was examined by Alan Williams, a medieval armour metallurgist at the Wallace Collection in London.

Could this corroded iron helmet found in 2009 in a Midlands antiques shop
be an extraordinary survival from the battle of Stamford Bridge in 1066?

Viking horned helmets are commonly held to be a fiction of recent centuries, since no such headgear is known to archaeologists, although a reconstruction of tapestry fragments found in the ship burial at Oseberg, Norway, shows what is clearly a sword-bearing figure wearing a horned helmet or head-dress.[1054]

Evidence from the *Anglo-Saxon Chronicle*,[1055] coins, and wills supports the proposition that body armour in the form of helmets and byrnies only became widespread amongst the English during the reform of the army by Æthelred the Unready,[1056] and representations in the Bayeux Tapestry which are held to be of chain-mail tunics may be quilted or padded jerkins or tunics[1057] – knee-length chain-mail will have been very heavy, and it is difficult to believe that wearers will have relished the restriction on movement imposed by such a cumbersome garment in the heat of battle when quick reflexes and dodging movements are likely to have been life-saving requirements. The sheer weight of chain mail will have quickly exhausted even the strongest warrior, which is perhaps why neither Egil nor Thorolf wore mail at the battle of *Brunanburh* in 937, if we can trust the account given in *Egil's Saga*.[1058] Furthermore, in his account of a later journey through Wales in 1188, Gerald of Wales ('Giraldus Cambrensis') makes a particularly interesting observation that in Gwynedd the natives used very long spears, and an iron coat of mail offered no resistance against such a weapon thrown at a short distance.[1059]

Some types of body armour and helmets are likely to have been produced from *cuir bouilli*, leather hardened by boiling and soaking in hot wax, which would have formed light but rigidly and surprisingly resilient protection. No archaeological or documentary

---

[1054] Campbell 1991: 150.
[1055] Sub anno 1008.
[1056] Brooks 1991: 216, who has concluded that in the tenth century English armies normally fought without helmets and byrnies against better-armed opponents, noting that the heriots (post-mortem lists of arms and valuables received from a lord) of English nobles do not normally mention body armour.
[1057] Burne 2002: 121.
[1058] Pálsson and Edwards 1976: 123.
[1059] Wright 1863: 438.

evidence of such material used for this purpose is known from this period, but this type of object – for example a leather cuirass – would not normally be expected to survive unless in waterlogged conditions,[1060] and contemporary illustrations are notoriously difficult to interpret. Indeed, the most practicable form of body protection may have been a padded tunic or doublet with insewn hard leather or even horn plaques, which would have been both light and flexible, and far less expensive to produce than mail armour. In the poem about the battle of Maldon in 991, spears, shields, and swords are mentioned among Byrhtnoth's troop, but the absence of references to body armour may indicate that the English wore none, or at least no metal armour.[1061]

The demand for helmets and mail for men who were to form the fighting contingents may show that the English forces of the late tenth century lacked the helmets and body armour regularly worn by the Viking invaders, a suspicion reinforced by the Maldon poem, in which only the Vikings are said to have had mail-shirts. But if helmets and chain mail were not commonly worn towards the end of the tenth century, they were at least as scarce early in the century. One reason may have been that armour was uncomfortable, impractical and unfashionable, and it should not be assumed that if English warriors at the battle of Tettenhall went into battle unarmoured, it was entirely the result of royal parsimony: the wearing of chain mail was probably a distinct disadvantage in the fast-moving action of the battlefield. Experience may have shown that nimbleness and stamina were of more importance than the notional but perhaps illusory benefits of weighty and cumbersome armour, which may have been worn only by leaders as a symbol of their status.[1062]

With one exception the wills of the great nobles of this period do not mention helmets and mail as part of their heriot payments to the king, whereas in later wills such items as well as weapons are regularly included.[1063] Clearly the thegn had military obligations: by a law of Cnut, who ruled from 1016 to 1035, the heirs of a thegn who stood nearest the king were required to provide him with four horses (two saddled), two swords, four spears and shields, a helmet, corselet, and fifty *mancuses* of gold, before they took their inheritance.[1064]

Unquestionably the main battle weapon of the early tenth century was the ubiquitous spear, carried by every warrior: the possession of a spear – or spears – and shield was the sign of free status. Indeed, the spear was the most important weapon of tenth-century warfare – its use is mentioned repeatedly in the poem describing the battle of Maldon, whereas swords appear to have played a much less significant role,[1065] and the Bayeux tapestry shows ranks of warriors with spears in both armies. Spears had the advantage that – in theory at least – they kept the enemy at a distance, and were not eschewed by the upper ranks in society, as is clear from the text of *The Battle of Maldon*, and they have been found in 'thanely' graves at Taplow and Broomfield, and in the regal burial at Sutton

---

[1060] Cuir bouilli is usually found used for medieval domestic items such as costrels, bombards, and knife sheaths.
[1061] For the use by the Danes of poisoned arrows and bronze helmets in a document dated c.1000 see Whitelock 1955: 843.
[1062] Lavelle 2010: 114.
[1063] Williams 2003: 80-83.
[1064] Stenton 1971: 489.
[1065] Brooks 1991: 210-214. Swords are found in only 11% of pre-9th century Anglo-Saxon graves and 20% of warrior graves from Jutland and southern Sweden, whilst spearheads are found in almost all: Jones 2011: 44.

Hoo.[1066] Both Viking and Anglo-Saxon warriors used a spear some 5'6" to 7'6" in length, tipped with an iron leaf-shaped or slender lozenge-shaped spearhead with a pronounced central rib, from four to twenty-four inches long, designed for throwing or thrusting. Some had blades of diamond cross-section to penetrate mail, or the leaf-shaped blades sometimes had sharp wings which may have been used to hook enemy shields, to catch and lock an opponent's weapon in hand-to-hand combat, stop a blade sliding down the shaft towards the user's hands, and to prevent a spear piercing an enemy so deeply that it could not be withdrawn. Sometimes the wings were attached separately to the shaft below the spearhead. The flat edges of wider spearheads were sharpened so that the weapon could also be used in a slashing action. Inlaid silver or copper decoration on the socket and flat of the blade was not uncommon on Viking spearheads, and it is possible that the spear-shaft may have been painted. Split sockets are usually characteristic of Anglo-Saxon spearheads, and rarely found on Viking weapons.[1067] Ash was a favoured wood for spear shafts since it grows straight and withstands impact without shattering.

A warrior had the choice of holding his spear overarm to thrust at the enemy or hurl it, or he could hold it underarm. To use it most effectively he would need to grip its shaft in both hands and put his full weight behind the thrust, but that would mean he could not use his shield. It is clear that the Anglo-Saxons usually fought with the spear in one hand and the shield in the other. Some Anglo-Saxon spears had cutting blades which must have required two hands to wield in the manner of a pole-axe. The shorter spears were generally used as missiles, and often had a barbed point, with longer spears used defensively, and some longer spears may have been used to display standards or banners: a spearhead from a grave at Welbeck Hill, Lincolnshire, has a large blade with the lower corners pierced as if for the attachment of decorative plumes or ribbons.[1068] Spears will rarely have been thrown

---

[1066] Swanton 1973: 3.

[1067] See especially Pollington 2002: 137-46.

[1068] Pollington 2004: 90. There is evidence that the Vikings carried into battle royal standards and battle banners, including the famed raven banner, which appears to have held some mystical qualities. Some Scandinavian banners are said to have been given names: ASC 'E' refers to the capture of the banner called Raven from the Danes in 878 (Swanton 1996: 77 and fn.14), and one carried before the king in 1066 was known as Land-ravager: Sturlason 1930: 226. The *Flateyjarbók* of Ólafssaga Tryggvasons (Ch. 186) records that one Viking banner 'was made with much fine work and resplendent craftsmanship. It was made in the form of a raven, and whenever the wind blew the banner it was as if the raven stretched its wings for flight': Pollington 2002: 90. A well-known illustration from the St Gall Psalter, dating from 890-920 – the period of the battle of Tettenhall – shows a group of mounted Carolingian warriors, some in armour of small overlapping plates, all helmeted, with spears raised over their shoulders, led by a single rider in armour with what seems to be a large three-dimensional hollow banner in the form of a fish-shaped dragon with flames emerging from its mouth: Bullough 1965: 182. The Irish *Three Fragments* mentions that in the second half of the 9th century a Scottish army chose to carry St Columba's crozier as their standard: O'Donovan 1860: 231. The ASC tells us that in 878 English forces seized a banner from the defeated Danes in Devon: *Dar wæs se guðfana genumen ðe hi raefen heton* ('there that banner was taken which they call "Raven"'): Pollington 1989: 151. In early European societies the raven was associated with war cults, and for Germanic warriors it had special associations with battle and with the cult of Óðinn, who was credited in mythology with having two particular ravens, Huginn ('thought'), and Muninn ('memory'), who sat at the ears of Óðinn and 'told him of tidings that they saw or heard' and on battlefields were known as prophets of victory, and by tradition the banners were woven or embroidered with the image of a raven, in many cases by women who were close relatives of the leaders who carried them, or by a sorceress, in order to ensure a harvest of enemy corpses for the war god (Smyth 1977: 269-70; Holland 2016: 7). The Danes apparently attributed magical properties to the banner, and regarded its capture with dismay. William of Malmesbury refers to Æthelstan's army unfolding in the wind standards and a hundred banners at the battle of *Brunanburh* in 937: Whitelock

at an enemy, for the owner will not only have lost his weapon, but it became available for use by the enemy. The rivet holding the head to the shaft was often designed to come free and deny the use of a thrown spear to the enemy, and to allow the iron head to be detached if necessary for use as a bayonet or dagger. Illustrations from Anglo-Saxon documents show that another common weapon was the *daroð* or dart, a short metal-tipped rod, of which ceorls may have carried two or three which were hurled at the foe before hand-to-hand fighting began.[1069]

On his left arm the right-handed warrior would carry a wooden shield, traditionally round, convex, and about a yard across, slung around the neck by a strap. Willow, poplar, lime and maple were the favoured wood for shields, but any light, springy wood might be used, such as pine. The shield was laminated from boards glued together,[1070] and a concave shield that bulged outwards was better able to resist blows. Shields were often faced with leather,[1071] probably painted,[1072] sometimes with a decorative motif, and generally reinforced with an iron rim-band. The central hand-grip was protected by a projecting central iron circular boss, known as the *rand*, attached by rivets, which often had a large protruding iron stud with a sharp-edged flat head on a short neck.[1073] Shields were used not only to parry blows and offer protection from enemy weaponry, but could be used offensively, with either the rim or the stud on the boss used to cause injury to the foe. Some high-status shields were also applied with metal shapes representing birds, beasts or fish, but whether these had any ritual significance is uncertain. Experiments have shown that shields were particularly susceptible to splitting, and were so important that it seems very possible that warriors went into battle carrying a spare. The very lowest social orders may have possessed cruder wooden, leather or wicker shields of roughly circular shape. It was not until the early eleventh century that the shield shape began changing to the kite shape well-known from the Bayeux Tapestry, and shields used by both sides at Tettenhall will have been round.[1074]

1955: 283. The standards illustrated on English coins and the Bayeux Tapestry are small, rectangular or triangular with tassels or ribbons on the trailing edge. The Bayeux Tapestry shows what seems to be a standard in the form of a flying winged dragon which may be King Harold's personal standard. The horn seems to have played some part in warfare, used for fanfares, alarms, and even for musical purposes: Pollington 2002: 191, 191, 195. The use of banners on the battlefield will have been crucially important, with raised banners providing a visual indication to warriors that their forces remained intact, and conversely when banners could not be seen, their position might well be at risk or have been overwhelmed. Banners will also have provided a gathering point for dispersed troops. In effect the banner represented the army's spirit and soul, and caused panic if it were lost. See also Jones 2010.
[1069] Pollington 1989: 144-5.
[1070] Watson 1994: 35-48. Marren 2006: 7 suggests that the boards of a shield were glued together with 'an unlikely-sounding but apparently effective rubbery mixture of cheese, vinegar and quicklime', but gives no source for this recipe.
[1071] King Æthelstan (924-39) issued an edict prohibiting the covering of shields with sheepskin: Pollington 1989: 135-6. Experiments have shown that a mixture of wood-ash soaked in milk, vinegar and water is effective in glueing leather to a wooden shield.
[1072] A runestone at Rønninge in Denmark mentions a man named 'Asgot of the red shield', and the shields recovered from the Gokstad ship in Norway were yellow and black.
[1073] See especially Stephenson 2002.
[1074] Brooks 1991: 214. The kite-shaped shield may have been designed primarily for use on horseback, and although normally regarded as a western European invention, was perhaps developed from the tall but flat-based infantry shields used in some Mediterranean and Middle East regions: Nicolle 1995: 83.

The Anglo-Saxon sword was a broad double-edged carefully balanced weapon weighing about three pounds with a hard and flexible blade of about three feet in length, used as a slashing instrument like a machete, the effects of which are often seen on mutilated skeletons from the period. Warriors of higher status and wealth on both sides would be identified by swords that were double-edged and pattern-welded with elaborate and expensive pommels, sometimes of gold inlaid with garnets of the type found in the Staffordshire Hoard. Many blades were formed from bars of metal repeatedly heated and hammered together into elaborate plaits to give a striking pattern when the finished blade was polished. This pattern welding was not only visually striking, but lessened the risk that the blade might shatter in combat. Archaeologists have calculated that as late as the tenth century nearly half of the swords so far excavated were produced by the time-consuming pattern-welding method. The sword was the standard aristocratic weapon and some were clearly of very considerable value and often became a family heirloom, handed down over many generations,[1075] perhaps to be seen as a status symbol of the nobility as well as a weapon: Anglo-Saxon burials have revealed a very large number of spears, whereas swords are relatively scarce, and invariably associated with high-status burials.[1076] The Viking double-edged sword, generally with a characteristic rounded pommel, was some 30"–35" long, sometimes pattern-welded. Many were imported from the Rhineland, and most had a heavy pommel which not only acted as a counterweight to the blade, but could be used at close quarters to deliver a disabling blow to the enemy.

Towards the end of the Anglo-Saxon period, the improving quality of iron ore meant that swords could be produced more cheaply, which in turn meant that more warriors could own one, and from about the beginning of the tenth century the pattern-welded blade, so highly valued for its visual appeal, seems gradually to have been replaced by new blades that were lighter and tougher.[1077] The weapon appears to have been more common in the south of England, for some 22 per cent of Dark Age graves in Kent contained swords, compared with only 3 per cent of Anglian graves in Northern England.[1078] Swords were carried in wooden, leather-covered scabbards, lined with oily fur or wool to keep the blade free of rust, suspended from the belt by supporting straps or from a shoulder-harness or baldric. Often richly decorated, the scabbard was another mark of high status.

The ubiquitous Viking battle-axe of the eleventh century may have been in use in the early tenth century, but probably not by the English, for the Danish army is described as 'the barbarian axe' by William of Malmesbury when writing in the twelfth century of the battle

---

[1075] Marren 2006: 8 suggests that 'a pattern-welded Dark Age sword was worth at least as much as a Ferrari, in modern terms, perhaps a quarter of a million pounds'. King Alfred bequeathed to his son-in-law Æthelred a sword worth 3,000 silver pennies, enough to purchase more than 100 oxen or 300 acres of land (Hindley 2006: 218), and the Will of Atheling Athelston, eldest son of King Ethelred (1015) left the sword which belonged to King Offa and a sword with a 'pitted' hilt and other property to his brother Edmund: Whitelock 1955: 548-9.
[1076] Brooks 2000: 140. McLynn 1998: 151 notes that evidence from Anglo-Saxon graves shows spears outnumbering swords by about twenty to one. Some of the best swords appear to have been given personal names: see, e.g., Pálsson and Edwards 1976: 123, 163, where swords called *Long*, *Adder* and *Dragvendil* are mentioned. Saxo Grammaticus, writing in the twelfth century, tells us that the sword of the legendary King Offa (not to be confused with the later Mercian king), who ruled over the Angles in their Continental home, probably in the latter half of the fourth century, was called *Skrep*: Fox 1955: 290. A sword named *Skofnung* ('scraper') is recorded in *Kormáks saga*, the Saga of Kormak the Poet.
[1077] Pollington 1989: 157; Williams 2014: 106-10.
[1078] Marren 2006: 8-9.

of *Brunanburh* in 937.[1079] There is little doubt that it was a multi-purpose tool used with both hands by the Vikings not just as a weapon (which was in reality impractical, since it needed much space, meaning its wielder was unable to shelter within a defensive formation),[1080] but to construct and repair their ships and to fell trees for encampments. Anglo-Saxon grave-goods, invariably including one or more spear-heads, sometimes include axe-heads which might be seen as throwing axes.[1081]

A weapon used by both Anglo-Saxons and Scandinavians was the *seax*, a type of single-edged short machete-like knife or sword with a small cross-guard between 14" and 30" long, carried at the belt and used as a cutlass. These weapons were often richly decorated with inlays of precious metals in geometrical patterns, and some carried inscriptions recording ownership. Most warriors probably carried a small knife or dagger, whatever other arms they had: thoughout history fighting men have carried home-made daggers of various types, and there is no reason to imagine that tenth-century warriors would have been any different.

There has been a general assumption that the Anglo-Saxons used bows and arrows, albeit not extensively.[1082] In early medieval society the bow was a weapon of the unfree or the semi-free, not of the noble or well-armed warrior, as evidenced by the absence of references to bows in the corpus of Anglo-Saxon laws, which is concerned mainly with the free and noble classes. The bow was, for some reason, seen primarily as a hunting weapon, a short bow drawn to the chest, not like the later longbow which was drawn to the ear, although the Vikings seem to have had less prejudice against the weapon.[1083] Archers are unlikely to have been used by either the English or the Danes in any great numbers, although references to arrows do appear in the Old English poems *Andreas, Juliana, Christ II, Solomon and Saturn, The Battle of Maldon* and *Beowulf* (but, significantly, not *The Battle of Brunanburh*, recording the battle fought only 27 years after Tettenhall). Reference in the Maldon poem to arrows could apply to either Vikings or Anglo-Saxons, and not necessarily to both. Despite such evidence, which is not extensive, the Bayeux Tapestry illustrates only a single Saxon archer, who is shown without armour and at a smaller size than the other well-armed warriors around him. With one exception, the Norman archers are also shown without armour, and relegated to the lower border. Henry of Huntingdon, writing some 50 years after the battle of Hastings, refers to William the Conqueror 'scorning the Saxons for their lack of archers'. The foreign association of the bow and arrow, specifically with Vikings rather than with Normans, might explain the connection between devils and archery in Old English poetry.[1084]

It is generally accepted that yew is the best wood for bows, but pre-Conquest England is unlikely to have been as heavily wooded as popular imagination supposes, and yew is not a common native tree. It is slow growing (but not as slow as some authorities claim) and does not spread rapidly, for it tends to shade out new growth from its own seeds. To manufacture bows in any quantity, yew trees would need to be cultivated or imported, and

---

[1079] Whitelock 1955: 283.
[1080] Griffith 1995: 174.
[1081] Swanton 1973.
[1082] On the minor role of bowmen in Anglo-Saxon England, see Manley 1985: 223-35; Bradbury 1985: 12-19.
[1083] Pollington 1989: 142; McLynn 1998: 151.
[1084] See Abraham 1994: 1-12, 16-17, and *The Old English Newsletter*, Vol. 28 No. 2 Winter 1995 7.

there is little evidence of any such cultivation or importation. In fact there is some evidence that bows were cut, if not from yew, then from dwarf-elm, ash, holly or hazel.

Whether troops carried haversacks or backpacks of some kind is unknown, but each will have had personal items of kit (perhaps even for shaving – most illustrations of Anglo-Saxons at this period show clean-shaven warriors), and it seems reasonable to imagine some sort of carrying pack. The proliferation of bronze strap-ends found by metal detectorists might suggest that as well as waist belts, such objects were used more widely, perhaps amongst other things on carrying packs, though weight must have been a factor to be considered during military campaigns.

17. Viking armies.

Historians have debated at length the size of the Viking fleets and armies and their impact on life in England,[1085] but even allowing for the understandable exaggeration of the English chroniclers, studies into the logistics of feeding men and horses suggests that warbands found it necessary to divide into modest raiding parties, but that the warbands themselves were large-scale armies transported by fleets of ships which may on occasions have numbered hundreds.

The *Anglo-Saxon Chronicle* often mentions the size of invading fleets, the smaller of which were said to number between 3 and 22 vessels, the larger between 80 and 350 ships. The vessels themselves, based on archaeological evidence such as the Gokstad ship from Oslo, are thought to have had crews of 30 to 32 oarsmen, but could carry many more men and even horses. Contemporary sources from widely separated parts of mainland Europe support the view that the fleets that transported the main Viking armies comprised between 50 and 250 ships, and that fleets of one or two hundred ships were not rare. Before about 840, Viking fleets were relatively small, if we are to believe those sources, but thereafter the size of war-bands increased: there were said to have been 63 ships in a fleet which sacked Nantes in 843; a fleet on the Seine in 843 had 120 ships; the fleet which attacked Canterbury and London in 851 reputedly numbered 350 ships; and 260 vessels are said to have made up two fleets which occupied the Seine in 861.[1086] In 892, a Viking fleet variously given in different versions of the *Anglo-Saxon Chronicle* as 200 or 250 ships brought a great army and its horses, and perhaps even wives and children, to Appledore.[1087] Until recent years it was considered unlikely that even such a great fleet would have carried over 1,000 troops,[1088] but the accounts mentioned above suggest that these Viking armies were quite possibly up to a few thousand strong, though attempts to analyse the likely size of enemy forces at such an early date are fraught with problems, since few authors of early accounts will have been eye-witnesses to the events they describe, and the compilers or their informants may, unwittingly or otherwise, have exaggerated figures to glorify victories or explain defeats.

The available evidence tends to support Stenton's hesitant conclusion that the 'large' Danish armies of 865 and 892 were probably 'in thousands rather than in hundreds',[1089] but not tens of thousands.[1090] The various sources agree that these armies were led by kings, whose title may have depended not on established settlements and kingdoms, but as leaders who were part of the Danish *stirpes regia*. It must not be forgotten that the Danish territories were not then a consolidated kingdom, and like other pagan Germanic rulers, Scandinavian kings may have been polygamous, with many of their sons styled as 'kings' who sought booty and fame outside their homeland.

[1085] See for example Sawyer 1957: 1-17; Sawyer 1962: 117-28; also generally Brooks 1979; Clarke 1999: 40-1, and now Hadley and Richards 2016: 24-5, 58-9.
[1086] Coupland 1995: 194-5.
[1087] ASC 'A' and 'E'; Swanton 1996: 84-5.
[1088] Sawyer 1962: 128.
[1089] Stenton 1971: 243, n.1. Smyth estimates that the Vikings who began King Alfred's last war by invading Kent in 892 in 250 ships could have totalled as many as 5,000 or 6,000 men (Smyth 1999: 8-9), but that was an exceptionally large fleet.
[1090] See especially Coupland 1995: 194.

Subordinate to the kings were the jarls or chieftans, and in the ninth and tenth centuries, authority in Scandinavia was shared by an unknown number of kings, jarls, chieftans and lords. The *Anglo-Saxon Chronicle* records that during the fighting in Wessex in the winter of 870-1, one king and nine Danish jarls were killed. In some, perhaps many, areas, power was not in the hands of a single ruler, but shared by several chieftans, each with his own men.[1091] In 918, in the 'second' battle of Corbridge on the Tyne, the Norse jarls were said to have fought in a separate body from their kings and from the young nobles, perhaps reflecting the differences in rank or status of the Norse leaders, or the presence of individual warbands who preserved their separate differences on the battlefield.

The *Anglo-Saxon Chronicle* sometimes names several Viking leaders in the same army (as at Tettenhall), from which it may be deduced that Viking armies fought in 'divisions', both in England and France. Neil Price notes that during the late ninth century several different armies were operating in Western Europe, each with an array of leaders, nationalities and objectives – fighting for money, land and political power, or for a combination of these. These forces may even have had completely different command structures, since an army fighting on the Loire told Frankish messengers that they had no commander but made their decisions on a communal basis, while a Danish army on a raid into Sweden is recorded as casting lots to decide on strategy. Viking armies sometimes fought each other or combined in temporary pacts, and there was certainly a continual interchange between them.[1092] Many Viking attacks may have been carried out by small forces, but they were capable of uniting into much larger armies when necessary, and these armies may have incorporated thousands, possibly several thousands, of troops.

While the late seventh-century Laws of Ine,[1093] a copy of which King Alfred appended to his own legislation, defined 'an army' (*here*) as a band totalling no more than 35 men,[1094] the word *here* in that context, as has been noted above, is probably best translated as 'raid'.[1095] The *micel here* or Great Army may have been 1,000 or more strong, a figure that is supported by calculations of the population capacities of Viking field fortifications, including winter camps. Such a relatively small force may seem insufficient to threaten an entire country, but battles were usually fought between armies of armoured and experienced Scandinavian mercenaries on the one hand, and hastily organised Anglo-Saxon militias on the other. Furthermore the Scandinavians had the advantage of surprise and mobility, while many terrified English people clearly perceived their pagan foe as agents of the Antichrist. We should also remember that on occasions the Great Army was actively assisted by various disaffected factions among the English.

Neil Price also reminds us that in contrast to the two-dimensional picture of pagan killers conveyed by the written sources, the Viking armies should be seen as a complex, shifting network of power structures and alliances, interacting on several levels with the peoples of

---

[1091] Sawyer 1993: 37. For most of the period between the 9th and the 17th century, the Danes were the leading power in Scandinavia, occupying the most fertile part of Scandinavia which also supportest the densest population. The authority of Danish kings relied on naval power, and their territory allowed easy access to the sea, by which they controlled the entrance to the Baltic and profited from Baltic trade: ibid.
[1092] Graham-Campbell 1994: 129.
[1093] 13: 1.
[1094] Abels 1998: 138 fn.38.
[1095] Abels 2003: 269.

England and Continental Europe.[1096] Although Continental sources often quote the numerical size of belligerent forces,[1097] the *Anglo Saxon Chronicle* tends to use adjectives such as *micel here*, *mycel hæthen here* 'large army, large heathen army' (865); *mycel sumor lida* 'large summer force' (871), and (tellingly using the definite article) *se micla here* 'the great army' (892). Moreover, the uniform mass of raiders described in the written sources as Vikings conceals a highly variable range of men (and perhaps women) of different nationalities, organization, leadership and motives: opportunistic Englishmen and troops from other countries were willing to fight for the Danes, presumably sensing that they were destined to defeat the English to become rulers of all England.[1098] In an important paper Richard Abels has concluded that in the late ninth century the Viking threat probably took the form of several different Viking *heres* (raiding armies) trying to take advantage of the campaigns of others, giving the impression of a 'single hydra-headed enemy' attempting to take over the kingdom. The objective of these *heres* seems to have been obtaining plunder (*feo*) to purchase land in East Anglia and Northumbria, with those who failed crossing the channel to serve as pirates there.[1099]

The *micel here*, the 'great army' of the Danes, a co-ordinated force of considerable strength, led by several kings and numerous jarls, started to arrive in East Anglia in 865. Parts of this force began to settle in the conquered areas of England, particularly in the north and east, and new Danish forces reached England in 871 and 879 to join the earlier army, doubtless explaining why the Continent was relatively untroubled by Viking attacks from 866 to 879.[1100] The following year this army left England to campaign in Francia, and returned to England in 891, fragmented by various campaigns and defeats.[1101] After wintering at *Cwatbrycge* in 895-6, the *micel here* dispersed into East Anglia, Northumbria and the region around the Seine.

But the *micel here* was not the only Viking army recorded in the *Chronicle*. It is clear that there was no single Great Army, but an amalgamation of forces that was in a state of continual change and division,[1102] and probably included a not insignificant proportion of English warriors, doubtless gambling that the opportunity for land and wealth was greater with the Danes than with the English, a hope that came very close to reality in 878 when King Alfred was forced to seek refuge at Athelney in the Somerset levels and the English were perilously close to annihilation by the Danes. In 871 a Great Summer Army came to Reading, and in 892 two Danish armies are recorded, one making a fortification at Milton,

---

[1096] Graham-Campbell 1994: 129. Michael Davidson has identified 16 cases of military alliance in Britain mentioned in apparently reliable sources from the reign of Alfred to the end of the 10th century, almost equally balanced between those involving alliances with Scandinavians, those involving alliances against Scandinavians, and those involving no Scandinavians. Anti-Scandinavian alliances are in fact the fewest of the 16. We might conclude (as Janet Nelson has observed in respect of the Continent) that rulers often fought against Scandinavians, but were equally willing to employ them, sometimes literally, for their own ends: Davidson 2001: 202.

[1097] Brooks 1979: 4. Two Viking raiding parties on the Seine in 865 numbered 200 and 500 warriors according to the *Annales Bertiniani*: Coupland 1995: 195.

[1098] Stenton 1970: 123.

[1099] Abels 2003: 278.

[1100] Clarke 1999: 41.

[1101] A close study of the *Annales Bertiniani* and other Frankish sources provides evidence that the disparate groups of Vikings that operated along the rivers of Francia in the second half of the ninth century often acted independently, but sometimes joined forces, at least temporarily, to seize larger targets, as attested by the well-recorded siege of Paris in 885-6: Abels 2003: 272.

[1102] See especially McKitterick 1995: 195.

the other at Appledore.[1103] The Vikings' success has been attributed in part to their ability to maintain their armies as coherent military forces for years at a time, whereas their opponents in Francia, Ireland, Scotland and the Anglo-Saxon kingdoms depended on small cores of royal retainers supplemented by irregular levies who could not be maintained in the field for long.[1104]

As noted elsewhere, it is important, though not always easy, to distinguish itinerant Viking warbands from the 'regular' forces of the Scandinavian kingdoms. As we have seen, by the 890s the Danes of York had divided their territories into three 'ridings' to allow them to undertake military campaigns on a continuous basis with a third of their forces.[1105]

Just as we have no firm information about the size of particular Viking armies and warbands, it is equally difficult to determine the numbers of those killed in battle. Estimates of enemy casualties are notoriously unreliable in any military campaign, and the *Anglo-Saxon Chronicle* is reticent in giving actual figures. In 837 the men of Brega, north of Dublin, routed a plundering war band of Vikings and 120 Vikings are said to have been killed. On two occasions we are given vague estimates: at the battle of Ashdown, one of a series of engagements fought in 871, 'many thousands' of Danes are said to have died, and in 894 'many hundreds' are said to have been killed near Chichester. On two other occasions we are given more precise figures. In 878 the leader of a fleet of 23 ships was killed at Countisbury in Devon with 800 men and 40 of his warband, and in 896, after the disbanding of the main Danish army, a small sea-borne band from East Anglia was attacked by vessels from Alfred's new fleet. 120 Danes from three Danish ships were killed, leaving a handful to row away in their ships. The figures suggest that those ships may each have had a crew of 50 to 60 men, but many large fleets may have had small vessels and ships laden with arms, provisions, horses and non-combatants. In 917, about 100 warriors from both sides are said to have died in fighting lasting several hours, and the *Annales Bertiniani* record that 240, 500, 700 and 1,200 Vikings were killed in four battles in Ireland.[1106]

Many Viking armies will have included the dreaded *berserker* and *ulfheðnir*. Both groups were held in fear and awe by their companions as well as their enemies. They were religious zealots with a fanatical devotion to the cult of Odin, and fought with naked ferocity to achieve one goal – death in battle. Their aim was not victory or personal honour, but the opportunity to achieve a glorious death in fighting (*vapndauðr*, 'weapon-death'), which would provide entry to Odin's heavenly hall.[1107] Before a fight they would induce into themselves a kind of fit or trance in which they were seized by a blood-lust which allowed them to slash and cut their way through the ranks of the enemy without the least regard for their own safety. Little wonder that *Egil's Saga* describes them as 'men that iron could never bite'.[1108]

[1103] Whitelock 1955: 185; Coupland 1995: 195.
[1104] Prker 2014: 31.
[1105] Higham 1993: 180.
[1106] Clarke 1999: 40.
[1107] Pollington 1989: 143. The sagas tell how the *beserkar* and *ulfheðnir* are said to have fought largely naked apart from their animal skins and oblivious to pain and injury: *beserkar* means 'bear-shirts' and *ulfheðnir* means 'wolf-coats': ibid.
[1108] Pálsson and Edwards 1976: 34.

18. Viking strategy and tactics.

For some decades prior to 865 the Viking strategy on the Continent and in Ireland had been to concentrate their activities on a particular river-basin, and use an off-shore or up-river island as a permanent wintering camp and a safe store for booty. But the 865 army developed a new strategy of moving camp each autumn to a new area to establish a base for the following year. Those camps were not, as before, newly constructed, but captured royal and administrative centres of the Anglo-Saxon kingdoms, such as York, Nottingham, Thetford, Reading, London, Torksey, Repton, Cambridge, Wareham, Exeter, Chippenham and Cirencester. Most of these places had existing defences, evidently unable to resist the Viking forces but which enabled the Vikings to defend themselves against siege, which tends to suggest that their great armies numbered thousands rather than hundreds of men. In 867, for example, the Danes wintered in the *geweorc* or fortification of Nottingham, presumably having surprised the local defenders before they could muster and man the ramparts, and were able to defy the besieging armies of the Mercian and West Saxon kings, a feat only possible if they had sufficient troops to maintain an effective defence force. A small force of Danes would be unlikely to choose a large fortified centre as winter quarters and a base for campaigning. At Nottingham, the enemy refusing to be drawn into a pitched battle (something the Danes were always anxious to avoid, for defeat so far from their home base would be particularly disastrous), a peace was concluded, probably by the payment to the Danes of tribute in the form of coin, precious metals and, almost certainly, provisions for men and horses.

The main explanation for the military achievements of the Danes is well-recorded by chroniclers in Europe, as well as English sources. The key lay in the speed with which their armies could travel not only across country from their riparian bases, but as occasion demanded, from England to the Continent and back again. Their ships were faster than any land army, and on land they seized horses and travelled without foot-soldiers and baggage trains, looting en route and retreating and making large detours to avoid contact with enemy forces. In the face of concerted attempts by a whole region to annihilate them, they would make their escape abroad, only to return when the enemy troops had returned to their fields and estates. Unlike the Anglo-saxons, the Vikings were full-time warriors, accustomed to fighting all the year round. Unless the Vikings could be denied the benefit of mobility, the English would always be in the weaker position. The answer was clear: a fleet capable of defeating the Vikings at sea, and fortified bridges and riverside towns to obstruct navigation upstream. The theory was difficult to put into practice, but King Alfred managed to co-ordinate the ship-building and fortress work necessary to gain the upper hand over the Danes.

Chivalry or Code of Battle is not a concept found in chronicles of the period, which record shameless acts of barbarity by both the English and the invaders, and despite recent attempts to rehabilitate the reputation of the Vikings, it is clear that the Scandinavian armies and warbands were unprincipled and ruthless in their military activities, with the Norse enjoying a fearsome reputation. Alfred Smyth has noted that Viking poetry 'reflects a taste for violence on the part of the Norse aristocracy which verged on the psychopathic'.[1109] It is also clear that the Vikings had no scruples about slaughtering clergy. They killed three Frankish bishops out of hand in 859, and any high-status prisoners kept for ransom would almost certainly be killed if the ransom were unpaid. During an attack on the inhabitants of the Somme basin in 884, 'The Northmen did not

---

[1109] Smyth 1984: 142.

desist from the slaying and taking captive of Christians, tearing down churches, razing fortifications to the ground and burning settlements. On all the streets lay the corpses of clerics, of nobles and of other lay people, of women, young people, and sucklings. There was no street or place where the dead did not lie, and it was for everyone a torment and a pain to see how Christian people had been brought to the point of extermination'.[1110] As if to emphasise how little respect the Vikings displayed for the Christian religion, Ælfheah, Archbishop of Canterbury, was captured and beaten to death with ox-bones by drunken Vikings in 1013 and became a martyr saint.[1111]

Other than a reference in *The Battle of Maldon*, the poem recording the battle between the English and the Danes at Maldon in Essex in 991 (where in any event part of the losing English army fled from the battlefield), there is little evidence that it was customary at the time for an army to fight to the death. Certainly the annals imply that significant elements of a defeated army often escaped to fight another day, as we are told was the case of the Scandinavians who fought at the battle of Tettenhall. It appears that conflicts would continue until one side or the other recognised that its opponents had achieved a clear victory by possession of the battlefield, with the death of the principal leader(s) seen as an irrelevance (as in the case of death of the usurper Æthelwold at the battle of the Holme c.903), and such possession may have signalled a tacit suspension of fighting whilst survivors made their escape and the victors plundered the wounded and dead for arms, jewellery, clothing, and any other spoil.[1112]

There is some slight evidence that the raising of a shield may have signalled non-hostility, akin to the modern white flag. This may at least have been a Scandinavian code of truce. The *Annals of Fulda* record how Frankish nobles entered a Viking fortress at Asselt on the banks of the Meuse after an exchange of hostages in 882. Once the Franks were inside, the Vikings closed the fortress gates, trapping the Franks, and followed the convention of lowering a raised shield.[1113]

It has been argued in the context of the Vikings in Ireland that before they arrived, warfare followed a curiously ritual pattern that included conventions such as the cessation of hostilities when the king was killed, a tradition that was neither understood nor followed by the Vikings.[1114] Battles were clearly bloodthirsty and violent, and there is little evidence that either side may have been restrained by the knowledge that acts of gratuitous barbarity were likely to be repaid with interest by the enemy in a future engagement. We

---

[1110] The annalist at St Vaast, cited in Smyth 1995: 129. We must remember, however, that the Anglo-Saxons themselves were no great respectors of religious communities outside their kingdoms: one is reminded of the slaughter of the monks of Bangor-is-y-Coed who had gathered to pray for a British victory before the battle of Chester in 615, although Bede says that they were treated as enemy combatants for their involvement: McClure and Collins 1994: 73-4; Charles-Edwards 2013: 132, 388-9.
[1111] Marren 2006: 19.
[1112] In the Welsh poem *Y Gododdin*, of which the greater part may date from the late 6th century, it is said that the Britons attacked the Anglo-Saxons at the battle of Catterick in 598 and fought against heavy odds for a week, except for truces on Friday and Saturday to count the dead (Williams 1953: 19-20), but it would be unsafe to place any weight on such a source, and whether truces were actually agreed is uncertain. It is also said that one of the duties of the king's house poet, one of 24 officers of the Welsh court, was singing *Unbeinyaeth Prydain* ('The Sovereignty of Britain') on the day of battle: ibid. 8-9.
[1113] Lavelle 2000: 43; Lavelle 2010: 320.
[1114] Sawyer 1982: 95.

cannot know whether it was customary to allow a beaten force to retreat or escape, or whether an army set out with the intention to destroy every last man of the enemy force, but it is evident that the English saw defeat in battle as God's punishment for the sins of the leader of the defeated army, which may be why so many clerical chroniclers were reluctant or unable to name the victors in many battles.[1115]

[1115] See Whitelock 1955: 262.

19. Viking allies.

Viking raiding parties were by definition marauding Scandinavian warbands interested only in securing booty, but they often included warriors from other countries, and we can suppose that many Englishmen joined their ranks, fearful, especially under the reign of King Alfred, that England would inevitably fall under Danish control, as it nearly did. Many defecting Englishmen may have anticipated favourable treatment from a Danish kingdom, though whether any rewards would have found their way to those Englishmen in such circumstances must be debatable. Even if England had fallen to the Danes, the Vikings may well have continued their age-old practices of raiding and looting.

Furthermore, it must not be assumed that the Vikings were always seen as the enemy. As early as 838 the Britons of Devon and Cornwall entered into an alliance with the Vikings against their West Saxon neighbours. In 878 Wessex was invaded by Vikings under Guthrum who may have recruited Ealdorman Wulfhere to their cause. He paid for his treachery by his loss from office and his inheritance was confiscated.[1116] Asser records how in 886 all the Angles and Saxons who had been 'with the pagans but not as captives' submitted to King Alfred.[1117] Most critically, Alfred's nephew Æthelwold, the son of his brother Æthelred, led an insurrection to seize the throne of Wessex from Edward the Elder which only ebded with the death of Æthelwold at the battle of the Holme c.903. But he was not the only member of an English royal family to act against an English king, for Brihtsige, an atheling (probably of the Mercian nobility), was killed fighting alongside Æthelwold,[1118] and there were doubtless other Englishmen of whom we have have no record who actively supported the Danish rulers and their campaigns. Indeed there is evidence that men with English names were fighting with Northumbrians against the English armies at the battle of Tettenhall.

Likewise in Wales the allegiance of Welsh rulers could change according to the circumstances. Rhodri Mawr ('Rhodri the Great') was one of the most forceful and successful kings of Wales whose territory was in the north-west of the country. He had fought against Viking warbands in 853 and 856, but raids into Wales intensified in the 870s, and according to the *Annals of Ulster* in 877 he was compelled to flee to Ireland.[1119] Returning in 878 he became king of Gwynedd, but that same year was killed fighting against the English in circumstances that remain unclear. Æthelred's defeat by Anarawd of Gwynedd at the battle of Conwy in 881 brought to an end any hope that Mercia could impose its authority on Gwynedd and though the area of Æthelred's overlordship in Wales contracted, Mercia continued to be a predatory power.[1120] Rhodri had left several sons – the precise number varies in different records – including Anarawd, a powerful ruler who was to be a key player in the region for over three decades. He sought to impose his authority over central and south Wales, which, with the 'power and tyranny of ealdorman Æthelred',[1121] led the kings of South Wales to seek the protection of King Alfred.[1122] Rhodri's sons were initially unwilling to submit to Alfred, and soon after 881 made a pact

---

[1116] S.362; Nelson 1999: I 53-4, 67; Yorke 2001: 35-6..
[1117] Nelson 1999: I 53.
[1118] Sawyer 1982: 99.
[1119] Todd 1867: lxxxiii.
[1120] Charles-Edwards 2013: 491.
[1121] From Asser's account of the submission of the southern Welsh kings to Alfred: Smyth 2002: 38.
[1122] Note, however, that Rhodri's son Cadell may have been ruling Dyfed at his death in 909 (or 910): Charles-Edwards 2013: 508; genealogy on 538.

with the Scandinavian kingdom of York, whose power extended across the Irish Sea to Dublin.[1123] But the alliance failed to prevent Viking attacks on Wales, and seems to have proved fragile, for it came to an end c.890,[1124] and before 893 Anarawd and his brothers are said to have sought an alliance with Alfred.[1125] They not only submitted to Alfred, but acquired warriors from him for use in his own aggressive campaigns.[1126] Indeed, they and those warriors they may have provided the Welsh forces which joined with the West Saxon and Mercian armies to besiege the Danes at Buttington in 893.

Thereafter there is little firm evidence that any of the Welsh kings fought in alliance with the Scandinavians – they were not part of the coalition of Scots, Danes and Strathclyde Britons who rose against and were defeated spectacularly by Æthelstan at the battle of *Brunanburh* in 937; indeed several are witnesses to his early charters, and all attended his court from time to time, with some participating in his campaigns in Scotland in 934.[1127] However, Idwal of Gwynedd and his brother joined a revolt by the north and the Norse of the northern Mercian Danelaw resisting English hegemony under the new king Edmund after Æthelstan's death in 939, but were killed in battle by Edmund's forces in 942.[1128] This is the period when a certain Wulfrun was the only hostage reported to have been captured by Olafr Guthfrithson when he took Tamworth in 940, an event of sufficient importance to be recorded in the 'D' version of the *Anglo-Saxon Chronicle*.[1129] She is usually assumed to be Wulfrun who endowed (or re-endowed) the monastery of Wolverhampton in 994, though that assumption may be ill-founded.[1130]

[1123] Charles-Edwards 2013: 491-2.
[1124] Charles-Edwards 2013: 526.
[1125] Anarwd's submission to Alfred is recorded in Asser's *Life*, but Smyth notes that there is no other evidence to support Alfred's overlordship of Gwynedd or Powys, and is unwilling to accept that Anarwd submitted to Alfred, observing that his English allies in 895 were more likely to be Mercian than West Saxon: Smyth 2002: 129.
[1126] Davies 1982: 106.
[1127] Higham 2002: 189.
[1128] Lloyd 1948: I 337; Higham 2002: 189, 193. The deaths of Idwal and his brother Elisedd at the hands of the Saxons are recorded in *Brut y Tywysogion* s.a. 941: Williams ab Ithel 1860: 20-1.
[1129] ASC 'D': Swanton 1996: 111 fn.12.
[1130] Williams, Smyth and Kirby 1991: 241.

20. Mounted forces or cavalry?

One particular question that has greatly exercised – and continues to exercise – historians is whether English and Scandinavian forces habitually used horses, and whether either side fought on horseback.

There is no doubt that English forces of the ninth and tenth centuries, as well as Viking armies and warbands, used horses. Asser tells us that in 885 the Vikings besieging Rochester had horses they had brought with them from Francia, and the *Anglo-Saxon Chronicle* records in 892 how the Danish great army came from Boulogne to Kent with horses in '200 (+50)' ships.[1131] The mobility of both Viking and English armies is demonstrated by entries in the *Anglo-Saxon Chronicle* recording the pursuit of the Danes from Essex to Buttington in 893, from East Anglia to Chester in the same year, and from the river Lea to *Cwatbrycge* in 895. The *Chronicle* records that at the siege of Buttington the Danes were so starved that they ate their horses; at the siege of Chester the English *fyrd* used the crops in the field as fodder for their horses; and in 895 the army rode (*rad*) after the Vikings. It is also clear that the Danes were using horses,[1132] indeed had stirrups and high saddles,[1133] and that the English had developed a mounted force to engage in pursuits, based on King Alfred's introduction of the requirement of the *fyrd* of nobles and their lesser-born followers to supply horses and sixty days' worth of provisions, in addition to their existing obligation to provide their own arms.

Though there is no doubt that both Vikings and the English employed horses for the rapid movement of infantry troops – mounted warriors appear in carvings on one of the pre-Conquest Abertemno stones from Angus in Scotland[1134] – we have little evidence to show whether military forces fought on horseback. The *Anglo-Saxon Chronicle* records in the poem of *The battle of Brunanburh* in 937 that 'the whole day long the West Saxons with mounted companies kept in pursuit of the hostile peoples ...',[1135] but that merely tells us that the victorious army pursued on horseback escapees from the battlefield.[1136] One recent scholarly analysis of the evidence has concluded that mounted warriors almost certainly could and did fight in battles at the beginning of the tenth century,[1137] and since the Carolingian Franks were well known for their deployment of mounted men in battle, and strategies and tactics adopted on the Continent tended to quickly be taken up in England, we can reasonably assume that both Anglo-Saxons and Vikings had heard of such a practice, and probably tried to emulate it, though academic opinion on the point is far from unanimous.[1138]

[1131] Keynes and Lapidge 1983: 86-7; Whitelock 1979: 201.
[1132] Clapham 1910: 287-93. ASC 'A' records that in 891 'the [Viking] raiding army went east; and King Arnulf with the East Franks and Saxons and Bavarians fought against the mounted raiding-army before the ships came, and put it to flight': Swanton 1996: 82.
[1133] Griffith 1995: 180. For a survey of studies relating to the use of stirrups see John Sloan, *The Stirrup Controversy*, 1994 (mediev-l@ukanvm.cc.ukans.edu).
[1134] The stone is Abertemno 2, the date of which remains the subject of academic debate.
[1135] Whitelock 1955: 201.
[1136] Cavill, Harding and Jesch 2000: 68. It is clear that despite their famous defeat, many enemy survivors managed to reach their ships and escape: Swanton 1991: 106-10.
[1137] Halsall 2003: 180-88; see also Williams 2008: 197-8. The early 7th-century Sutton Hoo helmet incorporates plaques showing a mounted rider with his spear raised and his horse trampling an enemy, but that cannot be taken as evidence that warfare then took place on horseback.
[1138] It is known that the Vikings fought on horseback in Francia: there is a reference to Viking cavalry at a battle near Maastricht in 891: Davis 1957: 174, citing a translation of the *Chronicles of Regino of*

One, admittedly late, source used in discussions about the use of horses in warfare in the pre-Conquest period is the account of the defeat of English forces near Hereford by a Welsh coalition force as recorded in the 'C' version of the *Anglo-Saxon Chronicle* for 1055, where 'before any spear was thrown the English people already fled, because they were on horse; and a great slaughter was made – about four hundred men, or five – and none in return',[1139] with Florence (John) of Worcester telling us that the English were ordered 'contrary to their custom, to fight on horseback', although the interpretation of this evidence has been debated.[1140] Two other pieces of evidence have been used to support the view that the English fought on foot at this period. The first is a pair of drawings illustrating the *Canterbury Hexateuch*, the earliest vernacular translation of the first six books of the Old Testament, probably dating to the second quarter of the eleventh century, where one illustration shows an army riding, the other the army dismounting to engage in battle. The second is the poem *Elene*, written by Cynewulf probably between 750 and 900, which makes clear reference to horses in the army, evidently warhorses, at the beginning of a campaign, but makes no mention of them during the battle itself, though that cannot be taken as proof that the army had dismounted.[1141]

Other clues to whether the Anglo-Saxons fought on horseback may perhaps be found in the type of horses available to the Carolingians and the Anglo-Saxons. At this period the 'great horse' of the Middle Ages was virually unknown in England: the indigenous horse of north-western Europe was probably little bigger, if at all, than a Shetland pony, standing perhaps no more than 10 hands, which would be too small to allow mounted troops to fight as cavalry.[1142] These horses were also relatively heavy-boned, slow and unresponsive. That meant that a rider could easily be unseated and dragged to the ground, where he would be especially vulnerable – it was obviously critical for warriors to stay on their feet. Small, slow, horses would almost certainly prove a liability in the melée of a battlefield, where instant responses were vital. It seems unlikely, therefore, that these diminutive horses would have had a significant role in early tenth century warfare (though by 1066 the situation may have been otherwise),[1143] and their value was probably limited to transporting troops, provisions and arms to the battlefield, and enabling fleeing troops to escape from the area if that should prove necessary. It may be that Carolingian forces had access to larger horses which made mounted warfare more advantageous in Francia.

The development of the saddle and spurs is also an important factor, for both would have been necessary for fighting on horseback. There is no archaeological evidence for the use of metal stirrups in England before the Viking age, and little evidence for their widespread use by the English before the eleventh century (although Carolingian illustrations from the late ninth and early tenth century show mounted Carolingians using stirrups),[1144] but the earlier use of rope or leather stirrups, which would leave no archaeological traces, cannot be ruled out. Little surviving physical evidence exists for the widespread use of saddles at this period, although again we would not expect objects of wood, leather and cloth to show

---

Prüm, ed. Kurze, 1890: 136 ff. In contrast to the Anglo-Saxons, the Franks relied on cavalry almost exclusively: ibid. 175 fn.2.
[1139] Swanton 1996: 186.
[1140] Stevenson 1853: 125; Freeman 1873: II 259; Lavelle 2010: 284..
[1141] Halsall 2003: 183-4.
[1142] Graham Campbell 1992: 78; see also Hayland 1994.
[1143] Glover 1996: 179-80.
[1144] See, for example, an illustration from the St Gall Psalter (890-920) showing mounted warriors: Bullough 1965: 182.

in archaeological contexts,[1145] but there is the testimony of various Old English poems to show that the saddle was by this time part of the warrior's normal equipment. But we might remember that horses had other uses, apart from serving as mounts for a cavalry force, for *in extremis* they could be killed and eaten, as we have seen happened at Buttington in 893, despite which many of the besieged Danes are said to have starved to death.[1146]

Further evidence that the Anglo-Saxon thegn, unlike Continental knights, generally fought on foot is shown by his byrnie, or mail tunic, which research has shown was designed primarily for infantry warfare and would have proved impractical when on horseback.[1147] But the small Anglo-Saxon horse was still valued, and even in the eleventh century the heriot (the right of the lord to take the best beast or chattel when a tenant died) payable in respect of thegns called for palfreys (light horses or small saddle-horses), rather than destriers (heavier warhorses or chargers).[1148] One authority has concluded after careful analysis of the evidence that can be extracted from the limited sources available: '... there is considerably more evidence for the idea that Anglo-Saxon warriors could fight mounted than there is for the idea that they always dismounted to fight'. He also concludes that Viking fighting methods brought about tactical changes in the way the English fought, with dismounted shield-wall warfare possibly more common in the later Anglo-Saxon period than earlier, and that like his Continental counterpart, the Anglo-Saxon warrior could and did fight on horseback when occasion demanded, just as he could dismount and fight on foot if that seemed appropriate.[1149] That Anglo-Saxon warriors could fight mounted does not of course mean that they did fight mounted, and the weight of scholarly opinion supports the idea that in 910 the battle of Tettenhall would not have involved warriors on horseback, though the matter is far from certain.

[1145] Graham Campbell 1992: 79.
[1146] ASC 'A'; Swanton 1996: 87.
[1147] Brooks 2000: 161.
[1148] Abels 1998: 198; but see also Lavelle 2010: 114-28.
[1149] Halsall 2003: 184-5.

21. Medical matters.

Weapons commonly used in the Anglo-Saxon period could cause fearsome injuries. Very few medieval battle cemeteries have been excavated, but one of the most famous is that of Visby, where in July 1361 a Danish army invaded the Swedish island of Gotland, defended by a hastily raised Swedish peasant army, which was annihilated. Three mass graves were excavated in the earlier part of the twentieth century, and over a thousand skeletons unearthed.[1150] The injuries to the skeletal remains varied from scratches and nicks on individual bones to dismemberment.[1151] The latter is illustrated by the presence of severed hands and feet, partial limbs and complete limbs. One individual had the lower halves of both left and right tibiae and fibulae completely severed, apparently by a single blow. The lower legs of the bodies were affected more than any other area of the body: about 65% of the cutting trauma involved tibiae.

The focus on the lower limbs doubtless reflects the use of shields and protective clothing for the trunk of the body, leaving the legs especially vulnerable to injury. Sword blows directed at the lower legs typically resulted in the chipping of bones on the tibia anterior crest. It seems very likely that these injuries are to be seen as evidence of an important feature of Danish fighting techniques of the period, and 'may well echo the wounds inflicted in earlier Anglo-Scandinavian battles fought on foot, such as Ashington, 1016, or Stamford Bridge, 1066'.[1152] Most of the Visby skeletons had received more than one wound, and many cuts were to the head, with wounds directed from above, and several crania showing marks of repeated cuts. It is clear that the head was a natural target in hand-to-hand fighting, but it is impossible to know how many of the cuts marked a coup-de-grâce when the victim lay helpless on the ground. It may also be noted that many serious wounds might leave no trace on bones. Data on nineteenth-century American army casualties wounded in engagements with Native Amercians show that stomach wounds (which might leave no trace on bones) proved fatal in almost two-thirds of cases, followed by those to the head, spine and chest, whereas wounded limbs often healed.[1153] But it should not be overlooked that in early medieval warfare the effects of wounds may not have been immediately apparent – the quick clean kill may have been the exception rather than the rule, with minor wounds often becoming infected and leading to a painful death.[1154]

Anglo-Saxon medical and surgical skills were both surprisingly advanced and alarmingly unsophisticated, as evidenced by surviving medical texts written in both Old English and Latin, and from skeletal evidence which shows that many who sustained serious injury survived for many years, although medical knowledge was much less advanced than in (for example) contemporary Byzantium and, especially, the Muslim world. Some 500 leaves of medical texts in Old English are known, almost certainly a small fraction of a very substantial body of vernacular medical literature which must once have existed.[1155] One of the major Old English medical works is the *Leechbook* of Bald', a collection of

---

[1150] Surprisingly, the graves included a considerable quantity of armour and chain mail, which one might have expected to be robbed for re-use or re-cycling before the bodies were buried.
[1151] A diagram showing an analysis of wounds to the limb-bones of skeletons from the mass graves at Visby will be found in Nicolle 1995: 256.
[1152] Strickland 2003: 173.
[1153] *Antiquity* 89: 940-954.
[1154] For a useful analysis see Pollington 2001: 220-22.
[1155] Lapidge et al 1999: 304-5.

medical texts possibly compiled during the reign of King Alfred, which provides treatments and remedies for a wide variety of conditions.[1156] A re-assessment of Anglo-Saxon medicine, treatments and remedies shows that while there were medical works of doubtful value – perhaps surprisingly, works copied from those of the classical world – which circulated among the literate, many of the various 'native' medical remedies from England and Ireland seem to have had real curative value, although there is also evidence that some seemingly bizarre wound dressings and the widespread belief that promoting pus would assist in healing injuries were positively harmful.[1157]

We might suppose (although there is no direct evidence) that major armies were supported by field surgeons and auxiliaries experienced in the treatment of the types of traumatic injuries likely to be met on the battlefield, who perhaps carried dressings, surgical instruments, medical paraphernalia and anaesthetic drugs known to the Anglo-Saxons, such as opium, hellebore and alcohol, although any such facility might have been intended to benefit the leaders, and the reality may have been that, as in Charlemagne's army, priests tended the wounded rank-and-file soldiers, and were better qualified to administer the last rites than to save a warrior's life.

Some treatments known to the Anglo-Saxons were undoubtedly helpful, and it is generally accepted that they were aware of the need to reduce and splint fractures to promote healing and prevent deformity. General surgery (though not associated with battles) on injured and gangrenous limbs is described in contemporary sources, with instructions on the amputation of limbs, recognising that the part to be amputated must extend to include some healthy tissue, a point insisted upon today. The closing of cuts and wounds by stitching with silk thread is recorded in the *Leechbook*, and a skull from a cemetery at Willoughby-on-the-Wolds, Nottinghamshire, bore a 2" linear injury, probably caused by a sword blow. Next to it was a neat trepanation scar, evidence that trepanation (cutting a hole in the skull) had been used to treat the effects of the injury: the patient had evidently survived long enough for the scar to heal over.[1158] Cauterisation (burning the body tissue with a hot iron) was used to encourage healing by assisting clotting and reducing blood loss, a horrifically painful treatment which produced severe scar tissue but in reality was of limited value in staunching the flow of blood.[1159]

Plants such as sage were used to clean wounds, and primitive methods of haemostasis (stopping or arresting blood circulation) were practised. Soot from cooking pots, horse dung and dried blood are all recorded as haemostatic agents, and the Scandinavians held the leek in high esteem for its healing qualities when applied to wounds.[1160] There are also occasional references to pressure bandages for haemorrhage. Post-operatively, there is mention of dressing the stump of an amputation with boiled sheep's marrow. Many remedies, however, will have been useless or positively harmful, for practitioners will have had no knowledge of the necessity to sterilize surgical knives and other instruments: the importance of cleanliness was simply not understood – we know next to nothing of the personal hygiene arrangements of Anglo-Saxons in general, and even less of those within tenth-century armies – which meant that even minor surgery probably led in many cases to avoidable deaths, with septicaemia turning many superficial wounds into fatal injuries.

[1156] Keynes and Lapidge 1983: 270 fn.220.
[1157] Pollington 2002: 221, and now Kirkham and Warr 2014, especially the chapter by Clasper.
[1158] Pollington 2002: 222.
[1159] Rubin 1989: 13-14.
[1160] Sturlason 1930: 199.

Deaths from slowly-developing septicaemia may have far outnumbered deaths on the battlefield caused by weapon injuries.

One of the most common surgical procedures was blood letting, based on the theory that excess blood in the body was harmful, a belief that lasted until fairly recent times. Magic and superstition played an important role in this procedure, and it was thought more beneficial to employ the treatment on certain days.[1161] Those conditions which failed to respond to treatment were evidently dealt with by magical practices, such as the recitation of traditional incantations that we now call charms – the Old English word for a charm is *galdor*, related to the word *galen* 'to sing'.[1162] Those who survived battle wounds could expect, at best, a prolonged recovery with possible after-effects including epilepsy, progressive blindness, deafness, paralysis, lameness, and so on. Little wonder that Anglo-Saxon and Viking armies took pains to avoid direct armed conflict.

[1161] Lapidge et al 1999: 430-1.
[1162] Lapidge et al 1999: 304-5; 96-7.

22. Treatment of defeated enemies.

There was no common practice during the Anglo-Saxon period for dealing with defeated enemy combatants.[1163] In the ninth and tenth century royal and noble prisoners taken prisoner in battle were often slain outright, or taken for ransom. Some men of high status recorded as being killed in battle are likely to have been captured and executed afterwards. Vikings who fell into English hands tended to be treated in the same way as common criminals and summarily executed. This was the fate of the Vikings whose two ships were swept ashore after a naval battle with the English off the south coast in 896.[1164] The Vikings were taken to King Alfred at Winchester, who ordered that they be hanged. Sometimes, if we are to believe what was written at the time, Viking survivors met a more gruesome end, such as being flayed alive,[1165] although no evidence has been found to support the widespread idea that some ancient church doors were covered with (and even retain traces of) human skin, supposedly from captured Vikings.[1166]

The fate of prisoners taken in battle lay entirely at the whim of the victor, and those of high status are likely to have been treated more harshly than others. Those of low status often had some value as chattels, to be sold: slaves were a valuable commodity not only in Anglo-Saxon England, but throughout the European mainland, and the market in English slaves on the continent is well recorded in Anglo-Saxon, Irish and Frankish sources.[1167] Like the Anglo-Saxons, the Vikings certainly treated captured enemies as slaves and booty. Bede relates how a Northumbrian nobleman called Imma who was captured fighting against Mercia after the battle of the Trent in 679 claimed to have been a poor married peasant who was merely delivering provisions to the enemy. His life was spared and his wounds treated so that he could be sold into slavery, though he was later able to buy his freedom.[1168]

There is little evidence that the adoption of Christianity introduced any concept of compassion on the battlefield. Bede tells how two heathen nobles captured in battle were allowed to accept baptism before they were executed so that their souls could be saved, allowing them to submit gladly to temporal death.[1169] In 914 the men of Gloucestershire and Herefordshire defeated a Danish army at the battle of Archenfield and cornered the survivors in an enclosure, taking hostages to guarantee the oaths of the Danes to leave peacefully, although we might assume that the English forces could easily have stormed the enclosure and killed the enemy.[1170] In 921, Edward the Elder slew all those who had put up armed defence of a fortification at Tempsford, but took prisoner all those who had

---

[1163] See especially Gillingham 2008.
[1164] Swanton 1996: 91.
[1165] Pollington 1989: 126.
[1166] Pepys records a visit to Rochester on 10th April 1661 where he saw the cathedral doors which were said to be covered with the skins of Danes, and similar traditions are found at Hadstock, Essex, and Westminster Abbey.
[1167] For slavery in the Viking age see Brink 2008a. In 821 Vikings seized and took into captivity 'a great number of women' from Howth peninsula, north of Dublin, and in 871 Viking raiders from Dublin returned from the British kingdom of Stathclyde with 'a great prey of Angles, Britons and Picts': HM March 2014 28. A fanciful account in the *Fragmentary Annals* tells how the sons of Ragnall mac Albdain travelled to Spain and Africa, returning c.866 with a number of African captives: Downham 2009: 267.
[1168] McClure and Collins 1999: 207-10.
[1169] McClure and Collins 1999: 198.
[1170] Swanton 1996: 98.

not fought.[1171] The *Liber Eliensis*, a Latin compilation of c.1170 derived from pre-Conquest sources, has an account of the battle of Maldon in 991 which tells how the Vikings left the battlefield with the head of Ealdorman Byrhtnoth, the heroic leader of the doomed English forces, who had been decapitated as he fought. The head was evidently retained as a trophy. Since the incident is recorded with some horror, it might be imagined that it was seen as an exceptional act of barbarity, but an analysis of early sources reveals other examples of Scandinavians placing the head of an enemy leader on a stake and using it for target practice.[1172]

However, there was one aspect of warfare with the Scandinavians that is said to have struck particular terror into English leaders. One gruesome aspect of their sacrifices to Óðinn, god of war, was what the Scandinvians supposedly termed *blóðorn*, or 'blood-eagle'. This was the grisly ritual in which the victim's lungs were torn out and spread like wings on his back. In 867 the Danes fought the English at York and captured king Ælla, who was then murdered. The Danish historian Saxo Grammaticus (c.1150-c.1220) gives an account of the death of the king: 'When they captured him, they ordered the figure of an eagle to be cut in his back, rejoicing to crush their most ruthless foe by marking him with the cruellest of birds. Not satisfied with imprinting a wound on him, they salted the mangled flesh. Thus Ælla was done to death'.[1173] *Ragnars saga* gives this account: 'King Ælla and his men took flight, but he was captured. [The Danish king] Ívarr was nearby at the time, and said that they should thus devise his death ... Let a skilled wood-carver mark out an eagle on his back as deep as may be, and let that eagle be reddened with his blood ... they caused a bloody eagle to be carved into the back of Ælla, and they cut away all of the ribs from the spine, and then they ripped out his lungs'.

Elsewhere, the text known as *Orkneyinga Saga* tells of the capture of Hálfdan háleg, son of king Haraldr of Norway, in the last decade of the ninth century, by the ruler of Orkney, Jarl Torf Einarr, who 'carved the bloody eagle on his back by laying his sword in the hollow at the backbone and hacking all the ribs from the backbone down to the loins, and drawing out the lungs; and he gave him to Óðinn as an offering for his victory'.[1174]

These texts have been held to be clear evidence of the ritual of the blood-eagle. In the case of both Ælla and Hálfdan, the defeated leaders were kings and were taken captive after battle, and both were ritually sacrificed in the same way. However, the *Orkneyinga Saga* was written c.1200, and Saxo Grammaticus was writing in the early thirteenth century, long after the events he purports to describe. Both sources are a mixture of myth and fact. Paddy Griffiths is probably correct in his conclusion that 'The whole blood-eagle phenomenon was entirely invented in the Iceland of the 1100s, and its only link with poets vaguely contemporary with the actual event is every bit as unsubstantiated as the technical details of just how the execution itself may have been carried out'.[1175]

Yet there is other evidence that might support the existence of *blóðorn*. In 870, king Edmund besieged the Danes under King Ívarr in their winter camp at Thetford, but the Danes joined battle, and Edmund was captured and killed. The chronicler Abbo of Fleury (c.945-1004) describes how Edmund was beaten, bound to a tree, shot full of arrows, and

---

[1171] Swanton 1996: 102.
[1172] Kennedy 1991: 63-8; McDougall 1993: 211-12.
[1173] Smyth 1977: 189; Ellis Davidson and Fisher 1980: II 160-1.
[1174] Smyth 1977: 191; Smyth 1984: 153-4.
[1175] Griffiths 1995: 35-6; see also Williams 2008: 196.

finally beheaded. Abbo says that after the shooting of javelins into his body, and with his body 'lacerated to the very marrow by the acutest tortures', the king still called out Christ's name. Ívarr then ordered Edward's head to be cut off, but 'The king was by this time almost lifeless, though the warm life-stream still throbbed in his breast. And he was scarcely able to stand erect. In this plight he was hastily wrenched from the blood-stained tree, his ribs laid bare by numberless gashes, as if he had been put to the torture on the rack, or been torn by savage claws, and was bidden to stretch forth his head ...'. The mention of ribs laid bare and of bones being exposed, and the use of the expression 'torn', might be seen as an account of a high-status victim subjected to the ritual of the blood-eagle.

Of particular interest, though not directly linked to any known battle, is the discovery in 2010 on the ancient Ridgeway, four miles north of Weymouth, of a mass grave containing 55 well-built skeletons. Scientific examination revealed that the bodies were those of tall, well-fed young males, most aged 17 to 25, with a few slightly older. Some had evidence of long-standing physical impairment and poor health, but there was no sign of earlier war wounds. By isotopic testing of their teeth enamel it was established that they all came from Scandinavia and immediately adjacent areas: one may have been from Iceland, and all had spent much of their lives in the Arctic Circle. One skull had distinctively Scandinavian horizontal grooves that had been filed on the front teeth. All the bodies had been savagely decapitated, and the absence of any brooches, pins or other clothing-related items suggests that they were naked when they were killed. Osteological examination of the bones showed that they had been decapitated from the front, facing their executioners. Most of their faces and many of their right ears had been mutilated, some had deep cuts to their jaws and collarbones, and others deep wounds to the pelvis, stomach and chest. One had wounds to his hands, evidence of a futile attempt to defend himself. The bodies had been thrown into an empty Roman quarry pit with the severed heads placed in a pile near the side. The improvised mass grave was then sealed with a layer of earth. Radiocarbon tests dated the bones to between 970 and 1025, and archaeologists concluded that they may have been the remains of Vikings executed by the English, or perhaps Danes slaughtered in the infamous St Brice's Day massacre. In the late summer or autumn of 1002, 'the king ordered to be slain all the Danish men who were in England [and] this was done on St Brice's Day (13th November)', although the *Anglo-Saxon Chronicle* explains or excuses his actions by recording that 'he had been informed that they would treacherously deprive him, and then all his counsellors, of life, and possess the kingdom afterwards'.[1176]

[1176] Boyle 2016.

23. Wales in the late ninth and early tenth century.

It is far from easy to extract a clear picture of events in Wales in the latter part of the ninth and early part of the tenth centuries from the tantalisingly incomplete, fragmentary, and in many ways contradictory written evidence.[1177] What is clear is that despite their hostility, there existed, as Alfred Smyth has emphasised, a recognition of a common Germanic society – enshrined primarily in similarities of common Germanic culture and oral literature – between English and Danes, which perhaps explains the rapid assimilation of Danish settlers into the Anglo-Danish society of the tenth and eleventh centuries (but perhaps places insufficient weight on the retention by the Hiberno-Scandinavians of their pagan religion well into the tenth century), whereas the Welsh were, perhaps surprisingly, seen as *Wealh*, 'foreigner', who 'would remain a foreign people whose impenetrable language and zealously guarded traditions prevented that same kind of acculturation which developed at so many levels between Christian English and pagan Dane.'[1178] Smyth also notes that in his *Life of Guthlac*, the biographer Felix, writing in the 730s or 740s, confirms early English hatred of the Welsh even – perhaps most particularly – in the circles of the holiest of holy men,[1179] and also military campaigns by the Welsh far into central, and perhaps even eastern, England, regarding them as 'implacable enemies of the Saxon race, troubling the nation of the English with their attacks, their pillaging and their devastations of the people'.[1180]

The ethnic barriers which existed between English and Welsh are further highlighted at about the same time by Bede's venomously racist attack on the Welsh (though not the Irish) clergy: he writes that 'Though, for the most part, the Britons oppose the English through their inbred hatred, and the whole state of the catholic Church by their incorrect Easter [dating] and their evil customs, yet being opposed to the power of God and man alike, they cannot obtain what they want in either respect'.[1181] Bede's views were perhaps influenced by Gildas's excoriation of the Britons for failing to join in the evangelisation of the pagan English, and his [Bede's] earlier description of the Welsh as 'that nation of heretics' and his justification of the slaughter of Christian Welsh clergy at the hands of the English at the battle of Chester in 613.[1182] Some degree of the supposed animosity between the English and Welsh recorded by Bede evidently survived well into the eighth century, but the realities of the changing political situation in England and Wales led to some gradual shifting of positions. That seems to be shown by evidence such as *St Mildburh's Testament*, which provides important information about the history of Much Wenlock abbey, founded c.685. A brief overview of that history is provided elsewhere in this volume, but suggests that during the reign of Wulfhere (657-674) and Ethelred (674-704), an Anglian dynasty took control, though not by force of arms, and reigned over a preponderantly Welsh-speaking population, successfully planting English settlers in the Welsh Marches, and enjoying a relatively peaceful coexistence and evolution with the native population, joining with their Welsh neighbours as necessary against their common Northumbrian enemies. Further evidence from the *Life of St Guthlac* points to a

---

[1177] For a general overview see Hill 2001: 173-82.
[1178] Smyth 1998: 30-1.
[1179] The first consecration of Chad as bishop by one English and two Welsh bishops was rescinded by Theodore and Wilfrid as illegitimate, since the Welsh were considered heretics and schismatics: Charles Edwards 2013: 396-410.
[1180] Smyth 1998: 31-2.
[1181] Book V 23; McClure and Collins 1994: 290.
[1182] Sherley-Price 1968: 102-4; Book II 2; McClure and Collins 1994: 73-4.

breakdown in that relationship, with a series of devastating Welsh raids over Mercia during the reign of Coenred (704-9), which continued intermittently throughout the eighth century, proof that 'in the age-long conflict for the domination of the marchlands the initiative in these years was with the Welsh',[1183] until Offa (757-96) built his dyke to firmly demarcate the frontier.[1184] In 816 Mercian armies under Cœnwulf (796-821) penetrated into Snowdonia, and in 818 Dyfed was harried, with the campaign against the Welsh continued by the king's brother and successor, Ceolwulf I (821-3).[1185]

From the end of the seventh century there were several separate kingdoms in Wales. The largest was Gwynedd, which probably encompassed the whole of north-west Wales, with several other kingdoms: Gwent, on the north side of the Severn estuary, Glywysing in south Wales, Dyfed in south-west Wales, Ceredigion and Ystrad Tywi in central west Wales (which were previously united as Seisllwg), and Powys, lying between Gwynedd and Mercia, but these were not monolithic territorial units, for on occasions there may have been more than one king in a single kingdom, and at other times kings seem to have controlled more than one kingdom. As occasion demanded, these kingdoms sometimes formed alliances under a single strong leader, such as Cadwallon ap Cadfan, king of Gwynedd, who was driven out of his kingdom by Edwin of Northumbria, but formed an unexpected alliance with the ruthless pagan King Penda of Mercia (c.626-55) to attack and defeat Edwin at the battle of Hatfield Chase c.633, only to be killed himself the following year at the battle of Heavenfield near Hexham.[1186] Indeed, the major political development in the eighth and ninth century was the growth in power of the kings of Gwynedd, which may have been the pre-eminent kingdom from an early date, but it is clear that the Vikings had long been a threat to all the Welsh kingdoms.

To the Vikings the Irish Sea was little more than an inland lake, and like Ireland, Wales was raided from the Irish Sea. Terse annalistic accounts record raids between 851 and 877.[1187] Anglesey was ravaged by Irish Vikings in 853-4 and in 856 Rhodri Mawr killed Orm, the leader of the Viking fleet, off Anglesey, for which Continental sources tell us that he won the gratitude of the Frankish king, Charles the Bald, who was suffering even more severely from Viking attacks.

The medieval forger of the so-called *Pseudo-Ingulph*, who is likely to have made use of genuine sources, some of which are now lost to us, says of events in 871 'Bürgred, king of the Mercians, was busily engaged with the Britons, who, by their frequent interruptions, disquieted the western borders of his kingdom of Mercia', which, if based on historical events, might suggest a pattern of attacks by the Welsh, though Charles-Edwards sees the Mercians taking 'every opportunity to pursue their objective of maintaining their power in Wales, probably taking advantage of Viking attacks on Gwynedd'.[1188] The 870s and 880s were decades characterised by English campaigns in North Wales.[1189] Bürgred himself was driven overseas in 873 by the Danish Great Army which partitioned Mercia in 877, leaving a client-king Ceolwulf in possession of 'English' Mercia. In 877 Rhodri Mawr, king of

---

[1183] Stenton 1970: 362.
[1184] Finberg 1964: 75, 77, 81. For military activity involving the Welsh during Offa's reign and earlier see Stenton 1970: 359-62.
[1185] Williams, Smyth and Kirby 1991: 83.
[1186] Williams, Smyth and Kirby 1991: 72.
[1187] Davies 1990: 50.
[1188] Charles-Edwards 2013: 486-6.
[1189] Griffiths 2001: 180.

Gwynedd, was defeated in battle in Anglesey and fled to Ireland.[1190] The Irish annals tell us that his enemies were Vikings from the group to which Orm had belonged, who were not only avenging Orm but protecting links with Dublin by conquering Anglesey.[1191]

If Asser is to be believed, the Vikings wintered in Dyfed in south-west Wales in 878, which often presaged a more permanent base: it would be surprising if Wales did not witness intense coastal raiding of the sort seen in Ireland at this period. In the same year King Alfred defeated the Danish Great Army at the battle of Edington, which led to the baptism of the Danish king Guthrum into the Christian faith. The *Annales Cambriae* tells us that in the same year 'Rhodri and his son Gwriad [were] killed by the Saxons', probably a force led by Ceolwulf, the ruler appointed by the Danes and memorably described in the partisan *Anglo-Saxon Chronicle*, originating in Wessex, as 'a foolish king's thegn', although there is evidence that he was in reality a powerful and successful ruler. In circumstances that remain cloudy Ceolwulf was succeeded by *ealdorman* Æthelred as ruler of Mercia the following year, but even though married to Alfred's daughter, Æthelflæd, he was never recognised as king by the West Saxons.[1192]

In the 880s Alfred may have been encouraging West Saxon contacts with Wales, and his attempts to improve learning and literacy attracted scholars from throughout Europe to his court, including Asser, a senior Welsh cleric who became Alfred's biographer and raised the profile of Alfred in Wales, and of Wales in Alfredian circles.[1193] If we can rely on Asser's *Life of Alfred*, the authenticity of which has been the subject of particularly vicious and unedifying academic dispute in recent years but is now generally accepted as trustworthy,[1194] possibly intended for a Welsh audience (an idea rejected in particularly scathing terms by Alfred Smyth),[1195] Alfred took a surprisingly active role in undermining Mercian control over the Welsh.

According to Asser, the southern Welsh kings feared attack from Gwynedd in the case of Dyfed, and Brycheiniog in the central south-east, and from 'the force and tyranny' of the Mercians under Æthelred in the case of Gwent and Glywysing in the far south-east. It was Æthelred who led the Mercian army against the Welsh of Gwynedd at the battle of Conwy in 881, hostilities resulting from a blood-feud between Mercia and Gwynedd which ended

---

[1190] Rhodri married the daughter of the king of Ceredigion, and seems to have acquired Powys in 855 and absorbed Ceredigion in 872. From the twelfth century he was known as Rhodri Mawr, from *mawr* 'great', alluding to his resistance to the Vikings and his expansion of Gwynedd: Williams, Smyth and Kirby 1991: 207; James 2001: 205; Davies 2003: 324.
[1191] Despite its English-sounding name, long influenced by association with Angles, Anglesey, first recorded in a Norse text of 1098, probably combines the Scandinavian personal name *Ongull* (whose identity is unknown) and Old Norse *ey* 'island'. Its ancient name was *Môn*, Latinized as *Mona*, of uncertain meaning: Wyn Owen and Morgan 2007: 7; Wyn Owen 2013: 325.
[1192] Hill 2001: 175; Charles-Edwards 2103: 488. In Mercia Æthelred's name appears after that of Ceolwulf II in the Mercian king-list preserved at Worcester: Smyth 1995: 389. The chronicler Æthelweard refers once to Æthelred as *ealdorman* (dux), and twice by the unambiguous title *rex*: Campbell 1962: 46, 49, 50.
[1193] Maund 2005: 77.
[1194] See especially Smyth 1995, a magisterial, if flawed, case arguing that 'Asser' is a late 10th or early 11th century forgery compiled in the late tenth century at the monastery of Ramsey. Those arguments have not found favour with most Anglo Saxon scholars: see e.g. Lapidge 2003: 44-47. A brief but balanced analysis of the evidence can be found in Abels 1998: 318-26.
[1195] Keynes and Lapidge 1983: 56-7; Smyth 2002: 130. Smyth finds the idea that the 'neologisms, Grecisms and archaic Latin ... to confuse and impress the most erudite scholars' could have been produced for a Welsh audience to be preposterous: Smyth 2002: 130.

in a Mercian defeat (called by the Welsh 'God's vengeance for Rhodri'), which marked the start of the collapse of Mercian authority in Wales,[1196] and during which Æthelred may have sustained injury that could explain what has been seen to be his gradually incapacitating ill-health. This was the period during which Æthelred's power in Wales was described by Asser as a military tyranny,[1197] but Æthelred's defeat at Conwy highlights the military strength of the Welsh of Gwynedd, capable of defeating a powerful Mercian army. Much of northern and eastern Mercia was now held by the Vikings, and it is possible that fears of attacks from the Danelaw led to some population drift southwards, perhaps into south Wales, which possessed good agricultural land. However, the kings of south Wales were weak and their borders difficult to defend, which led to them accepting the overlordship of Alfred, who represented a strong political force capable of resisting the Vikings and discouraging Æthelred's ambitions in the region. He was also overlord of the Mercians, of whom they were fearful, as they were of Anarawd ap Rhodri of Gwynedd and his brothers, the most powerful and politically effective group in Wales. From the death of his father Rhodri in 878 Anarawd was to prove the most powerful and significant figure in North Wales for more than three decades.[1198]

Æthelred of Mercia's submission to Alfred, rewarded by the grant of London to the *ealdorman* in 886 (which placed London in Mercian hands, though the *Anglo-Saxon Chronicle* account recording the event was careful to conceal that Æthelred was a Mercian, rather than a West Saxon), further cemented by Æthelred's political marriage to Alfred's daughter, emphasised that Wessex and Mercia were to be seen as strong allies. That seems to have been one factor which encouraged Anarawd, if Asser is to be believed, to enter an alliance with the Viking rulers of York.[1199] Anarawd's territory would have held great strategic importance for both the Danes and Hiberno-Scandinavians, providing them with strategically important unhindered access via Anglesey to the Irish Sea, linking the interests of Dublin and York via the trans-Pennine Roman roads between the Mersey and York.[1200] The other factor was how the Viking threat was perceived at the time: Anarawd must have calculated that a Viking victory over the English was all but inevitable, that the threat from Æthelred's Mercia was unremitting, and that he had little to gain from an alliance with the English king. The alliance might provide an explanation for the otherwise puzzling suggestion by Roger of Wendover that there were existing Viking settlements at and near Buttington in 893.[1201]

That idea is reinforced by entries in the Welsh annals (from manuscripts written long after) which mention Danes in Wales: the Welsh chronicle *Brenhinedd y Saesson* records under the year 890 (correctly 892): 'the Black Norsemen came again to Gwyn',[1202] an event also

---

[1196] Charles-Edwards 2001: 101, 491. Asser describes the power of Æthelred in Wales a militant tyrant, with the animosity between Gwynedd and Mercia is powerfully exemplified in the 10th-century poem *Armes Prydein*: Charles-Edwards 2013: 491.
[1197] Charles-Edwards 2013: 491.
[1198] Charles-Edwards 2013: 438.
[1199] Charles-Edwards 2013: 491-2, 526.
[1200] Stevenson 1959: 318; Davies 1982: 106; Williams, Smyth and Kirby 1991: 46; Davies 2003: 335; Charles-Edwards 2013: 490-1. There is considerable evidence of Roman saltworking at Middlewich but less at Northwich and Nantwich in the Roman period, though at Domesday these and other nearby places in Cheshire were clearly thriving salt-producing centres and the focus of established long-distance route-ways: VCH Cheshire I 198-211, 328-9. The significance of salt production to the Scandinavians is unclear.
[1201] Giles 1892: 231.
[1202] Jones 1971: 24-5.

recorded in *Brut y Tywysogion* which notes that in 890 'the Black Normans came a second time to Castle Baldwin'. That place can be identified as Hen Domen (also known as Old Montgomery, not to be confused with the present town of Montgomery), which lies at the strategically important ford of Rhydwhiman[1203] on the river Severn, some seven miles from the ford at Buttington.[1204] Neither chronicle indicates when the Danes first came to the area,[1205] but we have seen that there were Viking settlers in the Wirral and Southern Lancashire at this period,[1206] and that the Vikings had ravaged Gwynedd and other parts of Wales in the mid-890s.[1207]

Anarawd's alliance with the Northumbrians was to prove short-lived. He soon discovered that the Northumbrians were not to be trusted, and their repeated attempts to occupy North Wales are said to have led him to abandon the treaty c.890 and with his brothers negotiate a new alliance with King Alfred by 893.[1208] According to Asser, although Anarawd was received at court by Alfred and treated with greater respect than any of the other Welsh kings – Alfred indeed became his godfather – oppressive terms were imposed on him.[1209] One outcome of the treaty might have been Anarawd's support of the English at the siege of the Danish camp at Buttington in 893, where the armies of Wessex and Mercia are said to have been assisted by a contingent of Welsh forces.

After their defeat at Buttington the Danes regrouped at Shoebury and moved back to Chester, where they were attacked by the English and forced to retreat into Wales, eventually reaching Monmouthshire and Glamorganshire in 894, before eventually retreating from their fortification on the river Lea and wintering in 895-6 at *Cwatbrycge*.[1210] Gwynedd, Glywysing, Ceredigion, Dyfed, Ystrad Tywi, Brycheiniog, Gwent and Gwynllwg (the coastal area between the river Rhymney and Usk in Monmouthshire) were all ravaged in two raids in the mid-890s, both from the direction of Mercia.

Anarawd's alliance with Alfred, if true,[1211] means that by 896 Alfred had two leading Christian subordinates: his son-in-law Æthelred, *ealdorman* of the Mercians, and the king of Gwynedd, both of whom were subject to the same treaty arrangements,[1212] in addition to the allegiance of the southern Welsh kings. This arrangement was not without its dangers,

---

[1203] Rhydwhiman is the anglicised Welsh name Rhyd Chwima: Davies 2006: 23.

[1204] Both place-names were transferred to the new castle at Montgomery Trefaldwyn, which lies a little under two miles away, c.1224: Morgan 2001: 137-8; Owen and Morgan 2007: 328.

[1205] Williams ab lthel 1860a: 16-17; Downham 2009: 205.

[1206] Bu'lock 1972: 51.

[1207] Wendy Davies has concluded that at a later period, between c.960 and 1015, Scandinavians were actually controlling Gwynedd, either from the Isle of Man or Dublin or indeed from bases within Wales itself: the various members of the Gwynedd dynasty were referred to as 'holding' Gwynedd. They were not called 'kings', and were paying tribute to the Vikings: Davies 1990: 59

[1208] See Kirby 1971: 12-35; Charles-Edwards 2013: 491-2, 526.

[1209] Williams ab lthel 1860: 16; Stevenson 1959: 318; Jones 1971: 27; Davies 1982: 106; Williams, Smyth and Kirby 1991: 46; Davies 2003: 335. It is worth noting that Welsh rulers retained their kingship after submission to Alfred, whereas in West Saxon eyes Æthelred was not king of the Mercians, but *ealdorman*: Charles-Edwards 2013: 494.

[1210] Wainwright 1975: 75-6.

[1211] Alfred Smyth notes that the (West Saxon) *Anglo-Saxon Chronicle* would have been expected to trumpet such a remarkable military and political success, which it does not mention, and concludes after careful analysis that the account of Anarawd abandoning his allegiance with the Northumbrians and submitting to king Alfred 'can be dismissed as fiction': Smyth 1995: 358-62, 390.

[1212] Charles-Edwards 2001: 101-2; Charles-Edwards 2013: 489-90, 493-4.

for Alfred would have realised that he might be at risk if Æthelred and Anarawd were to combine forces against him, perhaps not the most obvious coalition given that it was Anarawd who had led his forces to victory over Æthelred's forces at Conwy in 881. Yet there is evidence that suggests that Alfred's settlement of the Welsh situation did face attack by his principal client rulers.

The *Annales Cambriae* records in 894 that 'Anarawd with the Angli came to ravage Ceredigion and Ystrad Tywi'.[1213] *Angli* was probably the expression used in place of the usual term *Saxones* to show that it was the Mercians rather than Alfred and the West Saxons who were involved in this campaign. The account may be seen as evidence of a joint action by Anarawd and Æthelred to make inroads into the various alliances with an increasing number of Welsh kings created by Alfred during the 880s (or possibly of an attempt to dislodge newly-arrived Scandinavians), and is a reminder that Æthelred was a powerful ruler prepared when necessary to challenge Alfred's client kingdoms, notwithstanding Alfred's overkingship, and was no passive vassal of his father-in-law.[1214] Certainly Asser refers to the 'power and tyranny' of ealdorman Æthelred that compelled the kings of South Wales to seek the protection of Alfred.[1215] Anarawd certainly received military support from the Mercians in the joint campaign of 894 to extend his power into south-west Wales, when Alfred chose not to support the heirs of Hyffaidd, the king of Demetia with whom he had an alliance but who had died in 893. It is clear that submission to the king of Wessex offered no automatic protection from the aggressive rulers of Gwynedd. One intriguing reference in the Anglo-Saxon Chronicles mentions the death in 896 of a certain Wulfric, described not only as the king's horse-thegn, but as the Welsh reeve.[1216] The term is unique, and Wulfric's powers and responsibilities unknown, but it has been suggested that he may have been bi- or even tri-lingual if he was required to administer taxes among the Welsh or Cornish.[1217] The office may have been a Mercian innovation, since a list of soldiery or officials with mounted men including 'those men who we call in English *wahlfaereld* [literally 'Welsh expedition']' to whom the grantees were excused from providing food and lodging are mentioned in a grant of privileges in 855 to the monastery of Blockley, Gloucestershire, during the reign of Mercia's King Burghred.[1218]

Little is known of other matters affecting the region at this period, but a reference in *Brenhinedd y Saesson* to England and Brycheiniog and Gwent and Gwynllwg being ravaged in 896[1219] hints at other actions about which we have no other details, and there were doubtless very many more which have been lost in history.

For almost a decade Anarawd and his brothers had been able to consolidate their holdings in north and central Wales, until the Viking leader Ingimund, driven from from Dublin in 901, defeated the Welsh near Llanfaes and sought refuge in Anglesey before he was forced out by the Welsh under Cadell ap Rhodri.[1220] Ingimund and his followers then moved to the Wirral, to occupy land supposedly granted by Æthelflæd. This seems to have been a

---

[1213] Williams ab Ithel 1860: 15.
[1214] Charles-Edwards 2013: 495-6, 507.
[1215] Smyth 2002: 38-9.
[1216] ASC 'A' *Wealhgefera*, 'B', 'C' and 'D' *Wealhgerefa*: Swanton 1996: 91. For a useful discussion of the *Chronicle* entries see Williams 2009a: 47-8.
[1217] Swanton 1996: 91.
[1218] S.207; Hill 2001: 182; Ray and Bapty 2016: 226, 409 fn.42.
[1219] Jones 1971: 19.
[1220] Wainwright 1975: 79-86; Downham 2009: 208; Charles-Edwards 2013: 496.

period when an upsurge in Viking settlement occurred in the wider region, including the Isle of Man,[1221] with Vikings drawn form much further afield – possibly including Brittany, the Shetlands and even Iceland – moving to the north-west. Anarawd continued to rule Gwynedd until his death in 916, when the Welsh chronicles commemorate him as king of the Britons, a title reserved for the most powerful Welsh kings.[1222]

The challenge by Anarawd to Alfred's support for his Welsh sub-kings in the 890s was to lead eventually, seemingly between 903 and 909, to Alfred's heirs and successors promoting overlordship over the Welsh, and the conquest of Dyfed by the Mercian alliance.[1223] By 910 it is likely that the Welsh kingdoms in the north of Wales were in allegiance with the Mercians, were unlikely to support any Danish incursions into Mercia, and may even have fought in support of the joint English army at the battle of Tettenhall,[1224] but the impact of the battle on Welsh history might be measured by the fact that it merits not even mention in a footnote in a recent magisterial study of the early medieval history of that nation.[1225] The creation of the *burh* at Chirbury on the Welsh border by Æthelflæd in 915 (probably January) and at *Cledmuþan*, probably Rhuddlan in north Wales, in 921 by her brother Edward the Elder, suggest a considerable English influence in, or domination over, this part at least of north Wales and concerns about attacks from both the Scandinavians and the Welsh during this period, concerns perhaps apparent in the disturbances that Edward was forced to quell at Chester immediately before his death in 924.[1226]

On the other hand the *burhs* could have reflected co-operation between the Welsh and English against a mutual enemy, the Vikings.[1227] Wendy Davies reminds us that 'the overwhelming tenor of the surviving written evidence is that it was the English who repeatedly launched attacks on Wales, and not the Welsh who attacked England. Despite popular belief, schoolbooks and the mythology that surrounds [Offa's] dyke, it is extremely difficult to find solid evidence of Welsh attacks on the English between the late seventh and mid-eleventh centuries'.[1228]

Charles-Edwards has identified three characteristics to mark the final phase of Welsh-Mercian relations in the quarter century between 893 and the winter of 918, shortly before Æthelflæd's daughter Ælfwynn was removed from Mercia in a *coup d'état* by her uncle Edward: the revival of Mercian power in Wales, the triumph of Merfyn Frych in all regions outside the South-East, and renewed Viking pressure on Gwynedd.[1229] Æthelred and Æthelflæd had evidently wished to maintain Welsh support, but also ensured they kept a visible reminder of Mercian supremacy. Both took an interest in Wales, suppressing activities which threatened the security of the border and assisting with defence against Viking attacks, though their authority in Wales was not unlimited: they could not raise

---

[1221] Charles-Edwards 2013: 500-501.
[1222] Maund 2002: 43-5.
[1223] Charles-Edwards 2001: 104-105.
[1224] Though Wainwright commented that 'relations between Mercia and the Welsh were not good', at least during the first two decades of the 10th century: Wainwright 1975: 90 fn.2. Wendy Davies has concluded that in the tenth century Welsh alliances with the Vikings were not uncommon, though no sources are cited: Davies 2003: 335.
[1225] Charles-Edwards 2013.
[1226] Griffiths 2001: 182-3.
[1227] Wainwright 2000: 26 fn.21; Maund 2005: 77.
[1228] Davies 1990: 67, but see Charles-Edwards 2001: 181-2.
[1229] Charles-Edwards 2001: 498, 102.

taxes, for example.[1230] One question arises from this: was the joint English army at the battle of Tettenhall supported by Welsh forces? If it was – which is quite possible, though there is not the slightest evidence – they were were almost certainly led or made available by Anarawd, the former ally of the Scandinavians. Indeed, Anarawd's brother Cadell ap Rhodri, probably holding Dyfed and Ystrad Tywi (both to become known as Deheubarth) died in 909 or 910.[1231] Could Cadell have been injured or fallen at Tettenhall? The answer is probably no, since there is no hint in Welsh chronicles that his death was violent.

A curious if violent incident occurred in at midsummer, 916, when (according to the *Mercian Register*) an Abbot Ecgbriht, 'though innocent', and his companions were killed, and three days later, presumably in response, Æthelflæd sent an army into Wales which destroyed *Brecenan mere* (Llangorse Lake, near Brecon) and captured the king's wife and 33 others.[1232] Nothing more is known of these events, but the implication is that Brycheiniog then possessed its own king under Æthelflæd, who was forced to demonstrate her authority in the area.[1233] We also have here confirmation that the force sent into Wales was not led by Æthelflæd herself.[1234]

The submission of Dyfed and Gwynedd to Edward the Elder in 918 may be seen as circumstantial evidence (though not accepted by Charles-Edwards)[1235] that Æthelflæd, described in both Irish and Welsh annals (both in later manuscripts) as queen,[1236] who died at Tamworth on 12th June 918, had secured during the second decade of the tenth century the submission of the brothers Hywel and Clydog of Dyfed, together with Idwal of Gwynedd, the three Welsh kings who held all of Wales except Brycheiniog, Glywysing and Gwent in the far south-east of Wales. Of those kingdoms it seems possible that by 914 the first had fallen under Mercian control, and the other two under West Saxon control. That would explain the attendance by Welsh kings at the Wessex court in the early tenth century, to judge from the witness lists to English charters, including king Tewdwr, son of Elisedd and ruler of Brycheiniog in 916.[1237] It would also explain why Edward paid forty pounds ransom to secure the release from Viking raiders of the Welsh bishop of Archenfield, after which the men of Hereford and Gloucester drove off the Vikings, killing a number of their leaders. The events were recorded by Æthelweard, who portrays the

---

[1230] Maund 2005: 77.

[1231] Lloyd 1948: II 332; Charles-Edwards 2013: 504. It is unlikely that Cadell is the same person as *Catol* who was campaigning in 903 in Pictland with two grandsons of Ívarr (Downham 2009: 209-10), but Anarawd and Cadell acted together to launch an invasion of Dyfed in 905: Maund 2000: 44-5; see also Charles-Edwards 2013: 504, 506.

[1232] Earle and Plummer 1892-9: I 100. Little is known of Ecgbriht, but he is likely to be the same person as Abbot Ecgberht who witnessed a charter of Æthelflæd (S.225, 13th century copy, in which she is called *regina* and illustrated in royal majesty) in 915: *Prosopography of Anglo-Saxon England* sub nom *Ecgberht*, accessed 12 September 2015.

[1233] Charles Edwards 2013: 505.

[1234] It is worth recording the comment of the 12th-century monk, politician and historian Aelred of Rievaulx, who records when writing of Æthelflæd that 'She herself fought against the Welsh': Sommerfeldt 2006: 108. The comment seems likely to derive from the incident at Llangorse Lake.

[1235] Charles-Edwards 2013: 498-9.

[1236] Williams ab Ithel 1860: 17; Jones 1971: 28-9. Æthelred, Æthelflæd and their daughter Ælfwynn are described by Davidson as 'quasi-regal subreguli, who were unable or unwilling to completely break off their ties with Edward [the Elder]': Davidson 2001: 204-5. Demonstrating which English personalities were significant to the Irish and Welsh at this period, Irish sources and the 13th-century *Annales Cambriæ* record the death of Æthelred and Æthelflæd, whereas the death of Edward the Elder is unmentioned: Woolf 2001: 89.

[1237] Davies 1982: 114.

Welsh as powerless against their attackers, who had 'ravaged in Wales everywhere along the coast where it suited them'.[1238]

The possibility of a Viking political overlordship in North Wales in the tenth century has been reinforced by evidence from Anglesey, including excavations near Llanbedrgoch in Anglesey of a settlement of Hiberno-Scandinavians which produced traces of links between Wales and Ireland.[1239] This was a period which saw a considerable immigration of Hiberno-Scandinavians from Ireland into north-eastern England between the Mersey and the Solway Firth. The first intimation of the new danger from that quarter is an account from Irish sources (perhaps based on the work of a Welsh analist writing in Latin, whose writings may lie behind the terse entries in the Welsh *Annales Cambriæ*)[1240] of settlement in the Wirral by Hiberno-Scandinavians led by Ingimund in the early years of the tenth century after they had been driven from Dublin in 901.[1241] One group, led by Ingimund, is said by a later section, perhaps eleventh century, of *The Fragmentary Annals of Ireland* (though its reliability is open to question),[1242] to have fled to North Wales, almost certainly Anglesey, but was forced out by Clydog ap Cadell after 'Ogmundr' was defeated by the Welsh at the battle of *Ros Melion*, as recounted in the Welsh *Annales Cambriae* and *Brut y Tywysogion*,[1243] and made its way into north-western England. From there Ingimund made some sort of arrangement with Æthelflæd – the few references to her husband, 'Edilfrid', said to be 'at that time in a disease ... and it was from this disease that Edeilfrid died',[1244] are noteworthy – who supposedly granted him land in the Wirral to settle, but in about 905 he attempted to seize Chester, seeing that 'the city was very wealthy, and the land around it choice'.[1245] The siege was the subject of a lengthy and entertainingly fantastical account – much, if not all, probably myth – in Irish annals.[1246] Æthelflæd, supposedly with the assistance of Christian Irish and Danes, repulsed the attack, said to have been made by both Norsemen and Danes, and refortified the town in 907, a measure clearly designed to help control the new settlers and protect Mercia from Ingimund's forces.[1247] Once again these actions are attributed to Æthelflæd alone, seen as further evidence of her husband's ill health. If *The Fragmentary Annals of Ireland* is to be believed, not long after Ingimund's attack on Chester '[they came] to wage battle again',[1248] though nothing more is known about the episode(s) which led to this brief but ominous record.

David Griffiths, reviewing in some detail the history of the wider area around Chester from the reign of Offa to the death of Edward the Elder, sees the Ingimund/Chester events as 'a

---

[1238] ASC 'A', 'C', and 'D'; EHD I 194; Pelteret 2009: 327.
[1239] Maund 2005: 81; Griffiths 2001: 179; Downham 2009: 207; Readknap 2008; Redknap 2009; Charles Edwards 2013: 501-2.
[1240] Wainwright 1975: 151.
[1241] Wainwright 1975: 131-61.
[1242] Maund 2005: 81, which points out that the north Welsh king is named as 'the son of Cadell son of Rhodri' presumably intending Hywel Dda, which would be impossible at this date.
[1243] Griffiths 2001: 179; Lavelle 2010: 140, 230; see also Charles 1934 16-18.
[1244] Wainwright 1975: 80.
[1245] VCH Cheshire: I 249.
[1246] O'Donovan 1860: 230-7. The inventive tactics used by the defenders included pouring boiling beer on the attackers and hurling bee hives against them.
[1247] VCH Cheshire: I 249; Wainwright 1975: 84, 153-4; Williams, Smyth and Kirby 1991: 160; Swanton 1996: 94. Wendy Davies has concluded that in the tenth century Welsh alliances with the Vikings were not uncommon, though no sources are cited: Davies 2003: 335.
[1248] O'Donovan 1860: 230-7; Wainwright 1975: 79-83; Quanrud 2015: 79.

product of the Irish annalistic tradition, which tended to stress the heathenism and barbarity of the Vikings', and points out the dangers of relying on events recorded only in one source –*The Fragmentary Annals* – implying that the legendary events involving the Vikings and Chester may be greatly embroidered, if not fiction, and preferring to see the new *burh* at Chester in the light of centuries of fluctuating Mercian control over the North Welsh border territory, especially the territory known to the Welsh as Tegeingl, between Chester and Rhuddlan.

We are told by William of Malmesbury in his *De Gestis Regum Anglorum* that Edward died suddenly from sickness at his estate at Farndon-on-Dee, twelve miles south of Chester, in 924, shortly after suppressing a putative Mercian and Welsh rebellion centred on Chester, in which he placed a garrison.[1249] If true (and we have no other evidence: the *Anglo-Saxon Chronicle* is silent on the point), the account suggests that the local population preferred an alliance with the Welsh rather than submission to the remote authority of Wessex.[1250] Passions long continued to simmer, with Rhuddlan, for example, temporarily recovered by the Welsh as late as the mid-eleventh century.[1251]

The account in *The Fragmentary Annals* may distract us from attempts by Æthelflæd in 907 to formally consolidate from Chester control of territory nominally under Mercian domination but with what Griffiths describes as 'the most decayed infrastructure of royal control',[1252] and to impose military authority from an ancient and strategic centre, dominating a direct route between Scandinavian Dublin and York, which would subjugate both the Scandinavians and the Welsh within the wider area: we should recall the critical alliance, perhaps made c.881, between Anarawd of Gwynedd and the Viking rulers of York,[1253] abandoned by the Welsh king c.890, and the Welsh annals which mention Danes in central Wales and Hen Domen.[1254]

It will be also remembered that Roger of Wendover (and Matthew Paris following him), in describing the events leading up to the siege at Buttington in 893, mentions 'countrymen [of the Danish Vikings] who dwelt in the western part of England', and 'the town they had built there [i.e. at Buttington]',[1255] with the *Anglo-Saxon Chronicle* reporting that after regrouping following their defeat at Buttington, Danish Viking forces returned to the north-west and took refuge in the fortification of the 'deserted city' of Chester, perhaps indicating that the place had been evacuated in the face of the Scandinavian advance.[1256] If Roger of Wendover is correct, the movement of Hiberno-Norse into the area after their expulsion from Dublin c.901 served to supplement an existing population of Scandinavians in the region, and their migration doubtless precipitated other medium-ranking leaders, some associated with the exiled Dublin family of Ívarr, others from elsewhere, to launch a new phase of settlement in the Irish Sea region, with landings on the

---

[1249] Giles 1847: 131.
[1250] Smyth 1995: 438-40; Griffiths 2001: 167, 182; Charles Edwards 2013: 500.
[1251] Griffiths 2001: 180-2.
[1252] Griffiths 2001: 2001.
[1253] Charles-Edwards 2013: 491-2, 526.
[1254] Jones 1971: 24-5. As noted elsewhere, there is a reference to the *pagani* recorded in the territory of the *Wreocensæte*, 'the people associated with the Wrekin' (which seems to have included what became the northern part of Shropshire as far as the Cheshire border), in a Mercian charter of 855: S.206; see Gelling 1992: 51, 83; also Whitelock 1955: I 90; 485-6; Finberg 1961: 48 no. 77. These *pagani* are usually seen as a raiding party rather than settlers.
[1255] Luard 1872: 431; Giles 1892: 231.
[1256] Giles 1892: I 231; ASC 'A'; Swanton 1996: 88; Griffiths 2001: 169.

coasts of Galloway, the Isle of Man, Cumbria, Westmorland, Lancashire, East Yorkshire, Anglesey, and the north coast of North Wales (as well as the Faeroes and the Cotentin Peninsula), to negotiate new settlements with local lords and to displace others, attested by surviving Old Norse place-names, sculpture, hoards, artifacts, and other archaeological evidence.[1257]

The great Cuerdale Hoard found near Preston in 1840, which included silver from Dublin and coins of c.902-5 from York, suggests that relations between the Vikings of the Irish Sea littoral and York were established very soon after 902.[1258] As noted above, the siege of Chester in 905 was said to have been carried out by both Norsemen and Danes (but with other Danes fighting with the English), a formidable and threatening coalition confronting the Mercians ostensibly ruling the area, and Charles Edwards has no doubt that 'Edward the Elder's *burh*-building activity in north-west Mercia in 919-21 may have been directed at enhancing royal power ... with Vikings in mind rather than the Welsh', and concludes that the mysterious 'battle of the New Fortress', recorded tersely in 921 in the *Annales Cambriæ*, could have been at Rhuddlan and could as easily have been Welsh allied with Edward against Vikings, as between the Welsh and the English,[1259] so not dismissing the supposed alliance between English rebels and the Welsh leading to the Chester uprising immediately before Edward's death in 924.[1260]

After the death in 918 of Æthelflæd, the dominant figure in western Britain north of the Brecon Beacons, and the abrupt removal of her daughter and successor Ælfwynn by Edward the Elder soon after, Mercia became effectively subsumed into Wessex, but rather surprisingly there seem to have remained separate administrative arrangements for the collection of tribute, one covering the West Saxon section and another for the Mercian section, a division which evidently persisted long after. Owain of Gwent was among the rulers who formally submitted to Æthelstan after he became king in 927.[1261] When King Eadred died in 955, his nephew Edwy became king of Wessex, but was seen as weak and troublesome by the Mercians and Northumbrians, who preferred Edwy's young brother Edgar. In November 957 the Mercians and Northumbrians renounced their allegiance to Edwy, and most of Wales went with Mercia, with Welsh tribute paid to Mercian officials. The following year fifteen-year old Edgar was signing charters as 'King of the Mercians and Northumbrians and Britons',[1262] and the division of taxation continued after Edgar also became king of Wessex on Edwy's death in 959. The situation remained unchanged in the second half of the tenth century after Mercia fell under the control of the powerful ealdormen Ælfhere and his brother-in-law Ælfric, and continued under earls Leofwin and Ælfgar in the eleventh century. Wales had effectively become divided between Gwent, which paid tribute to Wessex, and the neighbouring lands to the north which owed tribute to Mercia, a split which could be traced back to when Edward the Elder was overlord of Gwent and Æthelred and Æthelflæd were Lord and Lady of the Mercians.[1263]

[1257] Griffiths 2001: 35; ownham 2009: 84. Gillian Fellows-Jensen has suggested that the Norman Barony of Copeland and the Westmorland hamlet of Coupland both have Norse place-names incorporating ON *kaupa land*, 'bought land', suggesting that 'not only great estates, but small units of settlement passed into the hands of the Vikings in return for money': Fellows-Jensen 1985: 417, quoted in Griffiths 2015: 36.
[1258] Gooch 2012: 169; Charles Edwards 2013: 502.
[1259] Charles Edwards 2013: 499, 503.
[1260] Charles Edwards 2013: 500.
[1261] Whitelock 1961: 68-9.
[1262] Charles-Edwards 2013: 513; S.677; EHD 109.
[1263] Charles-Edwards 2013: 513-4.

There are various incidents and campaigns during the period which can be pieced together from brief documentary sources, and there were almost certainly many others, some probably significant, of which no evidence has survived, but it seems evident that in the late ninth and early tenth century the Danes and Hiberno-Scandinavians were not seen by the Welsh as natural allies, but at least some of the Welsh saw the Scandinavians as more amenable allies than the English, as evidenced by the poem *Armes Prydein* ('The Great Prophesy of Britain'), found in *The book of Taliesin*, an early fourteenth-century manuscript. The poem is not so much a prophesy as a two-hundred line violently anti-English call to arms and expression of hatred against the 'dung-gatherers of Thanet', perhaps responding to the appeasement of King Æthelstan by Hywel ap Cadell (Hywel Dda 'the Good'), dating from between 927 and 942:[1264]

'... and there will be reconciliation between the Cymry and the men of Dublin, the Irish of Ireland and Anglesey and Scotland, the Picts, the men of Cornwall and of Strathclyde will be made welcome among us ...'[1265]

The poem not only calls upon the Welsh and their allies, the non-Saxon peoples of the British Isles ('the men of Dublin' being York-based Norse who had recolonised Dublin after their expulsion in 901), to oppose the policies of Hywel Dda and rise against the English, but prophesies that the day will come when the English will be expelled from the land of Britain forever.

Though evidence for this period is confusing and contradictory, one respected authority has even concluded that between c.960 and 1015 Scandinavians were actually controlling Gwynedd, either from the Isle of Man or Dublin or indeed from bases within Wales itself: the various members of the Gwynedd dynasty were referred to as 'holding' Gwynedd. They were not called 'kings', and were paying tribute to the Vikings.[1266]

[1264] See especially Charles-Edwards 2013: 514, 519-35.
[1265] Williams 1953: 63; Davies 1982: 117.
[1266] Davies 1990: 59

24. Supposed tumuli in the Wolverhampton, Wednesfield and Tettenhall area.

Any study of the battle of Tettenhall must consider the number of supposed tumuli in the wider Wolverhampton area, since burial mounds have long been associated, in most cases incorrectly, with the burial of battle dead.[1267] Since none is known to have been excavated, it is impossible to know what number may have been man-made, and the Anglo-Saxons of the West Midlands (who would have no better knowledge than we have about tumulus-shaped mounds) would tend to label any mound with the appearance of a tumulus as a *hlāw*, often found as 'low' in place-names.[1268]

Whilst most tumuli are prehistoric, usually Bronze Age, in date, the pagan Anglo-Saxons, before they converted to Christianity in the seventh century, are known to have buried their dead in large mounds, sometimes re-using prehistoric tumuli. Artificial mounds were also created for other purposes in the Anglo-Saxon period, including meeting places and boundary markers. The concentration of mounds in the Wolverhampton area is of particular interest in the light of the place-name Wednesfield, with its pagan Anglo-Saxon connotations, and the possibility that the burial places of the dead from the battle of Tettenhall were marked by mounds raised over mass burials. It should be remembered that no supposed or suspected tumulus mentioned below has been scientifically explored; no reference to bones or grave deposits has been traced in association with any of the supposed tumuli; and no artifacts are recorded that may help to date any of the mounds. They could have been Bronze Age, early Anglo-Saxon, of natural formation, or artificially created for purposes unknown at any time from the prehistoric period. It should also be borne in mind that Bronze Age tumuli were generally constructed on skylines, not necessarily the highest point in the area, but a mound raised over the dead from a battle is likely to have been established close to the concentration of corpses. If any of the presumed tumuli in the area lay on low ground, that might increase slightly the remote possibility that they could be associated with the battle of Tettenhall.

The following is a list of supposed tumuli (none of which has been detected in LiDAR surveys) in the Wolverhampton/Wednesfield area:

Low Hill 2 miles north of Wolverhampton, on Bushbury Hill (SJ 9201),[1269] recorded as *La Lowe* 1287,[1270] *Lowe* 13th and 14th centuries, *le Lowe Hyll* 1545,[1271] *Le Lohill* 1612,[1272] *Low* 1686.[1273] This was a large tumulus (now destroyed) well-recorded on the hill at Bushbury. The mound is mentioned by Huntbach (1639-1705), who described it as 'very large',[1274] and it is recorded by Plot in 1686,[1275] although by the early nineteenth century it was barely visible.

[1267] To the north, two tumuli are recorded on Calf Heath near Four Ashes, and one on Rowley Hill, on the west side of the river Penk: Horovitz 1992: 20. A number of place-names in the Pattingham area (e.g. Kingslow, Stanlow) attest to the existence of others: Horovitz 2005: 343, 508.
[1268] In the 17th century Robert Plot believed the sandstone outcrop at Hints on Watling Street near Tamworth was a Roman tumulus which had become solidified with age: Plot 1686: 402-3.
[1269] Wolverhampton HER 2507.
[1270] SHC 1911 193.
[1271] SHC XI 289.
[1272] SHC IV NS 38.
[1273] Plot 1686: 409.
[1274] Erdeswick 1844: 349.
[1275] Plot 1686: 409.

Rumblelows (Farm) obsolete, in the manor of Wednesfield, 1½ miles north-east of Wolverhampton (SJ 925005),[1276] on the north side of the headwaters of Smestow Brook. The earliest spelling which has been traced is *Tromelow* c.1272.[1277] The first element in the name is from *þrēom*, the dative of Old English *þrēo* 'three', giving 'the three tumuli or mounds'. When the name was prefixed by *æt* 'at', the initial letter of the name became confused with the end of the preposition, which produced *æt Romelow*, rather than *æt Tromelow*. The name changed to Rumbelows (a name also found in other parts of the country) around the turn of the nineteenth century: the Wednesfield Tithe Map of c.1842 shows the name as *Rumbeloes*.[1278] No record of any tumuli in the area has been traced,[1279] and the farm itself lay in the approximate position marked by the southernmost part of Hallams Crescent in Fallings Park.[1280]

North Low at Wednesfield (SJ 944005).[1281] Huntbach (1639-1705) says that a tumulus here was visible 'near in lands croft-lodge',[1282] but Plot, writing in 1686, says that though there was previously a tumulus, in his time it had disappeared.[1283] North Low Field lay near Stafford Road (which may have been the early name for Amos Lane or Long Knowle Lane),[1284] upon the Old Heath: *Northlowefeld* is recorded in 1312, and *Norlowefeld Super le Oldehet* in 1347.[1285] Nordley Hill on the west side of Wednesfield (cf. Nordley Road) marks the position of Northlow Hill: Old English *law* sometimes becomes *–ley* in Staffordshire place-names, and *Northley Field* is recorded in 1667.[1286] Smallshire noted that 'No one could readily accept Mill Hill or Nordley Hill as being burial lows as they are igneous rock, but they may once have had lows upon them'.[1287] The summit of the hill at Nordley appears to lie under houses fronting East Avenue, though tumuli are often sited on the skyline rather than a true summit.

[1276] Wolverhampton HER 8700.

[1277] Horovitz 2005: 469.

[1278] Robert Dawson's detailed O.S. drawing, produced in 1816 (BL map collection), shows no features around what is named *Rumblands*: BL online gallery of first edition 1" O.S. draft surveys.

[1279] Rumblelows is not mentioned in the list of local sites where tumuli were still visible prepared by Huntbach (1639-1705): Shaw 1801 II: 150.

[1280] Land at Rumbelows was granted for the benefit of the chantry chapel at Willenhall in 1365 (SRO D593/B/1/26/19/17), with ten acres granted to Erdington's chantry of the chantry of St Leonard's, Bilston, in 1460 (Price 1835: 23). WJ, February 1906 41-7 contains an article on the planned estate at Fallings Park, with a detailed description and plan of the area. No reference is made to any historical features, and no evidence as to the location of the mounds can be traced on the map, or on 1816 draft 1" O.S. map produced by Robert in 1816 (BL map collection) or the the Tithe Map c.1842 (WSL S.MS.417/817). The Tithe Map shows *Bickford Harbour* on the south-west side of the crossroads to the south-east of Rumbleows Farm, also recorded in 1832-5 (SRO Q/Rut/3/5/1-4). The name may be of some antiquity: the word harbour occasionally derives from OE *eorþburg* 'earth fortification', and the name may be associated with *the Arbarleso* recorded in 1537 (SHC 1912 93), although that place is said to be in Gorsebrook. It is unclear whether the name might refer to ancient earthworks (a group of tumuli?) here. Could it refer to an ancient earthworks on *Woundon* (Dunstall Hill), overlooking the brook? The name Woundon may be from OE *wunden-dun* 'twisted hill', perhaps with reference to the banks and ditches of unrecorded earthworks.

[1281] Wolverhampton HER 352.

[1282] Shaw 1801 II: 150.

[1283] Plot 1686: 415.

[1284] Smallshire 1978: 53; 96.

[1285] SRO D593/B/1/26/6/2/4; SRO D593/B/1/26/6/2/17.

[1286] SRO D1798/666/62.

[1287] Smallshire 1978: 23.

South Low (SO 947993). *South Low Field* (also known as *Windmill Field*) is recorded as *Southlowefeld* in the early fourteenth century and lay at Mill Hill, Neachells Lane and Well Lane,[1288] with the windmill said by Huntbach to have been built near (not on) the low which was visible in his day, and supposedly situated just north of Planetary Road.[1289] Plot says in 1686 that the low 'lately had a windmill upon it, the low being there before as within memory', and believed it was associated with the battle of Tettenhall,[1290] but Wilkes, writing in the eighteenth century, claimed that the windmill was set on hard rock which extended several yards below the surface.[1291] As noted above, Smallshire commented that both North Low and South Low were on igneous rock, but may once have had tumuli on them.[1292] A steel pressings factory for A. E. Jenks & Cattell Limited is said to have been built on the site in the 1930s.[1293]

Dunnlow Flatt recorded near Northlow in Wednesfield in 1702.[1294] The name probably means 'the dun or brown tumulus', or the first element may be from the Old English personal name Dunna.

John *Lowe* is recorded in Wednesfield in 1451,[1295] probably from *The Low*, but possibly from Northlow, Southlow, Dunnlow, or some other unrecorded low.

The Low (Heath Town), recorded as a field-name on the 1840 Tithe Apportionment, at SO 933993. This is evidently to be associated with *Lyttyl Low*, recorded on *the Heath* of Wolverhampton in 1537,[1296] and *the great and little lowe in the heath grounds* mentioned by Huntbach (1639-1705), and evidently still visible when he was writing.[1297] *The Low* seems to have been within Churchfield on or near the summit of slightly rising ground which is now crossed by the northernmost of two railway lines south of New Cross hospital. The name *Great Low* implies that it was the largest in the area – it evidently lay on the highest point in the vicnity of Wednesfield, higher indeed than the village centre, but on the other hand may have been so-named to distinguish it from a smaller mound (*Lyttyl Low*) nearby.

Coplowe is associated with *Le Hylfeld* (Hillfield, one of the common fields of Willenhall) in 1463.[1298] The name incorporates Old English *copp* 'peak' with *hlāw*, so 'the tumulus

---

[1288] SRO D593/B/1/26/2/1-2; Wolverhampton HER 353. Well Lane is recorded in 1764 (Smallshire 1978: 53), and may be associated with John ate Walle recorded in 1513: SRO D593/B/1/26/6/7/14.
[1289] Shaw 1798: I 150; Smallshire 1978: 53; 96. The mill is shown on Robert Baugh's map of Shropshire, 1808.
[1290] Plot 1686: 415.
[1291] Shaw 1801 II: 150. Any tumulus could have been removed to create a firm foundation for the windmill.
[1292] Smallshire 1978: 23.
[1293] Smallshire 1978: 130.
[1294] Smallshire 1978: 97.
[1295] SRO D593/B/1/26/6/2/5.
[1296] Shaw 1801 II: 150; Hackwood 1908: 7; SHC 1912 93. Huntbach notes that Little Low lay 'in the heath grounds', presumably the area marked *Heath* to the east of Wolverhampton and south of what is now Heath Town on Yates' 1775 map of Staffordshire. Heath Town, in the 18th-century *Heath Houses* (Bowen's map of Staffordshire 1749), was formerly a manor called *Heath*, recorded in 1557: SHC 1928: 132-3. In the later 19th century it known as Wednesfield Heath.
[1297] Shaw 1801 II: 150.
[1298] SRO D593/1/26/6/39/10.

with the peak or pointed top', or (less likely) 'the tumulus on the pointed hill': there are few hills here.[1299]

At Stowheath lay *Stowman's Hill*,[1300] or *Stowmanslow*, sometimes said to have been a tumulus, recorded from 1686: Plot mentions 'Stowman's hill on the road betwixt Wolverhampton and Walsall, half a mile SW of the village of Nechells', believing it to have been the burial place of a Saxon or Danish king or noble.[1301] Wilkes says in the eighteenth century that *Stowman-low* had been removed to mend the roads, and was a stone pit, but nothing remarkable had been found in it.[1302] Mander notes that Stowmans Hill marked the meeting place of the townships of Wolverhampton, Bilston, Willenhall and Wednesfield,[1303] but the apparent size of the mound makes it unlikely that it was a tumulus or erected as a boundary marker, and it must have been adopted as a pre-existing prominent local landmark. It also marked the boundary between the Hundreds of Seisdon and Offlow. The age and derivation of the name are unknown.[1304]

The mound, which was evidently of considerable size, may have been a natural deposit of alluvial gravel, though it is noteworthy that Wulfrun's supposed charter of 994 and a survey of 1240 both use the ford over the river Tame here as a boundary mark, not Stowman's Hill. Had the prominent mound existed at the time, we might suppose it would have been utilised as the mark. Furthermore, the 1240 survey mentions an 'entrenched place of Wulfrini', probably a misreading of the name Wulfrun. The place, probably somewhere between the ford and Noose Lane in Wednesfield, has never been identified, but the description 'entrenched place' is unlikely to have been applied to Stowman's Hill.

Another intriguing name recorded in Wednesfield in the earlier fourteenth century is *Cauwet* (described as 'a small piece of land'), mentioned in 1313, *Kanwotes* (perhaps properly *Kauwotes*, *n* and *u* being frequently confused) in 1339, *le cawotes* (1346), and *the*

[1299] Though outside this area of study, a supposed tumulus adjoining Rushall Hall on the north side of Rushall in a low-lying and formerly wet situation may be mentioned. The mound is said to have produced many fragments of human bones mingled with 'Saxon coins': Willmore 1887: 249.
[1300] At SO 947982; Wolverhampton HER 2506.
[1301] 1686: 415.
[1302] Shaw 1798: I 38; Shaw 1801 II: 150. The hole was presumably the 'old Quarry Pit' (Moseley Hole?) mentioned in 1836: Price 1836: 16.
[1303] WA II: 90-1. The O.S. 1" map of 1895 shows the township boundary meeting point at crossroads a short distance to the west. Shaw 1801 II: 147 fn.3 suggests, without elaborating, that the names *Monmore*, *Lechmore* or *Lichmore*, *Stowman hill* and *Stowman lane* might be associated with the battle of Tettenhall.
[1304] On the various meanings of *stow* see Smith 1956: 35. No references to the name have been found before the 17th century (Plot 1686: 415), and there is no evidence that the name is of great antiquity: *Gibbet Lane* and *Gibbet meadow*, 2 acres adjoining *Stowman Lane* recorded c.1720 (SRO D440/99) might suggest that a gibbet stood on, or close to, Stowman Hill; see SRO D4407/77 for dating; *Stowman Hill* is recorded in Court Rolls in 1733 (WA II 91); and the field-name *Stowman hillpiece* is recorded in 1767 (SRO D4407/107 [SF124]); see also Price 1835: 16. The surname Stowmansell is found frequently in rent rolls from the early part of the seventeenth century, e.g. 1615 (SRO D593/J/22/7/14), 1620 (SRO D593/J/22/7/16), 1636 (SRO D593/5/22/7/19). If that is correct, the surname might perhaps be from the name of the hill, with the meaning 'the hill of the dweller(s) at the place called Stow', incorporating OE *mann* (EPNE ii 35), but possibly meaning 'the Mansell family from Stow', presumably the Stow from which Stow Heath took its name. But the references could be mistranscriptions of the name Normansell, a family prominent in the town at this period who lived at High Hall: Shaw 1801: II 163; Mander and Tildesley 1960: 61, 68, 93.

Cowats (1615).[1305] The name (the definite article may be noted) is not readily intelligible, but it may conceivably be a phonetic spelling of Old English **cwætt*, an element probably found in the name *Cwatbrycge* discussed elsewhere in this volume, almost certainly related to *quat*, a word used by Shakespeare meaning 'a pimple, a pustule, a small boil'.[1306] Such a word might have been applied to tumuli or burial mounds. Unfortunately it has not been possible to trace the location of the place(s).

Horselow, remembered in the name Horseley Fields 1 mile east of Wolverhampton.[1307] Recorded as *Horselawe* in 1204,[1308] Shaw gives, in chronological order, *Horslow*, *Horselowe-field*, *Horsehull-field*, and *Horseley-field*.[1309] The name is from Old English *hors* 'horse'. The tumulus had been obliterated by development by the eighteenth century.[1310]

Ablow, between Graisley and Wolverhampton, above Graisley Brook on the south-west side of Wolverhampton (SO 912978?).[1311] The earliest spelling to be traced is *Abbelowefeld* from 1361.[1312] Ablow Field covered 40 acres of unenclosed ground (according to one source enclosed c.1580)[1313] divided by Graisley Brook, and traces of the mound, 'a great low, or tumulus', were evidently still visible in the seventeenth century, when it was said to be 'near the turnpike on the Worcester road [i.e. the road to Penn], a little north of Grazeley brook', planted with a bush called Isley Cross or Iseley Cross.[1314] Local folklore which claims that the tumulus lies under St Paul's church[1315] seems to be based on little or no evidence. The mound is commemorated in the name Ablow Street, which appears to run slightly to the north of the former course of Grazeley Brook, which ran from the south-east to the north-west.[1316] Windmills were often located on mounds, and the old Goldthorn Windmill, a tower mill that appears to have stood at Blakenhall at the eastern end of what is now Grange Road, off Goldthorn Road until well into the twentieth century,[1317] may have replaced a much older mill, and was known as 'the windmill in Ablow Field', though it lay a good distance south of Ablow Street, which still exists.[1318] The first part of the name Ablow is evidently a personal name such as masculine

---

[1305] SRO D593/B/1/7/1/7; SRO D593/B/1/26/6/2/10; SRO D593/B/1/26/6/2/3; SRO D4407/85 [SF102].
[1306] CDEPN 487 sub. nom. Quatt.
[1307] At SO 9398; Wolverhampton HER 2503.
[1308] Horovitz 2005: 327.
[1309] 1801: II 150.
[1310] Shaw 1801 II: 150.
[1311] Wolverhampton HER 2505. The mound may be the supposed tumulus noted by Huntbach at *Hampton-town* mentioned in Shaw 1798: I 150.
[1312] WA DX/109/117/1.
[1313] Oliver 1836: 161.
[1314] Shaw 1798 I: 150; 1801 II: 163, 165; *172. The unexplained reference to a bush with the name of a cross is puzzling, and one would like to know more about the monument, about which nothing has been traced. It seems very possible, if not likely, that the handwriting of Huntbach, the original author (see Shaw 1798 I: 150; SHC 4th Series 11 72) was misread by Shaw or the printer, and that the name was actually [Gra]iseley [Cross]: written in 18th century script the words Cross and Bush might easily be confused.
[1315] Hackwood 1908: 7.
[1316] 1834 O.S.
[1317] Approximately SO 39909695. The mill is shown on Robert Dawson's Ordnance Survey map of 1816: BL.
[1318] Roper 1976: [22]. The mill is shown on Robert Baugh's map of Shropshire, 1808.

Ab(b)a or Æbba or feminine Æbbe or a shortened version of a personal name such as Eadbald or Eadburg.

Huntbach refers to a tumulus or tumuli (unidentified) 'at Hampton-town' (Wolverhampton),[1319] evidently sufficiently well-known to need no further description, but which could not be Ablow, which is mentioned separately.[1320] Nothing further is known of the mound.

Low Field recorded in Tettenhall in 1296[1321] and 1518 and said to have been 99 acres in 1613.[1322] It extended from what is now Coppice Lane to Wergs Road, but the precise location of the mound which gave its name to the field ('abutting upon a way leading from the Wergs to Stockwellend' according to a Court Roll of 1655)[1323] is now uncertain. According to Huntbach, although the mound had long been ploughed, it was still very visible in his day.[1324] Presumably because of its prominence, no early historian thought to give further details of its location. Tumuli were frequently on a skyline, so it is possible that the site lies beneath or near to the site of the present cricket club or at Danescourt House,[1325] which is on the highest point in the area, but the ground has been much affected by the creation of, amongst other things, the cricket field, a cemetery, and by the installation of field drainage at various times, and no evidence of any tumulus has been detected on aerial photographs.

Stonylowe in Tettenhall, traced in records only once, in 1296, the location of which is unknown.[1326]

Wightwick Mill mound(s). In his *History of Tettenhall*, published in 1894, J. P. Jones noted: 'Close to Wightwick Mill is a tumulus or burial mound, which would doubtless yield good results if explored; and on the opposite side of the road are some remains of a fort or fortification ... The tumulus at Wightwick is probably the burial place of many of those killed in this battle [i.e. the battle of Tettenhall], and traces of earthworks on the hill side adjacent to it suggest the locality of their camp', and in 1904: 'The presence of some large tumuli at Wightwick indicate the burial place of the slain, as well as the site of the battlefield. Some years ago I obtained permission from the late Colonel Henry Loveridge to explore the largest tumulus, but owing to the lack of funds; and worse still, an entire lack of interest in archaeology locally, the project had to be abandoned'.[1327] This

---

[1319] Shaw 1801 II: 150.
[1320] It is uncertain whether John *ate Lowe*, recorded in 1327 (Mander and Tildesley 1960: 7) or Alic' *Attelohende*, recorded in 1332 (SHC X 126), are to be associated with this feature.
[1321] *Lowefield*, SHC 4th Series XVIII 184.
[1322] VCH XXX 28; Wolverhampton HER 2511. VCH I 193 states that 'many human bones have been discovered' at Low Hill field, but the evidence cited does not support the claim, which appears unfounded.
[1323] Staffs SMR 2511. The 'way' may have been Danescourt Road.
[1324] Shaw 1801 II: 194. No reference to bones having been found has been traced.
[1325] ?SJ 884007. The curve near the west end of Danescourt Road might be thought to mark traces the perimeter of the lost mound, but Robert Dawson's map of Wolverhampton (probably the earliest detailed map of Tettenhall) produced for the O.S. in 1816 (BL map collection) shows that the road then meandered north-west from the site of what was to become Danescourt House (no building is shown on the site) to the junction of Wergs Road and Keepers Lane, rather than joining Wergs Road at that point.
[1326] SHC 4th Series XVIII 184.
[1327] WJ, October 1904 266.

tantalising reference to a tumulus and tumuli (and earthwork) must be of interest (if it can be relied upon), but can be seen only as strong evidence that more than one mound with the appearance of burial mounds, one larger than the other(s), existed near Wightwick Mill. We are given little information about their precise location or precise number. However, we have an important clue to the site of Jones's tumuli, for his reference to Colonel Loveridge consenting to an excavation implies that the mounds lay on his property.

Henry Loveridge (1810-92) was a successful local industrialist and businessman with a particular interest in art and design who lived in later life at Elmsdale (Hall),[1328] sometimes known as Viewlands, a grand house which still exists on the east side of and midway along Wightwick Bank, near what is now Wightwick Drive. In 1902 it stood in extensive grounds, with a carriage drive to Bridgnorth road which became Viewlands Drive.[1329] It seems safe to assume that the grounds incorporated the mystery mounds. The western boundary of Elmsdale is uncertain, but may have extended to the lower end of Grove Lane, now marked by the east end of Torvale Road, in which case our search can be narrowed to what still remains a sizeable block of land divided by Viewlands Drive on the north of Bridgnorth road, north-west of Wightwick Mill which stands on the opposite side of Bridgnorth road.[1330]

Our curiousity is further aroused by the conclusions of William Hutchinson, writing in 1904, who says: '... the writer ... ventures to think that the battle [of Tettenhall] took place between Compton and Wightwick, near the site which is marked by the presence of two large tumuli in the grass fields on the right side of the road, in which tumuli or 'lows', local tradition says the slaughtered Danes and Anglo-Saxons alike were buried, on the ground on which they fell'.[1331] Since Hutchinson was a Tettenhall man, we must suppose that the mounds to which he refers were on the right (west) side of Henwood Road travelling south from Tettenhall, and were those mentioned by J. P. Jones.

It seems clear that the supposed tumuli are to be associated with the mound on the west side of Henwood Road road opposite the mill explored in the 1920s by pupils from Wolverhampton Grammar School who found no artifacts. The mound is said, somewhat improbably, to have been surrounded by a ditch at least 15' deep and some 30' wide (measurements that must surely be incorrect), and a posthole on the perimeter was the only evidence of a structure. In 1955 Tettenhall Council arranged for a section to be cut through the mound before its imminent destruction. The section revealed fragments of brick and coal on an old turf line beneath mound debris. Yet the mound appears to have been in existence when the site was inspected in 1958 and 1974 by officers from the Royal Commission on Historical Monuments who describe it as 0.7 metres high with a diameter averaging 12 metres, with the ditch only visible as a slight scarping of the slope and the base [of the mound?] further scarped by ploughing. The 'excavation trench', presumably that made in 1955, had been left open, and was c.1 metre wide, 9 metres long and had been driven from the south-west to the centre of the mound where it had been enlarged into a

---

[1328] Loveridge had formerly lived at Claregate, at Stockwell End, and also owned the old farmhouse on Upper Green: Jones 1894: 4.
[1329] 1889-1891 1:10,560 O.S. map.
[1330] The 1889-1891 1:10,560 O.S. map shows a small roughly square copse in the approximate position of the east end of Torvale Drive (SO 876987) which might possibly mark the site of the mounds, though that is no more than speculation.
[1331] WJ, September 1904 240.

square pit. A red sandy soil containing small pebbles similar to natural sub-soil with traces of old turf lines and lenticulation was visible in the sides of the trench. Darker soil at the edge of the mound indicated the former ditch.[1332] Those reports tend to suggest that the mound was of relatively recent date.[1333] Certainly no references to any tumulus have been traced in early records, and the side of a river valley is not where one might expect to find an ancient burial mound. The area has now been subsumed beneath modern housing, though it is not impossible that traces have avoided destruction.

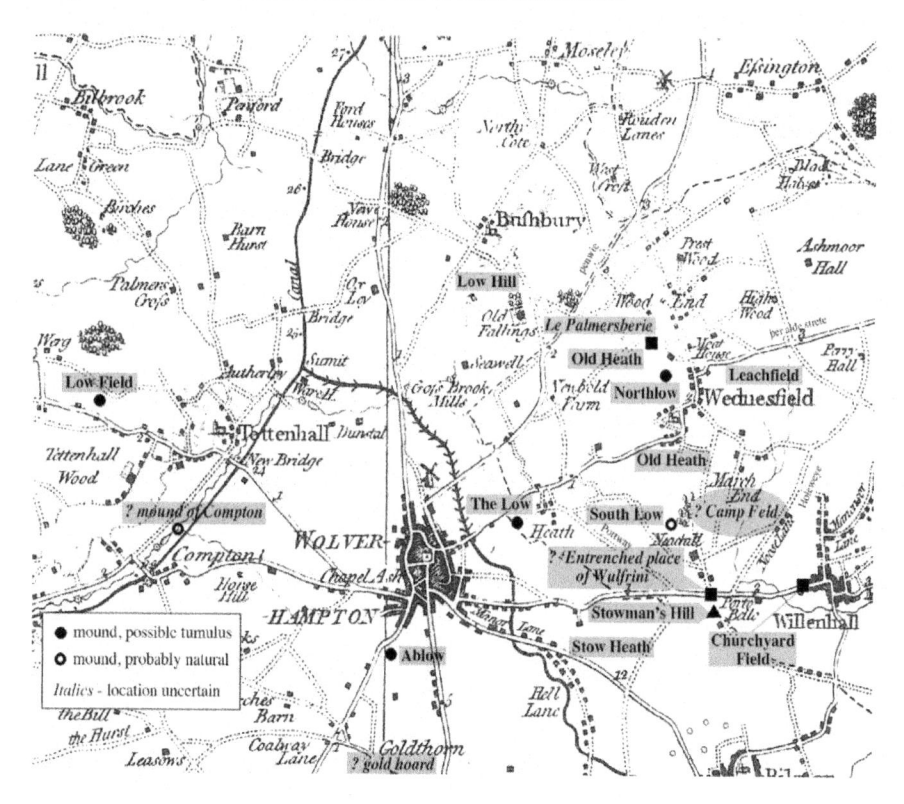

Extract from the first edition of William Yates' map of Staffordshire, 1775, with features mentioned in early records superimposed. The location of those shown in italics (especially *Camp Feld*) is uncertain, and they appear in their supposed position.

[1332] Wolverhampton HER 2566; grid reference 87550 98630. The record is somewhat confused, and it is not entirely clear when and by whom some of the measurements were made. The general view seems to have been that the feature was not ancient.

[1333] JNSFC 3 1965 49. This is clearly the mound at Compton excavated by amateurs in the early 1930s (perhaps the Grammar School pupils said to have dug in the 1920s?) which showed that it was of natural formation: in G. P. Mander's copy of Jones 1894 p.7 (in possession of author) is a manuscript note in the handwriting of GPM indicating that a supposed burial mound at Compton was explored in 193? [sic] and found to be a natural sand formation. JNSFC 3 1965 49 suggests that excavations of a mound near Wightwick Mill in 1955 (sic) showed it was of recent date. It is unclear whether these reports relate to the same mound.

No further information has been traced about the supposed earthworks on the bank above the Wightwick 'tumulus' or any fortification opposite (i.e to the east of) Wightwick Mill (if indeed the references relate to different features), which do not seem to have been noticed or mentioned by any other commentator. The latter can be probably be assumed to have been a natural feature or associated in some way with the construction of the nearby canal.

A mound called *Burni(l)delowe*, probably in Upper Penn, is recorded in the thirteenth century.[1334] The name appears to derive from *Brunhild's low*, Brunhild being an uncommon Anglo-Saxon personal name.[1335]

Roulowe Field in Lower Penn is recorded in 1316, and evidently lay near the road from Wolverhampton to Seisdon. The name is from Old English *ruh hlāw* 'rough mound or tumulus', perhaps meaning 'the overgrown mound or tumulus'.

In adition to the sites mentioned above, there are likely to have been other ancient mounds in the area which have long been destroyed, but which may be identifiable from documentary references to field-names incorporating Old English *hlāw*, usually found as 'low'.

[1334] SRO D593/B/1/17/1/3/10; Mander and Tildesley 1960: 8.
[1335] Searle 1897: 117. Reference has been made previously to the 'three lows on the common between Wombourn and Swin, placed in a right line that runs directly East and West? and about half a mile to the North of them is another, by the country people called Soldiers' hill. They are all large, and capable of covering a great number of dead bodies': Shaw 1798: I 38; see also Plot 1686: 397; Scott 1832: 329. No trace could be found of the mounds in the 1960s: NSJFS 1965 59.

25. Willenhall and its chapel.

We have seen that long before Domesday Book, Willenhall, a mile and a half south-east of Wednesfield, some two miles north-west of Wednesbury, was evidently a place of some importance: two charters[1336] of King Æthelbald of Mercia were attested at *Willanhalch*, usually identified as Willenhall in Staffordshire,[1337] as early as c.732, attested by the king and six and seven other witnesses respectively. These are some of the earliest references to any place in the county, and are of considerable significance, suggesting, if the identification of the place of attestation is correct (there is another Willenhall near Coventry, but it is very unlikely to be the place mentioned in the charters), that there was a high-status residence in what was probably a royal estate here in the first half of the eighth century of sufficient importance to serve as accommodation for the king and the important nobles and bishops in his retinue.[1338] An associated church is also likely to have existed at that time. David Roffe has concluded that Willenhall was clearly a royal vill, or part of one, in the eighth century,[1339] and Domesday Book records that the king retained an interest in Willenhall in 1086. It was evidently an important centre in the Middle Saxon period.[1340] Indeed, since it was in the Ancient Parish of Wolverhampton, it has been suggested that it (and Wednesfield) was once a member of Tettenhall.[1341]

Unfortunately the place-name Willenhall tells us little. Stebbing Shaw believed that the name was likely to be a corruption of *Winehale* (as it is actually recorded, typically corrupted, and also as *Winenhale*, in Domesday Book), incorporating Old English *win*, meaning 'toil, labour; fight, strive, struggle; conquer, gain; endure, suffer', and which he translated as 'victory', the name commemorating, he thought, 'that great battle which was fought hereabouts'.[1342] However, other early spellings make it clear that the place-name means 'the nook or corner of Willa',[1343] about whom we have no information of any kind, except that he lived before c.732, and the place-name can have no association with a battle which took place almost two centuries later. It is nevertheless of interest that Stebbing Shaw was willing to suppose that the great battle took place hereabouts.

After c.732 there is a complete silence about Willenhall until the eleventh century: it was not, despite a reference to the place in the preamble, included within Wulfrun's supposed endowment to the church of Wolverhampton, ostensibly in 994, since there is no boundary clause of the place, not because the charter was a post-Domesday forgery – it has now been shown to pre-date Domesday[1344] – but it is mentioned in Domesday when two hides were held as church property,[1345] perhaps having been exchanged for Bilston, a manor of

---

[1336] S.86 and S.87; Horovitz 2005: 578.
[1337] The charters are very similar, each being a grant by the king of the toll due on one ship at London to Mildred, abbess of Thanet.
[1338] S.86 is attested by the king and 7 nobles or bishops, S.87 by the king and 8 nobles or bishops, being those who witnessed the former plus one other.
[1339] Roffe 2014.
[1340] VCH IV 39.
[1341] Thorn and Thorn 2007.
[1342] Shaw 1801: II 147
[1343] Horovitz 2005: 578; CDEPN 680.
[1344] I am indebted to Dr David Roffe for making available his yet unpublished research into the Domesday estates of south Staffordsahire which, inter alia, establish that Domesday Book post-dates Wulfrun's charter.
[1345] The third endorsement made in the 11th or 12th century on the endorsement of the confirmation charter of Burton Abbey, which incorporates a copy of the will of Wulfric Spott, mentions, as well as

equal value. The rest of Willenhall, amounting to three hides, was held by the King in 1086, possibly ancient demesne of the Mercian rulers, or spoils recovered by King Æthelred from the dissolution of the Mercian ealdormanry on the banishment of Alfric, son of the notorious Elfhere.[1346] Willenhall therefore lay in the great Wolverhampton manor known as Stowheath, within the great *feld* or open plain from which Wednesfield took its name.

Any religious establishment at Willenhall must be of interest given the proximity of the place to Wednesfield and the possibility that it may have been in some way connected with, conceivably even created as a result of, the great battle. Domesday Book provides no evidence for any church at Willenhall, but is notoriously unreliable in that respect, since the purpose of the great survey took little interest in such matters. Any church existing in 732 may have been destroyed by the Danes, assuming it still existed into the later part of the ninth century, but as noted elsewhere in this volume, Beadugyth's stream mentioned in Wulfrun's grant formed the southern boundary of Willenhall, part of which was held by the church of Wolverhampton in 994 (if the spurious charter has been correctly dated), and may have been named after a religious, perhaps an abbess, in the late seventh century. Since her name is associated with the Willenhall area, it would not be surprising if she were connected with a church at that place: a Christian place of worship sited in an area possibly associated with pagan worship would be entirely appropriate. Indeed, evidence is adduced elsewhere in this volume which might identify Beadugyth as a late seventh-century abbess.

The chapel of St Giles at Willenhall is known to have been in existence by 1297,[1347] by tradition a chantry chapel built by and belonging to the Lords of the Manor of Stowheath,[1348] and is recorded as a chantry chapel in 1328, when it was granted various endowments by Richard and John Gervase.[1349] William, 7th Lord Lovell, held the lordship by 1441, and confirmed the original grant of Willenhall chantry in 1448.[1350] Of particular interest to us is a charter of 1365 relating to Rumblelows, the name meaning 'three mounds', on the north side of Wolverhampton near Dunstall, which includes the words *in quodam campo vocato Thromlowe inter terram cantarie de Stoweheth ex una parte et terram dicti Johanni de Ruyshale ex parte altera* ('... in a certain field called Thromlowe between the land of the chantry of Stowheath on the one side and the land of the said John

---

Waleshale and *Wodnesbyri*, two hides at *Wilenhale*, though none of those places was ever held by Burton abbey: Sawyer 1979: xxxvii.
[1346] WA II 89; Styles 1940: 58-9; VCH IV 39, 45; Hooke 1983: 66.
[1347] Patent Rolls 1297: Hackwood 1908: 32. The entry describes the church as Willenhall in Staffordshire, but it is just possible that it refers to Willenhall in Coventry. Mander and Tildesley 1960: 33 states that the church of St Giles was founded c.1300 by Richard and John Hampton, although no evidence is provided. The Great Pipe Roll of 1200-1201 lists *Wilenhale* and the abbot of *Wilenhale* (Chancellor's Roll of Third Year of King John, 1833, 49), but that is an error for abbot of *Lilleshall*: see SHC II 95, 103. The Levesons, associated with Willenhall since at least 1274, were greatly enriched by a grant of the lands of Lilleshall Abbey: TSAHS VI 1883: 15.
[1348] LMM I 1792: 341. An early lord of the manor was Robert Burnell (d.1292) of Acton Burnell in Shropshire, Bishop of Bath and Wells and Lord Chancellor of England 1274-1292: WA II: 106.
[1349] Shaw 1801 II: 174; SHC 1913 8-9; Tildesley 1952: 57; VCH III 325. Tildesley 1952: 57. Mander and Tildesley (1960: 33) say the chantry was founded in 1328, but it was evidently already in existence at that date: SHC 1913 8-9. By about 1394 at least 4 chantry chapels had been founded within the margins of Wolverhampton parish, including Willenhall, Bilston (Erdington Chapel), Pelsall (by 1311: Jenkins 1988: 45) and Hatherton: Price 1835: 23.
[1350] WA II: 105.

of Rushall on the other side').[1351] The reference is curious, and might imply that there was at this date a chantry chapel at Stowheath, which held the land which adjoined that being granted, but no chantry is known at Rumbelows, and it is clear that the chantry chapel of Stowheath was that of Willenhall: in a case heard in Chancery in 1795 it was claimed by the lords of the manor of Stowheath that the chapel of Willenhall had been founded and originally endowed by the lord or lords of the manor of Stowheath 'before time of memory'.[1352]

Chantry chapels – the word comes from Latin *cantana*, meaning a place for singing, specifically singing the Mass on behalf of departed souls – were created to allow prayers to be offered for the benefactor and others, so that their souls did not remain too long in the feared limbo-land of purgatory, a concept which took hold in the twelfth century, with the movement to found chantries gaining popularity in the thirteenth century.[1353] As in other places, chantries first appeared locally in the late twelfth century, but other than Burton Abbey, none is known in Staffordshire before the mid thirteenth century. From the 1240s they began to become far more common, and there were 20 in 1355.[1354] Willenhall chapel may well have originated, as stated by Hackwood and Tildesley,[1355] as a chapel of ease, established for the 'ease and comfort' of those living at some distance from the parish church,[1356] but by 1365 – and possibly much earlier – the chantry chapel certainly enjoyed, as noted above, the benefit of land at Rumbelows, perhaps including the site of three tumuli,[1357] which might conceivably be associated in some way with the battle of Tettenhall, and Richard Wilkes says of the chapel 'no date, or hint relating to it, was to be found; nor is any thing about it come to us by tradition'.[1358] That comment would suggest that the chapel was of some considerable age, for with other chapels the date of foundation is almost always on record. As we have seen, a chapel existed at Willenhall in the late thirteenth century, by 1328 it was a chantry, and it seems very possible that it was originally founded as such, even perhaps at a much earlier date.

There were three manors in Wolverhampton, two belonging to the church and one to the king. The church manors were those of The Deanery and the prebends, the the king's manor was that of Stowheath.[1359] Stowheath, a mile or so to the east of Wolverhampton, to the south of the road to Willenhall, is a name traced from at least 1272 (coincidentally,

---

[1351] SRO D593/B/1/26/6/19/17. I am indebted to Dr Philip Morgan of Keele University for this extract.
[1352] Attorney General –v– The Marquis of Stafford, 1795, Chancery cases. There were four chantries within the outer area of Wolverhampton parish: Bilston (founded in 1458), Pelsall (1312), Hatherton (before 1293) and Willenhall, with two others in St Peter's, Wolverhampton, one founded in 1311, the other mentioned in 1398: Price 1835: 22-3; Oliver 1836: 46; Hackwood 1908: 34; VCH III 325.
[1353] Gardiner and Wenborn 1995: 148.
[1354] VCH III 42. It should be noted that some chantries were private chapels rather than commemorative foundations: VCH III 42 fn.10.
[1355] Hackwood 1908: 32-3; Tildesley 1952: 57.
[1356] Friar 2000: 96. It was not until 1727 that St Giles church was consecrated for burials: Hackwood 1908: 79, 137.
[1357] If indeed the mounds were artificial, and not natural mounds, they are more likely to have been prehistoric than Anglo-Saxon. It is worth recording that 10 acres of land in 'the Rombelows in Hampton' were granted to Bilston chapel in 1460, having been founded two years earlier: Price 1835: 2-23.
[1358] Shaw 1801 II: 149.
[1359] Mander and Tildesley 1960: 25-6.

about the time of the earliest reference to Willenhall chapel)[1360] – and perhaps much older – and formerly applied to the manor formed probably in the early thirteenth-century by uniting the local royal manors of Bilston,[1361] part of Willenhall and one half of Wolverhampton, including the site of St Peter's church.[1362] *Stow* is an Old English word which may mean simply 'place', but often meant 'place of assembly', specifically 'holy place', often associated with a religious site or building. The most obvious derivation, if not from Willenhall chapel, is from the church founded or re-founded by Wulfrun, perhaps the predecessor to the present church, so 'the heath associated with the holy estate known as *stow*', but from the reference in 1365 to *cantarie de Stoweheth* 'the chantry of Stowheath', the place clearly provided income to support a chantry chapel at Willenhall.

The medieval capital messuage of Stowheath appears to have been at a moated site one mile to the south-east of Wolverhampton,[1363] and such sites often incorporated a church, though one has not been traced in records relating to the area. Although Hackwood, writing in 1908, felt that the chapel at Willenhall was neither 'a large or a magnificent structure, [but rather] a diminutive chapel constructed of timber ... some of its wall spaces, perhaps, were only of timber framed wattle and daub; and at most any building material of a more durable nature ... would be a plinth of stone masonry, and dwarfed at that',[1364] that is likely to have been mere conjecture, for there is particularly compelling evidence to the contrary: Richard Wilkes, the eminent and reliable historian who lived at Willenhall, saw fragments of an earlier (perhaps the original) building incorporated within the old Willenhall church in 1748 before it was rebuilt, from which he concluded that it had been a half-timbered building 'greatly ornamented, and must have been the gift of some rich man, or a number of such, the village then being thin of inhabitants; and ... they could not have been able to erect such a fabric; but no date or hint relating to it was to be found; nor has any thing about it come down to us by tradition.'.[1365] He was clearly impressed and perplexed by what he saw. Since an early lord of the manor of Stowheath was Ralph de Somery (c.1156-1211), Earl of Dudley, who in c.1204 exchanged it with King John (who consented in 1205 to the foundation of a Cistercian Abbey at Wolverhampton, a scheme which came to nothing)[1366] for the manors of Clent, Mere and Kingswinford, and the manor later passed to Robert Burnell (c.1239-1292), Lord Chancellor and said to be one of the most important church officials of the thirteenth century,[1367] it would not be especially surprising to find evidence of sumptuous ornamentation within any ancient fabric.

[1360] Horovitz 2005: 517.
[1361] The derivation and implications of the name Bilston (the place lies 2 miles south-east of Willenhall) should not be overlooked. In 895 it is recorded as *Bilsatena*, and between 994 and 1066 as *Bilsetnatun*, meaning 'the dwellers at Bil, indicating a tribal grouping which originated here or elsewhere. The meaning of Bil is uncertain: Horovitz 2005: 121.
[1362] WA II 103. Pasture called *Stow-brook* is recorded in 1458 (Price 1835: 23), but has not been located.
[1363] At SO928982. It was subsumed by the Chillington Iron Works: Cockin 2000: 561. It might be mentioned that the river Smestow, which rises near Showell and runs south to the river Stour, does not incorporate the element *stow*, but was originally Smestall, from OE *smeðe* 'smooth' or 'a smithy', with Mercian OE *steall* 'a place for catching fish' or 'stagnant water': Horovitz 2005: 498.
[1364] Hackwood 1908: 32; Shaw 1801: II 149.
[1365] Shaw 1801 II: 149. The building was then half-timbered, but it is not clear whether the fragments of fabric that impressed Wilkes were of timber or stone. It is said that when the church was rebuilt in 1750 it was 'so decayed that the inhabitants ... were in great danger of being killed': VCH III 69.
[1366] Styles 1940: 68-9.
[1367] 1274-1292: WA II 106.

What is curious is the location of Willenhall chapel, for as noted above the manor-house of the Lords of Stowheath is believed to have been on the moated site which lay on the south side of the road from Wolverhampton to Willenhall, a mile from Wolverhampton but over two miles from Willenhall.[1368] Still traceable well into the twentieth century, the moat was some 380 feet square when mapped in 1788,[1369] and evidently once a place of importance. If a chapel at Willenhall existed at an early date, that might explain why the capital messuage at Stowheath seems to have had no chapel – the lord made his prayers at his chantry chapel at Willenhall.

Many chapels were built at the roadside, often near bridges and fords, at shrines, and over holy wells. The only notable natural features at Willenhall appear to have been a number of springs that lay on the north side of a brook which flowed from the south-east side of Wolverhampton, one of which (according to Richard Wilkes) was noted for the cure of eye problems,[1370] and was (he claims) dedicated to St Sunday, 'no common saint'.[1371] Hackwood was unable to identify St Sunday,[1372] but occasional references elsewhere have been traced, and Leland mentions a former chapel of St Sonday by the castle at Newcastle under Lyme, having first written, and then deleted, the name St Salviour.[1373] St Sunday was in fact the same person as St Dominic (c.1170-1221, founder of the Order of Preachers or Black Friars): the error arose from confusion about *Sanctus Dominicus* ('St Dominic') and Latin *dies dominica* 'Sunday'.[1374]

The spring at Willenhall[1375] will therefore have been dedicated to St Dominic, a post-Conquest rather than Anglo-Saxon saint, and the church is in any event not at the site of the spring. That there is a St Giles church and St Sunday's well in Newcastle, and a St Giles chapel and St Sunday's well in Willenhall is evidently coincidence. The dedication does little to help us to date the foundation of Willenhall chapel: we do not know the age

---

[1368] At SO 927982. Mander notes that the ancient moated site at Stowheath lay near The Portway, the ancient road between Stafford and Warwick (and so to London): ibid.

[1369] Map of Wolverhampton township by Godsons of Brailes, 1788. See also WA II 103; Wolverhampton HER 2531.

[1370] Shaw 1801 II: 148, Appendix 17. The site of the spring appears to have been forgotten by 1862, when a correspondent to *The Willenhall Magazine* asked if anyone knew of its location, and a reply was published (p.114) from 'an old inhabitant' to say that it was 'supposed to have been somewhere near the back of the Wake-field', i.e. the field where the Wake was held. Hackwood 1908: 179 claims that the medieval Holy Well lay between the church and what was then known as the manor house.

[1371] Shaw 1801 II: 147-8. Wilkes is said to have raised a stone over the sulphurous spring with the inscription 'Fons occulis, morbisque cutaneis diu celebres, anno Domini 1728', with the arms of his family: Harwood 1844: 410.

[1372] Hackwood 1908: 91.

[1373] Toulmin Smith 1964: V 18-19. The dedication of the late 12th-century church of St Giles at Newcastle-under-Lyme was applied to the church as well as a chancel, and is first recorded there in 1493. An ancient well in Lower Street near the church was still known as St Sunday's well in the 20th century: Pape 1938: 26. Interestingly, John Topyn of Ripe mentions *Imagini sancti dominici vocat seint Sonday* when he made his will in 1493. Hackwood 1908: 93 claims that Robert Plot mentions the spring at Willenhall, but the quotation he gives includes wording not found in Plot: Plot 1686: 318.

[1374] See Pape 1938: 26. A Guild of St Sonday existed in Doncaster, and the expression may have been a personification of the Lord's Day.

[1375] The spring may have been the source of *Beadugipe-burne* 'Beadugyth's stream', mentioned in the boundary clause of Bilston and Wednesfield in the forged confirmation of Wulfrun's grant to the monastery of Wolverhampton: Hooke 1983: 72.

of the dedication to St Giles, a saint who cannot obviously be associated with battles,[1376] and we might perhaps expect any such origins to have been recorded in local tradition or mentioned in early records, though J. C. Tildesley, the Willenhall historian, reminds us that Giles de Erdington, who had been Dean of Wolverhampton for some forty years, died in 1268, and the dedication could well honour his memory.[1377] On the other hand, the earliest history of the chapel is now lost in history,[1378] perhaps suggesting that it was the oldest of the four other outlying Wolverhampton chantry chapels, and there remain unexplained oddities about Willenhall: the unexpectedly quality of the interior of the old church demolished in 1748, for example, as well as the legal tenure of several areas, including the centre of Willenhall, which was freehold, whereas one or other of the three large manors that made up the original parish of Wolverhampton was copyhold, an anomaly which has not been satisfactorily explained.[1379]

We might consider whether an earlier chapel on the same site could have been erected near the battlefield as a chantry chapel for the dead of the great battle of 910 on a site associated with Mercian royalty since at least 732, though it must be emphasised that there is not the slightest evidence to support the idea.[1380] However, the tradition of religious foundations established to celebrate victory in battle is long: Bede records in his *Historia Ecclesiastica* that after he had defeated Penda at the battle of Winwæd in 655, King Oswiu of Northumberland gave an *ex voto* offering of twelve small plots of land for monasteries,[1381] and c.1020 Cnut built a small minster on the site of his victory at Ashingdon (Essex). After the Conquest, churches were built to commemorate battles at Battle in Sussex (1066), Battlefield near Shrewsbury (1406), Towton in Yorkshire (1461), and Dadlington near Bosworth (1485). The practice can hardly be said to have been widespread, but an ingrained belief in the need to pray for the souls of those who died in battle evidently ran deep in the psyche of the ruling elite and its clergy. It would not be especially surprising if Willenhall had been chosen as the site of a commemorative chantry chapel with rich fittings founded at some date after c.1200 to honour and pray for the souls of the war dead of August, 910 (though it must be admitted that various medieval inquisitions into the administration of the chapel lands mention only benefits such as 'for the ease of the Inhabitants there being far remote from their prshe Church of Wolverhampton').[1382] We can almost certainly discount the possibility that a chapel was erected soon after the battle,

---

[1376] St Giles was supposedly a hermit in Saint-Gilles, near Arles, before the 9th century, and although very little is known about him, he became one of the most popular saints of Western Europe in the later Middle Ages, with over 150 churches in Great Britain dedicated to his honour. He was looked on as the patron of cripples and the indigent: Attwater 1965: 155. Alternatively, the dedication may have been associated with the grant of Wolverhampton by King Henry III to Giles of Erdington in 1258.

[1377] Tildesley 1952: 17-18.

[1378] VCH III 325.

[1379] Mander and Tildesley 1960: 26-7.

[1380] Domesday Book records the canons of Wolverhampton holding 2 hides in the royal estate of Willenhall in 1086: VCH IV 39, 45. The place may have been held by the crown since c.732, when King Æthelbald attested two charters there, or even before. As noted elsewhere in this volume, the woman named Beadugyth who gave her name to the nearby stream was of some importance, and may have been an abbesses, perhaps of a mixed monastery at or near Willenhall in the later seventh or early eighth century, possibly with Northumbrian roots, perhaps founded under the auspices of King Wulfhere, which may have been connected with another contemporary female Beorngyth and the church of Wolverhampton.

[1381] HE III, c. xxiv; John 1964: 13-14. Bede also records how a monastery was founded at Gilling in Yorkshire as atonement for the killing of King Oswine after an abortive battle in 642: HE III, c.xxiv.

[1382] Tildesley 1952: 58.

for there is little evidence for the creation of monasteries associated with battles in the later Anglo-Saxon period.[1383] Furthermore, it is unlikely that Willenhall then existed as a place of any significance, for the conflict might have come down to us as the battle of Willenhall.

[1383] Lavelle 2010: 304.

26. Accounts of the battle of Tettenhall.

It must be emphasised that there is no certain evidence relating to the battle of Tettenhall. The only information we have is from later English chronicles (no useful information has been traced in contemporary or near-contemporary Welsh or Irish chronicles,[1384] or in Scandinavian, Icelandic, Frankish and other Continental chronicles),[1385] but details of the conflict – and even its year – vary in those accounts. Whether any of those reports is based directly on first-hand eyewitness statements from those who may have been present at the battlefield, or whether they derive from anecdotal – or even invented – evidence set down by the chroniclers, either in good faith or knowing or suspecting that it was of doubtful veracity, is impossible to know. We must also understand that the early chroniclers derived their work from various sources, some now lost to us,[1386] and from earlier writers, so that most accounts are clearly derivative, perpetuating and doubtless in many cases adding to any errors in the accounts on which they were based. The chronicles are listed in the approximate chronological order (some cannot be dated with accuracy) in which they were written.

The primary source of information for the Anglo-Saxon period has long been, and remains, the so-called *Anglo-Saxon Chronicle*, in reality a term applied to a composite set of annals and written, unusually, in vernacular Old English rather than Latin, probably based on an original compilation put together in the late ninth century possibly under the auspices of Alfred the Great utilising earlier Latin annals, Bede's *Ecclesiastical History of the English People*, genealogies, lists of episcopal appointments and charters.[1387] The *Chronicle* seems to have been made available for copying and circulation in 892, with those copies eventually recopied, and new material about international, national and local events added from time to time.[1388] Copies survive in various forms, the most important identified for convenience as versions 'Ā', 'B', 'C', 'D', 'E', 'F', 'G', 'H', and 'I'. *Chronicle* 'F' is a bilingual

---

[1384] The later *Annales Cambriæ*, *Brenhinedd y Saesson* and *Brut y Tywysogion* (on which see Graves 1975: 296, 407) for example, have only one record relating to England in the first decade of the tenth century – the death of Bishop Asser, King Alfred's biographer and a Welshman.

[1385] See for example Fjalldal 2005.

[1386] From at least the time of Offa, Mercia had been a leading centre of literacy and learning: we should remember that King Alfred, bemoaning the lack of both in Wessex in the late 9th century, sought to remedy that situation by attracting Mercian scholars to the West Saxon court. Many of the places where Mercian muniments are likely to have been kept were destroyed long ago, including – but not limited to – Tamworth (the Mercian 'capital' from at least the time of Offa), Lichfield and Repton in 874-5 (by the Danish army based at Repton), unidentified monasteries and minsters in central and western Mercia in 910 (by a Scandinavian raiding army before the battle of Tettenhall), Pershore Abbey (by fire in 1002 and 1223), Hereford Cathedral (burnt by Gruffydd ap Llywelyn and his English allies in 1055), Gloucester Abbey (by fire in 1122), and most seriously St Peter's Abbey in Winchcombe, anciently associated with the archives of Æthelred and Æthelflæd in the later ninth and early tenth century (razed during the anarchy of Stephen's reign in 1151). We cannot know what irreplaceable manuscripts were lost in such destruction: see Ray and Bapty 2016: 166. James Campbell, while recognising that some sources have been lost (noting for example the East Anglian annals drawn upon in the F text of the ASC and certain accounts of 10th-century history used by William of Malmesbury and by Florence (John) of Worcester), has concluded that 'the Anglo-Norman historians were to a very large extent dependent on no works other than those which still survive. It is virtually certain that for large areas of Anglo-Saxon history the inquirer of c.1100 had no source apart from Bede or the wretched annals of one or more versions of the Chronicle': Campbell 1986: 216.

[1387] Gransden 1992: 201-2; Higham and Ryan 2013: 271-6.

[1388] Gransden 1996: 29-41; Bredehoft 2001: 4-6.

chronicle based on the same Kentish chronicle from which 'E' and 'Ā' (with a bar) were copied. It covers the period 1 AD to 1058 AD. *Chronicle* 'H'[1389] is a fragment, probably from a Winchester manuscript, covering the period 988 AD to 1268 AD, and 'I'[1390] from Christchurch, Canterbury, was written on an Easter table, and covers the period 988 AD to 1268 AD. Neither 'H' nor 'I' is therefore relevant to our interest in the period leading up to the first decade of the tenth century.[1391]

1. *Anglo-Saxon Chronicle* 'A'[1392] (the 'Winchester Manuscript'; in academic writings sometimes recorded as 'Ā', to distinguish it from another version known as 'A' which was a copy of the former before it left Winchester, and which was destroyed by fire in 1731, leaving only a few fragments, but not before it had been copied by Abraham Wheloc) covers the period 60 BC to 1070, and was probably begun at Winchester and continued there until the eleventh century.[1393] It is generally known as the Parker Chronicle, after the Elizabethan Archbishop of Canterbury into whose collection it came. The relevant entry (written in a hand identified by palaeographers as scribe 2b, writing probably between 911/914 and 930)[1394] reads:

[AN.] .dccccx. Her bræc se here on Norðhymbrum þone frið, 7 forsawon ælc frið þe Eadweard cyng 7 his witan him budan 7 hergodon ofer Mercna lond; 7 se cyng hæfde gegadrod sum hund scipa 7 wæs þa on Cent, 7 þa scipu foran be suðan east andlang sæ togeneshim. Þa wende se here þæt his fultumes se mæsta dæl wære on þæm scipum 7 þæt hie mehten faran unbefohtene þær þær hie wolden. Þa geascade se cyng þæt þæt hie ut on hergað foron, þa sende he his fird ægðer ge of Westseaxum ge of Mercum, 7 hie offoron ðone here hindan,[1395] þa he hamweard wæs, 7 him þa wið gefuhton 7 þone here gefliemdon 7 his fela þusenda ofslogon, 7 þær wæs Ecwils[1396] cyng ofslægen.[1397]

910 'Here the raiding-army in Northumbria broke the peace, and scorned every peace which King Edward and his councillors offered them, and raided across the land of Mercia. And the king had gathered some hundred ships, and was then in Kent; and the ships went east along the south coast towards him. Then the raiding-army imagined that the most part of his reinforcement was on these ships, and that they might go unfought wherever they wanted. Then when the king learned that they had gone out on a raid, he

---

[1389] BM Cotton MS Domitian A.ix.
[1390] BM Caligula A.xv.
[1391] See generally Whitelock 1979: 109-24, 145-6; Swanton 1996: xi-xxix.
[1392] Corpus Christi College, Cambridge, MS 173.
[1393] Swanton 1996: xxi; Gransden 1996: 38-9.
[1394] Bateley 1996: xxxiii; Stafford 2008: 108. The last annal in hand 2b is dated 911; but the identity and chronology of the various hands is an especially vexed issue, but hazards a date of c.915-c.930: Bateley 1996: xxxiii-xxxiv. Bredehoft notes that from 901 to 915 the annals in version A and in B and C are in remarkable agreement, though A was not kept up to date regularly and neither, it seems, was the B and C ancestor. Both texts, he concludes, rely on a single source which might be seen as the 'official copy', transcribed into A and into the B and C ancestor at different stages. He also notes Bateley's belief that A may have been updated around 912, which if correct would mean that the entry relating to the battle of Tettenhall would have been entered within (at most) 2 years of the battle: Bredehoft 2001: 64-5, 189 fn.8.
[1395] This wording echoes ASC 'A' recording the events at Buttington in 893: ... *Þa offoron hie þone here hindan æt Butting tune*: Earle and Plummer 1892-99: I 87. It may be noted that the word *offoron* in ASC 'A' may also be translated as 'intercept, fall upon, attack': Clark Hall 1960: 259.
[1396] Identified as *Eowils 1* in the *Prosopography of Anglo-Saxon England*, accessed 11 April 2010.
[1397] Bately 1986: 63-4.

sent his army both from Wessex and from Mercia, and they got in front of the raiding-army from behind when it was on its way home, and then fought with them and put the raiding army to flight, and killed many thousands of it; and King Eowils was killed there.[1398]

It will be noticed that no information is given about the area ravaged by the Scandinavian raiding-army and not the slightest clue as to the site of the battle.

2. The *Chronicon Æthelweardi*, a short Latin history produced by the noble *ealdorman* and chronicler Æthelweard, believed to have been written between 978 and 988, is the first history in England to be written by a layman – the only Latin work composed by an English layman before the fourteenth century – and incorporates the most valuable account of the battle. Æthelweard, the section of whose work from 893 to 946 is not derived from any known source, provides intriguing and often unique information, and the added detail on Mercian events and the upgrading of Æthelred, Lord of the Mercians, to *rex*, as opposed to the *Anglo-Saxon Chronicle* which consistently downgrades him to *hlaford*, 'lord, or ealdorman', might suggest that the lost copy of the *Chronicle* which Æthelweard used for his translation may have been housed at some Mercian centre in the tenth century before it came into his possession.[1399] What is clear is that, perhaps surprisingly, he had no access to entries found after 893 in the versions of the *Anglo-Saxon Chronicles* with which we are familiar today, or to the *Mercian Register*, as mentioned hereafter.[1400] Although it has been said that '[h]is Latin was poor, his chronology confused, and his transcription of proper names careless',[1401] his prose is now seen as learned Latin typical of the period, known to scholars as 'hermeneutic', though his elaborate vocabulary and convoluted syntax, or 'ornate pomposity', make translation problematic in some areas. The following extract under the year 909 (in a part of the text where the dates are one year too early) is from Henry Savile's printed transcription made in 1596 before the manuscript was badly damaged in the fire at Ashburnham House in 1731.[1402] Words and parts of words legible in the surviving fragments of the early text are shown in italics:

Annum post unum barbari pactum rumpunt Eaduuardum regem aduersus, nec non contra Ætheredum, qui tum regebat Northhymbrias partes, Myrciasque. Vastantur passim Myrciorum arua a tempestate prædicta et penitus usque ad Afne fluenta, ubi inchoat. Occidentalium terminus Anglorum nec non Myrciorum. Deinde transuehuntur occidentales / in partes per fluuium Sefern, illicque uastarunt non minimas prædas. Ast ubi *pedem retraxere* **domi** *ouantes spoliis opimus parte in eoa fluuii Sefern etiam transmeabant pontem ordine litterato qui uulgo Cantbricge nuncupatur. Statuta* **quippe** *acie tendebant repente ob***uio turmæ simul Myrciorum Occidentaliu**m**que. Insistunt pugnæ** *mora* **nec attent**a *in Vuodnesfelda campo***, Angli** *uictoriæ* **optinere** *numen***, Danorumque fugatur ex***ercitus telo oppresus. Facta hæc memorantur quinta in die mensis Augusti. Ibidemque ruunt reges tres eo****rum** **turbine**

[1398] Earle and Plummer 1892-9: II 126.
[1399] Campbell 1962: xlii; Barker 1967: 74-91; Smyth 1995: 476-7; Bredehoft 2001: 63-71. Janet Bateley also suggests that Æthelweard had access to a version of the *Chronicle* which was closer to the original than any other extant manuscript: see Bately 1986: lxxix. Æthelweard's wife was named Æthelflæd, a name especially associated with Mercia and the Lady of the Mercians. Her ancestry is unknown, but if she was from Mercia, that might help to explain the source from which her husband obtained detailed information about the history of Mercia not available to other chroniclers: Walker 2000: 119-20.
[1400] Bredehoft 2001: 65-6.
[1401] Marsh 1970: 157.
[1402] Savile 1596; Campbell 1962: xlii.

in *eodem* (uel cert*amine dicere fas est*) *scilicet Healfdene, Eyuuysl*[1403] *quoque,* nec *non Iguuar relicta ty*rannide tu*m ad aulam properauit inferni,* maioresque *natu eorum, duces ac nobiles* simul.[1404]

'After a year the barbarians broke the peace with King Eadweard, and with Æthelred, who then ruled the Northumbrian and Mercian areas. The fields of the Mercians were ravaged on all sides by the throng we spoke about, and deeply, as far as the streams of the Avon, where the boundary of the West Saxons and Mercians begins. Then they were transported across the river Severn into the west country, and there they ravaged great ravagings. But when rejoicing in rich spoil they returned towards home, they were still engaged in crossing to the east side of the river Severn over a pons to give the Latin spelling, which is called [C]antbricge] by the common people. Suddenly squadrons of both Mercians and West Saxons, having formed battle-order, moved against the opposing force. They joined battle without protracted delay on the field of Wednesfield; the English enjoyed the blessing of victory; the army of the Danes fled, overcome by armed force. These events are recounted as done on the fifth day of the month of August.[1405] There fell three of their kings in that same 'storm' (or 'battle' would be the right thing to say), that is Healfdene and Eywysl, and Inwær also hastened to the hall of the infernal one, and so did senior chiefs of theirs, both jarls and other noblemen.'.[1406]

[1403] Æthelweard was evidently following an independent source with a variant of the name: Campbell 1962: lix.

[1404] Campbell 1962: 52-3. Surviving fragments of the early text confirm the correct spelling of *Cantbrycge* – see also PN Sa 1: 57.

[1405] That is, St Oswald's Day.

[1406] Taken from Campbell 1962: 52-3, who has wrongly emended *[C]antbrycg* to *[C]uatbrycge* (see PN Sa I 57) and identified it as Bridgnorth. Whitelock 1979: 210 notes that 'Cantbricg is probably an error for Cuatbricg'. Henry Savile published the following translation of Æthelweard's account in 1596: 'After one year the barbarians break their compact with King Edward and Earl Ethelred who then ruled over the provinces of Northumberland and Mercia. The lands of the Mercians are laid waste on all sides by the aforesaid as far as the streams of the Avon where begins the frontier of the West Saxons and the Mercians. Thence they pass over the river Severn into the western regions and gain by means of their devastation no little booty. But when they had withdrawn homewards rejoicing in their rich spoils they passed over a bridge on the eastern side commonly called Cantbridge (Cautbridge), one troop of Mercians met them and battle ensued in the plain of Wednesfield, the English obtaining the victory. The Danish army fled overwhelmed by the darts of their enemies. These things were said to have been done on the fifth of August 911. These three kings fell in the turmoil of the battle namely Halfdene, Egwyse. Hingham. They lost their sovereignty and descended to the infernal kings and their elders and nobles with them': Savile 1596, as cited in Smallshire 1978: 21. It may be noted that Savile's translation incorrectly attributes the victory to a Mercian troop, rather than a joint Mercian and West Saxon (*occidentaliumque*) force. Campbell and Savile translate *Vuodnesfelda campo* as 'field of Wednesfield' and 'plain of Wednesfield' respectively, but Latin *campo* could also be translated as 'a place of battle, a theatre of action', which could be what Æthelweard intended. An alternative translation is to be found in Whitelock 1955: 193: '909 [for 910]: After one year the barbarians break their pact with King Edward and with Ethelred, who then ruled the district of Northumbria and Mercia. The fields of the Mercians are wasted on all sides by the aforesaid disturbances, right up to the River Avon, where begins the boundary of the West Angles [i.e. the Saxons] and the Mercians. Thence they cross over the River Severn into the western districts, and there obtained by plunder no little booty. But when, exulting in their rich spoils, they withdrew homewards, they crossed a bridge on the eastern side of the Severn, which is commonly called [?]antbricge. A battle-line was formed, and the troops of the Mercians and the West Saxons suddenly went against them. A battle ensued and the English without delay obtained the victory at Wednesfield, and the army of the Scandinavians was put to flight, overcome by weapons. These things are said to have been done on the fifth day of the month of August. And it may rightly be said that in the turmoil or encounter three of their kings fell, namely Healfdene and Eywysl, and also Ivar

3. The Latin *Annals of St Neots*, sometimes known as the *East Anglian Chronicle*,[1407] possibly compiled between c.985 and 1040,[1408] perhaps by Byrhtferth of Ramsey[1409] (died c.1012), is in part derived from Asser's *Life of Alfred*, surviving in a single manuscript written by an anonymous chronicler at Bury St Edmunds in the second quarter of the twelfth century, and records under the year 910, four years before the chronicle stops:

Anno DCCCCX bellum apud Wodnesfeldam, in quo ceciderunt *Eouuilsus* et *Healfdena*, reges paganorum, *et Ochter et Scurfa comites*, et *Othulfus* et *Bensingus* et *Anolafus niger* et *Thurfridus* et *Osfridus* et *Godefridus* [id est Gutheferth[1410]] et alius *Godefridus* et Eagellus[1411] et *Agamundus*, primates paganorum, et multi alii innumerabiles quasi arena maris.[1412]

'*In the year 910 a battle at Wednesfield, in which were killed Eowils and Halfdan, kings of the heathens, and jarls Ochter and Scurfa, and Othulf and Benesing and Anolaf the black and Thurferth and Osfrid and Godefridus [that is Guthfrith] and another Godefridus and Eagell and Agmund, the chief of the heathens, and many others as countless as the sands of the sea*'.[1413]

4. The *Mercian Register*, sometimes (and perhaps more appropriately) known as *The Annals of Æthelflæd*,[1414] is not an independent manuscript, but a set of annals for 902-924 incorporated into the *Anglo-Saxon Chronicle* versions 'B', 'C', and 'D' (all associated with Mercia in some way), the earliest of which ('B') perhaps written between 977 and 1000. The *Register* records the 910 battle in entries inserted into versions 'B', 'C' and 'D' of the *Anglo-Saxon Chronicle*, but is extraordinarily and inexplicably terse in its bland summary of the facts:

On þysum geare Engle 7 Dene gefuhtan æt Teotanheale. 7 Engle sige naman.[1415]

'*In this year the English and Danes fought at Tettenhall, and the English were victorious*'.

---

lost his sovereignty and hastened to the court of hell, and with them their more distinguished leaders and nobles.'. An important extract from the *Chronicon* was made by William Camden, the 16th-century antiquary: 'at [*Cwatbryge*] when the Danes passed over by filling off [?] laden with rich spoils, the west Saxons and Mercians receiv'd them with a bloody encounter in Woodnesfield in which Healden, Cinuil and Inguar, three of their Princes were slain': Camden 1695: 235.
[1407] Dumville and Lapidge 1985; Smyth 2002: 72-6; Hart 2006.
[1408] The date of compilation is the subject of continuing debate, with some scholars arguing for a late 10th-early or 11th century date, and others for a date between 1120 and 1140: Keynes and Lapidge 1983: 57, 199; Smyth 1995: 160-62; Lapidge et al 1999: 49.
[1409] Hart 2006.
[1410] The words in brackets are added above the name Godefridus in another hand: Stevenson 1959: 145.
[1411] Unlisted in the *Prosopography of Anglo-Saxon England*, accessed 11 April 2010.
[1412] Stevenson 1959: 144-5; see also Gale 1691: 174.
[1413] This chronicle alone adds the name Eagellus to the list of the slain enemy. The name appears to be unique in the Anglo-Saxon period, and is possibly a corrupt repetition of Eowils/Eyuuysl/Eowilisc/Ecwils/Auisle named in this and other accounts. The phrase *quasi arena maris* is biblical, and appears in Hosea chapter 1, Job chapter 6 and Isaiah 10.
[1414] The expression seems first found in Earle and Plummer 1892-99: I 92; Stafford 2008.
[1415] ASC 'B', from Thorpe 1861: 184. ASC 'C' reads *On þysum ge(a)re Engle 7 Dene gefuhton æt Teotanheale. 7 Engle sige namon* (Earle and Plummer 1892-99: 94-5; O'Keefe 2001: 75), and ASC 'D' *Her Ængle 7 Dene gefuhton æt Totanheale* (Cubbin 1996: 37).

5. *Anglo-Saxon Chronicle* 'B' and 'C' (the 'Abingdon Manuscripts')[1416] are eleventh century copies twice removed from an original now lost, which was probably sent to Abingdon after its refoundation in the mid-eleventh century. 'B' covers the period 1 AD to 977, and 'C' the period 60 BC to 1066. ASC 'B' reads as follows:[1417]

[An.] .dccccxi. Her bræc se here þone frið on Norðhymbrum þone frið, 7 forsawan ælc riht þe Eadweard cing 7 his witan him budan 7 hergodan ofer Myrcna lond; 7 se cyng hæfde gegadrod sum hund scipa 7 wæs þa on Cent, 7 þa scipu foran be suþan east 7lang sæ togeanes him. Þa wende se here þæt his fultomes wære se mæsta dæl on þæm scipum 7 þæt hie mihten faran unbefohtene þær ðær hie woldan. Þa geahsode se cing þæt þæt hie on heregað foron, þa sende he his fyrd ægþer ge of Westsexum ge of Myrcum, 7 hie offoran þone here hindan, þa he hamweard wæs, 7 him wiþ gefuhton 7 þone here geflymdon 7 his feala þusenda ofslogon, 7 þær wæs Eowils cing ofslægen,[1418] 7 Healfden[1419] cing, 7 Ohter[1420] eorl, 7 Scurfa[1421] eorl, 7 Oþulf[1422] hold, 7 Benesing[1423] hold, 7 Anláf[1424] se swearta,[1425] 7 Þurferð[1426] hold, 7 Osferð[1427] Hlytte, 7 Guðferð[1428] hold, 7 Agmund[1429] hold, 7 Guðferð.[1430]

911 [for 910]'Here the raiding-army in Northumbria broke the peace, and scorned every right which King Edward and his councillors offered them, and raided across the land of Mercia. And the king had gathered some hundred ships, and was then in Kent; and the ships went east along the south coast towards him. Then the raiding-army imagined that the most part of his reinforcement was on these ships, and that they might go unfought wherever they wanted. Then when the king learned that they had gone out on a raid, he sent his army both from Wessex and from Mercia, and they got in front of the raiding-army from behind when it was on its way home, and then fought with them and put the raiding army to flight, and killed many thousands of it; and King Eowils was killed there, and King Healfdene and Earl Ohter and Earl Scurfa, and Othulf the hold, and Benesing the hold, and Anlaf the Black (or infamous), and Thurfreth the hold, and Osfrith Hlytta, and Guthfrith the hold, and Agmund the hold and Guthfrith.'

[1416] BM Cotton MS Tiberius A.vi, and BM Cotton MS Tiberius B.i.
[1417] Thorpe 1861: I 184.
[1418] Bately 1986: 63-4.
[1419] Identified as *Halfdan 3* in the *Prosopography of Anglo-Saxon England*, accessed 11 April 2010. Exceptionally rare coins with the name Halfdan are now associated with the Danish Midlands and the 890s. He could be the person so-named who was killed at Tettenhall: Dolley 1978: 26.
[1420] Identified as *Ohtor 2* in the *Prosopography of Anglo-Saxon England*, accessed 11 April 2010.
[1421] Identified as *Scurfa1* in the *Prosopography of Anglo-Saxon England*, accessed 11 April 2010.
[1422] Identified as *Othulf 1* in the *Prosopography of Anglo-Saxon England*, accessed 11 April 2010. Anderson 1922: 400 suggests the name may perhaps be Eadulf.
[1423] Identified as *Benesing 1* in the *Prosopography of Anglo-Saxon England*, accessed 11 April 2010.
[1424] Identified as *Olaf 2* in the *Prosopography of Anglo-Saxon England*, accessed 11 April 2010.
[1425] OE *sweart* is translated as 'swarthy, dark, black; gloomy; evil, infamous': Clark Hall 1960: 329.
[1426] Identified as *Therferth 1* in the *Prosopography of Anglo-Saxon England*, accessed 11 April 2010.
[1427] Identified as *Osfrith 9* in the *Prosopography of Anglo-Saxon England*, accessed 11 April 2010.
[1428] Identified as *Guthfrith 4* in the *Prosopography of Anglo-Saxon England*, accessed 11 April 2010, or the identification may relate to the other Guthfrith: only one is listed in the *Prosopography of Anglo-Saxon England*.
[1429] Identified as *Agmund 1* in the *Prosopography of Anglo-Saxon England*, accessed 11 April 2010.
[1430] Thorpe 1861: I 182.

6. The relevant entries from *Anglo-Saxon Chronicle* 'C' (with 'B', one of the 'Abingdon Manuscripts', which records two battles) read:[1431]

[An.] dccccx. ... On þysum gere Engle 7 Dene gefuhton æt Teotanheale 7 Engle sige namon.[1432] ...

[An.] .dccccxi. Her bræc se here þone frið on Norðhymbrum 7 forsawan ælc riht þe Eadweard cing 7 his witan him budan 7 hergodon ofer Myrcna land. 7 se cing hæfde gegadorod sum hund scypa 7 wæs ða on Cent, 7 þa scipu foron be suþan east andlang sæ togenes him. Þa wende se here þæt his fultomes se mæsta dæl wære on þæm scypum 7 þæt hi mihten unbefohtone faran þær ðær hie woldon. Þa geahsode se cing þæt þæt hi on hergeað foron, þa sende his fyrde ægþer ge of Wessexum ge of Myrcum, 7 hie offoron þone here hindan,þa he hamweard wæs, 7 him þa wið gefuhton 7 ðone here geflymdon 7 his fela ðusenda ofslogon, 7 þær wæs Eowils cing ofslegen,7 Healfden cing, 7 Ohter eorl, 7 Scurfa eorl, 7 Oðulf hold, 7 Benesing hold, 7 Anláf se swearta, 7 Þurferð hold, 7 Osferð hlytte, 7 Guðferð hold, 7 Agmund hold, 7 Guðferð.[1433] ...

910 '*In this year English and Danes fought at Tettenhall, and the English took the victory.*'

911 [for 910]'*Here the raiding-army in Northumbria boke the peace, and scorned every right which King Edward and his councillors offered them, and raided across the land of Mercia. And the king had gathered some hundred ships, and was then in Kent; and the ships went east along the south coast towards him. Then the raiding-army imagined that the most part of his reinforcement was on these ships, and that they might go unfought wherever they wanted. Then when the king learned that they had gone out on a raid, he sent his army both from Wessex and from Mercia, and they got in front of the raiding-army from behind when it was on its way home, and then fought with them and put the raiding army to flight, and killed many thousands of it; and King Eowils was killed there, and King Healfdene and Earl Ohter and Earl Scurfa, and Othulf the hold, and Benesing the hold, and Anlaf the Black (or infamous), and Thurfreth the hold, and Osfrith Hlytta, and Guthfrith the hold, and Agmund the hold and Guthfrith.*'

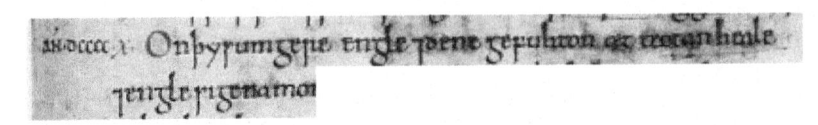

Extract from Anglo-Saxon Chronicle, version 'C', known (with version 'B') as the Abingdon Manuscript, *British Library MS Cotton Tiberius Bi, ff. 115v.-64*. The extract reads *AN DCCCCX On þysum gere Engle 7 Dene fuhton æt Teotanheale. 7 Engle sige namon* ': 910 In this year English and Danes fought at *Teotanheale*, and the English took the victory' (British Library).

7. *Anglo-Saxon Chronicle* 'D'[1434] (the 'Worcester Manuscript') is a mid-eleventh century manuscript taken from a lost original which was possibly located at York or Ripon, or

---

[1431] Thorpe 1861: I 185.
[1432] Earle and Plummer 1892-9: I 94.
[1433] Thorpe 1861: I 182; Bately 1986: 63-4.
[1434] BM Cotton MS Tiberius B.iv.

perhaps Gloucester,[1435] and covers the period 1 AD to 1080 AD. Its compiler had access to Northern material which could explain the extra detail it provides in some annals.[1436] The relevant entries (which record three battles) read:[1437]

N. .dccccix. Her Myrce 7 Westseaxe gefuhton wið þone here neh Teotanheale on .viii. idus Agustus, 7 sige hæfdon...

N. .dccccx. ... Here Ængle 7 Dene gefuhton æt Totanheale...

N. .dccccxi. Her bræc se here þone frið on Norðhymbrum, 7 forsawon ælc riht þe Eadweard cyning 7 his witan him budon, 7 hergoden ofer Myrcland. 7 se cyning hæfde gegaderod sum hund scipa, 7 wæs þa on Cent, 7 þa scipu foron besuðan east andlang sæ togeanes him. Þa wende se here þæt his fultum wære se mæsta dæl on þam scipum, 7 þæt hi mihton unbefohtene faran þær hi wolden. Þa geahsode se cyning þæt hi on hergeað foron. Þa sende he his fyrd ægðer ge of Westseaxum ge of Myrcum, 7 hy offoron þone here hindan, þa he hamweard wæs, 7 him wið þagefuhton, 7 þone here geflymdon, 7 his feola ofslogen, 7 þær wæs Eowilisc cyng ofslægen, 7 Healden cyng, 7 Other eorl, 7 Scurfa eorl, 7 Aþulf hold, 7 Agmund hold.[1438]

909'Here the Mercians and West Saxons fought against the raiding-army near Tettenhall on 6 August and had the victory.'

910 'Here the English and the Danes fought at Tettenhall...'

911 'Here the raiding-army in Northumbria broke the peace, and scorned every privilege which King Edward and his councillors offered them, and raided across the land of Mercia. And the king had gathered some hundred ships, and was then in Kent; and the ships went east along the south coast towards him. Then the raiding-army imagined that the most part of his reinforcement was on these ships, and that they might go unfought wherever they wanted. Then when the king learned that they had gone on a raid, he sent his army both from Wessex and from Mercia, and they got in front of the raiding-army from behind when it was on its way home, and then fought with them and put the raiding army to flight, and killed many of it. And there was killed King Eowils and King Halfdan, and Jarl Ohtor, and Jarl Scurfa,[1439] and Hold Athulf and Hold Agmund.'

The second of the consecutive triplicated accounts is so brief that it fails even to mention the victors in the battle. *Chronicle* 'D' alone gives the date of the conflict: *viii idus Agustus* (6 August).[1440]

8. The *Chronici Mariani Scotti* is generally, though possibly incorrectly, attributed to Marianus Scotus (1028-c.1083), an Irish monk and chronicler properly named Máel Brigte ('(Saint) Bridget's Servant'), who arrived in Europe in 1056 and served as a monk at

---

[1435] Gransden 1996: 39 suggests York, Worcester or Evesham.
[1436] Stafford 2008: 102.
[1437] Thorpe 1861: I 183, 185; Cubbin 1996: 37-8.
[1438] Cubbin 1996: 37-8.
[1439] The personal name Scurfa ('scab') is said to be found in the place-name Scruton in North Yorkshire, *Scurvetone* in Domesday Book (Ekwall 1960: 409; Watts 2004: 533), and in Sheraton, Durham, *Scurufatun* c.1050 (12th century): Fellows-Jensen 2008: 132.
[1440] Cubbin 1996: 37.

Cologne, Fulda and Mainz. The chronicle which bears his name, a history of the world to 1082, includes many additions drawn from Bede, Asser, lives of saints, and a version of the *Anglo-Saxon Chronicle* no longer extant, and was brought to England before 1095. It is of value because the compiler apparently followed his sources, and was widely known during the Middle Ages, used extensively, for example, by Florence of Worcester.[1441] The account of the battle of 910 is found in a section where the dating is significantly awry:

Anno D. 933 In Provincia Stafordensi in loco, qui dicitur Trottanhale, inter Anglos & Danos insigne prœlium actum est; sed Angli potiti sunt Victoria ...[1442]

'*AD 933. A great battle was fought between the English and the Danes at Trottanhale,*[1443] *in the province of Stafford, and the English were victorious ...*'.

9. *Anglo-Saxon Chronicle* 'E' (the 'Laud or Peterborough Manuscript')[1444] was copied in the eleventh to twelfth centuries at Peterborough from a chronicle sent from Canterbury based on 'D' or a version of it. It contains much interpolated material such as charters, events concerning the monastery of St Augustine, and Latin enties about local and national affairs. It covers the period 1 AD to 1153 AD. The relevant entry reads:

910 Her Engle here 7 Dene ge fuhton æt Teotan heale. 7 Æþered Myrcena ealdor forð ferde.[1445]

910 'Here the English raiding-army and the Danes fought at Tettenhall, and Æthelred, leader of the Mercians, died...'

It may be this account that has led to the belief that Æthelred died of wounds received in the battle, but he died in 911, and there is no evidence that his death was connected in any way with the battle – which cannot, of course, be seen as evidence that it did not. The account is notable for its failure to identify the victors at Tettenhall.

10. The *Chronicon ex Chronicis* of Florence (John) of Worcester is a chronicle of world history presumed to have been started by a monk of Worcester called Florence and completed by another monk named John in the late eleventh century and opening decades of the twelfth century.[1446] It records (under the year 911):

In provincia Stæffordensi, in loco qui dicitur Teotanhele, inter Anglos et Danos, insigne prœlium actum est, sed Angli potiti sunt victoria.[1447] **Eodum anno victoriosus rex Edwardus, centum naves coadunans, milites legit, naves conscendere jussit, sibique per terram iter facturo occurrere in Cantia præcepit. Interea Danorum**

[1441] Graves 452-3.
[1442] Hearne 1770: III 282.
[1443] The *e* in *Teottanhale* has evidently been misread as *r*.
[1444] Bodleian MS Laud 636.
[1445] Earle and Plummer 1892-9: I 95. The word *here* was usually applied to attacking armies, either Viking or invading English armies, and its use in this entry to refer to both English and Danish armies has been seen by Swanton as indicating that both armies were intent on invasion: Swanton 1996: xxxiv. That suggestion seems inexplicable.
[1446] Lapidge et al 1999: 188. Alfred Smyth has suggested that Byrthferth of Ramsey may have been responsible for the 10th-century section of Florence of Worcester: Smyth 2002: xix.
[1447] This sentence was evidently taken from the *Chronici Mariani Scotti*, and explains whyFlorence (John) of Worcester concludes that there were two battles

exercitus, qui Northhymbriam inhabitabunt, fœdere quod cum eo statuerant rursus dirupto, et omni rectitudine, quam ipse suique primates eis obtulerant, spreta, agros Merciorum ausu temerario depopulati sunt; æstimantes sane majus robur in navibus esse, et se quocunque vellent sine prœlio ire posse. Quod ubi rex audivit, exercitum West-Saxonum simul et Merciorum ad repellendos eos misit; qui cum illos a depopulatione revertentes, in campo qui lingua Anglorum Wodnesfeld dicitur comprehendissent, duos reges eorum Eowils et Halfdene, fratres regis Hinguari,[1448] comitesque duos, Ohter et Scurfa, novemque proceres nobiliores, multaque millia extinxerunt, cæterisque fugatis, omnem prædam excusserunt.[1449]

'*A great battle was fought between the English and the Danes at Teottanhele, in the province of Stafford, and the English were victorious. In the same year the victorious king Edward collected a hundred ships, and, selecting soldiers, ordered them on board, with instructions to meet him in Kent, whither he intended to go by land. In the meantime the army of the Danes who dwelt in Northumbria, having again broken the peace which they had concluded with him, and rejected all the civil rights which he and his nobles had offered to them, with rash boldness invaded the Mercian territory; for they thought that their great strength lay in their ships, and that they could go wherever they pleased without being obliged to hazard an engagement. When the king heard of this, he sent an army of West Saxons and Mercians to drive them back. This army met with them on their return from the scene of their devastations, at a place called in the English tongue Wodnesfeld, and slew their two kings, Eowils and Halfdene, brothers of king Hinguar, two earls named Other and Scurfa, nine of their chief nobles, and several thousand of their men besides; and putting all the rest to flight, they recaptured all the spoil.*'[1450]

11. The *Historia Regum* ('History of the Kings'), attributed almost certainly incorrectly to Symeon or Simeon of Durham, and probably written c.1129 at Sawley, Yorkshire, incorporates (like *Anglo-Saxon Chronicle* 'D' and 'E') passages based on the lost *Northern Annals*,[1451] and comprises two overlapping chronicles, one from 731 to 957, the other from 848 to 1129. The first, written after 1042, contains much material about Northumbria,[1452] and records under the year 910:

Anno DCCC.XAngli et Dani pugnaverunt apud Teotanbole [*sic,recte Teotanhale?*].[1453]

'*AD 910. The English and the Danes fought at Teotanbole [sic, recte Teotanhale?]*'.

[1448] Identified as *Ingvar1* in the *Prosopography of Anglo-Saxon England*, accessed 11 April 2010. It will be noted that Florence (John) of Worcester, unlike Æthelweard, does not say that Hinguar was killed.
[1449] Thorpe 1848: I 121. It is unclear how Chaney (1970: 37) reached the odd conclusion that *Wodnesfeld*, named in this extract, could perhaps be identified as Wanswell in Gloucestershire.
[1450] Stevenson 1853: 73-4. Thorpe 1849a: I 120 gives the spelling *Teotanheal*. It would appear that Florence (John) of Worcester has confused king Halfdene, who died in the battle, with Hálfdan, king of Northumbria who was killed in 877 by the Norwegian leader Bárðr at Strangford Lough on the coast of County Down in Northern Ireland – Bárðr's foster-son Eysteinn had been assassinated by Hálfdan in 875. It was this Hálfdan who was the brother of Ívarr [Hinguar] and son of Ragnarr loðbrók: Smyth 1977: 262-3.
[1451] Graves 1975: 297.
[1452] Gransden 1996: 148-51.
[1453] Hinde 1868: I 63.

The second chronicle, derived largely from Asser and Florence (John) of Worcester (and here based on *Chronici Mariani Scotti*), records:

Anno DCCCCXI In provincia Sterffordensi in loco qui dicitur Teotenhale inter Angles et Danos insigne prælium actum est; sed Angli potiti sunt victoria...[1454]

'AD 910. A famous battle was fought in the district of Stafford, at a place called Teotenhale, between the Angles and the Danes, where the Angles obtained the victory'.[1455]

It will be noted that the first account fails to mention the victorious side.

12. Henry of Huntingdon was formerly believed to have incorporated valuable material based on old folk-songs into his account of Anglo-Saxon history in his *Historia Anglorum*, the greater part of which was probably written between 1125-30, but that idea is now considered untenable, and some details in the *Historia Anglorum* not recorded elsewhere are held to be figments of the imagination.[1456] He recorded the battle of Tettenhall as two separate actions in the following terms:

Anno sequenti, exercitus Dacorum uenit in Merce predatum. Rex autem congregauerat centum puppes, et misit eas contra exercitum. Quas postquam comparuit exercitus putauit ab eis habere auxilium, et ut securius possent ire quoquo uellent. Porro rex misit exercitum post eos ex Westexe et Merce, qui consecuti sunt eos a tergo cum domum reuerterentur, et cum eis pugnauerunt. Bellum ingens commissum est. Contriuit autem Dominus infideles centricione magna, et ex eis multa milia mors cruenta deuorauit. Corrueruntque principes eorum in confusione et deuorati in puluere sordueruot. Occidit namque rex Haldene, et rex Eowils, et Uhthere consul, et Scurfa consul, et Oswlf hold, et Benesing hold, et Hanlaf niger, et Werferd hold, et Osferd hold, et Osferd hlytte, et Ahmund hold, et Gudferd hold, et alius Gudferd. Serui autem Domini uictoria tanta potiti, exultantes in Deum uiuum in hymnis et concentibus Dominum exercituum benedicebant.[1457]

The most recent translation of this is:

'In the following year [910], the Danish army came to ravage Mercia. The King gathered together a hundred ships and sent them against the army. When they appeared, the army thought they would receive aid from them, and would be able to proceed more safely wherever they wished. Next the King sent an army after them from Wessex and Mercia,

---

[1454] Arnold 1892: ii 122. Symeon (or Simeon) of Durham flourished in the early twelfth century. His main work is the *Historia Ecclesiae Dunelmensis*(History of the Church of Durham), which extends to 1096. Stevenson, in the preface of his translation of the *Historia Regum*, says: 'It is not probable that both these chronicles, which constitute the History of the Kings, are the work of Simeon of Durham; or, indeed, that they are to be ascribed to one and the same author. They contain statements which are contradictory the one to the other, and they vary in their chronology. It might be doubted, were we disposed to be sceptical, how far either of them is the production of the author whose name the whole now bears. Recent scholarship has suggested that the first chronicle's initial compilation was by Byrhtferth, a monk and teacher at Ramsey Abbey (north of Huntingdon), at the turn of the tenth century.' The second chronicle is based on the *Chronicon ex Chronicis* of Florence (John) of Worcester. See also Graves 1975: 292; Whitelock 1979: 127; Story 2003: 117-26.

[1455] Stevenson 1855: 500.

[1456] Graves 1975: 431-2.

[1457] Greenaway 1996: 300-302; see also Arnold 1879: 154.

which followed them from the rear as they turned back homewards, and attacked them. A huge battle commenced. But the Lord struck down the heathens in a great defeat, and bloody death consumed many thousands of them. Their leaders fell to the ground in confusion and were destroyed and made filthy in the dust. For there perished King Healfdene, King Eowils, Earl Ohter, Earl Scurfa, Othulf the faithful,[1458] *Benesing the faithful, Anlaf the Black, Thureth the faithful, Osfrith the faithful, Osfrith Hlytta, Agmund the faithful, Guthfrith the faithful,*[1459] *and another Guthfrith. The servants of the Lord, having gained such a great victory, exalted in the living God and blessed the lord of hosts in hymns and canticles.'*[1460]

A nineteenth century translation of the same text gives:

'*The next year [907] the Danish army entered Mercia, with intent to plunder; but the king had collected 100 ships, and dispatched them against the enemy. On their approach they were mistaken for allies, and the Danish army supposed that they might therefore march wherever they would. Presently, the king sent troops against them out of Wessex and Mercia, who fell on their rear, as they were retiring homewards, and engaged them in fight. A pitched battle ensued, in which the Lord severely chastised the heathen, many thousands of them meeting a bloody death, and their chiefs were confounded, and, falling, bit the dust. There were slain King Healfdene and King Ecwulf [Ecwils], and the earls Uthere and Scurf; with the Holds Othulf, Benesing, Anlaf [Olave] the Black, Thurferth, and Osferth, the collector of the revenue; and Agmund the Hold, the Guthferth the Hold, with another Guthferth. The servants of the Lord, having gained so great a victory, rejoiced in the living God, and gave thanks with hymns and songs to the Lord of hosts.'*[1461]

Of the second action Henry of Huntingdon records:

Sexto anno, Anglici at Daci pugnauerunt apud Totanhale. Quis autem cuneorum horrendos aggressus, ignitas collisiones, formidabiles tinnitus, feras irruptiones, miserabiles occasus, clamores hirrisonos, scriptis exequet? Tandem suos diuina pietas uictoria decorauit, Dacosque infideles cede simul et fuga dehonestauit.[1462]

'*In the sixth year [of Edward the Elder] the English and the Danes fought at Totanhale. But who may convey in writing the fearful attacks of the squadrons, the fiery clashes, the terrifying clang, the wild incursions, the wretched deaths, the blood-curdling shouts? In*

[1458] Greenaway 1996: 303 observes that this man does not appear in the ASC.

[1459] Greenaway 1996: 302 notes that only ASC 'B' and 'C' give the names of the slain. Henry's Osfrith the hold may not be a simple error on his part. Florence (John) of Worcester gives the first four names – Healdene, Eowils, Ohter and Scurfa – and says there were nine others (*nouemque proceres nobiliores*): ASC, however, gives only eight names after Scurfa. Like Henry, the Annals of St Neots gives a name extra to those in the surviving ASC version, but the name, Eagellus, is different from Henry's addition of Osfrith the hold. Curiously, it is not unusual for the chronicles to give details of the Danish slain, with no mention of the English who died. The ASC tells us that at the battle of Ashdown in 871, King Alfred led a force which defeated a Viking army. The dead included King Bagsecg, and jarls Osbern, Fraena, Harold, and two Sidrocs, but no English dead are named.

[1460] Greenaway 1996: 300-302.

[1461] Forester 1853: 163.

[1462] Greenaway 1966: 304.

the end divine compassion honoured His own with victory, and dishonoured the faithless Danes with slaughter and also flight.[1463]

13. The *Chronicle of Melrose*[1464] is an anonymous annalistic chronicle up to 1170, thought to have been the work of the monks of Melrose abbey. In two parts, the first, taken from Simeon of Durham's *Historia Regum*, finishes in 1140, in which year it was probably compiled, and has the following entry for the battle:

Anno dccc.xj. in provincia Stanfordensin, in loco qui dicitur Totenhale, inter Anglos et Danos insigne prœlium habetur, et tandem Angli victoria potiuntur.[1465]

'911. A celebrated battle was fought between the Angles and Danes in the province of Stamford [sic], at a place called Totenhale; and at last the Angles obtained the victory.'[1466]

14. William of Malmesbury, who died c.1143, was of mixed Norman and English parentage and the most important historian of Britain after the time of Bede until his own period. From childhood, when he was a Benedictine monk at Malmesbury, he devoted his life to Christian learning and the writing of history, for which he travelled throughout Britain and perhaps to Normandy, using a vast range of sources. Formerly considered to be a meticulous researcher and historian, in recent years his writings have come under more scrutiny, and been found wanting.[1467] Remarkably, he provides no specific details of the battle of Tettenhall, which is not even mentioned, nor of any other military conflicts of the early tenth century, which is all the more extraordinary since he will have used one or more versions of the *Anglo-Saxon Chronicle* and is known to have had access to Æthelweard's *Chronicon* which gives so much information, merely observing that:

'[King Edward]...devised a mode of frustrating the incursions of the Danes; for he repaired many ancient cities, or built new ones, in places calculated for his purpose, and filled them with a military force, to protect the inhabitants and repel the enemy. Nor was his design unsuccessful; for the inhabitants became so extremely valorous in these contests, that if they heard of an enemy approaching, they rushed out to give them battle, even without consulting the king or his generals, and constantly surpassed them, both in number and in warlike skill. Thus the enemy became an object of contempt for the soldiery and of derision to the king. ... Ethelfled, sister of the king and relict of Ethered, ought not to be forgotten, as she was a powerful accession to his party, the delight of his subjects, the dread of his enemeies, a woman of enlarged soul ... This spirited heroine assisted her

---

[1463] Greenway 1996: 304-5. The grandiloquent language suggests that Henry may have been drawing on a Latin praise poem, perhaps even a life of Æthelflæd (although he makes her the daughter Æðered (*sic*), not Alfred, and the sister, not mother of Ælfwynn), composed after the battle, and is vaguely reminiscent of Æthelweard's account of æðeling Edward's engagement with the Danes at Farnham in 893: 'There was no delay, the young men leaped against the prepared defences, and having slipped on their armour they duly exalted, being set free [from care] by the prince's arrival, like sheep brought to the pasture by the help of the shepherd after the customary ravaging' (Campbell 1962: 49), as well as *The Battle of Maldon*, the famous poem commemorating Byrhtnoth's defeat by the Vikings in 991.
[1464] Cotton MS Faustina B ix; Graves 1975: 412.
[1465] Stevenson 1835: 26.
[1466] Stevenson 1856: 95.
[1467] 'William is a treacherous witness: for all the praise heaped on him in modern times': Dumville 1992: 146. For useful summaries of modern views on William of Malmsbury's writings, see Graves 1975: 436-7; Gransden 1974-82: I 166-85.

brother greatly with her advice, was of equal service in building cities, nor could you easily discern, whether it was more owing to fortune or her own exertions, that a woman should be able to protect men at home, and to intimidate them abroad.'[1468]

The explanation for the paucity of specific information provided about the reign of Edward the Elder may be gleaned from remarks he gives about the complex campaign involving King Alfred and the Danes, which is simply ignored, with the estraordinary explanation that 'It has not been my intention to unfold the inextricable labyrinths of Alfred's labours, for the story of his doings year by year would only confuse the reader. To give the details of armies advancing and retreating, of rapine and slaughter, to follow Alfred in short all round the island would argue mental deficiency'.[1469]

15. Robert of Torigni (c.1110-86), otherwise Robertus de Monte, was abbot of Mont-Saint-Michel, and an important and respected twelfth-century chronicler[1470] best known as the last of three contributors to the *Gesta Normannorum Ducum* (Deeds of the Norman kings), written by William of Jumieges, enlarged by Orderic Vitalis and completed by Robert. Robert's entire account of the reign of Edward the Elder reads in full:

Edwardus rex Anglorum regnat xxiiij. annis, et pugnavit contra Dacos in Nordimbre, et in egressione Merce vicit eos gloriose, et occidit reges fortes. Vicit quoque Dacos apud Totenhale, et conquisivit Merce.[1471]

'Edward king of England ruled 24 years, and fought against the Danes in Northumbria, and leaving Mercia gloriously defeated and killed mighty kings. He defeated the Danes at Tettenhall and took over Mercia'.

It is supposed that Robert incorporated material from Henry of Huntingdon, but that is not evident in the terse account cited above, which is noteworthy not only for its brevity, but for the prominence given to one of only two events recorded by Robert for Edward's reign: the defeat of the Danes at Tettenhall and the takeover of Mercia.

16. Roger de Hoveden, who died c.1201, was probably born at Howden in Yorkshire. Little is known of his life, and there were others with the same name, but he may have been a professor of theology at Oxford, employed by Henry II in 1174 to administer Forest Laws. After Henry's death he appears to have joined the crusade of Richard I to the Holy Land, and began his history of England during the journey, basing the first part (to 1154) on Bede, Simeon of Durham and Henry of Huntingdon.[1472] He summarises the battle succinctly:

Anno DCCCCVII, in provincia Steffordensi, in loco qui dicitur Teotenhale, inter Anglos et Danos insigne prælium actum est; sed Angli potiti sunt victoria.[1473]

[1468] Giles 1847: 123-4. The Latin text can be found in Hardy 1840: 195-6.
[1469] Galbraith 1982: XI 15.
[1470] Graves 1975: 446-7; Gransden 1996: 261-3.
[1471] Howlett 2012: IV 14. Torigni's works were used as the basis to c.1172 for the historical works of Ralph de Diceto (died c.1202), elected dean of St Paul's, London, in 1180: Graves 1975: 418.
[1472] Graves 1975: 431; EHD 119; Gransden 1996: 225-30.
[1473] Riley 1853: I 61; Stubbs 1868: I 51.

'Anno 907, in the province of Stafford, in the place which is called Tettenhall, was a pitched battle between the English and the Danes; with the English enjoying the victory.'

17. The chronicler Roger of Wendover, who died in 1236, was a monk at St Albans who wrote an important history, probably between about 1219 and 1235,[1474] known as *Flores Historiarum* ('Flowers of History'), an 'original authority of considerable value', the pre-Conquest part of which incorporated the works Williams of Malmesbury, Florence (John) of Worcester and Henry of Huntingdon (and was perhaps adapted from an earlier compilation made at St Albans),[1475] and which formed the basis of the *Chronica majora* of Matthew Paris, commonly regarded as England's greatest medieval historian.[1476] Roger also seems to have had access to early annals, now lost, and records under the year 911:

Eodem anno Dani, Merciam hostiliter ingressi, prædas ibidem egerunt et rapinas; quod cum regi Eadwardo muntiatum fuisset, cum strepitu militari prædonibus obviavit, et in Wodensfeld, id est, in campo Wodeni, duospaganorum reges, Eowils et Haldene, cum duobus comitibus Scurfam et Other et novem eorum proceribus commisso prælio, interemit.[1477]

'In the same year the Danes entered Mercia, which they ravaged and plundered; on hearing of which, king Edward met the robbers with a military force, and engaging with them in battle at Wodensfeld, i.e. the field of Woden, he slew two of the pagan kings, Eowils and Haldene, with two earls, Scurfa and Other, and nine others of their chiefs.'[1478]

18. The *Chronica Johannis Wallingford*, a chronicle attributed to John of Wallingford, who was a friend of the chronicler Matthew Paris and who died in 1258, is an anonymous compilation from c.1225-50, which includes sections based on the 'lost Northummbrian chronicle', for which it is of particular value, incorporated into a chronicle written by John.[1479] The anonymous chronicle contains the following account, in translation, evidently based on that of Æthelweard's *Chronicon*:

'[909] ... the barbarians break their compact with King Eadward and also with Aethered, who then governed Northumbria and Mercia; the lands of the Mercians are laid waste on all sides by the aforesaid tempestuous hosts, as far as the river Afne [Avon], which forms the boundary between the West Angles and the Mercians. They pass thence towards the west to the river Severn and obtain no small booty by their ravages. They next withdraw homewards, rejoicing in the richness of their spoils, and pass over a bridge in regular order, on the eastern bank of the Severn, which is usually called Cantbricge. The troops of the Mercians and West Saxons meet them inbattle array: an engagement ensues without delay, and the Angles obtain the palm of victory on the plain of Wodnesfelda. The Danish army fled, being overwhelmed by darts. These events are recorded as occurring on the 5th day of August: and their three kings fell there in the tumultuous contest, so to speak, namely Healfdene, Eywysl, and Igwar. They left their rule which they had hitherto

---

[1474] Galbraith 1982: X 21.
[1475] Giles 1892: vi; Galbraith 1982: X 21.
[1476] Graves 1975: 441-2, 451-2.
[1477] Coxe 1841: 375.
[1478] Giles 1892: 238.
[1479] MS Cott. Julius Dvii 6; Graves 1975: 299, 450, 451-2. Confusion is caused by the existence of two chroniclers known as John of Wallingford. The other, also known as John de Cella, was abbot of St Albans 1195-1214.

exercised, and hastened to to the court of the infernal king, and many of their chiefs and nobles with them.'[1480]

In addition, in a further section giving a brief and vague account of Alfred's reign, the chronicle includes the following extraordinarypassage:

Quamobrem diversæ provinciæ in unum condicentes, petierunt a Rege Edwardo, ut eorum voluntati hostes prædicti traderentur, depontes in Regis + nono multas querlas de frequenti prædarum subreptione, de viarum interclusione, de Mercatorum spoliis, & de multis aliis in hunc modum erumpentibus, sed & in secretis que ad publicam non pertinent narrationem. Accepta itaque a rege licentia, unaqueque prouincia munitiones quibus se tuebantur delecit, non tamen sine graui bello et labore diutino, sub quo tempore deletum est opitimum eorum presidium in Mercia nomine Wistoche.[1481]

'*... various provinces agreeing together, asked King Eadward, in the ninth year of his reign [908], that [the Danes] should be given up to them to be dealt with as they might choose, testifying with bitter complaints that they had frequently carried off much plunder and blockaded the roads and robbed the merchants; and that indeed many others sallied forth for similar purposes, but secretly, and not in such way to call for public complaint. The king, therefore, having given permission, all the provinces pulled down the fortifications behind which the Danes defended themselves, though not till after much warfare and long-continued labour, during which their strongest post in Mercia, named Wistoche, was destroyed ... .*'[1482]

Wistoche remains unidentified, and the entire passage seems entirely fanciful.[1483]

19. Matthew Paris (c.1200-59), perhaps the greatest of England's medieval historians, was a monk of St Albans who may have studied in Paris. He travelled on a diplomatic mission to Norway in 1248, and on his return took up the mantle of Roger of Wendover, using and revising his work to 1234.[1484] He records of 910 in his *Chronica Majora*:

Eodem anno Dani, Merciam hostiliter ingressi, prædas ibidem egerunt et rapinas; quod cum regi Eadwardo intimatum fuisset, cum strepitu militari prædonibus obviavit, et in Wodenesfeld, id est, in campo Wodenii, duos paganorum reges, Eowils et Haldene, cum duobus comitibus, Scurfam et Other, et novem eorum proceribus, commisso prælio interemit.[1485]

'*In the same year the Danes entered Mercia, which they plundered and ravaged; on hearing of which King Edward met the robbers with a military force,, and engaging them in battle at Wednesfield, that is, the field of Woden, he slew two of the pagan kimgs, Eowils and Haldene, with two earls, Scurfa and Other, and nine other of their chiefs.*'

[1480] Stevenson 1854: 437.
[1481] Gale 1691: 538-9.
[1482] Stevenson 1854: 544.
[1483] Hart suggests that Wistoche may be Wistow in Huntingdonshire: Hart 2003: Vol. II, Book 1, 11-12.
[1484] Graves 1975: 441-2; Gransden 1996: 359.
[1485] Luard 1872: I 440.

20. The lesser-known but useful chronicle of Bartholomew de Cotton (died c.1298), a monk of Norwich who wrote in the late thirteenth century, and for the period 449–1066 is mainly an abridgement of Henry of Huntingdon, notes (under the year 918):

Anno xviii. Factum est prælium inter Anglos et Dacos ... et Angli Dei gratia vicerunt.[1486]

'Anno [9]18. An action was fought between the English and the Danes ... and the English by the grace of God were victorious.'

21. Peter Langtoft (died after 1307) was an English canon of Bridlington, historian and author of a chronicle in rhyming French verse. His metrical history of the Anglo-Saxon kings is said to have been taken from Geoffrey of Monmouth, Henry of Huntingdon, William of Malmesbury, and other well-known writers,[1487] but his account of each ruler is terse and garbled. Of the reign of Edward the Elder, Langtoft gives only a few lines, including the following:

**L'an disme de sun regne vint la chuvalerye
De Danemarche en Kent of molt graunt navye,
Iij. rays et Vj. dukes; Eduuard en Lyndseye
Oist la novele, sun hast requert et prie
Ke tost se hastent tuz, et il baner desplye.
A Treford en Norfolk les Daneys sunt unye;
Les iij. rays sunt tuez, des alters graunt partye
Retournent à lur nefs; Eduuard, Dieu mercye!
Unkes vint en bataille k'il n'avait la mestrie.**[1488]

*'In the tenth year of his reign came the chivalry
Of Denmark into Kent with a very great navy,
Three kings and six dukes; Edward in Lindsey
Hears the news, calls and prays his army
That they will all hasten at once, and he displays his banner.
At Thetford in Norfolk the Danes have engaged him;
The three kings are slain, the others in great part
Return to their ships; Edward, God be thanked!
Never came into battle, but he had the mastery.'*[1489]

It is difficult to know what to make of the account, which from its dating (910), the reference to a fleet at Kent, and to three kings and six dukes, might be seen to refer to the battle of Tettenhall (for which the name Thetford could be a misidentification),[1490] but the arrival and departure of the Danes by ship is inexplicable, and suggests (together with the reference to Lindsey) that the account may be a much-garbled version of the battle of the Holme, which probably took place in East Anglia, and which may not have directly involved Edward's forces.

[1486] Luard 1859: 21; Graves 1975: 416-7.
[1487] Graves 1975: 434.
[1488] Wright 1866: 322.
[1489] Wright 1866: 323.
[1490] Wright notes that other manuscripts give the place as Scheford, Teford and Teteford in Northfolk: Wright 1866: 322 fn.3.

22. The chronicle *Flores Historiarum*, long attributed to Matthew of Westminster, is now believed to have been written by various authors at various times, with the section to 1259 derived from Matthew Paris, and that Matthew of Westminster is an entirely imaginary person. The chronicle, which was continued in various hands to 1326, was printed in 1570, and gives the following account:

[911] Eodum anno Dani Merciam hostiliter nostiliter ingress, prædas ibidem egerunt & rapinas. Quod cum regi Eadvvardo nūciatum fuisset, cum strepitu military prædonibus obuiavit, & in Wodensfeilde, id est, in campo VVoden duos paganorum reges, Eovvils, & Haldeinum, cum duobus comitibus Scufam & Other, & nouem corum proceribus, commisso prąlio, inter-emit.[1491]

'[911] The same year the Danes ravaged Mercia and seized great plunder. King Edward gathered a force and engaged the raiding army at Wodensfeilde, that is, the field of Woden, and two pagan kings, Eovvils, & Haldeinus, together with two earls, Scufam and Other, and a great many others, were killed.'

23. Ranulph Higden was a monk at St Werburgh's Abbey, Chester, and author of the *Polychronicon*, or 'Chronicle of many ages', the standard work of general history in the fourteenth and fifteenth centuries, who died in about 1364.[1492] He tells us that:

Hoc anno in provincial Staffordensi apud Totenhale Angli vicerunt Dacos et postmodum apud Wodenisfeld rex Edwardus occidit de Dacis duos reges, duos comites, cum multis millibis Dacorum Northimbrensium.[1493]

'That year in the province of Stafford at Thotenhale the Englishmen overcame the Danes; and afterwards at Wodenesfeld king Edward slew of the Danes two kings, two earls, and many thousand Danish men from Northumbria.'

Higden's account was printed by William Caxton in his *Prolicionycion*, c.1482:

That yere in the prouince of Stafford at toten hale the englysshmen ouercome the danes and afterward at wodeynysfelde kyng Edward slough of the danes twey kynges twey erles and many thaousands of danes of northumberlond.[1494]

24. Richard of Cirencester was a monk at Westminster who died c.1401. His *Speculum historiale de gestis regum Angliæ* is a history of England from 447 to 1066, essentially a compilation from other chroniclers, including Roger of Wendover,[1495] from whom he extracted the following account:

Per idem tempus Dani Merciam hostiliter ingressi prædas ibidem egerunt et rapinas. Quod cum regi Edwardo intimatum fuisset, cum strepitu militari prædonibus obviavit, et in Wodeniesfeld, id est in Campo Wodenii, duos paganorum reges Edwils

---

[1491] Anon. 1570: 354.
[1492] Graves 1975: 429.
[1493] Lumby1876: VI 410-13.
[1494] Caxton 1482.
[1495] Graves 1975: 291.

et Haldene cum duobus comitibus Scurfam et Ether et novem eorum proceribus commisso prœlio interemit.[1496]

'... *the Danes entered Mercia, which they ravaged and plundered; on hearing of which, King Edward met the robbers with a military force, and engaging with them in battle at Wodensfeld, i.e. the field of Woden, he slew two of the pagan kings, Eowils and Haldene, with two earls, Scurfa and Other, and nine others of their chiefs.*'[1497]

25. John Trevisa, a chronicler who died in about 1412 who translated Ranulph Higden's *Polychronicon*, writes:

Þat yere in þe province of Stafford at Thotenhale þe Englisshe men overcome þe Danes; and afterward at Wodenesfeld kyng Edward slouw of þe Danes tweye kynges, tweye erles, and meny þowsand of men of Danes of Northumbelond.[1498]

'*That year in the province of Stafford at Tettenhall the English men overcame the Danes; and afterwards at Wednesfield king Edward slew of the Danes two kings, two earls, and many thousand Danish men of Northumbria.*'

26. The *Chronicon* of John Brompton, who flourished c.1437, has been described as 'An untrustworthy Chronicle, made up of extracts from Bede, Henry of Huntingdon, Higden and other well-known sources. It is not certain that Brompton [elected abbot of Jervaux in 1437] wrote it', and more recent research has shown that it is a later collection.[1499] The *Chronicon* (and Leland's *Collectanea*, which may have incorporated Brompton's account) records that the battle took place at *Wilmesford*, but no place called Wilmesford or Wilmsford has been traced.

27. The anonymous author of Harleian MS 2261, written in a hand of the 15th century, records:

Ynglische men hade victory of the Danes in this yeare, at Totenhale in Staffordshire. And after that kynge Edwarde did sl[ay] at Wodnesfelde 1j. kynges, 1j. erles, with mony thowsandes of the Danes of Northumbrelonde.[1500]

28. Robert Fabyan, a merchant and alderman who was sheriff of London in 1493, was the compiler of *The New Chronicles of England and France*, first published in 1516.[1501] His work contains the following account:

In the xii. yere of kynge Edwardes reygne, the Danys repentynge theym of theyr couenauntes before made, myndynge and entendyng ye breche of the same, assembled an hoost [host=army], and met wt the kynge in Stafford shyre, at a place called Toten halle; and soone after at Wodenesseylde; at whiche. ii. places the kynge

---

[1496] Mayor 1869: II 53, from the spurious chronicle of 'Richard of Cirencester', based (for this entry) on Roger of Wendover and the spurious 'Matthew of Westminster', which itself was largely taken from Matthew Paris.
[1497] Giles 1892: 238.
[1498] Lumby 1876: VI 413.
[1499] Gross 1900: 270; Hunter 1980: VIII 100.
[1500] Lumby 1876: VI 411-3.
[1501] Graves 1975: 420.

slewe. ii. kynges. ii. erlys,and many thoushādes of the Danys yt then occupied the countre of Northumberlande.[1502]

It will be noted that the account mentions two battles but fails to mention the victor in either.

29. *Holinshed's Chronicles* is the name given to a work which was compiled by various authors, with Raphael Holinshed (1529-80) responsible for the history of England before the Norman Conquest. The first edition of the work, published in 1577, gives the following account:

The yere next insuing, the Danes with a great armie entred into Mercia, to rob and spoile ye countrey, against whom king Edward sent a mightie host, assembled togither of the Westsaxons and them of Mercia, the which set vpon the Danes, as they were returning homeward, and slew of the[m] an huge multitude, together with their chief capitaines, and leaders, as king Halden, and kyng Eolwils, erle Vther, erle Scurfa, & divers other ...

After this, other of the Danes assembled the[m]selves togither, & in Staffordshire at a place called Tote[n]hal, fought with the Englishmen, & after great slaughter made on both parties, the Danes were overcome: and so likewise were they shortly after at Woodfield, or Wodenfield. And thus K. Edw. put the Danes to the worse in eche place commonly where hee came ...[1503]

The second edition of 1587, which was one of the major sources used by Shakespeare in a number of his plays, gives the following account:

The yeere next ensuing, the Danes with a great armie entered into Mercia, to rob and spoile the countrie, against whome king Edward sent a mightie host, assembled togither of the West Saxons& them of Mercia, which set vpon the Danes, as they were returning homeward, and slue of them an huge multitude, together with their chief capitaines and leaders, as king Halden, and king Eolwils, earle Uter, earle Scurfa, and divers other ...

After this, other of the Danes assembled themselves togither, and in Staffordshire at a place called Totenhall, fought with the Englishmen, and after great slaughter made on both parties, the Danes were overcome: and so likewise were they shortly after at Woodfield or Wodenfield. And thus king Edward put the Danes to the woorse in each place commonlie where he came ...[1504]

30. John Leland (c.1506-52), the distinguished antiquary, took holy orders and was appointed royal librarian and later king's antiquary by Henry VIII, spending ten years travelling the country visiting cathedrals and churches in search of antiquarian material. His work remained unpublished until 1710. Of the great battle he writes:

Anno 6. Reg: Sui Dani depredantes Merciam ab Edwardi exercitn in campo Wilmesford gloriose victi. Ubi ex Danis ceciderunt rex Alfdene, rex Eolwolpf, &

[1502] Ellis 1811: 177.
[1503] Holinshed 1577: I 219.
[1504] Holinshed 1587: II 150.

Uther consul, & Owlfholde, & Benesinghold, & Offerd, & Ahemundhold, & Gutferhold, & alius Gutferd, cum multis Danorum millibus.[1505]

'Year 6 of the reign. The Danes ravaged Mercia and Edward engaged them at the field of Wilmesford to achieve a glorious victory. There were killed king Alfdene, king Eolwolpf, and earl Uther, and Owlfholde, and Benesinghold, and Offerd, and Ahemundhold, and Gutferhold, and the other Gutferd, with many thousands of other Danes.'

Elsewhere Leland writes:

Anno DCCCCX°: bellum apud Wodnesfeldam, in quo ceciderunt Eouuilfus & Healfdena, reges paganorum, & multi alii primates paganorum.[1506]

'910: a battle at/near Wednesfield, in which ere killed Eowilfus and Healfdene, kings of the pagans, and a multitude of other pagan leaders.'

and subsequently (perhaps from the account of Roger de Hoveden):

In provincia Steffordensi in loco, Totenhale, inter Anglos & Danos insigne prælium actum est. Sed Angli potiti sunt Victoria.[1507]

'In the province of Stafford, in the place Tettenhall, was a pitched battle between the English and the Danes. With the English enjoying the victory.'

31. Richard Grafton (c.1511-1572), became King's Printer under Henry VIII and Edward VI, and was Member of Parliament for Coventry in 1562. He was imprisoned for sedition on more than one occasion, falling foul of the rapidly changing religious dogmas of the period. In 1568 he published his *Chronicle at Large, and Meere History of the Affayres of Englande, and Kinges of the Same, deduced from the Creation of the Worlde, vnto the First Habitation of thys Islande: and so by continuance vnto the First Yere of the Reigne of our Most Deere and Souereyne Lady Queene Elizabeth, collected out of sundry aucthors ...* Grafton's work was a valuable compilation from various authorities listed at the front of his *Chronicle*, but those authorities are not cited in the main text. He was criticised by John Stow, the cantankerous historian of London, who made much of minor errors in the work, but although little known today, the *Chronicle* contains material of interest to modern historians. The following extract is taken from the second edition, republished in 1809:

In the xij yere of [King Edward's] reigne the Danes repentyng them of theyr couenants before made, and mynding the breach of the same, assembled an hoste and met with the King in Staffordshire at a place called Toten hall, and soone after at Wodnesfield: At which two places the king slue two kinges, two Earles, and many thousands of the Danes that then occupyed the countrye of Northumberland.[1508]

32. John Foxe (c.1516-87), the English martyrologist and historian, a staunch Protestant, published the first English edition of his *Actes and Monuments* (more commonly known as *Foxe's Book of Martyrs*) in 1563, having worked on a Latin edition during his exile in

---

[1505] Hearne 1770: I 218.
[1506] Hearne 1770: III 219.
[1507] Hearne 1770: III 183.
[1508] Grafton 1809: 115.

Europe during the Marian persecutions. The second English edition, published in 1570, was well received by the Church, which ordered a copy to be installed in every cathedral, and became extraordinarily popular, eventually running to four editions. As well as his account of the lives of the church martyrs, Foxe included in his second edition a history of England which contains the following account, obviously extracted from the work of Richard Grafton published only two years earlier:

... aboute the xij. yeare [of Edward's] reigne, the Danes repenting them of their couenants, & minding to breake the same: assembled an hoste and met with the King is Staffordshire at a place called totenhall, and sone after at Wodnesfield: at which two places the king slew. ij kynges, ij.erles, and many thousands of Danes, that occupied the country of Northumerland.[1509]

33. William Lambarde (1536-1601) was an eminent lawyer and Member of Parliament who in 1570 achieved fame with the publication of the first English county history, the *Perambulation of Kent*. In about 1577 he completed his *Dictionarum Angliæ Topographicum & Historicum. An Alphabetical Description of the Chief Places in England and Wales; with an Account of the most Memorable Events which have distinguish'd them*, which was published posthumously in 1730. Lambarde's brief note on the great battle reads:

Kinge Edward, the Son of Alfrede, met a great Army of the Danes at Wodensfield in Mercia, wheare he Slew two of their Kinges, two Earles, and nine Noblemen, besides an infinite Multitude of common Souldiours.[1510]

34. David Powel was a historian whose book, *The Historie of Cambria, now called Wales: a Part of the Most Famous Yland of Brytaine, written in the Brytish Language about two hundreth years past*, was published in 1584. Based on the chronicle of Caradoc of Llancarvan (who died c.1147) with much supplementary material, it records, immediately before recording the death of 'Edelred, Duke of Mercia' (Æthelred died in 911), the following, which would seem to refer to the battle of Tettenhall:

About this time, Edward sent a great armie to Northumberland, which spoiled the countrie, and then returned home: neuertheless, the Danes followed them and destroyed a great part of Mercia. But within a while after, Edward gathered an armie, and giving them battell, ouerthrew them, and slue their kings Alden and Edelwulph, and a great number of their nobles.[1511]

35. In his monumental work *Britannia*, first published in 1586, William Camden (1551-1623), the eminent antiquary who taught himself Old English, writes in Latin in the third (1590) edition of his work:

[1509] Foxe 1570: Book III.
[1510] Lambarde 1730: 436.
[1511] Powel 1584 (reprinted London 1811: 36).The entry is said to be from the chronicle of Matthew of Westminster, who it was later discovered never existed. His chronicle is believed to have been that of Matthew Paris, but the entry cited is not found in Matthew's chronicle. The extract appears to be a garbled conflation of the battle of Tettenhall and the battle of the Holme, c.903, in which Edward's cousin Æthelwold was killed. The battle of the Holme is mentioned elsewhere (twice) by Powel, who gives Æthelwold's name as Edelwulph. Alden is presumably Eohric, the Danish king of East Anglia, who also died in the battle.

Theotenhall, hodie Tetnal, Danico cruore, anno 911. Ab EdWardo Seniore intinctum.

The last (1607) edition published during Camden's life was translated by Philemon Holland in 1610, probably under Camden's direction. The relevant extract reads:

Theoten Hall, which is by interpretation 'The habitation of Heathens or Pagans', at this day Tetnall, embrued with English bloud in the yeere 911 by King Edward the Elder in a bloudy battaile.[1512]

36. The reputation of the historian and antiquary John Stowe (c.1524-1605) is based largely on his *Survey of London*, published in 1598 and popular ever since, but in the later sixteenth century he was encouraged by Archbishop Matthew Parker to translate a number of medieval chronicles, and in 1605 published *The Annales of England*, in which he recorded that:

In the yeare 910 a battell was fought at Wodnesfæld, in Staffordshire, where Cowilfus and Healidene kings of the Pagans, with many Earles and nobles were slaine, but of the common people innumerable [sic].[1513]

37. In 1614 the eminent cartographer John Speed (1552-1629) published the first edition of *The Historie of Great Britaine Vnder the Conquests of the Romans, Saxons, Danes and Normans*. The following is his account of events in 910:

The truce yet lasting, the *Danes* in *Northumberland* were nothing quiet, to stay whose interruptions King *Edward* sent a great power, who harried the Country before them, and with much slaughter returned victorious. These daliances of Fortune made the *Danes* very desperate, and therefore to stay the rowling ball before it should pass their goale, they gathered their powers and entred *Mercia*, where with victory & spoile they raged for a time. But *Edward* to aid *Ethelred* his brother in law, and *Earle* of that *Prouince*, mustered his men, & at *Wodnesfield* neere *Wolfrune-hampton* in *Stafford-shire* gaue the battaile, wherein the *English* so behaued theselues that the two Pagan kings *Cowilfus* and *Healidine*, the two Earles *Vter* and *Scurfa*, besides other Nobles & Commons innumerable they slew; and now the clouds of these distemperatures being driuen backe, King *Edwards* Monarchy ascended the Horizon, and the *Sunne* of his power beganne to shine very bright, therefore he seeking to hold what he had got, set his thoughts to secure his towns with Castles and walles of defence.[1514]

38. Little is known about the life of Thomas Heywoode, but he was born in about 1574, the son of a rector in Lincolnshire, and probably attended the University of Cambridge, but did not take a degree. He combined acting with the writing of poetry and more than 220 plays. In *Gynaikon: or, Nine Bookes of Various Historie, Onelie Conuerning Women*, published in 1624, he writes:

Ethelredus duke of Mercia ... was generall to the king in all his expeditions against the Danes, in the last battaile that he fought against them at a place cald Toten Hall

---

[1512] Camden 1610. Camden's etymology of the name *Theotenhall* was mistaken, but adopted repeatedly by later historians.
[1513] Stowe 1605: 106.
[1514] Speed 1614: 361.

in Staffordshire, he gaue them a mightie auerthrow, but a greater at Wooddensfield where were slaine two Kings, two Earles, and of the soldiers many thousands which were of the Danes of Northumberland. In this battaile were the King and Elphleda [Æthelflæd] both present.[1515]

39. John Flood (1587-1652), a Jesuit missioner and church historian, wrote various works under the pseudonym Michael Alford or Griffith, including *Fides Regia Britannica Sive Annales Ecclesiæ Britannicæ* in four large volumes in Latin, published posthumously in 1653. His account of the battle of Tettenhall reads:

Erat adhuc Danus, aut Danorum saltem reliquiæ; in Merciis, hoc est, in ipsis Insulæ visceribus. Has ergò persequi, & unà omne factionis alimentum tollere; nè pro barbarorum libidene in flammas crumperet, Edoardus omninò decrevit. In Cornaviis, & agro Staffordiensi domicilium fixerant, locumque Theoten-hal, hoc est, infidelium seu paganorum aulem, inde nominaverant. Nunc Tetnal contractiūs dicitur. Ibi fides, cum perfidiâ, certavit insigniter, teste Hovedeno, qui annum prælii, locumque certaminis, & eventum ita paucis explicat.[1516]

40. John Milton, the poet, undertook careful research in the late 1640s, the period of the Commonwealth, to write a detailed history of pre-Conquest Britain, which remained unpublished until 1670, but was influential long thereafter. He summarises the events of the period around 910 in somewhat tortuous language:

King Edward raising great Forces out of West-Sex, and Mercia, sent them against the Danes beyond Humber; where staying five weeks, they made great spoil and slaughter. The king offer'd them terms of Peace, but they, rejecting all, enter'd with the next year into Mercia, rendering no less hostility than they had suffer'd; but at Tetnal in Staffordshire, saith Florent, were by the English in a set Battle overthrown. King Edward then in Kent, had got-together of Ships about a hundred Sail, others gon Southward, came back and met him. The Danes now supposing that his main Forces were upon the Sea, took liberty to rove and plunder up and down, as hope of prey led them, beyond the Severn. The King, guessing what might embold'n them, sent before him the lightest of his Army to entertain them; then following with the rest, set upon them in thir return over Cantbrig in Gloucestershire,[1517] and slew many thousands, among whom Ecwils, Hafden, and Hinguar thir Kings, and many harsh names in [Henry of] Huntingdon; the place also of this fight is variously writt'n, by Ethelwerd and Florent, call'd Wodensfield.[1518]

41. James Tyrrell (1642-1717), a grandson of James Ussher, the celebrated historian and Archbishop of Armagh (1581-1656), was a Whig lawyer, polemicist, historian and antiquary who published in 1697 the first of three volumes of *The General History of England, both Ecclesiastical and Civil; From the Earliest Accounts of Time, to the Reign of His Present Majesty, King William III*. The impressively detailed and astute history, uncompleted and little known today, contains the following account:

[1515] Heywoode 1624: 236.
[1516] Alford 1563: III 218.
[1517] Cambridge is a hamlet in Slimbridge, Gloucestershire, anciently *Hislingbruge*, on the river Cam which falls into the Severn. William Camden identified the place as *Cwatbrycge* (Camden 1695: 235), which is philologically impossible.
[1518] Milton 1695: 253-4.

Anno Dom DCCCCXI That the *Danish* Army in Northumberland not regarding the Peace which king *Edward* and his Son had made with them, again wasted the Province of the *Mercians*; but the King being then in *Kent*, had got together about 100 Ships, which sailed towards the South-East to meet them, and then the *Danes* supposing that the greatest part of the King's forces were in his Fleet, thought they might march safely whither they would without fighting; but so soon as the king understood they were gone out to plunder, hesent an Army consisting of *West Saxons* and *Mercians*, who followingthe *Danes* in the Rear, as they returned home met with them (in a place called Wednesfield,) and fought with them, routingand killing many Thousands of them, with *Eowils* and *Healfden* their Kings, with Several Earls and Chief Commanders of their Army;whose names I forbear to give, because I would tire my Reader as little as I could. ... Also in the Same Year, as *Florence* hath it, there was a remarkable Battle between the *English* and the *Danes* in Staffordshire, but the former obtained the Victory.[1519]

The only matter of note (other than the mistaken reference to two battles) is the mention of the Danes breaching a treaty made with Edward and his son, Æthelstan, who was born in 895. No other reference has been traced which mentions Æthelstan as a party to any treaty, which in any event is inconceivable, and the reference may have been intended to refer to Æthelred, Edward's brother-in-law.

42. Laurence Echard (1670?-1730) was chaplain to the bishop of Norwich and a notable historian who in 1707 published *The History of England; From the First Entrance of Julius Cæsar and the Romans, to the End of the Reign of King James the First, Containing the Space of 1678 years*, which became a standard work until superseded by the translations of Rapin de Theyras's *Histoire d'Angleterre*.[1520] His account of the battle is of particular interest, but though he gives some sources for his writings, none are shown for the following entry other than Henry of Huntingdon:

AD 912: But in the following Year they broke this [treaty] also, and furiously invaded *Mercia*, where they were met by the *English* at *Teoten hale*, or *Tetnal* in Staffordshire, and overthrown. King *Edward* was then in *Kent*, and had gather'd together about an hundred Sail of Ships, besides such as were sent to the Southward and met him at Sea. The *Danes* imagining that he had shipt off the Majority of his Forces, took the Liberty to rove about beyond the *Severn*, and whenever else the Hopes of Booty could invite them. Whereupon King *Edward* sent the lightest of his Army before, to divert the Enemy 'till he could come up; and then following with the main Body, he engag'd them in their Return at *Cantbridge* in *Glocestershire*, where he gave them a memorable Defeat.[1521] The Annals relate, that many thousands of them were slain, together with *Eowd* their King; but [Henry of] *Huntingdon* mentions two other kings *Haldene* and *Eolwulf*, besides *Uther* a Consul, and eight other Noblemen whose barbarous Names may without any Loss to the reader be omitted.[1522]

[1519] Tyrrell 1697: Book V 315-6. Between the entries for the two battle, Tyrrell notes that the *Annals of Winchcomb* record that Reginald succeeded Kings Eowils and Healfden. Reginald is Ragnall, who indeed took the throne at York in 919 or possibly earlier: Williams, Smyth and Kirby 1991: 205.
[1520] DNB 16 351-2.
[1521] As noted previously, early historians identified *Cwatbrycge* as Cambridge in Gloucestershire (Camden 1695: 235), which is philologically impossible.
[1522] Echard 1707: I 78.

The account, evidently based on Æthelweard's *Chronicon*, the only early source to mention *Cwatbrycge*, but placing the defeat of the Danes at Tettenhall rather than Wednesfield as named by Æthelweard, is notable for the idea, untraced elsewhere, that Edward divided his forces and sent 'the lightest of his Army' to divert the Danes before his main forces arrived to confront the Danes.

43. An important eighteenth-century publication was the six quarto volumes of over 4,800 pages compiled by Thomas Cox and Anthony Hall, with maps by Robert Morden, and the title *Magna Britannia Antiqua & Nova; or; a New, Exact and Comprehensive Survey of the Ancient and Present State of Great-Britain ... the whole being more Comprehensive and Instructive than Camden, or any other Author on this Subject ...*, published as volume V in 1730, though the title-page bears the date 1727. The relevant entry reads:

Wednesfield, a Place of great Note in our Histories, for a signal Victory which K. Edward sen. Obtain'd over the Danes, who in divers Parties harass'd the Land. Edward was no sooner settled on his Throne, but he provided an Army to subdue these his Enemies; and first meeting them at Theoten-Hall, now called Tetten-Hall, where they had settled their habitation (the Name importing, as Camden tells us, The Habitation of the Heathens) he encounter'd their Army, and after a sharp Fight, obtain'd a compleat Victory, and razed their City. This Destruction of their Brethren was no sooner heard by the Danes that possess'd Northumberland, but they, not regarding the League which they had lately made with King Edward, rais'd an Army, and to revenge the Death of their Countrymen, invaded Mercia, pillaging the Country all along as they marched. King Edward, not insensible of their Motions, brings a powerful Army, both of West-Saxons and Mercians, against them; and overtaking them in their March against this Village, which is at a small distance from Theoten-Hall, brought them to battle, and overthrew them, killing Covills and Hailden, two of their Kings, divers of their Nobles, and an innumerable Multitude of their common Soldiers. Of this great Slaughter, there are here no other remains but a Low in a Ground call'd South-Low Field, which has lately had a mill set upon it. There is a Field, also, call'd North-Low Field, in which there is no Low now; but doubtless there has been one if not more. The Danish or Saxon Nobles, slain in this Battle, are bury'd under them.[1523]

The entry contrives to make sense of the contradictory evidence by asserting that two battles took place, the first associated with Danes living at the supposed 'ancient city' at Wrottesley, an idea that has since proved baseless and the 'city' a chimera. As will be seen, the account was subsequently adopted by other commentators.

44. Tobias Smollett (1721-1771) was a Scottish poet, novelist and historian who considered his greatest work *A Complete History of England*, the third edition of which was published in 1758 and which included the following account:

Notwithstanding [the treaty of Tiddingford], which was concluded at Ickford, in Bucks, the peace of the kingdom was incessantly disturbed by the Northumbrians and Danes of Derby, Nottingham, Leicester, Lincoln and Stamford, who joined their forces, and ravaged their adjacent country. At length Edward, incensed by these hostilities, equipped a fleet, in order to infest their commerce and their coasts; and they supposing that the greatest part of his army was embarked, invaded his

---

[1523] Cox, Hall and Morden 1727: V 27.

territories with a strong body of forces, in full confidence of pillaging with impunity. But in their return they were attacked at Tetenhale, in Staffordshire, by the West Saxons and Mercians who defeated them in a pitched battle, which cost them the lives of two kings, a great number of principal officers, and many of their common men; a disaster which humbled the Danes to such a degree, that for some years they remained quiet at home, without attempting any new irruption.[1524]

The account is noteworthy for the claim that the Scandinavians who fought at Tettenhall were a raiding party from the 'Five Boroughs' of the east Midlands, rather than from Northumbria, though his conclusions are unsupported by the sources he cites.[1525]

45. In 1777-8 Joseph Strutt (1749-1892), an engraver turned artist, antiquary and writer, published two volumes of English history incorporating vast research. In volume II of *The Chronicle of England: or, a Compleat History, Civil, Military and Ecclesiastical, of the Ancient Britons and Saxons, from the Landing of Julius Cæsar in Britain, to the Norman Conquest*, he wrote of events in 910 in the following terms:

The following year [910], the Danes rejecting all offers of peace, entered Mercia, and retaliated the injuries which they had received, but being met by a strong party of Saxons, at Tetnal in Staffordshire, they were overthrown in a set battle. In the meantime king Edward was in Kent, and had collected about an hundred sail of ships, and was met by others which had been cruising upon the southern coasts. The Danes (hearing how Edward was employed, and imagining the greatest part of his army was sent on board the vessels) collected all the forces they could, and advancing beyond the Severn into Wessex, plundered every part of the country they passed through. The king, on hearing of their proceedings, marched against them with all expedition, and came up with them unexpectedly, at a place called Wodnesfield, in Staffordshire, as they were returning home: a bloody battle ensued, in which the Danes after a desperate resistance, were totally overcome, with the loss of some thousands of their army, together with Ecwils their king, and several others of their chief noblemen and leaders.[1526]

Strutt's account speaks of two battles, and mistakenly claims the Danes crossed the Severn into Wessex (Æthelweard says 'the west country'), which lay south of the Avon.

46. At the end of the eighteenth century, the great Staffordshirecleric, topographer and historian Stebbing Shaw (1762-1802), in the first volume of his *The History and Antiquities of Staffordshire* published in 1798, reached the following conclusion as to the battle, rather surprisingly omitting the widely-recorded names any of the Danes who died:

We will take a view of the deplorable remains of those bloody wars between the Saxons and the Danes. The principal of which may be esteemed those extensive ruins in Wrottesley park, which Plot takes to have been a British city, the whole containing a circuit of three or four miles, lying part in this county and part in Shropshire. But, upon further consideration, he believes them to be the remains of the old Theotenhall of the Danes, who having resided there some time, built themselves this city, or place

---

[1524] Smollett 1758: 186-7.
[1525] It should perhaps be noted that ASC 'A' records a king from the East Midlands killed in 920: Swanton 1996: 102.
[1526] Strutt 1778: II 43.

of habitation, which, in the year 907 (Roger of Hoveden's Annals, Part I; but 911 according to other historians) was finally demolished by Edward the elder, in a most signal and destructive victory.[1527] To revenge this fatal quarrel, another army of Northumbrians invaded Mercia in the same year, when King Edward, with a powerful force of West Saxons and Mercians, overtook them at the village of Wednesfield, near Theotenhall, and vanquished them again, with much slaughter. Of this there are no remains but a low, in a place called North Low-field, though the low is not now visible. These, doubtless, were cast up over some of the Kings or nobles then slain here; as was also Stowman's hill, on the road between Wolverhampton and Walsall, half a mile South-west of the village of Nechels.[1528]

47. In *A Topographical History of Staffordshire* published in 1817, William Pitt, an agronomist born at Tettenhall in 1749, provides no new information about the battle, simply recording that

A great battle is said to have been fought between Tettenhall and the Wergs, where, in a field called Low-hill-field, a large tumulus is still to be seen

and adding for good measure that in 911 Edward the Elder defeated the Danes at Tettenhall.[1529]

48. The London solicitor and prolific historian Sharon Turner (1768-1847) published, in the fourth (1823) edition of his well-researched *History of the Anglo-Saxons*, first issued in 1799-1805, a brief account of the conflict:

The Danes, fancying the great body of [Edward's] forces to be on the seas, advanced into the country to the Avon, and plundered without apprehension, and passed onwards to the Severn. Edward immediately sent a powerful army to attack them; his orders were obeyed. The Northerns were surprised in a fixed battle at Wednesfield, and were defeated, with the slaughter of many thousands. Two of their kings fell, brothers of the celebrated Ingwar, and therefore children of Ragnar Lodbrog, and many earls and officers. The Anglo-Saxons sung hymns of their great victory.[1530]

49. Johann Martin Lappenberg (1759-1819) was a German scholar who in 1834 published in German a detailed history of the Anglo-Saxon period in England, translated in 1845 by Benjamin Thorpe, the great Victorian Anglo-Saxonist. Lappenberg provides the following account of events in 910:

… the Northumbrians, either in agreement with their brethren in France, or of their own accord, seeing the favourable moment, when the greater part of the English army was on board the fleet, again violating the treaty, proceeded to the Severn, which river (after having collected a vast booty along its western bank) they crossed

---

[1527] The remains of the so-called British city are discussed elsewhere in this volume.
[1528] Shaw 1798: I 37.
[1529] Pitt 1817: 183.
[1530] Turner 1823: 165. Turner was evidently following Florence (John) of Worcester in suggesting that the kings who died were brothers of Ingvar. As noted previously, it would appear that the chronicler confused king Halfdene, who died in the battle, with Hálfdan, king of Northumbria who was killed in 877 at Strangford Lough on the coast of County Down in Northern Ireland: Smyth 1977: 262-3.

at the bridge of Cantbricge (Cambridge in Gloucestershire?).[1531] On receipt of this intelligence, Eadward immediately despatched an army of West Saxons and Mercians to expel the barbarians, who overtook them on their return laden with spoil at Wodnesfeld, where in the battle which took place, the Danish kings Eowils and Healfdene, brothers of Ingvar (of whom the English annals make mention thirty years earlier),[1532] the jarls Other and Scurfa, nine holds and men of note, besides a considerable number of common people were slain. The royal names mentioned on this occasion excite some suspicion, and justify the doubt whether the choniclers may not have blended the remembrance of some former battle with their account of the present one.[1533]

50. In 1850 Thomas Miller, a popular writer on historical and topographical subjects, published the second edition of his *History of the Anglo-Saxons from the Earliest Period to the Norman Conquest*, which mentions Edward the Elder's raid into Northumbria [in 909] and adds:

In the following spring, the Danes retaliated, and attacked Mercia on each side of the river Trent [*recte* Severn?]. While Edward was busy on the south-eastern coast, repairing and collecting together his ships, a rumour circulated amongst the Danes that he had gone to the opposite shore [*sic*] with his fleet. Misguided by these tidings, the Danish army passed across the country in the direction of the Severn, plundering every place they approached, and moving about in that irregular manner which showed that they were not apprehensive of any attack. Great was their surprise when they saw a powerful army approaching them; they discovered not the danger until it was too late to fly from it, for Edward was upon them, and there was no alternative but to fight. The battle took place at Wodensfield, and thousands of the Danes were slain, for, beside many earls and chiefs, they left two of their kings dead upon the field.[1534]

Rather surprisingly Sampson Erdeswick of Sandon (c.1528-1603), the father of Staffordshire historians, who completed his manuscript *Survey of Staffordhire* at the end of the sixteenth century, makes no reference at all to the battle.[1535]

[1531] As noted previously, early historians identified *Cwatbrycge* as Cambridge in Gloucestershire (Camden 1695: 235), which is philologically impossible.
[1532] See preceding footnote.
[1533] Thorpe 1845: 90.
[1534] Miller 1850: 200-201.
[1535] The preface in the 1820 edition of Erdeswick's *Survey* records that 'In 911, at Wednesfield, Edward the Elder defeated the Danes in a battle, in which two of their kings, two earls, and nine other chiefs, were slain; memorials of it are to be seen in South-Low-field; in North-Low-field the barrow has been levelled' (p.xii), and that 'In 910, Edward the elder sent a powerful army to attack the Danes. The Northumbrians were surprised into a fixed battle at Wodnesfield, Wednesfield, and were defeated with the slaughter of many thousand men. Two of their kings fell, Halfden and Eowils, the brother of the celebrated Ingwar, and many earls and officers. The Anglo-Saxons sung hymns on their great victory': p.288. Footnotes in Harwood's 1844 edition of Erdeswick also give battles between the English and the Danes at both Tettenhall and Wednesfield: Erdeswick 1844: 351, 392-3.

Chronicle	Chronicle date	Wintering of Danes 895-6	Reference to Tettenhall	Reference to Wednesfield	Battle date	Reference to Æthelflæd's burh
Anglo-Saxon Chronicle A (Parker/Winchester MS)	Before 924	æt Cwatbrycge [be Sæfern]	896	-	-	910	-
Anglo-Saxon Chronicle B (Abingdon MS)	c.977 x 979	æt Bricge	[for 895] 896	-	-	910	Bricge
Annals of St Neots ("the East Anglian Chronicle")	Before c.1012	-	-	-	Wodnesfeldam	910	-
Æthelweard	c.978 x 988	-	-	Vuodnesfelda campo	909 5th August	-
Anglo-Saxon Chronicle C (Abingdon MS)	c.1048	æt Bricge	896	æt Teotan heale	-	910	Bricge
Anglo-Saxon Chronicle D (Worcester MS)	c.1054	æt Brygce [be Sæfern]	896	neh Teotanheale	-	909	-
" " " " " " "	"	æt Brygce	896	æt Totanheale	-	910	-
" " " " " " "	"	-	-	-	911 6th August	-
William of Malmesbury	c.1100	-	-	-	-	-	-
Florence (John) of Worcester ("the Worcester Latin Chronicle")	d.1118	Locum qui Quattbrycge dicitur cwatbrycge	896	Teotanheal (Thorpe) Teottanhele (Stephenson)	in campo, qui lingua Anglorum Wodnesfeld dicitur	911	Brycge
Anglo-Saxon Chronicle E (Laud/Peterbororugh MS)	c.1121	Quadruge		Æt Teotan heale	-	910	-
Simeon of Durham ("Byrhtferth's Northumbrian Chronicle")	d. after 1129	-		✓	-	910	-
Chronicle of Melrose	1140	-		Totenhall	-	911	-
Roger of Hoveden	1148 x 1161	-		✓	-	907	Brige
Henry of Huntingdon	c.1130 x 1154	Quathruge iuxta sauernam		apud Totanhale	-	907	-
Roger of Wendover	c.1235	Quantebregge	896	-	Wodnesfeld	911	Bregges
Matthew Paris	d. c.1259	Quantbregge		-	Wodenesfeld	911	Bregges
Bartholomew de Colton	Late 13th century	Quantbregge		-	-	907	-
Ranulph Higden	d.1364	Brugge super Sabrinum		Totenhale/ Thotenhall	Wodenisfeld/ Wodenesfelde/ Wodemisfeld	-	Brugge super Sabrinam
John Trevisa	d.1412	brigge uppon Sevarne		Thotenhale	Wodenesfeld	-	Brygge/brigge uppon Sevarn
John Brompton	fl.1437	-		✓	-	911 (Plot 1686: 415)	-
MS Harleian 2261	15th century	brygges nye to Severne		Totenhale	Wodenesfelde	-	Brugg on Severne

Table showing early sources of information relating to the battle of Tettenhall.

27. Analysis of the documentary evidence relating to the battle of Tettenhall.

With such diverse accounts of the date and place of the battle(s) and the identification of the Scandinavian dead, how is the historian to rank the credibility of each account, particularly since none is contemporary?[1536] One approach is to consider the origins and likely veracity of each of the accounts, bearing in mind that the chroniclers borrowed from many different sources (few if any of which will have been contemporary), and in many cases from each other. But the events of 910 must be seen as only part of a complex scenario that for convenience we can take back to events of the previous year when a joint English army raided into the Danelaw. ASC 'A' records the event in the following terms:

[909] ... 7 þy ilcan gere sende Eadweard cyng firde ægðer ge of Westseaxum ge of Mercum, 7 heo gehergade swiðe micel on þæm norðhere, ægðer ge on mannum ge on gehwelces cynnes yrfe, 7 manega men ofslogon þara Deniscena 7 þær wæron fif wucan inne.[1537]

That is usually translated as:

' ... and in the same year King Edward sent an army both from Wessex and from Mercia, and it raided the north raiding-army very greatly, both men and every kind of property, and killed many men of those Danish, and were inside there for five weeks'.[1538]

However, what appears at first glance to be straightforward may be rather more complex, and it is necessary to analyse in some detail the precise vocabulary used by the chroniclers. The terms *norðhere* and *Deniscena*, translated as 'northern army' and 'Danish', in reality do little to identify any specific Scandinavian force or its location. For many generations – indeed, since the time of the Anglo-Norman historians – those terms have, perhaps too simplistically, been taken to apply to a Danish army from Northumbria, ruled from York. The traditional interpretation was necessarily influenced by earlier entries in the *Anglo-Saxon Chronicle* where Scandinavian settlement in England was restricted to areas north and east of Watling Street after it was established as the southern boundary of Danish territory in the treaty between Alfred and Guthrum at some date between 878 and 886.[1539]

John Quanrud, having methodically analysed the *Anglo-Saxon Chronicle*, concludes in a landmark study that whilst the term *se here* 'the army' is found throughout the work, often with words such as *micel* 'great', *scip* 'ship', and *hæðen* 'heathen' in the ninth and tenth centuries, the annal for 909 is unique: it is the only occasion in the entire *Chronicle* where the expression *norðhere* is used. Clearly the northern army was based somewhere within the Danelaw, but we are offered no clues to pin down any precise location, or even the general region or area. Quanrud suggests, very plausibly, that *norðhere* is a new term used for a new threat, namely the Hiberno-Scandinavians, or Irish Sea Vikings in north-west

---

[1536] Sadly, we possess nothing to equate with the 59-line poem known as *Das Ludwigslied*, probably written in the 930s, which celebrates the victory of Louis II of France over the Danes on 3rd August 881 at Saucourt-en-Vimeu, when the French army intercepted a Viking force returning to base with the spoils of war from their campaign in the Somme Region, an episode that has obvious parallels with the battle of Tettenhall only 30 years later.
[1537] Bateley 1986: 63.
[1538] Swanton 1996: 94-6.
[1539] Abrams 2001: 132.

England, who were to be distinguished from the other Scandinavian armies of York-ruled Northumbria.[1540]

Turning to the term *Deniscan* in the same *Chronicle* entry, which we have seen is translated, understandably for phonetic reasons alone, as 'Danish', it has been suggested that the word was never intended by the chroniclers to distinguish 'Danes' from 'Norwegians', and was almost certainly used in a loose sense to denote any Scandinavians or ally of the Scandinavians.[1541] Though a close study of the *Anglo-Saxon Chronicle* entries covering the period from 830 to 1000 suggests that English chroniclers on the whole applied the words 'Danes' and 'Northmen' with some precision, the West Saxons were confronted mainly by Danes, which explains why the *Chronicle* shows less familiarity with Norwegians or Norsemen than it does with the ubiquitous Danish enemy. Quite simply, the term *Deniscan* cannot be assumed to mean 'Danes of York'.[1542] Indeed, the evidence suggests that the five-week raid into the Danelaw by Edward and a joint West Saxon and Mercian force in 909 was intended to neutralise the dangers posed by an army formed by the Irish Sea Vikings in north-west England who may by then have launched attacks into Danish-held areas in the north and east of England, and perhaps into Wales and the north of English Mercia.[1543]

The *Anglo Saxon Chronicle* records that in 910 a raiding-army in Northumbria broke the peace, and scorned every privilege which King Edward and his councellors offered them.[1544] However, as Quanrud has pointed out, there are subtle but perhaps significant variations in the language used by different versions of the Chronicles to record this. *Anglo-Saxon Chronicle* 'B' and 'D', for example, say *Her bræc se here þone friðon Norðhymbrum* 'in this year was broken by the army the peace in Northumbria'. In *Chronicle* 'A', however, the word-order differs slightly: it begins *Her bræcse here on Norðhymbrum þone frið* 'in this year the army in Northumbria broke the peace'. The words *se here on Norðhymbrum* in *Chronicle* 'A' mirror exactly the words in an entry in the same *Chronicle* for 900, translated as 'the raiding-army in Northumbria', and it is possible that the later text, like that of 900, refers to the Danish army in York.[1545]

But if the version in the other Chronicles is to be preferred, then it was the peace in Northumbria that had been violated, and *se here* may be equated with the *norðhere* of the annal for 909, perhaps referring to a Scandinavian army based elsewhere in the north. The most likely identification must be the Hiberno-Scandinavians of the north-west. Though the Anglo-Saxon kingdom of Northumbria had effectively come to an end with the fall of York in 867, the term *Norðanhymbre* continued to be used long after for its former territories, which included northern England from the Irish Sea to the North Sea, demonstrated by a reference in the *Chronicle* in 919 to *Mameceaster on Norþhymbrum* 'Manchester in Northumbria'.[1546] It has been suggested that the compiler of *Chronicle* 'A'

[1540] Quanrud 2015: 77-9.
[1541] Downham 2007: xviii; Downham 2009: 143.
[1542] Quanrud 2015: 76.
[1543] On a strict reading of the *Chronicle* the English raid of 909 did not involve the Hiberno-Norse in the Wirral, eventually occupied by Ingimund and his followers after their expulsion from Dublin c.901, since it lay within Mercia, the Mersey (meaning 'boundary river') probably forming the border with Northumbria: Hill 1984: 56.
[1544] Swanton 1996: 96-7.
[1545] Bateley 1986: 62; Swanton 1996: 92.
[1546] Bateley 1986: 69; Quanrud 2015: 77.

deliberately modified the original text *þone frið on Norðhymbrum* of the primary version to read *se here on Norðhymbrum* as found in the other vernacular versions.[1547]

A further variation between *Chronicle* 'A' and the other *Chronicles* is found in the remainder of the sentence in which the above extracts occur. *Chronicle* 'A' says that the Scandinvian army had 'scorned every peace (or privilege)' – *forsawan ælc frið* – whereas the other *Chronicles* use the expression *ælc riht* 'every right'. Old English *richt* meant 'that which properly belonged to a person, that which might justy be claimed, a right, a due', whereas *frið* was something in the king's power to confer or bestow.[1548] Cyril Hart puts forward the persuasive idea that the compiler of *Chronicle* 'A' perhaps amended the text of the primary source to better enhance Edward's reputation as recorded in the primary source by referring to 'privileges' rather than 'rights' offered to the Northumbrians.[1549] If that suggestion is correct, then we might suspect that the same compiler could have amended the original source text as probably found in the other *Chronicles* to read *se here on Norðhymbrum* 'the army in Northumbria', which could well refer to a Hiberno-Scandinavian army.

The chronicler Æthelweard, of whom more shortly, in his Latin text says simply that the barbarians *pactum rumpunt* 'broke the pact'[1550] with King Edward, and with Æthelred 'who then ruled the Northumbrian and Mercian areas'. This wording has led to some academic discussion,[1551] since Æthelred is not known to have ruled any part of the Northumbria – indeed, all the evidence, including the failure of the *Chronicle* to refer even obliquely to such rule, is to the contrary – and we have no knowledge of the source of Æthelweard's comment.[1552] Quanrud follows Campbell in concluding that Æthelweard's words mean that Æthelred ruled the Northumbrian and Mercian areas. That is probably correct, but is not necessarily what Æthelweard is telling us, since an alternative (though admittedly less likely) reading is that together Edward and Æthelred ruled the Northumbrian and Mercian areas respectively: in other words, that it was Edward who ruled the Northumbrian areas, not Æthelred, as discussed elsewhere in this volume. That interpretation would not remove the difficulties, but would simply transfer the issues from Æthelred to Edward, since we have no knowledge that Edward ruled any part of Northumbria at this date.

If Æthelweard's statement is to be accepted at face value, and is not an aberration, the most likely area to have been subject to Edward's rule must be the north-west, a possibility perhaps supported by Stenton's observation that '[t]here is no reason to think that the English occupation of the north-west was affected by the decline of Northumbrian power in the eighth century, and the little evidence which exists suggests that the country west of the Pennine hills was still subject to English rulers when King Alfred died in 899',[1553] that is, only a decade before the battle of Tettenhall. It is very possible that at the time of

---

[1547] Quanrud 2015: 77-8.
[1548] BT.
[1549] Hart 1982: 254.
[1550] Campbell 1962: 52, where *pactum* is translated as 'peace', though 'break the peace' would normally be *pacem violere*.
[1551] For example Downham 2009: 88; Quanrud 2015: 79.
[1552] The section of Æthelweard's chronicle from 893 to 946 does not appear to derive from any source known to us: Campbell 1962: xlii. It is noteworthy that Campbell failed to comment on this curious entry.
[1553] Stenton 1960: 216.

Tettenhall the north-west was still under English overlordship, though if that were the case compelling evidence has yet to surface.[1554]

So what precisely was the *frið* or peace that was violated in 910? *Chronicle* 'A' is silent on the point, but we must conclude that it was some pact or treaty, perhaps the treaty of c.905 under which Edward made peace with the East Angles and Northumbrians of York at *Yttingaford* (Tiddingford, Bedfordshire).[1555] Versions 'A', 'B', 'C', and 'D' of the *Anglo-Saxon Chronicle* state that the treaty occurred 'just as King Edward decreed', but in a subtle variation version 'E' and the *Historia Regum Anglorum*, Part I, written in about 1129 by Simeon of Durham, state that Edward was 'compelled by necessity' to make the agreement.[1556] This may have been an attempt to prevent a coalition between the Danes of York and those from Dublin who had settled on the Wirral to reinforce the established body of Norse settled in the wider Lancashire and Cumbria region.[1557] Or the peace that was violated may have been another treaty of which we have no knowledge, perhaps even a pact concluded with the Hiberno-Norse in return for the land on which to settle supposedly granted to them by Æthelflæd, probably around the Wirral,[1558] or even a treaty concluded with Edward to bring an end to the devastating English raid of 909 into

---

[1554] It should not be overlooked that immediately before her death at Tamworth in June 918 Æthelflæd had received 'by pledge and oaths' the submission of the York-folk (*Eoforwicingas*), and may have been at Tamworth, on the border of the Danelaw, to accept the submission: such meetings were frequently held at boundaries: ASC 'C'; Swanton 1996: 105. The agreement with Viking York may be seen as evidence that Æthelflæd, rather than Edward, was perhaps the dominant influence north and west of a line from Cirencester to Northampton and on to Stamford: Charles-Edwards 2013: 498.

[1555] This is the view taken by Ryan Lavelle, who has pointed out that 'a significant proportion of the acts of submission or peacemaking (the line between them being very blurred) were associated with the same groups as those who undertook the hostile acts shortly thereafter', noting specifically the Tiddiford treaty followed some years later by every peace or every privilege 'being spurned by the Northumbrians': Lavelle 2012: 80-81.

[1556] Whitelock 1979: 278; Downham 2007: 85-6. The later 14th-century chronicler John of Fordun mentions a treaty between the kings of the Danes and Constantine of the Scots in about 903, but 'remaining faithful scarcely two years, they [the Danes] were led away by the treacherous promises of Edward and made peace with him against the Scots, to their own hurt. Nor did the stipulations of this covenant hold long; indeed, four years after, there sprang up some estrangement between them – by what chance, is not certain; but, it is believed, by Edward's wickedness, who made a hostile invasion of their territory, and wasted it with piteous slaughter for a whole month', as a result of which the Danes eventually renewed their treaty with Constantine: Skene 1872: 154-5. The alliance between Edward and the Danes against the Scots c.905 may be identified as the treaty of Tiddingford, with Edward's month-long expedition two years later representing his ravaging of Northumbria the year before the battle of Tettenhall. If that was the case, Fordun evidently believed that Edward's campaign into Northumbria was against 'the Danes' (i.e. Scandinavians), probably unaware of two factions (the Danes of York and the Hiberno-Norse) within the territory of the Northumbrian Scandinavians. The sources for the Scottish chonicler's statements are unknown, but he was doubtless influenced by his anti-English sentiments.

[1557] The loyalty of some English landowners may not have been beyond doubt, for a suit heard c.975 recorded in the *Liber Eliensis* suggests that Edward the Elder, after the conquest of the southern Danelaw, confiscated the lands of those Englishmen who had taken the Danish side in the recent war: Stenton 1970: 123.

[1558] In which case they had already breached any such treaty by attacking Chester, if the account of its siege is based on fact. Pelteret has concluded, that 'The treaty of Tiddingford was of great potential strategic significance because it protected the north-east flank of the West Saxon realm against their Anglo-Saxon [*sic*] neighbours, who could pose a serious threat if they joined with the Vikings in the towns later known as the Five Boroughs' (Baxter et al 2009: 323), a puzzling analysis that is difficult to explain.

Scandinavian territory. If any such treaty was with the Hiberno-Scandinavians of the north-west – which is very likely – it can be assumed that those who broke the peace and ravaged in England in 910 were those same Hiberno-Scandinavians. Such treaties seem typically to have involved 'the exchange of hostages, the reciprocal swearing of oaths and agreement of terms, in different combinations according to the particular circumstances, sometimes with further refinements such as the baptism of the Viking leaders'.[1559] The precise nature of the 'privileges' offered by Edward to avoid military action is unknown, but doubtless involved the offer of silver in the form of coin and bullion, the usual form of Scandinavain wealth, in which case we must wonder at the reason for the Scandinavian raid into Mercia in 910 if not for loot and plunder.

In this case the *Chronicle* tells us specifically that 'privileges' or inducements were offered not just by Edward, but by Edward and his advisors, before the battle of 910. It also implies that such privileges were offered after the raiding-army had broken the peace,[1560] but whether before or after hostilities had started, Edward clearly had forewarning that one at least of his existing treaties was effectively valueless, which we must imagine led him to warn his commanders that their troops should be poised for action at short notice. That would certainly help to explain the otherwise extraordinary speed with which those forces reacted to the Northumbrian incursion in 910, but adds to the puzzle of his association with his fleet off the south coast which clearly distracted Edward from the real threat from the Scandinavians. We must suppose that the situation which had led to the assembling of the fleet was thought to be real and serious, and may indeed have been both.[1561]

The most important authority for the events of 910 is indisputedly Æthelweard, a magnate, diplomat and chronicler from a noble background[1562] – he claimed to be the great-great-grandson of Æthelred (d.871), a brother of King Alfred – who became *ealdorman* of the south-western provinces, and from 992 to his death in 988 was the leading ealdorman of King Æthelred II *Unræd*. Cultured and learned, his Latin *Chronicon*, written between 978 and 988,[1563] was derived from a version of the *Anglo-Saxon Chronicle* no longer surviving, its later annals perhaps suggesting additions from a northern source, and which incorporated an account of the 890s which gave particular prominence to Æthelred, Lord of the Mercians, and may have preceded the postulated *Annals of Æthelflæd*, discussed below.[1564] Indeed, it may have been the original *Chronicle* from which the other versions ultimately derive, and he is likely to have had access to other chronicles, some now lost. His translation was dedicated to his German cousin Matilda, abbess of Essen, and was written in an elaborate form of Latin favoured in his day abounding with archaic and

---

[1559] Keynes 1986: 199. Æthelweard tells us that in 876 a treaty was made between Alfred and the Danes sealed by the giving of hostages and oaths made upon their sacred armlets, but adds that oaths on their armlets was something they never did again: Campbell 1962: 41-2. Whether the policy by Edward the Elder and Æthelred of Mercia to encourage the purchase from the Danes of estates within the Danelaw (or possibly to reward their thegns with land recovered from Danish control), including property in Derbyshire and Bedfordshire, between 906 and 911, is to be associated in any way with the treaty is unknown: Whitelock 1979: 546-7; Hill 1984: 47; Keynes 2001: 56.
[1560] ASC 'A' and 'D'; Swanton 1996: 96-7.
[1561] It is not inconceivable that the threat was posed by elements of the mysterious fleet which supported Æthelwold before the battle of the Holme in 903.
[1562] Identified as Æthelweard 23 in the *Prosopography of Anglo-Saxon England*, accessed 30 October 2014.
[1563] Campbell 1962: xiii. The sole surviving fragments are from a copy of early 11th century date: ibid.
[1564] Bredehoft 2001: 65-7; Stafford 2008: 114.

obscure words.[1565] Writing within 75 years or so of the battle, he may have had an opportunity to talk to veterans of the battle, or to others who remembered those who fought there.[1566] His chronicle, shown to be generally reliable where we are able to check it, provides valuable information not found in any other source. Without doubt it is the primary source for the battle of Tettenhall: it is some of the earliest evidence we possess for the events of 910, and the only source that provides any information about the activities of the Scandinvian raiding party immediately preceding the battle. That information is invaluable, albeit (as will be seen) in some respects not readily explicable. Without it, we would know little more than the date of a battle between the English and the Northumbrians at or near Tettenhall or Wednesfield in which the English were victorious, with not the slightest indication of events leading to the battle.

We have no knowledge of the exact source of Æthelweard's information, which was evidently unknown to other chroniclers at the time – or at least, no evidence has come down to us that others were aware of it. The surviving manuscript of his chronicle was virtually destroyed in the disastrous fire in the Cottonian library in 1731, but by the greatest good fortune had been printed in 1571, and comparison with the few charred fragments of the original suggests that the printed version was produced with a high degree of accuracy. The statement that the battle took place at *Wodnesfeld campo* 'the field of Wednesfield' must carry considerable weight, and the addition of the word *campo* should be particularly noted: it makes clear that if there was a place of habitation called *Wodnesfeld* in 910, the battle did not take place there, but on the great open plain from which *Wodnesfeld* took its name.[1567] It is noteworthy that the account in the *Annals of St Neots*, probably by Byrhtferth of Ramsey who died c.1012, a century or so after the battle, gives the site of the battle as *Wodnesfeldam*.[1568]

Æthelweard's *Chronicon* reminds us that remarkably detailed accounts of historical events had been compiled and were accessible to authors in the tenth century, and perhaps much earlier, but are now lost to us. In this case the source of Æthelweard's account of the Tettenhall campaign, assumed to be a version of the *Anglo-Saxon Chronicle*, quite possibly the most detailed – and hence most important – in existence, could well have been but one of such accounts no longer surviving, though we can suspect that Æthelweard is likely to have extracted the most significant information from his source(s). It can only be hoped that other chronicles might one day come to light from some unexpected source – just as Anglo-Saxon charters still occasionally emerge unexpectedly from long sleep in dusty archives and other repositories[1569] – to cast further light on events of this era.

Careful research extending back at least to the nineteenth century has established a hierarchy for the various versions of the *Anglo-Saxon Chronicle* and other chronicles, enabling historians to identify the chronology and relationship of the various manuscripts. We must recognise, however, that a careful forensic analysis of the limited documentary evidence may lead to conclusions which do not reflect the facts at the time, since scribes

---

[1565] Williams, Smyth and Kirby 1991: 30-31.
[1566] Campbell 1962: xxxii. In 994 Æthelweard was one of the negotiators of the treaty with the Danish army of Olafr Tryggvason, which had defeated the East Anglian army under ealdorman Byrhtnoth at Maldon in 991: Williams, Smyth and Kirby 1991: 30-1.
[1567] It is noteworthy that Æthelweard names two of the dead Scandinavians, compared with none named in *Anglo-Saxon Chronicle* 'C' and 'E', two in 'A', and several in 'B' and 'D'.
[1568] Stevenson 1959: 144.
[1569] See for example Brooks 2000a; 217-39 for a charter of Edgar granting land at Ballidon, Derbyshire, in 963.

writing a thousand or so years ago were not necessarily compiling authoritative and objective analyses of historical events for the benefit of future historians, but had a markedly different agenda which is likely to have imposed upon and distorted their writings. Furthermore, we cannot know how the information that reached the chroniclers originated – it would be surprising to learn that efforts were made soon after the battle to interview and set down in writing accounts from leading participants, although that idea cannot be ruled out, since the circulation of the *Anglo-Saxon Chronicle* two decades earlier will have served to emphasize the value of recording great historical events for posterity. However it occurred, some details of the battle were evidently available to the chroniclers, who incorporated them into their annals. That documentation must necessarily be scrutinised carefully because, quite simply, it is the only evidence we possess. There is no one definitive version of the *Anglo-Saxon Chronicle* because even the oldest manuscript (*Chronicle* 'A', the Parker Chronicle), is not in the form of the earliest text, and although all versions derive from a core text to 891, from the tenth-century onwards most of the surviving versions begin to develop an independent record of events.[1570]

Critical to any study of the early decades of the tenth century is the so-called *Mercian Register*, sometimes known as *The Annals of Æthelflæd*, a set of annals for 902-24 incorporated into the *Anglo-Saxon Chronicle* versions 'B', 'C', and 'D'. The entries begin with the death of Ealhswith – Alfred's Mercian widow and Æthelflæd's mother – and end with the accession of Æthelstan 'chosen king by the Mercians' in 924 and with his marriage of his (unnamed) sister overseas, then breaking off in versions 'B' and 'C'. 'D' identifies his un-named sister's husband as the king of the Old Saxons, with further entries for 925 and 926 ending with the marriage of another sister of Æthelstan to king Sihtric of York. It is sobering to reflect that without the *Mercian Register* we would know virtually nothing about Æthelflæd and her extraordinary military and diplomatic achievements during the first two decades of the tenth century: astonishingly, the single fact we learn from the main text of the *Anglo-Saxon Chronicle* is the year of her death. The *Mercian Register* is, however, just as important for what it does not mention as for what it does, for valuable inferences can sometimes be extracted from its silence. Neither should all statements in the *Register* be accepted uncritically – the submission of the folk of York conspicuously recorded immediately before Æthelflæd's death might be one example which raises doubts.

The *Mercian Register* has, deservedly, been the subject of exceptionally intensive academic study, and there are grounds for believing from the grammar of the Old English annals that a Latin, possibly poetic, *Gesta* or *Life* of Æthelflæd lies behind the entries.[1571] It is not difficult to believe that such *Gesta* could have been compiled at the behest of Æthelflæd herself, just as the Welsh bishop Asser has left us his *Vita Ælfredi regis Angul*

[1570] It is frequently said that the *Chronicle* has a strongly West-Saxon bias, and was written for a West-Saxon audience, but Simon Keynes has concluded that it was not written from a narrowly West-Saxon perspective, but in the knowledge that Mercia, Kent and Sussex were in the West-Saxon orbit: Keynes 1998: 39-41. It is difficult to reconcile that view when comparing the 'second continuation' of the *Chronicle* covering the early stages of Edward the Elder's campaign against the Danes (in the annals for 897-914), which has a decidedly West Saxon emphasis, and the events recorded by the *Mercian Register* covering the period 902-24 in ASC 'B', 'C', and 'D'.

[1571] Stafford 2008: 105-7. Szarmach has concluded that there are possible traces of such a poem in the chronicles of William of Malmesbury and Henry of Huntingdon: Szarmach 1998: 120-22; see also Stafford 2008: 105-6. The *Catalogi veteres librorum Ecclesiæ Dunelmi* at Durham contains a reference to *Elflēdes Boc*, which suggests that these annals once existed in the form of a book of Æthelflæd, recording her campaign against the Danes: Ward and Waller 1920: 110.

Saxonum, probably an unfinished draft of a *Life* (up to 893) of her father.[1572] Which versions in the *Anglo-Saxon Chronicle* retain a more complete set of the annals remains unclear.[1573] What is indisputable is that the *Register* gives particular and unique information about this critical period in Mercian history, or more accurately about Æthelflæd and her military activities in Mercia, but not about her husband (who is barely mentioned, and then only to record his death in 911 and to tell us that he was Lord of the Mercians and Ælfwynn's father), or her brother Edward the Elder, details not found in any other source and which must have a Mercian origin.[1574] The *Register* records the 910 battle in entries inserted into versions 'B', 'C' and 'D' of the *Anglo-Saxon Chronicle*, but is extraordinarily and inexplicably terse in its bland summary of the facts, which omits all background details and simply mentions a battle at Tettenhall between the English and Northumbrians, with an English victory,[1575] though astonishingly, 'D' even fails to record the victors in the momentous conflict (though the battle is recorded again in two further entries, in the second of which a fuller account is provided with the victors identified).[1576] The account is noticeably similar to the brief reference to the battle found in the *Historia Regum* ('History of the Kings'), attributed (probably wrongly) to Symeon or Simeon of Durham, probably written after 1042, and it is possible that this northern annal is based on version 'C' of the *Anglo-Saxon Chronicle*.[1577] Yet is is remarkable that an author who we must assume was a Mercian writing at or near the Mercian court, probably within a decade or so of the battle,[1578] should have had no access to other particulars about the great Mercian and West Saxon victory of 910 (far more details being known to and recorded by the West Saxon chroniclers, not least Æthelweard), a lacuna which seems to have received scant scholarly consideration and interpretation. Few conclusions can be extracted from an analysis of the brief entry in the *Mercian Register*, although it may be remarked that other campaigns or engagements by Æthelflæd are prefaced in the *Register* with the words 'with

---

[1572] See especially Smyth 2002.

[1573] See especially Szarmach 1998; Bredehoft 2001; Stafford 2008.

[1574] The absence of any reference to Æthelflæd in the *Mercian Register* before 912 could be seen as strong evidence that the supposed long-standing ailment which later Irish annals tell us afflicted Æthelred was greatly exaggerated, and that he played a far more prominent role in Mercian affairs than the chronicles might suggest.

[1575] It is clear that the chronicler(s) compiling ASC 'C' and 'D' believed that the great (un-named) battle in which the fallen Danes were named was not the same as the battle recorded in the *Mercian Register* at Tettenhall, since both chronicles refer to two separate battles. It is also worth noting F. T. Wainwright's observation on the precision of the scribe of the *Mercian Register* who 'was not altogether bound in his chronological arrangements by year-numbers. Comparison may be made with the annals for 910, 911, 912, and 913 where the *Mercian Register* commonly uses *Her* [here, at this date], *On þysum geare* [in this year], *þæs ilcan* [after the same], *Þa oðres geares* [the next year] and *Þa þæs opre geare* [then after the next year] to express chronological sequence': Wainwright 1975: 127-9.

[1576] Cubbin 1996: 37-8.

[1577] Arnold 1892: 122. Symeon (or Simeon) of Durham flourished in the early twelfth century. His main work is the *Historia Ecclesiae Dunelmensis*('History of the Church of Durham'), which extends to 1096. Stevenson, in the preface of his translation of the *Historia Regum*, says: 'It is not probable that both these chronicles, which constitute the History of the Kings, are the work of Simeon of Durham; or, indeed, that they are to be ascribed to one and the same author. They contain statements which are contradictory the one to the other, and they vary in their chronology. It might be doubted, were we disposed to be sceptical, how far either of them is the production of the author whose name the whole now bears. Recent scholarship has suggested that the first chronicle's initial compilation was by Byrhtferth, a monk and teacher at Ramsey Abbey (north of Huntingdon), at the turn of the tenth century.' The second chronicle is based on the *Chronicon ex Chronicis* of Florence (John) of Worcester. See also Whitelock 1979: 127; Story 2003: 117-26.

[1578] Stafford 2008: 102.

the help of God' or 'with God's help' or 'by the grace of God', which seem to have been used when the victory was hard-won,[1579] but no such words appear in the Tettenhall entry, from which we might assume that God's help had not been necessary when the West Saxons and Mercians had combined to form an invincible force.

But the brevity of the accounts mentioned above is surpassed by that in version 'E' of the *Anglo-Saxon Chronicle*, probably compiled from northern sources now lost, which records (in the same terms as the second entry recording the battle in *Chronicle* 'D') simply that 'the English raiding-army (*here*) and the Danes fought at Tettenhall', with 'E' adding that Æthelred, leader of the Mercians, died, implying (almost certainly wrongly) that the two events were linked, though we know that the battle took place in August 910 and that Æthelred died the following year.[1580] Curiously, the entry, one of very few in the *Chronicle* for this period, describes the English forces (without mentioning West Saxon and Mercians) as a *here*, a term usually meaning 'predatory band, troop, army', and used almost exclusively of Viking forces.[1581] Given the magnitude of the conflict we might have expected more to have been made of the battle: most notably, none of the entries based on the *Mercian Register* mentions Æthelred, or names the leader(s) of the English forces.

What is noteworthy is that a number of the annalists in the Common Stock of the *Anglo-Saxon Chronicle* are able to identify by name so many of the dead Northumbrians, from which it would appear that the English had a particularly detailed knowledge of their adversaries, and raises the intriguing possibility that the English annalists may have had access to some long lost Danish record.[1582] Notably, Æthelweard is the only source that tells us that three kings of the tyrants were killed, whom he names as *Healdene, Eywysl* and *Inwær*,[1583] with the other chroniclers who mention kings speaking only of two: the name *Inwær* is not recorded elsewhere. Of the chroniclers who mention *Healdene* and *Eywysl/Eowils*, all (except the *Annals of St Neots*) name the two kings first and in that order (with the *Annals of St Neots* reversing the order), which might imply that *Healdene* was a king of greater seniority/age/renown, and that *Inwær* was a lesser king.[1584] Whether these were kings in any real sense of the word rather than merely leaders of the raiding army is quite unknown. Of the *Anglo-Saxon Chronicles*, version 'A' identifies by name only one of the Danes killed in the battle, with only 'B' and 'D' giving a list of names.[1585] The sources that provide several names tend to give those names in the same general order, even if the names do not coincide precisely in different accounts, suggesting perhaps that the information derived ultimately from a single source.

[1579] Stafford 2008: 102.
[1580] Earle and Plummer 1892-99: I 95; Cubbin 1996: 37. One of the three accounts of the battle in ASC 'D' uses similar but not identical wording and does not mention the death of Æthelred: ibid. 97.
[1581] Clark Hall 1960: 179; Irvine 2004: 54, where *here* seems to be mistranslated.
[1582] For an analysis of the spellings of Norse names in ASC 'A' see Bately 1986: clxii-clxiii.
[1583] Multiple kings leading Danish raiding armies are recorded in 874, when kings Guthrum, Oscytel and Anund led a great army from Repton to Cambridge, where they settled for a year: ASC 'A': Swanton 1996: 75.
[1584] As noted elsewhere, the names of the dead kings match a trio of Viking leaders active in the 860s and 870s, and at least two of those kings (Hálfdan and Ívarr) were related, perhaps implying that the kings killed at Tettenhall were members of the same family which ruled Dublin before 902 and after 917: Downham 2009: 87.
[1585] Hart was satisfied that the three Danish kings, Healdene, Eywysl and Ivar, were from the Northern Danelaw, not East Anglia, inadvertently citing ASC 'A': Hart 1992: 34.

One name in particular listed in version 'B' and 'D' deserves special notice: that of Agmund the hold, who the *Annals of St Neots* picks out by describing him as *the chief of the heathens*. Wainwright questions whether this person is the same as the Scandinavian leader, probably of some standing, who gave his name to Amounderness (from *Agmundarnes*), an area in Lancashire bordering the Irish Sea between Chester and Carlisle, the name of which is recorded in a charter of the 930s, perhaps genuine but corrupted in transmission, but concludes that since the name Agmund is 'very common' in northern England, the question remains unresolved.[1586] He adds that 'if the identification could be accepted as proved it would be of considerable historical significance, for it would show the Lancashire Norsemen raiding into southern England and would imply a greater degree of military organisation than we have allowed'.[1587] Atkin observes that Wainwright failed to note the existence of the name Anlafr included in the list of enemy dead at Tettenhall, a name which also occurs in Lancashire place-names, but concedes that both names are fairly common in northern England.[1588] What is not so common is the existence of district and parish names incorporating both of those personal names.

Henry of Huntingdon's reference to *Osfrith the hold* as one of the dead Scandinavians may not be a simple error on his part. Florence (John) of Worcester gives the first four names – *Healdene, Eowils, Ohter* and *Scurfa* – and says there were nine others (*nouemque proceres nobiliores*). Anglo-Saxon Chronicle 'B' however, gives only eight names after *Scurfa*: *Othulf, Benesing, Anlaf, Thurfreth, Osfrith, Guthfrith, Agmund*, and another *Guthfrith*.[1589] Like Henry, the *Annals of St Neots* gives an additional name to those in the surviving *Anglo-Saxon Chronicle* version, but the name, *Eagell*, probably the *Eowils* recorded by Florence (John) of Worcester, is different from Henry's addition of *Osfrith the hold*. It is not possible to say whether these additional names are errors, or whether the chroniclers had additonal information not found elsewhere, but it seems likely that the authors had access to more complete information than other writers.[1590] Curiously, it is not unusual for the chronicles to give details of the Danish slain in battles, with no mention of the English who died.[1591] The *Anglo-Saxon Chronicle* tells us that at the battle of Ashdown in 871,

---

[1586] The charter (S.407) records the purchase 'from hateful servitude' by Æthelstan for the benefit of St Peter's church in York: Whitelock 1979: 547.

[1587] Wainwright 1975: 222-4; Fellows-Jensen 1989: 88.

[1588] Atkin 1997: 17. He might have added that the name Halfdan is also found in some northern place-names, e.g. Alston, Cumbria: CDEPN 11. See also Quanrud 2015: 82.

[1589] Thorpe 1861: I 184.

[1590] Lapidge et al 1999: 49. In 1834 Lappenberg concluded that the Danish kings Eowils and Healdene were the brothers of Ivar, recorded 30 years earlier, which led him to question whether the chroniclers recording the dead at Wednesfield may have incorporated inadvertently the names of those killed in some earlier campaign. He was presumably referring to Florence (John) of Worcester's conclusion (which was evidently erroneous) that kings Eowils and Halfdan were brothers of king Ivar, a statement evidently based on entries in the ASC for 878 which mention the brothers Halfdan, Ivar the boneless, and Ubba (the sons of Ragnar Lothbrok). Ivar was killed in 870, and Ubba in 878: see Stevenson 1853: 74; Swanton 1996: 70 fn.2, 75 fn.12.

[1591] It is sometimes claimed (see e.g. Walker 2000: 94-5; Carver 2010: 130) that the ailing Æthelred, who died in 911, may have sustained injuries in the battle of Tettenhall which eventually proved fatal (a belief perhaps based on the terse entry in ASC 'E' which records in the same sentence the battle, without naming the victors, followed by the death of Æthelred), which may be true, but there is no evidence that he took any part in the conflict, or that his death was connected with any battle wounds. He may well have been considerably older than Æthelflæd – we have no information about his date of birth, and he is first mentioned in 883, by which date he was probably principal ealdorman of the Mercians: Oxford DNB. It is probable that he led the Mercian forces to defeat at the battle of the

Alfred (later to become King) led a force which defeated a Viking army. The dead included King Bagsecg, and jarls Osbern, Fraena, Harold, and two men named Sidroc. That is mirrored by the complete absence of any information about the English dead.[1592]

We have seen that William of Malmesbury makes no mention of the battle of Tettenhall, nor indeed about most of the crucial military events in the early decades of the tenth century. That omission is curious and unexplained, made more perplexing by the fact that he is known to have used the chronicle of Æthelweard with its comparative wealth of detail, perhaps the actual manuscript virtually destroyed in 1731.

Before considering the chroniclers' accounts of the battle in more detail, it is appropriate to make a digression to discuss the Danes and the Irish North Sea Vikings or Hiberno-Scandinavians.

The identity of the Scandinavian groups which raided and settled in both Britain and Ireland in the ninth and early tenth century is clearly of considerable relevance in any investigation into the battle of Tettenhall. Until a century ago it was generally believed that the Danes were the dominant force in Ireland in the ninth century, but a claim put forward in 1900 that the Norwegians held that position has since been widely accepted. A theory is emerging and gathering scholarly support which maintains that the Northumbrians undertaking the raid of 910 culminating in the battle of Tettenhall were perhaps not York-based, as hitherto believed, but probably those of Scandinavian origin from north-west England, including Scandinavians who had been driven out of Dublin c.901, generally known as the Hiberno-Norse or Hiberno-Scandinavians or Irish North Sea Vikings.[1593] The theory has centred on the relationships, if any, between these Scandinavians and those who made their base in York.

In that respect there has been intensive research into the geographical origin and familial relationships, if any, of those Scandinavians who attacked and in some cases established settlements in Ireland in the ninth and tenth centuries. That exercise poses many difficulties, not least the problems created for a modern reader by expressions such as 'Dane and 'Danish', which imply an ethnic identity, an interpretation almost certainly not intended by the compilers of the *Anglo-Saxon Chronicle* to distinguish 'Danes' from 'Norwegians' and others. Particular difficulties arise from the fact that the names Denmark ('the march or borderland of the Danes') and Norway ('the North way') are unrecorded until

---

Conwy in 881 (Charles-Edwards 2013: 490-1), and if he were 30 at that date (it is unlikely that he was any younger), he would have been 60 when he died.

[1592] ASC 'A' and 'E': Swanton 1996: 70-71.

[1593] I am particularly indebted to Dr John Quanrud for providing a copy of his paper 'Taking Sides: North-western Vikings at the Battle of Tettenhall AD910' presented to a conference on 'The Vikings in the North East' organised by the Manchester Centre for Anglo-Saxon Studies on 13 April 2013, now published as Quanrud 2015. The paper sets out a revisionist position on the Viking presence in Britain at the end of the ninth and early tenth century, arguing that the Viking raid on Mercia in 910 was conducted by Hiberno-Scandinavian Vikings in the north-west, who were acting in opposition to the York-based vikings of the North-East, and that the mysterious treaty of Tiddingford which Edward the Elder entered into in 905 or 906 'by necessity' (according to ASC 'E') with a raiding army from East Anglia and with the Northumbrians was a pact whereby Edward allied himself with them against the Scandinavians of the north-west, who by that date were seen as dangerously militant rivals. This persuasive analysis may correctly reflect the events of the period, and though the cited evidence is not wholly unequivocal, the main arguments are accepted by the present author and have been incorporated into the text of this volume.

found in the English translation of the *History of Orosius* dating to the 890s, and the territories of Denmark, Norway and Sweden in the ninth century differed from the areas of the later medieval states. Denmark was the eastern islands of modern Denmark with the south-western parts of what is now Sweden, and Norway was the name given to the coasts on either side of Oslo Fjord.[1594] In short, the ethnic distinctions 'Danes' and 'Norwegians' were of little significance when describing Vikings in the ninth century, and are unlikely to have been recognised by Irish chroniclers in the ninth century. No word for Norway is found in Irish sources until the eleventh century, and the confused political situation in Scandinavia during the ninth and tenth centuries means that the use of the terms Danes and Norwegians is more appropriate to the mid-eleventh century than the ninth century, and the terms obfuscate rather than clarify the situation in that period. What is becoming very clear is that the term *Denisc* in this adjectival form is likely to have been used in the *Chronicle* to refer to Scandinavians in general, and cannot be taken to mean Danish in the modern sense of that word.[1595]

That idea, at least as far as the Common Stock of the *Chronicle* up to the last decade of the ninth century is concerned, is supported by the annal for 789 which record *iii. Scipu Norðmanna* 'Three ships of Northmen'[1596] reaching (according to the *Annals of St Neots*) Portland in Dorset, where they murdered the king's reeve. Three versions of the *Chronicle* add that the seamen were *of Hæreðalande* 'from Höthaland', a district in western Norway.[1597] The *Chronicle* adds that these ships were *ærestan scipu Deniscra monna þe Angelcynnes lond gesohton* 'the first ships of the Danish men which sought out the land of the English race'.[1598] Clearly *Denisc* refers here not to men who came from Danish lands, but from what is today Norway, but that does not mean that the terms were interchangeable: *Denisc* is the only adjectival form found in the *Chronicle*, and its use, as Quanrud has noted, is oddly uniform, for apart from the single example of *Norðmenn* in annal 789, neither *Dene* nor *Norðmenn* occur in any annals to the end of the ninth century, though both terms are found elsewhere, for example the *Old English Orosius* dating from Alfred's reign.[1599] That makes it unrealistic to attempt to differentiate between Viking groups of 'Danish' and 'Norwegian' ethnicity.[1600] Not until the historic submission of various leaders to Edward the Elder at Bakewell in 923 (if indeed such submission actually took place) do we find a reference to *Denisce ge Norþmen*, 'Danes and Norwegians'.[1601]

A further difficulty is that colour terms describing Vikings are found in Irish and Welsh chronicles of the period rather than terms for their place of origin or place of intermediate habitation to identify attacking forces. Terms found in Irish annals for different Viking

---

[1594] Fletcher 1997: 406.
[1595] Downham 2007: xviii; Quanrud 2015: 75-6.
[1596] ASC 'B', 'C', D' and 'E'; Thorpe 1861: I 96-7.
[1597] Sawyer 1962: 2.
[1598] Thorpe 1861: I 96-7; Bateley 1986: 29 (787 for 789).
[1599] Quanrud 2015: 76. The next occurrence in the ASC of the term *Norðmenn* after 789 is in the annal for 920, and so post-dated the compilation of the original Common Stock of the ASC: ibid.The Orosius, MS BL Additional 47967, written probably between 889 and 899 (Masdalen 2010: 17, citing Janet Bateley) gives the first recorded reference to Norway (*norðwey*) and Denmark (*denamearc*).
[1600] Downham 2009: 143. Cyril Hart noted what may be a significant record in this respect in the Appendix to the Chronicle of Florence (John) of Worcester where the pagan force active in England in 867 is said to have included *Danis, Norreganis, Suanis, Goutis et quarundum aliarum natione populis*, an identification 'not based on any known source': Hart 1983: 277.
[1601] ASC 'A'; Swanton 1996: 104.

groups in ninth and tenth century Ireland, Finn ('white/fair') and Dub ('black/dark'), have been used by scholars to support the idea of a conflict between Norwegian and Danish factions. That the label Finn described Norwegians and Dub described Danes has been accepted by Alfred Smyth, after researching in considerable detail the history of the Irish, Scottish and Northumbrian Vikings.[1602] Smyth believes that it was the Norwegians who seized Dublin in 853 (an action perhaps connected with entries in the *Brut y Tywysogion* recording at about this date an attack against Anglesey by the Black Pagans,[1603] and a record of the *pagani* in the territory of the *Wreocensæte*, 'the people associated with the Wrekin', in a Mercian charter of 855,[1604] suggesting that the *pagani* were Hiberno-Scandinavians rather than Danes), but after their leader Olafr died the descendants of Ivarr (identified by Smyth as a Dane) took control, and founded a new ruling dynasty in Dublin known as the Uí Ímar which would dominate much of the Irish Sea region into the eleventh century. He suggested that 'dark' refers to the 'new' groups and 'fair' to the 'old', a claim supported by Colmán Etchingham who holds that Vikings from Laithlinn were the 'old/fair foreigners' in Ireland before the 'new/dark foreigners' arrived.[1605] Donnchadh Ó Corráin, on the other hand, has argued that the royal dynasty came from Norway via the Scottish islands.[1606] Yet attempting to attribute the colour-terms 'fair' and 'dark', used in the ninth century, to ethnic disctinctions such as hair colour and dress is doubtless unwise, and the descriptions used, for example, in *The Fragmentary Annals of Ireland*, probably compiled in the eleventh century, doubtless reflect perceptions of Viking identities at that time as much as ninth-century realities.[1607]

Another approach is that of David Dumville, a leading authority on the period, who has argued that the labels 'dark' and 'fair' do not identify separate Norwegian and Danish groups active in Ireland, but refer to 'old and 'new' groups ruling Ireland in the ninth century, with the term 'dark' likely to refer to armies under the leadership of the dynasty of Ivarr, who died c.873 as 'king of the Northmen of all Ireland and Britons', and his kinsmen

---

[1602] See for example Smyth 1998.

[1603] ab Ithel 1860: 12-13.

[1604] S.206; see Gelling 1992: 83; also Whitelock 1955: I 90; 485-6; Finberg 1961: 48 no. 77.

[1605] To add to these uncertainties, the location of Laithlinn/Lochla(i)nn, a Celtic term – or perhaps two terms – applied to a Viking kingdom, mentioned in various Irish sources, has been hotly debated for over 150 years, with some identifying it with Hlaðir in Norway, and others the Northern and Western Isles of Scotland or even, very specifically, the viking site at Woodstown near Waterford. Etchingham 2007: 25. By the mid-11th century the term Lochlann seems to have been applied to Norway, which had then developed into a distinct political unit: Downham 2009: 15 fn.28.

[1606] Etchingham 2007: 11-32. There are 14 events involving 'dark foreigners' recorded in Irish Chronicles for 851, 853, 856, 867, 870, 875, 877, 877 (twice) 893, 917, 918, 921, 927 and 940. The notion of 'dark foreigners' in Wales may have been borrowed from Ireland, and they are found in Welsh Chronicles on five occasions, in 853, 867, 890/892 – when an attack is recorded apparently aimed at Gwynedd – and in 987 and 989. No reference to 'fair' foreigners has been found in Welsh Chronicles. The earliest source to identify 'dark' Vikings as Danes and 'fair' Vikings as Norwegian seems to be the *Fragmentary Annals of Ireland*, dating from between 1025 and 1075 (when relations between the two countries were not good), but the distinction perhaps arose as an attempt to enhance the reputation of the hero of the narrative. Other accounts prove contradictory: 12th-century Welsh sources tell us that the leaders of Vikings in Ireland were Norwegians, but later Icelandic sagas claim a Danish pedigree. In Gaelic poetry of the sixteenth and seventeenth centuries the term 'fair' foreigners is used of the 'old' English, and sometimes for Hebrideans, with 'dark foreigners' the description used for English military forces and colonists arriving in Ireland during the Tudor conquests: ibid.

[1607] The Appendix which forms part of the Chronicle of Florence (John) of Worcester records that the pagan force active in England in 867 included *Danis, Norreganis, Suanes, Goutis et quarundum aliarum natione populis*, an identification which 'is not based on any known source': Hart 1983: 277.

Hálfdan (his brother), Óláfr (possibly another brother), and Ásl, who were active in Dublin and elsewhere. Ivarr's family may have been leaders of the 'new' or dark foreigners. As will be seen, the names of Ivarr's kinsmen may be commemorated in the names of some of the Northumbrian dead at the battle of Tettenhall.[1608]

One thing is clear: *The Fragmentary Annals of Ireland* leaves an image that the 'Norwegians' were seen (at least in the eleventh century, though even that date is debated) as cowardly, brutal and entirely heathen, levying harsh tribute and breaking their oaths to the Irish, whereas the 'Danish' are remembered for their generosity and bravery. But the strongest words are reserved for the *Gall-Goídil*, initially described as Gaels who had been seduced by the Scandinavians into renouncing Christianity to take up pagan rites and plunder churches, then as the foster-children of Vikings who deserved to be killed, and finally as much worse than the original Scandinavians who wrought evil on the churches.[1609] Even worse than the heathen were the *Gall-Goídil*: they were apostates.[1610]

In 893 the *Annals of Ulster* record the major defeat of 'dark foreigners' at the hands of the English, which Claire Downham suggests was the siege of Buttington, with a contingent from Dublin perhaps fighting alongside the Northumbrians, since a party of Vikings left Dublin the same year. If that was the case, the Dublin contingent presumably joined other Scandinavians at Shoebury in Essex[1611] before the raiding army moved along the Thames to the Severn, or joined that group during its progress. Jarl Sihtric, who led one of the contingents from Dublin, has been tentatively identified with Sihtric, leader of a Northumbrian fleet that attacked Wessex the same year.

The grandsons of Ivarr returned to Ireland in 917 following their expulsion c.901, and that year were engaged in a great battle with the forces of Leinster at Ceann Fuait. Ragnall, grandson of Ivarr, is called 'King of the dark foreigners' by the *Annals of Ulster*, but was not to become King of York until 918, which tends to demolish the theory that the title 'king of the dark foreigners' is to be interpreted as 'king of the Danes of York'. Sihtric, who controlled Dublin after the battle of 917, may have been a brother or cousin of Ragnall. Both Sihtric (d.927) and Ragnall (d.921) were described in Irish Chronicles as 'king of the fair foreigners', suggesting that both had won recognition as leaders of the dynasty of Ivarr and overlordship of the 'old' foreigners of Ireland who may have remained on the island while Ivarr's family had been away in exile.

Whether it is appropriate to categorise these various leaders and their followers as Vikings is debatable – Smyth has emphasised how the original restricted application of that word was to North Sea pirates and to many who behaved as outlaws in the Scandinavian homelands[1612] – but the parameters of the definition are obviously indistinct, and the term is used in this work from time to time to mean simply Scandinavians of the late ninth and early tenth centuries.

[1608] See Quanrud 2015: 81, citing Etchingham 2014: 37.
[1609] The Old Irish word *Gaill*, originally meaning 'Gauls', by the 9th century had come to mean 'foreigners, strangers', applied to the Scandinavian invaders: Smyth 1998: 27-8.
[1610] Wainwright 1975: 149-50; Downham 2013: 117-20, 172. The name of Galloway was derived from that of the *Gall-Goídil*: Wainwright 1975: 149.
[1611] A rampart at Shoebury enclosing a semi-circular area, approximately 1495 feet across, adjacent to the sea may be the Viking camp of 893: Richards 1991: 23.
[1612] Smyth 1998: 39.

Reverting, then, to the chroniclers' accounts of the battle, one name of particular interest is that of Eowils, a king, the only Scandinvavian of 'many thousands' of those killed who is mentioned in *Anglo-Saxon Chronicle* 'A',[1613] from which we might assume that he was a figure of particular significance. The name is also found (as *Eywys*, *Auisle* and *Ecwils*) in other accounts of the battle. That unusual name is likely to be an Anglicised version of Old Norse *Ásl* or *Auðgísl* which appear as *Auisle* in Irish: the –g– in the Old Norse name is silent.[1614] *Ásl* was the name of an earlier Viking leader who may have been related to *Eowilisc/Eowils* – we have seen that three Vikings named *Healfdene*, *Ívarr* and *Auisle* (the first two related and the third – perhaps also related to the other two – murdered in 867) were active in Dublin and York in the 860s and 870s,[1615] and it has been suggested that kings *Eowils* (*Auisle*), and *Healfden* mentioned in the Chronicles, with king *Inwær* (*Ívarr*) recorded by Æthelweard, all of whom fell at Tettenhall, were also members of the same *Dubgaill* dynasty based at York.[1616] This supports the views of Alfred Smyth, who also placed these kings at York, with the caveat that 'We know nothing of the York rulers from the death of King Knútr in c.902 until the mention of two Danish kings, Eowils and Healfdan, who were slain, according to the *Anglo-Saxon Chronicle*, in a battle at Tettenhall'.[1617]

But since Smyth wrote those words, the scenario has changed, and as John Quanrud has pointed out, no evidence of any kind, numismatic or otherwise, has ever been found to link these kings to York. Indeed, Colmán Etchingham, carefully reassessing the use of the terms *Dubgaill* and *Finngaill* in contemporary sources, has concluded that 'When *Finngaill* reappears in the titles of kings in the tenth century, it seems to distinguish the Dublin-based and predominantly Norwegian portion of their domain from the York-Northumbrian

---

[1613] Swanton 1996: 96. The suggestion that *Eowilisc cyng* may be the Welsh name *Hywel*, since the Welsh are known to have fought occasionally with the Scandinavians, and the name *Eowel* is recorded in a will of Aethelgifu (S.1497) (Earle and Plummer 1892-9: II 126), can now be discounted. The fact that the *Chronicle* mentions this single king's name may however indicate that he was seen as particularly important.

[1614] Anderson 1922: 401 fn.1; Campbell 1962: 53; Smyth 1977: 147; Downham 2009: 87. I am grateful to Clare Downham for linguistic information about the name Eowils, in which she mentions advice from Martin Syrett and David Dumville, and refers to Alex Woolf (*Pictland to Alba*) and to the Irish/English version Daibhí Ó Croinín (*Early Medieval Ireland, 400-1200*). It should be noted that Ívarr grandson of Ívarr is said in the *Annals of Ulster* to have been killed in battle in 904: Downham 2009: 146. He is presumably Ivar II mentioned by Smyth as killed in 903 during a two-year campaign in Scotland culminating with a Scottish victory in Strathhearn: Smyth 1984: 197. There could of course have been other grandsons of Ivarr with the same name.

[1615] Downham 2009: 21.

[1616] Dumville 2005: 44. The possibility that the names of *Healfdene*, *Ívarr* and *Auisle* who were prominent Vikings active in the 860s and 870s became inadvertently incorporated by confusion into some early account of the battle of Tettenhall which was adopted by subsequent chroniclers cannot be entirely dismissed: Æthelweard names only three Scandinavians who died at Tettenhall, *Healfdene, Eyuuysl and Iguuar* (two of those names, of brothers *Healdene* and *Inwær*, and another unnamed third brother, are recorded by him in 879 arriving with forces in 30 ships which besieged an unidentified fortress in the south-west where the king of the barbarians and 800 of his men were killed, but the Danes held the battlefield: Campbell 1962: 42-3), names which appear grouped together (though not in that order) in the *Annals of Ulster* (Part 433, U863.4) as Amhlaim (*Healfdene*), Ímh (*Iguuar*) and Auisle (*Eyuuysl*): Campbell 1962: 52-3. It is of interest that Auisle and Sichfrith, two sons of Sitric Gáile (king of Dublin and York, who died in 927), are recorded in the *Annals of Clonmacnoise* as having fallen at the battle of *Brunanburh*, though the origins of the report are unclear: Downham 2009: 29, 193, 247, 274.

[1617] Smyth 1975-9: I 75.

and predominantly Danish portion'.[1618] If that conclusion is correct, kings *Healfdene*, *Auisle* and *Inwær* were almost certainly from the lineage of what had been a Dublin-based dynasty of primarily Norwegian descent whose fortunes had declined after internal dissent and military setbacks, whose elite were expelled from Dublin c.901,[1619] and who were unrelated to and often hostile to the Danish rulers based at York.[1620]

This identification must be greatly strengthened by the knowledge that these three names, as noted above, are identical with 'the names of the three Viking brothers from Dublin who were active in the 860s and 870s ... and they are no doubt here those of their children or grandchildren'.[1621] This would reinforce the evidence given above and mean that the Scandinavians at Tettenhall were Hiberno-Scandinavians – Irish Sea Vikings from the north-west – rather than a warband of York-based Northumbrians from the north-east. Further slight, if negative, evidence for a north-west connection with the Scandinavians at the battle of Tettenhall may be detected in the absence of coinage for *Healfdene*, *Auisle* and *Inwær*, for unlike the Danes of York, the Hiberno-Scandinavian rulers of the north-west did not mint their own coinage at that date.[1622]

It has been argued that other clues to the origins of the Scandinavian forces at Tettenhall may be found in the references to warriors with the title *hold* in accounts of the battle:[1623] *Anglo-Saxon Chronicle* 'A' mentions *Opulf hold*, *Benesing hold*, *Þurferð hold* and *Agmund hold*, and 'D' also names *Aþulf* (*Othulf*) *hold* and *Agmund hold*.

The term *hold* has been the subject of considerable academic research. *Hold* (Old English *holdas*, Old Norse *holdr*) was a title of honour introduced into East Anglia by the Scandinavians,[1624] denoting 'a nobleman of exalted class' of lower rank than an ealdorman (or jarl) but higher than a thegn, i.e. equivalent to that of high-reeve,[1625] used of men of great territorial power. The term occurs several times in contemporary accounts of the early Danish wars, with *holds* said to have been separately mentioned among the leaders who submitted to Edward the Elder in 914.[1626] In Old English texts the term is used only in reference to Scandinavians, and is thought to have developed from a Germanic stem. Significantly, it is not found in Danish or Swedish literary contexts but only in West Norse

---

[1618] Etchingham 2014: 37.

[1619] Tha anonymous *Chronicon Scottorum*, compiled at the monastery of Clonmacnoise c.1135, says the heathen were driven out of Dublin in 902 after abandoning a good number of their ships.

[1620] Woolf 2001: 93.

[1621] Dumville 2005: 44.

[1622] Edwards 1998: 57; Sheehan 2001: 53; Williams 2007: 202. The first Hiberno-Norse ruler known to have minted coinage was Ragnall, at some date in the second decade of the tenth century after he took over territories formerly under Danish rule in eastern England. The designs include what may be pagan elements: Quanrud 2015: 81.

[1623] Quanrud 2015: 81-2.

[1624] Thorpe 1861: II 76 fn.4.

[1625] In the eleventh-century 'Law of the Northumbrian Priests', which related to 'Northumbria and the territory of the Five Boroughs', the *hold* had the same wergeld as a king's high reeve, double that of a thegn, and 15 times that of a ceorl: Monsen and Smith 1932: 108 fn.1. In northern England a hold was 'a designation of exalted social rank reckoned in one document which has come down to us. See Thorpe 1861: II 76 fn.4; Whitelock 1955: 191 fn.9; Stenton 1971: 509; Clarke 1999: 38; Fletcher 2002: 51; Williams 2003: 34; Edmonds 2009: 7 fn.3; and especially Quanrud 2015: 82. It may be noted that in her translation of *Historia Anglorum* Greenway translates *hold* as 'faithful': Greenway 1996: 301-2.

[1626] Stenton 1971: 509. The basis for Stenton's statement is untraced.

(Norwegian), from which language it seems to have entered Old English.[1627] According to Norwegian law texts, the *holds* were free men in possession of allodial lands, that is estates over which there were no superior rights. An anonymous abbreviated skaldic poem which may be as early as the mid-tenth century mentions various men of high standing, *holds*, who accompanied *Eiríkr blóðøx* (Eric Bloodaxe), king of Northumbria, to Valhalla at his death in battle.[1628] Quanrud makes the point that a Norwegian derivation for the term *hold* must reinforce the likelihood that the enemy at Tettenhall were primarily Hiberno-Scandinavians rather than Danes of York,[1629] but his case is greatly undermined, if not demolished, by mention in the *Anglo-Saxon Chronicle* of two named Scandinavians, each described as a *hold*, who fell at the battle of the Holme c.903, and by a reference to *Þurferþ eorl 7 þa holdas* 'Jarl Thurferth and the holds' in 920, where those holds can only have been Northumbrians of York or East Anglia, and Danes of the East Midlands respectively.[1630]

Barbara Crawford has noted 'the use of different titles in the record of the battles of 911 [*sic*] where King Eowils and King Halfdan, Jarl Ohtor and Jarl Scurfa and Hold Athulf and Hold Agmund' are listed in the 'D' manuscript of the *Anglo-Saxon Chronicle* as having been killed. 'This gives a very nice demarcation of apparent hierarchy in the Norwegian-Danish armies in England at the time, but what factors dictated the use of their titles by such warriors is entirely unknown. It also shows that there were many 'kings' around in the British Isles in the tenth century. ... petty Norse warlords in the Western Isles and the Norse dynasty in Dublin continued to call themselves king ... '. In the late ninth century jarl was an Old Norse title which was 'the preserve of certain powerful dynasties in Norway as a family dignity (='earl', in origin 'a gentle, noble man, a warrior'), later equivalent to 'chief'.[1631] Not all those referred to as 'jarls' or 'kings' in accounts of the battle of Tettenhall are likely to have been accorded the same rank in Scandinavia, since titles acquired by leaders in exile cannot be taken as a reliable guide to status,[1632] and '[t]he

---

[1627] Quanrud 2015: 81-2. The Danish historians I. Steenstrup and Erling Monsen considered *hold* to be a Norse title: Monsen and Smith 1932: 63.

[1628] Yet Eric Bloodaxe, if not a convert, was evidently sympathetic of Christianity: under the title *Eiric rex Danorum*, he is named in the *Liber Vitae*, the 'Book of Life' of the community of St Cuthbert which lists those for whom special commemorative prayers were offered: Fletcher 1997: 392.

[1629] Gillian Fellows-Jensen has highlighted philological issues around the term *hold*, pointing out that in England the word was used of men of much higher status than the *höldar* in Norway, and noted that *holds* are named in company with Danish [*sic*] kings and jarls in the *Anglo-Saxon Chronicle*, which might suggest that the spelling reflects the etymologically related OE adjective *hold*, Old Danish *hold, huld*, meaning 'faithful, loyal': Fellows-Jensen 1989: 90. Those concerns incorporate the traditional and long-held assumption that the Scandinavians who fought at Tettenhall were Danes but, as Quanrud has observed, the philological difficulties evaporate if the Scandinavians were Hiberno-Scandinavians of Norwegian descent rather than Danes of York, and we should not be surprised if terms such as *hold* developed differently over time and in different kingdoms: Quanrud 2015: 81-2. Fellows-Jensen has also considered place-names which might serve as evidence for the *hold* term, and notes that Holderness, on the east coast between the North Sea and the Humber, appears to incorporate *höldr*, and may 'support the view that the hold in England can have been no mere freeman with rights over a small portion of allodial land': Fellows-Jensen 1989: 90. A valuable analysis of the Scandinavian *hold* is found in Quanrud 2015: 81-2.

[1630] Thorpe 1861: I 195; Swanton 1996: 94-5, 102. Wainwright held the name Thurferth to be Danish: Wainwright 1975: 302.

[1631] Crawford 2014: 67-8.

[1632] Swanton 1996: 72.

distinction between the ... 'kings' and the 'earls' slain at Tettenhall ... would be one of descent rather than power or possessions'.[1633]

The name *Healfden(a)*, identified as one of the three Scandinavian kings who died at Tettenhall, might provide some tenuous information about the bearer's parentage, for it is Anglo-Scandinavian *Healfdene* (or an anglicised form of Old Norse *Halfdanr*, Old Danish *Half(f)dan*), meaning 'half Dane',[1634] so perhaps implying the offspring of a mixed marriage between a Scandinavian (not necessarily a Dane) and a non-Scandinavian, possibly in this case the son of a Scandinavian whose wife could have been from England, Scotland or Ireland, though the name is so common that it was probably borne by many Scandinavians not of mixed parentage.

One particular curiosity deserving of mention is that of the fourteen names of the Northumbrian dead at the battle of Tettenhall mentioned in the various sources, no fewer than nine are or might be English (or at least anglicised) rather than Scandinavian: *Æthulf*,[1635] *Benesing*,[1636] *Werferd* (Wærfrith),[1637] *Agmund* (Agemund or Agamund),[1638] *Thurfridus* (Thurfrith or Thurferth),[1639] *Osferd* (Osfereth or Osfrith),[1640] *Eagellus* (Eigil or Egil),[1641] and *Gudferd* (Gusferth or Guthfrith)[1642] are all Anglo-Saxon names,[1643] and we are told that there were two men killed named *Osferd*,[1644] and two more named *Gudferd* – a total of eleven men with certain or probable English names, one of whom (*Gudferd*) was described as a *hold*, and another (*Osferd*) with the Old English nickname *hlytte* ('soothsayer, diviner, one who divines by casting lots'), evidently a cognate of Old Norse *hlutr*.[1645] Furthermore, the chronicler Æthelweard, writing in Latin, gives an Old English name *Halfdene* (Healfdene),[1646] translating (it is supposed) the Danish *Halfdan*,[1647] which appears as *Healden* in *Anglo-Saxon Chronicle* version 'D'. The implications of this are not immediately obvious. It seems possible that Scandinavians who had married English women might have given at least some of their children English names, but if so there is no evidence that this practice was widespread. Or we might suppose that the Northumbrian raiding army could have included a significant proportion of Englishmen, or more

---

[1633] A. Campbell, 'The Northumbrian kingdom of Raegnald', EHR lvii (1942), 86 n. 1, cited in Smyth 1977: 192. It has been suggested that the holds and jarls may have been local commanders based in the significant *burhs*: Hadley 2006: 56.
[1634] Reaney 1997: 212.
[1635] ASC ASC 'D'; Searle 1897: 76.
[1636] A name which may be unique – no other example has been traced – but Benson or Bensington, Oxfordshire, appears to derive from a postulated OE personal name *Benesa, formed from OE Bana, meaning appropriately 'killer, slayer, murderer': the place is recorded as *Bænesing tun* in ASC 'A' under the year 571, *Benesing tun* under the year 777 (ASC 'A': Watts 2004: 50; Insley 2013: 227). No evidence has been found to suggest a Scandinavian derivation.
[1637] ASC 'B'; Searle 1897: 474.
[1638] ASC 'B' and 'D'; *Annals of St Neots*; *Henry of Huntingdon*; Searle 1897: 63.
[1639] *Annals of St Neots*; Searle 1897: 448-9.
[1640] *Annals of St Neots*; Searle 1897: 372-3.
[1641] *Annals of St Neots*; Searle 1897: 224. The name may however be an attempted rationalisation of the name *Eouuilsus*, mentioned earlier in the same text: Whitelock 1959: 144-5.
[1642] *Annals of St Neots*; *Henry of Huntingdon*; Searle 1897: 272-3.
[1643] See generally Searle 1897.
[1644] By coincidence two of the dead Northumbrians named Osferd bore the same name as the person who may have led the West Saxon forces.
[1645] Toller 1898: I 546; Zoëa 1910: 203-4. The translation 'collector of revenues' is preferred, without explanation, by Monsen and Smith 1932: 63.
[1646] Campbell 1962: 53; Searle 1897: 284.
[1647] Fellows-Jensen 1994: 134.

specifically (and improbably) that some of the more high-ranking members of the Northumbrian force had English names.[1648] A more likely explanation, however, as Gillian Fellows-Jensen has suggested, is that some Scandinavian personal names were anglicised in Æthelweard's chronicle and in the primary text of the *Anglo-Saxon Chronicle*, with *Osferd*, for example, representing the Danish *Ásfrith*,[1649] a possibility strengthened by the description of Osferd as *hold*, the Scandinavian term of rank or status applied to some Scandinavians. That suggestion may be reinforced by Asser's *Life of Alfred* in which the names of some Danes who fell at the battle of Ashdown in 871 also seem to have been anglicised.[1650]

Evidence of other Englishmen fighting for the Scandinavians, specifically the Hiberno-Scandinavians, albeit some years after the battle of Tettenhall, has been detected in the report of two young noblemen brothers who were rewarded as *robusti bellatores* ('hard fighters') by Ragnall, the Norse leader from Dublin, after fighting under him at the battle of Corbridge in 918.[1651] It seems more likely that they had fought on the English side and that Ragnall had allowed them to keep their father's land after the battle.[1652] However, it was not unknown for Englishmen, including those of high rank, to ally and fight with the Scandinvians when it suited them, and Englishmen may well have fought alongside the Scandinvians at the battle of Tettenhall.[1653] As noted elsewhere, a suit heard c.975 recorded in the 12th-century *Liber Eliensis* implies that Edward the Elder, after the conquest of the southern Danelaw, confiscated the lands of those Englishmen who had taken the Danish side in the recent war.[1654] The value of the source is difficult to determine, and 'the recent war' is an opaque expression, but it might conceivably refer to the battle of Tettenhall.

If there were Englishmen within the Northumbrian raiding army – which is far from certain – we need to consider whether they could have been remnants of the English followers of Æthelwold, the cousin of Edward the Elder, who made a determined bid for power with a Northumbrian army after the death of Alfred in 899, as discussed elsewhere in this volume. Æthelwold was killed and his forces were defeated c.903 at the battle of the Holme. The list of dead who fought for Æthelwold is intriguing, for it includes Brihtsige (an English name) 'son of æðeling Beornoth' (another English name), perhaps members of

---

[1648] We can safely ignore the cryptic reference in the chronicle of Bartholomew de Cotton to the death at Tettenhall of King Celwlf, also an English name, evidently a rationalisation of Ecwulf (for Eowils) taken from a version of Henry of Huntingdon's chronicle, of which Bartholomew de Cotton's history was an abridgement: Luard 1859: 21; Forester 1853: 163; Gross 1900: 277.

[1649] Fellows-Jensen 1994: 134. Campbell noted that Æthelweard took an interest in the names of Norse leaders and their language and where appropriate changed and improved the versions of personal names found in the ASC: Campbell 1962: lix.

[1650] Smyth 2002: 20.

[1651] Mentioned in the *Historia de Sancto Cuthberto* ('History of Saint Cuthbert'): Wainwright 1975: 165-7; South 2002: 63. The editor of the latest scholarly edition of the *Historia* has concluded that it is probable that the author, working with separate references to the same battle, mistakenly created two battles at Corbridge, whereas there was probably only a single battle, in 918: South 2002: 8, 105, 106, 107; Downham 2009: 92-3. Evidence also survives which implies that after his conquest of the southern Danelaw in the 920s, Edward the Elder confiscated the lands of Englishmen who had supported the Danes in the recent war: Stenton 1970: 123.

[1652] Stenton 1971: 333 fn.4; Wainwright 1975: 170; South 2002: 63.

[1653] An ealdorman of Wiltshire, Wulhere, who may have been an uncle of the rebellious Æthelwold, gained notoriety as the only one of Alfred's ealdorman to defect to the Vikings at some date before 901: Yorke 2001: 35.

[1654] Stenton 1970: 123.

one of the families with a claim to the throne of Mercia.[1655] But if, as seems likely, the Scandinavians at Tettenhall were North Sea Scandinavians, it seems improbable, though not impossible, that any Englishmen who may have fought and died alongside them in 910 were amongst those Englishmen who seven years earlier had rallied to Æthelwold's cause, since the latter were part of a York-based campaign, to be distinguished from the Hiberno-Scandinavians of the north-west.

To revert to the battle of 910, it should be noted that notwithstanding the conflicting statements in the *Anglo-Saxon Chronicles* – 'A' and 'B' to a battle at an un-named place in 910; 'C' to a battle at Tettenhall in 910; 'D' to a battle at Tettenhall in 909 and another the following year, as well as a separate account which is clearly the battle of Tettenhall, in 911; 'E' to a battle at Tettenhall in 911; the *Mercian Register* to a battle in 910 at Tettenhall; Florence (John) of Worcester conflating the sources to refer to two battles, at Tettenhall and Wednesfield, in 911; and Æthelweard to a battle in 909 (for 910) at *Wodnesfield campo*, with Henry of Huntingdon recording two battles, one *apud* Tettenhall, and Roger of Wendover recording a battle in 911 at Wednesfield, with the *Annals of St Neots* giving the date of the battle as 910 – historians generally agree that there was but one single battle in the Tettenhall/Wednesfield area in 910, since the various references to two battles are readily explained as attempts by the chroniclers, doubtless unaware of the proximity of Tettenhall and Wednesfield, to reconcile and integrate disparate and seemingly contradictory source material – Æthelweard tells us it was fought at *Wodnesfelda* on 5th August, *Anglo-Saxon Chronicle* 'D' near Tettenhall on 6th August.[1656] It would be an astonishing and statistically inconceivable coincidence if two (or even more) major battles between the English and the Danes had occurred only a few miles apart on almost the same day in August in different years in a relatively obscure part of England, and the likelihood can be discounted. It is clearly indisputable that there was only a single major battle between the English and the Northumbrians in the Tettenhall/Wednesfield area in early August 910.

The site of the battle, however, is rather less straightforward. We have seen that those versions of the *Anglo-Saxon Chronicle* that name the location of the battle (i.e. as Tettenhall) are 'C', 'D' and 'E'. The palaeography of the three versions shows that 'C' was written in handwriting of the mid eleventh century,[1657] the 'D' manuscript is a consolidated document by various scribes, the oldest hand being no earlier than the second half of the eleventh century,[1658] and 'E' is a copy in a single hand up to 1121, with further additions in the same hand.[1659] So whilst it is very likely that those annals were recorded soon after the battle (the hand responsible for the entry in version 'A', which does not name the battle

---

[1655] Campbell 2001: 21-22. Beorhtsige is probably the man of that name who attested a charter of 898 (S.350): Yorke 2001: 36-37. He may have been associated with the *Eoforwicingas* ('York-folk') who in 918 promised by pledges and oaths to give loyalty to Æthelflæd, according to the *Mercian Register*. Wainwright wondered whether they were Danes or Angles, but came to no conclusion: Earle and Plummer 1892-99: I 105; Whitelock 1955: 198; Wainwright 1975: 337. The *Jomsvikingsaga* (set in the 10th century; written in the 13th century: John 1996: 139) assumes that those who 'joined the fellowship' of that mysterious band would not necessarily be Scandinavian, and early in the 11th century Wulfstan, Archbishop of York, accepted that an English thrall 'might run away from his lord, leave Christendom and become a Viking': Davis 1988: 168.
[1656] Darlington et al 1995-8: I 365 fn.8.
[1657] Whitelock, Douglas and Tucker 1961: xiii.
[1658] Whitelock, Douglas and Tucker 1961: xv; Cubbin 1996: lxxix.
[1659] Whitelock, Douglas and Tucker 1961: xvi.

site, appears to date from the period between c.915 and c.930, possibly between 924 and 927),[1660] we have no certain evidence of the dates when 'C', 'D' and 'E' were first written.

Æthelweard's *Chronicon* (dating from between 978 and 988), and the *Annals of St Neots* (dating from between 985 and c.1012),[1661] as well as Roger of Wendover, who had access to records now lost,[1662] all give the site of the battle as Wednesfield, or more precisely at *Vuodnesfelda campo*, 'the *feld* or place of battle known as the open land or battlefield associated with Woden',[1663] according to Æthelweard. Wednesfield is also named by Florence (John) of Worcester,who for good measure also mentions another battle in the same year at *Teottanhele*.[1664] The weight of evidence is thus seen to tilt convincingly in favour of Wednesfield (*campo*) as the scene of the battle, and 910 as the year.

Whilst the two accounts we are perhaps entitled to treat as the most trustworthy, that is Æthelweard and the *Mercian Register* incorporated into some versions of the *Anglo-Saxon Chronicle*, appear to name different but nearby places, a short word which appears in version 'D' of the *Anglo-Saxon Chronicle* (written, it must be remembered, no earlier that the second half of the eleventh century) before the name *Teotan heale* must be of particular significance. That word is *neh* (for *neah*), meaning 'near, close to'.[1665] The only evidence of the *Mercian Register* is found in the interpolations in versions 'B', 'C' and 'D' of the *Anglo-Saxon Chronicle*, and we may be entitled to believe that version 'D' (which alone of the versions gives a precise date for the battle, 6th August 909), is the more accurate, with the chronicler, evidently having access to a record (possibly compiled at York or Ripon,[1666] although some scholars rule out York and prefer a southern, possibly Gloucester, rather than a northern, origin)[1667] which was not available when the other versions were written, amalgamating the *Mercian Register* into chronological order rather than incorporating it wholesale as in versions 'B' and 'C'.[1668] That conflation would not have been easy, and explains why some events from the *Register* in version 'D' are omitted and why some are entered twice, for example the two accounts of the battle of Tettenhall, one entered under

---

[1660] Bateley 1986: xxxiii-xxxiv.

[1661] Hart 2006.

[1662] Lapidge et al 1999: 18. It is possible that Æthelweard, writing between 978 and 988, had access to a version of the *Chronicle* which was closer to the original than any other extant manuscript (see Campbell 1962: xiii; Bately 1986: lxxix; Smyth 1995: 459, 460), but Whitelock notes that whatever version he used, Æthelweard seems to have lacked the annals from 893 to 915: Whitelock 1955: 114. Smyth 1995: 474-7 argues that Stenton's speculation that Æthelweard's *Chronicon* was 'composed for an ealdorman of Somerset, or at least for some prominent thegn of this region', is unsupportable.

[1663] Campbell 1962: 53 translates *campo* as 'plain', but the word may well be from Latin *campus* 'battlefield, battle': see VEPN (BRACE-CÆSTER) 2000 135-6. Early manuscripts commonly use the word *campo* or *feld* for the sites of battles: see e.g. Morgan 2000.

[1664] Florence (John) of Worcester was evidently using, as might be expected, ASC 'D' (the Worcester Chronicle) as his source.

[1665] *909 Her Myrce 7 West Seaxe gefuhton wiþ þone here neh Teotan heale. On .viii. idus Agustus. 7 sige hæfdon...*: 'Here the Mercians and West Saxons fought against the raiding-army near Tettenhall on 8th ides [6th] of August and had the victory': Earle and Plummer 1892-90 95; Swanton 1996: 95.

[1666] Swanton 1996: xxv. The *Chronicle* was made in about 1050 and maintained at Worcester up to 1079. See also Stafford 2008: 102 fn.5.

[1667] John 1996: 193-4.

[1668] Earle and Plummer 1892-90: I lxxiii-lxxiv; Swanton 1996: xxv. The most recent editor of ASC 'D', G. P. Cubbin, credits Ealdred, bishop of Worcester from c.1046 to 1062, and bishop of York from 1061 to 1069, 'not just for the creation of the MS but, through the exchanges of materials involved, for giving a wider impulse to work on the Anglo-Saxon Chronicle generally in the late eleventh century': Cubbin 1996: lxxi.

the year 909, the other 910. The 'D' version has long been associated with Worcester (from which it takes its name),[1669] some 28 miles from Tettenhall, and might perhaps have incorporated local knowledge, although it may be additional information from the 'northern' records that provides specific evidence of the battle.[1670]

On balance, we might entertain the conclusion that the 'D' version of the *Anglo-Saxon Chronicle* is to be seen as a more reliable – or perhaps more accurately the least unreliable – guide to events in the first two decades or so of the tenth century. The word *neh* tells us that version 'D' of the *Chronicle* differs fundamentally from version 'C' (which is the only other version to name the battle site as Tettenhall) by informing us that the battle did *not* take place at Tettenhall, but somewhere nearby.

Furthermore, we should note that Henry of Huntingdon – said to have known 'a lot of legendary matter but little reliable information'[1671] – mentions two battles, which are clearly one and the same: in the first, Henry names the prominent Danes who were killed, a list similar to that in the *Anglo-Saxon Chronicle*; in the second (part of an interpolation from 'the old chronicles') Henry records a great battle, at which the English were victorious, between the English and the Danes *apud Totanhale*.[1672] This is usually read as 'at Tettenhall', but *apud* can be translated in various ways, including 'at', 'near', 'by', 'to', and 'towards'. It may be more accurate to translate *apud Totanhale* as 'in the Tettenhall area'.

Nowadays there is universal agreement among Anglo-Saxon scholars that there was one single major conflict between the English and the Danes in 910 (a conclusion supported by the evidence cited above), somewhere near Tettenhall[1673] – it would be stretching credulity to imagine two encounters between large forces within a few miles of each other at about the same date in the same small area – and the reference to *Vuodnesfelda campo* in Æthelweard's *Chronicon*,[1674] the fullest account of the circumstances leading up to the battle (though not the earlies reference to the battle, which is found in *Anglo-Saxon Chronicle* 'A' in a section perhaps written between c.915 and c.930, possibly c.924),[1675] entitles us to assume that we need to look to the east of Tettenhall, to an area in the direction of the field of Wednesfield, a topographical name which in the early tenth century may well have been attached to a sizeable open area extending some way towards, perhaps even once incorporating, Tettenhall – the present townships are only 3½ miles apart, with the estate boundaries only a mile from each other – rather than a place of

---

[1669] Swanton 1996: xxv. The *Chronicle* was made in about 1050 and maintained at Worcester up to 1079.

[1670] As evidence of particular northern knowledge, the 'D' *Chronicle* tells us that the marriage of Æthelstan's un-named sister in 924 was to the son of the king of the Old Saxons and has two following entries for 925 and 926 on Æthelstan's relations with the kings of Northumbria and other rulers of Northern and Western Britain: Stafford 2008: 102. However, academic debate continues on origins of the 'D' Chronicle: Eric John believed that details of events about the north of England and Scotland can be explained by the intermittent connection between the sees of Worcester and York 972-1062: see John 1996: 193-4 fn.2.

[1671] Whitelock 1955: 121. '[M]odern criticism ... has largely destroyed Henry's claims to rank as a first-rate historical authority, and neither in style, accuracy, nor fullness of detail is he worthy of any serious comparison with William [of Malmesbury]': Ward and Waller 1920: 166.

[1672] Arnold 1879: 154-7; Forester 1853: 163, 166.

[1673] E.g. Whitelock 1955: 192 fn.7, Stenton 1971: 323-4; Fisher 1973: 238; Campbell 1991: 160; Blair 1997: 77; Yorke 1999: 71-2.

[1674] See generally Campbell 1962.

[1675] Bateley1986: xxxiii-xxxiv.

habitation. But given its unique status, it is worthwhile analysing Æthelweard's account in more detail.

As discussed elsewhere, the reference to *Vuodnesfelda campo* is especially noteworthy, since the word *campo* is found nowhere else in Æthelweard's *Chronicon*: the majority of names are preceded by the formulaic *in loco* followed by a noun describing the subject of the name (monastery, town, island, province, territory, wood, land, ford, etc.) and 'which is commonly called' or 'which is called' or 'known as', with the name alone without qualifying words used for rivers or towns – and lesser places, without apparent pattern – such as London, York, Reading, Chippenham, Sheppey, Edington, Gloucester, Cirencester, Rochester, Southampton, Wedmore, and Carhampton. Some places in Britain are referred to in different places in the text both with and without the qualifying words.[1676] The qualifying words are used of no Continental towns or rivers. Why that wording was not used with *Vuodnesfelda* is not readily explicable, but more importantly we must question why Æthelweard chose to refer to *Vuodnesfelda campo* and not simply *Vuodnesfelda*.

One of the meanings of Latin *campo* is 'theatre of action, battlefield', but Æthelweard has already mentioned a battle, and the word *campo* is not found attached to the names of any other of the many battles or places he mentions, or indeed to other battle sites recorded by other early historians. Its unique use may be to emphasise its other meaning 'a level place, a large plain', to give 'the place called *Vuodnesfelda* in the large tract of level treeless land'.[1677] The element *felda* in *Vuodnesfelda* may have been used by Æthelweard to mean 'area of open ground' rather than 'battlefield',[1678] and *campo* must have been intended to supplement the name, presumably representing the literal translation of Old English *feld*, perhaps supporting the idea of an extensive area of open land known simply as *feld* incorporating Wednesfield to the east of Wolverhampton and extending to Finchfield (probably within *ðone feld* recorded in 985)[1679] or beyond to the west, with both such *feld*-names probably adopted after the battle, and the association with Woden as an ancestral figure rather than a pagan god perhaps arising as a result of the battle.[1680] Since Æthelweard does not say where *Vuodnesfelda campo* lay, we might assume that it was sufficiently prominent and well known to require no explanation, or that his source did not provide any details he could use to help locate the place, and was ignorant of its location.

On balance, the available evidence suggests that we might seek the site of the battle of Tettenhall somewhere on the estate known as Wednesfield, which until the 1860s contained some 3,700 acres and included Heath Town and New Invention.[1681] Its boundaries as set out in the forged confirmation of Wulfrun's charter show that in the tenth

---

[1676] For example Repton: Campbell 1962: 22, 40, 41.
[1677] This is made explicit in the chronicles of Roger of Wendover and Matthew Paris: Cox 1841: 375; Luard 1872: I 440; Luard 1890: I 482.
[1678] Clark Hall 1960: 113.
[1679] S.860; Hooke 1983: 63-5.
[1680] The northern (and possibly western) side of the *feld* appears to have been bounded by a great moor or marshland (remembered in the name Oxley Moor) known as *sæffan mor* (later Saltmoor) which extended north at least as far as the river Penk, and is crossed by the boundary of Cannock Forest in 1286. The name is likely to be associated with and derive from *seofan wyllan broc* (Seven Wells Brook, which gave its names to Showell, on which see JEPNS 39 (2007) 7-44): both *sæffan mor* and *seofan wyllan broc* are found in 985 in the forged grant of Wolverhampton and Trescott from King Æthelred to Wulfrun (S.860): Hooke 1983: 63-5; Horovitz 2005: 474-5; JEPNS 39 (2007) 7-44.
[1681] Smallshire 1978: 132.

or eleventh century it extended from Pool Hayes in the east to Showell in the west, and from Blackhalve and Ashmore in the north to Moseley Hole in the south, an irregular shape up to four miles across and two-and-a-half miles deep, and perhaps originally part of a much greater area, possibly incorporating Finchfield to the west.[1682] Its eastern boundary lay little more than a mile from the estate of Tettenhall – a record of 1228 mentions 'the neighbouring vills of Wodnesfelde and Tettenhall ...'[1683] – of which, with Wolverhampton and many other estates, it probably once formed part. Furthermore, we should not overlook the possibility that Wednesbury, some three miles from Wednesfield, once lay within the great open plain of *Wodnesfeld*, which would help to explain its name, and would mean that the *feld* would have been several miles or more across,[1684] providing a parallel with other vast Staffordshire *feld* estates at *Letocetum*/Lichfield, 12 miles to the north-east, Enville (with Enville Common), 10 miles to the south-west of Bridgnorth, and Morville, 4 miles east of Bridgnorth, which despite their modern spellings are ancient *feld* name, as well as Worfield, 3 miles north-east of Bridgnorth.[1685]

The inference of the above analysis may be that Æthelweard's *Vuodnesfelda campo* was intended to refer to an area called *Vuodnesfelda*, perhaps without a settlement, which lay within a sizeable tract of open ground, possibly originally of much greater extent, in which case we are forced to recognise the inescapable if unpalatable possibility that the battle of 910 may have been fought anywhere within a vast area, not necessarily close to the settlement of Wednesfield.[1686]

In that respect it is worth recording that Wednesfield lay within the medieval Forest of Cannock, a royal hunting area, not necessarily wooded, which certainly existed at the Norman Conquest,[1687] and possibly long before. Domesday assessed the estate of Wednesfield at five hides, with 6 villeins and 6 bordars, most if not all of whom will have had families. Shaw notes that at the Conquest 'the extent [of Wednesfield] was then very large',[1688] but until the eighteenth century Wednesfield had always been relatively insignificant in terms of population,[1689] and is not even shown on Christopher Saxton's 1577 map of Staffordshire or John Speed's 1610 map of the county, though both include many minor places.

Finally, it it noteworthy that events from this period in English history are all but ignored by writers in Britain outside England.[1690] Neither the *Chronicon Scotorum*, a valuable set of annals for early Irish history, nor the *Annals of Ulster* mention of any battle which

---

[1682] S.860; Hooke 1983: 63-5.
[1683] Smallshire 1978: 50.
[1684] It is susrprising to find that the location of *Wodnesfeld* was formerly debated by historians, even though the name was linked to that of Tettenhall. C. S. Taylor, for example, considered it may have been in the Cotswolds, perhaps Wanswell in Berkeley: Taylor 1892-3: 88.
[1685] Horovitz 2005: 17-21, 248, 361; PN Sa I: 213-4; 326-7.
[1686] The area between Wolverhampton and Wednesfield has long been known as Stowheath, a name of uncertain age which may conceivably predate the name Wednesfield.
[1687] VCH II 338. Tettenhall, in whole or part, lay within Tettenhall Wood, a detached part of Kinver Forest, some of which may have existed before 1086: VCH II 336, 343.
[1688] Shaw 1801: II 150.
[1689] In 1665-6 47 some 47 houses in Wednesfield paid Hearth Tax (WA I: 156-7) and in 1801 Wednesfield had a recorded population of 1,088: Smallshire 1978: 132.
[1690] It is not only writers outside England who overlook the battle: it is unmentioned in Sir Francis Palgrave's monumental two volumes on the Anglo-Saxon period and its institutions: Palgrave 1832.

might be identified as the conflict at Tettenhall;[1691] likewise the *Annales Cambriæ*, the *Brenhinedd y Saesson*, and *Brut y Tywysogion*, informative annals (at this period notably terse) on Welsh history.[1692] Apart from Robert of Torigni, who in the early twelfth century provides the briefest possible reference to Tettenhall,[1693] Continental writers are equally silent. Dudo of St Quinton, for example, the author of the Frankish *History of the Normans*, fails even to mention Edward the Elder, although he was a contemporary of Hrolf (better-known as Rollo), a Norse Viking of noble birth, the first ruler (from the year after the battle of Tettenhall) of the region of northern France (the country then under the rule of Charles, the son-in-law of Edward the Elder)[1694] which was to become Normandy, who conversely is mentioned in the *Anglo-Saxon Chronicle* versions 'E' and 'F' in 876.[1695] No Scandinavian sources (which all post-date the Norman Conquest) mention any battle which might be identifiable as the engagement at Tettenhall.[1696]

[1691] Hennessy 1866.
[1692] Ab Ithel 1860; Jones 1971; Jones 1973. See also Graves 1975: 286, 406-7, 406-7.
[1693] Howlett 2012: IV 14.
[1694] Stevenson 1848: 125.
[1695] Swanton 1996: 74.
[1696] One of the few references in Scandinavian sources which seems to relate to events of the early tenth century is a much-garbled account of battles in Cleveland and Scarborough involving the rebellious Æthelwold c.903: Smyth 1975-9: I 47-52. The prolific and respected 18th-century Danish historian Peter Friderich Suhm records in his 7-volume history of Denmark a battle in 911 at which kings Eowils and Hildein were killed, evidently taking his information from Matthew of Westminster, a mythical medieval chronicler whose works were later identified as those of Matthew Paris: Suhm 1776: 880. A review in Swedish of the English sources, with commentary, can be found in Suhm 1776: 93, 182, 881, 884.

28. Opinions as to the site of the battle of Tettenhall.

In the seventeenth century the Staffordshire historian John Huntbach of Featherstone (1639-1705, a nephew of Sir William Dugdale, the renowned antiquary and his mentor in antiquarian studies), who knew the area well, since his family home was the ancient moated house at Sewall,[1697] on the north side of Wolverhampton, mid-way between Tettenhall and Wednesfield, and who might be expected to have had a particular interest in the battle, recorded that: '...the place of battle was in the field between Tettenhall and the Wirges, where yet is to be seen a very great Tumulus where the bodies were buried; and, although the plough hath for many ages made furrows over it, yet it is very visible, and the field, called by the name of Low-hill field to this day.'[1698]

Notwithstanding this unhesitatingly confident identification, Huntbach could have had no knowledge of the actual site of the battle, but he was a local man, and it is not entirely inconceivable (but most improbable) that some residual folk-memory of the battle-site still persisted in the area, though we should remember that the sites of many battles of national importance, some far more recent than Tettenhall, have become completely lost to memory. However, Huntbach's assured assertion must be treated with circumspection, for he was not unequivocal in his opinion: in his entry for Wednesfield, Stebbing Shaw, the great Staffordshire historian, cites a contrary account provided by Huntbach: '[ancient historians say] the battle was here fought; for besides the name given to the place, there are many tumuli, or lowes, there ...'.[1699] There is no indication that Huntbach disagreed with the 'ancient historians', and his views as to the site(s) of the battle(s) were clearly and not unreasonably predicated on the mention of Tettenhall and Wednesfield in the extant histories, combined with the presence of what were believed to have been – and perhaps some were – ancient tumuli which were assumed to cover battle dead, an assumption for which little or no empirical evidence was available.

Dr Robert Plot, in his *The Natural History of Staffordshire*, published in 1686, built upon Holinshed's account of the battle, and concluded that there were two battles in the area, one at or near Wrottesley (which he extraordinarily and inventively held to be the site of an ancient city once occupied by Danes), and one at Wednesfield. He says: 'I come next to treat of such as are the deplorable remains of the bloody warrs 'twixt the Saxons and Danes: amongst which the first in order of time, are the ruins ... in Wrottesley park ... which upon second considerations I am inclined to believe, if Theotenhall doe import the habitation of heathens as Camden informs us, are no Roman antiquity, but the true remains of the old Theotenhall of the Danes, who I suppose having resided there for some time, built them this City or place of habitation, which ... in all probability was finally rased by Edward Senior in that signal victory he there obtained over them... To revenge whose quarrel, another army of them that possest Northumberland, breaking a league they had formerly made with King Edward, invaded Mercia in the very same year, pillageing the Country wherever they came: against whom king Edward bringing a powerful Army both of West Saxons and Mercians, overtook them in their return at the village of Wednesfield, not farr from Theotenhall, and overthrew them again in another bloody battle ... Of which great slaughter yet there are no more remains but a Low in the ground call'd South Low field, which has lately had a windmill set upon it, the Low being there before as within

---

[1697] Now remembered in Showell Road.
[1698] Shaw 1801 II: 194. There is no Tithe Apportionment for Tettenhall and the location of the field is uncertain.
[1699] Shaw 1801 II: 150.

memory. There is another ground here too call'd North-Low field, which no question heretofore has had also a Low in it, tho' now it be gone. Which doubtless were cast up over some of those kings, or Danish or Saxon nobles, then slain there; and so 'tis like was Stowman's hill on the road betwixt Wolverhampton and Walsall, half a mile SW of the village of Nechels.'[1700]

Francis Wise (1695-1767), a notable antiquary, mentions the battle, observing that 'the Saxon annals ... do not mark out the place, but Ethelward an old historian, tho' something later than the Annalist, tells us that it was Wodnesfeld', before adding the surprising comment: 'but where to look for that place [Wednesfield] I know not', highlighting the modest size and remote obscurity of the place even seven hundred years or more after the battle.[1701]

Between 1726 and 1731 the first English translation by Nicholas Tindal of the French edition of the generally well-researched 15-volume history of England by Paul de Rapin Thoyras (1661-1725), a former active soldier, was published, with copious footnotes. It proved very popular, and went through several editions in the first half of the eighteenth century.[1702] Under the year 907 the work records that '[The Danes] sued for peace [at Yttingaford]; which Edward readily granted them, on condition they would acknowledge him for sovereign as they had done his father, and the Normans return to France [*sic*]. This peace could not hold long between the neighbouring nations so exasperated against one another. It proved fatal to the Danes, who lost in very little time two battles. Edward, who knew how to improve his victories, took from them several towns in Mercia, and at length drove them quite out of the kingdom. Then it was that Ethelred, who had all along bravely seconded the king his brother-in-law, became in reality the earl of Mercia; but that was not long so. He died almost as soon as that whole province was united under his government. The first [battle] was at Wodnesfield. For the Danish army in Northumberland not regarding the peace which King Edward and his son [*sic*] had made with them, wasted against the province of Mercia. In this battle were slain several thousand Danes, with their Kings Ecwils and Healfden. They were succeeded by one Reginald [Ragnall]. The second battle was fought at Teotenhale, or Tetnel in Staffordshire.'[1703]

The eighteenth-century Staffordshire historian Dr Richard Wilkes (1690-1760)[1704] lived at Willenhall, close to Wednesfield, and so took a special interest in the battle. His observations and conclusions are set out out posthumously by Stebbing Shaw:

'Florence of Worcester, and Ralph Higden, say this battle was fought at or near Tettenhall; but Ethelwald [Æthelweard] will have it fought on the fifth of August, this year, at Wednesfelda, now Wednesfield, near Wolverhampton. Higden, I think, clears up the point, and assures us that the Danes were beat this year, at both these places, and that they came hither from Northumberland. Of both these battles there are yet some remains. In the liberty of Wednesfield, two of the common fields belonging to that village take their

---

[1700] Plot 1686: 415.
[1701] Wise 1742: 40-42.
[1702] Hill 2006: 117-8; the English translations give the author as Mr Rapin de Thoyras.
[1703] de Thoyras 1757: I 340-1. The account is notable for its suggestion that Ethelred became lord of the Mercians only after the battle of Tettenhall, and for the statement that the treaty of *Yttingaford* had been made by Edward and his son: Æthelstan, Edward's eldest son, was born about 895, and so would have been about 9 or 10 when the treaty was concluded: Williams, Smyth and Kirby 1991: 50-1. Neither statement is likely to be correct.
[1704] For a short biography see SHC 4th Series 11 84-93.

names from the lows that were raised over some of the generals, or perhaps over the two kings, the one being called North Low and the other South Low field. ... Our antiquaries have long endeavoured to find the place where the battle of Tettenhall was fought, but to no purpose. There are three lows on the common between Wombourn and Swin,[1705] placed in a right line that runs directly East and West? and about half a mile to the North of them is another, by the country people called Soldiers' hill.[1706] They are all large, and capable of covering a great number of dead bodies. There cannot be the least doubt but this place was the scene of action; for king Edward, to perpetuate the memory of this signal victory, I presume, here founded a church; called by the name of the place Wonbourn, now Wombourne; and took this whole parish out of the parish of Tettenhall, which before this battle extended as far as the forest of Kinver.[1707] These four lows were all thrown up by the soldiers immediately after the battle, and in all probability the single one contains the bodies of the two kings; who, being there placed on a hill, had a fine opportunity of viewing both armies, and from thence giving their orders to the several parts of them.'.[1708]

Evidently Wilkes's confident identification of Wombourne as the site of the battle was based on what he deemed to be the derivation of the place-name, for he adds:[1709] '...the participle *won*, or *win*, from *winnan* to fight, formerly was used for victory. ... *bourne* signifies a brook, so that the name of this place is very significant; for by it is meant that great and signal victory which king Edward here gained over the Northumbrian Danes, his inveterate enemies. I have sometimes thought that Swin, Old Swinford, and King's Swinford, all in this neighbourhood, were so called from some of the Danes; but if they were it must have been afterwards, when they became masters of the whole island [*sic*].' In fact the place-name Wombourne cannot be associated in itself with any battle: the name means 'the bourne or stream associated with the womb-like topographical feature'.[1710]

As we have seen, at the end of the eighteenth century Stebbing Shaw himself reached the following conclusion as to the battle and its site: 'King Edward, with a powerful force of West Saxons and Mercians, overtook [the Danes] at the village of Wednesfield, near Theotenhall, and vanquished them again, with much slaughter. Of this there are no remains but a low, in a place called North Low-field, though the low is not now visible. These, doubtless, were cast up over some of the Kings or nobles then slain here; as was also

---

[1705] Presumably Swindon, 1½ miles south of Wombourne. Scott 1932: 329 says 'Three lows are described [at Wombourne] as on the waste, now inclosed, between Wombourne and Swindon, in a right line E. and W. besides Soldiers'-hill, half a mile to the north'. These were presumably the lows on Wombourne Heath recorded by Plot, who thought they 'may have been raised over some eminent Roman Commanders': Plot 1686: 397. There seems little likelihood that the tumuli (if such they were) are to be associated with the battle of Tettenhall: Wombourne lies some 7 miles from Tettenhall and 10 from Wednesfield. Willmore 1908: 9 notes that 'in past times a number of ancient weapns have been dug up at Wombourne', but cites no source for his statement.

[1706] Gunstone could find no trace of any mounds in the 1960s: NSJFS 1965 59. The mounds evidently gave rise to the name Battlefield, applied to an area adjacent to the Stourbridge road south-east of Wombourne, and remembered in the name Battlefield Lane, which is probably of nineteenth century origin (Horovitz 2005: 106), and is not to be seen as evidence for any battle here.

[1707] No evidence has been found to support this statement, but Kingsley, a royal manor a mile south-west of Tettenhall, once held by the king (see VCH XX 29), was part of Kinver Forest. Kingsley Wood became Tettenhall Wood.

[1708] Shaw 1798: I 38.

[1709] Shaw 1798: I 38, footnote.

[1710] See Horovitz 2005: 586.

Stowman's hill, on the road between Wolverhampton and Walsall, half a mile South-west of the village of Nechels.'.[1711]

The Staffordshire section in the multi-volume compendium *The Beauties of England and Wales*, written by the Reverend Joseph Nightingale and published in 1813,[1712] says of Wednesfield that the place 'is remarkable as the scene of an engagement between Edward the elder and the Danes ... [t]he number and extent of the lows or tumuli, to be seen here, are decisive monuments of this important victory'.[1713] Of Tettenhall (wrongly named as Tatenhill, confusing the village of that name near Uttoxeter), he adds that 'a severe battle was fought in this neighbourhood, between the Danes and Edward the Elder, at the commencement of the tenth century'.[1714]

In *A Topographical History of Staffordshire* published in 1817, William Pitt, an agronomist born at Tettenhall in 1749, provides no new information about the battle, simply recording that 'A great battle is said to have been fought between Tettenhall and the Wergs, where, in a field called Low-hill-field, a large tumulus is still to be seen', adding for good measure that in 911 Edward the Elder defeated the Danes at Tettenhall.[1715]

Thomas Harwood's 1820 edition of Sampson Erdeswick's *Survey of Staffordhire*, first published in 1717, notes that 'In 910, Edward the Elder sent a powerful army to attack the Danes. The Northumbrians were surprised into a fixed battle at Wodensfield, Wednesfield, and were defeated with the slaughter of many thousand men. Two of their kings fell, Halfdan and Eowils, the brother of the celebrated Ingwar, and many earls and officers. The Anglo-Saxons sung hymns on their great victory'.[1716] The enlarged edition of 1844 notes that 'In 910 a battle was fought [at Tettenhall] between the Danes and Edward the Elder, in which the English were victorious',[1717] but confusingly also repeats verbatim the 1820 account.[1718]

George Oliver, curate of St Peter's, Wolverhampton, records in 1836 in his undistinguished church history an English victory over the Danes at Wednesfield, adding for good measure that 'The Danes were also overthrown in a field between Tettenhall and the Wergs'.[1719]

Towards the end of the nineteenth century the Ordnance Survey marked the '*Supposed Site of Battle Between the Danes & Saxons*' on its maps on the west side of New Cross canal bridge, south of the canal and north of the railway[1720] (both features now subsumed beneath modern development), probably on the west side of the junction of what are now Planetary Road and Manfield Road, but such battle-sites on early Ordnance Survey maps must be treated with considerable caution, for typically there is no evidence that the location was anything more than guesswork, probably based on the fact that the place was on a noticeable hill, and local folklore associated the reputed mounds of The Low and Southlow with the battle dead. Certainly there was no archaeological evidence to support

---

[1711] Shaw 1798: I 37.
[1712] Nightingale 1813: 864.
[1713] Nightingale 1813: 843-4.
[1714] Nightingale 1813: 864.
[1715] Pitt 1817: 183.
[1716] Harwood 1820: 288.
[1717] Harwood 1844: 350.
[1718] Harwood 1844: 392-3.
[1719] Oliver 1836: 4.
[1720] O.S. map of 1889, 1:2,500. The wording is centred on grid reference SO 99809390.

the identification, which in itself can carry no weight in any attempt to pinpoint the battle site.

The prominent Tettenhall ironmaster Colonel Thomas Thorneycroft (1822-1903) believed that the battle of Tettenhall took place on and around Tettenhall Green,[1721] but whatever his many other achievements, was no historian, and the reasons for his identification have not come down to us. George T. Lawley, the Bilston historian, concluded that a single battle had taken place where Tettenhall College now stands, on the edge of the ridge of Tettenhall Wood.[1722] Again, the basis for his conclusion is not known, but his view seems to have been followed in part by the Tettenhall historian J. P. Jones. In his *History of Tettenhall*, published in 1894, Jones writes: 'I believe there was only one battle, the distance between the two places [Tettenhall and Wednesfield] is only 3 miles. It probably began at Wednesfield, where the Danes and English first came into collision, and the Danes in retreating took up a position at Tettenhall. This is just such a position as a retreating force would take up, for it is a commanding ridge intersected by a high road, and it was here that the Danes probably received their defeat'. In 1902 Jones again summarised his views: '... collating the evidences which are extant I am forced to the conclusion that two battles were fought in this district AD 910-911. The records show that a Danish force landing on the East coast came down the river Trent and sacked Lichfield, while it is proved that another Danish force came up the Severn as far as Bridgnorth. These two forces effected a junction at Wednesfield, where they were defeated, and falling back upon Tettenhall were caught between the armies of the West Saxons and the Mercians and totally defeated. There is no doubt the battle was fought along the valley of the Smestow and ranged from Autherley to beyond Wightwick. The Danes after their defeat at Wednesfield would naturally fall back upon Tettenhall, as the position is just such a one as a retreating force would take up. They probably found that the commanding ridge at Tettenhall was occupied by the West Saxons, and so caught between the two armies their defeat was certain'.[1723]

Jones' conclusions may be entirely correct, but in reality serve as an outstanding example of a case built not on slender foundations, but upon no foundations at all. The use of the expressions 'evidences which are extant', 'forced to the conclusion', 'records show', 'it is proved', 'there is no doubt', 'would naturally', and so on are used without the slightest evidence or sources cited to support them, and Jones' opinion was evidently influenced by the not uncommon delusion that a major historical event must have taken place at or close to the author's home. It is a complete mystery where Jones obtained his information that a Danish force landed on the east coast, travelled along the Trent and sacked Lichfield, an episode entirely at odds with the earliest chronicles and otherwise completely unknown to history.

Our curiousity is further aroused by the conclusions of William Hutchinson, writing in 1904, who says: '... the writer ... ventures to think that the battle [of Tettenhall] took place between Compton and Wightwick, near the site which is marked by the presence of two large tumuli in the grass fields on the right side of the road, in which tumuli or 'lows', local tradition says the slaughtered Danes and Anglo-Saxons alike were buried, on the ground on which they fell'.[1724] Since Wightwick is further south than Compton, we must suppose

---

[1721] WJ, June 1904 163. Presumably Lower Green is meant.
[1722] Hancock 1991: 8.
[1723] WJ, October 1904 265-6.
[1724] WJ, September 1904 240.

that the so-called tumuli lay in the fields below the ridge on the west side of the road between Compton and Wightwick, although it is perforce unsafe to place much faith in an author who is able to write with such ambiguity. The only mound traced in this area is the one at Wightwick Mill mentioned elsewhere in this volume, and it is possible that Hutchinson's reference to 'two large tumuli' is in fact to the single mound at Wightwick Mill. However, it is not possible to exclude the possibility that other mounds lay nearby.

In 1908 William Page observed tersely in Volume One of the *Victoria History of the County of Stafford* that 'in 910 Edward the Elder met the Danes at Tettenhall and defeated them',[1725] and in the same year the prolific Black Country writer F. W. Hackwood decided that there were two battles between the Saxons and the Danes, one in 910 near The Wergs, the other in 911 at Heath Town, apparently basing his conclusions on the views of the Walsall solicitor and antiquary W. H. Duignan.[1726] Duignan, himself a capable scholar, is less than clear about the date and site of the battle, stating that 'On the plain at the foot [of Tettenhall ridge], in 910, a battle was fought between the Saxons and the Danes, which in the Chronicles is called the battle of Totanheale, though it was actually waged about a mile N. of Wolverhampton', adding elsewhere that the battle was fought in 911 (*sic*) 'on Wednesfield Heath (now Heath Town)', repeating the view of earlier writers that 'the dead were buried as usual under mounds, which in Huntbach's time still remained, and were known as North Low, South Low, the Little Low, the Great Low, Horselow, Tromelowe, and Ablow (many of these names survive), besides others which had then disappeared. It is therefore difficult to say whether 'the Low' [at Tettenhall] was a prehistoric tumulus, or a battle-mound'.[1727]

In 1960 an extensive history of Wolverhampton to the late nineteenth century was published by Wolverhampton Corporation. Based on a draft prepared but not completed by Geoffrey Mander, a well-respected medievalist and scion of the Mander family of Wightwick Manor, and completed by Norman W. Tildesley, a scholarly historian from Willenhall, the book wastes little time over the battle of 910: 'The Anglo Saxon Chronicle mentions the battle in which Edward the Elder defeated the Danes in 910 alternately as being fought at Tettenhall or at Wednesfield. Perhaps the truth is that it was fought midway between on the higher ground at Wolverhampton; but as this place was then nameless, so the suggestion is that theChronicle mentioned those lying near'.[1728]

A slim but useful history of Wednesfield incoporating materials collected by a class of the Workers' Educational Association was published in 1978 by John Smallshire, a local historian who had the benefit of detailed knowledge of the Wednesfield area and, as might be expected, a particular interest in the battle of Tettenhall. Having cited the principal historical sources relating to the battle, he reviewed the evidence and concluded with admirable pragmatism: 'There was a battle (if not two battles) and it raged either at Tettenhall or Wednesfield or at both places or near both. It is wise to take the view that the battle raged to and fro between and about these settlements, and the pinpointing of a battlefield near New Cross [presumably the Ordnance Survey designation] is obviously nonsense. Nevertheless the marshy land of March End, and Poole Hayes to Moseley Hole may well have formed the eastern limits of the battleground and the failure to mention Wolverhampton may throw the line of battle between the town site and Bushbury Hill. The

---

[1725] VCH I 219.
[1726] Hackwood 1908: 5-10.
[1727] Duignan 1902: 97, 151, 169.
[1728] Mander and Tildesley 1960: 3.

heights of Tettenhall and the marsh near Wednesfield are probably the other limits. Perhaps this main battle took place on the Heath from Stow Heath to Old Fallings. This could be argued from Shaw's siting of the burial lows, but we have no archaeological evidence. No one could readily accept Mill Hill or Nordley Hill as being burial lows as they are igneous rock, but they may once have had lows upon them'.[1729]

Various publications, including in particular Staffordshire trade directories and general historical and topographical works from the late eighteenth century onwards, briefly mention the battle(s),[1730] but merely regurgitate in different ways conclusions reached by earlier writers, and, unsurprisingly, provide no additional information that might help to identify the site of the conflict.

More recent national historians accept unanimously that there was a single battle, and invariably associate it with Tettenhall, though few profess to have considered the location of the battle in any detail. Sir Charles Oman, an authority on medieval history, made a careful analysis of the relevant source material before stating in 1913: 'I cannot doubt that the two battles are identical, and that 910 is the real date', and decided that the battle had taken place between Tettenhall and Wednesfield.[1731] The doyen of twentieth-century Anglo-Saxonists, Sir Frank Stenton, concluded that the Danes'were overtaken at last near Tettenhall in Staffordshire, where the English levies won a conclusive victory. The raiding army was annihilated, and among its leaders three Northumbrian kings were killed', and adds in a footnote that the clearest account of this campaign is given by Æthelweard, who gives a precise date for the decisive battle and states that it was fought *in Uuodnesfelda campo*, that is, near Wednesfield.[1732] Dorothy Whitelock, an especially distinguished scholar of the period and near-contemporary of Stenton, speaks of a single battle of Tettenhall.[1733] F. T. Wainwright, a respected authority on Mercian and Scandinavian military and political matters in the north-west Midlands during the late ninth and early tenth centuries, referred cautiously to a battle at 'Tettenhall (or Wednesfield)'.[1734] Eric John, a leading scholar of the Anglo-Saxon period, placed a single battle at Tettenhall,[1735] while Alfred Smyth, an academic with a particular interest in the events and personalities of the later ninth and early tenth centuries, mentions a single battle of Tettenhall,[1736] and Richard Abels, an expert on military matters of the same period, concludes that one battle took place at Wednesfield, near Tettenhall.[1737]

Finally, in our search for clues to the site of the battle, we might consider the views of the eminent historian of battlefields, A. H. Burne, who writes of the battle of *Brunanburh* which took place in 937: 'We should expect Æthelstan to take up a position on commanding ground and also on a ridge running roughly at right angles to the direction in which he was facing. The position should also be astride of the road by which he was

---

[1729] Smallshire 1978: 23.
[1730] For example, Samuel Lewis's *Topographical Dictionary of England*, 1849 IV 495 says of Wednesfield: 'Edward the Elder, in 911, defeated the Danes here, when two of their kings, two earls, and nine other chiefs, were slain; and there were formerly two barrows on the supposed site of the battle, one of which has been levelled'. No reference to the battle is made in the entry for Tettenhall.
[1731] Oman 1913: 496-7.
[1732] Stenton 1971: 323.
[1733] Whitelock 1955: 36.
[1734] Wainwright 1975: 88.
[1735] John 1996: 91.
[1736] Smyth 1977: 192 fn.10.
[1737] Abels 1991: 148-9.

advancing. These two features seem common to all Anglo-Saxon battles of which the sites can be identified. As regards the second point, I believe armies in those days were more wedded to existing roads than we are apt to imagine, but have not the space here to substantiate my argument. As regards the predeliction for commanding ground, I believe there were three reasons: (1) that a charge downhill would have more impetus than one on the level; (2) that movements of the enemy prior to the battle could be better observed; (3) a position on the higher ground tended to induce heightened morale in the occupiers of it. So I attach considerable importance to these two features - a position astride a road and on commanding ground'.[1738]

Whilst many of Burne's writings are now derided, and not all his opinions should be dismissed out of hand, it seems unlikely that an army in the late ninth or early tenth century (or indeed at any other period) will have carefully selected the most advantageous position with the expectation that the enemy would choose to attack it there. There was no rule or (as far as we know) convention that dictated when one army should engage with another. Burne studied the Anglo-Saxon battles of Mount Badon, Deorham, Ashdown, Ethandon, Maldon, Assingdon, Stamford Bridge and Hastings (though not Tettenhall), but his conclusions about the site of pre-Conquest battles are somewhat weakened by his identification of the site of the battle of *Brunanburh* as the east bank of the river Rother, near Rotherham (now held on philological evidence to be unlikely),[1739] and, even more, by supposition and speculation based almost entirely on his fabled and subesquently much ridiculed 'Theory of Inherent Military Probability'on which many of his conclusions were based.[1740] It is evident that many of Burne's views as to the site of Anglo-Saxon battles are built on the most doubtful arguments and founder for want of firm, or, indeed, in many cases, any evidence.[1741]

[1738] Burne 2002: 74-6.
[1739] JEPNS 36 (2003-4) 25-38.
[1740] Williams 2016: 36.
[1741] For completeness, it may be noted that Geffrei Gaimar (fl.1136-7), probably a secular clerk of Norman extraction, wrote a poetic history of England in Norman-French (the first work of English history written in French, largely a translation of a version of the *Anglo-Saxon Chronicle* and other works borrowed from Robert of Gloucester, but there is slight evidence that he had knowledge of an official version of the ASC: Lavelle 2010: 182) for a Norman family in Lincolnshire shortly before 1140, and mentions that King Edward beat the Danes at Tettenhall: *Ke Eadward si combati, li reis; Od les Engleis k'il assemble, A Thuetenhale les mata*: Petrie 1848: 807; Stevenson 1854: I 771. Variants of the history give the names *Tutenhale, Tenetehale,* and *Thenethale*. No other information about the battle is given: Hardy and Martin 1889: I 145; Vol. II: 111; Bell 1960: 248.

29. Clues to the site of the battle of Tettenhall?

During the Anglo-Saxon period, various terms meaning 'battlefield' are found in literary and poetic sources, wills, charters, saints' lives, histories and chronicles, including *æscstede, beaduwang, campstede, feld, folcstede, herefeld, meotudwang, meþelstede, sigewang, wælfeld, wælstow, wælwang, wig* and *camp*.[1742] Some of those expressions are rare, if not unique, but among the more common are *folcstede, wælfeld, wælstow* and *camp*.[1743]

In that respect perhaps the most interesting clue to have come to light in the search for the possible site of the battle of Tettenhall in the greater Tettenhall/Wednesfield area is a field-name recorded in Wednesfield in the early sixteenth century as *Camp Feld*,[1744] a name of unknown antiquity but possibly of great significance.[1745]

The Old English word *camp* (from Latin *campus*) was applied in the Anglo-Saxon period to 'open land or field' in Saxon areas of the South-East and the Home Counties,[1746] but in Northern (Anglian) areas, such as Wednesfield, the element could mean 'battle, fight, contest, dispute'.[1747] The word is well attested, found, for example, in the great Anglo-Saxon epic poem Beowulf, the manuscript dating from c.1000, where the context clearly shows that the meaning is 'battle', and in the *Anglo-Saxon Chronicle* poem describing the battle of *Brunanburh* in 937.[1748] Some examples of *camp* might appear in place-names where the meaning 'dispute' may be more appropriate, but the word – which led to several other battle-associated dithematic terms (for example *camp-dom* (warfare), *camp-had* (warfare), *camp-ræden* (state or condition of warfare), *camp-stede* (place of battle),[1749] *camp-wæpen* (battle weapon), *camp-weorud* (fighting-men), *camp-wered* (an army), *camp-wig* (a battle), *camp-wudu* ('war-wood' = a shield)[1750] – seems to have fallen out of use at an early period. That very few *camp* place-names have been interpreted with the meaning 'battle' may partly be due to excusable myopia on the part of the investigator: no pre-Conquest (and many post-Conquest) battles, even conflicts of considerable magnitude,

---

[1742] TOE I 598.

[1743] Clark Hall 1960: 64; Pollington 1993: 27.

[1744] SRO D593/B/1/26/6/7/14. Examination of the deed confirms that the spelling of the name is correct.

[1745] By coincidence, the only other Camp Field traced in Staffordshire is recorded in Wednesbury in 1763 (WLHC record 457), presumably associated with *Campfield Lane*, recorded between 1776 and 1834 (SRO D1317/1/13/1/1/1-8), doubtless remembered in Camp Hill lane and Camp Street to the south-west of Wednesbury church. No evidence has been traced to suggest that those names are of great antiquity. The *bury* element in the place-name Wednesbury supports the latter interpretation here, and provides further evidence for the former existence of a hill-fort. Scott, not always a reliable authority, could see no traces of any 'large graff' at Wednesbury in 1832: Scott 1832: 332. In June 2009 it was reported that two ditches had been revealed by archaeologists in St Mary's Road, Wednesbury, possibly of Iron Age or Anglo-Saxon date: Wolverhampton*Express & Star*, 11th June 2009.

[1746] Clark Hall 1960: 64; S.528; Earle 1888: 182-4.

[1747] EPNE i 79; OED; TOE I 598, citing *campstede*; see also Gardner 1968: 4,106-8; Gelling 1997: 74-8; VEPN 135-6. Cognates include Danish *camp*, Swedish *kamp*, and Norwegian and Icelandic *kapp*.

[1748] Clark Hall 1960: 64; *Beowulf* line 2505: Klaeber 1950: 94; ASC 'A'; Earle and Plummer 1892-99: i 106.

[1749] Found in the well-known poem describing the battle of *Brunanburh* in 937: ASC 'A'; Earle and Plummer 1892-99: i 109.

[1750] BT i 144.

have been precisely located, and researchers would therefore have no cause to associate the word *camp* meaning 'battle' with a historic, and perhaps unrecorded or unidentified, transitory event.[1751]

Camp was, it is true, later reintroduced in the early modern period from French as a term for a military encampment or fort, and its use with reference to significant ancient earthworks is widespread from at least the eighteenth century, but from the relatively early record of the name *Camp Feld* in Wednesfield, and the absence of any recognisable archaeological features which might mark ancient earthworks, it must be very unlikely that it refers here to some vanished fortification, nor is it a term that might be expected to be associated with one of the post-Conquest moated homestead sites in the area, of which there was an exceptional concentration in and around Wednesfield.[1752]

Like *camp*, the word *feld* (also, of course, found in the place-name Wednesfield) is of special interest. In Old English the term was used for a large area of open land (cf. African *veldt*), more specifically 'unencumbered ground ... land without trees as opposed to woodland, level ground as opposed to hills, or land without buildings', and it was only later, probably during the tenth century, that it developed the meanings 'arable land', and, in about the fourteenth century, 'an enclosed piece of land', usually a piece of land enclosed by hedges or fences.[1753]

However, as noted in the list of battlefield words cited above, *feld* meaning 'the ground on which a battle is fought' is well-attested in Old English.[1754] Margaret Gelling, a notable specialist in English place-names, observed that some *feld* names include sites of battles and synods, and it is likely that the unemcumbered and accessible nature of the ground was

---

[1751] It has been suggested that Campden (Gloucestershire), Compton (Derbyshire) and *Nordkampe* (Nottinghamshire) – all in Midland England – might contain OE *camp* 'battle, fight, contest': EPNE i 79. 8 examples of *camp* are found in OE charters according to the Langscape website, accessed 9 November 2014: 4 in Sussex, 2 in Surrey, 1 in Hampshire, and 1 in Gloucestershire.

[1752] It should be noted, however, that Dodgson suggests that *le Campfeld*, recorded c.1468 in Knutsford, Cheshire, is 'probably from ModE *camp*, 'a camp', and feld', a judgment possibly influenced by the late-recorded name Camp Green (*Camp Field* in 1847) in Rostherne, Cheshire, which might refer to earthworks believed to have existed in the area: Dodgson 1970: 58, 76. There seems to be no reason why the Knutsford name should derive from 'a camp' rather than 'a battle'; indeed it has been noted that if it referred to earthworks, it would be a very early example of that meaning: Parsons and Styles 2000: 135-6. A derivation from ME *campin* (OE *campian*) 'fight, contend; play at football' (cf. ME *campinge* 'football match') for *camp feld* in Wednesfield cannot be ruled out completely, but is most unlikely, even though the OE word *lāc* (perhaps found in Lachefield, the name of the open field in this area discussed elsewhere) had a number of meanings including sometimes 'play, sport'. Janet Bately has analysed the vocabulary of the Anglo-Saxon texts, and found no instance of the word *campian* in early West Saxon prose texts, but there are examples in Wærferth's translation of *Gregory's Dialogues*, the *Martyrology*, and the prose *Guthlac*, all apparently texts of Mercian origin: Bately 1990: 291.

[1753] EPNE i 166-8; Gelling and Cole 2000: 269-74. It has also been suggested the *feld* may have been used by English speakers to rename Welsh territorial districts, possible examples being Welsh *Ergyng* in south-west Herefordshire, which was anglicised to Archenfield; *Tegeingl* in north-east Wales, anglicised to Englefield; Ightfield in Shropshire, with an unexplained pre-English first element also found in the river-name Giht; as well as Lichfield, which derives from Old Welsh *Luitcoyt*: Lewis 2007: 137-40; Gelling 2000: 275. The place-name Wednesfield, however, incorporates two OE words; no pre-English name is known.

[1754] TOE I 598. Curiously, the earliest recorded use of the term applied to a battle in OED is c.1300.

what made a *feld* suitable for the purpose of military or ecclesiastical encounter.[1755] This meaning was evidently understood and in general usage in Anglo-Saxon England. Although one recent study has concluded that 'It is notable that the landscape feature by which we tend to define conflict locations in modern vocabulary – the field – is only very infrequently implied in conflict toponymy by its OE ancestor term, *feld* ...',[1756] the evidence hardly supports that claim. We might note the battle of 633 in which Edwin of Northumbria was killed by Penda of Mercia was fought at Hatfield or Heathfield;[1757] the battle of 634 where Oswald of Northumbria defeated Cadwallon of Gwynedd was fought at Heavenfield (*caelestis campus*) near Hexham;[1758] the battle of 641 in which Oswald was killed by Penda was fought (according to English sources) at *Maserfeld*,[1759] or (according to one Welsh source) at *maes cogwy*, 'field of Cogwy';[1760] the battle of 655 in which Penda was killed by Oswy of Northumbria was fought at *Winwædfeld*;[1761] and the battle of Englefield (*Englafelda*) was fought in 870 between the English and the Danes, in which the English were the victors.[1762] William of Malmesbury gives the name *Brunefeld* for the battle of *Brunanburh*, the famous conflict between a confederation of Vikings, Scots and Celts who fought the English in 937 probably near Bromborough in the Wirral,[1763] charters and chronicles from the twelfth century have *Bruningafeld*, and John of Fordun from the fourteenth century, as well as Walter Bower, have variants of *Brounyngfeld*.[1764] It is very likely that the *feld* element in some, most, or even all of these examples denotes the site of a battle,[1765] and rather than describing the topography, refers to a significant military encounter that took place there.[1766] We should also remember that the Latin chronicler Æthelweard tells us that the battle of 910 was fought at *Vuodnesfelda campo*, the only

---

[1755] Gelling and Cole 2000: 269-70; Cavill 2008: 317. 116 examples of *feld* are found in OE charters according to the Langscape website, accessed 9 November 2014. Most are in the southern part of the country, doubtless due to the paucity of charter evidence for the north of the country.

[1756] Williams 2016: 44. Williams suggests somewhat cryptically that *feld*-names may well form a special category, citing from 'the few examples' Englafield, Heavenfield, and Wodnesfield as having the hallmarks of what have been catgorised as 'iconic' names, and which 'carry special significance through the words from which they are compounded': Williams 2016: 54 fn.88.

[1757] Whitelock 1955: 621.

[1758] Whitelock 1955: 623. Bede says of Heavenfield: 'which name it formerly received as a presage of what was afterwards to happen': Giles 1892b: 110.

[1759] Whitelock 1955: 151.

[1760] From a stray englyn appended as stanza 111 to *Canu Heledd*, dating from the ninth century: Stancliffe 1995: 85.

[1761] Whitelock 1955: 152.

[1762] ASC 'A': Bately 1986: 48. It has been suggested that the name *Englafeld* may have been adopted well after the event 'as part of burgeoning efforts to build a sense of English nationhood in the later ninth century': Williams 2016: 37.

[1763] Whitelock 1955: 278. The site of the battle remains the subject of ongoing debate by historians.

[1764] Cavill 2008: 317.

[1765] Major ancient *feld* names are relatively scarce in the Midland counties, with none in Huntingdonshire, 2 in Cambridgeshire, 1 in Bedfordshire, 6 in Northamptonshire (Cavill 2008: 269-70), but several in Staffordshire (Horovitz 2005: 603), though there is of course no agreed definition of what constitutes a 'major' name, and many 'major' names may have developed from a minor name. Whether any of those names could have derived from a battle is another question.

[1766] It is difficult, in the light of the cited evidence, to accept William's observation that 'It is notable that the landscape feature by which we tend to define conflict locations in modern vocabularly – the field – is only very infrequently implied in conflict toponymy by its OE ancestor term, *feld*, and may well form a special category for that very reason', citing Englefield, Heavenfield and Wodensfield from the few examples in Britain which have the hallmarks of Morgan's 'iconic' names, carrying 'a special significance though the words with which they are compounded': Williams 2016: 44, 54 fn.88.

occasion where he uses the word *campo*, translated in the standard edition of his work as 'field'.[1767]

In the name *Camp Feld* at Wednesfield, the use of *Feld* may point towards an early coinage, since by the sixteenth century *feld* might be expected to have developed into Modern *field* – by at least the fourteenth century the word field is normal in this area, and indeed *Camp Feld* is the sole example of the spelling *feld* to have been traced from any period in Wednesfield, which speaks of some antiquity – though we cannot know whether it was first used to describe a large unenclosed open area or an enclosed area used for cultivation: pasture was normally described in Wednesfield as *medo* 'meadow'. To the south of Wednesfield (the north of the village has not been investigated in similar detail) in the early modern period the word field is found attached only to the areas of the great open fields, and *Camp Feld* might conceivably represent the ghost of a much earlier and much greater area of the same name over which the open fields were created.[1768]

This analysis, however, conceals one possible fly in the ointment. It would be unconscionable to fail to mention a reference in 1352 to meadow and pasture lands called *camp'* – the apostrophe should be noted – somewhere in Walsall (possibly at Rushall, on the north side of the town),[1769] barelyfour miles south-east of Wednesfield, implying that the word was also applied in the area to meadow and pasture (though it may, of course, refer to a battle-site, though that must be most unlikely), and the possibility that *Camp Feld* in Wednesfield carried the same meaning cannot be discounted, though combining in such case two elements (*camp+feld,* 'meadow/pasture' + 'open land') in this way might be thought tautologous and improbable. Furthermore, if *camp'* were a common name for pasture very many other cases would be expected, whereas this seems to be a rare example, not just locally, but even perhaps nationally. The explanation is likely to be that the document in which *camp'* appears is written in Latin (like the document in which *camp feld* is recorded, with the place-names in English), and given the apostrophe or superscript notation at the end of the word – a typical scribal indication of abbreviation – is simply a shortening of the widely found Latin *campo* or *campus* 'field'.[1770] English *camp* and Latin *camp'* (*campo, campus*), as noted above, are not entirely synonymous, and not to be confused. On balance the tiny inked scratch superscribed at the end of the word *camp'* in the Walsall document is probably sufficientfor it to be discounted in this discussion, but the appearance of this expression must necessarily weaken to some degree the idea that *Camp Feld* memorializes the great battle of 910.

[1767] Campbell 1962: 53. Latin *campus* is found in compounds with the meaning 'battle' or similar: *camp remansit cum* (c.1347) is given to mean 'victory rested with', and *camp apertus* (c.1142) 'pitched battle': Latham 1965: 66. In Ainsworth's *Thesaurus Lingæ Latinæ Compendiarius* (1830: 480), the definition of *campus* includes 'a plain field, a plain or down', and 'a military camp, or place of exercise'.

[1768] One eminent philologist has recently suggested that several examples of *campfeld* which appear in OE charters may be appropriately translated as 'battle-site or hill-fort' (P. R. Kitson, *Anglo-Saxon Charter Boundaries*, forthcoming, cited in Parsons and Styles 2000: 136), though the present author has failed to trace any example of *campfeld* on the Electronic Sawyer database of Anglo-Saxon Charters, accessed 14 October 2014.

[1769] WLHC 276/17.

[1770] RMLWL 66. We might note that the field-name *Campo de Tettenhall*, which James P. Jones took as evidence for a camp or ancient earthwork, is recorded in Tettenhall in medieval documents: Jones 1894: 7. The name means simply 'field of Tettenhall'.

In short, then, it is very possible, though far from certain, that the name *Camp Feld* in Wednesfield provides direct place-name evidence of the great conflict of 910. Though philologists might quibble that if the designation had survived from the tenth century the word *camp* would be expected to have been affected by normal West Midlands sound changes where the rounding of *a* before nasals is evident fairly early, so that *camp* would become *comp*, as *man* becomes *mon*, it has been observed that for some reason this particular word seems not to follow that process.[1771] It may be, therefore, that the name *Camp Feld* was coined during the Anglo-Saxon or Middle English period (when the word was still used of battlefields)[1772] at a time when the site of a great battle was still well remembered, but if that were the case we might question why the term 'battlefield' was not chosen, as in the case of Battlefield near Shrewsbury with reference to the battle of 1403. The answer is that 'battle' is a Middle English word from Old French *bataille*, derived from Latin *battalia*, meaning gladiatorial exercises, so is a post-Conquest term and not contemporary or near-contemporary with the conflict of 910. We may be entitled to assume that the name *Camp Feld* was adopted at a relatively early date, certainly long before it was set down in writing in 1513. Despite the somewhat equivocal evidence, no-one attempting to pinpoint the site of an ancient battle could hope to trace a more significant name than *Camp Feld*.

So where was *Camp Feld*? The reference has been found, once only, in a quitclaim[1773] of 1513 of 'a croft called the Brech [from Middle English *breche* 'land broken up for cultivation]'[1774] lying between Camp Feld and the lane leading to the brook' in Wednesfield.[1775] That leads us to an unavoidably lengthy and somewhat tedious examination of the historical topography locally.

The first problem is to identify 'the brook', a task not as straightforward as might first appear. The earliest large-scale Ordnance Survey maps of the late nineteenth century contain a wealth of detail, but post-date the large-scale industrialization to the south of Wednesfield which affected all aspects of the landscape, including watercourses, many of which must by then have been diverted or obliterated. Even the survey map produced by Robert Dawson for the Ordnance Survey in 1816, of inestimable value in any study of the history of Wednesfield, shows no watercourses around Wednesfield – even Waddens Brook is missing.[1776] Yet a careful study of suspiciously sinuous hedgelines and spot-heights taken across the area (but bearing in mind recent changes to the surface topography) has made it possible to identify the low-lying routes of two 'lost' watercourses, in addition to Waddens Brook. We now turn to a mind-numbingly detailed study of those watercourses.

Waddens Brook ran from north-west of Moat House Farm and through that moat southwards, passing near March End on the east side of Wednesfield to merge north of

---

[1771] Were it not for the typical spoon-shaped valley or *cumb* at Compton Holloway, south of Tettenhall, which clearly gave the place its name, we might wonder whether that place could have been connected in some way with the great battle.

[1772] MED 105.

[1773] A quitclaim is a legal instrument whereby the owner of land transfers all interest to a recipient and relinquishes ('quits') all rights in favour of the recipient.

[1774] *Brech* is a term widely found (usually as *bruche*) throughout the area in the medieval period.

[1775] SRO D593/H/3/392. The quitclaim is included in the Sutherland Collection Papers at Staffordshire Archives showing that the land was once in the ownership of the Sutherland-Leveson-Gower family, which held many properties in Staffordshire, including the Wednesfield area.

[1776] BL online gallery of first edition 1" O.S. draft surveys.

Portobello with a stream – the river Tame – with its source at Stow Heath flowing eastwards, via the ancient *Kirnesford* recorded in Wulfrun's charter,[1777] around the south of Willenhall village to form a headwater of the Tame.[1778] The name *Wademorebroke* and other names incorporating it are found several times in medieval deeds,[1779] but except for *Caldwall*, dealt with below, no other stream-name has been traced in the area.

We would seem safe in assuming that the name Waddens Brook, surprisingly untraced before 1889,[1780] is a corruption of *le Wademorebroke*, meaning 'the brook associated with the moorland or marsh with the wade or ford' (from Old English *wæð* and *mōr*).[1781] The name *Wademorebroke* is not found after the eighteenth century, and evidently evolved into Waddens Brook. Clearly *Wademor(e)* is to be associated with *Wademor next to the Willenhall-Wednesfield* road recorded in 1355,[1782] and *Wademorelone* (Wademorelane) recorded in Willenhall in 1367,[1783] which was probably the former name of the lane from March End (or possibly Broad Lane) to Willenhall, now Fibbersley and Wednesfield Road.[1784] *Wademorefordehende*, 'the end of the township towards *Wademoreforde*' in Willenhall is also found in 1368.[1785] As will be seen, *Wademoreforde* was possibly then further east, near the junction of Waddens Brook Lane and Broad Lane South.

Wademore was clearly a considerable area that extended southwards from the north side of what is now Waddens Brook Lane perhaps at least as far as Noose Crescent, the point where the stream crossed Noose Lane, and in the later thirteenth century was described as pasture enclosed with hedges and ditches, although at Domesday it seems to have been the site of an extensive area of woodland providing pannage, which developed into the larger area of woodland that by 1240 was known as the Priests' Wood (Prestwood).[1786] The area to the west of, and probably adjoining, *Wadmore* was *Southlowefield*, one of the great fields of Wednesfield. The precise location of the tumulus-like feature which gave its name to the field (also known as Windmill Field after a mill which stood on or close to the mound until at least 1808)[1787] is uncertain, but was probably just north of Planetary

---

[1777] Hooke 1983: 73-5.
[1778] 1:2,500 O.S. map 1889.
[1779] For example SRO D593/B/1/21/6/38/2.
[1780] 1:10,560 O.S. map 1889.
[1781] SRO D593/B/1/21/6/38/2; SRO D593/B/1/26/6/38/14. although of course many other streams and rivulets will have existed. Smallshire suggests that the name Waddens Brook may be derived from the surname Warin, citing *Warines Milnes* and (in 1376) *Waryn's Shute* (Smallshire 1978: 45, 47; *Warings Boradlands* [*recteBroadlands*?] is recorded in 1614: SRO D440/85[SF102]). That idea cannot be sustained. *Warynes Shute* recorded in 1376 was in Prestwood: Pat Rolls Ed. III 16 282.
[1782] SRO D593/B/1/26/6/3/15.
[1783] SRO D593/B/1/26/6/11/13.
[1784] The swine-fold mentioned as a boundary mark in Wulfrun's charter may have been in this general area: Hooke 1983: 71-3.
[1785] SRO D593/B/1/26/6/4/12.
[1786] VCH IV 45; Smallshire 1978: 44-5; Shaw 1801: II 150.
[1787] Job 1985; The mill is shown on Robert Baugh's map of Shropshire, 1808. *South Low field*, also known as *Windmill Field*, named after a supposed tumulus, lay at Mill Hill, Neachells Lane and Well Lane, with the mill, owned by Mr Hope, situated just north of Planetary Road: Smallshire 1978: 22, 53, 96. Mill Hill is marked on the 1889 1:10,560 O.S. map at 948991. There was waste belonging to the lord of the manor (the Earl of Bradord) in Well Lane and March End in 1702: Smallshire 1978: 94-5.

Road, and subsumed in the 1930s by the metal pressings factory of A. E. Jenks & Cattell Limited which was extended during the second World War.[1788]

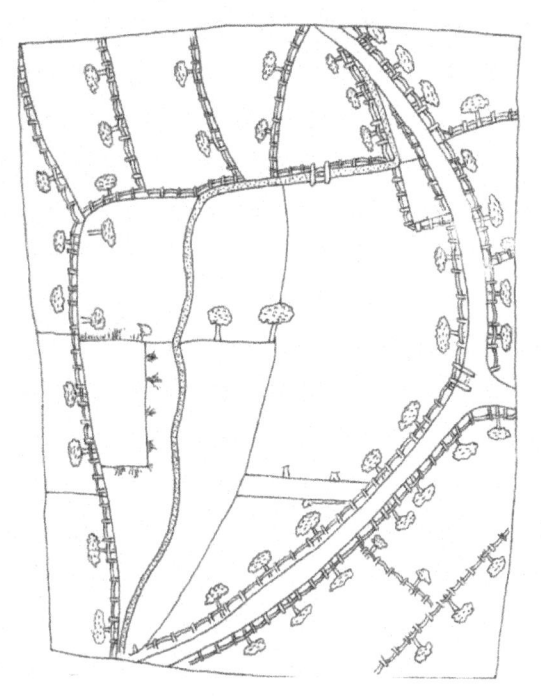

Re-drawn early seventeenth-century map (the 'Lilleshall Collection map') of the Fibbersley area south-west of Wednesfield, showing the junction of Noose Lane with the lane running south-east towards Willenhall. The rectangular field on the left may be *Kings Meadow* marked on a 1764 map of the area. Field-names and other writing on the original are not shown.

By fortuitous happenstance, an early map of an area to the south-east of Wednesfield has come to light in the vast Lilleshall Collection, recently acquired and carefully catalogued by Shropshire Archives.[1789] The archive was amassed by the Leveson-Gower family, who held land at Wednesfield, which explains the existence of a map of the area. The map, probably dating from 1590-1610 on palaeographical and other evidence,[1790] is the earliest known map of any part of Wednesfield, and deserving of particular study. Multicoloured and slightly worn, the Lilleshall Collection map, as we shall call it, is 17¼" x 15", drawn on parchment, and seems to have been trimmed or reduced with some loss to all sides, which probably explains why it carries no scale or title. One clue to its purpose may perhaps be gleaned from wording written across one of the fields towards the bottom of the map: *Parcell of the Mores wherein the destresse was taken*, implying that the area was the

---

[1788] Plot 1686: 415; SRO D593/B/1/26/6/2/1; Smallshire 1978: 53, 96, 130, 133; Wolverhampton HER 353.
[1789] SA collection number 972/7/1/48. The map has been digitised and published as a PDF file on the SA website, enabling it to be enlarged and studied in detail online.
[1790] Elements on the Wednesfield plan, including trees, fencing and colouring, mirror almost exactly a map probably to be associated with a lease dated 1603 of property in Claverley: SA 972/7/1/47 (plan); SA 972/2/1/87 (lease). The two maps appear to be by the same hand.

subject of a legal action for possession. Although schematic in nature and not easy to correlate precisely with later maps which were probably professionally surveyed, the Lilleshall Collection map is of particular interest (from our point of view) for a number of features, not least because the larger fields are labelled either *The great Mores* or *parcel of the Mores*, evidently the pasture called *le More* and *le More meadow alias Maggemedow* recorded in a quitclaim of 1517.[1791] Furthermore, the eye of faith may detect the words *Wadmore Lane* at the northern end of the lane which seems to be Fibbersley, the road from Broad Lane to Wednesfield Road, although the first word is admittedly very rubbed and indistinct. That lane may be associated with *Watmore Meadow* or *Walmore Meadow* – the handwriting is unclear – the name attached to a narrow strip of land at the northern end of Longer Moor, on the south side of Waddens Brook Lane and bisected by the brook, listed in the Tithe Apportionment of c.1842.[1792]

But the most obvious difference from later maps is the course of Waddens Brook as it is shown on the Lilleshall Map. On a later, more detailed map of 1764 in the Sutherland Collection,[1793] described in more detail below, the watercourse runs south-west from what is now Waddens Brook Lane from a point some distance east of the junction with Fibbersley road, following the course of a reversed-S hedgeline. On the Lilleshall Collection map, however, the stream runs southwards from what seems to be the junction of Waddens Brook Lane and Broad Lane, neither of which are shown on the map.[1794] The former seems to have been known as Offley Lane, which is so-named on the map, from a Mr Offley,[1795] who is also named.[1796] After a short distance the brook turns 90° westwards to run straight for some distance, with a simple footbridge about half way along (apparently at the point where a trackway crosses the hedgeline on the Sutherland Collection map, both hedgeline and trackway surviving to this day), before turning 90° south and taking a slightly sinuous course south to meet Noose Lane, so-named on the earlier map.

From this it is clear that in the early seventeenth century Waddens Brook took a different course from that shown on the Sutherland Collection map, the Tithe Map and on later Ordnance Survey maps. Indeed, the ford where the road to Willenhall crosses the stream, which almost certainly explains the name of the brook, may then have been close to the junction with Broad Lane. The brook is unnamed on the Lilleshall Collection map, labelled simply *The Brooke runninge from Wadmore ... [illegible]... Mores*, with a triangular field in the north-east corner adjacent to the stream labelled *Brooke meadowe*.[1797] In other words the watercourse was then known simply as *The Brooke* (note the definite article),

---

[1791] SRO D593/B/1/26/6/38/2.
[1792] See Smallshire 1978: 48.
[1793] SRO D593/H/3/392.
[1794] It is worth noting that the ancient boundary of Wednesfield appears to have followed the line of a *dīc* ('ditch; an excavated trench whose purpose was either defensive or for the drainage of water': EPNE i 131-2), Hooke 1983: 72-5. The *dīc* may have been the former course of Waddens Brook, part of which is shown on the Lilleshall Collection map.
[1795] Sir Thomas Offley held land in Wednesfield in 1576 (Smallshire 1978: 79), and John Offley is mentioned in a Conveyance of 1702: ibid. 94-5. The Offley lands are assumed to have been near Alfred Squire Road and Bolton Road: ibid. 94.
[1796] The *suinsete* or swine-fold mentioned in the forged charter of Wulfrun of 994 may have lain somewhere in this area: Hooke 1983: 73-5. It may be noted that Domesday Book records pannage at Wednesfield: VCH IV 45.
[1797] *Broke Meadowe*, presumably the same field, is recorded c.1535: SRO D593/B/1/26/6/8/2; Smallshire 1978: 77.

and in that respect it will be remembered that the quitclaim of 1513 which mentions *Camp Feld* records that it was next to a croft called *the Brech* near a lane leading to *the brook*. The lane we seek seems to have run only to the brook, rather than between two named places.*Wademorelone* (Waddens Brook Lane) led of course to the brook from both directions, but if the lawyer preparing the quitclaim in which *Camp Feld* is mentioned had intended to refer to that lane, he would surely have used its name. Since he would have been concerned to avoid ambiguity, we might assume there was at that time only one lane leading to the brook, and that it had no name, presumably because it was the only lane and it was not close to a place with a name with which to identify it, though medieval estate boundaries are notorious for their casual vagueness.

Noose Lane is shown on the Lilleshall Collection map curving south-west in a wide arc to meet the brook. It is noteworthy that the 1517 quitclaim includes pasture called *le Noses*, from which Noose Lane, so-named on the Lilleshall Collection map, takes its name. Normally we might expect a nose-shaped topographical feature such as a mound or hillock to explain the name, recorded from at least c.1299 as *le Nous*,[1798] but none exists in this area, and the name probably derives from a misdivision of Middle English *atten wāse* 'at the muddy or miry place', *wāse* having become modern 'ooze'.[1799] Confirmation of the derivation may be found in a deed of 1518 that mentions *le Noces* at *le Mores*.[1800]

The Lilleshall Collection map gives a fascinating and invaluable insight into this part of Wednesfield some four centuries ago. Many of the fields are described as *parcell of the Mores* or similar, with a large undivided area (through which runs the *oulde Lane*) named as *The great Mores*, adjoining Noose Lane, providing some idea of the seventeenth century, and perhaps much earlier, landscape, with smaller hedged fields and enclosures beginning to emerge as parts of the moor were taken into husbandry – so creating *breches* – but the map incorporates no direct evidence that might help to identify the site of the battle of Tettenhall, unless the name *Kings Meadow* on the Tithe Map c.1842 is to be given more significance than it might deserve.[1801] On the other hand, it does reveal the existence of a lane then already old running towards the brook in this area, and the reference to *The Brooke* adds perhaps some weight to the possibility that *Camp Feld* may have lain in this general area. It is a rather curious coincidence that the mysteriously-named *Kings Meadow* lies in the precise area in which we seek clues as to the site of the battle.

We now turn to the 1764 map mentioned above, which is included in a survey of sixteen parcels of Sutherland family landholdings, and was perhaps prepared as an enclosure map.[1802] It incorporates most of the area covered by the Lilleshall Collection map, but the latter includes land on the east of Waddens Brook which is not included in the Lilleshall Collection map.[1803] The Sutherland Collection map shows twelve fields with their

---

[1798] Smallshire 1978: 46.

[1799] EPNE ii 247.

[1800] SRO D593/B/1/26/6/38/12.

[1801] Other field-names incorporating King are supposedly connected by tradition with medieval rulers (see, e.g. Foxall 1980: 56), but is seems unlikely that the Wednesfield name is of great antiquity, though it may of course commemorate local tradition.

[1802] SRO D593/H/3/392. The map is impressively accurate when compared with the 1889 6" O.S. map, with the detail including gates in fields and individual trees.

[1803] The lane now known as Waddens Brook Lane is not shown on the Lilleshall Collection map, merely the southern boundary of the lane, against which properties were later built on purprestures at the eastern end, with the modern lane running on the north side of those properties, but we have Yates's map of Staffordshire, 1775, to confirm its existence at that date and the reference to *Wademorelone* in 1367 to show that it existed then.

acreage,[1804] the largest over 11 acres in area, the smallest on the eastern edge containing a building which was probably a house,[1805] together forming a bloc of over seventy acres, with each field, except the smallest, labelled *Longer Moor* or *Longer Moors*. The name may imply the existence of another, 'shorter', moor, perhaps *Wademore* which we have seen lay both to the north and south of Waddens Brook Lane. The age of the name *Longermore* is uncertain, but it may perhaps be the land recorded in 1382 in a feoffment relating to a piece of land at *Wademore* called *Le Longemedewe*.[1806] In 1517 a quitclaim[1807] of land in Wednesfield mentions *the More, the More Meadow alias Maggemedow* (possibly *Longermore* recorded in 1764), as well as a small plot of pasture called *the Noses*, clearly to be associated with Noose Lane. From this we seem to have tenuous evidence that *Camp Feld* may have lain in or near the moor and probably near the Wednesfield-Willenhall road, not far distant from Noose Lane.

Redrawn extract from the 1764 map of Sutherland property known as Longer Moor in Wednesfield, based on Smallshire 1978, page 61. The northern boundary is marked by Waddens Brook Lane, the eastern boundary by Fibbersley and Noose Lane. The eastern part of the field marked X is named *Kings Meadow* on nineteenth-century maps.

[1804] The boundaries of the fields within *Longer Moor* suggest that it was divided at an earlier date into three fields before being further subdivided. If *Camp Feld* lay in this area, it may have been the field on the east, adjoining the brook.

[1805] The TA c.1842 names the fields here as *Big House Pasture* and *Little House Pasture*: SRO S.MS.430/26.

[1806] SRO D593/B/1/26/6/6/3. A feoffment was a transfer of rights to land or property (the 'fee' or 'fief') which extinguished the rights of the grantor and allowed the grantee to sell or pass the rights to his heirs. It must be acknowledged that *Camp Feld* may have been disposed of after 1513 but before the Sutherland Collection map of 1764 (and Sir John Leveson, whose ancestors may have held *Camp Feld*, appears to have sold all his anciently inherited Staffordshire land in the late 16th century, except for one cottage in Wolverhampton: SRO D-868-1-67 (31/553)), in which case the suggested link with Longer Moor could not be sustained.

[1807] SRO D593/B/1/21/6/39/10. One of the parties was James Leveson, Merchant of the Calais Staple.

Longer Moor evidently lay within and to the west of an area enclosed on the north and east by Waddens Brook Lane, Fibbersley, and Noose Lane,[1808] and the western boundary seems to have been Waddens Brook. The north-western extremity reached what became Shed Farm, which at the turn of the nineteenth century lay in the bend of Waddens Brook Lane south of March End Road. Waddens Brook appears to have flowed south-east through the Moor, its line marked by a sinuous hedgerow, and the south-western boundary, which may have reached Watery Lane, seems to have followed the line of the brook. The central part of *Longer Moor* is identified as *March End* on William Yates's map of 1775, a name derived from *Marsh End*, meaning 'the end of the village towards the marsh', recorded as *Marshend Meadoe alias Launne Meadowe* in 1652,[1809] and found as *Merch* in the thirteenth century.[1810] Since we know that *Camp Feld* was separated from the lane leading to the brook by a croft called *the Brech*, is it possible that one of the fields on the central part of the west side of *Longer Moor*,[1811] on the east side of Waddens Brook, was formerly known as *Camp Feld*? The c.1842 Tithe Map of the larger area of what was Longer Moor shows mundane names (e.g. *Round Meadow, Far Piece, Big Field, The First Moor, The Second Moor*) for the individual fields, but we have seen that the central field on the west side,[1812] evidently sub-divided since 1764, is named, intriguingly, *Kings Meadow*,[1813] the significance of which is not known – it may perhaps have been occupied by a man surnamed King, although no evidence has been traced of a family of this name in the area – but there is no indication that the name is of any great age.[1814] Nevertheless, the name is strikingly out of place with the other names, and given its location it is tempting to speculate that it may have ancient origins.

Perhaps the most unexpected revelation from the two maps discussed above, apart from the way in which Waddens Brook has altered its course, is that local field-names, generally known for their longevity, changed from the early 1600s (the date of the Lilleshall Collection map) to the 1764 map, and again on the c.1842 Tithe Map, but all incorporate references to areas named Moor.[1815] As we have seen, the western boundary of *Longermore* in 1764 was seemingly Waddens Brook itself, land on the west side shown on the Lilleshall Collection map no longer forming part of it. At that period the word moor had two meanings, 'a marsh, fen or tract of low watery land', and 'a large heath, common or waste ground, where nothing but turf or other vegetables grow without cultivation'.[1816] In that respect we may recall part of the description of Wednesfield given in Smallshire's history of the area: 'To the direct east and south east of Wednesfield village runs Waddensbrook, tributary of the river Tame, itself a main feeder to the Trent. Much of

---

[1808] Fibbersley is recorded as *Fibrychelleye* in 1459 (SRO D593/B/1/26/6/12/27), *Fyburslye* in 1511 (SRO D593/B/1/26/6/7/9), and *Fibbersleys* in 1520 (SRO D593/B/1/26/6/38/10). The derivation of the name is uncertain, but it perhaps incorporates the ME name Filberd, from OF *Filuberht*, OG *Philibert*: Reaney and Wilson 1997: 168.
[1809] WLHC 35/1/10.
[1810] Mander and Tildesley 1960: 29.
[1811] At approximately SO 95659955, to the north-west of Willenhall Town Football Club.
[1812] Numbered 329 on the TA and Tithe Map: WSL S.MS.417/187. The Apportionment is WSL S.MS.430/26..
[1813] WSL S.MS.417/187; WSL S.MS.430/26; SRO D593/H/3/399. No other reference to the name has been traced.
[1814] A conspicuously rhomboid-shaped field labelled *parcel of the Mores* is shown on the Lillehall map in this approximate area.
[1815] For medieval field-names in the Wednesfield area see also Shaw 1801: I 150.
[1816] From two 18th century dictionaries, Barclay's *English Dictionary* and *A Compendious English Grammar*.

the area in the vicinity of the brook was formerly called the Moors or the Marsh, from which March End is derived, and an earlier hamlet called Moor End (now untraceable)'.[1817] What is clear is that this area was formerly an area of boggy pasture and meadow with woodland stretching along Waddens Brook, with the landscape accurately preserved by the name March End on the east side of Wednesfield, recorded from at least 1658,[1818] and probably much older still.

If we are correct in imagining that *Camp Feld* may have been somewhere in the general area of Waddens Brook, probably towards the west and not far distant from 'the brook', the theory may be strengthened by the fact that the Leveson-Gower deeds dating to the early decades of the sixteenth century, of which the 1513 quiclaim forms part, seem to relate, so far as the holdings can be identified, virtually exclusively to an area between Wednesfield and Willenhall. Since the name *Camp Feld* has been traced only once, it is likely that in 1513 the *feld* was relatively modest in size, but if the word *feld* had been adopted in the pre-Conquest period or soon after for a large area of open ground, *Camp Feld* was perhaps the surviving fragment of a much larger area of the same name, possibly integrated into adjoining fields in the sixteenth century.[1819] We might also suppose that it lay a little way from Wadmore, since areas adjoining the stream were long known as The Mores, and perhaps unlikely to be part of a *feld*.

It will be recalled that *Camp Feld* is mentioned in the extract which reads *a croft called the Brech lying between Camp Feld and the lane leading to the brook.* Running westwards from the central part of Noose Lane on the Lilleshall Collection map is a wide strip coloured blue and labelled *an oulde Lane in the Mores*, which heads directly towards the brook, but stops short at a boundary which seems to be the central spine field-line running north-east to south-west on the Sutherland Collection map. Any continuation would have reached the southern part of an almost rectangular field (an unusually regular shape) which seems to have formed part of the intriguingly named *Kings Meadow* mentioned previously. Possibly that was the lane mentioned in the quitclaim with which *Camp Feld* is to be associated – perhaps as a counterpart on the west side of Waddens Brook – with the *oulde Lane in the Mores*, which is difficult to identify but which may be what became the eastern part of Watery Lane, unmarked on the 1764 map.[1820]

Names incorporating *breche* (from Old English *bryche*, 'land broken up for cultivation', in the main a heathland term),[1821] were not uncommon in this part of Wednesfield. *Wadmore* lay on the north and south of Waddens Brook Lane, and *Tybotebruchenext to Wademorelone*, recorded in 1367,[1822] evidently adjoined that lane, but since it is mentioned

---

[1817] Smallshire 1978: 9. Could this be 'a certain hamlet ... called Mora' recorded in Wolverhampton (Stowheath) in 1242 (SHC 1911 144)? March End appears as *Marshend* on the 1st edition 1" O.S. map of 1834.
[1818] Smallshire 1978: 84.
[1819] No clue to the location of *Camp Feld* can be obtained from field-names in the Wednesfield TA of c.1842 (WSL S.MS.430/26).
[1820] Though the 1764 map has an intriguing field boundary. Curiously, on the first edition 1" O.S. map of 1834 Noose Lane stops at Watery Lane and does not continue further south, yet that continuation is shown on the Lilleshall Collection map and William Yates' map of Staffordshire, 1775. Watery Lane was not developed as a modern road until 1966: Smallshire 1978: 104.
[1821] PN Sa IV xviii.
[1822] SRO D593/B/1/26/6/11/13. Tibbots is a family name recorded in Wednesbury in 1773: SRO B/C/5/1773/167.

again as *Tibbots Bruche* in 1520,[1823] it is unlikely to be *the Breche* of 1513, for the name *Tibbots Bruche* would presumably have been used. A more likely candidate must be *le Wademore Bruche*, recorded in 1517 and as *Wadmore Birch* in 1627.[1824] If nothing else, the name *the Brech* indicates that *Camp Feld* probably lay a little distance from the Wednesfield, for land close to the village will have been taken into cultivation at an early date as part of the great open fields (unenclosed until c.1765),[1825] with the marginal and poorer land included at a later date, although we do not, of course, know the period at which *the Brech* was so-named: it may date from a relatively early period. Furthermore, the *feld* element in *Camp Feld* probably tells us that it was not part of Longer Moor, where names incorporating *field* – in this area probably implying cultivation – are not found. Our search for the site of *Camp Feld* must turn elsewhere.

The deed of 1627 that mentions *Wadmore Birch* also separately mentions *Hobs Gate at Wednesfield Townsgate*, the area on which Hart Road, south of March End Road, is said to have been created, on the west side of Wadmore. The reference to Hobs Gate might possibly support the idea mentioned above (though the evidence is admittedly slight) that the lane to the brook was a lane to the west of Wadden's Brook, in which case *Camp Feld* would perhaps be somewhere to the west, perhaps in the general area of Neachells.[1826]

That leads us to consider the first of the two 'lost' watercourses identified in the area to the south of the higher ground of Wednesfield village. Low spot heights and meandering field boundaries suggest that a watercourse may have run south-east from somewhere near Well Lane, though the only evidence detected on early maps is what might be slight traces of the southern end of the stream, which seems to have run into the moat of Merrill's Hall, then from its south-east corner to meet Waddens Brook on the north side of the former Merrill's Hole Colliery.[1827] What makes that watercourse of particular interest is the lane which ran south, parallel with Neachells Lane, from the site of the Falcon Inn in Waddens Brook Lane past Merrill's Hall, continuing south to meet the western part of Watery Lane. The lane has long been known as Merrill's Hall Lane, but the Merrill family are unrecorded in Wednesfield before the seventeenth century, and the name must be relatively modern. The site of Merrill's Hall is of some antiquity, with the ancient farmhouse of that name lying within a moat, recorded as L-shaped with arms of 130' and 50', but evidently once rectangular and very much larger,[1828] all now obliterated by modern development, and nothing more has been discovered about its origins or history. However, a deed of 1359

[1823] SRO D593/B/1/26/6/38/2; Smallshire 1978: 79. *Tibbots Bruche* is recorded with *Longheyen alias Longeypoles*, *Ardersleys*, *Thornhursts*, and *Fibbersleys* (SRO D593/B/1/26/6/38/10, SRO D593/B/1/26/6/38/11), all evidently in the same general area, if not adjoining each other.
[1824] SRO D593/B/1/21/6/39/10; Smallshire 1978: 79.
[1825] Smallshire 1978: 54.
[1826] Hob's Gate (not to be confused with Hobgate Road off Woden Road) is marked as the eastern end of field no. 586 on the west side of Merrill's Hall on the 1887-9 1:2,500 O.S. map. Hart Road is said to have been created on land known as Hob's Gate, recorded in 1627, supposedly associated with elves, goblins, fairies and devils, from OE *hob*, *hobbe* 'a hobgoblin': Smallshire 1978: 68, 79; Foxall 1980: 67. Hope's Gate works is said to have taken its name from Hob's Gate (VCH I 368; HER 2533; Smallshire 1978: 68, 79), or Hob Croft (WA I: 137), but a member of the prominent Hope family, long recorded in Neachells (see WA I: 135-47), is said to have owned the nearby windmill, and Hob is probably from a personal name, though OE *hobb(e)* meant 'a tussock of grass': Foxall 1980: 67; Field 1982: 105. Merrill's (or Merol's) Hall moated site which lay at the eastern end of Hart Road, now subsumed by modern development, has an obscure history, but Merrell is a local surname recorded from at least 1603: Smallshire 1978: 81.
[1827] 1887-9 O.S. 1:2,500 map; Smallshire 1978: 68.
[1828] Smallshire 1978: 68; 1:2,500 O.S. map 1889.

describing the boundaries of Neachels refers to the highway from Wednesfield to Birmingham (probably Neachells Lane) on one side of the estate and by *Stomfordeslone* (almost certainly a misreading of *Stonifordeslone* 'the lane with the paved ford') on the other,[1829] possibly to be identified as Merrill's Hall lane.

Neachells is an ancient estate recorded from at least 1293.[1830] The name is from Old English *$\bar{e}cels$ 'an addition, land added to an estate' (from $\bar{e}aca$ 'addition, increase'),[1831] probably here denoting the gradual clearance of land creating areas known as *breche*, of the type recorded in the 1513 quitclaim that mentions *Camp Feld*. The N in Neachells comes from *atten* 'at the', where the expression *atten ēcels* has become mis-divided.[1832] Neachells was evidently an area of some importance in the later medieval period, for no fewer than three moats are recorded in relatively close proximity, two (Old House Moat and Neachells Hall) on the west side of Neachells Lane opposite Watery Lane, and a third (Neachells Farm) on the west side further south.[1833] All traces of the moats and the buildings associated with them have now been subsumed beneath modern development. Land in *Le Echeles* between *Stomfordeslone* and the highway from Wednesfield to Birmingham and between *Muchelbruch* and the lane called *Bredenebruggelone* is mentioned in 1371.[1834] *Bredenebruggelone*, 'plankbridge lane', from Old English *breden* 'made of planks' and *brycg* 'a bridge', could then have been the older name for Watery Lane, which may have run only to Waddens Brook: it will be remembered that the Sutherland Collection map shows what may be the eastern end of that lane which does not continue west. *Muchelbruch*, 'the big(ger) *breche*', from Old English *mucel*, may have lain to the north or south of Watery lane and may possibly have been the *breche* associated with *Camp Feld* or at least not far from it, and in any event tells us that ground cleared for cultivation – *breche* – certainly existed in the immediate area by the later fourteenth century.

If the above identifications are correct, that leads to the possibility – though no more than a possibility – that *Camp Feld* lay somewhere close to Neachells and the stream that ran through it, which supports the tentative conclusion reached previously based on a consideration of the Sutherland Collection map and the 1764 map of Longer Moor. It will be recalled that the 1513 quitclaim that mentions *Camp Feld* is actually of 'a croft called the Brech lying between *Camp Feld* and the lane leading to the brook'. Since that croft is recorded in the Sutherland deeds we must suppose that it lay outside the Neachells estate, not known to have formed part of the Sutherland holdings, which evidently covered Longer Moor and several smaller areas scattered around Wednesfield.[1835] But there is no reason why *Camp Feld*, or indeed 'the lane leading to the brook', must have been within the Sutherland holdings, although if not, they were presumably not far distant. *Camp Feld*, therefore, was quite possibly near Merrill's Hall Lane (which seems to have formed the eastern boundary of Neachells), either on the west within Neachells, or on the east outside Neachells, and on the west side of Longer Moor, possibly near Watery Lane. And by a

---

[1829] Identified by Mander as 'the lane running north from the present Summerford', the identity of which is not readily apparent: WA II 91 fn3.
[1830] Horovitz 2005: 405.
[1831] Horovitz 2005: 405.
[1832] W. H. Duignan, writing in 1912, noted that a family in Wednesfield still used the surname Echelles, rather than Neachells: Duignan 1912: 89.
[1833] Brief details of the moats, which appear on Robert Dawson's survey of 1816 (BL map collection), are given in Smallshire 1978: 67. For the Hope family of Neachells see Smallshire 1978: 84-5.
[1834] Pat Rolls 32 Ed. III 95-6.
[1835] Smallshire 1978: 54, 57-61.

curious coincidence – if coincidence it be – the enigmatic *Kings Meadow* was also in the same area. Indeed, *Camp Feld* and *Kings Meadow* may not inconceivably have been the same place. And that is probably as close as we are likely to get to identifying the location of *Camp Feld*. On the other hand, it should be said, *Camp Feld* may have had no connection at all with either the battle (a case has been put forward elsewhere in this volume for a site anywhere within a great *feld* extending perhaps from Finchfield to Wednesbury) or with the Neachells area: both the lane and the brook with which it is recorded may have been elsewhere. It is left to others to form their own views.

The second of the 'lost' watercourses ran south from the spring at the head of Well Lane in Wednesfield village to join Waddensbrook somewhere to the south-east of Neachell Farm,[1836] and its course is less problematic: it is clearly shown on the 1927 1" Ordnance Survey map, but the area was then heavily industrialised, and it may have taken a rather different course in medieval times. The watercourse is probably to be associated with land in *Church Withies* called *Coed-Well Flatt* [sic], recorded in 1702.[1837] The Tithe Map c.1842 shows *Caldwell* as field 468 north-east of Neachells Hall and south-west of Wednesfield village, probably connected with *meadow called Caldwallemore* recorded in 1340.[1838] *Caldwell* is the common stream-name 'cold spring or stream', from Old English *cald wælle*. *Caldwell* and *Caldwallemore* will be mentioned again below.

The name *Church Withies*, though, is of particular interest and, with other place-names, helps to build up a more detailed picture of the area lying south of Wednesfield in the centuries following the battle of Tettenhall. That evidence includes in particular the field-name *Chirchezordesfeld at Walgrene* recorded in Wednesfield in 1399.[1839] The meaning of *Chirchezordesfeld* is clearly 'the field associated with the churchyard', with the element *feld* perhaps carrying its older sense of 'open ground', rather that its modern sense of an enclosed area of pasture or cultivation. The location of *Walgrene* has not been traced, but the spelling (if not an error for *Wallegrene*, from Mercian Old English *wælle* 'spring, well', which is very possible, perhaps referring to *Coldwall*) might point towards a possible derivation from Old English *wæl*, *wel* 'a corpse', usually found in a collective sense 'the slain',[1840] with Old English *grēne* 'a grassy area',[1841] so perhaps meaning here 'the grassy area associated with the slain'.[1842] The names John ate *Walle* (probably the spring in Well Lane, but possibly *Caldwall*) and Willi *Echeles* (Neachells) also occur in the 1399 deed, and may provide some support for a derivation of *Walgrene* from Old English *wælle* and

---

[1836] 1887-9 O.S. 1:2,500 map. The course of the watercourse can be traced from low spot heights obtained from www.daftlogic.com accessed 29 September 2015. The well (i.e. spring) of Wednesfield is recorded c.1272: SHC 1999 175.
[1837] Smallshire 1978: 95.
[1838] SRO D593/B/1/26/6/2/11.
[1839] SRO D593/B/1/26/6/6/15. The name *Churchyard Piece* is recorded as Field 21 in the Tithe Award of 1842, but adjoins the present Willenhall church, from which it takes its name, and can have no connection with *Chirchezordesfeld*.
[1840] EPNE ii 237 suggests that the word may be found in the name Wellesbourne in Warwickshire, with Mercian *wel* alternating with *wæl* in the spellings which are otherwise difficult to explain (see also PN Warwickshire 286), though Ekwall was evidently comfortable with the derivation 'Wealh's stream' or 'the stream of the Britons' (Ekwall 1960: 504), and Watts prefers OE *wæl*, *wel* 'a deep pool', or possibly the personal name Wealh: Watts 2004: 660. No deep pond is known or likely in the *Walgrene* area.
[1841] Other than in place-names the word *grēne* is unrecorded before 1300: EPNE i 209. Thomas of the Grene and John at Walle in Wednesfield are recorded in 1428: SHC XVII 121.
[1842] As noted, two of several Anglo-Saxon terms for a battlefield were *wælfeld* and *wælstow*: Clarke Hall 1960: 393.

also a clue to the general area in which we should seek *Chirchezordesfeld at Walgrene*, but the possibility that *Walgrene* is to be associated with the battlefield cannot be entirely discounted: it is true that Old English *wæl*, **wel* seems not to have been definitely traced in any other place-name, but (like *camp*) the explanation may be due to the ephemeral memory of most battle-sites, rather than philological reasons.

Other clues help us to identify *Chirchezordesfeld*, which is to be associated with *Chirchewythiesfeld* (which must be connected with Church Withies mentioned above) recorded in 1312,[1843] since it is found as *Chyrchewythyesfeld at Walgrene* in 1334,[1844] and *Churchwythas* extending on the *Churchway* (the latter a significant name) in 1615.[1845] The precise location of *Chirchezordesfeld* has not been identified, but we have seen that *Chirchewythesfeld* included land called *Caldwell*, recorded from 1340, north-west of Neachells Hall. The nature of the ground here may be gleaned from a reference to meadow called *Caldwallemore* in 1340, a name incorporating Old English *mōr*, indicating that the area around Caldwell was, or had been, a moor, or barren wasteland.[1846] That conclusion is reinforced by a reference in the Plea Rolls of 1428 to *a place in Chirchefeld at Cornewalle mores yate called Foulsiche medewe*.[1847] *Cornewalle* is probably a phonetic variation of *Caldwalle*, and the entry evidently refers to a meadow at *Foulsiche* (Old English *fūl sīc*, 'foul or dirty watercourse', a very common stream-name)[1848] at 'the gate to Caldwall moor'. That reference is supported by a conveyance of 1702 which mentions 'a place called Fullsuch', doubtless to be associated with a bridge recorded as *Fulebrig'* and *Folebrigge* between 1262 and 1271.[1849] The watercourse known as *Foulsiche*, wherever it ran – it may well have been the stream running south from Well Lane, with the bridge known as *Fulebrig'* on the lane south-west of Neachell Hall Farm – might conceivably be the brook linked to *Camp Feld*, in which case *Camp Feld* may, as posited above, have lain in the wider Neachells area.

The name Churchfield, one of the four great open fields of Wednesfield (evidently unenclosed until c.1765),[1850] to the south of New Cross,[1851] is of particular interest in this study, since it is not readily explicable, long predating the earliest church in Wednesfield, the church of St Thomas, consecrated in August 1750. It may simply record that the field was associated with the church of Wolverhampton, just as Deans Road records the interests of the Dean of Wolverhampton in the area.[1852] However, the existence of other

---

[1843] SRO D593/B/1/26/6/2/4.
[1844] SRO D593/B/1/26/6/2/6.
[1845] SRO D4407/85 [SF102]. Churchway may be the lane that ran west from Neachells Hall to the south of New Cross, or even of Neachells Lane itself: 1834 1" O.S. map. It is perhaps worth recording the apocryphal legend that the earliest church at Glastonbury was made from withies or wattles: Giles 1847: 22.
[1846] SRO D593/B/1/26/6/2/11; EPNE ii 42.
[1847] SHC XVII 121. Frustratingly, the translated extract from the Plea Rolls concludes with the words 'Several other pieces of land are here mentioned'.
[1848] See for example SHC 1909: 231; PN Sa III 209-10.
[1849] SHC 4th Series (1999) 36, 92.
[1850] Smallshire 1978: 54. The great fields of Wednesfield were Luchfield to the north-east, Windmill or Southlow Field to the south, Churchfield to the south-west, and Northlow Field to the north-west.
[1851] The deeds quoted in Smallshire 1978: 53, 94-5, seem to include land to the north and south of Wolverhampton road.
[1852] Smallshire 1978: 53, 56.

Church names here, including *Churchway*, makes that seem unlikely.[1853] The evidence, indeed, seems to imply the existence of a church in the area.

The 1399 deed in which the name *Chirchezordesfeld* appears describes it as adjoining an area of pannage called *hethelond*.[1854] Although there were many areas of heath in the area, Wednesfield Heath (marked *Heath* on William Yates' map of Staffordshire, 1775, and *The Heath* on Robert Dawson's Ordnance Survey drawing of 1816) gave its name to Heath Town, established in the mid-nineteenth century. The place known as *hethelond* might have been in the same area, or perhaps at Northlow Field: *Norlowefeld Super le Oldehet* is recorded in 1347,[1855] but it is impossible to know. One clue that must be relevant is that *hethelond* is described as an area of pannage, that is, an area of woodland providing acorns and beech mast for the feeding of pigs. But quite where woodland of this type existed in the area is difficult to say.

Before a new church was put up at Wednesfield the dead of the area would have been taken for burial to the churchyard at Wolverhampton,[1856] so the name *Chirchezordesfeld* cannot be explained as the burial-ground of local residents. But the name *Chirchezordesfeld* is of considerable archaeological significance, since if distant from a church such names were often applied to places where human bones had been discovered.[1857] The name implies that at some date before 1399 (the earliest *Chirche*–name given above is 1312), bodies were buried or bones were uncovered, presumably during the working of the land (and so not in areas of pasture or pannage), which were believed to be human, probably in or to the south of New Cross, within the open field called Churchfield.[1858] Furthermore, we are told that *Chirchezordesfeld* lay in *Walgrene*, with the possible derivation 'the grassy area associated with the slain'. The early reference to *Churchway*, 'the way to the church',[1859] is unexplained, but the evidence seems to point towards a place where bodies had been buried, or which marked the finding of skeletal

---

[1853] *Churchway* may conceivably have been the name of the most direct route to Wolverhampton church.
[1854] Smallshire 1978: 53.
[1855] SRO D593/B/1/26/6/2/4; SRO D593/B/1/26/6/2/17.
[1856] As confirmed by local Wills: see for example Smallshire 1978: 84.

[1857] See for example Foxall 1980: 58, which mentions fields named Church Yard in Alveley and Coreley (Shropshire), both remote from their parish churches, the first so-called because skeletons were once found there, and Horovitz 1992: 23, which notes *Churchyard Leasow*, perhaps *Churchyordfeld* recorded in 1494, by a large pit in countryside 2 miles west of Brewood. Another example of the name Churchyard referring to the discovery of bones is Wolverhampton Churchyard, a name in common use by 1686 for the Roman sites at Greensforge on Ashwood Heath, 7 miles south-west of Wolverhampton: Plot 1686: 406. The name Wolverhampton was applied to the place because Ashwood formed part of Wulfrun's endowment to Wolverhampton church c.994.
[1858] There is some uncertainty about the exact location of Churchfield, with contradictory opinions in Smallshire 1978: 53, 56, 79, 94, 95, but the evidence suggests it lay to the south of, but did not include, New Cross.
[1859] Could *Churchway* have been Strawberry Lane, which formerly continued west to meet Wolverhampton road between New Cross and Heath Town? The First Series O.S. 1" map shows the lane as a cul-de-sac, but later maps show the lane continuing south to meet Dean's Road near its junction with Julian Road. The First Series map (and Robert Dawson's 1816 survey drawing) show that from just south of the turn in the lane, another lane meandered north-west to join Wolverhampton Road to the south of New Cross. The age of those lanes lane is unknown – they may have marked the southern boundaries of Churchfield and (Wind)Mill Field, although field-boundaries running across the latter suggest that Deans Road was probably the boundary – but there is no reason to suppose they were not of some antiquity.

remains, perhaps even from a great conflict, on a site later marked by an early church, all memory of which is long lost. Is it coincidence that the area lies not far distant from Stow Heath,[1860] the *stow* element perhaps denoting an early religious foundation, and also a place of burial?[1861] The boundary between Churchfield on the west and Windmill Field (otherwise Southlow Field) on the east is unknown, but might possibly have been marked by the old footpath running south from the former Imperial Galvanized Iron Works, which lay near the junction of Well Lane and Wednesfield Way. If that is correct, *Chirchezordesfeld*, *Church Withies*, land called *Caldwell*, and *Walgrene* will all have lain to the west of that line, with *Camp Feld* (if the speculation given above could be correct) lying somewhere to the east.

Yet there is further slight evidence for the early history of this area that demands evaluation. That evidence is a hill in Churchfield with the name *Hildebaldes(c)hull* recorded in 1317 and again in 1348.[1862] The name is especially intriguing, and has left us with a significant mystery.

The hill-name clearly incorporates the male personal name Hildebald with the usual West Midlands form of Old English *hyll*.[1863] The two elements which make up the personal name in typical Germanic dithematic fashion (personal name + genitive *–es* + English generic) are Old German *hild*, 'war, battle', and Old German *b(e)ald*, 'bold, courageous, brave', so meaning 'battle-brave'.[1864] Both elements are commonly found in Anglo-Saxon personal names, Old English being a Germanic language – *hild* usually as a second element, described by a leading authority as a 'common theme' – but, most curiously and inexplicably, the two elements are rarely found recorded together in Old English.[1865] What is remarkable about the name is its rarity: few examples are recorded in England before the Conquest.

We know that that the hill called *Hildebaldes(c)hull*, or at least part of it, lay in Churchfield, which evidently incorporated an area of medieval ridge and furrow, said to have exceeded thirty acres[1866] and almost certainly very considerably more, south of New Cross, probably extending to Mill Field (*Northlow Field*) to the east, and the deeds that mention the name in 1317 and 1348 also mention (in the 1317 deed) *Echeles*, and (in the 1348 deed) two men, William son of Richard *del Echeles*, and Roger son of Wiliam *del Echeles*. In the earlier deed there is reference to a *selion* in *Hildebaldeshull*; in the later deed to *one selion in Chyrche[f]eld upon le Longeforlong in Hildebaldeschull* [*sic*]. *Selion* and *furlong* are both terms representing areas of cultivation, indicating that

---

[1860] Robert Dawson's drawing 1816 produced for the O.S. (BL map collection) shows Stow Heath on the south side of Willenhall Road at Moseley, but in the medieval period it is likely to have covered a large area to the north.
[1861] Hibaldstow in Humberside was adopted by the time of Domesday Book, the *stow* element marking the burial place of St Hygebald in the late 7th century Watts: 2005: 302.
[1862] SRO D593/B/1/26/6/2/5; SRO/B/1/26/6/15/14.
[1863] The single example in the *Prosopography of Anglo-Saxon England*, accessed 25 August 2015, is Hildebald, archbishop of Cologne c.784-818 and Charlemagne's influential friend and archchaplain.
[1864] Toller 1898: i 67; Insley 2013: 220, 222. Both *hild* and *b(e)ald* are well represented in names recorded in Searle 1897 and in the *Prosopography of Anglo-Saxon England*, accessed 25 August 2015.
[1865] Hildebald cannot be a Welsh, Scottish or Irish name.
[1866] Smallshire 1978: 56. The area is said to be marked as *House Piece* and *Bolton's Piece* on the 1842 Tithe Map: ibid.

Hildebaldes(c)hull was then cultivated.[1867] The later deed tells us that *Chyrche[f]eld* was in *Hildebaldeschull*, from which we must suppose that the latter was the name of a sizeable area of rising ground that incorporated at least some part, if not the whole, of *Chyrche[f]eld*.[1868] The quarrying, mining, industrial waste, reclamation and landscaping affecting the area over the last two centuries poses challenges when attempting to ascertain the surface topography several hundred years ago,[1869] but a pronounced and sizeable hill rising to 497' lies some 750' north-east of the junction of Deans Road and Friesland Road – higher indeed than the centre of Wednesfield, which is barely more than 480' – and (assuming that the ancient surface topography is reflected in the modern land surface, which might be unwise) must be the most likely candidate for *Hildebaldes(c)hull*, for it lies squarely within what we know of Churchfield.[1870] This may have been the site of the tumuli known as *The Low* (otherwise *Great Low*) and another known as *Littel Low* which seem from evidence from the Tithe Map to have lain some 650 feet to the south. From the high ground south of New Cross (which from its very regular and unnatural contours appears to have been substantially remodelled in recent years) the land slopes markedly east to Waddens Brook, broken by rising ground around Mill Hill, and an area of gradually rising land reaches over 442' in the Strawberry Lane area.[1871]

The rarity of the dithematic appellative Hildebald, combined with the rarity of hills in this area, might encourage the belief that what we have here, rather than a personal name, is a label attached to the most prominent hill on or near a battle site to commemorate the courageous deeds of the victors, so giving 'hill of the battle-brave'. Sadly, however, that idea collapses on philological grounds, for the hill-name is in the genitive singular form, showing it to be, extraordinarily, one of very few places recorded in England with the personal name Hildebald, which just happens to mean 'battle-brave'. What is clear is that whilst *hyll*-names with a masculine personal name are common, dithematic names are very rare, with only three examples recorded, and that *hyll*-names seem to date from the later period of Anglo-Saxon name formation.[1872]

[1867] *Le Longefurlong* is likely to be associated with *Longeforlong* in Wolverhampton recorded in 1349 and 1364. Two parties to the first deed are described as *de la heth*, and one to the second *atte Hethe*: SRO D593/B/1/26/6/17/3; SRO D593/B/1/26/6/19/1.

[1868] There is not the slightest ghost of the name detectable in the Tithe Apportionment, which shows that virtually all trace of ancient names had been replaced by the mid-19th century with prosaic names associated with heathland, mining, canals, railways, industry, quarries, marlpits, brewhouses, pubs, domestic buildings and gardens.

[1869] Another small area of raised ground can be identified between New Cross and Northlow Hill. The identification of the higher ground in the area is based on a close examination of Map 2, McC Bride et al 1997, and a particularly useful one-metre contour map produced by the O.S.

[1870] Heights taken from the daftlogic website, accessed 29 September 2015. The boundaries of Churchfield remaining uncertain, and it is unclear whether they encompassed New Cross itself, but it seems likely that the Wolverhampton road will have delineated the northern boundary. The highest ground in the area seems to be Nordley Hill, on the north-east side of New Cross hospital, which rises to 526'.

[1871] *The Low* is recorded as a field-name on the 1840 Tithe Apportionment, at SO 933993, and was probably 'the great lowe ... in the heath grounds': Shaw 1801: II 150. The description, quoted by Shaw from Huntbach (d.1705), is ambiguous, mentioning 'the Little lowe', still then visible, and 'the great lowe and the little lowe in the heath-grounds': ibid. The 'Lyttyl Lowe' at the Heath is recorded in 1537: SHC 1912: 93. Curiously, Plot 1686 mentions neither the great nor the little low.

[1872] Gelling and Cole 2000: 192. The 3 dithematic names are *Beornheard* (Barnsdale, Rutland), *Heardrēd* (Hartshill, Warwickshire), and *Wulfhere* (Wolvershill, Warwickshire): ibid.

The age of the personal name Hildebald cannot be determined – it was in use on the Continent at the end of the eighth century – but in England after the Conquest, Norman names (such as William, Robert, Richard, Ralph, Roger, Herbert, John, Hugo and Walter) were quickly adopted, and by 1317, when *Hildebaldeshull* is first recorded, Old English and imported Germanic personal names were greatly outnumbered by Norman names, though some Old English names, such as Edward, long retained their popularity.[1873] From this it is possible, though admittedly unlikely, that Hildebald is a post-Conquest rendering and rationalisation of the rare, though not unique, Old English personal name Hygeb(e)ald, of which a number of pre-Conquest examples have been traced,[1874] most of whom were probably churchmen, including a late 7th- or early 8th-entury abbot of Lindsey, and a bishop of Lindisfarne from 781 untilhis death in 803 during whose episcopacy Lidisfarne suffered the devastating attack by the Vikings in 893, the first recorded Viking assault on England,[1875] an episode recorded in a letter by Alcuin writing from the court of Charlegagne, and an attack which will surely have been known to Æthelred and Æthelflæd.[1876] There is not the slightest evidence that the hill-name *Hildebaldes(c)hull* in Wednesfield might be associated with any of these clerics. But why the name Hygebald might have been later understood as the Continental name Hildebald (if that is what happened) is not easy to explain.

So who was the Wednesfield Hygebald/Hildebald? Since his name became attached to a distinctive topographical feature mentioned in deeds more than three decades apart, we must suppose that he was of some renown (or infamy) or status locally. As we cannot know the period when the place-name was coined – though any hill-name created in the pre-Conquest period might have been expected to become abbreviated during the course of four centuries, in this case perhaps to Hibbelshull or even Huggshill or Hickshill or similar[1877] – the personal name was presumably well-known locally, with the hill-name adopted long after the Conquest, but it is difficult even to speculate about his identity. He may have been a landowner, agricultural worker, craftsman or artisan in this small and relatively obscure agricultural community,[1878] but unsurprisingly no such personal name is recorded in such local records as survive. That allows us to consider (with all the perils that conjecture poses) the engaging possibility that Hygebald could have been a prominent member in one of the divisions of the joint Mercian and West Saxon armies at the battle of Tettenhall who was remembered for his actions – even perhaps his death – on the battlefield, with his name attached to the hill where he fought and may have died.[1879]

[1873] Reaney 1997: xxii-xxiv.
[1874] Sweet 1885: 494.
[1875] Whitelock 1979: 844-6. The bishop is recorded in the *Prosopography of Anglo-Saxon England*, accessed on 23 November 2015, as Hygebald 2 and 3 respectively; Coates and Breeze 2000: 244. Searle records 6 men named Hygebeald, though the references are not necessarily to different people, and to two men named Hubald, all clerics: Searle 1896: 303, 310. ASC 'E' records that a Hygebald, about whom nothing is known, was killed in 710, but ASC 'D', supported by Gaimar, gives the name Sigbald: Whitelock 1961: 26; Greenway 1996: IV 223. A farmstead name *Hibaldestofte* is recorded in 963 in the West Riding of Yorkshire: PN WRY VIII (1962): 299. The name Hildebald is unmentioned in Jackson 1995. On the Continent the name has given rise to the later Hilboldt; in Belgium to Hildibald, Hillibold and Hellebold(us).
[1876] Preest 2002: 179.
[1877] Edmund McClure observed that '... Hygebald would naturally become Hygge or Hugga (represented in genitive form as Huggs, Hucks and Hicks) ...': McClure 1910: 133.
[1878] Domesday Book lists 6 villeins and 6 bordars with 6 ploughs (VCH IV 45), suggesting a population of perhaps 30 or so.
[1879] There is evidence that King Alfred employed mercenaries in his army: Asser says that 'many Franks, Frisians, Gauls, Vikings, Welshmen, Irishmen and Bretons' flocked to the King's court

Indeed, the supposed tumulus of *South Low* might even have marked his burial site, since the name *South Low* is untraced before the fourteenth century, perhaps implying that it replaced *Hildebaldeshull*, which has not been found after the fourteenth century.

That leaves us with the attractive idea that *Hildebaldes(c)hull* might conceivably represent a topographical war memorial unique in England, a hill-name coined at some date before the Conquest when the identity of at least one of the combatants (whose name might otherwise have been corrupted in memory with the passage of time) who had fought in the battle of Tettenhall was still remembered locally, a fighter destined to risk his life fighting against the pagan Northumbrians, whose actions became legendary in the area. And from the name *Hildebaldes(c)hull* we might, by an admittedly circular argument, have very tentative evidence that at least part of the battle of Tettenhall was fought at or close to *Hildebaldes(c)hull*, which might have been close, or even at, the site of the enigmatic *Camp Feld*, for the former lay within, and the latter either within or close to, Churchfield.[1880]

Yet the possibility that the name recorded in the fourteenth century might relate to a short-lived episode, however momentous, which occurred over four centuries earlier must almost certainly be discounted. Anglo-Saxon battle-sites are numerous, yet no comparable names have been traced elsewhere, and in any event a word denoting a battlefield is far more likely to have been attached to the area than an obscure personal name. And since the personal name in the hill-name had not become shortened in the usual way (as in Hibaldstow in Lincolnshire) by the date it is first found, the likelihood must be that it post-dates the Conquest and has a far more prosaic, and more recent, origin.

It is evident that most if not all of the pre-Conquest men named Hildebald and Hygebald were clerics (not unexpectedly, since most recorded names were those of nobles or churchmen attesting charters), which may have been a church-given name for a novitiate. A more likely – or, rather, less improbable – possibility, then, is that the eponymous Hygebald, far from being a tenth-century warrior, was a later churchman.

In that respect (and not overlooking the bishop of Lindisfarne who held office during the Lindisfarne attack in 893, an episode famed throughout northern Europe that would have had a particular resonance with Æthelred and Æthelflæd after the defeat of the Scandinavians at Tettenhall), we might consider in more detail Hygbald (sometimes Hybald or Hibald), the eighth-century abbot of Lindsey,[1881] the only man of this name

---

(Chapter 76; see also Williams 1999: 77), and the *Anglo-Saxon Chronicle* records that at a naval engagement between Alfred's fleet and the Danes in 896 a number of Frisians who were part of the English forces were killed, including three who are named and presumably held positions of some importance: Whitelock 1955: 189. It is known that Æthelstan had Scandinavians, including Egill Skallagrimsson if *Egil's Saga* is to be believed, amongst his forces at the battle of *Brunanburh* in 937: Pálsson and Edwards 1976: 118-31; Livingstone 2011; on mercenaries generally see also Halsall 2003: 111-8. There is no reason to imagine that Edward and Æthelred would not have employed mercenaries.

[1880] In that respect it is apposite to recall the words of John Smallshire: '... the pinpointing of a battlefield near New Cross is obviously nonsense' (Smallshire 1978: 23), and that Stebbing Shaw believed that the battle of Tettenhall took place close to Willenhall (Shaw 1801: II 147), though his belief was evidently based on an incorrect derivation of the place-name which he thought incorporated an OE word meaning 'victory'.

[1881] Identified as Hygebald 2 in the *Prosopography of Anglo-Saxon England*, accessed 4 December 2015.

sufficiently distinguished to have become a saint with a developed cult. Described as 'a very holy and abstemious man',[1882] little is known of his life, but he is said, notably, to have been a friend of St Chad,[1883] bishop of Lichfield, and to have had a dream which foresaw the death of Chad's brother, St Cedd, whose remains are also said to lie at Lichfield.[1884] Hygbald's monastery was at or near Hibaldstow near Scunthorpe,[1885] or at Bardney,[1886] both in Lindsey, 'territory sometimes under Northumbrian domination, sometimes Mercian'.[1887] He is remembered in the place-name Hibaldstow, first recorded in Domesday Book, which perhaps commemorates his burial place.[1888] Though the suggestion that Hygebald was a friend of Chad appears to derive from a misreading of Bede,[1889] it may have been a belief current and widely known in the early tenth century: the *Old English Martyrology*, an incomplete collection of over 200 hagiographies of saints or groups of saints, probably compiled in Mercia or by someone who wrote in Mercian Old English no earlier than the late ninth century, associates only four saints with the midlands area: Chad and Higebald, and (unknown to Bede) Guthlac and his sister Pege.[1890] Chad, Higebald and Guthlac are included in *Godes Sanctum, þe on Engla lande ærost reston* ('God's Saints who first lay in England'), generally known as the *Secgan*, a list of saints' burial places recorded in manuscripts of the early eleventh-century.[1891] From the *Anglo-Saxon Chronicle* we can see how important it was to the Anglo-Saxons to memorialise the burial-places of those deemed worthy of commemoration, and equally that the burial-places of those with a dishonourable reputation should quickly be lost to history.[1892] The evidence shows that Chad, Higebald and Guthlac were especially honoured within Mercia: Chad associated with Lichfield, Higebald (whose name follows Chad in the list) with Lindsey, and Guthlac with Crowland.

Since we have another *stow* name (in Stow Heath) and *Chirche–* field-names close to *Hildebaldes(c)hull*, we may be entitled to speculate about a link, albeit very tenuous, between St Hygebald (and his supposed friendship with the Mercian saint Chad) and Wednesfield, for it was of course from Bardney in Lindsey that St Oswald's relics were retrieved by Æthelflæd shortly before – perhaps less than twelve months before – the battle of Tettenhall (which took place on St Oswald's Day, 5th August) for reinterment at

---

[1882] He is presumed to have been the author of *Oratio Sancti Hygbaldi Abbatis* in the Royal Prayer Book: Sims-Williams 1990: 322-3.
[1883] Farmer 2003: 259.
[1884] Farmer 2003: 259; Thacker and Sharpe 2002: 520. The date and circumstances of Cedd's translation from Lastingham (Lincolnshire) to Lichfield are unknown: Thacker and Sharpe 2002: 520.
[1885] Stocker 1993: 101-22; Stocker and Everson 1993: 279.
[1886] Hart 1992: 241-2; Roberts 2001: 77; Thacker and Sharpe 2002: 539-40; Farmer 2003: 259; Blair 2005: 315-6. Hibaldstow and Bardney are 23 miles apart.
[1887] Roberts 2001: 77.
[1888] Cameron 1998: 63; Hadley 2000: 268-9.
[1889] Bede tells us that Hygebald was an abbot in the province of Bardney: McClure and Collins 1999: 178.
[1890] Roberts 2001: 77; Rauer 2013: 61, 226-7. Sources used by the *Old English Martyrology*, which is divided into monthly saints'-days, include the works of Bede, Aldhelm, Eddius, Adomnán, Gregory the Great, and Isidore of Seville, showing that the scribe had access to a significant library. Five principal manuscripts survive, but parts of January, and much of February and December are lost: Lapidge et al 1999: 303.
[1891] BL Stowe MS 944 f.34v.
[1892] A prime example from the period covered by this volume is *ætheling* Æthelwold, whose attempt to take the crown of Wessex from King Edward ended in his death (and that of his ally King Eohric of East Anglia) at the Holme c.903. We have no knowledge of the burial place of either.

Gloucester.[1893] We have seen that Æthelflæd and her husband were responsible for the active promotion of cults in the north Midlands, having 'espoused with enthusiasm the hagiographical legacy of the Mercian kingdom [and] ... especially concerned to rehouse royal saints in Mercian tradition in appropriate new communities within their newly fortified *burhs*.'[1894] Those saints and *burhs* included St Werburgh (Chester),[1895] St 'Bertelin' or Beorhthelm (Runcorn and possibly Stafford),[1896] St Oswald (Gloucester and Chester),[1897] St Alkmund (Shrewsbury),[1898] and possibly St Eadgyth (Tamworth) and (though not of royal stock) St Guthlac (Hereford), as well as St Mildburh at the abbey of Wenlock (where there was no *burh*).[1899] Of the four prominent Mercian saints, Chad had an existing dedication at Lichfield; Guthlac (buried at Crowland) seems to have been especially honoured at Hereford; and his sister Pega died in Rome and was buried there c.719.[1900] It would be idle to speculate whether, during the expedition in 909 to recover the relics of Oswald from Bardney, the mortal remains of Hygebald, the fourth saint, were also recovered from Hibaldstow, only 23 miles north of Bardney, readily accessible via Ermine Street, for reinterrment perhaps at Gloucester with Oswald – or even at the only other place which might conceivably bear his name, Wednesfield. Certainly not the slightest hint of such reinterrment can be detected in the *Secgan*, which records with convincing precision that Hygebald's body lies buried at *Cecesege/Cecesegi* (perhaps Hayes island) on the river *Oncel* (Ancholme),[1901] and the elaborate theory must be left in the air.

Though there is no evidence that a tenth-century *burh* may have existed in the Wednesfield area – which indeed is unlikely to have been seen as a prime site for a fortification – it is tempting nevertheless to speculate that a church for the souls of the English dead of the battle of Tettenhall could have been founded by Æthelred and Æthelflæd or a later ruler close to the battlefield at Wednesfield and dedicated (though he was admittedly not of royal stock) to St Hygbald,[1902] a church short-lived, to be abandoned, unrecorded, and lost

---

[1893] It is worth recording the observation of Clare Stancliffe and Eric Cambridge: '... there is also the complex question of whether Oswald was seen by his people, whose grasp of Christianity would at this stage have been tenuous, as being in some sense a sacral king, possibly one with a special relationship to Woden': Stancliffe and Cambridge 1996: 2.

[1894] Thacker 2001: 256. On the cult of St Oswald see generally Stancliffe and Cambridge 1996; for the New Minster at Gloucester see Heighway 2001. In 901 Æthelred and Æthelflæd donated land to the religious community at Much Wenlock and presented it with a valuable gold chalice in honour of St Mildburh (S.221); the body of St Werburgh was translated from Hanbury to Chester probably soon after its refortification in 907; and Æthelflæd probably also introduced the cult of St Oswald there at the same time. The remains of St Alkmund are also said to have been moved from Lilleshall to Derby, and supposedly from there to Shrewsbury (Foot 2006: 324), although the evidence is unclear: Blair 2002: 511, 549-50; Yorke 2003: 58; Lewis 2008: 114-5.

[1895] Thacker and Sharpe 2002: 557-8.

[1896] Walker 2000: 39; Thacker and Sharpe 2002: 515-6; Meeson 2015: 17.

[1897] Stancliffe and Cambridge 1995: 120, 246-7; Thacker and Sharpe 2002: 549-50.

[1898] St Alkhmund's was believed in the 12th century to have been founded by Æthelflæd: Eyton 1854-60: XI 355.

[1899] Foot 2000: 194; Thacker 2001: 256; Thompson 2002: 16; Meeson 2015: 17. It has been suggested that Æthelflæd may have been Eadgyth's great-niece: Meeson 2015: 18-19. In 901 Æthelred and Æthelflæd also donated a gold chalice to the abbey at Much Wenlock dedicated to St Mildburg: S.221; Finberg 1972: 148.

[1900] Farmer 2003: 419.

[1901] Liebermann 1889: II 7; Blair 2002: 539-40.

[1902] There are 4 Lincolnshire churches dedicated to the saint: Thacker and Sharpe 2002: 539-40. The 3 others are at Ashby, Manton and Scrawsby. All are clustered in and to the south-east of Scunthorpe.

to memory after the monastery of Wolverhampton was founded nearby to the west.[1903] But these musings, like so much of the preceding paragraphs, are incapable of proof, raise more questions than they answer, and indeed are unlikely to explain the name *Hildebaldes(c)hull*, for there is little evidence for the creation of monasteries associated with battles in the later Anglo-Saxon period.[1904] The identity of the eponymous Hygbald or Hildebald of Wednesfield – who in reality is more likely to have held the relatively lowly position of a Wednesfield agricultural tenant – will probably forever remain unresolved, but the existence of a hill with a rare name incorporating that of a prominent Mercian saint less than a mile from a settlement incorporating the name of a prominent pagan god must inevitably give cause for speculation.

Postscript:

The modern landscape of the area to the south of Wednesfield might usefully be recorded in some detail.[1905] The area south of Waddensbrook Lane, the north-western part of what was *Longer Moor* (the area immediately north of the road having been heavily developed with twentieth-century housing, and as far as we know devoid of any lane which might be linked to *Camp Feld*), is encroached upon by huge factory buildings occupied by Corus Steel. The Wolverhampton-Walsall boundary runs along the east side of those buildings and irregularly southwards to bisect the site, which slopes gradually to the south. Most of the rest of the area, bounded by Waddens Brook Lane, Noose Lane, Fibbersley and Watery lane, was (except perhaps for the north-eastern quadrant) formerly very heavily industrialised, with deep mines which remained in use until the end of the nineteenth century, to be replaced by clay and sand quarries. The Bentley Canal crossed the site from west to east from 1843 to 1953; from 1872 to 1931 a railway line crossed from north-west to south-east carrying passengers and freight between Wolverhampton and Walsall; and a mineral line ran north to south carrying coal, clay, etc. The sites of old coal shafts in the southern part of the area are shown on the 1889 and later Ordnance Survey maps, with large marshy pools marked on the 1938 map.

Most of the former Longer Moor (perhaps always meadow and never cultivated) is covered by undulating irregular rounded spoil mounds up to 60 feet or more high which rise on the west side of the site, covered in trees, bushes and short grass, close to the boundary with new factory buildings, and are reminders of the former collieries, factories and foundries. Lesser traces remain of earlier industrial use in the form of overgrown foundations and scatters of brick, with pools and ponds. There is a small caravan site on the south part of the site, and Willenhall Town Football Club lies on the south-east side, off Noose Lane. The north-east part of what was Longer Moor has a large expanse – several acres or more – of flat heathland covered in greyish-yellow grass, divided by what seem to be ancient hedgelines. The whole area is now preserved as the Fibbersley Local Nature Reserve, administered by Walsall Council, with a network of footpaths connecting irregular grassy spoil tips, wildflower meadows, marshes, copses and ponds.

The north-eastern part of Longer Moor, which, from an examination of early maps, seems to have survived the depredations of industrial activity relatively unscathed (though that impression could be deceptive), may provide some indication of how the rest of the moor

---

[1903] For evidence of an important proprietary church set up in the late 10th century of which no evidence remained in 1086 see Thompson 2002: 24.
[1904] Lavelle 2010: 304.
[1905] The description is based on a walk through the area on 5 August 2010, the eleven-hundredth anniversary of the battle of Tettenhall.

must have appeared over a thousand years ago, in which case it could have been an area to which both meanings of the word moor were appropriate: a large open heath, with areas close to the brook which were wet and marshy.[1906] As Smallshire has noted, 'Moorland is shown both on the Sutherland Collection field enclosure map of 1764 and the 1842 Tithe Map, between Noose Lane and Stubby Lane, with an extension below Nechells hamlet. It is all shown as south and east of March End'.[1907]

More detail can be added to the tenth-century topography of this area, for the boundary points of the Priests' Wood recorded in 1240 show that it encompassed an extensive area of woodland to the north-east, east and south-east of Wednesfield, from Burybrook north of Blackhalve Lane in the north, to Moseley Hole in the south.[1908] That area can be seen to exclude the land to the west with dolerite lying close to the surface, the type of landscape that would allow the growth of only small scrubby bushes, heather, bracken and gorse.[1909] In 1240 the Priests' Wood had evidently been in existence for at least two centuries, for a reference in Domesday Book to pannage (*silva pastilis*) at Wednesfield from a wood said to have been ¾ mile long by 660 yards wide held by the canons of Wolverhampton can be identified as the precursor of same woodland, and gave rise to the name Prestwood.[1910] The swinefold mentioned in Wulfrun's supposed 994 charter to the monastery of Wolverhampton was probably on the eastern edge of that area, perhaps near the point where Waddens Brook crossed Waddens Brook Lane, with the pigs enjoying pannage from the surrounding woodland.[1911] That woodland is still remembered in names such as Wood End, Wood Hayes and Prestwood. It seems likely that a significant area of woodland existed in the same area in the early tenth century, meaning that in 910 Waddens Brook formed a north-south band of marshy woodland on the east side of Wednesfield, marking the eastern boundary of the sparse heathland to the west.

To the west of the former Longer Moor, covering the former areas of Mill Hill and Neachells, is a large concentration of modern low-level factory and warehouse units forming industrial estates, and on the north side of the railway line, south of New Cross (the former site of Churchfield), a vast three-sided knoll rising quite steeply to 507', the highest point in the area (and the same height as the more gently-rounded dome of Nordley Hill to the north), covered with a large area of heavily undulating grassland with scattered irregular copses, evidently reclaimed and reshaped wasteland raised in height and lying above and obliterating both the former railway line that crossed the area and spoil tips from the former mines and factories that were concentrated hereabouts. To the north of that area is a dense concentration of modern low-rise factory units.

If the battle of Tettenhall did take place somewhere in this area, there is now no hope of identifying the ground surface on which the fighting occurred; the very slight chances of recovering physical evidence from any battle, such as late Anglo-Saxon military equipment or the recovery of human bones displaying signs of battle trauma, have almost

---

[1906] As indicated by the 1775 designation March End. The 1920 6" O.S. map shows a marshy area on the west side of Waddens Brook between the canal and the railway, but we cannot know to what extent surface conditions have been affected by the construction of both of those features and other industrial activities which are known to have taken place in the area.
[1907] Smallshire 1978: 48.
[1908] Smallshire 1978: 42, 45-6.
[1909] Smallshire 1978: 10.
[1910] VCH IV 45.
[1911] Hooke 1983: 72-5.

certainly been reduced to zero; and the ancient profile of the terrain can only partly be recreated with the help of early documentary and cartographic sources.

Should we have correctly identified at least the general location of the battle of Tettenhall, we must consider whether *The Low* and *South Low* (and possibly *North Low*, *Dunnlow* and *Little Low*) might have been burial mounds created to inter the dead from the battle, as believed locally since at least the seventeenth century. It is clear that at Mill Hill (the site of *South Low*), and the area to the north-east of Nordley Road, where North Low lay, local dolerite was at or close to the surface in the early twentieth century,[1912] and commentators have suggested that neither site would have been an obvious site for a tumulus. Yet it is evident from the number of moated sites in the area, including Merrill's Hall to the east of Mill Hill, probably fed by the small spring in Well Lane, and Neachells Hall to the south (where there were three moats close together), that there was sufficient depth of topsoil to create sizeable moats, probably clay lined. Furthermore, aerial photographs have revealed traces of medieval strip farming ('ridge and furrow') in Northlowfield, Mill Hill, and in Churchfield (in which lay *The Low*) to the south of New Cross, which shows that they must have had a reasonable depth of earth to allow agriculture in the medieval period.[1913] Nordley Hill and Mill Hill were prominent points in the local landscape, the type of highly visible location whose skyline was often chosen by prehistoric man for burial mounds.

There is no way of knowing whether all or any of *The Low*, *South Low*, *North Low*, *Dunnlow* and *Little Low* were artificial, and originated in the Bronze Age, the period from which most tumuli date, or even the pagan Anglo-Saxon period, from which period tumuli are far more rare, and their possible use as burial places in 910 is equally difficult to assess. The Old English word *hlāw* meant, in this area, 'a tumulus or tumulus-like mound' and the Anglo-Saxons would have had no means of knowing whether a prominent artificial-looking mound was natural or man-made. We have no comparable evidence from elsewhere to show that the dead from Anglo-Saxon battles were interred in existing prehistoric mounds, or that new mounds were raised over warriors interred in mass graves – or even that battlefield dead were normally buried. Indeed, there is stronger evidence that battle dead were simply left on the battlefield, and little evidence of mass graves.[1914]

Local folklore that speaks of these supposed lows as associated with the dead of the great battle was current in the late seventeenth century, but that idea may be little older, having developed when it became more widely known to antiquaries and local people from more readily available printed works that Wednesfield was one of the places named in early sources as the battle site, not least from Robert Plot's well-received *The Natural History of Staffordshire*, published in 1686. Even if the names are ancient, possibly pre-Conquest (*North Low* and *South Low* have not been traced before the fourteenth century; *The Low* before the eighteenth century; and *Dunnlow* is mentioned only once, in 1702), that cannot be taken as evidence that one or more of the features were artificial, since any tumulus-like feature might be termed a low. And if they were pre-Conquest, even prehistoric, they could well, like many others, have been robbed or levelled at any time for any number of reasons. Even if man-made there can be no way of knowing whether one or more may have been associated with the great battle. The matter must remain, probably for all time, unresolved.

[1912] Smallshire 1978: 16; and see especially the comprehensive data in McC. Bride et al 1997.
[1913] Smallshire 1978: 56.
[1914] It has been suggested that skeletons found neatly buried at Heronbridge, near Chester, might be the remains of participants in the battle of Chester in 615: Charles-Edwards 2013: 132, 388-9.

Finally, it is noteworthy that many Anglo-Saxon battles were fought close to Roman roads – one nineteenth-century authority bravely asserting that 'Nearly all the battles on English soil have been fought either across one or other of the old Roman roads, or in close proximity thereto',[1915] a claim largely supported in the case of Anglo-Saxon battles by recent research[1916] – and it must not be overlooked that a lost Roman road running from the Roman settlement and forts at Water Eaton (*Pennocrucium*) to Metchley Roman forts south-west of Edgbaston in Birmingham ran through or very close to Wednesfield. The precise course of that road can be traced to Slade Heath near Featherstone on the outskirts of Wolverhampton,[1917] two miles or so from Wednesfield, and a hint of the road might be detected in what is shown as *ye ould road from London to Salop* on a Sutherland Estate map of Prestwood Farm by William Forster dated 1661 running across Linthouse Lane parallel with Ridge Lane,[1918] but thereafter the line is lost and the precise course of the central section has never been identified, though its presumed route is marked on the fourth (and latest) edition of the Ordnance Survey map of Roman Britain. The ancient routeway running north-west/south-east known as The Portway, discussed elsewhere in this volume, may mark the approximate line of that road, and if prehistoric may even have been utilised by the Romans as part of the routeway joining the two major sites.

It must be added that though the existence of the Roman road or routeway may add to the weight of evidence favouring Wednesfield as the site of the great battle of 910, at least three other roads radiated south from the area around *Pennocrucium*, embracing a large arc extending from the Shropshire border to the road mentioned above, an area that includes Tettenhall, the other principal contender for the site of the great battle.[1919]

A large expanse of relatively level, open heathland, such as existed to the south of Wednesfield, will have provided a very suitable tenth-century battleground. Indeed, if it were chosen as the battlefield – though there is little evidence to show that battle sites at the time were chosen, as opposed to sites at which opposing parties happened to come into contact – the presence of a marsh and woods to the east could have been one reason: the English probably had sufficient numerical superiority to force the Danes into an area where woodland and marsh served to define its extent, denying the Danes escape in at least some directions, and allowing the English to deploy forces whose aim was to cut down the fleeing enemy attempting to retreat via the limited escape routes.

As noted previously, some historians, attempting to reconcile the claims of both Tettenhall and Wednesfield as the site of the battle,[1920] have suggested that Tettenhall may have been the scene of preliminary skirmishes leading up to the battle proper, possibly where the English launched their initial attack on the Scandinavians, forcing them east towards a full-

---

[1915] C.R.B. Barrett (Barrett 1896), cited in Bishop 2014: 71.
[1916] See especially Bishop 2014: 70-1, 120, 150-4; Marren 2006. A map of 7th-century battle sites and the Roman road system in northern England published in Higham 1993: 122 is especially illuminating.
[1917] Margary route 191; Margary 1967: 295.
[1918] Smallshire 1978: 32-3, 43, 45-6, 64. As noted elsewhere, an agreement between Robert de Essington and Robert de Wyston (1) and the Dean of Wolverhampton (2) mentions a high road called *Stamstre*, running from *Burybrook* and *Kirclesford* (Moseley Hole); a continuation of that road would follow Mattox Lane and Neachells Lane: ibid.
[1919] Horovitz 1992: 32-5.
[1920] A record of 1228 mentions 'the neighbouring vills of Wodnesfelde and Tettenhall ...': Smallshire 1978: 50.

scale confrontation closer to Wednesfield.[1921] Such a possibility cannot be dismissed, even if there is not the slightest evidence, apart from some duplicated – indeed, even triplicated – reports of the battle in the same source, superficially confusing but readily explicable as relating to a single event, to support it.

But the idea contrives unnecessarily to explain early references to both Wednesfield and Tettenhall, since historians now accept that there was but a single conflict at one place, and there is a ready explanation for the fact that in early accounts two places are associated with the battle: it is very likely to have taken place within a vast, sparsely-settled tract of open land called *feld*, part of which became known as *Wodnesfeld*, perhaps to commemorate the battle, and the nearest significant settlement with a church, probably already ancient serving a huge area including *Wodnesfeld*,[1922] would have been the minster at Tettenhall (an estate out of which, from inferences in Domesday Book, the estates of both Wednesfield and Wolverhampton may have been carved,[1923] in which case a battle at Wednesfield will indeed have taken place on *Woden's Feld* in the estate of Tettenhall), lying to the west, so giving rise to a conflict known, without contradiction, either as the battle of Wednesfield or the battle of Tettenhall.[1924] Furthermore, we are entitled to consider even negative evidence in placing the site of the battle: there is not the slightest trace of any early legends or other association of the ancient church of Tettenhall with any great battle, as might perhaps be expected had the engagement taken place there.[1925] Yet we should not overlook the unusual record in Domesday Book of the hide of land in Tettenhall held by the canons of Wolverhampton *est elemosina regis ad ecclesiam eiusdem ville* ('as King's alms to the church of the same vill'):[1926] one would wish to know what in particular may have led to the royal necessity for spiritual intercession.

If the above supposition might be correct, the names of both Tettenhall and Wednesfield could properly be justified to describe the site of the battle, just as the great battle of 1066

[1921] For example, Smallshire confidently assures us that 'There was a battle (if not two battles) and it raged either at Tettenhall or Wednesfield or at both places or near both. It is wise to take the view that the battle waged to and fro between and about these settlements ...': Smallshire 1978: 23.

[1922] Hooke 1993: 12. The origins of the church are uncertain, but it was clearly a pre-Conquest foundation. There was no church at Wednesfield. Whitelock 1955: 35 refers to the battle as at Tettenhall, although there is no evidence to suggest that she weighed up the competing locations.

[1923] Thorn and Thorn 2007.

[1924] As noted elsewhere in this volume, Dr David Roffe has concluded that *Wodnesfeld* was a vast royal estate stretching from Bushbury to Watling Street to Little Aston to Upper Penn, ecompassing Wednesbury and other estates such as Wolverhampton and Tettenhall, an immense irregular area of perhaps 100 square miles or more. The present author is sceptical about that claim.

[1925] Priests, implying a church, are recorded at Tettenhall in DB. The dedication of the church, a Royal Free Chapel, to St Michael (not an Anglo-Saxon saint) is first mentioned in 1247: VCH III 316; Thacker and Sharpe 2002. Some 5.75% of churches in England are dedicated to the saint: Jones 2007: 34.

[1926] VCH IV 45; the only other DB reference to *elemosina* in the entire county of Staffordshire relates to the canons of Stafford who held 3 hides there (VCH IV 44); Stafford, Wolverhampton and Tettenhall were all Royal Free Chapels. The entry recording *elemosina* at Tettenhall is made as if in clarification; the prinicpal manor of Tettenhall was known as *Tettenhall Regis*, and the church lands *Tenementa Clericorum*: Harwood 1844: 350-1. The same *elemosina* relates to a hide in Bilbrook, which lay in Tettenhall: VCH IV 45. At the time of DB property was normally held by military service performed by the king's tenants, measured by so many *knights' fees*, according to the number of knights the holder of the land was obliged to provide. Land could also be held by *serjeanty* (royal service, often in the royal household), or in the case of religious houses by *free alms*, i.e. spiritual service.

is named after Hastings, some nine miles from the site of the conflict on Senlac Hill, and the battle of Shrewsbury was fought in 1403 on Harlescott Old Field some two or three miles from that town.[1927] That would leave open the question why the name of *Heantune* (Wolverhampton, two miles south-west of Wednesfield) was not associated with the battle site. The most obvious reason is that in 910 *Heantune* may have been no more than a bleak and uninhabited hilltop, much like Bushbury, two miles to the north, or was the abandoned site of a former minster, probably of timber, that had decayed or been destroyed, possibly during the Viking incursions into Mercia in the 870s.[1928]

In summary, therefore, in the absence of further physical clues that may come to light, the chances of which must be negligible or worse for the reasons given above – given the almost complete industrial and commercial redevelopment over the wider area there is virtually no possibility that metal detectorists or redevelopment might one day reveal, for example, a concentration of late Anglo-Saxon military objects or Viking hack-silver or large numbers of preserved human bones with evidence of battle trauma – at present the

---

[1927] In a useful paper concentrating on medieval battles generally, Philip Morgan highlights how battlefields were what he describes as 'acidental landscapes', constructs created by both the actions of military forces, and of the participants and the local population, positing three stages to the establishment of a battlefield: firstly, the notion that a battle would have no name at all; secondly, a period of fluidity as to its name; and thirdly, only when ther battle had been recognised as important would it attract an 'official' name: Morgan 2000: 42-8; see also Lavelle 2010: 300, fn166, who notes that the theory seems to be a true of those battles that took place in the core territory of the West Saxon dynasty in the 9th century rather than those in their newly conquered territory in the 10th.

[1928] It is not inconceivable that any monastery at *Heantune* may have been destroyed by the Northumbrian raiding-army during the early stages of its campaign in 910 preceding the battle of Tettenhall. As an aside to this section, it is necessary to dispose of one of the more preposterous theories (of which there have been many) relating to the battle of Tettenhall: the idea that the Danes reached and/or escaped from the Tettenhall area by ships along Smestow Brook. No more than a moment's thought ought to be sufficient to dispel any such theory, but since the idea continues to be repeated, and has evidently gained some sort of credence, it is perhaps necessary to emphasise that the Danish army was travelling overland on its raiding expedition to the west of the river Severn immediately prior to the battle, and we are told that it crossed the Severn at *Cwatbrycge* (Quatford). It is of course possible that it could have acquired boats from the local populace, but any such boats are unlikely to have been of any size, in which case the raiding army would have required a considerable number. The Danes may have had the opportunity to acquire larger vessels, but Smestow Brook (a tributary of the river Stour which joins the Severn at Stourport-on-Severn, some 12 miles south of Quatford) is, and was most certainly in 910, a modest narrow meandering watercourse with numerous bends and (particularly in the summer months) shallows, with all kinds of obstructions, such as rocks, rapids, overhanging and fallen trees, and probably mills and fishtraps. The only means of propulsion could have been haulage – sails would have been of no benefit in those circumstances where sailing vessels were unable to sail against the wind, and masts would in any event have fouled waterside trees. In most places the sunken stream is not wide enough for oars, and boats would be moving against the current if travelling northwards, with trees and vegetation preventing haulage from the bank. To travel from the Severn to Tettenhall by water would, at best, involve a very slow and arduous journey of some 28 miles, with the Danes exposed at all times to attack from English forces. Self-evidently any boats could not have carried carts and horses. The success of the Viking warbands was attributable to the speed and flexibility of their movements across country, and their ability to avoid confrontation with enemy forces far from the Danelaw. The Danish raiding party of August 910 had travelled hundreds of miles in hostile territory in a looting expedition; it would have had no reason at all to attempt passage upstream along an insignificant and winding watercourse. Flight after the battle along a meandering watercourse, even if boats had been available and the watercourse passable, would have trapped the Danes in a slow-moving stream and exposed them to attack from either or both banks. Quite simply, the idea that the Danes travelled to or from Tettenhall by water is absurd.

best that can be made of the bewildering, contradictory and circumstancial evidence relating to the battle of Tettenhall is that a great military conflict is likely to have taken place somewhere to the north-east of Wolverhampton, perhaps on the south-west Wednesfield within the ancient open field of Churchfield, south of New Cross, on Sunday, 5th (or, less likely, Monday 6th) August 910, possibly on open ground still remembered as *Camp Feld* some six hundred years later, and a joint Mercian and West Saxon army achieved a devastating victory during which many Hiberno-Scandinavians, including three kings and many others of high-rank, some perhaps with English names, were killed, and many survivors forced to flee. Field-names in the area might hint, furthermore, at the former existence after 910 of a church set up on or close to the site of the battle, possibly even by Wulfrun herself, destined to vanish beyond memory, perhaps when the monastery of Wolverhampton was re-endowed by Wulfrun, supposedly in 994: one meaning of *Heantune*, found in the name Wolverhampton, is 'chief town', implying another, lesser, *tūn* elsewhere.[1929]

If the above conjecture about the battle site is correct, and (ignoring the possibility of a battlefield elsewhere in the great *feld* of Wednesfield) the battle of Tettenhall took place on the south side of Wednesfield, possibly on *Camp Feld*, close to the Roman road from Metchley to Water Eaton, the time has come when we should perhaps refer to the conflict as the Battle of Wednesfield. And if the location of *Camp Feld* (and perhaps *Churchyardfield* which may have been in close proximity) could be determined with certainty – which, with further research, is entirely possible – the battle site could be one of the very few – indeed, perhaps the only – Anglo-Saxon battlefield to be so precisely identified.[1930]

[1929] Horovitz 2005: 585-6.

[1930] The TA covering Northey Island in Essex contains no field-names which might offer clues to the site of the famed battle of Maldon, fought in 991 (see generally Cooper 1993), and there is a similar absence of place-names at Bromborough in Cheshire to indicate the location of the equally famous battle of *Brunanburh* in 937: Dodgson 1991: 178-9. It may be worth recording that one of the five Hundreds in Staffordshire is Cuttlestone, first recorded in Domesday Book, and meaning 'Cuðwulf's stone': Horovitz 2005: 221. Cuttlestone Bridge lies ½ mile south-west of Penkridge. 13 people with the name (including 3 moneyers) are mentioned in the pre-Conquest period, but others obviously existed. The *Prosopography of Anglo-Saxon England*, accessed 12 December 2014, lists *Cuðwulf 9* twice: as a witness to a charter from Æthelred and Æthelflæd of 901 granting land at Stanton Long and Caughley in Barrow, Shropshire in exchange for land at Easthope and Patton and a gold chalice (S.221); and as a beneficiary, described as a thegn, of a renewed grant of King Burgred by Æthelred of land in Marcliff in Cleeve Prior, Worcestershire, 'an ancient landbook having been carried off by the pagans', with an endorsement that Cuðwulf later granted the land to Worcester (S.222). The charter dates from between 883 and 911, the year following the battle of Tettenhall and the year of Æthelred's death. Could Cuðwulf, a thegn of Æthelred and Æthelflæd in 901, have been associated with, and given his name to the (re-named?) meeting-place, and/or his death have been connected with the battle of Tettenhall, Penkridge lying under 9 miles north-west of Wednesfield?

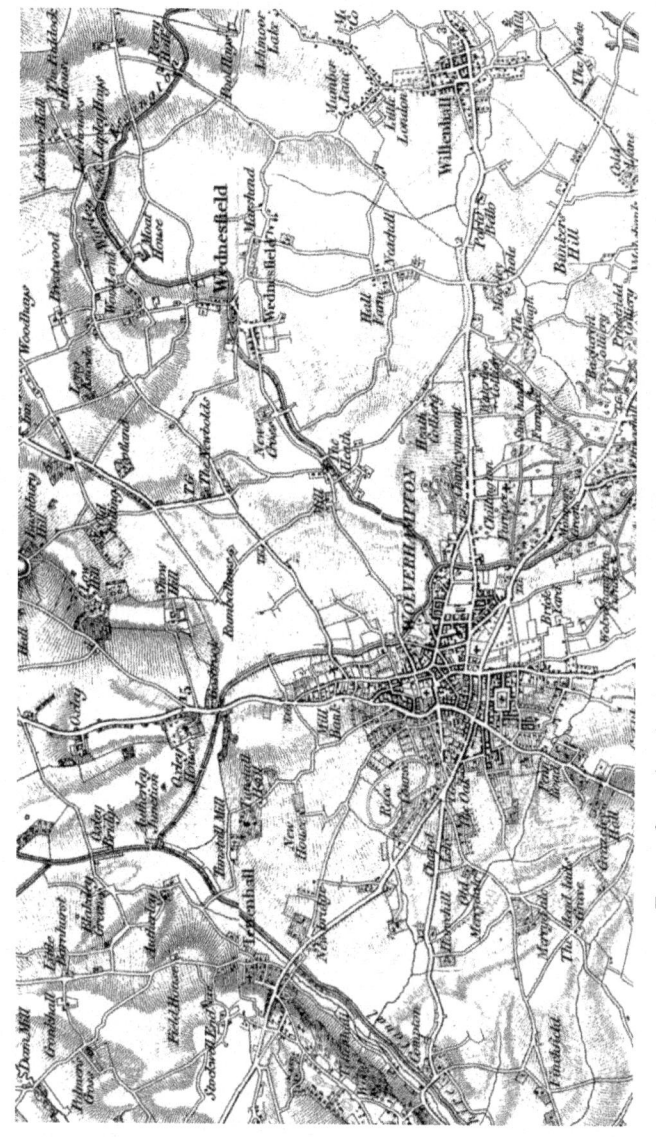

Extract from the First Edition One-Inch Ordnance Survey map of 1834 showing the area around Wolverhampton, including Tettenhall (to the west) and Wednesfield (to the east). Scale approximately two inches to one mile.

30. Archaeological evidence of the battle of Tettenhall.

So far as unequivocal archaeological evidence of the battle and the events leading up to it are concerned, it must be conceded at the outset that there is, so far as can be determined, none.[1931] The Tong Fragment, considered in the following chapter, may or may not date from the time of the battle, and even if it does, there can be no way of knowing whether there is any direct link with the conflict; likewise the Quatford spearhead, discussed in more detail in chapter 32.

The usual scavenging of battlefields after a battle will have meant that only smaller artifacts are likely to have been missed, though the rough surface of heathland and the soft surface of boggy areas may have concealed some larger pieces. Even the sites of battles of major national significance, such as Hastings, Culloden and Bosworth, have produced very little, if any, material traces, though in the latter case metal detecting has led to the re-identification of the likely site after metal artifacts were recovered during a major research project. It should come as no surprise that no recorded artefacts or other material (leaving aside for discussion elsewhere in this volume the vexed question of supposed tumuli) from the Wednesfield or Tettenhall area can be associated, even loosely, with the site of the battle of Tettenhall.

However, that has not prevented earlier authors from providing fascinatingly detailed reports of the conflict. Towards the end of the nineteenth century one respected local historian cites an un-named author: 'the Danes then retreated towards Wednesfield, where a bloody battle was fought, which raged for several hours, with little advantage to either army, when the Saxon were reinforced by Earl Kenwolf, and the contest was soon decided. The Danes were totally routed, leaving three kings dead upon the field. In this battle, while leading on the Saxons to the final charge, Earl Kenwolf fell mortally wounded'.[1932]

That quotation has been traced back to an account written by the Bilston historian G. T. Lawley in 1868,[1933] and is evidently a conflated version of the battle of Tettenhall and the battle of the Holme (still not certainly located), the latter fought c.903 when Abbot Cenwulf was killed fighting for Edward the Elder.[1934] F. W. Hackwood, the prolific Midland historical compiler, is the only other author who appears to mention Earl Kenwolf, and he notes that 'This Kenwolf, who is said to have been the greatest notable of the locality ... [was] seated on a good estate at Stowe Heath ...'.[1935] His note was evidently taken from Lawley's work, and since it arguably incorporates archaeological content it is worth reciting at some length an extract from that work to demonstrate the inventively nonsensical nature of what was written.

[1931] Plot records in 1686 what he describes as the brass head of the bolt of a Roman catapulta which was found in a wood at Bushbury called Burchen Lesow (Plot 1686: 403). Stebbing Shaw says the place where the object was found was then (1801) a field called Gun-birch, above the church, and suggested that the object 'had probably lain there from the time of the great battle fought in these parts about the year 907 [sic]': Shaw 1801 II: 181. In fact the object was almost certainly a Bronze Age celt or axe-head. A supposed 11th century Viking spearhead 16" long, seemingly associated with an oval mound some 75' long and about 7' high, was found in Great Barr (SP 05139437) in 1954: Gould 1957: 17; *Birmingham Post* 6th July 1954; BCSMR 2627.
[1932] Willmore 1887: 30.
[1933] Lawley 1868: 3-5.
[1934] Giles 1892: I 235; Swanton 1996: 92-4.
[1935] Hackwood 1908: 8.

Of a 'large Saxon manor house' at Ettingshall, he notes that 'the Saxon Hall ... was probably built by Ethelwolf, about the year 839, for we find that he gave it together with all lands, wardships and escheats, belonging to the manor of Stowheath, to Earl Gudolf, a very powerful nobleman; to be held by a kind of military tenure. He did not, however, remain in possession of this Hall more than six or seven years, being slain in battle by the Danes at Ockley, in Surrey, in 851. It then passed into the hands of Kedric Wolfeard, a valiant soldier, in great favour with the king, to whom he is supposed to have been related. During his life the Danes became very troublesome, so much so that Kedric had repeatedly to fight against them. He made a deep moat around the Hall, which he spanned by a rude movable draw-bridge, and he diverted the waters of the Hindbrook from its course, and caused it to flow in the moat as occasion required. The drawbridge which was made of wood, was so slightly constructed that its removal at sunset was easily performed. To Kedric succeeded Earl Kenwolf, who shared with Alfred the Great, many of his dangers and successes. In the year 909 the Hall was surrounded by an army of Danish invaders, but the approach of the Saxons, under Edward the Elder, saved it from destruction. ... [Here follows the account of the battle of Wednesfield recounted elsewhere in this volume] ... Edward the Confessor often visited this Hall when hunting and hawking in the neighbourhood. The family of "Ettings" was in possession of Stowheath Manor at the time of the conquest, and was dispossessed of them by William the Conqueror, who gave them to a Norman soldier, named Fitz Piers. ... As no evidence of the existence of this Hall after this period remains, it may reasonably be supposed that it was destroyed at the same time with many other Saxon halls and castles, during the Conqueror's reign. ... About 1760 a very interesting relic of this building was discovered. During some mining operations the workmen found a vaulted passage of stone work, about fifty feet in length by four feet in breadth, which they explored. In the passage several curious implements were found, among them a two-edged axe bearing in Saxon capitals the name "Cedric Wolfeard" with a crowned dragon underneath. Unfortunately, the workmen ignorant of the value of the implements, took no care of them, and the axe was taken home by one of the men and used as a wood chopper. The passage was also destroyed, without affording the antiquary an opportunity to examine it.'.[1936]

Apart from King Alfred, Edward the Elder, Edward the Confessor, and William the Conqueror – two of whom supposedly visited the hall – all the other named characters and the episodes in which they are said to have been involved are entirely fanciful,[1937] and the battle at Wednesfield is the only event which is known to have occurred. There is not the slightest evidence for any 'Saxon hall' at Ettingshall, and the extract is especially memorable for its creatively inventive account which is patently baseless.

Early historians have almost inevitably, and not unreasonably, associated the site of the battle with the surprisingly large number of supposed tumuli recorded in the Wolverhampton and Wednesfield area (with several at or near Wednesfield and at least one, and possibly more, at Tettenhall),[1938] and place-names recording the existence of other long-destroyed mounds. Tumuli are generally assigned to two periods in history: the Bronze Age and the pagan Anglo-Saxon period.

[1936] Lawley 1868 3-5.
[1937] The chronicler Bartholomew de Cotton names a King Celwlf as a Danish king who died fighting the English c.907, but no other reference to this figure has been traced in any early source.
[1938] See VCH I 193.

There is no obvious reason why the area to the east of Wolverhampton would have been especially attractive to Bronze Age peoples, whose burial mounds tend to be found on high ground where they can be seen in profile against the skyline or on false summits (such as the tumulus on Low Hill, south of Bushbury), although large groups were sometimes sited in river valleys.[1939] The lows to the east of Wolverhampton may conform loosely with that pattern – although there is of course no significant river in or near Wednesfield[1940] – but given what may be a pagan element in the place-names Wednesfield and Wednesbury we need to consider whether those supposed tumuli could be of pagan Anglo-Saxon origin. It is certainly conceivable that one or some or even all of the lows can be dated from the period between the earliest date of Anglian penetration into the West Midlands, probably in the mid-sixth century, and the introduction of Christianity in the area in the mid-seventh century, when we must assume that burial in such mounds came to an end – in other words, a period of no more than three or four generations. But tumuli that can be shown to date from that period in this area are extremely rare, and no pagan burial goods normally found with such burials are recorded in the area, though the fact that no excavations are known to have been made of any of these mounds means that the absence of such evidence proves little. For the moment we must assume, in the absence of other persuasive evidence, that by statistical probability these mounds are unlikely to date from the pagan Anglo-Saxon period.

But a third possibility – on which so many early historians have based their theories on the site of the battle of Tettenhall – is that the mounds, or some of them, are to be associated with the great battle of 910. The fact that all of the suspected tumuli have either been destroyed, or cannot be located with any precision, creates obvious difficulties for any researcher, but their distribution over a fairly wide area, and perhaps their bland names (which may of course in many cases be relatively recent) might tend to weigh against that possibility. Furthermore, there is little evidence that the English buried their own dead – even their military leaders – in such barrows after a conflict, and there is even less likelihood that the Christian victors carefully buried the vanquished pagans under cenotaph mounds.[1941] In addition, at least some of the 'ancient tumuli' (including that at Compton excavated in the early 1930s) are now believed to have been nothing more than hillocks of natural formation or relatively modern. No record (other than very tenuous evidence from the field-name *Chirchezordesfeld* in Wednesfield, discussed in the previous chapter) has been traced of any human bones having been found in the Tettenhall/Wednesfield area,

---

[1939] Grinsell 1953: 50-51.
[1940] It will be noted that the now destroyed supposed tumuli on Calf Heath near Four Ashes lay on relatively low ground on the north side of a stream: Horovitz 1992: 20-21. Since those mounds lay on Warren Heath, the possibility that they were not prehistoric, but associated with medieval rabbit warrens, cannot be excluded.
[1941] Deansley 1961: 342 states that there was a Christian duty to bury the dead [a duty that presumably did not extend to burying pagans]. Excavations at the site at Repton fortified by the great army of the Vikings who wintered here in 873-4 revealed a camp defended on one side by the river Trent, and on the other three sides by about 150 metres of ditch and earthwork defences incorporating as a gateway the church of St Wystan enclosing about 1.5 hectares, with the skeletal remains of a Viking chieftan and 250 other people, presumably Vikings, who appear to have died as a result of illness, since the skeletons showed no sign of injury. The burial was covered by a large mound. It has been suggested that the great army must have numbered fewer than 1000, given the small size of the camp, and the 100 metres of protected riverbank available to berth ships, suggesting a maximum of thirty to thirty-five ships, which had an average crew of 35: Abels 1998: 144, citing Peddie 1989: 75.

and it is in any event questionable whether the soil conditions locally, which tend to be sandy, could have preserved bones for over a thousand years.

What is especially noteworthy is that notwithstanding the construction of houses, churches, schools, factories, bridges, canals, cuttings, embankments, railways, roads, reservoirs, mines, quarries, drains, culverts and graves in the Tettenhall and Wednesfield areas over recent centuries, as well as the intensive cultivation of land on foot (where artefacts are more easily detected) over earlier centuries, no single reported case has been noted of any remains or artefacts that might conceivably be associated with the great battle.[1942] Organic materials, such as cloth, wood, leather, and horn, will have left no trace after a millennium in the ground, and it may be doubted whether stray finds of fragments of bone, or rusted and heavily corroded ironwork which might have been spearheads, swords, shield bosses or chain armour would have been recognised as such or been seen in any way as significant.

On the other hand, while it is questionable whether any ferrous metal might survive from the conflict[1943] (though the existence of the Quatford spearhead must be acknowledged), the chronicles tell us that the Danish army was laden with booty, to which must be added the personal jewellery and possessions of the warriors themselves, and since gold (and to a lesser degree silver) objects will survive untarnished and unchanged in the ground, it is perhaps surprising that not the slightest trace is recorded in the immediate area of Quatford or Tettenhall or Wednesfield of any artefact which might be associated with the battle, particularly given the increasing activity of metal detectorists in recent years.[1944]

Of the after-events of the battle we have no information, but it is possible that the local populace would have been conscripted to assist in the disposal of the bodies from both sides. It is important to emphasise that there is little evidence of mass burials at Anglo-Saxon battlefields, although in 1929 about 120 tidily arranged skeletons were found in a grave some 45' by 16' at Heronbridge, just south of Chester, believed to be combatants killed at the battle of Chester, fought in 613, so making it 'the earliest identifiable site of a major battleground in Britain'.[1945] Re-excavated in 2004, no dating evidence was found in the grave, but modern radiocarbon dating of the skeletons has provided a burial date consistent with the date of the battle. Bede records that at the battle of Chester King Æthelfrith of Northumbria defeated a hastily assembled army of Britons, seen by Bede as a

---

[1942] Though it is important to emphasise that that situation is in no way unusual so far as Anglo-Saxon battlefields are concerned: no human bones or military artefact that might be connected with the battle of Hastings have ever been found on the traditional battle site, with the exception of a corroded iron axe-head of doubtful authenticity which is now in the Battle Museum of Local History. The object was given a pre-17th century date by experts according to the *Time Team* television programme about the battle of Hastings aired on 1st December 2013.

[1943] An iron spearhead with decorated bronze socket (*sic*), is recorded from Stourton Farm, a little over a mile north-east of Kinver (SO 8585): Staffordshire Sites andMonuments Record 03645-MST3419; WAN 14: 2. Bi-metal weapons of this type are not common, but a number of Viking spear-heads found in the river Thames at the site of the old London bridge have sockets encrusted with silver and copper alloy, and of eight iron axe-heads recovered from the same location, two incorporated a copper-alloy sleeve in the socket: Anon. 1981. Both the English and the Danes sometimes decorated their spear-heads.

[1944] It is too early to consider the implications of the Staffordshire Hoard of gold and silver artefacts, most associated with arms and armour, which seem to date from c.650-670, found on the south side of Watling Street near Barracks Lane, south of Hammerwich, near Lichfield, in July 2009.

[1945] See especially Davies 2010 and the bibliography therein. For the date of the battle see Charles-Edwards 2013: 132, 288-9.

nation of heretics who refused to accept the authority of St Augustine and the Roman church. The Britons were accompanied by many monks – Bede says more than 2000 – from the nearby monastery at Bangor-on-Dee who were there to pray in support of the British army and were treated by Æthelfrith as enemy combatants. Bede claims that some 1,200 were slaughtered. All the Heronbridge skeletons were of males aged between 20 and 40, many with sword cuts to the head. The orderly way in which the bodies had been placed in the grave has been taken to indicate that they probably formed part of the victorious Northumbrian army. Two of the sleletons have been subjected to recent detailed analysis. One was in his early twenties, and had five injuries to the head, four of which could each have proved fatal. The other was aged about 40, and had four blade cuts to the skull, and a shallow cut by the right ear. Both had powerful arms, but that cannot be seen as evidence of weapons training, since many occupations will have led to a strong physique. The condition of the skeletons indicated that the bodies had been buried soon after death.[1946]

The deposit of vast quantities of human skulls and carefully separated skeletal bones discovered in the churchyard at Buttington near Welshpool in 1837, once believed to be victims of the siege of Buttington in 893, is discussed in more detail in chapter 2. Those remains are no longer thought to be connected with the events of 893, and probably have a monastic origin.

The building of South Benfleet railway bridge by the Thames opposite Canvey Island in 1855 revealed human bones and charred timbers preserved in the mud which were held to be associated with the siege of Benfleet in 894, when Londoners stormed the fortress of Hæsten, the Viking leader, and captured ships and goods and Viking womern and children. The charred timbers may have been from some of the ships that near-contemporary sources tell us were broken up and burned.[1947]

An early Anglo-Saxon cemetery at Eccles, Kent, produced six male interments, which may have been buried at the same time or individually over the course of perhaps a generation. The skeletons were of adults aged between 20 and 35, with one older, between 5' 8" and 6' 3" tall. All had cranial evidence of blows to the head. The cuts were clean, with no sign of fresh growth which would arise as the bone fused as the wound healed – a sign that if the victim survived his injuries, it was for less than five days, the usual length of time for such growth to begin. The skulls all had linear injuries to the brow, temple and crown (mostly on the left). Many appeared to have been caused by a downward vertical or angled chop, the longer (up to 6½") probably by blows from a sword, but one, 3" long, which had crushed and split the surrounding area, may have been caused by the thicker blade of an axe. One man had received some eleven blows to the head and a further five to the neck, ten to the back and three to the arms. Another had an iron projectile point lodged in his spine, which had entered his right side. The cranial injuries would have caused, at the very least, concussion and profuse bleeding. The impact of the cuts would have forced parts of the skull into the brain, driven deeper into the soft tissues by the thrust of the weapon's edge. The victim with the neck injuries would have died from the first blow to his neck, if indeed he had still been alive, which would have severed his brain stem. He had been brutally attacked and almost beheaded. In most cases shock to the brain would have caused

---

[1946] *The Times*, 21st February 2006; CA 202: 516-524.
[1947] Hodgkin 1939: II 663; Swanton 1996: 86.

a quick death. At most, the other victims could have survived for a few hours, unconscious and bleeding to death.[1948]

During strengthening measures carried out in 1950-1 by the National Coal Board to St Mary's church in Cuckney, some 7 miles north of Mansfield in Nottinghamshire, a mass burial was discovered under the nave of the present church and under the footings of an earlier Norman church. Some 200 skulls were counted, and in some places bodies are said to have been piled in mounds to a depth of 7 feet. All the skeletons appeared to be males. No dating evidence was found with the bones, and no cut marks or evidence of violent death was noted, but they were thought to represent a small section of a much larger battle pit, perhaps containing the dead from the battle of what Bede describes as *Heathfelth*, or Heathfield, which took place on 12th October 633 when Penda of Mercia and Cadwallon of Gwynedd defeated an army from Northumbria led by Edwin.[1949]

No archaeological evidence of any kind has been traced at Fulford of the great battle said to have been fought on 20 September 1066 between a Viking force under Earl Tostig and Harold Hardrada, king of Norway, and a joint Mercian and Northumbrian force led by Earl Edwin of Mercia and his brother, Earl Morcar of Northumbria, with great slaughter on both sides and the defeat of the English forces. However, the site of the battle is not given in the *Anglo-Saxon Chronicle* account, and the first reference to Fulford as the location does not appear until the twelfth century. Whilst that identification may be correct, in the 1950s, over 60 skeletons were discovered at Riccall, 10 miles to the south, including those of women and children.[1950] A water isotope examination of the teeth from 6 skulls revealed that they had probably spent their lives in Norway. Many of the skeletons showed traces of violent blows from sharp-edged or pointed weapons, and it is now believed that the bodies were those of Vikings associated with the Viking army. Possibly the battle took place near, or indeed at, Riccall, though the presence of women and children seems unlikely.

In 1996 some 43 skeletons were discovered heaped in a communal grave discovered during extension works at Towton Hall, almost certainly representing soldiery killed at the battle of Towton in 1461.[1951] The skeletons, which were found with a number of unidentified metal objects, were all male, with ages ranging from about 18 to about 45. The majority had wounds to the head, some with wounds to the top of the skull, and several displayed fatal blows to the back of the head. Many of the bodies had evidently suffered repeated blows to the head and face as they lay dying. A number of skeletons showed defensive injuries to the forearms and hands, but there were almost no leg injuries. One skeleton had shards of metal in its spine.

In general, it seems likely that after stripping the dead of arms, clothing, and indeed everything else which might be re-used or recycled, bodies of the slain enemy after battles in the Anglo-Saxon period were disposed of in the most practicable way possible, perhaps hauled into piles near where they fell, or dragged into pits and buried or even (especially in the case of the enemy) left exposed to be devoured by animals and birds, which might have been considered a suitably contemptuous gesture: the *Anglo-Saxon Chronicle* records in a poem commemorating the battle of *Brunanburh* in 937 that 'They [the victorious English army] left behind them the dusky-coated one, the black raven with its horned beak, to

---

[1948] Pollington 2002: 221-2.
[1949] See Revill 1975: 40-49. The site of the battle has not been located with certainty.
[1950] YAJ xl 301-7.
[1951] See Buck 2000.

share the corpses...'.[1952] A detailed account of the battle of Hastings, the *Carmen de Hastingae Proelio*, possibly written by Guy, Bishop of Amiens before May 1068, or much later by an unknown author, records that after the battle Duke William collected and buried the bodies of the dead Normans, but 'the corpses of the English, strewn upon the ground, he left to be devoured by worms and wolves, by birds and dogs'.[1953] That may have been a long-established battlefield convention.

Dead from the victorious side, particularly those of high rank, will have been treated with greater respect and, in the case of the battle of Tettenhall, may even have been taken to the nearest churchyard for burial, although at this period burial in a churchyard was not customary for all sections of society; it was perhaps 'only in the tenth century that the majority of people were for the first time told where they must bury their dead. This was also the time when certain individuals were forbidden from Christian burial in consecrated ground if they had been excommunicated or died without atoning for their sins', with the earliest surviving evidence for the consecration of churchyards also dating from the late tenth and eleventh centuries.[1954] Christians had a duty to pray for the souls of their dead warriors, and to recover their corpses for proper burial, but it was not until the tenth century, and then only gradually, that a proper burial was routinely given to battle victims by those with a shared culture.[1955]

It is said[1956] that Victorious heathen Vikings usually buried their dead on the battlefield on funeral pyres piled with weapons from both sides gathered from the battlefield so that their dead could take them into the afterlife, though the idea of huge pyres created on battlefields must be questionable, and no archaeological evidence has been traced of burned weapons. The custom is said to have ensured that Viking corpses could not be desecrated by the enemy.

[1952] EHD I 201. Writing some 60 years after the battle of Stamford Bridge which took place on 25th September 1066, when Harold defeated King Harald of Norway, the chronicler Orderic Vitalis claimed that 'Travellers cannot fail to recognise the field, for a great mountain of dead men's bones still lies there': Chibnall 1968-80: II 169. Despite that reference, not a single bone or weapon has otherwise been recorded from the area. Richard Bolton, a Staffordshire antiquary writing in the first quarter of the eighteenth century, records that certain fields near Checkley parish church were called *Nakedfields* in the late seventeenth and eighteenth centuries because the falllen victims of a battle against the Danes had been left unburied for sime time, adding that what grounds there might have been for the tradition he did not know (Woolf 2003: 348), but the story appears to have been based on a comment by Plot in 1686, who says of the three cross shafts at Checkley that '... the Inhabitants reporting them the memorials of three Bishops slain in a battle fought here about ¼ of a mile E.N.E. from the church, in a place still called Naked Fields, for that the bodies lay there naked and unburyed for some time after the fight ...': Plot 1686: 432. The supposed etymology for the field-names is baseless, but the later suggestion of a connection with the Danes (also baseless) is noteworthy.
[1953] Morrillo 1996: 51.
[1954] Hadley 2001: 36. It seems likely that cemeteries for those executed and others who were not buried in churchyards were a common feature of the Anglo-Saxon perid, but few have been identified: ibid. Later medieval sources suggest that those who were not permitted a churchyard burial included pagans, usurers, excommunicates, the indicted and strangers to the parish, as well as the concubines of clergy, and those who married without banns. Suicides were also forbidden burial in consecrated ground in the late Anglo-Saxon period unless madness led to the act, and many juries may have decided that death was due to madness or misadventure to enable the victim to have a churchyard burial: Hadley 2001: 50-51; Boyle 2016: 116.
[1955] Gillingham 2007.
[1956] Pollington 1989: 101.

It would be of great interest if we had early reports of mass graves, finds of weapons, or individual burials from the Anglo-Saxon period in the area between Quatford/Bridgnorth and Tettenhall/Wednesfield. Sadly, there is none.[1957]

However, a growing number of pre-Conquest coins and bronze objects, the latter very commonly including strap ends, mostly found by metal detectorists in recent years, may possibly include tangible evidence of a Viking presence in the region.[1958] A word of caution, however, is necessary about conclusions drawn from reported finds, for a preponderance of discoveries in one particular area may mean only that the area has been more intensively searched than other areas: the Portable Antiquities Scheme, for example, has a relatively high number of bronze strap ends reported from Worfield, doubtless reflecting the activities of a more concentrated campaign there by local detectorists, a willingness to properly record finds, and not least the size of the parish.[1959]

The so-called 'Age of Silver' in the north-west of England begins effectively in the early tenth century with the sudden influx of Scandinavian settlers dispossessed from Dublin in 901 supplemented by others from the Isle of Man, Scotland, and perhaps even Iceland and Scandinavia itself. The Vikings adopted silver for use in a commodity exchange system, and coins were valued not as coinagae *per se*, but for their silver content. From the late ninth century coins were minted by the Vikings themselves in the Danelaw, but those in the north-west produced no coins. Trace elements from silver objects found in hoards in southern Scandinavia show that they derived principally from Arabic silver coins.[1960]

The Portable Antiquities Scheme and the Fitzwilliam Museum in Cambridge maintain a record of coin finds listed under individual counties. In the case of Staffordshire and Shropshire such finds are modest in number, and it is likely that only a small proportion of finds discovered in recent years by, for example, metal detectorists, has been recorded, but there is a number of coins which have a special interest because they are not of English origin. Those coins are a fragment of a possible Islamic, arabic or near eastern coin, probably from the reign of Harum-al-Rashid (170-193AH, 786-809AD), from Sheinton (on the south side of the river Severn between Buildwas and Cressage);[1961] a French Merovingian coin of Louis the Pious (814-840) found at Wem;[1962] a fragment of an Islamic 'Abbāsid dirham, of al-Amin (809-13) or al-Ma'mun (813-33) found at an

---

[1957] Apart from the field-name *Chirchezordesfeld* discussed elsewhere in this volume, the only reference to human bones which has been traced in our area of interest is the account of skeletons found at the east end of Barnett's Hill, Bridgnorth mentioned previously, and an account, for which no authority is given, of human bones found 'on the common adjoining Abbot's-hill [Abbot's Castle Hill]' in Scott 1832: 323, 327. Presumably 'the common' refers to the meadows lying beneath the ridge of Abbot's Castle Hill, but Scott is not always a reliable authority. In 1809 a cave was exposed and cleared at the base of an overhanging rock at Burcote, 2 miles north-east of Bridgnorth, and disarticulated human and animal bones were discovered, including three human skulls on a rock ledge, all lacking the lower jaw: see Anon. 1824: 833-5.
[1958] See generally Hookway 2015.
[1959] However, for the large number of Anglo-Saxon strap ends found at the Viking camp at Torksey see Hadley and Richards 2016: 57-8.
[1960] Kershaw 2015: 151-2.
[1961] PAS record HESH-18E881. Below the reverse of the coin, which was found in March 2004, is 'Al-Fa dl'. The obverse is badly corroded and the mint indistinct.
[1962] PAS record LVPL1786.

unspecified location in Claverley;[1963] a Continental penny of 675-750 recorded from Compton;[1964] a fragment of a Near Eastern coin (?786-809) recorded from north of Much Wenlock;[1965] and a coin of Charles the Bald (840-877) reported to have been found at Hednesford.[1966] One or more of these modest pieces might be surviving evidence for the presence of the Danes in this area, since the Vikings will have had no interest in the age of the silver the coveted.

Single finds of 'Abbāsid dirhams characteristically date from the late ninth or early tenth century, and are found within the Danelaw: those from Torksey have been mentioned previously. The Claverley dirham is of particular significance since it appears to be the only example so far found outside the Danelaw.[1967] The Danish rulers of Northumbria only began minting from the 890s,[1968] and national coinages are not found in Scandinavia until the eleventh century, so the great majority of surviving coins that reached Scandinavia during the ninth and tenth centuries were of Islamic origin. Several hundred thousand dirhams have been found, singly or in hoards, from Russia to Ireland, of which more than 62,000 have been discovered in Scandinavia. The coins were obtained mainly from Arab merchants by northern traders who travelled through Russia to exchange their furs and slaves for silver coinage – according to Arab sources, the northern traders refused to accept anything other than silver coins for their goods.[1969]

The Croydon hoard, discovered in 1852, consisted of 175 English silver coins, the earliest dating from c.875, seven Carolingian deniers, and three 'Abbāsid dirhams (two of 786-809, the other 842-7), together with several silver ingots and fragments of hack silver. The hoard is dated fairly firmly to c.875. Dirhams are not found in Norway before the 890s, and 'No coins of the Abbasid caliphs are found in English deposits earlier than Croydon [i.e. 875]. By contrast, well over 100 ninth century dirhams have been found in Denmark, almost all from the first half of the century ... [A]s in Norway, many will only have arrived with the main influx of Kufic coins into Scandinavia in the very last years of the ninth and

---

[1963] Fitzwilliam Museum Corpus of Early Medieval Coin Finds 1995: 0128. This is presumably the 'Abbāsid dirham said to have been found 'near Bridgnorth' in Beckett 2003: 33. The Abbasid dynasty, whose capital was Baghdad, ruled the Arab world between 758-1258 AD.

[1964] Series E (secondary) (Type 4), mint and moneyer unknown, Fitzwilliam Museum Corpus of Early Medieval Coin Finds 1993.9234. This coin is doubtless to be associated with a penny of 675-750, Series A3 (Type 2a) (N40), mint and moneyer unknown, also recorded from Compton: Fitzwilliam Museum Corpus of Early Medieval Coin Finds 1993.9096. Metcalf 1977: 103 fn.6 observes that 'It is not clear from the sale catalogue whether this might be Compton 2 miles w. of Wolverhampton or Compton 5½ miles w. of Stourbridge'. The latter is presumably Compton 1 mile north-west of Kinver (SK 822828). Compton near Wolverhampton is perhaps the better known of the two, and it is likely that if the other place were the find site, the proximity to Kinver would have been mentioned, but the uncertainty about the coin find, and the find of the socketed spearhead from Stourton Farm near Kinver, should not be overlooked.

[1965] PAS record HESH-18E881.

[1966] Type Morrison and Grunthal 1063, mint and moneyer unknown, Fitzwilliam Museum Corpus of Early Medieval Coin Finds 1992.0251. It has been suggested that 'the concentration of single finds of Carolingian coins dating from the mid-eighth century in relatively discrete zones points to the existence of long-lived routes of exchange established well before the Vikings became a seriously destabilising factor in north-western Europe, and ... to the notion that Carolingian coinage played a bigger part in Anglo-Saxon monetary economies of the later eighth and ninth centuries than has previously been assumed': Story 2003: 251.

[1967] Beckett 2003: 33.

[1968] Higham 1993: 203.

[1969] Farrell 1982: 34-5.

the first half of the tenth century.'.[1970] With the Carolingian coins, the Kufic coins in the Croydon hoard support the evidence of the hack-silver and ingots that it was a Viking hoard with Danish, rather than Norwegian, connections. The Claverley dirham may have reached Scandinavia and found its way to England between c.875 and c.950.[1971]

Further evidence to suggest that the Claverley dirham may be more than an isolated find is a copper-alloy strap end found in 2010.[1972] The piece has been dated to 700-950, but of particular interest is a design that has been identified as Anglo-Scandinavian Trewhiddle style, strengthening the possibility (and it is no more than that) for an association of Claverley with Vikings recorded in the area in 895-6 and 910.

The Severn is known to have been used as a routeway by Vikings at various times, and a line drawn from Quatford to Tettenhall passes very close to both Claverley (4 miles from Quatford) and Compton (nearly 10 miles from Quatford), while Hednesford, which lies on the southern edge of the extensive heath and wooded uplands of Cannock Chase, is some 11 miles north-east of Tettenhall, in the general direction one might expect fleeing Scandinavians to take *en route* to the comparative if imaginary safety of the Danelaw. The general absence of recorded finds of Scandinavian hack-silver in the immediate area may, of course, be due to the failure of metal detectorists to recognise the significance of mutilated or fragmentary pieces of undecorated silver which are generally associated with the Vikings.[1973]

[1970] Brooks 2000: 78.
[1971] Brooks 2000: 68.
[1972] PAS record WMID-COBB26.
[1973] In 2000 two small silver ingots, one complete and one fragment, were found in Clive parish, Shropshire, The ingots (which are now on display in Ludlow Museum) have been identified as late ninth or tenth century in date. Clive is some 30 miles north-west of Tettenhall, in a direct line with Chester. For completeness, details of other artefacts from the period found in the area in which we are interested must be mentioned. In 2006 a complete cast copper alloy, and partly silvered, flat zoomorphic strap end, was found in Worfield (PAS record WMID-DFCCD4). The front of the piece is highly decorated in so-called Trewhiddle style (named after the Trewhiddle hoard, found in 1774 in an old tin mine at Trewhiddle, St Austell, Cornwall, which consisted of a number of silver artifacts with a large quantity of coins which dated the hoard to c.868: Webster and Backhouse 1991: 272-3). Typically, strap ends first appear in seventh-century pagan Saxon graves, but are mainly found in later Anglo-Saxon contexts and are usually dateable to the ninth century, as is this piece: see Wilson 1964: 169-71, 195-8, and 202-3, and plates XXX, XL, and XLII for similar strap ends. For the large number of Anglo-Saxon strap ends found at the Viking camp at Torksey see Hadley and Richards 2016: 57-8. Another copper alloy incomplete fragment, perhaps a terminal from a bracelet or armband, found in Worfield in 2013 has a design incorporating beasts identified as Anglo-Scandinavian in origin, dating from 750-1000 (PAS record HESH-A5C584), and another cast copper alloy flat zoomorphic strap end, incomplete and probably also decorated in Trewhiddle style, is recorded from Tong, Shropshire (PAS Record WMID-4CC935). This piece has been dated to the ninth century: see Wilson 1964: 202 and Plate XLII. Yet another fragmentary strap-end in Anglo-Scandinavian Borre-style known as 'vertebral ring chain', dating from the 10th century, was found in Albrighton in 2011: PAS record HESH-B84126. There is no evidence at all that any of these strap ends could have any association with the events of August 910, for the Anglo-Saxons had by then been well settled in the region for centuries, as can be inferred from the entries in Domesday Book for almost all villages in the area, and strap ends of this type are not particularly rare, or associated only with military use; they may well have been lost by a local landowner, churchman or traveller at any time during, or even well after, the ninth century – the quality of the first piece, with its silvered finish, indicates that it was likely to have been lost by a person of some wealth and status rather than a peasant artisan. On the other hand, the possibility that one or more of these pieces could have been lost by Anglo-Saxons or Scandinavians who were involved in events connected with the battle of 910

Coins from other lands were not allowed to circulate in Anglo-Saxon England, whereas the Vikings cared little about the types of coinage they acquired as long as they were of high quality silver that could be melted down or cut up for trading purposes, and Arabic coins were prized for their purity. It is very possible, therefore, that the Claverley dirham may have been lost by a Viking, perhaps during the Danish wintering at or near Quatford in 895-6, but it may be more likely that one or more of the coins from Claverley, Compton and Hednesford (especially the Claverley dirham) was part of the loot carried by the army *en route* from the river Severn prior to the conflict with the English in 910, although it must be recognised that all or any of those coins could have been lost at any time during the last 1,200 years or so.[1974]

It is noteworthy, however, that in the entire counties of Shropshire and Staffordshire, apart from three cigar-shaped silver ingots and one fragment, all found near Watling Street not far from the Roman site at *Letocetum* (Wall),[1975] all dating from the late ninth or early tenth century and important evidence of Scandinavians in the area at about the time of the battle of Tettenhall, the only finds we might possibly associate with Viking activity are a silver penny (c.895-c.910) issued by Danish settlers found in the Dovedale area in north-east Staffordshire,[1976] and the fragment mentioned previously from close to the river Severn at Sheinton. Especially surprising is the complete absence of any artifactual finds from the Quatford area which can be identified with certainty as Scandinavian (or indeed Anglo-Saxon) and dating from the late ninth century, bearing in mind that a Danish war band lay encamped there for several months in 895-6 under the watchful eyes of a nervous and sizeable English army.

Finally, the dirham from Claverley draws our attention to a particularly impressive pictorial representation of a battle in the form of a wall painting fifty-two feet long above the Norman north arcade in Claveley church, a royal chapel belonging to the Royal College of St Mary Magdalene at Bridgnorth Castle, which from the representations of arms, armour and clothing, has been dated to the early thirteenth century. The painting, of mounted warriors fighting with spears and swords, is the earliest and most extensive of any surviving medieval English royal painting scheme. Various theories have been put forward to explain ther iconography of the painting. For many years it was seen as a representation of the conflict between seven Christian virtues and seven pagan vices described in the fourth-century Roman poem, the *Psychomachia* by Prudentius,[1977] but a detailed survey of English medieval wall paintings has since concluded that the theory 'stumbles as heavily as

---

AD, however unlikely, cannot be ruled out completely: Worfield lies between Quatford and Tettenhall, and Tong was also the place where the Tong fragment, dealt with elsewhere in this volume, was found.

[1974] It has been suggested that 'the concentration of single finds of Carolingian coins dating from the mid-eighth century in relatively discrete geographical zones points to the existence of long-lived routes of exchange established well before the Vikings became a seriously destabilising factor in north-western Europe, and ... to the notion that Carolingian coinage played a bigger part in the Anglo-Saxon monetary economies of the later eighth and ninth centuries than has previously been assumed': Story 2003: 251. It is difficult to know to what extent this statement might apply to the West Midlands.

[1975] A cigar-shaped 7cm. silver ingot found in Shenstone parish in 2009 (PAS record WMID-F6EEFO); the cut and broken end of a cigar-shaped silver ingot found south of Watling Street on the east side of Shenstone (SK1205) in 2011 (PAS record WMID-OB3FC7); and one cigar-shaped 7cm silver ingot and half of another found in the Lichfield area in 2013 (PAS record WMID-C36B61). On Viking silver ingots, see Bean 2000; Kershaw 2015.

[1976] The coin is a St Eadmund penny, found in May 2009 (PAS record WMID-34C546).

[1977] Borenius and Tristram 1927: 48-9.

the falling riders it depicts', and rejects that interpretation, since the number of combatants does not match the number in the *Psychomachia*, and it is impossible to tell which horseman is a Vice or a Virtue.[1978] A more recent and exhaustively detailed study of the murals notes that Ranulf de Blondeville, Earl of Chester, became Sheriff of Shropshire and Keeper of Bridgnorth Castle, where he made extensive repairs. In 1218 he left on crusade, and it is persuasively argued that the painting, evidently the work of a local painter[1979] and interpreted as various biblical Holy Cross scenes and crusade imagery, dating perhaps to the second or third decades of the thirteenth century and painted over with stencil patterns in the fifteenth century, reflects widespread European themes including representations of Roman emperors and Charlemagne and the only surviving medieval mural of Roland, the latter a warrior for Christ well known in medieval Europe from the *Chanson de Roland*. The murals, it is suggested, may have been commissioned by Ranulph de Blondeville.[1980]

The interpretation of the painting must necessarily rest with specialists on the subject, but the extensive original paint losses and later repainting necessarily preclude any definitive conclusions, and we might wonder whether the painting originally portrayed in allegorical form the triumph of the English over the Danes[1981] – Christianity over paganism – conceivably based on the battle of Tettenhall some three centuries earlier, for the conflict is likely to have remained a vivid folk-memory in the locality into the early thirteenth century, and could well have been known to Ranulf de Blondeville. That idea might be reinforced by the fact that the church of Claverley was collegiate – and supported the clergy of Quatford. At the end of the twelfth or beginning of the thirteenth century the people of Claverley may have retained a distant memory derived from inherited folklore of a Scandinavian army (and possibly also an English army in pursuit) passing through Quatford and the Claverley area *en route* to the Tettenhall/Wednesfield area and of the conflict that followed. It was customary in the Middle Ages when illustrating historical events to show participants with contemporary clothing, arms and armour, and we should not expect artwork of that period to attempt to show either Anglo-Saxons or Vikings in ninth or tenth century garb. Yet attractive as the theory may be, there must be little doubt that the wider European themes mentioned above accurately explain the iconography of the murals.

Since the written sources tell us that the Danish army crossing the Severn in 910 was laden with booty, we might turn to consider the evidence for finds of pre-Conquest treasure in the greater Wolverhampton area.

The place-name *Goldhorde Style*, recorded on Rudge Heath in Claverley in 1615 and 1774,[1982] must be of special interest, since it is from Old English *gold-hord* 'gold hoard, gold treasure', applied to places where treasure has been found, so meaning here 'the stile where the hoard of gold was found'. Another reference to a gold hoard is found in the

---

[1978] Rosewell 2008: 94-5, who suggests that the same artist may have been responsible for the wall paintings at Claverley and Upton Cresset: ibid. 117.
[1979] Fragments of paintings at Upton Cressett, Shropshire, and Heightington, Worcestershire, are almost certainly by the painter of the Claverley mural: Barrett 2012: 158.
[1980] Barrett 2012: 129-68.
[1981] Barrett 2012 makes no mention of the battle of Tettenhall. An illustration in the manuscript Life of St Edmund, dating from 1125-50, in the Pierpont Morgan Library, shows three groups of mounted warriors, all wearing knee-length chain mail and conical helmets and carrying spears, attacking three groups of similarly armed warriors on horseback, and is said to represent the fight with the Danes: Rickert 1965: Plate 64.
[1982] Foxall 1980: 60; SA 330/25 (XBOY/5/6/R299833).

place-name Goldthorn Hill. The place lies 2 miles south-east of Wolverhampton, and is recorded as early as 1291 as *Golthordeshull*, from which it is evident that the modern name is a corruption of *gold-hord*.[1983] The place-name *Goltherdesbeuch* (probably meaning 'the batch (stream valley) at the place known as Gold Hoard') is recorded in 1296,[1984] and whilst its location cannot be identified with certainty, from other associated references to *Golthordeshull*[1985] in the same document it probably derived its name from the same hoard. It seems to have lain to the south or south-west of Wolverhampton within Kinver Forest (so suggesting that the hill was named after a spot on the western lower slopes of Goldthorn Hill), and is perhaps to be associated with *Hulhord* recorded in the Penn area in 1336,[1986] seemingly with the meaning 'hill where a hoard was found', although the word-order of the two elements is curious: *Hordhul* would normally be expected. It is noteworthy that all of these names, which seem to commemorate the same hoard of gold treasure found somewhere in Penn, presumably of some size and importance, lie roughly on a line from Quatford to Wednesfield.

It is obviously impossible to know more about the hoards after which these places were named, and if they or any of them were to be associated with the battle of Tettenhall. If they were – which on balance is unlikely, since silver rather than gold is normally found in Viking hoards, though Vikings missed no opportunity to acquire gold – it must remain a matter for speculation how the treasure came to be where it was found in or before the thirteenth century. Other place-names in the area, though not indicative of treasure, are *Burni(l)dlowe* recorded in the thirteenth century in Penn,[1987] perhaps meaning 'Brunhild's tumulus' or 'the low or tumulus associated with the burned hill', and *Roulowe Field* in Lower Penn recorded in 1316, which evidently lay near the road from Wolverhampton to Seisdon. The name is from Old English *ruh hlāw* 'rough mound or tumulus', perhaps meaning 'the overgrown mound or tumulus'. It is not impossible that one or both of these supposed tumuli was associated with one of the above hoards. Other place-names recording tumuli, or tumuli-like features, for example Rowley, Kingslow, Stanlow, and possibly Coplow, are not unusual in the wider area.[1988]

Other finds of treasure include a gold torc found at Fantley Hill to the west of the church at Pattingham in 1700.[1989] Torcs were heavy neckrings used in the Iron Age which came into fashion again in the Viking period. The find, of which no details exist, may be associated with the name *Goldthorn Acre* in Pattingham recorded in 1683.[1990]

[1983] See WA II: 41-2; Horovitz 2005: 279. Although the word *hord* was also used for a privy, that meaning is improbable in early place-names.

[1984] SHC 4th Series XVIII 185. Other *–beuch* names are recorded in the same area: ibid.

[1985] SHC 4th Series XVIII 185.

[1986] SHC 1928 34.

[1987] SRO D593/B/1/17/1/3/10.

[1988] Horovitz 2005.

[1989] Shaw 1801 II: 279; Gough's edition of Camden's *Britannia*, 1806: 500; Erdeswick 1844: 364. The torc was sold to a brazier in London who is said to have made a copy in brass which he passed off as the original when the authorities began to make enquiries. The original was supposedly 2 feet or 4 feet long (depending on the report), and weighed 3lbs 2ozs, which throws some doubt on whether it may have been an Iron Age torc, or possibly an Anglo-Saxon or Viking piece. Again in Pattingham, in 1780 a small gold ingot, some 2" long with a rounded top, was found by a youth on Golden Bank, the next field westwards to Fantley Hill. It was sold in Birmingham for £1. 18s. 0d. Torque House in Pattingham is recorded at some date between 1811 and 1856: SRO D3074/D/2/7/1-8.

[1990] Horovitz 2005: 279.

It is probably no more than curious coincidence that in the whole of Staffordshire (one of the larger counties in England) the examples cited above, and an unidentified field-name in Brewood recorded in 1453 as *Goldburynes*, 'burial place where gold was found',[1991] seem to be the only place-names so far traced incorporating the word 'gold', though it is right to add that detailed surveys of field-names in Staffordshire remain incomplete.

[1991] Oakden 1984: 47. It is unclear whether the name is to be associated with tumuli recorded at Calf Heath on the eastern edge of the parish: Plot 1686: 403; Horovitz 1992: 20.

31. The Tong Fragment.

A particularly evocative archaeological find that might possibly relate directly to the battle of Tettenhall was made in 1994 when Clive Rasdall, an experienced metal detectorist from Albrighton, picked up from earth excavated from a pipeline trench alongside the main A41 near the church at Tong, some seven miles north-west of Tettenhall, a small copper alloy fragment in the form of a legless dog/hound.[1992] A full-size photograph of the piece appears on the front cover of this volume.[1993]

The worn and tiny fragment is just under 1½" long, but clearly a piece of remarkably high quality, and exceptionally unusual in design. The head has a small projecting ear and large curved mouth with curled lip, with a small rounded protrusion underneath the bottom jaw. The neck curves backwards and the head bends back over the body. The tail is bent at right angles to enter the mouth. All of the limbs are missing, so it is uncertain whether it had two or four legs when made, but the stub of a foreleg suggests that it may originally have been raised and tucked into the body.

The body itself is divided into sections by raised lines across the jaw and (perhaps) shoulder, and the front haunch and the tail divide the body into separate areas. The whole piece has a dark green patina. The remains of dark grey enamel are clearly visible on two areas of the torso, with other traces on the rear haunch and neck, all incorporating marks from inlaid silver wire in a simple wavy pattern, with fragments of wire remaining embedded in the enamel over the haunch. It seems likely that all separate areas of the animal (with the exception perhaps of the jaws, tail and lower legsl) were originally enamelled. Similarly, the eye, which seems to have been formed by a circular depression within an almond shape, will almost certainly have been highlighted with some sort of coloured infill, but no trace can now be seen. The back of the piece, which shows evidence of vertical filing marks, has a single vertical rectangular staple on the left side (when seen from the back), but no trace of any other fixing. It must be assumed that the piece was affixed by a rod, possibly of squared section, running through the staple, though why the staple should be offset to one side is unclear. The quality of the workmanship points to a craftsman of remarkable skill, but the purpose the piece remains uncertain. Stokes describes it as a belt-fitting,[1994] and Redknap suggests that it may have been part of a cheekpiece from a harness,[1995] although the shallow staple opening makes it difficult to see how it could have been attached directly to leatherwork, and its use as a brooch cannot be ruled out. Given the uncertainty surrounding its original purpose, it is referred to here as the Tong fragment.

The piece can only be dated by comparing it with other similar designs with a known date period. The motif of a backward-facing animal, known in many regions and periods, may have had its origins as a talismanic emblem intended to avert evil (an apotropic symbol),

---

[1992] 34mm long, 23mm high and 7mm thick, weighing 6.86 grams: PAS record WMID-F8C502 (119280).
[1993] The author is particularly grateful to Clive Rasdall for allowing him to examine the find and for providing the photograph which has been used on the cover of this volume.
[1994] TSAHS LXX 1995 217, although in a letter to the finder in 1994 he also suggested that it may have been a brooch.
[1995] Redknap 2000: 91.

and is noticed in the work of late Roman craftsmen working in the Saxon region of Germany, with examples dating from the fifth and sixth century found in Sweden.[1996]

The Portable Antiquities Scheme has concluded that 'There is no doubt whatsoever that [the Tongfragment] dates to the period AD 875–950, as it is a perfect example of the so-called 'Jelling' style of Viking age art'.[1997] The style is usually termed Jellinge (with a final 'e') to distinguish it from Jelling in Jutland, the burial ground and complex established in the mid-tenth century by the Danish royal family, a style derived from designs found on a tenth-century silver cup or beaker found in the royal burial chamber at Jellinge.[1998]

Yet the confident assertion that the Tong fragment is a perfect example of Jellinge design may be open to debate. Typical Jellinge animals are non-representational, often with ribbon-like intertwined bodies, frequently decorated with transverse billets, rather than naturalistic: the Tong beast is notably naturalistic, with the body strikingly un-ribbonlike with no intertwining. Jellinge beasts generally have their heads shown in profile with open mouth, the upper jaw embellished with a curlicue (known as a lip-lappet), and almond shaped eye (as in the Tong piece), but also a head lappet or pigtail which may interlace with the body. The legs tend to emerge from spirally decorated front and rear haunches, of which there is no evidence on the Tong fragment, which displays a notably fleshy and well-rounded rear haunch.[1999] Indeed, Mark Redknap has suggested that the piece is 'Sub-Ringerike' [derived from Ringerike?] in style, dating from the eleventh-century.[2000]

The Ringerike style is notable for the distinctive profusion of extended, sometimes lightly fleshy, tendrils from its subject matter. The style emerged towards the end of the tenth century and lasted into the third quarter of the eleventh century.[2001] In that respect the decoration on the Ædwen brooch, found in Sutton in Cambridgeshire, is of interest. This silver disc brooch, so-named from an ownership inscription on the back, is divided on the surface into panels by petals drawn by a compass with applied conical bosses at the intersections. Of the four animals incorporated into the design, one quadruped has an almond-shaped eye and characteristic lobed snout. What is of particular interest are the parallel zig-zag lines on the neck and body (as found on the Tong brooch), and that the designs are also niello-inlaid (as on the Tong brooch). The Ædwen brooch is held to be a poorly implemented version of Viking Ringericke style of the early eleventh century.[2002]

There are certainly similarities in the pose of the Tong beast and that of a back-facing beast on a circular silver brooch from Espinge, Skane, southern Sweden, which has been

---

[1996] Ager 1996: 112. It is worth noting that some elements of the Tong fragment reflect forms found in 'quoit type' brooches and buckles focussed around the Severn estuary and tentatively associated with one of the 'border zone' British kingdoms of the late or post-Roman period: Halsall 2013: 261-2, citing Suzuki 2000.
[1997] PAS record WMID-F8C502 (119280), which cites an example of similar decoration in Wilson and Klindt-Jensen: 1966: page 105, fig 48. That depicts an ornament from a cross-shaft in the parish church at Collingham, Yorkshire. In reality, though the beast at Collingham has a backturned head biting part of the interlace design, there is little similarity with the Tong brooch.
[1998] TSAHS LXX 1995: 217; PAS Annual Report 1996.
[1999] An example of Jellinge design bearing similarities to the Tong brooch is found on a cross-shaft in the parish church at Collingham, Yorkshire, illustrated in Wilson and Klindt-Jensen 1966: 105 fig. 48.
[2000] Redknap 2000: 91.
[2001] Wilson and Klindt-Jensen 1980: 146.
[2002] Marzinzik 2013: 258-9.

described as 'The most completely typical Ringerike style animal on a piece of jewellery', and dated to c.1048.[2003] That has the typical Ringerike spiral designs forming the top of the legs, which are not found on the Tong fragment. Furthermore, a bronze sword cross-guard found recently some 15 miles off the coast of Pembrokeshire is decorated with interlaced animal bodies in late Viking style incorporating a head (though not a body) strikingly similar to that of the Tong fragment: it is shown in profile and has a long snout with terminal knop, short lower jaw with a downturn, almond eye and backset ear. The piece, which also has silver and niello inlay, is seen as the product of a Dublin workshop, and perhaps dates to the eleventh century.[2004]

What other comparable pieces to the Tong find are known from elsewhere? A circular beaded-frame gilt-bronze mount surrounding a back-facing beast recovered from the Gokstad ship-burial in Norway has some similarities with the Tong piece. The body is divided into panels, including over the haunch and front legs, each filled with a design of parallel lines. The neck and body are decorated with similar parallel lines. But unlike the Tong piece, the head is not long, and the mouth (which does not bite the tail, which curves down to the upper back) shows sharp teeth. The legs, especially the front, seem to have a similar configuration to the Tong piece, and may demonstrate how the missing limbs appeared originally on the Tong fragment. The date of the Gokstad pieces, which have been assigned to an individual craftsman of the Borre school of design (so-called from a major Viking cemetery with a ship burial and rich grave goods, including gilt-bronze harness mounts, dating from c.900),[2005] is not known, but the Gokstad ship, an oak-framed clinker built single sail sailing vessel some 23.3 metres long and dating from c.880, was buried c.900-5 (meaning the Gokstad brooch must pre-date 905), and contained skeletal remains of a man aged between sixty and seventy, together with a number of high quality grave goods, which indicate a very high status burial.[2006] The pieces recovered from the Gokstad burial bear no relation to any other Scandinavian style, and it has been suggested that they may be adaptations of an English model, though no such models have been identified, unless the Tong piece is, in reality, Anglo-Scandinavian in origin.

An undated bronze horse figure from Birka has its body divided into zones consisting of wide ribbons filled with interconnected Staffordshire knots (echoing the wavy-line pattern on the Tong animal), with the front and rear haunches marked with sub-circular plain areas.[2007] Those areas are mirrored in the Tong brooch, although the Birka horse does not have a back-turned head.

From England, a carved stone fragment identified as part of a length of pilaster or jamb for a doorway found in Palmer Lane, near the Cathedral and Priory of St Mary, Coventry, bears a particularly striking resemblance to the Tong piece. The carving is of an Urnes-style quadruped with a back-facing profile head, large in relation to its body, having a crest

---

[2003] Wilson and Klindt-Jensen 1980: 140, 135, Plate LXII c; Graham-Campbell 2013: 121, 198. The brooch was part of the largest silver hoard known from Scandinavia (excluding Gotland): ibid. 121.
[2004] Graham-Campbell 2013: 156-7.
[2005] Wilson and Klindt-Jensen 1980: 91-2, 118; Haywood 2000: 35.
[2006] Graham-Campbell andKidd 1980: 158-9; Haywood 2000: 82-3.
[2007] The zones appear to be undecorated in the black and white photographs in Wilson and Klindt-Jensen 1980: Plate xxiii b, and it seems unlikely that they were originally enamelled or similarly decorated.

on the back of the head and an elongated snout and almond-shaped eye.[2008] The lower parts of the legs are missing, but the tail curves up around the inner face of the rear legs. A ninth-century date has been proposed based on the fleshy plant-scroll in which the creature stands, and from the stance of the animal, with the body facing right and the head twisted backwards, similar to beasts on ninth-century cross-shafts from Gloucester St Oswald and Frome, and other evidence from the 'Cropthorne Group' of Anglo-Saxon sculpture at Wroxeter and Colerne in Wiltshire.[2009] Yet to highlight the difficulty in dating such carvings, the Coventry quadruped bears a striking similarity both to a carving on a runstone from Yttergärde, Uppland, Sweden, which is dated to the eleventh century,[2010] and to an architectural relief from Canterbury Cathedral (now in Canterbuy Heritage Museum) dated to the late eleventh or early twelfth centuty.[2011]

From York there is a bone trial piece decorated with a frieze of five quadrupeds, the central figure representing an animal which resembles the Tong beast with its tail in its mouth. The piece is said to be in the Trewhiddle style dating from the ninth or early tenth century.[2012] On one part of the Ramsbury Cross in Wiltshire (made up up fragments from two cross-shafts) are three carved roundels, one above the other, each containing a back-facing beast biting its tail, alternately facing left and right. The carvings have been dated by one commentator to 850-900,[2013] by another to the ninth century,[2014] and by a third probably to some date after the establishment of the see at Ramsbury in 906.[2015] Closer to the Tong area is a small grave slab with simple interlacing and an animal in profile with a backturned head and tail turned back across the body from an unrecorded site in Chester which has been dated to the early or middle ninth century.[2016]

Whilst the Tong animal cannot therefore be dated with any certainty,[2017] it seems to fall within a wide date range, the latter part of the ninth century to the latter part of the tenth century. As has been noted, 'objects with a very Scandinavian appearance, but apparently no exact parallels in these regions, such as the Tong brooch, are enigmatic at present'.[2018]

It is nevertheless tempting, and perhaps not unreasonable, to speculate that the piece might have been lost by one of the warriors who formed part of the Northumbrian army that fought the English in 910, even though there is no evidence to prove or disprove the theory. The fact that the artefact was found on the modern A41 road (the Tong by-pass), close to the old main road through Tong on the east side of the church, cannot be taken as firm proof that the road was in use in the pre-Conquest period: the brooch could have been

---

[2008] See Owen 2001: 218-9; the piece is now in the Herbert Art Gallery and Museum. The Urnes style is named from the 11th-century stave-church at Urnes on Sogne fjord, Norway, and originated in about 1050, continuing throughout the Viking world into the 12th-century.
[2009] Bryant 2012: 336-8, illustrations 585-91
[2010] Carroll et al 2014: 61.
[2011] Grape 1994: 41.
[2012] Anon. 1981: 47 and117; described in detail earlier in this chapter.
[2013] Fisher 1959: Plate 36A.
[2014] Wilson 1984: Plate 135.
[2015] Clapham 1964: 127, Plate 54.
[2016] Bu'Lock 1972: 48, Plate 8. The stone may have come from St Werburgh's church: ibid.
[2017] It is worth citing the observations of one authority on the period who, writing of Scandinavian grave-goods, observed that they were difficult to date, adding 'Iam sceptical in the matter of accurate typological dating in the Viking period, believing ... that it is difficult to date any object to a period within a hundred years if there is no documentary source to assist the dating': Wilson 1976: 397.
[2018] PAS Annual Report 2006: 70.

a valued heirloom or talisman that was lost long after it was made (it was clearly a special piece made with particular care and skill), but it is very possible that the routeway was in use in the Anglo-Saxon period, particularly since an incomplete copper alloy strap end, probably of ninth-century date, is also recorded from Tong.[2019] The find spot is very close to the line of a lost Roman Road that ran south from the Roman forts at Burlaughton on Watling Street towards Wrottesley Lodge Farm and on in the direction of The Walls, the Iron Age earthworks at Chesterton, passing to the west of Tong. That road (unrecorded by Margary and the Ordnance Survey) may well have remained in use as late as the tenth century or even later.[2020] The fact that the brooch was found on an ancient routeway that led westwards from Tettenhall and the Wednesfield area (and near a Roman road running north from Chesterton, which could have played some part in the events of 910) may be a coincidence, but a noteworthy coincidence nevertheless.

All that can be said is that the likely date of the Tong fragment does not preclude a connection with the battle, a possibility perhaps reinforced by the discovery of a fragmentary strap-end in Anglo-Scandinavian Borre-style known as 'vertebral ring chain', dating from the tenth century, found in Albrighton, two miles or so south-east of Tong, in 2011.[2021] We might speculate that one or both pieces may have been lost by Scandinavian warriors before or after the battle, or (even more improbably) by English fighters who had looted them from the enemy on the battlefield.

[2019] PAS record WMID-4CC935. It is of course possible, though hardly likely, that the strap-end and the Tong Fragment were lost at the same time.
[2020] The reference to *æt Twongan* in the will of the magnate Wulfric Spot c.1004 (S.1536; S.906) has been taken to refer to Tong in Shropshire (Ekwall 1960: 477), but is probably to be identified with Tonge in Leicestershire (Sawyer 1979: xxvii-xxviii). The creation of the College of St Bartholomew at Tong, converted into a collegiate church, was licensed in 1410: VCH Shropshire II 131.
[2021] PAS record HESH-B84126.

33. The Quatford Spearhead.

Despite records dating back over a thousand years which refer to events in or close to Quatford at the end of the ninth and early part of the tenth century, not the slightest material evidence such as coins, military equipment, or domestic items from this narrow time-frame has been discovered or reported from the wider area – with one single and possibly very relevant exception. That exception is an iron spearhead apparently found at Quatford at some date prior to 2015, probably before – but perhaps not long before – 2005. It is appropriate to give a short account of the object and its provenance.

By complete happenchance, in October 2015 the present author learned of an auction house near Cirencester offering for sale a spearhead with the following description: 'A large Viking iron spearhead, late 9th century, iron with overall patina, socket for fixing to wooden pole, 27cm (10.5ins) long. Found by a householder in Quatford, Shropshire. Presumed to date from the time of the viking camp at the crossing of the Severn near Quatford, established in 895. The mound of the camp can still be viewed'.[2022] The 'mound of the camp' presumably refers to Camp Hill, the Norman mound traditionally (and probably correctly) associated with the Viking wintering of 895-6. The author was able to acquire the object, hereafter called 'the Quatford spearhead', and it remains in his possession.

When acquired the spearhead was (and is) enclosed in a modern glazed frame bearing a printed label indicating that it was 'excavated by a householder in Quatford digging foundations for a conservatory in the area where a Viking camp and fortress once stood'. Extensive enquiries to establish the identity of the vendor and/or the finder of the spearhead and the location of the findspot and the date it was found have proved frustrating and unsuccessful.

If credible, the label tells that the object was revealed during domestic building work which we must suppose was being carried out well above the Severn flood levels and close to Camp Hill. Since no houses lie close to Camp Hill on its north or east side, the find was presumably made somewhere to the south of and not far from the earthwork.[2023]

The discovery may be supported by an intriguing comment in an antiquarian discussion website in which an unidentified contributor with an interest in the area recorded in 2005 that 'A friend of mine from Quatford found an old spearhead in her garden with some design on it'.[2024] It has not been possible to secure further details of this tantalising record or the place and date of the discovery or the object itself (which a sceptical observer might suspect to have been nothing more than a misidentified Victorian fence finial or similarly prosaic object), but both the Vikings and to a lesser extent the Anglo-Saxons sometimes decorated their spearheads. The Quatford spearhead, however, has no obvious pattern on it.

[2022] Dominic Winter Auctions, South Cerney, Cirencester, 15th October 2015; Lot 134.
[2023] A small cluster of old properties lie on the southern side of Camp Hill around the old ferry site. Further south is a mobile home park on which a number of properties were built in 2005, a date which may be significant in the light of a reference in that year to a spearhead from Quatford noted above.
[2024] http://www.themodernantiquarian.com/forum/?thread=19781&message=264967; author 'Hafod?' [*sic*].

The wide, leaf-shaped rust-coloured spearhead, with markedly rounded shoulders, in unusually – perhaps even suspiciously – well-preserved condition, is almost 11" long overall, with an 8" blade, well made with a distinct thickening to form a slight central rib on the blade, and a carefully forged 2¾" long socket some 9/16" in internal diameter, the exterior of the socket octagonally faceted longitudinally with a closed straight butt-joint (unlike most Anglo-Saxon spearheads, which usually have an open join) and a small slightly oval hole an eighth of an inch at its widest, ¼" from the socket end opposite the butt-joint. The socket has a slight circumferential groove adjoining a single plain circumferential collar of semi-circular profile at the point where the head and socket meet. The interior of the socket is empty, with traces of red oxide dust, and part of the open end is bent inwards and missing a small section opposite the rivet hole. The eye of faith might detect raised lines on one facet of the socket near the blade which may represent traces of decoration, and other facets have an irregular pock-marked surface which may have once carried decoration. The surface of the piece, in places pock-marked, has probably been lightly buffed to remove loose surface corrosion, and one side of the blade shows a few faint and fine scratches along the length of the blade possibly caused by a wire brush. One edge of the blade has small indentations which may have been made by heavy impact: they are too deep and patinated to have been caused accidentally or recently.

Early Viking spearheads were forged from iron, about 8" long, while later ones were as long as 24".[2025] Like sword blades, during the early Viking period some were made using pattern-welding techniques. Both blades and socket could be decorated with inlays of precious metals or with scribed geometric patterns. In cross-section, spear heads were slender-lozenge shaped or leaf-shaped, with a thick central rib. The head tapered smoothly to a sharp edge on either side of the rib. Some Viking spears could be magnificent works of art, with inlaid copper and silver designs on the rib, and leafy foliage decoration on the surface of the blade. After forming the head, the smith flattened and drew out the iron to create the socket, forming it around a mandrel and often welding the lapped join to form a socket (sometimes polygonal externally), though in some cases, the joint was left unwelded, as with the Quatford example. This can be compared with the open-cleft sockets of Anglo-Saxon spearheads, which frequently have decorative rings around the junction of the blade with the socket. A single rivet sometimes fixed an Anglo-Saxon spearhead to its wooden shaft, but is a feature more common on Viking spearheads. The rivets on surviving historical weapons are surprisingly slight. One literary source suggests that the rivet was designed to be easily be removed.[2026] That was probably to allow a spearhead to be easily detached for use when required as a short sword or bayonet. Researchers have also suggested that a weak rivet was to ensure that once thrown (and lost to the user), spears could not be re-used as a spear by the enemy.

Sockets on surviving Viking spears show that the wooden shafts were typically round in section, with a diameter of about ¾" to 1¼". Since very few shafts have survived there is little evidence to show their length, and the sagas are, for the most part, silent, but evidence from burials suggests that most were up to up to 6' 6" long,[2027] probably cut to suit the size of the user.[2028] Perhaps the best guess we can make is that the combined

---

[2025] See http://www.hurstwic.org/history/articles/manufacturing/text/viking_spear.htm, accessed 16 October 2015.
[2026] *Grettis saga* (chapter 48).
[2027] Pederson 2008: 206.
[2028] *Gisla saga* (chapter 6) mentions a spear-shaft so long that a man's outstretched arm could touch the rivet.

length of shaft and head of Viking age spears was 7-10ft, although one can make arguments for the use of spears having both longer and shorter shafts.[2029] A strong, straight-grained wood such as ash was used, and there is mention in the sagas of spear shafts reinforced with iron. The lower end was occasionally given an iron cap to help protect the end and to help balance the weapon, but the evidence is very slight, and they were not common.

The shape of the Quatford spearhead (a photograph of which appears on the spine of this book) parallels to a degree Viking spearheads dateable to the turn of the ninth century found in Denmark, though the style is not common, and an identical example has not been traced from Britain. Specifically, the Quatford piece is similar but not identical to a larger (19") high-status spearhead from a tenth-century site in Rønnebæksholm, Zealand, Denmark, with the socket encrusted with copper and silver decorated with simple geometric designs and interlace pattern.[2030] Another, smaller, spearhead with a blade of slender lozenge design (unlike the Quatford piece), but probably of the same date, from the ritual site at Tissø, Zealand, has an octagonal socket encrusted with silver in geometric and interlace patterns.[2031] Although the label attached to the Quatford spearhead describes it as large, the object is in reality modest in size compared with most Viking spearheads, which are generally very slender, and the socket of the Quatford example has an unusually small internal diameter, though some spearheads recovered from archaeological contexts are quite small: one saga mentions a *spjótsprika*, sometimes translated as 'puny spear',[2032] possibly for use by juveniles. The Quatford object is perhaps best described as a small spearhead or javelin-head,[2033] and its well-preserved condition might be explained if, for example, it had been wrapped in oiled or greased cloth or skin or was lost in a particular localized environment that protected it from corrosion and aided its preservation: many examples are recorded of Viking artefacts in remarkably fine condition, especially those immersed in water, which paradoxically seems in many cases to aid preservation.[2034]

Modern forgeries of ancient objects are not unknown, but the commercial value of genuine Viking spearheads is not great, and even if a forger possessed the necessary skills to produce an 'authentic' Viking spearhead with appropriate corrosion (which is very doubtful), any such exercise would be uneconomic. Objects from that period are notoriously difficult to copy, since the skills of Viking-age craftsmen have simply been lost in the modern world, and centuries-old corrosion is virtually impossible to fake. Furthermore, if the object is a deliberate attempt to deceive, one might have expected a faked ancient label (far easier to fabricate than a Viking spearhead), and a find spot rather better associated with a Viking presence than an obscure Shropshire village. Furthermore we have uncorroborated hearsay confirmation of a spearhead being found at Quatford in the late twentieth or early twenty-first century, and it is difficult to imagine any motive for inventing that claim. There is no obvious reason to doubt the statement. It would be hard to

---

[2029] Thompson 2004: 62-71, 85-6
[2030] Anon 1981: 154-5.
[2031] Anon 1981: 154-5.
[2032] *Laxdæla saga* (chapter 64); Smiley and Kellogg 2000: 396.
[2033] Logan Thompson draws attention to warriors carrying such javelins as depicted in the Bayeux Tapestry, and observes that 'The devastating effect of a javelin thrown at close quarters should not be underestimated. It need not be razor-sharp to be effective. ... It is easy to see how bodies of light infantry armed with such weapons could have softened up a shield wall before it came into contact eith its main enemy.': Thompson 2004: 66, 69.
[2034] Thompson 2004: 119-20.

offer a motive for a recent and invented provenance attached falsely to the Quatford spearhead: such a provenance is hardly likely to have materially affected its relatively modest value. On the balance of probability it seems possible, if unprovable, that the two spearheads are one and the same, since the website comment and the sale of the object both occurred within a few years, and no other type of artefact which might conceivably have been associated with the Vikings has been traced within a wide radius of Quatford.

To establish whether the object could be of Viking origin, photographs were submitted to Dr Kevin Leahy, National Adviser in Early Medieval Metalwork to the Portable Antiquities Scheme. He sought advice from Professor James Graham-Campbell, a leading expert on Viking weaponry,[2035] who felt the spearhead to be too flat and thin to have a Scandinavian origin, and saw no parallels in finds from Britain, but turned for a further opinion to Dr Anne Pedersen,[2036] an authority in Viking weaponry at the National Museum of Denmark in Copenhagen.[2037] Dr Pederson, in an exhaustive study of the photographs,[2038] noted the similarity in some respects to Norwegian spearheads from the Viking period, including some from Dublin (as will be seen, a point perhaps of particular

[2035] Emeritus Professor of Medieval Archaeology at University College London Institute of Archaeology, and a specialist in Viking, Late Celtic and Anglo-Saxon art and artefacts.
[2036] See Pederson 2008.
[2037] Thanks are due to Dr Leahy, Professor Graham-Campbell, and Dr Pederson for their learned opinions on the spearhead.
[2038] In an unpublished report dated 23 September 2016 (a synopsis of which follows with the kind permission of Dr Pederson), the similarity of the Quatford spearhead to weapons from Rønnebæksholm and Tissø, and with the general outline of a spearhead from Trelleborg, is noted, but Dr Pederson expressed concern about some differences. The Quatford spearhead resembles J.P. type G, type group IX, as categorized by Bergljot Solberg (in *Norwegian Spear-heads from the Merovingian and Viking Periods*, Bergen, 1984). That group is characterized by shoulders on the blade (or as in the case of IX.2 no clearly defined shoulders) and a short socket elongation into the blade; alternatively a ring-shaped elevation between socket and blade (variant IX.3). Blades are usually wide in comparison to other Scandinavian spearheads. The Quatford spearhead appeared to lack the socket elongation into the blade, and the transition from socket to blade seemed rather abrupt compared with type G spearheads, both on the faces and the sides. Moreover, the blade seemed remarkably flat and thin, lacking the typical shoulders of type G and showing a rather even curve at the widest point unlike the Trelleborg and Rønnebæksholm examples which are more angled. The blade appeared too wide (and rather too triangular in outline) for the subgroup IX.2 without shoulders. Furthermore, the socket of the Quatford spearhead is slightly longer than would have been expected for a type G, with the split seam of the socket a feature that Dr Pederson could not recall seeing in Danish spearheads, though it is apparently not uncommon, and some Dublin spearheads show similar splits. In the Quatford spearhead the split seam is consistent with a description of the suggested method of manufacture: 'After forming the head, the smith flattened and drew out the iron to create the socket, forming it around a mandrel and often welding the lapped join to form a socket, though in some cases, the joint was left unwelded', as with the Quatford example. Dr Pederson was uncertain whether that method applied to all Viking-age spearheads: on some Finnish spearheads, the blades appeared rather to have been inserted into the socket, the elongations on either side supporting the welded joint. Dr Pederson compared the Quatford spearhead with photographs in Pirkko-Liisa Lehtosalo-Hilander, 'Viking Age spearheads in Finland', *Society and Trade in the Baltic during the Viking Age*, Visby, 1985. She would have expected rivet holes at the sides of the socket, but in the Quatford example the single hole is on the face opposite the seam, although this feature had also been observed on a Dublin spearhead. Dr Pederson found no exact parallel for the Quatford spearhead in the Copenhagen collections, and whilst expressing serious doubts about a Viking, i.e. Scandinavian, origin, suggested that if it was indeed from the ninth or tenth century, it may have been made locally or by a smith copying the general type. Dr Pederson's conclusions were supported independently by her colleague, Dr Peter Pentz. Dental x-rays of the artifact kindly provided by Dr Christopher Burn revealed no evidence of pattern-welding.

significance), but with no exact parallels and was hesitant about ascribing a Scandinavian attribution to the object, concluding that if it does indeed date from the ninth or tenth century it may have been manufactured by a local ironworker based on Scandinavian weaponry.[2039] Although she did not say so explicitly, her report left open the possibility that the object might date from the end of the ninth or the beginning of the tenth century, and leads us to conclude that that it could conceivably be associated with the battle of Tettenhall, or at least that there is nothing to definitely exclude the possibility. It should be added that the weapon is very unlike Anglo-Saxon spearheads of the period with their split sockets, and the idea that it may have been lost by one of the English forces in the area in the late ninth or early tenth century can be ruled out.

In summary, therefore, if its recently claimed find spot is reliable (which we shall probably never know), the Quatford spearhead, evidently of some age, and perhaps dating from the time of the battle of Tettenhall, might be explained,in the light of expert opinion which is to a degree equivocal and in truth sceptical about its date and origin, as lost during the long wintering of the Danes at Quatford in 895-6, or alternatively (perhaps more likely given the possible Dublin association) could have been an object produced in Dublin by a local smith based on Viking designs, lost when Northumbrian forces, who were probably Hiberno-Norse who had been expelled from Dublin c.901 and settled soon after in north-west England, crossed the Severn in August 910 immediately before the battle of Tettenhall – it will be recalled that Æthelweard tells us that the Scandinavians were first attacked *repente* 'suddenly'[2040] by English forces as they were crossing the river at *Cwatbrycge* – or indeed at some other date at about that period when unrecorded parties of Scandinavians could have been in the area.

So the Quatford spearhead might – just possibly – be the only surviving physical evidence directly associated with the great battle of 910, and most poignantly with someone who actually fought – and perhaps died – there.

[2039] On supposedly distinctive 'Dublin type' spearheads from Viking sites in Ireland see now Harrison and Ó Floinn 2014, but note review in *Antiquaries Journal* 96 (2016) 451-2.
[2040] Campbell 1962: 53.

34. The prelude to the battle of Tettenhall.

Alfred the Great died on 26 October 899.[2041] That he intended his son Edward to take the crown is implied by a charter the previous year in which Edward is called king.[2042] Edward was indeed consecrated king on 8 June 900, but as David Dumville has observed, '[t]he chronology of the reign of Edward the Elder, and especially of its first decade, is severely problematic in detail',[2043] since the sources are sparse, incomplete, partisan, sometimes contradictory, and almost invariably enigmatic. There is little doubt, however, that the opening years of the tenth century were especially notable for the acute threat to Edward's crown, and indeed to the kingdom of Mercia, posed by his cousin Æthelwold, who made a determined bid for power after the death of Alfred, a power struggle which was to lead to open warfare between the principal rivals to the throne of Wessex.[2044] In the memorable words of Sir Frank Stenton, Edward 'was kept in unease by an enemy sprung from his own house'.[2045]

Born in 868, Æthelwold[2046] was Edward's cousin, the younger of two known sons of Alfred's elder brother, King Æthelred (the older was Æthelhelm, who seems to have died between c.885 and some date in the 890s),[2047] and had some claim to rank above Edward,[2048] but had been too young to succeed when his father died in 871. In Wessex at

---

[2041] A curious observation by the chronicler Ætheleard deserves mention. He tells us that in 899, prior to Alfred's death, 'there was a disturbance on a very great scale among the English, that is the bands who were then settled in the territories of the Northumbrians': Campbell 1962: 51. That comment was considered by Stenton, who felt that it revealed 'the instability of the peace which Alfred had made, and helps to explain the readiness with which the Northumbrians supported Æthelwold's claim.': Stenton 1970: 12-13.

[2042] S.350; Keynes 2001: 48. For the intriguing possibility that animosity between Alfred and Edward may have led Alfred to consider making Æthelstan his immediate heir, see Nelson 1991: 63-4. Alfred's youngest surviving son was Æthelweard, whose education seems to have differed from that of Alfred's other children, Edward and Ælfthryth, if we are to believe Asser, with the latter brought up at the royal court under Alfred's supervision, and Æthelweard was taught at the more intensive *schola* supervised by *magistri*: Yorke 2001: 27-9. Little is known about Æthelweard, but he had at least 2 sons who were killed at *Brunanburh*, and died c.921.

[2043] Dumville 1992: 10 fn54.

[2044] The older brother, Æthelhelm, died c.898: Ashley 1999: 468. It is worth noting that after King Alfred's death Edward married Ælfflæd, niece of Æthelwold and grand-daughter of King Æthelred, Alfred's older brother, a union that was within the prohibited degrees: Sharp 2001: 82.

[2045] Stenton 1971: 321.

[2046] Listed as Æthelwald 35 [*sic*] in the *Prospography of Anglo-Saxon England*, accessed 1st October 2016.

[2047] Yorke 2001: 30-31.Alfred's father, Æthelwulf, had left his sons Alfred, Æthelred, Æthelbald and Æthelbert royal estates, but it was recognised that whoever succeeded as king needed the bulk of those estates to rule effectively. Under the terms of an agreement made between Æthelwulf and Æthelred declared before the witan in about 870-871, Æthelhelm and Æthelwold were excluded from inheriting those estates, though they were entitled to the estates which King Æthelwulf had given to Æthelred and Alfred during their brother Æthelbald's lifetime, which may have been those estates bequeathed to Æthelhelm and Æthelwold in Alfred's will. Alfred right to bequeth his lands as he wished was upheld by the witan c.885, when it was made clear that he intended to leave the bulk of his inheritance to Edward, with relatively modest estates in the more remote parts of eastern Wessex to his two nephews. That would have proved problematic if either nephew had inherited the throne, for he would have held insufficient estates to support his position, though would not have fatally damaged the position of Æthelhelm and Æthelwold when Alfred's will was declared, for they were still senior æthelings: Keynes and Lapidge 1983: 173-83, 313-26; Yorke 2001: 30-1.

[2048] One obvious advantage enjoyed by Æthelwold is that he was born to a consecrated queen, Wulfyth, who is titled *regina* in her only appearance in a charter (S.340). The only surviving charter

that date there were no firmly established traditions surrounding royal succession: primogeniture was not established, and suitability and competence were seen as more important than the preservation of any specific line of descent, with adult males taking preference over children.[2049] Unlike the position in Francia, where Frankish kings divided their kingdoms equally between their sons,[2050] there was no accepted custom that the son of a king was bound to succeed his father; indeed, brothers had the same right to inheritance as sons, and the throne had often passed from uncle to nephew, brother to brother, cousin to cousin – Alfred's father had been the first son of a king to succeed directly to the throne in almost two centuries. Succession was ultimately in the hands of the *ealdormen*, the great men of the kingdom, and the acclamation of the people.[2051] But as senior *æðeling* (prince of the royal dynasty eligible for kingship),[2052] at Alfred's death Æthelwold believed himself to be the true successor to the West Saxon throne, a claim not without merit – in the words of Janet Nelson 'in the eyes of many Englishmen as well as Scandinavians this ætheling had claims stronger than Edward's own'[2053] – and enjoyed a not insignificant following ready to support his cause. However, Alfred had promoted Edward as his successor during his lifetime – even perhaps having Edward formally anointed as king before Alfred died.[2054] Under Alfred's will Æthelwold as a nephew conspicuously inherited fewer properties than Edward, and those estates lay in the eastern, or 'less important' part of Wessex.[2055] Indeed, on at least one occasion when king, Alfred had been forced to publicly deflect before the *witan* complaints from Æthelwold and his brother Æthelhelm about the size of their inheritance and defend the acquisition of estates he had acquired and his disposal of others, an action unlikely to have increased the affection for his nephews by their uncle.[2056] The frequency of Edward's name attesting charters (six, to Æthelwold's one), indicates that Edward often accompanied the king when he conducted business,[2057] and Edward's military experience – he is known, for example, to have led a section of the West Saxon *fyrd* when a Viking army was defeated at Farnham in 894[2058] – meant that he was suitably qualified to take up the reigns of power.[2059] He could also call on the support of his brother-in-law Æthelred with whom he had long co-operated in military campaigns resisting the Viking onslaught.[2060]

It was against that backdrop that Æthelwold, then 32 years old and probably a battle-hardened military commander, formally contested Edward's succession before the *witan*

---

witnessed by Æthelwold, probably of the 890s (S.356), is attested by Æthelwold immediately before Edward, both described as *filius regis*, inferring that Æthelwold was the senior of the two. Æthelhelm is unmentioned in the charter, which might indicate that he was then dead, for he is unrecorded after the declaration of Alfred's will: Yorke 2001: 31.

[2049] Yorke 2001: 30.
[2050] Horspool 2014:13.
[2051] Holland 2016: 25. An illuminating account of complex discussions and negotiations relating to the distribution of estates and rights of inheritance before and following the death of a king is recited in the will of King Alfred: Harmer 1914: 49-53; Keynes and Lapidge 1983: 173-8.
[2052] Dumville 1979.
[2053] Nelson 2008: 122.
[2054] A charter of 898 (S.350) is witnessed by Alfred as *rex Saxonum* followed by Edward as *rex*: Yorke 2001: 32.
[2055] Earle and Plummer 1892-99: II 115; Keynes and Lapidge 1983: 173-81.
[2056] Holland 2016: 26.
[2057] Yorke 2001: 31, though the vagaries of charter survival might have created a misleading impression.
[2058] Earle and Plummer 1892-99: II 108.
[2059] Yorke 2001: 32; Downham 2009: 80; Pelteret 2009: 325.
[2060] For a valuable analysis of the claims to succession on the death of Alfred see Yorke 2001.

(which would explain the seven-month delay in Edward's coronation), presumably expecting to enjoy significant support from the magnates of Wessex, and when that challenge came to nothing embarked on a course which could only be seen as full-scale rebellion.[2061]

With disaffected supporters he seised both the royal manors of Wimborne, (of particular significance not only for its control of north and west Wessex, but as the burial place of Æthelwold's father, and perhaps a centre of family power), and that (æt) Tweoxn eam (Twynham, the old name of Christchurch, ten miles away),[2062] 'against the will of the king and his counsellors (witena)'.[2063] For the witan to be involved we must assume that as well as disputing Edward's right to the throne, Æthelwold, deeply aggrieved by what he saw as his rightful title to the throne thwarted, had formally contested Edward's right to those two places, with the dispute heard by the witan and judgment given against him. From Wimbourne, Æthelwold – pointedly identified in Anglo-Saxon Chronicle 'A'as Edward's uncle's son, rather than æðeling – taunted Edward, who had hastened in pusuit of his rebellious cousin with a great army. Æthelwold and his supporters barricaded the gates of Wimbourne and were besieged by Edward, who evidently retained the loyalty of the greater part of the West Saxon army, which had camped at Baddanbyrig, the prehistoric earthworks now known as Badbury Rings, 3½ miles to the north-west at the strategic junction of four Roman roads.[2064] Whether Edward and Æthelwold had direct communication is unknown, but very unlikely. Æthelwold nevertheless made it known that he would either live or die at Wimborne, clearly a sham boast intended to deceive, since somehow and rather remarkably (and to Edward's great cost) he and his forces escaped in darkness, abandoning a former nun – very probably royal-born – who he had 'taken' unlawfully without Edward's permission and against the bishops' orders (possibly as a wife, according to Florence (John) of Worcester and Henry of Huntingdon),[2065] if the undoubtedly prejudiced Chronicle, keen to blacken Æthelwold's character, is to be believed.[2066] Æthelwold's female companion was seised by Edward and, according to the chroniclers, returned to her monastery.[2067]

Outriding Edward and his troops, the would-be usurper and his forces eventually reached Northumbria, presumably aware from earlier contacts that he would be well-received,the

---

[2061] See especially Lavelle 2009. Æthelhelm, Æthelwold's elder brother, had died a few years earlier.
[2062] The name (æt) Tweoxn eam means '(the place) betwixt the streams': Ekwall 1960: 483. On the burh at Twynham see Hill and Rumble 1996: 198-9.
[2063] On Wimborne and Christchurch see Smyth 1995: 437.
[2064] ASC 'A'; Swanton 1996: 92-3; Stevenson 1853: 72.
[2065] Stephenson 1853: 72; Greenway 1996: 299. Marrying without royal permission is said to have been one way for princely rebels in the 10th century to assert their defiance of a king: Holland 2016: 98. Alex Woolf has considered the 'constant intermarriage between the various royal houses of the ninth and early tenth century', and suggests that the identity of the nun was intended to bolster Æthelwold's claim to the throne, that she was probably a member of the west Saxon or Mercian royal house, and could have been Æthelgifu, King Alfred's daughter, who was abbess at Shaftesbury minster (Woolf 2001: 99-100), though Ryan Lavelle feels it unlikely that Æthelwold's route would have taken him through Shaftesbury: Lavelle 2009: 62-3.
[2066] Hart 1992: 513; Williams, Smyth and Kirby 1991: 33. This was an offence expressly provided for in the Laws: Earle and Plummer 1892-99: II 115. King Alfred had taken a stronger line than his predecessors against those responsible for the sexual assault of women, and nuns especially: Holland 2016: 31.
[2067] See for example Florence (John) of Worcester (Stephenson 1853: 72), and Roger of Wendover (Giles 1892: 235).

implication being that Mercia offered no possibility of aid and sanctuary, though there is, as we shall see, evidence of at least limited support from a Mercian faction.

Anglo-Saxon Chronicle 'D' tells us that Æthelwold 'sought out the raiding-army in Northumbria', generally assumed to mean the Danes of York (though we should note that the same expression is used of those who 'broke the peace' and were defeated at the battle of Tettenhall),[2068] which 'received him as king and submitted to him', the latter claim conspicuously omitted from version 'A', keen to play down his success.[2069] The claim was clearly ambiguous, and could have meant he was recognised as the true king of Wessex, or that he was received as king of York, both of which would have been anathema to Edward and the chronicler in Wessex. There is some evidence that Æthelwold was indeed promoted as the – or at least a – king of York, since a shared kingship cannot be ruled out,[2070] although that is a possibility disputed by some historians since we have have vague details of the kings who ruled York until c.905.

Roger of Wendover tells us that when Æthelwold reached Northumbria he invited the Danes to choose one of their number to fight against Edward and 'was presently installed in the royal dignity by them all',[2071] and Florence (John) of Worcester claims that when he reached Northumbria Æthelwold 'requested the Danes to allow him to join them, not so much in the capacity of a leader as of a comrade; they, very shortly afterwards, made him their king'.[2072] The *Annals of St Neots*, written between c.1120 and 1140, go so far as to describe *Adheluuoldus* as both *rex Danorum* and *rex paganorum*,[2073] but rumours that he had renounced his Christian faith were doubtless later propaganda.[2074]

Coins from York (including one found in the Silverdale Viking Hoard from North Lancashire in September 2011) bearing the name ALVALDVS REX, with the reverse using dies from the coinages of Siefred and Cnut, do not assist in resolving that point, since they may have been intended to maintain his claim to the throne of Wessex, or to confirm his kingship in York.[2075] The idea of shared kingship at York may, however, be evidenced by more than 3,000 coins from the Cuerdale hoard from the same York mint which show that Siefred of York, with his coins giving the Latin SIEFREDVS or the Anglicised SIEVERT, appears to have ruled York and been succeeded for a few years by Knútr (Cnut); indeed the kings – both probably Christian[2076] – seem to have ruled jointly for a short period, with Richard Hall raising the possibility that one or both may have ruled jointly with Æthelwold, though that idea was influenced by the belief that the three kings killed at Tettenhall were from York.[2077]

[2068] ASC 'A'; Swanton 1996: 96.
[2069] Swanton 1996: 92-3.
[2070] Dumville 1992: 10; Downham 2009: 79-82.
[2071] Giles 1892: 235. Simeon of Durham records that a certain Osberht, a prince in Northumbria, was expelled in 899. It is suggested in Earle and Plummer 1892-99: I 115 that the expulsion might account for the reception of Æthelwold.
[2072] Stevenson 1853: 72.
[2073] Stevenson 1959: 144.
[2074] Holland 2016: 32.
[2075] Gooch 2012: 59. Stenton's view that Æthelwold is unlikely to have been king of Northumbria, and that he is not necessarily to be associated with the Northumbrian coins bearing his name (Stenton 1971: 322 fn.2), is now seen as outdated: see Keynes and Lapidge 1983: 292, fn.11.
[2076] As evidenced by strong Christian and Frankish influences in both iconography and legends: Hall 2001: 189.
[2077] Hall 2001: 189; Downham 2009: 78-9; Gooch 2012: 48, 160.

Knútr reappears in later Norse sagas which relate that soon after his arrival at York, Æthelwold was challenged by a Viking of unknown origin[2078] named Cnut in battles to the north of Cleveland and at Scarborough, at the second of which Æthelwold (called *adalbrigt* in the sagas) is said to have been defeated.[2079] The supposed defeat of Cnut may merely reflect the rivalry, even hostility, between Cnut and Æthelwold, but if true would explain why Æthelwold then disappears from the histories for a time. What is unclear is the nature of the relationship between the Northumbrians of York (in general terms Danes) and the Hiberno-Scandinavians (in general terms Irish-Norwegians) of the north-west, but Siefred's death (Cnut's is unrecorded) seems to have caused great unrest in the Danish army and amongst the people in 'English' Northumbria (Bernicia).[2080] However, the chronicles imply that Æthelwold was seen in York as a formidable leader with a powerful following.[2081] As a Christian with a modest yet elite force at his command it would have been surprising if he had not received a warm welcome in Northumbria, where he surely inspired local leaders by promoting the idea of a unified country with himself as king.[2082]

Not only is there a lacuna in the records about Æthelwold's actions in the north, but about the steps, if any, that Edward may have taken to neutralise this full-blown rebellion which posed the greatest threat, not just to his kingdom, but the whole of England. It is hardly believable that no action was taken to erode the risk from Æthelwold and his forces, but easy to forget that military matters were only one aspect (if the most important) of Anglo-Saxon rulership, and other matters of state will have occupied the time of any ruler.[2083] At the very least it must be supposed that Edward – with Æthelred and Æthelflæd – ensured that the forces of Wessex and Mercia were in a state of high alert, prepared at short notice to meet the likely threat from the north. But Edward was doubtless confounded by intelligence from Northumbria which reported that Æthelwold appeared to have left the kingdom and disappeared. Edward, though nonplussed, may have been lulled into a false sense of security, and what he was almost certainly not expecting was a determined military incursion from a completely different part of the country.

[2078] See especially Downham 2009: 78-80. Logan has seen the presence of coins in the Cuerdale hoard bearing the joint names of Siefred and Cnut as further evidence that in the late ninth and/or early tenth century there was a period of joint kingship at York (Logan 1991: 159-60), but his dates for Cnut's rule on page 159 are evidently an inadvertent error for those of Ragnall. Siefred is unlikely to be the 'Sigeferth the pirate arrtived from the land of the Northumbrians' who attacked north Devon in 893 and/or the jarl *Sichfrith* recorded in Dublin the same year: Hall 2001: 189; Gooch 2012: 48.

[2079] These events are recorded in the c.1230 manuscript *Eyrbyggja Saga* misplaced within a section referring to events of 1066, but Alfred Smyth argues that *adalbrigt*, though described as a king of illustrious goodness who lived to old age, is perhaps to be identified with Æthelwold. The chronology is uncertain, however, and it is possible that Cnut did not obtain York until after Æthelwold's death: Smyth 1975: I 47-52; Hart 1992: 512-3. For *Eyrbyggja Saga* see Thorkelin 1788: 29; Sturlason 1930: 225.

[2080] Downham 2009: 81-2. Æthelweard tells us that after the death of Siefred there had been great unrest among English settlers in Northumbria: Campbell 1962: 51.

[2081] See Downham 2009: 81-2.

[2082] As noted previously, the chronicler Ætheleard records that in 899, prior to Alfred's death, 'there was a disturbance on a very great scale among the English, that is the bands who were then settled in the territories of the Northumbrians': Campbell 1962: 51. Stenton believed it revealed 'the instability of the peace which Alfred had made, and helps to explain the readiness with which the Northumbrians supported Æthelwold's claim.': Stenton 1970: 12-13.

[2083] One minor example is evidenced by diplomas recording specific meetings of the king with his counsellors in 900, 901 (at Southampton), 903, 904 (at Bickleigh, Devon), and 909: Rumble 2001: 235, citing Keynes 1994: 1141-5.

A few years later, probably in early 903 – the precise chronology is unclear and still debated[2084] – in circumstances which remain unexplained, Æthelwold is found in Essex (according to Simeon of Durham, Matthew Paris and Roger of Wendover having returned from Gaul, where he had hoped to gather a stronger force, presumably of Scandinavians)[2085] with an army which arrived in 'a great fleet' of uncertain origin. According to Florence (John) of Worcester he had 'returned to England from the parts beyond the sea, with a numerous fleet, some of which he had purchased, and the rest whereof he had got together from East Anglia'.[2086] That Æthelwold arrived in Essex by sea is confirmed by the *Anglo-Saxon Chronicle*.[2087] The ships could have been remnants or replacements of the warships built 'many years before' by the Danes of East Anglia and Northumbria which they had used to raid the Wessex coast in 896,[2088] but the accounts seem to suggest that they originated on the Continent, presumably crewed by Continental Vikings. With limited English support Æthelwold rather remarkably persuaded the English rulers of Essex (which had been ceded to the Danes under Alfred's treaty with Guthrum between 878 and 890) to submit to him and join his cause.[2089] This was a statement of the greatest political importance, demonstrating that he was recognised as controlling part of the kingdom of Wessex. He also induced the Danes of East Anglia to join him in a serious campaign against English Mercia and Wiltshire,[2090] reaching as far as the fortified *burh* at Cricklade (only 6 miles from Cirencester and a mere dozen miles from the historic West Saxon town of Malmesbury) and Braydon near Swindon, and 'thirsting for prey, destroyed everything with fire and sword',[2091] before crossing the Thames into Wessex, apparently meeting no resistance.[2092]

[2084] See Hart 1992: 26 fn.2. ASC 'D' dates Æthelwold's revolt to 901, his arrival by sea with a fleet in 904, and the battle of the Holme to 905: Swanton 1996: 91-3. If the date of the battle, 13th December (see below), is correct, that might mean Æthelwold had been 'at large' for several months before the conflict, which would have allowed Edward ample time to gather a great army, but that is not the impression we have from the sources.

[2085] Stevenson 1855: 518; Luard 1872: 436; Giles 1892: 235. Roger tells us that after fleeing from Wimborne, Æthelwold crossed to Gaul, hoping to return with a stronger force to confront Edward (ibid.), the *Book of Hyde* that he 'quitted England, and went to France' (Stevenson 1855: 518), and Grafton's *Chronicle* of 1569 says that '... the King pursued him so sharpely, that he constrayned him [Æthelwold] to leaue that Countrie, and so he sayled into Fraunce, and left Nonne behind him': Grafton 1809: 114. The early history of the Vikings in France is cloudy, but by 844 a great fleet of 54 ships, based at Noirmoutier on the Loire, sailed south to attack the Basque country: Price 2008a: 463. Clearly there was a significant Viking presence in France from at least the mid-9th century, and it is quite possible that Vikings from across the Channel were involved in Æthelwold's campaign: Lappenberg, in his history of the Anglo-Saxons, records that the battle of Tettenhall involved Northumbrians of their own accord or 'in agreement with their brethren in France' embarked on their untimately disastrous raid into Mercia: Thorpe 1845: 90.

[2086] Stevenson 1853: 72.

[2087] ASC 'A' and 'D': Swanton 1996: 92-3.

[2088] ASC 'C' and 'D'. Little research seems to have been undertaken on the identity of this fleet, which may have been a Viking fleet from the Continent.

[2089] There is no evidence that the English rulers of Essex were penalised for their insurrection, but it is difficult to imagine that they did not pay a price for supporting Æthelwold. Whether Æthelwold's forces included a contingent from the Hiberno-Norse of the north-west is unknown, but it must be unlikely, and they are unmentioned in the chronicles.

[2090] Smyth 1995: 436. Henry of Huntingdon tells us that the attack on Mercia took place the year following Æthelwold's arrival with a fleet: Forester 1853: 162.

[2091] Stevenson 1853: 73.

[2092] Giles 1892: 235. ODNB gives the date of the battle of the Holme as 13 December 902; Dumville believes it was probably fought in 904: Dumville 1992: 10.

This was no mere raiding army, and seems to have been a substantial invasion force which dared to move deep into Mercia and the western margins of Wessex, doubtless to demonstrate his strength and procure the support of other influential nobles. We are not told of his intentions, which remain unclear, but the route of his incursion is puzzling. Was he deflected by forces from Wessex and thwarted in his aim to strike deep into Wessex and seek the crown? We must suppose that West Saxon forces had been mustered to defend their territory, and with the support of divisions of the Mercian army closely monitoring Æthelwold's forces and ready, if reluctant, to challenge them in battle, succeeded in deflecting the invading forces to turn and make their way back to East Anglia, with the chronicles giving no hint of any direct opposition or military resistance to Æthelwold's incursion.

Edward responded, not by intercepting the enemy and attempting to engage directly with Æthelwold, as might be expected (but was not, in fact, the norm, and would in any event be ill-advised without the support of the Mercian forces), but by leading a raiding army into the southern Danelaw, ravaging as far as the Fens 'between the Dykes'[2093] and the river *Wusan* (perhaps the Ouse, though at that time the river Nene was also called the *Wusan*),[2094] the ancient boundary between Mercia and East Anglia to the east of Cambridge.[2095] This seems to have been something of a ritual dance, with two great armies ravaging enemy territory but careful to keep their distance, and one might detect signs that Edward, uncertain and fearful of the strength of the enemy, and unsupported by his Mercian allies (doubtless for reasons considered below), was reluctant to engage in full-blooded face-to-face warfare: Henry of Huntingdon says 'having hastily collected some troops, [Edward] followed [the enemy's] rear, ravaging the whole territory between the Dyke and the Ouse'.[2096] The extent of Edward's campaign is unknown, and we are left to wonder at the means by which each leader was kept apprised of the movements of the other, but Edward's forces will have been on high alert, ready for action at short notice, since Æthelwold's flight from Wimborne some three years' earlier, a period of the greatest anxiety for Edward.

Before starting the journey homeward with his spoils, Edward is said to have ordered it to be announced throughout the army that it was to stay in close formation, but the straggling Kentish contingent supposedly chose to ignore the order, despite no fewer than seven messengers sent to them,[2097] a tale not found in the *Annals of St Neots*, otherwise the *East Anglian Chronicle*. The claim, implying conduct akin to disobedient children, has been seen as an implausible and perhaps self-serving interpolation, inserted more than a decade after the event, to disguise guilt,[2098] a suspicion reinforced by other sources which maintain that Edward chose not to engage Æthelwold's forces, leaving the men of Kent to face the enemy, conduct which led to lasting resentment on the part of the people of Kent.[2099]

[2093] ASC 'A', 'B', 'C', 'D'; Whitelock 1961: 59-60. The dykes can be identified as the boundary earthworks now known as The Devil's Dyke and Fleam Dyke: Hart 1992: 26 fn.2; Swanton 1996: 94.
[2094] Hart 1992: 26-27, 513-4; Swanton 1996: 94.
[2095] Hart 1992: 26-27.
[2096] In his translation, Forester says, curiously, that the area ravaged was of the Mercians: Forester 1853: 162. However, that wording is not found in Petrie 1848: 742 (on which Forester claims to have based his translation); or Arnold 1879: 154; or Greenway 1996: 300-1.
[2097] ASC 'A'; Swanton 1996: 94.
[2098] ASC 'A'; Swanton 1996: 94; Hart 1992: 514-5. If the Kentish force constituted the withdrawing rearguard, it may have formed the vanguard in Edward's advancing army: Campbell 2001: 17.
[2099] Smyth believed the loyalty of the Kentish magnates may have been won by King Alfred by means of grants from derelict monastic estates: Smyth 1995: 446. Holland briefly discusses Alfred's

Whether Edward and Æthelwold each intended to face the other in full-scale battle must remain unresolved, but if Edward had decided to withdraw from an imminent battle with Æthelwold's forces (as claimed by Henry of Huntingdon, for example),[2100] the reasons can be readily understood: he had, we are told, raised only 'some' troops (the remainder probably taking defensive positions to protect Wessex from Æthelwold's incursion), and his forces were evidently without the support of the Mercian army under Æthelred and Æthelflæd which we must suppose had been simultaneously preoccupied on two fronts: the defence of their western regions against the attack by Æthelwold's great coalition army, and the monitoring of the turbulent Hiberno-Norse making their home on the north-western border of Mercia after their flight from Dublin and Anglesey.[2101] That will have left Edward in a critical situation, for his forces would have been understrength at a moment when they faced the very real prospect of annihilation, a scenario that would have left Mercia in turn exposed to defeat. As noted later in this chapter, we also have indirect and admittedly slight clues which might suggest a significant revolt in London and Oxford (the latter some 35 miles from Cricklade, reached by Æthelwold's forces), possibly implying that Æthelwold's intention had been to join with and reinforce that rebellion, in which case Edward and the rulers of Mercia will have been under very considerable pressure on a number of fronts. It is nevertheless curious – even perhaps ominous – that elements of the Mercian forces which we must imagine were closely monitoring Æthelwold's raid into Mercia did not (we must suppose) follow his forces on their return into East Anglia to reinforce Edward's army, though that may be reading too much into the sparse information we possess – or, more accurately, do not possess. Yet we may perhaps need to face the unthinkable possibility that Æthelred equivocated in providing support to his brother-in-law in resisting Æthelwold's insurrection. A leader of strong independence who according to Asser had when he felt it necessary acted against the interests of Alfred, his overlord,[2102] he may have seen this as an opportunity to break free of Edward' overlordship by striking some sort of accommodation with Æthelwold about a newly-shaped kingdom of England.[2103] This is an area where speculation could run riot.

---

willingness to entrust Edward with the title to what had been the kingdom of Kent: Holland 2016: 27. Hart suggests that Edward's subsequent (and third) marriage c.919 to Eadgifu, the daughter of ealdorman Sigehelm, who was killed in the battle, may have been a diplomatic gesture to placate his Kentish subjects: Hart 1992: 515. It may be noted that neither Roger of Wendover nor the *Annals of St Neots*, which dates the battle to 904, make any mention of the Kentish contingent at the Holme: Giles 1892: 235-6; Stevenson 1959: 144.

[2100] Forester 1853: 162.

[2101] It must be very possible that Æthelwold timed his military action deliberately to coincide with distractions caused on the north-west borders of Mercia by Ingimund and his Hiberno-Norse followers which prevented Mercian forces from reinforcing Edward's troops. It is even possible that Æthelwold and his Danish forces planned an alliance with the Hiberno-Norse which came to nothing. Furthermore, the possibility that at least some of the Mercian *witan* were to a degree sympathetic to Æthelwold's claim to the throne of Wessex, whilst certainly improbable, cannot be dismissed entirely: Æthelwold's military incursion seems to have been directed more at Wessex than Mercia, and we might see Mercian sympathies as an unlikely but not impossible explanation for the probable absence of Mercian forces supporting Edward's army against Æthelwold, and why the later treaty of Tiddingford discussed below was entered into by Edward 'by necessity'. Even close family loyalties could be broken when the need arose, though it is true that there is not the slightest hint of this in the sources for this period.

[2102] Asser tells us that the kings of Gwent and Glywysing feared the 'force and tyrany' of the Mercians under Æthelred turned to Alfred for protection: Smyth 2002: 38, 125.

[2103] We might note that a charter of 901 of Æthelred and Æthelflæd (S.221) gives both of them grander styles than usual, and makes no mention of Edward, which might be seen as evidence of an attempt at Mercian autonomy at the time of Æthelwold's insurrection.

The *Anglo-Saxon Chronicle*, whilst providing details of the battle with Æthelwold and his coalition forces, fails to identify the site. For that we must turn to two of the earliest sources, the chronicler Æthelweard and the *Mercian Register*. The former fails to mention the rebellious Æthelwold (a silence readily explicable since Æthelweard's grandfather was Æthelwold's brother Æthelhelm, who died c.898),[2104] and describes the enemy cryptically as 'the eastern enemy',[2105] without identifying the English forces but recording that 'a part of the Kentish gentry nearly all inclusive' fell, with *ealdormen* Sigewulf and Sigehelm, and names the barbarians (whose king 'Haruc' was killed) as victors who 'held the field with exultation'.[2106] The latter, in a remarkably terse entry, possibly abbreviated,[2107] simply records a battle between the people of Kent and the Danes (but also fails to mention Æthelwold or even identify the victors – a surprising omission since victory by the usurper would have led to a change of leadership in Mercia as well as Wessex – evidence perhaps that the Mercians were not directly involved in the battle, and even that the outcome was not necessarily welcomed by all Mercians),where the place is named (*æt tham*) *holme* (the name also noted by Æthelweard) from which the conflict has become known as the battle of the Holme.[2108]

According to Æthelweard, the only chronicler to provide a date, the battle occurred 'five days after the feast of the Holy Mother' (13th December) in 902,[2109] and *Anglo-Saxon Chronicle* 'A', 'B', 'C', and 'D' tell us that at the engagement 'they' were surrounded and attacked by Æthelwold's army, and a great battle ensued.[2110] The text is not free from ambiguity – possibly even deliberate – but 'they' are normally held to be the Kentish contingent (as specifically recorded in the *Mercian Register*, which records a battle between the people of Kent and the Danes, and by Henry of Huntingdon, Florence (John) of Worcester, and *TheChronicle of Melrose*),[2111] rather than Edward's main force, which we are led to suppose took no part in the conflict. Roger of Wendover presents us with a rather different picture, recording that before retiring homewards from the Fens 'with an immense booty', Edward pursued the fleeing Æthelwold towards East Anglia (implying that Æthelwold was then outside that area), where 'finding him with all his men prepared for battle in the plain between the two trenches' (clearly the dykes mentioned in the *Anglo-Saxon Chronicle*), claims that Edward's forces made a courageous attack and at the 'first onset' many leading figures (who he names) on both sides were slain. 'On learning that the bravest of his enemies were slain, King Edward wisely withdrew from the place of

---

[2104] Campbell 1962: 52; Ashley 1999: 468.
[2105] Campbell 1962: 52.
[2106] Campbell 1962: 52.
[2107] Thompson 2002: 12.
[2108] Campbell 1962: 52; Whitelock 1961: 59. The name of the battle site is also given in Florence (John) of Worcester and Simeon of Durham, the latter taken from the former: Stevenson 1853: 372; Stevenson 1855: 500. Hart suggests Holme in Huntingdonshire: Hart 1992: 515.
[2109] Campbell 1962: 52 fn2; but see Hart 1992: 26 fn2. Æthelweard provides no details of other events of the same year that might enable us to verify his dating of the battle.
[2110] Whitelock 1961: 59.
[2111] Whitelock 1961: 59; Forester 1853: 162; Stevenson 1853: 72-3; Stevenson 1856: 95; Greenway 1996: 304-5. *Anglo-Saxon Chronicle* ASC 'B' and 'C' mention a battle at the Holme between the men of Kent and the Danes in 903 (evidently incorporated *en bloc* from the *Mercian Register*) before recording in detail the great battle two years later: Thorpe 1861: I 180-1. Florence (John) of Worcester records the battle of the Holme in 904 where the men of Kent had the victory, and in more detail another battle in 905 which is clearly the battle of the Holme involving the men of Kent: Stevenson 1853: 72-3.

contest', which suggests that his main army was indeed involved in – or perhaps arrived too late to participate in – the battle.[2112]

The tenor of the accounts indicates that much about the battle of the Holme will forever remain unknown,[2113] but the likelihood is that the Kentish division, whether by accident or

---

[2112] Giles 1892: 235-6. Grafton's Chronicle, published in 1569, says of the Kentish contingent: 'Wherefore the Danes wayting theyr prayer, fell vpon them by bushments, and slue a great number of them, where-with the King was sore discontented. Soon after both the Armies met, wher eafter a long and cruell fight, Clyto [Latin 'prince, ætheling'] with a great number of the Danes were slaine': Grafton 1809: 114.

[2113] In an account of events at this period by Sir Winston Churchill in his *Divi Britannici: Being a Remark Upon the Lives of All the Kings of this Isle*, published in 1675, we are told that Gurmo [Guthrum, the Danish leader defeated by Alfred at Edington who accepted baptism and adopted the baptismal name of Athelstan, was a party to the treaty of Wedmore, and became king of East Anglia 879-90: Williams, Smyth and Kirby 1991: 148.], after his baptism, married King Alfred's sister Thyra, by whom he had issue Harold Blaatand who became King of Denmark and Knute who went to Ireland. East Anglia he bequeathed to his brother Eric [Eohric] and was buried at Haddon in Suffolk, which he hoped would become burial place of the East Anglian kings. Churchill continues with a wholly invented account of events surrounding the battle of the Holme (a battle mentioned again in the briefest of terms on pp.140-1) which is sufficiently extraordinary and fantastical (with numerous fictitious characters, and no mention of the Kentish forces) to deserve quoting verbatim, omitting lengthy and irrelevant flowery asides: 'Eric finding himself overmatch'd by his Contemporary King Edward, who as he was surnam'd the Elder, was questionless the Wiser, if not the Valianter Prince of the two, thought it necessary to ... tamper with Ethelbald, the Son of the late King Ethelbert, and Uncle to the present King Edward, who having been disappointed of the Succession by reason of his Minority, at the time of his Fathers death. Coming now to Age, thought himself sufficiently qualified for, and as well intituled to the Government, as King Edward himself ... so Ambition meeting with his Youth, incens'd his Passions to that degree, that he presently flew to Arms, declaring himself as much an enemy to his Country as his Competitor, by the commitment of several Outrages, that spoke him less sensible of Shame then danger: And that he might yet appear more an Enemy to himself than either, he as rashly quit his religion as his Loyalty, drawing many infamous Persons after him by the fame of his Apostacy. Eric publicly joined with him, and declar'd against the Peace made by his Predecessors. King Edward that had been sufficiently allarm'd by the Noise of this Conspiracy, before it came to its height, waited not their coming towards him, but met them half way, and at a place call'd St Edwards Ditch, famous for a Victory obtain'd by the English not long before, resolv'd to try his Title with them, dividing his Armies into two Battalions; the first led by himself, the other by Prince Athelstan his Son: Against which Eric (who had the marshalling the other side) drew up his army; but divided not as King Edward expected, with two great Wings, one to be commanded by himself, the other by Ethelbald, but after the manner of his Ancestors, made up three bodies, two whereof were all English, the third all Danes: And ... set the English against the English, and kept himself for the Reserve. The right Wing he left to be commanded by Ethelbald, who arrang'd against Prince Athelstan that had the left Wing of his Fathers Forces, and against King Edward that had the right Wing, he appointed one Cowulph, a Person of as deperate Fortune as Disloyal principles, descended by his Mothers side from the Earls of Chester, by the Fathers side from a bastard Dane, upon which account they afterward made him Titular King of Mercia: Eric with his Body of Danes stood to view the Field, and witness the gallant Madness of the English; whilst each man fell upon his Fellow, his Brother, his Father, or his Uncle: not fighting Foe against Foe, but Friend against Friend: each wound that each man gave together, letting out some of the same blood that run in his own Veins: wherein Fortune dispos'd the Battel. Even as himself could wish, for Ethelbald lost his life, and King Edward the day: whose Forces being totally routed, Eric suffer'd not his men to wipe off the blood from their Swords, til they brandish'd them in the Faces of the Mercians, where King Edward appear'd at the head of them as boldly, as if he had receiv'd no defeat before. Here the Interest of both Nations came the second time to the stake: For on the English side were engaged Ethelred, surnam'd Michill, or the great Duke of Mercia, Brother in law to King Edward, Sigeline Earl of Kent his Father in Law, Prince Athelstan his Son, Ethelmere Earl of

design – though it has been suggested that the Kentish men were perhaps insisting on their right to strike the first blow on the enemy[2114] – became separated from the main body of Edward's army, almost certainly without any Mercian element, and was attacked by Æthelwold's forces (or *vice versa*) which had united into a single army,[2115] doubtless including a contingent from Essex, in which case pitting forces from each side of the Thames against each other, though there is no evidence of this, fully expecting, not unreasonably, an easy victory. Florence (John) of Worcester indeed tells us that the Kentish men scorned the order to retire, and refusing Edward's entreaties, 'boldy persisted in their resolution' to confront the Danes,[2116] which may be an unjustified gloss on the events. Whatever the case, the battle was to prove Æthelwold's nemesis. Miraculously and inexplicably, against all the odds the men of Kent caused catastrophic losses to the enemy army, killing Æthelwold and Eohric, king of East Anglia, as well as many of their followers, in an extraordinary military achievement. The named dead on the Kentish side included two ealdormen, Sigewulf and Sigehelm,[2117] and several other men of high rank, including Abbot Cenwulf.[2118]

Chester, Wolnoth Earl of Devon and Dorset, Seaward the potent Earl of Somerset, and divers others of the greatest note amongst the English. On Eric's side appear'd Cowulph, Titular King of Mercia, Healidine the Victorious Vice-Roy of Northumberland, Stroeg Duke of Cumberland, Godfride Earl of Westmoreland, Colberne Earl of Yorkshire, a man of great strength, that they called him the Giant; these were reinforced by the new Supplies out of Denmark, under the Conduct of three famous Commanders, Uter, Iring, and Scurfa. The hopes Conceiv'd on either side was equal, as was their Courage; neither were their Forces disproportionate to their Hopes. The advantage of the Danes was the reputation of the last Victory, that of the English rested in their despair. Either side alike concern'd in the thoughts of Greatness or a Grave. But whilst they were fatally disputing the Ground they stood on, Fortune that for a while had turn'd her back on King Edward, declar'd for him, and by withdrawing her Presence out of the Danish Camp, left such an impression of Fear upon them, that one half Quit the Field, the other that stayed did yet worse: For laying hold of their own King (who out of Indignation of the approaching Repulse, had turn'd his Fury upon those that fled) they bought their own Peace, with the price of his Head: whereby the English recover'd back all of Mercia, and the greater part of East-Anglia, which were henceforth preserv'd as inseparable Members of the English Empire, till the Reduction of the whole under Knute: the Danes that fled thinking it enough to be able to make good Northumberland, as the parts about it; and being afterward back'd by the Scotch and Welch, whose business it was to hold up the War, they set up another King of the same name, though not of the same Race ... Eric the Second, by some writers call'd Sytherick, and by his Countrymen Sygefrid ...': Churchill 1675: 163-7. The sources (if any) used by Churchill remain untraced; his book – which makes no mention of the battle of Tettenhall – was not reprinted, and is now largely forgotten. Indeed, his contemporary and notable chronicler, Anthony A' Wood, remarked: '... in the said book, which is very thin and trite, are the arms of all the kings of England, which made it sell among novices, rather than for the matter therein.'

[2114] Earle and Plummer 1892-99: II 124. The 'right to strike the first blow' is not further explained, and the story was doubtless invented to put a noble gloss on the episode. A more likely explanation may be that the Kentish forces had been scavenging for supplies, having joined Edward's forces in haste.

[2115] Stevenson 1863: 73.

[2116] Stevenson 1853: 73.

[2117] As noted above, in about 919 Edward took as his third wife Eadgifu, the daughter of Sigehelm: Holland 2016: 45.

[2118] Swanton 1996: 92-4; Campbell 2001: 21-22; Stafford 2008: 110. For the battle of the Holme see Hart 1992: 26 fn.2, 511-15. Hart suggests that Cenwulf may have been from St Augustine's, Canterbury: Hart 1992: 514.

The list of dead from the East Anglian and Northumbrian forces is intriguing. It begins with Eohric, the only known reference to this king,[2119] and 'the *æðeling* Æthelwold whom they had chosen as king', then Brihtsige (an English name) 'son of *æðeling* Beorhnoth' (another English name).[2120] Brihtsige and Beorhnoth – doubtless'the two [un-named] princes of the English, soft of beard' (young adults) mentioned by Æthelweard[2121] – may have been members of one of the families with claim to the throne of Mercia[2122] or a descendant of King Æthelwulf of Wessex or his father King Ecgbehrt,[2123] and while there is little direct evidence of any widespread support for Æthelwold's campaign in either Mercia or Wessex, we have what may be evidence (discussed above and in more detail later in this chapter) of a degree of sympathy from a not insignificant Mercian faction for Æthelwold's cause.[2124] Also killed fighting for Æthelwold or the East Anglians were two holds named Ysopa and Oscetel, and 'much of the nobility on either side'.[2125] What is particularly remarkable is that the chronicler knew not only the names but also the ranks and relationships of the important dead on the Scandinavian as well as the English side.[2126] Equally noteworthy is the number of prominent chronicles – including in particular the *Mercian Register*, Æthelweard, Roger of Hoveden and William of Malmesbury – who, for whatever reason (Æthelweard's, as we have seen, almost certainly that Æthelwold was his ancestor; William of Malmesbury's that his work incorporated that of Æthelweard), chose to draw a veil over the very significant rebellion of Æthelwold, failing even to mention his name in their annals.

In spite of their losses, the *Anglo-Saxon Chronicle* records that 'it was the enemy that had possession of the place of slaughter'[2127] – not altogether surprising if they had faced only the Kentish forces – and Æthelweard tells us that 'in the end the barbarians were the victors, and held the field with exultation',[2128] meaning that Æthelwold's forces were technically the victors, even though their leaders had been killed, a remarkable outcome with Northumbrian and East Anglian losses reportedly greater than those of the Kentish contingent. The retention of the field of the battle was more than symbolic victory: it meant that Edward's forces – or the men of Kent – were unable to recover the spoils looted by Æthelwold during his ravaging campaign in Mercia. One struggles to imagine the scenario where the victors in a great battle have lost their leaders but retained domination of the battlefield and their booty, and we are left to wonder why Edward chose not to

---

[2119] Tyrrell tells of a long story by Polydore Virgil about Eohric who, after defeat in a great battle with Edward, returned home but was murdered by his people, who then split into two factions, both of which were forced to submit to Edward: Tyrrell 1697: Book V 323.

[2120] Brihtsige and Beorhnoth were perhaps members of one of the families with claim to the throne of Mercia (Walker 2000: 89; Yorke 2001: 36-7) or a descendant of King Æthelwulf of Wessex or his father King Ecgbehrt (Smyth 1995: 436), but there is little, if any, evidence of any widespread support for Æthelwold's campaign in either Mercia or Wessex. Beorhnoth may have been the great-grandfather of Byrhtnoth, famed for his role in the battle of Maldon: Hart 1992: 514 fn.10; Jayakumar 2008: 86.

[2121] Campbell 1962: 52.

[2122] See Yorke 2001: 36-7.

[2123] Smyth 1995: 436. Beorhnoth may have been the great-grandfather of Byrhtnoth, famed for his role in the battle of Maldon: Jayakumar 2008: 86.

[2124] However, as discussed later in this chapted, there is evidence that within a few years of the Holme, Edward was forced to deal with 'rebel subjects, and especially the citizens of London and Oxford': Giles 1893: I 236. Both places lay in Mercia.

[2125] ASC 'D'; Swanton 1996: 95; Campbell 1962: 52.

[2126] Thompson 2002: 11-12.

[2127] ASC 'A'; Swanton 1986: 94.

[2128] Campbell 1962: 52.

continue (or join) the action to eliminate the leaderless enemy forces, which we are led to believe had suffered significant losses. The ambivalent outcome is well recorded by Henry of Huntingdon, who adds laconically to his brief note of the events the informal aside: 'But as to the identity of the victors, the sources leave us in doubt, don't they?', a conclusion presumably shared by the *Mercian Register* which, as we have seen, leaves the victors unnamed.[2129] Whatever the truth, we can be certain that Edward, even though denied the physical spoils of victory, celebrated the death of Æthelwold with heartfelt satisfaction,[2130] and the battle is usually seen as a triumphant victory on Edward's part,[2131] for the loss of their leaders meant that the rebellion was effectively crushed.[2132] The magnitude of the episode is evident from its cryptic mention as one of the few terse entries in the *Mercian Register* at this period,[2133] even though the Mercians almost certainly played no part in the outcome – or at least not on Edward's side.[2134]

It is about this time – the date in unrecorded – that Edward took as his second wife Ælfflæd, a niece of Æthelwold (so making it within the prohibited degrees). Ælfflæd was consecrated and anointed with holy oil, so distinguishing her from her uncle, a renegade – who by by some improbable later accounts had even renounced his Christian faith and become a pagan[2135] – among Vikings. Edward's first wife Ecgwynn, mother of Æthelstan, may have died before 899, and it is possible Edward may have married Ælfflæd even before his father's death.[2136] It would be strange indeed if Edward had chosen to marry Æthelwold's neice during her uncle's rebellion.

Æthelwold's insurrection, unquestionably the greatest threat to Edward's reign, had been resolved – or almost resolved – in dramatic fashion, and must be seen as an astonishing outcome, perhaps secured by a relatively small section of Edward's forces. We might suppose that the most surprised participant in the entire campaign was Edward himself. Nevertheless, Æthelwold, with the support of representatives from practically all of the Danelaw, and probably with many disaffected Englishmen – including Mercians – hoping that his campaign would unseat Edward and bring them rich rewards and offices, had raided deep into central and south-west Mercia, and audaciously even within striking distance of Æthelred's principal centre at Gloucester.[2137] Æthelwold, far from the relative safety of the Danelaw, had demonstrated absolute confidence that his forces were capable of seeing off any challenge by armies from Wessex and Mercia, and posed the greatest risk to those kingdoms. Realising that those kingdoms were within his grasp, he had overturned

---

[2129] Whitelock 1961: 59; Greenway 1996: 304-5.

[2130] What happened to the bodies of Æthelwold and King Eohric is unrecorded, but since their forces retained control of the battlefield they may have been identified and buried where they fell to prevent them falling into the hands of the enemy.

[2131] For example, James Campbell notes that 'Edward ... won a victory, albeit a bloody one': Campbell 2001: 21.

[2132] There is no evidence that anyone in the Kentish contingent received any exceptional reward for their valour, or that the men of Essex were punished for their betrayal.

[2133] Whitelock 1961: 59.

[2134] Whitelock 1961: 59.

[2135] Holland 2016: 32. The rumours were almost certainly later propaganda, since the Danes of York were Christianised at the time of battle of the Holme.

[2136] Sharpe 2001: 82-3; Yorke 2001: 33-4. With Edward Ælfflæd had two sons, Edmund and Eadred, both to become kings, and two daughters: Bailey 2001: 122.

[2137] Æthelweard records that in 878 the Danes ravaged Mercia and occupied Gloucester [ASC says Chippenham: Swanton 1996: 76-7], leaving the following year to winter at Cirencester until they left for East Anglia the year after: Campbell 1962: 42-3; Swanton 1996: 76-7.

conventional thinking by proving that the son of an English king could lead a Danish army to further his ambitious military and political aspirations. In the words of Alistair Cambell, 'what the annals seem to be telling us is that in the years immediately after 899, the major influence towards the unification of England was not Alfred's son Edward, but his cousin Æthelwold. Had Æthelwold won the battle [of the Holme], England could, we may fairly guess, have been united in a different manner, involving much less warfare than ultimately proved to be the case ... Æthelwold might very well have been regarded as one of the greatest figures in our island story'.[2138] Martin Ryan has concluded that 'What is striking about Æthelwold's 'rebellion' is the level and range of support he was able to draw on: he could call on allies from Wessex, Northumbria, East Anglia and, probably, Mercia and Essex. For a time Æthelwold had a claim to be the most powerful ruler in England. Edward's apparent reluctance to engage him in battle will have been well founded'.[2139] That an English *ætheling* could lead a powerful army of both Scandinvians and English and perhaps Continental Vikings to challenge the dominance of Wessex and Mercia will have rocked military and political conventions to their foundations. Natural divisions between Scandinavians and English, pagans and Christians, those within and outside the Danelaw, would need to be rethought.

The vacumn left by the slaughter of the leaders of Northumbria and East Anglia and many other important officers and foot-soldiers from those kingdoms at the Holme evidently led to what seems to have been a crumbling of military capacity in York-based Northumbria, and, as we shall see, resulted eventually in the collapse of resistance against other more beligerent Scandinavians, notably Ragnall, the pagan Hiberno-Norse leader from Dublin, who appears to have seized York in 911, but was distracted by other campaigns, faced continuing resistance from the Christianised Danes of York, and did not take full control until 919. In the same way, the crumbling of East Anglian resistance to Edward was doubtless due in part to the lack of a king to lead them.

To add to the acute military threat posed by Æthelwold and his forces in the north, east, and west, early tradition, supported by Irish and Welsh chronicles, tells of the expulsion from Dublin in about 901 of the pagan Scandinavian elite, including Ingimund and significant numbers of his Hiberno-Scandinavian followers, that is, Scandinavians who had settled in Ireland, as well as some Irishmen, from the 60-year old Viking stronghold at the mouth of the river Liffey.[2140] Those expelled formed different groups, some going to France, others, including the King of Dublin, to north-west England, and another group travelling a shorter distance to Anglesey.[2141] In the words of the anonymous *Annals of Ulster*,[2142] there was an 'Expulsion of the Gentiles [= pagans][2143] from Ireland, from the fortress of Ath-cliath [Dublin] ... where they left a great number of their ships, and

---

[2138] Campbell 2001: 21; see also Williams, Smyth and Kirby 1991: 33; Smith 2012: 158-60.
[2139] Ryan 2013: 297.
[2140] The archaeological evidence from Dublin shows little evidence of any break in Scandinavian occupation in the years immediately following 902.
[2141] The *Annales Cambriæ* record that *Igmunt in insula Mon venit, et tenuit maes Ocmeliaun* [*Ysfeilion*]: Williams ab Ithel 1860: 16. Mon was probably Anglesey rather than the Isle of Man. *Ysfeilion* is probably to be identified as the area around Lanfaes, on the eastern horn of Anglesy, which stands for Llan Faes Ysfeilion, named after Ysfael ap Cunedda: AC 85 (1930) 333.
[2142] The *Annals of Ulster* (the English translation of the Latin name *Annales Ultoniensis*, a late 16th-century chronicle called the *Annate Senait*) is an annalistic history concentrating on Ulster (Graves 1975: 403), described by David Dumvilleas 'probably the most important single member of the Irish annalistic tradition': Dumville 1990: XVI 77.
[2143] Brink 2008: 5.

escaped half-dead [to North Wales], after having been wounded and broken'.[2144] That account is supported by a briefer record in the *Chronicon Scottorum*, an anonymous compilation of Irish annals.[2145] Driven out of North Wales by King Cadell, according to the *Three Fragments* (the only source for the story), Ingimund approached Æthelflæd, Lady of the Mercians, who was exercising power during the long illness of her husband, Æthelred,[2146] to seek land on which to settle. We are told that at his request Æthelflæd granted to Ingimund certain land (which is un-named, but probably on the peninsula now known as the Wirral, near Chester), an event not recorded in any English chronicles, including in particular the *Mercian Register*, which makes not the slightest reference to the Hiberno-Norse.[2147] Ingimund and his followers, who presumably arrived there c.903, supposedly remaind there 'for some time', but with other leaders and their followers coveted the wealth of Chester and the fertile land around it.[2148] The later Irish *Three Fragments* tells how, 'when [Ingimund] saw the wealthy city [of Chester], and the choice lands around it, he yearned to possess them. Ingimund came then to the chieftans of the Norwegians and the Danes; he was complaining bitterly before them, and said they were not well off unless they had good lands, and that they all ought to go and seize Chester and posess it with its wealth and lands'.[2149] At the instigation of Ingimund, then, the Hiberno-Scandinavians in the shape of the Danes, Norse and ex-patriot Irish forces attacked Chester.

The *Three Fragments* describes the siege and the legendary tactics used by the defenders.[2150] We are led to believe that Æthelflæd possessed an impressive intelligence network, and on becoming aware of the plot to launch an attack, had arranged for the

---

[2144] Higham 1993: 184. The entry purports to be of events in 903. What would appear to be the largest known hoard of Viking gold was discovered in the early 19th century on a small island in the river Shannon in Ireland. The gold weighed over 10lbs, and surviving descriptions of the objects, all arm rings, suggest that they were buried in the late 9th or early tenth century. The entire hoard was melted down in the 19th century: Graham Campbell and Kydd 1980: 34. It is not known whether the hoard was associated with the expulsion of the Hiberno-Scandinavian from Dublin.

[2145] Hennessy 1866.

[2146] Several sources provide compelling evidence that Æthelred suffered some sort of serious incapacitating illness or disability from at least 903 – indeed entries in the *Anglo-Saxon Chronicle* imply that from at least 902 Æthelflæd was acting on her own initiative, wielding authority and not merely influence – until his death in 911: see O'Donovan 1860: 227, 231, 233; Wainwright 1975: 79-84, 141, and 308, citing the *Three Irish Fragments* and Henry of Huntingdon; Lavelle 2010: 230, with extracts from the *Fragmentary Annals of Ireland*. ASC 'A' and 'C' record that it was Æthelflæd alone who built the *burh* at *Bremesbyrig* after the battle of Tettenhall in 910, and that in 909 and 910 Edward the Elder ordered the Mercian *fyrd* against the Danes, so far as we know without reference to Æthelred, who is not mentioned in connection with these campaigns: Swanton 1996: 94.

[2147] Curiously, Donnchadh Ó Corráin notes that 'When Dublin fell its rulers went to Scotland and to territories that had long been their dependencies', and how in 903 they were engaged in fierce warfare in southern Pictland, but makes no mention of Ingimund's settlement in the Wirral: Ó Corráin 2012: 431.

[2148] Coins from the Cuerdale hoard, deposited on the banks of the Ribble c.902-5 (Gooch 2012: 169), include silver pennies of Edward the Elder struck by 5 West Mercian moneyers, some associated with Chester, implying that moneyers were operating there during the late 9th century, perhaps from a *wic* outside the walls, as was the case at London: Lyon 2001: 75. It has also been suggested that the Chester mint may have originated in another Mercian centre (possibly Tamworth) and moved to Chester in 907: Griffiths 2001: 170. During Æthelstan's reign it was the most productive mint in England: ibid.

[2149] O'Donovan 1860: 226-7, 231-7; Radner 2008: FA429; and see especially Wainwright 1975: 131-62; Cavill, Harding and Jesch 2000: 19-59; Higham 1993: 184.

[2150] Wainwright 1975: 81-3.

Chester garrison to be strengthened.[2151] Nevertheless, Ingimund and his forces besieged the city and demanded its surrender. Rebuffed, he named a day for battle, and on the stated day attacked the city. The defenders sent word to Æthelred and Æthelflæd, the 'King of the Saxons' being 'in a disease and on the point of death', who advised them to engage the enemy in battle outside the city but to leave the gates open. Should the enemy have the upper hand the English were to retreat into the city and close the gates, trapping the enemy. This was done and many of the the enemy slaughtered within the city. Others outside the walls made hurdles under the shelter of which they attempted to break through the walls. Æthelred and Æthelflæd sent messengers to the Irish element among the enemy appealing to their honour and good nature (the author was of course Irish), urging them to change sides.[2152] Their entreaties were successful, and the Irish came to support the English defenders. Large numbers of the enemy were killed by rocks, beams, spears and javelins hurled down on them. Their comrades, however, managed to breach the walls. The defenders threw down large rocks to destroy the hurdles. The enemy placed posts under the hurdles. The defenders poured boiling water and beer onto the enemy 'so their skins were peeled off'. The enemy placed hides over the hurdles. The defenders hurled beehives at the besiegers, who eventually fled.[2153]

As F. T. Wainwright pointed out, the *Three Fragments* provides compelling evidence in its reference to Ingimund contacting other leaders about his plans to seize Chester that there were many colonies of Scandinavians and their followers settled in the region,[2154] and the reference in *The Annals of Ulster* to both Norwegians and Danes has been seen as evidence that a *hold* who held land by the Ribble estuary may, as noted above, have represented the authority of the Danish King of York at a site which the king could have provided in western Lancashire for the Irish Norse under Ivar II (who was killed in 903)[2155] and his brother Ragnall.[2156] The presence of Norwegian and Danish survivors from the siege of Chester, it has been suggested, would explain place-names such as Croxteth and Toxteth, as well as the Danish names Derby and Ormskirk, and that the *hold* of the Ribble estuary may have been Agmund who gave his name to Amounderness, a place-name incorporating the genitival form compounded with Norse *nes* 'headland' or from a stem-form of Agmund with Old English *hērness* 'area subject to authority.[2157] But the failed attack on Chester was evidently not the last word on Ingimund's ambitions: the *Three Fragments'* report of the siege of Chester ends cryptically: 'It was not long, however, until they came to fight again'.[2158] What prompted that comment is unrecorded, and nothing more is known about

---

[2151] Increasing the garrison could hardly explain the reference to the 'restoration' of Chester recorded in 907 (ASC 'C'); the events recorded in the *Three Fragments* were evidently based on events that necessitated its restoration, and so occurred in or before 907.

[2152] *Fragmentary Annals of Ireland*, FA301, 172; ASC 'B', 'C' and 'D', see Earle and Plummer 1892-99: I 95-105; II 116; Charles-Edwards 2013: 502-3; Griffiths 2015: 34. It has been suggested that the Ingimund saga was largely the product of the Irish annalistic tradition, which tended to emphasise the barbarity and heathenism of the Vikings: Griffiths 1995: 83-4. It is very possible that this incident explains the image of a tower found mainly on Chester-minted coins of the period: Karkov 2011: 128-9.

[2153] O'Donovan 1860: 226-7, 231-7; Radner 2008: FA429.

[2154] Wainwright 1975: 86.

[2155] Downham 2009: 261.

[2156] Higham 1993: 184.

[2157] Higham 1993: 184; Edmonds 2009: 7. Agmund is of particular interest to us, since he might conceivably be the *hold* of the same name killed at the battle of Tettenhall: Quanrud 2015: 82. For the idea that the Viking threat in the early 10th century was exaggerated in Irish annals see Griffiths 1995a: 84.

[2158] O'Donovan 1860: 237; Griffiths 2015: 34.

this episode, but Æthelred and Æthelflæd would have feared the next move by a powerful and belligerent neighbour. The comment may indeed be especially meaningful in our attempt to identify the Scandinavian or 'Northumbrian' protagonists at the battle of Tettenhall.

Though the account of the siege of Chester may be largely if not wholly mythical, the sudden flood of Hiberno-Scandinavians into the area to swell the existing Scandinavian population in the north-west was very real, and is discussed elsewhere in this volume. There is little doubt that the influx of a powerful dynasty of Hiberno-Scandinavians unsettled the political and military balance held by the two principal bodies of protagonists which had existed for several decades, namely the Danes of York in the north and the English kingdoms in the south.[2159] Wainwright rightly noted that the appearance of Ragnall 'added another element to the racial complex, and though we may speculate on possible repercussions we can be sure only that the arrival of the Norsemen disturbed whatever uneasy political balance then existed'.[2160]

In recent decades a new interpretation of those events has evolved from detailed research into place-names, stone sculpture, treasure hoards of hacksilver and coins, grave goods, and other archaeological finds in north-west England. That interpretation sees the expulsion of Ingimund as the trigger for a fundamental change to the balance of power within the Danelaw which in turn led directly to the battle of Tettenhall. The traditional view, held by historians for over a thousand years – or at least the view attributed to them – that the Northumbrians who were defeated by the English at Tettenhall were from the York-based kingdom, a view tacitly if not explicitly endorsed by the most eminent Anglo-Saxonists until the later part of the twentieth century,[2161] is now coming under increasing scrutiny and reassessment.

From the 1980s various scholars, including in particular Professor Nicholas Higham, after careful reassessment of the available evidence, especially the make-up and date of the Cuerdale hoard, have developed a revised scenario leading up to the battle of Tettenhall. The astonishing treasure, now believed to date from no later than c.905 (slightly earlier than previously believed), found in 1840 on the south bank of the river Ribble near Preston, is the largest hoard of Viking-age silver ever found in Western Europe.[2162]

[2159] Æthelweard tells us that Alfred had despatched Ealdorman Æthelnoth, who had led the West Saxon forces at Buttington and was evidently a crucial figure in English government at that time, as an emissary to York to negotiate a peace treaty after a huge Viking fleet from Boulogne reached Kent in 894, though the outcome of the meeting is unknown: Campbell 1962: 51; Downham 2009: 74. The event can be seen as evidence that diplomatic relations continued despite ongoing warfare.
[2160] Wainwright 1975: 163.
[2161] Those scholars included T. D. Kendrick, Sir Frank Stenton and Dorothy Whitelock: see Quanrud 2015: 87-8.
[2162] The hoard, consisting of 1,300 items of hack silver and bullion bars of characteristic Irish extraction, as well as several thousand silver coins, mainly from the Viking kingdoms of eastern England, with others from Alfred's Wessex, and others including Carolingian, Italian, Byzantine and Arabic issues, has been seen to imply some sort of alliance between Danish York and the Irish Norse. The hoard was seemingly deposited within a year or two of 905. The first documented coin hoard to be found in Britain may be some 80 Anglo-Saxon, Anglo-Scandinavian and Continental coins, thought to have been buried in AD 910–15, and discovered on 8 April 1611 on land at Little Crosby, 8 miles north-west of Liverpool, Lancashire, owned by William Blundell, who had determined to build a secret chapel and cemetery for the burial of fellow Catholics when, in the wake of the Gunpowder Plot of 1605, anti-Catholic feeling was at its height. The hoard was found during gravedigging. Blundell was fascinated by the find, perhaps seeing it divine endorsement for his burial

Included in the hoard was silver from Dublin and coins now redated to c.902-905 from York, from which it has been concluded that relations between the Vikings of the Irish Sea littoral and York were established very soon after 902.[2163] Higham has noted that the former made a point of attacking over the next decade only the rivals to the Northern army of York – the Scots, the kingdom of Strathcyde and the 'northern Saxons' of Bernicia. He has concluded that when Ingimund and his followers were expelled from Dublin in 902 the Danes of York were the senior partners in the alliance with Ingimund – as noted above, land on the Ribble estuary may even have been made available to the Irish Norse by the King of York[2164] – but as the power of the York-based Danes waned after the defeat of its forces at the Holme in 903, the Hiberno-Scandinavians of the north-west (who may or may not have been involved in the Holme campaign) became the more dominant party, doubtless due to the aggressive ambitions of the pagan and warlike dynasty that had fled Dublin and taken root on the Wirral, supporting and reinforcing a further group which is believed to have settled in Lancashire.[2165] Thereafter the relationship between the two Scandinavian groupings – the York-based Northumbrians and the Hiberno-Scandinavians of the north-west – may have rapidly deteriorated to the point of mutual hostility, if not hatred, doubtless aggravated by the conflicting religious tenets of the two groups.[2166]

But though the single and later claim in the *Three Fragments* (notably unmentioned in any English record, perhaps for the most obvious reason) that after his expulsion from Dublin Æthelflæd granted to Ingimund lands near Chester on which to settle has been – and is – generally accepted by historians, any such grant must be very doubtful, even if paralleled

---

ground, since most of the coins bore a cross and one coin, that of Louis the Pious (778–840), the legend 'Christiana religio'. Sadly, the coins were melted down to make a chalice and pyx, but Blundell made a comprehensive record in a notebook recording every coin with an engraving of 35 of the coins, enabling the British Museum to identify coins in their collections possibly struck from the same die as some coins in the hoard. The hoard included pennies from at least four series of Edward's coins minted c.910, all bearing the names of moneyers from south-east England. The coins were evidently deposited around or shortly after the date of the attack launched by Edward into Scandinavian-controlled territory in 909 or the battle of Tettenhall the following year, and in an area in which there was a concentration of Hiberno-Scandinavian settlement: Edwards 1998 42-5; Graham-Campbell 2001: 219-20. In 2002 a small hoard of a silver ingot and short rod reduced to hack-silver was found at Eccleston, 2 miles south of Chester and 50 miles from Wednesfield, and in 2004 a hoard of 22 silver flattened and bent Hiberno-Scandinavian arm rings was discovered at Huxley, 2½ miles south-west of Tarporley in Cheshire, some 40 miles from Wednesfield (and, perhaps not coincidentally, close to a Roman road leading to York). Since both hoards were coinless, they cannot be dated precisely, but a connection with Edward's raid of 909 cannot be ruled out: Wiliams 2009: 73-83; Redknap 2009: 34.
[2163] Charles Edwards 2013: 502.
[2164] Higham 1993: 184. However, the identity of that king is unmentioned, and at this period there is believed to have been a hiatus in the kingship of York.
[2165] See e.g. Fellows-Jensen 1985; Higham 1992; Higham 1993: 184-89. The place-name Coniston in Cumbria has been seen as possible evidence for Scandinavian kings active in the north-west: the name may incorporate *konungr* 'king' and refer to 'a small Scandinavian mountain kingdom': Ekwall 1922: 215; Quanrud 2015: 81.
[2166]Walker 2000: 90. We might note that both Norse and Danes are said to have been involved in the attempt by Ingimund to seize Chester c.905 if later and improbable Irish annals have a kernel of truth: O'Donovan 1860: 230-7. It is said that when the Hiberno-Norse who took York in 918 were eventually crushed by English forces in 964, the local Danes celebrated their English countrymen as liberators from their fellow Norse: Welsh 2002: 45. However, Clare Downham has argued that the supposed animosity between 'Hiberno-Norwegian' and 'Anglo-Danish' factions in English politics before 954 '... is largely a historiographical invention and not a Viking-Age reality': Downham 2009a: 138-48.

by a handful of episodes in Europe: for example Charles the Simple (879-929), King of the Western Franks at this time, allowed one group of Vikings to settle at a strategic river mouth in return for an undertaking to defend the area against other Vikings.[2167] Why the fervently Christian Æthelflæd and the ailing but equally devout Æthelred – supported by the Mercian *witan* – would have acquiesced, if not encouraged, a hostile and pagan enemy force and its followers to settle permanently within their borders as an ever-present and unpredictable threat is not easy to explain, especially since they could have not have contemplated such action without the tacit approval of Edward, effectively their overlord, approval which is almost unthinkable.

There is some slight evidence for a settled Scandinavian presence in the region by c.893,[2168] and possibly even earlier, but we must suspect that the Irish annals have misrepresented what was in reality a *fait accompli*, the occupation, peaceable or otherwise, in the early tenth century of land in and around the Wirral which Æthelflæd was then powerless to challenge, for Edward and Æthelred, and indeed Æthelflæd herself, were at that very moment distracted and preoccupied in putting down the formidable insurrection by the rebellious Æthelwold, who had led enemy forces deep into Mercia, looting and destroying and finally coming within a whisker of annihilating Edward and his forces to integrate southern and central England into a new united kingdom of England with himself as its ruler.[2169] It should not be overlooked that Æthelwold had raided deep into central and south-west Mercia, and was even within striking distance of Æthelred and Æthelflæd's favoured centre at Gloucester. They were faced with an acute and immediate military threat in the south, and though the dangers from the pagan military force to the north were very real and growing, the priority was to confront the immediate peril from Æthelwold and his forces to the south. These were perilous years indeed for Æthelred and Æthelflæd, as well as Edward. Yet a mysterious treaty concluded by Edward at about the time of Æthelflæd's supposed grant to Ingimund and his followers might possibly explain that grant.[2170]

Anglo-Saxon Chronicle 'A' and 'D' record in 905 or 906 'the peace at *Yttingaford*, just as King Edward determined, both with the East Anglians and with Northumbrians'.[2171]

[2167] Walker 2000: 91; Downham 2009: 208, citing Janet L. Nelson, 'The Frankish Empire', in Sawyer 1977: 41.

[2168] Giles 1892: 231.

[2169] One curiosity at this period is the mention in the Chronicles of an eclipse of the moon in 904 and the appearance of a comet in 905: ASC 'C' and 'D'; Swanton 1996: 93. There was an eclipse of the moon in 904, and lunar eclipses in 901, 902, 903, 905 and 907. ASC 'D' says a comet appeared on 20 October (Swanton 1996: 93); in 904 there was a comet towards the end of the year, and in 906 one was visible for nearly 6 months: Earle and Plummer 1892-99: II 117-8. Roger of Wendover and Matthew Paris note the appearance in 906 of a comet for nearly half a year (confirming the veracity of the date), shortly before a battle between the Danes and the English, in which many nobles from both sides fell: Giles 1892: 237; Luard 1872: 438. The battle has not been identified: the battle of the Holme is mentioned in an earlier passage. Lunar eclipses were relatively frequent, with two recorded in other sources in 904. While comets are rarities, confirmation of sightings in 905 is found in numerous early European, Chinese and Japanese texts: Kronk 1999: 144-5. Astronomical events were often seen by the Anglo-Saxons as portents of major occurrences.

[2170] As recorded in the Irish *Three Fragments*, Ingimund was expelled from Dublin c.901 and attempted to settle in Anglesey, before he was forced to leave and moved to the Chester area where he supposedly sought land on which to settle from Æthelflæd, who granted him land in the Wirral (O'Donovan 1860: 227; 231-7), perhaps c.905-6.

[2171] Swanton 1996: 94-5. ASC 'A' records cryptically, immediately before the treaty of Tiddingford, and in the same year, the death of a certain Alfred (identified as *Alfred 25* in the *Prosopography of*

Simeon of Durham records in a slightly different but perhaps significant account that in 906, 'King Edward, compelled by necessity (*necessitate compulsus*), confirmed a peace (*frið*) with the East Anglians and Northumbrians', a statement also found in one of the few terse entries relating to the first half of the tenth century in manuscript 'E' of the *Anglo-Saxon Chronicle*, which refers to a *frið* or treaty established 'from need' (*for neode*),[2172] both with the army of the East Angles and the Northumbrians.[2173]

Yttingaford is Tiddingford, a ford across the Ouzel at Linslade, Buckinghamshire,[2174] the river which defines part of the boundary between Buckinghamshire and Bedfordshire, which we can assume to have been on the boundary between English Mercia and Danish territory (perhaps hinting that Bedfordshire was then in Danish hands, and implying that the Mercians were also party to the agreement),[2175] since most treaties and many meetings between enemies were made at boundaries.[2176] Though the chroniclers refer to the other parties as the East Anglians and Northumbrians (or in the case of *Anglo-Saxon Chronicle* 'E' the armies of those two kingdoms, or the army of the East Anglians and with the Northumbrians – the text is ambiguous – perhaps implying the absence of a king or kings), those terms are perhaps not as readily intelligible as might be imagined. For example, the Danish-ruled territory of the 'Five Boroughs' is not generally considered to lie in either, though is almost certainly to be included in the terms. We are, it seems, expected to understand that the expressions are shorthand terms for 'those controlling the territory of the Northern Army, reaching as far north as Bernicia, west to the Cumbrian coast, and all of eastern England (excluding East Anglia) as far south as the Wessex border', and to 'those controlling the area roughly equating to modern Norfolk' respectively.[2177]

Little academic research appears to have been concentrated on this mysterious *frið* – separate treaties, one with the Northumbrians, the other with the East Anglians, can probably be discounted[2178] – and details are unknown. Historians have wisely chosen to

---

Anglo-Saxon England, accessed 15 August 2015), who was reeve at Bath, assuming that readers would know of Alfred, who was can suppose was a figure of importance, though nothing more is known about him. David Pelteret has noted that Bath then lay within Mercia, and Alfred's post was militarily sensitive: his death may well have had political and/or strategic significance: Pelteret 2009: 323.

[2172] Earle and Plummer 1892-9: I 95; Whitelock 1961: 60.
[2173] Stenton 1971: 322; Stevenson 1855: 482; Whitelock 1963: 60.
[2174] Tiddingford lies at the point where a significant routeway known in Anglo-Saxon times as *þēodweg* 'people's or public road' crossed the Ouzel, is the place where the parish boundaries of Leighton Buzzard, Linslade and Grove meet, and may be close to the unlocated site of Edward's *burh* at *Wigingamere*: Hill 1984: 55; Baker and Brookes 2013: 208. The place lies a few miles west of the source of the river Lea, the boundary between the kingdoms of Alfred and Guthrum agreed in 878, suggesting that the boundary was revised after that date, perhaps under the Tiddingford treaty itself: Dumville 1992: 10 fn.56.
[2175] Dumville 1992: 11-12. Bedfordshire, Huntingdonshire, Cambridgeshire and Northamptonshire have been seen as satellite regions of East Anglia settled by four Danish armies under King Guthrum, each ruled by its own earl and holds, with boundaries probably fixed before the end of the 9th century: Hart 1992: 13.
[2176] Swanton 1996: 94, which inadvertently identifies the place as *Teotanheale* (*sic*).
[2177] Hill 1984: 56, map 83.
[2178] ASC 'E'; Swanton 1996: 95. It will be noted that the *Chronicle* account tells us that Edward entered into a treaty with the raiding-army from East Anglia and with the Northumbrians: evidently there were two treaties, or there was a tripartite agreement: ibid. One of Edward's law codes, probably dating from before 917, refers to 'treaties' or 'peace-writings' (*friðgewritu*) in the plural and also acknowledges the same three-fold structure (greater Wessex, East Anglia and Northumbria) as the Tiddingford peace: Attenborough 1922: 121; Wormald 1999: 438-9.

eschew any discussion of its possible terms. After the death of Æthelwold at the battle of the Holme the records are conspicuous as much for what we are not told as for what is recorded, and one would like to know much more about the enigmatic agreement.[2179] We shall return to the Tiddingford treaty later in this chapter, but clues to help explain it may well lie in accounts of the battle of the Holme. Since 'King' Æthelwold of Northumbria, the leader and figurehead of the rebellion against Edward, as well as King Eohric of East Anglia, and many of their followers, had perished in the battle, it is normally seen as a victory for Edward. Certainly Edward, in his euphoria and relief over the death of his rebellious cousin, must have seen it in that way.

While that is one interpretation, even the pro-Wessex *Anglo-Saxon Chronicle* paints a rather different picture, reporting that Edward lost a number of his leading ealdormen and thegns as well as a bishop in the great slaughter on both sides adding, crucially, that the Danes retained possession of the field of battle, on which they celebrated their victory. Despite his unalloyed satisfaction over the death of Æthelwold, Edward will have been greatly alarmed to realise that the Danes had been sufficiently powerful, even after the devastating loss of their two leaders, to have driven his forces – if only the Kentish division, if indeed they were representative of Edward's authority – from the battlefield. Leaders were expendable; armies were not. He must have wondered when a new leader

---

[2179] Uncharacteristically, neither Earle and Plummer (1892-9) nor Stenton (1971) have any comment on the treaty. Grafton's *Chronicle* of 1569 records that following Æthelwold's death at the Holme '... the residue [of the Danes] constreyned to flie, and to crie and reeke for peace, which was graunted vnto them vpon certayne condicions, and besides that to pay yerely a certain summe of money in way of Tribute. After which peace so stablished with them, the King repayred Cities, Townes, and Castels, that by the sayde Danes were battered and broken': Grafton 1809: 115. In 1757 a translation of M. Rapin de Thoyras's generally well-researched French history of England records under the year 907 that '[The Danes] sued for peace [at *Yttingaford*]; which Edward readily granted them, on condition they would acknowledge him for sovereign as they had done his father, and the Normans return to France' [*sic*]. It is difficult to know what to make of the concluding words. An account of the Tiddingford treaty in *The Cambridge Medieval History* (1922: III 361) deserves mention. It says that the pact was 'on the terms that the old treaty between Alfred and Guthrum of 886 should be reconfirmed, and that the Danes, in the dioceses of London and Dorchester, should abjure heathendom and pay tithes and other church dues to the bishops'. The account has an interesting history. In his translation of J. M. Lappenberg's *England under the Anglo-Saxon Kings*, Benjamin Thorpe refers to Guthrum II as leader of the East Anglians in 906 when peace was made with Edward the Elder, based on his earlier work, *Ancient Laws and Institutes of England* (1840), which set out the *Laws of Edward and Guthrum* as the agreement in 906. He claimed that the medieval historian John of Wallingford recorded Guthrum II active in Edward's reign. Wallingford (d.1258) indeed records that "Gytrus' [Guthrum], at the request of 'Ealstan' [Æthelstan, Edward's son, born c.894], came from Denmark with a large body of men and submitted to King' Edward, from whom he received East Anglia, which had come under Edward's dominion, and Ealstan was aided by Gytrus in subduing all the rebellions that broke out in South Anglia and bringing the dissatisfied again under his father's yoke' (Stevenson 1854: 545; but see Gross 1900: 308), the latter comment perhaps reflected in the comment of Roger of Wendover that after the Treaty of Tiddingford 'Edward reduced to due obedience some of his rebel subjects, and especially the citizens of London and Oxford': Giles 1892: 236. Joseph Stevenson, who later translated Wallingford's chronicle (a translation from which the above extract is taken), disagreed, finding that Wallingford imagined that Guthrum I who made peace with Alfred (and whose death in 890 is well attested), left England for Denmark and returned in the reign of Æthelstan. Attenborough's *Laws of the Earliest English Kings* (1921) discussed the matter, referring to the German historian Felix Liebermann, who thought the preamble inauthentic and from the reign of Æthelstan. Patrick Wormald noted that from 1568 the authenticity of the *Laws* was unchallenged until Dorothy Whitelock published a study of the text (Whitelock 1941: 1-21). Rather than a contemporary record of the Tiddingford treaty, or from the time of Æthelstan, the *Laws* are now dated to around 1000, probably written by Wulfstan II, Archbishop of York, who died in 1023.

might emerge to unite and head the enemy forces of the Northumbrians of York and the Danes of East Anglia, still forces to be reckoned with, who had retained their war loot at the Holme. The risk of military annihilation might have been lessened, but was hardly removed, by the battle of the Holme. The strength of the Danes of East Anglia alone is well illustrated by the difficulties subsequently experienced by Edward and his sister in taking the Five Boroughs (Lincoln, Nottingham, Derby, Leicester and Stamford) and other centres in the East Midlands following the battle of Tettenhall, a costly and exhaustive campaign that was to last several long years. Yet there can be little doubt that the kingdom of York had sustained a devasting blow which seems to have left it effectively rudderless for a decade or more, until Ragnall took advantage of the vacuum to take control.

In Alistair Campbell's succinct observation: '[a]fter the death of the ætheling Æthelwold at the battle of the Holme and the conclusion of the peace of [Tiddingford] with the Norsemen of both East Anglia and Northumbria [in 905], the affairs of Northumbria are shrouded for several years in darkness'.[2180]

Yet perhaps not absolute darkness, for numismatic evidence is now suggesting that in the decade after Tiddingford, the Northumbrians of York faced political and economic decline, for the royal coinage was replaced after about 905 with an anonymous issue which lasted for about fifteen years with the name of York on one side and the inscription SCI PETRI MO ('St Peter's mint or money') on the other, with the absence of any regnal name and a decline in weight-standard of about half their original value, pointing towards an absence of clear leadership. This might be seen as a reduction in economic activity, partly as a result of the expulsion of Hiberno-Norse from Dublin after 901, and partly as an indication of the devastating losses suffered by the York-based army at the battle of the Holme and political circumstances following the peace of Tiddingford.[2181]

There may be a further reason for Northumbria's lack of military activity during that period, assuming – as seems likely – that it was not responsible for the ravaging of Mercia that led directly to the battle of Tettenhall. We might speculate that Edward, fearful of the threat posed by the beligerent Hiberno-Norse of the north-west, who seems to have attacked at this period only the rivals to the Northern army of York – the Scots, the kingdom of Strathcyde and the 'northern Saxons' of Bernicia[2182] – found himself with little option but to enter into a pact with the leaders of East Anglia and the Danish rulers of York, remnants of the forces of Æthelwold, who, though ostensibly allies of the Hiberno-Norse, and retaining wealth they had looted in their ravaging of Mercia before the battle of the Holme, were equally nervous – with good reason, as time was to prove – about the ever-increasing threat from Ragnall and Ingimund, militant paganswho were at that very moment, if we can believe the sources, flexing their military muscle besieging Chester.

Though little is known about the treaty of Tiddingford, it may be possible to extract slender clues from the sources which, while not revealing the slightest hint about what terms it may have contained, or the background to its realisation, throw some faint light on its creation. We have seen that Edward made the treaty with the Danes of York and East Anglia *for neode*, 'compelled by necessity', (as Simeon of Durham and *Anglo-Saxon Chronicle* 'E' record).[2183] What are we to make of this cryptic observation? It seems

---

[2180] Campbell 1942: 85.
[2181] Downham 2009: 86.
[2182] Higham 1993: 185.
[2183] Stenton 1971: 322; Stevenson 1855; Whitelock 1963: 60.

reasonably clear that Edward faced unusual pressures which forced him to accept concessions with which he was less than comfortable: rather more than a whiff of reluctance can be detected in the chroniclers' uncharacteristically frank comment about the treaty, which no doubt disguises a particularly complex situation barely hinted at by the terse and cryptic annals. The failure to provide further explanation might imply that the pressures on Edward would not necessarily show him in a good light, perhaps exposing the weakness of his position or even identifying doubts about the loyalty of his erstwhile allies and supporters. Simeon of Durham, Florence (John) of Worcester and Roger of Hoveden may be correct when they write that 'the pagans of East Anglia and Northumbria, perceiving that King Edward was invincible, made peace with him',[2184] but those chroniclers were writing centuries after the event, and their analysis might not only be exaggerated and partisan, but the opposite of the truth.

There is no difficulty in supposing that the treaty of Tiddingford was forced upon Edward. He had little alternative but to prevent by any means any alliance between the Danes of York and East Anglia, and the Hiberno-Scandinavians of the north-west, as occurred in 893 with devastating consequences for the English.[2185] If those enemy forces were to form a combined Scandinavian army, their overwhelming might would have posed the greatest risk to Edward and probably proved unstoppable. His own forces had lost many from their crack Kentish contingent. The battle of the Holme had clearly been a close run thing, and Edward was fortunate to escape unscathed with most of his forces intact. His priority now was to prevent any further military incursions into England from the Danelaw so that he and the rulers of Mercia could build up their forces and plan the tactics for their long and ambitious strategy to retake the territories occupied by the Scandinavians, a campaign that Edward lived to see fulfilled.

The treaty was possibly to balance a previous unreported treaty with the Hiberno-Norse, but their continuing military operations in and around Chester makes that unlikely, and we might be entitled to imagine that the terms of the Tiddingford treaty permitted Ingimund and his followers to retain land they had occupied in and around the Wirral, a concession later attributed in Irish annals (the *Three Fragments*) to Æthelflæd, since those annals treated Æthelflæd as 'queen of the Saxons' (and Æthelred as 'king'), and took virtually no interest in Edward, though Æthelflæd could well have acted as negotiator in any such arrangement.[2186] Certainly any such arrangement would have been anathema to Edward

---

[2184] Stevenson 1853: 73; Riley 1853: 60; Stevenson 1855: 500. The wording of the latter part of this passage might suggest that it was translated into English from another language.
[2185] Swanton 1996: 84-9.
[2186] O'Donovan 1860: 227, 231-7. The 'breaking of the peace' by the Northumbrians which we are told preceded the battle of Tettenhall almost certainly referred to the treaty imposed on the Northumbrians after Edward's damatic five-week raid the previous year, rather than the treaty of Tiddingford. It is worth recording an observation of the Scottish historian John Fordun, whose chronicle of the Scottish nation dates from 1363, who records that four years before what must have been Edward's incursion into Northumbia, the 'kings of the Danish nation, indeed more fickle than the wind', were 'led away by the treacherous promises of Edward, and made a peace with him against the Scots, to their own hurt. Nor did the stipulations of this covenant hold long; indeed, four years after, there sprang up some estrangement between them – by what chance, is not certain, by Edward's wickedness, who made a hostile invasion of their territory, and wasted it with piteous slaughter for a whole month': Skene 1872: 154-5. Fordun goes on to record that as a result the Danes sent messengers to King Constantine and persuaded him to renew their treaty with him, and that in 919 Constantine granted Eugenius, the son of Donald, his expected next heir, the lordship of Cumbria: ibid.

(and no less to Æthelred and Æthelflæd), and would explain his reluctance to conclude the treaty, but the idea can be no more than speculation.

What is also puzzling is the hiatus – perhaps as long as two or even three years – between the battle of the Holme and the Tiddingford treaty (assuming the treaty was the formal culmination of hostilities in that conflict, as Roger of Wendover implies when he records the battle of the Holme and adds that 'not long afterwards [Edward] made peace with the pagans at a place called Ittingeford'),[2187] for treaties were normally concluded immediately or very soon after a major battle. That delay is perhaps explained not only by the equivocal outcome of the battle, where the Scandinavian leaders and many, if not most, of their combatants were slaughtered though their forces held the battlefield, which technically gave them the victory, but while the Danes of York, as noted elsewhere, seem, from abundant numismatic evidence from the Cuerdale hoard, to have been ruled shortly before that time by a Christian king Siefred of York, probably briefly succeeded by (or even ruling jointly with) Knútr (Cnut), also probably Christian,[2188] the Danes of East Anglia may have had no king or kings,[2189] a situation which is unlikely to have assisted negotiations between the parties.

Treaties were imposed by the victor on the vanquished. Was Edward the victor at the Holme? Did the Scandinavians share his view? Certainly the death of his rebellious cousin will have caused him immense relief, and later chroniclers, as we have seen, had little doubt about Edward's invincibility, but by retaining the field of battle at the Holme the Scandinavians remained a continuing threat. With whom was Edward to negotiate any treaty if the king of East Anglia was now dead, any surviving leaders could not agree between themselves, and the ruler(s) of Northumbria, perhaps without a king or kings, proved inflexible? Would the treaty include any reference to the spoils taken by Æthelwold and Eohric during their ravaging through Mercia, strictly the property of the victors, but doubtless demanded by Edward? From whom were the spoils to be demanded? Did 'the Northumbrians' who were parties to the treaty include as a separate faction the Hiberno-Norse of the north-west (as might be evidenced by the 'scorning of every peace' by the Northumbrians who ravaged Mercia and were vanquished at the battle of Tettenhall in 910)? At the time those Hiberno-Norse were placing Mercian Chester and its environs under considerable military pressure and posing a growing threat to Æthelred and Æthelflæd's northern frontier. Bilateral treaties could be readily achieved; trilateral pacts, or those made between even more parties, were far more complicated, and even moreso when some of the parties had no formalised leadership. And how were the English leaders of Essex, who had thrown in their lot with Æthelwold (Essex had no king), to be dealt with? We have also seen that before his ravaging of Mercia, Æthelwold, according to Simeon of Durham, Matthew Paris and Roger of Wendover, had been in Gaul attempting to gather a stronger force, presumably of Scandinavians, and reached Essex with an army in 'a great fleet'. Amongst any such forces were, we might suppose, Vikings from Gaul, and Edward will have been all too aware of the continuing threat posed from across the Channel by mercenary elements ready to seize any opportunity to enrich themselves with captured loot. In addition, we cannot know what influence, if any, the recently arrived Hiberno-Scandinavian immigrants under Ingimund who were, we are led to believe,

---

[2187] Giles 1892: I 236.
[2188] Hall 2001: 189; Downham 2009: 78-9; Gooch 2012: 48, 60.
[2189] The last (un-named) king of East Anglia is said to have been killed in 917 when Edward led an English force against the Danish fortification at Tempsford, and so recovered the whole of eastern England as far north as the Welland: ASC 'A'; Swanton 1996: 101.

settling in the Chester area may have had on the treaty. The makings of the Holme came from an unexpected geographical quarter. The next threat might cause similar surprise.

Delays in concluding the Tiddingford treaty may be self evident, but are almost certainly not the full story – possibly not even part of it. One aspect, indeed, that has received little comment is an almost incidental and little-noticed record by Roger of Wendover (followed in the usual way by Matthew Paris) that immediately after concluding the treaty of Tiddingford, Edward 'reduced to due obedience some [sic] of his rebel subjects, and especially the citizens of London and Oxford'.[2190] Both places lay in Mercia on the very border with Wessex,[2191] and we might suppose (if Roger's account is to be trusted) that a serious insurrection – presumably against Edward rather than Æthelred and Æthelflæd – by a faction of 'rebel subjects' about which we have no information had taken place in south-east Mercia, which Edward attempted, not altogether successfully, to quell. The supposed rebellions in London and Oxford, if they occurred, might conceivably have resulted from sanctions imposed for their support of Æthelwold, for as well as military forces provided by the leaders of Essex,[2192] he had certainly received military assistance from factions of the Mercian aristocracy – some had given their life at the Holme in his cause – and there were probably many others who had been sympathisers, but whatever the case any rebellion and its aftermath will have added a further complication to any treaty at Tiddingford.

However, at this point it is important to emphasise that Roger's chronology of events at this period is clearly confused, for the account of rebel subjects in London and Oxford is followed immediately by a note recording the appointment of Benedict as Pope. Benedict IV was Pope from some date in the first half of 900 to the summer of 903. From this we must conclude that the reference to Benedict is a misplaced interpolation, or that the brief note of rebellion in London and Oxford (if true) has been misplaced. Furthermore, an entry for 905 records the appointment of Frithstan as bishop of Winchester, and Eadulf as bishop of Wells, but both elections took place in 909.[2193] Under the year 912 (recte 911) Roger records the death of Æthelred and the rule of his widow Æthelflæd of 'the entire province of the Mercians, except the cities of London and Oxford, which her brother king Edward retained to himself'.[2194] The wording is suspiciously close to the claim of rebellion by the

---

[2190] Coxe 1841: 370; Giles 1893: I 236; Luard 1872: I 436. The source of this entry has not been traced: it is found in Richard of Cirencester's *Speculum historiale de gestis regum Angliæ*, a history of England from 447 to 1066, but that is essentially a compilation from other chroniclers, including Roger of Wendover: Graves 1975: 291. Luard claims it derives from ASC 'E', sub anno 910 (Luard 1872: 437), but no such entry is found in ASC 'E'. It may be thought that the accounts are garbled and misplaced versions of Edward's recovery of London and Oxford after the death of Æthelred in 911, but that recovery is properly recorded in its correct sequence by both chroniclers.
[2191] Hill 1984: 56, map 85.
[2192] Originally recorded in AD 527, during the ninth century, Essex was part of a sub-kingdom that included Sussex, Surrey and Kent. Its territory was later restricted to lands east of the River Lea, and in 903 it lay to the east of London, between Kent and East Anglia. At some date between 878 and 886, the territory was formally ceded by Alfred to the Danelaw kingdom of East Anglia, under the treaty with Guthrum. After Edward's reconquest the king's representative in Essex was styled an ealdorman and Essex came to be regarded as a shire. An enduring mystery is how the English leaders in Essex were treated by Edward after the Holme, which is unmentioned by the chronicles. It is difficult to imagine that they were not harshly dealt with, but the Tiddingford treaty may have secured their immunity.
[2193] Giles 1892: I 236-7.
[2194] Giles 1892: I 230. Simeon of Durham records in the briefest of terms the battle of Tettenhall in 910, followed by the claim (also found in *Anglo-Saxon Chronicle* 'A', 'D' and 'E': Earle and Plummer

citizens of London and Oxford made by Roger of Wendover, which could have been based on a garbled version of that entry in which an unwarranted gloss had been added to explain why Edward should have 'taken' (the word implying the use of force, and so perhaps rebellion) London and Oxford after Æthelred's death. Clearly the sequence of entries – and their credibility – in the various chronicles must be treated with considerable caution. Yet the reference to rebel subjects has a ring of authenticity – it might seem an unlikely subject to invent without some evidence to support it – and the possibility that it may well record a significant if otherwise unremarked episode of Edward's reign cannot be discounted entirely.

If Roger's claim could be well-founded, one would wish to know far more about there bellious factions in Oxford and London, and evidently elsewhere. Several possibilities suggest themselves. Perhaps those places refused to support resistance to Æthelwold's claim to the throne and his military insurrection c.903, which might in turn imply more Mercian support for the would-be usurper than we have been led to imagine. That idea might be borne out by the *Mercian Register*, which we have seen records the battle of the Holme in the briefest terms, identifying the Danes as the adversary but failing to mention the not insignificant role of Æthelwold or identify the victors – puzzling omissions. With Æthelwold and his East Anglian allies threatening Mercia and Wessex, Edward (as ultimate ruler of both) will have been under enormous pressure and at great risk from a significant Mercian rebellion on the northern borders of Wessex and belligerent Danes to the north-east. To what extent Æthelred and Æthelflæd may have been party to the supposed rebellion involving Oxford and London must remain unknown, but it might be considered inconceivable for those centres, among other places, to have resisted the rulers of both Mercia and Wessex, and the fact that Edward was forced to take action – almost certainly military action – implies that the Mercian leaders may even have been tacitly, if not actively, supporting the rebels at the Holme, perhaps taking a pragmatic approach to the prospect of a victory by Æthelwold's forces.

Another possibility is that the rebellion was associated in some way with the subsequent Tiddingford treaty, which might explain the cryptic claim that it was made *for neode*, 'for necessity', the pressure perhaps coming from the rebellious group. It is not difficult to understand why the West-Saxon orientated *Anglo-Saxon Chronicle* would be silent on a sizeable rebellion which may have led to a military confrontation, perhaps even military action, between the forces of Wessex and Mercia. It is difficult, however, to believe that the disaffection in London and Oxford – if accepted as fact – may have been unrelated in some way to the otherwise unexplained grant by Edward in 903 of charters for two estates in the environs of London and Oxford, both within Æthelred's Mercia, and both charters originating with others from a gathering in 903 attended by Edward, Æthelred and Æthelflæd, and their daughter Ælfwynn, with some Mercian nobles and a number of bishops from Kent, Sussex, and Mercia, though none from Wessex.[2195] Whether that assembly was held before or after the battle of the Holme is unknown, but the presence of reprentatives from Kent, which had supported Æthelwold at the Holme, is noteworthy. Another charter attested by Edward that seems to have been drawn up the following year relates to an estate at Water Eaton, to the north of Oxford – again, in Mercia.[2196] The fact

---

1892-9: I 96-7) that 'King Edward took London and Oxford, and what pertained to it', though there is no reference to the death of Æthelred: Stevenson 1855: 482.

[2195] S.367, S.367a, and S.371; see Keynes 2001: 51-4.
[2196] S.361.

that Edward presided over the proceedings and was identified by the draftsman of the charter as successor to the old Mercian royal house must be of particular interest.

How much reliance should be placed on the tantalising reference to rebellion in London and Oxford cannot be known. It is true that no evidence (other than the anonymous chronicle incorporated in John of Wallingford's writings) has been traced to support Roger's claim, though the circumstantial evidence cited above might possibly add some credence to his brief account. A rebellion might also help to explain why immediately after the death of Æthelred in 911 Edward very pointedly 'succeeded to London and Oxford and all the lands that belonged thereto',[2197] (London having been granted by King Alfred to Æthelred in 885 or 886),[2198] and the recovery of London and Oxford recorded by the *Chronicle* in the same sentence,[2199] an action which – if Roger's claim might be correct – was doubtless intended to remove the possibility of any further acts of disaffection.

In assessing Roger of Wendover's accuracy as a historian, however – and we should recognise that with considerable skill he interwove into his text much information about events on the Continent – we cannot overlook an especially curious account found in the his chronicle (and that of Matthew Paris, based Roger's work),[2200] which records that in 906, shortly after the appearance of a comet for half a year (an observation which confirms that the date is correct, for a comet is known to have been visible in that year for nearly six months),[2201] a battle occurred 'between the Danes and the English, wherein many nobles of both peoples fell', and that the following year 'The great King Edward assembled a numerous army and reduced Essex, East-Anglia, Mercia, Northumbria, and many other provinces, which he wrested from the dominion of the Danes, who had long possessed them. He also reduced the Scots, the inhabitants of Cumberland, and those of Galloway, and after receiving the submission of their kings, he returned home with glory and honour'.[2202] Although both chroniclers mention the battle of the Holme explicitly, the battle of 906 seems to be another reference to that conflict, which Florence (John) of Worcester records (for a second time, the first the previous year) immediately after the comet episode.[2203] Roger's account, which appears the year before the restoration of Chester in 907, is stated by the editor of his chronicle to be taken from Florence (John) of Worcester, but the annal for 907 in Florence is blank,[2204] and the original source for Roger's account has not been traced: it may be a misplaced and garbled précis of events in 920 when Edward supposedly accepted the submission of the Scots, Northumbrians, and king of Strathclyde at Bakewell,[2205] but has similarities with the enconium to Edward which

---

[2197] ASC 'A'; Swanton 1996: 96. Further evidence of disaffection in south-east Mercia might be detected in the chronicle of John of Wallingford (d.1258) who recorded the putting-down of rebellions that broke out in 'South Anglia' during King Edward's reign: Stevenson 1854: 545. However, Wallingford's *Chronica* has been held to be 'A compilation of no value. The latter part is taken from Matthew Paris [whose work incoporated that of Roger of Wendover]': Gross 1900: 308.

[2198] ASC 'A', 'C', 'D', 'E': Swanton 1996: 80-81. The grant of London may have sealed Æthelred's marriage to Æthelflæd.

[2199] ASC 'A', 'D', 'E': Swanton 1996: 95-7.

[2200] Gransden 1996: 359.

[2201] Earle and Plummer 1892-99: Ii 117-8.

[2202] Luard 1872: 439; Coxe 1841: I 373; Giles 1892: 237. The entry for 905 records the appointment of new bishops which occurred in 909, suggesting that the battle of 906 may be a misplaced and duplicated reference to Tettenhall, which is mentioned specifically in an entry for 911: Luard 1872: I 440; Giles 1892: I 237.

[2203] Stevenson 1853: 73-4.

[2204] Luard 1872: I 439.

[2205] ASC 'A'; Swanton 1996: 104; but for doubts on such submission see Davidson 2001: 200-202.

appears in Florence (John) of Worcester's chronicle (which was used by Roger) before Edward's death at Farndon is recorded in 924.[2206] Nevertheless, it is true to say that no convincing explanation is readily available for the remarkable (and patently unbelievable) account of Roger's account of a wide-ranging campaign in 907.[2207] That insertion *en bloc* must inevitably cast doubt on Roger of Wendover's authority as a historian, at least for this period.

In 907, evidently in response to Ingimund's supposed attempt two years earlier to seize Chester, when it was reported that 'the city was very wealthy, and the land around it choice',[2208] Æthelflæd took the precaution of refortifying the city,[2209] a measure clearly designed to help control the new Scandinavian settlers and protect Mercia from Ingimund's forces.[2210] Remarkably, this is the first mention of Edward's sister and Æthelred's wife in the *Anglo-Saxon Chronicle* – she is inexplicably also unmentioned in connection with this episode in the *Mercian Register* which simply records the restoration of Chester[2211] – though there is ample evidence from charters and other sources that she had taken a leading role in ruling Mercia since the 880s, and particularly after the seeming incapacity of her husband from at least the early 900s and possibly earlier. As we have seen, the *Three Fragments'* report of the siege of Chester in 905 ends cryptically: 'it was not long until they came to wage battle again'.[2212] That comment might well, as Wainwright believed,[2213] refer to an attack on refortified Chester in or soon after 907, memorably if imaginatively described in the Irish *Three Fragments*, though there is no hint of any such action in other chronicles.

It may have been around this time that a collapse of power of an English elite at the hands of the Hiberno-Scandinavians in the north-west forced members of the old English aristocracy to leave the region. For some 200 years after the end of Roman rule in Britain the area that became Westmorland was probably part of the British kingdom which became known as Cumbria or Stathclyde, but c.600 the greater region of the north-west came into English hands, and was probably still ruled by a native English aristocracy when Alfred died in 899. But at some date before 915 – perhaps much earlier – an important nobleman, Ælfred, son of Brihtwulf, was forced to flee from an invasion of 'pirates', and

---

[2206] Stevensoon 1853: 79.
[2207] It is worth mentioning a letter (S.1444) dated between 900-909 from Denewulf, Bishop of Winchester (879-909) addressed to Edward concerning property in Beddington in Surrey, 10 miles south of London, which mentions that the estate had previously been plundered by 'heathen men', i.e. Vikings, and to a very recent severe winter: Whitelock 1979: 543-4; Rumble 2001: 236-7. It is said that most of the river of England were frozen for two months in 908, which if true may help date the Viking incursion: Brazell 1968: 8, citing Short 1749, who rarely gives authorities for his research.
[2208] VCH Cheshire: I 249. The report is no earlier than the eleventh century, and the mythical material it contains must cast considerable doubt over its reliability.
[2209] Ward 2001. If John (Florence) of Worcester is to be believed, her husband Æthelred was also involved in the rebuilding of Chester, notwithstanding his suspected long-term disabling illness: Stevenson 1853: 73.
[2210] VCH Cheshire: I 249; Wainwright 1975: 84; Williams, Smyth and Kirby 1991: 160; Swanton 1996: 94. Although the *Chronicle* tells us that in 893 Chester had been a deserted city (ASC 'A'; Swanton 1996: 88), it probably misrepresents the situation, for there is evidence that a mint may have been operating before Æthelflæd restored the defences, and indeed that it had existed in Alfred's later years. The precursor of the present cathedral may have been founded as early as 689: Lyon 2001: 75; Griffiths 2001: 169.
[2211] Whitelock 1961: 61
[2212] Griffiths 2015: 34.
[2213] Wainwright 1975: 85.

sought sanctuary with bishop Cutheard (900-915).[2214] He became St Cuthbert's 'faithful man', receiving estates between the Wear and the Tees and later leading a force against Ragnall of York.[2215] Others fleeing from Cumbria by 915, and possibly much earlier, included the Abbot of Heversham, the only early monastery known to have existed in Westmorland, who with others sought the protection against pirates of the St Cuthbert community. These 'pirates' were a manifestation of an influx into north-western England of Hiberno-Norwegians which was to have a profound impact on the whole political and social history of England.[2216]

Doubtless in response to the attack on Chester and the growing threat from Ragnall and the Hiberno-Scandinavians, in 909 a large force of West Saxons and Mercians, perhaps even with support from the East Anglian and Northumbrian Danes, and possibly including Welsh elements, launched a devastating five week strike against what the *Chronicle* calls the *norð here*, literally the 'north army'.[2217] The driving force behind the campaign is clear from the words of the *Anglo-Saxon Chronicle*, our primary source for the action: 'King Edward sent [i.e. it was not led by him] an army both from Wessex and from Mercia, and it raided the north raiding army very greatly, both men and every kind of property, and killed many men of those Danish and were inside there for five weeks'.[2218] The entry implies that Edward had command over the armies of both Wessex and Mercia, but probably indicates that he ordered the army of Æthelred and Æthelflæd to join his own forces. What is especially curious, however, and not readily explicable, is that neither the chronicler Æthelweard nor the *Mercian Register* make any mention of this major incursion into Northumbria,[2219] from which we might understand that Æthelred's health prevented him from leading the Mercian contingent.

This was the *Chronicle* emphasising Edward's over-riding authority which allowed him to order into action the Mercian army, if not led by Æthelred then probably headed by a leading Mercian *ealdorman*, as well as his own West Saxon forces led by a senior West Saxon *ealdorman* (and perhaps including Edward's son Æthelstan), and was a large-scale and ruthless incursion by the English into Scandinavian territory. Roger of Wendover and Florence (John) of Worcester are amongst those who add that the Scandinavians were cruelly harassed, with many slain, many others carried away into shameful captivity, and immense booty taken, an unusual criticism of English activity against the Northumbrians.[2220] Some chroniclers, such as Florence (John) of Worcester and Simeon of Durham, seem to associate the incursion as a response a breach of the peace the Danes had

---

[2214] Quanrud 2015: 83.
[2215] Charles-Edwards 2013: 482. This doubtless explains why Ragnall confiscated large territories in the lowlands of County Durham from the community of St Cuthbert to give to his protégés Scule and Onlafball and their followers: Higham 1993: 186.
[2216] Stenton 1970: 215-6; Wainwright 1975: 330-2. A curious observation by the chronicler Æthelweard deserves mention. He tells us that in 899, prior to Alfred's death, 'there was a disturbance on a very great scale among the English, that is the bands who were then settled in the territories of the Northumbrians': Campbell 1962: 51. Whether that comment might refer to the English in the north-west and be connected with the flight by the English aristocracy is unknown.
[2217] ASC 'A', 'B', 'C', and 'D'; Thorpe 1861: I 184-5.
[2218] Thorpe 1861: I 184-5; Bateley 1986: 63; Swanton 1996: 94-7; Cubbin 1996: 37. Whitelock gives instead '... both men and every kind of cattle ....' (Whitelock 1961: 61; Whitelock 1979: 213): OE *yrfe, ierfe* can mean both 'property' or 'cattle', but the latter seems rather less likely in this context. What is unarguable is that many captives were taken as slaves by the English army: Pelteret 1995: 70.
[2219] Whitelock 1961: 61; Campbell 1962: 52.
[2220] Giles 1892: 238; Stevenson 1853: 73.

made with Edward', generally assumed to mean the treaty of Tiddingford, the only treaty mentioned (a few years earlier) by those chroniclers.[2221] Indeed, Henry of Huntingdon refers to the treaty and the raid into Northumbria in consecutive sentences, with those events taking place in consecutive years, though he makes no mention of any breach of a treaty.[2222]

It must be said that the early sources which mention Edward's raid into Northumbria in 909 are singularly unhelpful. Of one thing we can be certain: the incursion must have been in response to some particularly significant event or provocative circumstanes – or was a key obligation under a significant treaty with others – since leading a raiding army into Northumbria for no less than five weeks was not an exercise that Edward will have undertaken lightly.[2223] It will have taken considerable forethought, with troops assembled from outlying areas, warriors armed and armoured, provisions and transport laid on, all at great expense. Any such operation deep within enemy territory will have carried great risk, only to be mitigated by meticulous logistical planning and strength of numbers. The various chronicle accounts provide little clue to explain the reason behind Edward's raid, but Roger of Wendover claims that the campaign was in response to a Northumbrian rebellion[2224] – the 'Danes' (meaning here, as we shall see below, Scandinavians, not necessarily of Danish nationality) are described as *rebellantes* – but we have no knowledge of any such uprising, and the English incursion has generally been seen as a major, aggressive and intentional provocation by the English, with limited or no resistence from the Scandinavians, who were presumably taken by surprise.

It is readily apparent that Edward's raid was no unjustified provocation, but a carefully considered reaction to significant circumstances or events in Northumbria of particular concern to the English. The main evidence for disturbances in or shortly before 909 is admittedly legendary and probably fanciful, found, as noted above, only in the later Irish *Three Fragments*, of military activity by a collaboration of Danes, Norse and ex-patriot Irish forces against Chester after its refortification in 907,[2225] and vague and terse reports of continuing warfare after the refortification in other sources. Wainwright, having studied that region at this period in considerable detail, concluded that the highly embroidered and dramatically entertaining description of the unsuccessful attack against the city was based on an episode or episodes which took place probably after its refortification in 907 (and certainly before Æthelred's death in 911), and that '[i]t is, indeed, highly probable that Chester was endangered by recurrent attacks between 907 and 911, for this area was not

---

[2221] For example Stevenson 1853: 73; Stevenson 1855: 500;

[2222] Forester 1853: 163.

[2223] It is right to add that Simon Keynes has taken the view that '... Edward himself seems to have broken the peace in 909 ...': Keynes 1999: 464.

[2224] Coxe 1841: I 373; Luard 1872: I 439. Clare Downham has suggested that any such rebellion may have been a response to the imposition of Æthelred's overlordship, or a perceived abuse of that overlordship: Downham 2009: 88. These various theories might seem to contradict the persuasive evidence that Æthelred had long suffered from some disabling illness which led to his wife taking on a more significant role in ruling Mercia (though she may have needed no such encouragement), and further responsibility might seem an unlikely imposition.On the other hand, the *Mercian Register*, a set of annals inserted into the *Anglo-Saxon Chronicle* intended to glorify the exploits of Æthelflæd, does not mention her name before 912, which might suggest that Æthelred was not especially incapacitated before his death in 911.

[2225] The *Chronicle of Melrose* records that Chester was rebuilt at the command of King Edward: Stevenson 1856: 95.

free from trouble for many years'.[2226] The threat against Chester was not only from the militant Hiberno-Norse from the Wirral driven from Dublin c.901, but from the longer established Norse of the north-west in southern Lancashire and Cumbria (i.e. in Northumbria), not only envious of the wealth in and around Chester, but anxious to dispossess the English from a militarily and commercially important centre controlling sea traffic from the Irish Sea. It would not be unreasonable to suppose (though there is no direct evidence) that Edward's raid was a response of the firmest kind to events in and around Chester and the area to the north in or shortly before 909. That idea may be supported by the absence of reports of any military activity by the Hiberno-Norse in that area in the years following, and if this analysis is correct, the identity of those Scandinavians who launched a heavy raid into Mercia the following year will be self-evident. The failure of the ambitious and aggressive Ragnall and his forces to take the vacant kingship of York at this period (he eventually secured York and became king in 919, the year before he died)[2227] is tellingly indicative of the fraught relationship between the Danes of York and the Hiberno-Scandinavians of the north-west.[2228]

That conclusion may be supported by a detailed consideration of the *Chronicle* accounts which might throw light on Edward's raid into Northumbria. The entry in *Anglo-Saxon Chronicle* 'D' which tells us that the campaign was against the *norð here*,[2229] literally 'north army', found only once in the entire Chronicle, is surprisingly problematic, with a number of possible interpretations, including 'army to the north', 'northern army', or 'army of the *norð*-men', the latter inferred from other terms incorporating *here* such as *sciphere* 'army of ships' and *hæðen here* 'army of pagans'. As John Quanrud has pointed out, nothing helps us to narrow down the geographical territory of the 'north army', but the expression may have been used deliberately 'to introduce a Viking army that was new on the scene (such as, perhaps, the Irish Sea Vikings in north-west England) and therefore needed to be distinguished from other Scandinavian armies,'[2230] though we cannot overlook that during his rebellion against Edward, Æthelwold fled from Wimbourne to *þone here on Norðhymbrum* 'the army in Northumbria', i.e. the army in York.[2231]

It is true that the *Chronicle* describes those who were killed in the English raid of 909 as *þara deniscra*, usually and understandably interpreted as 'those Danes' or 'those Danish',[2232] but it is apparent that the chroniclers did not intend, by the use of such terms, to distinguish Danes from Norwegians or other Scandinavians, and *Denisc* in this adjectival form was probably used to mean Scandinavians in general, an idea supported by other examples from the Chronicles where *Denisc* is found in contexts which can only

---

[2226] Wainwright 1975: 85; Higham 1993: 184. Unfortunately no source is cited for this episode, which is likely to be the legendary siege described in the *Three Fragments* which followed the refortification of Chester in 907: Wainwright 1975: 85; Griffiths 2015: 34.

[2227] Though 'his career is badly recorded and at some points is quite obscure' (Wainwright 1975: 163), no evidence has been traced to support the claim in Williams, Smyth and Kirby 1991: 205 that Ragnall became king of York between 910 and 914.

[2228] It should not be overlooked that if the location of the battle of *Brunanburh*, where a formidable coalition of Scots, Strathclyde Britons and Vikings from Dublin was defeated by Æthestan's forces in 937, has been properly identified as Bromborough (and the evidence is compelling: see Livingstone 2011), the significance of the Wirral in the early 10th century is considerably reinforced.

[2229] Thorpe 1861: I 185.

[2230] Quanrud 2015: 75.

[2231] ASC 'D'; Earle and Plummer 1892-9: I 93.

[2232] See, for example, Whitelock, Douglas and Tucker 1961: 61; Swanton 1996: 97.

refer to Norwegians.[2233] Quanrud, having analysed the use of this and similar terms in Old English sources has concluded that the expression *Denisc* 'may ... represent an editorial decision taken by [the Chronicle's] authors when compiling that work rather than reflecting standard usage over decades ...'.[2234] The term was not intended to distinguish between Viking groups of differing ethnicity, but was used for Scandinavian forces generally; the men of the *norð here* killed in the raid of 909 were not Danish in the modern sense of the word, or more specifically 'Danes of York'.[2235] Indeed, it seems that by the mid-tenth century the word Dane may have come to mean something akin to 'inhabitant of eastern England', and at the end of the century was evidently the term for what we would now call Scandinavians.[2236] In the same way, Abrams has suggested that *pagani* may have come to mean Scandinavians, whatever their religion, or was used as a convenient slur 'when no longer strictly descriptive'.[2237]

We have seen that the unique term *norð here* was probably coined for a new threat, namely the Hiberno-Scandinavians, or Irish Sea Vikings in north-west England, who were to be distinguished from the other Scandinavian armies of York-ruled Northumbria, generally described as the *Norþhymbre* in the Chronicle.[2238] Scandinavian settlements had been established in Ireland for more than a century with much intermarriage between the two peoples and an interchange of vocabulary, which can also be traced in the place-names of north-west England.[2239] Edward's raid was, we may reasonably suppose, intended to neutralise a newly-formed but impatiently belligerent pagan Hiberno-Scandinavian army with its core in the north-west, posing a serious threat not only to Edward, Æthelred and Æthelflæd, but the Danes of York. Indeed, there is good reason to imagine that the raid could have been one of the obligations accepted by Edward as part of a treaty with those same Danes.

That view is not inconsistent with the views of Nicholas Higham, who believed that the Northern Army attacked by Edward may have been based in Lancashire, albeit as a force subject to the rulers of York.[2240] Any reported rebellion might have been an insurrection by the Northern Army against the rulers of York, with Edward providing forces under the Treaty of Tiddingford – or some subsequent agreement – to put down the rebellion, though there is little evidence to support such theory. Certainly the kingdom of York was still weakened after the battle of the Holme some six years earlier, though still a force to be reckoned with, and it may have been an accord with the Mercian rulers to protect the Danes of York from the Hiberno-Norse that is to be associated with the decision of

---

[2233] Quanrud 2015: 75-6; Downham 2007: xviii.
[2234] Quanrud 2015: 76.
[2235] Quanrud 2015: 76.
[2236] ASC 'A' s.a. 942; Swanton 1996: 110; Boyle 2016: 117.
[2237] Abrams 2001a: 32.
[2238] Quanrud 2015: 77-8.
[2239] Stenton 1970: 216-8.
[2240] Higham 1992: 24; Higham 1993: 186. Higham notes that Æthelweard records that the York kings 'were forced to accept the superiority of the now fatally sick king Ethelred of Mercia' (Higham 1993: 186), but no such account has been traced in Æthelweard's writings, and the reference may be based on a misreading of Florence (John) of Worcester who tells us that the Danish kings were compelled to renew with King Edward the peace which they had broken: Thorpe 1848: 120. A small hoard of coins discovered in Shrewsbury in 1936, of which there were at least six coins of Edward the Elder, may be as late as 910, with coins associated with Winchester or Oxford. The hoard (with the Harkirke hoard from Little Crosby, Lancashire, found in 1611), may be associated with Edward's campaign of 909-10 against the Northumbrian Danes: Lyon 2001: 75.

Æthelred and Æthelflæd to promote the cult of the Northumbrian martyr-king Oswald (who died, it should be remembered, at the hands of the Mercian King Penda, albeit a pagan). That promotion doubtless strengthened diplomatic ties between Mercia and Northumbria – the Danes of York, then largely Christianised, presumably gratified that an ancestral martyred king was to become the focus of an important Mercian cult – which led almost a decade later to the submission of the York-folk to the overlordhip of Æthefiæd, if the *Mercian Register* is to be believed.

However, we need to consider comments made by Florence (John) of Worcester which may throw other light on the background to Edward's military campaign against the Northern Army, for his chronicle tells us that he ravaged Northumbria 'on the occasion of the Danes breaking the peace which they had concluded with him', and that Edward forced their kings '(whether they liked it or not) to renew ... the peace which they had broken', claims also made by Simeon of Durham.[2241] But those accounts were of course written long after the events of 909, and their trustworthiness must be suspect. Æthelweard mentions that in 910 Æthelred ruled the Northumbrian and Mercian areas[2242] (a curious claim discussed in more detail elsewhere in this volume), and Higham interprets this to mean that in 909 the Northumbrians of southern Lancashire were forced to accept the superiority of the ailing ruler.[2243]

This might be seen to support the idea that to balance the treaty of Tiddingford an equivalent treaty was entered into by the Hiberno-Scandinavians of the north-west, which may explain John of Fordun's claim that 'treacherous promises' of Edward led the 'Danes' to enter into a treaty with him against the Scots, which lasted only four years until Edward invaded their territory.[2244] Indeed, such a treaty may even have been part of the *quid pro quo* by which Æthelflæd supposedly allowed Ingimund and his followers to settle near Chester in or after 903, an arrangement to which, if it occurred at all, Edward must have given his approval. We might also speculate that the Cuerdale Hoard found in the Ribble valley, deposited within a few years of 902, which probably included over 7,500 coins, including Arabic, Frankish and Anglo-Saxon issues – more than two dozen carrying Edward's name, three associated with Chester and another perhaps with Shrewsbury[2245] – but mainly newly-minted coins from York (implying an alliance, or at least cooperation between Danish York and the Irish Norse),[2246] could have been hidden by Scandinavians fearing an imminent English threat, with those concealing it killed in the English raid. But the Ribble valley lay on the main route between the Hiberno-Scandinavians of the north-west and the Danes of York, and many other plausible theories have been advanced for the deposition of the treasure.[2247] Other unanswered questions relate to the 'many captives' taken in Edward's raid of 909. Were they taken (and traded) as slaves? As hostages? And if

---

[2241] Stevenson 1853: 73; Stevenson 1855: 500.
[2242] Campbell 1962: 52.
[2243] Higham 1993: 186.
[2244] Skene 1872: 154-5.
[2245] Lyon 2001: 75.
[2246] Higham 1992: 185.
[2247] Other reasons for the deposition put forward by John Quanrud are that the hoard was an army 'pay-chest' intended to reverse the Dublin expulsion of the Hiberno-Scandinavians; or tribute taken from the Danes of Northumbria and East Anglia by the Hiberno-Scandinavians after their expulsion from Dublin; or it might represent extortion on an unprecedented scale resulting from a treaty, perhaps that of Tiddingford, between the Anglo-Saxons and Danelaw rulers against the Hiberno-Scandinavians: Quanrud 2015: 88 footnote. On the Vikings of the Ribble see Lewis 2016: 8-25.

the latter, what became of them when the treaty was quickly broken?[2248] We simply do not know. Of the 'immense booty' we can be more certain, but ironically its loss was probably the motive for the breach of the treaty by the Northumbrians as soon as opportunity allowed.[2249]

As noted elsewhere, the identification of the boundary line between Mercia and Northumbria in 909/910 may be of critical importance to this study, for, as we have seen, the sources tell us that the Edward's raid of 909 was against 'the north raiding-army', and the conflict of 910 was with the (or a) Northumbrian raiding army – though whether later chroniclers would have had knowledge of Northumbrian/Mercian boundary adjustments made from time to time must be doubtful. Without setting aside the discussion above on the identification of the *Norþhymbre*, we may suppose that the chroniclers intended their readers to understand that the area attacked by Edward in 909 formed part of Northumbria, and the protagonists who invaded Mercia in 910 were from Northumbrian-controlled territory. If that is the case, that means that they were certainly from north of the Mersey – there is no record that Northumbria ever extended south of the river – and probably from north of the Ribble, in which case they are likely to have been joined by supporters and sympathisers from the area around the Wirral. If that analysis is correct, it is unclear whether the core of the enemy force at Tettenhall included Ingimund's followers from the Wirral area, though it would be reasonable to imagine that they probably supported enthusiastically the cause of their compatriots to the north, with whom they shared a broadly similar background, ancestry, pagan religion, loathing of and contempt for the English, and presumably (but not necessarily) political and military ambitions.

Whether Edward's attack on the Northern Army presaged, incorporated, or followed a West Saxon and Mercian expedition deep into the Danelaw that same year to recover the remains of the Northumbrian king St Oswald from Lincolnshire is uncertain, though it seems more realistic to imagine the expedition taking place after any treaty which concluded Edward's five-week campaign into Northumbria, for no chroniclers link the two episodes. Indeed, *Anglo-Saxon Chronicle* 'A' records only the five-week raid, without mentioning the recovery of the relics;[2250] 'C' and 'D' and the *Mercian Register* mention the recovery of the relics (which 'D' dates to 906) but make no mention of the five-week campaign;[2251] and 'E' fails to mention either event.[2252] Henry of Huntingdon records the recovery of Oswald's relics, but not the five-week raid;[2253] Florence (John) of Worcester, Simeon of Durham and Roger of Wendover all mention the two events – in Roger's account two years' apart – with the recovery of the relics first;[2254] and Matthew Paris records the recovery of the relics in 910, the year after Edward's raid into Northumbria,[2255] all of which suggests that that both were separate and distinct operations, although as noted below, they may not have been unconnected. The casual way in which the recovery of the

---

[2248] On hostages at this period see Lavelle 2006.
[2249] Traces of Edward's campaign of 909 might be detected in the Harkirk hoard, now lost, which from engravings included 9 coins of Edward the Elder: Lyon 2001: 75.
[2250] Forester 1853: 163; Swanton 1996: 94-6.
[2251] Whitelock 1961: 61; Swanton 1996: 94-5. It is perhaps worth noting that the *Mercian Register* simply records that St Oswald's body was brought from Bardney into Mercia – it does not mention Gloucester: ibid. Could the implication be that the relics were recovered but not taken to Gloucester for ceremonial interment until a fitting mausoleum and suitably lavish shrine had been completed?
[2252] Earle and Plummer 1892-99: I 95; Swanton 1996: 95.
[2253] Greenway 1996: 304-5.
[2254] Stevenson 1853: 72-3; Giles 1892: 238; Stevenson 1853: 73.
[2255] Luard 1872: I 439.

relics is recorded in all existing accounts implies that there was no opposition by the Northumbrians who ruled the area, presumably explained by some arrangement with those in power in York and almost certainly associated with the greatly weakened state of the kingdom of York after the loss of many leaders at battle of the Holme.[2256]

What we do know (if the *Mercian Register* and later chroniclers are to be believed – the episode is unmentioned in the Main Stock of the *Anglo-Saxon Chronicle*) is that a Mercian expedition made its way, almost certainly along Fosse Way, the Roman road running north-east to Lincoln,[2257] and travelled 10 miles further east to the ruined monastery at Bardney, deep within the Danelaw to the east of Lincoln, just within the borders of Lindsey, where bones of St Oswald, killed and dismembered by the pagan Penda at the battle of *Maserfelth* in 642, were exhumed.[2258] The holy relics had originally been taken to Bardney some time after 679 (the year of the battle of Trent, when King Æthelred[2259] of Mercia's victory brought it permanently under Mercian control), on the instructions of his wife Osthryth, Queen of Mercia – both of whom were buried there[2260] – and enshrined in a reliquary chest, despite the initial resistance of the monks who opposed the commemoration of Oswald, a king who was seen as an outsider.[2261] Bede describes how Oswald's lavish shrine had once been adorned with the king's gold and purple royal standard,[2262] and it was later set with precious gifts and embellishments bestowed by no less than King Offa of Mercia.[2263] It was to Bardney that King Æthelred had retired in 704 to become its abbot, and he was buried there in 716. Bardney stood as a shrine to the Mercian lordship of Lindsey, and from what Bede tells us had probably been a royal centre.[2264] William of Malmesbury records how the abbey had close links with Malmesbury abbey and prospered until the arrival of the Danes, after which the archbishops of York brought in canons.[2265]

[2256] ASC 'D' dates the Bardney expedition to 906; ASC 'C' says 909 (Swanton 1996: 94; Greenway 1996: 305); curiously, neither mentions the raid against Northumbria. The later date is now accepted as correct. Sawyer suggests that the relics may have been taken by force during the English raid of 909 (Sawyer 1998: 117), an idea supported by the Oxford DNB (sub nom Æthelflæd), but there appears to be little, if any, evidence for the idea. Roger of Wendover, followed by Matthew Paris, tells us that Edward's attack on Northumbria took place in 909, with the translation of St Oswald's relics the following year: Giles 1892: 238; Luard 1872: 439. Thompson concludes that 'events must have been more complex [than a raid to recover the relics]; holy human remains with a guaranteed pedigree were a valuable commodity, and the bones could equally have been stolen by someone in Lincolnshire and sold to the Mercians, or given into their hands for safekeeping' (Thompson 2002: 15), though neither idea seems more plausible than the conventional explanation. However, it should not be overlooked that in 903 relics of the 7th-century Breton saint St Judoc (Ludoe) were brought by monks from Ponthieu to be housed in the new monastery at Winchester: ASC 'F'; Thorpe 1861: I 76; Swanton 1996: 93.

[2257] Margary route 5f.

[2258] Academic opinion favours Oswestry as the site of *Maserfelth* (Stancliffe and Cambridge 1996), though Thacker finds strong reasons for placing it on the northern boundary of Lindsey, which incorporated Bardney: Thacker 1996: 99.

[2259] The association between Bardney and Æthelred will not have been lost on Æthelflæd, whose husband bore the same name.

[2260] Rollason 1978: 89.

[2261] Thacker 2001: 256; Thacker and Sharpe 2002: 69, 430.

[2262] McClure and Collins 1994: 126.

[2263] Hart 1992: 241; Thacker and Sharpe 2002: 64; Godman 1982: 35, cited by Adams 2013: 366. Oswald was generally seen as a martyr, though not perhaps by Bede: Thacker and Sharpe 2002: 39 fn.232.

[2264] Thacker 1985: 2-4.

[2265] Preest 2002: 198.

The royal monastery, in Danish-occupied Mercia – at this date it would seem that each of the future counties which constituted Danish Mercia was occupied by an independent Danish army[2266] – and set within a prehistoric ritual landscape with symbolic causeways in the Witham valley,[2267] had been in a state of decay after its sacking by the Danes in the 860s, though the survival of the relics suggests that it had not been completely destroyed, but in all likelihood kept intact, probably by a powerful layman rather that a clerical presence.[2268] The fragments of Oswald's bones recovered from his shrine – which itself with its valuable embellishments (if not previously looted) may have been carefully dismantled – were taken to Gloucester (a destination curiously unmentioned in the *Mercian Register*), passing along the causeway from the monastery and west towards and then along the Roman Fosse Way as far as Cirencester and then 18 miles north-west along the Roman road to Gloucester itself,[2269] for reburial with suitable reverence and ceremony in the intended and eventual sepulchre of Æthelred and Æthelflæd in St Peter's, later St Oswalds's, the modest but sumptuous monastery they had founded c.900 'with no expense spared'.[2270]

Oswald's relics were probably laid with due reverence in a separate sunken crypt near the east end of the church, suitably enriched with valuable adornments, perhaps including the reassembled shrine from Bardney, or elements from it.[2271] The solemn deposition of relics in an altar was formalised in carefully-ritualised ceremonies which were developed in the sixth and seventh centuries, whereby they were first deposited in a suitable sanctuary near the altar, and vigils kept before them. On the day of dedication they were baptised with a mixture of holy water and chrism (oil blessed on Maundy Thursday used in baptisms), and the altar similarly baptised. The cavity in which they were to be enclosed was anointed with chrism and the relics placed inside with three fragments of consecrated wafer. A slab was placed over the cavity and the relics sealed within it. The bishop then made the sign of the cross with chrism on the slab, and the whole basilica was sprinkled with holy water before mass was celebrated.[2272] A *palla* of rich textiles, similar to the one which had once covered Oswald's shrine in Bardney, probably covered the shrine.[2273] We have no knowledge of what took place when Oswald's relics were translated at Gloucester, but might assume that at least some of the ceremonial described above was adopted.

The translation of Oswald's bones was part of the revived interest, driven by Æthelred and Æthelflæd (and later taken up by Æthelstan),[2274] in the cult of royal martyr-saints in

---

[2266] Stenton 1970: 11-12 fn.4.
[2267] Everson and Stocker 2003: 271-88.
[2268] Rollason 1995: 189; and especially Thompson 2002: 15-18, which notes that carved stones from the site suggest that ecclesiastical activity continued between the late 9th and the late 11th centuries.
[2269] On routes within the Danelaw see Hart 1992; 528-32. In France, cases are known when the translations of saints' relics were made in procession during which cures were effected, and whenever the relics rested a cross was erected, and if there was no church one was built (Wood 2002: 176-7), though no parallels have been traced from pre-Conquest England.
[2270] See especially Thompson 2002: 12-18. Some of the relics appear to have been taken from Gloucester to Glastonbury: Thacker and Sharpe 2002: 549-550. The churches at Shrewsbury, Chester and Gloucester seem to have been remodelled on similar lines to the 'royal' and 'civic' churches at Winchester: Bailey 2001: 123.
[2271] Heighway 2001: 108-9.
[2272] Thacker 2002: 65-6. The ceremonial, essentially a funerary ritual, is based on that applicable to the translation of relics and dedication of a church. The early Gallician rite, certainly known in England, was more closely related to the ritual of baptism: ibid.
[2273] Thacker 2002: 64.
[2274] Thacker 1995: 121.

Mercia in the early tenth century, and probably followed the transfer of the relics of St Werburgh from Hanbury in Staffordshire to Chesterat some date after its refortification in 907.[2275] The veneration of Oswald, a saint of Northumbria, by the Mercian rulers might be thought curious, but in the words of Alan Thacker, they 'had espoused with enthusiasm the hagiographical legacy of the Mercian kingdom. They were especially concerned to rehouse royal saints in Mercian tradition in appropriate new communities within their newly fortified *burh*s. Especial honour was paid to Oswald, who although a king of Northumbria, had died fighting pagans, and had been ... especially patronised by the Mercian king Offa ...'.[2276] Oswald may have been chosen by Æthelred and Æthelflæd because of real or perceived dynastic connections between the royal house of Northumbria and Alfred's maternal ancestors.[2277] In the words of Meeson when writing of St Editha of Polesworth, 'Remains or relics ... might not have been translated ... in order to be better protected within the *burh*, but rather that ... they might afford better protection [against the Vikings] to the *burh*'.[2278]

The chronicles provide little information about eastern England at this period, but the recovery of the relics by a Mercian contingent (if that is what happened), seemingly unsupported by West Saxon forces, implies that the military situation was calm, and that some sort of pact had been negotiated with the Danelaw rulers to allow unhindered access for the recovery of the relics. Though we have no direct evidence, one authority has suggested that Bardney then lay within in an area which had seen, or was experiencing, internal and perhaps external strife and upheaval after defeat at the battle of the Holme, since there are examples from Francia, Ireland and England of the recovery of relics after Viking activity.[2279] It seems unlikely that a Mercian force would have travelled deep into the Danelaw had there been ongoing Viking activity, but the eastern seaboard (which

---

[2275] Thacker and Sharpe 2002: 557. The tradition of the transfer of the saint's relics in 875 has not been traced to an earlier date than Ranulph Higden's *Polychronicon* completed in 1352, and a more likely date for the translation is after the refortification of Chester in 907: Lewis 2008: 114-5. There is no evidence for the supposed transfer of the relics of St Alkmund to Shrewsbury (Hadley 2000: 228): the idea probably arose because the relics are said in an 11th-century *vita* to have been taken to the old church of Lilleshall, a manor held before the Conquest by Shrewsbury's St Alkmund's church. It is worth recording the Life of St Neot, a wholly fictional concoction about a certain Neot, claimed in the earliest (12th-century) version to have been a brother of King Alfred, seemingly born in Cornwall, who became an anchorite, made a pilgrimage to Rome, founded a monastery in Cornwall visited by King Alfred, and died there in the 870s. Alfred's retreat to Athelney and the legend of the burnt cakes is mentioned, with a dream by Alfred of warriors rallying to his support, as a result of which Alfred prayed to Neot on the eve of the battle of Edington, which saw Alfred victorious. Many years later the relics of Neot were stolen from his church in Cornwall after the sacristan was instructed to do so in a dream and delivered to the protection of a certain magnate Æðelricus and his very devout wife Æðelfled, and a church built at St Neots on the river Ouse: Smyth 1995: 330-1.
[2276] Thacker 2001: 256. On the cult of St Oswald see generally Stancliffe and Cambridge 1996; for the New Minster at Gloucester see Heighway 2001. In 901 Æthelred and Æthelflæd donated land to the religious community at Much Wenlock and presented it with a valuable gold chalice in honour of St Mildburh (S.221); the body of St Werburgh was translated from Hanbury to Chester probably soon after its refortification in 907; and Æthelflæd probably also introduced the cult of St Oswald there at the same time. The remains of St Alkmund are also said to have been moved from Lilleshall to Derby, and supposedly from there to Shrewsbury (Foot 2006: 324), although the evidence is unclear: Blair 2002: 511, 549-50; Yorke 2003: 58; Lewis 2008: 114-5. The earlier transfer of relics to protect them from Viking attacks is well recorded: the relics of St Columba were taken to Ireland, those of St Cuthbert from Lindisfarne, and those of Philibert from Noirmoutier: Downham 2009: 87 fn.150.
[2277] Nelson 1991: 53.
[2278] Meeson 2105: 18-19.
[2279] Downham 2009: 86-7.

seems to have attracted Vikings, perhaps Continental mercenaries, in a fleet fromGaul to support Æthelwold's campaign c.903) may have seen attacks from other parts of Britain or mainland Europe about which we know little – confusingly, while Florence (John) of Worcester tells us that in 918 (*recte* 917) 'The Danish inhabitants of East Anglia also presented themselves to [King Edward], and swore that neither by sea nor by land would they do anything to [his] prejudice',[2280] an East Anglian army is said to have been reinforced in a siege of Maldon in 921 by 'those Vikings whom they had enticed to help them'[2281] – with the eastern Danelaw perhaps subjected to attacks from the west by the militant Hiberno-Scandinavians, whose navy was of sufficient strength to defeat an Irish fleet in 912, as well as a rival fleet off the Isle of Man the following year (or 914).[2282] It is nevertheless noteworthy that Oswald's relics had remained intact and unmolested by the Danes despite their occupation of the region, implying that some presence had been maintained to preserve the relics, as noted above, though it should not be overlooked that the Danes of York were by this date largely Christianised.

Reverting to the situation in Mercia in 910, we have seen that the recovery of St Oswald's relics the previous year does not seem to have faced any opposition from the Northumbrians or the Danes of the Five Boroughs, which may be an indication of the considerable influence of Edward and Æthelred within the Danelaw, or at least part of it. One explanation for the peaceful recovery of the relics could have been the surprise – indeed, unprecedented – nature of the incursion to Bardney, which denied the Northumbrians the opportunity to gather in sufficient strength to challenge the English forces, but that seems unlikely. The situation is made no more clear by the puzzling and unexplained statement of William of Malmesbury who tells us that Æthelred and Æthelflæd translated Oswald's relics *quod omnis Mertia eorum pareret imperio*, 'because they had all Mercia under their power',[2283] and that following the account in *Anglo-Saxon Chronicle* 'A' that immediately after the death of Æthelflæd in 918 all the nation of the land of Mercia which was earlier subject toÆthelflæd turned to Edward, is a record that soon after the recovery of Nottingham in the same year 'all the people that was settled in the land of Mercia, both Danish and English, turned to him'.[2284] The second reference must surely refer to the area of 'Old' Mercia that had fallen within the Danelaw and been ruled by the Danes. In other words, the expression 'Mercia' had two meanings: 'English' Mercia and that area of Mercia settled by the Danes from c.878 and subject to what became known as the Danelaw. The *Chronicle* may be telling us that both parts of Mercia were now subject to Edward – and that both of those parts might have been ruled until then by Æthelred and Æthelflæd.

It has long been understood that after the English raid of 909 the vanquished Northumbrians of York quickly built up their military strength which enabled them to show their contempt for the treaty that had been so openly broken by Edward (or of a treaty that had been concluded to ensure that Edward ceased his ravaging) by launching a

---

[2280] Stevenson 1853: 77. The account continues: 'A Danish army from Cambridge came also, and made choice of [King Edward] for their lord and master: moreover, at [King Edward's] request, they took oaths to the same effect.': ibid.
[2281] ASC 'A'; Swanton 1996: 102. It is unclear whether this event is to be associated with the *Chronicle* account that in in 920 'Thurkytel jarl went over the sea to France, with the men who would follow him, with the peace and support of king Edward': Thorpe 1861: I 81.
[2282] Higham 1993: 185; Byrne 2005: 852.
[2283] Thacker 1995: 120; Preest 2002: 198.
[2284] ASSC 'A'; Swanton 1996: 104.

massed raid into Mercia in the summer of 910.[2285] Yet that traditional analysis might be fallacious, and the Northumbrians, badly mauled militarily after the battle of the Holme, were perhaps in no state to pose any real threat to Mercia and Wessex. On the contrary, they will have been anxious to secure the protection of those two kingdoms against the growing beligerence of their pagan rivals, the Hiberno-Scandinavians of the north-west. Those same Hiberno-Scandinavians posed a menacing threat to Mercia and Wessex, a threat which was soon to become reality.

The history of the kings of York at this period, though far from clear, is better documented than that of the rulers of the north-west (which is virtually non-existent), and the absence of any record associating *Halfdan*, *Eowils*, and *Ivar* with York might suggest they were more likely to have been from the north-west,[2286] though we cannot overlook numismatic evidence from the Cuerdale hoard which shows that Siefred and Cnut ruled York in the early years of the tenth century, and that both kings might indeed have ruled jointly, showing that joint kingship may not have been unusual.[2287] But other evidence for a Hiberno-Norse origin for *Halfdan*, *Eowils* and *Ivar* might be detected in the name of one of those kings, *Eowils*, which is the Anglicised version of Old Norse *Ásl* or *Auðgísl*, found as *Auisle* in Irish. Furthermore, as noted elsewhere, the names of the dead kings at Tettenhall match a trio of Viking leaders active in the 860s and 870s, especially in Ireland and Northern Britain, and at least two of those kings (*Hálfdan* and *Ívarr*) were related, perhaps implying that the kings killed at Tettenhall were members of the same family which ruled Dublin before 902 and after 917, since Norse children and grandchildren were often named after their fathers and grandfathers.[2288] The available evidence, though not conclusive, points towards the violation in 910 of *þonefrið on Norþhymbrum*, 'the peace in Northumbria', by a Hiberno-Scandinavian raiding party, which could properly be described as the *norðhere* or *se here onNorþhymbrum*, expressions found in the Chronicle.

It is worth making the point that Edward and Æthelred had long fought side-by-side against the Scandinavian threat. For example, even before he became king, *aetheling* Edward, besieging a Danish force at Thorney in 893 had fought alongside Æthelred, described as 'King' by Æthelweard.[2289] That probably helps to explain why scholars have tended to assume that Æthelred, Æthelflæd and Edward (and Edward's son *ætheling*Æthelstan), together fighting a common enemy or enemies, would have acted throughout in unison and harmony to an agreed strategy. But it is self-evident that each was – indeed, needed to be – a forceful and strong-minded military tactician and

---

[2285] This was a period during which there were Mercian land purchases within the Danelaw in Derbyshire and Bedfordshire in 906-10 'by the order of King Edward and also Ealdorman Æthelred along with the other ealdormen and thegns', which suggest that Edward was encouraging his thegns to buy estates in Danish territory: Whitelock 1955: 503; Higham 1997: 146; S.396.

[2286] If *Halfdan*, *Eowils*, and *Ivar* are properly to be identified as Hiberno-Scandinavian rulers in the north-west and not from Danish Northumbria as hitherto supposed, it appears not to have been recognised as such by any other historians of the period, or at least not recorded in unequivocal terms. It should not be overlooked, however, that Halfdan, identified as *Halfdan 3* in the *Prosopography of Anglo-Saxon England*, accessed 11 April 2010 may have been associated with exceptionally rare coins bearing the name Halfdan now associated with the Danish Midlands and the 890s. It is unlikely, but not inconceivable, that he was the person so-named who was killed at Tettenhall: Dolley 1978: 26.

[2287] Hall 2001: 189; Downham 2009: 78-9.

[2288] Downham 2009: 87, 258-9.

[2289] Campbell 1962: 49-50; ASC 'A'; Swanton 1996: 84-5. Thorney is perhaps to be identified as Iver, Buckinghamshire: Stenton 1971: 14-15. Æthelweard tells us that in 886 ealdorman Æthelred was instructed by Alfred to guard London after its garrison had been strengthened: Campbell 1962: 46.

commander, and it is no more certain that Edward will have agreed with his sister on all matters than it is that she will have agreed with her husband and brother. Indeed, from our knowledge of powerful families – perhaps of all families – we can be certain that there was friction, rivalry, disunity, discord and dissent (or worse) between the principal players, even if we have little direct evidence of the nature of that dissension.[2290] Violent disagreements between military commanders are recorded throughout history and into modern times. Furthermore, we should not overlook that the marriage of Æthelred and Æthelflæd – he probably considerably older than she – was a typical political union to cement the relationship between Wessex and Mercia (just as King Alfred had married Eahlswith, daughter of a senior Mercian ealdorman),[2291] and we have no knowledge of any deeper feelings – or lack of them – between the two.[2292] It is, however, noteworthy that the *Mercian Register*, clearly intended to record the achievements of Æthelflæd, makes no mention at all of Æthelred, other than to record his death and the dispossession of his daughter by Edward. William of Malmesbury, writing in the twelfth century, is our main source for the claim that after their daughter Ælfwynn was born, Æthelflæd refused the embraces of her husband since the birth had been so traumatic and she was unwilling to risk another.[2293] We may wonder whether the first claim had some basis, with the second a convenient if invented gloss, but William also tells us that the boy Æthelstan was fostered by Æthelred and Æthelflæd, perhaps to be seen as a surrogate son.

Since neither Æthelred nor Æthelflæd ever adopted a royal title or issued coinage in their names, Mercia is often seen (as shown above) to have been subservient to Wessex. The evidence that this was the case is, at the very least, debatable. For example, Alfred recognised Æthelred's rights in London. A charter of 901 of Æthelred and Æthelflæd,[2294] gives both of them grander styles than usual, and makes no mention of Edward, which might be seen as evidence of an attempt at Mercian autonomy. This was the time of Æthelwold's rebellion, which may have encouraged the Mercians to take steps to achieve their independence (and may indeed be associated in some way with the treaty of Tiddingford), but Mercia was certainly under Edward's overlordship by 903, when Æthelflæd and Æthelred are explicitly said to govern the Mercians by his authority.[2295] It has been claimed that Edward issued no separate charters for Mercia, rather endorsing those of Æthelred, though that claim is incorrect: an otherwise unexplained grant by Edward in 903 of charters for two estates in the environs of London and Oxford, both

---

[2290] One example of Æthelred acting against Alfred's interests is the joint campaign by Anarawd and Æthelred to make inroads into the various alliances with an increasing number of Welsh kings created by Alfred during the 880s: Charles-Edwards 2013: 495-6, 507; see also Cumberledge 2002. One comment worth recording is that of Bishop Wærferth of Worcester in connection with the attempt by his predecessors to recover an ex-monastic estate at Old Sodbury, Gloucestershire, which was returned to Worcester c.903: 'We would never get anywhere until Æthelred became lord of the Mercians': S.1446; Blair 2005: 306. Possible evidence of a dispute between King Alfred and his son Edward has been identified by Janet Nelson, who suggests that Alfred may have considered bypassing Edward to make Æthelstan his immediate heir: Yorke 2001: 32.
[2291] Williams, Smyth and Kirby 1991: 117.
[2292] It is worth recording that although King Alfred mentions 'my ealdormen' in his will, leaving each of them 100 *mancuses*, Æthelred is the only one mentioned separately, as the inheritor of a 'sword worth 100 *mancuses*': Keynes and Lapidge 1983: 173-8. A *mancus* probably represented 30 silver pennies or 1 gold penny: Hunt 2016: 67.
[2293] Giles 1847: 123.For independent evidence supporting William of Malmesbury's claim see Wood 1999: 158-9; Foot 2011: 34-7; 98.
[2294] S.221.
[2295] S.367.

within Æthelred's Mercia,[2296] and another attested by Edward that seems to have been drawn up the following year relating to an estate at Water Eaton, to the north of Oxford, again, in Mercia, have been noted elsewhere.[2297] But Æthelred was certainly leader, at least nominally, of the Mercian forces, which on occasions – and perhaps surprisingly – acted against West Saxon interests.[2298] We have already seen that the treaty of Tiddingford c.905 may have been forced upon Edward under pressure from his sister and brother-in-law. It is likely that Æthelred was respected by Alfred and Edward as (at most times) an ally rather than a subordinate, just as recent numismatic evidence suggests that Æthelred's predecessor Ceolwulf of Mercia is to be seen as a ruler of equal standing to Alfred, rather than a 'foolish king's thegn' as claimed by the *Anglo-Saxon Chronicle*,[2299] but subtle clues might infer long-standing tensions between Wessex and Mercia.[2300] It would be susprising, even in the absence of those clues, if such tensions had not existed.[2301]

The abrupt removal into exile of Ælfwynn, Edward's niece, from her position as Lady of the Mercians (a position confirmed by the *Mercian Register*, which refers to her being deprived of all authority in Mercia),[2302] also speaks of Edward's ambitions to extend his empire, or at least to greatly curtail the power of Mercia, as does the deliberate and symbolic dissection of Tamworth, putative capital of Mercia, with the boundary of Staffordshire and Warwickshireforced through very centre of the town when Mercia was shired, almost certainly during Edward's reign and under his direction, probably after Ælfwynn was removed from power after her mother's death in 918.[2303] At Edward's death in 924 the Mercians had the satisfaction of seeing Æthelstan, by tradition brought up at the Mercian court, crowned as his successor (after the sudden and unexplained death unconsecrated of Æthelstan's younger brother Ælfweard at Oxford within days of that of his father) despite the strong opposition of factions within Wessex, *Anglo-Saxon Chronicle* 'D' emphasising that 'Æthelstan was chosen as king by the Mercians'.[2304] Bitterness in Wessex is revealed by the refusal of the bishop of Winchester to witness any of

---

[2296] S.367, S.367a, and S.371; see Keynes 2001: 51-4.
[2297] S.361.
[2298] See for example the campaign by Æthelred and Ananrawd of Gwynedd against Ceredigion and Ystrad Tywi in central Wales in 895: Smyth 2002: 128-9. Smyth concludes, however, that it is highly unlikely that Alfred or Edward ever considered that south Wales 'belonged' to the West Saxon dynasty in any meaningful sense: ibid. 129. This seems to overlook the ransom paid by Edward when bishop Cameleac was abducted from Archenfield by Vikings in 917: ASC 'A' and 'D'; Swanton 1996: 98-9.
[2299] *The Times*, 11 December 2015, reporting on the Watlington Hoard.
[2300] Walker 2000: 77-8; see also Cumberledge 2002. The 'uneasy realtionship' and 'tension between Wessex and Mercia alongside their growing unity' is discussed in Stafford 2008: 112-4.
[2301] It is right to note that Wainwright, an astute analyst of this period and its personalities, sees only complete accord between Æthelflæd and Edward, and detects no trace of tensions between the two leaders: Wainwright 1975.
[2302] Whitelock 1961: 67.
[2303] Hill 2001: 144-59.
[2304] Swanton 1996: 105. Walker is mistaken in claiming that the *Mercian Register* records Ælfeard as succeeding as king of Wessex: Walker 2000: 124. It should not be overlooked that from an early date Ælfweard, son of Edward and Ælfflæd (neice of his rebellious cousin Æthelwold, and granddaughter of King Æthelred I, Alfred's older brother), took precedence over Æthelstan, the king's first-born by Ecgwynn, and was his designated successor and the preferred choice of the West Saxons until his convenient, and possibly suspicious, death 16 days after his father in 924, though no contemporary sources imply foul play: Smyth 1995: 437-8; Keynes 2001: 51; Thacker 2001: 253-4.

Æthelstan's charters, with the scribes in the New Minster conspicuously omitting Æthelstan's name from their list of West Saxon kings.[2305]

Furthermore, in theory at least decisions in Wessex and Mercia on matters ecclesiastical, property-related, juridical, tax-raising and military, and, most importantly of all, electing the king, were taken by the West Saxon and Mercian *witenagemots*, assemblies of the king or leading lord, sometimes accompanied by his wife and sons (and sometimes, as in the case of Æthelred and Æthelflæd, daughter), bishops and abbots, ealdormen of the shires and provinces, and a number of the king's or lord's friends and dependants (*ministri*). We have little knowledge of their workings, but early ecclesiastical councils speak of speeches and voting, though we may doubt whether a king's authority was ever seriously questioned, Æthelbold's challenge to Edward's entitlement to the crown after Alfred's death representing one notable exception.[2306] Alfred issued his law code with the counsel and consent of his *witan*, and one eminent authority felt able to write in the mid-ninteenth century: 'Alfred himself is called King of Mercia. Nothing was there effected without his consent; every decree, gift, and exchange, required his ratification. As far as we know, there was never any misunderstanding or disagreement between Alfred and his Earl [Æthelred]; and this arose from the strictly honourable character of his son-in-law, as well as from the close relationship between them. Æthelred was devoted body and soul to his lord and king; he entered with perfect sympathy with all Alfred's wise thoughts and schemes, and never sought to gratify his own ambition at the expense of the general unanimity'.[2307] The realism (and cynicism) of the present age forces us to look askance at such optimistically rose-tinted conclusions which conveniently overlook the fallout arising from power politics. The reality may have been very different, though it would be an exceptional, naive or fearless scribe who had the temerity to record even obliquely any discord in the ruling families. Æthelbold's rebellion was simply of too great a magnitude to allow the chroniclers, however partisan, to omit any mention of its occurrence, consequences, and satisfactory outcome, even if some came close.

To revert to the identity of the Northumbrians who fought at Tettenhall, far from clarifying the picture, the evidence, such as it is, that they were Hiberno-Scandinavians from the north-west rather than York-based Danes – proof which would struggle to satisfy a jury beyond reasonable doubt, but probably sufficient to satisfy a court on the balance of probabilities – has, unsurprisingly, further muddied the already murky waters, and it is fair to say that the little we thought we knew about the battle has become even more uncertain.[2308]

[2305] Holland 2016: 49.
[2306] See specially Stubbs 1880: I 145-66, who notes that in Wessex there is not one example of a king's son succeeding his father in Wessex between 685 and 839, and the picture in Mercia is much the same: ibid. 160. The Mercian *witenagemot* is known to have met at Risborough in 883, and another was held in 888. A full assembly met at Gloucester in 896, with another whose date is uncertain: Thorpe 1853: 122. A reference to West Saxon and Mercian councillors c.878 is found in a charter of 901 relating to land at Wylye, Wiltshire: S.362
[2307] Thorpe 1853: 122; Stubbs 1880: I 149.
[2308] To add even more uncertainty, Dawn Hadley has suggested that the Scandinavian forces at Tettenhall may have been local rulers in the north Midlands, noting that there is evidence to show that control over the east Midlands was fragmented, with coins minted in several places in the region in the late 9th and early 10th century for various rulers including an otherwise unknown Halfdan somewhere in the east Midlands c.900, as well as coins minted briefly for an Earl Sihtric at Shelford in the late 9th century, while the anonymous St Edmund coins minted at several places in that area might indicate that it was ruled by several individuals: Hadley 2006: 56. The idea is not implausible

There could, however, be one further piece of missing evidence which should not be overlooked. That is the location of a *burh* built by Æthelflæd, according to the *Mercian Register*, at *Bremesbyrig* very soon after the battle of Tettenhall.[2309] The speed with which Æthelflæd moved to create the *burh* (the fact that her husband is unmentioned seems to be further evidence of his long-term incapacity) would suggest that it was constructed in an area seen by Æthelflæd as exploited by the Scandinavian enemy. Sadly and frustratingly, *Bremesbyrig* remains to be identified.[2310] Of the next two *burhs*, that at *Scergeat* and *Cwatbrycge*, both built in 912, only the latter has been identified with reasonable certainty as Quatford on the river Severn near the western border of Mercia, which does little to help identify the protagonists at Tettenhall. A candidate for the site of *Scergeat* is discussed in Chapter 10.

What is clear is that around the latter part of June 910 a substantial warband which can loosely be described as of Scandinavian descent, probably Hiberno-Scandinvians though almost certainly containing other nationalities (perhaps including some with English names, if not Englishmen), launched a large-scale attack, almost certainly a looting expedition rather than an attempt at settlement, deep into West Mercia – the English attack on Northumbria the previous year is said to have lasted five weeks,[2311] and the Northumbrian raid into Mercia probably lasted at least as long, and perhaps considerably longer, given the time Edward and Æthelred would have needed to raise their forces from distant parts of their kingdoms, co-ordinate their march to the west Midlands, and intercept and confront the enemy. As noted previously, whether those Northumbrian raiders could properly be described as Vikings must be debateable.

Whatever the political situation, it is unclear what led the Northumbrians, whether from the north-west, or, less likely, York, to 'break the peace' – almost certainly (but not necessarily) the treaty concluded after Edward's raid into Northumbria the previous year[2312] – and undertake their ill-fated looting campaign which culminated in the battle of Tettenhall. It is worth noting that *Anglo-Saxon Chronicle* 'A' tells us that 'the raiding-army in Northumbria broke the peace and scorned every peace which King Edward and his councillors offered them',[2313] while Æthelweard's account records how 'the barbarians broke the peace with King Eadweard, and with Æthelred'[2314] (in a comment with added puzzling elements analysed in more detail in chapter 36 on *The Three Fragments*). The *Chronicle* account is yet another instance of its attempt to minimise, dismiss or ignore the role of Æthelred and his wife, whereas Æthelweard, with no such agenda, makes it clear that the Scandinavians were breaching a peace concluded not just with Edward, but also

---

(and ASC 'A' records the death of a king in the east Midlands in 920: Swanton 1996: 102), but there is no evidence of unified control within the Danes of the north-east Midlands (Stafford 1985: 112), and given the events leading up to the battle must be very unlikely.

[2309] ASC 'C' and 'D'; Swanton 1996: 94-5.

[2310] Curiously, Robert Fabyan tells us that Æthelflæd 'buylded a bridge ouer ye ryuer of Seuerne; whiche is, or was named Brymmysbury Bridge': Ellis 1811: 177. Frustratingly, the source of this intriguing comment (also found in other works, e.g. 'Thatarne Brimsbury [sic], the bridge upon Seuerne' in Heywoode 1627: 236) is unknown, but perhaps explained by *Brycge* (Quatford) following *Bremesbyrig* in *Chronicle* accounts, with the reference to the Severn an added gloss.

[2311] ASC 'A'; Swanton 1996: 94-6.

[2312] Quanrud 2015: 78-9. Tyrrell makes the curious comment that the Danes broke 'the Peace which King Edward *and his Son* [italics added] had made with them': Tyrrell 1697: 315. Æthelstan was born in 895, and the idea, untraced elsewhere, is inconceivable.

[2313] Swanton 1996: 96.

[2314] Campbell 1962: 52.

with Æthelred, providing further evidence that Æthelred, notwithstanding his debilitating illness, was actively involved in major events at the time. Certainly the reference to both Edward and Æthelred in the chronicles suggests that the peace that was broken is likely to have been that imposed on 'the kings' of the Northumbrian areas after the West Saxon and Mercian incursion the previous year, rather than any breach of the treaty of Tiddingford some five years earlier.

The most obvious, and perhaps correct, explanation is that the Northumbrian raid of 910 was a tit-for-tat mirror image of the ravaging into their territory by the English the year before so that the Northumbrians could replenish their depleted war chest, greatly diminished by the devastating English attack, in the same way that Edward ravaged Danish East Anglia even as the usurper Æthelwold was devastating English Mercia c.903. Edward's attack on Northumbria in 909 had led to large amounts of coin and treasure, 'immense booty', being paid to or looted by the English attackers.

One point unraised by historians is the possibility that those involved in the Northumbrian raid into Mercia were not necessarily those Northumbrians against whom Edward led his forces the previous year. Nothing in the chroniclers' accounts tells against the idea, but we are probably safe in concluding that the Northumbrians involved in both operations were by and large the same grouping.

The military incursion by the Northumbrians deep into the territory of their Mercian overlords who had exercised control over that area of the north-west for more than four decades was evidently intended to be a relatively short-lived retaliatory hit-and-run looting raid rather than an attempt to take and occupy territory. Who led those forces is unknown, but the possibility that it was Ingimund, the leader of the militant Hiberno-Scandinavians who settled in the Wirral in the early tenth century, cannot entirely be discounted: he is last heard of in or before 907 in connection with the siege of Chester,[2315] and the date and circumstances of his death are unrecorded, though the chroniclers accounts of a Northumbrian force might be thought to exclude those from the Wirral, which lay within Mercia.[2316] Indeed, Ingimund has been associated with Agmund, one of the Scandinavian leaders named amongst the fallen at the battle of Tettenhall, though any association must be very tenuous: it is far from certain that Ingimund(r) and Agmund (perhaps Old Norse Øgmundr) are the same name.[2317]

The *Anglo-Saxon Chronicle*, it is true, tells us that the Northumbrians were under the mistaken impression that Edward the Elder's main body of troops was moving east in a hundred ships (a typical euphemism for 'a large fleet') sailing east along the south coast to meet the King who was travelling to Kent, and the Northumbrians believed that 'they might go unfought wherever they wanted'.[2318] That may or may not have been the case, but the evidence indicates that Edward and his forces, supported by a substantial fleet, was

---

[2315] O'Donovan 1860: 237.

[2316] See generally Wainwright 1975. The possibility that Ragnall, who was among those expelled from Dublin in 902, may have led the raid cannot be excluded, but is unlikely: his whereabouts at the time are uncertain, but he appears to have been involved in campaigns in western and northern Scotland, the Scottish Isles and the Orkneys.

[2317] Downham 2009: 84.

[2318] Stevenson 1853: 75; Swanton 1996: 97. Henry of Huntingdon adds some confusing wording which is evidently a misunderstanding of the *Anglo-Saxon Chronicle*: Forester 1853: 163; Greenway 1996: 300-301 fn96. Walker suggests that Edward was in Kent collecting a fleet possibly to attack East Anglia, though the evidence to support that idea is not given: Walker 2000: 92.

headed towards Kent to deal with what must have been perceived as a significant military threat, perhaps seaborne[2319] – reminiscent of the huge Viking fleet from Boulogne which, according to Æthelweard, reached Kent in 894[2320] – or to launch a major campaign.[2321] No chronicler further illuminates that threat or possible campaign, but if real it was presumably resolved quickly and decisively by Edward, or (if a planned campaign) promptly abandoned. One would wish to know much more about this enigmatic fleet and its intentions, and the threat it was to deal with.

What is clear is that while Edward was believed to be in the south-east of England, a strong force of Scandinavians, almost certainly Hiberno-Norse (the deadliest and most feared of the invaders) from the north-west, presumably, but not certainly, those Northumbrians who had the previous year suffered a major humiliation from an English raiding army ravaging for five weeks far into their territory with apparent impunity, chose to launch a full-scale looting raid dangerously deep into Mercia, exposed to attack from English forces and far from the safety of Danelaw. If the English had created a sophisticated deception by releasing deliberately misleading information about the disposition of their forces, we might expect the *Chronicle* to have capitalised on the ingenious ruse and recorded the fact, although Eric John seems to imply that that is exactly what happened: 'They [the Danes] seem to have been misled by bogus intelligence ...'.[2322]

If the story of the Edward and his fleet was a ruse, it succeeded brilliantly, though quite how Edward could have predicted the consequential Scandinavian raid is difficult to explain, unless he had specific intelligence of their preliminary arrangements: such an expedition could not have been put in place overnight. We must conclude that the *Chronicle* account is to be accepted at face value, even if many questions remain unanswered: how, for example, did the authors of contemporary annals come to know what the Scandinavians believed about Edward's disposition when they planned their incursion into Mercia? The Scandinavians may have taken some comfort by imagining that

---

[2319]Raiding armies from East Anglia and Northumbria greatly harassed the south coast of Wessex in 896 (ASC 'A'; Swanton 1996: 90), and probably in other years, and it will be recalled that the 'great fleet' in which Æthelwold reached Essex during his rebellion c.903 is said to have come from Gaul:Stevenson 1855: 518; Luard 1872: 436; Giles 1892: 235.The Hiberno-Scandinavians of the north-west are known to have maintained a powerful fleet at this period: they defeated an Irish fleet in 912 and, led by Ragnall, a rival Norse fleet off the Isle of Man the following year: Wainwright 1975: 166; Higham 1993: 186. Or Edward's fleet may have been called out to deal with a fleet from the Continent, such as the fleet supposedly raised by Æthelwold, perhaps from Gaul, to support his armed but ill-fated insurrection which culminated in the battle of the Holme, or the 'very large fleet' (presumably from the Continent) that Æthelweard tells us reached 'in the estuary and the streams of the Severn' in 914: Campbell 1962: 53. In that respect a detailed history of the Anglo-Saxon period in England by Johann Martin Lappenberg, a well-respected German scholar, translated by Benjamin Thorpe, the eminent Victorian Anglo-Saxonist, and published in 1845, is of particular interest. Lappenberg writes of the events of 910: '... the Northumbrians, either in agreement with their brethren in France, or of their own accord, seeing the favourable moment, when the greater part of the English army was on board the fleet, again violating the treaty, proceeded to the Severn ...': Thorpe 1845: 90. The reference to the Northumbrians' brethren in France is unexplained, and Lappenberg's source untraced.

[2320] Campbell 1962: 51. It should not be overlooked that the Danes of East Anglia and Northumbria had a history of seaborne raiding: Florence (John) of Worcester describes how the pagans 'pillaged [Wessex] stealthily along the sea-coast, chiefly in long, swift ships, which they had constructed several years before': Stevenson 1853: 71.

[2321] For naval matters at this period see Lavelle 2010.

[2322] John 1996: 91.

should Edward manage to assemble a counter-force, he would be hesitant, to say the least, to engage them head-on, as seems to have been the case most notably when his cousin, Æthelwold, ravaged Mercia c.903. The apparent failure of the Mercian forces to intercept and confront the enemy raiding party ravaging Mercia (as it failed to do too, apparently, when Mercia was ravaged by Æthelwold) is readily understandable. The Scandinavian raiding-army was clearly of some considerable strength – the chronicles (with typical exaggeration) tell of thousands of the enemy killed in the forthcoming battle – but Æthelred and Æthelflæd could not risk, and had no need to risk, a full-blooded confrontation without the support of the West Saxon forces, and prudently awaited reinforcement by Edward's army.

It is indisputable that in the early tenth century – indeed, during much of the later Anglo-Saxon period – news travelled considerable distances far more quickly than we might imagine, though the mechanics of such dissemination are unclear and appear to have received little study. Word (if true) that Edward was in the furthest corner of south-east England and that his ships were sailing east along the south coast reached the Northumbrians with sufficient speed to allow them to assemble a force to raid into the southernmost parts of Mercia, and in turn news of that raiding expedition reached Edward sufficiently quickly to allow him to deal with the immediate threat (if real) in the south-east and muster the West Saxon and Mercian forces (and even perhaps support from the Danes of York and East Anglia and the Welsh)[2323] and co-ordinate their call-up and muster for battle in Staffordshire in sufficient order and with sufficient leadership, arms, supplies and morale to achieve a great military victory – and we might only wonder (in both senses of that word) at the means of communication and transfer of intelligence between various parts of the country in the map-free Anglo-Saxon period.[2324] We might also question whether the Hiberno-Scandinavians could have set up a decoy – or indeed primary, two-pronged – operation involving vessels off the south coast with the intention of distracting Edward and allowing them to raid at will within Mercia. Those same Hiberno-Scandinavians were to defeat an Irish fleet in 912, as well as a rival fleet off the Isle of Man the following year (or 914), probably with their fleet which may have been based at Preston, and with the assistance of the Danes of Yorkshire raided the Clyde area in that same year.[2325] The possibility that the greater threat to Edward in August 910 was an unmentioned fleet off the south coast should not be overlooked: it will be recalled, for example, that some sources refer to a fleet from Gaul participating in Æthelwold's incursion into the south of England c.903. But given the speed with which Edward responded to the Scandinavian raiding army, it seems more likely than not that he had ready-assembled forces prepared to rendezvous in the West Midlands to intercept and engage in full-scale battle with the enemy, knowing that this was a perfect opportunity to destroy it far distant from reinforcements. This was a do or die campaign: there would be no second chance if it failed.

[2323] See especially Davidson 2001: 202, where an analysis of the evidence has led to the conclusion that as on the Continent, English rulers at this period 'often fought against the Scandinavians, but were equally willing to employ them, sometimes literally, for their own ends'.

[2324] To take but one example, in 927 Æthelstan convened a meeting at Eamont near Penrith attended by kings and nobles of the West Welsh, Gwent, Bamburgh and the Scots (the assembly recorded, extraordinarily, only in ASC 'D': Swanton 1996: 107). Presumably the logistics depended on messengers travelling to the attendees under armed escort carrying official papers or warrants, but we possess no details of any such arrangements, or the means by which those attending found their way to the meeting place.

[2325] Wainwright 1975: 166; Higham 1993: 185; Byrne 2005: 852.

For the reasons outlined above we cannot deduce the route taken by the Scandinavian raiding party – perhaps it was via the southern Pennines and Derbyshire, or in the case of the Danes of York down the east of England through the relative safety of the Danelaw – but Æthelweard, the sole source of information available to us, tells us that it ravaged the fields of the Mercians on all sides, and deeply, 'as far as the streams of the Avon, where the boundary of the West Saxons and Mercians begins. Then they were transported across the river Severn into the West Country, and there they ravaged great ravagings ... [before] rejoicing in rich spoil they returned towards home' and crossed the Severn at *Cwatbrycge*.[2326]

We might suppose that the Scandinavian warband, with surprise on its side, cut a swathe through central and western Mercia – essentially south through the Cotswolds to the Avon, west across the Severn, and north along the March of Wales. What route they took during their looting is unknown – no documentary or archaeological evidence has been traced of their plundering, and how they navigated without maps remains unexplained – but they might well have used one of the major north-south Roman roads such as the road running south from Wigan via Northwhich, Middlewich and Whitchurch to *Pennocrucium* south of Penkridge, to Watling Street, before moving east to Ryknield Street or the Fosse Way, living off the land, looting food and supplies, appropriating portable treasures, burning and destroying churches, and sweeping up rich pickings from the concentration of well over twenty minsters and other wealthy churches clustered throughout the region. One obvious targets for the raisers would have been the religious centre at Lichfield, assuming it had recovered from Danish attacks from Repton in 873.[2327] The sumptuous and richly-endowed minster of St Oswald's at Gloucester (a town occupied by the Danes in 878,[2328] strongly associated with Æthelred and Æthelflæd who had treated the place as their favoured centre after the Danish invasions left the old Mercian capital of Tamworth dangerously exposed on the very edge of the Danelaw, and who transferred to it the relics of St Oswald the previous year), evidently escaped unscathed, since Æthelred was buried there the following year.[2329] Likewise the important Christian sites at Hereford and Worcester, and the great abbey and cult centre (and Mercian royal archive) at Winchcombe in Gloucestershire, which seems to have been favoured in the early ninth century by leading Mercians in preference to one in the Mercian heartland, having by then been fortified,[2330] were probably not attacked, with the Northumbrians concentrating on undefended and relatively isolated religious houses, rather than well-defended towns,[2331] including Cirencester and Bath,[2332] which were probably skirted and left untouched.

[2326] Campbell 1962: 52-3.
[2327] Three separate finds of complete Viking cigar-shaped silver ingots and a fragment of a fourth from the area (PAS records WMID-F6EEFO, WMID-OB3FC7, and WMID-C36B61), discussed elsewhere in this volume, serve as hard evidence for a Scandinavian presence in the late ninth or early tenth century, and their significance should not be underestimated.
[2328] Campbell 1962: 42.
[2329] Williams, Smyth and Kirby 1991: 83; Keynes 2001: 316. Part of a Danish army had camped at Gloucester in 877, and the place had defences by 914, perhaps before 902: VCH Gloucestershire IV 5-12.
[2330] Brooks and Cubitt 196: 155. It has been suggested that Æthelred may have had a historic family link to the Winchcombe: Cœnwulf, king of Mercia from 796 to 821, had been buried at Winchcombe, which he either founded or lavishly endowed.
[2331] Viking raiders invariably took a circuitous route when ravaging to avoid areas already devastated, and it should not be overlooked that Æthelwold's army which had ravaged Mercia as far as the southern Cotswolds only 7 years earlier may have looted these same areas.
[2332] Pelteret 2009: 323.

It must be said that no documentary or other proof of any kind has been traced of any loss or destruction to a religious house or other site in this wider area in or about 910, unless a corrupt memorandum dating between 883 and 911 which records an ancient landbook (the legal title to an estate) carried off from Marcliff in Cleeve Prior in Worcestershire by the pagans refers to an incident to be associated with the campaign.[2333] The absence of any written evidence of depradations by the Northumbrian raiding-army in 910 must serve to reinforce the idea that relatively insignificant places were the primary target, since attacks on more important sites would probably have left some record. After raiding around the lower reaches of the Severn, we are told that the Scandinavians moved westwards:[2334] the boundary between the West Saxons and Mercians ran along the river Avon, through Bath, and the raiding force clearly reached that river before crossing the Severn – Æthelweard's claim that it was transported across that river implies perhaps the use of boats rather than a bridge – travelling gradually northwards on the west side of the river.[2335] Throughout their raid, those at particular risk will have been dwellings of the upper echelons of society likely to house gold or silver valuables or coinage, villages and (especially) lesser minsters, monasteries, and smaller churches – a list of possible sites includes Polesworth, Wootton, Stratford, Blockley, Evenlode, Daylesford, Charlbury, Withington, Cirencester, Yate, Tetbury, Westbury, Berkeley, Dowdswell, Winchcombe, Cheltenham, Bishops Cleeve, Deerhurst, Tewkesbury, Bredon, Beckford, Fladbury, Twyning, Kempsey, Inkberrow, Acton Beauchamp, Bromyard, Moreton, Pershore, Wigmore, Bromfield, Stanton Lacy, Stoke St Milborough, Stottesdon, Church Stretton, Wroxeter, Diddlesbury, Barrow, Atcham, Morville and Much Wenlock[2336] – which could be pillaged for easily portable wealth, the local population at best intimidatedto provide accommodation, food and rations, at worst slaughtered, their houses, barns, ricks, and churches, and perhaps even their ripening crops and orchards, put to the torch, for reinforcing their reputation for barbarity and savagery was not the least of the aims of the raiders.[2337]

Moving quickly to avoid warnings reaching likely targets and enabling valuables to be hidden and their owners to flee, we might imagine smaller raiding parties branching off the main group and returning from outlying areas with captured booty, the main warband leaving a broad swathe of death and devastion in its wake. Valuably decorated artifacts such as books and reliquaries will have been torn apart and broken up to remove jewels

---

[2333] S.222; Finberg 1972: 107; Whitelock 1978: 101. The memorandum cannot be genuine in its present form: Sawyer 1972: 107.
[2334] Campbell 1982: 71; Foot 2006: 32-3.
[2335] Ravaging Hereford, according to Hill 1984: 56, but that seems unlikely. It might be wondered whether the raiding party deliberately avoided encroaching into West Saxon territory, though that seems unlikely, since the West Saxons and Mercians were working in unison against the Scandinavians from at least 910, after the battle of Tettenhall, and probably long before, though the Scandinavians may have gambled that the West Saxons would not have wished to respond to a raid into Mercia, hence their shock at meeting the combined English army at Tettenhall. It is worth recording that the bishop's residence at Ergyng (Archenfield) was captured by the Vikings in 914, but apart from St David's, no Welsh church is recorded as having been raided more than once, and most recorded raids seem to have been from Ireland: Pryce 1992: 25.
[2336] List based on attested and presumed monasteries to c.850 in Foot 2009: 32-3, with the addition of Anglo-Saxon churches likely to have existed at that date. To the list might be added the ancient Royal Free Chapels of Staffordshire, including Tettenhall, Wolverhampton, Penkridge, and Stafford, although we have no evidence of their existence at that date.
[2337] It is worth recording that William of Malmesbury speaks not only of the fertility of the crops, especially fruit trees, in the vale of Gloucester area, but records that it 'more than any other parts of England ... is close packed with vineyards, producing a greater yield than anywhere else and better tasting wine': Preest 2002: 197.

and precious metals, though if the Scandinavians recognised especially sacred objects they were sometimes kept intact to be ransomed to owners who held them far more precious than mere gold, silver and gems.[2338]

How long the raiding party had been inside Mercia is unrecorded, but the shortest route to the region around the Avon from the Mercian borders would be over 200 miles as the crow flies, and using trackways and the road system which existed in the early tenth century, combined with the meandering route probably adopted by the raiders, might give a distance of two or three times that figure. Assuming a maximum average of 10 miles a day (the distance calculated by military experts),[2339] we might guess that the expedition could have been campaigning for roughly a month and a half, or six or seven weeks (500 miles ÷ 10 miles a day), meaning that they would have crossed into Mercia in mid-July or thereabouts (which would have given Edward sufficient time to assemble his West Saxon forces and travel to Mercia), though it will be understood that those figures amount to little more than guesswork. That may be compared with Edward's raid into Northumbria the previous year which we are told lasted for five weeks.

It was during their return journey laden with booty, according to Æthelweard, that the Northumbrian raiding party moved towards the Severn-crossing at *Cwatbrycge*, doubtless having sacked the wealthy monastery at Much Wenlock, a mere eight miles away: it had been heavily endowed with scattered estates, and the gold chalice of 30 *mancuses* it had received nine years earlier from Æthelred and Æthelflæd was doubtless but a small portion of the portable wealth amassed by the house since its foundation in the later seventh century, though it may well have been despoiled when the Danes overran Mercia c.874.[2340] The chalice may indeed have been part of the 'rich spoil' over which the raiding party is said to have been rejoicing as it was returning home – it is unrecorded after 901.[2341]

There are various scenarios that can be put forward for the events centred on *Cwatbrycge* in August 910, just as the wheat was ripening but before it was cut. The joint West Saxon and Mercian army, perhaps two or three thousand strong, could have followed in the tracks of the Northumbrian raiding army as it looted from the Avon and northwards on the west side of the Severn. But by the time Edward became aware that the Northumbrian were raiding along the Avon, and had taken steps to assemble his West Saxon forces – Æthelred and Æthelflæd will have raised the Mercian forces at the first news of the enemy incursion – and those forces had assembled and grouped together, the Northumbrian are likely to

---

[2338] The mid-8th century *Codex Aureus*, a gospel book now in Stockholm but probably originating in Canterbury, bears an OE inscription recording that it was looted in the late 9th century by Vikings and recovered by ealdorman Ealfred and his wife who paid a ransom of gold to the heathen army and donated the book to Christ Church, Canterbury. As noted elsewhere, the illuminated manuscript known as the Lichfield Gospels may have found its way from the church of Llandeilo Fawr in Dyfed after payment of ransom. Any such arrangement could have had no connection with the Scandinavian road of 910: Llandeilo Fawr lies some 20 miles north of Swansea, far west of the area likely to have been ravaged in that year.
[2339] Lavelle 2010: 190.
[2340] S.221; TSAHS 4th Series I (1911) 4-8; Finberg 1972: 197. A *mancus* was equivalent to 30 silver pennies or 1 gold penny (Hunt 2016: 67), and the Much Wenlock chalice will have weighed the equivalent of more than 18 modern gold sovereigns: Blackburn 2007: 56.
[2341] Campbell 1960: 53. William of Malmesbury records that the abbey of Much Wenlock was deserted when Roger of Montgomery filled it with monks from Cluny at the end of the 11th century, the attacks of enemies (presumably meaning the Danes) and time having destroyed all the signs of the people of old: Preest 2002: 207.

have been heading homewards on the west side of the Severn. The time-frame must discount the idea that the West Saxons may have crossed the Severn, possibly at Gloucester or Worcester, both readily accessible from the south-west by Roman roads, and followed the Northumbrians to *Cwatbrycge*. These matters and alternative possibilities are considered in more detail in the next chapter.

From which direction the Scandinavians approached *Cwatbrycge* or which route they intended to take with their booty on their return to the Danelaw after crossing the Severn (if indeed they had any firm plans, for flexibility was essential for any raiding army operating deep inside enemy territory), is of course unknown, but the shortest route back into the relative but doubtful safety of Scandinavian territory (the boundary of which probably ran from the Mersey to and along the Dove and Trent, so excluding what became Staffordshire)[2342] would have taken them north-east, or north-west to the territory of the Hiberno-Scandinavians.[2343] Heading north or north-west from Quatford would have led the raiding party to the Roman road[2344] running north-west from Greensforge to Rudge Heath and Ackleton in the direction of *Uxacona* (Redhill) on Watling Street, the latter of course the major military road bisecting England from the south-east to the north-west. Crossing the Greensforge-Ackleton road in a northerly direction would have taken the raiders to Watling Street itself. Fom the Quatford area an early routeway may have run north towards Roughton and the south of Worfield, crossing the Roman road from Greensforge north of The Walls at Chesterton and continuing past the western edge of Patshull Park. It is not demonstrably implausible that an English force encamped at The Walls, which lies on the Greensforge Roman road, encouraged the Scandinavians to turn away from the Chesterton area and take a route to the north-east rather than the north.

Digressing for a moment to consider early routeways and the landscape in the area, Robert Dawson's map of 1815 produced for the Ordnance Survey shows a trackway from the south side of Quatford church, passing Hillhouse Farm on the west and continuing north towards Stanmore Farm.[2345] An early routeway running east from Quatford is better evidenced, for perambulations of Morfe Forest in 1298 and 1300 mention *Hethenedich* 'the heathy ditch' (discussed elsewhere in this volume) which ran from the fish-weir in the Severn to *Halyweyes-lydyat*,[2346] evidently near Gag's Hill, a mile or so east of Quatford, from where a path or trackway is clearly shown continuing eastwards, probably to Kingsnordley, on the map of Bridgnorth c.1560.[2347] Except for the length from Swancote

---

[2342] Hill 1984: 56. It is unclear how the boundaries on the map in Lapidge et al 1999: 519, with the Mercian border following Watling Street before turning north between Stafford and Shrewsbury, were established.
[2343] Jesch 2000: 2-3. Nicholas Higham has emphasised the importance of the Mersey as the sole frontier between English Mercia and the Northumbrians: Higham 1997: 146.
[2344] O.S. *Historical Map of Roman Britain*, 6th edition, 2011; the northern part of the road remains untraced. Another supposed Roman road from Greensforge crossing the Severn at Bridgnorth to Morville and along Corve Dale (Margary route 193) is not included here for reasons given elsewhere in this volume.
[2345] BL.
[2346] Eyton 1854-60: III 219; TSAHS LXX 1996 27.
[2347] A mile north-east of Kingsnordley is Six Ashes, believed to be *Onennau Meigion*, a point on the boundary of territory Owain Glyndwr intended to take after the overthrow of Henry IV. That boundary and *Onennau Megion* are mentioned in the so-called Tripartite Indenture of 1405. What is of interest to us here is that the boundary is said to follow 'an ancient road' between *Onennau Meigion* and the head of the river Trent.The boundary is shown on a map in Rees 1967: Plate 52, where the place is given as *Onnenau Meigion*, and the road to the north is shown to run through Pattingham, past the royal oak at Boscobel, and through Newport; see also Shaw 1798 I: 34-5. But if

to Bridgnorth (which may have replaced an earlier route created when Bridgnorth was established c.1101), the modern Bridgnorth to Wolverhampton road is likely to follow an ancient trackway, the north-eastern part of which may be a road or trackway recorded in the grant of Wolverhampton by King Æthelred II to Wulfrun in 985 AD.[2348] There is no means of knowing whether after crossing the Severn the Danes intended to pass near Tettenhall/Wednesfield, or whether an assault by, or knowledge of the presence of, the English army caused them to deviate from their intended route, but an ancient routeway known as *penwie*, recorded in the forged charter purporting to grant estates to the minster of Wolverhampton in 996 (*recte* 994) ran through Penn to the uplands of Cannock, its route marking the western boundary of Wednesfield,[2349] a fact that might associate it directly with the route of the Northumbrians prior to the battle of Tettenhall. In addition, and importantly, a Roman road, now lost, ran from Metchley between Edgbaston and Selly Oak south-west of Birmingham to Water Eaton south-west of Penkridge, running through or very close to Wednesfield, and may have been the Danes' intended destination. That route or *penwie* could conceivably have been used by English forces from the south-east to reach the Wednesfield area.

Turning to the nature of area on the east side of the Severn at *Cwatbrycge*, the tenth-century landscape of what became Morfe Forest is unknown, but the term forest was a later legal expression denoting a royal hunting area, not necessarily wooded, subject to forest law, rather than common law, and often denoted managed heath and woodland.[2350] Place-names and maps of the Forest made in 1582 and 1613[2351] suggest that Morfe, one of the longest surviving forests in the Marches outside the Forest of Dean, containing some 1200 acres to the north-east of Quatford in the middle of the fifteenth century,[2352] was then an area of heathland with few trees – the fact that the area is shown as a complete blank on the later map is misleading, for the earlier map shows what appear to be occasional saplings and tree stumps, crossed by a trackway heading north-east from Bridgnorth labelled 'the waye leadynge from the town of Bridge to ...' (the writing fades here to illegibility)[2353] – though there is some evidence that the area formerly contained much woodland: Leland records in about 1540 that Morfe was then 'a grounde hilly and welle woddyd ... [i]t was a forest or chace havynge deere, but now it hathe none'. He appears to have passed through the area during a time of woodland clearance, for a survey of 1556 claims that only 52 acres of woodland then remained,[2354] and in 1615 John Hatton of Claverley could say that he was familiar with the 'great waste common called Morfe Wood reputed to be a Forest but he never did knowe any deare to be there in his memorie, neither is theire any woode or underwood, but few trees in many miles compass'.[2355] In 1621 it was said that 'the woods of Morffe Forest are decayed, the land chiefly used as common,

---

it existed – the line has never been satisfactorily traced, and the road is probably mythical, with the intended line probably 'the ancient boundary': the Staffordshire border runs through Six Ashes – it could arguably have served a Northumbrian warband in 910 AD.

[2348] S.860; see Hooke 1983: 63-5.
[2349] S.1380; Hooke 1983: 46-8; 64-75.
[2350] The date when Morfe ceased to be a royal forest is uncertain, but is likely to have been in the 16th or 17th century.
[2351] PRO E178/4428 (reproduced in Rowley 1972: 104) and SA 4296.
[2352] Rowley 2001: 141.
[2353] PRO E178/4428, copy in SA. A lease of 1739 mentions 'the wast or forest of Morfe': Griffith 1880: 88-9. Nightingale 1818: 230 says of Morfe: 'It has not at present a single tree'.
[2354] Rowley 1972: 103.
[2355] Rowley 2001: 141.

very unsuitable for deer, and much of it let on lease'.[2356] On the other hand, Saxton's 1577 map of Shropshire shows woodland east of Bridgnorth, and Joan Blaeu's *Atlas Major* of 1665 shows similar areas of broken woodland as far south as Alveley, although it would be a mistake to see these as evidence of a heavily wooded area at those periods: it may signify no more than open heathland. A traveller in 1808 describes *the Morff* as 'a barren heath'.[2357] The nature of the topography might be hinted at by the description of the higher ground to the east of Quatford on the Bridgnorth map c.1560: 'Pleayne in the Forrest of Morfe'. We might suppose that in 910 the area was relatively flat rough wooded heathland criss-crossed by minor paths and tracks with isolated hamlets.

The language of *Anglo-Saxon Chronicle* version 'A' is ambiguous and unclear about how the English forces intercepted the Northumbrian raiding force, recording that 'they [the English] got in front of the raiding-army from behind when it was on its way home',[2358] perhaps meaning that the Mercian and West Saxon armies followed the route taken by the Scandinvians, or were even able to predict the route of the Scandinvian forces, allowing them to intercept the enemy or block their route. *Cwatbrycge* may have been a bridge of such importance that the English could foretell with some confidence that it would be the crossing chosen by the Scandinvians – especially if the water-level of the Severn was unseasonably high, which would preclude fording – perhaps knowing that it had been used in previous raids into the region which remain unrecorded, so that the English were able to carefully choreograph their surprise interception and lie in wait to ambush the enemy at a place selected for its particular tactical advantage. That supposition may be reinforced by the belief that the Scandinvians would normally endeavour at all costs to avoid pitched battle with the enemy, since they could not hope for reinforcements, and would be exposed to annihilation far from the Danelaw. Given the opportunity, we can be confident the Scandinvians would have chosen to flee from the English rather than face them in a decisive battle, had that option been available, and that their decision to stand and fight was almost certainly forced upon them by the unexpected arrival of more powerful and encircling English forces.

[2356] CSP Domestic, Edward VI, Vol. 10: 288.
[2357] Aitken 1808: 326. See especially Yates 1965: 148-52 for medieval settlement at Morfe.
[2358] Swanton 1996: 96.

34. The battle of Tettenhall – possible scenario.

Having reviewed the evidence, such as it is, relating to the battle of Tettenhall, we must move on to the most difficult step, that is attempting to assemble the pieces to recreate a coherent chronological account of events leading up to, during and after the battle. That will inevitably involve much use of words such as 'may', 'possibly', 'could', 'might', 'probably', and so on, for some of the evidence is confusing and, on the face of it, irreconcilable, and certainly insufficient to satisfy a burden of proof beyond reasonable doubt. Nevertheless, we can adopt informed speculation (an especially hazardous activity for any historian) about what may, on the balance of probabilities, have occurred, but it will be seen that even that lesser standard of proof is unattainable in many areas.

A powerful force of well-armed Northumbrians, divided into divisions led by kings including Eowils, Halfdan and 'Inguuar', or with the kings together in the same division and earls in another, as Asser tells us happened at the battle of Ashdown, probably (given the large number of *höldar*, or non-royal chieftans, mentioned in some accounts) Irish Sea Hiberno-Scandinavians,[2359] perhaps even members of the same family, the descendants of Ívarr who ruled Dublin before 901,[2360] has ravaged far into Mercia from the north-west. The raiding-army includes at least five (and perhaps many more) Englishmen – or at least men with English names, or names which were anglicised by the chroniclers – mounted on horses no bigger than Shetland ponies.

Burdened not with captured cattle or slaves to slow their progress, but with more readily-portable booty in the form of weaponry, coin, jewellery, gold and silver and other precious artefacts such as holy book covers cut into small pieces of 'hack-silver' or melted into small ingots, perhaps carrying flags, banners and standards, possibly with a supporting baggage train of sumpter animals and oxen-drawn carts to transport the heavier and bulkier campaign necessities such as tents, provisions, camp kitchens and utensils, as well as larger items of booty,[2361] (though some raiding armies preferred to travel light without the burden of a baggage train),the Northumbrian force is travelling northwards, averaging perhaps a dozen or so miles a day,[2362] or more if unburdened with pack-animals and carts, somewhere in what was to become Shropshire on the west side of the river Severn early in August, 910.[2363]

[2359] Woolf 2007: 140. Ryan sidesteps the thorny issue of the identity of the Scandinavian raiding army, referring only to 'the army in Northumbria': Higham and Ryan 2013: 299. In his recent and well-researched book on the Vikings, Philip Parker espouses the traditional view and describes the Scandinavian forces as 'Danish raiders': Parker 2014: 426.

[2360] Clare Downham personal communication 22nd March 2013; see also Anderson 1922: 401 fn.1; Downham 2009: 87. Ívarr, grandson of Ívarr, is said in the *Annals of Ulster* to have been killed in battle in 904, but it is very possible that there were other grandsons of the same name: Downham 2009: 146. As noted elsewhere in this volume, the idea that the Northumbrians at Tettenhall were from the north-west is perhaps strengthened by existence of the district of Amounderness and the parish of Anglezarke to the south-east of Amounderness, the district named from a certain Agmund, the parish from Anlaf, both personal names included among the dead at Tettenhall, though there is of course no evidence that either was the same person.

[2361] Packhorses could carry loads of up to 185 lbs, carts some 1,100 lbs: Lavelle 2010: 192. Horsedrawn carts were uncommon before the Conquest, and there is little evidence for the use of four-wheeled wagons at this period.

[2362] Lavelle 2010: 193.

[2363] Whether it was customary for the warbands to include females, or whether field kitchens, cooking equipment and rations, or even wet-weather gear, was carried, is unclear: *Egil's Saga* tells us that at the battle of *Brunanburh*, King Olaf's men set up many tents, which led the enemy to believe that the

At this juncture, it may be noted that while Viking armies invariably included Danes, neither the Danes of Northumbria nor the Hiberno-Scandinavians of Ireland and the north-west were Vikings *per se*. A pedant might indeed argue that the battle of Tettenhall was fought between the Anglo-Saxon English (the West Saxons and the Mercians jointly, possibly supported by contingents of Welsh – though no Welsh annals record any such support –and even perhaps by East-Anglian and Northumbrian Danes and mercenaries from other countries) against probably Hiberno-Scandinavians from the north-west, rather than the Danes of York, and not between English and Vikings.[2364] The raiding party may have included both Hiberno-Scandinavians and Danes of York, but there is evidence of animosity between the two factions perhaps even amounting to hatred, and there is some indirect evidence that the Scandinavians had Welsh and Britons from the north of England in their armies.[2365]

The Northumbrian raiding army, possibly several hundred strong – a larger force would be unwieldly and difficult to provision and support during a campaign of several weeks; a smaller force would be more flexible but susceptible to attack and destruction by a powerful enemy – is probably the response to the five-week *blitzkrieg* campaign by a joint Mercian and West Saxon army the previous year which ravaged, seemingly unchallenged, through Northumbria, probably that part to the north of the Mersey, killing many Northumbrians and returning with much booty.[2366] That raid was probably to neutralise a growing threat from the Hiberno-Scandinavians who had formed a large and powerful enclave with those already in the north-west after large numbers were expelled from Dublin c.901, as well as to replenish English coffers.

Apparently believing that King Edward was with a large fleet off Kent,[2367] and with the confidence that their force was sufficiently large and suitably armed and experienced to deal with any English attack far from the relative though perhaps hypothetical safety of Danelaw,[2368] the Northumbrians left their base or bases and made their way deep into into Mercia to spend some weeks ravaging and looting as far as the river Avon almost into Wessex before crossing to the west side of the Severn and into the Welsh borderland,

---

English forces were greater than they were, although the value of the *Saga* (written about 1230) as a source for events in the early tenth century has been questioned: Pálsson and Edwards 1976: 120. We might suppose that plunder of sufficient quantities of staples, such as bread, from locals in thinly populated areas might be difficult, but livestock will have been easy to purloin, kill and cook. Bad weather seldom features in the chronicles, but that may suggest that military forces carried wet-weather clothing, rather than stoical acceptance of cold, wind and rain.

[2364] Florence (John) of Worcester records that in 917 the Danes of East Anglia hired 'pirates' to reinforce their forces: Stevenson 1853: 77.

[2365] This conclusion is based on a detailed analysis by Professor Hywel Wyn Owen of the place-name Bretton, attached to a village in Flintshire close to the Cheshire border, which is held to incorporate the ON *Bretar* 'Britons', implying that Bretton was settled by Scandinavianised Welsh speakers: Wyn Owen 1994: 20-21; Wyn Owen: 2013: 324-5. One unexplained curiosity is the claim supposedly made by the renowned Danish historian Johannes C. H. R. Steenstrup (1844-1935) in his *Normannerne* (iii 13 et seq) that Danes from Hertfordshire (*sic*) may have taken part in the battle of Tettenhall: cited in Grueber and Keary 1893: liii. The claim may be related to Roger of Wendover's reference to a great slaughter of Danes in the neighbourhood of Luton and in Hertfordshire in 914; Giles 1892: 241.

[2366] It has been suggested that the English campaign may have been to put down a Danish rebellion: Luard 1872: I 349.

[2367] ASC 'A' and'D'; Swanton 1996: 96-7.

[2368] Graham-Campbell 1994: 140 map 2, and Hill 1984: 56 indicate that the Danes looted Hereforden route to *Cwatbrycge*, though the evidence is not given.

moving northwards towards the Severn crossing at *Cwatbrycge* (Quatford) on their way home. The raiding party may have found the river Severn at its dry summer level, fordable with care at a number of points, but a timber bridge, one of the few – indeed, perhaps the only – bridge across the Severn in this region lay alongside the ford at Quatford. The place was also the site of a camp at which a Danish warband had wintered 15 years earlier.[2369] The English forces who had kept careful watch on that camp for a period of several months will have come to know the area well, and it is very likely that some of those present in 895-6 were in the English armies in 910. The Northumbrians may also have utilised the Danish camp at *Cwatbrycge* after they reached the river in 910, but if Æthelweard's *Chronicon* is to be believed – and he had access to details unavailable to other authorities – they certainly crossed the river here, an important crossing point when water levels made the ford impassable, probably a frequent occurrence.[2370]

At this juncture we must confront an especially perplexing issue. Critical as Æthelweard's information is to our understanding of the events leading up to the battle of Tettenhall, his account leaves us perplexed about what might have occurred when the Northumbrians reached the crossing at *Cwatbrycge*. We have seen that his *Chronicon* reports that 'when rejoicing in rich spoil they [the Northumbrians] returned towards home, they were still engaged in crossing to the east side of the river Severn over a *pons* to give the Latin spelling, which is called *Cwatbrycge* by the common people. Suddenly squadrons of both the Mercians and West Saxons, having formed battle-order moved against the opposing force. They joined battle without protracted delay on the field of Wednesfield'. The wording is unambiguous – the battle occurred as the Northumbrians crossed the river at Wednesfield. Given the paucity of early evidence about the battle, it is inevitable that we should scrutinise forensically every expression he uses in his writings, but we may be unwise to place too much weight on every detail of his account, which (quite apart from his use of convoluted Latin of the period which is not easy to translate, as evidenced by the various versions offered by historians and linguists)[2371] is not always readily explicable: Wednesfield lies more than a dozen miles from the Severn, and there is no river (and of course no *pons*) at Wednesfield.[2372]

[2369] In 912 the Danish camp at *Cwatbrycge* was refortified, or a new fortification built on the site or nearby, by Æthelflæd: ASC 'A': Swanton 1996: 96.

[2370] Could this be seen as tentative evidence that the river level was high, denoting heavy rain upstream in the days before the battle?

[2371] An important extract was made by William Camden, the 16th-century antiquary: 'at [*Cwatbryge*] when the Danes passed over by filling off laden with rich spoils, the west Saxons and Mercians receiv'd them with a bloody encounter in Woodnesfield in which Healden, Cinuil and Inguar, three of their Princes were slain': Camden 1695: 235.

[2372] Tom Holland resolves the difficulty by concluding that the Vikings were ambushed at a river crossing near Tettenhall (Holland 2016: 41), but there is no river at or near Tettenhall. However, *sæffan mor* and *seofan wyllan broc* are found in 985 in the forged grant of Wolverhampton and Trescott from King Æthelred to Wulfrun (S.860). *Sæffan mor* was an extensive area of moorland or boggy ground extending from the north to the west of Wolverhampton, taking its name from *seofan wyllan brōc*, 'seven springs brook', a minor watercourse across or near Oxley Moor, 1½ miles north of Wolverhampton: Hooke 1983: 63-5; Horovitz 2005: 474-5; SHC V (i) 180; SHC 1924 330; see also JEPNS 39 (2007) 7-44. The possibility that this part of Æthelweard's *chronicon* may have resulted from a common scribal error known as *homeoteleuton*, whereby a scribe jumps from one word in his exemplar to another appearance of the same word, inadvertently omitting the text between, with the scribe here confusing *Sefern* (River Severn, with OE forms in OE including *Sæfern(e)*: Ekwall 1928: 358-60) and *seofan (wyllan broc)* is very unlikely, given the subsequent reference to *Cantbrycge* [*Cwatbrycge*] but cannot be overlooked, given the proximity of *seofan (wyllan broc)* and *Wodnesfeld* and its *feld*.

If read literally, Æthelweard tells us that the Northumbrians were first attacked *repente* 'suddenly' as they were crossing the Severn,[2373] and battle was joined at Wednesfield. In other words, the English attacked the Northumbrians during their crossing to the east bank of the Severn, and there was presumably some sort of unexplained hiatus before a 'formal' full-blooded pitched battle later took place a dozen or so miles to the east.[2374] That seems a decidedly improbable scenario. Æthelweard's *Chronicon* provides intriguing and often unique information, implying tantalisingly that the copy of the source unknown to us which he incorporated into his translation may have been a Mercia-centric account of events in the late ninth and early tenth century compiled at some Mercian centre in the early tenth century before it came into his possession.[2375] But his claim that the Northumbrians were attacked as they crossed the Severn is difficult to rationalise, and we are forced to treat itas muddled and incorrect. Perhaps, understandably unaware that Wednesfield is no short distance from Quatford/*Cwatbrycge*, he simply conflated the battle with whatever source was available to him about the crossing of the Severn and the site of the battle, and that wording must be missing from Æthelweard's source or that source was mistranscribed or mistranslated. Yet one explanation might be connected with the fact that it was two English armies, not one, which confronted the Northumbrians at Tettenhall: those of the Mercians and the West Saxons.

Those armies had been mustered as a matter of national emergency from throughout the two kingdoms. By what means that was achieved is quite unknown, but presumably relied on written proclamations (presumably of more ephemeral nature than formal charters and wills that survive from the period) distributed to reeves and other officers requiring all reservists to report to assembly places ready to make their way to congregate into larger groups at key regional locations, which would have necessitated a sizeable scriptorium in each kingdom and a well organised cohort of messengers to deliver the orders. The logistical arrangements necessary to collate and deliver those troops and their necessary arms and supplies – all in the absence of maps – can only be wondered at.

It seems reasonable to suppose that the Mercian army would have mustered and been ready for battle before the West Saxons (unless of course the latter had been following the Northumbrians as they looted and pillaged, which we have seen to be unlikely), who will have had much further to travel, and that they saw it as their role to marshall the Northumbrian forces whilst awaiting the arrival of their West Saxon allies. A confrontation with the Northumbrians at a Severn crossing may have been designed to press them to cross the Severn towards the approaching West Saxon army at some previously-agreed rendezvous – possibly at Wednesfield, a great *feld* on the Roman road leading north-west from Metchley, south of Birmingham. The Northumbrians will have been reluctant to

---

[2373] Campbell 1962: 53.

[2374] Richard Abels has concluded from Æthelweard's account of the battle that it can be seen as an example of how the English took advantage of the loot-encumbered Viking army, where 'the English awaited the enemy's crossing on the eastern shore [*sic*] rather than blocking their passage over the bridge' (Abels 1991: 148), but fails to explain how Wednesfield fits into the picture, evidently not realising that Wednesfield lies a good distance from the Severn.

[2375] Barker 1967: 74-91; Smyth 1995: 476-7; Stafford 2008: 114. Janet Bateley also suggests that Æthelweard had access to a version of the *Chronicle* which was closer to the original than any other extant manuscript: see Bately 1986: lxxix. Æthelweard's wife was named Æthelflæd, a name especially associated with Mercia and the Lady of the Mercians. Her ancestry is unknown, but if she was from Mercia, she may have played some part in the provision of source(s) from which he extracted detailed information about the history of Mercia not available to other chroniclers: Walker 2000: 119-20.

engage the Mercians, for the outcomes of such engagements were impossible to predict, and the Scandinavians had developed an aversion to such clashes unless there was no possible alternative. The risks for both sides were simply too great.

But this troubling section of Æthelweard's *Chronicon* might even cause us to wonder, indeed, whether another Wednesfield could have existed near *Cwatbrycge*. The idea is not completely preposterous. By the curious laws of serendipity, we have the ghost of what may be a Woden name recorded only two miles or so north of *Cwatbrycge*, and just three miles south-west of The Walls at Chesterton (which may have played some part in the events of August 910). That is the field-name *Wodendale*, recorded in the field of Swancote, in Worfield parish, in 1401 and subsequently.[2376] Uncharacteristically, the name is mentioned without particular discussion by Margaret Gelling, a leading expert on pagan place-names, in her survey of Shropshire place-names.[2377] It is not impossible that the first element was derived from the name Woden, as believed by one writer in 1824: 'In [Swancote] is a vale called Woden's Dale, supposed to have been frequented by the early Saxons, in their devotion to their idol of this name'.[2378] If that theory were correct we would expect to see a medial –s– in the spellings, but the forms found after 1401 all begin *We–*, and most have –*dd*–, which probably tell against any pagan association. The name remains unexplained, and indeed the vale is unidentified – it may be the valley through which the main road runs, or the valley between Swancote and Hoccum, or one of the pronounced secondary valleys which run from them[2379] – but interestingly by the early nineteenth century the name seems to have reverted almost to its earliest manifestation, by which date the 1401 spelling must surely have been lost in history. The survival of the Woden element in local memory (or its reinvention by local antiquaries) makes the name deserving of particular interest, especially since no other element can readily be put forward to explain it.[2380] It will be noted that Worfield and Swancote lie on or close to the route likely to have been taken by a military force moving from the Severn at Quatford towards Tettenhall and Wednesfield. But mention of Tettenhall as the site of the battle in the *Anglo-Saxon Chronicle*[2381] removes any possible doubt that the 'Woden's Field' we seek was evidently in the Tettenhall area and to be identified as Wednesfield.

Nevertheless, despite the problems with Æthelweard's account there may be unwritten subtexts buried deep within his *Chronicon*. Paul Dalton has analysed Anglo-Saxon negotiations at rivers, river islands and river-crossings and has emphasised their importance for treaty meeting places, concluding that peacemaking at these locations in the Anglo-Saxon period was 'an inevitable corollorary of the manner in which they were treated in warfare'.[2382] *Cwatbrycge* is of added significance not only as the site of the Danish wintering camp in 895-6, but as the meeting point from at least 1056 and almost certainly much earlier of three dioceses, Hereford, Worcester and Lichfield. Since ecclesiastical and secular boundaries usually coincided, there is a stong presumption that the place was the boundary between the *Hwicce* and *Western Hecani* or *Magonsætan*, and

---

[2376] PN Sa 6: 89. Other spellings are *Wedyndale Forlonge* 1491, *Weddendale Forlonge* 1498, *Weddale Forlonge* 1509, and *Weddendale* 1623: ibid.

[2377] PN Sa 6: 89. Dr Gelling's explanation in full is 'dæl [valley], first el[ement] uncertain': ibid.

[2378] Gregory 1824: 84.

[2379] No clue is offered by Robert Dawson's survey of the Bridgnorth area (BL map collection), produced for the O.S. in 1815.

[2380] One possible candidate for the first element might be OE *wēoden* 'weed, free from weeds' (MED 677), though the –*dd*– forms count against it, and the idea seems unconvincing.

[2381] ASC 'C' and 'D'.

[2382] Lavelle 2010: 321. Dalton gives examples of such rivers and islands in Lavelle 2010: 321 fn.30.

as such an early meeting place.[2383] Could the hiatus between the Northumbrians crossing the Severn and the battle at Tettenhall/Wednesfield be explained by a confrontation of the Northumbrians by Mercian forces while the former were encamped at the fortification at *Cwatbrycge*? The English forces may have formed a cordon around the Northumbrian camp while awaiting West Saxon reinforcements, and some sort of military engagement followed. Whatever the case, there are obviously omissions or garbling in Æthelweard's *Chronicon*, probably attributable (since Æthelweard is generally a sound chronicler) to the source he was using. It must be emphasised, however, that there is not the slightest evidence to support the idea, though Æthelweard 's account may be rationalised if we imagine that the Scandinavian raiding-army was indeed attacked initially at *Cwatbrycge* by the Mercian army but actually defeated at a battle elsewhere involving both the Mercian and West Saxon armies, though that can be no more than conjecture.

In that respect the account of the battle as given by Laurence Echard in 1707 must be of especial interest. In his well-researched but now little known history of England he tells us that the Danes having ravaged to the west of the Severn, 'King *Edward* sent the lightest of his Army before, to divert the Enemy 'till he could come up; and then following with the main Body, he engag'd them in their Return at *Cantbridge* in *Glocestershire*, where he gave them a memorable Defeat'.[2384] It is now certain that *Cantbridge* is *Cwatbrycge* (Quatford in Shropshire), and not Cambridge in Gloucestershire, but the account is notable for the suggestion, untraced elsewhere, that Edward divided his forces and sent 'the lightest of his Army' to divert the Danes before his main forces arrived to overthrow them at 'Tetnal'.[2385] The failure of Echard to disclose his sources must be a matter of singular regret, but there is no reason to imagine that he had access to information otherwise unknown to us, and it can be assumed that his account is no more than an astutely perceptive and plausible (but unprovable) analysis and interpretation of then published annals and chronicles: it would certainly have made good sense (if risky) for Æthelred and Æthelflæd to have used their forces to harass and confront the Danish raiding party – and even perhaps shepherd it to the Severn crossing at *Cwatbrycge* and beyond towards Wednesfield – until the main force of the West Saxon army arrived, and would account for Æthelweard's otherwise inexplicable account of the battle(s). Echard, indeed, may have come closest to explaining what actually happened in August 910 – but we shall never know.

At this point, we might return to the accounts of the battle in the *Anglo-Saxon Chronicle* in the light of a general observation made by Sir Frank Stenton in the Preface to his great work *Anglo-Saxon England*: '... the significance to be attached to an episode [in the *Chronicle*] turns on the interpretation given to a particular Old English word or phrase'.[2386] Here we need to consider one short but critical phrase from the *Anglo-Saxon Chronicle*. Version 'A' (the *Parker Chronicle*), and version 'D' (the *Worcester Chronicle*), tell us that

---

[2383] Finberg 1972: 225-7. A parallel may be found at Madeley in west Staffordshire, the meeting-place of Staffordshire, Shropshire and Cheshire, and a name which may derive from OE *mæþel* 'assembly, council' (cf. Madehurst, Kent). The bounds of Madeley recorded in 975 include *witena leage* 'the wood or clearing of the witan': Hooke 1983: 106-8.
[2384] Echard 1707: I 78.
[2385] Echard's account brings to mind Æthelweard's account of the siege of Buttington in 893, where we are told that 'King [*sic*] Æthelred of the Mercians was afterwards present with [the West Saxons], being at hand with a large army' (Campbell 1962: 50), implying that there was some delay before the Mercians arrived on the scene.
[2386] Stenton 1971: ix.

... *7 hie offoron ðone here hindan, þa he hamweard wæs ....*[2387] An accurate interpretation might throw more light on the circumstances leading up to the battle.

Not unusually, it is possible to translate the above phrase in different ways, since Old English words often carried more than one meaning. For example, Petrie and Sharpe in 1848 translate the phrase as '... and they [the English forces] overtook the [Danish] army as they were on their way homewards ...';[2388] Thorpe in 1861 gives '... and [the English] overtook the [Northumbrian] army when it was returning homewards ...';[2389] Garmonsway in 1953 says '... and they intercepted the [Northumbrian] host as it was on its way home ...';[2390] Whitelock in 1955 and 1961 says '... and they [the English army] overtook the Danish army when it was on its way home ...';[2391] Keynes and Lapidge in 1983 translate similar wording as '... they [the English forces] overtook the Viking army from the rear ...';[2392] and Swanton in 1996 translates as '... and they [the English army] got in front of the [Northumbrian] raiding-army from behind when it was on its way home'.[2393]

The critical expression we need to consider is *offoron ðone here hindan*.[2394] Taking each word in order, the first, *offoron*, is to be read as the Old English verb *offeran* (unconnected with modern 'overrran'), meaning 'to overtake (an enemy)'.[2395] The word seems to be formed from the preposition or adverb *foran* 'before, in front, forward; attack, overcome, capture',[2396] with the prefix *of-*,[2397] so herewith the meaning 'to come up with those who

---

[2387] Earle and Plummer 1892-9: I 96-7; Bately 1986: 63. In OE the symbol 7 represents an ampersand.
[2388] Petrie and Sharpe 1848: 375.
[2389] Thorpe 1861: I 78.
[2390] Garmonsway 1953: 96-7.
[2391] Whitelock 1955: 193; Whitelock 1961: 60.
[2392] Keynes and Lapidge 1983: 116, translating the account of the siege of Buttington in 893; Bateley 1986: 57.
[2393] Swanton 1996: 96.
[2394] The OE wording (with *offoron ... hindan*) echoes the *Chronicle* account of the events at Buttington in 893: ... *þa offoron hie þone here hindan æt Buttingtune* ... (Bateley 1986: 57), translated by Thorpe as '... they followed after the [raiding] army to Buttington ...' (Thorpe 1861: II 71), by Whitelock as '... they overtook the Danish army at Buttington ...' (Whitelock 1961: 57), and by Swanton as '... they overtook the raiding army from behind at Buttington ...' (Swanton 1996: 87). It will be remembered that the Danes at Buttington may well have taken refuge on an island near a ford, and were under siege from both sides of the river – 'in front and behind' – by English (and Welsh) forces. Interestingly, the only examples of *offoron* found in the whole of the ASC are in connection with the pursuit of the Danes before the siege of Buttington and before the battle of Tettenhall: Thorpe 1861: 169, 170, 184, 185. However, the words *hindan offaran* are found in ASC 'A', 'B', 'C' and 'D' in the account of the pursuit of Danish forces who returned after the siege of Buttington and sought refuge at Chester, where we are told that the English army ... *na hindan offaran* ... ('...could not overtake them from behind ...'): Thorpe 1861: I 170-1; Bateley 1986: 58; Cubbin 1996: 33; Swanton 1996: 88. The words are translated simply as '... could not overtake them ...' in Thorpe 1861: II 72; Whitelock 1961: 56; Whitelock 1979: 204.
[2395] Clark Hall 1960: 259.
[2396] Clark Hall 1960: 112.
[2397] Yoshinoba Niwa has analysed what he calls a 'common semantic feature' used in OE to define the meaning of a verb, giving as one example the prefix *of-*, which supplements verbs by connoting death caused by the action described by the verb, such as *of-slean*, *of-feallan*, *of-hnitan*, *of-hreosan*, *of-sceotan*, *of-stingan* ('to kill by striking; to die by falling; to die from a thrust; to fall down, to die in an attack; to be killed by a missile; to die from stabbing'). However, one exception to this practice specifically noted by Niwa is *offoron* found in the ASC in the account of the siege of Buttington,

are pursued, to overtake, to get near enough to attack, to reach and attack', or 'to go beyond, pass'.[2398] The second word is *ðone*, 'the', the third *here* '(raiding) army', the fourth *hindan*, an adverb, which (depending on the authority adduced) meant 'from behind, at the back, in the rear, behind',[2399] or 'to go beyond, pass',[2400] or 'to go behind, follow'[2401] Most translators ignore the word *hindan* in the cited extract, presumably treating it as tautologous.[2402]

The phrase may simply mean 'caught up with the rear of the (Danish) army', but the two words *hindan offoran* used together have been held to mean 'to intercept from behind, to cut off retreat',[2403] or 'to go beyond, pass' or 'to overtake'.[2404] *Hindan* and *offoran* are found in our text, but not together, or in that order. However, the meaning attributed to many Old English words is almost invariably derived by philologists from the context in which they appear, which means that the text determines the meaning. This can lead to circular arguments, and in this case raises the question: what does the word *hindan* contribute to the account? And is it possible to overtake unless from behind?[2405] If we accept that the word must add something to the text, Swanton's most recent translation might be considered the most accurate: '... and they [the English army] got in front of the [Northumbrian] raiding-army from behind', although the reading '... and they [the English army] caught up with the [Northumbrian] raiding-army from behind' may be preferred. We may understand the wording in the *Chronicle* to mean that the English did not intercept the Northumbrians from a different direction, but by following in their tracks (and we have seen that Henry of Huntingdon tells us that the West Saxons and Mercians fell on the rear of the Danish army),[2406] but in truth our understanding of the *Chronicle* account must remain uncertain, and the best interpretation of the wording in question may simply be the bland 'overtook' as adopted by Thorpe in his translation of 1860;[2407] 'intercept', preferred by Garmonsway in his workmanlike translation of the *Chronicle*, first published in 1953;[2408] or indeed 'came up with the rear of the enemy', as proposed by Ingram in 1823.[2409] Sadly, that exercise provides little help in clarifying the scenario leading up to the battle.

That the Northumbrians reportedly crossed the Severn at *Cwatbrycge* gives little clue to their identity – though the Northumbrians who wintered there in 895-6 had been Danes, not Hiberno-Norse – nor any evidence for their intended destination: they might have been

---

which has a non-cumulative relationship: Niwa 1991: 167-9; Niwa 1997: 167-78. One might suppose, though, that *offaran/offoran* could indicate 'death resulting from attack or interception'.

[2398] TOE II 1221. It may be noted that OE *ofirnan* is also given the meaning 'to overtake': Clark Hall 1960: 259.

[2399] Toller 1898: 536.

[2400] TOE II 1074.

[2401] TOE II 1074.

[2402] As the authors of TOE evidently believed, since they give identical meanings for *offaran*, *offeren*, and *hindan offaran*.

[2403] Clark Hall 1960: 259.

[2404] TOE II 1074; TOE I 346.

[2405] OE *ofrīdan* meant 'overtake by riding, overtake': Clark-Hall 1960: 260.

[2406] Forester 1853: 163; Arnold 1879: 154; Greenway 1996: 300-2.

[2407] Thorpe 1860: II 78. The same interpretation of *offoran hindan* is given in Wyatt 1948: 204.

[2408] Garmonsway 1953: 96. It is worth noting that Florence (John) of Worcester tells us that the English formed an army not to destroy the Northumbrians, but 'to drive them back': *Florenti Wigorniensis monachi Chronicon et chronicis: ab adventus Hengisti et Horsi in Britannia*, Sumptibus Societas, 1849: 121.

[2409] Ingram 1823: 128-9.

heading in a north-easterly direction intending to loot the wealthy churches in that area, for it is difficult to imagine that they would have resisted and left untouched what was to become Staffordshire, and in particular the area centred on Wolverhampton and Tettenhall and the area to the north which contained a unique concentration of Royal Free Chapels, institutions of uncertain antiquity (discussed in more detail in Appendix III of this volume), some of which perhaps represented conventional Middle-Saxon minsters founded or adopted as early family churches of Mercian royalty, delimiting the heartland of Middle Saxon Mercia, with the remainder being lesser churches of Anglo-Saxon date.[2410] But whether the Northumbrians had indeed intended to cross the Severn at *Cwatbrycge* remains uncertain. They may have camped at *Cwatbrycge* with the intention of continuing north along the west side of the Severn. Knowledge of the presence of a powerful English force may have been sufficient to encourage, if not force, them to deviate from their intended route. English forces either advancing from their rear or awaiting them somewhere on the west side of the Severn near *Cwatbrycge* may have left them with little choice but to cross the river and make a run for the nearest area of the Danelaw, some 30 or so miles to the north-east at Tamworth.[2411] But in reality the Danelaw could not represent safety: its borders were purely political and administrative, a hypothetical line on a non-existent map far removed from the Iron Curtain of the later twentieth century, with its physical barriers, watchtowers, and border guards. The Northumbrians would have known that just as the English had driven deep into the Danelaw in their raiding campaign the previous year, pursuit by English forces would have continued however far they made it into the Danelaw. Furthermore, the idea of their forces outrunning an English army was unthinkable. Quite simply, flight was pointless. It must be more likely that the Northumbrians were marshalled by surrounding English forces and had little choice but to take the only route left open to them: north-east towards Wednesfield.

The crossing of the Severn at *Cwatbrycge* (and of course the place-name itself) demonstrates that it was one of only a few bridges across the Severn, and if the war-band was indeed from the north-west it may have been making for Watling Street. Heading north or north-east it could not have failed to reach that Roman road. But we have seen that the most significant Roman road in the area, which must have been crossed by the Northumbrians after leaving *Cwatbrycge*, was that which follows the escarpment of Abbot's Castle Hill from the Roman forts at Greensforge, three miles south-east.[2412] The possibility that Mercian forces (or at least some part of them) had mustered at the hundredal meeting place of Seisdon, a mile from that road and just six miles north-east of Quatford, or – perhaps more likely – at The Walls at Chesterton, three miles further north-west, lying on the same Roman road, cannot be discounted if we accept Æthelweard's claim that the Northumbrians were attacked as they crossed the Severn.

A direct route towards Tettenhall/Wednesfield would have taken the Northumbrians across Morfe Common and via Claverley (having crossed the Roman road from Greensforge mentioned above) to Lower Penn,[2413] though they may have travelled well north or south

---

[2410] Jenkins 1988.
[2411] A defeat of the Scandinavians at Wednesfield will have taken place only 17 miles from the Danelaw.
[2412] O.S. *Historical Map of Roman Britain*, 6th edition, 2011.
[2413] A name of Celtic origin; the routeway named *penwie*, running north-east from Penn and along the western boundary of Wednesfield to the uplands of Cannock, mentioned in a forged charter of 994 (S.1380), attests to the age of the name and the importance of the place: Hooke 1983: 46-8, 64-76.

of that route.[2414] Possibly they used the medieval routeway from Seisdon to Wolverhampton, which almost certainly existed in the pre-Conquest period, since Seisdon, as noted, was a one of the five Staffordshire Hundred meeting place where local legal and administrative assemblies took place, with some participants travelling considerable distances, and Wolverhampton lay in Seisdon Hundred, and will have been connected to Seisdon by a well-used routeway.[2415] In the same way, since Claverley, in 1086 in Staffordshire but from the twelfth century in Shopshire, lay in the same Hundred, there was probably an ancient routeway from Claverley to Seisdon, which may have been used by the Northumbrians, although it must be recognised that we have next to no information about how Scandinavian (or, for that matter, English) armies navigated with remarkable skill without maps (or compasses) from one place to another, both by land and sea, perhaps hundreds of miles apart, in the early tenth century, and very little information (as opposed to speculation) about the precise routes used by such forces.

Whether or not the English engaged with the Northumbrians at *Cwatbrycge*, after travelling north-eastwards for ten miles or so the Northumbrians make contact with the main body of a powerful combined force of Mercians and West Saxons marshalled at very short notice in a remarkable feat of organisation by King Edward to deal with the enemy incursion. If (which is quite possible) the English forces were supported by troops from the allied Welsh kingdoms, they were probably led by Anarawd of Gwynedd, erstwhile ally (albeit many years earlier) of the Danes of York. If the treaty of Tiddingford with the Danes of Northumbria and East Anglia was designed to create a reciprocal coalition against the threat of the Hiberno-Norse of the north-west,[2416] we have no evidence that Danes from York and East Anglia provided support to the English forces, though their participation cannot be ruled out. If they were involved, it is understandable that the chroniclers are silent, and would not wish to dilute the English victory. It would not be surprising if representatives from the old 'English' Northumbrian aristocracy fought in support of the English,[2417] and even professional Continental merceneries may have been called upon, given the gravity of the situation.

[2414] The age of the road from Bridgnorth to Wolverhampton is uncertain. The western end (from Bridgnorth to Swancote?) may date from the creation of Bridgnorth in 1101, but the rest of the road to the east is likely to be much older, probably pre-Conquest, and could have been used by the Danes.
[2415] Seisdon is one of the few places in Staffordshire where a 'muster' name has been identified: fields to the east of the village were known as *Musters*, recorded from 1298 as *le moustowe*, from OE *(ge)mot-stow* 'assembly-place': Horovitz 2005: 48-9. The date of the shiring of Staffordshire and the creation of the Hundreds is not known, but may have taken place towards the end of the reign of Edward the Elder, who ruled 899-924, after the conquest of the Danish settlements in the east Midlands and East Anglia (see Horovitz 2005: 43-50), although many of the Hundred meeting places may have had a far longer history as places of assembly. Haslam 2005: 151 fn.135 posits the existence in Mercia of a shire-type system for the continuation and manning of *burhs* from the 890s or earlier, but see also Bassett 1996.
[2416] Downham 2007: 85-6.
[2417] A Welsh element at Tettenhall seems unlikely: there is no hint of the conflict in Welsh annals, though they were compiled long after and which are notable for the almost complete absence of English matters. The closest Welsh kingdom to the West Midlands was Gwynedd, the king of which from 878 to 916 was Anarawd ap Rhodri, who entered into an alliance with the Danes of York c.885 until c.890, but in 893 transferred his allegiance to King Alfred in his fight against the Danes: Charles Edwards 2013: 526. If there was a Welsh contingent at the battle of Tettenhall, it could well have been led by Anarawd: Campbell 1982: 160. In the late 9th century a 'Saxon' kingship became established in north-eastern Bernicia centred on Bamburgh, south of Lindisfarne, under Ecgberht II and his successor Eadwulf, who died in 913 and might have received West Saxon sponsorship: McGuigan 2015: 53. The kingdom seems to have been sufficiently powerful to have deterred any

Doubtless arrayed with standards and banners – the banner of the West Saxons is said to have been a golden wyvern, and that of the Mercians a golden dragon on a black background, although the evidence is unclear – we must suppose that the English forces will have camped nearby overnight.[2418] We cannot know the size of the two English armies, but it seems probable that the combined force, much if not most of which may have been mounted, was perhaps as many as a few thousand, but unlikely to have greatly exceeded that figure. Certainly the joint English force was very considerably larger than the Scandinavian raiding army.

Supported by a convoy of carts and pack-horses transporting arms, armour, tents, campaign furniture, bedding, mobile kitchens, victuals and provisions – when campaigning, kings and their nobles,with their own sizeable personal entourages,would have lived, slept and eaten in a manner appropriate to their status[2419] – the two English armies will have included blacksmiths to make repairs to any ironwork, farriers to keep the horses shod, carpenters to repair and maintain the carts and wagons, leatherworkers to maintain footwear, saddles and tents, and quartermasters and their clerks,[2420] cooks, ostlers, medics, scribes, armourers, and many other skilled craftsmen and artisans, such as *scops* to entertain with poems and tales, clerics, musicians, and even perhaps women in some roles, most of whom will have been expected to participate on the battlefield, if not as fighters then in lesser roles such attending the wounded: as late as the Crimean War it was not unusual for wives to accompany their men on campaign,[2421] and it is possible that some females, exceptionally, fought with the English (and Scandinavian) armies at Tettenhall.[2422] Most of the warriors are likely to have been between the ages of 18 or so and about 45, but some were probably younger – perhaps much younger – and some much older (Byrhtnoth, who lost his life at the fateful battle of Maldon in 991, was at least 60),[2423] although average life spans were considerably less in the tenth century, and older fighters are likely to have been afflicted with such common disabilities as arthritis, rheumatism, poor eyesight or deafness, any one of which which at that period would be a considerable – potentially fatal – impediment on any battlefield. All will have been aware that they were participating in a military operation of critical importance to the future of their homeland, perhaps much like the situation in 1940 during the Battle of Britain, when so much depended on so few. They will have left their cots, hamlets and towns many days previously, not knowing whether they would see their homes and kinsfolk again, and their families would have been only too aware that their departing brothers, sons and fathers were to be involved in one of the most crucial conflicts in living memory.

---

military challenge by the Danes of York until after the death of Eadwulf, when an Irish source records an invasion of Bernicia by a joint force of Danes and Norwegians: Higham 1993: 181, 185.

[2418] We have next to no information about how armies lived and were fed during campaigns.

[2419] Large or relatively large armies could not support themselves by foraging without dispersing, which would make them vulnerable to attack.

[2420] It is often said that only the clergy could read and write at this period, but it is very likely that scribes were also employed in the secular world.

[2421] Gillies 2016. The role of 'camp followers' with medieval armies has been little explored, andno evidence has been traced from the Anglo-Saxon period.

[2422] Pollington 2002: 83-5; see also Lavelle 2010: 13 and footnotes. Weapons have been recorded with female burials, but canot be seen as evidence that they were warriors: they have also been found in infant burials. According to the Byzantine historian Johannes Skylitzes, armed women were found amongst Scandinavian dead at the battle of 971 in which the Scandinavian ruler of Kiev attacked and was defeated by the Byzantines in Bulgaria.

[2423] Pollington 2001: 82.

Whatever their line of approach, the English forces would have enjoyed the critical tactical advantage of surprise on their side. In the decade since the death of King Alfred in 899, military strategy had changed somewhat. Between the siege of Buttington in 893 and the battle of Tettenhall there was only a single major land battle with the Danes, at the Holme c.903, fought – if we are to believe the chroniclers – almost by accident, though it is very likely that there were many lesser actions of which we have no knowledge.[2424] Whereas in the time of Alfred his clashes with the Vikings were not infrequent – in one year alone (871), Alfred fought no fewer than five, or possibly six, battles[2425] – his son Edward (and indeed the Scandinavians) displayed a clear reluctance for full-blooded combat with an enemy army, as illustrated only too well not only by the seemingly shambolic and defensive manoeuvres at the Holme when the rump of his army was attacked by Æthelwold's forces and only by good fortune killed Æthelwold and the king of the Danes, but also by Edward's raid into the Danelaw in 909 when he seems to have met no resistance. Full-scale hostilities, where the outcome was likely to be momentous, were to be avoided, with sieges the preferred military option. The Northumbrians, deep in enemy territory with no prospect of reinforcements, will have known that their situation was critical, and that they were facing their first full-blooded battle since the Holme, which could only end in a horrific death. Many, if not most, will have had no experience of serious warfare, but may have been comforted by the thought that death in battle allowed them passage to Vanhalla.

The Northumbrian raiding party reaching the Severn at Cwatbrycge in August 910, whilst well-armed and on its guard, may have little suspected that they were about to enter a carefully-planned ambuscade. By combining the armies of Mercians and West Saxons – a tactic adopted on previous occasions when occasion demanded, such as the aborted siege of the Danes at Nottingham in 868[2426] and the successful siege of a Scandinavian raiding army at Buttington in 893,[2427] and evidence of very considerable logistical and organisational skills, with the two armies presumably kept ready for action with enough horses, food and fodder for an expedition that might last for many weeks[2428] – Edward had

---

[2424] Marren 2006: 189. A naval encounter with the Danes took place in 896: ASC 'A'; Swanton 1996: 90.
[2425] Marren 2006: 187-8.
[2426] In 867, after the Danes had taken the fortification at Nottingham, King Burgred of Mercia asked King Æthelred of Wessex and his brother Alfred for support, and both armies joined forces and went to Nottingham and besieged the Danes, but terms were made between the English and the Danes, and the army from Wesex returned home: Swanton 1996: 69-71.
[2427] In 893 Welsh allies also fought with the joint English forces: ASC 'A': Swanton 1996: 87. We might note that in 910 it was the West Saxons who came, not for the first time, to support the Mercians – there is no record that the Mercians were ever called upon for assistance by the West Saxons.
[2428] In an analysis of the events leading up to the battle of Hastings, Frank McLynn has considered the logistical arrangements associated with the army of William the Conqueror remaining at Dives for a month, prohibited from plundering or living off the land on pain of death. From that we can extrapolate rough figures applicable to an army of, say, 3,500 men with 3,000 horses. A ration of 4 pounds of grain and a gallon of water a day would require the provision of at least 8 tons of unmilled wheat and 4,500 gallons of fresh water every day, assuming that the army subsisted on bread and water. In reality it is likely to have been well supplied with meat and wine. To sustain the above number of troops and horses for a month – which may be the approximate period during which the English forces were in the field in July and August 910 – would have needed perhaps 600 tons of grain together with some 400 tons of straw and 40 tons of hay. If, as was likely, the grain was baked into bread for the men or cooked into porridge, this would consume perhaps 120 tons of firewood at the rate of two pounds per day per man. If we can assume that a tent would have accommodated ten

clearly set out to ensure that any conflict with the Northumbrians must end decisively in his favour, for the defeat of a joint English army by the Northumbrians would have left England defenceless, exposed to rapid and complete domination by the enemy. The strategy was audatious but not without considerable risk. The English forces will have consisted of the great *fyrd* or *here* (the national military force of well-armed foot-soldiers), the *select fyrd* (an army of well-equiped and well-trained warriors, with one warrior provided by each five-hide unit of land), and the housecarls, mounted warriors who will have fought on foot.[2429]

There are, of course, very many aspects of matters affecting the area to the east of the Severn at Quatford in 910 about we know virtually nothing. The populations of the villages and hamlets in existence at that date are quite unknown, as are their trades and occupations and health: epidemics at this period were commonplace, and murrain affecting man and beast is well recorded in this general period.[2430] Floods, destructive fires, famine, harsh winters and other local disasters, accidents and illnesses, as well as lawlessness and family feuds, must have been commonplace, but are lost to history. In the same way there are many aspects of the battle about which we can have no knowledge. We do not know, for example, the weather conditions – the battle of Towton in 1461 was fought in a snowstorm with strong winds, which favoured the victor, Edward IV. We might expect a battle fought in early August to have been in fine, dry weather, but English summers are notoriously unpredicatble, and any assumption that the conflict took place in fine weather may be quite wrong.[2431]

Rather surprisingly, we know the names of none of those who fought with the joint Mercian and West Saxon armies at the battle of Tettenhall, and even the identity of the leaders is uncertain. The assumption that the West Saxon army was led by Edward the Elder (then aged about 38, and with not inconsiderable military experience),[2432] is questionable: of all the chroniclers mentioned in this study, only four actually give his name in connection with this episode,[2433] and their accounts are likely to be derivative.

---

men, some 350 tents, if of leather, would have required the hides of some 9,000 calves and the work of scores of tanners and leather workers. Again, good shelter would have been needed to ensure that the horses remained in sound condition, which would have meant the construction of prefabricated stabling. The minimum daily ration for horses would have been 10 pounds of grain (oats or barley) and a dozen pounds of hay per horse, together with five tons of dry straw for bedding and huge quantities of fresh water: if this were unavailable for even a short period, the horses could have fallen ill or died. 3,000 horses would have required 12,000 horseshoes and 72,000 nails, all of which would need to be made by hand – a total of perhaps eight tons of iron: McLynn 1998: 192-3. A force of 350 men with 300 horses would have required 10% of the listed necessities, still a formidable quantity.

[2429] See Hollister 1962: 7; 38-9; 138-9.
[2430] ASC 'A'; Swanton 1996: 89-90.
[2431] A warm and dry climate phase in north-west Europe between c.600 and c.900 has recently been identified from limestone formations in a cave near Ulapool in north-west Scotland, suggesting perhaps that August 910 may have been slightly warmer and drier than we might expect in later times: Baker et al 2015. The few clues to weather conditions at this period include a letter (S.1444) of 900x909 concerning land at Beddington, Surrey, which refers to cattle, including oxen, which had then survived a severe winter (Campbell 2001: 14), a claim by Florence (John) of Worcester that the winter of 914 (*recte* 913) was 'very long and severe' (Stevenson 1853: 75), and a statement in Æthelweard's *Chronicon* that the winter of 915 was the 'calmest' (*tranquillitas*) in living memory: Campbell 1962: 53.
[2432] Pelteret 2009: 325.
[2433] Ranulph Higden, Matthew Paris, Roger of Wendover and Bartholomew de Cotton. Sir Charles Oman also had no difficulty in stating that the two English armies were led by Edward: Oman 1913:

Indeed, *Anglo-Saxon Chronicle* 'C' and 'D' tell us that Edward 'sent his army' to intercept the Northumbrians, a phrase that tells us that he was not himself leading his forces; he was evidently distracted by the unexplained events in Kent of sufficient gravity to have led him to assemble a force and a fleet of no fewer than a hundred or so ships.[2434]

Though Edward certainly led the West Saxon army at the time of the battle of the Holme some seven years or so earlier, that reflected the status of his adversary, his own rebellious cousin, *ætheling* Æthelwold, against whom he could scarcely expect a subordinate to head the counter-attack (if indeed Edward intended to engage Æthelwold in battle at all: the evidence is equivocal). That struggle was deeply personal, and for anyone but Edward to lead his forces would have been unthinkable. In contrast, the enemy at Tettenhall was a 'mere' raiding army, and there was no reason for him to be personally involved at the denouement,[2435] though he may have been represented by family members. Certainly he would have been apprehensive about the outcome of the forthcoming clash, for the outcome at the Holme had defied all expectations. Edward's uncle, Æthelweard (then perhaps in his mid-30s), might have led or been part of the West Saxon forces,[2436] and it is very possible, if not likely, that Edward's son Æthelstan, then aged about 15, who according to William of Malmesbury spent his early years with Æthelflæd and Æthelred, played some part in the action, fighting with the Mercians if not the West Saxons. For an *aethelings*, experience of warfare was paramount, and participation in military campaigns occurred at a far younger age than might be supposed.[2437]

If not headed by a member of the royal family, one or more leading *ealdormen* will have headed the West Saxon forces: the most important duty of *ealdormen* – regional leaders – was to act as military commanders and lead their military forces, the *fyrd*, into battle,

---

497. For Edward's military prowess at the battle of Farnham in 893 (mentioned, it should be noted, only by Æthelweard and ignored by the ASC) see Campbell 1962: 49; Pelteret 2009: 325.

[2434] ASC 'C' and 'D': Swanton 1996: 96-7. The reference to 100 ships was doubtless a figure of speech to denote a large fleet. It will be recalled that during the siege of Buttington in 893 king Alfred was in Devon fighting a raiding ship-army.

[2435] The claim by William of Malmesbury in his account of the wars with the Danes that '[Edward] was, with his usual activity, present in every action' must be taken as hyperbole: Giles 1857: 117.

[2436] The date of his birth is uncertain, and he is believed to have died c.920-922. He was a beneficiary of the will of his father, Alfred the Great, made between 873 and 888: Whitelock 1955: 492-5.

[2437] As Sarah Foot has observed: 'As the eldest of the king's sons, an ætheling marked both for future rule, Æthelstan's education involved as much training in arms and military tactics as book-learning. On reaching manhood, he expected to play a direct role in current campaigns, perhaps increasingly so after his uncle's death in 911 ...': Foot 2011: 159. Edmund (921-46), Æthelstan's stepbrother, was 16 when he participated in the decisive battle of *Brunanburh* in 937, and only 12 when he accompanied the invasion of Alba in 934: Swanton 1996: 107; Holland 2016: 88. William of Malmesbury records that Æthelstan was made a knight at a very early age by his grandfather, Alfred, who gave him a scarlet cloak, a jewelled belt, and a Saxon sword with a gold scabbard. William also quotes a poem which says that Æthelstan '... practised the pursuit of arms at his father's orders. Nor in this did the duties of war prove him remiss ...': Whitelock 1955: 279. From this it is quite possible that Æthelstan was present at the battle, and it is not inconceivable that he could have headed the Mercian contingent, although William's sources are unknown and Dumville warns that William of Malmesbury's statement, unconfirmed elsewhere, should be treated with caution: ' ... William is a treacherous witness: for all the praise heaped on him in modern times, we must nonetheless recognise that his attitude to evidence is mediaeval and not ours.': Dumville 1992: 146; see also Stafford 2008: 113 fn.49; Frost 2011: 251-8. However, the presence of king's sons at battles is recorded elsewhere: Edward the Elder led English forces at the battle of Farnham in 894 at the age of 24 (Campbell 1962: 49), and Edmund, son of Edward the Elder, was 16 when he participated in the decisive battle of *Brunanburh* in 937 (Swanton 1996: 107). In the 10th century Otto III is known to have been on the field of battle against the Slavs at the age of 6: Campbell 2003: 6.

having mustered troops from a wide area.[2438] The leading West Saxon *ealdormen* in 910 are uncertain, given the absence of charters from that date which would have provided witness lists, but in 909 the most important non-ecclesiatical witnesses, described as *dux* (ealdorman), in West Saxon charters, are named as Osferth (Osfrith),[2439] Ordlaf,[2440] Beorhtulf (Beorhtwulf),[2441] Ordgar[2442] and Heahferth, in that order.[2443] Since witnesss were invariably listed in order of seniority, we must suppose that one or more of Osferth, Ordlaf and Beorhtulf must be the most likely candidate(s) to have led the West Saxon forces, just as the West Saxon army at the siege of Buttington in 893 was led by *ealdormen* Æthelhelm and Æthelnoth, who happen to be the only two witnesses described as *dux* (*ealdorman*), attesting even before the king's sons, in a charter from King Alfred of land at Chelworth in Wiltshire dating from between 871 and 899, perhaps c.892.[2444]

It is clear that Osferth, *ealdorman* of Sussex, Surrey, Kent, and possibly Essex, who evidently had royal blood – he was amongst those who received a bequest (of seven estates) in the will of Alfred the Great, who calls him his kinsman,[2445] and seems to have had some close family connection to King Edward[2446] – was a particularly prominent West Saxon, holding senior positions within Wessex from 898 to 934, and he must be the person most likely to have commanded the West Saxon forces in 910, when he was probably in his mid to late 30s.[2447] Of the other *ealdormen* mentioned above very little is known, and there is less likelihood that one or more led the West Saxon army, though some or even all may have been present at the battle.

[2438] Pelteret 2009: 323.
[2439] In the *Prosopography of Anglo-Saxon England*, accessed 11 April 2010, *Osfrith 8*, whose name appears in the witness list of some 34 charters, is said to be the brother of Edward the Elder, but although described in a charter of 904 as *frater regis*, 'brother of the king', that is probably a mistake, and neither Searle 1899: 342-3 nor Ashley 1999: 468 mention his name, which does not alliterate with the names of King Alfred's other sons. However, he does seem to have had some close familial relationship to Edward the Elder: in 909 he was described as *propinquus regis*, and in 929 he witnessed as *Osferth comes cum ducibus et ceteris optimatibus*. He usually headed the list of thegns in charters he witnesses from 898 to 904, after which he he nearly always led the list of ealdormen witnessing. He last appears as a witness in 934, and was probably over 60 years old when he died: Hart 1992: 124-5.
[2440] Possibly the Ordlaf who gave land to the church of Malmesbury in 901 (S.1205), perhaps to be identified as *Ordlaf 1* [of Wiltshire?], who flourished 898-909, according to the *Prosopography of Anglo-Saxon England*, accessed 11 April 2010.
[2441] Possibly the Beorhtwulf who was given land in Dorset and Somerset by King Alfred in 889 (S.347), identified as *Beorhtwulf 8* [of Dorset?], who flourished ?891-909, according to the *Prosopography of Anglo-Saxon England*, accessed 11 April 2010.
[2442] There is more than one person of this name recorded in the early tenth century, but *Ordgar 4* flourished 900-26 according to the *Prosopography of Anglo-Saxon England*, accessed 11 April 2010.
[2443] S.375; S.376; S.377; S.378; S.382; S.383.
[2444] S.356, described as spurious by Stevenson but authentic by Finberg: Sawyer 1968: 158; for a translation and discussion see Keynes and Lapidge 1983: 179-86, 326-333; also Birch 1887: II 210. Æthelhelm was presumably the beneficiary of that name who was one of three named individuals and unnamed ealdormen who each received a bequest of 100 *mancuses* in the will of King Alfred drawn up between 888 and 899: Harmer 1914: 51; Keynes and Lapidge 1983: 177.
[2445] He may have been from the family of Alfred's mother, Os*burh*, or been a son of Oswald who was perhaps a son of Alfred's brother Æthelred: Thorpe 1853: 224; Keynes and Lapidge 1983: 177, 322-3.
[2446] See Hart 1992: 124-5, 572-3. Hart suggests that Osferth could have been killed in 934 during the military campaign in Scotland under Æthelstan when he was perhaps in his 60s: ibid.
[2447] If Osferth was the leader of the West Saxon army, it is a curious coincidence that the Northumbrian dead included two leaders with the same name (Osferd).

It would have been unthinkable for Edward to have allowed his brother-in-law *ealdorman* Æthelred to lead the combined Mercian and West Saxon contingents – there was considerable centuries-old underlying enmity between the Mercians and the West Saxons,[2448] even though for the sake of self-preservation both armies had for at least half a century joined forces when necessary to meet the greater threat from the Northumbrians – but it is curious that the (West-Saxon slanted) *Anglo-Saxon Chronicle* fails to record the name of the victorious leader(s), which further suggests that it was not Edward who was at the head of the West Saxon forces. Just as Æthelstan may be part of the Mercian or West Saxon contingent, so Edward's second son Ælfweard, though not yet in his teens, might have been present with his father's forces.[2449]

Just as we can rule out the idea that the joint English army could have been led by Æthelred, so it is unrealistic to imagine a Mercian army under direct West Saxon control: the rivalry mentioned above would have made it equally impolitic to impose a West Saxon leader on the Mercian forces, and the two armies would have been seen as two separate forces. Despite his royal and Mercian connections, Edward's oldest son Æthelstan, aged about 15, was almost certainly too young to lead the Mercian army (although we might be surprised at his military experience even at that age), and however well-connected with the Mercian court, as a member of the West Saxon royal house he is in any event unlikely to have been placed in command of Mercian troops.

It seems fairly certain, therefore, that the the Mercians were under the command of a prominent Mercian *ealdorman*, as was the case at the siege of Buttington when Æthelred headed the Mercian contingent. But we cannot know whether Æthelred was even present at the battle in 910,[2450] for the later Irish *Three Fragments* (though of uncertain historical value) mentions repeatedly that he had long been suffering from some unidentified debilitating illness or ailment, and even describe him, more than once, and as early as 907, as close to dying,[2451] and that he eventually died as a result of his long-standing illness.[2452] His death in 911 is held by some (including Henry of Huntingdon, who had no access to those Irish annals),[2453] to be a result of longstanding illness, and by others to be the result of wounds inflicted during the battle, or perhaps some earlier conflict. Certainly no

---

[2448] Perhaps illustrated by the puzzling claim of Florence (John) of Worcester that on the death of Æthelflæd, Edward 'reduced' (normally meaning 'destroyed', but perhaps here 'occupied') Tamworth to force the inhabitants to submit to him, suggesting that their loyalty to Æthelflæd did not extend to the ruler of Wessex: Stevenson 1853: 78.

[2449] Ælfweard was the first-born son of Edward and his second wife Ælfflaed (the niece of the rebellious Æthelwold), who he married c.900: Sharp 2001: 82-3.

[2450] Walker concludes that victory 'had been achieved largely by Mercian forces under Lord Æthelred although with some West Saxon assistance'; that Æthelred may have been injured in the battle; and that there is no real evidence that he suffered incapacitating illness: Walker 2000: 93-5.

[2451] O'Donovan 1860: 227, 231, 233; Wainwright 1975: 80-81, 141, 154. The *Three Fragments* record Æthelred's illness when they tell of the legendary tactics by which the English foiled a Viking siege of Chester, which is generally associated with the terse entry in ASC 'C' for 907: 'Here Chester was restored': Wainwright 1975: 140-1; Swanton 1996: 94. It should be remembered, however, that the *Three Fragments* derives from a lost 15th-century manuscript probably based on an original source compiled c.1000, and its accuracy must be open to question.

[2452] O'Donovan 1860: 227; Wainwright 1975: 80-1, 140-2. Æthelred had reached power by 883, by which date he is hardly likely to have been less than 30 years of age, and perhaps considerably older. That would make him at least 58 when he died in 911. His death may have been unrelated to any long-term illness.

[2453] Forester 1853: 167; Greenway 1996: 307.

chronicler records his presence at the battle,[2454] and indeed the meagre evidence from the *Anglo-Saxon Chronicle* has been held to suggest that from at least 902 Æthelred's wife Æthelflæd was acting for much, if not all, of the time on her own initiative, wielding authority and not merely influence.[2455]

Had Æthelred led the Mercian forces, we might have expected the *Mercian Register* to have recorded his presence, which it does not, though that may be misreading the evidence, for the *Mercian Register* is deceptively misnamed, being neither a history of Mercia nor an account of Æthelred, but a set of annals covering the period 902 to 924 essentially (from 910) glorifying the exploits of Æthelflæd, a West Saxon, and the legitimacy of her rule – indeed, an alternative name adopted by historians for the *Register* is the *Annals of Æthelflæd*. It is inconceivable that Æthelred was not involved in significant events between 902 and his death in 911, but not a single one is mentioned in the *Register*.[2456] Furthermore, and quite remarkably, the Lord of the Mercians is unmentioned in the *Anglo-Saxon Chronicle* between 893 (the siege of Buttington) and his death in 911 (when he is described in version 'A' simply as *ealdorman*),[2457] a critical period of intense activity within Mercia.[2458] An illuminating example of the discord between the way he and his wife are treated by the *Register* is the death of each. We are told in the case of Æthelred only the year of his death, and nothing more. By contrast, in the case of Æthelflæd we are told where she died, the day and month and year of her death, the place where she was buried, in what part of the church there she was interred, and for how long she had held dominion with lawful authority over the Mercians. That must lead us to conclude that Æthelred's presence at Tettenhall may have gone similarly unrecorded. Quite simply, the evidence (such as it is) is equivocal: as Lord of the Mercians Æthelred would have been expected to lead the Mercian forces, and may have done so, but there seems to be evidence that his health had been declining for some years (he was to die the following year), and we shall never know.[2459] On the balance of probabilities, however, we might conclude that he did not.

Whether or not Æthelred was present at the battle of Tettenhall, we must consider whether Æthelflæd, then probably in her early 40s, was there herself, for by this date it seems that she had may have taken on her husband's role during his long infirmity, if we are to

---

[2454] The claim that Æthelred's participation in the Tettenhall campaign is recorded by Æthelweard (Williams 1999: 189 fn.9) is mistaken.

[2455] For example Æthelflæd appears to have acted as principal Mercian negotiator with Norse settlers on the Wirral, if the chronicles are to be believed: Bailey 2001: 113. In 909 and 910 Edward directed the Mercian *fyrd* against the Danes without apparent refence to the Mercian ealdorman who is unmentioned in connection with the campaigns of these years, and the building of a *burh* at Bremesbyrig (an unidentified site: see Bassett 2011: 17 fn.59) in 910 is explicitly attributed to Æthelflæd, not her husband, in the *Mercian Register*, our main source of knowledge of Æthelflæd's activities: Swanton 1996: 94-5.

[2456] In particular, the *Register* makes no mention of Edward's 5-week raid against the Northern Army by armies from both Wessex and Mercia recorded in the *Anglo-Saxon Chronicle*: Whitelock 1961: 61.

[2457] Swanton 1996: 96. ASC 'D' describes him as Lord of the Mercians: ibid.

[2458] The only mention of Æthelred in the *Mercian Register* apart from the record of his death is an entry recording that Ælfwynn was his daughter: Whitelock 1961: 62. Æthelweard the chronicler evidently incorporated into his writings a chronicle which included an account of the 890s which gave particular prominece to Æthelred in which he was seen as a king and effectively a campaigning equal with *ætheling* Edward: Campbell 1962: 49-51; Stafford 2008: 114.

[2459] Walker concludes that Æthelred led the Mercians at Tettenhall and may have received injuries from which he died in 911: Walker 2000: 94. No evidence is given to support either claim.

believe the later Irish sources. Could she have led the Mercian contingent in person, sword in hand? Though a West Saxon, Æthelflæd was able to call on local loyalties not only by virtue of her marriage to Æthelred and her undoubted personal abilities, but perhaps more importantly because her mother came from a noble Mercian family, and there is every reason to believe that the Mercians were proud to recognise her as 'their' ruler, albeit subject to her brother's overkingship.[2460] Nevertheless, it is most unlikely that she would have led her Mercian forces personally, even though leaders at that period were expected to take to the battlefield and display their personal valour, for it would have been as unthinkable for a woman to lead an Anglo-Saxon army as it would have been for Elizabeth I to have led her army or her fleet against the Spanish centuries later. Æthelflæd will have been well aware of her value to Mercia and to her brother as an outstanding military strategist and tactician, and that her death in battle – particularly in a conflict as pivotal as that at Tettenhall – would have left not only Mercia but the English nation as a whole, fatally weakened. We can be sure that even if she had wished to lead the Mercian army (which, in reality, we can probably discount), Edward would have denied permission. Indeed, no source suggests that Æthelflæd was personally involved in any direct military action in her lifetime, anywhere, at any time, though her military prowess became legendary, and the *Mercian Register* has been held to portray her 'as a ruler, engaged in the quintessentially kingly and masculine role of a war leader', though whether that leadership supposedly included direct participation in warfare is uncertain.[2461] But though unlikely that she led the Mercian contingent, it is very possible that, knowing the Northumbrian warband was heavily outnumbered by the English and victory virtually assured, she chose the satisfaction of witnessing the defeat of the enemy for herself. Had Æthelflæd been associated with the battle, we might have expected the *Mercian Register* to have mentioned it (which it does not), though the first record of Æthelflæd's achievements is later in that very same same year.[2462] Whether the *Register* records her achievements from the start of 910 or only after the battle of Tettenhall in August of that year is a question that must remain unanswered. But her presence at the battlefield, if only to inspire and lend encouragement to the Mercian forces, is quite possible.

The most obvious person to have led the Mercian forces, if not Æthelred or Æthelflæd, must be ealdorman Æthelfrith,[2463] who seems to have been descended from the West

---

[2460] There is some evidence that Æthelflæd was the last of a line of accomplished Mercian royal women: Pauline Stafford has concluded that throughout the ninth century queens in Mercia seem to have been quite prominent and powerful, while queens among the West Saxons seem deliberately to have been kept in obscurity: Stafford 1983: 140.
[2461] Stafford 2008: 103.
[2462] The mention of Æthelflæd in the *Anglo-Saxon Chronicle* (or more correctly the *Mercian Register*) is her construction of the *burh* at *Bremesbyrig* following the battle of Tettenhall.
[2463] Identified as *Æthelfrith 3*, who flourished 901-904/915, according to the *Prosopography of Anglo-Saxon England*, accessed 11 June 2010, which gives 11 recorded references (S.219, S.371, S.220, S.220, S.218, S.367, S.225, S.1441, S.361, S.367a, S.1280), and not to be confused with *Æthelfrith14*, flourished 901-909. *Æthelfrith 3*, who appears to have married a woman called Æthelgyth (daughter of Æthelwulf), was the father of Æthelstan 'Half King', Ealdorman Ælfstan of Mercia, Ealdorman Æthelwold of Kent and the South-East, and Ealdorman Eadric of Wessex. He is the only Mercian ealdorman known to have witnessed charters of Edward the Elder – in 904 he sought endorsement of his renewed charters from Edward as well as Æthelred (Walker 2000: 99) – and was supposedly still alive in the autumn of 915, when he is named as a witness in a spurious charter (S.225, probably a corrupt copy of an authentic early 10th-century document: Sawyer 1968: 127) dated 878 (but probably c.915), which purported to grant land in Berkshire (puzzlingly, for we should suppose Berkshire was then in Wessex, not Mercia) to Æthelflæd's *minister* (thegn) Eadric, who may have been another son of Æthelfrith: Hart 1992: 460-1, 569-70, 572 fn.6, 573, 581. Before

Saxon royal house and held estates in Somerset, Buckinghamshire and Middlesex, one of the three sub-*ealdormen* of Mercia in the closing years of the ninth century who were each allotted an area to govern under Æthelred and Æthelflæd. In 904 he had sought endorsement of his renewed charters from Edward as well as Æthelred, perhaps indicating a West Saxon interest in Mercia which would make Æthelfrith an acceptable, if not the prime, candidate to lead a Mercian force in alliance woth the West Saxon army.[2464] The other *ealdormen* were Æthelwulf, responsible for the western territories and perhaps central Mercia, and Ealhhelm, who had responsibility for Mercian territory bordering the Danelaw. Æthelfrith seems to have controlled the southern and eastern territories of Mercia, but after the turn of the ninth century references to Æthelwulf and Ealhhelm cease, and Æthelfrith seems to have come to the fore and taken over their ealdormanships.[2465] He appears to have been the only active *ealdorman* in Mercia during the campaign against the Danes, and as such may have served as Æthelflæd's leading commander.[2466] In that capacity we can reasonably suppose that, if still in good health (there is evidence, albeit dubious, that he was living in 915),[2467] he could have been put in charge of the Mercian forces.[2468]

Did Anglo-Saxon kings and leaders take a prominent position at the front of their forces and literally lead them into battle? There is no evidence (apart perhaps from later visual representations of Anglo-Saxon battles, which provide very doubtful historical evidence) to suggest that they did, and a good deal of circumstantial evidence to show that they did not.[2469] Any prominent figure at the front of an armed force, fighting on foot or even on horseback, no matter how well protected by his personal bodyguards, would be especially vulnerable and a particular target for the enemy, and the death or injury of a leader would almost invariably be seen as the defeat of his (or her) forces.[2470] Equally important, no-one in the vanguard of a battle force would be well placed to take an overview of the course of

---

[2464] 915, Æthelfrith last witnessed charters in 903 and 904, and is named as *Aðelferð comes* (S.367) and *Athelfrid ealdor man* (S.1280). It is possible that he was one of the 4 un-named *thegns* of Æthelflæd, memorably described in ASC 'C' as 'dear to her', who were killed inside the gates of Derby when it was successfully stormed by Mercian forces before Easter in 917: Swanton 1996: 101. Hart suggests that King Alfred may have taken the opportunity to appoint a West Saxon when some members of the Mercian nobility transferred their allegiance to the Danes: 1992: Hart 1992: 571-2. That may be correct, but the evidence he adduces relates to events which took place after Alfred's death. See also Keynes 1994: 1109-49; Cyril Hart, '*Æthelstan (fl.932-956)*', Oxford DNB 2004.
Walker 2000: 99.
[2465] Searle 1899: 300 states that 'no ealdorman was appointed as successor to Ælfric [who was banished in 985], and the great Ealdordom of Mercia became a memory of the past', citing E. W. Robertson, *Historical Essays*, Edinburgh, 1872, 183, but that is not strictly correct: Edwin, the last Earl of Mercia, was assassinated in 1071: Eyton 1881: 9, 32.
[2466] Hart 1992: 460-1, 569-70, 581. It should, however, be noted that most of the later charters attested by Æthelfrith relate to property in Hampshire, i.e. in Wessex, which may be seen as evidence that he was spending time there rather than in Mercia.
[2467] The table showing the family of Æthelstan 'Half King' in Hart 1992: 571 suggests that Æthelfrith died between c.915 and 925, but the evidence for the later date (perhaps due to confusion with charter S.225?) is unclear.
[2468] Æthelfrith may well have been one of 'four [un-named] thegns, who were dear to her [Æthelflæd]' killed when Derby was captured from the Danes in 917 (Swanton 1996: 101; Thompson 2002: 11-12), and it is very possible that one or more of the four fought at Tettenhall.
[2469] The Irish authors of the *Three Fragments* and the *Annals of Ulster* seem to have accepted that Æthelflæd was able to command her troops and her territory with authority: Wyatt 2009: 190.
[2470] A notable exception is the battle of the Holme, where Æthelwold and Eohric, leaders of the Northumbrian and East Anglian forces, were killed, but their armies retained possession of the battlefield and were thus technically the victors.

the battle. Though it is possible that a leader, well-protected by a heavy phalanx of loyal bodyguards from his personal household, will have taken a forward position to provide moral leadership and demonstrate his personal valour, we must perhaps suppose that a leader took a position further back from the first line to take in the tactical aspects of the conflict and give orders and encouragement to his troops. In fact although many kings, ealdormen and senior officials (including churchmen)[2471] are known to have died in early Anglo-Saxon battles (more kings died on the battlefield than in their beds), relatively few Anglo-Saxon kings were killed fighting at this later period. That in itself suggests that if a king were present at a battle, it was probably on the periphery of the fighting, allowing him to control his forces but take flight if the battle appeared to be turning against him.[2472] On the other hand, an Anglo-Saxon king was perforce a warrior king, and proving his prowess on the battlefield was paramount. We must assume that he would choose the moment to engage personally with the enemy in hand-to-hand fighting to demonstrate his valour, serve as an example to his troops, and, perhaps most importantly, provide material for songwriters and poets to commemorate his bravery as a warrior long after his death: the idea that posthumous fame is the finest memorial is a constant theme of the epic Anglo-Saxon poem *Beowulf*, as well as the fragmentary poetic account of the battle of Maldon in 991.[2473]

Whoever its leaders, we can be certain that in readiness for the forthcoming battle each of the two English armies will have been split into divsons, as at the battle of Ashdown in 871 when the English forces had been divided, with King Ethelred of Wessex fighting against two Danish kings, and his brother Alfred concentrating on the jarls' troop.[2474] Later in the same year Ethelred and Alfred headed two divisions to victory at the battle of Meretun.[2475] Again, at Buttington in 893 the Mercian contingent (doubtless sub-divided) concentrated on specific parts of the Danish forces and the West Saxon army (similarly divided) on the other part. The chronicles record how before the battle of the Holme c.903, Edward's Kentish contingent ignored orders to keep up with the main body of his army, sustaining heavy losses (though achieving an astonishing victory) when attacked by Æthelwold's forces.[2476] We can be certain that in the campaign of 910 the Danish army

---

[2471] In his Pastoral Letter to Wulfstan, the homilist Ælfric argued in the early 11th century that a priest who died in battle merited minimal burial rites: Thompson 2002: 85. Closer in time to the battle of Tettenhall, Abbot Cenwulf is recorded amongst the English dead at the battle of the Holme c.903: ASC 'A'; Swanton 1996: 94.

[2472] A review of Anglo-Saxon battles from 850 to 950 is sufficient to demonstrate that on many occasions English kings were present at battles but escaped unharmed when the Danes or Vikings were victorious: in 871, for example, King Æthelred and his son, Alfred, escaped unharmed from at least four battles won by the Vikings: see e.g. Marren 2006: 187-60. It is worth noting that there is no firm evidence that King Harold fought hand-to-hand during the battle of Hastings: Lawson 2003: 242.

[2473] Whitelock 1979: 319-24.

[2474] At the battle of Corbridge on the Tyne in 918, the Norse are said to have been in four divisons, with jarls fighting in a separate body from their kings and from the young nobles, with one divison held in reserve and out of sight, suggesting the presence of individual warbands who preserved their separate identities on the battlefield: see Wainwright 1975: 167-8; Smyth 1995: 34.

[2475] Whitelock 1955: 178; Smyth 2002: 18-20. The accounts of the battle also give the names of the fallen Danish earls, Sidroc the Old, Sidroc the Younger, Osbearn, Fræna, and Harold.

[2476] It has been suggested that if the Kentish force constituted the withdrawing rearguard, it presumably formed the vanguard in the attack on Æthelwold's forces (Swanton 1996: 94-5; Campbell 2001: 17), but the sources, though equivocal, suggest that Edward's army did not engage with Æthelwold's forces, and it was the slow-moving Kentish contingent which was attacked by Æthelwold and forced into battle.

was similarly formed into divisions, each led by a king or the next in rank, the jarls: at the battle of Corbridge in 918 the Northumbrians had four divisions, with one held in reserve in a concealed position.[2477] We might picture the Northumbrian force which crossed the Severn in 910 split in up to five divisions, led by kings Eowils, Halfdan and Ivar, and the two jarls, Ohtor and Scurfa (who are named among the dead after the battle), but there may of course have been more jarls (and even, possibly, more kings) who were not amongst those killed, though the magnitude of the defeat makes that unlikely. Since a number of Englishmen, or at least men with English names, appear to have fought on the Northumbrian side, we can only wonder whether there was a separate English division (or even more than one) fighting alongside the Northumbrians.

We might imagine English scouts and lookouts on various high points on both sides of the Severn, carefully tracking the progress of the Northumbrian army approaching from the west or south-west (or even the north-west, if the Danes had sacked Much Wenlock), and perhaps signalling the news to other vantage points by means of smoke or fire, for the Anglo Saxons are believed to have employed a sophisticated interconnected system of beacons in Hampshire,[2478] and there is no reason to suppose that such an early warning system did not cover most of Anglo-Saxon (and doubtless Northumbrian) administered England, though in reality we have little knowledge how military intelligence and other news was conveyed over vast distances in Anglo-Saxon times, and about the extraordinary way in which military forces were marshalled and managed to navigate across great tracts of England – a large part of a large island – to specific points without the use of map or compass.

Knowing that the Northumbrian are moving north-east, possibly using a route they had taken on other occasions previously, and perhaps *en route* to the notional but illusory safety of the Danelaw to the north or north-east, the English may have had lookouts on the higher ground of Tettenhall, Wolverhampton and Bushbury, and we can assume that Northumbrian raiding armies, particularly if laden with booty and travelling slowly, would have had their own scouts reconnoitering ahead of the main force to warn of hostile forces. Of one thing we can be reasonably certain, and that is that the Northumbrians were not expecting a confrontation with an English force, not only because their intelligence was that Edward the Elder was in the far south of England, but because full-scale warfare had not taken place for a generation or more.[2479] Even the battle of the Holme may have come about almost accidentally, with Æthelwolds's forces stumbling across the straggling Kentish division which had not kept up with Edward's main army. Full-blooded battles were perhaps seen as a thing of the past.

Turning to what is probably the most fundamental question relating to the battle of Tettenhall – the location of the battlefield – it is important to re-emphasise that the topography of the area is largely irrelevant in attempts to identify the precise site, or to the disposition of the opposing forces. There was, of course, no 'rule' that battles could only be fought on clear, level ground (many medieval battles are known to have been fought on sloping or irregular ground), and if either side took up position on high ground to seek a tactical advantage, the other side was under no obligation to launch an attack. The battle of Tettenhall should not necessarily be seen as a set piece example of the type of battle seen

---

[2477] Wainwright 1975: 168.
[2478] Hill 1984: 164.
[2479] A convenient list of Anglo-Saxon battles is provided in Marren 2006: 182-92.

in the later medieval period, or indeed the Roman period, when well-drilled troops faced an enemy in carefully regulated formations.

There has been a tendency for military historians (and others) to produce learned and sophisticated diagrams of troop dispositions and movements for Dark Age battles which are in reality based on nothing more than complete guesswork with no supporting evidence.[2480] The traditional Hollywood concept of armed warriors facing their opponents in neat ranks facing each other on an open, flat, dry grassy area may well be a fiction developed by contemporary chroniclers and poets (who are unlikely to have had any direct first-hand knowledge themselves) and later military historians (perhaps with even less knowledge), but it does seem probable that each side arranged its forces in a manner that would indicate when it was either losing or winning a battle, which would be more difficult, or even impossible, if the army were a scattered and ragged collection of independent units fighting on uneven ground where an overview was not possible.

The conflict near Tettenhall may have taken place anywhere in the area – indeed, perhaps at more than one place, with divisions and cohorts from each army fighting some distance from other sections – on any type of reasonably firm, even sloping, ground, but probably close to, or even on, a major routeway, accessible to the carts containing war gear and provisions. But the likelihood is that the battlefield will have been a relatively modest area – perhaps as small as a few dozen acres or so – not necessarily perfectly level or unbroken or free of trees and bushes, ditches and streams, but sufficiently clear of obstructions to allow each army to arrange itself in military formation against the other and so that both armies could easily assess which side was gaining the upper hand. Terrain that was rugged, or particularly wet or marshy, or heavily wooded or with other obstructions, such as pits, pools or ditches, is unlikely to have been chosen, unless those areas could have proved advantageous to a powerful force which was in a position to dictate the battle site. There would have been an almost infinite number of suitable sites in the Tettenhall and Wednesfield areas, though early-recorded place-names suggestive of flat open heath or moorland are, as might be expected, far more common in the Wednesfield area than the Tettenhall area.[2481]

For the most detailed account of the battle of Tettenhall we are greatly indebted, as we have seen, to the chronicler Æthelweard, who evidently had access to early sources which are now lost. His chronicle provides telling, if in part baffling, additional detail not contained in the standard sources, which are notably terse. Certainly his account has information about the prelude to the battle – for example the crossing of the Severn at [C]antbrycge – which is missing from every other chronicle, and Æthelweard was writing only two or three generations after the battle, when the nature of warfare is likely to have changed very little since the events of 910. As a noble rather than a scholar cleric, he was certainly more familiar with battlefield strategy, and as a senior *ealdorman* – indeed, the premier *ealdorman* of King Æthelred from 992 to Æthelweard's death c.998[2482] – must have have had personal experience of skirmishes or even more heavyweight clashes with the Danes.[2483]

[2480] See, for example, the otherwise informative Marren 2006, which includes 'as imagined' battle maps.
[2481] Valuable maps of the area, including contour maps, geological maps, and maps showing made ground, are to be found in McC Bride et al 1997.
[2482] Williams, Smyth and Kirby 1991: 30.
[2483] In 994 he was one of the negotiators of the treaty with the Danish army of Olafr Tryggvason: Williams, Smyth and Kirby 1991: 30-1.

An important piece of evidence as to the possible site of the battle of Tettenhall may be the pre-Conquest (perhaps even pre-historic) routeway from the south-east known as the Portway, which ran past Wednesfield and Stowheath. Roman Icknield Street, many lengths of which remain in use to this day, and which contingents of Mercians could have conveniently joined at any point, will have provided a direct routeway from the south to the West Midlands. The Portway may have followed, or even served as, part of the Roman (or even pre-Roman) road from *Pennocrucium* (Water Eaton) on Watling Street south of Penkridge to Metchley Roman forts south-west of Birmingham, an obvious route to the north-west for military forces intending to intercept Northumbrian forces moving northwards who would need to cross the Severn on their journey back to the Danelaw. So few crossing points existed on the Severn that it is very possible that *Cwatbrycge* was a bridge the English knew would almost certainly be used by the Northumbrians.[2484]

We do not know how long it took the Northumbrian force to travel from the crossing on the river Severn – they probably camped overnight *en route* – but it seems likely that on Saturday, 4th August,[2485] the English forces were in visual contact with the Northumbrian forces. The route the enemy took is of course unknown, but they may well used the ancient routeway known as *alde strete*, at a vast heathland area – which the Anglo-Saxons will have known as a *feld* – known to us as Wednesfield, perhaps at the place recorded in 1513 as *Camp Feld*. The location of *Camp Feld* has not been traced, but we have seen that it may have lain near Neachells, on the south side of Wednesfield and close to the ancient Portway, which ran to the south. Nearby lay South Low, a mound thought be a tumulus, which, together with other mounds known as North Low and The Low, south-east of New Cross, are traditionally associated with the battle as marking the burial of fallen warriors, although that tradition is probably groundless and seems to have developed many centuries after the battle.[2486] If that location might be correct, the area was probably scrubby heathland sloping gradually down to the grassy wet ground of the moors adjoining Waddens Brook to the east, an area that also included areas of woodland that were to become known as Prestwood.

If, as Æthelweard tells us, the battle took place on 5th August (*Anglo-Saxon Chronicle* 'D' says 6th August, but Æthelweard gives more details of the battle, and was evidently better informed),[2487] it will have been an especially significant date in the Mercian calendar, for it was not only a Sunday, but St Oswald's Day – the Northumbrian king and martyr had died

---

[2484] The Viking raiding army that wintered at *Cwatbrycge* in 895-6 were Danes, not Hiberno-Norse.

[2485] Contact between the main forces of the English and the Northumbrians may of course have been made before 5th August, with the actual conflict taking place on 5th. Æthelweard gives the date of the battle as 5th August, whereas ASC 'D' says 6th August. We cannot be certain which is correct, but Æthelweard's is the earlier and more detailed account, and the author of ASC 'D' may have misread *vii ides* as *viii ides*. The ides were, in the ancient Roman calendar, the 15th day of March, May, July and October, and the 13th day of the other months. Only very rarely do we have the precise date of Anglo-Saxon battles, although the battle of Maldon is known to have taken place on 11th August 991.

[2486] The proximity of Luchfield to Waddens Brook has already been noted. It is possible, though unlikely, that the name incorporates OE *lāc*, which had several meanings, including 'battle, strife'.

[2487] Swanton 1996: 95; Campbell 1962: 53. Curiously, the date of the battle is unrecorded by the *Mercian Register*, although 'Precision of dating within the year marks all entries between 912 and 920': Pelteret 2009: 322.

in battle at *Maserfelth* on that exact day some 379 years' earlier[2488] – and his cult, established before the end of the seventh century, had been aggressively promoted by Æthelred and Æthelflæd (motivated by the firm conviction that the relics of a saint would offer powerful protection against the Vikings),[2489] who had recovered his bones from Bardney in the Danelaw only a year or so before the battle to be installed in St Oswald's minster in Gloucester.[2490] The Mercians are sure to have had St Oswald firmly in mind and seen the date as highly propitious, though it is hard to imagine that they contrived to ensure that the great battle took place on that exact date, and it is curious that the saint's day is unrecorded in the Mercian Register, though the annalist had recorded the translation of the saint's relics the previous year, and found space to record the far more obscure Saint Ciriacus in 916.[2491]

Northumbrian progress north-east of Wolverhampton, perhaps along *alde strete*, could have been blocked by the English forces somewhere near Heath Town/New Cross, where *alde strete* and (if Duignan is correct in his supposition that the Portway forked at Moseley Hole) the southern branch of *portstrete*/Portway would appear to have intersected, barely half a mile from Wednesfield, and battle forced upon the Northumbrians nearby. That scenario, however, would have required very considerable forward planning by the West Saxon and Mercian commanders, combined with hour-to-hour intelligence from scouts and messengers tracking the Northumbrian movements and communicating reports to the English forces.[2492] The English armies would have been at little or no risk of premature attack by the Northumbrians, since, as we have seen, both English and Scandinavians customarily assiduously avoided such engagements, and the Northumbrians will have been all too aware that they were heavily outnumbered by the English forces.

A further scenario would be an approach by the joint West Saxon and Mercian army through the West Midlands, perhaps along Ryknield Street, meeting at a junction on the Roman road such as Metchley or some other prearranged point, with an attack by the English armies intercepting the Northumbrian forces as they approached from the south-west and passed close to Wednesfield, or an attack by one of the two English armies, with the other blocking any escape, near Heath Town/New Cross. But that possibility would largely depend on the English possessing prior knowledge of or being able to anticipate the route the Northumbrians intended to take (that the English forces happened to stumble across the Northumbrian army by chance can be discounted), and does not explain

---

[2488] It is impossible to believe that this auspicious date was not recognised at the time, and curious that if any of the chroniclers was conscious of the particular saint's day, he chose not to record it: not even the *Mercian Register* mentions St Oswald's Day, even though it mentions elsewhere the construction of the *burh* at Scergeat on the eve of the Invention of the Holy Cross in 912, and that 16th June was the festival of the far more obscure St Ciricius: Whitelock 1961: 62, 64.

[2489] Æthelred and Æthelflæd, fighting for survival against pagans, will have been especially attracted to a Christian king who died in battle against a pagan, probably in Mercia: see Stancliffe 1995: 84-96; Thacker and Sharpe 2002: 549-50; Meeson 2015: 19.

[2490] On *Maserfelth*, Oswald and his cult and relics see generally Stancliffe and Cambridge 1995. On St Oswald's minster at Gloucester see Heighway 2001.

[2491] Whitelock 1961: 64. A more cynical observer might also wonder whether, alternatively, the histories have been manipulated to ensure the victory occurred on the auspicious date.

[2492] Bede tells of the overthrow of king Æthelfrith of Northumbria by Rædwald of East Anglia who in 617 raised a large army and marched north before Æthelfrith had time to raise a full army. Æthelfrith and his forces were defeated at the battle of the River Idle. Although Æthelfrith had advanced to the southern border of Northumbria to meet the enemy, we are not told how he knew of Rædwald's approach and the route he was taking. There seems to have been a considerable degree of intelligence and planning about which we can only speculate.

Æthelweard's reference to an English attack on the Northumbrians as they crossed the Severn at *Cwatbrycge*, if indeed we should attach any credibility to that part of his account.

Yet another possibility, which would accord with Æthelweard's *Chronicon*, is that the English, in the knowledge that the Northumbrians (albeit Danes, not Hiberno-Norse) had used the Severn crossing at *Cwatbrycge* in the past, lay in wait for the Northumbrians at some suitable place nearby[2493] and launched an ambush on the enemy (perhaps as they were encamped at the fortification at *Cwatbrycge*) to drive them east from the Severn towards the West Saxon forces, though it is difficult to envisage fleeing Northumbrians, even unburdened by their pack animals and carts which they will surely have abandoned, outpacing English forces to reach Wednesfield before being forced to make a stand and take on the English.

Yet if we can rely on the chronicle accounts, the most straightforward scenario is that the combined West Saxon and Mercian armies crossed to the west side of the river Severn and tracked the Northumbrian forces until they caught up with them and harassed them them from the rear after they had encamped at *Cwatbrycge* to drive them eastwards before battle was joined at Wednesfield, possibly close to the Roman road running south-east from Water Eaton on Watling Street.

Why (if we are to believe every part of Æthelweard's account, which may be unwise) there may have been an interval between any initial attack at *Cwatbrycge* and the battle at Wednesfield is now impossible to explain, and possible xplanations are all flawed, but we can be certain that the Northumbrians, knowing that they were isolated far from friendly territory, will have been desperate to avoid an engagement with the full weight of two English armies, and realised that were fleeing for their lives. Likewise, the English forces, with no hope of reinforcements, would have been equally apprehensive about a full-scale battle against a sizeable army of well-armed Northumbrians, even if the English were numerically far superior. This was a confrontation between two heavily-armed forces where the stakes for each could not be higher, and the outcome was far from a foregone conclusion. The likelihood of emissaries from the two sides attempting to formulate some sort of negotiated settlement must be improbable: the English had little choice but to take a heaven sent opportunity to annihilate the greatest threat to their two kingdoms.[2494] A more likely explanation is that Æthelweard has, for whatever reason – perhaps a misunderstanding of his sources – condensed events, not realising that Wednesfield lies many miles from the Severn, or that his source was similarly confused. But the reality is that however much we might theorise, we can never know the precise sequence of events leading up to the great battle, which must remain a matter of frustrated conjecture.

The above scenarios surrounding the events leading up to the battle of Tettenhall are of course unsupported by evidence, and based upon speculation – the fact that *portstrete* and *alde strete*, for example, intersect at Wednesfield, which is named by some of the early

---

[2493] The earthworks known as The Walls at Chesterton (which lie on a Roman road from the south-east) some five miles north-west of Quatford and close to any route likely to be taken by the Danes after crossing the Severn would have been very suitable.

[2494] It will be remembered that according to *Egil's Saga* (the value of which as historical evidence is disputed), at the battle of *Brunanburh* in 937 the English marked out the battlefield was hazel poles, and it was only after days of prolonged negotiations which came to nothing that a battle took place: Pálsson and Edwards 1976: 118-25.

chroniclers as the site of the battle, may be no more than coincidence – and coincidences must always be a fearsome beartrap for historians. Yet so far as the idea that the battle may have taken place on or close to a routeway is concerned, we might consider the views (admittedly to be treated with considerable caution) of the battlefield historian A. H. Burne, who, having considered several Anglo-Saxon battles, writes of the site of the battle of *Brunanburh* which took place in 937: 'The position should ... be astride of the road by which [King Æthelstan] was advancing. [This feature] seem[s] common to all Anglo-Saxon battles of which the sites can be identified. ... I believe armies in those days were more wedded to existing roads than we are apt to imagine... So I attach considerable importance to ... a position [of a battlefield] astride a road ...'.[2495] That opinion is reinforced by more detailed research recently published by M. C. Bishop which is supported by a full analysis of Anglo-Saxon and other battles.[2496] As noted elsewhere, the suspected routes of a number of lost Roman roads branching from the principal Roman settlement at *Pennocrucium* appear to have run separately through Wrottesley Park Farm, Wrottesley Park, Upper Pendeford Farm, and Wednesfield (perhaps on the line of *portstrete* mentioned above), together embracing a wide arc from the west to the east of Wolverhampton, including both Tettenhall and Wolverhampton.

[*This study assumes that the English and Northumbrian forces spent the night before the conflict bivouaced at or near the site of the battle, but it is feasible that the two forces engaged when they came within sight of each other (as seems to have occurred at Hastings, though in that case each side was fully aware of the existence of the other), with the joint English forces, probably many times the size of the Scandinavian raiding party, simply sweeping down onto an unsuspecting enemy from several directions in a carefully orchestrated ambush at some carefully chosen location. That scenario may possibly be hinted at by Æthelweard who writes that the English 'joined battle without protracted delay'.[2497] Or the two forces may have camped some distance from the battlefield before the conflict took place. In either case the following scenario would need to be adjusted or heavily revised as necessary*].

Wherever the conflict took place, we are ignorant of even basic details of how the armies may have spent the night before the battle – whether one or both of the English armies or the Northumbrian forces spent it on the battlefield itself; what the sleeping arrangements were; what food was eaten and whether and where it was cooked, and by whom; what form any camp kitchens and utensils may have taken; what tentage and bedding (if any) was provided; and so on, but it is not difficult to imagine that warriors accustomed to discomfort will have had little rest, and the English forces will have spent at least some of the time hearing prayers from churchmen travelling with the army, with veteran warriors encouraging their younger inexperienced companions, and even perhaps professional *scops* reciting legendary and uplifting poetic stories, perhaps accompanied by musicians, although given the nature of the campaign, that may be a romanticised picture totally divorced from the harsh reality of the difficult conditions endured by conscripted warriors far from home about to confront a savage and merciless enemy. The English leaders will have had splendidly decorated tents, perhaps of leather, furnished in considerable luxury, for displays of wealth, even on military campaign, were expected at this period. Rank-and-file warriors may have been provided with lesser, relatively simple accommodation in

---

[2495] Burne 2002: 74-6.
[2496] Bishop 2014: 150-62.
[2497] Campbell 1962: 53.

linen tents of different sizes proofed with grease.[2498] If armour was a communal commodity carried with the tentage and other necessities it will have been distributed to the fighters, but many may have carried their own armour.[2499] Sunset on that day will have been about 8.45, but few will have taken to their beds at that time, perhaps their last night on earth.

Like warriors before and since, fighters on both sides will have been fearful about surviving the coming conflict as they gathered around camp fires, lingered over whatever rations had been made available from the camp kitchens or plundered en route, and nervously sharpened their spears and swords, ritually checked and re-checked their war gear, and made strained jokes and remembered past conflictsin an attempt to encourage their more fearful and nervous colleagues, many little more than juveniles. Waiting has always been the worst time for those facing battle. Their fears, hardly lessened by thoughts of the wealth they would share in any victory, will have been justified at a time when trivial flesh wounds and relatively minor internal injuries could become infection-riddled life-threatening abscesses, though we might suppose that natural resistence to infection will probably have been higher in the Anglo-Saxon period when all sections of society were exposed from birth to rancid and putrid food, contaminated drink and abysmal standards of hygiene. Those who survived childhood might expect to live into adulthood. Even if warriors survived their battlefield wounds, those who became disabled and unable to work could be reduced to destitution and know that their families might starve. The English troops will have been all too aware that with no possibility of reinforcements reaching them, that the Northumbrians would prove an especially ferocious enemy.

While many, if not most, Danes in the Christianised kingdom of York had probably adopted Christianity of a sort by this date, the Hiberno-Norse of the north-west were still militantly pagan.[2500] Indeed, we know that Osfrith, one of the Northumbrian leaders who died in the battle, had the byname *Hlytta*, which may have meant 'diviner, soothsayer',[2501] perhaps indicating the presence of a high-ranking pagan practitioner.[2502] If we cannot know to which gods they made have addressed their prayers and whether any sacrifices may have been made, we can guess that Woden was certain to have been one to whom they addressed their invocations. And the English leaders will have tried not to dwell on tales of barbaric Scandinavian tortures such as the legendary blood-eagle, as recorded for example in the twelfth-century *Orkneyinga Saga* which tells how in the last decade of the

---

[2498] Flax was widely cultivated in the Anglo-Saxon period: the OE word for flax was *līn*, and *līnen* meant 'made of flax': Clark Hall 1960: 220.

[2499] According to Æthelweard, at the battle of Farnham in 893 the forces of Alfred's son Edward included young men who 'slipped on their armour [*armis irrepti*]' and attacked the Danes, forcing them to flee: Campbell 1962: 49. However, *armis* could also mean 'weapons', and *irrepti* seems to have had the sense of 'sneak into', with *induo* meaning 'to slip on clothing' (Ashworth 1830; 327, 398), so the translation is not certain.

[2500] Richards 2003: 383. Paganism lasted for some decades or more with the Hiberno-Norse: Sihtric Cáech, the Hiberno-Norse king of York from 920, met Æthelstan at Tamworth on 30 January 926, when he sealed an accord recognising Æthelstan's superiority by accepting Christian baptism and marrying Æthelstan's sister, sometimes (probably wrongly: Sargent 2016) said to be Eadgyth, but soon after renounced his wife and reverted to paganism: Williams, Smyth and Kirby 1991: 215-6. Presumably 'Eadgyth' returned to Mercia: the *Book of Hyde* records her burial at Tamworth: Edwards 1866: 111.

[2501] Whitelock 1955: 193 fn.5.

[2502] Tacitus mentions horses kept in sacred groves, believed to be confidants of the gods, and used to predict battles: Owen 1981 citing Mattingly 1948: 10. Presumably the process involved high priests or soothsayers.

ninth century the son of king Haraldr of Norway was captured by the Scandinavian ruler of Orkney, Einarr, who 'carved the bloody eagle on his back by laying his sword in the hollow at the backbone and hacking all the ribs from the backbone down to the loins, and drawing out the lungs; and he gave him to Óðinn as an offering for his victory'.[2503] All had much to fear in the coming conflict. Both sides will have heard tales of atrocities reportedly committed by the foe, none perhaps exaggerated.

The night could hardly have been darker – a new moon would appear two days later[2504] – and sunrise on the Sunday morning of the battle will have been at 5.30, though most combatants doubtless enjoyed only fitful sleep – perhaps their last ever. The reek of stale sweat and soiled clothing – most combatants wearing apparel probably unremoved for days or even weeks – will have gone unnoticed to those long accustomed to both, and body lice will have been no more than – literally – a lifelong minor irritation. Unless the weather had remained fine, virtually everything will have been sodden.

What cooking and eating arrangements were made for an Anglo-Saxon army are unrecorded, as is the food made available before battles, but the lower ranks – those with any appetite – perhaps queued at one or more feeding points, or from carts moving amongst the fighters, for coarse loaves[2505] served with boiled meat (probably pork, beef, mutton or goat), a particular luxury for those on campaign, with some form of gruel or pottage (cereals or pulses boiled with vegetables or other flavourings), probably in turned sycamore bowls (which would not taint food), perhaps with eggs and cheese, supplemented by weak ale in wooden or horn beakers,[2506] representing the staple fare for the rank-and-file. The leaders will have been far better served, as befitted their status, with benches and tables, even if only lighter campaign furniture, and appetising food and wine in vessels of pottery or even precious metals: in 806 Charlemagne required that supplies and equipment of the king when on campaign were to be carried in carts, as were those of bishops, counts, abbots and nobles, and were to include flour, wine, pork and victuals in abundance, as well as a huge variety of specialist tools and equipment, and each count was required to provide fodder for the use of the army.[2507] Warfare took up a significant part of a ruler's life, and we can imagine well-established arrangements were in place to ensure that the necessities and indeed many luxuries were available to field forces and their leaders.

What sanitary arrangements, if any, will have existed are unknown: throughout history few accounts of warfare choose to mention such niceties, about which we are left to guess, but almost certainly far more unpleasant than we can possibly imagine. One matter most histories gloss over is the sheer stench of times past, especially surrounding armies and on battlefields, with dysentery and similar disorders rife given the lack of hygiene, putrid food, and polluted watercourses and ponds used for drinking when ale was unavailable.[2508]

[2503] Anderson 1922: 390; Smyth 1977: 191; Smyth 1984: 153-4.
[2504] Astropixels.com/ephemeris/phasecat/phases0901.html.
[2505] Loaves were generally of rye and barley, sometimes supplemented with beans and acorns in times of poor harvest. Wheat loaves were normally available only in the south: Niles 2009: 376.
[2506] Beer with hops as a preservative is recorded from the 9th century, but was not to become widespread for some centuries.
[2507] McKitterick 2008: 228, 272-3.
[2508] Notables amongst the vast numbers who died from dysentery included King John (18 October 1216) and Sir Francis Drake (27 January 1596).

We know nothing about what communication, if any, may have been made between the opposing military forces before the armies met, or how such communications may have been made, and we cannot even speculate about the likelihood of negotiations, or their subject matter, that may have taken place between enemy leaders on the day of battle,[2509] though research has shown that both English and Scandinavians are likely to have understood to a limited degree the language of the other,[2510] and interpreters may not have been required. As noted above, it is very possible that prior to the conflict envoys from both sides were in contact well before the armies reached the battlefield, and/or immediately prior to the battle. The presence of any Englishmen fighting with the Northumbrians would of course have made communication straightforward. Whatever the case, any negotiations which may have taken place evidently failed, and a military engagement became inevitable.

What procedure (if any) was traditionally adopted to begin a battle we do not know; nor when battle may have started, if there were indeed a 'normal' time. Daybreak or sunrise would have been obvious times, but we have no evidence to suggest that this was the case, though each side will have been ready to take on the enemy at short notice – neither side will have taken the risk of being attacked whilst unprepared. Tacit understandings may have existed that battle proper would not be joined until both sides had indicated their readiness.

Taking the generally-accepted view that mounted forces were not used when fighting by either side in the conflict (an assumption that may be misplaced), each army will have ensured that its baggage-train and horses were secured and well guarded, presumably a short distance from the field of battle, for it would be critically important for warriors who realised that their forces were about to be overwhelmed to have a ready means of escape: whatever the code of loyalty emphasised in poems and sagas of the time, in which warriors supposedly fought to the death in support of their lord, for there is ample evidence of fighters and their leaders fleeing the battlefield.

It would have made good sense for the captured booty carried by the Northumbrians to be secured by them with the horses, though many warriors could have chosen to keep silver, coin and other easily portable loot with them (assuming it had by then been shared out),

---

[2509] The author of the OE poem *The Battle of Maldon*, fought in 991, and which has indeed been compared in some respects with the battle of Tettenhall (Abels 1991: 148-9), records in detail dramatic conversations before the fateful engagement between a Viking messenger and Byrhtnoth, commander of the Anglo-Saxon army, asking for tribute from the English (which is scornfully refused), and for leave to cross unopposed a narrow causeway which the English can easily defend (which is, perhaps imprudently, granted): see generally Scragg 1991. Again, in *Egil's Saga*, written in about 1230, we are told that before the battle of *Brunanburh* in 937, messengers were sent from King Æthelstan to the enemy challenging them to a pitched battle, adding that the king wanted no plundering of his kingdom, and that whoever won should rule England. The battle was to be fought in a week's time, and whichever army arrived first should wait up to one week for the other. It was said to be the custom in those days that once a field of battle had been declared for a king, he could not honourably wage war until that battle had been fought. The enemy agreed those terms, ensured there was no looting, and waited for the appointed day before moving their army to the battlefield, the extent of which had been marked out by hazel rods by the English, but further discussions followed between the two leaders via envoys for some days before negotiations broke down and battle commenced: Pálsson and Edwards 1976: 118-22. We cannot know to what extent these authors were reflecting what actually happened – the *Maldon* poem is of uncertain date, and in the case of *Egil's Saga* the author was writing almost three centuries after the event.
[2510] Thompson 2002: 4, 29, citing Townend 2000: 90; Townend 2002.

even if that made fighting more difficult. Possibly there were long-standing conventions as to the disposition and security of booty if the warband met an enemy – perhaps all valuables were kept close to the kings, under their banners, so that warriors defending their leaders were also protecting their personal wealth – but the sources are silent, and if such conventions existed we cannot know their details.

We have no information about preaching or prayers which may have taken place before battles at this period, but it is said that both Frankish and English kings always took their religious relics or a portable shrine with them on their travels, even when they went into battle[2511] – one is reminded of the great gold cross, embellished with four large garnets, and the silver gilt strip bearing the beligerent Biblical inscription in Latin *[S]urge d[omi]ne [et] disepentur inimici tui et fugent qui oderunt te a facie tua* ('Rise up, O Lord, and may Thy enemies be scattered and those who hate Thee flee from Thy face') from the astonishing Staffordshire Hoard, perhaps dating from c.650-670, found in 2009 only seven miles from Wednesfield[2512] – and a communal blessing incorporating the traditional morale-boosting assurance to the assembled warriors that God was on their side will almost certainly have been given by one of the churchmen (perhaps even a bishop: William of Malmesbury tells how the bishop of Ramsbury, a former soldier who had fought for Edward the Elder, accompanied Æthelstan in the *Brunanburh* campaign in 937 'to fire his spirit in times of success and to put things right when misfortune occurred')[2513] travelling with the English forces, given the staunchly Christian leaders of both Wessex and Mercia.[2514] At the very least prayers were addressed specifically to the saints, including in particular Oswald, Mercia's most favoured Christian martyr, on whose special day battle was to be joined.

We have seen that if the chroniclers are to be relied upon the Northumbrians at Tettenhall must have been Hiberno-Scandinavians from the north-west, rather than Christianised, if not Christian, Danish forces from York, but it is unsafe to rely on the chroniclers' claims about the religious beliefs of either group: it must be remembered that they were writing long after the event; the earliest, Æthelweard, and Byrhtferth of Ramsey, author of the *Annals of St Neots*, some three or four generations after the battle, and the others centuries later, and *pagani* may have come to mean Scandinavians, whatever their religion, when all Scandinavians may have been mythologised as pagan savages, or the term was used as a convenient slur 'when no longer strictly descriptive'.[2515] As we have seen, the name of one of the dead protagonists at Tettenhall, *Osferd*, had the nickname *hlytte*, 'soothsayer,

---

[2511] Deansley 1961: 336-7.
[2512] The implication is that the cross, the epigraphy of which remains the subject of continuing academic debate – it may conceivably date to a later period than the bulk of the hoard – had some military association, perhaps being carried into battle. The first record of a warrior bishop fighting with English armies is bishop Ealhstan of Sherborne who acted as Egbert's general in Kent in 825, and who was one of the commanders who defeated the Danes on the river Parret in 845 and in 858 took a leading part in supplanting Ethelwulf by his son Ethelbald. Two West Saxon prelates fell in the battle of Charmouth in 835: Stubbs 1880: 236-7; Nelson 1999: I 66, fn105. Bishop Heahmund of Sherborne was killed at the battle of Merton in 870: Swanton 1996: 71-2. Only six years before Tettenhall, Abbot Cenwulf was killed at the battle of the Holme c.903: Swanton 1996: 95.
[2513] Preest 2002: 15.
[2514] The bishop of Lichfield in August 910 appears to have been Wigmund or Wilferth (unmentioned in Wharton 1691: 432), who acceded between 889 and 900, and died between 903 and 915 – possibly but probably not at the battle of Tettenhall; the bishop of Worcester was Waerfrith, who acceded in 873; and the bishop of Hereford was Eadgar, who acceded between 888 and 901: Powicke and Fryde 1961: 229, 233, 260, with recent amendments.
[2515] Abrams 2001a: 32.

diviner, one who divines by casting lots', perhaps implying a pagan practitioner, possibly even a high priest.

The beliefs of the pagans has been well studied, and even though the Danes based at York were nominally Christian,[2516] as polytheists many will have initially accepted Christ simply as one more god to be worshipped alongside the traditional deities. Pagans believed that half of those who died in combat, as selected by Odin, travelled to Valhalla, led by valkyries, while the other half went to the goddess Freyja's field *Fólkvangr*. In Valhalla (from Old Norse *Valhöll* 'hall of the slain') the dead would join the masses of those who had fallen in combat, including legendary Germanic heroes and kings, to spend the night feasting with other warriors before fighting alongside the gods at Ragnarok. Those who died in their beds went to Hel. Since the English chronicler Æthelweard tells us that the enemy kings slain at Tettenhall 'hastened to the hall of the infernal one', with the *Annals of St Neots* referring to 'the kings of the heathens', Henry of Huntingdon describing them 'the faithless Danes', and Roger of Wendover and Matthew Paris calling them 'the pagan kings', it is clear that those writers were in no doubt as to the pagan beliefs of the Northumbrian forces at Tettenhall. If that were the case, the Scandinavians at Tettenhall, probably pagan Hiberno-Norse, could well have begun the day by formally dedicating the enemy dead to Óðinn, just as in the 980s the Swedish King Erik the Victorious dedicated the army of his enemy Styrbjörn to Óðinn before a battle near Uppsala, and any such dedication before the fight at Tettenhall may have been accompanied by a ritual sacrifice.[2517]

We can be sure that like warriors throughout the ages, fighters from both sides, pagan or Christian, will have ensured that their irreplaceable sentimental keepsakes or devotional talismans, carried with certain belief of protection in battle, were secure from the devastating possibility of loss on the battlefield, feared perhaps even more than injury or death itself.

We cannot know whether the leader's stereotypical stirring speech to the troops, recorded in connection with battles throughout history and in almost every case probably a later invention, may have been made before the conflict, but declaiming or reciting heroic verse to incite warriors to martial deeds was supposedly the practice in many medieval communities, as by tradition in the case of the battle of Hastings when the warrior-*jongleur* Taillefer is said to have sung the traditional *Song of Roland* before the fighting began.

[2516] An early Danish ruler of York, Guthfrith, who became king c.882 and died in 895, became a Christian with the support of the Abbot of Carlisle, seemingly in a ceremony which incorporated pagan Scandinavian customs with Christian tradition. Guthfrith was evidently on good terms with the community of St Cuthbert, which he encouraged to return from exile and settled at Chester-le-Street c.883, and at his death in 895 he was buried beneath York minster: Owen 1981: 175-6; Fletcher 1997: 392. The archbishopric of York was held by Æthelbeald in 900, and by Hrothweard from some date between 904 and 928 until 931 (Powicke and Fryde 1961: 263), and while little is known about the see during these years, the Viking age cemetery under the minster shows uninterrupted Christianity within the city (Hindley 2006: 202). The Siefred/Cnut coins issued in York at the turn of the ninth century contain Christian crosses, and some even contain Christian inscriptions: *Mirabilia fecit* ('He has done marvellous things'), and *Dominus deus omnipotens rex* ('Lord God, almighty King'). From 905 coinage from the mint at York Minster (the church of St Peter), carried for some ten years Christian legends that abbreviate the Latin *Sancti Petri Moneta* ('St Peter's money'): Bailey 1980: 42; Logan 1991: 171. The most recent proposals suggest that the issue came to an end when the Norse pagan Ragnall captured York in 919.

[2517] Branston 1974: 39. Adam of Bremen, writing in the second half of the eleventh century, confirms the Swedish practice of sacrificing to Óðinn before hostilities, and such ritual may well have been a significant feature for a Danish army wintering in England: Smyth 1977: 223.

Other similar instances are attested in both French and Germanic tradition, and indeed certain texts of the Welsh Law of Hywel prescibe that the song *Unbeiniaeth Prydain* ('The Sovereignty of Britain') should be sung before going into battle.[2518]

Since the only extended description of an English army engaged in combat against the Scandinavians is the famous poem *The Battle of Maldon* (of uncertain date and origin) describing events in August 991, described as 'a work of literary imagination, heavily influenced by the convention of heroic poetry',[2519] and probably of doubtful historical value, we have little information about Anglo-Saxon battles. Nevertheless, Æthelweard tells us that on the battlefield at Tettenhall the English formed a 'battle-order',[2520] presumably the classic shield-wall of the time.[2521] Each army, with its forces split into divisions – Old English terms such as *eóred-heáp*, *eóred-þreát*, *eóred-weorod*, *scild-truma*, *truma* and *weorod* may have carried a much more precise meaning than simply 'troop' and 'company', which is how they are generally translated today[2522] – will have arrayed the first lines of its warriors, all fighting on foot, in close-formed ranks facing the enemy, with shields interlocked and spears pointing forwards.[2523] The *ealdormen* and other senior officers may have been on horseback to better enable them to see how the battle was developing and to give orders, but the vulnerabilty of horsemen to unseating by the enemy makes it more likely perhaps that they were on foot, like their troops. Some of those troops, like their leaders, could have been protected by mail tunics, but probably only the leaders would have worn simple conical iron helmets (others may have worn domed or conical helmets of hardened leather), and many – perhaps most – of the Northumbrian warriors will have been wearing mailshirts, based very much on the Frankish model. One area on which we have little evidence is footwear: curiously, some contemporary illustrations seem to show barefoot warriors, as well as ploughmen and other outdoor workers,[2524] though it must be improbable that warriors engaged in battle unshod.

The leaders of the English forces (perhaps with ealdorman Osferth leading the West Saxon army and ealdorman Athelfrith heading the Mercians) are probably positioned towards the front of their forces, possibly using portable platforms – perhaps their supply carts – to provide a better field of view, each with a personal retinue of bodyguards, for leaders will have been especially targeted by the enemy. Any clerics could have been in the same group, with special ceremonial battle-crosses, perhaps inscribed with suitably militaristic wording like the inscribed gold fragment from the Staffordshire Hoard. The Northumbrian

---

[2518] Jarman 1990: lxxxi.
[2519] Abels 1991: 147.
[2520] Campbell 1962: 53.
[2521] The poem *The Battle of Brunanburh*, written at the close of the tenth century to celebrate the great victory of Æthelstan over a formidable coalition of Constantine II of Scotland, Owain of Strathclyde and Olaf Guthfrithsson from Dublin in 937, includes the expression *bord-weal*, 'wall of shields', and Asser's description of the battle of Ashdown in 871 describes the two Viking armies and the two West-Saxon armies each forming shield-walls: Keynes and Lapidge 1983: 79. For a warrior to sling his shield onto his back during battle was apparently regarded as particularly heroic: Nicolle 1995: 78.
[2522] Lawson 2003: 168.
[2523] It has been suggested that in battle the Vikings formed a phalanx of men five or more ranks deep with the better-armed and armoured warriors forming the front ranks: Chartrand et al 2006: 92. It is worth noting that recent commentators have concluded that the concept of the *comitatus*, found in literary and poetic contexts to describe 'a group of usually young, male, suicidally loyal thegns who are devoted to a lord and serve him in a peripatetic retinue', is almost certainly a chimera: Harris 2015.
[2524] See for example Webster 2012: 180.

leaders, like their English counterparts with their personal guards, were probably also on foot. To what extent the leaders of each side wore their gold adornments and other signs of rank on the battlefield is unknown: the *Maldon* poem tells us that Earl Byrhtnoth, aged at least 60,[2525] was wearing his armrings, gold bands and robe, as well as his ornamented sword, during the fateful battle,though how much reliance can be placed on the poem continues to be debated,[2526] and it must be doubtful whether any leader will have impeded his fighting ability by wearing restrictive clothing and carrying weighty adornments which would not only prove a highly visible target for the enemy, but fetter movement and hasten exhaustion, perhaps one of the greatest issues faced by fighters in battle.

Expensively produced swords with double-edged pattern-welded blades, often with gold pommels inset with garnets, were a sign of rank, carried by nobles and other leaders, but wear on the sword-fittings from the Staffordshire Hoard might suggest in most cases they were status symbols reserved for ceremonial use rather than for hard use in battle. By the early tenth century improved manufacturing techniques had led to the production in larger quantities of utilitarian swords which were lighter and tougher, but equally effective as weapons,[2527] and many of the troops at the battle of Tettenhall may have been armed with such weapons, as well as seaxes, the Anglo-Saxon single-edged knife, similar to a Gurkha khukri, and an assortment of utilitarian weapons such as axes, hatchets, maces, clubs, cudgels, daggers, and crude handled-blades and spikes – anything, indeed, simple to manufacture, carry and handle and could inflict grievous injuries on an enemy, especially in close-quarter fighting.[2528]

Warriors on both sides are likely to have been chanting war-cries – what seems to be an unexplained Scandinavian battle-cry *núi nú* is recorded[2529] – shouting oaths and earthily obscene insults, taunting the enemy, doubtless screaming choruses of rousingly patriotic anthems, rhythmically banging their shields with their weapons to un-nerve and intimidate the enemy and to encourage the flow of adrenalin, masking their own nerves. Possibly some sort of alcoholic drink or drugs such as hallucinogenic fungi were available to mask fear, increase aggression, and dull the pain from injuries. It must not be forgotten that large numbers of soldiers in combat will soil themselves as part of the inborn fight-or-flight response.[2530] One telling and unusually candid observation recorded in the *Anglo-Saxon Chronicle* for 1003 describes Ealdorman Ælfric, leader of an English army, claiming illness and feigning vomiting as soon as the enemy came in sight, charitably interpreted by the chronicler as some unexplained cunning ruse,[2531] but we may prefer to treat the incident at face value and see it as a rational physical response to imminent involvement in particularly violent butchery.[2532]

[2525] Pollington 2001: 82.
[2526] Scragg 1991: 14-5, 24-5, 34-5.
[2527] Pollington 1989: 157.
[2528] William of Poitiers records how at the battle of Hastings the first wave of the Norman advance against the English was repulsed by the English host using various weapons and missiles including 'stones tied to sticks', and one is reminded of 'trench clubs' fashioned from chair legs studded with nails which were widely used in close-quarters fighting in the trenches during the First World War.
[2529] Wainwright 1975: 149.
[2530] Walsh 2014, which cites a study of over 2,000 servicemen in the South Pacific during the Second World War, of whom hundreds reported involuntary defecation as well as unrination.
[2531] ASC 'E' and 'F': Swanton 1996: 134-5.
[2532] Given tortures such as the notorious 'blood-eagle' inflicted by the Scandinvians on their enemies (discussed elsewhere in this colume), English leaders had much to fear.

In heathen and early Christian times it had been customary for a single warrior to hurl his spear over the heads of the opposing forces as a signal that the fighting should begin. That may have occurred at the battle of Tettenhall, for it is thought to have been common practice with the Vikings well into the medieval period,[2533] but other signals may have been recognised, such as the sounding of a horn (*Egil's Saga*, admittedly of doubtful historical value, mentions a war-horn used before the armies assembled for the battle of *Brunanburh*)[2534] or the raising of a banner, or indeed there may have been no formalities before hostilities began: the conflict commenced when one side launched an attack on the other. Whatever the means of ignition, the conflagration bursts into life, marked by each side moving in ranks closer to the enemy, the raising of banners and the launch from both sides of a fusillade of throwing darts or light spears over the heads of the leading ranks of the enemy into the body of the opposing force. Doubtless missiles as crude as stones and rocks were also hurled by skilled throwers into the enemy troops: many on both sides will have been proficient from an early age in the use of slings, widely illustrated in contemporary manuscripts and an underrated weapon of surprising accuracy, still used in urban warfare today. Slingshot could have been used with devastating consequences some distance from the opposing force, well before it came within spear range. Vast quantities of light spears, stones and missiles will have been carried to the battlesite and issued to the English forces; the Northumbrians, travelling light in raiding-party mode and not anticipating a major engagement with the enemy, were certainly far less well equiped to respond in kind.

At this point we might wonder whether one or both of the opposing forces may have unleashed (quite literally) a fearsome weapon: the war-dog or battle-hound – a concept enthusiastically endorsed by modern writers of historical fiction and film-makers[2535] – which could have been specifically trained to attack enemies on the battlefield.[2536] Such beasts, straining at their leashes, would have intimidated and created panic in the opposing force, and though far easier to kill than an adult human, would be of considerable psychological value to their handlers and their compatriots. Hunting was an important element in the life of the higher echelons of Anglo-Saxon England (and also, though to a lesser extent, in the Viking world), and hunting dogs, trained to bring down game, are well-recorded in the Anglo-Saxon period and are pictured in the Bayeux Tapestry. Dog skeletons or parts are found frequently in Anglo-Saxon burials, and occasionally in Viking graves,[2537] but despite good evidence that war-dogs were used in battle elsewhere by other early societies,[2538] they are completely unmentioned in contemporary Anglo-Saxon texts,

---

[2533] Pollington 1989: 140-1.
[2534] Pálsson and Edwards 1976: 122.
[2535] See for example 'The Last Kingdom' series of books by Bernard Cornwell.
[2536] For a rare reference from the late 10th century to hounds attacking a rider see Lavelle 2010: 290-1.
[2537] See for example various references in Brink and Price 2012. Dogs seem to have been far more common in Anglo-Saxon society than in Viking society.
[2538] See, for example, Karunanithy 2008 and Crabtree 2103, the former discussing, inter alia, the war dogs of the Celtic peoples and of ancient Egypt and the Middle East. Archaeological evidence shows that in the later Anglo-Saxon period the largest type of dog would have been about the size of a large modern Alsatian and resembled a modern deer-hound. These would have been used for hunting, fighting, or as guard-dogs, with smaller dogs, perhaps the size of a modern collie, used as sheep-dogs, and even smaller dogs to keep down rats and as lap-dogs. There seem to have been no recognised breeds, with all dogs classed as 'mongrels' (from OE *gemong* 'mingling'), but certain traits and characteristics were selected for breeding. The general OE word for a dog was *hund* (and equivalent ON *hundr*), which by the twelfth century had narrowed to mean a dog used for hunting. Curiously, the origin of the word 'dog' remains uncertain. The late, rare, OE word *docga* is recorded,

poems and artwork and by modern accounts of early medieval, and even later, warfare.[2539] This might be seen as evidence that the aggressive characteristics that could be developed in breeds such as the modern Rottweiler were not found in dogs of the later Anglo-Saxon period, but it is far from inconceivable – though admittedly unlikely – that experienced dog-handlers, perhaps professional hunters, and purpose-trained war-dogs may have had some role in Anglo-Saxon (and perhaps Viking) armies.

On the battlefield the fateful encounter in which the violent resolution of one side was to face the savage determination of the other evolves into barely-controlled fury. Probably with forces held in reserve, each side continues its advance up to the shield-wall of the enemy, moving methodically but decisively to ensure cohesion is maintained. To what extent the maintenance of the shield-wall was seen to be of critical importance in battles of the period, with the breach or collapse of an army's shield-wall traditionally indicative of imminent defeat, is unclear, but it is certainly widely recorded in poetic tradition. Asser records of the battle of Ashdown in 871 that 'the Pagans, dividing into two bands, prepared shield walls of equal size – for they had two kings and many earls – giving the middle part of the army to the two kings and the other to all the earls. The Christians [under Alfred and his brother Æthelred] seeing this also divided their army into two bands in precisely [the same way] and formed their shield walls no less swiftly'.[2540] At Maldon in 991 the Danes and English (if the poem is to be believed) formed opposing shield walls and the battle took the form of a number of clashes between the two formations – each clash preceded by an exchange of missiles.[2541] Wace writes of the battle of Hastings that the Normans advanced against the English 'in close order at their slow pace [*sereement, lor petit*

---

evidently deriving from *docce*, 'muscle', with the suffix *-ga* (also found in *frocga* 'frog' and *picga* 'pig', but why *docga* displaced the native *hund* remains unexplained. What is certain is that by the 16th century *dogge* was the common word for a canine. Good hounds were valued both as working animals and as companions and were often given as gifts by the *æþeling*-class: Alfred the Great, for example, sent a gift of a pair of fine hounds to the archbishop of Reims. The Laws of Hywel Dda (Hywel the Good), king of Deheubarth in south-west Wales in the 10th century and friend of King Æthelstan, record that 'the value of the king's deer-hound is 240d when trained, 120d untrained, 60d when 1 year old, 30d when a puppy in the kennel, and 15d from time of birth to when it opens its eyes.' The same Laws state that the king's greyhound, if trained, is worth 120d, and his lapdog 240d. Conversely, a free-holder's deer-hound or lap-dog is valued at 120d. A 'foreigner's' lap dog is, however, valued at only 4d, the same value put on a 'common house dog'. Furthermore 'whatever dog a stranger may possess, its value shall be the same as that of a 'dung-hill dog', i.e. 4 pence. It has been calculated that the 'hundgild' for the king's prize hunting-dog might represent at least £2,500 in modern terms.The remains of dogs are often found in Anglo-Saxon sites, usually from middens, but dog skeletons are not uncommon in pagan Anglo-Saxon graves, and have been held to be beloved pets accompanying their master or mistress to the next world. Similarly, Viking graves often contain one or more dogs. The Tjängvide image stone from Gotland clearly shows the arrival of a dead warrior into Valhalla. He is met by a Valkyrie, bearing a mead-horn, but behind her waits the warrior's faithful hound. The poetic Eddas record that the dog Garmr guarded the entrance to the underworld, as depicted on the Tjängvide monument. Dogs were found in large numbers in the Vendel Age graves in Sweden. By the Viking Age, fewer dogs are found in each grave. The Oseberg ship burial contained four dog skeletons despatched to accompany their mistress. The Gokstad ship contained six dogs interred with their master. The Ladby ship-burial on Funen, Denmark, contained the skeletons of four dogs and, most tellingly, a gilded bronze dog lead decorated in Jelling Style. The custom of sending a person's dogs with them to the afterlife must have been common.

[2539] Although a reference to two battle-hounds is found in the early Welsh poem Gododdin, centred on the battle of Catterick c.600, the expression is used in a poetic sense for two named warriors Jarman 1990: 16.
[2540] Asser 2002: 18.
[2541] Manley 1985: 225, who cites conflicting views about the historical value of the poem.

pas]'.[2542] Victory may have been determined by whichever side could best hold its nerve and endure a long and bloody mêlée. Indeed, there are claims, possibly apocryphal, that two forces could be locked in battle for hours, shield-wall to shield-wall, until one side breached its opponents' defences.[2543]

Hand-to-hand fighting will have followed any breach in the shield-wall, and we must imagine a violent and bloody clash with war-cries and shouts mixed with the sound of sword against bone, spear against flesh, with screams, wails, oaths, curses, cries, shrieks, moans and mumbled prayers from warriors with grievous wounds. Mild-mannered companionable warriors will have become roaring, bellicose, half-crazed animals, clubbing, stabbing, thrusting, impaling, beating, lunging, skewering, gouging, punching, biting, clawing, flailing, maiming and killing to survive, sometimes armed with rage alone. Both sides will have used the ubiquitous spear much as pikes were used in Civil War battles of the seventeenth century: to probe, jab, stab and thrust at any unprotected part of the enemy line, concentrating on the enemies' exposed heads and legs, for legs will have been unprotected, and an enemy brought to the ground could be quickly disarmed and slaughtered. All combatants will have only too aware that minor immobilising injuries to a foot, ankle or leg were likely to end in quick despatch by the enemy, and many will have chosen to continue fighting as best they could with shattered lower limbs and dreadful foot injuries, knowing that to stumble or fall would prove fatal.

The use of long spears, too, will have kept the enemy at a distance. Hurling full-sized spears far into the enemy ranks seems unlikely, for they were not particularly accurate unless used at very close quarters, and once thrown, its owner may have been weaponless. Spears were therefore hurled only when an enemy was at point blank range, with enemies fighting virtually hand-to-hand. Shorter spears could also be used as battle staves, wielded with both hands to deflect enemy blows and cause serious injuries with the iron-shod butt end.

There were probably well-practiced manoeuvres adopted by groups of fighters on the battlefield, but we have little knowledge of these from the written sources. As noted elsewhere, one tactic favoured by the Vikings for breaking through an enemy battle-line was the *svinfylking* or 'swine-array', so-called from its comparison with a charging boar. Experienced troops would form a tight wedge-shaped formation some ten rows deep and charge into the enemy, maintaining formation to force a break in the line of opposing troops. Whether the Northumbrians had any opportunity to carry out the manoeuvre at Tettenhall is of course unknown, but the English, knowing of the ploy, could have isolated and dealt with such a manoevre simply by closing ranks behind the wedge, and indeed are likely on occasion to have adopted the same tactic themselves.[2544] Warfare and violence had long been part of everyday life, and warriors on the battlefield will have been trained from an early age in the mastery of weapons and the finer points of warfare, including group tactics. This was a sophisticated age of learning, literature, poetry, philosophy, laws, religion, ironworking, goldwork, trade, commerce, fine needlework (for which England was famed) and so on, and there is no reason to imagine that the art of war was any less refined.

[2542] Jones 2011: 80.
[2543] Haywood 1995: 84.
[2544] Lavelle 2010: 279.

The battlefield will soon have been littered with the bodies of the wounded, writhing, twisting, shrieking and and moaning, with blood, gore, body parts, broken spears, knives, swords, shields, shoes, clothing and the general detritus of battle. Gruesome sights will have included decapitated corpses, appalling facial mutilations, horrific slash injuries exposing bone, muscle and sinew, severed limbs, exposed entrails and internal organs, dreadfully maimed and shocked fighters staggering but still wielding their weapons.[2545] Adrenelin will have masked the pain of fearful wounds, many combatants unaware that they had suffered injury – even mortal injury – until blood loss led to collapse and rapid death.[2546] Many uninjured fighters will have been severely dehydrated, weakening and breathless, with no hope of respite. The air will have been tainted with the stench of sweat, blood, exposed flesh, brains, urine, vomit and human faeces from eviscerated corpses and those whose bowels had emptied, often from fear alone, before they died,.

Doubtless there were countless acts of despicable cruelty, many of heroic bravery, and even perhaps a few of mercy, with particular savagery reserved for any traitorous Englishmen who might have fought with the Northumbrians.[2547] Fear will have driven some fighters to shameful cowardice. Amid this terrible carnage most warriors – including perhaps the leaders – will have had little idea whether their side was winning or losing, for on level ground their field of vision would have been greatly restricted; concentrating on personal survival and close combat with those of the enemy within striking distance will have been the priority. The superior size of the English forces – many times larger than the Northumbrian force – quickly annihilated much of the enemy raiding army and many, if not most, of its leaders, who were doubtless individually targeted. The disappearance of one or more raised banners held aloft by their compatriots, or the sounding of horns – or their silence – will probably have confirmed to the Northumbrianswhat they feared and expected from the moment they became aware of the strength of the English foe: that their forces were being crushed and it was time to abandon the fight and make an escape.[2548]

At this period, battles could last for hours – at the battle of Ashdown in 871 the entire army of the pagans is said by Asser to have been driven in flight until nightfall and into the following day until they reached the safety of their fortification,[2549] and at the battle of Hastings, exceptionally, there was nearly nine hours of fighting, readily explained by the size of the opposing forces – and were notionally decided according to which army retained possession of the battlefield, regardless of the casualties sustained. Even with its leaders dead an army could claim victory if its forces held the field of battle, as occurred most notably at the Holme just seven years or so earlier. We might imagine the battle of

---

[2545] Examples of skeletal remains from other battles show that some individuals survived horrific injuries, for example the skull of body 16 from the mass grave from the battle of Towton in 1461 showed a blade wound cutting through the lower jaw and teeth on the left side, but the wound had clearly healed and there was no evidence of infection: Jones 2011: 134-5.

[2546] Whilst battles which took place after the introduction of firearms produced terrible injuries, musket ball and bullet generally caused far smaller wounds than those caused in earlier periods by sword, spear and dagger.

[2547] Heroic values and Christian ideals as exemplified on the battlefield have been widely studied: see, for example, O'Keefe 1991 and more recently Abels 2006 and the valuable paper by Stephen J. Harris, 'Complicating the Old English Comitatus', Academia.edu, 24 August 2015.

[2548] The standards illustrated on English coins and the Bayeux Tapestry are small, rectangular or triangular with tassels or ribbons on the trailing edge. The Tapestry shows what seems to be a standard in the form of a flying winged dragon which may be King Harold's personal standard. The horn seems to have played some part in warfare, used for fanfares, alarms, and even for musical purposes: Pollington 2002: 191, 191, 195.

[2549] Smyth 2002: 20.

Tettenhall lasting perhaps one or two hours at most, but almost certainly considerably less – it was impossible for warriors to engage in close combat hand-to-hand fighting for more than a short time before exhaustion set in – and it is clear that the numerically superior English forces managed to destroy many of the enemy and drive the remaining Northumbrians (perhaps the bulk of the enemy forces, since Æthelweard tells us that notwithstanding the death of three kings and many chiefs, jarls and nobles, it was 'the army of the Danes' that fled) from the battlefield to achieve a decisive victory, doubtless signalled by raised standards and the sounds of horns or other loud instrument on the orders of a senior commander having overview of the field of battle.

Whilst the *Mercian Register* gives only the briefest – almost incidental – record of the battle,[2550] most military victories it records are qualified with the words 'by the grace of God' or similar. The absence of any such expression in its terse account of the engagement at Tettenhall implies that victory was not hard won – victory was evidently attributable in large part to the overwhelming might of the English forces, and on this occasion God's help had not been required: St Oswald had repaid those who had so recently honoured his bodily remains.

Surviving English forces doubtless re-assembled around their standards to ensure that they were ready to re-engage the enemy in the unlikely event that the fleeing Northumbrians might regroup to launch a counter offensive. It is very possible (from the speed with which the battle was decided) that the joint English army had been of sufficient size to corner the Northumbrians and force them onto a carefully selected site, perhaps somewhere to the south of Wednesfield, an area bounded by swampy ground and woodland to the east, confident that the difficult terrain would deny the Northumbrians escape routes in that direction, and allowing the English to deploy forces to block and cut down enemy elements attempting to break out via the remaining escape routes. But that, it must be emphasised, is mere speculation, and if Æthelweard is correct in his claim that the army of the Danes was forced to flee, any pursuit of the Northumbrian survivors may have been half-hearted.

Version 'A' of the *Anglo-Saxon Chronicle* records that 'many thousands' of Northumbrians were slain (an expression commonly found in battle accounts from the period), and even allowing for typical nationalistic hyperbole, there is every possibility that the number of dead did indeed run into many hundreds or more, a possibility increased by our knowledge that many Danish leaders (and perhaps English leaders and other Englishmen fighting with them)[2551] were killed – not necessarily cut down in the battle, but possibly captured and summarily executed[2552] – including three kings, *Eowils*, *Halfdan* and '*Inguuar*' (Inwær or

---

[2550] The battle is inexplicably unmentioned in Pauline Stafford's otherwise forensically detailed analysis of the text of the *Mercian Register* in Stafford 2008: 101-16.

[2551] There is little evidence that Englishmen fought with the Hiberno-Norse: the anonymous *Historia de Sancto Cuthberto* ('History of Saint Cuthbert') records that in 915 the Hiberno-Scandinavian leader Ragnall killed Eadred, a tenant of Bishop Cutheard, and many others at the battle of Corbridge. The land of Eadred was granted, surprisingly, to two young English noblemen, the sons of Eadred, who had fought well in the battle. It has been suggested that the noblemen, Esbrid and Elston, were *robusti bellatores* ('hard fighters'), fighting for Ragnall (Stenton 1971: 333 fn.4), but it is perhaps more likely that the two brothers had fought on the English side and Ragnall had allowed them to keep their father's land: Wainwright 1975: 166-7, 170; South 2002: 63.

[2552] As was Kind Edmund of East Anglia, captured by the Vikings in 869: Williams, Smyth and Kirby 1991: 125-6. The English did not always execute captured enemies: after the battle of Archenfield in 917 the remnants of a Danish raiding party were cornered by the men of

Ivar), two Jarls, *Ohtor* and *Scurfa*, six Holds – *Athulf, Agmund*,[2553] *Benesing, Thurfreth, Guthfrith*, and *Osfrith* – together (probably) with *Anlaf the Black, Osfrith Hlytta, Eagellus*, and another leader named *Guthfrith*.[2554] We have no certain information about any of these kings or the other Northumbrian and English leaders (who may have been Scandinavian leaders whose names have been anglicised), but since *Anglo-Saxon Chronicle* 'A' mentions only *Ecwils* having been killed, he was perhaps the foremost king. None of the chronicles mentions the dead – or even any of the participants – from the English armies, but this was not unusual: Asser, in his *Life* of King Alfred, names one of two kings of the pagans and five of their counts amongst the 'thousands' of Danish killed at the battle of Ashdown, fought in 871, but identifies no English dead.[2555] Even the chronicler compiling the *Mercian Register*, when famously recording Æthelflæd's recovery of Derby in 917 with the loss of 'four of her thegns, who were dear (*besorge*) to her',[2556] thought it unnecessary to identify those prominent thegns, but given the many Northumbrians who died at Tettenhall, even on the victorious side there must have been many injuries and fatalities.[2557] An unexplained mystery that continues to exercise historians is why the chroniclers imagined that their readership would be more interested in the names of dead Northumbrians than the identities of English leaders who were killed.

The dearth of Mercian and West Saxon charters for a decade or so after 909 means that we have no means of establishing, from the absence of their names on witness lists, which senior English figures may have been killed, but the lack of charters may not be unconnected entirely with the loss of English leaders on the battlefield rather than the vagaries of survival of documents from this period.[2558]

Notwithstanding the great slaughter, both Æthelweard and the *Anglo-Saxon Chronicle* record that the Danish army was put to flight,[2559] which tells us unambiguously that some – possibly even the greater part – of the Northumbrian army survived to make its escape. A sizeable number of the Northumbrian raiding force, evidently of sufficient numbers still to

---

Gloucestershire and Herefordshire but released after the Danes made oaths to depart and gave hostages: ASC 'A' and 'D': Swanton 1996: 98-9.

[2553] Agmund may have been the man of that name who is recorded as a *hold* of land in the Ribble estuary in the early years of the tenth century: Higham 1993: 184. Bigsby 1854: 386 suggests that Agmund may be the same person as Amund, one of three Danish kings who went from Repton to Cambridge in 874 (see Swanton 1996: 72), but that seems unlikely.

[2554] The name *Eagellus* may be a corruption of *Eowils* or its variants, including *Auisle*. It is not inconceivable that Ingimund, the leader of the Hiberno-Scandinavians who settled in the Wirral in the early tenth century, also fought in the battle. The date and circumstances of his death are unrecorded: he is last heard of c.905. See generally Wainwright 1975; Williams, Smyth and Kirby 1991: 160.

[2555] Those named by Asser were King Bædsecg, old Count Sidroc, young Count Sidroc, Count Osbern, Count Fræna, and Count Harold: Smyth 2002: 20-1.

[2556] Whitelock 1961: 65. *Besorge* is an uncommon word, implying care and anxiety in addition to love and value, which is perhaps why it was chosen by the chronicler instead of the more usual *leof*: Thompson 2002: 11.

[2557] Indeed, Cadell ap Rhodri, the brother of Anarawd of Gwynedd who might possibly have led a Welsh contingent supporting the English forces, died in 910, but it is unlikely that he died in battle, since his death is recorded without comment in the *Annales Cambriæ*. Anarawd and Cadell had acted together to launch an invasion of Dyfed in 905: Maund 2000: 44-5; see also Charles-Edwards 2013: 504, 506.

[2558] But see especially Keynes 2001: 55-6. It will be noted that the names Ordlaf and Beorhtwulf are not recorded after 909 (which may deceive us into imagining that they did not survive long thereafter), whereas Ordgar is known to have been alive in 926.

[2559] Campbell 1962: 53; ASC 'A', 'B', 'C', 'D'.

be considered an army, was able to flee to fight another day (though there is no evidence that they ever again reconstituted as a single force), and despite the ignomy of deserting their leaders in time of battle, evidently had little compunction about fleeing when the might of the English forces and the tide of battle became all to evident, thus hastening victory by the English.

There is of course nothing to tell us how the Northumbrian forces made their escape from the battlefield, or in which direction(s) they fled, but from the limited information we have of battles from this period there is little proof that it was customary for fleeing enemies to be pursued with particular vigour. Quite how a large number of the enemy managed to escape the Tettenhall battlefield is unclear, but by no means unusual and may even have been normal. Indeed, perhaps surprisingly, the convention seems to have been that those who disengaged were free to make their escape, and that killings were confined to the battlefield proper, though that may be far from the truth. In his account of the battle of Ashdown, Asser tells us that after achieving victory over the enemy, Alfred pusued the surviving Danish forces 'right on to nightfall and into the following day', and 'the Christians followed them till nightfall, cutting them down on all sides'.[2560] It will be remembered that despite their severely weakened state, many supposedly starving Danes encircled by English and Welsh forces at the siege of Buttington in 893 managed, extraordinarily, to break through enemy lines and eventually reached safety, having travelled far through hostile enemy territory. Again, after their supposedly complete defeat at the battle of *Brunanburh* in 937, the Viking remnants of a coalition army of Dublin Vikings, Scots and Strathclyde Britons led by Olaf Guthfritsson of Dublin, we are told by the *Chronicle* that 'the West Saxons with elite cavalry pressed in the tracks of the hateful nation, [and] with mill-sharp blades severely hacked from behind those who fled battle',[2561] enemy forces still managed to reach their ships and flee to Dublin.[2562] We have the impression that mopping-up operations after victory in battle may have been the exception rather than the rule, and in most cases achieved relatively little. It may be that the euphoria of victory saw the pursuit of a fleeing enemy as of secondary importance.

Yet there may be some important if indirect evidence for the capture alive of one or more enemy leaders or other fighters at the battle of Tettenhall. That evidence is the record of the names of the enemy dead. It seems improbable – but not entirely impossible – that detailed intelligence about individuals within enemy forces was already known to the English, though many of the higher-ranking enemy may have been known by reputation or even from previous face-to-face negotiations. But even had a list of senior enemy officers been available, who was to identify the bodies and link them to a name? The assumption must be that the English ensured that important enemies were captured alive so that detailed intelligence – vital to any army – could be extracted by whatever means. Since it seems unlikely that scribes were present on the battlefield – though we might reasonably assume that many of the English contingent could read, and that some at least could write – the prisoners were evidently forced to identify compatriot dead on the battlefield before being removed for interrogation elsewhere (or, perhaps more realistically, peremptorily

---

[2560] Keynes and Lapidge 1983: 79.
[2561] ASC 'A'; Swanton 1996: 108.
[2562] EHD I: 201. It has recently been suggested that the great battle of *Brunanburh* in 937 was a victory for the English only in the strict sense of holding the field, and is rather to be seen as a strategic victory for the northern kings which had calamitous consequences for the West Saxon *imperium*: Kevin Halloran, '*Brunanburh*: the defeat of empire', academia.edu website accessed 22 December 2014.

slaughtered) and their information carefully recorded. Who took down and kept the original records, and where – and what became of them – is of course unknown, but from other names and details found scattered throughout the chronicles, such documenting must have been a regular occurrence. An alternative idea, that the English chroniclers had access to some form of Scandinavian record with the names of their war dead at Tettenhall can be dismissed, since there is not the slightest evidence of any form of documentation created or used by the Scandinavians at this period.

If we are to believe the chronicler Henry of Huntingdon, who wrote in the early twelfth century and recorded the battle twice, after their victory in 910 'the English, the servants of the Lord, ... exalted in the living God and blessed the lord of hosts in hymns and canticles', adding later 'Who can find language to describe the fearful encounters, the flashing arms, the terrible clang, the hoarse shouts, the headlong rush, and the sweeping overthrow of such a conflict?'[2563] That may be no more than typical literary embellishment and hyperbole – one analysis describes Henry's material not found elsewhere as figments of the imagination[2564] – but if correct the first remark might indicate the presence of priests and monks with the English army[2565] (if the wording refers to the victorious armies and not to prayers offered more widely afterwards by Christian congregations): a canticle is a Prayer-Book hymn.[2566] Whatever the case it is possible to visualise some sort of Christian ceremony on the battlefield to thank providence for the great victory, and to offer special prayers to St Oswald, who had demonstrated in so dramatic a fashion his heavenly intercession in gratitude for the ritual translation of his relics and the promotion of his cult

---

[2563] Forester 1853: 163, 166; Greenaway 1996: 300-302. *Servi autem Domini victoria tanta potiti, exultantes in Deum vivum, in hymnis et concentibus Dominum exercituum benedicebant. ... Quis autem cuneorum horrendos aggressus, ignitas collisiones, formidabiles tinnitus, feras irruptiones, miserabiles occasus, clamores horrisonos scriptis exequetur? Tandem suos divina pietas victoria decoravit, et Dacos infideles cæde simul et fuga dehonestavit*: Arnold 1879: 155, 157.

[2564] Gross 1900: 292.

[2565] Ælfric the Homilist recorded c.1006 that under canon law a priest was forbidden, inter alia, to carry weapons and to fight in battle, and if he died in battle no mass might be sung or prayers said, although he might nonetheless be buried:*hit ne gebyraþ þam þe beoð gecorene Gode to þegngenne þæt hi geþwærlæcan sceolon on æniges mannes deaðe*: 'it does not benefit those who are chosen for serving God that they should concur in the death of any men': Thompson 2002: 183-6. That uncompromising warning was doubtless influenced by his personal experiences which would be regarded by many as unworldly, but was applicable only to churchmen, and not necessarily shared universally: ibid.

[2566] The expression canticle (from Latin *canticum*=chant) applied always to the *Benedicte* (O all ye works of the Lord, bless ye ...), and sometimes to the *Benedictus* (Blessed be the Lord ...), *Jubilate* (O be joyful ...), *Magnificat* (My sould doth magnify ...), *Cantate* (O sing ...), *Nunc dimittiss* (Lord, now lettest thou thy servant depart ...), *Deus misereatur* (God be merciful ...), the *Te deum* (We praise thee O God ...), the *Venite* (O come ...), and the Song of Solomon: OED. As noted elsewhere, Bede relates how at the battle between the Northumbrians and the Welsh near Chester, c.613, over 2,000 monks from Bangor-is-Coed had assembled close to the battlefield, with a protective escort, to pray for the Welsh army. The Northumbrian King Æthelfrith, noting their presence and learning of their intentions, treated them as combatants and ordered them to be slaughtered first. Their escort fled, and some 1,200 monks were massacred: McClure and Collins 1994: 73-4. Bede does not suggest that the presence of monks at a battlefield was unusual: rather the story is recorded because of the large numbers involved. There may have been nothing unusual about the presence of `priests and monks at a battle, but there is little evidence to support the idea that it may have been the normal practice for Christian armies to be supported by those offering prayers before and during battle. Florence (John) of Worcester tells how at the battle of Assandun in 1016 the bishop of Lincoln and an abbot Wulsi, both of whom had come to offer up prayers to God for the soldiers while they were fighting, were slain by the Danes: Stevenson 1853: 105.

by the Mercian rulers, though one supposes that the surviving participants of the battle, including the leaders, would have been exhausted and traumatised, and engaging in such ceremonial in the midst of the dead and dying may not necessarily have been their foremost priority.

If there had been any brief ceremony of thanksgiving and speechmaking, we would expect a hiatus while wounded and incapacitated Northumbrians (and especially any Englishmen fighting with the Northumbrians) were brutally despatched where they lay, doubtless after gratuitous torture of the most terrible kind, unless they were obviously of high rank and might be taken for ransom (though ramsoming by the English seems to have been the exception, possibly because the Scandinvians placed little value on those who were captured, even those of high rank), while injured Mercians and West Saxons and any other friendly forces will have been treated with such rudimentary medical skills as were available at the time, perhaps by local clergy or churchmen travelling with the army, with priority given to the higher echelons of the fighting force.

Uninjured warriors and non-combatants from the Mercian and West Saxon armies doubtless scavenged across the battlefield, rendering compassionate *coups de grâce* to moribund Englishmen, exacting retribution by mutilating enemy bodies, whether dead or alive, and seeking anything of value, from arms and armour to jewellery, coins, footwear, clothing, saddles and horse harness, for battlefield loot was a valuable perquisite of the victors.[2567] Whilst items such as clothing and footwear may have been retained by whoever recovered them, valuable metalwork, coins, gold, great swords and high-status military and other fittings will have gone to the English leaders, perhaps deposited at a central collection point for formal distribution by the battle leaders, though that idea may be unrealistically idealised. Local people are likely to have hastily evacuated a wide area around the battlefield as word spread of the first approach of the armies, for they could not know which side might be victorious, and medieval battlefields were places best avoided by civilians. Some daring souls might have ventured onto the battlefield whilst scavenging by the military forces continued, whilst others with medical knowledge may have been conscripted to render what assistance they could to the injured on the English side.

The Northumbrians, according to the chronicles, had been laden with booty on their journey back towards the Danelaw before the battle took place. As victors, the English forces took possession of those spoils, or at least that which was not in the hands of the fleeing enemy.[2568] We can suppose that some of the captured booty, which may or may not have been distributed amongst the Northumbrians before the battle, was divided amongst English company commanders to share with their men – amongst the earliest surviving 'rules' as to the distribution of booty are those attributed to the contemporary Welsh king Hywel Dda,[2569] which stipulate that the king received one-third, and the rest was divided between the soldiers, but the leader of the royal war band actually received a double share, as well as one-third of the king's share[2570] – who would, doubtless, in a mood of

---

[2567] The *Emcomium Emmae* or *Gesta Cnutonis Regis*, a Latin text of c.1041 in two versions written by a Flemish monk, refers to the English victors at the battle of Assandun in 1016 spending the night on the battlefield before stripping the dead and leaving the corpses to be devoured: Lavelle 2010: 306.
[2568] Florence (John) of Worcester specifically mentions the recovery of the booty: Stevenson 1853: 73-4.
[2569] Hywel ap Cadell ap Rhodri, better known as Hywel Dda, who ruled from about 910 to about 950, was one of the greatest Welsh rulers, who at the time of his death was the king of all west Wales.
[2570] Nicolle 1995: 246, but see Roderick 1959: 67-73; Maund 2000: 50.

celebration (no less at their survival than gratitude for the perquisites of battle), have grouped to assess their casualties. To the captured spoils would be added the enemy's weapons, armour, provisions, horses, and general military paraphernalia, also to be shared amongst the victors. Like victorious fighters before and since, the jubilant English will almost certainly have suffused their euphoria well into the night by feasting on the captured supplies and the consumption of strong drink accompanied by raucous patriotic singing, probably with ribald vocalisation. Residual adrenaline will have denied relaxation to many exhausted warriors in desperate need of rest and sleep. The proportion of English warriors who escaped injury in the battle must remain unknown, but given the English superiority in numbers was probably very high, though the knowledge that even the most minor wounds could easily become infected and prove fatal will have weighed heavily in the minds of those otherwise thankful to have survived the day.

While more seriously injured English (excluding, of course, any who may have fought with the Northumbrians, who would have been dispatched without mercy) and their allies of higher rank were being attended by field surgeons or monks and removed from the battlefield to a place of shelter, perhaps on blankets or hides or wicker stretchers or carts, the battlefield will have been searched well into twilight to identify the bodies of English nobles and magnates who had fallen in the conflict. Their corpses were perhaps removed to the nearest church – probably at Tettenhall[2571] – for burial in consecrated ground,[2572] though at this period the patchy evidence suggests that churchyard burial was still a privilege available only to professional religious and others able to meet the charges imposed by the church,[2573] but with the culture of comparatively unregulated burial practice away from a church giving way to church-associated burials. Coffin burial was far from universal, and most corpses are likely to have been buried in shrouds.[2574] But some of the bodies of anyEnglish elite from Wednesfield are likely to have been taken, perhaps after dismembering and flensing (boiling the flesh from the bones) for ease of transport and to avoid the stench of decomposition, on the long journey back to their local estate for burial there or in a church nearby.[2575] Corpses of the rank-and-file soldiery may have been left where they had fallen, though Christians had a duty to pray for the souls of their dead

---

[2571] It would be idle to speculate whether the great low or tumulus at Low Field, on high ground 1,000 yards west of Tettenhall church, may have covered the bodies of English dead removed from the battlefield.

[2572] It has been suggested that some Anglo-Saxon battle-sites, for example Reading and possibly Tettenhall, may have had minsters at an early date: Baker and Brookes 2013: 206, citing Blair 2005: 338, though the reference in Blair is untraced. The early history of Bushbury church, which is a little over 2 miles from Wednesfield, is not known, but it was in existence by 1351: VCH III 264. There is no evidence that it was a pre-Conquest foundation, although the churchyard has the base of a cross-shaft which is said to be Anglo-Saxon: Pevsner 1974: 320.

[2573] Thompson 2002: 31.

[2574] Thompson 30-31.

[2575] The body of the Mercian ealdorman Æthelwulf, who had evidently transferred his allegiance to Wessex, was 'carried away secretly' and taken to Derby in Mercia for burial after a Viking victory in Wessex in 871 (Campbell 1962: 37; Williams, Smyth and Kirby 1991: 36; Walker 2000: 38), and two princes were taken to Malmesbury for burial after the battle of *Brunanburh* in 937: Hill 2004: 141. King Harold's brother Tostig was buried at York after the battle of Stamford Bridge in 1066, and skeletons bearing weapon injuries found buried at the church of St Andrew in the city are believed to be some of the fallen in the battle of Fulford in the same year: Lawson 2003: 249. For the dismemberment of bodies for the purpose of burial some distance from the battlefield see Bagliani 2001: 327-9. Hooper 1998 is a valuable survey of evidence on Anglo-Saxon battlefield burial practice.

warriors, and to recover their corpses for proper burial,[2576] and over a period of days the corpses of recognisably English fallen may have been collected, stripped of clothing and effects, and, particularly if there was habitation nearby, dragged into natural depressions and covered with earth with minimal ceremony. It was not until the tenth century, and then only gradually, that a proper burial seems to have been routinely given to battle victims by those with a shared culture.[2577]

The widespread idea of large numbers of corpses being burned on great pyres is very unlikely: human cadavers are surprisingly difficult to reduce by fire, with well over 60% of a human body made up of water, and only 10% fat, and great quantities of dried wood would have been required. Burning a single corpse cannot be compared with burning many. In a thinly-populated area such as Wednesfield it is probably more realistic to imagine that stripped corpses and body parts, scattered over a wide area, were left to decompose naturally where they lay, to be consumed as they rotted and decayed by birds, animals, and insects, as seems to have happened after the battle of *Brunanburh*, if we can believe the account in the *Anglo-Saxon Chronicle*.[2578] This was at a period where the contamination of watercourses by liquids leaching from putrescent corpses was little understood. Following the battle of Stamford Bridge in 1066 the bleached bones of the slain and the skeletons of dead horses and their iron horseshoes are said to have lain on the battlefield for years, though we cannot know how much truth should be attached to such anecdotes, and whether any such bones were those of the Scandinavian forces only.[2579]

How the corpses of the pagan Northumbrian kings and other leaders were treated is unknown – there is evidence that heads of decapitated enemies were sometimes displayed on stakes after a battle,[2580] most famously that of king Oswald of Northumbria (so revered

---

[2576] Though there was a duty to care for the poor, which presumably extended to 'the body of a pilgrim, penitent, tramp or traveller found dead in a ditch', there is no evidence that the burial of Christians fallen in battle was a religious obligation: Thompson 2002: 84-5.

[2577] Gillingham 2007.

[2578] ASC 'A', which refers to corpses left for the raven, eagle, 'war-hawk', and wolf: Swanton 1996: 109. The victory poem commemorating the battle refers to the Danes leaving behind them 'the dusky-coated one, the black raven with its horned beak to share the corpses ... to enjoy the carrion' (Whitelock 1955: 201), and the raven which preyed on the corpses of the warriors was seen as a symbol of Óðin's acceptance of the sacrifice of the slain (Smyth 1995: 78-9).

[2579] McLynn 1998: 205. In the 12th century Henry of Huntingdon records a saying that 'The plain of [the battle of Maserfelt, at which Oswald was slain in 641 or 642] was whitened with the bones of saints' (Forester 1853: 100-101), but he was writing some half a millennium after the battle. There is no evidence of any recognised process to deal with the war dead after an Anglo-Saxon battle: even in cases of natural deaths we have no knowledge of who may have laid out the corpse, arrange the funeral, choose the grave-site, dig the grave, and design and arrange the installation of any memorialThompson 2002: 46.

[2580] A drawing of Noah's raven pecking a bearded human head impaled on a stake from the illustrated *Old English Hexateuch* (London, BL MS Cotton Claudius B iv, fol. 15r, produced in the second quarter of the 11th century in Canterbury) is reproduced in Thompson 2002: 139. The practice of mounting heads on stakes may not have been unusual: the OE vocabulary included *heafodstoccum* 'head-stakes', and some charters include head-stakes as boundary marks: Thompson 2002: 189, 193-5. There is evidence that in every hundred criminals' severed heads and hanged bodies were displayed in association with ancient earthworks and significant boundaries before deliberately disorganised burial in a 'heathen cemetery': Thompson 2002: 172-3. As late as 1006 the heads of decapitated Scots were displayed on the city walls of Durham after they had been washed and the hair combed: Thompson 2002: 193.

by Æthelred and Æthelflæd) after his defeat at *Maserfelth* in 642,[2581] when other parts of his dismembered corpse were buried on the battlefield, by tradition recovered several decades later by the wife of king Æthelred of Mercia, suggesting (if true, which must be very doubtful) that the grave had some kind of marker[2582] – but we can suspect that most enemy corpses were abused, mutilated and dealt with barbarically, perhaps simply left to rot or get eaten by wolves and ravens where they lay,[2583] or dismembered and fed to dogs and pigs as an expression of utter contempt, hatred and vengeance: horses, dogs and, especially, pigs were proscribed in canon law as repugnant within church precincts.[2584] But canon law, which goes into extraordinary detail about the most arcane rituals involving every aspect of dying and death, seems to have had little to say about the treatment of enemies killed in battle, though since thieves were evidently denied consecrated burial,[2585] it is clear that there was no Christian obligation to treat enemy dead – and especially pagan enemies – with the slightest dignity.[2586] Indeed, and understandably, the opposite seems to have been the norm.[2587] Moreover, there is strong evidence for widespread pig-breeding in Wednesfield and surrounding areas from later Anglo-Saxon and medieval period, and wild swine swine from Cannock Forest, in which Wednesfield lay, could well have been driven – or were naturally attracted – to the area after the battle to scavenge amongst the corpses and body parts of both sides.[2588] Pigs, able to consume every part of a human body

---

[2581] Stancliffe and Cambridge 1996, but note Alan Thacker's discussion of the idea that *Maserfelth* may have been somewhere on the periphery of Lindsey: Thacker 1996: 99. The *Liber Eliensis*, a Latin compilation of c.1170 derived from pre-Conquest sources, has an account of the battle of Maldon in 991 which tells how the Vikings left the battlefield with the head of Ealdorman Byrhtnoth, the heroic leader of the doomed English forces, who had been decapitated as he fought. The head was evidently retained as a trophy. Since the incident is recorded with some horror, it might be imagined that it was seen as an exceptional act of barbarity, but an analysis of early sources reveals other examples of Scandinavians placing the head of an enemy leader on a stake and using it for target practice.Kennedy 1991: 63-8; McDougall 1993: 211-12.
[2582] Stancliffe and Cambridge 1995: 104 and generally; Thompson 2002: 193-5. It was the relics of Oswald, by then sainted, which were translated from Bardney to Gloucester in 909: ASC 'C' and 'D': Swanton 1996: 94-5.
[2583] The leaving of the fallen enemy unburied on the battlefield is a frequent element in the writings of Dudo of Saint-Quintin (c.965-c.943), a Norman historian who wrote a history of the Normans. Wolves are believed to have existed in Britain large numbers in the Roman and Anglo-Saxon period, especially in the Welsh Marches: see especially Pluskowski 2009. William of Malmesbury tells how Edgar (959-75) demanded annual tribute of 300 wolves from the king of the Welsh: Giles 1847: 158. There is some evidence that wolves and ravens had learned to associate armies with food, and even said that they made an appearance on battlefields before fighting occurred: Holland 2016: 97 fn.5.
[2584] Thompson 2002: 176-7.
[2585] Thompson 2002: 176, citing S.886 of 995.
[2586] An eschatological homily, Oxford Bodl. Hatton MS 115, dating from the second half of the 11th century, incorporates a list of sexual sins which exclude the sinners from conventional burial, concluding that they are 'not even to be carried to the heathen pit (*hæþenum pytte*), but dragged without a coffin ...': Thompson 2002: 171-2. The *hæþenum pytt* was presumably the place where criminal's heads and hanged bodies were unceremoniously dumped after public display: Thompson 2002: 172-3.
[2587] It is worth recording that within a few years of the battle of Hastings, penance was officially imposed on all those who had fought there. For every man he had slain in battle the penitent was required to fast on bread and water for a year; for every man struck but not killed, 40 days of penance; for everyone not sure of the number they had slain, a day of penance for every week remaining to them for the rest of their lives. Those who had been motivated to fight by greed rather than the glory of God were to be treated as murderers, and sentenced to 3 years of fasting: Vincent 2011: 51-2.
[2588] Thompson 2002: 177. For evidence of pig-breeding in the Wednesfield area see TSAHS XLVIII (2015) 6-14. A reference to a *suinsete*, a rare OE compound meaning 'swinefold', probably on the

including the bones (but not hair and teeth),[2589] would have proved exceedingly efficient machines for disposing of putrescent corpses, and nutritious high-protein carrion was a valuable commodity not to be wasted.

Some days may have passed before the bulk of the English survivors from the battle of Tettenhall started on their journeys home, for there would be many tasks to be attended to, and the trauma of battle will have taken a heavy toll on those who by good fortune had escaped unscathed. Sheer exhaustion will soon have eclipsed the euphoria of victory. During the days that followed, demobilised fighters from Wessex and many Mercian troops, weary but cheered not least by their share of booty recovered from the enemy, probably made their way south-east along the Portway towards Ryknield Street, with others heading west, perhaps along Watling Street: English Mercia extended westwards to Offa's Dyke, well past the river Severn, and north as far as the river Trent,[2590] and many English warriors must have come from that region. We have also seen that a Welsh contingent may have fought alongside the English.[2591]

If – which must be unlikely – burial pits or mounds were created at or near the battlefield, wherever it may have been, none is known to us with any certainty, but if (which cannot be assumed) *Camp Feld* in Wednesfield might be associated with the site of the battle, such pits may have been marked by the field-name *Chirchezordesfeld*, as discussed elsewhere recorded in Wednesfield in 1399, or, possibly, by some of the lows or mounds in the area (unless they were of prehistoric, pagan Anglo-Saxon or natural origin), for the concentration of supposed lows in the area – *Wodnesfeld* – named by early chroniclers as the site of the battle, could be more than coincidence. If so, the mounds are unlikely to have been deliberately raised as monuments for any commemorative reason,[2592] but created by the sheer volume of the many interred corpses before the earth was placed over

---

east side of Wednesfield, is found in Wulfrun's charter purporting to be of 994 (Hooke 1983: 72-5), showing that pigs were being bred in artificial enclosures at the time the sources used to compile the charter were created, evidence reinforced by a reference in Domesday Book to pannage (*silva pastilis*) at Wednesfield from a wood ¾ mile long by 660 yards wide (VCH IV 45), probably giving rise to the name Prestwood, i.e. 'wood belonging to the canons of Wolverhampton'. It is not inconceivable that disposing of the dead from the battle of Tettenhall indirectly initiated widespread pig-breeding in the area.

[2589] It is said that pigs can consume 2lbs of flesh a minute.

[2590] There is no evidence that the Danelaw ever included part of what became Staffordshire: see Horovitz 2005: 50-52.

[2591] There is little evidence that intensive efforts were made to pursue and capture fleeing enemy warriors after Anglo-Saxon battles, although following the battle of *Brunanburh* the English are said to have pursued the enemy for a whole day. However, that poetic account is ambiguous, for the battle itself is also said to have lasted all day: Swanton 1996: 106-10.

[2592] We have seen elsewhere that the Scandinavian saga known as *Egil's Saga*, probably written c.1230, gives much detail about the battle of Vin Heath, held by some to be the battle of *Brunanburh*, where Æthelstan defeated a great alliance of Vikings, Strathclyde Welsh, and Scots. Whether the details provide any element of truth is still debated, but after the battle the Viking Egil is said to have returned to the battlefield to find his brother Thorolf's corpse, which was washed and prepared for burial 'according to custom'. A grave was dug on the battlefield and Thorolf was laid in it with all his weapons and other clothing and a gold bracelet placed around each of Thorolf's arms before he was covered with earth and stones: Pálsson and Edwards 1976: 119-127. It must be improbable, to say the least, that a Viking would have returned to a battlefield, identified his brother amongst the dead, and buried him there with treasure, but the tale is perhaps of interest for the idea that burial on a battlefield may have been customary, and that the body was not taken for burial elsewhere.

them.[2593] But whether the corpses of war dead will have been dragged to high ground for communal burial must very doubtful.

Trampled and blood-soaked, thebattlefield will have recovered quickly, with the site marked, if not by any impromptu man-made memorial,[2594] then at least by potassium-, phosphate-, and nitrate-loving plants and grass of a darker shade of green,[2595] starkly remembered in local folklore as the place, surely haunted by demons and other spirits of the dead and best avoided,[2596] where a barbaric, fearsome and gruesomely bloody clash once took place, but surprisingly – as with many significant battlefields, even those of relatively recent times – gradually fading from memory until even the general area where it occurred became lost to memory.[2597]

[2593] It should not be overlooked that there is no evidence of skeletons associated with either mound, though whether human bones might survive for a millennium or more in the soil of the area is uncertain.

[2594] See Osaka 2004: 96; Marafioti 2014: 211. There is no surviving contemporary memorial at any Anglo-Saxon battle site (Osgood 2005), or any evidence that such places were commemorated at the time with memorials. Asser says he himself saw 'a solitary quite stunted thorn tree' on the battlefield at Ashdown, at which the Danes were defeated by Alfred in 871, but he also refers to fighting around the tree, so was clearly no memorial planted afterwards: Smyth 2002: 19.

[2595] We are reminded that the sudden mania to improve the soil in the 1820s and 1830s led to vast quantities of different materials being fed into agricultural land, including salt, soot, hooves, woollen rags, and, above all, ground bone. Human and animal bones were gathered and shipped to England in huge quantities from the battlefields of Leipzig, Austerlitz, Waterloo, and elsewhere: in 1821 alone more than 3 million bushels were unloaded at Hull to be processed into granules by steam-powered machines before sale to farmers: *Nautical Register*, November 1822.

[2596]

[2597] Examples of crucial battles where even the region where they were fought remains uncertain are surprisingly common, including in particular *Brunanburh* and the Holme.

35. The aftermath of the battle of Tettenhall.

The battle of Tettenhall– often claimed to have been the last defeat of a Viking army by the English – has been seen as a pivotal episode in the relationship between the English and the Northumbrians, although it would be a mistake to imagine that the decades of intermittent raiding, burning, looting, sacking and slaughter by Scandinavian war-bands and armies suddenly came to an end, for it was almost certainly a Hiberno-Scandinavian army that had been defeated at Tettenhall, and many beligerent Scandinavians remained a force to be reckoned with within the Danelaw.

Yet English forces had achieved two great victories over enemy forces in the space of seven years, with the success at Tettenhall to add to the defeat of Æthelwold's forces c.903 against superior odds. Hand-in-hand with the frenetic *burh*-building operation that was gathering pace, Edward, Æthelred and Æthelflæd had refined the military tactics and strategies of their troops to turn them into powerful, confident and well-drilled armies, with warriors from Wessex and Mercia prepared and able to fight together and co-ordinate their strategy effectively against a common foe. Whether the protagonists at the battle of Tettenhall were the Hiberno-Norse of the north-west or the Danes of York, the English victory was resoundingly successful, for whilst they remained a continuing threat to Mercia and Wessex, there is no firm evidence that either faction undertook any serious military incursions into English territory (as opposed to armed resistance within areas of the Danelaw) thereafter in the campaign by Edward and Æthelflæd. Also noteworthy is the fact that no chronicle mentions any treaty or pact after the conflict at Tettenhall, as often followed a battle. Edward and his allies doubtless viewed the exercise as pointless, given the repeated breaches of previous treaties by the Northumbrians, including in particular the breach that culminated in the battle of Tettenhall, and more importantly with the death of the Scandinavian leaders there may have been no surviving Scandinavians of rank and authority with whom to negotiate.

In Mercia, Æthelflæd promptly set to work, presumably on her own initiative since her husband is unmentioned, to strengthen the system of Mercian *burhs*. A fortification at *Bremesbyrig*[2598] was built in the same year as the battle,[2599] though its location remains unidentified.[2600] If ever located it may help to show the area then perceived by Æthelflæd to be under the greatest threat.

Æthelflæd's long-ailing husband Æthelred, probably in his late 50s or 60s died at some date in 911. He had probably led the Mercians to defeat at the battle of Conwy in 881 (at which he may have sustained injuries which led to his increasing incapacity), so is likely to have been born before, possibly well before, the mid 850s, making him at least 56, and possibly much older, and his rule has inevitably but certainly unfairly been overshadowed

---

[2598] ASC 'C' and 'D': Swanton 1996: 94-5.
[2599] Lavelle notes that a Viking army from Brittany arrived in the river Severn in 910 after the battle of Tettenhall (Lavelle 2010: 341), but this event occurred in 917: ASC 'A'; Swanton 1996: 98. The date is confirmed by Welsh annals, such as the *Annales Cambriae*.
[2600] Swanton suggests the location was possibly Bromsberrow in Gloucestershire or Bromesberrow near Ledbury in Herefordshire: (Swanton 1996: 95 fn.13, followed by Walker 2000: 93), though both seem to be the same place. Bromsberrow near Ledbury is not on a main road or river, though it is close to a Roman road linking Gloucester and Hereford (Margary route 610), and lies near the meeting point of Herefordshire, Gloucestershire and Worcestershire.

by that of his widow.[2601] The place and date and cause of his death are unrecorded (though Henry of Huntingdon tells us that he had been ill),[2602] but he may have spent his final days at Gloucester, knowing that his end was near and determined to spend his final days in his most favoured (and perhaps ancestral) centre. Æthelflæd, married for at least 24 years, arranged for her husband's body to be interred in the monastery at Gloucesterto which St Oswald's relics had been translated only two years earlier.[2603] Æthelweard tells us that Æthelred was interred *in pace* 'in peace', a curious expression in that context which might have some deeper meaning, probably associated with Æthelred's supposed long-standing disabling illness.

At Æthelred's death Æthelflæd, ruler *de facto* of Mercia, became ruler *de jure*, with the title *Myrcna hlæfdige*, Lady of the Mercians, a title found in the *Mercian Register* (three times) but not once in the Common Stock of the *Anglo-Saxon Chronicle*.[2604] The administrative and ceremonial formalities by which Æthelflæd assumed the role are quite unknown, since no precedent is available, but presumably included a formal resolution by the Mercian *witan*. Edward wasted no time in removing from Mercia control of London

---

[2601] A rare – possibly unique – insight into the physical appearance of a leader of this period might be gleaned from a 13th-century collection of Welsh genealogies, perhaps derived ultimately from a tenth-century text, which mentions Edryd Long-Hair, king of Lloegr, who fought the Welsh at the battle of Cymrid Conwy in 881. Lloegr was a term used for part of Britain south of a line from the Humber to the Severn, excluding Cornwall and Devon, and came to be used for England as a whole. Edryd can only be Æthelred, who was defeated at the battle of Conwy, from which we might suppose that his hair was then unusually long – and that it was usual for warriors to keep their hair short: Charles-Edwards 2013: 490-1. Further insight into Æthelred's character may be gleaned from a charter of c.903 (S.1446) relating to an ex-monastic estate at Old Sodbury (Gloucestershire), which the bishops of Worcester had been trying to recover since the 840s, but 'could never get anywhere until Æthelred became lord of the Mercians': Blair 2005: 306; the case described more fully in Thompson 2002: 22-3. To what extent his increasing disability, unidentified in the absence of clues, affected his piety cannot be known, but we might assume that until his father-in-law Alfred died they had a rapport based in part on their respective physical disorders: it may be noted that Alfred, whose illnesses are well-recorded, makes no comment on Æthelred's state of health when recording a specific bequest to him of a sword worth 100 *mancuses* in his will drawn up between 888 and 899: Keynes and Lapidge 1983: 18, 76, 88-90, 91, 101, 131, 173-8, 255-6, 270, 316. From an extraordinary account published in 1675 of very doubtful historical value describing the battle of the Holme we learn of 'Ethelred, surnam'd Michill, or the great Duke of Mercia, Brother in law to King Edward': Churchill 1675: 163-6. 'Michill' is from OE *micel*, ME *michel* 'much, great, large', presumably intended to signify his stature rather than his status, though it should be noted that Æthelred was almost certainly not present at the battle of the Holme. For a perceptive analysis of early tenth-century Mercia and Æthelred's role, see Cumberledge 2002: 1-15.

[2602] Greenway 1996: 307.

[2603] There is evidence that Æthelred and Æthelflæd had re-established Gloucester as a significant town to replace Minsterworth, 4 miles south-west of Gloucester, one of a number of place-names which incorporates OE *worðig*, perhaps introduced from Wessex to Mercia 'through royal dynastic contacts to name places which were of particular significance to ruling families, and situated in a particular relation to other significant palces nearby': JEPNS 44 (2012) 36-43. There is some evidence that before that date Æthelred and Æthelflæd's favoured religious centre was Worcester, where they may originally have chosen to be buried, was Worcester: 18-20.

[2604] The expression *Myrcna hlæfdige* 'Lady of the Mercians', with *hlæfdige* meaning in that context a woman who ruled over subjects, is first found in the *Mercian Register* in 912: ASC 'B' and 'C'; Thorpe 1861: 186-7. The word *hlæfdige* is recorded from c.825 of a mistress in relation to her servants or slaves (OED), and its appearance in the *Mercian Register* suggests that it was adopted to suit a situation where, perhaps uniquely, the wife of a leading ealdorman (sometimes honoured with the title *hlaford*) had effectively taken on his role after his death: there was no female equivalent of an ealdorman.

and Oxford and 'all the lands belonging to them' (evidently including the later shires of Oxfordshire, Buckinghamshire, Middlesex and western Hertfordshire) granted to Æthelred by Alfred in 886 on his marriage to Edward's sister, the recovery of London and Oxford an ominous forestaste of his ambitions regarding Mercia.[2605] Indeed, Æthelflæd and the Mercian *witan* may have surrendered London and Oxford to Edward as a means of discouraging him from taking control over Mercia itself.

Nevertheless, the frenetic campaign of fortifying West Mercia began – or perhaps more correctly, continued. The conventional analysis of the *Mercian Register*, our only souce for events in Mercia at this period, is that Æthelflæd launched the crash programme of *burh*-building immediately after the battle of Tettenhall. Yet this traditional conclusion may be deeply flawed. We have seen that the title of the *Mercian Register* is a misnomer: in reality it is nothing of the sort, but essentially a record of the legitimacy of the rule of Æthelflæd and her achievements and God's support for her after she became Lady of the Mercians following the death of her husband in 911 (with the exception of a brief mention of the 'restoration' of Chester in 907 and a note recording her construction in 910 of the *burh* at *Bremesbyrig* immediately after the battle of Tettenhall).[2606] From 912 to her death in 918 the Register is exclusively concerned with Æthelflæd's role in the kingly and masculine activities of a war leader.

Of the achievements of Æthelred – indeed any facts about his life – both the *Anglo-Saxon Chronicle* and the *Mercian Register* are notable for their almost complete silence: extraordinarily, the former records only that he was present at the siege of Buttington in 893, and his death (but not his burial place) in 911– an inexplicable hiatus of some 18 years – with *Chronicle* 'A' describing him deprecatingly as *ealdorman* rather than Lord of the Mercians; the latter records his death as Lord of the Mercians (and burial place) and the dispossession of Ælwynn, his daughter, in 918 or 919.[2607] This can only be seen as a conscious effort by the West Saxon *Anglo-Saxon Chronicle* to expunge his memory and treat him (and during his life by extension his wife) as *persona non grata* (more surprisingly in the case of the *Mercian Register*, perhaps to be seen as evidence of West Saxon authorship, contrary to most authorities),[2608] emphasising instead the

---

[2605] ASC 'A', 'D' and 'E'; Swanton 1996: 95-7. It has been suggested that Æthelflæd may have surrendered the important and strategic territory of London and Oxford (and the burdensome need to defend them) in return for recognition of her authority by Edward, who might otherwise have been tempted to take control of Mercia: Walker 2000: 99. Extraordinarily, the *Livere de Reis de Engletere*, perhaps by the English chronicler Peter of Ickham (fl. c.1290), records that after Æthelred died 'the Mercians and East-Anglians and West-Anglians and Northumbrians came against [Edward the Elder] with the Danes and Scots and Welsh; but he vanquished them all and made them subject to him. And Ethelfleda, his sister … aided him': Glover 1865: 58-9. It is difficult to explain the basis for this startling and entirely fanciful record.
[2606] Whitelock 1961: 61-2.
[2607] ASC 'C' and 'D'; ASC 'D' and 'E'; Whitleock 1962: 56, 62, 67. Recording for posterity the burial place of an especially honoured individual was important, and the failure to provide such information must tell us something of how they were seen at their death. Information relating to Æthelredis scarce, but Florence (John) of Worcester and Roger of Wendover are among those who tell us that he was responsible with his wife for restoring Chester c.907-8 (Stevenson 1853: 73; Giles 1892: 237), and Æthelweard records that at the time of the battle of Tettenhall he was ruling Mercia (and, curiously, as discussed elsewhere, 'the Northumbrian areas'): Campbell 1962: 52.
[2608] See Pelteret 2009: 325, where the possibility is raised that the author of the *Mercian Register* – which shows an intimate knowledge of Edward (and his sister's) achievements, including place-names, dates, periods, sequences, etc., – may have been Æthelweard, the youngest son of King Alfred and Edward's brother, who died in 922, and who as a youth had been 'handed over to the

accomplishments of Alfred's eldest son and daughter. In the same way the *Anglo-Saxon Chronicle* records Edward's *burh*-building programme only from 912, the year after Æthelred's death, and none of the fortifications built by Edward, Æthelred and Æthelflæd between 907 and 914 is included in the *Burghal Hidage*, a document composed in the early tenth century (probably 914-919 or a little later) surviving in seven later manuscripts that lists 33 places which are held to have been fortified by that date, though it is true that most will have dated from the time of Alfred.[2609] The *Anglo-Saxon Chronicle* records the construction of only two fortifications (Warwick in 914 and Buckingham in 918)[2610] listed in the *Burghal Hidage*, meaning that without the survival of later copies of the *Hidage* we would be in almost complete ignorance of 31 of those *burhs*, dependent instead on meagre and incomplete evidence to be gleaned from other sources. It would be very unwise to rely on silences in the *Register* (and equally the *Anglo-Saxon Chronicle*) as negative evidence.

Æthelred and Æthelflæd had ordered the fortification of Worcester at some date in the 890s (the period during which Worcester and London – both in Mercia – were (re)fortified, neither fortification being mentioned in the chronicles),[2611] and had created what amounted to a *burh* by refortifying Chester in 907 (recorded in the *Mercian Register* but unmentioned in the Common Stock of the *Anglo-Saxon Chronicle*).[2612] Are we really to believe that after Alfred's intensive and extensive *burh*-building campaign beginning in the early 890s (as evidenced by the *Burghal Hidage*), the Mercians only began a similar programme from 910 (under Æthelflæd), and that Edward (who oversaw a truly frenetic scheme of fortification-building in the East Midlands as recorded in the *Anglo-Saxon Chronicle*) built no *burh* before 914?[2613]

We might reasonably suppose that from the 880s to his death, Æthelred (and Æthelflæd and Edward) was responsible for constructing many, possibly dozens, of unrecorded fortifications throughout Mercia, most (from place-name evidence not always easy to interpret precisely),[2614] probably (in the case of Æthelred and Æthelflæd) concentrated in the west of the kingdom, either constructing earthworks around existing settlements or refortifying other suitable sites such as prehistoric earthworks or incipient commercial centres. When her husband died, Æthelflæd almost certainly possessed considerable experience in the construction of fortifications, and even before his death was continuing the great scheme in Mercia by speedily constructing the *burh* at *Bremesbyrig* in 910

---

pleasures of literary study'. Æthelweard may well have accompanied Edward on his campaigns, and in other circumstances could have been Edward's successor. Entries in the Register are spasmodic after 919, perhaps pointing to a new hand: Stafford 2008: 107-8.

[2609] Hill and Rumble 1996: 11, 90, 124-7. One obvious example of a fortification not recorded in the *Anglo-Saxon Chronicle* or the *Mercian Register* must be Gloucester, with which Æthelred (and possibly Æthelflæd, through her Mercian mother and aunt) may have had a particular affinity (and which must have been fortified before 909 – possibly well before, since the Roman walls remained intact – when Oswald's relics were translated from Bardney: Bassett 1996: 156. Æthelweard tells us that Æthelred was buried in *arce dicta Gleaucestre* 'the fortress known as Gloucester' the following year: Campbell 1962: 53.

[2610] ASC 'C'; Swanton 1996: 98; ASC 'A'; Swanton 1996: 100.

[2611] S.223 (Finberg 1972: 106-7); S.1280 (Finberg 1972: 107; Bailey 2001: 117-8); S.1628 (Hill and Rumble 1996: 226-8). See also Brooks 1996: 143.

[2612] Whitelock 1961: 61.

[2613] Other sources provide evidence for *burhs*, such as a charter (S.372), which mentions the fortification at Porchester (listed in the *Burghal Hidage*) in 904: Hill and Rumble 1996; 8.

[2614] The OE word *burh* or related *byrig* carried various meanings in the later Anglo-Saxon period, including 'fortification', 'defended enclosure', 'fortified manor house', 'monastery'.

immediately after the battle of Tettenhall, Æthelred presumably being too frail to have become involved, and after his death in 911 (which probably explains the *burh*-building interruption) *Scergeat* (unidentified, but discussed in more detail in Chapter 10), built in May 912, and others at *Cwatbrycge*, almost certainly Quatford (summer 912),[2615] Tamworth (early summer 913),[2616] and Stafford (July 913). Florence (John) of Worcester tells us that the winter of 913 was very long and severe,[2617] which may explain why the *burh* at Eddisbury was not built until early summer 914,[2618] followed by Warwick (probably the first or second week of September 914), Chirbury (probably January 915), *Weardbyrig* (unidentified, early in 915),[2619] and Runcorn (late in 915).[2620]

We have seen that this period is often held to be the most intensive period of Mercian *burh*-building, when Edward's role in establishing fortifications was dwarfed by that of his sister, whose immediate priority after the battle of Tettenhall seems to have been to fortify central and western Mercia against Scandinavian (and possibly Welsh) attack by both land and water, most specifically via the Severn, a policy and programme perhaps much influenced by the events leading up to the battle and the route of the raiding army, with the exercise extending northwards to the Mersey estuary doubtless for the same reason. Wainwright has noted that Æthelflæd's *burhs* at Stafford and Tamworth, both dating from 913, were built within a few months of two of the few expeditions important enough to be recorded in the *Anglo-Saxon Chronicle* 'A', namely two raids by the armies of Leicester and Northampton, one of which which reached Hook Norton, the other Luton, and probably took place in April 913, rather than 917 as the *Anglo-Saxon Chronicle* records,

---

[2615] The *burh* at *Cwatbrycge* will have protected the strategic crossing over the river Severn and served to defend the area not only from Danish incursions, but from any threat from the Welsh: Æthelflæd will not have forgotten that some two decades previously Anarawd of Gwynedd had entered into an alliance, admittedly short-lived, with the Northumbrians of York, which must have posed a serious threat to Mercia and her father's West Saxon kingdom.

[2616] The *Mercian Register* records that 'by the grace of God, Æthelflæd, lady of the Mercians, went with all the Mercians to Tamworth, and built the borough there in the early summer...': Whitelock 1961: 62-3. The reference to 'all the Mercians' must mean the entire Mercian army, presumably to unseat a strong force of Danes, and the expression 'by the grace of God' is normally found in the *Register* when announcing a hard-fought military victory, though the Danes in possession of Tamworth may have fled when they realised the strength of the Mercian force, so allowing Æthelflæd to peacefully occupy the place, important as the traditional capital of the 'original or first Mercia': Hill and Rumble 1996: 19 fn.2; Brooks 1989: 161-2.

[2617] Stevenson 1853: 75.

[2618] The *burh* is probably the Iron-Age hilfort at Eddisbury, near Delamere, 10 miles east of Chester, where excavations in 1938 produced evidence for the rebuilding of the inner and outer ramparts, though a reassessment of that evidence has led to uncertainty about the dating of that reconstruction: Griffiths 2001: 174-6.

[2619] Interestingly, when Æthelflæd attested a charter at *Weardbyrig*, possibly in 915 (S.225), her daughter Ælfwynn is likely to have been in attendance: Bailey 2001: 116, 118-21. The evidence might imply that Æthelflæd was present at the construction of at least some, if not all, of her *burhs*. However, the date of the charter, 9th September 878, is clearly incorrect, and the charter held to be spurious, perhaps a corrupt copy of an authentic early 10th-century document (Sawyer 1968: 127, which dates it to 916). Bailey concludes that it must post-date the construction of the *burh* at *Weardbyrig* (Bailey 2001: 119), but that overlooks that the *burh* might well have been constructed at an existing place of that name.

[2620] In a detailed analysis of ASC 'A' for the years 912 to 920 David Pelteret raises the possibility that the author may have been Æthelweard, the youngest son of King Alfred and Edward's brother, who died in 922, and who as a youth had been 'handed over to the pleasures of literary study': Pelteret 2009: 325.

the juxtopisition of dates due to the chronological confusion of Edward's reign.[2621] The (?re)fortification of Tamworth, until then dangerously vulnerable at what had been the very edge of English Mercia, shows that by 913 Æthelflæd's forces had driven the Danes from the immediate area, and from that period the Danelaw boundary in the region is in a state of disintegration, though Tamworth seems to have marked the Mercian boundary for many years after.[2622] But without in any way diminishing Æthelflæd's achievements, the greater picture may disclose that her accomplishments reflect only what the chroniclers choose to tell us, and both her husband and brother may well deserve matching credit for the construction of earlier but unrecorded *burhs*.

But it was not only action on the military front that was being taken in connection with the conquest of the Danelaw. As noted elsewhere, there is a noticeable reduction in royal diplomas evidencing the transfer of land in the late ninth and early tenth century, with very few surviving from Alfred's reign and even fewer for the first decade of Edward's rule, followed by a complete and unparalleled absence between 909 and 925. David Dumville sees this as something more than the vagaries of survival of ephemeral archives, and surmises that Alfred and Edward were following a deliberate strategy of limiting grants of new bookland – land vested by a charter or diploma[2623] – which led to a complete cessation between 910 and 924. Possession of a royal diploma or charter gave presumptive title to land held by bookland but it would not be necessary for a king regranting land which had reverted to royal control to do anything more than hand over the original deed of grant without issuing a new diploma. In other words, the absence of diplomas shoulld not be seen as evidence that no royal grants were made, but that no *new* grants were made, so ensuring that royal assets were not diminished at a time when all resources were required to deal with the Scandinavian threat: the hiatus of bookland diplomas coincides exactly with the period during which the conquest of the southern and eastern Danelaw was taking place.[2624]

As Dumville notes, '[t]he events of 910 [the battle of Tettenhall] mark a turning point in Anglo-Scandinavian relationships; they may also mark the beginning of a decade and a half during which Edward's followers were rewarded for their military support with grants of land in the Danelaw', some likely to have been estates held by those Northumbrians who fell in the conflict [the assumption being that the Northumbrians in that conflict were the Danes of York, which could well be incorrect], with other Danish landowners dispossessed to allow English officials, especially ealdormen, to create an 'aristocracy of Southern orientation'.[2625] We might suppose that Æthelred and Æthelflæd granted similar bounties to Mercian nobles and others who had participated in the great victory or supported the ongoing campaign against the Danes. It must be admitted that such grants are not known to us, but there is evidence that though some Danish leaders and their followers (such as Jarl Thurcytel of Bedford and his compatriots)[2626] left England during the 'reconquest' of the Danelaw by Edward and Æthelflæd, most acknowledged Edward's

---

[2621] Wainwright 1975: 90; ASC 'A' 917; Swanton 1996: 98.
[2622] It will be seen that Æthelflæd died at Tamworth in 918, very soon after accepting the submission of the York-folk, suggesting (since treaties were customarily concluded on a boundary) that Tamworth then lay on the border of Northumbria and Mercia. That the boundary was little changed in 925 is shown by the record in the *Mercian Register* of the short-lived marriage that took place that year between Æthelstan's sister and Sihtric at Tamworth: ASC 'C'; Swanton 1996: 105.
[2623] Land vested without a charter was known as folkland.
[2624] Dumville 1992: 151-2.
[2625] Dumville 1992: 151-3.
[2626] ASC 'A'; Swanton 1996: 100.

position as king, with some Danish landowners retaining control of their estates, or at least receiving them back from Edward, in return for recognition of their law and customs, and, as noted elsewhere, some leaders, such as Earl Thurferth of Northampton, even retained their status after submission.[2627] At least one Danish leader was later assisted by Edward to leave the country with his followers to live amongst the Franks.[2628]

Reverting to the military position, what is especially noticeable is that during this period Edward and Æthelflæd were rarely, if ever, involved in joint campaigns against the Danes: each was responsible for a specific region and operated to a great degree independently, though there must have been co-ordination of military activities. Year-by-year, previous advances by Edward and his sister aimed at revanchism of the Danelaw were consolidated and the English frontier pushed gradually outwards. This was a massive logistical undertaking involving considerable planning to co-ordinate the activities not just of two significant armies, but also the mobile cohorts of pioneers, surveyors, engineers, drainage experts and navvies, with associated support facilities to obtain and deliver materials and ancillary services to maintain those creating the fortifications. In addition, the Mercian church, strongly supported by Æthelred and Æthelflæd, who undoubtedly shared the common belief that the Viking attacks were a scourge sent by God to punish Mercians for their sins, had long played an active role in *burh*-building, as revealed by an agreement that fortuitously survives from between 884 and 899 between Bishop of Waerferth of Worcester and Æthelred and Æthelflæd whereby the bishop was granted rights and dues within the new *burh* in Worcester in return for a substantial contribution towards its construction, which preserved his existing church.[2629]

As we have seen, the *burhs* built by Æthelflæd at Eddisbury, Chirbury, *Weardbyrig* and Runcorn[2630] were patently designed to protect Mercia from the Irish North Sea Hiberno-Scandinavians in and around the Wirral, but it was not only the English who had reason to fear the Irish Norse: the Danes of Northumbria were sufficiently disturbed by the threat from the newcomers (with good reason, as time was to prove) and so debilitated economically and militarily – probably from before the battle of Tettenhall, since a drop in coin quality has been identified from 905, perhaps reflecting economic decline linked to their defeat at the Holme and the demise of Viking Dublin as a major trading partner after the ejection of the Hiberno-Norse from Dublin c.901 – that they had neither the heart nor the means to countenance further aggressive action against the English, or offer support to their brethren in the region around the Five Boroughs who were open to attack by the Hiberno-Norse as well as the English. Æthelwold's disastrous bid for the English throne in 903 had left Northumbria kingless for more than fifteen years, an uneasy period for a kingdom not without significant residual power and influence. Equally importantly, there was a loosening of ties between the Danes in England and their kinsmen in Denmark.[2631]

[2627] Lapidge et al 2001: 136; Higham and Ryan 2013: 299-300.
[2628] In 917 Jarl Thurcytel 'sought out' Edward as lord, but we are told that 'almost' all of the principal men of Bedford joined him. Those who did not join him were doubtless the reason why Thurcytel 'with the peace and help of King Edward ... went across the sea to the land of the Franks with those men who wanted to follow him': ASC 'A' and 'D'; Swanton 1996: 100.
[2629] S.223; Brooks 1996: 143; Walker 2000: 195.
[2630] Swanton 1996: 98-9.
[2631] Dolley 1978: 26.

Little is known of the Danes of the Five Boroughs in the years immediately after 910,[2632] but as if to emphasise how the Scandinavian armies were essentially a many-headed Hydra, they took steps – perhaps even earlier, soon after the disastrous defeat at the Holme – to fortify Stamford, Leicester, Derby, Lincoln, Nottingham, Northampton, Huntingdon and Bedford (with Jarls Thurferth, Toli and Thurcytel controlling armies centred on the last three-named towns respectively),[2633] and by April 913 they – or possibly Hiberno-Scandinavians from the north-west, though that seems unlikely – were sufficiently confident, as noted above, to turn again to raiding and looting, with warbands from Northampton and Leicester raiding as we have seen into English Mercia and reaching Hook Norton in north Oxfordshire near the border with Warwickshire.[2634] Although the Danes in eastern England were fragmented and under no unified control, they retained the ability to take on the English forces, and the weakened state of Danish Northumbria meant that there was no power in northern England capable of effective resistance to the Hiberno-Scandinavian invaders from Ireland: there is little evidence that the York-based Northumbrians engaged in any serious campaigns.[2635]

Badly burned after their defeat at Tettenhall (if they have been correctly identified as the adversary at Tettenhall), the Hiberno-Scandinavians of the north-west turned their attention away from England, fearful of further confrontation with the might of the confident Mercian and West Saxon armies, and launched a second great wave of Viking attacks against Ireland which began in about 913 with the routing of an Irish fleet off the English coast and the following year destroying a rival fleet off the Isle of Man. The Hiberno-Scandinavian fleet was perhaps based in the Mersey or, at a safer distance from English forces, at Preston, at the mouth of the Ribble.[2636] As noted in Chapter 36, the arrival in Ireland of the remnants of a Viking fleet from Brittany (devastated and overrun by Scandinavians) that had entered the Severn estuary in 914,'utterly destroying everything at the river's side which they could lay their hands on', as Florence (John) of Worcester records,[2637] but also mentioned by Æthelweard who plays down the episode by noting that 'the fighting was not seriously protracted there in that year',[2638] prompted Ragnall, the powerful Norseman from Dublin, with his cousin or brother Sihtric Cáech (who was to marry Æthelstan's sister at Tamworth in 926), to return to Ireland to resettle Dublin on a new site (but not before entering the Severn estuary), and and with the help of reinforcements from the Breton Norse he temporarily captured York, and even issued coins at its mint in his name, heralding a period of still closer links between York and

---

[2632] Tyrrell records a curious tale that after the death of King Eohric of East Anglia at the battle of the Holme, c.903, certain Danish earls oppressed the people of East Anglia or incited them to take up arms against the West Saxons until the 18th year of Edward's reign (918), when he overcame them and the region was brought under his control: Tyrell 1697: Book V 313.
[2633] Stafford 1985: 112. Jarl Thurferth is not to be confused with Thurferth the hold killed at the battle of Tettenhall, since the Jarl is mentioned after the date of the battle.
[2634] Although recorded in *Chronicle* 'A' in 917. The 'significant juxtaposition' of dates is attributed to the 'chronological confusion' of the reign of Edward the Elder: Stafford 1985: 112-3.
[2635] Downham 2009: 86.
[2636] Hall 2001: 189.
[2637] Stevenson 1853: 75. This was the raid (also briefly recorded by Æthelweard: Campbell 1962: 53) where Norse survivors from a battle at Archenfield were released by the English and then made abortive attempts to land in Somerset before being driven to Flatholme, where many died of hunger before the rest escaped to Ireland: ASC 'A'; Swanton 1996: 98, 100.
[2638] Campbell 1962: 53.

Dublin.[2639] From a seemingly reliable Irish source we learn that this expedition to capture York was undertaken jointly by Danes and Norwegians, with similar joint enterprises alluded to in the vicinity of the Clyde in 913, a surprising development in the light of the brutal wars for the control of Dublin some half a century earlier and evidence of considerable importance, for any such alliance, doubted by many historians, will have been of considerable concern to Æthelflæd and Edward. Ragnall's authority was quickly asserted north of the Tyne, and a year later with a force of Breton Norse he attacked and defeated Eadwulf, king of Bernicia, where Ragnall became ruler, and thereafter was recognised as king of York.[2640] At the same time, the Scots, who had been resisting the York–Dublin Scandinavian dynasty since its members first made their piratical appearance in Scotland in the third quarter of the ninth century, submitted to that same dynasty.[2641]

Any alliance alluded to by the Irish annalists between the Irish Norse in exile and the Danes of York was probably a political and military necessity: the Irish annalists later speak of a military pact between a leader to be identified as Æthelflæd – though her name is not actually mentioned – and the northern Celtic kings which (if true) can only have been aimed at the Scandinavians.[2642] Yet as we have seen in the discussion of the *Three Fragments*, there must be considerable doubt about the existence of any reciprocal pact by Æthelflæd with the Picts and Scots. Given the existence on their eastern borders of yet unpacified Danes, and unpredictable and aggressive Hiberno-Scandinvians to the north and north-west, it is impossible to believe that Æthelflæd would have been ready or able or willing to support the Picts and Scots if they were attacked when those Scandinavians remained a grave threat.[2643]

Before the end of the decade Ragnall, as ruler of York, may even have accepted Edward the Elder as overlord of Northumbria, although the nature of any such overlordship cannot be known.[2644] It was during this period – perhaps c.917, though Irish sources differ as to the date – that Ragnall and Sihtric went to Ireland. Ragnall returned to York leaving Sihtric to consolidate Dublin as a major Viking centre. Norse kings then ruled York from 919 to 954 (interrupted by twelve years of English rule), with a Dublin-York axis which

---

[2639] Hall 2001: 190. Ragnall, one of the grandsons of Ivarr the Boneless, was expelled from Dublin in 902 and for the next four years harried the kingdoms of Strathclyde and Scotland. After the defeat of the Danes at the battle of Tettenhall he seized power in York and became king at some date between 910 and 914. In 914 he seised a large part of English Northumbria extending to the Tyne, and defeated an army raised against him by Constantine II of Scotland at the first battle of Corbridge. From 917-8 Ragnall was in Ireland to support his brother or cousin Sihtric Cáech. As has been noted, it is said that during that time Æthelflæd assembled a joint force of Mercians, Strathclyde Britons and Scots against him, but that seems doubtful. Æthelflæd was in negotiations with disaffected factions in York when she died in 918, enabling Ragnall to defeat the army of Constantine II at the second battle of Corbridge, and in 919 to overcome the opposition of York. On his death in 919, Ragnall was succeeded by Sygrygg Cáech (Sihtric Cáech): Williams, Smyth and Kirby 1991: 205. The Northumbrian coinage between 905 and 927 consists of coins in the name of St Peter, to whom York minster was dedicated. The coins are of differing weights, suggesting a decline from c.1.3 grams to c.97 grams or less, possibly as a result of the Danish defeat at Tettenhall, or the subsequent raids of the Hiberno-Scandinavian: Grierson, Blackburn and Travaini 1986: 322.
[2640] Clerigh 1910: 282-3; Higham 1993: 185-6; Byrne 2005: 852; Charles-Edwards 2013: 503.
[2641] Dumville 1992: 149.
[2642] Higham 1993: 185-6.
[2643] See especially Davidson 2001.
[2644] Downham 2009: 88.

marked a remarkable growth in trade, and a growing power which doubtless caused considerable concern to Edward and his successors.[2645]

While Æthelflæd had been creating her *burhs* in the West Midlands, Edward was undertaking a similar fast-moving programme in the east and south-east of the region and, having taken possession of London and Oxford in 911 on the death of Æthelred, concentrated on the recovery of East Anglia and the South-East Midlands. In 912 he built *burhs* at Hertford and Witham, between London and Colchester; in 915 constructed a new *burh* at Buckingham, which soon led to the submission of the Danes of Bedfordshire and Northamptonshire; and in 917 established a garrison at Maldon. Florence (John) of Worcester tells us that in 918 (*recte* 917) 'many of the English of East Anglia and Essex, who for nearly thirty years had been under the iron sway of the pagans, joyfully placed themselves under the king's protection. The Danish inhabitants of East Anglia also presented themselves to him ... A Danish army in Cambridge came also ...'.[2646] We are also told that a certain Turketil, a Danish chief from Buckingham, was not just permitted, but also assisted – though in what way is not explained – to leave for Gaul with his followers.[2647]

But in 916 Æthelflæd's *burh*-building programme had been interrupted by another threat. In midsummer of that year, according to the terse entries in the *Mercian Register*, an Abbot Ecgbriht, 'though innocent', and his companions were killed before midsummer on 16th June.[2648] The *Register* then adds a sentence: *Þyilcan dæge wæs Sċe Ciricius tīd ðroweres*,[2649] 'That same day it was the festival of St Ciricius the martyr'.[2650] Ciricius is an

---

[2645] Logan 1991: 161-2; Williams, Smyth and Kirby 1991: 22. Higham 1993: 185-6 has noted that intermarriage between the leaders of the Dublin Norse and the Great Danish Army had occurred towards the end of the ninth century, and that for a decade or so after 905 the Irish Norse attacked only the rivals of the Northern Army – the Scots, Strathclyde and the 'northern Saxons' of Bernicia, where the death of King Eadwulf in 913 prompted a Scandinavian invasion in 914.
[2646] Stevenson 1853: 77.
[2647] Stevenson 1853: 76.
[2648] Little is known of Ecgbriht, but he is likely to be the same person as Abbot Ecgberht who witnessed a charter of Æthelflæd (S.225) in 915: *Prosopography of Anglo-Saxon England* sub nom *Ecgberht* accessed 12 September 2015; Earle and Plummer 1892-9: I 100.
[2649] Thorpe 1861: I 191
[2650] ASC 'C'; Whitelock 1961: 64; Swanton 1996: 100. Information about Ciricius (*Giric mac Dúngail*, nicknamed *Mac Rath*, fl.878-889) is elusive and conflicting. From entries of doubtful value in versions A and D of the *Chronicles of the Kings of Scotland*, and the *Prose and Verse Chronicle* inserted in the *Chronicle of Melrose*, as well as a cryptic Irish poem *Prophesy of Berchán*, of dubious historical value, it is said that he was the son of Dúngal, killed his predecessor Aed son of Kenneth, reigned (with Eochaid map Rhun) as king of the Picts and Scots for 12 years, subdued all Ireland and nearly all England, and was the first to rid Scotland of Viking domination and give liberty to the Scottish church which had been in servitude to the Picts. He was remembered especially as a contemporary of Alfred the Great, a military leader and liberator of churches, whose territory extended from the farthest north of Britain down to Bernicia and Strathcylde, an area roughly equal to modern-day Scotland, and died in Dundurn in Strathearn, Perthshire, though the nature of his martyrdom is unrecorded. He was buried on Iona: Anderson 1922: 357-8, 363-5; Whitelock, McKitterick and Dumville 1982: 123-4; Hudson 1996: 85, 205-8, 241-2; Broun 1999: 140-3, 157, 162; Koch 2006: 523; Woolf 2007: 118-9; Marsden 2010: 167-75; Ashley suggests that Ciricius and Eochaid may have been defeated by their cousin, Donald II, and fled with other dispossessed Strathcyde Britons to northern Wales: Ashley 1999: 385. A church dedicated to the saint is said to have existed at Ecclesgreig in the Mearns, associated with St Andrew's Piory, in the late ninth century, and is recorded in 1200: Anderson 1822: 364. Various later Scottish chroniclers write of Giric as 'King Gregory the Great' who conquered half of England and all of Ireland. Evidently his

obscure saint, and mention of his name in the *Register* is baffling, but we must suppose he was of especial significance to the Mercians, though we have no further information.[2651] The entry (and references to God and his influence in events in the *Register*), does suggest, however, that the *Register* was compiled by a cleric, for whom the festival presumably had a particular relevance. Three days later – doubtless in response to the killings, with the *Register* emphasising the ability of the Mercian forces to react forcefully and with great speed – Æthelflæd sent an army into Wales which destroyed *Brecenan mere* (Llangorse Lake, near Brecon, known as Llyn Syfadden in modern Welsh)[2652] and captured the king's wife and 33 others.[2653] Nothing more is known of these events, but the implication is that Brycheiniog then possessed its own king who held power under Æthelflæd, and he had been responsible in some way for the abbot's death, forcing Æthelflæd to reinforce her authority in the area.[2654] The inference may be that some Welsh rulers were prepared to

---

memory was recognised, indeed commemorated, in Mercia at the time when Æthelflæd was promoting the cult of martyred royal saints within Mercia, with his feast-day of sufficient importance to be specifically mentioned in a little-regarded entry the *Mercian Register*, evidence that the saint was of considerable importance to the compiler of the *Register*. Whether it was intended to include Ciricius in that promotion is unknown, but his association with Bernicia ('English' Northumbria), with its links to Mercia and Wessex, is noteworthy, and there is a reference to the feast-day of the saint in 1407 at Bardney, from where St Oswald's relics had been translated to Gloucester in 909, showing that the saint's-day was still remembered at that date, though the record does, it is true, name the Roman martyrs Cyricus and Julitta, rather than Ciricius (Preest and Clark 2005: 360), presumably due to a confusion over names. Gerald of Wales mentions strange stories of the staff of St Ciricius/Cyric/Curig at St Germanus's church near Rhayader which had healing properties: Wright 1863: 335. It should be noted that some Cornish churches are dedicated to Cyricus and Julitta, and a Pope Ciricius, whose pontificate began in 384, also became a saint. All share the same feast-day. Swanton prefers to identify Cyricus as a child-saint martyred c.304 who is said to have appeared in a dream to Charlemagne, saving him from death by a wild boar: Swanton 1996: 100 fn.7.

[2651] Various dedications exist to St Ciricius or Cyr or Cyriac or Ciricus or Quircus for churches in the southern part of England (Wiltshire, Cambridgshire, Somerset, Devon and Cornwall), as well as two in Gloucestershire: Stinchcombe 3 miles east of Berkeley, and Stonehouse, 3 miles west of Stroud: Harris 2006: 451. Neither church appears to be of pre-Conquest origin. The saint is umentioned in the index to Thacker and Sharpe 2002, but is noted briefly by Wood 2002: 182.

[2652] The events should perhaps be related to the *Chronicle* account of 918 which records the death of Æthelflæd, and the takeover of Mercia by Edward, with three kings of the Welsh and 'all the Welsh people' turning to Edward: ASC 'A'; Swanton 1996: 98. However, Edward only gained power in Mercia after deposing Æthelflæd's daughter Ælfwynn, and any Welsh submission could not have occurred before 919: Charles-Edwards 2013: 498-9, 504-5. Charles-Edwards has noted that the timber for the crannog at Llangorse Lake, a construction perhaps unique in Wales, was felled between 889 and 893, probably in response to a new threat, perhaps the arrival of great Viking fleets from the Continent in 892: Charles-Edwards 2013: 494. However, a crannog would have offered meagre protection from Viking attack, shown by the ease with which it seems to have been taken by the Mercians. In that respect we may note the conclusion that crannogs in Ireland 'must have been the dwelling places of social groups of modest prosperity': O'Sullivan et al 2014: 62. The king's wife may have been staying on the artificial island of Llangorse crannog, which excavation has shown to have been a high-status residence: James 2001: 242.

[2653] Nora Chadwick suggested that Æthelflæd's raid into Brecon can best be explained as a blow at suspected Irish penetration of Brecon from Pembrokeshire, which was virtually an Irish kingdom, which enjoyed a close relationship with Brecon: Chadwick 1963: 348.

[2654] The king may have been Tewdwr ap Elise, the last historically attested king of Brycheiniog, whose reputation is not unsullied: he is said to have been forced to grant some of his lands as compensation for stealing funds due to the church: Ashley 1999: 159. It appears that the West Saxons had protected the south-east of Wales from Mercia, but had allowed most of the remainder of south Wales to be held under Mercian overlordship: Charles Edwards 2013: 505-7.

challenge Æthelflæd's authority, which might explain the location of some of her western *burhs*.

The account of matters surrounding the death of Abbot Ecgbriht should be compared with the ransom of 40 pounds said to have been paid by King Edward the following year for the release of Cameleac, the bishop of Llandaff, captured in *Ircinga felda* (Archenfield, in the Wye Valley, Herefordshire) and taken to their ships by a great raiding army from Brittany (said by Florence (John) of Worcester to have been the 'pagan pirates, who nearly nineteen years before had quitted Britain and gone to Gaul',[2655] presumably those who had wintered at *Cwatbrycge* in 895-6, though that claim can hardly imply that such raiding army had been engaged in no other campaigns during that interval) with two jarls, Ohtor and Hroald, which had ravaged the Severn estuary 'and utterly destroyed everything by the river's side which they could lay hands on', until driven off by 'the men from Hereford and from Gloucester and from the nearest strongholds', who put them to flight, driving them into an 'enclosure' (*pearroc*) until they agreed terms and gave hostages.[2656] The Viking force left the Severn but attempted to land near Watchet and at Porlock, but was repelled by the English, sustaining severe losses, with the survivors taking refuge on Steepholme until hunger drove them to Dyfed[2657] before they left for Ireland, presumably having received provisions from their enemies to help them on their way.[2658] It is clear that the threat to Mercia at this time came from several quarters, posing a serious military challenge to Æthelflæd and Edward, and was perhaps indicative of unrecorded troubles in the Marcher regions.[2659]

Before Easter 917 a co-ordinated campaign to push back the Danelaw boundaries was put into effect by Edward and his sister. While Edward advanced in the south in an offensive centred around Towcester, *Wigingamere* (unidentified)[2660] and Tempsford, in July Æthelflæd successfully ('with the help of God', wording indicating a hard-won victory) stormed 'Derby' – probably the Roman fort at Little Chester[2661] – albeit with the loss of four of her thegns 'who were dear to her', one of the few accounts in the *Anglo-Saxon Chronicle* to disclose any feelings of emotion, though it is noticeable that the four thegns are curiously un-named.[2662] The attack on Derby, the first direct assault on one of the major Danish fortifications by an English army, may have been timed to coincide with confused fighting around Towcester, Bedford, *Wigingamere* and Tempsford which involved Danes from Leicester and possibly Derby, perhaps leaving Derby with only a

---

[2655] Stevenson 1853: 75.
[2656] ASC 'A' and 'D'; Swanton 1996 98-100; Stevenson 1853: 75. One might have expected Archenfield to have been within Mercian territory, but the *Chronicle* describes the area as 'King Edward's domain': see Charles-Edwards 2013: 506.
[2657] Downham has questioned whether this entry implies that the people of Dyfed may have chosen to ally with the Vikings in the early years of the 10th century: Downham 2009: 211.
[2658] ASC 'A' and 'D'; Swanton 1996 98-100; Stevenson 1853: 75. The events should perhaps be related to the *Chronicle* account of 918 which records the death of Æthelflæd, and the takeover of Mercia by Edward, with three kings of the Welsh and 'all the Welsh people' turning to Edward: ASC 'A'; Swanton 1996: 98. However, Edward only gained power in Mercia after deposing Æthelflæd's daughter Ælfwynn, and any Welsh submission could not have occurred before 919: Charles-Edwards 2013: 498-9, 504-5.
[2659] ASC 'A' and 'D'; Swanton 1996: 98-9.
[2660] See for example Haslam 1997.
[2661] Birss and Wheeler 1985: 11.
[2662] On this episode see especially Thompson 2002: 11-12.

skeleton defence, an example of the successfully co-ordinated strategy of Æthelflæd and Edward.[2663]

At the beginning of 918 there remained four Danish strongholds between the Welland and the Humber still outside English control. Two of them, Stamford and Leicester, were occupied by Edward and Æthelflæd respectively during the first half of the year – *Anglo-Saxon Chronicle* 'C' tells us that Æthelflæd had peaceably taken control of the fortress of Leicester – a year after the occupiers had successfully campaigned against Edward – and subjected 'most' of its associated forces.[2664] During his campaign Edward may even have restored the former Danelaw rulers back to power at some of the *burhs* after they had promised him their allegiance,[2665] a suggestion strengthened by the *Anglo-Saxon Chronicle* which records enigmatically that in 918 Edward captured Nottingham, the earliest Danish centre in the region, probably occupied since 867,[2666] and 'ordered that it be improved and occupied, both with Englishmen and with Danish',[2667] evidence of some accommodation with the Danes in a fortification perhaps intended to resist the Hiberno-Scandinavians.

We must suppose that a sophisticated communication system of despatch riders existed to ensure that Edward and Æthelflæd each knew where the other was and would be at any particular time so that each could be made aware of any emergency in the other's kingdom, and it must have been an especially traumatic personal as well as military setback to Edward when messengers reached him at Stamford while he was 'settled in the seat there', having supervised the construction by his army of a second fortification on the south side of the river Welland and received the submission of all the people from the northern stronghold, to report the shocking news that Æthelflæd had died at Tamworth on 12th June 918,[2668] no older than 50.[2669] In the words of the *Anglo-Saxon Chronicle*, 'Æthelflæd ...

[2663] Wainwright 1975: 314-5; Walker 2000: 110. In his *Historie of Cambria* (1584), 47-8, (reprint of 1811: 39) David Powel gives a legendary account of the attack on Derby: 'Io. Castoreus reporteth this storie in this maner. Huganus Lord of Westwales, perceiuing King Edward to be occupied in the Danish warre, farre enough from him, gathered an armie of Brytaines, and entered the Kings land. Wherevpon Elfled, Ladie of Mercia, the sister of King Edward, came to Wales with a strong armie, and fought with the Welshmen at Brecknocke, and putting Huganus to flight, took his wife and 34. men captiues, and lead them with hir to Mercia. Huganus thus discomfited, fled to Derbie, and there being peaceablie receiued of the countriemen with fifteene men of warre, and two hundred souldiors well appointed, ioined himselfe with the Kings aduersaries the Danes, of which thing when Elfled was certified by the men of Derby, shee followed him with a great armie, and entred the gates of that towne, where Huganus resisted hir, and slue foure of hir chiefe officers. But Gwyane Lord of the Ile of Elie hir Steward, set the gates on fire, and furiouslie running vpon the Brytaynes, entred the towne. Then Huganus being ouermatched, and choosing rather to die by the sword, than to yield himselfe vnto a woman, was there slaine. This out of Castoreus.' The ultimate authority for this baseless legend is an author called Joannes Castoreus, that is, John (le) Bever, alias John of London, who flourished in 1310: note by Egerton Phillimore in *Y Cymmrodor*,X (1890) 116.
[2664] ASC 'A' and 'D'; Whitelock 1961: 66.
[2665] Some early 10th-century charters record in their witness-lists groups of Scandinavianised names perhaps representing those who were from Scandinavia or of Scandinavian descent allowed to keep their lands in and around Northampton and Cambridge in return for submitting to Edward in 917: Lavelle 2012: 74.
[2666] Higham 1993a: 113.
[2667] ASC 'A' (the entry wrongly dated 922); Swanton 1996: 104; Abrams 2001: 138.
[2668] ASC 'A'; Swanton 1996: 103.
[2669] Æthelflæd's father Alfred married in 868, and Æthelflæd was his oldest child, described as *coniux* (wife) of Æthelred in a Worcester charter of 887 (S.217): Dumville 1992: 18 fn.86. Skeletal evidence suggests that life expectancy (heavily skewed by the high proportion of deaths in childbirth and childhood) rose during the Anglo-Saxon period to 35.8 and 38.2 years for males and females

departed [died] ... 12 days before midsummer inside Tamworth'. What may have caused her death is unrecorded: whilst there is no hint of sickness or illness or indeed of any untoward or suspicious circumstances, neither is there is any suggestion that her death was sudden.[2670] It may be assumed that she was taken ill and died soon after, somewhere within the ancient square palace enclosure close to St Editha's church.[2671] In recording her death, version 'A' of the *Anglo-Saxon Chronicle* is careful not to describe her as Lady of the Mercians, as in 'B' and 'C', but as 'his [Edward's] sister'.[2672]

As discussed elsewhere in this volume, if later and dubious Irish accounts are to be believed, in about 918 Æthelflæd had assembled a coalition of Mercians, Strathclyde Britons and Scots to resist Ragnall, the Hiberno-Norse leader expelled with Ingimund's forces from Dublin in 901 and who in 914 had seized a large part of 'English Northumbria', otherwise Bernicia, which retained strong ties with Wessex and Mercia, and had ambitions to take York.[2673] The final act in Æthelflæd's life as recorded in the *Mercian Register* (but not, of course, the *Anglo-Saxon Chronicle*) is the submission to her by the *Eoforwicingas* ('York-folk'), a group not to be confused with Ragnall's Norsemen, but whose identity – whether Angles or Danes or Anglo-Danes – is not free from doubt,[2674] who had promised her – and some of them granted so by pledge, some comfirmed with oaths – that they would be at her disposition',[2675] an action (if historians are correct in accepting uncritically the account in the Æthelflæd-centric *Mercian Register* (our sole source for the claim, which is conspicuously entered immediately before the record of her death) that by a particular irony must be seen the high point of Æthelflæd's remarkable military career.[2676] Her presence at Tamworth – the place where early Mercian kings had their palace, and which Æthelflæd had successfully recovered from Danish control – is unexplained,[2677] but might have been directly related with the alleged sworn allegiance she had secured from the *Eoforwicingas*, doubtless because of their long-standing fear of the powerful pagan

---

respectively, with the gender differential persisting into the later Middle Ages, but those who survived their teens might expect to live considerably longer: Härke 1997: 135.

[2670] Thompson 2002: 1, 8-25. We might also note the sudden, unexplained and possibly suspicious death of Edward's son Ælfweard (preferred by the West Saxons as Edward's successor), who died shortly after his father in 924: Keynes 2001: 51.

[2671] On the early history of St Editha's church see Meeson 2015: 15-40, and for an outstanding study of the background to the death and buruial of Æthelflæd see Thompson 2002: 1-25 and generally.

[2672] Swanton 1996: 103.

[2673] Williams, Smyth and Kirby 1991: 205.

[2674] Whitelock 1961: 66-7; Wainwright 1975: 92, 337. The 'York-folk' are likely to have been the Christianised Anglo-Danes of York.

[2675] ASC 'C'; Whitelock 1955: 36; Swanton 1996: 101. The nature of the pledges, which evidently differed from oaths, is unclear, but the promise bythe *Eoforwicingas* may indicate that Æthelflæd, rather than Edward, was perhaps the dominant influence north and west of a line from Cirencester to Northampton and on to Stamford: Charles-Edwards 2013: 498. The *Eoforwicingas* had every reason to fear Ragnall: ASC 'D' and 'E' record that in 923 *Regnold cyning ge wan Eofer wic* 'King Ragnall won York': Earle and Plummer 1892-9: i 105; Swanton 1996: 105. As discussed in more detail elsewhere, an Irish tradition which assigns to Æthelflæd an important role which would readily explain the decision of the *Eoforwicingas* to choose her as their protector and ally is now considered baseless.

[2676] A very puzzling account is provided by Tyrrell, seemingly from a manuscript of Edmund de Hadenham in the collection of 'Mr Lambert', presumably the Kent historian and antiquary William Lambard, recording that in 918 'the Lady Elfleda, by the assistance of the King her brother, besieged the city of Canterbury, and taking it, slew a great many Danes that were therein': Tyrrell 1697: Book V 320. The identification of Canterbury is an obvious error.

[2677] One possibility is that Æthelflæd, having taken Nottingham, was planning to attack Lincoln, the last free Scandinavian stronghold south of the Humber. The date of its recapture is unrecorded.

Ragnall, with those fears highlighted by the important battle of Corbridge earlier in the year, for treaties were customarily concluded on boundaries.[2678] Whether that submission took place as claimed cannot be known: Downham, for example, suggests that Ragnall may have been welcomed by the Northumbrian Danes after Æthelflæd's death as a strong leader capable of resisting Edward's ambitions over Northumbria.[2679]

What is particularly noteworthy – indeed quite extraordinary – is that the submission, though perhaps not formalised (if indeed formalities were observed in such situations), had been made to Æthelflæd, and not to her brother Edward, the inference being that she had some kind of authority over the kingdom of York, or that the York-folk had real concerns about her brother.[2680] On the other hand Florence (John) of Worcester tells us that in 918 (*recte* 917) 'The Danish inhabitants of East Anglia also presented themselves to [King Edward], and swore that neither by sea nor by land would they do anything to [his] prejudice', a claim untraced elsewhere, but which would balance the submission of the York-folk to Æthelflæd.[2681] It would be invidious to wonder how Edward saw the alleged submission of the *Eoforwicingas* to his sister, and whether there may have been any connection with that event and his actions after her death, which seems to have created enough of a crisis in Northumbria to allow the take-over of York by the Hiberno-Norse, which meant that Edward and his successor (and Æthelflæd's foster-son) Æthelstan faced a hostile Scandinavian faction north of the Humber until matters came to violent climax at the battle of *Brunanburh* in 937.

Æthelflæd had by any standards been an exceptional personality. One notable modern authority could claim, with no intended hyperbole, that she had been 'the most remarkable woman in English political history' and 'England's founding mother'.[2682] With her husband,

---

[2678] Seven years later Tamworth remained the boundary: it was the placre where Sihtric, King of Northumbria 920-7, married 'Eadgyth' (in a short-lived arrangement) in 925: ASC 'D'; Swanton 1996: 105; Giles 1892: 245.
[2679] Downham 2009: 95.
[2680] One commentator has suggested that the submission to Æthelflæd rather than Edward can be simply explained: Mercia adjoined Northumbria, whereas at this time Edward was separated from Northumbria by Danish fortifications at Nottingham and Lincoln: Walker 2000: 111-12. The suggestion seems unconvincing.
[2681] Stevenson 1853: 77. The account continues: 'A Danish army from Cambridge came also, and made choice of [King Edward] for their lord and master: moreover, at [King Edward's] request, they took oaths to the same effect.': ibid.
[2682] Arnold 1879: 158; Tom Holland, *The Sunday Times*, 10 January 2016; Holland 2016: 95. On Æthelflæd's titles in various sources see Earle and Plummer 1892-99: II 118-9.It has been suggested that the OE poem *Judith*, an incomplete and damaged manuscript of some 350 lines dating perhaps from the later part of the tenth century, and written by the same scribe who was responsible for lines 1939b to 3182 of the *Beowulf* manuscript, may have been intended to commemorate the valiant deeds of Æthelflæd, though that idea has also been described as dubious: Szarmach 1998: 126 fn.23. The poem adapts the story of the Old Testament heroine of the same name and depicts the heroic code within a religious context, the heroine being the only character in OE poetry to engage actively in wielding a weapon (when she decapitates the drunken Holofernes of the Assyrians), and it is worthy of note that the greatest prose stylist of the Anglo-Saxon period, Ælfric the Homilist, had previously written a homily on Judith to teach the English the virtues of resistance to aggressors, which perhaps influenced the anonymous author of *Judith* to treat her as a national figure in the struggle of the English against the Danes: Treharne 2000: 196-211.Writing *c*.1130, Henry of Huntingdon declared Æthelflæd 'to have been so powerful that in praise and exaltation of her wonderful gifts, some call her not only lady, or queen, but even king' and follows this with a panegyric Latin poem describing her as 'worthy of a man's name' and, as noted above, 'more illustrious than Caesar': Forester 1853: 168 (in English); Arnold 1879: 158; Szarmach 1998: 122 (in Latin). Caradoc of Llancarvan gives the

a powerful, ambitious, and energetic ruler until incapacitated by illness or injury and probably unfairly relegated into his widow's shadow, she had taken an unusually active role in the rule of Mercia for some 27 years, not only witnessing charters but taking on a joint role in the matters covered by the documents, becoming, if we have read the evidence correctly, the senior partner in the relationship from the early years of the tenth century as his health gradually deteriorated, which doubtless created issues which we cannot begin to imagine. For a further seven years she ruled alone as a widow, proving to be a redoubtable military tactition and political leader in her own right, greatly feared by the Scandinavians, but also educated, learned, pious, energetic, visionary, and resolute, a zealous Christian devoted to St Peter, [2683] who with her husband had vigorously promoted throughout Mercia various royal saints and religious establishments – a true daughter of her father, himself an exceptional pious ruler and formidable military leader.[2684] With her ailing husband and determined brother she had achieved remarkable military success (including a memorable victory at Tettenhall), culminating in the effective collapse of the northern Danelaw. Unlike the majority of eligible Anglo-Saxon widows, after her husband's death she had remained unmarried,[2685] but continued apace with an astonishingly ambitious *burh*-building programme spread across the West Midlands; had gradually made inroads into the heavily militarised areas of the Danelaw bordering Mercia; and had died at the height of her powers.[2686] Her prominence may be explained in part by the relatively higher status which seems to have been accorded in the ninth and tenth century to Mercian queens than in neighbouring Wessex, possibly associated with the different succession arrangements in the two kingdoms,[2687] and by a select group of particularly competent loyal advisers whose abilities in all areas of statecraft and military strategy should not be overlooked.[2688]

Among her other later admirers was William of Malmesbury, describing her as a 'powerful accession to [Edward's] party, the delight of his subjects, the dread of his enemies, a

---

same Latin poem, which he says was set above her tomb: Powel 1584: 40. That poem may have been extracted from a poetic Latin account of the *gesta Adelfleda* from *Elfledes Boc*, an enigmatic lost manuscript, about which nothing more is known, recorded at Durham in a medieval catalogue: Szarmach 1998: 188-9, 122; Stafford 2008: 105-8.

[2683] Thompson 2002: 13-4, 18-9,25.

[2684] It is noticeable that after the death of Alfred in 899, Æthelred's charters and those of his wife make no reference to the consent of any overlord, with a few coming close to describing them as king and queen, using such periphrasis as 'holding, governing and defending the sole rule [*monarchia*] of the Mercians': Ryan 2013: 297. A useful itinerary of Æthelred and Æthelflæd is to be found in Bailey 2001: 116.

[2685] For a discussion of Æthelflæd's role see Wyatt 2009. A perceptive, if debatable, evaluation of Æthelflæd's life is to be found in Walker 2000: 96-121.

[2686] Tellingly, Welsh annals make no mention of the death of Æthelred, but record the death of *Aelfled regina* and *Eldfled vrenhines*, 'Queen Æthelflæd': Ab Ithel 1860: 17; Jones 1971: 28-9, though since the time of Offa the wives of Mercian kings had regularly borne the title *regina* in charters and also acted as witnesses in official documents, usually immediately after the king, another indication of their status: Stafford 1981: 3-27; Stafford 1983; Walker 2000: 114-6.

[2687] In Mercia the kingship rarely passed from father to son, but was generally in competition between rival dynasties, where the marriage of an erstwhile king might strengthen support from families close to the marriage alliance and a wife would carry considerable influence in the royal administration. West Saxon royal wives are far less prominent and were evidently of lesser status: Walker 2000: 114-6.

[2688] In a rare account of emotion and demonstrating personal relationships of this period we are told in the *Mercian Register* that in 917 four of Æthelflæd's thegns 'who were dear to her' were killed inside the gates during the recovery of Derby: Whitelock 1961: 64-5. One or more of those unnamed thegns may have fought at Tettenhall six years earlier.

woman of enlarged soul ... this spirited heroine assisted her brother greatly with her advice, was of equal service in building cities ... able to protect men at home and to intimidate them abroad'.[2689] Henry of Huntingdon recalled that she was said to have been so powerful that she was not only called lady or queen,[2690] but also king, in deference to her great excellence and majesty, which he honoured with a short tribute in verse,[2691] in which he described her as more illustrious than Cæsar (though his conclusions may have been distorted by his reliance on a version of the *Anglo-Saxon Chronicle* which incorporated the *Mercian Register* en bloc for the annal after 914, but lacked the West Saxon account of the years 914-20).[2692]

After her death Æthelflæd's body was probably removed first to a local church – perhaps St Editha's, to which relics of the saint, Æthelflæd's great aunt, may have been translated from nearby Polesworth by Æthelflæd herself in 913[2693] – before it was prepared (ritually washed, anointed with sweet-smelling spices and herbs, clothed, and shrouded in linen)[2694] for its journey to Gloucester, 66 miles away. In the meantime, messengers and senior *ealdormen* and officers will have travelled ahead to give word of the death and assist in the preparations for the obsequies. The courtege, with its wooden coffin, perhaps lead-lined and decorated with elaborately scrolled iron fittings,[2695] covered with a sumptuously-decorated pall and probably carried on a canopied unsprung two-wheeled cart, or even a

---

[2689] Giles 1847: 123-4.
[2690] It is telling that one of the last surviving authentic charters to which Æthelred was a party, dated 904, uses the phrases *Æþelrede 7 Æþelflæde ... hlafordum* 'Æthelred and Æthelflæd ... lords' and *Æþelred aldorman 7 Æþelflæd Myrcna hlafordas* 'ealdorman Æthelred and Æthelflæd lords of the Mercians': S.1280. Another charter dated 878 for 916 (S.225) describes Æthelflæd as *regine*, but is in part corrupt.
[2691] The Latin panegyric reads (Arnold 1879: The following translation is offered by Forester 158):   (1853: 168):

O Elfleda potens, O terror virgo virorum,	Heroic Elflede! Great in marshall fame,
Victrix naturæ, nomine digna viri.	A man in valour, woman though in name;
Te, quo splendidior fieres, natura puellam,	Thee warlike hosts, thee, nature too obey'd,
Te probitas fecit nomen habere viri.	Conqu'ror o'er both, though born by sex a maid.
Te mutare decet, sed solam, nomina sexus,	Chang'd be thy name, such honour triumphs bring,
Tu regina potens, rexque trophœa parans.	A queen by title, but in deeds a king.
Jam nec Cæsarei tantum meruere triumphi,	Heroes before the Mercian heroine quail'd:
Cæsare splendidior, virgo virago, vale.	Cæsar himself to win such glory fail'd.

[2692] Keynes 2001: 42. As a result, Henry was led to believe (wrongly) that Æthelflæd was ealdorman Æthelred's daughter.
[2693] Meeson 2015: 18-19. It is possible to imagine that in any illness before her death Æthelflæd chose to end her life within a church she knew well and had perhaps even refurbished to house the relics of a sainted member of her own wider family: ibid. 35-7. Embalming seems to have been largely unknown at this period, with even the use of externally applied substances such as myrrh and balsalm to disguise rather than delay the onset of decay uncommon, though some evidence for the process has been detected in archaeological contexts: ibid; Rodwell 1989: 39-41. A *līc-wake*, or night vigil with prayers, is likely to have been held over Æthelflæd's corpse during its time at Tamworth: Thompson 2002: 82-4.
[2694] Thompson 2002: 21, 33, 108-10, 115. The washing, clothing and shrouding of a corpse seems to have been common practice in episcopal circles in Mercia c.900: Thompson 2002: 20-21.
[2695] Thompson 2002: 124-6. Some coffins have been found with lids fitted with locks, and it has been suggested that with only the lid visible in the grave, they would have looked very like a door leading down into the earth: ibid. 125.

four-wheeled *wægen*,[2696] drawn by a pair or two of oxen or a team of horses, moved as quickly as the animals would allow rather than with the modern solemnity appropriate to such journeys, since embalming, though not unknown, was rarely practised in the early tenth century, and delays were to be avoided.[2697] With an honour-guard of armed warriors,[2698] the cavalcade would also be accompanied by her her personal entourage, sombre *ealdormen* and other Mercian officials, and perhaps her daughter Ælfwynn, though we have no information as to her whereabouts at the time of her mother's death and she may well have been elsewhere.

In the absence of major waterways, the funeral procession doubtless followed the straight Roman Ryknild Street – then barely maintained and far less impressive than it had been several centuries earlier – which ran six miles west of Tamworth directly to Gloucester via Droitwich, Worcester and Tewkesbury.[2699] Æthelflæd would quickly be interred with suitable reverence and afforded the distinction of a royal funeral with appropriate pomp and panoply[2700] – prayers, hymns, music and candles – in *þam east portice*, the east porticus (probably a crypt)[2701] of the 'New Minster', St Oswald's (the *Mercian Register* refers to St Peter's, the earlier dedication),[2702] her favoured religious foundation, built on a surprisingly modest but unusually elaborate scale from re-used Roman limestone masonry and sumptuously adorned by Æthelflæd and her late husband over some two decades where the bones of St Oswald had been brought in 909 and where she had laid her husband to rest

---

[2696] The *wægen*, from which the modern word wagon derives, is a conveyance rarely pictured in Anglo-Saxon art, unlike the common two-wheeled cart.

[2697] Embalming seems to have been largely unknown at this period, with even the use of externally applied unguents such as myrrh and balsalm to disguise rather than delay the onset of decay uncommon, though some evidence for the process has been detected in archaeological contexts: Rodwell 1989: 39-41; Thompson 2002: 20-21. William of Malmesbury tells how after his death Robert Bloet, bishop of Lincoln (1093-1123), was disembowelled so that his body 'might not pollute the air with foul smells', with his innards buried at Eynsham, the rest at Lincoln: Preest 2002: 212. The fact that the process was mentioned implies that it was not the norm.

[2698] Gild statutes from Exeter required an escort of 15 men to recover a member who fell ill within 60 miles, and a dead member 30 men, with 15 to 30 men accompanying the cart carrying a dying man or the corpse in Abbotsbury: Thompson 2002: 113-5.

[2699] Margary route 180. An alternative route would have been by road to Worcester, some 38 miles, and some 25 miles by water along the Severn to Gloucester.

[2700] Some idea of the elaborate ceremonies and rituals surrounding the burials of Æthelred and Æthelflæd may be seen in the charter (S.223) concluded by them at some date before 899 with bishop Werferth of Worcester which records in considerable detail the spiritual benefits they could expect in life and death in return for a financial contribution to the church, mainly fines extracted from the citizenry for breach of market rights and similar, suggesting that Worcester may have been their chosen place of burial before Gloucester was decided upon: Thompson 2002: 18-19.

[2701] ASC 'B', 'C' and 'D'; Thorpe 1861: I 192-3. The east porticus would normally mean the chancel, but probably means here a sunken crypt traced by archaeology adjacent to but seperate from St Oswald's, reminiscent of the 8th-century royal mausoleum at Repton: Heighway 2001: 109. The absence of grave-cuts suggested to excavators that the crypt could have housed either the tombs of Æthelred and Æthelflæd, or the shrine of St Oswald, or both, perhaps in the form of box-shrines: Thompson 2002: 17.

[2702] Whitelock 1961: 67; Thompson 2002: 16-17. From the reference in the *Mercian Register* Hunt concludes that Æthelflæd was buried in the Old Minster, St Peter's Abbey, founded within the Roman walls c.679 by Osric, ruler of the Hwicce (Hunt 2016: 121), overlooking that St Oswald's was so-named after the translation of the saint's relics (if not before), and was earlier St Peter's: Heighway 2001: 102, 108.

in 911.[2703] Mourners at her interment must have included her successor as Lady of the Mercians, Ælfwynn, with many Mercian *ealdormen*, bishops and senior clerics (who will have seen Æthelflæd to be a true Mercian, rather than Alfred's West Saxon daughter), and with Æthelflæd's nephew and foster-son Æthelstan,[2704] supported by senior nobles from Mercia and Wessex, and perhaps even contingents from Wales, York and Bernicia in attendance, if they managed to reach Gloucester in time.[2705] The assembled group, swollen by large numbers of grieving Mercians for whom Æthelflæd and Æthelred had been their saviours, will have been headed by Æthelflæd's brother King Edward, who will surely have struggled to retain his composure when leading the eulogies.[2706]

Although the precise chronology of events after Æthelflæd's death remains uncertain, it seems that Edward, evidently distrustful of the loyalty of the Mercians, promptly – perhaps even before Æthelflæd's body was removed from Tamworth[2707] – took advantage of her death and, as told by Florence (John) of Worcester, hastened to Tamworth (46 miles from

---

[2703] Szarmach 1998: 125 fn.19; Heighway 2001: 102-11; Thompson 2002: 18-25. St Oswald's had been founded by Æthelred and Æthelflæd 'with no expense spared' at some date between c.885 and 899: Heighway 2001: 103.

[2704] Æthelstan was to die at Gloucester ('snatched away from the world ... by an untimely death' according to William of Malmesbury: Preest 2002: 271), even perhaps at St Oswald's church, on 27 October 939, but was taken for burial to Malmesbury, his beloved and favoured abbey (which he had endowed with great riches and many relics, of which he was an assiduous collector), where he was buried under the altar next Aldhelm, the scholar and poet who died in 709 and was greatly admired by Æthelstan: Foot 2011: 186-7; Holland 2016: 74-5, 83. William of Malmesbury tells how before a battle Æthelstan lost his sword, but 'called upon the name Aldhelm and had been given his sword from heaven and thus snatched from the grasp of the enemy. Since that day he had bestowed upon the monastery [Malmesbury] several estates, many altar cloths, a gold cross, reliquaries also of gold, together with a piece of the Lord's cross ...': Preest 2002: 14, 271. For evidence from the time of Edward I that in the year of his coronation (925) Æthelstan seems to have made a grant of privileges to the church of St Oswald in accordance with 'the pact of paternal piety which formerly he pledged with Æthelred, ealdorman of the people of the Mercians' (that is, at some date between the deposition of Oswald's relics in 909 and Æthelred's death in 911), see Foot 2011: 34.

[2705] After her death, and her daughter's removal from power, with no other descendants to invest in its endowment Gloucester lapsed into relative obscurity, and was rarely visited by English kings. The golden age of St Oswald's had effectively come to an end, and even the site of the graves of Æthelflæd and her husband became lost to memory: Thompson 2002: 23-5. But if they fulfilled their obligations, the church community at Worcester will have prayed for her soul by singing *Laudate Dominum* three times a day and celebrating mass on Saturday: Thompson 1992: 25. It is difficult to reconcile the lapse of St Oswald's church into obscurity and the statement of William of Malmesbury that it was destroyed in succeeding times by the Danes, with Aldred, Archbishop of York and Worcester in 1061-2, founding another which was the chief of that city (Giles 1847: 124), and William's claim that Archbishop Thurstan of York (1119-40) – also responsible for the diocese of Worcester – took particular trouble to restore the shrine of St Oswald and enlarge the church, during which the graves and remains of Æthelred and Æthelflæd were supposedly discovered in the south porch: Hamilton 1870: 293; Preest 2002: 198. William's account shows that the shrine survived and was restored during the first half of the 12th century, even if we should treat with scepticism his claim that the remains of Æthelred and Æthelflæd were revealed.

[2706] The esteem in which Æthelflæd was held by the Mercian people is reflected in the popularity of her name among the Mercian (and other) nobility in the years after her death, including two future queens of England, Æthelflæd of Damerham, second wife of King Edmund I, and Æthelflæd*Eneda*, wife of King Edgar, as well as a number of noble ladies, including the wife of Æthelweard the chronicler: Walker 2000: 119-20. The *Prosopography of Anglo-Saxon England* (accessed 8 January 2017) records 30 women of that name, though some references may be to the same person.

[2707] In which case Edward will presumably have accompanied his sister's body on its journey to Gloucester.

Stamford) and 'reduced it to submit to him', or as recorded in *Anglo-Saxon Chronicle* 'A', after taking the stronghold of Tamworth, 'all the nations of the land of Mercia which was earlier subject to Æthelflæd turned to him', and the kings of Wales, *Howel* [Hywel], *Cledauc* [Clydog] and *Ieoþwel* [Idwal],[2708] and all the race of the Welsh sought him as their lord', before the *Chronicle* mentions Edward's move against Nottingham. Those listed kings ruled respectively the Welsh kingdoms of Powys, Dyfed – which probably included Ceredigion and Ystrad Tywi – and Gwynedd, which were added to the existing Welsh kingdoms over which Edward enjoyed overkingship.[2709] Charles-Edwards, analysing the language of *Anglo-Saxon Chronicle* 'A', concludes that the chronicler has linked two distinct political events: the submission of the Mercians who 'turned to' Edward, and the Welsh kings and all the Welsh people who 'sought him as their lord'. In both cases the *Chronicle* leads us to believe that the initiative came from those submitting rather than Edward. But the terms used can be differentiated: *cirran*, 'turn', is the standard and most neutral phrase used in the *Chronicle* for submissions, whereas to 'seek a lord' is a standard phrase for commending oneself to a lord, whether or not a king. Charles-Edwards argues that this shows that the Welsh kings and people were more empatically subject to Edward than were the Mercians. The situation can be distinguished from the submission by which Anarawd of Gwynedd and Æthelred of Mercia submitted to Alfred (if Asser is to be believed) on similar, if not identical, terms.[2710]

The *Chronicle* account would imply, at the very least, that the death of Æthelflæd had led to more than shock and grief on the part of the Mercians, and their loyalty to their Lady did not extend to her brother.[2711] Edward's action is, predictably, unmentioned by the *Mercian Register*, with the Mercians now finding themselves under the rule of the King of Wessex and necessarily circumspect about what might be written about their new ruler. Though we have no evidence of how the *ealdormen* and populace of Mercia viewed this development, it can be readily imagined: the realpolitik of the situation was accepted pragmatically, but Edward, the new commander-in-chief, is unlikely – to say the least – to have enjoyed widespread support, and almost certainly attracted a good deal of bitterness and hostility.[2712] It has indeed been suggested that Edward secured the necessary support from

---

[2708] Thorpe 1861: 195.

[2709] Stevenson 1853: 78; see also ASC 'A'; Swanton 1996: 103-4. It has been argued that evidence from Welsh sources suggests that the Welsh kings who submitted to Edward represented rulers over whom Æthelflæd had enjoyed overlordhip, a role inherited from her husband (Walker 2000: 107), though Charles-Edwards finds no evidence that the Welsh kings were transferring to Edward submissions previously made to Æthelflæd. From a close reading of the vocabulary used in ASC 'A' he has noted that after Æthelflæd's death the Welsh kings and people were more emphatically subject to Edward than were the Mercians, with no suggestion of any equality in the terms of submission which had, according to Asser, existed between Anarawd of Gwynedd and Æthelred of Mercia. Indeed, he thinks it possible that Anarawd's son Idwal did not submit to Edward before Charles-Edwards concludes that ASC 'A' compressed events: the Welsh kings could not have submitted to Edward before 919, and indeed Idwalprobably did so only after the mysterious battle of the 'New Fortress' (possibly Rhuddlan), recorded in typically cryptic fashion in the *Annales Cambriae* for 921, which was fought between the Welsh allied with Edward against the Vikings, or between the Welsh and the English: ASC 'A' 921; Swanton 1996: 103-4; Charles-Edwards 2001: 103; Charles-Edwards 2013: 498-500, 503.

[2710] Charles-Edwards 2013: 493-44, 498-9.

[2711] ASC 'A'; Swanton 1996: 103; Stevenson 1853: 78. Curiously, neither Roger of Wendover nor Matthew Paris mention Edward 'taking' Tamworth: Giles 1892; Luard 1872: I.

[2712] That picture is not necessarily shared by other commentators: see for example Walker 2000: 123-4, where the long period of co-operation between the formerly rival kingdoms is emphasised. Although Wainwright concluded that the removal of Ælfwynn meant that '[w]hatever the Mercians

important sections of Mercian society by promising a separate succession for Mercia after his death, an idea perhaps confirmed by what actually occurred when he died.[2713] As James Campbell has observed, at this period, 'Vikings or no Vikings, there remained an important and intransigent Mercian faction opposed to the West Saxon connection', which explains Edward's anxiety to achieve what was effectively a *coup d'état* to subsume Mercia into Wessex, and the delay in realising his aims.[2714]

Having recorded that all the nation of the land of Mercia which was earlier subject to Æthelflæd turned to Edward, it is puzzling to find a reference in the *Anglo-Saxon Chronicle* soon after the recovery of Nottingham in the same year recording that 'all the people that was settled in the land of Mercia, both Danish and English, turned to him'.[2715] As discussed later in this volume, that can surely refer only to 'Old' Mercian territory – that which lay south of the Humber, perhaps associated with the *Eoforwicingas* who had offered their loyalty to Æthelflæd shortly before her death – which had been within the Danelaw), and might tell us that Edward was succeeding not only to 'English' Mercia, but also to 'Old' Mercia, so perhaps serving as evidence that both were formerly under Æthelred's control and latterly held under Æthelflæd until her death. But the explanation is likely to be more prosaic: the submission was probably in respect of the last two of the Five Boroughs still in Danish hands – Stamford and Lincoln.[2716] Why the scribe chose not to name those places is inexplicable.

But tensions between Mercia and Wessex had long existed (and probably long continued),[2717] with distinct undertones of resistance, if not rebellion, by the Mercians, perhaps alarmed and suspicious about the circumstances surrounding Æthelflæd's sudden death and determined to maintain their independence as a kingdom, and might be discernible in the *Chronicle* accounts. If there was Mercian unrest, Ælfwynn's role is unknown, but it is difficult to imagine that she took no steps to protect Mercian interests, and certainly there is no evidence that the Mercians chose freely to submit to the direct rule of Edward – indeed the opposite seems to have been the case.[2718] Florence (John) of Worcester tells usthat having 'reduced' Tamworth (a puzzling phrase, for the word 'reduced' normally indicates destruction) to submit to him, Edward moved his army to Nottingham and had it repaired, stationing both English and Danes there.[2719]

---

thought about it, the inevitable had happened. Mercia and Wessex were united, and Mercia no longer existed as a separate state' (Wainwright 1975: 93), that exaggerated the position. For example, we learn that after Edward's death in 924 the Mercians chose Æthelstan as king (ASC 'D'; Santon 1996: 105), and the Mercians retained their own army which fought at *Brunanburh* (ASC 'A'; Swanton 1996: 108). Furthermore, there seem to have remained separate administrative arrangements for the collection of tribute, one covering the West Saxons and another for the Mercians, a division which evidently persisted long after, and the Mercian *witan* continued to meet and consider issues of concern to Mercia intermittently for several decades: see for example S.1447 (Robertson 1956: 91-3), a record dating from between 950 and 968 of a dispute involving estates; see also Smyth 1995: 441-2. But by the late tenth or early eleventh centuries Mercia existed, essentially, only in name. Edwin, the last Earl of Mercia, was assassinated in 1071: Eyton 1881: 9, 32.

[2713] Walker 2000: 205.
[2714] Campbell 1991: 161.
[2715] ASC 'A'; Swanton 1996: 104.
[2716] Oxford DNB *sub nom* Edward the Elder.
[2717] See, for example, Cumberledge 2002. The almost complete absence of references to Æthelred in the *Anglo-Saxon Chronicle* and even the *Mercian Register* may be evidence of how he was seen in Wessex.
[2718] For a plausible, if unprovable, account of these events see Walker 2000: 122-4.
[2719] Stevenson 1853: 78; see also ASC 'A'; Swanton 1996: 103-4.

The *Chronicle* accounts seem to tell us that even though Edward had taken control of Tamworth – evidently by force, or at the very least intimidation – the idea of a West Saxon king ruling Mercia was an unthinkable anathema to the Mercian *witan*, and it was some time before the shocked Mercians finally submitted, albeit grudgingly, to his authority,[2720] pointing to some degree of Mercian opposition and hostility,[2721] presumably led by Ælfwynn, to whom Æthelflæd's authority passed after her mother's death. At that date Ælfwynn was probably aged between 25 and 31[2722] – with her parents she witnessed three charters in 903,[2723] is mentioned in another in 904 (by which the bishop of Worcester grants property at Worcester to Æthelred and Æthelflæd for their lives and that of Ælfwynn, which has been seen to imply that it was intended that she would succeed to her parents' position),[2724] and had evidently taken on more responsibility after her father's death in 911.[2725] We have no knowledge of the role she played during this period, though she attested at least one charter in 916,[2726] but there is little doubt that from birth she received an education and upbringing appropriate for King Alfred's grad-daughter to ensure her competence to succeed to the mantle held by her parents, and was expected to step into her her mother's position – in which case she is the only known example in Anglo-Saxon England of a daughter succeeding her mother –and was recognised, at least by the Mercian *witan* and the general population of Mercia, as Lady of the Mercians, for the *Mercian Register* refers specifically to her authority over the Mercians, and Florence (John) of Worcester refers to Ælfwynn's Mercian kingdom – which will have increased

---

[2720] It is worth noting that at this period, 'Vikings or no Vikings, there remained an important and intransigent Mercian faction opposed to the West Saxon connection', which explains Edward's anxiety to achieve what was effectively a *coup d'état* to subsume Mercia into Wessex: Campbell 1991: 161. Walker suggests that the Mercians were probably won over by an assurance from Edward that at his death Mercia would be ruled by Æthelstan and Wessex by Ælfweard, but one suspects that any such unenforceable and unpredictable assurances are unlikely to have weighed seriously with a sceptical Mercian *witan*: Walker 2000: 124. Intriguingly, the late 14th-century *Book of Hyde* records that *Filium autem unicam Elfleda, nomine Elfwynam, rex Edwardus senior, potestate Merciorum ei adempta, duxit secum in Westsaxoniam* 'Elfleda's only daughter, named Elfwyna, was carried by King Edward the elder into West Saxony, when the government of the Mercians was taken from him [*sic*]': Edwards 1866: 61; Stevenson 1855: 514. The implication is that Ælfwynn was dispossessed when she resisted the surrender of Mercia to Edward after his sister's death.

[2721] Such animosity may have erupted in 924, when Edward was forced to put down a combined Mercian and Welsh uprising at Chester days before his death at Farndon: Giles 1847: 131; Griffiths 2001: 182.

[2722] Woolf 2001: 99 and Bailey 2001: 112-27, although an earlier age has been suggested since her mother Æthelflæd probably married in 883 (as revealed by a charter from the Worcester archives (S.218): Keynes and Lapidge 1983: 228) or 884 (Williams, Smyth and Kirby 1991); DNB says in or before 880; Staffordclaims, without citing sources, 887: Stafford 2003: 259.

[2723] Ælfwynn, identified as *Ælfwynn 2* in the*Prosopography of Anglo-Saxon England* (accessed 9 February 2016), unusually for a woman who was not a queen, queen-mother nor abbess, witnesses charters in 903 (S.367), 904 (S.1280) and 878 (for 916) (S.225): Keynes 2001: 52-4; Bailey 2001: 117-121. She seems to have played little part in administrative activities pertaining to Mercia before her deposition, but that picture may be distorted by the few charters that have survived from the period.

[2724] S.1280, probably authentic, relating to property in or near Worcester, on which see Walker 2000: 112, which perhaps overstates the evidence.

[2725] Bailey 2001: 118-22.

[2726] S.225, dated 878 (for 916), probably a corrupt copy of an authentic early 10th-century document: Sawyer 1968: 127.

substantially in size after her mother's conquests over the previous twelve months or so – after recording the death of Æthelflæd.[2727]

The Common Stock of the *Anglo-Saxon Chronicle*, though recording the death of Æthelflæd (extraordinarily, the only reference to this remarkable individual in the entire text), conspicuously ignores and makes no mention of Ælfwynn, but nearly six months or eighteen months after her mother's death (depending on the dating of the *Chronicle* entries),[2728] three weeks before midwinter she was seised on Edward's orders, 'deprived of all authority in Mercia', and 'led into Wessex',[2729] (words with an ominous ring), with Henry of Huntingdon pointedly explaining that Edward was more concerned with 'the policy than the justice of the act'.[2730] The abduction, presumably unannounced, and conspicuously unmentioned in *Anglo-Saxon Chronicle* 'A', is recorded with barely-concealed resentment by the *Mercian Register*, incorporated into versions 'B', 'C', and 'D', where the annalist tells of the abrupt deposition (but not identifying the abductor) not of her West Saxon mother's successor, but of the daughter of Æthelred, the Mercian-born 'Lord of the Mercians'.[2731] From this it could be inferred, and seems to be accepted by many scholars, that her actions, or perhaps inaction,[2732] did not meet the approval of her

---

[2727] Stevenson 1853: 78.

[2728] See Wainwright 1975: 127-9; Bailey 2001: 115-7; Pelteret 2009: 328. Florence (John) of Worcester tells us that it was only after Edward had stationed troops at Thelwall and Manchester in the autumn of 920 that he 'entirely deprived his niece Ælfwynn of her Mercian kingdom': Stevenson 1853: 78. ASC 'B', 'C' and 'D' record (in identical terms) the death of Æthelflæd 12 days before midsummer in 918, and the deposition of Æfwynn 3 weeks before Christmas the following year, with ASC 'A' recording Æthelflæd's death in 922 with no mention of Æfwynn: Thorpe 1861: 192-4. One reason for the confusion could be explained by the *Mercian Register* beginning its year with midwinter, with the *Anglo-Saxon Chronicle* using the September indiction: Bailey 2001: 115-7.

[2729] ASC 'C'; Whitelock 1961: 67; Swanton 1996: 105. Curiously, Florence (John) of Worcester erroneously records the removal of Ælfwynn following the restoration of Manchester, which occurred in 922: Stevenson 1853: 78; ASC 'A'; Swanton 1996: 104. The date has been wrongly corrected in ASC 'A': Bailey 2001: 117.

[2730] Forester 1853: 168.

[2731] ASC 'C'; Swanton 1996: 105. One commentator has concluded that Edward was in Tamworth in the summer of 918 to secure Ælfwynn's succession as ruler of Mercia by ensuring that the Mercian *witan* and those Welsh kings previously subject to Æthelflæd submitted to Ælfwynn's authority, but that after leading a Mercian and West Saxon force to capture Nottingham, Edward returned to Tamworth to deprive his niece of her authority since she was a 'young girl' who had failed to prove herself, and the Mercian *witan* believed it had little choice but to support Ælfwynn's removal in return for an assurance from Edward that Æthelstan would succeed him as ruler of Mercia: Walker 2000: 113-4, 122-4. That analysis may be correct, but Ælfwynn was hardly a young girl, and there is scant evidence to support it. It has been suggested that the Welsh kings could not have submitted to Edward before 919: Charles-Edwards 2103: 499. It may be noted that the chronicles record that in 920 a great raiding-army gathered from East Anglia, Essex 'and from the land of Mercia' to besiege the newly-built stronghold of *Wigingamere*, which repulsed the Danish attack: ASC 'A'; Swanton 1996: 101. The reference to 'the land of the Mercians' must refer to areas of Mercia occupied by Danes: Florence (John) of Worcester refers to the submission of all the Mercians and the Danish inhabitants of Mercia after Æthelflæd's death: Stevenson 1853: 78.

[2732] Walker concludes that Ælfwynn's removal can be explained by Edward's need for strong military leadership in Mercia: Walker 2000: 113. Certainly there is no evidence of any actions taken by Ælfwynn as Lady of the Mercians during her brief rule. Florence of Worcester and Simeon of Durham record how after Æthelflæd's death Edward sent an army of Mercians to repair Manchester (his first recorded act as Lord of the Mercians), evidently to stand between the Hiberno-Scandinavians in Ireland and the Danes in Yorkshire, and stationed 'valiant soldiers' there before depriving Ælfwynn of her authority: Stevenson 1853: 78; Stevenson 1855: 501. One cannot but suspect that the two events, if chronologically accurate, might be connected: perhaps Ælfwynn

uncle – doubtless her relative youth and perceived inexperience were seen as potential handicaps, or she showed unwanted and feisty resistance to her uncle's proposal effectively to subsume Mercia into Wessex – and she is then almost, but perhaps not quite, lost to history, probably remaining single and spending the rest of her life in a nunnery.[2733] It was probably shortly after Ælfwynn's deposition that Edward pointedly drove the boundary dividing the newly-shired counties of Staffordshire and Warwickshire directly through the

---

opposed her uncle's strategy, or was tardy in responding. This accords with the entry in ASC 'A' which records that in 923 (recte 922) a *burh* was built by Edward at Thelwall, and the Mercian army was ordered to 'improve' Manchester and man it: Swanton 1996: 104. No mention is made of Ælfwynn in that entry. Florence and Simeon's entries do not necessarily imply that the deposing of Ælfwynn could have resulted from her failure to commit forces to the project, since Manchester was probably refortified in 919, but possibly the following year or even later: Griffiths 2001: 177.

[2733] Foot 2011: 59. Alex Woolf has considered the 'constant intermarriage between the various royal houses of the ninth and early tenth century', the seizure of the unmarried Ælfwynn by her uncle, and the statement that William of Malmesbury that the young Æthelstan was brought up by the Mercian court in expectation of inheriting Wessex. He suggests that Æthelstan may have been betrothed to Ælfwynn, his first cousin, but that by the time he came of age the idea had become impossible in the new climate of religious reform tightening canonical restrictions on consanguinity of marriage following the death of Wærferth of Worcester, the most learned Englishman of his generation, in 915 or 916: Woolf 2001: 99-100. Ælfwynn is unrecorded in the chronicles after she was led away to Wessex, but is likely to have entered a nunnery, the customary fate of royal widows, unmarried princesses and other noble women removed from society but requiring security, such as her own aunt, Æthelgifu, King Alfred's daughter, who became abbess of Shaftesbury, in which case she may be the Ælfwynn who seems to have been a member of the royal family and may have been living as a lay sister in a nunnery, perhaps at Nunnaminster (Winchester) or Wilton (where two of Edward's daughters, Eadflæd and Æthelhild, were nuns), who is mentioned as a 'religious woman' in a charter of 948 (S.535) from King Eadred, although the charter does not mention any ties of kinship: see Dockray and Millar 2000: 70-76; Walker 2000: 114; Bailey 2001: 115-27, but also Keynes 2001: 57. Another of Edward's daughters, Eadburh, was a nun at Nunnaminster in Winchester: Bailey 2001: 122. For evidence supporting a curious theory that Ælfwynn married, and that one of her children was Wulfrun, captured by the Danes in 940, and possibly the same person as the benefactor of the monastery of Wolverhampton, see see SHC 1916 47-57, 62-6; WA I 289-91; and Wainwright 1975: 127. If the hypothesis is correct, Wulfrun would have been a great grand-daughter of King Alfred. The theory seems to be given some credence in VCH III 199, and it must be conceded that the *Burton Chronicle* describes her son Wulfric as *regali propinquus prosapiae* 'of near royal stock': SHC 1916: 10, 62-6. Modern scholars appear to have rejected – or overlooked – the theory, but see Hart 1975: 373. The *Prosopography of Anglo-Saxon England*, accessed 7 November 2014, lists 11 women named Wulfrun, some of whom are clearly the same person. It is worth recording a remarkable claim made by John Beaver or Bever (Latin *Fiberius* or *Castorius*), a Benedictine monk in Westminster Abbey, who flourished c.1320, who is cited in John Powel's edition of the *Historia Brittonum* of Caradoc of Llancarvan, that Ælfwynn was deprived of her authority by Edward for 'not making the King hir vncle (whome his mother had appointed gardian and ouerseer of hir) priuie to hir doings, had promised and contracted mariage with Raynald [Ragnall] King of the Danes': Powel 1584: 40. At about this time, according to Beaver, Leofred, a Dane [the name Leofred is English], and Gruffydh ap Madoc, brother-in-law to the prince of West Wales, came from Ireland with a great force, and intending to take all Wales and the Marches overran all the country to Chester before Edward learned of his plans. Vowing revenge, Edward and his sons with their private forces recaptured Chester, and with his forces split into two, with he and his son Æthelstan leading the first division and Edmund and Edred leading the second, chased the enemy to Walewode (Sherwood), where Æthelstan wounded and captured Leofred, and Edmund and Edred killed and decapitated Gruffydh. The heads of both Leofred and Gruffydh were displayed at Chester: Powel 1584: 40. Neither Leofred nor Gruffydh ap Madoc, or the events in which they were supposedly involved, are otherwise known to historians at this period. John Beaver or Castorius was held in some esteem by Leland, Stowe and Bale; his chronicle forms part of the Cottonian Collection, and has never been printed. There was a monk of St Albans of the same name who left writings of little value: Chalmers 1812: 268-9.

centre of Tamworth, the historic royal centre of Mercia – and perhaps explains the otherwise curious use of the word 'reduced', normally meaning 'destruction', by Florence (John) of Worcester.[2734] This action, evidently a pointed attempt to discourage Mercian separatism, is perhaps the most direct evidence for disunity between Edward and the Mercian rulers – and the Mercian ealdormanry – which may have been simmering for years, and evidently re-emerged on the death of Edward in what seems to have been a contested succession, with the Mercians successful in supporting the claim of Æthelstan with his strong Mercian links.

Yet Ælfwynn's rule of Mercia, however shortlived, deserves further analysis, since her deposition marked the end a brief interlude unique in Anglo-Saxon history, the seven years when Mercia was ruled by female rulers at a period dominated by warfare controlled by leaders in person. As the offspring of what may be seen as the most successful married partnership of the Anglo-Saxon period, it is surely the case that she had received the best possible schooling (alongside her nephew Æthelstan – probably some 2 to 8 years younger than Ælfwynn – if William of Malmesbury is to be believed)[2735] in statecraft, literary and biblical studies, and not least in military matters, and had gained considerable experience in the Mercian court to prepare for her important role in Mercian life.[2736] It is not difficult to imagine Ælfwynn proving to be an especially strong, independent, single-minded and successful Mercian leader (just as her mother, the daughter of Alfred, had inherited many of her father's strengths), but the paucity of references to her brief rule seem to suggest that that was not the case – or conversely that Edward was alarmed by her independent spirit. Whatever the case, the risk of her marriage to a powerful husband,[2737] and the undoubted loyalty of the Mercian *ealdormen* and military forces to Æthelflæd's heir, are likely to have been seen by Edward (and the West Saxon *witan*) as potential and unpredictable threats which required urgent attention, threats all the more real when assessed in the light of the supposed submission of the *Eorforwicingas* to Ælfwynn's mother (presumably perceived by the *Eorforwicingas* as more powerful and trustworthy than her brother) shortly before her death, a submission which would have very greatly increased the size – and strength and authority – of Mercia.

Whatever the situation, the York-folk had indeed been right to fear Ragnall, who took the opportunity in 919 to march south from Bernicia and seize York, so combining the last two insular Scandinavian armies in a united force to resist Edward's push north. It was seemingly as part of an attempt to reinforce Ragnall's forces at York that Sihtric, from Dublin, raided English Mercia c.919 and razed Davenport, probably the place of that name

---

[2734] Stevenson 1853: 78.Mercia was already hidated, with those hides grouped into provinces which Edward reorganised to support the principal fortifications from which Mercia was administered, revealed by the naming of the west Mercian shires with the formula '[name of central *burh*] + shire': Hill and Rumble 1996: 94. David Hill has suggested that Lichfield may also have been divided between two shires: ibid.
[2735] Foot 2011: 36. Bailey concludes that Ælfwynn was around 15 or 16 years of age in 903 (Bailey 2001: 120), which would make her about 30 or 31 in 918.
[2736] Latin may have been a subject reserved for boys intended for the churchYorke 2001: 28. For a useful analysis of the education of Edward and his sister Ælfthryth see Yorke 2001: 27-9. Curiously, Æthelflæd is unmentioned.
[2737] Bailey 2001: 122. Janet Nelson has raised the possibility that such a marriage may have taken place before her mother's death, and concluded that we are entitled to be suspicious about her fate, citing the mysterious disappearance of Charlemagne's nephews.

near Congleton, on the southern edge of the Danelaw.[2738] The attack may have been part of an attempt to raise 'Danish' Mercia in support of the Northumbrian cause, in which case Sihtric was unsuccessful. Edward's response, his first recorded action after the dispossession of Ælfwynn, was swift: he personally supervised in his capacity of King of Mercia and Wessex the construction of new strongholds in the same region at Thelwall and in the winter of the same year at Manchester ('in Northumbria'), the latter by a Mercian army.[2739] Manchester held a strategic position controlling the important Roman road between the Mersey and York,[2740] and its fortification was probably constructed after Ragnall's position had become more secure in York, and hence a greater threat to the English.

It was about this time – the year is unknown – that Edward took a new wife, his third, Eadgifu, daughter of Sigehelm, the heroic ealdorman of Kent who had taken on Æthelwold and Eohric and their forces and paid with his life whilst achieving an improbable victory at the Holme, effectively saving Edward and his kingdom from annihilation. Whether the marriage was a love-match or a diplomatic arrangement to appease the Kentish people is unknown, but Alfflæd, his second wife, was in typical fashion removed to a nunnery at Wilton.[2741]

If we are to accept the *Chronicle* record (and a careful analysis shows that for this period it was intended as an upbeat account promoting Edward's military accomplishments, just as the *Mercian Register* recited Æthlflæd's achievements), this was also a period of frenetic military activity in eastern England, with the Danes showing that they were prepared to use all means to resist Edward's forces. To address this, Edward, as noted earlier, had built a new *burh* at Towcester in 917 and another at *Wigingamere*, which remains unlocated. The Danes attacked Towcester but were repulsed, turning their attention to the Aylesbury area where they seised men and property. Embarking on their own *burh*-building exercise, Danes from Huntingdon and East Anglia constructed a fortification at Tempsford, and from there sent a force to take Bedford, but were repulsed. They then made an assault on a newly-built English fort at *Wigingamere*, but were again thwarted. Much other detailed information can be extracted from the Chronicles to show the rapidly evolving military situation and the ability of the Danes to regroup and turn their attention to new areas. Eventually Edward led an English force, drawn from the nearer *burhs*, against the newly-built Danish fortification at Tempsford, and in a great battle killed many of the defenders, including an unnamed king (presumably the successor of Eohric, killed at the Holme in 903), the last Danish king of East Anglia, and so recovered the whole of eastern England as far north as the Welland.[2742] After further military action which recovered Huntingdon and Colchester, 'a great tribe, both in East Anglia and in Essex, that was earlier under the control of the Danes, turned to him; and all the raiding army in East Anglia swore union with him: that they wanted all that he wanted, and would keep peace with all whom the

---

[2738] Higham 1993: 188.
[2739] Stevenson 1853: 78.
[2740] Higham 1993: 188; Griffiths 2001: 168-9. The site of *burh* at Thelwall remains uncertain; that at Manchester may have been the Roman fort at the confluence of the rivers Medlock and and Irwell: Higham 1993a: 113; Griffiths 2001: 177. It has been suggested that Edward may have founded a further *burh* at Penwortham, which now lies beneath the Norman castle: Higham 1993: 188.
[2741] Bailey 2001: 122; Holland 2016: 44-5.
[2742] ASC 'A'; Swanton 1996: 101.

king wanted to keep peace, both on sea and on land', and likewise the raiding-army from Cambridge.[2743]

The Northumbrians of York and East Anglia must have realised that further resistance against Edward was hopeless, and (if the *Chronicle* accounts are to be believed) his increasing military achievements reached a climax in 920,[2744] when at Bakewell in Derbyshire, a newly-built English *burh* close to the Northumbria/Mercia border, he received the submission of Constantine, king of the Scots, Ragnall of York, Ealdred of Bamburgh (ruler of all that remained of English Northumbria), and the submission of all the people of Northumbria, whether English, Danes, Norsemen and others, and of the king of the Strathclyde Welsh and all his people, though doubt has recently been cast on the likelihood that any meeting amounted to a 'submission'.[2745]

It may have been at this time that the Mercian boundary was moved north from the Mersey to the Ribble to incorporate territory in what became southern Lancashire known as 'between the Ribble and Mersey' (*inter Ripam et Mersham*)[2746] from the kingdom of York, since its hundredal organisation, hidation, assimilation into the diocese of Lichfield and idiosyncratic name all imply that it came into southern English hands.[2747] Although of no great value as a source of tax, this low-lying frontier region was of particular strategic significance, providing control of the Ribble estuary and the route between Dublin and York.[2748] The district is considered further in the next chapter.

The *Anglo-Saxon Chronicle* would have us believe that in little more than forty years after his father's kingdom had scarcely extended beyond the Somerset marshes, Edward had established himself as the most powerful ruler in all Britain.[2749] However, any accord

---

[2743] ASC 'A'; Swanton 1996: 103. The wording in the *Chronicle* suggests that sea-borne attacks against Edward's forces were viewed as a significant threat. An analysis of East Anglian coin finds has led Mark Blackburn to conclude that notwithstanding the claims in the *Anglo-Saxon Chronicle*, Edward may not have succeeded in imposing his authority in East Anglia as effectively as he had in the east midlands: Abrams 2001: 139.

[2744] Confusion has arisen over the date of the Bakewell 'submission', which is dated variously to 920, 921, 923, and 924: see e.g. Swanton 1996: 104. The confusion arises from misdatings resulting from later addition of minims in ASC 'A' to an initially correct date of 920: Bateley 1986: lviii, 69.

[2745] Green 1883: 217; Earle and Plummer 1899: II 131-2; and especially Davidson 2001: 200-211; Quanrud 2015: 78 fn. In a carefully researched study that deserves to be better known, Charles Truman Wyckoff put forward persuasive arguments to show that the Northumbrian Danes did not submit to an English overlord until the reign of Æthelstan: Wyckoff 1897: 1-12.

[2746] So-called in DB and *þære landabetwux Ribbel 7 Mærse* in the Will of Wulfric Spot c.1000: Sawyer 1979: xxiv, 53-6.

[2747] Higham 1993: 188; Charles-Edwards 2013: 503.

[2748] Sawyer 1979: xxiv; Higham 1993: 188. If the area had come into Mercian hands a decade earlier, we might have an explanation for the puzzling observation by the chronicler Æthelweard that in 909 (properly 910), in the prelude to the battle of Tettenhall, the Danes broke their pact not only with King Edward, but also with 'Æthelred, who then ruled the Northumbrian and Mercian areas': *Ætheredum,qui tum regebat Northhymbrias partes, Myrciasque*: Campbell 1962: 52. Interestingly, when an expedition led by ealdorman Æthelnoth of Wessex advanced on the Danes of York c.894, they are said by Æthelweard to have 'possessed large territories in the kingdom of the Mercians, on the western side of the place called Stamford': Stenton 1970: 9-10; Campbell 1962: 51. That area, corresponding with latterday Rutland (Swanton 1996: 88 fn.6), was evidently seen as Mercian, even though no longer under Mercian control.

[2749] We might note as an aside that in the late ninth and early tenth centuries there is a marked paucity in the issue of royal land charters. There are very few surviving documents from Alfred's reign, and even fewer for the first decade of his son, Edward the Elder. But from 910 to 925 we have a complete

which may have been made in 920 must have been fragile, and on Edward's death in 924 Sihtric, who had succeeded Ragnall on the latter's death in 920, seems to have taken territory in the eastern Midlands, if that is the inference to be drawn from coins issued from the mint at Lincoln portraying motifs identical with those from York. Terms between Sihtric and Edward's son and successor Æthelstan were agreed in 926, sealed by the marriage of Sihtric and Æthelstan's sister[2750] in a Christian ceremony at Tamworth (suggesting that Tamworth then marked the boundary between the territory of Sihtric and Æthelstan), but the following year Sihtric rejected both his wife and Christianity. Military conflict was only avoided by his death soon after, and in 927 Æthelstan 'succeeded to the kingdom of the Scandinavians'.[2751]

William of Malmesbury tells us that Edward died suddenly from sickness at Farndon-on-Dee, near Chester, in 924, shortly after quelling a Mercian and Welsh rebellion, having recovered significant areas of the Danelaw.[2752] Details of any such insurrection are unknown, but Edward's campaign into north-west Mercia might show that the simmering resentment at the West-Saxon takeover of Mercia after the death of Æthelflæd six years earlier was widespread, with more challenges to his authority than we might suppose. Furthermore, it is becoming increasingly apparent that the military successes against the Scandinavians made by Edward and Æthelstan by which the latter became king of all England were not without significant setbacks which remain unrecorded as such in the chronicles. Evidence of those significant ebbs and flows can be seen in the conferences which took place with northern rulers at Bakewell in 924,[2753] Tamworth (noted above) in 926,[2754] and Eamont Bridge (Westmorland), in 926,[2755] for such assemblies normally took

---

and unparalleled absence of royal charters, for reasons which remain unclear, but which are evidently not due simply to the vagaries of preservation: see Hart 1992: 293-301, and, especially, Keynes 2001: 55-6. David Dumville has suggested that we may not need to imagine that no royal grants of bookland (a land tenure which developed into a charter creating title to land with a perpetual right of free bequest, subject to any specific or general restrictions on alienation) were made during this period, but rather that no new land was booked, so that the royal resources were preserved at a time when the king needed all the means at his disposal to deal with the Viking threat, which must have occupied a considerable proportion of his time. The events of 910 marked the beginning of a decade and a half during which the followers of Edward were rewarded with grants of land in the Danelaw, as he attempted to encourage English settlement in areas formerly under Danish influence: Dumville 1992: 151-3; Lapidge et al 1999: 277-8; and especially Keynes 2001: 55. The dearth of charters means that we have little or no evidence (from witness lists) of prominent Mercians who may have participated in the battle of 910. The latest authentic charter of ealdorman Æthelred and Æthelflæd (ignoring those charters relating to Mercian estates issued by King Edward in the first decade of his reign) is to the church of Much Wenlock and is dated 901, with the names of 13 witnesses (in addition to the grantors) in the incomplete witness list, and is thus too early to provide evidence for the situation in 910: Finberg 1972: 148. One thing is apparent: while charters from Canterbury at this period display poor style grammar, those from Mercia, mainly Worcester (see for example S.1281 of 904), remained consistently well written in good Latin by competent scribes: Webster and Backhouse 1991: 261-2.

[2750] Later sources give the name Beatrix (a known Anglo-Saxon name) for Æthelstan's sister, or Eadgyth: Bailey 2001: 114; Williams, Smyth and Kirby 1991: 215-6; but see now TSAHS XLVIII (2015) 18-19.

[2751] Higham 1993: 189. Æthelstan's actions were resisted unsuccessfully by the Northumbrians, and at a meeting later in the year, perhaps at the ancient monastic site at Dacre, near the boundary of York and Strathclyde, their leaders recognised his superiority and 'renounced idolatry': ibid. 190.

[2752] Smyth 1995: 438-40; Griffiths 2001: 167, 182; Charles Edwards 2013: 500.

[2753] ASC 'A', Swanton 1996: 104

[2754] ASC 'D', Swanton 1996: 105.

[2755] ASC 'D', Swanton 1996: 107,

place on borders between kingdoms, in these cases the boundaries of the West Saxons and Mercians with the Scandinavians.[2756] That evidence is supported by coin hoards and individual coin finds which tend to confirm that the border with the Scandinavians fluctuated very dramatically. Nor should we overlook that immediately after Æthelstan's death in 939 Mercia was overrun by the Norseman Olaf who recaptured the so-called Five Boroughs in the north-east Midlands heavily settled by the Danes in the late ninth and early tenth century. The region was not restored to English control until 942, an event recorded in a poem that forms the annal for that year in the *Anglo-Saxon Chronicle*.[2757]

Of what importance in English history was the battle of Tettenhall?[2758] It can be no exaggeration to say that the future not just of Mercia, but of England and the British Isles, hung in the balance at dawn on the fifth of August 910, though in fairness that truism could be made about any number of Alfred's or Edward's battles, and probably many other major engagements during the Anglo-Saxon period, some of which are probably unknown to historians. F. T. Wainwright described the battle as 'one of the most significant events of [Edward's] reign', concluding that '[i]t would be difficult to exaggerate the calamity suffered by the Danish power at Tettenhall'.[2759] Sir Frank Stenton held that 'The battle of Tettenhall opened the way to the great expansion of the West Saxon kingdom which occurred in the following years. ... the Danish armies in Northumbria never recovered from the disaster of 910 ... [by 919] the king of Wessex had received the submission of every Danish army in southern England before the Irish Vikings descended in force on Yorkshire.'.[2760]

A victory by the Northumbrians at Tettenhall – wh possibly intended to soften-up areas of central and western Mercia in preparation for a full-blooded invasion of occupation – would have seen the destruction of the only military force capable of supressing the seemingly inexorable Scandinavian advance and led to the Scandinavianisation not only of all of England, but perhaps the whole of the British Isles. We can imagine the Hiberno-Scandinavians rapidly overrunning Mercia and Wessex, notwithstanding the emerging system of fortified *burhs* which in 910 was being expanded northwards and eastwards, for those few *burhs* could not have held out for long against sustained enemy attack, and with the English armies destroyed, could have expected no reinforcements. How the Hiberno-Scandinavians would have dealt with the Welsh of Cornwall, Wales and Strathclyde, and of course the Danes of York, are questions about which we can only speculate. But at the

---

[2756] Williams 2009: 82.
[2757] ASC 'A'; Swanton 1996: 110; Foot 2008: 131.
[2758] Not a great deal, according to some publications: *The Ordnance Survey Complete Guide to the Battlefields of Britain* [sic], by David Smurthwaite (Webb and Bower (Publishers) Limited, 1984), contains no mention of the battle. Graham-Campbell 1994, a superlative survey of the Viking world, shows the name Tettenhall on a single map, but the battle is unmentioned in the comprehensive text and in the chronological table on pages 8 and 9. Davies 2003, an outstanding survey of the period, contains a chronological table of events which fails to mention the battle of Tettenhall, as does the main text. In fairness, it is debatable whether the protagonists at Tettenhall should be described as Vikings.
[2759] Wainwright 1975: 88.
[2760] Stenton 1971: 323-4. Stenton views were based on the long-established belief that the defeated Scandinavians at Tettenhall were Danes of York, rather than the Hiberno-Norse of the north-west – and he may of course have been correct.

very least we can wonder whether the language that we (and a significant proportion of the world's population) speak today might be Scandinavian in origin.[2761]

But the defeat of the Northumbrian raiding army not only eliminated or incapacitated the principal enemy leaders and many of their followers, but delivered to the victors some or all of the plunder amassed by the Scandinavians during their ravaging, but also transferred to the English the weapons and jewellery normally carried or worn by the Scandinavians themselves. Such wealth will have replenished the coffers of the West-Saxons and Mercians to fund further military sorties and engagements, enabling them to construct more military *burhs*, and to fight off subsequent Scandinavian incursions. After the battle the larger Viking warbands appear to have turned their attention to mainland Europe.[2762]

The battle of Tettenhall was without doubt a pivotal point in the long conflict with the Scandinavians, a conflict of national importance in which a joint English army managed to intercept and defeat decisively what was almost certainly a much smaller but possibly better armed and armoured Scandinavian military incursion, and led directly to the gradual unification of England. It can properly be set against such landmark military engagements the battle of Hastings. It is surprising that the battle is so little known to this day.

[2761] We cannot of course be certain that the language arising out of a Viking-dominated Britain will have been Scandinavian. Scandinavians, even heavily reinforced by fellow immigrants from the European mainland, will have remained very much a minority population. Yet philologists are still debating how a relatively small influx of peoples we know as the Anglo-Saxons led to their language displacing that of the numerically superior Welsh-speaking natives in England.

[2762] Dramatic events were taking place across the Channel soon after the battle of Tettenhall. In 911 the army of Charles the Simple won a significant victory over the Vikings at Chartres, and in a treaty with their leader, Hrolf, better known as Rollo, Charles recognised their control over the area around the mouth of the Seine in return for Rollo's allegiance and baptism. The district around the lower Seine was formally ceded to the Vikings, and became known as the Duchy of the Northmen (Normandy): Davis 1957: 166; Coupland 1995: 201. This effectively ended Viking incursions up the Seine. In 914 the Vikings attempted to create another settlement in Brittany, but in 936 the Bretons drove them out, vitually ending Viking activity on the Continent: Haywood 1995: 52.

36. The enigma of the *Three Fragments* and other problems.

To help elucidate events which occurred in the early tenth century, it is necessary to consider what may be doubtful or peripheral evidence. In that respect the *Three Fragments (Fragmenta Tria Annalium Hiberniæ)*, an Irish manuscript source,[2763] may (or, on the other hand, may not) be of particular importance in any study of the battle of Tettenhall. One section of that manuscript that deserves particular analysis is generally held to refer to the battle or battles of Corbridge, which took place in the second decade of the tenth century.

Before attemptng to set the scene for those battles it must be emphasised that the relevant sources are muddled and often contradictory, with the chronology uncertain, but the key elements are set out by the anonymous author of the eleventh-century *Historia de Sancto Cuthberto* ('History of Saint Cuthbert').[2764] Briefly, we are told that Ragnall 'the king', with a great number of ships, seized the lands of Ealdred of Bamburgh, who fled north and persuaded Constantine II, king of the Scots, to join him in opposing Ragnall. The armies met at Corbridge, the 'heathen king' was victorious, Constantine put to flight, the Scots were scattered, and almost all the English nobles slain. The conquered territory was divided between two Scandinavian warriors, one notoriously hostile to Christianity until, after interrupting a church service, he was appropriately rewarded with a spectacular death. Some three years later Ragnall headed another army at Corbridge and was again victorious. From internal evidence the first battle has been dated between 913 and 915, the second to 917 or 918.[2765]

That is really all that the *Historia* tells us about the battle, but the so-called *Pictish Chronicle* notes that in the 18th year of the reign of Constantine (918) the battle of Tinemore was fought between Constantine and Ragnall, and the Scots were victorious. As a Scottish source we should not be unduly surprised at a claim of a Scots victory, even though the Scandinavians are believed to have suffered heavy losses, but the outcome of battles was often debatable.[2766]

In the Irish account known as *The War of the Gaedhil with the Gaill* ('The War of the Irish and the Norsemen') we are told that 'They [the Scandinavians] went ... to Alba [Scotland], and the men of Alba gave them battle, and they were slain there, that is Ragnall and Oittir'.[2767] This is evidently the same battle, but the account differs, crucially, in reporting Ragnall's death, and that of Ottir.[2768] In fact we know that Ragnall died in 920.[2769] Other Irish sources mention the battle, but in the briefest of terms. The so-called *Annals of the Four Masters* tell us simply that Oittir and the foreigners went from Waterford to Scotland, that Constantine son of Aedh gave them battle, and that Oittir and his followers were slain.[2770]

[2763] Bibliothèque Royale, Brussels, MS 5301-5320, fo. 33a-fo. 34b. See Wainwright 1975: 132-61 for a valuable critique of the manuscript.
[2764] Downham 2009: 91-5.
[2765] Wainwright 1975: 165-6.
[2766] See Williams, Smyth and Kirby 1991: 88.
[2767] Todd 1867: 235.
[2768] A late version of the text adds the name of Constantine to the dead (Wainwright 1975: 169), but he died in 952: Williams, Smyth and Kirby 1991: 88-9.
[2769] Williams, Smyth and Kirby 1991: 205.
[2770] Wainwright 1975: 168-9.

However, what seems to be a contemporary, or near-contemporary, account of an important battle is found in the *Annals of Ulster*, which records that Ragnall, king of the Dubhgall, left Waterford, where he had been in 917, with a force of Scandinavians which included Graggabai and *two* earls named Ottir – a point to which we shall return below. This campaign culminated in the battle of Corbridge, a strategic junction where Stanegate, a Roman road running south to York, is interrupted by the river Tyne, at which they fought against the men of Alba, led by Constantine II, and the English of Northern Northumbria 'on the banks of the Tyne among the North Saxons'. The Scandinavians were in four divisions: one under Guthfrith, grandson of Ivar; a second under the two Ottirs; a third under the young nobles; and the fourth, out of sight and held in reserve, under Ragnall himself. The men of Alba defeated the first three divisions and slew many of the Scandinavian warriors, including Ottir and Graggabai. Then Ragnall launched his reserves, and began to turn the tide, though we are told that no king or *mormaer*[2771] was killed, and the battle was only interrupted by darkness.[2772] The circumstances of this battle have been the subject of intensive scholarly debate as one of the most significant events in the history of the Vikings in Britain.

The Viking leader Ragnall (*Rögnvaldr ua Ímair*), was one of the grandsons of Ivarr the Boneless.[2773] He and his forces were eventually driven from Dublin by the Irish c.901 after a long period of internal dissent, evidently resulting from poor leadership and military setbacks. Those expelled split into groups, some going to France, some (like Ragnall) to the Isle of Man and Scotland, some to the north-west of England. As discussed in more detail in Chapter 33, one faction appears to have sailed to Anglesey, but was forced out by the Welsh and c.903 settled near Chester, probably in the Wirral, supposedly with the acquiescence, if not agreement, of Æthelflæd, and may have been part of a Hiberno-Scandinavian raiding army that was defeated by English forces at the battle of Tettenhall in 910.

Ragnall roamed the western seas and harried the kingdoms of Strathclyde and Northumbria until he took power in York at some date between 910 and 914, and even issued coins at its mint in his name.[2774] In 914 he seized a large part of English Northumbria extending to the Tyne, and, as we have seen, supposedly defeated Constantine II of Scotland at the first battle of Corbridge. From 917-8 he was in Ireland to support his cousin (by some authorities brother) Sihtric Cáech (*Sigtryggr ua Ímair*, Sihtric 'one-eyed', grandson of Ívarr the Boneless who died in 873),[2775] but in 918 defeated King Constantine II at the 'second' battle of Corbridge,[2776] and achieved his objective of reuniting the Dublin kingdom with York. Recent scholarship has shown that there was only one ('second') battle of Corbridge, the confused idea of two battles arising from an

---

[2771] An important officer of state: Wainwright 1975: 168.
[2772] Wainwright 1975: 168; Woolf 2001: 90.
[2773] Downham 2009: 267-8. *Healdene, Eywysl* and *Inwær*, the three Scandinavian kings said by Æthelweard to have died at the battle of Wednesfield/Tettenhall could well have been grandsons of Ivarr: Downham 2009: 87.
[2774] Williams, Smyth and Kirby 1991: 205; Hall 2001: 190. The Northumbrian coinage between 905 and 927 consists of coins in the name of St Peter, to whom York minster was dedicated. The coins are of differing weights, suggesting a decline from c.1.3 grams to c.97 grams or less, possibly as a result of the Northumbrian defeat at Tettenhall, or the subsequent raids of the Hiberno-Scandinavians: Grierson, Blackburn and Travaini 1986: 322.
[2775] Downham 2009: 257-8, 273-4.
[2776] Williams, Smyth and Kirby 1991: 205.

error based on a reading of the *Historia de Sancto Cuthberto*.[2777] In 919 Ragnall was recognised as king, and on his death in 920 was succeeded by Sihtric Cáech.

The various accounts of the battle are clearly difficult to reconcile, and as if this is not confusing enough, there have even been claims (reminiscent of accounts relating to the battle of Tettenhall) that there were no fewer than three separate battles of Corbridge involving two different Ragnalls.[2778] The editor of the latest scholarly edition of the *Historia de Sancto Cuthberto* has concluded that the author of the *Historia*, working with separate references to the same battle, mistakenly created two battles at Corbridge, whereas there was probably only a single battle, in 918.[2779]

At this point we can return to the *Three Fragments*, which survives in a single manuscript which is a copy of a copy made in 1643 by Dubháltach Mac Fir-Bhisigh (Duald MacFirbis) from a vellum manuscript which is now lost. The earliest version is therefore of the seventeenth century, and it is evident that the text has to some extent been modernised. Scholars now believe that the original text was compiled in the late eleventh- or twelfth-century.[2780] Understandably, historians have treated the work with suspicion, generally concluding that it is corrupt and untrustworthy, but one scholar, while acknowledging his lack of expertise in Irish sources, researched the history of the work (and its use by historians) in detail and was willing to accept that important material lies buried in the text. That scholar was F. W. Wainwright, who had a particular interest in the north-west Midlands in the late ninth and early tenth century, and who died tragically young in 1961, but not before publishing careful research in a number of papers which has proved invaluable to later researchers. Wainwright showed that the *Three Fragments* is based ultimately upon contemporary written accounts, and that some entries echo material in the early Welsh chronicles which tends to confirm the veracity of at least some of the Irish entries.[2781] He drew specific attention to a passage which seems to be allocated to 913 or thereabouts, and which gives a typically garbled and legendary description of a battle between Scandinavians and English as follows:

'There came in this year great hosts of the Black Galls ['Dark Foreigners', i.e. Danes] and Fair Galls ['Fair-Haired Foreigners', i.e. Norwegians] again into Saxonland, after setting up Sihtric, grandson of Imhar, as king. They challenged the Saxons to battle. And the Saxons did not indeed delay, but they came at once to meet the Pagans. A stubborn and fierce battle was fought between them, and great was the vigour, and strength, and emulation on both sides. Much of the blood of the nobles was spilled in that battle, but it was the Saxons that gained victory and triumph, after having made great havoc of the Pagans, for the king of the Pagans had contracted a disease, and he was carried from the battle to a neighbouring wood, where he died. But when Otter, the most influential Iarl that was in the battle, saw that his people were slaughtered by the Saxons, he fled to the dense woods which were in the neighbourhood, carrying with him the survivors of his people. Great parties of Saxons followed in pursuit of them, and they encompassed the wood round about. The Queen ordered them to cut all the wood down with their swords and axes. And they did so accordingly. They first cut down the wood, and [afterwards] killed all the

---

[2777] Downham 2009: 91-5.
[2778] Wainwright 1975: 164-5. See also Earle and Plummer 1899: II 130-1 for a useful summary of arguments and evidence for the existence of two Ragnalls.
[2779] South 2002: 8, 105, 106, 107; Downham 2009: 92-3; Downham 2012: 344.
[2780] Davidson 2001: 203.
[2781] Wainwright 1975: 79, 131-54, 150.

Pagans who were in the wood. In this manner did the Queen kill all the Pagans, so that her fame spread in every direction.'[2782]

If we accept at face value the battle account from the *Three Fragments*, we can conclude that it took place probably in Bernicia (as explained below), in the second decade of the tenth century. A large Scandinavian force came to 'Saxonland', after installing Sitric, son of Imhar, as king. A great battle followed, by implication involving Mercians supervised, if not led, by Æthelflæd, with the Scandinavians led by Jarl Ohtor. With the English gaining the victory, a Danish king was taken ill and carried from the battlefield to a nearby wood, where he died. Ohtor, the senior Jarl, fled with survivors to nearby woodland, pursued by English forces, who surrounded the wood. The queen ordered the woods to be cut down with swords and axes, which was done, and those Scandinavians who had been in the woods were killed. The queen's fame was widespread.

Sihtric, mentioned in the above account of the battle in the *Three Fragments*, can only be Sihtric Cáech. Exceedingly violent, Sihtric had a turbulent career. He may, as implied by Æthelweard, have been a Northumbrian.[2783] In 888 he killed his brother Sicfrith, and may have been amongst those who, following campaigns in Wessex, sailed to Dublin but failed to seize the Viking settlements.[2784] He is perhaps to be identified as Jarl Sihfric who led one of the contingents from Dublin in 893, perhaps fighting at the battle at which *Annals of Ulster* records in that year a major defeat of 'dark foreigners' at the hands of the English, and which Claire Downham suggests was the siege of Buttington, discussed in Chapter 2 of this volume.[2785] Sihtric was driven out of Ireland with other grandsons of Ívarr in 901. He may be the same person as the Sihtric active in the eastern Danelaw who ruled as an earl in Cambridgeshire,[2786] but the Danes of Cambridgeshire surrendered to King Edward in 917, and the fate of Sihtric is not recorded in English sources. However, in the same year he appeared with a fleet off Ireland, recapturing Dublin, and killed Niall Glúndubh (who ruled much of Northern Ireland) and 12 other kings at the battle of Islandbridge, near Dublin. A year later, as we have seen, Sihtric departed for York, where he became paramount ruler of York in 920 (and king in 921) on the death of his cousin – or brother – Ragnall,[2787] and demonstrated his authority by raiding, according to Simeon of Durham, as far south as Davenport in Cheshire – perhaps a market-place for a Danish settlement area: the name means 'market on the river Dane' – which was left in flames.[2788]

[2782] O'Donovan 1860: 244-6.
[2783] Downham 2009: 73.
[2784] Downham 2009: 73.
[2785] Downham 2009: 72.
[2786] Coins were issued in Cambridgeshire at this time bearing the legend SITRIC COMES and the mint name SCELDFOR (Shelford): Williams 2014a: 26.
[2787] We have little information about the appointment of Scandinavian kings in the 9th and 10th centuries. It may be that the kingship which Sitric held at that time was a military appointment as a leader in the Viking army rather than an appointment as ruler: see Rollason 2003: 213.
[2788] Stenton 1971: 329-30; PN Cheshire II: 301, citing Sagabook xiv 313; Downham 2009: 91, 97. Sihtric seems to have issued coins at Lincoln identical with those from York: Higham 1993: 188. Numismatists have suggested that the coins bearing his name, SITRIC REX, were struck at Lincoln, as also were those bearing the 'St Martin' legend; others, with the legend 'St Peter', were struck at York during his reign. After the death of Edward the Elder, Sihtric met Edward's successor Æthelstan at Tamworth on 30 January 926, when he sealed an accord recognising Æthelstan's superiority by accepting Christian baptism and marrying Æthelstan's sister, sometimes (but probably wrongly) named Eadgyth. That Tamworth was chosen as the meeting place may indicate that Sihtric's kingdom then extended much further south than has generally been recognised – in other words, that Æthelstan controlled far less territory than once thought, since such assemblies were frequently held

The account in the *Three Fragments* does not actually say that Sihtric Cáech was involved in the great battle: he may have been mentioned simply to set the date of the conflict, i.e. before 921, when he took the kingship of York. The un-named king who was carried fatally ill from the battlefield may have been another king, just as more than one Northumbrian king was killed at Tettenhall. The only other person named in the account is Otter, 'the most influential jarl', and he may hold the key to the identification of this incident. Just as Jarl Ohtor in the *Three Fragments* account is said to have died in battle, so of course a Jarl Ohtor is named as one of the dead after the battle of Tettenhall. However, the name is not uncommon, and others named Ohtor or similar are found in early tenth-century records, including the jarl of that name who with Hroald was leader of the great raiding army that reached the Severn estuary from Brittany in 914.[2789] Nevertheless, because of the reference to an earl Otter in the *Three Fragments*, and its place in the manuscript suggesting a date for the battle in the second decade of the tenth century, some historians have taken the view that it may relate to the battle of Tettenhall.[2790] Wainwright, however, argued persuasively that the Otter (Ohter) referred to in the *Three Fragments* could not be Ohtor slain at the battle of Tettenhall, since the account is preceded by a series of events which can be dated to the years 913-917, and that the account better fits what he saw as the second battle of Corbridge, though he acknowledged the conflicting accounts which might suggest that only one battle took place, in 918.

Since Wainwright published his thoughts in 1950,[2791] the events which precede the account in the *Three Fragments* have been correlated with other evidence, and seem to have occurred at some date between 907 and 918.[2792] In addition, the 'second' battle of Corbridge is already mentioned earlier in the *Three Fragments*, although, as Wainwright points out, it is not unusual for the same event to be recorded more than once (just as the battle of Tettenhall is recorded three times in *Anglo-Saxon Chronicle* 'D'), and may simply show that the compiler had access to more than one source. Furthermore, Sihtric mentioned in the *Three Fragments*, was not, as far as we know, at the 'second' (i.e. only) battle of Corbridge.

The first task is to identify the place, recorded as 'Saxonland', where the events recounted in the *Three Fragments* occurred. The place-name is unlocated, and not found anywhere else in the *Three Fragments*, but is used to refer to England in other early Irish chronicles covering the Danish wars:[2793] Scotland is normally referred to as 'Alba', as in the separate

---

on boundaries. But soon after the meeting Sihtric renounced his wife and reverted to paganism. 'Eadgyth' is said to have retired to a nunnery at Polesworth near Tamworth, where she was revered as a saint. Sihtric died in 927: Williams, Smyth and Kirby 1991: 215-6; Downham 2009: 273-4; Oxford DNB; but see now Sargent 2016.

[2789] ASC 'A' and ASC 'D' say 918 (for 917): Swanton 1996: 98-9. Æthelweard gives the date as 914, verified by his comment that in the following year Christmas Day fell on a Sunday, which it did in 914: Campbell 1962: xlii, 53. The Welsh *Brenhinedd Y Saesson* has the cryptic observation 'Otir came to the island of Britain' under the year 914 (Jones 1971: 8-9), and the *Annales Cambriæ* notes equally tersely that in 913 *Otter venit [in Britannia]*: Williams ab Ithel 1860: 17. The date of the raid is likely to have been 914, when remnants of the Severn raiding party reached Ireland. Any disparity in dates does not in any event greatly affect the conclusions in this chapter. From at least 878 the Bristol Channel provided a major entry point into western Britain for Viking fleets from Scandinavia, Brittany and Ireland ravaging at will around southern Wales: Smyth 2002: 124.

[2790] O'Donovan 1860: 245; Byrne 2005: 857.

[2791] Wainwright 1950: 156-73.

[2792] See McCarthy 2005. Dockray-Millar 2000: 67-8 dates the battle between 907 and 918.

[2793] See Todd 1867: 151. A discussion of early medieval words for England, the English and the Anglo-Saxons can be found in Reynolds 1985: 395-414.

and concluding part of the *Three Fragments*. Moreover, the corresponding account in the *Annals of Ulster*, said to be 'the only account ... that is at once detailed and trustworthy',[2794] tells us that the battle of 918 took place 'on the banks of the Tyne among the North Saxons (*la Saxanu tuaiscirt*)', literally 'the Saxons of the north'.[2795] From this we are entitled to understand that the events took place in English Northumbria, otherwise Bernicia, the land of the 'North Saxons'.

In the late ninth century a 'Saxon' kingship (in legend established by a group of Angles in the mid-sixth century), existed in north-eastern Bernicia, a kingdom north of the Tyne centred on Bamburgh, under Ecgberht II and his successor Eadwulf, a powerful figure, described by the chronicler Æthelweard as 'Reeve of the town called Bamburgh'.[2796] His death in 913 is recorded by Æthelweard and the Irish *Annals of Ulster* and *Annals of Clonmacnoise*, the Irish sources calling him 'King of the Saxons of the North'. The kingdom retained links – perhaps even an alliance – with Mercia and Wessex,[2797] as evidenced by a number of church dedications in the south of England to Northumbrian saints.[2798] It seems to have been sufficiently powerful to have deterred any military challenge by the Danes of York, but a power vacumn followed the death of Eadwulf which led, as we have seen, to Ragnall, victor at the battle of Corbridge in 918, taking power in York c.919. This 'English Northumbria' is evidently to be identified as the 'Saxonland' of the *Three Fragments*, with Corbridge, north of the Tyne, lying within that kingdom.

If 'Saxonland' is to be identified as Bernicia, we must consider whether Æthelflæd (for 'Etheldrida' and 'the Queen' can be only her)[2799] could have been at Corbridge in the far north of England, well past York, the heartland of hostile Danes (even if they might have been subject to the treaty of Tiddingford and weakened by defeat at Tettenhall if they are too be identified as the Scandinavians who fought there), in 918. The only information we have about her activities in that year comes from the *Three Fragments* and the *Anglo-Saxon Chronicle*. The former tells us that 'Etheldrida [Æthelflæd], through her own wisdom, made a treaty with the men of Alba [Scotland] and the Britons, that whenever the same race [the Scandinavians] should come and attack her, they would rise up and assist her; and that should they [the Scandinavians] come against them, she would assist them'; and the latter that before her death at Tamworth on 12th June, she had peaceably taken control of Leicester, and that the people of York had pledged their loyalty to her: 'the York-folk (*Eoforwicingas*) had promised her – and some of them granted so by pledge, some confirmed with oaths – that they would be at her disposition'.[2800]

[2794] Wainwright 1975: 172.

[2795] Wainwright 1975: 172-3.

[2796] Eadwulf may have taken the throne of York after the battle of Tettenhall if the three kings killed there were kings of York, which now seems unlikely.

[2797] Higham 1993: 181, 185; McGuigan 2015: 53..

[2798] For example at Wells, Somerset, where there is a dedication to St Cuthbert: McGuigan 2015: 53.

[2799] The *Three Fragments* describe Æthelred and Æthelflæd (*Edelfrid* and *Edelfrida*) as 'King' and 'Queen' of the 'Saxons', but such errors are characteristic of Irish (and Welsh) chronicles: Wainwright 1975: 142. The title 'queen' makes it clear that in Ireland and Wales Æthelflæd was regarded as holding a position of power and authority: the *Annals of Ulster* make no mention of the deaths of Alfred or Edward, but enters that of Æthelflæd and describe her as *famosissima regina Saxonum*: Wainwright 1975: 320. There is ample evidence of the serious incapacitating illness from which Æthelred was suffering from at least 907: O'Donovan 1860: 227, 231, 233.

[2800] ASC 'C': Swanton 1996: 105. Ragnall is conspicuously unmentioned. The identity of the *Eoforwicingas* has been much debated: see, for example, Wainwright 1975: 337, which concludes that they should probably be identified as the Danes of York seeking protection against the Hiberno-Norse.

Those claims call for comment. The first point is the statement that Æthelflæd made a treaty with the men of Alba and the Britons 'through her own wisdom', perhaps implying that she was acting on her own initiative and the pact was not necessarily sanctioned or endorsed by Edward, though that must be an unlikely – even inconceivable – idea. Yet we must question the likelihood of any reciprocal pact by Æthelflæd with the Picts and Scots.[2801] Given the existence on her eastern borders of intractably hostile Danes, and unpredictable and aggressive Hiberno-Scandinvians to the north and north-west, it is difficult to believe that Æthelflæd would have been ready or able or willing to support the Picts and Scots if they were attacked when those Scandinavians remained a grave threat. Moreover, since it was well understood that Æthelflæd, like her late husband, was effectively a *sub-regulus* of Edward – though there are also grounds for seeing the West Saxons merely as senior partners in the relationship[2802] – any such pact would surely have been with him, or with Edward and his sister jointly, and not with his sister alone. And crucially, and puzzlingly, the *Mercian Register*, ever-ready to highlight Æthelflæd's deeds and successes, makes no mention of any reciprocal treaty with the Picts and Scots (though, equally, it makes no mention of her name in connection with the victory at Tettenhall, though that may be explicable). We may be forced to doubt the likelihood of any pact as described in the *Three Fragments*, a conclusion that might be supported by other errors which confirm its untrustworthiness.[2803] One example from the saga is the claim that 'the king of the pagans' died in the battle, which does not fit with contemporary accounts of Ragnall's death in 921.

Other elements of the account in the *Three Fragments* seem equally implausible. It is difficult, if not impossible, to imagine, for example, what extraordinary circumstances may have led Æthelflæd to embark on a perilous military expedition deep into Northumbria at any time, but particularly in early 918, a critical period when co-operation with Edward was, as Wainwright himself recognised, crucial. Such a high-risk military incursion into the north of England, far from the safety of English Mercia and well beyond York, even in the light of any notional security which may have been afforded by the treaty of Tiddingford of 905 (as discussed below), and if the *Eoforwicingas* had indeed expressed their loyalty to her, and with the protection of a strong Mercian force. No such campaign – which could only have been undertaken with the sanction of King Edward, and, we must suppose, supported by West Saxon forces – is recorded in the *Anglo-Saxon Chronicle* (including version 'D', the Worcester Chronicle, which contains much Northern information), though crucial omissions from the *Chronicle* are not unusual, and it preferred to extol the successes of Edward, whilst ignoring his sister.[2804] It is impossible to imagine that Edward would have sanctioned such a campaign and provided military support at a time when he required all the military strength at his disposal to deal with the Danish

---

[2801] See especially Davidson 2001, which incorporates a brief but useful overview of military alliances from the reign of Alfred to the end of the 10th-century.

[2802] See for example Walker 2000: 77-9, 159-60, although charters refer to Æthelred as *subregulus et patricius Merciorum* (S.346; Earle 1888: 316-9), and 3 charters of 903 (S.367, S.367a, and S.371) issued by Edward relate, inter alia, to estates in the heart of Æthelred's territory, in the environs of Oxford and London, and record that Æthelred and Æthelflæd 'then held rulership and power (*principatum potestatemque*) over the race of the Mercians, under the aforesaid king [Edward] (*sub predicto rege*)': Keynes 2001: 52-4.

[2803] This conclusion is reinforced by Davidson 2001: 203, but belief in the pact is still widely held: see for example Holland 2016: 54.

[2804] For example the capture of Derby by Æthelflæd in July 917, which was the first of five great strongholds of the English Midlands to fall, is found only in version 'C' of the Chronicle.

threat in the East Midlands.[2805] The destruction of Mercian forces far from home would have put not only Mercia but his West Saxon kingdom at the greatest peril, allowing the Scandinavians to take over the whole of England. No Mercian campaign in Northumbria is recorded or even hinted at in the *Mercian Register*, which might be expected to reflect any great Mercian successes (though it does, as noted above, record the submission by the York-folk),[2806] nor is it mentioned in the chronicle of Simeon of Durham, who had a wealth of Northern material on which to draw.

But those various issues could arguably be set to one side in a scenario in which the overlordship of Northumbria was actually held by Æthelred. That pledges of loyalty were, as claimed, made in formal manner by the *Eoforwicingas* to Æthelflæd shortly before her death in June 918 might suggest that some major event had caused them to offer their submission to Mercia. The approach by the York-folk (to be distinguished from Ragnall's Norsemen) may be seen as evidence that before her death Æthelflæd, rather than Edward, was perhaps the dominant influence (as successor to Æthelred) north and west of a line from Cirencester to Northampton and on to Stamford, as suggested by Charles-Edwards.[2807] What is noticeable is that if real, the offer of submission of the *Eorforwicingas* to Æthelflæd shortly before her death was not, as far as we know, renewed in favour of Ælfwynn, doubtless considered an unknown quantity by the *Eorforwicingas*, though the Wessex chroniclers were reluctant – perhaps pathologically unable – to record any event that lauded Mercian, or more correctly Æthelflædian, successes. The *Anglo-Saxon Chronicle* does, however, record the 'turning' of not only Mercia, but 'all the people that was settled in the land of Mercia, both Danish and English', to Edward after Æthelflæd's death. We have seen elsewhere that the latter description is almost certainly 'Old' Mercia south of the Humber, perhaps the same territory as that of the *Eoforwicingas*.

The events that caused such consternation to the *Eoforwicingas* may indeed have been not only the threat from Ragnall, but not inconceivably a campaign by Æthelflæd and her forces into English Northumbria early in 918, even (if improbably) participating in the battle of Corbridge, a major event in the history of the Vikings, though with an inconclusive outcome.[2808] The idea, evidently supported by Wainwright after his research in the various sources,[2809] might reinforce the theory that Æthelred had taken control of Northumbria, or part of it, under the treaty of Tiddingford in 905, and that the York-folk were reiterating their loyalty to Æthelflæd, Æthelred's successor as ruler of Mercia. If that were the case, the entry might reinforce the theory that the Scandinavians fighting at the battle of Tettenhall had been Hiberno-Scandinavians from the north-west rather than Scandinavians from York, with a breach of that treaty by those same Hiberno-Scandinavians (perhaps recurrent attacks on Chester between 907 and 909, events thought 'highly probable' by Wainwright)[2810] provoking Edward's raid into Northumbria and a response from the Hiberno-Scandinavians in the form of a raiding-party ravaging central and western Mercia and culminating in the battle of Tettenhall.

[2805] It was not until 923 that Edward is said to have cemented his military successes at a great assembly at Bakewell where the Scots, Northumbrians (both English and Danish), Norwegians, and the Strathclyde Britons, and all their kings, chose him as their ruler: ASC 'A'; Swanton 1996: 104. Research has cast doubt on the veracity of this account: Wyckoff 1897: 1-12.
[2806] EHD 216.
[2807] Charles-Edwards 2013: 498.
[2808] For example the *Historio de Sancta Cuthberto* claims the battle was a victory for the Vikings, and the *Chronicle of the Kings of Alba* that it was a defeat: Downham 2009: 92.
[2809] Wainwright 1975: 175-9.
[2810] Wainwright 1975: 85.

However, such reflections are in truth pointless, since there is no direct, or indeed indirect, evidence in any English sources to support a claim that Æthelflæd was in Northumbria in 918. It was Constantine who fought against Ragnall at Corbridge, as confirmed by earlier and more trustworthy accounts in the *Annals of Ulster* and *The Chronicles of the Kings of Alba*,[2811] not Æthelflæd as claimed by implication in the *Three Fragments*, and Wainwright is almost certainly mistaken to suggest that Æthelflæd led the purported alliance – the *Three Fragments* indeed does not tell us that, but merely states that she instigated it. The record almost certainly derives from an unreliable saga which can be dated no earlier than the eleventh century, and can be of no historical value.[2812] The myth that Æthelflæd and her forces were involved in any military campaign at or near Corbridge in or about 918 must be laid to rest.

Nevertheless, we need to consider whether any other scenarios in which Æthelflæd played a part might account for the events recorded by the *Three Fragments*. In that respect it will be recalled that in 914 a Danish fleet carrying a great raiding army from Brittany had sailed into the Severn estuary under two jarls, Ohtor and Hroald, said by Florence (John) of Worcester to have been the 'pagan pirates, who nearly nineteen years before had quitted Britain and gone to Gaul',[2813] presumably those who had wintered at *Cwatbrycge* in 895-6 and later sailed to the Seine.

The strategy adopted by the Scandinavian raiders in the late ninth and early tenth century had been to concentrate on areas previously unaffected by campaigning and also unprotected by fortified *burhs* of the type established by Alfred, Æthelred, Edward and Æthelflæd in Wessex and Mercia from the 880s. Those unprotected areas offered slaves, grain and cattle for the taking, but the opportunity existed to loot towns such as Gloucester, Hereford and Worcester (though all had defences by this date), and especially wealthy but undefended ecclesiastical centres such as Much Wenlock and the myriad of lesser minster churches. On this occasion the raiding-army is said to travelled along the Severn and in the words of Florence (John) of Worcester 'immediately invaded the territory of the [Welsh], and utterly destroyed everything at the river's side which they could lay hands on', before taking Bishop Cameleac (*Cyfeiliog*) captive.[2814] He was probably bishop of *Ergyng* (Archenfield), a district just to the south of Ross-on-Wye, where he was captured, and King Edward paid a ransom of no less than forty pounds for his release, from which we can infer that the far south-east of Wales was within Edward's sphere of influence.[2815]

After moving into the Wye Valley, the Danes were confronted by English forces from Hereford and Gloucester 'and from the nearest strongholds' which put them to flight. Hroald was killed, and 'the other Jarl Ohtor's brother' and many other Danes died. The Danes were forced into a fenced enclosure and besieged until they provided hostages securing their promise to leave Edward's kingdom. To ensure his security, Edward arranged for troops to guard the coast from Cornwall to Avonmouth, but the Danes made two attempts to land, at Watchett and Porlock in Somerset, and were beaten back on both occasions, with the survivors forced to swim to their ships. Seeking safety on Flatholme island, they soon ran out of food, and after landing in South Wales sailed to Ireland.[2816]

[2811] Downham 2009: 149.
[2812] Downham 2007: 95 fn198.
[2813] Stevenson 1853: 75.
[2814] Stevenson 1853: 75.
[2815] Charles-Edwards 2013: 506. See also Ray and Bapty 2016: 274.
[2816] ASC 'A', 'C', 'D': see Whitelock 1955: 194-5; Bateley 1986: 65; Cubbin 1996: 39, Swanton 1996: 98-100. Æthelweard's *Chronicon* for the year 913 records: 'A fleet entered the mouth of the river

There is almost certainly much fictional embellishment (to say the least) in the *Three Fragments'* battle account – we have seen that the story has come to us at least fourth-hand from a manuscript made in 1643, doubtless gaining accidental or deliberate accretions and suffering deletions at each stage – but the fact that it refers to an unidentified major battle involving a personality (who is surely to be identified as Æthelflæd) and the Vikings in the second decade of the tenth century means that we must consider the report in some detail.[2817]

It is not impossible, though unlikely, that Æthelflæd ('the Queen' and 'Etheldrida') mentioned in the account from the *Three Fragments*, may well have been present herself in the Welsh Marches when the Vikings raiding into the Severn were confronted by the armies of Hereford and Gloucester in 914: she was effectively their commander-in-chief. In the *Anglo-Saxon Chronicle* accounts of the raid we are told that after Jarl Hroald and 'the other Jarl Ohtor's brother' had been killed, the Vikings were driven into an enclosure (*pearruc, pearroc*)[2818] and besieged until they gave hostages, and allowed to go free (to continue their warfare). The nature of the enclosure is uncertain, but the words used do not have any military connotations. Although there is a distinction between an enclosure and a wood, we are told that the wood was cleared with swords and axes, suggesting a copse or thicket rather than large trees. There might be little real distinction between a (fenced?) copse or thicket and an enclosure. However, the *Chronicle* account tells us that the besieged Vikings gave hostages and were released after undertaking to leave Edward's territory, whereas the *Three Fragments* says the Danes were killed.

One difficulty is that we are not told where the incident in which the clearing of the *pearroc* took place. The *Chronicle* refers to Edward's territory in its account, and it is Edward who paid the hefty ransom for the release of the captured bishop,[2819] but the boundary between Edward's territory and that controlled by the Mercians at this period is difficult to identify precisely.[2820] Since forces from Hereford and Gloucester, both in Mercia, were mustered, we may infer that the incident involving the fenced enclosure, if true, might have occurred within, or least close to, Mercian territory. If the action took place on West Saxon territory, the Mercian forces presumably took the fight to the Vikings, even though they may technically have been outside Mercian jurisdiction: political niceties such as notional borders are unlikely to have overridden military objectives of common interest to both kingdoms. From the *Chronicle* account we might

---

Severn, but no severe battle was fought there in that year. Lastly, the greater part of that army go to Ireland ...' (Giles 1901: 39), or 'After a year a very large fleet arrived on the shores of the English, in the estuary and streams of the Severn, but the fighting was not seriously protracted in that year. Then the major part of that army went to Ireland ...': Campbell 1962: 52-3. Doubtless this was the episode described by Simeon of Durham as occurring in 910, the same year as his entry for the battle of Tettenhall, as follows: 'In that year a large force of pirates attacked with cruel devastation round about the river Severn, but almost the whole of it quickly perished there': Whitelock 1955: 252. The dates in those various accounts are clearly incorrect. The raid is said to have been the last great Viking incursion from the Continent for some 60 years: Oman 1913: 500.

[2817] O'Donovan tentatively linked the account to the battle of Tettenhall, but recognised the difficulties: O'Donovan 1860: 245.
[2818] EPNE ii 60 states that in later OE the word came to mean 'ground enclosed with a fence, a small enclosure, a paddock'.
[2819] ASC 'A' and 'D'; Swanton 1996: 98-9. Charles-Edwards has concluded that between 893 and 918 the kingdoms of south-east Wales remained protected from Mercia under West Saxon overlordship, with the rest of south Wales held by Mercia. Brycheiniog, around the Wye valley, was probably subject to Æthelflæd in 914; it certainly was in 916: Charles-Edwards 2013: 506-7.
[2820] Charles-Edwards 2013: 506-7.

infer that the Mercian forces extracted oaths from the Vikings in favour of Edward, unless West Saxon forces, unmentioned in the *Chronicle*, were also involved in the campaign.

Yet Æthelflæd's presence at this encounter with the Danes, it must be said, is difficult to accept. We must also consider what caused her name to be included in the account of the 'second' battle of Corbridge in the *Three Fragments*. The answer may lie in her death. Very possibly the scribe of one of the early versions of the *Three Fragments* has attempted to integrate into its report of the battle of Corbridge a record of the death of Æthelflæd in 918, the same year as Corbridge. In the report of her death in the *Annals of Ulster* she is describes as as 'the famous Queen of the Saxons': *famosissima regina Saxonum*,[2821] an expression that has its counterpart in the *Three Fragments*. Her death is reported in the *Anglo-Saxon Chronicle* immediately following the claim that the *Eoforwicingas* had promised her their loyalty.[2822] That promise of obedience may have been recorded in greatly exaggerated form in the *Three Fragments* as a reciprocal treaty which included the Scots and Britons. That her death goes unmentioned in the *Three Fragments* is readily explicable: the manuscript ends abruptly shortly after mention of her supposed treaty with the Scots and Britons.[2823]

The idea that references to the battle of Tettenhall lie concealed within the text of the *Three Fragments* is not without some merit: the battle takes place in Saxonland (an English-controlled area) in the second decade of the tenth century; the Scandinavians are newly arrived in the area, in force, and a Scandinavian by the name of Ohtor is involved; many Scandinavians are slain; a king dies; and the English forces have the victory. Æthelflæd is associated with the event. But superficial similarities with the battle of Tettenhall are specious: there is not the slightest reason to suppose that the *Three Fragments* incorporates any allusion to the battle of Tettenhall, an event that occurred several years before both the battle at Corbridge and the Scandinavian raid into south Wales. At the very least, however, it is clear that the Irish annalist had no difficulty visualising the 'Queen of the Mercians' supervising her forces on the battlefield, proof indeed that Æthelflæd was recognised and accepted not only as a Queen, but also seen as a powerful, active and effective military leader, and (whether realistically or not) personally controlling her troops in the field, even by a contemporary chronicler far distant across the Irish sea.

The weight of evidence forces us to conclude that the account in the *Three Fragments* is a garbled, embroidered, legendary, and untrustworthy conflation which seems to intermix elements from a number of different episodes and events hundreds of miles apart, but all occurring within a few years, including the 'second' (i.e. only) battle of Corbridge in 918 and (possibly) the Danish raid into the Severn in 914 – the accidental merging of the two accounts by a confused Irish scribe is readily explained. Into that mix have been added references to the pledge of loyalty to Æthelflæd by the *Eoforwicingas* recorded in 918,[2824] with perhaps a *soupçon* extracted from the *Mercian Register* account of Æthelflæd sending forces to capture the royal crannog at Llangorse Lake with 34 hostages, including the queen, in retaliation for the killing of abbot Ecgberht and his companions in 916.[2825] The

---

[2821] Wainwright 1975: 320.
[2822] ASC 'C'; Swanton 1996: 105.
[2823] Wainwright 1975: 175.
[2824] Swanton 1996: 105.
[2825] ASC 'C'; Swanton 1996: 100, 105; Charles-Edwards 2013: 505-6, 548. A crannog was a group of structures built on made-up ground or timbers in a lake, and the OE word *pearroc* has also been used

above analysis may serve at least to eliminate the possibility that the *Three Fragments* might add anything to the evidence that has come down to us about the battle of Tettenhall. Yet some slight illumination of the period which might affect the conclusions set out above could possibly be extracted from other sources.

Military and political affairs in Mercia and Northumbria during the first decade of the tenth century have recently been subjected to intensive scholarly reinterpretation. Part of the evidence for that reappraisal is William of Malmesbury's puzzling comment in his *Gesta Pontificum Anglorum* ('Deeds of the Bishops of England') that Æthelred and Æthelflæd translated Oswald's relics from Bardney to Gloucester in 909 *quod omnis Mertia eorum pareret imperio,* 'because they had all Mercia under their power'.[2826] To that can be added a curious observation by the chronicler Æthelweard, who tells us that in 909 (properly 910), in the prelude to the battle of Tettenhall, the Danes broke their pact with *Eaduuarum regem aduersus, nec non contra Ætheredum,qui tum regebat Northhymbrias partes, Myrciasque,* 'King Eadweard, and with Æthelred, who then ruled the Northumbrian and Mercian areas'.[2827] The word *partes* 'area' is important, emphasising that we are dealing with only one (or possibly more) parts of Northumbria and Mercia. But it is not absolutely certain how Æthelweard's comment is to be interpreted: is he telling us that Edward ruled the Northumbrian areas, or that Æthelred ruled the Northumbrian and Mercian areas? The editorial insertion – found in Savile's transcript of 1596[2828] – of a comma after *partes* (which would not have been in the original manuscript) might be expected to be followed by a second main verb after *Myrciasque*,[2829] but the extract is now generally accepted by historians as meaning 'Æthelred, who then ruled the Northumbrian and Mercian areas'.[2830]

Although the comments of both William of Malmesbury and Æthelweard may have no factual basis – perhaps written from confusion in the mind of the author, or misinformation on which he was relying, or even a scribal slip – and a single unexplained comment might be dismissed as aberrant, a similar aside by two different chroniclers in two different contexts at two different periods centuries apart forces us to consider the issues in a different light, more especially since they relate to exactly the same narrow time frame, i.e.

---

of 'a fishing enclosure' in *la Parrok* in the Colne estuary, Essex: EPNE ii 60. Whilst a queen was captured at Llangorse crannog, no king is mentioned; the *Three Fragments* tells of the death of a king within a *pearroc*.

[2826] Hamilton 1870: 293; Thacker 1995: 120, fn.145; Preest 2002: 198. It is worth noting that in his translation of Henry of Huntingdon, Forester says, curiously, that the area in the Fens to the east of Cambridge ravaged by Edward before the battle of the Holme in 903 was 'of the Mercians': Forester 1853: 162. However, that wording is not found in Arnold 1879: 154.

[2827] Campbell 1962: 52. A surviving charter (S.226) purporting to grant land at Lench (Worcestershire) to St Mary's church, *Cronuchamme* (Evesham) by Edward the Elder, described as king of the Mercians, need not concern us: it is spurious, its witness list headed by king Ethelbert (860-6) and Eahlstan, bishop of Sherborne (824-67), whose dates fall within the reign of Burgred, king of Mercia: Stevenson 1959: 199; Finberg 1961: 367.

[2828] Savile 1596; Smallshire 1978: 20.

[2829] Nigel Coulton is thanked for his assistance in translating and commenting upon this passage. The almost complete destruction by fire in 1731 of the one early manuscript of Æthelweard's *Chronicon* means that we are unable to verify the accuracy of Savile's 1596 transcription, though the original text would have had no such punctuation.

[2830] Campbell 1962: 52. Any ambiguity may have been overstated: Campbell himself does not mention any issues.

909-910; in other words the approximate period which seems to be the subject of that part of the *Three Fragments* discussed above.[2831]

Æthelweard's use of sources is on the whole trustworthy, and William of Malmesbury is generally considered a reliable historian, even if his reputation is no longer as high as it once was.[2832] Æthelweard in particular was writing within 75 years or so – some three generations – of these events, had access to sources which are now lost to us,[2833] and might be expected to have had a good knowledge of the period. We are forced to conclude that the comments should be considered at face value, and that for some indeterminate period Æthelred evidently ruled both Northumbria – or at least part(s) of it – and Mercia.

In that respect it is important to properly identify those two areas. Put simply, they cover the entire Danelaw (excluding East Anglia): the area over which the Danes had control, bordered on the south and west by Mercia and the Thames.[2834] But the picture in the northwest is distinctly hazy. As Atkin has pointed out, the precise position of Æthelred's northern border is uncertain. Although Chester was unarguably within Mercia, the border with Northumbria to the north, as will be seen, is unclear.[2835] The statements by the two chroniclers therefore leave us with a puzzle. What we are not told by either author is how and when the Northumbrian area(s) – however that expression was then understood – in addition to Mercia, came to be ruled by Æthelred (and presumably, though not necessarily, later by Æthelflæd), and when that rule ceased.

William of Malmesbury's comment must be read in the light of what we know of the history of Mercia at this period. The northern boundary of greater Mercia in the 830s extended from the Humber to the Dee, but by the 870s the partition of the kingdom between the Danes and the English, formalised in the famous treaty between Alfred and Guthrum in or soon after 878, meant that the boundary more or less followed Watling Street but almost certainly took a more northerly course near Tamworth, running along the Trent and Dove to and along the Mersey, and in 909 that was still the position.[2836]

[2831] To add to the puzzle, it is worth recording that in his translation of Henry of Huntingdon, Forester says, curiously, that the area around the Dyke and the Ouse ravaged by Edward's forces following Æthewold's insurrection c.903 was the 'territory of the Mercians': Forester 1853: 162. However, that wording is not found in Petrie 1848: 742 (on whose work Forester claims to have based his translation); or in Arnold 1879: 154 or Greenway 1996: 300-1. Another puzzle is provided by a spurious charter (S.225, probably a corrupt copy of an authentic early 10th-century document: Sawyer 1968: 127) dated 878 (but probably c.915), which purports to be a grant by Æthelflæd to her *minister* (thegn) Eadric of land in Berkshire, though we might otherwise assume that Berkshire was then in Wessex, not Mercia: Hart 1992: 460-1, 569-70, 572 fn.6, 573, 581.
[2832] Gransden 1974-82: I 166-85; Dumville 1992.
[2833] Campbell 1962: 31; Keynes and Lapidge 1983: 189; Bateley 1986: lxxx-lxxxi.
[2834] Hill 1984: 56; Quanrud 2015: 77-8, which includes a short but useful note on the term *Norðanhymbre*. Nottingham, Lincoln, Stamford, Derby and Leicester, known collectively as the territory of the Five Boroughs, an expression first recorded in 942, lay within Northumbria.
[2835] Atkin 1997: 10.
[2836] Dumville 1992: 1-27, especially fn.105. The translated first provision of the treaty reads in full: 'Concerning our land boundaries: Up on the Thames, and then up on the Lea, and along the Lea unto its source, then straight to Bedford, then up on the Ouse unto Watling Street': White and Notestein 1915. The treaty has been used to support the view that the half of Staffordshire north of Watling Street lay within the Danelaw, but the treaty was hardly concerned with a region so far to the northwest: it probably served more modestly to manage the frontier between Wessex and Danish East Anglia: Abrams 2001: 132, 140 fn.1.

We have some evidence, then, that Æthelweard's statement that in 909 (properly 910), Æthelred ruled the Northumbrian and Mercian areas may have been intended to refer to Northumbria and Danish Mercia. That idea is supported by the *Anglo-Saxon Chronicle*, which after recording that in 921 (probably for 918) all the nation of the land of Mercia which was earlier subject to Æthelflæd turned to Edward, records that in the same year 'all the people that was settled in the land of Mercia, both Danish and English, turned to him',[2837] referring to the submission of the last two of the Five Boroughs still in Danish hands – Stamford and Lincoln, both within the Danelaw – from which it is clear that areas outside English Mercia but within 'Old' Mercia were still seen as Mercia.[2838] The comments of Æthelweard and William of Malmesbury, then, were possibly intended to relate to Danish, or 'Old', Mercia, in which case they are strikingly curious, may be of great significance, and deserve detailed analysis. John Quanrud (who accepts that Æthelweard is telling us that Æthelred ruled both the Northumbrian and Mercian areas), suggests that the comments have at least three possible explanations. First, the possibility that Æthelweard simply exaggerated Æthelred's influence; second, the 909 raid led to some form of capitulation at York, though Quanrud noted that there is no evidence for this, and felt the idea to be wholly untenable; or third, that the 'Northumbrian area' could refer to Æthelred's rule over the western territories of Northumbria.[2839]

Dealing with those possibilities in turn, Quanrud concluded that the first claim – that Æthelweard is mistaken – is most unlikely, for the reasons given above; the second implausible, not least because it is not even hinted at by the chroniclers; but the last claim – that Æthelred ruled over the western territories of Northumbria – might be supported by Stenton's conclusion that the English occupation of territory in the north-west was probably not affected by the decline of Northumbria in the eighth century, and there is slight evidence that western Northumbria could still have been under Mercian control in some form at Alfred's death in 899. Quanrud's view is that this area might be identified as that over which Æthelred exercised some authority, which if correct would mean that Edward's raid of 909 was against the territories of a newly established *norðhere* which, in addition to parts of what is now Cheshire, may have controlled bases in Lancashire and Cumbria.[2840] That in turn would mean that the peace violated by the Scandinavian army in 910 involved forces from the north-west and not the north-east of England.[2841]

That scenario follows the idea put forward two decades earlier by Higham, who surmised that by 909 the Northumbrians of southern Lancashire were forced to accept the superiority of the ailing ruler Æthelred,[2842] who had concluded a diplomatic accord with the rulers of 'Danish' Mercia which served to protect his eastern flank and allowed Æthelred to organise the translation of St Oswald's relics from Bardney without interference. The English raid into Northumbria in 909 was 'part of a carefully developed expansion of [Æthelred's] interests. It resulted in the isolated Danish leadership at York recognising [Æthelred] as king (or 'overking') – which may well mirror his status in the Mercian Danelaw. [Æthelred] had, therefore, by Christmas 909, attained considerable

---

[2837] ASSC 'A'; Swanton 1996: 104.
[2838] Oxford DNB *sub nom* Edward the Elder.
[2839] Quanrud 2015: 79.
[2840] It is worth recording that historians have suggested that the poetry attributed to Taliesin might indicate that the 6th-century Welsh kingdom of Powys extended into Cheshire and Lancashire, though the idea is not widely accepted: Dumville 1989: 221.
[2841] Quanrud 2015: 79.
[2842] Higham 1993: 186.

success in restoring the Mercian kingship to its ancient greatness.'[2843] If that analysis is correct – the scenario is compelling, entirely credible, and would explain the otherwise puzzling comments of Æthelweard and William of Malmesbury, as well as the recovery with impunity of St Oswald's relics from Bardney – we need to consider the extent of the territory in north-west Northumbria subject to Æthelred's overlordhip.

One district in particular must be an obvious candidate, and that is the area known with the singularly unimaginative but bureaucratically appropriate and catchy Latin name *inter Ripam et Mersham*, 'Between Ribble and Mersey'. This district, which extended well to the east of Manchester,[2844] emerged, probably in the early tenth century, as 'a kind of appendage to old Mercia, not quite English and not quite Danish',[2845] first recorded in the will of the Mercian nobleman and magnate Wulfric Spot c.1004 as *inter Ripam et Mersham*, a district-name still in use when Domesday Book was compiled, and eventually applied to what became, with the addition of Amounderness and other areas, the nucleus of Lancashire, which as a county was not to come into existence until 1182. The origins of *inter Ripam et Mersham* are obscure, but Ekwall concluded from early forms of both Northumbrian and Mercian place-names and dialects that the boundary may have shifted back and forth between Ribble and Mersey for some 300 years before the early tenth century,[2846] and a detailed analysis of the area by M. A. Atkin notes that it was more often seen as Mercian.[2847]

Whilst the Mersey had long (perhaps from c.600) formed the boundary between Mercia and Northumbria – the river-name indeed probably means 'boundary river', though the boundary is records is unclear[2848] – no certain pre-Conquest name-form survives,[2849] so it is not possible to speculate on the period it became recognised as a border, or indeed whether that boundary was that between Mercia and Northumbria, though Stenton was in little doubt that Æthelred's territory extended no further north than the Mersey.[2850] Yet significantly, from at least 850 to at least 1035 the district of *inter Ripam et Mersham* was evidently within the Mercian diocese of Lichfield, with the Ribble serving as the boundary with the see of York,[2851] and brief references to the district after 900 associate it with Mercia rather than Northumbria. That remained the case even after the emergence of the county of Lancaster in the twelfth century. Atkin speculates that Æthelflæd's policies may have done much to preserve the link with Mercia throughout a turbulent period.[2852] In that respect the location of the great Cuerdale hoard, originally consisting of up to 7,500 coins including some from West Mercian moneyers, discovered on the banks of the Ribble near its head of navigation must, together with its date of deposition (from mint-condition coins of Siefred and Cnut of York), evidently c.902-5 (slightly earlier than previously thought),

---

[2843] Higham 1993a: 110.
[2844] For a map showing the extent of *inter Ripam et Mersham* see Hill 1984: 141.
[2845] Warren 1987: 26.
[2846] Atkin 1997, especially 11; Griffiths 2001: 167-87, especially 181. Cyril Hart identified the Northern Danelaw as Yorkshire, excluding *inter Ripam et Mersham* and Amounderness, on his map of the Danelaw at some unspecified date, with a heavy line marking the Mersey: Hart 1992: 9, 14, 19.
[2847] Atkin 1997: 10-11.
[2848] Ekwall 1928: 289-90.
[2849] Ekwall 1928: 289-90.
[2850] Stenton 1971: 321.
[2851] Hill 1984: 148; Atkin 1997: 10.
[2852] Atkin 1997: 11.

be of particular significance.[2853] If the above historical analysis is correct, the hoard may have been concealed on the very border of Mercia.

At what date the area may have fallen under the control of the English is difficult to determine – most authorities suppose it was in or soon after 920, when the rulers of Northumbria and Strathclyde submitted to Edward[2854] – but since Edward's raid against the territory of the Northumbrian Army (generally understood to have lain at least in part within *inter Ripam et Mersham*)[2855] took place in 909, supposedly in response to a rebellion, it is not impossible that control passed to him in that year, perhaps by the treaty that concluded the incursion, evidently entered into with particular reluctance by at least some of the Scandinavian kings if Florence (John) of Worcester is to be believed.[2856] Another possibility is that control passed under the treaty of Tiddingford c.905-6, and is perhaps to be linked to the implausible claim in the *Three Fragments* (but nowhere else) that Æthelflæd granted land in the Wirral to Ingimund and his followers. Higham has indeed recorded the idea that a site on or near the Ribble estuary, where a *hold* (perhaps the eponymous Agmund who gave his name to Amounderness), represented the authority of the King of York, may have been placed at the disposal of the Hiberno-Norse under Ivar II (killed in 904) and his brother Ragnall.[2857] That site, if *inter Ripam et Mersham*, would have adjoined the land occupied by the Hiberno-Norse under Ingimund, and would tie in with the overlordship of Æthelred and Æthelflæd of the whole of that area, with the remainder of Northumbria perhaps held by Edward.[2858]

Though the *Anglo-Saxon Chronicle* tells us specifically that in 922 Manchester– in an area perhaps settled by Danes who 'had made their way to the Cheshire Plain from the Danelaw proper along valleys that cut through the Pennine Chain'[2859] – was in Northumbria, Atkins argues that the claim should perhaps not be taken too literally, and points to the relatively few Scandinavian place-names nearby as an indication that it may have lain outside the area of colonization from York.[2860] Simeon of Durham records Sihtric's raid which left Davenport, 7 miles south-east of Manchester, aflame in 920, which tells us that the place was then seen as lying within Mercia. The attack doubtless led to the refortification of Manchester in 922.[2861] Indeed, the relative dearth of archaeological, sculptural, numismatic and place-name evidence for Scandinavian occupation in that 'moss-ridden frontier region ... of no particular value in terms of its tax revenue',[2862] when compared with that from south of the Mersey and north of the Ribble,[2863] might suggest that *inter Ripam et Mersham* was treated by Æthelred as a

---

[2853] Graham-Campbell 2001: 220-3; Lyon 2001: 75; Gooch 2012: 169.

[2854] For example Sawyer 1979: xxiv; Higham 1993: 188; Higham 1993a: 113-4; Atkin 1997, especially 11; Griffiths 2001: 181. Sawyer notes that Amounderness, north of the Ribble, was granted to the Archbishop of York in 934 (S.407), and shows that this region was being granted out in large blocks; the district *inter Ripam et Mersham* may have been the subject of a similar grant: Sawyer 1979: xxiv.

[2855] See maps in Hill 1984: 56; Higham 1993: 187; Griffiths 2001: 168.

[2856] Stevenson 1853: 73.

[2857] Higham 1993: 184.

[2858] If that scenario, however improbable, might be correct, it would be understandable that no details of the treaty are provided in the chronicles, with Edward embarrassed by its brief life.

[2859] Fellows-Jensen 1997: 79.

[2860] Atkin 1997: 11-12; Fellows-Jensen 1997: 77-92.

[2861] ASC 'A'; Swanton 1996: 104.

[2862] Higham 1993: 188.

[2863] On which see especially Atkin 1997: 16; Graham-Campbell and Philpott 2009. As well as the Cuerdale hoard on the Ribble, two other mixed hoards are recorded from *Inter Ripam et Mersham*:

buffer area to separate the Hiberno-Norse of Cumbria and those of the Wirral, and was not an especially favoured area for Hiberno-Norse settlement.[2864] Griffiths notes that the old Mercian/Northumbrian border was becoming obsolete even before Æthelflæd's death in 918, presumably implying that the Ribble had become accepted as the new boundary.[2865] *Inter Ripam et Mersham* may have been seen as an unattractive area which neither the Mercians nor the Northumbrians felt worth the effort to fight over, which would have made any overlordhip granted to Æthelred more tolerable to the Northumbrians.

The area north of the Ribble – said to have been a major focus of interest in the early tenth century[2866] – is Amounderness, with an uncertain history (but from the presence of Scandinavian inflectional forms a Scandinavian-speaking environment at some stage in its history)[2867] and a name commemorating a certain Agmund, coined (if Wainwright is correct) between 900 and 930,[2868] and comes to prominence in a famous grant of 934 by Æthelstan to the church of St Peter of York of Amounderness, an area 'of no small size' which he had acquired by purchase with his own money, supposedly (and probably) from the Scandinavians, since the land granted to St Peter's was expressed to be 'without the yoke of hateful servitude', presumably referring to its previous control by the pagans.[2869] If Wainwright's dating is right, Agmund (Old Norse *Agmundr*), who may well have been a contemporary of Ingimund, could be the *hold* of that name amongst those killed at the battle of Tettenhall. Though the name was very common,[2870] there are probably no other place-names, and certainly no districts of similar size to Amounderness, incorporating the personal name, and the individual after whom the district was named was evidently a prominent personality. It is difficult to escape the conclusion that he was the same person as the *hold* at Tettenhall. The idea is made no less likely by the existence of the parish of Anglezarke in Chorley, Lancashire, within *inter Ripam et Mersham*, south-east of Amounderness, and so-named from a prominent Viking named Anlaf, an archaic, pre-1000 form of the name Óláfr.[2871] A chieftan named Anlaf was also of course amongst those

---

the Harkirk (Lancashire) hoard, on the west coast, and the Warton, Lancashire, hoard further east: ibid.

[2864] Note however the views of F. T. Wainwright who concluded that 'the Wirral was less heavily peopled by the Norsemen than were the districts north of the Mersey, and ... the settlement was not characterized by organised violence ... [but the Norsemen] were numerous enough to influence decisively the history and character of these western regions': Wainwright 1975: 329.

[2865] Griffiths 2001: 181.

[2866] Griffiths 2001: 181.

[2867] Watson 2011: 125-41; JEPN 47 (2015) 106.

[2868] Wainwright 1975: 222-3. The area is one of four major territorial divisions alon the Irish Sea coast which bear names of Scandinavian origin, the others being Allerdale, Copeland and Furness: Winchester 1985: 99.

[2869] S.407; Whitelock 1979: 548-51; Higham 1993: 192; Blair 2005: 313-4; Griffiths 2105: 35. The charter, whilst corrupt, probably as an authentic basis: Blair 2005: 313-4. The bounds of the area ran from the Irish Sea along the Cocker to its source, along Dunshop stream to the river Hodder, and along the Hodder to the sea: Whitelock 1979: 548-51. Though it is clear from place-names that the area was strongly Scandinavianised, there is no direct evidence that the area granted by Æthelstan was purchased from Scandinavians: Wainwright 1975: 194. John Insley has suggested that Æthelstan's grant could have initiated the gradual process of language shift from Norse to English: JEPNS 47 (2015) 107.

[2870] Wainwright 1975: 223 fn.3.

[2871] PN Yorkshire (West Riding) VII 59; Wainwright 1975: 185; Atkin 1997: 14; Watts 2004: 14. The name is recorded from 1202

killed at Tettenhall, though it should be stressed that, like Agmund, the name Anlaf was not uncommon in northern England.[2872]

The nature of the alleged uprising that led to the 909 raid is unknown, if indeed it occurred at all, but might perhaps have been associated with those continuing attacks on Chester by the Hiberno-Norse, or the harassment of clergy and others in Cumbria further north. It will be recalled that the 909 raid culminated in the renewal of treaty obligations previously imposed on the Northumbrians, for we are told that the kings of the Northern Army were 'compelled, whether they wished it or not, to renew with king Edward the peace which they had broken'.[2873] The reference to 'kings' (in the plural) is especially striking, for Northumbrian kings were of course killed at Tettenhall, but Siefred and Cnut seem to have ruled at York until c.901 but are unrecorded thereafter,[2874] and no Viking king in England is clearly iderntified from 910 until 918, although we have references to jarls ruling individual fortified centres.[2875]

The importance of the reference should not be exaggerated, but adds to the weight of evidence pointing towards the Tettenhall Northumbrians as Hiberno-Norse from the north-west. Kings Halfdan, Eowils, and Ivar, all killed at Tettenhall, could have been ruling north-west England jointly, or possibly each ruling a different part of that area. The kings compelled to renew their treaty obligations after the 909 raid may have acknowledged, inter alia, Æthelred's dominance over at least part of north-west Northumbria, and recognised the Mercian leader as their overlord, perhaps supported by oaths sworn on their sacred rings and the payment of coin and treasure by way of tribute.[2876]

That the battle of Tettenhall involved the Hiberno-Norse of the north-west is reinforced by the location of a cluster of *burhs* created between 914 and 921 at Eddisbury, Runcorn, Thelwall, Manchester, Rhuddlan, and probably several other unrecorded places in the region, clearly designed to protect Chester and degrade what must have been seen as a significant threat from those Northumbrians of the north-west.[2877] They would be the

---

[2872] Atkin 1997: 17. Atkin mentions the 'Viking host' that swept across Mercia in 910 and their defeat at the battle of Tettenhall, but concludes that the idea that they were Hiberno-Norse from the western side of the Pennines is unproven: Atkin 1997: 17.
[2873] Stevenson 1853: 73.
[2874] Siefred and Cnut, attested from numismatic evidence, seem to have held power in the late 9th and early 10th century: Hall 2001: 189. Logan has seen the presence of coins in the Cuerdale hoard bearing the joint names of Siefred and Cnut (who he thought otherwise unrecorded, but Cnut is perhaps the Cnut who is said to have fought Æthelwold during Æthelwold's insurrection against Edward in 901), as further evidence that in the late ninth and/or early tenth century there was a period of joint kingship at York (Logan 1991: 159-60), but his dates for Cnut's rule on page 159 seem to be an inadvertent error for those of Ragnall. Or it may be that the three kings were not rulers, but simply leaders of the Viking army – it is possible that York had no kings during this period, which might account for the production in York of coinage in the name of St Peter but with no royal name (see Rollason 2003: 213), or the kings may have been rulers of the North Midlands rather than kings in Northumbria (Hadley 2006: 55). In about 900 an otherwise unknown King, Halfdan, was ruling somewhere in the north-east Midlands, and coins were being struck in his name: Stafford 1985: 112. It is not inconceivable that this was Halfdan who died in the conflict near Tettenhall, but we seem to have no information about kings of the Five Boroughs c.910. That the Viking force which landed in East Anglia in 865-6 was under joint leadership is touched upon briefly in Richards et al 2004: 99.
[2875] Downham 2012: 344.
[2876] We might wonder whether the great Cuerdale Hoard of Viking silver could have been part of tribute gathered to meet Edward's demands – or concealed from his forces.
[2877] Higham 1993: 187.

successors, albeit of a different ethnic mix, of those Northumbrians north-west of the Pennines over whom King Æthelred of Mercia (not to be confused with the later Lord of the Mercians) could have exercised some authority after the collapse of Anglo-Saxon Northumbria in 867, the area, as noted above, that might have been still subject to English rulers at the end of the tenth century.[2878] The enduring power and continuing threat of the Hiberno-Norse in the north-west is demonstrated by references to their ships defeating the earliest-recorded Irish fleet 'on the coast of England' in 913[2879] and (led by Ragnall, according to the *Annals of Ulster*) crushing a rival Viking fleet under Barid, son of Oitir, off the Isle of Man in 914,[2880] the latter showing that major clashes between rival Norse factions were not unknown, and that those in the north-west had maintained and were crewing a powerful fleet or fleets: to Scandinavians the preservation of their longships will have been a cultural and military imperative. It seems reasonable to assume that other fleets existed in the region and that other naval engagements and lesser clashes occurred that have gone unrecorded.

But there is yet another possible scenario to explain the comments of Æthelweard and William of Malmesbury, which takes us even further back to the supposed grant by Æthelflæd of land in the Wirral to Ingimund, the leader of the Hiberno-Norse expelled from Dublin c.901. If such an arrangement was made – we have seen that it is only recorded in the Irish *Three Fragments* and by no English sources, and indeed the idea seems improbable, invented much later to explain a *fait accompli* by Ingimund – it is surely reasonable to assume that some substantial *quid pro quo* was secured.[2881] That *quid pro quo* may have been the imposition on Northumbria (or at least the somewhat hybrid district of *inter Ripam et Mersham*) of the lordship of Æthelred, as seems to be suggested by Downham,[2882] an arrangement which had come to an end in (or by) 910, presumably as a result of the English incursion into Northumbria the previous year, or whatever action by the Northumbrians may have precipitated that raid. Downham cites as evidence of that loss Æthelweard's description of Æthelred as *Myrciorum superstes* 'Lord of Mercians', without mentioning the Northumbrians, when recording his death in 911, though the term might accurately be read as 'Lord of English and Danish Mercia'.[2883] Or as suggested above the area might have formed the basis of the treaty of Tiddingford or that concluding Edward's raid of 909. If that were the case the Scandinavians evidently felt little compunction in flexing their military muscle besieging Chester, apparently renewing their attacks after it was refortified in 907, though those attacks may well have come from local Mercian-controlled areas.[2884] If such overlordship had come into existence, it is clear the treaty did

---

[2878] Stenton 1970: 216.
[2879] Ó Cróinín 2013: 268.
[2880] *Annals of Ulster* 913.5 and 914.4; Wainwright 1975: 166. Higham says that the first battle is said to have taken place off the coast of Northumbria (Higham 1993: 186), although the *Annals of Ulster* refers only to the coast of England. Ragnall's fleet was presumably harboured in the Mersey estuary, with Thingwall, a significant place-name derived from ON *þing-vollr* 'open space where the assembly meets', only several to the north (Cavill, Harding and Jesch 2000: 5-6, 62), though it has been suggested that that it may have been based at Preston on the river Ribble: Hall 2001: 189, citing Higham 1992: 28.
[2881] Any such arrangement might, for example, have required the Northumbrians to grant sanctuary to high-status English refugees, such as Christian clergy, from the territory of the Hiberno-Norse of the north-west, as recorded at some date before – perhaps well before – 915: Stenton 1970: 215-6; Charles-Edwards 2013: 482.
[2882] Downham 2009: 88.
[2883] Downham 2009: 88.
[2884] Wainwright 1975: 85.

not last, for the Hiberno-Norse proved immediately to be aggressive and troublesome. On balance, the idea must be seen to be unproven.

Yet another idea, floated by Downham, and perhaps supported by cryptic references in the *Three Fragments* discussed above, is that Æthelred (or Edward)[2885] may have become established as overlord of 'English Northumbria' in the north-east until 910, although the nature of such overlordship is unclear.[2886] As we have seen, in the late ninth century a 'Saxon' kingship existed in north-eastern Bernicia, a kingdom north of the Tyne centred on Bamburgh with historic links with Mercia and Wessex.[2887] Downham thought any lordship over English Northumbria by Æthelred seemed unlikely because the death in 913 of Eadwulf of Bernicia,[2888] in some sources called 'king', was so widely reported – it is recorded by Æthelweard, and in the Irish *Annals of Ulster* and *Annals of Clonmacnoise*, the Irish sources calling him 'King of the Saxons of the North' – that it is difficult to believe Eadwulf, said in the *Historia de Sancto Cuthberto* have been a favourite (*dilectus*) of Alfred the Great, could have achieved such fame had he ruled for only three years.[2889] And if Æthelred had ruled 'English Northumbria' before 910, it is unclear how he lost the overlordship before that year.

But other evidence supporting the idea might possibly be detected in the supposed submission of the York-folk (*Eoforwicingas*) to Æthelflæd only days before her unexpected death at Tamworth in June 918.[2890] What is especially noteworthy is that the submission, recorded only in the *Mercian Register*, and evidently arising from the fear of Ragnall in neighbouring Bernicia, was made to Æthelflæd, rather than her brother Edward, as might be expected. That might infer that she then had some kind of superior authority over the kingdom of York, or at least over Danish Mercia (and, as discussed above, an inherited rule over north-west Northumbria). Any such authority might well have derived, in part at least, from the Tiddingford treaty, with the *Anglo-Saxon Chronicle*, not untypically, leaving unmentioned such crucial developments since they related to Mercia and deflected attention from Edward.

We have seen that claims of a reciprocal treaty supposedly entered into by Æthelflæd to protect the Britons and the men of Alba against the Norsemen, an idea mentioned in the *Three Fragments* and readily supported by Wainwright (who believed such pact was probably made in 918, the year of her death),[2891] cannot reasonably be given credence. However, a cryptic observation by the chronicler Æthelweard recording in 899 'a disturbance on a very great scale among the English, that is the bands who were then settled in the territories of the Northumbrians' was seen by Stenton as evidence that the real danger that confronted Alfred and Edward was not from the disunited Danes of the

---

[2885] Logan 1991: 161-2; Williams, Smyth and Kirby 1991: 22. Higham 1993: 185-6 has noted that intermarriage between the leaders of the Dublin Norse and the Great Danish Army had occurred towards the end of the ninth century, and that for a decade or so after 905 the Irish Norse attacked only the rivals of the Northern Army – the Scots, Strathclyde and the 'northern Saxons' of Bernicia, where the death of King Eadwulf in 913 prompted a Scandinavian invasion in 914.
[2886] Downham 2009: 88.
[2887] For example at Wells, Somerset, where there is a dedication to St Cuthbert.
[2888] Eadwulf may have taken the throne of York after the battle of Tettenhall if the three kings killed there were kings of York, which now seems unlikely.
[2889] Downham 2009: 88.
[2890] ASC 'C'; Swanton 1996: 105.
[2891] Wainwright 1975: 175-9.

east Midlands, but from the remote and (at that time) aggressive kingdom of York,[2892] presumably assuming that the 'disturbance' was fomented by the Danes of York, though as we have seen, that risk seems to have been greatly reduced by the Northumbrian defeat at the Holme,[2893] and Æthelweard's reference almost certainly refers to Bernicia, 'English Northumbria' centred on Bamburgh, which could have lain behind the 'disturbance'. Indeed, the 'disturbance on a very great scale' might well have been associated with the arrival of the usurper Æthelwold in York in 901 and his attempt to raise forces to his cause. It is possible to imagine that many Englishmen 'settled in the territories of the Northumbrians' may have been attracted to his cause. Æthelweard may have been deliberately coy about disclosing any further details of the great disturbance; he was equally discreet, if not disingenuous, about the nature of the battle of the Holme when Æthelwold, Æthelweard's ancestral relative, lost his life.

A further scenario, as touched upon above, is that the treaty of Tiddingford with the Northumbrians of York and the rulers of East Anglia c.905, under which, according to the *Anglo-Saxon Chronicle*, '... they confirmed the peace at Tiddingford, just as King Edward determined, both with the East Anglians and with Northumbrians', and 'King Edward, from necessity, confirmed peace both with the raiding army from East Anglia and with the Northumbrians',[2894] left the Northumbrians (and the East Anglians) under English control. The treaty presumably marked the formal resolution of Æthelwold's insurrection, or followed some other military campaign or event unrecorded in the chronicles which would typically preface a treaty. Other than the two Scandinavian parties, no details of the accord are known.[2895]

The idea that the treaty could have transferred control of the whole of Northumbria (and East Anglia) to Edward and/or Æthelred might seem unlikely, but our understanding of the period may be unduly influenced by the (almost?) complete absence of any record of any such arrangements: it seems inconceivable that such a momentous event could have gone (virtually) unrecorded by the chroniclers, though significant voids in the documentary evidence for this period can easily be proved. Yet the idea might readily explain the final section of the *Three Fragments*, if the account from that misleading source might contain any grain of truth, for as noted above we are told that Æthelflæd had secured a mutual alliance with the Britons and the *men of Alba* (the Picts and the Scots), she to assist them and they to assist her against the Norse, and that her new allies proceeded to attack positions held by the enemy. No other chronicle mentions that pact, and we must be entitled to question the likelihood of any reciprocal pact by Æthelflæd with the Picts and Scots. Given the existence on her eastern borders of intractably hostile Danes, and unpredictable and aggressive Hiberno-Scandinvians to the north and north-west, it is hard to believe that Æthelflæd would have been ready or able or willing to support the Picts and

---

[2892] Campbell 1962: 51. Æthelweard's comments may be associated with an unexplained report by Simeon of Durham of the expulsion of one Osbrith 'from the kingdom' in the same year: Downham 2009: 82.
[2893] Stenton 1970: 12-13.
[2894] ASC 'A', 'D', 'E'; Swanton 1996: 94-5. A slightly different translation for 'A' and 'D' is provided in Whitelock 1961: 60: '... the peace was established at Tiddingford, just as King Edward decreed, both with the East Angles and the Northumbrians'. The laws of Edward (II Edward, 5.2) stipulate that certain legal provisions in eastern and northern England shall be 'in accordance with the provisions of the treaties' (*friðgewritu*, literally 'peace-writing'): Hadley 2012: 376.
[2895] Curiously, ASC 'D' records that in 906 (*sic*) St Oswald's relics were translated from Bardney before mentioning the Tiddingford treaty: Cubbin 1996: 37.

Scots if they were attacked when those Scandinavians remained a grave threat.[2896] But that scenario is thrown into a wholly different light if we envisage the existence of a pact with aMercian overlordship controlling the Danes of York, and might provide a straightforward and credible explanation for the claim made in the *Three Fragments*. It would admittedly also fit with the submission to Æthelflæd of the *Eoforwicingas* in 918, as recorded in the *Anglo-Saxon Chronicle*,[2897] although doubt has been cast on such submission.

We have seen that the Tiddingford treaty was evidently concluded reluctantly by Edward, doubtless because it was only two years or so since Æthelwold and his clique, together with his York-based Northumbrian allies, in hand with King Eohric of East Anglia and his forces, had come within a whisker of unseating him, taking both his kingdom and his life. Edward will have had scores to settle, but having technically lost the battle of the Holme and many of his Kentish forces (but arguably won the war), would not necessarily be negotiating from a position of strength, though both he and his enemies may have thought otherwise: Simeon of Durham, Florence (John) of Worcester and Roger of Hoveden may be correct when they write that 'the pagans of East Anglia and Northumbria, perceiving that King Edward was invincible, made peace with him.'.[2898] Their conclusion was doubtless based on a spectacular defeat achieved by only a small part of Edward's forces. But those chroniclers were writing long after the battle, and their analysis might not only be exaggerated, but completely wrong.

Edward's hand may have been forced at Tiddingford by Æthelred and Æthelflæd, only too aware of the looming threat from the Hiberno-Norse on their north-west border and fearful of a co-ordinated attack by an alliance of those forces with the Danes of York. Furthermore, they were perhaps alarmed at the thought of Edward himself taking control of Danish Mercia after his victory at the Holme, which he doubtless saw as his of right, but which, with Wessex, would have dominated their kingdom. There is also the possibility, mentioned elsewhere in this volume, that Æthelred (even perhaps Æthelflæd) may have ben hesitant in providing support to Edward in his clash with Æthelwold, notwithstanding the close familial relationship, seeing the rebellion as an opportunity to expand the role of Mercia in a reorganised country shared with a new ruler, in which case the treaty of Tiddingford will have involved daunting negotiations with multifarious parties. That might help explain the terse entry in the *Mercian Register* which records the battle of the Holme 'between the people of Kent and the Danes', downgrading the episode to a local confrontation with with no mention of Æthelwold and his Northumbrian forces or his East Anglian and Essex allies – nor indeed of Edward.[2899]

It may be relevant that the wording of the Chronicle entries recording the Tiddingford treaty seems to tell us that 'they confirmed the peace ... just as King Edward determined'.[2900] 'They' were clearly not the Northumbrians or East Anglians, who are mentioned immediately after, but could have been Æthelred and Æthelflæd (whom the Wessex Saxon chroniclers were customarily disinclined, indeed pathologically unable, to identify explicitly), a conclusion possibly supported by the fact that the treaty was

---

[2896] See especially Davidson 2001.
[2897] ASC 'C'; Swanton 1996: 105.
[2898] Stevenson 1853: 73; Riley 1853: 60; Stevenson 1855: 500. The wording of the latter part of this passage might suggest that it was translated into English from another language.
[2899] Whitelock 1961: 59.
[2900] It is right to add that the passage has also been interpreted as: 'And that same year the peace was established at Tiddingford, just as King Edward decreed, both with the East Angles and the Northumbrians': Whitelock 1961: 60. That would dispose of the unexplained 'they'.

completed on the Mercian boundary, though it is noteworthy that neither Æthelred nor Æthelflæd seem to have been parties, though one or both may have been, but unmentioned.[2901] A ruler's wife, it is true, would not be expected to be party to such a pact, but there were few rulers' wives of the calibre of Æthelflæd, who by any measure had achieved a status more akin to joint ruler: we have examples of charters attested by both Æthelred and Æthelflæd,[2902] and indeed some by Æthelflæd alone.[2903] It is probably fair to say that her recorded achievements (clearly very much less than the whole story) far and perhaps unfairly outshone in his later years those of her once-powerful husband, gradually – if we are to believe later annals – incapacitated by poor health, and were in no way comparable with the very limited powers (though not necessarily influence) of late Anglo-Saxon queens, or kings' wives.[2904]

Tensions between Edward and his brother-in-law (and sister) might be detectable in the Tiddingford accord, and in the fact that, apart from Edward concluding it 'for need' and 'by necessity', we are told so little about it. Both Roger of Wendover and Matthew Paris (whose work was based on Roger's chronicle) claim that Edward's campaign into Northumbria in 909 was in response to a Northumbrian rebellion.[2905] If true – and both chroniclers were writing long after the event – it is not difficult to imagine that any such rebellion could well have been occasioned by or arisen from Æthelred and Æthelflæd's control of Danish Mercia or north-west Northumbria (or even north-east Northumbria) under the treaty of Tiddingford. Since we only have two enigmatic references to provide dubious support for the idea that Danish Mercia or north-west Northumbria may have been controlled by Æthelred and Æthelflæd, we might imagine that the arrangement was relatively short-lived. But the translation of St. Oswalds' relics to Gloucester in 909 may have sealed an accord with Northumbria, whereby the Mercian rulers effected a diplomatic coup by raising to cult status in Mercia, with the full approval, if not encouragement, of the Northumbrians, the corporeal remains of one of Northumbria's most significant Christian martyrs, whose kingdom was immense and who was lauded by Bede as 'the most Christian king'. The translation might well have held considerably more significance than hitherto supposed.

A potential date for the ending of any control enjoyed by Æthelred over Danish Mercia and/or north-west Northumbria must be 911, when Æthelred died – Æthelweard, having previously described him as ruling the Mercian and Northumbrian areas, then describes him as 'Lord (*superstes*) of the Mercians', with no mention of Northumbria[2906] – and Edward promptly demonstrated his ability to clip his sister's wings by taking back London and Oxford 'and all the lands which belonged thereto' from Mercian control (or as the *Anglo-Saxon Chronicle* puts it, 'succeeded' to those towns and land).[2907] A more likely date, however, is 918, when the *Mercian Register* tells us that the *Eoforwicingas* or York-

---

[2901] Hill 1984: 56.
[2902] For example S.221 (901), S.223 (884x901),
[2903] For example S.224 (900), S.225 (916).
[2904] Asser records that in 9th-century Wessex 'the people ... do not even permit [the king's wife] to be called a queen but only the wife of the king', though Nelson observes that in Mercia several queens are attested: Nelson 2006: 69.
[2905] Coxe 1841: I 373; Luard 1872: I 439.
[2906] Campbell 1962: 53.
[2907] ASC 'A'; Swanton 1996: 96. The transfer of London and Oxford did not effect the border between Mercia and Wessex which continued to be recognised as the Thames, and may have been a concession to Edward who might otherwise have taken control of Mercia (Walker 2000: 99), though that probably underestimates Edward's authority over (but not support within) Mercia.

folk offered their submission to Æthelflæd shortly before her death. The expression *Eoforwicingas* (literally 'York-folk',[2908] with *Eoforwic* the Anglo-Saxon name of York), has a transparent meaning, but has never been satisfactorily explained, and seems to have received little academic discussion. Its solitary mention in the *Mercian Register* does not allow us to draw any firm conclusions – we know not whether the 'folk' were English or Danes or a combination of both – but it seems reasonable to assume that it had some distinctive meaning, possibly a term used for a faction of the ruling elite at York who held sway over Northumbria south of the Humber, that is 'Old' Mercia (an idea supported by Sir Frank Stenton),[2909] and were sufficiently alarmed by Ragnall's aggression that they felt need of protection by a powerful ally. That submission is perhaps more readily explicable if Æthelflæd were already in notional control of at least some parts of Danish (as well as English) Mercia and north-west (and even north-east) Northumbria. Important evidence for her control over Danish Mercia might possibly be detected in *Anglo-Saxon Chronicle* 'A', which having casually noted the death of Æthelflæd, described merely as '[Edward's] sister', the occupation of Tamworth and the submission by three Welsh kings and all the race of the Welsh who sought (*sohton*) him as king,[2910] followed by the capture of Nottingham,[2911] records (in wording that seems to have received little analysis or even notice by historians) the submission (*cierde*) to Edward of all the nation in the land of the Mercians which had been subject to Æthelflæd, before telling us, almost as an afterthought, that *him cierde eall þæt folc to þe on Mercna lande ge seten wæs, ægþer ge Denise ge Englisc*, 'all the people who had settled in Mercia, both Danish and English, submitted to him'.[2912] The words used by the Chronicle may repay more detailed analysis.

Old English *cierde* is from the verb *ci(e)rran*, which had a number of meanings, including 'submit, reduce, regard, translate, persuade, convert', but perhaps more generally 'turn, return, change'.[2913] It is noteworthy that *cierde* in that exact form is exceptionally rare in *Anglo-Saxon Chronicle* 'A', from which the above extracts have been taken – the only two examples are the ones in those extracts, which Whitelock translates as 'submit'.[2914] An alternative translation (preferred by Swanton) is 'turn',[2915] a word chosen perhaps by the scribe deliberately to emphasise (unlike the word 'submit') that both areas were changing, without military intervention, to West Saxon control. At the very least, we are led to believe that the word that applied to 'English' Mercia also applied to 'all the people who had settled in Mercia, both Danish and English'. And therein lies a further difficulty. What area should we understand by that expression?

[2908] Swanton 1996: 105.
[2909] Stenton 1971: 329. Stenton also observed, puzzlingly, that 'So far as is known, no proposal of the kind [made to Æthelflæd] was ever made to King Edward ...', even though subsequently noting that 'the English frontier had at last been carried to the Humber': ibid. 329-31.
[2910] Whitelock 1961: 67; Swanton 1996: 103; Thorpe 1861: I 194-5.
[2911] Nottingham and Lincoln were the last free Scandinavian strongholds south of the Humber, and Æthelflæd probably had Lincoln (unmentioned in the *Anglo-Saxon Chronicle*) in her sights at the time of her death.
[2912] ASC 'A'; Thorpe 1861: I 195; Swanton 1996: 103-4, where the entry is dated 922, which is obviouslt incorrect: Æthelflæd died in 918. It is unclear whether Ælfwynn was deprived of control in Mercia before or after the submission to Edwardby the Mercians and others mentioned in the Chronicle, but the former seems more likely.
[2913] Clark Hall 1960: 68.
[2914] The meaning 'submit to' is also preferred by Pelteret: Pelteret 2009: 330.
[2915] Swanton 1996: 103-4.

East Anglia as a kingdom was of course readily identifiable and well-known to the chroniclers, but was not viewed as part of Mercia,[2916] and the territory known from 942 as the Five Boroughs (*Burga fife*)[2917] was not yet considered a coherent and recognisable area. Mercia settled by both Danish and English is, we must assume, all of greater Mercia (excluding 'English' Mercia which had never fallen under Danish rule), which had extended as far as the Humber (and thus far into territory held by the Northumbrians, including Bardney).[2918] The expression can surely refer only to 'Old' Mercian territory which had been within the Danelaw, a term not recorded before c.1050.[2919] It seems clear that the expression 'Mercia' had two distinct meanings: 'English' Mercia was the area which remained under English control after the treaty of Alfred and Guthrum c.878, and 'Old' Mercia or 'Danish' Mercia, which was that area of Mercia south of the Humber that fell within Danish control.[2920] The entry in the Chronicle might tell us that Edward was merely succeeding to both 'English' Mercia and 'Old' Mercia, the whole or part of which had been under Æthelred's control until his death and latterly under Æthelflæd's control until her death, and perhaps for a short time under the control of her daughter Ælfwynn, though any presumption that Ælfwynn inherited her mother's interest may be misplaced.

However, if the rule of Æthelred and Æthelflæd had been so dramatically extended over Danish Mercia and elsewhere in north-west Northumbria (and/or Bernicia), it must be conceded that the silence on the subject by, especially, the *Mercian Register* (which fails even to mention the Tiddingford accord, perhaps implying that it had no relevance for Æthelred and Æthelflæd), is difficult to explain, and the northern chroniclers give no hint at any such arrangement, though they were notably, indeed extraordinarily, selective in what they recorded. Of the momentous battle of the Holme, for instance, Simeon of Durham simply tells of a victory by the Kentish men against 'a multitude of Danish pirates', but there is no mention of Æthelwold, nor his rebellion, nor his ravaging of Mercia, nor his key role in the battle, nor his death in the fighting,[2921] and the *Annals of St Neots* makes no mention of the treaty of Tiddingford, nor the recovery of the relics of St Oswald from Bardney, nor any incursion by the English into Northumbria, nor any raid by the Northumbrians into Mercia leading to the battle of Tettenhall. Indeed, the only two events recorded in those Annals between Æthelwold's defeat at the Holme and the battle of Tettenhall are the death of Edward's mother (905) and the death of the bishop of Sherborne (910).[2922] And the *Anglo-Saxon Chronicle* is, of course, notoriously silent on Mercian affairs.

The theories advanced above to explain the otherwise puzzling comments made by William of Malmesbury, Æthelweard and the *Anglo-Saxon Chronicle* would seem to be the least unlikely, though in reality may be very wide of the mark, and we must recognise that the precise and doubtless manifold reasons behind the curious comments from the two

---

[2916] Although East Anglia submitted to Mercia c.730 during the Mercian Supremacy, the defeat of Mercia by Wessex at the battle of Ellendun in 825 encouraged the East Anglians to re-establish their independence soon after.
[2917] ASC 'A', 'B', 'C', 'D'; Thorpe 1861: I 208-9.
[2918] Stenton 1971: 331.
[2919] OED; Holman 2001; Hart 1992; Hadley 2012.
[2920] Hill concludes without explanation that the *Eoforwicingas* were Danes within an area from the west coast to the east coast north of a line from the Mersey to the Humber as far north as Kirkby Lonsdale: Hill 1984: 59, map 95.
[2921] Stevenson 1855: 500.
[2922] Stevenson 1956: 144.

chroniclers, and how they might relate to enigmatic and improbable references in the *Three Fragments* (if at all), may forever remain unexplained.

Appendix I

The Morfe 'tumuli'.

In 1742 an account was published in the official journal of the Royal Society of London recording the partial excavation by the Reverend Thomas Stackhouse, minister of St Mary Magdalen in Bridgnorth, of five 'Sepulchral Tumuli' upon Morfe near Bridgnorth in July 1740.[2923]

Burial mounds are not unusual in this region, though it would be an exaggeration to suggest that they are common.[2924] What is remarkable about this supposed burial ground, however, is the arrangement of the five mounds, which are shown in a crude plan in the report to be set out in a quincunx pattern like the five spots on dominoes. In addition, the tumuli appear to have been enclosed by a bank – or perhaps a ditch (the drawing and report are unclear, but the enclosure is shaded like the mounds, so a bank may be more likely) – forming a more or less square enclosure. Allowances must be made for artistic licence, but some degree of accuracy might be assumed from the fact that dimensions have been added to the drawing to show that the boundary bank or ditch was 33 yards long on the north and south, and 36 yards on the north and west. The central mound was apparently the largest, being some 27' in diameter, the others 24'. It was trenched by Stackhouse from north to south, and the south-east mound cut through diagonally, but the excavations were interrupted by local people who 'flocked to the Place in great Numbers ... [and] ... spread a Report ... that by a Discovery made by some ancient Writings, we dug there for Treasure', which led to further work being abandoned and the refilling of the excavations.

These supposed tumuli, which are not independently recorded elsewhere,[2925] appear to have been destroyed by the early nineteenth century, so none of these facts can now be checked – even the location of the mounds is now lost – but if the report is to be relied upon, the arrangement of the mounds and the boundary bank or ditch will have formed an extraordinary and perhaps unique feature of the early landscape. The excavations (only two mounds were explored) produced what seems to have been a heel bone, a number of

---

[2923] PSRSL, No. 464 (May, June, July 1742), 134-6. The suggestion that Stackhouse's account was based on an excavation by the Reverend Richard Cornes, minister of St Mary's church in Bridgnorth from 1687 to 1726 (see articles about the discovery of Cornes' manuscript in *Bridgnorth Journal*, 21st and 29th August 1980), is misconceived: the manuscript is evidently entitled 'A short topographical account of Bridgnorth, in the county of Salop, taken from the original papers of the late Rev Richard Cornes, late Minister of the Parish of St Mary Magdalane, Bridgnorth, to which are added some remarkable occurrences and natural observations, 1739, Sat Plaruifse Proorst' [*ibid.*], from which it is clear (quite apart from the date of the excavation, which is after Cornes' incumbency) that the manuscript is not that of Cornes himself.

[2924] A possible Bronze Age barrow is recorded not far distant on the west side of the Severn at SO72339090 (ADS), and the field-name *Founslow* or *Fonslow* is recorded south of Eardington on the 1842 Tithe Map, perhaps incorporating OE *hlāw* 'a mound, a tumulus', generally found as low: the field appears to incorporate a pronounced headland.

[2925] Camden's *Britannia* 1806 III: 19: 'On the table-land at Morf were in the last century several tumuli, now levelled by the plough, but held by good authority to be British'; see also Eyton 1854-60 III 213; Hartshorne 1841 100. '... [U]p to about the year 1824 there were five tumuli or ancient burial mounds arranged like the five spots on a domino on the higher ground of [Morfe] forest, but these have all been levelled by the plough': Watkins Pitchford 1932. These accounts are clearly based on the original report by Thomas Stackhouse, who would seem to have taken a particular interest in burial mounds: a work entitled *Illustration of the Tumuli, or ancient Barrows*, by Thomas Stackhouse (presumably the excavator of the Morfe mounds) was published in London in 1806.

unidentifiable 'petrified' bones, and a small corroded iron egg-shaped object with a hole in one end, tentatively identified as 'the boss of a sword'.

Whilst the exact location of the curious feature is unknown,[2926] we do know from the 1742 report that it lay 'upon Morfe', and are also told that 'the soil is a strong gravel', and that upon excavating sections from two of the mounds to a depth of seven feet, rock was reached.

A plan of the mounds on Morfe Common as published in the *Philosophical Transactions*, May-July 1742.

The expression 'upon Morfe' does not enable us to identify even the general area with any certainty, but since the report is given prominence in a Victorian history of Bridgnorth,[2927] and we know that local people flocked to the excavations in great numbers, it seems reasonable to assume a location not far distant from that town. The forest of Morfe appears to have extended at least from Enville, some 5 miles east of Quatt, where we find Morfe Hall Farm, Morfe House Farm and Morfeheath Farm, almost to the Severn itself. However, evidence of what was known as Morfe near Bridgnorth in the 1740s is available from a map of Morfe Forest made in 1613,[2928] from John Ogilby's 1675 map of the road from Quatford to Bridgnorth (which is shown running across an unfenced highway labelled 'Pasture Ground called Morf Comon Heath or Forest'), from Baugh's map of

---

[2926] The only clue in the original report is a statement that the mounds lay in an area where the soil was strong gravel overlying sandstone, which evidently lay close to the surface. Hartshorne 1841: 99 and 223 mentions the '... nearly undiscernible tumuli which Mr Stackhouse opened about a century ago ...' and '... no vestiges of these Tumuli now appear, as the land is all under plough ...'. It seems likely that nineteenth and twentieth century writers who mention the tumuli preferred to disguise their ignorance as to their precise location. Local information suggests that they may have lain at or near Queen's Parlour, 'a secluded amphitheatre, ending in a jutting promontory of craig [sic]', on the east side of the Hermitage caves (TSAHS I 1878: 168), although the basis for that belief is uncertain. On of the highest points in the area may be a raised linear feature, boomerang-shaped in plan, which appears clearly in aerial photographs, 250 feet or so to the north-west of the roundabout junction of the B4363 (Hermitage Hill road) and the A454 (Stanmore road). The feature is probably natural in origin, and no cropmarks have been discerned in the area.
[2927] Bellett 1855: 5-7.
[2928] SA 4296.

522

Shropshire made in 1808 (which shows the Common extending from Rindleford, two miles north-east of Bridgnorth, almost to Bobbington, five miles south-east of Bridgnorth),[2929] and more particularly from John Rocque's map of Shropshire, published in 1752. That shows *The Morf Common* as a strip of high ground roughly parallel to the Severn running south-east from the outskirts of Bridgnorth towards Gags Hill.[2930] There is no indication on these maps, nor on the detailed Enclosure Map of the area produced in 1812,[2931] of any feature thereabouts that might represent the mounds, and an examination of aerial photographs and local field-names has revealed no clue to their location. The area, which rises steeply from the Severn, falls away gently to the east, with the crest of the ridge affording far-reaching views towards the Shropshire hills to the west. The ridge holds a commanding position over any crossing of the Severn at Quatford, which lies within half a mile of the summit. Wherever the mounds were located in the area, they seem likely to have lain on the higher ground, quite possibly in a prominent position on the skyline. The highest points in the area (at over 400') seem to be along the crest of the ridge above and to the south of the caves of The Hermitage,[2932] although on the ground the summit of the rounded hill west of Swancote Cottages seems higher. Aerial photography has failed to disclose any traces of the mounds, it is remotely possible that the site was a where a covered reservoir was created in the 1970s, an amenity that would have destroyed any evidence of earlier remains.[2933] The 1742 description might point towards Anglo-Saxon 'princely burials', high-status burials dating from the early seventh century marked by earth mounds 30' to 65' in diameter and up to 9' high, located in prominent positions, so as to see from and be seen, but it might be unlikely to find such monuments in this area.[2934]

The nature, age and origin of the mounds remain unresolved. If they were ancient, they seem to be unparalleled elsewhere, for no other reference has been traced to a dice-like pattern of five tumuli surrounded by a square bank or ditch. However, tumuli arranged in geometric patterns are not completely unknown. Thomas Bateman's nineteenth-century excavation of the great mound of Gib Hill, near Arbor Low stone circle in Derbyshire, two miles from the Staffordshire border, showed that the present mound was constructed over

---

[2929] The Hon. John Byng, en route from Enville to Bridgnorth, records in 1793 '... after passing the six-ashes [Six Ashes near Bobbington] which divide the counties of Stafford and Salop, upon a high bleak country, call'd (I believe) in the map, Morfe Forest: – and now finding a wide turfy road I could trot briskly along; and quickly came in sight of Bridgnorth.': Andrews 1936: 226.

[2930] Morfe Forest is said to have extended 'from Morfe to Romsley, thence to Alveley and Hampton Loade, then up the river bank, past Quatford, to the mouth of the Worfe, from thence to Allscote, Chesterton, Shipley, Abbot's Hill, and Gospel Ash, and so back to Morfe. This outline would surround a district about nine miles long by seven broad': Watkins-Pitchford 1932: 2. A small-scale map showing the boundaries of Morfe Forest in 1808 is to be found in Mason 1957.

[2931] SA QE/1/2/29.

[2932] The prehistoric earthworks of Burfe Castle lie on a hill that rises to a little over 400', but the hill is almost three miles from Bridgnorth, a distance that probably rules out any likely site for the Morfe mounds.

[2933] As noted elsewhere, the c.1560 map of Bridgnorth shows a gibbet to the south of The Hermitage with the note 'the olde Diche under the gybet' and a thumbnail sketch of two uprights and a crosspiece set on a mound with 'St Nicholas Oake' shown nearby to the east. Ogilby's road book of 1675 shows *Gallowes* in approximately the same position: Ogilby 1675 Plate 13. Eyton 1854-60 III: 19 mentions *Gibbet Hill*. 'The gibbet stood near the old Quatford road – a road which is very little used now – in the second field on the right, just after you have turned off the Stourbridge road just above St James' Priory': Watkins-Pitchford 1932: 24. It is not impossible that the mounds may have been connected in some way with the gibbet.

[2934] Lapidge et al 1999: 376.

four smaller mounds arranged in a square.[2935] Hoon Mount, the tumulus, probably a platformed bell-barrow, giving rise to the place-name Hoon in Derbyshire, 2 miles north of Tutbury and a mile or so north of the river Dove which forms the boundary with Staffordshire, lies within a square ditch.[2936] An Iron-Age barrow at Arras, Yorkshire, was surrounded by a square ditch, and numerous barrows with 'square trenches' have been noted on Raccal and Skipwith Commons in the East Riding of Yorkshire.[2937] Those tumuli will have been prehistoric rather than Anglo-Saxon.

The mounds on Morfe Common might have been a relatively recent feature of the landscape, evidently virtually treeless since the seventeenth century,[2938] possibly pillow mounds, artificial earthworks created as rabbit warrens or 'coney-garths'. Warrens certainly existed at an early date[2939] in the area, described in 1739 as '...formerly covered with stately oaks, but now an open plain...', with short turf and a racecourse,[2940] for in 1764 *The Gentleman's Magazine* mentions that during the first half of the eighteenth century the treeless slopes of the hillside between High Rock and Hermitage, on the east side of Bridgnorth, were enclosed and utilised as a private rabbit warren, and there are a number of references to the 'lodge warren in the forest of Morfe' in 1791.[2941] Arguably those reports help to demolish the idea that the mounds were warrens, since the author of the report of the 1742 excavations mentions that local people 'were much alarmed, and flocked to the Place in great Numbers, expecting ... to have seen Wonders; but being disappointed, they soon spread a Report over the Country, that by a Discovery made by some antient Writings, [the excavators] dug there for Treasure, by which [the excavators] were greatly enriched; To prevent the further Concourse of the People, &c., [the excavators] were glad to fill up the Trenches, and leave the other Tumuli unexamined'. It seems improbable that both the excavators and locals would have mistaken a rabbit warren for tumuli at a time when warrens were still much in use and not uncommon, and indeed warrens, as we have

---

[2935] Grinsell 1953: 226.
[2936] JEPNS 35 2002-3 45-8.
[2937] Grinsell 1953: 26.
[2938] Watkins-Pitchford 1932: 23.
[2939] A lease of 1658 mentions a new warren adjoining an old warren: SA X5586/2/1/367.
[2940] TSAS IX 1886 196. In the same year it was said that '... a considerable tract below the Hermitage [in Bridgnorth] seems to have been used as a rabbit warren and belonged to the Lord of the Manor of Worfield ... a dwellinghouse and appurtenances or lodge ... upon the forest of Morfe and all the warren of conies or parcel of waste used for a warren extending and lying in length between a certain rock or mountain called Pendlestone Rock, near the town of Bridgnorth, on the north part thereof, and the highway leading from Bridgnorth through the late hospital of St James's near the said town of Bridgnorth on the south part thereof, and in breadth from the late Hermitage there and the top of the mountain above the said Hermitage heretofore called broad ditch on the east part [presumably 'the olde Diche' marked on the c.1560 map of Bridgnorth] and the town of Bridgnorth on the west part thereof, and also all that warren of conies or parcel of waste ground being part of the wast or forest of Morfe aforesaid lying adjacent to the old warren extending itself to Gatacre highway on the north, and to a place called round Hill and Ewe tree Hill on the south [Round Hill Side and Yewtree Hill appear on the 1842 Tithe Map], and to a footway coming from the said Town of Bridgenorth': Jewett et al 1894: 72. The warrener's lodge was presumably The Lodge, marked on the 1833 First Edition 1" O.S. map at what is now The Grove. The racecourse on Morfe is recorded by 1690 and lay near Stourbridge Road and Green Lane. After 1811 race meetings moved to Innage, where they continued until 1830.
[2941] See for example SA 5586/2/1/493; Watkins-Pitchford 1932: 23-4. The rabbit is said to have been introduced to Britain by the Normans, and by the late Middle Ages artificial warrens were widespread: rabbits breed with proverbial rapidity and do well on the poorest ground. Norden tells us that 'As for Warrens of Conies, they ... require no rich ground to feed in but meane pasture and craggy grounds are fittest for them': Beresford and St. Joseph 1979: 71.

seen, had been created in the same area within the previous forty years or so, or perhaps much more recently – certainly well within living memory.[2942] Furthermore, circular pillow-mounds, if they existed, must have been very uncommon – almost all were '... low rectangular or ovoid mounds ...',[2943] and the size of the mounds on Morfe – up to 27' in diameter – might rule out any connection with rabbits.[2944]

So far as the few finds from the mounds are concerned, no clue can be offered as to the nature of the 'small corroded iron egg-shaped object with a hole in one end'. Of pagan Anglo-Saxon tumuli it is said that 'nearly all those which have so far been explored have contained primary extended skeletons ... the men were normally accompanied with shields of which the iron umbos remain ...',[2945] but an umbo or shield boss would be considerably larger than an egg, if 'egg-shaped' is also to be understood as 'egg-sized', as a suggested sword boss would be.

Since the origin of the Morfe mounds is unknown, the possibility that they were associated in some way with the wintering of the Danes in the area in 895-6 must be considered. As the Danes are known to have stayed in the area towards the end of the ninth century and passed through early in the tenth century, they were perhaps revisiting an area familiar to their predecessors, and they or those predecessors may have been associated with, or even the creators of, the mystery mounds, for it is said of the Danes that 'for notable men burial mounds were to be thrown up as memorials'.[2946] That remark was written in the 1230s, but there is ample archaeological evidence to show that in the ninth century Danes in the Midlands of England buried their dead beneath mounds.[2947]

When the Danes abandoned their heathen practices is not known, but there is evidence of the rapid adoption of Christianity throughout York-based Northumbria by the end of the ninth century – as noted elsewhere, Guthfrith, king of York (c.883-95) was almost certainly a Christian, for he was buried in York Minster[2948] – and heathenism probably ceased to be a powerful force among them during the reign of Edward the Elder (899-924).[2949] The Danes of York in the early tenth century were Christianised, if not Christians. Certainly the Danes plundered and sacked minsters within the Danelaw, but there is no evidence that they sought to impose paganism, and seem to have had no interest

---

[2942] Sandybury, half a mile to the east of Quatford, is a name of uncertain age (*Sandy Berry* 1815 O.S. survey by Robert Dawson, BL map collection), which may be from dialect *bury/berry*, meaning 'a rabbit hole' (EDD I 456), so 'sandy warren', but whether the place may be associated with the tumuli is unresolved.

[2943] Williamson 2007: 31.

[2944] It is however worth noting the now destroyed supposed tumuli on Calf Heath near Four Ashes which lay on relatively low ground on the north side of a stream: Horovitz 1992: 20-21. Since those mounds lay on Warren Heath, the possibility that they were not prehistoric, but associated with medieval rabbit warrens, cannot be excluded.

[2945] Grinsell 1953: 27-8.

[2946] Snorri Sturluson, *Ynglingasaga* 8: see Hollander 1964: 11-12.

[2947] Price 2008.

[2948] Williams, Smyth and Kirby 1991: 148.

[2949] Wainwright 1975: 282. The Seine Vikings were still pagan in the mid-890s: Abels 1988: 164 fn.101. We should also remember that Sihtric, King of York from 920 to 926, married the sister of King Æthelstan in a Christian ceremony at Tamworth in 926, but soon after renounced both his marriage and Christianity: Higham 1993: 189.

in restricting or prohibiting Christianity: after the recovery of the Danelaw no reconversion was necessary.[2950]

The supposed barrows on Morfe Common might be compared with the only known Scandinavian cremation cemetery in England, at Heath Wood, Ingleby, some 3 miles east of Repton in Derbyshire.[2951] Repton, lying on the east bank if the river Trent, was the site of the great mausoleum church of the Mercian kings, which was incorporated into the D-shaped 1¼ acre defences of a Danish stronghold when the Danes moved from Lindsey and wintered there in 873-4. A mass grave in Repton churchyard containing the disarticulated remains of 249 bodies, some 20% of which were female,[2952] has been associated with the Danish occupation of 873-4, since the male bones appeared to be particularly robust and non-local in character and from bodies aged between 15 and 45 or more, although they showed little evidence of battle trauma. By contrast, the female bones have been identified as a different population group, perhaps Mercian. An alternative theory is that the remains may represent the reburial of bones from the existing graveyard.[2953]

The cemetery at Ingleby consists of at least 59 mounds on rising ground on the south side of the river Trent.[2954] Fewer than half of the mounds have been excavated, but those that have were originally 20' to 25' in diameter (comparable with the Morfe mounds) and between 10" and 4' in height, covered by 'false cairns' (stone cappings) 15' to 20' in diameter. The mounds are arranged in four distinct groups with a few isolated barrows lying between them. The grouped mounds may have been arranged around particular barrows, which acted as a focal point (which echoes the arrangement of four mounds surrounding one mound on Morfe Common). At least eight of the mounds (six of which had an encircling ditch) were empty, and it was at one time thought that they may have served as monumental cenotaphs, although that suggestion is now doubted.[2955] None of the excavated mounds containing cremations had a surrounding ditch, but some contained unburned animal bones, thought to represent sacrificial offerings (although the acidity and sandy nature of the soil had not assisted the preservation of organic material), and there were many iron nails. It was a common Scandinavian practice to include animals as grave offerings, and Scandinavian burials typically include nails and other iron objects (and we may note the enigmatic egg-shaped iron object found in one of the two mounds excavated on Morfe Common). There is some evidence that sections of iron-rivetted planking had been used, perhaps as biers, in the Ingleby burial ritual.

The grave goods at Ingleby have affinities with finds from the area around North Jutland, from where those buried at Ingleby may have originated. At least five of the mounds overlay a substantial unweathered V-section ditch, possibly contemporary with the

---

[2950] Lawrence 1965: 54; see also generally Abrams 2001a.
[2951] A useful survey of Viking burial sites in Scandinavia and England can be found in AJ 84 (2004) 93-99 and in Griffiths and Newman 2009: 13-15.
[2952] There is some slight evidence that these women are of a different physical type from the males, raising the intriguing possibility that they may have been native English camp followers who had formed an association with the Vikings: Graham-Campbell 1994: 129.
[2953] Welch 2001: 156; AJ 84 (2004) 103. A further re-evaluation of the charnel bone assemblage has led to the suggestion that there may be evidence of weapon injury, and that the bodies were drawn from a single population: AJ 84 (2004) 111 fn.188.
[2954] At SK 342259.
[2955] AJ 84 (2004) 100; see also Hadley 2006.

cemetery, but a prehistoric origin cannot be ruled out.[2956] Several of the mounds lay directly on the natural bedded sandstone underlying the site (as appeared to be the case of the mounds on Morfe Common), and had been constructed from sand and cobbles evidently removed to expose the sandstone. The empty and cremation mounds may reflect a mix of co-existing Christian and pagan beliefs, with the Christianised Danes buried nearby at Repton, where a number of burials east of the church included a male skeleton with a massive cut to the top of its left leg. The body had been buried with a sword, a silver Thor's hammer amulet, a boar's tusk and a jackdaw bone, all pagan attributes,[2957] but the mounds have also been seen as a Viking war cemetery where those who died locally were buried, and to which the ashes of Vikings who had died elsewhere were taken for burial.[2958]

The Morfe 'tumuli', if such they were, clearly had a number of characteristics also found in the Ingleby mounds. The mounds at both places lay on high ground overlooking a major river.[2959] Both groups of mounds lay on sandstone bedrock and were of similar size and shape. The central, larger, mound of the quincunx on Morfe may have been a 'focal point', of which a number are thought to have been identified in the groupings at Ingleby. The enigmatically documented metal finds from Morfe might tend to indicate that the mounds were tumuli. Is is possible that the Morfe mounds are properly to be associated in some way with the Danish wintering at Cwatbrycge in 895-6? The fact that only five mounds are recorded would not be unexpected if they relate to the occupation of a fighting force of some hundreds of men for a period of several months.

Certainly no earlier historians have voiced any doubts as to the likely antiquity of the quincunx, but no reference to the mounds has been traced earlier than the 1742 excavation report – indeed that is the sole reference to the existence of the mounds that we know of, since all later reports are based on that account – and it would perhaps be surprising that such an unusual feature, if ancient, had not been remarked upon by earlier writers and historians or noted, even tangentially, in early records or had led to a descriptive field-name. The fact that they seem to have remained unremarked and un-named is curious. However, there is documentary evidence that the area was wooded until at least the mid-sixteenth century – Leland, for example, describes Morfe in the 1540s as 'a grounde hilly and welle woddyd ... [i]t was a forest or chace havynge deere, but now it hathe none'[2960] – and it is not impossible that five ancient mounds may have been obscured by dense undergrowth and vegetation until the area was cleared. The absence of earlier references to the feature, including any possible clues in local field-names, whilst frustrating, cannot be taken as evidence that it was not of ancient origin.

There are, though, other possible explanations for the Morfe mounds.

[2956] The ditch may have been part of a Viking defensive position, in which case we may need to consider whether, if the mounds on Morfe Common might have been Viking, there could also be a similar fortification in the same area.
[2957] MA 39 (1995) 51-70.
[2958] AJ 84 (2004) 1106-7. For Viking mortuary practices see especially Price 2008.
[2959] 'Certainly elevated positions were often chosen for Viking/Scandinavian graves and form one of the main class of site ...': Hall 1995: 53; Griffiths and Newman 2009: 21. Many of the first generation of Viking settlers on the Isle of Man were buried in prominent mounds sited on low hills overlooking the sea, for example at Ballateare and Cronk Moo`r: Richards 1991: 102-9.
[2960] Toulmin Smith 1964: II 96.

Bowmen had formed an increasingly important component of English post-Conquest armies, shown by their famous military victories such as Agincourt. Trained bowmen were considered critical elements within local and national forces. English freemen were required by the Assize of Arms of Henry III to own and use bow and arrows, an obligation extended the following year to villeins and serfs between the ages of 16 and 60, with the Statute of Winchester in 1275 requiring all males under a certain rank to practice archery from the age of 7. Over the centuries archery practice became a normal part of everyday life,[2961] but became of particular importance with the looming threat of a Spanish invasion in the 1580s. That threat lies behind a record of payments in the Bridgnorth Chamberlain's Accounts for 'making 2 paire of buttes' somewhere in or near Bridgnorth in 1588, and 'the dressinge and skowringe of two callivers' (a caliver being a large pistol or blunderbuss), with the same Accounts recording payments for 'wine and sugar vpon mr Bromley at the trayninge the first daie', 'to iiijor men for carienge of Byrches into morffe for the bower', 'to Charles for making the bower', 'for carienge of Cushions, boordes, forms, stooles to the bower in morffe', for the provision of '2 sugar loves bestowed upon Mr Bromley at the trayninge in Morffe', and '2 gallons of brued wine with rose water and sugar upon my ladie Bromley and others the same time in Morffe'.[2962]

Whether or not the butts are to be associated with the bower on Morfe is unclear. Archery butts at this period tended to be placed on common land on the outskirts of a village or town, and generally took the form of mounds or banks of earth or turf some 6' to 24' across and 3' to 9' high to form backstops against which the targets or 'marks' were affixed. Sometimes the targets were placed on flat tops formed on the mounds. Butts were usually set up in opposed pairs facing north and south so that archers did not have to shoot into the sun. Archers shot at these targets from distances of up to 240 yards – Henry VIII set the minimum distance at 220 yards. One account of 1583 lists materials used in the construction of butts – some were evidently reinforced with timber – and refers, perhaps significantly, to ditching in front of butts. A nineteenth-century account notes that turf from a heath or common was preferred for the construction of butts because its fibres made it tougher than common turf.[2963] We cannot say where the butts were set up – the name Bowmanshill attached to a level plateau between Bridgnorth and Quatford, on the south-west side of Stanmore Hall, is noteworthy but has not been traced before the nineteenth century[2964] – though butts on Morfe might account for the mystery mounds.[2965]

[2961] Six of the Earl of Huntingdonshire's archers in 1346 were tenants from his manor of Worfield: Ayton 2011: 32.

[2962] TSAHS X (1887) 148-9; *Manuscripts of the Earl of Westmoreland, and others*, HMSO, 1885: 431; *Report of the Royal Commission on Historical Manuscripts, Part 4*, 1906: 431. The entries include payments for such things as renting horses, paving streets, press money, harness repairs, cleaning prisons, repairing buildings and for a Robin Hood performance. It is impossible to know whether the entries were recorded in correct chronological sequence or transcribed from loose receipts in random order. Lady Bromley may have been Joan, wife of Sir George Bromley of Hallon, prominent lawyer, landowner, politician and judge, Recorder at Bridgnorth, and sometime leader of the Council of the Marches of Wales (Somerset 1994: 632-3), but in 1679 Francis Bromley, esq., Francis Wolridge or Wolryche and Edward Bromley, gent., possessed Morfe, though they had sold a great part and intended to sell the rest: *Manuscripts of His Grace the Duke of Norfolk, Vols 2-3*, HMSO 1903: 310.

[2963] Roth 2012, unpaginated.

[2964] The name is first recorded as Bowman Hill in 1838 (PN Sa 6: 81), and as Beaumont hill in 1841 (Leighton 1841), and is perhaps a relatively recent appellation from a corruption of French *beaumond* 'beautiful hill' (185; Kaye 1973: 76), though a derivation from 'bowmen' cannot be discounted. It is worth recording that during the Civil War in 1642 the Parliamentary force holding Bridgnorth was awaiting the Earl of Essex and his army, but were surprised by a Royalist army commanded by

Yet the truth is that we have no evidence that the butts were set up on, or even near, Morfe. What is indisputable, though, is that five years before the Spanish Armada threatened England a bower was erected on Morfe, complete with cushioned seats and benches from which some sort of training could be reviewed by Lady Bromley and others, for whom refreshments in the form of wine and sugar were provided.[2966] The expression 'bower' is usually understood to mean an arbour or structure made from arched branches,[2967] a meaning confirmed here by the references to 'the carienge of burches [presumably birch branches: the word burches is not found in the *Oxford English Dictionary*] into morffe for the bower' as noted above. We might suppose that any such audience area may have been raised to give a better view, which could perhaps explain the five mounds: the four corner mounds might, for example, have provided support for uprights forming the frame of the covering structure, with the central mound – said to have been 27' in diameter – used as a platform on which seating was arranged.

Another possible, though less likely, explanation for the Morfe mounds is that they were associated with the gibbet that existed from at least 1300.[2968] The most helpful evidence to show its location is the crude though valuable c.1560 map of Bridgnorth, which shows a typical gibbet of two uprights and a crosspiece standing on a prominent mound somewhere to the south of The Hermitage. A close study of the map shows that a road or trackway formerly crossed the steep Wolverhampton road south of The Hermitage and ran south-east to the edge of the escarpment where it joined another trackway (marked by Severn Street and St Nicholas Road) that ran east from the town. A short distance to the south another trackway ran from the town, now marked by a footpath. The gibbet seems to have stood between the junction of those two trackways and to the west of 'St Nicholas Oake', evidently a prominent and notable tree to the north of the crest of the escarpment.[2969] Gibbets were invariably placed in a conspicuous position on a prominent thoroughfare with the rotting bodies of executed criminals serving as a terrible warning to miscreants,

---

Prince Maurice. Royalist musketeers routed the Parliamentary cavalry outside the town, but when the musketeers attempted to ford the river Parliamentary archers drove them back under a hail of arrows: Norcroft 1642: 6. Essex Falls (by tradition – unrecorded by Bellet 1856 – named after the Earl of Essex, but see Burne 1883: 425; PN Sa 6: 82) lies on the north-west side of Bowman's Hill.

[2965] The field-name *The Five Butts* recorded in Worfield in 1838 (TA; PN Sa 6: 86) would normally be taken to derive from the word *butts* applied in Shropshire to field strips lying at right angles to the main strips (Foxall 1980: 7), but might also refer to archery butts.

[2966] J. Allen B. Somerset has suggested that he entries seem to show that Lady Bromley, with others, was a spectator at some event such as a Robin Hood play or game (a payment to 'them which plaied Robin Hood' is mentioned in the accounts), rather than a review of the musters: Somerset 1994: 633. References to 'trayninge' in the accounts are of little help: such training may have been rehearsals for a play, archery practice at the new butts, or some other enterprise, but the entries, and the date, seem to suggest a military connection. Lady Bromley may have been the wife of Sir George Bromley, Chief Justice of Chester, of Hallon (Worfield), who held estates in the area and died in 1588 aged 63: DNB. Worfield church has recumbent effigies of Sir George and his wife.

[2967] Barclays English Dictionary, 1742.

[2968] Bellett 1856: 212.

[2969] Bellet 1856 makes no mention of the tree or the saint, the 4th-century bishop of Myra who became one of the most universally venerated saints in both East and West, chosen as patron saint of Constantinople and the Byzantine Empire, Moscow and the Russian Empire, Holland, Norway, eastern Italy, Lorraine and New Amsterdam (Manhattan, NewYork), and the protector of the weak against the strong, the poor against the rich. He was patron saint of various trades and professions, and is said to have saved three unjustly condemned men from death (Farmer 2003: 385-6), hence his veneration by condemned prisoners and his association with gallows and gibbets.

and the gibbet at Bridgnorth is likely to have stood on the skyline on a trackway that ran south-east towards Gag's Hill following the edge of the escarpment.[2970]

The least unlikely explanation for the Morfe quincunx, therefore, may be that it was the vestiges of a structure erected in 1588 to provide temporary shelter for Mrs Bromley and others to review some form of 'training' on Morfe, perhaps lasting for a number of years, before it was abandoned and forgotten, or that it was associated with the creation in the same year of butts to facilitate regular archery practice on the high and easily accessible ground above Bridgnorth in the light of alarm caused by the threat of an imminent Spanish invasion.[2971] That, however, is no more than speculation, and for the present the nature and origin of the Morfe mounds must remain unresolved, as must the date on which the remaining unexcavated mounds were deliberately levelled and their very location lost to history.[2972]

[2970] The trackway evidently ran along the crest of the escarpment, and is shown on the c.1560 map of Bridgnorth and the 1613 map of Morfe Forest: SA 4296.

[2971] In that respect The Butts, some 1½ miles north-west of Norbury in Shropshire may be noted. Three earthwork mounds here have been identified as rare survivals of archery butts. The northernmost mound was insignificant – roughly circular, some 2' high and some 18 yards in diameter – and covered in vegetation: HER 01860.

[2972] It is said that the mounds were visible until 1824: Watkins-Pitchford 1932: 3.

Appendix II

Ancient Sites.

Four ancient sites in our area of interest are worthy of brief comment for their possible connection with the battle of Tettenhall. The first is the mysterious 'ancient city' at Wrottesley Park, on high land overlooking the Staffordshire-Shropshire border two miles or so west of Tettenhall. The second is the former earthwork which lay at the north-west end of a long escarpment known as Abbot's Castle Hill, which has long formed the boundary of Staffordshire and Shropshire. The third is the ancient site known as The Walls at Chesterton; and the fourth is Burf Castle, a mile and a half east of Quatford.

(i) Wrottesley

Dr Robert Plot, in his great *The Natural History of Staffordshire*, published in 1686, was one of the first to record in print the site at Wrottesley. He writes of:

'...that Noble antiquity near Wrottesley in this County, where there yet remains, either the foundations of some ancient British City, or other fortification, of great extent, it including above a moyety of Wrottesley, and part of Pateshull, Pepperhill and Bonningal parks; also some parcell of the two Commons of Kingswood and West-bach, the whole containing in circuit about 3 or 4 miles, lyeing part in Staffordshire and part in Shropshire ... within the limits whereof there are several partitions yet visible, running divers ways like the sides of streets, tho' hard to be fully traced, because unterrupted both by the mattock and plow, the foundations being dayly dug up by the former, to mend high-ways, make inclosures, and pavements; and then all levell'd by the latter: which together with the large hinges for doores, an antique dagger, that have been found here, and some of the stones squared; make me rather think it some ruinated City, than a fortification only : otherwise I could have been content to have thought it some such Brittish vallum, or encampment, ... or at lest I could have thought it same Camp of the Danes, who ... were overthrown at ... Tettenhall not farr off; the whole, or greatest part of it, being in that parish at this very day : but that the parallel partitions within the out wall, whole foundations are still visible, and represent streets running different ways, put it I think out of doubt, that it must have been a City, and that of the Britans, for that I could hear of no name it ever had, nor have the Inhabitants hereabout any tradition concerning it, of any sort whatsoever, somewhat whereof would certainly have been preserved, had it either been Roman; or so late as either the Saxon, or Danish conquests of this nation ...'[2973]

... which upon second considerations I am inclined to believe, if Theotenhall doe import the habitation of heathens as Camden informs us, are no Roman antiquity, but the true remains of the old Theotenhall of the Danes, who I suppose having resided there for some time, built them this City or place of habitation, which in the year of our Lord 907 ... [or] 911 in all probability was firmly rased by Edward Senior in that signal victory he there obtained over them ...'[2974]

[2973] Plot 1686: 394.
[2974] Plot 1686: 415.

The account suggests that Plot saw the so-called foundations with his own eyes, but he was not the first to mention them, for the antiquary Sir William Dugdale, in a questionnaire in his own handwriting dating from c.1680, notes 'the vast ruins in Wrotesley Parke'.[2975]

Plot's published account was to have a significant if unfortunate impact on Roman studies, for eighteenth and nineteenth century authorities on the period who almost certainly made no examination of the area mistakenly identified the remains with some degree of confidence as the Roman sites of either *Uxacona* or *Viroconium*.[2976]

Few traces of any such 'city' have been recorded independently by other writers (although many repeat or give a potted version of Plot's description, and Stebbing Shaw says 'the most visible traces of the ancient camp, or town, are in some fields a little West of the farm-house, now called Wrottesley lodge; where I saw several stones dug from thence; but very few are now prominent on that heathy ground, which has the appearance of an entrenchment on the West side of it'),[2977] and it seems improbable, if not inconceivable, that a settlement of any magnitude could disappear without trace. Finds of iron hinges and a dagger (if such they were) mentioned by Plot are remarkably scant evidence for the existence of a 'city', and it is noteworthy that no coin finds, invariably noted by local farmworkers on ancient sites, are mentioned. Furthermore, a most detailed map of the Wrottesley Estate made in 1634[2978] makes no mention of any such remains, and the place-name evidence on that map does not point towards the existence of any ancient features: the name *The Trench* which appears on the map on the west side of the park, is unlikely to refer to any archaeological feature.

A careful examination of the ground, early records and aerial photographs has failed to reveal the slightest evidence to support the existence of Dugdale and Plot's 'vast ruins', and it seems very likely that what they saw was no more than the baulks or headlands left between agricultural clearances created from the sandstone rubble and friable slabs which lie very close to the surface here and which may have appeared as what Plot describes as 'partitions'.[2979] In that respect it is of interest that in 1919 it was noted that 'Today little remains but heaps of rough sandstone collected along the field divisions and hedges by the industrious agriculturalist'.[2980] Today the area is remarkable only for a number of thick drystone walls of sandstone rubble, and a large circular mound of stones 300 yards or so to the south of Wrottesley Lodge Farm, which appears to have been formed by the dumping of field stones during recent times, but might have a much older history. Nevertheless, the notation 'Supposed British Town (Site of)' appears on the south side of Wrottesley Lodge Farm on 6" Ordnance Survey maps between 1886 and 1924, though Ordnance Survey records show that their field officers had failed to detect any significant features on the

---

[2975] SHC 4th Series 11 163. Dugdale was at Wrottesley on 9th April 1663 during his heraldic visitation of Staffordshire (SHC II (ii) 24), and may well have seen the 'ruins' or been told about them during his visit. See also Woolf 2003: 349.
[2976] Harwood 1820: 265; Anon. 1756: xxxi. *Uxacona* is now identified as Redhill on Watling Street, and *Viroconium* is Wroxeter near Shrewsbury.
[2977] Shaw 1801 II: 194.
[2978] SRO D3548/1.
[2979] John Huntbach, the Staffordshire historian born in 1639, writing in the eighteenth century, says: '[i]f I may give my conjecture, I think that those vast ridges of stones in Wrottesley park, Pepperhill park, and Patshull park, were collected and laid in that order by [the Danes in 911] ..., it being their main camp, and upon so high a ground, that it overlooks all the country ...': Shaw 1801 II: 194.
[2980] SHC 1919 184.

ground.[2981] Investigations published by Wolverhampton Archaeology Group in 2006 reinforce the impression that the underlying sandstone has been affected by frost action and that there is no evidence of permanent human habitation at any early period.[2982]

It should be noted however that a Roman road running from Pennocrucium [Water Eaton] on Watling Street has been traced to the high point to the south of Wrottesley Lodge Farm,[2983] where it probably changed direction to head south towards the earthwork at The Walls at Chesterton, and another road may have joined it from the west, marked by tracks and roads in and to the west of Patshull Park. Roman coins and brooches have been found at Wrottesley and Wrottesley Lodge Farm, and a Romano-British site has been recorded at nearby Pepperhill across the Shropshire border to the west.[2984]

(ii) Abbot's Castle

Abbot's Castle Hill is another site of equal mystery. The name[2985] is now applied to the high escarpment, some two miles long and looking out over Shropshire towards the Severn, centrally breached by a road at Tinker's Castle which runs to Seisdon, the assembly point of one of the five Staffordshire Hundreds, situated (unusually) near the county boundary.[2986] This breach forms a notable physical gap in the ridge, which itself marks the boundary between Shropshire and Staffordshire.[2987] Early historians recorded evidence of earthworks on the ridge. Robert Plot, writing in the 1680s, says:

'Near Seasdon in this County upon the edge of Shropshire, at a place now call'd Abbots or rather Ape-wood Castle, without all doubt there was a very ancient, and no less considerable fortification; it standing very lofty on a round Promontary, and having a vast prospect to the South-West into Shropshire, at which very place tho' the entrenchment be but small, yet the whole steep ridge of the boundary bank all along 'twixt it and Chasphill, for a mile together, having hollows cut into the ground, over which 'tis thought anciently

---

[2981] In a letter to the present author dated 29th January 1971, the Archaeological Division of the O.S. confirmed that they held no evidence to support the notation.
[2982] It is right to add that this is not the conclusion reached by the Group.
[2983] Grid Reference SJ 8300.
[2984] An absurd reference to traces of a Druid grove at a high place, where mysterious rites were supposed to have been celebrated, using as an altar a large slab of stone upon which no hammer or chisel had been used, is recorded at Wrottesley in 1904. Unsurprisingly, nothing more is known of this supposed monument, or its location, but the reference to an unworked stone slab is noteworthy: WJ, June 1904 157.
[2985] The name has no connection with any abbot. It is recorded as *Aquardescastell* (1295), *Aguardescastel* (1295), *Aquardescastel* (1295), *Akewardes castel* (1298), *apewardes castel* (1301), *Apeward* and *Apeis Castle* (15th century), *Abbots or rather Ape-wood Castle* (1686), *Abbots Castle Hill* (1752), *Abbots Castle* (1775): Horovitz 2005: 78-9. The element *castel(l)* is found in Welsh, Cornish, OE, Old French, and ME, from Latin *castellum* 'a fort', but is usually a post-Conquest element introduced by the Normans. Occasionally it is from OE *ceastel* 'a heap of stones', but that is not likely here, unless connected with the numerous pits recorded on the ridge, which could have been caused by stone extraction. *Aquard-* and *Aguard-* may, given the *castel* element, be from the Old French personal names Achart, Aquart, which are probably from Old German Agihard, Akihart. The change from Aq- or Ag- to Ap- is curious, and may perhaps be explained as misreading, but see PN Sa 6: 12-13.
[2986] Though more centrally placed if, as seems likely, the pre-Conquest Hundred stretched as far as the river Severn.
[2987] But an earlier boundary in pre-Conquest times may have run along the Severn to the west: see Eyton 1881: 2-4; TSAS LVII 1961-4 157-60.

they set their Tents, the whole seems but one continuous fortification, the two hills at each end being the principal bastions: which I am also inclined to believe to have been a British work ...'.[2988]

Later historians variously incorporate Plot's observations in their own works, but Nathanial Spencer visited the earthworks in the 1770s, and says that 'after we examined it with great exactness, we are convinced that is is not so old [as the Roman period], but most probably was thrown up by the Britons, during their war with the Saxons'.[2989] Sadly, he provides no evidence to support those conclusions. In October 1903 William Hutchinson, a geographer from Wolverhampton, published a description based on a personal inspection of the site:

'[From the cottage known as Tinker's Castle] leave the highway [no direction is given, an unfortunate though typical oversight for this geographer], and passing close in front of the castle, go along a narrow grassy lane ... and you perceive on the right a deep gully some twenty yards wide, closed at the end and evidently artificial, proceed further along the ... lane with the pine trees on the right ... you are walking along the dividing line between Staffordshire and Salop. In about half a mile the lane comes to an end, and you enter the plantation and keep straight on along a slightly raised and not much used path ... you presently observe a large circular hollow ten yards in diameter and three of four feet deep in the middle; twenty yards further on ... another, and another, and then to one fourteen yards in diameter and six or seven feet deep – then to others ten yards in diameter, succeeded by larger ones even sixteen yards in diameter, and nine feet deep, and so on, the larger and smaller occurring irregularly for the distance of about a mile – all along the crest of the ridge and in a tolerably straight line; the writer counted upwards of forty of them. Some of these singular saucer-like hollows have been almost levelled up by successive growths of brake ferns which have grown within them, and their outlines rendered indistinct, still they are there; others are very perfect, they run in a line West to East with the trend of the hill; at the West end there is the deep gully spoken of, and another answering to it at the East end; moreover a long ditch or fosse runs close in front of them on the South side, in some places three or four feet deep and likely enough formerly deeper, and two or three yards wide, with a continuous bank in front which form now the path on which the visitor walks. Now this remarkable series of circular pits, with their fosse or ditch, and vallum or bank, are the real castle – or camp'.[2990]

No earlier detailed study of the earthworks is known, but we seem to have the name of one of the two other works recorded by J. Luker of Bobbington in 1756 on the side of Whittemore Hill at the south-eastern end of the ridge near the ancient diamond-shaped stone known as The Warstone (which lies at the former junction of the Staffordshire and Shropshire boundaries):[2991] the end of the ridge is recorded in a perambulation of 1293 as

---

[2988] Plot 1686: 397.
[2989] Spencer 1772: 425.
[2990] WJ, October 1903. Hutchinson concluded that the circular pits were clearly the remains of prehistoric pit dwellings, a supposition almost certainly mistaken. LiDAR surveys show several depressions on the south side of the county boundary running north-west from the boundary junction with Tinker's Castle Road.
[2991] Shaw 1801: II 278; VCH XX 64, 185. Scott mentions 'Near to the hoar-stone [at the east end of the escarpment] ... [at] Wittimoor-hill are two small camps': Scott 1832: 328 fnU. LiDAR surveys reveal a rectangular double-ditched earthwork, roughly 450' by 200' with square corners and no obvious entrance, within a band of woodland, on the north side of and parallel with the road north-east of Upper Whittimere at SO 832932. The site lies a few yards north of the lost Roman road from Greensforge. No other earthwork has been untraced in the area.

Bekwynesburynesse, 'the nose or promontory of Bekwin's fortification'. The same perambulation perhaps enables us to locate the site of the original 'Abbot's Castle', presumably an earthwork at the north-west end of the ridge, around which the Staffordshire-Shropshire boundary forms a conspicuous curlicue. The nature of the earthworks is puzzling, for the crest of the ridge forms a boundary itself, and a linear fortification along the crest, which could easily be bypassed on either side, would create an odd defensive structure. Sir Cyril Fox noted that for hundreds of years, perhaps from the age of Penda (632-54), the Mercians built 'Short Dykes' as and when circumstances required in the central march, covering such outliers as the Long Mynd and Wenlock Edge, many of them dug across ridgeways leading from the Welsh highlands into the English plain, and others aligned across the heads of fertile valleys, which he saw as evidence of efforts made by the Mercians to control or provide warnings of attack from this difficult country, and to protect their steadings in its valley.[2992] The ditch and bank along Abbot's Castle Hill do not have the characteristics of these Short Dykes, and the feature may perhaps best be seen as an early estate boundary, or the earthworks may be associated with the Roman road from Greensforge to (and beyond) The Walls at Chesterton which runs along the southern flank of Abbot's Castle Hill towards the summit of the escarpment: the well-recorded circular pits could have been created when the hard breccia[2993] was extracted for the construction of the Roman road.

One intriguing account of this area exists which deserves to be set out in full. In about 1894, the Bilston historian G. T. Lawley wrote a series of articles for *The Midland Weekly News*, including a piece on the battles of Tettenhall and Wednesfield, blending genuine historical evidence with wildly speculative reconstructions incorporating invented individuals and specific local sites, in which he writes: 'On the plateau of the rear of the escarpment [at The Wildmoor on Abbot's Castle Hill] is still to be seen, in a good state of preservation, the ancient camp, containing an area of not more than two or three acres, now covered by a thicket of old Scotch pines and larches, and well protected by a steep ditch. It is approached from the village of Seisdon by a narrow and very ancient way ... approach along which was defended by a secondary, or outlying camp, the traces of which are not so well defined as those of the principal one. From the latter the distance westward to the entrenched banks, alluded to by Dr Plott, is about seven hundred yards, and here the plateau is terminated by an abrupt declivity, having at each end a round projecting knoll, admirably adapted for defensive purposes, and now known by the euphonious names of Knaves Castle and Tinkers Castle'.[2994] The 'ancient camp' described by Lawley was almost certainly the moated site at Wolmore,[2995] known as Wildmoor in the nineteenth century, but his less well-defined 'secondary or outlying camp' remains unidentified.[2996]

(iii) The Walls at Chesterton

One particularly significant military fortification lies close to a line drawn between Quatford and Tettenhall/Wednesfield, and that is the impressive multivallate earthwork known as The Walls at Chesterton in the parish of Worfield, five miles north-east of

---

[2992] Fox 1955: 285-7.
[2993] Hull 1869: 44-5.
[2994] Lawley 1894.
[2995] Shown in Moat Coppice at SO 822949 on the 6" O.S. map of 1886-91.
[2996] As has been noted, there is an account, for which no authority is given, of human bones found 'on the common adjoining Abbot's-hill [Abbot's Castle Hill]' in Scott 1832: 323, 327.

Quatford, on the Roman road that runs north-west from Greensforge.[2997] It occupies a slightly elevated position in an area of undulating land, within an angled, steep-sided bend of the Stratford Brook, a tributary of the river Worfe, and is roughly D-shaped in plan. Its overall dimensions are about 370 yards north-south by 670 yards north west-south east. The western and southern ramparts of the fortification, which has two, and in some places more, concentric ditches, form a right angle. The southern side is built above sandstone cliffs, which also protect the south-east and north-east approaches. The defensive circuit encloses an area of some 22 acres. The interior is defined by a single rampart with steep internal and external faces. The back of the rampart has been reduced in height by ploughing along much of the southern side. An outer rampart was constructed on the western side of the earthwork which also has a steep outer face and is separated from the inner rampart by a rock-cut ditch. Along the southern and eastern parts of the circuit the rampart is bounded externally by natural cliffs formed by the Stratford Brook. These cliffs formed additional lines of defence, and in places have been quarried to enhance their defensive appearance. Around the northern and western parts of the circuit the rampart is bounded by a broad external ditch, which has been largely infilled and is now mainly visible as a shallow depression. The present entrance, with a complete lack of defences, is towards the west end of the north bank, but is likely to be relatively modern.[2998]

Stebbing Shaw gives the following account in 1798: 'Here is perhaps as complete a Roman camp as any on this island. Its situation is on a hill, with a brook running close under it on the South and South-west sides, where the perpendicular face of a rock makes it inaccessible in every part, except the gate-way, where a cut has been made for the horse to go to water, and the army to come to it from the road, which lies at a distance of 2 or 300 yards. The four gate-ways are yet very visible, and the whole area within the bank is about 25 acres. The whole is generally called the Walls of Chesterton'.[2999]

Gough's edition of Camden's *Britannia*, published in 1806, includes a detailed description of the earthworks, and observes that 'There have been four gates or entrances into it: one in the middle of the north front from Chesterton, another in the middle of the west, a third in the south-east, and a fourth in the north-east corner. The odd position of the two last take advantage of the declivities in the rock…'.[3000] A wide break in the northern part of the west bank may mark an ancient entrance, but is not recorded in early accounts of the place, and there is no obvious trackway approaching the fortification at this point. To the east of the entrance, the external ditch has been recut and partially modified by modern drainage channels.

In 1908 The Walls was described as 'a large entrenched area following the hill-side except on the north where the ground falls gently away. This latter side has a vallum and fosse of considerable strength, describing an arc; from the interior the vallum rises 10ft, descending

---

[2997] The site lies at SO 786966; SMR PRN 00433. On the name The Walls see PN Sa 6: 74, 83.

[2998] Gale, writing in 1719, says that the outer bank may have been levelled for the farm buildings at Chesterton: Gough's *Britannia*, 1806. Hardwicke shows what appears to be a large mound to the north-east of this entrance on his plan of the site, and says that 'at each side of the entrance, as a guard thereto, is a high artificial mount of earth, that on the west side is at this day [1822] known by the name of Spy Bank, where it is presumed sentinels' tents or exploratories were placed to give alarm on the enemy's appearance, it being sufficiently high to comprehend a distant view of the surrounding country...': Hardwicke 1882.

[2999] Shaw 1798: I 30. See also Scott 1832: 321-5.

[3000] Camden 1806: III: 19; the place is unmentioned in Gibson's 1695 edition of *Britannia*. VCH Shropshire I 377-8 states that the entrance at the north-east is 'a modern way for farm carts'.

26ft into a fosse 9ft in depth. The entrance on this side is a simple opening; the entry at the eastern extremity, on the brow of the hill, is a modern way for farm carts, the greater part of the site being under the plough. On the western side these works are continued, but the greater depth of the hill-side has been utilized, giving the vallum a height of 22ft; the fosse below and the breastwork above are weak, being 4ft and 2ft respectively. The south and east are contained within a protecting curve of the river Worf; on the south the natural rock and declivity of the hill have needed no artificial work, the precipitous sides girded by the river precluding any assault. At the south-eastern corner a tongue of land fashioned by the bend of the river is at a slightly lower level and is severed from the main camp by an agger 13ft in height; in this is a means of egress to the external plateau, and from the latter a path – at the western angle – covered by the agger, descends to the stream beneath. Between this gateway and the broken vallum on the north the hill-side, 80ft in height, is crested by a rampart. Although of a simple character the site is so admirably chosen that the position is of great strength and convenience'.[3001]

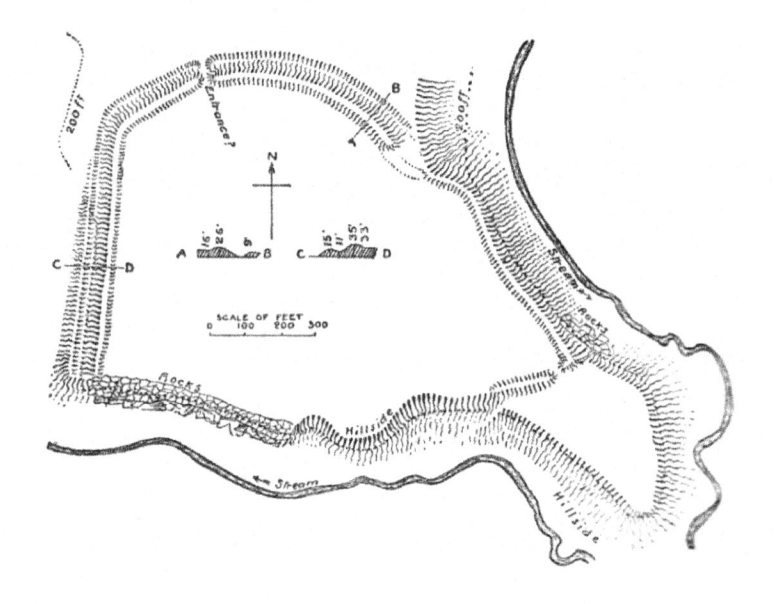

A plan with cross-sections of Chesterton Walls, from Volume 1 of the *Victoria History of the County of Shropshire*, 1908, page 378.

Along parts of the inner and outer faces of the recut ditch, revetment walls are visible. They are built of roughly coursed sandstone blocks and stand to a height of 2'. A wall faced in a similar manner, with a core of river cobbles and sandstone blocks, was constructed on top of the rampart which defines the interior. The wall, which now survives in discontinuous lengths and is partly embanked, is between 7'6" and 11'6" wide and stands up to 3' in height. This wall, or breastwork, noted by the antiquary J. B. Blakeway in the early nineteenth century, is impossible to date, but might conceivably be contemporary with a later occupation of the hillfort, and may well account for its name,

---

[3001] VCH Shropshire I: 37-8.

though the Shropshire Sites and Monuments Record describes the walling as modern. The interior of the fortification, once divided into five fields, which was reduced to three in 1886,[3002] and to two by 1908, is now an undivided gently undulating area. At the southeastern corner a tongue of land fashioned by the bend of the river is at a slightly lower level, and is severed from the main camp by a bank 13' in height.[3003]

The fortification lies on the north side of the Roman road from Greensforge which continues north-west through Ackleton, with another road running from the earthworks towards Roman forts at Burlaughton on Watling Street, passing through or near Tong. The nature of the earthworks suggests that they date from the early Iron-Age, but were doubtless utilised by the Romans, although no archaeological finds which might help to date the fortification are recorded.[3004] A gold ring and several Roman coins are said to have been found in the neighbourhood in the first half of the ninteenth century, but are now lost,[3005] and in any event cannot be taken as evidence of occupation, whatever their age might have been.

The earthworks would have served as a particularly suitable ready-made base for English forces overseeing the Danes who wintered at *Cwatbrycge* in 895-6, and if the combined English army which ambushed the Scandinavians returning with booty in 910 had planned its tactics in advance, as opposed to simply pursuing and intercepting the enemy and engaging in battle wherever that occurred, The Walls would have offered a position of considerable military strength at which the English could have mustered, rested and provisioned their forces prior to engagement with the enemy. Given the importance of the Severn crossing at *Cwatbrycge*, it is possible that the English were able to predict with a degree of certainty the route the Scandinavians were likely to take on their return to Northumbria, and The Walls could conceivably qualify as one of the infinite possible candidates for Æthelflæd's elusive *burh* built at *Scergeat* in 912 (considered in more detail in Chapter 10 of this volume): The Walls lies 1½ miles from the ancient Staffordshire boundary, which might be taken as tentative evidence of a connection with a shire boundary possibly implied by the place-name, though Staffordshire and Shropshire were probably not created as shires until a slightly later date. Certainly an existing fortification such as this would be easier to convert into a *burh* by means of a substantial timber palisade, and many *burhs* lie (as here) on a Roman road. From its mention (as *Stonystrete*) in a perambulation of 1298[3006] we have evidence that the road was likely to have been in use in the pre-Conquest period, and The Walls would have been a strategically valuable site to regulate the Severn crossing at *Cwatbrycge*, less than five miles distant, forming a strong base from which those creating Æthelflæd's *burh* at *Cwatbrycge* could be defended.

[3002] 1886-90 6" O.S. map.
[3003] VCH Shropshire I: 377-8.
[3004] See TSAS II 346-7, 359; VCH Shropshire I 377; Hardwicke 1882-3: 11-16; Mander 1908: 265-8. Hardwicke 1882-3: 15 mentions 'the entrenchments and tumuli, probably British, on Rudge Heath' opposite the north-east point of The Walls. No such features have been traced, and it may be that Hardwick misinterpreted the 'free warren in Rudge Heath' recorded in 1662 (SA 2028/1/5/17), the 'ancient warren [on a large waste called Rudge heath] for conies and a warrener's lodge', recorded c.1733 (SA 330/13): no relevant features are detectable in LiDAR surveys. Warren House and Warren Farm lie to the east of The Walls. The road from Rudge Heath to Sutton Maddock has the appearance of a Roman road, deviating in typical Roman fashion to avoid a difficult crossing of the river Worfe between Folley and Stableford, before continuing on its original alignment, and appears on Roque's 1752 map of Shropshire.
[3005] Mander 1908: 266.
[3006] TSAS LXXI (1993) 27.

On the other hand, apart from Lyng and Langport in Somerset, which are slightly less than six miles apart, no other Anglo-Saxon *burhs* lie only five miles apart. Furthermore, unlike most Mercian *burhs*, The Walls does not lie on a major river (it is some four miles from the Severn), but there is a watercourse that runs along its eastern and southern boundary, and not all Mercian *burhs* lie on a major river, Chirbury being but one example. If *Scergeat* were to be seen as a temporary *burh* to cover the Severn to the west, it would have become obsolete with the building of *Cwatbrycge* later the same year, which would explain why it disappears from the historical records. But it must be recognised that there are hundreds, if not thousands, of existing earthworks in Western Mercia that might be the site of *Scergeat*, and as many, if not more, of which no trace survives. The likelihood that The Walls can be identified as *Scergeat* must be considered extremely remote, yet it would be surprising if it had not been used at some period during the unsettled times in this region at the end of the ninth and beginning of the tenth centuries, even if only briefly.

(iv) Burf Castle

Burf Castle[3007] is a partially destroyed one-and-a-half acre double-banked roughly rectangular earthwork with a south-east entrance on the summit of a high escarpment overlooking the Severn a little over a mile to the east of Quatford. The site has never been excavated, and no finds have been recorded from the vicinity, but the earthwork remains are readily discernible and have the appearance of an Iron-Age hillfort.[3008] The name Burf is from Old English *burh* 'fortification'. The *–h* often developed into modern *–f* (as in the pronunciation, though not the spelling, of words such as *laugh* and *tough*), which has led to *burh* becoming Burf instead of Borough, especially in Shropshire, with examples such as Abdon Burf and Clee Burf (both with hillfort earthworks), and in some cases *–f* becomes *–th*, giving names such as The Berth, a low-lying prehistoric earthwork 7 miles north-west of Shrewsbury.

[3007] VCH Shropshire I 379-80. The name is from OE *burh* 'fortified place', with the common dialectical confusion between *f* and *th*. The name may perhaps be found in the surname *de Burgh'* recorded in 1327, and *de Bury* and *ate Bury*, recorded 1344-60: PN Sa 6: 23.
[3008] Hartshorne believed the earthworks to be Danish, dating from the wintering of the Danes in 895-6: Hartshorne 1841: 201-2. The crop-mark of a quadrant-shaped enclosure 500 yards west of Gags Hill (at SO 75159045), seemingly without an entrance, may be associated with recent pig-farming in this area.

Appendix III

The Royal Free Chapels, Wulfrun and the early history of Wolverhampton.

One particular curiosity of the area encompassing Wolverhampton, Tettenhall, Quatford and Bridgnorth is the unusual concentration of those churches known as royal free chapels. In 1318 nine such churches were listed in a mandate of Edward II:[3009]

St Martin le Grand, London[3010]
St Oswald, Gloucester
St Cuthburga, Wimborne
St Mary Magdalene, Bridgnorth
St Mary, Shrewsbury
St Peter (formerly St Mary),[3011] Wolverhampton
St Michael (probably formerly St Mary), Tettenhall
St Michael (formerly St Mary), Penkridge[3012]
St Mary, Stafford (formerly St Bertelin [Beorhthelm])[3013]

To this number can be added All Saints, Derby and St Mary in the castle, Hastings.[3014] St Lawrence's church at Gnosall also became a royal free chapel, apparently at some date after the reign of King Stephen, and during the reign of Edward III St George's, Windsor, and St Stephen's, Westminster, were created royal free chapels. The church of St Editha at Tamworth came to be regarded as a royal free chapel in the fourteenth century, but may have enjoyed that status at a much earlier date. Indeed, it may have been endowed with the saint's relics by Æthelflæd herself c.913.[3015]

The precise rights of these chapels is uncertain, for post-Conquest records use vague expressions such as 'customs', and land held 'liberally and freely', 'perpetually', and 'without perturbation', but the chapels were 'free' in the sense of exempt from all exactions and charges, and, crucially, had no parochial duties of their own.[3016] Almost all were centred on a college of secular canons, and it is evident that of the nine chapels listed, over half are in the West Midlands, and two, Tettenhall and Wolverhampton, are only two miles apart. Penkridge lies some 15 miles from Wolverhampton; Quatford some 21 miles. The churches of Tettenhall, Wolverhampton, Penkridge and Quatford, with Gnosall (a church which is particularly grand and impressive for such a small place, and was evidently of

---

[3009] Styles 1936: 56. In his study of collegiate churches, Paul Jeffery lists the following early Royal Free Chapels: Blyth (Nottinghamshire), Bosham, Bridgnorth, Gnosall, London (St Martin), Oxford (St George), Penkridge, Pevensey, Shrewsbury (St Juliana), Shrewsbury (St Michael's), Shrewsbury (St Mary's), Stafford, Steyning, Tettenhall, Wallingford, Wimborne, and Wolverhampton. The following Royal Free Chapels became monasteries in the twelfth century: Bromfield (Shropshire), Dover, Gloucester (St Oswald), Waltham (Essex): Jeffery 2004: 455-6. On the Royal Free Chapels of Staffordshire and the West Midlands see now especially Jenkins 1989 and Sargent 2012.
[3010] Created a Royal Free Chapel in the reign of Henry II: VCH III 321; VCH London II 555.
[3011] Recorded as St Mary in DB : VCH IV 45.
[3012] The cult of St Michael spread from Gaul to Celtic Britain in the 7th century: Finberg 1964: 57. '..the dedication to St Michael was a favourite one for early churchyards': Gould 1993: 5.
[3013] Thacker 1985: 18.
[3014] Styles 1936: 56.
[3015] Styles 1936: 56; Meeson 2015: 17.
[3016] Denton 1970: 8-14; Sargent 2012: 267-8.

considerable importance) could be encompassed in a circle of 12-miles radius.[3017] The freedom enjoyed by the Royal Free Chapels, as they came to be known after the Conquest,[3018] has been taken to indicate that they were held direct from the king, and enjoyed enviable exemption from diocesan jurisdiction and interference, an exemption they tended to protect aggressively when necessary. Some, if not all, may have their origins in grants by a powerful king or kings able to impose an irregular component into a regulated religious structure at a distant time, perhaps when the traditional constitution of the English church was yet developing, though there is no evidence that they might all date from even roughly the same period.

That a great proportion of the free chapels is concentrated in the West Midlands may be coincidental, but could imply that a particularly powerful Mercian ruler lay behind at least some of the foundations. Few records survive to throw any light on the matter. St Oswald's of Gloucester is said to have been founded or refounded by Æthelflæd, Lady of the Mercians c.900,[3019] and though Quatford church was built by Roger de Montgomery and Adeleya his wife in 1086, an earlier church may have existed: as noted elsewhere, Æthelflæd built a *burh* there in 912.[3020] Gnosall was by tradition founded by Wulfhere, king of Mercia 658-75, and is said to have been a royal free chapel by Æthelflæd,[3021] but the evidence for that claim is unclear. A charter[3022] of Edward the Confessor to the church of Wolverhampton, refounded by Wulfrun at some date after 994, formally elevated it to a free chapel.[3023]

It would be unsafe to rely on the traditions recorded in the fourteenth century that Tettenhall had been founded by king Edgar (957-75),[3024] and similar attributions to Shrewsbury[3025] and Penkridge recorded in the sixteenth century, the latter perhaps deriving from a visit there by Edgar in 958, when he issued two charters, in one of which Penkridge is described as *in loco famoso qui dicitur Pencric* 'in that famous place [or minster church – the word *loco* was sometimes applied to minsters][3026] which is called *Pencric*'.[3027] In fact a footnote in the *Liber Niger* of Archbishop John Alan or Allen of Dublin stated that Penkridge church was founded by King Eadred, Edgar's uncle, which if true might possibly explain the enigmatic reference to the famous place, and would date the

---

[3017] Wolverhampton and Penkridge (as well as Tong) are among minsters in Staffordshire, Shropshire and Herefordshire mentioned in the will of Wulfgeat of Donington, c.1000: S.1534.
[3018] Blair 2005: 309.
[3019] VCH Gloucestershire II 84-7.
[3020] ASC 'C'; Swanton 1996: 96; Eyton 1854-60: I 109.
[3021] Royds 1909: 139.
[3022] S.1155.
[3023] Styles 1940: 60.
[3024] Dugdale 1817-30: Vol. 6 Part III 1467; Jenkins 1988: 56. The earliest reference to its status as a royal free chapel is a declaration by Henry II in 1247: VCH III 316. It may be noted that Erdeswick (followed by Dugdale) suggests that Wulfrun was Edgar's sister, and it was Edgar who founded a chapel of 8 portionaries at Wolverhampton at the request of his dying sister in about 970: Erdeswick 1844: 354-5.
[3025] Owen and Blakeway 1825: II 302, who consider the assertion 'very unlikely'. It may be noted that St Chad's church in Shrewsbury also claimed, unsuccessfully, to be a Royal Free Chapel: ibid. 186.
[3026] Lewis 2008: 120, citing Blair 2005: 110; 217 fn.135. A minster at Penkridge certainly existed by c.1000: S.1534; Whitelock 1930: 54-5, 166.
[3027] S.667. The other charter is S.677. Both charters relate to estates outside Staffordshire. Penkridge was founded by c.1006, when it is mentioned in the will of Wulfgeat (SHC 1916 119-21; Whitelock 1930: 54-6, 163-7; VCH III 298). For a useful analysis of the background to the charters and the role of Penkridge, see Lewis 2008: 104-29.

foundation to 946-55.[3028] However, it seems probable that somewhere described as 'a famous place [or minster]' is likely to have been of some antiquity at the time it was so described.[3029] By the fourteenth century, two priests were required to say mass for the souls of the kings of England as founders of Penkridge church[3030] in a way that suggests the custom was already ancient at that time, and the kings for whom prayers were offered are probably to be understood as pre-Conquest kings. It may be noted that a nineteenth century history of Penkridge[3031] observes that '[T]he Church of Penkridge is of a very ancient foundation, but opinions vary as to the date of its earlier existence. According to one record, it was founded by King Edgar, in the year 964, but according to another, and perhaps more reliable authority, Ethelfleda, the daughter of King Alfred and the Lady of Mercia, conferred, at a much earlier date than 964, upon Penkridge Church, the distinction of a Royal Free Chapel'. Frustratingly, the author fails to identify the 'more reliable authority'. Domesday Book merely tells us that Penkridge had been held by Edward the Confessor, but we shall see that it is likely that the church of Penkridge was of much greater antiquity.[3032]

The church of St Mary in Stafford was formerly dedicated to St Bertelin, whose cult may have been well-established when Æthelflæd built her *burh* in Stafford in 913.[3033] There are traditions that Wolverhampton was founded by Wulfhere in 659, and in the sixteenth century King Edgar was believed to have been the founder, having (it was said) given the land to Wulfgeat, Wulfrun's kinsman,[3034] but no evidence has been traced to support either tradition. During the course of a papal enquiry of 1262 into its origins, the dean and chapter claimed, with wild extravagance and a notable absence of evidence, but doubtless in good faith, that the liberty of their church as a free chapel had been enjoyed, as all the king's chapels, 'ever since the Kingdom of England attained to the Christian faith and worship, and before any bishops were created there'.[3035]

The royal free chapel of Quatford transferred to Bridgnorth in 1101 together with borough status, Quatford being one of only two boroughs recorded in the Domesday Shropshire folios, the other being Shrewsbury itself, though others are likely to have existed.[3036] Quatford's prebends supplied the incomes of the lord's clerks who ran his household, with their holders either personally or via deputies maintaining a perpetual round of worship in which intercession for the founder and his family was a significant feature.[3037] Why should

---

[3028] SHC 1950-1 3.

[3029] The expression is found in other 9th and 10th century charters, but was used sparingly: there are nine examples in the 9th century (Canterbury, Tamworth and Bath in Mercia, and Kingston (Surrey), Mereworth and Wye (both in Kent) in Wessex), and in the 10th century are charters of Æthestan issued at Exeter, Eadred at Somerton and Edgar at Woolmer. The expression is restricted in the 11th century to monastic communities receiving royal donations or of the location of lands granted: Lewis 2008: 119. Royds 1909: 139 claims (without quoting any sources) that Penkridge was founded and made a royal free chapel either by Æthelflæd or Edgar.

[3030] CPR 1348-50 360.

[3031] Tildesley 1886: 10.

[3032] Jenkins 1989: 24.

[3033] Thacker 1985: 19. Researching the history of St Mary's church is not helped by the theft of its charters in the 13th century: Styles 1940: 74.

[3034] Hooke and Slater 1986: 16. Wulfgeat appears to have had some interest in Wrottesley in Tettenhall which had become lost by 1086: ibid.

[3035] Styles 1940: 87; SHC 1924 268-72.

[3036] Domesday Book cannot be relied upon as evidence for boroughs: it is likely that were not mentioned in the great record.

[3037] Dickinson 1979: 264.

Quatford church, which, as we have seen, was founded (or refounded) in 1086, have been made a royal free chapel (presumably by William the Conqueror or apredecessor)? In fact there is not the slightest evidence that William created any royal free chapel, and it is possible that the status was transferred from some earlier foundation at Quatford. But if that were the case, why should Quatford have been chosen as the site of a royal free chapel?

The most obvious explanation is that the place, recorded in the *Anglo-Saxon Chronicle* as *Brycge* or *Quatbrycge* and discussed in detail in earlier chapters of this volume, had a particular strategic and commercial interest as a principal crossing point of the river Severn, and chapels were often sited at such crossings, for bridges and fords were frequently the scene of accidents, especially in times of flood, with travellers likely to have taken comfort from prayers said before a crossing, or offering thanks for a crossing successfully made. We must also remember that the Danes established a wintering camp probably at or close to Quatford in 895, and the place evidently became of some importance when Æthelflæd had a *burh* constructed there in 912, though whether she built a chapel there is open to question, since it seems likely that the *burh* at *Cwatbrycge* was little more than a fortified enclosure, rather than an incipient urban centre, though a bridge-head settlement with commercial ambitions cannot be ruled out.

Can any light can be thrown on the origins of the royal free chapels by any common link between those listed above? Of the royal free chapels listed by Jeffery, all (except Derby) lie outside the Danelaw, and several – London,[3038] Gloucester,[3039] Wimborne,[3040] Wallingford,[3041] Quatford (replaced by Bridgnorth)[3042] and Derby (as well as Tamworth) – are in places known to have been occupied by the Danes, with the remainder in areas likely to have suffered from Danish raids. Shrewsbury (which some have identified as a possible

---

[3038] According to Tanner's *Notitia Monastica*, the chapel was founded by Ingelricus and his brother in 1056, possibly on the site of an earlier community originally founded by Victred or Wythred, king of Kent, c.700. Its freedom from Episcopal jurisdiction which later characterised royal chapels is recorded in a charter of William I in 1068, which conferred numerous privileges, but St Martin's only became a royal free chapel in the reign of Henry II: VCH III 321 fn.14.

[3039] A Danish army spent part of the winter of 877 at Gloucester: Heighway 2001: 102.

[3040] Wimborne was founded by Cuthburga, sister of King Ine, in 718. When King Æthelred was mortally wounded in a nearby battle with the Danes in 871, his body was brought to Wimborne for burial. After the destruction of the convent by the Danes c.1013, a college of secular canons was established by Edward the Confessor, and later became a Royal Free Chapel: Coulstock 1993.

[3041] The Danes burned Wallingford in 1006: Swanton 1996: 137.

[3042] Groom 1992: 21 states, without citing any source, that 'St Mary Magdalene was the castle chapel to which the status of royal free chapel pertaining to Quatford church was transferred. St Mary's parish crosses the Severn and that part west of the river covers little more than the area of the castle'. Other authorities have concluded that St Mary's chapel, Bridgnorth, became a royal free chapel: Barrow 2004: 47. The history of Quatford church is not without interest. In 1086 Roger de Montgomery, Earl of Shrewsbury, exchanged his Shropshire estate of Millichope for Eardington (which was then part of Quatford), then held by the church of St Mildburh of Wenlock, and in the same year a borough is recorded and a collegiate church was founded at Quatford. On his death in 1094 Earl Roger was succeeded by his second son Hugh, who at some date between 1094 and 1098, with his younger brother Arnulf, granted the church to the French abbey of La Sauve Majeure near Bordeaux. Earl Roger's eldest son Robert succeeded High as Earl in 1098 and the church was again granted to La Sauve, but on this occasion with the provision, common at this period, that the collegiate status be abolished: a monk replaced each canon on his death, and received his prebend: TSAS LVII 1961-4: 41. It should be noted that when the collegiate community of Quatford was transferred to Bridgnorth it moved from the diocese of Hereford to the diocese of Coventry and Lichfield: Barrow 2004: 47.

site of the *burh* of *Scergeat* constructed by Æthelflæd in 912)[3043] lies on the Severn, the course of which was probably followed by the Danes on their way to Buttington near Welshpool in 893, and Wolverhampton and Tettenhall (and possibly Penkridge, some 15 miles to the north) are associated with the English victory over the Danes in 910, and might previously have suffered at the hands of the Danes. Tamworth was the ancient royal capital of Mercia until it fell under Danish control in the 880s. One might speculate that these chapels have their origins in pre-Conquest royal foundations, perhaps dating from the late ninth/early tenth century, marking particular and notable victories over or deliverence from the Danes.[3044] If that is the case, we need to consider who may have initiated the creation of these various honoured chapels.

If the chapels are indeed to be associated with the Danish depredations, they must be later than the start of the Scandinavian raids, i.e. post 793 (when the attack on Lindisfarne was actually by Norwegians), although there is no reason to suppose that they must all have been created at the same time or by the same hand. One king who exerted power over both Wessex and Mercia, and had a particular and personal interest in Quatford, was Alfred, who might possibly have been there for at least some of the time during the Danish wintering of 895-6, since his forces may have joined Mercian forces pursuing the Danes to the place, the river Lea lying in Mercian territory, in which case he doubtless took the opportunity to travel in the area, and may have been associated in some way with one or more of the churches of Quatford, Penkridge, Tettenhall or Wolverhampton, if such had then existed. Certainly he knew Wimborne well, for it was a royal residence, and his brother, King Æthelred I, was buried there in 871.[3045] Gloucester, with Winchester, was the political centre of Alfred's kingdom which encompassed both Mercians and West Saxons from about the early 880s, and a place for which we can suppose Alfred had a particular affection.[3046] If not Alfred, his son-in-law and daughter, Æthelflæd and Æthelred,[3047] or Alfred's son Edward the Elder (or indeed a combination of them) could have been responsible for the creation of the royal free chapels, although it must be conceded that the lack of any reference in early documents or traditions to the source of their foundation does not assist the arguments for that case, and tends to point to earlier foundations. In addition, one might expect any church founded by Æthelflæd to be dedicated to one of the Saxon saints she was keen to promote, and even as Alfred's daughter and latterly Lady of the Mercians it may be doubted whether she carried the authority necessary to found a church free from diocescan control.

[3043] Shrewsbury was a *civitas* and centre of power in 901 (when Ealdorman Æthelred and his wife Æthelflæd, together with a number of Mercian nobles, are known to have stayed), and probably long before, and would appear to have been fortified before c.905, since coinage dating from that period is known (Bassett 1991: 1; Lyon 2001: 75-6; Bassett 1991: 1), and mints were only permitted in fortified places. No evidence has been traced to support the statement in TSAS 1937-8 98 that Shrewsbury possessed a mint at the time of Alfred the Great (d.899). For more detailed discussion of *Scergeat* see also chapter 10 of this volume.

[3044] Beresford 1883: 44 suggests that the collegiate centres of Derby, Stafford, Gnosall, Penkridge, Wolverhampton, Tettenhall, Chester, Shrewsbury, and possibly Tamworth, were founded in the tenth or early eleventh century.

[3045] Thacker 2001: 250. Æthelred's son, Æthelwold, Edward the Elder's cousin and rival, used Wimborne as his base in his attempt to take the throne after Alfred's death: ibid.

[3046] Keynes 2001: 45.

[3047] According to William of Malmesbury the royal free chapel of Gloucester was founded in the time of King Alfred by Æthelred and Æthelflæd, which would place the foundation between c.885 and 899. There is circumstantial evidence of a charter of Æthelstan dated 925 or 926 which provides support for William's claim: Heighway 2001: 103.

A short history of the diocese of Lichfield by William Beresford, published in 1883,[3048] notes that 'the origin of the royal associations of these collegiate churches is obscure. It would seem to be owing as much to Wulfhere as to Ethelfleda'. Frustratingly, the evidence for this opinion is not given, but that possibility has been explored in some detail by Dr Robin Studd,[3049] who has concluded that the late medieval claims that Edgar founded the royal free chapels at Penkridge, Tettenhall, Gnosall and Shrewsbury seem very doubtful, and may be compared with the many grammar schools supposedly founded by King Edward VI in the sixteenth century, and that the Royal Free Chapels mentioned above were in reality probably assisted in the recovery of their lost and ancient estates by the help of Edgar, who came to be regarded as their original founder.

Is there any evidence that might help throw light on the early history of the cluster of royal free chapels in Staffordshire? Specific and valuable information is provided from a Bull of Pope Clement IV (1265-68), preserved among the archives of the royal free chapel of Bridgnorth, which shows that Henry III had complained to the Pope that before diocesan bishops had been constituted in England, the kings of that realm had founded and endowed in it many churches, which, ever since the date of their foundation, had been absolutely free and immune from the jurisdiction of archbishops, bishops, and all other inferior ordinaries, and that down to recent times such churches had enjoyed full liberty. The Bull confirms that the Pope readily accepted and recognised those claims.[3050]

If such a claim is to be believed, then we must look back to a time before the mid-seventh century, when bishops of Mercia were first established, and the most likely candidate for the foundation of at least some of the royal free chapels in the West Midlands must be (as supposed by Beresford) Wulfhere, the Christian son of the pagan King Penda. He married the Christian Kentish princess Eormenhild in about 660, and during his life gave much land throughout his kingdom for the foundation of monasteries with generous endowments.[3051] But he retained estates where his own private churches were established, and the royal free chapels exempt from episcopal interference might be seen as surviving evidence of those estates and churches. It was under Wulfhere that the English church's first synod was organised under Archbishop Theodore of Canterbury in 672 at Hertford, and it was at this synod that the decision was taken to organise the church into smaller dioceses. It is possible that some of the older royal free chapels date from the period immediately prior to that synod, in which case those chapels of the West Midlands may have been some four centuries old at the date of the Norman Conquest. Anne Elizabeth Jenkins, in a wide-ranging study of the Royal Free Chapels in the West Midlands, has concluded that they may represent early family churches of Mercian royalty, delimiting the heartland of Middle Saxon Mercia, with the majority originating as conventional Middle-Saxon minsters and the remainder lesser churches of Anglo-Saxon date.[3052]

That idea might be supported by a study of the entries recording Edward the Confessor's holdings in Domesday Book that has identified what may be a pattern perhaps dating back

---

[3048] Beresford 1883: 43,
[3049] I am particularly grateful to Dr Studd for making available a copy of his unpublished paper 'Staffordshire Royal Free Chapels: a search for origins'.
[3050] TSAS XLVI 1931-2 iv, citing Owen and Blakeway 1825: II 188. However, the note in Owen and Blakeway (p.187) states that the Bull was seemingly of Pope Clement V (1305-1314).
[3051] Wulfhere's only daughter was Werburgh (died 700x707), abbess of Ely and later sanctified, to whom churches are dedicated in various parts of the country: Williams, Smyth and Kirby 1991: 21-2; Blair 2002: 557.
[3052] Jenkins 1988.

to the seventh century, and provides evidence for the early expansion of the Mercian kingdom westwards from Tamworth and Lichfield, the core of the 'original' Mercia (the *Ærest Myrcnaland*) mentioned in the mysterious document known as the Tribal Hidage, probably dating from the eleventh century but incorporating material which is much earlier. That advance was occurring in the mid-seventh century, after an alliance between King Penda of Mercia and Cadwallon of Gwynedd which led over several decades to Mercian expansion to the Severn and beyond, with new minsters established at places such as Much Wenlock, founded c.680.[3053] This alliance between the Mercians and the Welsh allowed the creation of a network of royal minsters on the western side of the Mercian heartland, probably before the end of the first decade of the eighth century, a pattern also followed by the kings of Kent and Northumbria. The very size of some of the Mercian minster communities at or soon after the time of Domesday tends to speak of their great antiquity: Stafford had thirteen canons, St Mary's, Shrewsbury, eleven, Penkridge nine, Wolverhampton seven, Tettenhall five, and Gnosall had four, while Derby had seven clerks. Such sizeable foundations suggest a fairly lengthy period of growth: Lichfield cathedral itself, founded in 669, had only seven more canons at the Conquest than St Mary's, Stafford.

It is probable that there were hundreds of minsters in England before the end of the seventh century, and perhaps dozens in Mercia, some of them royally connected. Studd has observed that there was a noticeable concentration of these royal minsters and their estates in Staffordshire by 910, when there were at least five, and probably six, and perhaps more – more than in any other county – all concentrated in the three southern hundreds. This may point to a survival from the days of the independent Mercian kingdom of at least the eighth century, and probably the seventh, when extensive estates were granted to Wilfrid by King Wulfhere, some of which were to form the basis of Lichfield's original episcopal holdings.[3054] We may also note that the church at Stone is by long tradition associated with King Wulfhere,[3055] and although the evidence is doubtful,[3056] Stone certainly held extensive estates from an early date. From the size of their *parochia* (their attached territories in which parochial duties were exercised and dues collected) it seems likely that a number of pre-Conquest minsters existed in Staffordshire, but we cannot know whether any were both royal and free from episcopal oversight at this time. Studd suggests that possible early minsters include Pattingham, held by the crown in 1086 but perhaps initially dependent on Tettenhall, and Wombourne, Kinver, Brewood and Walsall (St Matthew's). Further north, Stoke on Trent may have been an early minster. Little evidence is available to support the theory, but it has a sizeable parochia, a fragmentary Anglo-Saxon cross-shaft, and a persuasive place-name.[3057] Studd also points out that archaeological investigations at Tamworth have identified a pre-Conquest church beneath the present structure adjacent to the site of the palace of the Mercian kings, similar to the arrangement

---

[3053] Many monasteries from this period are known only from incidental references. The only incontrovertible early evidence for the house of Much Wenlock, for example, is found in a letter of St Boniface c.675-754: Campbell 1986: 51.
[3054] VCH III 2, 140.
[3055] The earliest known names of the iron-age hillfort, 1 mile north-west of Stone (SJ 8835) are *Wulfcestre ... le Buri* and *Wlferecestria* recorded in the 13th century. The name is explained by Leland, who writes c.1540: 'not ver far from Stone priori appereth the place wher King Woulphers castel or manor place was ... Ther appere great dikes and squarid stones': Toulmin-Smith 1964: V 20.
[3056] See however Sargent 2012.
[3057] From OE *stoc*, often found with the meaning 'monastery, cell': Horovitz 2005: 610.

found at Winchester, which was probably surrounded by a typical Anglo-Saxon *vallum monasterium*.[3058]

In addition, Alan Thacker has concluded that the very large *parochia* of secular minsters established in pre-Viking Mercia often exercised rights over co-extensive areas centred on a royal tun, whereby the religious income corresponded with the civil dues collected by the royal officials. As perpetual communities they may have undertaken an administrative role under the king. These foundations 'can still be indentified with some certainty in the Mercian heartlands, where the well-known group of royal free chapels in Staffordshire, Shropshire, and Derbyshire long preserved their large ancient parishes and collegiate status...'.[3059] Most pertinently, Thacker suggests that such foundations might have had royal treasuries, which if true would have made them especially attractive to Danish depredators in the ninth and tenth centuries. Other evidence of seventh century foundations in the West Midlands has been detected by Robin Studd[3060] in the Chronicle of St Werburgh's Abbey at Chester, a fifteenth century copy of a thirteenth century original based on material supplied by Gerald of Wales, which records that in 689 Wulfhere's younger brother, Ethelred, King of the Mercians, founded a collegiate church in the suburbs of Chester with the assistance of 'Wilfric, bishop of Chester'. There was no bishop of Chester at that time, and the name Wilfric is otherwise unrecorded, but it is believed that Wulfhere invited St Wilfrid, bishop of York, to spread the gospel in Mercia in 666-9, and Studd suggests that we might identify Wilfric as Wilfrid (sometimes known as Wilfrith),[3061] who later spent another period of exile in Mercia, from 691 to 702, possibly as bishop of Leicester,[3062] where he continued to visit minsters he had established and founded new ones. If Wilfrid was the founder of St John's, Chester, its date would be between 666 and 669 or in the decade following 691.

As we have seen, pre-Conquest Staffordshire contained much ancient Crown land, and the statements and policies of later kings provides evidence of a particularly long and close relationship between the crown and the chapels. Certainly such evidence as there is indicates a pre-Conquest date for their foundation,[3063] but only in the case of Wolverhampton does evidence exist, albeit of questionable authenticity, of its foundation (or refoundation). For Wolverhampton we are fortunate to have detailed published studies of the early history of the town and its church.[3064] It is unnecessary to detail here the valuable information contained in those publications, but there is other evidence which might serve to supplement those studies.

[3058] Studd also asserts that at Penkridge, Tettenhall, Stafford and Wolverhampton there are 'clear indications' of substantial monastic compounds, but other than citing property boundaries which might mark a possible earthwork around Wolverhampton church, mentioned in Hooke and Slater 1986: 38-9, the evidence is not presented. A map of Penkridge dated 1754 (VCH V facing p.104) shows a curving line of buildings to the south-west of the church which might just conceivably mark a very small section of an ancient *vallum monasterium*. The curved boundaries at Tettenhall have been mentioned elsewhere in this work, but are unlikely to be an early monastic boundary, and no evidence has been traced by the present writer for any monastic compound at Stafford.
[3059] Thacker 1985: 2
[3060] See 'Staffordshire Royal Free Chapels: a search for origins', supra; Meeson 2015: 15-17.
[3061] Searle 1897: 496.
[3062] Powicke and Fryde 1961: 232; Williams, Smyth and Kirby 1991: 236-8.
[3063] Except in the case of Bridgnorth, which did not exist at the time of Domesday.
[3064] Hooke 1983; Hooke and Slater 1986; Hooke 1993: 12-15.

It is well recorded that by a charter of 985[3065] King Æthelred granted to Wulfrun lands at *Heantune* ('high or chief *tūn*'). Wulfrun subsequently endowed a church there, supposedly in 994, apparently towards the end of her life.[3066] Although Æthelred's grant is the earliest record of the place that became known as Wolverhampton, it cannot of course be assumed that the absence of documentary evidence of the name *Heantune* prior to 985 means that the place did not exist before that date. Later property boundaries and the suggestive name Berry Street, possibly from Old English *burh* 'a fortification, a monastic enclosure', have led to speculation that an earthwork, perhaps of Iron-Age date, but more likely a *vallum monasterium*,[3067] may have lain on the prominent headland on which the town lies.

It has been suggested that the 985 grant by Æthelred to Wulfrun of land at *Heantune* and *Treselcotum* (Wolverhampton and Trescott) might be associated with the dissolution of the Mercian Ealdormanry on the banishment of ealdorman Alfric, son of Elfhere, who exercised considerable influence over Edgar of Mercia from 955, and even more so after Edgar's death in 975. As King of the Mercians and Northumbrians from 957, and of the English from 959, Edgar was a champion of monastic reform, while Elfhere was a ruthless exponent of the secular religious communities of canons. Although the struggle is hardly mentioned by the *Anglo-Saxon Chronicle*, it is clear that the dispute was fuelled by political ambitions.[3068] We know that King Edgar visited the area, for we have seen that he attested charters at Penkridge, 'that famous place', in 958.[3069]

To place Æthelred's grant to Wulfrun in its historical context, the years following the grant were marked by a great murrain which affected England, and ravaging by the Danes which culminated in the defeat of the English at the battle of Maldon in 991, leading to the payment of tribute to the Danes amounting to no less than ten thousand pounds. A heavy tax was raised to meet that payment, which would have required a careful survey of taxable capacity.[3070] The following years saw many clashes with the Danes, and a large Danish fleet reached London in 994, the supposed date of Wulfrun's grant, but the citizens successfully repulsed the attack. That forced the enemy to transfer its attention to other parts of southern England, which suffered greatly, and led the English to agree a truce with a payment to the Danes of sixteen thousand pounds tribute, a vast sum.[3071] Clearly these were years of great threat to England and Æthelred.

Our evidence for Wulfrun's grant to the church of *Hamtun* (Wolverhampton) is itself a subject of some curiosity. The confirmation of the grant was incorporated in a manuscript history of the church of Lichfield, *Historia Ecclesiae Lichfeldensis*, written in 1575 by an unknown author. The original is lost, but two copies survive, one made in 1661 by Thomas

---

[3065] In a twelfth century copy: S.860.
[3066] The tentative evidence for an early church on or close to the site of the battle of Tettenhall (so-called), on the south side of Wednesfield, even perhaps founded by Wulfrun, is discussed elsewhere in this volume. Any such church might explain a derivation of *Heantune* as 'chief *tūn*'.
[3067] See Hooke and Slater 1986: 39-40. There is a number of examples of the re-use of prehistoric hillforts as sites for monasteries and minsters, a classic example being Breedon on the Hill in Leicestershire. Hillforts could be considered 'public buildings' of the prehistoric period, the equivalent of Roman forts and fora, ownership of which seems to have devolved onto local rulers during the Anglo-Saxon period, and which in some cases (especially in the case of the Saxon Shore forts) were used for early churches: see Parsons 2001; especially 55-6.
[3068] Styles 1936: 58-9.
[3069] S.667. See especially Lewis 2008: 104-23.
[3070] VCH IV 5.
[3071] Whitelock 1955: 212-4

Barlow, Provost of The Queen's College, Oxford, the other a copy of Barlow's text made the following year for William Paul, Dean of Lichfield. The anonymous author of the *Historia* describes the discovery of the charter 'written in Saxon characters on parchment ... found in the rubble of a wall lapped in a sheet of lead'[3072] during rebuilding works at St Peter's church, Wolverhampton, in about 1560,[3073] by which Wulfrun, a 'noble matron and religious lady' endowed lands which were part of the grant made to her in 985 by King Æthelred. According to a Chancery suite of c.1572 John Leigh,[3074] one of the vicars choral, had delivered the confirmation of the charter to the Dean's steward, William Green.[3075] What appears to have been a defective copy of the confirmation was supposedly copied by Sir William Dugdale or Roger Dodsworth in 1640 (and printed in Dugdale's *Monasticon Anglicanum*), when it seems to have been in the possession of the Dean and Chapter of the Royal Chapel of Windsor. Sir Henry Spelman is believed to have made another and independent copy of all except the last two paragraphs and the names of the witnesses,[3076] but thereafter the charter is lost to history.

The charter,[3077] undoubtedly a later forgery based on earlier records, purports to be a confirmation by Sigeric,[3078] Archbishop of Canterbury, of a grant by Wulfrun of estates that had evidently been acquired (not necessarily at the same time) by Wulfrun or her family. As usual, the formal parts of the charter are in Latin, and the description of the estates is in Old English. The date, 996, must, from internal evidence, be incorrect, and was probably intended to be 994, and the fact that the estates in the charter are listed in virtually the same order as they appear in Domesday Book, which has been seen as the most reliable record available of the early possessions of the minster at the time the charter was fabricated, has led scholars to give it a post-1086 date.[3079]

[3072] *Dotatio et confirmation literis Saxonis in pergameno conscripta, in ruderibus muri, reperta est, lamina plumbea inclusa, circa annum Domini millesimum quintisimum sexagesimum*: WA 194 fn.1.
[3073] VCH III 321 fn.1, citing Wharton 1691: 444 seq., see also WA I 12 194-5; SHC 4th Series 11 9. The supposed discovery of ancient charters hidden in walls has a long tradition: '...charters and dignities, which they had found in the old walls of the monastery [of Medeshamstede (Peterborough)], which the monks had formerly hidden, when the Danes came, and would slay them...': *La Geste de Burch (Historia Vetus Coenobii Petriburgensis)*, in Mellows 1949: 210-11. At Abingdon the chatters and relics of the abbey were preserved in secret hiding places from a fury which left nothing standing but the walls: Finberg 1972: 206-7, citing *Chronicon Monasterii de Abingdon*. William Harrison, the Elizabethan clergyman and historian/topographer, relates the tale (recorded by Matthew Paris) of how a cache of ancient books and rolls, written in the British language, was supposedly discovered in a cavity in a wall of St Albans abbey, but adds in a marginal comment 'I doo believe this to be a lie': Chamberlin 1986: 31; Clanchy 1993: 149. Although the Wolverhampton charter is a later forgery, the circumstances of its supposed discovery may be true, though no ready explanation is available for the concealment of a document within a church wall.
[3074] 'Sir' John Leigh was a celebrated Wulfrunian, lauded by Holinshed for his charity. He was born in Shifnal and is recorded in Wolverhampton in the early 1500s, where he remained as a minister for 60 years. He spent £20 of his own money and laboured himself to improve the highways of the town, left benefactions to the poor and, according to Holinshed 'he lyvyd nyghe one hunderyd yeres': WA I 86-7.
[3075] C 2/Eliz I/L.12/50.
[3076] Mander and Tildesley 1960: 13, 58.
[3077] S.860; Mander and Tildesley 1960: 13.
[3078] Translated from Ramsbury in 990, after which he went to Rome for his pallium: Whitelock 1955: 212. He died on 28th October 994: Powicke and Fryde 1961: 210.
[3079] Hooke 1993: 12-13. The charter is usually held on internal evidence to have been intended to carry the date 994: see SHC 1916: 114-5; Sawyer 1968: 391. For the suggestion that Wulfrun's charter was a 12th century forgery utilising boundaries from a pre-Conquest survey, see VCH III 321. Simon Keynes has concluded that though spurious, the charter is based on an authentic gift,

However, recent research has thrown important new light on the charter, and a slight digression is appropriate to explain that research. A forensic analysis of the structure and palaeography of the Staffordshire entries in Domesday Book by Dr David Roffe has concluded that the charter is a composite document which may be an endorsement, an extract from a schedule of benefactors, or something similar, evidently earlier than Domesday Book, which has utilised the charter for its compilation. The key to that important conclusion is the Domesday entry for *Hocintvne* (Ogley Hay) paired with *Iltone* (Hilton, in Shenstone). The entry for *Hocintvne* is clearly a post-rubrication addition to the Domesday entry for the holdings of the canons of Wolverhampton (which explains why, atypically, it is not ruled through in red), so accounting for the disruption in order. The entry describes the holding as 1 hide, waste – *In HOCINTVNE i hid' Wasta* – and is evidently an interpolation added in a secondary hand, with the last word, *Wasta*, added by yet another scribe, confirmed by yet another hand. In other words, the main scribe wrote the entry for Hilton, and it was then noticed that *Hocintvne*, which preceded it in the charter, had been omitted. A terse entry for *Hocintvne* was then added, so that whilst the charter lists *Ocgintun/Ogintune* and *Hiltun* (in that order), Domesday Book gives *Iltone* and *Hocintvne* (i.e. in reverse order).This means that the main scribe, or his sources, drew on the charter, and Domesday Book was not the basis for its compilation. A comparison may usefully be made to demonstrate the order in which the estates appear in each source (and the spellings of those estates), with the list from the charter taken from its preamble:

Charter[3080]		Domesday Book[3081]	
1	Hamtune	1	Hantone
2	Earnleie	2	Ernlege
3	Espich	3	Haswic
4	Bilsetnatun	-	– [2 hides in *Billestune* held by the king: SHC IV 38]
5	Willenhal	5	Wodnesfelde
6	Wodensfeld	6	Winenhale
7	Weoleshale [for Peoleshale=Pelsall]	7	Peleshale
8	Ocgintun[3082]	8	Iltone
9	Hiltun	9	*Hocintvne* [a later interpolation]
10	Hagenþorndun	10	Hargedone
11	Kinwaldestun(e)	11	Chenwardestone
12	Hyltun	12	Haltone
13	Feoþerstan	13	Ferdestan

Supposedly witnessed by King Æthelred and attested by the archbishops of Canterbury and York, twelve bishops, eleven abbots, five dukes, two deacons, one count and five

---

combining 'elements derived from a papal privilege and from a royal diploma issued in the mid 990s': Hooke 1993: 11. It seems likely that the monks included in the charter those OE boundary clauses they had access to after that date, for the charter included Rodbaston in its estate at Kinvaston, although Kinvaston is listed separately at Domesday: Hooke 1993: 13. Ann Williams suggests, without further details, that the charter may date from the time of Archbishop Sigeric's successor Ælfric, who went to Canterbury from Ramsbury on 21st April 995 and died on 16 November 1005: Williams 2003: 177 fn.121.

[3080] Hooke 1983: 64-85.
[3081] Alecto 1988.
[3082] A careful analysis of the bounds of *Ocgintun/Ogintune* as they appear in Wulfrun's charter suggests that they may incorporate Hilton (in Shenstone). Curiously and uncharacteristically, Duignan failed to identify this Hilton, believing that the references to the name in Wulfrun's charter and Domesday Book were erroneously duplicated entries relating to another Hilton near Featherstone: Duignan 1888: 10; Duignan 1902: 79.

thegns,[3083] the confirmation of Wulfrun's charter records that for the memory of her husband and her own soul and for the offences of her kinsman Wulfgeat she gave land to the church *quod in moderno nunc tempore constructum est* 'which was constructed now in modern times', but subsequently continues that it held *loca urbana, oppida, vel rustica rura, sicuti omnia præfatum tuum monasterium Hampton detinuita priscis temporibus* '...all urban places, towns and rural areas, as thy aforesaid monastery of Hampton held all these from former times...'.[3084] This odd and garbled (and suspicious) language strongly suggests the existence of an earlier religious house (perhaps devastated by the Danish raids of the ninth and early tenth century) which Wulfrun had reorganised and endorsed, though how much earlier is uncertain.

It should not be overlooked that Wulfrun's grant to the monastery of Wolverhampton was an endowment to support the minster church – it did not include any part of the estate of *Heantune* granted to her by King Æthelred, which we must suppose was the subject of another grant that has not come down to us. In particular, the grant included a block of land to the east of Wolverhampton, made up of Wednesfield, Bilston, and part of Willenhall, which subsequently formed part of the manor of Stowheath, discussed further below. If the endowment had been to a new church, and not an existing church, Wulfrun might have been expected to have included land from Æthelred's grant upon which the church could be built. We must suppose that the church was already established on crown land which formed part of the royal grant to Wulfrun, or on land granted by the crown at an earlier date, a supposition perhaps supported by the status of the church as a royal free chapel, which implies a royal foundation, and tells against a foundation by Wulfrun herself.

There was unquestionably an extensive royal estate centred on what we now know as Wolverhampton before Domesday – quite possibly long before – and in that respect it is apposite to record the conclusions of David Dumville, who notes that in the mid- and later tenth century we find kings in possession of former monasteries, and granting lands which

---

[3083] Sigeric, archbishop of Canterbury, died on 28th October 994: Whitelock 1955: 214; see also Keynes 1991: 112 fn.75. Two of the witnesses, Ealdwulf, archbishop of York, and Godwine, bishop of Rochester, appear not to have been appointed until 995 (Powicke and Fryde 1961: 263, 248), but see SHC 1916: 114-5.

[3084] SHC 1916 105-15; Hooke and Slater 1986: 23; Dugdale 1817-30: Vol. 6 Part III 1444. The author of the charter, in referring cryptically to the sins of Wulfrun's kinsman Wulfgeat, a reference that has caused considerable speculation amongst historians, may have identified the thegn, correctly or not, with Wulfgeat, a West Saxon (said by Florence (John) of Worcester to be the son of Leofeca or Leoveca, about whom nothing is known), whose estates, with those of his wife, were forfeited in 1006 for 'the unjust judgments and arrogant deeds which he had committed': Hart 1975: 366-7. A diploma of 1008 (S.918) alleges that Wulfgeat and his wife were accused by 'the people' of 'the worst of crimes ... because of their misdeeds': Williams 2003: 70. It is unclear whether he is to be identified as Wulfgeat 'my beloved thegn' named among the king's leading counsellors in a charter by King Æthelred to St Mary's, Abingdon (S.937), made between 990 and 1006, but perhaps in 999 (Whitelock 1955: 537-9; Williams 2003: 34), in which case it is difficult to see how Wulfrun's grant could be dated 994. Indeed, Ann Williams has suggested that the foundation charter could date from the time of Sigeric's successor, Ælfric (21st April 995-1005): Williams 2003: 177 fn.122. Whitelock has observed that it is unlikely that Wulfgeat could be Wulfgeat of Donington, whose undated Will leaves (inter alia) four bullocks to Wolverhampton, as well as two each to Penkridge and Tong (Whitelock 1930: 54-5; 163-7), or Wulfgeat of Ilmington, Warwickshire, a correspondent of Ælfric the homilist, since both were probably Mercian thegns, whereas Wulfgeat son of Leofeca (who she identifies as the Wulfgeat mentioned in Wulfrun's grant) appears to have been a West Saxon: Whitelock 1981.

had been or may be argued to have once been ecclesiastical estates.[3085] The size of Tettenhall, [Wolver-] *Heantune* and Wednesfield at Domesday – one virgate, one hide and five hides respectively – does not provide any support for the argument that *Heantune* was not in existence in 910 (the date of the battle of Tettenhall), and whilst Tettenhall was evidently a minor holding at Domesday, held by the King, and included Bescot to the east of Wednesbury,[3086] it was perhaps one of the leading and most important estates in Staffordshire by the late Anglo-Saxon period, and possibly earlier, with the royal estate containing Compton, Wightwick, Old Perton (granted by Edward the Confessor to Westminster Abbey), Trescott, Bilbrook, Oaken, Wrottesley, Pendeford and Codsall, and probably Wolverhampton, which evidently included Willenhall, Bilston,[3087] Wednesfield, Pelsall, Kinvaston, Hilton, Featherstone and Bradley, and probably Wednesbury, Bloxwich, Shelfield and Bescot, which all lay within the Ancient Parish of Walsall.[3088]

The manorial divison of Wolverhampton was extremely complex, with two principal manors, the Deanery manor of the collegiate church and the royal manor of Stowheath. The Deanery manor included part of Codsall, Lutley, Ogley Hay, Pelsall, a small part of Willenhall, the northern part of Wolverhampton and most of Wednesfield,[3089] and Stowheath appears to have been formed early in the 13th century by uniting the royal manors of Bilston, Willenhall, and one half of Wolverhampton.[3090] It was held by Ralph de Somery, Earl of Dudley c.1204 when it was exchanged with King John for the manors of Mere, Swinford and Clent,[3091] but there is no evidence to show how and when it came into the hands of the Earl. The royal holding of Wolverhampton is not mentioned in Domesday Book, but from later evidence has been estimated at 3 hides.[3092] Isaac Taylor's 1751 map of Wolverhampton shows the boundary between the Deanery manor and Stowheath running in a meandering fashion following roads and property boundaries on the east side of St Peter's church. Stowheath covered a large part of Willenhall (including Short Heath, New Invention, Sandbeds, Little London and Portobello), all of Bilston except Bradley, and a considerable part of Wolverhampton, as far west as The Halfway House on Tettenhall Road and as far east as Clarkes Lane and High Road, Lane Head, which formed its boundary.[3093]

No evidence has been found to show that the name Stowheath was used prior to the creation of the enlarged royal manor, but that does not mean it was not, and the word *stow*,

---

[3085] Dumville 1992: 39-40.

[3086] I owe the reference to Bescot to Dr David Roffe.

[3087] As noted elsewhere, the derivation and implications of the name Bilston should not be overlooked. In 895 it is recorded as *Bilsatena*, and between 994 and 1066 as *Bilsetnatun*, meaning 'the dwellers at Bil, indicating a tribal grouping which originated here or elsewhere. The meaning of Bil is uncertain: Horovitz 2005: 121.

[3088] These conclusions are based on a detailed analysis of the Staffordshire entries in Domesday Book (Thorn and Thorn 2007), where it is suggested that 'the really ancient royal estates besides Tamworth were only Kingswinford, Trentham, Penkridge and Tettenhall'. The posited vast royal estate of Tettenhall will have lain to the south of and adjoined the huge estate of Penkridge, which perhaps included Brewood, Cannock, Gnosall, Whiston, Pillaton, Mitton, Stretton, Water Eaton, Gailey, Otherton, Great Saredon, Coppenhall, Shareshill, Levedale, Rodbaston, Little Saredon, and Bickford: ibid. Both blocs will have lain at the northern part of the territory of the *Pencersætan*, 'the people associated with the Penk'. See also Jenkins 1988.

[3089] Mander and Tildesley 1960: 25-6.

[3090] Shaw 1801 II: 165; WA II 103; see also SHC 1911 143-4.

[3091] Shaw 1801 II: 166.

[3092] SHC 1919 167-8.

[3093] Hackwood 1908: 148; Tildesley 1952: 99.

as noted elsewhere, was used in the Anglo-Saxon period to denote not only 'a place', but more specifically 'a place of assembly, a holy place'.[3094] We should be cautious about being mis-led by the supposed religious associations, but it is possible that the simplex *stow* element was adopted in the pre-Conquest period with the more usual meaning 'holy place'. No evidence has been traced to show that the element was used to denote an area removed from but belonging to a church, and we may have evidence here of a formerplace of worship in the area.

By the thirteenth century the prebendal holdings in the Deanery manor of Wolverhampton and the royal manor of Wolverhampton were so interlocked by inter-marriage of the families of the six prebendal priests priests who held land scattered both within and outside the town that they came to be regarded as a third manor held by the Leveson family.[3095] To complicate the matter even further, there were in addition to these three manors a number of islands of freehold land in various places throughout the town centre.[3096]

It seems reasonable to assume that the early chroniclers had particular information which caused them to name Tettenhall and/or Wednesfield as site of the battle of 910 rather than *Heantune*, or nearby Bushbury, which was also a pre-Conquest settlement, with the priests of Wolverhampton probably serving there before it became a separate parish in the twelfth century,[3097] and the explanation may lie in the preceding paragraph, which suggests that Wednesfield, as well as Wolverhampton, probably lay within and formed part of the ancient estate of Tettenhall.

If there were no church at Tettenhall in 910, we might consider the possibility that it was built to commemorate the great battle. Perhaps surprisingly, few examples of pre-Conquest royal gifts of land for monasteries to celebrate victory in battle have been traced, but Bede records in his *Historia Ecclesiastica* that after he had defeated Penda at the battle of Winwæd in 655, King Oswiu of Northumberland gave an *ex voto* offering of twelve small plots of land for monasteries,[3098] and c.1020 Cnut built a small minster on the site of his victory at Ashingdon (Essex). The practice can hardly be said to have been widespread, but the status of Tettenhall's church (like that at nearby Wolverhampton) as a Royal Free Chapel suggests strongly that it may have been a place of particular importance in the Anglo-Saxon period. The church was collegiate, and Stebbing Shaw notes in 1801 that 'though there are now no remains of this college, yet I am informed that some part of the fabric was standing, some years ago, near the East end of the church'. The church was almost completely destroyed by fire in 1950 and rebuilt.

[3094] EPNE ii 159-60.In the post-Conquest period *stow* appears to have developed into meanings which are difficult to identify precisely, but in some areas may have denoted a track or passage or place where animals were gathered: ibid.
[3095] Hooke and Slater 1986: 33. It may be noted that various manors in the land of the clergy of Wolverhampton, if Domesday Book is to be trusted, seem to have been drawn out of the hundred in which they lay geographically and placed in that where their holder had his principal manor or manors, as happened in other counties, so that, for example, Kinvaston, Hatherton and Pelsall, listed in Seisdon Hundred in 1086, were have been detached from it: Thorn and Thorn 2007.
[3096] Hooke and Slater 1986: 33. The islands of freehold land lay mainly in Dudley Street, Bilston Street and Cock Street (now Victoria Street), all to the south of the church. Their history is unknown.
[3097] Mander and Tildesley 1960: 25-6.
[3098] HE III, c. xxiv; John 1964: 13-14. Bede also records how a monastery was founded at Gilling in Yorkshire as atonement for the killing of King Oswine after an abortive battle in 642: HE III, c.xxiv.

One feature at Tettenhall which does not seem to have attracted previous attention is the parallel curving boundaries, now marked by roads including Stockwell End, Lothians Road and Sandy Lane, clearly marked on Robert Dawson's survey of Wolverhampton and the surrounding area made in 1816,[3099] seemingly with their radius at or close to the church, which curve around from west to north-east, some 400 and 500 yards from the church. The boundaries echo in some respects the curving boundaries identified around St Peter's church in Wolverhampton,[3100] and with the eye of faith may represent the ghost of a typically curvilinear Anglo-Saxon monastic enclosure boundary, or *vallum monasterium*, which generally measured between 150 and 300 metres across,[3101] possibly suggesting (if ancient) that Tettenhall may have been an important Christian site in the pre-Conquest period.[3102] There is evidence of circular enclosures, some of considerable size, around early Celtic Christian sites, and it is not inconceivable that we may have here a religious site dating back to the earliest years of Christianity in Mercia. However, it would be very unusual for any early boundary to attach to a religious site near the foot of a bluff; no maps of the field boundaries pre-dating the late 19th century have been traced; and the appearance of antiquity in the boundaries might be no more than a chimera.[3103]

Bushbury poses particular problems for the historian, for the name appears to mean 'Bishops' fortification or manor-house'.[3104] This could only be the bishopric of Lichfield, founded in the 660s, but no such bishop is known to have had any connection with Bushbury, which surely tells us that the connection must have been very ancient, at such an early date that it has escaped memory, or that the place once formed part of a larger estate held by the bishop. The earliest reference to the place-name is found in the spurious grant by Wulfrun to the church of Wolverhampton supposedly dating from c.994,[3105] where Bushbury is mentioned as a meeting point of *Wodnesfeld*, *Hamtun* and *Byscopesbyri*, in the boundary description of Bilston and Wednesfield.[3106] The word *byri* generally had the meaning 'fortification', often with reference to a prehistoric earthwork, and Bushbury lies on the side of a particularly prominent hill with far reaching views to the west, which would be a natural site for an earthwork. However, no record has been traced of any earthworks on the hill. Another meaning of *byri* was 'monastery', from the *vallum monasterium* which surrounded monastic buildings, but the meaning 'Bishop's

---

[3099] BL map collection.

[3100] See Hooke and Slater 1986: 38-9.

[3101] Blair 2005: 198. The existing boundaries, some of which are now followed by roads, may be parallel to boundaries of an 'inner' [original?] circuit, now untraceable, but it must be conceded that the 'complete' boundary would run across the cliff edge above Tettenhall church, which seems unlikely.

[3102] It is unclear whether the area encompassed by the boundaries lay within the manor of Tettenhall Clericorum (which included land extending from Old Hill to the north and north-east of the church incorporating Aldersley and Barnhurst), as described in VCH XX 18-19.

[3103] It is worth noting that in 1686 Plot records that '... at Tetnall also in Staffordshire upon the Hill above the Church, the Springs rise within 3 yards of the surface, where the Wells near the Church 20 yards below, are all betwixt 20 and 30 yards deep; so that the Springs on the Hill, lye at least 40 yards higher than those in the Vale, though they are not distant above 200 yards...': Plot 1686: 86. In Tettenhall churchyard are two of the most venerable yews trees in the area – indeed they are said to be the oldest yew trees in the West Midlands They were measured by the Ancient Yew Group in 1999, who recorded one male tree with a girth of 22' 9" and one female tree with a girth of 22' 4". In 1873 the two largest yews were 20' and 24' in circumference: JBAA 1873: 106-7.

[3104] Horovitz 2005: 166.

[3105] Shaw 1801 II: 176.

[3106] Hooke 1983: 72.

monastery' can be discounted. *Burh* could also mean 'fortified manor house', and that may be the meaning here.

The seventeenth-century historian John Huntbach, who lived at Featherstone, two miles north-east of Bushbury, noted that at Domesday the canons held one yardland at Bushbury, but those canons were from Wolverhampton, which as a Royal Free Chapel was not subject to the bishop's jurisdiction, and that connection does not help to explain the name.[3107] Wedgwood, whose opinions must always be treated with respect, had no doubt that Bushbury parish was formerly part of Wolverhampton, founded perhaps not long before 1291.[3108] The unravelling of the pre-Conquest history of Bushbury might throw much light on the early history of Wolverhampton, with which it may have had ancient links, but at present the evidence on which any such history might be based has proved elusive. It may not be inappropriate to remember that there were bishops of Mercia even before Chad (670-3) – Bede mentions Trumhere (c.658-62), appointed by Wulfhere, and Jaruman (662-67)[3109] – but they are said to have had no fixed seat, though they may have had residences. So little is known about the early Mercian bishops that it would be difficult to identify a period when one or more may have been associated with Bushbury. The most obvious solution is that Bushbury once formed part of Brewood parish (in Cuttlestone Hundred), which adjoins it and was an ancient holding of the bishop of Lichfield, who had a manor house at Brewood, and at an earlier period perhaps also at Bushbury, though the southern part of Bushbury may have formed part of Wolverhampton. The Domesday entry for Bushbury records one virgate there belonging to Essington, in Cuttlestone Hundred, but all of Bushbury, including that virgate, may have been in Seisdon Hundred.[3110]

The grant from King Æthelred to Wulfrun included a large tract of land more than three miles deep and over three miles wide extending on the east and south to the boundary of Bilston and Sedgley (which is mentioned in the grant, proof that both of those estates had been marked out before 985), including Upper Penn and Finchfield, and reaching to Gorsebrook in the north. The royal grant also included the estate of Trescott, although the bounds are not given. From Domesday Book and other sources we can see that the crown subsequently retained rights in Tettenhall (with Wightwick, Compton, Codsall, Bilbrook, Perton, Bilston, and Bescot to the east of Wednesbury), Wednesbury ('with its dependencies'), Bloxwich, Shelfield, Willenhall, and Stowheath. It has been surmised that Wolverhampton may indeed have served as a *villa regalis*, 'royal vill', in this area in the early Anglo-Saxon period with the minster deliberately founded on the royal estate long before Wulfrun's re-endowment of the new minster church,[3111] though that role may have fallen on Tettenhall.

David Roffe's researches show that Wolverhampton and Wednesfield, part of Willenhall, and perhaps the southern part of Bushbury, formed a consolidated core. Pelsall, Ogley Hay and Hilton near Shenstone are associated with Wednesbury to the east, a royal manor in 1086 and apparently so at the Conquest. Only Bloxwich and Shelfield, are named in Domesday, but traces of others can be detected from later records. Wednesbury church

---

[3107] SHC 4th Series 11 72; see however, Mander and Tildesley 1960: 26.
[3108] SHC 1916 197. Mander and Tildesley 1960: 14 says '... it is a matter of speculation how far the ownership of the church [of Wolverhampton] extended to the north, as we know it did extend, into what became Bushbury parish'. The Hundred boundary bisects the parish of Bushbury, which indicates that the parish is of more recent date than the Hundred.
[3109] McClure and Collins 1999: 152, 397.
[3110] Thorn and Thorn 2007.
[3111] Hooke and Slater 1986: 25.

was at Walsall in the thirteenth century with the whole of the vill held by the king, and, like Bentley and probably Darlaston, seems to have been part of Wednesbury at Domesday. Before then, the manor evidently extended beyond the lands of the king, with Aldridge, Great Barr and Shenstone all held by Robert d'Oilly at Domesday. In the thirteenth century those three settlements as well as Wednesbury were in the hands of his successors. Pelsall, Ogley Hay, and Shenstone fit neatly into this complex, as does Wolverhampton's land in Willenhall, which was perhaps part of the manor before the Conquest

In brief, four distinct tenurial blocs can be associated with Wolverhampton in 1086, namely the three royal manors of Wednesbury, Willenhall and Tettenhall and the bishop of Lichfield's manor of Brewood, with evidence that the three royal manors had long been closely associated, with key evidence provided by Bilston and Bescot to the east held by Tettenhall, an otherwise inexplicable anomaly which must represent the ghost of an earlier structure.[3112]

Moving away from the tenurial history of Wolverhampton, it may be possible to detect other clues that help to throw light on the history of Wolverhampton's church. The present fabric incorporates no trace of any Anglo-Saxon work, and the greater part of the structure dates from the re-building which took place in the mid and late fifteenth century.[3113] However, 'remains of very remote antiquity' are recorded by Stebbing Shaw near the collegiate church: '... at the south-west corner of the churchyard ... are still to be seen handsome and spacious rooms or vaults, about 30 feet square, with strong and massy groins meeting in the centre at the top, the whole unmutilated and very perfect stone-work. These might have formed part of the base story of a building of considerable magnitude. The walls are of great thickness, near three yards, in which are still visible the remains of doorways or passages. On the East and west sides are some small remains of carved cornice stones. When the assizes were held in this town, in queen Elizabeth's time, the same were used as a prison for the felons who were tried in the town-hall nearly adjacent.'[3114]

[3112] I am idebted to Dr Roffe for allowing me to summarise part of his conclusions set out in Roffe 2014. Wolverhampton may have formed the core of a vast royal holding known known simply as ðone feld 'the open land', which included the estates listed in the four tenurial blocks identified by Dr Roffe.

[3113] We cannot know whether the structure may have been associated with the discovery of Wulfrun's charter 'written in Saxon characters on parchment ... found in the rubble of a wall lapped in a sheet of lead' during rebuilding works at St Peter's church, Wolverhampton, in about 1560: VCH III 321 fn.1. It should be remembered that in 1204 Henry II gave his consent for the foundation of a Cistercian Abbey at Wolverhamton in place of his free chapel, with the archbishop to be wholly responsible for the foundation of the new abbey, the king having granted him wide freedom from many taxes and burdens, as well as the deanery and prebends, the manors of Wolverhampton and Tettenhall and associated woodland for the use of the new abbey. The monks were also granted timber and other rights, subject to 5 priests praying in perpetuity for the soul of the king, his ancestors and successors. Monks were established at Wolverhampton while consent for the new monastery was obtained from the Cistercian Order, but the death of the archbishop in 1205 led to the abandonment of the plan; the king's grants were cancelled, and he resumed possession of the church: Styles 1940: 69; VCH II 323; Mander and Tildesley 1960: 47-8.

[3114] Mander and Tildesley 1960: 47-8. For the town hall, an ancient building known as the Wadehall, a Tudor building known as High Hall, demolished in 1841, the Market Cross [markethouse] built in 1532, and 'another independent building of antiquity called The Roundabout', all in High Green, see WJ March 1907;WA I 15 et seq; Mander and Tildesley 1960: 36, 78-9, 95.

The vaults were presumably located between the town hall in High Green and the south-west corner of the church, and existed until 'only a few years' before 1836.[3115] Their age and original purpose are unknown, and no plans or drawings are known to exist.[3116] These very substantial remains must once have been part of some significant structure, from their monumental scale almost certainly of religious origin. If not fragments of the foundations of Archbishop Hubert Walter's ill-fated Cistercian monastery, plans for which were abandoned at his death in 1205, could they have been associated with Wulfrun's refoundation of the church c.994? The idea seems improbable, but the existence of two early churches on the same site has parallels elsewhere in the Midlands. Excavations in the centre of Stafford in 1950s revealed the remains of another early church just to the west of St Mary's (dating from the late thirteenth or early fourteenth century), identified as that dedicated to the mysterious St Bertelin. The excavators suggested that a wooden church on the site had been replaced by a stone church no later that the eleventh century, with the two churches later used simultaneously. Another example is at Winchcombe, north-east of Cheltenham, where in the mid eleventh century the abbey church and the church of St Peter stood close to each other. Steven Basset has suggested that when the church at Winchcombe, along with other churches in the diocese of Worcester, was refounded c.969, the original building may have been too small, which necessitated the building of another church nearby, with the old one retained for other functions.[3117] A similar situation existed at Worcester, where Bishop Oswald founded a new church near the ancient cathedral. It is not impossible that the vaults near Wolverhampton church were associated with Wulfrun's refounded church dating from the early eleventh century.

Other tentative clues to an even earlier earlier period in the history of Wolverhampton may be extracted from other evidence. In the boundary clauses of the 985 grant to Wulfrun, and in the confirmation of her supposed grant c.994, there are references to a female named Beorngyth.[3118] Those references are to *Byrngyðe stan* (in the 985 grant) and *beorgipes s[t]anes strete* (in the spurious 994 confirmation) – 'Beorngyth's stone' and 'the paved road associated with Beorngyth's stone'.[3119]

[3115] Foundations exposed when a property was built (near the present war memorial) may have been associated with the early remains: Mander and Tildesley 1960: 48-9; see also Isaac Taylor's map of 1750; Shaw 1801 II: 161-2; Oliver 1836: 6; Lewis 1849: IV 646.

[3116] It is unlikely that the vaults were associated with the building known as *le Wadehall*, which stood further east in Lichfield street south of the church and was used for church courts in 1508. The origin of the building is unknown, but it appears to have been a cloth hall or guildhall, the name perhaps from ME *wæde* 'garment': most of the building was destroyed in the eighteenth century, but a brick (i.e. Tudor or later) chimney breast at the rear which survived until 1859 carried four shields carved into an irregularly-shaped recessed plaster panel some 3' wide. At the top was the Royal Arms in use during the period 1509-1603, surrounded by the Garter. Below were the arms of the Drapers' Company, the City of London and the Merchants of the Staple.WA I 15-17, with plan and photograph; Mander and Tildesley 1960: 36, 48. Of the pre-existing building we have little information, but it stood on the west side of the passage between the churchyard and the art gallery, now public gardens, and seems to have been c.14' deep, possibly with an upper storey. After mentioning the ancient vaults Mander and Tildesley 1960 notes cryptically: 'I understand that something of this nature was laid bare at the time when Mr F. T. Back's frontage (by the war memorial) was built and it seems a pity it did not receive a rather different treatment at that time': ibid. 48.

[3117] Jenkins 1988: 39-40.

[3118] Stenton 1970: 332.

[3119] Hooke 1983: 64-5, 72-5.

What can we say about this mysterious feature known as Beorngyth's stone? From its place in the sequence of boundary landmarks mentioned in the charter it appears to have lain close to, and on the west side of, the meeting place of early trackways which marked the focal point of Wolverhampton minster.[3120] Since the Anglo-Saxons had a wide and precise vocabulary, we might assume that the stone was exactly that: a natural rock or *stān*, rather than a man-made object for which a word such as *gebēacen* or *gemyndstōw* ('monument') or *rōd* or *trēow* ('cross'), or *stapol, bēam* or *syl* ('column, pillar'), might be expected. We can assume that it must have been a particularly striking object to have been named after an individual, perhaps an especially impressive example of the relatively common glacial erratics or boulders found scattered throughout the area.

In that respect we might consider a massive and unusual natural tapering pinnacle of smooth felsite, of irregular squarish section some two feet across at the base and over 9 feet tall,[3121] which was found on the east side of Graisley Brook, less than a mile from St Peter's church, when brick pits were dug behind Oak Street in Merridale, formerly Old Merrydale,[3122] west of Wolverhampton, and subsequently transported to the West Park, some half a mile from the place of its discovery, when the park opened in 1881.[3123] There it was set upright in a concrete base, where it still stands. There is no evidence on the stone, apart from some parallel grooves towards the top of the column probably caused by glacial movement, of any markings that may be man-made, but the possibility – and it is no more than a possibility – must be considered that this could be the very stone associated with one of Wolverhampton's earliest named individuals, perhaps used at an early period to mark a holy site,[3124] although it must be more likely that the stone was buried in the geological period by glacial activity and lay recumbent and undisturbed until revealed by Victorian workers excavating for brick clay. But if it is not Beorngyth's stone, there is no other known candidate, and the stone appears to have been discovered in the (very

---

[3120] Hooke 1983: 65. Hooke 1993: 15 questions whether the stone might have been a forerunner of the cross, if not the cross itself.

[3121] The stone is set upright, and it is uncertain how much of the base lies below ground. According to an attached plaque, the stone was carried in one of the ice ages from the Arenig range in Merionethshire.

[3122] First edition 1" O.S. map of 1834. The 6" O.S. map of 1889-1890 shows *Old Brick Kilns* between Oak Street and Merridale Road, and the improbably-named *Harbour Terrace* to the south of the brick kilns and east of Merridale Road. If not ironical (sand pits are shown to the south-west), it is highly improbable that the name possibly derives from OE *eorþburg* 'earth fortification'. Oak Street was so-named from a house called The Oaks: White 1834: 58.

[3123] PMSANRP, ref. WMwvWVxx039. The circumstances surrounding the discovery of the stone, and the date it was found, remain unclear. WC June 1st 1881 says that the pillar was 'found in a brickyard at the bottom of Brickkiln Lane, not far from the cemetery'. The cemetery lay to the south of Oak Street.

[3124] It may be noted that a chapel of a hermitage, with a burial ground and adjacent croft, is recorded on the south-west side of Wolverhampton in 1550, evidently *the Hermytage chapell or Chapel of the Rood* mentioned in the 1546 chantry returns, with 'Chapell' repeatedly mentioned in a survey of 1609, probably some distance west of Tup Street (now North Street), and perhaps near the junction of Broadmeadow and Ablow fields. The survey refers to land in Broadmeadow field 'shutting down from the Chapell' and to land in Ablow field 'abutting at the north end on the field hedge at the Chapell'. The chapel by tradition gave its name to Chapel Ash: Wolverhampton HER 13394; TSSAHS XXXVII 1995-6 122; Horovitz 2005: 183. The *Chapel of the Rood* (from ME *rōde* 'cross, crucifix, gallows, pole': see Rumble 2006) probably took its name from the crucifixion, but as the name is exceptionally unusual – the name Chapel of the Holy Rood is more usual, but still very rare – there may have been a cross associated with the chapel from which it took its name. The possibility that it was the cross now in the churchyard of St Peter's church, less than half a mile distant, may not be entirely fanciful.

approximate) location suggested by the 985 and spurious 994 charters. If nothing else, the West Park stone proves that huge erratics lay hereabouts, and it may have been a similar monolith that was known as Beorngyth's stone.

We cannot know how common the name Beorngyth may have been in the Anglo-Saxon period, but the *Onomasticon Anglo-Saxonicum*, an exhaustive compilation of Anglo-Saxon personal names extracted from all known sources, lists only five places where the name has been recorded:[3125]

1. The reference to Beorngyth's stone in the 985 grant from King Æthelred to Wulfrun. Importantly, the name is, as we have seen, also found (in 'the paved road associated with Beorngyth's stone') in Wulfrun's charter c.994, which is overlooked by the *Onomasticon*.

2. The *Liber Vitae Dunelmensis*, a complex manuscript, the original core of which is a fair copy made in the 840s of what was probably a composite exemplar from the seventh century (possibly in the reign of King Ecgfrith of Northumbria, 670-85) as a list of several hundred names of benefactors associated with a Northumbrian church, probably Jarrow or Durham,[3126] which mentions four times the name of a later seventh century nun Beorngyth under the heading *Nomina reginarum et abbatissarum* ('names of queens and abbesses'). The fact that her name appears four times indicates four benefactions rather than four different Beorngyths.

3. A charter of 681 which survives only in a cartulary of Bath abbey, in which the name appears in its Latinised form *Bernguidi*, described as a 'venerable abbess'.[3127] This Beorngyth was, with *Folcburh* (*Folcburgi*), who was probably the *decana*, the equivalent of the prioress, of the convent,[3128] granted 20 hides of land by the river Cherwell by Æthelmod, with the grant (one of the earliest charters referring to Mercia)[3129] attested by King Ethelred of Mercia (son of King Penda and brother of King Wulfhere, who died in 675) and archbishop Theodore.[3130] The location of the religious establishment to which this Beorngyth was attached is uncertain: Sir Frank Stenton suggested that it lay in the neighbourhood of Oxford,[3131] many writers claim that it was at Bath,[3132] Elizabeth Briggs suggests that the monastery was that of Barking (see below),[3133] while S. E. Kelly suggests

---

[3125] Searle 1897: 99.
[3126] Sweet 1885: 154-5; Yorke 2003: 116; Rollason et al 2004; Rollason and Rollason 2007. In about 1100 a list principally of monks of Durham Cathedral Priory was appended to the *Liber*, which was continued until the 16th century. Several thousand names of lay persons were added throughout the middle ages
[3127] S.1167; Whitelock 1955: 444. Listed as *Beorngyth 1* in the *Prosopography of Anglo-Saxon England*, accessed 7 November 2014.
[3128] Hunt 1893: 262.
[3129] Whitelock 1955: 444. Æthelmod was probably a member of the Hwiccan royal family, perhaps King of the Hwicce, although he is not styled King in the charter. He may have been the son of Osric, reigning jointly with his uncle, Oshere.
[3130] S.1167; Whitelock 1955: 444; Stenton 1970: 51 fn.4. The grant does not mean that Beorngyth was being given empty land awaiting exploitation; 20 hides meant that the estate was due to pay a large tribute to the king, or, if he wished to alienate it, to some beneficiary: Sawyer 1998: 145.
[3131] Stenton 1970: 225.
[3132] E.g. Searle 1897: 105; Williams, Smyth and Kirby 1991: 62; Gwara and Ehwald 2001: 51.
[3133] Briggs 2004: 79-80. Hildelith (who died after 717), abbess of Barking, founded by 675, was in close touch with Wenlock abbey, for it was she who first informed St Boniface about the vision of the monk of Wenlock: Finberg 1972: 215, 216; Thacker and Sharpe 2002: 538; Yorke 2003: 26-7.

a minster in the area where the land lay, perhaps Eynsham near Oxford, the existence of which in the eighth and ninth centuries has now been confirmed by archaeology.[3134]

4. A grant of land at *Slæpi* (possibly Islip, Northamptonshire) made to the same Beorngyth (again written *Berguidi*), *venerabilis abbatissæ*, by Wigheard, with the consent of King Wulfhere of Mercia, in a spurious charter purporting to date from 670-71, but almost certainly also of 681, since the witnesses are identical with those in the charter of land by the Cherwell mentioned above, and one, Bosel, was bishop of Worcester from 680 to 691.[3135] As we have seen, Wulfhere was a Christian, unlike his father, Penda,[3136] and came to exert more authority over England than any previous king. It was Wulfhere, the first king of Mercia to be baptised, who granted land at Lichfield to bishop Wilfrid in the 660s to build the first Mercian cathedral, where Chad established his seat in 669, and it was under Wulfhere's aegis that the first general synod under the English church was summoned by Archbishop Theodore at Hertford in 672. This reorganised the structure of the church into smaller, less tribally-based dioceses, which led in due course to a change in the administrative base of England, with the dioceses becoming adminstrative centres. It is clear that Wulfhere was instrumental in encouraging the spread of the gospel and supporting religious foundations.[3137]

5. A certain Beorngyth was a nun of the double monastery of Barking abbey who corresponded with St Aldhelm (?640-709).[3138] Aldhelm was educated under Theodore, archbishop of Canterbury, and became the foremost scholar of the seventh century after Bede, becoming abbot of Malmesbury, and founding monasteries in Dorset and Bradford-on-Avon. When the West Saxon see was divided in 706, Wessex 'west of Selwood' was given to Aldhelm, who built a great cathedral at Sherborne. He was author of a number of Latin works in prose and verse on the merits of chaste living, who thought so highly of Hildelith, abbess of Barking, that at some date between about 685 and 705 he dedicated to her and nine other named nuns, including *Berngitha* (Beorngith) a Latin prose work *De Laudibus Virginitate*. The work praises their study of holy books and their cultural attainments, which included problems of history and allegory, as well as the intricacies of grammar and metre, and commends their celibate life, while condemning the fine clothing which had become fashionable for the clergy: scarlet tunics with striped silk sleeves, red fur shoes, and curled hair, with, instead of the modest dark veil, coloured headdresses with flowing ribbons.[3139]

Is it fanciful to imagine that some, even perhaps all, of these references to Beorgyth, are to the same person?[3140]

[3134] Stenton 1970: 225; Kelly 2008: 79-85.
[3135] S.1168; Whitelock 1955: 444; Powicke and Fryde 1961: 260; Sawyer 1968: 344. The charter may be the oldest English private deed in existence: Whitelock 1955: 444.
[3136] Whose name may well be remembered in Pendeford, some two miles north-west of Wolverhampton: Horovitz 2005: 431.
[3137] Both of Wulfhere's wives entered monasteries and became abbesses: Williams, Smyth and Kirby 1991: 210, 240.
[3138] Searle 1897: 99; listed as *Beorngyth 2* in the *Prosopography of Anglo-Saxon England*, accessed 7 November 2014.
[3139] Godfrey 1961: 204; Stenton 1970: 228; Schulenburg 1998: 204; Scott and Ehwald 2001: 53-4.
[3140] Certainly the Beorngyth mentioned in the two charters of 681 has been identified as the dedicatee of Aldhelm: Gwara and Ehwald 2001: 51.

Since her name was associated with a stone and a routeway, the Wolverhampton Beorngyth was clearly a prominent local personality, perhaps an important landowner and/or associated with a religious community, and although it must be emphasised that there is not the slightest direct evidence that she could be the same person as *Bernguidi* recorded in 681 (evidently of some age to be described as *venerabilis*), it is a possibility that cannot be ignored. It has been suggested that *Bernguidi* was an Englishwoman who retained Frankish connections through her deputy, Folcburh.[3141]

It may be that we have here some very tenuous evidence that Beorngyth could have been an early, perhaps the first, religious of Wolverhampton, who moved to (or, perhaps less likely, from) Bath or Barking or Eynsham, or elsewhere, in the later seventh or early eighth century.There is of course no way of knowing, but there are certainly parallels in this region and at this period for this scenario, perhaps the most well known being St Werburgh, daughter of King Wulfhere, who succeeded her great aunt Æthelthryth, grandmother Seaxburh and mother Eormenhild as fourth abbess of Ely, and who was reputedly given authority over all Mercian monasteries and later, at the request of her uncle, King Ethelred, reformed monasteries of nuns throughout England.[3142] She also established new monasteries at Trentham and Hanbury in Staffordshire, and at Weedon in Northamptonshire, dying c.699.[3143] She may well have been a contemporary of the Wolverhampton Beorngyth.

If Beorngyth was indeed the first abbess of Wolverhampton (and the founder of a church is perhaps more likely to have been honoured and remembered than subsequent abbesses), it would indicate that a religious site existed at Wolverhampton in the later seventh century.[3144] And if our Wolverhampton Beorngyth (who may have been of royal blood) should be the same person as *Bernguidi* mentioned in the charters of 681, could we have very tenuous evidence which might indeed identify a King of Mercia who may have been associated with the earliest religious site at Wolverhampton? Since Wolverhampton minster is one of the royal free chapels, we can assume that it was of royal foundation, perhaps founded prior to the synod of Hertford in 672. The King of Mercia from 658 to 675 was Wulfhere. If Beorngyth was *venerabilis* in 681, we might suppose she was of

---

[3141] Before *Mildburh* ruled it, the monastery of Much Wenlock was in charge of Abbot Æthelheah and an abbess with the Frankish name Liobsind (Yorke 2003: 27), and the first abbess of bath, Berta, bore a Frankish name (see Sims-Williams 1975: 8). Contacts with Francia in the second half of the 7th century were via abbesses at religious houses in Anglo-Saxon Gaul (such as Chelles, near Paris), known for their learning, and Bede mentions that many people in the mid- and late-7th century went from Britain to live in the Frankish monasteries, and also sent their daughters to such houses to be educated and become nuns. Chelles supplied nuns and books for teaching and the foundation of convents in England. These Frankish contacts seem to have diminished and eventually ceased as more religious houses for women were established in England: Yorke 2003: 27; Rollason, Piper and Harvey 2004: 80.

[3142] Yorke 2003: 20.

[3143] Other royal abbesses of this period are Cyneburga who married a Northumbrian prince and later ruled a convent at Castor in Northamptonshire, dying c.680, and Cuthberga, wife of King Aldfrid of Northumbria who later became a nun and founded the nunnery of Wimbourne, dying c.725: Attwater 1965: 340.

[3144] Perhaps associated with the remarks of Florence (John) of Worcester, who tells us that King Wulfhere, who died in 675 'abolished and thoroughly eradicated the worship of idols from all parts of his dominions, caused the name of Christ to be preached in every corner of his kingdom, and built churches in many places': Stevenson 1853: 24. It was under Wulfhere's aegis that the first general synod of the English church was summoned by Archbishop Theodore at Hertford in September 672. This reorganised the episcopal structure of the church into smaller, less tribally-based dioceses.

some age and had been at Barking or Bath for some years, in which case it may not be unreasonable to suppose that she was at Wolverhampton some decades before that date, i.e. the 660s (or possibly after 681).

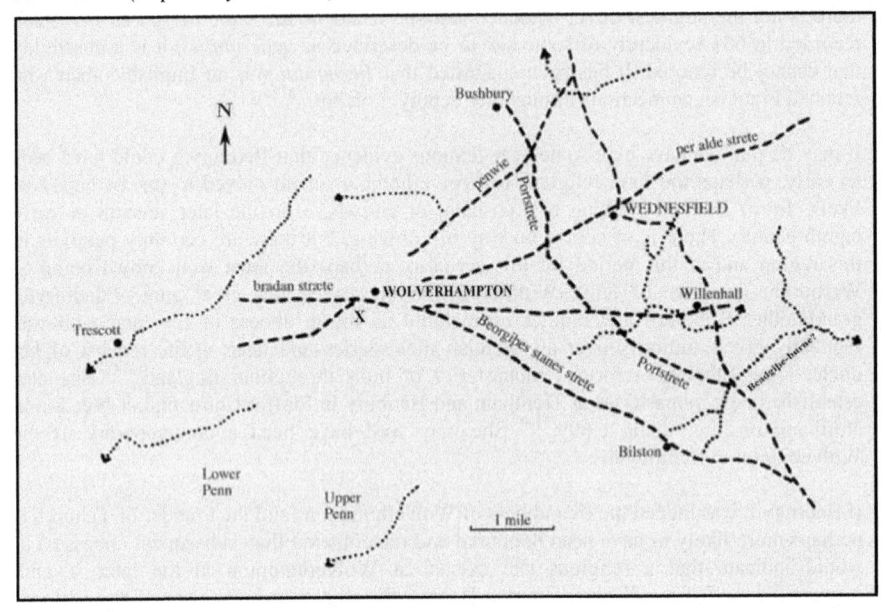

Map showing pre-Conquest routeways in the Wolverhampton area and the likely location of *Byrngyðe stan* ('Beorngyth's stone'), *beorgiþes s[t]anes strete* ('the paved road associated with Beorngyth's stone'), and *Beadgiþe-burne* ('Beadugyth's stream'), referred to in late tenth-century charters, based on Hooke 1983: 47. The fine dotted lines denote streams. **X** marks the spot on the south-west side of Wolverhampton where a large natural stone pillar, now erected in Wolverhampton's West Park, was found c.1881.

The possibility that Beorngyth alluded to in Wulfrun's grant of c.994 may be the same person as the abbess recorded in the *Liber Vitae Dunelmensis* may well be strengthened by other evidence. In the boundary clause of Wednesfield and Bilston in the confirmation of Wulfrun's grant there is a reference to *Beadgiþe-burne* 'Beadugyth's stream', which appears to have flowed to the east of Bilston.[3145]

[3145] Hooke 1983: 74-5. Mander (WA II 90-93) suggests that the watercourse is the Bilston brook (otherwise the Bourne), near The Lunts, a north-flowing stream which forms the southern boundary of Bilston and Willenhall (and becomes the river Tame at Walsall), possibly the river of the same name shown on Michael Drayton's decorative map of 1615, and mentioned in his poem *Polyolbion* of the same date: at the end of his '12th song' (p.208), having described the Smestall, tributary of the 'Stowr', he adds 'Nor shall the little Bourne have cause the Muse to Blame, From these Staffordian Heathes that strives to catch the Tame ...'. If Mander is correct, it is difficult to imagine how such an insignificant watercourse gained such fame, unless perhaps from its association with Beadugyth. Lawley 1836: 3 says that the stream passed through Bilston and then eastwards through Willenhall, where 'the bed of this stream was discovered a few years ago, in digging out the foundations for some buildings'. Hackwood suggests that a spring beneath Sedgley Beacon which gave its name to Spring Vale, and was 'the famous Spring known as the Lady Wulfruna's', fed a stream that flowed eastwards to Willenhall to meet the Tame: Hackwood 1908: 92-3. He was apparently led astray by a comment made in Lawley 1893: 174-5, which seems to be based on an anonymous reference to Wulfrun's Well in Gorsebrook (although it describes the well as south, rather than north, of Wolverhampton), rather

The name Beadugyth has been traced in only three sources:

1. In the stream-name in Wulfrun's charter c.994.[3146]

2. In the *Liber Vitae Dunelmensis*.[3147]

3. As a stream-name (*beadegyðe wyllan* 'Beadugyð's spring or stream') in the bounds of Beoley in Worcestershire (some 18 miles south-east of Wolverhampton) in one version of a charter to Pershore Abbey of 972.[3148]

It will be seen that two of the three records of the name are in the very charter and the same Durham records in which the name Beorngyth appears.[3149] Indeed, the name Beadugyth (mentioned twice in the *Liber Vitae Dunelmensis*, which lists thousands of names) not only appears in the very same part of the section of the *Liber* as the name Beorngyth, but amongst the four references to Beorngyth.[3150]

Coincidence can prove deceptively fatal quicksand for a historian, but it might not be unreasonable to suspect that both Beorngyth and Beadugyth recorded in the *Liber*, who appear to have had links with the church of Jarrow or Durham, were associated – probably as abbesses – with an earlier religious house or houses at or near Wolverhampton in the late seventh century. The foundation of monasteries and minsters was pioneered by the king and his nobles, while nunneries and double houses were commonly set up by queens and royal princesses, usually on estates under their control.[3151] It is now known that in the middle and later Saxon period it was the norm for cathedrals and monasteries to comprise not just one church but a tight-knit group of two or more separate churches and other sepulchral and liturgical foci, often set out in linear formation, which came to be physically conjoined. The principal church generally carried a dedication to one of the apostles, with another component of the group dedicated to St Mary (to whom

---

than Spring Vale north of Deepfields (*Spring Vale* 1834 O.S.), where no other reference to Wulfrun's Spring has been traced. The derivation and implications of the name Bilston should not be overlooked. In 895 it is recorded as *Bilsatena*, and between 994 and 1066 as *Bilsetnatun*, meaning 'the dwellers at Bil, indicating a tribal grouping which originated here or elsewhere. The meaning of Bil is uncertain: Horovitz 2005: 121. It may be noted that an extent of Wolverhampton c.1249 includes in its attached hamlets and estates Dunstall (the site of Wulfrun's Well), Willenhall and Bilston: VCH IV 44 fn.61.

[3146] Overlooked by Searle 1897.

[3147] Searle 1897: 81.

[3148] BL Cotton Vitellius Dvii 29v-30v – see Stokes 2009: 55, 64. It is difficult to draw even tentative conclusions from this fleeting reference, but the comparative proximity of Beoley to Wolverhampton is noteworthy.

[3149] Sweet 1885: 154-5. The name has the spelling Badugyth. No person of this or a similar name is listed in the the *Prosopography of Anglo-Saxon England*, accessed 7 November 2014

[3150] Although it has been suggested that *Byrngyðe/beorgiþe/Beadugyth*are likely to refer to the same person (Hooke 1983: 48; Hooke and Slater 1986: 20), that possibility can be dismissed. Alexander Rumble has pointed out that the names have 'the same deuterotheme (OE –gyð) but different protothemes (OE Beorn– and Beadu–), and it is likely that two related women, with alliterative and reduplicative names, are commemorated in the [boundary features] concerned': *Nomina* 10 (1986) 177-9.

[3151] Parsons 2001: 55. For a discussion of the term 'double house' when applied to religious houses of both men and women see Katharine Sykes, 'Canonici Albi et Moniales: Perceptions of the Twelfth-Century Double House', in *Journal of Ecclesiastical History*, 60, No. 2 (April 2009): 233-45.

Wolverhampton church was dedicated).[3152] The isolated house for women was not a normal feature of early English monasticism; indeed there may have been none. Most, if not all, monasteries founded in the late seventh or early eighth century (including Repton, Much Wenlock, Bardney, Whitby, Ely, Wimborne, Coldingham, Barking, the original monastery of Gloucester, and probably Bath) were joint establishments of men and women, with a house for females and an adjacent community of men. Archbishop Theodore of Canterbury recognised establishments of this kind as an English institution, which he disliked but tolerated. Abbesses were often royal widows or daughters,[3153] and 'double monasteries' housing both nuns and monks were always presided over by an abbess, rather than an abbot.[3154] John Blair had noted that early monastic heads, above all princesses and noblewomen, formed a category of local saints. Kings and aristocrats who transferred huge landed resources to ministers controlled by their kinswomen created what he calls a 'holy cousinhood' of female saints whose cults – almost fifty are known – endured for centuries in obscure minsters, with many such cults known outside their immediate contexts. 'The status of these ladies as virgins (or holy mothers) and monastic rulers ... was doubtless reinforced by genuine regard within communities for heads whose impact had been formative and who were remembered with reverence and affection. ... [but] long term survivial and record of [their cults] could have been at the mercy of external and later circumstances'.[3155]

Is it possible that Wolverhampton may have originated as the site of a religious community, perhaps a double house, which existed in the latter part of the seventh century, perhaps founded at the instigation of Wulfhere, with Northumbrian roots?[3156] We should remember not only that the Mercian King Penda was killed by the Northumbrians at the battle of the Winwæd in 655, and that for over two years the kingdom of Mercia was directly subject to the Northumbrians, but that Chad himself was appointed bishop of the Northumbrians before he was made bishop of Mercia, and King Ethelred (who ruled 674-704) married the daughter of Oswiu, King of Northumbria. It was Wulfhere who granted land at Lichfield in the 660s on which Chad built his cathedral. It would not be in the least surprising to find Northumbrian connections in Mercia. Wolverhampton indeed may have been a daughter house of another foundation, as Wenlock may have been of Iken ('Icanho') founded in 654.[3157] By the close of the ninth century double monasteries were going out of favour, and many transformed themselves into colleges of secular clerks, as seems to have

---

[3152] Rodwell et al 2008: 49-50.
[3153] Hild of Whitby was a kinsman of Oswiu, King of Northumbria, and Ælfflæd, her successor, was his daughter. Wimborne was founded by two sisters of Ine, King of Wessex; Ely was founded by Æthelthryth, and she and her successor Seaxburg were daughters of Anna, King of the East Angles. Mildburh, abbess of Wenlock, and Mildthryth, abbess of Minster in Thanet, were daughters of Merewalh, King of the Magonsætan. Most of their houses were destroyed by the Danes in the ninth century: Stenton 1970: 162.
[3154] James 2001: 184.
[3155] Blair 2002a: 460-1.
[3156] A possible association with Wulfhere is of particular interest in the light of a local tradition that he was connected with the original foundation of the monastery of Wolverhampton c.659: Hooke and Slater 1983: 16. The tradition appears to be relatively recent, since it is not mentioned by Dugdale, and may well have arisen as a result of a false etymology of the place-name based on the phonological similarity of the name Wulfhere to Wolver–: see for example Beresford 1883: 43. The present church is mainly of mid- to late-fifteenth century date, with the earliest part the four arches which support the tower, which were probably constructed in the thirteenth century: Mander and Tildesley 1960: 178.
[3157] Finberg 1972: 197-8.

occurred at many houses including Gloucester and probably Much Wenlock.[3158] It is at least possible that the canons of Wolverhampton recorded in Domesday Book represented a community of monks which had once formed part of a mixed foundation.[3159]

We might also note that Beadugyth's stream mentioned in Wulfrun's grant formed the southern boundary of Willenhall, part of which was held by the church of Wolverhampton in 994 (if the spurious charter has been correctly dated), and which had been visited by King Æthelbald of Mercia c.732 when he attested two charters there.[3160] Evidently there was a place in Willenhall in the earlier part of the eighth century with facilities suitable for accommodating the king and his extensive retinue. In that respect we should note that Wulfrun's charter to Wolverhampton minster states in its preamble that the estates granted thereby include Willenhall, although no boundary clause is included in the body of the document, perhaps because when the charter was forged the monks had no boundary clause available to copy.

It may be assumed that Beadugyth who gave her name to the nearby stream was of some importance – if she is indeed the person so-named in the *Liber Vitae Dunelmensis*, she is, with Beorngyth, listed under the rubric 'queens and abbesses'. Might we suspect that she was an abbess, even the founder, if not of Wolverhampton (and her name, we should remember, is associated with a stream that formed the boundary of the lands of Wolverhampton minster), then perhaps of a mixed monastery at or near Willenhall in the later seventh or early eighth century,[3161] possibly with Northumbrian roots, perhaps founded under the auspices of King Wulfhere, which may have been connected with Beorngyth and the church of Wolverhampton? Could any such foundation have been the place where Æthelbald and his retinue executed a charter c.732? Since the name Beadugyth appears so closely associated with that of Beorngyth in the *Liber Vitae Dunelm*, we might fairly assume that the women were contemporaries, and since the Anglo-Saxons at this period, certainly at the highest levels of society, were in the habit of giving their children alliterative first names, it is not impossible that Beadugyth and Beorngyth were closely related, perhaps mother and daughter.[3162]

The possibility of a seventh-century foundation for the church of Wolverhampton (as well as other royal free chapels in the area) is given added weight by research carried out in the 1980s by Anne Jenkins, who has argued that the royal free chapels of South Staffordshire 'were founded in the seventh and eighth centuries as the administrative centres of large royal estates, or early tribal areas, with which the parochiae of the churches often came to be co-terminous', and that those institutions exercised ecclesiastical jurisdiction over areas far more extensive than their later parishes.[3163] That situation might well explain a request

---

[3158] Finberg 1972: 197-8.
[3159] Stenton 1970: 228-9.
[3160] S.86 and S.87. Hookeobserves that *meidenesford*, which Wulfrun's charter mentions as a boundary mark in the south-east of Bilston, is 'probably an allusion to *Beadgiþ* or a similar lady connected with the minster': Hook 1983: 73-5.
[3161] The foundation of Much Wenlock is generally dated to the last quarter of the seventh century: Yorke 2003: 27; see also Finberg 1964: 66-82. The map of 'minsters housing women to c.850' in Foot: 2006: 175 shows a concentration of sites in the central Midlands, particularly the southern part, but there is a noticeable blank area from Repton in the north to Hanbury in the south, and from Wenlock in the west to Castor in the east.
[3162] As noted above, Alexander Rumble believes it likely that two women were related:*Nomina*10 (1986) 177-9.
[3163] Jenkins 1989: 24.

by Pope Leo III in a letter to Coenwulf, king of the Mercians, in 802 to respect the authority of archbishop Æthelheard in the dioceses '*tam episcoporum quam monasteriorum*', and by a statement made by the bishop of Coventry in the early part of the twelfth century concerning the church of Wolverhampton: *Hec quidem ecclesia de Wlfr[unehamptona] una erat antiquitus de propriis regis capellis que ad coronam spectabant*.[3164] It should not be overlooked that a hill named *Hildebaldeshull* is recorded twice in Wednesfield, probably on the south-west side of the village, in the early fourteenth century. The name is unexplained, and may (though probably does not) have religious associations.

The origins of the early tribal groups in the West Midlands remains uncertain, but they appear to have been established by the end of the seventh century,[3165] and several are listed in the *Tribal Hidage*, which mentions 34 kingdoms and tribal territories with an assessment of each in hides. The text survives in an eleventh-century manuscript which is much later than the material it contains. The people known as the *Wreocansaetan* ('the dwellers associated with the Wroxeter or the Wrekin'), who are listed in the Hidage, appear to have occupied an area extending from Wroxeter to beyond Chester. In a single reference in a charter of 849 we hear of the *Pencersaetan*, ('the dwellers associated with the Penk'), unmentioned in the Hidage. Anne Jenkins has detected evidence that Penkridge, transferred from the Romano-British civil settlement of *Pennocrucium*, where Watling Street crosses the river Penk two miles to the south, encompassed both Cannock and Rugeley, as well as Shareshill, Coppenhall, Stretton, Dunston, Congreve, Longridge, Lapley, Bednall, Brocton, and Acton Trussell (where a very substantial Roman villa is being excavated), and perhaps other places.[3166] That extensive area may be identifiable in the territory of the *Pencersaetan*, the northern part of which may be seen as the holding of Penkridge church identified by Jenkins. The territory of the *Pencersaetan*, long and narrow, perhaps included Stafford, Cannock, Tettenhall, Wolverhampton, and Willenhall in the north.[3167] All we know for certain is that the southern boundary of the *Pencersaetan* lay near Cofton Hackett and Alvechurch in Worcestershire (both places are named in the 849 charter where the boundary is mentioned) and their territory evidently adjoined that of the *Tomsaetan* ('the dwellers associated with the Tame'), whose territory, also long and narrow, may have extended from Repton in the north to King's Norton in the south, and included Lichfield, with the river Trent perhaps forming its eastern boundary.[3168]

We know also that by 860 the *Wreocensaetan* seem to have been under the authority of the bishop of Lichfield, while the *Hwicce* (listed in the Tribal Hidage), with their territory in parts of what became Worcestershire and Gloucestershire, had a bishop based at Worcester, and the *Magonsaetan* (whose territory lay to the west of the *Hwicce*) had one at Hereford.[3169] Since the *Pencersaetan* lay to the east of the *Wreocensaetan*, it is clear that they too fell within the orbit of the bishop of Lichfield.[3170] It seems possible that Penkridge

---

[3164] Denton 1970: 139-40. Denton also notes that the English royal free chapels bear a distinct resemblance to the Carolingian *Pfalzkapellen* ('palace-chapels') with their subordinate and perhaps prebendal *Fiskalkapellen* ('treasury-chapels'): ibid.
[3165] Brown and Farr 2001: 91.
[3166] Jenkins 1989: 25-32.
[3167] Hart 1977: 50.
[3168] Hart 1977: 50, 54; Hooke 1983: 12; Hooke 1992: 47-8; Hooke 1993: 12.
[3169] Charles-Edwards has suggested that the territory of the *Wreocensaetan* may have been split between the sees of Lichfield and Hereford, since the medieval diocesan boundary ran across the Wrekin, though that may be a later extension of Hereford northwards: Charles-Edwards 2013: 388.
[3170] See Bassett 2000a: 114.

was at some period the principal church in the territory of the *Pencersaetan*, but since it lay at the northern end of a sizeable area, another church may have ministered to those in the southern part of the territory. Whatever the case, Jenkins makes a persuasive case for both the antiquity and continuity of the administrative units upon which, as Anglo-Saxon minsters, the royal free chapels were based.[3171]

Finally, to add further evidence, albeit slight, to the possibility that Wolverhampton minster was a seventh century foundation, we may note that six of the nine royal free chapels, including Tettenhall, Penkridge and Wolverhampton, are or were dedicated to St Mary, in respect of whom there appears to have been an increased devotion by the late eighth and early ninth century. Such dedications may well help support arguments for a Middle Anglo-Saxon origin for those foundations.[3172]

In conclusion, there is no obvious reason why the minster of Wolverhampton could not have been founded under the patronage of the Mercian King Wulfhere in the later part of the seventh century, perhaps with high-born abbesses named Beorngyth and Badugyth, who may have had Frankish connections, with Beorngyth later moving to (or having moved from) another monastery, possibly Bath. The minster may have been destroyed during the Danish depredations of the later ninth century, which would perhaps explain why chroniclers record the battle of Tettenhall, which may have taken place at Wednesfield, rather than the battle of Wolverhampton, which (as a minster community) then lay in ruins, to be refounded by Wulfrun almost nine decades later, but that must remain entirely a matter for speculation. But if the conjecture is correct (and proof will almost certainly forever remain lacking), the early history of Wolverhampton could be pushed back well over three centuries earlier than previously suspected.

A drawing (with figure to show scale) showing two elevations of the felsite pillar, some nine feet high, found in 1881 in Oak Street, Wolverhampton, and now in West Park, Wolverhampton. Could this be Beorngyth's stone, mentioned in a grant of Wolverhampton and Trescott by King Aethelred in 985 AD and in the spurious charter of Wulfrun to the church of Wolverhampton? It is not known how much of the stone lies below ground.

[3171] The age, derivation and implications of the name Bilston should not be overlooked. In 895 it is recorded as *Bilsatena*, and between 994 and 1066 as *Bilsetnatun*, meaning 'the dwellers at Bil, indicating a tribal grouping which originated here or elsewhere. The meaning of Bil is uncertain: Horovitz 2005: 121.
[3172] Cramp 1977: 210.

Appendix IV.

The Wolverhampton cross-shaft.

The ancient sandstone column or cross-shaft on the south side of St Peter's church in Wolverhampton, probably the oldest monument in the area, is deserving of particular attention, since it is generally held to be pre-Conquest in date. Relatively little known outside the region, it is listed by Martin Carver with no less than the Sutton Hoo treasures and the Lindisfarne Gospels as examples of what the Anglo-Saxons could achieve with a wide range of materials when they wanted to.[3173] As we have seen, St Peter's church itself was founded or, more properly (and possibly as evidenced by the existence of the ancient cross-shaft) probably refounded – perhaps following destruction in 874, when the Danes overran Mercia – by Wulfrun in or about 994. The present church incorporates no evidence of any Anglo-Saxon work, but that is unsurprising: the greater part of the fabric dates from the re-building which took place in the mid and late fifteenth century. It is to be noted, however, that no archaeological evidence of unequivocal Anglo-Saxon occupation has been recorded from Wolverhampton.

The cast of the Wolverhampton cross-shaft and capstone, made in 1880, in the Victoria and Albert Museum, showing the irregular profile of the undecorated lower part of the column. The apparent curve in the pillar is the result of photographic distortion, but the curious 'waist' near the base is clearly defined.

[3173] Carver 1989: 81.

The cross-shaft raises a number of questions. Where was the stone quarried? Where was it made? Where was it carved? Is the carving contemporary with the manufacture of the column? What date can be attributed to the carving? When was it set up? By whom? Why was it set up? Is it in its original position? If the monument is incomplete, what form did it originally take? What is its recorded history? Are there other parallels elsewhere?

The column, some 14' high with a knop or capstone some 9" deep, has a lower diameter of 30" reducing to 22" beneath the knop.[3174] Unlike the pre-Conquest cross-shafts of the North Staffordshire area, which are of local stone, generally millstone grit,[3175] the Wolverhampton pillar is of a pale red medium-grained sandstone, quite unlike the softer and more coarsely-grained local red and yellow sandstone. Gerald Mander, the Wolverhampton antiquary, suggested that from its marked entasis it may have originated as a re-used Roman column from Viroconium, some 25 miles to the west of Wolverhampton, where he traced parts of two columns, not *in situ*, with similar dimensions to the Wolverhampton pillar,[3176] but the main type of stone used at Wroxeter is Hoar Edge Grit from between Harnage and Cardington.[3177] Other ancient columns have long been thought to be reused Roman columns, for example the pillar of Eliseg near Valle Crucis abbey in Clwyd,[3178] with its now illegible inscription indicating a *terminus ante quem* of 854, once believed to have been a Roman column from Chester or Wroxeter, but recently shown to be of local sandstone, the nearest source of which is probably less than two miles away.[3179] Sandstone of various types is found throughout the wider Wolverhampton area, but evidence from Gloucestershire, Herefordshire, Shropshire, Warwickshire and Worcestershire indicates that in those counties only in a few cases do examples of Anglo-Saxon stone sculpture lie above the geological strata from which they are presumed to derive, and most carved stones have been transported from their source

---

[3174] Anon. 1989 gives the height of the shaft as 3.5 metres above the plinth, with its widest diameter approximately 76cms (=29.92"), tapering to 55cms (=21.65"). Browne gives the circumference the pillar to be about 86 inches, which would give a diameter of a little under 27½": Browne 1885: 184-94.

[3175] TNSFC LXXXI 1946-7 162.

[3176] TNSFC LXXXII 1947-8 125. The re-used Roman columns at the entrance to Wroxeter churchyard have a maximum diameter of approximately 19", and less pronounced entasis. If the pillar is indeed a reworked column from elsewhere, that in itself would make it unusual: Bailey 1980: 238 records that little detailed research has been conducted into the material used by Viking-age sculptors, but 'in general it is not difficult to show [in respect of sculpture in northern England] that outcrops of the relevant type of stone can be found in the vicinity of the carving. Frequently the distance involved is less than a mile; rarely is it more than ten miles', although the Easby Cross from North Yorkshire is made from stone that probably originated at Whitby, some 50 miles to the east: Davies and Kennedy 2009: 148. There are few parallels for the re-use of Roman columns in the Anglo-Saxon period: scholars are undecided whether a short column from the church of St Pancras in Canterbury may have been robbed from a nearby Roman ruin or represents an early example of Anglo-Saxon workmanship: Eaton 2000; colour plate 25. Given the ready availabilty of sandstone in Wolverhampton and the surrounding region, it is difficult to explain why a pillar should have been brought from elsewhere, although it must be recognised that the local sandstone does not weather well. It is said that cylindrical pillars from a ruined building at the Roman site at *Uxacona* (Redhill, on Watling Street east of Telford) were taken to Lilleshall Hall at some date before 1767 (Gordon Cartlidge 1937-8: 26), although that claim must be entirely without foundation.

[3177] TSAHS LXXIX 2004 188.

[3178] A column with inscriptions linking the royal dynasty of Powys to Vortigern, Maximus, and Germanus, which Clapham 1930: 133-4 takes to be 9th century, a central date for the type. Nancy Edwards concludes that it was erected during the second half of the 8th and first half of the 9th centuries: Edwards 2009: 168.

[3179] Edwards 2009: 153.

rock, in some cases over considerable distances – in one case at least 50 miles – though that may in part reflect the lack of quality building stones along the Severn valley.[3180] It is also worth recording that the decorated square-section collared cross-shaft which stood in the churchyard at Wroxeter until the eighteenth century, fragments of which are now built into the fabric of thechurch there, does not utilise Roman stone readily available within yards of the church (two columns of which form a gateway to the churchyard), but is of oolitic limestone from the Cotswold Hills in Gloucestershire or Worcestershire, and was probably already carved when transported to Wroxeter.[3181]

In fact petrological examination of the Wolverhampton column shows it to be of the Helsby Sandstone Formation, Sherwood Sandstone Group, Triassic (CRB),[3182] found in various locations, but possibly here from the prominent west-facing escarpment of the Mid-Cheshire Ridge which runs south from Runcorn via Frodsham and Utkinton to Beeston Castle, or (less likely) from an outlier at Leek, in either case a minimum of 50 miles from Wolverhampton, though other lesser outcrops lie closer, such as those at Napley Heath on the Staffordshire-Shropshire border 5 miles north-east of Market Drayton and some 30 miles from Wolverhampton, and at Clive, 8 miles north of Shrewsbury and some 35 miles from Wolverhampton.[3183] Columns and fragments displayed in the Roman Gardens at Chester, including one on which weathering has highlighted the diagonal strata, have a superficial similarity to the Wolverhampton column, though at Wolverhampton the shaft tapers almost barbarously compared with the subtle entasis of typical Roman columns. Wherever its origin, it must have taken considerable skill and effort to extract a monolith weighing several tons and transport it to its present position. Whether it was carved at the quarry or on its original site (if indeed it stands in its original position) must remain a matter of speculation, although distortions in the carving of the higher part, mentioned later, may point, rather improbably, to the carving having been carried out after the pillar had been erected (though not necessary on its present site), and transporting a heavily carved monolith weighing several tons would have risked damage to the carvings.

It is generally assumed that the cross shaft has been in its present position since it was first erected. Steele reports a small excavation in 1948 which revealed that the pillar did not lie on natural rock, but on a moveable stone, confirming conclusions reached in 1873 and 1877.[3184] The 1948 excavation was carried out by Michael Rix and Gerald Mander and concluded that the pillar was suported on a huge rounded plinth with the remains of an outside circle of roughish but large stones which appeared to form steps, all resting on rubble and mortar which lay directly on a glacial deposit of sand and pebbles.[3185] A report published after further archaeological excavations by Birmingham University Field

---

[3180] Bryant et al 2012: 44.
[3181] Bryant 2012: 314-5, Plate 792-3.
[3182] Hawkes and Sidebottom forthcoming; Floyd 2015: 78, 173, 244.
[3183] Floyd 2015: 78, 173, 244.
[3184] The Rev. J. H. Iles reported in 1873 that a hole had been dug at the base of the pillar but no other steps had been found, nor had the surface of the ground been added to at all: the pillar was where it was first placed: JBAA 29 (March 1873: 29); Steele 1947-8: 125.
[3185] TNSFC LXXXII 1947-8 125. Rix and Mander's findings are said to have confirmed Lynam's conclusion of 1877 (ibid.), presumably in JBAA 1877: 38. It is unclear whether Lynam may have conducted his own excavation, perhaps when the plaster cast was created in 1877. In 1941 the British Museum was sufficiently concerned about damage from German bombing raids in 1941 to encourage the local Council to protect the monument with sandbags and iron sheeting, as a result of which the Borough Engineer recommended the erection of a protective 13' 6" brick wall around it, but there is no evidence that this was done: Whitehouse 1995: 48.

Archaeology Unit in August 1992 concluded that the shaft was erected on or near its present position 'during the early medieval period' (whatever that expression might mean), and may have been raised to a higher level in the mid nineteenth century.[3186] That conclusion might be supported by the discovery of human bone fragments in deposits adjoining the foundations of the cross, since it seems unlikely that the cross was originally sited in what was a churchyard. However, the fragments were found at the side of the sandstone blocks surrounding the base of the shaft, rather than from beneath those blocks, or indeed from beneath the shaft itself (an area which could not be fully explored), and the material (and the blocks) may have been put in place long after the column was first erected. Furthermore, an engraving of Wolverhampton church published in 1801[3187] shows that the column was then at a much higher level than the door of the porch, i.e. at about its present level.[3188] Pape noted that all of the early cross-shafts found in situ in the North Staffordshire area appear to have been placed to the south of the church, not far from the priest's door towards the east end of the church,[3189] whereas the Wolverhampton shaft lies south of the church near the west end, though even if the column stands in its original position the church may not stand precisely on its original foundations. There is further evidence discussed towards the end of this chapter which may support the idea that the pillar may not stand in its original position.

Repairs to the column have been carried out from time to time, some probably unrecorded, but an 1834 is mention of the '... ancient stone cross or pillar, lately repaired ...'.[3190] One would like to know more about this cryptic reference and the nature of the repair, but nothing more is known. In the 1950s remedial work on the shaft included cleaning to remove the heavy carbon deposits on the surface left by centuries of aerial pollution,[3191] and a programme of conservation was undertaken in 1993/4 by Richard Marsh Conservation of Bristol. Further intensive conservation work was carried out in 1998.[3192]

[3186] Hughes and Buteux 1992: 3, which failed to mention the comprehensive work carried out in 1989. Since the plaster cast in the Victoria andAlbert Museum shows what appears to be the full depth of the column, the supporting stones around the base must have been removed in 1877, when the cast was made, with the column supported and stabilised by other means. Indeed, Mander records in 1932 the recent removal of ivy which had been collecting around the base, which had revealed 'an imposingly large and solid rounded block of stone at the bottom of the structure. Above this a grotesquely ugly modern conglomeration of rubble has been accumulated' (WA I 12 362). If the shaft was indeed relocated in the nineteenth century (which seems unlikely, and no record of what would have been a major engineering exercise has been traced in local newspapers), the most likely date may be 1877. During the 1993 excavation a halfpenny of George II (1738) was found in the rubble surrounding the base of the shaft: Hughes and Buteux 1992: 3. An engraving of the unfenced column which forms the frontispiece to Oliver 1836 shows the base of the sandstone supporting structure level with the base of adjoining chamber tombs.
[3187] Shaw 1801 II: facing 155.
[3188] It may be worth recording that the churchyard was unenclosed in 1699: WA I 88.
[3189] Pape 1945-6: 25-49.
[3190] Calvert and West 1834: 17.
[3191] The cross-shaft was washed down with water and the capstone repaired in 1952: Whitehouse 1995: 50; Cockin 2000: 670. A reference in Calvert and West 1834: 17 mentions the '... ancient stone cross or pillar, lately repaired ...'. One would like to know more about this cryptic reference to repairs.
[3192] The conservation was carried out by Cliveden Conservation Workshop Limited of Taplow, including an investigation into the stability of the shaft, which was found to be tilting to the south. Non-destructive acoustic testing showed that the column was not homogenous through its vertical and horizontal planes, but was structurally stable. As the supporting plinth around the base of the shaft was opened up three different mortars were identified in its construction, and it was felt that it had been created predominantly from pieces of dressed red sandstone, probably waste from the

For detail of the carving on the shaft we are indebted to a single cast taken for the Plaster Gallery of the South Kensington (now Victoria and Albert) Museum in 1880 by Sergeant Bullen of the Royal Engineers (which can have been no easy task),[3193] and an extended drawing based on this cast prepared by a 'competent lady draughtsman', Miss Dorothy B. Martin of the Royal College of Art, published in 1913 by the Society of Antiquaries.[3194] On the basis of that drawing the deeply carved designs were for convenience divided by Michael Rix into five main zones and two minor zones, designated A-G:[3195]

A. About half-way up the shaft are two certain and three posible pendant triangles some 18" long, suspended from a cable moulding some 2½" deep, containing animals or foliage decoration. The first two triangles (numbered 5 and 4) are so weathered that nothing can be identified – even the frames are largely undetectable – but the third (numbered 3) has faint traces of what may be a symmetrical pattern of ropework or foliage, the fourth (numbered 2) incorporates what may be a forward-looking beast with notably bifurcated tail, and the fifth (numbered 1) what could be a parrot-like bird facing left with a pronounced circular eye and short down-curved beak. Very unusually, the frame around the latter appears to have been carved after the figure: the frame is interrupted on the left side by what appears to be some part of the overlying figure.

B. Immediately above are five lozenge-shaped panels about 19" deep each containing a long-necked four-legged beast with its head turned back, with bird-like creatures occupying the ten triangular spaces between the lozenges. The first and third animals are very similar, with upturned curved tails, perhaps intended as a pair, as with the second and fourth, while the fifth is a variation of the figures of the first pair, with a down-turned tail. The ten triangular spaces in the borders house what may have been five similar back-facing birds in the upper row, but in the lower row the figures are very uncertain.

---

nineteenth century restoration of St Peter's church. It was concluded that the shaft sits on its original circular base stone. The plinth was rebuilt after the area had been carefully cleaned and stabilised, with the stones reinstated in their original position where possible. Those which were completely degraded were replaced with other pieces of the same period found during the archaeological excavation. The mortar repairs to the shaft made in 1993-4 were found to be weathering at a different rate to the stone on the column, and were therefore removed and replaced with a hydraulic lime mortar of the same strength as the stone of the column. The capstone was removed to expose three vertical fractures roughly equidistant around the neck of the column which were found to have undergone intensive repairs in the past, including three delta metal staples or cramps across the three fractures. The staples and a central dowel were replaced with stainless steel copies, and a socket in the top of the column, an irregular polygonal-circle 180mm wide and 145 mm deep, was filled with stone pieces and mortar. A lead capping sheet was placed over this work, and the capstone, with its three separate pieces (which can be identified in the earliest illustrations of the shaft) secured each to its neighbour with long and wide stainless steel staples, replaced on the same alignment as it was when removed, secured by the stainless dowel set into the top of the column and threaded nut: Anon. 1989.

[3193] Acq. No. REPRO. 1880-117; Victoria & Albert Museum, *Register of Reproductions*, III (1879-83); Victoria & Albert Museum, *Casts from the Antique* (1882-4); Hawkes and Sidebottom forthcoming. It is clear that no attempt was made to remove the sandstone blocks and rubble surrounding the base of the shaft before the cast was taken.

[3194] PSA xxv; Baldwin Brown 1937: 273; Rix 1960: 71.

[3195] Rix 1960:72-3. Rix's slightly eccentric designations have been retained, but the descriptions of the carvings have been revised in the light of close examination of the plaster cast in the Victoria and Albert Museum.

C. A band of acanthus leaves some 7" deep bordered above and below by plain moulding.[3196]
D. A band some 19" deep containg boldly cut scrolling foliage.
E. Five panels, some circular and others lozenge-shaped, or with both straight and curved frames, in a zone 16" deep linked by large rosettes, each panel containing alternately a bird or a beast, each with its body facing to the left and with its head turned backwards. The first figure is a bird with its wings folded against its body and a parrot-like beak, the second is a fox-like animal in a naturalistic pose in profile with all the legs shown, the third a slender long-tailed bird with an angel-like wing shown above the body, the fourth what appears to be a seated animal biting its own back, and the fifth a grotesque bird with a small body, thin neck and large head with open beak.
F. A narrow decorative fillet.
G. A zone of scrolled plant forms with lobed tendrils and trifurcated terminals some 13" deep similar to zone D.

The capstone – with a vertical crack which is recorded in the earliest illustrations dating from the later eighteenth century – and generally assumed to be contemporary with and of the same stone as the column, has a flat base with sides flaring to an undecorated double roll moulding, the upper thicker than the lower, and a concave profile to a flat top. The lower edge is crisp, forming almost a right angle with its flat base, and it appears to have been laid on the flat top of the column: there is, curiously, no evidence that the capstone incorporates any form of recess or collar or other arrangement to prevent lateral movement. No Anglo-Saxon parallels for the capstone have been traced elsewhere.

To supplement Rix's analysis of the decorative arrangement, we have an especially valuable description of the monument provided by the Reverend. G. F. Browne which is included in a paper published in 1885 discussing the early font at Wilne, Derbyshire.[3197] With the aid of ladders, Browne was able to study the Wolverhampton carvings in situ and at close quarters (though hampered by constant drizzle), and recorded that 'The very fine but sadly decayed [cross-shaft] in the churchyard at Wolverhampton is a great puzzle. It stands 12 feet high on a pedestal of stones covered in ivy ... sixty-four inches from the bottom a raised belt of rope is cut on the pillar, from which raised bands descend forming five triangles, in each of which is a large animal or bird, about a foot high. The animal which has perished least is a nondescript. Immediately above the rope band is a remarkable tier of subjects, 19 inches wide, the girth of the pillar being about 86 inches. By means of bars crossing each other at about 55°, the belt is divided into five diamond-shaped areas, in each of which a large quadruped is sculptured, the small triangles above and below the intersection of the bars also containing a bird or a beast each. Thus there are in all 15 figures in this belt, five large and ten small. A large boss is placed at the intersection of the bars, and their ends are lost under a conventional leaf; these details look late. ... Next above comes a belt of acanthus leaves, 7 inches wide. Above that again a belt 19 inches wide filled with spiral scrolls, alternatively branching off to left and right. Whether the scrolls carry animals in them or only leaves or fruit, cannot now be determined with

---

[3196] Acanthus decoration, found towards the end of the ninth century, is said to exemplify the Carolingian influence which shaped the future of Anglo-Saxon art in the tenth century: Webster and Backhouse 1991: 280. The acanthus vine was a symbol of redemption of sin, and is used frequently in the Middle Ages as a device to indicate the joining of heaven and earth: Karkov: 2008: 228.
[3197] The font is described in the official listing (10.11.671) as a re-used Anglo-Saxon cross-shaft.

certainty; many years ago birds could be discovered in the scrolls and roses.[3198] Then another belt 17 inches wide with animals much decayed. At the top is a heavy cap, on the bevelled surface of which there are signs of interlacing work. The whole column tapers gently upwards ... So far as I could see the animals were not hampered and fettered as in other cases ...'.[3199]

Browne's first-hand and careful examination of the cross-shaft is of especial value, and his reference to interlace work on the 'bevelled surface' of the capstone (presumably referring to the upper surface, though the likelihood of any decorative scheme on the unseen top edge might be surprising) is unmentioned by any other commentator, including modern conservation specialists who have removed and carried out work on the capstone and produced detailed reports, evidently because Browne took the trouble to use ladders for his fastidious survey and was probably within inches of the capstone, and presumably because weathering of the capstone has since removed any traces of a design, is of particular note.[3200] There is no reason to doubt the information he provides – he was an eminent and respected authority on early sculptured stone crosses and a meticulous recorder[3201] – but it must remain a matter of regret that we have no further details of the design he mentions.[3202]

At this point we should recognise that the fine drawing published in 1913 must be treated with considerable caution, for it is very clear that the 'competent draughtwoman' was not recording what was then to be seen on the column, but rather recreating, based on a considerable degree of speculation and artistic licence, an intelligent suggestion (but not perhaps from a scholar with any knowledge of Anglo-Saxon sculpture) of what form the original decoration may have taken, for a study of the plaster cast created in 1880 shows that the carving was even then very eroded. No less troubling is the observation that 'Where the carving was too worn even in this reproduction, it was reconstructed on the basis of surviving details'.[3203] Indeed, a perceptive account from the earlier part of the nineteenth century records that 'The block [i.e. the column] being set contrariwise to its

---

[3198] This comment is unexplained, but no earlier detailed drawing of the carving has been traced.

[3199] Browne 1885: 184-94. Browne's paper contains an engraving of a back-facing animal (perhaps with a bird's head) from Band B of the Wolverhampton column, and draws attention to the similarity between the bird in his engraving and birds in the border of the Bayeux tapestry above the word *castellum* (which in reality are very different), though he is careful to avoid dating the shaft to that period, discussing events in the Wolverhampton region in the tenth century: ibid.

[3200] No design can be made out in close-up photographs of the weathered capstone taken during the conservation carried out in 1989, but the eye of faith might possibly detect traces of a design incorporating a horizontal line of rings or circles on the lower part of the capstone in Plate XVI in Parsons 1971.

[3201] George Forrest Browne (1833-1930), a Cambridge graduate, was ordained in 1858, became a teacher and priest, was appointed Disney Professor of Archaeology at Cambridge 1887-92, and eventually became bishop of Bristol in 1897. An extraordinarily prolific academic author and noted speleologist, he was President of the Alpine Club in 1905. Browne's papers in respected archaeological journals included studies of the early sculptured stones of Cheshire and the Sandbach crosses: Hawkes 2002: 182.

[3202] Browne's examination of the column was made after the plaster cast taken for the Victoria and Albert Museum in the 1870s, and though a photograph of the column on the museum website shows indistinct markings which might conceivably be traces of decoration, no obvious interlace could be detected by Dr Holly Trusted, Senior Curator of Sculpture at the museum, kindly reported in letter of 14th September 2016. The cast is currently inaccessible while renovation work to the gallery is carried out.

[3203] Hawkes and Sidebottom forthcoming.

quarry bed, the weather has acted greatly on its surfaces, and by ploughing them out in grooves and holes, has produced marks and indentations which have so much the appearance of the carver's work, that, at first sight, it appears much more richly wrought than a closer examination proves it to have been."[3204]

An extended drawing made in 1913 of the supposed ornamentation on the Wolverhampton cross-shaft, reproduced from *The Proceeding of the Society of Antiquaries*, Vol. XXV, 2nd Series, with the numbering and lettering of the decorative elements added by Rix.

A study of the plaster cast (which we now know may not be an accurate representation in all areas) illustrates the degree to which erosion had affected the carving by the late nineteenth century, and emphasises that many of the opinions as to the date of the column have been based on questionable evidence found in the above-mentioned drawing. Many of those conclusions may well have been very different if based on a less speculative illustration.[3205] What is clear, however, is that the sculptural decoration on the pillar was, in the main, of particularly high quality, both in design and execution, with the carved

---

[3204] Hall 1865: 28, citing Ewan Christian, *Report on the Proposed Restoration of Wolverhampton Church*, 1852. Christian was architect to the Ecclesiastical Commissioners. A photograph of the plaster cast on the Victoria and Albert Museum website shows a distinct long diagonal scar on the lower part of the column which is not obvious on the column itself.

[3205] For example, the 1913 drawing shows clearly five vandykes with carvings in each, whereas the plaster cast provides evidence for three; though they are likely to have existed there is no trace of the other two.

work deeply cut and the sculptural forms well rounded, even if T. D. Kendrick felt compelled to describe the work as 'a crowded display of finicky decoration'.[3206] We might suppose that the original design was carefully marked out on a flexible skin or cloth, allowing adjustments to be made to ensure that the conjoined rings and lozenges fitted exactly into the circumference of the tapering shaft (no easy task, and far more difficult than on a flat surface), before the design was transferred to the stone. The whole work displays a controlled exhuberance, with complex spirals of coiled foliage incorporating decorative tendrils in repetitively precise patterns, as well as the lively birds and beasts which inhabit the various panels, with bands of five components – lozenges, coiled vine scrolls, back-facing birds and beasts, and more scrolls – decreasing in size towards the top, all set above five hanging triangular pennants or vandykes. The design in its entirety is unquestionably a masterpiece of early art, but that is not to saythat the work is free from incongruities. For example, the 1913 drawing shows the birds and beasts in band E (the second band from the top) enclosed in circular frames. From a study of the plaster cast it is evident, assuming the cast is accurate, that at least two of the frames on the right-hand side of the drawing are far from circular, but take the form of a debased hexagon, with some sections almost straight and others curved. It is difficult to know what to make of these quirks, which are clearly not the result of differential weathering, but they might suggest that the carving could have been carried out when the column was in a vertical position, with the higher levels more difficult to work accurately, or even horizontally with that area underneath, though that is pure speculation.

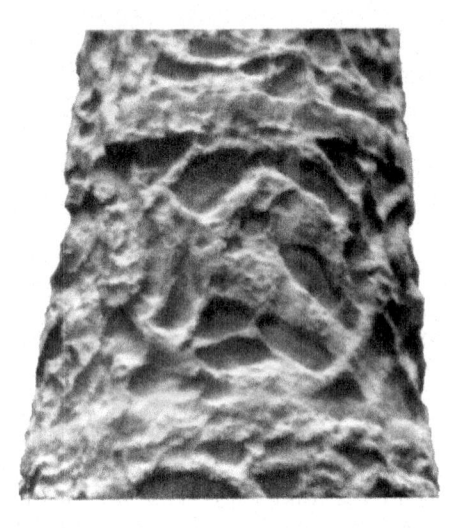

A photograph of the upper section of the cast of the Wolverhampton cross-shaft (the central roundel of Band E in the previous illustration) showing the irregular shape of the framing surrounding a back-facing bird.

The dating of monuments such as cross-shafts is perforce based on analogies between the decoration on the shaft and that of ornament in other dated media such as manuscripts and metalwork, but such methods are often viewed with suspicion by archaeologists and historians, and the science is admittedly inexact. The interpretation of early medieval

---

[3206] Kendrick 1949: 72.

animal art is much debated. Thompson has observed that 'distinguishing between the ornamental and the significant, the traditional and the innovative, the indigenous and the alien, can be a thankless task, based often on intuition as much as any other criterion ... Decorating something ... with plants, animals or human beings brings it to life, investing it with some of the force of the living things depicted'.[3207] Respected authorities on early art and sculpture have not managed to reach a consensus as to the date to the Wolverhampton shaft.

The first published detailed description of the cross can be traced to 1794, when it was noted that 'In the church-yard [of Wolverhampton], almost fronting the South porch, or principal entrance, is a round pillar, about 20 feet high, covered with rude carvings, divided into several compartments. On the North-West face, at the bottom, in the spandrils of a kind of arch, are cut a bird and beast looking back at each other. Above, divided by a narrow band, are other similar figures, or dragons with fore-feet and long tails, in lozenges. Above them, a band of Saxon leaves, and, in lozenges, birds and roses. Over these, a narrow band, and then, in lozenges, beasts or griffins. Another band, and a compartment of rude carvings, and then a regular plain capital. Whether it supported a cross is uncertain. The bottom of the pillar has stone-masonry worked round it to keep it upright. Whether this is a Danish or a Saxon monument is not exactly determined. There is one somewhat like it in Leek church-yard ... and others ruder in that of Checkley, in the same county'.[3208]

Stebbing Shaw, the Staffordshire historian, adopting part of this description, says of the pillar in 1801: 'Whether this is a Danish or Saxon monument is not exactly determined',[3209] but the impressively accurate engraving which appears in his work is nevertheless confidently entitled 'Danish Monument'.[3210] Dr George Oliver, in his undistinguished account of Wolverhampton and its church published in 1836, concluded that 'on the most mature deliberation ... I have ventured to decide that the column was erected by Wulhere, king of Mercia [658-74], in the 7th century, in commemoration of a great victory over the Mercians, which placed him on the throne',[3211] a conclusion typically devoid of any type of evidence. He ventured to suggest that it was extremely probable 'that our pillar was manufactured out of a gigantic rough stone idol, which had existed on the spot from time immemorial; for it is formed of a single block, and is of the soft grit found in the immediate neighbourhood',[3212] a short but fanciful statement which manages to incorporate at least four errors.

When the British Archaeological Association Congress met at Wolverhampton in 1872, Mr E. Roberts expressed the opinion that the pillar was of no later date than the tenth century, with the sculpture 'showing signs of late Norman or transitional feeling', but the baluster shape of the column, he felt, suggested that the work had been carried out on a pillar of earlier date.[3213] Mr G. M. Hills, a respected architectural historian, gave an

---

[3207] Thompson 2002: 132-3.
[3208] By 'R.G.' (Richard Gough, 1735-1809, the noted antiquary and topographer) in GM, August 1794, 714. The description is notable for its accuracy, and for the perceptive analysis of the decoration, which appears to assume a pre-Conquest date.
[3209] Shaw II 1801: 161.
[3210] Shaw II 1801: between 156 and 157.
[3211] Oliver 1936: 140, 169.
[3212] George Oliver (1782-1867) was the arrogant, unpopular, and incompetent Perpetual Curate of St Peter's church in Wolverhampton from 1834 to 1846, and a prolific author of topographical and Masonic works: Mander and Tildesley 1960: 174-5.
[3213] *The Atheneum*, 2339 (24 August 1872) 252.

account not altogether easy to follow, recording 'certain open spaces in the lower part, and then certain figures in the form of half a lozenge. Five of these could be traced half way up, leaving five spaces below for a figure under a canopy. In one of these spaces there were distinct traces of a figure. The figures to be traced above those canopies showed it could not be Danish ... in one the ox of St Luke, in the second the angel of St Matthew, and in the third the lion of St Mark, and in the fourth the emblem of St John, while the fifth was filled with scroll work ... from the absence of a symbol in the fifth canopy ... the crucifixion [might be assumed].' On one panel he 'fancied he saw the remains of a cross, immediately to the right of where the figure would be traced'. He had examined the top of the column and found evidence of provision for the insertion and fixing of other stone, probably a cross, and had no doubt that it was Norman work belonging to the twelfth century.[3214] If he noticed any carving on the capstone he chose not to mention it.

As early as 1877 Charles Lynam questioned the view that the pillar was twelfth century Norman work.[3215] He observed that, while not presuming to contradict a twelfth century origin, 'if such be the date, the whole spirit of its design is altogether of another character to that found in any corresponding work of the same period in the county', and pointed out that the profile of the shaft was certainly not Norman, but of classic type and with classic entasis.

Professor L. Dietrichson expressed the view in about 1880 that there was no semblance of Norse or Danish workmanship on the shaft, and pointed to the cable ornament as as sign of Norman work.[3216]

In 1913 Professor W. R. Lethaby concluded that the column, 'traditionally known as the Danes cross rises from a round stone, 7 ft in diameter, and its form is that of a cylinder, 2 ft 6 in in diameter, tapering towards the neck. Almost the entire surface of the shaft is covered with sculptured ornament of about the year 1150 to 1175 ...'.[3217]

In 1930 Sir Alfred Clapham took the view that the monument was of pre-Conquest date, observing that its decoration combined the Carolingean acanthus (generally dated to the tenth century) with the Anglian beast. He also observed that the vine scroll of Northumbria was still surviving in Mercia and Wessex in the ninth century, and in its most degraded form as a series of circles and rosettes containing rearward-looking beasts it is found on a shaft at Ramsbury, which seems to date from the early tenth century. He felt that the lack of examples in stone-carving was to some extent compensated for by the survival of certain ivories such as crosiers of the tau-form, which he dated to the first half of the eleventh century.[3218]

[3214] JBAA 1873: 106-7. A useful photograph of the column (Plate 3, page 107 of the report) shows vertical striations and marks on the lower part. An earlier part of the report seems to be a misplaced note about the base of the column. It reads 'A hole had been dug to discover if any steps lay beneath the surface, but no other steps had been found; nor had the surface of the ground been added to at all. The pillar was where it was first placed, and where a cross would normally be placed – at the summit of a hill.': ibid. 105.

[3215] JBAA 1877: 38.

[3216] WA I 12 (March 1932): 361-2. In fact cable work is not uncommonly found on Anglo-Saxon sculptural works.

[3217] Lethaby 1913: 158-9.

[3218] Clapham, 1930: 129-131, who notes that the tau-form of crozier survived the Norman Conquest in England but became increasingly uncommon. A dated example is represented on the tomb of

Gerald Mander considered the antiquity of the cross shaft in 1932, and with typical thoroughness corresponded with Clapham, who pointed out that the form and type of decoration was quite unknown in twelfth century England, while the cable ornament, though rare, could be found in both the early and late Anglo-Saxon periods. Mander concluded that 'it can now be attributed with some certainty and even finality to the late Saxon period, and the time of foundation of the church, shortly before 994, offers a very suitable date'.[3219]

Professor G. Baldwin Brown held in 1937[3220] that 'Cylindrical shafts displaying figures under arches or sunk in niches we have got to know as early forms, and they make their appearance at all periods presenting some of their best carved work that comes into view. One piece stands out as by far the most ambitious of this kind, and one of the chefs-d'œvre of the school, complimented, as every Saxon piece of out-of-the-way merit is sure to be, by the attribution to [the twelfth century]. This is the Wolverhampton pillar, best known from the fact that there is a cast of it in the Victoria and Albert Museum. It is a monument of the same general form as the enriched pillars that we have met with so early at Glastonbury and Reculver, and which we find later at Masham in Yorkshire and at other places especially in Mercia. Wolverhampton is called from Wulfruna, sister of Ethelred II [*sic*], who founded a college here in 996. The present fine church of St Peter occupies the site of the religious buildings connected with this foundation, and the enriched pillar may be reasonably claimed as an actual survival of these. It is about 12 ft high and its circumference in the lower part is 8 ft, while it tapers till the upper diameter is little more than half the lower one. This tapering is very Saxon and does not suggest [a twelfth century date]. The enrichment is in a style which in the case of most of it has a certain affinity with the work we have already got to know at Breedon-on-Hill and Fletton by Peterborough. Here are lively animals on a small scale disporting themselves amidst the stems and leaves of a foliage that in general effect resembles that on the base at the panel at Hovingham as well as some of the Breedon work. The animals turn back their heads in a manner that is very marked and characteristic of the Saxon period. A date of the late [tenth century] would suit it well enough. The one reason (besides its artistic excellence) for putting the monument as late as this is the appearance on it of the acanthus ornament in the form of stiff upright leaves that encircle it as well as in that of scrolls and flourishes. It is true that the acanthus makes no appearance in Saxon decorative stone-work in general, till we come to the curious Thrybergh stone, but it is freely used in other forms of art in Saxon times and can quite easily be accepted here. It must be noted that this Wolverhampton acanthus is of a type which resembles the Norman version of the motive, and does not suggest the crude and tentative handling which we found at Thrybergh. ... The original monument is very much blackened by weathering, and this gives a special value to the reproduction in the Victoria and Albert Museum. ... [With] the enriched shafts and pillars at Sandbach and Stapleford (Notts.) ... these monuments may be regarded as Mercian specialities.'[3221]

Abbot Isarn of St Victor, Marseilles, and another in the tomb of Abbot Morard of St Germain, Paris, who died in 1014.
[3219] WA I 12 (March 1932): 361-2.
[3220] Baldwin Brown 1937: 272-3.
[3221] This comment is hardly material if the shaft is a re-used Roman column. The Stapleford cross has a similar profile to the Wolverhampton shaft, with the lower part round in section with small squarish panels of profuse but crude interlace decoration, divided by double horizontal ring moulding. The upper part is square section above three horizontal rings around the shaft, with upward-curving mouldings above the rings, forming four rectangular panels, three contaning interlace work, but the one on the south containing a strange flat figure which might be an angel. The top of the cross is

T. D. Kendrick, writing in 1838 and 1949,[3222] concluded that the Wolverhampton shaft was unquestionably the noblest monument that has come down to us from the pre-Alfredian sculptures of the West Saxon supremacy, illustrating, better than all else, the gaily ornate style of the period of King Æthelwulf of Wessex (839-58) or his sons Athelbald and Alfred,[3223] a style that sought so often to express itself in the terms of the then fashionable Continental art. He believed there was nothing quite like it in England, though it was possible that the heavily decorated round-shaft crosses in the north, such as that at Masham, may to some extent reflect an analogous contemporary taste in another province.[3224] He felt that part of the decorative treatment was characteristic of the ninth century, noting that the column is 'the only carving in England to give adequate impression of the southern Continental 'Baroque' art of the mid-9th century', and in his view the object should be placed late in the ninth century. It had tenth-century traits (a date which had been suggested by Rosemary Cramp), the birds in some of the triangular fields being very similar to those that appear, for example, on the Canterbury censer-cover, which is usually considered to be of tenth-century date, and believed '[a] date within twenty-five years of 900 would be perfectly acceptable for the Wolverhampton Pillar'.[3225]

In 1952 Talbot-Rice mentioned the pillar briefly in his survey of English art from the late ninth to the end of the twelfth century, simply observing that Carolingian ornament, predominant in illustration and used frequently on figured slabs, is also to be seen from time to time on crosses, citing that at Wolverhampton. He observed that it is extremely hard to say whether individual examples were derived from old Northumbrian prototypes or were the result of an independent tenth-century influence from the Continent.[3226]

Lawrence Stone expressed the view in the mid 1950s that '... the round-shafted crosses at Masham in Yorkshire, and more particularly at Wolverhampton, are two of the largest monuments of the [ninth century]. The Wolverhampton cross, itself possibly a re-used Roman column from Uriconium [*Viroconium*], with its horizontal zonal divisions, its rich decorative patterns, its contorted and rampant Mercian animals, its fleshy Frankish acanthus scrolls and its ornamental triangular pendants, provides an extraordinary combination of motifs drawn from a wide range of sources but all welded into a whole by reduction to lush surface pattern'.[3227] He added that 'The first round-shaft cross of which we know is that at Reculver which, it has been suggested, took its inspiration from the carved pillar known to the Carolingian Rhineland. Another type, however, appears in the ninth century, of which the best example is the Mercian pillar at Wolverhampton, which may be dated to the middle of the century'.[3228]

---

missing. The shaft has been assigned to the same 11th-century group as the Leek shaft: Kerr and Kerr 1982: 72.
[3222] Kendrick 1938: 192.
[3223] Ethelwulf succeeded his father in 839, and was deposed by his eldest son Ethelbald in 856. Another son, Ethelred, was king from 865-871, succeeded by Alfred, the youngest son, who reigned from 871 to 899.
[3224] The decoration of the shaft at Masham includes animalistic figures in one of the encircling bands of arcading, but otherwise bears little resemblance to the decoration on the Wolverhampton column. It has been assumed to be part of a staff rood cross with a tapering square-section upper part surmounted by a large cross-head, part of which survives: Collingwood 1927: 6-7.
[3225] Kendrick 1938: 192-3; Kendrick 1949: 71-2, Plate XLVI.
[3226] Talbot-Rice 1952: 136.
[3227] Stone 1955: 238.
[3228] Stone 1955: 239.

In 1974 Nikolaus Pevsner published the Staffordshire volume in his esteemed series on the buildings of England, recording his opinion that the Wolverhampton cross-shaft was of mid-ninth century date, the rather wild acanthus ornament betraying Carolingian inspiration,[3229] and John Roper suggested subsequently that the shaft may be an indication of royal patronage, to be seen as evidence of Christian activity at Wolverhampton prior to Wulfrun's foundation of the minster.

In his detailed survey of Anglo-Saxon art published in 1984, David Wilson, describing the Wolverhampton column as 'a chronological enigma', observed that: 'One of the grandest [Anglo-Saxon] monuments is ... so worn that it is now virtually impossible to distinguish the details of the ornament. This is the Wolverhampton round-shaft. Here is displayed (and can still be faintly seen, particularly on the cast taken in the 1880s [sic] for the Victoria and Albert Museum) something of the same panelled style seen in the Canterbury Bible and on the Trewhiddle horn mounts and the same or related animal ornament. It also bears an acanthus-like leaf ornament which is clearly derived from Carolingian prototypes'.[3230]

In 1992 Professor Rosemary Cramp noted that the the column showed even in its worn condition a quality of carving and distinction of iconography unmatched in cross sculpture in the Midlands. She believed it obvious that it had been put up to commemorate some major event, and that the classical appearance was perhaps emphasised because it seemed to be a Roman column re-used, but was mainly produced by the crisp zones of plant ornament. The decoration was much more like Carolingian than English work, since rosette centerings are common on Carolingian stucco and ivories, and if the bronze screens from the palatine chapel at Aachen were accepted as a Carolingian copy of the antique then they parallel the method of binding with rosettes the inhabited and plain running scrolls on the Wolverhampton column. Nevertheless the Palatine scroll was still partly a vinescroll, and the Wolverhampton foliage more like the acanthus border on the mid-ninth century ivory from Metz. The birds and beasts in the lozenges, Anglian in type, were to be compared with Breedon, at least in their placing. Though so worn as to show no minor detail, the absence of a camouflaging growth of plant scroll at Wolverhampton was more like English work of the ninth century than of the later tenth, and she cited as an example the ivory penner from London, or the Corpus Christi Bede, CCCC 183. The reason she was uncertain whether a ninth-century date might be assumed was the stance of the small birds in zone B reaching down and pecking with exaggeratedly open beaks, an attitude common in tenth- to early-eleventh century manuscripts such as the Bosworth psalter, and also on metalwork such as the Canterbury censer cover. If the Wolverhampton column were to be dated a century earlier it would represent the earliest surviving example of this design. There was no evidence that crosses were set up at the foundation of monasteries except those, usually with inscriptions, associated with monastic burial grounds, but the Wolverhampton column could be an imitation of Continental carved columns, for example that at Trier, dated 958. She felt the Wolverhampton piece was a royal monument, an 'exotic outlier' from the main sphere of Wessex art, which had no obvious copies in the area unless one the crude round shafts of the West Midlands are derived from its form, but even in that group the top of the shaft differs. Built into the south porch at Avebury is an undatable fragment of an architectural sculpture with similar stiff acanthus as on zone C at Wolverhampton. She cited round shafts in Wessex such as the ninth-century example from Winchester with palmette trees and stag, or the possibly eleventh-century shaft from

---

[3229] Pevsner 1974: 315.
[3230] Wilson 1984: 105.

Yetminster (Dorset), but preferred to see the Wolverhampton shaft as 'a revival of the antique in the tenth century rather than a precocious ninth-century copy of Carolingian work', concluding that 'the case must rest as not proven'.[3231]

Cramp also cautioned that 'Rix's reconstruction with a square-sectioned shaft above the collar is no more certain than that the shaft was simply capped by a cross head in the manner of the Trier shaft',[3232] and subsequently observed that the Wolverhampton column, possibly of the ninth/tenth century, 'has been seen as a royal monument, and it may be noted that William of Malmesbury recorded that King Edgar was originally buried in capitulo, translated ... as 'in a column', before the church at Glastonbury ... [which] was traditionally a Celtic foundation, had a variety of recorded funerary monuments, and may well have kept the ancient tradition of marking royal graves with a column'.[3233]

More recently, Richard Jewell has expressed the view that the cross-shaft is the finest surviving example of tenth- and eleventh-century Anglo-Carolingian Winchester-style decorative sculpture, a tenth-century successor to the friezes at Breedon on the Hill, and which, like them, has no sculptural parallels in the south of England.[3234] Dominic Tweddle considers that the decoration on band B on the column is reflected to a degree in the decoration on a square-section cross shaft from Cross on Tees, North Yorkshire, which has been held to be 'more closely related to southern English fashions than those of Northumbria. Both the semi-naturalistic animals and the leaf forms of the scrolls, for example, lie close in spirit to those of the south-west Mercia material, even if the detailing is different.'[3235] He sees the column as the best example of a significant new form of cross shaft, consisting of a round shaft of circular section and columnar form, introduced in the ninth century, but concedes that its decoration, consisting of animal and plant ornament is unusual, and suggests that it is likely that this type, which in its pure form was never common, was intended to be a Christian version of the triumphal columns of the Roman emperors in Rome and Constaninople,[3236] while Karkov and Brown suggest that 'the cylindrical shape of the ninth century monuments that once stood at Reculver and Dewsbury, and still stand at Mallam and Wolverhampton, with the decoration arranged in horizontal registers were in all probability intended to replicate the triumphal monumental columna of the Roman world'.[3237] John Hunt, dating the column to the late ninth or tenth century, notes that it reflects influences from the south of England and Carolingian Europe, and that the cable-moulding, lozenge-shaped panels with characteristically Mercian

---

[3231] Cramp 1992.

[3232] Cramp 1975: 187-9; 245. The Trier pillar is in the centre of the *Haupmarkt*, or main square, and is in the form of a cylindrical stone column surmounted by a capital and cross which supposedly signifies the rights of the town to hold a market: see Baldwin Brown 1937: 106-7 and plate XXVIII. Nancy Edwards has noted that there were pillars topped by crosses at an early date in the Holy Land, with a large marble column surmounted by an iron cross recorded just outside Jerusalem c.570, and a column near the Holy Sepulchre, mentioned by Adomnán and Bede, which had an image of Christ on the top crowned by a cross. Edwards surmises that an *ampulla* from the Holy Land dated to the 6th century which includes a depiction of a pillar with a cross on top may have been the type of portable souvenir which could have inspired the introduction of round shafted crosses in England: Edwards 2009: 170.

[3233] Cramp 2006: 31.

[3234] Jewell 2001: 262. The worn base frieze on the slab from Hovingham, North Yorkshire, is reminiscent of band E of the Wolverhampton column: Collingwood 1927: 43, 72.

[3235] Dominic Tweddle in Webster and Backhouse 1991: 153.

[3236] Webster and Backhouse 1991: 242.

[3237] Karkov and Brown 2003: 78-9.

'Anglian beasts', foliage, and bird and beast carvings suggests a decorative scheme perhaps based on some kind of processional cross with applied metal plaques.[3238]

In summary, the above opinions can conveniently be tabulated as follows:

Gough	1794	pre-Conquest
Oliver	1836	7th century
Roberts	1872	10th–12th century
Hills	1872	12th century
Dietrichson	c.1880	Norman
Lethaby	1913	1150–1175
Clapham	1930	9th century – 1050
Mander	1932	late 10th century
Baldwin	1937	late 10th century
Kendrick	1938	9th century
Talbot-Rice	1952	–
Stone	1955	mid-9th century
Rix	1960	c.850
Pevsner	1974	mid-9th century
Cramp	1975/2006	9th–10th century
Wilson	1984	875–925
Tweddle	1991	9th century
Jewell	2001	10th–11th century
Karkov and Brown	2003	9th century
Hunt	2014	late 9th–10th century

It will be seen that the majority of more recent expert opinion, inevitably conflicting in many areas, dates the cross-shaft somewhere between c.800 and 1100, with the emphasis centering around the ninth century.

The undecorated lower part of the Wolverhampton shaft and its tapering shape are certainly reminiscent of the widely-spread group of Anglo-Saxon cross-shafts found as far south as Chebsey in mid-Staffordshire and north into Cumbria (taking in the Eliseg pillar) which Collingwood categorised as 'Staff Rood Crosses',[3239] characterised by roughly triangular pendants, such as those on cross shafts from Stanwick in the North Riding of Yorkshire, and at Leek, both perhaps dating from the year 1000 or later.[3240] However, the Wolverhampton shaft is atypical in its decoration, for there is no obvious trace of interlace or knotwork decoration, and the decoration is, unusually, in horizontal bands, rather than the far more common arrangement where the design is vertical on square or rectangular section shafts. We have seen that G. F. Browne recorded in the 1880s that on the bevelled

---

[3238] Hunt 2014: 33.
[3239] Collingwood 1927: 5.
[3240] Triangular pendants or 'vandykes' are commonly found as decorative devices to fill the space between an area of decoration on a column, shaft or globular object and the undecorated part, or to mark the edge of a metal mount on a cylindrical object, or to act as a terminal to a decorated or shaped area, for example the cross shafts at Sockburn, Lastingham, Brompton and Hawkser, all in Yorkshire: Bailey 1980: 188. Well-known examples are the great silver-mounted drinking horns and maplewood bottles from Sutton Hoo; the stave-built wooden bucket from grave 600 at Mucking in Essex, dating from the 6th century, which incorporates vandykes with face masks; the drinking horns from Prittlewell, c.610; and the drinking horn with silver mount incorporating vandykes with helmeted figures from the richly-furnished 7th century grave at Taplow in Buckinghamshire.

surface of the heavy cap were signs of interlacing work, though no such details are visible today, and interlace may once have existed within one of the badly worn vandykes. Most signficantly, and as noted by Browne, there is no evidence of any human representation or inscription, and the capstone has no exact parallel elsewhere, for the 'staff rood crosses' are in one piece and have an upper section, above a plain or multiple banded or decorated collar – the 'collared derivative round shaft' in Cramp's classification[3241] – that develops into a square cross-section with curved swags, a feature for which there is no evidence on the Wolverhampton shaft, for the nature of the top section (if any) is unknown.

In his widely-researched paper on the column published in 1960,[3242] Michael Rix, carefully analysing the stylistic evidence, held that the horizontal bands of decoration and the pendant triangles were reminiscent of a processional cross, and raised the possibility that an exchange of gifts between Charlemagne and Offa might have led to the introduction into England of a metalwork treasure that could have provided inspiration for the Wolverhampton cross. He suggested that the Leek shaft might have been a direct descendant of the Wolverhampton column, and drew parallels with other works of art, inluding Anglo-Saxon sculpture, metalwork and ivories, concluding that the column probably dated from c.850 AD. Yet whilst Rix's dating might be correct, there must be considerable doubt about some of his supposed parallels. For example, he likens the panels in band B to the decoration on a brooch dated from about 874 found at Beeston Tor in Staffordshire in 1926, and in particular notes that the beast by the tip of the pin on the smaller brooch has a trifurcating tail as has what has been identified as a bull (which seems to be without the usual wings) in one of the pendant triangles. In fact the supposed bull, which might be one of the best preserved parts of the sculpture, has what appears to be a bifurcating tail, the lower part of which ends in a fish tail, but the beast on the brooch (which, contrary to Rix's claim, has little resemblance to the beasts on the Wolverhampton shaft) has a tail that consists of three separate round-ended petals.[3243] The design of the brooches from Beeston has little or no similarity to the designs of the Wolverhampton shaft. In the case of the triangular pendants or vandykes, Rix cites the Copenhagen Fragment (which he illustrates), a metal collar seemingly from a wooden crozier or pastoral stave, probably of Irish origin, which he says is clearly seen to consist of a series of pendant triangles, but which we can see has commonly-found curvilinear decoration terminating in four round-ended pendants. A far closer parallel would be the silver-gilt mount from the Taplow drinking horn, dating from the early sixth century.[3244] Rix's paper serves, in fact, to emphasise the difficulty in identifying parallels for the designs on the Wolverhampton cross.

A superficial resemblance to the animals and birds which appear in the deep cutting of the Wolverhampton carvings is found in the well-known group of architectural friezes from the church at Breedon on the Hill in Leicestershire, some 35 miles from Wolverhampton, which are held to date from the late eighth or early ninth century, and in the birds and beasts on the cross-shaft of the late eighth or early ninth century from Croft-on-Tees in North Yorkshire.[3245] The tapering square-section Easby cross from North Yorkshire, dated to c.800-20, has a variety of decorative forms, including interlace and figural heads, but one side has a panel showing birds in a vine scroll with similarities to the Wolverhampton

---

[3241] Cramp 1984: xiv-xv.
[3242] Rix 1960: 71-81.
[3243] Rix 1960: 74; Webster and Backhouse 1991: 269-70.
[3244] Webster 2012: 58.
[3245] Cramp and Lang 1977 (unpaginated).

carvings, and indeed the corners of the column carry cable moulding similar to the cable band on the Wolverhampton shaft.[3246]

The evidence from Western Mercia seems to indicate that at least by the ninth century, sculpture, especially in the form of crosses, was found not only at central minster sites, but at monastic dependencies and probably elsewhere.[3247] In the West Midlands a style developed from at least c.800 and continued throughout the ninth century, paralleled on the continent, in which sculpture, metalwork and manuscripts incorporating animals became increasingly widespread during that century, and sculptural carvings, found across most of south-west Mercia and Wessex (like the Wolverhampton cross shaft) are notable for the absence of human figures.[3248] Cable moulding, once thought to exclude an Anglo-Saxon date for the Wolverhampton column, is in fact not uncommon in Anglo-Saxon sculpture: as noted previously, two cross-shafts with cable-moulding from St Oswald's Priory, Gloucester, have been given a date-range of the late 8th to the early 11th century, with c.850 perhaps the most likely date.[3249] Although as noted above 'staff-rood' crosses are found in Northern England as far south as Chebsey, with outliers in Wales, not a single round-shafted Anglo-Saxon column is found in Gloucestershire, Herefordshire, Shropshire, Warwickshire or Worcestershire,[3250] again emphasising the unique form of the Wolverhampton column. Nancy Edwards, discussing the Pillar of Eliseg, observes that the round-shafted cross is a unique form in Wales (apart from the later shaft near Corwen), and notes rather bravely that '[t]hough there were Anglo-Saxon round-shafted crosses of ninth-century date, none is known from north-west Mercia, where surviving monuments may be dated to the tenth or eleventh centuries', adding that other ninth-century crosses from elsewhere in Anglo-Saxon England could have partly inspired the form of the Eliseg Pillar.[3251] There is no mention of the Wolverhampton column.

Not all monumental stone columns stood outdoors. The fragmentary Reculver cross-shaft has been referred to by some of the authorities cited earlier. That fragment (now preserved in the crypt of Canterbury cathedral) is believed to have been carved from an old Roman column and was erected originally behind the altar at Reculver. The stylistic evidence and Carolingian parallels for the draped figures of saints or evangelists have led to a suggested late eighth- or early ninth-century date. With a strong Mercian tradition of stone sculpture in the eighth century, it has been suggested that the cross was set up while Reculver was under Mercian control. The minster at Winchcombe in Gloucestershire, associated with King Coenwulf (796-821), who may have founded it, is likely to have been the king's chief minster – it held his family deeds, and he was buried there – and could have housed an altar dedicated to the Holy Cross. Reculver would seem to have been another of Coenwulf's minsters (his brother Cuthred had been king of Kent until he died in 807), and

---

[3246] Broad outer cable moulding appears on the corners of two sections of cross-shaft, one with cable-moulded horizontal panel dividers, one from St Oswald's Priory, Gloucester, and the other probably part of the same cross which was amongst the hundreds of wagon-loads of stones and rubble removed from the Priory for road repair in 1655-6. A date-range of the late 8th to the early 11th century has been proposed for the shaft, with c.850 perhaps the most likely date: Bryant 2012: 221-4.
[3247] Bryant 2012: 22. Of particular interest is a fragment from the church at Llanrhaeadr-Ym-Mochnant, near Oswestry, 41cms x 30cms, apparently hollowed out at some date, of what seems to have been a cylindrical cross-shaft in 'striking red sandstone', originally some 90cms (3') in diameter and dated to the 9th century: Higham 2002: 174.
[3248] Hunt 2009: 200.
[3249] Bryant 2012: 221-4.
[3250] Bryant 2012: 49.
[3251] Edwards 2009: 169.

it has been suggested that the erection of a massive cross there may have reflected Winchcombe's influence.[3252]

By comparison with other decorative elements from sculpture, metalwork, manuscripts and textiles it may be possible to suggest the earliest probable date for the Wolverhampton sculpture, but it is far more difficult to postulate an actual date, for archaic designs may have been resurrected by sculptors many decades or even centuries after they were originally introduced, just as the various styles of post-Conquest medieval architecture continued in use into modern times.[3253] Furthermore, the particular shape, size and iconography of the carvings at Wolverhampton, greatly exacerbated by their eroded condition, make comparisons from artefactual designs problematic. However, a close parallel with some of the animal designs may be detected in a small ivory reliquary casket dating from c.900 from St Peter's at Salzburg, now held in the Metropolitan Museum of Art in New York. The casket contains backward-looking animals with narrowing torsos in similar poses in diamond- or lozenge-shaped frames on the face of the main box, and indeed what appear to be studs at the angles of the lozenges on the casket are mirrored in the carved foliates on the angles of the lozenges on the Wolverhampton shaft, although those are placed where adjoining lozenges meet. The casket has backward-facing birds in circular foliage frames similar to, but not identical with, the Wolverhampton carvings, on the front of the sloping roof of the box. The carving on the casket, which is rather less exuberant in design than the Wolverhampton carving, 'displays a very characteristic late Carolingian combination of foliage work, animal forms, and earlier circular patterns. After the increasing adoption of Roman formal language transmitted via Byzantium, earlier stylistic trends were beginning to make themselves felt again here. The earlier language had never become entirely extinct; nor was it, like the art of the Court School, restricted to a relatively limited circle. It remained particularly strong in the artistic centers outside the court, where it continued to prevail in later times'.[3254]

[3252] Kelly 2008a: 68-9, 80-1; Webster 2012: 90. John Leland was clearly impressed by the column when he visited Reculver in 1540, for he records: 'Yn the enteryng of the quyer ys one of the fayrest and the most auncyent crosse that ever I saw, a ix footes, as I ges, yn highte. It standeth lyke a fayr columne. The base greate stone ys not wrought. The second stone being rownd hath curiously wrought and paynted the images of Christ, Peter, Paule, John and James, as I remember. Christ sayeth [I am the Alpha and the Omega]. Peter sayeth, [You are Christ, son of the living God]. The saing of the other iij when painted [was in Roman capitals] but now obliterated. The second stone is of the Passion. The third conteineth the xii Apostles. The iiii hath the image of Christ hanging and fastened with iiii nayles and [a support beneath the feet]. the hiest part of the pyller hath the figure of a crosse.': Leland 1540: IV 59-60. Fragments of a similar column have been found at Hillborough, a mile south-west of Reculver: Kelly 2008a: 68-9.

[3253] The portal arch of the church of Saint-Marie-des-Dames at Saintes (Charente-Maritime), France, incorporates back-facing beasts within sub-circular roundels connected by animal-head bosses, has been dated to the mid-12th century: Sourchal 1968: 61. Very similar decoration is found on the portal arch of the church of Auley-de-Saintonge, Collégiale Saint-Pierre-de-la-Tour, dated to c.1130: Duby 1979: 90.

[3254] Backes and Dölling: 1969: 133. Some elements of design at this period may have derived from examples of richly patterned Islamic textiles which reached the West, and in that respect we might note the detail of rows of small beaded medallions containing beasts in a richly worked chasuble from the parish church of St Catherine's in Maaseik, Belgium, probably made in England in the late eighth or early ninth century, which incorporates flat embroidery of threads wrapped with gold, with variously coloured silk threads, the earliest known example of a technique known as *opus anglicanum* (English work): Wilson 1984: 108; Ford 1988: 175; Nees 2002: 126-7, which gives an illustration.

One of the birds on the Easby panel bears close comparison to the same subject depicted on a Carolingian ivory panel of the ninth century in the Vatican Museums,[3255] which shows birds in lobed vine scroll panels, which in turn echoes the carving on the Wolverhampton cross-shaft. Furthermore, the Vatican panel has a border incorporating at intervals an acanthus decoration identical to that in Band C of the Wolverhampton shaft. This must be seen as important evidence for the dating of the Wolverhampton shaft, for the panel combines in a single object three significant elements also found in the Wolverhampton carvings: gracefully sinuous lobed vine scrolls forming circular frames; active beasts and birds, one back-facing; and a border incorporating acanthus leaves, with a bold single acanthus forming a centrepiece to the upper frame. Carolingian panels of the mid- and later-ninth century often incorporated acanthus decorated borders,[3256] for example in a ninth-century German ivory panel of Christ in Majesty from the FitzWilliam Museum in Cambridge[3257] which has in the spandrels the symbols of the three evangelists (which may also have been found on the Wolverhampton column), with the fourth, St Matthew, appearing as himself, the whole framed in a border of formal acanthus leaves very much like the band on the Wolverhampton cross. Other comparable decoration may be seen in the framing border of the well-known illustration of Æthelstan presenting the volume of Bede's *Life of St Cuthbert*, probably dating to c.934.[3258] The birds and beasts of zone E of the Wolverhampton column seem to be echoed in the decorative border of an ivory panel from a (late?) eighth-century Anglo-Saxon casket, now in the Bayerisches Nationalmuseum in Munich, where vine scrolls contain backward-looking birds and animals biting the scroll terminals which take the form of bunches of grapes or leaves.[3259] The foliate scrolls in bands D and G have a close parallel in the design of interconnected complex scrolls containing birds and beasts which are found on the sword sheath covered in stamped gold probably given to Essen c.1000 by the abbess Matilda, a grand-daughter of Otto I by his English wife.[3260] Another similar inhabited scroll is found on a border of a gospel book of Odbert, dating from 986-1008.[3261]

But we have more relevant and dramatic parallels for major elements on the Wolverhampton cross far closer to home than Salzburg. Within 50 miles of Wolverhampton are two famed and closely studied Anglo-Saxon cross-shafts and associated cross fragments which incorporate several sculptural ingredients with the closest affinity to the Wolverhampton shaft. These are at Sandbach in south-east Cheshire where two carved stone shafts of medium-fine yellow sandstone (not dismilar to the stone of the Wolverhampton column) have been re-erected in the market place, having been reconstructed from pieces recovered from as far away as Tarporley (12 miles to the west) and Oulton Park (3 miles north-east of Tarporley). It is miraculous that those fragments survive. One of the shafts is topped by the remains of a cross-head from a third, now lost and smaller, monument, with the fragments of three further shafts and a coped tombstone set in the nearby churchyard. The shafts are of a type associated with important pre-Viking ecclesiastical enclosures: Sandbach may have been an early minster. In the Middle Ages,

---

[3255] Davies and Kennedy 2009: 148-9.
[3256] Swarzenski 1974: Figs. 32-34, 36, 45-6; Duby 1986: 38; Chastel 1994: 66, 68.
[3257] Collection ref: M.14-1904 (Applied Arts).
[3258] Brown 2007: 109 Plate 79.
[3259] Beckwith 1974: 26; Campbell 1991: 117. The central motif in the lower border happens to be a bull's head.
[3260] Swarzenski 1974: plate 44, no. 100; Campbell 1982: 171.Matilda was also a distant relative of the chronicler Æthelweard, to whom he dedicated his translation of the *Anglo-Saxon Chronicle* which contains valuable information relating to the battle of Tettenhall: Campbell 1962: xii-xiii..
[3261] Swarzenski 1974: plate 69, no. 160.

and was certainly the centre of a large parish, and whilst little is known about the scale of such important early churches or of the buildings associated with them, it is clear that they were often associated with large and impressive sculptured crosses, but we have no evidence of the original site of those at Sandbach.[3262]

The crosses and associated fragments have been subjected to meticulous study by Jane Hawkes, to whom we are indebted for a painstaking analysis of their sculptural repertoire. What is clear is that designs on the southernmost (and shorter) of the two tapering square-section crosses, some 10½' high, incorporate significant elements found on the Wolverhampton column. Vertical cable moulding forms the corners of the shaft, and each side is divided into geometrical compartments, with a row of vertically-arranged linked lozenge frames (rather than lozenges in a horizontal band as at Wolverhampton) on stones I to IV on the south-east face. Like the lozenges on the Wolverhampton column, those frames incorporate bosses at the intersections and at each of the side angles of the rhomboids, but enclose human figures and the outline of a prancing heraldic beast with a back-turned head, evidently very similar to beasts in B and E of the Wolverhampton column. Within the triangles formed between the lozenges and outer border are human figures and scrolled foliate decoration, and a backward-turning ribbon beast with its body entwined in interlace and a prancing beast with fore- and hind-quarters and a small curled lapper emerging from the back of the neck.[3263]

Though puzzlingly omitting even the slightest reference to the Wolverhampton cross-shaft in her extensive researches, despite parallels with that column and the Sandbach monuments noted by earlier commentators,[3264] Hawkes places considerable emphasis on the geometric frames and panels at Sandbach within which specific carvings are placed, commenting on 'the visually prominent effect of the framework and its unique status (not just at Sandbach, but within the extant Anglo-Saxon sculpture generally)', and notes that '[t]he use of lozenge shapes intersected by prominent bosses ... is rare in [Anglo-Saxon] sculptural contexts, but it is not unusual in metalwork contexts' (citing the late ninth-century fuller brooch and the late eighth-century Tassilo Chalice in the Benedictine monastery at Kremsmunster, Austria, with its rhomboids and bosses on the stem beneath prominent interlinked circular frames on the bowl and foot, its decoration strongly influenced by English work, and perhaps the work of a Continental artist trained by an [unknown] Anglo-Saxon master),[3265] and observes that 'the act of compartmentalising the decoration seems to have been the foremost principle of design. To enclose the decoration regardless of the disposition and shape of the frame, to incorporate all possible varieties of frame, was such a primary consideration that the distinctive layout may not even be a reflex of cultural or regional indentity'.[3266] The animals contained within and flanking the lozenges find their best parallels in Mercian and southern English work of the ninth century rather the later eighth'.[3267]

[3262] VCH Cheshire I 276-7.
[3263] Hawkes 2002: 97-103, 138-9, 164.
[3264] See for example VCH Cheshire I 276-7.
[3265] Campbell 1982: 109; Hawkes 2001: 96, 236. Patrick Wormald also notes that the Gandersheim Casket [from Gandersheim Abbey in Germany], and the Rupert Cross [from Bischofshofen near Salzburg] show strong English influence, if not of English manufacture, demonstrating the Anglo-Saxon impact on Continental culture, though they cannot be associated with any personality: Campbell 1981: 107.
[3266] Hawkes 2001: 235-6.
[3267] Hawkes 2002: 94.

Again in the context of the Sandbach crosses, Hawkes raises the possibility that '[t]hrough the use of rare and up-to-date iconographic schemes, the centres responsible ... may have been consciously expressing links with specific centres of prestige in the Carolingian world', noting that historically that is not entirely unfeasible: during the reign of the Mercian kings Offa (757-96) and Coenwulf (796-821), the height of the Mercian Supremacy, there was constant contact with the Carolingian court, particularly between 787 and 803 when papal envoys accompanied those from Gaul when the Mercian see was elevated to the status of an archbishopric, reduced by Coenwulf in 803.[3268] The contacts so established, with visits to and from papal representatives and Carolingian regal and ecclesiastical dignitaries, would have provided every opportunity for the transmission of knowledge relating to the production of images in the Carolingian world, especially those produced in royal foundations. For the iconographic sources of the crosses we must look to the gospel-books, ivories, and textiles brought back to the Lichfield diocese, and to designs of mosaics and sarcophagi recorded or described by pilgrims and traders from Rome and beyond.

The Carolingian empire is named after Charles Martel ('The Hammer'), bastard son of Pepin II, who with his son Pepin III the Short (751-68) greatly strengthened and enlarged the Frankish kingdom. On Pepin's death his son Charles (Charlemagne) continued the Frankish expansion, and on Christmas Day 800 was crowned Holy Roman Emperor by a Pope, with the papacy under his control. Charlemagne, with great energy, consolidated his kingdom, which extended to Byzantium, and it is from that period that Byzantine influences in Frankish and English art are found. Under Charlemagne's rule and with his personal encouragement the visual arts flourished to an extent unknown in the west since the end of the old Roman Empire. Byzantine sculptorscreated no monumental works of a kind found in ancient Egypt, Greece and Rome, preferring to work in ivory or precious metals of unparalleled richness and technical virtuosity on a smaller scale, as with ivory carvings deeply undercut to give their designs better prominence. Their churches avoided representations of the human form, with sculpture limited to pillars, low partitions and altar frontals with interlacing patterns, birds and geometrical fugures.Carolingian art, adopting elements of Byzantine iconongraphy, was marked by the strong personality of Charlemagne and the active involvement of his court in artistic creation, with sculptural objects such as reliquaries richly decorated with antique arrangements derived from Roman and early Christian triumphal forms foreshadowing the monumental iconography of the great Romanesque portals. Since the Carolingians had no flourishing artistic tradition of their own they turned abroad, as Charlemagne had done for some of his scholars, such as Alcuin from England. Italy was their most obvious choice for art, and in that respect Nancy Edwards considers that the form of the Anglo-Saxon round-shafted cross was probably derived in part from Roman victory colums such as Trajan's Column, the Column of Marcus Aurelius, or the Roman column which was salvaged and set up in the Roman forum in 608 to praise the exploits of the Byzantine Emperor Phocas, all of which will have been notable landmarks seen by later travellers in Rome.[3269]

Another influence on Anglo-Saxon art and sculpture was the early Christian art of the British Isles: it was Irish and Anglo-Saxon missionaries who had brought the Christian faith to parts of the Carolingian empire, and with it their own tradition of art. British art that existed on the Continent even before the time of Charlemagne was further replenished

---

[3268] It is worth recording that Coenwulf led a Mercian army into Snowdonia in 816, perhaps via the West Midlands.
[3269] Edwards 2009: 169-70.

from England during the Carolingian Renaissance itself. The earliest school of Carolingian painting at this period was not monastic, but attached to the court of Charlemagne and is traditionally known as the 'Ada School' (which lasted for some three decades) from a poem at the end of one manuscript which refers to a certain 'Ada the handmaid of God', perhaps a sister of Charlemagne. Seven complete manuscripts of the Ada School survive, all lavishly written in gold and silver, with opulent full-page illustrations.[3270] One, the Lorsch Gospels, contains an illustration of Christ in Majesty. The border consists, unusually, of lozenges with small circles at the intersections and angles, and is quite clearly a two-dimensional reprentation of a decorative metal frame with the circles denoting studs.[3271] The Gospels have been placed in the early ninth century, reinforcing Hawkes' dating of the Sandbach crosses.[3272]

Hawkes speculates that the Sandbach sculptures might be seen as the articulation of the continuing aspirations of the senior clergy in the region in the early years of the ninth century after Lichfield lost its archbishopric, and that specific prestigious Carolingian images of ecclesiastical authority were being adopted as part of that agenda, an idea that fits with what is known of the Mercian royal and ecclesiastical establishment of the late eighth- and early ninth centuries anxious to imitate artefacts both prestigious and Carolingian.[3273] The craftsmen responsible for the Sandbach crosses may have been consciously expressing their links with specific centres of prestige in the Carolingian world. Like Sandbach, Wolverhampton, of course, lies within the Mercian diocese of Lichfield.

The emphasis placed by Hawkes on the lozenge framing at Sandbach, said to be of 'unique status', is of exceptional significance and has an especial relevance in the light not only of the sequence of lozenges containing animal figures on the Wolverhampton cross-shaft, but of the emphatic horizontal bands of frame-shapes on the column, which would make it, with Sandbach, the only known example of Anglo-Saxon sculpture with lozenge framework and prominent bosses at intersections and angles as part of its design. The back-facing beast[3274] within a lozenge frame with distinctive bosses on the South Cross at Sandbach is mirrored exactly in back-facing beasts within lozenges in Band B at Wolverhampton, and the bold tree scrolls enclosing birds and beasts on the North Cross have close parallels with Bands D, E and G on the Wolverhampton column, though human figures carved at Sandbach are not to be found – or at least have not been recognised – at Wolverhampton.[3275] Vertical heavy cable moulding is found forming the arris on both the North and the South Cross – which clearly originate from the same sculptural centre – echoing the pronounced horizontal cable moulding at Wolverhampton. All these are surely

---

[3270] It may be noted that a number of illustrations from the Ada School incorporate prominent representations of decorative pillars: Dodwell 1993: 51, 53, 55, 57.

[3271] The figure of Christ in the centre of the picture is surrounded by a decorative circle of 10 saints, with roundels at top, bottom, left and right containing representations of the evangelists: an eagle (John), a winged man (Matthew), a winged ox (Luke), and a winged lion (Mark): Dodwell 1993: 132.

[3272] Dodwell 1993: 50-2, 132. It is noteworthy that in a copy of the illustration dating from 950-70 the border lozenges are replaced by a frame of acanthus, also prominent on the Wolverhampton column: Dodwell 1993: 133.

[3273] Hawkes 2002: 144-5.

[3274] It is worthy of note that in the early 20th century the beast was tentatively identified as a bull (also said to appear on the Wolverhampton column), an idea no longer held to be tenable: Hawkes 2002: 96-7.

[3275] Hawkes 2002: 88, 162-4, 166.

the closest parallel that can be made between the Wolverhampton cross-shaft and any other Anglo-Saxon sculpture.[3276]

It is difficult, if not impossible, to believe that the mastermind responsible for the crosses at Sandbach was unaware of the Wolverhampton column, and/or vice versa, though it must be possible that both are to be associated with another cross or crosses (or indeed other sculptural form) no longer existing. In that respect Hawkes has identified evidence of a close relationship between a number of sculptural pieces from Bakewell and the centre responsible for the Sandbach monuments,[3277] which perhaps implies a connection between the Bakewell school of sculpture and the Wolverhampton cross-shaft, though we should not overlook that there remain very significant differences between the designs and iconography at Sandbach and Wolverhampton, not least of course the square section of the Sandbach crosses and the round section and horizontal bands of the Wolverhampton column.[3278] But of one thing we can be confident: the similarities can be no coincidence. Similar lozenge designs in any area of Anglo-Saxon art are extremely rare. The strong evidence of Carolingian influence in the Wolverhampton cross-shaft iconography and likelihood of a date (very) broadly contemporary with the Sandbach crosses, of which the North Cross has been convincingly dated by Hawkes to 'the early decades of the ninth century' and the South Cross to 'a slightly later date within the ninth century',[3279] enables us to accept that the Wolverhampton column is to be set around the same broad time-frame as the South Cross, that is very roughly c.800-c.850. The lozenges on the South Cross might be explained if the designs on the Wolverhampton column became known to the workshop from which the Sandbach crosses originated only after the North Cross had been completed.

Problems remain, however. We cannot know, for instance, which of the Sandbach and Wolverhampton monuments influenced the other(s), if at all, or whether there may have been other crosses now lost with similar designs which may have served as an exemplar, or taken their inspiration from, those crosses, or either of them. But the unified design of the Wolverhampton column and the range of disparate carvings on the Sandbach crosses imply perhaps that it was the Wolverhampton cross from which designs were copied by the Sandbach sculptor rather than vice versa, since the Sandbach designs might have led to figural notifs on the Wolverhampton column. If that is correct, the Wolverhampton column could have been set up decades – even a century or more – before the Sandbach crosses, but contemporary norms have always been a dominent influence in the history of art, whatever the medium, and point towards a date roughly around the mid-ninth century for the Wolverhampton column,[3280] with the rosettes at the angles and junctions perhaps

---

[3276] The recently-published *Corpus of Anglo-Saxon Stone Sculpture: Lancashire and Cheshire* makes no connection between the Sandbach crosses and the Wolverhampton column, the latter awaiting analysis in a pending volume of the Corpus (Hawkes and Sidebottom (forthcoming)), but prefers a date in the 10th century, or possibly earlier, for the Wolverhampton column: Bailey 2011: 34.
[3277] Hawkes 2002: 72, 87. Illustration of a pre-Viking cross-shaft and sculptured stones at Bakewell appear in Dornier 1977: 222-3 and Higham and Ryan 2013: 295.
[3278] Rosemary Cramp has placed the Wolverhampton column in a southern English group ('Group 5') which relates to West Saxon and Mercian crosses and architectural sculpture from Wolverhampton to Winchester: Dornier 1977: 192.
[3279] Hawkes 2002: 28.
[3280] This analysis was written before the publication of Hawkes and Sidebottom (forthcoming), but has benefited from sight of a pre-publication draft of the detailed entry relating to the Wolverhampton cross-shaft (for which the present author is indebted to Professor Hawkes) which recognises the difficulties in dating the monument, but proposes a date in the tenth century, possibly

replicating or echoing the decorative rivets in earlier Irish and Anglo-Saxon brooches from the mid-seventh to the ninth centuries, a detail that becomes more prominent in the ninth century, or more especially the studs holding metal strips on objects such as a reliquary casket or similar devotional object, like the (later) example from St Peter's, Salzburg, mentioned previously.[3281] But if the above analysis is correct, it remains puzzling that the exceptionally lavish Wolverhampton column seems to have had so little influence on sculptural design elsewhere in the region, perhaps implying (though negative evidence must always be suspect) the existence of other Anglo-Saxon monuments long since destroyed or decayed.

It has generally been assumed that the existing column may represent the lower part of a tapering cross-shaft which was originally perhaps twice the height, possibly with a now-lost upper shaft surmounted by a cross-head,[3282] although it must be emphasised that the nature of the decoration, and the separate knop or capstone, now devoid of ornate decoration, but perhaps originally with interlace decoration on its bevelled surface,[3283] means that there are few parallels with which to compare it, making any suggested reconstruction entirely speculative.[3284] The thick and heavy capstone has a flat base which forms a significant overhang on the pillar, turning sharply into an outcurving profile reaching a simple horizontal roll moulding at its widest point before the profile curves inwards and upwards to a flat top. That top is considerably larger in diameter than the column below, from which we might question whether it is likely that a stone cross formed from separate components, assumed to have surmounted the monument, will have been structurally sound when placed in an exposed position, although a mortice and tenon could be secured by running lead between the two, which was the method employed at Bewcastle.[3285] It has been assumed that any cross head is likely to have been similar to that

---

early in that century [i.e. roughly contemporary with the battle of Tettenhall]. The draft also concludes that the shaft is in its original position, and that there is no evidence that Wulfrun founded or refounded any monastery at Wolverhampton, or that there was a pre-existing centre there before she was granted estates in the area in 985, but is subject to modification before publication.

[3281] Hawkes 2002: 96. But as Rosemary Cramp has observed, 'the mere importation of objects in other media that could have served as models does not entirely explain the Lichfield [angel] and other Mercian pieces', and cites Beckwith's conclusion that the inescapable conclusion was that 'the artists were Greeks working in a full living tradition': Rodwell et al 2008: 74.

[3282] See in particular Rix 1960: 71-81, which includes an artistic pictorial reconstruction showing the shaft topped by a slender tapering decorated four-sided shaft and round-headed cross-head, to form a particularly impressive version of the Staff Rood Cross. But since the Wolverhampton shaft is unique, we have no parallels to provide clues as to the original design, and if there was another section, what form it may have taken. There is no scientific evidence to show that the capstone itself is original, or of the same stone as the shaft. Shaw writes that 'whether [the column] supported a cross is uncertain': Shaw 1801 II: 161. The acerbic anonymous and learned reviewer of Dr George Oliver's undistinguished *An Historical and Descriptive Account of the Collegiate Church of Wolverhampton in the County of Stafford* for GM,July 1836: 387-94 had little doubt that the pillar was a sepulchral monument commemorating Wulfrun. Oliver himself noted that the column, 'a cylindrical, or rather a pyramidal [*sic*] column' had a cross '... down to a very recent period ...', and '... was graced with a cross on its summit, within the memory of man' (Oliver 1836: 138, 144), but all his statements must be treated with considerable caution. On jointed insular stone crosses see Mac Lean 1995.

[3283] Browne 1885: 190.

[3284] The Cross of Irbic at Llandough-juxta-Cogan, Glamorgan (mentioned in Rix 1960: 78), has a separate thick central knop, square in plan, above a square section shaft, with decorated horizontal bands, and an incomplete square-section shaft above, but the design of the monument, dating from the late 10th or 11th century, is very different from, and very much shorter than, the Wolverhampton shaft: Lord 2003: 42.

[3285] Bailey 1980: 242.

at Cropthorne, though that can be, at best, no more than guesswork. But if there is, as suggested above, an incontestible connection between the decorative scheme of the cross-shafts at Sandbach and that at Wolverhampton, it may be that (as at Sandbach), the Wolverhampton column was indeed topped with a carved stone cross-head similar to Cropthorne rather than a tapering shaft with an integral cross-head which has been suggested in reconstruction drawings.[3286] However, there is nothing to suggest that the head of the Wolverhampton shaft was likely to take the form of either the Sandbach cross(es) or the staff-rood crosses of the north, and the Carolingian association might point towards a Carolingian-style cross-head. The well-known Lechmere Stone, a small free-standing tapering four-sided Anglo-Saxon block from Hanley Castle, Worcestershire, dated to the first half of the ninth century, contains on one face a sculpted wheel-headed cross on a stepped base. The shaft is of two bellied sections separated by a collar; a second collar separates the top of the shaft from the head, which is a complete circle containing an equal-armed cross with incurving rounded terminals to the arms.[3287] That might hint at the type of cross-head which once surmounted the Wolverhampton column.

The Wolverhampton cross-shaft (known in the nineteenth century as The Clark's Pillar,[3288] the Danish Cross,[3289] or the Danes Cross,[3290] and in the early twentieth century as The Danes' Pillar, attributed by one writer to an association with 'the defeat of the Danes at Tettenhall in the 7th century [sic]',[3291] is perhaps but a fragment of what must have been in its entirety a spectacular monument, almost certainly painted in bright colours[3292] and

---

[3286] See for example Rix 1960: 80.
[3287] Bryant 2012; 357-60; Plates 635-45.
[3288] Parson and Bradshaw 1818: cxc. It may be noted that *Clerkmonnesmedwe* is recorded in 1344 in Willenhall (SRO D593/B/1/26/6/10/7), possibly to be associated with the modern Clarke's Lane, Willenhall.
[3289] JBAA 1889: 187.
[3290] Lethaby 1913: 158-9.
[3291] Muirhead 1920: 224.
[3292] 'There are, however, sufficient survivals [of traces of colour on Viking-age sculpture] to assure us that colouring was the normal treatment.': Bailey 1980: 26. For a study of original polychrome decoration on Anglo-Saxon free-standing sculptured crosses, see Cather, Park and Williamson 1990: 216, and for a painting showing a reconstruction of the larger Sandbach Cross, brightly coloured as it might have appeared in the 9th century, see the frontispiece to Hawkes 2002. The decoration of sculpture, including free-standing stone crosses, at this period seems to have involved the use of gesso or plaster base applied directly to the stone over which was added the colour scheme, perhaps of black, red, brown, white and blue. Whilst many designs were doubtless drawn or incised freehand directly on to the stone, there is strong evidence that templates or stencils were also used, since repeated designs on a number of monuments have been found to be of identical size and shape. In addition to painting, there may have been other types of decoration. The cross at Reculver in Kent has a number of small holes which might indicate that metal decorative treatments, possibly even jewellery or paste, were affixed to such monuments: ibid. 26; 246-7; 254. Evidence from the large boss at the centre of a cross-head from Sandbach strongly suggests that a metal appliqué once surrounded or enclosed the boss, and other holes in the cross may have contained decorative inserts: Hawkes 2002: 146. The Wolverhampton cross-shaft shows no obvious evidence of any such holes in the sculpted area (except a neatly drilled hole about 1" in diameter some two feet from the top which might be related to conservation work undertaken in the 1990s), but the plaster-cast in the Victoria and Albert Museum shows a number of holes in the bodies of the birds and beasts, including one in the centre of the body of the right-facing beast in band B above and to the right of the 'bull' vandyke, which appear too regular in size and shape to be explained by weathering. Some holes may have been filled in the original cross since the cast was taken. There are also two conical depressions close to the base of the plaster cast, about an inch deep and an inch or so across, with rounded bases. The two holes are not at the same level, and are not opposite each other, but are almost certainly artificial.

possibly even gilded and jewelled, perhaps with decorative metalwork, probably visible from many miles away, testifying to the power and wealth of whoever was responsible for commissioning and erecting it, and leads us to consider what may have prompted such a display of devotion.

In his analysis of Anglo-Saxon sculpture in the North Midlands,[3293] P C Sidebottom concluded that the western limits of what he classed as the South-Western regional school extended to Sandbach. He believed that the geographical limit could also be detected in present-day Staffordshire, since all the monuments of that school were contained in north-east Staffordshire, with the south-west of the county almost devoid of free-standing monuments, for, apart from isolated examples of carved stone fragments of possible Anglo-Saxon origin, there are no monuments in this area other than the Wolverhampton cross-shaft. The latter, said to be unique in England, could therefore safely be assumed to be unrelated to any school he had identified [a conclusion now in need of qualification]. The absence of sculpture in the south-west of his research area showed that it was unlikely that the diocese of Lichfield was responsible for the pre-Conquest schools of sculpture in the research area, suggesting that the monuments were perhaps produced, or organised, by monasteries or other ecclesiastical houses. The problems linking major ecclesiastical houses with free-standing monuments were, he felt, twofold. Firstly, much depended on when this occurred, since the influence of ecclesiastical houses was probably greatly diminished, if not in some cases extinguished, when they, and their lands, were seized by Scandinavian settlers. They were less likely, as a result, to have been responsible for a major exercise in the creation and installation of monumental cross shafts (unless these were demanded by the secular elite) until the 'monastic revival' in the tenth and eleventh centuries. Secondly, the existence of some religious houses before the Viking settlement may have gone unrecorded, with a new and reorganised provision appearing in, and after, the later tenth century.

How then can the Wolverhampton shaft fit into the known history of Wolverhampton? If it be accepted as late eighth- to mid-ninth century in date, it must be conceded that we have little documentary evidence for the pre-Conquest history of what became Wolverhampton, though what we do possess contains much valuable information. It has been suggested elsewhere in this volume that a minster church may have been established, possibly within a prehistoric fortification, in the late seventh or early eighth century, perhaps serving an extensive estate with scattered lands, although some doubt has been cast on the existence of any prehistoric earthwork.[3294]

In that respect we might consider in the briefest terms the political and ecclesiastical situation in West Mercia for the half century or so after 780.[3295] That brevity is in part forced upon us insofar as the ecclesiastical situation within Mercia is concerned, for in the two centuries after the death of Bede in 735 very little is known about the bishopric of Lichfield or its clergy, not least because from the 870s the Lichfield area, lying at the very edge of English Mercia against the Danelaw, was for several decades at the mercy of the

---

Furthermore, the plaster-cast of the column shows two larger and deeper depressions close to the base, but not opposite each other, although whether they are cast from the pillar itself is unclear.

[3293] Sidebottom 1994: 163-4.

[3294] Hooke and Slater 1986: 15-17. The dating would fit with the late 7th century date for Beadugyth/Beorngyth posited elsewhere. The boundaries of the supposed hillfort may however simply represent the boundary of a particularly large but typically curvilinear *vallum monasterii*, which generally measured between 150 and 300 metres across: see e.g. Blair 2005: 198.

[3295] See especially Walker 2000: 22-42; Keynes 2001.

Danes. We have a list of bishops who came after Chad, but that list is not certain, details of their dates are in many cases unsettled, and we know very little of their lives and deeds, or even whether they were based at Lichfield.[3296] The dissolute king Ceolred of Mercia (709-16) had been buried at Lichfield, but later rulers were buried elsewhere. The fourteenth-century Lichfield Chronicle contains no local pre-Conquest traditions, with almost all references to that period taken from the writings of Bede and William of Malmesbury, and even manages to misidentify Lichfield's one archbishop as Adulfus.[3297]

No account of this period can overlook the importance of one of the greatest figures of the age, Alcuin of York (c.735-804), the dominant intellectual of the time of Charlemagner and Offa. As Patrick Wormald observed, 'That Alcuin was English is one of the most important facts in the history of relations between Britain and the Continent in the early Middle Ages'. Educated in the cathedral church of York, where he wrote a poetic account of its history which has been called 'the first historical epic in the extant Latin literature of the medieval West', he travelled to Rome and Francia, and in 781 was appointed master of the court school of Charlemagne, king of the Franks, and became a central figure in the Carolingian Renaissance. He returned to England on occasions, and was in Northumbria from 790 to 793, but most of his last years were spent on the Continent, where he died in 804 as abbot of St Martin's, Tours. He was one of the foremost grammarians, liturgists and theologians of Charlemagne's Europe, and about 300 of his letters, many to English kings, prelates and noblemen, survive. They form a major source for English history of the period. Alcuin symbolises the continuing English commitment to the Continental Church which had begun with Willibord. As Patrick Wormald observed, 'almost all the evidence for the richness and vigour of Anglo-Saxon culture in the age of Offa comes from the Continent, not, as in the age of Bede, from England *and* the Continent.'[3298]

A convenient starting point for reviewing what little is known about the ecclesiastical situation in Mercia between 780 and 850 might be 786, during the later reign of Offa (757-96), when a party of papal missionaries arrived in England after negotiations with Offa, Pope Hadrian (772-95) and Charlemagne, and a constant flurry of diplomatic activity with the Carolingian court took place (and continued for some decades) which led to the elevation of Lichfield as a new archbishopric (with its province, according to William of Malmesbury, including the sees of Hereford, Worcester, Leicester, Linsdey and East Anglia),[3299] and Hygeberht's appointment as archbishop at the 'contentious synod' of Chelsea in 787.[3300] This was the culmination of the long-standing enmity between Offa and archbishop Jænberht of Canterbury (765-92), who had long supported the claims of Kent to independence from Mercia. The new archbishopric, acknowledged by an annual

---

[3296] On those uncertainties see Haddan and Stubbs 1871: III 614 fn.a., and generally to p.660 for details of Mercian Witenagemots and charters. For a collection of episcopal lists for the sees of Wessex, East Anglia and Mercia compiled according to Keynes c.810 (Cotton MS Vespasian B.vi, f. 108v) see Keynes 2001: 311-2. The list for Mercia, however (without dates), concludes with Hunberht who (according to Powicke and Fryde 1961: 233) was not consecrated until 828/830 and acceded in 830; see also Searle 1899: 130-35; SHC 1916: 136.
[3297] Wharton 1691: 423-33; Gould 1993: 8. Ealdwulf (bishop) succeeded Hygeberht (archbishop) at Lichfield: Powicke and Fryde 1961: 233. The Lichfield Chronicle was written by Alan of Ashbourne during the first half of the 14th century and published in Wharton 1691; I 423 et seq, but wrongly ascribed to Thomas Chesterfield: VCH Staffordshire III 140.
[3298] Wormald 1981: 107; Williams, Smyth and Kirby 1991: 38.
[3299] Nicholas Brooks has pointed out anomalies in William's account: Brooks 1984: 118-9. The creation of Lichfield as an archbishopric copied the see of York, elevated to an archbishopric in 735.
[3300] Cubitt 1995: 230-1; Godfrey 2016.

donation by Offa to the Pope of 365 *mancuses*, greatly enhanced the authority of its seat at Lichfield, close to Offa's palace at Tamworth and the Mercian royal mausoleum at Repton, whilst reducing the power of Canterbury. Thereafter joint synods were held by Lichfield and Canterbury, with Canterbury retaining supremacy until Jænberht's death, when Hygeberht became foremost prelate.

Whilst expanding and asserting ruthless control over a vast kingdom, Offa had not overlooked his religious responsibilities. He patronised monasteries established in different parts of his realm (e.g. *Medehamstede* and Crowland), founded others (e.g. Winchcombe, St Albans and Bedford), took control of religious houses in sensitive locations (e.g. Bath, Cookham and possibly Glastonbury), and prevailed upon Pope Hadrian to grant special privileges in respect of at least some of these minsters to himself and his wife.[3301] Offa died in July 796, a momentous year for Mercia. In April Offa's son-in-law Æthelred, king of the Northumbrians, had been killed, and Offa's son and nominated successor Ecgfrith (who had been consecrated by Hygeberht) died unexpectedly five months after his father. This opened the way for a continuation of the dynastic rivalry and instability in Mercia even during the long reigns of its recent kings: Offa was not closely related to his predecessor and succeeded the murdered Æthelbald only after victory in a civil war.[3302] And so it went on, with Mercian kings gradually losing authority over parts of their kingdom, which led to loss of revenue, and loss of more authority. This allowed the resurgence of Wessex and a weakened Mercia found it difficult to resist the major Viking assaults when they came.

Cœnwulf (796-821),[3303] a distant cousin and *thegn* of Offa, gained the support of the Mercian *ealdormen* (and the Mercian Church) and succeeded Offa's son as king of Mercia, but was faced with active dissent, most notably in Kent and East Anglia. A revolt in Kent was led by Eadberht Præn, the notorious and opportunistic scion of the Kentish royal kindred loathed by Offa, who drove out the pro-Mercian archbishop of Canterbury. Eadberht was captured, mutilated, blinded and imprisoned. Released in 811, his fate is unknown. At the same time East Anglia under Eadwald broke free of Mercian control. But Cœnwulf was still a power to be reckoned with, and quickly restored Mercian rule over both Kent and East Anglia. He also responded forcefully to Welsh aggression, with the Welsh annals recording the death of Caradog, King of Gwynedd, at the hands of the English near Offa's Dyke. But defensive action was also necessary: in 801 Mercia was invaded by the weak king Eardwulf of Northumbria, and Cœnwulf was forced to lead a large army on a long campaign before peace was restored.

The following year Æthelmund of Mercia (possibly *ealdorman* of the Hwicce) invaded Wessex with his forces, evidently a reaction to the return from exile of Egbert as king of Wessex after the death of the Mercian-backed Beotric. The action was a disaster. Æthelmund was killed and his forces routed.[3304]

[3301] Lapidge et al 1999: 340-41.
[3302] After analysing charters of the 9th-century Mercian kings, Keynes has considered whether each may have come to power as a reflection of 'a protracted rivalry between representatives of at least three different dynasties, each with names alliterating on a particular letter of the alphabet ['C', 'B' and 'W']': Keynes 2001: 314-23; see also Walker 2000: 29-42.
[3303] Said by Beresford to have been worthless with little time for religion, perhaps even hindering the preaching of the gospel in his kingdom (Beresford 1883: 41), but no sources are cited for these fanciful claims. See also Williams, Smyth and Kirby 1991: 83.
[3304] Walker 2000: 25-8.

In 802 the archbishopric of Lichfield was revoked by the Pope (archbishop Hygeberht having resigned) after embassies were sent to Rome by Cœnwulf,[3305] who (according to Studd) 'demonstrated hostility to the archiepiscopal see of Lichfield from the outset of his reign'[3306] and found Jænberht's successor archbishop Æthelheard more amenable to Mercian aspirations, proposing an annulment but suggesting a single archbishopric at London. The Pope chose to restore a single archbishopric, but at Canterbury, perhaps the most conspicuous indication of Mercia's slide from supremacy, and Cœnwulf's hold over Kent was weakened with the appointment of Wulfred, a Mercian, as archbishop of Canterbury in 805.[3307]

Wulfred, following his predecessor Æthelheard, used every opportunity to consolidate Canterbury's holdings, taking steps to deal with abuses such as the existence of 'proprietory churches' in the hands of powerful lay nobles and their families, who held the right to nominate abbots and abbesses to such houses. By the Synod of Chelsea in 816 that right was transferred to the bishops, but the measure was of limited success, with 'proprietory churches' continuing to prove a problem until the twelfth century. The provision of the council forbidding monasteries to grant leases of their property to laymen for more than the term of one life must have caused anxiety to innumerable noblemen holding monastic lands under arrangements made in an earlier generation.[3308] These reforming controls struck directly at royal interests since Cœnwulf and members of his family controlled a number of important and wealthy abbeys. Wulfred's attempt to wrest the Kentish houses of Minster-in-Thanet and Reculver, held by the king's sister, Cwœnthryth, abbess of Winchcombe, from Mercian control and his powerful assertion of episcopal rights led to conflict with Cœnwulf and Wulfred's deposition from the archbishopric between 817 and 821, the year of Cœnwulf's death.[3309] Wulfred was forced to surrender his claims, together with a large estate and heavy fine, before he was restored to office.[3310]

It was c.802, during the time of Cœnwulf, that a body of priests, deacons and clerks who were clearly secular clergy, an innovation perhaps due to Carolingean influence, is mentioned at Worcester in a charter witness list.[3311] Carolingian influences – including those relating to stone sculpture – were evidently to be found within Mercia in the early ninth century, having been established (or continued) by Offa, who from at least 786 had maintained direct links (not always cordial) with Charlemagne, king of the Franks and from 800 emperor of the West, with the legatine Council attended by the Pope's legates held in Mercia in 786 under Offa's auspices, as mentioned above.[3312]

At his death Cœnwulf – the last Mercian ruler considered important enough for his death to be recorded in the *Annals of Ulster* until Æthelflæd in 918 – was buried at Winchcombe, which he had lavishly endowed (and which he or Offa may have founded, the place having

---

[3305] See especially Whitelock 1979; 89, 866-9.
[3306] Studd 1982: 30.
[3307] Though Stenton aduced abundant evidence that Mercian overlordship of Kent ended with the death of Offa: Stenton 1970: 64.
[3308] Stenton 1971: 236-8.
[3309] On the dispute between Cœnwulf and Wulfred see Haddan and Stubbs 1871: 586-7; Walker 2000: 28-9.
[3310] Walker 2000: 29.
[3311] Mayr-Harting 1972: 245. The charter is S.154, for which Meyr-Harting gives the impossible date 799: Sawyer 1968: 110.
[3312] Williams, Smyth and Kirby 1991: 188-9.

been fortified no later than the early ninth century),[3313] but from a charter of 825 we learn that after he died 'many disagreements and innumerable disputes arose among leading persons of every kind – kings, bishops and ministers of the churches of God – concerning all manner of secular affairs, so that in various places the churches of Christ were greatly despoiled, in goods, lands, revenues, and all matters', an indication perhaps of the traumatic reaction to 'the passing of a strong ruler who had kept faction and discord in check', and merely one indication of the internal disintegration of the Mercian regime.[3314] Cœnwulf's brother Ceolwulf (821-3), in the earliest recorded English ceremony of consecration, was made king of Mercia in 821, but the auspicious beginnings of his reign ended in disaster, and in mysterious circumstances he was 'deprived of his kingdom'.[3315] This was also a time of external threats to Mercia: a series of diplomas issued by kings of the Mercians from 792 to 822 refer to repeated Viking incursions in Kent, and mention the existence of a Viking camp,[3316] with a further raid on Sheppey in 835.[3317]

Ceolwulf died in 823, to be succeeded by Beornwulf (823-6), who actively sought to secure support for his new dynasty. In 824 he held a synod at *Clofesho* (an important place still unidentified)[3318] to resolve the long-running dispute with archbishop Wulfred of Canterbury (who was suspended between 817-21) over the religious houses at Minster-in-Thanet and Reculver.[3319] Present was Nothelm, a papal messenger, perhaps to help broker a deal. The synod was of sufficient importance to merit mention in the *Anglo-Saxon Chronicle*. At a further synod at *Clofesho* the following year presided over by Beornwulf the dispute was finally settled. It was during Beornwulf's rule that the see of Lichfield was supposedly reorganised by Bishop Aedeluald or Æthelwald (818-29) to include the introduction of canons in accordance with the teachings of Chrodegang of Metz.[3320] It is of passing interest that bishop Æthelwald wrote his name in the form of an acrostic, like Carolingian scholars, in the Book of Cerne, an illuminated manuscript probably written at Lichfield,[3321] further evidence of Carolingian influence. In 825 Beornwulf was defeated by Ecgberht of Wessex at the battle of *Ellendun* (Wroughton in Wiltshire, well outside Mercia, showing that Beornwulf was the aggressor), which brought Mercia under West Saxon control and marked the end of Mercian supremacy. In Wessex the conquest of

---

[3313] Brooks and Cubitt 1996: 155; Lapidge et al 1999: 340. Cœnwulf's sister Cwœnthryth was abbess of Winchcombe, and his son Cynehelm, who Cœnwulf had hoped would succeed him, was buried at Winchcombe c.812: Walker 2000: 29.
[3314] S.1435, recording a settlement of the Council of *Clofesho* in 925, extract translated in Keynes 2001: 311 fn.5.
[3315] This was the period during which by tradition the 7 year old Cynehelm (St Kenelm), son of King Cœnwulf, almost certainly baseless, murdered by his jealous sister: Keynes 2001: 313. It is likely that Cœnwulf 'hallowed' Kenelm (who is unlikely to have been the king's son) to the throne (as Offa did for his own son), for a letter dated 798, allegedly from the Pope to 'King Kenelm' names Kenelm and gives his age as 12. In 799, Kenelm witnessed a deed of gift of land to Christ Church, Canterbury, and from 803 onwards his name appears on a variety of charters. He probably died in 811, for his name is unmentioned thereafter. This suggests that Kenelm was 25 years old when he died. It also seems that Kenelm's sister, Cwenthryth (Quendryda), had entered the church at the time of her father's death and was the abbess of Minster-in-Thanet: Williams, Smyth and Kirby 1991: 98; Walker 2000: 29-30 Keynes 2001: 316.
[3316] S.134; S.160; S.168; S.177; S.186; S.1264.
[3317] ASC 'A' and 'E'; Swanton 1996: 62-3.
[3318] Cibitt 1995: 27-8, 36-8.
[3319] Whitelock 1979: 90.
[3320] Brown 2001: 287. The evidence is preserved only in the later *Lichfield Chronicle* (Wharton 1691), much of which is fanciful.
[3321] Deansley 1961: 246.

Mercia led to Ecgberht being hailed as one of the greatest figures in English history.[3322] The following year Beornwulf was killed attempting to stem a revolt in East Anglia and succeeded by one of his *ealdormen*, Ludeca. In 829 Hunberght succeeded Æthelwald as bishop of Lichfield, but again we have little information about his career.

Ludeca (and five of his *ealdormen*) was himself killed by a faction of his East Anglian countrymen – the second successive Mercian ruler to die in this way – after a short and little-known rule,[3323] and Wiglaf (827-9, 830-c.838) took power, but was expelled from his kingdom by Ecgberht, who even issued coins minted in London bearing the legend *Rex M[erciorum]*, King of the Mercians, and went on to lead his victorious army north through Mercia to receive the submission of the Northumbrians at Dore near Sheffield. Wiglaf, whose kin-group may have been based on the territory of the *Tomsæte* centred on Tamworth since their family burial place was Repton,[3324] regained power at the Mercian revival in 830 in circumstances which remain cloudy, but was not of the Mercian royal line. Nevertheless, he wielded considerable power, for he quickly threw off West Saxon overlordship and had re-established his authority in Mercia in 830. By 831 his rule extended into Middlesex, and in 836 he held a synod at Croft in Leicestershire attended by the archbishop of Canterbury and all the southern bishops. He seems to have died c.838, and was succeeded by his son Wigmund, with Mercia passing to a rival dynasty in 840 with the succession of Beorhtwulf (840-52), of uncertain lineage.[3325]

In 851 the Mercian army was put to flight by a Viking force, said to have arrived in 350 ships, which stormed London, though if the *Anglo-Saxon Chronicle* is to be believed, Mercia seems to have escaped unscathed, with the Vikings crossing the Thames into Wessex where they ravaged until defeated by Æthelwulf at *Acleah*. The reality is that the Vikings were quick to recognise and exploit weakened kingdoms, and Mercia was certainly weakened at this time. It would be very surprising if numerous and significant unrecorded Viking attacks had not taken place against Mercia, actions which may have led Burgred (852-74), a kinsman who had succeeded Beorhtwulf as king of Mercia in 852, to seek a closer alliance with Wessex.[3326] In 853 he and king Æthelwulf of Wessex (839-58) allied to launch a joint assault against the Welsh.[3327] This was a time when recorded Viking attacks were increasing, with Scandinavian raiders in Anglesey and in the Wrekin area in the mid-850s, and it it is possible that their Welsh campaign was at least in part intended to deal with a Viking presence there. An alliance between Wessex and Mercia was sealed by the marriage of Burgred to the daughter of king Æthelwulfafter Easter 853.

Bishop Tunberht succeeded as bishop of Lichfield in about 842, an office he held until some time between 857-62, but though his name appears in several charters, we have little

---

[3322] Stenton 1971: 232.
[3323] See Keynes 2001: 313 fn.11; Walker 2000: 34.
[3324] Walker 2000: 34.
[3325] Williams, Smyth and Kirby 1991: 59-60; Walker 2000: 36-7. Beresford gives some details of an assembly held by Wiglaf in 851 (*sic*), with various participants, known and unknown, citing as his authority Ingulph, but the *Historia Monasterii Croylandensis* formerly attributed to Ingulph, Benedictine Abbot of Croyland (d.1109), is now recognised as a 13th or 14th century forgery, generally known as the *Pseudo-Ingulph*, though the forger may have made use of genuine sources, some of which are now lost to us.
[3326] In 849 Wiglaf's grandson Wigstan (St Wigstan) was murdered by Beorhtwulf at what became known in his memory as Wistowe ('Wigstan's stow or holy place') in Leicestershire, an act that led to later legends: Williams, Smyth and Kirby 1991: 59-60, 78, 236; Walker 2000: 38-9.
[3327] Williams, Smyth and Kirby 1991: 68.

information about his life. In 868 the Danish Great Army moved west as far Nottingham, where it repulsed a joint Mercian and West Saxon siege, and in 874 reached Repton, where it showed its disdain of the Mercian royal line by pointedly establishing its wintering camp at Repton, the revered mausoleum of the Mercian royal family, and looted throughout the region, which was at peril of complete subjection.[3328] Burgred fled to Rome, and Ceolwulf II (874-9),[3329] who probably came to some accommodation with the Danes (and was described in the West Saxon *Anglo-Saxon Chronicle*, almost certainly unfairly, as 'a foolish king's thegn' and presented as a puppet of the Danes), became the last independent king of Mercia, which was partitioned by the Danes during his reign. The period from c.855 will, we might suppose, have been a time of great instability in the West Midlands, and unlikely to have seen any resurgence of church building or the installation of Christian monuments.

The bald but necessarily selective facts (if facts they be) as set out above hardly allow us even to guess at any particular time-window in that period during which an exceptionally suptuous cross-shaft might have been commissioned and erected in the West Midlands, or indeed allow us to eliminate periods when such action might perhaps be ruled out, but in political and ecclesiastical terms the most likely period for for the creation of the southern Sandbach and Wolverhampton crosses (and doubtless others which almost certainly existed, long since destroyed or decayed), is rather obviously after the raising of the see of Lichfield to an archbishopric under Offa in 787 to create a major liturgical focus centred on the cathedral church and perhaps promoting political aspirations through the propaganda of royal dedications elsewhere, leading to the 'sudden explosion of stone carving' during the time of the Mercian supremacy in the early ninth century under king Cœnwulf of Mercia (796-821), which neatly ties in with Hawkes' dating of the southerly Sandbach cross, the most relevant for these researches.[3330]

Hawkes speculates that the loss of its archiepiscopal status may have led the senior clergy in the region to articulate their unextinguished aspirations by invoking prestigious Carolingian images of ecclesiastical authority, an idea in keeping with what is known of 'the tendencies of the Mercian royal and ecclesiastical hierarchies of the late eighth and early ninth centuries to imitate things prestigious and Carolingian'.[3331] Nothing recorded in the *Anglo-Saxon Chronicle* during the three decades between c.823 and c.855 (that is, during the reigns of Ecgberht and Æthelwulf, Kings of Wessex, the former conquering Mercia and imposing his superiority over the Northumbrians in 829, the year Bishop Hunberght succeeded to the see of Lichfield), provides any clues to suggest that the 'sudden explosion' continued into those reigns, though it will readily be appreciated that our knowledge of the region during this period is meagre indeed, and it must be very likely (as shown, for example, by Hawkes' dating of the later north cross at Sandbach) that the practice of erecting such monuments had become well established and relatively widespread, if not increasing. Evidence suggests that Offa was involved in the patronage of book production,[3332] and Lichfield was a notable centre of learning in the early ninth century (as evidenced by, for example, the Book of Cerne, mentioned above, a sophisticated and elaborate illuminated insular or Anglo-Saxon Latin personal prayer book

---

[3328] Beresford 1883: 36; Williams, Smyth and Kirby 1991.
[3329] Williams, Smyth and Kirby 1991: 78.
[3330] Bryant and Hare 2012: 46.
[3331] Hawkes 2002: 145.
[3332] Brown 2001: 284.

with Old English components probably produced at Lichfield in the 820s-840s).[3333] The high standard of erudition in the diocese, and the teaching of Greek and Hewbrew, doubtless explains why Alfred the Great was later to turn to Mercia for scholars adequately educated to support his reforms.

Any attempt to analyse the iconography of the Wolverhampton column must now take account of the remarkable discovery of Anglo-Saxon sculpture made in 2003, less than 15 miles from Wolverhampton. During excavations in the Gothic nave of Lichfield cathedral, three conjoining broken pieces of a bas-relief limestone panel were found, carved in pristine detail with the figure of an angel retaining traces of polychrome decoration, including a trace of gold. The panel is believed to represent the archangel Gabriel, and is thought to be one half of an Annunciation scene that was probably part of a shrine-chest associated with the cult of St Chad, who was interred at Lichfield in 732. Whether the damage to the panels was deliberate or accidental cannot be known, but from the Roman period onwards damaged or redundant liturgical furnishings were not infrequently buried, intact or deliberately broken, inside or close to religious buildings, both by pagans and Christians.[3334]

Of particular interest to this study is that the curled locks and staring eyes of of the angel have been held to derive from the classical Greek tradition heavily influenced by Byzantine art, with the remarkable series of Anglo-Saxon stone carvings from Breedon (Leicestershire), Castor and Fletton (Peterborough), and Peterborough itself – all closely linked in their foundation history – displaying eastern Christian traditions, and to be compared with 'Continental figures in manuscripts and ivories reflecting the cultural renaissance of Charlemagne and his successors'.[3335] The Lichfield angel has been tentatively ascribed on art-historical grounds to the late eighth- or early-ninth century, that is to the latter part of the reign of Offa, around the time of the elevation of Lichfield to achiepiscopal status in 787, or perhaps during the reign of his successor Cœnwulf.

An analysis of the iconography of the angel notes that the production of innovative and technically accomplished sculptures has long been recognised as dependant on the highest patronage and access to eastern models, and that somehow, in the period of Byzantine iconoclasm, craftsmen preserved and adapted the essential elements of the Graeco-Roman heritage. Those craftsmen, it is believed, are likely to have been Greeks, who are recorded at the Carolingian court, and Offa was well placed to attract them to his kingdom, not only to produce works themselves, but to train local sculptors. These foreign craftsmen would possess the expert skills to provide sculpted decoration of the highest quality at important churches or new religious foci – the Lichfield angel, uniquely, is part of a sumptuous shrine at a major cathedral, which at the time it was created could have been an archbishopric – with the iconography of works including commemorative monuments revealing different traditions and styles of workmanship.[3336] One sculpted panel from Breedon showing two figures has been said to be 'inexplicable in the context of Anglo-Saxon sculpture or of contemporary Carolingian work being a more faithful imitation of Hellenistic syle than even the ivories of Charlemagne's reign'.[3337]

[3333] Cambridge University Library MS L1.1.10; Brown 2001, especially 28-1...
[3334] Rodwell et al 2008: 59-60.
[3335] Brown 2001: 285; Rodwell et al 2008: 67.
[3336] Rodwell et al 2008: 74.
[3337] Jewell 2001: 252.

The iconography of the angel, like the Ruthwell cross and Anglo-Saxon sculpture from Wirksworth (both of the eighth or early ninth century) and Hovingham (early ninth century), has been held to derive from an early Christian, sixth-century model of late antique eastern Mediterranean origin. In that respect it should not be overlooked that figural stone sculpture is exceptionally rare on the Continent in the seventh to tenth centuries, which again might imply that the iconography of the Wolverhampton column, notable for the complete absence of figural forms, has its origins on the Continent.[3338] The Wolverhampton column and the Lichfield angel – two outstanding examples of Anglo-Saxon stone sculpture– could well be more or less contemporary, or separated at most by two or three decades, and possibly even share a similar inconographic ancestry, with skilled craftsmen of the same eastern nationality converting the designs with the greatest skill into three dimensions at or close to Lichfield: the stone block from which the angel has been carved is from what was probably a Roman quarry south-west Lincolnshire, within a few miles of Ancaster, near Grantham,[3339] some 65 miles north-east of Lichfield, but it may be supposed that it was transported, perhaps via the Trent and local rivers, in its unworked state to avoid damage to any carving during transit, to be marked out and sculpted at a workshop at or near Lichfield. The postulated existence of eastern masons of exceptional ability in that area in the late eighth or early ninth century might well serve to resolve some of the questions relating as to the nature of the Wolverhampton column, of equal stature, as unique, and quite possibly of the same period, as the Lichfield angel, which also happens to be the nearest certain example of Anglo-Saxon sculpture to Wolverhampton.[3340] That contiguity may be more than coincidence, and it is curious that the outstandingly detailed expert analysis of every aspect of the Lichfield angel should have left unmentioned the Wolverhampton column.[3341]

What is clear, however, is that in the late eighth or early ninth century the shrine of St Chad at Lichfield was reconstructed, probably with the simple wooden *theca*, or chest containing his relics, in the form of a wooden coffin in the shape of a house described by Bede, encased in a sumptuous sculpted limestone reliquary chest of a design unparalleled in Britain. It seems very likely that at a slighter later date a monumental column was erected less than 15 miles away at Wolverhampton with a design also unique in Britain. It might not be fanciful to suppose that the Church of Lichfield was responsible for both these examples of singular and outstanding Anglo-Saxon art.[3342]

[3338] Rodwell et al 2008: 67, 76.

[3339] The quarry was certainly being quarried in the second half of the 10th century, providing material for the many mid-Kesteven grave-covers found throughout west Lincolnshire and into Nottinghamshire and even at Derby, with cross-shafts produced in the 11th century, but a mid-9th century cross-shaft and two roundels from Edenham, Lincolnshire, some 16 miles south of Ancaster, are also recorded: Rodwell et al 2008: 58.

[3340] An Anglo-Saxon sculptural figure built in to the walls of the vestry at the north-west end of Eccleshall church, 20 miles north-west of Wolverhampton, probably of St Chad carrying a cross and walking alongside a horse, is comparable with sculptures from Sandbach; Leek, Chesterton, Alstonefield, Checkley, and Ilam (Staffordshire); and Bakewell and Norbury (Deryshire): Hawkes 2002: 139-41. Another sculpted slab at Eccleshall is probably a later grave-cover. A small incomplete Anglo-Saxon cylindrical cross-shaft with square upper section stands in Chebsey churchyard, 2 miles east of Eccleshall.

[3341] Just as the county town, Stafford, was called in one memorable expression in the 1970s 'the town that forget its castle' after the little-known Norman castle was revealed, so Wolverhampton might properly be called 'the town with the forgotten Anglo-Saxon masterpiece'.

[3342] It should be noted, however, that Sidebottom has concluded that the diocese of Lichfield is unlikely to have been the authority sesponsible for stone sculpture in the region (Sidebottom 1994: 163), though that conclusion pre-dates the discovery of the Lichfield angel.

Certain aspects of the Wolverhampton column should not pass unmentioned, however. It has been argued, perhaps surprisingly, that stone crosses were not necessarily erected in connection with the act of Christian worship. Peter Lord, discussing such monuments, writes that: '... the period at which [the manuscript known as the Gospels of St Chad] was in Llandeilo [c.830] is of great significance in itself. It coincides with a substantial change in the nature of the stone monuments which form the largest record of the visual culture of the period. In the ninth century the carving in the round of free-standing stone crosses was added to the tradition of the earlier period of incised decoration and inscription on the face of slabs'. Lord further suggests that the use of the word 'cross' to describe the later monuments, though an accurate description of their physical shape, may be misleading, arguing that it is unlikely that they had any role in worship similar to the way that a rood became the focus of devotion in the church buildings of the later Middle Ages. The Lives of the saints incorporate extensive evidence for the veneration of relics, but make no mention of the large and sophisticated stone monuments of the early medieval period, which could be seen as evidence that they were not foci for devotion in the same way. Where those monuments were located in close proximity to churches, they do not show any consistent spatial relationship to buildings which might be expected if they formed part of the normal Christian rites, and many of the crosses from a religious context, as evidenced on occasions by their inscriptions, were doubtless memorials to leading clerics, although the majority were evidently secular memorials, sometimes serving as burial monuments.[3343]

That view can be contrasted with that of Richard Bailey, who reminds us that from the ninth century we have the poem *De abbatibus*, which describes altar crosses covered with gold plate embedded with emeralds, and there are other literary descriptions of eighth century crosses at York and Hereford encrusted with gold, silver and jewels. He concludes that such richly decorated crosses formed a central role in the elaborate ritual of the Anglo-Saxon church, and that the stone crosses of the period were probably attempts by their sculptors to produce versions of those ornate crosses in stone. He suggests two reasons to explain why Anglo-Saxon masons chose to create these enormous crosses. The first relates to an international perception; the second is more deeply embedded in the Anglo-Saxon psyche.

Bailey points out that the Anglo-Saxon religious establishment is likely to have been aware through pilgrims' tales of a series of replica crucifixion crosses which had been erected on Golgotha hill. The first of these, probably set up by Constantine, was apparently in metal and was relatively plain. There are references to a gem-studded cross in the time of Theodosius between 417 and 440, which may be a new cross or decorative work on the earlier cross. In 620 this was replaced by a gem-encrusted silver cross, the *crux gemmata*, which was to become a highly potent symbol which travelled westwards in artistic representations. This great jewelled cross is also a central image in two of the major poems of the Anglo-Saxon period, *The Dream of the Rood* and *Elene*. Anglo-Saxon and insular

---

[3343] Lord 2003: 30. Barbara Yorke has noted how the monastery at Whitby commemorated the dead through stone monuments, and reminds us that Rosemary Cramp has suggested that an early example of a plain stone cross from Whitby, probably dating from the seventh century, may have been inspired by the wooden cross associated with King Oswald, the uncle of Abbess Ælfflaed of Whitby, and that the monastery may have pioneered the development of the standing-stone cross. Yorke also notes that nunneries in particular have produced some striking examples of monumental crosses that were a focus of prayers and liturgy as well as serving to commemorate families (Yorke 2003: 117-8), a comment that may have particular relevance in the case of the Wolverhampton cross-shaft.

sculptors were, according to Bailey, adopting a well-defined religious precedent in recreating their metalwork crosses in stone: they were effectively replicating the cross of Golgotha in Britain.

The second explanation suggested by Bailey relates to the prestigious status of the metalworker and jeweller, as evidenced for example by the finds from Sutton Hoo which emphasise that late pagan society expressed its achievements through magnificent jewellery. Liturgical metalwork such as chalices, shrines and bookcovers all testify to the continued high status of metalwork as an appropriate means to celebrate God and his word and to glorify his saints. Just as manuscripts incorporated metalwork-derived elements in their decoration, it may well be that sculptors for very good theological and social reasons sought in the same way to express the importance of their craft by creating monumental representations of crosses in stone, as evidenced by such examples as the Sandbach and Wolverhampton crosses.[3344]

The evidence from the Sandbach crosses in particular points towards the erection of a magnificent monumental, and perhaps commemorative, cross at Wolverhampton in or about the second quarter of the ninth century, possibly at the site of a minster which was re-endowed by Wulfrun c.994. It would perhaps be pushing the hypothesis too far to consider whether it may have been intended as a replacement for Beorngyth's stone, which could have been a natural pillar possibly associated with an earlier religious site in Wolverhampton. What is notable about the decoration on the shaft at St Peter's is the complete absence of human representations (other than in the somewhat cryptic and probably erroneous account prepared by G M Hills in 1872 which refers to 'distinct traces of a figure', presumably human, unmentioned by any other commentator), with no trace of any motifs which could have military connotations. Indeed, one might assume that there is nothing in the decorative scheme which could be seen as overtly religious (which might explain why it escaped the iconoclasm of the sixteenth and seventeenth centuries). However, we must recognise that Anglo-Saxon iconography which seems puzzling today had a significance that was likely to be readily apparent to its contemporary audience. Perhaps surprisingly, Anglo-Saxon crosses carved with human figures are comparatively rare, and the fact that the Wolverhampton shaft dispays no such representations – or at least none that can be identified on the eroded surface – is by no means unusual.[3345] As noted previously, figural stone sculpture is exceptionally rare on the Continent in the seventh to tenth centuries, reinforcing the idea that the iconography of the column has its origins in the Carolingian empire.[3346]

Jane Hawkes has observed that the plant scroll can be seen as a multivalent symbol that encompasses Christ, the Church founded in him, the sacraments of that Church, the life of faith leading to salvation, and eternal life itself, deriving from the association of the plant with the vine and its fruit with grapes, the source of wine that is one of the crucial elements of the Eucharist. Representations of the vine, widely found in Anglo-Saxon art and sculpture, had their roots in the biblical text of John's Gospel (15: 1-5), where, at the Last Supper, Christ explained his self-identification with the vine:

'I am the true vine and my Father is the husbandman. Every branch in me that beareth not fruit, he taketh away, and every branch that beareth fruit, he purgeth it that it may bring

---

[3344] Bailey 1990: 2; Bailey 2003: 237-8.
[3345] Hawkes 2003: 352.
[3346] Rodwell et al 2008: 67, 76.

forth more fruit ... Abide in me, and I in you. As the branch cannot bear fruit of itself, except it abide in the vine; no more can ye, except ye abide in me. I am the vine, ye are the branches: He that abideth in me, and I in him, the same bringeth forth much fruit: for without it ye can do nothing.'[3347]

Even the framework within which sculptural elements are found in Anglo-Saxon art has been interpreted to carry religious meaning far from obvious to a modern audience. Hawkes has concluded of the Sandbach crosses that '[w]hen lozenge-shaped frames with distinctive bosses are featured in an iconographically significant context in Early Christian art ... ... it is generally accepted that the distinctive frame does not function simply as a compositional devise [sic] dividing the field of decoration, but has a symbolic function integral to the iconographic language of the scheme: it expresses the harmonic fourfold nature of the cosmos centred on the Creator-Logos 'Christ', with the circular features at the angles of the lozenges emphasising the four cardinal points of the universe'. She notes other research that demonstrates that such ideas were current not only in Carolingian exegis and manuscript art, but 'were also well-established in earlier Hiberno-Latin literature and received visual expression in Insular art, specifically by means of the distinctive lozenge shape with its quarternial connotations.'[3348] The lozenge-shaped frame found in Insular art of the eighth and ninth centuries and uncommonly repeated in the Sandbach crosses serves not only as a decorative compartmental division, but creates the effect of a series of X-shape *chi*-crosses (so-called from the initial letter of Greek ΧΡΙΣΤΟΣ = Kristos = Christ) that run vertically along the length of the shaft,[3349] and as an endless horizontal encircling band at Wolverhampton.

It is true that what seems to be a bull can be identified in one vandyke on the Wolverhampton column, but the others are very eroded, making any identification particularly problematic. If we are correct in identifying a bull (and it is possible that damage to the stonework misleads the eye, and even that some of the carvings may have been 'enhanced' since they were first carved: the 'bull' seems to have no exact parallels in Anglo-Saxon art, sculpture or metalwork, for the horns of bulls found in manuscript and sculptural art of the later Anglo-Saxon period are normally shown upright), it seems possible that the vandykes originally contained the emblems of the evangelists,[3350] which were a bull or ox, often with wings (St Luke), a man or angel (St Matthew), a lion, often with wings (St Mark), and an eagle (St John).[3351] A close examination of the plaster cast of the shaft in the Victoria and Albert Museum reveals only two definite vandyke frames, one containing the supposed bull, and another adjoining it on the right, and perhaps traces of a third, which is surprising, given the boldness of the carving of the frames which survive.[3352] Although the drawing of the carvings on the pillar made in 1913 shows birds

---

[3347] Hawkes 2002: 91.
[3348] Hawkes 2002: 97-8.
[3349] Hawkes 2002: 101.
[3350] Masefield 1918.
[3351] Cronin 1995: 111-19. An eagle on a branch with its head turned to the right appears on the head of the Ruthwell Cross, and a bird identified as an eagle is found on a crucifixion panel on stone IV at Sandbach: Hawkes 2002: 134. The eagle was the bird of battle, 'eager for flesh', and so the biblical idea that 'where the body is, there the eagles will gather': Ó Carragáin 2000: 202-4.
[3352] Although the area is badly weathered, the surviving undulations in what we may suppose was one of the other vandykes might, with the eye of faith, appear to have a degree of symmetry, and although it is not possible to discern any disctinct pattern, there may be vague similarities to the design on a pillar-cross with circular cross head from Penally, Pembrokeshire, dated to the early 10th century (Bebb 2007: I 101), and a grave slab excavated at St Oswald's minster, Gloucester, which is

in three of the vandykes, the plaster-cast provides no evidence to support that interpretation, apart from what may be one parrot-like bird to the right of the 'bull'. In that respect we may note that in the later Anglo-Saxon period, representations of eagles often appeared parrot-like, and an eroded winged lion might appear to resemble a bird.[3353] However, the parrot-like carving, with a large round bulging eye, has a curious configuration, appearing to sit on a thick horizontal branch-like projection, and the identification as a bird must be open to doubt. The significance, if any, of the number five in the iconography of the column (a row of five motifs in each of the decorative bands with five vandykes) is unclear – perhaps an allusion to the five wounds (hands, feet and side) of Christ.

Details of the plaster-cast of the Wolverhampton cross-shaft showing (left) the vandyke frame enclosing a carving which is generally held to be a bull, and (right) the frame containing a bird-like shape. The way in which the second carving extends across the left-hand side of the double lines of the framing is particularly noteworthy.

It will be recalled that Sidebottom considered that a 'secular elite' could have have been responsible for the construction of sculptural crosses in the West Midlands, specifically the Wolverhampton cross-shaft.[3354] Who might be those secular elite? Simon Keynes has

---

decorated with inhabited plant-scrolls, described by Wilson as a highly competent piece of carving (Wilson 1984: 195-6; Walker 2000: 109).

[3353] See, for example, the transverse arm of the cross-head, probably of ninth-century date, from St Michael's church, Cropthorne, Worcestershire (Walker 2000: 32); the eagle fibula known as the Gisela Jewel, c.1000, in the Mittelrheinisches Landesmuseum, Mainz (Backes and Dölling 1969: 184-5), and another (?) example of the same brooch from Mainz c.1025: Swarzenski 1974: Plate 25, fig.56. It is of interest that the (c.12th century?) font at Llanfair Clydogau in Cardiganshire has representations of the four evangelists in the conventional form of the manuscript tradition, but the shape of the symbols suggests that the carver had seen few, if any, manuscript examples, since the eagle of St John was clearly based on a crow or raven: Lord 2003: 85.

[3354] It is worth recording that no connections have been traced between the Sandbach area and Wolverhampton in the pre-Conquest period.

identified 13 ealdormen recorded between c.798 and 884 whose careers span two or three reigns and who may have been appointed by the king and given responsibility for one of the former satellite provinces integrated into the enlarged kingdom of Mercia, or were themselves the hereditary or chosen leaders of the extended Mercian world who owed their positions to the standing they enjoyed locally.[3355] Any of those could have been responsible for the erection of carved Christian crosses, possibly but not necessarily associated with minsters, but various other candidates with local connections must also be considered, though the exercise is, in truth, unlikely to provide many answers to the unresolved questions.

From the tentative dating of the Wolverhampton pillar to the earlydecades of the ninth century we must exclude Beorngyth, mentioned in Wulfrun's charter, for (if the speculation elsewhere in this volume as to her identity is correct), the shaft is evidently of a much later period. King Æthelbald is known to have stayed nearby at Willenhall c.732,[3356] but again must be ruled out for the same reason. As noted elsewhere, a hill named *Hildebaldeshull* is recorded twice on the south-west side of Wednesfield in the early fourteenth century, and remains unexplained. The personal name Hildebald is exceptionally rare, but Hygebald was a seventh-century bishop of Lindsey. Bede records his holiness, and he was said to be a friend of St Chad and was told about a vision of the soul of Chad being led to heaven by the soul of his brother Cedd with a band of angels. He became a hermit and a Mercian saint.[3357] It is very difficult to imagine any connection, however indirect, between the saint and the Wolverhampton cross-shaft, though his connection with Chad and status as a Mercian saint should not be overlooked.

We might therefore consider other individuals who may have been responsible for erecting the cross at Wolverhampton, recognising that some unrecorded devout magnate and benefactor might equally well have sponsored the not insignificant expense associated with its quarrying, design, sculpting, haulage, decoration, installation and dedication.

King Edgar (959-75) is known to have stayed with his councillors in Penkridge, a mere 12 miles north of Wolverhampton, in 958 (when he was king of the Mercians and Northumbrians, and before he became king of all England in 959), and was known as 'the Peaceable' because of the absence of warfare and internal dissent during his reign,[3358] but perhaps more notably as patron of the monastic reform movement, which entailed the immense transference of land from lay to ecclesiastical control (which later provoked considerable resentment), and who, although pious, was not notably religious in his personal life.[3359] Not only was he at Penkridge (and possibly visited Wolverhampton), with that visit falling only slightly outside flexible margins of the postulated time-frame for the Wolverhampton cross shaft, but as noted previously William of Malmesbury recorded that Edgar was originally buried *in capitulo*, translated … as 'in a column', before the church at Glastonbury, traditionally a Celtic foundation, which had a variety of recorded funerary monuments, and may well have kept the ancient tradition of marking royal graves with a column.[3360] Possibly Edgar is to be associated with at least some monumental cross-shafts

---

[3355] Keynes 2001: 314-23.
[3356] S.86 and S.87.
[3357] Listed as Hygebald 2 in the *Prosopography of Anglo-Saxon England*, accessed 7 May 2016. Hygebald was also the name of the eighth-century abbot of Lindsey who reported the Viking raid on Lindisfarne in 793 to Alcuin and died in 803.
[3358] Whitelock 1955: 46.
[3359] Williams, Smyth and Kirby 1991: 123-5.
[3360] Cramp 2006: 31.

of this period. Yet the likely date of the Wolverhampton cross-shaft would seem to rule out Edgar as the driving force behind the creation of the Wolverhampton column, unless the sculptor chose to base at least some of his work on older designs existing 50 miles to the north in the Sandbach area, though as discussed above the Wolverhampton shaft may well pre-date the later of the two Sandbach crosses.

King Æthelred (978-1016) held estates near Wolverhampton. After reducing the influence of the reformed churches, he repented and encouraged the flowering of the church. He is self-evidently associated with Wolverhampton, for it was he who granted ten *cassati* of land in [Wolver-] *Heantune* and one *manentia* of land in Trescott to Wulfrun in 985,[3361] but again his reign post-dates the likely date of the Wolverhampton column.

Of Wulfrun herself we have little information, and although she is of a later period than the assumed date of the Wolverhampton cross-shaft, her prominence in the history of the area makes it necessary to consider her life, such as we know it.[3362] She was a wealthy noblewoman of Mercia who founded (or, more properly, refounded) the minster of St Mary at Wolverhampton. Her self-evidently strong links with Wolverhampton remain unexplained. Her background has led to much confusion. Florence (John) of Worcester says she was the wife of ealdorman Ælfhelm, and mother of Alfgiva of Northamptonshire, wife of Cnut.[3363] Sir William Dugdale claimed that she was a sister of King Edgar (a claim often repeated in later histories), but he gives no authority. Edgar's wife was named Ælfthfryth, the same name as Wulfrun's daughter, which might suggest some relationship. Plot says she was the daughter of Aldhelm, Duke of Northampton.[3364] He gives no authority, but was evidently following Florence (John) of Worcester.[3365] Both Dugdale and Plot appear to have been mistaken.

Wulfrun's charter which endowed the church, almost certainly a spurious invention of a later but pre-Domesday Book period with elements of authenticity, describes her as 'the noble matron and religious woman Wulfrun'.[3366] She is generally assumed to be the Wulfrun whose capture when Olafr Guthfrithson took Tamworth in 940 was of sufficient importance to be recorded as an exceptional entry in the 'D' version of the *Anglo-Saxon*

[3361] S.860. See also Williams, Smyth and Kirby 1991: 27-9; Keyes 1980.
[3362] Whitelock 1930: 44, 152-3, 164-5; Williams, Smyth and Kirby 1991: 241. Her family tree can be found in Swanton 1996: 295. Dugdale says she was the sister of King Edgar, but gives no authority for the statement, Plot that she was the widow of Althelm, Duke of Northampton, but again there is no authority for the claim: Plot 1686: 416-7. For an ingenious but doubtful (and unprovable) theory that Wulfrun may have been a daughter of Ælfwynn, who was the only child of Ealdorman Æthelred and Alfred's daughter Æthelflæd, and 'was deprived of all control of Mercia, and was led into Wessex' (ASC 'C'; Swanton 1996: 105) by her maternal uncle Edward the Elder in 919 following the death of her mother the previous year, and thereafter disappears from history, presumed to have spent the remainder of her life as a religious, see SHC 1916 47-57, 62-6; WA I 289-91; and especially Bailey 2001. If the hypothesis is correct, Wulfrun would have been a great grand-daughter of King Alfred. The theory seems to be given some credence in VCH III 199, and it must be conceded that the Burton Chronicle describes her son Wulfric as *regali propinquus prosapiae* 'of near royal stock' (SHC 1916: 10). Modern scholars appear to have rejected – or overlooked – the theory, but see Hart 1975: 373. The *Prosopography of Anglo-Saxon England*, accessed 7 November 2014, lists 11 women of this name, some of whom are clearly the same person.
[3363] Stevenson 1853: 112. Whitelock suggests that Ælfhelm was Wulfric's brother, and that Florence has confused Ælfgifu's mother with her grandmother: Whitelock 1930: 152-3.
[3364] Plot 1686: 416.
[3365] Whitelock 1930: 152.
[3366] Duignan 1888: 7; SHC 1916: 105-115.

Chronicle (incorrectly under the year 943, where Olafr is named as Anlafr),[3367] since the name Wulfrun was not common, and her son held land in Tamworth and was connected with the religious community there.[3368] Dorothy Whitelock has suggested that the reference to her capture at Tamworth may have been due to the interest taken at York (where the 'D' version of the Chronicle could have been compiled) in the mother of the man who later became ealdorman of Northumbria. It is however possible that she was remembered in her own right as a member of one of the great Mercian families – certainly the *Chronicle*, by giving no further information about Wulfrun at the time of her capture, assumes that readers would know her identity, which shows that she must have been a woman of importance, and Hart has suggested that she was probably related to the royal line.[3369] Since the charter itself is almost certainly spurious, we should remember that its date is also suspect, and any authentic charter on which it might have been based could have been dated up to nine years earlier, or indeed some years later.[3370]

Apart from Wulfruna's Well, a spring in Gorsebrook Road, Wolverhampton, presumably *St Wilfrune's Spring* (her elevation to sainthood should be noted) recorded in Song 12 of Michael Drayton's topographical poem and associated map *Polyolbion* of 1613[3371] which (together with 'the meadows below' called *Wolvern meadows*, seemingly 'Wulfrun's meadows')[3372] is by tradition associated with Wulfrun, no other places in Wolverhampton – or indeed elsewhere – are anciently connected with her name.[3373]

[3367] The entry in ASC 'D' is placed under 943, but it is evident that the capture of Wulfrun occurred before the recovery of the Five Boroughs which is dealt with in the preceding entry, apparently confusing the recently arrived Olafr (Sihtricson) with Olafr (Guthfrithson), who was involved in the fight for the Five Boroughs in 940: Swanton 1996: 111 fn.12. The fact that the sole reference to her capture is in the ASC 'D' may have been due to the interest taken at York, where the body of the text may well have originated, in the mother of the man (Aelfhelm) who later became ealdorman of Northumbria 993x1006: Whitelock 1959: 70-88; Hart 1975: 258-9. Olafr Gothfrithson, King of Dublin 934-41, King of York 939-41, succeeded his father Gothfrith as King of the Vikings of Dublin in 934. In 937 he attempted with Constantine II, King of the Scots, to take the kingdom of York, but was defeated by Æthelstan of Wessex at the battle of *Brunanburh*. On Æthelstan's death in 939 a second, successful, attempt was made. In 940 Olafr attacked Mercia, razing Tamworth (and capturing Wulfrun) and seizing the Five Boroughs (Leicester, Lincoln, Stamford, Nottingham and Derby). He died in 941. See Williams, Smyth and Kirby 1991: 190.

[3368] Whitelock 1930: 152.

[3369] Hart 1975: 373. Stevenson has noted that Romsley, left by Wulfric to Burton Abbey, was bequeathed with the landing-stage pertaining to it to Ealdorman Æthelmer (inadvertently called Ælfhelm), a son of Ealdorman Æthelweard the chronicler (a descendant of King Æthelred, and elder brother of King Alfred), by a female relative who was probably named Wulfrun: TSAS 4th Series I 1911 20-21. However, the estate was *Rameslege* (Brede in Sussex): S.911.

[3370] Ann Williams suggests, without further details, that the charter may date from the time of Archbishop Sigeric's successor Ælfric, who went to Canterbury from Ramsbury on 21st April 995 and died on 16 November 1005: Williams 2003: 177 fn.121.

[3371] Mander and Tildesley 1960: 4; SE 691.

[3372] Shaw 1801 II: 175, 186.

[3373] But note the reference at some date in the thirteenth century before 1269, discussed later in the chapter, to a place in the Wednesfield area described as the *fossatum Wulfrini* 'the entrenched place of Wulfrini'. We may note that Wollerton, a township in Hodnet in Shropshire, is said to incorporate the personal name Wulfrun (PN Sa 1: 319-20), but the age of the name is unknown and we cannot know whether this may be the Wulfrun associated with Wolverhampton. A salthouse in Newton-by-Middlewich, Cheshire, is said by Bu'Lock to be an estate mentioned in the will of Wulfric Spot, named *Woluernepool* (Ollerpool(e), lost), held to derive from his mother Wulfrun (Bu'Lock 1972: 66), but no such name is found in Wulfric's will (Sawyer 1979: xv-xxxviii). The explanation is that despite scholarly opposition John Dodgson felt Ollerpool(e) (and Wormald, Yorkshire West Riding)

Wulfrun's estates seems to have lain chiefly in Staffordshire, but she may have had strong ties with Worcestershire.[3374] She was married, though the name of her husband is not known.[3375] Since one of her sons, Wulfric Spot (who died between 1002 and 1004), is known unusually as Wulfric son of Wulfrun, she was perhaps of higher rank than her husband, or her husband may have died young. Her other son, Ælfhelm, was appointed ealdorman of Northumbria in 993 by Æthelred II, but in 1006 he fell foul of the king and was murdered, on the king's orders, by Eadric Streona. His sons, Wulfheah and Ufegeat, were blinded, but his daughter survived to become the wife of King Cnut and mother of King Harold. The spurious confirmation by Sigeric, Archbishop of Canterbury, of Wulfrun's charter to the monastery of Wolverhampton, was dated 996, clearly in error for 994, since Sigeric died on 28th October 994,[3376] which further confirms its status as a later forgery. The charter states explicitly that Wulfrun's daughter Ælfthfryth was dead, but does not make clear whether Wulfgeat (named as Wulfrun's kinsman and discussed previously in this volume), or Wulfrun's un-named husband, who is also mentioned, was alive or not, though these details, and even the supposed date of the charter, must be treated with great caution, given its spurious nature.[3377]

Wulfrun's date of birth is not known, but if we assume that she was a woman of some maturity and fame when her capture is recorded at Tamworth in 940, it seems unlikely that she was much younger than 30, in which case she would have been 84 or more in 994 (and of course older still if she was captured after the age of 30). That would have been exceptional longevity at a time when 60 was seen as a great age for a tenth-century *ealdorman*, and few *ealdormen* of the period survived beyond 55.[3378] Had Wulfrun been of such remarkable age when she supposedly made her endowment in 994, we would surely expect to see the fact recorded in the charter. It seems more likely that the Wulfrun captured at Tamworth was not the Wulfrun associated with Wolverhampton, but it may have been her mother. Or perhaps any charter from Wulfrun was made after 985 but well before 994.

Some clues as to Wulfrun's identity may be found in three charters by Oswald, bishop of Worcester (and later York). The first is dated 966 and leases to Eadric, Oswald's thegn, land at Alveston, Upper Stratford, and other places in Warwickshire for three lives. The

---

derived from the OE feminine personal name Wulfrūn, and notes that Wulfric Spot, whose mother was Wulfrūn, held land at Newton-by-Middlewich. The earliest spelling available for Ollerpool(e) is *Woluernepool* (1260-90): PN Cheshire 2: 244-5.

[3374] A Wulfrun is named as a witness to 5 charters all leasing land in Worcestershire with Wulfrun named as the second life and the reversion to the church of Worcester: S.1301 (962), S.1310 (966), S.1323 (969), S.1334 (977), S.1350 (985): the *Prosopography of Anglo-Saxon England*, accessed 7 November 2014. These dates could well suggest that the witness Wulfrun was the benefactor of the minster of Wolverhampton.

[3375] A charter dating from between 978 and 1016 says that Ærnketel (a Scandinavian name) and Wulfrun (written as *Wlfron* and *Wlfroun*), his wife, make known to King Æthelred and to the faithful in Yorkshire and Nottinghamshire that they give land at Hickling and Kinoulton (Nottinghamshire) and Lockington (Yorkshire) to Ramsey monastery: S.1493; Thorpe 1865: 531-2. This Wulfrun can be ruled out as the Wulfrun associated with Wolverhampton: the *History of Ramsey* says that Ærnketel and Wulfrun lived about Edgar's time: Pearson 1870: 18; Raftis 1957: 8-9. Willis 1718: 152 notes that amongst those interred in the abbey are 'Arnketel, and Wlfron his Wife, who both died An. 1013, and were parents to Æthelstan the fourth Abbat ...'. See also Wise and Noble 1881: 57.

[3376] Powicke and Fryde 1961: 210.

[3377] Wulfgeat's will makes it clear that he had an interest in Wrottesley: S.1534; Whitelock 1930: 56-7.

[3378] Hart 1975: 288; 355.

rubric names the recipients as Eadric and Wulfrun (presumably the second life).[3379] The second is dated 977, again to his thegn Eadric, of land at Tiddington, Warwickshire, for three lives, with Wulfrun named in the Worcester entry as second life.[3380] The third is dated 985, to his thegn Eadric, for three lives of land at Tiddington and Alveston, with the rubric again naming Wulfrun as the second life.[3381] It seems likely that Eadric was closely related to the Wulfrun named in these charters; indeed Hart has suggested that he may have been her brother.[3382] In 1004 a charter by Æthelmær mentions his (male) cousin Leofwine, his kinsman Godwin, and a kinsman Wulfrun, who has left him an estate called *Rameslege* and its harbour. *Rameslege* has been identified as Brede in Sussex.[3383]

Wulfrun does not appear to have been alive when her son Wulfric's will was drawn up before 1004, perhaps unsurprisingly as she could have been well into her 90s or even older at that date if we are to associate her with the capture at Tamworth. The statement in a grant of three hides at Abbot's Bromley to her son Wulfric in 996 that Wulfric had been given the place by his mother does not prove that she was either alive or dead at that date.[3384]

What clues might we use when attempting to identify Wulfrun's husband?

1. If we are correct in assuming that he was a person of considerable authority, it is unthinkable, even given our incomplete records relating to the tenth century, that he would have escaped mention completely.

2. Judging from wills and charters that have survived, sons normally inherited, with provision made for the widow during her widowhood and for the daughters at marriage.[3385] It is very likely that Wulfrun received some of her estates from her husband, and in due course some were granted to one or more of her children. Is there any evidence from some decades prior to 994 of a figure of authority who held estates that might be connected with Wulfrun and her children?

3. In the Anglo-Saxon period parents commonly used names for their children which alliterated with, or incorporated parts of, or were the same as, their own.[3386] The names of Wulfrun's children (Ælfhelm, Ælfthfryth and Wulfric) suggest that we might be seeking a husband with a name beginning Ælf– or Wulf–.

[3379] S.1310; Hart 1975: 80-81.
[3380] S.1334; Hart 1975: 82.
[3381] S.1350; Hart 1975: 82-83.
[3382] Hart 1975: 83. In the nineteenth century Charles H. Pearson investigated the genealogy of Earl Godwin and Earl Harold and made a case that Wulfrun was a kinswoman of the infamous Eadric Streona, a Shropshire magnate who rose to prominence in the reign of Æthelred the Unready (whose daughter he married), and became ealdorman of Mercia, but was eventually executed for his repeated perfidy (Williams, Smyth and Kirby 1991: 113-4). In that paper, it was suggested that Wulfrun was the ancestress of those leaving land to Earl Godwin and Earl Harold: see Pearson 1870: 15-36; also Sawyer 1979: xxi-xxiii, xxxix-xliii; Williams, Smyth and Kirby 1991: 181 *sub nom* Morcar; Insley 2000: 40 fn.37.
[3383] S.906; Whitelock 1930: 151-60.
[3384]
[3385] Loyn 1963: 180.
[3386] For example, St Wulfstan (1012?-1095) is said to have been given the first part of his name from that of his mother, Wulfgifu, and the second part from his father, Æthelstan.

In summary, we should perhaps identify an important figure with the name Ælf– or Wulf–, who held property later held by Wulfrun or her children, who is likely to have died several decades before Wulfrun, and who had no other recorded wife. One candidate in particular fulfils those criteria: Wulfsige *Maur*, otherwise Wulfsige the Black.

Little is known about Wulfsige. There is even uncertainty about the epithet *Maur* (which is not an Old English word), but Bridgeman has plausibly suggested that it derives from the Latin *Maurus* 'dark, swarthy', so 'Wulfsige the swarthy'. As it happens, in 962 there is a reference to *Wulfsige cognomina Blaca* 'Wulfsige known as the Swarthy'. By three charters dated 942, he received from Edgar, presumably as a reward for his loyalty, a large block of territory on either side of the river in the upper Trent valley in Staffordshire and Derbyshire.[3387] It is clear that he was of very considerable importance, and from wording at the end of the 942 charters it would appear that the lands were conferred on him as reward for some military service.[3388] He is probably Wulfsige *the blaca* who once held Abbot's Bromley, as recorded in the will of Wulfric Spot.[3389] The estate probably passed from Wulfsige to Wulfrun, and it may not be too fanciful to imagine that Wulsige was Wulfric's father (and Wulfrun's husband), or his maternal grandfather (and Wulfrun's father).[3390] According to the thirteenth century annals of Burton Abbey, Wulfric's endowment consisted of the whole of his paternal inheritance, worth seven hundred pounds, but those annals must be treated with caution, and Sawyer has suggested that Wulfric may have owed his rank and wealth to his mother, who may have been a sole heiress, rather than his father,[3391] but his brother, Ælfhelm, who became Ealdorman of Northumbria by 993, and his family, owned many of the estates that had belonged to Wulfsige, as well as many owned by Wulfric, which is consistent with some close kinship.[3392] Wulfsige may have been dead by 956, when some farms in Branston were granted to King Eadmund's son and eventual successor King Eadwig.[3393]

There are other possible candidates for Wulfrun's husband. One is Wulfhelm, a thegn who received estates in Marchington, Little Aston and Great Barr from King Eadwig in 957, although he was not of sufficient seniority to witness that king's charters. He rose to prominence after Edgar's revolt in 957, and was evidently a senior thegn, subscribing to most of the charters issued by Edgar as king of the Mercians, and continued to witness after Edgar succeeded to the whole of the kingdom in 959, but gradually lost seniority until rising in 962 to be one of the most important thegns in the country. He ceases to be a witness in 963, and we may assume that he died in that year or soon thereafter. Since the

---

[3387] Williams 2003: 33, 58, but see also Hart 1975: 376. It is possible that charters in the name of Wulfsige dating between 938 and 946 may relate to other men of the same name.
[3388] SHC 1916 83.
[3389] Hart 1975: 202. The estate, held jointly by Wulfsige and a certain Æscbyrht, passed to three men named Eadhelm, Alfred and Æthelwold, before it came into the possession of Wulfrun: Hart 1975: 206.
[3390] Hart 1975: 175-6. In 963 Wulfgeat, perhaps Wulfrun's kinsman mentioned in her will, attests Edgar's charters in 964 and 970, and was granted lands at Darlaston, Staffordshire, and Upper Arley, Worcestershire, by Edgar: Williams 2003: 33, 35, 58. Hart 1975: 373 thought it likely that an estate at Austrey in Warwickshire granted to a thegn named Wulfric in 958 which was in Wulfric Spot's possession when he founded Burton Abbey was held by Wulfric, the father of Wulfric Spot, and thus (presumably) the husband of Wulfrun. Wulfric Spot married Ealhswith, about whom we know nothing.
[3391] Sawyer 1979: xl, xliv-xliv. It is noteworthy that Wulfric made no bequest to his mother's own foundation at Wolverhampton.
[3392] Sawyer 1979: xliii.
[3393] SHC 1916 83.

Marchington estate descended to Wulfric Spot, we may make a connection with Wulfric, if not with his mother.[3394]

Another candidate as Wulfrun's husband is the Wulfric who was granted Austrey in Warwickshire in 958 by King Edgar. Since this estate was in the hands of Wulfric Spot in 1004, it is possible, as Hart believes, that Wulfric was Wulfric Spot's father (and Wulfrun's husband), or another close relative. Given the number of men of this name in the tenth century, it is difficult to assemble any further details of his life.[3395]

Whoever was Wulfrun's husband – and it is quite likely that he was none of the above, and very possible that Wulfrun's wealth (and power) were indeed inherited – Wulfrun herself was clearly of sufficient means and status, and had self-evident links with and affection for the church of Wolverhampton, to make her a plausible candidate responsible for sponsoring the construction and installation of the Wolverhampton cross-shaft, though she lived at a time that falls well outside the range of likely dates for the cross. Alternatively, the clergy of Wolverhampton may have thought it fitting to erect a cross to the memory of Wulfrun after her death, which probably occurred c.1000.[3396]

Such monuments to benefactors are rare but not unknown. A narrative in a forged charter, probably with an authentic basis, dating from the late eleventh century and purportedly dating from between 781 and 796, provides an interesting description of a stone monument with a cross 'in the manner of the ancients' which marked the burial place of Wiferd and Alta, a married couple who had granted 15 hides of land to the Worcester church in the late 8th century.[3397] The monument, about which we have no further details, stood within the cathedral precincts until the mid-eleventh century when it was pulled down to make room for an enlargement of St Peter's, the old cathedral church, and was presumably a notable landmark, for it was chosen by bishop Oswald (961-92) as the site from which to preach during the construction of the new cathedral of St Mary's. The burial of Wiferd and Alta was directly related to their social status and their patronage of the Worcester church, and the comment that the monument was 'in the manner of the ancients' might suggest that

---

[3394] Hart 1975: 368-9.

[3395] Hart 1975: 373.

[3396] Clues as to the identity of Wulfrun are few, but as noted elsewhere in this volume, there is a reference at some date in the thirteenth century before 1269 (possibly in 1240) to a place (a boundary mark in a survey of Prestwood, which seems to coincide in part with the eastern boundary of Wednesfield as set out in Wulfrun's supposed charter of 994) to the east of Wolverhampton, probably somewhere between *Kirclesford* or *Kirnesford* (a ford over the river Tame at Moseley Hole) and *Horestan* (near the junction of Fibbersley and Broad Lane South), described as the *fossatum Wulfrini*' the entrenched place of Wulfrini': Mander and Tildesley 1960: 28; Smallshire 1978: 45; Hooke 1983: 72-5. Wulfrini is surely to be identified, through the correction of a typical misreading of minims, as Wulfrun, the name Wulfrini being otherwise unrecorded and given her connection with the area. It has been suggested, somewhat improbably, that it may have lain in the Blackhalve area, or somewhere in Short Heath:(Mander and Tildesley 1960: 28), butSmallshirethought that it may have been in the Noose Lane/Portobello area: Smallshire 1978: 45. It is of interest that the ford was used as a boundary mark, when the place was the site of Stowman's Hill (Moseley Hole was the pit created when the gravel mound was destroyed for roadmaking), which might have been a more prominent landmark had it existed at the time.

[3397] Post finem autem uite illorum, lapidum structura, more antiquorum, super sepulchrum eorum, opera artificioso, cum croce dominica, ob monumentum largitatis et monimenum animarum ipsorum, compisita est: 'After the end of their lives, as memorial to their munificence and monument to their souls, a structure of stone with a cross to the lord, in the manner of their ancients, was skilfully built above their grave': *Hemingi chartularium*, 342.

such monuments were considered archaic by the late eleventh century.[3398] Here we have clear evidence that towards the end of the eighth century it was not unknown for major benefactors to a church to be buried there and commemorated by a prominent monumental cross. It does not seem implausible to imagine the practice continuing some two centuries later, with the prominent benefactor to Wolverhampton church interred at her foundation (or refoundation), with the site marked by an elaborately carved cross of suitable splendour, in which case we might suppose that the Wolverhampton cross-shaft was erected early in the eleventh century, soon after the death of Wulfrun, although the practice would evidently have been seen as unfashionable at the end of the century.[3399] It cannot be proved, but in the absence of further information about matters affecting Wolverhampton in the pre-Conquest period Wulfrun might be thought to be a leading candidate to be associated with the cross, though the design of the column would be so archaic that the idea can probably be discounted.

Other explanations for the existence of monumental crosses might be found in examples from mainland Europe. In France, for example, cases are known when the translations of saints' relics were made in procession during which cures were effected, and whenever the relics rested a cross was erected, and if there was no church one was built,[3400] though no parallels for this have been traced from pre-Conquest England.

Tweddle has put forward the idea that the Wolverhampton cross-shaft may have been designed as a 'triumphal column', a view supported by Karkov and Brown and by Cramp's belief that it was erected to commemorate some major event or was perhaps a royal monument,[3401] but (apart from the battle of Tettenhall) we have no information at all about major events, or in truth lesser events, at or near Wolverhampton (except for Æthelbald's stay at Willenhall c.732[3402] and Edgar's visit to Penkridge in 958) before about the year 1000, including the foundation (as opposed to Wulfrun's apparent (re)foundation) of the minster at Wolverhampton. If not associated with Wulfrun's grant, is it conceivable that the cross is to be associated in some way with the battle of 910, the only notable event in the area of which we are aware even though it falls outside the broad dating of the monument as suggested above? In that respect we may note that Nancy Edwards has concluded, in a detailed discussion of the Pillar of Eliseg, that '[t]he cross symbol – and by extension the free-standing cross – was essentially a sign of victory, as the Old English *sigbecn* ['emblem of victory, trophy, cross (of Christ)'] inscribed in runes on the Bewcastle cross makes clear', and concludes that '[t]he form of the Eliseg cross would have been appropriate to record the victory of Eliseg over the English', though not necessarily at or near the site of the cross.[3403]

Crosses associated with battlefields are recorded by early writers. Bede[3404] tells us that King Oswald helped with his own hands to erect a cross and prayed for God's protection

---

[3398] Hare 2014.
[3399] Tinti 2010: 314.
[3400] Wood 2002: 176-7.
[3401] Cramp 1975: 187-9; 245. William of Malmesbury records a series of stone crosses standing along the Fosse Way which he says marked bishop Aldhelm's funeral procession in 709 (34 miles from Doulting to Malmesbury, via Bath), with many miracles recorded at those crosses: Hamilton 1870: 383-4; Blair 2005: 480.
[3402] S.86 and S.87.
[3403] Edwards 2009: 169; Charles-Edwards 2013: 414.
[3404] HE III 2.

before the battle of Heavenfield,[3405] near Hexham, in 634, but as Adomnán, the earliest source for the battle, does not mention a cross, it is possible that Bede, and perhaps popular tradition, attributed a cross erected later to mark the site of the battle as having been set up before the battle. The monks of Hexham began the custom of an annual pilgrimage to the battle-field on the anniversary of Oswald's death and distributed splinters from the wooden cross as miracle-working relics. Bede expressly relates that because of the popularity of the pilgrimage the brethren had recently constructed a church on the site. Fragments of the wooden cross were later held by Durham priory according to a fourteenth-century relic list.[3406]

The Bewcastle cross, some six miles north of Hadrian's Wall to the north-east of Brampton, is a shaft dating from c.700 which incorporates three figure panels and a lengthy runic inscription which may have been altered in the nineteenth century, with the result that most of its letters cannot now be read, although the phrase 'this victory monument' and 'kyniburga' have been traced. Kyniburga was the wife of Aldfrith, who ruled Northumbria from 685 to c.704, and the cross is likely to be associated with that king.[3407] The expression 'victory monument' might suggest a battle marker.

Evidence of other crosses commemorating battles from the Anglo-Saxon period is scant, but Talbot-Rice states that King Ecgbert set up a cross at Caistor in Lincolnshire to commemorate his victory over Mercia in 927 [*sic*], but that nothing of the cross is known to have survived.[3408] The cross was mentioned in 1831, when *The Gentleman's Magazine* noted 'a most unequivocal token of this victory [by Egbert of Wessex over Wiglaf of Mercia, in 827] remains in an inscribed stone which was dug out of the Castle hill [at Caistor] by some labourers in the year 1770; from which we learn that Egbert piously dedicated his spoils to God at the foot of the cross … This memorial is now in the museum at Lincoln. It is a flat grey stone about a foot broad by two feet and a half wide, and appears to have been intended to fix in a wall. The letters are uncouth, and the inscription considerably defaced'.[3409] White's *Directory* of 1834 suggests that the inscription read *cruci spolium, quod Egbert rex in honorem*. The authenticity of this alleged antiquity must remain very uncertain.

At least 13 fragments of sculptured stone recovered from the foundations of the early church (possibly of Anglo-Saxon origin) of St Barnabus at Bromborough are of particular interest, not least as a result of their chequered and unfortunate history. The original church (located in a distinctive sub-circular churchyard, probably indicative of great antiquity)[3410] was demolished in 1827-8 and the fragments placed in the foundations of its replacement, itself pulled down in 1867 when the pieces were recovered and placed on the lawn of the rectory, but dispersed in 1909 and most lost. From photographs it is evident that the fragments consisted of pieces of cross-shaft, cross head, slabs, a round-headed gravemarker, socket stones and other fragments featuring various designs with Norse, Scottish and Northumbrian influences, and dating from the tenth and eleventh century.[3411]

[3405] Seemingly fought at Rowley Burn, 3 miles south of Hexham and referred to by the Old Welsh name *Cantscaul* 'young warrior's enclosure': *Nomina* 31 (2008) 155.
[3406] Stancliffe and Cambridge 1995: 63 fn.145; 168.
[3407] Kerr and Kerr 1982: 21-3
[3408] Talbot-Rice 1952: 137, citing W. E. St Lawrence Finny, 'The Church of the Saxon coronation at Kingston', *Surrey Archaeological Collections* xlviii (1943) 3.
[3409] GM 1831 Vol. CI 204.
[3410] Mainwaring Estate map c.1755; Tithe Map 1840.
[3411] Bailey 2010: 52-7.

Three stones were re-erected in the churchyard in 1958 to create a Celtic cross. Bromborough is one of the locations – arguably the strongest contender – put forward as the site of the battle of *Brunanburh* in 937, and we might wonder whether the church – and/or perhaps some kind of sculpted stone memorial – may have been set up to commemorate what is seen as one of the the most significant Anglo-Saxon battles before 1066.

Elsewhere, Battle Abbey in Sussex and Battlefield Church in Shropshire commemorate the battle of Hastings in 1066 and the battle of Shrewsbury in 1403 respectively, both built soon after those battles.[3412] Building of a chantry chapel appears to have started in 1483 on the battlefield after the battle of Towton in 1461, but no traces remain above ground and it is uncertain whether it was ever completed.[3413] An earlier example may be Ashington church in Essex, which might be the site of the battle of Assandun in 1016, where the 'flower of England' fell, and where by 1020 Cnut had raised a small minster built of stone and lime to have perpetual masses said for 'the souls of the men who were there slain',[3414] and near Cuckney in Nottinghamshire, a chapel at Edwinstowe may mark the spot where the Northumbrian King Edwin (St. Edwin) was killed by the pagan King Penda of Mercia in 633.[3415]

But even though the Wolverhampton pillar has what could be interpreted in the Anglo-Saxon period as patent and overt Christian associations, it is difficult to believe that a sculptural monument erected after the battle of Tettenhall will have failed to incorporate a symbolic reference, specifically in the form of warriors and/or arms and/or an inscription, to the great victory. The available evidence leads us to conclude that the column is not to be associated with the great battle which must have taken place almost within its shadow.
If, therefore, the cross had been erected before 910, we may have a possible explanation for the decision of the Danes to cross the Severn at *Cwatbrycge* immediately prior to the battle of Tettenhall. It might be imagined that the sumptuous Wolverhampton shaft was a celebrated landmark identifying a (later?) wealthy minster which attracted the attention of the Danes during their looting expedition in the later ninth and early tenth centuries, and the English army was able to attack the Danes as they approached (or had left) the minster in search of booty. On the other hand, the fact that no chroniclers refer to *Heantune* in accounts of the battle must be significant. If that place was an important religious focal point in the early tenth century, one might have expected the battle to have been named the battle of *Heantune*, and to find other references to the place before Wulfrun's late tenth-century endowment. Is it possible that an earlier minster church had decayed and/or been destroyed by the Danes, to the extent that *Heantune* had effectively ceased to exist?

Is there any other evidence of Christian memorials to the battle of Tettenhall? Tettenhall is a mile or so north-west of Wolverhampton, Wednesfield a mile or so north-east of Wolverhampton. The villages are just over three miles apart, with the parish boundaries less than two miles from each other. It may also be noted that the two manors of Tettenhall were each held by the church and the king. It would not be surprising if the victorious English decided to commemorate their victory with the erection of a church, and a church

---

[3412] William the Conqueror is said to have pledged the battlefield of Hastings to the church even before the battle began, with the site subsequently given to the monks of Marmoutier on the Loire on the understanding that they would build an abbey there: Vincent 2011: 51.
[3413] Gravett and Turner 2003: 77.
[3414] Burne 2002: 97; Blair 2005: 356; Marren 2006: 180-1.
[3415] Wood 1999: 216.

certainly existed at Tettenhall (and indeed Wolverhampton) at the time of Domesday. It is very possible that the church at Tettenhall predates – perhaps long pre-dates – the battle of Tettenhall,[3416] but if not in existence in 910, it may have been chosen as a religious site to commemorate the battle and offer prayers for the dead, although we have no evidence – in particular no early traditions – that that was the case. Indeed, in 1401 a jury of local residents concluded that the church had been founded by King Edgar (959-75), and he did indeed visit Penkridge in 958. Later juries in 1546 and 1548 ascribed the foundation, very curiously, to Edward III.[3417] There is no reason to imagine that the earlier jury was better informed than the later ones. No church is recorded at Wednesfield before a chapel was built c.1745, though the cryptic field-names *Chirchewythiesfeld* found in 1312 and *Chirchezordesfeld* in 1399 are discussed elsewhere in this volume. One of the medieval great fields of Wednesfield was Churchfield, which may be connected with those names.

The existence of the Wolverhampton cross-shaft also raises questions about the origins of the minster, for it has been thought that crosses, which were very common in areas evangelised by Irish missionaries, including Mercia,[3418] were set up to mark religious sites until a church could be erected. An eighth-century biography of St Willibald records how, in Somerset, a visiting priest would preach and celebrate the Mass at a cross set up outside a lord's hall, and that it was the custom of the Saxon race that, on many of the estates of the nobles and good men, there was not a church but the standard of the Holy Cross, dedicated to our Lord and reverenced with great honour, which mights suggest that many churches occupy sites which were already established as centres of local administration long before the arrival of minster priests.[3419] Had a church existed at Wolverhampton at the time the cross was commissioned, one might perhaps have expected the donor to enrich or enlarge the church rather than erect a sumptuously carved outdoor cross – which he or she may indeed have done. The purpose to be served by erecting an elaborately ornate Christian cross outside an existing church must be open to debate, and we might conclude that it is

---

[3416] VCH XX 3 suggests that there may have been a church at Tettenhall in 975. No evidence is provided, but the statement is probably based on Tanner's comment in Dugdale's *Monasticon Anglicanum*, 1830 VI iii 1467, that Tettenhall was a collegiate church and one of the King's free chapels, founded before the Conquest, perhaps as early as the reign of King Edgar's reign (959-75), as recorded in an Inquisition of 1401: VCH XX 18.

[3417] VCH III 315-6.

[3418] Stancliffe 1995: 90-91, citing Hill 1966: 126-99 ff., and Huneberc's *Life of Willibald*. Higham 1993: 160-61 has observed that 'The tradition of stone carving was imported from Frankia in the 670s ... Free standing stone crosses were first made in Northumbria in the first half of the eighth century. The origins of this type of monument are obscure. There was a tradition of cross-carved slabs within the Celtic Church and Northumbrian sculpture of this period occurs at several sites where these were extant (such as the Hirsel, Coldstream, and Addingham). However, these monuments were no more than one of several influences on Northumbrian sculptors. The more important prototypes were probably metal or ivory miniatures imported from the Mediterranean, which were then translated (and massively enlarged) into the medium of stone for the first time in Northumbria. ... The technique spread rapidly thence throughout England and to Ireland, Scotland and the Isle of Man, where local sculptors developed their own preferred styles and decorations – with the development of the ring-headed cross and decorative spirals particularly favoured by Irish patrons .... Free-standing crosses may have served a variety of functions. A schematic monastic plan in the eighth-century Irish Book of Mulling portrays a rampart-enclosed monastic precinct within which were several crosses and churches. The retrospectively named St John's Cross at Iona is an eighth-century example of just such a cross within a monastic precinct. Northumbrian monasteries were similarly enclosed and some contained paired or grouped churches, or a church and separate baptistry – as at Hexham and Jarrow – so it seems probable that crosses were distributed within Northumbrian religious precincts in a similar fashion. As such they were presumably intended to encourage meditation and private prayer.'

[3419] Friar 2000: 119.

unlikely, though not iconceivable, that a cross would be set up at a place which already had a church.[3420] However, a reference to St Oswald, archbishop of York 971-92, having to preach from the stone memorial cross in the churchyard of Worcester cathedral mentioned previously when he was bishop of Worcester because the building had insufficient space for the crowds who flocked to hear him reminds us that at least one, and probably more, of the great cathedrals had an outside cross, which seemingly served as a focus for preaching to an overspill audience, though whether such crosses may have pre-dated the cathedral itself is not known: the cross at which Oswald preached at Worcester no longer exists.[3421]

Another possibility that deserves to be considered is that the cross-shaft is of post-Conquest date, incorporating typically Romanesque and earlier motifs. What cannot be overlooked in this study is the remarkable corpus of outstanding twelfth-century ecclesiastical carvings found in (and well beyond) Herefordshire, which has come to be known as the Herefordshire School of Romanesque Sculpture. That corpus includes virtually all of the elements found on the Wolverhampton cross-shaft, including interlinked roundels, back-facing birds and beasts, spiralling foliage, and horizontal rope cabling – carvings from the long-demolished twelfth-century church at Shobden, Herefordshire, for example, incorporated all of those elements.[3422] Wolverhampton lies within the area covered by the Herefordshire School – a northern outlier is a dragon on the south base of the western crossing arch of the collegiate church of St Lawrence at Gnosall (like Wolverhampton a Royal Free Chapel), a piece related to the heads of five serpentine dragons at St Cassian's minster church at Chaddesley Corbett, Worcestershire, and similar to a dragon head at the former Bell Inn, Alveley. It would be unwise to dismiss the possibility, albeit very remote, that the Wolverhampton column could be a Continental Romanesque piece associated with the Herefordshire School in archaic style, perhaps adopting elements known from Sandbach.[3423]

[3420] Boniface (c.675-754) complained that worship at crosses was detracting from church attendance: Stancliffe 1995: 91 fn.42. On the other hand, the well-preserved state of some early cross shafts suggests that they have been spared exposure from the elements, and may originally have been placed within a building. Indeed, there is some evidence that a free-standing carved stone cross some nine feet high, perhaps dating from the ninth or early tenth century, fragments of which are now in the crypt of Canterbury cathedral, stood in front of the chancel arch at the Anglo-Saxon church at Reculver, wantonly destroyed in the early nineteenth century: Backhouse, Turner and Webster 1984: 40-41; Kelly 2008a: 69-70. It would be of great interest to know whether there might be any connection between the Wolverhampton cross-shaft and the vaulted stone rooms, 'remains of very remote antiquity', mentioned elsewhere in this volume, which lay near the south-west corner of the church until the early 19th century.
[3421] Zaluckyj 2001: 128.
[3422] Thurlby 1999: 71-86.
[3423] See generally Thurlby 2013. The church of Wolverhampton was granted to the bishop and cathedral church of Lichfield after the death of Roger, bishop of Salisbury in 1139. Roger, a renowned patron of architecture, who had seised it from the monks of Worcester intended to restore the building, though no such restoration is known: VCH Staffs. III 321-3; see also Stalley 1971; Thurlby 1982; Thurlby 2008a; Thurlby 2008b. In that respect various sculptural fragments from Reading Abbey and Hyde Abbey, Winchester c.1125-50, are of interest, including a column from a doorway at Reading decorated with beasts within coupled rings joined by clasps and spandrels filled with floral motifs, inspired by precious oriental silks, much copied during this period: Zarnecki, Holt and Holland 1984: 167-73. Some Continental churches exhibit sculptural decoration not entirely dissimilar to that of the Wolverhampton shaft, for example Santa Maria, Pomposa (Emilia-Romagna), Northern Italy, with vine scrolls twining around numerous figures.

In that respect we are reminded, as noted elsewhere that Henry II gave his consent in 1204 for the foundation of a Cistercian abbey at Wolverhamton with archbishop Hubert Walter to be wholly responsible for the foundation, the king having granted him wide freedom from taxes and burdens, as well as the deanery and prebends, the manors of Wolverhampton and Tettenhall and associated woodland. The monks were also granted timber and other rights and were established at Wolverhampton pending consent for the new abbey from the Cistercian Order, but the death of the archbishop in 1205 led to the abandonment of the plan; the king's grants were cancelled, and he resumed possession of the church, [3424] but we have no information as to any work that may have been carried out in connection with the proposed abbey. A spectacular stone cross would have served as a fitting monument to celebrate the foundation of the planned church. Most of the elements found on the Wolverhampton column are to be seen in French and Italian churches dating from the tenth to the twelfth centuries. It may also be noted that from the 1430s the church of Wolverhampton came under the jurisdiction of the joint deaneries of Windsor and Wolverhampton, with William Dudley the first such dean at a time when the church was being rebuilt. The arrangement was formalised and made permanent by Edward IV in 1480.[3425] Yet there can be little reason to suppose that a grand Romanesque cross in archaic style could have been installed, for example, by Hubert Walter to commemorate the creation of his planned abbey, or by William Dudley to mark the link with Windsor.[3426]

Finally, it is appropriate to record some puzzling aspects in relation to the Wolverhampton column. In particular, it is surprising, to say the least, to find that its existence seems to have gone completely unnoticed – or at least unremarked – until comparatively recent times.[3427] Inexplicably overlooked both by the antiquary Sir William Dugdale (1605-86), who indeed had close associations with the church at Wolverhampton, writing an account of the its historical constitution,[3428] and by the indefatigable Robert Plot in his great *The Natural History of Staffordshire*, published in 1686 (although he almost certainly stayed at the High Hall at High Green near the church whilst researching his book, visiting the church to examine the tomb of John Lane, and also collected material on other lesser carved shafts in the county, including Leek, Draycot, Chebsey, Checkley and Ilam, some of which are illustrated in his work), no mention of the the monument has been traced in the papers of either John Huntbach (1639-1705) or Richard Wilkes (1690-1760), both of whom were respected antiquaries living within a few miles of Wolverhampton and who will have known the town, the church and (we must suppose) the cross-shaft well.[3429]

[3424] Styles 1940: 69; VCH III 323. The ancient stone vaults to the south of the church recorded by Stebbing Shaw and mentioned elsewhere in this volume may, it has been suggested, have been vestiges of the cellarage of the abandoned monastery: Mander and Tildesley 1960: 48.
[3425] VCH III 325.
[3426] For example, the fragment of a nook-shaft with foliage decoration from York c.1180 (Zarnecki 1984: 200); sculptures, including especially a column from a doorway, from Reading Abbey (ibid. 167-73); and even the prolific sculptural columns in Monreale Cathedral near Palermo, Sicily, begun in 1174 and completed c.1200, which although not mirroring precisely the motifs of the Wolverhampton column, display an equally exhuberant style.
[3427] The column is unmentioned by John Leland, but his *Itinerary* did not take him past Wolverhampton: Mander and Tildesley 1960: 58.
[3428] 'Some Account of Wolverhampton', in Erdeswick 1717: 221-4; Broadway 2006: 102.
[3429] Mander and Tildesley 1960: 98, 106; Greenslade 1982: 72. Huntbach left detailed notes on the tombs and the despoiling of the chancel during the Civil War, and included notes on the archaeology of the area: ibid. Curiously, In his edition of Camden's *Britannia*, Richard Gough (1735-1809), a prolific topographer, followed Plot and mentioned lesser cross shafts in Staffordshire but not Wolverhampton (Gough 1806: II 498), although he may have been the author ('R.G.') of a detailed description of the cross shaft published in GM 1794 64 (ii) 714-5.

The column seems first to be recorded in the 1742 edition of the *Topographical Account of Great Britain* by 'a gentleman',[3430] which describes the monument, perhaps significantly, not as a column but a cross,[3431] and is first pictured in an illustration of St Peter's church which appears on Isaac Taylor's well-known map of Wolverhampton of 1751. The rather crude illustration shows a cylindrical column with a doughnut-shaped capstone set in a plinth consisting of a double tier of circular steps. The pillar is drawn with a vague suggestion of decoration, but no detail can be made out.

The fact that early references to the pillar cannot be traced, and that in the early nineteenth century no local legends or folklore relating to the pillar could be recorded,[3432] is difficult to explain, for the monument must have been striking and conspicuous, long known to the local populace including 'gentlemen of learning' who would have taken some pride in their local monumental sculpture, and we might expect it to have been widely-known to, and acclaimed by, early antiquaries, scholars, travellers, artists, and others.[3433] That it remained unmentioned is baffling; even perhaps suspicious.

All that can be said at present is that there is no firm archaeological evidence to show that the pillar has stood undisturbed in its present position since the pre-Conquest period – it may have been set on the natural surface cleared for that purpose at almost any period – and, remarkably, there is no documentary evidence of its existence prior to the mid-eighteenth century. A dispassionate observer might indeed wonder whether it could conceivably have originated elsewhere and been set up in the seventeenth or early eighteenth century. The idea that Anglo-Saxon crosses might have been moved and repositioned has been considered by Jane Hawkes, who notes that the two reassembled crosses at Sandbach can be assumed to have stood in their existing socket stones in Sandbach market place since 1585, but there is no evidence that this was their original position, and there may have been sculptured crosses already in the area which, with the rise of early antiquarian interest in 'ancient' monuments, were gathered together and re-

---

[3430] The work, written by Daniel Defoe (who died in 1731), was first published between 1724-7, but rights to republish were secured by the printer and novelist Samuel Richardson (1689-1761) who printed various revised and enlarged editions from 1738 to 1761: see Rogers 1998, especially Appendix A.

[3431] '... in the churchyard is a very old Stone Cross.': Richardson 1975: 350. Nathanial Spencer records in 1772 that 'an ancient stone cross was standing in the church yard, which we are persuaded has stood there ever since the church was founded': Spencer 1772: 424. GM April 1780: 165 notes that 'There are remains of a ... curious pillar in Wolverhampton church-yard, about 20 feet high, as it was in the year 1735, said to have had a cross on it formerly, the whole now very ruinous. – Query as to cross?...'. The enigmatic 1735 reference has not been traced, but the 1780 comment may explain Oliver's remark in 1836 noted previously that within living memory the column had a cross on its summit: Oliver 1836: 138. Rix's unequivocal statement (Rix 1963: 18) that the upper part of the cross shaft was destroyed in the 16th century at the Reformation may be correct, but no evidence has been traced to support it. It is worth noting that in October 1642, the church was occupied for 5 days by royalist soldiers under the papist Thomas Leveson, who engaged in considerable wanton destruction, including the plundering of the ancient church muniments. The chancel was wrecked and the roof stripped of its lead, not repaired until 1685: Mander and Tildesley 1960: 79, 98.

[3432] Oliver 1836: 138-9.

[3433] Perhaps explained because the town was not on the itinerary of early antiquaries: William Camden seems not to have visited the place (Gough 1806: 495), and John Leland bypassed the town: Mander and Tildesley 1960: 58.

erected to serve the same purpose, possibly to mark the Royal Charter to the town in 1578 allowing it to hold two annual fairs and a weekly market where the crosses now stand.[3434]

Undestandably, experts on the history of early sculpture examining the Wolverhampton cross-shaft over the last century-and-a-half have focussed on its carvings. Overlooked – or at least unmentioned – by earlier commentators is the undecorated part of the column, but that area may be of some considerable significance. Noticeable on both the column and the plaster-cast are what seem to be wide facets which begin at the cable ornament, suggesting that it may have been worked from a square or polygonal cross section, or was deliberately shaped with facets. That on the east face suggests that the shaft may at some time in its life have been dragged and worn, though that may be a false conclusion: the lowest part of the column is of course concealed by the sandstone rubble collar.

Perhaps more significantly, immediately below the carved area, seen particularly clearly on the cast in the Victoria and Albert Museum (a photograph of which is reproduced at the start of this chapter) and on one of the most accurate drawings of the shaft, published in 1872 (which appears as the frontispiece to this work), is a narrowing or 'waist', of very slight hour-glass profile, with the upper margin slightly rounded, and the lower edge forming a slight but marked regular horizontal step around the pillar.[3435]

At least four possible, if equally unlikely, explanations suggest themselves to explain the 'waist' on the column.

The first is that it marks an area where some decorative feature or even an inscription – not necessarily contemporary with the existing sculptural work on the column, but perhaps much later or even earlier – has been deliberately erased by iconoclasts at some time during its history, though it would be futile to speculate further on that intriguing possibility.[3436] Whatever has been effaced presumably (though not necessarily) ran around the entire circumference of the pillar, and may have been slightly more deeply cut in the central area, though whether to the same depth as the surviving carvings is uncertain. As previously noted, Rosemary Cramp has reminded us of the 'ancient tradition of marking royal graves with a column', and that crosses were set up at the foundation of monasteries, usually with inscriptions, associated with monastic burial grounds.[3437]

[3434] Hawkes 2002: 27. Wolverhampton's first market charter was granted by Henry III in 1258. Sidebottom has noted that all but one of Cheshire's Anglo-Saxon round-shafts stand in the grounds of large stately residences, concluding that their distribution results from the acquisition and subsequent recycling by local landowners in the 17th and 18th centuries from church sites, though the idea is contested by Bailey: Sidebottom 1994: 152-3; Bailey 2011: 37.

[3435] Evident in the engraving in Shaw II 1801, in a sepia drawing from the later 18th century (WSL SV-XII-107 (45/10115), and in the photograph (Plate 124) in Wilson 1984: 106. It is worth recording a curious comment by Oliver in 1836: 'A series of pointed arches is said to have encompassed the column below the carved work'. As Perpetual Curate of the adjoining church Oliver will have been very familiar with the shaft, but was seemingly referring to the spaces between the zig-zags of the decorated vandyke panels.

[3436] Nevertheless, it would be understandable if any column celebrating, for example, the proposed but stillborn new monastery of Hubert Walter, plans for which were abandoned in 1205, had any commemorative inscription effaced. Any idea that an inscription may have commemorated the battle of Tettenhall must be entirely fanciful.

[3437] Cramp 2002; Cramp 2006: 2001.

The second is that it was caused over very many years by abrasion from grazing animals such as sheep and cattle, or from the sharpening of tools or weapons, though it must be conceded that apart from a handful of doubtful cases of crosses in moorland settings there are few, if any, obvious parallels for such wear. For much of its life (but not necessarily from the outset) the ground level around the shaft could have been at the level of the slight ledge marking the lower margin of the waist – with the column set in the ground, possibly on a great mound – and nothing to protect the shaft above from physical abrasion. That would mean that the ground level around the shaft was once much higher, unlikely in its present position, so implying that it has at some time been relocated. Alternatively, a series of circular graded steps extending to the lower edge of the waist might be envisaged, but in that case the top level of any steps must have been very much higher – perhaps more than six feet – than the present ground level, which also tells against the column being in its original position.[3438]

The idea of steps is based not only on the 1751 thumbnail engraving which shows graded circular steps at the base of the column,[3439] but in part on the assumption that some reliable means of ensuring the stability of the column must have been in place when (and where) it was first erected: other Anglo-Saxon cylindrical crosses (e.g. the Pillar of Eliseg and the gritstone Clulow Cross in Cheshire, near the Staffordshire border) are set in round holes formed in purpose-made square or rectangular base stones, with no evidence of a reinforcing collar or cairn.[3440] That a column weighing several tons or more topped by a sizeable capstone such as the Wolverhampton column (and presumably with a substantial and heavy cross-head) would be free-standing in an especially exposed location without some form of secure lateral stabilisation at the base can be ruled out. Excavations at the Wolverhampton cross in 1993 showed that the large roughly-shaped circular sandstone base-stone (which – perhaps significantly – differed from the stone of the column: one might perhaps have expected a complete 'kit' to have been assembled at the outset from the same material), had been hollowed out to form a basin-like depression into which the column had been set,[3441] although there is no evidence to say what profile the underside of the base of the column takes, or whether traces of a tenon to fit a base-stone are to be found. Setting a monumental upright column in a stone basin seems an unlikely technical solution to secure the stability of the column for many generations. All that can be said is that at some date (probably after 1751) a crude low collar of mortared irregular sandstone rubble was set up on the unsophisticated base-stone around the column, reaching some four or five feet above ground level (shown in a confusing variety of forms in illustrations from the mid-eighteenth century onwards), but that primitive arrangement is very unlikely to be of great age.

[3438] A drawing of the pillar probably dating from the late 18th century clearly shows the irregular profile of the lower part of the shaft: WSL SV XII 107. Mander suggests that until the early 1930s, when it became the responsibility of the Borough of Wolverhampton, the greater part of the churchyard, including the Saxon pillar, was shut off by a wall or iron railings (WA II 82), though no such wall or railings seem to be shown in 18th and 19th century drawings and engravings.

[3439] The engraving appears on Isaac Taylor's map of Wolverhampton; see also Staffordshire Views Collection in WSL, especially SV XII.91, SV XII.95a, SV XII.102a, SV XII.107, SV XII.108a, SV XII.108b, SV XII.109a.

[3440] At Disley (Lyme Hall) in Cheshire a base for a pair of round shafts was found buried in the churchyard, and a similar base is recorded at Ecclesfield in the same county: Sidebottom 1994: 153, 156.

[3441] WMANS 34 (1993) 107-8.

A third possibility – if hardly likely – is that the narrowing of the column and the distinct shelf at the base of the area might mark where something flat and flexible was once attached, possibly a curved metal plaque or collar or suchlike – decorated and even jewelled – or some kind of decorative banner or embroidery wrapped around the column and displayed on special occasions, though the idea would seem to have no obvious parallels elsewhere.

Fourthly, but improbably, the column may have been worn by scrapings made by or for the benefit of those who attached to it particular sanctity, perhaps as a result of publicised miracles at the site. Dust from such objects was often venerated by believers.

In summary, therefore, the enigmatic waist-profile on the Wolverhampton column – which might date from a period long after (or not inconceivably well before) the carving on the shaft – however caused, and the crude collar of mortared rubble at its base, might arguably be seen as evidence that the column is not in its original position.[3442] In that respect we might remember Stebbing Shaw's record in 1801 (cited previously in this chapter) of 'remains of very remote antiquity' near the collegiate church in the form of '... handsome and spacious rooms or vaults ... [which] might have formed part of the base story of a building of considerable magnitude ... walls ... of great thickness, near three yards ...',[3443] a description which must surely indicate a very substantial structure, almost certainly a great church. We should be wise keep an open mind as to the location of the shaft before the mid-eighteenth century and the date when it was placed in its present position.

When the present condition of the carving is compared with the cast in the Victoria and Albert Museum made in 1880, it is clear (if the cast is accurate, which is far from certain, although those responsible were certainly skilled)[3444] that the decorative designs have further eroded significantly in little more than a century.The wear on the carvings is usually attributed to the acidic and corrosive atmosphere to which the pillar has been exposed, certainly from the eighteenth century, as a result of the various industrial processes carried out in the area. The rate at which this type of stone is affected by such corrosion is unclear. Indeed, whether or not the resulting chemical crust embedded in the surface of the stone damages or serves to protect the stone is uncertain, since some authorities argue that cleaning stained stonework makes the surface more friable and vulnerable to oxidisation and bacteria, which can lead to further degradation. Whatever the case, the carving (especially immediately below the capstone) might seem to have deteriorated more in the last century-and-a-quarter than in the preceding millennium or so. That may be entirely consistent with the polluted atmosphere to which it has been exposed, but might also suggest that the shaft could at one time have been protected from weathering, for example within a building. The matter is clearly deserving of further enquiry.

As a footnote, it must be of some interest that one of the earliest references to the Wolverhampton column calls into question the nature of the monument. A Swedish

---

[3442] The present author is unaware of any information about the lowest part of the column concealed by the rubble collar. It is worth recording that the Anglo-Saxon High Cross near the south-west corner of Bakewell church has been found to have been placed in its present position no earlier than 1030, and probably after the early 12th century: *Archaeology and Conservation in Derbyshire*,10 (2013) 18-19.
[3443] Mander and Tildesley 1960: 47-8.
[3444] The cast was evidently taken without disturbing the rubble base collar, for the base of the cast coincides with the visible base of the actual column.

traveller and commentator, R. R. Angerstein, recorded c.1754: 'In the churchyard [at Wolverhampton] stands a pillar that formerly supported a catholic saint, but in the time of Cromwell the statue was pulled down...'.[3445] The statement is intriguing, and presumably derives from information provided by a local informant. Since the Civil War (during which such monuments are known to have been damaged or defaced) had taken place only a century earlier, and Wolverhampton church was occupied for five days in Ocotober 1642, not by Cromwell's men but by Royalist forces under Colonel Thomas Leveson, a prominent and hot-headed recusant Catholic, whose troops caused very considerable damage and destruction in that short time, with the church chest broken open and rifled, tombs destroyed, memorial brasses ripped away, muniments destroyed, and even an attempt remove a heavy bronze statue of a Leveson ancestor to be smelted into cannon, it is very possible that the cross-shaft was also attacked: there is certainly evidence that the chancel was wrecked by the stripping of lead.[3446] It is at least possible that there was local folk memory explaining the incomplete column, particularly since there is some evidence that in the medieval period statues of kings, warriors, and saints were indeed mounted on tall pillars,[3447] as was the Roman practice which must have been known to the Anglo-Saxons, though whether any such folk memory reflects the true facts must remain a matter for speculation.[3448] But even if Angerstein's informant was correct, it is of course still possible that the column originated as part of a monumental Christian cross and was only used for other purposes long after it was first set up.

Finally, we may note for completeness that traces of two other possible pre-Conquest monuments are said to lie a short distance from Wolverhampton. In the churchyards of

---

[3445] Berg 2001: 43-4. The entry is accompanied by a very crude and inexact bird's-eye view of Wolverhampton church and a representation of a cylindrical column (without, it may be noted, any capstone) standing on a base of four circular graduated steps.

[3446] Mander and Tildesley 1960: 79-80. The iconoclasm of the 1550s should not be overlooked: 'The Puritans and fanatics now had their chance to do all the harm and destruction they were able against the beauty and craftsmanship of centuries. Wolverhampton was a conservative place given to the old ways of life; but this offered little protection against the march of events.': Mander and Tildesley 1960: 53. 'Images' at Wolverhampton church were taken down in 1539, set up again in 1555, and again taken down in 1559: Harwood 1844: 355: fn.

[3447] Notably, a late 9th-century manuscript, perhaps from St Gallen, incorporates an illustration of what seems to be a sculpture of a warrior with spear and shield atop a pillar: Dodwell 1993: 82. Strong 1990: frontispiece, shows a detail from a propaganda painting c.1570 from the National Portrait Gallery of Henry VIII on his deathbed, with a view through a window of soldiers destroying statues of saints and pulling down an image of the virgin or a female saint set on a tall cylindrical pillar standing on a stepped and chamfered square base.

[3448] The well-known Anglo-Saxon cross-shafts at Sandbach are first recorded, somewhat enigmatically, in 1585, but not mentioned again in subsequent accounts of Sandbach until the later 17th century, which is generally seen as confirmation that the shafts had been torn down by the iconoclasts of the early 17th century: certainly they had been dismantled, with pieces scattered around the Sandbach area, by the 1660s: Hawkes 2002: 15-20. The recovery of fragments, many re-used as building materials, from various locations, and the benevolence of Sir John Grey Egerton of Oulton Park, where some of the fragments were located, enabled the enlightened townspeople to reassemble the crosses in 1816: ibid. If the Wolverhampton cross shaft stands in its original position, we might wonder how, in a centre of population, it managed to avoid damage by iconoclasts in the sixteenth and seventeenth century. The answer may be its discrete sculptural repertoire, or even its sheer size, although with the removal of the supporting sandstone rubble at its base it would not have been difficult to topple it.

Penn and Bushbury are short fragments of circular stone cross-shafts which have been held to date from the eleventh century.[3449]

[3449] Hooke and Slater 1986: 20-1 and 24, although it is unclear how a short undecorated stump is to be dated with such precision. The Penn cross-shaft, said to have been discovered in 1912 beneath a later churchyard cross, is of sandstone heavily marked with traces of white mortar, has a diameter of 30½"; that at Bushbury, of fine-grained sandstone with a smooth finish and little evidence of weathering, just over 24".

Bibliography.

Abels 1991: Richard Abels, 'English Strategy, Tactics and Military Organisation in the Late Tenth century', in Scragg 1991: 143-55.

———1998: Richard Abels, *Alfred the Great: War, Kingship and Culture in Anglo-Saxon England*, London& New York: Longman.

———2003: Richard Abels, 'Alfred the Great, the micel hæðen here and the Viking threat', in Reuter 2003: 265-280.

———2006: Richard Abels, '"Cowardice"and Duty in Anglo-Saxon England, *Journal of Military History*, IV, 29-49.

Abels and Morillo 2005: Richard Abels and Stephen Morillo, 'A Lying Legacy: A Preliminary Discusion of Images of Antiquity and Altered Reality in Medieval Military History', *Journal of Medieval Military History* 3 1-13.

ab Ithel 1860: John Williams ab Ithel (ed.), *Brut y Tywysogion; or The Chronicle of the Princes*, London: Longman, Green, Longman, and Roberts.

Abraham 1994: Lenore Abraham, 'The Devil, the Yew Bow, and the Saxon Archer', *Proceedings of the PMR Conference* (1994) 16/17.

Abrams 2001: Lesley Abrams, 'Edward the Elder's Danelaw', in Higham and Hill 2001: 128-43.

——— 2001a: Lesley Abrams, 'The conversion of the Danelaw', in Campbell et al 2001: 31-44.

Adams 2013: Max Adams, *The King in the North: the Life and Times of Oswald of Northumbria*, London: Head of Zeus Limited.

Ager 1996: Barry Ager, 'A quoit brooch style belt-plate from Meonstoke, Hampshire', in ASSAH 9 1996 111-114.

Aitken 1808: John Aitken, *The Atheneum Magazine of Literary and Miscellaneous Information*, Vol. 3, January-June 1808, London: Longman, Hurst, Rees, and Orme.

Alexander 2100: Caroline Alexander, *Lost Gold of the Dark Ages*, Washington: National Geographical Society.

Alford 1653: Michael Alford or Griffith [real name John Flood], *Fides Regia Britannica Sive Annales Ecclesiæ Britannic*, Liege: Anglo Societas Iesu Theologo.

Allen Brown 1992: R. Allen Brown, *Castles from the Air*, London: The Promotional Reprint Company Limited.

Allies 1852: Jabez Allies, *On the Ancient British, Roman, and Saxon Antiquities and Folk-Lore of Worcestershire*, London: J. H. Parker; Worcester: J. Grainger.

Anderson 1864: John Corbet Anderson, *Shropshire: its Early History and Antiquities*, London: Willis and Southeran.

Anderson 1925: Alan Orr Anderson, *Early Sources of Scottish History AD500 to 1286*, Edinburgh: Oliver and Boyd.

Anderson 1977: J. J. Anderson, *Cleanness*, Manchester: Manchester University Press.

Anderson 1980: William Anderson, *Castles of Europe, from Charlemagne to the Renaissance*, London: Ferndale Editions.

Anderson 1982: Marjorie O. Anderson, 'Dalriada and the creation of the Kingdom of the Scots', in Whitelock, McKitterick and Dumville 1982: 106-32.

Andrews 1936: C. Bruyn Andrews (ed.), *The Torrington Diaries: Containing the Tours through England and Wales of the Hon. John Byng*, Vol. III, London: Methuen & Co. Ltd.

Anon 1570: *Flores Historiarum: per Matthæum Westmonasteriensem Collecti Præcipuè de rebus Britanni cis ab exordio mundi vsque ad Annum Domini 1307*, London: Thomæ Marshij.

Anon. 1756: *A New and Accurate Description of the Present Great Roads and the Principal Cross Roads of England and Wales, etc...*, London: R. & J. Dodsley.

Anon. 1824: *The Shropshire Gazetteer*, Wem: T. Gregory.

Anon. 1981: *The Vikings in England and their Danish Homeland*, London: The Anglo-Danish Viking Project. [A Catalogue to accompany the exhibitions held in Brede-Copenhagen, Århus and York in 1981 and 1982.]

Anon. 1998: *The Conservation of the Wolverhampton Saxon Coss Shaft and Cap Stone*, Taplow: Cliveden Conservation Workshop Limited.

Armitage 1912: Ellen S. Armitage, *Early Norman Castles of the British Isles*, London: John Murray.

Arnold 1879: Thomas Arnold (ed.), *Henrici Archidiaconi Huntendunensis Historia Anglorum: The History of the English*, London: Longman & Co., Trübner & Co., Oxford: Parker & Co., Cambridge: Macmillan & Co., Edinburgh: A. & C. Black and Douglas & Foulis; Dublin: A. Thom.

———— 1892: Thomas Arnold (ed.), *Rerum Britannicarum Medii Aevi Scriptores; or, Chronicles and Memorials of Great Britain and Ireland during the Middle Ages*, Vol II, 75, Part II, London: Longman & Company.

Arnold 2006: Martin Arnold, *The Vikings: Culture and Conquest*, London: Hambledon Continuum.

Ashley 1999: Mike Ashley, *The Mammoth Book of British Kings & Queens*, London: Constable Publishers.

Atkin 1997: M. A. Atkin, "The Land between Ribble and Mersey' in the Early Tenth Century', in Rumble and Mills 1997: 8-18.

Attenborough 1922: F. L. Attenborough (ed and trans.), *The Laws of the Earliest English Kings*, Cambridge: Cambridge University Press.

Attwater 1965: Donald Attwater, *The Penguin Dictionary of Saints*, Harmondsworth: Penguin Books Ltd.

Auden 1906: Thomas Auden, *Memorials of Old Shropshire*, London: Bemrose & Sons.

Ayton 2011: Andrew Ayton, 'Military Service and the Dynamics of Recruitment', in Bell et al 2011: 9-61.

Babington 1865: Churchill Babington (ed.), *Polychronicon Ranulph Higden, together with the English translations of John Trevisa and of an unknown writer of the fifteenth century*, Vol. I, London: Longman, Green, Longman, Roberts and Green.

Bachrach 2007: Bernard S. Bahrach, '"A Lying Legacy" Revisited: The Abels-Morillo Defense of Discontinuity', in *Journal of Medieval History* V 207 153-82.

Backes and Dölling 1969: Magnus Backes and Regine Dölling, *Art of the Dark Ages*, New York: Harry N. Abrams, Inc.

Backhouse, Turner and Webster 1984: Janet Backhouse, D. H. Turner and Leslie Webster (eds.), *The Golden Age of Anglo-Saxon Art, 966-1066*, London: British Museum Publications Limited.

Bagliani 2001: Agostino Paravicini Bagliani, 'The Corpse in the Middle Ages', in Lineham and Nelson 2001: 327-41.

Bailey 1980: Richard N. Bailey,*Viking Age Sculpture in Northern England*, London: William Collins & Co. Ltd.

———— 1990: Richard N. Bailey, *The Meaning of Mercian Sculpture*, Leicester: University of Leicester.

———— 1996: Richard N. Bailey, *'What Mean These Stones?' Some Aspects of Pre-Norman Sculpture in Cheshire and Lancashire* (Toller Memorial Lecture, 1995, reprinted in *Bulletin of the John Rylands University Library of Manchester*, 78.i (1996) 21-46.

———— 2003: Richard N.Bailey, "What mean these stones': Some Aspects of pre-Norman Sculpture in Cheshire and Lancashire', in Scragg 2003: 213-40.

———— 2011: Richard N.Bailey, *Corpus of Anglo-Saxon Stone Sculpture, Volume IX: Lancashire and Cheshire*, Oxford: Oxford University Press for the British Academy.

Bailey 2001: Maggie Bailey, 'Ælfwynn, second lady of the Mercians', in Higham and Hill 2001: 112-27.

Baker 2010: Nigel Baker, *Shrewsbury: An Archaeological Assessment of an English Border Town*, Oxford: Oxbow Books.

Baker and Howe 1998: Peter S. Baker and Nicholas Howe (eds), *Words and Works: Studies in Medieval English Language and Literature in Honour of Fred C. Robinson*, Toronto, Buffalo and London: University of Toronto Press.

Baker and Brookes 2013: John Baker and Stuart Brookes, *Beyond the Burghal Hidage: Anglo-Saxon Civil Defence in the Viking Age*, Leiden: Koninklijke Brill NV.

────── 2016: John Baker and Stuart Brookes, 'Landscapes of Violence in Early Medieval Wessex: Towards a Reassessment of Anglo-Saxon Strategic Landscapes', in Lavelle and Roffey 2016: 70-86.

Baker et al 2015: Andy Baker, John C. Hellstrom, Bryce F. J. Kelly, Gregoire Mariethoz and Valerie Trovet, 'A composite annual-resolution stalagmite record of North-Atlantic climate over the last three millennia', *Scientific Reports*, 5, article number 10307, 11 June 2015.

Baldwin and Whyte 1985: J. R. Baldwin and I. Whyte (eds), *The Scandinavians in Cumbria*, Edinburgh: Scottish Society for Northern Studies.

Baldwin Brown 1937: G. Baldwin Brown, *The Arts in Early England, Part II Saxon Sculpture*, London: John Murray.

Barber 1999: Richard Barber, *Myths and Legends of the British Isles*, Woodbridge: The Boydell Press.

Barker 1967: E. E. Barker, 'The Anglo-Saxon Chronicle used by Æthelweard', in *Historical Research*, 40, issue 101 (May 1967), 74-91.

Barker 1993: Philip Barker, *The Techniques of Archaeological Excavation*, London: B. T. Batsford.

Barrett 1896: C.R.B. Barrett, *Battles and Battlefields in England*, London: A. D. Innes and Co.

Barrett 2012: Christopher Barrett, 'Roland and Crusade Imagery in an English Royal Chapel: early thirteenth-century wall paintings in Claverley Church, Shropshire', in *The Antiquaries Journal*, 92 (2012), 129-68.

Barrow 2004: Julia Barrow, 'Clergy in the Diocese of Hereford in the Eleventh and Twelfth Centuries', in Gillingham 2004: 37-54.

Barrow and Wareham 2008: Julia Barrow and Andrew Wareham (eds.), *Myth, Rulership, Church and Charters: Essays in Honour of Nicholas Brooks*, Aldershot: Ashgate Publishing Limited.

Bassett 1989: Steven Bassett (ed), *The Origins of Anglo-Saxon Kingdoms*, London and New York: Leicester University Press.

────── 1991: Steven Bassett, 'Anglo-Saxon Shrewsbury and its churches', in *Midland History* Vol. XVI 1991 1-21.

────── 1996: Steven Bassett, 'The administrative landscape of the diocese of Worcester in the tenth century', in Brooks and Cubitt 1996: 147-73.

────── 2000: Steven Bassett, 'Anglo-Saxon Birmingham', in *Midland History*, xxv 1-27.

────── 2000a: Steven Bassett, 'How the west was won: the Anglo-Saxon takeover of the West Midlands', in ASSAH 11 (2000) 107-18.

────── 2007: Steven Bassett, 'Divide and Rule? The Military Infrastructure of Eighth- and Ninth-Century Mercia', *Early Medieval Europe* 15.

────── 2008: Steven Bassett, 'The Middle and Late Anglo-Saxon Defences of Western Mercia', ASSAH 15 180-239.

────── 2011: Steven Bassett, 'Anglo-Saxon Fortifications in Western Mercia', in *Midland History*, 36, No.1 (Spring 2011), 1-23.

Bately 1986: Bately, J. M. (ed.) *The Anglo-Saxon Chronicle: A Collaborative Edition, Vol. 3, MS A*, Cambridge: D. S. Brewer.

────── 1990: Janet Bately, 'The Compilation of the Anglo-Saxon Chronicle, 60 BC to A.D. 890: Vocabulary as Evidence', in Stanley 1990: 261-97.

Baugh and Cox 1982: G. C. Baugh and D. C. Cox, *Monastic Shropshire*, Shrewsbury: Shropshire Libraries.

Baxter et al 2009: Stephen Baxter, Catherine Karkov, Janet L. Nelson and David Pelteret, *Early Medieval Studies in Memory of Patrick Wormald*, Farnham: Ashgate Publishing Limited.

Bean 2000: C. Bean, 'Appendix: Silver Ingots from Ness, Wirral', in Cavill, Harding and Jesch 2000: 17-18.

Bebb 2007: Richard Bebb, *Welsh Furniture 1250-1950: A Cultural History of Craftsmanship and Design*, 2 vols., Kidwelly: Saer Books.

Beckett 2003: Katherine Scarfe Beckett, *Anglo-Saxon Perceptions of the Islamic World*, Cambridge: Cambridge University Press.

Beckwith 1974: [John Beckwith, introduction by], *Ivory Carvings in Early Medieval England 700-1200*, London: Arts Council of Great Britain, for The Victoria and Albert Museum.

Bell 1960: Alexander Bell (ed.), *L'Estoire des Engleis*, Anglo-Norman Text Society 14-16, Oxford: B. Blackwell.

Bell et al 2011: Adrian Robert Bell and Anne Curry, with Adam Chapman, Andy King and David Simpkin (eds), *The Soldier Experience in the Fourteenth Century*, Woodbridge: The Boydell Press.

Bellett 1855: Rev G Bellett, *The Antiquities of Bridgnorth*, Longman, Brown, Green & Longmans.

Bennett 2013: Matthew Bennett, *Campaigns of the Norman Conquest*, Abingdon: Routledge.

Beresford 1883: William Beresford, *Diocesan Histories: Lichfield*, London: Society for Promoting Christian Knowledge.

———1909: William Beresford (ed.), *Memorials of Old Staffordshire*, London: George Allen & Unwin Limited.

Beresford 1988: Maurice Beresford, *New Towns of the Middle Ages: Town Plantation in England, Wales and Gascony*, Gloucester: Alan Sutton Publishing.

Beresford and Finberg 1973: M. W. Beresford and H. P. R. Finberg, *English Medieval Boroughs: A Hand-List*, Newton Abbot: David & Charles.

Beresford and St. Joseph 1979: M. W. Beresford and J. K. St. Joseph, *Medieval England: An Aerial Survey*, 2nd edition, Cambridge: Cambridge University Press.

Berg 2001: Torsten and Peter Berg (trans.), with an Introduction by Professor Marilyn Palmer, *R. R. Angerstein's Illustrated Travel Diary 1753-1755: Industry in England and Wales from a Swedish Perspective*, London: Science Museum.

Bethell 1970: Dennis Bethell, 'The Lives of St Osyth of Essex and St Osyth of Aylesbury', in *Analecta Bollandiana*, Vol. 88, 75-127.

Biddle 1976: Martin Biddle, 'Towns', in Wilson 1976: 99-150.

Biddle and Kjølbye-Biddle 2001: Martin Biddle and Birthe Kjølbye-Biddle, 'Repton and the 'great heathen army', 873-4', in Graham-Campbell *et al.*, 2001 45-96.

Bigsby 1854: Robert Bigsby, *Historical and Topographical Description of Repton, in the County of Derby*, London: Woodfall and Kinder.

Bintley and Williams 2015: Michael T. J. Bintley and Thomas J. T. Williams (eds), *Representing Beasts in Early Medieval England and Scandinavia*, Woodbridge: The Boydell Press.

Birch 1885-93: Walter De Gray Birch, *Cartularium Saxonicum: A Collection of Charters Relating to Anglo-Saxon History*, 4 vols., London: Whiting & Company Limited.

Bird 1977: A. J. Bird, *History on the Ground*, Cardiff: University of Wales Press.

Birkett and Lee 2014: Tom Birkett and Christina Lee (eds), *The Vikings in Munster: Language, Myths and Finds*, Nottingham: Centre for the Study of the Viking Age.

Birss and Wheeler 1985: R. Birss and H. Wheeler, 'Roman Derby: Excavations 1968-83', *Derbyshire Archaeological Journal*, 105.

Bishop 2014: M. C. Bishop, *The Secret History of the Roman Roads of Britain*, Barnsley: Pen and Sword Military.

Blackburn 2001: M. Blackburn, 'Expansion and control: aspects of Anglo-Scandinavian minting south of the Humber', in Graham Campbell et al 2001: 125-42.

——— 2007: Mark Blackburn, 'Gold in England during the 'Age of Silver' (Eighth to Eleventh Centuries)', in Graham-Campbell and Williams 2007: 55-98.

Blackburn and Dumville 1998: M. A. S. Blackburn and D. N. Dumville (eds.), *Kings, Currency and Alliances:History and Coinage of Southern England in the Ninth Century*, Woodbridge: Boydell Press.

Blackwell 1985: Anthony Blackwall, *Historic Bridges of Shropshire*, Shrewsbury: Shropshire Libraries.

Blair 2002: John Blair, 'A Handlist of Anglo-Saxon Saints', in Thacker and Sharpe 2002 495-565.

———2002a: John Blair, 'A Saint for Every Minster? Local Cults in Anglo-Saxon England', in Thacker and Sharpe 2002: 455-94.

———2005: John Blair, *The Church in Anglo-Saxon Society, Oxford*: Oxford University Press.

Blair 1997: Peter Hunter Blair, *Anglo-Saxon England*, London: The Folio Society.

Blair and Millard 1992: J. Blair and A. Millard, 'An Anglo-Saxon Landmark Rediscovered: the Stanford/Stan Bricge of the Dunklington and Witney Charters', *Oxoniensia* LVII.

Blake and Lloyd 2000: Steve Blake and Scott Lloyd, *The Keys to Avalon*, Shaftesbury: Element Books Limited.

Bocock 1923: E. W. Bocock, *Shropshire Place-Names*, Shrewsbury: Wilding & Son Limited

Borenius and Tristram 1927: T. Borenius and E. W. Tristram, *English Medieval Painting*, Paris: Pegasus Press.

Bourke 1995: Cormac Bourke (ed.), *From the Isles of the North: Early Medieval Art in Ireland and Britain*, Belfast: H.M.S.O.

Boyce et al 2010: L. Boyce, L. Heidemann Lutz, S. Kleingärthur, P. Kruse, L. Mather, A. B. Sørensen (eds.), *Arkæologi i Slesvig/Archæologie in Schleswig*, Neumünster: Wachholtz.

Boyd Dawkins 1873: W. Boyd Dawkins, 'On some human bones found at Buttington, Montgomeryshire', in *Montgomeryshire Historical and Archaeological Collections*, Vol. VI 1873 141-5.

Boyle 2016: Angela Boyle, 'Death on the Dorset Ridgeway: The Discovery and Excavation of an Early Medieval Mass Burial', in Lavelle and Roffey 2016: 109-21.

Bradbury 1985: Jim Bradbury, *The Medieval Archer*, New York: St Martin's.

———1992: Jim Bradbury, *The Medieval Siege*, Woodbridge: Boydell Press.

Brazell 1968: John Harold Brazell, *London Weather*, London: H.M.S.O.

Bredehoft 2001: Thomas A. Bredehoft, *Textual Histories: Readings in the Anglo-Saxon Chronicle*, Toronto, Buffalo and London: University of Toronto Press.

Brenesel, Drout and Gravel 2005: Barbara Brenesel, Michael D. C. Drout and Robyn Gravel, 'A Reassessment of the efficacy of Anglo-Saxon medicine', in *Anglo-Saxon England*, 34 (2005) 183-95.

Brereton 1996: S. Brereton, *Wednesfield Archaeological Survey*, Oxford Archaeological Unit, Report No. 963/3; WVSURV 897/93.

Briggs 204: Elizabeth Briggs, 'Nothing But Names: The Original Core of the Durham *Liber Vitae*', in Rollason et al, 2004.

Brighton 1942: Rev. F. Brighton, *Pattingham*, Dudley: E. Blocksidge (Dudley) Limited.

Brink 2008: Stefan Brink, 'Who were the Vikings?', in Brink and Price 2008: 4-7.

——— 2008a: Stefan Brink, 'Slavery in the Viking Age', in Brink and Price 2008: 49-56.

Brink and Price 2008: Stefan Brink (ed), in collaboration with Neil Price, *The Viking World*, London: Routledge.

Brook 1955: George Leslie Brook, *An Introduction to Old English*, Manchester: Manchester University Press.

Brooks 1964: Nicholas Brooks, 'The Unidentified Forts of the Burghal Hidage', in *Medieval Archaeology* VII 74-90.

———1979: Nicholas Brooks, 'England in the Ninth Century: the Crucible of Defeat', *Transactions of the Royal Historical Society*, 5th Series 29 1-20.

———1984: Nicholas Brooks, *The Early History of the Church of Canterbury from 597 to 1066*, Leicester: Leicester University Press.

———1989: Nicholas Brooks, 'The formation of the Mercian kingdom', in Bassett 1989: 159-70.

———1991: Nicholas Brooks, 'Weapons & Armour', in Scragg 1991: 208-19.

———1996: Nicholas Brooks, 'The administrative background to the Burghal Hidage', in Hill and Rumble 1996: 128-50.

———2000: Nicholas Brooks, *Communities and Warfare 700-1400*, London& Rio Grande: The Hambledon Press.

———2000a: Nicholas Brooks, *Anglo-Saxon Myths: State and Church 400-1066*, London& Rio Grande: The Hambledon Press.

Brooks and Bassett 1996: Nicholas Brooks and Catherinee Cubitt, *St Oswald of Worcester: Life and Influence*, London and New York: Leicester University Press.

Broun 1999: Dauvit Broun, *The Irish Identity of the Kingdom of the Scots in the Twelfth and Thirteenth Centuries*, Woodbridge: The Boydell Press.

Brown 1992: R. Allen Brown, *Castles from the Air*, London: Promotional Reprint Company Limited.

Brown 2001: Michelle P. Brown, 'Mercian Manuscripts? The 'Tiberius' Group and Its Historical Context', in Brown and Farr 2001: 278-91.

——— 2007: Michelle P. Brown, *Manuscripts from the Anglo-Saxon Age*, London: The British Library.

Brown and Farr 2001: M. P. Brown and C. A. Farr (eds.), *Mercia: An Anglo-Saxon Kingdom in Europe*, London& New York: Leicester University Press.

Browne 1885: Reverend G. F. Browne, 'On a Supposed Inscription upon the font at Wilne', *Proceedings of the Derbyshire Archaeological Society*, VII, 184-94.

Bruce-Mitford 1975: Rupert Bruce-Mitford (ed.), *Recent Archaeological Excavations in Europe*, London& Boston: Routledge & Kegan Paul.

Bryant et al 2012: Richard Bryant with Michael Hare and contributions by C. Roger Bristow, Edward Freshney, Carolyn Heighway, Emily Howe, Elizabeth Okasha, David N. Parsons, and Jeffrey West, *Corpus of Anglo-Saxon Stone Sculpture, Volme X, The Western Midlands: Gloucestershire, Herefordshire, Shropshire, Warwickshire and Worcestershire*, Oxford: Oxford University Press for The British Academy.

Buck 2000: Jerry Buck, *Blood Red Roses: The Archaeology of a Mass Grave from the Battle of Towton 1461*, Oxford: Oxbow Books.

Bullough 1965: Donald Bullough, *The Age of Charlemagne*, London: Elek Books Limited.

Bu'lock 1972: J. D. Bu'lock, *Pre-Conquest Cheshire 383-1066*, Chester: Cheshire Community Council.

Burke 1884: Bernard Burke, *The General Armory of England, Scotland, Wales and Ireland: A Registry of Armorial Bearings from the Earliest to the Present Time*, London: Harrison& Sons.

Burne 1883: Charlotte Sophia Burne, *Shropshire Folk-Lore: A Sheaf of Gleanings, Part 2*, London: Trübner & Co.

Burne 2002: Alfred H. Burne, *The Battlefields of England*, London: Penguin Books.

Burton 1738: Robert Burton, *The Anatomy of Melancholy, by Democritus Junior*, London: B. Blake.

Buteux 1995: Victoria Buteux, 'Archaeological Assessment of Quatford, Shropshire', in *Central Marches Historic Towns Survey*, Archaeological Data Service Website.

Byrne 2005: F. J. Byrne, 'Ireland before the battle of Clontarf', in Moody et al 2005: 852-61.

Calvert and West 1834: Frederick Calvert and William West, *Picturesque Views and Descriptions of Cities, Towns, Castles, Mansions, and other objects of interesting feature, in Staffordshire*, Birmingham: William Evans.

Camden 1610: William Camden, *Britain; or A Chorographicall Description of the Most Flourishing Kingdomes, England, Scotland, and Ireland, and the Ilands adioyning, out of the Depth of Antiquity*, translated by Philemon Holland, London: George Bishop and John Norton.

——— 1971: *Camden's Britannia 1695: A Facsimile of the 1695 edition published by Edmund Gibson*, Newton Abbot: David & Charles (Publishers) Limited.

Cameron 1987: Kenneth Cameron, *Place-Name Evidence for the Anglo-Saxon Invasion and Scandinavian Settlements: Eight Studies Collected by Kenneth Cameron*, Nottingham: English Place-Name Society.

———1998: Kenneth Cameron, with contributions by John Insley, *A Dictionary of Lincolnshire Place-Names*, Nottingham: English Place-Name Society.

Campbell 1962: A. Campbell (ed.), *The Chronicles of Æthelweard*, London, Edinburgh, Paris, Johannesburg, Toronto and New York: Thomas Nelson and Sons Limited.

Campbell 1982: James Campbell (ed.), *The Anglo-Saxons*, Oxford: Phaidon.

——— 1986: James Campbell, *Essays in Anglo-Saxon History*, London: The Hambledon Press.

——— 1991: James Campbell (ed.), *The Anglo-Saxons*, London: Penguin Books.

——— 2001: James Campbell, 'What is not known about the reign of Edward the Elder', in Higham and Hill 2001: 12-24.

——— 2003: James Campbell, 'The Placing of Alfred', in Reuter 2003: 3-26.

Campbell and Williams 2007: J. Graham Campbell and Gareth Williams (eds), *Silver Economy in the Viking Age*, Walnut Creek: Left Coast Press.

Cantor 2001: Norman F. Cantor, *In the Wake of the Plague: The Black Death and the World it Made*, London: Simon & Schuster UK Limited.

Carr 1994: Tony Carr, *Shrewsbury: A Pictorial History*, Chichester: Phillimore & Co. Limited.

Carroll 2010: Jayne Carroll, 'Coins and the Chronicle Mint-names, History, and Literature', in Jorgensen 2010: 243-74.

Carroll and Parsons 2013: Jayne Carroll and David N. Parsons (eds), *Perceptions of Place: Twenty-First-Century Interpretations of English Place-Name Studies*, Nottingham: English Place-Name Society.

Carroll et al 2014: Jayne Carroll, Stephen H. Harrison and Gareth Williams, *The Vikings in Britain and Ireland*, The British Museum Press.

Carver 1980: M. O. H. Carver (ed.), *Medieval Worcester: An Archaeological Framework*, Transactions of the Worcestershire Archaeological Society, 3rd Series, Vol. 7.

——— 1989: Martin Carver, *Underneath English Towns: Interpreting Urban Archaeology*, London: FitzHouse Books.

——— 2003: Martin Carver (ed), *The Cross Goes North: Processes of Conversion in Northern Europe, AD300-1300*, Woodbridge: York Medieval Press/The Boydell Press.

——— 2010: Martin Carver, *Birth of a Borough: An Archaeological Study of Anglo-Saxon Stafford*, Woodbridge: Boydell.

Carver, Sanmark and Semple 2010: Martin Carver, Alex Sanmark and Sarah Semple (eds), *Signals of Belief in Early England: Paganism Revisited*, Oxford: Oxbow Books.

Cather, Park and Williamson 1990: S. Cather, D. Park and P. Williamson (eds.), *Early Medieval Wall Painting and Painted Sculpture in England*, Oxford: BAR British Series.

Cavill 2004: Paul Cavill (ed), *The Christian Tradition in Anglo-Saxon England: Approaches to Current Scholarship and Teaching*, Cambridge: D. S. Brewer.

——— 2008: Paul Cavill, 'The site of the battle of *Brunanburh*: manuscripts and the maps, grammar and geography', in Padel and Parsons 2008: 303-19.

——— 2010: Paul Cavill, 'The Place-Name Debate', in Livingstone 2010: 311-33.

——— 2015: Paul Cavill, 'The Battle of *Brunanburh* in 937: Battlefield Despatches', in Harding, Griffiths and Royles 2015: 95-108.

Cavill, Harding and Jesch 2000: P. Cavill, S. E. Harding and J. Jesch, *Wirral and its Viking Heritage*, Nottingham: English Place-Name Society.

Caxton 1482: William Caxton, *Prolicionycion*, Westminster.

Chadwick 1963: Norah K. Chadwick, 'The Celtic Background of Early Anglo-Saxon England', in Jackson et al 1963: 323-52.

Chalmers 1812: Alexander Chalmers, *The General Biographical Dictionary: A New Edition*, London: J. Nichols & Son [et al].

Chamberlin 1986: Russell Chamberlin, *The Idea of England*, Thames and Hudson.

Charles 1934: Bertie George Charles, *Old Norse Relations with Wales*, Cardiff: University of Wales Press.

——— 1938: B. G. Charles, *Non-Celtic Place-Names in Wales*, London: University College.

Charles-Edwards 2001: T. M. Charles-Edwards, 'Wales and Mercia, 613-918', in Brown and Farr 2001: 89-105.

——— 2013: T. M. Charles-Edwards, *Wales and the Britons 350-1064*, Oxford: Oxford University Press.

Chartrand et al2006: R. Chartrand, K. Durham, M. Harrison and I. Heath, *The Vikings: Voyagers of Discovery and Plunder*, Oxford: Osprey Publishing.

Chastel 1994: André Chastel, *French Art: Prehistory to the Middle Ages*, Paris: Frammarion.

Chibnall 1968-80: Marjorie Chibnall (trans. and ed), *The Ecclesiastical History of Orderic Vitalis* (Oxford Medieval Texts, 6 vols), Cambridge: Cambridge University Press.

—— 1991: Marjorie Chibnall (ed.), *Anglo Norman Studies XIII: Proceedings of the Battle Conference 1990*, Woodbridge: Boydell & Brewer.

—— 1992: Marjorie Chibnall (ed.), *Anglo Norman Studies XIV: Proceedings of the Battle Conference 1991*, Woodbridge: Boydell & Brewer.

—— 1994: Marjorie Chibnall (ed.), *Anglo Norman Studies XVI: Proceedings of the Battle Conference 1993*, Woodbridge: Boydell & Brewer.

—— 2000: Marjorie Chibnall, *Piety, Power and History in Medieval England and Normandy*, Aldershot: Ashgate Publishing Limited.

Church 2008: S. D. Church, 'Paganism in Conversion-Age Anglo-Saxon England: The Evidence of Bede's *Ecclesiastical History* Reconsidered', in *The Journal of the Historical Association*, Vo. 93 (2), No. 310: 162-80.

Churchill 1675: Sir Winston Churchill, *Divi Britannici: Being a Remark Upon the Lives of All the Kings of this Isle, from the Year of the Lord 2855. Unto the year of Grace 1660*, London: Francis Eglesfield.

Clapham 1910: J. H. Clapham, 'The Horsing of the Danes', *English Historical Review*, Vol. xv 1910, 287-93.

Clapham 1930-1934: Sir Alfred Clapham, *English Romanesque Architecture*, 2 vols, Oxford: Oxford University Press.

Clark 1874: G. T. Clark, 'Bridgenorth, Oldbury, and Quatford', *Archaeologia Cambrensis: The Journal of the Cambrian Archaeological Association*, V (4th Series) XX 263-77.

—— 1884: G. T. Clark, *Medieval Military Architecture in England*, 2 Vols., London: Wyman and Sons.

—— 1889: G. T. Clark, 'Contribution towards a complete list of moated mounds or *burh*s', *Archaeological Journal*, March 1889, 197-217.

Clark 2006: Linda Clark, *Identity and Insurgency in the Late Middle Ages*, Woodbridge: The Boydell Press.

Clarke 1999: H. B. Clarke, 'The Vikings', in Maurice Keen (ed.), *Medieval Warfare: A History*, Oxford: Oxford University Press: 36-58.

Clark Hall 1914: John R. Clark Hall, *Beowulf: A Metrical Translation*, Cambridge: Cambridge University Press.

—— 1960: J. R. Clark Hall, *A Concise Anglo-Saxon Dictionary*, Toronto: University of Toronto Press.

Clark-Maxwell and Hamilton Thompson 1927: W. G. Clark-Maxwell and A. Hamilton Thompson, 'The College of St Mary Magdalene, Bridgnorth, with some account of its Deans and Prebendaries', *Archaeological Journal*, lxxxiv 1-23.

Clasper 2014: John Clasper, 'The Management of Wounds in the Middle Ages', in Kirkham and Warr 2014: 17-42.

Clay 1914: Rotha Mary Clay, *The hermits and Anchorites of England*, London: Methuen & Co.

Clerigh 1910: Arthur Ua Clerigh, *The History of Ireland to the Coming of Henry II*, I, London: T. Fisher Unwin.

Coates 1998: R. Coates, 'Æthelflæd's Fortification of Weardburh', *Notes & Queries*, CCXLIII (1998) 8-12.

—— 2012: Richard Coates, '*Worthy* of great respect', in Journal of the English Place-Name Society, 44 (2012) 36-43.

Coates and Breeze 2000: Richard Coates and Andrew Breeze (with a contribution by David Horovitz), *Celtic Voices, English Places; Studies of the Celtic Impact on Place-Names in England*, Stamford: Shaun Tyas.

Cockin 2000: Tim Cockin, *The Staffordshire Encyclopaedia*, Barlaston: Malthouse Press.

Collingwood 1927: W. G. Collingwood, *Northumbrian Crosses of the Pre-Norman Age*, reprinted in 1989: Felinfach: Llanerch Enterprises.

Contamine 1986: Philipe Contamine, *War in the Middle Ages*, Oxford: Basil Blackwell Limited.

Cooper 2006: Alan Cooper, *Bridges, Law and Power in Medieval England*, Woodbridge: The Boydell Press.

Cooper, Ripper and Clay 1994: Lynden Cooper, Susan Ripper and Patrick Clay, 'The Hemington Bridges', *Current Archaeology*, 140 Vol. XII No. 8, November 1994.

Cornwell 2009: Bernard Cornwell, *Azincourt*, London: HarperCollins.

Coulstock 1993: Patricia H. Coulstock, *Collegiate Church of Wimborne Minster*, Ipswich: Boydell Press.

Coupland 1995: Simon Coupland, 'The Vikings in Francia and Anglo-Saxon England to 911', in McKitterick 1995: 190-201.

Cox, Hall and Morden 1727: Thomas Cox, Anthony Hall and Robert Morden, *Magna Britannia Antiqua & Nova; or; a New, Exact and Comprehensive Survey of the Ancient and Present State of Great-Britain ... the whole being more Comprehensive and Instructive than Camden, or any other Author on this Subject* ..., London: Eliz. Nutt.

Coxe 1841: Henry O. Coxe, *Rogeri de Wendover Chronica, Sive Flores Historiarum, Nunc Primum Edidit*, Vol. I, London: Sumptibus Societatis.

Crabtree 2013: Pam J. Crabtree, 'A Note on the Role of Dogs in Anglo-Saxon Society: Evidence from East Anglia', in *International Journal of Osteoarchaeology*, John Wiley & Sons Online Library.

Cramp 1975: Rosemary Cramp, 'Anglo-Saxon sculpture of the Reform period', in D. Parsons (ed.), *Tenth-Century Studies: Essays in Commemoration of the Millenium of the Council of Winchester and Regularis Concordia*, London 187-9.

——— 1977: Rosemary Cramp, 'Schools of Mercian sculpture', in Dornier 1977: 191-233.

——— 1984: Rosemary Cramp, *Corpus of Anglo-Saxon Stone Sculpture in England: General Introduction*, Oxford: Oxford University Press for British Academy.

——— 1992: Rosemary Cramp, *Studies in Anglo-Saxon Stone Sculpture*, London: Pindar Press.

——— 2006: Rosemary Cramp, *Corpus of Anglo-Saxon Stone Sculpture, Vol. VII, South-West England*, London: British Academy.

Cramp and Lang 1977: R. J. Cramp and J. T. Lang, *A Century of Anglo-Saxon Sculpture*, Newcastle-Upon-Tyne: Frank Graham.

Cranage 1903: D. H. S. Cranage, *An Architectural Account of the Churches of Shropshire*, Wellington: Hobson & Co.

Crawford 2003: Barbara E. Crawford, 'The Vikings', in Davies 2003a: 41-71.

——— 2014: Barbara E. Crawford, 'The Kingdom of Man and the Earldom of Orkney', in Sigurðsson and Bolton 2014: 65-80.

Croinín 2005: Dáibhi Ó Croinín (ed.), *A New History of Ireland: Prehistoric and Early Ireland*, Cambridge: Cambridge University Press.

Cronholm 1833: Abraham Cronholm, *Forn-Nordiska*, Lund: C. W. K. Gleerup.

Cronin 1995: James Cronin, 'The Evangelist Symbols as Pictorial Exegesis', in Bourke 1995: 111-17.

Croom 1989: Jane M. Croom, 'The Pre-Medieval and Medieval Human Landscape and Settlement Pattern of South-East Shropshire', unpublished University of Birmingham Ph.D. thesis, 1989.

——— 1992: Jane M. Croom, 'The Topographical Analysis of Medieval Town Plans: The Examples of Much Wenlock and Bridgnorth', in *Midland History*, XVII,16-38.

Cross 1971: F. L. Cross (ed.), *The Oxford Dictionary of the Christian Church*, London: Oxford University Press.

Cruttwell 1801: Rev. C. Cruttwell, *Tours Through the Whole Island of Great Britain, Divided into Journeys, Interspersed with Useful Observations*, London: G. and J. Robinson.

Cubbin 1996: G. P. Cubbin (ed.), *The Anglo-Saxon Chronicle: A Collaborative Edition, Volume 6: MS D*, Cambridge: D. S. Brewer.

Cubitt 1995: Catherine Cubitt, *Anglo-Saxon Church Councils c.650-c.850*, London and New York: Leicester University Press.

Cumberledge 2002: Nicola Cumberledge, 'Reading between the Lines: the Place of Mercia within an Expanding Wessex', *Midland History*, XXVII, 1-15.

Cutler, Hunt and Rátkai 2009: Richard Cutler, John Hunt and Stephanie Rátkai, 'Saxon *Burh* and Royal Castle: Re-Thinking Early Urban Space in Stafford', *Transactions of the Staffordshire Archaeological and Historical Society*, XLIII (2009) 39-85.

Darlington et al 1995-8: Reginald R. Darlington, Patrick Mc Gurk and J. Bray (ed and trans), *The Chronicle of John of Worcester*, 3 vols., Oxford: Clarendon Press.

Davidson 2001: Michael R. Davidson, 'The (Non) Submission of the Northern Kings', in Higham and Hill 2001: 200-211.

Davies 1982: Wendy Davies, *Wales in the Early Middle Ages*, Leicester: Leicester University Press.

——1990: Wendy Davies, *Patterns of Power in Early Wales*, Oxford: Oxford University Press.

——2003: Wendy Davies, 'Alfred's Contemporaries: Irish, Welsh, Scots and Breton', in Reuter 2003 323-37.

——2003a: Wendy Davies (ed.), *From the Vikings to the Normans*, Oxford: Oxford University Press.

Davies 2002: H. Davies, *Roman Roads in Britain*, Stroud: Tempus.

Davies 2006: John Davies, 'Rhyd Chwima – the Ford at Montgomery – Aque Vadum de Mungumeri', in *Montgomeryshire Collections*, 94 (2006) 23-6.

Davies 2010: Sean Davies, 'The Battle of Chester and Warfare in Post-Roman Britain', in *The Journal of the Historical Association*, Vol. 95 (2), No. 318, 144-58.

Davies and Kennedy 2009: Glyn Davies and Kirstin Kennedy, *Medieval and Renaissance Art: People and Possessions*, London: V & A Publishing.

Davis 1957: R. H. C. Davis, *A History of Medieval Europe: from Constantine to Saint Louis*, London: Longmans.

——1988: R. H. C. Davis, *A History of Medieval Europe*, 2nd edition, Harlow: Pearson Education Limited.

——1989: R. H. C. Davis, 'Did the Anglo-Saxons have warhorses?' in Hawkes 1989: 141-44.

——1991: R. H. C. Davis, *From Alfred the Great to Stephen*, London& Rio Grande: The Hambledon Press.

Deansley 1961: Margaret Deansley, *The Pre-Conquest Church in England*, London: Adam & Charles Black.

Deegan and Scragg 1989: Marilyn Deegan and D. G. Scragg (eds.), *Medicine in Early Medieval England*, Manchester: Manchester Centre for Anglo-Saxon Studies.

Denton 1970: J. H. Denton, *English Royal Free Chapels: A Constitutional Study*, Manchester: Manchester University Press.

de Thoyras 1757: *The History of England; written in French by M. Rapin de Thoyras. Translated in English by N.Tindal*, 4th eition, London: T. Osborne and J. Shipton, et al.

Dickinson 1979: J. C. Dickinson, *An Ecclesiastical History of England, from the Norman Conquest to the Eve of the Reformation*, London: Adam and Chales Black.

Dockray-Millar 2000: Mary Dockray-Millar, *Motherhood and Mothering in Anglo-Saxon England*, Basingstoke: Palgrave Macmillan.

Dodgson 1970: J. McN. Dodgson, *The Place-Names of Cheshire: Part II: The Place-Names of Bucklow Hundred and Northwich Hundred*, Cambridge: Cambridge University Press.

—— 1991: John McNeal Dodgson, 'The Site of the Battle of Maldon', in Scragg 1991: 170-9.

Dolley 1978: Michael Dolley, 'The Anglo-Danish and Anglo-Norse Coinages of York', in Hall 1978: 26-31.

Dornier 1977: A. Dornier (ed.), *Mercian Studies*, Leicester: Leicester University Press.

Downham 2008: Clare Downham, 'Vikings in England', in Brink and Price 2008: 341-9.

——— 2009: Clare Downham, *Viking Kings of Britain and Ireland: The Dynasty of Ívarr to AD 1014*, Edinburgh: Dunedin Academic Press Limited.

Downham 2009a: Clare Downham, "Hiberno-Norwegians' and 'Anglo-Danes': Anachronistic Ethnicities and Viking-Age England', *Medieval Scandinavia*, 19 (2009) 139-69.

——— 2011: Clare Downham: 'Viking identities in Ireland: it's not all black and white', (online: Academia.edu).

——— 2013: Clare Downham, 'No horns on their helmets? Essays on the Insular Viking Age', (online: Academia.edu), University of Aberdeen: Celtic, Anglo-Saxon and Scandinavian Studies I.

Dresvina and Sparks 2012: Juliana Dresvina and Nicholas Sparks (eds), *Authority and Gender in Medieval and Renaissance Chronicles*, Newcastle upon Tyne: Cambridge Scholars Publishing.

Duby 1979: George Duby, *L'Europe Au Moyen Âge: Art Roman, Art Gothique*, Paris: Arts et Métiers Graphiques.

——— 1986: George Duby, *History of Medieval Art 980-1440*, London: George Weidenfeld and Nicolson Limited.

Duckers and Duckers 2006: Peter and Anne Duckers, *Castles of Shropshire*, Stroud: Tempus Publishing Limited.

Duffy 2005: S. Duffy (ed), *Medieval Dublin 6: Proceedings of Friends of Medieval Dublin Symposium 2004*, Dublin: Four Courts Press.

Dugdale 1817-30: Sir William Dugdale, Roger Dodsworth, John Stevens, John Caley, Sir Henry Ellis, Bulkeley Badinel, and Richard C. Taylor, *Monasticon Anglicanum: A History of the Abbies and other monasteries, Hospitals, Frieries, and Cathedral and Collegiate Churches, with their Dependencies, in England and Wales*, 6 Vols. in 8, London: Longman, Hurst, Rees, Orme & Brown.

Duignan N/D [1888]: W. H. Duignan, *The Charter of Wulfrun to the Monastery at "Hamtun" Wolverhampton*, Wolverhampton: John Steen & Co.

——— 1902: W. H. Duignan, *Some Notes on the Place-Names of Staffordshire*, London& New York: Henry Frowde.

——— 1912: W. H. Duignan, *Warwickshire Place-Names*, London: Henry Frowde.

Dukes 1844: Thomas Farmer Dukes, *Antiquities of Shropshire*, Shrewsbury: John Eddowes.

Dumville 1976: David Dumville, 'The Anglian collection of royal genealogies and regnal lists', *Anglo-Saxon England*, 5, 23-50.

——— 1979: D. N. Dumville, 'The ætheling: a study in Anglo-Saxon constitutional history', *Anglo-Saxon England*, 8 (1979) 1-33.

——— 1983: D. N. Dumville, 'Brittany and 'Armes Prydein Vawr'', *Etudes Celtiques*, Vol 20 (1983), 145-59.

——— 1989: David Dumville, 'The origins of Northumbria: some aspects of the British background', in Bassett 1989: 213-22.

——— 1992: David N. Dumville, *Wessex and England from Alfred to Edgar*, Woodbridge: The Boydell Press.

——— 2005: David N. Dumville, 'Old Dubliners and new Dubliners in Ireland and Britain: A Viking Age story', in Duffy 2005: 78-93.

——— 2008: David N. Dumville, 'Vikings in Insular chronicling', in Brink and Price 2008: 350-76.

Dumville and Lapidge 1985: David Dumville and Michael Lapidge (eds.), *The Anglo-Saxon Chronicle 17: The Annals of St Neots with Vita prima sancti Neoti*, Cambridge: D. S. Brewer.

Dunn 2000: Diana Dunn (ed.), *War and Society in Medieval and Early Modern Britain*, Liverpool: Liverpool University Press.

Dyer 1972: James Dyer, 'Earthworks of the Danelaw Frontier', in Fowler 1972: 222-36.

Dyer and Slater 2000: Christopher Dyer and T. R. Slater, 'The Midlands', in Palliser 2000: 609-638.

Dymond 1900: Charles W. Dymond, 'On the identification of the site of 'Buttingtune' of the Saxon Chronicle, Anno 894', in *Collections Historical and Archaeological relating to Montgomeryshire and its border*, Vol. XXI 1900 337-46.

Earle 1888: John Earle, *A Hand-Book to the Land-Charters, and other Saxonic Documents*, Oxford: Clarendon Press.

Earle and Plummer 1894-99: Charles Plummer and John Earle, *Two of the Saxon Chronicles Parallel*, Oxford: Oxford University Press.

Eaton 2000: Tim Eaton, *Plundering the Past: Roman Stonework in Medieval Britain*, Stroud: Tempus Publishing Limited.

Echard 1707: Laurence Echard, *The History of England; From the First Entrance of Julius Cæsar and the Romans, to the End of the Reign of King James the First, Containing the Space of 1678 years*, London: Jacob Tonson.

Ede 1962: J. F. Ede, *History of Wednesbury*, Wednesbury: Wednesbury Corporation.

Edgeworth 2014: Matt Edgeworth, 'Enmeshment of Shifting Landscapes and Embodied Movements of People and Animals', in Leary 2014: 49-62.

Edwards 1866: Edward Edwards (ed), *Liber monasterii de Hyda: Comprising a Chronicle of the Affairs of England, from the Settlement of the Saxons to the Reign of Cnut, and a Chartulary of the Abbey of Hyde, in Hampshire*, London: Longmans, Green, Reader, and Dyer.

Edwards 1998: B. J. N. Edwards, *Vikings in North-West England*, Lancaster: University of Lancaster.

Edwards 2009: Nancy Edwards, 'Rethinking the Pillar of Eliseg', *Antiquaries Journal* 89 2009 143-77.

Edwards and Lane 1992: N. Edwards and A. Lane (eds), *The Early Church in Wales and the West*, Oxford: Oxbow Books.

Ekwall 1922: Eilert Ekwall, *The Place-Names of Lancashire*, Manchester: Manchester University Press.

——— 1928: Eilert Ekwall, *The Oxford Dictionary of River Names*, Oxford: Oxford University Press.

——— 1959: Eilert Ekwall, *Etymological Notes on English Place-Names*, Lund: C. W. K. Gleerup.

———1960: Eilert Ekwall, *The Concise Oxford Dictionary of English Place-Names*, 4th edition, Oxford: Oxford University Press.

Ellis 1811: Henry Ellis (ed), *The New Chronicles of England and France, in Two Parts, by Robert Fabyan, named by himself the Concordances of Histories, reprinted from Pynson's Edition of 1516, etc.*, London: F. C. and J. Rivington, etc.

Ellis Davidson 1964: H. R. Ellis Davidson, *Gods and Myths of Northern Europe*, London: Penguin Books.

Ellis Davidson and Fisher 1980: Hilda Ellis Davidson and Peter Fisher, *Saxo-Grammaticus: The History of the Danes*, Woodbridge: D. S. Brewer.

Elmore Jones and Blunt 1955-7: F. Elmore Jones and C. Blunt, 'The tenth-century mint "æt Weardbyrig"', *British Numismatic Journal*, 28 (1955-7) 494-8.

Erdeswick 1717: Sampson Erdeswick, *A Survey of Staffordshire: Containing the Antiquities of the County, with a Description of Beeston Castle in Cheshire*, London: E. Curll.

———1844: Thomas Harwood (ed.), *A Survey of Staffordshire, Containing the Antiquities of that County, by Samuel Erdeswick*, London: B. Nicholls & Son.

Erskine and Williams 2003: Erskine and Williams (ed), *The Story of Domesday Book*, Chichester: Phillimore & Co. Lt.

Etchingham 2007: Colmán Etchingham, 'The location of historical Laithlinn/Lochl(i)nn: Scotland or Scandinavia', in Ó Flaithearta 2007: 11-32.

——— Etchingham 2010: Colman Etchingham, 'Laithlinn, 'Fair Foreigners' and 'Dark Foreigners': the identity and provenance of Vikings in ninth-century Ireland', in Sheehan and Ó Corráin: 2010.

——— Etchingham 2014: Colman Etchingham, 'Names for the Vikings in Irish Annals', in Sigurðsson and Bolton 2014: 23-38.

Evans 2004: T. A. Ralph Evans (ed.), *Lordhip and Learning: Studies in Memory of Trevor Aston*, Woodbridge: The Boydell Press.

Everson and Stocker 2003: P. Everson and D. Stocker, 'The Straight and Narrow Way: Conversion of the Landscape in the Witham Valley', in Carver 2003: 271-88.

Eyton 1854-60: R. W. Eyton, *Antiquities of Shropshire*, London: John Russell Smith; Shifnal: B. L. Beddow.

―――1881: R. W. Eyton, *Domesday Studies: An Analysis and Digest of the Staffordshire Survey*, London: Trubner.

Falkus and Gillingham 1987: Malcolm Falkus and John Gillingham (eds.), *Historical Atlas of Britain*, London: Kingfisher Books.

Farrell 1982: R. T. Farrell (ed.), *The Vikings*, London and Chichester: Phillimore & Co. Ltd.

Featherstone 1997: Donald Featherstone, *Warriors and Warfare in Ancient and Medieval Times*, London: Constable and Company Limited.

Featherstone 2001: Peter Featherstone, 'The Tribal Hidage and the Ealdormen of Mercia', in Brown and Farr 2001: 23-34.

Fellows-Jensen 1985: Gillian Fellows-Jensen, *Scandinavian Settlement Names in the North-West*, Copenhagen: Københavns Universitet.

――― 1989: Gillian Fellows-Jensen, 'Amounderness and Holderness', in Peterson and Strandberg 1989: 57-94.

――― 1994: Gillian Fellows-Jensen, 'Danish Names in England', in Rumble 1994: 125-140.

――― 1994: Gillian Fellows-Jensen, 'Scandinavians in Cheshire: a Reassessment of the Onomastic Evidence', in Rumble and Mills 1997: 77-92.

――― 2008: Gilliam Fellows-Jensen, 'Grimston Revisited', in Padell and Parsons 2008: 125-35.

Field 1982: John Field, *English Field Names: A Dictionary*, Newton Abbot: David & Charles (Publishers) Limited.

Finberg 1964: H. P. R. Finberg, *Lucerna: Studies of some problems in the early history of England*, London: Macmillan & Co. Ltd.

―――1972: H. P. R. Finberg, *The Early Charters of the West Midlands*, Leicester: Leicester University Press.

Fisher 1959: E. A. Fisher, *An Introduction to Anglo-Saxon Architecture and Sculpture*, London: Faber and Faber.

Fisher 1973: *The Anglo-Saxon Age, c.400-1042*, London: Longman Group Limited.

Fitzhugh and Ward 2000: William W. Fitzhugh and Elisabeth I. Ward (eds), *Vikings: The North Atlantioc Saga*, Washington and London: Smithsonian Institution Press.

Fjalldal 2005: Magnús Fjalldal, *Anglo-Saxon England in Icelandic Medieval Texts*, Toronto, Buffalo and London: University of Toronto Press.

Fleming 1985: R. Fleming, 'Monastic Lands and England's Defence in the Viking Age', *English Historical Review*, 100, 247-65.

Fletcher 1997: Richard Fletcher, *The Conversion of Europe: From Paganism to Christianity 371-1386 AD*, London: HarperCollins Publishers.

Fletcher 2002: R. Fletcher, *Bloodfeud: Murder and Revenge in Anglo-Saxon England*, London: Penguin Books.

Floyd 2015: P. A. Floyd, *Building Stones and Stone Buildings in Staffordshire*, Ilfracombe: Arthur H. Stockwell Limited.

Foot 2000: Sarah Foot, *Veiled Women: Female Religious Communities in England, 871-1066*, II, Aldershot: Ashgate Publishing.

――― 2006: Sarah Foot, *Monastic Life in Anglo-Saxon England c.600-900*, Cambridge: Cambridge University Press.

――― 2008: Sarah Foot, 'Where English Becomes British: Rethinking the Contexts for *Brunanburh*', in Barrow and Wareham 2008: 127-44.

Foote and Wilson 1970: Peter Foote and David M. Wilson, *The Viking Achievement*, Sidgwick & Jackson Limited.

Ford 1988: Boris Ford (ed.), *The Cambridge Guide to the Arts in Britain: Prehistoric, Roman and Early Medieval*, Cambridge: Cambridge University Press.

Forester 1853: Thomas Forester, *The Chronicle of Henry of Huntingdon*, London: Henry G. Bohn.

―――1854: Thomas Forester (trans), *The Ecclesiastical History of England and Normandy by Orderic Vitalis*, London: Henry G. Bohn.

———1854a: Thomas Forester (trans), *The Chronicle of Florence of Worcester, with Two Continuations, comprising Annals of English History, from the Departure of the Romans to the Reign of Edward I*, London: Henry G. Bohn.

Forster 1941: M. Forster, *Der Flussname Themse und Seine Sippe*, Munich: Sitzungsberichte der Bayerischen Akademie der Wissenschaften, Philhist. Abteilung.

Fouracre and Ganz 2008: Paul Fouracre and David Ganz (eds.), *Frankland: The Franks and the World of the Early Middle Ages: Essays in Honour of Dame Jinty Nelson*, Manchester and New York: Manchester University Press.

Fowler 1972: P. J. Fowler (ed.), *Archaeology and the Landscape: Essays for J. V. Grinsell*, London: John Baker.

Fox 1955: Sir Cyril Fox, *Offa's Dyke: A Field Survey of the Western Frontier Works of Mercia in the Seventh and Eighth Centuries A.D.*, London: Oxford University Press for the British Academy.

Foxall 1980: H. D. G. Foxall, *Shropshire Field-Names*, Shrewsbury: Shropshire Archaeological Society.

Foxe 1570: John Foxe, *Actes and Monuments of these latter and perilous days, touching matters of the Church, wherein are comprehended and described the great persecutions and horrible troubles that have been wrought and practised by the Romish prelates, specially in this realm of England and Scotland, from the year of our Lord 1000 unto the time now present; gathered and collected according to the true copies and writings certificatory, as well of the parties themselves that suffered, as also out of the bishops' registers, which were the doers thereof; by John Foxe*, London: John Day.

Freeman 1873: Edward Augustus Freeman, *The History of the Norman Conquest: Its Causes and Its Results*, Oxford: The Clarendon Press.

Friar 2000: Stephen Friar, *The Companion to the English Church*, London: Chancellor Press.

Fritze and Robinson 2002: Ronald H. Fritze and William Baxter Robinson (eds.), *Historical Dictionary of Late Medieval England 1272-1485*, Westport: Greenwood Press.

Fryde and Reitz 2009: N. Fryde and D. Reitz (eds.), *Walls, Ramparts and Lines of Demarcation: Selected Studies from Antiquity to Modern Times*, Munster: Lit Verlag.

Galbraith 1982: V. H. Galbraith, *Kings and Chroniclers: Essays in English Medieval History*, London: The Hambledon Press.

Gale 1691: Thomas Gale, *Historia Britannicae, Saxonicae, Anglo-Danicae, Scriptores XV Ex Vetustis Cod. MSS. Edit Opera*, Oxford.

Gardiner and Coates 1987: M. Gardiner and R. Coates, 'Ellingsdean, a Viking battlefield identified', *Sussex Archaeological Collections*, 125 (1987) 251-2.

Gardiner and Rippon 2007: Mark Gardiner and Stephen Rippon (eds.), *Medieval Landscapes*, Macclesfield: Windgather Press.

Gardiner and Wenborn 1995: Juliet Gardiner and Neil Wenborn, *The History Today Companion to British History*, London: Collins & Brown Limited.

Gardner 1968: Thomas J. Gardner, *Semantic Patterns in Old English Substantival Compounds*, Hamburg [no publisher given].

Garmonsway 1953: G. N. Garmonsway (trans), *The Anglo-Saxon Chronicle*, London: J. M. Dent & Sons Ltd.

Garner 1844: Robert Garner, *The Natural History of the County of Stafford; Comprising its Geology, Zoology, Botany, and Meteorology; also its Antiquities, Topography, Manufactures, etc.*, London: John Van Voorst.

Gelling 1982: Margaret Gelling (ed.), *Offa's Dyke Reviewed by Frank Noble*, Oxford: BAR Reports Series 114.

——— Gelling 1982b: Margaret Gelling, 'Some meanings of *Stōw*', in Pearce 1982: 187-96.

——— Gelling 1983: Margaret Gelling (ed.), *Offa's Dyke Reviewed by Frank Noble*, Oxford: BAR Reports Series 114.

——— Gelling 1984: Margaret Gelling, *Place-Names in the Landscape*, London: J. M. Dent & Sons Limited.

────── Gelling 1987: Margaret Gelling, 'Further Thoughts on Pagan Place-Names', in Cameron 1987: 99-114.

────── 1997: Margaret Gelling, *Signposts to the Past: Place-Names and the History of England*, Chichester: Phillimore & Co. Ltd.

Giles 1847: J. A. Giles, *William of Malmesbury's English Chronicle*, London: Henry G. Bohn.

──────1892: J. A. Giles (trans.), *Roger of Wendover's Flowers of History*, I, London& New York: George Bell & Sons.

──────1892b: J. A. Giles, *The Venerable Bede's Ecclesiatical History of England. Also the Anglo-Saxon Chronicle*, London: George Bell & Sons.

──────1901: J. A. Giles, *Old English Chronicles*, London: George Bell & Sons.

Gillies 2016: Midge Gillies, *Army Wives: From Crimea to Afghanistan: the Real Lives of the Women Behind the Men in Uniform*, London: Aurum Press Ltd.

Gillingham 2004: John Gillingham (ed), *Anglo-Norman Studies XXVL: Proceedings of the Battle Conference 2003*, Woodbridge: The Boydell Press.

────── 2007: John Gillingham, '"Holding to the Rules of War (*Bellica Iura Tenentes*)": Right Conduct before, during and after Battle in North-Western Europe in the Eelventh Century', *Anglo-Norman Studies*, 29 (2007) 1-15.

────── 2008: John Gillingham, '*Fontenoy and after: pursuing enemies to death in France between the ninth and eleventh centuries*', in Gouracre and Ganz 2008: 242-265.

Glover 1865: John Glover (ed.), *Le Livere de Reis de Brittanie e Le Livere de Reis de Engletere*, London: Longmans, Green, Reader, and Dyer.

Glover 1996: Richard Glover, 'English Warfare', in Morillo 1996: 174-88.

Godden and Lapidge 1991: Malcom Godden and Michael Lapidge (eds), *The Cambridge Companion to Old English Literature*, Cambridge: Cambridge University Press.

Godfrey 1961: C. J. Godfrey, *The Church in Anglo-Saxon England*, Cambridge: Cambridge University Press.

────── 2016: C. J. Godfrey, 'The Archbishopric of Lichfield', *Studies in Church History*, Vol. 1 (2016) 145-53.

Godman 1982: Peter Godman (ed), *De potificibus et sanctis Euboricensis Ecclesiæ: The Bishops, Kings, and Saints of York*, Oxford: Clarendon Press.

Gooch 2012: Megan Laura Gooch, 'Money and Power in the Viking Kingdom of York', unpublished PhD Thesis, Durham University.

Goodall 2011: John Goodall, *The English Castle*, London: Yale University Press for Paul Mellon Centre for Studies in British Art.

Gordon Cartlidge 1937-8, J. E. Gordon Cartlidge, *The Gates of Oakengates*, Telford: Jean Beard.

Gough 1806: Richard Gough (translated and enlarged by), *Britannia: or, A Chorographical Description of the Flourishing Kingdoms of England, Scotland, and Ireland, and the Islands Adjacent, from the Earliest Antiquity. By William Camden*, 4 Vols., London: John Stockdale.

Gould 1957: J. Gould, *Men of Aldridge*, Bloxwich: Geoff J. Clark.

Grafton 1569: Richard Grafton, *Grafton's Chronicle; or, History of England, to which is added his Table of the Bailiff's, Sheriffs, and Mayors, of the City of London, from the year 1189, to 1558, inclusive*, 2 Vols, London: J. Johnson; F. C. and J. Rivinton; T. Payne; Wilkie and Robinson; Longman, Hirst, Rees and Orme; Cadell and Davies; and J. Mawman.

Graham Campbell 1992: James Graham Campbell, 'Anglo-Scandinavian Equestrian Equipment in Eleventh Century England', in Chibnall 1992 77-90.

────── 1992a: James Graham-Campbell (ed), *Viking Treasure from the North-West: Cuerdale Hoard in its Context*, Liverpool: National Museums and Galleries on Merseyside, Liverpool.

────── 1994: James Graham-Campbell (ed.), *Cultural Atlas of the Viking World*, New York: Facts on File Inc.

────── 2001: J. A. Graham-Campbell, 'The northern hoards: from Cuerdale to Bossall/Flaxton', in Higham and Hill 2001: 212-229.

────── 2013: James Graham-Campbell, *Viking Art*, London: Thames& Hudson.

Graham-Campbell et al2001: James Graham-Campbell, Richard Hall, Judith Jesch and David N. Parsons (eds), *Vikings and the Danelaw: Papers from the Proceedings of the Thirteenth Viking Congress, Nottingham and York, 21st-30th August 1997*, Oxford: Oxbow Books.

Graham-Campbell and Kidd 1980: James Graham-Campbell and Dafydd Kidd, *The Vikings*, London: British Museum Publications.

Graham-Campbell and Philpott 2009: James Graham-Campbell and Robert Philpott (eds), *The Huxley Viking Hoard: Scandinavian Settlement in the North-West*, Liverpool: National Museums Liverpool.

Graham-Campbell and Williams 2007: James Graham-Campbell and Gareth Williams (eds), *Silver Economy of the Viking Age*, Walnut Creek: Left Coast Press Inc.

Gransden 1974-82: Antonia Gransden, *Historical Writing in England*, 2 vols., London: Routledge & Kegan Paul.

——— 1992: Antonia Gransden, *Legends, Traditions and History in Medieval England*, London: The Hambledon Press.

Grape 1994: Wolfgang Grape, *The Bayeux Tapestry: Monument to a Norman Triumph*, Munich and New York: Prestel.

Graves 1975: Edgar B. Graves (ed), *A Bibliography of English History to 1485, based on The Sources and Literature of English History from the earliest times to about 1485 by Charles Gross*, Oxford: The Clarendon Press.

Gravett and Turner 2003: Christopher Gravett and Graham Turner, *Towton 1461: England's Bloodiest Battle*, Oxford: Ospey Publishing Limited.

Green 1884: J. R. Green, *The Conquest of England*, London: Macmillan & Co.

Greenway 1996: Diana Greenway, *Henry, Archdeacon of Huntingdon: Historia Anglorum: the History of the English People*, Oxford: Clarendon Press.

Gregory 1992: K. J. Gregory (ed.), *Fluvial Geomorphology of Britain*, New York.

Grierson, Blackburn and Travaini 1986: Philip Grierson, Mark A. S. Blackburn and Lucia Travaini, *Medieval European Coinage I: The Early Middle Ages (5th – 10th Centuries)*, Cambridge: Fitzwilliam Museum.

Griffith 1868: George Griffith, *Ribbesford and Other Poems*, Wolverhampton: Griffith.

——— 1880: George Griffith, *Reminiscences and Records during ten years' residence in the Midland Counties from 1869 to 1880*, Madeley: John Randall; Bewdley: George Griffith.

Griffith 1995: Paddy Griffith, *The Viking Art of War*, London: Greenhill Books; Mechanicsburg: Stackpole Books.

Griffiths 1995a: David Griffiths, 'The North-West Mercian *Burh*s: A Reappraisal', in ASSAH 8 1995 75-86.

——— 2015: David Griffiths, 'A Brief History and Archaeology of Viking Activity in North-West England', in Harding, Griffiths and Royle 2015: 33-49.

Griffiths and Newman 2009: David Griffiths and Rachel Newman, 'The Archaeological Background', in Graham-Campbell and Philpott 2009: 13-23.

Grimm 1880: Jacob Grimm (James Steven Stallybrass, trans), *Teutonic Mythology*, Cambridge: Cambridge University Press.

Grinsell 1953: L. V. Grinsell, *The Ancient Burial-Mounds of England*, second edition, London: Methuen & Co. Limited.

Groom 1992: Jane N. Groom, 'The Topographical Analysis of Medieval Town Plans: the Examples of Much Wenlock and Bridgnorth', *Midland History*, Vol. XVII.

Gross 1900: C. Gross, *The Sources and Literature of English History from the Earliest Times to about 1485*, London: Longmans, Green, & Co. [Now superseded by Graves 1975.]

Grueber and Keary 1893: Hubert A. Grueber and Charles Francis Keary, *A Catalogue of Coins in the British Museum, Anglo-Saxon Series, Part II*, London: B. Quaritch, for the Trustees of the British Museum.

Guizot 1826: François Guizot, *Collection de mémoires relatifs à l'histoire de France: depuis la fondation de la monarchie Française Jusqu'au 13e siecle et des notes*, Paris: Chez. J.-L.-J. Briere.

Hackwood 1908: Frederick W. Hackwood, *The Annals of Willenhall*, Wolverhampton: Whitehead Brothers.

Haddan and Stubbs 1871: Athur West Haddan and William Stubbs (eds), *Councils and Ecclesiastical Documents Relating to Great Britain and Ireland*, 3 vols., Oxford: The Clarendon Press.

Hadley 2000: D. M. Hadley, *The Northern Danelaw: Its Social Structure, c.800-1100*, Studies in the Early History of Britain, Leicester: Leicester University Press.

────── 2001: D. M. Hadley, *Death in Medieval England: An Archaeology*, Stroud: Tempus Publishing Limited.

────── 2006: D. M. Hadley, *The Vikings in England: Settlement, Society and Culture*, Manchester: Manchester University Press.

────── 2008: Dawn M. Hadley, 'The Creation of the Danelaw', in Brink and Price 2008: 375-8.

Hadley and Ten Herkel 2013: D. M. Hadley and Lotty Ten Terkel (eds), *Everyday Life in Viking-Age Towns; Social Approaches to Towns in England and Ireland, c.800-1100*, Oxford: Oxbow Books.

Hadley and Richards 2002: D. Hadley and J. D. Richards (eds), *Cultures in Contact: Scandinavian Settlement in England in the Ninth and Tenth Centuries*, Turnhout: Brepols N.V.

Hadley and Richards 2016: Dawn Hadley and Julian D. Richards, with contributions by Hannah Brown, Elizabeth Craig-Atkins, Diana Mahoney-Swales, Gareth Perry, Samantha Stein and Andrew Woods, 'The Winter Camp of the Viking Great Army, AD 872-3, Torksey, Lincolnshire', *Antiquaries Journal*, 2016 (96), 23-67.

Haldane 2008: A. R. B. Haldane, *The Drove Roads of Scotland*, Edinburgh: Birlinn.

Hall 1865: Frederick Hall, *A Short Historical Account of the Collegiate Church of St. Peter, Wolverhampton*, Wolverhampton: William Parke.

Hall 1978: R. A. Hall (ed.), *Viking Age York and the North*, London: Council for British Archaeology.

Hall 1981: R. Hall, 'Markets of the Danelaw', in *The Vikings in England and their Danish Homeland*, London: The Anglo-Danish Viking Project, 95-140.

Hall 1995: Richard Hall, *Viking Age Archaeology in Britain and Ireland*, Princes Risborough: Shire Publications Limited.

────── 2001: Richard Hall, 'A Kingdom Too Far: York in the Early Tenth Century', in Higham and Hill 2001: 188-99.

Halliwell-Phillipps 1881: James Orchard Halliwell-Phillipps, *A Dictionary of Archaic and Provincial Words*, London: J. R. Smith.

Halsall 2003: Guy Halsall, *Warfare and Society in the Barbarian West, 450-900*, Abingdon: Routledge.

Hamilton 1870: N. E. S. A. Hamilton (ed), *Willelmi Malmesbiriensis Monachii de gentis Pontificum Anglorum*, London, Oxford and Cambridge: Longman & Co., and Trübner & Co; Parker & Co; Macmillan & Co.

Hancock 1991: Geoffrey Hancock, *A Tettenhall History*, Tettenhall: Broadside.

Harding, Griffiths and Royles 2015: Stephen Harding, David Griffiths and Elizabeth Royles (eds.), *In Search of Vikings: Interdisciplinary Approaches to the Scandinavian Heritage of North-West England*, London: CRC Press.

Hardwicke 1882-3: William Hardwicke, 'An Account of the Roman Encampment at Chesterton, Co. Salop. By the late William Hardwicke. Communicated by Hubert Smith, F.R.H.S.', in *The Reliquary*, XIII (1882-3) 11-16.

Hardy 1840: Thomas Duffy Hardy, *Willelmi Malmesbiriensis Monachi Gesta Regum Anglorum atque Historia Novella*, Vol. I, London: Sumptibus Societis.

Hardy and Martin 1889: Thomas Duffus Hardy and Charles Trice Martin (eds.), *Lestorie des Engles Solum Translacion Maistre Geffrei Gaimar*, Vol. II, HMSO.

Hare 2014: Michael Hare, 'Hemming's Crosses', in Owen-Crocker and Thompson 2014.

Härke 1997: H. Härke, 'Early Anglo-Saxon Social Studies', in Hines 1997: 125-70.

Harmer 1914: F E. Harmer, *Select English Historical Documents of the Ninth and Tenth Centuries*, Cambridge: Cambridge University Press.

────── 1989: Florence E. Harmer, *Anglo-Saxon Writs*, second edition, Stamford: Paul Watkins.

Harris 2006: Brian L. Harris, *Harris's Guide to Churches and Cathedrals*, London: Ebury Press.

Harrison 1993: Mark Harrison, *Anglo-Saxon Thegn A.D. 449-1066*, Oxford: Osprey Publishing Limited.

Harrison 2004: David Harrison, *The Bridges of Medieval England: Transport and Society 400-1800*, Oxford: Oxford University Press.

Harrison and Ó Floinn 2014: Stephen H. Harrison and Raghnall Ó Floinn, *Viking Graves and Grave-Goods in Ireland*, Dublin: National Museum of Ireland.

Hart 1975: C. R. Hart, *The Early Charters of Northern England and the North Midlands*, Leicester: Leicester University Press.

────── 1977: C. R. Hart, 'The Kingdom of Mercia', in Dornier 1977: 43-61.

────── 1982: C. R. Hart, 'The B text of the Anglo-Saxon Chronicle', *Journal of Medieval History*, 8, 241-299.

────── 1983: C. R. Hart, 'The early section of the Worcester Chronicle', *Journal of Medieval History*, 9 251-315.

────── 1992: Cyril Hart, *The Danelaw*, London and Rio Grande: The Hambledon Press.

────── 1995: Cyril Hart, 'The *Aldwerke* and Minster at Shelford, Cambridgeshire', ASSAH 8 (1995) 43-68.

────── 2003: Cyril Hart, Learning and Culture in Late Anglo-Saxon England and the Influence of Romsey Abbey on the Major English Monastic Schools, New York: Edwin Mellor Press.

────── 2006: Cyril Hart, *Byrhtferth's East Anglian Chronicle: A Comparative Edition and Translation of the Old English and Latin Annals*, New York: Edwin Mellen Press.

────── 2006a: Cyril Hart, *Byrhtferth's Northumbrian Chronicle: A Comparative Edition and Translation of the Old English and Latin Annals*, New York: Edwin Mellen Press.

Hartshorne 1841: Charles Henry Hartshorne, *Salopia Antiqua: Or, An Enquiry from Personal Survey into the 'druidical', Military and Other Early Remains in Shropshire and the North Welsh Borders with Observations Upon the Names of Places and A Glossary of Words Used in the County of Salop*, London: John W. Parker.

Harvey 2014: Sally Harvey, *Domesday: Book of Judgement*, Oxford: Oxford University Press.

Harwood 1820: Thomas Harwood (ed.), *A Survey of Staffordshire, Containing the Antiquities of that County, by Samuel Erdeswick*, London: John Nichols & Son.

────── 1844: Thomas Harwood (ed.), *A Survey of Staffordshire, Containing the Antiquities of that County, by Samuel Erdeswick*, London: J. B. Nichols & Son.

Haslam 1984: Jeremy Haslam (ed.), *Anglo-Saxon Towns in Southern England*, Chichester: Phillimore & Co. Limited.

────── 1987: Jeremy Haslam, 'Market and Forterss in the Reign of Offa', *World Archaeology*, 19: I 76-93.

────── 1997: Jeremy Haslam, 'The Location of the *Burh* of *Wigingamere* – A Reappraisal', in Rumble and Mills 1997: 111-30.

────── 2005: Jeremy Haslam, 'King Alfred and the Vikings: Stategies and Tactics', ASSAH 13 (2005) 121-54.

Hawkes 1989: Sonia Chadwick Hawkes (ed.), *Weapons and Warfare in Anglo-Saxon England*, Oxford: Oxford University Committee for Archaeology.

Hawkes 2002: Jane Hawkes, *The Sandbach Crosses: Sign and Significance in Anglo-Saxon Sculpture*, Dublin: Four Courts Press Limited.

────── 2003: Jane Hawkes, 'Sacraments in Stone: The Mysteries of Christ in Anglo-Saxon Sculpture', in Carver 2003: 351-70.

Hawkes and Sidebottom (forthcoming): Jane Hawkes and Philip Sidebottom, *Corpus of Anglo-Saxon Stone Sculpture: Derbyshire and Staffordshire*, London: British Academy.

Hayland 1994: Ann Hayland, *The Medieval Warhorse from Byzantium to the Crusades*, Stroud: Alan Sutton.

Haywood 1995: John Haywood, *The Penguin Historical Atlas of the Vikings*, London: Penguin Books Limited.

────── 2000: John Haywood, *Encyclopaedia of the Viking Age*, London: Thames& Hudson Limited.

Hearne 1744: Thomas Hearne, *The Itinerary of John Leland the Antiquary*, Oxford: James Fletcher & Joseph Pote.

────── 1770: Thomas Hearne (ed), *Joannis Lelandi: Antiquarii De Rebus Britannicis Collectaneacvm Thomæ Hearnii Prefatione Notis et Indice ad Editionem primam*, Vol. III, London: Impensis Gul and Jo, Richardson.

Heighway 2001: Caroline Heighway, 'Gloucester and the new minster of St Oswald', in Higham and Hill 2001 102-11.

Hennessy 1866: W. M. Hennessy, *Chronicon Scotorum: A Chronicle of Irish Affairs from the earliest times to AD 1135*, London: Longman, Green, Reader & Dyer.

Heywoode 1624: Thomas Heywoode, *Gynaikon: or, Nine Bookes of Various Historie, Onelie Concerning Women: Inscribed by the names of the nine Muses: The Fifth Booke inscribed Terpeschore. Intreating of Amazons: and other Women famous either for Valour, or from Beautie*, London: Adam Islip.

Hickey and Puppel 1997: Raymond Hickey and Stanisław Puppel (eds), *Language, History and Linguistic Modelling: A Festschrift for Jack Fisiak on his 60th Birthday, Vol. I: Language History*, Berlin and New York: Mouton de Gruyter.

Higham 1992: N. J. Higham, 'Northumbria, Mercia and the Irish Sea Norse, 893-926', in Graham Campbell 1992a: 21-30.

────── 1993: N. J. Higham, *The Kingdom of Northumbria A.D. 350-1100*, Stroud: Alan Sutton.

────── 1993a: N. J. Higham, *The Origins of Cheshire*, Manchester: Manchester University Press.

────── 1997: N. J. Higham, 'The Context of *Brunanburh*', in *Names, Places and People: an Onomastic Miscellany for John McNeal Dodgson*, Stamford: Paul Watkins, 144-156.

────── 2002: N. J. Higham, *King Arthur: Myth-making and History*, London: Routledge.

────── 2007: N. J. Higham (ed.), *Britons in Anglo-Saxon England*, Woodbridge: Boydell Press.

Higham and Hill 2001: N. J. Higham and D. Hill (eds.), *Edward the Elder899-924*, London: Routledge.

Higham and Ryan 2011: Nicholas J. Higham and Martin J. Ryan (eds),*Place-Names, Language and the Anglo-Saxon Landscape*, Woodbridge: The Boydell Press for the Manchester Centre for Anglo-Saxon Studies.

Higham and Ryan 2013: Nicholas J. Higham and Martin J. Ryan, *The Anglo-Saxon World*, New Haven and London: Yale University Press.

Hill 1984: David Hill, *An Atlas of Anglo-Saxon England*, Oxford: Basil Blackwell.

────── 2001: David Hill, 'Mercians: Dwellers on the Boundary', in Brown and Farr 2001: 173-82.

Hill 1996: R. Hill, 'Christianity and geography in early Northumbria', *Studies in Church History* 3 126-99.

Hill 2004: Paul Hill, *The Age of Athelstan: Britain's Forgotten History*, Stroud: Tempus Publishing Limited.

────── 2006: Paul Hill, *The Anglo-Saxons: The Verdict of History*, Stroud: Tempus Publishing Limited.

Hill and Sharp 1997: David Hill and Sheila Sharp, 'An Anglo-Saxon Beacon System', in A. R. Rumble and D. Hill (eds.), *Names, Places and People: An Onomastic Miscellany in Memory of John McNeal Dodgson*, Stamford: Paul Watkins.

Hill and Rumble 1996: David Hill and Alexander R. Rumble (eds.) *The defence of Wessex: The Burghal Hidage and Anglo-Saxon fortifications*, Manchester& New York: Manchester University Press.

Hill and Worthington 2003: David Hill and Margaret Worthington, *Offa's Dyke: History and Guide*, Stroud: Tempus Publishing Limited.

Hinde 1868: John Hodgson Hinde (ed), *Symeonis Dunelmensis Opera et Collectanea*, London: Whittaker &Co; T. and W. Boone; Bernard Quarich; Edinburh; Blackwood and Sons; Durham: Andrews and Co. (for the Surtees Society).

Hindley 2006: Geoffrey Hindley, *A Brief History of the Anglo-Saxons*, London: Constable & Robinson Limited.

Hines 1997: John Hines (ed), *The Anglo-Saxons from the Migration Period to the Eighth Century: An Ethnographic Perspective*, Woodbridge: The Boydell Press.

Hinton 1977: David A. Hinton, *Alfred's Kingdom: Wessex and the South 800-1500*, London: J. M. Dent & Sons Limited.

——— 1984: David A. Hinton, 'The Towns of Hampshire', in Haslam 1984: 149-65.

——— 1984: David A. Hinton, *Archaeology, Economy and Society: England from the Fifth to the Fifteenth Century*, London and New York: Routledge.

Holinshed 1577: Raphael Holinshed, *The Chronicles of England, Scotland and Ireland*.

——— 1587: Raphael Holinshed, *The Chronicles of England, Scotland and Ireland*.

Hollander 1964: L. M. Hollander (trans), *Snorri Sturluson. Heimskringla. History of the Kings of Norway*, Austin: University of Texas Press.

Holland 2016: Tom Holland, *Athelstan: The Making of England*, Allen Lane/Penguin Books.

Hollister 1962: C. Warren Hollister, *Anglo-Saxon Military Institutions*, Oxford: Oxford University Press.

Holman 2001: Katherine Holman, 'Defining the Danelaw', in Graham-Campbell et al 2001: 1-12.

Hooke 1983: Della Hooke, *The Landscape of Anglo-Saxon Staffordshire: the Charter Evidence*, Keele: University of Keele.

——— 1990: Della Hooke, *Worcestershire Anglo-Saxon Charter-Bounds*, Woodbridge: Boydell.

——— 1992: Della Hooke, 'Early Units of Government in Herefordshire and Shropshire', in *Anglo-Saxon Studies in Archaeology and History*, 5, 47-64.

——— 1993: Della Hooke, 'Wolverhampton: The Foundation of the Minster', in Maddison 1993: 11-15.

——— 2002: Della Hooke, 'Early Units of Government in Herefordshire and Shropshire', in ASSAH 5 49-64.

——— 2006: Della Hooke, *England's Landscape: The West Midlands*, London: Collins/English Heritage.

Hooke and Slater 1986: D Hooke and T R Slater, *Anglo-Saxon Wolverhampton and its Monastery*, Wolverhampton: Wolverhampton Borough Council.

Hookway 2015: Esme Nadine Hookway, 'An Archaeological Analysis of Anglo-Saxon Shropshire AD 600-1066', unpublished MRes thesis, University of Birmingham.

Hooper 1989: Nicholas Hooper, 'The Anglo-Saxons at War', in Hawkes 1989: 191-202.

Hooper 1998: Jennie Hooper, "The Rows of the Battle Swan': The Aftermath of the Battle in Anglo-Saxon Art', in Strickland 1998: 82-9.

Horovitz 1992: David Horovitz, *Some notes on the history of Brewood in Staffordshire, with an account of the escape of Charles II after the battle of Worcester on 3rd September 1651*, Brewood: David Horovitz.

——— 2005: David Horovitz, *The Place-Names of Staffordshire*, Brewood: David Horovitz.

——— 2010: David Horovitz: *Notes and Materials on the battle of Tettenhall 910 A.D., and other researches*, Brewood: David Horovitz.

——— 2015: David Horovitz, 'Buttington and Buttington (or vice versa): a tale of two names', *Journal of the English Place-Name Society*, 47 (2015) 38-54.

Horspool 2014: David Horspool, *Alfred the Great*, Stroud: Amberley Publishing.

Howlett 2012: Richard Howlett (ed), *Chronicles of the Reigns of Stephen, Henry II, and Richard I*, Cambridge: Cambridge University Press.

Howlett and Coxah 1992: C. E. Howlett and M. Coxah, *An Archaeological Evaluation of Hay Farm, Eardington, Shropshire, on behalf of Redland Aggregates Limited*, Oxford: Tempvs Reparatvm Archaeological and Historical Consultants Limited.

Hudson 1996: Benjamin T. Hudson, *Prophesy of Berchán: Irish and Scottish High-Kings of the Early Middle Ages*, Westport: Greenwood Press.

Hughes and Buteux 1992: Gwilym Hughes and Simon Buteux, *Wolverhampton Cross Shaft, an Archaeological Assessment*, August 1992, Birmingham: Birmingham University Field Archaeology Unit.

Hulbert 1825: *Museum Europæum; or Select Antiquities, Curious Beauties, and Varieties, of Nature and Art, in Europe*, Shrewsbury: C. Hulbert.

Hull 1869: Edward Hull, *The Triassic and Permian Rocks of the Midland Counties of England*, London: Longmans, Green and Co.

Hunn 2000: J. R. Hunn, 'Hay Farm, Eardington, Shropshire: an Iron-Age and Romano British Enclosure', in Zeepvat 2000: 119-44.

Hunt 1893: William Hunt, *Two Chartularies of the Priory of St Peter at Bath*, London: Harrison& Sons.

Hunt 2009: John Hunt, 'A Figure Sculpture at Upton Bishop, Herefordshire: Continuity and Revival in Early Medieval Sculpture', *Antiquaries Journal* 89 (2009) 179-214.

────── 2014: John Hunt, 'Grave Goods, Gospels and Carvings', *West Midlands History*, 2, issue 3 (Autumn 2014) 31-3.

────── 2016: John Hunt, *Warriors, Warlords and Saints: The Anglo-Saxon Kingdom of Mercia*, Alcester: West Midlands History Limited.

Ingram 1823: Reverend James Ingram, (trans), *The Saxon Chronicle: AD 1 to AD 1154*, London: Longman, Hurst, Rees, Orme, and Brown.

Insley 2000: Charles Insley, 'Politics, Conflict and Kinship in Early Eleventh-Century Mercia', in *Midland History*, 25, No. 1 (2000) 28-42.

Insley 2013: John Insley, 'Personal names in place-names', in Carroll and Parsons 2013: 209-49.

Irvine 2004: S. Irvine (ed), *The Anglo-Saxon Chronicle: A Collaborative Edition, MS E*, Cambridge: D. S. Brewer.

Isaac 2007: G. R. Isaac, 'Armes Prydain Fawr and St. David', in J. Wyn Evans and Jonathan M. Wooding (eds), *St David of Wales. Cult, Church and Nation*, Studies in Celtic History, 24, Woodbridge: Boydell Press, 161-8.

Jackson 1879: Georgina F. Jackson, *Shropshire Word Book: A Glosary of Archaic and Provincial Words, etc., used in the County*: London: Trübner & Co.

Jackson 1953: K. H. Jackson, *Language and History in Early Britain*, Edinburgh: Edinburgh University Press.

Jackson 1995: Peter Jackson (ed), *Words, Names and History: Selected Writings of Cecily Clark*, Cambridge: D. S. Brewer.

Jackson at al 1963: Kenneth Jackson, Peter Hunter Blair, Bertram Colgrave, Bruce Dickins, Joan and Harold Taylor, Christopher Brooke and Nora K. Chadwick, *Celt and Saxon: Studies in the Early British Border*, Cambridge: Cambridge University Press.

James 1879: Samuel B. James, *Worfield on the Worfe*, London and Derby: Bemrose and Sons.

James 2001: Edward James, *Britain in the First Millennium*, London: Arnold.

Jarman 1990: A. O. H. Jarman, *Aneirin: Y Goddinn: Britain's Oldest Heroic Poem*, Llandysul: Gomer Press.

Jayakumar 2008: Shashi Jayakumar, 'Eadwig and Edgar: Politics, Propaganda, Faction', in Scragg 2008: 83-103.

Jeffery 2004: Paul Jeffery, *The Collegiate Churches of England and Wales*, London: Robert Hale.

Jenkins 1989: Anne E. Jenkins, 'The Early Medieval Contexts of the Royal Free Chapels of South Staffordshire', unpublished M.Phil thesis, Birmingham University.

Jeremiah 1998: Josephine Jeremiah, *The River Severn: A Pictorial History from Shrewsbury to Gloucester*, Chichester: Phillimore & Co. Ltd.

Jermy 1992: K. E. Jermy, 'Longford and Langford as Significant Names in Establishing Lines of Roman Roads', in *Britannia* 23 228-9.

Jermy and Breeze 2000: A. Breeze and K. E. Jermy, 'Welsh *ffordd* "road" in English Place-Names, particularly as an indicator of a Roman road', *Transactions of the Shropshire Archaeological and Historical Society* 75 109-10.

Jesch 2000: Judith Jesch, 'Scandinavian Wirral', in Cavill, Harding and Jesch 2000 1-10.

Jewell 2001: Richard Jewell, 'Classicism of Northumbrian Sculpture', in Brown and Farr 2001: 246-62.

Jewett et al 1894: L. F. W. Jewett, J. C. Cox and J. R. Allen, *The Reliquary and Illustrated Archaeologist*, London: Bemrose & Sons.

Job 1985: Barry Job, *Staffordshire Windmills*, Birmingham: Midland Wind and Watermills Group.

John 1992: Eric John, 'The Point of Woden', in ASSAH 5 (1992) 127-34.

────── 1996: Eric John, *Reassessing Anglo-Saxon England*, Manchester: Manchester University Press.

────── 2004: Eric John, 'The Annals of St Neots and the Defeat of the Vikings', in Evans 2004: 51-62.

Jones 1894: James P Jones, *A History of the Parish of Tettenhall*, John Steen & Co.

Jones 1971: Thomas Jones (trans.), *Brenhinedd y Saesson or The Kings of the Saxons*, Cardiff: University of Wales Press.

────── 1973: Thomas Jones (trans), *Brut y Tywysogyon, or The Chronicle of the Princes*, Cardiff: University of Wales Press.

Jones 2006: Charles Jones: *The Forgotten Battle of 1066*, Stroud: Tempus Publishing Limited.

Jones 2010: Robert W. Jones, *Blooded Banners: Martial Display on the Medieval Battlefield*, Woodbridge: Boydell Press.

Jones and Mattingly 1990: Barri Jones and David Mattingly, *An Atlas of Roman Britain*, Oxford: Basil Blackwell Limited.

Jorgensen 2010: Alic Jorgensen (ed), *Reading the Anglo-Saxon Chronicle: Language, Literature, History*, Turnhout: Brepols.

Jurkowski 2006: Maureen Jurkowski, 'Lollardy in Coventry', in Clark 2006: 145-64.

Karkov 2008: Catherine E. Karkov, 'The Frontispiece to the New Minster Charter and the King's Two Bodies', in Scragg 2008 224-41.

Karkov and Brown 2003: Catherine E. Karkov and George Jardin Brown (eds.), *Anglo-Saxon Styles*, New York: State University of New York Press.

Karkov, Keeper and Jolly 2006: Catherine E. Karkov, Sarah Larratt Keeper and Karen Louise Jolly (eds), *The Place of the Cross in Anglo-Saxon England*, Woodbridge: The Boydell Press.

Karunanithy 2008: David Karunanithy, *Dogs of War: Canine Use in Warfare from Ancient Egypt to the Nineteenth Century*, Brookings: Yarak Publishing.

Kaye 1973: Ruth Lincoln Kaye, *Thomas Lincoln of Taunton, Jospeh Hadley of Kellogg, and 144 Related Colinial Families*, Professional Print Co.

Kennedy 1991: Alan Kennedy, 'Byrhtnoth's Obits and Twelfth-Century Accounts of the Battle of Maldon', in Scragg 1991: 59-78.

Kelly 2008: S. E. Kelly, 'An early minster at Eynsham, Oxfordshire', in Padel and Parsons 2008: 79-85.

Kelly 2008a: Susan Kelly, 'Reculver Minster and its Early Charters', in Barrow and Wareham 2008, 67-82.

Kendrick 1938: T. D. Kendrick, *Anglo-Saxon Art to A.D. 900*, London: Methuen & Co.

────── 1949: T. D. Kendrick, *Late Saxon and Viking Art*, London: Methuen & Co.

Kerr and Kerr 1982: Nigel Kerr and Mary Kerr, *A Guide to Anglo-Saxon Sites*, St Albans: Granada Publishing Limited.

Kershaw 2015: Jane Kershaw, 'Viking-Age Silver in North-West England: Hoards and Single Finds', in Harding, Griffiths and Royles 2015: 149-64.

Kerslake 1875: Thomas Kerslake, 'St Ewen, Bristol and the Welsh Border, Circ. AD577-926', *Journal of the British Archaeological Association*, XXXI, 153-179.

Keynes 1980: Simon Keynes, *The Diplomas of King Æthelred, 978-1016*, Cambridge: Cambridge University Press.

―――― 1986: Simon Keynes, 'A tale of two kings: Alfred the Great and Æthelred the Unready', *Transactions of the Royal Historical Society*, 36 195-217.

―――― 1991: Simon Keynes, 'The Historical Context of the Battle of Maldon', in Scragg 1991: 81-113.

―――― 1994: Simon Keynes, 'The West Saxon Charters of King Æthelwulf and his Sons', *English Historical Review*, cix, 1109-49.

―――― 1998: Simon Keynes, 'King Alfred and the Mercians', in Blackburn and Dumville 1998: 39-41.

―――― 1999: Simon Keynes, 'England in the Tenth Century', in Reuter 1999: 457-88.

―――― 2000: Simon Keynes, 'England c.900-1016' in Reuter 200: 456-84.

―――― 2001: Simon Keynes, 'Edward, King of the Anglo-Saxons', in Higham and Hill 2001 40-66.

Keynes and Lapidge 1983: Simon Keynes and Michael Lapidge, *Alfred the Great: Asser's Life of King Alfred and other contemporary sources*, London: Penguin Books Limited.

Keynes and Smyth 2006: Simon Keynes and Alfred P. Smyth, *Anglo-Saxons: Studies presented to Cyril Roy Hart*, Dublin& Portland: Four Courts Press.

Kirkham and Warr 2014, Anne Kirkham and Cordelia Warr (eds.), *Wounds in the Middle Ages*, Aldershot: Ashgate.

Kirwan 2014: Mark Kirwan, 'The Viking Age in Ireland: An Overview', in Birkett and Lee 2014: 4-6.

Klaeber 1950: Fr. Klaeber (ed.), *Beowulf and the Fight at Finsburg*, 3rd edition, Lexington: D. C. Heath and Company.

Koch 1978: H. W. Koch, *Medieval Warfare*, London: Bison Books Limited.

Koch 2006: John T. Koch, *Celtic Culture: A Historical Encyclopedia, I, A-Celti*, Santa Barbara: ABC-CLIO.

Kronk 1999: Gary W. Kronk, *Cometography: A Catalog of Comets: Vol. I, Ancient–1799*, Cambridge: Cambridge University Press.

Laflin 2001: Susan Laflin, 'Roman Roads and Ford Names in Shropshire', *Transactions of the Shropshire Archaeological and Historical Society* 76 1-10.

Laing 1982: Lloyd and Jennifer Laing, *Britain Before the Conquest: Anglo Saxon England*, London: Paladin/Grafton Books.

Lambarde 1730: William Lambarde,*Dictionarum Angliæ Topographicum & Historicum. An Alphabetical Description of the Chief Places in England and Wales; with an Account of the most Memorable Events which have distinguish'd them*, London: Fletcher Gyles.

Lapidge 1982: M. Lapidge, 'Byrhtferth of Ramsey and the early sections of the *Historia Regum* attributed to Simeon of Durham', *Anglo-Saxon England* 10 97-122.

―――― 2003: Michael Lapidge, 'Asser's reading', in Reuter 2003 44-7.

Lapidge et al 1999: M. Lapidge, J. Blair, S. Keynes, and D. Scragg (eds.), *The Blackwell Encyclopaedia of Anglo-Saxon England*, Oxford: Blackwell Publishers Limited.

Larson 2001: A.-C. Larson (ed.), *Vikings in Ireland*, Roskilde: Viking Ship Museum.

Lavelle 1993: Ryan Lavelle, *Fortifications in Wessex c.800-1016: the Defences of Alfred the Great against the Vikings*, Osprey Publishing.

―――― 2000: Ryan Lavelle, 'Peace and Negotiation: Strategies for Co-existence in the Middle Ages and the Renaissance', in *Arizona Studies in the Middle Ages and the Renaissance*, 4, Arizona: University of Arizona.

―――― 2006: Ryan Lavelle, 'The Use and Abuse of Hostages in Later Anglo-Saxon England', *Early Medieval Europe*, 14, 269-96.

―――― 2009: Ryan Lavelle, 'The Politics of Rebellion: The Ætheling Æthelwold and West-Saxon Royal Succession, 899-902', in Skinner 2010: 51-80.

―――― 2010: Ryan Lavelle, *Alfred's Wars: Sources and Interpretations of Anglo-Saxon Warfare in the Viking Age*, Woodbridge: The Boydell Press.

―――― 2012: Ryan Lavelle, 'Representing Authority in Early Medieval Chronicle: Submission and Rebellion and the Limits of the Anglo-Saxon Chronicle', in Dresvina and Sparks 2012: 61-101.

Lavelle and Roffey 2016: Ryan Lavelle and Simon Roffey (eds), *Danes in Wessex: The Scandinavian Impact on Southern England, c.88-c.1100*, Oxford: Oxbow Books.

Lawley 1868: G. T. Lawley, *A History of Bilston*, Bilston: Price & Beebee.

―――― 1894: G. T. Lawley, 'Wolverhampton in the 10th Century' [a reprinted series of articles first published in *The Midland Weekly News*, c.1894; copy in Wolverhampton Archives].

Lawrence 1965: C. H. Lawrence (ed.), *The English Church and the Papacy in the Middle Ages*, London: Burns & Oates.

Lawson 2003: M. K. Lawson, *The Battle of Hastings 1066*, Stroud: Tempus Publishing Limited.

Leary 2014: Jim Leary (ed), *Past Mobility: Archaeological Approaches to Movement and Mobility*, Farnham: Ashgate Publishing Limited.

Legg 1993: Rodney Legg, *Steepholm: Legend and History*, Wincanton: Wincanton Press.

Leighton 1841: William Allport Leighton, *A Flora of Shropshire*, London: John Van Voorst.

Leonard 2004: John Leonard, *Churches of Shropshire and their Treasures*, Logaston: Logaston Press.

Lethaby 1913: W. R. Lethaby, 'Old Crosses and Lychgates', *Proceedings of the Society of Antiquaries*, XXV NS 158-9.

Lewis 2007: C. P. Lewis, 'Welsh Territories and Welsh Identities in Late Anglo-Saxon England', in Higham 2007: 130-43.

―――― 2008: C. P. Lewis, 'Edward, Chester and Mercia', in Scragg 2008 104-23.

Lewis 2016: Stephen M. Lewis, 'Vikings on the Ribble: Their Origins and *Longphuirt*', in *Northern History*, 53 (2016), Vol. 1.

Licence 2011: Tom Licence, *Hermits and Recluses in English Society*, Oxford: OxfordUniversity Press.

Liebermann 1889: F. Liebermann, *Die Heiligen Englands. Angelsächsisch und Lateinisch*, Hanover: Hahn'sche Buchhandlung.

Lilley 2000: Keith D. Lilley, 'Urban Landscape and the Cultural Politics of Territorial Control in Anglo-Norman England', in *Landscape Research*, 24 1999.

―――― 2002: Keith D. Lilley, *Urban Life in the Middle Ages: 1000-1450 (European Culture and Society)*, Basingstoke: Palgrave MacMillan.

Linehan and Nelson 2001: Peter Linehan and Janet L. Nelson (eds.), *The Medieval World*, Abingdon: Routledge.

Livingston 2011: Michael Livingston (ed.), *The Battle of Brunanburh: A Casebook*, Exeter: University of Exeter Press.

Lloyd 2008: David Lloyd, *The Origins of Ludlow*, Little Logaston: Logaston Press.

Llwyd 1832: Richard Llwyd, *The History of Wales, written originally in British by Caradoc of Llancarvan; translated into English by Dr Powell; augmented by W. Wynne, etc. ... by Richard Llwyd, Gent*, Shrewsbury: John Eddowes.

Loades 2003: David Loades (ed.), *Reader's Guide to British History*, 2 vols, London and New York: Fitzroy Dearborn.

Logan 1991: F. Donald Logan, *The Vikings in History*, London: Routledge.

Lord 2003: Peter Lord, *The Visual Culture of Wales: Medieval Vision*, Cardiff: University of Wales Press.

Loyn 1963: H. R. Loyn, *Anglo-Saxon England and the Norman Conquest*, London: Longmans Green and Co. Ltd.

―――― 1976: Henry Lloyn, *The Vikings in Wales: The Dorothea Coke Memorial Lecture in Northern Studies*, London: University College.

Luard 1859: Henry Richard Luard (ed.), *Bartholomæi de Cotton Monachi Norwicensis: Historia Anglicana; (A.D. 449-1298)*, London: Longman, Green, Longman, and Roberts.

―――― 1872: Henry Richard Luard (ed.), *Matthæi Parisiensis Monachi Sancti Albani, Chronica Majora*, London: Longman & Co., Trübner & Co., Oxford: Parker & Co., Cambridge: Macmillan & Co., Edin*burgh*: A. & C. Black, Dublin: A. Thom.

────── 1890: Henry Richard Luard (ed.), *Flores Historiarum, Vol. I: The Creation to A.D.1066*, London: Longman & Co.

Lumby 1876: Joseph Rawson Lumby (ed.), *Polychronicon Ranulph Higden, together with the English translations of John Trevisa and of an unknown writer of the fifteenth century*, Vol. VI, London: Longman & Co., Trübner & Co., Oxford: Parker & Co., Cambridge: Macmillan & Co., Edin*burh*: A. & C. Black, Dublin: A. Thom.

Lundskær-Nelson 1993: TomLundskær-Nelson, *Prepositions in Old and Middle English: A Study of Prepositions, Syntax and the Semantics of* At, In *and* On *in Some Old and Middle English Texts*, Odense: John Benjamin Publishing Compeny for Odense University Press.

Lyon 2001: Stewart Lyon, 'The Coinage of Edward the Elder', in Higham and Hill 2001: 67-78.

Mac Airt and Mac Niocaill 1983: S. Mac Airt and G. Mac Niocaill (eds.), *The Annals of Ulster (To AD 1131)*, Dublin: Dias.

Mac Lean 1995: Douglas Mac Lean, 'Technique and Control: Carpentry Constructed Insular Stone Crosses', in Bourke 1995: 167-175.

MacLean 2008: Simon MacLean, 'Making a difference in tenth-century politics: King Athelstan's sisters and Frankish queenship', in Fouracre and Ganz 2008: 167-90.

McClure 1910: Edmund McClure, *English Place-Names in their Historical Setting*, London: Society for the Promotion of Christian Knowledge.

McGuigan 2015: Neil McGuigan, 'Neither Scotland nor England: Middle Britain c.850-1150', unpublished PhD thesis, University of St Andrews.

Maddison 1993: J. Maddison (ed.), 'Medieval Archaeology and Architecture at Lichfield', *The British Archaeological Association Conference Transactions for the year 1987*, Leeds: W. S. Maney and Son Limited.

Mander 1908: Gerald P. Mander, 'Chesterton Walls', in WJ, October 1908: 265-8.

Mander and Tildesley 1960: Gerald P. Mander and Norman W. Tildesley, *A History of Wolverhampton to the Early Nineteenth Century*, Wolverhampton: Wolverhampton Borough Council.

Manley 1985: J. Manley, 'The archer and the army in the late Saxon period', *Anglo-Saxon Studies in Archaeology and History*, 4.

Marafioti 2014: Nicole Marafioti, *The King's Body: Burial and Succession in Late Anglo-Saxon England*, Toronto, Buffalo, London: University of Toronto Press.

Marren 2006: Peter Marren, *Battles of the Dark Ages*, Barnsley: Pen & Sword Military.

Marsden 1996: John Marsden, *The Fury of the Northmen: Saints, Shrines and Sea-Raiders in the Viking Age, A.D. 793-878*, London: Kyle Cathie Limited.

────── 2010: John Marsden, *Kings, Mormaers, Rebels: Early Scotland's Other Royal Family*, Ediburgh: John Donald Publishers Ltd.

Marsh 1970: Henry Marsh, *Dark Age Britain: Some Sources of History*, Newton Abbott: David & Charles.

Marten 2008: Lucy Marten, 'The Shiring of East Anglia: an alternative hypothesis', *Historical Research*, 81, issue 211, 1-27.

Martin 1985: G. H. Martin, 'Domesday Book and the Boroughs', in Sawyer 1985: 143-63.

Marzinzik 2013: Sonja Marzinzik, *Masterpieces: Early Medieval Art*, London: The British Museum Press.

Masdalen 2010: K.-O. Masdalen, *Uden Tviv-med fuldkommen Ret. Hvor lä Sciringes heal?*, Arendal: Aust-Agder Kulturhistorike Senter.

Masefield 1918: Charles Masefield, *The Little Guides: Staffordshire*, London: Methuen.

Mason 1957: J. F. A. Mason, *The Borough of Bridgnorth 1157-1957*, Bridgnorth: Bridgnorth Borough Council.

────── 1961-4: J. F. A Mason, 'The Norman Earls of Shrewsbury: Three Notes', *Transactions of the Shropshire Archaeological Society* Vol. LVII.

────── 2003: J. F. A. Mason, 'The Battle of Tettenhall', in Loades 2003: II: 1263-4.

Mason and Barker 1961-4: J. F. A. Mason and P. Barker, 'The Norman Castle at Quatford', *Transactions of the Shropshire Archaeological Society* Vol. LVII 37-63.

Mattingly 1948: H. Mattingly (trans), *Tacitus on Britain and Germany*, London: Harmondsworth.

Maund 2000: Kari Maund, *The Welsh Kings: The Medieval Rulers of Wales*, Stroud: Tempus Publishing Limited.

———— 2005: Kari Maund, "Dark Age' Wales c.383 – c.1063', in Morgan 2005: 51-88.

Mawer and Stenton 1927: A. Mawer and F. M. Stenton, *The Place-Names of Worcestershire*, Cambridge: Cambridge University Press.

Mayor 1869: John E. B. Mayor, *Ricardi de Cirencestria Speculum Historiale de Gestis Regum Angliæ*, London: Longmans, Green & Co.

McC. Bride et al 1997: D. Mc.C. Bride, M. J. Brown and P. J. Hooker, *Integrated Urban Environmental Survey of Wolverhampton: British Geological Survey Technical Report WE/95/49.* [No place of publication given]

McCarthy 2005: Daniel P. McCarthy, *Irish Chronicles and their chronology*, Dublin: Trinity College.

McClure and Collins 1994: Judith McClure and Roger Collins (eds.), Bede: *The Ecclesiastical History of the English People*, Oxford: Oxford University Press.

McDougall 1993: Ian McDougall, 'Serious entertainment: a particular type of Viking atrocity', *Anglo-Saxon England*, 22 (1993) 189-230.

McGurk 1998: P. McGurk (ed. and trans.), *The Chronicles of John of Worcester*, Vol. III, Oxford: Oxford University Press.

McKitterick 1995: Rosamond McKitterick, *The New Cambridge Medieval History, Vol. II c.700-c.900*, Cambridge: Cambridge University Press.

———— 2008: Rosamund McKitterick, *Charlemagne: The Formation of a European Identity*, Cambridge: Cambridge University Press.

McLynn 1998: Frank McLynn, *1066: The Year of the Three Battles*, London: Jonathan Cape.

Meaney 1966: Audrey Meaney, 'Woden in England: A Reconsideration', in *Folklore* 77(2) 105-115.

———— 2002: Audrey L. Meaney, 'Anglo-Saxon Idolators and Ecclesiasts from Theodore to Alcuin; A Source Study', in *Anglo-Saxon Studies in Archaeology and History*, 5, 103-25.

———— 2006: Audrey L. Meaney, 'Old English legal and penitential penalties for 'heathenism'', in Keynes and Smyth 2006: 127-158.

Meeson 2015: Bob Meeson, 'The Origins and Early Development of St Editha's Church, Tamworth', TSAHS XLVIII (2015) 15-40.

Mellows 1949: W. T. Mellows (ed.), *The Peterborough Chronicle of Hugh Candidus*, London: Oxford University Press.

Metcalf 1977: D. M. Metcalf, 'Monetary affairs in Mercia in the time of Æthelbald', in Dornier 1977 87-106.

———— 1989: 'Large Dangelds in Relation to War and Kingship: Their Implications for Monetary History, and Some Numismatic Evidence', in Hawkes 1989: 179-90.

Miller 1850: Thomas Miller, *History of the Anglo-Saxons, from the Earliest Period to the Norman Conquest*, London: David Bogue.

Monsen and Smith 1932: Erling Monsen (ed) and A. H. Smith (trans), *Heimskringla, or the Lives of the Norse Kings, by Snorre Sturlason*, Cambridge: W. Heffer and Sons.

Middlefell 1995: Alfred Middlefell, *The Story of the Ancient Parish of Berkswich*, Part 2, Baswich: Berkswich Local History Group.

Miles 2005: David Miles, *The Tribes of Britain*, London: Weidenfeld & Nicolson.

Mills 1997: A. D. Mills, 'Three Difficult English Place-Names Reconsidered', in Rumble and Mills 1997: 241-46.

Milton 1695: John Milton, *The History of Britain: That Part Especially Now Call'd England; From the First Traditional Beginning Continu'd to the Norman Conquest; Collected out of the Ancientest and Best Authors Thereof*, London: R. Scot, R. Chiswell, R. Bentley and G. Sawbridge.

Monsen and Smith: Erling Monsen and Albert High Smith (eds): *Snorre Sturlason: Heimskringla or The Lives of the Norse Kings*, Cambridge: W. Heffer and Sons.

Moody et al 2005: Theodore William Moody, Dáibhi Ó. Cróinin, Francis X. Martin, and Francis John Byrne, *A New History of Ireland: Prehistoric and Early Ireland*, Oxford: Oxford University Press.

Morgan 2000: Philip Morgan, 'The Naming of Battlefields', in Dunn 2000: 34-52.

Morgan 2001: Richard Morgan, *A Study of Montgomeryshire Place-Names*, Llanrwst: Gwasg Carreg Gwalch.

Morgan 2005: Prys Morgan (ed), *Wales: An Illustrated History*, Stroud: Tempus Publishing Limited.

Morillo 1996: Stephen Morillo (ed.), *The Battle of Hastings*, Woodbridge: The Boydell Press.

Morris 1976: John Morris (gen. ed), *Domesday Book: Staffordshire*, Chichester: Phillimore & Co. Ltd.

────── Morris 1986: John Morris (gen.ed), *Domesday Book: Shropshire*, Chichester: Phillimore & Co. Ltd.

Morriss 2005: Richard K. Morriss, *Roads: Archaeology and Architecture*, Stroud Tempus.

Muirhead 1920: Findlay Muirhead, *The Blue Guides: England*, London& Paris: MacMillan & Co. Ltd.

Murchison 1839: Frederick Impey Murchison, *The Silurian System: Founded on Geological Researches in the Counties of Salop, Hereford, Radnor, Montgomery, Carmarthen, Brecon, Pembroke, Monmouth, Gloucester, Worcester and Stafford*, Part I, London: John Murray.

Musson and Spurgeon 1988: C. R. Musson and C. J. Spurgeon, 'Cwrt Llechrhyd: A Moated Site in Powys', in *Medieval Archaeology*, XXXII (1988) 97-109.

Naismith, Allen and Screen 2014: Rory Naismith, Martin Allen and Elina Screen (eds), *Early Medieval Monetary History: Studies in Memory of Mark Blackburn*, Farnham: Ashgate Publishing Limited.

Naismith 2014: Rory Naismith, 'Prelude to Reform: Tenth-Century English Coinage in Perspective', in Naismith, Allen and Screen 2014: 39-84.

Nees 2002: Lawrence Nees, *Early Medieval Art*, Oxford: Oxford University Press.

Nelson 1991: Janet Nelson, 'Reconstructing a royal family: reflections on Alfred, from Asser chapter 2', in Wood and Lund 1991.

────── 1999: Janet L. Nelson, *Rulers and Ruling Families in Early Medieval Europe: Alfred, Charles the Bald, and Others*, Aldershot: Ashgate Variorum.

────── 2006: Janet Nelson, 'The queen in ninth-century Wessex', in Keynes and Smyth 2009: 69-77.

────── 2008: Janet Nelson, 'The First Use of the Second Anglo-Saxon *Ordo*', in Barrow and Wareham 2008: 117-126.

Nicolle 1995: David Nicolle, *Medieval Warfare Source Book Volume I: Warfare in Western Christendom*, London: Arms and Armour Press.

Nightingale 1813: Joseph Nightingale, *The Beauties of England and Wales or, Original Delineations, Topographical, Historical, and Descriptive, of Each County, Vol. XIII – Part II: Staffordshire*, London: Longman & Co.

────── 1818: Joseph Nightingale, *Shropshire; or, Original delineations, topographical, historical and descriptive of that county*, London: J. Harris.

Niles 1991: John D. Niles, 'Pagan survivals and popular belief', in Godden and Lapidge 1991: 126-41.

────── 2009: John D. Niles, 'Trial by ordeal in Anglo-Saxon Englans: what's the problem with barley?', in Baxter et al 2009: 369-82.

Ní Mhaonaigh 2001: Máire Ní Mhaonaigh, 'The Outward Look: Britain and Beyond in Medieval Irish Literature', in Linehan and Nelson 2001: 381-397.

Niwa 1991: Yoshinobu Niwa, *The Function and Development of Prefixes and Particles in Three Early English Texts – The Beginning of the Phrasal Verb*, Vol. I, Tokyo: Kinseido.

────── 1997: Yoshinobu Niwa, 'Cumulative phenomena between prefixes and verbs', in Hickey and Puppel 1997: 167-78.

Noble 1983: Frank Noble, *Offa's Dyke Reviewed by Frank Noble*, edited by Margaret Gelling, B.A.R. British Series 114, Oxford B.A.R.

Norcroft 1642: John Norcroft, *Exceeding Joyfull Newes From his Excelence the Earle of Essex*, London.

North 1994: J. J. North, *English Hammered Coinage, Vol. 1., Early Anglo-Saxon to Henry III - c.600-1272*, 3rd edition, London: Spink & Son.

Ó Carragáin 2009: Éamonn Ó Carragáin, 'Chosen arrows, first hidden then revealed: the Visitation-Archer sequence as a key to the unity of the Ruthwell Cross', in Baxter et al 2009: 185-204.

Ó Corráin 2008: Donnchadh Ó Corráin, 'The Vikings and Ireland', in Brink and Price 2008: 428-33.

Ó Cróinín 2103: Dáibhí Ó Cróinín, *Early Medieval Ireland, 400-1200*, London and New York: Routledge.

O'Donovan 1860: John O'Donovan, *Annals of Ireland: Three Fragments Copied from Ancient Sources by Dubhaltach Mac Firbisigh*, Dublin: University Press.

Ó Flaithearta 2007: Mícheál Ó Flaithearta (ed.), *Proceedings of the Seventh Symposium of Societas Celtologica Nordica*, Uppsala Universitet.

O'Keefe 1991: Katherine O'Brien O'Keefe, 'Heroic values and Christian ethics', in Godden and Lapidge 1991: 107-25.

——— 2001: Katherine O'Brien O'Keefe (ed), *The Anglo-Saxon Chronicle: A Collaborative Edition, Vol. 5: MS. C*, Cambridge: D. S. Brewer.

O'Sullivan et al 2014: Aidan O'Sullivan, Finbar McCormick, Thomas R. Kerr, and Lorcan Harney (eds), *Early Medieval Ireland AD400-1100 – The Evidence from Archaeological Excavations*, Dublin: Royal Irish Academy.

Oakden 1984: J. P. Oakden, *The Place-Names of Staffordshire, Part 1, Cuttlestone Hundred*, Nottingham: The English Place-Name Society.

Oda 2010: Tetsuji Oda, 'The Sound Symbolism of sc- in Old English Heroic Poetry', in Oda and Eto 2010: 55-90.

Oda and Eto 2010: Tetsuji Oda and Hiroyuki Eto (eds), *Multiple Perspectives on English Philology and History of Linguistics: A Festschrift for Shoichi Watanabe on his 80th birthday*, Berne: Peter Lang.

Ogilby 1675: John Ogilby, *Britannia, Volume the First: Or, An Illustration of the Kingdom of England and Dominion of Wales: By a Geographical and Historical Description of the Principal Roads thereof*, London: the author.

Oliver 1836: George Oliver, *An Historical and Descriptive Account of the Collegiate Church of Wolverhampton in the County of Stafford*, Wolverhampton & London: T. Simpson.

Oman 1913: Charles Oman, *England Before the Norman Conquest; Being a History of the Celtic, Roman and Anglo-Saxon Periods Down to the Year A.D. 1066*, London: Methuen & Co. Ltd.

——— 1924: Sir Charles Oman, *A History of The Art of War in the Middle Ages: Volume I: 378-1278 A.D.*, London: Methuen & Co.

Osaka 2004: Elizabeth Osaka, 'Memorial Stones or Gravestones?', in Cavill 2004: 91-102.

Osgood 2005: Richard Osgood, *The Unknown Warrior: An Archaeology of the Common Soldier*, Stroud: Sutton Publishing Limited.

Owen 1981: Gale R. Owen, *Rites and Religions of the Anglo-Saxons*, U.S.A.: Barnes & Noble.

Owen 2001: Olwyn Owen, 'The strange beast that is the English Urnes style', in Graham-Campbell et al 2001 203-22.

Owen and Blakeway 1825: H. Owen and J. B. Blakeway, *A History of Shrewsbury*, 2 vols, London: Harding Lepard & Co.

Owen and Morgan 2007: Hywel Wyn Owen and Richard Morgan, *Dictionary of the Place-Names of Wales*, Llandysul: Gomer Press.

Owen-Crocker and Thompson 2014: Gale R. Owen-Crocker and Susan D. Thompson, *Towns and Topography: Essays in Memory of David H. Hill*, Oxford: Oxbow Books.

Padel and Parsons 2008: O. J. Padel and David N. Parsons (eds.), *A Commodity of Good Names: Essays in Honour of Margaret Gelling*, Donington: Shaun Tyas.

Page 1970: R. I. Page, *Life in Anglo-Saxon England*, London: B. T. Batsford Ltd.

Palgrave 1832: Sir Francis Palgrave, *The Rise and Progess of the English Commonwealth: Anglo-Saxon Period*, 2 vols., London: John Murray.

―――― 1851: Sir Francis Palgrave, *The History of Normandy and of England*, London: John W. Parker and Son.

Palliser 2000: D. M. Palliser (ed.), *The Cambridge Urban History if Britain, Vol. I 600-1540*, Cambridge: Cambridge University Press.

Pálsson and Edwards 1976: Hermann Pálsson and Paul Edwards (trans.), *Egil's Saga*, Harmondsworth: Penguin Books.

Pannett 1981: David Pannett, 'Fish Weirs of the River Severn', in T. Rowley (ed.), *The Evolution of Marshland Landscapes*, Oxford: Oxford University Press.

―――― 1989: David Pannett, 'The River Severn at Wroxeter', *Transactions of Shropshire Archaeological and Historical Society*, LXVI 1989 48-55.

Pantos 1999: Aliki Pantos, 'Meeting-Places in *Wilvaston* Hundred, Cheshire', *Journal of the English Place-Name Society*, 31 (1988-9), 91-112.

Pantos and Semple 2004: Aliki Pantos and Sarah Semple, *Assembly Places and Practices in Medieval Europe*, Dublin: Four Courts Press.

Pape 1938: Thomas Pape, *Newcastle-under-Lyme in Tudor and Stuart Times*, Manchester: Manchester University Press.

―――― 1945-6: T. Pape, 'The Round-Shafted Pre-Norman Crosses of the North Staffordshire Area', in *Transactions of the North Staffordshire Field Club*, Vol. LXXX, 25-49.

Parker 1966: D. W. Parker, 'Old English Goldhordus: A Privy or just a Treasurehouse?', *Notes & Queries*, Sept. 1996 257-8.

Parker 2014: Philip Parker, *The Northemen's Fury: A History of the Viking World*, London: Jonathan Cape.

Parson and Bradshaw 1818: W. Parson and T. Bradshaw, *Staffordshire General and Commercial Directory*.

Parsons 1975: David Parsons (ed.), *Tenth-Ventury Studies: Essays in Commemoration of the Millennium of the Council of Winchester and Regularis Concordia*, London& Chichester: Phillimore & Co. Ltd.

Parsons 2001: D. Parsons, 'The Mercian Church: Archaeology and Topography', in Brown and Farr 2001 51-66.

Parsons and Stenton 1958: E. J. S. Parsons and Sir F. Stenton, The *Map of Great Britain A.D. 1360 known as the Gough Map*, London: Bodleian Library & Royal Geographical Society.

Parsons and Styles 2000: D. N. Parsons and T. Styles, *The Vocabulary of English Place-Names (BRACE-CÆSTER)*, Nottingham: Centre for English Name-Studies.

Partridge 1966: Eric Partridge, *Origins: A Short Etymological Dictionary of Modern English*, Abingdon: Routledge.

Partridge 1982: A. C. Partridge, *A Companion to Old and Middle English Studies*, New Jersey: Barnes& Noble Books.

Patterson 1982: Orlando Patterson, *Slavery and Social Death: A Comparative Study*, Harvard: Harvard University Press.

Pearce 1982: S. M. Pearce, *The Early Church in Western Britain and Ireland*, British Archaeological Reports 102.

Pederson 2008: Anne Pederson, 'Viking weaponry', in Brink and Price 2008: 204-11.

Peddie 1989: John Peddie, *Alfred the Good Soldier: His Life and Campaigns*, Bath: Millstream Books.

―――― 1999: John Peddie, *Alfred: Warrior King*, Stroud: Sutton Publishing Limited.

Peers 1921-2: C. R. Peers, 'Harlech Castle', *Y Cymmrodor*, 1921-2.

Pelteret 1995: David A. E. Pelteret, *Slavery in Early Medieval England, from the Reign of Alfred until the Twelfth Century*, Woodbridge: The Boydelll Press.

—— 2009: David A. E. Pelteret, 'An anonymous historian of Edward the Elder's reign', in Baxter et al 2009: 319-36.

Peterson and Strandberg 1989: L. Peterson and S. Strandberg (eds), *Studia Onomastica: festskrift till Thorsten Andersson den 23 februari 1989: With English Summaries*, Stockholm: Almqvist and Wiksell.

Pevsner 1958: Nikolaus Pevsner, *The Buildings of England: Shropshire*, Middlesex: Penguin Books Limited.

——1974: Nikolaus Pevsner, *The Buildings of England: Staffordshire*, Middlesex: Penguin Books Limited.

Pitt 1817: William Pitt, *A Topographical History of Staffordshire, Including its Agriculture, Mines and Manufactures*, Newcastle-under-Lyme: J. Smith.

Pluskowski 2009: Alexander Pluskowski, *Wolves and the Wilderness in the Middle Ages*, Woodbridge: Boydell Press.

Plot 1686: Robert Plot, *The Natural History of Staffordshire*.

Pollington 1989: Stephen Pollington, *The Warrior's Way: England in the Viking Age*, London: Blandford Press.

—— 2002: Stephen Pollington, *The English Warrior: From Earliest Times to 1066*, Hockwold-cum-Whinton: Anglo-Saxon Books.

Poole 1912: Reginald Lane Poole, *The Exchequer in the Twelfth Century*, Oxford: The Clarendon Press.

Powel 1584: David Powel, *The Historie of Cambria, now called Wales: a Part of the Most Famous Yland of Brytaine, written in the Brytish Language aboue two hundredth years past, translated into English by H. Lloyd, Gentleman; corrected, augmented, and continued out of records and best approved authors, by Dauid Powel*, London: John Harding.

Powell 2002: Steve Powell, *Subterranean Shropshire*, Stroud: Tempus Publishing Ltd.

Preest 2002: David Preest, *William of Malmesbury: The Deeds of the Bishops of England (Gesta Pontificum Anglorum)*, Woodbridge: The Boydell Press.

Preest and Clark 2005: David Preest (trans) and James G. Clark (ed), *The Chronica Maiora of Thomas Walsingham, 1376-1422*, Woodbridge: The Boydell Press.

Pretty 1989: Kate Pretty, 'Defining the Magonsæte', in Bassett 1989: 171-83.

Previté-Orton 1957: C. W. Previté-Orton, *The Shorter Cambridge Medieval History*, Vol. I, London: Cambridge University Press.

Price 1835: Joseph Price, *An Historical Acount of Bilston from Alfred the Great to 1831*, Bilston: The Author.

Price 2008: Neil Price, 'Dying and the Dead: Viking Mortuary Behaviour', in Brink and Price 2008: 257-73.

Price 2008a: Neil Price, 'The Vikings in Spain, North Africa and the Mediterranean', in Brink and Price 2008: 462-69.

Price 2014: Neil Price, 'Belief & Ritual', in Williams, Pentz and Wemhoff 2014: 163-95.

Pryce 1992: Huw Price, 'Ecclesiastical Wealth in Early Medieval Wales', in Edwards and Lane 1992: 22-32.

—— 2003: Huw Pryce, 'The Christianisation of Society', in Davies 2003: 139-167.

Purton 1998: Peter Purton, 'The siege castles at Arundel', *Postern*, Vol. 18 13-414.

Quanrud 2015: John Quanrud, 'Taking Sides: North-West England Vikings at the Battle of Tettenhall', in Harding, Griffiths and Royles 2015: 71-93.

Radner 2008: Joan N. Radner (trans.), *The Fragmentary Annals of Ireland*, University of Cork: CELT (Corpus of Electronic Texts Online)

Raftis 1957: James Ambrose Raftis, *The Estates of Ramsey Abbey: A Study in Economic Growth and Organisation,* Toronto: Pontifical Institute of Mediaeval Studies.

Raffield 2010: Benjamin Paul Raffield, "Inside that fortress sat a few peasant men, and it was half-made': A Study of Viking Fortifications in the British Isles, AD793-1066', unpublished MPhil Dissertation, University of Birmingham.

―――― 2013: Ben Raffield, 'Antiquaries, Archaeologists, and Viking Fortifications', *Journal of the North Atlantic*, No. 20: 1-29

Rahtz 1977: Philip Rahtz, 'The Archaeology of West Mercian Towns', in Dornier 1977: 107-29.

Ramsay 1898: James Henry Ramsay, *The Foundations of England*, London: S. Sonnenschein & Co. Ltd.

Randall 1863: John Randall, *Handbook to the Severn Valley Railway*, London: Virtue Brothers and Co.

Rauer 2013: Christine Rauer (trans. and ed.), *The Olde English Martyrology: Edition, Translation and Commentary*, Cambridge: D. S. Brewer.

Ray and Bapty 2016: Keith Ray and Ian Bapty, *Offa's Dyke: Landscape and Hegemony in Eighth-Century Britain*, Oxford: Windgather Press for Oxbow Books.

Reaney 1997: P. H. Reaney, *A Dictionary of English Surnames*, 3rd edition, Oxford: Oxford University Press.

Redknap 2000: Mark Redknap, *Vikings in Wales: An Archaeological Quest*, Cardiff: National Museum of Wales.

―――― 2008: Mark Redknap, 'The Vikings in Wales', in Brink and Price 2008: 401-10.

―――― 2009: Mark Redknap, 'Silver and Commerce in Viking-Age North Wales', in Graham-Campbell and Philpott 2009: 29-41.

Rees 1967: William Rees, *An Historical Atlas of Wales from Early to Modern Times*, London: Faber and Faber.

Rees 1997: Una Rees (ed.), *The Cartulary of Lilleshall Abbey*, Shrewsbury: Shropshire Archaeological & Historical Society.

Renn 1973: D. F. Renn, *Norman Castles in Britain*, London: John Bakers Publishers Limited.

Reuter 1999: Timothy Reuter (ed.), *The New Cambridge Medieval History III: c.900-c.1024*, Cambridge: Cambridge University Press.

―――― 2003: Timothy Reuter (ed.), *Alfred the Great: Papers from the Eleventh-Centenary Conferences*, Aldershot: Ashgate.

Revill 1975: S. Revill, 'King Edwin and the battle of Heathfield', *Transactions of the Thoroton Society*, No. 779.

Reynolds 1985: Susan Reynolds, 'What do we mean by "Anglo-Saxon" and the "Anglo-Saxons"', *Journal of British Studies*, 24, 395-414.

―――― 2008: Susan Reynolds, 'Compulsory purchase in the Earlier Middle Ages', in Fouracre and Ganz 2008: 28-43.

Richards 1991: Julian D. Richards, *English Heritage Book of Viking Age England*, London: B. T. Batsford/English Heritage.

―――― 2003: Julian D. Richards, 'Pagans and Christians at the Frontier: Viking Burial in the Danelaw', in Carver 2003: 383-95.

―――― 2005: Julian D. Richards, *The Vikings: A Very Short Introduction*, Oxford: Oxford University Press.

Richards et al 2004: Julian D. Richards, Pauline Beswick, Julie Bond, Marcus Jecock, Jacqueline McKinley, Stephen Rowland and Fay Worley, 'Excavations of the Viking Barrow Cemetery at Heath Wood, Ingleby, Derbyshire', *The Antiquaries Journal*, 84 (2004) 23-116.

Richardson 1975: Samuel Richardson (ed), *A Tour of Great Britain, 1742, by Daniel Defoe*, Vol. 8, Richardsoniana (17), Garland Publishing: New York and London.

Richmond 1996: Velma Bourgeois Richmond, *The Legend of Guy of Warwick*, London: Routledge.

Rickert 1965: Margaret Rickert, *Painting in Britain in the Middle Ages*, Harmonsworth: Penguin Books Limited.

Riggings and Evans Jones 1910: Richard Riggings and Basil Evans Jones, 'A History of the Parish of Llanmerewig', *Collections, Historical and Archaeological, Relating to Montgomeryshire*, 35, 81-128.

Rigold 1986: S. E. Rigold, *Lilleshall Abbey, Shropshire*, London: English Heritage.

―――― 1995: S. E. Rigold, 'Structural Aspects of Medieval Timber Bridges', in *Medieval Archaeology* xxxix 1995 48-91.

Riley 1853: Henry T. Riley (trans), *The Annals of Roger de Hoveden*, 2 vols., London: H. G. Bohn.

―――― 1860: Henry T. Riley (ed), *Munimenta Gildhallæ Londiniensis: Liber Albus, Liber Custumarum, et Liber Horn: Vol. II, Part II, containing Liber Custumarum, with Extracts from the Cottonian MS. Claudius, D II*, London: Longman, Green, Longman, and Roberts.

Rivet and Smith 1979: A. F. Rivet and C. Smith, *The Place-Names of Roman Britain*, B. T. Batsford Limited.

Rix 1960: Michael Rix, 'The Wolverhampton Cross Shaft', *Archaeological Journal*, 117 71-81.

―――― 1963: Michael Rix, 'Wolverhampton's Oldest Work of Art', *Wolverhampton Magazine*, 1963.

Roberts 2001: Jane Roberts, 'Hagiography and Literature: The Case of Guthlac of Crowland', in Brown and Farr 2001: 69-86.

Robertson 1956: A. J. Robertson, *Anglo-Saxon Charters*, Cambridge: Cambridge University Press.

Robinson 1923: J. Armitage Robinson, *The Times of Saint Dunstan*, Oxford: Clarendon Press.

Robinson 1980: D. H. Robinson, *The Wandering Worfe*, Albrighton: Waine Research Publications.

Roderick 1959: A. J. Roderick (ed.), *Wales Through the Ages, Vol. I, From the Earliest Times to 1485*, Llandybie: Christopher Davies (Publishers) Limited.

Rodwell et al 2008: Warwick Rodwell, Jane Hawkes, Emily Howe and Rosemary Cramp, 'The Lichfield Angel: a spectacular Anglo-Saxon painted sculpture', *Antiquaries Journal*, Vol. 88 (2008) 48-108.

Roesdahl 1991: Else Roesdahl, *The Vikings*, London: Guild Publishing.

Roffe 2014: David Roffe, 'Sitting on the fence: the Staffordshire Hoard find site in context', Haskins Society Conference paper, Carleton College, Minnesota, 8th November 2014.

Rogers 1998: Pat Rogers, *The Text of Great Britain: Theme and Design in Defoe's Tour*, London: Associated University Press.

Rollason 1978: D. Rollason, Lists of saints' resting-places in Anglo-Saxon England', *Anglo-Saxon England*, 7 (1978) 61-94.

―――― 1995: David Rollason, 'St Oswald in Post Conquest England', in Stancliffe and Cambridge 1995: 164-77.

―――― 2003: David W, Rollason, *Northumbria 500-1100: Creation and Destruction of a Kingdom*, Cambridge: Cambridge University Press.

Rollason et al 2004: David W, Rollason, A. J. Piper, Margaret Harvey and Lynda Rollason (eds.), *The Durham Liber Vitae and its Context*, Woodbridge: The Boydell Press.

Rollason and Rollason 2007: D. W. Rollason and Lynda Rollason, *Durham Liber Vitae*, London: The British Library.

Roper 1976: John Roper, *Wolverhampton As It Was, Volume III*, Nelson: Hendon Publishing Co. Ltd.

Rosewell 2008: Roger Rosewell, *Medieval Wall Paintings in English and Welsh Churches*, Woodbridge: The Boydell Press.

Roth 2012: Erik Roth, *With a Bended Bow: Archery in Medieval and Renaissance Europe*, Stroud: Spellmont.

Rowley 1972: Trevor Rowley, *The Shropshire Landscape*, London: Hodder and Stoughton.

―――― 1983: Trevor Rowley, *The Norman Heritage 1066-1200*, London: Routledge & Kegan Paul plc.

―――― 2001: Trevor Rowley, *The Welsh Border: Archaeology, History and Landscape*, Stroud: Tempus Publishing Limited.

Royds 1909: Gilbert Twemlow Royds, 'The Five "Royal Free Chapels" of the County', in Beresford 1909: 138-61.

Rubin-1989: Stanley Rubin, 'The Anglo-Saxon Physician', in Deegan and Scragg 1989 7-15.

Rumble 1994: Alexander Rumble (ed.), *The Reign of Cnut, King of England, Denmark and Norway*, London: Leicester University Press Limited.

―――― 2001: Alexander R. Rumble, 'Edward the Elder and the Churches of Winchester and Wessex', in Higham and Hill 2001: 230-47.

―――― 2006: Alexander R. Rumble, The Cross in English Place-names: Vocabulary and Usage', in Karkov, Keeper and Jolly 2006: 29-42.

Russell, Hurley and Eogan 2014: Ian Russell, Maurice F. Hurley and James Eogan (eds), *Woodstown: A Viking-Age settlement in Co. Waterford*, Dublin: Four Courts Press.

Ryan 2013: Martin J. Ryan, 'Conquest, Reform and the Making of England', in Higham and Ryan 2013.

Salisbury 1995: Chris Salisbury, 'The excavation of Hemington Fields', *Current Archaeology*, 145 (XIII) 1, November 1995.

Sandred 1963: Karl Inge Sandred, *English Place-names in –stead, II*, Uppsala: Almqvist & Wiksells Boktryckeri-A-B.

Sargent 2012: Andrew Sargent, 'Lichfield and the Lands of St Chad', unpublished PhD Dissertation, Keele University.

―――― 2016: Andrew Sargent, 'A Misplaced Miracle: The Origins of St Modwynn of Burton and St Eadgyth of Polesworth', *Midland History*, 41 (2106) 1: 1-19.

Savile 1596: Henry Savile, *Rerum Anglicarum scriptores post Bedam*, London.

Sawyer 1957: P H Sawyer, 'The Density of the Danish Settlement in England', *University of Birmingham Historical Journal* VI 1-17.

―――― 1962: P H Sawyer, *The Age of the Vikings*, London: Edward Arnold Publishers Limited.

―――― 1962: P H Sawyer, 'Fairs and market in early medieval England', in Skyum-Nielsen and Lund 1981: 153-70.

―――― 1977: P H Sawyer (ed), *The Oxford Illustrated History of the Vikings*, Oxford: Oxford University Press.

―――― 1979: P H Sawyer (ed), *Charters of Burton Abbey*, Oxford: Oxford University Press for The British Academy.

―――― 1982: P. H. Sawyer, *Kings and Vikings*, London: Methuen & Co. Ltd.

―――― 1983: P. H. Sawyer, 'The Scandinavian Background', in Scragg 1993 33-42.

―――― 1985: Peter Sawyer, *Domesday Book: A Reassessment*, London: Edward Arnold.

―――― 1998: Peter Sawyer, *From Roman Britain to Norman England*, 2nd edition, Abingdon: Routledge.

―――― 2013: Peter Sawyer, *The Wealth of Anglo-Saxon England*, Oxford: Oxford University Press.

Sayles 1964: G. O. Sayles, *The Medieval Foundations of England*, London: Methuen & Co. Ltd.

Schulenburg 1998: Jane Tibbetts Schulenburg, *Forgetful of the Sex*, Chicago: University of Chicago Press.

Scott 1832: William Scott, *Stourbridge and its Vicinity*, Stourbridge: J. Heming.

Scott and Ehwald 2001: Scott Gwara and Rudolf Ehwald (eds), *Aldhelmi Malmesbiriensis: Prosa de virginitate: cum glasa Latina atque anglosaxonica St. Aldhelm*, Turnhout: Brepols Publishers NV.

Scragg 1991: Donald Scragg (ed.), *The Battle of Maldon AD 991*, Oxford: Basil Blackwell in association with The Manchester Centre for Anglo-Saxon Studies.

―――― 2003: Donald Scragg (ed.), *Textual and Material Culture in Anglo-Saxon England: Thomas Northcote Toller and the Toller Memorial Lectures*, Woodbridge: D. S. Brewer 213-40.

―――― 2006: Donald Scragg, *The Return of the Vikings: The Battle of Maldon 991*, Stroud: Tempus Publishing Limited.

―――― 2008: Donald Scragg (ed.), *Edgar, King of the English 959-975*, Woodbridge: Boydell Press.

Searle 1897: W. G. Searle, *Onomasticon Anglo-Saxonicum: A List of Anglo-Saxon Proper Names from the time of Beda to that of King John*, Cambridge: Cambridge University Press.

―――― 1899: W. G. Searle, *Anglo-Saxon Bishops, Kings and Nobles: The Succession of the Bishops and the Pedigrees of the Kings and Nobles*, Cambridge: Cambridge University Press.

Semple 1998: Sarah Semple, 'A Fear of the Past: The Place of the Prehistoric Burial Mound in the Ideology of Middle and Later Anglo-Saxon England', *World Archaeology*, 30:1, 109-26.

———— 2013: Sarah Semple, *Perceptions of the Prehistoric in Anglo-Saxon England: Religion, Ritual and Rulership in the Landscape*, Oxford: Oxford University Press.

Sharma 1997: P. Vallabh Sharma, *Environmental and Engineering Geophysics*, Cambridge: Cambridge University Press.

Sharp 2001: Sheila Sharp, 'The West Saxon tradition of dynastic marriage: with special reference to Edward the Elder', in Higham and Hill 2001: 79-88.

Sharp 2016: Tony Sharp, 'Chronicles, Treaties and *Burhs*; the Burghal Hidage and the *Mercian Register*', academia.edu website, accessed 10 February 2016.

Sheehan 2001: J. Sheehan, 'Ireland's Viking Age hoards: sources and contacts', in Larson 2001: 51-59.

Sheehan and Ó Corráin: 2010: John Sheehan and Donnchadh Ó Corráin (eds.), The Viking Age: Ireland and the West: Papers from the Proceedings of the 15th Viking Conference, Cork, 18-27 August 2008, Dublin.

Sherley-Price 1968: Leo Sherley-Price (trans.), *Bede: A History of the English Church and People*, Harmondsworth: Penguin Books Limited.

Short 1749: Thomas Short, *A General Chronological History of the Air, Weather, Seasons, Meteors, in Sundry Places and Different Times, etc.*, London: T. Longman and A. Millar.

Sidebottom 1994: Philip Charles Sidebottom, 'Schools of Anglo-Saxon Stone Sculpture in the North Midlands', unpublished PhD thesis: University of Sheffield.

Sigurðsson and Bolton 2014: Jón Viðar Sigurðsson and and Timothy Bolton (eds), *Celtic-Norse Relationships in the Irish Sea in the Middle Ages800-1200*, Leiden and Boston: Brill.

Sims-Williams 1975: P. Sims-Williams, 'Continental Influence at Bath Monastery in the Eleventh Century', in *Anglo-Saxon England* 4 (1975).

———— 1990: Patrick Sims-Williams, *Religion and Literature in Western England, 600-800*, Cambridge: Cambridge University Press.

Skene 1872: William F. Skene (ed), *John of Fordun's Chronicle of the Scottish Nation*, Vol I, Edinburgh, republished in facsimile by Llanerch Publishers, 1992.

Skinner 2009: Patricia Skinner (ed), *Challenging the Boundaries of Medieval History: The Legacy of Timothy Reuter*, Turnhout: Brepols Publishers.

Skyum-Nielsen and Lund 1981: Niels Skyum-Nielsen and Niels Lund (eds), *Danish Medieval History: New Currents*, Copenhagen: Museum Tusculanum Press.

Slater 1988: T. R. Slater, *Medieval Composite Towns in England: The Evidence from Bridgnorth, Shropshire*, School of Geography, University of Birmingham, Working Paper Series, 41.

———— 2007: Terry R. Slater, 'The Landscape of Medieval Towns', in Gardiner and Rippon 2007 11-26.

Smallshire 1978: John L. Smallshire, *Wednesfield: the Field of Woden - Research into the History of Wednesfield*, Wolverhampton: The Workers' Educational Association.

Smiley and Kellogg 2000: Jane Smiley (preface) and Robert Kellogg (introduction), *The Sagas of the Icelanders: A Selection*, London: Viking Penguin.

Smith 1956: A. H. Smith, *English Place-Name Elements*, 2 Vols., Cambridge: Cambridge University Press.

Smith 1967: Brian S. Smith, *The Dougharty Family of Worcester, estate surveyors and mapmakers, 1700-60*, Worcester Historical Society, New Series No. 5, Miscellany II: 138-180.

Smith 1999: Brendan Smith (ed.), *Britain and Ireland, 900-1300: Insular Responses to Medieval European Change*, Cambridge: Cambridge University Press.

Smith 2012: Scott Thompson Smith, *Land and Book: Literature and Land Tenure in Anglo-Saxon England*, Toronto, Buffalo and London: University of Toronto Press.

Smollett 1758: Tobias Smollett, *A Complete History of England from the Descent of Julius Cæsar, to the Treaty of la Chapelle, 1748*, London: James Rivington and James Fletcher.

Smyth 1975-9: Alfred Smyth, *Scandinavian York and Dublin: The History and Archaeology of Two Related Kingdoms*, 2 vols., Dublin: Templekieran Press.

———— 1977: Alfred P. Smyth, *Scandinavian Kings in the British Isles 850-880*, Oxford: Oxford Universitry Press.

———— 1984: Alfred P. Smyth, *Warlords and Holy Men*, Edinburh: Edinburh University Press.

———— 1995: Alfred P. Smyth, *King Alfred the Great*, Oxford: Oxford University Press.

———— 1998: Alfred P. Smyth (ed), *Medieval Europeans: Studies in Ethnic Identity and National Perspectives in Medieval Europe*, Basingstoke: Macmillan Press Limited.

———— 1998a: Alfred P. Smyth, 'The Emergence of English Identity, 700-1050', in Smyth 1998: 24-53.

———— 1999: Alfred P. Smyth, 'The Effect of Scandinavian Raiders on the English and Irish Churches: A Preliminary Reasessment', in Smith 1999: 1-38.

———— 2002: Alfred P. Smyth, *The Medieval Life of King Alfred the Great: A Translation and Commentary on the Text Attributed to Asser*, Basingstoke: Palgrave.

Somerset 1994: J. Allen B. Somerset (ed), *Records of Early English Drama, 2: Shropshire: Editorial Apparatus*, Toronto, Buffalo and London: University of Toronto Press.

Sommerfeldt 2006: John D. Sommerfeldt, *Aelred of Rivaulx: On Love and Order in the World and the Church*, New York: The Newman Press.

Sourchal 1968: François Sourchal, *Art of the Early Middle Ages*, London& New York: Harry N. Abrams, Inc.

South 2002: Ted Johnson South, *Historia de Sancto Cuthberto*, Cambridge: D. S. Brewer.

Speed 1614: John Speed, *The Historie of Great Britaine Vnder the Conquests of the Romans, Saxons, Danes and Normans*, London: John Sudbury and George Humble.

Spencer 1772: Nathanial Spencer, *The Complete English Traveller*, London: J. Cooke.

Sprague 2007: Martha Sprague, *Norse Warfare: Unconventional Battle Strategies of the Ancient Vikings*, New York: Hippocrene Books Inc.

Stafford 1981: Pauline Stafford, 'The King's Wife in Wessex 800-1066', *Past & Present*, 91: 3-27.

———— 1983: Pauline Stafford, *Queens, Concubines and Dowagers: The King's Wife in the Early Midle Ages*, London: B. T. Batsford Limited.

———— 2008: Pauline Stafford, "The Annals of Æthelflæd': Annals, History and Politics in Early Tenth-Century England', in Barrow and Wareham 2008: 101-16.

Stalley 1971: R. A. Stalley, 'A 12th-Century Patron of Architecture: A Study of the Buildings Erected by Roger, Bishop of Salisbury', *Journal of the British Archaeological Association*, 3rd Series, xxxiv (1971) 62-83.

Stancliffe 1995: 'Where was Oswald Killed?', in Stancliffe and Cambridge 1995: 84-96.

Stancliffe and Cambridge 1995: Clare Stancliffe and Eric Cambridge (eds.), *Oswald: Northumbrian King to European Saint*, Stamford: Paul Watkins.

Stanley 1990: E. G. Stanley (ed.), *British Academy Papers on Anglo-Saxon England*, Oxford: Oxford University Press for The British Academy.

Stafford 1985: Pauline Stafford, *The East Midlands in the Early Middle Ages*, Leicester: Leicester University Press.

———— Stafford 2003: Paulin Stafford, 'Succession and inheritance: a gendered perspective on Alfred's family history', in Reuter 2003: 251-64.

Steele 1948: H. J. Steele, 'A Photographic Survey of the Pre-Conquest Carved Crosses of Staffordshire, with an Account of the Wolverhampton Pillar', *Transactions of the North Staffordshire Field Club*, LXXXII (1947-8) 116-125.

Stenton 1970: Dorothy M. Stenton (ed.), *Preparatory to Anglo-Saxon England: The Collected Papers of Frank Merry Stenton*, Oxford: Oxford University Press.

Stenton 1971: F. M. Stenton, *Anglo-Saxon England*, 3rd edition, Oxford: Oxford University Press.

Stephenson 2002: I. P. Stephenson, *The Anglo-Saxon Shield*, Stroud: Tempus Publishing Limited.

Stevenson 1835: Joseph Stevenson (trans.), *Chronica de Mailros e Codice Unico in Bibliotheca Cottoniana Servato, Nunc Iterum in Lucem Edita*, Edinburgh: Typis Societatis Edinburgensis.

———— 1853: Joseph Stevenson (trans.), *Florence of Worcester*, facsimile: Lampeter: Llanerch Enterprises [with the author given as Joseph Stephenson].

───── 1854: Joseph Stevenson (trans.), *The Church Historians of England, Vol. II, Part II*, London: Seeleys.

───── 1855: Joseph Stevenson (trans.), *The Church Historians of England, Vol. III, Part II, Containing the Historical Works of Simeon of Durham*, London: Seeleys.

───── 1856: Joseph Stevenson, *The Church Historians of England, Vol. IV (I)*, London: Seeleys.

Stevenson 1959: W. H. Stevenson (ed.), *Asser's Life of Alfred*, Oxford: Oxford University Press.

Stocker 1993: D. Stocker, 'The Early Church in Lincolnshire: a study of the sites and their significance', in Vince 1993: 101-22.

Stokes 2009: Peter A. Stokes, 'King Edgar's Charter for Pershore (AD 972)' in *Anglo-Saxon England*, 37 (2009) 31-78.

Stone 1955: Lawrence Stone, *Sculpture in Britain: The Middle Ages*, Harmondsworth: Penguin Books Limited.

Story 2003: Joanna Story, *Carolingian Connections: Anglo-Saxon England and Carolingian Francia, c.750-870*, Aldershot: Ashgate Publishing Limited.

Stowe 1605: John Stowe, *The Annales of England: The race of the Kings of Brytaine after the received opinion since Brute, &c.*, London: G. Bishop and T. Adams.

Strahler 1963: Arthur N. Strahler, *The Earth Sciences*, New York, Evanston & London: Harper & Row.

Strickland 1998 Matthew Strickland (ed.), *Armies, Chivalry and Warfare in Medieval Britain and France: Proceedings of the 1995 Harlaxton Symposium*, Stamford: Shaun Tyas.

───── 2003: Matthew Strickland, *War and Chivalry: The Conduct and Perception of War in England and Normandy*, Cambridge: Cambridge University Press.

Strutt 1778: Joseph Strutt, *The Chronicle of England: or, a Compleat History, Civil, Military and Ecclesiastical, of the Ancient Britons and Saxons, from the Landing of Julius Cæsar in Britain, to the Norman Conquest. With a Compleat View of the Manners, Customs, Arts, Habits, &c. of those People*, London: Walter Shropshire.

Stubbs 1868: William Stubbs (ed.), *Chronica Magistri Rogeri de Houedene*, London: Longmans, Green, Reader, and Dyer.

───── 1880: William Stubbs, *The Constitutional History of England, in its Origin and Development*, Oxford: Clarendon Press.

Studd 1982: Robin Studd, 'Pre-Conquest Lichfield', *Transactions of the South Staffordshire Archaeological and Historical Society for 1980-1981*, Vol. XXII, 24-34.

Sturlason 1930: Snorre Sturlason, *Heimskringla: The Norse King Saga*, London: J. M. Dent & Sons Ltd.

Styles 1936: Dorothy Styles, 'The Early History of the King's Chapels in Staffordshire', *Transactions of the Birmingham Archaeological Society*, Vol. LX 1936 57-95.

Suhm 1776: Peter Frederick Suhm, *Critisk Historie af Danmark udi den hedenske Tid, fra Odin til Gorm den Gamle*, Vol. III, Copenhagen: Brodrene Johann Christian& Georg Christopher Berling.

Sutcliffe 1993: S. Sutcliffe, 'The cult of St Sitha in England: an introduction', *Nottingham Medieval Studies*, 37, 83-9.

Suzuki 2000: Seiichi Suzuki, *The Quoit Brooch Style and Anglo-Saxon Settlement*, Woodbridge: Boydell Press.

Swanton 1973: M. J. Swanton, *The Spearheads of the Anglo-Saxon Settlements*, Royal Archaeological Institute.

Swanton 1996: Michael Swanton, *The Anglo-Saxon Chronicle*, London: J M Dent.

Swarzenski 1974: Hanns Swarzenski, *Monuments of Romanesque Art*, London: Faber and Faber.

Sweet 1885: Henry Sweet, *The Oldest English Texts*, London: Oxford University Press for The Early English Text Society.

Swift 2008: Katherine Swift, *The Morville Hours*, London: Bloomsbury Publishing

Symonds 1872: William Samuel Symonds, *Records of the Rocks; Or, Notes on the \geology, Natural History and Antiquities of North & South Wales, Devon, and Cornwall*, London: John Murray.

Szarmach 1998: Paul E. Szarmach, 'Æthelflæd of Mercia: *Mise en page*', in Baker and Howe 1998: 105-26.

Taylor 1892-3: C. S. Taylor, 'The Danes in Gloucestershire', *Transactions of the Bristol& Gloucestershire Archaeological Society*, 17 (1892-3) 68-95.

Taylor 1979: Christopher Taylor, *Roads and Tracks of Britain*, London: J. M. Dent & Sons Limited.

Taylor 2000: Simon Taylor (ed), *Kings, Clerics and Chronicles in Scotland, 500-1297: Essays in honour of Marjorie Ogilvie Anderson on the occasion of her ninetieth birthday*, Dublin: Four Courts Press.

Tengvik 1938: G. Tengvik, *Old English Bynames*, Nomina Germanica, Uppsala: Almqvist & Wiksells Boktryckeri-A-B.

Thacker 1985: Alan Thacker, 'Kings, Saints, and Monasteries in Pre-Viking Mercia', in *Midland History* Vol. 10 1985 1-25.

────── 1995: Alan Thacker, '*Membra Disjecta*: the Division of the Body and Diffusion of the Cult', in Stancliffe and Cambridge 1995: 97-127.

────── 2001: Alan Thacker, 'Dynastic Monasteries and Family Cults: Edward the Elder's sainted kindred', in Higham and Hill 2001: 248-63.

────── 2002: Alan Thacker, 'The Making of a Local Saint', in Thacker and Sharpe 2002: 45-74.

Thacker and Sharpe 2002: Alan Thacker and Richard Sharpe (eds.), *Local Saints and `Local Churches in the Early Medieval West*, Oxford: Oxford University Press.

Thomas 2003: Rodney M. Thomas, *William of Malmesbury*, Woodbridge: The Boydell Press.

Thompson 1983: F. H. Thompson (ed.), *Studies in Medieval Sculpture*, London: The Society of Antiquaries of London.

Thompson 1990: Kathleen Thompson, 'Robert de Bellême Reconsidered', in Chibnall 1991: 263-90.

Thompson 2002: Victoria Thompson, *Dying and Death in Later Anglo-Saxon England*, Woodbridge: The Boydell Press.

Thompson 2004: Logan Thompson, *Ancient Weapons in Britain*, Barnsley: Pen & Sword Military.

Thorkelin 1788: Grimr Jonson Thorkelin, *Bibliotheca Topographica Britannica No. XLVIII, Containing Fragments of English and Irish History in the Ninth and Tenth Century, Translated from the Original Icelandic*, London: John Nichols.

Thorn and Thorn 2007: Caroline Thorn and Frank Thorn, *Staffordshire* [online introduction notes and commentary on the Phillimore Edition of Domesday Book for Staffordshire, https://hydra.hull.ac.uk/resources/hull:554, accessed 19 October 2015].

Thorpe 1845: Benjamin Thorpe (trans.), *A History of England under the Anglo-Saxon Kings, Translated from the German of Dr. J. M. Lappenberg*, London: John Muray.

────── 1848: Benjamin Thorpe (trans), *Florenti Wigorniensis monachi Chronicon et chronicis: ab adventus Hengisti et Horsi in Britannia*, London: Sumptibus Societatas.

────── 1853a: Benjamin Thorpe, *Florenti Wigorniensis Monachi Chronicon ex Chronicis*, London.

────── 1853: B. Thorpe, *The Life of Alfred the Great, Translated from the German of Dr. R. Paull*, London: Henry G. Bohn.

────── 1861: Benjamin Thorpe (ed.), *The Anglo-Saxon Chronicle, According to the Several Original Authorities*, London: Longman, Green, Longman, and Roberts.

────── 1865: Benjamin Thorpe, *Diplomatarium Anglicum ævi Saxonici: A Collection of English Charters from the reign of King Æthelberht of Kent AD DCV to that of William the Conqueror*, London: Macmillan & Co.

Thurlby 1982: M. Thurlby, 'A Note on the Twelfth-Century Sculpture from Old Sarum Cathedral', *Wiltshire Archaeological and Natural History Magazine*, lxxxvi (1982) 93-7.

────── 1999: M. Thurlby, *The Herefordshire School of Romanesque Sculpture*, Almeley: Logaston Press.

────── 2008a: M. Thurlby, 'Sarum Cathedral as rebuilt by Roger, Bishop of Salisbury, 1102-1139: the state of research and open questions', *Wiltshire Archaeological and Natural History Magazine*, 101 (2008) 130-40.

———— 2008b: M. Thurlby, 'Reflections on the Herefordshire School of Romanesque Sculpture', *Ecclesiology Today*, 40 (2008) 20-29.

Thurlby and Coplestone-Crow 2013: Malcolm Thurlby and Bruce Coplestone-Crow, *The Herefordshire School of Romanesque Sculpture,with an Essay on The Anarchy in Herefordshire*, Logaston: Logaston Press.

Tildesley 1886: James Carpenter Tildesley, *A History of Penkridge in the County of Stafford*, London: Hamilton, Adams & Co.

Tildesley 1952: Norman W. Tildesley, *A History of Willenhall*, Willenhall: Willenhall Urban District Council.

Timmins 1899: H. Thornhill Timmins, *Nooks and Corners of Shropshire*, London: Elliot and Stock.

Tinti 2010: Francisca Tinti, *Sustaining Belief: The Church of Worcester from c.870 to c.1100*, Aldershot: Ashgate Publishing Limited.

Todd 1867: J. H. Todd, *The War of the Gaedhil with the Gaill, or the Invasion of Ireland by the Danes and other Norsemen*, London: Longmans, Green, Reader, and Dyer.

Toller 1898: T. Northcote Toller (ed.), *An Anglo-Saxon Dictionary based on the manuscript collections of the late Joseph Bosworth*, Oxford: Oxford University Press.

Tolstoy 2008: Nokoli Tolstoy, 'When and where was Armes Prydein composed?', *Studia Celtica*, XLII (2008), 145-9.

Toulmin Smith 1964: Lucy Toulmin Smith (ed.), *The Itinerary of John Leland in or about the years 1535-1543*, 5 vols., London: The Centaur Press.

Townend 2000: M. Townend, 'Viking Age England as a Bilingual Society', in Hadley and Richards 2000: 89-105.

———— 2005: Matthew Townend, *Language and History in Viking Age England: Linguistic Relations between Speakers of Old Norse and Old English*, Turnhout: Brepols N.V.

Treherne 2000: Elaine Treharne (ed.), *Old and Middle English: An Anthology*, Oxford: Blackwell Publishers Ltd.

Trinder 2005: Barrie Trinder, *Barges and Bargemen: A Social History of the Upper Severn Navigation*, Chichester: Phillimore & Co. Ltd.

Turner 1823: Sharon Turner, *The History of the Anglo-Saxons: Comprising the The History of England from the Earliest Period to the Norman Conquest*, 4th edition, I, London: Longman, Hurst, Rees, Orme, and Brown.

Tyler 2010: Ric Tyler, *Wednesfield High School: An Archaeological Desk-Based Assessment*, Birmingham Archaeology, University of Birmingham, July 2010, PN 2102b.

———— Tyler 2010a: Ric Tyler, *The Braybrook Centre, Wood End, Wednesfield: An Archaeological Desk-Based Assessment*, Birmingham Archaeology, University of Birmingham, July 2010, PN 2102c.

Tyrrell 1697: James Tyrrell, *The General History of England, Both Ecclesisatical and Civil; From the Earliest Accounts of Time, to the Reign of His Present Majesty King William III*, London: W. Rogers, etc.

Vergil 1555: Polydore Vergil, *Anglica Historia*.

Vince 1993: Alan G. Vince (ed), *Pre-Viking Lindsey*, Lincoln: City of Lincoln Archaeological Unit.

Vincent 2011: Nicholas Vincent, *A Brief History of Britain 1066-1485: The Birth of the Nation*, London: Constable and Robinson Limited.

Wainwright 1950: F. T. Wainwright, 'The Battles of Corbridge', *Saga Book of the Viking Society*, XIII: 156-73.

———— 1962: F. T. Wainwright, *Archaeology and Place-Names and History: An Essay on Problems of Co-Operation*, London: Routledge & Kegan Paul.

———— 1975: F. T. Wainwright (H. P. R. Finberg (ed.)), *Scandinavian England*, Chichester: Phillimore & Co. Ltd.

———— 2000: F. T. Wainwright, 'North-West Mercia A.D. 871-924' in Cavill, Harding and Jesch 2000 19-42.

Walker 2000: Ian W. Walker, *Mercia and the Making of England*, Stroud: Sutton Publishing Limited.

Walsh 2014: Chris Walsh, *Cowardice: A Brief History*, Princeton: Princeton University Press.

Walvin 2006: James Walvin, *Atlas of Slavery*, Harlow: Pearson Education Limited.

Wanklyn 1988: M. D. G. Wanklyn, 'Severn Navigation in the Seventeenth Century: Long Distance Trade of Shrewsbury Boats', in *Midland History*, XIII 1988.

Ward 2001: Simon Ward, 'Edward the Elder and the re-establishment of Chester', in Higham and Hill 2001: 160-6.

Ward and Waller 1920: *The Cambridge History of English Literature*, Vol. I, Cambridge: Cambridge University Press.

Warner 1903: R H Warner, 'Eardisley and its castle', *Transactions of the Woolhope Naturalists Field Club for 1903*.

Warren 1987: Wilfred Lewis Warren, *The Governance of Norman and Angevin England*, 1066-1272, Stanford: Stanford University Press.

Wasey 1865: George Leigh Wasey, *Our Ancient Parishes, Or a Lecture on Quatford, Morville & Aston Eyre 800 Years Ago*, Bridgnorth: Clement Edkins.

Watkins-Pitchford 1932: W. Watkins-Pitchford, *Morfe Forest and Some of its People*, Shepshed: F. B. Foxall.

———— 1935: W. Watkins-Pitchford, *Bygone Traffic on the Severn with Special Reference to the Port of Bridgnorth*, (reprinted 2000), Shepshed: Rev and Mrs F. B. Foxall.

———— 1937: W. Watkins-Pitchford, 'The Old Castle at Quatford', in *Bridgnorth Journal*, October 1937.

Watson 1994: Jacqui Watson, 'Wood Usage in Anglo-Saxon Shields', in ASSAH 7 (1994) 35-48.

Waton 2011: Richard Watson, 'Viking Age Amounderness: a reconsideration', in Higham and Ryan 2011: 125-41.

Webster and Backhouse 1991: Leslie Webster and Janet Backhouse (eds.), *The Making of England: Anglo-Saxon Art and Culture A.D. 600-900*, London: British Museum Press.

Welch 2001: Martin Welch, 'The Archaeology of Mercia', in Brown and Farr 2001 147-59.

Welfare and Swan 1995: H. Welfare and V. Swan, *Roman Camps in England: the Field Archaeology*, London: HMSO.

Welsh 2002: Frank Welsh, *The Four Nations: A History of the United Kingdom*, London: HarperCollinsPublishers.

West 1983: John West, *Town Records*, Chichester: Phillimore & Co. Ltd.

West 1983a: Jeffrey K. West, 'A Carved Slab Fragment from St. Oswald's Priory, Gloucester', in Thompson 1983: 41-53.

Westwood 1985: Jennifer Westwood, *Albion: A Guide to Legendary Britain*, London: Granada Publishing Limited.

Wharton 1691: [H. Wharton], *Anglia Sacra sive Collectio Historiarum, Partim antiquitus, partim recenter scriptarum, de Archiepiscopis & Episcopis Angliæ, a prima Fidei Christianæ susceptione as Annum MDXL*, vol. I, London: Richard Chiswel.

White 1834: 58. William White, *History, Gazetteer and Directory of Staffordshire*.

White and Barker 1998: Roger White and Philip Barker, *Wroxeter: The Life and Death of a Roman City*, Stroud: Tempus Publishing Limited.

White and Notestein 1915: Albert Beebe White and Wallce Notestein (eds), *Source Problems in English History*, New York: Harper and Brothers.

Whitehouse 1995: Sue Whitehouse, 'The Saxon Cross, St. Peter's Churchyard, Wolverhampton', *The Blackcountryman*, Vol. 28 No.4 48-51.

Whitelock 1930: Dorothy Whitelock (ed. and trans.), *Anglo-Saxon Wills*, Cambridge: Cambridge University Press.

———— 1941: Dorothy Whitelock, 'Wulfstan and the so-called Laws of Edward and Guthrum', *English Historical Review*, LVI 1-21.

———— 1955: Dorothy Whitelock (ed.), *English Historical Documents, c.500-1042* Vol. I, London: Eyre & Spottiswood.

——— 1959: Dorothy Whitelock, 'The Dealings of the Kings of England with Northumbria in the Tenth and Eleventh Centuries', *Anglo-Saxon Studies ... presented to Bruce Dickins*, ed. P. Clemoes.

——— 1961: Dorothy Whitelock (ed), with David C. Douglas and Susie Tucker, *The Anglo-Saxon Chronicle: A Revised Translation*, London: Eyre and Spottisoode.

——— 1972: Dorothy Whitelock, 'The pre-Viking age church in East Anglia', *Anglo-Saxon England*, 1.

——— 1979: Dorothy Whitelock (ed.), *English Historical Documents, c.500-1042* Vol. I, second edition, London: Eyre Methuen.

——— 1981: Dorothy Whitelock, *History, Law and Literature in tenth- and eleventh-century England*, London: Variorum Reprints.

Whitelock, McKitterick and Dumville 1982: Dorothy Whitelock, Rosamund McKitterick and David Dumville (eds), *Ireland in Early Medieval Europe: Studies in Memory of Kathleen Hughes*, Cambridge: Cambridge University Press.

Wiggins and Field 2007: Alison Wiggins and Rosalind Field (eds.), *Guy of Warwick: Icon and Ancestor*, Woodbridge: D. S. Brewer.

Williams 1953: Gwyn Williams, *An Introduction to Welsh Poetry, from the Beginnings to the Sixteenth Century*, London: Faber and Faber Limited.

Williams 1995: Ann Williams, *The English and the Norman Conquest*, Woodbridge: The Boydell Press.

——— 1999: Ann Williams, *Kingship and Government in Pre-Conquest England*, Basingstoke: Macmillan Press Limited.

——— 2003: Ann Williams, *Æthelred the Unready: The Ill-Counselled King*, London: Hambledon and London Limited.

——— 2009a: Ann Williams, 'Offas Dyke: a monument without a history?', in Fryde and Reitz 2009: 31-56.

Williams 2001: Gareth Williams, 'Military Institutions and Royal Power', in Brown and Farr 2001: 295-309.

——— 2007: Gareth Williams, 'Kingship, Christianity and coinage: monetary and political perspectives on silver economy in the Viking Age', in Campbell and Williams 2007: 177-214.

——— 2008: Gareth Williams, 'Raiding and Warfare', in Brink and Price 2008: 192-203.

——— 2009: Gareth Williams, 'Hoards from the Northern Danelaw from Cuerdale to the Vale of York', in Graham-Campbell and Philpott 2009: 73-83.

——— 2013: Gareth Williams, 'Towns and identities in Viking England', in Hadley and Ten Herkel 2013.

——— 2014: Gareth Williams, 'Warfare & Military Expansion', in Williams, Pentz and Wemhoff 2014: 78-115.

——— 2014a: Gareth Williams, 'Coins and Currency in Viking England, AD 865-954', in Naismith, Allen and Screen 2014: 13-38.

Williams 2010: Howard Williams, 'Remembering elites: Early Medieval stone crosses as commemorative technologies', in Boyce et al 2010: 13-32.

Williams 2015: Thomas J. T. Williams, "For the Sake of Bravado in the Wilderness': Confronting the Bestial in Anglo-Saxon Warfare', in Bintley and Williams 2015: 176-204.

——— 2016: Thomas J. T. Williams, 'The Place of Slaughter: Exploring the West Saxon Battlescape', in Lavelle and Roffey 2016: 35-55.

Williams ab Ithel 1860: John Williams ab Ithel, *Rerum Britannicarum Medii Ævi Scriptores, or Chronicles and Memorials of Great Britain and Ireland during the Middle Ages: Annales Cambriæ*, London: Longman, Green, Longman, and Roberts.

——— 1860a: John Williams ab Ithel, *Brut y Tywysogion; or, The Chronicle of the Princes*, London: Longman, Green, Longman, and Roberts.

Williams, Pentz and Wemhoff 2014: Gareth Williams, Peter Pentz and Matthias Wemhoff (eds), *Vikings: Life and Legend*, London: The British Museum

Williams, Smyth and Kirby 1991: Ann Williams, Alfred P. Smyth and D. P. Kirby, *A Biographical Dictionary of Dark Age Britain: England, Scotland and Wales c.500-c.1050*, London: B. A. Seaby Limited.

Williamson 2007: Tom Williamson, *Rabbits, Warrens and Archaeology*, Stroud: Tempus.

Willis 1718: Browne Willis, *An History of the Mitred Parliamentary Abbies and Convential Cathedral Churches*, London: R. Gosling.

Wilson 1964: David M. Wilson, *Anglo-Saxon Ornamental Metalwork 700-1100 in the British Museum*, London: Trustees of the British Museum.

——— 1976: David M. Wilson (ed.), *The Archaeology of Anglo-Saxon England*, London: Methuen & Co. Ltd.

——— 1984: David M. Wilson, *Anglo-Saxon Art, from the Seventh-Century to the Norman Conquest*, London: Thames and Hudson.

——— 1989: David M. Wilson, *The Vikings and their Origins*, London: Thames and Hudson.

Wilson 1992: David Wilson, *Anglo-Saxon Paganism*, London: Routledge.

Wilson and Klindt-Jensen 1980: David M. Wilson and Ole Klindt-Jensen, *Viking Art*, second edition, London: George Allen and Unwin.

Winchester 1985: A. Winchester, 'A multiple estate: A framework for the evolution of settlement in Anglo-Saxon and Scandinavian Cumbria', in Baldwin and Whyte, 1985: 89-101.

Wise 1742: Francis Wise, *Further Observations Upon the White Horse and Other Antiquities in Berkshire, with An Account of Whiteleaf-Cross in Buckinghamshire*, Oxford: Thomas Wood.

Wise and Noble 1881: J. Wise and W. M. Noble, *Ramsey Abbey: Its Rise and Fall*, London: Simpkin Marshall.

Wood 1999: Michael Wood, *In Search of England: Journeys into the English Past*, London: Viking.

Wood 2002: Ian Wood, *Constructing Cults in Early Medieval France: Local Saints and Churches in Bergundy and the Auvergne 400-1000*, in Thacker and Sharpe 2002: 155-87.

Wood and Lund 1991: I. Wood and N. Lund (eds), *People and Places in Northern Europe, 500-1000*, Woodbridge: Boydell Press.

Woolf 2001: Alex Woolf, 'View from the West: An Irish perspective on the West Saxon dynastic practice', in Higham and Hill 2001: 89-101.

——— 2007: Alex Woolf, *From Pictland to Alba 789-1070*, Edinburgh: Edinburgh University Press.

Woolf 2003: Daniel Woolf, *The Social Circulation of the Past: English Historical Culture 1500-1730*, Oxford: Oxford University Press.

Wormald 1981: Patrick Wormald, 'The Age of Offa and Alcuin', in Campbell 1981: 101-31.

——— 1999: P. Wormald, *The Making of English Law: King Alfred to the 12th Century, i: Legislation and its Limits*, Oxford: Oxford University Press.

Wright 1855: Thomas Wright (trans. and ed.), *The History of Fulk Fitz Warine, an Outlawed Baron in the Reign of King John*, London: The Warton Club.

——— 1863: Thomas Wright (ed.), *The Historical Works of Geraldus Cambrensis containing The Topography of Ireland, and the History of the Conquest of Ireland, translated by Thomas Forester, Esq., M.A.; and The Itinerary Through Wales, and The Description of Wales, translated by Sir William Colt Hoare, Bart.*, London: H. G. Bohn.

——— 1866: Thomas Wright (ed.), *The Chronicle of Pierre de Longtoft in French Verse, from the Earliest Period to the Death of King Edward I*, London: Longmans, Green, Reader, and Dyer.

Wright 2004: James Wright, *Castles of Nottinghamshire*, Nottingham: Nottinghamshire County Council.

Wyatt 1948: Alfred John Wyatt, *An Anglo-Saxon Reader, Edited with Notes and Glossary*, Cambridge: The University Press.

Wyatt 2009: David Wyatt, *Slaves and Warriors in Medieval Britain and Ireland, 800-1200*, Leiden and Boston: Koninklijke Brill NV.

Wyckoff 1897: Charles Truman Wyckoff, *Feudal Relations between the Kings of England and Scotland under the Plantagenets*, Chicago: Chicago University Press.

Wyn Owen 1994: Hywel Wyn Owen, *The Place-Names of East Flintshire*, Cardiff: University of Wales Press for the Board of Celtic Studies of the University of Wales.

────── 2013: Hywel Wyn Owen, 'English place-names in Wales', in Carroll and Parsons 2103: 323-53.

Yorke 1988: Barbara Yorke, *Bishop Æthelwold, His Career and Influence*, Woodbridge: Boydell & Brewer Ltd.

────── 1995: Barbara Yorke, *Wessex in the Early Middle Ages*, London: Leicester University Press.

────── 1999: Barbara Yorke, *The Anglo-Saxons*, Stroud: Sutton Publishing.

────── 2001: Barbara Yorke, 'Edward as Ætheling', in Higham and Hill 2001 25-39.

────── 2003: Barbara Yorke, *Nunneries and the Anglo-Saxon Royal Houses*, London & New York: Continuum.

Zaluckyj 2001: Sarah Zaluckyj, *Mercia: the Anglo-Saxon Kingdom of Central England*, Logaston: Logaston Press.

Zarnecki, Holt and Holland: Goerge Zarnecki, Janet Holt and Tristram Holland (eds.), *English Romanesque Art 1066-1200*, London: Arts Council of Great Britain, in association with Weidenfeld and Nicolson.

Zeepvat 2000: R. Zeepvat (ed), *Three Iron-Age and Romano-British Rural Settlements on English Gravels*, BAR (British Series) 312, Oxford.

Zoëga 1910: Geir T. Zoëga, *A Concise Dictionary of Old Icelandic*, Oxford: Clarendon Press.

Index.

Abbot's Castle Hill, 42, 89, 182, 350, 427, 532, 534, 536
Abels, Richard, 13, 77, 116, 167, 183, 186, 188, 191, 192, 204, 205, 214, 223, 310, 345, 422, 447, 526
Ablow, 237, 238, 309
Acton Beauchamp, 414
Acton Trussell, 567
Ada School, 591
adalbrigt, 371
Adam's Grave, 165
Adelais, 100
Adeleya, 542
Ælfflaed, abbess of Whitby, 604
Ælfhelm, 610, 611, 612, 613
Ælfric, 83, 166, 231, 437, 438, 452, 480, 551, 552, 610
Ælfwynn, 227, 228, 231, 261, 406, 407, 476, 477, 484, 485, 486, 487, 488, 489, 519, 520, 609
Æthelbald, King (716-57), 20, 102, 104, 105, 161, 166, 181, 242, 247, 566, 608, 615
Æthelbeald, archbishop of York, 166, 449
Æthelflæd, Lady of the Mercians (d.918), 1, 19-21, 24, 26, 32, 35, 57, 65, 82, 104, 106, 107, 113, 115-35, 141, 145, 146, 223-31, 249, 251, 253, 261, 282, 285, 288, 298, 333-4, 341, 381, 383, 384, 394, 398-409, 413, 415, 421, 422, 432-8, 442, 460, 466, 468-85, 487, 488, 493, 497, 499, 501-10, 512, 514-20, 539, 541-5, 609
Æthelfrith, King of Northumbria (604-17), 436, 437, 442, 459
Æthelgifu, 369, 489
Æthelhelm, 24, 26, 367, 375, 433
Æthelhild, 489
Æthelmær, 612
Æthelmund, 597
Æthelnoth, 24, 26, 33, 383, 433
Æthelred, King of Mercia (675-704), 104, 401, 514
Æthelred, King of Northumbria (774-9, 790-96), 597
Æthelred, King of Wessex (865-71), 47, 187-8, 210, 283, 367, 454, 545
Æthelred, Lord of the Mercians (d.911), (see also Ethelred, surnam'd Michill), 19-24, 26, 29, 30, 34, 35-9, 104, 106, 107, 113, 115, 117, 119, 127, 128, 135, 162, 192, 200, 223-8, 231, 249, 251-2, 257, 270, 281, 287, 288, 331, 332, 334, 341, 379, 381-3, 385, 391-6, 398, 399, 402, 403, 404-9, 412-5, 424, 430, 432-8, 442, 460, 463, 466-9, 471, 472, 474, 478, 481, 482, 484, 485, 487, 488, 492, 493, 501-4, 507-20, 544, 545, 610, 612
Æthelred, king of England (978-1016), 194, 196, 243, 417, 441, 549-52, 556, 560, 609, 611
Æthelstan, King of England (924-39), 8, 20, 82, 83, 93, 169, 170, 173, 187, 190, 193, 198, 199, 232, 285, 288, 300, 305, 310, 332, 381, 405-7, 432-4, 437, 444, 445, 447, 473, 480, 484, 486, 489, 490, 492, 493, 499, 512, 526, 545, 588, 610-12
Æthelswith, 20
Æthelthryth, 562, 565
Æthelweard, chronicler, 20, 24, 26, 33, 41, 82, 84-6, 93, 94, 162, 166, 171, 175, 183, 195, 223, 228, 251, 252, 258, 261, 263, 274, 278, 281, 283, 284, 287, 289, 293, 296-301, 305, 310, 314, 366, 378, 383, 398, 399, 405, 409, 413, 415, 421-4, 427, 431, 432, 435, 440-3, 449, 450, 458, 468, 470, 492, 497, 499-501, 504, 507, 509, 510, 514-16, 520, 588, 610
Æthelweard, brother of Edward the Elder, 468, 469
Æthelwold, 188, 193, 210, 270, 283, 297, 303, 367-80, 385, 387, 388, 407, 410-12, 430, 437, 439, 466, 491, 513, 516, 517, 520, 545, 599, 613
Æthelwulf, 20, 27, 378, 437, 462, 581, 600
Agmund, 253, 254, 255, 256, 260, 288, 294, 295, 296, 382, 410, 419, 457, 511, 512
Alba, 293, 496, 497, 500-3, 515, 516
Alcuin, 590, 596, 608
Aldridge, 557, 641

669

Alfred, King of Wessex 871-99), 19-26, 28, 33-7, 39, 47-9, 115-7, 127, 134, 169, 171, 173, 187, 188, 190, 191-3, 200, 203-7, 210-12, 216, 218, 221, 223-7, 249, 253, 257, 260, 261, 279, 281, 283, 285, 289-93, 297, 310, 319, 331, 344, 367, 369, 371, 373, 380, 383, 385-7, 394, 395, 403, 406-8, 428, 430, 432, 433, 437, 438, 468, 470, 475, 478, 485, 489, 490, 492, 501, 504, 508, 509, 515, 543, 545, 579, 581, 609, 610, 613
Alfred, reeve of Bath, 384-5
Alfred, who opposed Æthelstan, 192
Alfric, 243, 549
Alkmund, 95, 334, 403
Allerdale, 512
Alstigus, 23
Alveley, 57, 59, 71, 72, 97, 328, 418, 524
Amos Lane, 152, 155, 157, 178, 234
Amounderness, 288, 382, 419, 510, 511, 512, 639
Anarawd, 26, 28, 32, 37, 132, 210, 224, 225, 226, 227, 228, 230, 406, 428, 457, 470, 485
Ancaster, 603
Anglesey, 16, 26, 27, 35, 79, 85, 169, 222-4, 226, 229, 231, 232
Anglezarke, 419, 512
Anglo-Saxon Chronicle, 3, 8, 12, 13, 19-21, 28, 35, 36, 38, 47, 48, 49, 57, 78, 82, 93, 105, 107, 115, 116, 122, 150, 170, 171, 174, 188, 190, 193, 196, 203, 204, 211-3, 223, 225, 249-57, 261, 278-89, 293-300, 303, 311, 332, 348, 381, 385-8, 394, 395, 397, 400, 407, 409, 410, 418, 423, 424, 432, 434, 435, 442, 452, 456, 458, 462, 470, 478, 485, 501, 502, 505, 506, 515, 517, 519, 520, 549, 588, 610
Anker, river, 120
Anlaf, 288, 419, 512
Annales Bertiniani, 205
Annales Cambriae, 28, 30, 223, 226, 229, 466, 485
Annales Ultoniensis, 380
Annales Vedastini, 17
Annals of Æthelflæd, 435
Annals of Clonmacnoise, 293, 501, 515
Annals of St Neots, 253, 260, 278, 284, 288, 290, 296, 298, 299, 370, 374, 449, 520, 637, 648
Annals of St Vast, 34
Annals of the Four Masters, 496
Annals of Ulster, 23, 27, 29, 169, 210, 292, 293, 302, 380, 382, 419, 438, 497, 499, 501, 504, 506, 515
Annate Senait, 380
Apley, 58
Appledore, 23, 203, 206
Arabic coins, 47, 350, 353, 383, 399
Archenfield, 15, 36, 218, 228, 313, 407, 414, 477, 504
archers, 201, 529
archery, 201, 529, 531
Arley, 57, 59, 86, 113, 613
army-service, 14
Arras, 17, 525
Arundel, 42, 43, 76, 656
Ashdown, 186, 187, 206, 260, 288, 311, 438, 450, 458, 462
Ashford, 19
Ashmore, 154, 155, 302
Assandun, 460, 617
Asser, 19, 28, 41, 187, 188, 190, 193, 210-12, 223-5, 249, 253, 259, 297, 331, 411, 450, 454, 456, 457, 465, 485, 518
Atcham, 75, 76, 414
Ath-cliath (Dublin), 380
Athelney, 19, 26, 190, 205, 403
Auisle, 16, 253, 293, 294, 405, 457

Avebury, 582
Avon, river, 120, 252, 276, 413-5, 420, 561
Badbury, 369
Badger, 92, 94
Bakewell, 290, 393, 492, 493, 503, 592
Baldwin Brown, G., 573, 580, 583
Ballyscyles, 157
Baltic, 14, 204
Bamburgh, 428, 492, 496, 501, 515, 516
Bangor-is-Coed, 208, 459
banners, 198, 419, 429, 448, 452, 455
Bardney, 333, 401, 403, 442, 463, 476, 507, 509, 516, 520, 565
Barlow, Thomas, 550
Barnes, 112, 654, 655
Barnet's Hill, 44, 45
Barrow, 44, 94, 128, 172, 341, 414, 544
Bartholomew de Cotton, 265, 297, 344, 432
Bassett, Steven, 89, 94, 117, 120, 435, 545, 567
Bateley, Janet, 18, 93, 250, 251, 279, 280, 290, 299, 395, 422, 425, 492, 504, 508
Bath, 243, 386, 413, 414, 543, 560, 562, 563, 565, 568
Bayeux Tapestry, 77, 185, 194, 195, 196, 199, 201, 455
beacons, 117, 439
Beadugyth, 243, 247, 563, 564, 566, 595
Beadugyth's stream, 563
Beckford, 414
Bede, 3, 100, 103, 169, 171, 208, 218, 221, 247, 249, 261, 262, 267, 314, 333, 346, 348, 401, 442, 459, 554, 556, 561, 562, 582, 583, 588, 615
Bedford, 75, 118, 127, 129, 134, 473, 477, 491
Bednall, 567
Beeston Berrys, 49
Bellimore, 157
Benedicte, 459
Benesing, 253, 254, 255, 259, 260, 288, 294, 296, 457
Benfleet, 23, 24, 347
Bentley, 154, 158, 335, 557
Beoley, 564
Beorhthelm, 334, 541
Beorhtsige, 298
Beorngyth, 247, 558, 560-4, 566, 568, 595, 605, 608
Beorngyth's stone, 558, 559, 560, 563
Beornoth, 297
Beornwulf, 599
Beresford, William, 82, 112, 113, 122, 525, 545, 546, 565
Berkeley, 302, 414, 476
Bernicia, 371, 384, 386, 388, 428, 474, 475, 479, 490, 499, 501, 515, 516, 520
Berrington, 143
Bertelin, 334, 541, 543, 558
Berth, The, 540
Bescot, 553, 556, 557
Bevere, 49
Bewdley, 37, 59, 93, 103
Bickford, 234, 553
Bilsetna, 161
Bilsetnatun, 161, 551
Bilston, 159, 161, 179, 234, 236, 242, 243, 244, 245, 308, 343, 536, 552-7, 563, 566
Biscay, 17
Bishops Cleeve, 414

671

Black Galls, 498
Black Mountains, 77
Blackhalve Lane, 178, 336
Blaeu, John, 418
Blockley, 226, 414
blóðorn, 219
blood-eagle, 219, 452
Bloxwich, 553, 556
Blyth, 76, 541
Bobbington, 524, 535
Bolton, Richard, 319, 329, 349
Bonningale, 532
Bordeaux, 16, 544
Borewardes Croft, 158
borough, 26, 43, 63, 71, 73-80, 91, 93, 94, 95, 100, 111, 112, 118, 122, 125, 127-30, 543, 544
Borough-work, 102, 115
Borre-style, 352, 361
Bosworth psalter, 582
Boulogne, 23, 33, 212, 383, 411
bow, 190, 194, 201
Bowman's Hill, 63
bowmen, 201, 529
Bradley, 3, 553
Braydon, 372
bread, 420, 430, 446, 464
Brecenan mere, 228, 476
breche, 155, 316, 323, 325
Bredon, 414
Breedon, 549, 580, 582, 583, 585, 602
Bremesbury, 145
Bremesbyrig, 132, 145, 255, 381, 409, 435, 436, 466, 468, 469
Brenhinedd y Saesson, 27, 30, 38, 224, 226, 249, 303
Bretons, 19, 193, 331, 495
Bretton, 28, 420
Brewood, 4, 9, 156, 328, 356, 547, 553, 556, 557
Bridge Acre, 111, 112
bridges, 1, 18, 35, 48, 50, 56-9, 61, 62, 74, 75, 79, 80, 82, 84, 86-115, 118, 120-8, 134, 149, 153, 160, 190, 207, 246, 252, 277, 307, 325, 344, 346, 347, 418, 421, 422, 427, 441, 446, 544
bridgework, 14
Bridgnorth, 1, 11, 24, 39, 41-6, 50, 53-6, 71-107, 110-13, 120-2, 125, 127, 130, 147, 148, 239, 252, 308, 350, 351, 353, 354, 416, 417, 428, 522-5, 541, 543, 544, 546, 548
Brihtsige, 210, 297, 378
Bristol, 15, 27, 35, 500, 572
Britannia, 270, 274, 355, 426, 500, 522, 537, 620
Britons, 28, 43, 132, 169, 174, 208, 210, 218, 221, 222, 227, 231, 291, 326, 346, 420, 458, 474, 475, 479, 501-3, 506, 515, 516, 535
Brocton, 567
Bromesberrow, 132, 466
Bromfield, 414
Brompton, John, 100, 267, 278
Bromsberrow, 132, 466
Bromyard, 414
Bronze Age, 127, 233, 337, 343, 344, 345, 522
Broomy Leasow, 41, 96
Broughton, 147
Brown Clee, 71, 126

Brunanburh, 8, 158, 173, 187, 188, 193, 196, 198, 201, 211, 212, 293, 310-12, 314, 332, 341, 348, 397, 419, 432, 443, 444, 447, 450, 452, 458, 462, 464, 480, 486, 610, 617
Brut y Tywysogion, 23, 27, 30, 225, 229, 249, 303, 627, 666
Brycge, 35, 41, 57, 82, 111-3, 121, 122, 127, 128, 278
Brycheiniog, 30, 38, 210, 223, 225, 226, 228, 476, 505
Buckingham, 118, 127, 469, 475
Buellt, 31
Bunker's Hill, 178
Burcote, 147, 350
Burf Castle, 42, 46, 61, 82, 126, 532, 540
Burghal Hidage, 117, 118, 124, 127, 142, 469, 629, 631, 645, 660
Burgred, King of Mercia (852-74), 20, 341, 430, 507
burh, 1, 46, 47, 57, 65, 72, 74, 77, 82, 101, 107, 113, 115-36, 142, 145-7, 155, 164, 182, 227, 230, 231, 278, 334, 381, 386, 409, 435, 466, 469, 470, 472, 475, 481, 489, 491, 492, 539, 540, 542, 543, 544, 545, 549, 555
Burhall, 147
Burlaughton, 361, 539
Burne, A.H., 113, 196, 310, 311, 444, 617
Burni(l)delowe, 241
Burrington, 143
Burry Holm, 49
Burton Abbey, 242, 244, 610, 613
Burton Chronicle, 489, 609
Burton-on-Trent, 19
Bushbury, 152, 153, 155, 159, 164, 178, 179, 233, 309, 339, 340, 343, 345, 439, 461, 554-6, 626
Butting tune, 11, 23, 250
Buttington, 1, 23-37, 49, 91, 107, 142, 183, 211, 212, 214, 224, 225, 230, 250, 292, 383, 425, 430, 432-4, 438, 458, 499, 545
Buttington Tump, 24
butts, 529, 531
Bylet, 59, 60, 99, 111, 112
Byrhtferth of Ramsey, 92
Byrngyðe stan, 558, 563
Byzantium, 16, 168, 215, 383, 429, 587, 590, 602, 644
Cadwallon, 314, 348, 547
Caernarvon, 27, 76
Caldwall,, 153, 317
Caldy, 49
Calf Heath, 233, 345, 356, 526
Camden, William, 150, 270, 621
Cameleac, 15, 407, 477, 504
Camp Feld,, 312, 321, 325, 332, 341
camp followers, 190
Camp Hill, 41, 95, 96, 312
Campbell, James, 8, 18, 20, 21, 24, 26, 33, 38, 82, 84, 93, 105, 166, 171, 183, 188, 195, 196, 204, 205, 213, 214, 223, 251, 252, 261, 281, 283, 284, 293, 296-301, 315, 359, 366, 367, 371, 373, 375, 377, 379-84, 388, 395, 399, 405, 409, 411, 413, 414, 420, 422, 428, 431, 432, 439, 450, 458, 468, 486, 487, 492, 494, 500, 505, 507, 508, 511, 516, 527, 547, 588
Cannock, 158, 179, 302, 352, 553, 567
canon law, 463
Canterbury, 14
Cantern Brook, 85
captives, 210, 218, 395, 399, 459
Caradoc of Llancarvan, 270, 480, 489
Caradog, King of Gwynedd, 597
Carolingia, 18, 195, 198, 212, 213, 351-3, 383, 567, 574, 581, 582, 583, 587, 588, 592
Carton, 93, 103

673

Carver, Martin, 38, 87, 90, 91, 100, 120, 127, 179, 288, 569
Castle Hill, 42, 43, 82, 89, 91, 111, 112, 120, 122, 350, 534, 536
Castlecroft, 151
Castor, 562, 566, 602
cavalry, 1, 24, 34, 212, 213, 214
ceastel, 151, 534
Cedd, St, 333
Cella, John de, 263
Celtic Church, 618
Celtic fields, 87
Ceolwulf, 20, 106, 222, 223, 407, 599, 601
Ceolwulf II, 20, 106, 223
Ceredigion, 26, 28, 35, 37, 222, 223, 225, 226, 407, 485
Chanson de Roland, 354
chantry, 81
Charlbury, 414
Charlemagne, 20, 190, 216, 329, 354, 446, 585, 627
Charles the Simple, 34
Charles the Bald, 20, 38, 105, 115, 222, 351, 653
Charles-Edwards, T.M., 16, 24, 26, 102, 133, 168, 170, 208, 210, 211, 222-8, 230-2, 282, 289, 337, 346, 382, 395, 406, 457, 467, 474, 476, 477, 479, 485, 488, 492, 503, 504, 505, 506, 514, 567
charm, 217
Checkley, 349, 578, 620
Chelles, 562
Chelmarsh, 59, 104, 125
Cheltenham, 414, 558
Chepstow, 23
Cheshire, 3, 19, 21, 28, 30, 76, 78, 118, 119, 132, 145, 156, 224, 229, 230, 313, 341, 384, 394, 420, 424, 499, 509, 610, 623, 628
Chester, 3, 21, 24, 30, 34, 74, 95, 102, 103, 118, 144, 145, 146, 156, 158, 166, 177, 178, 208, 212, 221, 225, 229, 230, 282, 288, 334, 337, 346, 352, 354, 360, 381, 382, 383, 384, 388, 389, 393, 394, 395, 396, 397, 399, 403, 410, 413, 434, 449, 459, 468, 470, 477, 489, 493, 497, 503, 508, 513, 514, 545, 548, 567, 570
Chesterton, 36, 89, 92, 148, 181, 416, 423, 427, 443, 524, 532, 534, 536, 537, 538
Chetton, 71
Chibnall, Marjorie, 43, 75, 76, 91, 111, 349, 634, 641, 663
Chirbury, 32, 120, 121, 136, 142, 145, 146, 227, 470, 472
Chirchezordesfeld, 326-8, 345, 350, 464, 618
Christchurch, 127, 250, 369
Christian, 4, 12, 15, 17, 20, 22, 113, 115, 119, 160, 163-73, 183, 185, 189, 193, 208, 221, 223, 225, 229, 243, 261, 345, 349, 353, 371, 385, 445, 449, 452, 455, 459, 460, 463, 481, 493, 499, 514, 526, 528, 543, 546, 555, 561, 576, 582, 583, 604, 617, 618, 625
Christianity, 1, 15, 23, 103, 162-71, 189, 218, 233, 292, 295, 345, 354, 445, 449, 493, 496, 526, 555
Chrodegang of Metz, 599
Chronici Mariani Scotti, 256, 257, 259
Chronicle of Melrose, 261, 278, 375, 396, 475
Chronicles of Regino of Prüm, 34, 213
Chronicles of the Kings of Alba, 503, 504
Chronicon Æthelweardi, 251
Chronicon Scottorum, 294, 381
Church Field, 156
Church Stretton, 414
Church Withies, 326, 327, 329
Churchfield, 160, 235, 327, 328, 329, 330, 332, 336, 337, 341, 618
Churchill, Sir Winston, 376, 377
Churchyardfield, 341
Cirencester, 23, 207, 266, 267, 282, 301, 362, 372, 379, 391, 402, 413, 414, 479, 503

Ciricius, St, 475
Cistercians, 245, 557, 558, 620
Clapham, Sir Alfred, 71, 212, 360, 570, 579, 580, 584
Clark, G. T., 46, 53, 54, 55, 65, 68, 70, 73, 76, 79, 84, 86, 95, 128, 161, 250, 254, 312, 426, 476, 594
Claverley, 42, 55, 72, 88, 97, 147, 148, 318, 351, 352, 353, 354, 417, 427, 629
Cleeve Prior, 15, 341, 414
Clent, 245, 553
Cliff Coppice, 46, 87, 126
climate, 431, 489, 629
Clive, 352, 357
Clulow Cross, 623
Clun, 104
Clydog, 228, 229, 485
Clyttwic, 485
Cnut, 49, 166, 169, 170, 192, 193, 197, 247, 371, 390, 449, 510, 513, 554, 609, 611, 617
Coates, Richard, 135
Coelwulf, 20
Coenwulf, 20, 102, 567, 586, 590, 599
Cœnwulf, 222, 413, 597, 598, 599, 601, 602
Coffin burial, 461
coins, 14, 18, 36, 78, 80, 89, 169, 177, 187, 193, 207, 283, 350, 351, 353, 383, 384, 410, 419, 448, 472, 494, 513, 533
Colberne, 377
Collingwood, R.G., 581, 583, 584, 635
Colne, river, 49, 114, 507
Colwick near Holme Pierrepoint, 101
common burdens, 14, 102
Compton, 239, 240, 308, 313, 316, 345, 351, 352, 353, 553, 556
Congreve, 567
Constantine, 88, 193, 282, 389, 474, 492, 496, 497, 504, 604, 610
Continent, the, 48, 170, 205, 331, 372, 411, 412, 476, 495, 505
Conwy, 20, 210, 223, 226, 289, 466, 467
Cooper, Alan, 91, 93, 105, 106, 109, 111, 341
Copeland, 231, 512
Coplow, 355
Coppenhall, 553, 567
Corbridge, 204, 297, 438, 439, 457, 474, 480, 496, 497, 498, 500, 501, 503, 504, 506
Cornes, Rev. Richard, 522
Cornovii, 102
Cornwall, 26, 210, 232, 352, 403, 467, 494, 504, 662
corpses, 17, 45, 168, 198, 208, 233, 349, 455, 461, 462, 465
Cotton, Bartholomew de, 265, 297, 344, 432
Cottonian Collection, 489
Coven, 177, 178
Cowulph, 377
Cramp, Rosemary, 568, 581-5, 604, 608, 615
crannog, 476, 506
Cressage, 88, 350
Cricklade, 127, 372
Croom, Jane, 50, 72, 87, 96, 97, 98, 105, 108, 122
Cropthorne, 360, 594, 607
Cuckhamsley Hill, 172
Cuckney, 348, 617
Cuerdale hoard, 370, 371, 381, 383, 390, 405, 510, 511, 513
Culloden, 343
Cumbria, 231, 282, 288, 384, 389, 394, 397, 509, 512, 513, 584
Curtle(s)ford, 158

675

Cuthbert, 166, 295, 297, 395, 403, 449, 457, 496, 501, 515, 588
Cuthburga, 541, 544
Cwatbrycge, 1, 18, 24, 34-43, 47, 48, 50, 57, 69, 79-88, 92-6, 100- 6, 111-15, 118-21, 124-8, 132-5, 141, 145, 173, 182, 205, 212, 225, 237, 274, 278, 340, 413, 415, 416, 418, 420-8, 430, 441, 443, 528, 539, 540, 544, 617
Cwatt, 82, 83
Cwicchelmes hlaew, 172
Cwœnthryth, abbess of Winchcombe, 598
Cymrid Conwy, 467
Cynehelm (Kenelm), 599
Cyricbyrig, 120, 129
Dalton, Paul, 423
Danelaw, 13, 19, 21, 35, 36, 39, 107, 117, 118, 132, 146, 165, 167, 180, 181, 193, 224, 279, 280, 282, 283, 287, 297, 340, 350, 351, 352, 373, 379, 383, 389, 399, 400, 401, 403-5, 411, 413, 416, 418, 420, 427, 430, 437, 439, 441, 442, 460, 464, 466, 477, 478, 480, 481, 491, 493, 499, 508, 509, 510, 526
Danery, The, 107
Danes, 1, 12, 13, 16-43, 46-50, 53-5, 57, 61, 71, 82, 84, 86, 92, 93, 100-3, 107, 115, 118, 121, 123, 127, 132-4, 142, 145, 147, 150, 165, 167-9, 181, 183, 185, 187, 188, 190, 193, 197, 198, 201, 204-12, 218-25, 229-32, 239, 243, 252-300, 304-11, 314, 332, 338, 340, 343, 344, 346, 349, 351, 354, 366, 370, 372, 376, 377, 380-402, 404, 408, 409, 411-13, 417, 420, 424, 425, 428, 430, 435, 437, 438, 441-3, 445, 448-50, 460, 462, 466, 468, 472-5, 477, 478, 480, 486, 488, 489, 491, 492, 494, 498, 499, 501, 502, 504-8, 515-7, 520, 526-8, 532, 533, 544, 550, 565, 569, 579, 594, 617
Danescourt, 151, 238
Danesford, 45, 46, 87, 101, 147
Danes' Pillar, 594
Danish Camp, 41, 66
Danish Cross, 594
Dark Foreigners, 498, 638
Darlaston, 178, 557, 613
Davenport, 490, 499, 511
Daylesford, 414
De Laudibus Virginitate, 561
Deanery, 107, 244, 553, 554
dedications, 75, 95, 114, 123, 172, 246, 247, 339, 501, 515, 541
Dee, river, 27, 132, 145, 230, 347, 493, 508
Deerhurst, 49, 414
Defoe, Daniel, 621
Deheubarth, 132, 228
Delamere, 119, 470
Denisc, 290, 397
Deniscena, 279
Denmark, 14, 167, 199, 289, 290, 303, 351, 364, 387, 472
Derby, 19, 119, 135, 146, 334, 382, 388, 403, 437, 462, 473, 477, 478, 502, 508, 541, 544, 545, 547, 610
Derbyshire, 18, 19, 20, 76, 180, 182, 283, 313, 405, 413, 492, 524, 527, 548, 613
Derwent, river, 195
Devon, 8, 24, 26, 118, 198, 206, 210, 371, 432, 467
Dewsbury, 583
Diceto, Ralph de, 262
Diddlesbury, 414
Dietrichson, Professor L., 579, 584
Diminsdale, 154
dirhams, Arabic, 47, 350, 351, 352, 353
Ditton Priors, 105
Dodsworth, Roger, 550, 637
dog, 452

Domesday Book, 3, 43, 59, 63, 71, 73-80, 82, 84, 96, 97, 111, 121, 129-30, 133, 135, 150, 159, 164, 179, 181, 182, 242, 243, 247, 256, 319, 329, 331, 333, 336, 339, 341, 352, 464, 510, 543, 546, 550, 551, 553-6, 566, 609
Dorchester, 387
Dougharty, Joseph, 137, 138, 139, 140, 146
Dove, river, 21, 182, 416, 508, 525
Dowdswell, 414
Dowles, 59, 93
Downham, Clare, 23, 28, 29, 31, 33, 166, 167, 218, 225, 226, 228, 229, 280-2, 290, 292, 293, 297, 368, 370, 371, 383, 385, 388, 390, 396, 398, 403, 405, 410, 419, 428, 473, 474, 480, 496-500, 503, 504, 514-16
Drayton, Michael, 563, 610
Droitwich, 105, 179
Dub, 291
Dubgaill, 293
Dubhgaill, 27
Dublin, 8, 15, 16, 21, 22, 28, 29, 30, 35, 132, 168-70, 187, 206, 211, 218, 223-6, 229, 230, 232, 280, 282, 289, 291-5, 297, 350, 359, 380, 381, 384, 388, 397, 399, 410, 419, 420, 458, 472-5, 479, 490, 492, 497, 499, 514, 515, 542, 610, 628
Dudmaston, 62, 84, 108, 130
Dudmaston Mill, 62
Dudo of St. Quentin, 38
Dugdale, Sir William, 304, 533, 542, 550, 552, 565, 609, 618, 620
Duignan, W.H., 159, 178, 180, 309, 325, 442, 551, 609
Dumbarton, 16
Dumville, David, 19-21, 28, 34, 118, 128, 188, 261, 291, 293, 294, 367, 370, 372, 380, 386, 432, 475, 478, 493, 508, 509
Dunklington, 86
Dunnlow, 164, 235, 337
Dunston, 567
Dyfed, 15, 16, 28, 210, 222, 223, 225, 227, 228, 415, 457, 477, 485
Eadflæd, 489
Eadgifu, 374, 491
Eadgyth, 334, 445, 493, 499
Eadmund, 49, 353, 613
Eadred,, 457, 489, 542
Eadric the Wild, 78
Eadwulf, 428, 474, 475, 501, 515
Eagell, 253, 288
Eagellus, 253, 260, 296, 457
Eahlstan, 507
Eahlswith, 406
Ealhhelm, 19, 437
Ealhswith, 20, 285, 613
Eardington, 58, 62, 63, 73-5, 81, 87-9, 93-6, 98, 99, 101, 103-5, 108, 113, 124-31, 522, 544
Eardisley Camp, 80
Easby cross shaft, 570, 585, 588
East Anglia, 18, 19, 22, 23, 30, 31, 34, 37, 47, 113, 117, 165, 167, 171, 205, 206, 212, 270, 287, 289, 294, 372, 373, 377, 380, 386-8, 391, 399, 410, 412, 428, 442, 475, 488, 491, 492, 508, 513, 516, 517
East Anglian Chronicle, 253
Easthope, 71, 341
Eaton-under-Haywood, 74
Ecgberht, 428, 501, 600, 601
Ecgbriht, 228, 475
Echard, Laurence, 273, 424, 638
eclipses, 385

Ecwils, 250, 253, 260, 272, 293, 305
Eddisbury, 118, 119, 120, 145, 470, 472, 513
Edgar, King of England (959-75), 231, 542, 543, 546, 549, 583, 608, 609, 611, 613, 614, 618
Edgeworth, Matt, 55, 97, 638
Edington, 19, 223, 301, 403
Edmund, 20, 167, 169, 187, 200, 219, 354, 408, 432, 489
Edryd, 467
Edward the Elder, King of Wessex (899-924), 11, 15, 19, 20, 21, 23, 44, 45, 49, 76, 99, 111, 116-8, 127, 134, 169, 188, 191, 193, 210, 218, 220, 227-31, 250, 252, 254-6, 258, 260-2, 264, 266-74, 276, 277, 279-86, 289, 290, 294, 297, 303-7, 309-11, 331, 332, 343, 367, 368, 370, 372-5, 377-81, 384-90, 393-400, 404, 405, 407, 409-12, 415, 418, 420, 424, 428, 430-7, 439, 466-8, 470-5, 477-80, 484-94, 499, 501-5, 507-20, 526, 532, 541-6, 609, 627
Edward the Confessor, 73, 103, 128, 344, 542-4, 546, 553,
Egil's Saga, 158, 187, 193, 196, 206, 332, 419, 443, 447, 452, 464
Ekwall, 84, 137, 151, 361, 369, 421
Ekwall, Eilert, 23, 42, 82-5, 98, 155, 162, 256, 326, 384, 510
Elfhere, 243, 549
Elfledes Boc, 285, 481
Eliseg pillar, 570, 584, 615, 623
Ellendun (battle of), 599
Emsger, 49
English Northumbria, 492, 497, 503, 515
Enville, 523, 524
Eoforwicingas, 282, 298, 479, 480, 486, 501-3, 506, 515, 517, 518, 520
Eohric, King of East Anglia, 188, 270, 376, 378, 379, 387, 491, 517
Eowils, 250, 251, 253-6, 258, 259, 260, 263, 264, 267, 277, 288, 293, 295, 297, 303, 307, 405, 419, 439, 457, 513
Ergyng, 313, 414, 504
Essex, 18, 23, 29, 31, 34, 44, 71, 77, 102, 114, 156, 162, 208, 212, 247, 292, 341, 372, 390, 393, 433, 475, 488, 507, 541, 549, 554, 584, 617
Etchingham, Colmán, 291, 293
Ethelbert, 507
Etheldrida, 501, 505
Ethelmere, 377
Ethelred, surnam'd Michill (see also Æthelred, Lord of the Mercians), 467
ethnic distinctions, 290
Evenlode, 414
Evesham, 256, 507
Ewdness, 42, 147
Exeter, 117, 124, 207, 543, 650
Eyton, R.W., 37, 41, 42, 45, 46, 50, 53, 55, 56, 63, 68, 70, 72, 74, 76, 79, 83, 92-7, 99, 100, 103, 107, 111, 114, 122, 125, 127, 128, 416, 437, 486, 522, 524, 534, 542
Eywys, 293
Eywysl, 252, 287, 497
Fair Galls, 498
Fair-Haired Foreigners, 498
Farnham, 49, 195, 261, 368, 432, 629, 650
Featherstone, 183, 304, 338, 551, 553, 556
Fellows-Jensen, J., 231, 256, 288, 295-7, 384, 639
felsite pillar, Wolverhampton, 559, 568
Fens, 373, 507
feoh, 37
Fibbersley, 317, 318, 319, 321, 322, 335, 614
field-names, 158, 341
Finberg, H.P.R., 27, 35, 82, 93, 97, 103, 104, 135, 169, 222, 230, 291, 415, 424, 433, 493, 507, 541, 550, 560, 565, 566
Finchfield, 162, 556

678

Finland, 16
Finn, 291
Finngaill, 293
Five Boroughs, 19, 132, 282, 294, 388, 404, 472, 473, 508, 513, 610
Fladbury, 414
Flatholme, 49, 477, 504
fleets, 19, 23, 29, 33, 37, 92, 143, 193, 203, 206, 207, 222, 276, 283, 292, 332, 372, 383, 390, 391, 404, 410-22, 420, 432, 436, 473, 499, 504, 505, 549
Fletton, 580, 602
floods, 50, 60, 86, 100, 108
Florence (John) of Worcester, 13, 31, 34, 41, 42, 49, 78, 100, 121-6, 143, 257-60, 276, 278, 286, 288, 290, 291, 299, 372, 375, 377, 389, 391, 393, 395, 398-400, 426, 434, 460, 468, 484, 488, 511, 517, 552, 562, 609
Folcburh, 560, 562
folklore, 23, 64, 101, 237, 307, 337, 354, 465, 621
food, 15, 18, 24, 104, 190, 413, 430, 444-6, 504
Fordun, John of, 193, 282, 314, 389, 399, 660
fortress, 18, 23, 25, 31, 32, 34, 35, 69, 89, 91, 93, 102, 115, 118, 207, 208, 293, 347, 362, 380, 469, 478
fortresswork, 14
fossatum Wulfrini, 158, 610, 614
Fosse Way, 401, 402, 413
Founslow, 127, 522
Fox, Sir Cyril, 23, 24, 59, 116, 172, 200, 536, 640
Fragmentary Annals, The, 218, 229, 230, 291, 292, 381
Francia, 14-7, 21, 23, 34, 38, 105, 106, 115, 171, 205, 212, 403, 562
Frankish annals, 38
Franks, 19, 20, 34, 38, 170, 183, 193, 208, 212, 213, 331, 385, 640
frið, 250, 254-6, 280-2, 386, 405
Friezeland, 154
Frigg, 166
Frisians, 19, 170, 193, 331
Fulford, 189, 348, 462
Fulk Fitz Warine, 79
Furness, 512
Fye, river, 41
fyrd, 116, 183, 191, 212, 254, 256, 368, 381, 431, 433, 435
Gadstone Ford, 58
Gags Hill, 53, 88, 416, 524, 531, 540
Gags Rock, 53
Gailey, 553
Gall-Goídil, 292
Gateholm, 49
Gaul, 90, 372, 390, 411, 541, 562
Gauls, 19, 193, 292, 331
geat, 53, 125, 143, 146
Gelling, Margaret, 2, 3, 19, 27, 31, 35, 55, 82-5, 95, 111, 123, 125, 134, 135, 144, 145, 148, 162-5, 169, 230, 291, 312-4, 423
Gentleman's Magazine, The, 28, 525, 578, 593, 616
Geology, 1, 58
gesta Adelfleda, 481
Gib Hill, 524
gibbet, 45, 55, 236, 524, 530
Giraldus Cambrensis, 91
Giric mac Dúngail, 475
Gironde, 16, 108
Glamorganshire, 31, 225

Gloucester, 18, 20, 23, 39, 40, 74, 86, 90, 91, 103, 107, 143, 146, 228, 256, 299, 301, 311, 334, 360, 379, 385, 402, 403, 408, 413, 416, 442, 467, 476, 477, 482, 484, 504, 505, 507, 541, 542, 544, 545, 565, 566, 586, 606
Gloucester Abbey, 249
Gloucestershire, 7, 23, 24, 36, 39, 49, 85, 132, 150, 218, 258, 272, 277, 313, 406, 413, 466, 467, 542, 567, 586
Glyndwr, Owain, 416
Gnosall, 541, 542, 545, 546, 547, 553
Godebold, 95
Godfride, 377
gods, 163, 165, 167-73, 175, 198, 219, 449
Gokstad, 199, 203, 359, 453
gold, 38, 104, 107, 166, 180, 184, 188, 197, 200, 334, 341, 346, 354-6, 381, 401, 403, 415, 432, 448, 451, 460, 465, 539, 587, 588, 604
Goldthorn, 179, 237, 355
Goltho, 77
Gospels of St Chad, 604
Goths, 13, 168
Gotland, 14, 173, 215, 359
Gough, Robert, 37, 82, 111, 355, 537, 578, 584, 620, 641, 655
Grafton, Richard, 269
Grafton's Chronicle, 372, 376, 387
Graggabai, 497
Grammaticus, Saxo, 200, 219
Grassholm, 49
Grateley Code, 190
graves, 167, 197, 200, 215, 337, 346, 350, 352, 484, 528, 583, 608
Grazeley, 237
Great Army, Danish, 18, 23, 30, 165, 204, 205, 222, 223
Great Barr, 343, 557, 613
Great Saredon, 553
Greece, 590
Greeks, 593, 602
Greenland, 16
Greensforge, 88, 89, 92, 147, 177, 181, 182, 328, 416, 427, 536, 537, 539
Gruffydd ap Llewelyn, 78, 249
Gurmo, 376
Guthfrith, 166, 168, 193, 253-5, 260, 288, 296, 449, 457, 497, 526
Guthrum, 47, 166, 210, 223, 279, 287, 376, 386, 387, 508
Gwent, 31, 38, 222, 223, 225, 226, 228, 231
Gwespyr, 145
Gwynedd, 16, 26, 28, 35, 78, 132, 196, 210, 211, 222-8, 230, 232, 291, 314, 348, 407, 428, 457, 470, 485, 547
Gwynllwg, 31, 38, 225, 226
hacksilver, 47, 383
Hackwood, F.W., 179, 235, 237, 243-6, 309, 343
Haddon, 376
Hadley, Dawn, 41, 296, 333, 349, 403, 408, 513, 516, 527
Hæsten, 23, 24, 38, 347
Hampton Loade, 97, 524
Hamstead, Big, Little and Church, 125
hām-stede, 125
Hamstodeshul, 95, 125, 126
Hanbury, 30, 103, 334, 403, 562, 566
Hanley Castle, 594
Hardwicke, William, 44, 53, 44, 63-5, 78, 81, 111, 112, 537, 539
Harkirke hoard, 398

Harold Blaatand, 376
Harold, King, 77, 78, 167, 199, 260, 289, 348, 349, 438, 456, 462, 611, 612
Harpsford, 131
Harpswood, 131
Harrison, William, 95, 109, 113, 550
Hart, Cyril, 13, 14, 27, 38, 86, 103, 253, 281, 287, 290, 291, 299, 324, 333, 369, 371-4, 377, 386, 401, 433, 437, 489, 493, 508, 510, 520, 552, 567, 609-14
Hartlebury, 148
Hartshorne, William, 69, 70, 72, 78, 81, 179, 522, 523
Harwood, Thomas, 246, 277, 307, 638, 644
Hastings, 7, 188, 189, 201, 311, 340, 343, 346, 349, 430, 438, 450, 454, 456, 463, 495, 541, 617
Hawkes, Jane, 575, 589, 590-4, 601, 605, 606, 621, 622, 625
Hay, The, 95, 126, 130, 131
Haye House, 99
Healdene,, 260, 287, 288, 497
Healfden, 254, 255, 293, 296, 305
Healidine, 377
Heantune, 158, 340, 341, 549, 552-4, 609, 617
Heath Town, 152, 154, 178, 235, 301, 309, 328, 442, 443
Heathen's Ditch, 53, 55
Heavenfield, 314, 616
Hecani, 102, 103, 423
Hedeby, 15
Heimskringla, 188
Hen Domen, 27, 225, 230
Hengest dune, 172
Henry I, 42, 43, 76, 78, 80, 91, 92, 95, 111, 122
Henry III, 247, 546, 654
Henwood Road, 239
Hereford, 23, 63, 73, 77, 78, 93, 94, 99, 102, 103, 115, 117, 123, 124, 134, 143, 155, 178, 213, 228, 413, 414, 420, 423, 448, 477, 504, 505, 544, 567, 604
Hereford Cathedral, 249
Herefordshire School, 619, 663, 664
Hermitage, 44, 45, 56, 58, 87, 91, 523, 534, 525
Heronbridge, 337, 346
Hertford, 34, 118, 127, 134, 475, 546, 561, 562
Hethenedich, 53, 55, 56, 416
Hexham, 314, 616, 618
Heywoode, Thomas, 132, 271, 272, 409, 645
Hiberno-Norse, 22, 167, 170, 282, 371, 384, 388, 389, 397, 405, 445, 472, 480, 511, 512, 513
Hiberno-Scandinavians, 168, 229, 283, 289, 294, 295, 297, 381, 383, 399, 412, 416, 420, 449, 494, 503
Higden, Ranulph, 30, 266, 267, 278, 403, 432, 628
High Hall, Wolverhampton, 236, 557
Higham, Nicholas, 15, 20, 120, 134, 167, 169, 192, 206, 351, 381-4, 388, 395, 397-9, 404, 405, 411, 412, 416, 429, 457, 472, 474, 475, 478, 491-3, 499, 501, 509-13, 515, 526, 618, 627, 628
Highgate, 92
Hildebald, 329, 330, 331, 332, 335, 608
Hildebaldes(c)hull, 329
Hildelith, abbess of Barking, 560, 561
Hill House Farm, 53
Hillborough, 587
Hillhouse Farm, 119, 416
Historia de Sancto Cuthberto, 297, 457, 496, 498, 515
Historia Ecclesiae Dunelmensis, 259, 286
Historia Ecclesiae Lichfeldensis, 549
Historia Ecclesiastica gentis Anglorum, 3, 247, 554

Historia Regum, 174, 258, 259, 261, 282, 286
Hlytta, 254, 255, 260, 445, 457
hold, 96, 105, 126, 198, 244, 254, 255, 256, 259, 260, 271, 282, 288, 294-6, 305, 382, 389, 454, 457, 500, 511, 512, 583
Holinshed's Chronicles, 130, 268
Holme, Battle of the, 101, 177, 188, 193, 210, 270, 283, 295, 297, 343, 372, 375-7, 380, 384, 385, 387-90, 393, 398, 401, 403, 405, 411, 430, 438, 439, 448, 465, 467, 472, 491, 507, 516, 517, 520
Hooke, Della, 43, 86, 93, 97, 103, 105, 111, 152, 155, 159, 162, 178-80, 243, 317, 319, 336, 339, 417, 424, 464, 543, 548, 549, 550-2, 554-6, 558, 559, 563-7, 595, 614, 626
Hope, 19
Horselow, 237, 309
horseshoes, 431, 462
Houghton, A.W.J., 3, 88-90, 92
Hoveden, Roger de, 78, 143, 262, 269
Howel, 485
Hroald, 500, 505
Hrothweard, archbishop of York, 449
human bones, 28, 32, 236, 328, 336, 340, 345-7, 350, 465, 536
Humber, 18, 272, 295, 467, 478-80, 508, 519
Hun(c)deus, 34
Huntbach, John, 233-5, 237, 238, 304, 309, 330, 533, 556, 620
Huntingdon, 35, 42, 100, 118, 143, 201, 259, 260, 262, 267, 272, 273, 278, 285, 286, 288, 296-8, 300, 369, 372-5, 379, 381, 396, 400, 410, 449, 459, 462, 473, 480, 482, 491, 507, 508, 520
Hutchinson, William, 239, 308, 309, 535
Hwicce, 20, 94, 102, 103, 135, 423, 560, 567, 597
hydrology, 1, 58
Hygeb(e)ald, 331
Hygeberht, 596, 597, 598
Hywel, 28, 132, 228, 229, 232, 293, 420, 450, 461, 485
Hywel Dda, 453, 461
Iceland, 15, 16, 169, 219, 220, 227, 350
Idwal, 228, 485
Iken, 103, 565
Ine, King, 173, 191, 204, 544, 565
Ingimund, 30, 226, 229, 280, 380, 382-4, 388, 394, 399, 400, 410, 457, 479, 512, 514
Ingleby, 167, 527, 528
Inkberrow, 414
inter Ripam et Mersham, 492, 510, 511, 512, 514
Inwær, 252, 287, 293, 294, 457, 497
Iona, 475, 618
Iring, 377
Irishmen, 15, 19, 193, 331, 380
Iron Age, 48, 87, 116, 119, 120, 126, 181, 195, 312, 355
Isle of Man, 28, 225, 227, 231, 232, 350, 404, 411, 412, 497, 528, 618
Ivarr the Boneless, 474, 497
Jænberht, 596, 598
Jellinge, 358
Jenkins, Anne E., 72, 243, 427, 541, 542, 543, 546, 553, 558, 566, 567, 568
Jewell, Richard, 583, 584
Jones, J.P., 27, 29, 38, 89, 92, 150, 151, 197, 199, 224, 225, 226, 228, 230, 238-40, 303, 308, 339, 454, 455, 481, 500
Judith, 480
Juthwal, 485
Kelly, S.E., 560, 561, 619
Kempsey, 414
Kendrick, T.D., 383, 577, 581, 584
Kenelm, (Cynehelm), 599599

Kent, 14, 18, 20, 23, 25, 33, 71, 171, 200, 203, 212, 250, 254-6, 258, 270, 272, 273, 285, 347, 373, 375, 377, 378, 383, 410, 420, 424, 432, 433, 437, 448, 543, 544, 547, 549, 594
Kings Meadow, 320, 321, 322, 323, 326
King's Orchard, 120
King's Swinford, 306
Kingslow, 233, 355
Kinvaston, 551, 553, 554
Kinver, 83, 302, 306, 346, 351, 355, 547
Kirclesford, 158, 178, 338, 614
Kirnesford, 158, 317, 614
Knaves Castle, 536
Knightwick Bridge, 72
Knowle, 58, 178
Knute, 377
Knútr, 293, 370, 390
La Sauve Majeure, 544
Ladby, 453
Lambarde, William, 270, 649
Lancashire, 19, 28, 193, 225, 231, 282, 288, 382-4, 397, 398, 492, 509, 510, 512, 628
languages, 22
Lapley, 567
Lappenberg, J.M., 276, 288, 372, 387, 411
Lastingham, 333, 584
Lavelle, Ryan, 30, 115, 127, 134, 183, 184, 186, 187, 197, 208, 213, 214, 229, 282, 340, 381, 400, 411, 415, 419, 423, 455, 466, 478
Lawley, George T., 157, 308, 343, 344, 536, 563
Le Sauve Majeure, 101
Lea, 18, 34, 35, 36, 37, 48, 127, 134, 212, 225, 386
Leechbook, 215, 216
Leek, 578, 581, 584, 585, 620
Leicester, 19, 118, 388, 470, 473, 477, 478, 501, 508, 548, 610, 628
Leigh, Sir John, 107, 550, 665
Leighton, 31, 89, 386
Leland, John, 69, 80, 81, 132, 143, 246, 268, 417, 489, 528, 547, 621
Lemore Mount, 80
Lethaby, W.R., 579, 584, 594
Letocetum, 146, 164, 177, 182
Leveson family, 316, 318, 321, 323, 554, 621
Liber Eliensis, 186, 219, 282, 297, 463
Liber Vitae Dunelmensis, 560, 563, 564, 566
Lichfield, 15, 63, 93, 94, 99, 102, 154, 156, 163, 164, 176, 180, 181, 182, 249, 302, 308, 313, 333, 334, 346, 353, 413, 415, 423, 448, 490, 492, 510, 544, 546, 547, 549, 555-8, 561, 567, 590, 591, 593, 595, 596, 598-603, 619
Lichfield angel, 602, 603
Lichfield Gospels, 15, 415
LIDAR surveys, 46, 54, 89, 124, 233, 535
Life of St Guthlac, 221
Lilleshall, 95, 96, 108, 243, 318, 319, 320, 322, 323, 334, 403, 570
Lincoln, 19, 166, 167, 274, 334, 388, 401, 460, 473, 479, 480, 483, 486, 493, 499, 508, 509, 519, 610, 616
Lindisfarne, 12
Liobsynde, 103
Little Chester, 146
Little Low, 164, 235, 309, 337
Little Quatford, 41, 107
Little Saredon, 553
Little Shrawardine, 133, 134, 141, 142, 145

Little Wenlock, 94
Llandaff, 477
Llandeilo, 15, 415, 604
Llandeilo Fawr, 15, 415
Llandough-juxta-Cogan, 593
Llandrinio, 31
Llangorse, 228, 476, 506, 507
Lloegr, 467
Llyn Syfadden, 476
Lockington-Hemington, 91, 109
Loire, 16, 23, 49, 105, 115, 204, 372, 617
London, 3, 4, 16, 18, 19, 21, 25, 30, 34, 37, 41, 66, 88, 90, 97, 114, 116, 127, 131, 164, 166, 177, 178, 195, 203, 207, 224, 242, 246, 269, 270, 276, 301, 338, 346, 355, 381, 387, 392, 406, 467, 468, 475, 478, 518, 522, 541, 544, 553, 558, 582, 627, 628
Longer Moor, 319, 321, 322, 324, 325, 335, 336
Longermore, 321, 322
longphort, 16
Longridge, 567
longship, 14
Lorsch Gospels, 591
Loveridge, Henry, 238, 239
Low Field, 234, 235, 238, 274, 461
Low Hill, 233, 345
Luchfield, 155, 156, 327, 441
Ludeca, 600
Ludlow, 77, 79, 89, 352
Lutley, 553
Lyminge, 14
Lyminster, 42
Lynam, Charles, 571, 579
Madeley, 94, 424, 642
Magonsaete, 102, 103
Magonsæte, 134, 144, 146
Maine, Normandy, 76
Mallam, 583
Malmesbury, William of, 41, 109, 193, 198, 200, 230, 261, 278, 285, 289, 314, 401, 404, 406, 432, 481, 489, 490, 493, 507, 508, 510, 514, 545, 583, 608
Malverley, 59
Manchester, 118, 119, 146, 280, 289, 488, 491, 510, 511, 513
Mander, Gerald P., 4, 43, 44, 158, 159, 161, 178, 179, 236, 238, 240, 241, 243, 244, 246, 247, 309, 322, 325, 539, 550, 553, 554, 556-8, 563, 565, 570-2, 578, 580, 584, 610, 614, 620, 621
March End, 152, 154, 309, 316, 317, 322-4, 336
Marcliff, 15, 341, 414
Marianus Scotus, 256
Maserfeld, 314
Masham cross shaft, 580, 581
Mason, J.F.A., 41, 53, 55, 81, 82, 83, 89, 94, 96, 99, 100, 112, 113, 524
Medehamstede, 104
medical texts, 215
Mediterranean, 17, 23, 199, 618
Medway, river, 90
Meigion, 113, 416
Mercia, 11, 14, 18-20, 23, 24, 30, 32, 40, 50, 94, 102, 104, 107, 115, 117, 118, 127, 128, 135, 142, 143, 145, 163, 164, 169, 171, 181, 192, 210, 218, 222-5, 227, 229, 231, 242, 250-2, 254, 255, 256, 259, 260, 262, 264, 267, 268, 270-4, 276, 279, 280, 283, 285, 286, 289, 298, 304, 305, 314, 340, 348, 367, 370, 372, 373, 378, 379, 385, 386, 388, 389, 393-402, 404, 406, 408, 410, 412, 413, 415, 416, 419, 420, 422, 428, 430, 436, 437, 445, 463, 464, 466, 467, 468, 470, 472, 473, 476-81, 485-

8, 490, 492-4, 501-15, 517-20, 540, 542-9, 555, 556, 560-2, 565, 566, 569, 578-80, 583, 586, 609, 610, 612, 616-8
Mercian Register, 115, 118-20, 132, 228, 253, 285, 286, 287, 298, 299, 375, 379, 394, 395, 400, 407, 409, 435, 467, 475, 476, 487, 488, 502, 503, 506, 515, 520
Mere, 245, 553
Merewalh, 102, 103, 104, 565
Merfyn, 26, 227
Merridale, 559
Merrill family, 324
Merrill's Hall, 324, 325, 337
Merrill's Hole Colliery, 324
Mersea Island, 31, 34, 49
Mersey, river, 21, 116, 132, 224, 229, 280, 400, 416, 420, 491, 492, 508, 510, 511
micel here, 204, 205
Middlewich, 30, 224, 610
Mildburh, 73, 74, 94, 103, 104, 107, 221, 334, 403, 562, 565
Mildthryth, abbess of Minster in Thanet, 565
Mill Hill, 234, 235, 310, 317, 330, 336, 337
Millichope, 74, 96, 105, 108, 544
Milton, 23, 205, 272, 652
Milton, John, 272
mint, 30, 113, 166, 294, 350, 351, 370, 381, 388, 394, 449, 473, 493, 497, 499, 510, 545
Mitton, 553
Modwenna, St, 113
Monmore, 161, 178, 236
Monmouth, 93, 653
Montgomery, Roger de, 71, 75, 79, 82, 95, 99, 100, 105, 108, 133, 542, 544
Moor End, 152
Moor Farm, 96, 130
Mor Brook, 71, 99, 130, 131
Moreton, 414
Morfe Common, 50, 54, 55, 427, 523, 525, 527, 528
Morfe Forest, 44, 45, 50, 53, 55, 60, 61, 99-101, 128, 130, 416, 417, 523, 524
Morfe Hall Farm, 523
Morfe House Farm, 523
Morfeheath Farm, 523
Morgannwg, 30
Morville, 87-9, 103, 105, 113, 123, 176, 302, 414, 416
Mose, 53
Moseley Hole, 152, 158, 178, 236, 302, 309, 336, 338, 442, 614
motte-and-bailey castle, 76
mounted forces, 1, 212
Much Wenlock, 87, 104, 107, 221, 334, 351, 403, 414, 415, 493, 504, 547, 562, 565, 566
Muchall, 152
nails, 431, 527
Nantes, 16, 203
Nantwich, 30, 224
Neachells, 153, 160, 178, 180, 235, 317, 324-7, 336-8, 441
Nennius, 7, 108
Netherton, 56, 95, 99, 100, 107
New Cross, 152, 154, 160, 235, 307, 309, 327-30, 332, 336, 337, 341, 441, 442, 443
New Invention, 180, 301, 553
Nightingale, Joseph, 307, 417
Noose Lane, 158, 180, 236, 317-9, 320-3, 335, 336, 614
Norðanhymbre, 280, 508
norðhere, 279, 280, 405, 509
Nordley, 97, 152, 154, 158, 234, 310, 330, 337

Norman-French, 23, 136, 311
Normans, The, 23, 27, 70, 72, 74, 77-9, 112, 144, 185, 201, 225, 271, 303, 305, 349, 387, 454, 525, 534, 636, 661
Norse, 3, 12, 13, 22, 28, 29, 132, 166, 167, 169, 170, 181, 188, 192, 201, 204, 207, 230, 231, 279, 280, 282, 289, 293-8, 303, 371, 372, 374, 380-4, 388, 389, 396, 398, 399, 404, 405, 410, 411, 435, 438, 445, 449, 457, 466, 472-5, 479, 494, 501, 511-17, 579
North Low, 154, 234, 235, 276, 306, 309, 337, 441
Northern Army, 19, 386, 398, 400, 475, 513, 515
Northey Island, 49, 86, 341
Northgate Museum, 50, 55
Northicote, 178
Northumbria, 11, 12, 18, 19, 20, 22, 23, 30, 31, 33, 34, 37, 38, 48, 117, 165, 166-8, 192, 193, 205, 250, 252, 254-6, 258, 262, 266, 267, 276, 279-82, 294, 295, 300, 314, 346, 348, 351, 369, 370, 372, 380, 386-9, 391, 393, 395-401, 403, 405, 409, 410, 420, 428, 442, 463, 472-4, 476, 479, 480, 491, 492, 494, 497, 501-4, 507-11, 513-8, 520, 526, 539, 547, 560, 562, 565, 579, 583, 610, 611, 613, 616, 618, 627
Northwich, 30, 224
Norton Canes, 164
Norway, 12, 167, 168, 196, 199, 219, 264, 289-91, 295, 348, 349, 351, 359, 360, 446
Norwegians, 12, 13, 15, 16, 21, 189, 280, 289-92, 371, 381, 382, 395, 397, 429, 474, 498, 503
Norwich, 41, 73, 265, 273
Nottingham, 3, 4, 9, 18, 19, 118, 127, 134, 207, 388, 430, 473, 478-80, 486, 488, 508, 519
nova domus, 43, 65, 73, 76, 77, 80, 111
Nunnaminster, 489
Nuthurst, 19
oaths, 23, 36, 218, 282, 283, 292, 298, 451, 454, 479, 501, 506, 513
Óðinn, 165, 167, 168, 169, 171, 172, 219, 446
Offa, 249, 597
Offa's Dyke, 136
Offa's Dyke, 23, 24, 25, 27, 31, 32, 102, 103, 120, 127, 132, 145, 373, 464, 508
Offlow, 182, 236
Ogilby, John, 45, 88, 523, 524
Ogley Hay, 164, 553, 556
Ohter, 254, 255, 258, 260, 288, 500
Ohtor, 254, 256, 295, 439, 457, 477, 499, 500, 504, 505, 506
Olaf, 20, 21, 187, 254, 419, 458
Olafr (Guthfrithson), 211, 610
Olafr (Sihtricson), 610
Old Camp, 138, 139, 140
Old House Moat, Wednesfield, 325
Old Perton, 553
Old Sodbury, 406, 467
Old Swinford, 306
Oldbury, 54, 55, 121, 130, 147, 178, 634
Oliver, George, 237, 244, 307, 558, 572, 578, 584, 593, 621, 622, 627
Onennau Megion, 416
Onomasticon Anglo-Saxonicum, 560, 659
Orderic Vitalis, 43, 75, 76, 91, 111, 122, 262, 349
Ordheah, 24, 29
Orosius, 115, 290
Oseberg, 453
Osfrith, 254, 255, 260, 288, 296, 433, 445, 457
Oslofjord, 13
Oswy, 314
Otherton, 553
Othulf, 253, 254, 255, 260, 288, 294
Otter, 498, 500

Ottir, 496, 497
Ougeres Klif, 126
Ouse, river, 55, 97, 373, 403, 508
Oxford, 3, 4, 64, 83, 94, 102, 262, 288, 392, 398, 401, 406, 407, 437, 468, 475, 500, 518, 541, 550, 560, 628
paganism, 162, 163, 166, 167, 170, 173, 354, 445, 500, 526
pagans, 1, 12, 15, 19, 26, 40, 150, 162, 169, 170, 171, 173, 189, 210, 341, 345, 349, 380, 388, 389, 397, 414, 445, 502, 517
Palmeresberie, 155, 158
Pannett, David, 58, 59, 100
Panpudding Hill, 42, 121, 122
Paradise, 69
Paris, 16, 30, 106, 123, 143, 205, 230, 264, 267, 270, 278, 303, 372, 385, 390, 393, 400, 432, 449, 518, 550, 562, 580
Parker Chronicle, 250, 285, 424
Parret, river, 24, 26, 448
Parva Quatford', 41
Patshull, 532
Pattingham, 125, 148, 233, 355, 416, 547, 631
Paul, William, 237, 305, 423, 541, 550
Peada, 163
Pee, Ralph, 58, 59, 61
Pelsall, 152, 243, 244, 551, 553, 554, 556
Pembrokeshire, 25, 49, 359, 476, 606
Penda, 38, 102-4, 113, 163, 247, 314, 348, 536, 546, 547, 554, 560, 561, 565, 617
Pendeford, 163, 177, 444, 553, 561
Penk, river, 155, 177, 233, 301, 553, 567
Penkridge, 30, 152, 177-9, 341, 413, 417, 441, 541-3, 545-9, 552, 553, 567, 568, 608, 664
Penn, 152, 164, 179, 237, 241, 339, 355, 427, 556, 626
Pennocrucium, 30, 164, 177-9, 181, 338, 413, 441, 444, 534, 567
penwie, 152, 179, 181
Pepperhill, 532, 533, 534
Perry Hall, 154, 159
Pershore Abbey, 249, 414, 564
Peterborough, 104, 128, 257, 550, 580, 602
Pevsner, Nikolaus, 62, 66, 67, 582, 584
Pictish Chronicle, 496
pigs, 328, 336, 463, 464
Pillaton, 553
Pitt, William, 276, 307, 656
place-names, 16, 28, 83-5, 94, 98, 105, 112, 125, 137, 141, 147, 148, 150-2, 155, 157, 162, 164, 165, 169, 170, 172, 173, 175, 182, 225, 231, 233, 234, 288, 295, 312, 326, 341, 344, 345, 355, 356, 382, 383, 398, 423, 440, 510, 511, 512
plague, 36, 37
pledges, 298, 479, 503
Plot, Robert, 151, 233-6, 241, 246, 275, 278, 304-6, 318, 328, 330, 343, 349, 356, 383, 532-5, 555, 609, 620
Polesworth, 113, 403, 414, 482, 500
Pont de L'Arche, 106
porridge, 430, 446
Portobello, 152, 154, 158, 317, 553, 614
Portway, 178, 179, 181, 246, 338, 441, 442, 464
Portwey, 155
Powel, David, 270, 478
Powys, 3, 23, 26, 78, 132, 211, 222, 223, 485, 509, 570
Prestwood, 154, 155, 157, 177, 178, 317, 336, 338, 441, 464, 614
Prestwood Road, 157

687

privileges, 281, 283, 544
prostitute, 190
Quanrud, John, 9, 13, 229, 279-81, 288-90, 292-5, 382-99, 409, 492, 508, 509
Quatford, 1, 41-50, 53-63, 65-88, 90-113, 119-35, 141, 144, 145, 147, 148, 173, 181, 182, 340, 343, 346, 350, 352-5, 362-4, 366, 416, 417, 421-4, 427, 443, 470, 523, 524, 526, 536, 540-5
Quatford Castle, 42, 63, 65, 66, 67, 72, 76
Quatford church, 72, 73, 75, 77, 86, 94, 96, 105, 107, 125, 544
Quatford Minore, 107
Quatford Parva, 107
Quatford spearhead, 362, 364
Quatone, 84
Quatt, 72, 82-5, 89, 93, 96-8, 101, 107, 237, 523
Rackham Bank, 42
Radnor, 104, 653
Rædwald, 442
Raffield, 47, 48, 69, 656, 657
Ragnall, 166, 169, 218, 292, 294, 297, 305, 371, 380, 382, 383, 388, 395, 410, 449, 457, 473, 474, 479, 489, 490, 492, 493, 496, 497, 499, 501-4, 511, 513, 515
Ramsbury Cross, 360
Ramsey, 49, 92, 223, 253, 257, 259, 284, 286, 449, 611
Ranulph Higden, 30, 266, 267, 278, 403, 432, 628
rations, 430, 431
ravens, 198, 348, 462, 607
Ray and Bapty, 24, 25, 103, 134, 143, 504
Reading, 40, 41, 187, 205, 207, 301, 458, 461, 619, 620
Reculver, 580, 581, 583, 586, 587, 594, 598, 599, 619
Redhill, 89, 181, 570
relics, 7, 15, 30, 107, 166, 333, 400-4, 442, 448, 467, 476, 483, 507, 509, 516, 520, 541, 550, 604, 616
Repton, 18, 20, 30, 41, 47, 61, 127, 167, 181, 207, 249, 287, 301, 345, 413, 457, 527, 528, 565-7, 597, 600, 601
Rhodri Mawr, 16, 27, 28, 132, 210, 222-4, 226, 228, 229, 428, 457, 461
Rhuddlan, 227, 230, 231, 485, 513
Rhydwhiman, 27, 70, 134, 225
Ribbesford, 72
Ribble, river, 381, 382-4, 399, 400, 457, 473, 492, 510-12, 628
Richards Castle, 77
Ringerike, 358, 359
rivers, 14-8, 21, 25, 43, 46, 48, 60, 61, 90, 95, 97, 106, 108, 116, 124, 146, 181, 205, 301, 423, 491
Rix, Michael, 571, 573, 576, 583-5, 593, 621, 658
Robert de Bellême, 42, 43, 71, 73, 75, 78-82, 99, 111, 113, 114, 120-2
Robert of Torigni, 262, 303
Rochester, 90, 212, 301, 552
Rocque, John, 87, 524
Rodbaston, 551, 553
Roffe, David, 75, 76, 129, 164, 242, 339, 551, 553, 556, 557
Rollason, David W., 402, 499, 513, 560, 562
Roman road, 17
Roman roads, 17
Romanesque, 619, 634, 662, 664, 668
Romans, 10, 17-9, 30, 47, 49, 68, 71, 76, 86-93, 98, 101, 105, 108, 109, 112, 116, 118, 126, 144-8, 158, 164, 167, 177-82, 184, 186, 220, 224, 233, 304, 306, 328, 338, 341, 343, 347, 353, 358, 361, 384, 394, 401, 402, 413, 416, 417, 427, 440, 441, 443, 444, 466, 476, 477, 483, 491, 497, 532, 534-7, 539, 549, 567, 570, 580-3, 587, 590
Rome, 20, 23, 26, 193, 403, 550, 583, 590
Roper, John, 237, 582
Roughton, 89, 416

688

Roulowe Field, 241, 355
Rowley Hill, 233
Royal Free Chapels, 2, 427, 541, 542, 546, 548
Royal Peculiar, 73
royal saints, 334, 403, 476, 481
Rudge Heath, 89, 182, 354, 416, 539
Rumblelows, 234, 243
Runcorn, 116, 120, 145, 334, 470, 472, 513
Rushock Hill, 24
Russia, 16, 351
Ruthwell cross, 603
Ryknield Street, 180, 413, 442, 464
saddles, 213, 214
sæffan mor, 301, 421
Salopia Antiqua, 69, 70, 644
salt, 30, 104, 105, 224
Saltmoor, 301
Sandbach, 580, 588-91, 594, 595, 601, 605, 606, 609, 619, 625, 644
Sandy, 49, 526, 555
Sandybury, 53, 526
Sashes, 127
Savile, Henry, 251, 252, 507, 659
Saxonland, 498, 499, 500, 501, 506
Scandinavians, 12, 13, 15-7, 21, 22, 28, 30, 74, 118, 142, 166, 167, 170, 182, 193, 204, 205, 216, 219, 221, 224-30, 232, 252, 280, 282-4, 288, 289, 292-8, 332, 338, 341, 352, 353, 366, 368, 380, 382-4, 389, 390, 394-7, 399, 405, 408-12, 414, 416, 419-22, 424, 426-8, 430-1, 439, 441-3, 445, 447, 448, 455-8, 460, 461, 463, 466, 471-4, 478, 488, 493-9, 501-3, 512, 514, 517, 539
scaru, 137, 141
scearu, 137, 141
Scergeat, 1, 118, 119, 132-5, 141, 143, 145, 146, 470, 539, 540, 545
Scomer, 49
Scotland, 8, 16, 78, 170, 177, 193, 212, 232, 291, 293, 296, 300, 350, 410, 431, 433, 474, 475, 496, 497, 500, 501, 618
Scots, 8, 187, 282, 314, 384, 388, 389, 393, 399, 458, 465, 468, 474, 475, 479, 492, 496, 502, 503, 506, 515, 516, 610, 627
Scott, W., 42, 63, 68, 156, 178, 241, 306, 312, 350, 535, 536, 537, 561
scræf, 137, 140, 143
Scredington, 137, 141
sculpture, 166, 231, 360, 383, 570, 575, 578, 582, 583, 585, 586, 587, 594, 605, 606, 618
Scurfa, 253-6, 258-60, 264, 267, 268, 271, 277, 288, 295, 377, 439, 457
Scutchamer Knob, 172
Seawall, 148, 152
Seaward, 377
seaxes, 451
Sedgley Beacon, 563
Seine, 16, 34, 37, 38, 49, 105, 106, 108, 115, 203, 205, 495, 526, 640
Seisdon, 182, 236, 241, 355, 427, 428, 534, 536, 554, 556
select fyrd, 116, 431
Seven Books of History Against the Pagans, 115
Severn, 11, 18, 23-8, 31, 34-8, 41-6, 48-50, 53, 54, 56, 57-63, 67, 68, 70, 71, 80-108, 110-15, 118, 120-34, 137, 141, 142, 145, 152, 181, 182, 222, 225, 252, 272, 273, 276, 292, 308, 340, 350, 352-4, 358, 362, 366, 411, 413-6, 418, 419-27, 430, 439, 440, 441, 443, 444, 464, 466, 467, 470, 477, 500, 504-6, 522, 523, 534, 539, 540, 544, 545, 547, 617
Severn Bore, 108
Shaw, Stebbing, 148-52, 156, 157, 160, 178, 234-8, 241-6, 275, 276, 302, 304-7, 310, 317, 322, 330, 332, 343, 355, 416, 533, 535, 537, 553, 555, 557, 558, 572, 578, 593, 610, 622, 624
Shelfield, 553, 556

689

Shenstone, 353, 551, 556
shield, 185, 187, 190, 192, 194, 197-9, 208, 214, 346, 450, 453, 526
shield-wall, 185, 187, 214, 450, 453
Shifnal, 550
Shoebury, 23, 225, 292
Short Heath, 154, 158, 553, 614
Showell, 148, 152, 160, 179, 245, 302, 304
Shrawardine, 70, 133, 134, 135, 141, 142, 144, 145
Shrewsbury, 28, 31, 69, 70, 74, 75, 78-80, 87, 88, 91, 95, 103, 107, 109, 121, 133, 135, 136, 142, 145, 247, 316, 334, 340, 398, 403, 416, 540-7, 617, 628
Shropshire, 3, 4, 31, 37, 42-5, 50, 54, 59, 63, 64, 69, 72-5, 77, 78, 81-3, 86-9, 94, 95, 97, 98, 100, 104, 111, 112, 114, 120, 121, 124, 125, 129, 130, 132, 133, 134, 135, 145, 157, 163, 230, 235, 237, 243, 275, 313, 317, 318, 328, 338, 341, 350, 352-4, 362, 418, 419, 423, 424, 524, 532, 534, 535, 537-44, 548, 586, 610, 612, 617, 627, 628
Shugborough, 146
Sidebottom, 595, 607, 660
Sidebottom, P. C., 622
Siefred, 166, 193, 370, 371, 405, 449, 510, 513
Sigehelm, 374, 491
Sigeline, 377
Sigeric, Archbishop of Canterbury, 550
Sihtric, 20, 33, 285, 292, 408, 445, 473, 474, 490, 493, 497-500, 511, 526
silver, 38, 78, 146, 187, 193, 198, 200, 231, 283, 346, 350-3, 355, 357-9, 363, 364, 381, 383, 413, 419, 448, 513, 528, 584, 604
Simeon of Durham, 20, 121, 123, 143, 173, 174, 258, 259, 261, 262, 278, 282, 286, 370, 372, 386, 388, 390, 395, 399, 400, 488, 499, 503, 505, 511, 516, 517, 520
Sims-Williams, Patrick, 94, 102, 103, 333, 562
Sittingbourne, 23
skeletons, 44, 45, 64, 200, 215, 220, 328, 337, 345, 346, 347, 348, 350, 462, 465, 526
Skilgate, 137, 141
Skokholm, 49
Slade Lane, 48, 81, 97, 101, 124-6
Sladeford, 81, 87, 97, 101
Slater, T.R., 120, 121, 543, 548, 549, 552, 554-6, 564, 565, 595, 626
slings, 190, 452
Smallshire, John, 152-8, 160, 177, 178, 180, 234, 235, 252, 301, 302, 309, 310, 317-29, 332, 336-9, 507, 614
Smalman, John, 57, 63-7, 69, 70, 72, 76-80, 97, 99, 128
Smestall, river, 160, 245, 563
Smestow Brook, 148, 152, 234, 340
Smyth, Alfred, 13, 20, 21, 26, 28-30, 33-5, 41, 92, 93, 168, 169, 171, 193, 198, 203, 207, 208, 211, 219, 221, 223-5, 229, 230, 251, 253, 257, 258, 276, 284, 291-3, 296, 299, 303, 305, 310, 369, 371-3, 378, 380, 394, 403, 406, 407, 422, 438, 441, 445, 446, 449, 457, 462, 474, 475, 479, 486, 487, 493, 496, 497, 500, 515, 526, 546, 560, 561, 608, 609, 610, 612
Somerset, 19, 26, 112, 150, 205, 299, 433, 437, 492, 501, 504, 515, 540, 618
Somery, Ralph de, 245, 553
Sonday, St, 246
soothsayer, 296, 445, 449
Southlow, 156, 164, 235, 327, 329
Sow, river, 120
Speed, John, 130, 271, 302, 661
Spy Bank, 537
St Albans abbey, 25, 550
St Alkmund, 95, 334, 403
St Asaph, 134
St Bertelin, 334, 541, 543, 558
St Cedd, 333

690

St Chad, 221, 333, 542, 556, 561, 565, 604
St Ciricius, 475
St Cuthburga, Wimborne, 541
St Cynehelm (Kenelm), 599
St Mary Magdalene, Bridgnorth, 72
St Mary's, Stafford, 507, 543, 547, 544, 558, 614
St Milburh, 74, 544
St Mildburh's Testament, 104, 221
St Modwenna, 113
St Nicholas Oake, 524
St Nicholas's Oak, 530
St Oswald, 252, 333, 334, 360, 400, 401, 403, 404, 442, 460, 467, 476, 483, 484, 509, 516, 520, 541, 542, 586, 606, 619
St Oswald's, Gloucester, 484
St Peter's, Salzburg, 593
St Peter's church, Wolverhampton, 550
St Peter's, Wolverhampton, cross-shaft, 2, 5, 358, 547, 569, 570, 572, 576, 577, 582-6, 588, 592-4, 607, 608, 614, 615, 618, 619, 626
St Sythe, 95, 113
stabling, 431
Stackhouse, Rev. Thomas, 522, 523
Staff Rood Crosses, 584
Stafford, 4, 20, 72, 78, 93, 118, 120, 145, 177, 178, 234, 244, 246, 250, 256-9, 263, 266, 267, 269, 271, 285, 286, 299, 300, 309, 334, 377, 416, 432, 436, 470, 473, 481, 487, 513, 524, 541, 543, 545, 547, 548, 558, 567, 593
Staffordshire, 4, 7, 19-21, 63, 89, 97, 113, 126, 132, 137, 141, 145, 146, 150, 154, 158, 164, 178-80, 182, 184, 191, 234, 235, 240, 242, 243, 244, 267, 268, 269, 272, 273, 275, 276, 277, 302, 304, 305, 307, 310, 312, 314, 316, 320, 321, 323, 328, 341, 346, 349, 350, 353, 356, 359, 403, 407, 412, 416, 417, 424, 427, 428, 448, 451, 464, 489, 524, 532-5, 539, 541, 542, 546-8, 551, 553, 555, 562, 566, 570, 572, 578, 582, 584-6, 611, 613, 620, 623
Staffordshire Hoard, 164, 451
Staines, 112
Stamford, 19, 26, 41, 127, 195, 196, 215, 261, 274, 282, 311, 349, 388, 462, 473, 478, 479, 485, 486, 492, 503, 508, 509, 610
Stancliffe, Clare, 314, 334, 403, 442, 463, 616, 618, 619
Stanlow, 233, 355
Stanmore Farm, 87, 416
Stanmore Hall, 529
Stanton, 19, 341, 414
Stanton Lacy, 414
Steepholme, 49
Stenton, Sir Frank, 3, 19, 23, 24, 25, 26, 49, 82, 91, 103, 158, 162-4, 171, 173, 174, 178, 191, 193, 194, 197, 203, 205, 281, 282, 294, 297, 299, 300, 310, 367, 371, 383, 386-8, 395, 398, 402, 405, 424, 457, 494, 499, 509, 510, 514-6, 558, 560, 561, 565, 566
Stephen, 249
Stoke on Trent, 547
Stoke St Milborough, 414
Stonylowe, 238
Stottesdon, 414
Stowheath, 152, 154, 157, 159, 160, 178, 180, 236, 243-6, 302, 310, 317, 323, 329, 333, 344, 441, 552, 553, 556
Stowman's Hill, 158, 160, 236, 614
Strata Marcella, 29
Stratford, 72, 103, 414, 537, 611
Stratford Brook, 537
Stratford-upon-Avon, 72, 103
Strathclyde, 8, 16, 132, 187, 232, 393, 458, 465, 474, 475, 479, 492-4, 497, 503, 511, 515

straw, 77, 430
Strawberry Lane, 152, 328
Strengate, 132, 143
Stretton, 553, 567
Stroeg, 377
Stroud, 72,
Studd, Robin, 546-8
Sturluson, Snorri, 168, 187, 526, 646
Sully, 49
superstition, 217
Sussex, 18, 100, 247, 285, 313, 433, 549, 610, 612, 617
Sutherland Collection, 158, 316, 319, 320, 321, 323, 325, 336
Sutherland Estate, 157, 177, 338
Sutton Hoo, 37, 44, 46, 198, 212, 569, 584, 605
Sutton Maddock, 89, 539
Swancote, 88-90, 92, 416, 428
Swedes, 13, 16
sword, 165, 167, 186, 190, 194, 196, 200, 201, 216, 219, 347, 359, 363, 372, 432, 446, 451, 454, 455, 478, 523, 528
Sygefrid, 377
synod' of Chelsea, 596
Taliesin, 232, 509
Tame, river, 153, 162, 236, 317, 322, 563, 567, 614
Tamworth, 20, 39, 107, 115-7, 120, 123, 124, 135, 145, 211, 228, 233, 249, 282, 334, 381, 407, 413, 427, 434, 445, 470, 473, 478, 479, 483, 484, 487, 488, 493, 499, 501, 508, 515, 526, 541, 543-5, 547, 553, 609-12, 652
Taylor, Isaac, 41, 42, 90, 302, 553, 558, 621
Tees, 18, 395, 583, 585
Telford, 89, 149, 570
Telford, Thomas, 149
Teme, 72
Tempsford, 55, 97, 218, 477, 491
Tenbury, 72
Tengvik, G., 83, 663
tents, 419, 429, 431, 445, 537
Tetbury, 414
Tettenhall, 1, 3, 1, 7, 8, 9, 11, 22, 54, 82, 89, 93, 115, 118, 132, 133, 141, 142, 147-52, 154, 156, 159, 163-6, 169, 170, 172, 177, 181, 182, 185, 195, 197, 198, 208, 210, 227, 228, 233, 235, 236, 238, 239, 242, 244, 249, 253-7, 262, 263, 267, 269, 270, 272, 274, 276-9, 281, 282, 284, 286-9, 292-312, 316, 320, 326, 331-3, 335-41, 343-6, 349, 350, 352-5, 357, 361, 366, 367, 372, 381-4, 388, 389, 393, 400, 405, 408-10, 415, 417, 419-21, 423, 424, 427, 428, 430, 431, 435, 436, 438-41, 444, 447-9, 451, 452, 456, 458, 461, 466, 468, 472-4, 481, 492, 494-8, 500-3, 505-7, 512, 513, 515, 520, 532, 536, 541-3, 545-9, 553-7, 567, 568, 588, 594, 615, 617, 618, 620
Tettenhall Clericorum, 151
Tettenhall Regis, 151
Tewkesbury, 23, 414, 483
Thacker, Alan, 103, 114, 333, 334, 339, 401-4, 407, 442, 507, 541, 543, 545, 548, 560, 630, 631, 663
Thames, 16, 23, 24, 26, 34, 41, 49, 90, 127, 292, 346, 347, 372, 508, 518
Thanet, 48, 49, 164, 232, 242, 565
The Danes' Pillar, 594
Thelwall, 145, 489, 491, 513
Theodore, Archbishop of Canterbury, 221, 546, 560-2, 565, 653
Thor, 166, 167, 528
Thornbury, 143
Thorneycroft, Thomas, 308
Thorpe, Benjamin, 39, 82, 93, 121, 150, 253-6, 258, 276-8, 290, 294, 295, 372, 387, 397, 398, 408, 411, 425, 426, 433, 475, 611

Thoyras, Paul de Rapin, 305
Three Fragments, 1, 30, 198, 381, 382, 384, 394, 396, 397, 409, 434, 438, 474, 496, 498-502, 504-8, 514-6, 521
Thunor, 169
Thurfreth, 254, 255, 288, 457
Thyra, 376
Ticklerton, 74
Tiddingford, 274, 282, 289, 374, 385-92, 396, 398, 399, 407, 410, 428, 501-3, 511, 514-8, 520
Tilbury Camp, 151
Tildesley, J.C., 158, 159, 161, 178, 179, 236, 238, 241, 243, 244, 247, 309, 322, 543, 550, 553, 554, 556-8, 565, 578, 610, 614, 620, 621
Tinkers Castle, 536
Tong, 1, 343, 352, 357-9, 360, 361, 539, 542, 552
Tong Fragment, 343, 357, 361
Topographical History of Staffordshire, 276
Torigni, Robert de, 262, 303
Torksey, 41, 47, 48, 207, 351
Tostig, 78, 348, 462
Towcester, 116, 119, 477, 491
tower coinage, 144, 382
Towton, 247, 348, 431, 455, 617, 632, 642
tradition, 30, 96, 103, 104, 166, 173, 186, 193, 198, 208, 230, 239, 243-5, 247, 308, 320, 334, 349, 380, 382, 403, 441, 449, 450, 454, 463, 479, 532, 542, 543, 547, 550, 559, 565, 583, 604, 607, 608, 610, 616, 618
treaties, 19, 33, 34, 170, 225, 273, 276, 279, 282-4, 289, 305, 383, 385-91, 396, 399, 400, 404, 407, 409-11, 423, 428, 441, 466, 480, 495, 501-3, 506, 508, 511, 513-8, 520
Trent, river, 21, 41, 47, 61, 91, 101, 109, 113, 127, 152, 153, 162, 181, 218, 308, 322, 345, 401, 416, 464, 508, 527, 547, 567, 613
Trentham, 553, 562
Trescott, 301, 421, 549, 553, 556, 568, 609
Trevisa, John, 267, 278, 628
Trewhiddle, 352, 360, 582
Tribal Hidage, 547, 567
tribute, 18, 19, 28, 38, 207, 225, 231, 232, 292, 399, 447, 486, 513, 549, 560
trimoda necessitas, 102, 115
Trimpley, 59
Tripartite Indenture, 416
tufa, 70, 71, 72, 77, 81
tumuli, 2, 44, 233-5, 237-9, 244, 304, 306-8, 337, 343-5, 355, 356, 522-6, 528, 539
tumulus, 68, 126, 172-4, 233-8, 240, 241, 276, 304, 307, 309, 317, 330, 332, 337, 345, 355, 441, 461, 522, 525
Tunberht, 600
Turner, Sharon, 276, 617, 619, 628
Tuter's Hill, 148
Tweddle, Dominic, 583, 584, 615
Twyning, 414
Uhtred, 19
Unbeiniaeth Prydain, 450
Underhill, 159, 178
Upton Cresset, 87, 354
Uter, 377
Uxacona, 89, 181, 416, 570
Valhalla, 295, 449, 453
vallum monasterium, 548, 549, 555, 595
Valor Ecclesiasticus, 94, 99
Victoria and Albert Museum, 573, 580, 582, 594, 606, 622, 624
Vignats, 75

Viking, 1, 7, 9, 11-6, 28, 30, 32-4, 37, 38, 41, 47, 48, 53, 55, 61, 62, 69, 75, 97, 101, 102, 106, 115, 117, 120, 143, 146, 166, 167, 169, 170, 183, 187, 191-8, 200, 203-8, 210, 212-4, 218, 222, 224, 226- 30, 257, 260, 279, 282, 283, 287, 289-94, 298, 303, 340, 343, 345-50, 352, 353, 355, 358-60, 362-4, 366, 368, 371, 372, 381-3, 394, 397, 403, 411, 413, 420, 422, 425, 434, 441, 447, 449, 450, 458, 466, 472-6, 479, 493-5, 497, 499, 500, 505, 512, 513, 527, 528, 548, 570, 594, 627
villa regalis, 556
Viroconium (see also Wroxeter), 18, 58-60, 86, 88-90, 144, 360, 414, 533, 567, 570, 571
Vuodnesfelda campo, 154, 175, 251, 252, 278, 299-301, 314
Wace, 454
Waddensbrook, 152, 153, 156, 157, 177, 316, 317, 319, 320, 321, 322-6, 330, 335, 336, 441
Wadmore, 317, 319, 323, 324
Wærferth, 313, 406, 489
Wainwright, F.T., 20, 21, 23, 26, 27, 30, 31, 142, 145, 169, 225-7, 229, 286, 288, 292, 295, 297, 298, 310, 381-3, 394, 396, 397, 407, 410, 434, 438, 439, 451, 457, 470, 471, 478, 479, 485, 486, 488, 489, 494, 496, 497, 498, 500-6, 512, 514, 515, 526
Wales, 1, 3, 16, 21, 23, 26-30, 34, 35, 78, 81, 88, 91, 104, 108, 123, 132, 142, 145, 170, 177, 181, 196, 210, 221-32, 270, 280, 291, 307, 313, 380, 407, 461, 475, 476, 478, 484, 489, 494, 497, 500, 501, 504, 505, 506, 548, 586, 627
Walgrene, 326, 327, 328
Walker, Ian, 29, 32, 34, 142, 251, 288, 378, 385, 407, 410, 422, 434, 437, 468, 472, 478, 480, 481, 485-9, 502, 518, 607
Wallingford, 124, 263, 387, 393, 541, 544
Wallingford, John of, 263
Walls, The, 89, 181, 182, 416, 423, 427, 443, 532, 534, 536, 537, 539, 540
Walsall, 4, 152, 179, 236, 276, 305, 307, 309, 315, 335, 547, 553, 557, 563
Walter the smith, 95, 128
Walter, Hubert, 74, 95, 96, 108, 128, 130, 314, 331, 558, 620
Wansdyke, 165, 173
war-dogs, 453
Wareham, 124, 127, 207
warren, 525, 526, 539
Warstone, The, 535
Warwick, 118, 120, 145, 178, 246, 470, 657, 658, 666
Warwickshire, 3, 19, 72, 94, 97, 148, 178, 326, 407, 473, 489, 552, 586, 611, 613, 614
Wasey, George Leigh, 41, 50, 56, 57, 67, 70, 72, 78, 81, 95, 99, 107, 108, 123, 129
Water Eaton, 30, 177, 178, 338, 341, 417, 441, 443, 534, 553
Watery Lane, 153, 180, 322-5
Watkins-Pitchford, W., 42, 45, 46, 54, 55, 65, 67, 68, 71, 77, 81, 82, 99, 107, 122, 524, 525
Watling Street, 19, 21, 30, 35, 89, 146, 164, 177-82, 233, 279, 339, 346, 353, 361, 416, 427, 441, 443, 508, 534, 539, 567, 570
Weardbyrig, 145, 470, 472
weather, 431
Wedmore, treaty of, 19, 301
Wednesbury, 163, 164, 170, 172, 175-9, 242, 302, 312, 323, 339, 345, 553, 556, 557, 638
Wednesfield, 1, 54, 84, 115, 147, 152-8, 160, 162-4, 169, 170, 172-82, 233-6, 242-3, 252-3, 264, 267, 274, 276-8, 284, 288, 298-313, 315-28, 330-3, 335-9, 341, 343-6, 350, 354, 355, 361, 366, 384, 417, 421-4, 427, 440-4, 456, 461, 464, 497, 536, 549, 552-6, 563, 567, 568, 608, 610, 614, 617
Wednesfield Heath, 154
weir, 53-6, 59, 60, 62, 95-8, 100, 101, 105, 108, 134, 416
Welland, river, 26, 41, 390, 478, 491
Welsh, 8, 12, 15, 16, 22-4, 26-8, 31-2, 35, 37, 38, 41, 42, 70, 78, 79, 83, 103, 104, 108, 113, 123, 132, 134, 142, 143, 145, 187, 193, 208, 210, 213, 221-32, 249, 290-3, 303, 313, 314, 329, 380, 384, 395, 406, 412, 414, 420, 425, 428, 430, 450, 457-9, 461, 464-8, 470, 476, 477, 481, 485, 488, 492-5, 497, 498, 500, 501, 505, 509, 519, 534, 536, 547, 616
Welshmen, 19, 26, 78, 193, 331, 478
Welshpool, 11, 23, 29, 31, 37, 545

Wendover, Roger of, 25-7, 30, 35, 41, 49, 84, 123, 124, 224, 230, 263, 264, 267, 278, 298, 299, 369, 370, 372, 374, 385, 390, 395, 396, 400, 432, 449, 468, 518
Wenlock Edge, 71, 87, 91, 92, 96, 102, 536
Wenlock, Little, 94
Werburgh, 30, 103, 334, 360, 403, 546, 548, 562
Werferd, 259, 296
Wergs, 7, 149, 238, 276, 307, 309
Wessex, 18-20, 26, 29, 33, 37, 47, 48, 115-7, 127, 134, 135, 164, 181, 191-3, 204, 210, 223-6, 228, 230-2, 251, 254-6, 259, 260, 279, 292, 367, 369, 370, 372, 378, 379, 383, 386, 387, 391, 395, 405-8, 420, 430, 433, 434, 437, 438, 462, 464, 466, 476, 479, 486-9, 494, 499, 501, 504, 508, 515, 517, 518, 543, 545, 561, 565, 579, 582, 586, 609, 610, 616
West Saxons, 18-20, 23, 26, 34, 187, 212, 223, 226, 252, 256, 258, 268, 276, 277, 280, 299, 304, 306, 308, 395, 407, 413, 414, 420, 421, 428-30, 432, 434, 436, 460, 476, 479, 486, 502, 545
Westbury, 136, 143, 145, 414
Westerna, 102, 103
Westminster, 71, 267, 270, 303, 489, 541, 553
Westmorland, 170, 231, 394, 493
Whiston, 553
Whitelock, Dorothy, 3, 12, 19, 27, 35, 49, 82, 83, 115, 116, 118, 143, 169, 174, 185, 187, 188, 190, 193, 197, 198, 200, 201, 206, 209, 212, 230, 250, 252, 259, 283, 286, 288, 291, 294, 298, 299, 300, 310, 314, 332, 339, 375, 379, 383, 386-8, 395, 397, 405, 425, 432, 435, 438, 445, 462, 475, 476, 478, 479, 504, 505, 512, 516, 517, 542, 549, 550, 552, 560, 561, 608-12, 627
Whittemore Hill, 535
Widsith, 13
Wightwick, 43, 151, 238-41, 308, 309, 553, 556
Wigingamere, 119, 386, 477, 488, 491
Wigmore, 414
Wildmoor, The, 536
Wilkes, Richard, 152, 235, 236, 244-6, 305, 306, 620
Willanhalch, 164, 242
Willenhall, 1, 152-4, 159-61, 164, 181, 234-6, 242-7, 305, 309, 317-9, 321-3, 326, 329, 332, 335, 552, 553, 556, 557, 563, 566, 567, 594, 608, 615
William of Malmesbury, 41, 109, 193, 198, 200, 230, 261, 278, 285, 289, 314, 401, 404, 406, 432, 481, 489, 490, 493, 507, 508, 510, 514, 545, 583, 608
Williams ab Ithel, John, 23, 28, 225, 226, 228, 500, 627, 666
Wilne, Derbyshire, 574
Wilton, 491
Wiltshire, 26, 165, 297, 360, 372, 408, 433
Wimborne, 369, 372, 541, 544, 545, 565, 635
Winchcombe, 115, 249, 413, 414, 558, 586, 597, 598, 599
Winchester Farm, 88
Windmill Field, 235, 317, 329
Windsor, 620
Wininicas, 103
Winwædfeld, 314
Wirksworth, 603
Wirral, 8, 22, 28, 30, 35, 225, 226, 229, 280, 282, 314, 381, 384, 385, 397, 400, 410, 435, 457, 472, 497, 512, 514, 629, 633, 648
Wise, Francis, 305, 611
Wistoche, 264
witan, 250, 254-6, 369, 385, 408, 424, 468, 486, 487, 488
witenagemots, 408
Withington, 414
Woden, 1, 154, 162, 163, 164, 169-73, 175, 264, 267, 299, 324, 339, 423, 446
Woden's Dale, 423
Wodendale, 423
Wodnesbeorg, 172

Wollesford, 157
Wollmore, 157
Wolnoth, 377
Wolverhampton, 1, 2, 4, 5, 43, 44, 149, 151, 152, 154-6, 158-65, 177-81, 233-47, 276, 302, 304, 305, 307, 309, 312, 318, 321, 323, 327, 328, 330, 335, 336, 338-41, 344, 345, 351, 354, 355, 417, 427, 428, 439, 441, 442, 444, 464, 489, 534, 535, 541-3, 545, 547-59, 561-70, 572, 576-8, 580-6, 588, 592-5, 605, 607-11, 613-5, 617-21, 623-5, 628
Wolverhampton cross-shaft, 2, 5, 358, 547, 569, 570, 572, 576, 577, 582-6, 588, 589, 591-5, 604, 607-9, 614, 615, 618, 619, 626
Wombourne, 306, 547
Wood End, 154, 156, 336
Wood Hayes, 154, 177, 336
Woolf, Alex, 20, 228, 293, 294, 349, 369, 419, 475, 487, 489, 497
Wootton, 55, 99, 414
Worcester, 18, 21, 23, 26, 34, 37, 46, 49, 73, 75, 86, 90, 92, 94, 99, 103-5, 111, 113, 117, 120-4, 135, 145, 179, 181, 223, 237, 255-7, 278, 288, 298-300, 305, 341, 394, 395, 406, 416, 423, 424, 448, 469, 472, 478, 483, 486, 487, 489, 493, 502, 504, 558, 561, 567, 609, 611, 614, 619
Worcester, Florence (John) of, 13, 31, 34, 41, 42, 49, 78, 100, 121-4, 126, 143, 257-60, 276, 278, 286, 288, 290, 291, 299, 372, 375, 377, 389, 391, 393, 395, 398-400, 426, 434, 460, 468, 484, 488, 511, 517, 552, 562, 609
Worcester, William of, 111
worðig, 135, 141
worðign, 135, 136, 141, 143
Worfield, 43, 45, 63, 71, 72, 97, 148, 163, 350, 352, 416, 525, 536
Worthen, 136, 143
Worthenbury, 143
Wrekin, 27, 28, 35, 102, 104, 169, 230, 291, 567
Wr(e)ocensæte, 27, 28, 35, 134, 144, 146, 230, 291
Wrottesley, 177, 274, 275, 304, 444, 532-4, 543, 553, 611
Wrottesley Lodge Farm, 534
Wrottesley Park, 177, 444, 532
Wroxeter (see also Viroconium), 18, 58, 59, 60, 86, 88, 89, 90, 360, 414, 533, 567, 570, 571
Wulfgeat, 542, 543, 552, 611, 613
Wulfhere, 104, 163, 166, 210, 221, 247, 542, 543, 546, 547, 548, 556, 560-2, 565, 566, 568
Wulfred, 598, 599
Wulfric Spot, 492, 510, 611, 613, 614
Wulfrini, 158, 236, 610, 614
Wulfrun, 2, 155, 158-60, 162, 178, 179, 180, 236, 242, 243, 245, 301, 317, 319, 328, 336, 341, 417, 464, 489, 541-3, 549-52, 555-8, 560, 563, 564, 566, 568, 569, 582, 593, 605, 608-15, 617
Wulfruna's Well, 610
Wulfsige the Black, 613
Wulfyth, Queen, 367
Wye, river, 23, 104, 477, 504, 505, 543
Yate, 414
Yetminster, Dorset, 583
yew trees, 201, 555
York, 18, 20-2, 26, 33, 165, 166, 168, 169, 192, 206, 207, 211, 219, 224, 230, 231, 255, 256, 279, 280, 282, 288, 289, 292-5, 298-301, 360, 370, 371, 380, 382-4, 387, 388, 395, 398, 401, 404, 405, 408, 409, 412, 413, 419, 420, 428, 445, 449, 462, 466, 470, 473, 474, 479, 484, 492-4, 497, 499-503, 509-13, 515-7, 519, 526, 548, 551, 552, 587, 604, 610, 611, 619, 620, 627, 628
Yorke, Barbara, 114, 165, 171, 193, 297, 298, 300, 334, 367, 368, 378, 403, 560, 562, 566, 604
Yorkshire, 4, 8, 19, 148, 181, 231, 247, 256, 258, 262, 358, 412, 488, 494, 510, 512, 525, 554, 570, 580, 581, 583-5, 611
Ystrad Marchall, 29
Ystrad Tywi, 28, 35, 37, 225, 226, 228, 407, 485

'How these curiosities would be quite forgot, did not such idle fellows as I am put them downe!' – John Aubrey, Antiquary, 1626-1697.

Lightning Source UK Ltd.
Milton Keynes UK
UKOW05n0640060317
295905UK00004B/23/P

Spittle feyldes

Bishopesgate

S. Botolph

Aldgate

East Smithfyeld

Towre Posterne

S. Katherynes

Bellyns / Lion kaye / Custom h. / The to...

LONDON

A HISTORY IN MAPS

LONDON

A HISTORY IN MAPS

By Peter Barber

with notes on the engravers by Laurence Worms
edited by Roger Cline *and* Ann Saunders

The London Topographical Society *in association with* The British Library • 2012

This is Publication No. 173 of the
London Topographical Society

First published in 2012 (reprinted 2013) by
The London Topographical Society
3 Meadway Gate
London NW11 7LA
and
The British Library
96 Euston Road
London NW1 2DB

© text London Topographical Society
© illustrations British Library unless otherwise stated

Every effort has been made to contact all copyright holders. The publishers would be grateful if copyright holders whom we have been unable to contact would make themselves known.

ISBN 978 0 9020 8760 6 (LTS)
ISBN 978 0 7123 5879 8 (BL)

FRONT ENDPAPER: Extract from John Norden, *A Guide for Cuntrey men ... by the helpe of wich plot they shall be able to know how farr it is to any street. As allso to go unto the same, without forder troble* (London: Peter Stent, 1653). Copperplate engraving. 51.2 × 72 cm. Maps Crace I.33. Reproduced at approximately its true scale

BACK ENDPAPER: William Daniell, *A View of the East India Docks 1808*. Coloured aquatint. 55.8 × 87.9 cm. Maps K. Top. 21.31-5c Port. II. Tab. Reproduced at approximately two-thirds scale

DESIGNED AND PRODUCED IN GREAT BRITAIN
BY OBLONG CREATIVE LTD
PRINTED AND BOUND IN CHINA

CONTENTS

Editorial vii

London: A History in Maps viii

Section One **The Walled City 50–1066** 1
   1.1 Within the Walls 1
   1.2 A Renaissance Vision 10
   1.3 London from Bankside 16
   1.4 The First Maps 27
   1.5 The London Reality 48

Section Two **London Reborn** 51
   2.1 Rebuilding the City 51
   2.2 The City and Westminster 62
   2.3 Profiting from Development 68
   2.4 The Coming of the West End 73
   2.5 London Life 86

Section Three **'Sweet, Salutarie Air': London's Countryside** 104
   3.1 London's Villages 104
   3.2 From Noble Mansion to Gentleman's Villa 116
   3.3 'Sweet, Salutarie Air' 126

Section Four **Out of Sight: The East End and Docklands** 140
   4.1 London's Workshop 141
   4.2 The Coming of the Docks 156

Section Five **The Age of Improvement** 168
   5.1 The Demands of Commerce 168
   5.2 Regency Grandeur 186

Section Six **The Mean Streets of Victorian London** 218
   6.1 Unbridled Growth 218
   6.2 Hard Times 228
   6.3 The Coming of the Railways 240
   6.4 Sewage and London-wide Government 248
   6.5 Open Spaces, Health and Social Harmony 256
   6.6 New Roads for Old 264
   6.7 Stanfords for Maps 270

Section Seven **Metroland** 282
   7.1 Different Londons 282
   7.2 Be a Sport… 296
   7.3 Imperial Grandeur 306
   7.4 Getting Around 312
   7.5 A to Z 326
   7.6 Destruction from the Air 337

Section Eight **Maps in Modern London** 344
   8.1 Convulsions 344
   8.2 London Resurgent 352
   8.3 London Present and Future 364

Index 375

THE LONDON TOPOGRAPHICAL SOCIETY

The following publications reproduce in full those items included in the exhibition.

1. Van den Wyngaerde's View of London, *c.* 1550 (Topographical Society of London), 1881–2: 52.5 × 295.5 cm, on 7 sheets 80 × 59.5 cm, with sheet of text. (See No. 151.)

2. Plan of London, *c.* 1560, attributed to Hoefnagel (T.S.L. 1882–3): from Braun and Hogenberg's *Civitates Orbis Terrarum*, second state showing Royal Exchange, 35.5 × 49 cm, on sheet 56.6 × 74.5 cm.

4. Visscher's View of London, 1616 (T.S.L. 1883–5): 42 × 216.5 cm, on 4 sheets 59 × 78 cm. (See 'Notes on Visscher's View of London, 1616' by T. F. Ordish, *L. T. Record*, VI, 39.)

8. Kensington Turnpike Trust Plans, 1811, by Salway, of the road from Hyde Park Corner to Counter's Bridge (1899–1903): 52.5 × 1711 cm, in colour, 30 sheets and title-page 61 × 69 cm. (See 'Notes on Salway's Plan', by W. F. Prideaux, *L. T. Record*, III, 21, and V, 138.)

12. Hollar's West-Central London, *c.* 1658, a bird's eye-view (1902): 33.5 × 44 cm on 43 × 59 cm. (See 'Hollar's Map', W. R. Lethaby and R. Jenkins, *L. T. Record*, II, 109.)

14. Kip's View of London, Westminster and St James's Park, 1710 (1903): *c.* 134 × 208 cm on 12 sheets 56 × 61 cm. (See No. 161.)

15. Morden and Lea's Plan of London, 1682, also known as Ogilby and Morgan's Plan (1904): 150.5 × 238 cm on 9 sheets 56 × 76.5 cm and 3 sheets 56 × 38.5 cm. (See Morden and Lea's Plan of London', by W. L. Spiers, *L. T. Record*, V, 117.)

17. Map of Elizabethan London, formerly attributed to Ralph Agas (1905): 71.5 × 183 cm on 8 sheets 59.5 × 44 cm.

18. Faithorne and Newcourt's Map of London, 1658 (1905): map *c.* 82.5 × 180.5 cm on 6 sheets 51 × 64 cm and 2 sheets 51 × 31.5 cm, and title on 4 pieces.

19. Hollar's Long View of London, 1647 (1906–7): 46 × 233.5 cm in 7 pieces on 6 sheets 64.5 × 48.5 cm.

22. Hollar's 'Exact Surveigh', 1667 (1908, 1909): 54.5 × 82.5 cm on 2 sheets 64.5 × 48.5 cm.

24. The Palace of Whitehall, View from the River, 1683 (1909): 35.5 × 62.5 cm on sheet 61 × 89 cm. (See 'View of the Palace of Whitehall', by W. L. Spiers, *L. T. Record*, VII, 26.)

34, 36, 37, 41, 42, 43 and 44. Rocque's Plan of London, 1746 (1913–19): 203 × 387.5 cm, with key, on 49 sheets 43 × 57 cm. (See 'Rocque's Plan of London', by H. B. Wheatley, *L. T. Record*, IX, 15.)

48. Tallis's Plan of Bond Street (1921): 12 pages 14.5 × 23 cm. (See 'Tallis's Street Views of London', by E. B. Chancellor, *L. T. Record*, XII, 67. See also No. 110.)

54. A London Plan of 1585 (1925): 57 × 98 cm on sheet 63.5 × 91 cm, folded.

95 and 96. A Survey of the Parliamentary Borough of St Marylebone, including Paddington and St Pancras, 1834, engraved by B. R. Davis (1962–3): slightly reduced scale, 103 × 86.5 cm on 2 sheets 50.5 × 92.5 cm.

104. Hollar's 'Exact Surveigh', 1667 (1966, extra publication): 54.5 × 82.5 cm on sheet 63.5 × 88 cm. Replacing No. 22.

106. Horwood's Plan of London, 1792–9 (1966, extra publication, a memorial to the work of the London Survey Committee): 221 × 406 cm, iv + 32 sheets 62.5 × 58.5 cm; includes variant plates from sheets A1 and B1.

110. *John Tallis's London Street Views*, 1838–40 and 1847, with introduction by Peter Jackson (1969, extra publication): 20 × 28.5 cm, full cloth; published by Nattali and Maurice in association with the London Topographical Society. (See Nos 48 and 160.)

112. Hollar's Long View of London from Bankside, 1647 (1970, extra publication): 47 × 236.5 cm on 7 sheets 63.5 × 48 cm. (Replacing No. 19.)

118 and 119. Thomas Milne's Land Use Map of London and Environs in 1800, with an introduction by Dr G. B. G. Bull (1975–6): north and south sections each 51 × 103 cm on 3 sheets, iii + 6 sheets 61 × 42 cm in folder, available in colour and in black and white.

122. *The A to Z of Elizabethan London*, compiled by Adrian Prockter and Robert Taylor with introductory notes by John Fisher (1979): 31 × 22 cm, Linson, published concurrently by the Society and by Harry Margary in association with Guildhall Library.

126. *The A to Z of Georgian London*, with introductory notes by Ralph Hyde (1982): 30.5 × 22 cm, Linson, uniform with 122, published concurrently by the Society and by Harry Margary in association with Guildhall Library.

130. Charles Booth's Descriptive Map of London Poverty 1889, with an introduction by Dr David A. Reeder (1984): in colour, 93 × 117.5 cm on ii + 4 sheets averaging 51 × 64 cm in folder.

131. *The A to Z of Regency London*, with introduction by Paul Laxton and index by Joseph Wisdom (1985, extra publication): 30.5 × 22 cm, Linson, uniform with 122, published concurrently by the Society and by Harry Margary in association with Guildhall Library.

135. *The London Surveys of Ralph Treswell*, ed. by John Schofield, illustrated with all of Treswell's London plans, several in colour (1987): 28 × 23 cm.

145. *The A to Z of Restoration London* (The City of London, 1676), with introductory notes by Ralph Hyde and index by John Fisher and Roger Cline (1992): 30.5 × 22 cm, Linson, uniform with 122, published concurrently by the Society and Harry Margary in association with Guildhall Library.

150. *Joel Gascoyne's Engraved Maps of Stepney*, 1702–04, with an introduction by W. Ravenhill and D. Johnson (1995); 8 sheets 54.5 × 62.5 cm in folder + with an explanatory booklet.

151. *The Panorama of London circa 1544*, by Anthonis van den Wyngaerde, ed. Howard Colvin and Susan Foister (1996): 34 × 48.5 cm.

153. *The Whitehall Palace Plan of 1670*, by Simon Thurley (1998): hardback, 55 pp., 31 × 23 cm.

159. *Tudor London – a Map and a View*, ed. Ann Saunders and John Schofield (2001): paperback, 57 pp., 30 × 22 cm.

160. *John Tallis's London Street Views 1838–1840*, with the revised and enlarged views of 1847. Introduction and biographical essay by Peter Jackson (2002): hardback, 305 pp., 20 × 29 cm. (See Nos 48 and 110.)

161. Jan Kip's View of London, Westminster and St James's Park 1720, with an introduction by Ralph Hyde and keys by Peter Jackson (2003): 131 × 192 cm on 12 map sheets each *c.* 51 × 69 cm. (See No. 14.)

164. *The London County Council Bomb Damage Maps 1939–1945*, with an introduction by Robin Woolven, ed. Ann Saunders, published in association with London Metropolitan Archives (2005): 215 pp., 37 × 27 cm.

EDITORIAL

From November 2006 to March 2007 an exhibition on London was held at the British Library. Selected and organised by Peter Barber, Head of Maps, it proved to be the most visited British Library exhibition to that date. Since it was arranged in conjunction with the British Library's publication of *London: A Life in Maps* by Peter Whitfield, there was no catalogue, not even a handlist giving the captions; the lack was keenly felt by those attending.

The Council of the London Topographical Society, realising the need, decided to publish the captions with every item illustrated in part or in whole. The British Library readily co-operated in the venture and it now appears with an introduction by Mr Barber. We hope that the volume will become a milestone in the representation of London's growth and development, besides being appreciated as a beautiful volume.

The Society thanks the British Library for its partnership and all those other Libraries, institutions and individuals who have so generously and readily allowed reproduction of items in their collections. The book has been designed by Derek Brown and his team at Oblong.

The Society hopes that you will enjoy this book and from it come to a deeper understanding of London's development.

Ann Saunders
Editor

LONDON: A HISTORY IN MAPS

Over the past 2000 years London has developed from a small town, fitting snugly within its walls, into one of the world's greatest and most dynamic cities. The exhibition of 2006–07, and now this book, illustrate and help to explain the transformation. Side-by-side with the great, semi-official but sanitised images of the whole city, there are the more utilitarian maps and plans of the parts — actual and envisaged — which perhaps present a more truthful picture. Some maps played a part in the story by acting as spurs for major developments, others simply reflected change. But the maps and panoramas are far more than topographical records. They all have something unique to say about the images, concerns, assumptions, ambitions and prejudices of their makers and their age: occasionally revealing attitudes which were too crass to be put into writing. Collectively they constitute a uniquely revealing life of London and Londoners.

Note: except where otherwise stated the measurements are those of the sheet and not of the mapped or engraved area within the neat lines. 15 cm are approximately 6 inches. Each entry ends, where appropriate, with the British Library shelfmark or manuscript number.

SECTION ONE
THE WALLED CITY 50–1666

1.1 WITHIN THE WALLS

London was founded by the Romans in about 50 AD and acquired its walls between 190 and 225. Despite some expansion south of London Bridge, and to the North and West along the Strand, London remained essentially within its walls until after 1550.

Before about 1480 its standard image was of a walled town, its particular identity being revealed through the depiction of a few key buildings. This became a symbol, to be seen on medals and municipal seals as well as illustrating texts on parchment. In the late Roman period, the walls and the Thames were sufficient to identify London. Notable buildings, like St Paul's and the Tower, with London Bridge and the town gates, were being added by the thirteenth century.

1.1 A symbolic view of London with a fence partly substituting for walls, *c.* 1450. Cotton MS Claudius E.iv.f.4

DID JULIUS CAESAR STOP AT ST PANCRAS?

In 55 and 54 BC, a century before the foundation of London, Julius Caesar made brief forays into England. William Stukeley (1687–1765), physician, parson, antiquary and a pioneer of modern archaeology, became convinced that he had established a large encampment around St Pancras church. This plan, superimposing the camp's supposed outlines onto a map of the area as it was in 1749, visualises his fantasy. The earthwork shown in the drawing, supposedly a royal British palace, with the Roman walled city of London in the distance, is probably only the remains of a moated medieval rectory. But old St Pancras church does incorporate late Roman brickwork.

1.1.1a   William Stukeley, 'Caesar's Camp at Pancras called the Brill' [1749]. Ink and watercolour on paper. 33 × 20.3 cm. Maps Crace XIV.48

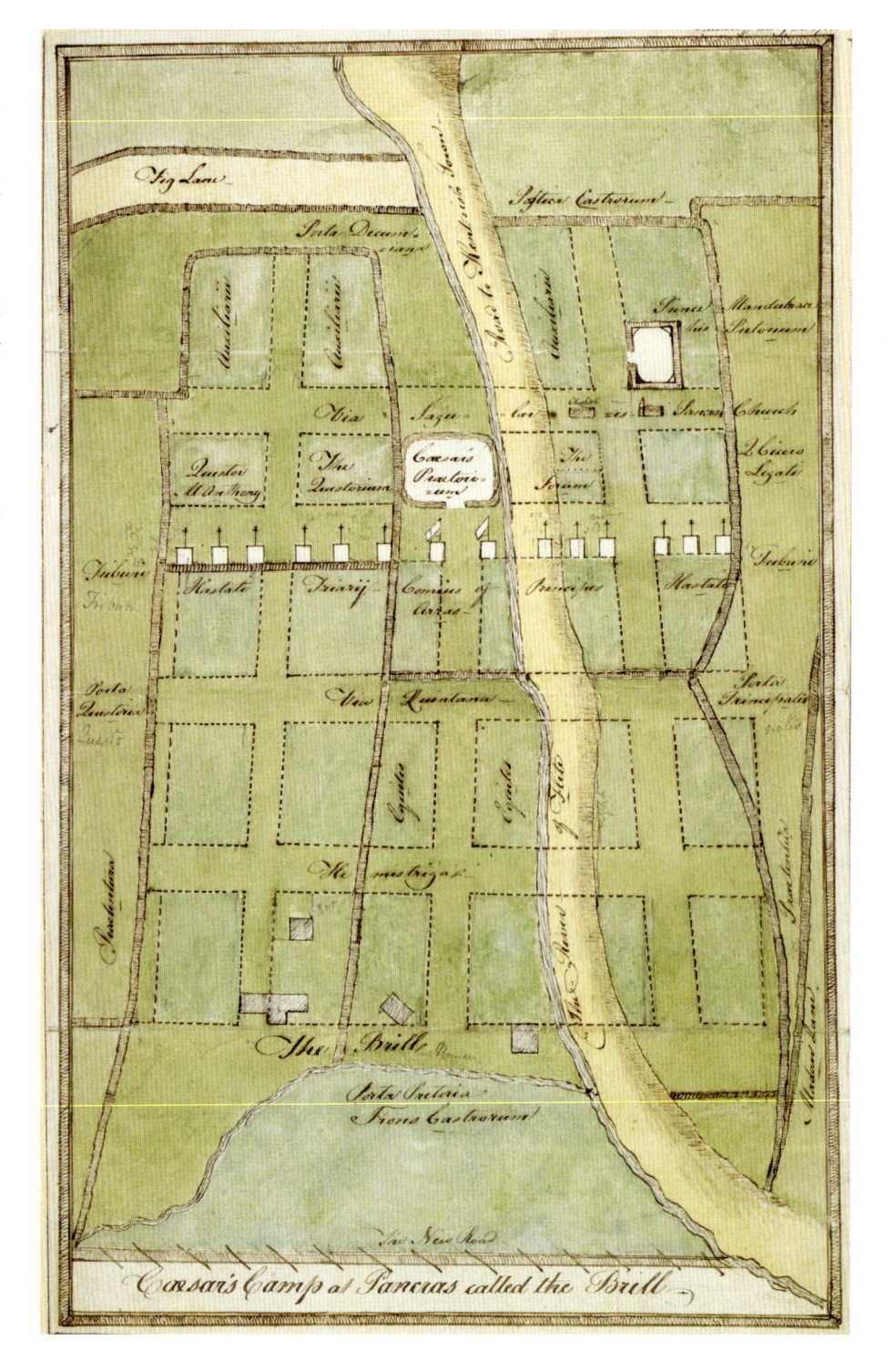

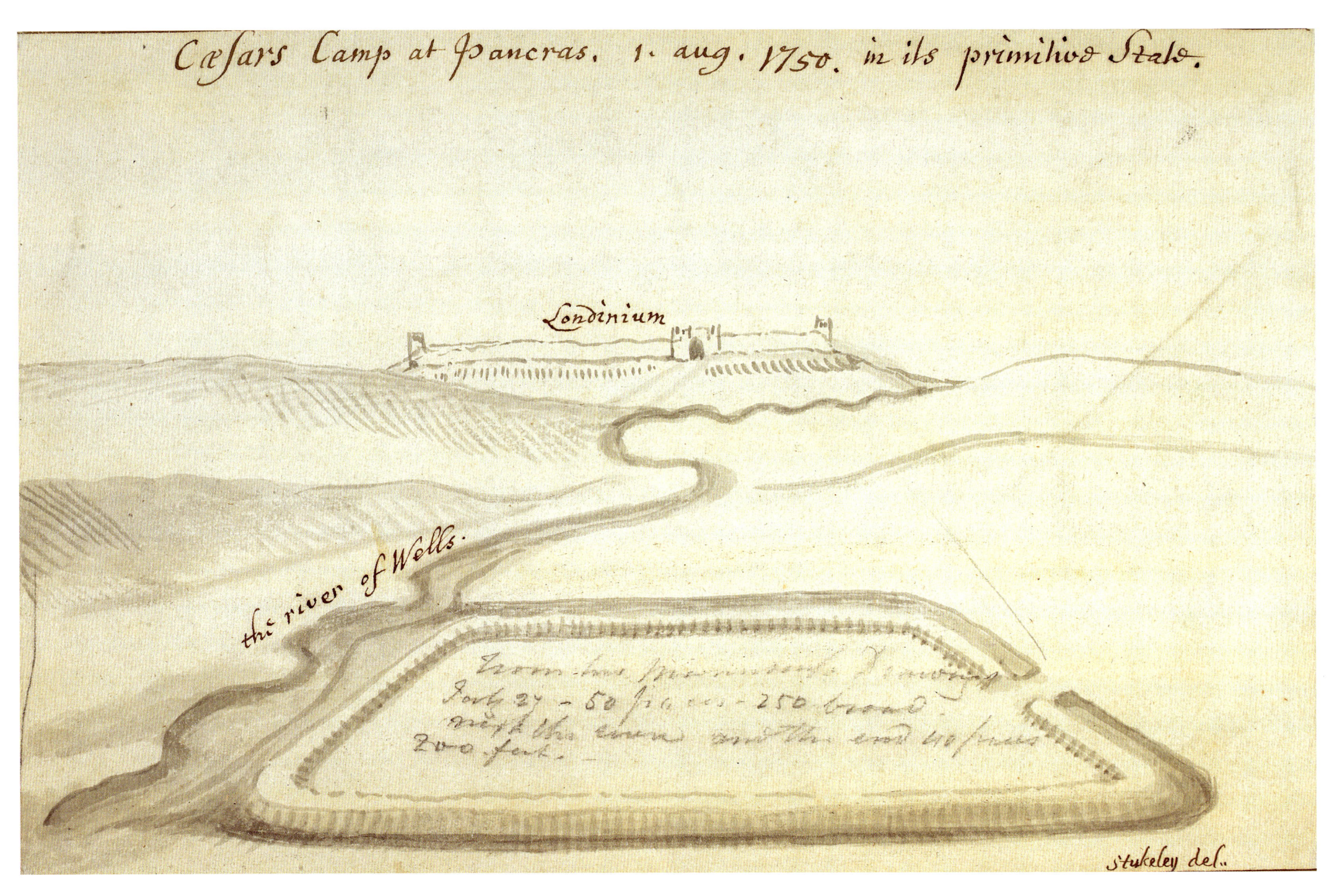

1.1.1b   William Stukeley, 'Caesars Camp at Pancras, 1. aug. 1750. in its primitive State.' Ink and pencil drawing. 16.5 × 26 cm. Maps Crace XIV.47

THE EARLIEST IMAGE OF LONDON

This medal contains the earliest known representation of London. It commemorates London's surrender to Constantius I Chlorus, whose forces had just defeated the usurper Allectus in 296. The features, though standardised, resemble reality with the city shown walled in the characteristic Roman way on the north bank of the Thames. There is a galley on the Thames. Constantius is portrayed as an Emperor (and 'restorer of eternal light') on horseback, spear in one hand, sceptre in the other. Before him kneels the personification of London, which he had saved from being sacked. Fragments of the Roman wall of London survive.

OBVERSE   REVERSE

1.1.2   Gold medallion of 10 aurei struck in Trier in 297 AD. Diameter 4 cm. From the Arras hoard (1922). Musée des Beaux Arts, Arras. [Electrotype, the British Museum]

LONDON FROM CONSTANTINE TO KING ALFRED

London was important enough to merit the establishment of an imperial mint in 285 but physical decay and a loss of the technological skills necessary to maintain the all-important port facilities followed the withdrawal of Roman forces from Britain in 407.

1.1.3a   Bronze follis of Constantine I, struck in London ('PLN') c. 310. Diameter 2.5 cm. Private collection

By 500 the area within the walls seems to have been deserted. Commercial activity eventually resumed in a more easily managed area to the West on the banks of the Thames where a new settlement, Londonwic (today commemorated in the name Aldwych or 'old town'), was established. The recently discovered gold coin, or *mancus*, of King Coenwulf of Mercia of about 805 explicitly mentions it ('VICO LVNDONIAE').

1.1.3b   Gold *mancus* of Coenwulf of Mercia, Londonwic, c. 805–10. Diameter 2.1 cm. British Museum: Registration number 2006,0204.1

Some administrative activity continued in a small area in the north-west of the walled city, to this day still called Aldermanbury, and this is probably what is referred to in the silver penny of King Egbert of Mercia of 828–29 referring to the town of London ('LUNDONIA CIVIT').

1.1.3c   Silver penny of King Egbert of Mercia, London, 828–29. Diameter 2 cm. British Museum: Registration number 1893, 1204.208

Repeated attacks by the Vikings forced Londoners back within the walls, and by the end of the ninth century, beautifully designed coins incorporating the London monogram were being struck in the name of King Alfred 'the Great' within the walls of a reviving city that was never again to look back.

1.1.3d   Silver penny of King Alfred, London, c. 890. Diameter: 1.9 cm. British Museum: Registration number 1935, 1117.412

A SYMBOL FOR LONDON

From about 1190, when its first mayor was elected, until 1967 the City Corporation used the same seal (re-engraved after the Great Fire). It showed St Paul with drawn sword and the banner of England and, on the other side, the most famous early Londoner, Thomas à Becket, depicted as Archbishop of Canterbury. Both are shown protecting a walled city dominated by its churches and towers.

1.1.4 Diameter: 7.5 cm. Seal lxviii.18 & 19

7

A CHURCH-DOMINATED CITY

Matthew Paris was mostly confined to his Benedictine abbey at St Albans but his well-developed mapmaking abilities enabled him to make mental pilgrimages to the Holy Land starting from London at the bottom left. Matthew adopts an artificial, map-like viewpoint based on the view from Highgate. Secular London is represented by London Bridge, the Thames, the city gates and the Tower. The Church however dominates with St Paul's, the important priory of Holy Trinity Aldgate, St Mary-le-Bow, Lambeth, the London home of the Archbishop of Canterbury and Westminster squeezed in at the right. The locations are broadly correct even though Westminster is shown as if within the walls of the City and lack of space has forced Matthew Paris to place the Tower on the south side of the Thames.

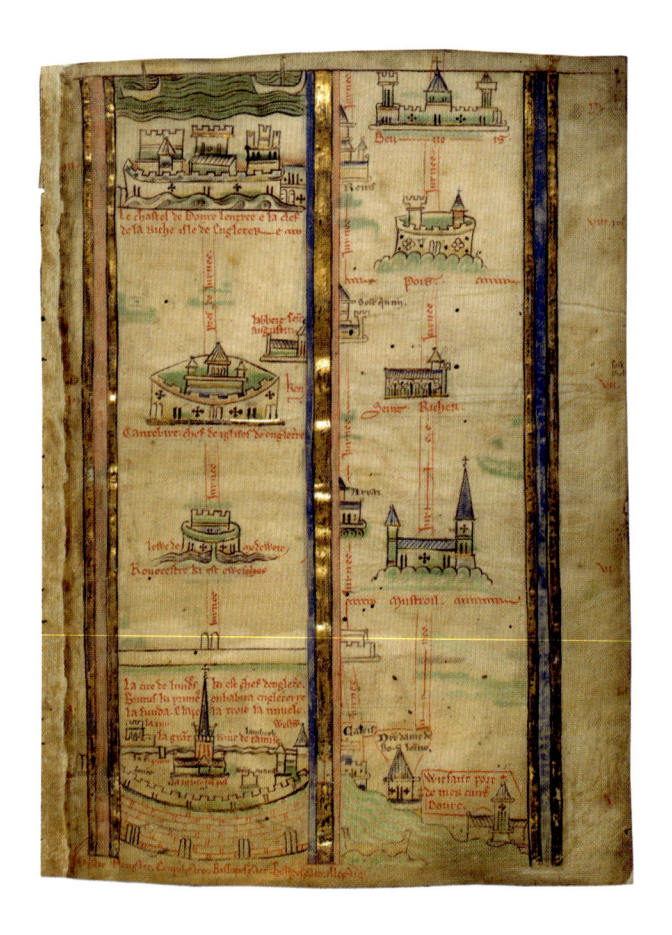

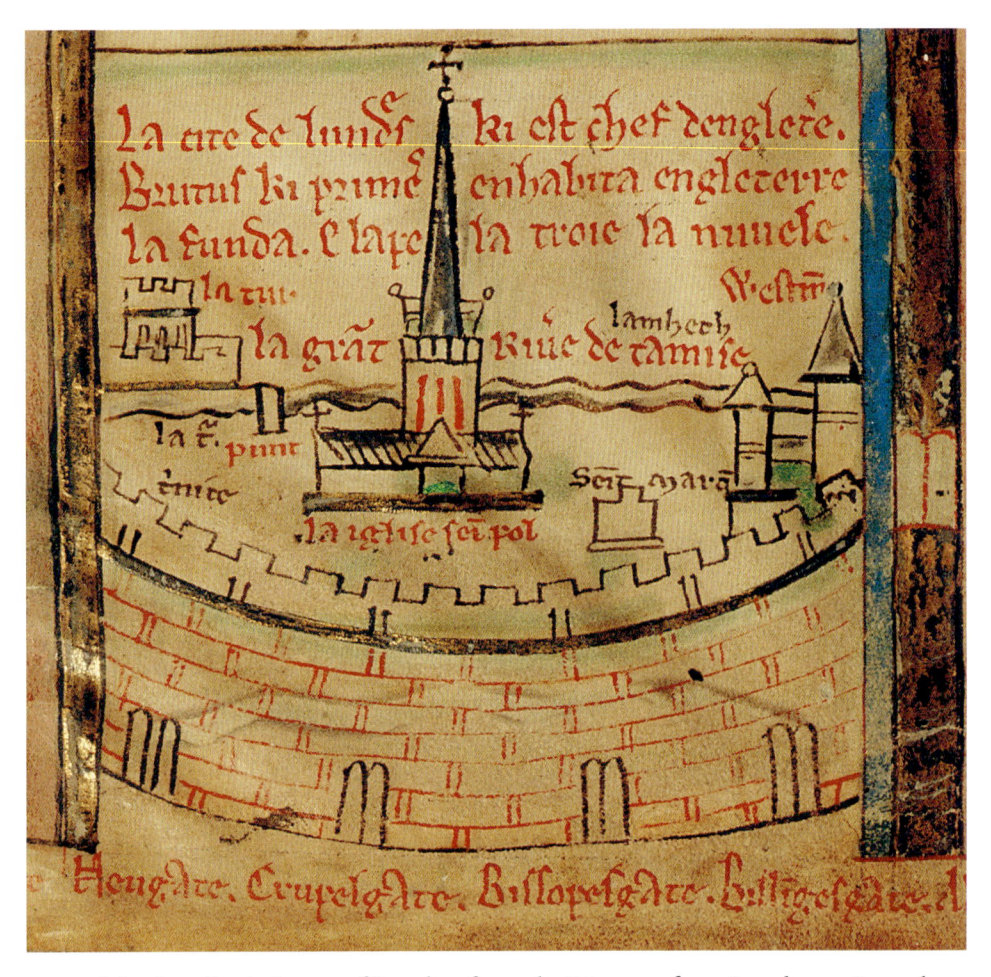

1.1.5 Matthew Paris, image of London from the Itinerary from London to Jerusalem, c. 1250. 8.5 × 5.5 cm on sheet measuring 39.5 × 29.5 cm. Royal MS 14.C.VII fol. 2

THE CITY GATES

In this plan from another itinerary of the route to Jerusalem, Matthew Paris views London from the south, across the Thames, concentrating on the City walls and gates. He shows a selection in the correct sequence except that Ludgate and Aldersgate are confused and Aldgate is not shown.

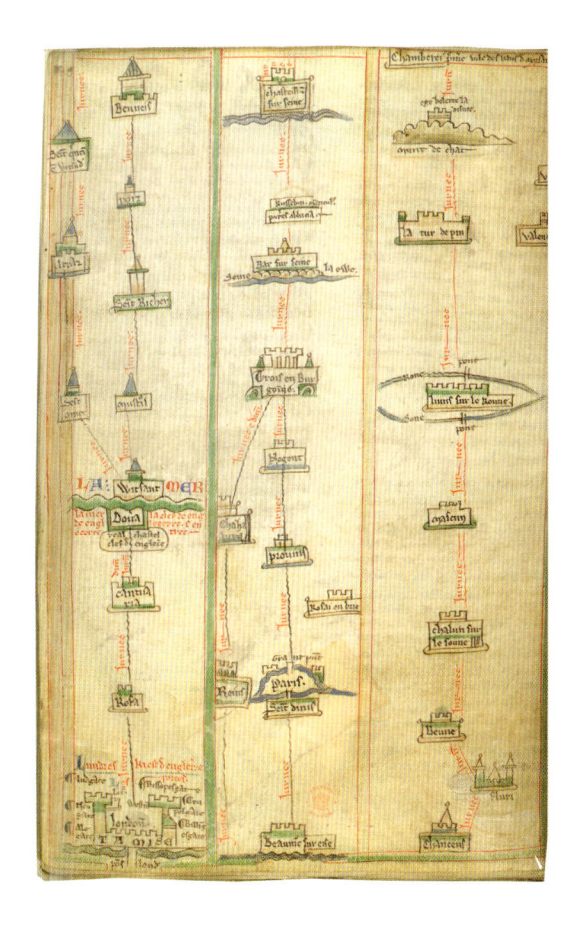

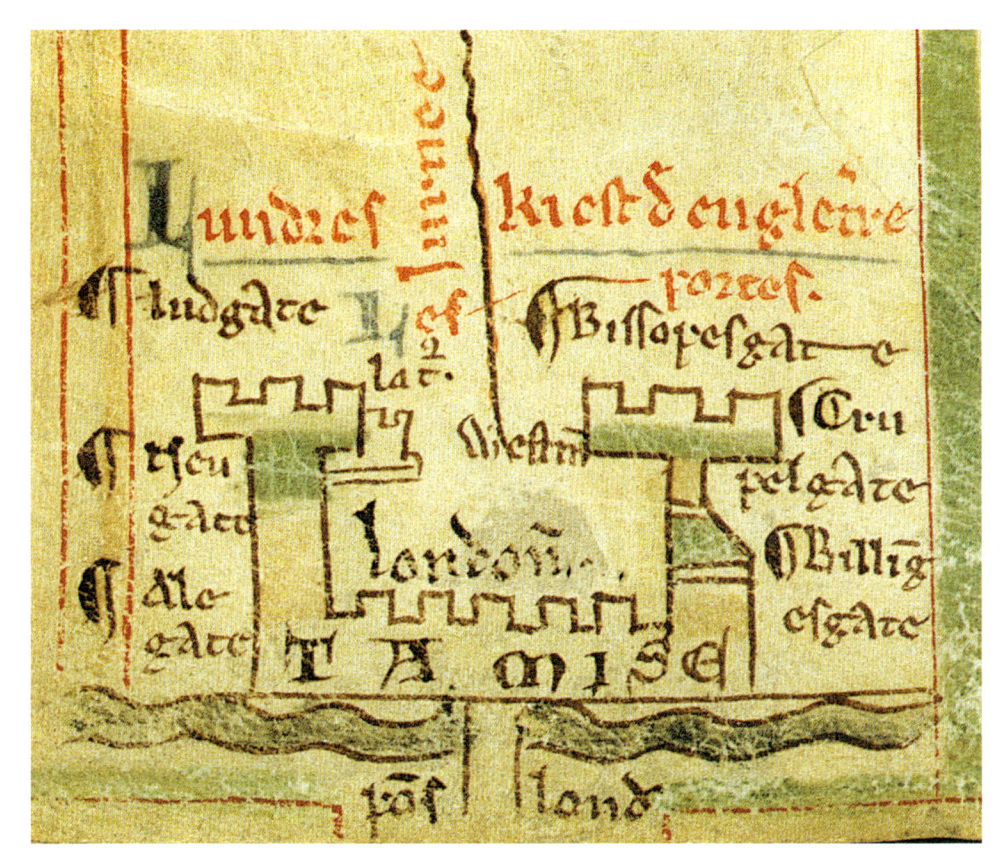

1.1.6 Matthew Paris, image of London from the Itinerary from London to Jerusalem, *c.* 1250. 6 × 7 cm on sheet 35.5 × 22.5 cm. Cotton MS Nero D.i fol. 182ᵛ

1.2 A RENAISSANCE VISION

From about 1480, when artistic realism was belatedly beginning to take hold in England, a new image emerged which prevailed until about 1550. It showed London looking upstream from the Thames, often as if viewed from an artificial, raised viewpoint east of the Tower. This was how foreigners would have first seen the city unless they came by road from Dover and it may first have been created by an Italian — Italian mapmakers were working in London at least as early as 1438. The overall structure of the bird's-eye view resembled popular Italian printed views of towns like Florence as seen on the 'Catena' view of 1500 now in the Kupferstichkabinett of the Staatsmuseum in Berlin. No full-size originals survive, but views inspired by it are known in manuscript paintings, engraved copies of lost paintings and as vignettes on early maps.

1.2a   Ribbon development spreading from the walls towards Wapping, Mile End, Shoreditch, Borough High Street and the Strand, 1538 [Detail showing 'London' from a map showing proposals for Anne of Cleves voyage to England] 5.5 × 9.5 cm Cotton MS Augustus I.ii.64

1.2b A symbolic version from the Lily map of Great Britain and Ireland, 1546 1.5 × 2.2 cm on map measuring 51.5 × 72 cm. K. Top. 5.1

This was the first separately printed map of the British Isles. George Lily, although spending much of his life as a Catholic exile in Rome (where the map was produced), was a Londoner by birth and the son of the humanist William Lily, highmaster of St Paul's School. He died at Canterbury in 1559.

1.2c A related image with swallows around the steeple of St Paul's and the characteristic tower of old St Mary-le-Bow in front. From a Netherlandish map of Great Britain and Ireland, 1548–49. Private collection, USA

A ROYAL CITY

The London shown in the background to this illustration of the poet Duke of Orleans in the Tower is that of Edward IV, who commissioned this copy of his poems. The Tower and London Bridge emphasise that the city is well-defended, the numerous church spires, that it is pious. The arcaded customs' house, with ships outside, that it is prosperous and the green of Tower Hill hints that it is spacious. The banners with the royal standard above the White Tower imply that it is under royal control: in that respect, the reality was rather different.

1.2.1 [Poésies de Charles, Duc d'Orléans, father of Louis XII of France], *c.* 1480. 39 × 58 cm. Royal MS 16.F.II, f.73

13

ARRIVING BY RIVER

The appearance of the ships in the foreground suggests that the original painting, then owned by the earl of Hardwicke, but which cannot now be traced, was created in about 1540. Though several details were misunderstood or carelessly copied by the engraver, it gives an impression of the city as it would have appeared to a visitor arriving by river before the destruction by lightning of the cathedral spire in 1561. Gothic St Paul's Cathedral dominated the city and old London Bridge, completed in 1209, with its chapel and houses acted as much as a defensive structure as a means of communication.

1.2.2   J. Wood, *South-East view of the City of London Engrav'd from a very Antient Picture*, 1754. Engraving with etching 38 × 57.5 cm Maps K. Top. 21.58

1.3 LONDON FROM BANKSIDE

From about 1550 a new image of London emerged. It showed the city as if viewed from the tower of Southwark Cathedral (though in reality such a wide view is impossible). It may have originated in a panoramic painting by the Flemish artist, Antonis van Wijngaerde, prepared for Whitehall Palace in about 1540, the preparatory drawings for which still survive. Simplified woodcut images, possibly designed by an emigré French printer, Giles Godet, of London from Bankside were circulating even before the destruction by lightning of the steeple of St Paul's in 1561. By 1567 the image was popular enough to be included as a detail in an advertisement illustrating lottery prizes. The view remains the iconic image of London and has been given a fresh lease of life following the opening of Tate Modern on Bankside.

1.3.a Anon. Detail from a drawing in the Wijngaerde album showing St Paul's from what may be a preparatory drawing for, or a copy of, a panoramic painting of London in Whitehall Palace, c. 1545, Ashmolean Museum, Oxford. Maps 184.f.2 (2)

Although little of the life of Antonis van Wijngaerde is known, his travels through Europe can be traced from many surviving topographical drawings. The fine arts inevitably required royal or aristocratic patronage at this time and the similar views he produced elsewhere in England, in Italy, Spain, and the southern Netherlands suggest that he perhaps accompanied Philip II on his travels. He died in 1571.

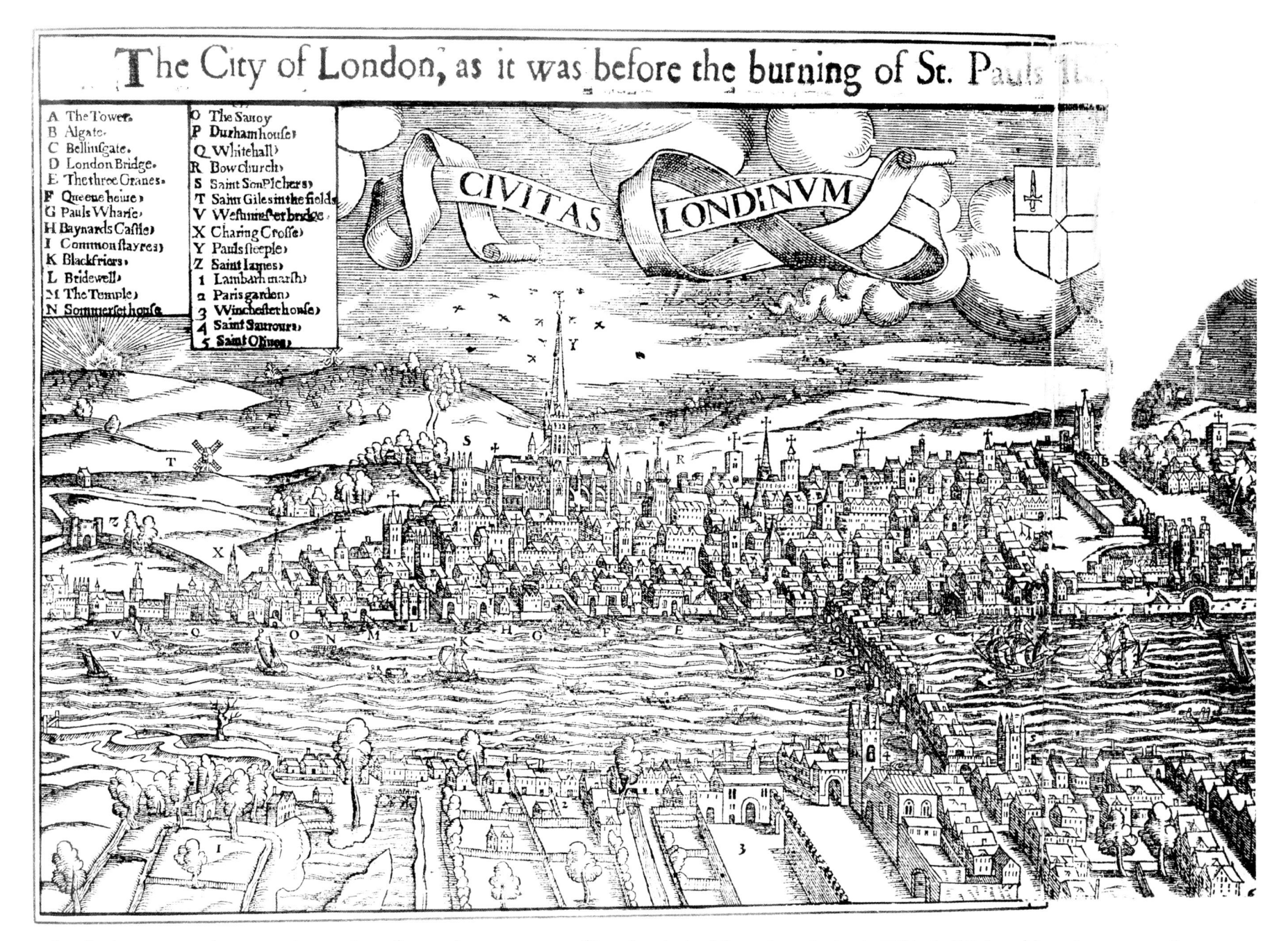

1.3.b   Early seventeenth-century impression of a woodcut panorama of London derived from the painting in Whitehall Palace (?), perhaps originally published by Giles Godet of London, *c.* 1560, showing the spire of St Paul's before it burnt down. 26 × 37.7 cm. Pepys Library, Magdalene College, Cambridge

Godet is numbered among the enormous number of refugees who have come to London over the years to escape religious persecution elsewhere. He was granted letters of denization in 1551, became a Brother of the London Stationers' Company in 1555, and was living in Blackfriars in 1568 with his daughter and two male employees, both of whom also 'came for religeon'.

17

A BIRD'S-EYE VIEW OF HENRY VIII'S LONDON

Wijngaerde, a Flemish artist, was probably commissioned to create a panorama of London for Whitehall Palace by Henry VIII in the years when, flush with money from the dissolved monasteries, the King was employing large numbers of foreign craftsmen. This is a preliminary sketch, intended for a lost painting. There are simplifications (for instance, the nave of St Paul's has been halved in size), confusions (St Giles's Cripplegate is given the tower of St Mary-le-Bow) and gaps (Whitehall Palace is omitted). For all that, the panorama gives a good — and unique — impression of early Tudor London still with its monastic buildings.

1.3.1   Anthonis van den Wijngaerde, [Panorama of London and Westminster, 1540 (?)]. Reproduced from facsimile published by the Topographical Society of London, 1881–82 an 1996 (publication nos 1 and 151). 53 × 254 cm. Maps 184.f.2 (1)

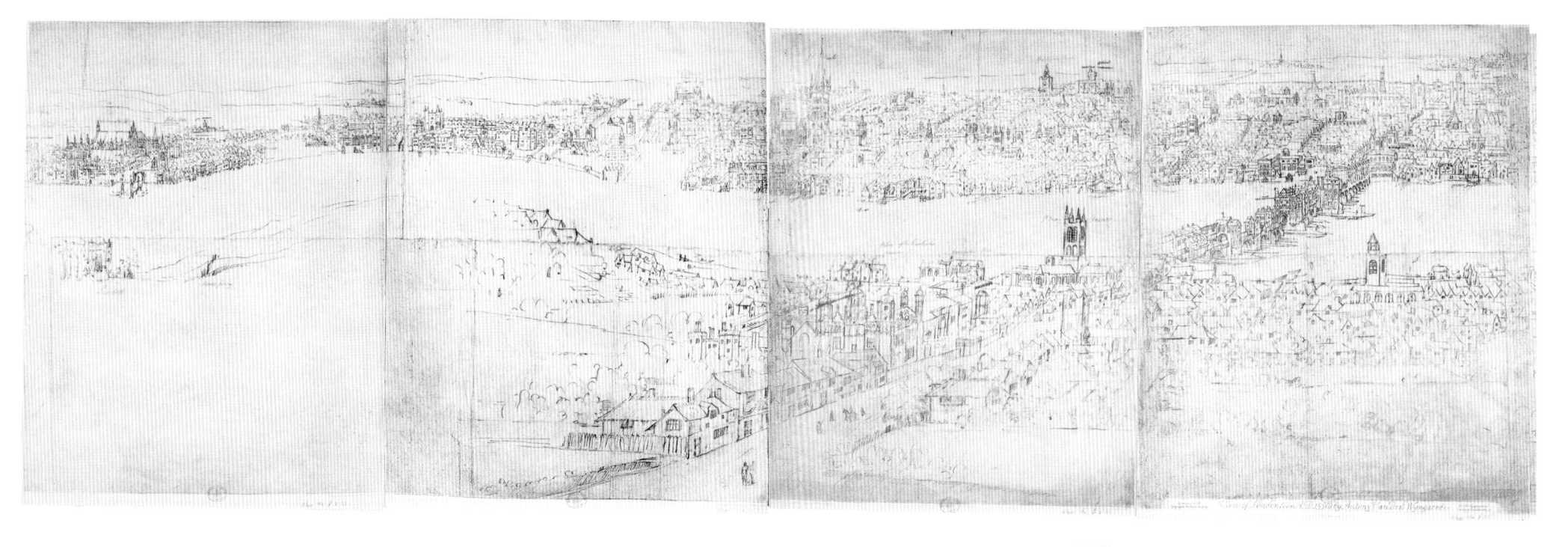

19

LONDON IN THE YEAR OF THE ARMADA

William Smith has combined a profile view of London with a perspective view of Whitehall and Westminster. Neither was original. The city view is probably derived from a mural by Wijngaerde in Whitehall Palace, while the bird's-eye view seems ultimately to be copied from the 'Copperplate Map'. Smith shows St Paul's without its spire; south of the river, to the left of what is now Southwark Cathedral, he emphasises the large palace of the bishops of Winchester, of which only the west wall now survives. Further west, there are bull and bear-baiting pits but not yet theatres.

1.3.2   William Smith, view of London, Westminster and Southwark from *A Particular Description of England*, 1588. 29 × 54 cm Sloane MS 2596, f.52

The herald, topographer and playwright William Smith came originally from Cheshire, but became a freeman of London and a member of the Haberdashers' Company in the 1570s, at which time he wrote his earliest known work — *A breffe discription of the royall citie of London* (Guildhall MS 2463). He then lived in Nuremberg for a number of years before finally settling in London for the last thirty years of his life. He became Rouge Dragon Pursuivant at the College of Arms in 1597 and was buried at the church of St Alfege, London Wall, in 1618.

LONDON.

CELEBRATED THROUGHOUT THE WORLD...

Intended for the homes of the seriously wealthy, the title and decoration of this panorama, extending from Whitehall to east of the Tower, play on the city's prosperity and fame. The artist may never have visited London. The image is derived from older printed views and shows the city as it was in about 1600. Among the grandeur there are some of the 2000 licensed watermen rowing their boats up and down an unrealistically wide Thames, cowherds driving cows for milking, the gatehouse of London Bridge adorned with the severed heads of traitors and a perhaps not too accurate depiction of Shakespeare's Globe in Southwark.

1.3.3   Claes Jansz. Visscher, *Londinum Florentissima Britanniae Urbs Toto Orbe Celeberrimum Emporiumque*. Copperplate engraving, Amsterdam: Jodocus Hondius Jr, 1616. 65 × 218 cm. Maps C.5.a.6

Warke

REMEMBERED IN EXILE...

This extremely accurate panorama of the 'royal seat' of London from Milbank towards Greenwich, inspired by John Norden's panorama of 1600, was etched in Antwerp, Hollar's refuge from the Civil War. It is based on earlier observations from Southwark Cathedral and other points: two preliminary drawings still survive. The second Globe theatre, rebuilt in 1614 can be seen on the South Bank, though it is wrongly entitled 'Beere bayting', while the Hope theatre, where bear-baiting did take place, is entitled 'The Globe'. The allegorical figures refer to London's trade, fame, more ambiguously to the ethics of its ruling elite. Old Father Thames, is shown at the bottom right and at the bottom left there is the seated figure of Justice carrying her attributes of a sword and scales. Seated between representations of wealth (merchandise and coins spilling out of a cornucopia) and legality (the Crown and the book of the Law), her scales are tipped towards Law and the Crown as against merchant wealth. An 'objective' view of London is thus transformed into implied criticism of a city seduced by its wealth into treason towards its rightful lord.

1.3.4   Wenceslaus Hollar, *Serenissimae Mariae invictissimae Magnae Britanniae … Regis … filiae … hunc amoenissimum celeberrimi Londinensis emporii ac sedes regalis aspectum D.C.Q. Cornelius Danckers … Wenceslaus Hollar delineauit, et fecit Londini et Antverpiae*, 1647. 53 × 241.5 cm. Maps 162.h.4

Wenceslaus Hollar (1607–77) born in Prague, but a Londoner for the greater part of his life, is remembered as one of the finest of all urban artists, needing no further comment. But it is perhaps worth recalling Aubrey's remarks in his *Brief Lives* that he was by nature 'very short-sighted' and that 'when he tooke his landskapes, he, then, had a glasse to helpe his sight'.

AN ALTERNATIVE VIEW

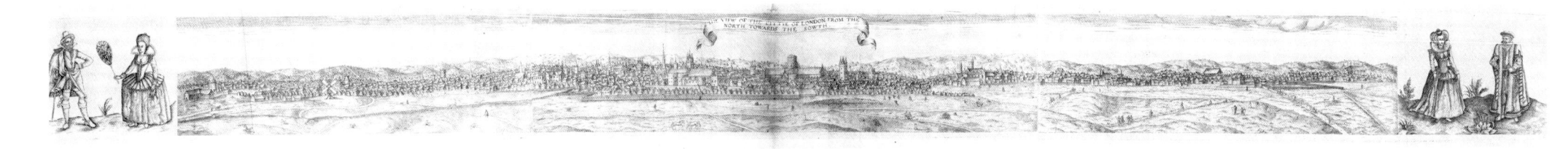

There were alternatives to the view of London from Bankside. A few were centred on Cheapside in the middle of the City, and there was this extremely rare view from the North, extending from Shoreditch to Westminster. Based on a drawing of 1597/8 and taken from a standpoint a little north of Clerkenwell, it gains in importance from showing one of London's two earliest theatres, built in 1576–77. Debate still rages over whether the circular building with a flag at the extreme left is the Theatre, demolished in 1598 and whose timbers were re-used for the Globe, or the longer-lived Curtain.

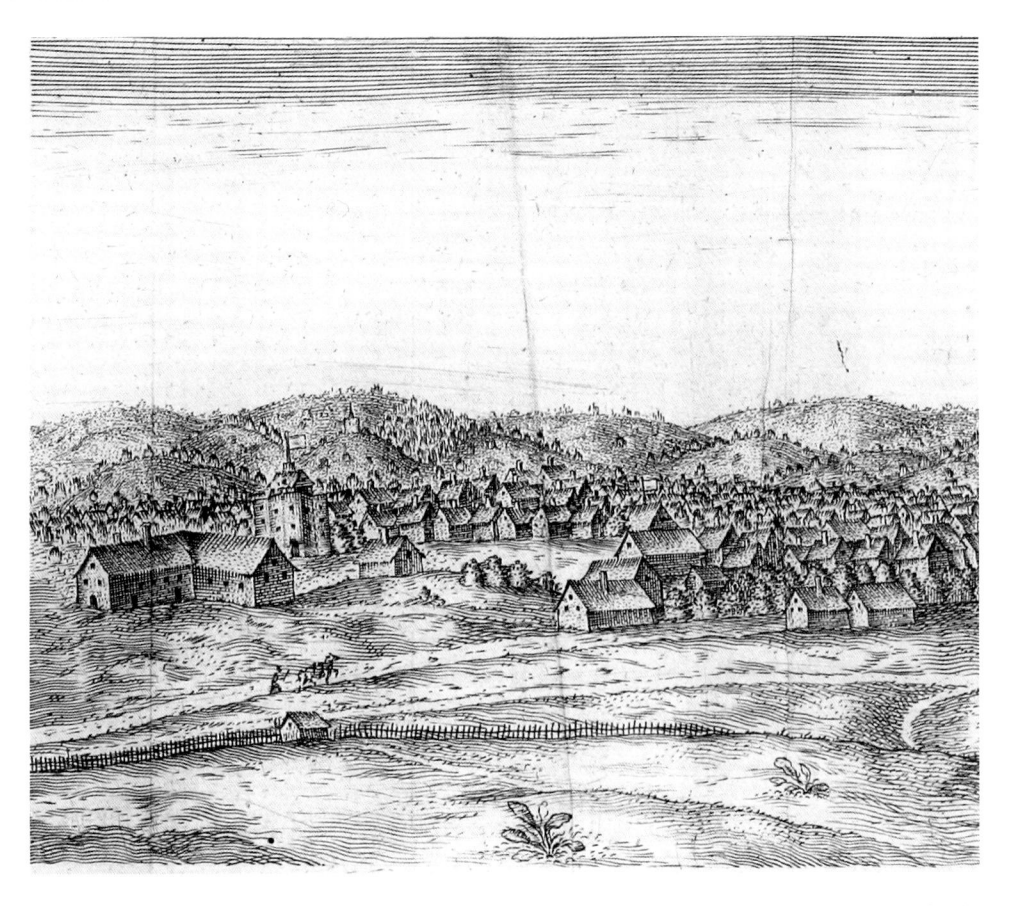

1.3.5   John Norden (?), *The View of the Cittye of London from the North towards the Sowth* (London, c. 1615). 16.5 × 129 cm. Burden Collection

The view is plausibly attributed to John Norden, estate surveyor, topographer, county mapmaker and devotional writer — known for much similar work as well as his textbook *The Surveyors' Dialogue* (1607). Originally from Somerset, he died in the parish of St Giles in the Fields, where he had lived for many years, in 1625.

1.4 THE FIRST MAPS

The earliest surviving printed maps of London portray a bustling, prosperous and well-ordered city. All derived from a common source but they emitted radically different messages. The first shows a royal city on an off-shore island, dependent on foreign merchants for its prosperity. The derivatives, sometimes incorporating minor additions and corrections, depict an ancient mercantile city, its wealth dependent on British merchants. The dramatic expansion of London to the East and West, spurred by a six-fold increase in population to about 400,000 between 1550 and 1650, led to calls for a new survey from 1618. Only Newcourt and Faithorne's reached publication in 1658 but Faithorne's friend and rival, Wenceslas Hollar, was at work on what would have been a magnificent map when the Great Fire intervened.

A FRAGMENT OF THE FIRST PRINTED MAP

No impressions and only three of the original fifteen copperplates are known from the earliest detailed printed map of London. These survived because the backs were re-used for paintings shortly after 1600. The map was probably commissioned from a foreign surveyor for presentation to Mary Tudor's husband, Philip II, by German merchants in London as part of their struggle to maintain their privileges after 1554. It was probably engraved and printed abroad. The map was an extremely expensive and perishable luxury item, printed in small numbers for display in prestigious locations. All knowledge of the map had been lost in England by 1618.

1.4.1   Copperplate showing the area around St Paul's Cathedral in about 1556–58, on the back of a painting of the Tower of Babel by a member of the circle of Martin van Valkenborch, *c.* 1600. 36.8 × 49 cm. Anhaltische Gemäldegalerie, Dessau, Germany

A CITY PROTECTED BY THE CROWN — AND BY GERMAN MERCHANTS

A bird's-eye view superimposed on a plan, the Copperplate Map represented the cutting edge of mid-sixteenth century mapmaking. The exaggerated size of the fields for laying out cloth to the North hint at commercial wealth based on the wool trade. This is linked to royal protection — the palaces and even the royal barge ('Cymbula Regia') are named — and to the German merchants whose extensive headquarters, the Steelyard (on the site of Cannon St Station), is also named. There is no mention of the Germans' rivals, the City livery companies (though their halls are depicted), or of Blackwell Hall where they did business.

The location of the three surviving plates on the complete map

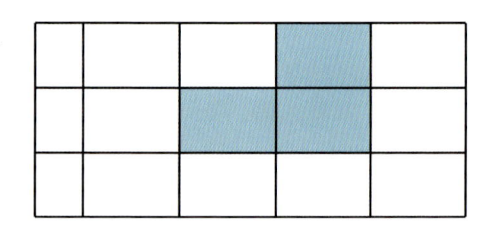

1.4.2   Recent impressions and re-drawings from the surviving copperplates. City of London, London Metropolitan Archives

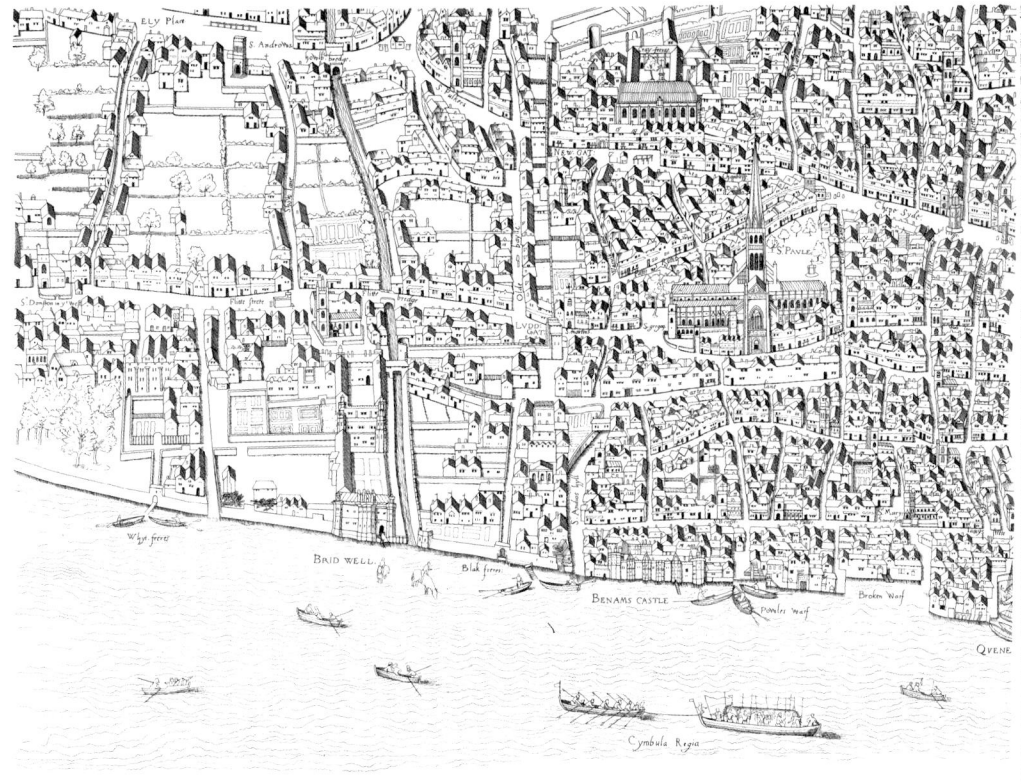

29

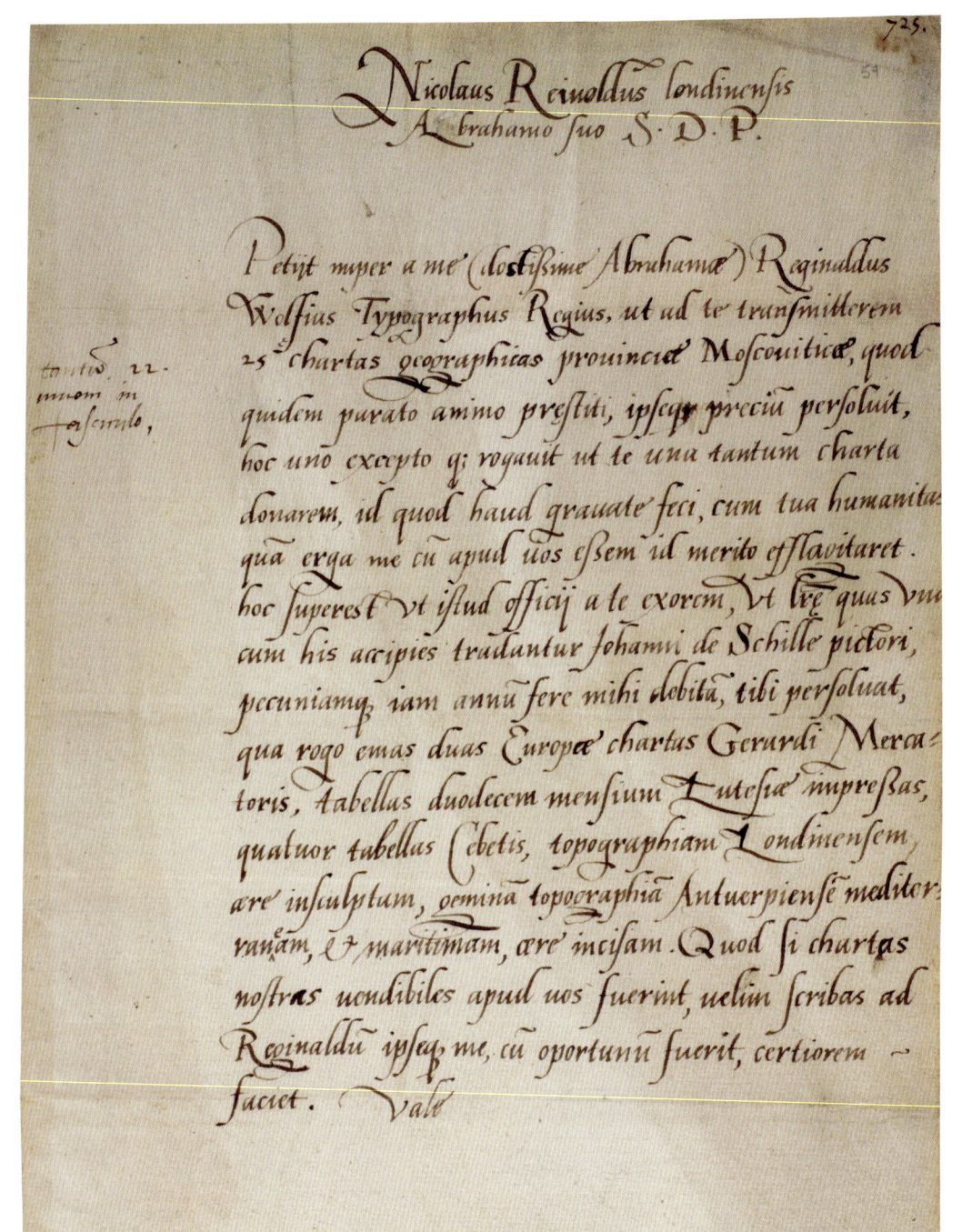

A REQUEST FOR THE COPPERPLATE MAP

This beautifully written letter, dateable to 1562/3, from the English mapmaker Nicholas Reynolds to the Flemish mapmaker and publisher, Abraham Ortelius, who was to publish the first modern atlas a few years later, provides firm evidence that the Copperplate Map reached publication. It also suggests that it was printed and published abroad. Reynolds promises to send Ortelius twenty-five examples of his own recently published map of Muscovy (of which only one example is now known to survive), but he asks Ortelius to send him several maps. Among them (lines 15–16) is a copy of 'the topography of London engraved on copper' [*topographiam Londinensem aere insculptum*].

1.4.3 Letter of Nicholas Reynolds to Abraham Ortelius, London [1562–63], 29.5 × 21 cm. Add. MS 63650 Q

Although Reynolds describes himself as a Londoner on the map of Muscovy, quite who he was remains open to debate — he may be the *Nicholas Reignoldes* who hailed from 'the dominion of the King of France' and was naturalized in January 1562, but equally he may be identified with the *Nicholas Reignolds* who became a freeman of the Goldsmiths' Company by patrimony (which would imply English birth) in 1567.

LONDONERS FIGHT BACK

This relatively cheap woodcut map known as the 'Agas Map' after Ralph Agas, who was wrongly believed to be its creator, was produced in considerable numbers soon after 1561 to adorn merchants' homes. A few years later the woodblocks were clumsily altered to accommodate the Royal Exchange. All three surviving examples date from about 1633 and show the arms of Charles I. While the image is a close but reduced-size and simplified copy of the Copperplate Map showing a spireless St Paul's Cathedral, the text panels proudly boast London's antiquity, wealth and natural advantages, without mentioning any foreigners.

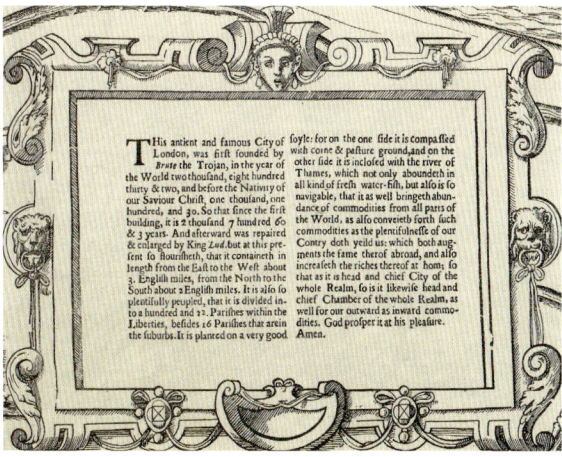

1.4.4 Anon., after the Copperplate Map, *Civitas Londinvm*, c.1633. 72.4 × 184.2 cm. City of London, London Metropolitan Archives

THE COPPERPLATE MAP IN MINIATURE

This is how the Copperplate Map image has come down to us. It shows London with some ribbon development beyond the walls but virtually no suburbs. The texts imply that London owes its prosperity to the league of German merchants known as the Hansa. The original state of 1572 even ignored the Royal Exchange, opened a few years earlier by the Hansa's arch enemy Sir Thomas Gresham. This was belatedly included in the second edition of 1574 though St Paul's continued to be shown with the spire that it had lost in 1561. Business is business but respect for the externals of religion alters.

1.4.5   *Londinum feracissimi Angliae regni metropolis* from Georg Braun and Frans Hogenberg, *Civitates Orbis Terrarum* (Cologne, 1574), [edition of 1623] 31.75 × 48 cm. Maps C.29.e.1 volume 1, map 1

1.4.5a   Detail from *Londinum feracissimi Angliae regni metropolis* from Georg Braun and Frans Hogenberg, *Civitates Orbis Terrarum* (Cologne, 1574), [edition of 1623] 31.75 × 48 cm. Maps C.29.e.1 volume 1, map 1

1.4.5b   Detail from the first edition of 1572 showing the Cornhill area before the insertion of the Royal Exchange [G.3603]

LONDINVM FERACISSIMI ANGLIAE REGNI METROPOLIS

Hæc est regia illa totius Angliæ ciuitas LONDINVM, ad fluuium Thamesin sita: Cæsari, vt plures exiftimant, Trinobantum municeps: ædium multarum gentium coniunctis nobilitata, ædeis domib. ornata templis, exclesia ædibus, ciuium ingenis, virtute omnium artium doctrinarumque re præstantibus, perreclebris. Denique, omnium rerum copia atque opum excellentia mirabilis: funebri in eam totius orbis opes ipsæ Thamasis, onerarijs nauibus per sexcenta millia passuum, ad vrbem præter alueo nauicabilis vsquam.

STILLIARDS, Hansa, Gothica dicto, conuentum, vel congregationem fonans, muitarum ciuitatum est confœderatarum Societas, tum ob præstita Regibus ac Ducib. beneficia: tum ob securam terra marique, mercatura tractationem, tum denique ad tranquillam Rerumpub. pacem, & ad modestam adolescentum institutionem conseruandam, instituta: plurimos Regum, ac Principum, inprimis Angliæ, Galliæ, Daniæ, ac Magni Moscouiæ, nec non Flandriæ, ac Brabantiæ Ducum priuilegijs, ac immunitatib. ornatam fuit. Habet ea quatuor Emporia, Contores quidam vocant, in quibus ciuitatum negotiatores resident, suaque mercatus exercent. Hor. alterum huic Londini, Domestica œconomia, hoc est ædibus domum Guldhallæ Teutonica, qui vulgo Stilliard, nuncupat.

LONDON BECOMES A EUROPEAN COMMERCIAL CENTRE

In the early sixteenth century the English had to market their wool and cloth through the exchange or Bourse of Antwerp. Sir Thomas Gresham, a leading London Merchant Adventurer, resented this and the privileges bestowed on foreign merchants in London. He succeeded in getting these restricted and in financing the creation in the course of the 1560s of the Royal Exchange, surmounted by his family's symbol of the grasshopper.

1.4.6 Frans Hogenberg [Exterior of the Royal Exchange from Cornhill], c. 1570. 21.5 × 30 cm. K. Top. 24.11–a–2

35

THE EXPANDING SUBURBS

Newcourt's twelve-sheet map reveals how much London had expanded East as well as West since the 1550s. Possibly surveyed in the mid-1640s in preparation for Royalist attacks and afterwards selectively updated, and decorated with the arms of the 'Great Twelve' livery companies, it shows the Covent Garden development of the 1630s, the new houses around St James's Park and the great noble houses and gardens on the Strand as well as a gaming house near Piccadilly. By contrast no specific information is given about the poor hamlets east of the Tower, apart from a lime kiln that gave Limehouse its name. For all its superficial modernity, however, as recent research has shown, the map is misleading in several ways. It omits the large defensive ramparts beyond the walls dating back to the Civil War, which contemporaries could not have avoided, and it shows St James's Park as full of trees, even though Cromwell had had them chopped down. Most provocatively of all, the map is dominated by representations of St Paul and Westminster Abbey. Until recently these had been used as stables and St Paul's Cathedral was in a state of collapse. At the foot of the map there is a long text and genealogical table demonstrating London's supposed Trojan origins, Newcourt, it seems, was not presenting the sober reality of Cromwellian London but the idealised London of his dreams.

1.4.7   Richard Newcourt (surveyor) and William Faithorne, Sr (engraver), [*An Exact Delineation of the Cities of London and Westminster and the Svbvrbs Thereof, Together with the Burrough of Southwark and all the Throughfares, Highwaies, Streetes, Lanes & Common Allies within the same Composed by a Scale and Ichnographically described by Richard Newcourt of Somerton in the Countie of Somerset Gentleman. 1658*], Late edition of about 1661. 87 × 183.5 cm Maps Roll 17.a.3

The engraver of the map was the elder William Faithorne (1621–1691), a Londoner who joined the King's forces at Oxford at the time of the Civil War, was captured at the siege of Basing House in 1645 and spent a period of exile in France. The surviving records of Hoare's Bank show a payment to Faithorne of £5. 7*s*. 6*d* from Samuel Pepys, who had known Faithorne since at least 1662, in September 1690.

THE MOST BEAUTIFUL MAP OF LONDON THAT NEVER WAS

From at least 1660, Hollar, presumably aware of the limitations of his friends Faithorne and Newcourt's map, worked on what he intended to be a 5 feet by 10 feet (150 × 300 cm), twenty-four-sheet, bird's-eye map of London showing every principal building as it actually was, plotted onto a ground plan. This is the unique example of the only surviving sheet. It shows the most fashionable part of London around the newly-constructed Covent Garden piazza and was probably intended to accompany the printed prospectus and appeal to subscribers of which a single copy is known. Hollar had made considerable progress with the map by the time of the Great Fire.

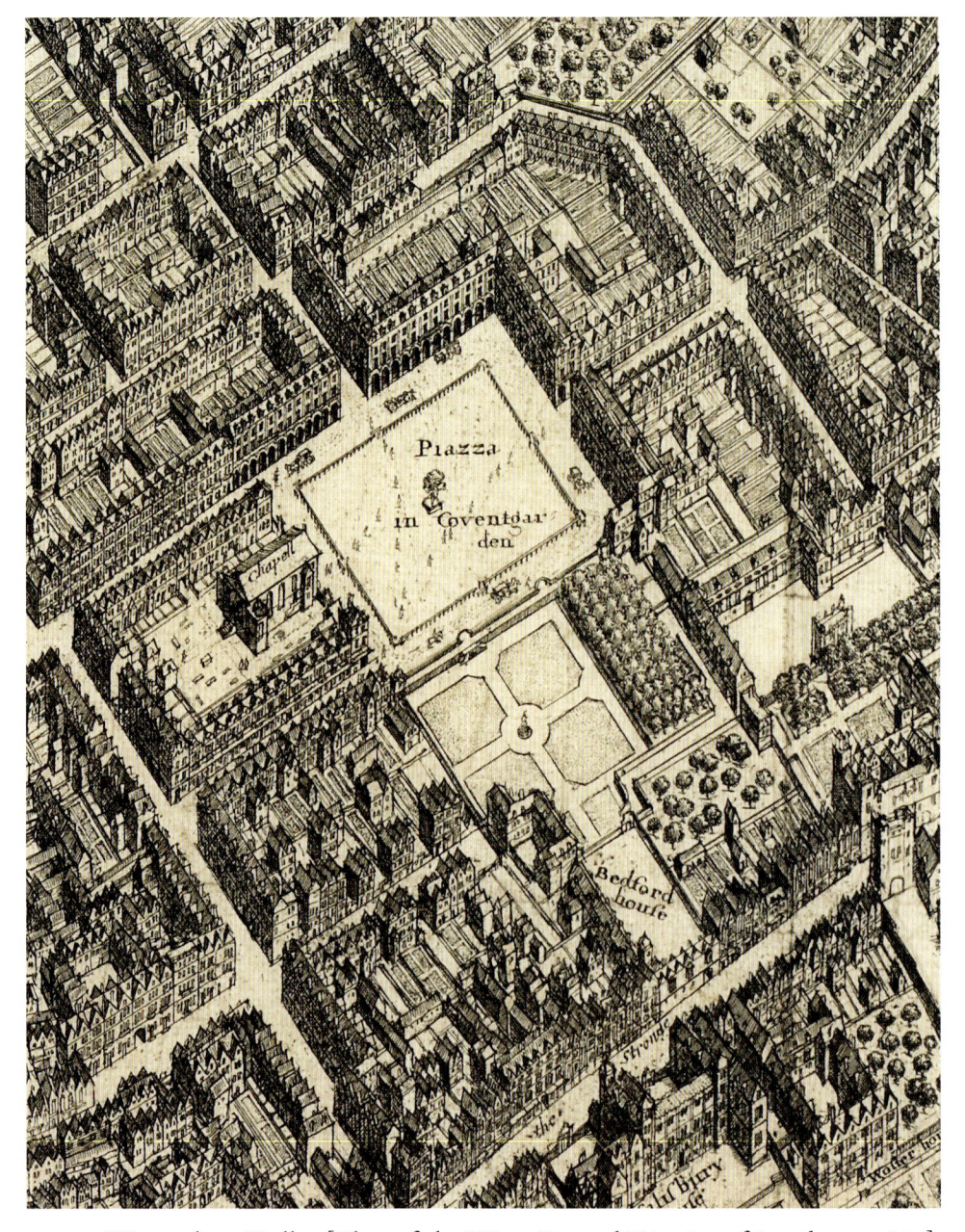

1.4.8 Wenceslaus Hollar [Plan of the West Central District of London *c.* 1660]. 34.4 × 45.5 cm. Trustees of the British Museum

S. Giles

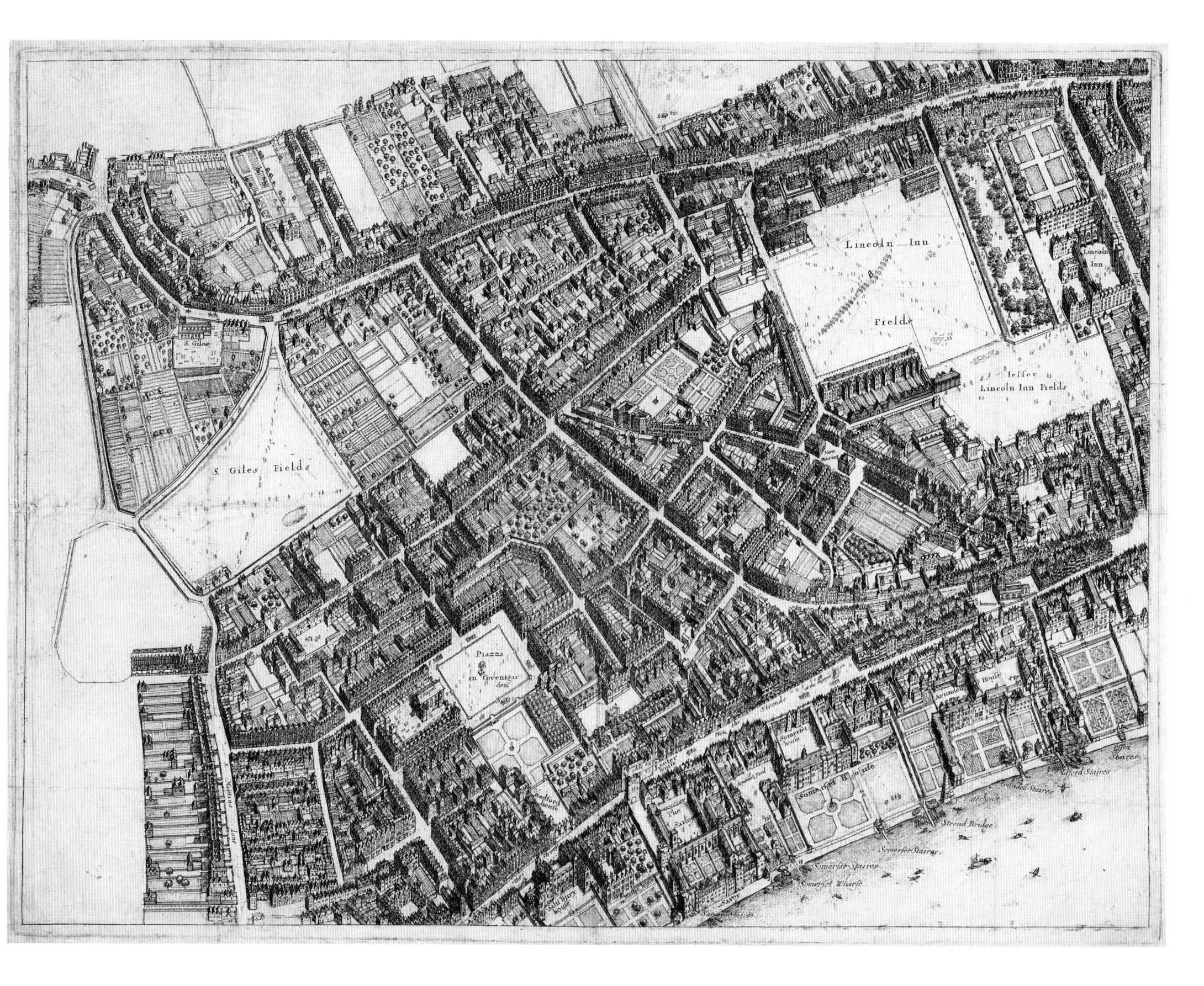

Lincoln Inn

Fields

Lincoln Inn

Lesser
Lincoln Inn Fields

S. Giles Fields

Piazza in Covent Garden

Bedford house

Arundell House

Strande

Somerset house

Savoy

Salisbury house

Somerset Wharfe
Somerset Staires
Strond Bridge
Dudley Staires
Arundell Staires
Milford Staires
Essex Staires

A LAST GLIMPSE

This great seal, in use from 1663 to 1672, shows Charles II on horseback before a panorama of London copied from the Visscher print of 1616. The work of Thomas Simon, perhaps the greatest native-born British medallist ever, it provides a last glimpse of the pre-Fire city.

1.4.9 Thomas Simon, reverse side of third seal of Charles II. diameter 15 cm Seal xxxix.2

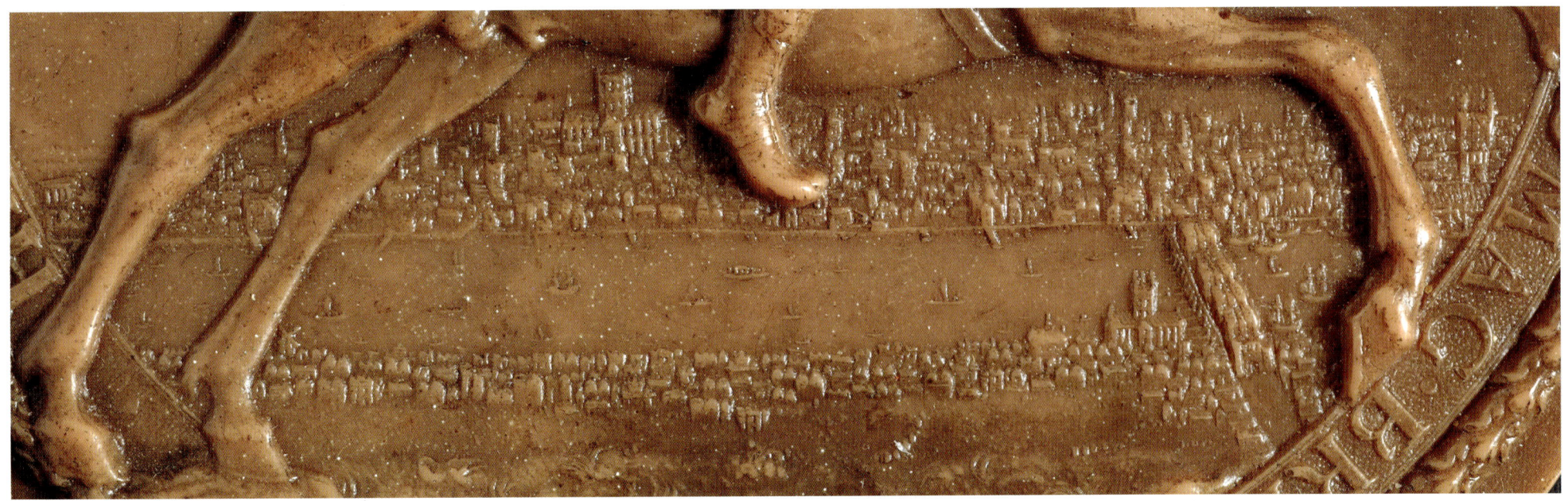

Simon (1618–65) was baptised at the French Protestant Church on Threadneedle Street, the son of a London merchant of French descent and his Guernsey-born wife. He became a freeman of the Worshipful Company of Goldsmiths in 1646 and Chief Engraver to the Mint two years later. Such was his skill that he continued to be employed to engrave the seals of state after the Restoration, despite having produced the Great Seal of the Commonwealth under Cromwell — and having depicted Cromwell on the coinage.

A WITNESS TO THE GREAT FIRE

Between 2 and 6 September 1666, two-thirds of the city of London was destroyed by fire. Though Samuel Pepys's account is better known, his friend John Evelyn also described the events in a diary compiled from notes taken at the time. Here he recalls the 'calamitous spectacle … the skie … like the top of a burning Oven … the noise & crakling & thunder of the impetuous flames, the shrieking of Women & children … the fall of towers, houses & churches … London was but is no more'.

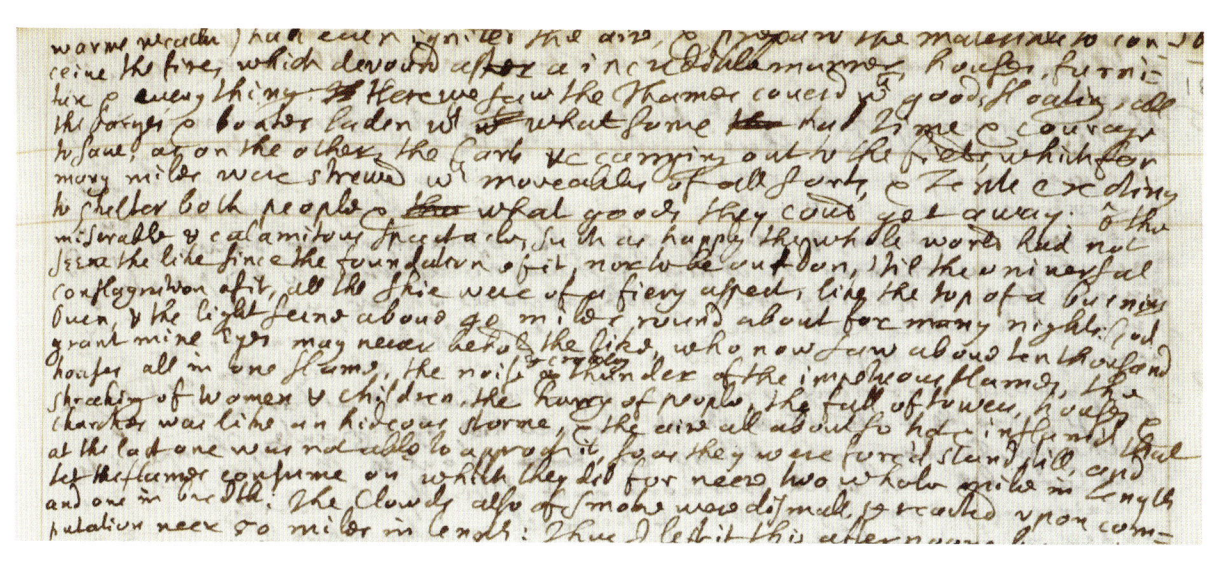

1.4.10   Diary of John Evelyn for 3 September 1666. 24 × 38 cm. Add. MS 78323

John Evelyn (1620–1706) is remembered for much else besides, but in a London context we recall not only his gardens at Deptford, but that he wrote the first English book on pollution (*Fumifugium* 1661), that he served as a commissioner of sewers, and as a committee-man for licensing hackney coaches, for reforming the streets, for repairing St Paul's Cathedral and for re-planning London after the Great Fire.

MAKING MONEY FROM THE FIRE

The Great Fire made news throughout Europe. This Dutch news sheet was compiled in stages from September 1666. Dots have been etched onto the copperplate of an existing map of London to show the extent of the destroyed area and flames added to a reduced version of Hollar's panorama. The Fire started in a bakery in Pudding Lane and, appropriately, the print shows a lamenting baker standing next to the depiction of the Fire which is surmounted by images of his loaves. Behind him a father pays a carter to transport his family and worldly goods to safety. Evelyn had commented on 'carts &c carrying out to the fields which for many miles were strewed with moveables of all sorts & Tents … to shelter both people & … goods'.

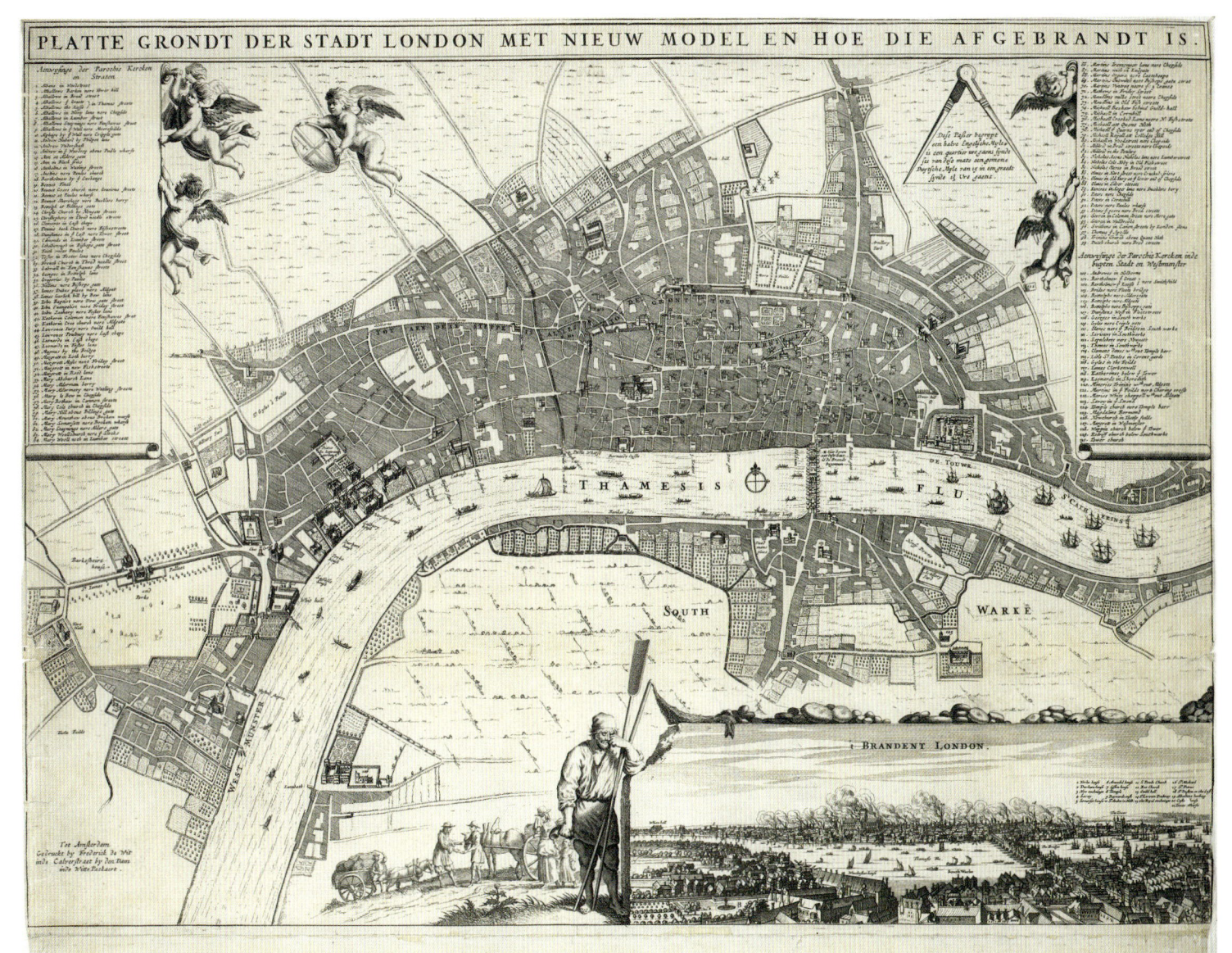

1.4.11   *Platte Grondt der Stadt London met nieuw model en hoe die afgebrandt is* (Amsterdam: Frederick de Witt, 1667). 59.5 × 54 cm. Maps Crace 1.49

FIRST IDEAS FOR A REBUILT CITY

This manuscript reduction by John Leake, from the original six-sheet survey undertaken on orders from the City Corporation in December 1666, is the only part that has survived. It was drawn in January and then revised in March 1667 for presentation to the King and the commissioners responsible for the rebuilding. As well as showing the extent of the Fire, it contains the first tentative proposals for the new city. As well as the sites of major buildings, and the widths of the existing streets at major junctions, brown shading shows improvements such as the beginnings of a straight new road from Guildhall to the Thames, some street widenings particularly near St Paul's and a regularised river front.

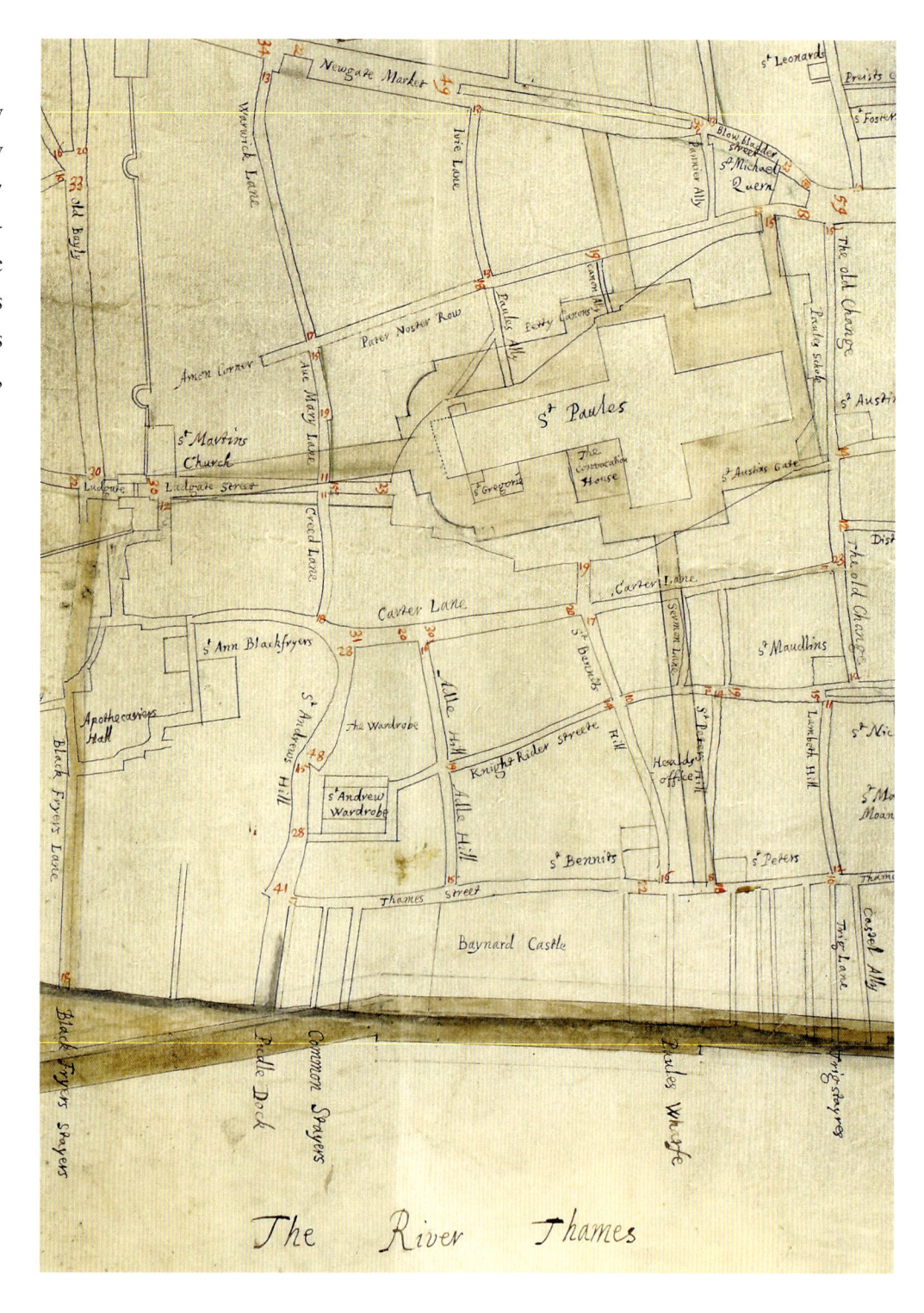

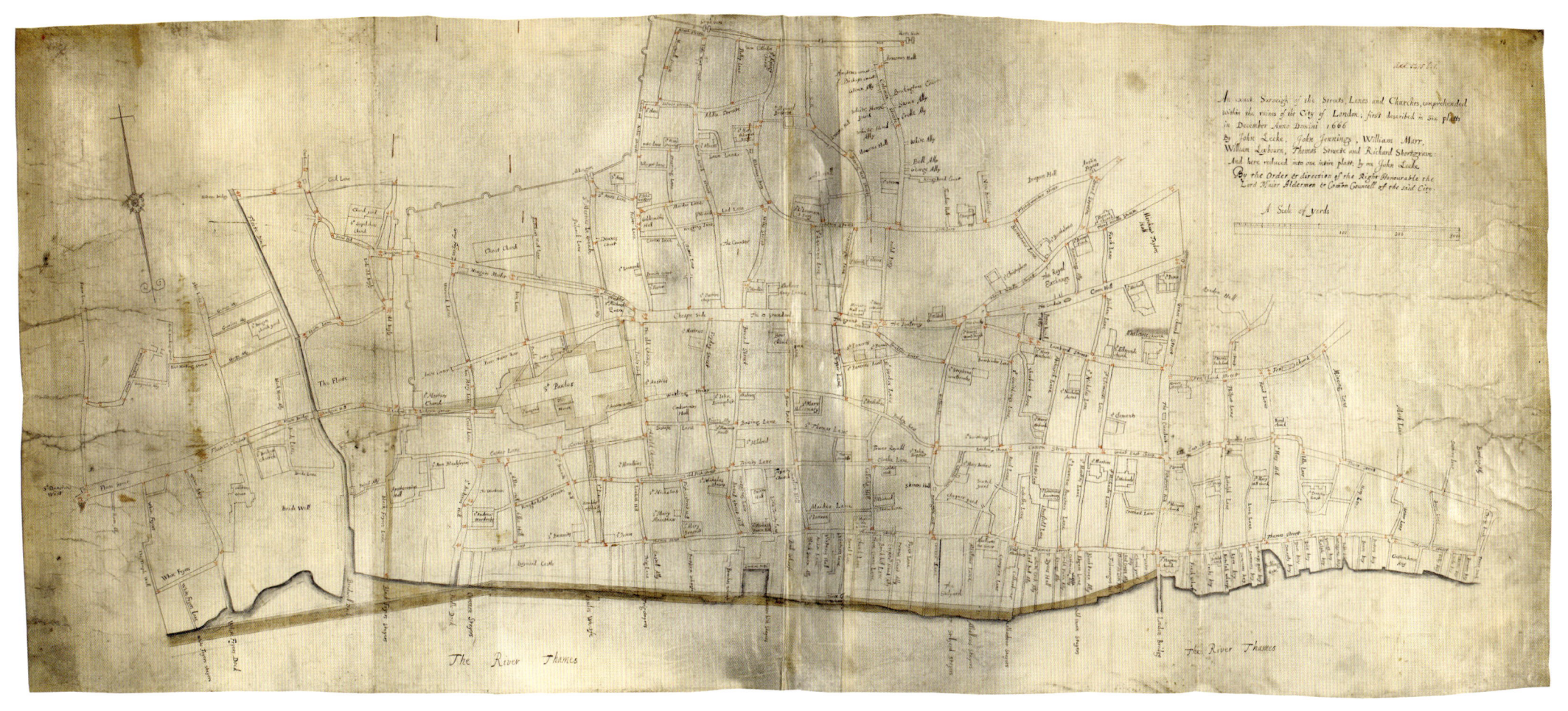

1.4.12   John Leake, 'An exact Surveigh of the Streets, Lanes, Churches comprehended within the ruines of the City of London', January–March 1667. 58 × 134 cm. Add. MS 5415.1.E

John Leake was a London mathematical practitioner who, among other things, designed an elaborate sundial for erection in Leadenhall Street — and later became first master of the new Mathematical School at Christ's Hospital in 1673.

AFTER THE FIRE

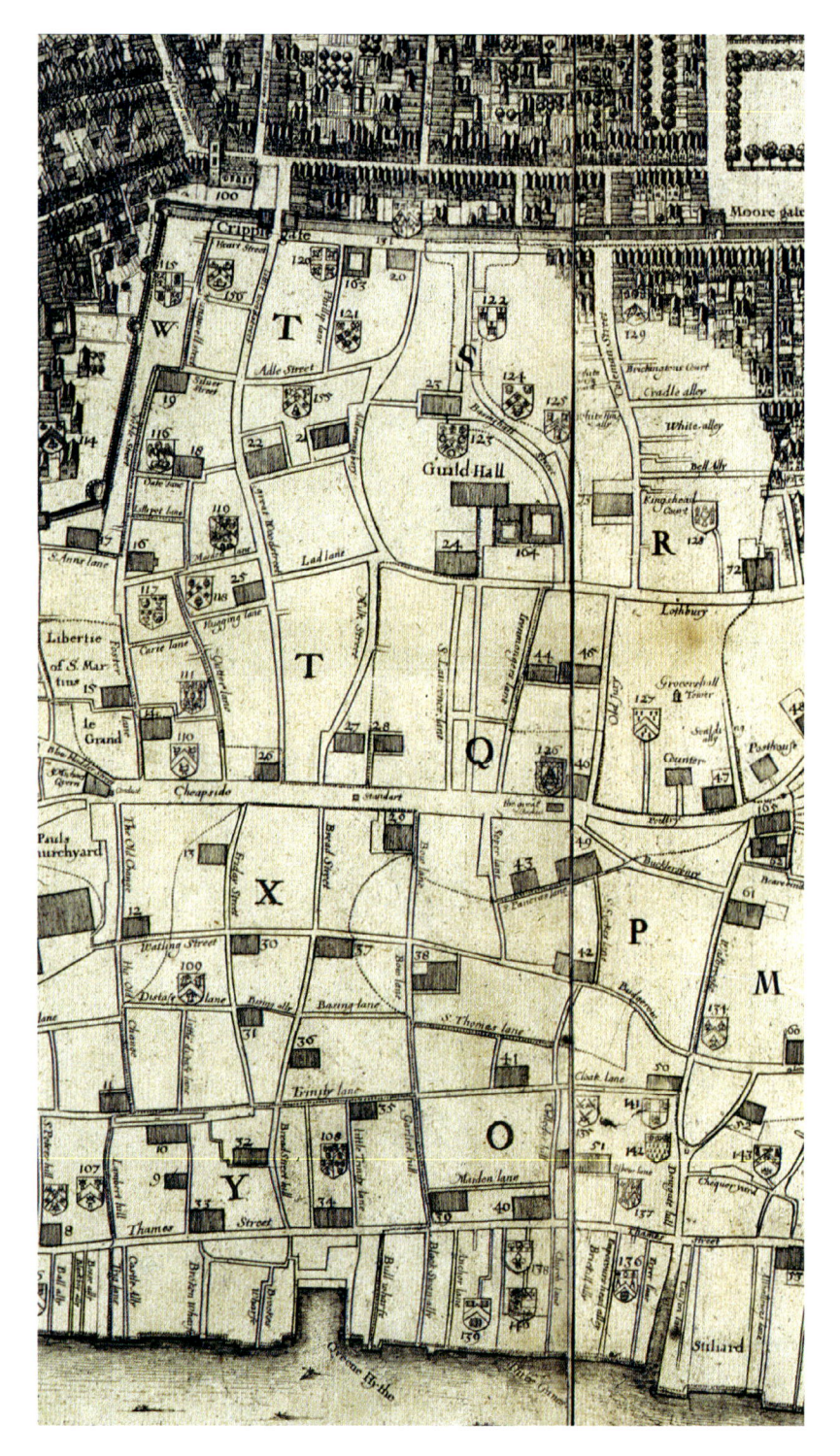

Soon after the Fire, six skilled surveyors led by a distinguished mathematician, John Leake, were commissioned to draw up plans of the devastated area. The six-sheet survey, undertaken in December 1666, was presented to Charles II the following March. Hollar was commissioned to prepare a two sheet printed version, at a scale of about 27.5 inches to the mile (1:2300) and he probably copied Leake's reduced plan (1.4.12). To demonstrate the City's defiant resolve to continue as normal, ward boundaries are shown and the sites of the livery halls are indicated by their arms. Beyond, Hollar has included what remained valid of the 'Great Map' of London that he still hoped to publish. Ultimately it was not the Fire but changing ideas of what constituted a good map that seems to have put paid to his map. The new scientific spirit held that a ground plan was preferable to the bird's-eye view which Hollar had mastered to perfection.

1.4.13   Wenceslaus Hollar, *An Exact Svrveigh of the Streets Lanes and Chvrches Contained within the Rvines of the City of London First Described in Six Plats* [1667] (London: Nathaniel Brooke, 2nd edn, 1669). 56 × 84 cm. Maps Crace 1.50

The publisher of the map was Nathaniel Brooke, a second-generation London bookseller. Like thousands of Londoners he had lost his premises (at the sign of the Angel on Cornhill) in the Great Fire and was now working from temporary premises off Bishopsgate. Sometimes referred to as Major Brooke, presumably from service in the Civil War, he is further remembered as the publisher of the *Musaeum Tradescantianum; or, a Collection of Rarities preserved at South-Lambeth neer London* (1656) — the first museum catalogue to appear in England — adorned with portraits of the Tradescants by Hollar. He petitioned unsuccessfully against other publishers pirating the map.

AN EXACT SVRVEIGH OF THE STREETS LANES AND CHVRCHES CONTAINED WITHIN THE RVINES OF THE CITY OF LONDON FIRST DESCRIBED IN SIX PLATS BY IOHN LEAKE, IOHN IENNINGS, WILLIAM MARR, WILL. LEYBVRN, THOMAS STREETE & RICHARD SHORTGRAVE in Dec. A. 1666. BY THE ORDER OF THE LORD MAYOR ALDERMEN AND COMMON COVNCELL OF THE SAID CITY.
Reduced here into one intire plat, by Iohn Leake, the City Wall being added also; The places where the Halls stood are exprest by Coats of Armes, & all the Wards divided by pricks & Alphabet
The Prospect of this City, as it appeared from the opposite Southwarke side in the fire time.
The Right Honourable S. William Turner the Lord Major. A. 1669.
Hatton Garden
Smith Field
Moore fields
Moore gate
Aldersgate
Newgate
Ludgate
Bridewell
Paules Churchyard
Guild Hall
Tower hill
East Smith field
THE RIVER THAMES
Part of Southwarke
a Scale of Feet,
Published with the description of the Wards, by the care Industrie and Charge of Nathanaell Brooke Stationer, and are to be Sould at his shop at the Angell, in the second Yard of Gresham Colledge leading from Bishopsgate street.

1.5 THE LONDON REALITY

There were many important aspects of London that were reflected not in the sanitised printed maps meant for public consumption but in private, hand-drawn plans commissioned for a very restricted number of users. These included plans showing water conduits and analysing lawless districts where neither the writ of the King nor the City Corporation ran. There had always been more industry (and noise, discomfort, disease and smells) than was reflected in the printed maps. After 1550, however, rapid population growth transformed London from the relatively spacious city portrayed in printed maps to a jumble of over-crowded houses, often in multiple occupation and overlooking open drains, built over former gardens and connected to nearby lanes by narrow, insanitary passages

LIBERTIES AND LAWLESSNESS IN SOUTHWARK

Following the Reformation, Henry VIII tried to restrict the rights to sanctuary in former monastic and other religious precincts. He commissioned maps to identify them. This, perhaps the earliest surviving London street plan and still quite recognisable (with East at the top), depicts one of the most lawless parts of London. Neither King nor City exercised full authority in Southwark with its maze of manors, liberties and precincts, taverns, jails, hospitals and markets, most of them with their own, varied, rights and immunities. The daggers mark the limits of the City's jurisdiction while royal jurisdiction is shown to be limited to the park around the royal manor house on the West (bottom) side of Borough High Street. The pillory in the middle of the road and Marshalsea Prison on the east side are just a gesture to law-enforcement. Theatres were to flourish in this environment and even Henry proved unable to cope: London's last 'liberties', or self-governing lawless enclaves, were finally suppressed only in the nineteenth century.

1.5.1   Anon. [Plan of Borough High Street, Southwark, *c.* 1542]. 83.1 × 58.4 cm. The National Archives PRO MPC 64

KEY

1   River Thames
2   London Bridge
3   St Thomas's Hospital
4   The Tabard Inn
5   Marshalsea Prison
6   King's Bench Prison
7   Royal Manor House (Suffolk House)
8   Winchester House
9   Southwark Cathedral (as it now is)

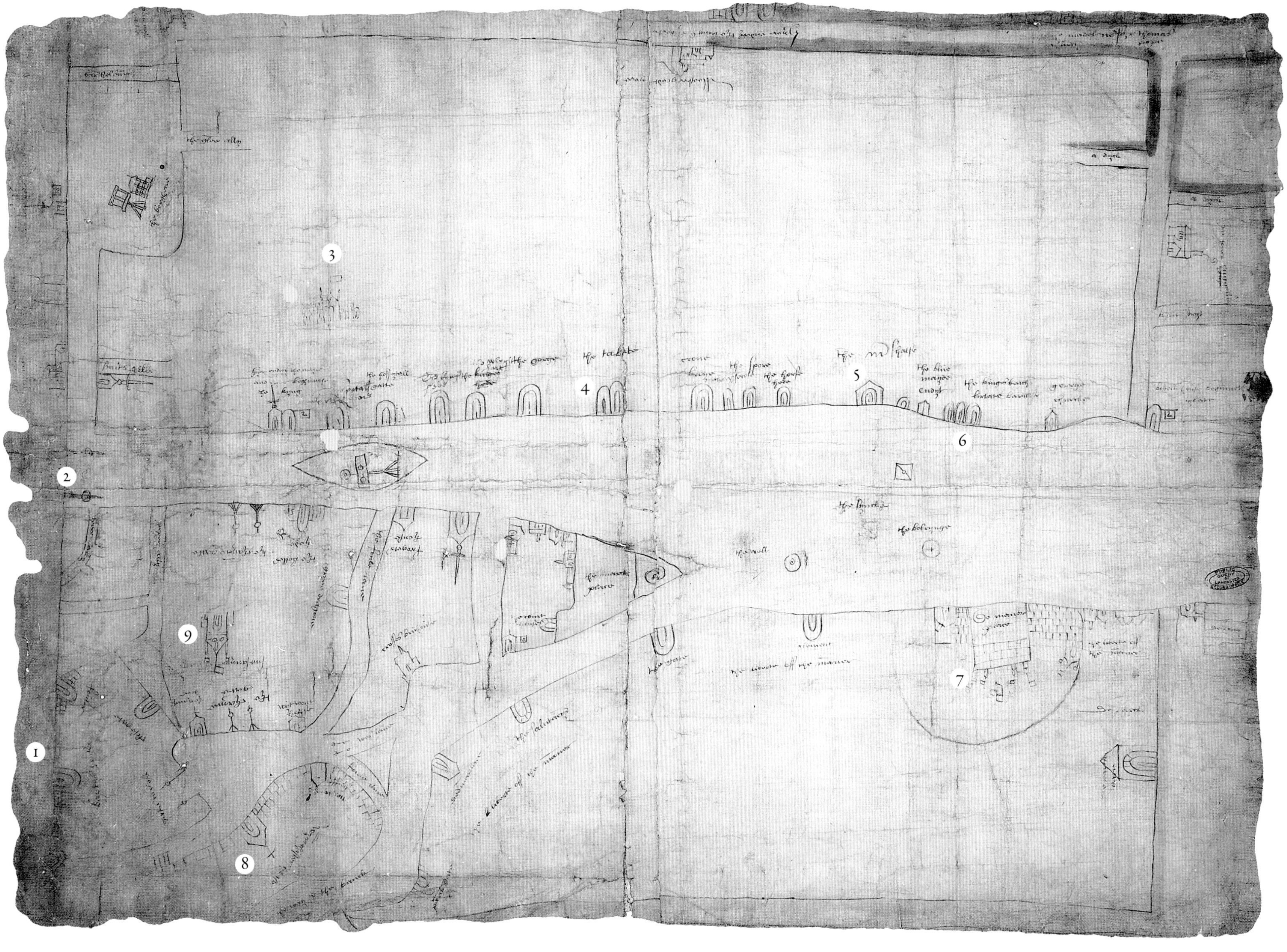

3
4
5
6
2
9
1
8
7

PUBLIC SPLENDOUR PRIVATE SQUALOR

As London's population grew so living quarters became more cramped. Livery companies like the Clothworkers needed, as landlords, to know what conditions were really like. This plan, with East at the top, shows a warren of passages and courts separating two- and three-storey half-timbered buildings bordering the Fleet (now Farringdon Street) at the bottom (West) and Fleet Prison ('Flete') at the right (South). While Lady Wood enjoyed a spacious house and garden, the privies of her tenants, in contravention of a 1531 law, emptied into the Fleet degrading it from a river to a 'diche'. For a Victorian plan of the same site see 6.3.2.

1.5.2   Ralph Treswell, plan of houses along Fleet Lane [now 16 Fleet Lane, 16–21 Farringdon Street, Modern Court], 1612. 49.5 × 36.8 cm. Clothworkers' Company Plan Book, 47. Courtesy of the Clothworkers' Company

Ralph Treswell, originally from St Albans, was trained as a painter but came increasingly to concentrate on work as one of the earliest modern surveyors. He was a senior member of the Painter-Stainers' Company and became senior common councilman for the ward of Aldersgate in the City of London, where he lived.

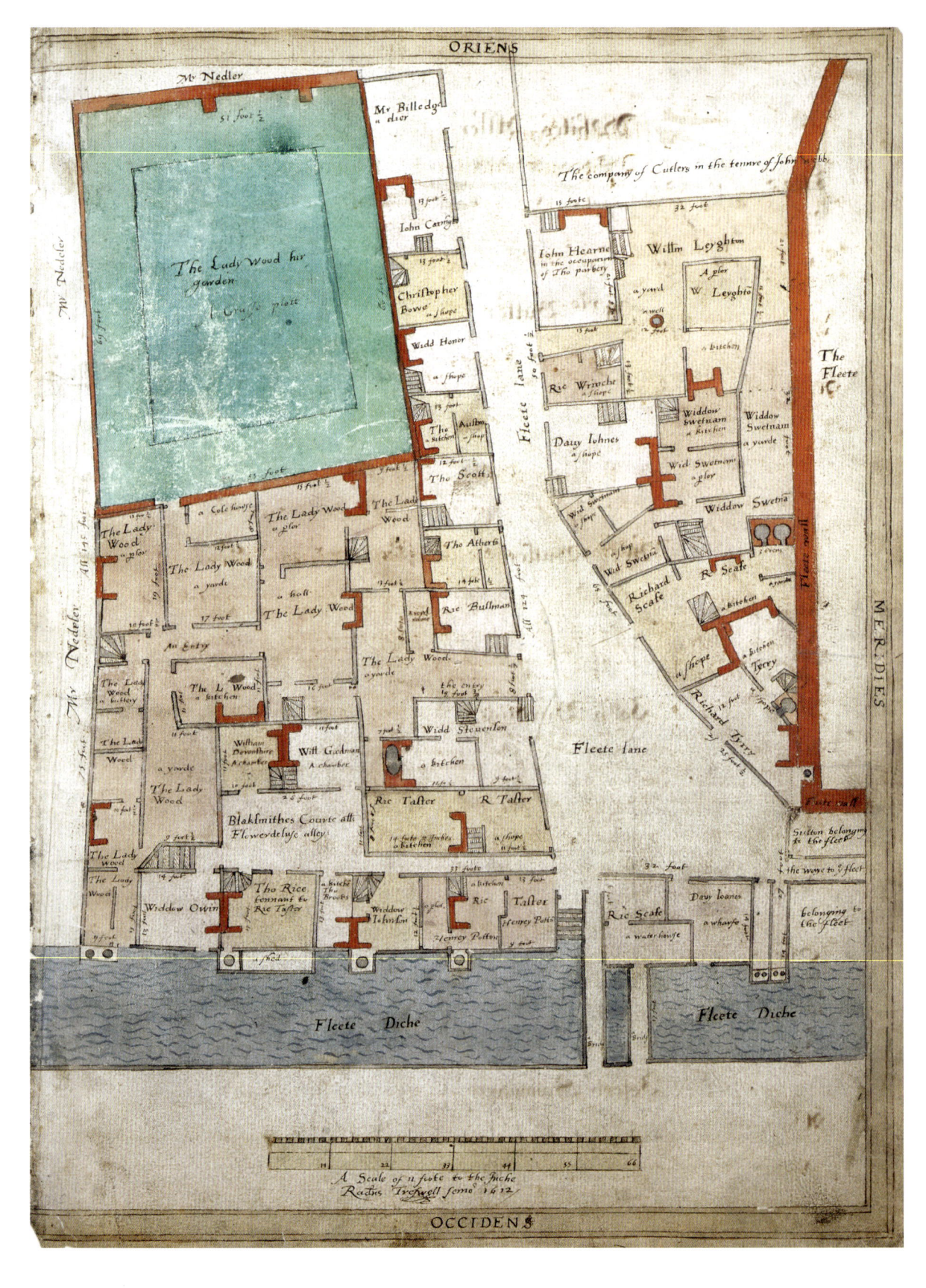

Detail from William Morgan's map of London and Westminster including the Monument ('Pillar') and ward boundaries

SECTION TWO
LONDON REBORN

The great maps of Ogilby, Morgan and Rocque encapsulated the period of London's triumphant recovery from the Great Fire and its emergence as a centre of European civilisation. Ogilby and Morgan's map of 1676 was very English and generally sober, Rocque's of 1746 cosmopolitan and in tune with the latest French scientific and decorative fashions. But the West End could not have been developed without the assistance of larger-scale manuscript estate plans. Handy printed maps were also produced to tempt the tourist, or to enable the merchant to do business in the Royal Exchange. Still others recorded, for future use, the way in which the government had suppressed the mob in 1780. Otherwise maps on the whole ignored the poor.

2.1 REBUILDING THE CITY

In the wake of the Fire a spate of visionary proposals for a new city were submitted. They took no account of expense and existing property rights, however, and the danger that the City might be entirely abandoned unless it was speedily rebuilt: many merchants had moved to the new western suburbs before the Fire and many did so in the immediate aftermath, never to return. The continuing participation of leading figures from the recently established Royal Society like Robert Hooke and Christopher Wren ensured that the rebuilding would nevertheless reflect some of the rationalist ideals of Baroque Europe. The new City, which had been substantially rebuilt by 1675, was embellished by brick buildings, some widened roads, a handsome monument to the Fire and eventually by the spires of the new churches, many designed by Wren and his assistant Nicholas Hawksmoor.

GRAND IDEAS

Within days of the Fire Christopher Wren and many others, including John Evelyn and Richard Newcourt, submitted revolutionary ideas, influenced by foreign models, for the rebuilding of the City. This rare print, published in Wren's lifetime, was the source of numerous later copies. It shows a canalised Fleet River, a series of piazzas and a business quarter centred on the Royal Exchange. Many have regretted the failure to act on Wren's ideas. However, as Joshua Reynolds commented much later, their 'effect might have been … rather unpleasing: the uniformity might have produced weariness, and a slight degree of disgust'.

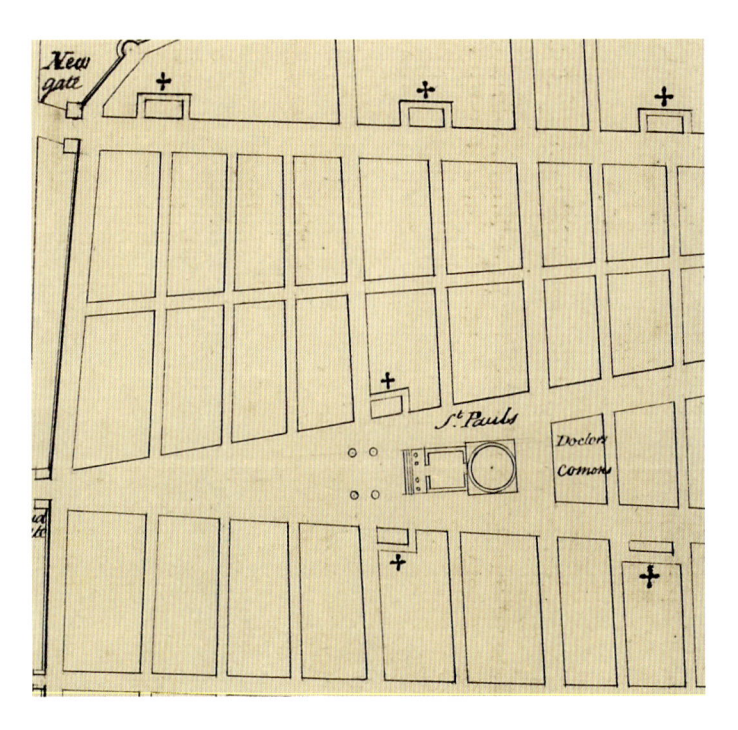

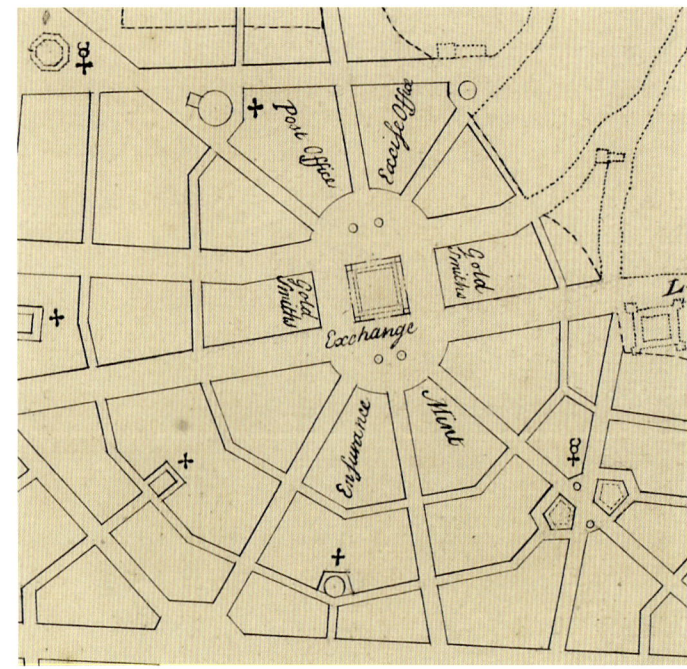

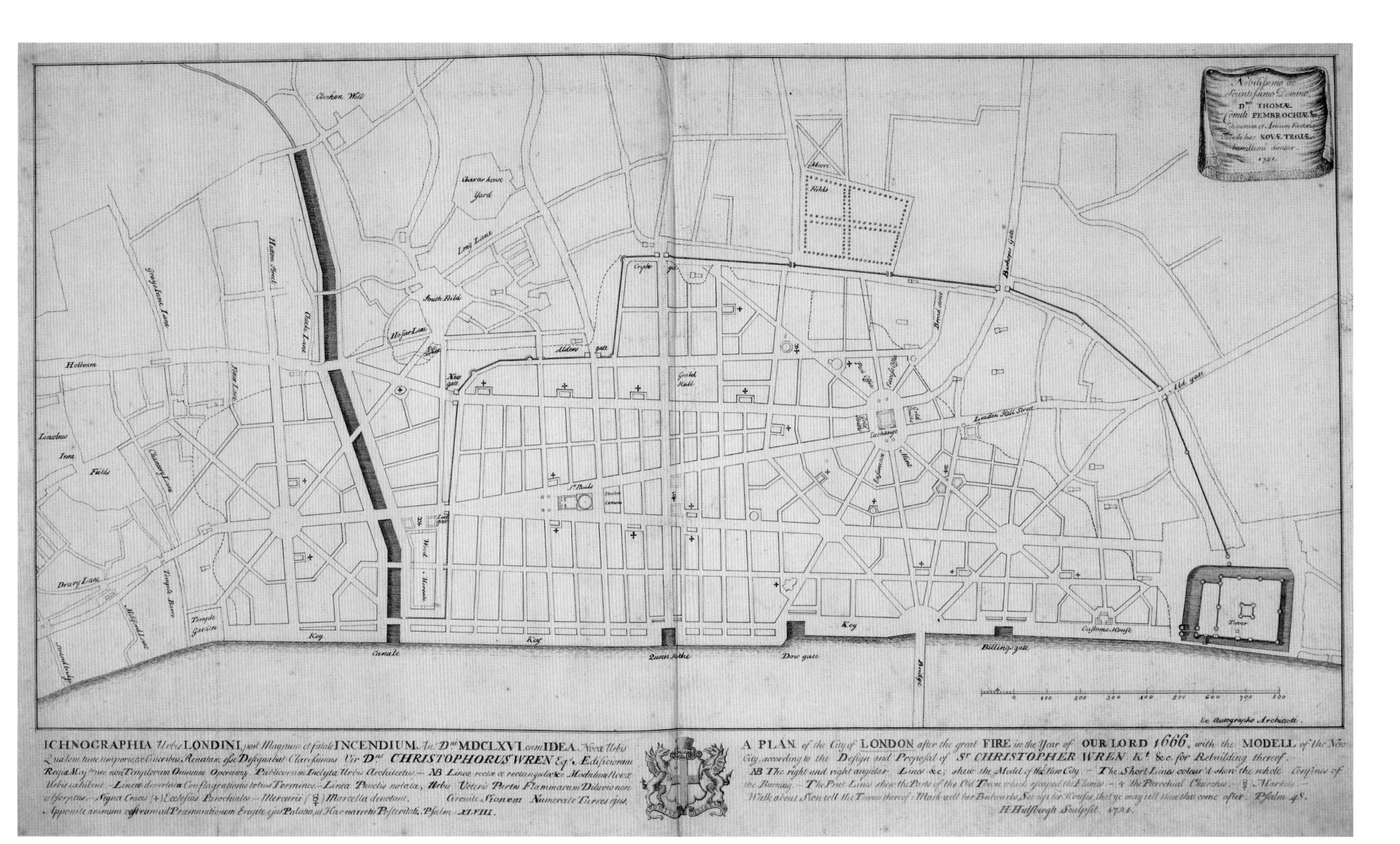

2.1.1   H. Hulsbergh (engraver), *Plan of the City of London after the great Fire in the year of our Lord 1666; with the modell of the New City according to the Design and Proposal of Sir Christopher Wren, Knt., etc. for rebuilding thereof … ex autographo architecti 1721* [Proof without title text which has been added in manuscript] engraving. 43.2 × 74 cm. Maps K. Top. 20.19-3

Henry Hulsbergh came originally from Amsterdam. He specialised in architectural work and was working with Nicholas Hawksmoor on a project to engrave plates of all Wren's principal works when he was struck down by a paralytic fit. It left him incapable of further work and he was supported through the two years of this illness by the members of the Lutheran Church in the Savoy, where he was buried in 1729.

THE SPIRES OF THE CITY CHURCHES

One of the most original architects that Britain has produced, Nicholas Hawksmoor was Christopher Wren's assistant in the 1690s. They were both involved in the design of the tower and steeple of St Bride's [Bridget's] Church off Fleet Street, which was to be completed in 1701–03. Hawksmoor probably drew this delicate sketch for the steeple. The steeples were to add a Baroque flourish to the skyline of London for centuries. St Bride's is not only the highest of the Wren steeples. It is also said to have provided the model for the traditional British wedding cake.

2.1.2 Nicholas Hawksmoor (?), 'St Bridget', *c.* 1695 Pencil sketch. 29 × 12.2 cm Maps K. Top. 23.10-c

AN ANCIENT AND MODERN MONUMENT

At 202 feet or just over 60 metres, the Monument to the Great Fire is still the world's tallest isolated stone column. A combination of observatory with telescope and classically-inspired memorial, with complex allegorical carved images and Latin inscriptions at its base, it is one of the few completed works to have something of the radicalism of the initial proposals for rebuilding the City.

This is not surprising since it was the brainchild of the multi-talented scientist Robert Hooke and his close friend Christopher Wren. Hooke's drawing shows the final design, with a flaming urn rather than a phoenix or statue surmounting the pillar.

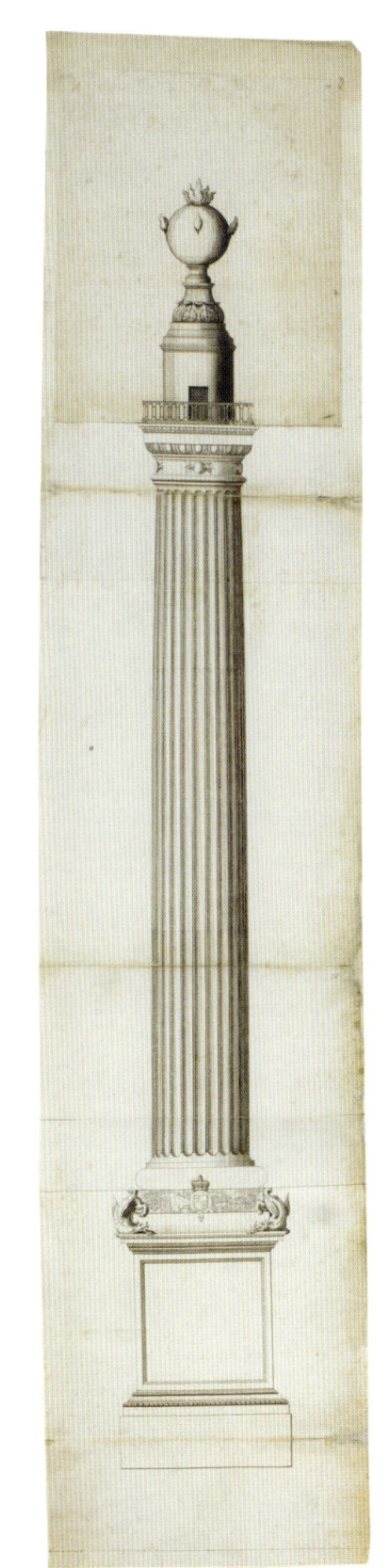

2.1.3   Robert Hooke (?) [final design for the Monument, 1675] 126 × 27 cm. Additional MS 5238.78

HOW WAS LONDON SURVEYED?

The preliminary sketches for Ogilby and Morgan's map would have looked like this. The sheet records the statistician and mapmaker Gregory King's daily progress in mapping lanes, alleys and buildings east of the Tower. King, who had mapped much of London and Westminster for Ogilby and Morgan and had proposed the scale for the completed map, used chains, a rod and measured angles with a theodolite as recommended by Ogilby's assistant, William Leybourne in the 1674 edition of his book *The Complete Surveyor* based, as he stated, on his own experience in mapping London after the Fire. A brief diary on the right records King's work schedule ('7 [June] survey afternoon sans assistance; 8 Saturday survey from 10 to 6 sans assistance') and visits to Whitehall, Windsor, Lambeth and Epsom. The finished survey, dated 1687, is in Guildhall Library [Map Case 290].

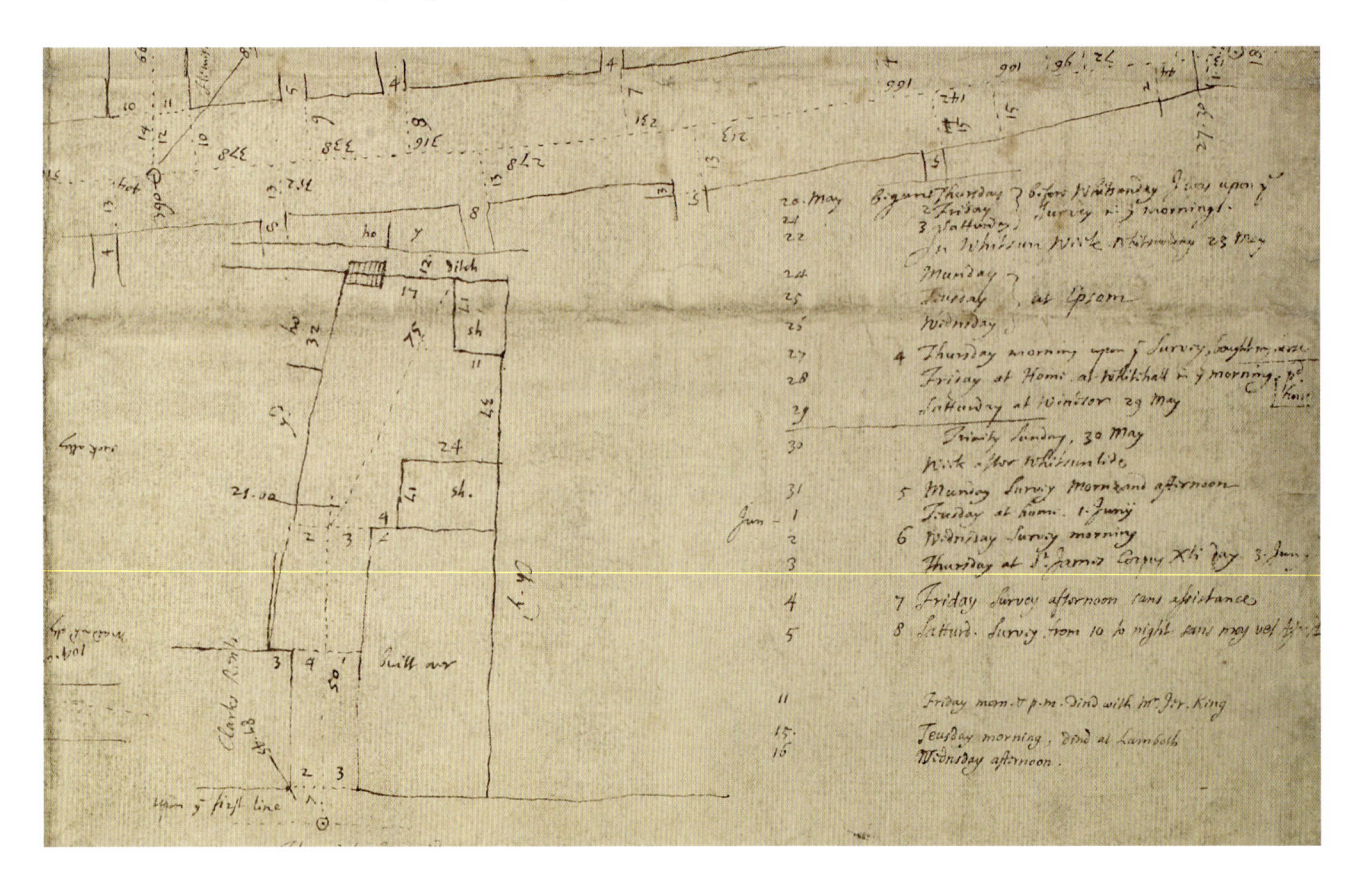

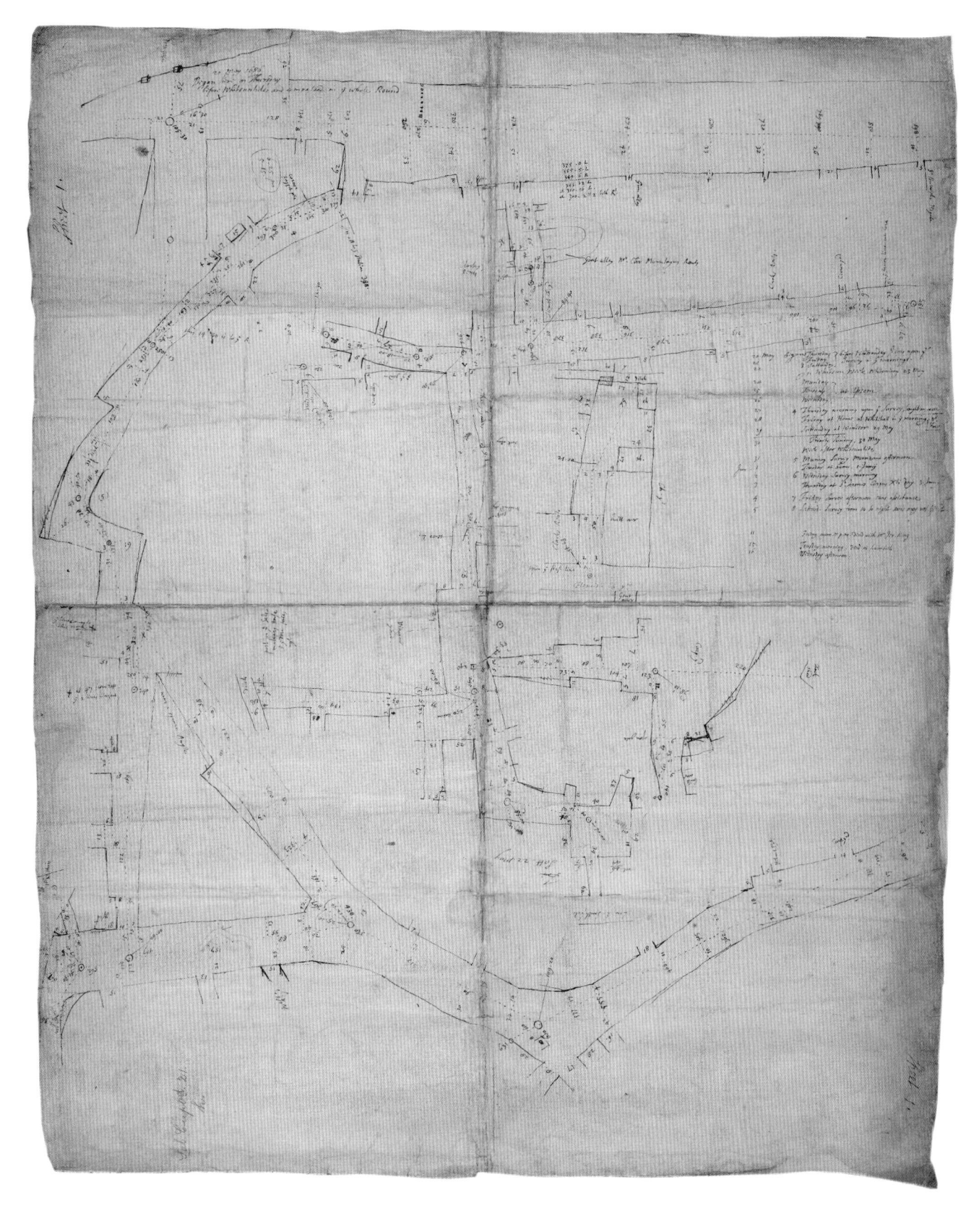

2.1.4 Gregory King, sketches with diary (middle of right side) for a survey, executed in collaboration with Edward Bostock Fuller, of the Precinct and Hospital of St Katharine by the Tower, 20 May – 16 June 1686. 51 × 43 cm. Sloane MS 3254 A.5

BACK IN BUSINESS

This is a scientific marvel, organised by John Ogilby, a colourful Scottish entrepreneur, bankrolled by City merchants, created by England's best surveyors, closely supervised by the scientist Robert Hooke and buttressed by information from a preceding written survey. The very large scale of 100 feet to the inch (1:1200) enabled every house and numerous boundaries to be depicted and an accompanying booklet identified almost every nook and cranny. Mapping in plan ('ichnographically') provided the precision desired by bureaucrats and businessmen and approved of by the scientifically-minded scientists and amateurs of the recently-founded Royal Society. It was this new idea of what a good plan should be and not the Fire of London that probably finally put paid to Hollar's dream of creating a bird's-eye map of the capital. Hollar did contribute to this plan — but only the elaborate compass star, the ships on the Thames and a few other decorative elements. A plan of the City for the City it is a sober celebration of its almost complete rebuilding just 10 years after the Fire. It does not extend to Westminster, the site of the government, and almost the only figurative decoration shows the Artillery Ground and the train bands, which in the 1640s had been used against the Crown.

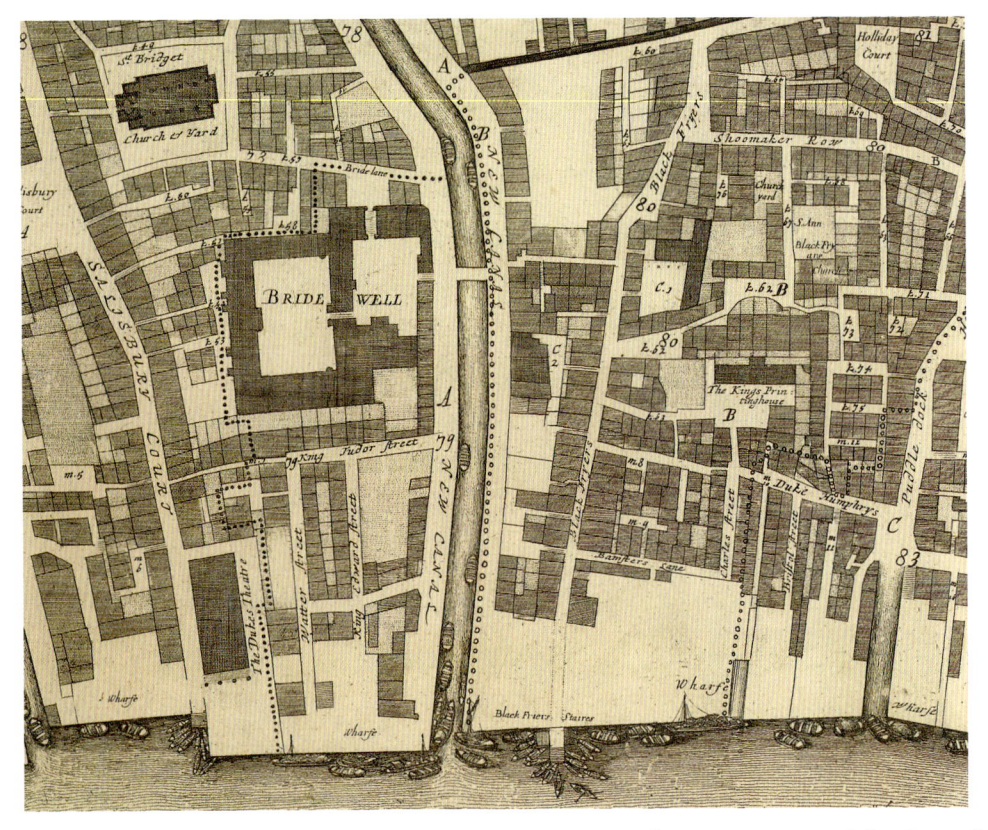

2.1.5   John Ogilby and William Morgan, *A Large and Accurate Map of the City of London Distinct from Westminster and Southwark, Ichnographically Describing all the Streets, Lanes, Alleys. Courts, Yards, Churches, Halls, Houses &c At the Scale of an Hundred Foot in an Inch. Actually Survey'd and Delineated by John Ogilby Esq, His Majesties Cosmographer, 1677* [sic] (London: 1676). Engraved and etched map. Title and date added in manuscript 148 × 253 cm. Maps Crace II.61

John Ogilby (1600–76) was born near Dundee and was in turn dancing-master, perhaps soldier, the founder of the first theatre in Dublin, poet, translator, and finally publisher and printer of lavish editions of the classics. Ruined financially by the Great Fire in 1666, in which he lost the bulk of his stock, he became a surveyor to the City of London and ended a flamboyant career with a dramatic intervention into cartographic publishing. He is buried at St Bride's, Fleet Street. William Morgan, who assisted with the map in spite of his absence from the title (see opposite), was another of the King's cosmographers. Morgan was Ogilby's wife's grandson by an earlier marriage.

A LARGE AND ACCURATE MAP OF THE CITY OF LONDON.

Ichnographically Describing all the Streets, Lanes, Alleys, Courts, Yards, Churches, Halls and Houses, &c. Actually Surveyed and Delineated. By JOHN OGILBY, Esq; His Majesties Cosmographer. 1677

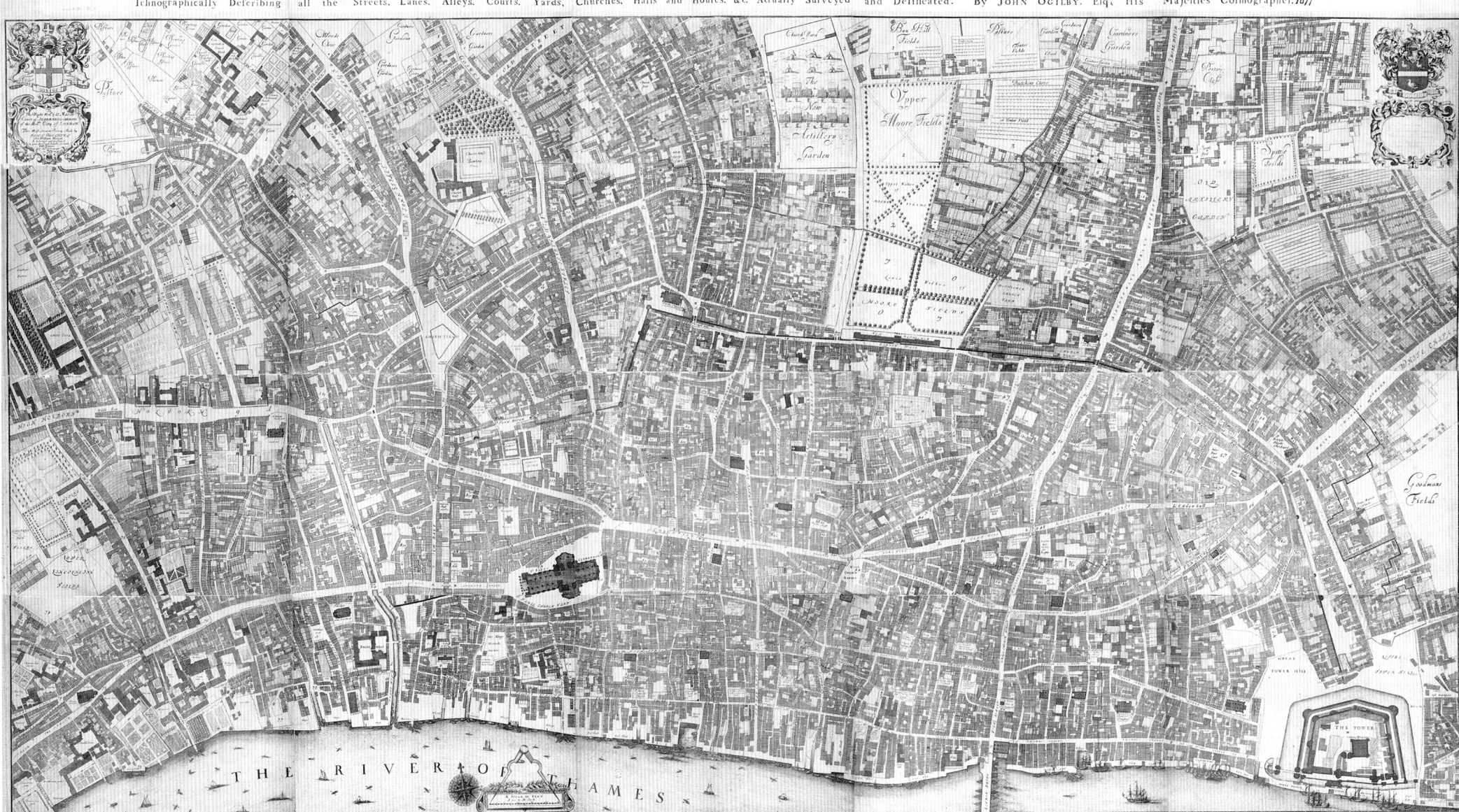

CELEBRATE!

This flamboyant map, combining separate detailed surveys of the City, Westminster and Southwark with an extremely accurate post-Fire panorama, was meant for public display. The mathematical plan therefore gives way to the depiction in elevation of the principal buildings (with an imaginative vision of a rebuilt St Paul's) and to large engraved views of Whitehall Palace (in particular), the Queen's palace of Somerset House and Westminster Abbey.

In 1681–82, after a turbulent period of Whig ascendancy, Charles II was reasserting the power of the Crown and he plays a central role on the map. He is shown receiving the subscription book of the survey from Morgan's deceased associate, Ogilby, and there are statues of him and his father at the upper corners. The extensive lists of princes, privy councillors, ministers, peers, bishops, masters of Cambridge and Oxford Colleges and office-holders of all sorts reflect the royal ascendancy as well as financial support for Morgan. Only views of the Royal Exchange, Guildhall and Mercers' Hall relate to the City and Morgan comments waspishly on the miserliness of the several livery companies which had failed to sponsor his map despite receiving prospectuses from him. Map, panorama and grand and miniaturised views glorify not the London of the merchants but the capital of the resurgent British monarchy.

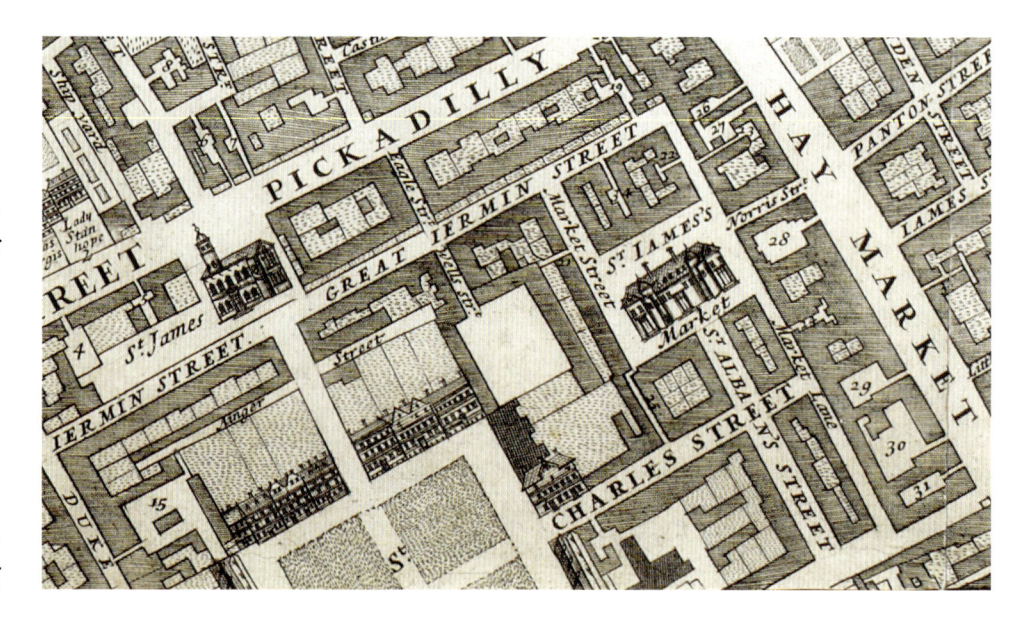

2.1.6 Willliam Morgan, *London &c actually survey'd* (London: 1682). 157 × 245 cm. Maps Crace II.58

61

2.2 THE CITY AND WESTMINSTER

John Ogilby's ground plan of the City of 1676 served as a discreet reminder that the City was back in business after its Great Fire. There were however to be two further great fires in 1691 and 1698 which destroyed almost all of the rambling Palace of Whitehall, hitherto the largest — and ugliest — palace in Europe, which had been at the heart of court and government. The court and court life moved to what had previously been a subsidiary palace in the increasingly prestigious new suburb of St James's. By then the cities of London and Westminster had grown together and were spreading northwards, with the population and social life being increasingly concentrated outside the City.

FROM WHITEHALL PALACE TO 'WHITEHALL'

This plan of Whitehall Palace, with West at the top, was drawn in preparation for its proposed transformation by Wren. The blue washed walls show the public and royal areas and the red, the lodgings and offices occupied by courtiers, ministers and the royal household, identified by letters and numbers. After the fires, which spared Inigo Jones's Banqueting House but put an end to the rebuilding plans, the nascent civil service moved into Henry VIII's undamaged sports complex to the west ('The Tennis Court', 'The Cockpit', 'Tilt Yard') on a supposedly temporary basis which has lasted to this day.

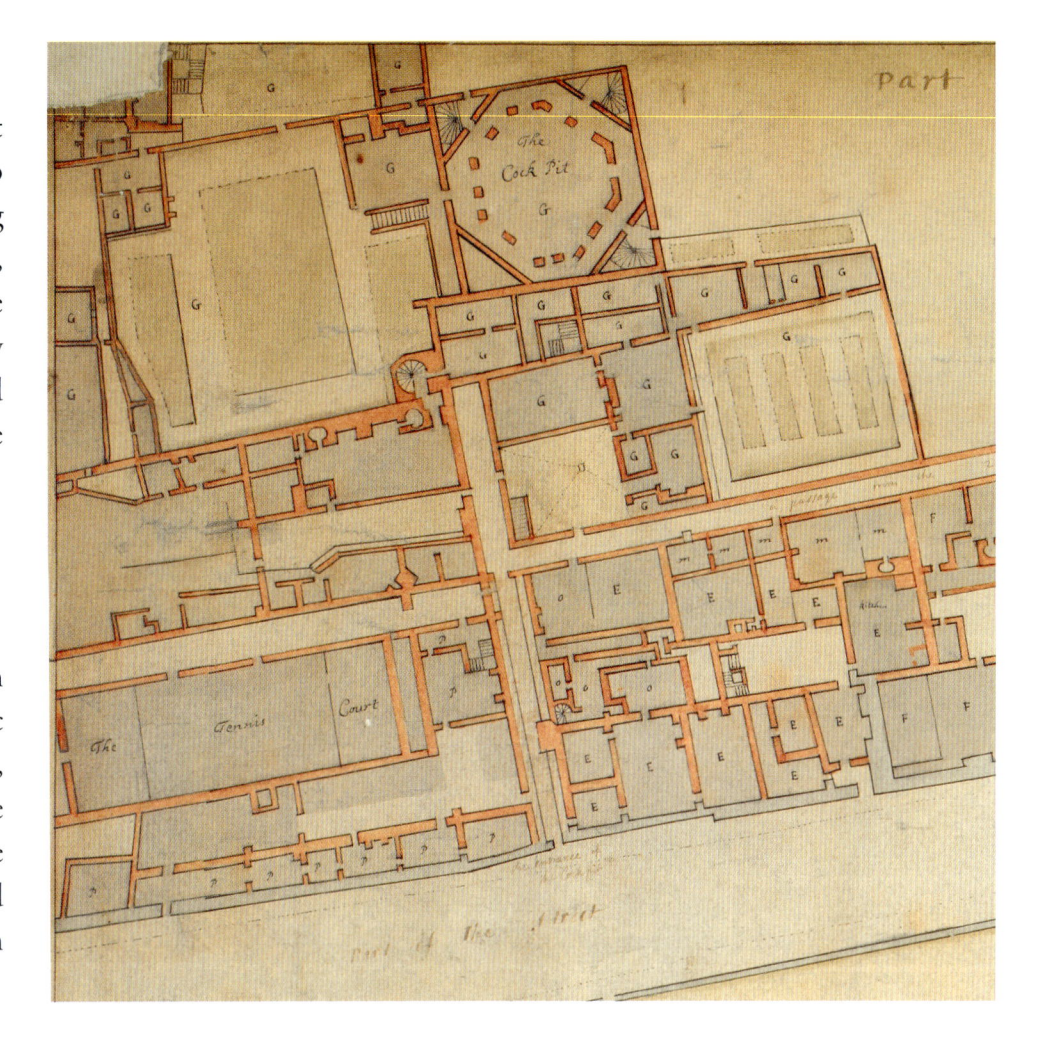

2.2.1 Office of Works draughtsman after Ralph Greatorex, 'Plan of the Palace of Whitehall', *c.* 1670. Ink and watercolour on paper. 71 × 85.6 cm. Maps Crace XI.65

63

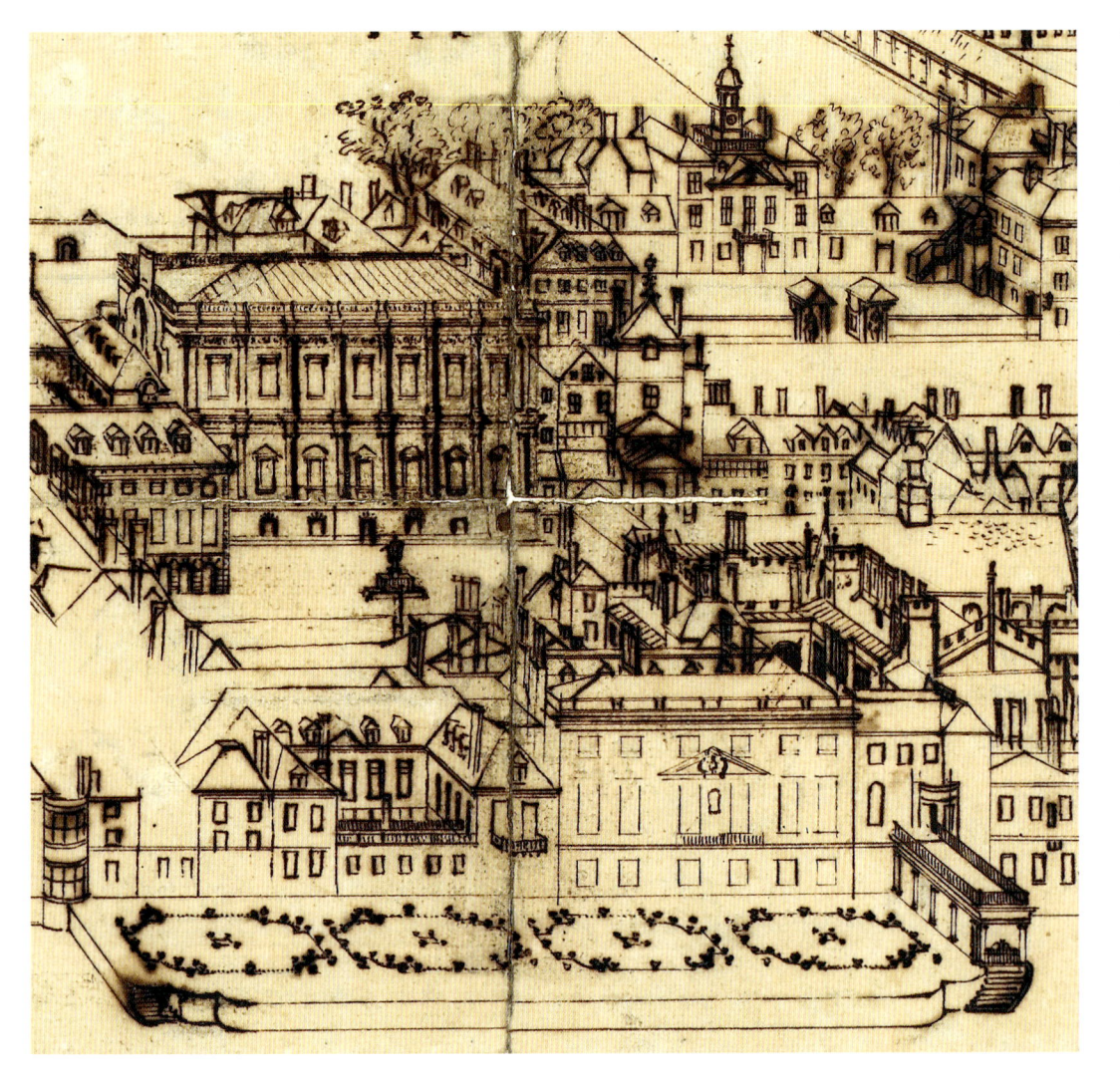

THE LAST DAYS OF WHITEHALL PALACE

Whitehall Palace as it was between the fires of 1691 and 1698 is seen from the same viewpoint as the plan. While the river front has been transformed by Wren's creation of new apartments and a terrace with flower beds for Queen Mary (the steps on the right still exist), the Great Hall, the riverside ranges to the right, the Privy Garden, the Cockpit, the Great Covered Tennis Court (of which fragments also survive) and the Banqueting House are as they were in 1670, when the plan (2.2.1) was drawn. St James's Palace (right) and the predecessor of Buckingham House (centre) can be seen in the background.

2.2.2   Leendert Knyff [A bird's-eye view of Whitehall Palace from the east 1695–97]. 33.6 × 48.8 cm. British Museum

Knyff (1650–1722) was born at Haarlem in the Netherlands, the son of the painter Wouter Knijff. He was working in London from at least 1681 and apart from views of this type he is also remembered as a portraitist and still-life painter. He was buried in the New Chapel, Broadway, in the parish of St Margaret's Westminster.

65

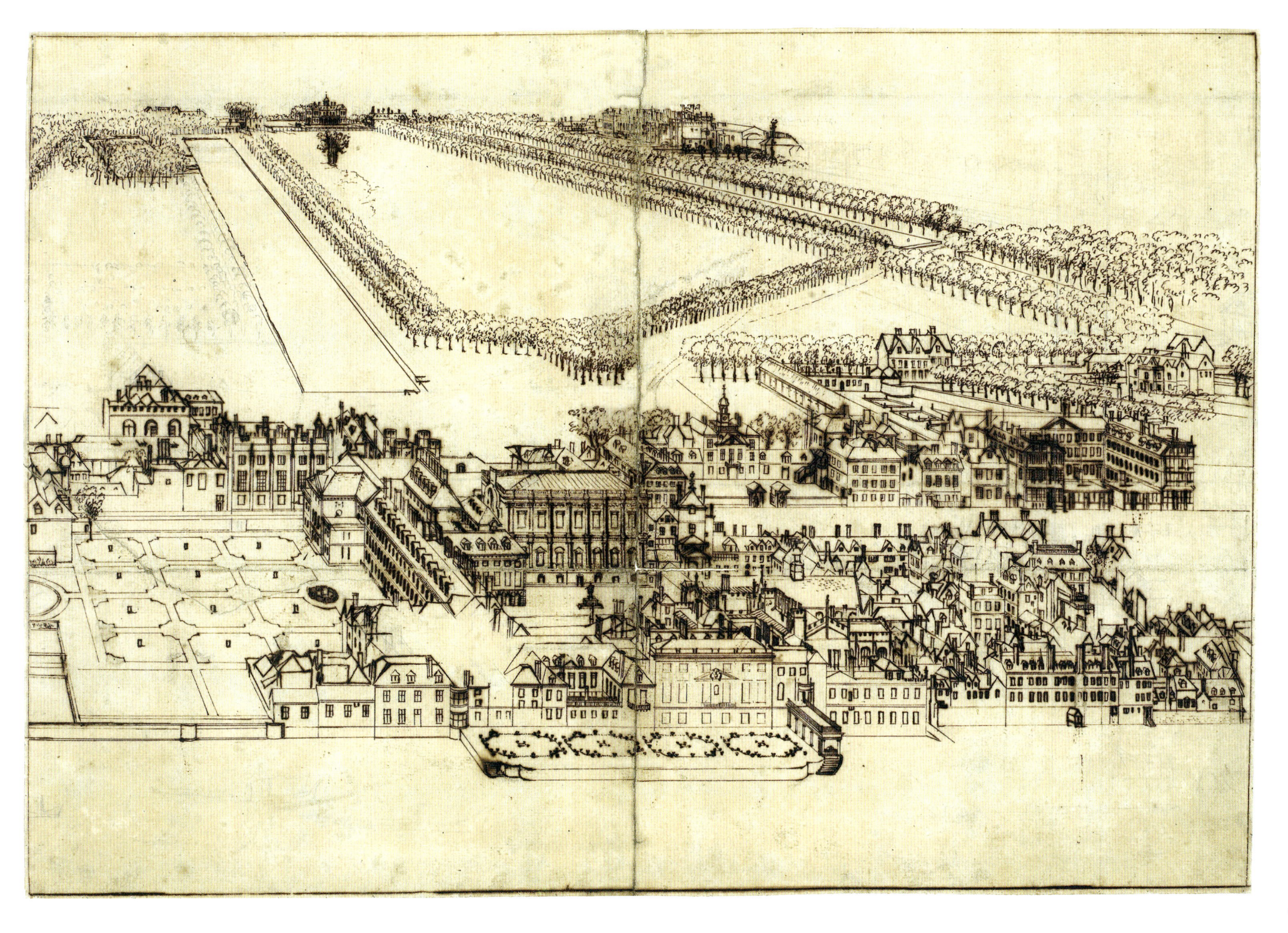

A NEW PERSPECTIVE

Seen from the roof of Buckingham House, St Paul's and the City are only a distant presence. The elegant new houses and churches of Westminster and the West End are much more prominent. To the left are the palaces lining the Mall and behind them, the recently-built St James's neighbourhood with St James's Square at its heart and Piccadilly beyond. The Dutch-born Kip, a loyal Hanoverian, shows the King and Prince of Wales in their coaches in Green Park followed by an escort of horse. St James's Park is the epicentre of fashion. Well-dressed ladies and gentlemen parade, buy fresh milk and salute the sedan chair carrying Lady Rachel Russell, the widow of a Whig martyr, Lord William Russell, who had lost his life under James II. Courtesans look for custom in the wilderness to the right. On the other side of the park wall, the poor beg.

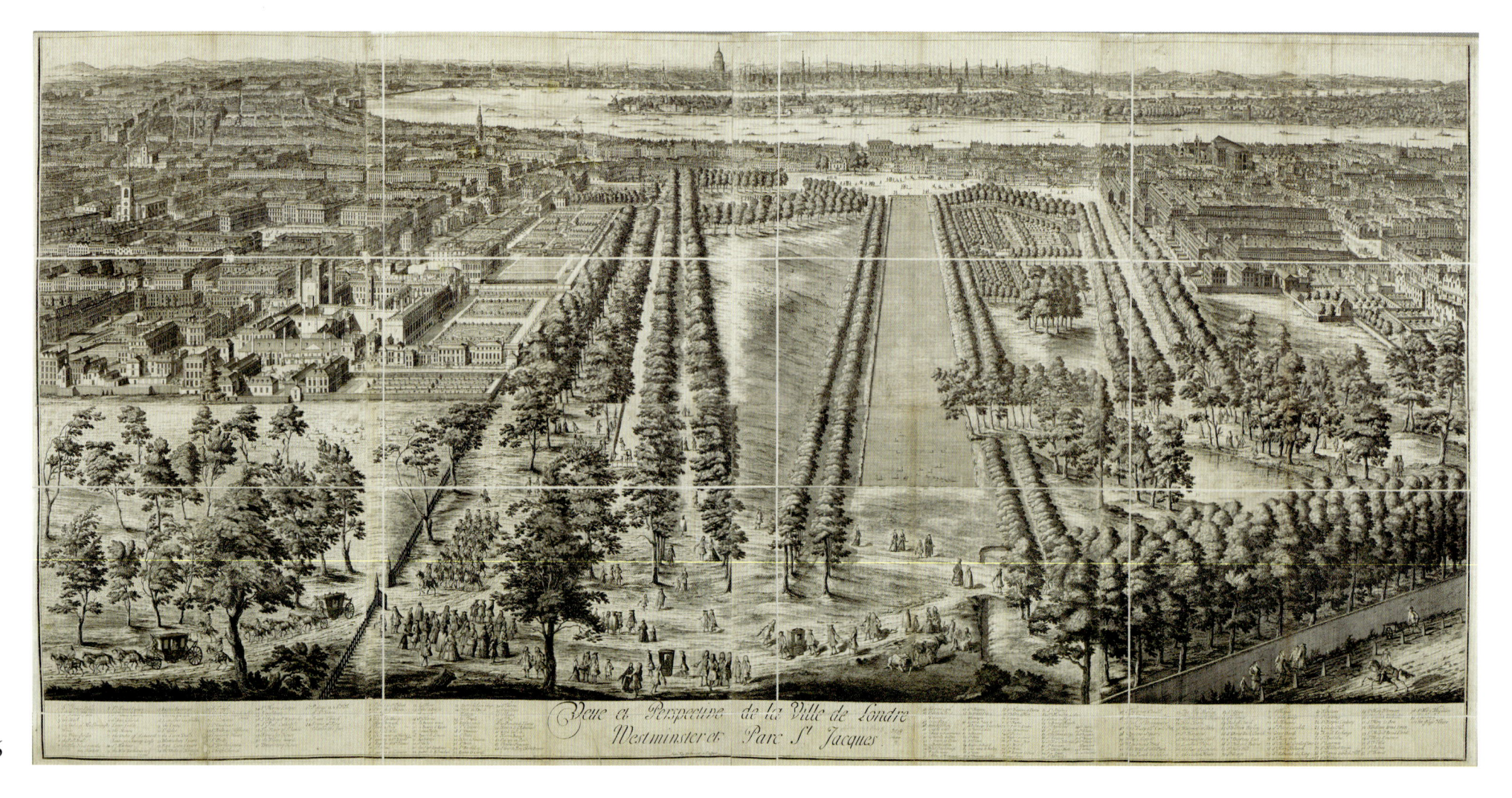

2.2.3 Jan Kip *Veue et Perspective de la Ville de Londre* [sic] *Westminster et Parc St Jacques* (London, 1720; edition of *c.* 1728 showing Gibbs spire of St Martin's in the Fields of 1726). Engraving. 103 × 208 cm. Maps *3518 (9)

Kip came from Amsterdam and almost certainly arrived in London in the wake of William of Orange. He immediately established a reputation as an engraver of architectural prospects and views, often working with Lendert Knyff. He was buried at St Margaret's Westminster in 1721.

2.3 PROFITING FROM DEVELOPMENT

After 1660, the built-up area of London mushroomed. Existing laws could not prevent it, but they could be exploited to raise money for the government by way of fines. The royal and noble owners of the vast surrounding landed estates soon realised that they did not have the money to build the houses needed to meet the demand. So they employed enterprising middlemen to seek out and issue cheap leases for relatively short periods of years to builders. The builders incurred the risk and got a short-term return on their money; the landlords got a return in the longer term and patterns of development and land ownership were set which have in large part endured to modern times.

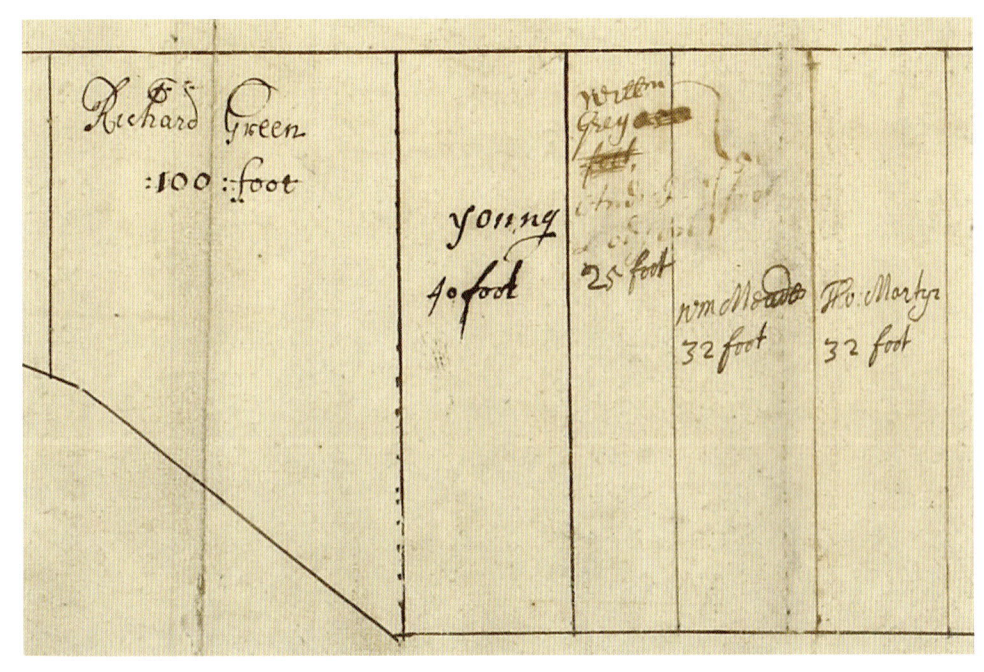

Detail from a proposal for a street near St James's Palace, 1688 (shown in full on p. 70)

RETROSPECTIVE PLANNING PERMISSION

Despite proclamations forbidding building beyond the City walls except along existing highways, John Carter had built a row of houses on Hares Marsh, east of Brick Lane. This plan, with South at top, illustrates the situation. Now he wanted to build more, even though the area was muddy, impassable for coaches and distant from any church. The warrant allows him to do so, on condition that he use brick and stone, and paves and drains the road, since the alternatives presented 'a greater Nuisance'. The government got money from fines and payments for the warrant and Carter got his new houses.

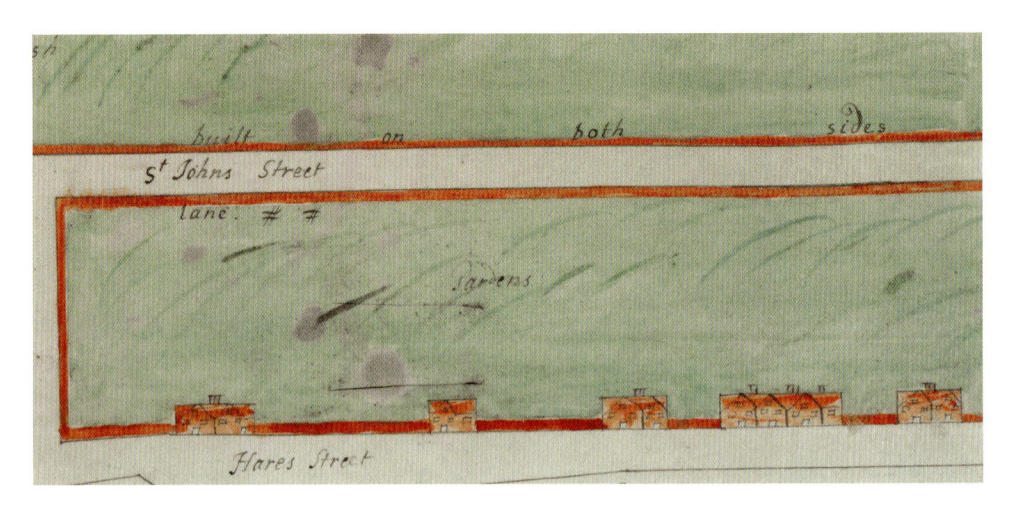

2.3.1   Anon., 'John Carters ground in Stepney containing eight akers, two roodes and seaven perche measured in June 1671' accompanying Privy Seal warrant, 29 July 1671. Ink and washes on vellum. 48 × 63 cm. Harley MS 7344 art. 72

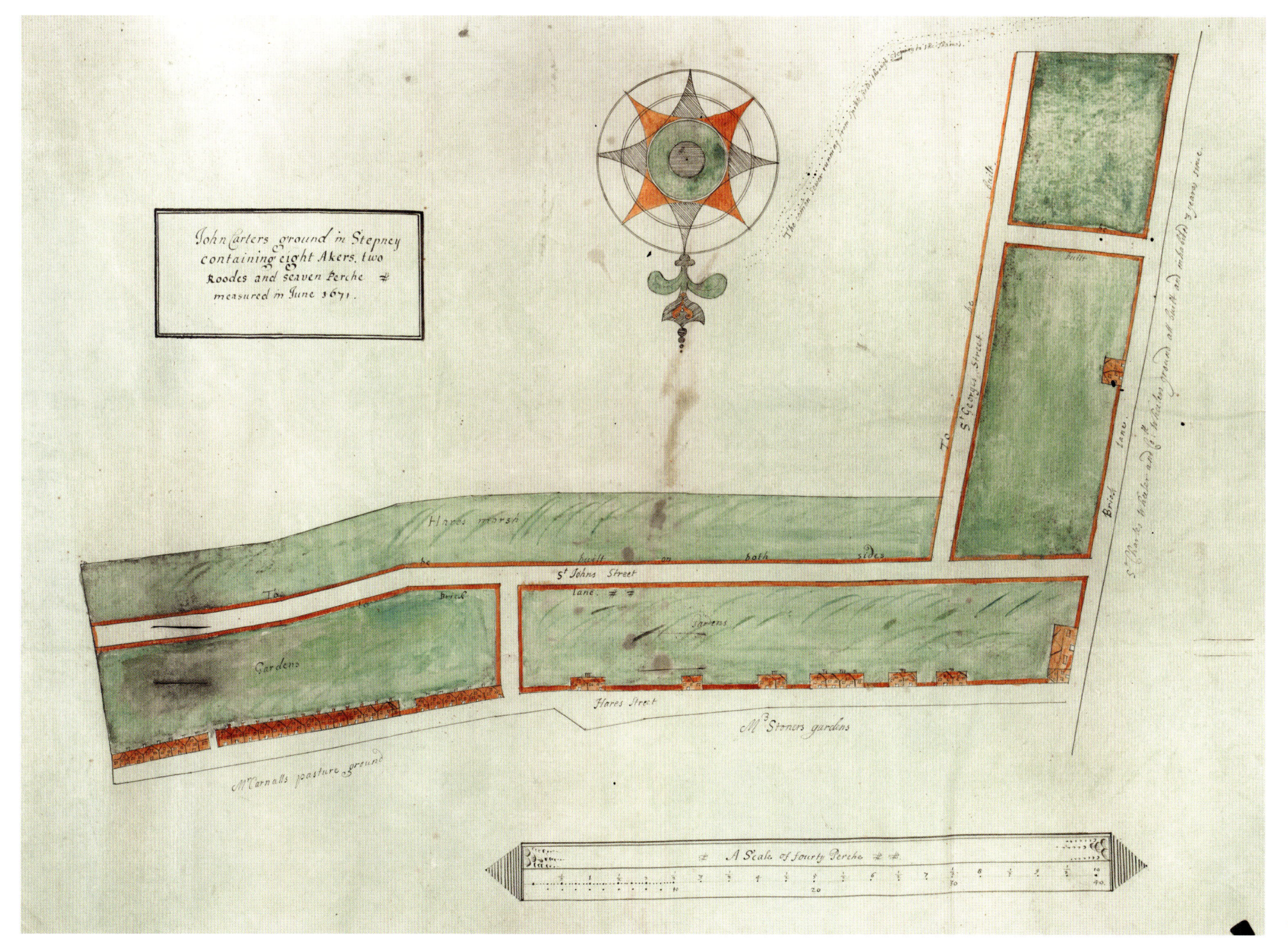

John Carters ground in Stepney
containing eight Akers, two
Roodes and seaven Perche
measured in June 1671.

Hares marsh

be built on both sides

St Johns Street lane

The Ditch

Gardens

Gardens

Hares Street

Mr Tarnalls pasture ground

Mr Stoners gardens

To St Georges Street

Brick lane

A Scale of fourty Perches

DEVELOPMENT ON THE CHEAP

In 1688 James II tried to finance the building of a new Wren- or Hawksmoor-designed royal mews north of St James's Palace by creating a road stretching up to Piccadilly inside Green Park. On his behalf, Richard Frith, a leading developer commemorated in Frith Street, Soho, offers 99-year leases on building plots of varying sizes to tradesmen contributing goods or services worth £200 or more towards the construction of the mews. The tradesmen enter their names, parishes, professions and the value of their goods and services below, while the sketch-plan gives the names of the leaseholders of the variously-sized building plots on each side of the proposed road. In December the King fled and the project came to nothing. The mechanism, however, was the key to London's growth as much in the Wembley of the 1930s as in St James's in the 1680s.

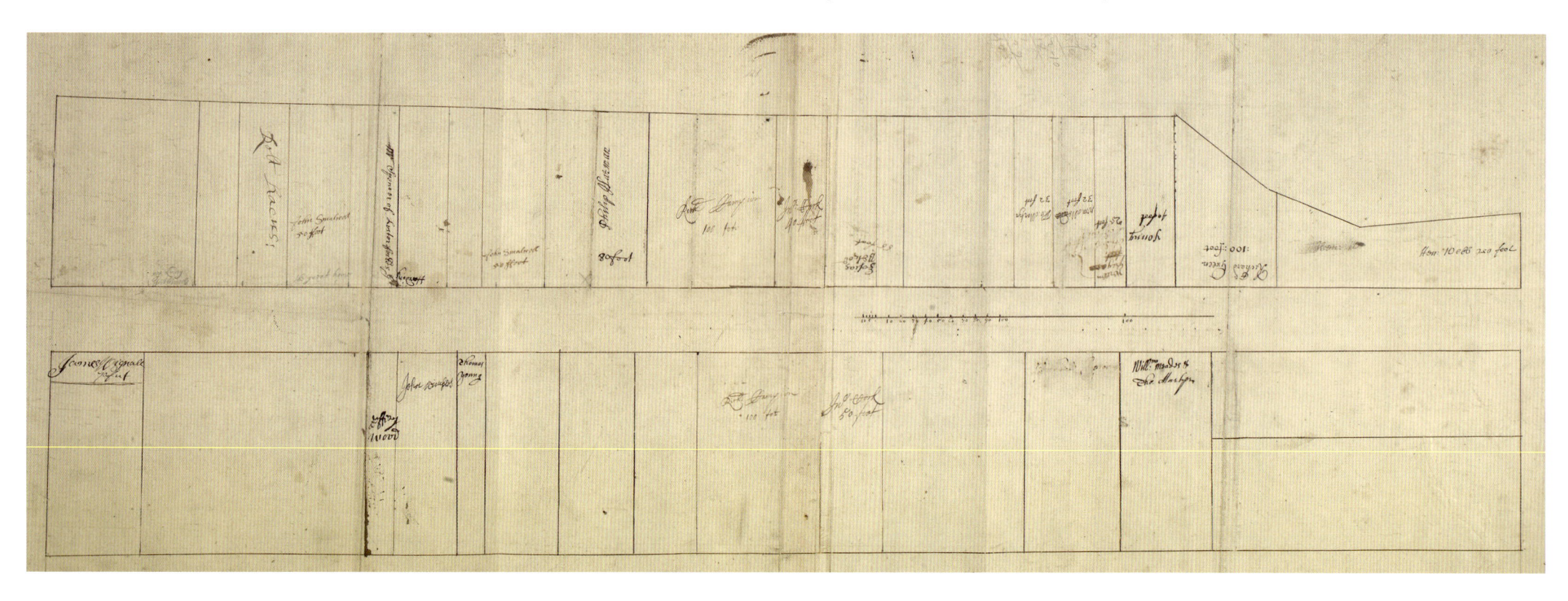

2.3.2 'Proposalls made and agreed on Betwene Richard Frith of St Martins in the Fields, And the severall and respective Tradesmen hereunto subscribing' [1688] with plan. 43 × 29 cm and (plan) 35.5. × 104 cm. From the papers of Francis Gwynne, a long-serving Under-Secretary of State. Add. MS 16370.115, 116

TAKE WHAT YOU CAN GET

It was not easy to find takers for land on the less attractive estates. This advertisement for building plots on land owned by Lord Somers, just north of what is now Euston Road, contains regulations concerning the appearance of the buildings to be erected. Suggested street names are inked in, some of which, like Ossulton Street, have endured. There is nevertheless a touch of desperation in the wording relating to the sort of people who might be interested. For all the fine words of the regulations, the agent of Lord Somers, Jacob Leroux, was pessimistic about there being any takers in the middle of a wartime recession. His fears were realised. Exceedingly modest houses were built, predominantly for poverty-stricken French and Spanish political refugees. In about 1880 many were demolished to make room for a railway goods yard, which in its turn gave way to the new British Library in the course of the 1980s and 1990s.

2.3.3 *A Plan of ground to be lett on building leases for 95 years at Sommers Place*, c. 1800. 37 × 24 cm. Maps K. Top. 28.17

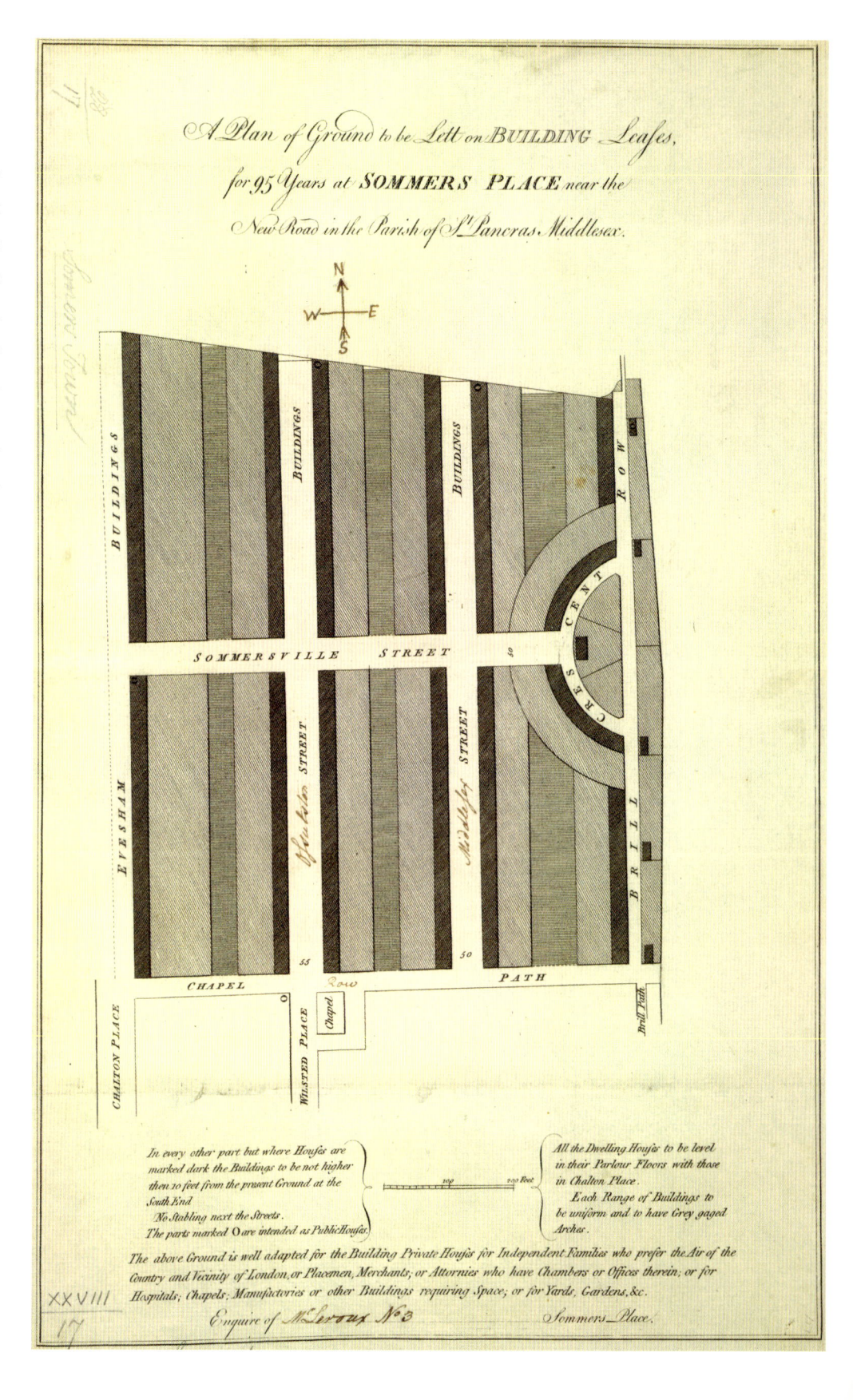

2.4 THE COMING OF THE WEST END

From the 1630s, the fields west of the city walls were rapidly built over. The Earl of Bedford's estate centred around the Italian-influenced Covent Garden piazza was the initial magnet, but after 1660 it was replaced by St James's, which took its name and attraction for the wealthy from the nearby royal palace and park. By the later 1720s the Mayfair estate of the Grosvenor family around Grosvenor Square was being built up. Before 1800 the Portman and Portland estates north of Oxford Street and the Bedford estate in Bloomsbury had largely been developed. From 1815 the other Grosvenor estate in Pimlico followed. They have remained prestigious while Soho and Covent Garden declined into raffishness and restaurants.

Detail from Ralph Treswell's map of the lands between Piccadilly and Oxford Street (shown in full on page 75)

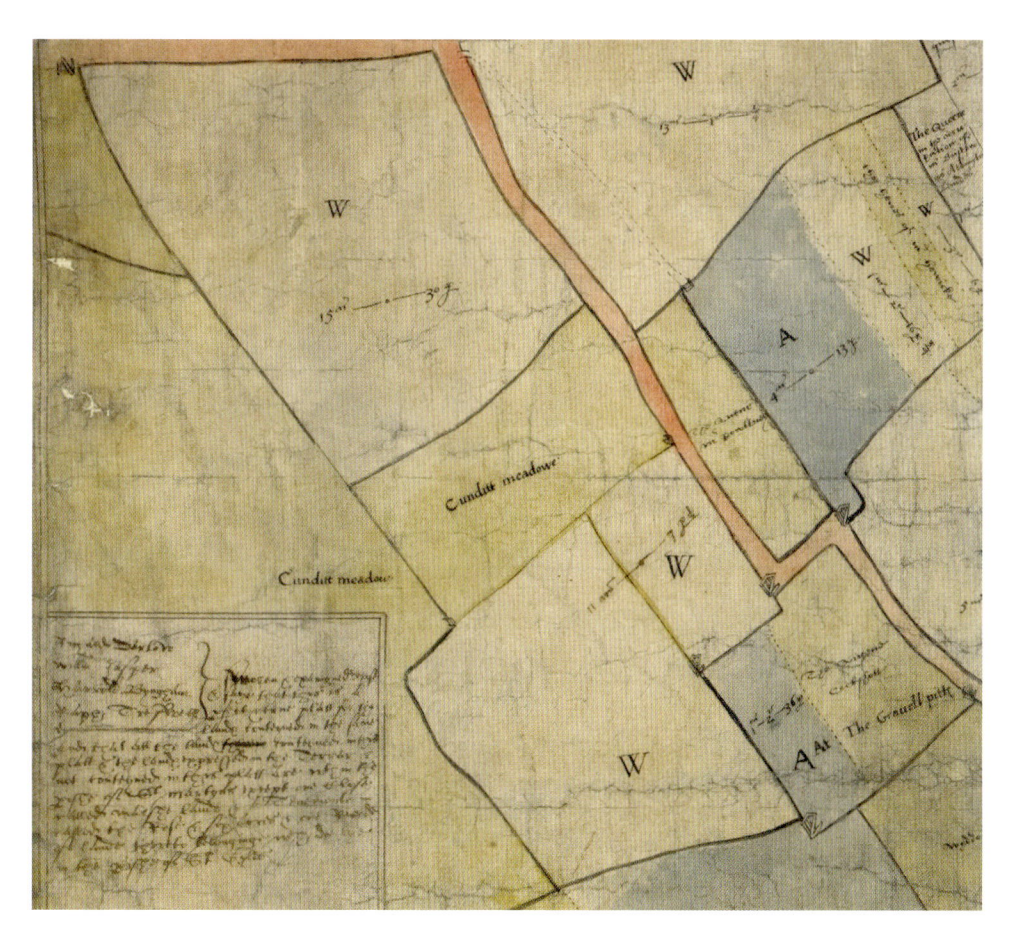

THE FIELDS BENEATH

In 1585 Ralph Treswell produced this map to clarify a dispute over grazing land in Geldings Close, near today's Oxford Circus. The map, an early example of a local map drawn to a consistent scale, presents the first accurate image of the West End, over 100 years before it was built over. Of particular note are the two 'Conduit Meadows' through which, since 1236, lead pipes from sources in Hyde Park had run to keep London supplied with water. The City continues to own the land, commemorated in the modern Conduit Street.

2.4.1   Ralph Treswell [Map of lands between Piccadilly and Oxford Street], 1585. Ink and washes on paper. 56 cm × 81.5 cm The National Archives. Maps MPB 1 (from PRO E.178-139)

Oxford Street is at the top, the village of St Giles in the Fields (now in the shadow of Centre Point) top right, linked by St Martin's Lane to St Martin's in the Fields with the royal mews (now the National Gallery) bottom right, and Cockspur Street and Haymarket going up from there to Piccadilly ('The way from Colebrook to London') which goes down towards the bottom left. The course of the other roads can be followed on modern maps.

OCCIDENS / ORIENS

The Waye frome Uxbridge to London

Cundits meadow
Cundit meadow

Goldingers dales
The Queenes

The fielde called St Gilles fielde

St Martins fielde

Windmill fielde

At the Gravell pitts

St James fielde

The Waye from Colbroke to London
The Way to Charing

The Mewes
The Mewes clos

CHANGING FASHIONS

In 1678 Arundel House, the riverside mansion of the dukes of Norfolk and former home of the great art collector, Thomas, Earl of Arundel, followed most of the grand palaces of the Strand in being demolished. This redevelopment plan shows streets and a new Norfolk House designed by Hooke with a grand courtyard for coaches as an entrance and a small garden overlooking the Thames. Covent Garden was already losing its prestige, however, and the pull of the West End proved too strong. The whole site is covered with houses on Morgan's map of 1682. The new Norfolk House was eventually built in St James's Square.

2.4.2 Anon., 'The ground plot of Arundell house and gardens', *c.* 1678. Ink and washes on paper. 60.5 × 48 cm Maps K. Top. 21.10-4

'Behold that narrow street which steep descends,
Whose building to the slimy shore extends;
Here Arundel's fam'd structure rear'd its frame,
The street alone retains the empty name;
Where Titian's glowing paint the canvas warm'd
And Raphael's fair design, with judgment charm'd,
Now hangs the bellman's song and pasted here
The coloured prints of Overton appear.'

John Gay, *Trivia*, 1716

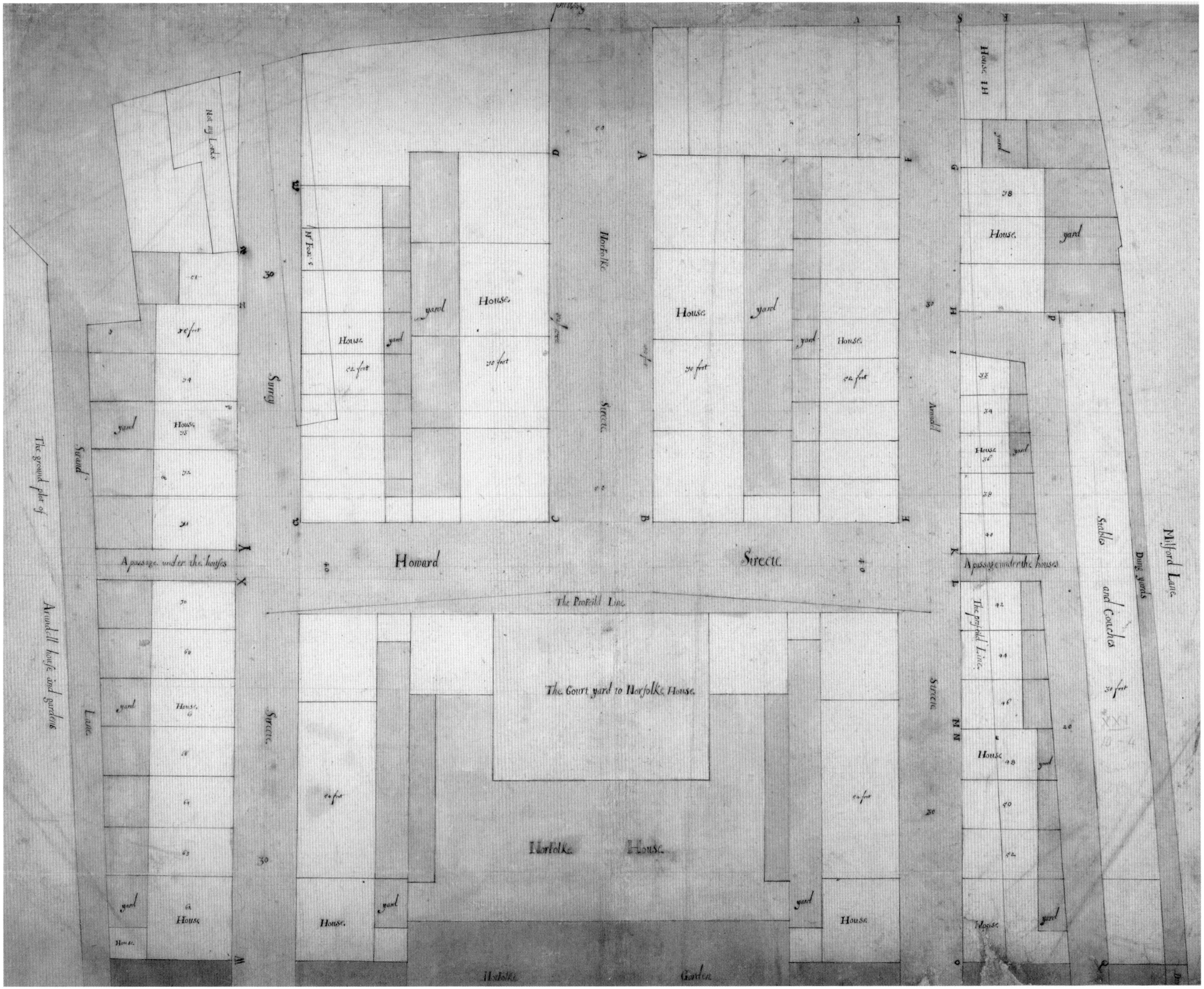
The ground plot of Arundell house and gardens
Strand Lane
Surrey Street
Norfolke Street
Howard Street
Arundell Street
Milford Lane
A passage under the houses
The Profeild Line
The Court yard to Norfolke House
Norfolke House
Norfolke Garden
Stables and Coatches
Dung yards
House
yard

2.4.3 Plan of St James's Square, 1725–28. 54 × 75 cm. Ink and watercolour on paper
Add. MS 5024.3

THE HEIGHT OF ELEGANCE

The occupants of St James's Square, uniquely among the residents of the West End, owned and did not lease their houses. As this schematic plan shows, it was occupied almost exclusively by the nobility. Among them were the Dukes of Chandos, Kent and Norfolk. Sir Spencer Compton was Speaker of the House of Commons. The Duke of Chandos, who had earned a fortune while financing the Duke of Marlborough's campaigns during the War of the Spanish Succession, is now best known as Handel's patron.

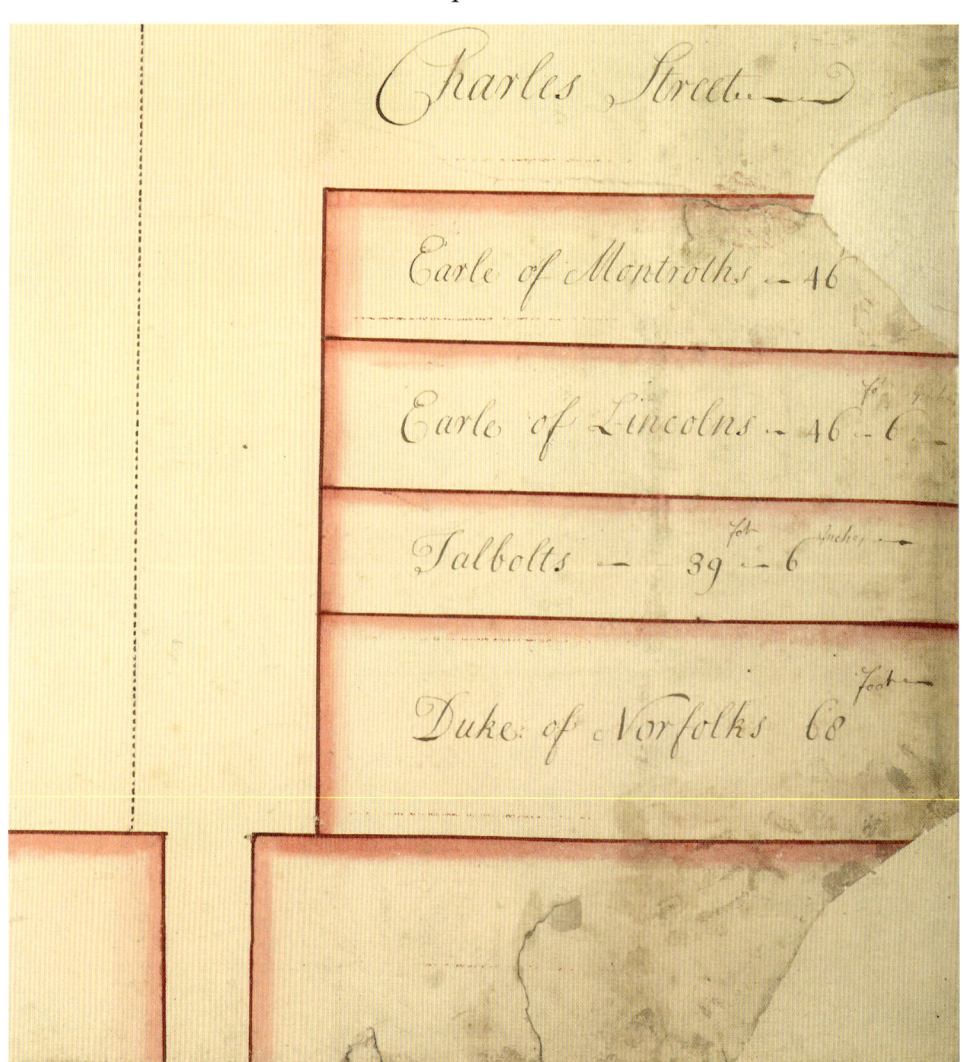

Mr Trotmans — 27 ft

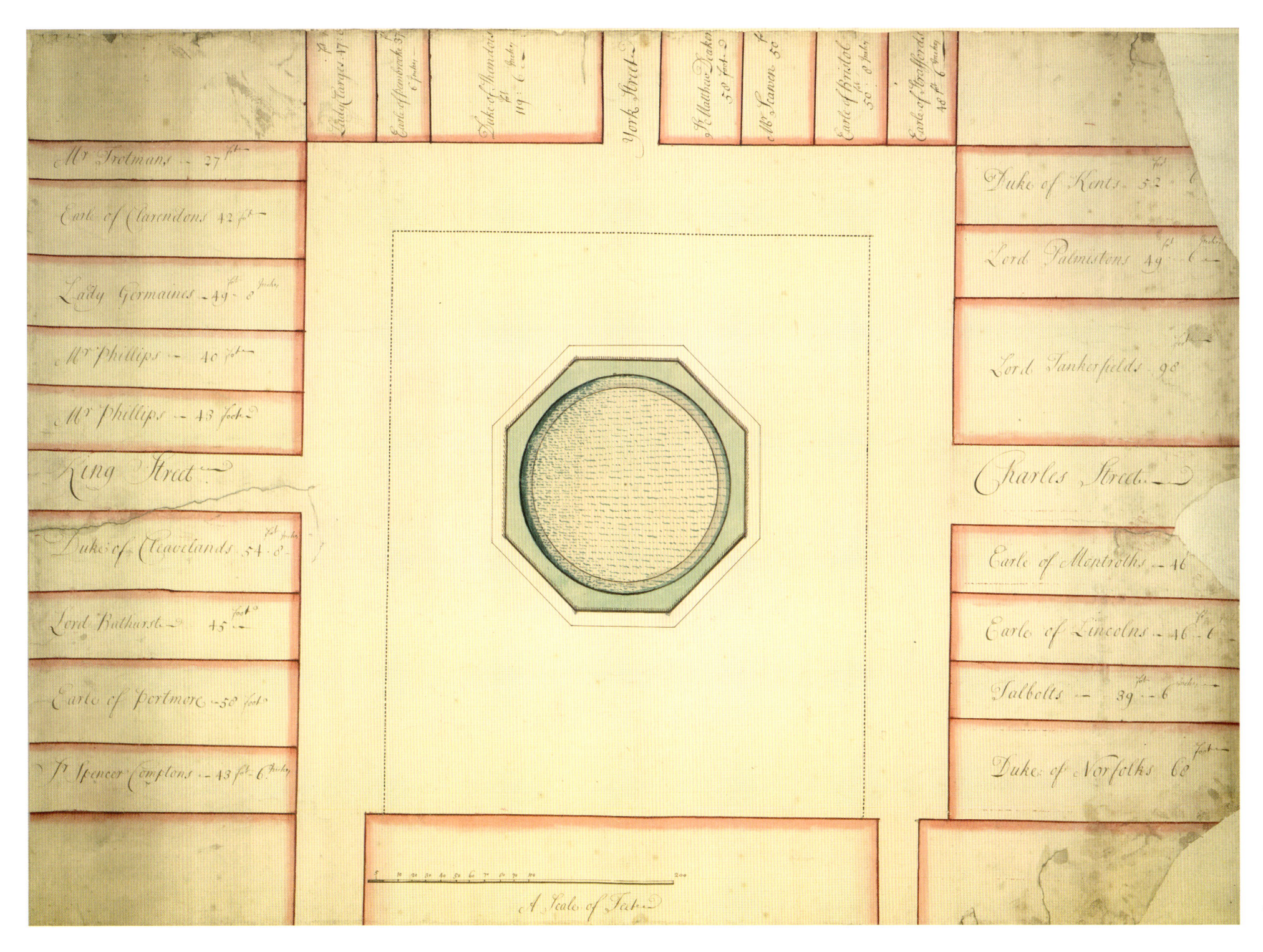

Earle of Clarendons — 42 ft

Lady Germaines — 49 - 0

Mr Phillips — 40 ft

Mr Phillips — 43 feet

King Street

Dukes of Cleavelands — 54 - 8

Lord Bathurst — 45 feet

Earle of Portmore — 50 feet

Sr Spencer Comptons — 43 ft - 6 Inch

Lady Ranges 47
Earle of Pembroke 37
Duke of Montrose 119 - 6
York Street
H. Matthew Deakin 50 feet
Mr Lanor 50
Earle of Bristol 50 - 0
Earle of Strafford 40 ft - 6

Duke of Kents — 52

Lord Palmistons — 49

Lord Tankerfields — 98

Charles Street

Earle of Montroths — 46

Earle of Lincolns — 46 - 6

Talbotts — 39 - 6

Duke of Norfolks — 60 ft

A Scale of Feet

HANDSOME INTERIORS

The Earl of Strafford owned one of the few early St James's Square houses that still survives. An idea of its splendid interiors can be garnered from this sketch by the carpenter Charles Griffiths for an elaborate fireplace in one of its back parlours. The receipt for the £12 that he received for his work still survives. Much of Lord Strafford's wealth came from the East End where he was lord of the manor of Stepney and heir to the owner of the East India Dock. His family name is commemorated in Wentworth Street.

2.4.4   Drawing for a fireplace in Strafford House, St James's Square, 1719. 33 × 22.5 cm. Add. MS 63474, f. 125ᵛ. (The image has manuscript writing showing through from the reverse side of the original drawing)

LAVISH LIFE-STYLES

Richard Graham, Viscount Preston, a leading diplomat and politician, was an early resident of 21 King (now Soho) Square which had been developed by Richard Frith and Gregory King from 1677. These bills from his private papers give a flavour of the life-style of the first residents of the new West End squares. They include, with builders', grocer's, cook's, laundryman's and water bills, bills for portraits by the artist Jacob Huysmans, and a coachman's bill mentioning journeys to Pall Mall and Whitehall.

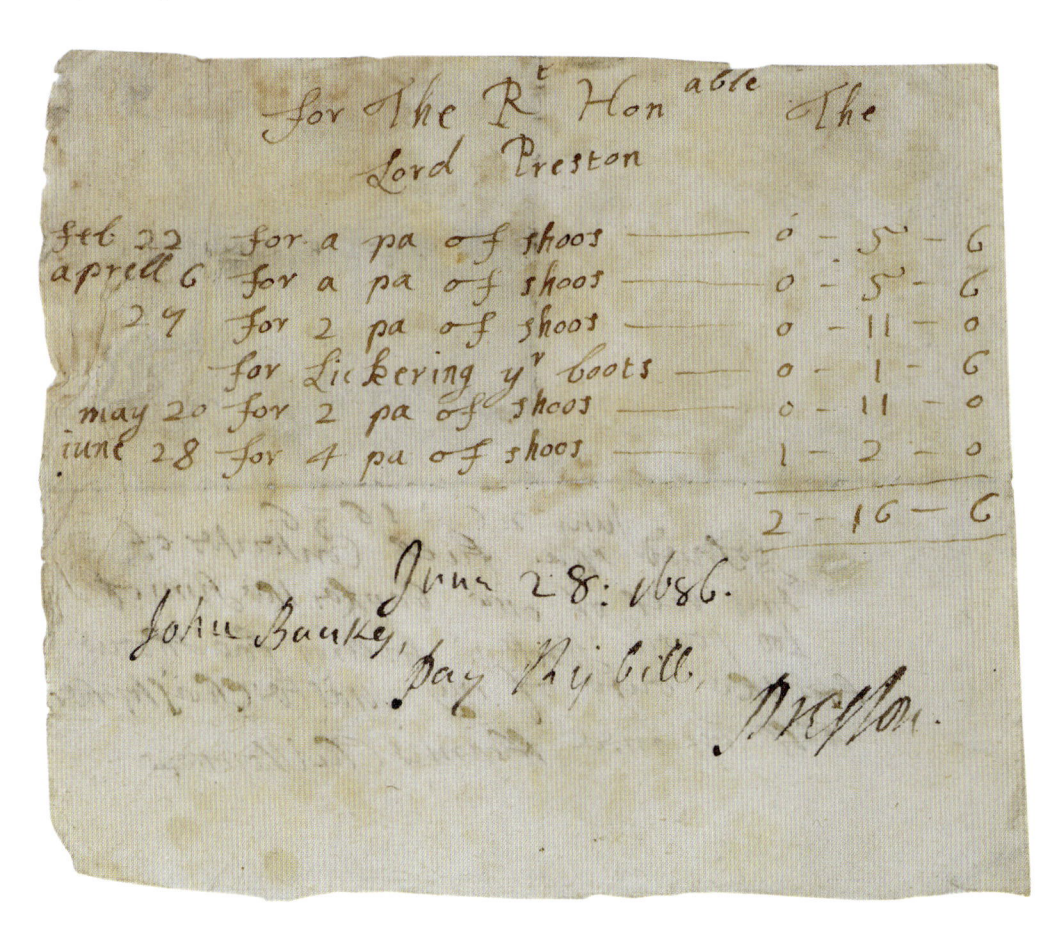

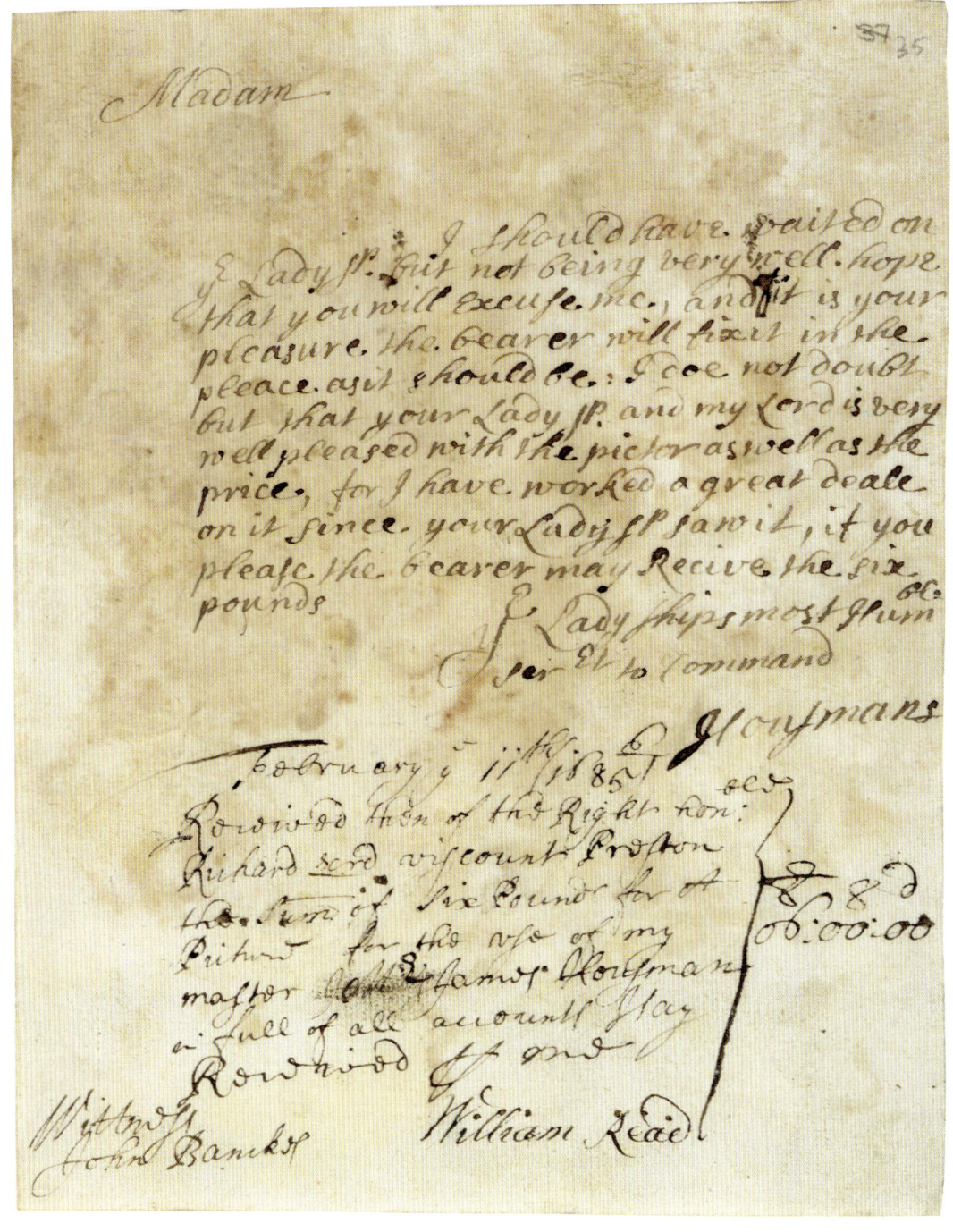

2.4.5   Miscellaneous household bills from the Preston Papers, 1685–67. Add. MS 63777 ff. 11, 15, 34, 35, 37, 40, 42, 45ᵛ, 57ᵛ–8, 62, 66, 77ᵛ, 84, 109, 113.

THE EARLIEST MAP OF MAYFAIR AND BELGRAVIA

In 1665 a young City lawyer, Alexander Davies, unexpectedly died of the plague. He left a disputed 100 acre estate stretching from the Thames to Oxford Street, debts from trying to develop his Thames-side lands without assistance from a middleman like Richard Frith, lands that he had consequently been forced to lease out — and a baby heiress, Mary. This rough map, thickly annotated with legal notes on the differing tenures of parts of the estate and showing what are now Oxford Street, Park Lane, Piccadilly, Knightsbridge and 'Pimplico', helped to disentangle the mess. After failing to marry Lord Berkeley, the owner of the fields that are not coloured on the map, in 1677 Mary married a Cheshire squire, Sir Thomas Grosvenor. Their descendant, the Duke of Westminster, still owns most of the estate, now better known as Mayfair, Belgravia and Pimlico. But because the Berkeley and Davies estates were never to be integrated, it is still difficult for strangers to find their way from Grosvenor Square to Berkeley Square.

2.4.6   Anon. [Map of the Davies estate in the parishes of St Martin and St Margaret Westminster], *c.* 1665. 135 × 64 cm. Ink and coloured washes on parchment. Add. MS 38104

NORTH ←

THE EMERGENCE OF MAYFAIR

Mary Davies eventually went insane. Her trustees probably commissioned the original of this map, which shows the situation in about 1723, the Grosvenor lands being shown in pink. Several pieces of land had already been sold off (including the sites of Chelsea Hospital and Buckingham House). Alexander Davies's Thameside house had been completed as Grosvenor House. Much of the rest of the estate was leased to the Chelsea Waterworks Company and was to remain as open fields until after 1800. Plans for the development of Mayfair around a new Grosvenor Square were well advanced, but not yet in their final form.

2.4.7 Anon. 'Map of the Grosvenor estate in St George's Parish as it was in the year 1723' [Nineteenth-century copy]. 70.5 × 81 cm. Watercolour on paper. Maps Crace X.20

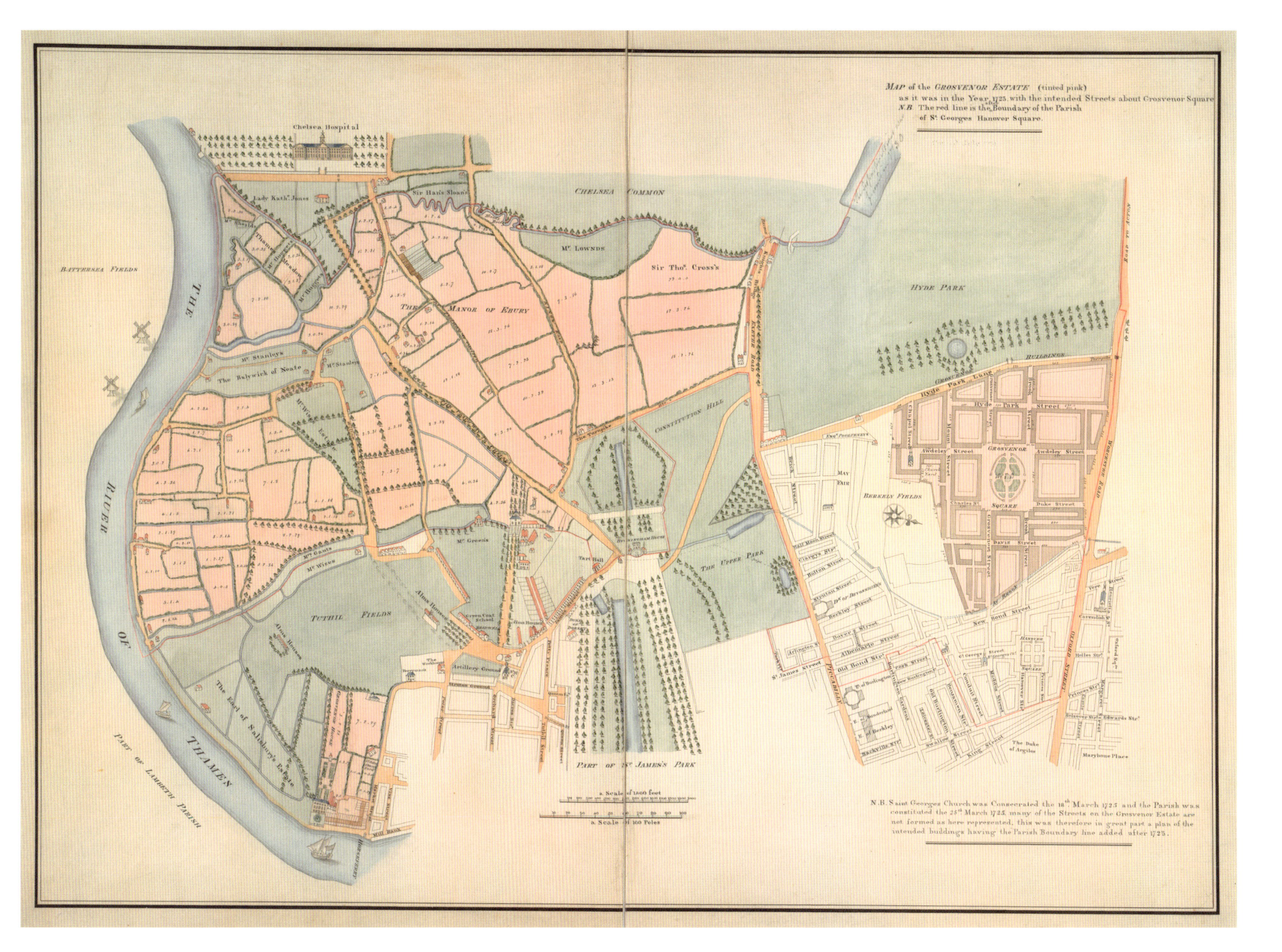

MAP of the GROSVENOR ESTATE (tinted pink) as it was in the Year 1725, with the intended Streets about Grosvenor Square
N.B. The red line is the Boundary of the Parish of St Georges Hanover Square.

N.B. Saint Georges Church was Consecrated the 18th March 1725 and the Parish was constituted the 25th March 1725, many of the Streets on the Grosvenor Estate are not formed as here represented, this was therefore in great part a plan of the intended buildings, having the Parish Boundary line added after 1725.

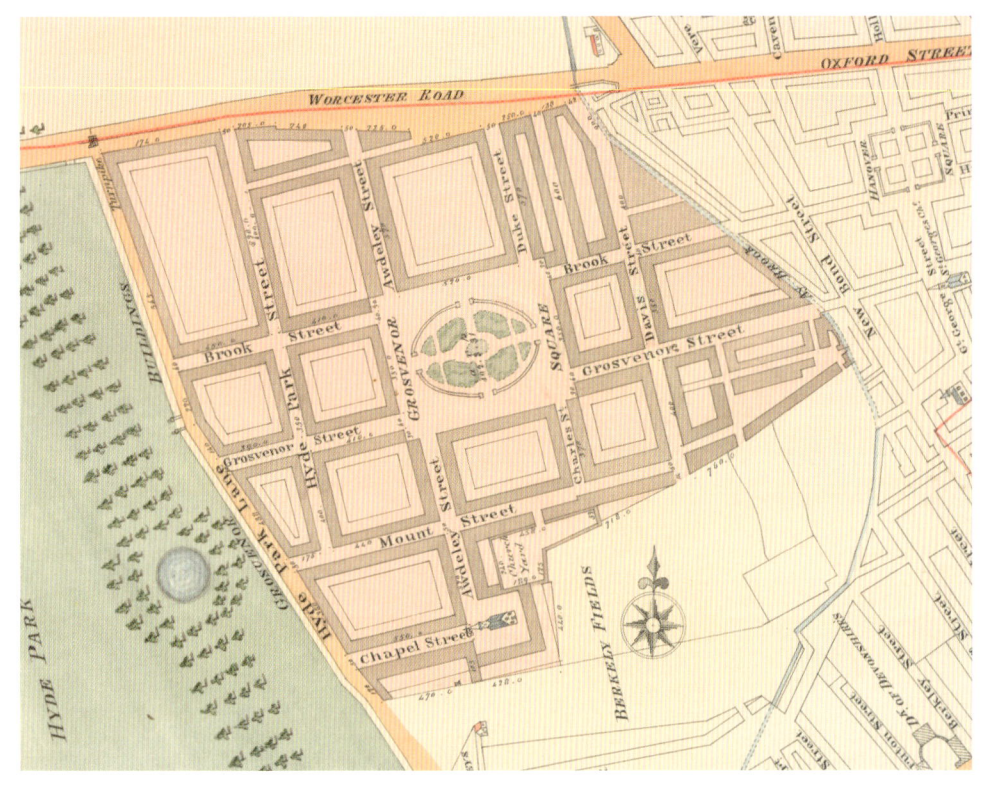

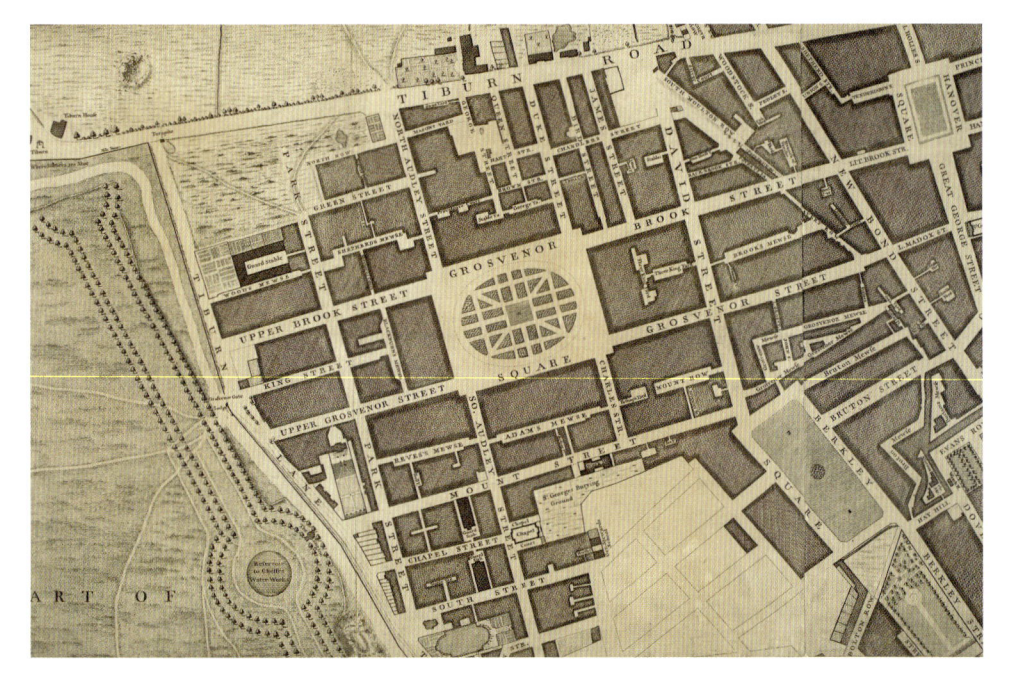

2.5 LONDON LIFE

By 1746 London was Europe's largest city, its opulence buttressed by profits from the City, now the world centre for international trade. London had much to offer its residents and, increasingly, tourists. The wealthy and the middle-classes mingled in pleasure gardens, like Vauxhall and Ranelagh, its elegant shops and numerous theatres, and visited proto-museums like Sir Hans Sloane's collections and the Physic Garden in Chelsea. Looking on enviously but generally impotently from the grime and stench of the rookeries were the destitute, gin-sodden, and short-lived poor. Recently-founded hospitals, almshouses, chapels and workhouses salved the consciences of their social betters, but the mob remained a radical element which exploded onto the streets in the Gordon Riots of 1780.

Mayfair as projected in 1723

Mayfair as built, 1746 (John Rocque, *Plan of the Cities of London and Westminster*)

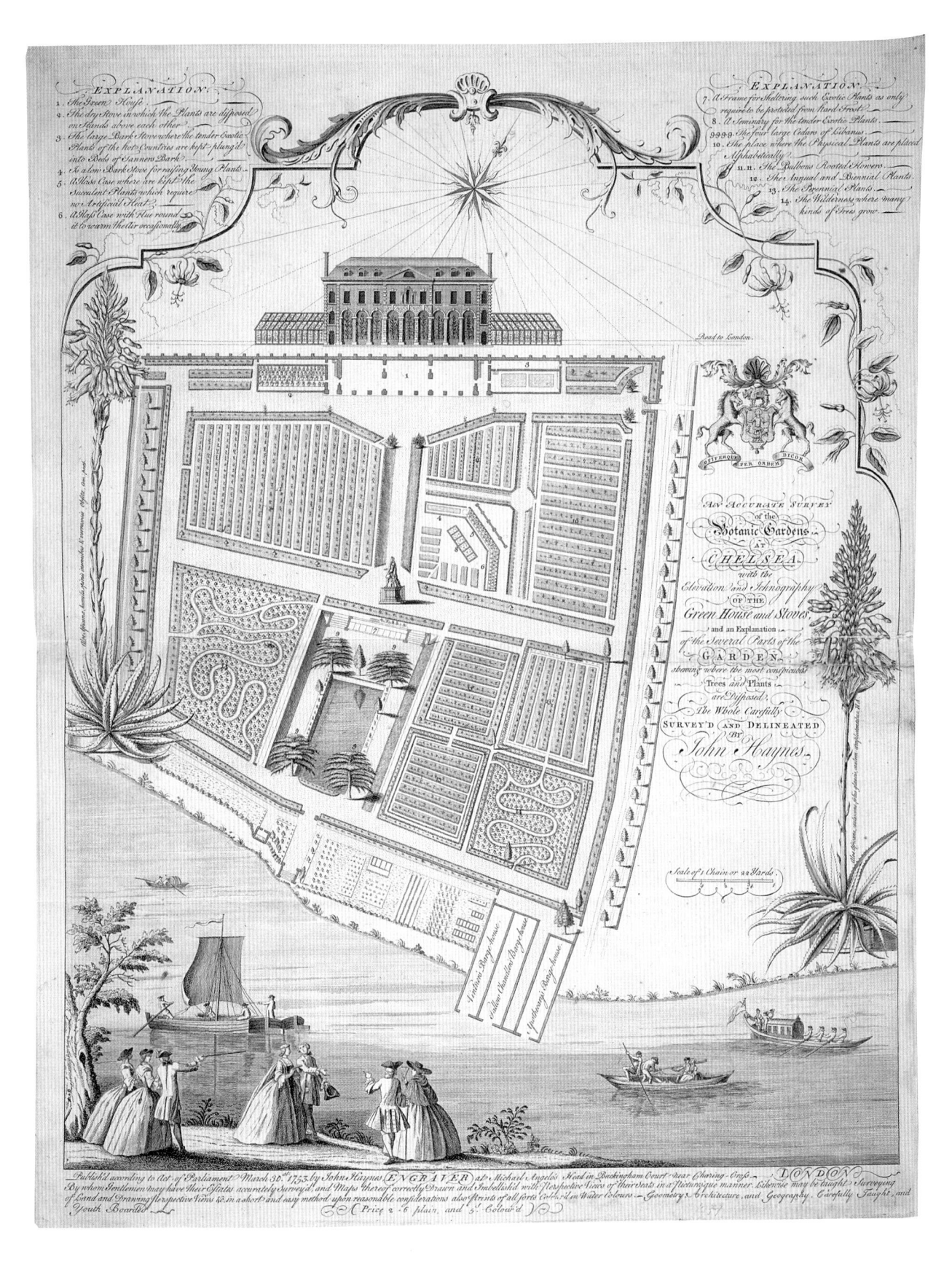

SOPHISTICATED PLEASURES

Almost as popular with the fashionable elite as pleasure gardens like Ranelagh, was the nearby Chelsea Physic Garden. In 1713 Sir Hans Sloane, the lord of the manor of Chelsea, had presented the Garden's freehold to the Worshipful Company of Apothecaries which had founded it in 1673. Accordingly, Sloane's statue by Rysbrack was erected in the centre. The original is now in the British Museum of which Sloane was to be the effective founder. In a successful effort to appeal to the desired sort of visitor, John Haynes conveys the Garden's elegance, exclusivity and the contemporary fascination with botany (the founder of the modern classification of plants, the Swede, Carl Linnaeus, had visited and been impressed by the garden). In the text below the map Haynes uses the image to advertise his skills and services as an estate surveyor.

2.5.1   John Haynes, *An Accurate Survey of the Botanic Gardens at Chelsea*, 1753. Engraving. 62 × 48 cm. Maps K. Top. 28.4-p

John Haynes, land surveyor and engraver, is probably to be identified with the John Haines who was apprenticed to Sutton Nicholls (see 2.5.6 below) in 1716. He probably worked both in York (where is said to have been born) and in London, where he died in 1772.

MAPS IN SOCIETY

Eighteenth-century maps often took unexpected forms, appearing as educational games, on screens, as interior decorations and in miniaturised form on business cards and medals. Some were printed on fabric. Such maps supported the silk weavers of Spitalfields and often had practical uses because of their durability and flexibility. A few fabric maps, however, like this example, were specifically manufactured as fans. Such novelties would doubtless have provided a subject for discussion at polite assemblies, in pleasure gardens or at the theatre. The street information was ultimately derived from Rocque's great map.

2.5.2   Richard Bennett, *A New & Correct Plan of London, including all the New Buildings &c.* (London: *c.* 1760) Engraved map on silk mounted on fan with ivory and bone telescopic sticks [Clarke & Co]. 29 × 48 cm. Private collection, image courtesy of Sotheby's

Richard Bennett, who produced the map, became a freeman of the Merchant Taylors' Company, as his father had been before him, in 1754. His brother, Thomas Bennett, was a well-known engraver of sheet music.

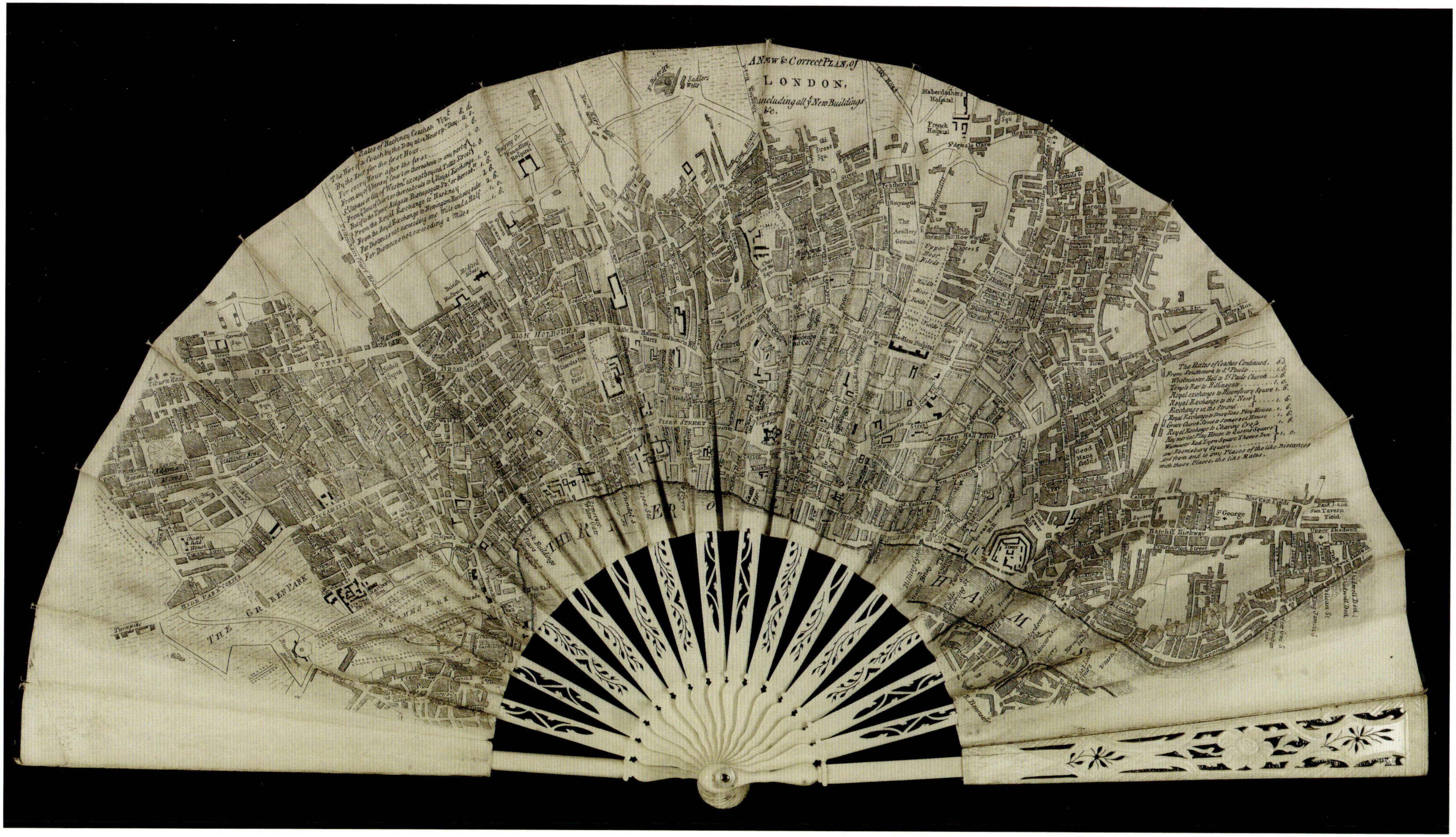
A New & Correct PLAN, of
LONDON,
including all ye New Buildings &c.

BIGGER AND BETTER THAN PARIS

In the early eighteenth century there was rivalry between Paris and London for the title of the largest city in western Europe. This map, published at a time when England was at war with France, proved conclusively that London was bigger. John Rocque was the ideal person to undertake the work. A trained surveyor and, he claimed, originally a skilled garden designer, he was probably born in France but raised in Geneva. He used distinctively French conventions in his mapping. This was a mapping language that the French would understand and would reinforce the unpalatable message of London's superiority.

From 1738, supported by the Royal Society and the City Corporation, he used the most accurate surveying instruments and techniques of the time to map London and Westminster. Demonstrating its seriousness, the map dispenses with views. Within the elegant rococo frame, you can see the expanding West End and industry along the Thames, but also such characteristic eighteenth-century institutions as almshouses, workhouses, lunatic asylums, hospitals of different kinds (the Foundling as well as Guy's Hospital), pleasure gardens like Ranelagh in Chelsea and lesser ones like Merlin's Cave in Clerkenwell, schools, churches, a variety of chapels — and the gallows at Tyburn (today's Marble Arch).

2.5.3 John Rocque engraved by John Pine, *Plan of the Cities of London and Westminster and the Borough of Southwark* (London: John Tinney and John Pine, 1747). Scale: 200 feet to the inch [1:2400]. 198 × 387 cm. Maps *3480 (293)

John Pine (1690(?)–1756), the engraver and co-publisher of the map, was generally considered the finest English engraver of his time. He was apprenticed to the silver engraver, John Roy Arnold, in 1709, simply described as the son of a gentleman of London. He was a close friend of William Hogarth, who introduced his portrait as the fat Friar in the painting *O the Roast Beef of Old England (The Gate of Calais)* 1748. Pine was thenceforth known as 'Friar' Pine, somewhat to his annoyance. John Tinney, (1706–61) the other publisher, was, like Pine, a London-born member of the Goldsmiths' Company and numbered the exquisite engravers Anthony Walker and William Woollett among his apprentices.

LAMBS

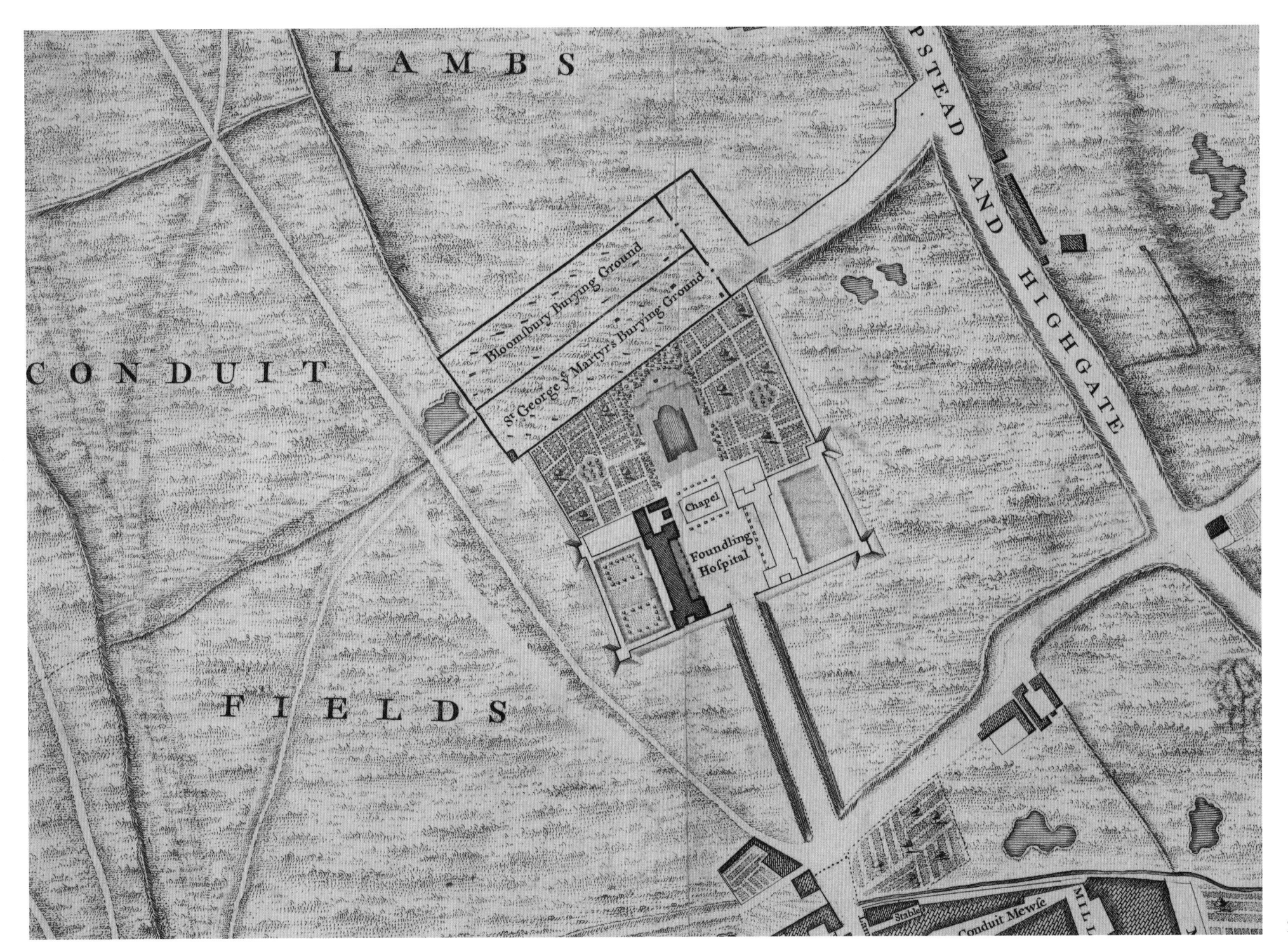

CONDUIT

Bloomsbury Burying Ground

St George ye Martyr's Burying Ground

Chapel

Foundling Hospital

PSTEAD AND HIGHGATE

FIELDS

Stable

Conduit Mewse

FOR THE FRENCH VISITOR TO LONDON

British culture became an object of European admiration from about 1740 and as its capital, London became a target for foreign visitors. This is one of the earliest foreign maps to cater for them. Visitors are encouraged to visit Ranelagh, the 'Theatre Pantomique' near the New River Head in Islington and the cabinet of natural history of 'Chevalier Sloane' — the predecessor of today's Natural History Museum — in Chelsea. There are many mistranslations, however, revealing that Le Rouge, a leading French map publisher, was not all that familiar with London, or with English, himself.

2.5.4 Georges Louis Le Rouge, [Plan of London with list of locations] (Paris: Le Rouge, *c.* 1750). 25 × 32 cm [map] 23 × 30.5 cm [explanatory sheet] Maps cc.5.a.412

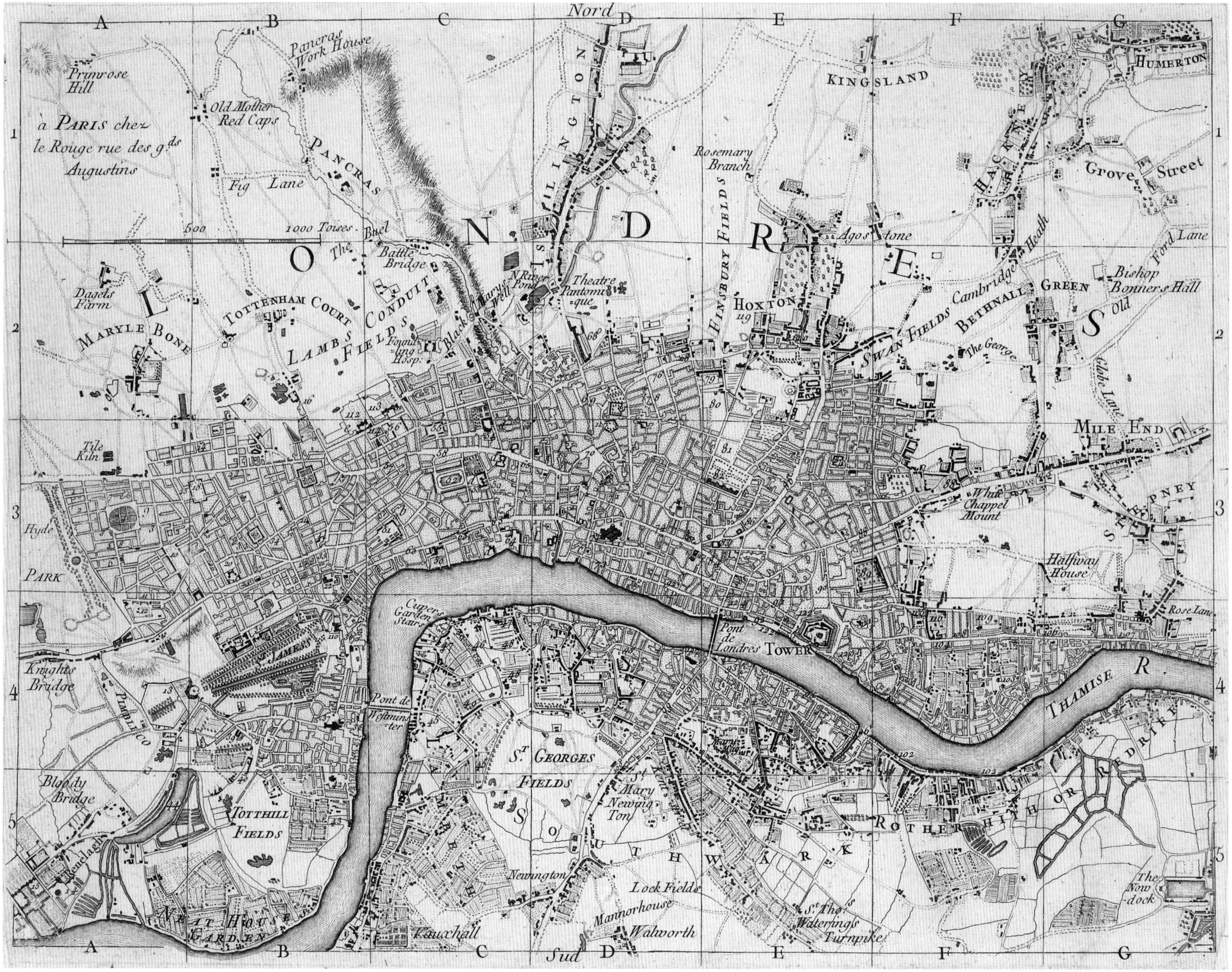
Nord
Sud
a PARIS chez
le Rouge rue des g.ds
Augustins
LONDRES
500
1000 Toises
Primrose Hill
Old Mother Red Caps
Pancras Work House
PANCRAS
Fig Lane
ISLINGTON
KINGSLAND
HUMERTON
Rosemary Branch
FINSBURY FIELDS
HACKNEY
Grove Street
Agos stone
Ford Lane
The Battle Bridge
Theatre Pantomi que
N River Pond
HOXTON
Cambridge Heath
BETHNALL GREEN
Bishop Bonners Hall
Dagets Farm
MARYLE BONE
TOTTENHAM COURT
LAMBS CONDUIT FIELDS
Found-ling Hosp.
SWAN FIELDS
The George
Old
Globe Lane
Tile Kiln
MILE END
Whit Chappel Mount
STEPNEY
Hyde PARK
Halfway House
Rose Lane
Cupers Garden Stairs
Pont de Londres
TOWER
THAMISE R
Knights Bridge
PIMLICO
Pont de Westminster
St. GEORGES FIELDS
St. Mary Newing Ton
Bloody Bridge
TOTTHILL FIELDS
SOUTHWARK
ROTHERHITH OR REDRIFE
Ranelagh
Newington
Lock Fields
Mannorhouse
Walworth
Vauxhall
St. Thos. Waterings Turnpike
The New dock
NEAT HOUSE GARDEN

RANELAGH

Opened in 1742, Ranelagh Gardens remained one of the centres of London's social life until shortly after 1800 when its grounds were incorporated into those of Chelsea Hospital which nowadays accommodate the Chelsea Flower Show every May.

2.5.5a *The Perspective View as Intended to be finish'd of the Amphitheatrical Building and part of the Garden in which it is Erected in Chelsea. Designed by William Jones Archt.* (London: 1742). Engraving. 41 × 69.5 cm. Maps K. Top. 28.4-t

2.5.5b Anon., *A Survey of the Mansion House, Amphitheatre, Gardens and Lands belonging to the Proprietors of Ranelagh...* (London: 1777). 51 × 70 cm. Engraved map. Maps cc.5.a.356

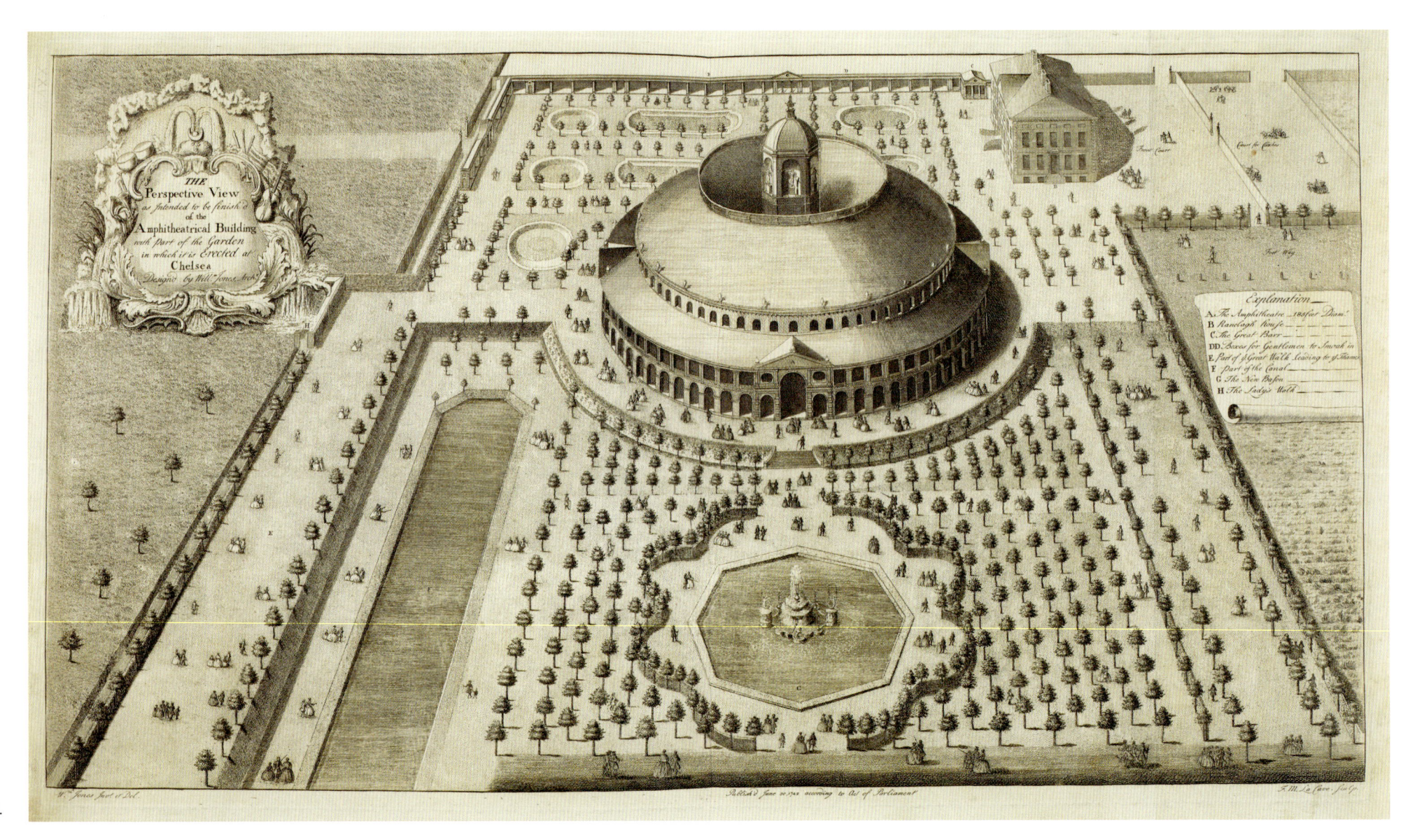

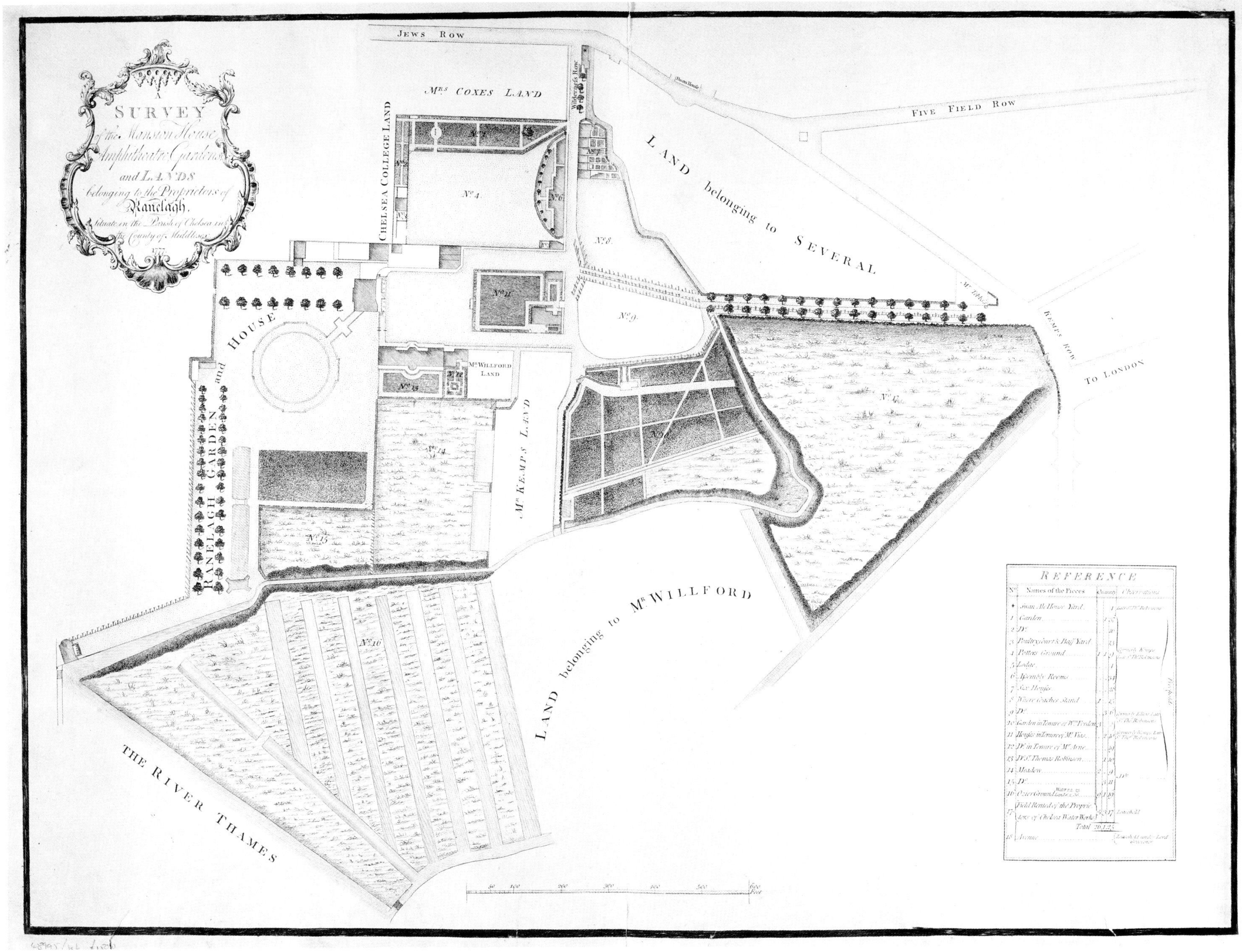
A SURVEY
of the Mansion House Amphitheatre, Gardens and LANDS
belonging to the Proprietors of Ranelagh.
Situate in the Parish of Chelsea in the County of Middlesex
JEWS ROW
Mrs COXES LAND
CHELSEA COLLEGE LAND
FIVE FIELD ROW
LAND belonging to SEVERAL
RANELAGH GARDEN and HOUSE
Mr WILLFORD LAND
Mr KEMPS LAND
KEMPS ROW
TO LONDON
LAND belonging to Mr WILLFORD
THE RIVER THAMES
No 4
No 8
No 9
No 11
No 13
No 14
No 15
No 16
REFERENCE
No. Names of the Pieces
* Swan Ale House Yard
1 Garden
2 Do
3 Poultry Court & Bass Yard
4 Potters Ground
5 Lodge
6 Assembly Rooms
7 Six Houses
8 Where Coaches Stand
9 Do
10 Garden in Tenure of Wm Fordon
11 Houses in Tenure of Mr Vias
12 Do in Tenure of Mr Arne
13 Do Sr Thomas Robinson
14 Meadow
15 Do
16 Ozier Ground
17 Field Rented of the Proprietors of Chelsea Water Works
Total 26.1.25
18 Avenue
Freehold
Leasehold
Feet

A COSMOPOLITAN CENTRE

Even if an increasing number of wealthy businessmen now lived amidst the pleasures of the West End, the City remained the main business quarter. It continued to be centred on the rebuilt Royal Exchange and in the nearby coffee houses like Lloyd's where maritime insurance deals were struck. The Royal Exchange was a cosmopolitan place, with each 'nation', or regional group of traders, having its specified position under the arcades of the building as is indicated in the bottom line of text on this view.

2.5.6 Thomas Taylor, *A View of the Inside of the Royal Exchange in Cornhill, London as it now is 1712*. Engraving. 52 × 59 cm Maps K. Top. 24.11-k

This view was engraved by Sutton Nicholls (1668–1729), born at Eltham, for the Fleet Street printseller Thomas Taylor. Nicholls was trained by Philip Lea (see 3.1.1. below), is remembered for his own maps and a fine panoramic view of London, and in particular for some striking early views of the London squares, engraved from his own drawings.

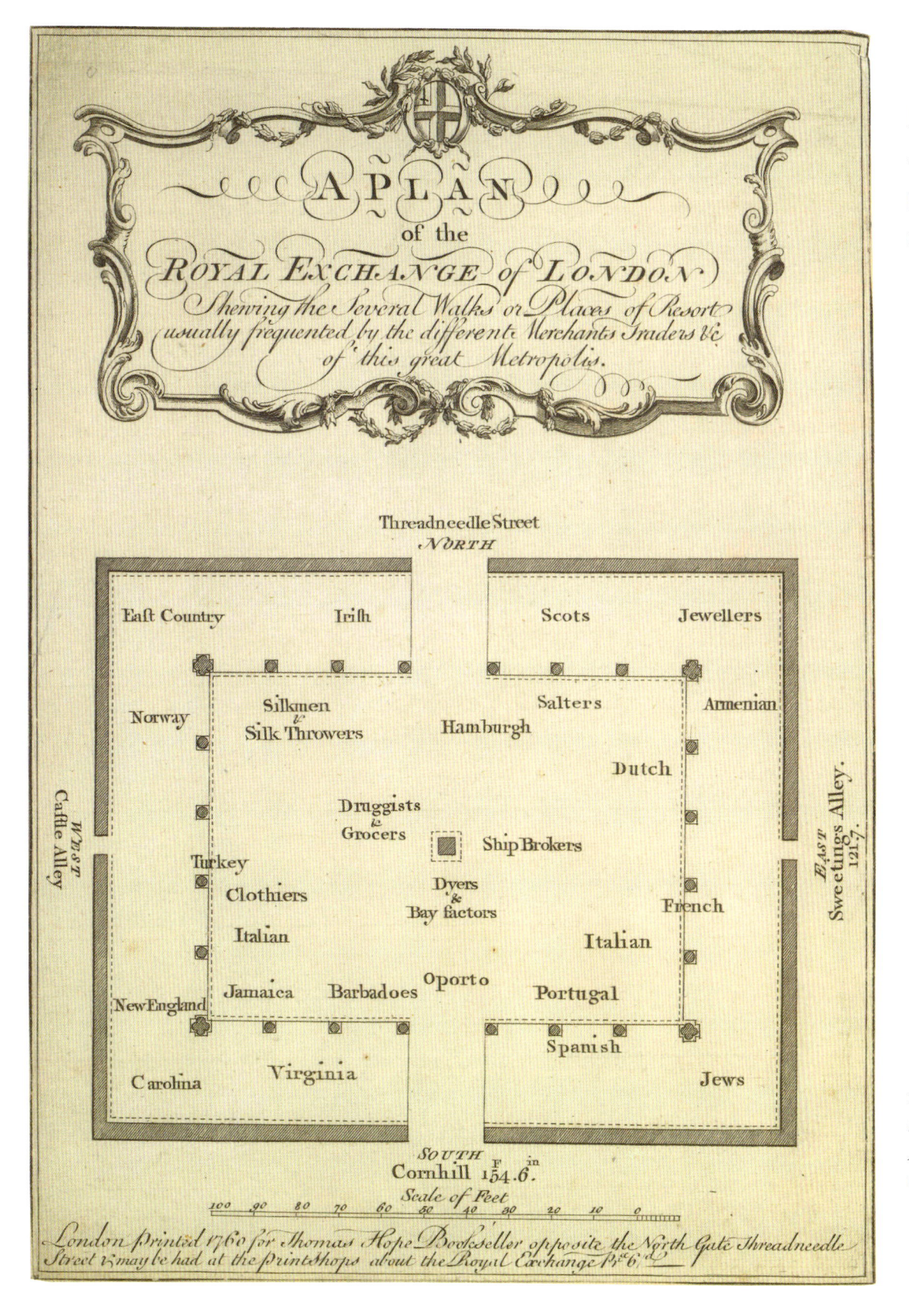

HOW TO LOCATE A MERCHANT

This plan was on sale near the Royal Exchange and seems to have been intended to enable strangers to find particular groups of merchants.

2.5.7   Thomas Hope, *A Plan of the Royal Exchange of London shewing the several Walks or Places of Resort usually frequented by the different Merchants, Traders &c. of this great Metropolis*, 1760. 27 × 20 cm. Maps Crace VIII.63

A GEORGIAN WHO'S WHO

The Pantheon on Oxford Street near today's Oxford Circus was opened in 1772 as a magnificent 'winter Ranelagh'. After running into difficulties it was converted in 1791 into a handsome theatre which was burnt down only a year later. This is the only known view of its interior. The power structure of late eighteenth-century England is laid bare in the plan of the boxes. Near the royal box can be seen the boxes of Thomas Coutts, the royal banker, and of Warren Hastings, a controversial administrator of British India. The Prince of Wales and his circle of government opponents own the boxes to the left, closest to the stage. The site is now occupied by a Marks and Spencer store.

2.5.8a   Anon., 'The Inside of the Kings Theatre Pantheon Drawn from the stage 1791'. Watercolour. 28.5 × 26 cm. Maps K. Top. 25.20-1-b

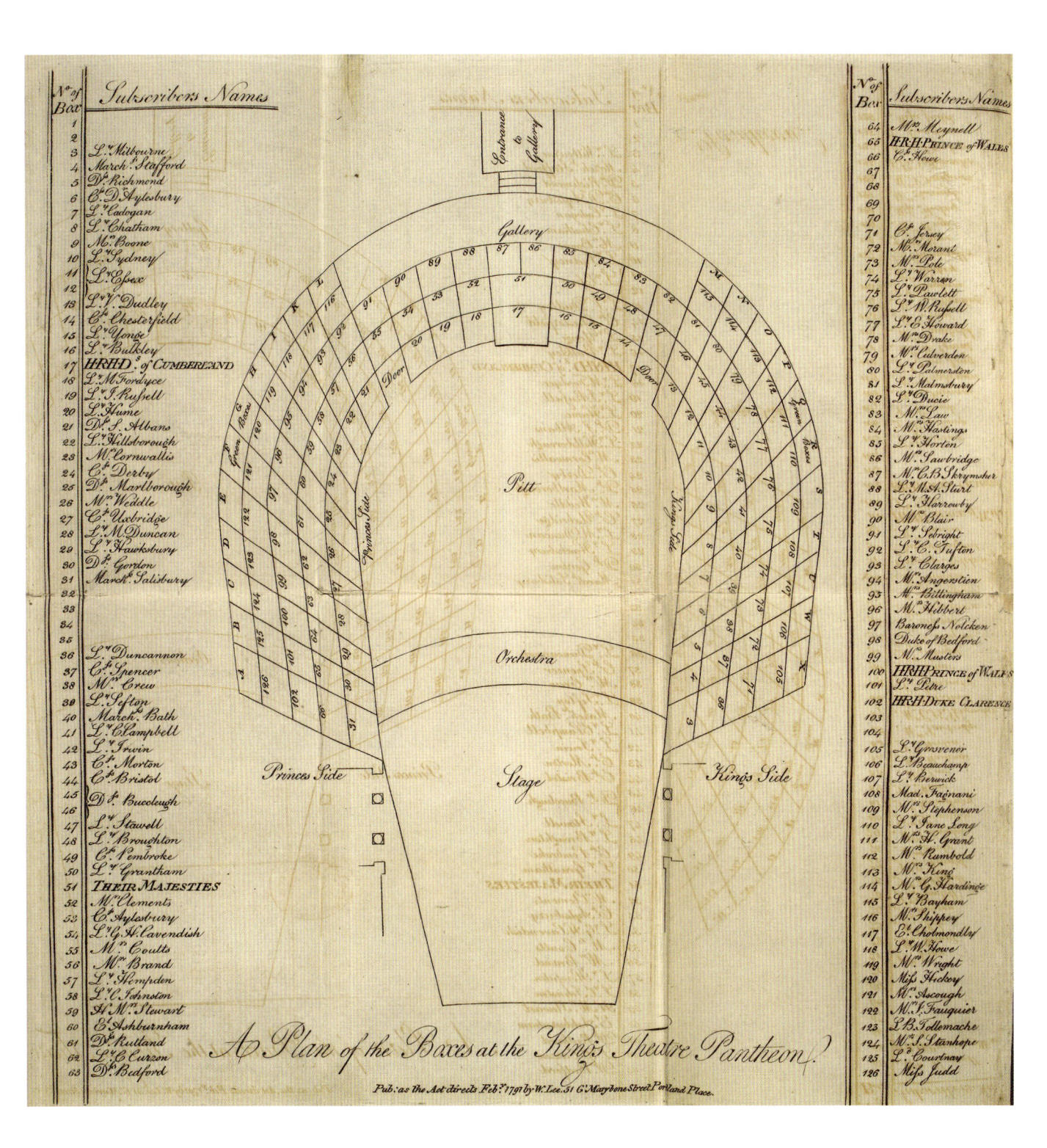

2.5.8b *Section of the Boxes at the King's Theatre Pantheon with the Alphabetical List of Subscribers to the King's Theatre Pantheon: with references to their different boxes* (London: H. Reynell, 1791).
37 × 33 cm. 118.b.38 (2). Maps K. Top. 25.20-1-d

THE MOB INTERVENES

In the first week of June 1780 the London mob, led by an extreme Protestant, Lord George Gordon, and ostensibly protesting at a proposed law to alleviate the harsh laws against Roman Catholics, wreaked havoc in Holborn, the City, Southwark and the East End. They looted and torched Catholic chapels, the houses of known Catholics (as here) and those of their supposed supporters, including the Lord Chief Justice. Newgate and other prisons, and distilleries were destroyed. Over 400 people are said to have been killed or injured. The rioters were only halted when they tried to take the Bank of England.

2.5.9 James Heath after Francis Wheatley, *The Riot in Broad Street on the Seventh of June 1780* (London: 1790). Engraving. 47 × 61 cm. Maps K. Top. 22.9

The artist Francis Wheatley (1747–1801) was the son of a London tailor. He studied initially under a neighbour in Covent Garden — Daniel Fournier, who described himself as somewhat improbably as an '*a la mode* beefseller, shoemaker and engraver. Drawing master and teacher of perspective'. Wheatley is chiefly remembered for his frequently reproduced series of paintings of *The Cries of London*, exhibited at the Royal Academy and engraved and published in pairs from 1793. The engraver, James Heath (1757–1834), the son of a London bookbinder, was appointed Historical Engraver to George III in 1794.

THE RIOT IN BROAD STREET, ON THE SEVENTH OF JUNE 1780.

SUPPRESSION

In 1780 the police did not exist and British forces were engaged worldwide in a major war. The Gordon Riots induced an initial stunned paralysis before the government placed huge encampments of troops and militia in Hyde Park, St James's Park and the British Museum gardens. These kept the West End quiet. Troops were also massed in trouble spots like the Bank of England. Armed detachments and night patrols on foot and horseback eventually restored calm. Afterwards the authorities had recent maps annotated to serve as a guide for the future — this example was meant for George III.

2.5.10 'Disposition of the Troops and Patroles in and about London during the Riots in 1780'. Annotated copy of Carington Bowles's *Reduced New Pocket Plan of the Cities of London and Westiminster with the Borough of Southwark … 1780*. Printed map annotated in ink and watercolour. Add. MS 15533, f. 40

Carington Bowles (1724–93) was a member of a distinguished London print-selling dynasty, taking over the famous family shop in St Paul's Churchyard from his uncle. It was the leading place to buy prints in London for over a century.

DISPOSITION of the TROOPS and PATROLES in and about LONDON during the RIOTS in 1780.

SECTION THREE
'SWEET SALUTARIE AIR': LONDON'S COUNTRYSIDE

From 1600 towns, villages and countryside on both sides of the Thames were drawn into London's economic orbit. They facilitated its transportation through the hay supplied for horses and its meat supply through the pasture for cows and sheep en route for Smithfield market. They provided wheat and vegetables for its inhabitants and (at least for the wealthier citizens) health and social standing through spacious country villas surrounded by well-wooded parks. Their importance led the region to be accurately mapped as decoration for the merchant's parlour and as a very early aid to economic planning. Not surprisingly the region was also one of the first to be mapped by the young Ordnance Survey in about 1800 when foreign invasion threatened.

3.1 LONDON'S VILLAGES

Whether a place gets mapped depends on its perceived importance. Before 1680 the ancient towns and villages now absorbed in Greater London were rarely considered important enough to be mapped in their own right, though they did feature, with surrounding fields, on estate, manorial and route maps. From the 1680s, as the villages became socially and economically integrated into the London region, this changed. They were shown like stars surrounding the central sun of London, which had previously been depicted only with the villages of Middlesex, north of the Thames. The villages were also mapped in the context of the feeding and defence of the capital. Nevertheless, despite their increasing integration with London, most of the villages were still surrounded by fields in 1850.

NORTH END

HAMPSTEAD HEATH

Spaniards gate
Kenwood House
KENWOOD
HAMPSTEAD PONDS

Childs Hill Lane
CHILD'S HILL

The Cow House

Blind Lane
Fortune Green

HAMPSTEAD

West End Lane
Shoot up hill Lane

Mr Ketterichs
Pound Street

LONDON AT THE CENTRE

London was placed at the centre of a map of the surrounding countryside for the first time in a map of 1683. A few years later Philip Lea unashamedly copied the plan of one of his rivals and published it as his own. In terms of content it is entirely unoriginal, being based on older county maps. Surrounding towns and villages are shown unrealistically as consisting of a single street and there are numerous omissions with some parks being shown but not others. Cunningly Lea distinguishes between 'Gentlemens Houses' and 'Ordinary Houses' probably to flatter 'gentlemen' subscribers to the map, which was still being republished in 1730.

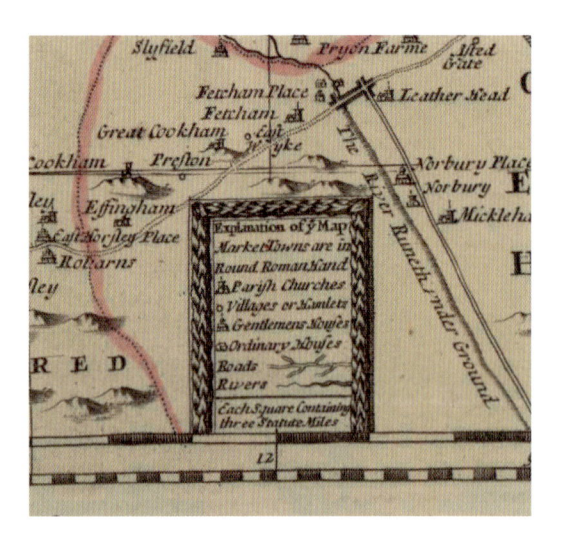

3.1.1 Philip Lea, *A Mapp containing the Townes Villages Gentlemens Houses Roads Rivers Woods and other Remarks for 20 Miles Round London* (c.1690). Engraved map. 72.5 × 59 cm. Maps Crace XIX.10

Philip Lea (1660–1700), originally from Bridport, Dorset, made and sold maps, globes and mathematical instruments from his shop on Cheapside. Among his customers was Samuel Pepys, for whom he coloured maps. The map he copied was one made by his old master, Robert Morden — but as the two frequently worked in partnership and owned equal shares in a number of publications (including 2.1.6, William Morgan's great map of 1682), the arrangement was presumably an amicable one.

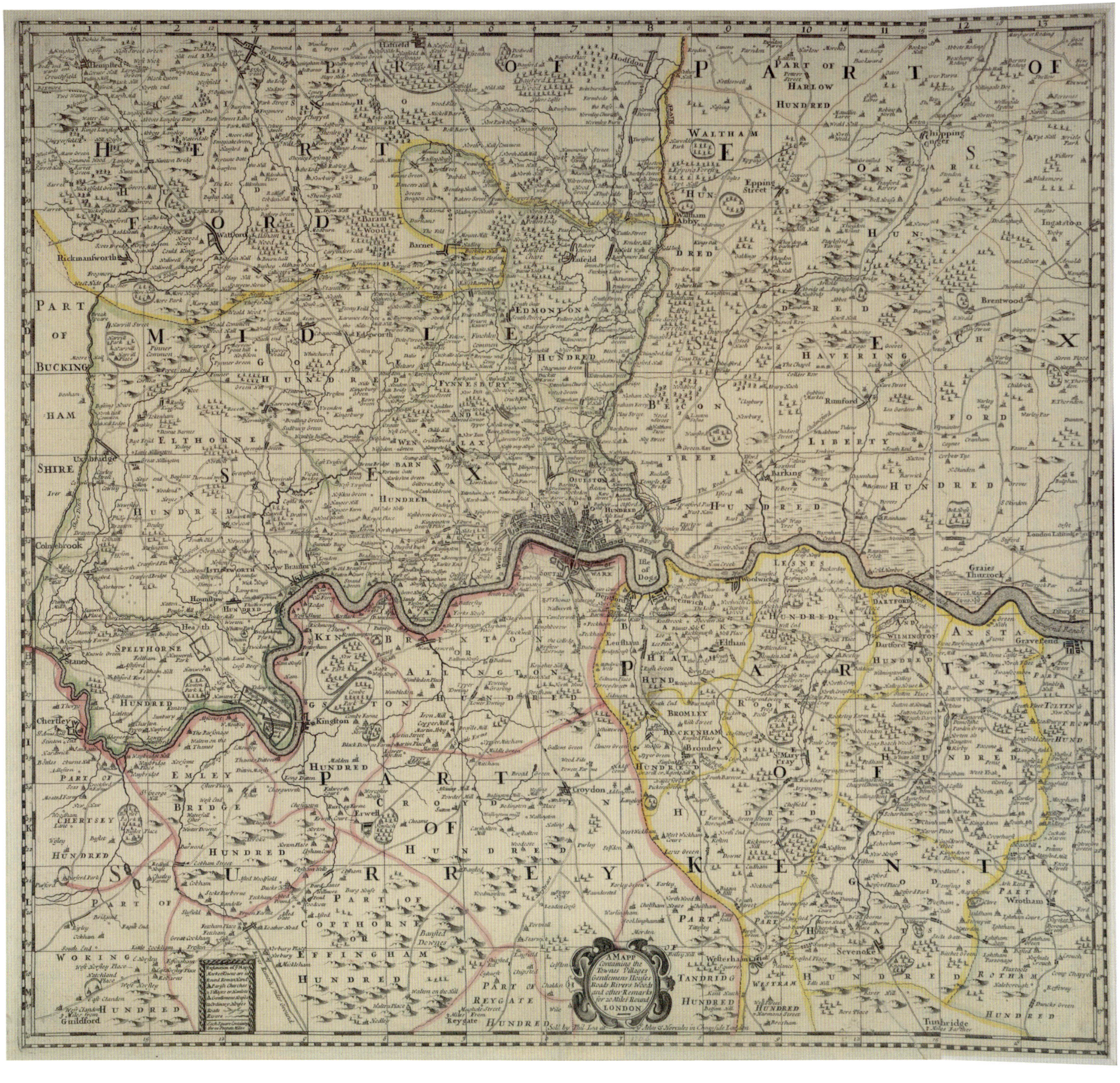

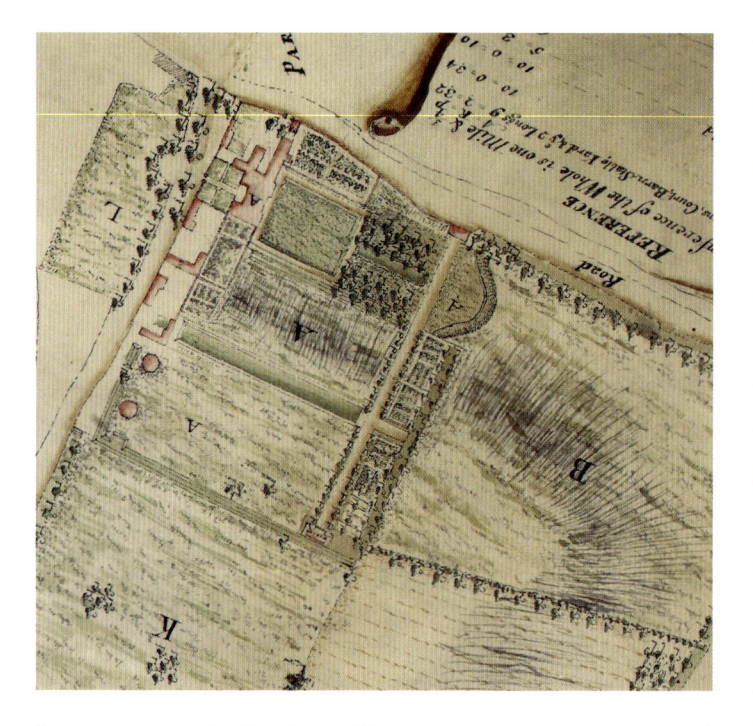

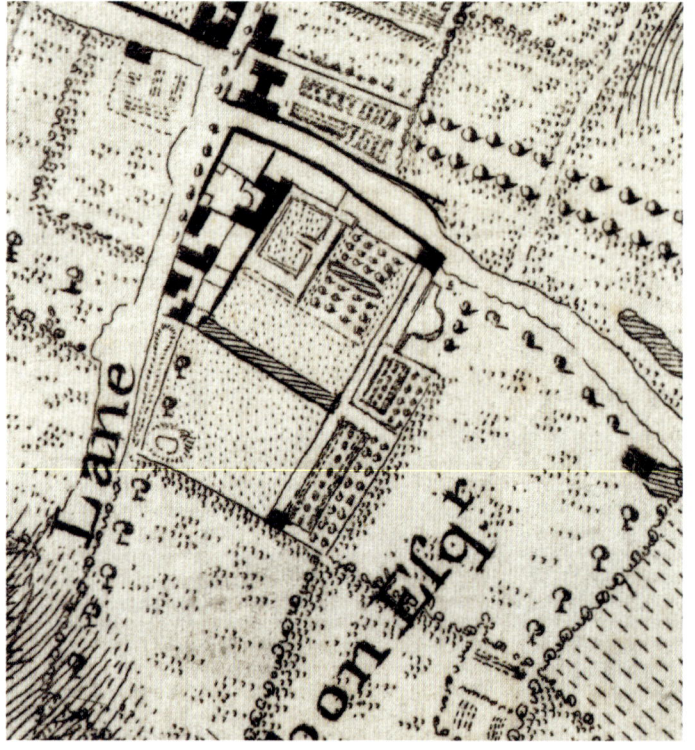

USING VANITY TO FINANCE A GRAND SURVEY

Rocque helped to finance his great map of the environs of London by surveying individual private estates. The surveys pandered to the vanity of their owners. This example shows the 'spacious house with gardens and lands,' purchased by Edward Gibbon, a successful merchant, where his grandson, the historian of the same name, was born in 1737. The survey was commissioned by the historian's father, who was also persuaded to subscribe to the great map of the environs of London, which contains a miniaturised version of the plan. It is dominated by the title panel which reduces the surrounding plans of the small estate to insignificance. The panel abounds with flattering references to Rocque's patron. It is surmounted by the Gibbon coat of arms and adorned with the figures of Minerva and Neptune alluding to Edward's wisdom and patriotism. Rocque evidently knew his man. The historian commented that 'several undertakings which had been profitable in the hands of the Merchant (his grandfather) became barren or adverse in those of the Gentleman (his father)'.

Details, showing part of Gibbon's estate, from Rocque's manuscript survey (above) and his printed map (below)

3.1.2   'A Survey of the House Gardens & Grounds at Putney Belonging to Edward Gibbon Esqr. Surveyed and Drawn by I. Rocque 1744'. Ink and watercolour on vellum. 53 × 63 cm. Add. MS14411

A Survey of the House, Gardens & Grounds at Putney Belonging to Edward Gibbon Esq.

Surveyed & Drawn by I. Rocque 1744

REFERENCE	A	R	P
The Circumference of the Whole is one Mile & ¼			
A the House, Gardens, Court, Barn, Stable Yard & Co Long	9	2	32
B Sweep Field	10	0	24
C Park Field	10	0	10
D Hop Garden Field	5	2	4
E Garden Field	6	3	36
F Lower Doves	5	0	29

REFERENCE	A	R	P
G Upper Dove	4	3	4
H Bears Den Hall	9	0	12
I Spring Field	9	0	16
K	9	3	25
L Little Sweep Field	2	0	5
M Long Croft	11	0	6
Total	92	1	33

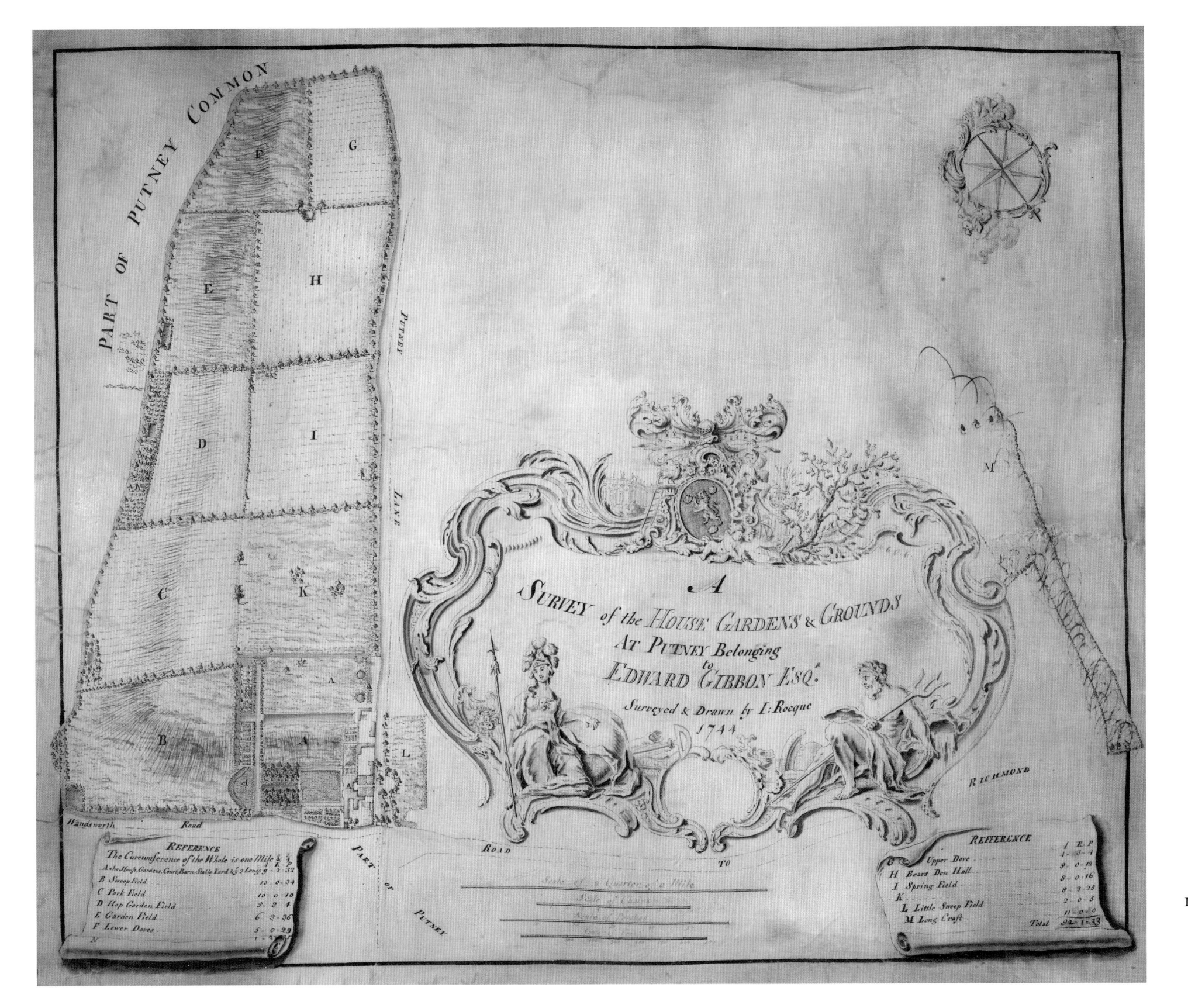

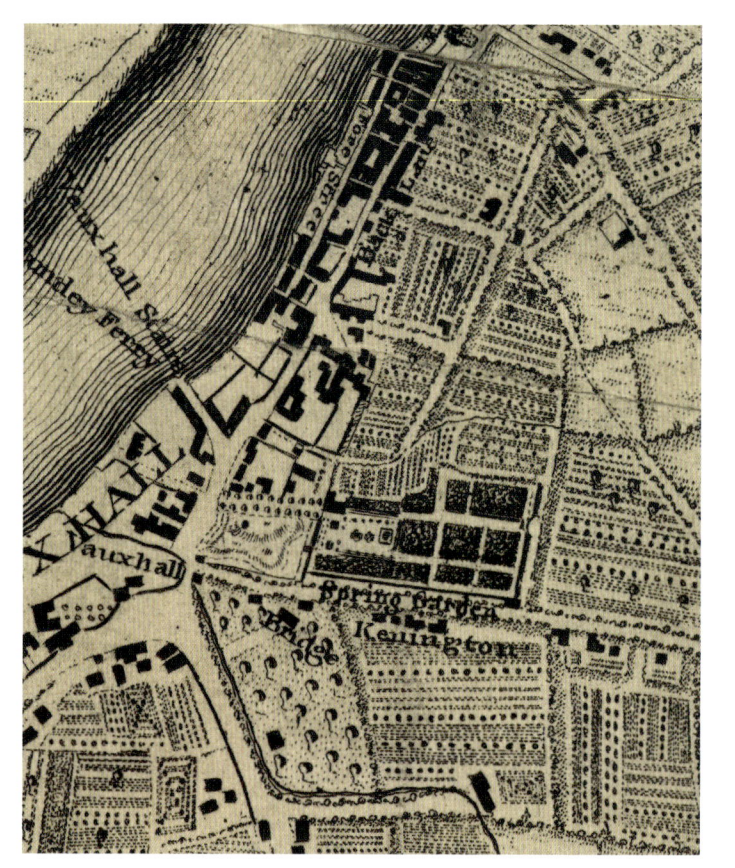

THE VILLAGES IN DETAIL

This is the first printed map to contain detailed plans of all the individual villages around London. Rocque, who did not have the support of the Royal Society or the Corporation of London for this map, seems to have gambled on the assumption that there would be enough wealthy Londoners prepared to purchase maps showing their country estates to make such a map commercially viable. The map combines the conventions of the estate surveyor to distinguish various sorts of land-use (e.g., gardens, orchards, ploughed land, pasture, and woods) with the those of the French-trained military surveyor to depict physical relief (hills, rivers) though details like field boundaries are not reliable. The result was a totally new sort of map, dedicated to the architect Earl of Burlington, whose London home is now the Royal Academy and whose still-surviving Palladian country house in Chiswick he had mapped in the previous decade. At the top Rocque can be seen surveying with a theodolite from a City church tower.

3.1.3 John Rocque engraved by Richard Parr, *An Exact Survey of the Citys of London, Westminster ye Borough of Sout'wark and the Country near ten miles round* (London: 1746). Engraved and etched map. 190 × 257 cm. Maps K. Top. 6.87-5

Rocque, who died in 1762 having survived the loss of all his stock in a fire in 1750, also produced large-scale plans of other towns — Bristol 1743, Exeter 1744, Shrewsbury 1746, Dublin 1756, Kilkenny 1758 and Cork 1760 — as well as county surveys of Shropshire, Middlesex, Armagh, Dublin, Berkshire and Surrey. His brother, Bartholomew Rocque, was a horticulturalist who wrote a number of tracts on the cultivation of improved grass strains — his farm is clearly marked on the map at Walham Green. The engraver, Richard Parr, came from Weymouth and was apprenticed to the London engraver William Hulett for a fee of twenty guineas in 1722. He was buried at St Andrew Undershaft in 1753.

An Exact Survey of the CITYS of LONDON WESTMINSTER y Borough of SOUTWARK and the COUNTRY NEAR TEN MILES ROUND BEGUN IN 1741 & ENDED IN 1745 by JOHN ROCQUE LAND SURVEYOR & ENGRAU'D BY RICHARD PARR

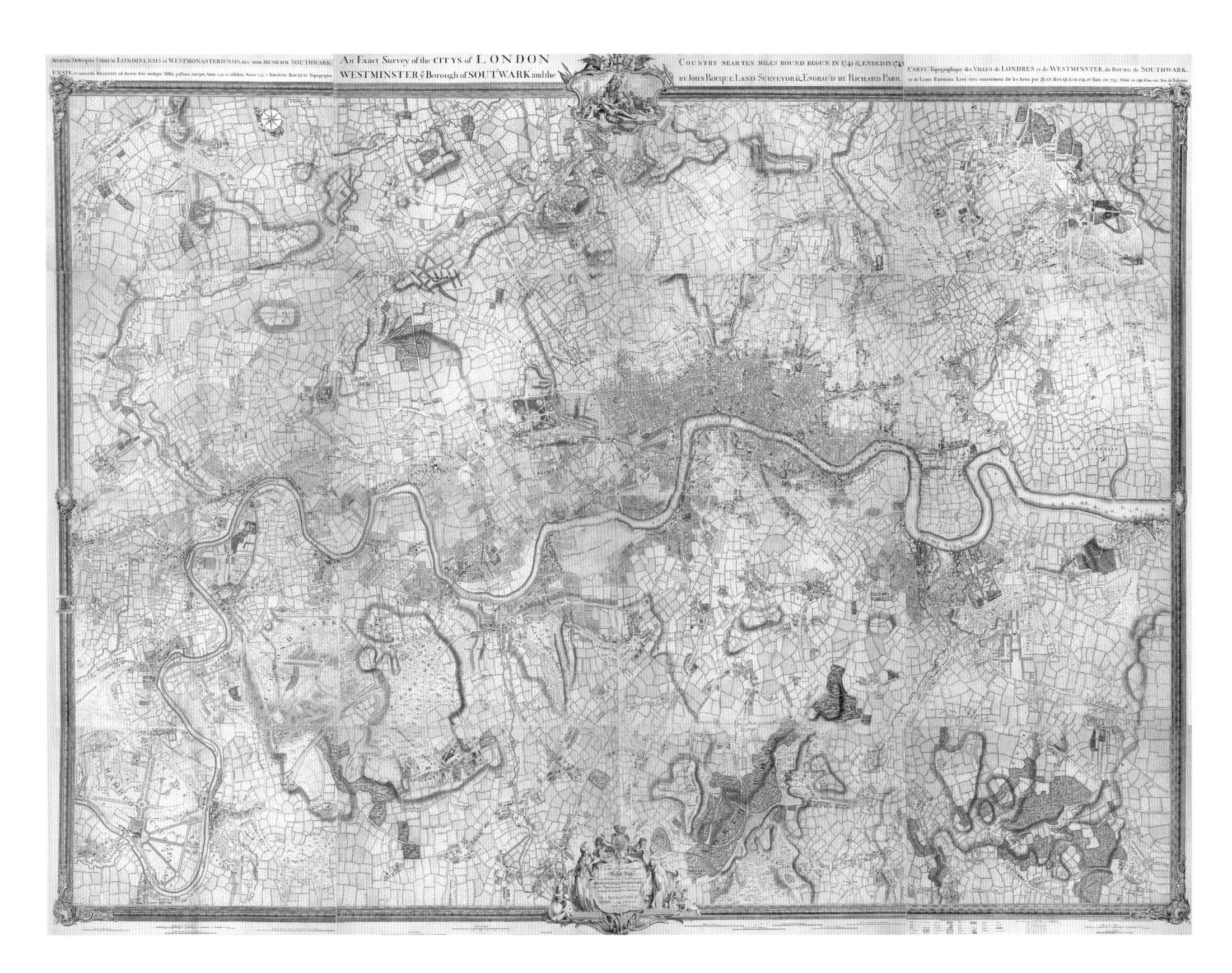

HOW THE COUNTRYSIDE SERVED LONDON

Thomas Milne was a skilled estate and county mapmaker. He had access to Ordnance Survey mapping long before it was published and he used it to create this trailblazing thematic map. Through letters (*a* for enclosed arable, *m* for enclosed meadow and pasture, *p* for paddocks and little parks, *g* for enclosed market gardens, *caf* for common arable field etc.) and the standardised use of colour he shows how, moving out of London westwards along the Thames, clay and gravel pits for bricks and roads were succeeded by nurseries and market gardens to feed Londoners, pasture and meadows for their milk and hay for their horses before reaching the parks and paddocks of wealthy Londoners' country homes. Ordnance Survey may have thwarted the map's publication: the British Library owns the unique complete example, presented to George III.

3.1.4   Thomas Milne *Land Use Plan of London & Environs in 1800*. Engraved map with watercolour washes. 72 × 90 cm [mapped area] 102 × 111 cm [whole sheets]. Maps K. Top. 6.95

Little is known of Milne beyond the record of his work, but he had premises in Knightsbridge at this time, had previously worked closely with William Faden (see 4.2.3 below), and was, like Faden, a member of the Society of Civil Engineers.

Ealing Common
EAST ACTON
WORMHOLT BARNS
SHEPHERDS BUSH
GUNNERSBURY MANOR
ABBOTS KENSINGTON
KENSINGTON
NORTH END
EARLS COURT
Tothill Fields
TURNHAM GREEN
CHISWICK GARDENS
RICHMOND GARDENS
KEW GARDENS
WALHAM GREEN
SANDFORD
PARSONS GREEN
Battersea Bridge
Putney Bridge
Barnes Common
MORTLAKE
Mortlake Common
NINE ELMS
SOUTH LAMBETH
STOCKWELL
Clapham Common
BATTERSEA RISE
Wandsworth Common
ALLFARTHING
Brixton Causeway

A GOVERNMENT SURVEY

Early Ordnance surveyors wanted to demonstrate their skills even in their unpublished work. You can see much detail that would not normally be found on a map at this scale, like accurate field boundaries, the ridge and furrow of open fields, the smallest water channels and even the plans of large buildings. Industrial features like the Limehouse Cut opened in 1770, locks and ropewalks receive due attention. This map was updated before publication in reduced form in 1806 to show the new docks. But the landowners who dominated parliament ensured that some information that often got onto commercial maps, like land ownership, was omitted.

3.1.5 [Lt Col W. Twiss], Neat drawing of East London and the Lea Valley etc at 3 inches to the mile [1:21120] sent for engraving 1799 [published 1806]. Ink and watercolour on paper. 80 × 89 cm. Maps OSD 131

William Twiss was a career military engineer, appointed to the Ordnance Office as early as 1760. In the course of a long career he constructed fortifications in Gibraltar, Portsmouth, Quebec and Dover, as well as being largely responsible for the construction of the chain of Martello Towers along the Kent and Sussex coast. He retired to Bingley in Yorkshire, where he was customarily carried about in a sedan-chair by two liveried servants until his death at the age of 82 in 1827.

115

3.2 FROM NOBLE MANSION TO GENTLEMAN'S VILLA

George Robertson, A View of Wanstead in the County of Essex, The seat of the Rt. Honble the Earl of Tylney. Engraved by James Fittler (London: John Boydell, 1781) 39.9 x 52.5 cm. Maps K. Top 13.30-d

From Saxon times London was surrounded by vast estates that had been donated to the Church. Following the Reformation the monastic estates passed into the hands of secular families. Occasionally the owners built themselves mansions, sometimes on the site of former monasteries, like the dukes of Northumberland at Syon House. Eventually most estates were subdivided or sold off, providing space for gentlemen's villas and small parks which survived until most gave way to urban housing in the later nineteenth century. The original landowning families continue to be commemorated in street names, while the villages became objects of affection and nostalgia for the London gentlemen who lived in or near them.

SAXON HAMPSTEAD

During the Saxon period, the Church acquired vast landholdings around London. In one of the few authentic documents showing how this happened, King Ethelred confirms his grant in 986 of five 'mansae' of land in 'Hamstede' to Westminster Abbey. Most of the charter is in Latin but the passage written in small letters in Anglo-Saxon between lines 6 and 10 takes the place of a modern map. The boundaries of the donated land are described so clearly that they can still be traced on the ground with some confidence. Part of the boundary can be seen on Hampstead Heath.

3.2.1 Confirmation (*c.* 988) of charter by Ethelred the Unready bestowing land in Hampstead on newly-founded Westminster Abbey, 986. Ink on parchment. 33.5 × 33.5 cm. Stowe Charter 33

The descriptive text reads:

'First at Sandgate [Sandy Heath], go east to the wood-clearing of Bedegar [near Kenwood Dairy]; then south to the dwelling of Deormod; from the dwelling of Deormod to Middle Hampstead [near South End Green]; so forth along the hedge to the rush field [at Chalk Farm]; from the rush-field west by the marsh to the barrow [Primrose Hill?]; from the barrow west along the boundary to the stony thicket; from the thicket to Watling Street; so north along Watling Street to the boundary stream [Kilburn]; from the boundary stream again east along the boundary to Sandgate'.

THE ANCIENT MANORS

This vast map of the manor of St John of Jerusalem, extending from Aldersgate Street to Hornsey Lane, illustrates the immense size of most of the ancient manors around London. The map was made to enable the manor's administrators to keep control of changes in tenancies and land use, from which they profited through fines and fees. Accordingly it shows boundaries and names occupants. Pencil annotations indicate developments up to the 1860s, such as the line of Camden Road and a reference to Thomas Cubitt, the first modern building contractor, who had developed Belgravia and Bayswater. But everywhere there is open land.

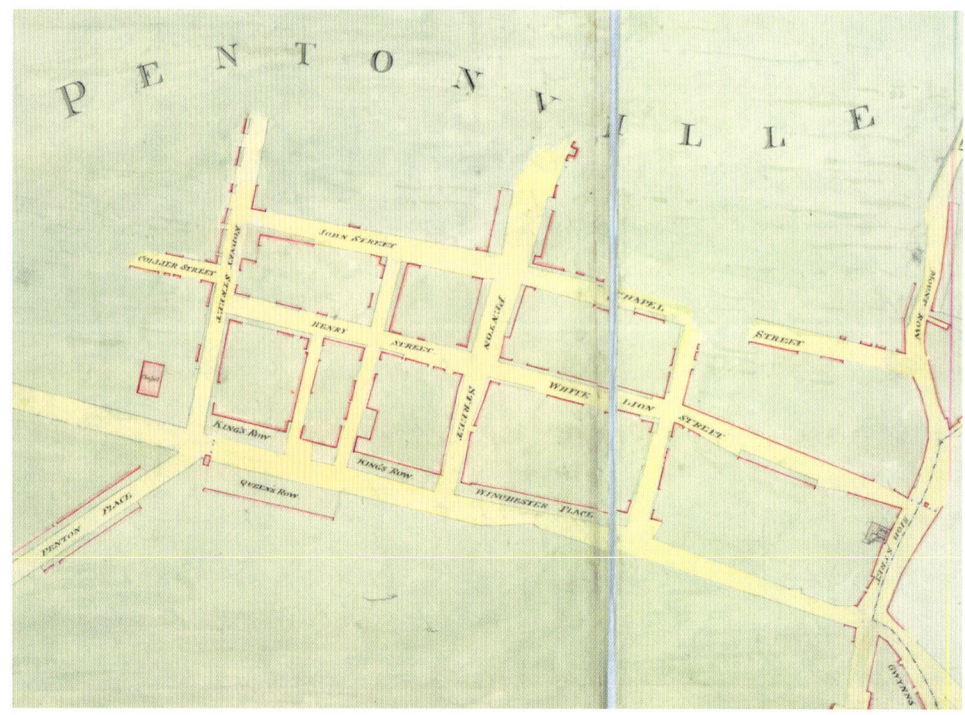

3.2.2 [Thomas Denton?], 'A plan of the manor of St. John of Jerusalem', c. 1810. Ink and watercolour on paper. 431.5 × 124 cm. Add. MS 31323 MM and YY (extracts). The large size of this plan is represented in relation to a human figure on the left

119

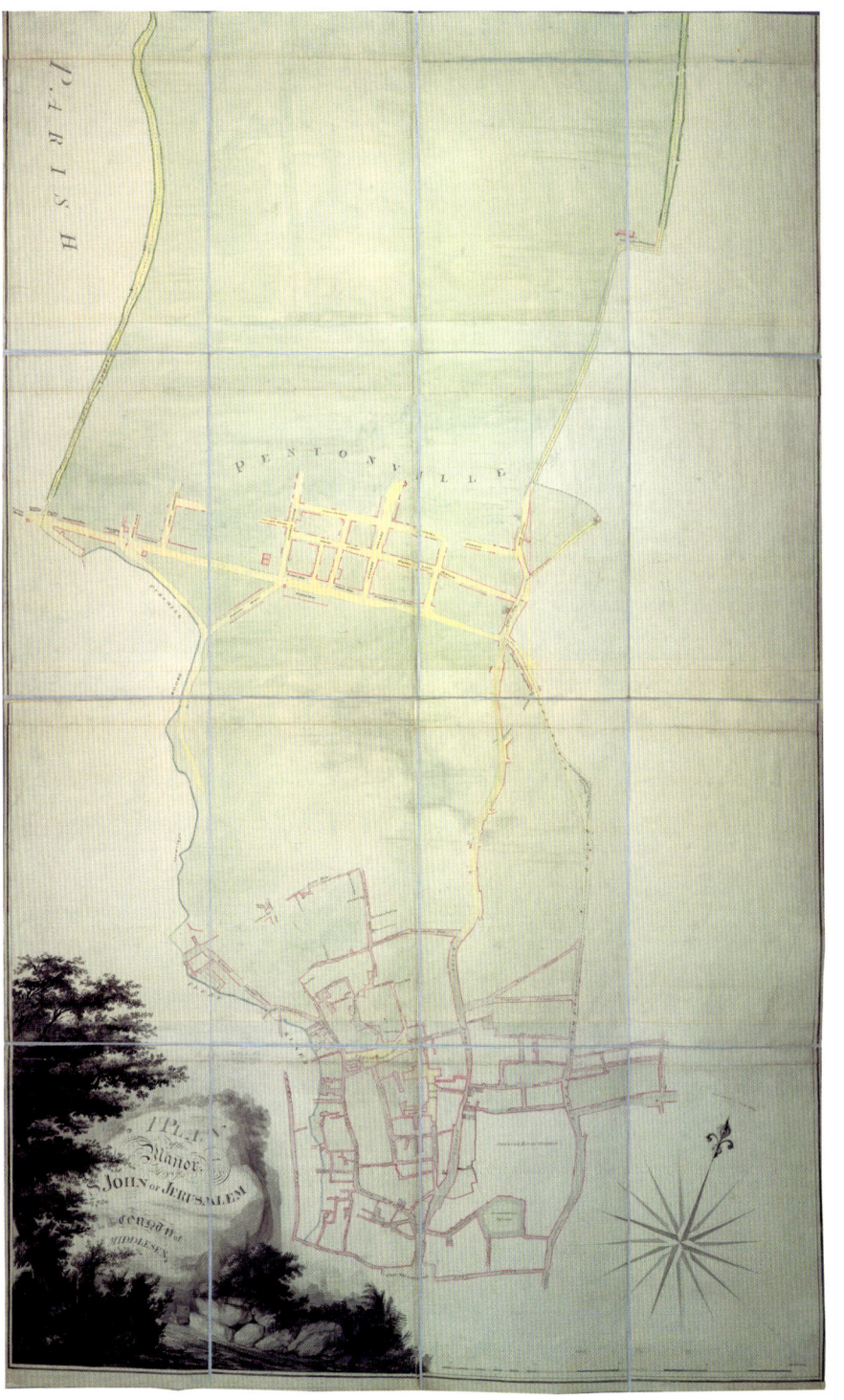

WHAT A LORD OF THE MANOR NEEDED TO KNOW

The land around London was divided up into large manors. In 1787 the 2nd Earl Spencer commissioned a map to clarify his holdings and rights as lord of the manor of Wimbledon. Manorial mapping was inward-looking. There is a concentration on tenants, owners, land-use, acreages and the precise depiction of boundaries. London is ignored and, since Lord Spencer was not interested in the area's military potential, no physical relief is depicted. Among the named house-owners in 'Wimbledon Town' is William Wilberforce. Following his spiritual awakening and judging Wimbledon to be too distant from town, Wilberforce had in fact just sold his house, in order to live closer to Westminster and the parliamentary struggle for the abolition of slavery.

3.2.3 John Corris, 'A Plan of Putney Parish with parts of the parishes of Wimbledon and Mortlake within the Manor of Wimbledon also of the West Common and part of Wimbledon Park in the Parish of Wandsworth in the County of Surrey', 1787. Ink and colour washes on vellum. 114 × 69 cm. Add. MS 78153 D

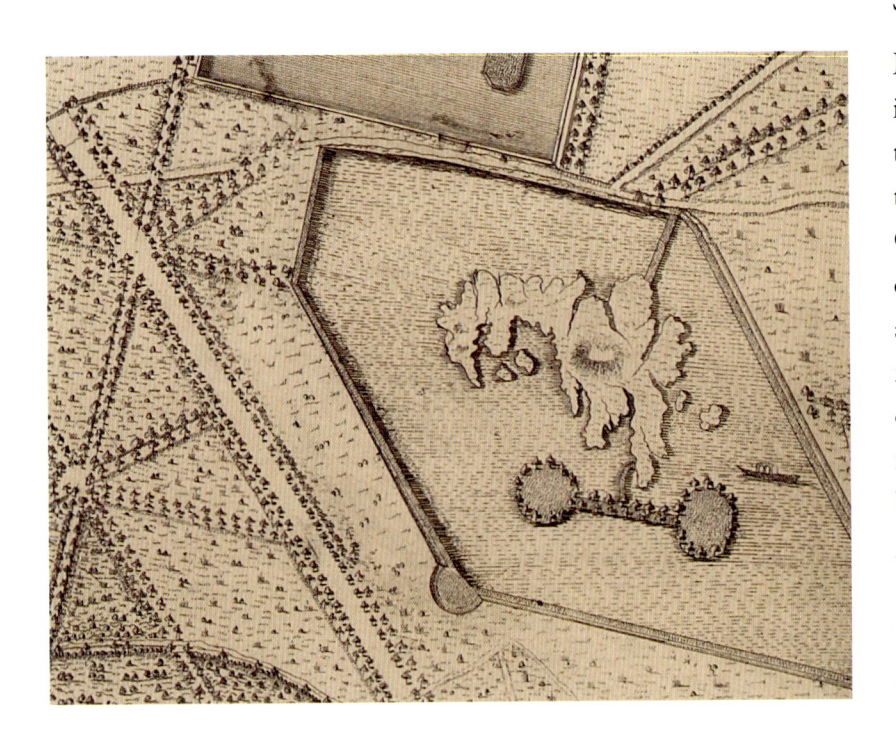

STATELY SPLENDOUR

Like several other great houses in the vicinity of London, Wanstead House lay in the middle of an enormous estate that before the Reformation had belonged to the Church. In 1735 the 1st Earl Tylney commissioned John Rocque to depict the gigantic mansion recently designed for him by the leading Palladian architect Colen Campbell and its extensive formal gardens. As far as the gardens were concerned, Rocque seems to have worked from the plans rather than the reality and some features, such as the pond in the shape of a map of Great Britain, seem never to have existed. Such details, however, did not matter. The print capitalises on the splendour attaching to the recently-ennobled Earl to divert attention from his relatively humble origins: the Earl's grandfather, Josiah Child, who had bought the estate, had been no more than a successful City merchant banker. At the same time the print advertised Rocque's skills and paved the way for a cartographic career that flourished until his death in 1762. When Wanstead House was demolished in the course of 1822–24 its fixtures and fittings were used to embellish a host of smaller houses in the neighbourhood of London.

3.2.4 John Rocque: *Plan of the house, gardens, park & plantations of Wanstead in the County of Essex, the seat of the Right Honourable the Earl Tylney*, 1735. 69 × 106.5 cm. Maps K. Top. 13.30 – a 11 Tab

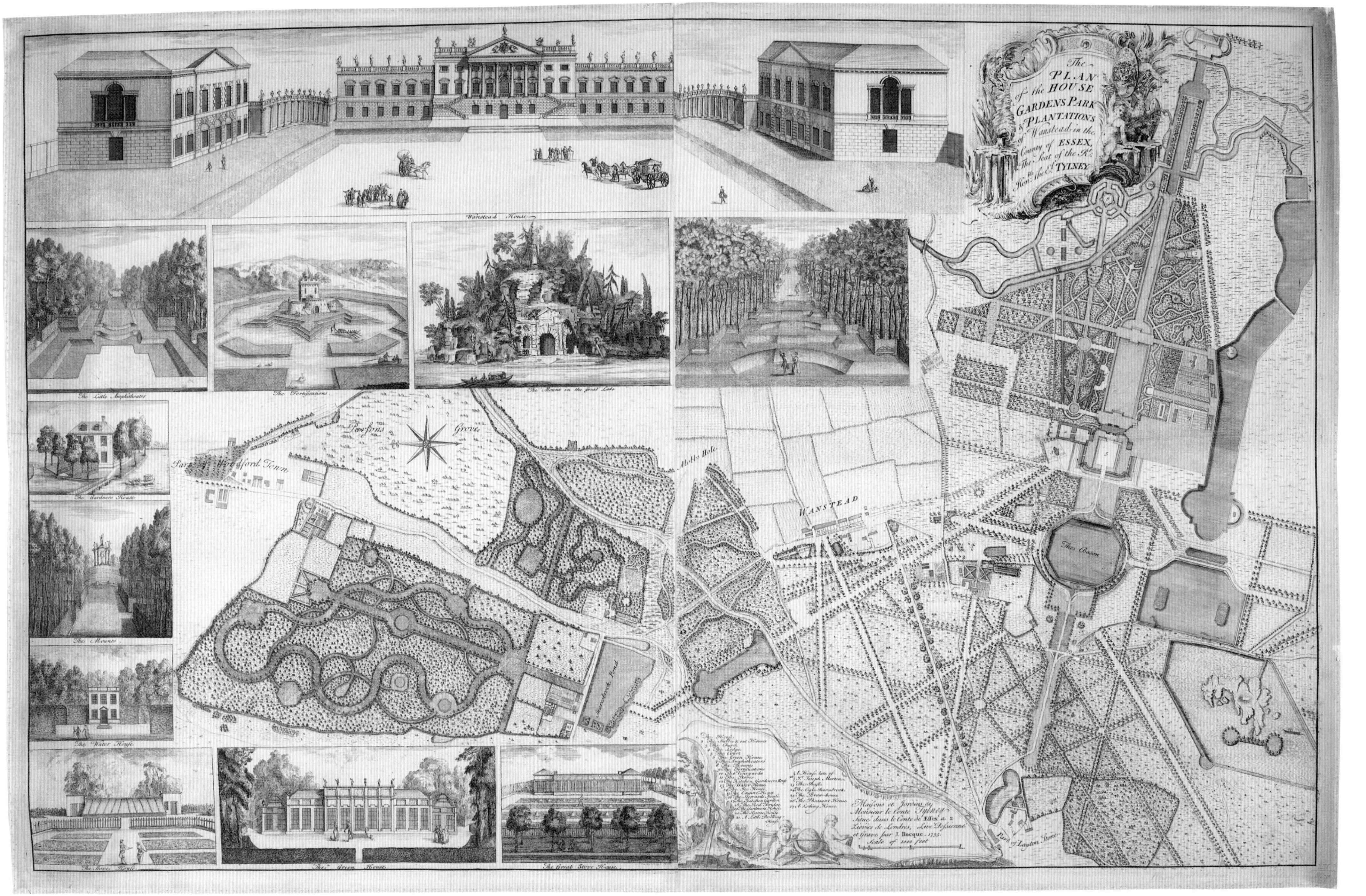

FROM GREAT ESTATE TO GENTLEMAN'S PARK

After 1700 many of the great estates surrounding London disappeared, though the families often retained residual rights and influence as lords of the manor. This sale catalogue, with plans by Isaac Messeder, illustrates the process by which great noble estates made way for merchants' villas and their 'parks'. Messeder, a particularly active estate surveyor with offices in town, was happy to create printed plans for auctioneers' catalogues as well as ornate coloured manuscript estates on vellum for property owners. The next generation of estate surveyors frequently also worked as commercial estate agents, sometimes creating firms which survive to this day.

3.2.5 *A Catalogue of all the demesne lands of the most noble William, Duke of Powis deceased situated in the parish and within the manor of Hendon ... which ... will be sold by Mr Langford at his house in the great piazza in Covent Garden on Tuesday and Wednesday the 19 and 20 October 1756.* 24 × 29 cm. Maps K. Top. 29.20-d. Open at lot 17 with an annotation stating that it had been purchased by 'Mr Bingley'

The Messeder family came from Bushey in Hertfordshire, not far from Hendon, and much of their work was carried out in this area to the north and west of London. By the 1760s they were themselves the proprietors of a large estate of 288 acres at nearby Willesden.

The Second Day's Sale.
LOT 14.

Numbers referring to the Plan.	Names of the Land.	Quality of the Lands.	Quantity of the Lands. Acr. Ro. Per.	Yearly Value. £. s. d.

Daniel Weedon, Tenant by Lease for 21 Years from *Michaelmas* 1739,

To a Parcel of Land near *Burrows*.

98	Barn Field (in which is a Barn)	Meadow	6 2 8	
99	The 5 Acre Silk Field	Meadow	6 0 6	} 49 18 0
100	The 8 Acre Silk Field	Meadow	8 3 20	
101	The 14 Acre Silk Field	Meadow	16 0 37	

Acres 37 2 31

N. B. This Lot and Lot 15 are let together to Mr. *Weedon*, at £. 108 0 0, per Ann.

To be put up at the Sum of £. 1200.

There are in this Lot 143 Trees of Oak, and 15 of Elm Timber, valued at £. 50.

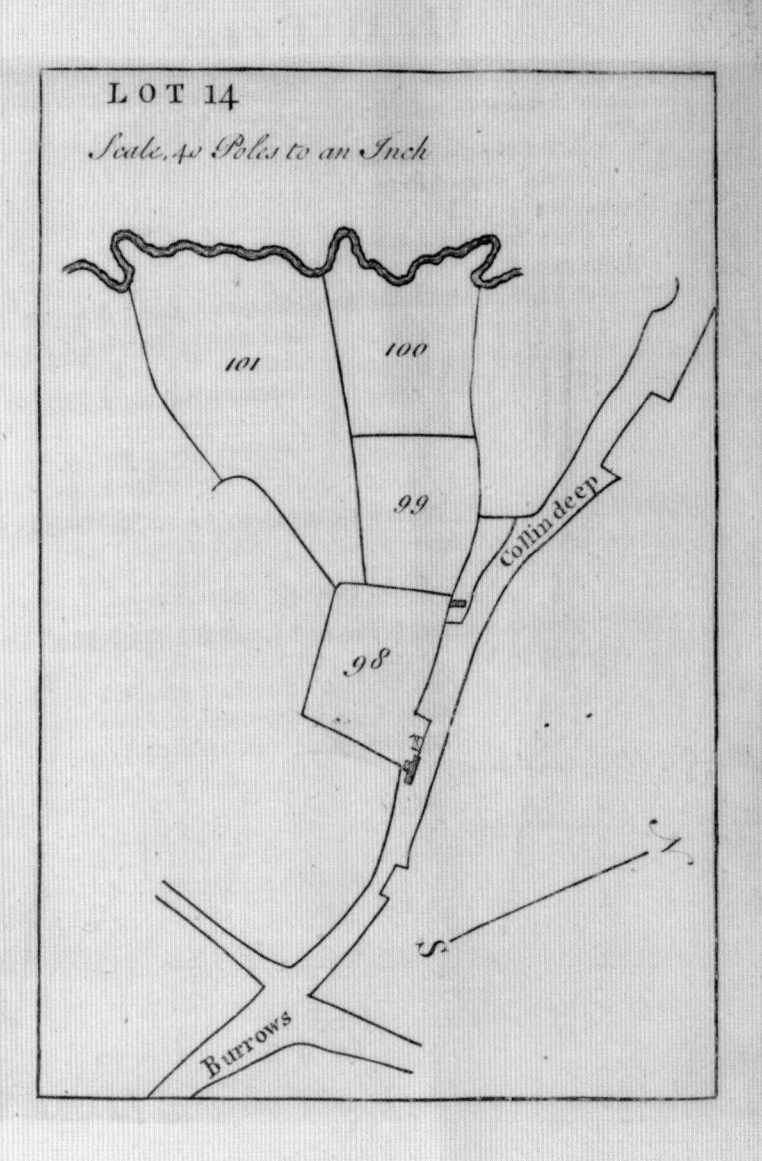

1510 Mr Bingley

LOT 14
Scale, 40 Poles to an Inch

3.3 'SWEET, SALUTARIE AIR'

Such was London's death rate, particularly among children, until about 1870 that without mass immigration the city itself would have died. Successful Londoners tried to safeguard their family's health by acquiring country houses in the vicinity. For similar reasons, schools flourished there. Views from the surrounding hills (and the fact that sewage flowed downhill) particularly appealed to some; vicinity to the royal court and to the River Thames to others. These suburban houses were week-end and holiday homes, with their owners living in town for most of the time, until, from about 1800, improved road surfaces enabled them to commute daily from the countryside. The nineteenth century saw the wealthier residents of the more prestigious villages fighting, often successfully, to keep London at bay.

3.3a George Scharf, 'On Shooters Hill', 1826 showing a variety of coaches on the road. Watercolour. 14 × 22.5 cm. Add. MS 36849A no. 38

George Johann Scharf (1788–1860) was born in Bavaria. His father's business ruined by the European wars, he became a peripatetic artist before eventually enlisting in the British army and serving at Waterloo. He arrived in London in 1816 and was before long befriended by the lithographic printer Charles Joseph Hullmandel (see 5.1.6a and 5.1.6b), who gave him his first important work. Scharf's son, Sir George Scharf (1820–95) became first Secretary of the National Portrait Gallery and it was in his private rooms over the Gallery that Scharf senior died in 1860.

on Shooters Hill. g.S. 1826

THE RUSTIC IDYLL

Highgate had been popular with successful City merchants since before 1500. This print helps to explain why. There were extensive views to London and, being on a hill, as the antiquary and mapmaker John Norden had noted in 1593, the air was sweet and salutary. The contented farm-workers in the foreground, working in the fields of Charles Fitzroy, Lord Southampton and lord of the manor of Tottenhall, whose villa can be seen in the middle distance, add to the impression of a rustic idyll. Amazingly the view (with more trees) can still be enjoyed by visitors to Kenwood.

3.3.1 George Robertson, *A North View of the Cities of London and Westminster, with part of Highgate, taken from Hampstead Heath near the Spaniards*. Engraved by Daniel Lerpinière (London: John Boydell, 1780). 47.5 × 60.5 cm Maps K. Top. 21.53

The artist George Robertson was the son of a London wine-merchant. Under the patronage of William Beckford, he studied in Italy and later worked in Jamaica. Returning to London, he became drawing-master at a boarding-school for young ladies in Bloomsbury and also served as president of the Society of Artists. He was still under the age of forty when he died at Newington Butts in 1788.

The publisher John Boydell (1720–1804) began his career selling prints from a portfolio as he walked the streets of London. He rose to become the greatest art-publisher of his day and served as Lord Mayor of London in 1790–91. Daniel Lerpinière (1734–84), the engraver of the view, was born in London — a third generation Huguenot. He was one of Boydell's best hands, earning as much as 150 guineas for his print of *The Relief of Gibraltar* in 1784.

A NORTH VIEW of the CITIES of LONDON and WESTMINSTER, with part of HIGHGATE taken from Hampstead Heath, near the Spaniards.

Published June 10th 1780 by John Boydell Engraver in Cheapside London.

AN ELEGANT SUBURBAN VILLA

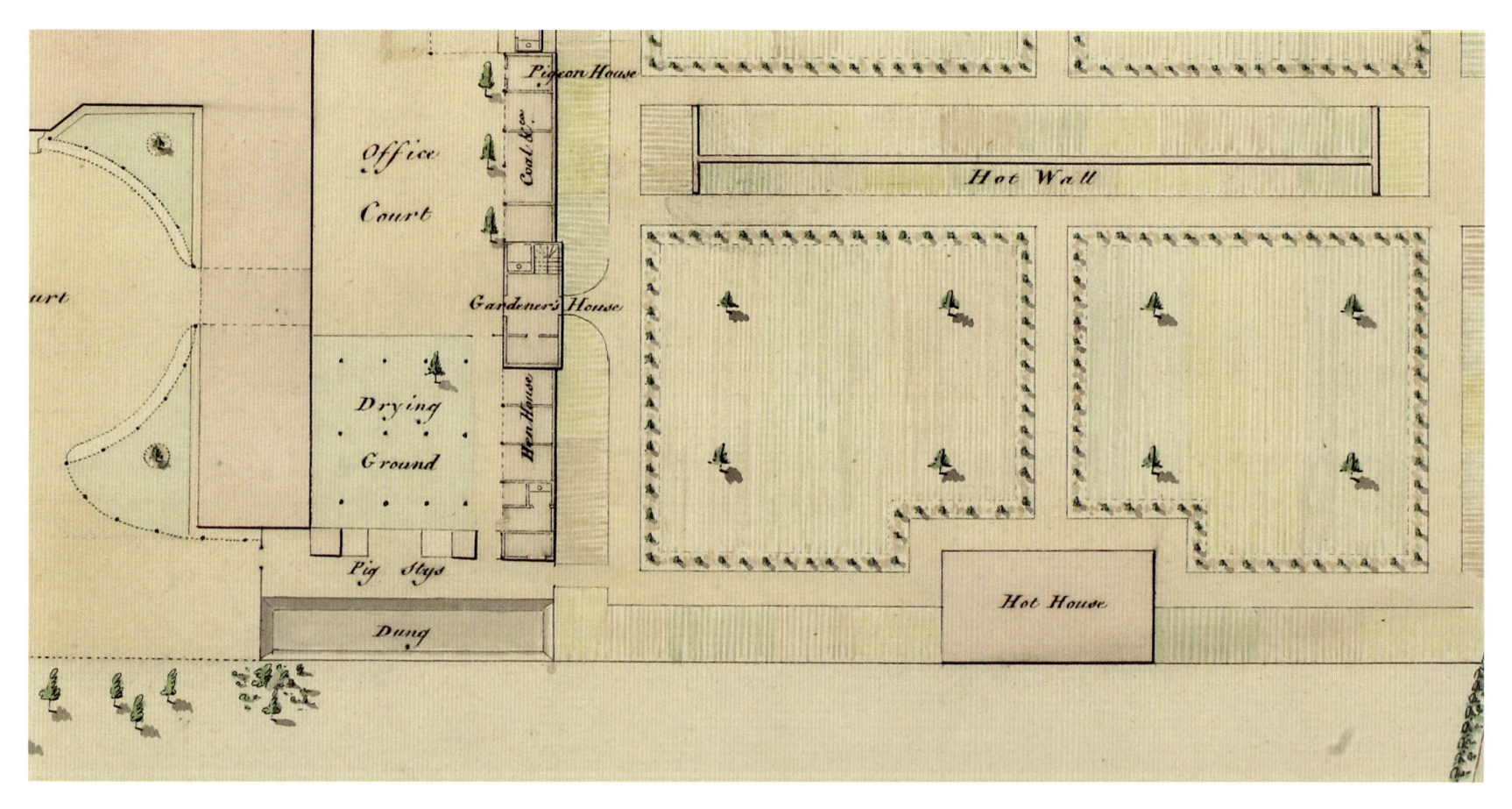

This is one of three drawings by the architect Henry Holland showing the suburban villa that he had just built for himself near Chelsea. It was popularly called 'The Pavilion' after the Royal Pavilion in Brighton that he had designed for the Prince of Wales. Set in 21 landscaped acres, including 3 acres of garden, it resembled the villas being created in increasing numbers all around London. The dung, pig sty and hen house in the forecourt were typical rustic touches and the adjoining park included a lake and pasture for cattle and sheep. The house is commemorated in a street name.

3.3.2   Henry Holland, 'Mr Holland's House in Sloane Street', 11 August 1790. Ink and watercolour on paper. 51 × 67 cm. Maps K. Top. 28.4-dd-3

Henry Holland (1745–1806), was born in Fulham, the son of a prosperous Georgian builder. His other distinctive contributions to the London landscape included Brooks's Club in St James, 'Hans Town' (Sloane Street, Cadogan Place and Hans Place), the rebuilding of Carlton House in Pall Mall, York House (now Dover House) in Whitehall, and East India House, as well as the Theatre Royal (Drury Lane), the Covent Garden Theatre, the Albany on Piccadilly, etc.

Mr. Holland's House in Sloane Street
General Plan, Includes about 3 Acres of Ground.

Pleasure Ground

The House

Approach from Sloane Street

Court

Office Court

Stable Yard

Drying Ground

Gardener's House

Pig Styes

Dung

Kitchen Garden

Hot Wall

Hot House

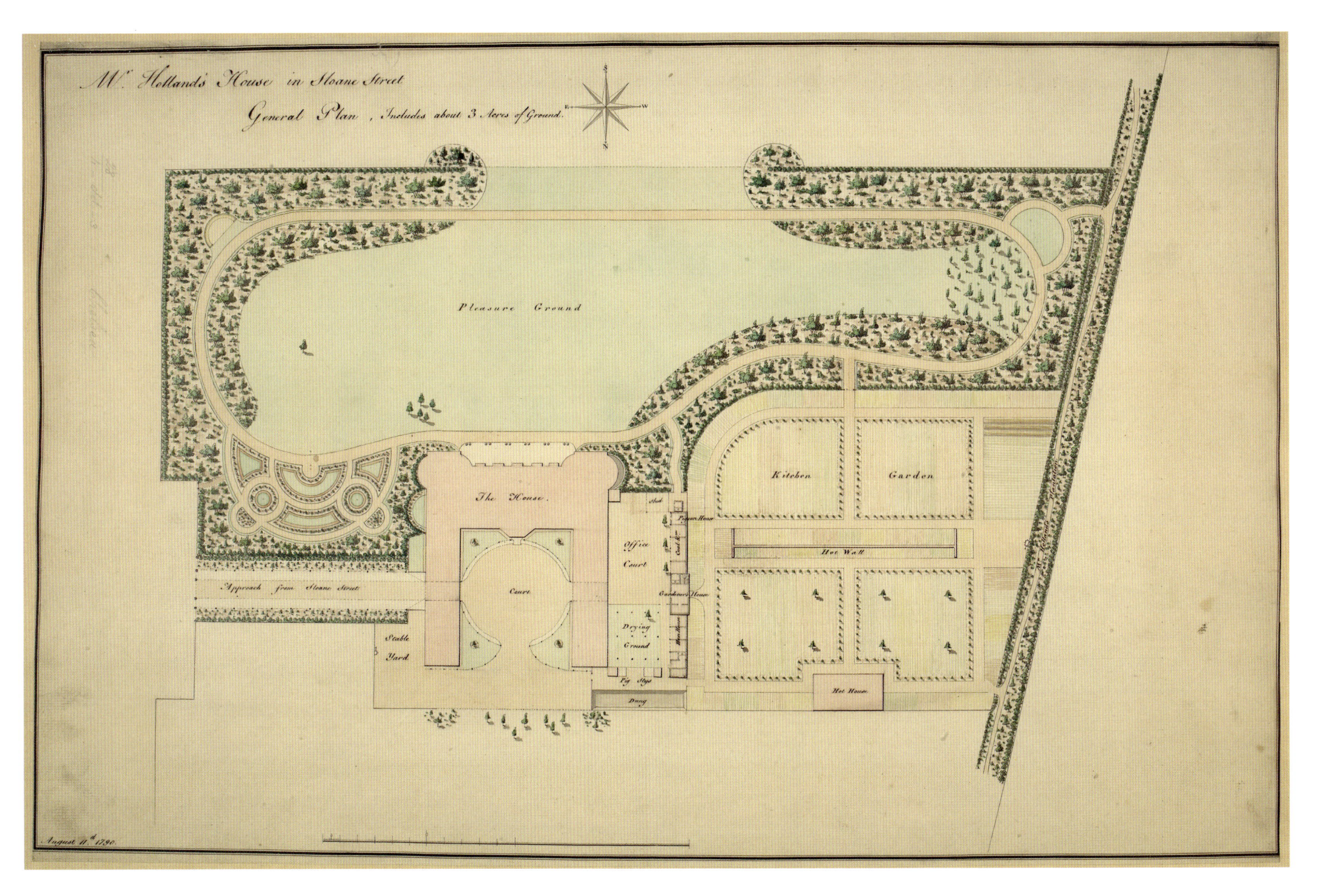

August 11th 1790

A HEALTHY EDUCATION

Because of their relatively healthy situation, the villages around London abounded in boarding schools for the children of prosperous Londoners. The Scottish philosopher David Hume was involved in founding this 'academy' in what had once been an elegant house with a 12 acre formal garden in Notting Hill. At a starting price of 30 guineas (£31. 10. 00 or £31.50) a year, it claimed to combine the best features of French and British education. Moreover it offered cricket, fives, skittles, and a riding school with a small exercise track for the less academic.

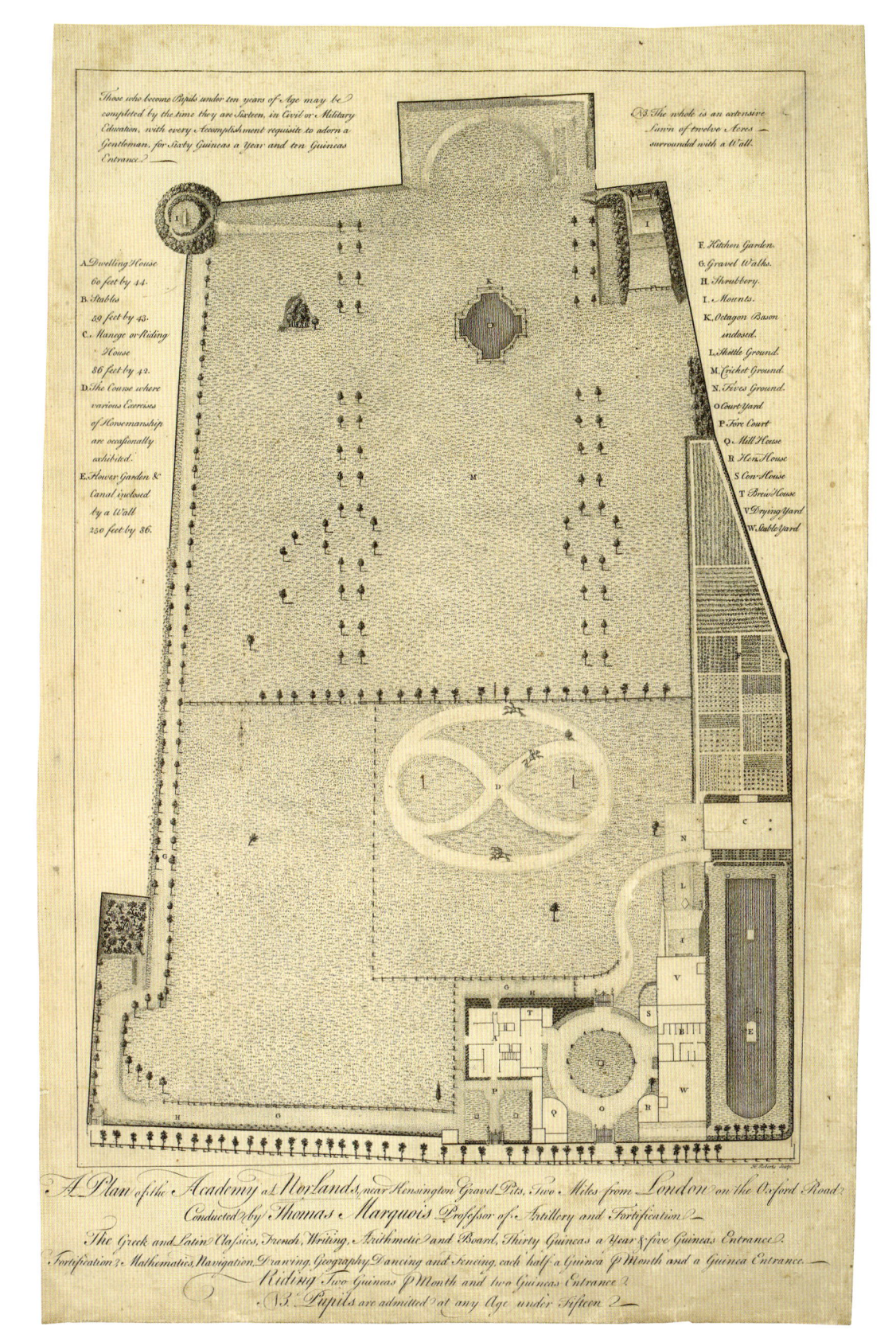

3.3.3   *A Plan of the Academy at Norlands, near Kensington Gravel Pits, … Conducted by Thomas Marquois*; engraved by H. Roberts, *c.* 1762. 51 × 33 cm. Maps K. Top. 30.11-1

The first principal, Thomas Marquois, styled himself a 'Professor of Artillery and Fortification'. He was the inventor of the Marquois Parallel Scales, which enjoyed a considerable vogue, but had originally been apprenticed to the Huguenot map-engraver Paul Fourdrinier in 1742. The engraver, Henry Roberts, originally from Pembrokeshire, was a versatile hand known for a great variety of work. His apprentices included the distinguished engravers Edward Rooker and Thomas Bonnor.

PAROCHIAL PRIDE

From about 1790 — just at the time when they were ceasing to be true rural villages and daily commuting was becoming possible for wealthier residents — the first, separate maps of London's villages began to be published, sometimes as illustrations to local histories which were just putting in their appearance. The nostalgic tone of the histories was frequently reflected in picturesque marginal decoration on the maps. These trade cards of Smith & Bye and Thomas Starling appeal to the parish-pump loyalties of the city gentlemen who fancied themselves as rural squires. Both contain miniaturised versions of maps, one of Clerkenwell by James Tyrer and the other of Islington commissioned by the Vestry, that first appeared in 1805–06. Benjamin Smith & Joseph Bye add pretty corner decoration while Starling indicates his own house.

3.3.4a Trade card of Smith & Bye 'Map, Historical and Writing Engravers' incorporating a miniature plan of Clerkenwell, c. 1805. Engraved map on card. 12.5 × 8.5 cm. Maps 188.v.25

Joseph Bye was the son of a London printer and, like James Tyrer, an apprentice of the Islington engraver Benjamin Baker, who was to become chief engraver to the Ordnance Survey. Smith was the son of an engraver of the same name. Both Smith and Bye were convicted of forgery at Dover in 1817 and condemned to death.

3.3.4b   Trade card of T. Starling 'Map, Chart & Plan Engraver', incorporating miniature map of Islington, 1818. Engraved map on card. 12.5 × 8.2 cm. Maps 188.v.26

Thomas Starling (1796–1850) was himself born in Islington — a member of an extensive family of engravers, printers and booksellers. He featured in a trial at the Old Bailey in 1828 when a canvasser he employed for selling a larger plan of the parish was prosecuted for embezzling the subscriptions.

135

IMPROVED ROADS

The Kensington Turnpike Trust was formed by Act of Parliament in 1725 to care for several important roads to the west of London. In 1811 it commissioned Joseph Salway to create a detailed record of everything under its management. This sheet shows the parish church, houses and shops lining the high street of the still rural village of Kensington. Although turnpike trusts had been heavily censured for their neglectful ways, road surfaces were improving. Regular coach services were already running from outlying villages as far away as Deptford to central London.

3.3.5 Joseph Salway, Kensington High Street and Kensington Church Street from the Kensington Turnpike Trust Drawings, 1811. Ink and watercolour on paper. 74 × 128.5 cm. Add. MS 31325, ff. 27ᵛ–28

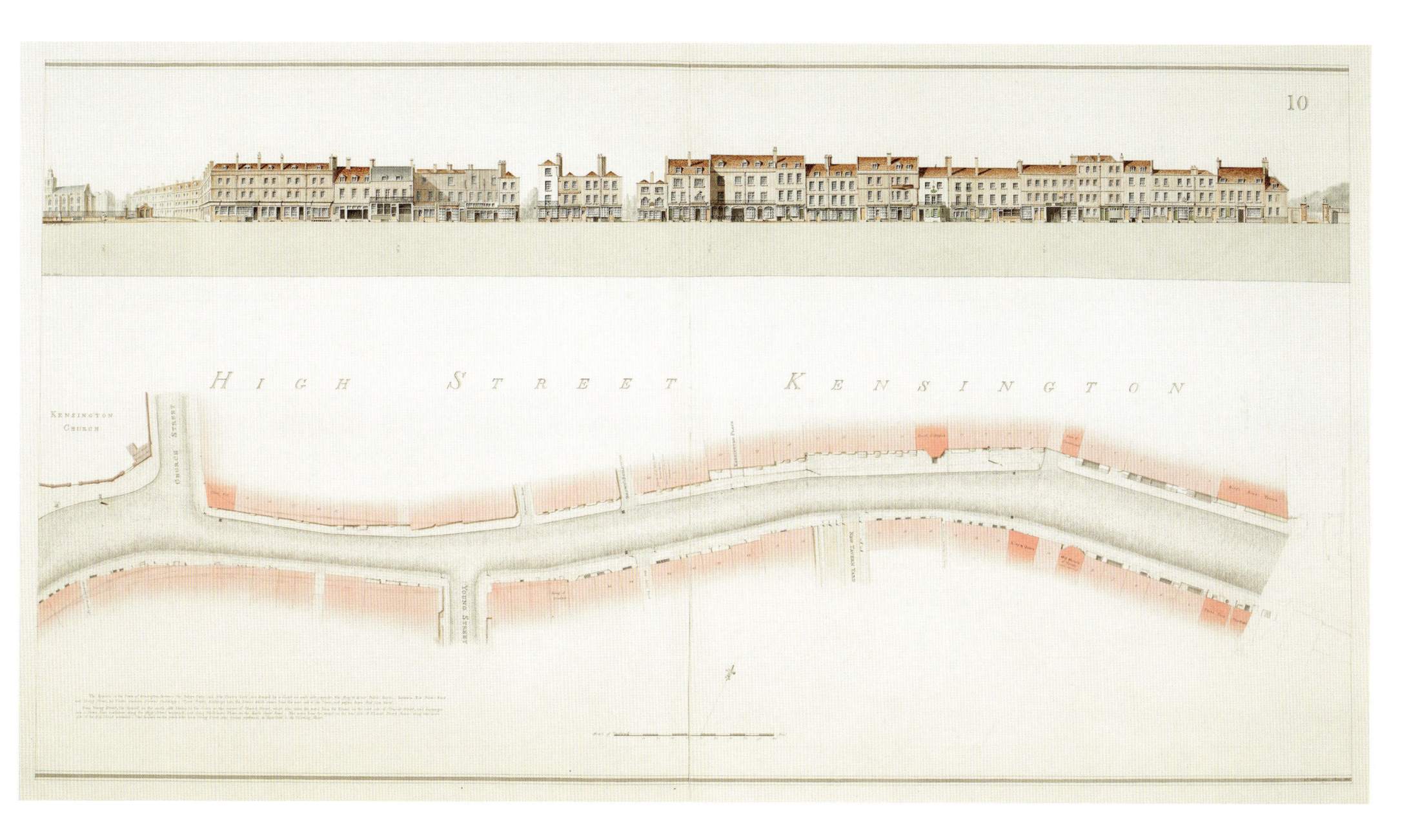

HIGH STREET KENSINGTON

STILL RURAL

The most striking thing about this map is that, despite the enormous growth in the size of London since the 1740s, the surrounding villages are still by and large surrounded by open country. A close study will show brickfields and fingers of ribbon development, however, and the wealthy owners of suburban villas were now commuting to town on a daily basis. Smith's map is notable for the number of the upper middle-class villa owners whom he mentions. He also includes important information on tracks and footpaths which foreshadow later developments, but which are often not shown on the First Edition Ordnance Survey maps.

3.3.6   Charles Smith, *Map of Country Twelve Miles round London* September 1822. Engraved W. R. Gardner. 74 × 85.5 cm. Maps 3479 (124)

Charles Smith was one of the best-known mapsellers of his time and himself something of a London landmark. He had premises at No. 172 Strand, on the corner of Surrey Street, for upwards of fifty years, and was still there in 1851, still publishing maps (with the assistance of his daughter Charlotte) at the age of eighty-three. The family firm survived on into the twentieth century.

The map was engraved by William Robert Gardner. *The Times* of 21 September 1829 reported that 'extensive forgeries had lately been detected' and that Gardner, aged about forty and of 'a very prepossessing exterior and agreeable manners', was thought to have fled the country with perhaps £10,000 obtained with forged bills. He had left home on 29 July 1829 with an eight-year-old son, and was later seen at London Docks seeking passage to New York. His wife and three other children were left behind, claiming to know nothing. He was never seen again.

MAP OF THE COUNTRY TWELVE MILES ROUND LONDON

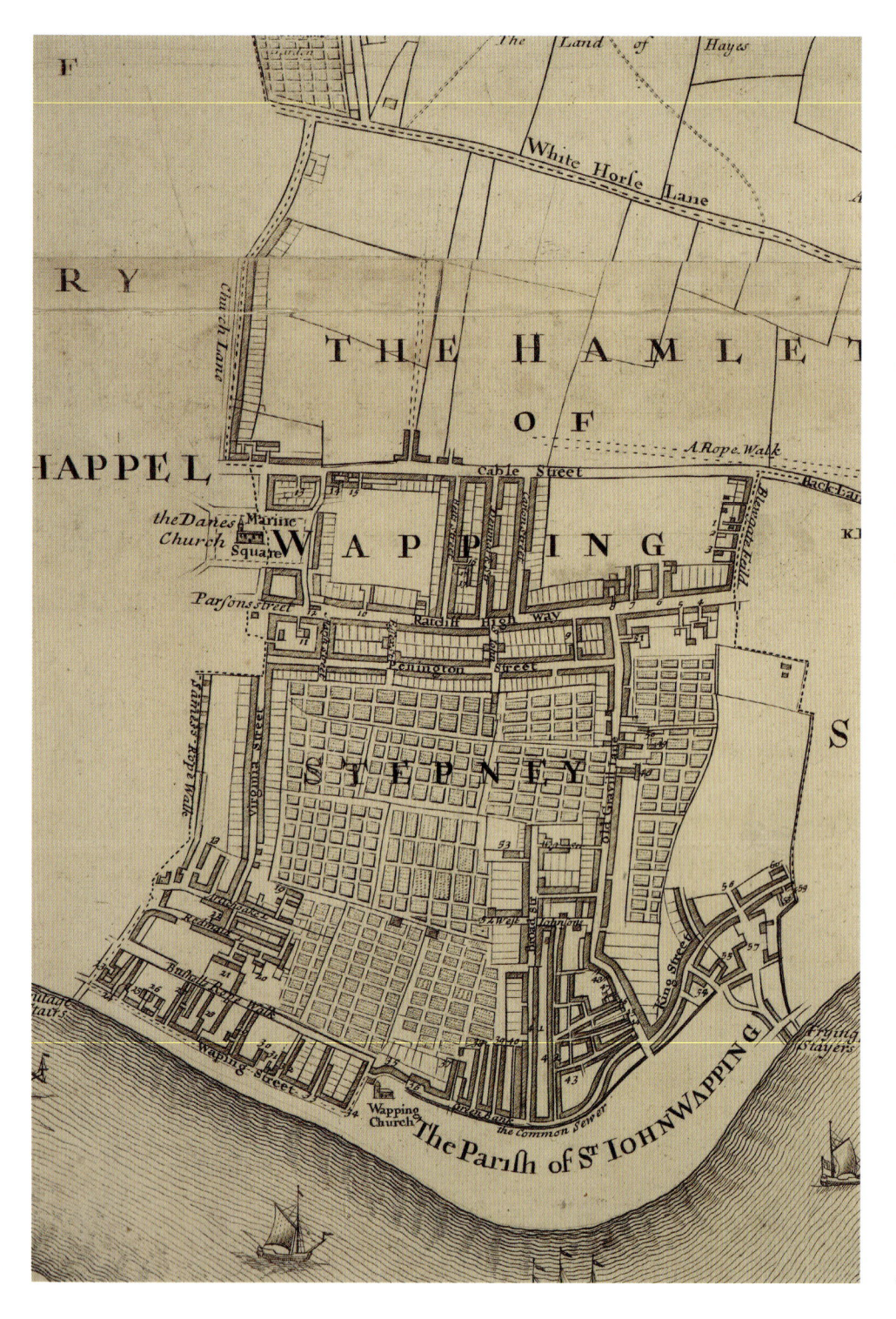

SECTION FOUR
OUT OF SIGHT: THE EAST END AND DOCKLANDS

The East End generated the profits that were spent in the West End, but before the 1650s it was ignored on printed maps of London, which stopped at the Tower. The East End was long a socially mixed area and its mapping reflects this. Boundary disputes between the royal dockyards and the prosperous inhabitants led the village of Deptford to be mapped as early as 1623. By contrast, the poorer hamlets east of the Tower only got mapped in detail 80 years later, as a means of coping with the consequences of rapid population growth. Mapping really came to the fore in the East End from the 1790s, however, as an essential first step in the development of massive new docks.

Joel Gascoyne, *An Actuall Survey of the Parish of St Dunstan*, 1703 (detail)

4.1 LONDON'S WORKSHOP

The East End developed on both sides of the Thames in the course of the sixteenth century to deal with the increased number of ships coming to and leaving from London. Cheek-by-jowl with pockets of wealth and elegance, ships anchored and unloaded, were repaired and fitted out there. The docks employed about a quarter of the London workforce by 1700. Related trades, like victualling and rope-, tar- and chart-making, with their workshops, came into being. The land to the North was agricultural but there were mills along the River Lea. The working population expanded dramatically and, amidst gross overcrowding, came to include the poorest immigrants.

4.1a   George Scharf, 'on the River Thames, Bermondsey', 1827. Watercolour. 23 × 14 cm. Add. MS 36489A no. 108

For George Scharf see 3.3a above.

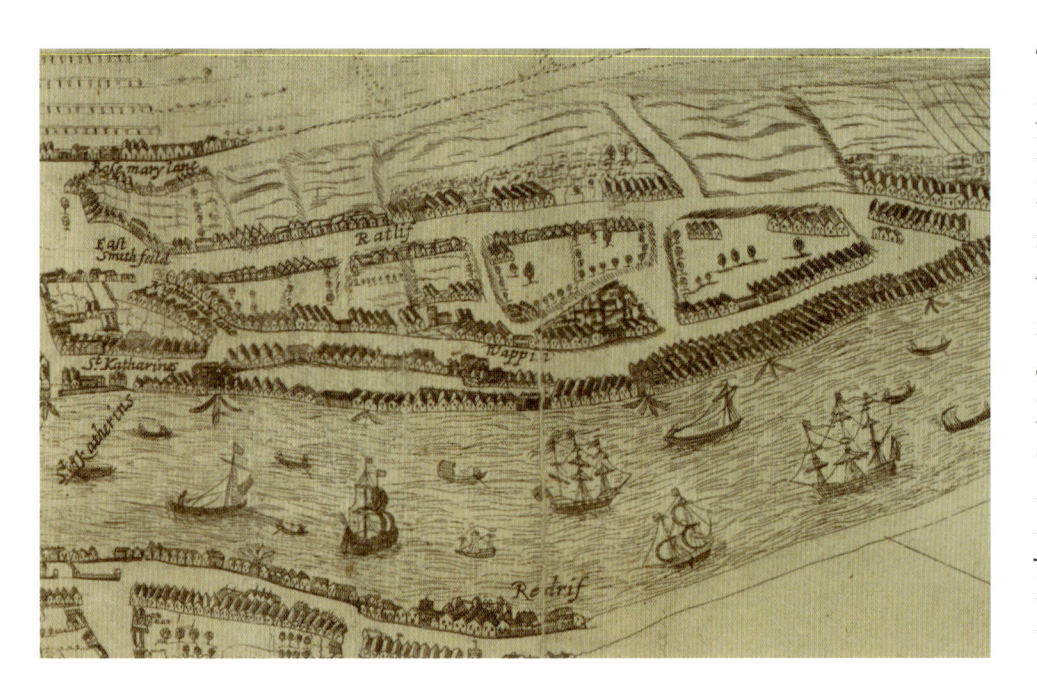

ON THE MAP BUT LITTLE-KNOWN

This is the first map to show the Thames-side hamlets. The map, with its phonetic, almost cockney-sounding, place-names ('Wappin'; 'Algate'; 'Old Pallas Yard') was compiled from earlier maps and when it reaches the unmapped East End it is suddenly mute. Only the names of the hamlets are given, apart from Whitechapel's Petticoat Lane [now officially Middlesex Street] (silk weavers were already working in Spitalfields) and Wentworth Street, (the family name of the lords of the manor), and Ratcliffe [Highway]. But numerous ships east of the Tower hint at the area's commercial importance. Since the 1590s this had encouraged the growth of a cottage industry of manuscript chart-making that, despite increasing competition from printed charts, was to continue until the 1730s. Documents among the papers in the British Library of Henry Johnson, the owner of the East India dock at Blackwall and a director of the East India Company, show that in 1689 alone the Company imported more than £900,000 of goods net of all taxes (BL Add. MS 22185 fols 17^v–18).

4.1.1 Thomas Porter, *The Newest & Exactest Mapp of the most Famous Citties London and Westminster, with their Suburbs; and the manner of their Streets* (London: Robert Walton, [1654]). Engraved map. 28.7 × 79 cm. Maps Crace I.34

Of Thomas Porter little is known, but he is probably not to be identified with the quarrelsome contemporary playwright of that name who killed his best friend in a duel. The present Thomas Porter is also known for his book *A compendious view, or cosmographical, and geographical description of the whole world*. It was intended, he wrote, 'cheifly [sic] for those who want, either time to read, or money to buy, many books'. Like the map, it was published by Robert Walton (1618–88) who came originally from Northamptonshire. Apprenticed to a London copperplate-printer at the age of fourteen, his shop at the sign of the Globe and Compasses in St Paul's Churchyard was one of only handful in London where maps could be bought at this time.

BURSTING AT THE SEAMS

In the fifty years after 1650 the population of the East End mushroomed. Working-class Wapping, Ratcliffe, Limehouse and Poplar, full of mariners and shipwrights, grew together along the shore of the Thames. By 1700 the population of these hamlets was already as great as Bristol, England's third largest city, but most of the area still formed part of the ancient parish of St Dunstan, Stepney. These disorganised and potentially riotous and even revolutionary masses, most of whom did not belong to the Church of England, placed great strains on the infrastructure and caused considerable uneasiness to the predominantly Anglican authorities.

In 1702, the vestry of St Dunstan commissioned a parish map from Joel Gascoyne, a local chart-maker turned land surveyor, so that it could get a clear picture of the situation and begin to tackle the underlying problems. The original manuscript map on vellum, now badly damaged, survives in the ownership of the Museum of Docklands, but it soon appeared in printed form so as to be available to the numerous individuals concerned in dealing with the problems. The grid of impossibly narrow streets shown in Stepney did not exist in reality but gives an impression of the unrestrained development of poor-quality lanes that was typical of the time and which worried the authorities. By contrast, as the map also shows, prosperous country villages like Mile End Old Town and Bethnal Green, occupied by wealthy merchants and retired naval officers, were to still to be found in the empty agricultural north of the parish.

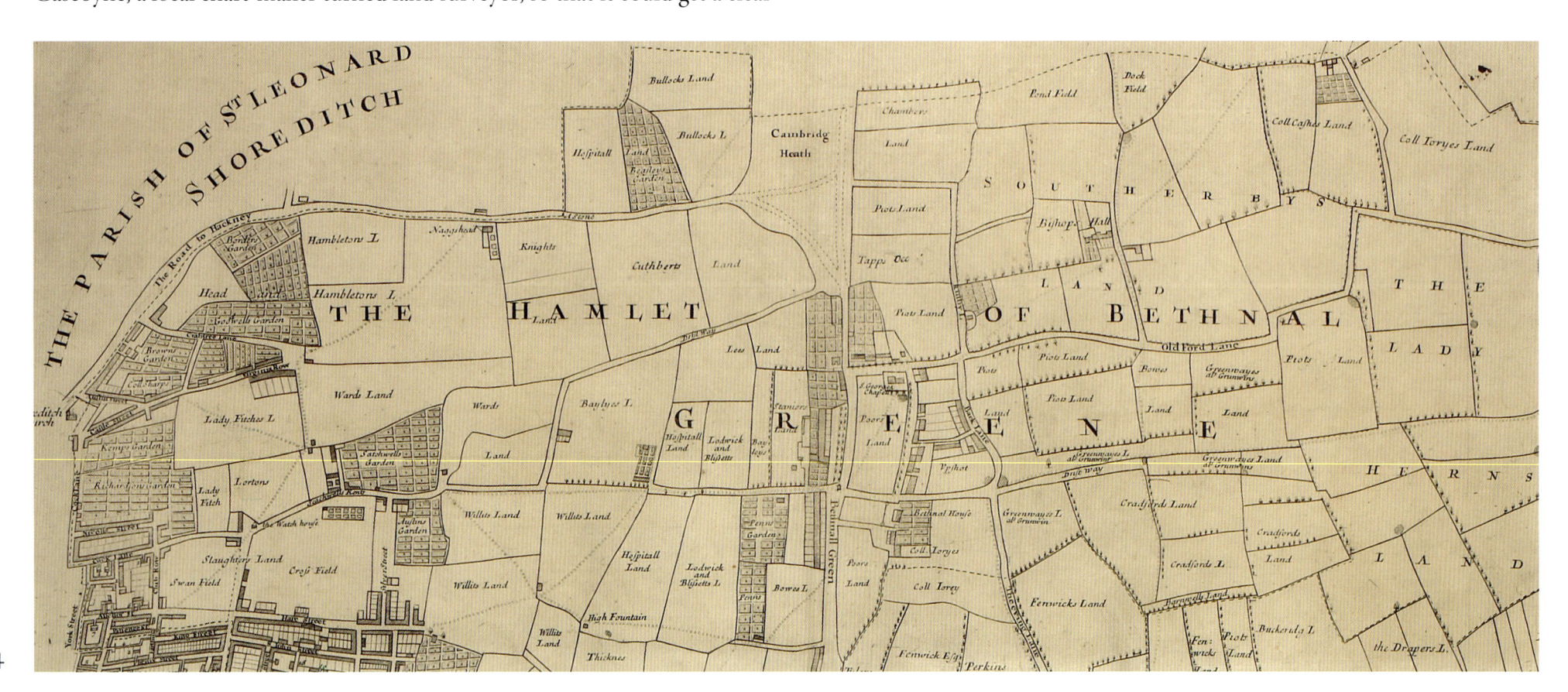

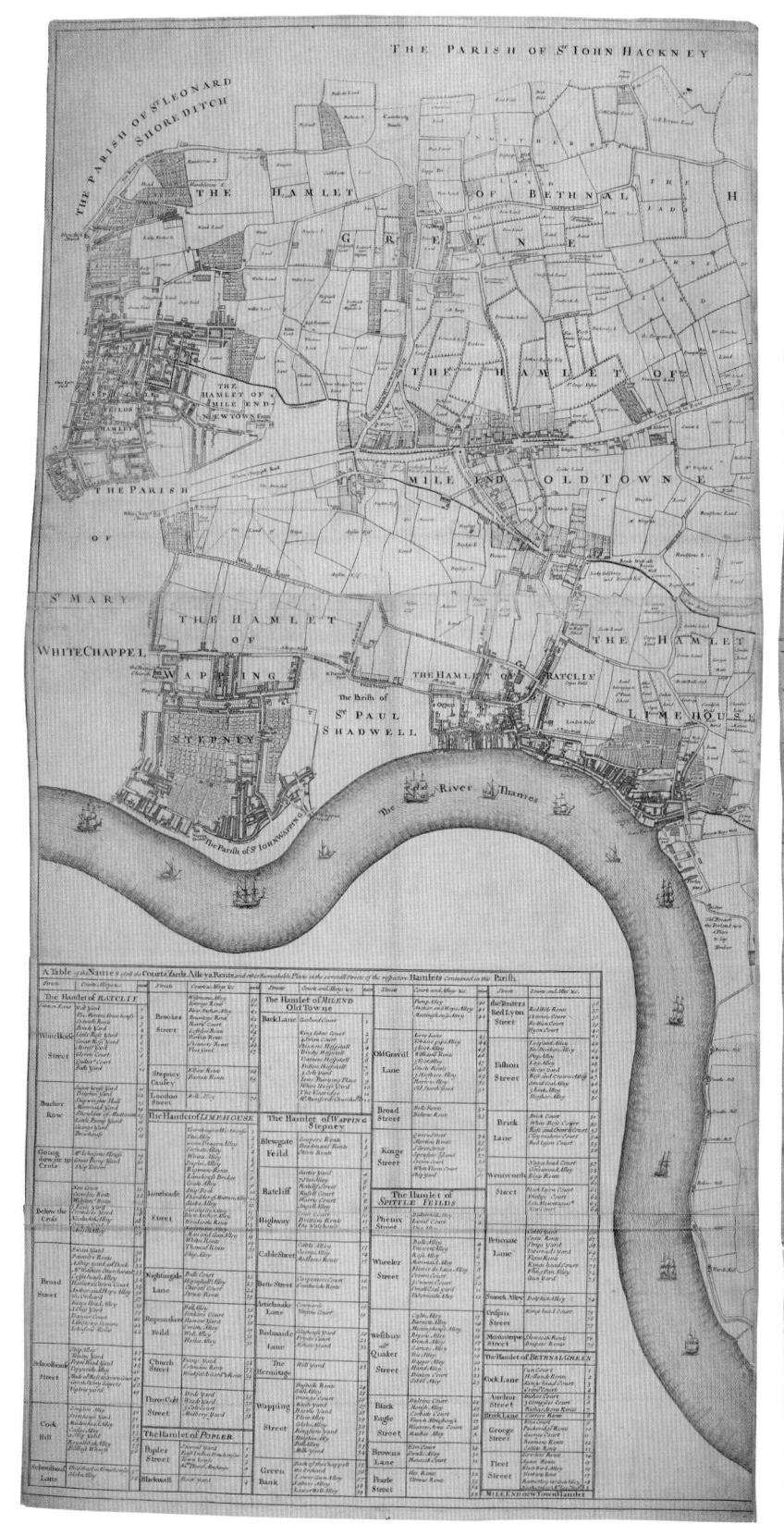

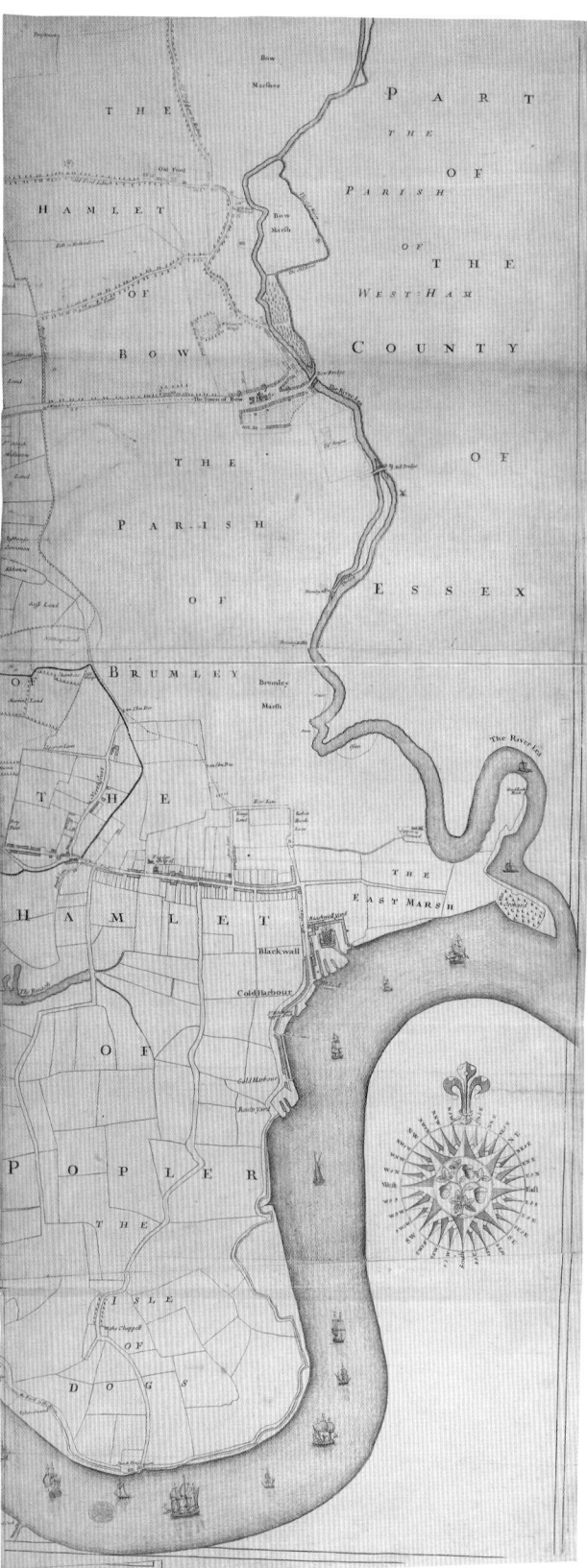

4.1.2 Joel Gascoyne, *An Actuall Survey of the Parish of St Dunstan alias Stebunheath Being one of the Ten Parishes in the County of Middlesex adjacent to the City of London, Describing exactly the Bounds of the Nine Hamlets in the said Parish*. Engraved by John Harris, 1703. 124 × 108.7 cm. Maps K. Top. 28.18-b

Joel Gascoyne (1650–1705) was the son of ship's master from Kingston upon Hull. Apprenticed to the London chart-maker, John Thornton, in 1668, Gascoyne worked for a number of years as a chart-maker in Wapping before switching to land-surveying. He worked in Cornwall for a number of years, there producing the first large-scale map of the county, before returning to London to map the Tower Hamlets.

GUILTY MERRIMENT IN BLACKWALL

Gascoyne's map shows 'Blackwall Yard', then the only wet dock on the Thames. Although it mainly serviced East Indiamen, Royal Navy ships were also built and refitted there. Three weeks after issuing this order, the Navy Board and its secretary, Samuel Pepys (whose signature can be seen bottom right), visited the Yard's owner, Henry Johnson, to monitor progress 'and at his house eat and drank and mighty extraordinary merry (too merry for me, whose mother died so lately: but they know it not, so cannot reproach me thereon, though I do reproach myself).' [Diary, 28 March 1667] The order was cancelled with lines following payment.

4.1.3   Order to Mr Frear to pay Henry Johnson £135 for work to be done on HMS Portland signed by members of the Navy Board, 5 March 1666/7 and later receipted. 30 × 19 cm. Add. MS 22183, f.8

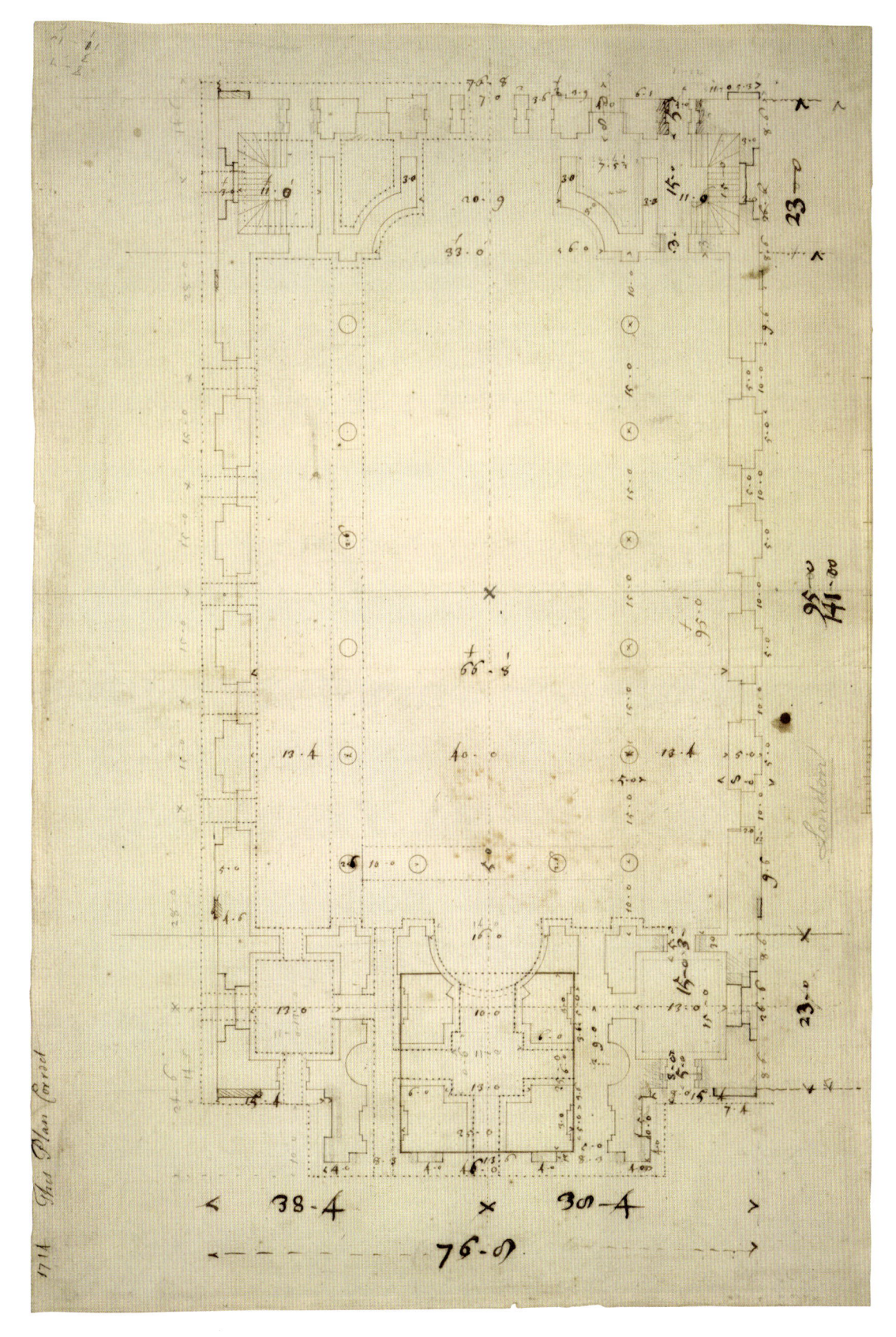

ANGLICAN SPLENDOUR IN SPITALFIELDS

One way of bringing order to the East End was to establish smaller and more effective parishes, which at the time still provided for the secular administration as well as the spiritual welfare of their neighbourhoods. In 1711 Spitalfields became a parish in its own right. Determined to impress the largely Calvinist population of French weavers with the majesty and power of Anglicanism, a government quango commissioned Nicholas Hawksmoor to design a new parish church with 'a solemn and awfull appearance'. This is a preliminary design, in his own hand, for the interior of Christ Church Spitalfields, which is widely regarded as his masterpiece. The design lacks the pillared screen in front of the chancel as built in the 1720s. After decades of neglect the church has recently been restored to its original splendour.

4.1.4   Nicholas Hawksmoor, '1714 This plan correct' [Preliminary ground plan of interior of Christ Church Spitalfields]. Ink and pencil on paper. 45 × 30.5 cm. Maps K. Top. 23.11-h

LIFE AND DESTRUCTION IN RATCLIFF

On 23 July 1794 a massive fire destroyed hundreds of houses and public buildings in the riverside hamlet of Ratcliffe. Until then it had changed little since being mapped by Gascoyne, who had begun his career as a maker of manuscript charts in these streets. This commemorative map shows the extent of the fire and distinguishes the individual buildings. Amidst the numerous warehouses, the timber yard, rope grounds and malt house, were a school, almshouses, a tavern and a cow yard. At the bottom left the mapmaker includes a view of the Shadwell Water Works where he had drawn the plan.

4.1.5 William Frazer, *A Correct Ground Plan of the Dreadful Fire at Ratcliff … on Wednesday July 23d 1794 … The whole laid down reduced to a scale from a survey, and humbly dedicated to Sir Thomas Coxhead, Knt, M.P. By Wm Frazer* (Ratcliff, 1794). Engraved map with watercolour. 54.3 × 74.8 cm. Maps *3495 (131)

A Correct Ground Plan of the Dreadful Fire at Ratcliff, which began at Mr. Cloves, Barge Builder, Cock Hill, on Wednesday July 20th, 1794, 3 o'Clock P.M. and extended the Wind blowing from S.W. to N.E. to Ratcliff Square, by which Conflagration, 453 Dwelling Houses, and upwards of 20 Public Buildings were destroyed. — The Whole laid down Reduced to a Scale from a Survey, and Humbly Dedicated to Sir Thomas Corbead Knt. M.P. By Wm. Frazer.

SHADWELL WATER WORKS

SCALE OF FEET

RIVER THAMES

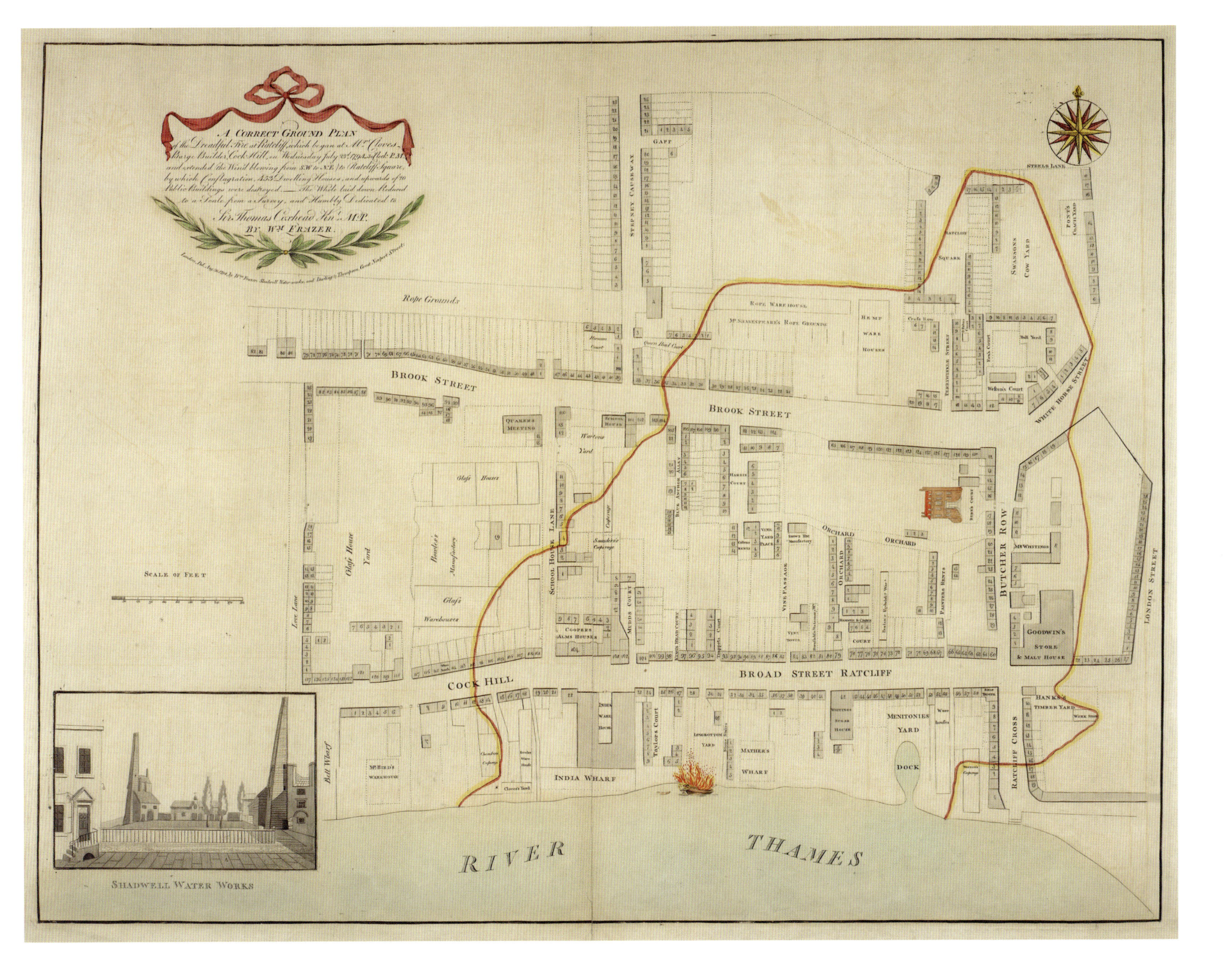

LIVING CHEEK BY JOWL WITH THE NAVY IN DEPTFORD

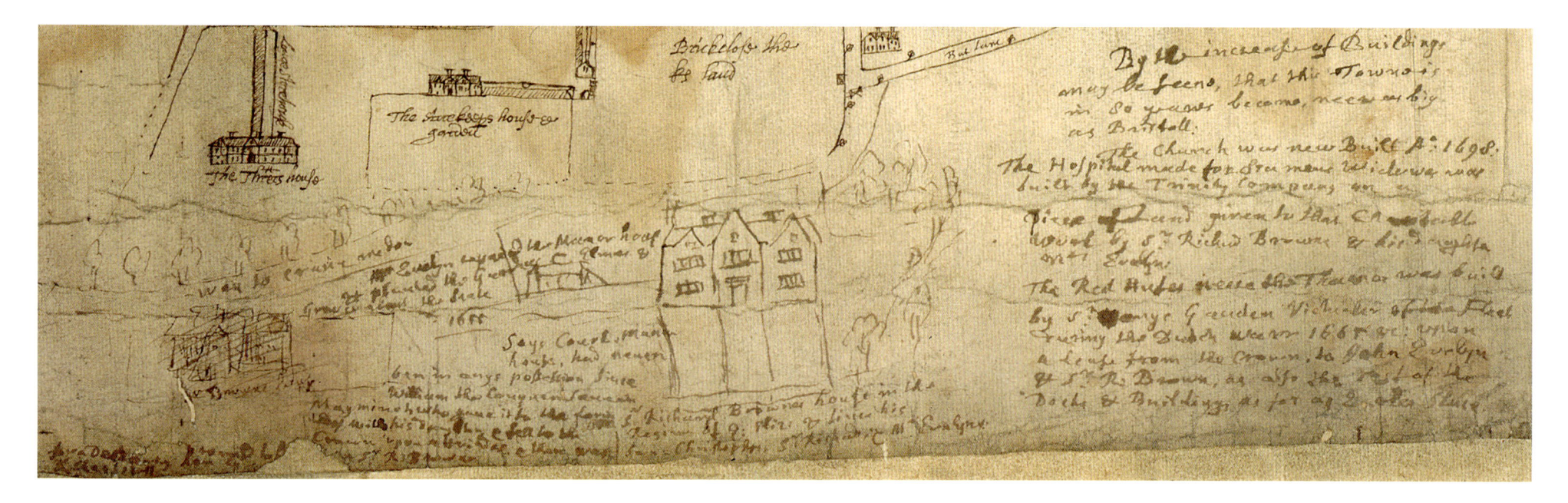

This early, damaged plan of Deptford was probably intended to clarify the boundary of the royal dockyard which Henry VIII had established in 1513. The town also included various private wharves and docks, East India Company land and the homes of naval captains and the diplomat Sir Richard Browne. Browne's son-in-law, the diarist John Evelyn, later annotated the plan with comments on Deptford's recent growth — '… the Town is in 80 yeares become neere as big as Bristoll' — and a drawing of his elegant home, Sayes Court House, which had its magnificent garden vandalised by Peter the Great of Russia when staying there in 1698.

4.1.6   Anonymous plan of Deptford, 1623 [date below scale bar]. Ink on paper. 52 × 73 cm. Add.Ms 78629 A

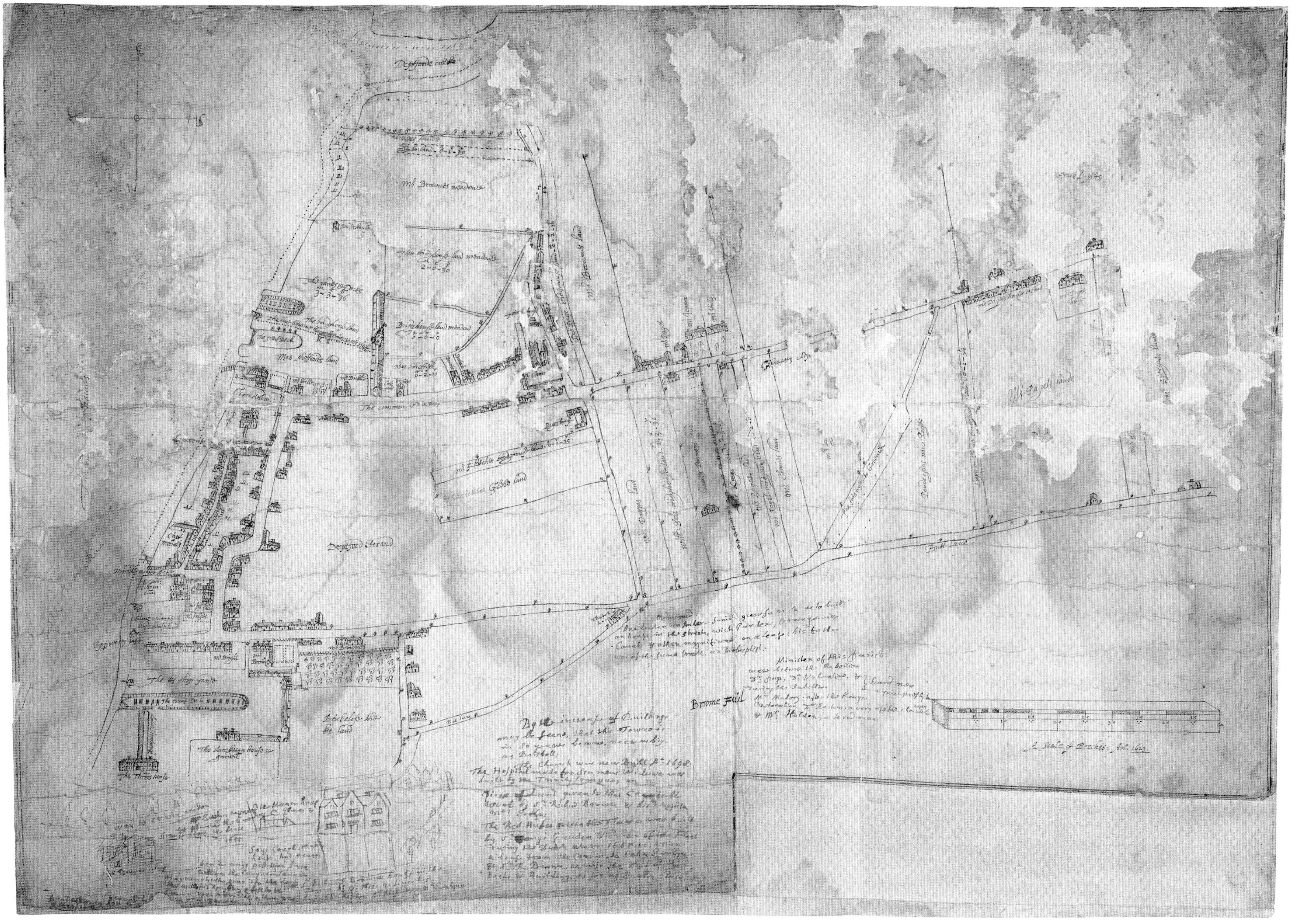
Mr Brownes meadowe
Deptford Strand
The common Street
Broome Feild
The Church was new Built Ao: 1698.
A Scale of Perches: Ano 1623

ELEGANCE IN WEST HAM

West Ham, close to the area redeveloped for the 2012 Olympic Games, was an elegant village in the eighteenth century. This view, probably by Jean Baptiste Chatelain, a French artist who specialised in elegant suburban scenes, shows prosperous inhabitants strolling in the spacious churchyard by the medieval parish church of All Saints. The nearby terrace of houses must have been built fairly recently. The scene would not have been out of place in a country village near the more fashionable west of London.

4.1.7 Jean-Baptiste Chatelain (?), [View of West Ham village, *c.* 1750]. Ink and wash on paper. 38.5 × 59.2 cm. Maps K. Top. 13.39-a

Doubt persists as to whether Chatelain was born in London or Paris — or whether Chatelain was even his real name. He was, however, one of the finest draughtsmen of the period and much in demand by the London print-sellers. He worked only when he had to and according to John Boydell (see 3.3.1 above) 'would often come for half an hour receive sixpence go and spend it amongst bad women in Chick Lane and Black-boy Alley'. He died in 1758 after a debauch at the White Bear in Piccadilly.

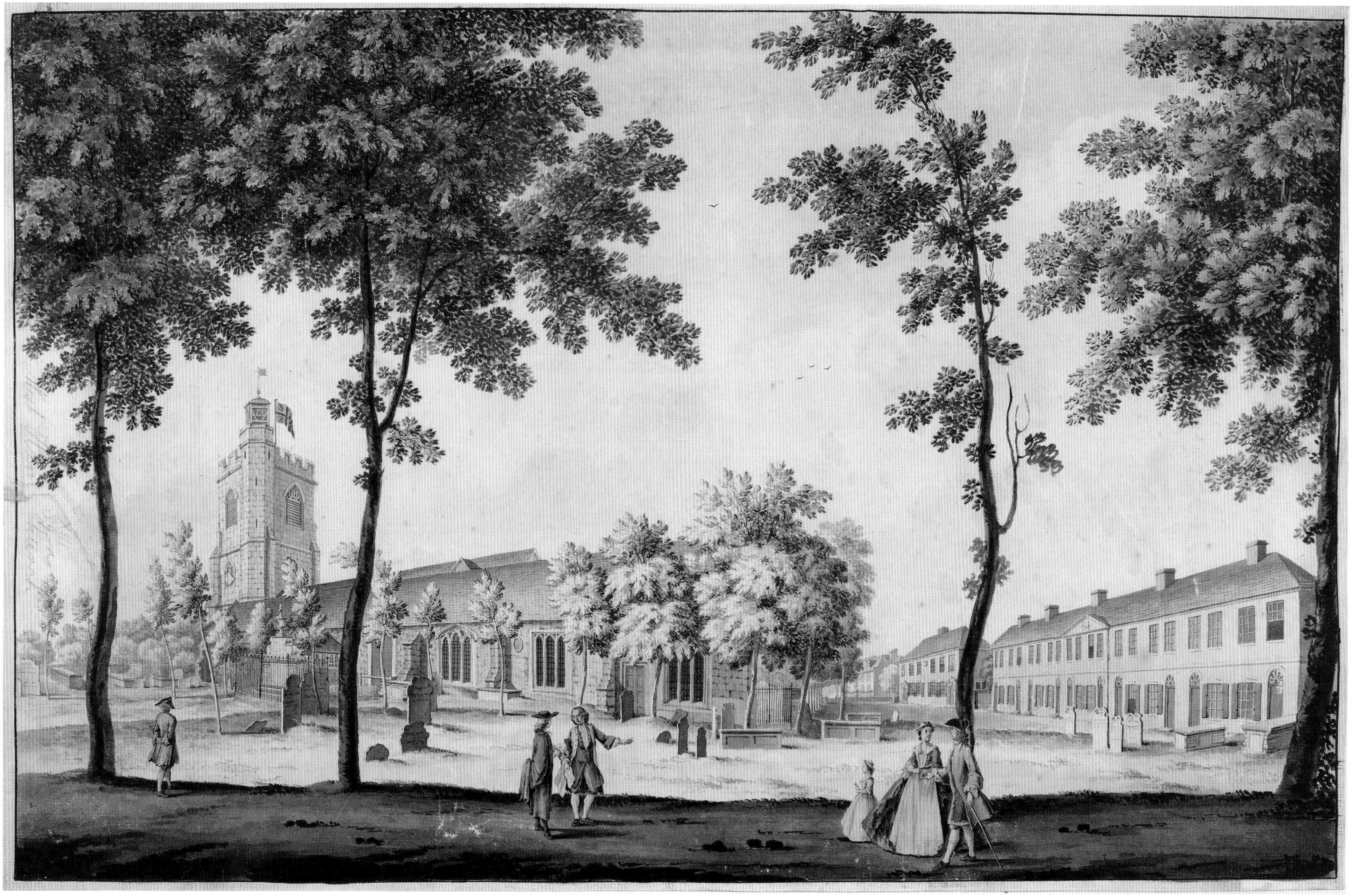

ON THE BOUNDARY BETWEEN WEALTH AND POVERTY

Eighteenth-century Shoreditch stood between prosperous Islington and poverty-stricken Spitalfields. Despite a lawless and licentious past, there had been growing signs of gentility with the development of Hoxton Square (1683) and the stylish rebuilding of St Leonard's (1736–40). This beautifully engraved map by a Huguenot surveyor-architect from Soho, listing all landowners and tenants and describing residents' civic duties, was probably commissioned to facilitate superior development to the North. It contains notes on manorial dues, window and land tax and on past donations by the rich for the poor. To emphasise the positive qualities of the neighbourhood, medicinal springs like St Agnes le Clear ('an antient spring (now a cold bath) much frequented for cure of Rheumatick Pains etc.'(no. 30)) are selected for special mention. But no less than six almshouses are listed, including (no. 6) what is now the Geffrye Museum, and nos 17 and 47 'Rose & Crown alias Sound Arse Alley' and 'Blunderbus alias Spread Eagle Court' suggest that poverty and Shoreditch's licentious legacy might yet thwart the striving for gentility.

Chassereau, who had worked in Charleston, Carolina, for a time, also surveyed a Suffolk estate owned by a City trust, the income for which was devoted to educating poor children in East London. That map was printed so that each of the numerous trustees could have a copy.

4.1.8 Peter Chassereau, *An Actual Survey of the Parish of St Leonard in Shoreditch, Middlsex, taken in the year 1745*. Engraved map. 56 × 72 cm. Maps Crace XVI.4

The map was engraved by James Cole of Hatton Garden. Cole was born in London in the late seventeenth century and was apprenticed into the Leathersellers' Company in 1709. His indenture was cancelled and he had to be re-apprenticed a year later because he was discovered to be only thirteen years of age. Later in life he too became involved in City affairs, serving on the Court of Assistants of the Leathersellers before his death in 1749.

155

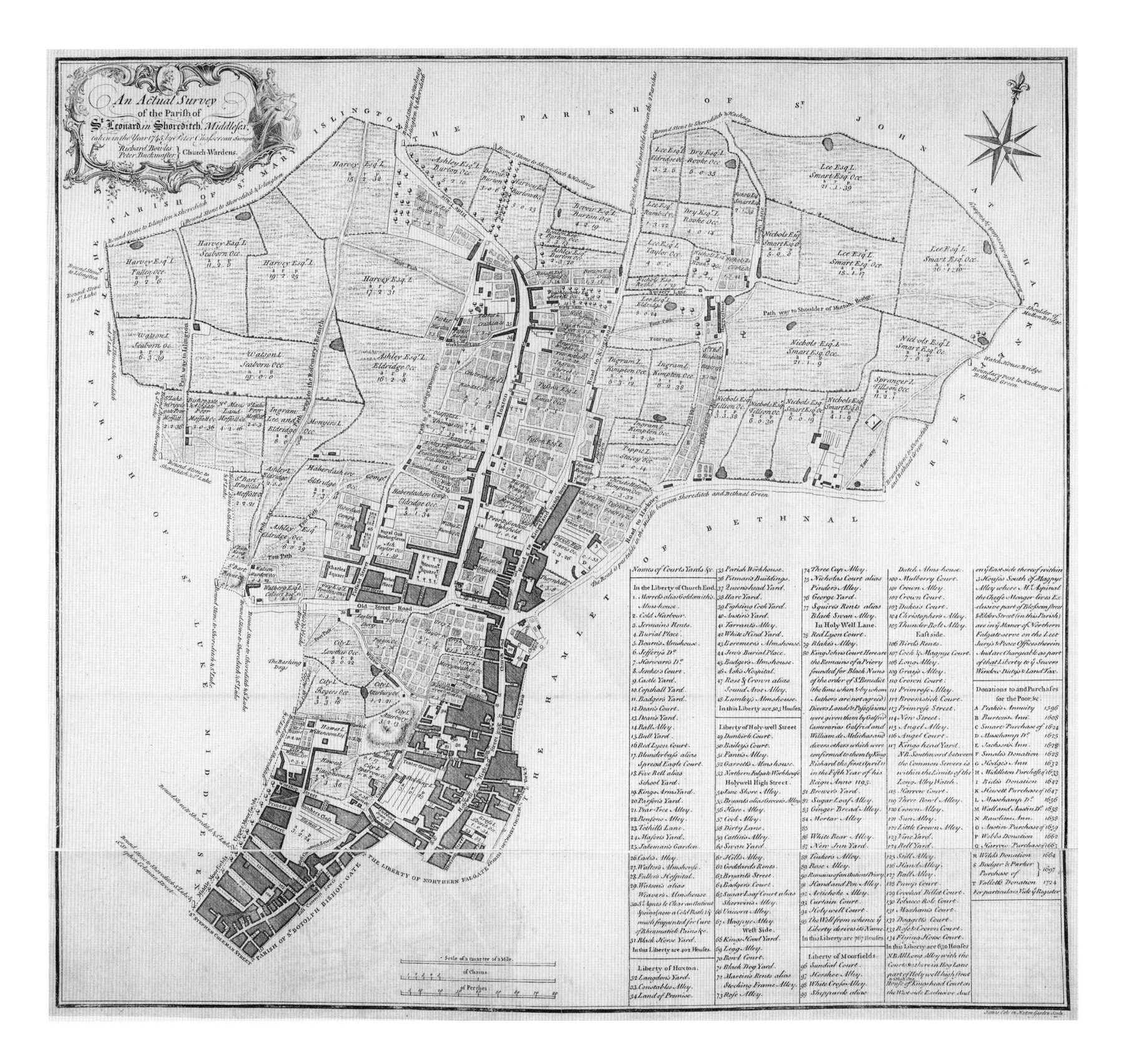

4.2 THE COMING OF THE DOCKS

A dramatic increase in sea-borne trade, size of ship and pilfering in the late eighteenth-century came close to throttling London as a world-class port. There simply was not enough room on the Thames for all the ships bringing their wares to London and insufficient security for their cargoes. From 1793 there was growing merchant pressure to create purpose-built, enclosed wet dockyards with secure bonded warehouses in Wapping where ships could be unloaded, their goods stored and the customs formalities completed. Otherwise, the merchants threatened to divert their ships to the new docks in Liverpool and Manchester. The City of London was afraid of losing important revenues if the docks were built in Wapping and, in a spoiling tactic, collaborated with the West Indies merchants and proposed that new docks be built on virgin land, further away from the City, in the Isle of Dogs. The competition between the two schemes generated a pamphlet war that was accompanied by many plans illustrating the differing proposals. The City of London hoped that Parliament would tire of the rivalry and would sanction neither scheme but nevertheless in 1799 Parliament sanctioned both new docks. Within a few years a new road, Commercial Road, linked them with the City. The docks were a source of patriotic pride during the Napoleonic wars. Few thought of those rendered homeless in the process.

William Daniell, *A View of the East India Docks*, 1808 (detail)

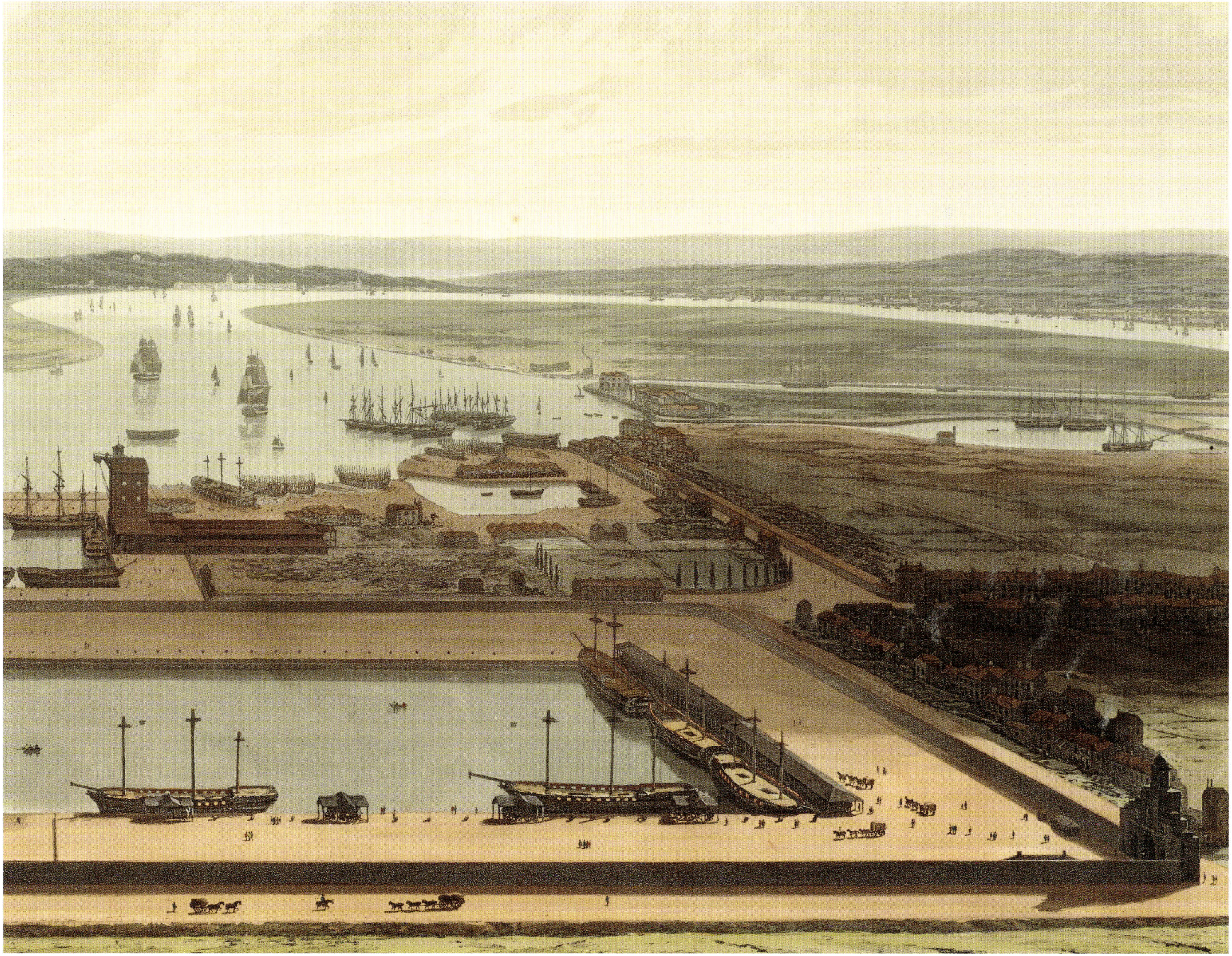

THE NEED FOR NEW DOCKS

In May 1799, when Parliament was debating whether to support the creation of new docks in Wapping ('The London Docks') or the Isle of Dogs ('The West India Docks') a group of merchants led by William Vaughan, who championed the Wapping option, sent this map to George III. Manuscript additions to the printed plan show how ships traditionally anchored according to size in the Pool of London, east of the Tower. Numerous lighters (small cargo boats) then transported their wares the often considerable distance to a limited number of Legal Quays near Custom House. By 1790 ships often waited weeks to be unloaded.

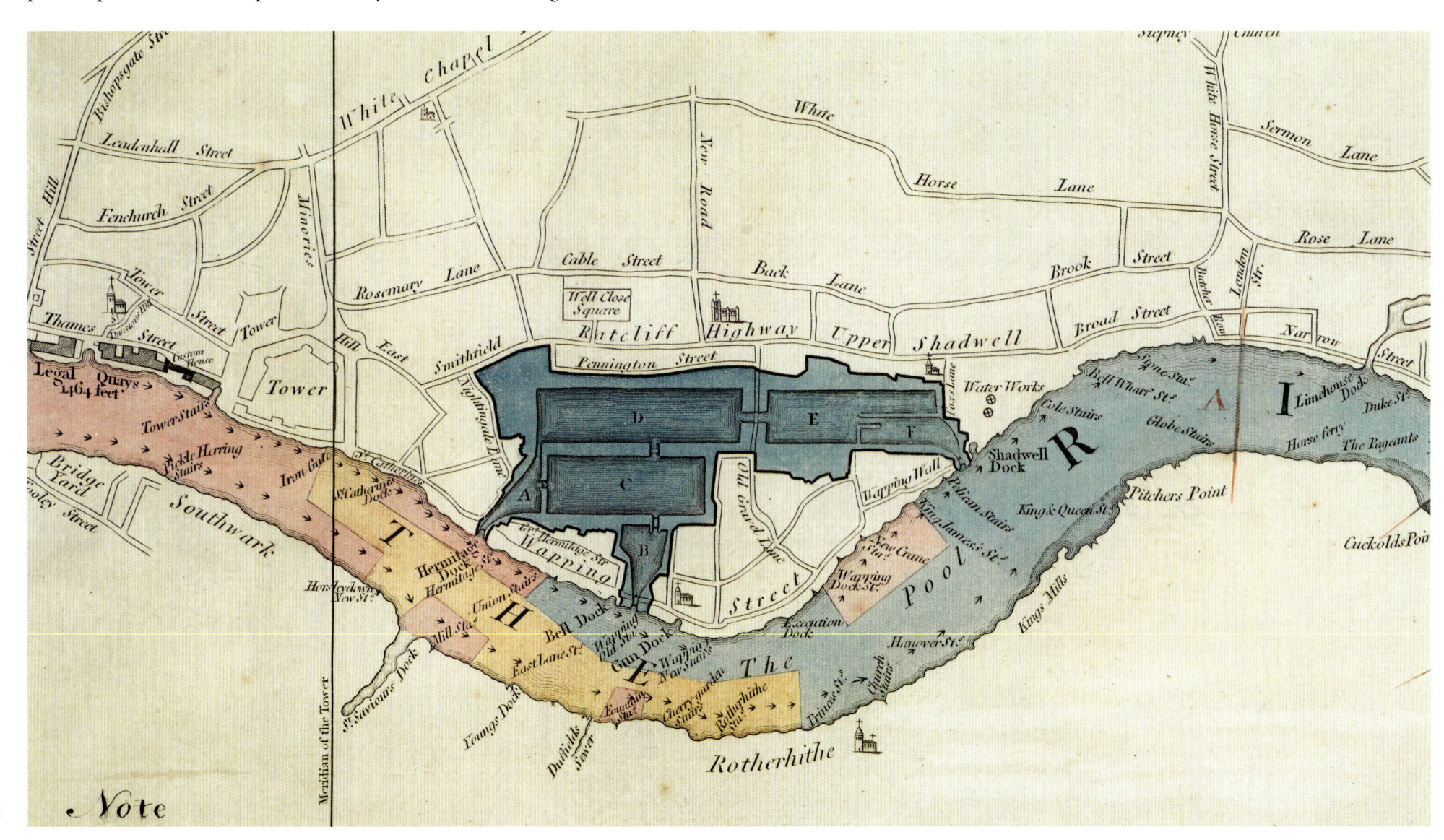

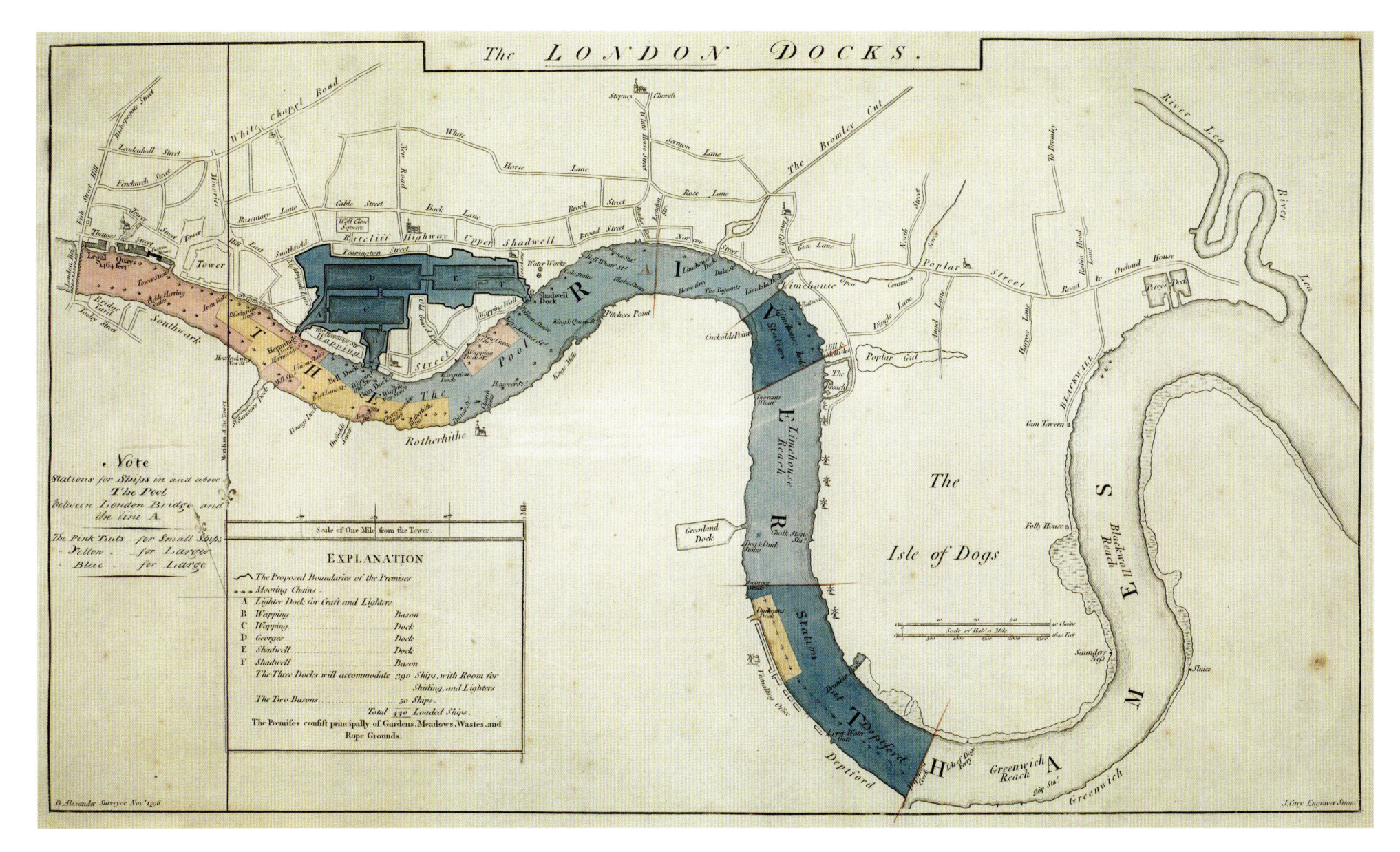

4.2.1 [William Vaughan], 'The Merchant Plan of the London Docks 1799' using Daniel Alexander, *The London Docks* (London: John Cary, 1796) as a base map. Ink and watercolour over an engraved base map. 33 × 54 cm. Maps K. Top. 21.18-1

The architect and engineer Daniel Asher Alexander (1768–1846) was born in Southwark and educated at St Paul's School and the Royal Academy. He became Surveyor to the London Dock Company in 1796 and for the next thirty-five years the whole landscape of the docks was constructed to his designs. Among the first to raise the standing of professional architects, he made the distinction 'a builder supplies the bricks, and an architect supplies the brains'.

John Cary (1755–1835), the engraver of the map, was the son of a Wiltshire maltster. He came to London at the age of fifteen to be apprenticed to the map-engraver William Palmer. One of the best-known of all English mapmakers — the clarity of his engraving universally admired — his premises on the Strand were a London landmark for nearly forty years.

HELPING TO EASE THE CONGESTION

From the 1780s, the East India Company erected a number of large and architecturally rather distinguished warehouses near its headquarters, East India House, in the City of London. Some still survive. Goods were taken to them straight from the Legal Quays, where unloading was permitted, without having to go through Custom House first. Excise duty was paid on sale. This provided the model for the warehouses that were to be built besides the West India and London docks. The existence of these warehouses meant that the East India Docks, which opened in 1808, were not supplied with warehouses.

4.2.2.a [CWC of Sloane St?] 'General Plan of part of the City of London showing in what situation the buildings are erected'. Ink and watercolours on paper. IOR H/763 A. p.7

ELEVATION *of the Front of the Warehouses, in* FENCHURCH STREET.

4.2.2b [CWC of Sloane St?] 'Elevation of the Front of the Warehouses in Fenchurch Street' [of the East India Company], May 1806. Ink and watercolours on paper. 34 × 50 cm. IOR H/763 B f.7

THE HUMAN COST

In May 1799, at the time of the parliamentary debate on the proposed docks, this plan was sent to George III in the hope of persuading him to order his supporters to vote for the London Docks at Wapping. The outlines and area are superimposed on the existing lay-out. The marginal notes imply that the development cost would be moderate (the rival, Isle of Dogs, scheme would have involved virtually no demolitions). Most of the site was open land, the notes argue, and the houses and tenements for which compensation (to the owners not residents) would be payable were old, decrepit and occupied by 'the Poorest Classes': 5000 people ultimately lost their homes.

4.2.3 Daniel Alexander, *Plan of the Proposed London docks* (London: William Faden, 1797). Annotated May 1799. Engraved map with manuscript annotations.
52.8 × 73 cm Maps K. Top. 21.22-1

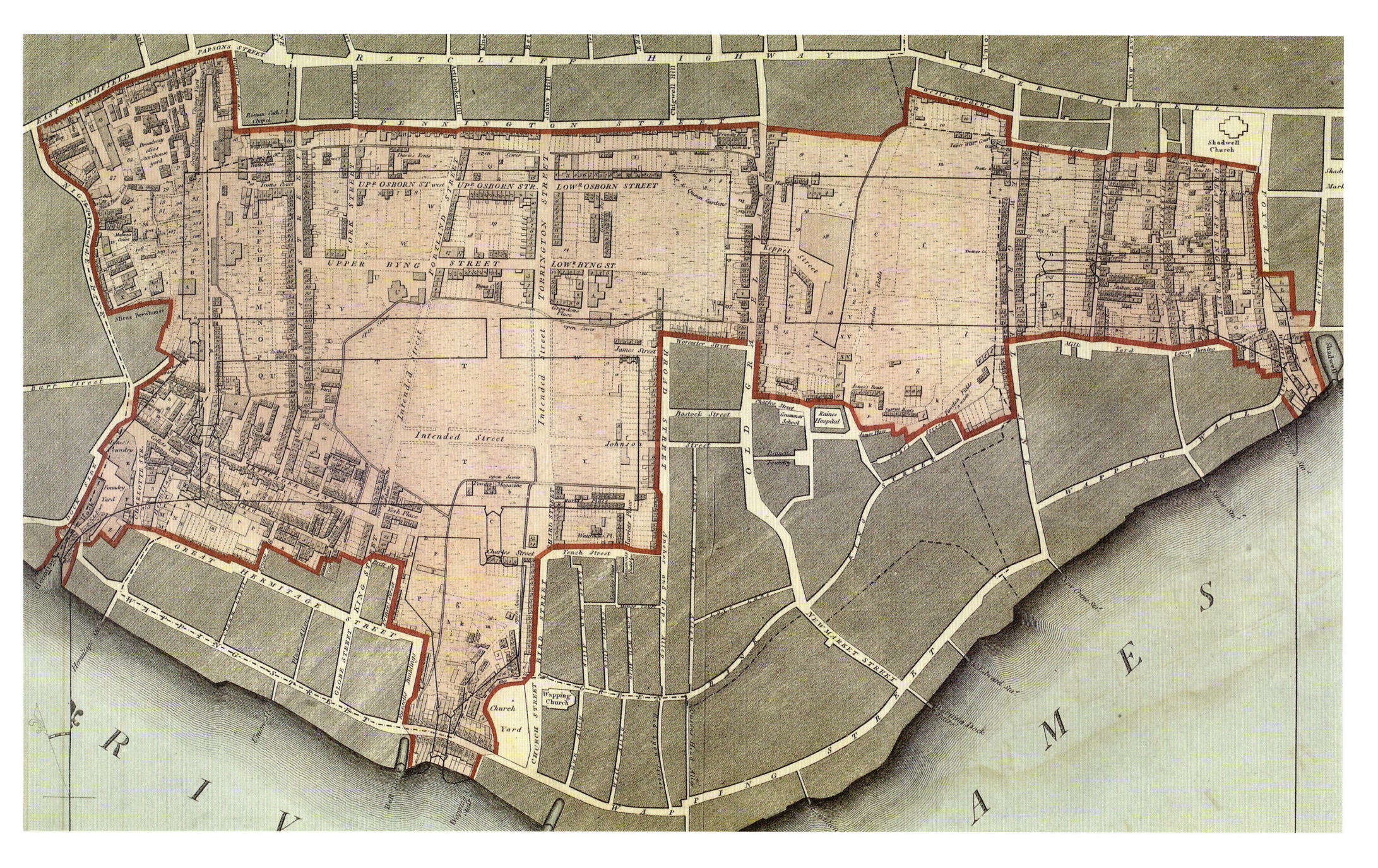

For Alexander see 4.2.1 above. The map was produced by William Faden (1749–1836), the son of a London printer. Himself a member of the (Smeatonian) Society of Civil Engineers, Faden became Geographer to the King and was the finest London mapmaker of his day — involved in mapping almost every major infrastructure project. Unlike many of his colleagues in the map trade, he prospered in a financial sense — retiring to a handsome estate at Shepperton.

THE FINISHED JOB

William Daniell executed a number of magnificent large aquatints of the newly completed docks. This shows the walled East India Docks, the work of John Rennie and Ralph Walker, looking south over the Isle of Dogs (right) towards Greenwich with the winding River Lea to the left. The East India Docks, unlike the West India and London Docks, had no warehouses constructed next to them. Beyond them can be seen the Brunswick Dock, also known as Perry's Dock, of 1789 and further to its right the original East India Dock, also known as Blackwall Yard, the first and for long the only wet dock on the Thames, created by Henry Johnson in 1661. Blackwall Basin, leading to the West India Docks, is visible still further to the right. The O2 Arena now occupies the tip of the promontory on the far side of the river.

4.2.4   William Daniell, *A View of the East India Docks* 1808. Coloured aquatint. 55.8 × 87.9 cm. Maps K. Top. 21.31-5c Port. II. Tab

William Daniell was born at Kingston-on-Thames in 1769, the son of an innkeeper. He studied under his uncle, the painter Thomas Daniell, and accompanied him on an extensive tour of India between 1786 and 1793 — the work from which established his reputation. His most famous publication work was the *Voyage round Great Britain*, a magnificent series of views around the British coastline published between 1814 and 1825. He died in Camden Town in 1837.

A VIEW OF THE EAST INDIA DOCKS.

GETTING THE GOODS TO THE CITY

Splendid though the new docks were, it was realised from the first that a road would have to be created to enable the goods to be brought as directly and speedily as possible from the warehouses (or in the case of East India Company from the docks themselves) into the City. A company was established to create the road and Luffman, who specialised in news maps, was commissioned to publicise its proposals. At the same time he includes a plan of the magnificent West India Docks, opened in 1802. The road was particularly wide by the standards of the time. 200 years later it remains the principal road link between the City and Docklands.

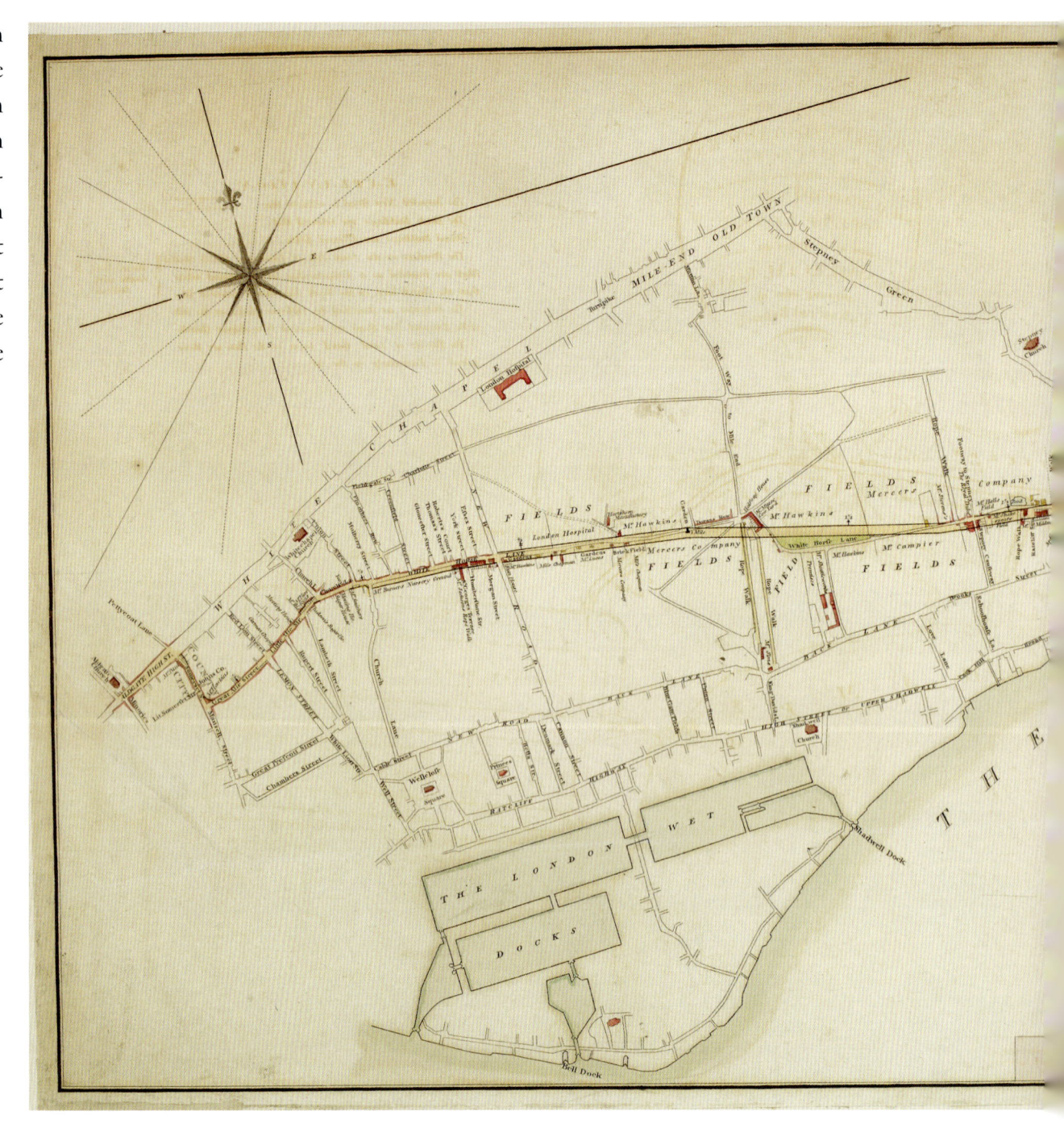

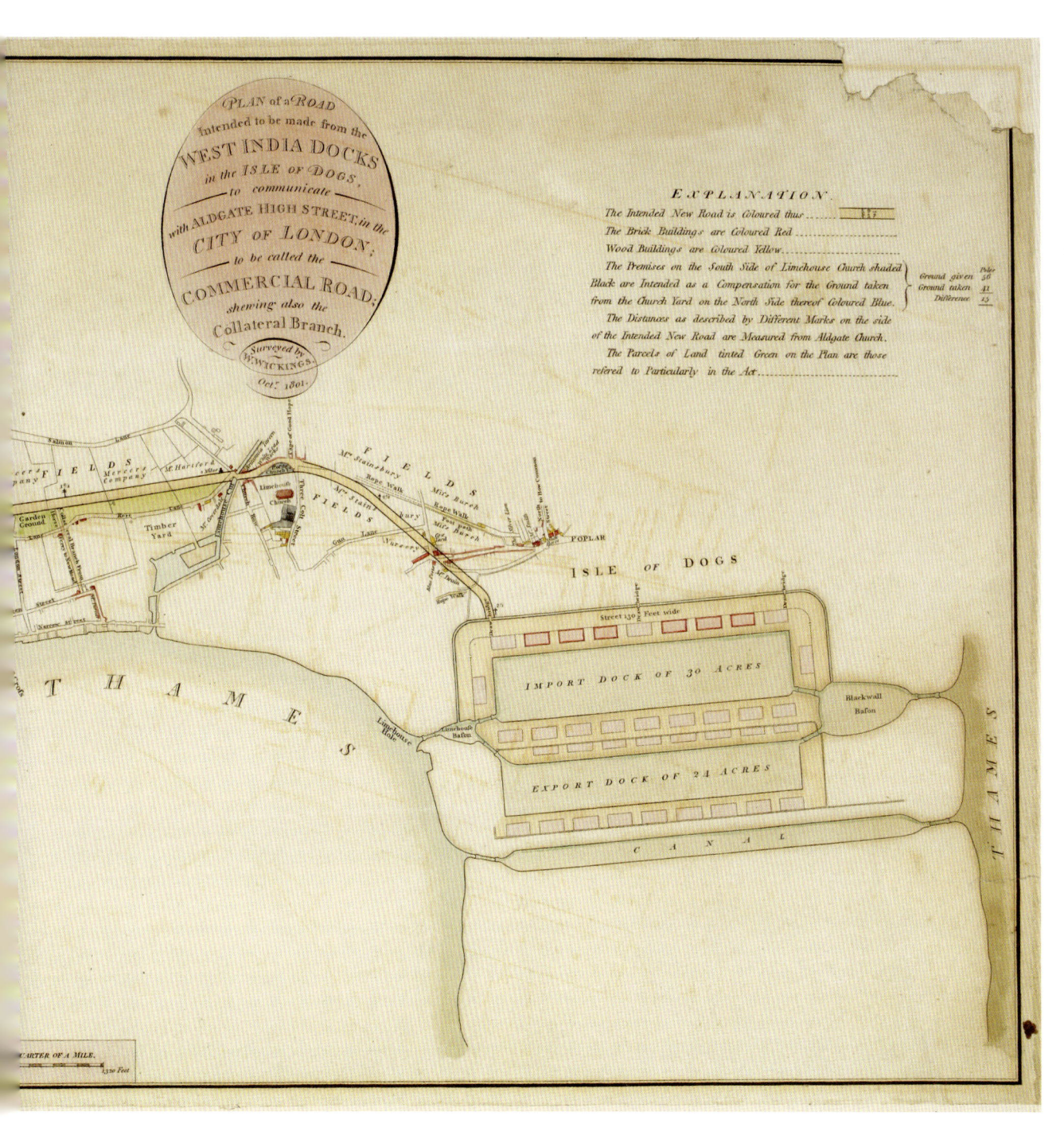

4.2.5 *Plan of a Road intended to be made from the West India Docks in the Isle of Dogs, to communicate with Aldgate High Street in the City of London; to be called the Commercial Road … Surveyed by W. Wickings October 1801* (Luffman, October 1801). Printed map with watercolour. 50.6 × 63.5 cm. Maps 3495 (24)

John Luffman (1751–1821) was not just an interesting mapmaker but a man with determined views on individual liberty. Born in London, he had himself lived in the West Indies, publishing his *A brief account of the island of Antigua: together with the customs and manners of its inhabitants, as well white as black; as also an accurate statement of the food, cloathing, labor, and punishment, of slaves* on his return in 1788. It became one of the earliest key texts in the struggle for the abolition of slavery.

SECTION FIVE
THE AGE OF IMPROVEMENT

London was transformed between 1750 and 1850. For the first and only time the King and government, as well as private speculators, the City Corporation and numerous other administrative bodies responsible for the built-up area attempted to emulate Paris, Munich and Berlin in consciously creating a magnificent city. This involved the creation of detailed maps and hand-drawn and printed preparatory plans and led to the publication of commemorative maps, views, peepshows and panoramas that reflected the contemporary craze for visual thrills. In the 1790s, when the population was just under a million, Richard Horwood produced a wall map showing every house in London. By 1851, with a population approaching 2.5 million, such a map had become unrealisable.

5.1 THE DEMANDS OF COMMERCE

Napoleon famously branded the British a nation of shopkeepers and, as the Horwood Map shows, nowhere was this truer than Regency London. In order to make it more effective as a commercial centre, new bridges had been created at Westminster and Blackfriars. These were followed after 1813 by new Vauxhall, Waterloo, and Southwark bridges and London Bridge was rebuilt. New roads were created to by-pass London, cut through the ancient fabric to ease inner city traffic congestion, tunnel under the Thames and open up the area south of the Thames for development. By 1850 London was a city transformed by the needs of business.

Detail from Richard Horwood, *Plan of the Cities of London and Westminster* (1799)

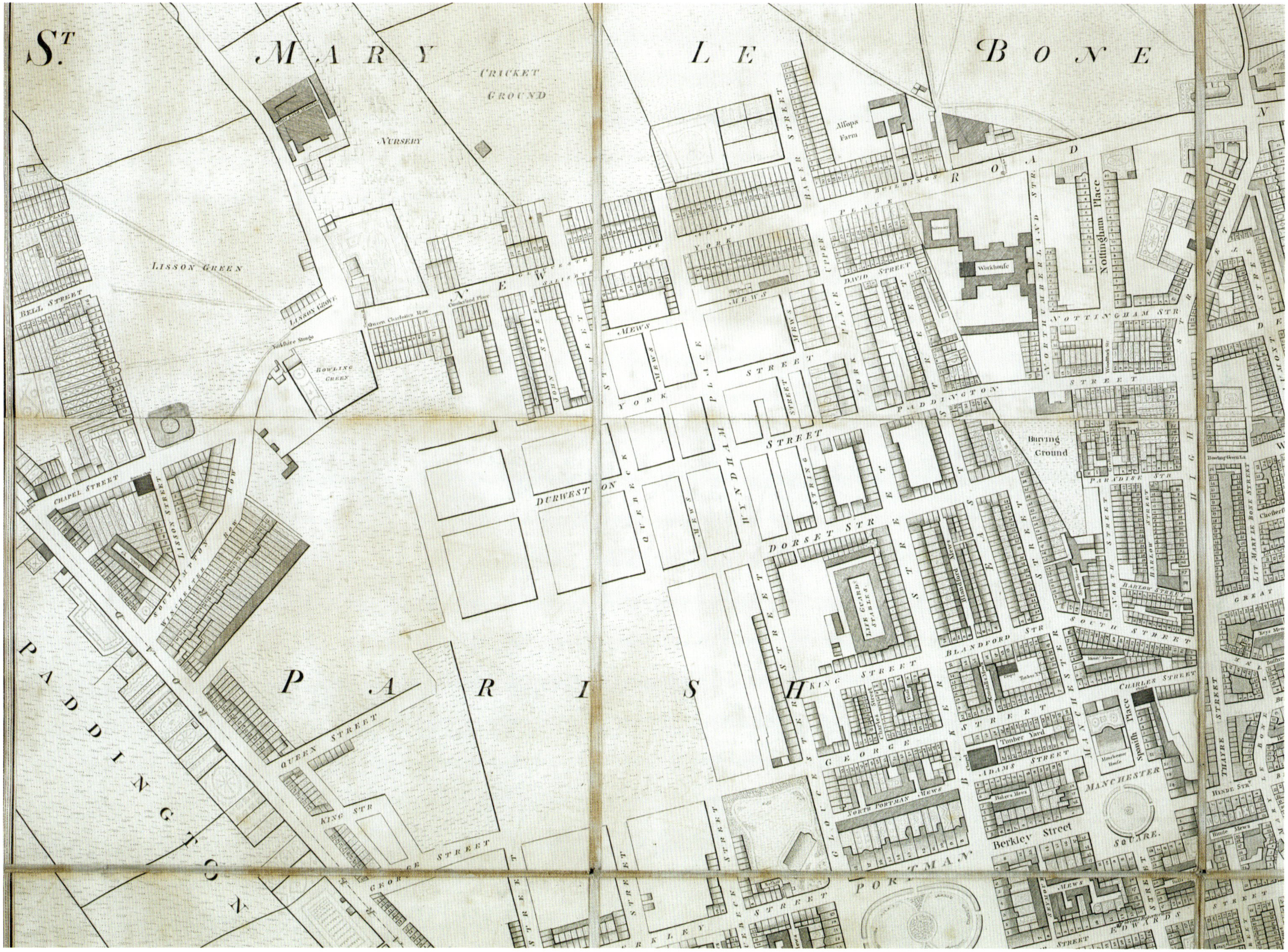
St. MARY LE BONE PARISH
PADDINGTON
CRICKET GROUND
NURSERY
LISSON GREEN
BOWLING GREEN
Workhouse
Burying Ground
NEW ROAD
PADDINGTON STREET
YORK STREET
DURWESTON
DORSET STR
BLANDFORD STR
KING STREET
GEORGE STREET
QUEEN STREET
CHAPEL STREET
LISSON STREET
BAKER STREET
BELL STREET
Nottingham Place
Spanish Place
Timber Yard
Berkley Street
MANCHESTER SQUARE
CHARLES STREET
SOUTH STREET
NORTH PORTMAN MEWS
PORTMAN
HIGH STREET
LIFE GUARD STABLES
Allsops Farm

MADE FOR A NATION OF SHOPKEEPERS

Horwood's enormous map is at about the same scale as Rocque's map of London. Commenced in 1790 but only completed nine years later, it was the last map that attempted to show every house on a single surface (albeit of thirty-two sheets) — a task made easier following the gradual introduction of house numbering from 1762. Its size shows how much London had grown since 1746, particularly south of the River. While, in addition to numerous private subscriptions, Rocque was supported by the City Corporation and Royal Society, Horwood who also depended on subscriptions, received a loan of £500 (which he managed to repay) from the Phoenix Assurance Company to enable him to complete the map. The Company had good commercial reasons for supporting the mapping since it enabled its managers to pinpoint and approximately assess the risks of properties that were insured or applying for insurance. In another sign of changing times, Horwood names the big breweries, tanneries and vinegar manufacturers but only a few homes of the nobility (though the copy owned by the British Library was owned by the Duke of Northumberland). The map was repeatedly updated over the coming decades, but not by Horwood who in 1803 died in poverty in Liverpool which he had just surveyed.

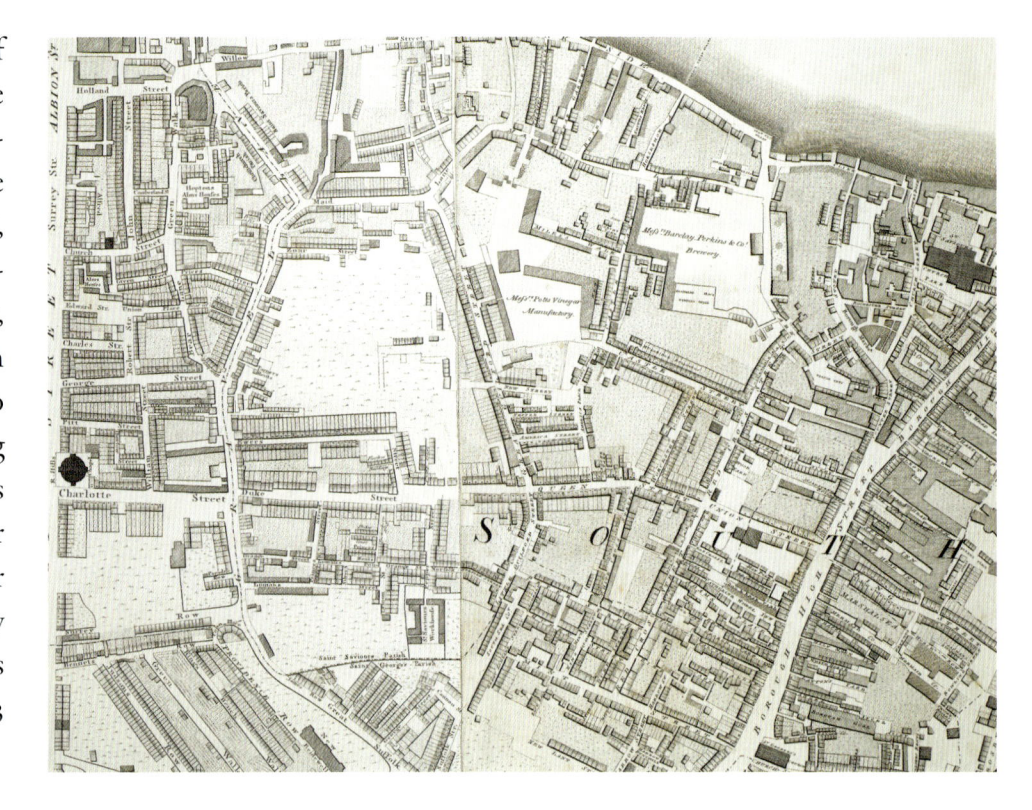

5.1.1   Richard Horwood, *Plan of the Cities of London and Westminster, the Borough of Southwark and parts adjoining, shewing every house*, 1st edition, 1799. Engraved map. 224 × 408 cm. Maps C.24.f.7

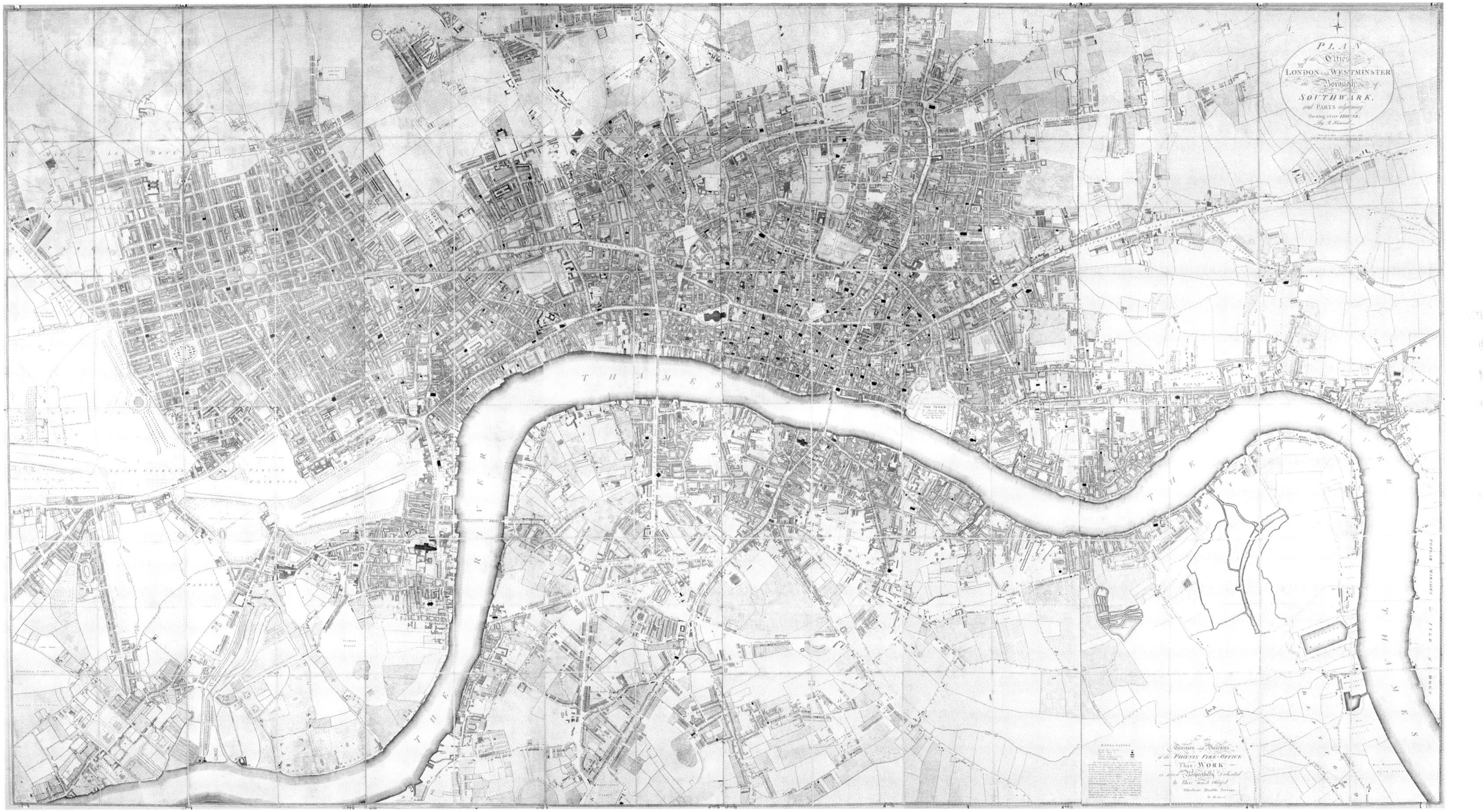
PLAN
of the Cities of
LONDON and WESTMINSTER
the Borough of
SOUTHWARK,
and PARTS adjoining
Shewing every HOUSE.
THAMES
PHENIX FIRE-OFFICE
This WORK
Respectfully
Obedient Humble Servant

A RIVAL TO HORWOOD?

The British Library possesses several hand-drawn sheets of what seem to be drafts for another detailed survey of London. At the same scale as Horwood's and undertaken perhaps a little later, they are sufficiently different in style not to be his work. Notes in a mid-nineteenth century hand on the back of some of the maps suggest that they were the work of or were executed for William Faden, who published extensively revised versions of Horwood's map in 1807, 1813 and 1819 but the information on the sheets seems too early even for the 1807 edition. Another endorsement states that the sheets were the work of Thomas Milne who completed his Land-Use map (see section 3) in these years. On balance this seems more likely. Ralph Hyde has suggested that the map may have been the one promised, but never delivered, by John Lockie to accompany his detailed gazetteer, *The Topography of London*, first published in 1810. This sheet shows the area around the British Library. Another group shows South London around St George's Fields. There may well have been links between the work of the Ordnance Survey, Horwood and Milne, and their maps reflect the vitality of London around 1800 — and hint at an awareness of the associated problems and the need to deal with them.

5.1.2 [Thomas Milne?], Extract showing Somers Town from the neat draft of an unfinished [?] map of London, *c.* 1800. Ink and wash on paper. 60.4 × 45.1 cm. Maps Crace XIV.40* (3)

Lord Southampton's Arms
Gloucester Place
St. Pancras Ch.
Church Yard
Sidney Street
Bridgewater Street
Granville Street
Clarendon Street
Hampden Street
Hampden Street
Polygon
Phœnix Street
Crescent
Chapel Path
Bethel Chapel
Chalton Street
Middlesex Street
Tottenham Court Turnpike
St. James's Chapel
Burying Ground
St. Pancras Female Charity School
William Str.
Frederick Str.
Sommers Place
Charles Str.
Brook Str.
Southampton Place
Tottenham Court
Tottingham Place
Grafton Street
Fitzroy Square

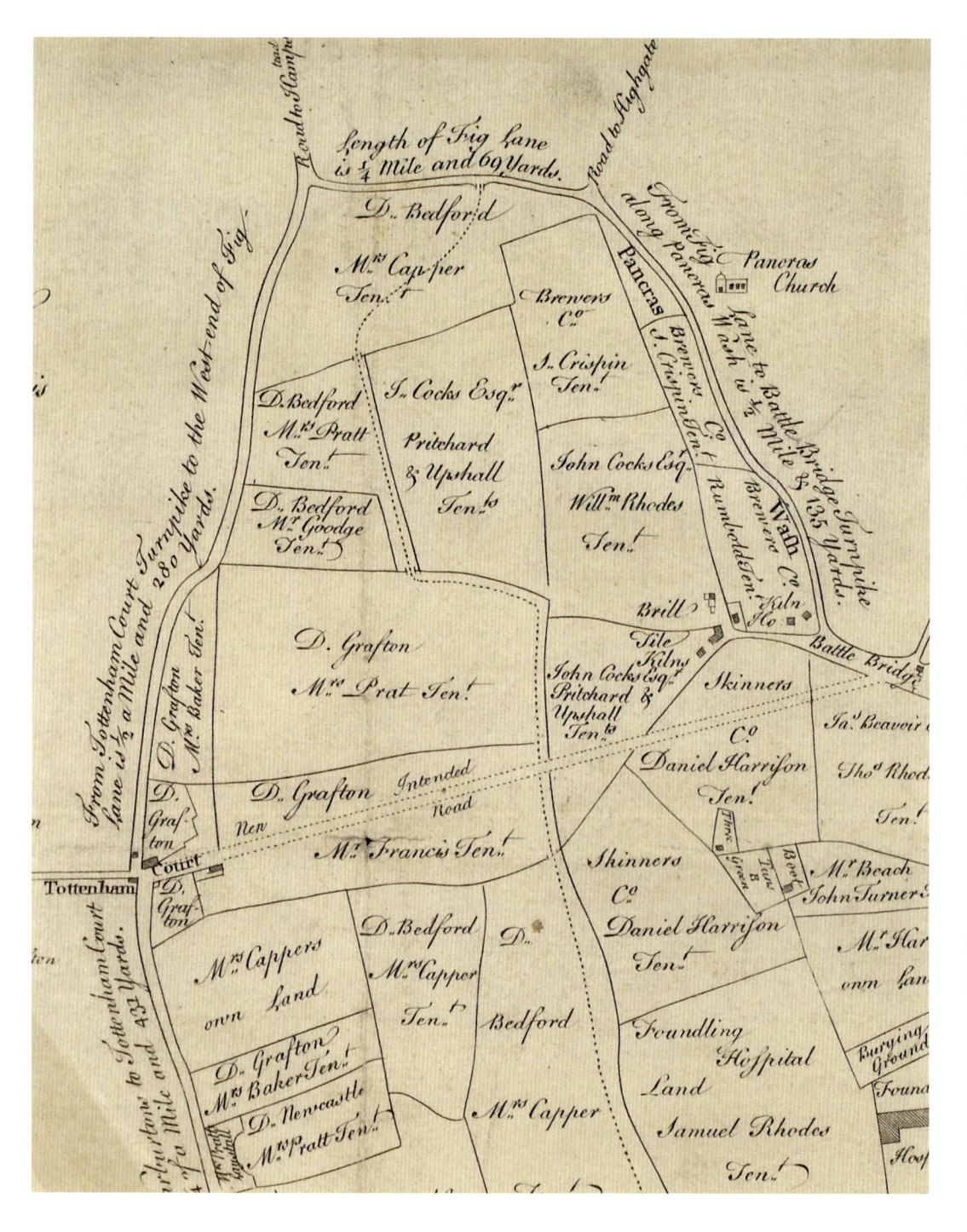

LONDON'S FIRST BY-PASS

In 1755 a consortium supported by the Duke of Grafton won permission to construct London's first 40 feet (13 metre) wide by-pass or 'New Road', now known as Marylebone, Euston, Pentonville and City roads. The widespread interest was reflected in plans like this which were produced for popular periodicals of this time. As well as the obvious advantages to West End residents from decreasing congestion and diverting animals on their way to Smithfield from their elegant streets, the New Road offered eventual development opportunities to the landowners such as Lord Somers, Mr Goodge or the Skinners Company named on this plan. By 1820 most were commemorated in the names of the generally middle or, north of the road, lower middle class 'towns', 'villes' or streets that had taken the place of the fields.

5.1.3   Thomas Marsh, *A Plan of the New Intended Road from Paddington to Islington* [*c.*1755]. Printed. 24.2 × 50 cm. Maps K. Top. 22.14-b

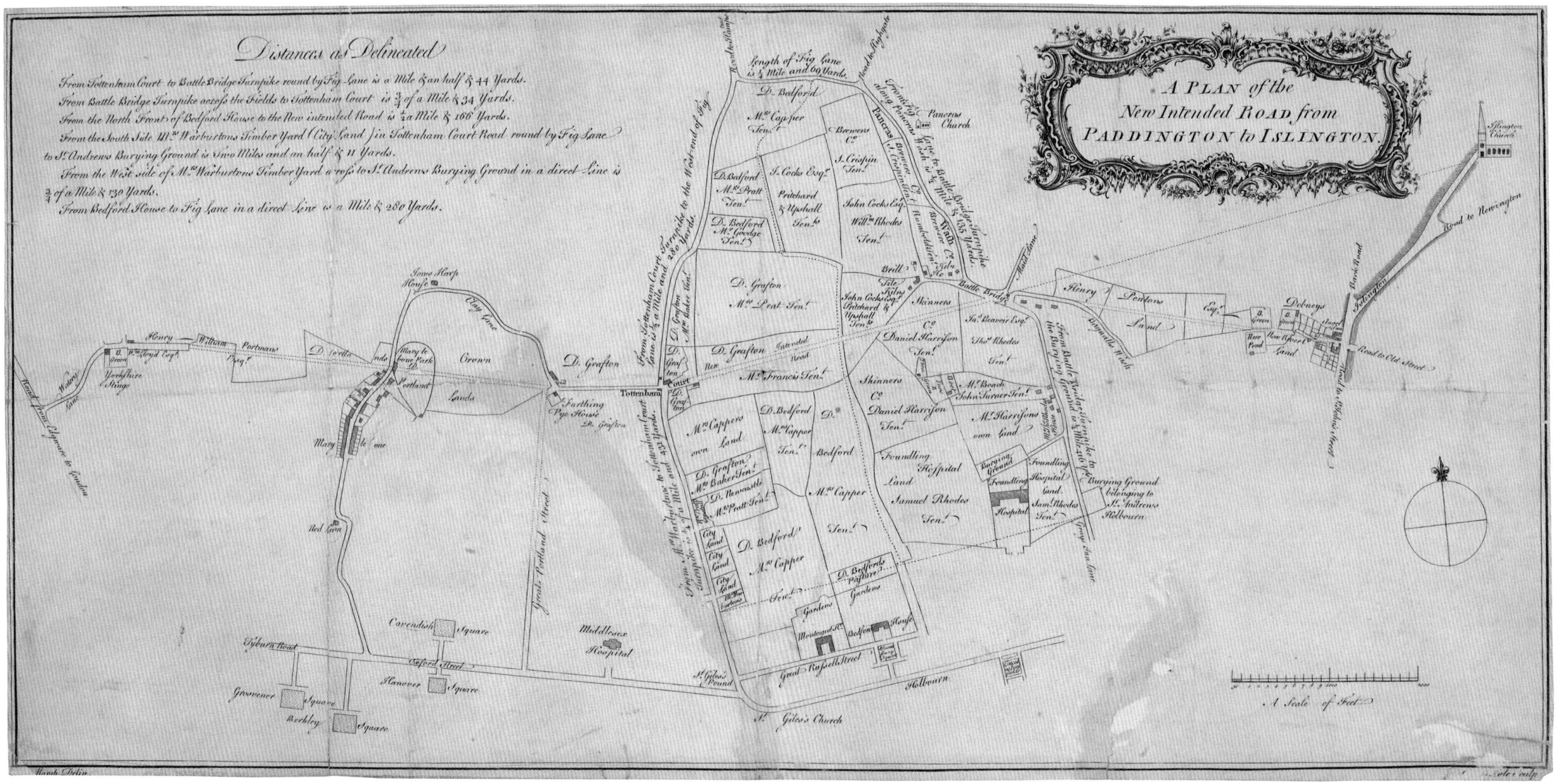
A PLAN of the New Intended ROAD from PADDINGTON to ISLINGTON.
Distances as Delineated
From Tottenham Court to Battle Bridge Turnpike round by Fig Lane is a Mile & an half & 44 Yards.
From Battle Bridge Turnpike across the Fields to Tottenham Court is ¾ of a Mile & 34 Yards.
From the North Front of Bedford House to the New intended Road is ¼ a Mile & 166 Yards.
From the South Side Mr. Warburtons Timber Yard (City Land) in Tottenham Court Road round by Fig Lane to St. Andrews Burying Ground is Two Miles and an half & 11 Yards.
From the West side of Mr. Warburtons Timber Yard across to St. Andrews Burying Ground in a direct Line is ¾ of a Mile & 130 Yards.
From Bedford House to Fig Lane in a direct Line is a Mile & 280 Yards.
Jews Harp House
Clay Lane
Crown Lands
D. Grafton
Tottenham Court
Farthing Pye House
Yorkshire Stingo
Red Lion
Great Portland Street
Cavendish Square
Middlesex Hospital
Tyburn Road
Oxford Street
Hanover Square
Grosvenor Square
Berkley Square
St. Giles's Pound
Great Russell Street
Holbourn
St. Giles's Church
Montague Ho.
Bedford House
Gardens
D. Bedfords Pasture
City Land
D. Bedford Mr. Capper
Mr. Cappers own Land
D. Grafton Mr. Baker Tent.
D. Newcastle Mr. Pratt Tent.
D. Grafton Mr. Peat Tent.
D. Grafton Intended Road
New
Mr. Francis Tent.
D. Bedford Mr. Pratt Tent.
D. Bedford Mr. Goodge Tent.
Mr. Capper Tent.
D. Bedford
J. Cocks Esqr.
Pritchard & Upshall Tent.
Brewers Co.
S. Crispin Tent.
John Cocks Esqr. Willm. Rhodes Tent.
Pancras Church
Pancras
Length of Fig Lane is ¾ Mile and 69 Yards
Road to Highgate
Brill
Tile Kilns
Skinners Co.
Daniel Harrison Tent.
Jno. Beaveir Esqr.
Thos. Rhodes Tent.
Mr. Beach John Turner Tent.
Mr. Harrisons own Land
Foundling Hospital Land Samuel Rhodes Tent.
Burying Ground
Foundling Hospital
Foundling Hospital Land Saml. Rhodes Tent.
Burying Ground belonging to St. Andrews Holbourn
Battle Bridge
Henry Pentons Land Esqr.
Dobneys
Islington Church
Road to Newington
Back Road
Islington
Road to Old Street
A Scale of Feet

SOUTH LONDON OPENS UP

As well as roads, the years after 1750 witnessed a spate of bridge-building. Having been served by only one bridge for 1700 years, central London had no fewer than six by 1830. The first new bridge was at Westminster, long-projected but only completed in 1750 to the designs of the Swiss engineer Charles Paul Dangeau de la Beyle ('Charles Labelye'). This elegant map was probably presented to George II's influential younger son, William, Duke of Cumberland, some time before the bridge opened in order to win his support for a parliamentary act providing for the creation of new roads. It demonstrates how roads leading from the new bridge could improve communications to the coast and Deptford and open the area south of the Thames for development. The proposed turnpike roads, indicated in yellow are now major roads and 'Newington' is better known as Elephant and Castle. Full development was unleashed with the opening of Blackfriars Bridge in 1769.

5.1.4 Anon. [Plan of roads south of River Thames, *c.* 1745]. Ink, gilt and watercolours on vellum. 46.5 × 66 cm. Maps K. Top. 27.48-2

A Scale of Yards.
THE RIVER THAMES
LAMBETH
PALACE
LAMBETH Church
St GEORGES FIELDS
St Georges Church
NEWINGTON
WALWORTH
Turn Pike
St Mary Magdalene Bermondsey
LONDON BRIDGE
Kennington Lane
To Clapham
To Croydon
To SUSSEX
Kent Street
THE KENT ROAD
NEW CROSS
Peckham Lane
To Lewisham
WOODPECKER LANE
DEPTFORD
His Majesties Ship Yard
Ship Yards
Mary Rotherhith
To Greenwich
To Black Heath
Loving Edwards Lane
Little Brown Lane
Butt Lane

AN ARCHWAY TO THE NORTH

The most dramatic example of road improvements north of London was the building of a bridge carrying Hornsey Lane high over a newly constructed stretch of the Great North Road that bypassed Highgate. The steep gradients of Highgate Hill had long been regarded as an obstacle to commerce. The original plan was for the new road to be carried under the ridge east of Highgate through a tunnel, but this collapsed in spectacular fashion in April 1812 and a year later it was replaced by a bridge resembling a Roman aqueduct designed by John Nash and known as 'the Archway'. A considerable engineering feat (and far more effective, initially, than the road beneath), it was to be demolished in 1900 and replaced by a modern road bridge constructed a little to its south.

5.1.5   Augustus Charles Pugin engraved by J. Hill, *View of the Excavated Ground for Highgate Archway*, 1812 (London: Rudolph Ackermann, 1 October 1813). Coloured aquatint. 38.1 × 45 cm. Maps K.Top 30.1-1-g

Augustus Charles Pugin (1762–1832) was born in Paris and arrived in London as a young man at the outbreak of the French Revolution. He worked as a draughtsman for John Nash before developing his independent career as an artist. His record of the interiors of the major London buildings, published by Ackermann as *The Microcosm of London* between 1808 and 1810, is as handsome a record as exists of London 200 years ago. His son, Augustus Welby Northmore Pugin (1812–52), was the celebrated architect of the interiors of the Houses of Parliament. The publisher, Rudolph Ackermann (1764–1834), originally from Saxony, is remembered principally as the publisher of lavish colour-plate books, but he was also a carriage designer (he designed Nelson's funeral carriage in 1806), a manufacturer of paints and waterproof materials, a charity fund-raiser, and a major supporter of Simon Bolivar and the struggle for independence in South America.

Drawn by A. Pugin. Engraved by J. Bill.

179

OLD LONDON GIVES WAY TO NEW

For all its picturesque qualities, by the mid-eighteenth century Old London Bridge was regarded as an obstacle to trade because of the narrowness of the roadway and of its piers which were dangerous to navigate and regularly caused the Thames to freeze. Between 1757 and 1762 the old buildings on the bridge were demolished but continuing problems and its ever worsening condition led Parliament in 1821 to sanction the creation of a new London Bridge designed by John Rennie. Because it was positioned a little to the west of the old bridge, major demolition work was needed at both ends. The Corporation commissioned the German-born artist George Scharf to record their progress. He originally created these novel panoramas of men at work as watercolours which were destroyed in 1941. Luckily they were popularised at the time through excellently produced lithographs and Scharf's preparatory drawings still survive in the possession of the British Museum and the British Library. The doomed Wren church of St Michael's Crooked Lane dominates the northern view which shows the end of old London Bridge at the right. The southern view shows the condemned east side of old Borough High Street. Scharf portrays each of the shop fronts in minute detail. The new bridge was opened on 1 August 1831.

For George Scharf see 3.3a above. His printer, Charles Joseph Hullmandel (1789–1850), was born in Mayfair, the son of a German composer and a French aristocrat who had escaped from France on the eve of the revolution. He was introduced to the new printing technique of lithography by its inventor, Alois Senefelder, and rapidly became one of the leading exponents of this new technique, not only producing some of the first artistically successful lithographic prints but also popularising the process through his books.

5.1.6a George Scharf lithographed by C. Hullmandel, *A View of the Northern Approach to London Bridge while in a state of progress shewing St Michael's Church, Crooked Lane, since taken down: taken on the spot, June 1830*. 56 × 156 cm. Maps 3520 (8)

5.1.6b George Scharf lithographed by C. Hullmandel, *A View of High Street Southwark being the Ancient Roadway leading from Old London Bridge taken July 1830 previous to its Removal for the New Line of Approach*. 56 × 156 cm. Maps 3520 (7)

A VIEW of the Northern Approach to LONDON BRIDGE while in a state of progress shewing St MICHAEL'S CHURCH, Crooked Lane, since taken down; taken on the spot, June, 1830.

A VIEW OF HIGH STREET SOUTHWARK being THE ANCIENT ROADWAY leading from OLD LONDON BRIDGE taken July, 1830, previous to its Removal for the New Line of Approach.

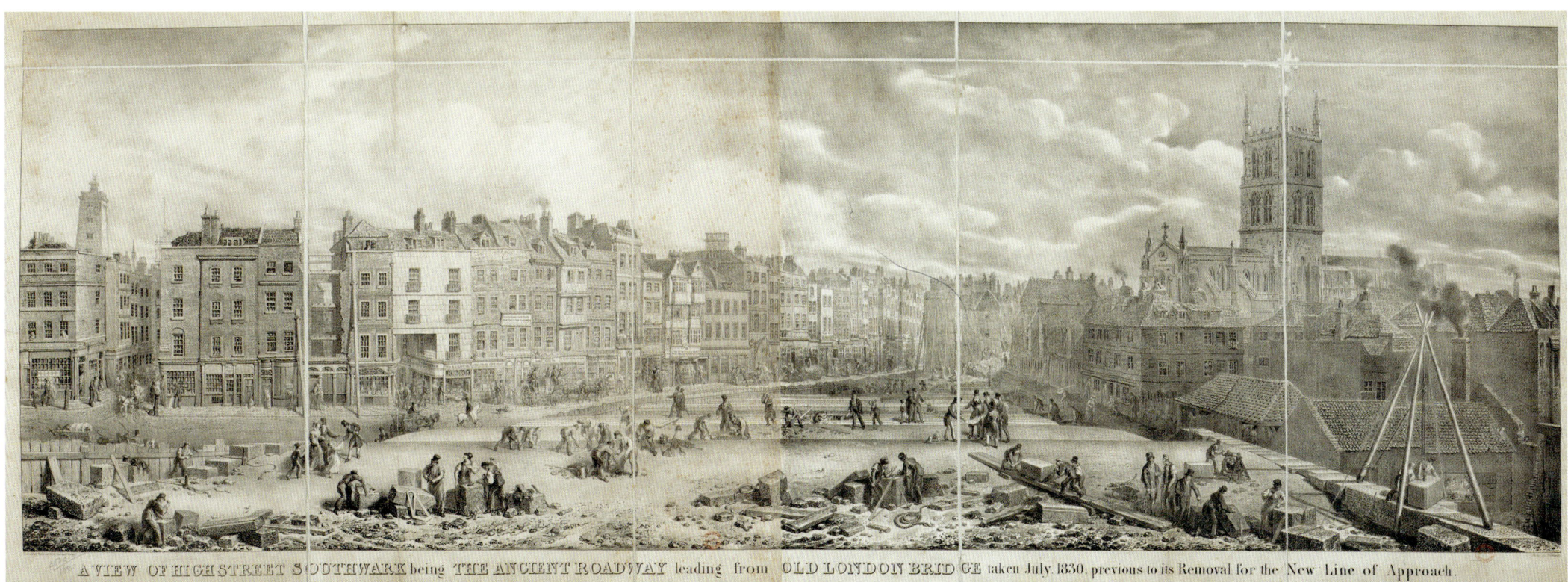

5.1.6c George Scharf, pencil sketch of demolition work at Crooked Lane for access road to new London Bridge, June 1830. 23 × 14 cm. Add. MS 36489 A no. 51

5.1.6e George Scharf 'Old Murphy and Starling Jacque': one of the bricklayers and his dog. Watercolour. 23 × 14 cm. Add. MS 36849 A no. 62

5.1.6d George Scharf, pencil sketch of men at work on new London Bridge. 23 × 14 cm. Add. MS 36489 A no. 61

183

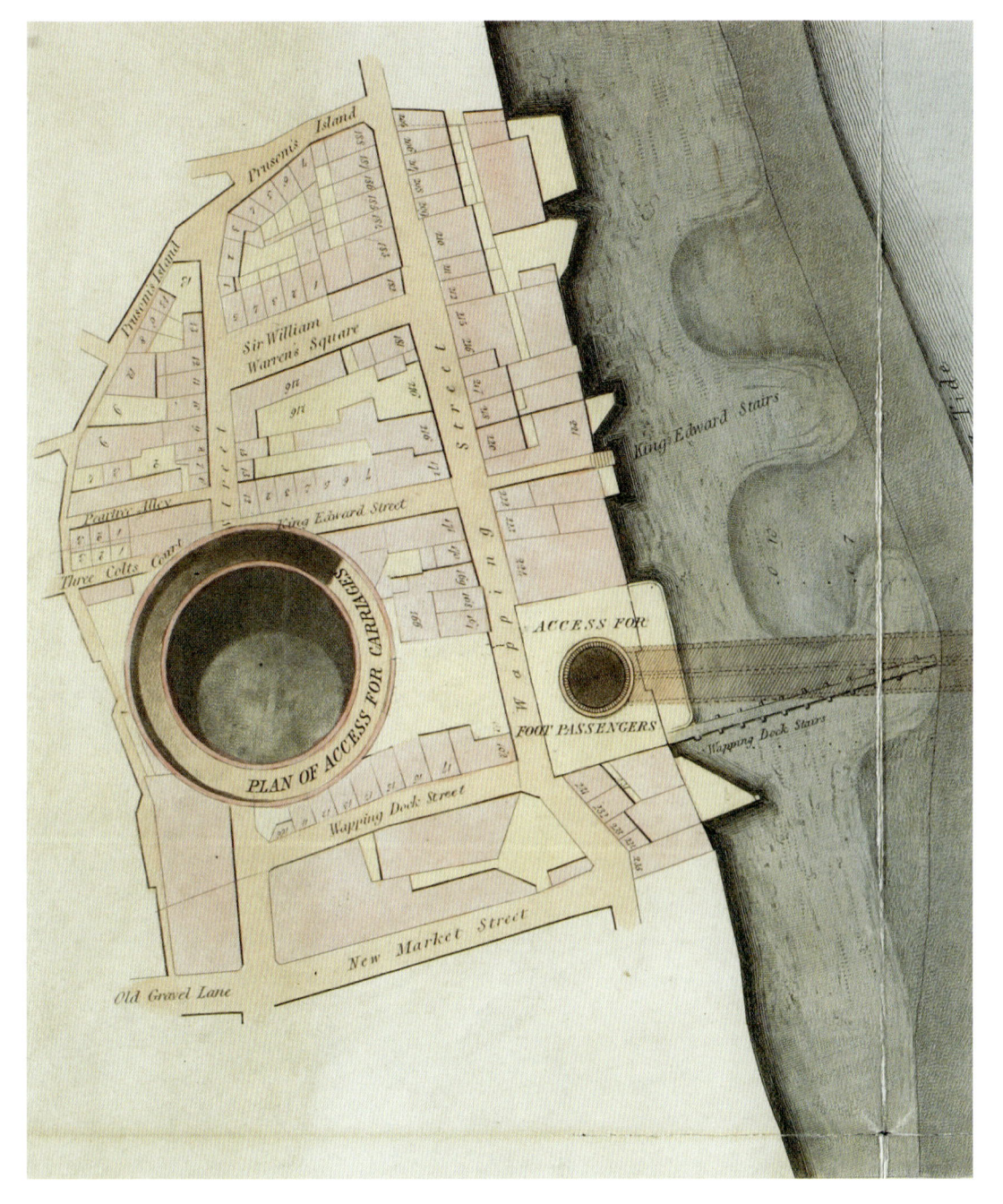

A TUNNEL UNDER THE THAMES

In 1825 work began on the first tunnel in the world to be built under a navigable river. Designed by Marc Isambard Brunel and his son Isambard Kingdom Brunel and linking Wapping to Rotherhithe, it was intended for road traffic. It was one of the wonders of the time and this plan is typical of the innumerable commemorative maps and views that charted its progress. A manuscript note in the middle of the Thames reflects the initial excitement: 'Progress of the Tunnel in May 1827 when Baron Humbold [the famous explorer and scientist Alexander von Humboldt] descended in the Diving Bell'. Marc Brunel descended at the same time, however, to mend a hole in the tunnel. Further complications followed and completion was delayed until 1842. The tunnel was never used for road transport: since 1867 railway trains have run through it and it is now part of the East London Line of the London Overground.

5.1.7 Anon. *Thames Tunnel c.* 1825(?). Coloured engraving. Maps 3710 (11)

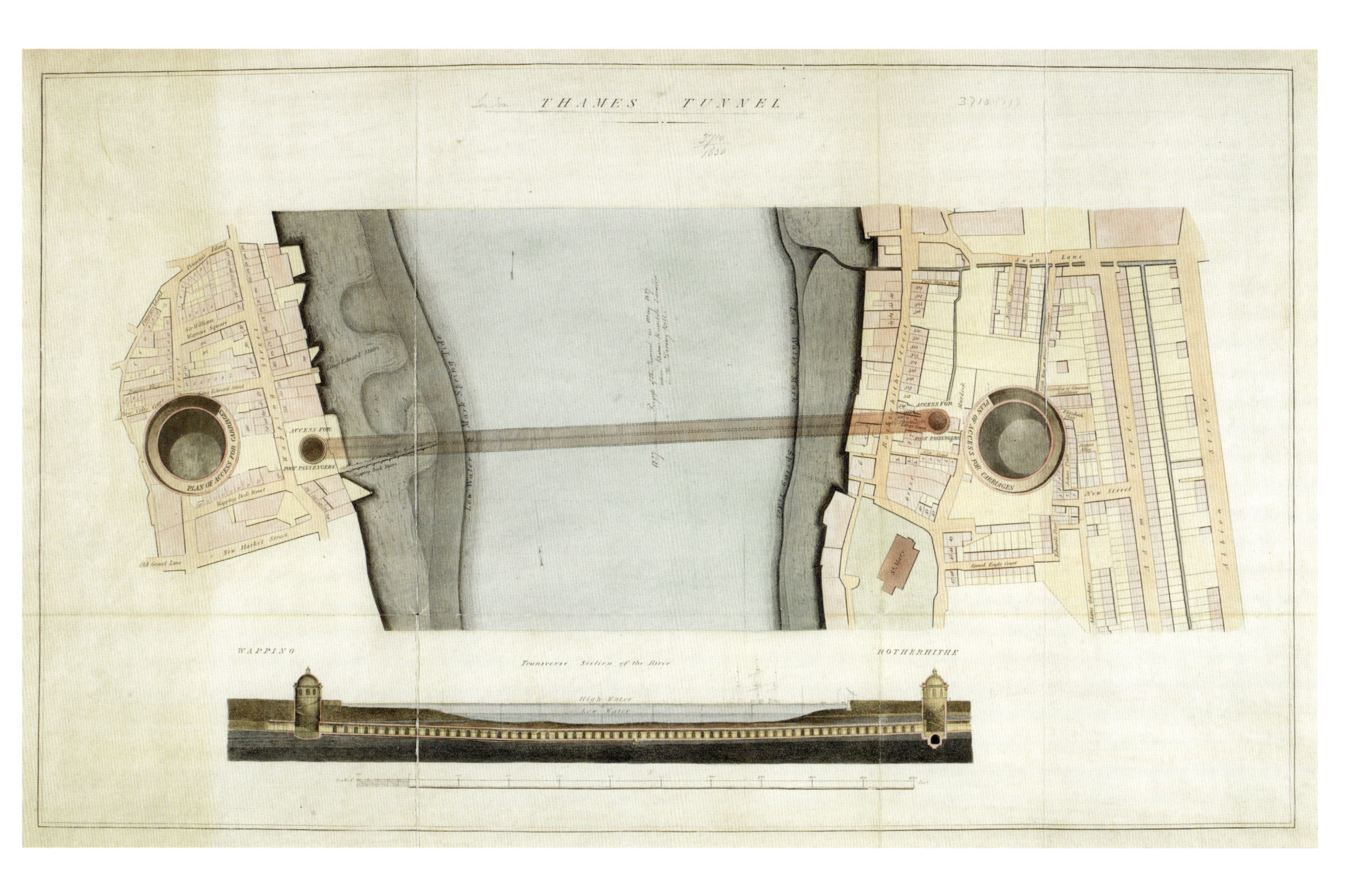

THAMES TUNNEL

WAPPING

Transverse Section of the River

ROTHERHITHE

5.2 REGENCY GRANDEUR

A PALACE ON THE THAMES

In 1768 the fashionable Scottish-born architects Robert and James Adam leased the site of the Bishop of Durham's former riverside mansion off the Strand not far from Charing Cross. Influenced by Emperor Diocletian's palace in Split, by 1774 they had created a central block of terraced houses surrounded by three other terraces on top of enormous arches overlooking the Thames It was the first attempt in London to disguise what was in reality a housing estate, composed of numerous private dwellings, as a palace. Robert and James Adam named the development the Adelphi after the Greek for 'Brothers'. This is the only-known original plan, probably presented to George III in 1771 when the brothers were seeking parliamentary permission to create an embankment. Despite a difficult start, the Adelphi ultimately proved a commercial success. The main block was demolished and replaced by an office block in 1936 and only a few houses on the periphery still survive, though these include the elegant headquarters of the Royal Society of Arts.

Private initiatives to create a dignified setting for a world city, like the Adelphi development of the Adam brothers, were emulated by government particularly in the development of government offices at Somerset House, a ceremonial archway at Hyde Park Corner, and in the development of Regent's Park, Regent Street and Trafalgar Square. These were the only official attempts at the comprehensive redevelopment which characterised other European capitals such as Paris, Berlin and Vienna. The government had additional, more down-to-earth, objectives: notably to prevent the wealthier areas such as Mayfair from being contaminated by the poverty and vulgarity of Soho and Covent Garden and to ensure the prosperity of, and thus a high level of income for the government from, the newly-developed Crown lands.

5.2.1 [Unique surviving manuscript plan for Adelphi by the Adam brothers], 1768. Ink on paper. 46 × 61.5 cm. Maps K. Top. 22.7-a

YORK BUILDINGS

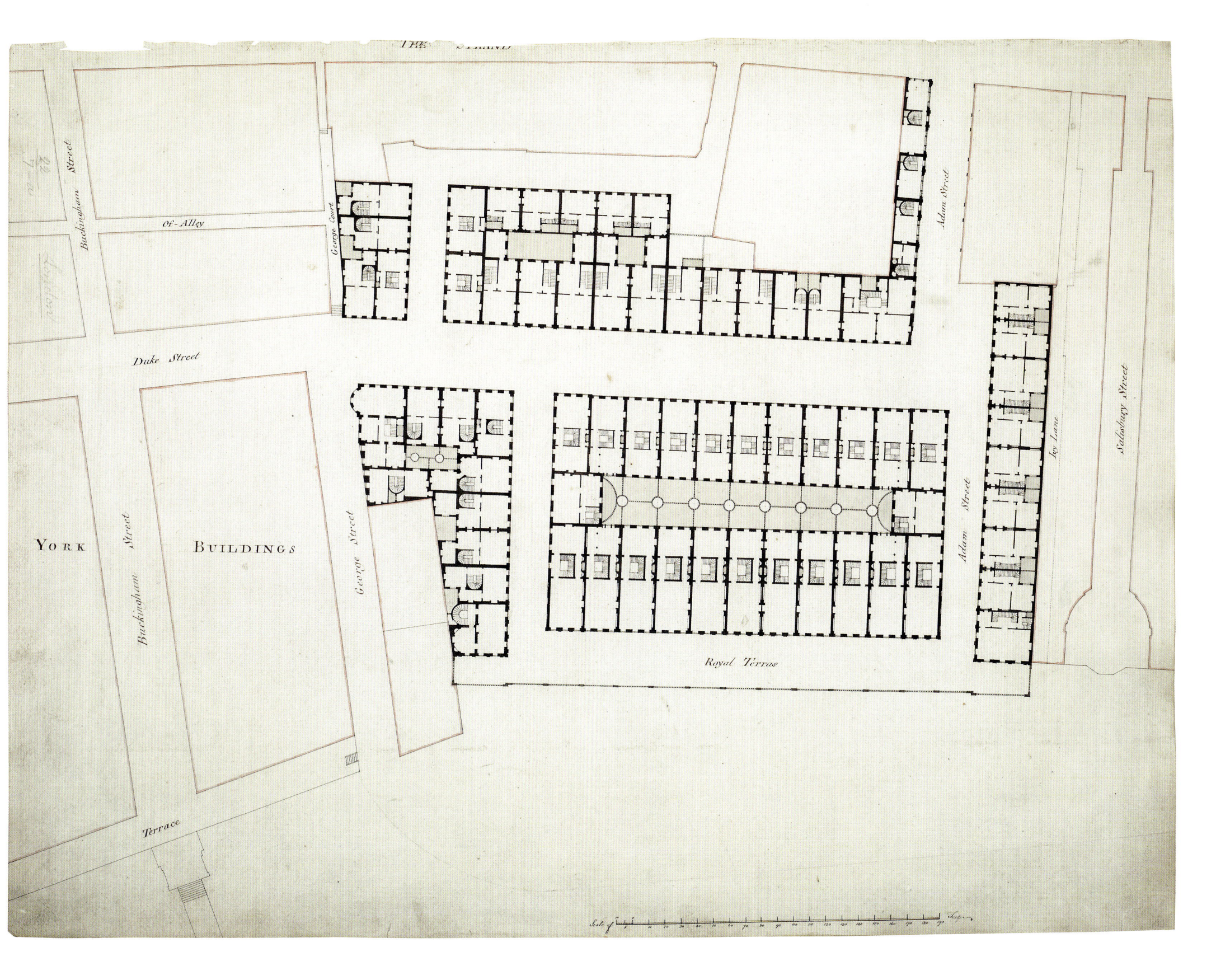

Buckingham Street
Of- Alley
Duke Street
Buckingham Street
Terrace

George Court
George Street

Adam Street
Ivy Lane
Salisbury Street

Royal Terrace

A RIVERSIDE PANORAMA

This gives an idea of the impression that the Adam brothers sought to create with the Adelphi. The Royal Terrace is shown above the arches which had been created over the steep bank to the Thames. The arches, used as storage vaults, became the haunt of beggars and criminals. The embankment was the first to be created on the Thames. In the distance can be seen St Paul's and Blackfriars Bridge which had been completed in 1769. With the sole exception of Somerset House, built by the Adams' rival William Chambers, the Adelphi did not influence later developments along the Thames. Nash, however, was to adopt the notion of disguising private houses as palaces for the terraces bordering Regent's Park.

5.2.2   Benedetto Pastorini, *View of the South Front of the New Buildings called Adelphi formerly Durham Yard*, c. 1774. Engraving. 51.5 × 82 cm. Maps K. Top. 22.7-b

Benedetto Pastorini was originally from Italy but settled in London early in life, marrying Alice Kelly at St James Westminster in 1770. He was employed as a decorator of ceilings but also established a career as a printmaker, working with many of the leading artists and architects of the day. He collaborated with the Adam Brothers in the publication of their *Works in Architecture* (1778 on) and became one of the founding governors of the Society of Engravers in 1803.

VIEW of the *SOUTH FRONT* of the New Buildings called ADELPHI, formerly DURHAM YARD; and also that part of the Cities of LONDON & WESTMINSTER which extends along the RIVER THAMES to the MONUMENT.

The above Print exhibits the Royal Terras, the Houses, and Openings of the Streets leading to the Strand; Together with the Wharfs, Arcade, and entrances to the Subterraneous Streets, and Warehouses of the Adelphi, which is a private Undertaking of Mess.rs ADAM, designed by them, and begun to be carried into Execution in July 1768, Being so contrived as to keep the Access to the Houses, level with the Strand, and distinct from the Traffic of the Wharfs and Warehouses.

Published according to Act of Parliament.

A GRAND ENTRANCE TO LONDON

From about 1770, Hyde Park Corner at the junction of Green Park and Hyde Park was seen as the natural site for a grand entrance to London from the West. In November 1778 Robert Adam submitted a series of designs including this one, incorporating royal statues and decorative references to England, Scotland, the Crown and Parliament. Standing at the end of the Knightsbridge Turnpike, the brick and stucco arch, despite its grand appearance, was to accommodate a toll gatherer's lodge (to the left) and a weigh house for carts (to the right). His proposals, costed at £3,050, were, however, not accepted. It was only between 1825 and 1827 that Decimus Burton created the existing screen and arch.

5.2.3   Robert Adam [Elevation and plan of proposed arch at Hyde Park Corner, November 1778]. Ink and wash on paper. 51 × 67.2 cm. Maps K. Top. 27.26-c-2

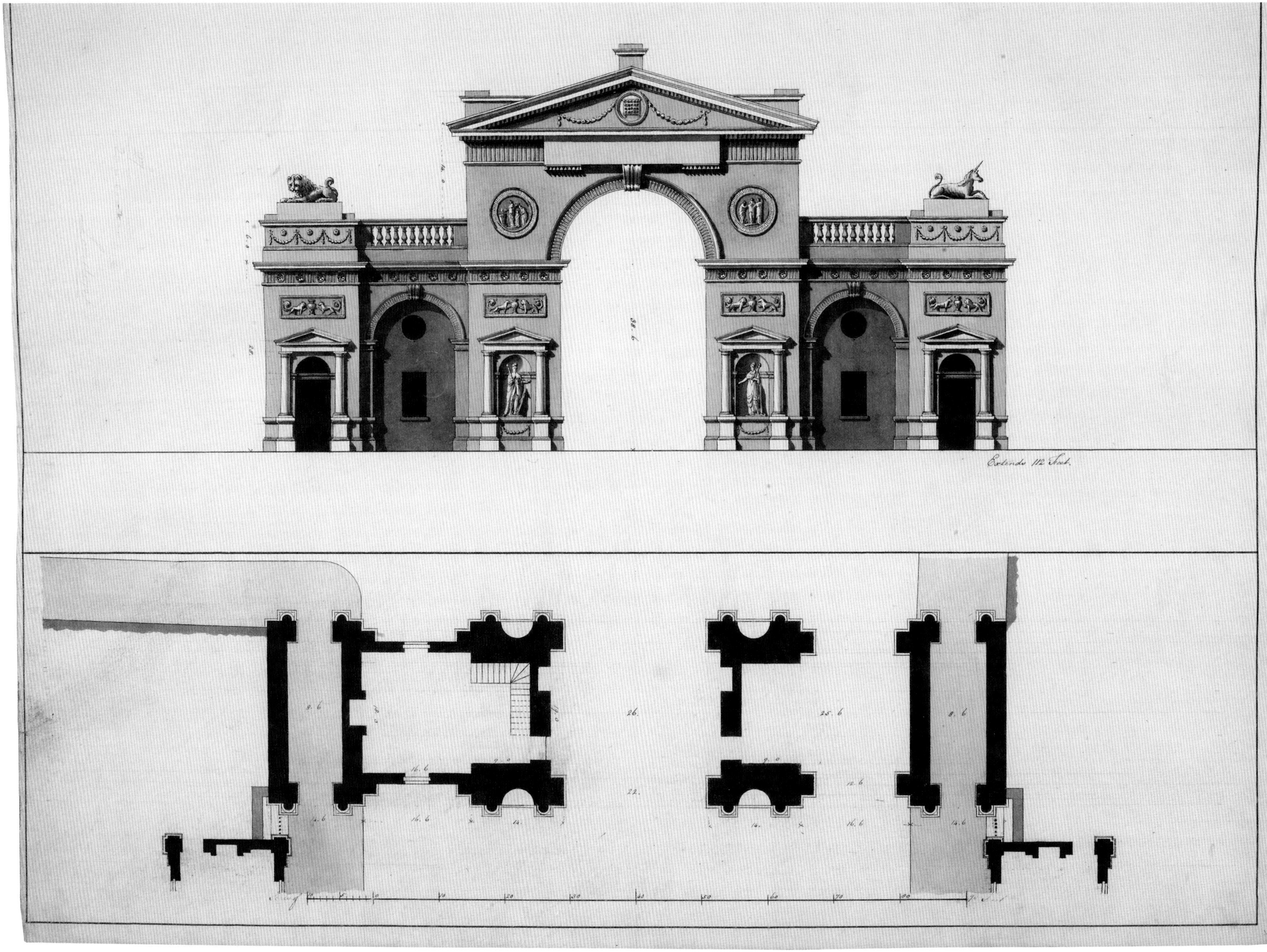
Extends 112 Feet.

A DEVELOPMENT OPPORTUNITY

In 1794 the grounds of Marylebone Park, Crown (royal) land with the circular boundaries of a medieval hunting park, were leased out for farming. High-class developments were already near completion on the Portman, Portland and Southampton (Grafton) estates to the south and east and St John's Wood was slowly emerging as London's first garden suburb. The government thus knew that in 1811, when the leases fell in, Marylebone Park would present an ideal opportunity for profitable development. Planning could not start too early. This survey was printed so that it could be circulated to architects, with a prize of £1000 for the best development scheme.

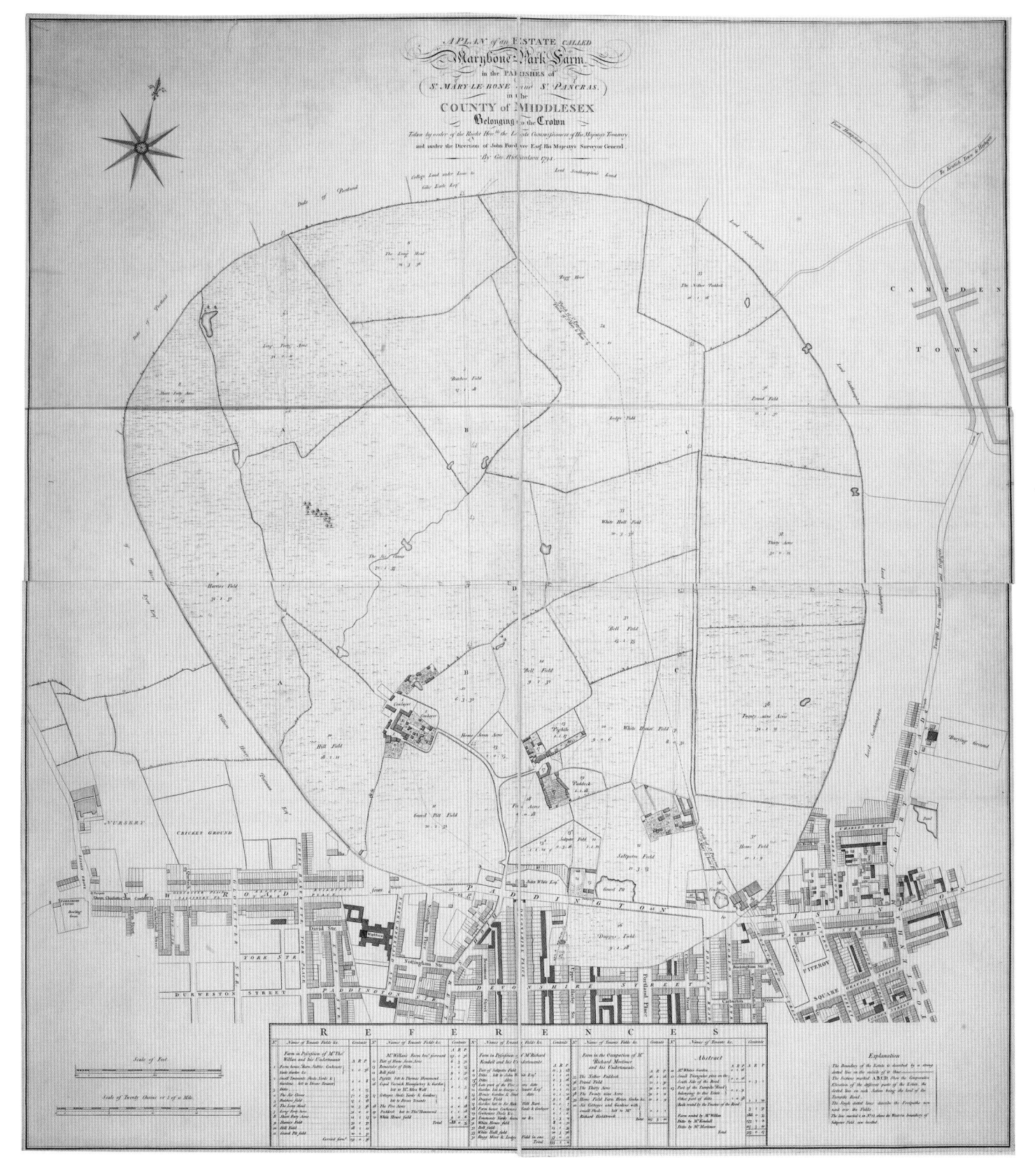

5.2.4   George Richardson, *A plan of an Estate called Marybone Park Farm, in the parishes of St. Mary-le-bone and St. Pancras in the county of Middlesex, belonging to the Crown* (London: William Faden, 1794). Engraved map. 108.2 × 102 cm. Maps Crace XIV.28

A VIEW ACROSS MARYLEBONE PARK

For much of his career, Samuel Hieronymous Grimm, a talented Swiss artist, was employed by wealthy and cultured members of the English gentry to depict houses, antiquities and landscapes. In precisely the months when George Richardson was surveying Marylebone Park, Grimm drew this view of the same neighbourhood looking to the North, with the hills of Hampstead and Highgate beyond, for the Rev. Richard Kaye. A coach is shown travelling along what is now Marylebone Road.

5.2.5 Samuel Hieronymous Grimm [A view across Marylebone Park towards Hampstead, Primrose Hill and Highgate from Devonshire Place, 1793]. Ink and wash on paper. 19 × 27 cm. Additional MS 15542, f.136

Grimm (1733–94) arrived in Covent Garden in 1768 after a spell in Paris — and there remained for the rest of his life. The antiquary Francis Grose referred to him thus in 1777 — 'He is nearly the best draughtsman in London. His expenses will be very moderate … This Grim is a very modest, well behaved man and will do as he is bid and not give himself those impertinent airs frequently assumed by artists much his inferiors in abilities.'

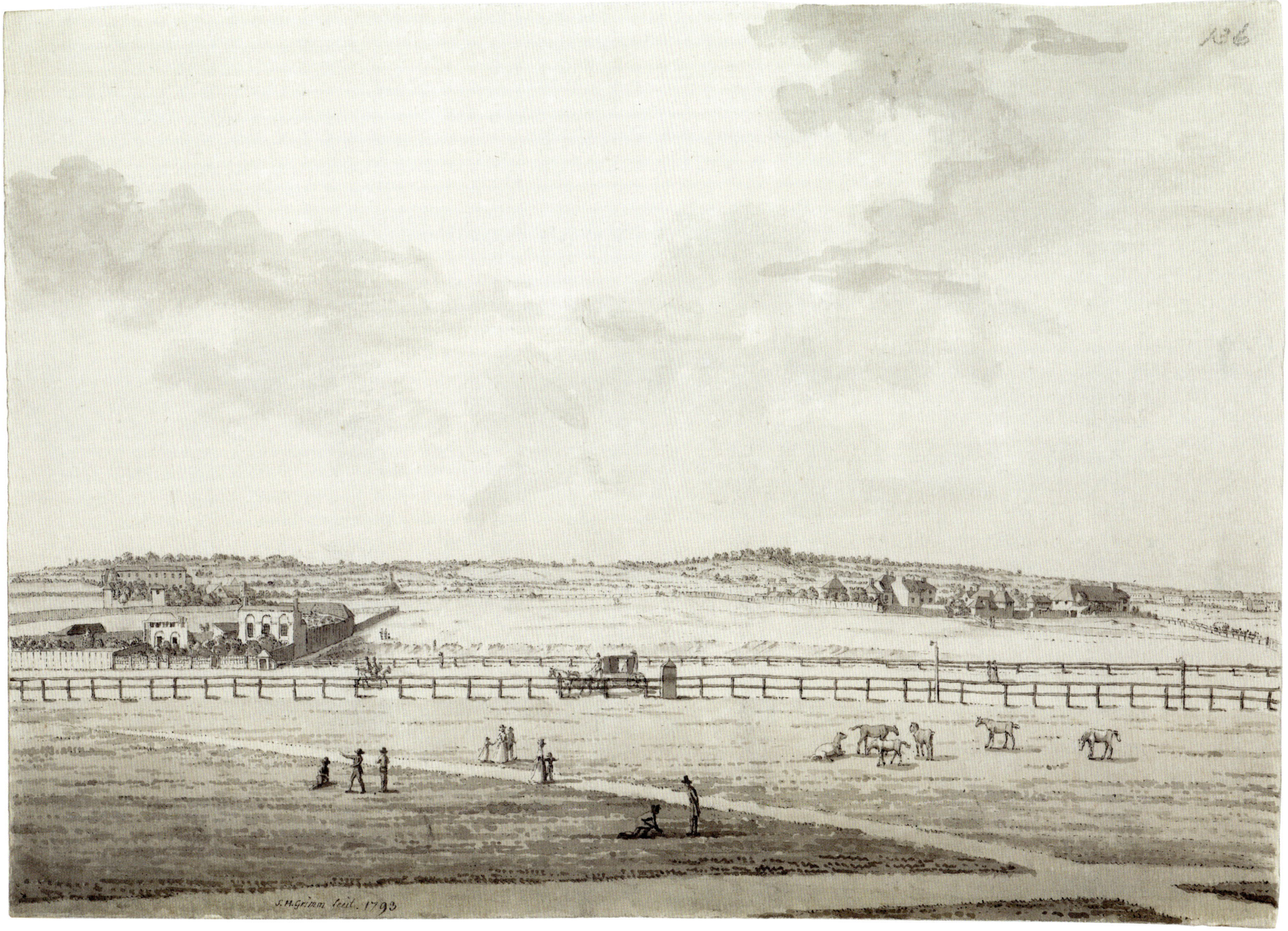

136
S.H.Grimm fecit. 1793

AN INITIAL VISION

Initial attempts to find a developer were unsuccessful. In 1811, however, John Nash, the Prince Regent's favourite architect, drew up a plan, of which this is a revised version. He hoped to create an upper-class garden suburb, with access only from the prosperous districts to the south, with a miniature royal palace, handsome terraces, circuses, crescents, a new church, markets, a barracks, 56 detached villas hidden among the greenery, a sinuous lake and a picturesque canal linking Paddington to the Docks. He predicted profits of nearly £60, 000 for the Crown Estates in return for an expenditure of £12,000. The plan was immediately accepted and work started.

5.2.6 John Nash, *Plan of an Estate belonging to the Crown called Marybone Park Farm upon A Design for letting it out on Building Leases*. From John White, Jr., *Some Account of the proposed improvements of the Western Part of London By the formation of the Regent's Park, the New Street, the New Sewer Illustrated by a variety of Plans*, 2nd ed., 1815. Aquatint. 22.7 × 29 cm. 10350 d.12

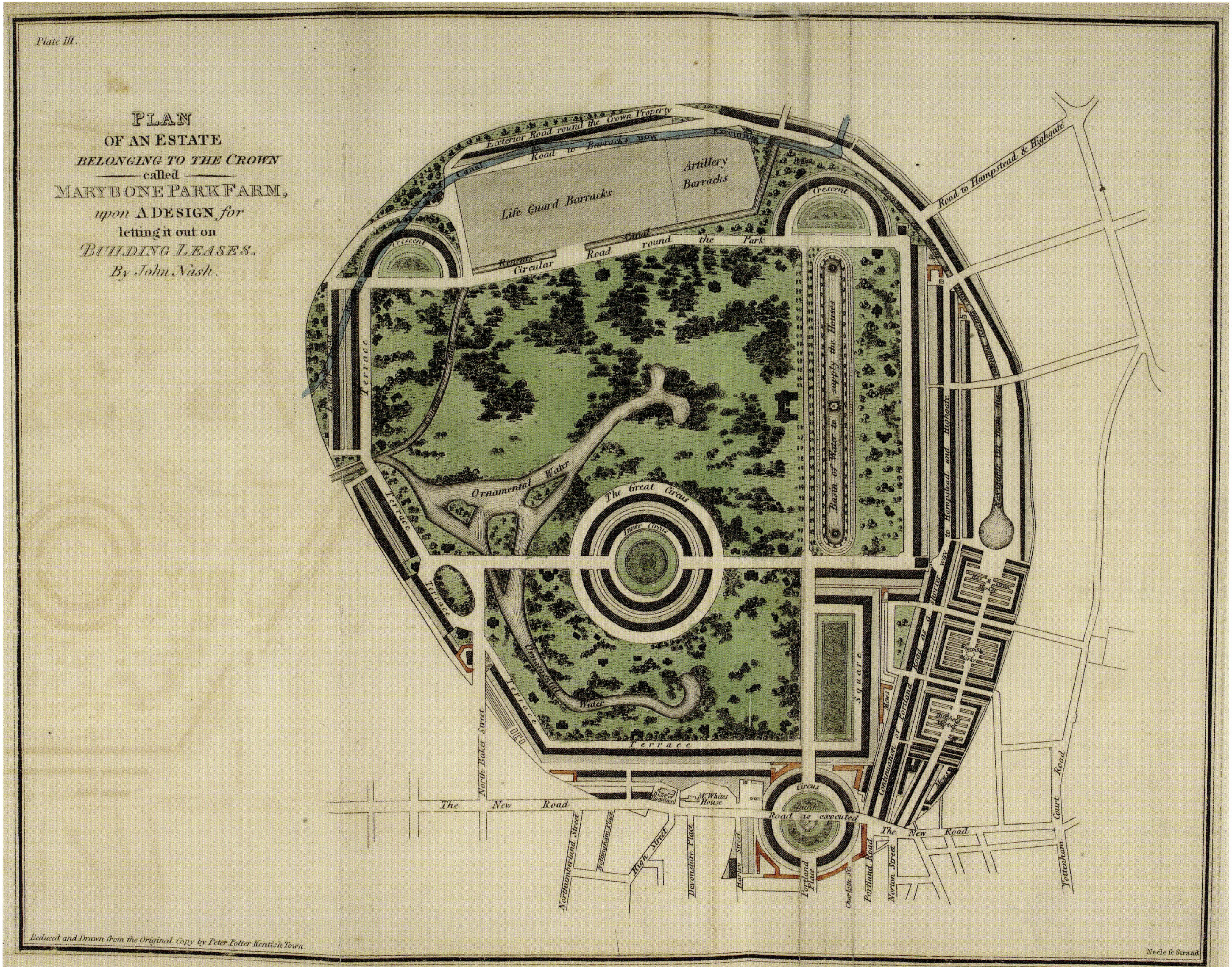
Plate III.
PLAN
OF AN ESTATE
BELONGING TO THE CROWN
called
MARYBONE PARK FARM,
upon A DESIGN for
letting it out on
BUILDING LEASES.
By John Nash.
Exterior Road round the Crown Property
Canal
Road to Barracks now Executing
Life Guard Barracks
Artillery Barracks
Crescent
Crescent
Regents Canal
Circular Road round the Park
Road to Hampstead & Highgate
Terrace
Terrace
Terrace
Terrace
Terrace
Ornamental Water
Ornamental Water
The Great Circus
Inner Circus
Basin of Water to supply the Houses
Road to Hampstead and Highgate
Square
Mews
Continuation of Portland Road as shown
Circus
Road as executed
The New Road
The New Road
North Baker Street
Northumberland Street
High Street
Devonshire Place
Harley Street
Portland Place
Portland Road
Norton Street
Tottenham Court Road
M. Whites House
Reduced and Drawn from the Original Copy by Peter Potter Kentish Town.
Neele sc Strand

FLOWERS AT THE CENTRE

Things did not go smoothly when work began on Regent's Park in 1811. In the end, the villas were reduced to a mere eight (seriously diminishing the expected profits), the canal, church and barracks repositioned and the royal villa omitted. More positively, in 1828 a Zoological Garden arose on part of the original barracks site. There were particular problems with the double circus at the centre. The houses were never built and after being considered as a site for the new King's College, in 1840 the ground was leased to the Royal Botanic Society whose proposals are illustrated here. Kew Gardens were not yet open to the public.

5.2.7 [James Basire after Decimus Burton?] *Design for laying out the Inner Circle of the Regents Park as a Garden for the Royal Botanic Society of London referred to in the Report of Messrs Burton & Marnock dated 15th July 1840.* Aquatint. 34 × 45 cm. Maps Crace XVII.66

James Basire (1796–1869) was the fourth London engraver of that name and represented the fifth generation of a London engraving family descended from the Huguenot refugees, Jacques Basir and his wife Magdelaine Lair. Basire's own son, also James, was his apprentice at this time but, after a spell in debtors' prison, broke the family tradition by moving to Bristol, where he worked as a draughtsman.

DESIGN FOR LAYING OUT THE INNER CIRCLE OF THE REGENTS PARK.
as a GARDEN for the
ROYAL BOTANIC SOCIETY OF LONDON.

Referred to in the Report of Messrs. Burton & Murnock, dated 15th July, 1840.

REFERENCE

- A Linnean Arrangement
- B Jussieuean D°. examples of
- C Medical Collection
- D Plants used in Agriculture
- E Plants used in the Arts and Manufactures
- F Experimental Garden
- G British Plants, on Banks, with Rockwork, Water, &c.
- H Border for Florist Flowers, Annuals, &c.
- I Mounds for shelter, and to give variety and interest to the Garden, with beds of American Plants
- K Mound with large Reservoir, for supplying the Garden with Water
- L Engine House for supplying the above Reservoir
- M Lake
- N Grottos and Seats
- O Open Seats, in Recesses, among the Planting
- P Bridge
- Q Geographical Arrangement
- R Borders for choice Flowers
- S Entrance to Covered Way to Winter Garden, or Conservatory
- T Back Yard for Composts, and to be sufficiently large to contain Carts, and other Vehicles for the conveyance of Plants on Exhibition Days
- V Back Yards with open Sheds Underground Passage to D°
- U Underground Passage to Lawn
- W Curator's House
- X Store Room attached to Agricultural Ground

The Trees and Shrubs throughout the Garden to be arranged according to the Natural System of Jussieu.

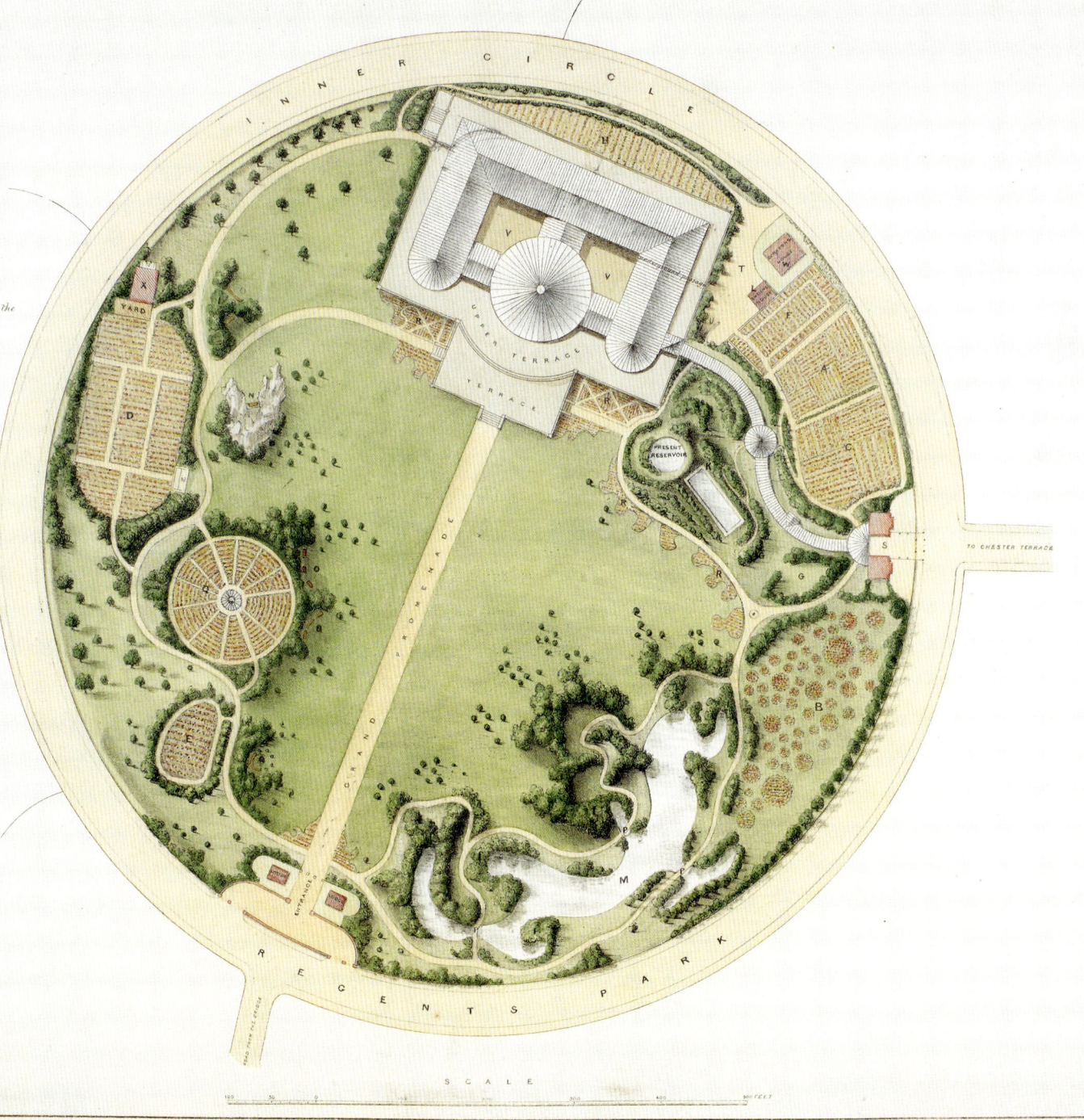

THE FINAL RESULT

This 360 degreee panorama shows the periphery of Regent's Park as finally completed in 1830 — and looking very different from even Nash's revised plan of 1815. There were fewer terraces but also some unplanned features like the Colosseum and Diorama which catered for the public appetite for visual illusions. Street entertainers and a Steam Washing Company cart complete the scene. As if to mark their approval of the Park's final appearance, William IV and his queen, riding with a military escort in an open carriage, jovially doff their hats to the public.

5.2.8   Richard Morris, *Panoramic View round the Regents Park by Richard Morris author of essays on landscape gardening* (London: Rudolph Ackermann, 1831). Coloured aquatint. 13.6 × 593 cm. BL Maps 14.a.29

201

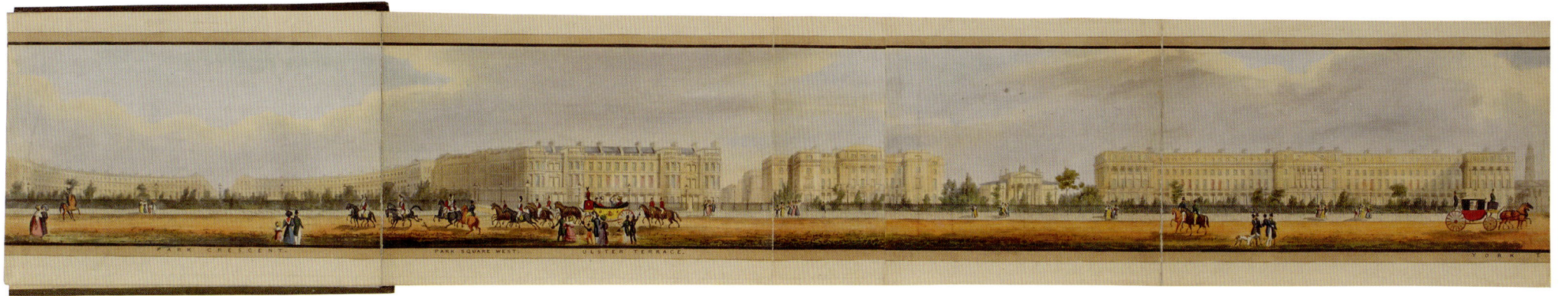

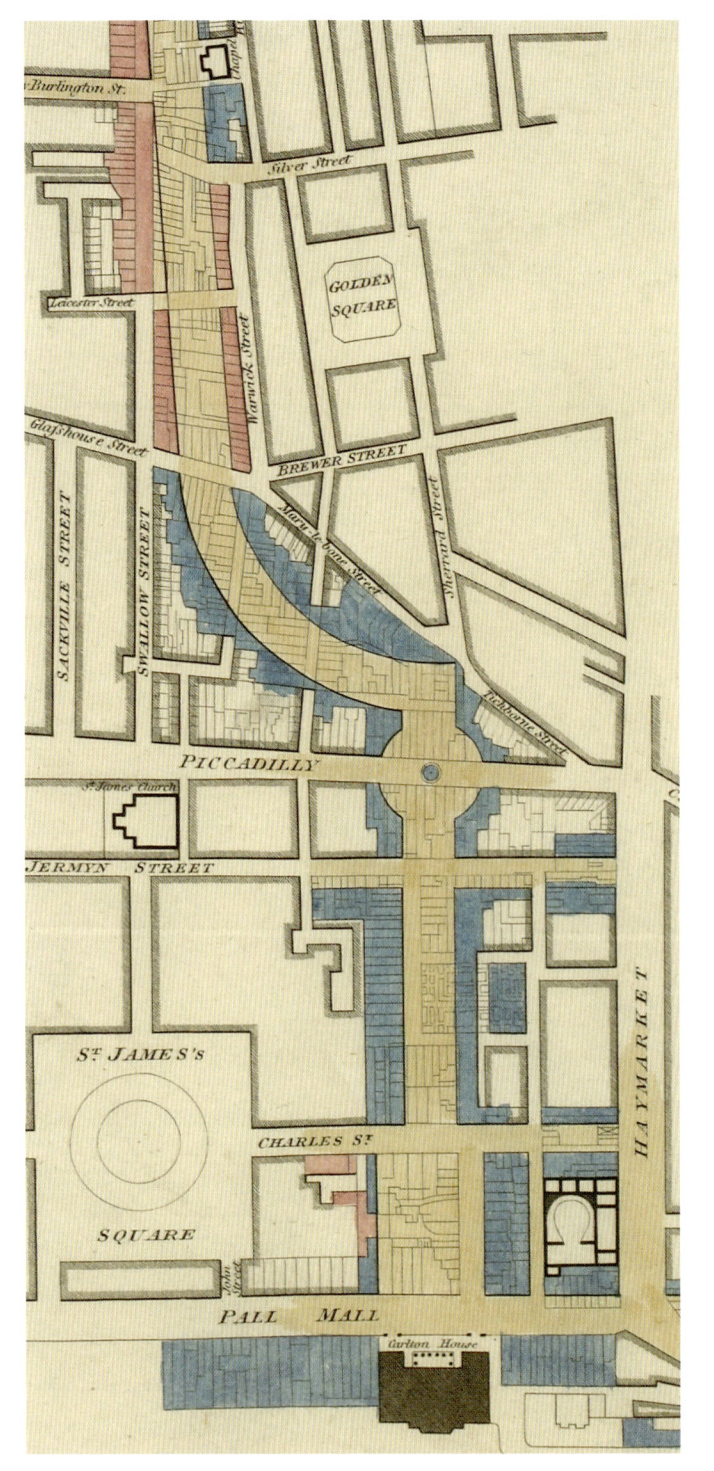

THE GENESIS OF REGENT STREET

It was always accepted that Regent's Park would never be a success unless a direct link to Westminster was provided for its residents. This offered Nash an opportunity to build a grand colonnaded street, modelled on the rue de Rivoli in Paris, from Carlton House, the Prince Regent's palace, to his new villa in the Park. The road did not, however, follow the most direct route from Piccadilly to the new Park. There were three principal reasons for this and they are clarified on this plan which distinguishes between Crown land (coloured blue) and private land (coloured pink). First, fashion demanded that the road be enlivened by a crescent. Secondly, by placing it at the start of the route, additional buildings would be erected on land owned by the Crown. Thirdly, and of perhaps greatest importance, by drawing the line a little to the West of what was to become Piccadilly Circus, the road would prevent the prosperous West End from being contaminated by down-at-heel Soho. Regent Street has acted as a *cordon sanitaire* between the louche and the elegant ever since. It has been said by the architectural historian J. Mordaunt Crook that 'the sinuous line of Regent Street was … the developer's line of maximum profit'.

5.2.9 Anon. *Plan, presented to The House of Commons, of a Street proposed from Charing Cross to Portland Place, leading to the Crown Estate in Mary-le-Bone Park. Ordered by the House of Commons to be printed 10 May 1813*. Printed Map. 52 × 67.2 cm. Maps K. Top. 22.4-2

PLAN, presented to The House of Commons, of a STREET proposed from Charing Cross to Portland Place, leading to the Crown Estate in Mary-le-Bone Park,— On a reduced Scale.

PLAN of a STREET, proposed from Portland Place to Charing Cross, leading from the Crown Estate in Mary-le-Bone Park, and affording a broad and uninterrupted access from the Houses of Parliament and other Public Buildings in Westminster, to all the principal Streets in the West & North West part of the Town between Pall Mall and the New Road.

For widening the entrance to Pall Mall, and continuing Pall Mall to the Portico of St Martins Church.

For widening the narrow part of Cockspur Street.

For continuing Charles Street St James's Square into the Haymarket.

For widening Jermyn Street, And improving the purlieus of Carlton House.

NB. The parts shaded with a Blue Colour, are Crown Property.

Ordered by the HOUSE OF COMMONS to be printed 10th May 1815.

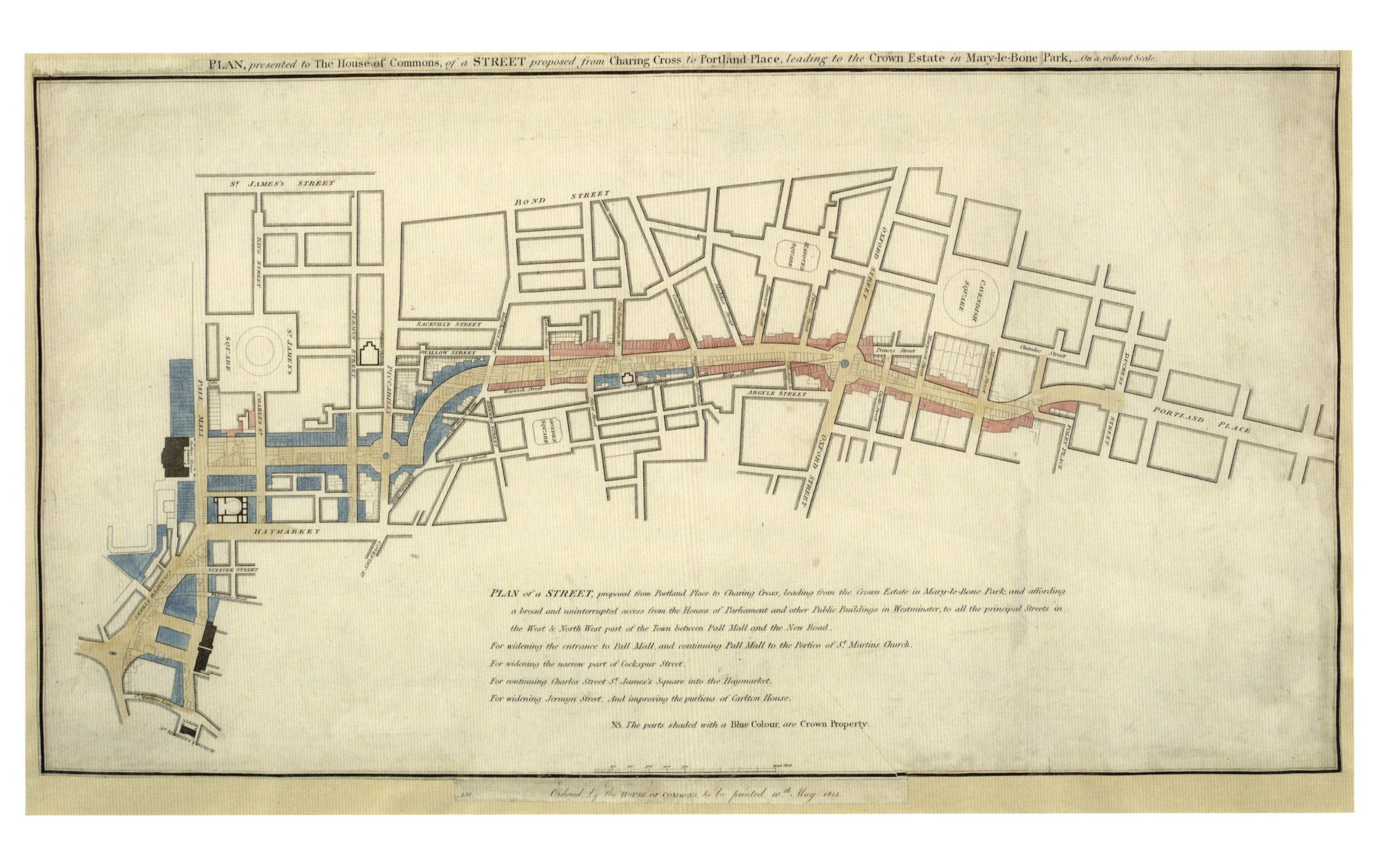

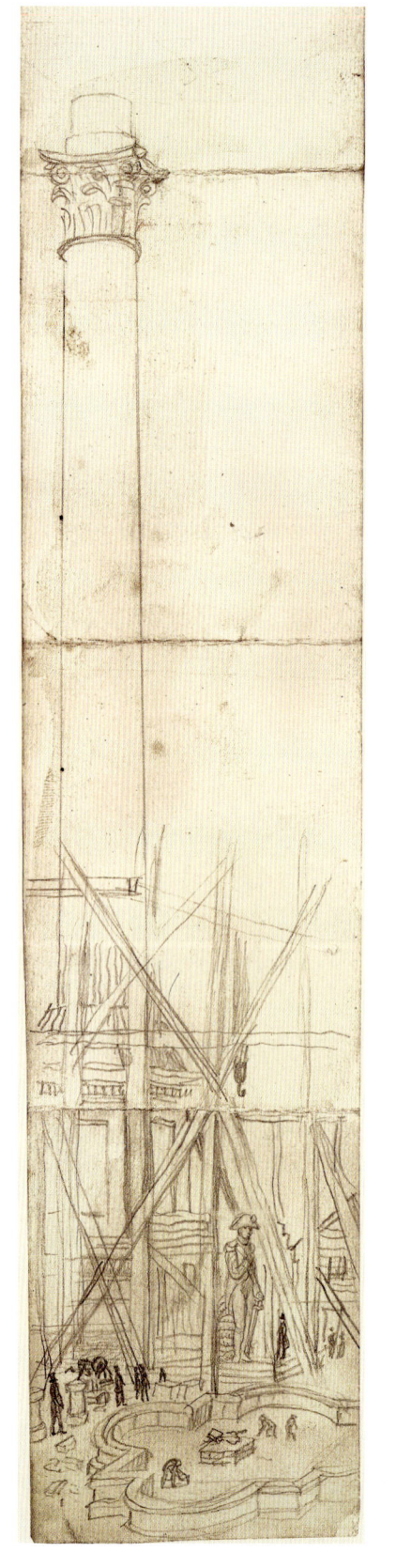

THE ORIGINS OF TRAFALGAR SQUARE

Nash's plans extended beyond Carlton House and Pall Mall all the way to Westminster. This plan shows the land that the government needed to purchase to realise the scheme for a grand square east of a rebuilt Pall Mall. An imitation Greek temple at the centre housing the Royal Academy was to stand between statues of George III and George IV with wide roads radiating out to the British Museum, (which was then being rebuilt in a piecemeal, incremental fashion), the Strand and Parliament. Ultimately the government failed to provide money for the new Royal Academy. A cheaper alternative, Nelson's Column, originally meant for Greenwich, took its place almost as an afterthought, in 1835, and with it the name Trafalgar Square.

5.2.10a   George Scharf [pencil sketch of the statue of Nelson at the foot of the column, 1835]. 37.5 × 7.5 cm. Add. MS 36489 A no. 68

For George Scharf see 3.3a above.

5.2.10b   James Basire, *Plan of the Proposed Improvements at Charing Cross, St Martin's Lane and Entrance to the Strand* (Ordered by the House of Commons to be Printed, 12th May 1826; Luke Hansard). Printed map with watercolour. 41 × 51 cm. Maps Crace XVII.38

For James Basire see 5.2.7 above. He was routinely employed to produce official maps for parliamentary reports, etc., the delineation of postal boundaries, etc. For Luke Hansard see 6.5.3 below.

Plate III.

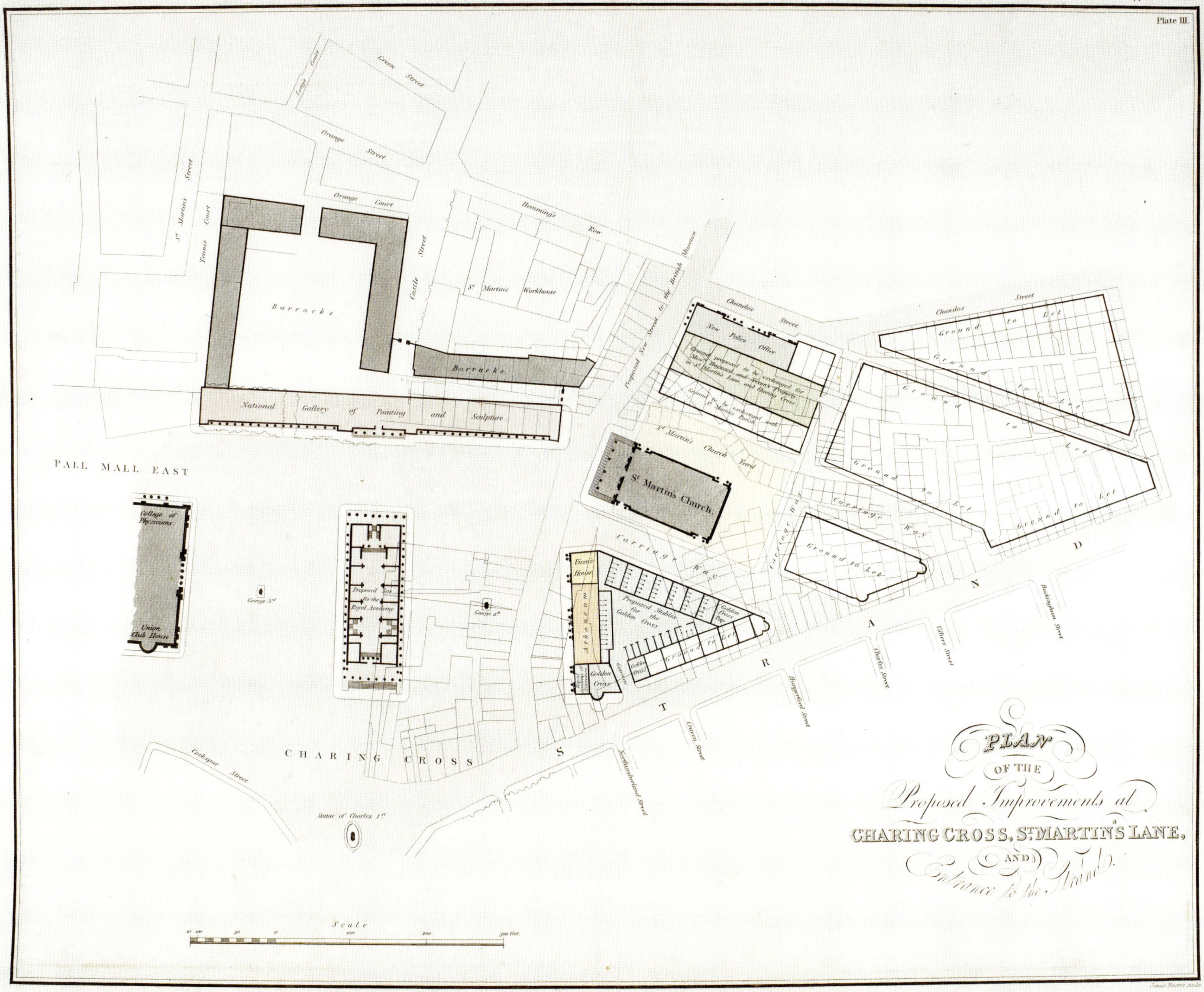

James Basire sculp.

368. Ordered by The HOUSE OF COMMONS, to be Printed, 12th May 1826.

Luke Hansard & Sons Printers.

LONDON FROM ABOVE

From about 1790, perhaps as a consequence of the craze for ballooning, the traditional panorama was joined by any number of optical tricks aiming at giving the illusion of viewing places from a great height from within the confines of buildings such as the Colosseum on Regent's Park. This peepshow selects the top of the commemorative column to George IV's brother, 'The Grand Old Duke of York', the Commander-in-Chief of the British army, who had died in 1827. The column had been erected on the site of Carlton House which had been demolished in 1826 following George IV's decision to make Buckingham Palace into his principal residence. The column was intended to be the focal point of the grand route to Regent's Park, but this view centres on the area to the East towards Blackheath and Greenwich, and particularly the now numerous bridges over the Thames.

5.2.11   *C. A. Lane's Telescopic View of London and the Thames, from the Duke of York's Column, Carlton Gardens* (London, 1851(?)). Engraved panorama. 16 × 20 × 50 cm (depth). HS. 74/2087

Charles Augustus Lane (1802–82) was born in Lambeth. He was described on the 1851 Census simply as a forty-nine-year-old manufacturer of fancy goods, living with his wife Susannah at 46 Stanhope Street, St Pancras. He published a similar peepshow of the interior of the Great Exhibition, but subsequently became a house-agent.

AN OVERVIEW

A COSMORAMIC VIEW OF LONDON.

This view is taken from a point south of Elephant and Castle. In common with most such panoramas, it exaggerates the size of important buildings and church steeples for ease of identification. Particularly noteworthy are Nash's rebuilt Buckingham Palace, Trafalgar Square, the anticipated appearance of the Houses of Parliament as rebuilt after the 1834 fire, the new bridges over the Thames and London's first railway coming into London Bridge Station. The eagle-eyed will make out the new Archway near Highgate on the northern horizon. The view went through several editions with a variety of different titles.

5.2.12 Edward Wallis, *A Cosmoramic View of London*, 1843. Coloured steel aquatint. 45.5 × 105 cm. Maps STL 382

The view was the work of John Henry Banks (1816–79), an inventive and resilient engraver and printer whose life was one of perpetual financial difficulty. He appeared in bankruptcy proceedings in four different decades, was imprisoned at least twice for debt, and yet was still taking out patents for improved printing processes as late as the 1870s. Few men can have known London better — born in Marylebone, he lived at various times in his necessarily peripatetic life at King's Cross, Holborn, St Giles, Clerkenwell, Islington, Lambeth, Covent Garden, Battersea and Wandsworth. His publisher Edward Wallis (1787?–1868) was one of the leading London producers of pictorial material, including maps, games and jigsaw puzzles.

REGENCY SPLENDOUR

This map reflects the elegance aspired to by well-to-do Regency Londoners — and something of the evangelical piety, secularism and pleasure-seeking that existed side by side with it. It was the work of a skilled surveyor and artist and of a leading antiquary who was also editor of one of the most popular guides to London. By the 1830s the great estates south and west of Regent's Park had been fully developed. The Regency developments did not work out as planned, however. Regent Street ultimately culminated not in Carlton House, which was demolished in 1826, but in the elegant clubs of Waterloo Place and the Duke of York's Column. The lay-out of Regent's Park was radically simplified. Meanwhile Thomas Cubitt, the first professional large-scale commercial builder and developer, was beginning to build over the Bishop of London's Bayswater estates and neo-classicism, the neo-gothic and evangelism came together to adorn the district with many new churches. They are illustrated here — together with secular institutions, such as the recently-founded and aggressively 'godless' University College, and a few amusements such as the Colosseum and the Diorama. Property ownership remained the key factor in the further development of London, however, and the owners of estates of all sizes, particularly in the long, narrow and still largely rural parish of St Pancras, extending up to Highgate Village, are all identified by numbers.

5.2.13   F. A. Bartlett and B. R. Davies, *Topographical Survey of the Borough of St Marylebone as incorporated & defined by Act of Parliament 1832 … and Plans & Elevations of the Public Buildings. Engraved by B. R. Davies from Surveys & Drawings by F. A. Bartlett under the direction of J. Britton*, 1834 [Revised edn, 1837] Steel engraving with watercolour. 70 × 102 cm. Maps Crace XIV.1

The engraver Benjamin Rees Davies (1789?–1872) was the son of a Holborn tailor. When he was apprenticed to John Lodge in 1803 he joined an unbroken master-apprentice line of map-engravers in the Merchant Taylors' Company that stretched back to the seventeenth century. The map-making tradition in London was a cumulative one and Davies was one of its finest exponents, much employed in making quasi-official maps for the Post Office directories, etc. (see 6.1.3 below).

THE PROFITS OF COMMERCE

Between 1838 and 1840 the mapmaker John Tallis produced a series of detailed street views, embellished with steel-plate engravings. The owners had to pay a guinea to have their shops named and the wrappers of each part contained details of the properties shown so that the completed work could be used as a directory. Although Tallis did not succeed in covering the whole city, his *Street Views* provide invaluable information about the appearance of early Victorian London extending from the elegance of Regent Street to the relative poverty of the East End. *Grimstone's Eye Snuff Manufactory* adds a suitably Dickensian touch to this view of a corner of Broad Street in Bloomsbury.

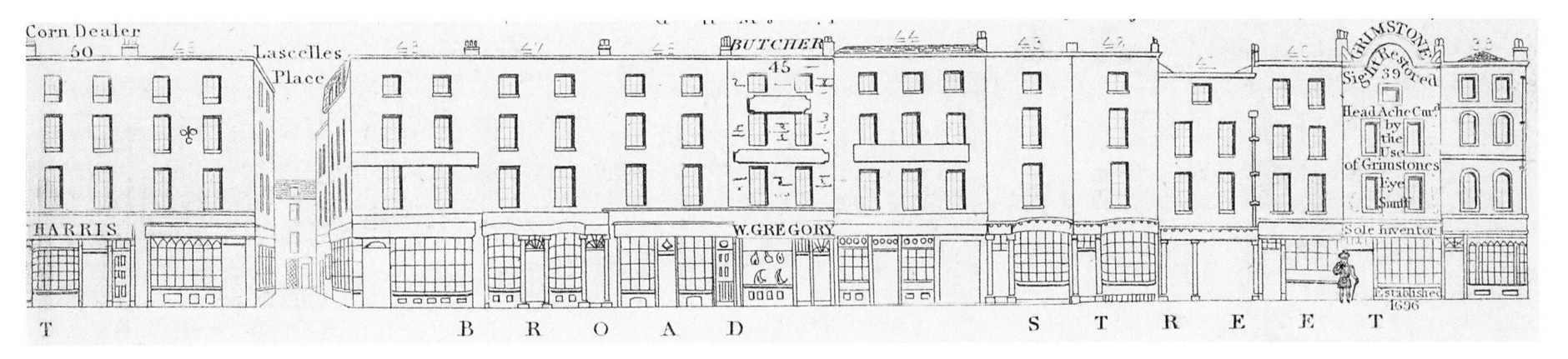

5.2.14 John Tallis, *Tallis's London Street Views*, 1838–40. Part 26. 15.5 × 75 cm. Maps C.7.a.34

John Tallis (1792–1842) was originally a bookseller at Stourbridge in Worcestershire. By about 1820 he had moved to London and there came to specialise in the publication of popular works published in weekly or monthly installments, of which the best-known is perhaps Thomas Dugdale's *Curiosities of Great Britain*. He built up a national distribution network which became international when his son and successor, also John Tallis, opened a New York office in 1849. The London street views are said to have been drawn by the artist and surveyor Charles Bigot (d. 1865).

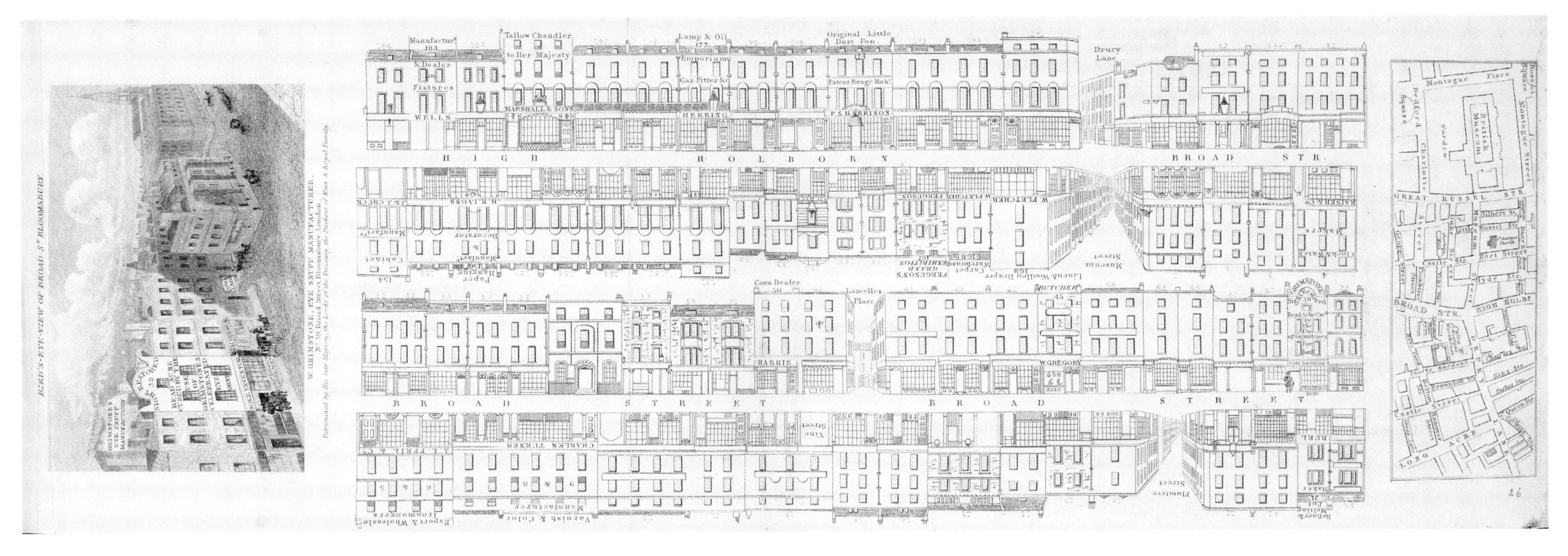

BIRD'S-EYE-VIEW OF BROAD ST BLOOMSBURY.

W. GRIMSTONE, EYE SNUFF MANUFACTURER,
N.º 39, Broad Street, Bloomsbury, London.
Patronized by His late Majesty, the Lords of the Treasury, the Duchess of Kent, & Royal Family.

213

A LAST LOOK AT REGENCY LONDON

It took Christopher and John Greenwood three years to survey this detailed and beautifully engraved map which captures all of the changes that had taken place since the first edition of Horwood's map in 1799. Belgravia is under development by Thomas Cubitt and the built-up area extends southwards towards Stockwell, Camberwell and Peckham. The numerous parish, vestry and liberty boundaries reveal the impossibility of centralised planning for London. The map was cynically republished by the Greenwoods' successor, Edward Ruff, in 1851 to cash in on the popularity of the Great Exhibition, and shows the exhibition area, some railways and Victoria Park, but it had not been systematically revised since 1830.

5.2.15   [Christopher and John Greenwood; engraved by Josiah and James Neele] *Map of London from Actual Survey comprehending the Various Improvements to 1851* (Edward Ruff & Co., 1851). Steel engraving with watercolour. 127 × 188 cm Maps Crace VII.265

The brothers Christopher and John Greenwood were the sons of a Yorkshire grazier. Their ambitious plan to survey the whole country was never completed, but they did produce fine maps of thirty-three English and four Welsh counties between 1815 and 1830 before financial failure overtook them. Christopher (1786–1855) struggled on until 1840, when his stock-in-trade was dispersed at auction. He died in obscurity in Dalston, while John (1791–1867) returned to Yorkshire to find a career in making local estate maps. Their engravers, James and Josiah Neele, were also brothers — the sons of the prolific and successful mapmaker Samuel John Neele (1758–1824) of the Strand. Unresolved problems over his will laid additional financial pressures on them and their own partnership was formally dissolved in 1829. Josiah (1804–76) was declared insolvent in 1837. Ruff (1812–86) was primarily a stationer, born in Brixton, and with premises off Fleet Street. He specialised in map-mounting, spring-rollers, varnish and tracing-paper manufacture — and was able to retire in prosperity.

MAP
of
LONDON
From Actual Survey
HUMBLY DEDICATED TO
Her most Gracious Majesty
QUEEN VICTORIA.
REFERENCE to the PARISHES &c.

INTERNATIONAL BUT VERY BRITISH

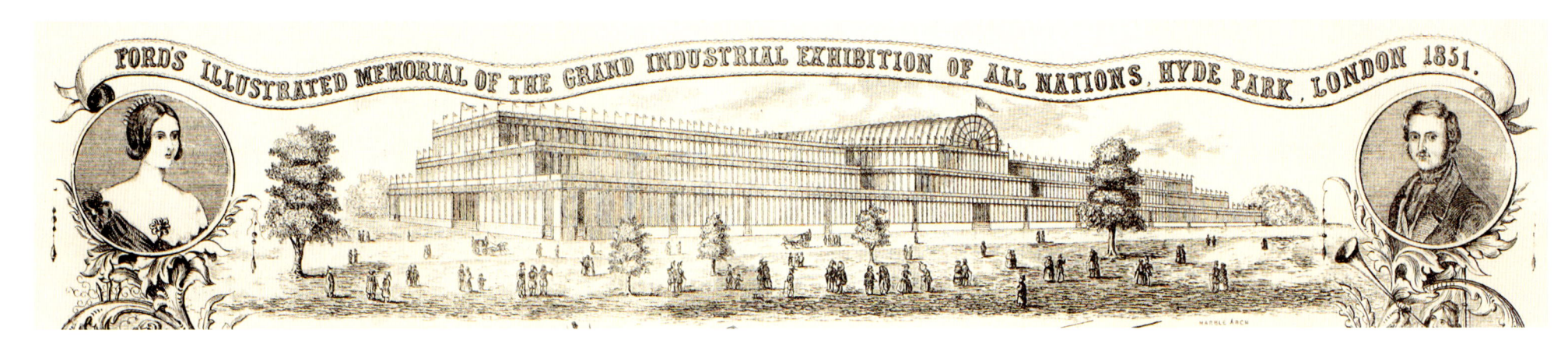

The Great Exhibition of 1851 marked the climax of efforts to present London as a world city. Oriented to the West so that Hyde Park and the Crystal Palace are at the top, this map is lined with depictions of the peoples of the world. They stand beneath Britannia and Fame, however, and the other illustrations reveal loyalty to the values of Victorian England with portraits of Victoria and Albert, and vignettes of buildings associated with the constitution, the law, education, Anglicanism, the theatre and commerce. Predictably the panorama of Bank of England, Royal Exchange (the third on the site) and Mansion House, the home of the Lord Mayor, at the bottom reflect the wealth and continuing commercial importance of the City.

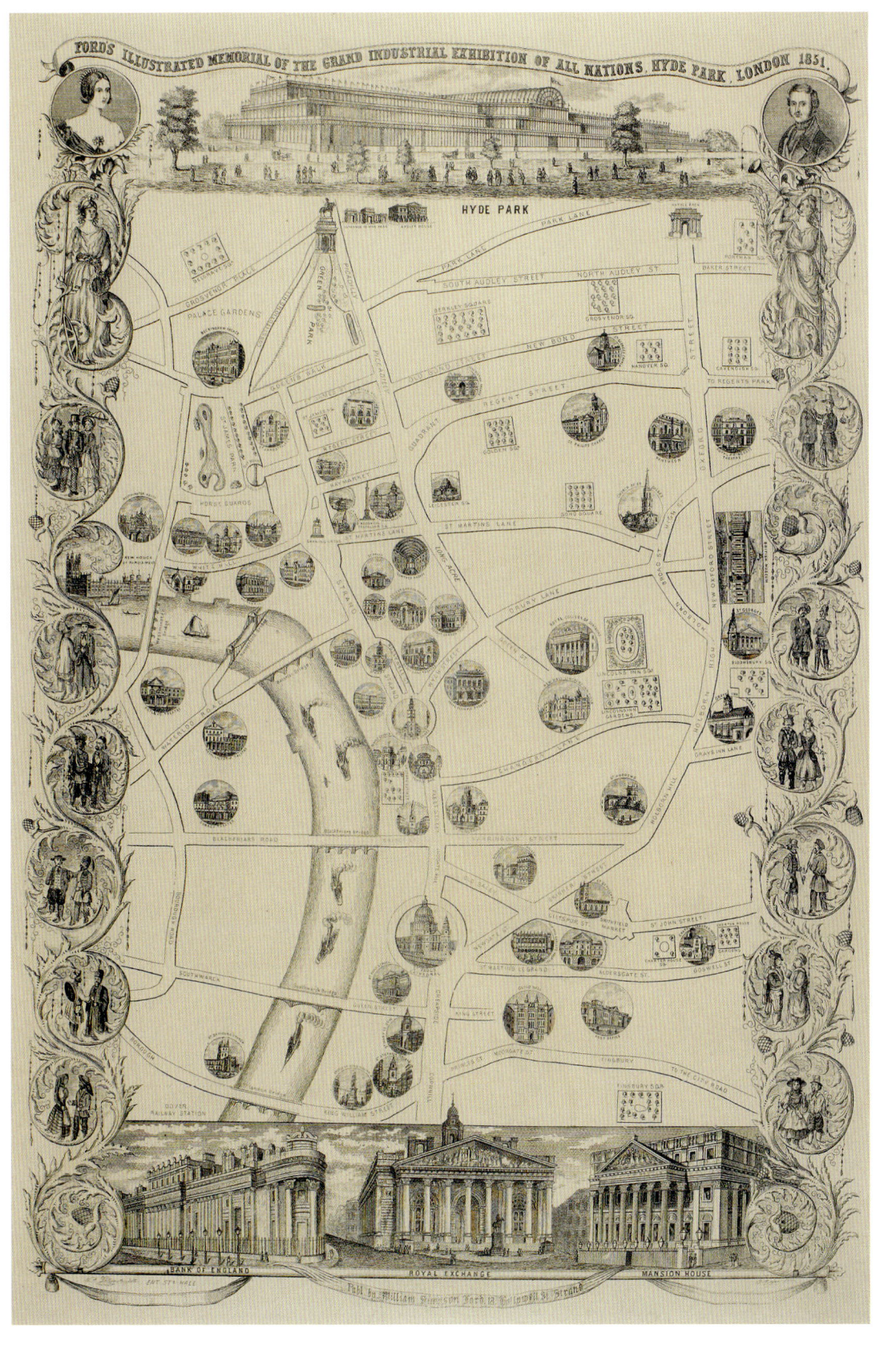

5.2.16   [William Simpson Ford] *Ford's Illustrated Memorial of the Grand Industrial Exhibition of all Nations, Hyde Park, London 1851.* Printed Map. 72 × 49.4 cm. Maps Crace VII.267

William Simpson Ford was a printseller with premises in Holywell Street off the Strand. He came originally from Lancashire and in 1851 was living over the shop with his wife Ann and two young sons.

SECTION SIX
THE MEAN STREETS OF VICTORIAN LONDON

Maps played a major role in Victorian London. As well as recording the face of a city that more than doubled in size and underwent significant administrative changes, maps were used to identify and analyse the causes of many of the metropolis's social problems, to suggest solutions and to monitor progress on the ground. It is no exaggeration to say that to some extent Londoners owed the improved health, housing, environmental and social provisions that they enjoyed by the time of Queen Victoria's death in 1901 to the clarity and succinctness with which a good map can present information.

6.1 UNBRIDLED GROWTH

London more than doubled in size and population between 1851 and 1901. Some influential Londoners were mentally prepared for this. Opposition from the City Corporation and other local vested interests, however, prevented the creation of the over-arching single authority for the whole London area that some radical reformers wished for. The desperate need to create a new sewage disposal system made possible the creation, in 1855, of the Metropolitan Board of Works. However, it was not directly elected and had very limited powers. In 1889 a County of London was founded within the Board's boundaries administered by an elected London County Council — but initially with no additional powers. In the meanwhile the built-up area had spread far into Essex and what was left of Middlesex.

E. Stanford, *A Map of the County of London...*
(London: E. Stanford, 1898). Detail

THE MARCH OF BRICKS AND MORTAR

George Cruikshank's cartoon, of robot-like houses and brick-ovens laying waste the countryside and putting terrified haystacks to flight as they advance on the heights of Hampstead, well represents the apprehension and powerlessness felt by middle classes owners of 'rural' parks and villas in the vicinity of London in face of what seemed to be irresistible urbanisation. In the year that this cartoon appeared, the first attempts were made to develop Hampstead Heath, leading to a campaign that was to continue until the passage of an act of parliament in 1871 ensuring the survival in perpetuity of Hampstead Heath as a public open space.

6.1.1 George Cruikshank, *London Going out of Town — or — the March of Bricks and Mortar* (1829) Hand-coloured printed cartoon from *Scraps and Sketches* (London: Reeves & Turner 1882). 37.7 × 36 cm. LR 271.a.7

A life more complex and contradictory than that of George Cruikshank (1792–1878) would be difficult to imagine, a hard-living moralist as convivial as he was quarrelsome. He remains one of the greatest English graphic satirists. Born and raised in Bloomsbury, he always remembered that his 'life school was in the street' of his native London.

LONDON going out of Town — or — The March of Bricks & mortar!

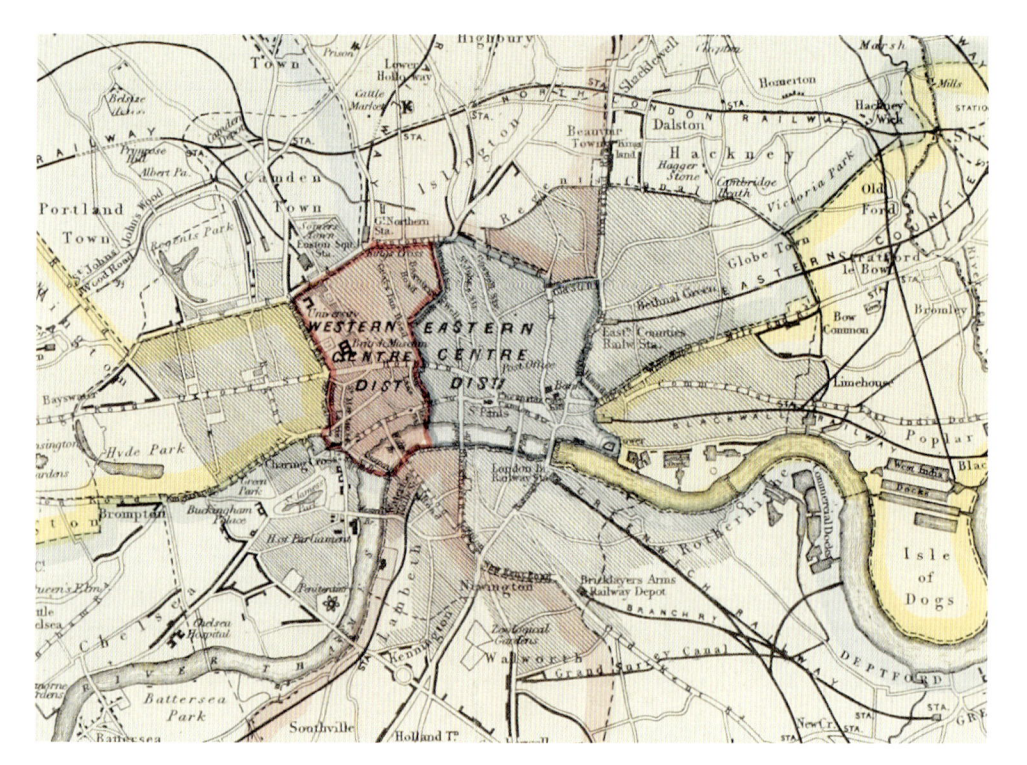

GREATER LONDON BEFORE ITS TIME

The postal reformer Rowland Hill was ahead of many of his contemporaries in thinking of the London region and the built-up area as a single district (though the Metropolitan Police area had been similarly defined in 1829). In 1855 Hill chaired a committee which decided that, to improve delivery times, local sorting offices should be created within a 12-mile radius of the General Post Office in the City. Each area was given a letter reflecting its geographical relationship to central London according to the points of the compass. Only two small districts, Eastern Centre and Western Centre, were totally urbanised. The new system came into operation in 1857. By 1870 suburbia had spread to areas beyond the 12-mile circle but those areas remain excluded from the compass point lettering system. The system included North-Eastern and Southern postal districts, no longer in use today.

6.1.2 *Sketch Map of the London Postal District with its subdivisions* (London: E. Stanford, 1856). Lithographed map. 68 × 69 cm. Maps 3485 (12)

The mapmaker and publisher Edward Stanford (1827–1904) was the son of a tailor and draper of Holborn Hill, educated at the City of London School. He trained as a printer and stationer but came to specialise in map production. He founded Stanford's Geographical Establishment in 1857 and was soon the leading map-retailer in London. The business survives in Long Acre, Covent Garden to the present day.

SKETCH MAP
OF THE
LONDON POSTAL DISTRICT
WITH ITS
SUBDIVISIONS
1856.

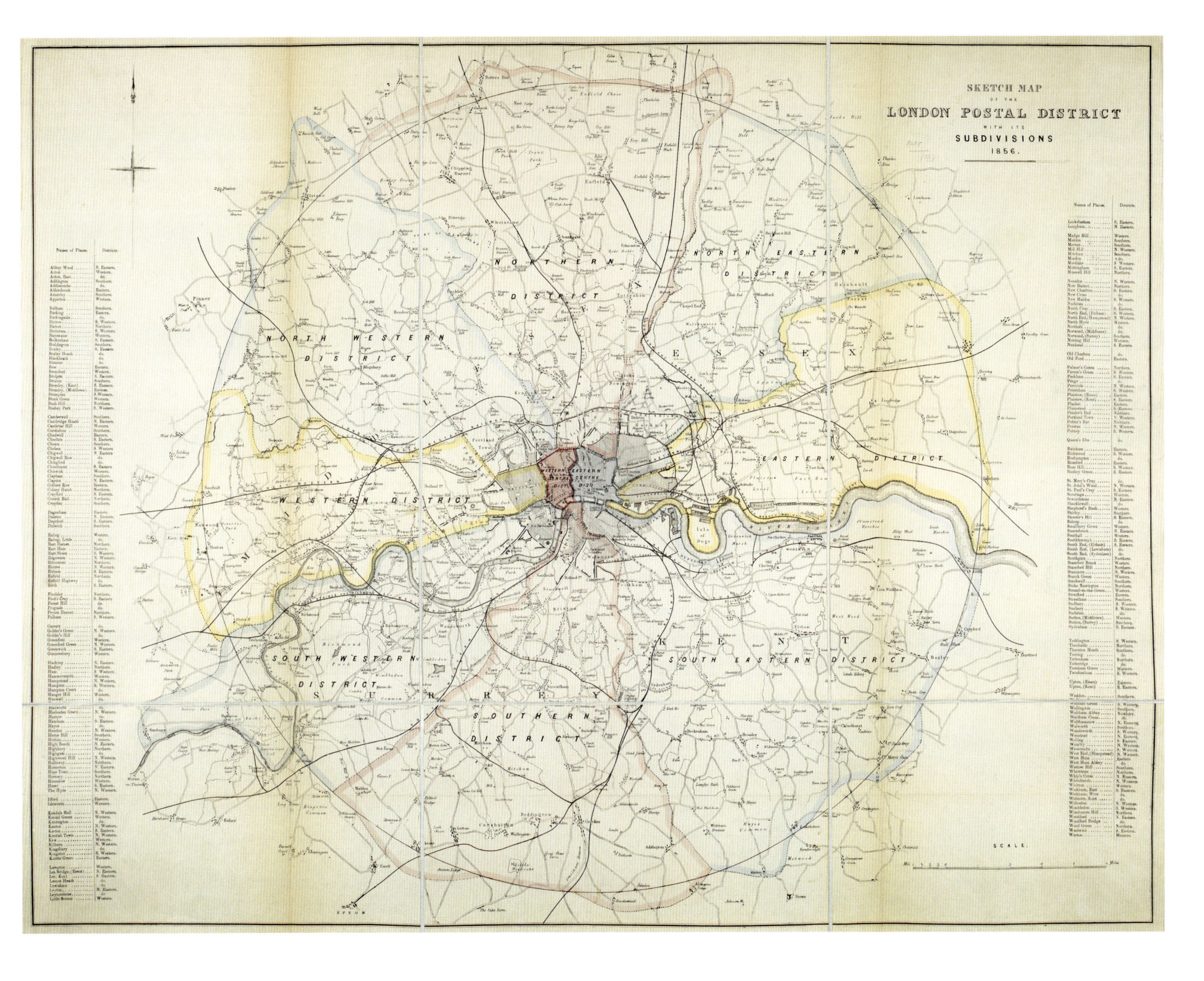

THE REALITY OF LONDON

In comparison with the generous boundaries of the London Postal District, the built-up area of London in the 1850s seems minute. It effectively stops at Regent's Park, Hyde Park, Battersea, Blackwall, Islington and Kentish Town. Its population was now 2.3 million with only 300,000 people living in the surrounding countryside. In the following year the first London-wide authority, the Metropolitan Board of Works, was to be created but it was dependent on the existing vestries which elected its members and it had few powers. The City retained its independence, despite its declining population, and a complicated network of other bodies remained responsible for different aspects of Londoners' lives.

6.1.3   *Davies's New Map of the British Metropolis the boundaries of the boroughs, county court districts, railways, and modern improvements* (London: E. Stanford [1854]). Steel-plate printed map. 97 × 94 cm. Maps 3480 (142)

For Benjamin Rees Davies see 5.2.13 and for Edward Stanford 6.1.2 above.

DAVIES'S NEW MAP OF THE BRITISH METROPOLIS

A COUNTY IN NAME ONLY

A county of London administered by the London County Council was created in 1889. This map, highlighting the constituent district boards of works (replaced by boroughs in 1899), exudes civic pride. A table at the top right gives details of its population — approaching 4.5 million. However the LCC's boundaries, being those of the Metropolitan Board of Works, took no account of the enormous growth of London since 1855. There were an additional 2 million people in the built-up area beyond the county (and the map)'s borders. Moreover the LCC's powers were as limited as those of its predecessor: numerous other, often conflicting, bodies were still involved in the administration of London as the table makes clear.

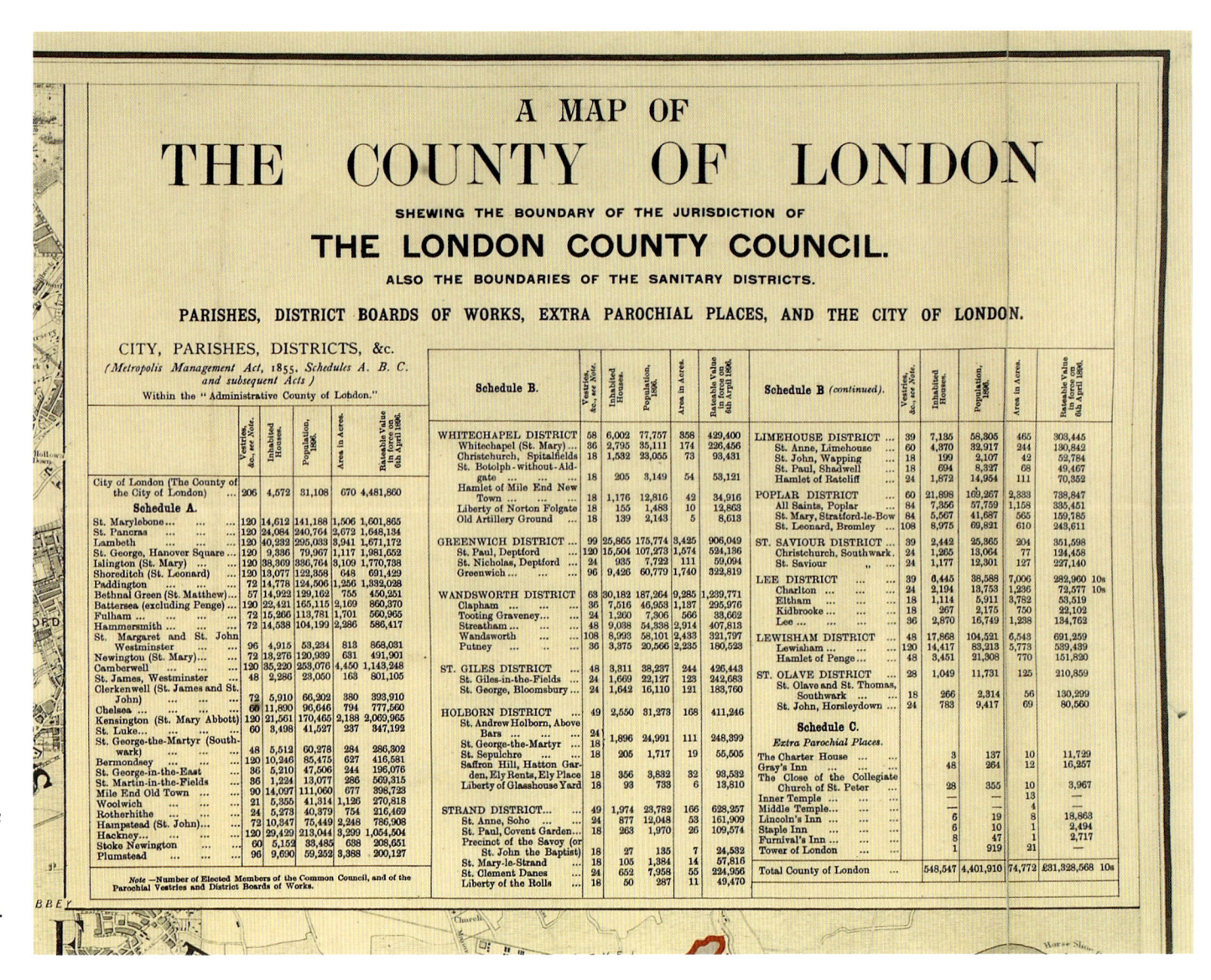

6.1.4 E. Stanford, *A Map of the County of London shewing the boundary of the jurisdiction of the London County Council also the boundaries of the sanitary districts* (London: E. Stanford, 1898). Chromo-lithographed map. 68.5 × 102.2 cm. Maps 3485 (120)

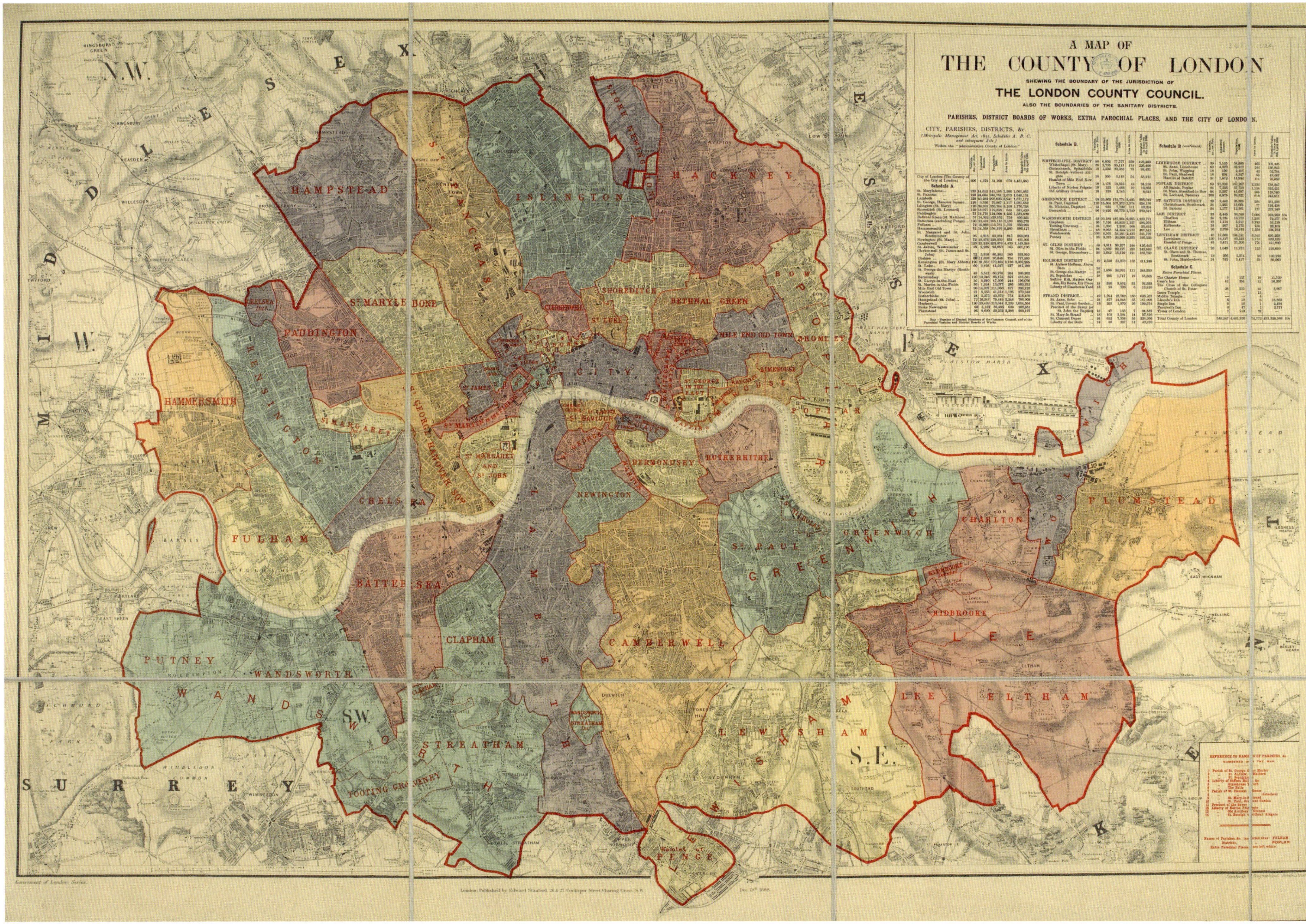

A MAP OF
THE COUNTY OF LONDON
SHEWING THE BOUNDARY OF THE JURISDICTION OF
THE LONDON COUNTY COUNCIL.
ALSO THE BOUNDARIES OF THE SANITARY DISTRICTS.
PARISHES, DISTRICT BOARDS OF WORKS, EXTRA PAROCHIAL PLACES, AND THE CITY OF LONDON.
N.W.
MIDDLESEX
ESSEX
SURREY
KENT
S.W.
S.E.
HAMPSTEAD
ST PANCRAS
ISLINGTON
HACKNEY
ST MARYLEBONE
PADDINGTON
KENSINGTON
HAMMERSMITH
SHOREDITCH
BETHNAL GREEN
MILE END OLD TOWN
BROMLEY
POPLAR
LIMEHOUSE
CITY
ST LUKE
CLERKENWELL
ST JAMES
ST MARGARET AND ST JOHN
ST GEORGE HANOVER SQR.
CHELSEA
FULHAM
BATTERSEA
LAMBETH
NEWINGTON
BERMONDSEY
ROTHERHITHE
ST PAUL
GREENWICH
CHARLTON
PLUMSTEAD
WOOLWICH
LEE
KIDBROOKE
ELTHAM
CAMBERWELL
CLAPHAM
PUTNEY
WANDSWORTH
STREATHAM
TOOTING GRAVENEY
LEWISHAM
PENGE

6.2 HARD TIMES

London had been notoriously smoky, foggy, smelly, noisy, insanitary and overcrowded since 1550 but living conditions in early Victorian London were in some respects possibly worse than they had been hundreds of years earlier. London lacked the infrastructure and at first, the knowledge, to cope with the consequences for the inhabitants, rich and poor, of industrialisation, mass immigration from Britain's countryside and abroad, overcrowding and hitherto unknown illnesses, notably cholera. The Victorian period, however, was the golden age of the thematic map that depicted the geographical spread of features or phenomena that were as often social, ethnographical or medical as physical. Such maps identified, illustrated and dramatised London's numerous problems, and sometimes incidentally, sometimes intentionally, increased the pressure on decision-makers to take action.

Detail from Henry Vizetelly, *The Grand Panorama of London from the Thames* (London: Charles Evans, 1844)

HELL ON EARTH?

John Loveday, the Phoenix Assurance Company's surveyor of risks, altruistically published these early printed fire insurance plans, for the use of all fire insurance companies. He introduced colouring conventions that were to become standard with pink for brick, yellow for timber, yellow-ochre for brick and timber and blue for glass. Such plans give a detailed picture of the horrendous living conditions endured in parts of London in early Victorian times. Here, on the south bank of the Thames, a dwelling house (R) is shown only a stone's throw away from an enormous (200 feet long) old timber building serving as a tar and turpentine store (M). Directly opposite is a large sea biscuit bakery with no less than eight ovens (O). On the other side of the lane to the left (North) by the Thames and behind the dwelling house are further tar and turpentine stores housed in brick buildings (D, U), nestling cheek-by-jowl with buildings (E, F) containing two 26 horse-power engines running millstones that were in operation 24 hours a day. Directly behind the dwelling house are large gas works (B) and stagnant and presumably stinking water from a blocked-up former mill stream.

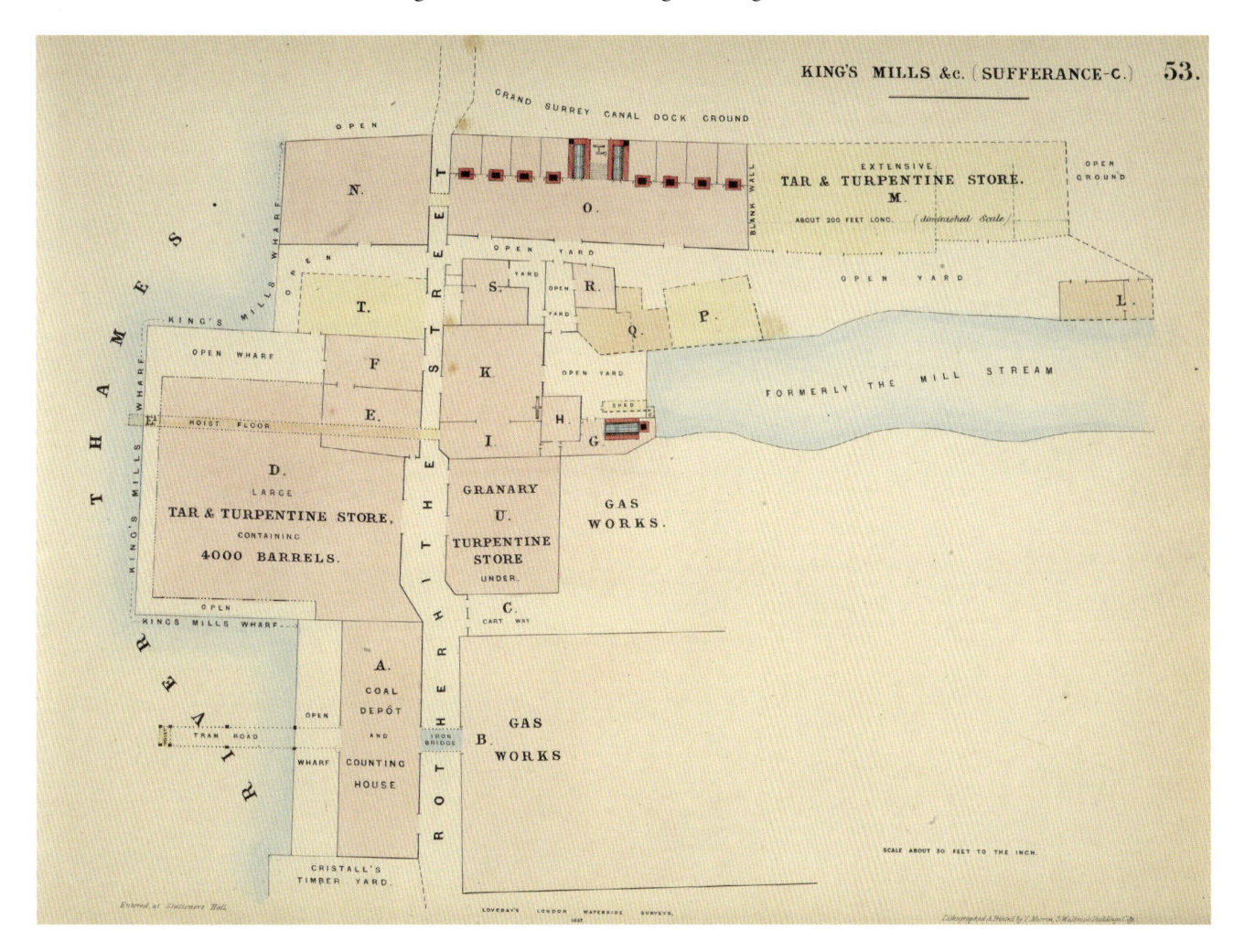

6.2.1   John Thomas Loveday, 'Kings Mills Wharf, Warehouses, Granary and Sea-Biscuit Bakery' from Loveday's *London Waterside Surveys for the use of Fire Insurance Companies*... Lithographed by T. Morrow. (London, 1857) Lithograph with watercolour. 28.5 × 77 cm. (opening) Maps 4 b.1, page 53

The plans were lithographed and printed by Thomas Morrow (1817–78), himself no stranger to life at the margins of the Victorian city — he was born in Whitechapel and lived at Mile End before moving out to Tottenham.

229

LONDON DIRT

In order to tempt readers away from the *Illustrated London News* in 1844 the editor of the *Pictorial Times*, Henry Vizetelly, commissioned a 12-foot (4 metre)-long *Grand Panorama of London and the Thames from Westminster to St Katharine's Dock*. Soon afterwards the panorama was issued as a separate publication, selling for 1 shilling and sixpence (7.5p). It harks back to Visscher's panorama of 1616 in format, but this London is one of warehouses, steamboats, gas works and factory chimneys, most of them identified, growing in number as one proceeds eastwards. One can almost feel the dirt, dust and pollution.

6.2.2   Left section of Henry Vizetelly, *The Grand Panorama of London from the Thames* (London: Charles Evans, 1844). Woodcut. 16.5 × 396 cm. Maps 42.a.30

Henry Richard Vizetelly (1820–94), journalist and publisher, was the son and grandson of London printers who claimed descent from an ancient Venetian family. First trained as a wood-engraver, he had helped found the *Illustrated London News* before setting up the *Pictorial Times*. He worked as a journalist in Paris for much of his life but returned to London, resumed publishing, and became a hero of the fight for a free press by bringing out translations of the best of recent European fiction (including the novels of Flaubert, Daudet, Dostoievsky and Tolstoy). He subsequently suffered imprisonment and humiliation for publishing those of Zola — novels branded at the time by the Solicitor-General as works of 'bestial obscenity'.

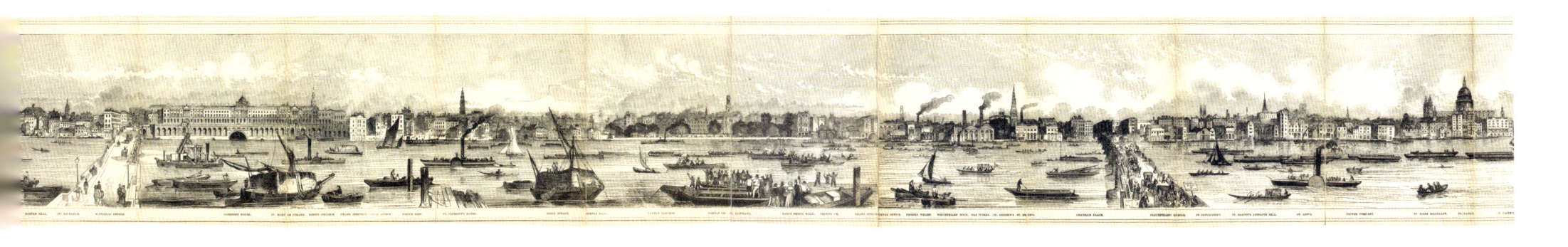

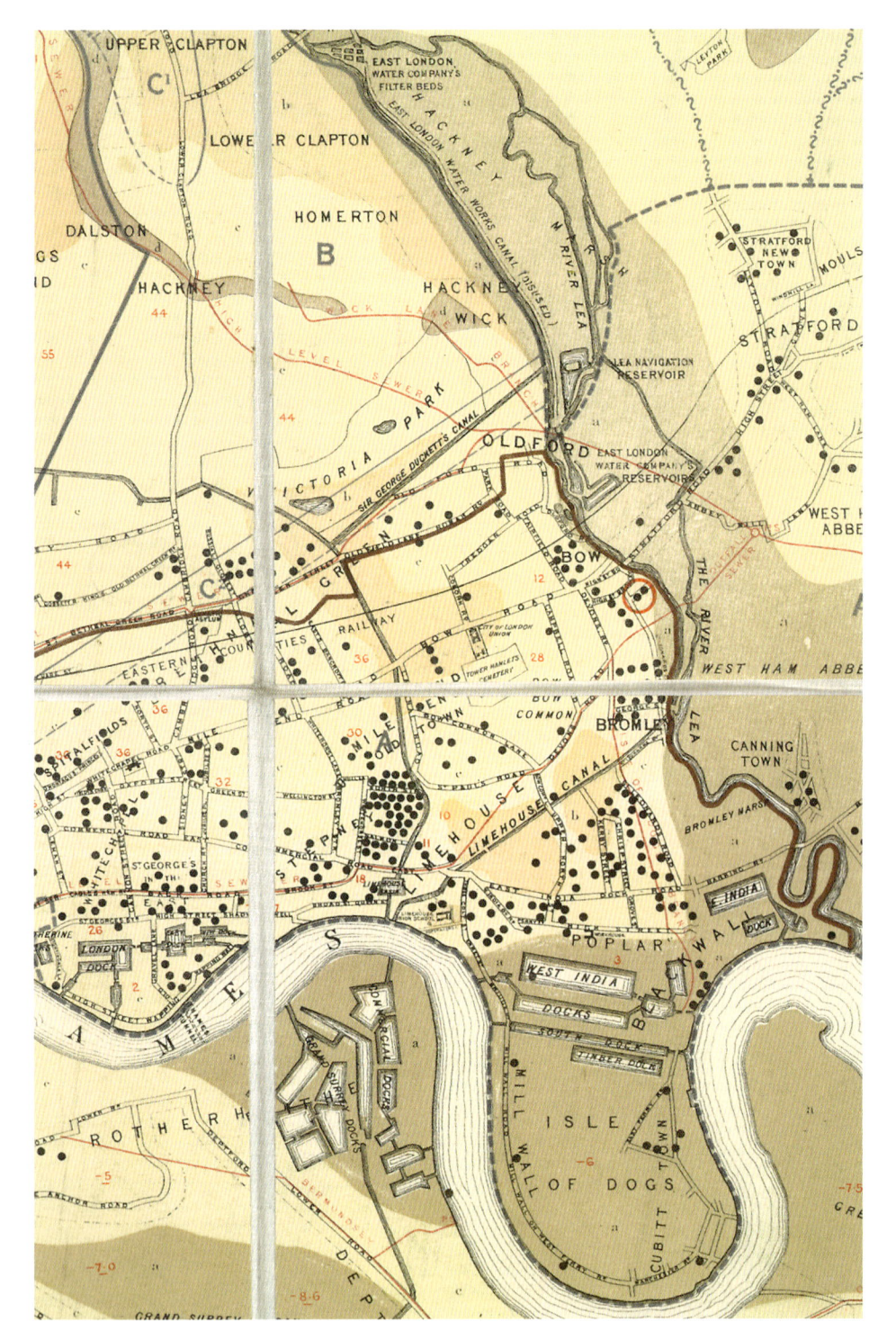

MAPPING THE CAUSE OF CHOLERA

Cholera first ravaged London in 1832. There were repeated outbreaks in the following years. In the mid-1850s, Dr John Snow, utilising an outbreak in the Soho area as a test case, had produced strong arguments, supported by maps, suggesting that the disease was carried in sewage-infested water. The weight of medical opinion, however, was unconvinced, considering the maps to be partisan and misleading and debates continued as to the causes of cholera. A detailed official report was produced immediately after another severe outbreak in the East End in 1866. The compiler of the accompanying map used one of the earliest accurate geological maps of London to investigate various hypotheses. One was that the disease was air-borne and linked to the nature of the soil, hence the need for the geological map which, however, showed no correlation between soil type and incidents of cholera. Another theory was that the fault lay with the pipes used by the water companies, so a red line marks the boundaries of the respective water companies, again without demonstrating any connection. But the map did convincingly demonstrate that all the victims had drunk water supplied from the Old Ford reservoir of the East London Water Company at Bow, as indicated by the broken dark grey line (the area east of the River Lea was still rural, explaining the paucity of black dots there). The map thus helped to confirm the truth of John Snow's controversial theories, and finally led to action being taken.

6.2.3 *Map showing the distribution of Cholera in London and its Environs from June 27th to July 21st 1866 Map 1* (Day & Son, 1867). From the [9th] Report of the Medical Officer of the Privy Council for 1866. Signed by J. N. Radcliffe. Coloured lithograph, 61 × 87.5 cm. Maps 3485 (41)

The map was among the last of the productions of the firm of Day & Son — the firm founded by William Day and Louis Haghe in the 1820s and the most famous and artistically successful London lithographic printing-house of the period. For all the magnificent work the firm had produced, the business failed later in 1867.

TO ILLUSTRATE MR RADCLIFFE'S REPORT.
MAP I.
MAP
SHOWING THE DISTRIBUTION OF
CHOLERA
IN
LONDON AND ITS ENVIRONS,
FROM JUNE 27TH TO JULY 21ST 1866.
REFERENCE.
The earliest deaths from Cholera (June 27th)
Deaths from Cholera & Choleraic diarrhœa from June 30th to July 21st
Limits of the East London Water Companys supply. Where continuous the line shows the district (B) supplied from the Lea Bridge Reservoirs. Where broken the line shows the districts (A) supplied from the Old Ford Reservoirs. Where both dotted and broken the line indicates a locality which is partly supplied from Old Ford. Where the line is drawn by notes of interrogation (???) it indicates rural districts supplied to an uncertain and comparatively small extent from Old Ford. The slighter marked continuous and broken lines indicate districts (C) supplied indifferently and to an undetermined extent from both the Lea Bridge and the Old Ford Reservoirs.
Shows the district in which the Metropolitan Main Drainage System was not in operation in July 1866.
Simple red figures express in feet the average elevation (e.g. 82) or depression (e.g. -79) of the several Registration Districts within which they stand as compared with Trinity High Water mark, and similar figures underlined (e.g. 97 or -8.6) express the actual elevation or depression of the spot where they stand.
Boundary line of houses Metropolitan Area and immediate environs
Shows the Metropolitan Main Sewers
J. N. Radcliffe.
GEOLOGICAL REFERENCE.
(The Geology from the Map of Mr Mylne and from the Geological Survey.)
Alluvium & Peat a
Brick Earth b
Gravel & Sand c
London Clay d
Pebble-bed e
Striped Sands f
Shelly Clays g
Sands & Mottled Clays h
Thanet Sand i
Chalk j
Scale 2 Inches to 1 Mile.
TOTTENHAM
HORNSEY
HIGHGATE
HAMPSTEAD
WALTHAMSTOW
LEYTON
WANSTEAD
ILFORD
STRATFORD
HACKNEY
ISLINGTON
KENTISH TOWN
HOXTON
BOW
WEST HAM
BARKING
PLAISTOW
MARYLEBONE
REGENT'S PARK
HYDE PARK
HAMMERSMITH
BROMPTON
CHELSEA
WESTMINSTER
BERMONDSEY
ROTHERHITHE
POPLAR
ISLE OF DOGS
NORTH WOOLWICH
GREENWICH
CHARLTON
PLUMSTEAD
DEPTFORD
NEW CROSS
BLACKHEATH
LEWISHAM
LEE
ELTHAM
PECKHAM
CAMBERWELL
KENNINGTON
BRIXTON
CLAPHAM
BATTERSEA
FULHAM
BARNES
PUTNEY
WANDSWORTH
ROEHAMPTON
CHISWICK
THAMES
Day & Son (Limited) Lith London WC

POVERTY IN LONDON

Charles Booth, a wealthy Liverpool businessman, was sceptical about a socialist claim in 1885 that a quarter of the London population lived in extreme poverty, so he employed teams of young people to investigate. Partly through interviews and partly from census returns and School Board visitors' records, they concluded that the true figure was 30%. The findings were entered by hand onto a very detailed 'Master Map' using seven colour categories ranging from black for 'Lowest class, vicious, semi-criminal', through blues, purple, pink and red to gold for wealthy. Significantly, perhaps, there was no category for excessive, ill-gotten, semi-criminal wealth. This sheet shows the variety to be found in Westminster. The published report and maps which appeared from 1891 were taken seriously. The first Council houses were built shortly afterwards.

6.2.4   Sheet 34, showing part of Westminster, from the 'Master Map' of London poverty. Watercolour on sheets of the 1st edition (1869) Ordnance Survey, 25-inches-to-a-mile (1:2500) map. 64.2 × 48 cm. Museum of London. 27.120/1 ah (Courtesy of the City of London, Museum of London)

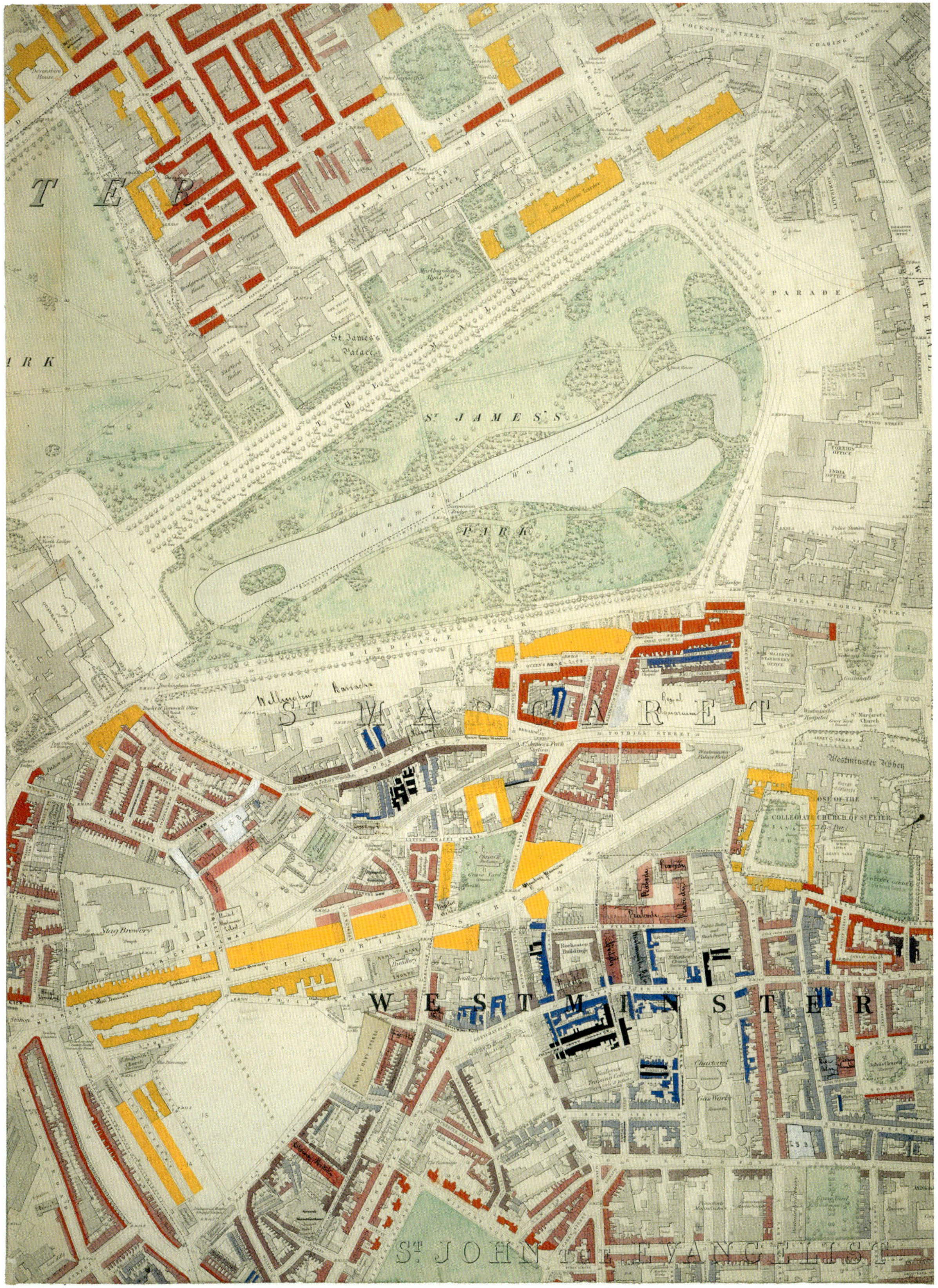
St. James's Palace
St. JAMES'S
PARK
PARADE
BIRDCAGE WALK
GREAT GEORGE STREET
St. MARGARET
Westminster Abbey
Stag Brewery
WESTMINSTER
St. JOHN THE EVANGELIST

ARRIVING FROM ABROAD

From 1881 up to 7000 poor Jews a year, escaping Tsarist persecution in Russia and Poland, found refuge in the East End. Their strange appearance, customs, Yiddish language and readiness to take on jobs at subsistence wages aroused hostility. This map was designed by the person who was responsible for Booth's poverty maps and, like them, it was based on School Board visitors' statistics. It accompanies a book that sought to present a balanced picture. The map itself, however, fails to achieve that objective. The title itself gives the impression that the area shown must have been predominantly Jewish. That this was not the case would only have been apparent from closer examination for which the casual viewer may not have had time. By featuring the few streets that were already 95% Jewish, moreover, and showing them in colours which on Booth's Poverty Maps verged on 'vicious semi-criminal poverty', it transmitted alarmist messages about the character and morals of the Jewish inhabitants, about the future of the district and probably fuelled the racism that led to the passing of the 1905 Aliens Act aimed at reducing Jewish immigration to a trickle. In fact, at the time the overall Jewish presence in Stepney was only 18% and it never seems to have exceeded that percentage.

6.2.5   George E. Arkell, *Jewish East London* in C. Russell and H. S. Lewis, *The Jew in London: A Study of Racial Character and Present-Day Conditions being two essays prepared for the Toynbee Trustees* (London: T. Fisher Unwin, 1900). Chromo-lithographed map. 38 × 56 cm. (within neat lines) 04034.ee.33

George Edward Arkell (1857–1926) was born in Pimlico — the son of a London cab-driver — there can be few better basic qualifications for mapping London. He worked originally in publishing, but by this period was employed as a private secretary. He conducted numerous interviews for Booth — speaking to tailors, hatters, boot-makers, wood-workers and others — and toured the poorer streets (escorted by policemen) to make notes. Notebooks, sketch-maps, and letters survive in the library of the London School of Economics.

Jewish East London

This Map shows by Colour the proportion of the Jewish population to other residents of East London, street by street, in 1899.

EXPLANATION OF COLOURING.

Proportion of Jews indicated

- 95% to 100%
- 75% and less than 95%
- 50% and less than 75%
- 25% and less than 50%
- 5% and less than 25%
- Less than 5% of Jews.

NOTE.—In all streets coloured blue the Jews form a majority of the inhabitants; in those coloured red, the Gentiles predominate.

ARRIVING FROM THE SHIRES

The 1891 first edition of Booth's report on life and labour in London included some rather more conventional maps, such as this one, derived from the 1881 census, showing the percentages of Londoners who had been born in other parts of Britain. In the outer suburbs and in Kensington they constituted up to 60% of the total population. If this seems surprising for such affluent areas, one only needs to refer back to the Poverty Map of Westminster (page 235) where the mews behind the grand houses are shown as occupied by the poor who were almost certainly servants: the former country people on this map seem to a great extent also to have been domestic servants. Immigration from the countryside was an age-old phenomenon, though the serious agricultural depression at the time probably increased the numbers. It serves as a reminder that throughout its history London has kept going only thanks to newcomers.

6.2.6 *A Map of London showing the proportion of the inhabitants of each registration sub-district in 1881, born in other parts of the United Kingdom* (1891) from Charles Booth, *Life and Labour in London* (London: Macmillan & Co., 1891) 35 × 44 cm. 08275.bb.5 vol. 2

A MAP OF LONDON
SHOWING THE PROPORTION OF THE INHABITANTS
OF EACH REGISTRATION SUB-DISTRICT IN 1881,
BORN IN OTHER PARTS OF THE UNITED KINGDOM.

Under 20 per cent.
From 20 to 30 per cent.
" 30 " 40 "
" 40 " 50 "
" 50 " 60 "

NOTE.—The statistics upon which this map is based are given in appendix B.7.

6.3 THE COMING OF THE RAILWAYS

Railways arrived on the fringes of London from 1836. It was a further 20 years before they were allowed to penetrate the inner city. The opportunity was taken for slum clearance and comprehensive redevelopment, but in the process there was devastation. Nearly 37,000 Londoners lost their homes between 1859 and 1867. Newly constructed working-class suburbs only became viable with the introduction of subsidised workmen's tickets in the 1860s and even then it was the clerks who benefited. The livelihoods of the labourers and other casual workers who had lost their homes through the clearances depended on them being available for employment in the inner city. Slum clearance meant that the remaining slums just became even more crowded.

THE FIRST RAILWAY STATIONS

In 1846 the publishers of the newly-founded *Illustrated London Advertiser*, playing on the popularity of railways, tried to whip up custom by offering subscribers this free map, an amended version of one published in 1842. By 1846 there were already eight stations around London, though none was permitted into the centre. Six are depicted along the sides of the map, generally and rather confusingly identified by the names of their destinations rather than by the actual names (e.g. Euston Station is called Birmingham). The London panorama at the top includes a fantasy railway bridge. At the bottom there is a daunting array of statistics about London derived from the 1841 census.

6.3.1 George Biggs, *The Railway Bell and the Illustrated London Advertiser Map of London* (London: 1846). Wood engraving. 78.5 × 96 cm. Maps Crace VII.251

THE RAILWAY BELL AND
ILLUSTRATED LONDON ADVERTISER
MAP of LONDON
PUBLISHED AT 335, STRAND, OPPOSITE SOMERSET HOUSE.
SCALE OF ONE MILE
BIRMINGHAM RAILWAY
REGENTS PARK
HYDE PARK
SERPENTINE RIVER
GREEN PARK
VICTORIA PARK
LONDON DOCK
WEST INDIA DOCKS
ISLE OF DOGS
BATTERSEA FIELDS
GRAND SURRY CANAL
DOVER
SOUTHAMPTON
PRESENTED GRATUITOUSLY to the SUBSCRIBERS of the RAILWAY BELL and ILLUSTRATED LONDON ADVERTISER
1819
1819

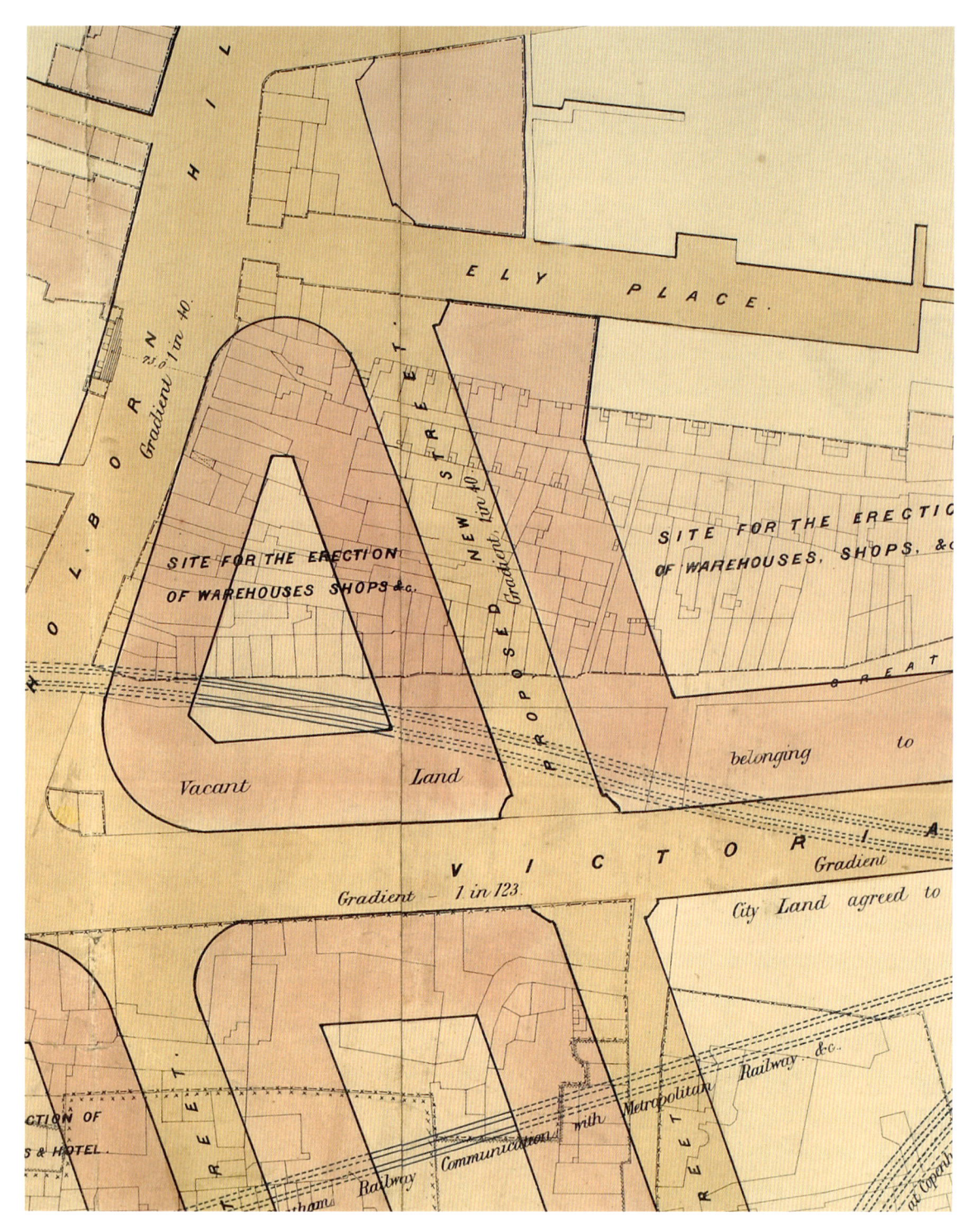

STATIONS IN PLACE OF SLUMS

Railways and railway stations forced themselves into the centre of London from 1860. This radical proposal shows a new station, approximately on the site of today's City Thameslink station, and other street improvements intended to expand and improve access Smithfield, then as now London's main meat market. To give an idea of the demolition work involved, the plans are superimposed in pink and yellow on a map showing the existing situation. This included the location of some of London's worst slums or 'rookeries', like Saffron Hill formerly on the banks of the Fleet Ditch, where Dickens placed Fagin's den. When building started on a variant of these ideas, only the owners of the buildings were compensated. No provision was made for the people who lost their homes. They moved to the surviving slums which became worse.

6.3.2   J. A. Cumming, *Proposed Plan for improving the approaches to the Metropolitan Meat Market, Smithfield and Railway Stations, and for reducing the acclivities of Holborn Hill, Skinner Street &c.* (1860). Coloured printed map 76.1 × 106 cm. Maps 3495 (61)

PROPOSED PLAN
FOR IMPROVING THE APPROACHES TO THE
METROPOLITAN MEAT MARKET, SMITHFIELD,
AND
RAILWAY STATIONS,
AND FOR
REDUCING THE ACCLIVITIES OF HOLBORN HILL, SKINNER STREET, &c.

L. A. Bunning, Architect.
Guildhall, 15th Oct.r 1860.

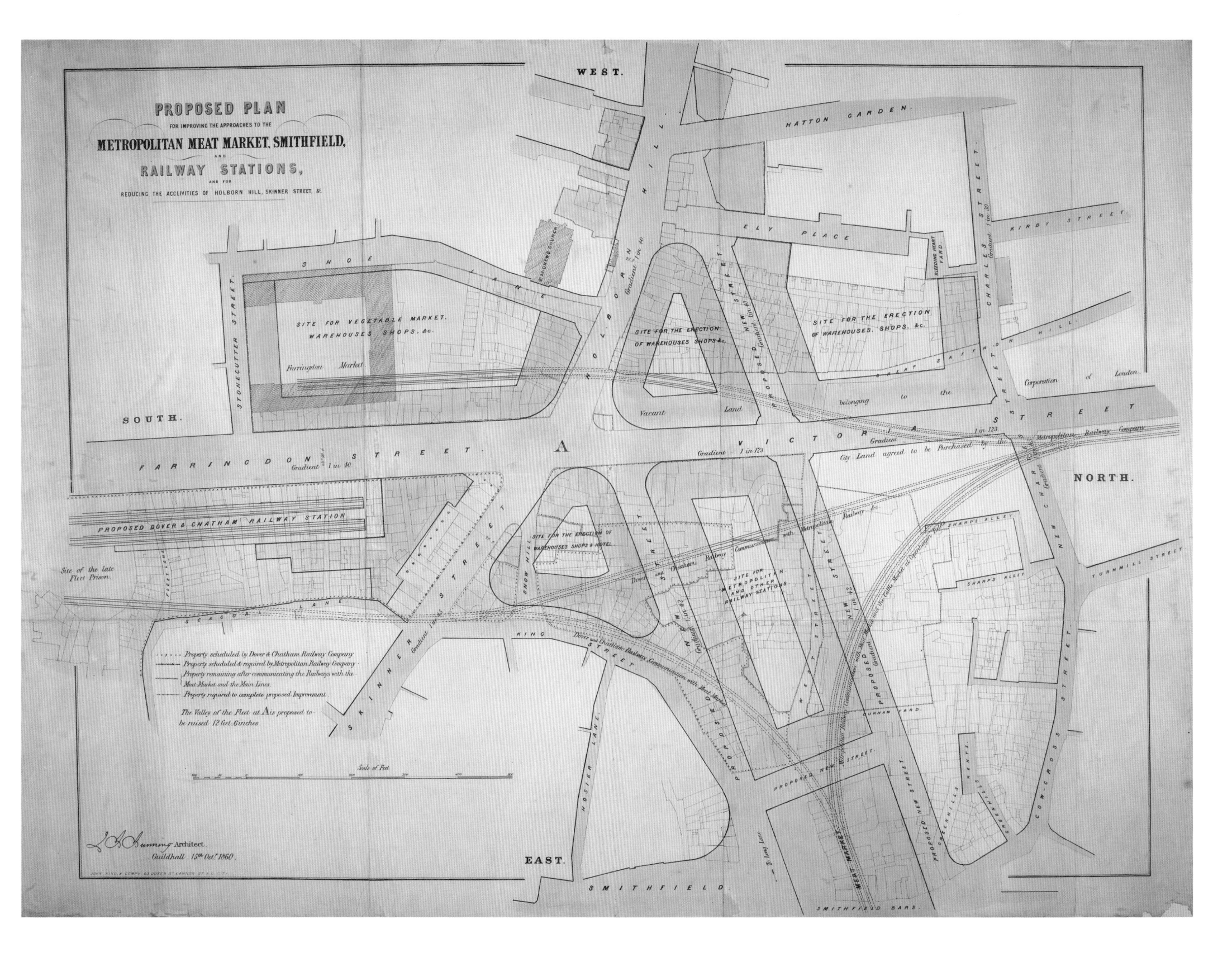

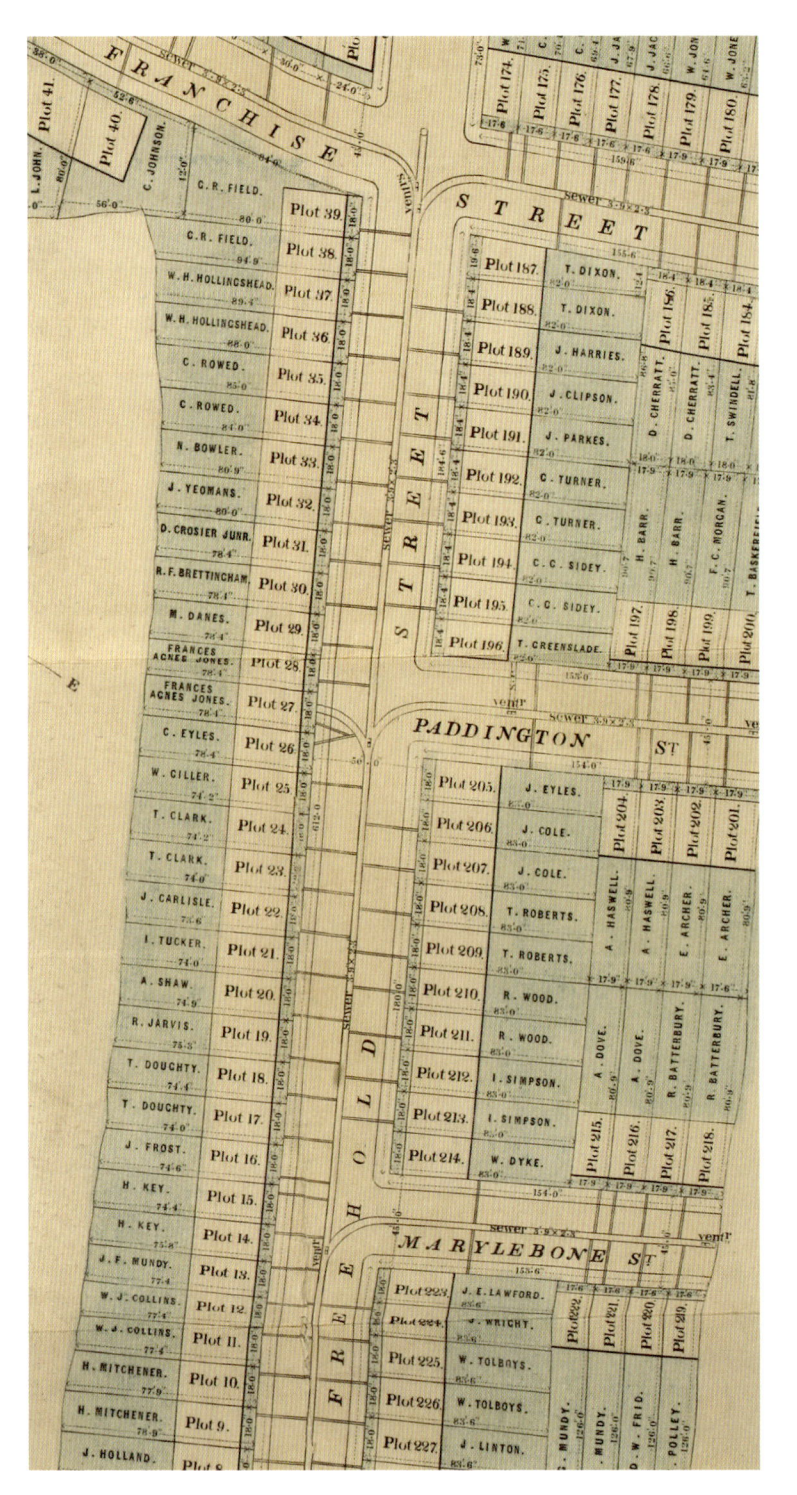

RAILWAY DEMOCRATISATION

Even after the passing of the 1832 Reform Act, the vote was limited to wealthy male property owners. Railways however brought reasonably-priced building land, a short distance from town, within reach of lower middle-class Londoners and offered them the hope of political emancipation. The political parties, which were gradually being transformed into the mass organisations that we know today, were quick to sense that this could be turned to their advantage. Land (the ancestors of today's building) societies linked to the political parties came into existence to buy land, build houses and make loans available to so that London clerks could buy them. The St Pancras, Marylebone and Paddington Freehold Land Society bought two meadows bordered by Hornsey Road and Seven Sisters Road in Islington. 'Reform', 'Franchise', 'Liberty', and 'Freehold' Streets reflect the Society's political aspirations. These were to be realised under the terms of the 1867 Reform Act. Once built however, the streets soon received the more prosaic names of Alsen, Andover, Victor, and Durham.

6.3.3 *Plan of the Long Lands Estate: the Property of the St Pancras, Marylebone and Paddington Freehold Land Society 1851*. Lithographed map with watercolour. 62.5 × 48 cm. Maps 3465 (2)

The map was produced by the engraver and printer Charles George Sidey (1818–63), a young Londoner whose ownership of two plots in Freehold Street is marked on the map. His own life demonstrates the movement out to the suburbs — born close to the City in the parish of St Luke Old Street, living in Camden Town with his wife and two young children in 1851, and farther out still at Finchley by 1861.

PLAN
OF THE
LONG LANDS ESTATE,
THE PROPERTY OF THE
ST PANCRAS, MARYLEBONE AND PADDINGTON
FREEHOLD LAND SOCIETY.
1851.

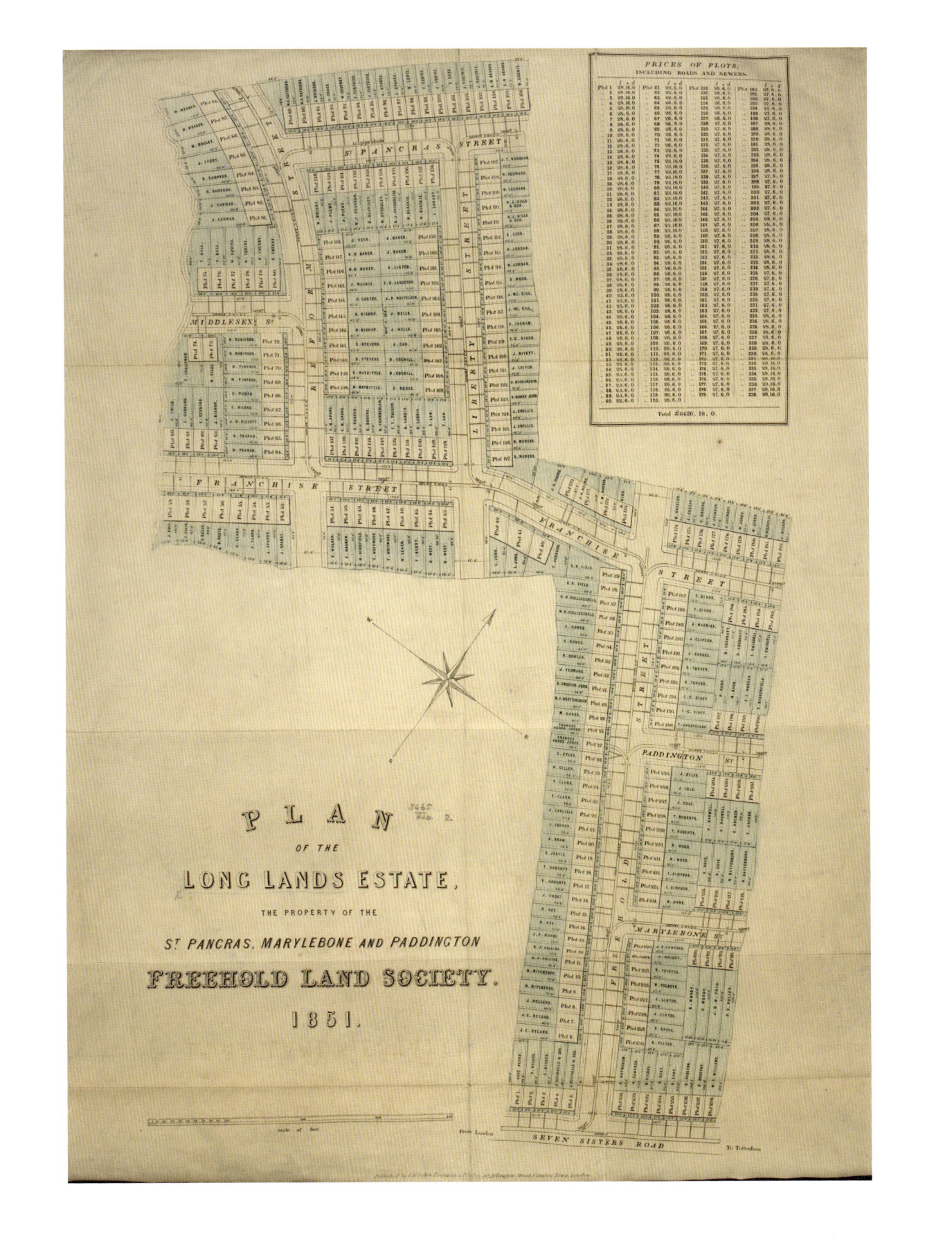

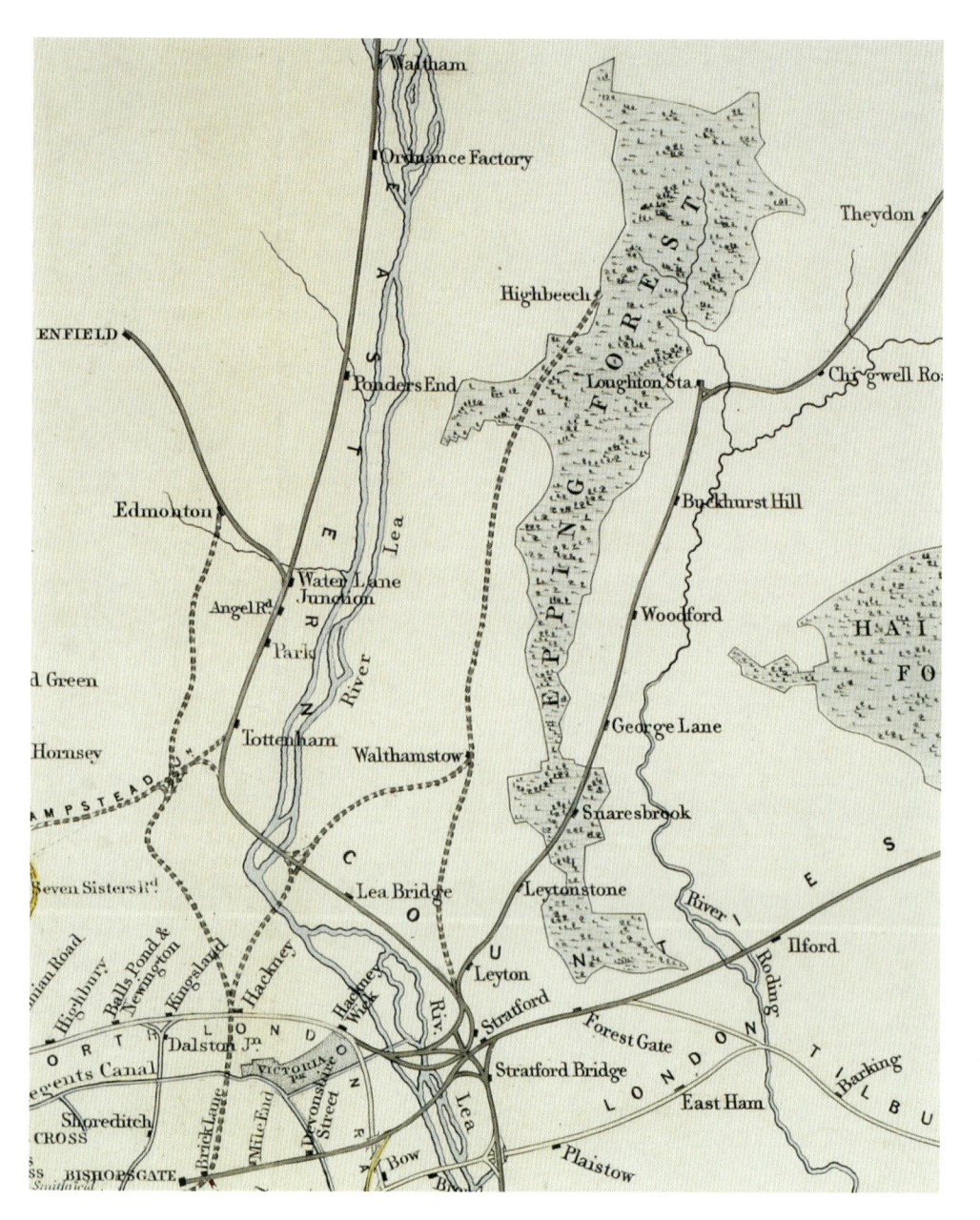

RAILWAYS, SUBURBS AND OPEN SPACES

By 1867 the railways had expanded far outside London and cheap, two-penny, workers' tickets had been introduced. Working-class suburbs were soon to be built close to the new stations, with the character of country villages like Tottenham being radically altered in the process. This map emphasises the railway lines, including some that were still only projected, like the Highgate to Alexandra Palace line, at the expense of all but the most essential geographical features. Significantly these include major open spaces like the South London commons and Epping Forest — the 'lungs of London' — which the predominantly middle-class Commons Preservation Society had just begun fighting to preserve, primarily, they said, for the benefit of the labouring classes.

6.3.4 *Macaulay's Metropolitan Railway Map* (1867 edn). Lithographed map. 42.7 × 52.5 cm. Maps 3480 (201)

Zachary Macaulay was born in the East Indies about 1815 and worked as Secretary to the Railway Clearing House. Although he died in 1860, copyright in his maps of the London and British railway systems was inherited by his widow, Mary Macaulay, and the maps continued to appear in his name for many years. The present map was drawn by J. E. Dawson and John Bockett and first published in 1859. Bockett was born in Bloomsbury about 1826 and in 1861 was a clerk at the Railway Clearing House, living in Kentish Town and supplementing his income by acting as an agent for chemical apparatus.

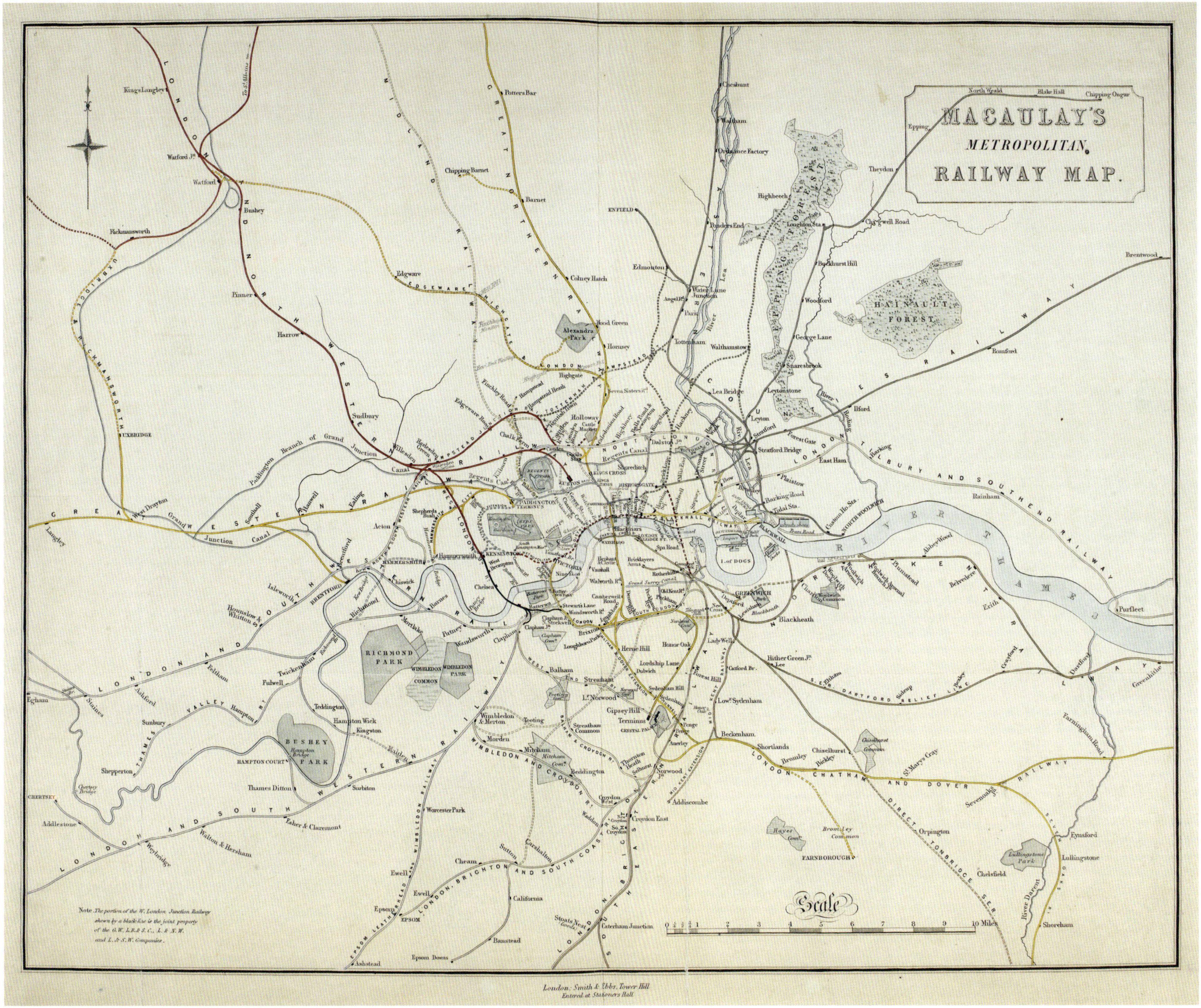
MACAULAY'S
METROPOLITAN
RAILWAY MAP.
Note. The portion of the W. London Junction Railway shewn by a black line is the joint property of the G.W., L.B.&S.C., L.&N.W. and L.&S.W. Companies.
Scale
1 2 3 4 5 6 7 8 9 10 Miles
London: Smith & Ebbs, Tower Hill.
Entered at Stationers Hall.
RIVER THAMES
RICHMOND PARK
WIMBLEDON COMMON
BUSHEY PARK
HAINAULT FOREST
EPPING FOREST

6.4 SEWAGE AND LONDON-WIDE GOVERNMENT

From 1830 the increasing use of flush toilets caused the flooding of private cesspools and of the fragile sewers intended for rainwater, turning the Thames into one enormous cesspool. Londoners found themselves drinking their own sewage. Realistic remedies were proposed but these — including detailed preliminary mapping of the terrain and subsequently the creation of a new city-wide system of adequate sewers — were beyond the powers and resources of the patchwork of authorities that then administered London. Against intense opposition, the first London-wide body, the Metropolitan Board of Works was created in 1855. Given adequate powers after parliament had endured the 'Great Stink' emanating from the Thames in 1858, the Board commissioned Joseph Bazalgette to construct a new drainage system.

THE GREAT STINK

In July 1858 the odours from the Thames became so overpowering that Parliamentarians in the Palace of Westminster decided to abandon their sittings. The magazine *Punch* produced a cartoon showing a skeleton representing Death rowing over a River Thames littered with sewage and dead animals with the caption 'The "Silent Highway"-man. "Your money or your life!"'. It perfectly summarised the situation: either money was found for the building of adequate sewers, or Londoners would die.

6.4.1 'The "Silent Highway"-Man', *Punch,* 10 July 1858

PUNCH, OR THE LONDON CHARIVARI, July 10, 1858.

THE "SILENT HIGHWAY"-MAN.
"Your MONEY or your LIFE!"

ENVISAGING AN EMBANKMENT

John Martin is best known as the painter of vast panoramas of cataclysms, but he had an abiding interest in metropolitan improvements aimed at sparing London from such disasters. This plan illustrates how sewage could be intercepted before reaching the Thames by an enormous sewer that would carry the waste to the countryside to be recycled for agricultural purposes. An embankment, with a road above was to be carried over this new sewer. Martin's ideas anticipated the achievements of Bazalgette, but though Martin lobbied extensively, there was not yet a London-wide authority with the powers to realise his ideas.

6.4.2 John Martin, *Thames and Metropolis Improvement Plan First Division. Improvement of the Drainage of the Metropolis, and preservation of the sewage for agricultural purposes* [Third map, showing Westminster, Milbank and Battersea] from *Principle of intercepting the Sewage of the Metropolis and conveying it into the country for agricultural purposes* (1846). Lithograph. 50 × 73 cm. Maps 24.e.27

THAMES AND METROPOLIS IMPROVEMENT PLAN.

FIRST DIVISION.

IMPROVEMENT OF THE DRAINAGE OF THE METROPOLIS, AND PRESERVATION OF THE SEWAGE FOR AGRICULTURAL PURPOSES.

This Map shows the mode of diverting the Sewage, the Line of Embankment and Public Walks, improved Lines of Communication, &c. in the Three Sections of the Western or Westminster District.

JOHN MARTIN,
30, Allsop Terrace, New Road, London,
March, 1846.

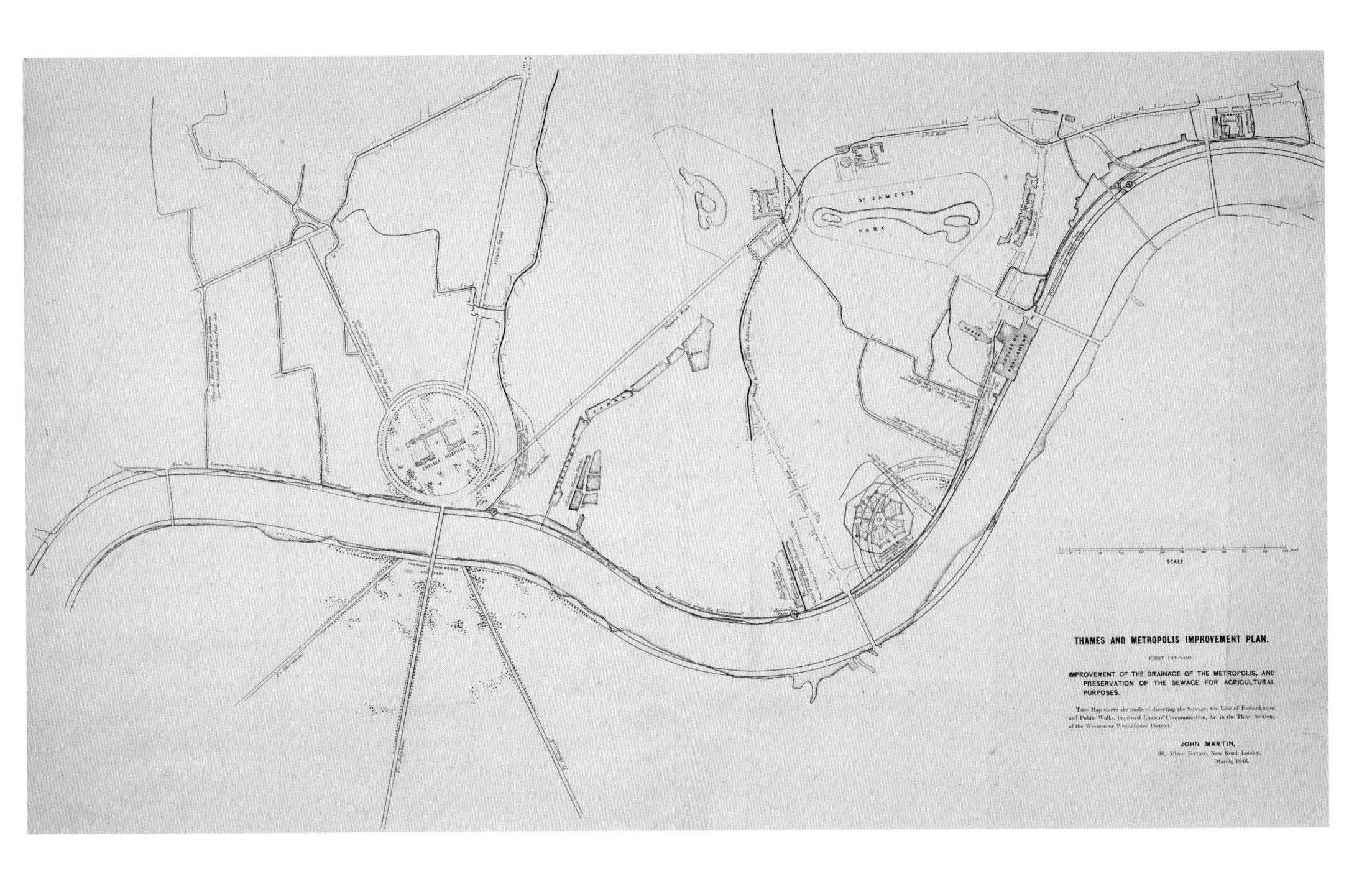

THE 'SKELETON' SURVEY OF LONDON

An essential preliminary to the building of sewers was the creation of a very detailed map showing the slightest differences in levels. Commissioned by the new Metropolitan Board of Sewers, the first London-wide body of any kind, it was surveyed and printed by the Ordnance Survey between 1848 and 1851. Hostility from commercial map publishers led by James Wyld Jr, who was also a Member of Parliament and who was toying with the idea of producing yet another updated version of Horwood's map, prevented the Ordnance Survey for many years from providing anything more than the 'Skeleton' outlines illustrated here.

6.4.3   Extract from sheet 448 of the 'Skeleton Plan of London at 5 feet to the mile' [1:1056] (Southampton: Ordnance Survey, 1848–51)

AN EMBANKMENT AND SEWER FOR CHELSEA

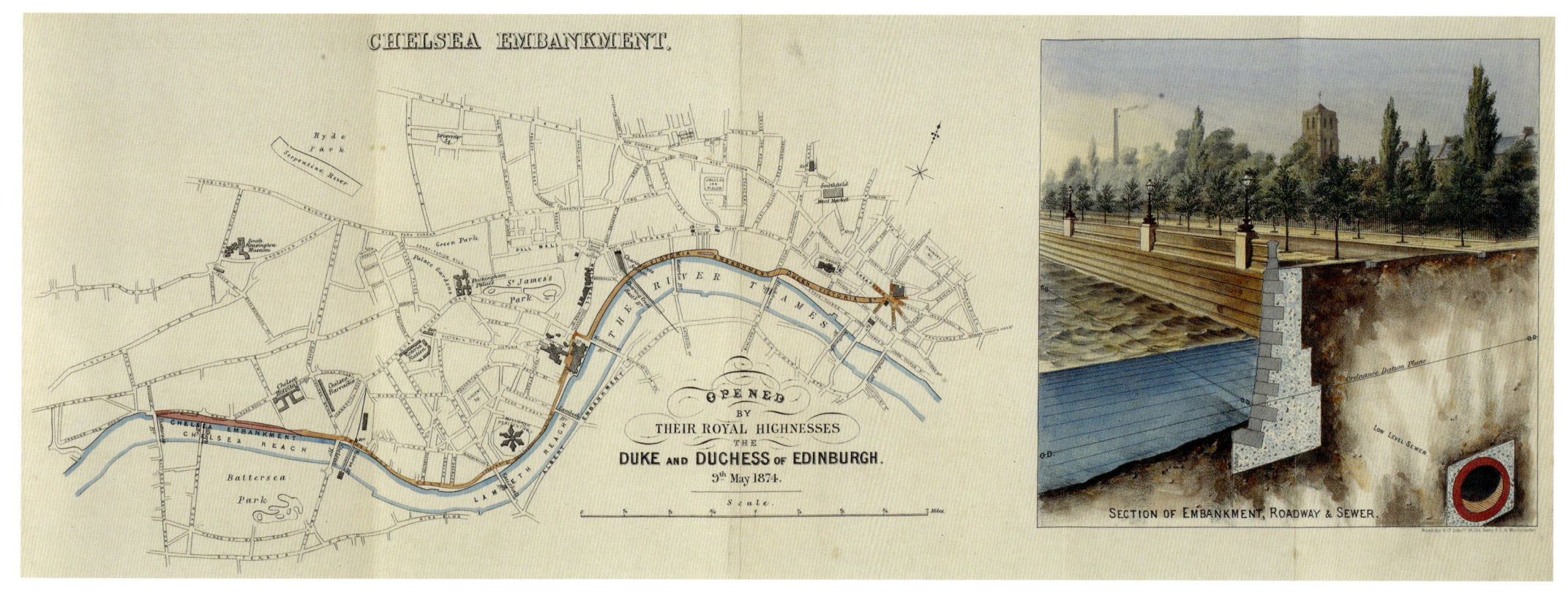

Joseph Bazalgette worked as an engineer for various London-wide bodies from 1849 to 1889. He was responsible not only for creating miles of sewers and embankments but also bridges and new roads such as Shaftesbury Avenue. The Chelsea Embankment, built between 1871 and 1874, was the third and last of his great embankments. It carried the low level intercepting sewer from Battersea Bridge to Chelsea Hospital and also spared Cheyne Walk from excessive traffic and flooding. This plan and section, showing the new road and the sewer beneath, form part of an elaborate booklet commemorating the Embankment's opening. Bazalgette was knighted soon afterwards.

6.4.4. *Chelsea Embankment, opened by their Royal Highnesses the Duke and Duchess of Edinburgh on May 9th, 1874* [An account of the works, with a plan.] Coloured lithograph. 26 × 84 cm. C.193.b.54

The plan was lithographed by Standidge & Co., the City of London firm headed by Harriet Standidge (1805–75). Born Harriet Burford at Stratford-le-Bow, she married the lithographic printer William Standidge (see item 6.5.3) in 1830, was widowed in 1850 and — left with at least seven children to raise — she took on the business herself. By 1871 she was employing fourteen men and a number of boys and the firm had become one of leading specialist printing-houses. She died at West Ham in 1875.

SECTION OF EMBANKMENT, ROADWAY & SEWER.

6.5 OPEN SPACES, HEALTH AND SOCIAL HARMONY

Considerations of sanitation and social peace came together in debates about graveyards and open spaces. The disgusting state and overcrowding of City graveyards had been a scandal long before the government ordered their closure in 1852. The need to improve living conditions in the East End if further social unrest was to be avoided lay behind the creation of Victoria Park in the 1840s. In the 1870s and 1880s a series of strikes and violent working class marches led local government leaders to fear that a socialist revolution would break out unless the masses were tamed by healthy air and natural beauty. They also knew that well-managed open spaces could only improve the rateable value of the neighbouring districts. An impressive tally of parks, commons and elegant new cemeteries resulted.

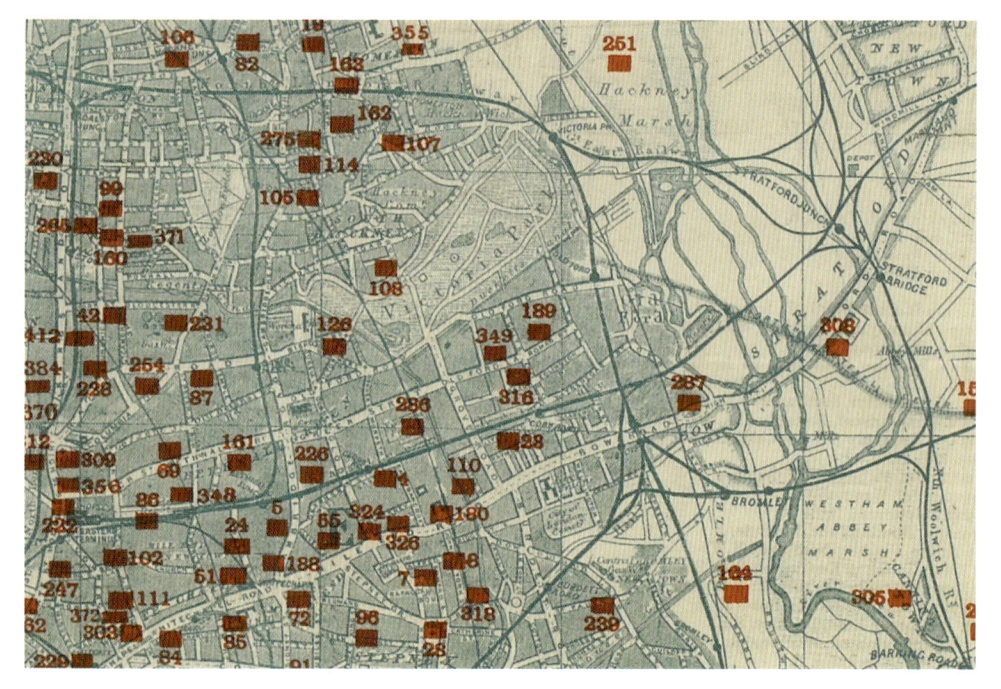

Detail from *Map of London. Work of Metropolitan Public Gardens Association* (1900). For the full map, see p. 263

CHURCHYARD INTO GARDEN

In 1852 inner-city graveyards were closed for burials. Among the oldest and most crowded were the two next to Old St Pancras church, one having served the old church for centuries and the other serving as an overflow for St Giles in the Fields churchyard. From 1850 the whole neighbourhood had been blighted through its vicinity to King's Cross and St Pancras stations. Much land had been lost to the railway. This plan attempts to convert the redundant churchyards into a much needed open space for a crowded working-class neighbourhood. The churchyards were disrupted by the building of the railway into St Pancras and the novelist Thomas Hardy, then working as an architect on this railway project, positioned displaced gravestones around a tree which still survives (as The Hardy Tree). The gardens finally opened, to a different design and with a fountain presented by the philanthropic Baroness Burdett-Coutts, in 1891.

6.5.1 [Henry Hewitt Bridgman, Architect] *Suggestion for laying-out as memorial-grounds St. Pancras and St. Giles Burial Grounds* (1876). Chromolithograph. 62.5 × 78.5 cm. Maps 3495 (65)

The architect and surveyor Henry Hewitt Bridgman was born in Torquay in 1845, the son of a timber merchant. He spent his working life in London, married Elizabeth Codner, the daughter of a City of London cordwainer, lived locally in Camden Square and died at St Pancras in 1898.

SUGGESTION
FOR
LAYING-OUT AS MEMORIAL-GROUNDS
ST. PANCRAS AND ST. GILES BURIAL GROUNDS.

All Subscriptions in aid of the carrying out of this Plan are to be sent to
THOS. ECCLESTON GIBB,
Vestry Clerk of St. Pancras,
Vestry Hall,
St. Pancras, London, N.W.
Cheques to be crossed National Bank, Camden Town.
By order of the Vestry.

Henry Hewitt Bridgman, A.R.I.B.A.
Architect,
71, Pratt St, London N.W.

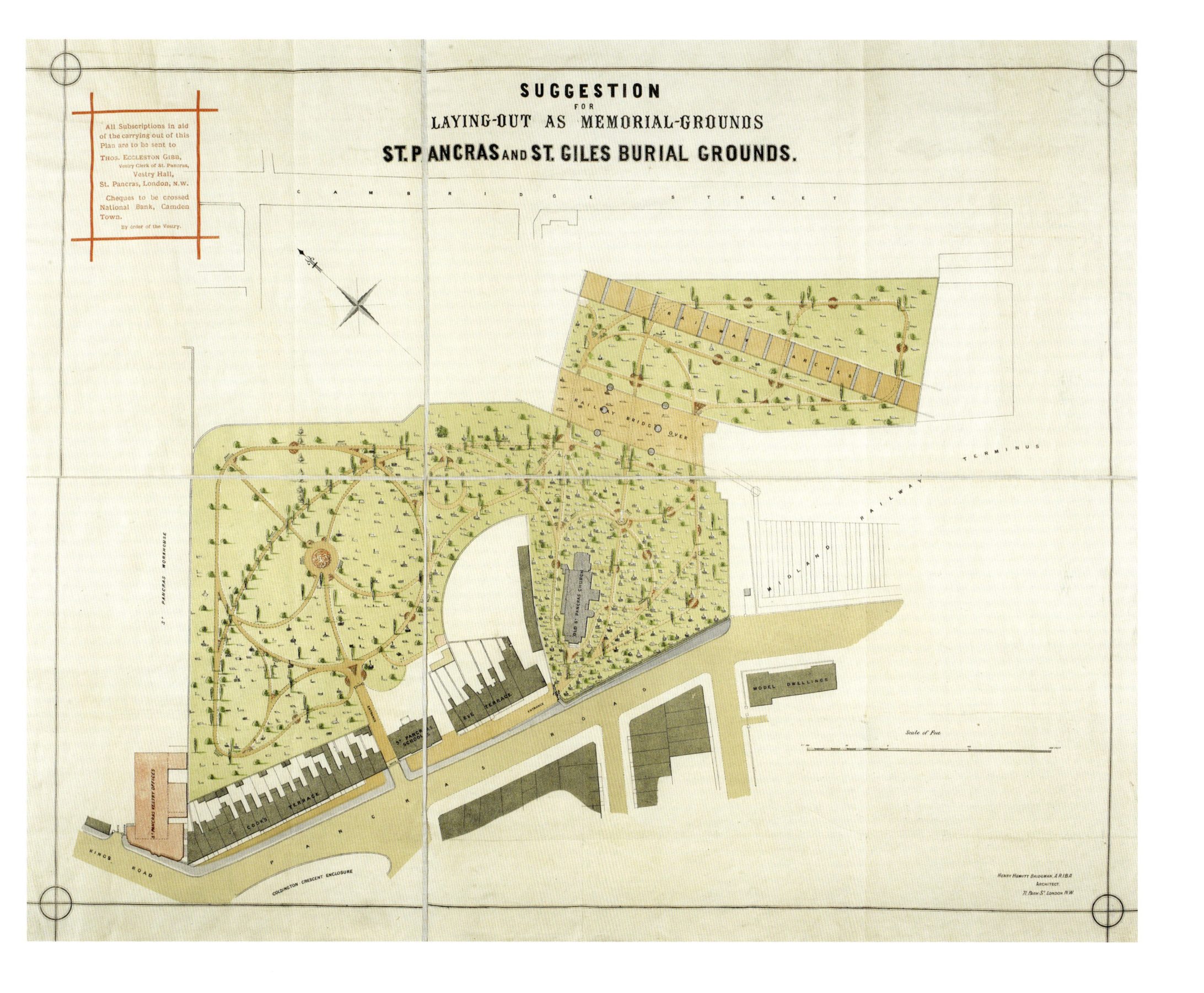

A FINE AND PRIVATE PLACE

Kensal Green Cemetery was created in the early 1830s. It was the first of the privately-owned cemeteries and was intended to be an attractive open space offering tranquillity for repose, reflection and commemoration. The grand entrance arch and the Anglican and Dissenters' chapels shown on this early plan were built in the fashionable Greek Revival style, while the grounds were laid out in a picturesque style similar to the original planting of Regent's Park. The cemetery's social acceptability became assured after two of George III's children decided to be buried there in the 1840s.

6.5.2   C. B. Bowman, *Plan of the General Cemetery at Kensal Green in the Harrow Road* [1839?]. Lithograph. 25.7 × 37 cm. 695.l.14 (50)

The plan was published in the name of the solicitor, Charles Broughton Bowman, the first Secretary of the General Cemetery Company. He died relatively young late in 1840, not long after the plan was published, and his pillared memorial capped with an urn is one of the most distinctive early graves at Kensal Green — and now a Grade II listed monument.

PLAN
of the
General Cemetery
at
Kensal Green
in the
Harrow Road.

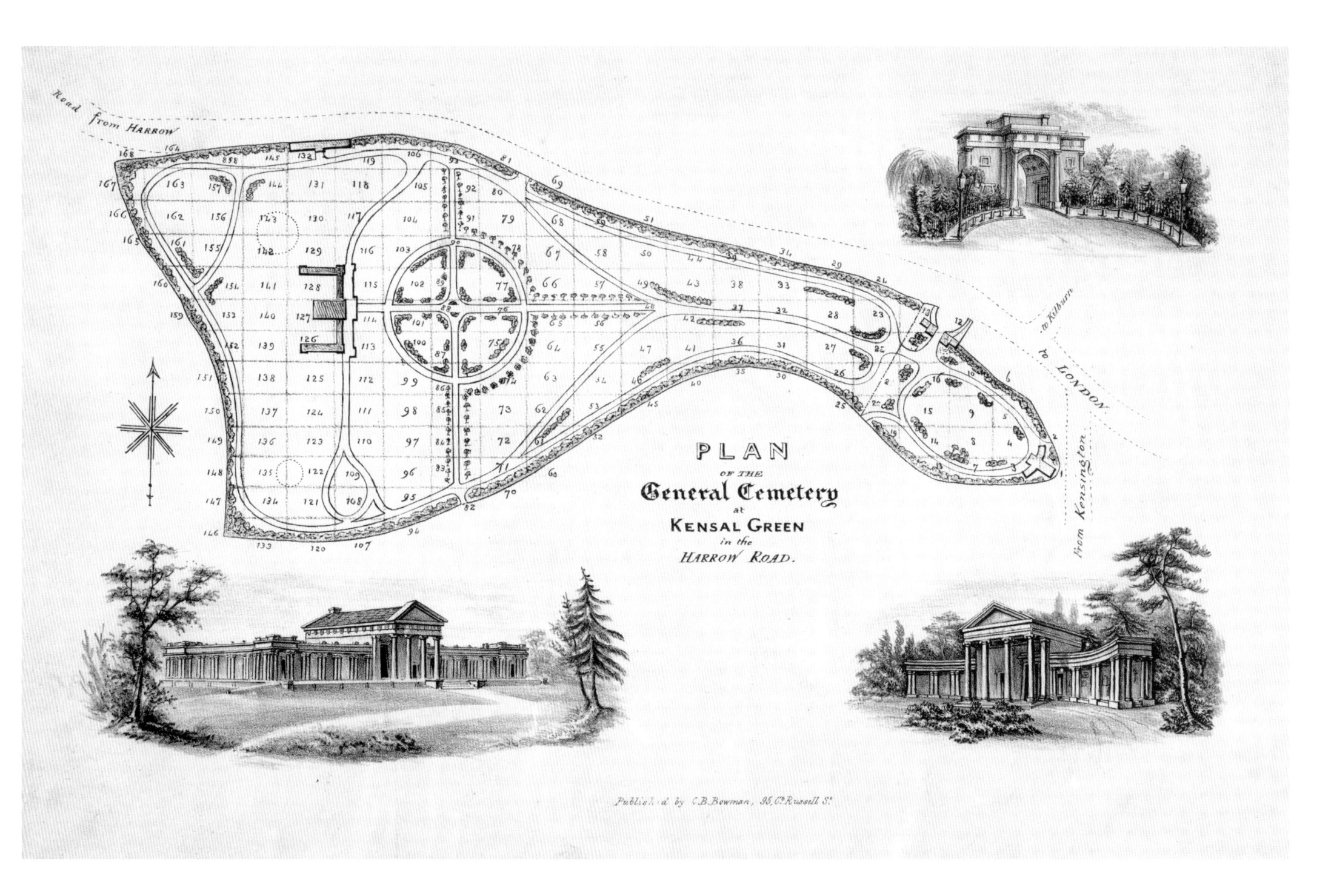

A PARK FOR THE EAST END

This plan was drawn up following Parliament's decision to create a park in Hackney at a time of political and social unrest when much social legislation aimed at bettering living and working conditions was being introduced. The park was designed by Nash's most talented pupil, James Pennethorne, as an East London equivalent of Regent's Park. It was to have similar picturesque planting and, initially, as shown here, villas scattered around its margins. Later a lake was added. Its 290 acres were purchased from the proceeds of the sale of the home of the Prince Regent's brother, the Duke of York. The park opened in 1845. By 1900 no self-respecting London borough was without its park.

6.5.3   James Pennethorne and Thomas Chawner, *Plan for laying out the proposed Eastern Park to be called Victoria Park*, 1841. Lithograph with watercolour. 25.7 × 37 cm. Maps Crace XIX.43

The map was printed by the firm founded by Luke Hansard (1752–1828), whose name remains synonymous with the official parliamentary record. Hansard himself came from Norwich, but his son and grandson, whose names appear on the map and who by now headed the largest printing-house in the capital, were both Londoners born. The lithography was executed by a specialist, William Standidge, of Cornhill.

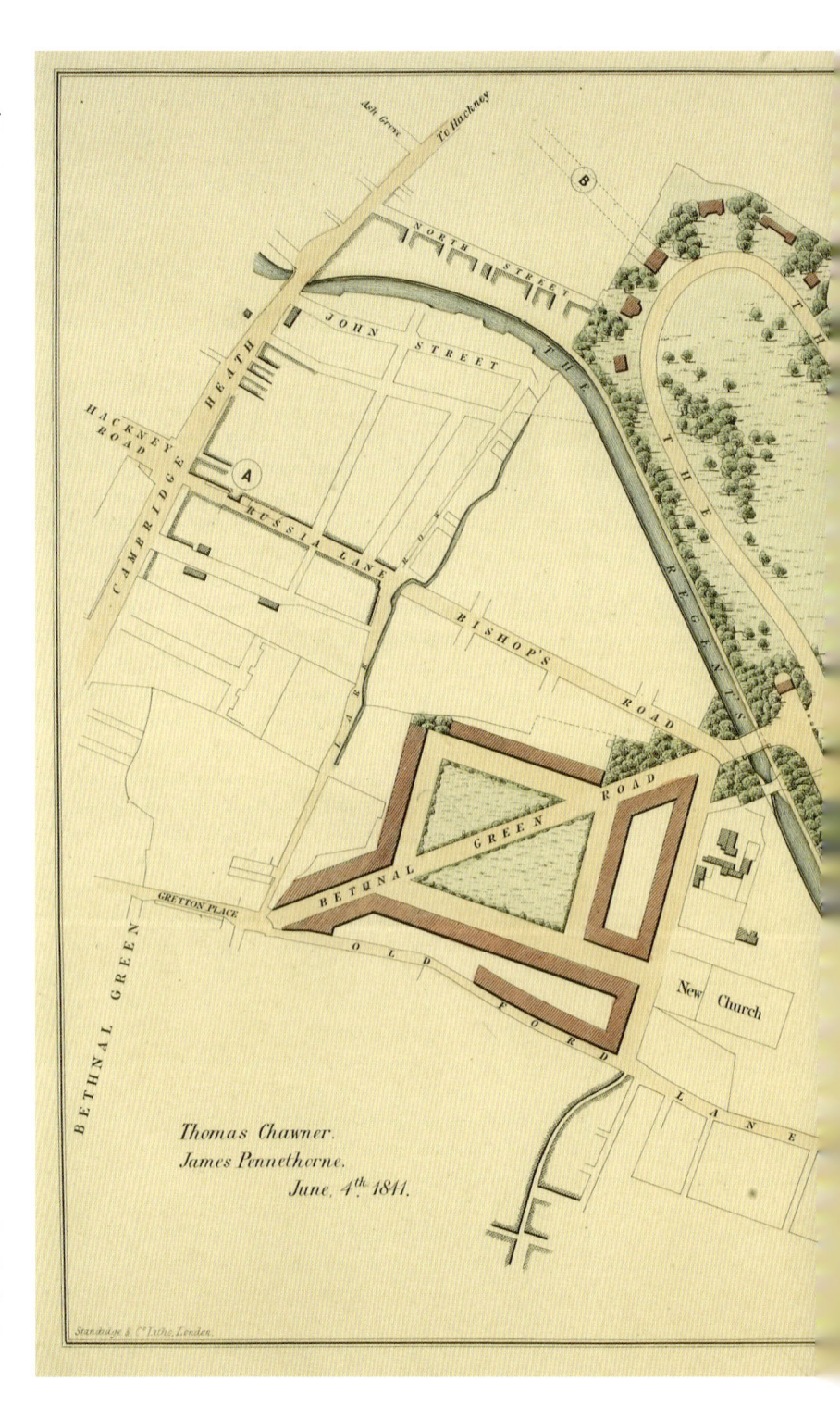

APPENDIX.—18TH REPORT WOODS, FORESTS, & LAND REVENUES.

APPENDIX N° 20.

PLAN
FOR LAYING OUT THE PROPOSED
Eastern Park,
TO BE CALLED
VICTORIA PARK.

Scale of Feet.

Ordered by the House of Commons to be Printed, 21st June, 1841.

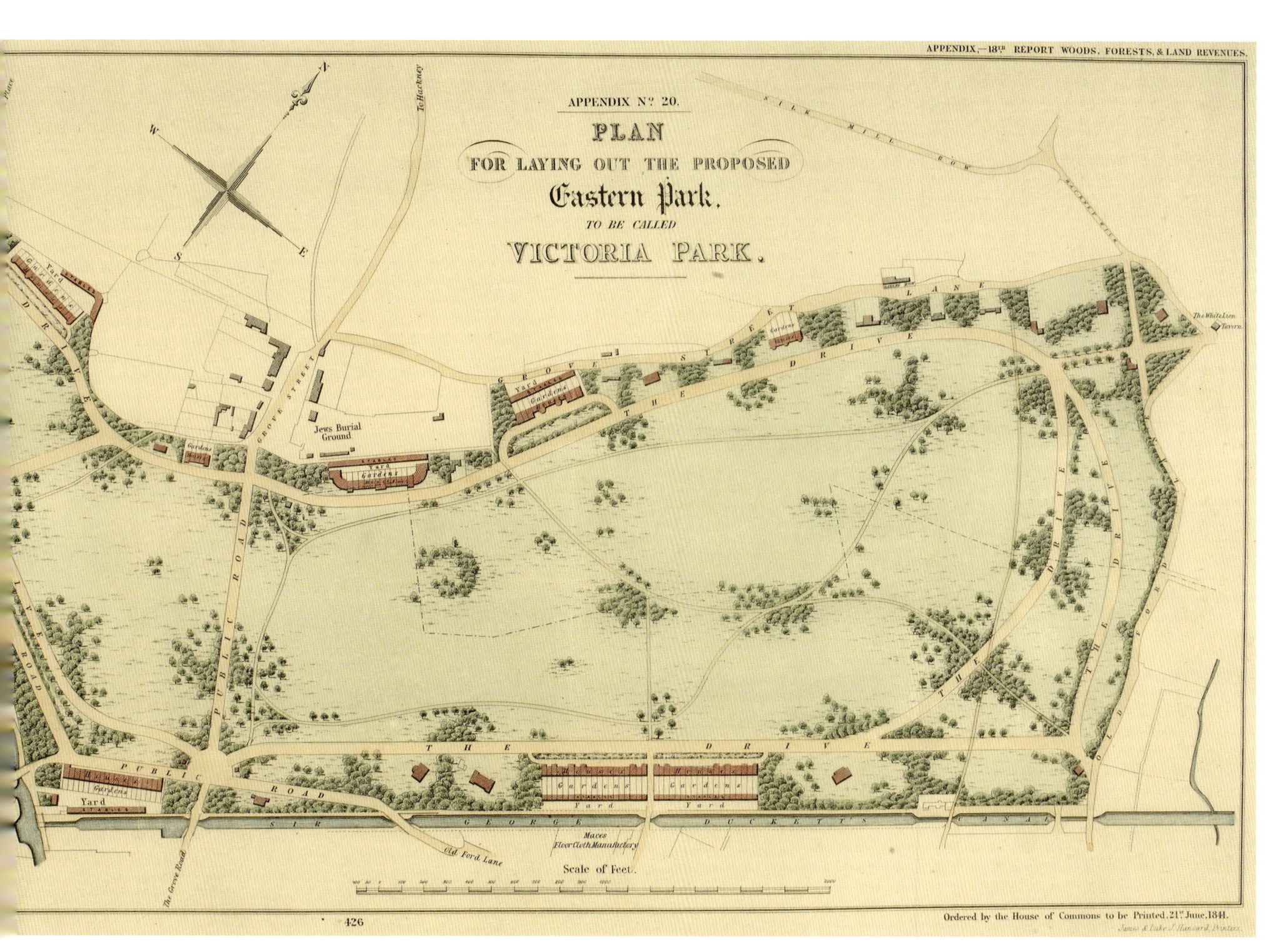

SAVING THE SQUARES

While a number of amenity societies like the Commons' Preservation and the Open Spaces societies fought to preserve large open spaces like Hampstead Heath and Epping Forest from development from the 1860s, the Metropolitan Public Gardens Association has concentrated on saving smaller spaces such as town squares and churchyards. The numerous red squares on this plan show its considerable achievements between its foundation in 1882 and 1900. In reality the Association's impact was a little less dramatic than it appears since the plan includes enormous open spaces which it helped others to save and it does not distinguish between those and minute City churchyards. The threat of development moreover continued to the 1920s when, despite the Association's best efforts, the whole of Mornington Crescent and the southern part of Euston Square were built over.

6.5.4 *Map of London. Work of the Metropolitan Public Gardens Association November 1882 to December 1900* (London: E. Stanford, 1900). Chromolithograph. 50.5 × 60.7 cm. Maps 3485 (135)

MAP OF LONDON

WORK
OF THE
METROPOLITAN
Public Gardens Association

November, 1882, to December, 1900.

83, Lancaster Gate, W.

Scale of Miles

THE INDEX, TO WHICH THE RED NUMBERS REFER, IS PRINTED ON THE BACK OF THE MAP

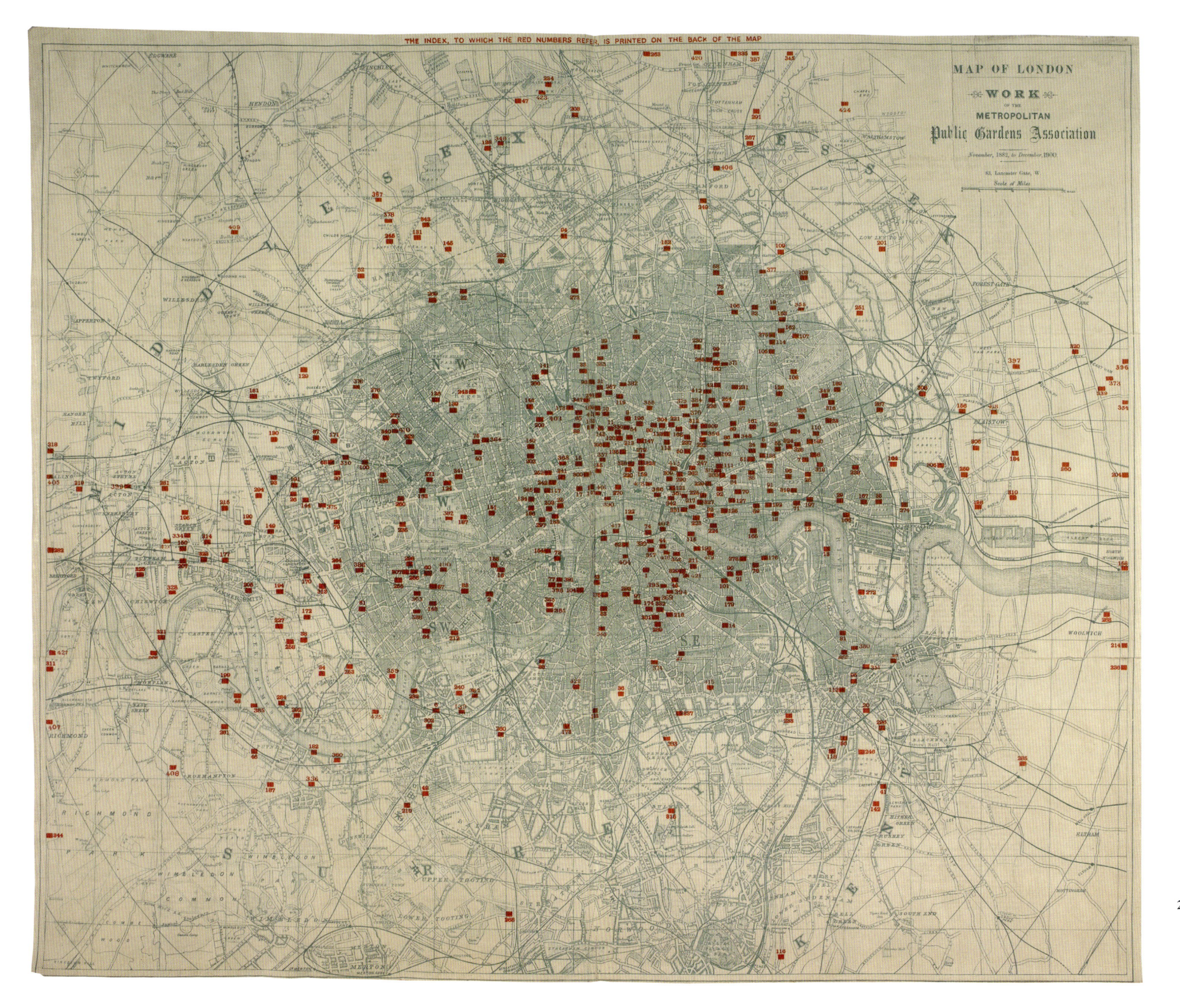

6.6 NEW ROADS FOR OLD

The later Victorian and Edwardian years saw the creation of many new streets to improve communications in central London. Some, like Shaftesbury Avenue (1877–86), named after the philanthropic 8th Earl of Shaftesbury, were also slum-clearance projects with the government now stipulating that those rendered homeless be re-housed, though this led to delays in completion and complaints from the developers. At the other extreme was The Mall (1903–11), with Admiralty Arch and the Victoria Memorial, which were intended to provide an appropriately imperial processional route between Buckingham Palace and Trafalgar Square. Yet other proposals, like Kingsway (1900–05), saw grand avenues being created while networks of ancient and picturesque, but insanitary buildings and lanes, with a few exceptions, were demolished.

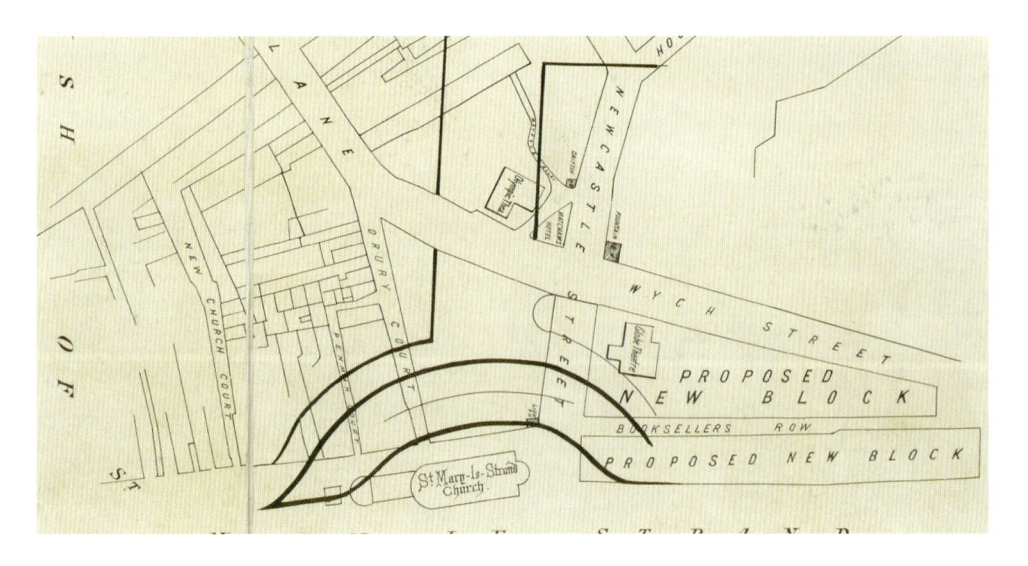

KINGSWAY

The idea for a wide road connecting Holborn to the Strand, now known as Kingsway, was first mooted in the early 1890s. As well as improving communications and providing a grand avenue, it would eradicate some of the worst remaining slums. These included Wych Street, one of the last lanes still with pre-Great Fire houses, which gave way to Aldwych once work started in 1900. Wych Street would have survived had this early plan been implemented. In the end only the sixteenth-century 'Old Curiosity Shop' in Portsmouth Street was saved because of its supposed links with Charles Dickens. But, in contrast to earlier redevelopments, those rendered homeless were re-housed.

6.6.1 Alfred Ahrenfeld, *The London Improvements Bill. In Parliament. Session 1893: Plan of the London County Council showing the new streets from Southampton Row to the Strand proposed to be made and property to be acquired by the Council along the route.* Chromolithograph. 42.1 × 87.1 cm. Maps 3495(71)

Alfred Ahrenfeld (1837–1901) was a Fleet Street lithographic draughtsman, the son of a Swiss commercial agent and a young woman from Liverpool. Although born in Liverpool, Ahrenfeld had lived in London since early childhood.

THE LONDON IMPROVEMENTS BILL.

IN PARLIAMENT
SESSION—1893.

Plan of the London County Council showing THE NEW STREETS from SOUTHAMPTON ROW TO THE STRAND proposed to be made, and property to be acquired by the Council along the route.

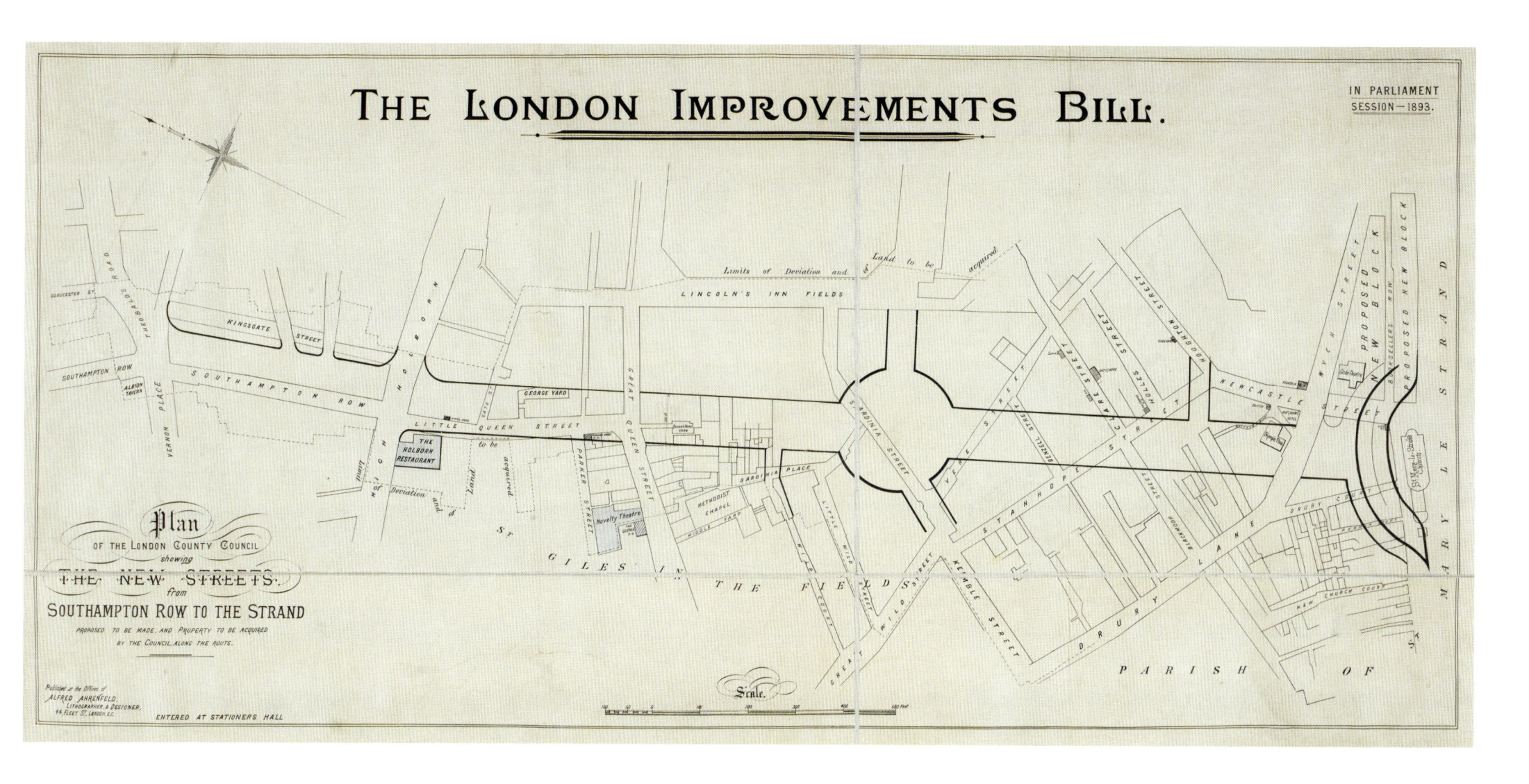

A RELIC OF OLD LONDON

The Society for Photographing Relics of Old London was founded in order to ensure the creation of reliable images of ancient buildings that were in danger of demolition. In some cases the buildings were demolished only months after the photographs were taken; in others, the danger never materialised. In others still, as with Wych Street, demolition took place a generation later in 1903.

6.6.2   Wych Street looking towards St Clement Danes, in about 1875. Photographed by Alfred and John Bool for The Society for Photographing Relics of Old London [Album, 1875–86], photograph 7.22 × 17 cm. Tab.700.b.3

Alfred Henry Bool and his younger brother John were born in Pimlico in 1844 and 1850 respectively, the sons of the sculptor John James Bool and his French wife Eugenie. Their father abandoned sculpture to become a farmer in Hampshire, but his sons were among the earliest photographic artists to work in London. Later in life, Alfred lived in Fulham and taught photography and painting. John became a portrait painter as well as a photographer.

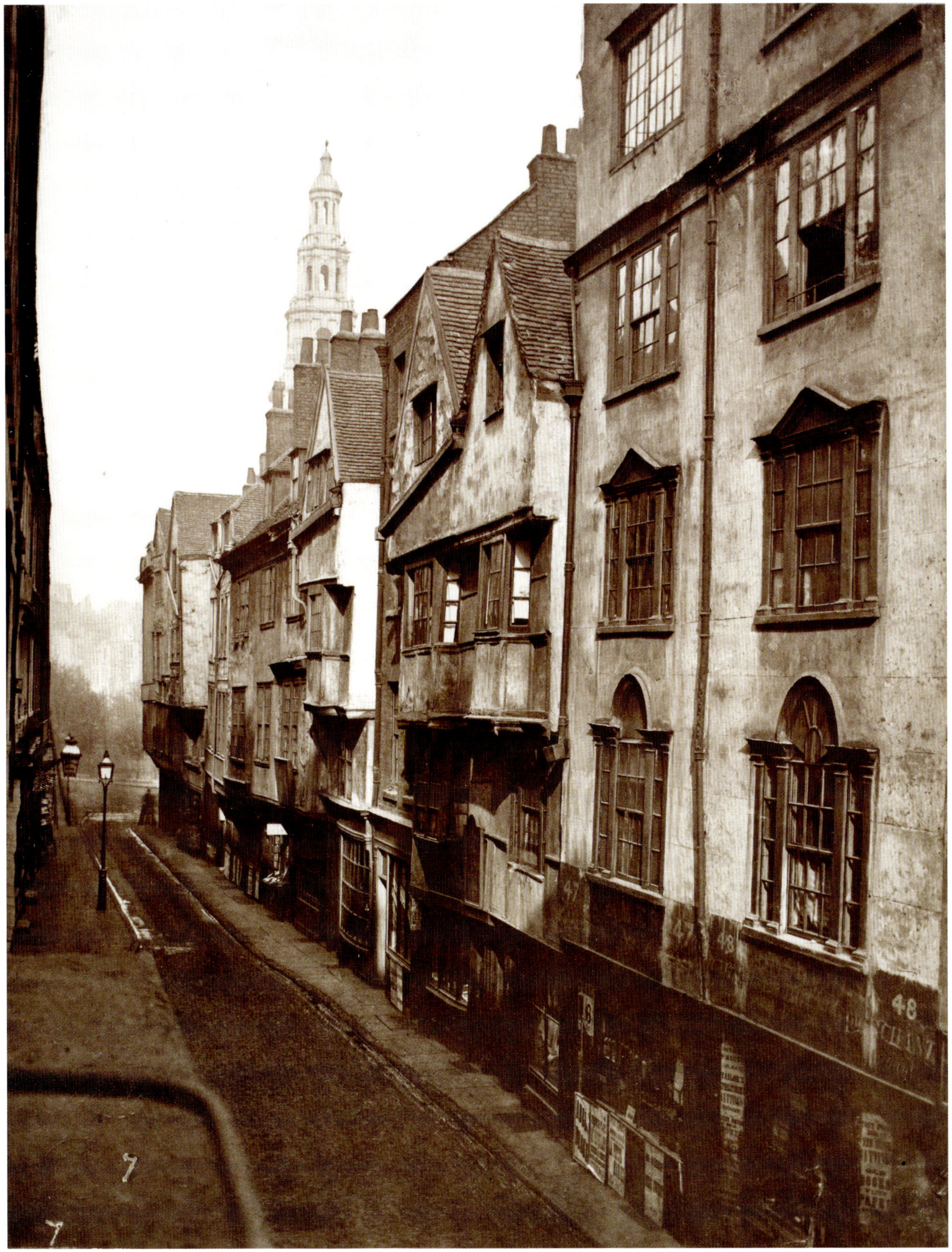

'... WE SHOULD HAVE A ROW WITH THE QUEEN ...'

With this confidential letter, Reginald Brett (later 2nd Viscount Esher), the newly-appointed Permanent Secretary at the Board of Works, tries to win the support of John Burns, a leading LCC councillor and the MP for Battersea, for a bold idea. Enclosing a plan of the area between Trafalgar Square and the Mall, Brett writes that 'I should like to alter the carriage way and have it down the centre of the Mall — the two centre alleys — and keep the side alleys for pedestrians …'. Enticingly, he mentions that if his proposals were implemented, the London County Council would have its long-desired 'Hotel-de-Ville' on the north side of The Mall and adds extra spice by mentioning conspiratorially, 'We should have a row with the Queen possibly but I think it might be done.' It was — but only in 1911: ten years after the Queen's death.

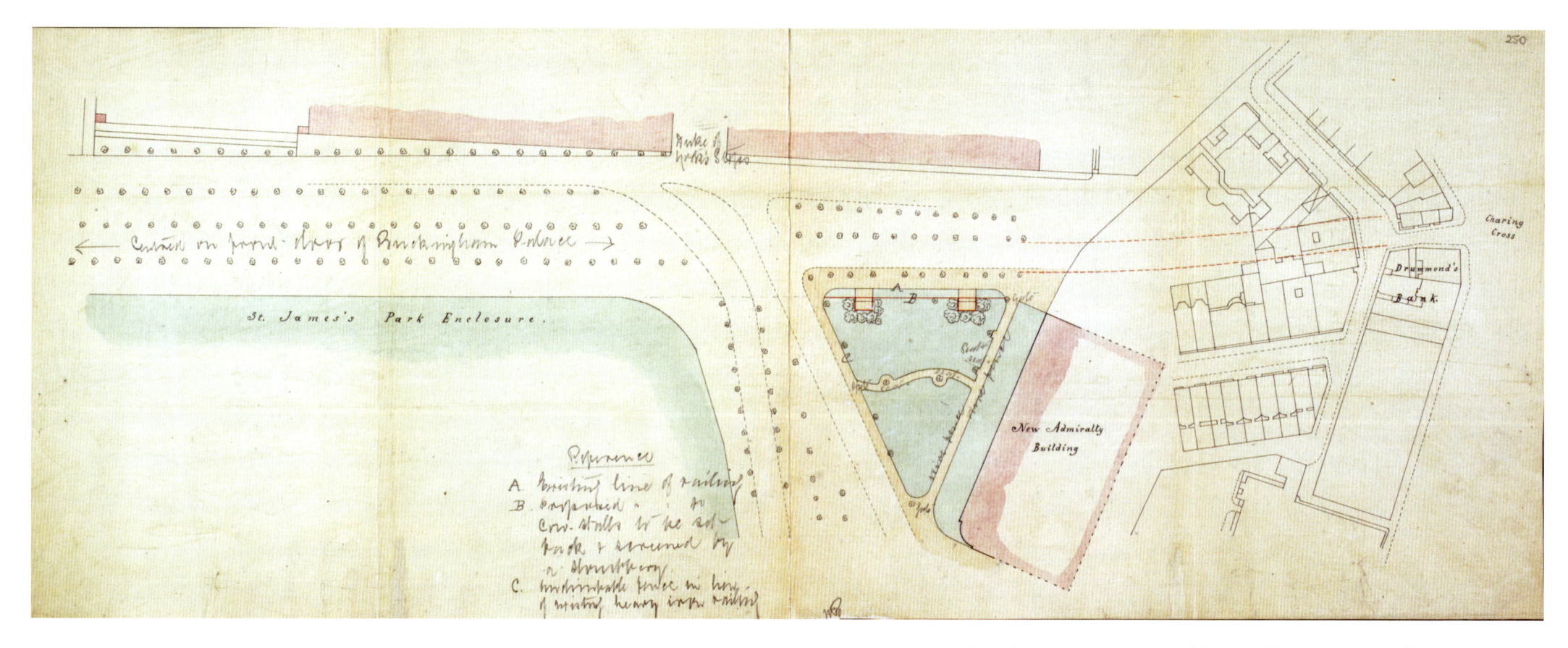

6.6.3 Annotated Ordnance Survey plan of the Trafalgar Square-Mall area., 25.5 × 67 cm. Add.46295 f. 249ᵛ; letter of Reginald Brett to John Burns, 26 November 1895. 18 × 11.5 cm. Add.46295 ff.247ᵛ–8

for the same reasons.

I do hope you will like the suggestion, for I had the devil of a fight to get the piece thrown open to the public.

When we open out the Mall into Charing X which I hope to do in about 4 years time — this garden will be a great feature.

Then I hope that this Office will move into a new building to the South of the Mall on ground on which Spring Garden now stand — and that the L.C.C will build on the North side of the Mall their Hotel de Ville — It will be a magnificent culminating point to that drive — I should like to alter the carriage way and have it down the centre of the Mall — the two centre alleys — and keep

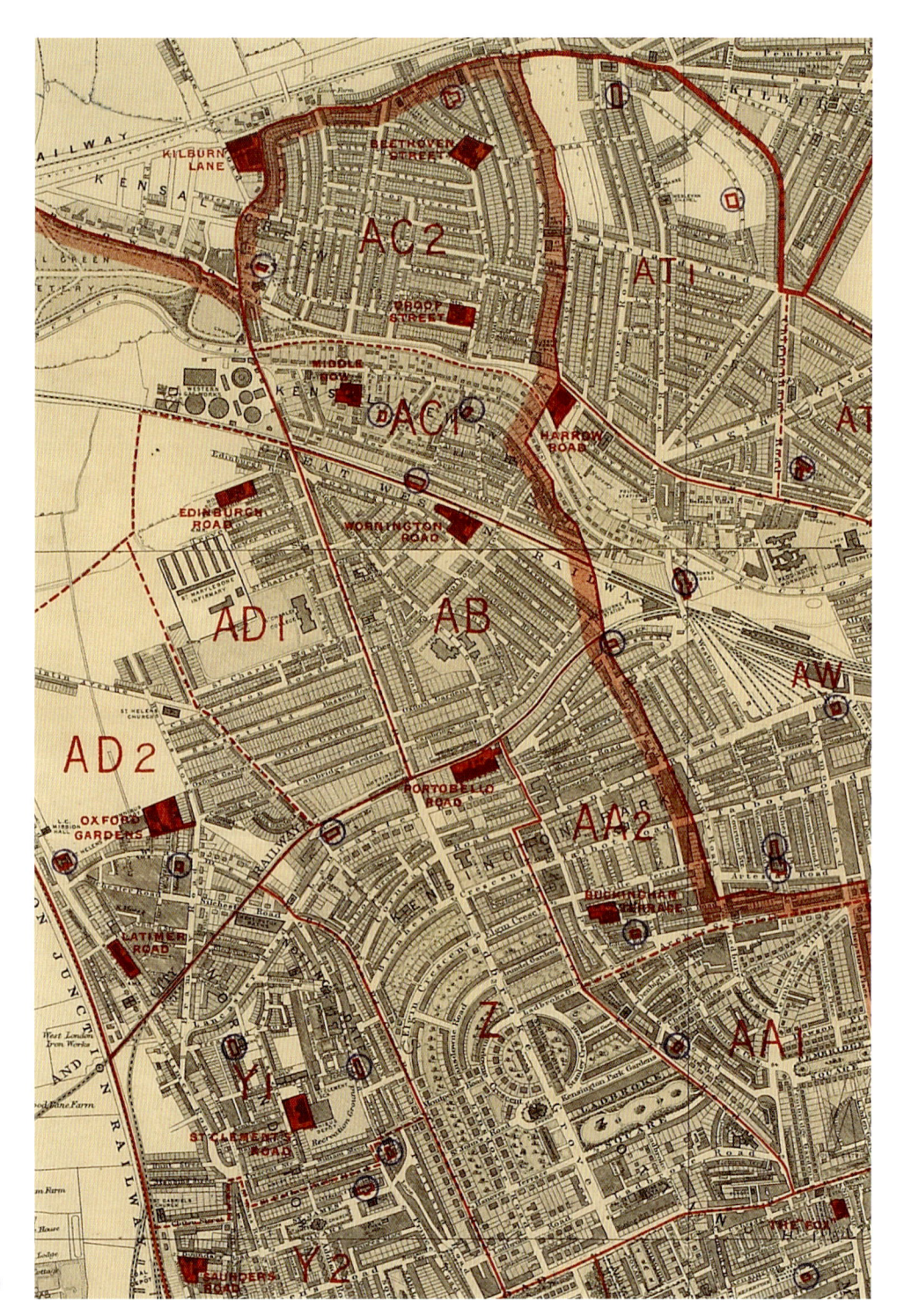

6.7 STANFORD'S FOR MAPS

In part because of opposition from commercial map publishers, Ordnance Survey was prevented for many years after 1851 from producing the detailed maps for London that it created for other cities. Edward Stanford (see 6.1.2 above) filled the gap with his elegant and informative *Library Map of London* at a scale of 6 inches to the mile (1:10560), first published in 1862. It and the succeeding editions provided the map onto which the Metropolitan Board of Works and later the London County Council superimposed all manner of additional information in their endeavours to analyse and improve the amenities, education and health of Londoners.

Extract from E. Stanford, *School-board Map of London* (London: E. Stanford, 1892 edn). (For the whole map, see p. 277)

THE ADMINISTRATOR'S MAP OF LONDON

Profiting from the absence of a detailed Ordnance Survey map of London, Edward Stanford published the first edition of his 24 sheet *Library Map of London* in 1862. He updated the outlines of the Ordnance Survey 'Skeleton' survey of 1848–51, adding a lot of information, for instance about ownership and commercial buildings, that no Ordnance Survey map would have carried. There were several revised editions over the next 40 years.

6.7.1 *Stanford's Library Map of London and its suburbs* (London: E. Stanford, 1891 edn), sheet 11. Lithograph. 37.7 × 45.4 cm. Maps 9.e.10

ON 24 SHEETS WITH AN INDEX MAP
SHEET II.
KEY TO ADJOINING SHEETS
STANFORD'S LIBRARY MAP OF LONDON AND ITS SUBURBS
G
H
e
f
Artillery Ground
MILE END NEW TOWN
WHITECHAPEL ROAD
COMMERCIAL ROAD EAST
GOODMAN'S FIELDS
BLACKWALL RAILWAY
TEMPLE
BLACKFRIARS
SOUTHWARK BRIDGE
LONDON BRIDGE
THE TOWER
TOWER BRIDGE
ST KATHARINE DOCKS
LONDON DOCKS
The Jetty
SHADWELL NEW BASIN
WAPPING
UPPER POOL
BOROUGH ROAD
BETHLEHEM LUNATIC ASYLUM
BERMONDSEY
SCALE: 6 Inches to 1 Eng. Statute Mile; or 1 Inch to 880 Feet; or as 1:10560 on the Ground.
London: Published by Edward Stanford 26 & 27 Cockspur Street, Charing Cross. S.W.

GAS RIVALRIES

This is the sort of simple map that formed the basis for thematic maps of the London area before the appearance of Stanford maps. By the 1840s gas was being widely used to light shops, theatres and private houses as well as streets. There was fierce competition between the gas companies. Several serviced the same district, such as Oxford Street and Tottenham Court Road, and often indulged in unethical tactics to attract and retain custom. This map attempts to clarify the situation, presumably so that residents would know what, if any, alternatives to their current suppliers were available. It has a familiar ring today.

6.7.2 *A skeleton map Shewing the Districts occupied by The Metropolitan Gas Companies* (1849). Lithograph. 51 × 62 cm. Maps 3485 (2)

The map was lithographed by the ambitious young London printer Daniel Grant, originally from South Shields. By 1861, the year in which he became a Fellow of the Royal Geographical Society and still in his early thirties, he was employing sixty-eight men and fifty boys. In 1880 he became Member of Parliament for Marylebone and has a further claim on London's history in being the original publisher of Gustave Doré's searing images of the Victorian city in *London : A Pilgrimage* in 1872.

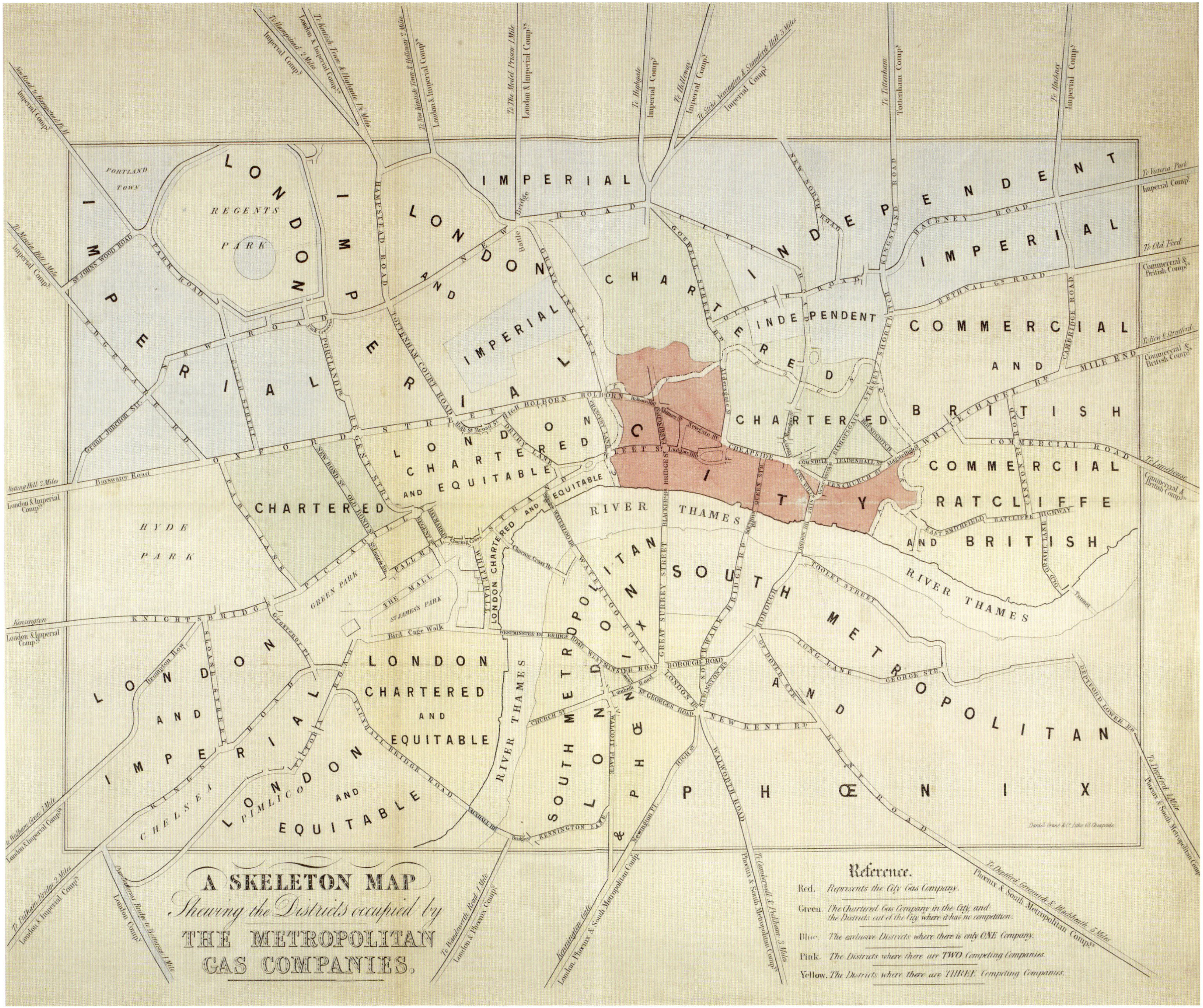

A SKELETON MAP
Shewing the Districts occupied by
THE METROPOLITAN GAS COMPANIES.
Reference.
Red. Represents the City Gas Company.
Green. The Chartered Gas Company in the City, and the Districts out of the City where it has no competition.
Blue. The exclusive Districts where there is only ONE Company.
Pink. The Districts where there are TWO Competing Companies.
Yellow. The Districts where there are THREE Competing Companies.
IMPERIAL
LONDON IMPERIAL
LONDON AND IMPERIAL
INDEPENDENT
CHARTERED
INDEPENDENT
IMPERIAL
COMMERCIAL AND BRITISH
CHARTERED
CITY
LONDON CHARTERED AND EQUITABLE
CHARTERED
COMMERCIAL RATCLIFFE AND BRITISH
REGENTS PARK
PORTLAND TOWN
HYDE PARK
GREEN PARK
ST JAMESS PARK
RIVER THAMES
SOUTH METROPOLITAN
LONDON AND IMPERIAL
LONDON CHARTERED AND EQUITABLE
LONDON PIMLICO AND EQUITABLE
CHELSEA
SOUTH METROPOLITAN
LONDON & PHŒNIX
SOUTH METROPOLITAN AND PHŒNIX
Daniel Grant & Co. Litho 63 Cheapside

273

THE PROVISION OF ELECTRICITY

Electricity revolutionised London from the mid-1870s. As well as providing bright lighting for streets and theatres, it also powered lifts and escalators. Allied to the improvements in building techniques, it made possible the creation of the first department stores, purpose-built large hotels and office buildings. Initially electricity companies sprang up in an unplanned and haphazard way. This map depicts the districts for which they were responsible. The underlying Stanford map provides for far greater precision than had the base map for the gas provision map of 1849.

6.7.3   *Stanford's Map of London shewing the areas granted to the electric light supply companies under the Electric Lighting Acts, 1882 & 1888* (London: E. Stanford, 1890). Chromolithograph. 67 × 94 cm. Maps 3485 (98)

STANFORD'S MAP OF LONDON SHEWING THE AREAS GRANTED TO THE ELECTRIC LIGHT SUPPLY COMPANIES.
UNDER THE ELECTRIC LIGHTING ACTS, 1882 & 1888.

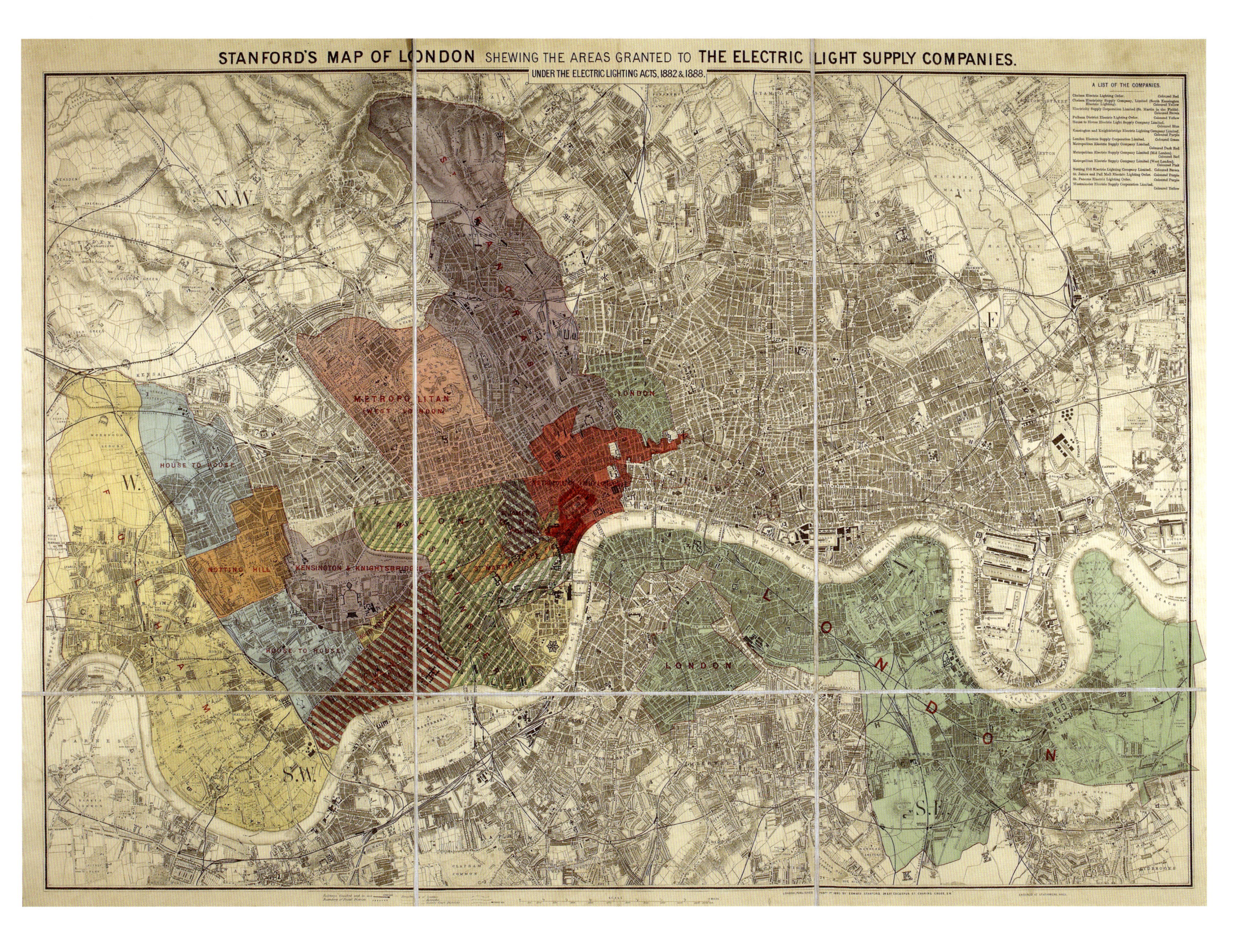

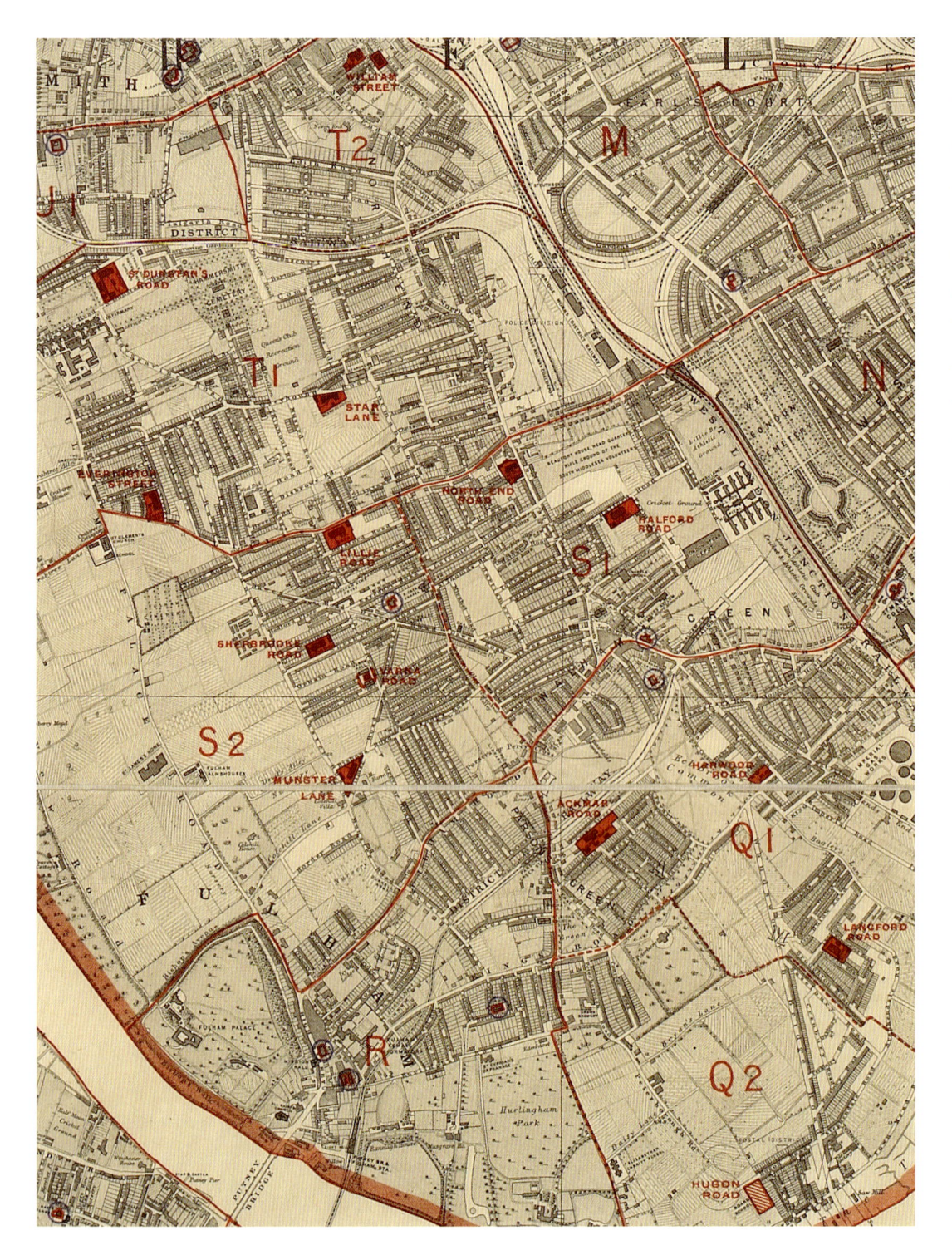

ENSURING SCHOOLS FOR ALL

The 1870 Education Act made education compulsory for all children between the ages of 5 and 13. In the Metropolitan Board of Works area the Act was administered by the School Board for London. It ensured that schools were built where they were needed. Stanford's 'Library Map', periodically updated, was the means by which progress could be checked. It was overlaid with symbols distinguishing between existing Board schools, temporary and planned Board Schools, and the voluntary, faith, schools. This map, showing the Chelsea division, dates from the year after free schooling was introduced. Tall, red-brick, slate-roofed Board schools, with separate entrances for boys, girls and teachers, an odour of stale vegetables and floor polish and external lavatories in the playgrounds are still a familiar sight, though many now serve different purposes.

6.7.4   Edward Stanford, *School-Board Map of London: Chelsea* (London: E. Stanford, 1892 edn). Chromolithograph. 79 × 73 cm. Maps 3990 (3)

CHELSEA

WHERE HOSPITALS ARE NEEDED

Maps like the cholera map demonstrated that diseases were most prevalent in the poorest districts like Whitechapel, Mile End, Limehouse, Soho and Southwark. This map created by Dr Frederick Mount, the Inspector-General of Hospitals (and Vice-President of the Statistical Society of London) shows that these were precisely the areas where there was no medical provision in terms of general and special hospitals (crosses). Poor law institutions and lunatic asylums are indicated by stars and circles.

6.7.5 [Frederick Mount], *The Lancet Map of Medical London 1881: Distribution of Medical Relief within the Metropolitan Area. London, 1881* (London: E. Stanford, published by John Croft, May 1881 to accompany an article in *The Lancet* of 16 July 1881). Chromolithograph. 37.5 × 52 cm. Maps 3485 (74)

THE LANCET MAP OF MEDICAL LONDON 1881.

Distribution of Medical Relief within The Metropolitan Area London, 1881.

KEEPING TRACK OF THE DEMON DRINK

It was only in 1903 that a reliable map was produced of the places where intoxicating drinks were sold. The Local Government and Taxation Committee of the LCC commissioned it in response to a memorial presented by the London United Temperance Council. The public houses are printed in black on a green base map. This sheet illustrates the gulf between the wealthy, living on the Portland, Portman and Bedford estates where public houses were barely tolerated and Soho where they proliferated, and were doubtless enjoyed by some residents of the neighbouring estates.

6.7.6 *Map shewing the situation of all premises licensed for the sale of intoxicating liquors in the County of London Section 1* (London: E. Stanford for the LCC, 1903). [Detail] Chromolithograph, Maps 3485 (178)

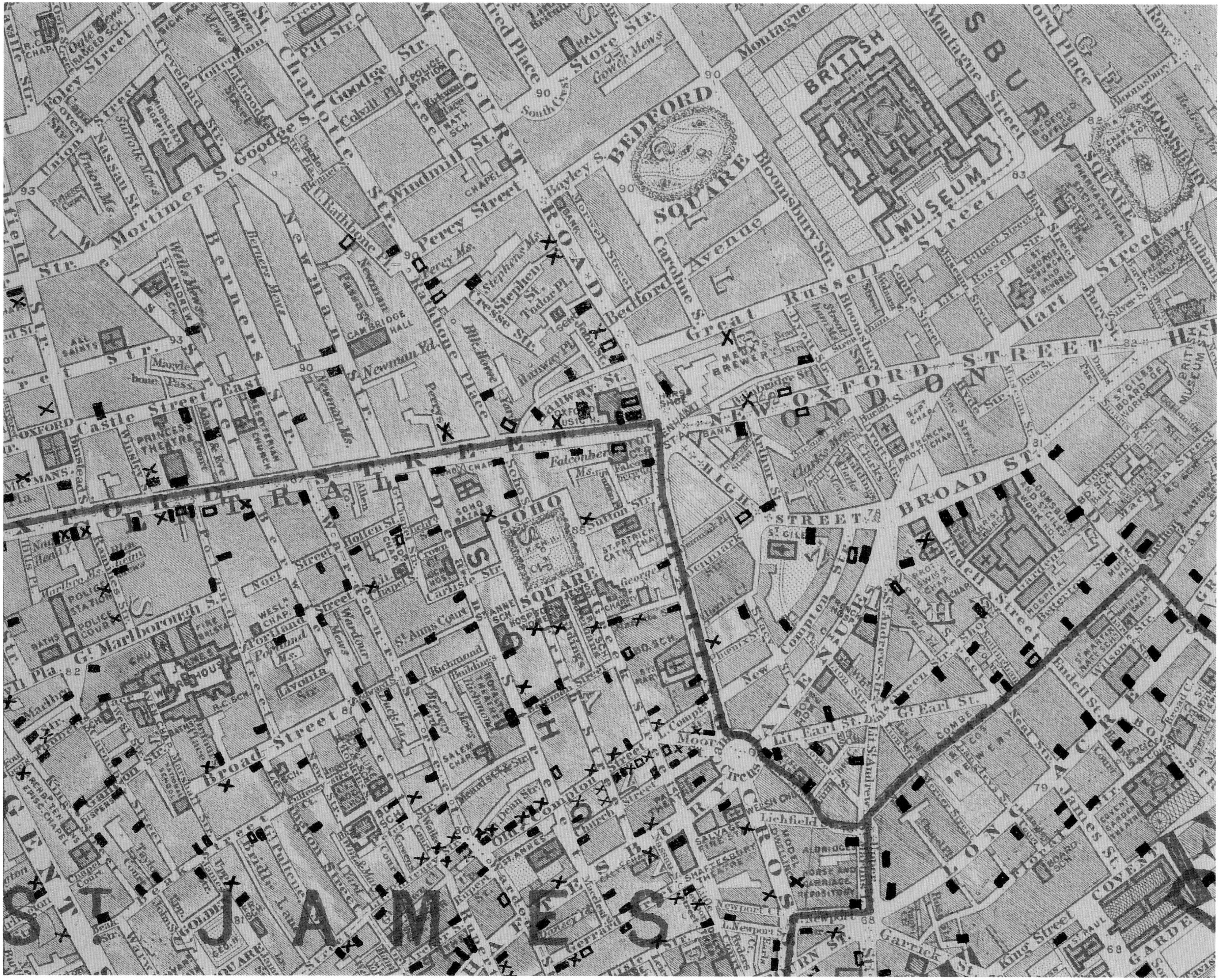

BRITISH MUSEUM
BEDFORD SQUARE
Bloomsbury Str.
Great Russell Street
Oxford Street
NEW OXFORD STREET
BROAD ST.
High Street
SOHO SQUARE
Gt Marlborough St.
Broad Street
Mortimer St.
Goodge St.
Percy Street
Windmill St.
Charlotte St.
Rathbone Place
Castle Street East
Berners Str.
Newman Str.
Hanway St.
Dean Str.
Compton Street
Wardour Str.
Endell Street
Long Acre
Garrick St.
King Street
Circus
Newport Market
ST. JAMES

SECTION SEVEN
METROLAND

Between 1850 and 1945 London changed beyond recognition as a result of the interplay between population pressures, new means of transport, a revolution in building techniques, raised social expectations and a new, leisure ethos. Buildings spread deep into the countryside until Green Belt legislation was passed to save what remained. Distinct types of suburb developed. More than ever, particular types of buildings reflected the differing functions of the institution that they housed, from department stores to museums. Maps had to change radically in appearance to be of real use in this changed environment. Some of the most distorted maps, like Harry Beck's Tube map, were so effective that they became symbols for the new London.

7.1 DIFFERENT LONDONS

By the early twentieth century there was a variety of Londons. The depopulated centre was increasingly given over to business and pleasure. The inner suburbs were full of clerks like Charles Pooter, proudly enjoying their recently-acquired middle-class status and the benefits of bourgeois life. Beyond them, the superior outer suburbs were springing up on the site of dismembered parks and villas. Still further out, enormous council housing estates or private garden suburbs evolved to provide quasi-rural amenity and social harmony, as the Metropolitan (and other) Railways and light industry pushed deep into the countryside. In 1938, in a reaction to the rapid suburbanisation of the whole South-East, the surviving London countryside received statutory protection in the form of the first, rather timid, Greenbelt Act.

Extract from Patrick Abercrombie, *Greater London Plan: Master Plan 1944*

283

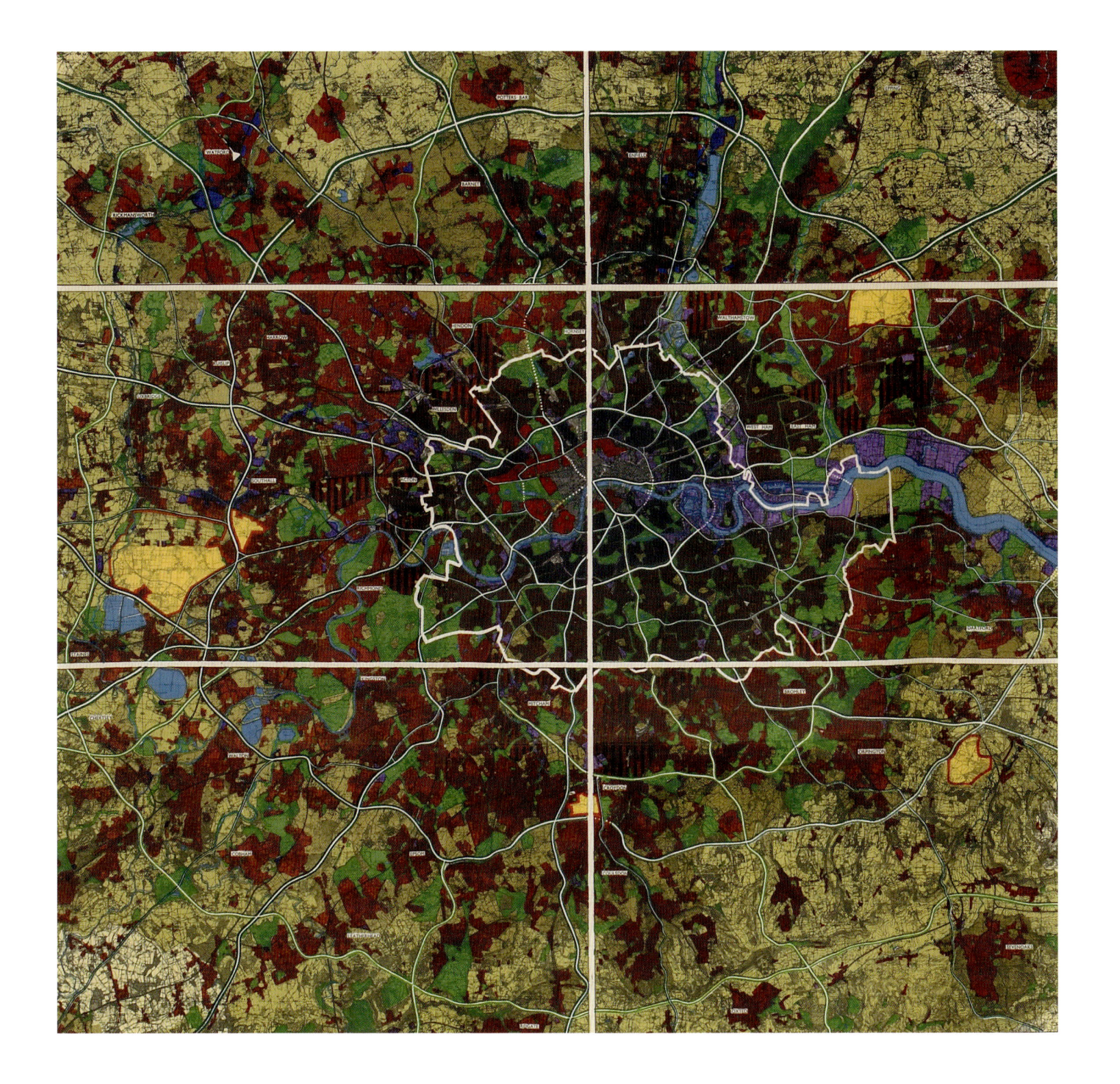

THE INNER CITY: WHO OWNS WHAT?

In order to do its work, the LCC needed to know the names of property-owners within its area. Business-use was coming to predominate there and population was in decline by 1910. No Ordnance Survey map contained such information: property-owners who still dominated Parliament in the 1890s would not have considered including it. The introduction of universal male suffrage, which finally ended the dominance of the landed classes in Parliament in 1906 and the election of a reforming Liberal administration seems to have encouraged the LCC to take matters into its own hands. This highly detailed map of the surroundings of Bunhill Fields in Finsbury, copied from a smaller-scale survey completed in 1910, itself compiled from a wide variety of sources, is annotated to show even the smallest property holding in an area just beyond the City.

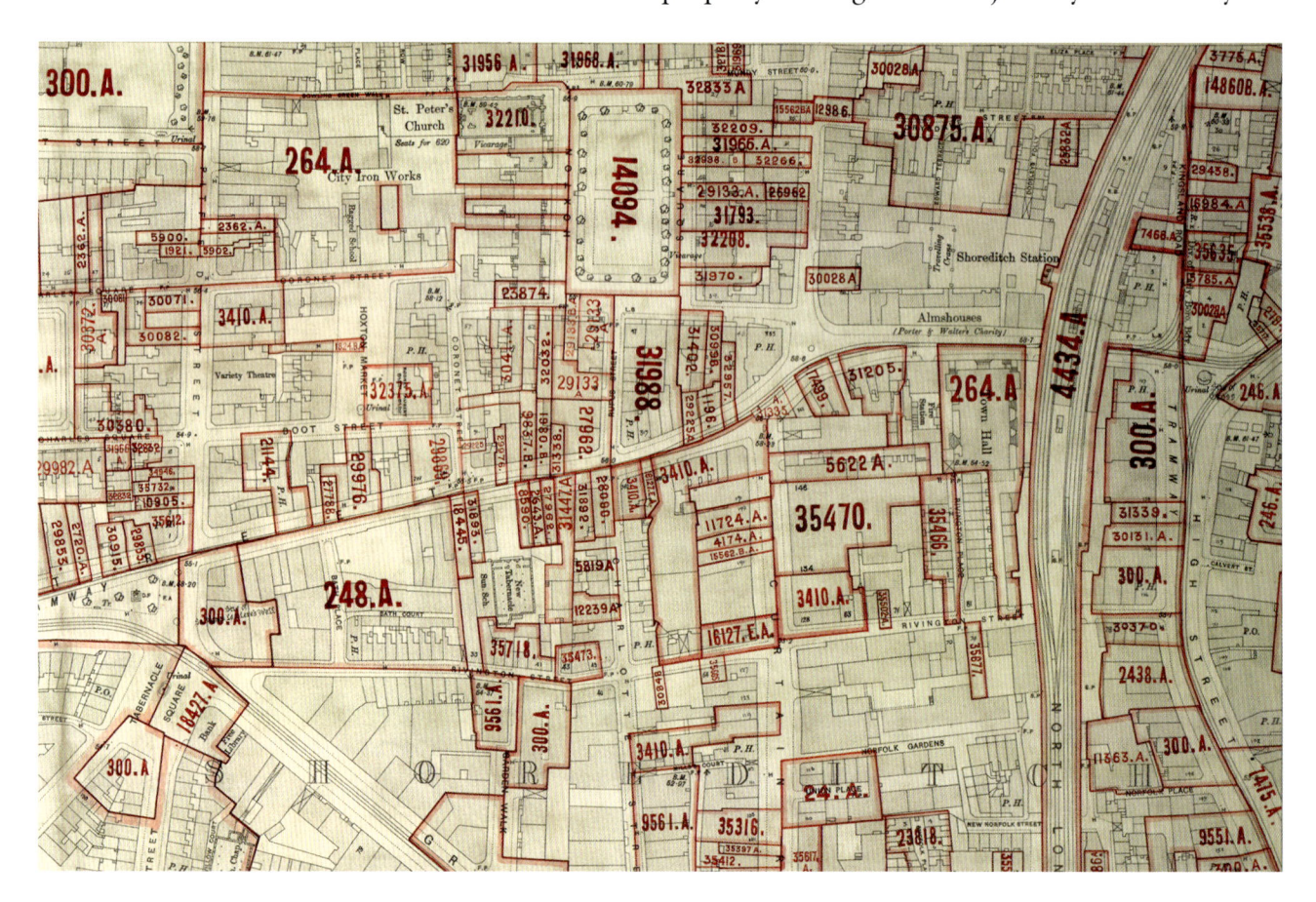

7.1.1   LCC 'Ground Plan' for the Bunhill Fields area, with numbered boundaries added in red to a 5 foot to the mile [1:1056] 2nd edn Ordnance Survey map, 1910–15. 70.5 × 98 cm. City of London, London Metropolitan Archives

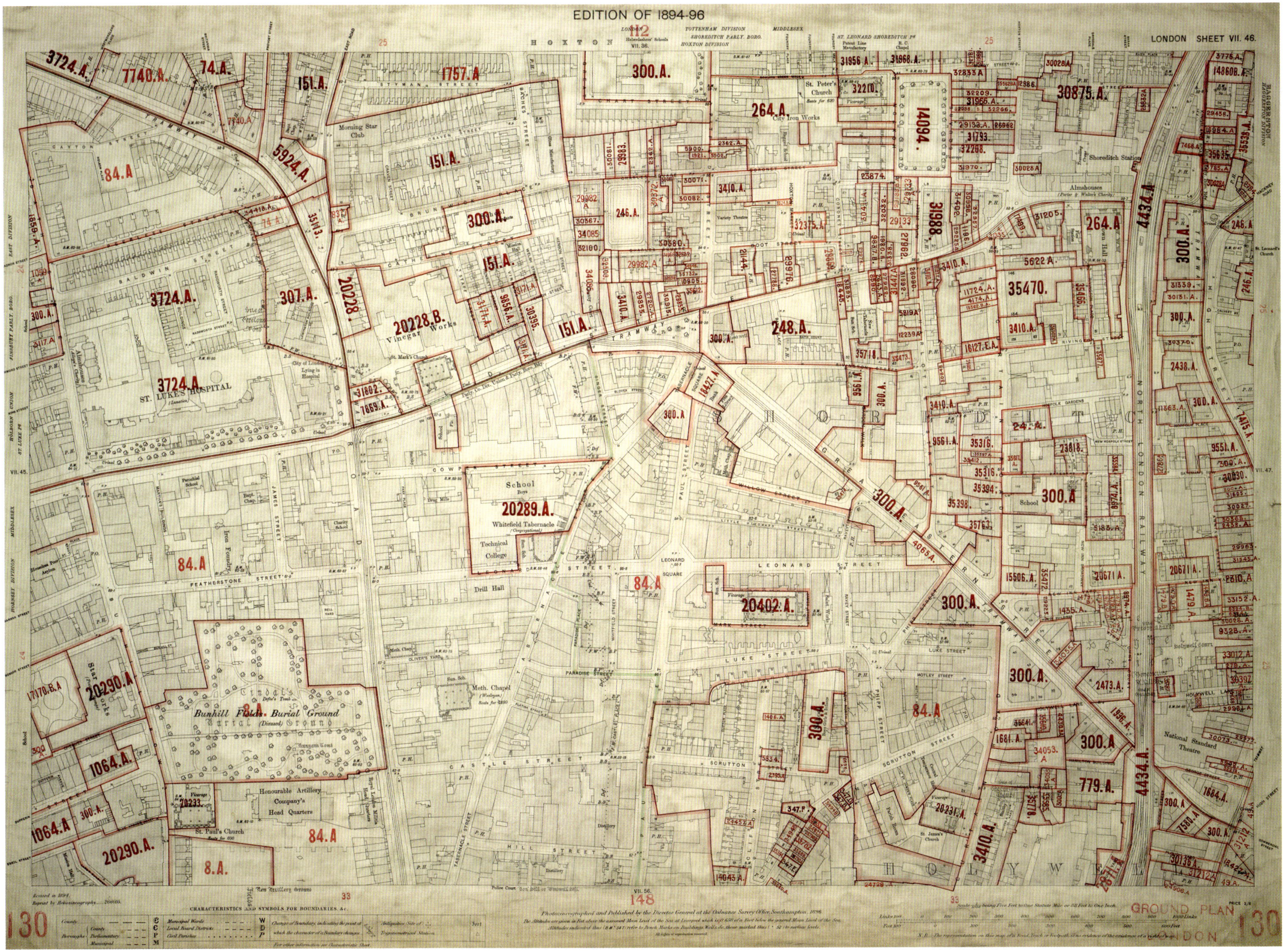
EDITION OF 1894-96
LONDON SHEET VII. 46.
HOXTON
SHOREDITCH
HOLYWELL
St. Peter's Church
City Iron Works
Shoredith Station
Almshouses
Morning Star Club
Vinegar Works
St. Mark's Church
St. Luke's Hospital
School
Whitefield Tabernacle
Technical College
Drill Hall
Leonard Square
Leonard Street
Luke Street
Scrutton Street
Castle Street
Paradise Street
Featherstone Street
Bunhill Fields Burial Ground
Honourable Artillery Company's Head Quarters
St. Paul's Church
National Standard Theatre
North London Railway
Meth. Chapel
Distillery
St. James's Church
CHARACTERISTICS AND SYMBOLS FOR BOUNDARIES &c.
GROUND PLAN
130

THE INNER SUBURBS: SOCIAL LIFE AND RELIGIOUS APATHY IN HOLLOWAY

This map by a church warden proudly depicts the streets near the Holloway home of Charles Pooter, the fictional author of the *Diary of a Nobody*. Presumably in return for their Anglican owners' donations towards the cost of publishing the map and in recognition of their attendance at church, the local shops, theatre and educational establishments, like Holloway College, are named. As a result the plan gives an idea not only of the geography and boundaries of the area but also of the social life of its residents. Pooter patronised [Peter] Jones's elegant department store and perhaps also the rather expensive 'Crown Bazaar' which had only two prices: 2/6 (12.5p) and 5/- (25p). The text at the foot of the plan recalls the years 1876–77 when the vicar 'went to the people as they would not come to him and preached in the streets' and it depicts the new church of 1884 that was built as a result of his endeavours. Things were not as they appeared however. Ten years later the church was evidently still starved of funds and little respected by some of the local community. It lacked a proper church tower, mission hall, school and parsonage and the text laments that 'the church front has been sadly disfigured by mischievous boys and therefore requires gates for its protection'. It is a reminder that anti-social behaviour is not just a twenty-first-century phenomenon and that, contrary to the stereotype, most Victorian Londoners were not regular church-goers.

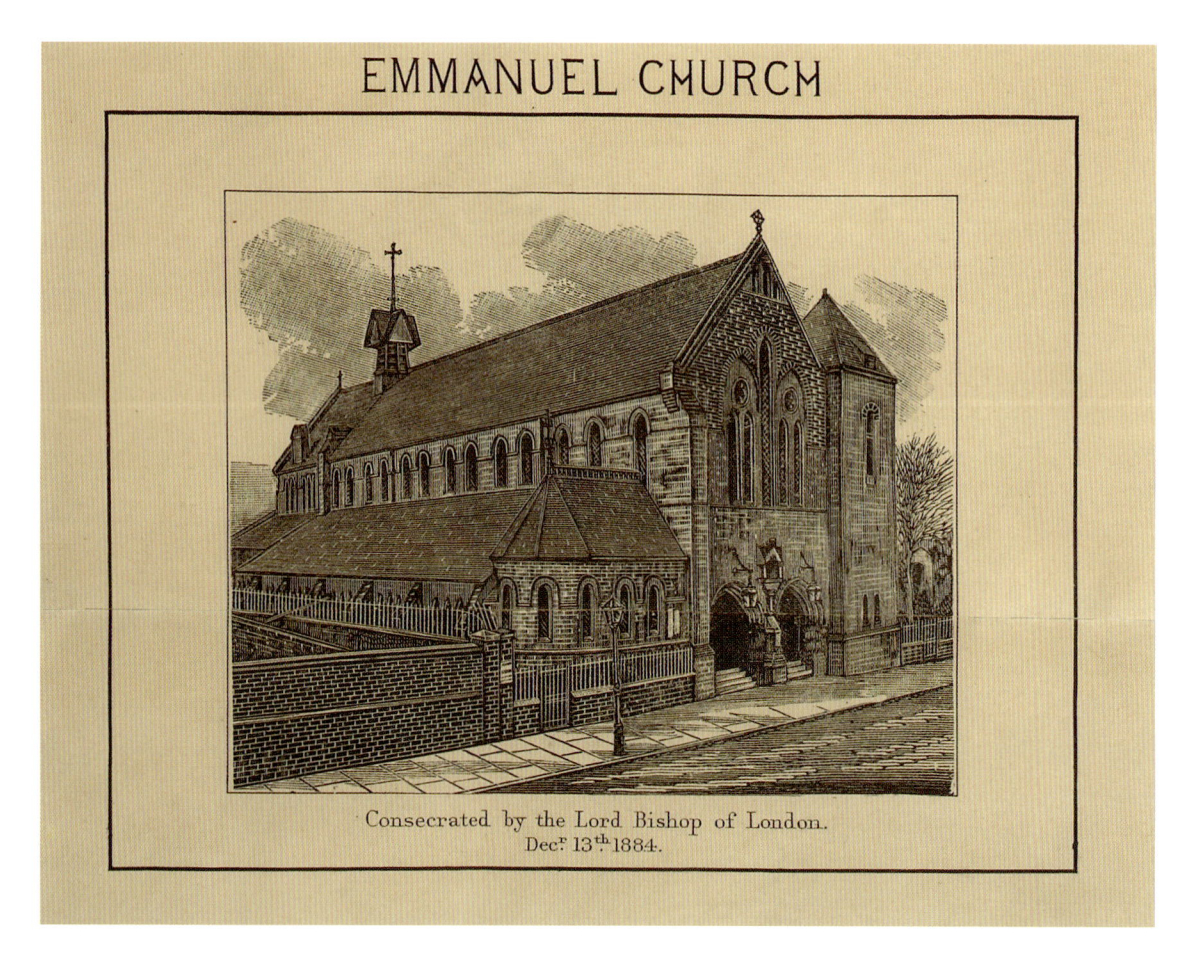

EMMANUEL CHURCH

Consecrated by the Lord Bishop of London.
Dec.r 13th 1884.

7.1.2   Ralph Welland, *Map of Emmanuel Parish, Holloway*, 1894 (Holloway: Thomas H. Bloom, 1894). Chromolithograph. 65.8 × 43.6 cm. Maps 3495 (72)

The map was designed and engraved by Ralph Welland. He was born in Islington in 1847 and was, like his father James and his uncle George before him (and his daughter Frances after him), a professional map engraver — although here plainly working in his spare time for the good of the parish. He lived locally in Isledon Road. His neighbour in Sussex Road, Thomas Henry Bloom, who published the map in his capacity as churchwarden, came originally from Norfolk, married Florence Wright from Balham, and was employed as a clerk on the railways. The beleaguered vicar, Henry Bloomer, to whom the map is dedicated, came from the Midlands, married Edith Sarah Jecks, the daughter of a bank clerk from Lambeth, and left her with at least six children to bring up alone on his early death in 1906.

287

THE OUTER SUBURBS: VILLAS GIVE WAY TO STREETS

This plan is taken from an 1880 sales brochure for a late-eighteenth-century house, The Elms, and its estate in Muswell Hill. The accompanying photographs show its owners and their friends enjoying the spacious grounds. The estate agents assumed that it would succumb to development as had by then most of the fields between London and Muswell Hill. A proposed road is shown dividing the estate in two. In the event, a private buyer was found. But when the buyer sold the house in 1900, the estate agents' assumption was realised, the house and estate going to a developer, James Edmonson. Shops and the suburban houses of Duke's Avenue now cover the site.

7.1.3 The Elms, Muswell Hill sale catalogue, August 1880. Chromolithograph. 49.2 × 61 cm. Maps 137.a.11, vol. 2 no. 3

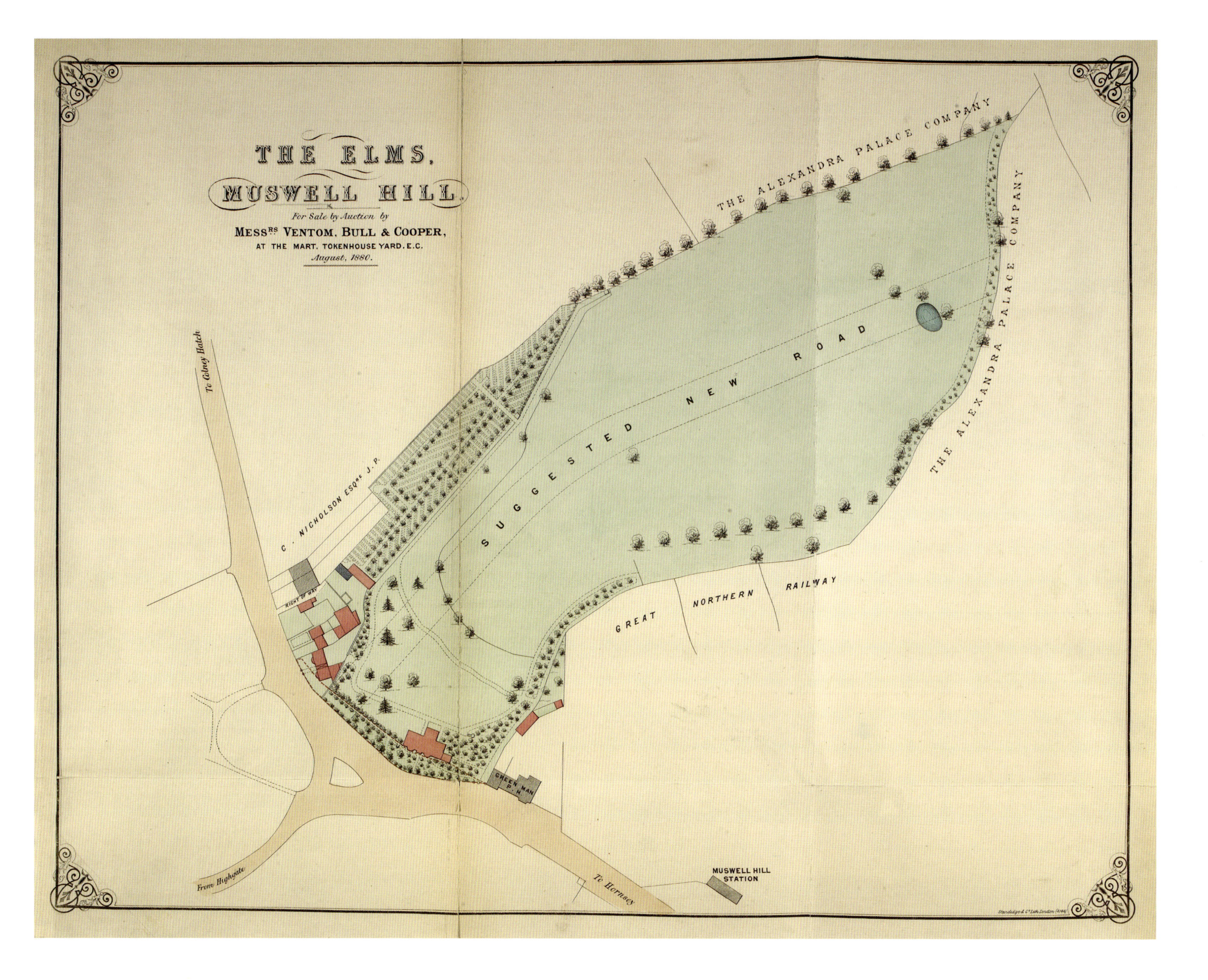

THE ELMS,
MUSWELL HILL.

For Sale by Auction by

MESSRS VENTOM, BULL & COOPER,
AT THE MART, TOKENHOUSE YARD, E.C.
August, 1880.

THE ALEXANDRA PALACE COMPANY

THE ALEXANDRA PALACE COMPANY

SUGGESTED NEW ROAD

C. NICHOLSON ESQRE J.P.

RIGHT OF WAY

GREAT NORTHERN RAILWAY

GREEN MAN P.H.

To Colney Hatch

From Highgate

To Hornsey

MUSWELL HILL STATION

METROLAND

After opening its line to High Wycombe to passenger traffic from 1906, the Great Central Railway Company copied the tactics of the Metropolitan Railway in its efforts to encourage Londoners to move to country districts near its stations. This schematic plan was supplied free to passengers and to people thinking of moving out to the new suburbs. Distances are distorted, in a way that was to become familiar in twentieth century commercial cartography, giving the impression that Aylesbury was little more than a stone's throw away from Marylebone Station. The Railway Company's publicists have also decided, without any obvious factual evidence for the assertion, that the region that it served was 'London's most healthy Residential Area' and have adorned the plan with evocative photographs of then rural villages like Wembley and Rickmansworth. The Underground connections beyond Marylebone suggest that the new commuters would have no difficulty in reaching their London offices wherever they were in the capital. Future residents would have the best of town and country. The back of the plan is covered with advertising for builders and estate agents.

7.1.4 [Great Central Railway Company] *London's most Healthy Residential Area served by the Great Central Railway Co.* (c. 1910). 49.9 × 63.4 cm. Maps 3487 (34)

London's Most Healthy Residential Area served by the Great Central Rly. Co.

Main Line to the North, Sheffield, Manchester, Etc.

CALVERT — VERNEY JCTN. — WINSLOW ROAD — GRANDBORO ROAD — QUAINTON RD — WADDESDON MANOR — AKEMAN ST — WADDESDON — WESTCOTT — WOTTON — WOOD SIDING — BRILL — HADDENHAM — AYLESBURY — STOKE MANDEVILLE — LITTLE KIMBLE — WENDOVER — PRINCES RISBORO' — GT HAMPDEN — GT MISSENDEN — CHESHAM — LITTLE MISSENDEN — BRADENHAM PARK — SAUNDERTON — CHENIES — CHALFONT RD — AMERSHAM — SHARDELOES — HUGHENDEN MANOR PARK — CHORLEY WOOD — WEST WYCOMBE — RICKMANSWORTH — HIGH WYCOMBE — JORDANS — CHALFONT ST GILES (For Milton's Cottage) — MOOR PARK — SANDY LODGE — BEACONSFIELD — Wm Penn's Meeting House and Burial Place — BEACONSFIELD GOLF LINKS HALT — NORTHWOOD — HALL BARN — HAREFIELD — PINNER — BULSTRODE PARK — RUISLIP RESERVOIR — HARROW-ON-THE-HILL — GERRARDS CROSS — LANGLEY PARK — DENHAM GOLF HALT — NORTH HARROW — WEMBLEY PARK — BURNHAM BEECHES — DENHAM — RUISLIP & ICKENHAM — NEASDEN — WILLESDEN GREEN — KILBURN & BRONDESBURY — WEST HAMPSTEAD — NORTHOLT — WEMBLEY PARK — FINCHLEY RD — STOKE POGES (Scene of Grey's Elegy) — UXBRIDGE — SOUTH HARROW — SUDBURY & HARROW RD — WEMBLEY HILL — SWISS COTTAGE — MARLBORO' RD — ST JOHNS WOOD RD — MARYLEBONE TERMINUS GT CENTRAL Subway Connection — Metropolitan Rly — BAKER ST — To the City, Met Rly — Bakerloo Ry (Tube) — To the West End, Waterloo, Elephant & Castle Etc — EDGWARE ROAD — To Kensington, Hammersmith, Etc.

GET A COPY OF "THE HOMESTEAD."

KNAPP, DREWETT & SONS LTD LITHO KINGSTON-ON-THAMES

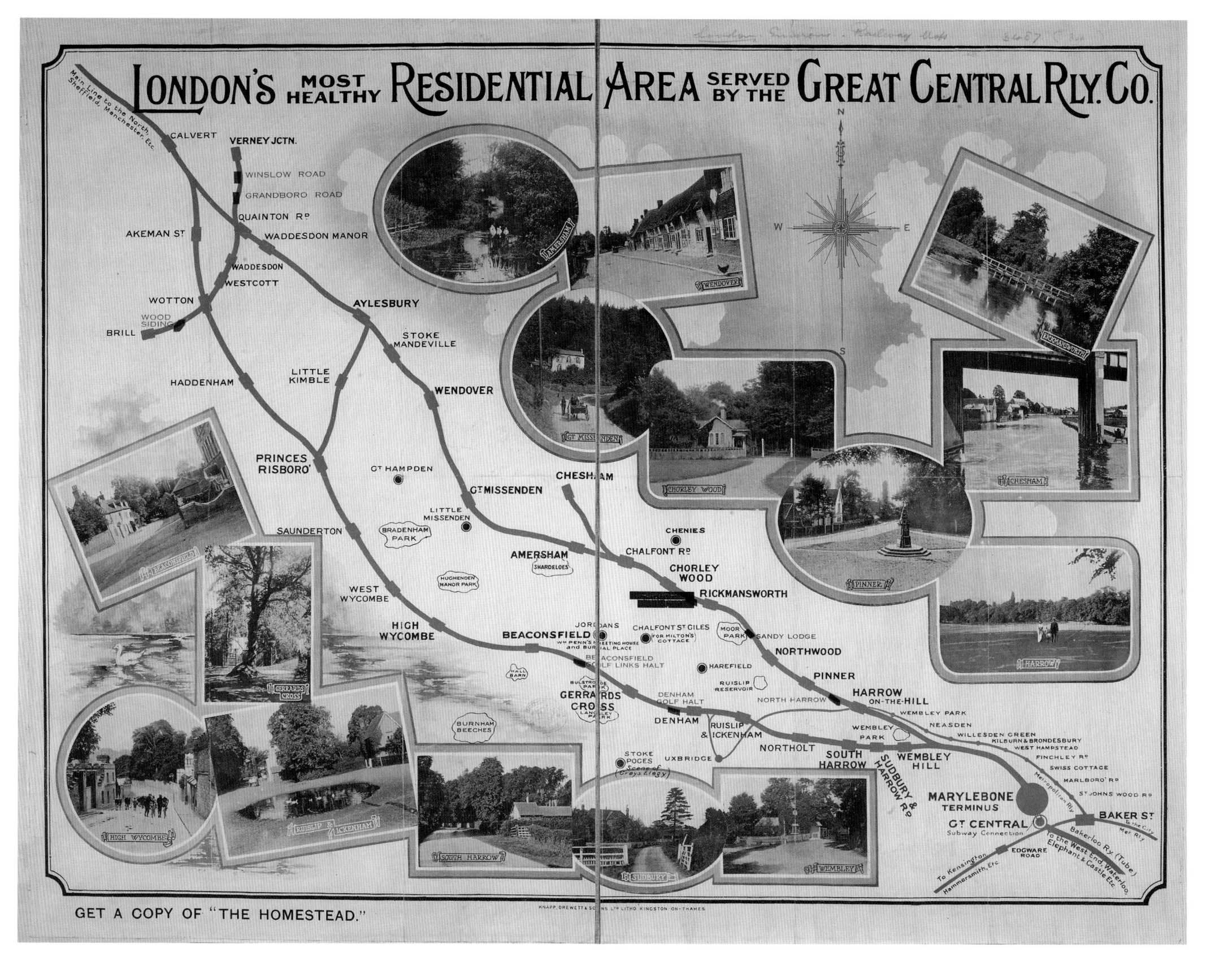

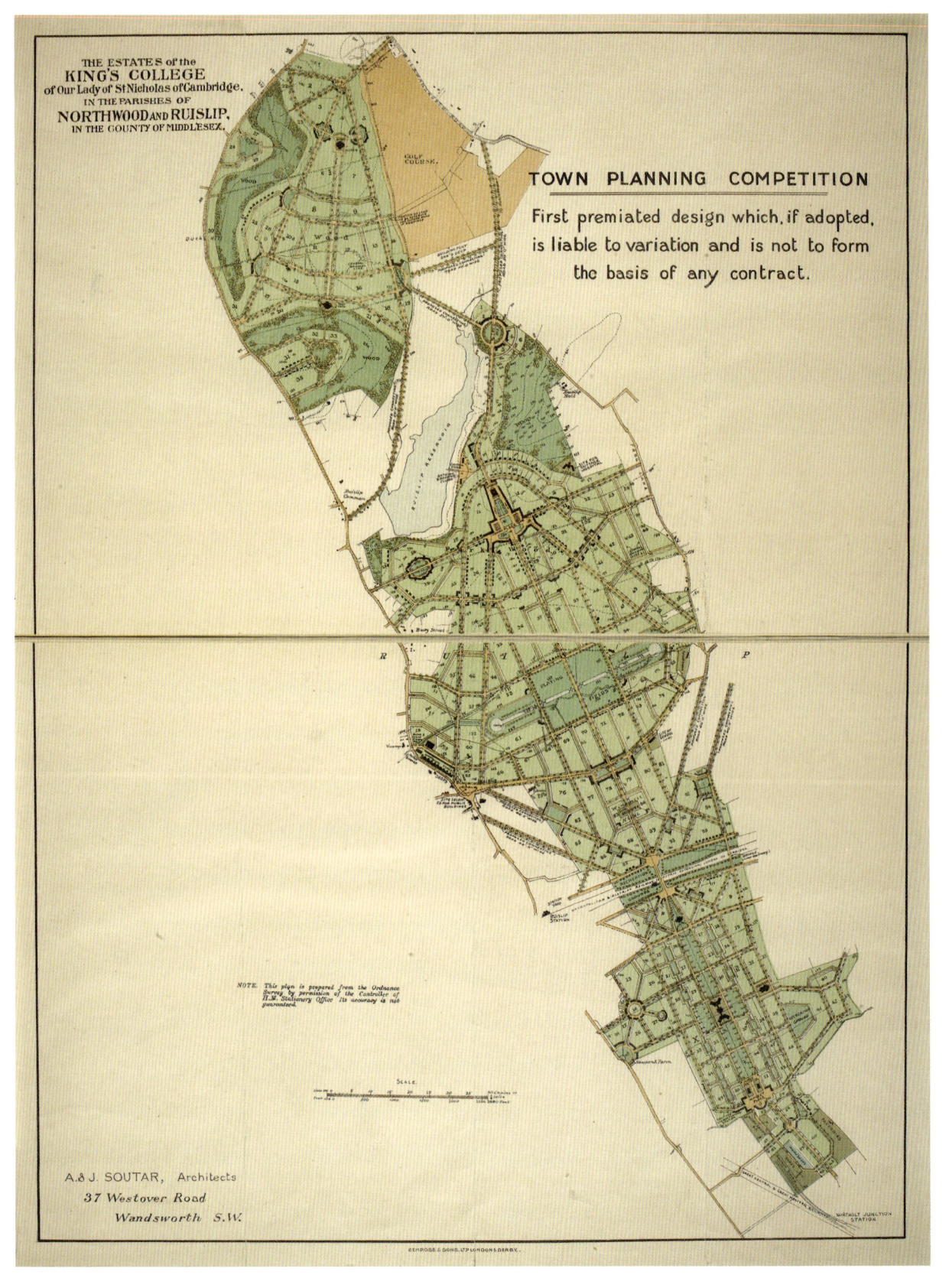

SOCIAL HARMONY IN RUISLIP

The garden suburb can be traced to the development of St John's Wood around 1800, but from 1900 socialist planners like Raymond Unwin viewed it primarily as a mechanism for achieving social harmony in a happy, because green and healthy, social community. As Unwin wrote in the 1907 *Prospectus* accompanying the earliest plans for Hampstead Garden Suburb, 'We desire to do something to meet the **housing problem**, by putting within the reach of working people the opportunity of taking a cottage with a garden within a 2d fare of Central London, and at a moderate rent … in cleaner air, with open space next to their doors, with gardens where the family labour would produce vegetables, fruit and flowers, the people would develop a sense of home life and interest in nature which forms the best security against the temptations of drink and gambling…'. These cottages would be built close to homes for the wealthy because 'we desire to promote a **better understanding** between the members of the classes who form our nation.' Though particularly associated with Hampstead Garden Suburb, there were several other garden suburbs like this prize-winning project near Ruislip Manor station on the Metropolitan Line. Bright green colours emphasise the optimism, and the open spaces, woods, and water its environmental philosophy while church, library, club and golf course show the sort of virtuous activities expected of the future residents. Much of this was realised after 1914, though not as stylishly as in Hampstead.

7.1.5a   A. & J. Soutar Architects, *The estates of the Kings College … in the parish of Northwood and Ruislip … Town Planning Competition: First premiated design …* (1911). Chromolithograph. 64.5 × 50.6 cm. Maps 3465 (10)

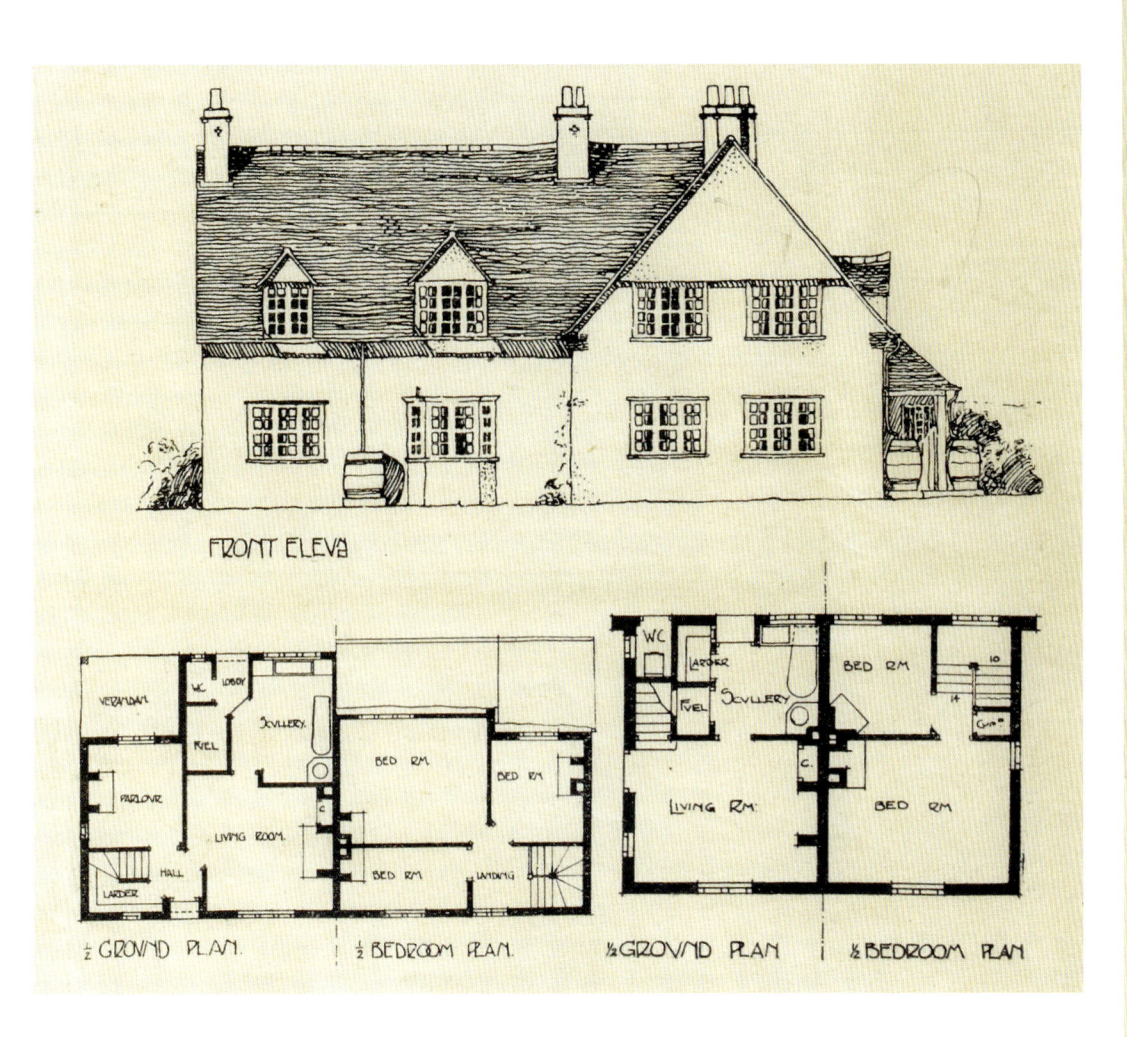

7.1.5b Barry Parker and Raymond Unwin, *Hampstead Tenants Limited: Preliminary sketch plan shewing proposed development of land at Hampstead Garden Suburb* (March 1907). Plan with elevations and plans of cottages and Prospectus. 42.5 × 27.5 cm (plan and elevations); 26 × 20.5 (prospectus) Maps 3479 (106)

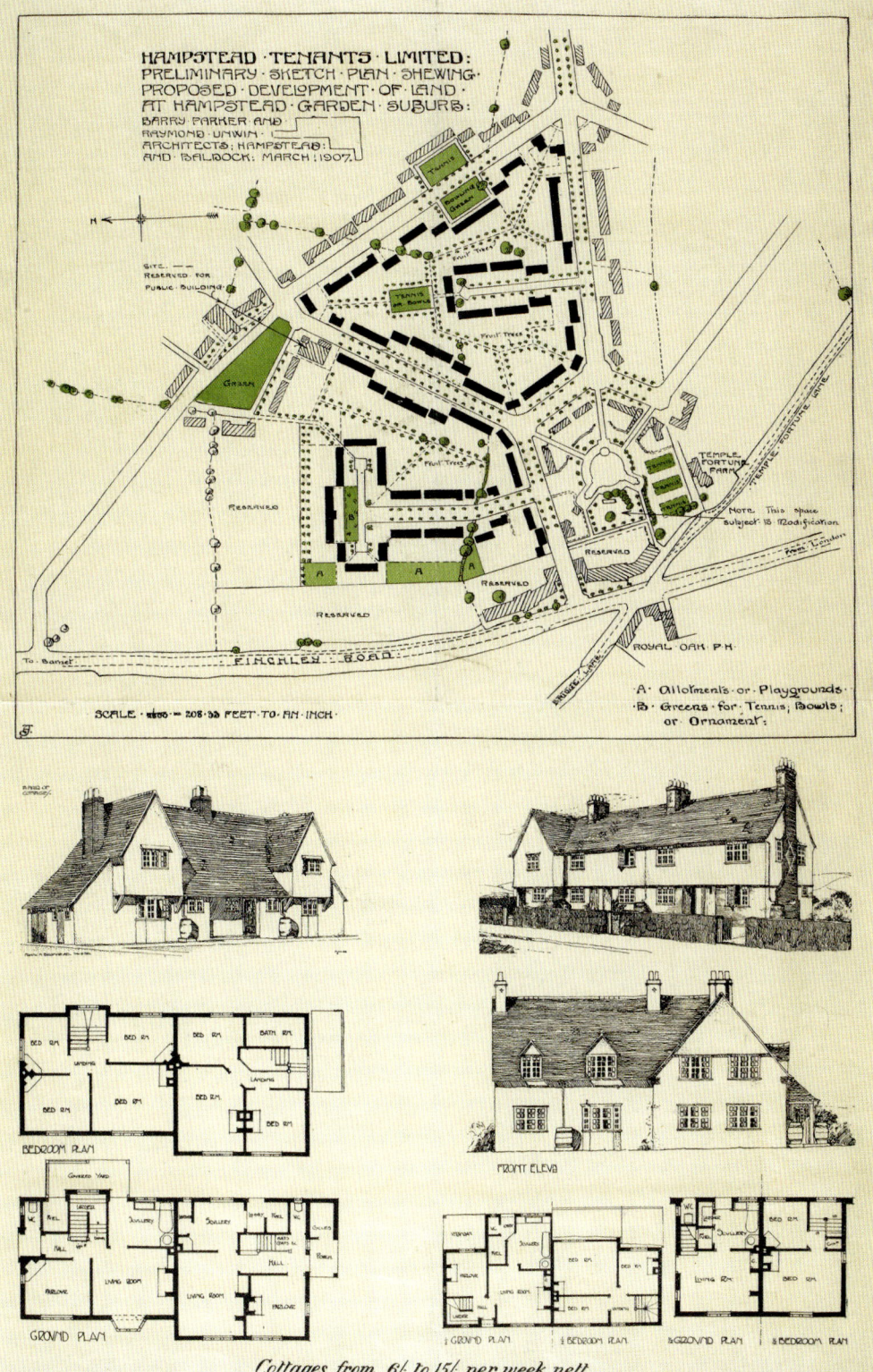

THE COMING OF THE GREEN BELT

In 1944 a team led by Professor Patrick Abercrombie compiled a lengthy and highly influential report on London's future. Its authors believed that, through timely planning, a prosperous and socially-integrated new London could be created from the bombed-out ruins of the old. The seemingly endless expansion of suburbia was a major concern. Open spaces are shown here in colours ranging from yellow to dark green, incidentally revealing how much greenery there was in central London. A timid Greenbelt Act, the first attempt to limit the growth of London since Stuart times, had already been passed in 1938. The report called for more stringent protection of open spaces and also recommended that in place of yet more suburban development, existing market towns around London be developed as satellite towns. These are depicted as orange circles. The plan also paid attention to transport, including air transport. What was to become Heathrow Airport is picked out in bright yellow.

7.1.6 *Greater London Plan. Master Plan 1944*, from Patrick Abercrombie, *Greater London Plan* (London: HMSO, 1945). 102 × 105 cm. Maps 199. f.2

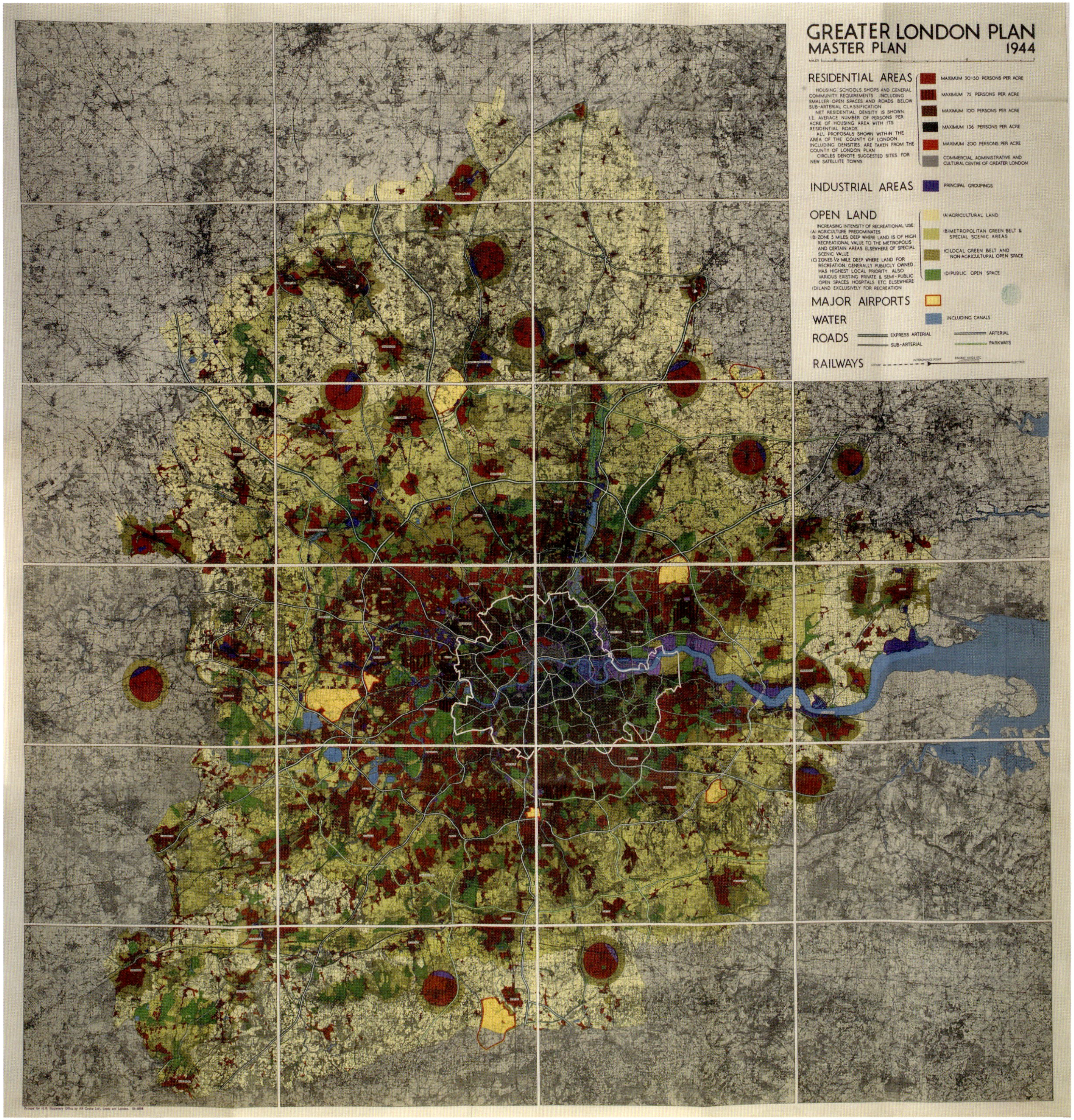
GREATER LONDON PLAN
MASTER PLAN 1944
MILES
RESIDENTIAL AREAS
HOUSING SCHOOLS, SHOPS AND GENERAL COMMUNITY REQUIREMENTS . INCLUDING SMALLER OPEN SPACES AND ROADS BELOW SUB-ARTERIAL CLASSIFICATION
NET RESIDENTIAL DENSITY IS SHOWN I.E. AVERAGE NUMBER OF PERSONS PER ACRE OF HOUSING AREA WITH ITS RESIDENTIAL ROADS
ALL PROPOSALS SHOWN WITHIN THE AREA OF THE COUNTY OF LONDON, INCLUDING DENSITIES, ARE TAKEN FROM THE COUNTY OF LONDON PLAN
CIRCLES DENOTE SUGGESTED SITES FOR NEW SATELLITE TOWNS
MAXIMUM 30-50 PERSONS PER ACRE
MAXIMUM 75 PERSONS PER ACRE
MAXIMUM 100 PERSONS PER ACRE
MAXIMUM 136 PERSONS PER ACRE
MAXIMUM 200 PERSONS PER ACRE
COMMERCIAL ADMINISTRATIVE AND CULTURAL CENTRE OF GREATER LONDON
INDUSTRIAL AREAS
PRINCIPAL GROUPINGS
OPEN LAND
INCREASING INTENSITY OF RECREATIONAL USE:
(A) AGRICULTURE PREDOMINATES
(B) ZONE 5 MILES DEEP WHERE LAND IS OF HIGH RECREATIONAL VALUE TO THE METROPOLIS AND CERTAIN AREAS ELSEWHERE OF SPECIAL SCENIC VALUE
(C) ZONES 1/2 MILE DEEP WHERE LAND FOR RECREATION, GENERALLY PUBLICLY OWNED, HAS HIGHEST LOCAL PRIORITY. ALSO VARIOUS EXISTING PRIVATE & SEMI-PUBLIC OPEN SPACES HOSPITALS ETC. ELSEWHERE
(D) LAND EXCLUSIVELY FOR RECREATION
(A) AGRICULTURAL LAND
(B) METROPOLITAN GREEN BELT & SPECIAL SCENIC AREAS
(C) LOCAL GREEN BELT AND NON-AGRICULTURAL OPEN SPACE
(D) PUBLIC OPEN SPACE
MAJOR AIRPORTS
WATER
INCLUDING CANALS
ROADS
EXPRESS ARTERIAL
SUB-ARTERIAL
ARTERIAL
PARKWAYS
RAILWAYS

7.2 BE A SPORT...

From about 1870 most Londoners at last had money and, thanks to the introduction of Saturday half-holidays and bank holidays, sufficient time for regular sport and other forms of recreation. Cycling and later, for the wealthy, motor cars became crazes. Indeed, many Londoners first got to know the suburbs where they were later to live from their saddles when these districts still formed part of the Essex, Middlesex, Kent and Surrey countryside. On the outskirts of London sports clubs, utilising formerly agricultural land and with members drawn from the locality, became common, their matches and fund-raising activities helping to bond the residents of the new middle-class suburbs. Ramblers took advantage of the commons, heaths and woods around London that had been saved by amenity societies like the Commons Preservation Society. While the Ordnance Survey produced maps geared for ramblers, tyre and sportswear manufacturers tried to attract business by sponsoring maps for cyclists and cricketers.

Extract from *Harrison's Bicycle Road Map of Middlesex* (London: Gall & Inglis, 1883)

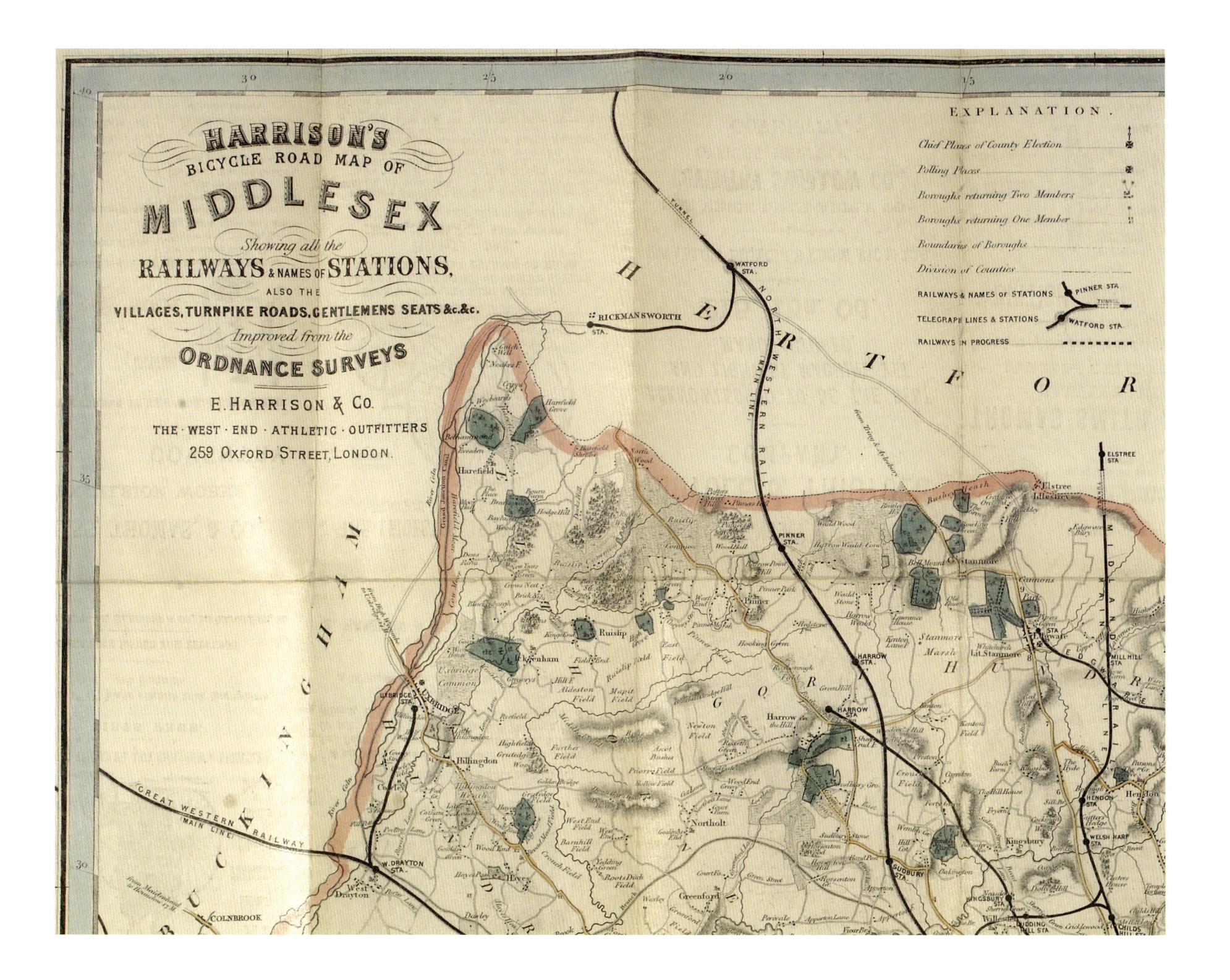

HARRISON'S
BICYCLE ROAD MAP OF
MIDDLESEX
Showing all the
RAILWAYS & NAMES OF STATIONS,
ALSO THE
VILLAGES, TURNPIKE ROADS, GENTLEMENS SEATS &c. &c.
Improved from the
ORDNANCE SURVEYS

E. HARRISON & Co.
THE · WEST · END · ATHLETIC · OUTFITTERS
259 OXFORD STREET, LONDON.

EXPLANATION.

Chief Places of County Election	
Polling Places	
Boroughs returning Two Members	
Boroughs returning One Member	
Boundaries of Boroughs	
Division of Counties	
RAILWAYS & NAMES of STATIONS	
TELEGRAPH LINES & STATIONS	
RAILWAYS IN PROGRESS	

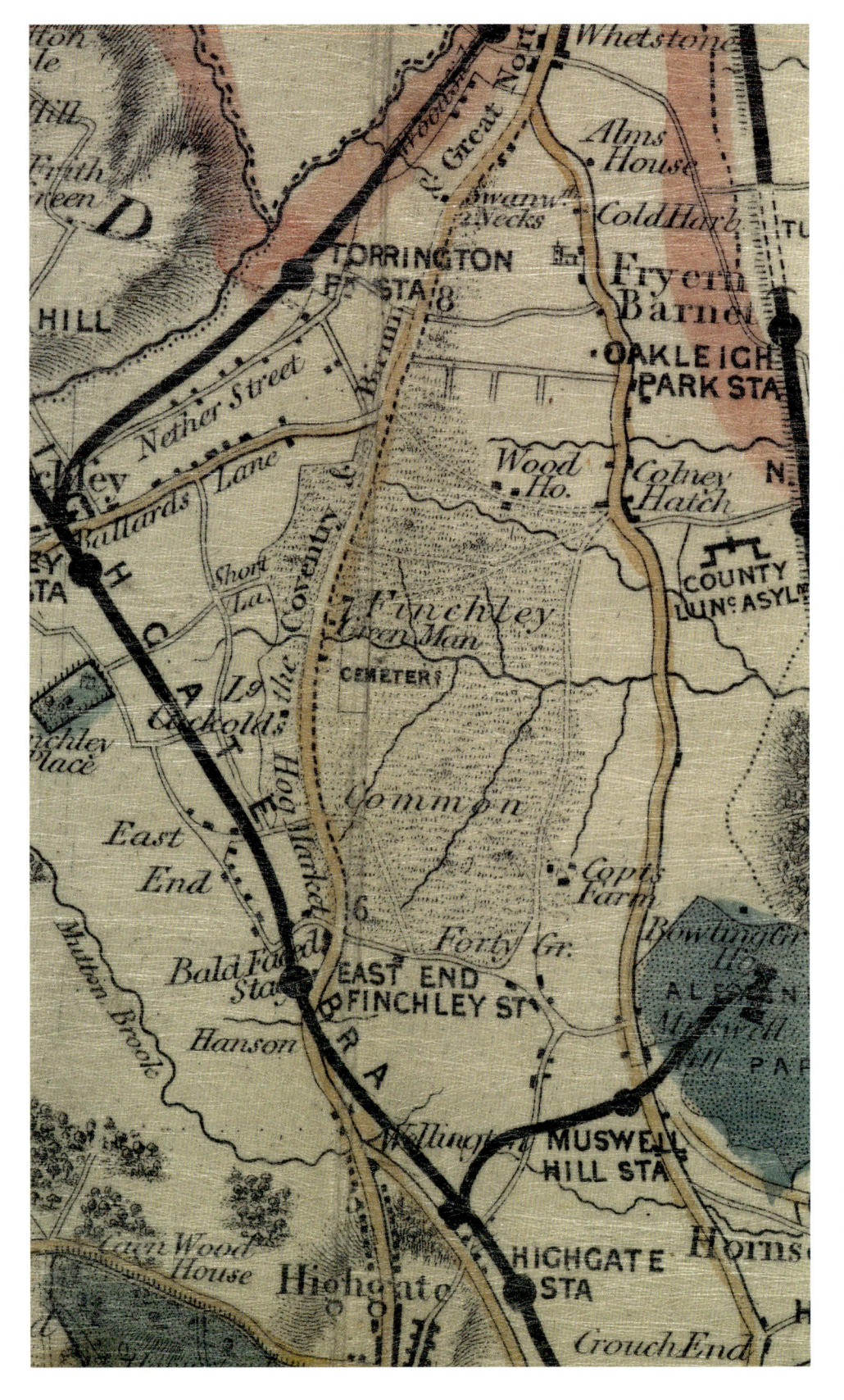

CYCLING TRICKERY

Mapmakers were quick to cash in on the popularity of cycling. This claims to be a purpose-made and up-to-date cycling map. A superficial glance shows railways and even the recently opened Alexandra Park and Palace. A closer look, however, reveals obsolete references in the title to 'Villages, Turnpike Roads, Gentlemens Seats &c &c' and features like Finchley Common that had disappeared more than 60 years earlier. In fact the map had originally been published in John Cary's *New English Atlas* in 1809. It cost the owners of the copperplate little to reprint it for the sportswear outfitters, Harrison's, camouflaged with appropriate advertisements but with relatively few other alterations, to accompany the printed guidebook. After all, the course of the main roads had not changed and the plates were still being reprinted, this time for car drivers, as late as the 1930s …

7.2.1 *Harrison's Bicycle Road Map of Middlesex showing all the Railways & names of Stations Also the Villages, Turnpike Roads, Gentlemens Seats &c &c improved from the Ordnance Surveys* (London: Gall & Inglis, 1883). Engraving. 53.5 × 72 cm. Maps 9.a.22

"CHALLENGE" BICYCLES & TRICYCLES. SINGER & CO., COVENTRY.
HARRISON'S BICYCLE ROAD MAP OF MIDDLESEX
Showing all the RAILWAYS & NAMES OF STATIONS, ALSO THE VILLAGES, TURNPIKE ROADS, GENTLEMENS SEATS &c. &c.
Improved from the ORDNANCE SURVEYS
E. HARRISON & CO.
THE WEST END ATHLETIC OUTFITTERS
259 OXFORD STREET, LONDON.
EXPLANATION.
HERTFORDSHIRE
BUCKINGHAMSHIRE
ESSEX
SURREY
LONDON
ALL BICYCLISTS AND TRICYCLISTS SHOULD HAVE
BOWN'S "ÆOLUS"
ADJUSTABLE BALL BEARINGS FITTED TO THEIR MACHINES, AND NO OTHERS.
THOMAS HOUGH, FLORENCE WORKS, MANDER ST., PENN ROAD, WOLVERHAMPTON.
THE SPECIAL "FLORENTINE" BICYCLE, (BALL BEARINGS TO BOTH WHEELS), Price £8. 15s., has rapidly grown in public favour the last four years, and will be the most popular Machine for 1883. Price Lists and Testimonials free.
AGENTS LONDON: Messrs. E. HARRISON & CO., 259 Oxford St. MANCHESTER: THOMAS HUDSON, 63 Shudehill CANADA: WATSONS, PELTON, & CO., MONTREAL
"CHEYLESMORE" TRICYCLE. As supplied to H.R.H. PRINCE OF WALES.
COVENTRY MACHINISTS' COMPANY LD. WORKS: COVENTRY.
Illustrated Lists sent on receipt of One Stamp.
Branches MANCHESTER: 9 VICTORIA BUILDINGS. LONDON: 15 HOLBORN VIADUCT. BIRMINGHAM, &c. &c.
The SPECIAL CLUB and CLUB RACER BICYCLES.
Longitude East from London

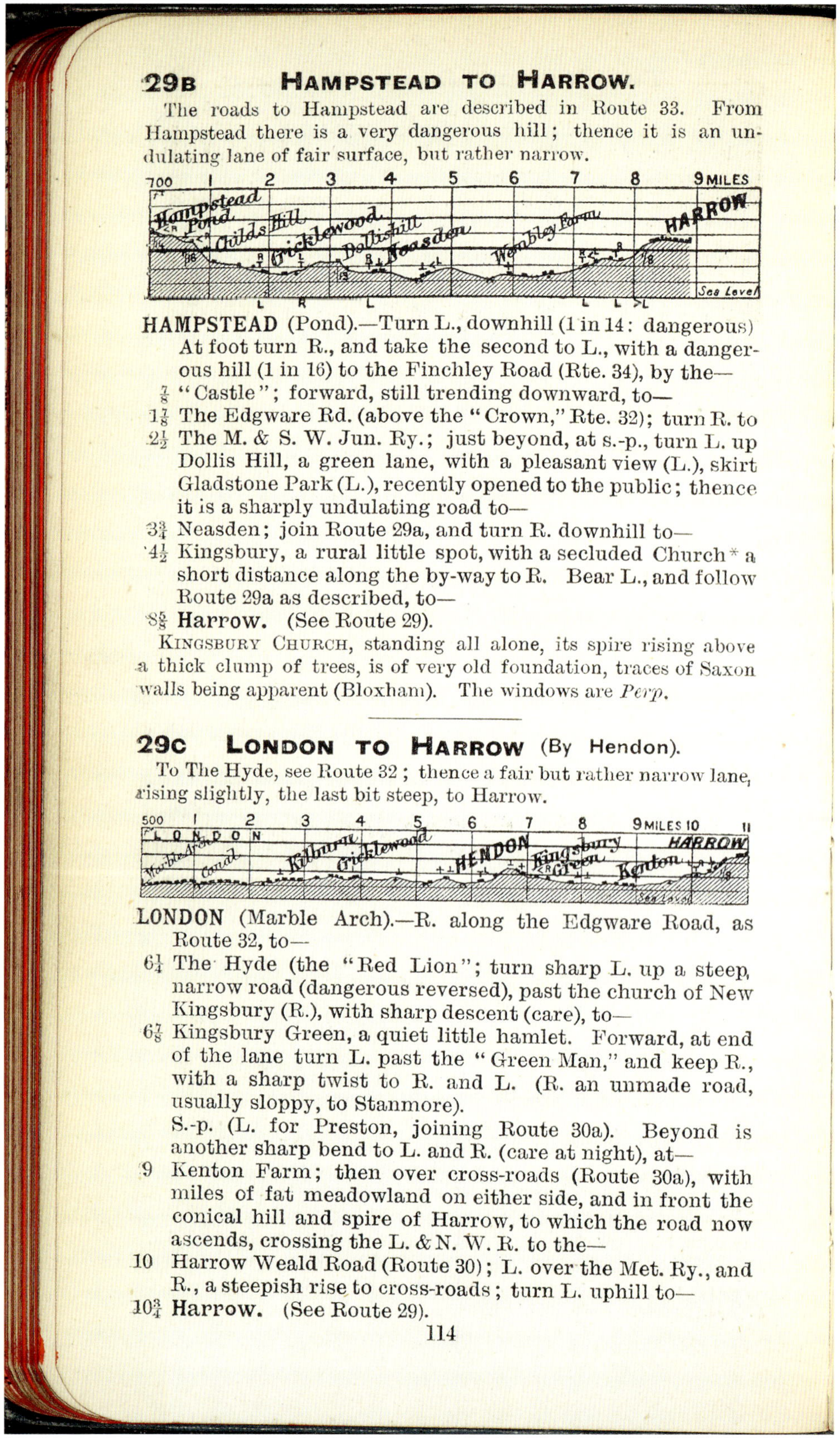

BEARING THE CYCLIST IN MIND

This book, though it had the same publisher as Harrison's map, treats the cyclist with respect. The text and maps are carefully tailored to their users' particular interests, giving details, for instance of the regular cyclists' 'meet' at Woodford as well as the usual tourist information about the sights to be seen along the way, illustrated by photographs. Most important of all, the miniature diagrams give an idea of the gradients, and alternative routes for those who preferred to avoid steep hills.

7.2.2 Arthur C. Armstrong and Harry R. G. Inglis, *Short Spins round London with 286 maps and plans* [*The Contour Road Books*] (London & Edinburgh: Gall & Inglis, 1906). 16 × 17.5 cm. 010349.de.7

WHO'S FOR CRICKET?

From about 1850 farmers near London often allowed urban sports clubs, like the one from Holloway College (see 7.1.2), to play on their land. During the economic recession of the 1880s the clubs got the chance to lease the fields, which would otherwise have been built over. The landowners were happy, since the playing fields enhanced the value of the surrounding properties. The matches and tournaments in their turn provided a social focus for the residents of the new suburbs. This was the background to the Crouch End Playing Fields which attracted enough players to make it worthwhile for a cricket bat manufacturer to subsidise the production costs of this map through an advertisement.

7.2.3 *Hopsons Handy Map of the Crouch End Cricket Fields* (London: Playing Fields Association, 1897). Chromolithograph. 32 × 51 cm. Maps 4050 (1)

Hopson's Handy Map of the Crouch End Cricket Fields

Price 2d.

Playing Fields Association — Hornsey C.C. &c

Entered at Stationers' Hall.

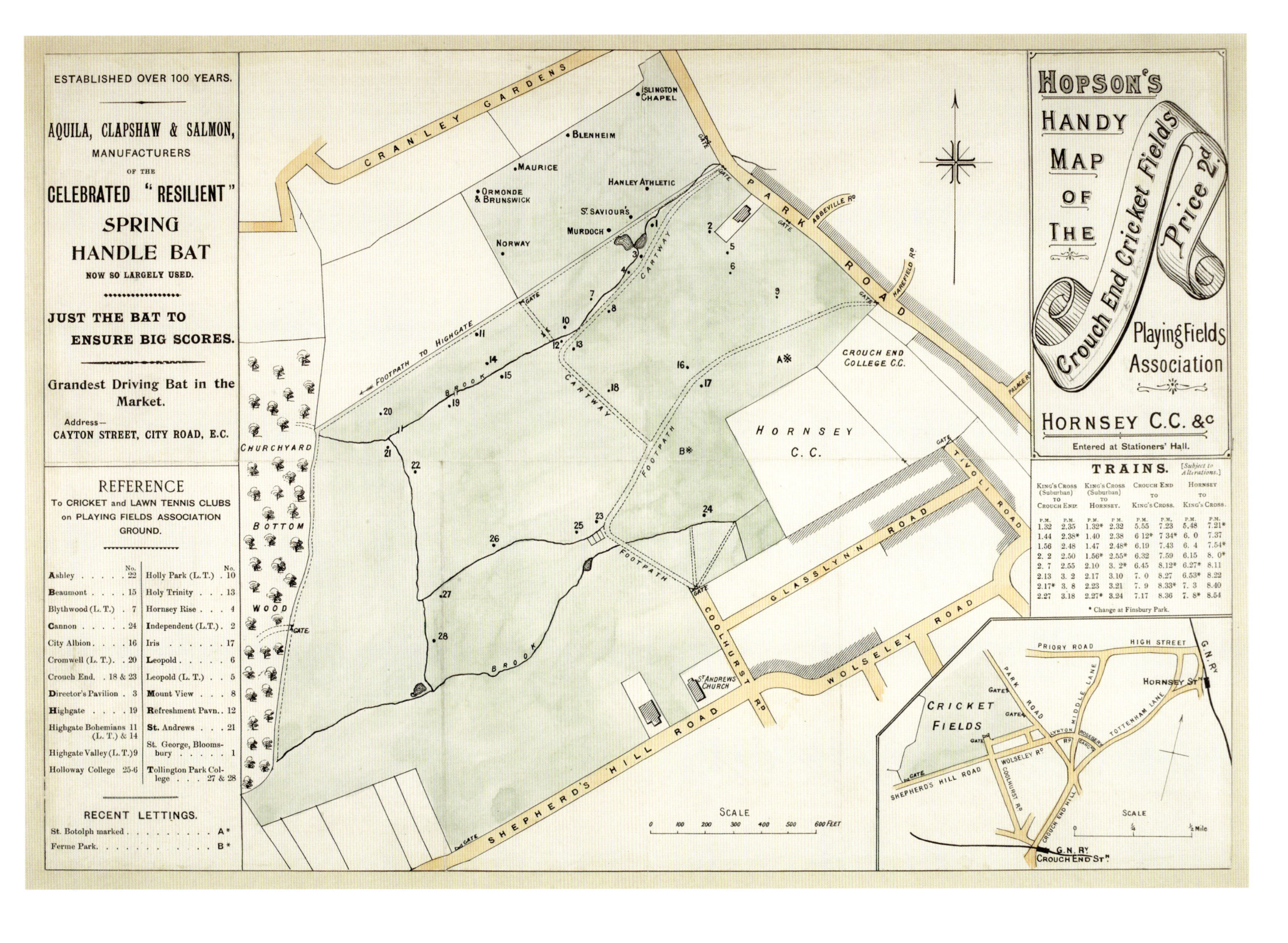

ESTABLISHED OVER 100 YEARS.

AQUILA, CLAPSHAW & SALMON,
MANUFACTURERS OF THE
CELEBRATED "RESILIENT"
SPRING HANDLE BAT
NOW SO LARGELY USED.

JUST THE BAT TO ENSURE BIG SCORES.

Grandest Driving Bat in the Market.

Address—
CAYTON STREET, CITY ROAD, E.C.

REFERENCE
To CRICKET and LAWN TENNIS CLUBS on PLAYING FIELDS ASSOCIATION GROUND.

Club	No.	Club	No.
Ashley	22	Holly Park (L.T.)	10
Beaumont	15	Holy Trinity	13
Blythwood (L.T.)	7	Hornsey Rise	4
Cannon	24	Independent (L.T.)	2
City Albion	16	Iris	17
Cromwell (L.T.)	20	Leopold	6
Crouch End	18 & 23	Leopold (L.T.)	5
Director's Pavilion	3	Mount View	8
Highgate	19	Refreshment Pavn.	12
Highgate Bohemians (L.T.)	11 & 14	St. Andrews	21
Highgate Valley (L.T.)	9	St. George, Bloomsbury	1
Holloway College	25-6	Tollington Park College	27 & 28

RECENT LETTINGS.
St. Botolph marked .... A*
Ferme Park .... B*

TRAINS. [Subject to Alterations.]

King's Cross (Suburban) to Crouch End	King's Cross (Suburban) to Hornsey	Crouch End to King's Cross	Hornsey to King's Cross
P.M. P.M.	P.M. P.M.	P.M. P.M.	P.M. P.M.
1.32 2.35	1.32* 2.32	5.55 7.23	5.48 7.21*
1.44 2.38*	1.40 2.38	6.12* 7.34*	6.0 7.37
1.56 2.48	1.47 2.48*	6.19 7.43	6.4 7.54*
2.2 2.50	1.56* 2.55*	6.32 7.59	6.15 8.0*
2.7 2.55	2.10 3.2*	6.45 8.12*	6.27* 8.11
2.13 3.2	2.17 3.10	7.0 8.27	6.53* 8.22
2.17* 3.8	2.23 3.21	7.9 8.33*	7.3 8.40
2.27 3.18	2.27* 3.24	7.17 8.36	7.8* 8.54

* Change at Finsbury Park.

Map features: Cranley Gardens, Islington Chapel, Blenheim, Maurice, Ormonde & Brunswick, Hanley Athletic, St Saviour's, Norway, Murdoch, Park Road, Abbeville Rd, Harefield Rd, Palace Rd, Footpath to Highgate, Brook, Cartway, Crouch End College C.C., Hornsey C.C., Bottom Wood, Churchyard, St Andrews Church, Coolhurst Rd, Tivoli Road, Glasslynn Road, Wolseley Road, Shepherd's Hill Road.

Scale: 0–600 Feet.

Inset: Cricket Fields — Priory Road, High Street, Park Road, Middle Lane, Lynton Rd, Wolseley Rd, Tottenham Lane, Coolhurst Rd, Shepherds Hill Road, Crouch End Hill, G.N. Ry Hornsey Stn, G.N. Ry Crouch End Stn. Scale: ¼–½ Mile.

THE FIELDS DISAPPEAR

The Commons and Footpaths Preservation Society encouraged its members, while on walks, to annotate the Society's copies of Ordnance Survey maps in red ink to indicate the course and state of the footpaths and stiles, and to show footpaths not marked on the printed map. They were also expected to update the map. This rambler, near Ruislip in about 1906, did as he was told and red lines are to be seen particularly at the left, but he also found urban development encroaching from all sides. At the top is the inked-in course of the Metropolitan Railway and on the left of the Great Western & Great Central Joint Railway. Around Ruislip itself pencil marks indicate newly-built residential roads. Ickenham Marsh at the bottom left is painted in green, though, to highlight the need to preserve a feature of particular importance.

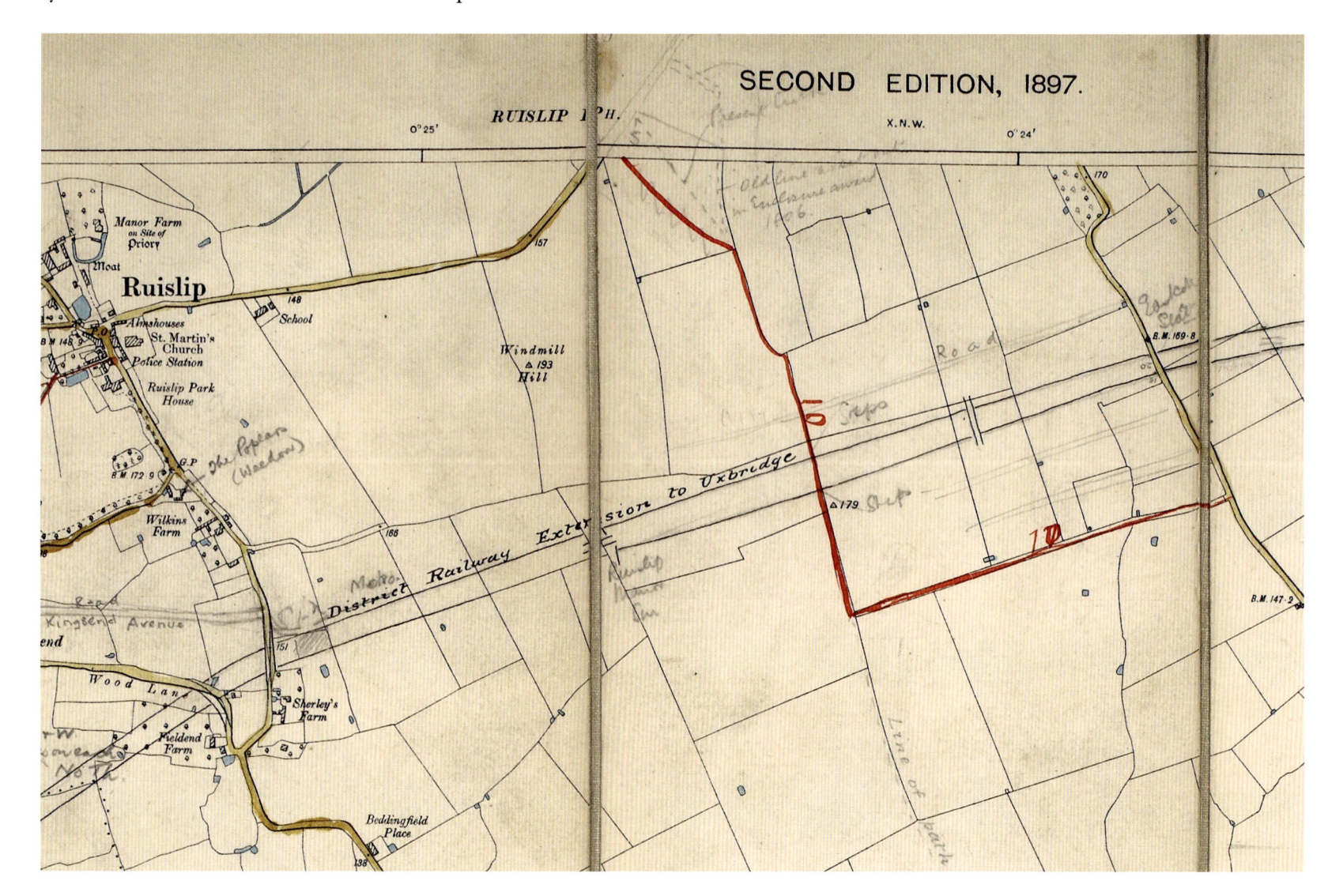

7.2.4 2nd edition Ordnance Survey 6-inch map Middlesex sheet X. SW (1897) annotated for the Commons and Footpaths Preservation Society in about 1906. Printed map with pencil, ink and watercolour annotations. 39.9.x.57 cm.
Maps C.44.b.68

SECOND EDITION, 1897.

MIDDLESEX. SHEET X. S.W.

RUISLIP PH.

PINNER PH.

LON. 0° 26' W. 0° 25' XV. N.W. 0° 24' LON. 0° 23' W.

NORTHOLT PH.

Surveyed in 1863-64. Revised in 1894.
Reprint 100/98.

CHARACTERISTICS AND SYMBOLS

County Boundary
Parish Boundary
Contours { Instrumental 200 ; Sketched 225
Antiquities, Site of +
Arrow, showing direction of flow of water
Trigonometrical Station △

For other information see Characteristic Sheet.

Price 1s.

Scale—Six Inches to One Statute Mile or 880 Feet to One Inch = 1/10560

10 Chains 5 0 10 20 30 40 50 60 70 80 Chains } 1 Mile
40 Perches 20 0 40 80 120 160 200 240 280 320 Perches
1000 Feet 500 0 1000 2000 3000 4000 5000 5280 Feet
1 Furlong 0 ¼ ½ ¾ 1 Mile

Heliozincographed from 1/2500 Plans and Published at the Ordnance Survey Office, Southampton.

N.B.—The representation on this map of a Road, Track, or Footpath, is no evidence of the existence of a right of way.

The Altitudes are given in Feet above the assumed Mean Level of the Sea at Liverpool, which is 0·650 of a Foot below the general Mean Level of the Sea.

Altitudes indicated thus (↑B.M. 54·7) refer to Bench Marks on Buildings, Walls, &c., those marked thus (·) preceded or followed by the height to surface levels.

SHEET X.

N.W.	N.E.
S.W.	S.E.

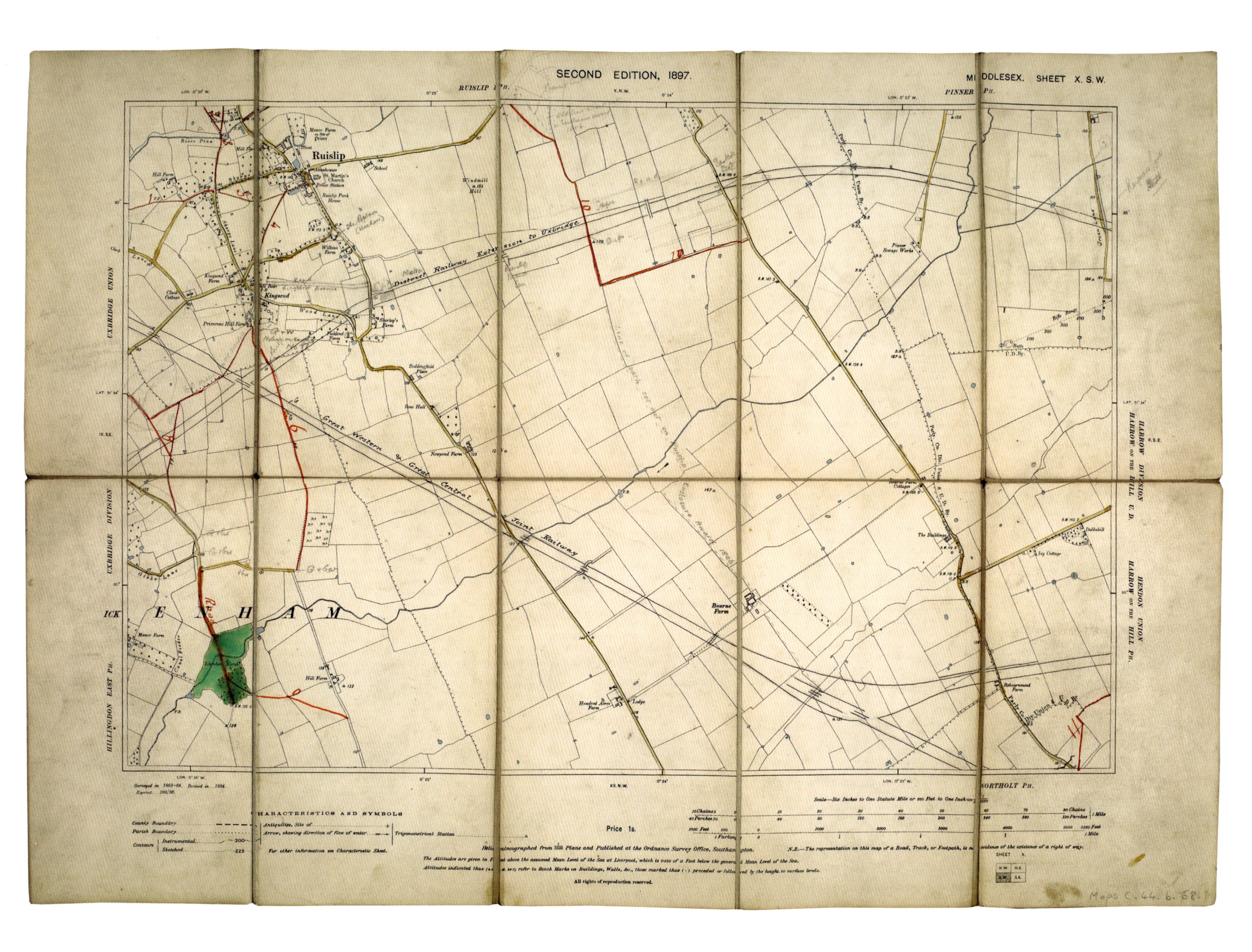

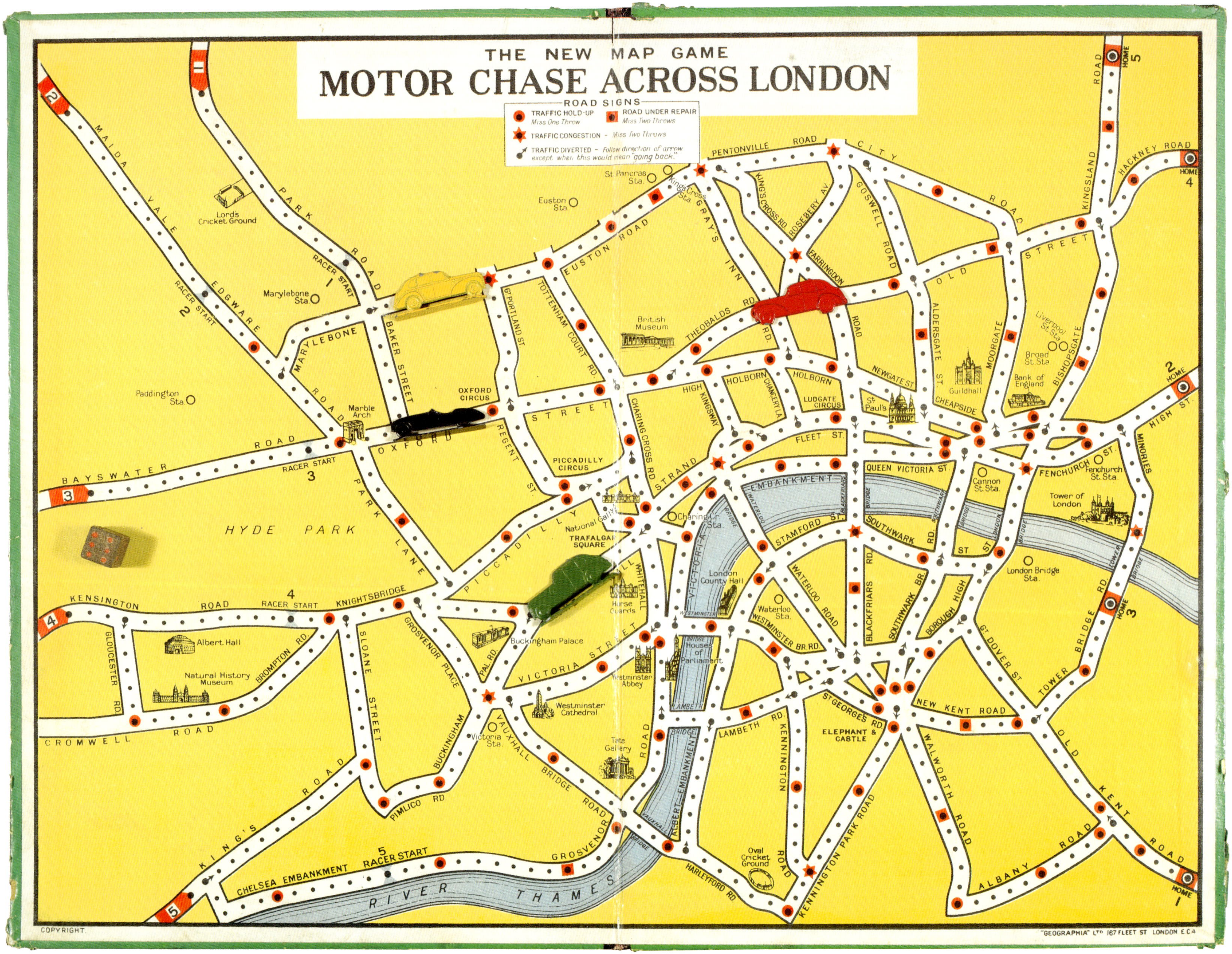
THE NEW MAP GAME
MOTOR CHASE ACROSS LONDON
ROAD SIGNS
TRAFFIC HOLD-UP Miss One Throw
ROAD UNDER REPAIR Miss Two Throws
TRAFFIC CONGESTION – Miss Two Throws
TRAFFIC DIVERTED – Follow direction of arrow except when this would mean "going back."
MAIDA VALE
PARK ROAD
EDGWARE ROAD
MARYLEBONE ROAD
BAKER STREET
EUSTON ROAD
PENTONVILLE ROAD
CITY ROAD
KINGSLAND ROAD
HACKNEY ROAD
HOME 5
HOME 4
HOME 2
HOME 3
HOME 1
RACER START 1
RACER START 2
RACER START 3
RACER START 4
RACER START 5
Lords Cricket Ground
Marylebone Sta.
Paddington Sta.
Euston Sta.
St Pancras Sta.
Kings Cross Sta.
GRAYS INN ROAD
KING'S CROSS RD.
ROSEBERY AV.
GOSWELL ROAD
FARRINGDON ROAD
OLD STREET
British Museum
THEOBALDS RD.
TOTTENHAM COURT RD.
GT PORTLAND ST.
OXFORD CIRCUS
OXFORD STREET
REGENT ST.
Marble Arch
BAYSWATER ROAD
HYDE PARK
PARK LANE
PICCADILLY
PICCADILLY CIRCUS
CHARING CROSS RD.
HIGH HOLBORN
KINGSWAY
CHANCERY LA.
LUDGATE CIRCUS
St Paul's
NEWGATE ST.
ALDERSGATE ST.
MOORGATE
Guildhall
CHEAPSIDE
Liverpool St. Sta.
Broad St. Sta.
Bank of England
BISHOPSGATE
FLEET ST.
STRAND
QUEEN VICTORIA ST.
Cannon St. Sta.
FENCHURCH ST.
Fenchurch St. Sta.
MINORIES
HIGH ST.
Tower of London
EMBANKMENT
National Gallery
TRAFALGAR SQUARE
Charing Cr. Sta.
STAMFORD ST.
SOUTHWARK ST.
WATERLOO ROAD
BLACKFRIARS RD.
SOUTHWARK BR. RD.
BOROUGH HIGH ST.
London Bridge Sta.
TOWER BRIDGE RD.
London County Hall
Waterloo Sta.
WESTMINSTER BR. RD.
WHITEHALL
Horse Guards
Buckingham Palace
KENSINGTON ROAD
KNIGHTSBRIDGE
GROSVENOR PLACE
GLOUCESTER RD.
Albert Hall
Natural History Museum
BROMPTON RD.
SLOANE STREET
CROMWELL ROAD
VICTORIA STREET
Westminster Abbey
Houses of Parliament
Westminster Cathedral
Victoria Sta.
VAUXHALL BRIDGE ROAD
BUCKINGHAM PALACE RD.
PIMLICO RD.
KING'S ROAD
Tate Gallery
ALBERT EMBANKMENT
LAMBETH RD.
KENNINGTON ROAD
ST GEORGE'S RD.
ELEPHANT & CASTLE
NEW KENT ROAD
GT DOVER ST.
OLD KENT ROAD
WALWORTH ROAD
KENNINGTON PARK ROAD
Oval Cricket Ground
HARLEYFORD RD.
ALBANY ROAD
GROSVENOR ROAD
CHELSEA EMBANKMENT
RIVER THAMES
COPYRIGHT
"GEOGRAPHIA" LTD 167 FLEET ST LONDON E.C.4

THE COMING OF THE CAR

Cars were eventually to transform both London's road infrastructure and, by shrinking the distances, the mentalities of Londoners who needed no longer feel stranded in the remotest suburbs. But when this map was thought up they were still a comparative rarity. The board is covered by a realistic but simplified street plan and the penalties are equally realistic: players missed turns if they got caught up in traffic hold-ups, congestion or road-works and there were diversions. In those days, high-speed motor chases across town were also feasible, though doubtless frowned on by the authorities.

7.2.5   *The new map game: motor chase across London* (London: Geographia, 1925). 37.5 × 50 cm. Maps 162 p. 9

I LOVE TO GO AWANDERING

Between the Wars, Ordnance Survey made a great effort to increase its sales by commissioning attractive pictorial covers for its one-inch to the mile Popular Edition series from commercial artists such as Ellis Martin (1881–1977). These featured the users for whom the map was intended — and the one inch to the mile maps were best suited to ramblers and tourists. Although this design was used for maps throughout the country, it seems to show a scene in the south-east of England with rambling, cycling, the bus and the private car combined in a single image.

7.2.6   Ordnance Survey, *Ordnance Survey 'one-Inch' Map. Special Popular Edition. Hertford and St Albans* (cover) (Southampton: Ordnance survey, 1932). 19.3 × 11 cm

7.3 IMPERIAL GRANDEUR

Some purpose-built buildings, like churches, theatres, clubs and some shops, existed long before 1800. From 1860, however, the introduction of wrought-iron and later steel framed buildings and of electricity made possible the creation of new, larger types of urban buildings. These fully reflected the confidence of their builders and provided the somewhat overblown grandeur that an imperial city required. Grand hotels and restaurants rubbed shoulders with new monster department stores, banks and the headquarters of insurance companies, while a whole new museum quarter arose in South Kensington. Tourists came to gawp, map in hand, while insurance companies insisted on the full disclosure of fire risks in plans supplied to them. Inner London continues to be dominated by their even larger though plainer successors.

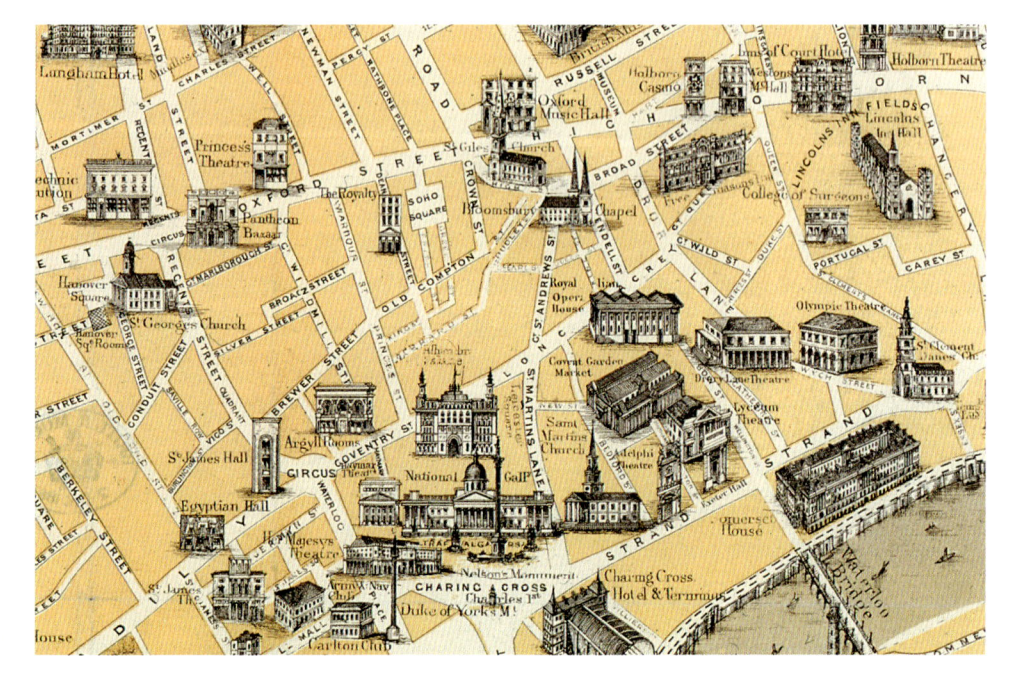

CHURCHES AND MUSIC HALLS

This precursor of the modern tourist map depicts London's traditional sights and, genuflecting towards middle class values, numerous administrative, commercial, educational and religious buildings. But its creator was much more interested in popular amusements, including not only mainstream theatre, and older entertainments like the Colosseum, the Egyptian Hall, and the circus-like Astley's, but the newer working class rage, the music hall. More of these, such as the Canterbury, the Oxford or Gatti's, are shown than any other group. The first purpose-built grand restaurants, office buildings and department stores were being built when this map was being published, but already it was possible to guess the functions of many buildings from their distinctive exteriors.

7.3.1 *Illustrated Map of London or Stranger's Guide to the Public Buildings, Theatres, Music Halls & all Places of Interest* (London: Smith and Son, 1867). Chromolithograph. 50.5 × 65 cm. Maps 3480 (203)

ILLUSTRATED MAP of LONDON

OR STRANGER'S GUIDE TO THE PUBLIC BUILDINGS, THEATRES, MUSIC HALLS, & ALL PLACES OF INTEREST.

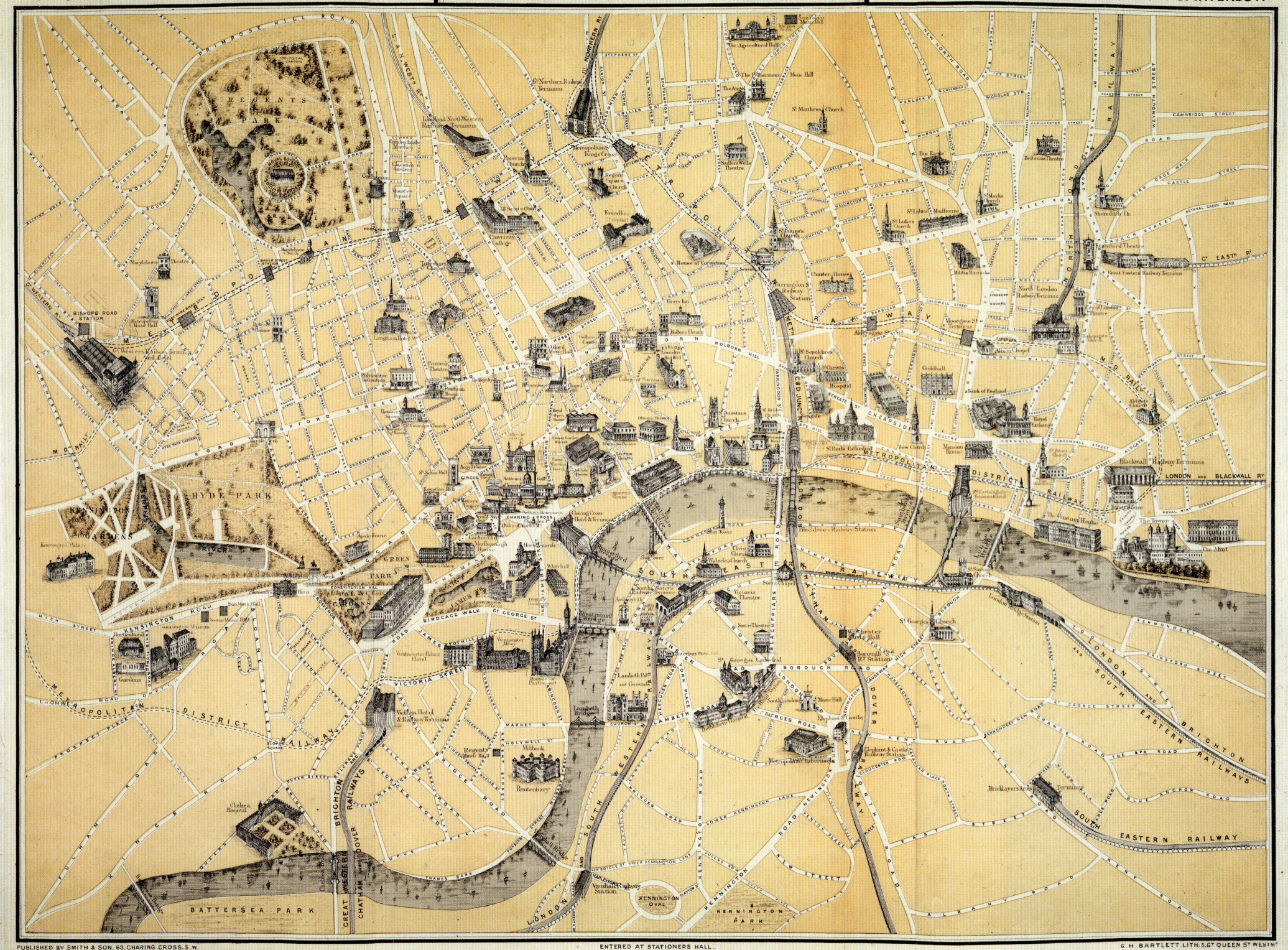

LAND FOR THE ARTS AND SCIENCES

Part of the enormous profit of £186,000 made by the Great Exhibition of 1851 was used to purchase these 87 acres in South Kensington. They were to provide a home for institutions that would further the Exhibition's objectives of 'increasing the means of industrial education and extending the influence of science and art upon productive industry'. Over the following decades these vague words materialized into a large number of purpose-built museums and further education institutions such as the Royal Albert Hall, the Royal College of Music, the Science, Natural History and Victoria and Albert Museums, the Royal College of Organists and Imperial College.

7.3.2 *Plan of Estates in the parishes of Kensington and St Margaret's Westminster ... Purchased by Her Majesty's Commissioners for the Exhibition of 1851* (London: Day & Son, *c.* 1853). Lithograph. 48 × 72 cm. Maps Crace X.15

Plan of Estates
IN THE PARISHES OF
KENSINGTON
AND
St MARGARETS WESTMINSTER,
IN THE COUNTY OF
MIDDLESEX.
Purchased by
HER MAJESTY'S COMMISSIONERS
FOR THE
EXHIBITION OF 1851.

Note.

The Green color indicates the Commissioners' Estate, the different properties composing it being enclosed in boundary lines of various colors, viz.

Gore House Estate	Blue
Villars Estate	Red
Harrington Estate	Yellow
Smith's Charity Estate	Brown

The Light Brown color indicates the different roads intersecting and bounding the Estate, the whole of them, with the exception of the Kensington Road on the North, having been newly constructed by the Commissioners.

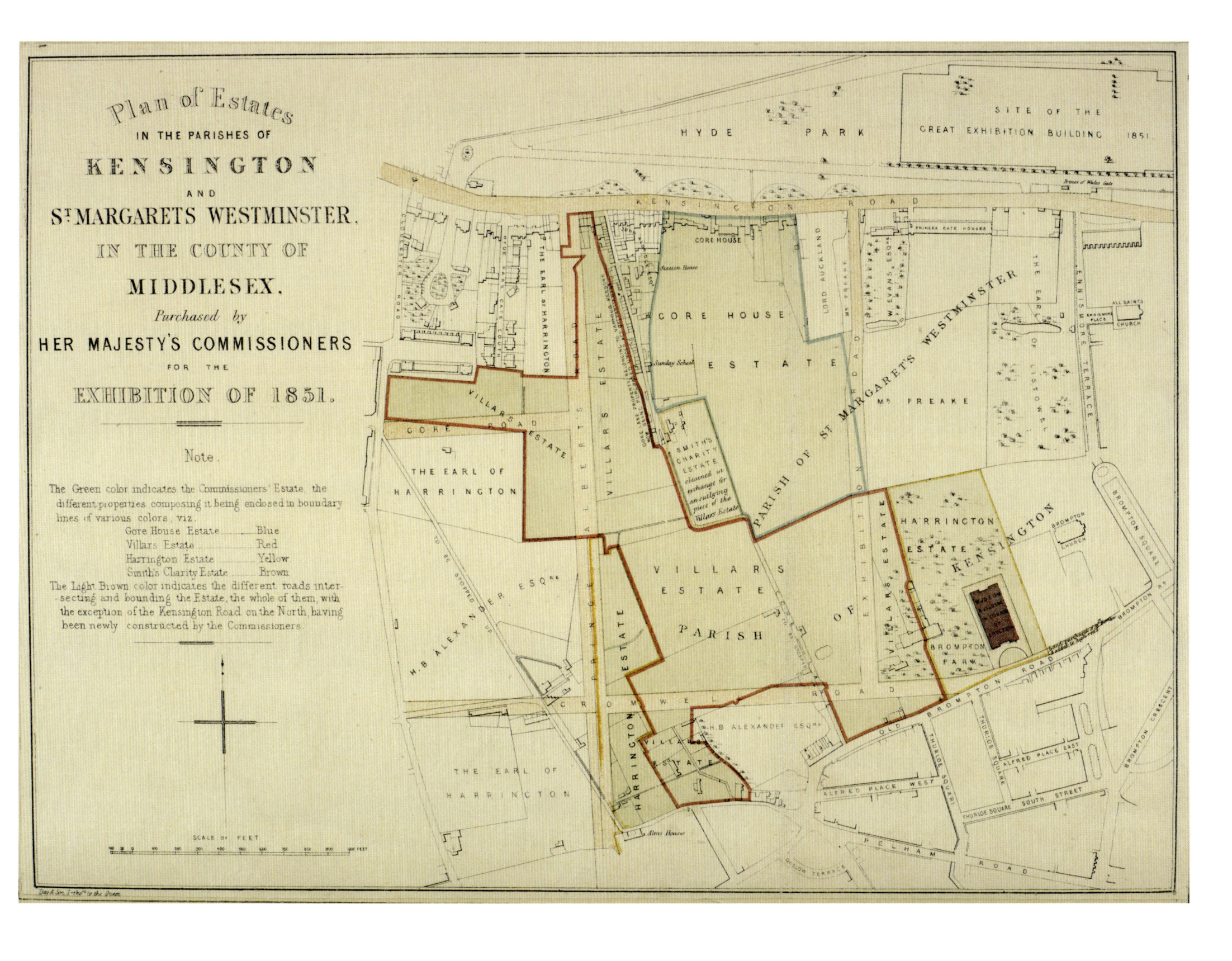

SCALE OF FEET

HARROD'S

The coming of electricity and wrought-iron framing made possible the erection of large department stores lit by electric light and serviced by lifts and escalators. The grandest was Harrod's. It was being rebuilt in 1901 and this fire insurance plan was presumably created in part from the architects' plans. No information that might in any way be relevant for the assessment of risks could be concealed from the Goad company's surveyors. The plan distinguishes between the different building materials — glass is blue, timber yellow and brick pink — and also the functions of the different areas. The grocery and provisions, drugs, butcher's, furniture, fancy drapery and kitchenware departments and the floral hall and restaurants are all to be seen.

7.3.3 Charles Goad Ltd, 2nd edition. plan sheet A 14 [South Kensington] (September 1901). Chromolithograph 63.5 × 53 cm. Maps 145.b.23

Charles Edward Goad (1848–1910) was born in Camberwell, the son of a plumber. He emigrated to Canada in 1869 and there worked as a railway engineer before hitting upon the masterly idea of combating the ever-present danger of fire by providing detailed plans showing every detail that might be of service — street-widths, building materials, thickness of walls, internal dimensions, positions of doors and windows, sources of water, position of fire appliances, etc. His company was founded in Montreal in 1875 and the London office, which was to become the hub of a worldwide concern, opened in 1886. Goad's fire-insurance plans (still being produced) did much to cement London's place as the home of the world insurance industry.

7.4 GETTING AROUND

The first omnibus ran through the streets of London in 1829 and in 1863 the first underground line opened but Londoners had been using cabs and, before them, boats on the Thames, for centuries. Maps promising to protect their purchasers from being overcharged by cab- and watermen first appeared soon after 1700. Monuments to misanthropy, they became one of the commonest types of London map. Tube maps evolved from the late nineteenth century to become, at the hands of Harry Beck, and divorced from most of the characteristics of orthodox maps, a worldwide symbol of London. Humbler diagrammatic maps encouraged the growing number of fans to catch a tram to football and cricket matches.

Extract from Underground Electric Railways of London (Joshua Riddle & Co., 1907)

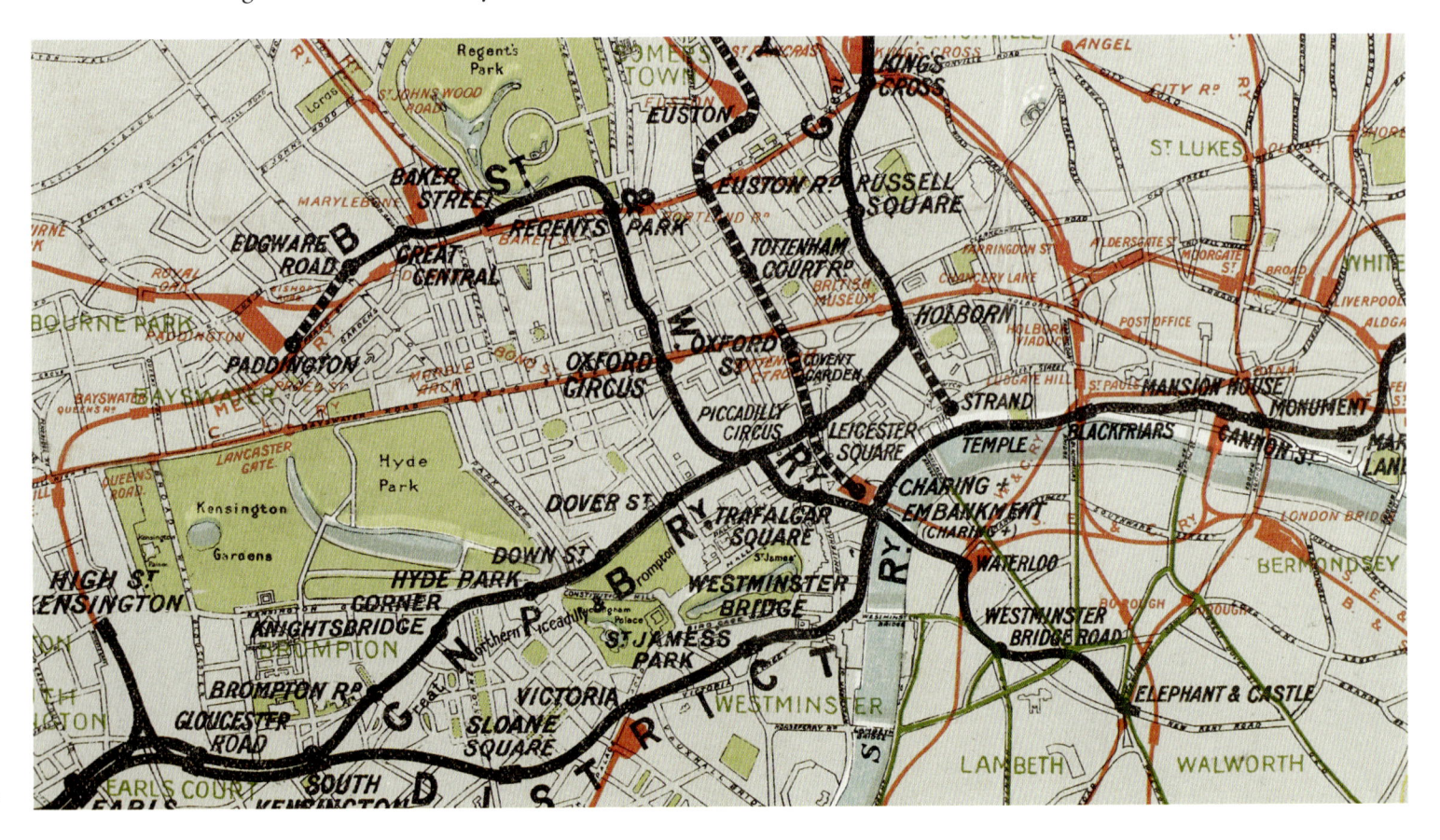

HOW MUCH WILL IT COST?

This map, published by the widow of its original maker, combines views of important buildings, an up-to-date town plan, a brief history of London, a detailed and referenced street index with over 1000 names — and a list of the rates and fares for coachmen and watermen, giving prices for a large number of journeys by land and water. A contemporary visitor to London could scarcely have asked for more …

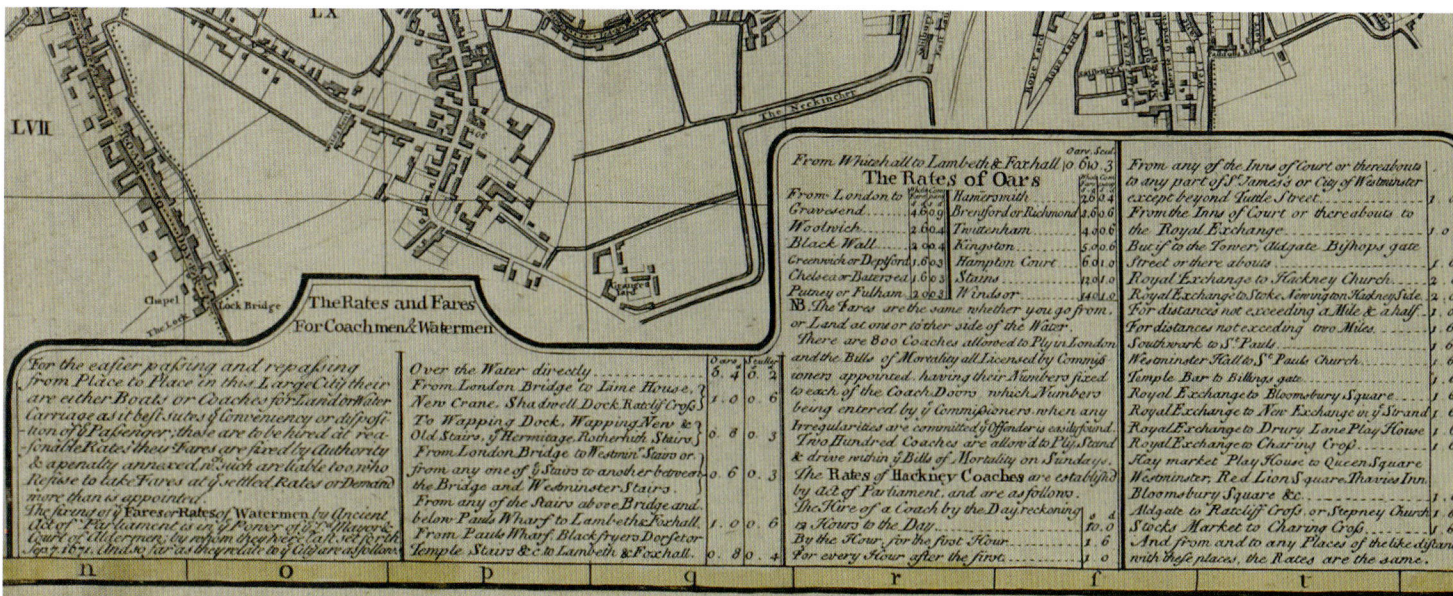

7.4.1 Elizabeth Foster, *A New and exact Plan of the Cities of London and Westminster & the Borough of Southwark to this present year 1738…* (1752). Copperplate engraving. 57.2 × 154.9 cm. Maps Crace III.110

The map was engraved by Emanuel Bowen, Geographer to George II. Born in Wales, Bowen became one of the leading London mapmakers of his time, yet despite a lifetime of hard work and endeavour he died in 1767 in poverty and 'almost blind through age'.

ROAD CLOSED

This map of central London is presented as a puzzle. The aim was to find the single route that would enable a traveller on horseback or in a carriage to reach St Paul's Churchyard from the Strand without finding his path blocked by road repairs. The map was on sale for a shilling (5p) — with a key. Some things never change.

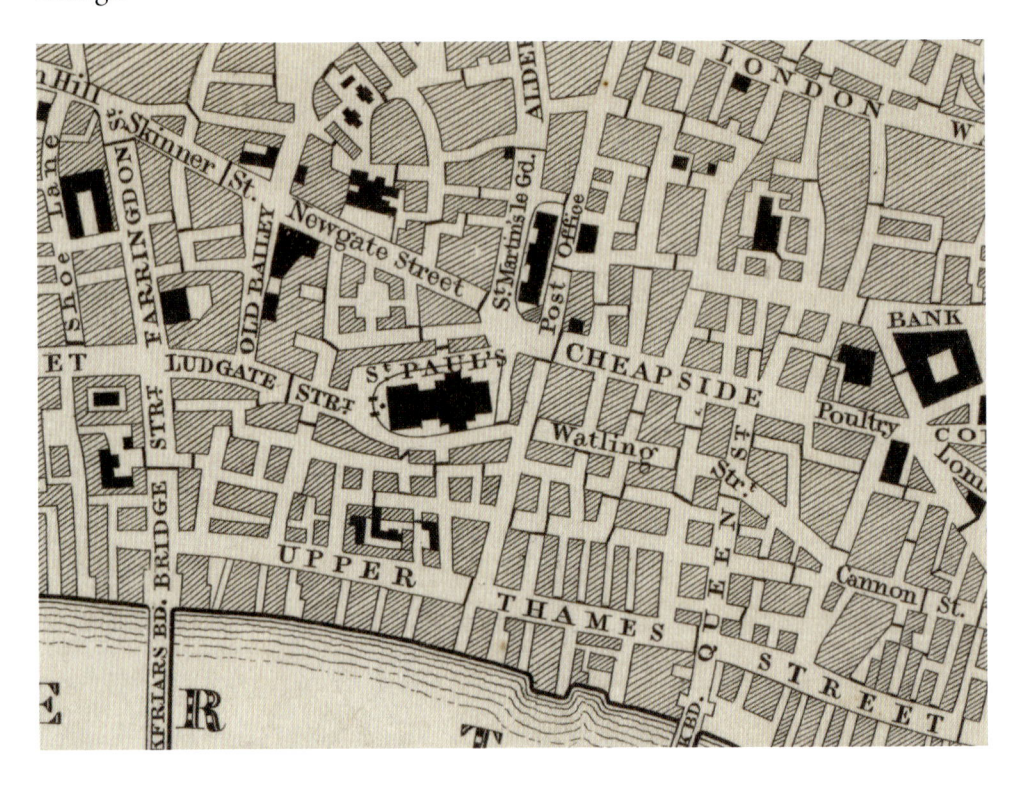

7.4.2   Charles Ingrey and F. Waller. *Labyrinthus Londinensis Or The Equestrian Perplexed* (London, 1830). Steelplate engraving. 21 × 28.6 cm Maps Crace VI.214

The publisher Charles Ingrey (1800?–41) had a Lithographic Printing Office in the midst of the disruption at No. 310 Strand, his exasperation perhaps the worse in that much of his recorded output was of plans relating to road improvement schemes and maps to show 'the practicability, utility and benefit of railroads'. His neighbour and co-publisher, Frederick Waller, a stationer at 49 Fleet Street, was no doubt similarly affected.

LABYRINTHUS LONDINENSIS,
or
THE EQUESTRIAN PERPLEXED.

Mending our Ways, our ways doth oft-times mar,
So thinks the Traveller by Horse or Car,
But he who scans with calm and patient skill
This "Labyrinthine Chart of London," will
One Track discover, open and unbarred,
That leads at length to famed St Paul's Church Yard.

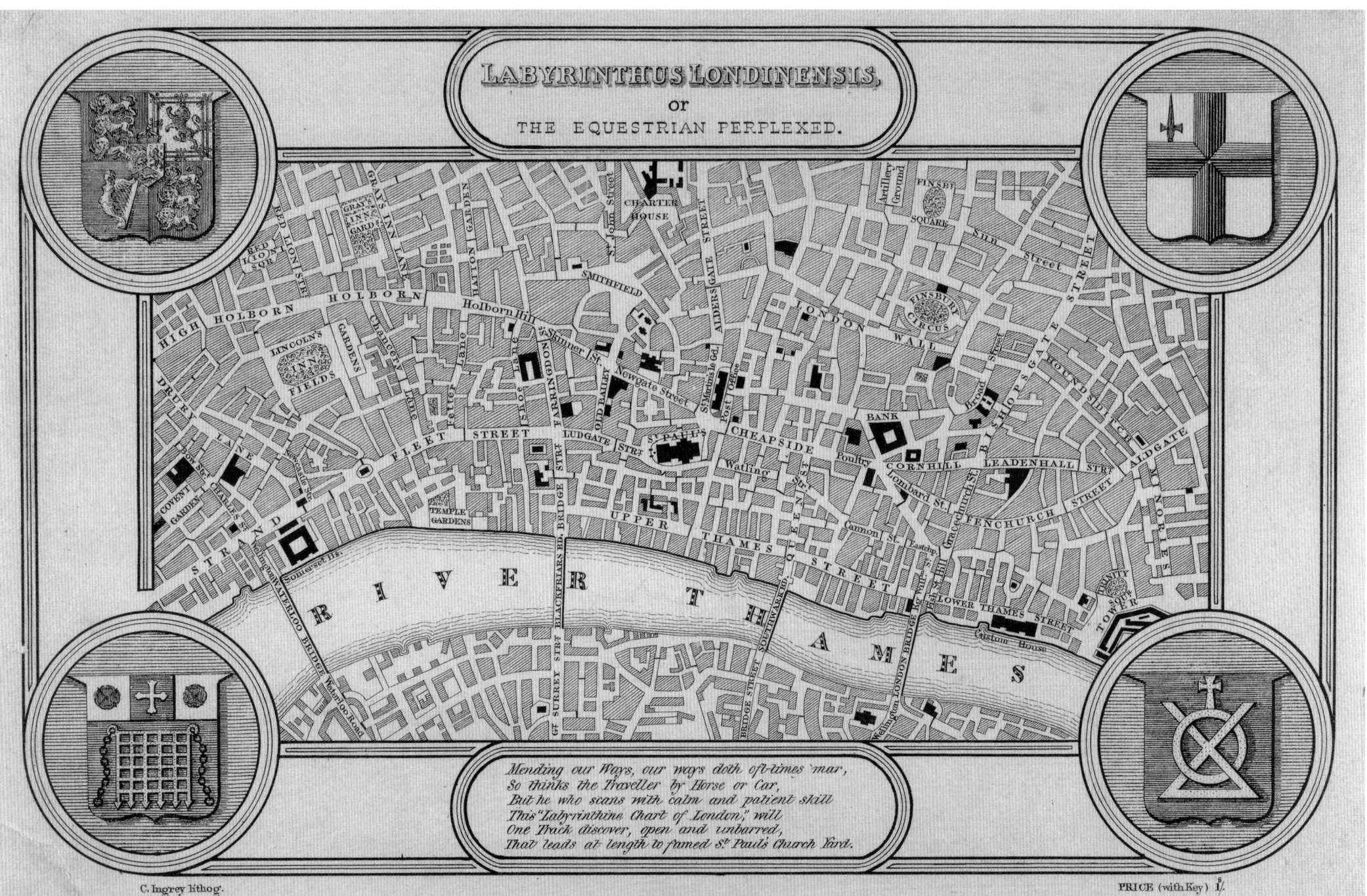

C. Ingrey lithog.

PRICE (with Key) 1/.

A PUZZLE

Suggested by the Stoppages occasioned by repairing the Streets. The object is to find a way from the Strand to St Paul's, without crossing any of the Bars in the Streets supposed to be under repair.

Published by C. Ingrey, 310, Strand, and F. Waller, 49, Fleet Street, London.

PAYING THE RIGHT FARE

Maps giving cab and boat fares were particularly useful before the introduction of meters. But their appearance has varied. This mapmaker places distinctively coloured circles at one and at two miles' distance from the main railway terminals (distances from King's Cross being yellow, Paddington pink and so on). The text on the inside cover gives the latest official cab prices per mile and per hour, with information on what to do in case of disputes. However, the small print reminding its users that 'allowance must be made for the winding of the streets' was a gift to an argumentative cabman. It pinpointed the map's core weakness and turned it from being a means of getting value for money into a near-guarantee of a stand-up row with any determined cab-driver.

7.4.3 *Reynolds's Distance Map of London* (London: Reynolds, *c.* 1859). Lithograph. 33 × 59 cm. Maps C.44.a.25

James Reynolds (1817–76) was born in Islington, the son of a printer. From his premises at 174 Strand he published at least ten separate maps of London. He lived over the shop and is recorded there on the 1851 Census with his wife, Mary, two small children, his widowed mother, a younger brother Robert, also employed in the business, and two female servants.

REYNOLDS'S DISTANCE MAP OF LONDON,
FOR ASCERTAINING CAB FARES & SHEWING THE DISTANCES IN EVERY DIRECTION FROM THE RAILWAY STATIONS &c.

THIS MAP IS DIVIDED INTO SQUARE SECTIONS EACH OF WHICH REPRESENTS A QUARTER OF A MILE THE DISTANCES FROM THE RAILWAY STATIONS ARE SHOWN BY CIRCLES DRAWN ROUND EACH AT DISTANCES OF ONE AND TWO MILES IN CALCULATING THE DISTANCE FOR CAB FARES ALLOWANCE MUST BE MADE FOR THE WINDING OF THE STREETS.

LONDON, PUBLISHED BY JAMES REYNOLDS, 174, STRAND

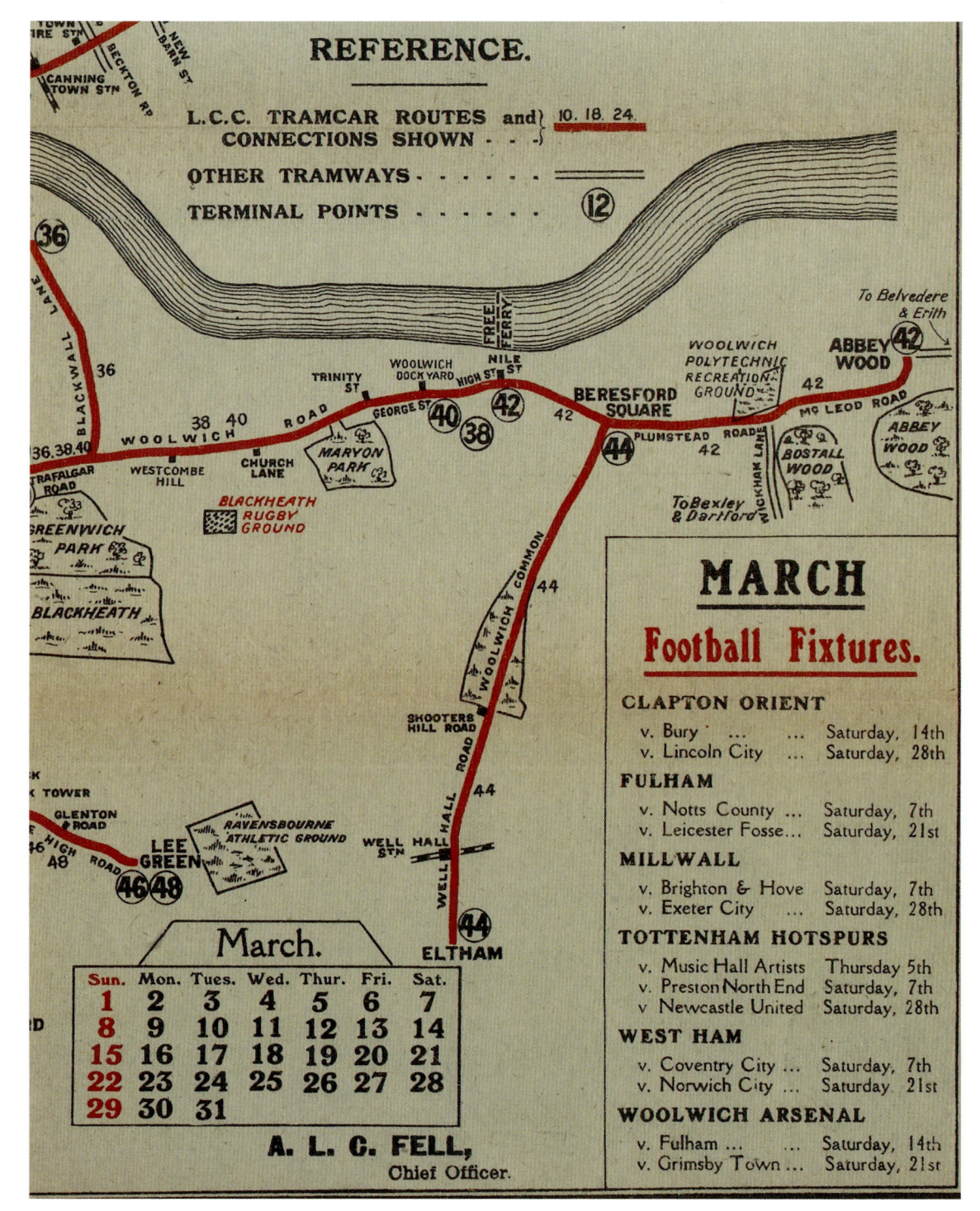

GETTING THERE BY TRAM

Working people took the tramcar or, as they would have called it, the 'car'. By consulting the monthly timetable, illustrated with a diagrammatic map, they could see both what was happening as well as how to get there. In March 1914, Tottenham Hotspur had three fixtures (one against 'Music Hall Artists') and it would cost a fan a penny halfpenny (0.62p) to get to the stadium. Alternatively there was the spring bulb display at the Royal Horticultural Hall in Westminster or a pony show at the Royal Agricultural Hall in Islington. The map was tailored to meet peoples' needs and thereby to entice them into using the tram. Apart from tram routes, only stations, parks and sports grounds were shown.

7.4.4 *London County Council Tramways and through running connections* (March 1914). 33 × 59 cm. Maps Y 814

LONDON COUNTY COUNCIL TRAMWAYS
AND THROUGH RUNNING CONNECTIONS.

INTERESTING EVENTS DURING MARCH

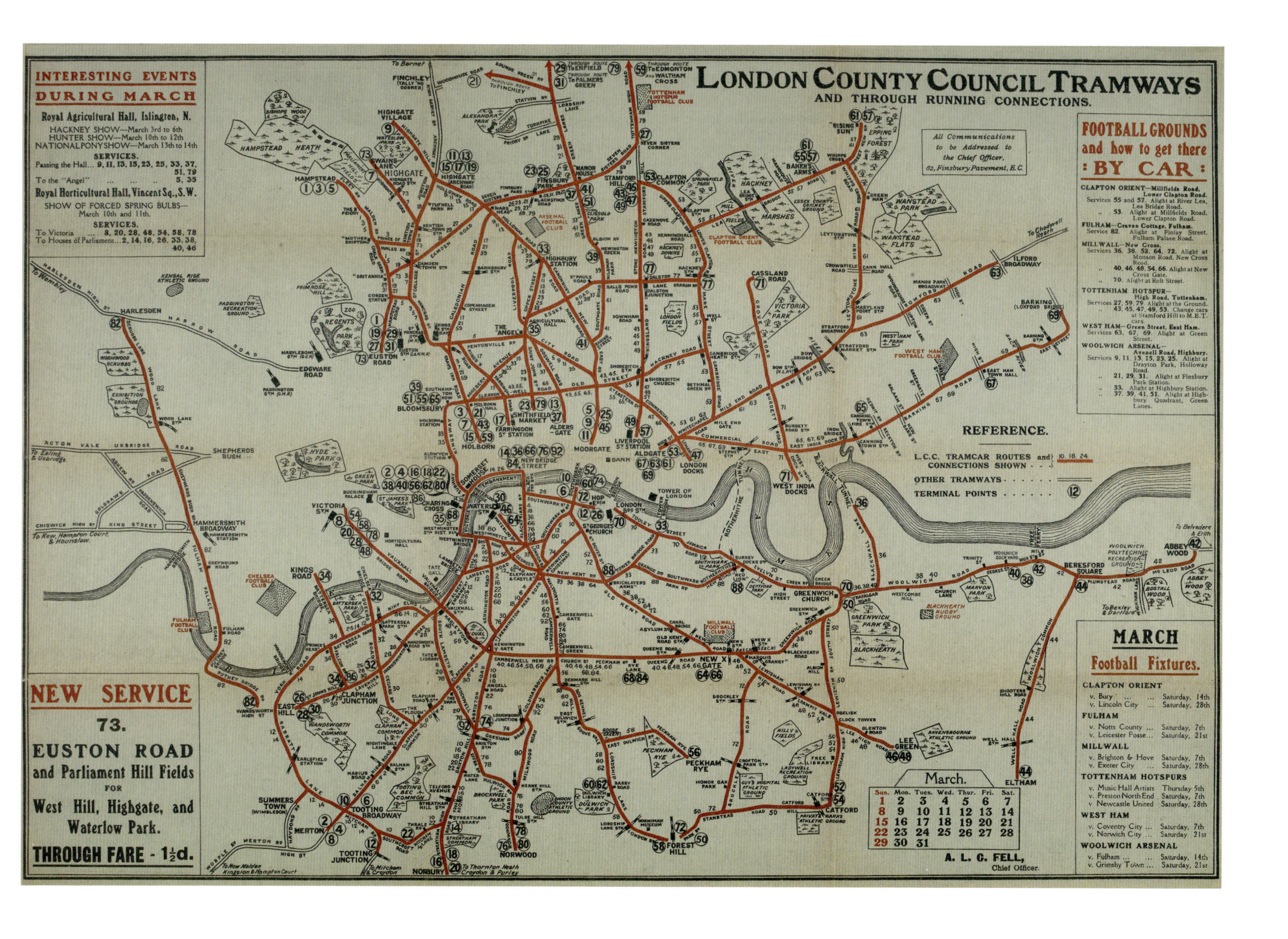

Royal Agricultural Hall, Islington, N.
HACKNEY SHOW—March 3rd to 6th
HUNTER SHOW—March 10th to 12th
NATIONAL PONY SHOW—March 13th to 14th

SERVICES.
Passing the Hall ... 9, 11, 13, 15, 23, 25, 33, 37, 51, 79
To the "Angel" ... 5, 35

Royal Horticultural Hall, Vincent Sq., S.W.
SHOW OF FORCED SPRING BULBS—
March 10th and 11th.

SERVICES.
To Victoria ... 8, 20, 28, 48, 54, 58, 78
To Houses of Parliament ... 2, 14, 16, 26, 33, 38, 40, 46

NEW SERVICE
73.
EUSTON ROAD
and Parliament Hill Fields
FOR
West Hill, Highgate, and
Waterlow Park.
THROUGH FARE - 1½d.

All Communications to be Addressed to the Chief Officer, 62, Finsbury Pavement, E.C.

REFERENCE.
L.C.C. TRAMCAR ROUTES and CONNECTIONS SHOWN
OTHER TRAMWAYS
TERMINAL POINTS 12

FOOTBALL GROUNDS and how to get there :BY CAR:

CLAPTON ORIENT—Millfields Road, Lower Clapton Road.
Services 55 and 57. Alight at River Lea, Lea Bridge Road.
" 53. Alight at Millfields Road, Lower Clapton Road.

FULHAM—Craven Cottage, Fulham.
Service 82. Alight at Finlay Street, Fulham Palace Road.

MILLWALL—New Cross.
Services 36, 38, 52, 64, 72. Alight at Monson Road, New Cross Road.
" 40, 46, 48, 54, 66. Alight at New Cross Gate.
" 70. Alight at Bolt Street.

TOTTENHAM HOTSPUR—High Road, Tottenham.
Services 27, 59, 79. Alight at the Ground.
" 43, 45, 47, 49, 53. Change cars at Stamford Hill to M.E.T. cars.

WEST HAM—Green Street, East Ham.
Services 63, 67, 69. Alight at Green Street.

WOOLWICH ARSENAL—Avenell Road, Highbury.
Services 9, 11, 13, 15, 23, 25. Alight at Drayton Park, Holloway Road.
" 21, 29, 31. Alight at Finsbury Park Station.
" 33. Alight at Highbury Station.
" 37, 39, 41, 51. Alight at Highbury Quadrant, Green Lanes.

MARCH Football Fixtures.

CLAPTON ORIENT
v. Bury ... Saturday, 14th
v. Lincoln City ... Saturday, 28th

FULHAM
v. Notts County ... Saturday, 7th
v. Leicester Fosse ... Saturday, 21st

MILLWALL
v. Brighton & Hove ... Saturday, 7th
v. Exeter City ... Saturday, 28th

TOTTENHAM HOTSPURS
v. Music Hall Artists ... Thursday 5th
v. Preston North End ... Saturday, 7th
v. Newcastle United ... Saturday, 28th

WEST HAM
v. Coventry City ... Saturday, 7th
v. Norwich City ... Saturday, 21st

WOOLWICH ARSENAL
v. Fulham ... Saturday, 14th
v. Grimsby Town ... Saturday, 21st

March.

Sun.	Mon.	Tues.	Wed.	Thur.	Fri.	Sat.
1	2	3	4	5	6	7
8	9	10	11	12	13	14
15	16	17	18	19	20	21
22	23	24	25	26	27	28
29	30	31				

A. L. C. FELL,
Chief Officer.

TAKING THE UNDERGROUND

From 1863, when the first underground train ran, mapmakers tried to create clear and informative maps for users. This one shows some awareness of their particular requirements. The centre of town is depicted at a larger scale than the suburbs. The underground lines owned by Underground Electric Railways Co. of London Ltd which financed this map, superimposed over a simplified and faded town plan, are emphasised in black. The thin red lines show the underground and overground lines owned by other companies. No visual distinction is made between the different UERL lines, and interchanges are not clearly marked. Worst of all, the lines follow the geography and snake around, making the sequence of stations and general direction difficult to remember.

7.4.5 *Underground Electric Railways of London* (Johnson, Riddle & Co., [1907]). 33.2 × 40.3 cm. Maps 3485 (170)

UNDERGROUND ELECTRIC RAILWAYS OF LONDON

HAMMERSMITH, PICCADILLY, KINGS CROSS, FINSBURY PARK
(G.N. PICCADILLY & BROMPTON RAILWAY.)

Hammersmith.
Barons Court.
Earls Court.
Gloucester Road.
South Kensington.
Brompton Road.
Knightsbridge.
Hyde Park Corner.
Down Street.
Dover Street.
Piccadilly Circus.
Leicester Square.
Covent Garden.
Holborn.
Russell Square.
Kings Cross.
York Road.
Caledonian Road.
Holloway Road.
Gillespie Road.
Finsbury Park.

BAKER STREET AND WATERLOO RAILWAY.

Elephant & Castle.
Westminster Bridge Road.
Waterloo.
Embankment—
Charing Cross.
Trafalgar Square.
Piccadilly Circus.
Oxford Circus.
Regent's Park.
Baker Street.

CHARING CROSS, EUSTON & HAMPSTEAD RAILWAY.
(Open June, 1907.)

Charing Cross.
Leicester Square.
Oxford Street.
Tottenham Court Road.
Euston Road.
Euston.
Camden Town.
Chalk Farm.
Belsize Park.
Hampstead.
Golders Green.

Castle Road.
Kentish Town.
Tufnell Park.
Highgate.

THE DISTRICT RAILWAY.

MAIN LINE.

Ealing Broadway.
Ealing Common.
Mill Hill Park.
Chiswick Park.
Turnham Green.
Ravenscourt Park.
Hammersmith.
Barons Court.
West Kensington.
Earls Court.
Gloucester Road.
South Kensington.
Sloane Square.
Victoria.
St. James's Park.
Westminster.
Charing Cross.
Temple.
Blackfriars.
Mansion House.
Cannon Street.
Monument.
Mark Lane.
Aldgate East.
St. Marys.
Whitechapel.

EXTENSIONS.

South Harrow.
Sudbury Hill.
Sudbury Town.
Perivale-Alperton.
Park Royal.
North Ealing.

Hounslow Barracks.
Heston Hounslow.
Hounslow Town.
Osterly and Spring Grove.
Boston Road.
South Ealing.

South Acton.

Putney Bridge.
Parson's Green.
Walham Green.
West Brompton.

High Street

321

BY UNDERGROUND TO THE EMPIRE EXHIBITION

This colourful map, embellished with decoration imitating sixteenth- and seventeenth-century maps, plays havoc with cartographic conventions in order to get people to and around the British Empire Exhibition at Wembley. Most of the map is occupied with a depiction of the 220 acre exhibition site in plan and picture. London is turned into a suburb of Wembley. The whole of the London underground system is compressed into the bottom third of the map. No attempt is made to include a street plan. Each line has a different colour, the central area is enlarged, and many stations distant from Wembley are omitted. But overall the Underground system still looks like a half-finished plate of spaghetti.

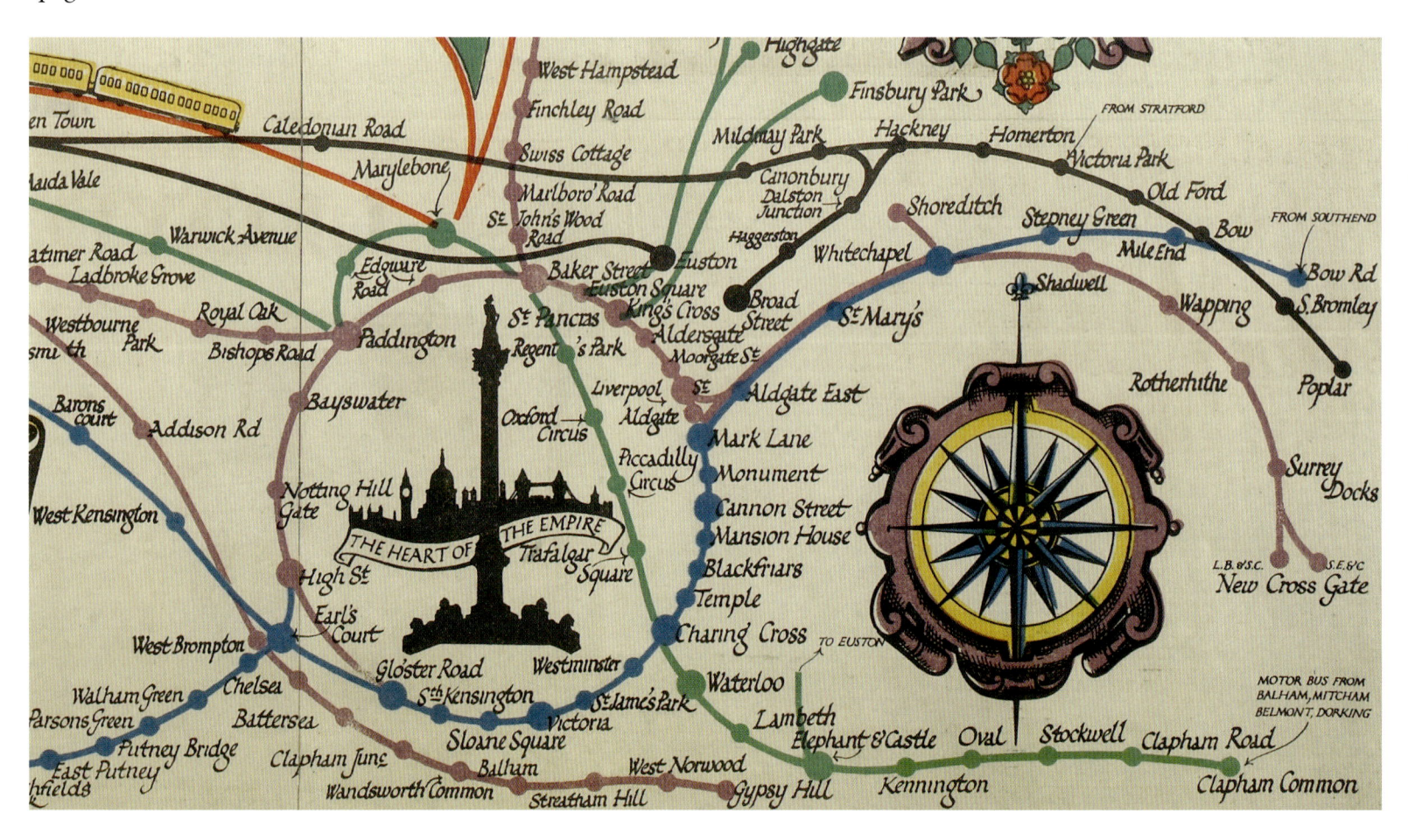

7.4.6   Kennedy North, *British Empire Exhibition 1924. Wembley Park April – October* (London: Dobson, Molle and Co., 1923). 50 × 74.2 cm. Maps 3465 (16)

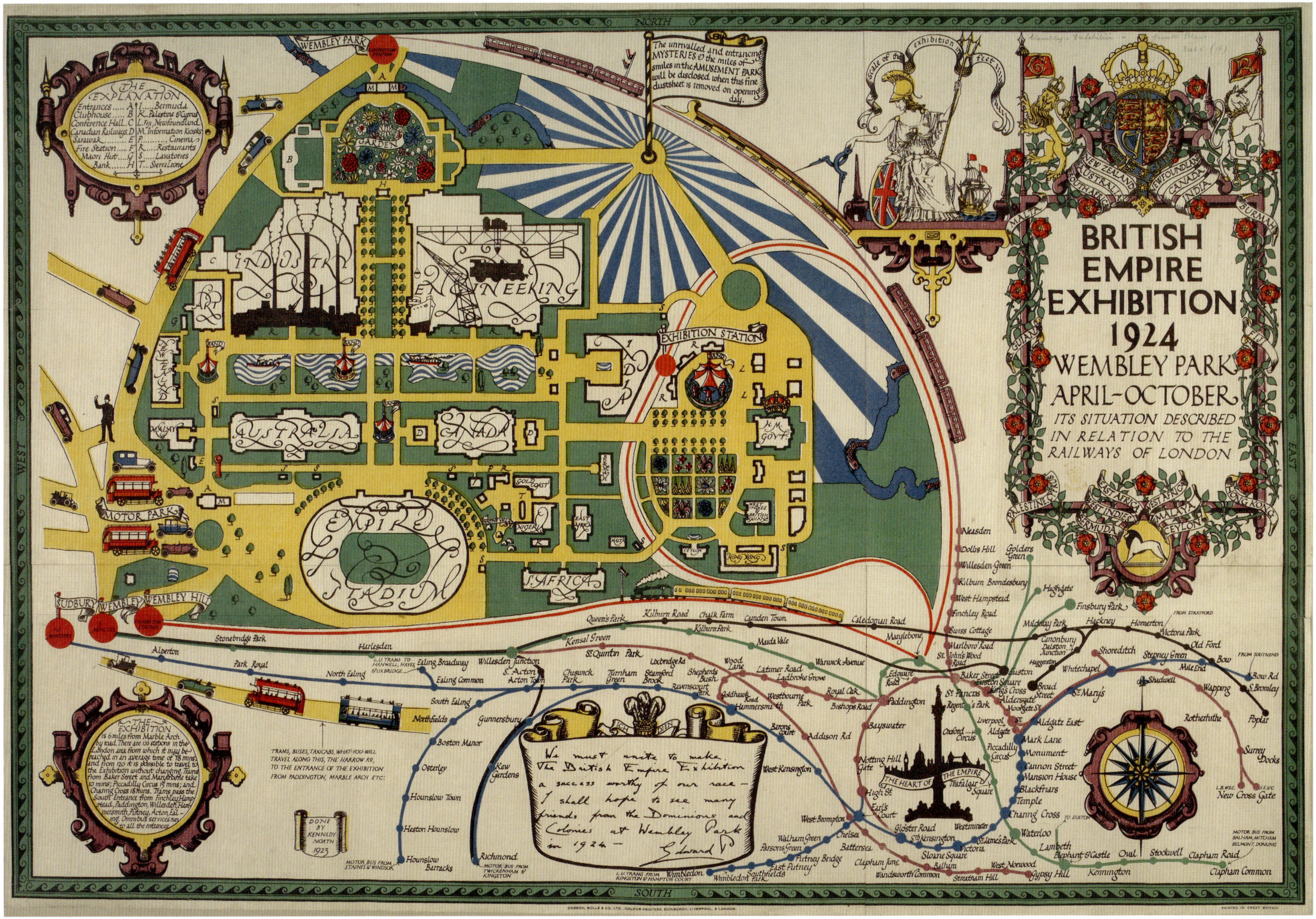
BRITISH EMPIRE EXHIBITION 1924
WEMBLEY PARK
APRIL-OCTOBER
ITS SITUATION DESCRIBED IN RELATION TO THE RAILWAYS OF LONDON
NORTH
SOUTH
EAST
WEST
THE EXPLANATION
Entrances ..... A
Clubhouse ..... B
Conference Hall.. C
Canadian Railways D
Sarawak .... E
Fire Station ..... F
Maori Hut .... G
Bank ...... H
I ..... Bermuda
K. Palestine & Cyprus
L. Fiji, Newfoundland
M. Information Kiosks
P .... Cinema
R .... Restaurants
S ..... Lavatories
T ... Sierra Leone
The unrivalled and entrancing MYSTERIES & the miles of smiles in the AMUSEMENT PARK will be disclosed when this fine dustsheet is removed on opening day.
INDUSTRY
ENGINEERING
ART
AUSTRALIA
CANADA
INDIA
EMPIRE STADIUM
S. AFRICA
H.M. GOVT.
HONG KONG
EXHIBITION STATION
WEMBLEY PARK
MOTOR PARK
SUDBURY
WEMBLEY
WEMBLEY HILL
THE EXHIBITION is 6 miles from Marble Arch by road. There are 126 stations in the London area from which it may be reached in an average time of 18 mins; and from 120 it is possible to travel to the Exhibition without changing. Trams from Baker Street and Marylebone take 10 mins; Piccadilly Circus 15 mins; and Charing Cross 18 mins. Trams pass the South Entrance from Finchley, Hampstead, Paddington, Willesden, Hammersmith, Putney, Acton, Ealing. Omnibus services run to all the entrances.
TRAMS, BUSES, TAXICABS, WHAT-YOU-WILL TRAVEL ALONG THIS, THE HARROW RD, TO THE ENTRANCE OF THE EXHIBITION FROM PADDINGTON, MARBLE ARCH ETC:
DONE BY KENNEDY NORTH 1923
We must unite to make The British Empire Exhibition a success worthy of our race — I shall hope to see many friends from the Dominions and Colonies at Wembley Park in 1924 — Edward P.
THE HEART OF THE EMPIRE
Trafalgar Square
NEW ZEALAND
AUSTRALIA
SOUTH AFRICA
NEWFOUNDLAND
CANADA
INDIA
MALTA
BURMA
GUIANA
FIJI
PALESTINE
WEST INDIES
BERMUDA
EAST AFRICA
WEST AFRICA
MALAYA
CEYLON
HONG KONG
Stonebridge Park
Harlesden
Alperton
Park Royal
North Ealing
L.U. TRAMS TO HANWELL, HAYES & UXBRIDGE
Ealing Broadway
Ealing Common
Willesden Junction
S. Acton
Acton Town
South Ealing
Northfields
Boston Manor
Osterley
Hounslow Town
Heston Hounslow
Hounslow Barracks
MOTOR BUS FROM STAINES & WINDSOR
Gunnersbury
Kew Gardens
Richmond
MOTOR BUS FROM TWICKENHAM & KINGSTON
Queen's Park
Kilburn Road
Chalk Farm
Camden Town
Caledonian Road
Kilburn Park
Kensal Green
Maida Vale
St. Quintin Park
Uxbridge Rd
Chiswick Park
Turnham Green
Stamford Brook
Ravenscourt Park
Shepherds Bush
Wood Lane
Latimer Road
Ladbroke Grove
Warwick Avenue
Goldhawk Road
Hammersmith
Westbourne Park
Royal Oak
Bishops Road
Barons Court
Addison Rd
West Kensington
West Brompton
Walham Green
Parsons Green
Chelsea
Battersea
Putney Bridge
East Putney
Southfields
Wimbledon Park
Wimbledon
L.U. TRAMS FROM KINGSTON & HAMPTON COURT
Clapham Junc.
Wandsworth Common
Neasden
Dollis Hill
Golders Green
Willesden Green
Kilburn Brondesbury
West Hampstead
Finchley Road
Swiss Cottage
Marlborough Road
St. John's Wood Road
Marylebone
Edgware Road
Paddington
Bayswater
Notting Hill Gate
High St.
Earl's Court
Gloster Road
S. Kensington
Sloane Square
Victoria
St. James's Park
Westminster
Baker Street
Euston Square
Regent's Park
St. Pancras
King's Cross
Euston
Oxford Circus
Piccadilly Circus
Charing Cross
Waterloo
Temple
Blackfriars
Mansion House
Cannon Street
Monument
Mark Lane
Aldgate East
Aldgate
Moorgate St.
Aldersgate
Liverpool St.
Broad Street
Highgate
Finsbury Park
Mildmay Park
Canonbury
Dalston Junction
Haggerston
Hackney
Homerton
FROM STRATFORD
Victoria Park
Old Ford
Bow
FROM SOUTHEND
Bow Rd
S. Bromley
Poplar
Shoreditch
Whitechapel
Stepney Green
Mile End
Shadwell
St. Mary's
Wapping
Rotherhithe
Surrey Docks
New Cross Gate
Lambeth
Elephant & Castle
Oval
Stockwell
Clapham Road
Clapham Common
Kennington
Balham
West Norwood
Gypsy Hill
Streatham Hill
MOTOR BUS FROM BALHAM, MITCHAM, BELMONT, DORKING
DOBSON, MOLLE & CO. LTD., COLOUR PRINTERS, EDINBURGH, LIVERPOOL & LONDON.
PRINTED IN GREAT BRITAIN

A SYMBOL FOR LONDON

Harry Beck, a temporary draughtsman laid off by the Underground Railway Company in 1931, spent his enforced leisure designing an easy-to-understand tube map that would meet passengers' needs. Thinking of diagrams and perhaps influenced by the simple, clear lines of contemporary Art Deco, he abandoned the cartographer's usual priorities of distance, direction and terrain, concentrating instead on the sequence of stations and interchanges, all centred on the Central Line which is shown mainly as a straight horizontal line. He enlarged the central area and ignored ground features but for a schematic Thames. The rest of the map, the manuscript version of which dates back to 1931, was constructed using only straight lines at 45° and 90° angles. Beck got his job back. His plan became a symbol for London.

7.4.7 [Harry Beck] *Railway Map* (London Passenger Transport Board, 1935). 15.1 × 22.8 cm. Maps 3485 (247). Reproduced by kind permission of Transport for London

TO CHESHAM AMERSHAM GREAT MISSENDEN WENDOVER AYLESBURY
RICKMANS-WORTH
WATFORD
CROXLEY GREEN
MOOR PARK & SANDY LODGE
NORTHWOOD
NORTHWOOD HILLS
PINNER
NORTH HARROW
HARROW ON THE HILL
WATFORD JUNCTION
WATFORD (HIGH STREET)
BUSHEY AND OXHEY
CARPENDERS PARK
HATCH END FOR PINNER
HEADSTONE LANE
HARROW & WEALDSTONE
KENTON
PRESTON ROAD
STANMORE
CANONS PARK
QUEENSBURY
KINGSBURY
NEASDEN
DOLLIS HILL
WILLESDEN GREEN
KILBURN & BRONDESBURY
WEST HAMPSTEAD
FINCHLEY ROAD
SWISS COTTAGE
MARLBORO ROAD
ST. JOHNS WOOD
MARYLEBONE
UXBRIDGE
ICKENHAM
RUISLIP MANOR
RAYNERS LANE
WEST HARROW
HILLINGDON (SWAKELEYS)
RUISLIP
EASTCOTE
NORTHWICK PARK
SOUTH KENTON
NORTH WEMBLEY
WEMBLEY PARK
WEMBLEY FOR SUDBURY
STONEBRIDGE PARK
HARLESDEN
WILLESDEN JUNCTION
KENSAL GREEN
QUEENS PARK
KILBURN PARK
MAIDA VALE
WARWICK AVENUE
SOUTH HARROW
SUDBURY HILL
SUDBURY TOWN
ALPERTON
PARK ROYAL
NORTH EALING
EALING BROADWAY
EALING COMMON
EAST ACTON
WEST ACTON
NORTH ACTON
WOOD LANE
SHEPHERDS BUSH
LATIMER ROAD
WESTBOURNE PARK
ROYAL OAK
LADBROKE GROVE
PADDINGTON
PADDINGTON PRAED STREET
EDGWARE ROAD
BAYSWATER
NOTTING HILL GATE
UXBRIDGE ROAD
HOLLAND PARK
QUEENS ROAD
LANCASTER GATE
MARBLE ARCH
BOND STREET
BAKER STREET
REGENTS PARK
GREAT PORTLAND ST.
OXFORD CIRCUS
ACTON TOWN
SOUTH ACTON
SOUTH EALING
NORTHFIELDS
BOSTON MANOR
OSTERLEY
HOUNSLOW EAST
HOUNSLOW CENTRAL
HOUNSLOW WEST
CHISWICK PARK
TURNHAM GREEN
GUNNERSBURY
STAMFORD BROOK
KEW GARDENS
RICHMOND
RAVENSCOURT PARK
GOLDHAWK ROAD
HAMMERSMITH
BARONS COURT
ADDISON ROAD
WEST KENSINGTON
EARLS COURT
HIGH STREET KENSINGTON
GLOUCESTER ROAD
SOUTH KENSINGTON
SLOANE SQUARE
WEST BROMPTON
WALHAM GREEN
PARSONS GREEN
PUTNEY BRIDGE
EAST PUTNEY
SOUTHFIELDS
WIMBLEDON PARK
WIMBLEDON
HYDE PARK CORNER
KNIGHTSBRIDGE
GREEN PARK
PICCADILLY CIRCUS
VICTORIA
ST. JAMES PARK
WESTMINSTER
EDGWARE
BURNT OAK (WATLING)
COLINDALE
HENDON CENTRAL
BRENT
GOLDERS GREEN
HAMPSTEAD
BELSIZE PARK
CHALK FARM
HIGHGATE
TUFNELL PARK
KENTISH TOWN
CAMDEN TOWN
MORNINGTON CRESCENT
EUSTON
EUSTON SQUARE
WARREN STREET
GOODGE STREET
TOTTENHAM COURT ROAD
COVENT GARDEN
LEICESTER SQUARE
TRAFALGAR SQUARE
STRAND
CHARING CROSS
TEMPLE
ALDWYCH
HOLBORN (KINGSWAY)
RUSSELL SQUARE
CHANCERY LANE (GRAYS INN)
POST OFFICE
KINGS CROSS ST. PANCRAS
ANGEL
FARRINGDON
ALDERSGATE
MOORGATE
OLD STREET
BANK
MANSION HOUSE
BLACKFRIARS
CANNON STREET
MONUMENT
MARK LANE
ALDGATE
ALDGATE EAST
LIVERPOOL STREET
ST MARYS
WHITECHAPEL
STEPNEY GREEN
MILE END
BOW ROAD
SHOREDITCH
SHADWELL
WAPPING
ROTHERHITHE
SURREY DOCKS
NEW CROSS GATE
NEW CROSS
LONDON BRIDGE
BOROUGH
ELEPHANT & CASTLE
WATERLOO
LAMBETH NORTH
KENNINGTON
OVAL
STOCKWELL
CLAPHAM NORTH
CLAPHAM COMMON
CLAPHAM SOUTH
BALHAM
TRINITY ROAD (TOOTING BEC)
TOOTING BROADWAY
COLLIERS WOOD
SOUTH WIMBLEDON (MERTON)
MORDEN
COCKFOSTERS
ENFIELD WEST (OAKWOOD)
SOUTHGATE
ARNOS GROVE
BOUNDS GREEN
WOOD GREEN
TURNPIKE LANE
MANOR HOUSE
FINSBURY PARK
ARSENAL (HIGHBURY HILL)
HOLLOWAY ROAD
CALEDONIAN ROAD
DRAYTON PARK
HIGHBURY & ISLINGTON
CANONBURY & ESSEX ROAD
ESCALATOR CONNECTION BETWEEN BANK AND MONUMENT STATIONS
TO BROMLEY WEST HAM PLAISTOW UPTON PARK EAST HAM BARKING UPNEY BECONTREE HEATHWAY DAGENHAM HORNCHURCH UPMINSTER BRIDGE UPMINSTER SOUTHEND
REFERENCE
DISTRICT LINE
PICCADILLY LINE
BAKERLOO LINE
MORDEN-EDGWARE LINE
CENTRAL LONDON LINE
METROPOLITAN LINE
NORTHERN CITY LINE
INTERCHANGE STATIONS
LONDON UNDERGROUND TRANSPORT
H.C.BECK

7.5 A TO Z

The beginnings of the A to Z can be traced back to seventeenth-century sheet maps for strangers to the capital. By the early nineteenth century, following the enormous growth of London, the street index became a separate volume until in the 1850s maps and index were brought together in a handy small atlas format. By the early twentieth century, road atlases had taken on their modern characteristics, open spaces being compressed and the width of streets enlarged. One of the earlier publishers of these atlases was an energetic Hungarian, Alexander Gross. In 1936 his daughter, Phyllis Pearsall, under his direction, published the first mass-produced A to Z.

Extract from *Collins' Illustrated Atlas of London* (London: H. G. Collins, 1854)

PL. 18. ST PAUL'S (AND BANK) TO E. COUNTIES' RAIL.Y TERM.S SHOREDITCH, AND KINGSLAND ROAD.

THE EARLIEST STREET GUIDE TO LONDON

In 1623 an enterprising mapmaker, John Norden, realised that a street guide to London was needed and could be profitable. Deleting the date, he reprinted a map he had created to illustrate a book in 1593, even though it did not include the new suburbs. The map already had lists of the most important streets and buildings reerenced from a to z and from 1 to 22. Norden now completed the street listing by adding new entries from 23 to 95. Thousands of copies were probably printed and used to destruction: only one example of the 1623 edition and a handful of this reissue of 1653 have survived.

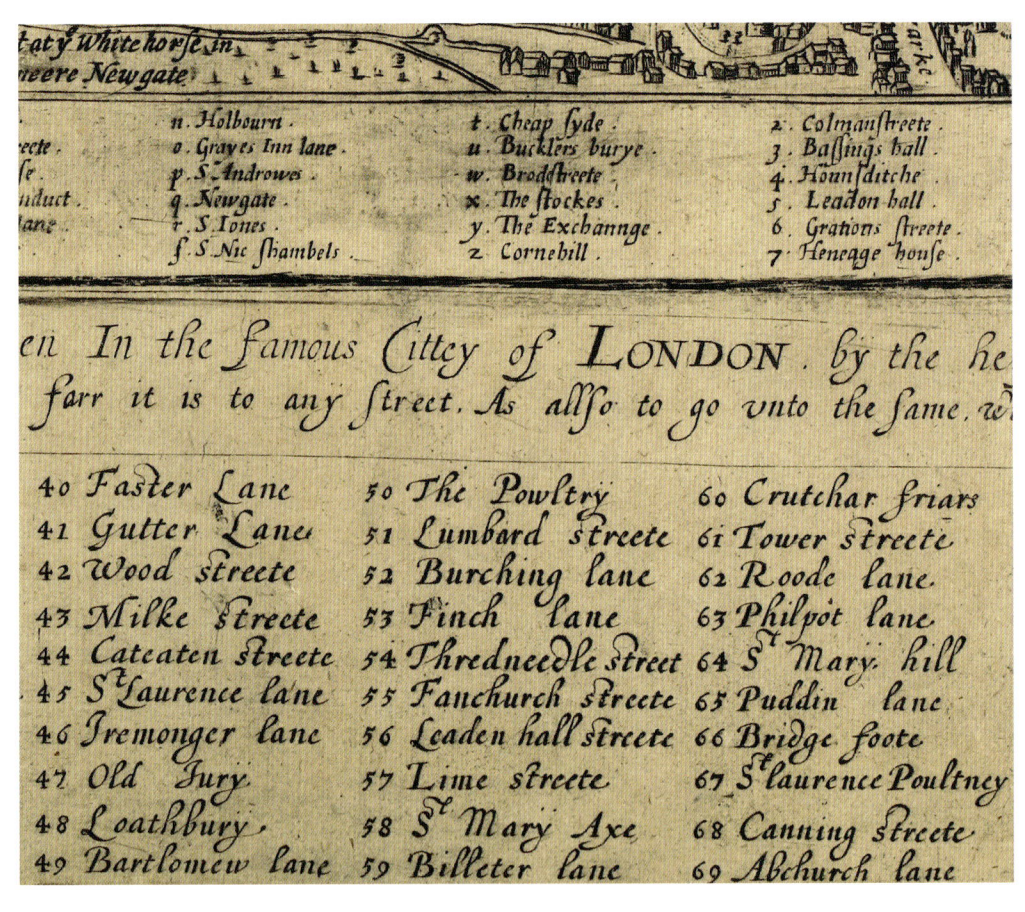

7.5.1 John Norden, *A Guide for Cuntrey men ... by the helpe of wich plot they shall be able to know how farr it is to any street. As allso to go vnto the same, without forder troble* (London: Peter Stent, 1653). Copperplate engraving. 51.2 × 72 cm. Maps Crace I.33

For Norden see 1.3.5 above. Peter Stent (1613?–65) came originally from Hampshire and was apprenticed to Elizabeth Lowe, widow of the London copperplate-printer George Lowe, in 1627. By the 1640s his shop in Giltspur Street probably had the largest stock of any of the handful of London printsellers. He died of the plague in the Great Plague of 1665.

LONDON

A guide for Cuntrey men In the famous Citty of LONDON, by the helpe of wich plot, they shall be able to know, how farr it is to any street. As allso to go vnto the same, without forder troble. Anno 1653.

✢ Long lane	30 The Posterne	40 Faster Lane	50 The Powltry	60 Crutchar friars	70 St Swithens lane	80 Garlicke hill	90 Lambeth hill
⊙ St Johnstreete	31 Litle More feild	41 Gutter Lane	51 Lumbard streete	61 Tower streete	71 St Clements lane	81 Boo lane	91 Old Chaunge
⊙ Turnboule streete	32 Showe Lane	42 Wood streete	52 Burching lane	62 Roode lane	72 Dowgate	82 Trynitie lane	92 Distaff lane
23 Goulding lane	33 Fleete lane	43 Milke streete	53 Finch lane	63 Philpot lane	73 Walbrooke	83 Soper lane	93 Carter lane
24 Red crosstreete	34 Warwick lane	44 Cateaten streete	54 Thredneedle street	64 St Mary hill	74 Cloake lane	84 Bredstreete	94 Pie Corner
25 Beech lane	35 Pater noster Roe	45 St Laurence lane	55 Fanchurch streete	65 Puddin lane	75 Budge Roe	85 Watling streete	95 Cow lane
26 White crosse steete	36 Petecannons	46 Iremonger lane	56 Leaden hall streete	66 Bridge foote	76 St Sythes lane	86 Friday streete	
27 Chisil streete	37 Paules Crosse	47 Old Iury	57 Lime streete	67 St Laurence Poultney	77 St Pantlins	87 Old fish streete	
28 Grub streete	38 Blacke Fryers	48 Loathbury	58 St Mary Axe	68 Canning streete	78 Whittington Colledge	88 Fishstreete hill	
29 More Lane	39 St Martens	49 Bartlomew lane	59 Billeter lane	69 Abchurch lane	79 St Thomes Apostles	89 Nighfryday streete	

329

THE GRID REFERENCE

By 1800, London maps containing long lists of street names were relatively common (see, for example, 7.4.1). Since 1738 some mapmakers, as in this example, had squared the map and identified streets by reference to the number of the relevant square, a step towards the grid system used on the modern *A–Z*. As early as 1676, however, William Morgan, realising the impossibility of including references to all London street names on a single map, had published a separate booklet with the names of buildings and streets referred to on his and Ogilby's great map of London (see 2.1.5). The Companion to Langley and Belch's map of London of 1812 contained no fewer than 10,000 names.

7.5.2 *Tegg's New Plan of London &c. with 360 references to the principal streets &c. 1830* (London: T. Tegg, 1830). Copperplate engraving. 51.1 × 71.8 cm. Maps Crace VII.230

Thomas Tegg (1776–1846) was the son of a Wimbledon grocer and one of the most colourful members of the nineteenth-century book trade. His nightly auctions were for many years a popular feature of London life and his philosophy was one of piling high and selling cheap. He specialised in cheap reprints of works no longer in copyright, scooping up remainders (describing himself as 'the broom that swept the booksellers' warehouses') and mass-producing the cheap and cheerful. The seventeenth-century façade of his premises at 73 Cheapside survives laid out as an ornamental flower-bed in the Pines Garden at St Margaret's Bay in Kent.

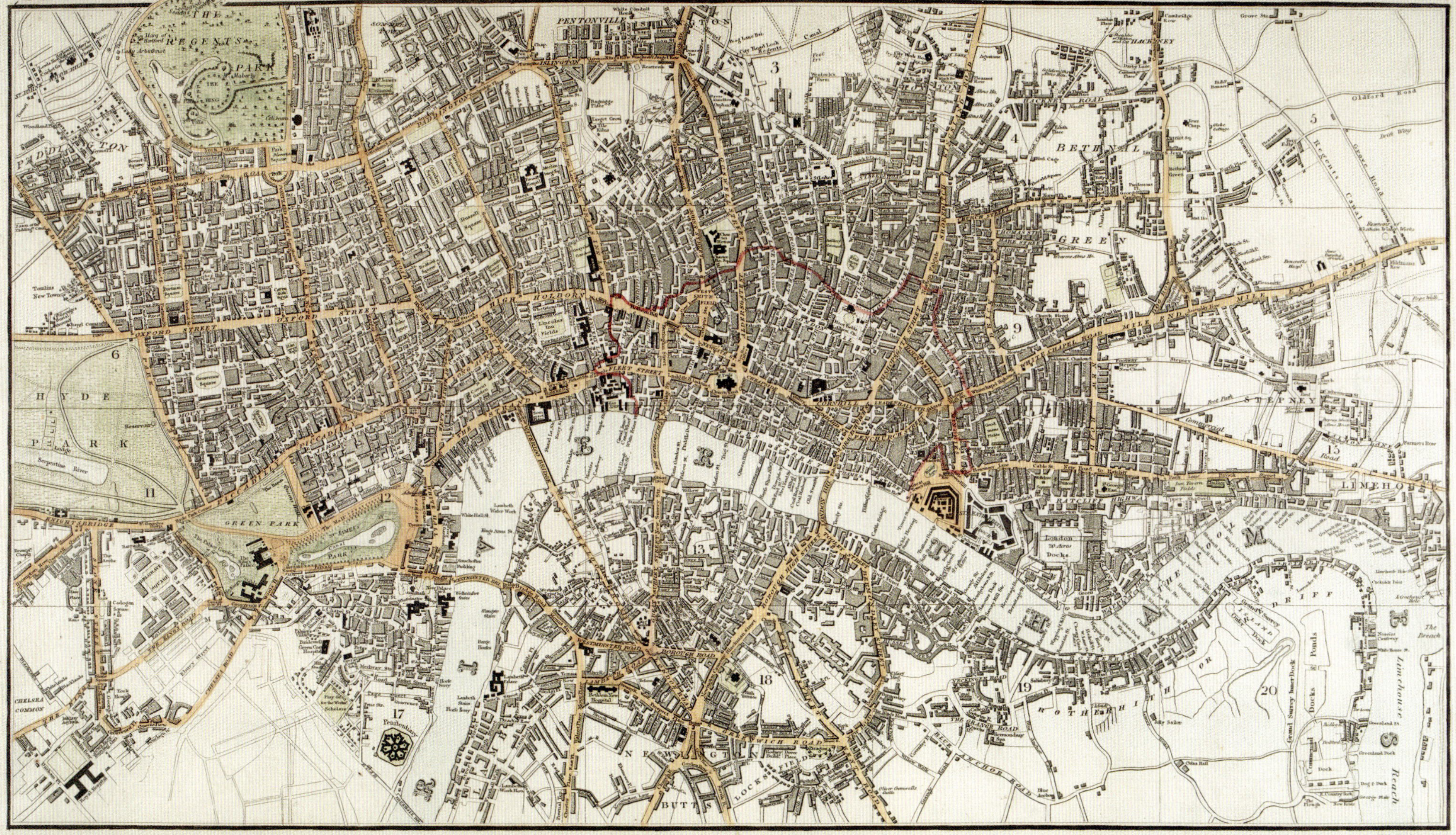

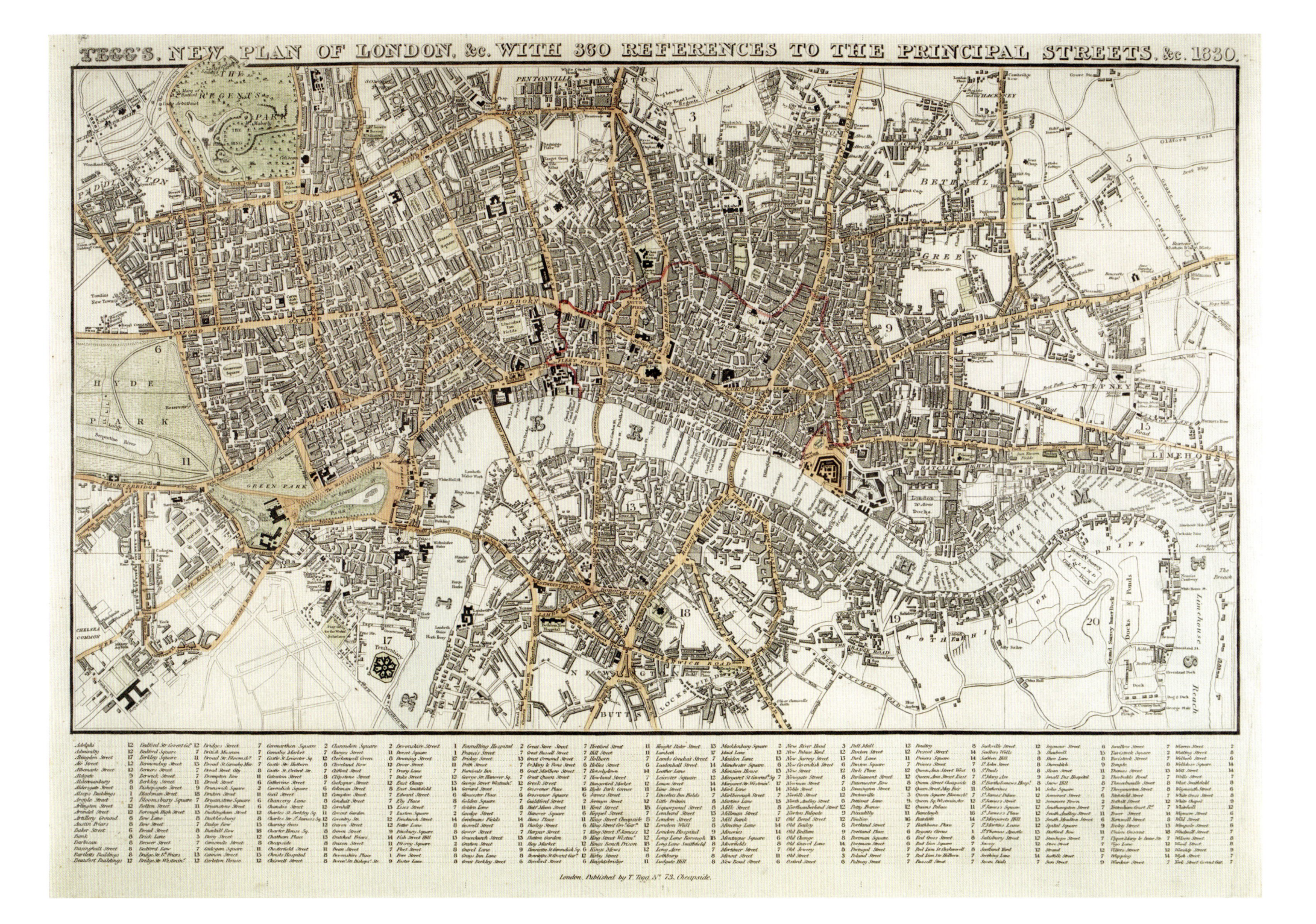

THE STREET ATLAS

Henry Collins seems to have had the idea of re-uniting the street map and the street index in a single indexed atlas, and one, moreover, that was small enough to be carried around in a spacious pocket. There is an extensive index and the maps, adorned with charming vignettes of important buildings, are reproduced at a large enough scale for even alleys to be seen and named. The only weakness is that the maps contain no indications of orientation and only a few have North at the top. Despite the frustration that this must have caused users, the atlas was regularly reprinted.

7.5.3 *Collins' Illustrated Atlas of London with 7000 references in 36 Plates of the Principal Routes between St Paul's and the Suburbs from A Survey made expressly for this work by R. Jarman Esq.* (London: H. G. Collins, 1854). Steel engraving. 20 × 29 cm. Maps 15.b.18

Henry George Collins was baptised at St Martin-in-the-Fields in 1808 and was originally a bookbinder before turning to map-publishing in the 1840s. His map-publishing career was a relatively short one, his stock being dispersed at auction in 1858. He was also a patentee of electro block printing and retired to Witham in Essex. The draughtsman and engraver Richard Jarman (1807–77) was born in Whitechapel, had premises in Bartholomew Close and also produced Collins' Standard map of London. He emigrated to Australia in 1857 and had a successful career in Hobart.

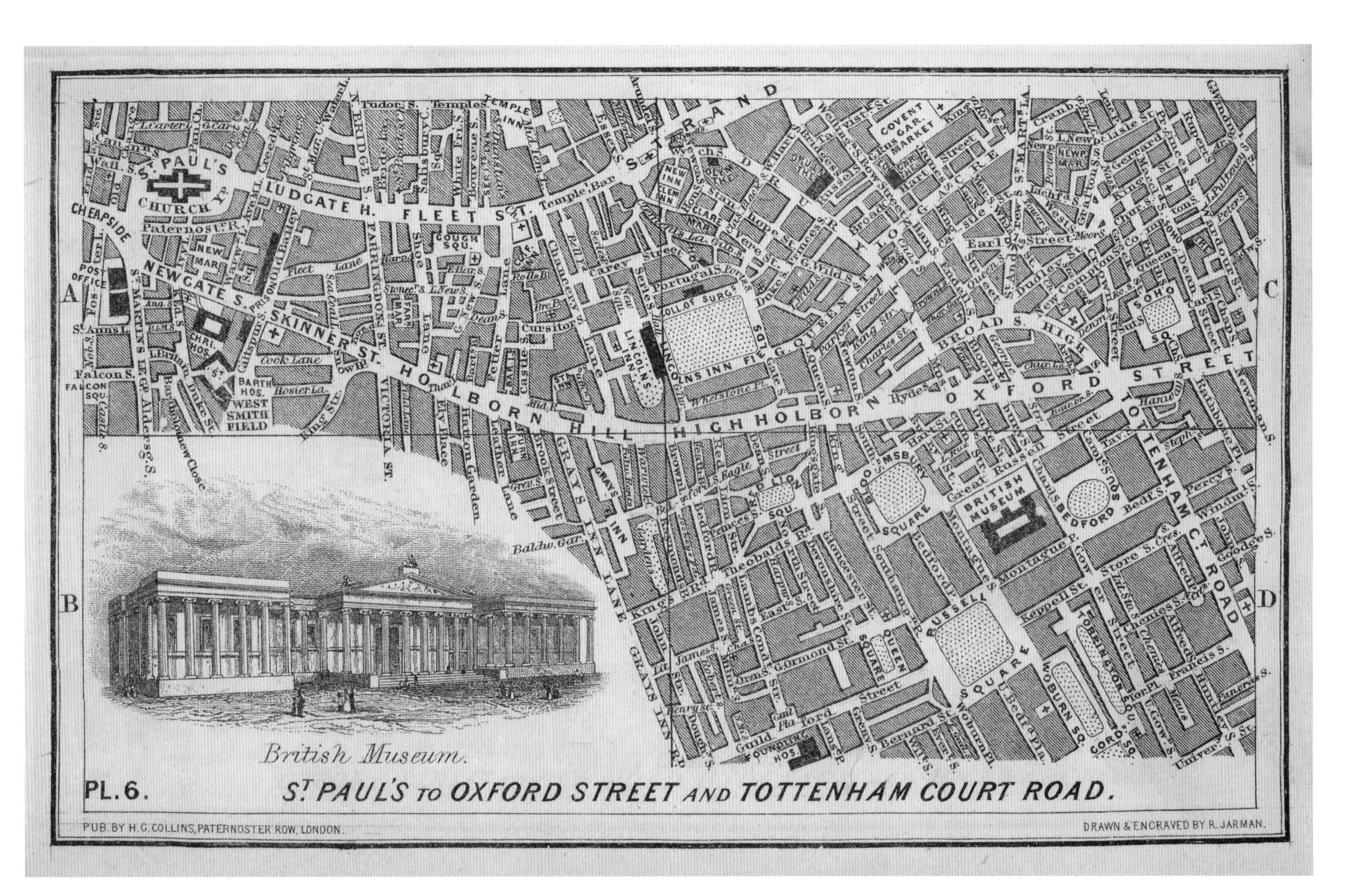

PL. 6. ST PAUL'S TO OXFORD STREET AND TOTTENHAM COURT ROAD.

British Museum.

PUB. BY H.G. COLLINS, PATERNOSTER ROW, LONDON.   DRAWN & ENGRAVED BY R. JARMAN.

 Continued on Pages 21&22

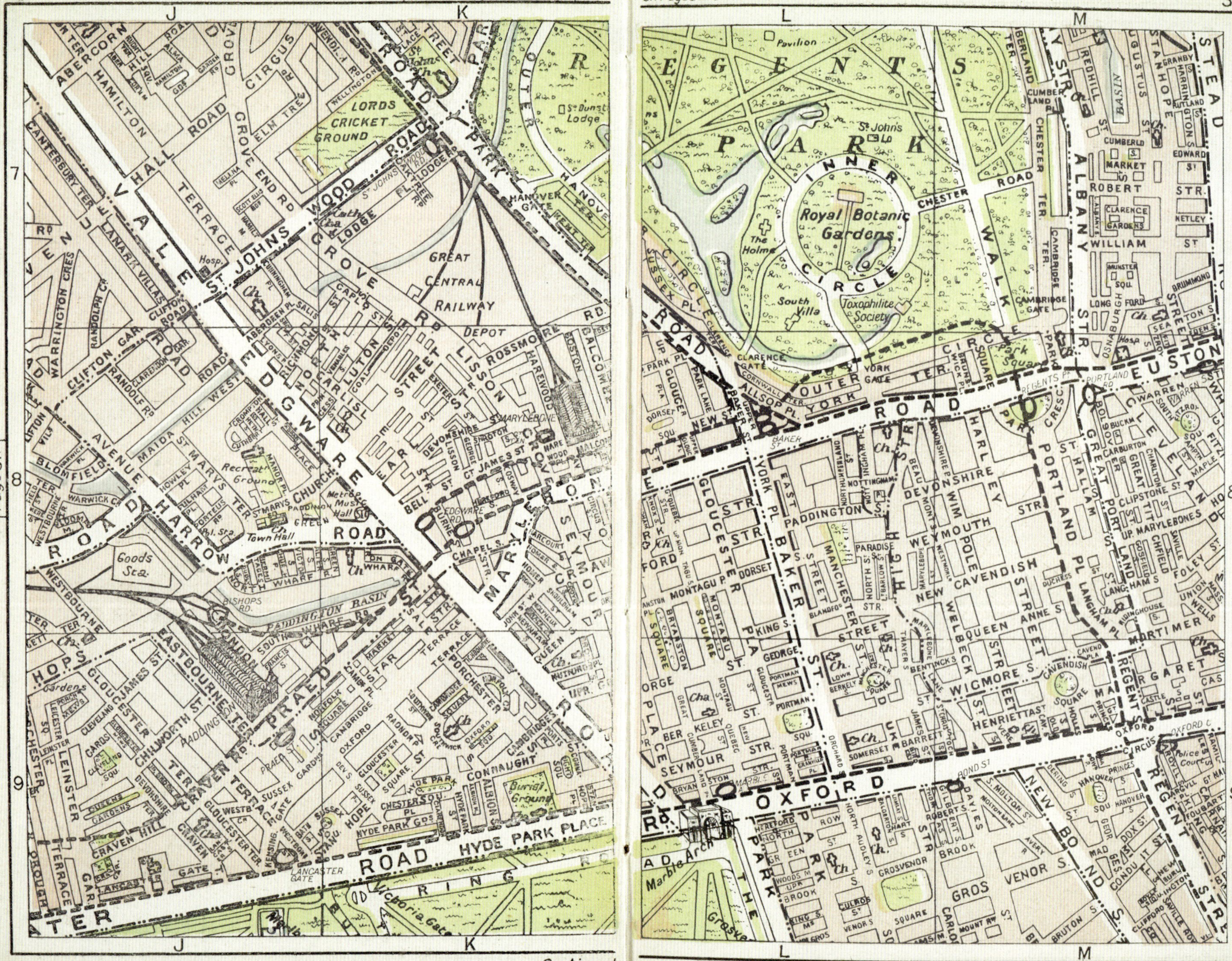

0 ¼ ½ Mile Continued on Pages 43&44. Railways & Staˢ Underground Staˢ
Tram & Omnibus Routes

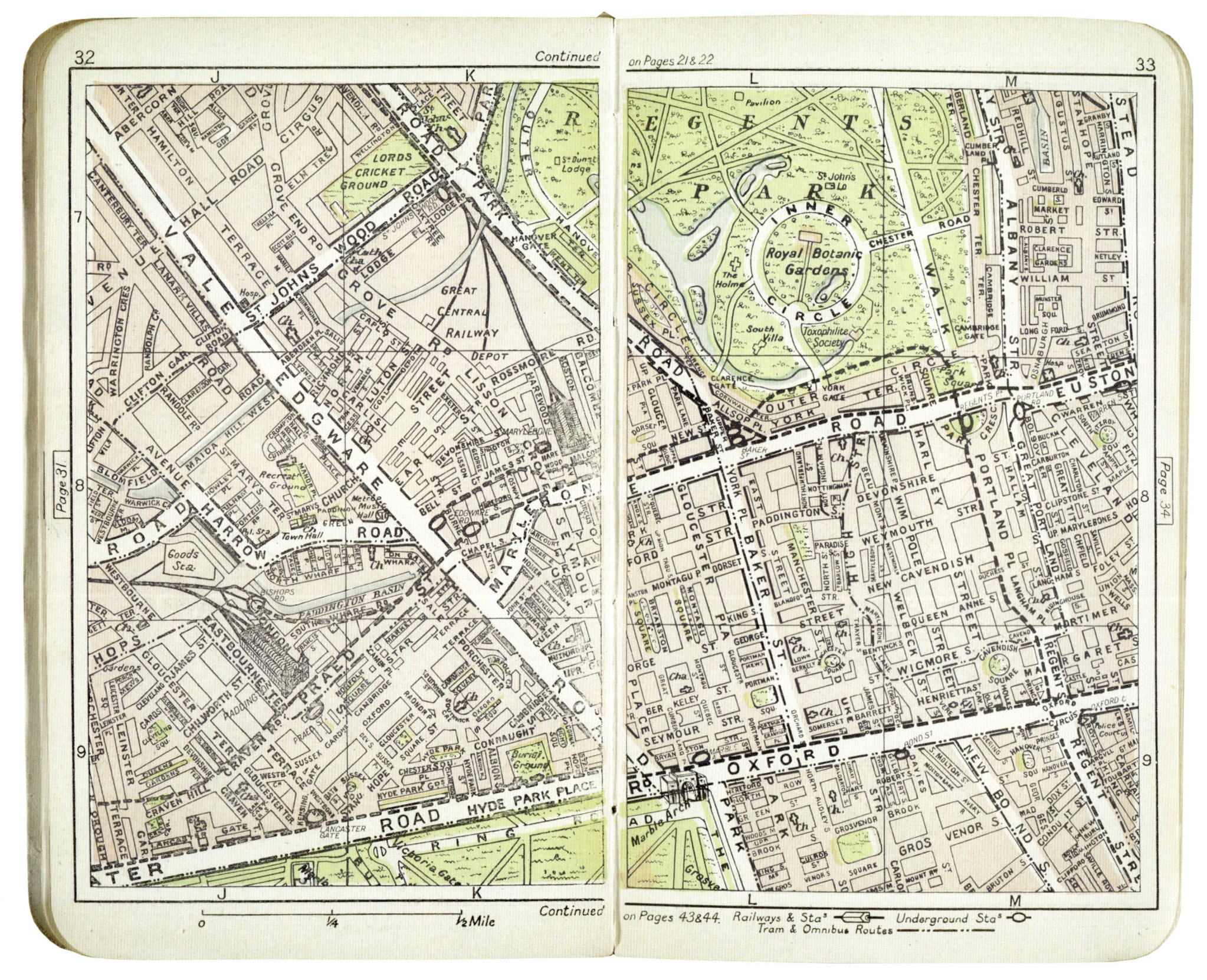

AN A to Z?

Sandor Grosz (Alexander Gross) was an enterprising Hungarian-Jewish émigré who founded the *Geographia* map publishing company. In 1913 he decided to follow the lead of other companies like Philips' in its *ABC Guide to London* of 1911 by producing a London street atlas. In order to improve legibility, he, like Philips, exaggerated the width of streets at the expense of nearby open spaces. He also included full grid references in the index. Although (unlike Philips) there was the occasional vignette of a building, essentially this was an *A to Z* before its time. Gross was the father of Phyllis Pearsall, the publisher of the first *A to Z*.

7.5.4 Alexander Gross, *Geographia New Atlas and Guide to London with Index containing over 8000 street names* (London: Geographia, 1913). 18 × 23 cm (opening) Maps 15.a.11

THE *A to Z*

Phyllis Pearsall published the first *A to Z* atlas in 1936 under the direction, she states on the title-page, of her father Alexander Gross. Though he was then a US resident, they communicated via cable. There was nothing new about the concept of the atlas and even the information on house-numbers in long streets had been seen earlier, but the area covered was much expanded to take account of London's growth since 1918. Mrs Pearsall was an energetic walker of streets, and claimed to have got her information from notes taken during her walks. But reliable information on new street names and even street numberings was available from local town halls without the need for such efforts. First editions are very rare: a testimonial to the *A to Z*'s usefulness and Phyllis Pearsall's marketing skills.

7.5.5 [Phyllis Pearsall], *Geographers' A to Z clear and up-to-date Atlas to London and Suburbs with House Numbers* (London: Geographers' Map Co., *c.* 1946). 17.8 × 19 cm. Maps 197.b.40. Front cover image used with the knowledge and permission of Geographers' A–Z Map Co. Ltd

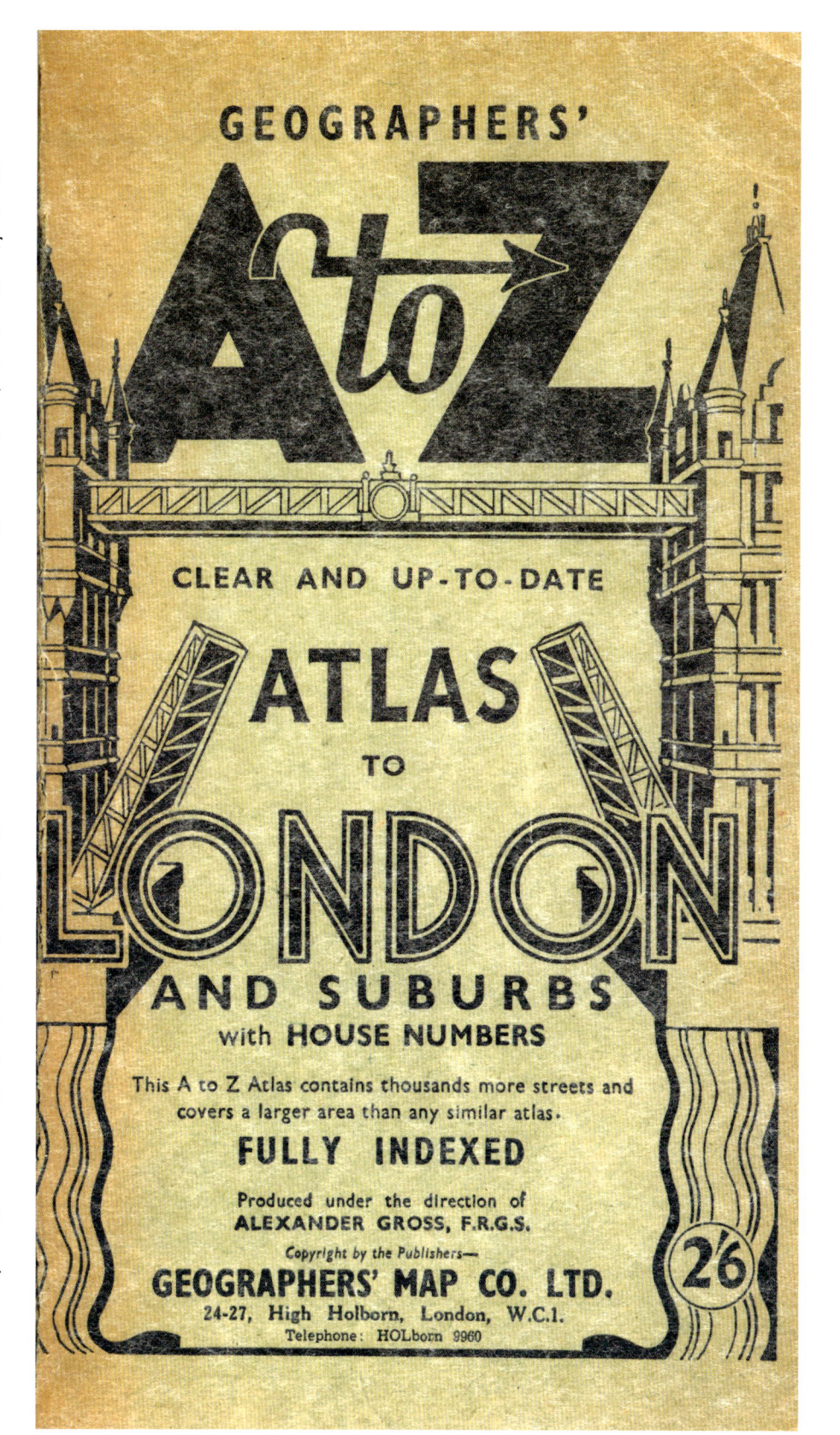

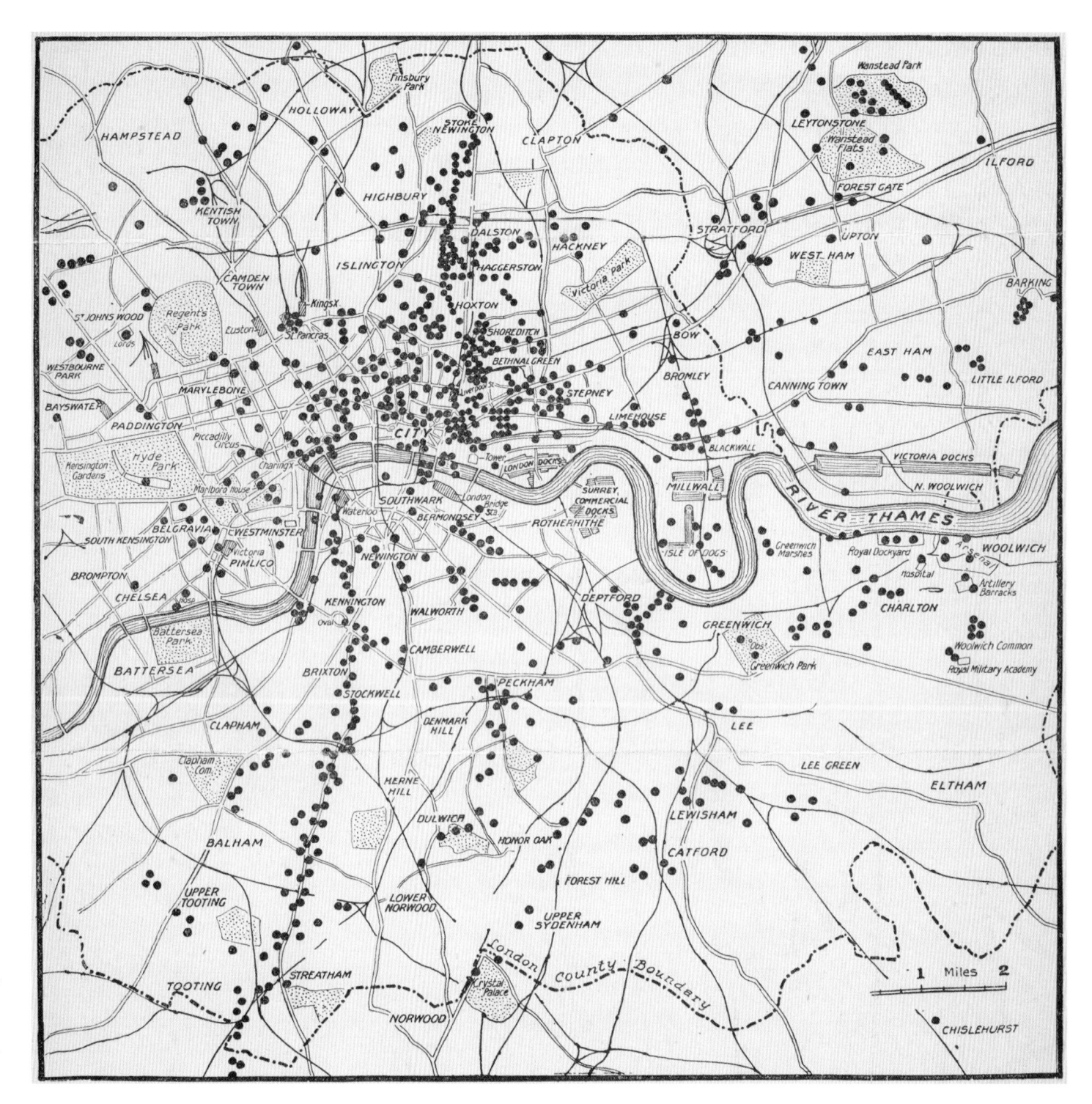

7.6.1 *The Daily Mail Map of Zeppelin and Aeroplane Bombs on London* (From *Daily Mail*, 31 January 1919). 20 × 19.8 cm (within neatlines). Maps 3485 (263)

7.6 DESTRUCTION FROM THE AIR

Despite persistent fears from the 1870s that socialist revolution would devastate London as it had devastated Paris in 1870–71, it was to be aerial bombardment after 1900 that did so. Foreshadowed by Zeppelin raids between 1915 and 1918, the threat was at its greatest during the Blitz of 1940–41 and again in 1944 and 1945 when pilotless V1s and V2s rained down on London. Official maps identified and quantified in awe-inspiring detail the damage done by German bombs throughout London, while German maps seized during the closing months of the war revealed Nazi invasion plans and the London buildings and installations that their aircraft had targeted.

THE FIRST LONDON BOMBS

Zeppelin airships first raided London on 31 May 1915 and became familiar sights until 1917 when the Germans replaced them with bomber planes. The pattern of bombings on this map (*facing page*) reflects the fact that the airmen followed the major roads on their way to and from the capital. In contrast to the Second World War, the Germans mainly targeted central London in order to damage civilian morale, ignoring the docks. The myth of their impact on London was out of all proportion to the physical damage that they actually inflicted.

LIVING THROUGH THE BOMBING

The most sustained period of Zeppelin attacks came in the autumn of 1915. As a change from essays on their summer holidays, the boys of Princeton St Elementary Schools near Bedford Row, Holborn, were asked to write down their impressions of the Zeppelin raids of 8 September and 13 October on the days after they happened. On 8 September a single Zeppelin, the L13, almost single-handedly caused more than half the total damage inflicted by all the raids against Britain in 1915. After the War, the headmaster presented the essays to the British Museum.

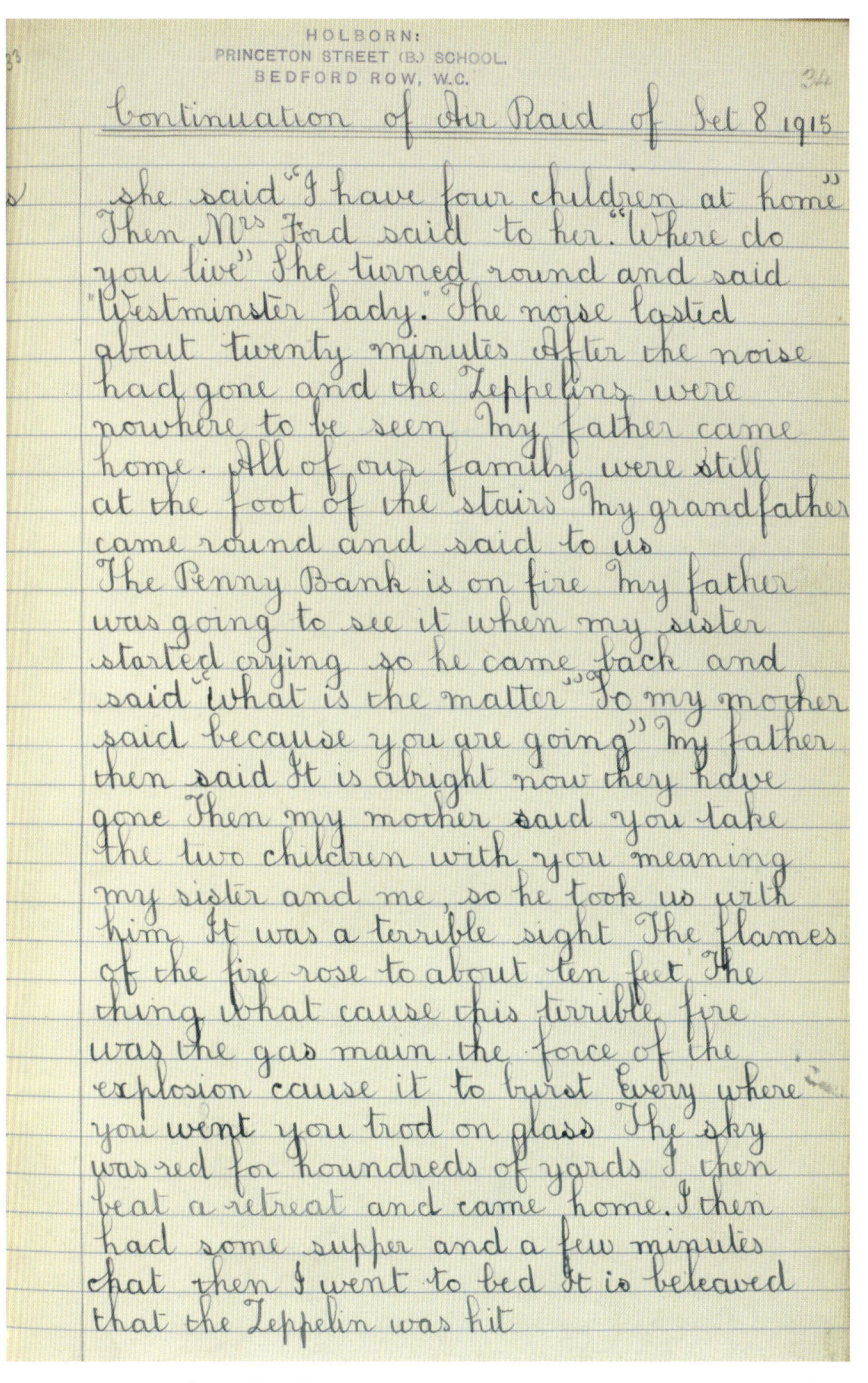

7.6.2 Essays of pupils of Princeton St Elementary Schools near Bedford Row, Holborn, 1915. 33 × 40 cm. Add. MS 39257

PREPARING FOR THE FALL OF LONDON

Following a successful *Blitzkrieg*, the Germans speedily overran Belgium and France in May and June 1940. They then turned to Britain. In preparation for the invasion, the British government ordered all signs to be removed from London streets. In August 1940 this special map was prepared for the German forces. It is copied from Ordnance Survey data. Street names have been added — but only for the through routes. At that time the German High Command expected that no more information would be required. Their troops would speedily sweep through the capital to complete their conquest of Great Britain.

7.6.3   Generalstab des Heeres: Abteilung für Kriegskarten und Vermessungswesen, *Militärgeographische Angaben über England. Mappe 8 London Stadtplan von London Verkehrsplan von London und Umgebung* (2nd edn, 30 August 1940). 94.1 × 74.9 cm. Maps 236.a.85

ROAD
UPPER STREET
Canonbury
ST PANCRAS
HIGH STR.
Dalston
KINGSLAND ROAD
MARE STR.
Haggerston
Hoxton
PENTONVILLE RD.
CITY ROAD
GOSWELL RD.
KING'S CROSS RD.
FARRINGDON RD.
ALDERSGATE
HOLBORN
NORTON FOLGATE
CAMBRIDGE ROAD

DESTRUCTION FROM THE AIR (1)

This special edition of the *Luftwaffe*'s official journal from the Front Line dates from the height of the Battle of Britain in October 1940. It contains maps and views of the Germans' principal targets along the River Thames and particularly in Docklands. These are outlined in red on a map copied from the Ordnance Survey 6-inches to the mile (1:10,560) map (left) and on an aerial photograph of the same area (right), derived from German reconnaissance flights undertaken during the so-called 'Phoney War' of autumn 1939. The targets include Abbey Mills Pumping Station, West Ham and Bow Power Stations and the Bromley-by-Bow Gasworks. Setting targets was one thing, actually hitting them, however, was another and the German success-rate was mixed.

7.6.4 Special edition of the *Frontnachrichtenblatt der Luftwaffe*, Blue series (Berlin: Oberbefehlshaber der Luftwaffe, Führungsstab IC, October 1940). 33.5 × 63.5 cm. Maps 46.c.24

Zielgebiet II London

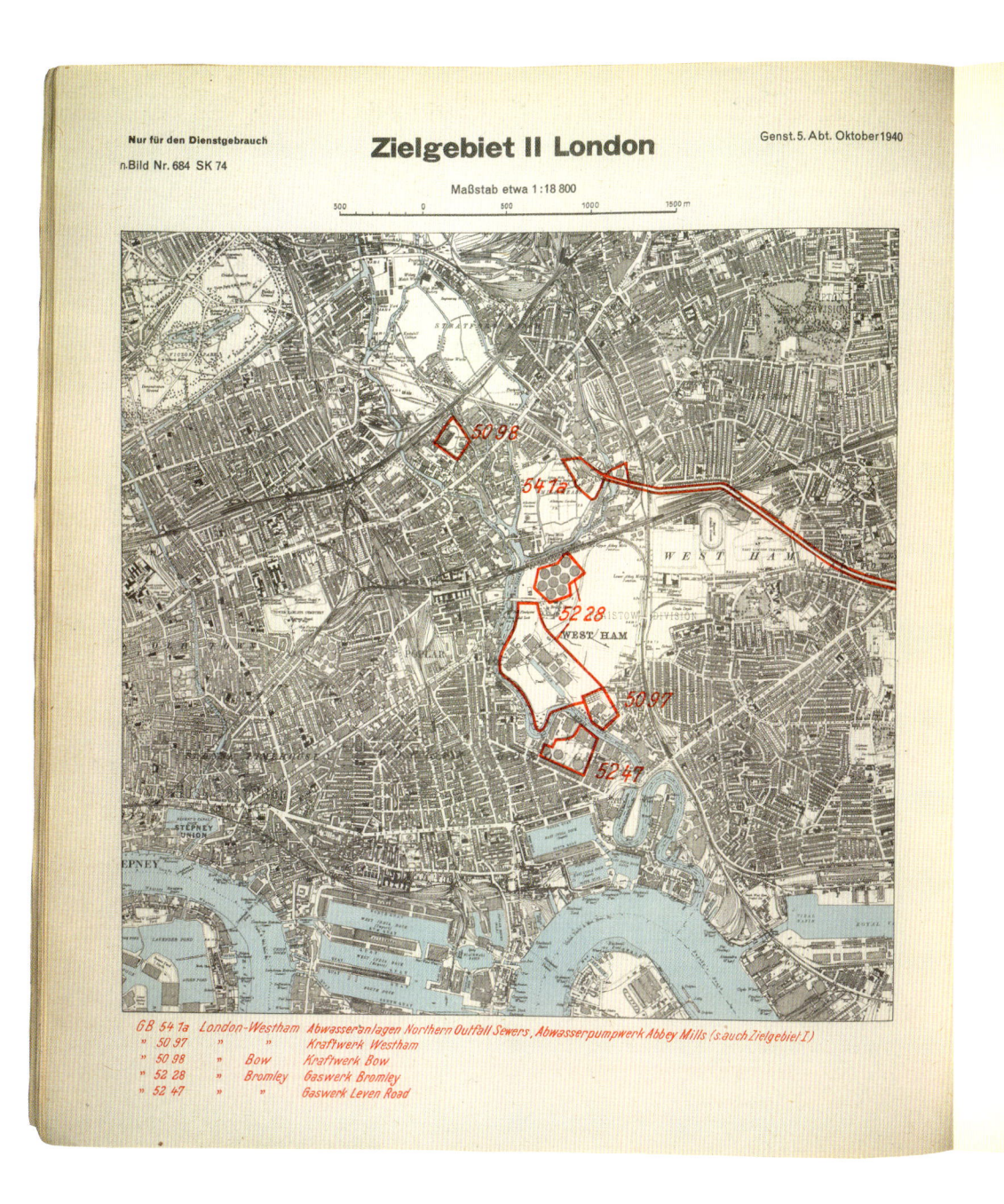

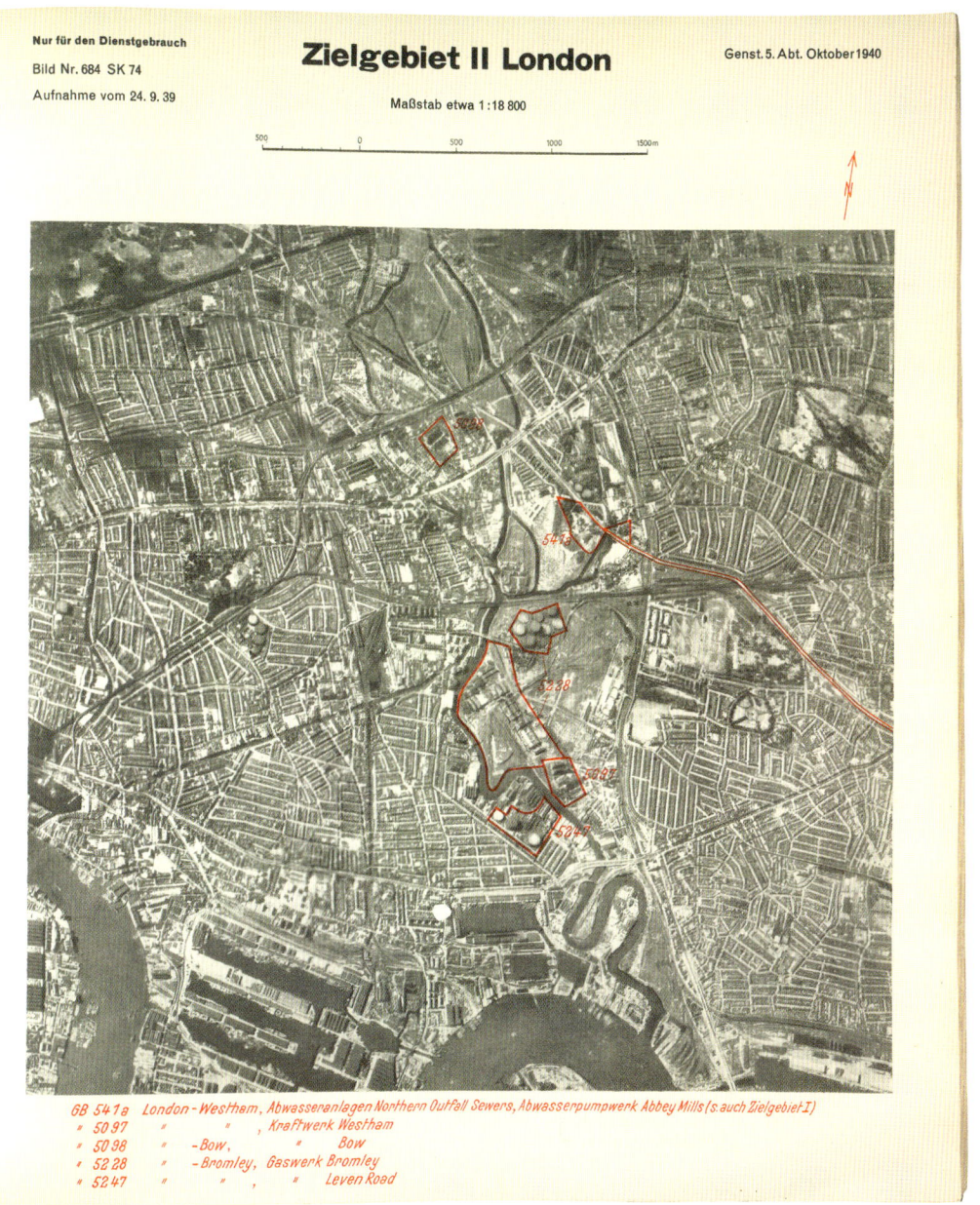

Nur für den Dienstgebrauch
n.Bild Nr. 684 SK 74
Genst. 5. Abt. Oktober 1940
Maßstab etwa 1:18 800

GB 54 1a London-Westham, Abwasseranlagen Northern Outfall Sewers, Abwasserpumpwerk Abbey Mills (s. auch Zielgebiet I)
" 50.97 " " Kraftwerk Westham
" 50.98 " Bow Kraftwerk Bow
" 52.28 " Bromley Gaswerk Bromley
" 52.47 " " Gaswerk Leven Road

Zielgebiet II London

Nur für den Dienstgebrauch
Bild Nr. 684 SK 74
Aufnahme vom 24.9.39
Genst. 5. Abt. Oktober 1940
Maßstab etwa 1:18 800

GB 54 1a London-Westham, Abwasseranlagen Northern Outfall Sewers, Abwasserpumpwerk Abbey Mills (s. auch Zielgebiet I)
" 50.97 " " , Kraftwerk Westham
" 50.98 " -Bow, " Bow
" 52.28 " -Bromley, Gaswerk Bromley
" 52.47 " " , " Leven Road

DESTRUCTION FROM THE AIR (2)

From early 1941, district surveyors went on site immediately after air raids to assess the severity of damage to individual buildings. There were six categories, ranging from total destruction (black) to minor blast damage (yellow). Tracings of 25 inch to the mile Ordnance Survey sheets were appropriately coloured on the spot and then transcribed onto these master maps in the War Damage Survey Section of the LCC Architects' Department. From 1944 the damage done by V1s and V2s was also recorded (circles). The maps were intended to identify areas for post-war reconstruction, but they are also witnesses to the suffering of Londoners, particularly East-Enders with houses near the docks.

7.6.5   LCC War Damage map, sheet 78. 76 × 104.5 cm. City of London, London Metropolitan Archives

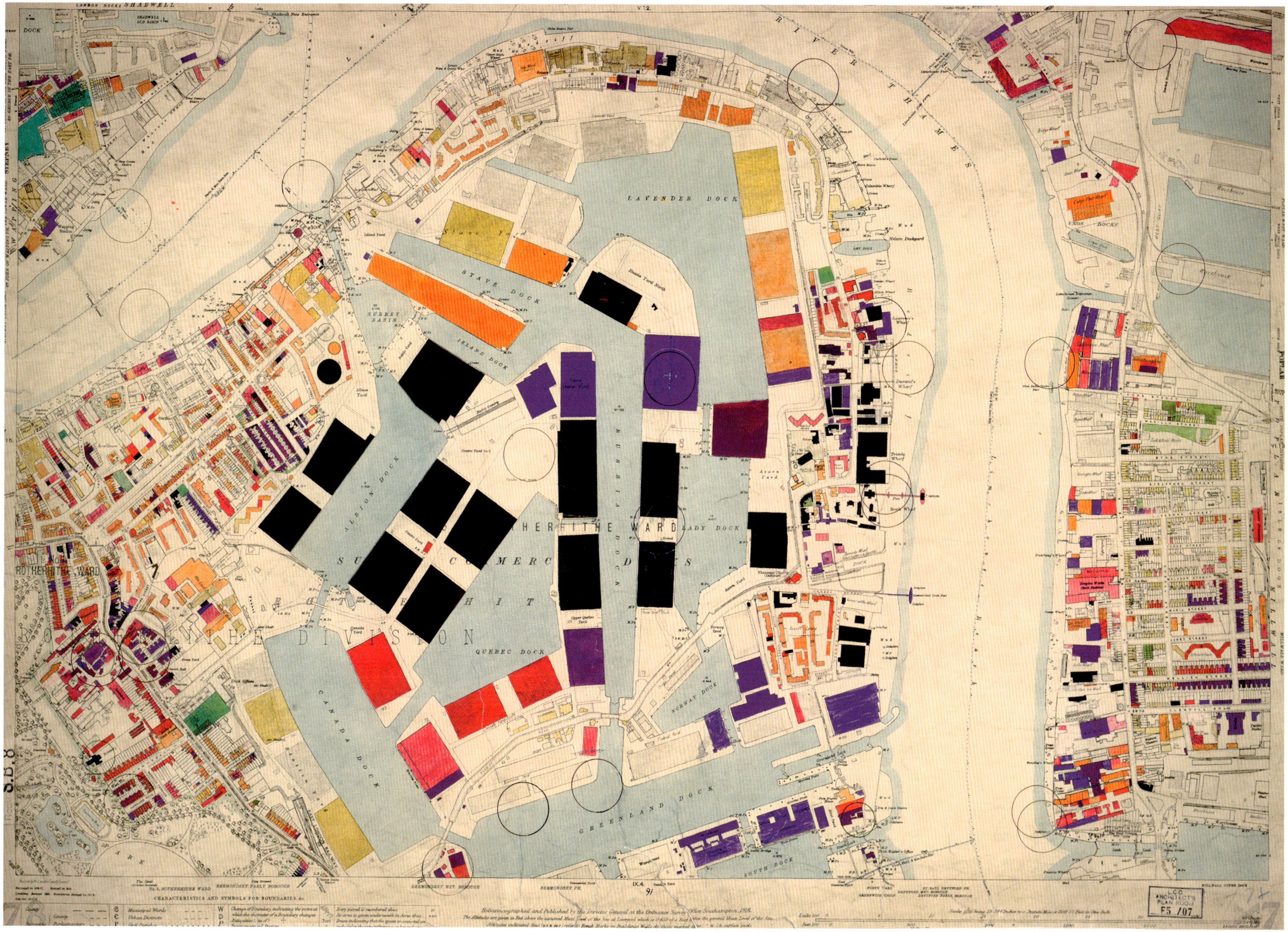
LAVENDER DOCK
STAVE DOCK
ISLAND DOCK
SURREY BASIN
ALBION DOCK
RUSSIA DOCK
QUEBEC DOCK
CANADA DOCK
GREENLAND DOCK
NORWAY DOCK
SOUTH DOCK
ROTHERHITHE WARD
LCC ARCHITECT'S PLAN ROOM F5 /07

SECTION EIGHT
MAPS IN MODERN LONDON

Maps continue to be involved in the warp and weft of London life. Commercial mapping has reflected Londoners' changing attitudes and passing fashions as well as boosting tourism and business. The council and the commercial planner have expressed their values and aspirations through bold maps and rose-tinted elevations. Since 2000 current and future problems have been tackled with the help of digital maps of unsurpassed analytical sophistication and diversity produced cheaply and easily using Geographical Information Systems. Their low price and relative ease of production have also had the effect of democratising map making, rendering it easier for the disadvantaged and for minorities to present viewpoints which often question the assumptions of the majority or highlight problems which might otherwise be glossed over. Panoramas and plans can now be combined in the same operating systems to assess the impact of proposed developments. Aerial panoramas, as artificial and subjective as any traditional map, are currently transforming Londoners' hitherto map-based perceptions of their surroundings.

8.1 CONVULSIONS

London emerged from the Second World War badly battered. Recovery was slow and the next sixty years saw population decline, the annihilation of London's industry and docks, and the loss of empire. 'Comprehensive redevelopment' and tower blocks caused at least as many social problems as they were intended to resolve. Racial conflict spilt out into street violence and street crime seemed worse than ever before. Life for the homeless and unemployed was as hard as it ever had been in Dickensian London. Under Margaret Thatcher London became the only world city not to have any over-arching administration following the abolition of the Greater London Council.

345

MAKING A FRESH START

For contemporaries, the Blitz was as much of a turning point as the Great Fire, as the reproduction of Hollar's post-Fire plan of 1667 as the frontispiece for this report makes clear (see 1.4.12 for the original). The priority was again London's speedy reinstatement as 'the centre of the World's commerce'. The orange area 'where Development may be considered imminent' shows the bombed-out districts which are particularly obvious north of St Paul's Cathedral. The grey area, with buildings left relatively untouched, was where 'rebuilding may be considered improbable'. Brown marks churches and places of historical interest. The few buildings marked in this way betray the official lack of interest in the built heritage. In the event, redevelopment was not as speedy as after 1666. But since 1975 more of the City has been demolished and rebuilt, largely with skyscraper office blocks, than was destroyed in the Blitz, including the area where in 1944 rebuilding was considered to be improbable.

8.1.1 F. J. Forty, *Report of the Improvements and Town Planning Committee … on the draft proposals for the Post-War Reconstruction in the City of London. Plan 1A: Opportunities and Considerations in the Redevelopment of the City of London.* (London: Corporation of London: Public Health Department, 24 July, 1944). 34 × 99 cm. Maps 59.e.17. Courtesy of the City of London

CORPORATION OF THE CITY OF LONDON
OPPORTUNITIES AND CONSIDERATIONS
IN THE REDEVELOPMENT OF THE CITY OF LONDON
PLAN NUMBER 1A
TOWN PLANNING SURVEY 1943
REFERENCE
AREAS WHERE REDEVELOPMENT MAY BE CONSIDERED IMMINENT.
AREAS WITHIN THE CITY OF LONDON WHERE IMMEDIATE REBUILDING MAY BE CONSIDERED IMPROBABLE including fully framed and semi-framed buildings.
PLACES OF WORSHIP AND BUILDINGS OF HISTORIC INTEREST within the City of London.
OPEN SPACES. All categories.
RIVER THAMES.
Redevelopment means generally the erection of a new building or the material alteration of an existing building.
Sites uncoloured represent land occupied by other buildings, streets, etc.
For existing Railways and Major Subways, see Plan No. 1B.
The information on this plan is as accurate as possible at the time of its preparation, but nothing herein implies or indicates proposals of the Corporation in relation to any site, nor can anything herein be cited as evidence of the condition or structure of a building or of the use of land; or of a right of way or of title to property or land.
W.F.B.L./R & F/1944
RIVER THAMES
The Tower
F. J. FORTY B.Sc., M.Inst.C.E
CITY ENGINEER
GUILDHALL, E.C.2
SCALE
Reproduced from the Ordnance Survey Map, with the sanction of the Comptroller of H.M. Stationery Office.
CHARLES SKIPPER & EAST LTD., Printers & Lithographers, LONDON, E.C.2.

COMPREHENSIVE REDEVELOPMENT

The 1960s was the great age of 'comprehensive redevelopment'. Spurred by an idealistic determination to improve inner-city living conditions, it was perhaps over-influenced by the Swiss architect Le Corbusier's theories of 'vertical garden cities' and assumptions about the need for inner city motorways to improve communications and commerce. The ideas found expression in this plan of 1969 for the redevelopment of the historic centre of Brixton, a poor area with a large immigrant community and high unemployment levels where rioting was to break out in 1981 and again in 2011. The plan shows a major motorway tearing its way through the town centre, with the local population being decanted into tower blocks. The brutalist way in which the plan is drawn (finely executed delicate black lines would have conveyed the information just as well) reflects the belief in revolutionary modernity of the time: the Labour Prime Minister, Harold Wilson, was talking proudly of the 'white heat of technological revolution' following the supposed stagnation of thirteen years of Conservative government. These proposals, drawn up just a year after the much-publicised collapse of a residential tower block at Ronan Point in Canning Town, were not implemented.

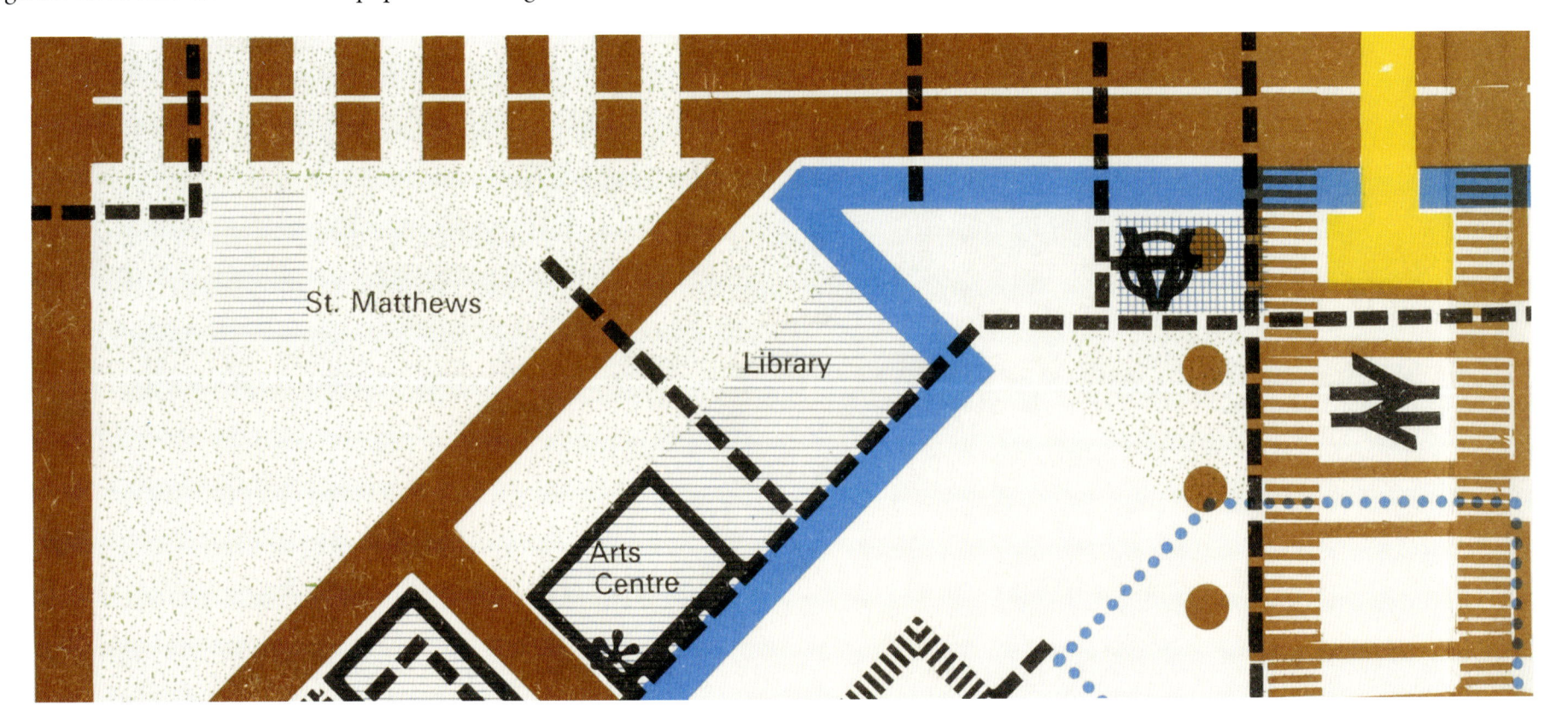

8.1.2 London Borough of Lambeth, *Brixton Town Centre Redevelopment Proposals* (June 1969). 21 × 29.7 cm and 29.5 × 41 cm. Maps 36.d.10 (part). Courtesy of the London Borough of Lambeth

4.c Preferred Solution

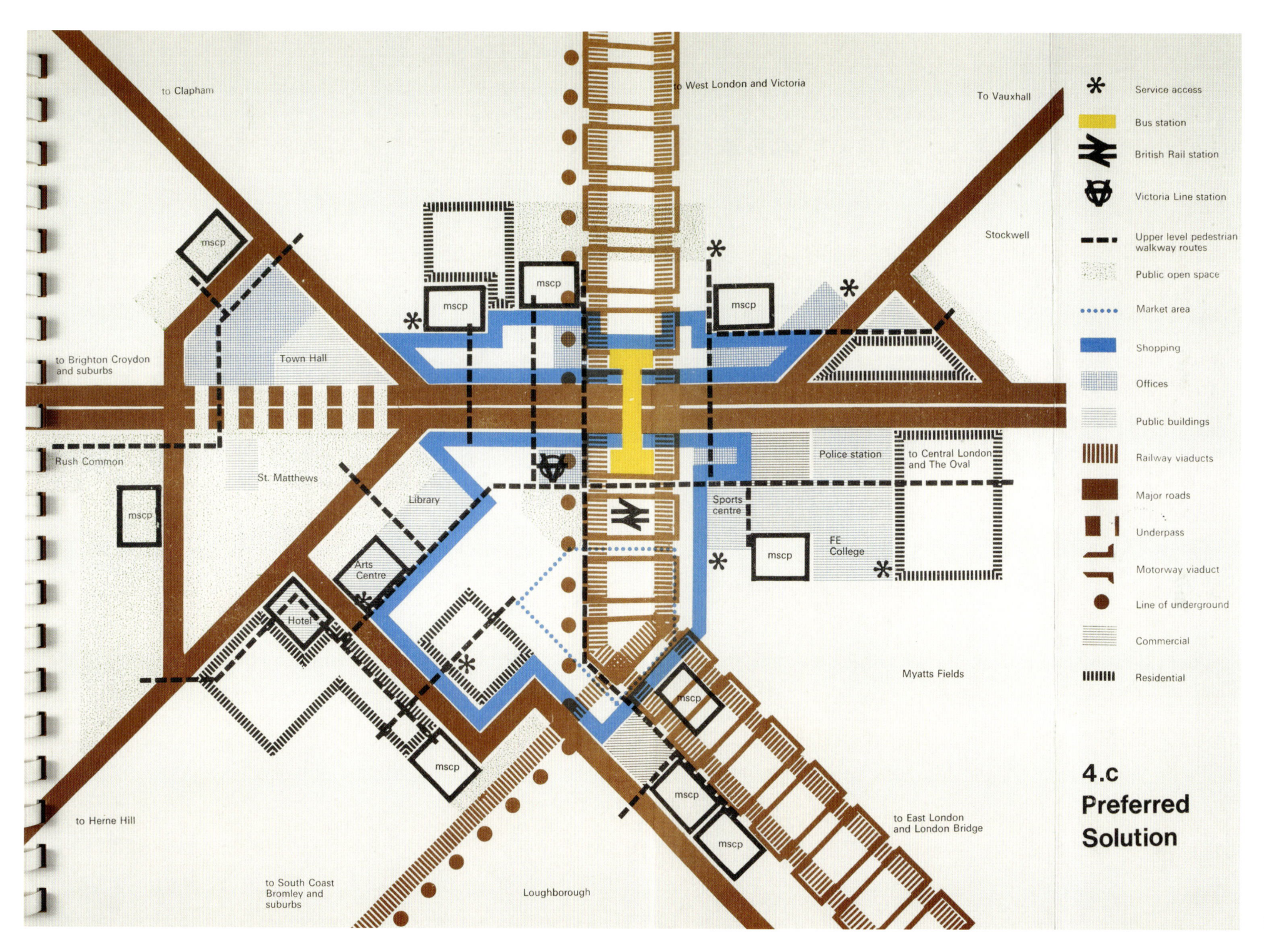

DISLOCATION AND UNEMPLOYMENT

In the 30 years after 1960 more than a million Londoners lost their jobs as factories and docks closed and London's industrial base shrank dramatically. This cheaply-produced official plan of Camden Town and Somers Town in 1986 was freely available in public libraries at the time. Far from being an objective depiction of the street pattern, with a guide to shops and services, the key to the plan reveals it to have been produced primarily for the unemployed. Red dots mark where Camden citizens could go to find work (Employment Exchanges), get benefit (Unemployment Benefit Office), get advice on the problems that followed the loss of a regular income (housing aid, social services, law and community centres and Citizens' Advice Bureaux), get treatment for physical and psychological ills (clinics) and where they could while away their jobless days (community centres). The mass production of these plans reflects the number of people whom Council officers felt needed the information that they contained.

8.1.3   Camden Council, *Camden Town Neighbourhood Guide* (London: London Borough of Camden, June 1986). 30 × 21 cm. Maps Y. 1590 (part). Courtesy of the London Borough of Camden

HOMELESSNESS

Homelessness again became a serious problem from the late 1980s as the stock of council housing dried up, private housing failed to fill the gap and social security payments for sixteen- and seventeen-year-olds were abolished. It has been estimated that there could be as many as 100,000 homeless people in London. The television charity, Comic Relief, financed the publication of this guide in 1996. There is an almost Victorian grimness to the descriptions of some of the hostels.

8.1.4   Resource Information Service, *Emergency Hostels Map Book* (1996), pp. 6–7: Arlington-West End House and Bondway Nightshelter. 29.7 × 21.4 cm. Maps 215. f.5

Arlington - West End House

91 Dean Street
W1

Male   Ages : 18-65 (Ave. 33)   **0171-437 3703**

How to get there : From Tottenham Court Rd tube: take the Oxford St exit, turn left & walk along Oxford St. Dean St is the 2nd turning on the left. The entrance to the hostel is in a small alley, Diadem Court, which is the 2nd turning off Dean St on the right. From Piccadilly Circus tube: take exit 4 & walk along Shaftesbury Avenue. Dean St is about 400 yards along on the left hand side by McDonalds. Walk up Dean St. Entrance is in Diadem Court which is on the left hand side of the street.

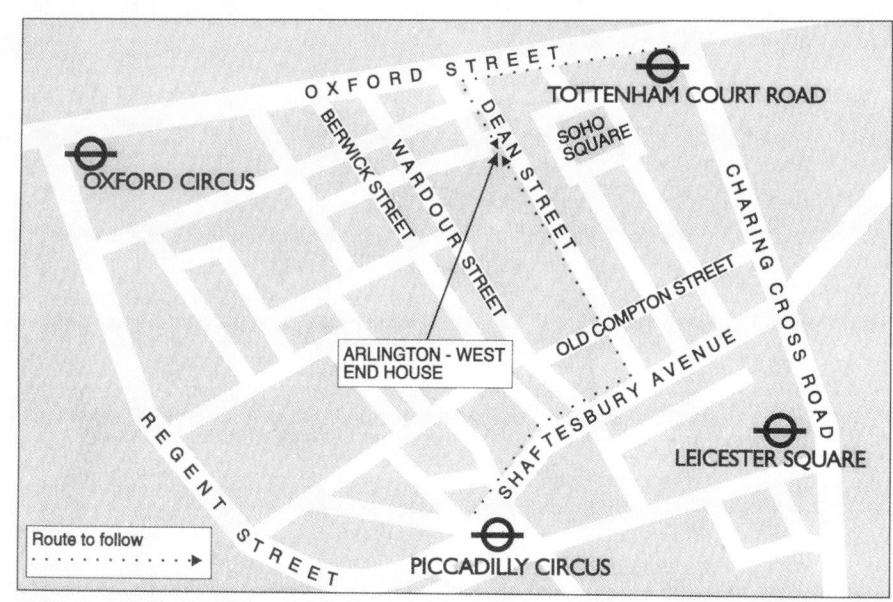

Public Transport : Tottenham Court Road or Piccadilly Circus tubes. Buses to Oxford Street: 73, 25, 8, 55, 176, N73, N79. Buses to Shaftesbury Avenue: 38, 14, 22.

Opening Hours : Self or agency referrals. Phone 24 hours a day to check vacancies or go to the door. 24 staff provide 24 hour cover.

Target Group : Single homeless men.

Description : 129 spaces in single and shared accommodation. Cheap canteen for all meals. No self catering facilities.

Page 6   Resource Information Service

Bondway Nightshelter

35-43 Bondway
SW8

Male   Ages : 30+ (Ave. 50)   **0171-582 6202/3**

How to get there : From Vauxhall tube: take exit 3 (Bondway East Side) which is straight ahead at the top of the escalators and then on the right. When you come out on to Bondway turn left. The Bondway Shelter is about 100 yards along, past the Refugee Council offices and the Centrepoint hostel. The Shelter has a large red door and a buzzer.

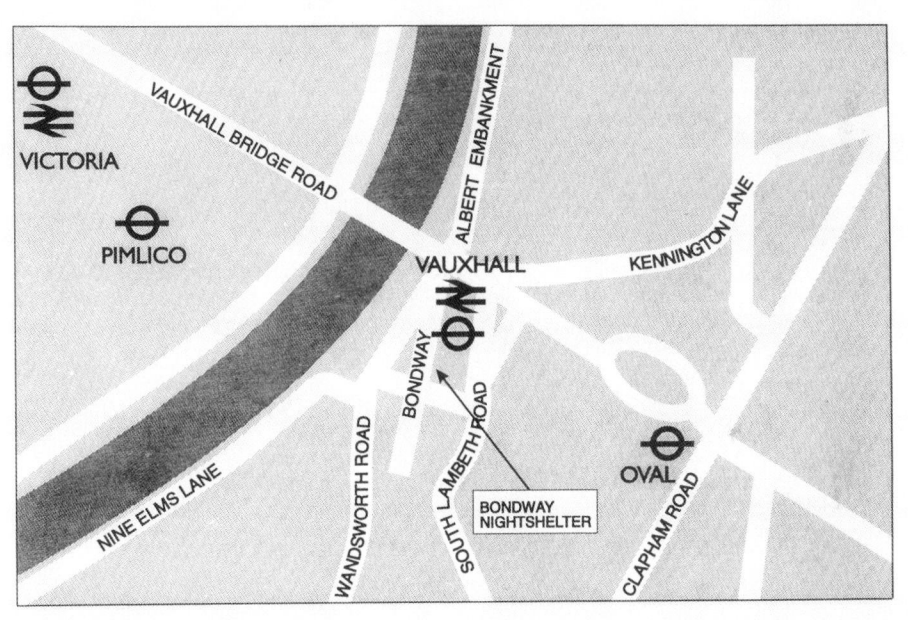

Public Transport : Vauxhall tube/BR. Buses: 44, 77a, 344. Buses to Vauxhall Bridge: 36, 36b, 88, 322.

Opening Hours : Self or voluntary agency referrals. Do not accept statutory agency referrals. Phone or turn up at the door 24 hours a day to check for vacancies. 24 hour access. 8 staff and 17 volunteers provide 24 hour waking cover.

Target Group : Single homeless men over 30, particularly those who are vulnerable due to ill health or alcohol problems.

Description : 95 spaces in 3 dormitories divided into cubicles. All meals provided. No self catering facilities.

Resource Information Service   Page 7

8.2 LONDON RESURGENT

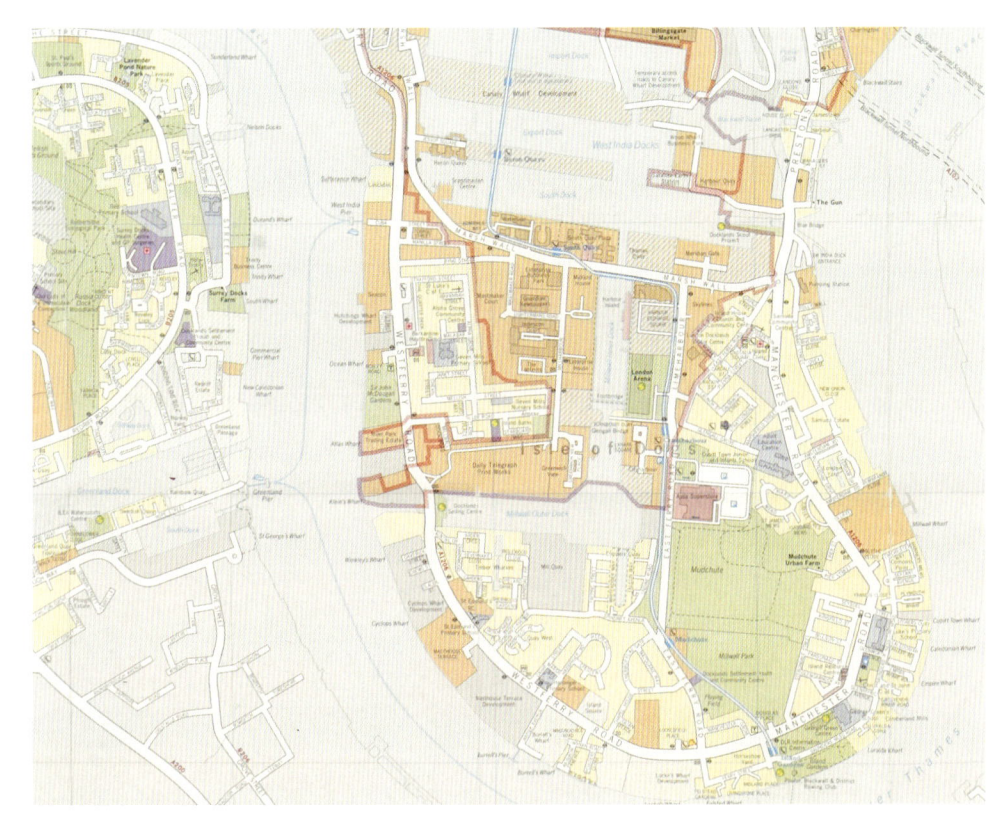

Extract from Geoprojects Docklands and Greenwich (Henley: Geoprojects, 1989)

There has been a lot that is positive about London since 1945. The growth of tourism and financial services has largely balanced the loss of heavy industry. The London Olympics of 1948, the Festival of Britain of 1951, 'Swinging' and 'Cool' London of the 1960s and 1990s attracted millions of visitors. The City, and more recently the Docklands development, have successfully fought to retain London's position as one of the world's leading financial centres — though much of it is no longer British-owned and its primacy remains continuously under threat. The Clean Air Acts of the 1950s, the disappearance of factories and factory chimneys, the conservation movement and gentrification of large areas of the inner London area since 1970 have made London a far pleasanter place in which to live than it has been since 1500.

A TORCH AMIDST THE GLOOM

The London Olympics of 1948 were held amidst the ruins and austerity of Post-War London. Just over 4000 athletes from 59 countries participated, excluding Germany and Japan which were not invited. Contestants were asked to bring their own food, because of UK rationing. This map reflects the Games' modest spirit. No buildings — not even an Olympic village — were specially created. The Games were centred on Wembley Stadium with other existing locations, mainly in central and west London, including the Guinness Sports Ground at Park Royal and the Polytechnic's Sports Ground at Chiswick. The Games nevertheless raised spirits and were a great success, with some records being broken.

8.2.1 Geographia, *Daily Telegraph Map of the Olympic Games Venues* (London: Hutchinson, 1948). 50.6 × 75.9 cm. Maps 245.a.60

E S S E X
M I D D L E S E X
L O N D O N
TOTTENHAM HOTSPUR F.C.
HARRINGAY
WALTHAMSTOW AVENUE F.C.
SUDBURY LYONS SPORTS GRD
WEMBLEY
HIGHBURY ARSENAL F.C.
ILFORD F.C.
PARK ROYAL GUINNESS SPORTS GRD
VICTORIA & ALBERT MUSEUM
BRENTFORD F.C.
EARL'S COURT
DULWICH HAMLET F.C.
FULHAM F.C.
CHISWICK POLYTECHNIC SPORTS GROUND
HERNE HILL
CRYSTAL PALACE F.C.

THE END OF AUSTERITY

The Festival of Britain of 1951, commemorating the centennial of the Great Exhibition, was the first occasion when Londoners could sense the impending end of austerity, particularly at the Festival Pleasure Gardens (Battersea Fun Fair). The Festival, however, was in many ways a deeply serious event in the tradition of the Great Exhibition. The South Bank Exhibition included didactic displays on numerous aspects of Britain and the life of its peoples — including power and production (4), discovery (6), transport (7) and television (10), which was still a luxury product. Only the Royal Festival Hall (13) still survives of the numerous new buildings created for the event.

8.2.2   *Picture Plan and Guide to 1951 South Bank Exhibition*, from Geographia, *"All in One" Map Guide Festival London (London: Geographia, 1951)*. 18.5 × 23 cm. 010349.n.71

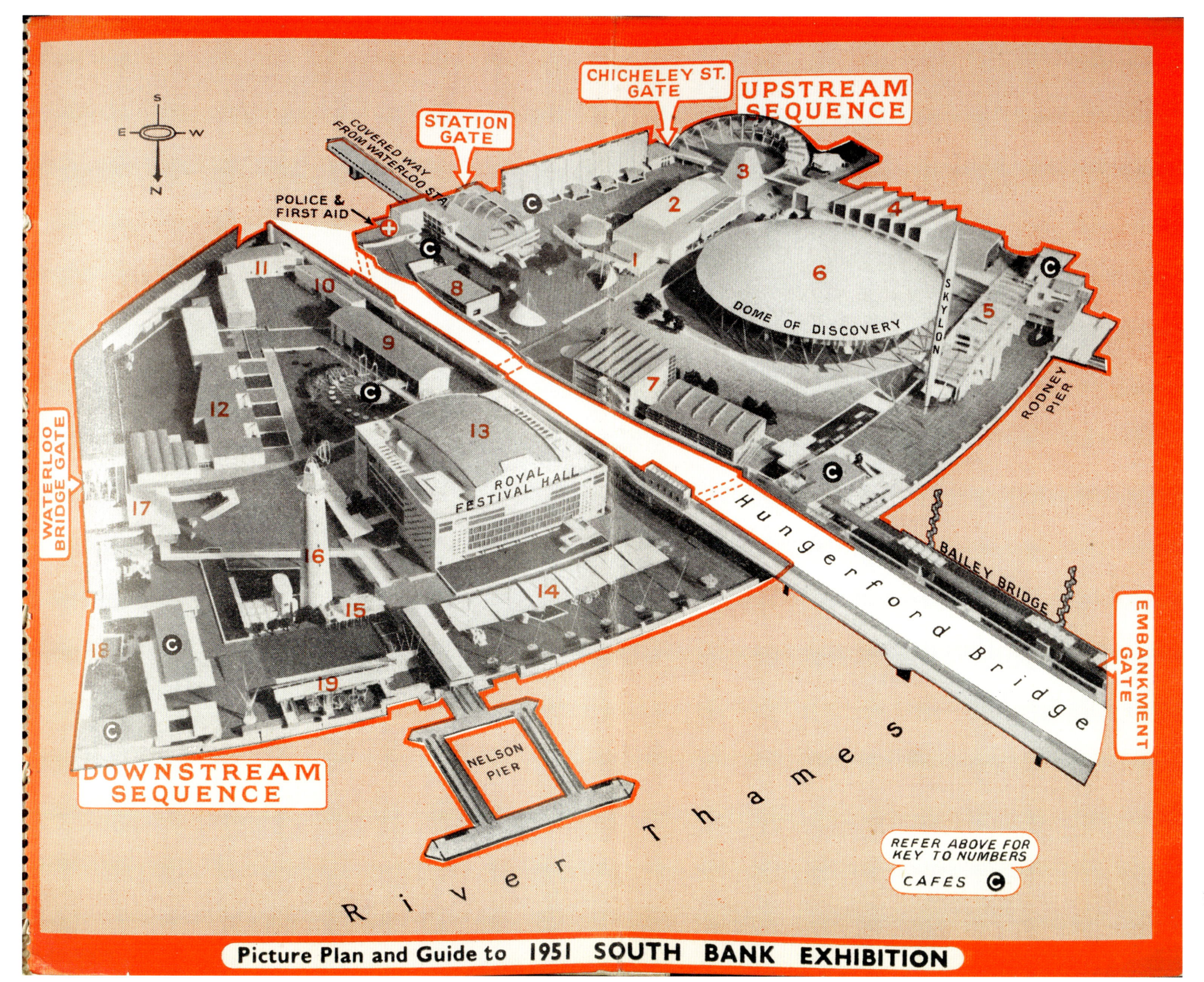

Picture Plan and Guide to 1951 SOUTH BANK EXHIBITION

'SWINGING LONDON'

'Crowds cram into Carnaby Street on anyday in the summer but pack tightest of all on a Saturday … The crowds know that however many boutiques open elsewhere … there's still nothing like the place where it all began'. The 1960s saw the invention and flowering of 'Swinging London' centred on Carnaby Street in Soho. The world tourism which it attracted helped to offset the effects of London's industrial decline as did 'Cool Britannia' 30 years later. This psychedelic street panorama, a distant descendant of Tallis's Victorian street scenes (see 5.2.14), captures the spirit of the time.

8.2.3   Malcolm English, *A Saturday Morning I* from Tom Salter, *Carnaby Street* (Walton-on-Thames: M. & J. Hobbs, 1970). Between pp. 33 and 40. 21 × 78 cm. X.809.8375. Copyright courtesy of the artist / The Bridgeman Art Library

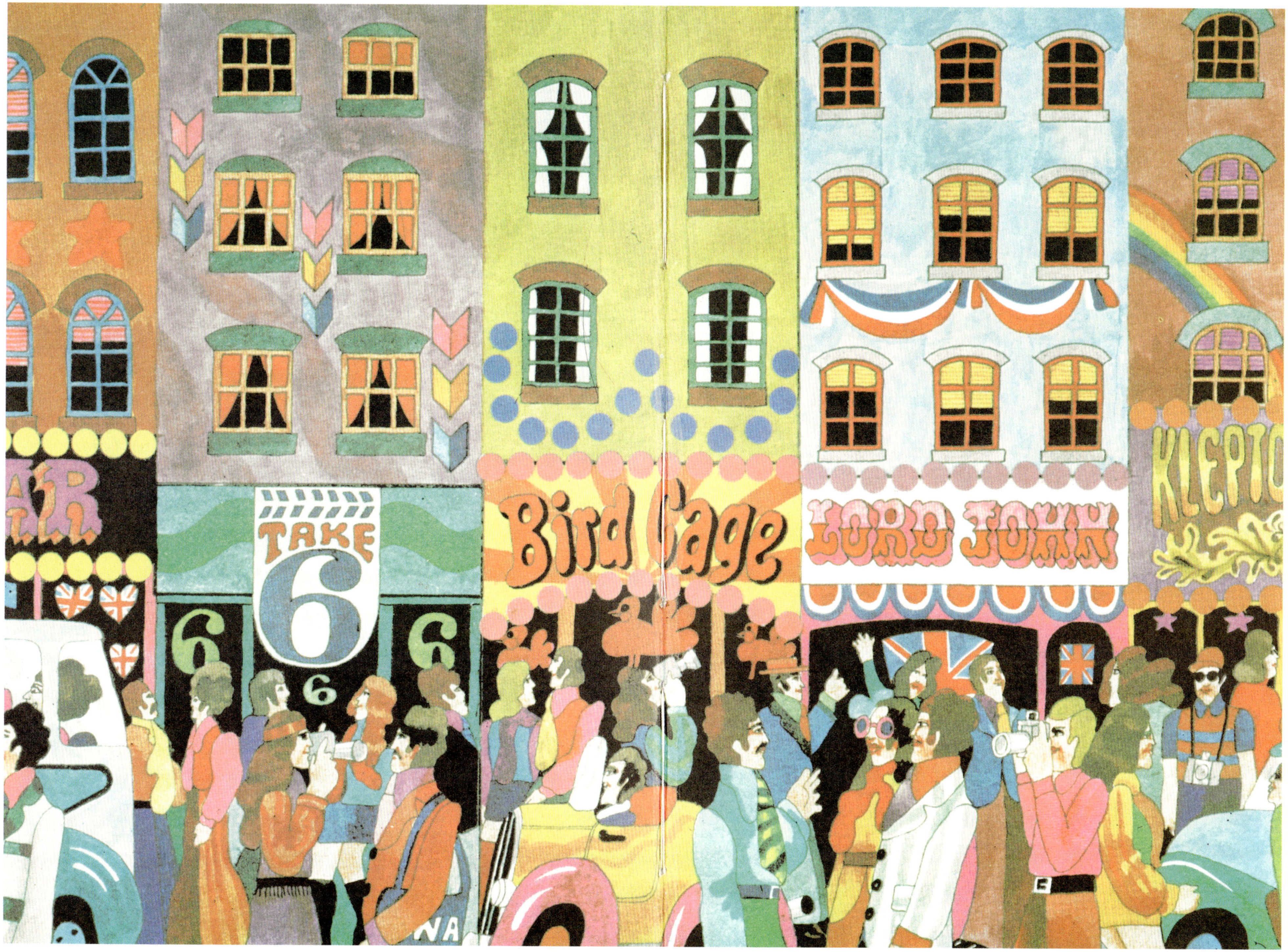
TAKE
6
Bird Cage
LORD JOHN

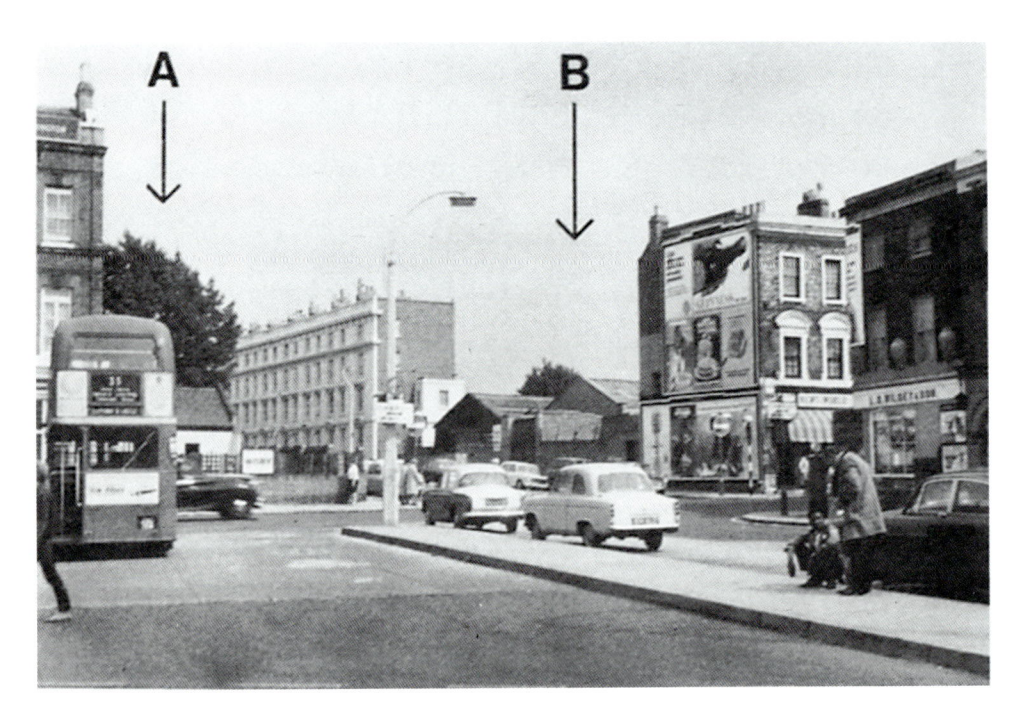

CONSERVATION AND GENTRIFICATION

This set of plans, aimed at enhancing Clapham Old Town and created by the same department that was responsible for the plans of the same year for redeveloping Brixton, typifies a more sensitive awareness of the urban environment. The conservation mentality can be traced back to at least the 1830s. Since the 1970s, however, as manifested in the rediscovery of districts like Clapham, Battersea, Wandsworth, Islington and Hackney by young, upwardly mobile middle-class bankers, stockbrokers, entrepreneurs and media people and in the creation of statutory conservation areas, town trails through historic centres, urban farms and 'green' linear parks and walkways, it has had a dramatic and positive effect on hitherto neglected inner city areas.

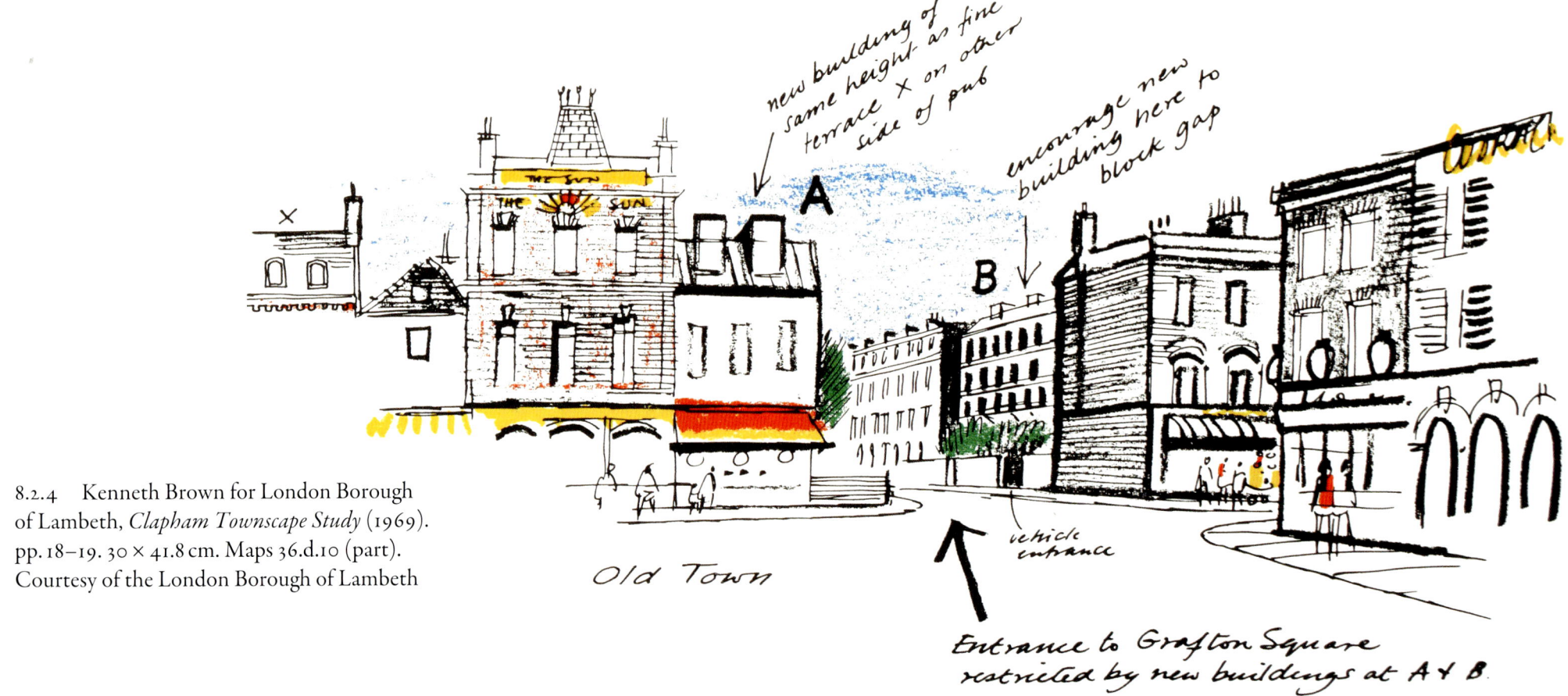

8.2.4 Kenneth Brown for London Borough of Lambeth, *Clapham Townscape Study* (1969). pp. 18–19. 30 × 41.8 cm. Maps 36.d.10 (part). Courtesy of the London Borough of Lambeth

4. Old Town

This also still retains some remnants of its original village character especially looking south towards the common. The feeling of place is increased by the bus terminus in the square – the red buses themselves making a welcome splash of colour. Old Town contains some good buildings (which are noted in the full Townscape report) notably Nos. 39 – 43, three very handsome houses of 1705 with fine doorways. Maintenance is however urgently needed on No. 43.

Unfortunately, there is a bad **leakage of space** on the west side, at the entrance to Grafton Square (see photos 17a, 18a, 18b) where the road seems unnecessarily wide creating an unpleasant gap and leaving the large south terrace of Grafton Square visually isolated like a stranded liner.

A **new building** on the vacant side adjacent to the Sun pub, would help to close the gap (A in 18a, 18c,). Also new building of a height comparable with the Grafton Square terrace should be encouraged at B. (18a, 18c, 18b).

The **central space** of Old Town is at present very bleak and uninviting. The effect is intensified by the hideous concrete lamp standards and the discrepancies in scale of the surrounding buildings – Maritime House being a particular offender (see 17a).

The bleakness would be relieved if semi-mature trees were planted in a cluster north of the bus stand. This would help to carry through the character of the adjacent Common and soften the disharmony in scale of the surrounding buildings. On a slightly raised central island and perhaps combined with a new bus shelter, the trees would then provide a focus which is missing today (17b). The floorscape too needs treatment. At present this is just a wasteland of tarmac. The centre might be slightly raised and paved while the ugly concrete lamp standards should be replaced by more elegant metal standards of a better design.

17a View from west side showing over-wide entrance to Grafton Square and bleak appearance of central space.

17b How the situation might be improved.

Further views showing space leak at entrance to Grafton Square

18a

18b

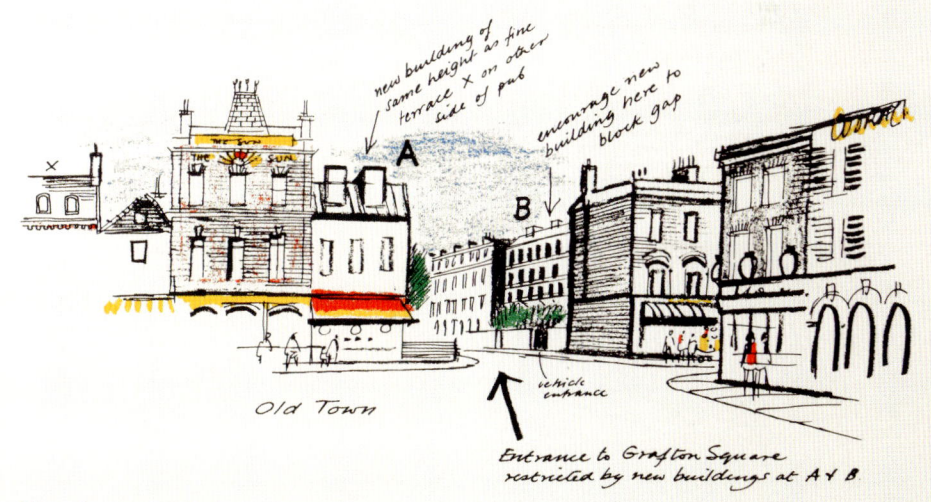

18c Space contained.

STAYING ON TOP?

Through a ruthless adoption of the latest technology and continuous demolition and rebuilding, the City has helped to offset the effects of London's industrial decline. This map of 1995 locates and distinguishes between the accountants, banks, commodity brokers, fund managers, insurance companies, Lloyds brokers and solicitors as well as between the hotels and restaurants that constitute the modern City. The halls of the ancient livery companies may still be indicated, but this map's sponsorship by European branches of two American-owned companies underlines the fact that the City is now supranational and more than ever dependent on international trends and finance.

8.2.5 The Clever Map Company, *The Wall Street Journal Europe: Financial Map of the City in association with IBM* (1995). 20 × 10 cm. Maps X. 5784

361

DOCKLANDS DEVELOPMENTS

In 1981 the last of the docks closed and the Thatcher government established the London Docklands Development Corporation to redevelop the 8.5 mile area, free from local government controls. This rather attractive tourist map, with its clean lines and bright colours, shows some of the actual and proposed developments by 1989. Pastel shades indicate the intended mixture of employment, residential, retail, education and community use and ecological open spaces that were to take the place of the run-down old docks. Like all maps, however, this one is selective and it conceals as much as it reveals. It neither defines the sorts of 'Employment' that would be available nor the price-brackets of the new homes. As a result, the needs of the existing community of dock workers have been tactfully swept under the carpet — together with the realities of the unemployment and relocation that many of them had to face. Developments like Canary Wharf have nevertheless enabled London to survive as a financial centre by offering office space at half the City rents and have thereby indirectly and eventually benefited all Londoners.

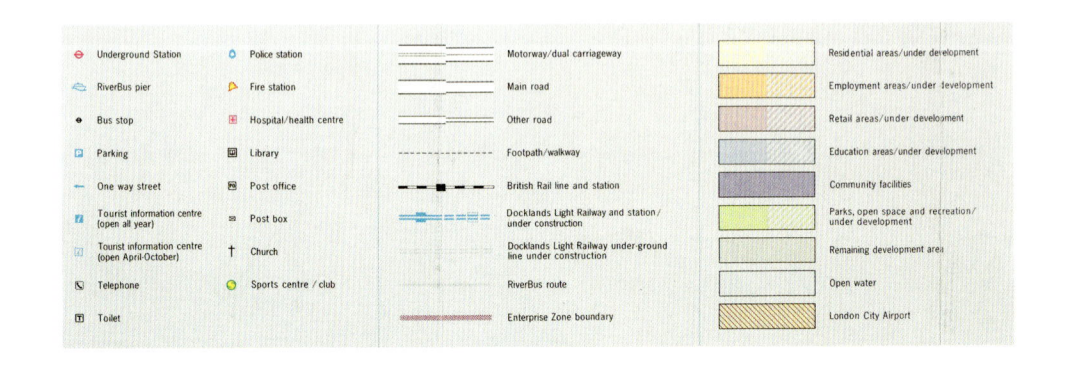

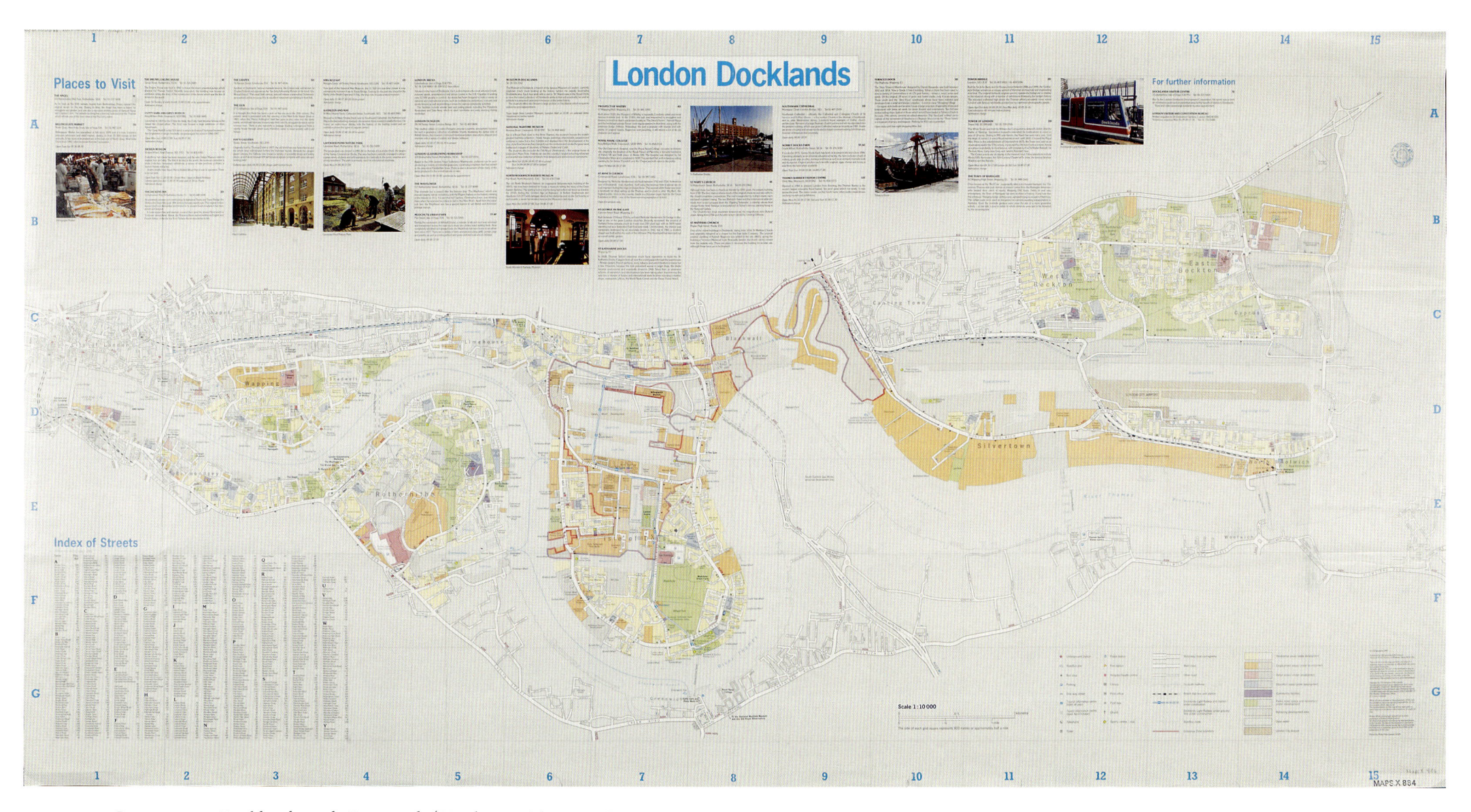

8.2.6   Geoprojects, *Docklands and Greenwich* (Henley-on-Thames: Geoprojects, 1989). 64.6 × 138.5 cm. Maps X. 884

8.3 LONDON PRESENT AND FUTURE

The London of today is buoyant. Self-government has been restored, culture is booming, population increasing and the preparations for the 2012 Olympics have involved the cleansing and redevelopment of some of the grimmest parts of London. It can also boast an enviable degree of racial harmony despite a continuing potential for conflict. There are challenges aplenty, not least in planning for the consequences of climate change and population increase without devastating the greenery that has been one of London's greatest bonuses. London's continuing financial pre-eminence must be defended and managed without destroying London's architectural and cultural heritage. Maps play a vital role in meeting these and most other challenges while continuing to reflect and highlight the Londoner's world view.

HARMONISING PAST AND FUTURE

In order to provide sufficient office space to remain competitive, the City has had, ever more creatively, to grow upwards. This has put at risk many of the traditional views that Londoners and tourists hold dear and particularly the view of St Paul's from the River Thames lovingly described in the early 1800s by the poet William Wordsworth. This official discussion document of 2005 uses the latest mapping techniques in an attempt to illustrate how space for future high-rise developments can be provided without prejudicing historic views toward the City.

8.3.1   Greater London Authority. *London Plan, London View Management Framework Draft Supplementary Planning Guidance*, SPG 2005 (April 2005), pp. 114–15. 29.5 × 43 cm. 232.b.98. Courtesy GLA

Waterloo Bridge

12B.2 Waterloo Bridge: the downstream pavement – at the centre of the bridge

224 The primary landmark associated with the view experienced from the centre of the bridge is St Paul's Cathedral. Secondary landmarks include St Bride's church and the cupola of the Old Bailey, while Tower 42, 30 St Mary Axe and the Barbican towers are also prominent in the background.

Assessment Point 12B.2

Camera Location
Centreline of bridge
National Grid Reference
530793 180535, height
16.55m AOD [Estimated]
Height of camera 1.60m

Date and time of photograph
26/10/04 13:54

Significant view from Assessment Point 12B.2 (central section)

Significant view from AP12B.2 (left)

Significant view from AP12B.2 (right)

Protected Vista

225 The important view of St. Paul's Cathedral experienced from the centre of the bridge will be managed by geometric definition. The Landmark Viewing Corridor is asymmetrical to account for the western towers of the cathedral.

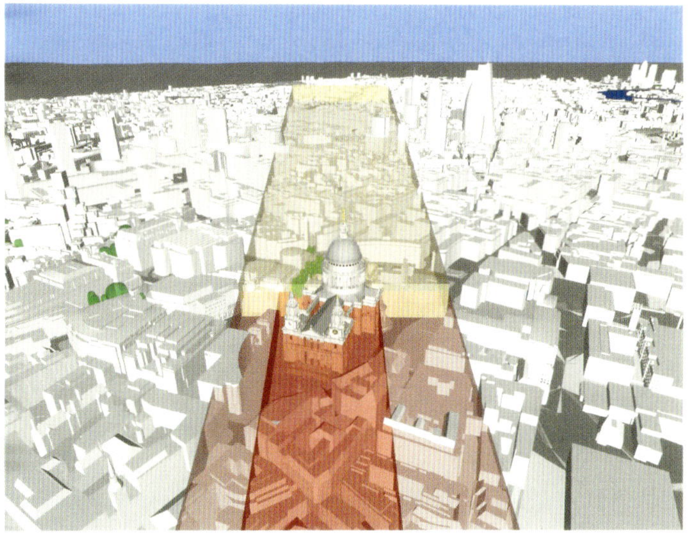

Protected Vista from Assessment Point 12B.2 to St Paul's (aerial view)

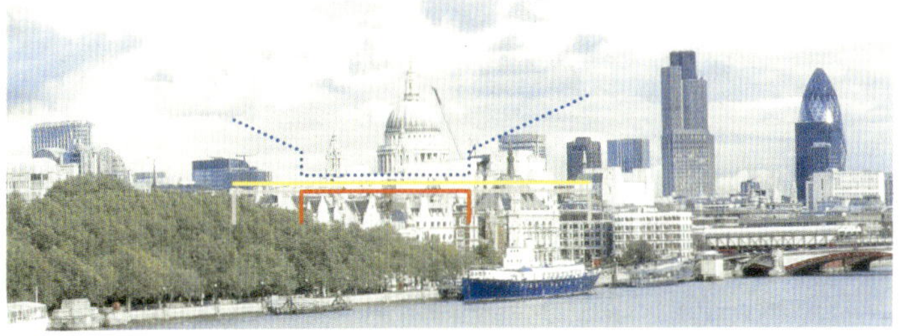

Protected Vista from Assessment Point 12B.2 to St Paul's (telephoto view)

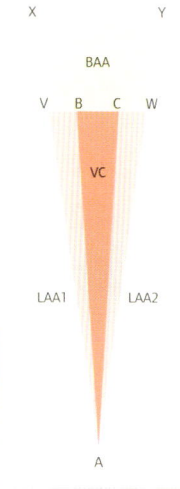

Location of Defining Point (OS)

A	530724E	180651N
B	532034E	181198N
C	532066E	181110N
V	532018E	181241N
W	532091E	181044N
X	534284E	182273N
Y	534484E	181731N

Height of Defining Point (AOD)

	viewing corridor (VC)	lateral assessment area 1 (LAA1)	lateral assessment area 2 (LAA2)	background assessment area (BAA)
A	16.5	16.5	16.5	
B	45.9	45.9		
C	45.9		45.9	
V		45.9		52.1
W			45.9	52.1
X				114.4
Y				114.4

NEW LONDONERS

This map is compiled from the latest census data using a Geographical Information System which enables statistics with a spatial element to be plotted onto a digital base map. The map is centred on the Thames, shown as a sinuous line in the middle. It illustrates the population distribution of one of the latest waves of mass immigration, in this case from southern Asia. Though there are concentrations in the same East End areas occupied before them by French Huguenot silk weavers and the Jewish tailors and furniture makers, the maps reveals that southern Asians are now to be found throughout the built-up area of Greater London. Like all immigrants, and despite occasional frictions, they provide services that established Londoners can, or will, not provide and contribute enormously to the cultural variety and vibrancy that distinguishes modern London.

8.3.2 *South Asian Immigrants Residing in London, 2001*

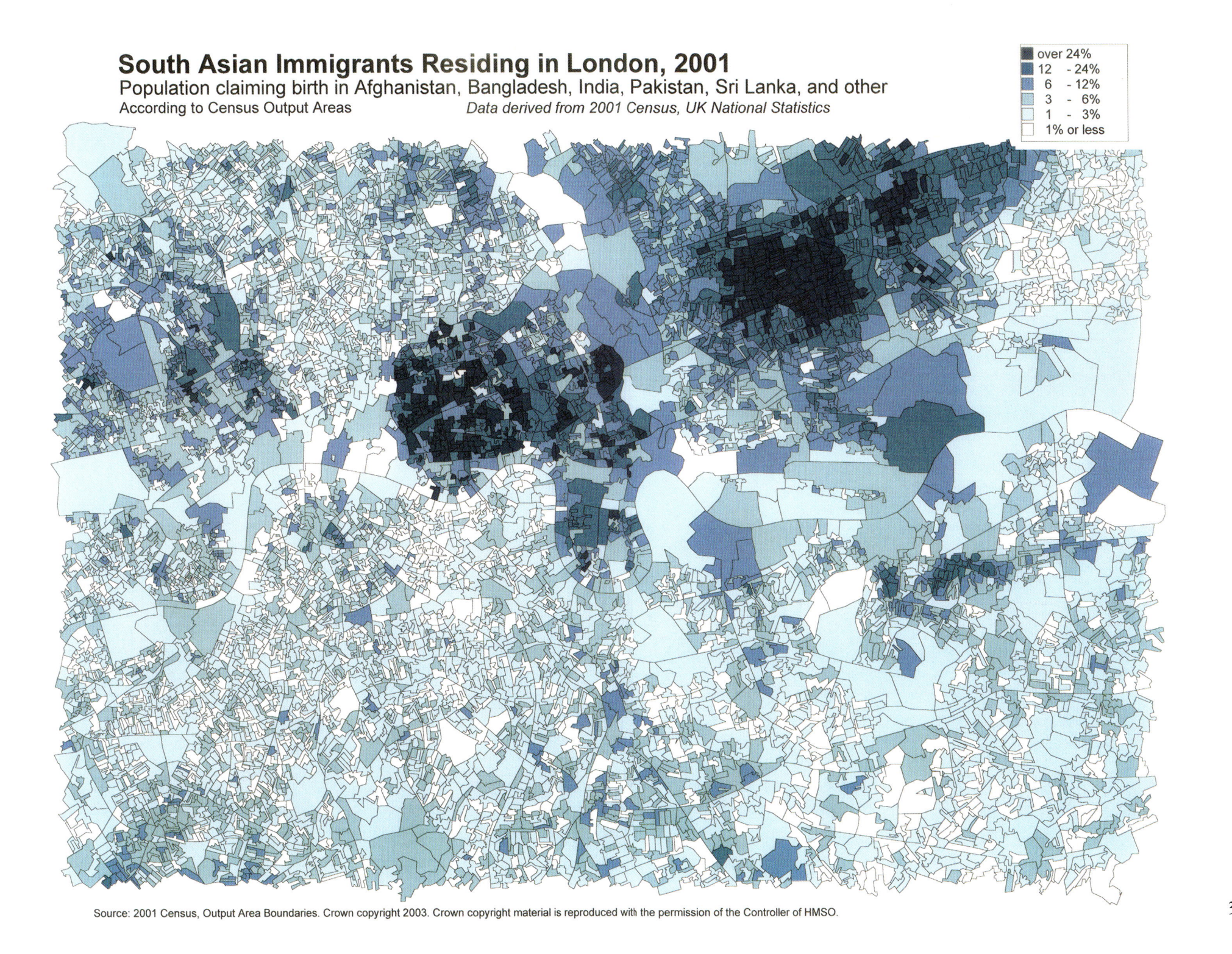

South Asian Immigrants Residing in London, 2001
Population claiming birth in Afghanistan, Bangladesh, India, Pakistan, Sri Lanka, and other
According to Census Output Areas *Data derived from 2001 Census, UK National Statistics*

- over 24%
- 12 - 24%
- 6 - 12%
- 3 - 6%
- 1 - 3%
- 1% or less

Source: 2001 Census, Output Area Boundaries. Crown copyright 2003. Crown copyright material is reproduced with the permission of the Controller of HMSO.

A WARNING FOR THE FUTURE

The government has announced that the future expansion of London will be mainly along the so-called Thames Gateway, lining the shores of the Thames from the Isle of Dogs towards Southend, and in the Lea Valley, the main site for the 2012 Olympics. This map of 2005, commissioned by a variety of agencies concerned with London's development and plotting a variety of data onto a base map, presents an alarming picture of the threat of flooding to precisely these areas: a threat likely to increase if global warming continues and which it will cost a lot of money to overcome.

8.3.3 Thames Gateway Partnership and others, *Residual Flood Damage Risk within zone 3*, 2005. (Courtesy of www.thames-gateway.org.uk)

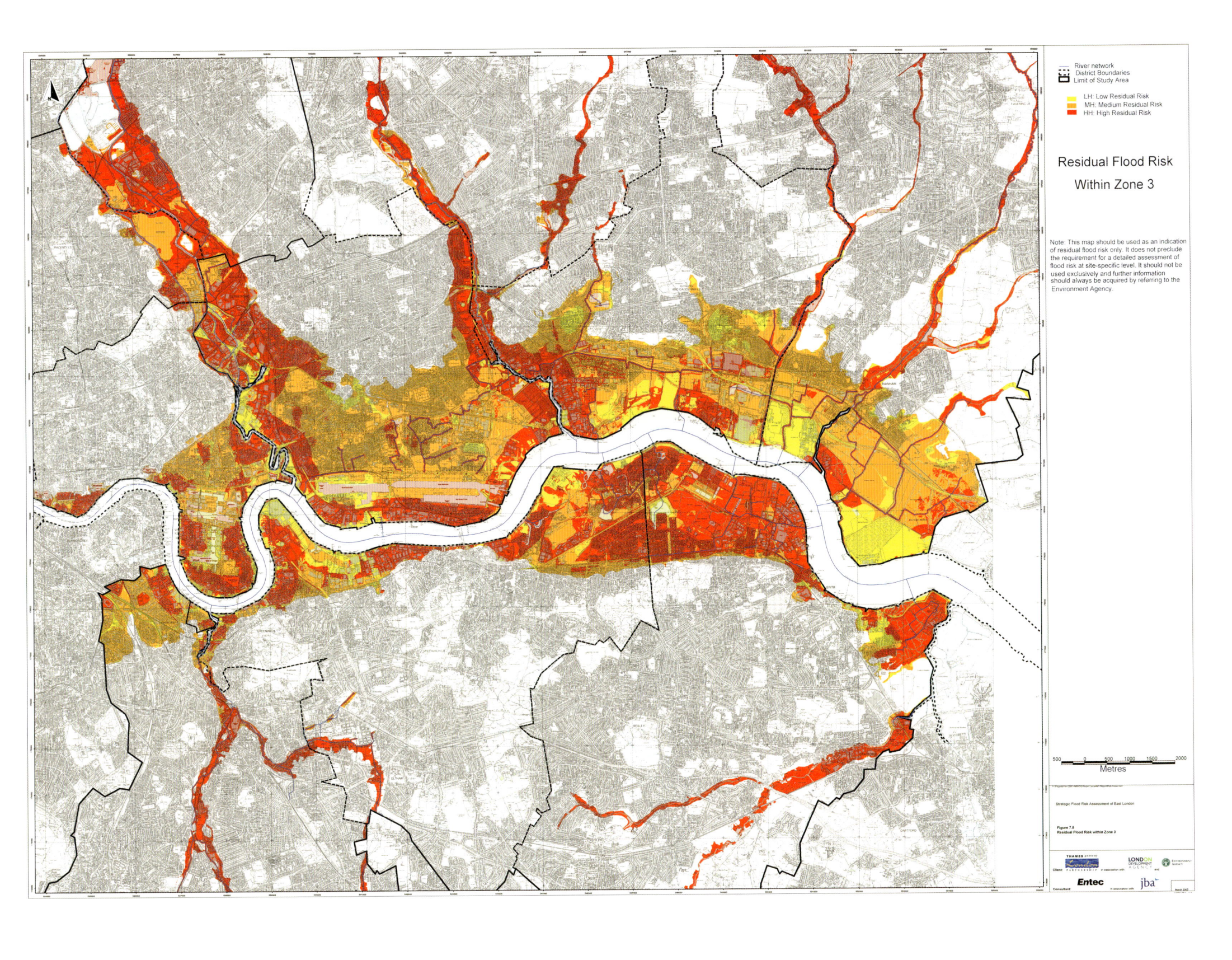

Residual Flood Risk Within Zone 3

BRINGING LONDON TOGETHER

The London transport network has expanded considerably since 1990 after thirty years of relative neglect. It had to, in order to provide the mass communications with the City that were essential for the success of the Docklands development and, more recently, not just to ensure the success of the 2012 Olympics but also to underpin the redevelopment, in the context of the Games, of a hitherto neglected part of the East End.

8.3.4   Plan showing the extent of the London Underground and overground railway systems in 2012. 29.5 × 32 cm. (© TfL). Reproduced by kind permission of Transport for London

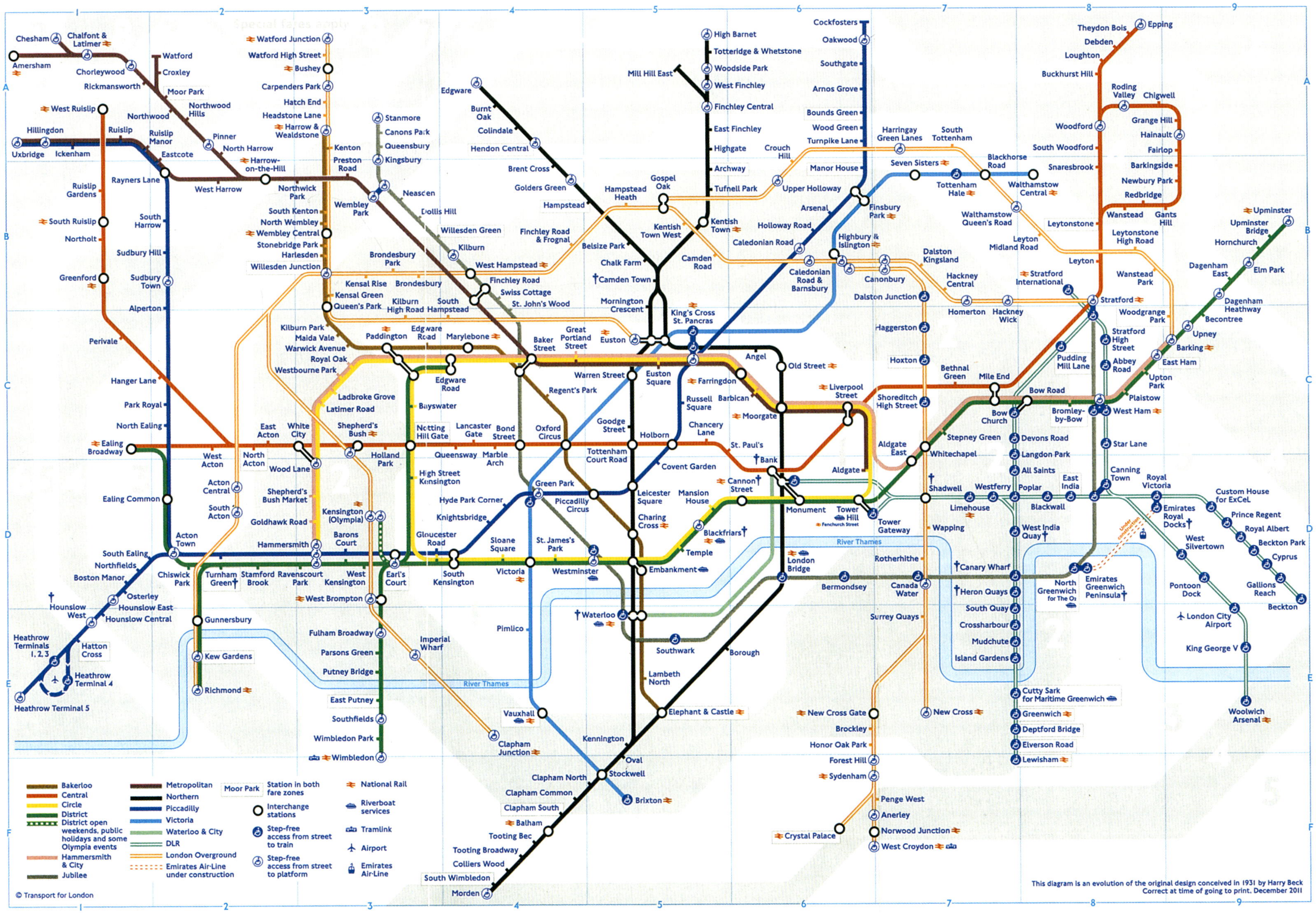

Chesham
Chalfont & Latimer
Amersham
Chorleywood
Rickmansworth
Watford
Croxley
Moor Park
Northwood
Northwood Hills
Pinner
North Harrow
Harrow-on-the-Hill
West Harrow
Rayners Lane
Eastcote
Ruislip Manor
Ruislip
Ickenham
Hillingdon
Uxbridge
West Ruislip
Ruislip Gardens
South Ruislip
Northolt
Greenford
Perivale
Hanger Lane
Park Royal
North Ealing
Ealing Broadway
Ealing Common
South Harrow
Sudbury Hill
Sudbury Town
Alperton
West Acton
North Acton
East Acton
White City
Acton Central
South Acton
Acton Town
South Ealing
Northfields
Boston Manor
Osterley
Hounslow East
Hounslow Central
Hounslow West
Hatton Cross
Heathrow Terminals 1, 2, 3
Heathrow Terminal 4
Heathrow Terminal 5
Chiswick Park
Turnham Green
Stamford Brook
Ravenscourt Park
Gunnersbury
Kew Gardens
Richmond
Watford Junction
Watford High Street
Bushey
Carpenders Park
Hatch End
Headstone Lane
Harrow & Wealdstone
Kenton
South Kenton
North Wembley
Wembley Central
Stonebridge Park
Harlesden
Willesden Junction
Northwick Park
Preston Road
Wembley Park
Stanmore
Canons Park
Queensbury
Kingsbury
Neasden
Dollis Hill
Willesden Green
Kilburn
West Hampstead
Finchley Road
Swiss Cottage
St. John's Wood
Brondesbury Park
Brondesbury
Kensal Rise
Kensal Green
Queen's Park
Kilburn High Road
South Hampstead
Kilburn Park
Maida Vale
Warwick Avenue
Royal Oak
Westbourne Park
Paddington
Edgware Road
Marylebone
Baker Street
Great Portland Street
Euston
Regent's Park
Ladbroke Grove
Latimer Road
Shepherd's Bush
Wood Lane
Holland Park
Notting Hill Gate
Bayswater
Queensway
Lancaster Gate
Marble Arch
Bond Street
Oxford Circus
Shepherd's Bush Market
Goldhawk Road
Hammersmith
Kensington (Olympia)
Barons Court
West Kensington
Earl's Court
West Brompton
High Street Kensington
Gloucester Road
South Kensington
Hyde Park Corner
Knightsbridge
Sloane Square
Victoria
St. James's Park
Green Park
Piccadilly Circus
Leicester Square
Charing Cross
Embankment
Westminster
Fulham Broadway
Parsons Green
Putney Bridge
East Putney
Southfields
Wimbledon Park
Wimbledon
Imperial Wharf
Clapham Junction
Pimlico
Vauxhall
Edgware
Burnt Oak
Colindale
Hendon Central
Brent Cross
Golders Green
Hampstead
Hampstead Heath
Gospel Oak
Finchley Road & Frognal
Belsize Park
Chalk Farm
Camden Town
Camden Road
Kentish Town West
Kentish Town
Mornington Crescent
King's Cross St. Pancras
Warren Street
Euston Square
Goodge Street
Tottenham Court Road
Holborn
Covent Garden
Russell Square
Chancery Lane
Farringdon
Barbican
Moorgate
St. Paul's
Bank
Mansion House
Cannon Street
Temple
Blackfriars
Monument
Tower Hill
Fenchurch Street
Tower Gateway
Aldgate
Aldgate East
Liverpool Street
Old Street
Angel
Waterloo
Southwark
Borough
Lambeth North
Elephant & Castle
Kennington
Oval
Stockwell
Brixton
Clapham North
Clapham Common
Clapham South
Balham
Tooting Bec
Tooting Broadway
Colliers Wood
South Wimbledon
Morden
Mill Hill East
High Barnet
Totteridge & Whetstone
Woodside Park
West Finchley
Finchley Central
East Finchley
Highgate
Archway
Tufnell Park
Crouch Hill
Upper Holloway
Holloway Road
Caledonian Road
Caledonian Road & Barnsbury
Highbury & Islington
Canonbury
Dalston Junction
Dalston Kingsland
Haggerston
Hoxton
Shoreditch High Street
Arsenal
Finsbury Park
Manor House
Turnpike Lane
Wood Green
Bounds Green
Arnos Grove
Southgate
Oakwood
Cockfosters
Harringay Green Lanes
South Tottenham
Seven Sisters
Tottenham Hale
Blackhorse Road
Walthamstow Central
Walthamstow Queen's Road
Leyton Midland Road
Leytonstone High Road
Wanstead Park
Hackney Central
Homerton
Hackney Wick
Stratford International
Stratford
Leyton
Leytonstone
Snaresbrook
South Woodford
Woodford
Buckhurst Hill
Loughton
Debden
Theydon Bois
Epping
Roding Valley
Chigwell
Grange Hill
Hainault
Fairlop
Barkingside
Newbury Park
Redbridge
Wanstead
Gants Hill
Upminster
Upminster Bridge
Hornchurch
Elm Park
Dagenham East
Dagenham Heathway
Becontree
Upney
Barking
East Ham
Upton Park
Plaistow
West Ham
Woodgrange Park
Stratford High Street
Abbey Road
Pudding Mill Lane
Bethnal Green
Mile End
Bow Road
Bow Church
Bromley-by-Bow
Stepney Green
Whitechapel
Devons Road
Langdon Park
All Saints
Shadwell
Limehouse
Westferry
Poplar
East India
Blackwall
Canning Town
Star Lane
Royal Victoria
Custom House for ExCeL
Prince Regent
Royal Albert
Beckton Park
Cyprus
Gallions Reach
Beckton
West Silvertown
Pontoon Dock
London City Airport
King George V
Woolwich Arsenal
Emirates Royal Docks
Emirates Greenwich Peninsula
Under construction
North Greenwich for The O2
Canary Wharf
Heron Quays
West India Quay
South Quay
Crossharbour
Mudchute
Island Gardens
Cutty Sark for Maritime Greenwich
Greenwich
Deptford Bridge
Elverson Road
Lewisham
Wapping
Rotherhithe
Canada Water
Surrey Quays
Bermondsey
London Bridge
New Cross Gate
New Cross
Brockley
Honor Oak Park
Forest Hill
Sydenham
Penge West
Anerley
Crystal Palace
Norwood Junction
West Croydon
River Thames
River Thames
Bakerloo
Central
Circle
District
District open weekends, public holidays and some Olympia events
Hammersmith & City
Jubilee
Metropolitan
Northern
Piccadilly
Victoria
Waterloo & City
DLR
London Overground
Emirates Air-Line under construction
Moor Park
Station in both fare zones
Interchange stations
Step-free access from street to train
Step-free access from street to platform
National Rail
Riverboat services
Tramlink
Airport
Emirates Air-Line
© Transport for London
This diagram is an evolution of the original design conceived in 1931 by Harry Beck
Correct at time of going to print. December 2011

ALL CHANGE AT ST PANCRAS

King's Cross and St Pancras form an important element in London's fight to remain a world commercial centre. As in Docklands, the redevelopment of a run-down inner city area offers commercial as well as community benefits. Locals should gain from an improved environment as old buildings are renovated and former railway land developed for housing, while speedy transport links with the continent, and cheaper office rental costs should attract businesses and benefit the British economy as a whole. This drawing reflects initial thoughts from as long ago as 1988.

8.3.5 *King's Cross 1988. King's Cross Master Plan* [Bird's-eye view of King's Cross from the South] (London: London Regeneration Consortium [Skidmore], 1998). 52.1 × 51.6 cm. Maps 223.c.87 and 88

373

SELECT READING LIST ON HISTORIC MAPS OF LONDON

This list excludes the numerous maps, atlases and volumes, particularly *The London Topographical Record*, published annually by the London Topographical Society since its foundation in 1880, for which see http://www.topsoc.org/publications. It also excludes works on historic maps of districts of London, including ward maps.

A. BIBLIOGRAPHIES

James Howgego, *Printed Maps of London circa 1553–1850* (Folkestone: Dawson, 1978). Second edition of the standard bibliography which first appeared in 1964

Ralph Hyde, *Printed Maps of Victorian London 1851–1900* (Folkestone: Dawson, 1975)

Lucinda Boyle with Ralph Hyde, *London: A Cartographic History 1746–1950: 200 years of folding maps* (Wycombe: Countrywide, 2002)

B. MONOGRAPHS

Felix Barker and Peter Jackson, *A History of London in Maps* (London: Barrie and Jenkins, 1990)

Claire Dobbins, *London Underground Maps: Art, Design and Cartography* (London: London Transport Museum, 2012)

Simon Foxall, *Mapping London: Making Sense of the City* (London: Black Dog, 2007)

Ken Garland, *Mr Beck's Underground Map: A History* (London: Capital Transport, 1994)

Philippa Glanville, *London in Maps* (London: The Connoisseur, 1972)

Geraldine Edith Mitton, *Maps of Old London* (London: Adam & Charles Black, 1908)

Peter Whitfield, *London: A Life in Maps* (London: British Library, 2006)

C. WEBSITES

Images of the maps in the Crace Collection, British Library Online Gallery: http://www.bl.uk/onlinegallery/onlineex/crace/

High resolution images including maps and views of London from the Crace Collection: British Museum: Search the Collection database: http://www.britishmuseum.org/research/search_the_collection_database.aspx

Listing of online images of historic maps of London, often with commentaries (from Map History, a website run by Tony Campbell, former Map Librarian, British Library): http://www.maphistory.info/imagebi.html#eng

Images, including maps, from London Metropolitan Archives and Guildhall Art Gallery: http://collage.cityoflondon.gov.uk/collage/app

GIS plotting contemporary data on Rocque's 1746 map of London and Westminster (Locating London's Past: a collaborative project of the Universities of Hertfordshire and Sheffield and Museum of London Archaeology): http://www.locatinglondon.org/

INDEXES

Where a subject appears on both sides of a pagespread, only the left-hand page is noted.
Bold numbers indicate the most significant entries where there are many.

INDEX OF PEOPLE

Abercrombie, Patrick 282, 294
Ackermann, Rudolph 178, 200
Adam, Robert and James 186, 188, 190
Ahrenfield, Alfred 264
Alexander, Daniel Asher 159, 162
Alfred, King 5
Allectus 4
Anne of Cleves 10
Arkell, George Edward 236
Armstrong, Arthur C. 300
Arnold, John Roy 90
Arundel, Thomas Duke of 76
Aubrey's Brief Lives 25

Baker, Benjamin 134
Banks, John Henry 209
Bartlett, F. A. 211
Basire, James 198, 204
Bazalgette, Joseph 248, 250, 254
Beck, Harry 282, 312, 324
Becket, Thomas à 6
Beckford, William 128
Bedford, Earl of 73
Bennett, Richard and Thomas 88
Berkeley, Lord 82
Biggs, George 240
Bigot, Charles 212
Bingley, Mr 124
Bloom, Thomas H. 287
Bloomer, Henry 287
Bockett, John 246
Bonner, Thomas 133
Bool, Alfred and John 266
Booth, Charles 234, 236, 238
Bowen, Emanuel 313
Bowles, Carington 102
Bowman, Charles Broughton 258
Boydell, John 128, 152
Braun, Georg 32
Brett, Reginald 268
Bridgeman, Henry Hewitt 256
Britton, John 211
Brooke, Nathaniel 46
Brown, Kenneth 358

Browne, Sir Richard 150
Brunel, Marc and Isambard 184
Burdett-Coutts, Baroness 256
Burlington, Earl of 110
Burns, John MP 268
Burton, Decimus 190, 198
Bye, Joseph 134

Campbell, Colen 122
Canterbury, Archbishop of 6
Carter, John 68
Cary, John 159, 298
Chambers, William 188
Chandos, Duke of 78
Charles I 31
Charles II 40, 46, 60
Chassereau, Peter 154
Chatelain, Jean Baptiste 152
Chawner, Thomas 260
Child, Josiah 122
Clarke & Co. 88
Coenwulf, King of Mercia 5
Cole, James 154
Collins, Henry George 326, 332
Compton, Sir Spencer 78
Constantine 5
Constantius I Chlorus 4
Corbusier 348
Corris, John 121
Coutts, Baroness Burdett 256
Coutts, Thomas 98
Coxhead, Sir Thomas MP 148
Croft, John 278
Cromwell, Oliver 36
Crook, J. M. 202
Cruikshank, George 220
Cubitt, Thomas 118, 210, 214
Cumberland, William, Duke of 176
Cumming, J. A. 242

Daniell, Thomas and William 164
Davies, Alexander 84
Davies, Benjamin Rees 211, 224
Davies, Mary 82, 84

Dawson, J. E. 246
Day, William 232
de la Beyle, Charles 176
de Witt, Frederick 43
Denton, Thomas 118
Dickens, Charles 212, 242, 264
Diocletian, Emperor 186
Doré, Gustave 272
Dugdale, Thomas 212
Durham, Bishop of 186

Edinburgh, Duke of (in 1874) 254
Edmonson, James 288
Edward IV 12
Egbert, King of Mercia 5
English, Malcolm 356
Esher, Viscount 268
Ethelred, King 116
Evans, Charles 230
Evelyn, John 41, 52, 150

Faden, William 112, 162, 172, 193
Faithorne & Newcourt 38
Faithorne, William 37
Fitzroy, Charles 128
Ford, William Simpson 217
Forty, F. J. 346
Foster, Elizabeth 313
Fourdrinier, Paul 133
Fournier, Daniel 100
Fox, Charles James 98
Frazer, William 148
Frear, Mr 146
Frith, Richard 70, 81
Fuller, Edward Bostock 57

Gardner, W. R. 138
Gascoyne, Joel 140, 144, 146
Gay, John 76
George II 176, 313
George III 100, 204, 258
George III, maps presented to 102, 112, 158, 162, 186
George IV 204, 206
Gibbon, Edward 108

Goad, Charles Edward 310
Godet, Giles 16
Goodge, Mr 174
Gordon, Lord George 100
Grafton, Duke of 174
Graham, Richard 81
Grant, Daniel 272
Greatorex, Ralph 62
Greenwood, Christopher and John 214
Gresham, Sir Thomas 32, 34
Griffiths, Charles 80
Grimm, Samuel Hieronymous 194
Grose, Francis 194
Gross, Alexander 326, 335
Grosvenor, Sir Thomas 82
Grosz, Sandor, *see* Gross
Grove, John 15
Gwynne, Francis 71

Haghe, Louis 232
Handel, Frederick 78
Hansard, Luke 204, 260
Hardy, Thomas 256
Harris, John 145
Harrison, E. & Co. 296, 298
Hastings, Warren 98
Hawksmoor, Nicholas 51, 53, **54**, 70, **147**
Haynes, John 87
Heath, James 100
Henry VIII 18, 48, 62, 150
Hill, J. 178
Hill, Rowland 222
Hogarth, William 90
Hogenberg, Frans 32, 34
Holland, Henry 130
Hollar, Wenceslaus **24**, 27, **38**, 42, **46**, 346
Hondius, Judocus Jr 22
Hooke, Robert 51, 55, 58, 76
Hope, Thomas 97
Horwood, Richard **168**, **170**, 172, 214, 252
Hulett, William 110
Hullmandel, Charles Joseph 126, 180
Hulsbergh, Henry 53
Humbold, Baron 184

375

Hume, David 132
Huysmans, Jacob 81
Hyde, Ralph 172

Inglis, Harry R. G. 300
Ingrey, Charles 314

James II 70
Jarman, Richard 326, 332
Johnson, Henry 142, 146, 164
Jones, Inigo 62
Jones, William 94
Julius Caesar 2

Kaye, Rev. Richard 194
King, Gregory 56, 81
Kip, Jan 66
Knyff, Leendert 64, 67

Labelye, Charles 176
Lane, Charles Augustus 207
Langford, Mr 124
Langley & Belch 330
Le Rouge, Georges Louis 92
Lea, Philip 96, 106
Leake, John 44, 46
Leroux, Jacob 72
Lerpinière, Daniel 128
Leybourne, William 56
Lily, George 11
Linnaeus, Carl 87
Lockie, John 172
Lodge, John 211
London, Bishop of 210, 286
Louis XII 12
Loveday, John 229
Lowe, George 328
Luffman, John 166

Macaulay, Zachary 246
Marlborough, Duke of 78
Marquois, Thomas 133

Marsh, Thomas 174
Martin, Ellis 305
Martin, John 250
Mayor of London 6, 128
Messeder, Isaac 14
Milne, Thomas 112, 172
Mordant Crook, Joseph 202
Morden, Robert 106
Morgan, William 51, 58, 60, 76, 106, 330
Morris, Richard 200
Morrow, Thomas 229
Mount, Frederick 278

Nash, John 178, 188, 196, 200, 202, 204, 208, 260
Neele, Josiah and James 214
Nelson, Horatio 178, 204
Newcourt, Richard 27, 36, 52
Nicholls, Sutton 87, 96
Norden, John 24, 128, 328
Norfolk, Duke of 76, 78
North, Kennedy 322
Northumberland, Duke of 116, 170

Ogilby, John 51, 56, 58, 60, 62, 330
Orleans, Duke of 12
Ortelius, Abraham 30

Palmer, William 159
Paris, Matthew 8
Parker, Barry 6, 293
Parr, Richard 110
Pastorini, Benedetto 188
Pearsall, Phyllis 326, 335
Pennethorne, James 260
Pepys, Samuel 37, 41, 106, 146
Peter the Great 150
Philip II 16, 27
Philips 335
Pine, John 90
Pooter, Charles 282, 286
Porter, Thomas 143
Powis, Duke of 124

Preston, Viscount 81
Prince of Wales 98, 130
Prince Regent (later George IV) 196, 202
Pugin, Augustus Charles 178

Radcliffe J. N. 232
Rennie, John 164, 180
Reynell, H. 99
Reynolds, James 316
Reynolds, Joshua 52
Reynolds, Nicholas 30
Richardson, George 193, 194
Roberts, Henry 133
Robertson, George 128
Rocque, John 51, 88, 90, 105, 108, 110, 122, 170
Rooker, Edward 133
Ruff, Edward 214
Russell, Lady Rachel 66
Russell, Lord William 66
Rysbrack 87

Salway, Joseph 136
Scharf, George Johann 126, 141, 180, 182, 204
Senefelder, Alois 180
Sheridan, Richard Brinsley 98
Sidey, Charles George 244
Simon, Thomas 40
Sloane, Sir Hans 86, 92
Smith, Benjamin 134
Smith, Charles 138
Smith, William 20
Snow, Dr John 232
Somers Town 73, 172, 350
Somers, Lord 72, 174
Sotheby 88
Soutar, A. & J., Architects 292
Southampton, Lord 128
Spencer, Earl 120
Standidge, William 254, 260
Stanford, Edward 218, 222–26, 262, 270–80
Starling, Thomas 134
Stent, Peter 328

Strafford, Earl of 80
Stukeley, William 2

Tallis, John 212, 356
Taylor, Thomas 96
Tegg, Thomas 330
Thornton, John 145
Tinney, John 90
Treswell, Ralph 50, 74
Twiss, Lt Col William 114
Tylney, Earl 116, 122
Tyrer, James 134

Unwin, Raymond 292

van Valkenborch, Martin 27
Vaughan, William 158
Victoria, Queen 218, 268
Visscher, Claes Jans 22, 40, 230
Vizetelly, Henry 230

Walker, Anthony 90
Walker, Ralph 164
Waller, Frederick 314
Wallis, Edward 209
Walton, Robert 143
Weedon, Daniel 125
Weiland, Ralph 287
Westminster, Duke of 82
Wheatley, Francis 100
White, John 196
Wickings, William 167
William IV 200
Wilberforce, William 120
William of Orange 67
Winchester, Bishop of 20
Wingaerde, Anthonis van den 16, 18, 20
Woollett, William 90
Wren, Sir Christopher 51, **53**, 54, 70, 180
Wyld, James MP 252

York, (Grand Old) Duke of 206, 260

GENERAL INDEX

A to Z 326, 335
Abbey Mills Pumping Station 340
ABC guide to London 335
Adelphi 186, 188
Admiralty Arch 264
Albany, The 130
Albertopolis 308
Alcohol 280
Aldermanbury 5
Aldersgate 9, 50, 118
Aldgate 9, 42
Aldwych 5, 264
Alexandra Park/Palace 246, 298
Aliens Act 1905 236
All Saints, West Ham 152
Allegorical Figures 24
Amsterdam 53, 67
Antwerp 24, 34
Apothecaries' Company 87
Archway 178, 208
Armada, Spanish 20
Arras Hoard 4
Artillery Ground 58
Arts, Royal Society of 188
Arundel House 76
Ashmolean Museum 16
Asians 366
Astley's 306

Babel, Tower of 27
Balham 287
Ballooning 206
Bank of England 102, 216
Bankside 16, 26
Banqueting House 62
Bartholomew Close 332
Basing House 37
Battersea 209, 224, 250, 268
Battersea Bridge 254
Battersea Park 224
Bayswater 118, 210
Bear Baiting 24
Bedford Estate 73, 280
Bedford Row, Holborn 332
Belgravia 82, 116, 214
Benedictine Abbey at St Albans 8
Berkeley Square 82
Bermondsey 141
Bethnal Green 144, 260
Bird's-eye view 28, 64
Bishopsgate 46
Black-boy Alley 152
Blackfriars 17
Blackfriars Bridge 168, 176, 188, 231
Blackheath 206

Blackwall 142, 224
Blackwall Yard 146, 164
Blackwell Hall 28
Blitz 337, 346
Bloomsbury 73, 128, **212**, 220, 246
Blunderbus Court 154
Board Game 304, 314
Bombing 336
Borough High Street 48, 180
Bow 232
Brick Lane 68
Brill, The 2
British Empire Exhibition 1924 322
British Library 72, 180
British Museum 87, 102, 180, 204, 337
Brixton 138, 214, 221, **348**, 358
Broad Street 100, 212
Broadway 64
Bromley-by-Bow Gas Works 340
Brooks's Club 130
Brunswick Dock 164
Buckingham House/Palace 66, 84, 206, **208**, 264
Building Insurance 170, 229
Building Societies 244
Bull and Bear Baiting 20
Bunhill Fields 284
Burden Collection 26
Burial Grounds 256
Buses 312
Bushey 124

Cadogan PLace 130
Camberwell 138, 214, 311
Camden Road 118
Camden Square 256
Camden Town 164, 244, 350
Canary Wharf 362
Canning Town 348
Cannon Street Station 28
Carlton House 130, 202, 204, 206, 210
Carnaby Street 356
Cars 305
Catena view 10
Catholics 100
Cemetery 258
Centre Point 74
Chalk Farm 117
Chalton Street 72
Charing Cross 186, 202, 204
Cheapside 26, 106, 330
Chelsea 86, 90, 92, 130, **254**, 276
Chelsea Embankment 254
Chelsea Hospital 84, 94, 251, 254
Chelsea Waterworks Company 84
Cheyne Walk 254, **256**

Chick Lane 152
Chiswick House 110
Cholera 232, 278
Christ Chuch, Spitalfields 147
Christ's Hospital 45
Churchyards 256
City Churchyards 262
City Corporation 6, **44**, 48, 90, 110, 168, 170, 180, 218, 346
City of London School 222
City Road 174
City Thameslink Station 242
Civil Unrest 86, 100, **102**, **144**, 256, 337
Civil War 24, 36
Civitas Londinvm 31
Clapham Old Town 138, **358**
Clean Air Acts 352
Clerkenwell 90, 134, 209
Clever Map Co. 361
Cloth laying out in fields 28
Clothworkers' Company 50
Cockpit, Whitehall Palace 62, 64
Cockspur Street 74
Coffee Houses 96
Colebrook 74
College of Arms 20
Cologne 32
Colosseum, Regent's Park 200, 206, 210, 306
Comic Relief 350
Commercial Road 156, 167
Commons and Footpaths Preservation Society 246, 262, 296, **302**
Complete Surveyor 56
Conduit Meadows 74
Conduit Street 74
Contour Road Book 300
Cool Britannia 356
Cool London 352
Copperplate map 20, 28, 30
Cornhill **32**, **34**, **96**, 260
Cosmorama 208
Cotton MS 9
County of London 218, 226
Covent Garden Theatre 130
Covent Garden 36, **38**, 73, 76, 100, 124, 186, 194, 209, 222
Crace Collection 58, 62, 84, 97, 106, 143, 154, 172, 193, 204, 214, 217, 240, 260, 308, 313, 314, 330
Cricket 300
Cries of London, The 100
Crooked Lane 182
Crouch End 300
Crown Estate 186, 192, 196, 202
Crystal Palace, Hyde Park 216
Custom House 158, 160

Customs' House (15th Cent) 12
Cycling 296, 298, 300

Daily Mail 336
Daily Telegraph 352
Dalston 214
Deptford 41, 136, 140, 150, 176
Development of Land 36, 51, **68–72**, 76, 81–84, 118, 144, 154, 168, 174, 176, **192**, 220, 288, 344, 348, **362**
Devonshire Place 194
Diary of a Nobody 286
Diorama, Regent's Park 200, 210
Displacement (Re-Housing/Compensation) **162**, 242, 264, 350
Docklands 140, 156, 196, 342, 362
Docklands Museum 144
Dover 10
Drury Lane 130
Duke of York's Column 207, 210
Duke's Avenue, Muswell Hill 288
Dulwich 138
Dundee 58
Durham Yard 188

East End 100, 140, 144, 147, 212, 232, 256, 260, 342
East India Company 142, 146, 150, 160, **166**
East India Dock 80, 157, 160, **164**, 166
East India House 130, 160
East London Line, London Overground 184
East London Water Company 232
Eastern Park 260
Education Act 1870 276
Egyptian Hall 306
Electricity Supply 274
Elephant & Castle 176, 208
Eltham 96
Embankment of Thames 188, 250, 254
Emmanuel Church, Holloway 286
Employment 350
Engineers, Civil 112, 163
Engravers, Society of 188
Epping Forest 115, **246**, **262**
Epsom 56
Euston Road 72, 174
Euston Square 262
Euston Station 240
Exact Surveigh 44, 46

Fabric, maps on 88
Fans, maps on 88
Fare-checking maps 312, 316
Farringdon Street 50
Fenchurch Street 161
Festival of Britain 1951 352, 354
Financial map of the City 361

Finchley 244, 298
Finsbury 284
Fire of 1794 in Ratcliffe 148
Fire of London 1666 38, 42–46, 51, 56, 58, 62
Fires of 1691 and 1698 62, 64
Fleet Lane 50
Fleet Prison 50
Fleet River/Ditch 50, 52, 242
Fleet Street 54, 214, 314
Flooding 368
Florence 10
Food Supply 104
Footpaths 138, 302
Foundling Hospital 90
Freehold Land Society 244
French Weavers 147
Frith Street 70
Fulham 130, 266
Fulham Bridge 108
Fumifugium 1661 41

Gall & Inglis **298**, 300
Games 304, 314
Garden Suburb 192, 282, 292
Gas Supply 272
Gates of the city 8
Geffrye Museum 154
Geldings Close 74
General Cemetery Company 258, 328
General Post Office 352
Gentrification 352
Geographers' Map Co. 335
Geographia 335, 352
Geoprojects 352, **363**
German Maps for WW2 338, 340
German Merchants 28, 32
Globe & Compasses 143
Globe Theatre 22, 24
Goldsmiths' Company 30, 90
Gordon Riots 86, **100**, **102**
Gothic St Paul's Cathedral 14
Grafton Estate 192
Graveyards *see also* City Churchyards 256
Great Central Railway 290
Great Exhibition 207, 214, **216**, 308
Great Hall, Whitehall Palace 64
'Great Map' of London 46
Great North Road 178
Great Seal of the Commonwealth 40
Great Stink 248
Great Twelve Livery Companies 36
Great Western and Great Central Joint Railway 302
Greater London Authority 364
Greater London Council 344
Greater London Plan 1944 294
Green Belt 282, 294
Green Park 70, 190
Greenwich 24, 164, 204, 206

Grid Reference for Maps 330
Grosvenor Estate 73, 84
Grosvenor House 84
Grosvenor Square 82, 84
Ground Plan 284
Guildhall 60
Guildhall Library 31, 56
Guy's Hospital 90

Haberdashers' Company 20
Hackney 115, **260**, **358**
Hackney Coaches 41
Hampstead 116, 194, 220
Hampstead Garden Suburb 292
Hampstead Heath 116, **128**, 220, 262
Hampstead Tenants Ltd 293
Hans Town/Place 130
Hansa 32
Hares Marsh 68
Harley collection 68
Harrod's 310
Harrow Road 259
Hatton Garden 154
Haymarket 74
Healthy Living 126, **256**, **290**, 352
Heathrow Airport 294
Hendon 124
Highgate 8, **128**, **178**, 194, 208, 210, 246
HMS Portland 146
Hoare's Bank 37
Holborn 100, 209, 211, **212**, 264
Holborn Hill 222, 242
Holloway 286
Holloway College 286, 300
Holy Trinity Church Aldgate 8
Holywell Street 217
Homelessness 350
Hope theatre 24
Hopson's handy map 300
Hornsey Lane 118, 178
Hornsey Road 244
Hospitals 278
Hotel-de-Ville for LCC 268
Houses of Parliament 178, 204, 208, **228**, 248
Housing, Municipal **234**, 282
Hoxton Square 154
Huguenot 128, 133, 154, 198, 366
Hyde Park 74, 102, 190, 216, 224
Hyde Park Corner 186, 190

Ickenham 302
Illustrated London Advertiser 240
Illustrated London News 230
Immigration (*see also* Tourism) 238, **366**
Imperial College 308
Improvement Plans 250, 264, 372
Industry 48, 90, 114, 141, 142, 217, **228**, 230, 282, 308, 311, 344, 350, 352, 356, 360

Insurance for buildings 229, 311
Interiors of buildings 80, 88, 98, 147, 178, 207
Invasion 338
Isle of Dogs 115, 156, 162, 164, 368
Islington 92, 119, 134, 154, 174, 209, 224, 287, 316, 318, 358
Italian mapmakers 10

Jerusalem (*see also* St John of) 9
Jews 236, 366
Johnson, Riddle & Co. 312, **320**
Justice 24

Kensal Green Cemetery 258
Kensington 133, **136**, 238, 308
Kensington Turnpike 136
Kent 78
Kentish Town 224, 246
Kenwood 128
Kew Gardens 198
Kilburn 117
King (now Soho) Square 81
King Street 44
King's College 198, 292
Kings Cross 209, 316
Kings Cross Station 256
Kings Mills Wharf 229
Kingston 164
Kingsway 264
Knightsbridge 82, 112
Knightsbridge Turnpike 190

Labyrinthus Londinensis 314
Lambeth 8, 56, 209, 287, 348
Lancet, The 278
Land Use Plan/Map 112, 172
Lea, River 141, 164, 232
Leadenhall Street 45
Leathersellers' Company 154
Legal Quays 158, 160
Liberties **48**, 214
Library Map of London 270, 276
Lightning 16
Lily map of Great Britain and Ireland 11
Limehouse 36, 144, 278
Limehouse Cut 114
Livery Companies 36
Lloyd's 96, 360
Londinium 3
London Bridge 1, 8, 12, **14**, 22, **180**
London Bridge rebuilt 168, 182
London Bridge Station 208
London County Council 218, **226**, **264**, **268**, 270, 280, 284, 318, 342
London Dock **158**, **160**, **162**, 164
London Dock Company 159
London Docklands Development Corporation 362
London Metropolitan Archives 284

London Plan 2005 364
London Postal District 222, 224
London School of Economics 236
London United Temperance Council 280
Londonwic 5
Long Acre 222
Long Lands Estate 245
Ludgate 9
Lunatic Asylums 278
Lutheran Church in the Savoy 53

Magdalene College, Cambridge 17
Mall, The **66**, **264**, **268**
Manors 80, 87, **118**, 120, 124, **128**, 154
Mansion House 216
Marble Arch 90
Marks & Spencer 98
Marshalsea Prison 48
Martello Towers 114
Marylebone **193**, 209, **211**, 244, 272
Marylebone Park 192, 194
Marylebone Road 174, **194**
Marylebone Station 290
Master Map of London Poverty **234**, 236
Mayfair 73, 82, **84**, 180, 186
Medical Relief 278
Mercers' Hall 60
Merchant Adventurer 34
Merchant Taylors' Company 88, 211
Merlin's Cave 90
Metroland **282**, **290**
Metropolitan Board of Sewers 252
Metropolitan Board of Works **218**, **224**, 226, 248, 270, 276
Metropolitan Gas Companies 272
Metropolitan Police Area 222
Metropolitan Public Gardens Association 262
Metropolitan Railway 282, 292, 302
Microcosm of London 178
Middlesex Street 142
Midland Railway 256
Mile End 10, 229, 278
Mile End Old Town 144
Millbank 24, 250
Mint, The 40
Monument 51, **55**
Mornington Crescent 262
Mortlake 121
Motor Chase Across London 304
Multi-storey car parks 349
Musaeum Tradescantianum 46
Muscovy 30
Museum of Docklands 144
Museum of London 234
Museums area, Kensington 306
Music Halls **306**, 318
Muswell Hill 288

National Archives 74
National Gallery 74
National Portrait Gallery 126
Natural History Museum 92, 308
Navy Board 146
New River Head 92
New Road 174
Newgate prison 100
Newington 128, 176
News Maps 165
Norfolk House 76
Norlands 133
Northwood 292
Notting Hill 132
Nuremberg 20

O2 Arena 164
Old Bailey 135
Old Curiosity Shop 264
Old Ford 232
Old Palace Yard 142
Olympic Games 1948 352
Olympic Games site 2012 152, 368
Omnibus 312
Open Spaces Society 262
Ordnance Survey 104, 112, 114, 134, 138, 172, 234, 242, 252, 268, 270, 298, 302, 338, 340, 342
Ownership of Property 284
Oxford 37
Oxford Circus 74, 98, 272
Oxford Street 73, 74, 82, 98, 272

Paddington 174, 196, 244, 316
Painter-Stainers' Company 50
Pall Mall 81, 130, 204
Panorama 16–24, 42, 208, 230, 240
Pantheon 98
Paris 8, 89, 90
Park Lane 82
Park Royal 352
Pavilion, The 130
Peckham 138, 214
Peep-Show 207
Pentonville 118
Pentonville Road 174
Pepys Library 17
Perry's Dock 164
Peter Jones department store 286
Petticoat Lane 142
Phoenix Assurance Company 170, 229
Photography 266
Physic Garden 86
Piccadilly 36, 66, 70, 74, 82, 130, 152, 202
Pictorial Times 230
Pimlico 73, 82, 236, **251**, 266
Plague, Great 328
Playing Fields Association 300
Pleasure Gardens 86, 94, 354

Pool of London 158
Poplar 144
Portland Estate 73, 192, 280
Portland Place 202
Portman Estate 73, 192, 280
Portsmouth Street 264
Post Office Directory 211
Postal Districts 222
Poverty 234
Prague 25
Pre-Fire city 40, 264
Preston Papers 81
Primrose Hill 117, 194
Princeton Street, Holborn 336
Privy Garden 64
Pudding Lane 42
Punch 248
Putney 108, 121

Queen Street 44
Queen's Palace 60

Railway Bell 240
Railway Clearing House 246
Railways 240, 246
Rambling 296
Ranelagh 86, 90, 92, 94
Ranelagh, winter version 98
Ratcliff(e) 142, 144, 148
Reform Acts 1832, 1867 244
Reformation 48
Regency 168, 186, **210**, 214
Regent Street 186, 196, 202, 210, 212
Regent's Park 186, **196–202**, 206, 210, 224, 258
Relics 266
Ribbon Development 10, 32, 138
Richmond Terrace 228
Rickmansworth 290
Road Repairs 314
Roads 136, **264**
Romans 1
Rome 11
Ropewalks 114
Rose & Crown Alley 154
Rotherhithe 184
Rouge Dragon Pursuivant 20
Royal Academy 100, 110, 159, 204
Royal Agricultural Hall 318
Royal Albert Hall 308
Royal Barge 28
Royal Botanic Society 198
Royal College of Music 308
Royal College of Organists 308
Royal Exchange 31, 32, **34**, 51, 52, 60, 69, 90, **96**, 216
Royal Festival Hall 354
Royal Geographical Society 272
Royal Horticultural Hall 318
Royal Society 51, 58, 90, 110, 170

Royal Society of Arts 186
Royal Terrace, Adelphi 188
Ruislip 302
Ruislip Manor 292

Saffron Hill 242
St Agnes le Clear spring 154
St Albans 50
St Alfege, London Wall 20
St Andrew Undershaft 110
St Bride, Fleet Street 54, 58
St Clement Danes 266
St Dunstan, Stepney 140, 144
St George's Fields **172**, 176
St Giles in the Fields 26, 74, 209, 256
St Giles, Cripplegate 18
St James, Westminster 188
St James's 62, 66, 70, 73
St James's Palace 70
St James's Park 36, 67, 102, 235
St James's Square 66, 76, 78, 80
St John of Jerusalem, Manor of 118
St John's Wood 192, 292
St Katharine by the Tower 57
St Katharine's Dock 230
St Leonard, Shoreditch 154
St Luke, Old Street 244
St Margaret, Westminster **64**, **67**, 308
St Margaret's Bay, Kent 330
St Martin's in the Fields 67, 70, 74, 82, 332
St Martin's Lane 74, 204
St Mary-le-bone, *see* Marylebone
St Mary-le-Bow 8, 11, 18
St Michael, Crooked Lane **180**, 183
St Pancras 2, 193, **210**, 244, **256**
St Pancras Church, Old 256
St Pancras Station 256, 372
St Paul the Apostle 6
St Paul's Cathedral rebuilt 60
St Paul's Cathedral spire lost 31, 32
St Paul's Cathedral 1, 8, **16**, 18, 20, 27, **36**, **41**, 44, 188
St Paul's Churchyard 102, 143, 314
St Paul's School 11, 18
Sayes Court House 150
School Board for London 234, 236, 270, **276**
Schools (*see also* Education Act) 132, **276**
Science Museum 308
Seal, Great 40
Seven Sisters Road 244
Sewage 126, **248**, **250**
Shadwell 148
Shaftesbury Avenue 254, 264
Shepperton 163
Shooters Hill 126
Shops 86, 170
Shoreditch 10, 26, 154
Short Spins around London 300
"Silent Highway" -man 248

Silk Weaving 142
Skeleton Map 242, **252**, 270, **272**
Skinner Street 242
Skinners' Company 174
Slavery 120, 167
Sloane MS 20
Sloane Street 130
Smeatonian Society 163
Smith & Bye 134
Smith & Son 306
Smithfield Market 104, 174, **242**
Society for Photographing Relics of Old London 266
Society of Artists 128
Soho 73, 81, 186, 202, 232, 278, 280, 356
Somerset House 60, **186**
Sound Arse Alley 154
South Kensington 306, 308
South London 176, 246
Southampton Estate 192
Southampton Row 264
Southwark 22, 48, 100, 278
Southwark Bridge 168
Southwark Cathedral 16, 20, 24
Spaniards, The 128
Spitalfields 88, 142, 147, 154
Sport 296
Spread Eagle Court 154
Stanhope Street, St Pancras 207
Stationers' Company 7
Statistical Society 278
Steam Washing Company 200
Steelyard 28
Stepney 68, 80, 114, 140, **144**
Stockwell 214
Strand 1, 76, 138, 159, 186, **204**, 214, 217, **264**, 314, 316
Stranger's Guide 306
Strategic Views of St Paul's 365
Stratford-le-Bow 115, 254
Street Guides 328–35
Street Views 212
Subscriptions to maps 106, 170
Suburbs 36, 51, 143, **286**, **288**
Surrey Street 138
Surveyors' Dialogue, The 26
Swinging London 352, 356
Syon House 116

Tate Modern 16
Tennis Court, The 62, 64
Thames Gateway 368
Thames (*see also* Embankment) 3, 8, **16–24**, 58, 82
Thames Tunnel 184
Thames, Old Father 24
Theatre Pantomique 92
Theatre Royal Drury Lane 130
Theatres 86
Threadneedle Street 40
Tilt Yard 62

379

Topography of London 172
Tottenhall Manor 128
Tottenham 229, 246
Tottenham Court Road 272
Tottenham Hotspur Football 318
Tourism/Visitors 14, 51, 86, 92, 128, 300, 305, **306**, 312, 344, 352, 356, 362, 364, 366
Tower Hamlets 145
Tower Hill 12
Tower of Babel 27
Tower of London 1, 8, **12**, 22, 36
Toynbee Trustees 236
Trafalgar Square 186, **204**, 208, 264, 268
Traitors, severed heads 22
Trams 318
Trier 4
Trivia 76
Trojan origins 36
Tyburn 90

Underground Railways 320, 370

University College 210
Vauxhall 86
Vauxhall Bridge 168
V-bombs 337, 342
Victoria and Albert Museum 308
Victoria Memorial 264
Victoria Park 214, 256, 260
View from the North 26
Views 194, 364
Vignette 332
Vikings 5
Villages round London **104**, **106**, 110, 132
Visitors, *see* Tourism
Voyage Round Great Britain 164

Walham Green 110
Wall Street Journal 360
Walls of the City 1, 3, 4, 9
Wandsworth 121, 209, 358
Wanstead House 122
Wapping 142, 144, 156, **158**, 162, **184**

War Damage map 342
War, WW1 336
War, WW2 338–44
Warehouses 148, 156, **160**, 166, 230, 330
Waterloo Bridge 168
Waterloo Place 210
Watermen 22
Watling Street 117
Weavers, French Silk 88, 142, 147, **366**
Wembley 70, 290, **322**, 352
Wentworth Street 80, 142
West Central District Map 38
West End 51, 66, 73, 74, 76, 78, 81, 90, 96, 102, 40, 174, **202**, **351**
West Ham 152, 254
West Ham Power Station 340
West India Docks 158, 160, 164, **166**
West India Trade 156
Westminster Abbey 60, 116
Westminster Bridge 168, **176**, 228
Westminster, Palace of 248

Westminster 8, 202, 204, 230, **234**, 238, 250, 318
White Bear, Piccadilly 152
White Tower 12
Whitechapel 142, 229, 278
Whitehall 20, 22, 56, 130
Whitehall Palace 6, 18, 20, 60, **62**, 64
Willesden 124
Wimbledon 120, 330
Windsor 56
Woodcut Panorama of London 17
Woodford 300
Wool Trade 28
Workmen's railway tickets 240, 246
Works in Architecture 188
Wych Street 264, 266

York House (Dover House) 130
York, Duke of, Column 207, 210

Zeppelin Raids 336
Zoological Garden 198

380

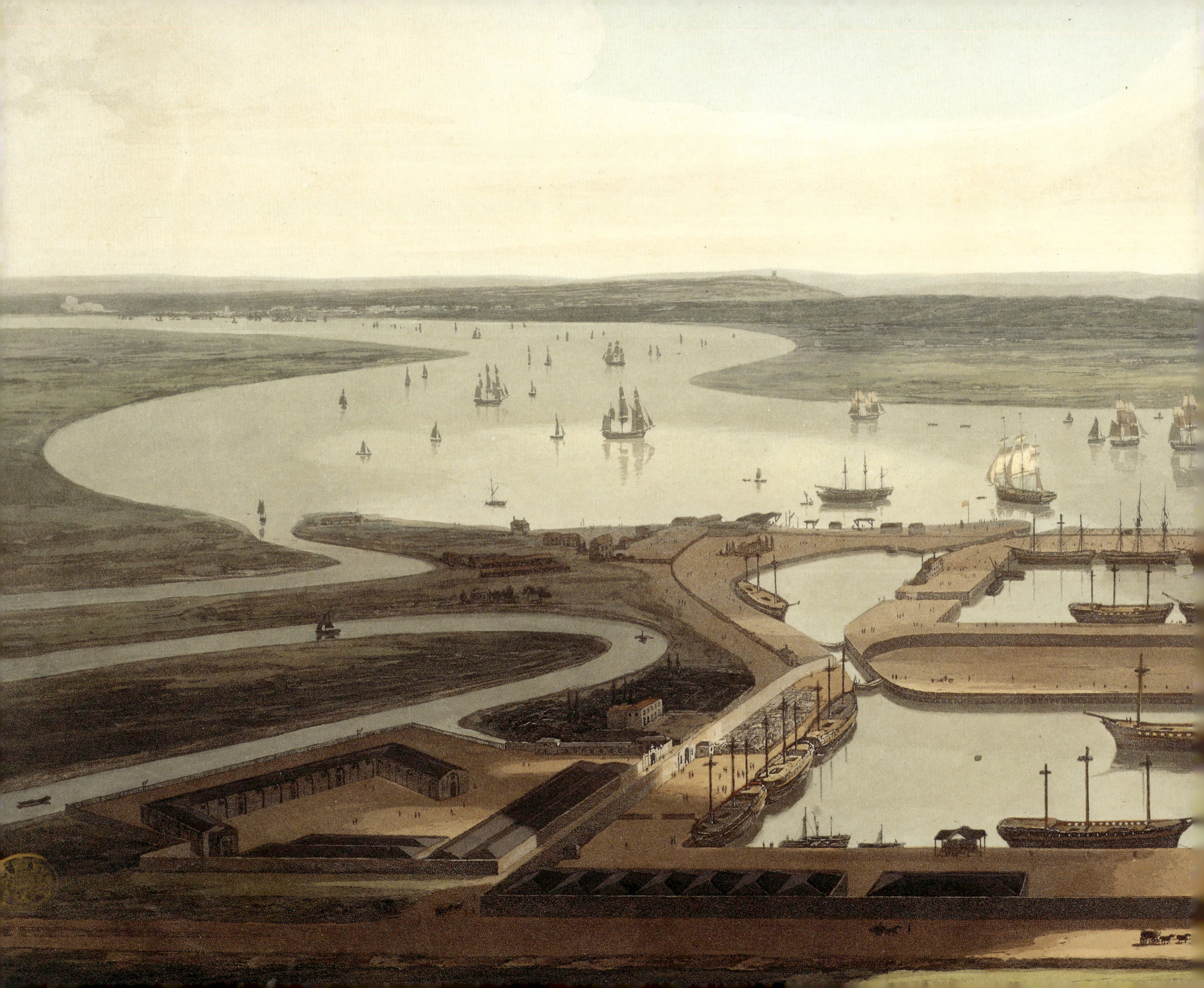